Christine Maxwell
Czeslaw Jan Grycz

NEW RIDERS' OFFICIAL
INTERNET
YELLOW
PAGES

NEW RIDERS
PUBLISHING

New Riders Publishing, Indianapolis, Indiana

New Riders' Official Internet Yellow Pages

By Christine Maxwell and Czeslaw Jan Grycz

Published by:
New Riders Publishing
201 West 103rd Street
Indianapolis, IN 46290 USA

Printed in the United States of America   6 7 8 9 10

Maxwell, Christine.

   New Riders' Official Internet Yellow Pages / Christine Maxwell, Czeslaw Jan Grycz. — 2nd ed.

      p.   cm.

   Includes bibliographical references (p.) and index.

   1. Internet (Computer network) — Directories.   I. Grycz, Czeslaw

Jan.   II. New Riders Publishing.   III. Title.

TK5105.875.I75M368   1994b

011'.3 — dc20

                                                            94-34785

                                                                CIP

Warning and Disclaimer

This book is designed to provide information about the Internet. Every effort has been made to make this book as complete and as accurate as possible, but no warranty or fitness is implied.

The information is provided on an "as is" basis. The authors and New Riders Publishing shall have neither liability nor responsibility to any person or entity with respect to any loss or damages arising from the information contained in this book or from the use of the disks or programs that may accompany it.

Publisher
Lloyd J. Short

Associate Publisher
Tim Huddleston

Product Development Manager
Rob Tidrow

Marketing Manager
Ray Robinson

Director of Special Projects
Cheri Robinson

Managing Editor
Matthew Morrill

About the Authors

Christine Maxwell is Director of Internet Research and Development and Publisher of McKinley Group, Inc. (The McKinley Group specializes in Internet directory publishing and helping companies attain a strong market presence on the Internet.) She also is President and CEO of Research on Demand Inc., a Berkeley based information broker company. Maxwell has been in the information brokering business more than 12 years. Previously, she worked in senior positions In International scientific and educational publishing. She also is a trained elementary school teacher and has taught for several years in British public schools.

Maxwell has written several books including *The Pergamon Dictionary of Perfect Spelling* and *Spelling...Spelling Basics*. Maxwell particularly likes to focus her writing skills on books that deal with problems of information access. Her eclectic background has proved well-suited to exploring all the riches of the Internet and helping those riches to become more accessible to everyone.

Czeslaw (Chet) Jan Grycz is the Director of Advisory Board and Database Development for the McKinley Group. He also is a lecturer in the School of Library Science and Information Technology at the University of California at Berkeley Extension, where he teaches two of the required courses in the Certificate of Publishing program. Grycz also is on permanent faculty of the Denver Publishing Institute, and has conducted workshops and lectured throughout the world, especially in Central and Eastern Europe.

Grycz is an author, consultant, writer, and editor. His special interests are in developing electronic models for publishers, especially in distributed digital network environments. He was instrumental in initiating the 1992 "Red Sage" project, a collaborative electronic publishing effort involving the University of California at San Francisco, Springer-Verlag Publishers, and AT&T Bell Laboratories. In 1994, he helped consolidate a partnership between the University of California System and the Institute for Electrical and Electronics Engineers (IEEE) to similarly prototype electronic publishing mechanisms for engineering information.

Lead Editor
Lisa Wilson

Production Editors
Cliff Shubs
Amy Bezek
Suzanne Snyder
Sarah Kearns

Copy Editors
Rob Lawson
Tad Ringo
Steve Weiss
Lillian Yates

Book Production
Roger S. Morgan
Matthew Morrill
Lisa Wilson

Indexer
Suzanne Snyder

Graphics Image Specialists
Dennis Sheehan
Jeff Yesh

Publisher's Assistant
Melissa Lynch

Editorial Assistant
Karen Opal

Trademark Acknowledgments

All terms mentioned in this book that are known to be trademarks or service marks have been appropriately capitalized. New Riders Publishing cannot attest to the accuracy of this information. Use of a term in this book should not be regarded as affecting the validity of any trademark or service mark.

Acknowledgments

We would like to thank the individuals who have tirelessly assisted us in making the major changes needed to bring about this second edition of our directory. In particular, we are very grateful to the McKinley Group's Managing Editor, Susanna Camp, for her dedication, professionalism, and extremely hard work. We would also like to sincerely thank our Editorial Advisory Board for its expert evaluation assistance. Special thanks are also due to:

Alex Cohen for both his excellent technical and surfing support; Patrick de Harveng and Suresh Thakur for their invaluable help in programming and developing our database.

Wes Thomas of Mondo for his much-appreciated surfing skills.

Rick Wilson, Intelligent Tool & Eye, San Francisco, for his vision in creating a much improved design.

Laurie Abbott for her special expertise on OPACs.

We would also like to thank the following people for their help in specific areas:

Jim Terragno and Steve Macintosh: Online Systems Specialists

Helene Atkin: Public Relations

We are very conscious of the important work that was accomplished by all the other experts who "surfed" the Internet on our behalf, gathering resources from all over the world in an ever-growing range of subject areas. Other surfers helped in sorting, cataloging, and verifying the massive amounts of data and Internet URLs that were ultimately e-mailed to our Berkeley, California, headquarters, where all the entries were assembled.

Creating a directory such as this involves much professionalism and an equal amount of generous volunteerism! The following Internet Specialists contributed both in abundance:

Kasey Asberry
John Barrie
Andrew Bernick
Matisse Enzer
Antonella Fruscione
Jack Kessler
Joel Kohn
Sean Malloy
Robert Porter
Tony Safina

We also wish to acknowledge the important contributions of the following individuals who helped us locate additional resources and shared their Internet navigational experiences with us:

John Bernard Condant
Anna Couey
Larry Dieterich
Nancy Gusack
Craig Harris

Joel Levine
Judy Malloy
Joe Paska
Brian Tanaka
Eric Theise
Caius van Nouhuys
Marla Wilson
Bob Zimmerman

For their special efforts, we are indebted to Lisa Bornstein and Barbara Lee Williams, our Consulting Editors. We would also like to express much gratitude to the rest of the editorial staff:

Judith Abrams
Kathleen Benafel
Theresa Bergen
Will Crain
Nicholas Cronbach
Diane Gibbs
Helen Yoon

Putting together a book that literally has no beginning, no middle, and no end (until it is all assembled) poses a particularly tough challenge. Our special thanks go to Darek Milewski, for his unstinting technical support.

We wish to acknowledge the numerous administrative and data-entry-related services supplied by the following individuals, without whose assistance, total dedication, and perseverance this project would not have been possible. Special thanks are due to:

Jeremy Bled
Robyn Gregg
Stephanie Gregg
Hillary Hayden
Kaethin Prizer
Lisa Sorenson

Thanks are also due to:

Yu-ling Chang
Michael Coleman
Greg Drinkwater
Apolinar Flores
Roberta Kane
Dayhawk Kim
David Schneer
Irene Sidera
Neal Skapura

Among our friends at New Riders, we would like to thank Cheri Robinson, Director of Special Projects. Special thanks also go to Matthew Morrill and his team of talented editors, in particular the editing team of Lisa Wilson, Cliff Shubs, Amy Bezek, Suzanne Synder, and Sarah Kearns. Special thanks also goes to Roger Morgan, our page layout specialist.

Thanks are also due to *The McKinley Group* and *Stokes•Hayden, Inc.*, both of Berkeley, California, for their technical and office support and to The Wladyslaw Poniecki Foundation for providing Internet access and connecitivity for the project. (The latter nonprofit organization will continue to provide a registry service for new listings.)

Finally, we would like to give special thanks to our long-suffering spouses, Roger and Monica, and to our children, Xavier, Yuri, and Giselle Malina, and Stefan and Krysia Grycz, for putting up once again with our long absences from family life. A special thank you also to Isabel and David Hayden for their inestimable contributions, which included database development and logistical help, and to Ian Maxwell for his advice and support during the many months it took to compile this work.

Disclaimer

An environment as dynamic as the Internet, where change occurs continually, can never be fixed in a book such as this. While every effort has been made to check the factual information contained in this directory, we are very conscious that many changes will have inevitably taken place between the time of this compilation and the date of its publication. We therefore welcome and solicit reader feedback in correcting inaccuracies or in suggesting improvements and additions for subsequent editions of this directory. Forms have been provided at the back of the directory for these purposes. We look forward to your comments.

Table of Contents

Foreword

Once the preserve of the research and education community, the global Internet has emerged from its academic cocoon to become a vital new infrastructure for electronic commerce. As the pages of this book vividly illustrate, an almost unfathomable wealth of information and services lies below the rolling surface of the Internet ocean.

Navigating its waters and mining its riches are still tasks for the hardy and the brave—not unlike the pioneers who blazed trails across the endless prairies of the American West. But even the unruly frontiers must someday be settled, and the authors of this much-needed guide provide a civilizing influence on the exponentially growing global Internet. New with names such as gopher, World Wide Web, Archie, Mosaic, and Wide Area Information Service (WAIS) are emerging as the basis for new information-browsing and indexing tools. Stable information repositories are emerging that can be cataloged and indexed in various ways. Distributed searching tools based on intelligent agents, Knowbot™ programs, and the like are appearing in both the research and commercial worlds.

Although still somewhat novel today, the application of computers to everyday living and commerce, particularly in connection with the Internet, provides a basis for new product development over the next few years. Mail-enabled applications will increase in popularity, as will combinations of print and online advertising and order fulfillment. Monetary transactions are also finding fertile ground in the Internet landscape.

It should be very apparent to anyone reading this book that the Internet community has diverse interest and skill, which, by their very heterogeneity, suggest an extraordinary breadth of potential. So much communication today is carried digitally that it seems all but inescapable that computer-managed communication and application services will become the norm.

Although the future of the Internet and its technology is still difficult to discern with certainty, it is now deeply embedded not only in the US telecommunications infrastructure, but also in that of other nations. As a global telecommunications service provider and key player in the development of the US Internet infrastructure, MCI Corporation is deeply aware of the needs of Internet users. This massive, globe-girdling, and exponentially growing resource offers almost unlimited opportunities for information service providers and users. In keeping with MCI's network philosophy, MCI is committed to helping the networking technology, including the global Internet.

Vinton Cerf
President, The Internet Society
Senior Vice President, Data Architecture
MCI Corporation

Introduction

In the first edition of this directory, we wrote that INFORMATION ACCESS and PEOPLE ACCESS are what the "Internet" is all about. The Internet now has 10 times as much traffic as six months ago, and 50 times as many information and data resources. Every month, approximately 1 million new subscribers sign on to the Internet. This traffic, along with the daily increase in the enormous volume of information available on the Internet, has made it virtually impossible—even for a proficient Internet user—to zero in easily and quickly on the best resources. Once you get to a site, you now must navigate through increased layers of intermediate menu structures before actually reaching the information required. This is true for all disciplines, regardless of what time of day (or night) you are searching.

This Internet Reference Work is for Internet Novices and Experts Alike

Whether novice or expert, readers soon discover how helpful it is to have this value-added directory (and its updates) close at hand while searching the Internet.

The entries chosen for this second edition still represent only a fraction of the resources available on the Internet. We have striven to correct omissions of coverage in some areas and have expanded the range and scope of many others, as well as reassessing resources originally listed in the first edition. In many cases, we have replaced old listings with brand new entries judged to be of superior quality in both content and coverage.

Key Features from the First Edition

Listed below are features that were carried over from the first edition because readers reported finding them particularly useful.

Embedded Index: A unique feature of *New Riders' Official Internet Yellow Pages* is that entries are repeated under their relevant keyword headings. The directory therefore functions as its own index.

Provision of Non-Technical, Factual Resource Descriptions: Short descriptions and profiles for each resource are written in non-technical, plain English.

Template Format: Descriptive fields are consistent with the first edition: Title, Short Description, Keywords, Sponsor, Audience, Contact, Details, Notes , and URL (Internet address).

Titles of Listings: Sorted alphabetically by a series of keywords as well as by title.

Keywords: Provided to help readers focus quickly on the most relevant resources suitable to a given inquiry.

Audience Fields: These are provided to help organize and classify Internet resources for specific audiences and constituencies.

Short Descriptions and Profiles: The content of each resource has been carefully analyzed, enabling precise, factual descriptions for each resource to be compiled.

User Info: Additional navigation information is provided (where applicable) to assist the reader in accessing a resource as efficiently as possible.

Details: This field identifies whether access to a selected resource is free of charge or has a cost associated with it. Resources can be moderated, and have image, sound or multimedia files.

Internet addresses (or URLs): These are supplied at the bottom of each listing to give quick and easy access to each resource. Whenever available, alternative addresses are given to ensure that as many people as possible can navigate their way to a given resource, even if they don't have a high-speed modem or sufficient bandwidth to be able to access such sites using more sophisticated search tools like Lynx or Mosaic. (See Chapter 5 for an explanation of these and other Internet Access Tools.)

Expanded Features in the Second Edition

International Editorial Advisory Boards Provide Independent The Assessment of Resources. Following the well-established scientific publishing tradition of "peer review," we have greatly expanded our teams of experts and editorial advisors to help review and evaluate the Internet resources published in this new edition. We are particularly pleased that editors representing the Advisory Board of Annual Reviews—the premier international review body of published articles in 57 scientific disciplines—and world-class editors from leading international scientific and educational journals have agreed to serve on newly established Editorial Advisory Boards. Their participation helps us provide the quality-assurance factor that is so vital for today's Internet users.

Each resource listed in this directory has been reviewed and carefully evaluated. We have put into place a system to allow for ongoing evaluations of resources by our Advisory Boards. This system focuses on rating the relative importance of resources, according to a set list of criteria. This is the source of the Subject/Topic Ranking System (STAR) described in detail in Chapter 3. The ranking system is unique and is of inestimable value to professionals and individuals who want to proceed directly to the most useful resources in their interest areas.

Even with artificially intelligent "knowbots"(TM) executing automated resource searches, a directory providing an independent review of Internet resources is essential. For example, if you were to search the Internet for resources dealing with "accounting," you would end up with a list of over 2,000 references! Your productivity would decrease rather than increase while you searched for what you needed—exactly the opposite of what the Internet promises and can deliver!

Increased Selection of Internet Resources. We have increased the selection of listings in this second edition by 45 percent, and have updated the navigational instructions for all the listings appearing in the first edition. One of the most challenging realities of the Internet today continues to be its volatility. Resources made available by a provider one day may be moved or transported to another network site the next day. It is, therefore, quite difficult to keep up with these changes. Until the Internet matures and stabilizes, constant surveillance is necessary. We continue to provide that surveillance on a daily basis in our efforts to produce the most up-to-date information available in subsequent editions of this directory.

More International Resources. The Internet continues to expand globally, even as it penetrates into more communities and remote locations in the United States. Mindful of the global reach of the Internet, we have gone to special lengths to expand the number of international resources listed. In addition, our Advisory Boards are international in scope and have been specifically requested to help us identify international Internet resources wherever they exist and to evaluate them for us.

Commercial Access to the Internet Gives Business a Competitive Advantage

The recent opening of the Internet information highway for commercial use has resulted in far-reaching opportunities for every kind of business—both large and small. Companies can research new markets and track existing ones, increase their level of direct customer contact, make new business connections, and get instant feedback (through e-mail) from internal staff and customers alike.

With the use of the Internet, communities no longer need to be defined entirely by where people live and where businesses are situated. Individual consumers find that shopping on the Internet is an exploding field, and opportunities abound for learning, being entertained, and pursuing every kind of hobby or interest imaginable.

The Two-Way Flow of Information

The Internet is "interactive." This means it is two-directional. People use the Internet to access information, but they also use it to provide information for others to seek out and find.

It is important for both individuals and businesses to realize that the higher the quality of information provided to the Internet, the greater the value received back. In keeping with this simple truth, we want to encourage readers to provide us with feedback on existing and new listings. We have provided in Appendix G a series of forms titled "Making Your Voice Heard."

The forms cover:

- How to register an Internet resource
- How to correct a listing
- How to list an advertisement

The comprehensive cataloging of Internet content can never be completed. It is impossible to get "ahead" of the Internet: we can only strive consistently and conscientiously to locate and document in this directory the best resources in every field of endeavor. To that end, we constantly are adding to our Advisory Boards, whose members are at the cutting edge of their given fields.

The Internet is a new world community, with businesses now joining educational and research institutions in embracing its electronic reach. On the Internet, people help one another from across the world—working collaboratively to solve problems, sharing insights, or providing each other with information, solutions, and fresh ideas. The Internet contains a treasure trove that needs to be open to all people. We are committed not only to providing the best information about the contents of the Internet, but also to setting quality standards by which those contents can be evaluated and used.

Finally, the special format we have devised for all entries in the directory ensures that readers do not drown in information overload, but are able to swim gracefully and precisely to where they need to go.

The Elements of the Internet

Some people draw a diagram of a cloud to
represent the Internet. In fact, it is a hierarchical
assembly of networks: a network of networks.
It could be diagrammed in schematic form like this:

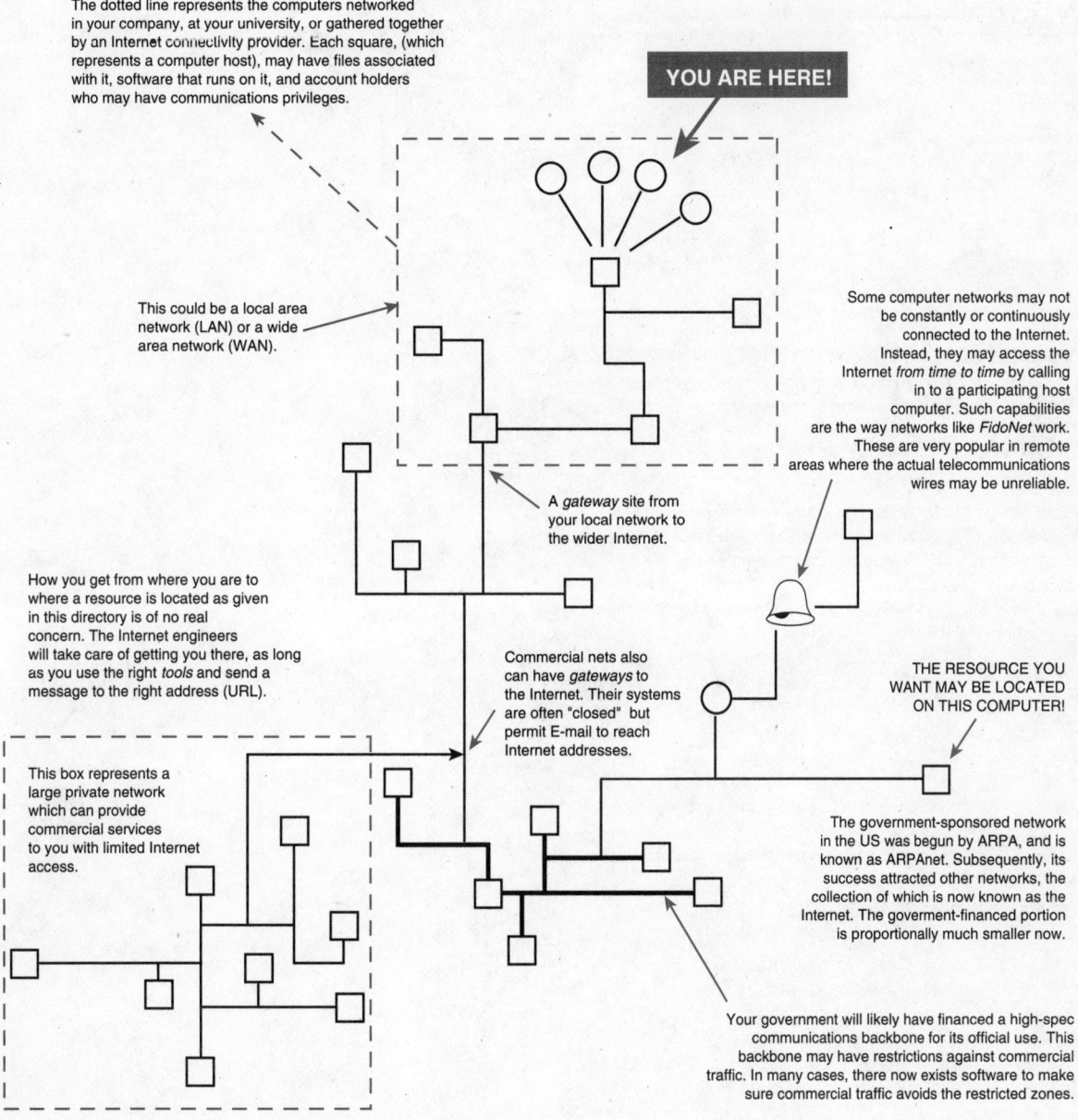

The dotted line represents the computers networked
in your company, at your university, or gathered together
by an Internet connectivity provider. Each square, (which
represents a computer host), may have files associated
with it, software that runs on it, and account holders
who may have communications privileges.

YOU ARE HERE!

This could be a local area
network (LAN) or a wide
area network (WAN).

Some computer networks may not
be constantly or continuously
connected to the Internet.
Instead, they may access the
Internet *from time to time* by calling
in to a participating host
computer. Such capabilities
are the way networks like *FidoNet* work.
These are very popular in remote
areas where the actual telecommunications
wires may be unreliable.

A *gateway* site from
your local network to
the wider Internet.

How you get from where you are to
where a resource is located as given
in this directory is of no real
concern. The Internet engineers
will take care of getting you there, as long
as you use the right *tools* and send a
message to the right address (URL).

Commercial nets also
can have *gateways* to
the Internet. Their systems
are often "closed" but
permit E-mail to reach
Internet addresses.

THE RESOURCE YOU
WANT MAY BE LOCATED
ON THIS COMPUTER!

This box represents a
large private network
which can provide
commercial services
to you with limited Internet
access.

The government-sponsored network
in the US was begun by *ARPA*, and is
known as ARPAnet. Subsequently, its
success attracted other networks, the
collection of which is now known as the
Internet. The goverment-financed portion
is proportionally much smaller now.

Your government will likely have financed a high-spec
communications backbone for its official use. This
backbone may have restrictions against commercial
traffic. In many cases, there now exists software to make
sure commercial traffic avoids the restricted zones.

1

Making the Internet More Accessible

The second edition of *New Riders Official Internet Yellow Pages* has expanded original features and added new ones to make it even easier to access the Internet. These upgraded features continue to set the standard for ease of use among content-specific Internet directories.

With thousands of resources being added to the Internet daily from locations around the world, it has become more crucial and urgent than ever before to have informative and concise guideposts to the content and the value of each Internet resource.

Increased Number of Listings

This second edition contains 45 percent more listings than the first edition. Given the constant increase in substantive information that is coming onto the Internet, our resource specialists and editorial advisory boards felt it imperative to provide a high level of increased coverage in this second edition.

Every effort has been made to mirror the breadth of the Internet's coverage and to take into account the major new content areas of commerce and business. Resources that pertain to people of all ages, cultures, and religious persuasions, as well as those that originate from other countries and focus on international issues have been carefully sought out to ensure broad coverage.

Expanded International Coverage

The largest increase in Internet access is coming from countries outside the United States. This increased international Internet activity is reflected in the quality of resources being put onto the Internet from many countries around the world. Representative examples of international resources include:

CEDAR (Central European Environmental Data Request) Facility

CEDAR (Central European Environmental Data Request) Facility

This gopher site provides information about the environmental and scientific community in Central and Eastern Europe (CEE), with access to environmental information located throughout the world on various international computer networks and hosts.

Keywords: Europe, EEC, Environment

Sponsor: The International Society for Environmental Protection, and The Austrian Federal Ministry for Environment, Youth and Family (BMUJF)

Audience: Environmentalists, Educators, Students, Urban Planners

Contact: cedar-info@cedar.univie.ac.at

Notes: CEDAR Marxergasse 3/20, A-1030 Vienna, Austria Tel.: +43-1-715 58 79

`gopher://pan.cedar.univie.ac.at`

Medical and Biological Research in Laboratories Institutions (Israel)

Medical and Biological Research in Laboratories Institutions (Israel)

A descriptive listing of medical research and diagnostic laboratories in Israel. This site also has information on medical research being carried out in Israeli universities and hospitals.

Keywords: Medical Research, Biological Research, Israel

Audience: Medical Researchers, Biomedical Researchers, Medical Professionals

Profile: MATIMOP, The Israeli Industry Center for Health Care Research And Development, is a non-profit service organization, founded by an Israeli association of hospitals, universities, and other medical researchers, aiming their activities at promoting cooperation of Israeli entrepreneurs and manufacturers with qualified business firms abroad. This gopher details specific medical and biological research projects in progress in every department of every major Israeli health care institution: including universities, The General Federation of

A
B
C
D
E
F
G
H
I
J
K
L
M
N
O
P
Q
R
S
T
U
V
W
X
Y
Z

Labour, public hospitals, government-municipal hospitals, government hospitals, as well as medical and biological research in the Israeli laboratories and research institutes.

Contact: rdinfo@matimop.org.il

`gopher://gopher.matimop.org.il`

Refined Keyword List

The keyword list has been carefully refined to take into account all new resources that have been added.

- Appendix A provides a complete list of keywords under which resources have been organized.

- All resources continue to be listed alphabetically by title, as well as under the keyword headings associated with their content. A new page design makes the directory easier for readers to quickly locate specific resources, while simultaneously discovering other potentially relevant ones.

Expanded Audience Fields

The audience fields also have been refined and expanded to take into account the increasing breadth and complexity of the directory. An additional 300+ audience categories have been added. Appendix B provides a complete list of audience fields under which the resources have been organized.

Expanded Ratings

The criteria for rating entries have been extended and clarified. (See Chapter 3 for detailed information.) A rating system using stars and four levels has been instituted to make each resources value instantly visible and easily understood. This system is called STAR (Subject and Topic Access Rater).

A star rating appears at the top right of the entry. If an entry does not have a star, the resource is either quite narrow in scope and likely to change rapidly in coverage, is experimental, or is in development. The resource also might have come to our attention with insufficient time for a proper evaluation. In the latter case, the resource was judged by us to be of sufficient importance to be listed while the evaluation process is underway.

Expanded Coverage of Resources that Contain Image, Sound, and Multimedia Files

The expanding acceptance of the World Wide Web has resulted in a major increase in the availability of files with images, sounds, and multimedia. The following is an example of this:

Leonardo Electronic Almanac

Leonardo Electronic Almanac

⭐⭐⭐⭐

The Leonardo Electronic Almanac (LEA) is a monthly, edited journal and an electronic archive dedicated to providing current perspectives in the art, science, and technology domains.

Keywords: Art, Multimedia, Music, Electronic Media

Sponsor: International Society for the Arts, Sciences, and Technology

Audience: New Media Artists, Researchers, Art Educators, Art Professionals

Profile: LEA is an international, interdisciplinary forum for people interested in the use of new media in contemporary artistic expression, especially involving 20th century science and technology. Material is contributed by artists, scientists, philosophers and educators. LEA is published by the MIT Press for Leonardo, the International Society for the Arts, Sciences, and Technology (ISAST).

Contact: Craig Harris
           craig@well.sf.ca.us

Details: Costs, Moderated, Images, Sounds, Multimedia

`mail to:journals-orders@mit.edu`

`ftp://mitpress.mit.edu/pub/Leonardo-Elec-Almanac`

Improved Appendices

In this second edition, the appendixes have been improved to offer more information. They are as follows:

- Appendix A—List of Keywords. All keywords are now listed alphabetically, with referenced page numbers alongside.

- Appendix B—List of Audience Fields. All audience fields are now listed alphabetically, with referenced page numbers alongside.

- Appendix C—Internet Service Providers. Appendix C offers a list of Internet access providers.

- Appendix D—Glossary. Provides an expanded glossary of terms.

- Appendix E—Further Readings. This appendix offers an expanded reading list.

- Appendix F—A Whimsical Tour of the Internet. This appendix provides numerous suggestions about where to travel on the Internet

- Appendix G—Making Your Voice Heard. This is a new section that has evolved to make it easy for readers to register reader feedback, to register new listings, update a current listing, recommend a listing, or apply to become an Internet resource evaluator.

- Appendix H—List of Advertisements.

Improved Library Listings

Emphasis has been placed on expanding the coverage of those major Internet library resources that are superior gateways to thousands of other national and international online public access catalogs, known as OPACs. The following is an example:

Libraries

MELVYL

MELVYL is the University of California's catalog of books and periodicals for the university and the California State Library. It also permits access to database systems around the world.

Keywords: Libraries, Databases, OPACS, Internet
Surfers

Audience: General Interest, Students, Teachers,
Librarians

Producer: University of California

Contact: Genny Engel, MELVYL System Users
Services
email:gen@dla.ucop.edu

Profile: The MELVYL system is a centralized
information system that can be reached
from terminals in libraries at all nine
campuses of the University of California.
The system can also be reached by any
terminal or microcomputer with dialup
access to UC computers connected to
the MELVYL system. The system includes
a library card catalog database, a
periodicals database, article citation
databases, and other files.

Details: Free

Notes: All these databases are searched using
the same basic commands.

`telnet://melvyl.ucop.edu`

Advertising

In recognition of the growing presence of
commerce and business on the Internet, we
have decided to allow advertisements to
appear in this directory. In keeping with the
low key approach to the presence of
commercial messages on the Internet,
advertisements have been restricted to an
unobtrusive and informative style. The
intention is to make them subsidiary to the
directory text itself. Advertisements appear in
the directory with a tinted background and
are not rated.

A
B
C
D
E
F
G
H
I
J
K
L
M
N
O
P
Q
R
S
T
U
V
W
X
Y
Z

A
B
C
D
E
F
G
H
I
J
K
L
M
N
O
P
Q
R
S
T
U
V
W
X
Y
Z

2

The Internet Has Resources of Interest to Everyone

A common vision is developing in the US and around the world that views the Internet as a vital purveyor of information. The new resources listed in this second edition have been chosen because they:

- Help to expand the contents of resources into new fields not yet covered in the first edition
- Provide expanded coverage of existing subject areas
- Provide updated or more complete coverage of selected subject fields

Every day, people confront situations in which they are required to find some piece of information. Businesses, individuals, organizations, and schools are learning that they all can benefit from having the ability to access the global resources available on the Internet.

The following examples demonstrate the breadth and depth of content. Thumbing through the directory listings will give readers an immediate feel for the breadth of topics covered from A-Z.

Global Change Information Gateway

Global Change Information Gateway

This gateway was created to address environmental data management issues raised by the US Congress, the Administration, and the advisory arms of the Federal policy community. It contains documents related to the UN conference on Environment and Development.

Keywords: UN, Environment, Development, Oceans, Atmosphere

Audience: Environmentalists, Scientists, Researchers, Environmentalists

Details: Free

Select from menu as appropriate.

`gopher://scilibx.ucsc.edu`

ACM SIGGRAPH Online Bibliography Project

ACM SIGGRAPH Online Bibliography Project

This is a collection of computer-graphics bibliographic references.

Keywords: Multimedia, Interactive, Computer Graphics, Programming

Sponsor: Association of Computing Machinery (ACM), Special Interest Group on Computer Graphics (SIGGRAPH)

Audience: Developers, Designers, Producers, Educators, Programmers, Graphic Artists

Profile: The goal of this project is to maintain an up-to-date database of computer-graphics literature, in a format that is accessible to as many members of the computer-graphics community as possible. The database includes references from conferences and workshops worldwide and from a variety of publications dating back as far as the late-19th century. The majority of the major journals and conference proceedings from the mid-1970s to the present are listed.

Contact: bibadmin@siggraph.org

Details: Free, Moderated, Multimedia

`ftp://siggraph.org/publications`

Many Internet resource sites contain such a variety of resources that, any one group of individuals might access the same resource and be able to find totally different information and adapt it to their own particular advantage.

Astronomy

Astronomical Information on the Internet

This FTP site contains pointers to potentially relevant resources available via the Internet.

Keywords: Astronomy, Astrophysics, Astronomical Software, Astronomical Instrumentation

Sponsor: European Space Organization (ESO) and Space Telescope European Coordinating Facility (ST-ECF)

Audience: Astronomers, Physicists, Students (college, graduate), Educators

Profile: This is the entry point for most astronomical resources available online categorized by function. More than 100 resources are accessible concerning general astronomical information, software, and publications. The following are just a few examples of the resources available as of January 1994:

- Online publications from CERN, SISSA, STSCI, NASA, PASP, Cfa, and so on.
- Conferences and meetings
- Metereological information
- Access to over 30 observatories and institutes
- Data archives from over 20 previous and current satellite missions, observatories, and astronomy data centers
- Astronomical images
- Astronomical software
- Jobs

Contact: Hans-Martin Adorf
adorf@eso.org

Details: Free, Moderated; Image, Sound, and Multimedia files available.

`ftp://ecf.hq.eso.org/pub/WWW/astro-resources.html`

Business and Commerce Come to the Internet

The Internet has started to make substantive changes to conventional ways of doing business. However there is still a long way to go before it becomes a place where people feel comfortable doing business and buying or selling products and services. The issues of security, private fiscal transactions, and appropriate pricing mechanisms need to be resolved before the Internet market place fulfills its global potential.

For many companies, the Internet already represents a good, cheap communications link to geographically distant work sites. Technology companies (and increasingly, other types of companies), see the Internet as providing an excellent communications channel between customers and vendors, allowing for expanded and improved customer support, at the same time as it enables operational efficiencies. Publishers by the hundreds (self-publishers and professional publishers alike), and companies with consumer products and services, are making their catalogs available on the Internet, allowing anyone with an Internet connection to peruse them and order desired titles, products and services. Some, like The Online Bookstore, even make the complete text of many books available online.

Online Books

Online BookStore (OBS)

★ ★ ★

Offers full text (fiction and nonfiction) in a variety of electronic formats, free and for a fee.

Keywords: Online Books, Books, ShareWord, Fiction, Nonfiction Books

Sponsor: Editorial Inc./OBS

Audience: General Public, Reading Enthusiasts

Profile: Started in 1992, the OBS offers a variety of full-text titles.

Contact: Laura Fillmore
laura@editorial.com

Details: Costs, Moderated, Images, Multimedia

User Info: To subscribe to the list, send an e-mail message requesting a subscription to the URL address below.

`http://marketplace.com/0/obs`

No single marketing, or advertising channel is going to reach 100 percent of the Internet market; but even a fraction of that market can represent millions of people. Those companies who can quickly master the rules of online commerce and find a niche market to exploit, can immediately do very good business on the Internet. Many are already doing so.

In line with this growing business emphasis, many commercial sites have been the focus of close scrutiny by other companies, to analyze and keep a close eye on what is succeeding and why. At this time, some companies have developed "home pages" (the opening menu item at all www sites). They often contain a solid body of information of general business interest and are also equipped with instrumentation by which the home page producer can learn how many searches page have been made to the home . (In Chapter 7, the section "Understanding Internet Addresses" will help to clarify further the type of information one can glean from an Internet (URL) address.) An example of a company's home page is given below.

AT&T

AT&T Bell Laboratories WWW Information Page

★ ★

This web site provides information on research and development at AT&T Bell Laboratories.

Keywords: Telecommunications, Technology, AT&T, Cellular Technology

Sponsor: AT&T Bell Laboratories

Audience: Engineers, Educators, Communications

Specialists

Contact: webmaster@research.att.com

Details: Free

`http://www.research.att.com`

Advertising Comes to the Internet

Fun, games, hobbies, sports, and recreation are to be found in abundance on the Internet.

As resistance to traditional advertising on the part of Internet users diminishes, new opportunities for advertising are increasing. The advantages for advertising on the Internet are the opportunity to present more information—unlike advertisements in traditional media. The Internet culture encourages vendors to offer significant amounts of information about the product or service being advertised. There is no lead time between the placement of an ad and its being immediately received by an enormous percent market.

Many shopping malls are beginning to spring up on the Internet. An example of one is shown below. These shopping malls offer a series of services, such as press release services and are busy developing other innovative ways to curry favor with businesses and Internet browsers alike.

Internet Shopping Network

Internet Shopping Network

A shopping network on the Infobahn

Keywords: Business, Electronic Commerce

Sponsor: Internet Shopping Network

Audience: Business Users, Commercial Internet Users, General Public

Profile: The Internet Shopping Network aims to conduct research and develop products and services that commercialize the Internet, for the purpose of retailing and mass merchandising. The stores within this network offer approximately 20,000 products from 1000 vendors.

`http://www.internet.net`

Telemedia, Networks, and Systems Group

Telemedia, Networks, and Systems Group

A list of commercial services on the Web (and Net).

Keywords: Business, Electronic Commerce

Sponsor: MIT Laboratory for Computer Science, Cambridge, MA 02139

Audience: Business Professionals, Commercial Internet Users, General Public

Profile: This list of commercial Internet services is well-maintained and frequently updated.

Contact: hhh@mit.edu

`http://tns-www.lcs.mit.edu/`
`commerce.html`

`http://tns-www.lcs.mit.edu`

Resources of Interest to . . . Businesses

Virtually any resource can be viewed as having potentially useful business applications, and useful market intelligence. The following Internet resources point to the variety of information that can be found.

Business

Business News-Singapore

This gopher site focuses on business in Singapore.

Keywords: Singapore, Economics, Business

Audience: Economists, Business Professionals

Details: Free

`gopher://gopher.cic.net/11/e-serials/`
`alphabetic/b/business-news`

`http://gopher.cic.net`

Environment

ESRI (Environmental Systems Research Institute)

Environmental Systems Research Institute, Inc. is the world leader in GIS technology. ARC/INFO is ESRI's powerful and flexible flagship GIS software.

Keywords: Geographic Information Systems (GIS), Environment, Software, Computers

Audience: Geographers, Environmentalists, Computer Users

Details: Costs

For product information, call (909) 793-2853, X1475.

For training information, call (909) 793-2853, X1585, or fax (909) 793-5953.

`mailto:ajackson@esri.com`

Sun Microsystems, Inc.

Sun Microsystems, Inc.

This site provides a directory of Sun Microsystems products and services, including a company profile, announcements, financial statements, marketing reports, and international sales and support access.

Keywords: Computer Systems, Sun Microsystems

Sponsor: Sun Microsystems, Inc., Mountain View, California, USA

Audience: Sun Microsystems Users

Profile: Languages: English

Contact: webmaster@sun.com.

Details: Free

`http://www.sun.com`

Resources of Interest to . . . People of All Ages and Cultures

With people from all over the world rushing on to the Internet, it is important to realize that its content mirrors that of the people who use it.

One can discover and access thousands of diverse resources from all over the world, as exemplified below:

Chicano Culture

Chicano/LatinoNet

An electronic mechanism that brings together Chicano/Latino research, as well as linguistic minority and educational research efforts being carried out at the University of California and elsewhere. It serves as a gateway between faculty, staff, and students who are engaged in research and curricular efforts in these areas.

Keywords: Culture, Race, Hispanics

Sponsor: Chicano Studies Research Center, University of California at Los Angeles

Audience: Students, Mexican-Americans, Latinos

Contact: Richard Chabran Chabran@latino.sscnet.ucla.ed

Details: Free

`gopher://latino.sscnet.ucla.edu`

un.wcw.doc.eng

This is a read-only conference comprised of official UN documents for the United Nations Fourth World Conference on Women: Action for Equality, Development and Peace, scheduled to take place at the Beijing International Convention Center, Beijing, China, from 4-15 September 1995. The documents are provided by the official Conference Secretariat, are posted as received by the UN Non-Governmental Liaison Service (NGLS).

Keywords: Women, Development (International), Peace, UN, World Conference on Women

Audience: Women, Activists, Non-Governmental Organizations, Feminists

Contact: United Nations Non-Governmental Liaison Service/Edie Farwell ngls@igc.apc.org, efarwell@igc.apc.org

Details: Costs, Moderated

User Info: Establish an account on the nearest APC node. Login, type c for conferences, then type go un.wcw.doc.eng.

For information on the nearest APC node, contact:
APC International Secretariat IBASE
E-mail: apcadmin@apc.org

`telnet://igc.apc.org`

NativeNet

NativeNet

Provides information about and discusses issues relating to indigenous people around the world, including threats to their cultures and habitats (for example, rainforests).

Keywords: Indigenous People, Environment, Anthroplogy

Audience: Anthropologists, Environmentalists, Indigenous People

Contact: Gary S. Trujillo gst@gnosys.svle.ma.us

Details: Free

User info: To subscribe to the list, send an e-mail message requesting a subscription to the URL address below.

`mailto:gst@gnosys.svle.ma.us`

Resources of Interest to . . . Disabled

Many resources on the Internet are especially useful for disabled people. Examples of such resources are:

Cornucopia of Disability Information (CODI)

Cornucopia of Disability Information (CODI)

★★★

A large collection of disability-related information available via gopher.

Keywords: Disabilities, Health

Sponsor: State University of New York (SUNY) at Buffalo

Audience: Disabled People, Activists, Rehabilitation Counselors, Health Care Professionals

Profile: This site provides a wide variety of information resources concerning people with disabilities, ranging from legal information to a directory of computer resources aimed at the disabled consumer. Includes state, local, and national information and government documents such as the Americans with Disabilities Act. Also has links to many other related resources on the Internet, such as the National Rehabilitation Information Center.

Contact: Jay Leavitt
leavitt@ubvmsb.cc.buffalo.edu

`gopher://val-dor.cc.buffalo.edu`

Disability Information

★★★★

A collection of information about and links to sources of disability-related information from around the world. Includes archives of many related mailing lists and electronic newsletters, as well as legal and technical help for the disabled, and information about the Parkinson's Disease Information Exchange Network.

Keywords: Disabilities, Health, Diseases

Sponsor: Computing & Information Services at Texas A&M University, Galveston, Texas, USA

Audience: Disabled People, Rehabilitation Counselors, Health Care Professionals, Activists

Contact: Computing & Information Services at Texas A&M University
gopher@tamu.edu

`gopher://gopher.tamu.edu/.dir/disability.dir`

National Library of Medicine Gopher

World Health Organization (WHO)

★★★★

This gopher provides information about the National Library of Medicine, the world's largest single-topic library.

Keywords: Medicine, Health, World Health

Sponsor: National Library of Medicine, Massachusetts

World Health Organization, Geneva, Switzerland

Audience: Health-care Professionals, Medical Professionals, Researchers

Profile: The National Library of Medicine (NLM) cares for over 4.5 million holdings (inncluding books, journals, reports, manuscripts, and audio-visual items). The NLM offers extensive online information services dealing with clinical care, toxicology, environmental health, and basic biomedical research, It has several active research and development components, including an extramural grants program, houses an extensive history of medicine collection, and provides several programs designed to improve the nation's medical library system.

Contact: R. P. C. Rodgers
rodgers@nlm.nih.gov
akazawa@who.ch

Details: Free

`gopher://el-gopher.med.utah.edu`

`gopher://gopher.who.ch`

Resources of Interest to . . . Children and Teachers

As education moves into the 21st century students of all age groups and ability levels (and their teachers) will find enormous quantities of resources on the Internet to:

- Support independent as well as cooperative learning efforts

- Provide tools and projects to promote connectivity with classrooms and individuals worldwide

- Supply information about any topic or curriculum issue

K12Net is an example of a strong educational resources. It is a loosely organized network of school-based electronic bulletin board systems throughout North America, Australia,

Europe, and the former USSR, which share curriculum-related conferences, making them available to students and educators at no cost. Other examples of the breadth and depth of educational resources accessible over the Internet are:

EDNET

EDNET

★★★★

This forum explores the educational potential of the Internet.

Keywords: Education, Internet

Audience: Students, Educators

Profile: This independent, unmoderated mailing-list interest group is open and free of charge to all participants. Ednet links educators with common interests, and introduces students to a number of fields and sources of information, while offering criticism and suggestions.

Contact: Prescott Smith
pgsmith@educ.umass.edu

Details: Free

User info: To subscribe to the list, send an e-mail message to the address shown below consisting of a single line reading:

SUB Ednet YourFirstName YourLastName

To send a message to the entire list, address it to:
ednet@nic.umass.edu.

`gopher://ericir.syr.edu/00/AskERIC/FullText/Lists/Messages/`

`EDNET-List/README`

`mailto:listserv@nic.umass.edu`

K12 Net

K12 Net

★

Decentralized network of school-based bulletin board systems (BBSs).

Keywords: Education (K-12), Networks

Audience: Educators (K-12), School Children

Profile: K12 Net provides millions of teachers, students, and parents in metropolitan and rural areas throughout the world with the ability to meet and talk with each other to discuss educational issues, exchange information, and share resources on a global scale.

Contact: Jack Crawford, Janet Murray

jack@k12net.org or jmurray@psg.com

Details: Free

`gopher://woonext.dsrd.ornl.gov/11/Docs/k12net`

Today students range in all ages, with many older adults continuing in life-long education or retraining. Administrators, parents, teachers, and educational planners will find here the tools needed to transform their schools into environments that avail themselves of the Information Age with vital forums in cyberspace where ideas can be explored, designs shared, and solutions developed.

Resources of Interest to . . . Researchers, Academics, and the Intellectually Curious

The Internet was founded, originally, to provide operational efficiencies to researcher and academics so they could connect with each other at various remote sites and laboratories. As the Internet grew, this successful pattern was replicated by countries around the world and has resulted in the Internet becoming the single largest network in the world.

The resources now available over the Internet have the potential to fulfill a researcher's highest aspirations or create their worst nightmare. A cyberspace "heaven and hell" where the information one seeks is probably there, but the effort to find it is often equivalent to that needed to find a needle in a haystack!

Further examples of the international nature of many Internet resources are shown below.

LabStat

LabStat

The public database of the Bureau of Labor Statistics.

Keywords:	Economics, Labor, Census Data
Sponsor:	United States Government, Bureau of Labor Statistics
Audience:	General Public, Statisticians, Researchers
Profile:	LABSTAT provides current and historical data, as well as numerous press releases. This site is composed of individual databases (in flat file format) corresponding to each of 26 surveys.
Contact:	labstat.helpdesk@bls.gov.
Details:	Free
	Login: anonymous; use e-mail address as password.

Notes:	For each news release published by the Bureau of Labor Statistics, the two most current are stored in the /news.release directory. The documentation provides a list of the abbreviations used to identify the news releases, and a description of the sub-directories available to the user.

`ftp://stats.bls.gov`

The Growth of Online Public Access Catalogs (OPACS)

A recent development within the library community has been the rush to put library catalogs online, (known as OPACS). Libraries have for the past several years engaged themselves in the process of converting paper library card catalog systems to computerized ones. The advent of being able to access OPACS on the Internet allows libraries to reach beyond their normal constituencies, and provide considerably more flexible searching capabilities than were available from the paper card catalogs. This makes their collections accessible to the widest number of researchers, academics, and the intellectually curious from anywhere in the world.

Following is the listing for the Internet Library of Congress Catalog. Having access to this, on one's computer means having the collections catalog of the largest library in the world at one's desk. At present, it does not mean you have actual books themselves, although efforts to provide textual matter behind the catalog citations are taking place in various experimental sites in many libraries around the world.

The most visible of the online public access catalogs (OPACs) are contained in the HYTELNET list and the Yale Directory of Internet Libraries. Between these two, alone, there is a huge amount of information readily accessible to anyone with telnet or gopher capabilities on their computer.

Yale Directory of Internet Libraries is a comprehensive listing of worldwide libraries (of which HYTELNET is subset) that provides connection information for all its entries (usually automatic-just hit return) via telnet or gopher and provides subject information for many of its entries, and for all of its major academic research entries.

HYTELNET

HYTELNET

A shareware application database directory to libraries

Keywords:	Computer Systems, Libraries, Shareware
Audience:	General Audience
Profile:	HYTELNET is a guide to library catalogs from the Americas, Europe
Contact:	Peter Scott
aa375@freenet.carleton.ca	
Details:	Free
Notes:	HYTELNET is in English, but the interface to some international

`gopher://gophlib@gopher.yale.edu`

Yale Directory of Internet Libraries

Yale Directory of Internet Libraries

An online directory of international library catalogs with

Keywords:	Libraries
Sponsor:	Yale University, New Haven, Connecticut, USA
Audience:	General Audience
Profile:	The Yale Directory of Internet Libraries is a comprehensive
Notes:	The Yale Directory of Internet Libraries is in English, but the

`gopher://gophlib@gopher.yale.edu`

Resources of Interest to...Cybernauts of All Persuasions.

The diversity of resources can be clearly seen in Appendix G, "A Whimsical Tour of the Internet." We hope you will enjoy this compilation as a fun expression of some of the more lighthearted directory listings to be found among these pages.

Suffice it to say that whatever your interests, whatever your concerns, wherever your imagination leads you, the Internet is ready to satisfy your curiosity and to empower you with information you can put to productive, entertaining, educational, or profitable use.

The following examples should serve to wet anyone's appetite for information.

Astronomy

Center for Extreme Ultraviolet Astrophysics

A department of the University of California at Berkeley devoted to research in extreme ultraviolet astronomy. It is the ground-based institution of EUVE (the Extreme Ultraviolet Explorer), a NASA satellite launched in 1992.

Keywords: Astronomy, Astrophysics, EUVE, NASA, Satellite

Sponsor: NASA and University of California at Berkeley

Audience: Astronomers, Astrophysicists

Profile: Provides access to details about the EUVE Guest Observer (EGO) Center, the EUVE Public Archive of Mission Data and Information, satellite operation information, and so on. The EUVE Guest Observer Center provides information, software, and data to EUVE Guest Observers.

Contact: egoinfo@cea.berkeley.edu
archive@cea.berkeley.edu

Details: Free

`http://cea-ftp.cea.berkeley.edu`

UC Berkeley Museum of Paleontology and the WWW Subway

UC Berkeley Museum of Paleontology and the WWW Subway

This web site provides a multimedia museum display from UC Berkeley's Museum of Paleontology. Also features an interactive Subway, a tool linking users to other museums and WWW sites around the world.

Keywords: WWW, Museums, Paleontology

Sponsor: University of California at Berkeley, Museum of Paleontology, Berkeley, California, USA

Audience: Paleontologists, Internet Surfers, General Public

Contact: David Polly, Robert Guralnick
davip@ucmp1.berkeley.edu
robg@fossil.berkeley.edu

`http://ucmp1.berkeley.edu/subway.html`

Women

Women's Wire

Women's Wire is an online interactive network focusing on women's issues and interests.

Keywords: Networking, Women's Issues, Online Services

Audience: Women, Internet Users

Profile: This service acts as an international clearinghouse for resources and networking on a broad range of topics including news, politics, careers, education, parenting, health, and arts. Provides e-mail and access to thousands of resources, including Usenet newsgroups.

Details: Costs

Access via an easy-to-use graphical interface for Macintosh and Windows platforms, or a text-based interface for DOS and Unix platforms. Local access numbers available throughout the US and in most countries.

`mailto:info@wwire.net`

MUDs

MUD

A discussion list for the exchange of information about new and recommended Multiuser Dungeons and Dragons (MUDs).

Keywords: MUDs, Games

Audience: MUD Users

Contact: Joseph Wisdom
jwisdom@gnu.ai.mit.edu

Details: Free

User Info: To subscribe to the list, send an e-mail message requesting subscription to the URL address below.

`mailto:jwisdom@gnu.ai.mit.edu`

alt.romance.chat

alt.romance.chat

A Usenet newsgroup providing discussion about the romantic side of love.

Keywords: Chat Groups, Romance

Audience: General Public

User Info: To subscribe to this Usenet newsgroup, you need access to a newsreader.

`news:alt.romance.chat`

rec.arts.tv

rec.arts.tv

A Usenet newsgroup providing information and discussion about past and present TV shows and related trivia.

Keywords: Television, Trivia

Audience: General Public, Television Viewers, Trivia Enthusiasts

User Info: To subscribe to this Usenet newsgroup, you need access to a newsreader.

`news:rec.arts.tv`

Online Career Center

Online Career Center

The Online Career Center gopher provides access to job listings and employment information to member companies and to the public.

Keywords: Employment, Internships

Sponsor: Online Career Center

Audience: Job Seekers

Profile: Online Career Center is a not-for-profit organization funded by its member companies. It is devoted to distributing and exchanging employment and career information between its member companies, human resource professionals, and perspective employees.

Contact: OCC Operator
occ@msen.com

`gopher://gopher.msen.com`

Blues

Blues-L

A mailing list for the discussion of Blues music and the culture surrounding the genre of the Blues.

Keywords: Blues Music, Musical Genres

Audience: Blues Enthusiasts

Contact: listserv@brownvm.brown.edu

Details: Free

User Info: To subscribe to the list, send an e-mail message to the URL address below, consisting of a single line reading:

SUB blues-l YourFirstName YourLastName

To send a message to the entire list, address it to:
blues-l@brownvm.brown.edu

Notes: To receive the list in digest form: once you get acknowledgment from the listserver that you are on the list, send another message to the URL address below with the message:

SET Blues-L Dig

mailto:listserv@brownvm.brown.edu

Cards

Cards

This list is for people interested in collecting, speculating, and investing in baseball, football, basketball, hockey, and other trading cards and/or memorabilia. Discussion and want/sell lists are welcome.

Keywords: Trading Cards, Collectibiles, Memorabilia

Audience: Sports Card Collectors, Sports Card Traders, Memorabilia Collectors

Contact: Keane Arase
cards-request@tanstaafl.uchicago.edu

Details: Free

To subscribe to the list, send an e-mail message requesting a subscription to the URL address below.

To send a message to the entire list, address it to:cards@tanstaafl.uchicago.edu

Notes: The list is open to anyone.

mailto:cards-request@tanstaafl.uchicago.edu

3

The Role of the Editorial Advisory Boards

The second edition of *The New Riders Official Internet Yellow Pages* includes an expanded and simplified star rating system for Internet resources. These stars act as guides to the size and relative importance of each resource.

Criteria developed in cooperation with our Editorial Advisory Boards has been tailored for rating specific varieties of Internet data resources. Those that apply, for example, to a Gopher-compliant database will not necessarily apply to an electronic discussion group. Tailored ratings help you save time, and focus on those listings that are most likely to help you keep up-to-date when you're in a hurry. Information resources on the Internet adjust rapidly to the real world—that means they are continually changing. By concentrating on the resources ranked with a high number of stars, the reader who is pressed for time will find the most comprehensive or dynamic sources of information.

About Our Editorial Advisory Boards

Because the emphasis (and distinguishing feature) of this directory is on the content and value of Internet resources, the Editorial Advisory Boards, composed of recognized specialists in specific subject areas, has been formed to help evaluate the listings selected for publication in this directory.

Getting expert advice about the information you find is always helpful, but often not readily available. Being confident in the reliability of information on an expanding Internet may be more difficult as the Internet includes an ever-expanding array. If you know a specific data provider or the author of the materials you chose to download to your computer, you may feel comfortable about the reliability of the information. If you, as millions of other Internet users, will be referring to resources about which you actually know very little about, then a guide to help you may be crucial. In many instances, predictably, you will have no idea whether the information available is valid, biased, complete, or trustworthy.

In the print world, scientific publishers have developed mechanisms for "peer review," by which articles and manuscripts were subjected to a rigorous evaluation process by the author's peers who are experts in the subject. This process ensured objectivity and critical judgment.

Similar conventions can be applied to the evaluation of Internet resources. Members of the Editorial Advisory Boards are asked to help evaluate Internet resources within their specific areas of expertise. It is intended that the combined judgments of such experts will help save you time. The STAR (H) ratings system informs you of the relative merit assigned a resource.

Gaining the cooperation of external specialist evaluators is an expanding and ongoing process because the evaluation and ranking of resources is one of the most important contributions that can be made to fulfill the promise of the Internet to its various constituencies.

Coverage

Because it would be impractical to establish advisory boards for all the keywords under which individual listings may be found, "umbrella" fields have been established. These are the following:

- Business
- Communications
- Economy
- Education
- Energy
- Engineering
- Government and Politics
- Health and Family
- Humanities and Arts
- Information Science
- International Affairs
- Law
- Life Sciences
- Materials Sciences and Technology
- Physical Sciences
- Popular Culture
- Recreation and Sports
- Religion and Spirituality
- Science (General)
- Social and Behavioral Sciences

The process of evaluating Internet resources "by hand," so to speak, is laborious, but we feel there is no technological substitute for it. Some listings arrived too late for formal review, but were deemed important enough to be included in the directory; these listings have no stars.

The Rating System

Working with our Editorial Advisory Boards, we have developed criteria for rating specific varieties of Internet data resources; this is particularly important as the criteria that is relevant, for example, to a gopher compliant database will not necessarily apply to an electronic discussion group. Tailored ratings help you save time, and allow you to focus on those listings that are most likely to keep you up-to-date.

If a resource has been given a single STAR ★, it has been judged important enough to be included in our directory. A single star designation usually indicates that the information provided in the resource is:

- quite specific in scope
- likely to change rapidly in coverage
- under development

The single STAR ★ ratings are important and valuable resources, and often represent the wide range of coverage represented by Internet resources. The following examples testify to this.

Multimedia

Multimedia, Telecommunications, and Art Project

A project to promote online art that will be implemented as gopher site and on the World-Wide Web.

Keywords: Multimedia, Electronic Art, Telecommunications

Sponsor: CISR (Centre for Image and Sound Research), Vancouver, B.C., Canada

Audience: Artists, Writers

Contact: Derek Dowden
Derek_Dowden@mindlink.bc.ca

For more information, send an e-mail message to the URL address below.

Details: Free

`mailto:Derek_Dowden@mindlink.bc.ca`

rec.pets

rec.pets

A Usenet newsgroup providing information and discussion about pets and pet care.

Keywords: Pets, Animals

Audience: Pet Owners

To subscribe to this Usenet newsgroup, you need access to a newsreader.

`news:rec.pets`

Economics

CERRO (Central European Regional Research Organization)

CERRO provides access to information about the economic restructuring of Central Europe, including a discussion list, papers, news summaries, and pointers to other gophers in Central Europe.

Keywords: Central Europe, Economics, News

Audience: Economists, Researchers, Journalists

Contact: gunther.maier@wu-wien.ac.at

Details: Free

`gopher://osiris.wu.wein.ac.at`

Evaluation Criteria

Other resources may be given higher ratings. This will indicate that they provide access to proportionally larger amounts of information or are resources of significance. They might:

- contain essential or unique information
- have been developed in a particularly careful way
- be the product of established and reputable entities

If a resource has been assigned a greater number of stars, this means that the Editorial Advisory Boards found the following:

- the resource is more focused or part of a clearly defined subject area
- the resource has important institutional backing
- the resource contained essential or unique information

The following are examples:

Astrophysics

Center for Extreme Ultraviolet Astrophysics

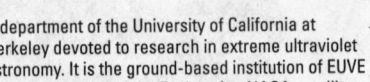

A department of the University of California at Berkeley devoted to research in extreme ultraviolet astronomy. It is the ground-based institution of EUVE (the Extreme Ultraviolet Explorer), a NASA satellite launched in 1992.

Keywords: Astronomy, Astrophysics, EUVE, NASA, Satellite

Sponsor: NASA and University of California at Berkeley

Audience: Astronomers, Astrophysicists

Profile: Provides access to details about the EUVE Guest Observer (EGO) Center, the EUVE Public Archive of Mission Data and Information, satellite operation information, and so on. The EUVE Guest Observer Center provides information, software, and data to EUVE Guest Observers.

Contact: egoinfo@cea.berkeley.edu, archive@cea.berkeley.edu

Details: Free

`http://cea-ftp.cea.berkeley.edu/`

The highest, or 4-star, rating is reserved for resources of truly outstanding merit. Information in these resources might:

- contain unique information not found anywhere else
- be prepared by institutions or agencies of considerable stature
- point to a wide range of additional resources on the Internet
- consist of layer upon layer of detailed information about a given topic

The following are some examples of 4-star Internet resources, which are important both as resources and as pointers to hundreds of other related materials and files.

Politics

White House Information Service

An outstanding database of current White House information, from 1992 to the present.

Keywords: White House, Politics, President (US), Database

Sponsor: Texas A & M University

Audience: General Public

Profile: Much of the older information on this site was obtained from the clinton@marist.bitnet listserv list or the alt.politics.clinton Usenet newsgroup, both of which receive the information indirectly via the MIT White House information server. Newer and current material is received directly from the MIT distribution list. The menu includes a searchable database and headings such as Domestic Affairs (Health Care, Technology, and so on), Press Briefings and Conferences, the President's Daily Schedule, and many more.

Contact: whadmin@tamu.edu

Details: Free

```
gopher://tamuts.tamu.edu/11/.dir/
president.dir
```

Black/African Related Online Information

Black/African Related Online Information

This is a list of online information storage sites that contain a significant amount of information pertaining to Black or African people, culture, and issues around the world.

Keywords: Culture, Race, Africa, African Studies

Sponsor: AfriInfo

Audience: Students, African-Americans, Africans

Contact: McGee

Contact: mcgee@epsilon.eecs.nwu.edu

Details: Free

```
ftp://ftp.netcom.com/pub/amcgee/
my_african_related_lists/afrisite.msg
```

Music Resources

University of California Santa Barbara Virtual Library

This source provides detailed lists of Internet music resources.

Keywords: Music Resources

Sponsor: University of California at Santa Barbara

Audience: Musicians

Profile: This site contains lists pointing to music resources on the Internet, including ftp sites, gopher servers, newsgroups, and list servers.

Details: Free

Path is The Subject Collections/The Arts Collections/Music

```
gopher://ucsbuxa.ucsb.edu
```

4

Getting Connected: What Are the Basics?

In theory, getting connected to the Internet is relatively easy. It can, however, be frustrating. In this chapter, we've tried to organize the information you'll need to begin accessing the Internet with a minimum of frustration.

The essential components of connecting to the Internet are not complicated. You will need the following:

- Hardware (personal computer, modem, and hard drive)
- Software (telecommunications software, TCP/IP software, and virus protection software)
- Access to the Internet

Hardware

- A personal computer. This can be of any size or type. It doesn't need to be a fancy model with bells and whistles—a computer that can run a conventional communications program will suffice.

- A modem. This device converts what is typed on a personal computer into signals that can be transmitted across standard telephone wires or data lines. (Modems usually are distinguished by their speed of transmission, which is rated at bits per second, or baud rate. The higher the baud rate, the faster the transmission.)

  If you simply intend to exchange e-mail, a modem with relatively low transmission speeds, like 2400 baud will suffice. Today's modems, however, deliver considerable functionality for their price. Purchasing a modem with the highest available baud rate you can afford is advisable. This means that the transferring and receiving of files can be done much more quickly.

- A hard drive. The hard drive is where you store the files of information taken off the Internet. Buying a hard drive with the most capacity is highly advisable. If you become active in one or more discussion groups, you will quickly find yourself storing a large number of messages. It is likely that the more interesting and complex files and any image or sound files will take up a great deal of space. The prices of hard-disk storage have dropped substantially, and sizes formerly reserved for institutional use (1 gigabyte or more) are now popular for individual purchase.

Software

- A telecommunications program. Communications programs are software programs that permit your computer to send data across a modem. In an increasing number of business and office environments, local area networks (LANS) are being established, through which Internet access is available. If you work from home, you will need a software program to permit your home computer to make a phone connection across telephone lines to another computer connected directly to the Internet.

  Frequently, the people who specialize in modems can recommend an appropriate communications software program. They also can answer questions about setup and provide initial trouble-shooting help.

- TCP/IP software. Standard communications programs are useful for connecting your computer to a variety of online services and bulletin board systems. They also make it possible to connect your computer to other computers.

  If you intend to spend much time on the Internet, however, you will need an additional set of enabling software tools. This is the software that permits the transmissions from your computer to conform to the widely adopted standard for communicating on the Internet. This is known as TCP/IP (Transfer Control Protocol/Internet Protocol). Check the Internet Resources listed in this directory to help you understand how to get the software tools you need.

  Fortunately, a variety of packages are available; many are inexpensive, and many are even free. Check with your software vendor about the specific programs you will need for your model computer. Ask for the software that will help you establish a SLIP (Serial Line Internet Protocol) or a PPP (Point-to-Point) connection to the Internet. Also look around for various commercially available packages that include all the software you will need for Internet connectivity. Increasingly, the IP tools come bundled with the major communications software packages that are available, or they can be provided by your Internet service provider.

- Virus Protection Software. Computer viruses can be conveyed on program files that are downloaded to your computer. Because the Internet holds many programs that will be of interest to you, it is wise to purchase high-quality virus protection software. This software scans incoming files and uses a variety of methods to identify files that might harbor viruses that could harm or disable your computer. No virus protection software is foolproof, so you should be cautious about the files you download onto your hard disk. Caution, coupled with high-quality virus protection software, can protect your investment.

Access to the Internet

All Internet users must establish an Internet address. To do so, you must contact a company specializing in providing Internet communications access. Known as Internet Providers, many are listed in Appendix C of this directory. You must pay one of the Internet providers a monthly fee for an electronic account. (This is just like having to pay the phone company for your telephone number.)

Electronic accounts also can be obtained from universities or research institutions (if you happen to be affiliated with one), or from businesses (many companies are already installing or investigating electronic networking). You might want to check these sources, as they might be able to supply you with additional information and assistance for your particular set of requirements.

Differences Between Providers

When looking around for an authorized access account to the Internet, it is important to be aware that some electronic network providers give subscribers access to a suite of services easily confused with the real Internet. Some might provide restricted gateways to the Internet, but not to the full suite of Internet access tools. Be sure to know what you are getting as you investigate the various access points to the Internet.

There is tremendous ongoing volatility in the marketplace for online connectivity and services. There are, however, identifiable differences among certain providers. One group of companies only provides Internet connectivity, another group provides access to a set of individual online databases, and yet another group provides proprietary online

database access *and* a minimum of e-mail access to the Internet. These differences can be confusing, since many of the services seem to overlap.

- Internet Providers. Providers who were once primarily interested in the technical aspects of providing Internet connectivity exclusively to institutions are now beginning to compete with one another for the individual customer. This means that they are providing a greater degree of customer service, troubleshooting, software installation advice, and general hand-holding. These are the companies providing basic access.

- Service Providers. Companies like CompuServ, America Online, GEnie, and Prodigy (all headquartered in the US), Minitel (headquartered in France), and other producers in other countries provide broad menus of electronic services, which they package in an overall user-interface. These companies may not, however, actually be on the Internet. In most cases, they still only provide e-mail access to the Internet, allowing customers to send and receive electronic mail from anyone anywhere on the Internet. This is called providing a gateway to the Internet.

  Minitel in France allows full access to the Internet from Minitel, but not vice versa. As of the time of this writing, Delphi is the only commercial access provider with a full Internet gateway. CompuServ has just given notice that it will also be going to full Internet connectivity. America Online has a partial gateway. It is obvious that the trend is for commercial providers to open up more gateways to the Internet.

- Proprietary Database Vendors. These are companies like Dialog, Data Star, Questel, Orbit, Mead (Nexis/Lexis), and CD Plus (now part of CD Plus).

Business Connectivity

Businesses wanting to use the Internet for commercial or operational advantage must understand the types of available connections to the Internet. While most individual consumers will be satisfied with a SLIP connection, businesses may require greater throughput speeds, particularly if they want to connect their companys local area networks (and thus provide Internet access to all of their employees at one time.)

Universities and large corporations rent dedicated lines from the phone company that are directly connected to the Internet. These lines come in different categories, depending on the speed with which communications can be passed through the wires. This is commonly described as bandwidth. The smallest of these is a 56 KB line, but you can also lease 128 KB transmission capability, all the way up to T1 and T3 speeds.

The educational aspects of Internet connectivity have also spurred an interest in ISDN (Integrated Switching Data Network), which has the capability to provide both data and video channels. The prices for these connections vary enormously (in one sample quotation, including distance education, prices ranged from $45 to $2,500 per month). It is worth spending some time comparing services and vendors with your requirements and needs to obtain the right level of service and connectivity for the best price.

Client/Server Programs

The way one works on a personal computer and the way one works on the Internet are different. Because these differences are fundamental to understanding how the Internet works, we want to close this chapter by addressing some of them.

People used to working with personal computers know that their application programs reside on their computers hard disk and that document files are created every time a Save command is issued. The interaction from the user to the program and from the program to the saved documents seems instantaneous even if it actually isn't.

The Internet's various computer nodes are connected to disks containing numerous programs. Each of the computer nodes is governed by a set of programs. On the Internet, you have the option of running a local program, downloading a program from a remote computer, or, in some cases, actually running a program on a distant computer. This is the case, for example, with the online public access library catalogs (OPACs) in which the actual searching of a very large library database is done by a program located at the site of the OPAC.

For many activities, it doesn't matter whether a program is available locally or at a distance, but imagine the scale of the Internet and the millions of users sending commands and instructions to distant programs, and you can envision some of the traffic bottlenecks and time lags that could result.

This situation has led to the development of a variety of software programs known as client/server. While it isnt necessary to know about client/server technology in any detail, you may run across the term, and it is useful to have a general understanding of what it means because using these new programs can result in a more efficient use of the Internet.

In general, data providers on the Internet realize they can't anticipate all the various equipment configurations and models that may be used to access information. Instead, they have concentrated on establishing standards to provide the information in consistent, regularized, and reliable formats.

Programmers can produce software specific to individual computer platforms when they know that the servers they intend to access contain information in predictable formats. Once servers are known to be reliable, client software can be designed to conform to the special needs of individual hardware configurations. Thus, the Internet access tools described in the following chapter are available for a wide variety of computers. This is why we can talk about SLIP connections and Gopher software later, confident that readers who have Macintosh computers will be able to find client software appropriate for their computers, while DOS users will be able to find similar software for the various operating systems, including OS/2 and Windows, which are particular to their computers.

5

Internet Access Tools

Considering the size of the Internet, the numbers of computers connected to it (over three million at press time), and the sheer amount of data and information resources available, it's easy to imagine that it's impossible to get around on the Internet without getting lost. Although it's true that the Internet's scale and volume are enormous, there are a number of software tools available that help overcome the problems and make it possible and certainly easier to move around.

The following section describes the most common Internet Access Tools. The descriptions are not intended to be definitive, but descriptive. For detailed or technical information you might want to consult books that focus specifically on the How-Tos of the Internet. Appendix E, "Further Readings," gives a list of useful books in this regard.

Moving into and onto the Internet puts one into *cyberspace*, the term coined by William Gibson in his science fiction classic, *Neuromancer*. Cyberspace refers to an electronic place where people and programs work, learn, and coexist. Each of the tools described here have a specialized set of capabilities to help you navigate your way around cyberspace when your computer is connected to the Net.

Telnet

Telnet is one of the earliest Internet Access Tools. This software permits a connection to be made to a remote computer to read the directory of files located on that remote computer and use its programs. Using Telnet software, an authorized user can log on to a computer and have much the same access to it as if he were actually sitting at his own keyboard console.

To use Telnet, you need to know the Internet address of the computer to which you want to establish a connection. If you don't know its address, but do know its common name, you can sometimes use the name in place of the formal Internet address. Simply type the word `telnet` followed by the sequence `ComputerName.ComputerLocation` all in one line with no spaces. For example:

`telnet: olorin.uchicago.edu`

The Internet Telnet software is a tool that has proven to be beneficial to scientific and engineering research and development. This tool makes it possible for people all over the world to work together and share resources in ways otherwise unthinkable without the connectivity that the Internet provides.

Guest Access to Remote Computers

Most computers on the Internet are protected by passwords (at minimum, their important files are protected by some security measures). Only authorized users can have access to protected files. Many of the computers that allow a Telnet connection will permit temporary access (usually restricted to some specific set of functions). In such cases, you might be asked to supply your computer account as a password. In other cases, you will be asked to use the word anonymous or guest as a login. You might have to try several options before being successfully connected to the remote computer. Reading the information on your screen returned by the remote computer during a Telnet session also can provide information about procedures established at a given site.

Telnet-How To

Telnet-How To

An introduction to telnet, an Internet access tool.

Keywords: Internet Tools, Telnet

Sponsor: SURAnet Network Information Center

Audience: Internet Surfers

Contact: info@sura.net

Details: Free

           File is: pub/nic/network.service.guides/
           how.to.telnet.guide

`ftp://ftp.sura.net`

Viruses

It is crucial to point out that most computer viruses are obtained from downloaded program files. Viruses don't come attached to documents or text files but are exclusively associated with executable or program files. If you intend to use FTP (or any other Internet Access Tool) to download executable files to your own computer, make absolutely certain that you know the reliability of the source of the executable program, and that your own computer is protected by a sufficiently capable virus protection program that will scan, evaluate, and intercept all incoming files to check for viruses.

Telnet is a useful command structure with which to interact with computers on the Internet. Many commercial programs now incorporate basic Telnet programming structures, making it possible to use this facility from a variety of telecommunications software programs.

Virus-L

Virus-L

Virus-L is a forum for the discussion of computer virus experiences, protection software, and other virus-related topics. It includes archives and files that list a number of viruses, trojan horses, and pirated programs for the IBM PC.

Keywords: Computer Viruses, Security

Audience: Computer Users

Contact: Kenneth R. van Wyk
luken@vax1.cclehigh.edu

Details: Free

To subscribe to the list, send an e-mail message to the URL address below consisting of a single line reading:

SUB virus-l YourFirstNameYourLastName

To send a message to the entire list, address it to: virus@lehigh.edu

`mailto:listserv@lehigh.edu`

Internet Tools

Telnet-How To

An introduction to Telnet, an Internet access tool.

Keywords: Internet, Tools, Telnet

Audience: Internet Users

Producer: SURAnet Network Information Center

Contact: info@sura.net

Details: Free

User Info: File is: pub/nic/network.service.guides/
how.to.telnet.guide

`ftp://ftp.sura.net`

FTP (File Transfer Protocol)

FTP is more specific. Its special job is retrieving (downloading) files from remote computers. An FTP Internet Access Tool also enables you to place (upload) files on a remote computer. The files that are transferred can be text files, application programs, binary code, software updates, various utilities, and any of an assortment of helpful or useful computing aids.

To use an FTP Access Tool, you need to know the computer address of the site to which you want to have access, or its common name. Many FTP sites are listed in this directory

because they represent a popular way of archiving information that is frequently requested and often downloaded.

Although FTP sites often require passwords, many have been established for the purpose of archiving files, programs, and utilities that are specifically produced for the benefit of the Internet community as freeware (no cost for obtaining or using them for non-commercial purposes). These are known as Anonymous FTP sites, and they enable you to log in with *anonymous* as your login name, and the computer account as the password. Because many of these Anonymous FTP sites are popular, you might experience difficulty logging them at the first try. Persevere, because the information available on many of the Anonymous FTP sites is quite useful.

The difference between an FTP Internet Access Tool and a Telnet tool is that some of the functions for exchanging files have been incorporated into the FTP software. Anything done by FTP software can be done during a Telnet session. The FTP software simply incorporates the command language into various menu items or selections, making it easier for individuals without a working knowledge of Internet protocols to download or upload files.

What you will receive upon login will be a directory listing of the files available. You will need to scroll through these file names looking for items of interest. Many FTP sites have organized files into general categories, but FTP is not designed to provide anything more elaborate than a file name for your guidance. It is a powerful, but simple, retrieval tool.

You should know whether the file you want to move is an executable program or a text file. If it is an executable program, it frequently needs to be identified as a *binary* file, as contrasted with an *ASCII* or *text* identification appropriate for readable files. The FTP software can sometimes make a judgement about what is appropriate (based on a series of algorithms), but if you can supply the information, the transfer may go more smoothly.

FTP FAQ

FTP FAQ

Common questions and answers about FTP (File Transfer Protocol), FTP sites, and anonymous FTP. General information for the novice FTP user.

Keywords: FTP, Internet Reference

Audience: Students, Computer Scientists, Researchers

Contact: Perry Rovers
perry.rovers@kub.nl

`ftp://ftp.ifh.de/pub/FAQ/ftp.faq`

Using FTP requires an individual to know (or learn) what resource is available at which site. There is another Internet Access Tool that has been developed to index all FTP sites, producing a long list of file names and addresses, and which can be enormously useful to those who want to look for specific programs or files and learn where the files actually are located. This service is known as Archie.

Archie

Archie is a software program with a specific function on the Internet. Archie's job is to query all the registered anonymous FTP sites on the Internet in a standardized manner and to create a composite index of the files located on these sites, arranging them in alphabetical order. Because there are thousands of anonymous FTP sites, it could be impossible to find a specific file if you didn't know where it was located. Archie solves the problem by producing a single comprehensive index. Now, if you know a file name, Archie can tell you where such a file is located.

Archie is a software tool that—on an ongoing basis—scans anonymous FTP sites and builds an index of those sites, making it easier to find specific items.

Internet Tools

Archie

A description of Archie, an electronic directory service for the Internet, which allows the user to find files remotely.

Keywords: Internet Tools

Audience: Internet Users

Producer: Computing Centre, McGill University, Montreal, Quebec, Canada

Contact: archie-group@archie.mcgill.ca

Details: Free

User Info: File is: pub/archie/doc/whatis.archie

Archie is accessible on the Internet. Directions and instructions can be obtained from the Internet resources listed in the appropriate sections of the directory.

Gopher

Gopher is an extremely popular Internet tool, representing an improved level of ease of use. Gopher was developed at the University of Minnesota. Once connected to a gopher site, you are provided with an opening menu, followed by a practically unlimited number of submenus. Gopher permits you to access data without knowing precisely what you are looking for. In other words, gopher navigation is based on an inquiry about a subject and does not depend on your knowledge of computer addresses or locations, making it an ideal introductory tool for new Internet users. The links among the gopher sites are more or less invisible to the user, which has made gopher a very popular Internet Access Tool.

Most of the Internet tools can be retrieved from FTP sites. These types of tools often are also carried on local sites, so you might check with your local administrator to find out if a copy is already available to you through your home account provider.

Internet Tools

gopher

A guide to using gopher, an Internet access tool that locates and retrieves resources using a graph of menus.

Keywords: Internet Tools

Audience: Internet Users

Contact: gopher@boombox.micro.umn.edu

Details: Free

User Info: File is: pub/gopher/00README

`ftp://boombox.micro.umn.edu/pub/gopher`

You should locate the appropriate gopher software for your particular computer so that you can pursue those gopher sites that are of interest to you. Frequently, the same site that provides the actual Internet tools will have ancillary files available that provide explanations, demonstrations, or operations manuals.

Internet Tools

Gopher FAQ

Answers to frequently asked questions (FAQs) about gophers from the USENET newsgroup comp.infosystems.gopher

Keywords: Internet Tools, Gopher

Audience: Internet Users

Contact: Paul Lindner
lindner@boombox.micro.umn.edu

Details: Free

User Info: File is: pub/usenet/news.answers/gopher-faq

`ftp://pit-manager.mit.edu/pub`

Veronica

Veronica is a gopher service analagous to Archie for anonymous FTP sites. The difference is that Veronica has been designed to locate keywords at the various gopher sites that have been established on the Internet. Going to a Veronica site can speed up a search for information. Veronica usually contains information about a large number of sites dealing with a specific keyword, permitting the user to find an Internet resource location that is specific to her interests quickly, rather than making her go through a hierarchical path-searching process.

Veronica is an augmentation of gopher and provides keyword searches of the titles of gopher items. This is a major help to finding where a given file or program not only can be found among the various gopher Internet sites but also can be retrieved. You can often get to Veronica by going through a normal gopher client, either your own or one supplied by your Internet service provider if you don't have your own.

Internet Tools

Veronica Introduction

Veronica (Very Easy Rodent-Oriented Net-wide Index to Computerized Archives) is an Internet access tool that locates titles of gopher items by keyword search.

Keywords: Internet Tools, Veronica

Audience: Internet Users

Details: Free

User Info: File is: pub/comp.archives/bionet.software/veronica

`ftp://cs.dal.ca`

Wide Area Information Servers (WAIS)

WAIS is another information locating tool that enables users to search and access different types of information from a single interface. The information being sought can be in any format (for example, text, sound, or images) and can reside anywhere on the network.

When WAIS finds the information, it ranks the results and delivers a document with the search matches ranked by relevance. You can use the results of your search to modify your original search even further. Thus, if the fourth-ranked file is closer to what you want than the first-ranked file, you can add it to your query parameters, saying, in effect, Get me more like this but including this topic.

WAIS is an example of a tool that provides an enhanced retrieval mechanism through ranking of items according to their relevance to a constructed query.

Internet Tools

WAIS

WAIS (Wide Area Information Servers) is an Internet access tool that retrieves resources by searching indexes of databases.

Keywords: Internet Tools, WAIS

Audience: Internet Users

Details: Free

User Info: Read wais/README first.

`http://www.wais.com`

World Wide Web (WWW)

Another characteristic of the Internet is its capability to link documents at one location with files at another. This type of network linking is known as *hypertext*, and a special tool has been developed to pursue hypertextual links among disparate files.

World Wide Web (WWW) is an Internet software tool for network navigation similar to gopher. It also is menu-driven. Unlike gopher, WWW follows hypertext links between related sources rather than files related to one another by server identification. WWW enables you to pursue the strands of a web of information distributed across the Network. Using WWW you might locate an interesting document, notice a citation in it, and use WWW to look up the source document.

This popular Internet navigation software can be obtained from a site in Europe.

Internet Tools

World Wide Web (WWW)

World Wide Web (WWW) is an Internet application tool that retrieves resources through a hypertext browser of databases.

Keywords: Internet Tools, World Wide Web

Audience: Internet Users

Producer: CERN (European Laboratory for Particle Physics)

Details: Free

User Info: Documents and guides are in: pub/www/doc

`http://info.cern.ch`

Though a relative newcomer, WWW holds great promise for navigating the Internet electronically.

Cello and Lynx

Cello and Lynx are useful interfaces to WWW because they are powerful, small, and simple programs. As a result, they are good introductory tools to the World Wide Web of databases on the Internet. The look and feel of these programs is text-based. They lack the elegance of a more polished program like Mosaic, but the navigation capabilities are quick, and the programs provide straightforward and easy ways of obtaining information from WWW sites.

Cello

Cello

A DOS-based Internet browser incorporating WWW (World-Wide Web), Gopher, FTP, Telnet, and usenet.

Keywords: Internet Tools, Cello, DOS

Audience: Internet Surfers

Details: Free

```
ftp://fatty.law.cornell.edu/pub/ldd/
cello
```

```
gopher://fatty.law.cornell.edu
```

```
http://fatty.law.cornell.edu/cello/
cellotop.html
```

Cello FAQ

A site containing common questions and answers about Cello, a multipurpose Internet browser which allows access to the myriad information resources of the Internet. It supports World Wide Web, Gopher, FTP, CSO/pf/qi, and Usenet News retrievals natively, and other protocols (WAIS, Hytelnet, Telnet, and TN3270) through external clients and public gateways.

Keywords: Internet Tools, Internet Reference

Sponsor: Cornell Law School, New York, USA

Audience: Students, Computer Scientists, Researchers.

```
http://www.law.cornell.edu/cello/
cellofaq.html
```

Lynx FAQ

A resource providing common questions and answers about Cello, a distributed hypertext browser with full WWW capabilities.

Keywords: Internet Reference

Sponsor: University of Kansas, Distributed Computing Group, Kansas, USA

Audience: Students, Computer Scientists, Researchers

Contact: Garrett Blythe, Lou Montulli
doslynx@falcon.cc.ukans.edu,
montulli@mcom.com
lynx-help@ukanaix.cc.ukans.edu

```
http://ftp2.cc.ukans.edu/about_lynx
```

```
http://ftp2.cc.ukans.edu/lynx_help
```

```
http://ftp2.cc.ukans.edu/lynx_writeup
```

Mosaic

Mosaic was developed by the National Center for Supercomputing Applications at the University of Chicago at Urbana-Champaign, Illinois. It is among the most popular of the recently available Internet searching tools. It comes in many flavors for various computing platforms. Be sure to download the version of Mosaic that matches your computer.

Internet Tools

Mosaic

Mosaic provides a network-distributed hypermedia system for information discovery. It is Internet-based and is free for academic, research, and internal use.

Keywords: Internet Tools, Mosaic

Audience: Internet Users

Contact: mosaic-x@ncsa.uiuc.edu

Details: Free

User Info: File is: Mosaic/README.Mosaic

```
ftp://ftp.ncsa.uiuc.edu
```

Mosaic understands the protocols of many of the most-used graphical user interfaces. It unifies the searching capacities of many Internet retrieval tools and adds the capability to display images in a variety of graphic formats. This means that Mosaic can retrieve a variety of image files and show them to you on your computer even if you don't own the original graphics program from which the images were generated. Of course, your computer must be able to display graphics (that is, it must have a windowing capability of some sort).

Mosaic is very popular due to its flexibility and its comprehensiveness as an Internet navigator and retriever of a wide variety of types of files. As with many such specialized tools, finding out what can be retrieved by Mosaic can be a problem. Just before publication of this directory, an Internet announcement heralded the appearance of World Wide Web (Worm) WWW(W). The worm accomplishes a function similar to that of Veronica. It scours the Internet, locating WWW sites and indexing their contents so

---

that people can more easily find information they are seeking.

Mosaic

Mosaic Home Page

This is the welcome page to the National Center for Supercomputing Applications (NCSA) World Wide Web server, which features the Mosaic application. Mosaic provides a network-distributed hypermedia system for information discovery. It is Internet-based and is free for academic, research, and internal commercial use.

Keywords: Internet Tools, Mosaic, WWW

Audience: Internet Surfers

Contact: mosaic-x@ncsa.uiuc.edu

Details: Free

```
http://www.ncsa.uiuc.edu/SDG/
Software/Mosaic/NCSAMosaicHome.html
```

Newsreaders

Newsreader programs have been created specifically to give people easy ways to read postings made to specific Usenet newsgroups, a specific variety of electronic discussion group. Usenet is a type of loosely organized network, stemming from the period in the Internet's development when programmers designed software for their own use. The programs created to make it easy to keep in touch with one another on a variety of topics became known as *newsgroups*, which became very popular and proliferated. Newsreader software was created when the number of newsgroups grew to unmanageable proportions.

Newsreaders are programs that permit you to specify those newsgroups that are of interest to you. Having been configured in this manner, the program then collects information only from the specified sources, making it a burdenless process to keep abreast of one or several discussions at a time. There is a way to post messages to newsgroups through e-mail (see the following example).

Internet

E-mail Usenet

E-mail Usenet allows the user to post to a newsgroup via e-mail.

Keywords: Internet, Services, E-mail, Usenet

Audience: Internet Surfers

Details: Free

```
mailto://hierarchy-group-
name@cs.utexas.edu
```

The following listing contains instructions on retrieving newsreader software. Routine postings on Usenet lists contain information about subscribing to them. Comprehensive and frequently updated lists of currently active newsgroups also are available. These form a dynamic and active portion of the Internet. Changes are frequent, with some newsgroup topics emerging while others are dying off for lack of sustained interest.

Newsreaders

Usenet Newsreaders

Usenet newsreader programs have been created to give people ways to read the thousands of Usenet newsgroups available on the Internet. Among the most popular are: tin, rn, nn, and trn.

Keywords: Newsreaders, Usenet

Audience: Internet Users

Profile: The rn interface uses full-screen display with direct positioning. It includes reading, discarding, and/or processing of articles based on user-definable patterns, and the ability of the user to develop customized macros for display and keyboard interaction.

trn allows readers to follow "threads of discussions" in newsgroups. Trn can be obtained from ftp.coe.montana.edu in the /pub/trn directory, from uunet in the news subdirectory, and from many other archive servers world-wide.

"nn" is different in that it presents a menu of article subject and sender-name lines, allowing you to preselect articles to read. nn is also a very fast newsreader

tin" is a reader that operates with threads, has different article organization methods, and is full-screen oriented. tin also works on a local news spool and has an extensive list of features.,

User Info: rn software can be obtained from: ftp://lib.tmc.edu
trn can be obtained from: ftp://ftp.coe.montana.edu in the /pub/trn directory and from manyother Archie servers worldwide.
nn can be obtained via anonymous FTP from: ftp://dkuug.dk, uop.uop.edu
tin can be retrieved by accessing the newsgroup: news:alt.sources

Details: Free

Notes: Each of thse newsreaders can be access from a variety of sources. Further information regarding tin is available from Iain Lea (iain%anl433.uucp@Germany.EU.net).

See the URL information given in the User Info.field above.

Usenet is not centrally organized, so there is no control over who gets a particular newsfeed or how individual articles are sent out. But the bottom line is that whatever your interest may be, there's bound to be a discussion group dedicated to that very subject.

Finger: Finding People on the Internet

Finger helps you locate other people on the Internet. The Finger tool can provide the e-mail addresses, full name, telephone numbers, and other information about a particular user at a specified site. Because Finger enables you to search the user log on a computer connected to the Internet, you can find someone's e-mail address provided you know the name of the computer he or she uses. Even if you don't know a person's login name, you can type part of a person's name and Finger will produce a list of possibilities.

Finger

Finger Database

This service allows access to a database facility via finger.

Keywords: Internet Services, Finger (Internet Database)

Audience: Internet Surfers

Contact: http://www.usyd.edu.au

Details: Free

`http://www-ns.rutgers.edu/htbin/finger`

Service or resource providers on the Internet will often provide help facilities that explain the service or resource. Such is the case with the Internet Finger Database. It is worth trying an address a few times if at first you dont succeed in getting through. You also can experiment with the possibility of reaching a resource using other Internet tools if the first tool doesn't work.

Internet Services

Finger Database

This service allows access to a database facility via Finger.

Keywords: Internet, Services, Finger

Audience: Internet Users

Details: Free

`finger://help@dir.su.oz.au`

Finger enables you to access other types of information contained in text files. For instance you can reach NASA's *Headline News* by typing:

`finger://nasanews@space.mit.edu`

Or you can find the *Top 40* on the pop music charts by typing:

`finger://buckmr@aix.rpi.edu`

STAR (Subject and Topic Access Rater)

What each of these electronic Internet Access Tools lacks is an evaluation of the resource by subject experts. In that context, the STAR ratings are an important Internet access tool because they provide an analytical judgement in a familiar format.

Brown University Library

Brown University Library

The Brown libraries contain approximately 1.5 million volumes, including historical archives of early American imprints and biomedical engineering holdings.

Keywords: Libraries, Research

Audience: General Public, Researchers

Contact: Howard Pasternick blips15@brownvm.brown.edu

Details: Free

Notes: At the Brown logon screen: tab to command field, Enter Dial Josiah, tab to Josiah choice on the screen.

`telnet://brownvm.brown.edu`

`telnet://library.brown.edu`

`http://www.brown.edu/facilities/university/library/library.html`

6

Internet Addresses Explained

Each of the resources listed in *The New Riders' Official Internet Yellow Pages* includes at least one Internet address referred to as a Uniform Resource Locator (URL). The URL appears at the bottom of each listing and is the unique electronic address on the Internet that identifies the location of that specific site and the method(s) for gaining access to it.

It is common now to refer to Internet addresses as URLs. *The New Riders' Official Internet Yellow Pages* adopts this standard for all addresses listed.

Communications on the Internet

Information moves across the Internet in much the same way as mail moves through post offices. Just as your letter is carried in a mail truck, your electronic message is transported through a packet-switching network. In either instance, the message travels along with thousands of other unrelated messages. In the case of the Internet, the destination computer picks up and reassembles the pieces of your message before delivering it to your personal mailbox.

The Internet URL is made up of specific address parts that guarantee a unique address code for each information packet or file. The Transmission Control Protocol (TCP) is the set of rules guaranteeing that packets sent through the Internet are properly packaged, efficiently transmitted, and properly received at their destination.

Understanding Internet Addresses

When you first see an Internet URL, it can appear incomprehensible, as in the following example:

```
telnet://purple-
crayon.media.mit.edu:8888
```

Instead of separating parts of an address by lines as on an envelope, an Internet address separates elements typographically using periods, slashes, and colons. Just as the world is divided up into continents, countries, and regions, Internet addresses are divided up into domains and subdomains. Countries have domain names, and these are known as top-level domains. India's domain name is *in*, for example, Japan's is *jp*, and the United Kingdom's is *uk*.

Internet addresses are built up from left to right, beginning with the most specific piece of information (a users personal and individual identification) and proceeding to the most general (the highest level domain within which the user can be found).

URLs provide one additional important piece of information. They identify the access tools you need to use when attempting to reach a particular Internet resource. These tools have been explained in more detail in the chapter on Internet access tools. They have names like telnet, gopher, FTP, MOSAIC, and WAIS. To reach a specific Internet resource, you need to know which primary access tool will gain you access to it.

Thus at the beginning of each URL address in this directory, the first item of information identifies the appropriate tool to use in accessing that particular resource. Depending on your software, you may have to type the research tool words as commands. These may be summarized as follows:

- telnet://—use a standard telnet tool to access the resource.

- gopher://—use any of the variety of gopher software that is available for your computer.

- ftp://—use File Transfer Protocol tools.

The situation, however, is different for mailto or http. The tools for accessing those types of resources instruct you on how to proceed.

- mailto:—use telnet or standard e-mail management software. (Do not type the word mailto.)

- http://—use Mosaic.

Dissecting a Uniform Resource Locator (URL)

Following is a typical URL address and a description of what each element means.

```
telnet://purple-
crayon.media.mit.edu:8888
```

The :// that follows the research tool is the standard way of separating the name of the research tool from the remainder of the URL address. If your host computer runs UNIX (which most host computers do), then for research tools like telnet and gopher you do not need to physically type :// into the computer when you are trying to access the resource. Instead, you leave a space between the command and the address.

`purple-crayon.media.mit.edu` actually is a specific computer! On the Internet, computers have distinguishing numerical identifiers, known as IP addresses (for example, 18.85.0.48). These addresses are hard to remember, so to make things simpler, the computers have also been assigned easier-to-remember names. Both the name of the

to-remember names. Both the name of the computer and its IP number can be used interchangeably in an Internet address. At each major site, a computer acts as a domain name server, which translates any alphabetic IP address into its proper numerical one.

In this example, the purple-crayon computer is located on a subnet of other computers that are all collected together in the network media. In turn, the subnet media is located at mit, which stands for the Massachusetts Institute of Technology, located in Boston Massachussetts.

The .edu at the end of the address reveals that this address represents an educational institution. Certain types of messages (for example, those that are strictly business or commercial) are prohibited from traveling from computers dedicated to research or teaching. Similarly, you cant use military computers to exchange stock market information. While the laws regarding appropriate use have relaxed over time, the individual institutional policies governing these uses, and—perhaps more important—the culture of the Internet user community, is very good at policing itself and taking violators to task. This is especially true for those who appear to be posting messages of a purely marketing or advertising content.

Within the US, higher level domains have been established that are based on different kinds of organizations instead of on geographical location. These include .com (commercial), .edu (education and research), .gov (government agencies), .mil (military), .net (network support centers), and .org (other organizations).

Because the Internet began in the United States, *users* within the US do not presently need to identify the top-level domain *us* in an Internet address. As usage of the Internet continues to expand internationally, it eventually may be necessary to add this final suffix to addresses even within the US. It is, however, required for countries outside the United States. If the example were an address within the educational sector of the Czech Republic, it would be written with the final suffix showing the top-level domain of that country.

Finally, the :8888 is the port number. This instructs your computer to connect not only to a specific address, but to one special port at that address. Whereas Mosaic sites and Telnet sites might not include any port numbers at all, gopher servers have been designated to use port 70. If you were typing the command at a UNIX prompt, it would look like this:

```
telnet purple-crayon.media.mit.edu
8888
```

Notice that spaces separate those parts of the address that were marked as colons in the URL.

The Internet addressing system may seem complicated at first, but after a while, you will begin to recognize domain names and be able to tell not only where resources lie, but which types of organizations they are associated with.

7

E-Mail
on the
Internet

Sending and receiving electronic mail (e-mail) is one of the Internet's most frequently used functions. At one time, it was thought that letter-writing would go the way of the horse and buggy, but e-mail has revived and transformed it into something new.

Instead of being delivered by the Post Office, e-mail messages are sent directly to your computer. This not only vastly accelerates the speed with which messages can be transmitted, but provides numerous advantages to individuals as well as businesses.

People use e-mail for the same reasons they use postal mail. In addition, e-mail can be used to transfer and receive copies of files and document; to subscribe to electronic discussion groups, electronic journals, and electronic newsgroups; to obtain free copies of computer software; and to obtain copies of sounds, graphics, and multimedia over the Internet. E-mail is not only faster, but the cost is a fraction of what it is to send and receive mail through traditional means.

There are any number of useful e-mail management software packages available. Many have built in functions that facilitate sending and receiving messages, attaching other files from your computer, and replying to messages that you might have received. With speed and convenience, however, come the danger of new forms of miscommunication.

Using the Reply Function

Most e-mail software packages permit you to easily reply to an incoming message. Every message has a header. The header contains information about the time a message was sent, where it came from, and what path it took to reach you. When you use the Reply function built in to the software, it assumes you want to respond to the sender and uses the information from the header to address your reply.

While this is easy, there are two common situations you should be cautious about.

cc: [carbon copies]. Some software picks up the names of any individuals who have been copied on the original incoming message, or you may have received a copy of a message sent to someone else. Know how your e-mail software treats a "reply." Some packages pick up only the address of the original sender; others pick up all the names of those receiving the message. You may (or may not) want your reply to go to all the individuals who received the original message. Be sure to check which it is that you want.

ListServs. Similarly, when a message comes to you from an electronic discussion group, it is sent by the software that provides mail management functions for a list of individuals. The most common of such software is known as ListServ or MajorDomo. If you post a message to the list management software, the message is sent to all subscribers to the list. But if you use the Reply function, your message also goes to everyone on the discussion list. If you don't want that to happen, pay particular attention to the address line before sending your message

Perhaps the only true drawback of e-mail is that the system is not secure. This means that others may be able to read the mail you send or receive. If you want your mail to remain private, don't risk sending it e-mail.

E-mail Software Programs

To be able to write and receive e-mail messages, you need to have an e-mail software program. The purpose of this software is to enable you to see incoming e-mail messages and to provide an editor for outgoing messages. Check with your local computer software support staff for advice on which e-mail software is most suitable for you.

Using E-mail To Subscribe to ListServs, Mailing Lists, and Discussion Groups

Any listing that has a URL beginning with `mailto:` can be subscribed to via e-mail. Simply "write" to the contact person of the resource, and they "write back." It is just like sending a letter through the post office, except it all happens electronically.

To subscribe to a ListServ group, you first need to send an e-mail message to the URL address. Sometimes the transaction takes place between software programs. Other times, you will be dealing directly with someone. Knowing the difference between a list that has a moderator and one that is controlled by software is useful. You can usually tell by the URL. If the address contains the information listserv@, the resource is handled by a computer; if it contains the information -request@ there is an intermediary who handles the subscription and information requests and maintains the distribution list manually.

Other mailing lists and discussion groups can be subscribed to simply by sending a message to the contact e-mail address supplied.

A Note on Passwords. Security issues on the Internet have frequently made headline news. Individual Internet users can minimize their risks of being victimized by installing and using virus protection software on their computers and by choosing a password that is not easily determined. Passwords also should be changed frequently.

ListServs. ListServs are software programs that enable and maintain e-mail discussion groups. Each ListServ is dedicated to a specific topic. ListServ software permits Internet users to subscribe to a list. After you do so, you will receive copies of any message sent to the list.

To subscribe to a ListServ list, send an e-mail message to the software (called, *ListServ*) that governs the subscription requests and maintains the distribution records for the discussion list in which you are interested. The software governing a list will be located on the same computer host on which a particular discussion group is located. The subscription request is sent as a message containing the single line: `<SUB ListName YourFirstName YourLastName>`

(Substitute your real first name and your real last name for the phrases YourFirstName and YourLastName above.)

To unsubscribe is easier. Send a message containing the single line: `UNSUB ListName>`

In this case, the computer software will determine your first name and last name based on the records it has kept about who has subscribed to the list. It is, however, important to send these messages from the same computer from which you subscribed in the first place, otherwise the records wont match.

To send a message to everyone on the list, simply address an e-mail message to the list instead of to the ListServ software. Thus, if you wanted to join a list called Wonderful-L located at rloc.bernard.edu, you would send a subscription request to: `ListServ@rloc.bernard.edu`

If you intended to send a message to all the subscribers of the list you would address your message to: `Wonderful-L@rloc.bernard.edu`

The computer host, domain, and type (everything following the @ sign) are identical in both instances. You simply are addressing the software manager (ListServ) in the first case, and the distribution list (Wonderful-L) in the second.

ListServs are free. You do not need to pay a subscription fee. But there may be a price associated with subscribing to too many ListServs (or ones that are very active). You should be aware that some ListServs generate a lot of interest and a lot of mail. If you subscribe to several ListServs, be prepared for a substantial increase in mail. This can be difficult to review, but it can also take up disk space on your own computer until you can decide whether or not you wish to keep individual messages. Keep records of the lists to which you have subscribed so that you can easily unsubscribe from a list that inundates you with more messages than you care to (or are able to) handle.

Bulletin Board Systems (BBSs). Newsgroups distributed worldwide are broken down into the following seven traditional classifications. Each newsgroup is geared to a specific subject. Some newsgroups may literally have thousands of subscribers whereas others may exist with only a dozen or so subscribers.

news	Groups concerned with the news about network and administration topics.
soc	Groups that primarily address social issues and socializing.
talk	Groups largely debate-oriented that tend to feature long exploratory discussions on individual topics with little resolution.
misc	Groups that address themes that are not easily classified under any other headings, or that incorporate themes from multiple headings.
sci	Groups concerned with discussing practical knowledge, usually related to research in or the application of established sciences.
comp	Groups that discuss topics of interest to computer professionals and hobbyists. Hardware and software systems are also discussed.
rec	Groups oriented toward the arts, hobbies, and recreational activities.

In addition, there is a rapidly growing category of newsgroups with alternative grouped names. These involve subjects or communities that are less formal and less traditional, such as the following:

alt	Groups that deal with ephemeral, frivolous, or highly controversial topics.
biz	Groups that are for business and commercial topics.
Ieee	Groups that are for discussions related to engineering and electronics.
k12	Groups that are for discussions of primary school educational topics.

BBSs are software tools for providing bulletin board services. BBSs differ only slightly from e-mail ListServs. Any given BBS can provide e-mail, but it will also provide access to collections of data and documents that are available for downloading. BBSs offer an alternative to ListServs in that you can choose whether you want to obtain information from a BBS, whereas by subscribing to a ListServ you automatically receive all messages from the ListServ. Non-Internet BBSs frequently involve a fee for access, while most Internet-based BBS are free.

Usenet (Users Network). Usenet refers to a worldwide collection of thousands of computers (not all on the Internet) that host and receive Usenet newsgroup information and exchanges. Youll find many of these in *The New Riders' Official Internet Yellow Pages* as they have become immensely popular. There are thousands of newsgroups that function as forums for the exchange of questions and answers by their users concerning a selected topic.

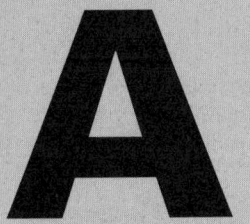

AACIS-L (American Association for Collegiate Independent Study)

AACIS-L (American Association for Collegiate Independent Study)
★

The focus of this list is on correspondence, independent study, and distance learning.

Keywords: Education (Adult), Education (Distance), Education (Continuing)

Sponsor: American Association for Collegiate Independent Study (AACIS)

Audience: Faculty Administrators

Details: Free

User Info: To subscribe to the list, send an e-mail message to the URL address shown below consisting of a single line reading:

SUB aacis-l YourFirstName YourLastName

To send a message to the entire list, address it to: aacis-l@bgu.edu

`mailto:listserv@bgu.edu`

AARNet Guide

AARNet Guide
★

This is the Australian Network Sites and Resources Guide.

Keywords: Internet, Internet Guides, Australia

Sponsor: Australian Academic and Research Network

Audience: Internet Surfers

Details: Free

Files are in: pub/resource-guide

`ftp://aarnet.edu.au/pub/resource-guide`

ABC Programming Language

ABC
★

Discussion of the ABC Programming Language and its implementations.

Keywords: Programming Languages, ABC Programming Language

Audience: Programmers

Contact: Steven Pemberton
abc-list-request@cwi.nl

Details: Free

User Info: To subscribe to the list, send an e-mail message requesting a subscription to the URL address below.

To send a message to the entire list, address it to: ABC@cwi.nl

`mailto:abc-list-request@cwi.nl`

ABI/Inform

ABI/Inform
★ ★ ★

ABI/Inform is a comprehensive source for business and management information, containing abstracts from close to 1,000 publications and the full-text from over 100 publications. The database covers trends, corporate strategies and tactics, management techniques, competitive information and product information

Keywords: Business, Business Management, Management

Sponsor: UMI, Ann Arbor, Michigan, US

Audience: General Public, Researchers, Librarians

Profile: A few of the thousands of business subjects that can searched in ABI/Inform include: company news and analysis, market conditions and strategies, employee management and compensation, international trade and investment, management styles and corporate cultures, and economic conditions and forecasts.

Contact: CDP Technologies Sales Department (800)950-2035, extension 400

User Info: To subscribe, contact CDP Technologies directly

`telnet://cdplus@cdplus.com`

Abolitionism

Johns Hopkins University Library
★ ★ ★

The library's's holdings are large and wide-ranging and contain significant collections in many fields.

Keywords: Literature (English), Economics, Classics, Drama (German), Slavery, Trade Unions, Incunabula, Bibles, Diseases (History of), Nursing (History of), Abolitionism

Audience: General Public, Researchers, Librarians, Historians

Details: Free

`telnet://jhuvm.hcf.jhu.edu`

The University of Illinois at Chicago Library
★ ★ ★

The library's holdings are large and wide-ranging and contain significant collections in many fields.

A
B
C
D
E
F
G
H
I
J
K
L
M
N
O
P
Q
R
S
T
U
V
W
X
Y
Z

Keywords: Health Science, Chicago, Industry, Slavery, Abolitionism, Roosevelt (Franklin D.)

Audience: General Public, Researchers, Librarians, Historians

Details: Free

User Info: Expect: introductory screen, Send: Clear key; Expect: UIC flame screen, Send: Enter key; Expect: Logon screen, Send: DIAL PVM; Expect: PVM (Passthru) screen, Send: Type: Move cursor to NOTIS and press Enter key Response: One line message about port in use Type: Enter key

`telnet://uicvm.uic.edu`

U.S. Civil War Reading List

★ ★ ★

A major directory on abolitionism, providing access to a broad range of resources (library catalogs, databases, and servers) via the Internet.

Keywords: History (US), Abolitionism

Audience: General Public, Historians

Profile: The Suggested Civil War Reading List contains 61 books, several of them with multiple volumes, as well as an 11-hour documentary film and a CD of Civil War era songs. The material is sorted into general categories: General Histories of the War, Causes of the War and History to 1861, Slavery and Southern Society, Reconstruction, Biographies and Autobiographies, Source Documents and official Records, Unit Histories and Soldiers' Reminiscences, Fiction, Specific Battles and Campaigns, Strategies and Tactics, The Experience of Soldiers.

Contact: Stephen Schmidt
whale@leland.Stanford.edu

`http://www.cis.ohio-state.edu/ hypertext/faq/usenet/civil-war-usa/ reading-list/faq.html`

Abortion

Abortion and Reproductive Rights

★ ★ ★

A major directory on abortion, providing access to a broad range of related resources (library catalogs, databases, and servers) via the Internet.

Keywords: Abortion, Activism, Women's Issues

Sponsor: The WELL Computer Conference System

Audience: Activists, Feminists

Profile: Choice-Net Report is a weekly update on reproductive rights issues distributed through E-mail, Women's Wire, gopher.WELL.com, Usenet groups alt.activism, talk.abortion, soc.women, and other Internet channels.

Details: Free

`http://gopher.well.sf.ca.us`

alt.feminism

A Usenet newsgroup providing information and discussion about feminism.

Keywords: Feminism, Women's Studies, Abortion, Activism

Audience: Women, General Public, Feminists

User Info: To subscribe to this Usenet newsgroup, you need access to a newsreader.

`news:alt.feminism`

table.abortion

A Usenet newsgroup providing information and discussion about all sides of the abortion issue.

Keywords: Abortion, Women's Issues, Health

Audience: Women, Activists, Health Care Professionals

Details: Free

User Info: To subscribe to this Usenet newsgroup, you need access to a newsreader.

`news:table.abortion`

Women.health

This conference features articles, documents, news, announcements, policy statements, and other information about women's health around the world. Topics include breast cancer, ovarian cancer, alcohol, abortion, pregnancy, sterilization of women, pesticides, Quinacrine, HIV, disability.

Keywords: Women, Abortion, AIDS, Disability, Feminism, Health

Audience: Activists, Family Planners, Health Professionals, Non-Governmental Organizations, Women

Details: Costsosts

User Info.: Establish an account on the nearest APC node. Login, type c for conferences, then type go women.health. For information on the nearest APC node, contact: APC International Secretariat IBASE.

E-mail: apcadmin@apc.org

`telnet://igc.apc.org`

Academia

Academia Latinoamericana de Espanol

This program is specifically designed for those interested in learning to speak Spanish through a fully immersive trip to Ecuador.

Keywords: Spanish Language, Education (Bilingual)

Sponsor: Academia Latinoamericana de Espanol, Quito, Ecuador

Audience: Researchers, Students, Language Teachers

Contact: Webmaster
webmaster@comnet.com

`http://www.comnet.com/ecuador/ learnSpanish.html`

Academic Freedom Statements

A major directory on academic freedom, providing access to a broad range of related resources (library catalogs, databases, and servers) via the Internet.

Keywords: Academia

Audience: Professors, Students (College/Graduate), General Public

Profile: An online collection of general academic freedom statements, including the Statement on the Rights and Freedoms of Students. Examples of statements include: Academic Freedom and Artistic Expression; an official statement of the American Association of University Professors; The Lima Declaration on Academic Freedom and Autonomy of Institutions of Higher Education; an international declaration by the World University Service; A Statement on the Freedom to Read, Queen's University (Canada); The Yale University (Connecticut) Policy on Freedom of Expression.

Contact: J.S. Greenfield
greeny@eff.org

`gopher://gopher.ef.org/00/CAF/ academic/README`

Academic Institution Information of Western Countries

A major directory of information on academic institutions, providing access to a broad range of related resources (library catalogs, databases, and servers) via the Internet.

Keywords: Academic Research, Information Retrieval, Academia

Audience: Students, Educators, Researchers

Profile: Includes information on financial aid, and address for academic institutions in Australia, Canada, Europe, New Zealand, and Hong Kong.

`gopher://ifcss.org/11/cal-aeic/info-World.Inst`

Academic Job Listings All Over the World

A major directory on academic institution information, providing access to a broad range of related resources (library catalogs, databases, and servers) via the Internet.

Keywords: Academia, Employment

Audience: Academics, General Public

Contact: Prentiss Riddle
cwis@rice.edu

`gopher://riceinfo.rice.edu/11/Subject/Jobs`

alt.usage.english

A Usenet newsgroup providing information and discussion about English grammar, word usages, and related topics.

Keywords: Lexicology, Academia, Linguistics, Education

Audience: English Educators

User Info: To subscribe to this Usenet newsgroup, you need access to a newsreader.

`news:alt.usage.english`

CAF Archive

A source of information relating to Computers and Academic Freedom (CAF).

Keywords: Education, Computers, Academia

Audience: Educators, Researchers

Contact: kadie@eff.org

`http://www.eff.org/CAF/cafhome.html`

The English Server

A large and eclectic collection of humanities resources.

Keywords: Humanities, Academia, English, Popular Culture, Feminism

Sponsor: Carnegie Mellon University English Department, Pittsburgh, Pennsylvania, USA

Audience: General Public, University Students, Educators (College/University), Researchers (Humanities)

Profile: Contains archives of conventional humanities materials, such as historical documents and classic books in electronic form. Also offers more unusual and hard-to-find resources, particularly in the field of popular culture and media. Features access to many humanities and culture-related online journals such as Bad Subjects, FineArt Forum, and Postmodern Culture. Also has links to a wide variety of related Internet sites and resources.

Contact: Geoff Sauer
postmaster@english-server.hss.cmu.

`gopher://english-server.hss.cmu.edu`

`http://english-server.hss.cmu.edu`

The MIT Press Online Catalogs

A descriptive listing of recent books and current journals published by the MIT Press.

Keywords: Academia, Books, Publishing, Technology

Sponsor: The MIT Press, Cambridge, Massachusetts, USA.

Audience: Researchers, Scholars, University Students, Technical Professionals

Profile: Contains a keyword-searchable index of books published in the years 1993 to 1994, as well as current journals covering computational and cognitive sciences, architecture, photography, art and literary theory, economics, environmental science, and linguistics.

Contact: ehling@mitpress.mit.edu

Notes: Coverage: 1993 to present; updated semiannually. MIT Press can also be accessed by calling (800) 356-0343.

`http://www-mitpress.mit.edu`

`gopher://gopher.mit.edu`

Research Databases and Resources by Subject

A collection of databases on over forty subjects, ranging from Anthropology to Women's Studies.

Keywords: Databases, Academia

Sponsor: University of California at Berkeley

Audience: Researchers, General Public

Contact: Gopher Manager
gophcom@infolib.lib.berkeley.edu

`gopher://umslvma.umsl.edu/Library/Subjects/Biology/Bioformt/Biodbs`

`gopher://infolib.lib.berkeley.edu`

Academics

Academic Computing Training & User Support

This directory is a compilation of information resources focusing on academic computer training and user support.

Keywords: Computing, Academics

Audience: Computer Users

`ftp://una.hh.lib.umich.edu/70/inetdirsstacks/acadcomp:kovacsm`

Academic Institution Informations of Western Countries

A major directory of information on academic institutions, providing access to a broad range of related resources (library catalogs, databases, and servers) via the Internet.

Keywords: Academics, Information Retrieval

Audience: Students, Educators, Researchers

Profile: Includes information on financial aid, and address on academic institutions in Australia, Canada, Europe, New Zealand, and Hong Kong.

`gopher://ifcss.org/11/cal-aeic/info-World.Inst`

Accounting

Financial Economics Network (FEN)

A mailing list dedicated to recent research in financial economics.

Keywords: Accounting, Economics, Finance

Audience: Business Professionals, Investors, Economists, Accountants

Contact: Wayne Marr
Email:marrm@clemson.clemson.edu

Profile: FEN is the largest network of business and economics scholars and practitioners in the world. FEN is a 40+-channel electronic network linking teachers, scholars, and practitioners in investment banks, banks, companies of all sizes, government agencies, international agencies, and universities.

User Info: Access to the network is free, but you must request a subscription to be included in the mailing list.

Details: Free, Moderated

`URL:mailto:marrm@clemson.clemson.edu`

NAARS (National Automated Accounting Research System)

The National Automated Accounting Research System (NAARS) library, provided as a service by agreement with the American Institute of Certified Public Accountants (AICPA) contains a variety of accounting information.

Keywords: Accounting, Auditing, Filings, Publications

Audience: Accountants

Profile: The NAARS library contains annual reports of public corporations and accounting literature and publications for the accounting professional. Annual reports are annotated with descriptive terms assigned by the AICPA. These terms allow the user to search for annual report footnotes that illustrate one or more recognized accounting practices.

Contact: Mead New Sales Group at (800) 227-4908 or (513) 859-5398 inside the US, or (513) 865-7981 for all inquiries outside the US.

User Info: To subscribe, contact Mead directly.

A B C D E F G H I J K L M N O P Q R S T U V W X Y Z

A
B
C
D
E
F
G
H
I
J
K
L
M
N
O
P
Q
R
S
T
U
V
W
X
Y
Z

To examine the Nexis user guide, you can access it at the ftp site of the University of Texas at Austin at the URL address: ftp://ftp.cc.utexas.edu

The files are in: /pub/ref-services/LEXIS

`telnet://nex.meaddata.com`

`http://www.meaddata.com`

Utah Valley Community College Library

The library's holdings are large and wide-ranging and contain significant collections in many fields.

Keywords: Accounting, Automobiles, Cabinetry, Child Care, Drafting, Electronics, Home Building, Local History, Refrigeration, Air Conditioning

Audience: General Public, Researchers, Librarians, Document Delivery Professionals

Details: Free

User Info: Expect: Login; Send: Opub

`telnet://uvlib.uvcc.edu`

Accri-l

Accri-l

A mailing list providing information on anesthesia and critical care resources available via the Internet.

Keywords: Health Care, Medical Treatment, Medicine

Audience: Health Care Professionals, Health Care Providers

Contact: A.J. Wright

meds002@uabdpo.dpo.uab.edu

User Info: To subscribe, send an e-mail message to the URL address below consisting of a single line reading:

SUB accri-l YourFirstName YourLastName

To send a message to the entire list, address it to: accri-l@uabdpo.dpo.uab.edu

`mailto:listserv@uabdpo.dpo.uab.edu`

ACDGIS-L

ACDGIS-L

GIS discussions for German speakers.

Keywords: Germany, Geographic Information Systems, Geography

Audience: Germans, Geographers, Cartographers

Details: Costs

Inquire through wigeoarn@awiwuw11.bitnet

`mailto:acdgis-l@awiwuw11.bitnet`

ACEN (Art Com Electronic Network)

ACEN (Art Com Electronic Network)

A conference on the WELL for art, technology, and text-based artworks.

Keywords: Art, Literature (Contemporary), Multimedia

Sponsor: Art Com Electronic Network

Audience: Artists, Musicians, Writers

Profile: Started in 1986, ACEN is a seminal art BBS that includes actual artworks, discussion on topics such as software as art, and on line published works by John Cage, Fred Truck, Jim Rosenberg, Judy Malloy, and others.

Contact: Carl Loeffler artcomtv@well.sf.ca.us

User Info: To participate in a conference on the WELL, you must first establish an account on the WELL. To do so, start by typing: **telnet://well.sf.ca.us**

`telnet://well.sf.ca.us`

ACLU

ACLU Free Reading Room

A gopher site containing information relating to the ACLU (American Civil Liberties Union), including the current issue of the ACLU newsletter, Civil Liberties; a growing collection of recent public policy reports and action guides; Congressional voting records for the 103rd Congress; and an archive of news releases from the ACLU's national headquarters.

Keywords: ACLU, Civil Liberties, Congress (US), Activism

Sponsor: ACLU (American Civil Liberties Union)

Audience: Privacy Activists, Civil Libertarians, Activists

Contact: infoaclu@aclu.org

`gopher://aclu.org`

ACM SIGGRAPH Online Bibliography Project

ACM SIGGRAPH Online Bibliography Project

★★★★

This is a collection of computer-graphics bibliographic references.

Keywords: Multimedia, Interactive, Computer Graphics, Programming

Sponsor: Association of Computing Machinery (ACM), Special Interest Group on Computer Graphics (SIGGRAPH)

Audience: Developers, Designers, Producers, Educators, Programmers, Graphic Artists

Profile: The goal of this project is to maintain an up-to-date database of computer-graphics literature, in a format that is accessible to as many members of the computer-graphics community as possible. The database includes references from conferences and workshops worldwide and from a variety of publications dating back as far as the late-19th century. The majority of the major journals and conference proceedings from the mid-1970s to the present are listed.

Contact: bibadmin@siggraph.org

Details: Free, Moderated, Multimedia

`ftp://siggraph.org/publications`

`Acoustical Engineering`

Accoustical Engineering

CEC

A mailing list for the CEC (Canadian Electro-Acoustics Community).

Keywords: Engineering, Acoustical Engineering, Canada, Canadian Electro-Acoustics Community

Audience: Engineers

Contact: Peter Gross grosspa@qucdn.queensu.ca

Details: Free

User Info: To subscribe to the list, send an e-mail message to the URL address below, consisting of a single line reading:

SUB cec YourFirstName YourLastName

To send a message to the entire list, address it to: ced@qucdn.queensu.ca

`mailto:listserv@qucdn.queensu.ca`

Activism

Abortion and Reproductive Rights

A major directory on abortion, providing access to a broad range of related resources (library catalogs, databases, and servers) via the Internet.

Keywords: Abortion, Activism, Women's Issues

Sponsor: The WELL Computer Conference System

Audience: Activists, Feminists

Profile: Choice-Net Report is a weekly update on reproductive rights issues distributed through E-mail, Women's Wire, gopher.WELL.com, Usenet groups alt.activism, talk.abortion, soc.women, and other Internet channels.

Details: Free

`http://gopher.well.sf.ca.us`

ACLU Free Reading Room

A gopher site containing information relating to the ACLU (American Civil Liberties Union), including the current issue of the ACLU newsletter, Civil Liberties; a growing collection of recent public policy reports and action guides; Congressional voting records for the 103rd Congress; and an archive of news releases from the ACLU's national headquarters.

Keywords: ACLU, Civil Liberties, Congress (US), Activism

Sponsor: ACLU (American Civil Liberties Union)

Audience: Privacy Activists, Civil Libertarians, Activists

Contact: infoaclu@aclu.org

`gopher://aclu.org`

Act-up

A mailing list for discussion of the work being done by various Act-Up chapters worldwide.

Keywords: AIDS, Health Care, Activism

Audience: AIDS Activists, Health Science Researchers

Contact: Lenard Diggins
act-up-request@world.std.com

User Info: To subscribe to the list, send an e-mail message to the URL address below.

To send a message to the entire list, address it to: act-up-request@world.std.com

`mailto:act-up-request@world.std.com`

Activ-L

A mailing list for the discussion of peace, empowerment, justice, and environmental issues.

Keywords: Peace, Justice, Environment, Activism

Audience: Activists, Students

Contact: Rich Winkel
harelb@math.cornell.edu

User Info: To subscribe to the list, send an e-mail message to the URL address below consisting of a single line reading:

SUB activ-l YourFirstName YourLastName.

To send a message to the entire list, address it to: active-l@mizzou1.missouri.edu

`mailto:listserv@mizzou1.missouri.edu`

alt.activism

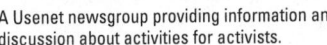

A Usenet newsgroup providing information and discussion about activities for activists.

Keywords: Activism

Audience: Activists

User Info: To subscribe to this Usenet newsgroup, you need access to a newsreader.

`news:alt.activism`

alt.censorship

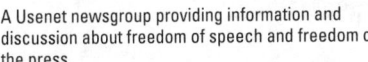

A Usenet newsgroup providing information and discussion about freedom of speech and freedom of the press.

Keywords: Censorship, Freedom of Speech, Constitution (US), Activism

Audience: Press, Students, Educators, Activists

User Info: To subscribe to this Usenet newsgroup, you need access to a newsreader.

`news:alt.censorship`

alt.feminism

A Usenet newsgroup providing information and discussion about feminism.

Keywords: Feminism, Women's Studies, Abortion, Activism

Audience: Women, General Public

User Info: To subscribe to this Usenet newsgroup, you need access to a newsreader.

`news:alt.feminism`

Amend2-discuss

A mailing list for discussion of the implications and issues surrounding the passage of Colorado's Amendment 2, which revokes any existing homosexual civil rights legislation and prohibits the drafting of any new legislation.

Keywords: Activism, Gay Rights, Lesbians, Bisexuality

Audience: Gay Rights Activists

Contact: amend2-mod@cs.colorado.edu

User Info: To subscribe to the list, send an e-mail message to the URL address below consisting of a single line reading: subscribe amend2-discuss

`mailto:majordomo@cs.colorado.edu`

Amend2-info

Colorado voted in an amendment to their state constitution which revokes any existing gay/lesbian/bisexual civil rights legislation and prohibits the drafting of any new legislation. This moderated list is for information on the implication and issues of this amendment.

Keywords: Activists, Gay, Lesbian, Bisexual, Constitutional Amendments, Colorado, Civil Rights

Audience: General Public, Gays, Lesbians, Bisexuals, Activists

Contact: amend2-info@cs.colorado.edu

User Info: To subscribe to the list, send an e-mail message requesting a subscription to the URL address below.

To send a message to the entire list, address it to: amend2-info@cs.colorado.edu

`mailto:majordomo@cs.colorado.edu`

Amnesty International

A site containing information about Amnesty International, an organization focused strictly and specifically on human rights around the world.

Keywords: Government, Human Rights, Politics (International), Activism

Sponsor: Amnesty International

Audience: Students, Activists

Contact: Catherine Hampton
ariel@netcom.com

`ftp://ftp.netcom.com/pub/ariel/www/human.rights/amnesty.international/ai.html`

AR-news

A public news wire for items relating to animal rights and animal welfare.

Keywords: Activism, Animal Rights

Audience: Activists, Animal Lovers

Contact: Ian Lance Taylor, Chip Roberson
taylor@think.com or csr@nic.aren.com

User Info: To subscribe to the list, send an e-mail message to the URL address below.

To send a message to the entire list, address it to: ar-news@think.com

Notes: Appropriate postings to ar-news include posting a news item, requesting information on some event, or responding to a request for information. Discussions on ar-news are not allowed.

`mailto:ar-news@think.com`

A B C D E F G H I J K L M N O P Q R S T U V W X Y Z

AR-talk

An unmoderated list for the discussion of animal rights and related issues, such as animal liberation, consumer product testing, cruelty-free products, vivisection and dissection, and vegan lifestyles.

Keywords: Activism, Animal Rights

Audience: Activists, Animal Lovers, Researchers

Contact: Ian Lance Taylor, Chip Roberson

taylor@think.com or csr@nic.aren.com

User Info: To subscribe to the list, send an e-mail message to the URL address below.

To send a message to the entire list, address it to: ar-talk@think.com

`mailto:ar-talk-request@think.com`

ARlist

An open, unmoderated mailing list to provide a forum for discussing action research and its use in a variety of disciplines and situations. Topics include philosophical and methodological issues in action research, the use of action research for evaluation, actual case studies, and discourse on increasing the rigor of action research.

Keywords: Activism, Research, Politics

Audience: Activists, Researchers

Profile: Arlist is an open unmoderated mailing list to provide a forum for discussing action research and its use in a variety of disciplines and situations. It is usually (but perhaps not always) cyclic, participative, and qualitative.

Contact: Bob Dick
arlist@psych.psy.uq.oz.au

Details: Free

User Info: To subscribe to the list, send an e-mail message to the URL address below.

To send a message to the entire list, address it to: arlist@psych.psy.uq.oz.au

`mailto:arlist-request@psych.psy.uq.oz.au`

`ftp://psych.psy.uq.oz.au/dir/lists/arlist`

Arts Wire

A national communications network for the arts located on the Meta Network.

Keywords: Art, Writing, Activism, Music

Sponsor: New York Foundation for the Arts

Audience: Art Activists, Art Organizations, Artists, Composers, Foundations, Government Arts Agencies, Writers

Profile: Arts Wire provides immediate access to news, information, and dialogue on conditions affecting the arts and artists, as well as private conferences for organizations. Core features include Money, a searcable resource of grant

deadlines; Hotwire, a summary of arts news; and conferences about new music, interactive art, literature, AIDS, and Latino art.

Contact: Judy Malloy
artswire@tmn.com

`telnet://tmn.com`

freedom

Mailing list of people organizing against the Idaho Citizens Alliance antigay ballot initiative.

Keywords: Gay Rights, Activism, Gays

Audience: Gays, Lesbians, Bisexuals, Idaho Citizens, Activists

Details: Free

User Info: To subscribe to the list, send an e-mail message to the URL address shown below consisting of a single line reading:

SUB freedom YourFirstName YourLastName.

To send a message to the entire list, address it to: freedom@idbsu.idbsu.edu

`mailto:listserv@idbsu.idbsu.edu`

HungerWeb

This web site focuses on the political, economic, agricultural, and ethical implications of world hunger.

Keywords: World Health, Activism

Sponsor: Oxfam

Audience: Activists, Financial Planners

Contact: Daniel Zalik
Daniel_Zalik@cs.brown.edu

Details: Free

`http://www.hunger.brown.edu/oxfam`

Mother Jones

A web site containing online electronic issues of Mother Jones magazine (and Zine), making possible instant electronic feedback to the publishers regarding articles.

Keywords: Zines, Ethics, Public Policy, Activism

Sponsor: Mother Jones

Audience: Students, General Public

Contact: Webserver
webserver@mojones.com

`http://www.mojones.com/motherjones.html`

People Using Networks Can Have an Impact on Government

Statement by community networker Anne Fallis, who emphasizes the need for easy-to-use interfaces and inexpensive access to worldwide information. She lists many examples of local communities using networking.

Keywords: Community, Networking, Activism

Audience: Activists, Policymakers, Community Leaders, Network Users

Contact: Anne Fallis
afallis@silver.sdsmt.edu

Details: Free

`http://nearnet.gnn.com/mag/articles/oram/bio.fallis.html`

Qn

A mailing list for Queer Nation activists and for anyone interested in Queer Nation, an activist group devoted to furthering gay rights. The purpose of qn is to network among various Queer Nation chapters, to discuss actions and tactics to bring about Queer Liberation.

Keywords: Homosexuality, Gay Rights, Activism

Audience: Gay Rights Activists, Political Activists

Contact: Roger Klorese
qn-request@queernet.org

Details: Free

User Info: To subscribe to the list, send an e-mail message requesting a subscription to the URL address below.

To send a message to the entire list, address it to: qn@queernet.org

`mailto:qn-request@queernet.org`

Stonewall25

A mailing list for discussion and planning of the "Stonewall 25," an international gay/lesbian/bisexual rights march in New York City on Sunday, June 26, 1994, and the events accompanying it.

Keywords: Gay Rights, Lesbian, Bisexual, Activism

Audience: Gays, Lesbians, Bisexuals, Activists

Contact: stonewall25-request@queernet.org

Details: Free

User Info: To subscribe to the list, send an e-mail message requesting a subscription to the URL address below.

To send a message to the entire list, address it to: stonewall25@queernet.org

`mailto:stonewall25-request@queernet.org`

talk.origins

A Usenet newsgroup providing information and discussion about evolution versus creationism.

Keywords: Evolution, Creationism, Activism

Audience: General Public, Evolutionists, Creationists, Activists

Details: Free

User Info: To subscribe to this Usenet newsgroup, you need access to a newsreader.

`news:talk.origins`

Ada (Programming Language)

info-Ada

Discussion of the Ada programming language.

Keywords: Programming Languages, Ada (Programming Language)

Audience: Programmers

Contact: Karl A. Nyberg
Karl@grebyn.com

Details: Free

User Info: To subscribe to the list, send an e-mail message requesting a subscription to the URL address below

`mailto:info-Ada-request@sei.cmu.edu`

ADA-Law

ADA-Law

A mailing list for the discussion of the Americans with Disabilities Act (ADA) and other disability-related legislation both in the US and abroad.

Keywords: Disabilities, Law (US)

Audience: Disabled People, Legal Professionals

Contact: wtm@bunker.afd.olivetti.com

User Info: To subscribe to the list, send an e-mail message to the URL address below consisting of a single line reading:

SUB ADA-Law YourFirstName YourLastName.

To send a message to the entire list, address it to: ADA-Law@vm1.nodak.edu

`mailto:listserv@vm1.nodak.edu`

Ada-sw

Ada-sw

A list for users who access and contribute software to the Ada Repository on SIMTEL20.

Keywords: Programming

Audience: Programmers

Details: Free

User Info: To subscribe to the list, send an e-mail message requesting a subscription to the URL address below.

To send a message to the entire list, address it to Ada-sw@wsmr-simtel20.army.mil

`mailto:ada-sw-request@wsmr-simtel20.army.mil`

ADD (Attention Deficit/ Hyperactivity Disorder)

ADD-parents

A mailing list intended to provide support and information to parents of children with Attention Deficit/Hyperactivity Disorder.

Keywords: Parenting, ADD (Attention Deficit/ Hyperactivity Disorder)

Audience: Parents, Educators, Health Care Providers

Contact: add-parents-request@mv.mv.com

User Info: To subscribe to the list, send an e-mail message to the URL address below.

To send a message to the entire list, address it to: add-parents@mv.mv.com

`mailto:add-parents-request@mv.mv.com`

ADLTED-L (Canadian Adult Education Network)

ADLTED-L (Canadian Adult Education Network)

The Canadian Adult Continuing Education Network list is a broad, worldwide discussion group.

Keywords: Education (Adult), Education (Distance), Education (Continuing)

Sponsor: Canadian Adult Education Network

Audience: Researchers, Educators, Faculty Administrators

Details: Free

User Info: To subscribe to the list, send an e-mail message to the URL address shown below, consisting of a single line reading:

SUB alted-l YourFirstName YourLastName

To send a message to the entire list, address it to: adlted-l@ureginal.bitnet

`mailto:listserv@uregina1.uregina.ca`

Adoption

Adoptees

The adoptees mailing list is a forum for discussion among adult adoptees of any topic related to adoption.

Keywords: Adoption

Audience: Adoptees

Contact: adoptees-request@ucsd.edu

User Info: To subscribe to the list, send an e-mail message to the URL address below.

To send a message to the entire list, address it to: adoptees@ucsd.edu

Notes: This list is not intended to be a general discussion forum for adoption among non-adoptees.

`mailto:adoptees-request@ucsd.edu`

Adoption

A mailing list for discussion of anything and everything connected with adoption.

Keywords: Adoption

Audience: Adoptees, Adoptive Parents

Contact: adoption-request@think.com

User Info: To subscribe to the list, send an e-mail message to the URL address below consisting of a single line reading:

SUB adoption YourFirstName YourLastName.

To send a message to the entire list, address it to: adoption@think.com

`mailto:listserv@think.com`

Bethany Christian Services

A major directory on adoption, providing access to a broad range of related resources (library catalogs, databases, and servers) via the Internet.

Keywords: Adoption, Christianity, Pregnancy, Abortion Rights

Sponsor: Bethany Christian Services, Grand Rapids, Michigan, USA

Audience: Pregnant Women

Profile: The gopher server of Bethany, a pro-life, pro-family agency reaching out to women with unplanned pregnancies and adoptive couples. Contains a large amount of information about national and international adoption, the adoption process, African-American adoptions, and adoption of children with special needs. Also contains information for pregnant women, such as birth father rights and responsibilities, pregnancy counceling, and so on.

Contact: gophermaster@bethany.org

`gopher://gopher.bethany.org/11`

Birthmother

A mailing list for any birthmother who has relinquished a child for adoption.

Keywords: Adoption

Audience: Parents, Adoptees

Contact: nadir@acca.nmsu.edu

Details: Free

To join the mailing list, send a message to the URL address below with your E-mail address and brief information about your situation (i.e. bmom who relinquished x years ago and does/does not have contact, has/has not been reunited).

`mailto:nadir@acca.nmsu.edu`

Adult/Distance Education

Adult/Distance Education

This directory is a compilation of information resources focused on adult/distance education. The directory is sponsored by The American Association for Collegiate Independent Study, and focuses on correspondence, independent study and distance learning.

Keywords: Education (Adult), Education (Distance), Education (Continuing)

Audience: Educators, Researchers

Details: Free

`ftp://una.hh.lib.umich.edu/70/`
`inetdirsstacks/disted:ellsworth`

Adv-Eli

Adv-Eli

Adv-Eli discusses the latest advances in electrical engineering. It is sponsored by the IEEE Student Branch of Santa Maria University (Chile).

Keywords: Electrical Engineering, Engineering, Electronics

Audience: Engineers, Educators, Students

Contact: Francisco Javier Fernandez
ffernand@utfsm

Details: Free

User Info: To subscribe to the list, send an e-mail message to the URL address shown below consiting of a single line reading:

SUB adv-eli YourFirstName YourLastName

To send a message to the entire list, address it to: adv-eli@loa.disca.utfsm.cl

`listserv@loa.disca.utfsm.cl`

Adv-Elo

Adv-Elo

Discusses the latest advances in electronics. Sponsored by the IEEE Student Branch of Santa Maria University (Chile).

Keywords: Electrical Engineering, Engineering, Electronics, Technological Advances

Audience: Engineers, Educators, Students

Contact: Rodrigo E. Rodriguez
rrodrigu@utfsm

Details: Free

User Info: To subscribe to the list, send an e-mail message to the URL address shown below consiting of a single line reading:

SUB adv-elo YourFirstName YourLastName

To send a message to the entire list, address it to: adv-elo@loa.disca.utfsm.cl

`listserv@loa.disca.utfsm.cl`

Advanced Product Centers (APC)

APC-Open

A mailing list for the interchange of information relevant to Advanced Product Centers (APC).

Keywords: Advanced Product Centers

Audience: APC-OPEN Members

Contact: Fred Rump
fred@compu.com

User Info: To subscribe to the list, send an e-mail message requesting a subscription to the URL address below.

To send a message to the entire list, address it to: apc-open@compu.com

Notes: Membership restricted to APC-OPEN members or those specifically invited.

`mailto:apc-open-request@compu.com`

Advanced Workshops

MICnews

Microcomputer and advanced workstation computing news relevant to the computing populace at the University of California, Los Angeles (UCLA).

Keywords: Microcomputing, Advanced Workshops, UCLA

Sponsor: Microcomputer Information Center, UCLA

Audience: UCLA Students

Contact: Bob Cooper
csmibob@mvs.oac.ucla.edu

Details: Free

User Info: To subscribe to the list, send an e-mail message to the URL address below, consisting of a single line reading:

SUB micnews YourFirstName YourLastName

To send a message to the entire list, address it to:
micnews@uclacn1.ucla.edu

`mailto:listserv@uclacn1.ucla.edu`

Advertising

Apollo Advertising

A major directory on advertising, providing access to a broad range of related resources (library catalogs, databases, and servers) via the Internet.

Keywords: Advertising, Business

Audience: Advertisers, Business Professionals, General Public

Profile: A new web service for advertisers and information providers, which maintains the philosophy that consumers will choose to look for goods and services where it is easy and convenient to locate them. This involves the development of a database of short advertisements, many having hypertext links to more substantial advertisements. These can range from text documents to hypermedia commercials. The Apollo directory can be searched, using logical sorting methods, to identify items of interest. Additional information, including hypermedia, may be connected to the entries. This service encompasses short, stand-alone advertisements, as well as entries with hypertext links to other Internet resources.

Contact: apollo@apollo.co.uk

`gopher://apollo.co.uk`

Communication and Mass Communication Resources

An archive of materials related to mass communications and the media.

Keywords: Mass Communications, Media, Journalism, Telecommunications, Advertising

Sponsor: The University of Iowa

Audience: Mass Communications Students and Teachers, Journalists, Broadcasting Professionals

Contact: Karla Tonella
Karla_Tonella@uiowa.edu

`gopher://iam41.arcade.uiowa.edu`

The Branch Mall, an Electronic Shopping Mall

Branch Information Services offers shopping to customers and leases storefronts and electronic catalogs to vendors.

Keywords: Mall, Shopping, Gifts, Advertising, Mailorder

Sponsor: Branch Information Services

Audience: Consumers, Merchants

Contact: Jon Zeeff
jon@branch.com

Details: Free

Notes: Free for consumers.

`http://branch.com`

Advisory

INTER-L

A list for members of the National Association of Foreign Student Advisors.

Keywords: Advisory, Education (Bilingual), Educational Policy

Sponsor: National Association of Foreign Student Advisors (NAFSA)

Audience: Foreign Students, NAFSA Members

Details: Free

User Info: To subscribe to the list, send an e-mail message to the address below consisting of a single line reading:

`mailto:listserv@vtm1.cc.vt.edu`

AEC

Architecture, Building

This directory is a compilation of information resources focused on architecture.

Keywords: Architecture, Building, Construction, AEC

Audience: Architects, Builders, Civil Engineers

Contact: J. Brown

Details: Free

`ftp://una.hh.lib.umich.edu/70/`
`inetdirsstacks/archi:brown`

AEDNET (Adult Education Network)

AEDNET (Adult Education Network)

★★★★

This is an international electronic network for those involved in distance education.

Keywords: Education (Adult), Education (Distance), Education (Continuing)

Sponsor: Adult Education Network

Audience: Educators, Researchers, Faculty Administrators

Details: Free

User Info: To subscribe to the list, send an e-mail message to the URL address shown below consisting of a single line reading:

SUB aednet YourFirstName YourLastName

To send a message to the entire list, address it to:
AEDNET@alpha.acast.nova.edu

`mailto:listserv@alpha.acast.nova.edu`

Aeronautics

Aelflow

A mailing list for the discussion of aerospace and aeronautical engineering.

Keywords: Aerospace, Aeronautics, Engineering

Sponsor: The Aerospace Engineering Fluid Group

Audience: Engineers, Educators, Students

Contact: Dr. Yakov Cohen
aer8601@technion.ac.il.edu

Details: Free

User Info: To subscribe to the list, send an e-mail message to the URL address shown below consiting of a single line reading:SUB aelflow YourFirstName YourLastName

To send a message to the entire list, address it to: Aelflow@technion.ac.il ed

`listserv@technion.ac.il edu`

Aeronautics

★★

A moderated discussion-group dealing with atmospheric flight, aerodynamics, flying qualities, simulation, structures, systems, propulsion, and design human factors.

Keywords: Aeronautics

Audience: Aeronautical Engineers

Contact: aeronautics-request@rascal.ics.utexas.edu

User Info: To subscribe to the list, send an e-mail message to the URL address below.

To send a message to the entire list, address it to:
aeronautics@rascal.ics.utexas.edu

Notes: The aeronautics mailing list is a news-to-mail feed of the sci.aeronautics newsgroup. Subscribers can participate in real-time with the main group.

`mailto:aeronautics-`
`request@rascal.ics.utexas.edu`

Aeronautics (History of)

Massachusetts Institute of Technology Library

★★★★

The library's holdings are large and wide-ranging and contain significant collections in many fields.

Keywords: Aeronautics (History of), Linguistics, Mathematics (History of), Microscopy, Spectroscopy, Aeronautics, Mathematics, Glass

Audience: General Public, Researchers, Librarians, Document Delivery Professionals

Details: Free

User Info: Expect: Mitek Server..., Send: Enter or Return; Expect: prompt, Send: hollis

`telnet://library.mit.edu`

European Space Agency

A major directory on aeronautics, providing access to a broad range of related resources (library catalogs, databases, and servers) via the Internet.

Keywords: Space Science, Aeronautics

Audience: Space Science Researchers

Profile: The home page of the European Space Agency, including information about ESA's mission, specific ESA programs (Science, Manned Spaceflight and Microgravity, Earth Observation, Telecommunications, Launchers), and issues related to the space and aeronautics industry.

Contact: webmaster@esa.it

`http://www.esrin.esa.it`

Massachusetts Institute of Technology Library

The library's holdings are large and wide-ranging and contain significant collections in many fields.

Keywords: Aeronautics (History of), Linguistics, Mathematics (History of), Microscopy, Spectroscopy, Aeronautics, Mathematics, Glass

Audience: General Public, Researchers, Librarians, Document Delivery Professionals

Details: Free

User Info: Expect: Mitek Server..., Send: Enter or Return; Expect: prompt, Send: hollis

`telnet://library.mit.edu`

Princeton University Library

The library's holdings are large and wide-ranging. They contain significant collections in many fields.

A
B
C
D
E
F
G
H
I
J
K
L
M
N
O
P
Q
R
S
T
U
V
W
X
Y
Z

A
B
C
D
E
F
G
H
I
J
K
L
M
N
O
P
Q
R
S
T
U
V
W
X
Y
Z

Keywords: China, Japan, Classics, History
(Ancient), Near Eastern Studies,
Literature (American), Literature
(English), Aeronautics, Middle Eastern
Studies, Mormonism, Publishing

Audience: General Public, Researchers, Librarians,
Document Delivery Professionals

Details: Free

User Info: Expect: Connect message, blank screen,
Send: <cr>; Expect: #, Send: Call 500

`telnet://pucable.princeton.edu`

Rascal Aviation Archives

A major directory on aeronautics, providing access
to a broad range of related resources (library
catalogues, databases, and servers) via the Internet.

Keywords: Aeronautics, Aviation

Audience: Aviators, Aeronautical Engineers

Contact: rdd@rascal.ics.utexas.edu

`ftp://rascal.ics.utexas.edu/explore-me/Aviation-stuff`

Spacelink

This contains information about NASA and its
activities, including a large number of curricular
activities for elementary and secondary science
classes.

Keywords: NASA, Aeronautics, Education (K-12)

Audience: Students (K-12), Educators, General
Public

Details: Free

`telnet://newuser@spacelink.msfc.nasa.gov`

Ssi_mail

A moderated list for topics related to Space Studies
Institute programs—past, present, and future.

Keywords: Space Studies, Space Science,
Aeronautics

Audience: Space Students, Space Scientists

Contact: Mitchell James
mjames@link.com
mitchellj@aol.com

Details: Free, Moderated

User Info: To subscribe to the list, send an e-mail
message requesting a subscription to
the URL address below.

To send a message to the entire list,
address it to: ssi_mail@link.com

Notes: Archives available.

`mailto:listprocessor@link.com`

Aerospace

Aerospace Engineering

This directory is a compilation of information
resources focused on aerospace engineeering.

Keywords: Aerospace, Engineering, Aviation, Space

Audience: Aerospace Engineers, Space Scientists

Profile: This is a guide to Internet resources that
contain information pertaining to
aerospace engineering. Originally the
guide was to cover the area of
aerospace engineering as applied to
lower atmospheric flight. However, it is
difficult to narrow the sites down to
specific subject areas. As the guide
evolved, sites were included with a
broader scope of information.The guide
is by no means comprehensive and
exhaustive; there are sites that are not
included and those the authors were not
aware of, and they welcome
suggestions. The directory lists sites on
FTP, Gopher, Listserv, OPAC, Telnet,
Usenet, and WWW.

Details: Free

`ftp://una.hh.lib.umich.edu/70/
inetdirsstacks/aerospace:potsiedalq`

DMS/FI Market Intelligence Reports

DMS/FI Market Intelligence Reports is the
largest collection of unclassified defense and
aerospace information available from any single
source.

Keywords: Defense, Aerospace

Sponsor: Forecast International/DMS, Newtown,
CT, USA

Audience: Defense Analysts

Profile: This file contains the most comprehensive and up-to-date full-text data and
analysis for the industry and provides
users with valuable information on
defense budgets, aerospace and
weapons programs, power systems,
companies (US and international),
agencies, or countries that are involved
in the aerospace/defense industry. File
589 contains a great deal of information
relative to civil and commercial
programs. Reports provide detailed and
extensive information such as forecasts,
major activity, funding, inventories,
location, and much more. This
information is gathered from such
diverse sources as government
documents, civil and defense journals,
manufacturers, and field interviews with
key industry people. This database is
vital to anyone involved in market
research, business development, or
program management in the aerospace/
defense industry.

Contact: Dialog in the US at (800) 334-2564, Dialog
internationally at country-specific
locations.

User Info: To subscribe, contact Dialog directly.

Notes: Coverage: Current; updated weekly.

`telnet://dialog.com`

Jane's Defense & Aerospace News/Analysis

This file provides articles that summarize, highlight,
and interpret worldwide events in the defense and
aerospace industry.

Keywords: Defense, Aerospace, News Media

Sponsor: Jane's Information Group, Alexandria,
VA US

Audience: Aerospace Industry Professionals

Profile: The database contains the complete text
of the following publications: Jane's
Defense Weekly, International Defense
Review, Jane's Intelligence Review
(formerly Jane's Soviet Intelligence
Review), Interavia Aerospace Review,
and Jane's Airport Review. File 587 also
contains the complete text of DMS
newsletters, which ceased publication in
1989.

Contact: Dialog in the US at (800) 334-2564, Dialog
internationally at country-specific
locations.

User Info: To subscribe, contact Dialog directly.

Notes: Coverage: 1982 to the present; updated
weekly.

`telnet://dialog.com`

Lockheed Missiles & Space Company

A web site containing information about Lockheed
Missiles and Space Company, a major aerospace
and defense company specializing in the
development of space systems, missiles and other
high technology products. Includes company
information and press releases.

Keywords: Defense, Aerospace

Sponsor: The Lockheed Palo Alto Artificial
Intelligence Center

Audience: Aerospace Industry Professionals

`http://www.lmsc.lockheed.com`

McDonnell Douglas Aerospace

A web site providing information about McDonnell
Douglas, including a company profile and related
discussion about technology.

Keywords: Aerospace, Space, Aviation, Technology

Audience: Aerospace Engineers

Contact: Zook@pat.mdc.com

`http://pat.mdc.com`

af

af

A mailing list for discussion of AudioFile, a client/server, network-transparent, device independent audio system.

Keywords: Audio Electronics, Electrical Engineering

Audience: Audio Enthusiasts, Electrical Engineers

Contact: af-request@crl.dec.com

User Info: To subscribe to the list, send an e-mail message to the URL address below.

To send a message to the entire list, address it to: af@crl.dec.com

`mailto:af-request@crl.dec.com`

Africa

Africa in the CIA World Fact Book

A gopher site containing geographical and political information about individual countries in Africa.

Keywords: Africa, Intelligence, Project Gutenberg

Sponsor: Project Gutenberg

Audience: Africans, General Public

`gopher://hoshi.cic.sfu.ca/11/dlam/cia/Africa`

Africa-n

A moderated mailing list dedicated to the exchange of news and information on Africa, including correspondence from many sources worldwide.

Keywords: News Media, Africa

Audience: Africans, Students

Contact: Faraz Rabbani
frabbani@epas.utoronto.ca

User Info: To subscribe to the list, send an e-mail message to the URL address below consisting of a single line reading:

SUB africa-n YourFirstName YourLastName

To send a message to the entire list, address it to: africa-n@utoronto.bitnet

`mailto:listserv@utoronto.bitnet`

African Art Exhibit and Tutorial

This web site provides images of African art and an overview of African aesthetics.

Keywords: Art, Africa, Cultural Studies

Sponsor: University of Virginia

Audience: Artists, Art Students, Educators, Historians

`http://www.lib.virginia.edu`

African Education Research Network

This gopher contains various links to African studies programs at select universities, and other archived information of interest to the African studies scholar.

Keywords: Cultural Studies, Africa, African Studies

Sponsor: Ohio University, African Education Research Network

Audience: Students, African-Americans, Africans

Contact: Milton E. Ploghoft
mperdreau@ohiou.edu

Details: Free

`gopher://gopher.ohiou.edu/00/dept.servers/aern`

Black/African Related Online Information

This is a list of online information storage sites that contain a significant amount of information pertaining to Black or African people, culture, and issues around the world.

Keywords: Culture, Race, Africa, African Studies

Sponsor: AfriInfo

Audience: Students, African-Americans, Africans

Contact: McGee
mcgee@epsilon.eecs.nwu.edu

Details: Free

`ftp://ftp.netcom.com/pub/amcgee/my_african_related_lists/afrisite.msg`

MDEAFR

The Middle East and Africa (MDEAFR) library contains detailed information about every country in the Mideast and Africa. Structured for those who want to follow the unfolding events in the Gulf states, as well as in North and South Africa, this library contains a broad array of sources, including international research reports from InvestextR.

Keywords: News, Analysis, Companies, Middle East, Africa

Audience: Journalists, Business Professionals

Profile: The MDEAFR library contains a wide array of pertinent sources. Among the information sources are newspapers and wire services, trade and business journals, company reports, country and region background, industry and product analysis, business opportunities, and selected legal texts. News sources range from the world-renowned Associated Press and Christian Science Monitor to the regionally important Jerusalem Post and Africa News. Company information is contained in the EXTEL cards as well as ICC. Providers of country background and industry analysis include Associated Banks of Europe, Bank of America, Business

International, IBC USA, and the US Department of Commerce. Customers interested in new business opportunities can check OPIC and Foreign Trade Opportunities (FTO).

Contact: Mead New Sales Group at (800) 227-4908 or (513) 859-5398 inside the US, or (513) 865-7981 for all inquiries outside the US.

User Info: To subscribe, contact Mead directly.

To examine the Nexis user guide, you can access it at the ftp site of the University of Texas at Austin at the URL address: ftp://ftp.cc.utexas.edu

The files are in: /pub/ref-services/LEXIS

`telnet://nex.meaddata.com`

`http://www.meaddata.com`

Northwestern University Library

The library's holdings are large and wide-ranging and contain significant collections in many fields.

Keywords: Africa, Wright (Frank Lloyd), Women's Studies, Art, Literature (American), Contemporary Music, Government (US State), UN Documents, Music

Audience: General Public, Researchers, Librarians, Document Delivery Professionals

Details: Free

User Info: Expect: COMMAND:, Send: DIAL VTAM

`telnet://nuacvm.acns.nwu.edu`

South Africa

A major directory on Africa, providing access to a broad range of related resources (library catalogues, databases, and servers) via the Internet.

Keywords: Africa, South Africa

Audience: General Public

Profile: South Africa's home page, containing information about different regions and major cities, weather conditions, vital statistics, and information about the University of South Africa.

Contact: Aleksandar Radovanovic
radova@osprey.unisa.ac.za

`http://osprey.unisa.ac.za/0/docs/south-africa.html`

African American Studies

soc.culture.african.american

A Usenet newsgroup providing information and discussion about African American culture.

Keywords: African American Studies, Sociology, Minorities

Audience: Sociologists, Researchers, General Public

A
B
C
D
E
F
G
H
I
J
K
L
M
N
O
P
Q
R
S
T
U
V
W
X
Y
Z

Details: Free

User Info: To subscribe to this Usenet newsgroup, you need access to a newsreader.

`news:soc.culture.african.american`

African Studies

African Education Research Network

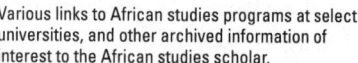

Various links to African studies programs at select universities, and other archived information of interest to the African studies scholar.

Keywords: Culture, Race, Africa, African Studies

Sponsor: Ohio University, African Education Research Network

Audience: Students, African-Americans, Africans

Contact: Milton E. Ploghoft
mperdreau@ohiou.edu

Details: Free

`gopher://gopher.ohiou.edu/00/dept.servers/aern`

Black/African Related Online Information

★★★★

This is a list of online information storage sites that contain a significant amount of information pertaining to Black or African people, culture, and issues around the world.

Keywords: Culture, Race, Africa, African Studies

Sponsor: AfriInfo

Audience: Students, African-Americans, Africans

Contact: McGee
mcgee@epsilon.eecs.nwu.edu

Details: Free

`ftp://ftp.netcom.com/pub/amcgee/my_african_related_lists/afrisite.msg`

Afrikaans

Harvard UniversityLibrary

★★★★

The library's holdings are large and wide-ranging and contain significant collections in many fields.

Keywords: Afrikaans, Alchemy, Arabic Culure (History of), Celtic Philology, Congo Languages, Folklore, Hebraica, Mormonism, Numismatics, Quakers, Sanskrit, Witchcraft, Arabic Philology

Audience: General Public, Researchers, Librarians, Document Delivery Professionals

Details: Free

User Info: Expect: Mitek Server..., Send: Enter or Return; Expect: prompt, Send: hollis

`telnet://hollis.harvard.edu`

Agence FrancePresse International French Wire

Agence FrancePresse International French Wire

 ★★★

Agence FrancePresse International French Wire provides full-text articles in French relating to national, international, business, and sports news.

Keywords: News Media, Europe, Third World, French

Sponsor: Agence FrancePresse, Paris, France

Audience: Market Researchers, Journalists, Francophiles

Profile: Agence FrancePresse distributes its French service worldwide, including Western and Eastern Europe, Canada, northern and western Africa, the Middle East, Vietnam, French Guiana, the West Indies, and the French Pacific islands. Agence FrancePresse International French Wire has extensive coverage of the European countries, including every aspect of economic, political, and general business news. It also provides excellent industrial and market news from both developed countries and from theThird World.

Contact: Dialog in the US at (800) 334-2564; Dialog internationally at country-specific locations.

Details: Costs

User Info: To subscribe, contact Dialog directly.

Coverage: September 1991 to the present; updated daily.

`telnet://dialog.com`

Aging

AgeLine

★★★

The AgeLine database is produced by the American Association of Retired Persons (AARP) and provides bibliographic coverage of social gerontology—the study of aging in social, psychological, health-related, and economic contexts.

Keywords: Gerontology, Retirement, Public Policy, Aging

Sponsor: American Association of Retired Persons, Washington, DC, USA

Audience: Retired Persons, Health Care Providers, Researchers

Profile: AgeLine covers the delivery of health care for the older population and its associated costs and policies, as well as public policy, employment, and consumer issues. Literature covered is of interest to researchers, health professionals, service planners, policy makers, employers, older adults and their families, and consumer advocates.

Contact: Dialog in the US at (800) 334-2564; Dialog internationally at country-specific locations.

Details: Costs

User Info: To subscribe, contact Dialog directly.

Notes: Coverage: 1978 to the present (selected coverage back to 1966); updated bimonthly.

`telnet://dialog.com`

agora

agora

★★★★

A forum for Hungarian speakers to discuss a wide variety of subjects.

Keywords: Hungary

Audience: Hungarian Speakers

Contact: Zoli Fekete
fekete@bcvms.bc.edu

Details: Free

Inquiries and contributions to the list can be sent to the personal address of the contact above (place word AGORA in the subject field), or to the world.std.com address below (place word $SEGIT in the subject field).

`mailto:agora@world.std.com`

Agoraphobia

Panic

★

This is a support group for panic disorders. Discussion involving phobias resulting from panic (agoraphobia and others). Also a place to meet people who have gone through the disorder as well.

Keywords: Panic Disorders, Agoraphobia

Audience: Panic Disorder Sufferers

Contact: Panic-Request@gnu.ai.mit.edu

Details: Free

User Info: To subscribe to the list, send an e-mail message requesting a subscription to the URL address below.

To send a message to the entire list, address it to: panic@gnu.ai.mit.edu

`mailto:Panic-Request@gnu.ai.mit.edu`

Agriculture

agmodels-l

★★

A forum for the discussion of agricultural simulation models of all types. Issues include plant growth, micro-meteorology, soil hydrology, transport, farm economy, and farm systems.

Keywords: Agriculture, Farm Economy

Audience: Agronomists

Contact: Jerome Pier
jp@unl.edu

User Info: To subscribe to the list, send an e-mail message to the URL address below consisting of a single line reading:

SUB agmodels-I YourFirstName YourLastName

To send a message to the entire list, address it to: agmodels-I@unl.edu

`mailto:listserv@unl.edu`

AGRICOLA

The AGRICOLA database of the National Agricultural Library (NAL) provides comprehensive coverage of worldwide journal literature and monographs on agriculture and related subjects.

Keywords: Agriculture, Animal Studies, Botany, Entomology

Sponsor: US National Agricultural Library, Beltsville, MD, USA

Audience: Agronomists, Botanists, Chemists, Entomologists

Profile: Related subjects include: animal studies, botany, chemistry, entomology, fertilizers, forestry, hydroponics, soils, and more.

Contact: Dialog in the US at (800) 334-2564, Dialog internationally at country-specific locations.

User Info: To subscribe, contact Dialog directly.

Notes: Coverage: 1970 to the present; updated monthly.

`telnet://dialog.com`

Agricultural Guide

A specialized guide, entitled "Not Just Cows," to the Internet/Bitnet resources in agriculture and related science.

Keywords: Agriculture, Internet, Internet Guide

Sponsor: University of North Carolina

Audience: Internet Surfers

Contact: Wilfred Drew

Details: Free

`ftp://sunsite.unc.edu/pub/docs/about-the-net/libsoft/agguide.dos`

`gopher://sunsite.unc.edu`

`http://sunsite.unc.edu/pub/docs/about-the-net/libsoft/agguide.dos`

Agriculture

This directory is a compilation of information resources focused on agriculture.

Keywords: Agriculture, Economics

Audience: Farmers, Agronomists, Agriculturalists

Contact: Wilfred Drew
drewwe@snymorva.cs.snymor.edu

Details: Free

`ftp://una.hh.lib.umich.edu`

`gopher://snymorvb.cs.snymor.edu`

Agriculture, Veterinary Science & Zoology

This directory is a compilation of information resources focused on agriculture, veterinary science, and zoology.

Keywords: Agriculture, Veterinary Science, Zoology

Audience: Farmers, Agronomists, Veterinarians, Zoologists

Details: Free

`ftp://una.hh.lib.umich.edu/70/inetdirsstacks/agvetzoo:haas`

AGRIS International

This database serves as a comprehensive inventory of worldwide agricultural literature that reflects research results, food production, and rural development.

Keywords: Agriculture, Rural Development, Food Production, Development

Sponsor: US National Agricultural Library, Beltsville, MD, USA

Audience: Agronomists, Market Researchers, Agricultural Economists

Profile: Designed to help users identify problems involved in all aspects of world food supply, the file corresponds in part to Agr Index, published monthly by the Food and Agriculture Organization (FAO) of the United Nations. Subject coverage focuses on many topics: general agriculture; geography and history; education, extension, and advisory work; administration and legislation; economics, development, and rural sociology; plant production; protection of plants and stored products; forestry; animal production; aquatic sciences and fisheries; machinery and buildings; natural resources; food science; home economics; human nutrition; pollution; and more.

Contact: Dialog in the US at (800) 334-2564

Details: Costs

User Info: To subscribe, contact Dialog directly.

`telnet://dialog.com`

Biosis Previews

The database encompasses the entire field of life sciences and covers original research reports and reviews in biological and biomedical areas. This includes field, laboratory, clinical, experimental and theoretical work. The traditional areas of biology,

including botany, zoology and microbiology are covered, as well as the related fields such as plant and animal science, agriculture, pharmacology and ecology.

Keywords: Biology, Botany, Zoology, Microbiology, Plant Science, Animal Science, Agriculture, Pharmacology, Ecology, Biochemistry, Biophysics, Bioengineering

Sponsor: Biosis

Audience: Librarians, Researchers, Students, Biologists, Botanists, Zoologists, Scientists, Taxonomists

Contact: CDP Technologies Sales Department (800)950-2035, extension 400

User Info: To subscribe, contact CDP Technologies directly

`telnet:\\cdplus@cdplus.com`

Food Industry Investext

The world's largest database of company, industry, topical, and geographic analysis.

Keywords: Food Industry, Agriculture

Sponsor: Thomson Financial Networks, Boston, MA US

Audience: Business Professionals, Market Researchers

Profile: The database is composed of more than 320,000 full-text reports written by analysts at 180 investment banks and research firms worldwide. The research can be used for a wide range of business intelligence activities, including competitive analysis, evaluation of companies, and strategic planning. Coverage includes 14,000 companies worldwide and 53 industry groups.

User Info: To subscribe, contact Dialog directly.

Notes: Coverage: July 1982 to the present; updated daily.

`telnet://dialog.com`

Iowa State University

The library's holdings contain significant collections in many fields.

Keywords: Agriculture, Veterinary Medicine, Statistics, Labor, Soil Conservation, Film

Audience: General Public, Researchers, Librarians, Document Delivery Professionals

Details: Free

User Info: Expect: DIAL, Send: LIB

`telnet://isn.iastate.edu`

Ogphre - SunSITE

A collection of Internet resources organized by subject. Particular strengths include agriculture, religious texts, poetry, creative writing, and US politics. The ftp site has a set of more general Internet guides.

Keywords: Agriculture, Politics (US), Religion, Internet

Sponsor: The University of North Carolina - Chapel Hill and Sun Microsystems, USA

Audience: General Public, Internet Surfers, Researchers

Contact: Darlene Fladager, Elizabeth Lyons
           Darlene_Fladager@unc.edu
           Elizabeth_Lyons@unc.edu

`gopher://sunsite.unc.edu`

`ftp://sunsite.unc.edu`

University of Maryland, College Park

The library's holdings are large and wide-ranging and contain significant collections in many fields

Keywords: Agriculture, Coastal Marine Biology, Fisheries, Water Quality, Oceanography

Audience: Researchers, Students, General Public

Contact: Janet McLeod
           mcleod@umail.umd.edu

Details: Free

User Info: Expect: Login; Send: Atdu

`telnet://info.umd.edu`

University of Puerto Rico Library

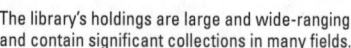

The library's holdings are large and wide-ranging and contain significant collections in many fields.

Keywords: Computer Science, Education, Nursing, Agriculture, Economics

Audience: Researchers, Students, General Public

Details: Free
           After Locator: telnet://, press Tab twice. Type DIAL VTAM.
           Enter NOTIS. Press Return. On the blank screen, type LUUP.

`telnet://136.145.2.10`

University of Wisconsin River Falls Library

The library's holdings are large and wide-ranging and contain significant collections in many fields.

Keywords: Agriculture, Education, History (US)

Audience: Researchers, Students, General Public

Details: Free

User Info: Expect: Service Name, Send: Victor

`telnet://davee.dl.uwrf.edu`

USDA Agricultural Extension Service

Includes information from the USDA (United States Department of Agriculture) Extension Service, National Agriculture Library, and Americans Communicating Electronically (ACE)

Keywords: Agriculture

Audience: Farmers, Agriculturalists, Educators

Details: Free

`gopher://cyfer.esusda.gov`

Washington State University at Puyallup Library

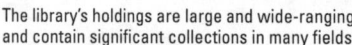

The library's holdings are large and wide-ranging and contain significant collections in many fields.

Keywords: Agriculture, Scientific Research

Audience: Researchers, Students, General Public

Details: Free

User Info: Expect: Login; Send: Lib

`telnet://wsuvm1.cscwsu.edu`

AIDS

Act-up

A mailing list for discussion of the work being done by various Act-Up chapters worldwide.

Keywords: AIDS, Health Care, Activism

Audience: AIDS Activists, Health Science Researchers

Contact: Lenard Diggins
           act-up-request@world.std.com

User Info: To subscribe to the list, send an e-mail message to the URL address below.
           To send a message to the entire list, address it to: act-up-request@world.std.com

`mailto:act-up-request@world.std.com`

Aids

A forum for the discussion of AIDS, predominantly from a medical perspective, but also with some discussion of political and social issues.

Keywords: AIDS, Medicine, Politics

Sponsor: UCLA

Audience: AIDS Researchers, AIDS Activists, Health Care Providers

Contact: Daniel R. Greening
           aids-request@cs.ucla.edu

User Info: To subscribe to the list, send an e-mail message to the URL address below.
           To send a message to the entire list, address it to: aids@cs.ucla.edu

`mailto:aids-request@cs.ucla.edu`

AIDS Treatment News

A newsletter on AIDS treatment.

Keywords: AIDS, Health, Medicine

Sponsor: IGC (Institute for Global Communications)

Audience: AIDS Researchers, Health Workers, AIDS Sufferers

Profile: This newsletter contains interviews, reports on new and existing treatment modalities, announcements of clinical drug testing trials, and more.

Contact: atn@igc.apc.org

Details: Free

`gopher://odie.niaid.nih.gov/11/aids`

AIDS/HIV Information

A clearinghouse for AIDS/HIV-related information. Contains Internet connections to WWW and gopher servers, and archives of AIDS server FAQ's, including an archive of AIDS treatment news.

Keywords: AIDS, Medicine, Health

Sponsor: Queer Resources Directory, USA

Audience: AIDS Sufferers, Gays, Activists

Contact: QRD Staff
           QRDstaff@vector.casti.com

Details: AIDS Treatment News

`http://vector.casti.com/QRD/.html/AIDS.html`

AIDSLINE

The AIDSLINE database is a bibliography of research and clinical information as well as health policy issues concerning AIDS. The citations in AIDSLINE are primarily derived from MEDLINE, Health Planning & Administration, CancerLit, CATLINE, AVLINE, the meeting abstracts from the International Conferences on AIDS, the Symposia on Non-human Models of AIDS, and AIDS-related abstracts from the Annual Meetings of the American Society of Microbiology.

Keywords: AIDS, Medicine

Sponsor: U.S. National Library of Medicine

Audience: AIDS Researchers, Epidemiologists, Clinicians, AIDS Sufferers

Contact: CDP Technologies Sales Department (800)950-2035, extension 400

User Info: To subscribe, contact CDP Technologies directly

`telnet://cdplus@cdplus.com`

National Institutes of Health Gopher

Provides access to a broad range of National Institutes of Health (NIH) resources (library catalogues, databases) via the Internet.

Keywords: Health, AIDS, Molecular Biology, Grants

Sponsor: National Institutes of Health

Audience: Health Professionals, Molecular Biologists, Researchers

Profile: This gopher provides access to NIH resources, including institute phone books and calendars, library catalogs, molecular biology databases, the full text of the NIH Guide for Grants and Contracts, files containing AIDS and cancer information and more.

Contact: gopher@gopher.nih.gov

Details: Free

User Info: Expect: Login; Enter: Gopher

`telnet://gopher.nih.gov`

`gopher://gopher.nih.gov`

`gopher://odie.niaid.nih.gov`

South East Florida AIDS Information Network (SEFAIN)

Contains a wide range of information on AIDS research(ers), organizations, and services in searchable databases.

Keywords: AIDS, Medicine

Sponsor: This project is sponsored in part by the National Library of Medicine

Audience: Medical Professionals, Scientists, Educators, Health Care Providers

Details: Free

Select L on main menu, then select 1 on next menu

`telnet:// library@callcat.med.miami.edu`

Women.health

This conference features articles, documents, news, announcements, policy statements, and other information about women's health around the world. Topics include breast cancer, ovarian cancer, alcohol, abortion, pregnancy, sterilization of women, pesticides, Quinacrine, HIV, disability.

Keywords: Women, Abortion, AIDS, Disability, Feminism, Health

Audience: Activists, Family Planners, Health Professionals, Non-Governmental Organizations, Women

Details: Costs

User Info: Establish an account on the nearest APC node. Login, type c for conferences, then type go women.health. For information on the nearest APC node, contact: APC International Secretariat IBASE.

E-mail: apcadmin@apc.org

`telnet://igc.apc.org`

Aikido

Aikido Information

An FTP site containing aikido dojo addresses from around the world, plus a calendar of events, FAQs, and lists of books and periodicals related to aikido.

Keywords: Aikido, Martial Arts, Sports, Japan

Sponsor: University of California at San Diego, San Diego, CA, USA

Audience: Martial Arts Enthusiasts

Contact: aikido@cs.ucsd.edu

Details: Free

`ftp://cs.ucsd.edu/pub/aikido`

aikido-l

A discussion group and information exchange on the Japanese martial art Aikido.

Keywords: Aikido, Martial Arts, Sports, Japan

Sponsor: Gerry Santoro

Audience: Martial Arts Enthusiasts

Contact: aikido-l-request@psuvm.psu.edu

User Info: To subscribe to the list, send an e-mail message to the URL address below consisting of a single line reading:

SUB aikido-l YourFirstName YourLastName

To send a message to the entire list, address it to: aikido-l@psuvm.psu.edu

`mailto:listserv@psuvm.psu.edu`

Physical Education & Recreation

A collection of information on sporting and recreational activities from aikido to windsurfing.

Keywords: Sports, Recreation, Aikido, Cycling, Scuba Diving, Windsurfing

Audience: Sports Enthusiasts, Fitness Enthusiasts

Contact: ctcadmin@ctc.ctc.edu

`gopher://ctc.ctc.edu`

Air Conditioning

Utah Valley Community College Library

The library's holdings are large and wide-ranging and contain significant collections in many fields.

Keywords: Accounting, Automobiles, Cabinetry, Child Care, Drafting, Electronics, Home Building, Local History, Refrigeration, Air Conditioning

Audience: General Public, Researchers, Librarians, Document Delivery Professionals

Details: Free

User Info: Expect: Login; Send: Opub

`telnet://uvlib.uvcc.edu`

Airplanes

Airplane-clubs

A mailing list for discussion of all matters relating to the management and organization of groups operating aircraft.

Keywords: Airplanes, Aviation

Audience: Aviators

Contact: Matthew Waugh airplane-clubs-request@dg-rtp.dg.com

User Info: To subscribe to the list, send an e-mail message to the URL address below.

To send a message to the entire list, address it to: airplane-clubs@dg-rtp.dg.com

`mailto:airplane-clubs-request@dg-rtp.dg.com`

Alaska

Information About Alaska

This collection contains information on Alaska's government and politics, as well as historical documents about Alaska's neighbors, Russia and Canada. It also has cultural information, including literature and sports in the Land of the Midnight Sun.

Keywords: Alaska, Travel

Sponsor: University of Alaska Computer Network (UACN), Alaska, USA

Audience: Alaskans, Travelers, General Public

Contact: Douglas Toelle sxinfo@orca.alaska.edu

`gopher://info.alaska.edu`

A B C D E F G H I J K L M N O P Q R S T U V W X Y Z

A
B
C
D
E
F
G
H
I
J
K
L
M
N
O
P
Q
R
S
T
U
V
W
X
Y
Z

Alchemy

Harvard UniversityLibrary

The library's holdings are large and wide-ranging and contain significant collections in many fields.

Keywords: Afrikaans, Alchemy, Arabic Culure (History of), Celtic Philology, Congo Languages, Folklore, Hebraica, Mormonism, Numismatics, Quakers, Sanskrit, Witchcraft, Arabic Philology

Audience: General Public, Researchers, Librarians, Document Delivery Professionals

Details: Free

User Info: Expect: Mitek Server..., Send: Enter or Return; Expect: prompt, Send: hollis

`telnet://hollis.harvard.edu`

Aldus Pagemaker

PAGEMAKER

The PageMaker ListServ is dedicated to the discussion of desktop publishing in general, with emphasis on the use of Aldus PageMaker. The list discusses PageMaker's use in both the PC and Macintosh realms. The list also maintains an extensive archive of help files that are extremely useful for the modern desktop publisher.

Keywords: Desktop Publishing, Aldus Pagemaker, IBM PC, Macintosh

Audience: Desktop Publishers, Computer Users

Contact: Geoff Peters gwp@cs.purdue.edu

Details: Free

User Info: To subscribe to the list, send an e-mail message to the URL address shown below consisting of a single line reading:

SUB pagemaker YourFirstName YourLastName

To send a message to the entire list, address it to: gwp@cs.purdue.edu

`mailto:listserv@cs.purdue.edu`

Alex

Alex Description

An NIR (Network Information Retrieval) description of Alex, an Internet access tool.

Keywords: Internet Tools, Internet, Alex

Audience: Internet Surfers

Details: Free

`ftp://alex.sp.cs.cmu.edu/usr0/anon/ doc/NIR.Tool`

Aliens

alt.alien.visitors

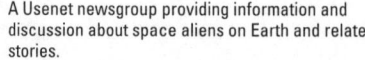

A Usenet newsgroup providing information and discussion about space aliens on Earth and related stories.

Keywords: UFOs, Aliens, Extraterrestrial Life

Audience: Alien Enthusiasts

User Info: To subscribe to this Usenet newsgroup, you need access to a newsreader.

`news:alt.alien.visitors`

The University of California Search for Extraterrestrial Civilizations

A web site containing information on the UC Berkeley SETI Program, SERENDIP (Search for Extraterrestrial Radio Emmisions from Nearby Developed Intelligent Populations), an ongoing scientific research effort aimed at detecting radio signals from extraterrestrial civilizations. Details about the program and updates on current research activities are also accessible.

Keywords: Extraterrestrial Life, Astronomy, Aliens

Audience: Astronomers, Physicists, Students, Educators, Engineers, General Public

Contact: Dan Werthimer sereninfo@ssl.berkeley.edu

Details: Free

If Mosaic is available, use the http address below. Otherwise, please send a request for information to the contact address provided.

`http://sereninfo.ssl.berkeley.edu`

Alife

Alife

The alife mailing list is for communications regarding artificial life, a formative interdisciplinary field involving computer science, the natural sciences, mathematics, and medicine.

Keywords: Artificial Life, Science, Mathematics

Sponsor: UCLA

Audience: Scientists, Biologists, Mathematicians

Contact: alife-request@cognet.ucla.edu

User Info: To subscribe to the list, send an e-mail message to the URL address below.

To send a message to the entire list, address it to: alife@cognet.ucla.edu

`mailto:alife-request@cognet.ucla.edu`

Allergies

National Institute for Allergy & Infectious Disease (NIAID)

This is a resource into other databases for searching many medical fields, such as the NIAID network userlist or a databank of AIDS-related information.

Keywords: Medicine, Infectious Diseases, Allergies

Sponsor: NIAID

Audience: Health Care Professionals, Researchers, Students

Contact: Brent Sessions sessions@odie.niaid.nih.gov

Details: Free

`gopher://gopher.niaid.nih.gov/1`

Alliance Marketing Systems

Alliance Marketing Systems

Develops marketing strategies for new business on those in need of turn-around. Designs advertising/marketing plans to prequalify the buying public.

Keywords: Business Marketing, Sales

Audience: Business Professionals, Marketing Professionals, Sales Executives

Details: Costs

`mailto:prftmaker@secretsams.win.net`

Allied and Alternative Medicine (AMED)

Allied and Alternative Medicine (AMED)

The Allied and Alternative Medicine database covers the fields of contemporary and alternative medicine.

Keywords: Medicine, Alternative Medicine

Sponsor: Medical Information Service, British Library, Boston Spa, West Yorkshire, UK

Audience: Doctors, Nurses, Health Care Providers, Medical Practitioners, Health Care Industry, General Public

Profile: The AMED database will be of interest to all those who need to know more about alternatives to conventional medicine, such as doctors, nurses and other medical practitioners, therapists, health care libraries, specialist colleges, self-help groups, and the pharmaceutical industry. Coverage includes acupuncture, homeopathy, hypnosis, chiropractic, osteopathy, psychotherapy, diet therapy, herbalism, holistic treatment, traditional Chinese medicine, occupational therapy, physiotherapy, rehabilitation, ayurvedic medicine, reflexology, iridology, moxibustion, meditation, yoga, healing research, and the Alexander Technique.

Contact: Data-star through Dialog in the US at (800) 334-2564; Dialog internationally at country-specific locations.

Details: Costs

User Info: To subscribe, contact Dialog directly.

`telnet://dialog.com`

Alloys

METADEX

International literature covering metals and alloys.

Keywords: Material Science, Metals, Alloys

Sponsor: Materials Information, a joint information service of ASM International and the Institute of Materials

Audience: Materials Scientists, Researchers

Profile: Contains more than 925,000 records from the international literature on metals and alloys concerning processes, properties, materials classes, applications, specific alloy designations, intermetallic compounds and metallurgical systems. Updated monthly.

Contact: paul.albert@neteast.com

User Info: To subscribe contact Orbit-Questel directly.

`telnet://orbit.com`

Almost 2001 Archive

Almost 2001 Archive

Archive of transcripts of Almost 2001, a series on computer communications of the future, produced by NBC (National Broadcasting Company).

Keywords: Computers, Communications, Internet

Sponsor: The WELL (Whole Earth 'Lectronic Link)

Audience: Computer Users, Internet Surfers

Details: Free, Moderated

User Info: To participate in a conference on the WELL, you must first establish an account on the WELL. To do so, start by typing: telnet://well.sf.ca.us

`gopher://gopher.well.sf.ca.us//11/`
`Communications/2001`

alpha-osf-managers

alpha-osf-managers

This list is intended to be a quick-turnaround trouble shooting aid for those who administer and manage DEC Alpha AXP systems running OSF/I.

Keywords: Computer Systems, Computer Administration

Sponsor: Oakridge National Laboratory

Audience: Computer Programmers

User Info: To subscribe to the list, send an e-mail message to the URL address below consisting of a single line reading: subscribe alpha-osf-managers.

Notes: Alpha-osf-managers archived at ftp/kpc.com: /pub/list/alpha-osf-managers

`mailto:majordomo@ornl.gov`

Alspa Computer

Alspa

Discussion by users of the CP/M machines made by (now defunct) Alspa Computer, Inc.

Keywords: Computers, Alspa Computer, Inc., CP/M

Audience: CP/M Users

Contact: Brad Allen
alspa-users-request@ssyx.ucsc.edu

Details: Free

User Info: To subscribe to the list, send an e-mail message requesting a subscription to the URL address below.

To send a message to the entire list, address it to: alspa-users@ssyx.ucsc.edu

`mailto:alspa-users-`
`request@ssyx.ucsc.edu`

alt.3d

alt.3d

A Usenet newsgroup providing information and discussion about three-dimensional imaging.

Keywords: Imaging, 3-D

Audience: Graphic Artists, Artists

User Info: To subscribe to this Usenet newsgroup, you need access to a newsreader.

`news:alt.3d`

alt.activism

alt.activism

A Usenet newsgroup providing information and discussion about activities for activists.

Keywords: Activism

Audience: Activists

User Info: To subscribe to this Usenet newsgroup, you need access to a newsreader.

`news:alt.activism`

alt.alien.visitors

alt.alien.visitors

A Usenet newsgroup providing information and discussion about space aliens on Earth and related stories.

Keywords: UFOs, Aliens, Extraterrestrial Life

Audience: Alien Enthusiasts

User Info: To subscribe to this Usenet newsgroup, you need access to a newsreader.

`news:alt.alien.visitors`

alt.aquaria

alt.aquaria

A Usenet newsgroup providing information and discussion about the aquarium as a hobby.

Keywords: Aquariums, Fish, Hobbies

Audience: Aquarium Keepers, Fish Lovers

User Info: To subscribe to this Usenet newsgroup, you need access to a newsreader.

`news:alt.aquaria`

alt.artcom

alt.artcom

A Usenet newsgroup providing information and discussion about contemporary art and technology. Discussion ranges from GIF files to Australian alternative cinema.

Keywords: Art, Technology

Audience: Artists, Writers

User Info: To subscribe to this Usenet newsgroup, you need access to a newsreader.

`news:alt.artcom`

A B C D E F G H I J K L M N O P Q R S T U V W X Y Z

A
B
C
D
E
F
G
H
I
J
K
L
M
N
O
P
Q
R
S
T
U
V
W
X
Y
Z

alt.arts.nomad

alt.arts.nomad

A Usenet conference that focuses on group disembodied art projects.

Keywords: Art

Sponsor: Media Arts, Banff Centre, Canada

Audience: Artists

`news:alt.arts.nomad`

alt.atheism

alt.atheism

A Usenet newsgroup providing information and discussion about atheism.

Keywords: Religion, Divinity, God

Audience: Philosophers, Clergy, Atheists

User Info: To subscribe to this Usenet newsgroup, you need access to a newsreader.

`news:alt.atheism`

alt.bbs

alt.bbs

A Usenet newsgroup providing information and discussion about computer BBS systems & software.

Keywords: BBS, Cyberspace, Computers

Audience: BBS Users

User Info: To subscribe to this Usenet newsgroup, you need access to a newsreader.

`news:alt.bbs`

alt.beer

alt.beer

A Usenet newsgroup providing information and discussion about beer and ale.

Keywords: Beer

Audience: Brewers, Beer Enthusiasts

User Info: To subscribe to this Usenet newsgroup, you need access to a newsreader.

`news:alt.beer`

alt.binaries.pictures.cartoons

alt.binaries.pictures.cartoons

A Usenet newsgroup devoted to cartoon illustrations.

Keywords: Cartoons

Audience: Animators, General Public, Animation Enthusiasts

User Info: To subscribe to this Usenet newsgroup, you need access to a newsreader.

`news:alt.binaries.pictures.cartoons`

alt.bonsai

alt.bonsai

A Usenet newsgroup providing information and discussion about Bonsai gardening.

Keywords: Bonsai Trees, Japan, Gardening, Landscaping

Audience: Gardeners, Bonsai Enthusiasts

User Info: To subscribe to this Usenet newsgroup, you need access to a newsreader.

`news:alt.bonsai`

alt.books.reviews

alt.books.reviews

A Usenet conference devoted to reviews of books, especially science fiction and computer science books.

Keywords: Literature (General), Computer Science, Science Fiction, Books

Audience: General Public, Publishers, Educators, Librarians, Booksellers

Profile: Alt.books.reviews (a.b.r. for short) is a forum for posting reviews of books of interest to readers, school and public librarians, bookstores, publishers, teachers and professors, and others who desire an "educated opinion" about particular books. This is an unmoderated newsgroup.

Contact: sbrock@csn.org.

Details: Free

To participate in a Usenet newsgroup, you need access to a newsreader

Notes: The reviews in alt.books.reviews are archived at csn.org. Ftp to csn.org; login: anonymous; password: your complete E-mail address. At the ftp prompt, type: cd pub/alt.books.reviews

`news:alt.books.reviews`

alt.california

alt.california

A Usenet newsgroup providing information and discussion about California and Californian lifestyles.

Keywords: California

Audience: Californians, General Public

User Info: To subscribe to this Usenet newsgroup, you need access to a newsreader.

`news:alt.california`

alt.callahans

alt.callahans

A Usenet newsgroup providing information and discussion about Callahan's bar for puns and fellowship.

Keywords: Humor, Word Play

Audience: Punsters, Comedians

User Info: To subscribe to this Usenet newsgroup, you need access to a newsreader.

`news:alt.calahans`

alt.caving

alt.caving

A Usenet newsgroup dedicating to discussions of caving and related issues, including cave locations, equipment, spelunking techniques, and other caving information.

Keywords: Spelunking, Caves

Audience: Spelunkers

User Info: To subscribe to this Usenet newsgroup, you need access to a newsreader.

`news:alt.caving`

alt.censorship

alt.censorship

A Usenet newsgroup providing information and discussion about freedom of speech and freedom of the press.

Keywords: Censorship, Freedom of Speech, Constitution (US), Activism

Audience: Press, Students, Educators, Activists

User Info: To subscribe to this Usenet newsgroup, you need access to a newsreader.

`news:alt.censorship`

A
B
C
D
E
F
G
H
I
J
K
L
M
N
O
P
Q
R
S
T
U
V
W
X
Y
Z

alt.chinese.text

alt.chinese.text

★

A Usenet newsgroup providing information and discussion about Chinese language software.

Keywords: Chinese Language, Language Software

Audience: Chinese, Linguists, Computer Users

User Info: To subscribe to this Usenet newsgroup, you need access to a newsreader.

news:alt.chinese.text

alt.christnet

alt.christnet

★

This Usenet newsgroup is a gathering place for Christian ministers and other users.

Keywords: Religion, Christianity, Bibles, Divinity

Audience: Christians, Ministers

User Info: To subscribe to this Usenet newsgroup, you need access to a newsreader.

news:alt.christnet

alt.christnet.bible

alt.christnet.bible

★

A Usenet newsgroup providing information and discussion about bible discussion and research.

Keywords: Bibles, Christianity, Religion, Divinity

Audience: Biblical Scholars, Bible Readers

User Info: To subscribe to this Usenet newsgroup, you need access to a newsreader.

news:alt.christnet.bible

alt.config

alt.config

★

A Usenet newsgroup providing information and discussion about alternative subnet discussions and connectivity.

Keywords: Internet, Computer Networks, Connectivity

Audience: Network Administrators

User Info: To subscribe to this Usenet newsgroup, you need access to a newsreader.

news:alt.config

alt.conspiracy

alt.conspiracy

★

A Usenet newsgroup providing discussion about conspiracy and paranoia.

Keywords: Conspiracy, Paranoia

Audience: Paranoid Persons, General Public

User Info: To subscribe to this Usenet newsgroup, you need access to a newsreader.

news:alt.conspiracy

alt.cult-movies

alt.cult-movies

★

A Usenet newsgroup providing information and discussion about popular movies.

Keywords: Film, Popular Culture

Audience: Film Enthusiasts, Critics

User Info: To subscribe to this Usenet newsgroup, you need access to a newsreader.

news:alt.cult-movies

alt.cyberpunk

alt.cyberpunk

★

A Usenet newsgroup providing information and discussion about the high-tech low-life.

Keywords: Computers, Cyberspace

Audience: Hackers, Cybernauts, General Public

User Info: To subscribe to this Usenet newsgroup, you need access to a newsreader.

news:alt.cyberpunk

alt.drugs

alt.drugs

★

A Usenet newsgroup providing information and discussion about the use of mind, body, and behavior drugs, and about popular drug awareness.

Keywords: Drugs

Audience: Drug Users, Drug Educators

User Info: To subscribe to this Usenet newsgroup, you need access to a newsreader.

news:alt.drugs

alt.fan.monty-python

alt.fan.monty-python

★

A Usenet newsgroup providing an electronic fan club for those wacky Brits.

Keywords: Humor, Entertainment, Comedy, Satire

Audience: Monty Python Enthusiasts, General Public

User Info: To subscribe to this Usenet newsgroup, you need access to a newsreader.

news:alt.fan.monty-python

alt.fan.rush-limbaugh

alt.fan.rush-limbaugh

★

A Usenet newsgroup providing information and discussion about Rush Limbaugh, a politically conservative American figure.

Keywords: Limbaugh (Rush), Politics (Conservative), Comedy

Audience: Rush Limbaugh Enthusiasts

User Info: To subscribe to this Usenet newsgroup, you need access to a newsreader.

news:alt.fan.rush-limbaugh

alt.fashion

alt.fashion

★

A Usenet newsgroup providing information and discussion about all facets of the fashion industry.

Keywords: Fashion Industry, Style

Audience: Designers, General Public

User Info: To subscribe to this Usenet newsgroup, you need access to a newsreader.

news:alt.fashion

alt.feminism

alt.feminism

★

A Usenet newsgroup providing information and discussion about feminism.

Keywords: Feminism, Women's Studies, Abortion, Activism

Audience: Women, General Public

User Info: To subscribe to this Usenet newsgroup, you need access to a newsreader.

news:alt.feminism

A
B
C
D
E
F
G
H
I
J
K
L
M
N
O
P
Q
R
S
T
U
V
W
X
Y
Z

alt.folklore.computers

alt.folklore.computers

A Usenet newsgroup providing information and discussion concerning stories and anecdotes about computers.

Keywords: Computers, Folklore

Audience: Computer Users, Storytellers

User Info: To subscribe to this Usenet newsgroup, you need access to a newsreader.

`news:alt.folklore.computers`

alt.folklore.urban

alt.folklore.urban

A Usenet newsgroup providing information and discussion about urban legends and urban myths.

Keywords: Urban Studies, Folklore

Audience: Story Tellers, General Public

User Info: To subscribe to this Usenet newsgroup, you need access to a newsreader.

`news:alt.folklore.urban`

alt.guitar

alt.guitar

A Usenet newsgroup providing information and discussion about guitar playing.

Keywords: Guitar, Musical Instruments

Audience: Guitarists

User Info: To subscribe to this Usenet newsgroup, you need access to a newsreader.

`news:alt.guitar`

alt.housing.nontrad

alt.housing.nontrad

This newsgroup is for discussion of all forms of "nontraditional housing," including cohousing and communes.

Keywords: Community, Housing, Communes

Audience: General Public, Community Activists

Details: Free

User Info: To subscribe to this Usenet newsgroup, you need access to a newsreader.

`news:alt.housing.nontrad`

alt.hypertext

alt.hypertext

A Usenet newsgroup devoted to hyperfiction and hypertext documents. Postings range from information about and reviews of both recent hyperfiction and recent nonfiction hypertext documents, to information and/or reviews of software for creating hypertext.

Keywords: Literature (General), Hyperfiction, Hypertext

Audience: General Public, Writers, Computer Programmers

Details: Free

User Info: To subscribe to this Usenet newsgroup, you need access to a newsreader.

`news:alt.hypertext`

alt.kids-talk

alt.kids-talk

A Usenet newsgroup that provides a place for the pre-collegiate to chat.

Keywords: Chat Groups, Children, Education (K-12)

Audience: Students (K-12)

User Info: To subscribe to this Usenet newsgroup, you need access to a newsreader.

`news:alt.kids-talk`

alt.music.alternative

alt.music.alternative

A Usenet newsgroup providing information and discussion about alternative music.

Keywords: Musical Genres, Rock Music

Audience: Alternative Music Listeners, Musicians

User Info: To subscribe to this Usenet newsgroup, you need access to a newsreader.

`news:alt.music.alternative`

alt.music.progressive

alt.music.progressive

A Usenet newsgroup providing information and discussion about progressive music, including the groups Marillion, Asia, King Crimson, and many others.

Keywords: Musical Genres, Pop Music

Audience: Progressive Music Listeners

User Info: To subscribe to this Usenet newsgroup, you need access to a newsreader.

`news:alt.music.progressive`

alt.pagan

alt.pagan

A Usenet newsgroup providing information and discussion about paganism and religion.

Keywords: Paganism, Religion

Audience: Cult Members, Religion Students

User Info: To subscribe to this Usenet newsgroup, you need access to a newsreader.

`news:alt.pagan`

alt.peeves

alt.peeves

A Usenet newsgroup providing information and discussion about peeves, complaints, and whining.

Keywords: Humor, Comedy

Audience: General Public, Complainers

User Info: To subscribe to this Usenet newsgroup, you need access to a newsreader.

`news:alt.peeves`

alt.personals.ads

alt.personals.ads

A Usenet newsgroup providing a forum for singles.

Keywords: Personals, Singles

Audience: Singles

User Info: To subscribe to this Usenet newsgroup, you need access to a newsreader.

`news:alt.personals.ads`

alt.politics.clinton

alt.politics.clinton

A Usenet newsgroup providing information and discussion about President Bill Clinton and the White House. Perspective tends to be anti-Clinton.

Keywords: Politics (US), Clinton (Bill)

Audience: Politicians, General Public

User Info: To subscribe to this Usenet newsgroup, you need access to a newsreader.

`news:alt.politics.clinton`

A
B
C
D
E
F
G
H
I
J
K
L
M
N
O
P
Q
R
S
T
U
V
W
X
Y
Z

alt.politics.election

alt.politics.election

A Usenet newsgroup organized to help people in the process of running for office.

Keywords: Politics (US), Government

Audience: Politicians, Campaign Managers

User Info: To subscribe to this Usenet newsgroup, you need access to a newsreader.

news:alt.politics.election

alt.politics.libertarian

alt.politics.libertarian

A Usenet newsgroup providing information and discussion about the libertarian ideology.

Keywords: Libertarian Party, Politics

Audience: Libertarians, Politicians

User Info: To subscribe to this Usenet newsgroup, you need access to a newsreader.

news:alt.politics.libertarian

alt.rap

alt.rap

A Usenet newsgroup providing information and discussion for fans of rap music, including talk about rap performers, new albums, concerts and other aspects of rap.

Keywords: Musical Genres, Rap Music

Audience: Rap Listeners, Rappers

User Info: To subscribe to this Usenet newsgroup, you need access to a newsreader.

news:alt.rap

alt.religion.kibology

alt.religion.kibology

A Usenet newsgroup consisting of followers of a god named Kibo, who is, in fact, a human being living in Boston. This newsgroup is highly humorous and hardly religious.

Keywords: Satire, Humor, Religion

Audience: Kibologists

User Info: To subscribe to this Usenet newsgroup, you need access to a newsreader.

news:alt.religion.kibology

alt.rock-n-roll

alt.rock-n-roll

A Usenet newsgroup providing information and general discussion about Rock & Roll.

Keywords: Musical Genres, Rock and Roll Music

Audience: Rock Music Listeners

User Info: To subscribe to this Usenet newsgroup, you need access to a newsreader.

news:alt.rock-n-roll

alt.rock-n-roll.metal

alt.rock-n-roll.metal

A Usenet newsgroup providing information and discussion about heavy metal music.

Keywords: Musical Genres

Audience: Heavy Metal Listeners

User Info: To subscribe to this Usenet newsgroup, you need access to a newsreader.

news:alt.rock-n-roll.metal

alt.romance.chat

alt.romance.chat

A Usenet newsgroup providing discussion about the romantic side of love.

Keywords: Chat Groups, Romance

Audience: General Public

User Info: To subscribe to this Usenet newsgroup, you need access to a newsreader.

news:alt.romance.chat

alt.security.pgp

alt.security.pgp

A Usenet newsgroup providing information and discussion about the Pretty Good Privacy package, a privately-developed encryption technique.

Keywords: Privacy, Encryption, Security, Firewalls, Computers

Audience: Internet Surfers

User Info: To subscribe to this Usenet newsgroup, you need access to a newsreader.

news:alt.security.pgp

alt.sex

alt.sex

A Usenet newsgroup with many categories providing discussion about sex.

Keywords: Sex

Audience: Adults

User Info: To subscribe to this Usenet newsgroup, you need access to a newsreader.

news:alt.sex

alt.sexual.abuse.recovery

alt.sexual.abuse.recovery

A Usenet newsgroup providing information and discussion about sexual abuse recovery and helping others deal with traumatic experiences.

Keywords: Sexual Abuse, Psychotherapy

Audience: Victims

User Info: To subscribe to this Usenet newsgroup, you need access to a newsreader.

news:alt.sexual.abuse.recovery

alt.tasteless

alt.tasteless

A Usenet newsgroup providing information and discussion about tasteless jokes.

Keywords: Humor, Comedy

Audience: General Interest, Jokers

User Info: To subscribe to this Usenet newsgroup, you need access to a newsreader.

news:alt.tasteless

alt.usage.english

alt.usage.english

A Usenet newsgroup providing information and discussion about English grammar, word usages and related topics.

Keywords: Lexicology, Academia, Linguistics, Education

Audience: English Educators

User Info: To subscribe to this Usenet newsgroup, you need access to a newsreader.

news:alt.usage.english

Alternate Tuning Mailing List

Alternate Tuning Mailing List

This mailing list is intended for exchanging ideas relevant to alternate tunings.

Keywords: Musical Instruments, MIDI

Sponsor: Mills College

Audience: Musicians

Profile: This list deals with just intonation, paratactical tunings, experimental music instrument design, non-standard equal temperaments, MIDI tuning system exclusive specifications, concert postings, non-Western tunings, and the experimental tunings of such people as Harry Partch, Lou Harrison, Martin Bartlett, James Tenney and others.

Contact: Greg Higgs
Higgs@Mills.edu

Details: Free

User Info: To subscribe to the list, send an e-mail message to the URL address below, consisting of a single line reading:

SUB tuning YourFirstName YourLastName

`mailto:listproc@varese.mills.edu`

Alternates

Alternates

A mailing list for people who advocate and/or practice an open sexual lifestyle. Its members are primarily bisexual people and their significant others. It serves as a forum and support group for adult men and women who espouse their freedom of choice and imagination in human sexual relations, no matter what their orientaion.

Keywords: Sexuality, Bisexuality, Sexual Orientation

Audience: Bisexuals, General Public

Contact: alternates-request@ns1.rutgers.edu

User Info: To subscribe to the list, send an e-mail message requesting a subscription to the URL address below.

To send a message to the entire list, address it to:
alternates@ns1.rutgers.edu

`mailto:alternates-request@ns1.rutgers.edu`

Alternative Management

AltInst

A mailing list for proposing and critiquing alternative institutions and ways of life. Topics include alternative ways to run conversations, countries, households, markets, offices, romances, and schools.

Keywords: Institutions, Alternative Management

Audience: General Public

Contact: Robin Hanson
altinst-request@cs.cmu.edu

Details: Free

User Info: To subscribe to the list, send an e-mail message requesting a subscription to the URL address below.

To send a message to the entire list, address it to: altinst@cs.cmu.edu

Notes: AltInst is open to people from any political persuasion, but general political flaming/discussion is forbidden.

`mailto:altinst-request@cs.cmu.edu`

Alternative Medicine

Allied and Alternative Medicine (AMED)

The Allied and Alternative Medicine database covers the fields of contemporary and alternative medicine.

Keywords: Medicine, Alternative Medicine

Sponsor: Medical Information Service, British Library, Boston Spa, West Yorkshire, UK

Audience: Doctors, Nurses, Health Care Providers, Medical Practitioners, Health Care Industry, General Public

Profile: The AMED database will be of interest to all those who need to know more about alternatives to conventional medicine, such as doctors, nurses and other medical practitioners, therapists, health care libraries, specialist colleges, self-help groups, and the pharmaceutical industry. Coverage includes acupuncture, homeopathy, hypnosis, chiropractic, osteopathy, psychotherapy, diet therapy, herbalism, holistic treatment, traditional Chinese medicine, occupational therapy, physiotherapy, rehabilitation, ayurvedic medicine, reflexology, iridology, moxibustion, meditation, yoga, healing research, and the Alexander Technique.

Contact: Data-star through Dialog in the US at (800) 334-2564; Dialog internationally at country-specific locations.

Details: Costs

User Info: To subscribe, contact Dialog directly.

`telnet://dialog.com`

Alternative Medicine, The Definitive Guide

A one-stop reference covering common health problems and leading alternative therapies.

Keywords: Alternative Medicine, Medicine, Health Care

Sponsor: Future Medicine Publishing, Inc.

Audience: General Public, Health Care Professionals

Profile: Spanning a global effort of 4 years and including input from nearly 400 health care professionals, this one-stop reference offers 1100 pages of in-depth explanations to 43 of the leading alternative therapies. In addition to covering over 200 of the most common health problems, this site offers a wide range of choices for maintaining and regaining your health, highlighted with graphic illustrations. This is truly the "Voice of Alternative Medicine."

Details: Costs

`mailto:futuremd@crl.com`

Alternative Press

Prog-Pubs

A mailing list for people interested in progressive and/or alternative publications and other media. Discussions include issues pertaining to all kinds of small-scale, independent, progressive, and/or alternative media, including newspapers, newsletters, and radio and video shows.

Keywords: Media, Alternative Press, Communications

Audience: Students (college/university), Independent Media Professionals

Contact: prog-pubs-request@fuggles.acc.virginia.edu

Details: Free

User Info: To subscribe to the list, send an e-mail message requesting a subscription to the URL address below.

To send a message to the entire list, address it to:prog-pubs@fuggles.acc.virginia.edu

`mailto:prog-pubs@fuggles.acc.virginia.edu`

Altlearn (Alternative Approaches to Learning Discussion)

Altlearn (Alternative Approaches to Learning Discussion)

A discussion list that is broadly concerned with learning strategies at all levels.

Keywords: Education (Adult), Education (Distance), Education (Alternative)

Sponsor: Alternative Approaches to Learning Discussion

Audience: Educators, Administrators, Researchers

Details: Free

User Info: To subscribe to the list, send an e-mail message to the URL address below, consisting of a single line reading:

SUB Altlearn YourFirstName YourLastName

To send a message to the entire list, address it to: altlearn@sjuvm.bitnet

`mailto:listserv@sjuvm.bitnet`

AM/FM

AM/FM

A mailing list for the AM/FM Online Edition, a monthly compilation of news stories concerning the UK radio industry.

Keywords: Radio, United Kingdom, Communications

Audience: Radio Enthusiasts (UK), Communications Specialists, Students (College, University)

Contact: Stephen Hebditch listserv@orbital.demon.co.uk

User Info: To subscribe to the list, send an e-mail message to the URL addres below, consisting of a single line reading:

SUB am/fm YourFirstName YourLastName

To send a message to the entire list, address it to: AM/FM@orbital.demon.co.uk

`mailto:listserv@orbital.demon.co.uk`

AMALGAME

AMALGAME

A resource containing Macintosh demos and XFCN PrintZ files on the subject of health.

Keywords: Health

Sponsor: University of Montreal

Audience: Medical Researchers

Contact: benoit@medent.umontreal.ca

Details: Free

`ftp://amalgame.Medent.Umontreal.Ca`

Amazons International

Amazons International

An electronic digest newsletter for and about Amazons (physically and psychologically strong, assertive women who are challenging traditional ideas about gender roles, femininity, and the female physique).

Keywords: Gender, Feminism, Women's Issues

Audience: Women, Feminists, Writers, Art Historians

Profile: The digest is dedicated to the image of the female hero in fiction and in fact, as it is expressed in art and literature, in the physiques and feats of female athletes, and in sexual values and practices; it also provides information, discussion, and a supportive environment for these values and issues.

Contact: Thomas Gramstad amazons-request@math.uio.no

Details: Free

User Info: To subscribe to the list, send an e-mail message requesting a subscription to the URL address below.

To send a message to the entire list, address it to: amazons@math.uio.no

`mailto:amazons-request@math.uio.no`

Ambulatory Care

University of Texas Health Science Center at San Antonio Library

The library's holdings are large and wide-ranging and contain significant collections in many fields.

Keywords: Allied Health, Dentistry, Nursing, Veterinary Science, Ambulatory Care, Obstetrics/Gynecology, Pediatrics

Audience: Researchers, Students, General Public

Details: Free

User Info: Expect: Login, Send: LIS

`telnet://athena.uthscsa.edu`

Amend2-discuss

Amend2-discuss

A mailing list for discussion of the implications and issues surrounding the passage of Colorado's Amendment 2, which revokes any existing homosexual civil rights legislation and prohibits the drafting of any new legislation.

Keywords: Activism, Gay Rights, Lesbians, Bisexuality

Audience: Gay Rights Activists

Contact: amend2-mod@cs.colorado.edu

User Info: To subscribe to the list, send an e-mail message to the URL address below consisting of a single line reading: subscribe amend2-discuss

`mailto:majordomo@cs.colorado.edu`

Amend2-info

Amend2-info

Colorado voted in an amendment to their state constitution which revokes any existing gay/lesbian/bisexual civil rights legislation and prohibits the drafting of any new legislation. This moderated list is for information on the implication and issues of this amendment.

Keywords: Activists, Gay, Lesbian, Bisexual, Constitutional Amendments, Colorado, Civil Rights

Audience: General Public, Gays, Lesbians, Bisexuals, Activists

Contact: amend2-info@cs.colorado.edu

User Info: To subscribe to the list, send an e-mail message requesting a subscription to the URL address below.

To send a message to the entire list, address it to: amend2-info@cs.colorado.edu

`mailto:majordomo@cs.colorado.edu`

AmerCath (History of American Catholicism)

AmerCath (History of American Catholicism)

This mailing list focuses on the history of American Catholicism.

Keywords: Catholicism, Christianity, Religion

Sponsor: Jefferson Community College, University of Kentucky, Louisville, KY, USA

A B C D E F G H I J K L M N O P Q R S T U V W X Y Z

A
B
C
D
E
F
G
H
I
J
K
L
M
N
O
P
Q
R
S
T
U
V
W
X
Y
Z

Audience: Researchers, Educators, Students, Catholics

Profile: Since AMERCATH can be accessed internationally, it thus forms a global network of people who research and teach the history of American Catholicism. AMERCATH facilitates communication among faculty, students, and researchers.

Contact: Anne Kearney
jccannek@ukcc.uky.edu

Details: Free

User Info: To subscribe to the list, send an e-mail message to the address below, consisting of a single line reading:

Sub AmerCath YourFirstName YourLastName

To send a message to the entire list, address it to: AmerCath@ukcc.uky.edu

`mailto:listserv@ukcc.uky.edu`

America

America

For people interested in how the United States is dealing with foreign trade policies, congressional status, and other inside information about the government that is freely distributable.

Keywords: Foreign Trade, Government (US), Congress (US), Business (US)

Audience: General Public, Researchers, Journalists, Political Scientists, Students

Contact: subscribe@xamiga.linet.org

User Info: To subscribe to the list, send an e-mail message to the URL address below, consisting of a single line reading:

SUB america YourFirstName YourLastName

To send a message to the entire list, address it to: america@xamiga.linet.org

Notes: This list has monthly postings that are generally in large batches, with posts exceeding a few hundred lines.

`mailto:subscribe@xamiga.linet.org`

American Banker Full Text

American Banker Full Text

This database corresponds to the authoritative print publication American Banker.

Keywords: Banking, International Finance, Foreign Trade

Sponsor: American Banker-Bond Buyer, New York, NY, USA

Audience: Financial Analysts, Bankers

Profile: Specific coverage is given to local, regional, and international financial services, technology applications, legal commentary and court actions, international trade, government regulations, Washington events, marketing of financial services, general economic overviews, personnel issues, and profiles and movements of industry personnel. Statistical rankings of all types of financial institutions (from thrifts to commercial banks, US and worldwide) are included beginning with the October 1987 editions. Other special features include quarterly bank earnings, results of American Banker surveys, and the complete text of speeches and articles by the industry professionals that are unavailable in the printed paper.

Contact: Dialog in the US at (800) 334-2564; Dialog internationally at country-specific locations.

Details: Costs

User Info: To subscribe, contact Dialog directly.

`telnet://dialog.com`

American Chemical Society

American Chemical Society

This is the gopher site of the American Chemical Society.

Keywords: Chemistry, Chemical Engineering

Sponsor: The American Chemical Society

Audience: Chemists, Chemical Engineers

Profile: This site contains supplemental material pages from the Journal of the American Chemical Society. Instructions for authors' submissions are also to be found here, as well as general information about the Society.

Contact: Gopher Operator
gopher@acsinfo.acs.org

Details: Free

`gopher://acsinfo.acs.org`

American Drama

University of Chicago Library

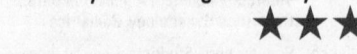

The library's holdings are large and wide-ranging and contain significant collections in many fields.

Keywords: English Bibles, Lincoln (Abraham), Kentucky & Ohio River Valley (History of), Balzac (Honore de), American Drama, Cromwell (Oliver), Goethe, Judaica, Italy, Chaucer (Geoffrey), Wells (Ida, Personal Papers of), Douglas (Stephen A.), Italy, Literature (Children's)

Audience: General Public, Researchers, Librarians, Document Delivery Professionals

Details: Free

User Info: Expect: ENTER CLASS, Send: LIB48 3;
Expect: CONNECTED, Send: RETURN

`telnet://olorin.uchicago.edu`

American Hockey League

American Hockey League

This list is for people interested in discussing and following the activities of The American Hockey League.

Keywords: Sports, Hockey

Audience: Hockey Enthusiasts, Sports Enthusiasts

Contact: ahl-news-request@andrew.cmu.edu

Details: Free

User Info: To subscribe to the list, send an e-mail message requesting a subscription to the URL address below.

To send a message to the entire list, address it to: ahl-news@andrew.cmu.edu

`mailto:ahl-news-request@andrew.cmu.edu`

American Studies

Summit of the Americas Internet Gopher

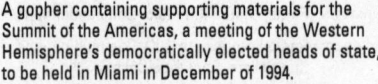

A gopher containing supporting materials for the Summit of the Americas, a meeting of the Western Hemisphere's democratically elected heads of state, to be held in Miami in December of 1994.

Keywords: American Studies, International Relations, Haiti, Latin America

Sponsor: The Florida University Latin American and Caribbean Center

Audience: Government Officials, Journalists, NGOs, General Public

Contact: Rene Ramos
summit@SERVAX.FIU.EDU

`gopher://summit.fiu.edu`

Americana

soc.culture.usa

A Usenet newsgroup providing information and discussion about the culture of the United States.

Keywords: Americana, Sociology, Popular Culture

Audience: Sociologists, General Public

Details: Free

User Info: To subscribe to this Usenet newsgroup, you need access to a newsreader.

`news:soc.culture.usa`

Americana (Western)

University of the Pacific Library

The library's holdings are large and wide-ranging and contain significant collections in many fields.

Keywords: Pharmacology, Americana (Western)

Audience: Researchers, Students, General Public

Details: Free

User Info: Expect: Login, Send: Library

`telnet://pacificat.lib.uop.edu`

Williams College Library

The library's holdings are large and wide-ranging and contain significant collections in many fields.

Keywords: Americana (History of), Graphic Arts, Printing (History of), Performing Arts, Printing

Audience: General Public, Researchers, Librarians, Document Delivery Professionals

Contact: Jim Cubit

Details: Free

User Info: Expect: Mitek Server..., Send: Enter or Return; Expect: prompt, Send: hollis

`telnet://library.williams.edu`

Americans with Disabilities Act

Americans with Disabilities Act

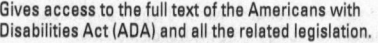

Gives access to the full text of the Americans with Disabilities Act (ADA) and all the related legislation.

Keywords: Disabilities, Legislation (US), Government (US)

Audience: General Public, Disabled People, Differently Abled People, Politicians, Journalists, Students

Profile: The purpose of ADA is to provide a clear and comprehensive national mandate to end discrimination against individuals with disabilities and to bring them into the economic and social mainstream of American life; to provide enforceable standards addressing discrimination against individuals with disabilities; and

to ensure that the federal government plays a central role in enforcing these standards on behalf of individuals with disabilities.

Details: Free

`gopher://val-dor.cc.buffalo.edu/11/.legislation/`

Amiga

Amiga CD-ROM

For Amiga users who are interested in CD-ROM drives and discs.

Keywords: Computers, Amiga, CD-ROM

Audience: Computer Users, Amiga Users

Contact: ben@ben.com

Details: Free

User Info: To subscribe to the list, send an e-mail message requesting a subscription to the URL address below.

To send a message to the entire list, address it to: cdrom-list@ben.com

`mailto:cdrom-list-request@ben.com`

Amiga Files

Archive of files of interest to Amiga users.

Keywords: Amiga

Audience: Computer Users, Amiga Users

Details: Free

`ftp://archive.umich.edu`

AMOS

For the AMOS programming language on Amiga computers. Features source, bug reports, and help from users around the world, but mainly from European users. Most posts will be in English, but there are no language limitations.

Keywords: Computers, Programming Languages, AMOS, Amiga

Audience: Programmers, Computer Users, Amiga Users

Contact: subscribe@xamiga.linet.org

Details: Free

User Info: To subscribe to the list, send an e-mail message to the URL address below, consisting of a single line reading:

SUB YourFirstName YourLastName

To send a message to the entire list, address it to: amos@xamiga.linet.org

`mailto:subscribe@xamiga.linet.org`

comp.sys.amiga

A Usenet newsgroup providing information and discussion about Amiga systems. There are many categories within this group.

Keywords: Computer Systems, Amiga

Audience: Computer Users, Amiga Users

User Info: To subscribe to this Usenet newsgroup, you need access to a newsreader.

`news:comp.sys.amiga`

amlat.mujeres

amlat.mujeres

This conference serves as a forum for interchange between organizations and women's movements in Latin America and the Caribbean.

Keywords: Women Issues, Latin America, Caribbean, Feminism

Audience: Women, Feminists, Activists

Contact: Agencia Latinoamericana de Informacion
info@alai.ec
uualai@ecuanex.ec

Details: Costs

User Info: Establish an account on the nearest APC node. Login, type c for conferences, then type: go amlat.mujeres

For information on the nearest APC node, contact: APC International Secretariat, IBASE.

E-mail: apcadmin@apc.org

`telnet://igc.apc.org`

Amnesty International

Amnesty International

A site containing information about Amnesty International, an organization focused strictly and specifically on human rights around the world.

Keywords: Government, Human Rights, Politics (International), Activism

Sponsor: Amnesty International

Audience: Students, Activists

Contact: Catherine Hampton
ariel@netcom.com

`ftp://ftp.netcom.com/pub/ariel/`

`http:www/human.rights/amnesty.international/ai.html`

An NREN That Includes Everyone

An NREN That Includes Everyone

In this article, community networker Tom Grundner (founder of Free-Net), advocates a National Community Network, one that treats patients looking for health care information as researchers. He advocates expanding our definition of educational access to include people of all ages—senior citizens as well as kindergarteners.

Keywords: Community Networking, Networking, Government (US)

Audience: Activists, Policymakers, Community Leaders

Contact: Tom Grundner
tmg@nptn.org

Details: Free

Notes: This document contains hypertext links to the NPTN (National Public Telecomputing Network).

```
http://nearnet.gnn.com/mag/articles/
oram/bio.grundner.html
```

Analog Equipment

Analog Heaven

The Analog Heaven mailing list caters to people interested in vintage analog electronic music equipment. Topics include items for sale, repair tips, equipment modifications, ASCII & GIF schematics, and a general discussion of new and old analog equipment. There is an FTP/Gopher site located at cs.uwp.edu with discussions on various machines, a definitive guide to Roland synths, patch editors, modification schematics, and GIFs/JPEGs of vintage synths, as well as a few sound samples of some of the gear itself.

Keywords: Music, Synthesizers, Sequencers, Analog Equipment, Electronic Music

Audience: Electronic Music Enthusiasts, Musicians

Contact: Todd Sines
analogue-request@magnus.acs.ohio-state.edu

Details: Free, Sound files available.

User Info: To subscribe to the list, send an e-mail message requesting a subscription to the URL address below.

To send a message to the entire list, address it to:
analogue@magnus.acs.ohio-state.edu

```
mailto:analogue-
request@magnus.acs.ohio-state.edu
```

Analysis

CANADA (Canadian News and Information Library)

The Canadian News and Information library (CANADA) contains Canadian legal news, business and company information.

Keywords: News, Analysis, Companies, Canada

Audience: Canadians

Profile: The CANADA library contains respected Canadian news publications such as The Toronto Star, The Vancouver Sun, Ottawa Business News and the Montreal Gazette. The CANADA library also offers Canadian company profiles, country reports, and Canada's financial database, CANCORP Plus.

Contact: Mead New Sales Group at (800) 227-4908 or (513) 859-5398 inside the US, or (513) 865-7981 for all inquiries outside the US.

User Info: To subscribe, contact Mead directly.

To examine the Nexis user guide, you can access it at the ftp site of the University of Texas at Austin at the URL address: ftp://ftp.cc.utexas.edu

The files are in: /pub/ref-services/LEXIS

```
telnet://nex.meaddata.com
```

```
http://www.meaddata.com
```

ENVIRN (Environment Library) ★★★

The Environment (ENVIRN) Library contains a variety of environment-related news and legal information.

Keywords: News, Analysis, Law, Environment

Audience: Environmental Researchers, Business Professionals

Profile: The ENVIRN library contains a combination of environmental information that can provide critical insight into environmental hazards, EPA ratings, specific company investigations, evaluations on potentially hazardous chemicals, and parties responsible for cleanup of specific hazardous sites. Additionally, ENVIRN provides a wealth of environment-related information—legislation, regulations, and court and agency decisions at both the federal and state levels; news; the Environmental Law Reporter, and American Law Reports.

Contact: Mead New Sales Group at (800) 227-4908 or (513) 859-5398 inside the US, or (513) 865-7981 for all inquiries outside the US.

User Info: To subscribe, contact Mead directly.

To examine the Nexis user guide, you can access it at the ftp site of the University of Texas at Austin at the URL address: ftp://ftp.cc.utexas.edu

The files are in: /pub/ref-services/LEXIS

```
telnet://nex.meaddata.com
```

```
http://www.meaddata.com
```

FEDTAX (Federal Tax Library)

The Federal Tax library offerers a comprehensive, up-to-date collection of tax-related materials, including case law, agency materials, legislative and regulatory materials, and so on.

Keywords: Law, Analysis, Tax

Audience: Lawyers

Profile: The Federal Tax library offers a comprehensive, up-to-date collection of tax-related materials. This library includes federal and state tax case law, Internal Revenue Service rulings and releases, state tax administrative decisions and rulings, the Internal Revenue Code, federal tax regulations, international news and treaties, tax looseleaf services, tax periodicals, tax law reviews, tax dailies, pending state legislation, and state property records.

Contact: New Sales Group at 800-227-4908 or 513-859-5398 inside the US, or 1-513-865-7981 for all inquires outside the US.

User Info: To subscribe, contact Mead directly.

To examine the Lexis user guide, you can access it at the ftp site of the University of Texas at Austin at the URL address: ftp://ftp.cc.utexas.edu

The files are in: /pub/ref-services/LEXIS

```
telnet://nex.meaddata.com
```

```
http://www.meaddata.com
```

INSURE (Insurance) ★★★

The Insurance (INSURE) library contains specific full-text and abstract news and legal information sources focusing on the insurance industry.

Keywords: News, Analysis, Law, Insurance

Audience: Insurance Professionals, Lawyers

Profile: The INSURE library contains leading insurance industry news sources, legal and regulatory materials from NILS Publishing Company's INSURLAW, analyst reports on the insurance industry from InvestextR, and insurance company financial reports. Federal and state case law and federal regulations are also available.

Contact: Mead New Sales Group @ (800) 227-4908 or (513) 859-5398 inside the US, or (513) 865-7981 for all inquiries outside the US.

User Info: To subscribe, contact Mead directly.

To examine the Nexis user guide, you can access it at the ftp site of the University of Texas at Austin at the URL address: ftp://ftp.cc.utexas.edu

The files are in: /pub/res-services/LEXIS

`telnet://nex.meaddata.com`

INVEST (Investment News and Information)

★ ★ ★

The INVEST library contains company and industry research reports provided through the Investext(R) database. These reports are created by industry experts who are employed for their accurate and insightful evaluation. Only the most recent 12 months of data will be displayed.

Keywords: Companies, Financials, Analysis

Audience: Business Researchers, Analysts, Entrepreneurs

Profile: INVEST is categorized by type. Selections can be made using these categories: Industry (more than 50 industries are available), State (where a specific company is located), Country (Country in which the company is located), US Broker or International Broker. The INVEST library provides an automatic display following the selection of a file. For industry reports, a menu will appear providing definitions as they relate to the industries. All remaining files will provide a confirmation of the file selected.

Contact: Mead New Sales Group at (800) 227-4908 or (513) 859-5398 inside the US, or (513) 865-7981 for all inquiries outside the US.

User Info: To subscribe, contact Mead directly.

To examine the Nexis user guide, you can access it at the ftp site of the University of Texas at Austin at the URL address: ftp://ftp.cc.utexas.edu

The files are in: /pub/ref-services/LEXIS

`telnet://nex.meaddata.com`

`http://www.meaddata.com`

LAWREV (Law Review Library)

★ ★ ★

The Law Review library contains law reviews, American Bar Association publications, American Institute of Certified Public Accountants periodicals, and other materials. The present focus concentrates on both state and national issues of legal significance.

Keywords: US Law, Analysis, Law Reviews, Journals

Audience: Lawyers

Profile: The Law Review library currently consists of over 70 law reviews, several American Bar Association publicatons and American Institute of Certified Public Accountants periodicals, an Environmental Law Institute publication, ALR and LEd2d articles, two leading

legal indices and a number of Warren Gorham & Lamont tax journals. The present focus concentrates on both state and national issues of legal significance.

Contact: New Sales Group at 800-227-4908 or 513-859-5398 inside the US, or 1-513-865-7981 for all inquires outside the US.

User Info: To subscribe, contact Mead directly.

To examine the Lexis user guide, you can access it at the ftp site of the University of Texas at Austin at the URL address: ftp://ftp.cc.utexas.edu

The files are in: /pub/ref-services/LEXIS

`telnet://nex.meaddata.com`

`http://www.meaddata.com`

MARKET (Markets and Industries News and Information)

★ ★ ★

The Markets and Industries News and Information (MARKET) library contains sources covering developments in a wide variety of markets and industries.

Keywords: News, Analysis, Industry, Marketing

Audience: Business Professionals, Researchers

Profile: The MARKET library contains a wide selection of sources ranging from trade and industry sources to InvestextR industry reports to company profiles. To round out the offering, MARKET also covers advertising, marketing, public opinion polls, market research, public relations, sales and selling, promotions, consumer attitudes, trends and behaviors, demographics, product announcements and product reviews. In addition, Predicasts Overview of Markets and Technology (PROMT), Marketing and Advertising Reference Service (MARS), US and International Forecast Databases (UFRCST and IFRCST) and the US Time Series (USTIME), all from Information Access Company, are available.

Contact: Mead New Sales Group at (800) 227-4908 or (513) 859-5398 inside the US, or (513) 865-7981 for all inquiries outside the US.

User Info: To subscribe, contact Mead directly.

To examine the Nexis user guide, you can access it at the ftp site of the University of Texas at Austin at the URL address: ftp://ftp.cc.utexas.edu

The files are in: /pub/ref-services/LEXIS

`telnet://nex.meaddata.com`

`http://www.meaddata.com`

MDEAFR

★ ★ ★ ★

The Middle East and Africa (MDEAFR) library contains detailed information about every country in the Mideast and Africa. Structured for those who want to follow the unfolding events in the Gulf states, as well as in North and South Africa, this library contains a broad array of sources, including international research reports from InvestextR.

Keywords: News, Analysis, Companies, Middle East, Africa

Audience: Journalists, Business Professionals

Profile: The MDEAFR library contains a wide array of pertinent sources. Among the information sources are newspapers and wire services, trade and business journals, company reports, country and region background, industry and product analysis, business opportunities, and selected legal texts. News sources range from the world-renowned Associated Press and Christian Science Monitor to the regionally important Jerusalem Post and Africa News. Company information is contained in the EXTEL cards as well as ICC. Providers of country background and industry analysis include Associated Banks of Europe, Bank of America, Business International, IBC USA, and the US Department of Commerce. Customers interested in new business opportunities can check OPIC and Foreign Trade Opportunities (FTO).

Contact: Mead New Sales Group at (800) 227-4908 or (513) 859-5398 inside the US, or (513) 865-7981 for all inquiries outside the US.

User Info: To subscribe, contact Mead directly.

To examine the Nexis user guide, you can access it at the ftp site of the University of Texas at Austin at the URL address: ftp://ftp.cc.utexas.edu

The files are in: /pub/ref-services/LEXIS

`telnet://nex.meaddata.com`

`http://www.meaddata.com`

NEWS (General News)

★ ★ ★

The General News (NEWS) library includes more than 2,300 sources. Full-text news from national and international newspapers, magazines, newsletters, and wire services and abstract information are both available.

Keywords: News, Analysis, People, Companies

Audience: Journalists, General Public

Profile: The General News (NEWS) library contains a number of publications and wire services of general interest, as well as others that specialize in particular areas of business . The NEWS library is organized into individual files, group files by source or subject, and user-defined combination files for full-text information sources. Abstracts are also available as individual files or can be searched together in one group file. The NEWS

A B C D E F G H I J K L M N O P Q R S T U V W X Y Z

library includes such prestigious full-text sources as the New York Times and more than more than 30 major newspapers from around the US and the world.

Contact: Mead New Sales Group at (800) 227-4908 or (513) 859-5398 inside the US, or (513) 865-7981 for all inquiries outside the US.

User Info: To subscribe, contact Mead directly.

To examine the Nexis user guide, you can access it at the ftp site of the University of Texas at Austin at the URL address: ftp://ftp.cc.utexas.edu

The files are in: /pub/ref-services/LEXIS

`telnet://nex.meaddata.com`

`http://www.meaddata.com`

NSAMER (North and South America Library)

★★★★

The North and South America library contains detailed information about every country in North and South America (except the United States). The US-Canada Free Trade Agreement, the North American Free Trade Agreement, relations with Mexico and events in such countries as Brazil, Peru, and Nicaragua are among the topics covered by a variety of business, news and legal sources. International research reports from InvestextR are also included. The United States is not covered in this library.

Keywords: News, Analysis, Companies, North America, South America

Audience: Journalists, Business Professionals

Profile: The North and South America library contains a broad array of sources. Among the information sources are newspapers and wire services, trade and business journals, company reports, country and region backgrounds, industry and product analyses, business opportunities, and selected legal texts. News sources range from the world-renowned Washington Post and Christian Science Monitor to the regionally important Toronto Star and Latin American Newsletters. Canadian Business and Maclean's represent a portion of the array of business and trade journals. Company information is contained in the EXTEL cards as well as ICC. Providers of country background and industry analyses include Associated Banks of Europe, Bank of America, Business International, IBC USA and the US Department of Commerce. Among the specialized resources are IBC's Mexico and Brazil Services as well as BI's Business Latin America. Researchers interested in new business opportunities can check OPIC and Foreign Trade Opportunities (FTO).And selected legal texts covering the US-Canada Free Trade Agreement and other international agreements planners and advisors to better assess the business climate in North and South America.

Contact: Mead New Sales Group at (800) 227-4908 or (513) 859-5398 inside the US, or (513) 865-7981 for all inquiries outside the US.

User Info: To subscribe, contact Mead directly.

To examine the Nexis user guide, you can access it at the ftp site of the University of Texas at Austin at the URL address: ftp://ftp.cc.utexas.edu

The files are in: /pub/ref-services/LEXIS

`telnet://nex.meaddata.com`

`http://www.meaddata.com`

SPORTS (Sports News)

 ★★★

The Sports News (SPORTS) library contains a variety of sports-related news and information.

Keywords: News, Analysis, Sports, Biographies

Audience: Sports Enthusiasts, Journalists

Profile: The SPORTS library is a specialized news library that contains the full text of Sports Illustrated and The Sporting News and selected sports-related stories from many major US newspapers and wire services. Biographical information and 1992 Olympic facts are also part of this library.

Contact: Mead New Sales Group at (800) 227-4908 or (513) 859-5398 inside the US, or (513) 865-7981 for all inquiries outside the US.

User Info: To subscribe, contact Mead directly.

To examine the Nexis user guide, you can access it at the ftp site of the University of Texas at Austin at the URL address: ftp://ftp.cc.utexas.edu

The files are in: /pub/ref-services/LEXIS

`telnet://nex.meaddata.com`

`http://www.meaddata.com`

STATES (States Library)

 ★★★

The combined States library contains case law, code and agency materials from the 53 individual US state libraries (50 states plus the District of Columbia, Puerto Rico and the Virgin Islands), all in the same library.

Keywords: Law, Analysis, Case, States

Audience: Lawyers

Profile: The combined States library contains case law, code and agency materials from the 53 individual state libraries (50 states plus the District of Columbia, Puerto Rico and the Virgin Islands), all in the same library. The States library also features many large group files which allow several individual files to be accessed in the same search. Many of the group files involve case law, including files that cover all state case law available on the LEXIS service plus ALR material and files that combine all federal and state case law available on the LEXIS service.

Contact: Mead New Sales Group at (800) 227-4908 or (513) 859-5398 inside the US, or (513) 865-7981 for all inquiries outside the US.

User Info: To subscribe, contact Mead directly.

To examine the Nexis user guide, you can access it at the ftp site of the University of Texas at Austin at the URL address: ftp://ftp.cc.utexas.edu

The files are in: /pub/ref-services/LEXIS

`telnet://nex.meaddata.com`

`http://www.meaddata.com`

TOPNWS (Top News)

 ★★★

The Top News (TOPNWS) library contains today's news today for selected key sources from around the world.

Keywords: News, Analysis

Audience: Journalists, General Public

Profile: In the Top News (TOPNWS) library newswires are collected and updated every 60 minutes. Newspapers and other daily publications are updated throughout the day on the day of publication. Transcripts are updated within three hours of broadcast. Two weeks worth of data from more than 40 major publications may be searched as individual files or in specialized group files. The TODAY group file contains today's published information from all sources. the 2WEEK group file expands the window of current information from all sources to two weeks. Specialized section files, designed to be like sections of a newspaper, contain stories from each publication that pertain to the section or topic selected.

Contact: Mead New Sales Group at (800) 227-4908 or (513) 859-5398 inside the US, or (513) 865-7981 for all inquiries outside the US.

User Info: To subscribe, contact Mead directly.

To examine the Nexis user guide, you can access it at the ftp site of the University of Texas at Austin at the URL address: ftp://ftp.cc.utexas.edu

The files are in: /pub/ref-services/LEXIS

`telnet://nex.meaddata.com`

`http://www.meaddata.com`

Animal Rights

AR-news

 ★★

A public news wire for items relating to animal rights and animal welfare.

Keywords: Activism, Animal Rights, Veterinarians

Audience: Activists, Animal Lovers

A

Contact: Ian Lance Taylor, Chip Roberson
taylor@think.com or csr@nic.aren.com

User Info: To subscribe to the list, send an e-mail message to the URL address below.

To send a message to the entire list, address it to: ar-news@think.com

Notes: Appropriate postings to ar-news include posting a news item, requesting information on some event, or responding to a request for information. Discussions on ar-news are not allowed.

`mailto:ar-news@think.com`

AR-talk

 ★★

An unmoderated list for the discussion of animal rights and related issues, such as animal liberation, consumer product testing, cruelty-free products, vivisection and dissection, and vegan lifestyles.

Keywords: Activism, Animal Rights

Audience: Activists, Animal Lovers, Researchers

Contact: Ian Lance Taylor, Chip Roberson
taylor@think.com or csr@nic.aren.com

User Info: To subscribe to the list, send an e-mail message to the URL address below.

To send a message to the entire list, address it to: ar-talk@think.com

`mailto:ar-talk-request@think.com`

Animal Science

Biosis Previews

The database encompasses the entire field of life sciences and covers original research reports and reviews in biological and biomedical areas. This includes field, laboratory, clinical, experimental and theoretical work. The traditional areas of biology, including botany, zoology and microbiology are covered, as well as the related fields such as plant and animal science, agriculture, pharmacology and ecology.

Keywords: Biology, Botany, Zoology, Microbiology, Plant Science, Animal Science, Agriculture, Pharmacology, Ecology, Biochemistry, Biophysics, Bioengineering

Sponsor: Biosis

Audience: Librarians, Researchers, Students, Biologists, Botanists, Zoologists, Scientists, Taxonomists

Contact: CDP Technologies Sales Department (800)950-2035, extension 400

User Info: To subscribe, contact CDP Technologies directly

`telnet://cdplus@cdplus.com`

Animal Studies

AGRICOLA

 ★★★

The AGRICOLA database of the National Agricultural Library (NAL) provides comprehensive coverage of worldwide journal literature and monographs on agriculture and related subjects.

Keywords: Agriculture, Animal Studies, Botany, Entomology

Sponsor: US National Agricultural Library, Beltsville, MD, USA

Audience: Agronomists, Botanists, Chemists, Entomologists

Profile: Related subjects include: animal studies, botany, chemistry, entomology, fertilizers, forestry, hydroponics, soils, and more.

Contact: Dialog in the US at (800) 334-2564, Dialog internationally at country-specific locations.

User Info: To subscribe, contact Dialog directly.

Notes: Coverage: 1970 to the present; updated monthly.

`telnet://dialog.com`

Animal Welfare

NetVet Veterinary Resources

 ★★★

An Internet server for veterinary and animal resources.

Keywords: Veterinary Medicine, Animal Welfare, Animals

Sponsor: Washington University, St. Louis, Division of Comparative Medicine

Audience: Veterinarians, Animal Lovers

Profile: A collection of veterinary and animal-related computer resources that includes archives of animal legislation and regulation, listings for colleges of Veterinary Medicine, conference information, and animal-related databases, including the Electronic Zoo. Also has links to other animal and veterinary-related systems.

Contact: Dr. Ken Boshert
ken@wudcm.wustl.edu

`gopher://netvet.wustl.edu`

`http://netvet.wustl.edu`

Animals

Animals

 ★

This directory is a compilation of information resources focused on animals.

Keywords: Animals, Electronic Media

Audience: Animal Lovers, Veterinarians, Activists

Contact: Ken Boschert
ken@wudcm.wustl.edu

Details: Free

`ftp://una.hh.lib.umich.edu/70/`
`inetdirsstacks/animals:boschert`

NetVet Veterinary Resources

 ★★★

An Internet server for veterinary and animal resources.

Keywords: Veterinary Medicine, Animal Welfare, Animals

Sponsor: Washington University, St. Louis, Division of Comparative Medicine

Audience: Veterinarians, Animal Lovers

Profile: A collection of veterinary and animal-related computer resources that includes archives of animal legislation and regulation, listings for colleges of Veterinary Medicine, conference information, and animal-related databases, including the Electronic Zoo. Also has links to other animal and veterinary-related systems.

Contact: Dr. Ken Boshert
ken@wudcm.wustl.edu

`gopher://netvet.wustl.edu`

`http://netvet.wustl.edu`

rec.equestrian

 ★

A Usenet newsgroup providing information and discussion about all things pertaining to horses.

Keywords: Horses, Equestrians, Animals, Sports

Audience: Horse Riders, Horse Trainers, Horse Owners

User Info: To subscribe to this Usenet newsgroup, you need access to a newsreader.

`news:rec.equestrian`

rec.pets

 ★

A Usenet newsgroup providing information and discussion about pets and pet care.

Keywords: Pets, Animals

Audience: Pet Owners

User Info: To subscribe to this Usenet newsgroup, you need access to a newsreader.

`news:rec.pets`

B
C
D
E
F
G
H
I
J
K
L
M
N
O
P
Q
R
S
T
U
V
W
X
Y
Z

A
B
C
D
E
F
G
H
I
J
K
L
M
N
O
P
Q
R
S
T
U
V
W
X
Y
Z

rec.pets.cats

A Usenet newsgroup providing information and discussion about domestic cats.

Keywords: Pets, Animals

Audience: Cat Owners

User Info: To subscribe to this Usenet newsgroup, you need access to a newsreader.

`news:rec.pets.cats`

rec.pets.dogs

A Usenet newsgroup providing information and discussion about dogs.

Keywords: Pets, Animals

Audience: Dog Owners

User Info: To subscribe to this Usenet newsgroup, you need access to a newsreader.

`news:rec.pets.dogs`

Animation

ANIME-L

This discussion list covers animation news, with a special emphasis on Japanese "animedia."

Keywords: Animation, Film, Japan

Audience: Animation Enthusiasts, Animators

Details: Free

User Info: To subscribe to the list, send an e-mail message to the address below, consisting of a single line reading:

Sub anime-l YourFirstName YourLastName

To send a message to the entire list, address it to: anime-l@vtvm1.cc.vt.edu

`mailto:listserv@vtvm1.cc.vt.edu`

OTIS (Operative Term Is Stimulate)

An image-based electronic art gallery.

Keywords: Art, Graphics, Electronic Art, Animation

Audience: Graphic Artists

Profile: OTIS is a public-access library containing hundreds of images, animations, and information files.

Within the sunsite ftp, the directory is: / pub/multimedia/pictures/OTIS. Use the bin command to insure you're in binary transfer mode.

`ftp://sunsite.unc.edu`

rec.arts.anime

A Usenet newsgroup providing information and discussion about Japanese animation fen.

Keywords: Animation, Fen, Japan

Audience: Animators

Details: Free

User Info: To subscribe to this Usenet newsgroup, you need access to a newsreader.

`news:rec.arts.anime`

Annealing

Anneal

A mailing list for the discussion of simulated annealing techniques and analysis, as well as related issues such as stochastic optimization, Boltzmann machines, and metricity of NP-complete move spaces.

Keywords: Mathematics, Simulation, Annealing

Sponsor: UCLA

Audience: Mathematicians, Physicists

Contact: Daniel R. Greening anneal-request@cs.ucla.edu

User Info: To subscribe to the list, send an e-mail message to the URL address below.

To send a message to the entire list, address it to: anneal@cs.ucla.edu

Notes: Membership is restricted to those doing active research in simulated annealing or related areas.

`mailto:anneal-request@cs.ucla.edu`

Annual Reports

CIA World Factbook

Annual report of CIA (Central Intelligence Agency) research in over 247 nations.

Keywords: CIA, Intelligence, Annual Reports

Audience: Governments, Lawyers, FBI

Details: Free

`gopher://marvel.loc.gov`

Anthropology

Anthropology, Cross Cultural Studies, & Archaeology

This directory is a compilation of information resources focused on anthropology, cross cultural studies, and archaeology.

Keywords: Anthropology, Cultural Studies, Archaeology

Audience: Anthropologists, Archaeologists, Students, Educators

Contact: G. Bell

Details: Free

`ftp://una.hh.lib.umich.edu/70/ inetdirsstacks/anthro:bell`

Indigenous

A collection of various on-line resources about indigenous peoples.

Keywords: Indigenous Peoples, Anthropology

Audience: Reseachers, Anthropologists

Details: Free

`ftp://netcom.com`

NativeNet

Provides information about and discusses issues relating to indigenous people around the world, including threats to their cultures and habitats (e.g. rainforests).

Keywords: Indigenous People, Environment, Anthroplogy

Audience: Anthropologists, Environmentalists, Indigenous People

Contact: Gary S. Trujillo gst@gnosys.svle.ma.us

Details: Free

User Info: To subscribe to the list, send an e-mail message requesting a subscription to the URL address below.

`mailto:gst@gnosys.svle.ma.us`

Smithsonian Institution Natural History Gopher

The Smithsonian Natural History Gopher Server provides access to data associated with the Institutions museum collections (natural history and anthropology).

Keywords: Smithsonian, Natural History, Anthropology

Sponsor: Museum of Natural History, Smithsonian Institution, Washington, DC.

Audience: Anthropologists, Biologists, Natural History Scientists, Researchers

Profile: With over 120 million collections and 135 professional scientists, the National Museum of Natural History is one of the worlds largest museums devoted to natural history and anthropology. This server provides access to data associated with the collections, and to information and tools for the study of the natural world. The Department of Vertebrate Zoology includes checklists of known species names. Currently the Mammal Species of the World have been posted. Plans to expand this to include Amphibians, Fishes, and so on, are under way.

Contact: Don Gourley
don@smithson.si.edu

Details: Free

`gopher://nmnhgoph.si.edu`

Anti-Semitism

The Israel Information Service

A gopher server containing information on Israel.

Keywords: Israel, Middle East, Political Science, Anti-Semitism, Holocaust, Archaeology

Sponsor: Israeli Foreign Ministry

Audience: Israelis, Jews, Tourists, General Public

Profile: This server features updates on the Middle East peace process, including text of the latest Israel-PLO accord, as well as general political, diplomatic, cultural and economic information on the state of Israel. Also includes archives on archaeology in Israel, anti-Semitism and the Holocaust, and current excerpts from Israeli newspapers.

Contact: Chaim Shacham
shacham@israel-info.gov.il

`gopher://israel-info.gov.il`

Antiquarian Books

Indiana University Libraries

The library's holdings are large and wide-ranging and contain significant collections in many fields.

Keywords: Literature (English), Literature (American), 1640-Present, British Plays (19th-C.), Western Americana, Railway History, Aristotle (Texts of), Lafayette (Marquis de), Handel (G.F.), Austrian History, Antiquarian Books, Rare Books, French Opera (19th-C.), Drama (British) ,

Audience: General Public, Researchers, Librarians, Document Delivery Professionals

Details: Free

User Info: Expect: User ID prompt, Send: GUEST

`telnet://iuis.ucs.indiana.edu`

ANU (Australian National University) Asian-Settlements Database

ANU (Australian National University) Asian-Settlements Database

A searchable database containing abstracts of theses and research studies provided by the Asian Institute of Technology, relating to issues of demography and social geography in Asia.

Keywords: Asian Studies, Demography, Geography

Sponsor: The COOMBSQUEST Social Sciences & Humanities Information Facility at ANU (Australian National University), Canberra, Australia

Audience: Asia Studies Instructors, Demographers, Geographers

Contact: Dr. T. Matthew Ciolek
coombspapers@coombs.anu.edu.au

Details: Free

`gopher://cheops.anu.edu.au/Coombs-db/ANU-Asian-Settlements.src`

`http://coombs.anu.edu.au/WWWVL-AsianStudies.html`

ANU (Australian National University) Buddhism Database

ANU (Australian National University) Buddhism Database

A searchable database of messages from the BUDDHA-L listserv, an academic forum for the discussion of Buddhism. It currently contains archives for messages posted in 1993-94.

Keywords: Religion, Asian Studies, Buddhism

Sponsor: COOMBSQUEST Social Sciences & Humanities Information Facility at ANU (Australian National University), Canberra, Australia

Audience: Buddhists, Religious Studies Instructors, Asian Studies Educators

Contact: Dr. T.Matthew Ciolek
coombspapers@coombs.anu.edu.au

`gopher://cheops.anu.edu.au/Coombs-db/ANU-Buddha-1.src`

`http://coombs.anu.edu.au/WWWVL-AsianStudies.html`

ANU (Australian National University) Demography and Publications Database

ANU (Australian National University) Demography and Publications Database

A WAIS database of publications on demography by researchers from Australian National University.

Keywords: Demography

Sponsor: Research Schools of Social Sciences & Pacific and Asian Studies, ANU (Australian National University), Canberra, Australia

Audience: Demographers

Contact: demography@anu.edu.au

`waissrc:/Coombs-db/ANU-Demography-Publications.src`

`gopher://cheops.anu.edu.au/7waissrc/Coombs-db/ANU-Demography-Publications.src`

ANU (Australian National University) Vietnam-SciTech-L Database

ANU (Australian National University) Vietnam-SciTech-L Database

A WAIS database of information on the development of science and technology in Vietnam

Keywords: Vietnam, Science, Technology

Sponsor: Australia Vietnam Science-Technology Link

Audience: Vietnamese, Scientists, Technology Professionals

Contact: Vern Weitzel

vern@coombs.anu.edu.au

`waissrc:/Coombs-db/ANU-Vietnam-SciTech-L.src`

`gopher://cheops.anu.edu.au/7waissrc/Coombs-db/ANU-Vietnam-SciTech-L.src`

APC-Open

APC-Open

A mailing list for the interchange of information relevant to Advanced Product Centers (APC).

A B C D E F G H I J K L M N O P Q R S T U V W X Y Z

A
B
C
D
E
F
G
H
I
J
K
L
M
N
O
P
Q
R
S
T
U
V
W
X
Y
Z

Keywords: Advanced Product Centers (APC)

Audience: APC-OPEN Members

Contact: Fred Rump
fred@compu.com

User Info: To subscribe to the list, send an e-mail message requesting a subscription to the URL address below.

To send a message to the entire list, address it to: apc-open@compu.com

Notes: Membership restricted to APC-OPEN members or those specifically invited.

`mailto:apc-open-request@compu.com`

ApE-info

ApE-info

★★

A mailing list for the discussion of the scientific visualization software package ApE, its usage, development, and implementation.

Keywords: Computers, Visualization, Science

Audience: ApE Software Users, Computer Programmers

Contact: Jim Lick
ape-info-request@ferkel.ucsb.edu

User Info: To subscribe to the list, send an e-mail message to the URL address below.

To send a message to the entire list, address it to: ape-info@ferkel.ucsb.edu

`mailto:ape-info-request@ferkel.ucsb.edu`

APEX-J (Asia-Pacific Exchange Electronic Journal)

APEX-J (Asia-Pacific Exchange Electronic Journal)

★

An electronic journal about the Pacific Rim.

Keywords: Asian Studies

Sponsor: Published by the University of Hawaii at Kapiolani Community College, Hawaii, USA

Audience: Educators, Students

Contact: Jim Shimabukuro
JamesS@Hawaii.edu

Notes: login anonymous;password your email address; cd outgoing; get file.name; bye

`ftp://ftp.hawaii.edu`

API Energy Business News Index (APIBIZ)

API Energy Business News Index (APIBIZ)

Worldwide coverage of commercial, financial, marketing and regulatory information affecting the petroleum and energy industries.

Keywords: Petroleum, Business

Sponsor: The American Petroleum Institute - Central Abstracting and Information Services

Audience: Researchers, Librarians

Profile: Twenty-two major news and economics publications are the primary sources for worldwide coverage of information affecting the petroleum and energy industries. Contains more than 600,000 records. Updated weekly.

Contact: paul.albert@neteast.com

User Info: To subscribe contact Orbit-Questel directly.

`telnet://orbit.com`

APL (Programming Language)

APL-L

★

Discussion of the APL language, its implementation, application, and use. Contributions on teaching APL are particularly welcome.

Keywords: Programming Languages, APL (Programming Language)

Audience: Programmers

Contact: David G. Macneil
dgm@unb.cat

Details: Free

User Info: To subscribe to the list, send an e-mail message to the URL address below, consisting of a single line reading:

SUB APL-L YourFirstName YourLastName

To send a message to the entire list, address it to: PL-L@cis.vutbr.cs

`mailto:listserv@cis.vutbr.cs`

Apngowid.meet

Apngowid.meet

★

A conference on plans by Asia Pacific regional women's groups for the United Nations Fourth World Conference on Women to be held in Beijing in September 1995.

Keywords: Women, Asia, Pacific, Feminists, Development, United Nations, World Conference on Women

Audience: Women, Feminists, Nongovernmental Organizations

Contact: AsPac Info, Docu and Communication Committee
AP-IDC@p95.f401.n751.z6.g

Details: Costs, Moderated

Establish an account on the nearest APC node. Login, type c for conferences, then type: go apngowid.meet.

For information on the nearest APC node, contact: APC International Secretariat, IBASE

E-mail: apcadmin@apc.org

`http://www.igc.apc.org/igc/www.women.html`

Apollo Advertising

Apollo Advertising

★★

A major directory on advertising, providing access to a broad range of related resources (library catalogs, databases, and servers) via the Internet.

Keywords: Advertising, Business

Audience: Advertisers, Business Professionals, General Public

Profile: A new web service for advertisers and information providers, which maintains the philosophy that consumers will choose to look for goods and services where it is easy and convenient to locate them. This involves the development of a database of short advertisements, many having hypertext links to more substantial advertisements. These can range from text documents to hypermedia commercials. The Apollo directory can be searched, using logical sorting methods, to identify items of interest. Additional information, including hypermedia, may be connected to the entries. This service encompasses short, stand-alone advertisements, as well as entries with hypertext links to other Internet resources.

Contact: apollo@apollo.co.uk

`gopher://apollo.co.uk`

Apple Computer

Apple II Files

★

This FTP site contains the archive of files relating to Apple II computers.

Keywords: Apple Computers, Computers

Audience: Programmers, Computer Users, Apple II
            Users

Details: Free

`ftp://archive.umich.edu`

Apple Computer Higher Education Gopher Server

This directory is maintained by Apple Computer to provide information about products from Apple Computer.

Keywords: Computer Systems, Computer-Aided
            Instruction, Apple Computer

Sponsor: Apple Computer, Cupertino, CA

Audience: General Public

Profile: This directory also contains promotional
            material, such as Apple Press Releases,
            extensive product information, Apple
            publications, regional market
            information, higher education marketing
            Information and support information.

Contact: feedback@info.hed.apple.com

`http://www.apple.com`

Apple Computer WWW Server

A web site containing information about Apple Computer. The resource is designed to provide timely product information, including press releases on Apple's technology and research. Also contains links to Freeware and Shareware sites, and includes information for developers and programmers.

Keywords: Computer Systems, Technology, Apple
            Computer, Shareware

Audience: General Public

`http://www.apple.com`

comp.sys.apple2

A Usenet newsgroup providing information and discussion about Apple II systems. There are several categories within this group.

Keywords: Computer Systems, Apple Computer

Audience: Computer Users, Apple II Users

User Info: To subscribe to this Usenet newsgroup,
            you need access to a newsreader.

`news:comp.sys.apple2`

AppWare Programming Language

AppWare-info

A forum for discussion of issues relating to AppWare software. Topics include simple programming questions, tips for program efficiency, quirks of, and complaints about, the environment or tools, the process of writing new ALMs or functions, third party enhancements, and any other question.

Keywords: Programming Languages, AppWare
            Programming Language

Sponsor: Novell Inc.

Audience: AppWare Users, Computer Programmers

Contact: Novell Inc.
            appware-info@serius.uchicago.edu

User Info: To subscribe to the list, send an e-mail
            message to the URL address below.

            To send a message to the entire list,
            address it to: appware-
            info@serius.uchicago.edu

`mailto:appware-info-request@serius.uchicago.edu`

`ftp://serius.uchicago.edu`

Aquaculture

University of Maine System Library Catalog

The library's holdings are large and wide-ranging and contain significant collections in many fields.

Keywords: Ucadian Studies, St. John Valley (History
            of), Canadian-American Studies,
            Geology, Aquaculture, Maine

Audience: General Public, Researchers, Librarians,
            Document Delivery Professionals

Contact: Elaine Albright, Marilyn Lutz

Details: Free

User Info: Expect: login, Send: ursus

`telnet://ursus.maine.edu`

University of Maryland System Library

The library's holdings are large and wide-ranging and contain significant collections in many fields.

Keywords: Medicine (History of), Nursing,
            Pharmacology, Microbiology,
            Aquaculture, Aquatic Chemistry,
            Toxicology

Audience: General Public, Researchers, Librarians,
            Document Delivery Professionals

Contact: Ron Larsen

Details: Free

User Info: Expect: Available Services menu; Send:
            PAC

`telnet://victor.umd.edu`

Aquariums

alt.aquaria

A Usenet newsgroup providing information and discussion about the aquarium as a hobby.

Keywords: Aquariums, Fish, Hobbies

Audience: Aquarium Keepers, Fish Lovers

User Info: To subscribe to this Usenet newsgroup,
            you need access to a newsreader.

`news:alt.aquaria`

Aquatic Biology

The University of Notre Dame Library

The library's holdings are large and wide-ranging and contain significant collections in many fields.

Keywords: Music (Irish), Ireland, Botany (History
            of), Ecology, Entomology, Parasitology,
            Aquatic Biology, Universities (History of),
            Paleography

Audience: General Public, Researchers, Librarians,
            Document Delivery Professionals

Details: Free

User Info: Expect: ENTER COMMAND OR HELP:,
            Send: library; To leave, type x on the
            command line and press the enter key.
            At the ENTER COMMAND OR HELP:
            prompt, type bye and press the enter
            key.

`telnet://irishmvs.cc.nd.edu`

Aquatic Chemistry

University of Maryland System Library

The library's holdings are large and wide-ranging and contain significant collections in many fields.

Keywords: Medicine (History of), Nursing,
            Pharmacology, Microbiology,
            Aquaculture, Aquatic Chemistry,
            Toxicology

Audience: General Public, Researchers, Librarians,
            Document Delivery Professionals

Contact: Ron Larsen

Details: Free

User Info: Expect: Available Services menu; Send:
            PAC

`telnet://victor.umd.edu`

Aquatic Science

Aquatic Sciences and Fisheries

This database is a comprehensive database on the science, technology, and management of marine and freshwater environments.

A
B
C
D
E
F
G
H
I
J
K
L
M
N
O
P
Q
R
S
T
U
V
W
X
Y
Z

Keywords: Aquatic Science, Marine Biology

Sponsor: US National Oceanic and Atmospheric Administration (NOAA)/Cambridge Scientific Abstracts, Bethesda, MD, US

Audience: Marine Biologists, Environmentalists

Profile: The database corresponds to the print Aquatic Sciences and Fisheries Abstracts; Part 1: Biological Sciences and Living Resources; Part 2: Ocean Technology, Policy, and Non-Living Resources; and Part 3: Aquatic Pollution and Environmental Quality. ASFA includes citations to 5,000 primary journals, monographs, conference proceedings, and technical reports.

Contact: Dialog in the US at (800) 334-2564, Dialog internationally at country specific locations.

User Info: To subscribe, contact Dialog directly.

`telnet://dialog.com`

rec.aquaria

A Usenet newsgroup providing information and discussion about pet fish and aquaria.

Keywords: Fish, Aquatic Science

Audience: Fish Enthusiasts

Details: Free

User Info: To subscribe to this Usenet newsgroup, you need access to a newsreader.

`news:rec.aquaria`

AR-news

AR-news

A public news wire for items relating to animal rights and animal welfare.

Keywords: Activism, Animal Rights, Veterinarians

Audience: Activists, Animal Lovers

Contact: Ian Lance Taylor, Chip Roberson

taylor@think.com or csr@nic.aren.com

User Info: To subscribe to the list, send an e-mail message to the URL address below.

To send a message to the entire list, address it to: ar-news@think.com

Notes: Appropriate postings to ar-news include posting a news item, requesting information on some event, or responding to a request for information. Discussions on ar-news are not allowed.

`mailto:ar-news@think.com`

AR-talk

AR-talk

An unmoderated list for the discussion of animal rights and related issues, such as animal liberation, consumer product testing, cruelty-free products, vivisection and dissection, and vegan lifestyles.

Keywords: Activism, Animal Rights

Audience: Activists, Animal Lovers, Researchers

Contact: Ian Lance Taylor, Chip Roberson taylor@think.com or csr@nic.aren.com

User Info: To subscribe to the list, send an e-mail message to the URL address below.

To send a message to the entire list, address it to: ar-talk@think.com

`mailto:ar-talk-request@think.com`

Arabic Culture (History of)

Harvard University Library

The library's holdings are large and wide-ranging and contain significant collections in many fields.

Keywords: Afrikaans, Alchemy, Arabic Culure (History of), Celtic Philology, Congo Languages, Folklore, Hebraica, Mormonism, Numismatics, Quakers, Sanskrit, Witchcraft, Arabic Philology

Audience: General Public, Researchers, Librarians, Document Delivery Professionals

Details: Free

User Info: Expect: Mitek Server..., Send: Enter or Return; Expect: prompt, Send: hollis

`telnet://hollis.harvard.edu`

Arabic Philology

Harvard University Library

The library's holdings are large and wide-ranging and contain significant collections in many fields.

Keywords: Afrikaans, Alchemy, Arabic Culure (History of), Celtic Philology, Congo Languages, Folklore, Hebraica, Mormonism, Numismatics, Quakers, Sanskrit, Witchcraft, Arabic Philology

Audience: General Public, Researchers, Librarians, Document Delivery Professionals

Details: Free

User Info: Expect: Mitek Server..., Send: Enter or Return; Expect: prompt, Send: hollis

`telnet://hollis.harvard.edu`

Arachnophilia: Florida Institute of Technology's WWW server.

Arachnophilia: Florida Institute of Technology's WWW server.

Provides pointers to information resources and search tools around the Web. Specifically for use by educators and researchers.

Keywords: Internet Tools

Audience: Educators, Researchers

Contact: www@sci-ed.fit.edu

Details: Free

`http://sci-ed.fit.edu`

Archaeology

Anthropology, Cross Cultural Studies, & Archaeology

This directory is a compilation of information resources focused on anthropology, cross cultural studies, and archaeology.

Keywords: Anthropology, Cross Cultural Studies, Archaeology

Audience: Anthropologists, Archaeologists, Students, Educators

Contact: G. Bell

Details: Free

`ftp://una.hh.lib.umich.edu/70/`
`inetdirsstacks/anthro:bell`

Archaeology, Historic Preservation

This directory is a compilation of information resources focused on archaeology, historic preservation, and heritage conservation.

Keywords: Archaeology, Historic Preservation

Audience: Archaeologists, Historians, Architects

Details: Free

`ftp://una.hh.lib.umich.edu/70/`
`inetdirsstacks/archpres:stott`

The Israel Information Service

A gopher server containing information on Israel.

Keywords: Israel, Middle East, Political Science, Anti-Semitism, Holocaust, Archaeology

Sponsor: Israeli Foreign Ministry

Audience: Israelis, Jews, Tourists, General Public

Profile: This server features updates on the Middle East peace process, including text of the latest Israel-PLO accord, as well as general political, diplomatic, cultural and economic information on the state of Israel. Also includes archives on archaeology in Israel, anti-Semitism and the Holocaust, and current excerpts from Israeli newspapers.

Contact: Chaim Shacham
shacham@israel-info.gov.il

`gopher://israel-info.gov.il`

Archie

Archie ★

A description of Archie, an electronic directory service for the Internet, which allows the user to find files remotely.

Keywords: Internet Tools, Archie

Sponsor: Computing Centre, McGill University, Montreal, Quebec, Canada

Audience: Internet Surfers

Contact: archie-group@archie.mcgill.ca

Details: Free

File is: pub/archie/doc/whatis.archie

`ftp://archie.ans.net`

Archie Demo ★

A Telnet demonstration of Archie, an Internet access tool.

Keywords: Internet Tools, Archie

Audience: Internet Surfers

Details: Free

Notes: login; Send: archie

`telnet://archie@archie.ans.net`

Archie Hypertext Servers ★

A list of hypertext Archie servers around the world.

Keywords: Internet Tools, Archie

Sponsor: NEXOR

Audience: Internet Surfers

Contact: Martijn Koster
m.koster@nexor.co.uk

Details: Free

`http://web.nexor.co.uk.archie.html`

Archie Manual ★

A reference manual for Archie, an Internet access tool.

Keywords: Internet Tools, Archie

Audience: Internet Surfers

Contact: R. Rodgers, Nelson N. Beebe
rodgers@maxwell.mmwb.ucsf.edu
beebe@math.utah.edu

Details: Free

File is: pub/archie/doc/archie.man.txt

`ftp://archie.ans.net`

Architecture

ArchiGopher ★★

A server dedicated to architectural knowledge. It includes The Kandinsky archive and the Palladio archive as well as images such as Hellenic architecture.

Keywords: Art, Architecture

Sponsor: University of Michigan, College of Architecture and Urban Planning

Audience: Architects, Artists

Contact: Wassim M. Jabi
wjabi@libra.arch.umich.edu

`gopher://libra.arch.umich.edu`

Architecture, Building ★

This directory is a compilation of information resources focused on architecture.

Keywords: Architecture, Building, Construction

Audience: Architects, Builders, Civil Engineers

Details: Free

`ftp://una.hh.lib.umich.edu/70/`
`inetdirsstacks/archi:brown`

Art & Architecture ★★

This directory is a compilation of information resources focused on art and architecture.

Keywords: Art, Architecture

Audience: Artists, Architects, Art Historians, Architectural Historians

Details: Free

`ftp://una.hh.lib.umich.edu/70/`
`inetdirsstacks/artarch:robinson`

McGill University, Montreal Canada, INFOMcGILL Library ★★★

The library's holdings are large and wide-ranging and contain significant collections in many fields.

Keywords: Architecture, Entomology, Biology, Science (History of), Medicine (History of), Napolean, Shakespeare (William)

Audience: Researchers, Students, General Public

Contact: Roy Miller
ccrmmus@mcgillm (Bitnet)
ccrmmus@musicm.mcgill.ca (Internet)

User Info: Expect: VM logo; Send: Enter; Expect: prompt; Send: PF3 or type INFO

`telnet://vm1.mcgill.ca`

Universite de Montreal UDEMATIK Library ★★★

The library's holdings are large and wide-ranging and contain significant collections in many fields.

Keywords: Art, Architecture, Economy, Sexology, Social Law, Science, Technology, Literary Studies

Audience: Researchers, Students, General Public

Contact: Joelle or Sebastien Roy
udematik@ere.umontreal.ca
stemp@ere.umontreal.ca
roys@ere.umontreal.ca

User Info: Expect: Login; Send: Application id INFO

`telnet:// udematik.umontreal.ca`

University of New Mexico Unminfo Library ★★

The library's holdings are large and wide-ranging and contain significant collections in many fields.

Keywords: Photography (History of), Architecture, Native American Affairs, Land Records

Audience: Researchers, Students, General Public

Contact: Art St. George
stgeorge@unmb.bitnet

Details: Free

User Info: Expect: Login; Send: Unminfo

`telnet://unminfo.unm.edu`

University of Rochester Library ★★

The library's holdings are large and wide-ranging and contain significant collections in many fields.

Keywords: Architecture, Art History, Photography, Literature (Asian), Lasers, Geology, Statistics, Optics, Medieval Studies

Audience: Researchers, Students, General Public

Details: Free

User Info: Expect: Login; Send: Library

`telnet://128.151.226.71`

University of Wisconsin at Milwaukee Library ★★

The library's holdings are large and wide-ranging and contain significant collections in many fields.

Keywords: Art, Architecture, Business, Cartography, Geography, Geology, Urban Studies, Literature (English), Literature (American)

A
B
C
D
E
F
G
H
I
J
K
L
M
N
O
P
Q
R
S
T
U
V
W
X
Y
Z

Audience: Researchers, Students, General Public

Details: Free

User Info: Expect: Login, Send: Lib; Expect: vDIAL prompt, Send: Library

`telnet://uwmcat.lib.uwm.edu`

Archive of Biology Software and Data

Archive of Biology Software and Data

★★★★

The main area of concentration of this archive is molecular biology. It contains software for the Macintosh, MS-DOS, VAX-VMS, and UNIX platforms.

Keywords: Health, Biology, Molecular Biology

Sponsor: Indiana University

Audience: Biologists, Students

Contact: archive@bio.indiana.edu

Details: Free

Notes: It is recommended that the file Archive.doc be transferred and read first. This file gives considerable information about and instructions for using the archive.

`ftp://ftp.bio.indiana.edu`

Archosaurs

dinosaur

★

Discussion of dinosaurs and their reptilian contemporaries.

Keywords: Dinosaurs, Archosaurs

Audience: Dinosaur Enthusiasts, Paleontologists

Contact: John Matrow
dinosaur-request@donald.WichitaKS.NCR.COM

Details: Free

User Info: To subscribe to the list, send an e-mail message requesting a subscription to the URL address below.

To send a message to the entire list, address it to: dinosaur-request@donald.WichitaKS.NCR.COM

`mailto:dinosaur-request@donald.WichitaKS.NCR.COM`

Argentina

Argentina

★★

Mailing list for general discussion and information about Argentina, including Argentine culture and politics.

Keywords: Argentina, Politics, Culture

Sponsor: Carlos G. Mendioroz

Audience: Spanish Speakers, Students

Contact: Carlos G. Mendioroz
argentina-request@ois.db.toronto.edu

User Info: To subscribe to the list, send an e-mail message to the URL address below.

To send a message to the entire list, address it to:
argentina@ois.db.toronto.edu

`mailto:argentina-request@ois.db.toronto.edu`

Aristotle (Texts of)

Indiana University Libraries

★★

The library's holdings are large and wide-ranging and contain significant collections in many fields.

Keywords: Literature (English), Literature (American), 1640-Present, British Plays (19th-C.), Western Americana, Railway History, Aristotle (Texts of), Lafayette (Marquis de), Handel (G.F.), Austrian History, Antiquarian Books, Rare Books, French Opera (19th-C.), Drama (British) ,

Audience: General Public, Researchers, Librarians, Document Delivery Professionals

Details: Free

User Info: Expect: User ID prompt, Send: GUEST

`telnet://iuis.ucs.indiana.edu`

University of Pennsylvania PENNINFO Library

★★★

The library's holdings are large and wide-ranging and contain significant collections in many fields.

Keywords: Church History, Spanish Inquisition, Witchcraft, Shakespeare (William), Bibles, Aristotle (Texts of), Fiction, Whitman (Walt), French Revolution, Drama (French), Literature (English), Literature (Spanish)

Audience: Researchers, Students, General Public

Contact: Al DSouza
penninfo-admin@dccs.upenn.edu
dsouza@dccs.upenn.edu

Details: Free

User Info: Expect: Login; Send: Public

`telnet://penninfo.upenn.edu`

ARlist

ARlist

★★

An open, unmoderated mailing list to provide a forum for discussing action research and its use in a variety of disciplines and situations. Topics include philosophical and methodological issues in action research, the use of action research for evaluation, actual case studies, and discourse on increasing the rigor of action research.

Keywords: Activism, Research, Politics

Audience: Activists, Researchers

Profile: Arlist is an open unmoderated mailing list to provide a forum for discussing action research and its use in a variety of disciplines and situations. It is usually (but perhaps not always) cyclic, participative, and qualitative.

Contact: Bob Dick
arlist@psych.psy.uq.oz.au

Details: Free

User Info: To subscribe to the list, send an e-mail message to the URL address below.

To send a message to the entire list, address it to: arlist@psych.psy.uq.oz.au

`mailto:arlist-request@psych.psy.uq.oz.au`

`ftp://psych.psy.uq.oz.au/dir/lists/arlist`

Armadillo's World Wide Web Page

Armadillo's World Wide Web Page

This site provides resources and instructional material for an interdisciplinary Texan culture course.

Keywords: History (US), Texas, Cultural Studies, Education

Sponsor: Rice University, Houston, Texas, USA

Audience: Educators, Students

Contact: armadillo@rice.edu

`http://chico.rice.edu/armadillo`

ars magica

ars magica

★★

A mailing list for the discussion of White Wolf's role-playing game, Ars Magica.

Keywords: Role-Playing, Games

Audience: Role-playing Enthusiasts, Game Players

Contact: ars-magica-request@soda.berkeley.edu

User Info: To subscribe to the list, send an e-mail message to the URL address below.

To send a message to the entire list, address it to: ars-magica-request@soda.berkeley.edu

Notes: Also available upon request as a nightly digest.

`mailto:ars-magica-request@soda.berkeley.edu`

Art

ACEN (Art Com Electronic Network)

A conference on the WELL for art, technology, and text-based artworks.

Keywords: Art, Literature (Contemporary), Multimedia

Sponsor: Art Com Electronic Network

Audience: Artists, Musicians, Writers

Profile: Started in 1986, ACEN is a seminal art BBS that includes actual artworks, discussion on topics such as software as art, and on line published works by John Cage, Fred Truck, Jim Rosenberg, Judy Malloy, and others.

Contact: Carl Loeffler
artcomtv@well.sf.ca.us

User Info: To participate in a conference on the WELL, you must first establish an account on the WELL. To do so, start by typing: telnet://well.sf.ca.us

`telnet://well.sf.ca.us`

African Art Exhibit and Tutorial

This web site provides images of African art and an overview of African aesthetics.

Keywords: Art, Africa, Cultural Studies

Sponsor: University of Virginia

Audience: Artists, Art Students, Educators, Historians

`http://www.lib.virginia.edu`

alt.artcom

A Usenet newsgroup providing information and discussion about contemporary art and technology. Discussion ranges from GIF files to Australian alternative cinema.

Keywords: Art, Technology

Audience: Artists, Writers

User Info: To subscribe to this Usenet newsgroup, you need access to a newsreader.

`news:alt.artcom`

alt.arts.nomad

A Usenet conference that focuses on group disembodied art projects.

Keywords: Art

Sponsor: Media Arts, Banff Centre, Canada

Audience: Artists

Details: disembodied art projects.

Notes: Art

`news:alt.arts.nomad`

ArchiGopher

A server dedicated to architectural knowledge. It includes The Kandinski archive and the Palladio archive as well as images such as Hellenic architecture.

Keywords: Art, Architecture

Sponsor: University of Michigan, College of Architecture and Urban Planning

Audience: Architects, Artists

Contact: Wassim M. Jabi
wjabi@libra.arch.umich.edu

`gopher://libra.arch.umich.edu`

Art & Architecture

This directory is a compilation of information resources focused on art and architecture.

Keywords: Art, Architecture

Audience: Artists, Architects, Art Historians, Architectural Historians

Details: Free

`ftp://una.hh.lib.umich.edu/70/`
`inetdirsstacks/artarch:robinson`

Art-support

A UK Mailbase forum for the discussion of art-related matters.

Keywords: Art, Fine Arts

Audience: Artists, Art Enthusiasts, Art Students

Notes: Login guest; password mailbase

`gopher://mailbase@mailbase.ac.uk`

`mailto:art-support-`
`request@mailbase.ac.uk`

`telnet://mailbase.ac.uk`

artist-users

A discussion group for users and potential users of software tools from Cadence Design Systems.

Keywords: Computers, Computer Art, Art

Sponsor: Cadence Design Systems

Audience: Computer Artists

Contact: Jeff Putsch
artist-users-request@uicc.com

User Info: To subscribe to the list, send an e-mail message to the URL address below.

To send a message to the entire list, address it to: artist-users-request@uicc.com

Notes: This mailing list is bi-directionally gatewayed to the Usenet newsgroup

`mailto:artist-users-request@uicc.com`

Arts

An umbrella arts conference on the WELL.

Keywords: Art, Music, Dance

Audience: Artists, Dancers, Musicians, Photographers

Profile: A genereal arts conference thet includes listings of show opportunities, books, and events, as well as discussion about art and art criticism.

Contact: Tim Collins

Notes: To participate in a conference on the WELL, you must first establish an account on the WELL. To do so, start by typing: telnet well.sf.ca.us

`telnet://well.sf.ca.us`

Arts Wire

A national communications network for the arts located on the Meta Network.

Keywords: Art, Writing, Activism, Music

Sponsor: New York Foundation for the Arts

Audience: Art Activists, Art Organizations, Artists, Composers, Foundations, Government Arts Agencies, Writers

Profile: Arts Wire provides immediate access to news, information, and dialogue on conditions affecting the arts and artists, as well as private conferences for organizations. Core features include Money, a searcable resource of grant deadlines; Hotwire, a summary of arts news; and conferences about new music, interactive art, literature, AIDS, and Latino art.

Contact: Judy Malloy
artswire@tmn.com

`telnet://tmn.com`

California Museum of Photography: Network Exhibitions

This is a collection of digital images for educational and general use.

Keywords: Photography, Art, Education

Sponsor: University of California, Riverside, California, USA

Audience: Photographers, Artists, Educators (esp. K-12), Historians

Profile: The California Museum of Photography is in the process of selecting groups of images from the collections as thematic exhibitions. Instead of displays on the walls, these exhibitions comprise a group of digital images with associated text. Particular emphasis is on the utility of these images in class projects for elementary and secondary school students. However, the digital images also have potential value for more advanced scholarly research in preparation of papers in the Humanities, Social Sciences and the Arts.

Contact: Russ Harvey
russ@cornucopia.ucr.edu

`gopher://gopher.ucr.edu`

comp.graphics

A Usenet newsgroup providing information and discussion about computer graphics, art, animation and more.

Keywords: Computer Graphics, Art

Audience: Computer Users

User Info: To subscribe to this Usenet newsgroup, you need access to a newsreader.

`news:comp.graphics`

Conference about Virtual Reality (The)

A conference on the WELL about cyberspace and virtual reality.

Keywords: Virtual Reality, Art, Cyberspace

Audience: Artists, Computer Programmers, Cyberpunks

Contact: Peter Rothman
avatarp@well.sf.ca.us

`telnet://well.sf.ca.us`

ecto

Information and discussion about singer/songwriter Happy Rhodes, and other music, art, books, and films of common (or singular) interest.

Keywords: Music, Art, Rhodes (Happy)

Audience: Music Enthusiasts, Art Enthusiasts

Contact: Jessica Dembski
ecto-request@ns1.rutgers.edu

Details: Free

User Info: To subscribe to the list, send an e-mail message requesting a subscription to the URL address below.

To send a message to the entire list, address it to: ecto-request@ns1.rutgers.edu

`mailto:ecto-request@ns1.rutgers.edu`

Electronic Cafe

A seminal art and telecommunications group that specializes in video transmission.

Keywords: Art, Video, Telecommunications

Audience: Artists

Profile: This combines performance, communication, and community outreach by making telecommunications equipment available in a cafe-style artists' space.

Contact: Kit Galloway and Sherrie Rabinowitz, 1641 18th St., Santa Monica, CA 90404, USA

`mailto:ecafe@netcom.com`

FineArt Forum

A monthly newsletter that includes listings of art and technology events, showcases, conferences, and jobs.

Keywords: Art, Multimedia

Sponsor: The International Society for the Arts, Sciences, and Technology

Audience: Art Educators, Art Professionals, Artists

Profile: Published by the National Science Foundation Engineering Research Center for Computational Field Simulation, Mississippi State University. FineArt Forum has provided timely information to a large international audience since 1988. The subscriber list consists of individuals working in the realm where art, science, and technology converge. Issues provide information about conferences and competitions, calls for presentations and research, and notices about performances. FineArt_Online is both an archive of FineArt Forum, ISEA News, Leonardo Electronic News, and a variety of longer postings. In January 1994 it began posting an online gallery.

Contact: Paul Brown
brown@erc.msstate.edu

User Info: To subscribe, send E-mail to: brown@erc.msstate.edu, with the message

SUB FAST; also give your name, postal address, and E-mail address.

`http://www.msstate.edu/Fineart_Online/home.html`

IMAGELAB

An unmoderated bulletin board for the discussion of image databases in libraries. Its purpose is to raise questions, solicit input, and share ideas. Another function of the list is to serve as a clearinghouse to announce image databases.

Keywords: Images, Art

Sponsor: University of Arizona Library

Audience: Arts Community

Contact: Stuart Glogoff

User Info: To subscribe to the list, send an e-mail message to the URL address shown below consisting of a single line reading:

SUB imagelab YourFirstName YourLastName

`listserv@arizvm1.ccit.arizona.edu`

Images from Various Sources

This site serves as a link to some 35 image archives throughout the world. A wide variety of images is available, with a particularly large number of weather, geological, and biological collections from government and private sources.

Keywords: Computer Graphics, Photography, Art

Sponsor: The University of Alaska

Audience: General Public

Contact: Douglas Toelle
sxinfo@orca.alaska.edu

Details: Free, Images

`gopher://gopher.uacn.alaska.edu`

`http://info.alaska.edu:70`

Interactive

A conference on Arts Wire about interactive art that includes a library of artists' statements about artworks, texts, and publications, as well as discussion.

Keywords: Art, Interactive Art

Sponsor: New York Foundation for the Arts

Audience: Artists, Writers

Contact: Anna Couey, Judy Malloy
couey@tmn.com, jmalloy@tmn.com

`telnet://tmn.com`

Internet Art Gallery

An online art collection in the form of JPEG files, including the works of 85 artists ranging from Dali to Van Eyck.

Keywords: Art, Fine Art, Art History

Sponsor: New York State Education Department

Audience: Artists, Art Students, Art Teachers, General Public

Contact: Steve Richter, George Casler
steve@unix5.nysed.gov
gcasler@unix5.nysed.gov

`gopher://unix5.nysed.gov`

ISEA (Inter-Society on Electronic Arts) Online

An online forum for discussion of topics related to ISEA-94, the 5th International Symposium on Electronic Art which will take place in Finland in August, 1994.

Keywords: Art, Electronic Art, Technology

Audience: Artists, Art Enthusiasts

Details: Free

`ftp://ftp.ncsa.uiuc.edu`

Kaleidospace

This is a new web server that provides a multimedia showcase for artists, performers, CD-ROM authors, musicians, writers, animators, filmmakers and software developers.

Keywords: Art, Computer Art, Multimedia

Audience: Artists, Performers, CD-ROM Authors, Musicians, Writers, Animators, Filmmakers, Software Developers

Profile: This site was created to support independent artists. The site has similarities to other web servers such as IUMA, but differs in that it works with all kinds of artists, and that it processes orders for the artist's material.

Contact: Jeannie Novak, Peter Markiewicz jeannienov@aol.competerm@ewald.mbi.ucla.edu

`http://kspace.com`

`http://fire.kspace.com`

Leonardo Electronic Almanac

The Leonardo Electronic Almanac (LEA) is a monthly, edited journal and an electronic archive dedicated to providing current perspectives in the art, science and technology domains.

Keywords: Art, Multimedia, Music, Electronic Media

Sponsor: International Society for the Arts, Sciences, and Technology

Audience: New Media Artists, Researchers, Developers, Art Educators, Art Professionals

Profile: LEA is an international, interdisciplinary forum for people interested in the use of new media in contemporary artistic expression, especially involving 20th century science and technology. Material is contributed by artists, scientists, philosophers and educators. LEA is published by the MIT Press for Leonardo, the International Society for the Arts, Sciences, and Technology (ISAST).

Contact: Craig Harris craig@well.sf.ca.us

Details: Costs, Moderated, Images, Sounds, Multimedia

`mail to:journals-orders@mit.edu`

`ftp://mitpress.mit.edu/pub/Leonardo-Elec-Almanac`

Muchomedia Conference

A conference on the WELL about multimedia with topics ranging from products and software to multimedia for beginners.

Keywords: Multimedia, Art

Audience: Artists, Computer Programmers, Producers

Contact: Douglas Crockford crock@well.sf.ca.us

To participate in a conference on the WELL, you must first establish an account on the WELL. To do so, start by typing: telnet well.sf.ca.us

`telnet://well.sf.ca.us`

naplps-list

This is a mailing list for people interested in NAPLPS graphics.

Keywords: Computer Graphics, Art

Audience: Graphic Artists, Artists

Contact: Dave Hughes oldcolo@goldmill.uucp

`naplps-list@oldcolo.com`

Northwestern University Library

The library's holdings are large and wide-ranging and contain significant collections in many fields.

Keywords: Africa, Wright (Frank Lloyd), Women's Studies, Art, Literature (American), Contemporary Music, Government (US State), UN Documents, Music

Audience: General Public, Researchers, Librarians, Document Delivery Professionals

Details: Free

User Info: Expect: COMMAND:, Send: DIAL VTAM

`telnet://nuacvm.acns.nwu.edu`

NYAL (New York Art Line)

A gopher containing selected resources on the arts.

Keywords: Art, Audio-Visual Materials, Multimedia, Computer Art

Sponsor: Panix Public Access Unix & Internet Gopher Server, New York, USA

Audience: Artists, Art Enthusiasts

Profile: NYAL features a wide variety of arts resources. The primary focus of this site is visual art, particularly in the New York city area. Information includes online access to selected galleries, image archives, and New York city arts groups. Beyond visual art, information on dance, music, and techno art (with a special section on Internet art) is also available. It also features links to various electronic journals, museums, and schools.

Contact: Kenny Greenberg kgreen@panix.com

`gopher://gopher.panix.com`

`http//gopher.panix.com/nyart/Kpage/kg`

OTIS (Operative Term Is Stimulate)

An image-based electronic art gallery.

Keywords: Art, Graphics, Electronic Art, Animation

Audience: Graphic Artists

Profile: OTIS is a public-access library containing hundreds of images, animations, and information files.

Within the sunsite ftp, the directory is: /pub/multimedia/pictures/OTIS. Use the bin command to insure you're in binary transfer mode.

`ftp://sunsite.unc.edu`

rec.arts.fin

A Usenet newsgroup providing information and discussion about the visual arts. Discussions range from archival materials to Ansel Adams, Mary Cassat and Andy Warhol.

Keywords: Art, Fine Art

Audience: Artists, Art Educators, Art Professionals

User Info: To subscribe to this Usenet newsgroup, you need access to a newsreader.

`news:rec.arts.fin`

rec.photo

A Usenet newsgroup providing information and discussion about photography.

Keywords: Photography, Art, Crafts

Audience: Photographers, Artists

User Info: To subscribe to this Usenet newsgroup, you need access to a newsreader.

`news:rec.photo`

rec.video

A Usenet newsgroup providing information and discussion about video.

Keywords: Video, Art, Film, Computer Art

Audience: Cinematographers, Video Artists

User Info: To subscribe to this Usenet newsgroup, you need access to a newsreader.

`news:rec.video`

Rosen Sculpture Exhibition

This web site contains various examples of sculpture movements.

Keywords: Art, Fine Arts

Sponsor: Visual Resources Curator of the Department of Art at Appalachian State University, Boone, North Carolina, USA

Audience: Art Educators, Art Students

`http://www.acs.appstate.edu/art`

A B C D E F G H I J K L M N O P Q R S T U V W X Y Z

A
B
C
D
E
F
G
H
I
J
K
L
M
N
O
P
Q
R
S
T
U
V
W
X
Y
Z

UCSB Library Reference Guide

A list of art references including indexes, dictionaries, bilbiographies and biographical materials.

Keywords: Art, History (World), Libraries

Sponsor: University of California at Santa Barbara

Audience: Artists, Historians, Librarians

`gopher://ucsbuxa.ucsb.edu`

Universite de Montreal UDEMATIK Library

The library's holdings are large and wide-ranging and contain significant collections in many fields.

Keywords: Art, Architecture, Economy, Sexology, Social Law, Science, Technology, Literary Studies

Audience: Researchers, Students, General Public

Contact: Joelle or Sebastien Roy
udematik@ere.umontreal.ca
stemp@ere.umontreal.ca
roys@ere.umontreal.ca

User Info: Expect: Login; Send: Application id INFO

`telnet://udematik.umontreal.ca`

University of Northern Iowa Library

The library's holdings are large and wide-ranging and contain significant collections in many fields.

Keywords: Art, Business Information, Education, Music, Fiction

Audience: Researchers, Students, General Public

Contact: Mike Yohe
yohe@uni.edu

Details: Free

User Info: Expect: Login; Send: Public

`telnet://infosys.uni.edu`

University of Wisconsin at Milwaukee Library

The library's holdings are large and wide-ranging and contain significant collections in many fields.

Keywords: Art, Architecture, Business, Cartography, Geography, Geology, Urban Studies, Literature (English), Literature (American)

Audience: Researchers, Students, General Public

Details: Free

User Info: Expect: Login, Send: Lib; Expect: vDIAL prompt, Send: Library

`telnet://uwmcat.lib.uwm.edu`

Virginia Commonwealth University Library

The library's holdings are large and wide-ranging and contain significant collections in many fields.

Keywords: Art, Biology, Humanities, Journalism, Music, Urban Planning

Audience: Researchers, Students, General Public

Details: Free

User Info: Expect: Login; Send: Opub

`telnet://vcuvm1.ucc.vcu.edu`

WWW Paris

A web site created as a collaborative effort among individuals in both Paris and the United States.

Keywords: Paris, Culture, Art, Travel, French, Tourism

Audience: Students, Educators, Travelers, Researchers

Profile: Contains an extensive collection of images and text regarding all of the major monuments and museums of Paris, including maps of the Metro and the RER; calendars of events and current expositions; promotional images and text relating to local department stores; there is also a visitors' section with up-to-date tourist information on hotels, restaurants, telephones, airport schedules, a basic Paris glossary, and the latest weather images. Includes an extensive collection of links to other resources about Paris and France, and a selected bibliography of history and architecture in Paris.

Contact: Norman Barth, Eric Pouliquen
nbarth@ucsd.edu
epouliq@ucsd.edu

`http://meteora.ucsd.edu/~norman/paris`

Art & Architecture

Art & Architecture

This directory is a compilation of information resources focused on art and architecture.

Keywords: Art, Architecture

Audience: Artists, Architects

Details: Free

`ftp://una.hh.lib.umich.edu/70/`
`inetdirstacks/artarch:robinson`

Art Com Magazine

Art Com Magazine

A newsletter about art and technology (subjects covered include robotics, artists' software, hyperfiction) that is guest-edited by individual artists.

Keywords: Computer Art, Literature (Contemporary), Technology, Hyperfiction

Sponsor: Art Com Electronic Network

Audience: Artists, Writers

Contact: Fred Truck
fjt@well.sf.ca.us

User Info: To participate in a conference on the WELL, you must first establish an account on the WELL. To do so, start by typing: telnet://well.sf.ca.us

`mailto:artcomtv@well.sf.ca.us`

Art Exhibitions

Smithsonian Online

Located on America Online (with partial access by ftp), this allows online access to the Institution's resources.

Keywords: Museums, Art Exhibitions

Sponsor: Smithsonian Institution, Washington DC

Audience: Educators, Students, General Public

Profile: Smithsonian Online includes resources for teachers and students in the form of bulletin boards about Smithsonian museums, photographs, listings of events in Washington and other communities, and excerpts from Smithsonian and Air & Space/ Smithsonian.

`ftp://photo1.si.edu`

Art History

Internet Art Gallery

An online art collection in the form of JPEG files, including the works of 85 artists ranging from Dali to Van Eyck.

Keywords: Art, Fine Art, Art History

Sponsor: New York State Education Department

Audience: Artists, Art Students, Art Teachers, General Public

Contact: Steve Richter, George Casler
steve@unix5.nysed.gov,
gcasler@unix5.nysed.gov

`gopher://unix5.nysed.gov`

University of Rochester Library

The library's holdings are large and wide-ranging and contain significant collections in many fields.

Keywords: Architecture, Art History, Photography, Literature (Asian), Lasers, Geology, Statistics, Optics, Medieval Studies

Audience: Researchers, Students, General Public

Details: Free

User Info: Expect: Login; Send: Library

`telnet://128.151.226.71`

Artificial Intelligence

Artificial Intelligence, Expert Sys., Virtual Reality

This directory is a compilation of information resources focused on computer science research, artificial intelligence, expert systems, and virtual reality.

Keywords: Computer Science, Artificial Intelligence, Expert Systems, Virtual Reality

Audience: Computer Scientists, Engineers

Details: Free

`ftp://una.hh.lib.umich.edu/70/ inetdirsstacks/csaiesvr:kovacsm`

Computists' Communique

A weekly newsletter serving professionals in artificial intelligence, information science, and computer science.

Keywords: Artificial Intelligence, Information Science, Computer Science

Audience: Computer Scientists, Information Scientists, Computists International Members

Profile: Content is career oriented and depends partly on contributions from members. The moderator filters submissions, reports and comments on industry news, collects common knowledge about academia and industry, and helps track people and projects. The Communique is only available to members of Computists International, a networking association for computer and information scientists. It is an association for mutual mentoring about grant and funding sources, information channels, applications, text, software publishing, and the sociology of work.

Contact: Kenneth I. Laws laws@ari.sri.com

Details: Costs, Moderated

`mailto:laws@ari.sri.com`

Artificial Life

Alife

The alife mailing list is for communications regarding artificial life, a formative interdisciplinary field involving computer science, the natural sciences, mathematics, and medicine.

Keywords: Artificial Life, Science, Mathematics

Sponsor: UCLA

Audience: Scientists, Biologists, Mathematicians

Contact: alife-request@cognet.ucla.edu

User Info: To subscribe to the list, send an e-mail message to the URL address below.

To send a message to the entire list, address it to: alife@cognet.ucla.edu

`mailto:alife-request@cognet.ucla.edu`

Artificial Life

A forum for the accumulation and dissemination of information about all aspects of the Artificial Life enterprise. Services provided include an FTP site containing preprints and software, a bibliographic database on Artificial Life, and links to various Usenet services.

Keywords: Artificial Life, Chaos Theory

Sponsor: MITPress, Cambridge, Massachusetts, USA

Audience: Mathematical Biologists, Researchers, Theoretical Biologists

Contact: Chris Langton cgl@santafe.edu

`http://alife.santafe.edu`

artist-users

artist-users

A discussion group for users and potential users of software tools from Cadence Design Systems.

Keywords: Computers, Computer Art, Art

Sponsor: Cadence Design Systems

Audience: Computer Artists, Graphics Designers

Contact: Jeff Putsch artist-users-request@uicc.com

User Info: To subscribe to the list, send an e-mail message to the URL address below.

To send a message to the entire list, address it to: artist-users-request@uicc.com

Notes: This mailing list is bi-directionally gatewayed to the Usenet newsgroup

`mailto:artist-users-request@uicc.com`

Asat-eva (Distance Education Evaluation Group)

Asat-eva (Distance Education Evaluation Group)

This mailing list addresses issues in evaluating all forms of distance learning and programs.

Keywords: Education (Adult), Education (Distance), Education (Continuing)

Sponsor: Agricultural Satellite Corporation

Audience: Educators, Administrators, Researchers

Details: Free

User Info: To subscribe to the list, send an e-mail message to the URL address below, consisting of a single line reading:

SUB asat-evaYourFirstName YourLastName

To send a message to the entire list, address it to: asat-eva@unlvm.unl.edu

`mailto:listserv@unlvm.unl.edu`

ASCII

Gopher-Based ASCII Clipart Collection

A collection of more than 500 individual pictures.

Keywords: ASCII, Clipart

Sponsor: Texas Tech Computer Sciences Gopher Server

Audience: Computer Users, General Public

Contact: Abdul Malik Yoosufan gripe@cs.ttu.edu

Details: Free, Images

`gopher://cs4sun.cs.ttu.edu`

`ftp://ftp.cs.ttu.edu:/pub/asciiar`

Asia

apngowid.meet

A conference on plans by Asia Pacific regional women's groups for the United Nations Fourth World Conference on Women to be held in Beijing in September 1995.

Keywords: Women, Asia, Pacific, Feminists, Development, United Nations, World Conference on Women

Audience: Women, Feminists, Nongovernmental Organizations

A
B
C
D
E
F
G
H
I
J
K
L
M
N
O
P
Q
R
S
T
U
V
W
X
Y
Z

A
B
C
D
E
F
G
H
I
J
K
L
M
N
O
P
Q
R
S
T
U
V
W
X
Y
Z

Contact: AsPac Info, Docu and Communication Committee
AP-IDC@p95.f401.n751.z6.g

Details: Costs, Moderated

Establish an account on the nearest APC node. Login, type c for conferences, then type: go apngowid.meet.

For information on the nearest APC node, contact: APC International Secretariat, IBASE.

E-mail: apcadmin@apc.org

`http://www.igc.apc.org/igc/`
`www.women.html`

Asia-Pacific

 ★★★★

The database covers the business, economics, and new industries of the Pacific Rim nations, including East Asia, Southeast Asia, the Indian Subcontinent, the Middle East, Australia, and the Pacific Island nations.

Keywords: Asia, Pacific, Business, Economy

Sponsor: Aristarchus Knowledge Industries, Seattle, WA, USA

Audience: Market Researchers, Economists, Market Analysts

Profile: Records are of two types: main records consisting of abstracts or citations for journal articles and other publications; and company thesaurus records. Detailed abstracts are provided for selected journal articles, monographs, selected papers in conference proceedings, dissertations, and government documents. Shorter citations with briefer indexing are provided for a wide variety of journal articles, newspapers, government documents, and annual report publications. Asia-Pacific also includes an extensive Corporate Thesaurus subfile, which provides detailed coverage of the corporate players in the Pacific Rim, including thousands of companies traded on the stock exchanges of Southeast and East Asia.

Contact: Dialog in the US at (800) 334-2564; Dialog internationally at country-specific locations.

Details: Costs

User Info: To subscribe, contact Dialog directly.

`telnet://dialog.com`

Asian American FAQ

 ★★

Document of FAQs for the soc.culture.asian.american Usenet newsgroup. Includes information concerning terminology, publications, dating, and references.

Keywords: Asia, Asian Studies

Audience: Students, Asian-Americans, Asians

Contact: Bryan Wu
bwu@panix.com

Details: Free

`ftp://rtfm.mit.edu/pub/usenet/`
`soc.culture.asian.american/`
`FAQ_for_soc.culture.asian.american`

Asian and Pacific Economic Literature

 ★★★

A list of economic literature covering Asia and the Pacific region.

Keywords: Asia, Pacific, Economics

Audience: Economists, Business Professionals

Details: Free

`ftp://coombs.anu.edu`

Asian Pacific Business and Marketing Resources

 ★

A forum on business and marketing in the Pacific Rim region.

Keywords: Asia, Pacific, Business, Management

Audience: Business Professionals, Market Researchers

Details: Free

`gopher://hoshi.cic.sfu.ca/11/dlam/`
`business/forum`

Chiba University Gopher

 ★

The Chiba University gopher, including files from the university's library.

Keywords: Japan, Asia, Libraries

Sponsor: Chiba University, Chiba, Japan

Audience: Japan Residents, Computer Programmers, Librarians, Linguists

Contact: hasimoto@chiba-u.ac.jp

`gopher://himawari.ipc.chiba-u.ac.jp`

University of Hawaii Library

★★

The library's holdings are large and wide-ranging and contain significant collections in many fields.

Keywords: Asia, European Documents, Book Arts, Hawaii

Audience: General Public, Researchers, Librarians, Document Delivery Professionals

Details: Free

User Info: Expect: enter class, Send: LIB

`telnet://starmaster.uhcc.hawaii.edu`

University of Michigan Library

 ★★

The library's holdings are large and wide-ranging and contain significant collections in many fields.

Keywords: Asia, Astronomy, Transportation, Lexicology, Math, Zoology, Geography

Audience: Researchers, Students, General Public

Contact: info@merit.edu

Details: Free

User Info: Expect: Which Host; Send: Help

`telnet://cts.merit.edu`

Asian American Studies

soc.culture.asian.american

 ★

A Usenet newsgroup providing information and discussion about Asian American culture.

Keywords: Asian American Studies, Sociology

Audience: Sociologists

Details: Free

User Info: To subscribe to this Usenet newsgroup, you need access to a newsreader.

`news:soc.culture.asian.american`

Asian Studies

ANU (Australian National University) Asian-Settlements Database

 ★★★

A searchable database containing abstracts of theses and research studies provided by the Asian Institute of Technology, relating to issues of demography and social geography in Asia.

Keywords: Asian Studies, Demography, Geography

Sponsor: The COOMBSQUEST Social Sciences & Humanities Information Facility at ANU (Australian National University), Canberra, Australia

Audience: Asia Studies Instructors, Demographers, Geographers

Contact: Dr. T. Matthew Ciolek
coombspapers@coombs.anu.edu.au

Details: Free

`gopher://cheops.anu.edu.au/Coombs-db/`
`ANU-Asian-Settlements.src`

`http://coombs.anu.edu.au/WWWVL-`
`AsianStudies.html`

ANU (Australian National University) Buddhism Database ★★★

A searchable database of messages from the BUDDHA-L listserv, an academic forum for the discussion of Buddhism. It currently contains archives for messages posted in 1993-94.

Keywords: Religion, Asian Studies, Buddhism

Sponsor: COOMBSQUEST Social Sciences & Humanities Information Facility at ANU (Australian National University), Canberra, Australia

Audience: Buddhists, Religious Studies Instructors, Asian Studies Educators

Contact: Dr. T.Matthew Ciolek coombspapers@coombs.anu.edu.au

```
gopher://cheops.anu.edu.au /Coombs-
db/ANU-Buddha-1.src
```

```
http://coombs.anu.edu.au/WWWVL-
AsianStudies.html
```

APEX-J (Asia-Pacific Exchange Electronic Journal) ★

An electronic journal about the Pacific Rim.

Keywords: Asian Studies

Sponsor: Published by the University of Hawaii at Kapiolani Community College, Hawaii, USA

Audience: Educators, Students

Contact: Jim Shimabukuro JamesS@Hawaii.edu

Notes: login anonymous;password your email address; cd outgoing; get file.name; bye

```
ftp://ftp.hawaii.edu
```

Asian American FAQ ★★

Document of FAQs for the soc.culture.asian.american Usenet newsgroup. Includes information concerning terminology, publications, dating, and references.

Keywords: Asia, Asian Studies

Audience: Students, Asian-Americans, Asians

Contact: Bryan Wu bwu@panix.com

Details: Free

```
ftp://rtfm.mit.edu/pub/usenet/
soc.culture.asian.american/FAQ
```

```
_for_soc.culture.asian.american
```

AskERIC Virtual Library

AskERIC Virtual Library ★★★★

This gopher is part of a federally-funded system to provide public access to educational resources.

Keywords: Education (K-12), Computer-Aided Learning, Libraries, Electronic Books

Sponsor: Educational Resources Information Center (ERIC)

Audience: K-12 Teachers, Administrators

Profile: This gopher contains a wide range of educational aids including pre-prepared lesson plans, guides to Internet resources for the classroom organized by subject, updates on conferences for educators, and archives of education-related listservs. Also allows access to outside gophers, libraries, and sources of electronic books and journals.

Contact: Nancy A. Morgan nmorgan@ericir.syr.edu askeric@ericir.syr.edu

```
gopher://ericir/syr.edu
```

ASSETS (Real Estate Tax Assessor and Deed Transfer Records)

ASSETS (Real Estate Tax Assessor and Deed Transfer Records) ★★★

The Real Estate Tax Assessor and Deed Transfer Records (ASSETS) library contains information compiled from real property records.

Keywords: Real Estate, Property, Taxes

Audience: Lawyers

Profile: The ASSETS library contains a variety of real estate information, including asset ownership, property address, owner's mailing address, assessed valuation, current market value, and recent property sales and deed transfers. Information is collected from county tax assessors' and recorders' offices nationwide and compiled by TRW REDI Property Data. The ASSETS library also contains a variety of boat and aircraft registration information.

Contact: Mead New Sales Group at (800) 227-4908 or (513) 859-5398 inside the US, or (513) 865-7981 for all inquiries outside the US.

User Info: To subscribe, contact Mead directly.

To examine the Nexis user guide, you can access it at the ftp site of the University of Texas at Austin at the URL address: ftp://ftp.cc.utexas.edu

The files are in: /pub/ref-services/LEXIS

```
telnet://nex.meaddata.com
```

```
http://www.meaddata.com
```

Assignees

LEXPAT (Patents US) ★★★

The LEXPAT library contains the full text of US patents issued since 1975, the US Patent and Trademark Office Manual of Classification, and the Index to US Patent Classification. The approximately 1,500 patents added to the library each week appear online within four days of their issue.

Keywords: Patents, Inventors, Assignees, Litigants

Audience: Lawyers, Business Researchers, Analysts, Entrepreneurs

Profile: LEXPAT may be searched by individual files for the full text of utility, design or plant patents, or you can combine the files in one 'omni' search. The Manual, Index and Class files can be used to supplement your full-text patent searches. LEXPAT is a valuable tool for both patent professionals and for anyone who needs to access to technical information. More than 80 percent of the information contained in patents is unavailable in any other form.

Contact: Mead New Sales Group at (800) 227-4908 or (513) 859-5398 inside the US, or (513) 865-7981 for all inquiries outside the US.

User Info: To subscribe, contact Mead directly.

User Info: To examine the Nexis user guide, you can access it at the ftp site of the University of Texas at Austin at the URL address: ftp://ftp.cc.utexas.edu

The files are in: /pub/ref-services/LEXIS

```
telnet://nex.meaddata.com
```

```
http://www.meaddata.com
```

ASTRA-UG

ASTRA-UG ★★

A mailing list for the discussion of Italian and European GIS (Geographical Information Systems).

Keywords: GIS (Geographic Information Systems), Europe, Italy

Audience: Geographers, Cartographers, Europeans

Details: Free

User Info: To subscribe to the list, send an e-mail mesage to the URL address below, consisting of a single line reading:

SUB ASTRA-UG YourFirstName YourLastName

```
astra-ug@icnucevm
```

A
B
C
D
E
F
G
H
I
J
K
L
M
N
O
P
Q
R
S
T
U
V
W
X
Y
Z

Astronomy

Astronomical Information on the Internet ★★★★

This FTP site contains pointers to potentially relevant resources available via the Internet.

Keywords: Astronomy, Astrophysics, Astronomical Software, Astronomical Instrumentation

Sponsor: European Space Organization (ESO) and Space Telescope European Coordinating Facility (ST-ECF)

Audience: Astronomers, Physicists, Students (college, graduate), Educators

Profile: This is the entry point for most astronomical resources available online categorized by function. More than 100 resources are accessible concerning general astronomical information, software, and publications. The following are just a few examples of the resources available as of January 1994:

- On-line Publications from CERN, SISSA, STSCI, NASA, PASP, Cfa, and so on.
- Conferences and meetings
- Metereological information
- Access to over 30 observatories and institutes
- Data archives from over 20 previous and current satellite missions, observatories,and astronomy data centers
- Astronomical images
- Astronomical software
- Jobs

Contact: Hans-Martin Adorf

adorf@eso.org

Details: Free, Moderated; Image, Sound, and Multimedia files available.

`ftp://ecf.hq.eso.org/pub/WWW/astro-resources.html`

Astronomical Publications Resources (APR) ★★★★

Contains pointers to many relevant resources available via the Internet.

Keywords: Astronomy, Astrophysics, Physics

Sponsor: Space Telescope Science Institute

Audience: Astronomers, Physicists, Students (college, graduate), Educators

Profile: APR is a useful starting point to most of the astronomical publication resources available online. It is conviently divided by type of access (gopher, wais, www, telnet, ftp). As of January 1994, resources include:

- Astrophysics Preprints—SISSA
- ADC Documents
- NOAO News
- NRAO Preprint Database
- STECF Newsletter
- STELAR ApJ, ApJS, AJ, PASP, A&A, A&AS, MNRAS, and JGR Abstracts
- STScI Preprint Database
- IAU Circulars Astronomical Union
- CfA Index of ApJ, AJ, PASP
- DIRA2 Database
- Electronic Journal of Astronomical Society of the Atlantic

Contact: rrpss@stsci.edu

Details: Free, Moderated

`http://stsci.edu/net-publications.html`

`gopher://stsci.edu`

Astronomical Software Resources (ASR) ★★★★

Contains pointers to many relevant resources available via the Internet.

Keywords: Astronomy, Astrophysics, Astronomical Software

Sponsor: Space Telescope Science Institute

Audience: Astronomers, Physicists, Students (College, Graduate), Educators

Profile: ASR is a useful starting point to most of the astronomical software resources available on line. It is conviently divided by type of access (www, wais, gopher, telnet, ftp). As of January 1994, resources include:

- Computer Software Management and Information Center
- IRAF Information System
- Software Support Laboratory SSL
- Starlink Help Browser
- Space Telescope Science Data Analysis System (STSDAS)
- FITS Archive
- NAG Bulletin Board Services
- Numerical Recipes Software
- STSDAS Software
- Working Group on Astronomical Software Archives
- FITS Documents

Contact: rpss@stsci.edu.

Details: Free, Moderated; Image, Sound, and Multimedia files available.

`http://stsci.edu/net-software.html`

Astronomy ★

This directory is a compilation of information resources focused on astronomy.

Keywords: Astronomy, Astrophysics, Space

Audience: Astronomers, Astrophysicists, Space Enthusiasts

Details: Free

`ftp://una.hh.lib.umich.edu/70/inetdirsstacks/astron:parkmiller`

Astrophysics Data System (ADS) ★★★★

A distributed processing software that provides its users with access to over 190 astronomical catalogs and approximately 125,000 astronomical abstracts.

Keywords: Astronomy, Astrophysics,

Sponsor: Smithsonian Astrophysical Observatory

Audience: Astronomers, Physicists, Students (College, Graduate), Educators

Profile: ADS is a suite of information management, manipulation, visualization, and access tools that facilitate user selection of, and access to, data in a distributed environment. These data can be imported to or exported from analysis systems through the use of the ASCII and FITS I/O standards. ADS also provides direct access to the HEASARC Browse tool, NSSDC's Online Data and Information Service (NODIS), the NASA/IPAC Extragalactic Database (NED), SIMBAD (Set of Identifications, Measurements, and Bibliography for Astronomical Data). The user is able to access all of this information via a simple-to-use Graphical User Interface (GUI).

Contact: ads@cuads.colorado.edu

Details: Free, Image files available.

Notes: To become a registered user and get ADS, request a registration form from ads@cuads.colorado.edu.

`http://adswww.colorado.edu/adswww/adshomepg.htlm`

CADC (Canadian Astronomy Data Center) Home Page ★★★

The CADC maintains archives of scientific data from the Hubble Space Telescope and the Canada France Hawaii Telescope. It also serves as a distribution point for various astronomy-related software packages.

Keywords: Astronomy, Hubble Telescope

Sponsor: Dominional Astrophysical Observatory, Victoria, British Columbia, Canada

Audience: Astronomers

Contact: Dennis Crabtree crabtree@dao.nrc.ca

`http://ucluelet.dao.nrc.ca`

Canopus

Newsletter of the Space Science and Astronomy Technical Committee of the American Institute of Aeronautics and Astronautics. Its objective is to provide an insider's perspective on issues in space science and astronomy.

Keywords: Space Science, Astronomy

Sponsor: NASA (National Aeronautics and Space Administration)

Audience: Astronomers, Space Scientists

Contact: William W. L. Taylor
wtaylor@nhqvax.hq.nasa.gov

Details: Costs

User Info: To subscribe to the list, send an e-mail message to the URL address below.

`mailto:wtaylor@nhqvax.hq.nasa.gov`

Center for Extreme Ultraviolet Astrophysics

A department of the University of California at Berkeley devoted to research in extreme ultraviolet astronomy. It is the ground-based institution of EUVE (the Extreme Ultraviolet Explorer), a NASA satellite launched in 1992.

Keywords: Astronomy, Astrophysics, EUVE, NASA, Satellite

Sponsor: NASA and University of California at Berkeley

Audience: Astronomers, Astrophysicists

Profile: Provides access to details about the EUVE Guest Observer (EGO) Center, the EUVE Public Archive of Mission Data and Information, satellite operation information, and so on. The EUVE Guest Observer Center provides information, software, and data to EUVE Guest Observers.

Contact: egoinfo@cea.berkeley.edu, archive@cea.berkeley.edu

Details: Free

`http://cea-ftp.cea.berkeley.edu`

Earth and Sky

This is a weekly publication of transcripts of earth science and astronomy radio programs aired daily on the Earth & Sky Radio Series, hosted by Deborah Byrd and Joel Block.

Keywords: Earth Sciences, Astronomy

Audience: General Public, Earth Scientists, Astronomers

Contact: majordomo@lists.utexas.edu

Details: Free

User Info: To subscribe to the list, send an e-mail message to the URL address shown below consisting of a single line reading:

SUB earth-and-sky YourFirstName YourLastName

To send a message to the entire list, address it to: earth-and-sky@lists.utexas.edu

`mailto:majordomo@lists.utexas.edu`

Extraterrestrials

A forum for academics, scientists and others interested in questions about the existence of intelligent life in the universe.

Keywords: Astronomy, Extraterrestrial Life, Space

Sponsor: University of Kent at Canterbury, United Kingdom

Audience: Scientists, Astronomers, General Public

Contact: Dr. Peter Moore
pgm@ukc.ac.uk

User Info: To subscribe to the list, send an e-mail message to the URL address shown below consisting of a single line reading:

SUB extraterrestrials YourFirstName YourLastName

To send a message to the entire list, address it to:
extraterrestrials@mailbase.ac.uk

`mailbase@mailbase.ac.uk`

IUCAA (Inter-University Centre for Astronomy and Astrophysics)

The IUCAA was set up to promote the growth of active groups in astronomy and astrophysics in India. The Centre runs vigorous visitor programs involving short and long-term visits of scientists from India and abroad.

Keywords: Astronomy, Astrophysics, Physics, Education

Sponsor: Centre for Astronomy and Astrophysics (IUCAA)

Audience: Researchers, Astronomers, Physicists, Students

Contact: Postmaster
amk@iucaa.ernet.in

`http://iucaa.iucaa.ernet.in/welcome.html`

Library of Congress, Astronomy, Astrophysics, and Physics Resources

Pointers to important remote databases relating to astronomy and physics.

Keywords: Astronomy, Astrophysics, NASA

Sponsor: Library of Congress, Washington, DC

Audience: Astronomers, Educators (Post-Secondary), Physicists, Students

Profile: The Library of Congress has pointers to many important remote databases including Astronomy, Astrophysics, and Physics Journals, the Aerospace Directory from Rice University, The American Astronomical Society, The Astronomical Internet Resources Directory, The Cold Fusion Bibliography, The Electromagnetic Wave Research Institute of NRC (Florence, Italy), LANL Physics Information, The Lunar/ Planetary Institute Database of Geology, Geophysics, and Astronomy, The NASA Extragalactic Database, The NASA Network Applications and Information Center (NAIC), The National Institute of Standards and Technology (NIST), The Physics Resource Directory from University of California, Irvine, and The Space Telescope Electronic Information System (STEIS).

Contact: lcmarvel@seq1.loc.gov

Details: Costs

User info: Can be accessible via telnet:// marvel.loc.gov (login: marvel).

`gopher://marvel.loc.gov/11/global/sci/astro`

NASA/IPAC Extragalactic Database (NED)

Contains positions, basic data, and over 500,000 names for 250,000 extragalactic objects, as well as some 450,000 bibliographic references to 21,000 published papers, and 25,000 notes from catalogs and other publications.

Keywords: Astronomy, Databases

Sponsor: Jet Propulsory Lab/ Infrared Processing and Analysis Center

Audience: Astronomers, Scientists

Profile: Uses a VT100 or X-based interface.

Contact: G. Helou, B. Madore, M. Schmitz
ned@ipac.caltech.edu

Details: Free

User Info: Telnet to URL address below; Expect: login; Send: ned

Notes: sshare@cscns.comservice@cscns.com

`telnet://ned@ned.ipac.caltech.edu`

`ftp://ned.ipac.caltech.edu/pub/ned`

sci.astro

A Usenet newsgroup providing information and discussion about astronomy.

Keywords: Astronomy, Space

Audience: Astronomers

User Info: To subscribe to this Usenet newsgroup, you need access to a newsreader.

`news:sci.astro`

A
B
C
D
E
F
G
H
I
J
K
L
M
N
O
P
Q
R
S
T
U
V
W
X
Y
Z

A
B
C
D
E
F
G
H
I
J
K
L
M
N
O
P
Q
R
S
T
U
V
W
X
Y
Z

Sci.astro.fits

Discussions of the Flexible Image Transport System (FITS), a widely used standard for transporting astronomical data.

Keywords: Astronomy

Audience: Astronomers

Details: Free, Images

User Info: To subscribe to this Usenet newsgroup, you need access to a newsreader.

`news:sci.astro.fits`

Sci.astro.hubble

Information about all subjects concerning NASA's Hubble space telescope.

Keywords: Hubble Telescope, Astronomy, Space, NASA, Stargazing, Telescopes

Audience: Astronomers, General Public, Science Teachers, Stargazers

Contact: Paul A. Scowen
scowen@wfpc3.la.asu.edu

Details: Free, Moderated, Images

User Info: To subscribe to this Usenet newsgroup, you need access to a newsreader.

`news:sci.astro.hubble`

Sci.astro.planetarium

A group catering to the planetarium operations community.

Keywords: Astronomy, Planetariums

Audience: Educators, Astronomers, Planetarium Operators

Details: Free

User Info: To subscribe to this Usenet newsgroup, you need access to a newsreader.

`news:sci.astro.planetarium`

The Curiosity Club

This web site offers both an astrophysics exploration and a playspace for young scientists

Keywords: Astronomy, Mythology, Children

Sponsor: Center for Extreme Ultraviolet Astrophysics, Berkeley, California, and The San Francisco Unified School District,San Francisco, California

Audience: Educators,Students,Astronomers,

Contact: Kasey Rios Asberry
jasberry@sfsuvax1.sfsu.edu

Details: Free

`http://nisus.sfusd.k12.ca.us/curiosity_club/bridge1.html`

The University of California Search for Extraterrestrial Civilizations

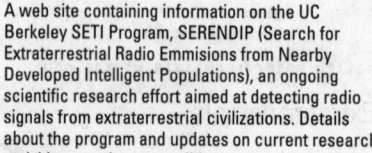

A web site containing information on the UC Berkeley SETI Program, SERENDIP (Search for Extraterrestrial Radio Emmisions from Nearby Developed Intelligent Populations), an ongoing scientific research effort aimed at detecting radio signals from extraterrestrial civilizations. Details about the program and updates on current research activities are also accessible.

Keywords: Extraterrestrial Life, Astronomy, Aliens

Audience: Astronomers, Physicists, Students, Educators, Engineers, General Public

Contact: Dan Werthimer
sereninfo@ssl.berkeley.edu

Details: Free

If Mosaic is available, use the http address below. Otherwise, please send a request for information to the contact address provided.

`http://sereninfo.ssl.berkeley.edu`

University of Michigan Library

The library's holdings are large and wide-ranging and contain significant collections in many fields.

Keywords: Asia, Astronomy, Transportation, Lexicology, Math, Zoology, Geography

Audience: Researchers, Students, General Public

Contact: info@merit.edu

Details: Free

User Info: Expect: Which Host; Send: Help

`telnet:// cts.merit.edu`

Astrophysics

Astronomical Information on the Internet

This FTP site contains pointers to potentially relevant resources available via the Internet.

Keywords: Astronomy, Astrophysics

Sponsor: European Space Organization (ESO) and Space Telescope European Coordinating Facility (ST-ECF)

Audience: Astronomers, Physicists, Students (College, Graduate), Educators

Profile: This is the entry point for most astronomical resources available online categorized by function. More than 100 resources are accessible concerning general astronomical information, software, and publications. The following are just a few examples of the resources available as of January 1994:

- Online Publications from CERN, SISSA, STSCI, NASA, PASP, Cfa, and so on.
- Conferences and meetings
- Metereological information
- Access to over 30 observatories and institutes
- Data archives from over 20 previous and current satellite missions, observatories,and astronomy data centers
- Astronomical images
- Astronomical software
- Jobs

Contact: Hans-Martin Adorf
adorf@eso.org

Details: Free, Moderated. Images, Sounds, and Multimedia files available.

`ftp://ecf.hq.eso.org/pub/WWW/astro-resources.html`

Astronomical Publications Resources (APR)

Contains pointers to many relevant resources available via the Internet.

Keywords: Astronomy, Astrophysics, Physics

Sponsor: Space Telescope Science Institute

Audience: Astronomers, Physicists, Students (College, Graduate), Educators

Profile: APR is a useful starting point to most of the astronomical publication resources available online. It is conviently divided by type of access (gopher, wais, www, telnet, ftp). As of January 1994, resources include:

- Astrophysics Preprints—SISSA
- ADC Documents
- NOAO News
- NRAO Preprint Database
- STECF Newsletter
- STELAR ApJ, ApJS, AJ, PASP, A&A, A&AS, MNRAS, and JGR Abstracts
- STScI Preprint Database
- IAU Circulars Astronomical Union
- CfA Index of ApJ, AJ, PASP
- DIRA2 Database
- Electronic Journal of Astronomical Society of the Atlantic

Contact: rrpss@stsci.edu

Details: Free, Moderated

`http://stsci.edu/net-publications.html`

`gopher://stsci.edu`

Astronomical Software Resources (ASR)

★★★★

Contains pointers to many relevant resources available via the Internet.

Keywords: Astronomy, Astrophysics, Astronomical Software

Sponsor: Space Telescope Science Institute

Audience: Astronomers, Physicists, Students (college, graduate), Educators

Profile: ASR is a useful starting point to most of the astronomical software resources available on line. It is conviently divided by type of access (www, wais, gopher, telnet, ftp). As of January 1994, resources include:

- Computer Software Management and Information Center
- IRAF Information System
- Software Support Laboratory SSL
- Starlink Help Browser
- Space Telescope Science Data Analysis System (STSDAS)
- FITS Archive
- NAG Bulletin Board Services
- Numerical Recipes Software
- STSDAS Software
- Working Group on Astronomical Software Archives
- FITS Documents.

Contact: rpss@stsci.edu.

Details: Free, Moderated, Image, Sounds and Multimedia files available.

`http://stsci.edu/net-software.html`

Astronomy

This directory is a compilation of information resources focused on astronomy.

Keywords: Astronomy, Stars, Astrophysics, Space

Audience: Astronomers, Astrophysicists, Space Enthusiasts

Contact: A. Park, J. Miller

Details: Free

`ftp://una.hh.lib.umich.edu/70/`
`inetdirsstacks/astron:parkmiller`

Astrophysics Data System (ADS)

★★★★

A distributed processing software that provides its users with access to over 190 astronomical catalogs and approximately 125,000 astronomical abstracts.

Keywords: Astronomy, Astrophysics, Astronomical Software, Astronomical Catalogs

Sponsor: Smithsonian Astrophysical Observatory

Audience: Astronomers, Physicists, Students (college, graduate), Educators

Profile: ADS is a suite of information management, manipulation, visualization, and access tools that facilitate user selection of, and access to, data in a distributed environment. These data can be imported to or exported from analysis systems through the use of the ASCII and FITS I/O standards. ADS also provides direct access to the HEASARC Browse tool, NSSDC's Online Data and Information Service (NODIS), the NASA/IPAC Extragalactic Database (NED), SIMBAD (Set of Identifications, Measurements, and Bibliography for Astronomical Data). The user is able to access all of this information via a simple-to-use Graphical User Interface (GUI).

Contact: ads@cuads.colorado.edu

Details: Free, Image files available.

To become a registered user and get ADS, request a registration form from ads@cuads.colorado.edu.

`http://adswww.colorado.edu/adswww/`
`adshomepg.htlm`

Center for Extreme Ultraviolet Astrophysics

★★★

A department of the University of California at Berkeley devoted to research in extreme ultraviolet astronomy. It is the ground-based institution of EUVE (the Extreme Ultraviolet Explorer), a NASA satellite launched in 1992.

Keywords: Astronomy, Astrophysics, EUVE, NASA, Satellite

Sponsor: NASA and University of California at Berkeley

Audience: Astronomers, Astrophysicists

Profile: Provides access to details about the EUVE Guest Observer (EGO) Center, the EUVE Public Archive of Mission Data and Information, satellite operation information, and so on. The EUVE Guest Observer Center provides information, software, and data to EUVE Guest Observers.

Contact: egoinfo@cea.berkeley.edu, archive@cea.berkeley.edu

Details: Free

`http://cea-ftp.cea.berkeley.edu/`

IUCAA (Inter-University Centre for Astronomy and Astrophysics)

The IUCAA was set up to promote the growth of active groups in astronomy and astrophysics in India. The Centre runs vigorous visitor programs involving short and long-term visits of scientists from India and abroad.

Keywords: Astronomy, Astrophysics, Physics, Education

Sponsor: Centre for Astronomy and Astrophysics (IUCAA)

Audience: Reseachers, Astronomers, Physicists, Students

Contact: Postmaster amk@iucaa.ernet.in

`http://iucaa.iucaa.ernet.in/`
`welcome.html`

Library of Congress, Astronomy, Astrophysics, and Physics Resources

★★★★

Pointers to important remote databases relating to astronomy and physics.

Keywords: Astronomy, Astrophysics, NASA

Sponsor: Library of Congress, Washington, DC

Audience: Astronomers, Educators (Post-Secondary), Physicists, Students

Profile: The Library of Congress has pointers to many important remote databases including Astronomy, Astrophysics, and Physics Journals, the Aerospace Directory from Rice University, The American Astronomical Society, The Astronomical Internet Resources Directory, The Cold Fusion Bibliography, The Electromagnetic Wave Research Institute of NRC (Florence, Italy), LANL Physics Information, The Lunar/Planetary Institute Database of Geology, Geophysics, and Astronomy, The NASA Extragalactic Database, The NASA Network Applications and Information Center (NAIC), The National Institute of Standards and Technology (NIST), The Physics Resource Directory from University of California, Irvine, and The Space Telescope Electronic Information System (STEIS).

Contact: lcmarvel@seq1.loc.gov

Details: Costs

User info: Can be accessible via telnet:// marvel.loc.gov (login: marvel).

`gopher://marvel.loc.gov/11/global/`
`sci/astro`

NSSDC (National Space Science Data Center)'s Online Data & Information Service

The NSSDC (National Space Science Data Center) is the NASA facility charged with archiving the data from all of NASA's science missions.

Keywords: Space, Astrophysics, Software, NASA, Science

Sponsor: NASA

Audience: Scientists, Space Scientists, Astronomers, Engineers

A
B
C
D
E
F
G
H
I
J
K
L
M
N
O
P
Q
R
S
T
U
V
W
X
Y
Z

Profile: This resource contains information about NASA's missions and analysis of their data.

Details: Free

User Info: Expect: Login, Send: nssdc

See the menu entries in your particular area of interest.

`telnet://nssdc.gsfc.nasa.gov`

Physics

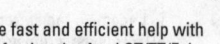

A newly created digest covering current developments in theoretical and experimental physics. Topics might include particle physics, plasma physics, or astrophysics.

Keywords: Physics, Astrophysics, Plasma Physics

Audience: Physicists, Astrophysicists

Contact: Mike Miskulin
physics-request@qedqcd.rye.ny.us

Details: Free

User Info: To subscribe to the list, send an e-mail message requesting a subscription to the URL address below.

To send a message to the entire list, address it to: physics@qedqcd.rye.ny.u

`mailto:physics-
request@qedqcd.rye.ny.us`

AT&T

AT&T Bell Laboratories WWW Information Page

This web site provides information on research and development at AT&T Bell Laboratories.

Keywords: Telecommunications, Technology, AT&T, Cellular Technology

Sponsor: AT&T Bell Laboratories

Audience: Engineers, Educators, Communications Specialists

Contact: webmaster@research.att.com

Details: Free

`http://www.research.att.com`

att-pc+

A mailing list for users and potential users of the AT&T PC 63xx series of systems.

Keywords: Computers, AT&T

Audience: Computer Programmers

Contact: Bill Kennedy
bill@ssbn.wlk.com

User Info: To subscribe to the list, send an e-mail message to the URL address below.

To send a message to the entire list, address it to: att-pc+@ssbn.wlk.com

Notes: Sub-lists are maintained for MS-DOS-only and Simul-Task mailings as well as the full list for items of general interest. Membership must be requested and mail path verification is required before membership is granted.

`mailto:att-pc+@ssbn.wlk.com`

Atari

ST viruses

This list is to provide fast and efficient help with computer viruses infecting the Atari ST/TT/Falcon only.

Keywords: Computer Viruses, Atari

Audience: Computer Users

Contact: r.c.karsmakers@stud.let.ruu.nl

Details: Free

User Info: To subscribe to the list, send an e-mail message requesting a subscription to the URL address below.

To send a message to the entire list, address it to:
r.c.karsmakers@stud.let.ruu.nl

`mailto:r.c.karsmakers@stud.let.ruu.nl`

Atmosphere

Global Change Information Gateway

This gatewas was created to address environmental data management issues raised by the US Congress, the Administration, and the advisory arms of the Federal policy community. It contains documents related to the UN conference on Environment and Development.

Keywords: UN, Environment, Development, Oceans, Atmosphere

Audience: Environmentalists, Scientists, Researchers, Environmentalists

Profile: [profile needed]

Details: Free

Select from menu as appropriate.

`gopher://scilibx.ucsc.edu`

Atmospheric Science

National Oceanic & Atmospheric Administration (NOAA), Office of Environmental Safety and Health, Department of Energy

The NOAA catalog provides keyword access to sources of environmental information in the US. Gopher for resources pertaining to health and environmental safety.

Keywords: Environment, Oceans, Atmospheric Science, Health, Environmental Safety

Sponsor: National Oceanic & Atmospheric Administration (NOAA), Department of Energy (USA)

Audience: Environmental Scientists, Researchers, Environmentalists, Epidemiologists, Public Health Officials

Profile: [profile needed]

Details: Free

`gopher://scilibx.ucsc.edu`

`gopher://gopher.ns.doc.gov`

Purdue University Library

The library's holdings are large and wide-ranging. They contain significant collections in many fields.

Keywords: Economics (History of), Literature (English), Literature (American), Indiana, Rogers (Bruce), Engineering (History of), Aviation, Earth Science, Atmospheric Science, Consumer Science, Family Science, Chemistry (History of), Physics, Veterinary Science

Audience: General Public, Researchers, Librarians, Document Delivery Professionals

Contact: Dan Ferrer
dan@asterix.lib.purdue.edu

Details: Free

User Info: Expect: User ID prompt, Send: GUEST

`telnet://lib.cc.purdue.edu`

AUC TeX

auc-TeX

Discussion and information exchange about the AUC TeX package, which runs under GNU Emacs.

Keywords: Computers, TeX, AUC TeX, Emacs

Audience: Computer Users

Contact: Kresten Krab Thorup
auc-tex-request@iesd.auc.dk

A
B
C
D
E
F
G
H
I
J
K
L
M
N
O
P
Q
R
S
T
U
V
W
X
Y
Z

Details: Free

User Info: To subscribe to the list, send an e-mail message requesting a subscription to the URL address below.

To send a message to the entire list, address it to: auc-tex@iesd.auc.dk

`mailto:auc-tex-request@iesd.auc.dk`

Audio Electronics

af

A mailing list for discussion of AudioFile, a client/server, network-transparent, device-independent audio system.

Keywords: Audio Electronics, Electrical Engineering

Audience: Audio Enthusiasts, Electrical Engineers

Contact: af-request@crl.dec.com

User Info: To subscribe to the list, send an e-mail message to the URL address below.

To send a message to the entire list, address it to: af@crl.dec.com

`mailto:af-request@crl.dec.com`

rec.audio

A Usenet newsgroup providing information and discussion about audio products, including troubleshooting advice.

Keywords: Audio Electronics, Stereo Electronics

Audience: Stereo Owners, Music Listeners

User Info: To subscribe to this Usenet newsgroup, you need access to a newsreader.

`news:rec.audio`

rec.music.cd

A Usenet newsgroup providing information and discussion about Compact Discs.

Keywords: Music, Audio Electronics

Audience: Compact Disc Users

User Info: To subscribe to this Usenet newsgroup, you need access to a newsreader.

`news:rec.music.cd`

rec.music.makers.synth

A Usenet newsgroup providing information and discussion about synthesizers.

Keywords: Music, Audio Electronics

Audience: Synthesizer Users

User Info: To subscribe to this Usenet newsgroup, you need access to a newsreader.

`news:rec.music.makers.synth`

Audio Reproduction

Bass

The purpose of this list is to discuss the reproduction and enjoyment of deep bass, primarily in consumer audio.

Keywords: Audio Reproduction

Audience: Stereo Enthusiasts, General Public

Contact: bass-request@gsbcs.uchicago.edu

Details: Free

User Info: To subscribe to the list, send an e-mail message requesting a subscription to the URL address below.

To send a message to the entire list, address it to: bass@gsbcs.uchicago.edu

Notes: Ownership of a subwoofer is not required—membership is open to anyone with an interest in deep bass reproduction.

`mailto:bass-request@gsbcs.uchicago.edu`

Audio-Visual Materials

NYAL (New York Art Line)

A gopher containing selected resources on the arts.

Keywords: Art, Audio-Visual Materials, Multimedia, Computer Art

Sponsor: Panix Public Access Unix & Internet Gopher Server, New York, USA

Audience: Artists, Art Enthusiasts

Profile: NYAL features a wide variety of arts resources. The primary focus of this site is visual art, particularly in the New York city area. Information includes online access to selected galleries, image archives, and New York city arts groups. Beyond visual art, information on dance, music, and techno art (with a special section on Internet art) is also available. It also features links to various electronic journals, museums, and schools.

Contact: Kenny Greenberg kgreen@panix.com

`gopher://gopher.panix.com`

`http//gopher.panix.com/nyart/Kpage/kg`

Auditing

NAARS (National Automated Accounting Research System)

The National Automated Accounting Research System (NAARS) library, provided as a service by agreement with the American Institute of Certified Public Accountants (AICPA) contains a variety of accounting information.

Keywords: Accounting, Auditing, Filings, Publications

Audience: Accountants

Profile: The NAARS library contains annual reports of public corporations and accounting literature and publications for the accounting professional. Annual reports are annotated with descriptive terms assigned by the AICPA. These terms allow the user to search for annual report footnotes that illustrate one or more recognized accounting practices.

Contact: Mead New Sales Group at (800) 227-4908 or (513) 859-5398 inside the US, or (513) 865-7981 for all inquiries outside the US.

User Info: To subscribe, contact Mead directly.

To examine the Nexis user guide, you can access it at the ftp site of the University of Texas at Austin at the URL address: ftp://ftp.cc.utexas.edu

The files are in: /pub/ref-services/LEXIS

`telnet://nex.meaddata.com`

`http://www.meaddata.com`

AUGLBC-L

AUGLBC-L

The American University Gay, Lesbian, and Bisexual Community (AUGLBC) is a support group for lesbian, gay, bisexual, transsexual, and supportive students. The group is also connected with the International Gay and Lesbian Youth Organization (known as IGLYO).

Keywords: Gays, Lesbians, Bisexuality, Transsexuality, Sexuality

Audience: Gays, Lesbians, Bisexuals, Transsexuals, Students (college)

Contact: Erik G. Paul

User Info: To subscribe to the list, send an e-mail message to the URL address below, consisting of a single line reading:

SUB AUGLBC-l YourFirstName YourLastName

To send a message to the entire list, address it to: AUGLBC-l@american.edu

`mailto:listserv@american.edu`

Australia

AusGBLF

An Australian-based mailing list for gays, bisexuals, lesbians, and friends.

Keywords: Australia, Gays, Lesbians, Bisexuality

Audience: Gays, Lesbians, Bisexuals

Contact: zglc@minyos.xx.rmit.oz.au

Details: Free

User Info: To subscribe to the list, send an e-mail message requesting a subscription to the URL address below.

To send a message to the entire list, address it to:
ausgblf@minyos.xx.rmit.oz.au

```
mailto:ausgblf-
request@minyos.xx.rmit.oz.au
```

AusRave (Australian Raves)

A regional rave-related mailing list covering the Australian continent. AusRave contains both discussions and informational postings.

Keywords: Music, Raves, Australia

Audience: Ravers (Australian)

Contact: Simon Rumble
ausrave@lsupoz.apana.org.au

Details: Free, Moderated

User Info: To subscribe to the list, send an e-mail message requesting a subscription to the URL address below.

To send a message to the entire list, address it to:
ausrave@lsupoz.apana.org.au

Notes: The mailing list Best of AusRave provides information only.

Postings to AusRave are not archived, but the list does have an FTP site at:
elecsun4.elec.uow.edu.au

```
mailto:ausrave-
request@lsupoz.apana.org.au
```

Australia

Full-text versions of Australian legislation.

Keywords: Australia, Law (International)

Audience: Australians, Environmentalists

Details: Free

Notes: Select from menu as appropriate

```
gopher://wiretap.spies.com
```

Australian Environmental Resources Information Network (ERIN)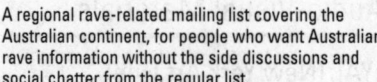

This gopher contains a wide range of Australian environmental information.

Keywords: Environment, Australia, Ecology

Audience: Environmentalists, Ecologists, Researchers, Australians

Profile: Coverage includes biodiversity, protected areas, terrestrial and marine environments, environmental protection and legislation, international agreements, and general information about ERIN.

Contact: gopher@erin.gov.au

Details: Free

```
gopher://kaos.erin.gov.au
```

```
http://kaos.erin.gov.au/erin.html
```

Best-of-AusRave (Australian Raves)

A regional rave-related mailing list covering the Australian continent, for people who want Australian rave information without the side discussions and social chatter from the regular list.

Keywords: Music, Raves, Australia

Audience: Ravers (Australian)

Contact: Simon Rumble
best-of-ausrave-request@lsupoz.apana.org.au

Details: Free, Moderated

User Info: To subscribe to the list, send an e-mail message to the URL address below, consisting of a single line reading:

SUB ausrave YourFirstName YourLastName

To send a message to the entire list, address it to: best-of-ausrave@lsupoz.apana.org.au

```
mailto:best-of-ausrave-
request@lsupoz.apana.org.au
```

ELISA (Electronic Library Service)

An information delivery service of the Library of the Australian National University.

Keywords: OPAC System, Australia

Sponsor: Australian National University

Audience: General Public

Profile: This information delivery service contains Australian mirrors of major gopher directories, and is a national entry point for Australian gopher services.

Contact: infodesk@info.anu.edu.au

Details: Free

```
gopher://info.anu.edu.au
```

news: aus.films

Discussion of films and the film industry from an Australian perspective.

Keywords: Film, Australia

Audience: Australia Enthusiasts, Film Enthusiasts

Details: Free

User Info: To subscribe to a Usenet newsgroup, you need access to a "newsreader."

```
news:aus.films
```

Resodlaa (Research SIG of the Open and Distance Learning Association of Australia)

The purpose of this list is to foster electronic discussion, symposia, and conferences on topical issues in distance education and open-learning research.

Keywords: Education (Adult), Education (Distance), Education (Continuing), Australia

Sponsor: Research Special Interest Group (SIG) of the Open and Distance Learning Association of Australia

Audience: Educators, Administrators, Researchers

Details: Free

User Info: To subscribe to the list, send an e-mail message to the URL address below ,consisting of a single line reading:

SUB resodlaa YourFirstName YourLastName

To send a message to the entire list, address it to: resodlaa @usq.edu.au

```
mailto:listserv@usq.edu.au
```

Austrian History

Indiana University Libraries

The library's holdings are large and wide-ranging and contain significant collections in many fields.

Keywords: Literature (English), Literature (American), 1640-Present, British Plays (19th-C.), Western Americana, Railway History, Aristotle (Texts of), Lafayette (Marquis de), Handel (G.F.), Austrian History, Antiquarian Books, Rare Books, French Opera (19th-C.), Drama (British) ,

Audience: General Public, Researchers, Librarians, Document Delivery Professionals

Details: Free

User Info: Expect: User ID prompt, Send: GUEST

```
telnet://iuis.ucs.indiana.edu
```

Autocrossing

autox

A mailing list for the discussion of autocrossing and other SCCA (Sports Car Club of America) Solo events.

Keywords: Automobiles, Autocrossing

Sponsor: SCCA (Sports Car Club of America)

Audience: Autocross Drivers

Contact: autox-request@autox.team.net
autox-request@hoosier.cs.utah.edu

User Info: To subscribe to the list, send an e-mail message to the URL address below.

To send a message to the entire list, address it to: autox-request@autox.team.net

Also available upon request as a digest.

`mailto:autox-request@autox.team.net`

`mailto:autox-request@hoosier.cs.utah.edu`

Automobiles

autox

A mailing list for the discussion of autocrossing and other SCCA (Sports Car Club of America) Solo events.

Keywords: Automobiles, Autocrossing

Sponsor: SCCA (Sports Car Club of America)

Audience: Autocross Drivers

Contact: autox-request@autox.team.net
autox-request@hoosier.cs.utah.edu

User Info: To subscribe to the list, send an e-mail message to the URL address below.

To send a message to the entire list, address it to: autox-request@autox.team.net

Notes: Also available upon request as a digest.

`mailto:autox-request@autox.team.net`

`mailto:autox-request@hoosier.cs.utah.edu`

BMW

This is a discussion of cars made by BMW. Both regular and digest forms are available.

Keywords: BMW, Automobiles

Audience: Automobile Enthusiasts, Automobile Racers, BMW Enthusiasts

Contact: Richard Welty
bmw-request@balltown.cma.com

Details: Free

User Info: To subscribe to the list, send an e-mail message requesting a subscription to the URL address below.

To send a message to the entire list, address it to: bmw@balltown.cma.com

`mailto:bmw-request@balltown.cma.com`

British-Cars

This is a discussion of owning, repairing, racing, cursing, and loving British cars, predominantly sports cars, with some talk of Land Rovers and sedans. Also available as a digest.

Keywords: Automobiles

Audience: British Automobile Enthusiasts, Automobile Enthusiasts

Contact: Mark Bradakis
british-cars-request@autox.team.net
british-cars-request@hoosier.cs.utah.edu

Details: Free

User Info: To subscribe to the list, send an e-mail message requesting a subscription to the URL address below.

To send a message to the entire list, address it to: british-cars@autox.team.net

`mailto:british-cars-request@autox.team.net`

datsun-roadsters

A mailing list for discussing any and all aspects of the owning, showing, repairing, driving, and so on, of Datsun roadsters.

Keywords: Datsuns, Automobiles

Audience: Datsun Owners, Automobile Enthusiasts

Contact: Mark J. Bradakis
datsun-roadsters-request@autox.team.net
datsun-roadsters-request@hoosier.utah.edu

Details: Free

User Info: To subscribe to the list, send an e-mail message requesting a subscription to the URL address below.

To send a message to the entire list, address it to: datsun-roadsters-request@autox.team.net

`mailto:datsun-roadsters-request@autox.team.net`

Fordnatics

This unmoderated forum discusses high-performance Fords or Ford-powered vehicles, focusing on modifications and driving techniques for competition or track use.

Keywords: Automobiles, Fords

Audience: Automobile Enthusiasts, Ford Drivers, Racers

Details: Free

User Info: To subscribe to the list, send an e-mail message requesting a subscription to the URL address below.

To send a message to the entire list, address it to: fordnatics@freud.arc.nasa.gov

`mailto:fordnatics-request@freud.arc.nasa.gov`

Miata

An open forum for Mazda Miata owners.

Keywords: Automobiles

Audience: Drivers

Details: Free

User Info: To subscribe to the list, send an e-mail message requesting subscription to the URL address below.

`mailto:miata-request@jhunix.hcf.jhu.edu`

Mustangs

A forum for the discussion of technical issues, problems, solutions, and modifications relating to late-model (1980 and later) Ford Mustangs.

Keywords: Automobiles

Audience: Drivers

Details: Free

User Info: To subscribe to the list, send an e-mail message requesting a subscription to the URL address below.

`mailto:mustangs-request@cup.hp.com`

Porschephiles

This list is for people who own, operate, work on, or covet various models of Porsche automobiles. Discussion topics include features, functionality, and purchasing advice.

Keywords: Porsche, Automobiles, Sports Cars

Audience: Porsche Owners, Sports Car Owners, Automobile Mechanics

Contact: porschephiles-request@tta.com

Details: Free

User Info: To subscribe to the list, send an e-mail message requesting a subscription to the URL address below.

To send a message to the entire list, address it to: porschephiles@tta.com

`mailto:porschephiles-request@tta.com`

Quattro

A mailing list for discussions pertaining to Audi automobiles, especially the AWD (all wheel drive) Quattro models. It also includes news, opinions, maintenance procedures, and parts sources.

Keywords: Automobiles

A B C D E F G H I J K L M N O P Q R S T U V W X Y Z

A
B
C
D
E
F
G
H
I
J
K
L
M
N
O
P
Q
R
S
T
U
V
W
X
Y
Z

Audience: Automobile Enthusiasts

Contact: David Tahajian
           quattro-request@aries.east.sun.com

Details: Free

User Info: To subscribe to the list, send an e-mail
            message requesting a subscription to
            the URL address below.

            To send a message to the entire list,
            address it to:
            quattro@aries.east.sun.com

`mailto:quattro-`
`request@aries.east.sun.com`

rec.autos.driving

A Usenet newsgroup providing information and
discussion about driving, traffic laws, and car
buying.

Keywords: Automobiles

Audience: Drivers, Automobile Buyers

User Info: To subscribe to this Usenet newsgroup,
            you need access to a newsreader.

`news:rec.autos.driving`

rec.autos.sport

A Usenet newsgroup providing information and
discussion about automobile competition.

Keywords: Automobiles, Automobile Racing, Sports

Audience: Automobile Racing Enthusiasts

User Info: To subscribe to this Usenet newsgroup,
            you need access to a newsreader.

`news:rec.autos.sports`

rec.autos.tech

A Usenet newsgroup providing information and
discussion about the technical aspects of
automobiles.

Keywords: Automobiles, Technology

Audience: Automobile Users

User Info: To subscribe to this Usenet newsgroup,
            you need access to a newsreader.

`news:rec.autos.tech`

rec.autos.vw

A Usenet newsgroup providing information and
discussion about Volkswagon products.

Keywords: Automobiles

Audience: Volkswagon Drivers

User Info: To subscribe to this Usenet newsgroup,
            you need access to a newsreader.

`news:rec.autos.vw`

Stealth

Discussion of anything related to Dodge Stealth and
Mitsubishi 3000GT cars.

Keywords: Automobiles

Audience: Car Enthusiasts

Contact: stealth-
           request%jim.uucp@wupost.wustl.edu

Details: Free

User Info: Expect: Username prompt, Send: tcucat

            To subscribe to the list, send an e-mail
            message requesting a subscription to
            the URL address below.

            To send a message to the entire list,
            address it to: stealth-
            request96jim.uucp@wupost.wustl.edu

`mailto:stealth-`
`request%jim.uucp@wupost.wustl.edu`

Utah Valley Community College Library

The library's holdings are large and wide-ranging
and contain significant collections in many fields.

Keywords: Accounting, Automobiles, Cabinetry,
           Child Care, Drafting, Electronics, Home
           Building, Local History, Refrigeration, Air
           Conditioning

Audience: General Public, Researchers, Librarians,
           Document Delivery Professionals

Details: Free

User Info: Expect: Login; Send: Opub

`telnet://uvlib.uvcc.edu`

Autopoiesis

(The) Observer

The central scope of the group covers the theory of
autopoiesis (of Humberto Maturana and Francisco
Varela) and enactive cognitive science. The
extended scope includes applications of the above
theoretical work and other relevant work (e.g.
systems theory, cognitive science, phenomenology,
artificial life, and so on). This is an edited electronic
newsletter issued (approximately) twice monthly.

Keywords: Autopoiesis, Systems Theory, Cognitive
           Science

Audience: Systems Theorists, Researchers

Contact: Randall Whitaker
           rwhit@cs.umu.se

User Info: To subscribe to the list, send an e-mail
            message to the URL address below
            consisting of a single line reading:

            SUB the observer YourFirstName
            YourLastName

            To send a message to the entire list,
            address it to: rwhit@cs.umu.se

`mailto:listserv@cs.umu.se`

Aviation

Aerospace Engineering

★★★★

This directory is a compilation of information
resources focused on aerospace engineeering.

Keywords: Aerospace, Engineering, Aviation, Space

Audience: Aerospace Engineers, Space Scientists

Profile: This is a guide to Internet resources that
           contain information pertaining to
           aerospace engineering. Originally the
           guide was to cover the area of
           aerospace engineering as applied to
           lower atmospheric flight. However, it is
           difficult to narrow the sites down to
           specific subject areas. As the guide
           evolved, sites were included with a
           broader scope of information.The guide
           is by no means comprehensive and
           exhaustive; there are sites that are not
           included and those the authors were not
           aware of, and they welcome
           suggestions. The directory lists sites on
           FTP, Gopher, Listserv, OPAC, Telnet,
           Usenet, and WWW.

Details: Free

`ftp://una.hh.lib.umich.edu/70/`
`inetdirstacks/aerospace:potsiedalq`

Aviator

★

A mailing list for users of Aviator™, the flight-
simulation program from Artificial Horizons, Inc.

Keywords: Aviation, Simulation, Computers

Audience: Software Users

Contact: Jim Hickstein
           aviator@icdwest.Teradyne.com

Details: Free

User Info: To subscribe to the list, send an e-mail
            message requesting a subscription to
            the URL address below.

            To send a message to the entire list,
            address it to:
            aviator@ICDwest.Teradyne.COM

Notes: Aviator runs on Sun workstations with
           the GX graphics accelerator option. Its
           charter is simply to facilitate
           communication among users of Aviator.
           It is not intended for communication with
           the "providers" of Aviator. All mail
           received at the submission address is
           reflected to all the subscribers of the list.

`mailto:aviator-`
`request@ICDwest.Teradyne.COM`

Current Weather Maps and Movies

★★★

This web site is updated hourly, and provides links
to downloadable software sites instrumental in
accessing interactive weather browsers.
International information is available, and visual and
infrared maps are supplied from satellites.

Keywords: Weather, Meteorology, Aviation

Sponsor: Michigan State University, Michigan, USA

Audience: General Public, Oceanography, Pilots

Contact: Charles Henrich
henrich@crh.cl.msu.edu

`http://rs560.cl.msu.edu/weather`

McDonnell Douglas Aerospace
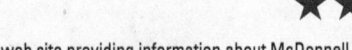

A web site providing information about McDonnell Douglas, including a company profile and related discussion about technology.

Keywords: Aerospace, Space, Aviation, Technology

Audience: Aerospace Engineers

Contact: Zook@pat.mdc.com

`http://pat.mdc.com`

News, Weather, and Travel Advisories

A major directory of news, weather, and travel advisories, providing access to a broad range of related resources (library catalogues, databases, and servers) via the Internet.

Keywords: Travel, Weather, Aviation

Sponsor: Kennesaw State College, Georgia, USA

Audience: General Public, Travellers

Profile: This collection includes CNN news sources, the National Weather Service Forecast, and the US State Department Travel Advisory, among other sources.

Details: Free

`gopher://kscsuna1.kennesaw.edu`

Purdue University Library

The library's holdings are large and wide-ranging. They contain significant collections in many fields.

Keywords: Economics (History of), Literature (English), Literature (American), Indiana, Rogers (Bruce), Engineering (History of), Aviation, Earth Science, Atmospheric Science, Consumer Science, Family Science, Chemistry (History of), Physics, Veterinary Science

Audience: General Public, Researchers, Librarians, Document Delivery Professionals

Contact: Dan Ferrer
dan@asterix.lib.purdue.edu

Details: Free

User Info: Expect: User ID prompt, Send: GUEST

`telnet://lib.cc.purdue.edu`

Rascal Aviation Archives

A major directory on aeronautics, providing access to a broad range of related resources (library catalogues, databases, and servers) via the Internet.

Keywords: Aeronautics, Aviation

Audience: Aviators, Aeronautical Engineers

Contact: rdd@rascal.ics.utexas.edu

`ftp://rascal.ics.utexas.edu/explore-me/Aviation-stuff`

Aviation Industry

TRANS (The Transportation Library)

The Transportation library contains federal transportation cae law, statutes and agency decisions.

Keywords: Transportation Law, US Government Regulations, Aviation Industry, Railroad Industry, Trucking Industry

Audience: Lawyers

Profile: The Transportation library contains federal transportation case law, statutes and agency decisions. The major emphasis of the library is on three modes of transportation (aviation, railroad and trucking) and how those modes are regulated by the federal government. Agency decisions are provided from the Interstate Commerce Commission, Department of Transportation and the National Transportation Safety Board (NTSB).

Contact: New Sales Group at 800-227-4908 or 513-859-5398 inside the US, or 1-513-865-7981 for all inquires outside the US.

User Info: To subscribe, contact Mead directly.

To examine the Lexis user guide, you can access it at the ftp site of the University of Texas at Austin at the URL address: ftp://ftp.cc.utexas.edu

The files are in: /pub/res-services/LEXIS

`telnet://nex.meaddata.com`

Ayurveda

Ayurveda

Ayurveda is the ancient science of life that originated in India. This mailing list provides information about Ayurveda, such as lectures, workshops, and stores that sell Ayurvedic herbs.

Keywords: Spirituality, Ayurveda, India

Audience: General Public

Contact: ayurveda-request@netcom.com

Details: Free

User Info: To subscribe to the list, send an e-mail message requesting a subscription to the URL address below.

To send a message to the entire list, address it to: ayurveda@netcom.com

`mailto:ayurveda-request@netcom.com`

A
B
C
D
E
F
G
H
I
J
K
L
M
N
O
P
Q
R
S
T
U
V
W
X
Y
Z

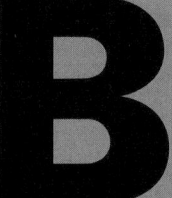

ba-Firearms

ba-Firearms

This list is an announcement and discussion of firearms legislation and related issues. The ca- list is for California statewide issues; the ba- list is for the San Francisco Bay Area and gets all messages sent to the ca- list. Prospective members should subscribe to one or the other, generally depending on whether they are San Francisco Bay Area residents.

Keywords: Firearms, Gun Control Legislation, San Francisco Bay Area

Audience: Politicians, General Public, Gun Users, San Francisco Bay Area Residents

Contact: Jeff Chan
ba-firearms-request@shell.portal.com

Details: Free

User Info: To subscribe to the list, send an e-mail message requesting a subscription to the URL address below.

To send a message to the entire list, address it to: ba-firearms@shell.portal.com

mailto:ba-firearms-request@shell.portal.com

ba-Liberty

ba-Liberty

This list is an announcement of local Libertarian meetings, events, activities, and so on. The ca- list is for California statewide issues; the ba- list is for the San Francisco Bay Area and it gets all messages sent to the ca- list. Prospective members should subscribe to one or the other, generally depending on whether or not they are San Francisco Bay Area residents.

Keywords: Libertarian Party, Politics, San Francisco Bay Area

Audience: Libertarians, Political Scientists, Politicians, General Public

Contact: Jeff Chan
ba-liberty-request@shell.portal.com

Details: Free

User Info: To subscribe to the list, send an e-mail message requesting a subscription to the following URL address.

To send a message to the entire list, address it to: ba-liberty@shell.portal.com

mailto:ba-liberty-request@shell.portal.com

ba-Poker

ba-Poker

Discussion of poker as it is available to residents of and visitors to the San Francisco Bay Area (broadly defined), in home games as well as in licensed card rooms. Topics include upcoming events, unusual games, strategies, comparisons of various venues, and player "networking".

Keywords: Poker, Card Games, San Francisco Bay Area

Audience: Poker Players

Contact: Martin Veneroso
ba-poker-request@netcom.com

Details: Free

User Info: To subscribe to the list, send an e-mail message requesting a subscription to the URL address below.

To send a message to the entire list, address it to: ba-poker@netcom.com

mailto:ba-poker-request@netcom.com

ba-Sappho

ba-Sappho

Ba-Sappho is a San Francisco Bay Area lesbian mailing list intended for local networking and announcements. Ba-Sappho is not a discussion group.

Keywords: Lesbians, San Francisco Bay Area

Audience: Lesbians

Contact: ba-sappho-request@labrys.mti.sgi.com

Details: Free

User Info: To subscribe to the list, send an e-mail message requesting a subscription to the following URL address.

To send a message to the entire list, address it to: ba-sappho@labrys.mti.sgi.com

mailto:ba-sappho-request@labrys.mti.sgi.com

ba-Volleyball

ba-Volleyball

This list is used for announcements about San Francisco Bay Area volleyball events, clinics, tournaments, and so on.

Keywords: Volleyball, San Francisco Bay Area, Sports

Audience: Volleyball Enthusiasts

A
B
C
D
E
F
G
H
I
J
K
L
M
N
O
P
Q
R
S
T
U
V
W
X
Y
Z

Contact: ba-volleyball-request@klerk.cup.hp.com

User Info: To subscribe to the list, send an e-mail message requesting a subscription to the URL address below.

To send a message to the entire list, address it to: ba-volleyball@klerk.cup.hp.com

`mailto:ba-volleyball-request@klerk.cup.hp.com`

ba.general

ba.general

A Usenet newsgroup providing general information and discussion about the San Francisco Bay Area.

Keywords: California

Audience: Tourists, Visitors, Bay Area Residents

User Info: To subscribe to this Usenet newsgroup, you need access to a newsreader.

`news:ba.general`

Baby Boomer Culture

30something

★★

A mailing list for discussion of the TV show 30something.

Keywords: Television, Baby Boomer Culture

Audience: Television Viewers, Baby Boomers

Contact: Marc Rouleau
30something-request@fuggles.acc.virginia.edu

User Info: To subscribe to the list, send an e-mail message to the URL address below. To send a message to the entire list, address it to:
30something@fuggles.acc.virginia.edu

`mailto:30something-request@fuggles.acc.virginia.edu`

Backstreets

Backstreets

★

Discussion of Bruce Springsteen's music.

Keywords: Rock Music, Springsteen (Bruce), Musical Groups

Audience: Bruce Springsteen Fans

Contact: Kevin Kinder
backstreets-request@virginia.edu

Details: Free

User Info: To subscribe to the list, send an e-mail message requesting a subscription to the URL address below.

To send a message to the entire list, address it to: backstreets@virginia.edu

`mailto:backstreets-request@virginia.edu`

Bagpipes

Pipes

★

A mailing list of people interested in any topic related to bagpipes, most generally defined as any instrument where air is forced manually from a bellows or bag through drones and/or over reeds. All manner of Scottish, Irish, English, and other instruments are discussed.

Keywords: Musical Instruments, Bagpipes

Audience: Bagpipe Enthusiasts

Contact: pipes-request@sunapee.dartmouth.edu

Details: Free

User Info: To subscribe to the list, send an e-mail message requesting a subscription to the URL address below.

To send a message to the entire list, address it to:
pipes@sunapee.dartmouth.edu

`mailto:pipes-request@sunapee.dartmouth.edu`

Balloon Art

Balloon Sculpting

★

This list is for the discussion of balloon sculpting. Anyone interested in balloon art is welcome to join. New sculpture designs and suggestions for improving old ones are exchanged. Other topics discussed include entertaining with balloons, health issues, various types of balloons, and book reviews.

Keywords: Balloon Art

Audience: Balloon Artists, Balloonists

Contact: Larry Moss
balloon-request@ent.rochester.edu

Details: Free

User Info: To subscribe to the list, send an e-mail message requesting a subscription to the URL address below.

To send a message to the entire list, address it to: balloon@ent.rochester.edu

`mailto:balloon-request@ent.rochester.edu`

Ballooning

Balloon

This is a list for balloonists of any sort. Discussion covers all types of balloons including hot air, gas, commercial, or sport, and just about anything related to ballooning.

Keywords: Ballooning, Hot Air Balloons

Audience: Balloonists

Contact: Phil Herbert
balloon-request@lut.ac.uk

User Info: To subscribe to the list, send an e-mail message requesting a subscription to the URL address below.

To send a message to the entire list, address it to: balloon@lut.ac.uk

`mailto:balloon-request@lut.ac.uk`

Ballroom Dancing

Ballroom

Discussion of any aspect of ballroom dancing, including places to dance, special events, clubs, ballroom dance music, dances, and steps.

Keywords: Ballroom Dancing, Dancing

Audience: Ballroom Dancers

Contact: Shahrukh Merchant
ballroom-request@athena.mit.edu

Details: Free

User Info: To subscribe to the list, send an e-mail message requesting a subscription to the URL address below.

To send a message to the entire list, address it to: ballroom@athena.mit.edu

`mailto:ballroom-request@athena.mit.edu`

Baltic Republics

Balt-L

★

A forum devoted to communications to and about the Baltic Republics of Lithuania, Latvia, and Estonia.

Keywords: Lithuania, Latvia, Estonia, Baltic Republics

Audience: Researchers, Baltic Nationals

Contact: Jean-Michel Thizy
jmyhg@uottawa.edu

Details: Free

User Info: To subscribe to the list, send an e-mail message to the URL address below, consisting of a single line reading:

SUB balt-l YourFirstName YourLastName

`mailto:listserv@ubvm.cc.buffalo.edu`

Mideur-l

A list containing the history, culture, politics, and current affairs of those countries lying between the Mediterranean/Adriatic and the Baltic Seas, and between the German/Austrian borders and the former Soviet Union.

Keywords: Soviet Union, Baltic Republics, Eastern Europe, News

Audience: Political Scientists, Researchers, Historians, General Public

Contact: Jan George Frajkor
mideur-1@ubvm.cc.buffalo.edu

Details: Free

User Info: To subscribe to the list, send an e-mail message to the URL address below consisting of a single line reading:

SUB mideur-l YourFirstName YourLastName

To send a message to the entire list, address it to: mideur-1@ubvm.cc.buffalo.edu

`mailto:listserv@ubvm.cc.buffalo.edu`

Balzac (Honore de)

University of Chicago Library

The library's holdings are large and wide-ranging and contain significant collections in many fields.

Keywords: English Bibles, Lincoln (Abraham), Kentucky & Ohio River Valley (History of), Balzac (Honore de), American Drama, Cromwell (Oliver), Goethe, Judaica, Italy, Chaucer (Geoffrey), Wells (Ida, Personal Papers of), Douglas (Stephen A.), Italy, Literature (Children's)

Audience: General Public, Researchers, Librarians, Document Delivery Professionals

Details: Free

Expect: ENTER CLASS, Send: LIB48 3;
Expect: CONNECTED, Send: RETURN

`telnet://olorin.uchicago.edu`

Banking

American Banker Full Text

This database corresponds to the authoritative print publication American Banker.

Keywords: Banking, International Finance, International Trade

Sponsor: American Banker-Bond Buyer, New York, NY, USA

Audience: Financial Analysts, Bankers

Profile: Specific coverage is given to local, regional, and international financial services, technology applications, legal commentary and court actions, international trade, government regulations, Washington events, marketing of financial services, general economic overviews, personnel issues, and profiles and movements of industry personnel. Statistical rankings of all types of financial institutions (from thrifts to commercial banks, US and worldwide) are included beginning with the October 1987 editions. Other special features include quarterly bank earnings, results of American Banker surveys, and the complete text of speeches and articles by the industry professionals that are unavailable in the printed paper.

Contact: Dialog in the US at (800) 334-2564; Dialog internationally at country-specific locations.

Details: Costs

User Info: To subscribe, contact Dialog directly.

`telnet://dialog.com`

Banking News Library

The Banking News library provides you with specific banking industry sources. More than 40 full-text documents and selected full-text sources that focus on the banking related news and issues.

Keywords: Banking, Financial News, Regulation

Audience: Journalists, Banking Industry Analysts

Profile: This library contains news, Investext Industry Reports, and legal/ regulatory information. Also included in an abstract file is the Financial Industry Information Service (FINIS). The S&L file includes documents from newspapers and magazines which are specific to the S&L crisis.

Contact: Mead New Sales Group at (800) 227-4908 or (513) 859-5398 inside the US, or (513) 865-7981 for all inquiries outside the US.

User Info: To subscribe, contact Mead directly.

Notes: To examine the Nexis user guide, you can access it at the ftp site of the University of Texas at Austin at the URL address: ftp://ftp.cc.utexas.edu

The files are in: /pub/ref-services/LEXIS

`telnet://nex.meaddata.com`

`http://www.meaddata.com`

Bankruptcy

BKRTCY (Bankruptcy Library)

The Federal Bankruptcy library is a comprehensive collection of primary and secondary legal research materials pertaining to bankruptcy issues.

Keywords: Law, Filings, Bankruptcy

Audience: Lawyers, Bankers

Profile: The Federal Bankruptcy library is a comprehensive collection of primary and secondary legal research materials that includes case law, rules, statutory and regulatory materials, legal publications, accounting literature, and other resources pertaining to bankruptcy issues.

Contact: New Sales Group at (800) 227-4908 or (513) 859-5398 inside the US, or (513) 865-7981 for all inquires outside the US.

User Info: To subscribe, contact Mead directly.

To examine the Lexis user guide, you can access it at the ftp site of the University of Texas at Austin at the URL address: ftp://ftp.cc.utexas.edu

The files are in: /pub/ref-services/LEXIS

`telnet://nex.meaddata.com`

`http://www.meaddata.com`

Barron's Guide to Accessing On-Line Bibliographic Databases

Barron's Guide to Accessing On-Line Bibliographic Databases

A comprehensive listing of publicly-accessible online libraries, including login instructions for each site.

Keywords: Libraries, Databases

Sponsor: University of North Texas

Audience: Researchers, Library Users, Librarians

Contact: Billy Barron
billy@unt.edu

`gopher://alf.zfn.uni-bremen.de/Allgemeine`

Base de Dados Tropical (BDT)

Base de Dados Tropical (BDT)

Base de Dados Tropical (Tropical Data Base) is a collection of information related to biodiversity and biotechnology.

Keywords: Biodiversity, Biotechnology, Brazil

Sponsor: Fundacao Tropical de Pesquisas e Tecnologia "Andre Tosello", Campinas, SP, Brazil

Audience: Biotechnologists, Scientists, Researchers

Contact: manager@bdt.ftpt.br

Details: Free

`gopher://bdt.ftpt.br`

A B C D E F G H I J K L M N O P Q R S T U V W X Y Z

Base-Jumping

Base-Jumping

An open discussion of fixed-object skydiving. Topics include equipment, sites, packing techniques, and related publications.

Keywords: Skydiving, Sports

Audience: Skydivers

Contact: base-request@lunatix.lex.ky.us

Details: Free

User Info: To subscribe to the list, send an e-mail message requesting a subscription to the URL address below.

To send a message to the entire list, address it to: base@lunatix.lex.ky.us

Notes: Membership is open to anyone who has made at least one base jump or skydive.

`mailto:base-request@lunatix.lex.ky.us`

Baseball

Minors

Issues affecting minor league baseball, including new stadium standards, minor league franchise status and changes, road trips and groups, schedules, team and league status, players and teams to watch, and collectibles.

Keywords: Baseball, Minor League

Audience: Minor League Baseball Fans

Details: Free

User Info: To subscribe to the list, send an e-mail message requesting subscription to the URL address below.

`mailto:minors-request@medrant.apple.com`

Professional Sports Schedules

Sports schedules for major professional sports.

Keywords: Sports, Baseball, Hockey, Football, Basketball

Sponsor: Colorado University, Boulder, CO

Audience: Sports Fans, Football Fans, Hockey Fans, Baseball Enthusiasts, Basketball Enthusiasts

Profile: The Colorado University gopher maintains an interactive online database of schedules for all major US professional sports teams (NBA, NFL, NHL, NBA). The database is indexed by both team name and dates of games, and can be searched accordingly.

Contact: gopher@gopher.colorado.edu

Details: Free

`gopher://gopher.colorado.edu/11/professional/sports/schedules`

rec.sport.baseball

A Usenet newsgroup providing information and discussion about professional baseball.

Keywords: Baseball, Sports

Audience: Baseball Fans, Sports Fans

User Info: To subscribe to this Usenet newsgroup, you need access to a newsreader.

`news:rec.sport.baseball`

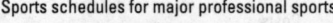

Basketball

Professional Sports Schedules

Sports schedules for major professional sports.

Keywords: Sports, Baseball, Hockey, Football, Basketball

Sponsor: Colorado University, Boulder, CO

Audience: Sports Fans, Football Fans, Hockey Fans, Baseball Enthusiasts, Basketball Enthusiasts

Profile: The Colorado University gopher maintains an interactive online database of schedules for all major US professional sports teams (NBA, NFL, NHL, NBA). The database is indexed by both team name and dates of games, and can be searched accordingly.

Contact: gopher@gopher.colorado.edu

Details: Free

`gopher://gopher.colorado.edu/11/professional/sports/schedules`

rec.sport.basketball.college

A Usenet newsgroup providing information and discussion about college basketball.

Keywords: Basketball, College, Sports

Audience: Basketball Fans, Sport Fans

User Info: To subscribe to this Usenet newsgroup, you need access to a newsreader.

`news:rec.sport.basketball.college`

rec.sport.basketball.pro

A Usenet newsgroup providing information and discussion about professional basketball.

Keywords: Basketball, Sports

Audience: Basketball Fans, Sports Fans

User Info: To subscribe to this Usenet newsgroup, you need access to a newsreader.

`news:rec.sport.basketball.pro`

Basque Studies

University of Nevada at Reno Library

The library's holdings are large and wide-ranging and contain significant collections in many fields.

Keywords: Basque Studies, Nevada , UN Army Map Service, Patents

Audience: General Public, Researchers, Librarians, Document Delivery Professionals

Details: Free

Expect: login, Send: wolfpac

`telnet://wolfpac.lib.unr.edu`

Bass

Bass

The purpose of this list is to discuss the reproduction and enjoyment of deep bass, primarily in consumer audio equipment.

Keywords: Audio Reproduction

Audience: Stereo Enthusiasts, General Public

Contact: bass-request@gsbcs.uchicago.edu

Details: Free

User Info: To subscribe to the list, send an e-mail message requesting a subscription to the URL address below.

To send a message to the entire list, address it to: bass@gsbcs.uchicago.edu

Notes: Ownership of a subwoofer is not required—membership is open to anyone with an interest in deep bass reproduction.

`mailto:bass-request@gsbcs.uchicago.edu`

Bbones

Bbones

A list discussing the construction of e-mail backbones for organizations and campuses.

Keywords: E-mail, Networking

Audience: Internet Surfers

Contact: mail-bbones-request@yorku.ca

Details: Free

User Info: To subscribe to the list, send an e-mail message requesting a subscription to the URL address below.

To send a message to the entire list, address it to: mail-bbones@yorku.ca

`mailto:mail-bbones-request@yorku.ca`

A B C D E F G H I J K L M N O P Q R S T U V W X Y Z

BBS

alt.bbs

A Usenet newsgroup providing information and discussion about computer BBS systems and software.

Keywords: BBS, Cyberspace, Computers

Audience: BBS Users

User Info: To subscribe to this Usenet newsgroup, you need access to a newsreader.

`news:alt.bbs`

Government-Sponsored Electronic Bulletin Boards

★★★★

A list of U.S. Government-sponsored electronic bulletin boards (BBSs) for various agencies and departments.

Keywords: Government (US Federal), Law (US Federal), BBS

Sponsor: United States Government

Audience: General Public, Researchers

Profile: EBBs provide a wide and ever-changing assortment of government information, including text files, statistics, software, and graphics. Some of the information also is available in printed form. Depository librarians may find government-sponsored EBBs useful in answering reference questions and in obtaining electronic versions of government publications, regardless of whether those publications were distributed to depository libraries.

Details: Free

`gopher://gopher.ncsu.edu`

bcdv

bcdv

★

A mailing list to discuss issues related to bicycling in the greater Philadelphia metropolitan region, and the advocacy work of the Bicycle Coalition of the Delaware Valley (BCDV), including current efforts to ensure that an appropriate amount of Federal ISTEA and Congestion Mitigation and Air Quality grants are spent on removing barriers to bicycling.

Keywords: Bicycling

Audience: Bicyclists

Contact: bike-request@bcdv.drexel.edu

Details: Free

User Info: To subscribe to the list, send an e-mail message requesting a subscription to the URL address below.

To send a message to the entire list, address it to: bike@bcdv.drexel.edu

`mailto:bike-request@bcdv.drexel.edu`

Bears

Bears

A mailing list in digest format for gay and bisexual men who are bears themselves and for those who enjoy the company of bears. The definition of "bears" encompasses men who are variously cuddly, furry, perhaps stocky, or bearded. Mail.bears is designed to be a forum to bring together folks with similar interests for conversation, friendship, and sharing of experiences.

Keywords: Gays, Bisexuality

Audience: Gays, Bisexuals

Contact: Steve Dyer, Brian Gollum
bears-request@spdcc.COM

Details: Free

User Info: To subscribe to the list, send an e-mail message requesting a subscription to the URL address below.

To send a message to the entire list, address it to: bears@spdcc.COM

`mailto:bears-request@spdcc.COM`

Beer

alt.beer

A Usenet newsgroup providing information and discussion about beer and ale.

Keywords: Beer

Audience: Brewers, Beer Enthusiasts

User Info: To subscribe to this Usenet newsgroup, you need access to a newsreader.

`news:alt.beer`

rec.crafts.brewing

A Usenet newsgroup providing information and discussion about making beers and meads.

Keywords: Beer, Crafts

Audience: Beer Brewers

User Info: To subscribe to this Usenet newsgroup, you need access to a newsreader.

`news:rec.crafts.brewing`

Behavior

PsycINFO

PsycINFO is a leading research database providing bibliographic access to the international literature in psychology, as well as the related behavioral and social sciences.

Keywords: Psychology, Psychiatry, Behavioral Science

Sponsor: American Psychological Association

Audience: Social workers, Psychologists, Psychiatrists, Librarians, Students

Contact: CDP Technologies Sales Department (800) 950-2035, extension 400

User Info: To subscribe, contact CDP Technologies directly

`telnet:\\cdplus@cdplus.com`

Behavioral Science

Eastern Washington University Library

The library's holdings are large and wide-ranging and contain significant collections in many fields.

Keywords: Education, Music, Social Science, Behavioral Science

Audience: Researchers, Students, General Public

Details: Free

`telnet:// wsduvm12.csc.wsu.edu`

University of Texas at Austin Library

The library's holdings are large and wide-ranging and contain significant collections in many fields.

Keywords: Music, Natural Science, Nursing, Science Technology, Behavioral Science, Social Work, Computer Science, Engineering, Latin American Studies, Middle Eastern Studies

Audience: Researchers, Students, General Public

Details: Free

Expect: Blank Screen, Send: Return; Expect: Go, Send: Return; Expect: Enter Terminal Type, Send: vt100

Notes: Some databases are restricted to UT Austin users only.

`telnet://utcat.utexas.edu`

Washington University Library

The library's holdings are large and wide-ranging and contain significant collections in many fields.

Keywords: Technology, Literature (German), Social Science, Behavioral Science

Audience: Researchers, Students, General Public

Contact: services@wugate.wustl.edu

Details: Free

Expect: Login; Send: Services

`telnet://wugate.wustl.edu`

A B C D E F G H I J K L M N O P Q R S T U V W X Y Z

A
B
C
D
E
F
G
H
I
J
K
L
M
N
O
P
Q
R
S
T
U
V
W
X
Y
Z

Bel Canto

Bel Canto

A mailing list for the discussion of the music, lyrics, and shows of the group Bel Canto, and solo projects of group members, or even the work of related artists if appropriate.

Keywords: Musical Groups, Music

Audience: Music Enthusiasts

Contact: dewy-fields-request@ifi.uio.no

Details: Free

User Info: To subscribe to the list, send an e-mail message requesting a subscription to the URL address below.

To send a message to the entire list, address it to: dewy-fields@ifi.uio.no

`mailto:dewy-fields-request@ifi.uio.no`

Belgium

BFU (Brussels Free Universities)

The gopher server of the Brussels Free Universities VUB /ULB is the national entry point for EMBnet in Belgium and provides links to university library systems and EMBnet databases.

Keywords: Computing, EMBnet, Belgium, Europe

Audience: Scientists, Biologists, Biotechnologists

Contact: support@vub.ac.be

Details: Free

`gopher://gopher.vub.ac.be`

Beloved

Beloved

A mailing list for the discussion of the Beloved, an English pop group with strong ambient and techno influences.

Keywords: Musical Groups, Music

Audience: Music Enthusiasts

Contact: Jyrki Sarkkinen beloved-request@phoenix.oulu.fi

Details: Free

User Info: To subscribe to the list, send an e-mail message requesting a subscription to the URL address below.

To send a message to the entire list, address it to: beloved@phoenix.oulu.fi

`mailto:beloved-request@phoenix.oulu.fi`

Berlin Wall

9nov89-l

A discussion list relating to recent events in the former German Democratic Republic.

Keywords: German Democratic Republic, Germany, Berlin Wall

Audience: Researchers, Political Scientists

Contact: Axel Mahler

Contact: axel@avalanche.cs.tu.berlin.de

User Info: To subscribe to the list, send an e-mail message to the URL address shown below, consisting of a single line reading:

SUB 9nov89-l YourFirstName YourLastName

To send a message to the entire list, address it to: 9nov89-1@tubvm.cs.tu.berlin.de

`mailto:listserv@tubvm.cs.tu-berlin.de`

Berne Convention Implementation Act of 1988

Berne Convention Implementation Act of 1988

An act to amend Title 17, United States Code, to implement the Berne Convention for the Protection of Literary and Artistic Works, as revised in Paris on July 24, 1971, and for other purposes.

Keywords: Legislation (US), Government (US), Politics (US), Copyright

Audience: Lawyers, Students, Politicians, Journalists

Details: Free

`gopher://wiretap.spies.com/00/Gov/Copyright/US.Berne.Convention.txt`

Best of the Web '94

Best of the Web '94

This web site highlights those places that were judged as the best sites (based on the criteria of quality, versatility, and power) on the World Wide Web.

Keywords: Internet, WWW

Audience: Internet Surfers

Contact: Brandon Plewe plewe@acsu.buffalo.edu

Details: Free

`http://wings.buffalo.edu/contest`

Best-of-AusRave (Australian Raves)

Best-of-AusRave (Australian Raves)

A regional rave-related mailing list covering the Australian continent, for people who want Australian rave information without the side discussions and social chatter from the regular list.

Keywords: Music, Raves, Australia

Audience: Ravers (Australian)

Contact: Simon Rumble best-of-ausrave-request@lsupoz.apana.org.au

Details: Free

User Info: To subscribe to the list, send an e-mail message to the URL address below, consisting of a single line reading:

SUB ausrave YourFirstName YourLastName

To send a message to the entire list, address it to: best-of-ausrave@lsupoz.apana.org.au

`mailto:best-of-ausrave-request@lsupoz.apana.org.au`

BETA

BETA

A discussion forum for BETA users. BETA is a modern object-oriented programming language.

Keywords: Programming Languages, Object-Oriented Programming, BETA

Audience: Programmers

Contact: Elmer Soerensen Sandvad usergroup-request@mjolner.dk

Details: Free

User Info: To subscribe to the list, send an e-mail message requesting a subscription to the URL address below.

To send a message to the entire list, address it to: usergroup@mjolner.dk

`mailto:usergroup-request@mjolner.dk`

Bethany Christian Services

Bethany Christian Services

A major directory on adoption, providing access to a broad range of related resources (library catalogs, databases, and servers) throughout the Internet.

Keywords: Adoption, Christianity, Pregnancy

Sponsor: Bethany Christian Services, Grand Rapids, Michigan, USA

Audience: Pregnant Women

Profile: The gopher server of Bethany, a pro-life, pro-family agency reaches out to women with unplanned pregnancies and adoptive couples. It contains a large amount of information about national and international adoption, the adoption process, African-American adoptions, and adoption of children with special needs. Also contains information for pregnant women, such as birth father rights and responsibilities, pregnancy counseling, and so on.

Contact: gophermaster@bethany.org

`gopher://gopher.bethany.org/11`

BiAct-L

BiAct-L

A discussion list for bisexual activists.

Keywords: Bisexuality, Activism

Audience: Bisexual Activists

Contact: Elaine Brennan
EL406010@brownvm.brown.edu

Details: Free

User Info: To subscribe to the list, send an e-mail message requesting a subscription to the URL address below. Directions for posting to the list will be sent to you when you are added to the list.

`mailto:EL406010@brownvm.brown.edu`

Bible

alt.christnet

This Usenet newsgroup is a gathering place for Christian ministers and users.

Keywords: Religion, Christianity, Bible, Divinity

Audience: Christians, Ministers

User Info: To subscribe to this Usenet newsgroup, you need access to a newsreader.

`news:alt.christnet`

alt.christnet.bible

A Usenet newsgroup providing information and discussion about bible discussion and research.

Keywords: Bible, Christianity, Religion, Divinity

Audience: Biblical Scholars, Bible Readers

User Info: To subscribe to this Usenet newsgroup, you need access to a newsreader.

`news:alt.christnet.bible`

Bible (King James Version)

★★★

The Bible (King James Version) includes the complete text of the modern Thomas Nelson revision of the 1769 edition of the King James version of the Bible.

Keywords: Bible, Religion, Christianity

Sponsor: Thomas Nelson Publishers, Nashville, TN, USA

Audience: Christians, Theologians, Historians, Moralists

Profile: The King James version originated from translations ordered by King James of England in 1604 at the Hampton Court Conference. Both the Old and New Testaments are included in this version. Records in the database represent both chapters and verses.

Contact: Dialog in the US at (800) 334-2564, Dialog internationally at country specific locations.

Details: Costs

User Info: To subscribe, contact Dialog directly.

`telnet://dialog.com`

Bibles

Johns Hopkins University Library

★★★

The library's holdings are large and wide-ranging and contain significant collections in many fields.

Keywords: Literature (English), Economics, Classics, Drama (German), Slavery, Trade Unions, Incunabula, Bibles, Diseases (History of), Nursing (History of), Abolitionism

Audience: General Public, Researchers, Librarians, Document Delivery Professionals

Details: Free

`telnet://jhuvm.hcf.jhu.edu`

University of Pennsylvania PENNINFO Library

★★★

The library's holdings are large and wide-ranging and contain significant collections in many fields.

Keywords: Church History, Spanish Inquisition, Witchcraft, Shakespeare (William), Bibles, Aristotle (Texts of), Fiction, Whitman (Walt), French Revolution, Drama (French), Literature (English), Literature (Spanish)

Audience: Researchers, Students, General Public

Contact: Al DSouza
penninfo-admin@dccs.upenn.edu

dsouza@dccs.upenn.edu

Details: Free

Expect: Login; Send: Public

`telnet://penninfo.upenn.edu`

Bibliographies

Bibliographies of US Senate Hearings

The US Senate produces a series of committee hearings, prints, and publications as part of the legislative process. The Documents department at North Carolina State University contains files for the 99th through 103rd Congresses, which also can be searched through a WAIS searchable database.

Keywords: Senate (US), Politics (US), Legislation (US), Bibliographies, Government (US)

Audience: General Public, Journalists, Students, Politicians, US Citizens

Contact: Jack McGeachy
Jack_McGeachy@ncsu.edu

Details: Free

`gopher://dewey.lib.ncsu.edu/11/`
`library/disciplines/government/senate`

Music Library Association Mailing List

★★★

This is a mail distribution service for the Music Library Association (MLA).

Keywords: Music Library, Bibliographies

Sponsor: Indiana University

Audience: Music Librarians

Profile: The services provided for the MLA include mail distribution, mail archiving, and file/document serving. This is a list server implementation, and the list managers intend that these services be used for various activities of the MLA that can benefit by wide-scale distribution, such as announcements of deadlines for NOTES and the MLA Newsletter, news items, general inquiries about MLA activities, and so on.

Contact: Ralph Papkhian
Papakhi@iubvm.ucs.Indiana.edu

Details: Free

User Info: To subscribe to the list, send an e-mail message to the URL address below, consisting of a single line reading:

SUB mla-u YourFirstName YourLastName

`mailto:listserv@iubvm.ucs.Indiana.edu`

Style Sheets from the Online Writers' Workshop.

This gopher provides information and examples on how to write bibliographies using three formats: MLA (Modern Language Association), Old-MLA, and APA (American Psychological Association).

Keywords: Bibliographies, Writing, Lexicology

Sponsor: University of Illinois at Urbana-Champaign

A
B
C
D
E
F
G
H
I
J
K
L
M
N
O
P
Q
R
S
T
U
V
W
X
Y
Z

Audience: Writers, Students (High School/College/University)

Contact: Dr. Michael Pemberton
michaelp@ux1.cso.uiuc

gopher://gopher.uiuc.edu

Bicycling

bcdv

A mailing list to discuss issues related to bicycling in the greater Philadelphia metropolitan region, and the advocacy work of the Bicycle Coalition of the Delaware Valley (BCDV), including current efforts to ensure that an appropriate amount of Federal ISTEA and Congestion Mitigation and Air Quality grants are spent on removing barriers to bicycling.

Keywords: Bicycling

Audience: Bicycling Enthusiasts

Contact: bike-request@bcdv.drexel.edu

Details: Free

User Info: To subscribe to the list, send an e-mail message requesting a subscription to the URL address below.

To send a message to the entire list, address it to: bike@bcdv.drexel.edu

mailto:bike-request@bcdv.drexel.edu

Bikecommute

This list's discussion centers around bicycle transportation and the steps necessary for improved bicycling conditions in (sub)urban areas. Participants include local members (Silicon Valley) as well as a few national organizations (League of American Wheelmen, Bikecentennial, and the Bicycle Federation of America).

Keywords: Bicycling

Audience: Bicyclists

Contact: bikecommute-request@bike2work.eng.sun.com

Details: Free

User Info: To subscribe to the list, send an e-mail message requesting a subscription to the URL address below.

To send a message to the entire list, address it to: bikecommute@bike2work.eng.sun.com

mailto:bikecommute-request@bike2work.eng.sun.com

Bikepeople

Bicycle activists, primarily from Santa Cruz County, CA, discuss bicycle issues on local, state, and national levels. Public hearings and government meetings are announced and reported on, and messages occasionally are cross-posted with the bikecommute mailing list.

Keywords: Bicycling

Audience: Activists, Bicyclists

Contact: Kevin Karplus
karplus@ce.ucsc.edu

Details: Free

User Info: To subscribe, send an e-mail message requesting a subscription to the URL address below.

mailto:karplus@ce.ucsc.edu

Biking

Information on biking events and maintenance, including an FAQ from rec.bicycles.

Keywords: Sports, Bicycling, Fitness

Audience: Bicyclists, Fitness Enthusiasts

Contact: Joern Yngve Dahl-Stamnes
dahls@fysel.unit.no

Details: Free

ftp://ugle.unit.no/local/biking

Biking in Canada

A repository of information for bicyclists, including utility programs, events, FAQs, and how-to guides; some with Canadian-specific details.

Keywords: Sports, Bicycling, Canada

Sponsor: Habitat Ecology Division at the Bedford Institute of Oceanography

Audience: Cyclists, Fitness Enthusiasts

Contact: sysop@biome.bio.ns.ca

Details: Free

gopher://gopher.biome.bio.dfo.ca/pub/biking

ebikes

New York City Bicycle discussion list.

Keywords: Bicycling, New York

Audience: Bicyclists

Contact: Danny Lieberman
ebikes-request@panix.com

Details: Free

User Info: To subscribe to the list, send an e-mail message requesting a subscription to the URL address below.

To send a message to the entire list, address it to: ebikes-request@panix.com

mailto:ebikes-request@panix.com

Velo News Experimental Tour de France Web Page

This web site provides background information on the Tour de France, including press coverage from this year's race.

Keywords: Bicycling, Sports

Sponsor: Velo News

Audience: Bicyclists, Sports Fans

Contact: VeloNews@aol.com

http://cob.fsu.edu/velonews/

World Cycling Championship 1994

This web site contains information about events surrounding the 1994 World Cycling Championship.

Keywords: Bicycling

Audience: Bicyclists, Sports Fans

http://www-worldbike.iunet.it/

BiFem-L

BiFem-L

A mailing list for bisexual women and bi-friendly women.

Keywords: Bisexuality

Audience: Bisexual Women

Contact: Elaine Brennan
listserv@brownvm.brown.edu

Details: Free

User Info: To subscribe, send an e-mail message requesting a subscription to the URL address below, consisting of a single line reading:

SUB BiFem-L YourFirstName YourLastName

To send a message to the entire list, address it to: BiFem-L@brownvm.brown.edu

mailto:listserv@brownvm.brown.edu

Big Dummy's Guide

Big Dummy's Guide

A comprehensive guide to the Internet for people with little or no experience with network communications.

Keywords: Internet, Internet Guides

Sponsor: Electronic Frontier Foundation

Audience: Internet Surfers

Contact: Shari Steele
ssteele@eff.org

Details: Free

Notes: Big Dummy's Guide to the Internet is available in: /pub/Net_info/Big_Dummy, in several versions. The basic text version is bigdummy.txt

ftp://ftp.eff.org

Big-DB

Big-DB

Discussions pertaining to large databases (generally greater than 1 million records) and large database management systems such as IMS, DB2, and CCA's Model/204.

Keywords: Databases, Database Management

Audience: Database Users, Database Managers

Contact: Fareed Asad-Harooni
big-DB@midway.uchicago.edu

Details: Free

User Info: To subscribe to the list, send an e-mail message requesting a subscription to the URL address below.

`mailto:big-DB@midway.uchicago.edu`

Bilingual Education Network

Bilingual Education Network

This gopher site contains bilingual and bicultural, ESL (English as a Second Language), and Foreign Language resources and curriculum guidelines.

Keywords: ESL (English as a Second Language), Education (Bilingual)

Sponsor: California Department of Education, California, USA

Audience: Educators, Administrators, Parents

`gopher://goldmine.cde.ca.gov`

Biochemistry

Biosis Previews

The database encompasses the entire field of life sciences and covers original research reports and reviews in biological and biomedical areas. This includes field, laboratory, clinical, experimental, and theoretical work. The traditional areas of biology, including botany, zoology, and microbiology are covered, as well as the related fields such as plant and animal science, agriculture, pharmacology, and ecology.

Keywords: Biology, Botany, Zoology, Microbiology, Plant Science, Animal Science, Agriculture, Pharmacology, Ecology, Biochemistry, Biophysics, Bioengineering

Sponsor: Biosis

Audience: Librarians, Researchers, Students, Biologists, Botanists, Zoologists, Scientists, Taxonomists

Contact: CDP Technologies Sales Department (800)950-2035, extension 400.

User Info: To subscribe, contact CDP Technologies directly.

`telnet://cdplus@cdplus.com`

University of Texas Health Science Center at Tyler Library

The library's holdings are large and wide-ranging and contain significant collections in many fields.

Keywords: Biochemistry, Cardiopulmonary Medicine, Cell Biology, Family Practice, Molecular Biology

Audience: Researchers, Students, General Public

Details: Free

Expect: Username Prompt, Send: LIS

`telnet://athena.uthscsa.edu`

Biodiversity

Base de Dados Tropical (BDT)

Base de Dados Tropical (Tropical Data Base) is a collection of information related to biodiversity and biotechnology.

Keywords: Biodiversity, Biotechnology, Brazil

Sponsor: Fundacao Tropical de Pesquisas e Tecnologia "Andre Tosello," Campinas, SP, Brazil

Audience: Biotechnologists, Scientists, Researchers

Contact: manager@bdt.ftpt.br

Details: Free

`gopher://bdt.ftpt.br`

Biodiv-L

This list discusses technical opportunities, administrative and economic issues, and practical limitations and scientific goals, leading to recommendations for the establishment of a biodiversity network. Individual contributions are requested, not only as to network capabilities but also as to existing databases of interest to biodiversity.

Keywords: Biodiversity

Audience: Ecologists

Contact: listserv@bdt.ftpt.ansp.br

Details: Free

User Info: To subscribe to the list, send an e-mail message to the URL address below, consisting of a single line reading:

SUB biodiv-l YourFirstName YourLastName

To send a message to the entire list, address it to: biodiv-l@bdt.ftpt.ansp.br

Notes: For those interested in receiving a summary of all contributions that have been sent to this list, please send the following message get biodiv-l readme.first to the URL address shown below.

`mailto:listserv@bdt.ftpt.ansp.br`

Bioengineering

Biosis Previews

The database encompasses the entire field of life sciences and covers original research reports and reviews in biological and biomedical areas. This includes field, laboratory, clinical, experimental and theoretical work. The traditional areas of biology, including botany, zoology, and microbiology are covered, as well as the related fields such as plant and animal science, agriculture, pharmacology, and ecology.

Keywords: Biology, Botany, Zoology, Microbiology, Plant Science, Animal Science, Agriculture, Pharmacology, Ecology, Biochemistry, Biophysics, Bioengineering

Sponsor: Biosis

Audience: Librarians, Researchers, Students, Biologists, Botanists, Zoologists, Scientists, Taxonomists

Contact: CDP Technologies Sales Department (800) 950-2035, ext. 400.

User Info: To subscribe, contact CDP Technologies directly.

`telnet://cdplus@cdplus.com`

Biographies

Bowker Biographical Directory

This is a collection of biographical directories that correspond to certain Bowker print publications.

Keywords: Biographies

Sponsor: R.R. Bowker, a Reed Reference Publishing Company, a division of Reed Publishing (US) Inc., New Providence, NJ, US

Audience: General Public, Writers, Researchers

Profile: The database corresponds to the Bowker print publications as follows: American Men and Women of Science, covering over 122,500 leading US and Canadian scientists and engineers in the physical, biological, and related sciences; Who's Who in American Art, covering some 7,000 North American artists, critics, curators, administrators, librarians, historians, collectors, and dealers; and Who's Who in American Politics, covering over 25,400 American political decision-makers at all levels from federal to local government.

A
B
C
D
E
F
G
H
I
J
K
L
M
N
O
P
Q
R
S
T
U
V
W
X
Y
Z

A
B
C
D
E
F
G
H
I
J
K
L
M
N
O
P
Q
R
S
T
U
V
W
X
Y
Z

Contact: Dialog in the US at (800) 334-2564, Dialog internationally at country specific locations.

Details: Costs

User Info: To subscribe, contact Dialog directly.

`telnet://dialog.com`

SPORTS (Sports News)

The Sports News (SPORTS) library contains a variety of sports-related news and information.

Keywords: News, Analysis, Sports, Biographies

Audience: Sports Enthusiasts, Journalists

Profile: The SPORTS library is a specialized news library that contains the full text of *Sports Illustrated* and *The Sporting News* and selected sports-related stories from many major US newspapers and wire services. Biographical information and 1992 Olympic facts also are part of this library.

Contact: Mead New Sales Group at (800) 227-4908 or (513) 859-5398 inside the US, or (513) 865-7981 for all inquiries outside the US.

User Info: To subscribe, contact Mead directly.

To examine the Nexis user guide, you can access it at the ftp site of the University of Texas at Austin at the URL address: ftp://ftp.cc.utexas.edu

The files are in: /pub/ref-services/LEXIS

`telnet://nex.meaddata.com`

`http://www.meaddata.com`

Supreme Court Judges

Biographies from the sitting Justices, and a few former Justices.

Keywords: Judiciary, Supreme Court, Judges, Biographies

Audience: General Public, Lawyers, Judges, Journalists

Details: Free

`gopher://info.umd.edu`

Bioinformatics

Bioinformatics

★★★

This gopher server provides data and software related to bioinformatics, including public-domain software for biology and mirror storage for the main databases of the Human Genome Project and Molecular Biology.

Keywords: Bioinformatics, Biology, Molecular Biology

Sponsor: Weizmann Institute of Science, Israel

Audience: Scientists, Biologists

Contact: lsprilus@weizmann.weizmann.ac.il

Details: Free

`gopher://bioinformatics.weizmann.ac.il`

`http://bioinformatics.weizman.act.il`

Marshall University School of Medicine (MUSOM) RuralNet Gopher

A gopher server dedicated to the improvement of rural health care.

Keywords: Rural Development, Health Care, Medical Treatment, Bioinformatics

Sponsor: Marshall University School of Medicine

Audience: Health Care Professionals, Medical Students, Rural Residents

Profile: A collection of health care resources, with particular emphasis on rural health care. Includes listings of clinical resources by subject area, information on state and federal rural health care initiatives, and links to local and national health and education services.

Contact: Mike McCarthy, Andy Jarrell mmccarth@muvms6.wvnet.edu, jarrell@musom01.mu.wvnet.edu

`gopher://ruralnet.mu.wvnet.edu`

Virus Gopher Server

This server contains names of virus families/groups and members now available online from the Australian National University's bioinformatics facility.

Keywords: Viruses, Bioinformatics, Biology

Sponsor: Research School of Biological Research, Australian National University, Canberra, Australia

Audience: Researchers, Biologists, Health Professionals

Details: Free

`gopher://life.anu.edu.au`

Biological Research

CVNet (Color and Vision Network)

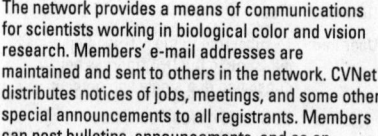

The network provides a means of communications for scientists working in biological color and vision research. Members' e-mail addresses are maintained and sent to others in the network. CVNet distributes notices of jobs, meetings, and some other special announcements to all registrants. Members can post bulletins, announcements, and so on.

Keywords: Optics, Biological Research, Psychology

Sponsor: York University, North York, Ontario, Canada

Audience: Psychologists, Color/Vision Researchers

Contact: Peter K. Kaiser cvnet@vm1.yorkU.ca

Details: Free

User Info: To subscribe, send an e-mail message requesting a subscription to the URL address below.

`mailto:cvnet@vm1.yorkU.ca`

Medical and Biological Research in Laboratories Institutions (Israel)

A descriptive listing of medical research and diagnostic laboratories in Israel. This site also has information on medical research being carried out in Israeli universities and hospitals.

Keywords: Medical Research, Biological Research, Israel

Audience: Medical Researchers, Biomedical Researchers, Medical Professionals

Profile: MATIMOP, The Israeli Industry Center for Health Care Research And Development, is a non-profit service organization, founded by an Israeli association of hospitals, universities, and other medical researchers, aiming their activities at promoting cooperation of Israeli entrepreneurs and manufacturers with qualified business firms abroad. This gopher details specific medical and biological research projects in progress in every department of every major Israeli health care institution including universities, The General Federation of Labour, public hospitals, government-municipal hospitals, and government hospitals, as well as medical and biological research in the Israeli laboratories and research institutes.

Contact: rdinfo@matimop.org.il

`gopher://gopher.matimop.org.il`

Neuron

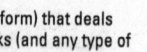

This is a moderated list (in digest form) that deals with all aspects of neural networks (and any type of network or neuromorphic system). Topics include both connectionist models (artificial neural networks) and biological systems ("wetware").

Keywords: Neural Networks, Biological Research

Audience: Neuroscientists, Neurobiologists

Contact: Peter Marvit neuron-request@cattell.psych.upenn.edu

Details: Free

User Info: To subscribe to the list, send an e-mail message requesting a subscription to the URL address below.

Notes: Back issues and limited software are available through FTP from cattell.psych.upenn.edu. The Digest is gatewayed to Usenet's comp.ai.neural-nets.

`mailto:neuron-request@cattell.psych.upenn.edu`

Biology

Archive of Biology Software and Data

 ★★★★

The main area of concentration of this archive is molecular biology. It contains software for the Macintosh, MS-DOS, VAX-VMS, and UNIX.

Keywords: Health, Biology, Molecular Biology

Sponsor: Indiana University

Audience: Biologists, Students

Contact: archive@bio.indiana.edu

Details: Free

Notes: It is recommended that the file ARCHIVE.DOC be transferred and read first. This file gives considerable information about and instructions for using the archive.

`ftp://ftp.bio.indiana.edu`

Bioinformatics

 ★★★

This gopher server provides data and software related to bioinformatics, including public-domain software for biology and mirror storage for the main databases of the Human Genome Project and Molecular Biology.

Keywords: Bioinformatics, Biology, Molecular Biology

Sponsor: Weizmann Institute of Science, Israel

Audience: Scientists, Biologists

Contact: lsprilus@weizmann.weizmann.ac.il

Details: Free

`gopher://`
`bioinformatics.weizmann.ac.il`

`http://bioinformatics.weizman.act.il`

Biomedical Computer Laboratory (BCL)

 ★★★

A resource for biomedical computing.

Keywords: Health, Biomedical Research, Biology, Medicine

Sponsor: Washington University School of Medicine

Audience: Medical Researchers, Biologists

Profile: A significant portion of the activities at BCL are supported by the National Center for Research Resources' Biomedical Research Technology Program (BRTP), which promotes the application of advances in computer science and technology, engineering, mathematics, and the physical sciences, to research problems in biology and medicine by supporting the development of advanced research technologies.

Contact: Kenneth W. Clark info@wubcl.wustl.edu

Details: Free

Notes: login; Send: anonymous

Investigators wishing to explore the possibility of interactions with BCL at Washington University should send e-mail (preferred).

`ftp://wubcl.wustl.edu`

bionet.molbio.genbank.updates

 ★

A Usenet newsgroup providing information and discussion about the GenBank Nucleic acid database.

Keywords: Molecular Biology, Biology, Genetics

Audience: Molecular Biologists, Researchers

User Info: To subscribe to this Usenet newsgroup, you need access to a newsreader.

`news:bionet.molbio.genbank.updates`

bionet.software

★

A Usenet newsgroup providing information and discussion about software for use in biological research.

Keywords: Computers, Biology

Audience: Students, Educators, Biologists

User Info: To subscribe to this Usenet newsgroup, you need access to a newsreader.

`news:bionet.software`

Biosis Previews

★★★

The database encompasses the entire field of life sciences and covers original research reports and reviews in biological and biomedical areas. This includes field, laboratory, clinical, experimental, and theoretical work. The traditional areas of biology, including botany, zoology, and microbiology are covered, as well as the related fields such as plant and animal science, agriculture, pharmacology, and ecology.

Keywords: Biology, Botany, Zoology, Microbiology, Plant Science, Animal Science, Agriculture, Pharmacology, Ecology, Biochemistry, Biophysics, Bioengineering

Sponsor: Biosis

Audience: Librarians, Researchers, Students, Biologists, Botanists, Zoologists, Scientists, Taxonomists

Contact: CDP Technologies Sales Department (800)950-2035, extension 400.

User Info: To subscribe, contact CDP Technologies directly.

`telnet:\\cdplus@cdplus.com`

BOING (Bio-Oriented INternet Gophers)

 ★★★★

A searchable gopher index, BOING is used to search through the titles of items in bio-gopher space and to access the items returned.

Keywords: Biology, Health, Medicine

Audience: Health Professionals, Biomedical Researchers, Students (college, graduate)

Details: Free

`gopher://gopher.gdb.org`

CSU Entomology WWW Site

 ★★★★

A web site containing online photos of insects, entomology educational programs, and extensive Internet entomology links.

Keywords: Bioscience, Biology, Entomology

Sponsor: Colorado State University, Denver, Colorado, USA

Audience: Students, Researchers, Entomologists

Contact: Lou Bjostad lbjostad@lamar.colorado.edu

`http://www.colostate.edu/Depts/`
`Entomology/ent.html`

Drosophila Information Newsletter

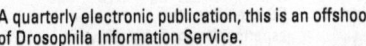 ★

A quarterly electronic publication, this is an offshoot of Drosophila Information Service.

Keywords: Drosophila, Biology, Genetics

Audience: Biologists, Geneticists

Contact: Kathy Matthews matthewk@ucs.indiana.edu

Details: Free

User Info: To subscribe, send an e-mail message to the address below consisting of a single line reading:

SUB drosophila-information-newsletter YourFirstName Your Last Name

To send a message to the entire list, address it to:

drosophila.information.newsletter@ucs.indiana.edu

`mailto:listserv@iubvm.ucs.indiana.edu`

EMBnet (European Molecular Biology Network)

 ★★★★

A group of European Internet sites that provide computational molecular biology services to both national and international researchers.

Keywords: Biology, Bioscience, Molecular Biology

Sponsor: The EC Funding Program (BRIDGE)

Audience: Biologists, Molecular Biologists, Researchers

A
B
C
D
E
F
G
H
I
J
K
L
M
N
O
P
Q
R
S
T
U
V
W
X
Y
Z

Contact: Rodrigo Lopez, Robert Herzog
rodrigol@biotek.uio.no,
rherzog@ulb.ac.be

`http://biomaster.uio.no/embnet-www.html`

Harvard Biosciences Online Journals

★★★★

A resource containing selected online journals and periodicals in biology and medicine. Includes peer-reviewed e-journals, journal indexes, and databases.

Keywords: Biology, Bioscience, Molecular Biology

Sponsor: Harvard Biolabs, Harvard University, Cambridge, Massachusetts, USA

Audience: Biologists, Molecular Biologists, Researchers

Contact: Keith Robinson, Steve Brenner
krobinson@nucleus.harvard.edu
s.e.brenner@bioc.cam.ac.uk

`http://golgi.harvard.edu/journals.html`

Institute for Molecular Virology

★★★

A unique virology resource for students, scientists, computer visualization experts, and the general public.

Keywords: Disease, Viruses, Biology

Sponsor: University of Wisconsin-Madison, Madison, Wisconsin, USA

Audience: Virologists, Biologists, Researchers

Contact: Stephen Spencer
sspencer@rhino.bocklabs.wisc.edu

`http://www.bocklabs.wisc.edu/Welcome.html`

Interactive Frog Dissection Kit

★

An interactive simulation of the dissection of a computer-generated frog.

Keywords: Biology, Simulation, Interactive Learning

Sponsor: Lawrence Berkeley Laboratory-Whole Frog Project, Berkeley, California, USA

Audience: Students, Educators, Biologists

Contact: David Robertson
dwrobertson@lbl.gov

Notes: Copyrighted (commercial uses require permission)

`http://george.1b1.gov/ITG.hm.pg.docs/dissect/info.html`

Johns Hopkins Genetic Databases

★★★

This gopher provides electronic access to documents pertaining to computational biology and a number of different genetic databases.

Keywords: Genetics, Molecular Biology, Medicine, Biology

Sponsor: Johns Hopkins University

Audience: Geneticists, Researchers, Scientists, Molecular Biologists

Profile: The databases accessible from this entry point include GenBank, Swiss-Prot, PDB, PIR, LiMB, TFD, AAtDB, ACEDB, CompoundKB, PROSITE EC Enzyme Database, NRL_3D Protein-Sequence-Structure Database, Eukaryotic Promoter Database (EPD), Cloning Vector Database, Expressed Sequence Tag Database (ESTDB), Online Mendelian Inheritance Man (OMIM), Sequence Analysis Bibliographic Reference Data Bank (Seqanalref), and Database Taxonomy (GenBank, Swiss-Prot). The gopher also provides direct links to other gophers with information relevant to biology.

Contact: Dan Jacobson
danj@mail.gdb.org

Details: Free

`gopher://merlot.welch.jhu.edu`

McGill University, Montreal Canada, INFOMcGILL Library

★★★

The library's holdings are large and wide-ranging and contain significant collections in many fields.

Keywords: Architecture, Entomology, Biology, Science (History of), Medicine (History of), Napoleon, Shakespeare (William)

Audience: Researchers, Students, General Public

Contact: Roy Miller
ccrmmus@mcgillm (Bitnet) or
ccrmmus@musicm.mcgill.ca (Internet)

Expect: VM logo; Send: Enter; Expect: prompt; Send: PF3 or type INFO

`telnet:// vm1.mcgill.ca`

MegaGopher

★

This is the gopher at the University of Montreal. It supports the software and information requirements for the MegaSequencing project. It also serves as a repository of data for organellar genome and molecular evolution research and acts as the focal point for the GDE (Genetic Data Environment) package.

Keywords: Biology, Canada

Audience: Biologists

Contact: Tim Littlejohn
tim@bch.umontreal.ca

Details: Free

`gopher://megasun.bch.umontreal.ca`

MGD (Mouse Genome Database)

★★

This site provides a comprehensive database of genetic information on the laboratory mouse.

Keywords: Biology, Genetics

Sponsor: The Jackson Laboratory

Audience: Biologists, Researchers, Educators, Students

Contact: mgi-help@informatics.jax.org

Details: Free

Notes: Contact Mouse Genome Informatics User Support by telephone at (207) 288-3371, X 1900, or by FAX at (207) 288-2516.

`http://www.informatics.jax.org/mgd.html`

National Science Foundation Center for Biological Timing Vertebrate Museum and Virus Gopher Server

★★★

This gopher accesses investigative research pertaining to various aspects of biological timing. The goal of this gopher is to make the Museum's Collections information available over the Internet. This server contains names of virus families/groups and members now available online from the Australian National University's bioinformatics facility.

Keywords: Biology, Vertebrates

Sponsor: Reasearch School of Biological Research, Australian National University, Canberra, Australia

Audience: Biologists, Educators, Researchers

Profile: The center combines the efforts of several universities pertaining to research in biological timing. This includes Vistudies, the internal timing mechanisms that control cycles of sleep and waking, hormone pulsatility, neural excitability, and reproductive rhythmicity. Investigators are involved with research from behavior testing to molecular genetics.

The center also supports educational and outreach programs to industry, universities, and high schools. The center also hosts an annual scientific symposium and a number of mini-symposias.

Details: Free

`gopher://gopher.virginia.edu/11/pubs/biotimin`

NIBNews - A Monthly Electronic Bulletin About Medical Informatics

★

Disseminates information about Brazilian and Latin American activities, people, information, events, publications, software, and so on, involving computer applications in health care, medicine, and biology.

Keywords: Health Care, Biology, Brazil, Latin America, South America, Medicine

Audience: Health Care Professionals, Biologists

Contact: Renato M. E. Sabbatini
sabbatini@bruc.bitnet

Details: Free

e-mail a short notice to

`mailto:sabbatini@ccvax.unicamp.br`

Smbnet (Society for Mathematical Biology Digest)

Keywords: Mathematical Biology, Biology

Audience: Mathematical Biologists, Biologists

Contact: Ray Mejia

Details: Free

User Info: To subscribe to the list, send an e-mail message to the URL address below consisting of a single line reading:

SUB smbnet YourFirstName YourLastName

To send a message to the entire list, address it to: smbnet@fconvx.ncifcrf.gov

mailto:listserv@fconvx.ncifcrf.gov

SOCINSCT (Social Insect Biology Research List)

SOCINSCT is dedicated to communication among investigators active in the discipline of social insect biology.

Keywords: Biology, Insect Biology

Audience: Biologists, Researchers (college, graduate)

Profile: It is restricted to discussions of research at the university level. Social insects (bees, wasps, ants, and termites) are the main interest but information can include any area of sociobiology, or solitary bees and wasps. Such areas could include: orientation, navigation, adaptation/selection/evolution, superorganism concept, behavior, physiology and biochemistry, pheromones, flight and energetics, taxonomy and systematics, ecology, genetics, pollination, and nectar/pollen biology. Announcements of meetings and professional opportunities, requests for research help, sharing of literature references, sharing research topics and discussion of ideas are welcome.

Contact: Erik Seielstad
erik@acspr1.acs.brockport.edu

Details: Free

User Info: To subscribe to the list, send an e-mail message to the address below consisting of a single line reading:

SUB socinsct YourFirstName YourLastName

To send message to the entire list, address it to: socinsct@albany.edu

mailto:listserv@albany.edu

taxacom

Discussion list on biological systematics.

Keywords: Biology

Audience: Biologists

Contact: James H. Beach
beach@huh.harvard.edu

Details: Free

User Info: To subscribe to the list, send an e-mail message to the URL address below, consisting of a single line reading:

SUB taxacom YourFirstName YourLastName

To send a message to the entire list, address it to:
taxacom@harvarda.harvard.edu

mailto:listserv@harvarda.harvard.edu

US Geological Survey Server

This resource containis publications, USGS research programs, technology transfer partnerships, and fact sheets about geology.

Keywords: Biology, Geology, Natural Science

Sponsor: US Geological Survey

Audience: Biologists, Geologists, Researchers, Naturalists

Contact: Systems Operator
webmaster@info.er.usgs.gov

http://info.er.usgs.gov

Vertebrate Museum

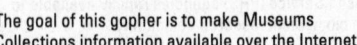

The goal of this gopher is to make Museums Collections information available over the Internet.

Keywords: Vertebrates, Biology

Sponsor: The Museum of Vertebrate Zoology, University of California at Berkeley

Audience: Natural Scientists, Biologists, Researchers

Details: Free

gopher://ucmp1.berkeley.edu

Virginia Commonwealth University Library

The library's holdings are large and wide-ranging and contain significant collections in many fields.

Keywords: Art, Biology, Humanities, Journalism, Music, Urban Planning

Audience: Researchers, Students, General Public

Details: Free

Expect: Login; Send: Opub

telnet://vcuvm1.ucc.vcu.edu

Virus Gopher Server

This server contains names of virus families/groups and members now available online from the Australian National University's bioinformatics facility.

Keywords: Viruses, Bioinformation, Biology

Sponsor: Research School of Biological Research, Australian National University, Canberra, Australia

Audience: Researchers, Biologists, Health Professionals

Details: Free

gopher://life.anu.edu.au

WWW Biological Science Servers

A web site containing Internet links to many gopher servers and other web sites pertaining to bioscience.

Keywords: Bioscience, Biology

Sponsor: U.S. Department of the Interior Survey

Audience: Biologists, Researchers.

Contact: Systems Operator
webmaster@info.er.usgs.gov

**http://info.er.usgs.gov/network/
science/biology/index.html**

Biomechanics

Biomch-L

This list is intended for members of the International, European, American, Canadian, and other Societies of Biomechanics, and for members of ISEK (International Society of Electrophysiological Kinesiology), as well as for all others with an interest in the general field of biomechanics and human or animal movement.

Keywords: Biomechanics, Kinesiology, Movement

Sponsor: International Society of Biomechanics

Audience: Kinesiologists

Contact: Ton van den Bogert
listserv@nic.surfnet.nl

Details: Free

User Info: To subscribe to the list, send an e-mail message to the URL address below, consisting of a single line reading:

SUB biomch-l YourFirstName YourLastName

To send a message to the entire list, address it to: biomch-l@nic.surfnet.nl

Notes: To obtain technical help, send the command send biomch-l guide to listserv@nic.surfnet.nl.

mailto:listserv@nic.surfnet.nl

Biomedical Research

Biomedical Computer Laboratory (BCL)

A resource for biomedical computing.

Keywords: Health, Biomedical Research, Biology, Medicine

A B C D E F G H I J K L M N O P Q R S T U V W X Y Z

Sponsor: Washington University School of Medicine

Audience: Medical Researchers, Biologists

Profile: A significant portion of the activities at BCL are supported by the National Center for Research Resources' Biomedical Research Technology Program (BRTP), which promotes the application of advances in computer science and technology, engineering, mathematics, and the physical sciences to research problems in biology and medicine by supporting the development of advanced research technologies.

Contact: Kenneth W. Clark
info@wubcl.wustl.edu

Details: Free

Expect: login; Send: anonymous

Notes: Investigators who want to explore the possibility of interactions with BCL at Washington University should send e-mail (preferred).

`ftp://wubcl.wustl.edu`

MEDLARS (MEDical Literature Analysis and Retrieval System)

★★★★

MEDLARS is the computerized system of databases and databanks pertinent to biomedical research and patient care, including MEDLINE, the largest and one of the most-used biomedical databases ever.

Keywords: Medicine, MEDLINE, Biomedical Research

Sponsor: National Library of Medicine

Audience: Health Care Providers, Scientists, Biomedical Researchers

Profile: The computer files can be searched either to produce a list of publications (bibliographic citations) or to retrieve factual information on a specific question. MEDLARS comprises two computer subsystems, ELHISS and TOXNET (TOXicology data NETwork), on which reside over 40 online databases containing about 16 million references. MEDLINE is the largest database and corresponds to three print indexes: Index Medicus, Index to Dental Literature, and Internatonal Nursing Index.

Details: Costs

User Info: To subscribe to the service, send e-mail requesting an account to: medlars@nlm.nih.gov

An account is needed for entry and a fee is charged for use. Many university library computers have free link to the MEDLINE database.

`telnet://medlars.nlm.nih.gov`

NIH (National Institute of Health)

★★★★

This server is a network-based computer service operated by the Division of Computer Research and Technology (DCRT) to distribute information for and about the NIH (National Institutes of Health).

Keywords: NIH, Health Sciences, Biomedical Research, Medicine

Sponsor: Division of Computer Research and Technology (DCRT), National Institute of Health

Audience: Scientists, Biomedical Researchers, Health CareProfessionals, General Public

Profile: This server provides Internet access to information about NIH health and clinical issues (including CancerNet and a variety of AIDS information), NIH-funded grants and research projects, and a variety of research resources in support of NIH and worldwide biomedical researchers. The major molecular biology databases (GenBank, SWISSPROT, PIR, PDB, TFD, Prosite, LiMB), for example, can be accessed through keyword searches from this gopher.

Details: Free

`gopher://gopher.nih.gov`

NIH Grant Line (Drgline Bulletin Board)

★★★★

The purpose of the NIH Grant Line is to make program and policy information from the Public Health Service (PHS) agencies rapidly available to the biomedical research community.

Keywords: Biomedical Research, NIH, Grants

Sponsor: The National Institute of Health

Audience: Scientists, Researchers, Students

Profile: Most of the research opportunity information available on this bulletin board is derived from the weekly publication *NIH Guide for Grants and Contracts* and consists of notices, RFAs, RFPs (announcements of availability), numbered program announcements, and statements of PHS policy. The information found on the NIH Grant Line is grouped into three main sections: short news flashes that appear without any prompting shortly after you have logged on, bulletins that are for reading, and files that are intended mainly for downloading. The E-Guide is available for electronic transmission each week. The material consists predominantly of statements about the research interests of the PHS agencies, institutes, and national centers that have funds to support research in the extramural community. Currently under development are two new files: one will be a monthly listing of new NIH Awards, and the other will be an order form to obtain NIH publications from DRG's Office of Grants Inquiries.

Details: Free

To access the NIH Grant Line, telnet to the URL address below and when a message has been received that the connection is open, type: ,GEN1 (the comma is mandatory). At the INITIALS? prompt, type BB5 and at the ACCOUNT? prompt, type CCS2

The NIH Guide to Grants and Contracts also can be accessed through gopher:// helix.nih.gov/11/res/nih-guide

`telnet://wylbur.cu.nih.gov`

The Tumor Gene Database

 ★★

A database containing information about genes associated with tumorigenesis and cellular transformation.

Keywords: Genetics, Diseases, Biomedical Research, Databases

Sponsor: Department of Cell Biology, Baylor College of Medicine

Audience: Biomedical Researchers

Contact: David Steffen, Ph.D.
steffen@bcm.tmc.edu

`gopher://mbcr.bcm.tmc.edu`

University of Texas Southwestern Medical Center Library

 ★★

The library's holdings are large and wide-ranging and contain significant collections in many fields.

Keywords: Biomedical Research

Audience: Researchers, Students, General Public

Details: Free

Expect: Login, Send: TIntutsw; Expect: Password, Send: Library

`telnet://library.swmed.edu`

Biomedicine

MEDLINE

MEDLINE is a major source of bibliographic biomedical literature. The MEDLINE database encompasses information from three printed indexes (Index Medicus, Index to Dental Literature and the International Nursing Index) as well as additional information not published in the Index Medicus.

Keywords: Biomedicine, Dentistry, Nursing, Medicine

Sponsor: U.S. National Library of Medicine

Audience: Librarians, Researchers, Physicians, Students

Contact: CDP Technologies Sales Department (800) 950-2035, ext. 400

User Info: To subscribe, contact CDP Technologies directly

`telnet://cdplus@cdplus.com`

sci.engr.biomed

 ★

A Usenet newsgroup providing information and discussion about the field of biomedical engineering.

Keywords: Biomedicine, Engineering (Biomedical)

Audience: Engineers (Biomedical), Biomedical Researchers

Details: Free

User Info: To subscribe to this Usenet newsgroup, you need access to a newsreader.

`news:sci.engr.biomed`

The National Library of Medicine (NLM) Online Catalog System

★★★★

Catalog of library holdings.

Keywords: Medicine, Health Sciences, Biomedicine, Rare Books

Sponsor: National Library of Medicine

Audience: Health Professionals, Medical Educators, Students

Profile: The National Library of Medicine (NLM) is the world's largest biomedical library with a collection of over 4.9 million items. NLM is a national resource for all US health sciences libraries and fills over a quarter of a million interlibrary loan requests each year for these libraries. The library is open to the public, but its collection is designed primarily for health professionals. The library collects materials comprehensively in all major areas of the health sciences. Housed within the library is one of the world's finest medical history collections of pre-1914 and rare medical texts, manuscripts, and incunabula.

Contact: ref@nlm.nih.gov

Details: Free

The NLM can be accessed also through the WWW at http://www.nlm.nih.gov

`telnet://locator@locator.nlm.nih.gov`

University of Texas at Galveston (Medical Branch) Library

★★

The library's holding's are large and wide-ranging and contain significant collections in many fields.

Keywords: Health Sciences, Biomedicine, Nursing

Audience: Researchers, Students, General Public

Details: Free

Expect: Login, Send: Library

`telnet://ibm.gal.utexas.edu`

Biophysics

Biosis Previews

★★★

The database encompasses the entire field of life sciences and covers original research reports and reviews in biological and biomedical areas. This includes field, laboratory, clinical, experimental, and theoretical work. The traditional areas of biology, including botany, zoology, and microbiology are covered, as well as the related fields such as plant and animal science, agriculture, pharmacology, and ecology.

Keywords: Biology, Botany, Zoology, Microbiology, Plant Science, Animal Science, Agriculture, Pharmacology, Ecology, Biochemistry, Biophysics, Bioengineering

Sponsor: Biosis

Audience: Librarians, Researchers, Students, Biologists, Botanists, Zoologists, Scientists, Taxonomists

Contact: CDP Technologies Sales Department (800) 950-2035, ext. 400.

User Info: To subscribe, contact CDP Technologies directly.

`telnet://cdplus@cdplus.com`

Bioscience

CSU Entomology WWW Site
★★★★

A web site containing online photos of insects, entomology educational programs, and extensive Internet entomology links.

Keywords: Bioscience, Biology, Entomology

Sponsor: Colorado State University, Denver, Colorado, USA

Audience: Students, Researchers, Entomologists

Contact: Lou Bjostad
lbjostad@lamar.colorado.edu

`http://www.colostate.edu/Depts/`
`Entomology/ent.html`

EMBnet (European Molecular Biology Network)

★★★★

A group of European Internet sites that provide computational molecular biology services to both national and international researchers.

Keywords: Biology, Bioscience, Molecular Biology

Sponsor: The EC Funding Program (BRIDGE)

Audience: Biologists, Molecular Biologists, Researchers

Contact: Rodrigo Lopez, Robert Herzog
rodrigol@biotek.uio.no,
rherzog@ulb.ac.be

`http://biomaster.uio.no/embnet-`
`www.html`

Harvard Biosciences Online Journals
★★★★

A resource containing selected online journals and periodicals in biology and medicine. Includes peer-reviewed e-journals, journal indexes, and databases.

Keywords: Biology, Bioscience, Molecular Biology

Sponsor: Harvard Biolabs, Harvard University, Cambridge, Massachusetts, USA

Audience: Biologists, Molecular Biologists, Researchers

Contact: Keith Robinson, Steve Brenner
krobinson@nucleus.harvard.edu,
s.e.brenner@bioc.cam.ac.uk

`http://golgi.harvard.edu/`
`journals.html`

Poisons Information Database

★★

Directories of antivenoms, toxicologists, poison control centers, and poisons from around the world.

Keywords: Medical Research, Bioscience

Sponsor: Venom and Toxin Research Group, Department of Anatomy, National University of Singapore, Singapore

Audience: Biologists, Researchers, Medical Professionals, Toxicologists

Contact: Professor P. Gopalkrishnakone
antgopal@leonis.nus.sg

`http://biomed.nus.sg/PID/PID.html`

WWW Biological Science Servers

★★★

A web site containing Internet links to many gopher servers and other web sites pertaining to bioscience.

Keywords: Bioscience, Biology

Sponsor: U.S. Department of the Interior Survey

Audience: Biologists, Researchers.

Contact: Systems Operator
webmaster@info.er.usgs.gov

`http://info.er.usgs.gov/network/`
`science/biology/index.html`

Biosym Technologies Software

Biosym

★

For users of Biosym Technologies software, including the products Insight II, Discover, Dmol, Homology, Delphi, and Polymer. The list is not run by Biosym.

Keywords: Biosym Technologies Software, Software

Audience: Software Users

A B C D E F G H I J K L M N O P Q R S T U V W X Y Z

A
B
C
D
E
F
G
H
I
J
K
L
M
N
O
P
Q
R
S
T
U
V
W
X
Y
Z

Contact: Reinhard Doelz
dibug-request@comp.bioz.unibas.ch

Details: Free

User Info: To subscribe to the list, send an e-mail message requesting a subscription to the URL address below.

To send a message to the entire list, address it to:
dibug@comp.bioz.unibas.ch

`mailto:dibug-request@comp.bioz.unibas.ch`

Biotechnet Electronic Buyer's Guide

Biotechnet Electronic Buyer's Guide

Biotechnet is a global computer network created specially for research biologists. It is intended to be a valuable source of information and data, a communications resource, a forum to foster the exchange of current ideas, and an international marketplace for relevant goods and service.

Keywords: Molecular Biology, Electrophoresis, Chromatography

Audience: Molecular Biologists, Chemists, Laboratory Suppliers

Profile: One of the services offered by Biotechnet is the Electronic Buyer's Guide, which is divided into five individual databases for specific product categories: Molecular Biology, Electrophoresis, Chromatography, Liquid Handling, and Instruments & Apparatus. After selecting one of the guides at the prompt, you can search through each database to find either product names and applications or the name and address of the company that manufactures the product you wish to locate.

Details: Free

Notes: Password: bguide

`telnet://biotech@biotechnet.com`

Biotechnology

Base de Dados Tropical (BDT)

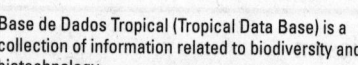

Base de Dados Tropical (Tropical Data Base) is a collection of information related to biodiversity and biotechnology.

Keywords: Biodiversity, Biotechnology, Brazil

Sponsor: Fundacao Tropical de Pesquisas e Tecnologia "Andre Tosello," Campinas, SP, Brazil

Audience: Biotechnologists, Scientists, Researchers

Contact: manager@bdt.ftpt.br

Details: Free

`gopher://bdt.ftpt.br`

Health Periodicals Database

This source covers a broad range of health subjects and issues.

Keywords: Health, Biotechnology, Medicine, Nutrition

Sponsor: Information Access Company, Foster City, CA, US

Audience: Health Professionals, Dieticians, Librarians

Profile: The database provides indexing and full text of journals covering a broad range of health subjects and issues including: prenatal care, dieting, drug abuse, AIDS, biotechnology, cardiovascular disease, environment, public health, safety, paramedical professions, sports medicine, substance abuse, toxicology, and much more.

Contact: Dialog in the US at (800) 334-2564, Dialog internationally at country-specific locations.

User Info: To subscribe, contact Dialog directly.

Notes: Coverage: 1988 to the present; updated weekly.

`telnet://dialog.com`

ICGEBnet

This is the information server of the International Centre for Genetic Engineering and Molecular Biology (ICGEB), Trieste, Italy.

Keywords: Molecular Biology, Biotechnology, Italy, Europe

Audience: Molecular Biotechnologists, Molecular Biologists

Profile: The primary purpose of the ICGEB computer resource is to disseminate the best of currently available computational technology to the molecular biologists of the ICGEB research community.

Contact: postmaster@icgeb.trieste.it

Details: Free

`gopher://icgeb.trieste.it`

IST BioGopher

This is the gopher server of the National Institute for Cancer Research (IST) and of the Advanced Biotechnology Center of Genoa, Italy.

Keywords: Cancer, Biotechnology, Italy, Europe

Audience: Biologists, Medical Researchers

Profile: The server includes data from the Interlab Project Databases (biological materials availability in European laboratories) and the Bio-Media Bulletin Board System (biotechnology researchers, projects, fundings and products).

Contact: gophman@istge.ist.unige.it

Details: Free

`gopher://istge.ist.unige.it`

Birds

TitNeT Titnews Titnotes

The network of the International Tit Society (TITS),

Keywords: Ornithology, Birds

Sponsor: International Tit Society

Audience: Bird Watchers

Profile: The network of the International Tit Society (TITS), Titnet posts three formal series: TITNET, which is the listing of e-mail subscribers, and includes their e-mail addresses, institutional affiliations, and research interests; TITNEWS, which is the forum for exchange concerning academic activities, and consists of single-topic issues and multiple announcements; and TITNOTES, which is the forum for exchange of information about tits (and other hole-nesting birds).

Contact: Jack P. Hailman
jhailman@vms.macc.wisc.edu.

Details: Free

User Info: To subscribe, send an e-mail message requesting a subscription to the URL address below. Provide: Full name, e-mail address, institutional affiliation, species studied, and topics studied.

`mailto:jhailman@vms.macc.wisc.edu`

titnet (Paridae and Hole-nesting Bird Discussion List)

Promotes communication among scientists working on tits (Paridae) and other hole-nesting birds.

Keywords: Birds, Ornithology

Audience: Bird Watchers

Profile: Titnet is a publication listing e-mail addresses of conference members. Titnews contains announcements and discussions of activities such as bibliographic systems and hence serves as the e-mail newsletter. Titnotes contains material on the biology of the birds and hence serves as a kind of e-mail journal.

Contact: Jack P. Hailman
jhailman@macc.wisc.edu

Details: Free

User Info: To subscribe to the list, send an e-mail message requesting a subscription to the URL address below.

To send a message to the entire list, address it to: jhailman@macc.wisc.edu

Notes: Send full name, mailing address, which is forwarded to Dr. Ficken for PARUS INTERNATIONAL, e-mail address(es), species studied, and types of studies (population dynamics, general ecology, vocalizations, nesting, behavior, and so on.).

`mailto:jhailman@macc.wisc.edu`

Birthmother

Birthmother

A mailing list for any birthmother who has relinquished a child for adoption.

Keywords: Adoption

Audience: Parents, Adoptees

Contact: nadir@acca.nmsu.edu

Details: Free

User Info: To join the mailing list, send a message to the URL address below with your e-mail address and brief information about your situation (i.e. bmom who relinquished x years ago and does/does not have contact, has/has not been reunited).

`mailto:nadir@acca.nmsu.edu`

Bisexuality

Alternates

A mailing list for people who advocate and practice an open sexual lifestyle. Its members are primarily bisexual people and their significant others. It serves as a forum and support group for adult men and women who espouse their freedom of choice and imagination in human sexual relations, no matter what their orientaion.

Keywords: Sexuality, Bisexuality, Sexual Orientation

Audience: Bisexuals, General Public

Contact: alternates-request@ns1.rutgers.edu

User Info: To subscribe to the list, send an e-mail message requesting a subscription to the URL address below.

To send a message to the entire list, address it to: alternates@ns1.rutgers.edu

`mailto:alternates-request@ns1.rutgers.edu`

Amend2-discuss

A mailing list for discussion of the implications and issues surrounding the passage of Colorado's Amendment 2, which revokes any existing homosexual civil rights legislation and prohibits the drafting of any new legislation.

Keywords: Activism, Gay Rights, Lesbians, Bisexuality

Audience: Gay Rights Activists

Contact: amend2-mod@cs.colorado.edu

User Info: To subscribe to the list, send an e-mail message to the URL address below, consisting of a single line reading: subscribe amend2-discuss

`mailto:majordomo@cs.colorado.edu`

Amend2-info

Colorado voted in an amendment to their state constitution which revokes any existing gay/lesbian/bisexual civil rights legislation and prohibits the drafting of any new legislation. This moderated list is for information on the implication and issues of this amendment.

Keywords: Activists, Gay, Lesbian, Bisexuality, Constitutional Amendments, Colorado, Civil Rights

Audience: General Public, Gays, Lesbians, Bisexuals, Activists

Contact: amend2-info@cs.colorado.edu

User Info: To subscribe to the list, send an e-mail message requesting a subscription to the URL address below.

To send a message to the entire list, address it to: amend2-info@cs.colorado.edu

`mailto:majordomo@cs.colorado.edu`

AUGLBC-I

The American University Gay, Lesbian, and Bisexual Community (AUGLBC) is a support group for lesbian, gay, bisexual, transsexual, and supportive students. The group also is connected with the International Gay and Lesbian Youth Organization (known as IGLYO).

Keywords: Gay, Lesbian, Bisexual, Transsexual, Sexuality

Audience: Gays, Lesbians, Bisexuals, Transsexuals, Students (college)

User Info: To subscribe to the list, send an e-mail message to the URL address below, consisting of a single line reading:

SUB AUGLBC-I YourFirstName YourLastName

To send a message to the entire list, address it to: AUGLBC-I@american.edu

`mailto:listserv@american.edu`

AusGBLF

An Australian-based mailing list for gays, bisexuals, lesbians, and friends.

Keywords: Australia, Gay, Lesbian, Bisexuality

Audience: Gays, Lesbians, Bisexuals

Contact: zglc@minyos.xx.rmit.oz.au

Details: Free

User Info: To subscribe to the list, send an e-mail message requesting a subscription to the URL address below.

To send a message to the entire list, address it to: ausgblf@minyos.xx.rmit.oz.au

`mailto:ausgblf-request@minyos.xx.rmit.oz.au`

Bears

A mailing list in digest format for gay and bisexual men who are bears themselves and for those who enjoy the company of bears. The definition of "bears" encompasses men who are variously cuddly, furry, perhaps stocky, or bearded. Mail.bears is designed to be a forum to bring together folks with similar interests for conversation, friendship, and sharing of experiences.

Keywords: Gay, Bisexuality

Audience: Gays, Bisexual Men

Contact: Steve Dyer, Brian Gollum bears-request@spdcc.COM

Details: Free

User Info: To subscribe to the list, send an e-mail message requesting a subscription to the URL address below.

To send a message to the entire list, address it to: bears@spdcc.COM

`mailto:bears-request@spdcc.COM`

BiAct-L

A discussion list for bisexual activists.

Keywords: Bisexuality, Activism

Audience: Bisexual Activists

Contact: Elaine Brennan EL406010@brownvm.brown.edu

Details: Free

User Info: To subscribe to the list, send an e-mail message requesting a subscription to the URL address below. Directions for posting to the list will be sent to you when you are added to the list.

`mailto:EL406010@brownvm.brown.edu`

BiFem-L

A mailing list for bisexual women and bi-friendly women.

Keywords: Bisexuality

Audience: Women, Bisexuals

Contact: Elaine Brennan listserv@brownvm.brown.edu

Details: Free

User Info: To subscribe, send an e-mail message requesting a subscription to the URL address below, consisting of a single line reading:

SUB BiFem-L YourFirstName YourLastName

To send a message to the entire list, address it to: BiFem-L@brownvm.brown.edu

`mailto:listserv@brownvm.brown.edu`

A B C D E F G H I J K L M N O P Q R S T U V W X Y Z

A
B
C
D
E
F
G
H
I
J
K
L
M
N
O
P
Q
R
S
T
U
V
W
X
Y
Z

Bisexu-L ★

This list is for the discussion of issues of bisexuality and the civilized exchange of relevant ideas, opinions, and experiences between members of all orientations. There is no discrimination on the basis of orientation, religion, gender, race, and so on.

Keywords: Bisexuality, Gender

Audience: Bisexuals, General Public

Contact: Bill Sklar
listserv@brownvm.brown.edu

Details: Free

User Info: To subscribe to the list, send an e-mail message to the URL address below, consisting of a single line reading:

SUB Bisexu-L YourFirstName YourLastName

To send a message to the entire list, address it to: bisexu-l@brownvm.brown.edu

`mailto:listserv@brownvm.brown.edu`

BITHRY-L ★

This list is for the theoretical discussion of bisexuality and gender issues. It is not a social group, a support group, or an announcement or news forum.

Keywords: Bisexuality, Gender

Audience: Bisexuals, Sex Therapists, Psychologists, Psychiatrists

Contact: Elaine Brennan
listserv@brownvm.brown.edu

Details: Free

User Info: To subscribe to the list, send an e-mail message to the URL address below, consisting of a single line reading:

SUB bithry-l YourFirstName YourLastName

To send a message to the entire list, address it to: bithry-l@brownvm.brown.edu

`mailto:listserv@brownvm.brown.edu`

DC-MOTSS ★

DC-MOTSS is a social mailing list for the gay, lesbian, and bisexual folks who live in the Washington Metropolitan Area—everything within approximately 50 miles of The Mall.

Keywords: Gay, Lesbian, Bisexuality, Washington DC

Audience: Gays, Lesbians, Bisexuals, Washington DC Residents

Contact: DC-MOTSS-request@vector.intercon.com

Details: Free

User Info: To subscribe to the list, send an e-mail message requesting a subscription to the URL address below.

To send a message to the entire list, address it to: DC-MOTSS-request@vector.intercon.com

`mailto:DC-MOTSS-request@vector.intercon.com`

gay-libn ★

A network for gay, lesbian, and bisexual librarians.

Keywords: Libraries, Gay, Lesbian, Bisexuality

Audience: Librarians, Gays, Lesbians, Bisexuals

Details: Free

User Info: To subscribe to the list, send an e-mail message to the URL address below consisting of a single line reading:

SUB gay-libn YourFirstName YourLastName

To send a message to the entire list, address it to: gay-libn@vm.usc.edu

`mailto:listserv@vm.usc.edu`

Ne-social-motss ★

Announcements of lesbian/gay/bisexual social events and other happenings in the Northeastern US.

Keywords: Social Events, Lesbian, Gay, Bisexuality

Audience: Lesbians, Gays, Bisexuals

Contact: ne-social-motss-request@plts.org

Details: Free

User Info: To subscribe to the list, send an e-mail message requesting a subscription to the URL address below.

`mailto:ne-social-motss-request@plts.org`

NJ-motss ★

Mailing list for gay, lesbian, and bisexual issues in New Jersey.

Keywords: Gay, Lesbian, Bisexuality, New Jersey

Audience: Gays, Lesbians, Bisexuals

Contact: majordomo@plts.org

Details: Free

User Info: To subscribe to the list, send an e-mail message to the URL address below consisting of a single line reading:

SUB NJ-motss YourFirstName YourLastName

To send a message to the entire list, address it to: NJ-motss@plts.org

`mailto: majordomo@plts.org`

NJ-motss-announce ★

Announcements of interests to New Jersey's gay, lesbian, and bisexual population.

Keywords: Gay, Lesbian, Bisexuality, New Jersey

Audience: Gays, Lesbians, Bisexuals

Contact: majordomo@plts.org

Details: Free

User Info: To subscribe to the list, send an e-mail message to the URL address shown below consisting of a single line reading:

SUB NJ-motss-announce YourFirstName YourLastName

To send a message to the entire list, address it to: NJ-motss-announce@plts.org

`mailto:majordomo@plts.org`

OUTIL (Out in Linguistics) ★

The list is open to lesbian, gay, bisexual, transsexual linguists and their friends. The only requirement is that you be willing to be out to everyone on the list. The purposes of the group are to be visible and to gather occasionally to enjoy one another's company.

Keywords: Linguistics, Gays, Lesbians, Bisexuality, Transsexuals

Audience: Linguists, Gays, Lesbians, Bisexuals, Transsexuals

Contact: Arnold Zwicky
outil-request@csli.stanford.edu

Details: Free

User Info: To subscribe to the list, send an e-mail message requesting a subscription to the URL address below.

To send a message to the entire list, address it to: outil@csli.stanford.edu

`mailto:outil-request@csli.stanford.edu`

soc.bi ★

A Usenet newsgroup providing information and discussion about bisexuality.

Keywords: Bisexuality, Social and Behavioral Science

Audience: Bisexuals, Bisexual Activists, Sociologists, Social Scientists

Details: Free

User Info: To subscribe to this Usenet newsgroup, you need access to a newsreader.

`news:soc.bi`

soc.motss ★

A Usenet newsgroup providing information and discussion about homosexuality.

Keywords: Homosexuality, Gays, Lesbians, Bisexuality

Audience: Gays, Lesbians, Bisexuals

Details: Free

User Info: To subscribe to this Usenet newsgroup, you need access to a newsreader.

`news:soc.motss`

Stonewall25

A mailing list for discussion and planning of the "Stonewall 25," an international gay/lesbian/bisexual rights march in New York City on Sunday, June 26, 1994, and the events accompanying it.

Keywords: Gay Rights, Lesbian, Bisexuality, Activism

Audience: Gays, Lesbians, Bisexuals, Activists

Contact: stonewall25-request@queernet.org

Details: Free

User Info: To subscribe to the list, send an e-mail message requesting a subscription to the URL address below.

To send a message to the entire list, address it to: stonewall25@queernet.org

`mailto:stonewall25-request@queernet.org`

bit.general

bit.general

A Usenet newsgroup providing information and discussion about Bitnet or Usenet. Contained in the bit. category are many bit.listserv discussion lists.

Keywords: Internet, Bitnet

Audience: General Public, Internet Surfers

User Info: To subscribe to this Usenet newsgroup, you need access to a newsreader.

`news:bit.general`

Bitnet

LIST REVIEW SERVICE

Explores e-mail distribution lists (primarily bitnet and ListServ lists).

Keywords: E-mail, Bitnet, Listserv

Audience: E-mail Users

Profile: Akin to book and restaurant reviews, each issue begins with a narrative description of usually one weeks worth of monitoring, then presents simple statistical data, such as the number of messages and lines, number of queries and nonqueries, number of subscribers and countries represented, list owner, location, and how to subscribe.

Contact: Raleigh C. Muns
srcmuns@umslvma.bitnet

Details: Free

User Info: To subscribe, send an e-mail message to the address below, consisting of a single line reading:

SUB listreviewservice YourFirstName YourLastName

To send a message to the entire list, address it to:

`listreviewservice@kentvm.kent.edu`

`mailto:listserv@kentvm.kent.edu`

NetMonth

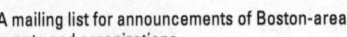

An independant guide to Bitnet.

Keywords: Bitnet, Networking

Audience: Computer Users, Internet Surfers

Contact: Philip Baczewski
nmonthed@vm.marist.edu

Details: Costs

User Info: To subscribe, send an e-mail message to the address below, consisting of a single line reading:

netmonth YourFirstName YourLastName

To send a message to the entire list, address it to: netmonth@vm.marist.edu

`mailto:listserv@vm.marist.edu`

BIVERSITY

BIVERSITY

A mailing list for announcements of Boston-area events and organizations.

Keywords: Boston

Audience: Boston Residents

Contact: liz@ai.mit.edu

Details: Free

User Info: To subscribe to the list, send an e-mail message requesting a subscription to the URL address below.

`mailto:liz@ai.mit.edu`

BKRTCY (Bankruptcy Library)

BKRTCY (Bankruptcy Library)

★★★★

The Federal Bankruptcy library is a comprehensive collection of primary and secondary legal research materials pertaining to bankruptcy issues.

Keywords: Law, Filings, Bankruptcy

Audience: Lawyers, Bankers

Profile: The Federal Bankruptcy library is a comprehensive collection of primary and secondary legal research materials that includes case law, rules, statutory and regulatory materials, legal publications, accounting literature, and other resources pertaining to bankruptcy issues.

Contact: New Sales Group at (800) 227-4908 or (513) 859-5398 inside the US, or (513) 865-7981 for all inquires outside the US.

User Info: To subscribe, contact Mead directly.

To examine the Lexis user guide, you can access it at the ftp site of the University of Texas at Austin at the URL address: ftp://ftp.cc.utexas.edu

The files are in: /pub/ref-services/LEXIS

`telnet://nex.meaddata.com`

`http://www.meaddata.com`

Black/African Related Online Information

Black/African Related Online Information

This is a list of online information storage sites that contain a significant amount of information pertaining to Black or African people, culture, and issues around the world.

Keywords: Cultural Studies, Race, Africa, African Studies

Sponsor: AfriInfo

Audience: Students, African-Americans, Africans

Contact: McGee
mcgee@epsilon.eecs.nwu.edu

Details: Free

`ftp://ftp.netcom.com/pub/amcgee/my_african_related_lists/afrisite.msg`

Blacksburg Electronic Village Gopher

Blacksburg Electronic Village Gopher

The Blacksburg Electronic Village is a project to link an entire town in southwestern Virginia with a 21st-century telecommunications infrastructure. This infrastructure will bring a useful set of information services and interactive communications facilities into the daily activities of citizens and businesses.

Keywords: Community Networking, Networking, Telecommunications

Sponsor: Town of Blacksburg, Virginia, USA

Audience: Activists, Policymakers, Community Leaders, Government

A B C D E F G H I J K L M N O P Q R S T U V W X Y Z

A
B
C
D
E
F
G
H
I
J
K
L
M
N
O
P
Q
R
S
T
U
V
W
X
Y
Z

Profile: This community gopher server, run by the town of Blacksburg, contains information about Blacksburg and how it is building its electronic infrastructure. It includes a list of Blacksburg-area BBSs, instructions for local residents to get an account on the town's BBS, and a section called "Village Schoolhouse."

Details: Costs

`gopher://morse.cns.vt.edu`

Blindness

Blind News Digest

This is a moderated mailing list in digest format that deals with all aspects of visual impairment and blindness.

Keywords: Blindness, Disabilities

Audience: Blind People, Health Care Providers, Therapists

Contact: wtm@bunker.afd.olivetti.com

Details: Free

User Info: To subscribe to the list, send the message:

SUB BlindNws YourFirstName YourLastName to listserv@vm1.nodak.edu

Or send e-mail requesting a subscription to wtm@bunker.afd.olivetti.com

`mailto:wtm@bunker.afd.olivetti.com`

BlindFam

This is not readable★★

The Blindness and Family Life mailing list is devoted to a discussion of the day-to-day impact of this disability on families, and the patterns of domestic life associated with blindness.

Keywords: Blindness, Disabilities, Family

Audience: Blind People, Families, Health Care Professionals, Therapists

Contact: Roger Myers, Patt Bromberger Meyers@ab.wvnet.edu, Patt@squid.tram.com

User Info: To subscribe, send an e-mail message to the URL address below, consisting of a single line reading:

SUB BlindFam YourFirstName YourLastName.

To send a message to the entire list, address it to: BlindFam@sjuvm.stjohns.edu

`mailto:listserv@sjuvm.stjohns.edu`

Disability-Related Resources

★★

A collection of information that includes newsletters for deaf/blind issues, electronic resources for the deaf, and a section on Chronic Fatigue Syndrome.

Keywords: Disabilities, Deafness, Blindness, Chronic Fatigue Syndrome

---

Sponsor: University of Washington DO-IT Program

Audience: Deaf and Disabled People, Health Care Professionals

Contact: Sheryl Burgstahler, Ph.D. doit@u.washington.edu

`gopher://hawking.u.washington.edu`

Blues

Blues (St. Louis Blues)

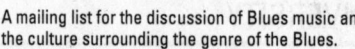

Provides information, game reports, stats, discussion, and more on the St. Louis Blues of the National Hockey League.

Keywords: Hockey, Sports

Audience: Hockey Enthusiasts

Contact: Joe Ashkar blues@medicine.wustl.edu

User Info: To subscribe to the list, send an e-mail message requesting a subscription to the URL address below.

To send a message to the entire list, address it to: blues@medicine.wustl.edu

`mailto:blues@medicine.wustl.edu`

Blues-L

★

A mailing list for the discussion of Blues music and the culture surrounding the genre of the Blues.

Keywords: Blues Music, Musical Genres

Audience: Blues Enthusiasts

Contact: listserv@brownvm.brown.edu

Details: Free

User Info: To subscribe to the list, send an e-mail message to the URL address below, consisting of a single line reading:

SUB blues-l YourFirstName YourLastName

To send a message to the entire list, address it to: blues-l@brownvm.brown.edu

Notes: To receive the list in digest form: once you get acknowledgment from the listserver that you are on the list, send another message to the URL address below with the message: SET Blues-L Dig

`mailto:listserv@brownvm.brown.edu`

BMW

BMW

This is a discussion of cars made by BMW. Both regular and digest forms are available.

Keywords: BMW, Automobiles

Audience: Automobile Enthusiasts, Automobile Racers, BMW Enthusiasts, Automobile Mechanics

Contact: Richard Welty bmw-request@balltown.cma.com

Details: Free

User Info: To subscribe to the list, send an e-mail message requesting a subscription to the URL address below.

To send a message to the entire list, address it to: bmw@balltown.cma.com

`mailto:bmw-request@balltown.cma.com`

BMW Motorcycles

This is a discussion of all years and models of BMW motorcycles.

Keywords: BMW, Motorcycles

Audience: Motorcycle Enthusiasts, BMW Enthusiasts

Contact: bmw-request@rider.cactus.org

Details: Free

User Info: To subscribe to the list, send an e-mail message requesting a subscription to the URL address below.

To send a message to the entire list, address it to: bmw@rider.cactus.org

`mailto:bmw-request@rider.cactus.org`

Boating

The Nautical Bookshelf

Catalog and ordering information for Nautical Bookshelf's collection of books on Sailing and other water sports.

Keywords: Boating, Power Boating, Sailing, Sports

Sponsor: Nautical Bookshelf

Audience: Boating Enthusiasts, Sailors

Contact: staff@nautical.com

`gopher://gopher.nautical.com`

Boise State University Library

Boise State University Library

The library's holdings are large and wide-ranging and contain significant collections in many fields.

Keywords: Jordan (Len, Senatorial Papers of), Church (Frank, Senatorial Papers of), Poetry (American)

Audience: General Public, Researchers, Librarians, Document Delivery Professionals

Details: Free

Notes: Expect: login; Send: catalyst

`telnet://catalyst.idbsu.edu`

A
B
C
D
E
F
G
H
I
J
K
L
M
N
O
P
Q
R
S
T
U
V
W
X
Y
Z

Bong (Depeche Mode)

Bong (Depeche Mode)

Bong is for the discussion of the mostly electronic band Depeche Mode and related projects like Recoil. Depeche Mode incorporate synth-pop, industrial dance, Kraftwerkian electro, ambient, techno, and rock influences in a dark blend of innovative alternative music.

Keywords: Musical Groups, Pop Music, Electronic Music

Audience: Pop Music Enthusiasts, Depeche Mode Enthusiasts, Musicians

Contact: Colin Smiley
bong-request@lestat.compaq.com

Details: Free

User Info: To subscribe to the list, send an e-mail message requesting a subscription to the URL address below.

To send a message to the entire list, address it to: bong@lestat.compaq.com

`mailto:bong-request@lestat.compaq.com`

Bonsai

alt.bonsai

A Usenet newsgroup providing information and discussion about Bonsai gardening.

Keywords: Bonsai Trees, Japan, Gardening, Landscaping

Audience: Gardeners, Bonsai Enthusiasts

User Info: To subscribe to this Usenet newsgroup, you need access to a newsreader.

`news:alt.bonsai`

Bonsai

This list has been set up to facilitate discussion of the art and craft of bonsai (the Oriental art of miniaturizing trees and plants into forms that mimic nature) and related art forms.

Keywords: Bonsai Trees, Japan, Gardening, Landscaping

Audience: Bonsai Enthusiasts, Horticulturists, Gardeners

Contact: Dan@foghorn.pass.wayne.edu

Details: Free

User Info: To subscribe to the list, send an e-mail message to the URL address below, consisting of a single line reading:

SUB bonsai YourFirstName YourLastName

To send a message to the entire list, address it to: bonsai@cms.cc.wayne.edu

Notes: Everyone interested, whether novice or professional, is invited to subscribe.

`mailto:listserv@cms.cc.wayne.edu`

Book Arts

University of Hawaii Library

The library's holdings are large and wide-ranging and contain significant collections in many fields.

Keywords: Asia, European Documents, Book Arts, Hawaii

Audience: General Public, Researchers, Librarians, Document Delivery Professionals

Details: Free

Expect: enter class, Send: LIB

`telnet://starmaster.uhcc.hawaii.edu`

Book Reviews

alt.books.reviews

A Usenet conference devoted to reviews of books, especially science fiction and computer science books.

Keywords: Literature (General), Computer Science, Science Fiction, Book Reviews

Audience: General Public, Publishers, Educators, Librarians, Booksellers

Profile: Alt.books.reviews (a.b.r. for short) is a forum for posting reviews of books of interest to readers, school and public librarians, bookstores, publishers, teachers and professors, and others who desire an "educated opinion" of a book. This is an unmoderated newsgroup.

Contact: sbrock@csn.org.

Details: Free

To participate in a Usenet newsgroup, you need access to a "newsreader."

Notes: The reviews in alt.books.reviews are archived at csn.org. Ftp to csn.org; login: anonymous; password: your complete e-mail address. At the ftp prompt, type: cd pub/alt.books.reviews

`news:alt.books.reviews`

Book Review Index

This database contains references to more than 2.5 million citations to reviews of approximately 1.5 million distinct book and periodical titles.

Keywords: Book Reviews, Periodicals, Publications

Sponsor: Gale Research, Inc., Detroit, MI, USA

Audience: Publishing Professionals, Writers, Researchers

Profile: The database covers every review published since 1969 in nearly 500 periodicals and newspapers. Each record includes the author and title of the work being reviewed, journal name, date of review, and page number.

Document type indications are also included if the work is a periodical; a reference work; a children's book, periodical, or reference book; or a young adult book, periodical, or reference book. Book Review Index corresponds to the print publication of the same name. Periodicals indexed range from the Harvard Business Review to the Center for Children's Books: Bulletin, and from the American Scholar to Psychology Today. General interest magazines such as *Ms.*, *Time*, *The New Yorker*, and *Atlantic* are covered, as are specialized periodicals like *Flying*, *Yachting*, and *National Genealogical Society Quarterly*.

Contact: Dialog in the US at (800) 334-2564, Dialog internationally at country specific locations.

Details: Costs

User Info: To subscribe, contact Dialog directly.

`telnet://dialog.com`

Erofile

This newsletter provides reviews of the latest books associated with French and Italian studies in fields such as literary criticism, cultural studies, film studies, pedagogy, and software.

Keywords: Italian Studies, French Studies, Book Reviews

Audience: French Students, Italian Students, Book Reviewers

Details: Free

`mailto:erofile@ucsbuxa.ucsb.edu`

Books

Books In Print

This is a major source of information on books currently published and in-print in the United States.

Keywords: Books, Publications

Sponsor: R.R. Bowker, New York, NY, US

Audience: General Public, Writers, Researchers

Profile: The database provides a record of forthcoming books, books in-print, and books out-of-print. Scientific, technical, medical, scholarly, and popular works, as well as children's books, are included in the file. The file corresponds to several print publications: Books in Print, Subject Guide to Books in Print, Books in Print Supplement, Paperbound Books in Print, Forthcoming Books, Law Books in Print, Subject Guide to Forthcoming Books, and Scientific and Technical Books & Serials in Print. Records in Books In Print include basic bibliographic information (author, title, publisher, date), as well as L.C. card number, International Standard Book Number (ISBN), and price.

A
B
C
D
E
F
G
H
I
J
K
L
M
N
O
P
Q
R
S
T
U
V
W
X
Y
Z

Contact: Dialog in the US at (800) 334-2564, Dialog internationally at country specific locations.

User Info: To subscribe, contact Dialog directly.

`telnet://dialog.com`

Books Online

 ★★★

This web site contains hundreds of full-text online books, including many classics such as *Anna Karenina* and *The Complete Works of William Shakespeare*. Also provides links to other book resources and has a searchable index.

Keywords: Books, Electronic Media

Audience: Readers, Literary Scholars

Contact: spok@cs.cmu.edu

`gopher://calypso-2.oit.unc.edu/11/`
`sunsite.d/book.d`

`http://www.cs.cmu.edu/Web/books.html`

Electronic Books

 ★★

A collection of books available as ASCII text files, including classics of antiquity (Aristotle, Virgil, Sophocles, the Bible), as well as more contemporary works of fiction and nonfiction by authors ranging from Dostoevsky to Martin Luther King, Jr.

Keywords: Books, Online Books, Literature (Contemporary), Literature (General)

Sponsor: The Blacksburg Electronic Village (BEV) at Virginia Tech

Audience: General Public, Historians

Contact: BEV Gopher Administrators gopher@gopher.vt.edu

`gopher://gopher.vt.edu`

Moon Travel Handbooks

 ★★

Moon Publications' gopher features a travel newsletter, as well as excerpts and ordering information for their travel guides.

Keywords: Travel, Books

Sponsor: Moon Publications

Audience: International Travelers, General Public

Contact: gopher@moon.com

Notes: Also see Moon Publications' hypertext exhibit, Big Island of Hawaii Handbook, at http://bookweb.cwis.uci.edu:8042.

`gopher://gopher.moon.com`

Mystery

 ★

This mailing list reviews and discusses mystery and detective fiction, including works on film, television, and radio.

Keywords: Mystery Fiction, Detective Fiction, Books

Audience: Mystery Enthusiasts

Details: Free

User Info: To subscribe to the list, send an e-mail message requesting a subscription to the URL address below.

`mailto:mystery-request@introl.com`

Online BookStore (OBS)

 ★★★

Offers full text (fiction and nonfiction) in a variety of electronic formats, free and for a fee.

Keywords: Online Books, Books, ShareWord, Fiction, Nonfiction Books

Sponsor: Editorial Inc./OBS

Audience: General Public, Reading Enthusiasts

Profile: Started in 1992, the OBS offers a variety of full-text titles.

Contact: Laura Fillmore laura@editorial.com

Details: Costs

User Info: To subscribe to the list, send an e-mail message requesting a subscription to the URL address below.

`mailto:laura@editorial.com`

Publishing

 ★★

This directory is a compilation of information resources focused on publishing.

Keywords: Publishing, Books

Audience: Publishers, Book Dealers, Book Readers

Details: Free

`ftp://una.hh.lib.umich.edu/70/`
`inetdirsstacks/publishing:robinson`

rec.arts.books

 ★

A Usenet newsgroup providing information and discussion about a wide variety of books.

Keywords: Books

Audience: Readers, Writers

Details: Free

User Info: To subscribe to this Usenet newsgroup, you need access to a newsreader.

`news:rec.arts.books`

rec.arts.comics.misc

 ★

A Usenet newsgroup providing information and discussion about comic books and graphic novels.

Keywords: Comic Books, Books

Audience: Comics Enthusiasts, Readers, Writers

Details: Free

User Info: To subscribe to this Usenet newsgroup, you need access to a newsreader.

`news:rec.arts.comics.misc`

The MIT Press Online Catalogs

 ★★

A descriptive listing of recent books and current journals published by the MIT Press.

Keywords: Academia, Books, Publishing, Technology

Sponsor: The MIT Press, Cambridge, Massachusetts, USA.

Audience: Reseachers, Scholars, University Students, Technical Professionals

Profile: Contains a keyword-searchable index of books published in the years 1993 to 1994, as well as current journals covering computational and cognitive sciences, architecture, photography, art and literary theory, economics, environmental science, and linguistics.

Contact: ehling@mitpress.mit.edu

Notes: Coverage: 1993 to present; updated semiannually. MIT Press can also be accessed by calling (800) 356-0343.

`http://www-mitpress.mit.edu`

`gopher://gopher.mit.edu`

Books (Antiquarian)

Princeton University Online Manuscripts Catalog Library

 ★★

The library's holdings are large and wide-ranging. They contain significant collections in many fields.

Keywords: Books (Antiquarian), Dickens (Charles), Disraeli (Benjamin), Eliot (George), Hardy (Thomas), Kingsley (Charles), Trollope (Anthony)

Audience: General Public, Researchers, Librarians, Document Delivery Professionals

Details: Free

            Expect: VM370 logo, Send: <cr>; Expect: Welcome screen, Send: folio <cr>; Expect: Welcome screen for FOLIO, Send: <cr>; Expect: List of choices, Send: 3 <cr>; To exit: type: logoff

`telnet://pucc.princeton.edu`

Bosnia

BosNet

 ★

BosNet is a group/forum run by volunteers. Its goals are to present and distribute information relevant to the events in/about the Republic of Bosnia-Herzegovina (RB&H) and to initiate and coordinate various initiatives, and so on.

Keywords: Bosnia, Herzegovina

Audience: Bosnians, Political Scientists, Students

Contact: listproc@cu23.crl.aecl.ca

Details: Free

User Info: To subscribe to the list, send an e-mail message requesting a subscription to the URL address below.

To send a message to the entire list, address it to: BosNet@cu23.crl.aecl.ca

Notes: The contributions/opinions presented on BosNet do not necessarily reflect the personal opinions of the moderator or the member(s) of the Editorial Board. To participate in a discussion on a specific topic related to RB&H, please consider Usenet newsgroup soc.culture.bosna-herzegovina.

`mailto:listproc@cu23.crl.aecl.ca`

Boston

BIVERSITY

A mailing list for announcements of Boston-area events and organizations.

Keywords: Boston

Audience: Boston Residents

Contact: liz@ai.mit.edu

Details: Free

User Info: To subscribe to the list, send an e-mail message requesting a subscription to the URL address below.

`mailto:liz@ai.mit.edu`

Boston Bruins

This list is for discussion of the Boston Bruins of the National Hockey League and their farm teams. Also available as a digest.

Keywords: Boston, Hockey, Sports

Audience: Hockey Enthusiasts, Boston Residents, Sports Enthusiasts

Contact: Garry Knox
            bruins-request@cristal.umd.edu

Details: Free

User Info: To subscribe to the list, send an e-mail message requesting a subscription to the URL address below.

To send a message to the entire list, address it to: bruins@cristal.umd.edu

`mailto:bruins-request@cristal.umd.edu`

Botanical Taxonomy

The University of Minnesota Library System (LUMINA)

The library's holdings are large and wide-ranging and contain significant collections in many fields.

Keywords: Immigration (History of), Ethnic Studies, Horticulture, Equine Research, Botanical Taxonomy, Quantum Physics, Native American Studies, Holmes (Sherlock)

Audience: General Public, Researchers, Librarians, Document Delivery Professionals

Contact: Craig D. Rice
            cdr@acc.stolaf.edu

Details: Free

`telnet://lumina.lib.umn.edu`

Botany

AGRICOLA

The AGRICOLA database of the National Agricultural Library (NAL) provides comprehensive coverage of worldwide journal literature and monographs on agriculture and related subjects.

Keywords: Agriculture, Animal Studies, Botany, Entomology

Sponsor: US National Agricultural Library, Beltsville, MD, USA

Audience: Agronomists, Botanists, Chemists, Entomologists

Profile: Related subjects include: animal studies, botany, chemistry, entomology, fertilizers, forestry, hydroponics, soils, and more.

Contact: Dialog in the US at (800) 334-2564, Dialog internationally at country-specific locations.

User Info: To subscribe, contact Dialog directly.

Notes: Coverage: 1970 to the present; updated monthly.

`telnet://dialog.com`

Biosis Previews

The database encompasses the entire field of life sciences and covers original research reports and reviews in biological and biomedical areas. This includes field, laboratory, clinical, experimental, and theoretical work. The traditional areas of biology, including botany, zoology, and microbiology are covered, as well as the related fields such as plant and animal science, agriculture, pharmacology, and ecology.

Keywords: Biology, Botany, Zoology, Microbiology, Plant Science, Animal Science, Agriculture, Pharmacology, Ecology, Biochemistry, Biophysics, Bioengineering

Sponsor: Biosis

Audience: Librarians, Researchers, Students, Biologists, Botanists, Zoologists, Scientists, Taxonomists

Contact: CDP Technologies Sales Department (800) 950-2035, ext. 400.

User Info: To subscribe, contact CDP Technologies directly.

`telnet://cdplus@cdplus.com`

CP

Topics of interest to the group include the cultivation and propagation of CP's (carnivorous plants), field observations of CP's, sources of CP material, and CP trading between members. The discussion is not moderated, and usually consists of short messages offering plants for trade, asking CP questions and advice, relating experiences with plant propagation, and so on. The group also maintains archives of commercial plant sources and members growing lists.

Keywords: Carnivorous Plants, Botany

Audience: Horticulturists, Botanists

Contact: Rick Walker
            walker@hpl-opus.hpl.hp.com

User Info: To subscribe to the list, send an e-mail message to the address below consisting of a single line reading:

SUB CP YourFirstName YourLastName

To send a message to the entire list, address it to: CP@hpl-opus.hpl.hp.com

`mailto:listserv@hpl-opus.hpl.hp.com`

The University of Kansas Library

The library's holdings are large and wide-ranging and contain significant collections in many fields.

Keywords: Botany, Chinese Studies, Cartography (History of), Kansas, Opera, Ornithology, Joyce (James), Yeats (William Butler), Walpole (Sir Robert, Collections of)

Audience: General Public, Researchers, Librarians, Document Delivery Professionals

Contact: John S. Miller

Details: Free

Expect: Username, Send: relay

`telnet://kuhub.cc.ukans.edu`

Botany (History of)

The University of Notre Dame Library

The library's holdings are large and wide-ranging and contain significant collections in many fields.

Keywords: Music (Irish), Ireland, Botany (History of), Ecology, Entomology, Parasitology, Aquatic Biology, Universities (History of), Paleography

Audience: General Public, Researchers, Librarians, Document Delivery Professionals

Details: Free

Expect: ENTER COMMAND OR HELP:, Send: library; To leave, type x on the command line and press the enter key. At the ENTER COMMAND OR HELP: prompt, type bye and press the enter key.

`telnet://irishmvs.cc.nd.edu`

Bowker Biographical Directory

Bowker Biographical Directory ★★

This is a collection of biographical directories that correspond to certain Bowker print publications.

Keywords: Biographies

Sponsor: R.R. Bowker, a Reed Reference Publishing Company, a division of Reed Publishing (US) Inc., New Providence, NJ, US

Audience: General Public, Writers, Researchers

Profile: The database corresponds to the Bowker print publications as follows: American Men and Women of Science, covering over 122,500 leading US and Canadian scientists and engineers in the physical, biological, and related sciences; Who's Who in American Art, covering some 7,000 North American artists, critics, curators, administrators, librarians, historians, collectors, and dealers; and Who's Who in American Politics, covering over 25,400 American political decision-makers at all levels from federal to local government.

Contact: Dialog in the US at (800) 334-2564, Dialog internationally at country specific locations.

Details: Costs

User Info: To subscribe, contact Dialog directly.

`telnet://dialog.com`

Boy Scouts

Eagles ★

This list provides a forum for Boy Scouts, Scouters, and former Scouts who are gay/bisexual to discuss how they can apply pressure to the BSA to change their homophobic policies.

Keywords: Boy Scouts, Gays, Lesbians

Audience: Gays, Lesbians, Boy Scouts, Former Boy Scouts

Contact: eagles-request@flash.usc.edu

Details: Free

User Info: To subscribe to the list, send an e-mail message requesting a subscription to the URL address below.

To send a message to the entire list, address it to: eagles-request@flash.usc.edu

`mailto:eagles-request@flash.usc.edu`

Boyler-Moore Theorem Prover

nqthm-users ★

Discussion of theorem proving using the Boyler-Moore theorem prover, NQTHM. Offers lore, advice, information, discussion, and help.

Keywords: Computer Programs, NQTHM, Boyler-Moore Theorem Prover

Audience: NQTHM Theorem Users

Contact: nqthm-users-request@cli.com

Details: Free

User Info: To subscribe to the list, send an e-mail message requesting a subscription to the URL address below.

To send a message to the entire list, address it to: nqthm-users@cli.com

`mailto:nqthm-users@cli.com`

BPM

BPM ★

This list is for novice and professional DJs. Discussion often covers music releases, DJing techniques, and turntable maintenance.

Keywords: Disk Jockeys, Music

Audience: Disk Jockeys, Music Enthusiasts

Contact: Simon Gatrall bpm-request@andrew.cmu.edu

Details: Free

User Info: To subscribe to the list, send an e-mail message requesting a subscription to the URL address below.

To send a message to the entire list, address it to: bpm@andrew.cmu.edu

`mailto:bpm-request@andrew.cmu.edu`

Brain Research

Neurosciences Internet Resource Guide ★★★

A comprehensive Internet resource addressing biological, chemical, medical, engineering, and computer science aspects of neurobiology.

Keywords: Neurobiology, Neuroscience, Brain Research

Sponsor: The University of Michigan School of Information and Library

Audience: Neuroscientists, Neurobiologists

Profile: This resource provides links to journal articles, tutorials on neuroimaging and neurobiology, moderated newsgroups, and international forums, all of which address issues surrounding the field of neuroscience.

Contact: Sheryl Cormicle, Steve Bonario sherylc@sils.umich.edu, sbonario@umich.edu

`http://http2.sils.umich.edu/Public/nirg/nirg1.html`

Brazil

Base de Dados Tropical (BDT) ★★

Base de Dados Tropical (Tropical Data Base) is a collection of information related to biodiversity and biotechnology.

Keywords: Biodiversity, Biotechnology, Brazil

Sponsor: Fundacao Tropical de Pesquisas e Tecnologia ÒAndre TornselloÓ, Campinas, SP, Brazil

Audience: Biotechnologists, Scientists, Researchers

Contact: manager@bdt.ftpt.br

Details: Free

`gopher://bdt.ftpt.br`

Brasil ★

This is a mailing list for general discussion about and information on Brazil. Portuguese is the main language of discussion.

Keywords: Brazil, Portuguese Language

Audience: Brazilians, Portuguese Speakers

Contact: B. R. Araujo Neto bras-net-request@cs.ucla.edu

Details: Free

User Info: To subscribe to the list, send an e-mail message requesting a subscription to the URL address below. Include your name, e-mail, phone number, address, and topics of interest.

To send a message to the entire list, address it to: bras-net@cs.ucla.edu

`mailto:bras-net-request@cs.ucla.edu`

NIBNews - A Monthly Electronic Bulletin About Medical Informatics ★

Disseminates information about Brazilian and Latin American activities, people, information, events, publications, software, and so on, involving computer applications in health care, medicine, and biology.

Keywords: Health Care, Biology, Brazil, Latin America, South America, Medicine

Audience: Health Care Professionals, Biologists

Contact: Renato M. E. Sabbatini
SABBATINI@BRUC.BITNET

Details: Free

E-mail a short notice to:

`mailto:sabbatini@ccvax.unicamp.br`

BRIDGE

BRIDGE

An online public access catalog, this PALS-based resource provides access to the collections of two institutions, St. Boniface University and the Manitoba General Hospital.

Keywords: Medicine, Library

Sponsor: St. Boniface University, and the Manitoba General Hospital Libraries

Audience: Health Professionals, Students, Medical Educators

Details: Free

`telnet://BE@umopac.umanitoba.ca`

Brit-Iron

Brit-Iron

The purpose of this list is to provide a friendly forum in which riders, owners, and admirers of British motorcycles can share information and experiences. A list of parts sources and shops that repair these classic machines is maintained. All makes are welcome, from AJS to Vellocette.

Keywords: Motorcycles

Audience: British Motorcycle Enthusiasts, Motorcycle Enthusiasts

Contact: cstringe@indiana.edu

Details: Free

User Info: To subscribe to the list, send an e-mail message requesting a subscription to the URL address below.

To send a message to the entire list, address it to: Brit-Iron@indiana.edu

`mailto:Brit-Iron@indiana.edu`

Britain

British Online Yellow Pages

A directory of British firms and organizations; searches of the database are possible by firm, location, or product.

Keywords: Britain, Business (British)

Sponsor: British Telecom

Audience: General Public, Market Researchers

Details: Free

`telnet://sun.nsf.ac.uk`

veggies

Vegetarian matters in Britain.

Keywords: Vegetarianism, Britain, Food

Audience: Vegetarians

Details: Free

User Info: To subscribe to the list, send an e-mail message requesting a subscription to the URL address below.

To send a message to the entire list, address it to: veggies@ncl.ak.uk

`mailto:veggies-request@ncl.ac.uk`

Britannica Online

Britannica Online

This web site provides an information service for Encyclopaedia Britannica, Inc. Its database allows for keyword searches, and also includes experimental articles.

Keywords: Information Retrieval, Databases

Sponsor: Encyclopaedia Britannica, Inc.

Audience: Researchers, Educators, Students

Contact: support@eb.com

Details: Costs

`http://www.eb.com`

British

British-Cars

This is a discussion of owning, repairing, racing, cursing, and loving British cars, predominantly sports cars, with some talk of Land Rovers and sedans. Also available as a digest.

Keywords: Automobiles, Britiain

Audience: British Automobile Enthusiasts, Automobile Enthusiasts, Automobile Mechanics

Contact: Mark Bradakis
british-cars-request@autox.team.net, british-cars-request@hoosier.cs.utah.edu

Details: Free

User Info: To subscribe to the list, send an e-mail message requesting a subscription to the URL address below.

To send a message to the entire list, address it to: british-cars@autox.team.net

`mailto:british-cars-request@autox.team.net`

British National Register of Archives

A multi-volume electronic guide to accessing a wide-variety of archival materials and repositories in the United Kingdom.

Keywords: United Kingdom, History, Business (British), Information Retrieval

Sponsor: Coombspapers Social Sciences Research Data Bank at ANU (Australian National University).

Audience: Researchers, Anglophiles, Archioists

Contact: Dr. T. Matthew Ciolek
tmciolek@coombs.anu.edu.au

`gopher://coombs.anu.edu.au`

`ftp:/coombs.anu.edu.au/coombspapers/otherarchives/uk-nra-archives/`

`http://coombs.anu.edu.au/CoombsHome.html`

British Commonwealth Law

University of Texas at Austin Tarlton Law Library

The library's holdings are large and wide-ranging and contain significant collections in many fields.

Keywords: British Commonwealth Law, Constitutional Law, Law (International), Human Rights

Audience: Researchers, Students, General Public

Details: Free

Expect: Login, Send: Library

`telnet://tallons.law.utexas.edu`

British Plays (19th-C.)

Indiana University Libraries

The library's holdings are large and wide-ranging and contain significant collections in many fields.

Keywords: Literature (English), Literature (American), 1640-Present, British Plays (19th-C.), Western Americana, Railway History, Aristotle (Texts of), Lafayette (Marquis de), Handel (G.F.), Austrian History, Antiquarian Books, Rare Books, French Opera (19th-C.), Drama (British) ,

Audience: General Public, Researchers, Librarians, Document Delivery Professionals

Details: Free

Expect: User ID prompt, Send: GUEST

`telnet://iuis.ucs.indiana.edu`

A
B
C
D
E
F
G
H
I
J
K
L
M
N
O
P
Q
R
S
T
U
V
W
X
Y
Z

Broadcasting

FM-10

A discussion of modifications, enhancements, and uses of the Ramsey FM-10 and other BA-1404 based FM Stereo broadcasters; some discussion of the FM pirate radio, as well.

Keywords: Radio, Broadcasting

Audience: Broadcasters, Radio Broadcasters

Details: Free

User Info: To subscribe to the list, send an e-mail message requesting a subscription to the URL address below.

To send a message to the entire list, address it to: fm-10@dg-rtp.dg.com

`mailto:fm-10-request@dg-rtp.dg.com`

Multicast

Discussion of multicast and broadcast issues in an open systems interconnection environment.

Keywords: Multicasting, Broadcasting

Audience: Multicasters, Broadcasting Professionals

Details: Free

User Info: To subscribe to the list, send an e-mail message requesting subscription to the URL address below.

`mailto:multicast-request@arizona.edu`

Brown University Library

Brown University Library

The Brown libraries contain approximately 1.5 million volumes, including historical archives of early American imprints and biomedical engineering holdings.

Keywords: Libraries, Research

Audience: General Public, Researchers

Contact: Howard Pasternick
blips15@brownvm.brown.edu

Details: Free

Notes: At the Brown logon screen: tab to command field, Enter Dial Josiah, tab to Josiah choice on the screen.

`telnet://brownvm.brown.edu`

`telnet://library.brown.edu`

BTHS-ENews-L

BTHS-ENews-L

This list provides an open forum for students, teachers, and alumni of Brooklyn Technical High School.

Keywords: New York, Education (K-12)

Audience: Teachers, Students, Educators

Contact: listserv@Cornell.edu

Details: Free

User Info: To subscribe to the list, send an e-mail message to the URL address below, consisting of a single line reading:

SUB BTHS-ENews-l YourFirstName YourLastName

To send a message to the entire list, address it to: BTHS-ENews-l@Cornell.edu

`mailto:listserv@Cornell.edu`

Buddhism

ANU (Australian National University) Buddhism Database

A searchable database of messages from the BUDDHA-L listserv, an academic forum for the discussion of Buddhism. It currently contains archives for messages posted in 1993-94.

Keywords: Religion, Asian Studies, Buddhism

Sponsor: COOMBSQUEST Social Sciences & Humanities Information Facility at ANU (Australian National University), Canberra, Australia

Audience: Buddhists, Religious Studies Instructors, Asian Studies Educators

Contact: Dr. T.Matthew Ciolek
coombspapers@coombs.anu.edu.au

`gopher://cheops.anu.edu.au /Coombs-db/ANU-Buddha-l.src`

`http://coombs.anu.edu.au/WWWVL-AsianStudies.html`

Budget

Budget of the United States (1994)

Provides the full-text of the 1994 budget of the United States.

Keywords: Budget, Government (US), Finance

Audience: Politicians, Lawyers, Journalists, Economists, Students, US Citizens

Details: Free

Notes: This document is over one megabyte in size and thus takes a couple of minutes to load onto the screen.

`gopher:// wiretap.spies.com/00/Gov/US-Gov/budget.94`

Bugs-386bsd

Bugs-386bsd

This list is for 386bsd bugs, patches, and ports.

Keywords: Operating Systems, 386bsd

Audience: Computer Operators, Computer Scientists, Computer Engineers

Contact: bugs-386bsd-request@ms.uky.edu

Details: Free

User Info: To subscribe to the list, send an e-mail message requesting a subscription to the URL address below.

To send a message to the entire list, address it to: bugs-386bsd@ms.uky.edu

Notes: Requirement to join: an interest in actively working on 386bsd to improve the operating system for use by yourself and others.

`mailto:bugs-386bsd-request@ms.uky.edu`

Builder Xcessory

BX-Talk

BX-talk has been created for users of Builder Xcessory (BX) to discuss problems (and solutions) and ideas for using BX, which is a graphical user interface builder for Motif applications, and is sold by ICS. Note that this list is not associated with ICS (the authors of BX) in any way.

Keywords: Builder Xcessory, Graphical User Interfaces

Audience: Graphics Experts, Computer Operators

Contact: Darci L. Chapman
bx-talk-request@qiclab.scn.rain.com

Details: Free

User Info: To subscribe to the list, send an e-mail message requesting a subscription to the URL address below.

To send a message to the entire list, address it to: bx-talk@qiclab.scn.rain.com

Notes: This list is unmoderated.

`mailto:bx-talk-request@qiclab.scn.rain.com`

Building

Architecture, Building

This directory is a compilation of information resources focused on architecture.

Keywords: Architecture, Building, Construction, AEC

Audience: Architects, Builders, Civil Engineers

Contact: J. Brown

Details: Free

```
ftp://una.hh.lib.umich.edu/70/
inetdirsstacks/archi:brown
```

Bulgaria

CEE Environmental Libraries Database

A directory of over 300 libraries and environmental information centers in Central Eastern Europe that specalize in, or maintain significant collections of information about, the environment, ecology, sustainable living, or conservation. The database concentrates on six Central Eastern European countries: Bulgaria, Czech Republic, Hungary, Romania, Slovakia, and Poland.

Keywords: Central Eastern Europe, Environment, Sustainable Living, Bulgaria, Czech Republic, Hungary, Romania, Slovakia, Poland.

Sponsor: The Wladyslaw Poniecki Charitable Foundation, Inc.

Audience: Environmentalists, Green Movement, Librarians, Community Builders, Sustainable Living Specialists.

Profile: This database is the product of an Environmental Training Project (ETP) that was funded in 1992 by the US Agency for International Development as a 5-year cooperative agreement with a consortium headed by the University of Minnesota (US AID Cooperative Agreement Number EUR-0041-A-002-2020). Other members of the consortium include the University of PittsburghÕs Center for Hazardous Materials Research, The Institute for Sustainable Communities, and the World Wildlife Fund. The Wladyslaw Poniecki Charitable Foundation, Inc., was a subcontractor to the World Wildlife Fund and published the Directory of Libraries and Environmental Information Centers in Central Eastern Europe: A Locator/ Directory . This gopher database consists of an electronic version of the printed directory, subsequently modified and updated online. Access to the data is facilitated by a WAIS search engine that makes it possible to retrieve information about libraries, subject area specializations, personnel, and so on.

Contact: Doug Kahn, CEDAR
kahn@pan.cedar.univie.ac.at

```
gopher://gopher.poniecki.berkeley.edu
```

Business

ABI/Inform

ABI/Inform is a comprehensive source for business and management information, containing abstracts from close to 1,000 publications and the full-text from over 100 publications. The database covers trends, corporate strategies and tactics, management techniques, competitive information and product information

Keywords: Business, Business Management, Management

Sponsor: UMI, Ann Arbor, Michigan, US

Audience: General Public, Researchers, Librarians

Profile: A few of the thousands of business subjects that can searched in ABI/ Inform include: company news and analysis, market conditions and strategies, employee management and compensation, international trade and investment, management styles and corporate cultures, and economic conditions and forecasts.

Contact: CDP Technologies Sales Department (800) 950-2035, ext. 400

User Info: To subscribe, contact CDP Technologies directly

```
telnet://cdplus@cdplus.com
```

API Energy Business News Index (APIBIZ)

Worldwide coverage of commercial, financial, marketing and regulatory information affecting the petroleum and energy industries.

Keywords: Petroleum, Business

Sponsor: The American Petroleum Institute - Central Abstracting and Information Services

Audience: Researchers, Librarians

Profile: Twenty-two major news and economics publications are the primary sources for worldwide coverage of information affecting the petroleum and energy industries. Contains more than 600,000 records. Updated weekly.

Contact: PAUL.ALBERT@NETEAST.COM

User Info: To subscribe contact Orbit-Questel directly.

```
telnet://orbit.com
```

Apollo Advertising

A major directory on advertising, providing access to a broad range of related resources (library catalogs, databases, and servers) through the Internet.

Keywords: Advertising, Business

Audience: Advertisers, Business Professionals, General Public

Profile: A new web service for advertisers and information providers that maintains the philosophy that consumers will choose to look for goods and services where it is easy and convenient to locate them. This involves the development of a database of short advertisements, many having hypertext links to more substantial advertisements. These can range from text documents to hypermedia commercials. The Apollo directory can be searched, using logical sorting methods, to identify items of interest. Additional information, including hypermedia, may be connected to the entries. This service encompasses short, stand-alone advertisements, as well as entries with hypertext links to other Internet resources.

Contact: apollo@apollo.co.uk

```
gopher://apollo.co.uk
```

Asia-Pacific

The database covers the business, economics, and new industries of the Pacific Rim nations, including East Asia, Southeast Asia, the Indian Subcontinent, the Middle East, Australia, and the Pacific Island nations.

Keywords: Asia, Pacific, Business, Economy

Sponsor: Aristarchus Knowledge Industries, Seattle, WA, USA

Audience: Market Researchers, Economists, Market Analysts

Profile: Records are of two types: main records consisting of abstracts or citations for journal articles and other publications; and company thesaurus records. Detailed abstracts are provided for selected journal articles, monographs, selected papers in conference proceedings, dissertations, and government documents. Shorter citations with briefer indexing are provided for a wide variety of journal articles, newspapers, government documents, and annual report publications. Asia-Pacific also includes an extensive Corporate Thesaurus subfile, which provides detailed coverage of the corporate players in the Pacific Rim, including thousands of companies traded on the stock exchanges of Southeast and East Asia.

Contact: Dialog in the US at (800) 334-2564; Dialog internationally at country-specific locations.

Details: Costs

User Info: To subscribe, contact Dialog directly.

```
telnet://dialog.com
```

A B C D E F G H I J K L M N O P Q R S T U V W X Y Z

Asian Pacific Business and Marketing Resources

A forum on business and marketing in the Pacific Rim region.

Keywords: Asia, Pacific, Business, Management

Audience: Business Professionals, Market Researchers

Details: Free

```
gopher://hoshi.cic.sfu.ca/11/dlam/
business/forum
```

British National Register of Archives

A multi-volume electronic guide to accessing a wide variety of archival materials and repositories in the United Kingdom.

Keywords: United Kingdom, History, Business(British), Information Retrieval

Sponsor: Coombspapers Social Sciences Research Data Bank at ANU (Australian National University).

Audience: Researchers, Anglophiles, Archivists

Contact: Dr. T. Matthew Ciolek tmciolek@coombs.anu.edu.au

```
gopher://coombs.anu.edu.au
```

```
ftp:/coombs.anu.edu.au/coombspapers/
otherarchives/uk-nra-archives/
```

```
http://coombs.anu.edu.au/
CoombsHome.html
```

Business Dateline

The database contains the full-text of articles from more than 350 local and regional business publications from the United States and Canada.

Keywords: Business, Regional Business, Market Research

Sponsor: UMI, Louisville, KY, USA

Audience: Business Analysts, Market Researchers, Writers

Profile: Sources include city business journals, daily newspapers, regional business magazines, and wire services. Subjects include city economic conditions, new product announcements, manufacturing methods, executive profiles, quality control, company histories, market conditions, service industries, regulations, litigation, and legislation.

Contact: Dialog in the US at (800) 334-2564, Dialog internationally at country specific locations.

Details: Costs

User Info: To subscribe, contact Dialog directly.

```
telnet://dialog.com
```

Business News-Singapore

This gopher site focuses on business in Singapore.

Keywords: Singapore, Economics, Business

Audience: Economists, Business Professionals

Details: Free

```
gopher://gopher.cic.net/11/e-serials/
alphabetic/b/business-news
```

```
http://gopher.cic.net
```

Business Sources on the Net

A list of business-related Internet resources organized by subject.

Keywords: Business

Audience: Business Professionals

Profile: A project undertaken by librarians at Kent State to catalog business-related Internet resources, this guide currenty has 13 chapters on aspects ranging from accounting to statistics.

Contact: Leslie M. Haas lhaas@kentvm.kent.edu

```
gopher://refmac.kent.edu
```

Business Wire

The database contains the unedited text of news releases from over 10,000 diverse news sources: companies, public relations firms, government agencies, political organizations, colleges and universities, and research institutes.

Keywords: Business, Finance, and Industry

Sponsor: Business Wire, San Francisco, CA, USA

Audience: Business Analysts, Market Researchers, General Public

Profile: Approximately 90 percent of all releases carried by Business Wire are business/financial related, covering essentially every category of business and industry. News releases include all information on earnings, dividend announcements, mergers and acquisitions, major contract awards, new products, new security offerings, takeovers, restructurings, and more. Business Wire transmits the full, unedited text of these releases, complete with financial statements and other details that are not generally made available by the press. In addition, all releases carry the name and telephone number of a contact person within that company. Also contains news on other subjects, such as entertainment, travel, sports, politics, medicine and science, and lifestyles.

Contact: Dialog in the US at (800) 334-2564, Dialog internationally at country specific locations.

Details: Costs

User Info: To subscribe, contact Dialog directly.

```
telnet://dialog.com
```

Business, Economics

This directory is a compilation of information resources focused on business and economics.

Keywords: Business, Economics

Audience: Business Professionals, Business Students, Economists

Details: Free

```
ftp://una.hh.lib.umich.edu/70/
inetdirsstacks/govdocs:tsangaustin
```

BUSREF (Business Reference)

The Business Refernce (BUSREF) library contains a variety of reference materials covering business and industry.

Keywords: Reference, Business, Government

Audience: Business Professionals, Business Analysts

Profile: The BUSREF library contains company directories, reference publications, information on business opportunities, and biographical information on political candidates, Congressional members, celebrities, and international decision makers.

Contact: Mead New Sales Group at (800) 227-4908 or (513) 859-5398 inside the US, or (513) 865-7981 for all inquiries outside the US.

User Info: To subscribe, contact Mead directly.

To examine the Nexis user guide, you can access it at the ftp site of the University of Texas at Austin at the URL address: ftp://ftp.cc.utexas.edu

The files are in: /pub/ref-services/LEXIS

```
telnet://nex.meaddata.com
```

```
http://www.meaddata.com
```

Chemical Industry Notes

Citations to worldwide chemical business news.

Keywords: Chemistry, Business

Sponsor: Chemical Abstracts Service, American Chemical Society

Audience: Researchers, Librarians, Chemists

Profile: Contains worldwide chemical business news related to production, pricing, sales, facilities, products and processes, corporate activities, government activities, and people. Contains over 950,000 records. Update weekly.

Contact: PAUL.ALBERT@NETEAST.COM

User Info: To subscribe contact Orbit-Questel directly.

```
telnet://orbit.com
```

CommerceNet

An open, internet-based infrastructure for electronic commerce, created by a coalition of Silicon Valley organizations.

Keywords: Business, Electronic Commerce

Sponsor: CommerceNet, Inc. 800 El Camino Real, Menlo Park, CA 94025

Audience: Business Professionals, Commercial Internet Users, General Public

Profile: Services include basic enabling services required by virtually every user and application (generic directories, secure multimedia messaging, network access control, and payment facilities). Applications include a framework for the development of compelling applications and services targeted to electronic commerce among companies in the region. Applications are designed to address the varied business and community needs of CommerceNet users; these are developed by third-party providers, in compliance with protocols established by CommerceNet. Connectivity is high-quality and affordable, with minimal on-site equipment or network expertise required of the user.

Contact: feedback@commerce.net

`http://www.commerce.net`

Computer-Mediated Marketing Environments

 ★★

A web site devoted to research aimed at understanding the ways in which computer-mediated marketing environments (CMEs), especially the Internet, are revolutionizing the way firms conduct business.

Keywords: WWW, Information Retrieval, Internet, Marketing, Business

Sponsor: Vanderbilt University, Owen Graduate School of Management, Nashville, Tennessee, USA

Audience: General Public, Entrepeneurs, Financial Planners, Marketers

Contact: Donna Hoffman, Tom Novak hoffman@colette.ogsm.vanderbilt.edu, novak@moe.ogsm.vanderbilt.edu

`http://colette.ogsm.vanderbilt.edu`

D&B - Duns Financial Records Plus

★★★

This database provides up to three years of comprehensive financial statements for over 650,000 private and public companies.

Keywords: Finance, Business, Dun & Bradstreet

Sponsor: Dun & Bradstreet Information Services, Parsippany, NJ, USA

Audience: Business Professionals

Profile: Information provided includes balance sheet, income statement, and 14 of the most widely used business ratios for measuring solvency, efficiency, and profitability. A companyÕs financial position can be compared to those of others in the same industry as determined by industry norm percentages. In addition, there are over 1.2 million records included that contain company history and operations background only. DFR also contains company identification data, such as company name, address, primary and secondary SIC codes, D-U-N-S number, and number of employees. Textual paragraphs cover the history and operations background of a firm. Coverage: Current; updated quarterly.

Contact: Dialog in the US at (800) 334-2564, Dialog internationally at country-specific locations.

Details: Costs

User Info: To subscribe, contact Dialog directly.

`telnet://dialog.com`

D&B - Dun's Electronic Business Directory

 ★★★

This database provides online directory information for businesses and professionals throughout US.

Keywords: Finance, Business, Dun & Bradstreet

Sponsor: Dun & Bradstreet Information Services, Parsippany, NJ, USA

Audience: Business Professionals, Business Analysts

Profile: A full directory listing is provided for each entry, including address, telephone number, SIC codes and descriptions, and number of employees. The file covers both public and private US companies of all sizes and types. Fifteen broad business categories are indexed as industry groups: agriculture, business services, communication, construction, finance, insurance, manufacturing, mining, professional services, public administration, real estate, retail, transportation, utilities, and wholesale. Data for the file is compiled and maintained primarily through Dun & BradstreetÕs intensive credit interviewing process. Dun's staff of 1,300 business analysts actively interviews millions of entrepreneurs each year. This information is supplemented with data from large-volume telemarketing and direct mail campaigns. Coverage: Current; updated quarterly.

Contact: Dialog in the US at (800) 334-2564, Dialog internationally at country-specific locations.

Details: Costs

User Info: To subscribe, contact Dialog directly.

`telnet://dialog.com`

D&B - European Dun's Market (EDMI)

 ★★★★

This database presents detailed information on over 2.5 million businesses located in 26 European countries.

Keywords: Dun & Bradstreet, Europe, Business

Sponsor: Dun & Bradstreet Information Services, Parsippany, NJ, USA

Audience: Business Professionals

Profile: EDMI provides directory listings, sales volume and marketing data, and references to parent companies. Companies are selected for inclusion based on sales volume, national prominence, and international interest. Names, addresses, SIC codes, D-U-N-S numbers, and other data are given in each record. Both public and private companies are included.

Contact: Dialog in the US at (800) 334-2564, Dialog internationally at country-specific locations.

User Info: To subscribe, contact Dialog directly.

Notes: Coverage: Current; updated quarterly.

`telnet://dialog.com`

Delphes European Business

 ★★★

This is a French database that provides information on international markets, products, industries, and companies from a European perspective.

Keywords: Business, Europe

Sponsor: Chamber of Commerce and Industry of Paris and The French Assembly of the Chambers of Commerce and Industry, Paris, France

Audience: Business Professionals

Profile: Abstracts are produced by approximately 60 local organizations grouped into two networks, CCIP (Chamber of Commerce and Industry of Paris) and ACFCI (French Assembly of the Chambers of Commerce and Industry), which collect and consolidate the information into the Delphes database. Delphes contains bibliographic citations and informative abstracts from over 900 European trade journals, newspapers, and business periodicals, in French, English, Italian, German, or Spanish. Titles are in the original language; abstracts are in French. A comprehensive classification scheme in English, French, and Spanish is used to index documents covered. Geographic coverage is 45% France, 35% Europe, and 20 percent is devoted to other countries. In addition, about 1,000 new books, corporate and business directories, and reports are reviewed each year.

A B C D E F G H I J K L M N O P Q R S T U V W X Y Z

A
B
C
D
E
F
G
H
I
J
K
L
M
N
O
P
Q
R
S
T
U
V
W
X
Y
Z

Contact:	Dialog in the US at (800) 334-2564, Dialog internationally at country-specific locations.
User Info:	To subscribe, contact Dialog directly.
Notes:	Coverage: 1980 to the present; updated weekly.

`telnet://dialog.com`

Dun & Bradstreet Corporation

Dun and Bradstreet's home page contains examples of existing services, services in development, and business and financial information, advising and so on.

Keywords:	Finance, Business
Audience:	General Public, Business Professionals
Profile:	Files include company news, related industry information, product descriptions, and discussions of IBM's services.

`http://www.corp.dnb.com`

e-europe

The electronic communications network for doing business in Eastern Europe. Its purpose is to help these countries in their transition to market economies.

Keywords:	Eastern Europe, Economics, Business
Audience:	Business Profesionals, Investors, Economists
Contact:	James W. Reese r505040@univ scvm or e-europe@pucc.princeton.edu
Details:	Free
User Info:	To subscribe to the list, send an e-mail message to the URL address shown below consisting of a single line reading:
	SUB e-europe YourFirstName YourLastName
	To send a message to the entire list, address it to: e-europe@indycms.iupui.edu

`mailto:listserv@indycms.iupui.edu`

econ-dev

This mailing list is for sharing with economic development professionals who are helping small, innovative companies compete in the new global environment.

Keywords:	Economic Development, Business
Audience:	Economic Development Experts, Business Professionals
Contact:	majordomo@csn.org
Details:	Free

User Info:	To subscribe to the list, send an e-mail message to the URL address shown below consisting of a single line reading:
	SUB econ-dev YourFirstName YourLastName
	To send a message to the entire list, address it to: econ.dev@csn.org

`mailto:majordomo@csn.org`

Esbdc-l

A mailing list intended to facilitate discussion between small business development centers, focusing on such topics as performance standards, business behavior, products, specific industry information access, deficit reduction plans, and private cost sharing.

Keywords:	Business, Small Business
Sponsor:	Association of Small Business Development Centers, USA
Audience:	State Officials, Educators, Certified Public Accountants, Investors
User Info:	To subscribe to the list, send an e-mail message to the URL address below consisting of a single line reading:
	SUB esbdc-l YourFirstName YourLastName
	To send a message to the entire list, address it to: esbdc-l@ferris.bitnet

`mailto:listserv@ferris.bitnet`

EUROPE (European News Library)

The Europe library contains detailed information about every country in Eastern, Central, and Western Europe.

Keywords:	Business, Europe
Audience:	Business Researchers, Analysts, Entrepreneurs, Regulatory Agencies
Profile:	EUROPE is designed for those who need to monitor countries of the European Community, the European Free Trade Association, or emerging European market economies. This library includes a wide array of sources: Among the information sources are: newspapers and wire services, trade and business journals, company reports, country and region background, industry and product analyses, business opportunities, and selected legal texts. News sources range from the world-renowned Financial Times and Reuters to the regionally important PAP and CTK newswires. EIS's European newsletters and Euroscipe from Coopers and Lybrand help analyze the legal and business environment in Western Europe. Company information is contained in the EXTEL cards as well as ICC.
Contact:	Mead New Sales Group at (800) 227-4908 or (513) 859-5398 inside the US, or (513) 865-7981 for all inquiries outside the US.

User Info:	To subscribe, contact Mead directly.
	To examine the Nexis user guide, you can access it at the ftp site of the University of Texas at Austin at the URL address: ftp://ftp.cc.utexas.edu
	The files are in: /pub/ref-services/LEXIS

`telnet://nex.meaddata.com`

`http://www.meaddata.com`

GC-L

Project for international business and management curricula.

Keywords:	Business, Management, Language
Sponsor:	Global Classroom
Audience:	Linguists, Language Teachers, Language Students, International Business Educators
Details:	Free
User Info:	To subscribe to the list, send an e-mail message to the address below, consisting of a single line reading:
	SUB gc-l YourFirstName YourLastName

`mailto:listserv@uriacc.uri.edu`

International Business Machines

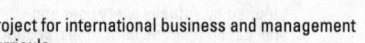

This is IBM's main WWW server and it contains extensive links to information about the company and its products.

Keywords:	Computers, Business
Audience:	General Public
Profile:	Contains: Industry Solutions, Products and Services, Technology information and News about the company.
Contact:	mail to: askibm@www.ibm.com

`http://www.ibm.com`

Internet Shopping Network

A shopping network on the Infobahn

Keywords:	Business, Electronic Commerce
Sponsor:	Internet Shopping Network
Audience:	Business Users, Commercial Internet Users, General Public
Profile:	The Internet Shopping Network aims to conduct research and develop products and services that commercialize the Internet, for the purpose of retailing and mass merchandising. The stores within this network offer approximately 20,000 products from 1000 vendors.

`xxx@xxx.xxx`

Materials Business File

Covers all commercial aspects of iron and steel, non-ferrous metals and non-metallic materials.

Keywords: Materials Science, Business, Iron, Steel

Sponsor: Materials Information, a joint information service of ASM International and the Institute of Materials

Audience: Materials Scientists, Researchers

Profile: Articles are abstracted from over 2,000 worldwide technical and trade journals to create more than 65,000 records. Updated monthly.

Contact: PAUL.ALBERT@NETEAST.COM

User Info: To subscribe, contact Orbit-Questel directly.

`telnet://orbit.com`

National Export Strategy

This site provides the complete text of a report presented to Congress by the Trade Promotion Coordinating Committee, describing ways to develop U.S. export promotion efforts.

Keywords: Commerce, Trade, Exports, Business

Sponsor: United States Government, Trade Promotion Coordinating Committee

Audience: Exporters, Business Professionals, Trade Specialists

Details: Free

`ftp://sunny.stat-usa.gov`

`http://sunny.stat-usa.gov`

National Technology Transfer Center (NTTC)

A federally-funded national network to apply government research to commercial applications.

Keywords: Technology, Research and Development, Business, Industry, Defense, Government (US)

Sponsor: National Technology Transfer Center

Audience: Business Professionals, Entrepreneurs, Manufactures, Technology Enthusiasts

Profile: Features state-by-state listings of agencies designed to facilitate the adaptation of new technologies to industry. Also provides updates on conferences, and a current list of Department of Defense projects soliciting private assistance from small businesses. Allows limited access to NTTC databases.

Contact: Charles Monfradi cmonfra@nttc.edu, info@nttc.edu

`gopher://iron.nttc.edu`

`http://iridium.nttc.edu/nttc.hmtl`

NetEc

An electronic forum for published academic papers relating to economics.

Keywords: Economics, Business

Audience: Economists, Business Professionals

Contact: netec@uts.mcc.ac.uk

Details: Free

User Info: To subscribe to the list, send an e-mail message to the address below, consisting of a single line reading:

SUB netec YourFirstName YourLastName

To send a message tothe entire list, address is it to: netec@hasara11.bitnet

`mailto:listserv@hasara11.bitnet`

Overseas Business Reports

Full-text of U.S. International Trade Administration reports, discussing the economic and commercial climate in various countries around the world.

Keywords: Business, Trade, Commerce

Sponsor: U.S. Government, International Trade Administration

Audience: Business Professionals, Trade Specialists, Investors

Details: Free

`gopher://umslvma.umsl.edu/11/library/govdocs/obr`

Special Chemicals Update Program

Comprehensive reports covering 32 specialty chemical industry segments.

Keywords: Chemistry, Business

Sponsor: Chemical Marketing Research Center

Audience: Librarians, Researchers, Chemists

Profile: Coverage of chemical industry segments, plus more than a dozen reports of general interest on the management of specialty chemical businesses.

Contact: PAUL.ALBERT@NETEAST.COM

User Info: To subscribe, contact Orbit-Questel directly.

`telnet://orbit.com`

St. Petersburg Business News

Contains a digest of business information extracted from Russian and St. Petersburg morning newspapers, stock exchange reports, reports from the News own correspondents.

Keywords: Business, St. Petersburg

Audience: Russians, Business Professionals

Contact: Elena Artemova esa@cfea.ecc.spb.su spbeac@sovamsu.sovusa.com

Details: Costs

User Info: To subscribe to the list, send an e-mail message to the URL address below, consisting of a single line reading:

SUB spbeac YourFirstName YourLastName

`mailto:listserv@sovamsu.sovusa.com`

State Small Business Profiles

This site contains Small Business Administration reports, which provide statistics on the small business sector in each state.

Keywords: Business, Statistics, United States

Sponsor: U.S. Government, Small Business Administration, in conjunction with the Reference Department of the Thomas Jefferson Library of the University of Missouri-St. Louis

Audience: Business Professionals, Researchers

Profile: The 1993 State Business Profiles bring together an array of statistics on the small business sector in each state. Included is data on small business income and employment trends; women-owned and minority-owned businesses; business closings and formations; and state exports.

Contact: Raleigh Muns srcmuns@umslvma.umsl.edu

Details: Free

Notes: For additional information, call the Small Business Administration toll free at (800) 359-2777, or the SBA District Office in Washington, D.C. at (202) 205-6600.

`gopher://umslvma.umsl.edu/11/library/govdocs/states`

Telemedia, Networks, and Systems Group

A list of commercial services on the Web (and Net)

Keywords: Business, Electronic Commerce

Sponsor: MIT Laboratory for Computer Science, Cambridge, MA 02139

Audience: Business Professionals, Commercial Internet Users, General Public

Profile: This list of commercial Internet services is well-maintained and frequently updated.

Contact: hhh@mit.edu

`http://tns-www.lcs.mit.edu/commerce.html`

`http://tns-www.lcs.mit.edu`

The Management Archive

This is an electronic forum for management ideas and information.

Keywords: Management, Business, Economics

A B C D E F G H I J K L M N O P Q R S T U V W X Y Z

Audience: Managers, Business Professionals, Economists

Profile: The Archive arranges working papers, teaching materials, and so on, in directories by subject. All materials in the Archive are fully indexed and searchable. If you have material that you would like to see receive worldwide network exposure and distribution, submit them to the Archive.

Contact: Jim Goes
goes@chimera.sph.umn.edu

Details: Free

Expect: login, Send: anonymous; Expect: password, Send: your e-mail address.

`ftp://chimera.sph.umn.edu`

The Teleputing Hotline And Field Computing Source Letter

A leading voice in covering telephone connections worldwide. Plans to expand coverage of a worldwide revolution called Field Computing.

Keywords: Business, Telecomputing, Telecommunications

Audience: Industry, Telecommunications Experts, Business Professionals

Profile: Field Computing involves linking workers outside the office—in sales, repair, and delivery functions—to central computer systems with handheld terminals and wireless data networks. The Teleputing Hotline has covered this trend since its inception.

Contact: Dana Blankenhorn
MCI: 409-8960 GEnie: nb.atl CompuServe

Details: Costs

User Info: To subscribe to the list, send an e-mail message requesting a subscription to the URL address below.

`mailto:sfer request@mthvax.cs.miami.edu`

Total Quality Management Gopher

A collection of materials relating to the elimination of defects through comprehensive quality control in industry, government, and universities.

Keywords: Quality Control, Management, Business

Sponsor: The Clemson University Department of Industrial Engineering, Clemson, South Carolina, USA

Audience: Managers, Administrators

Contact: quality@eng.clemson.edu

`gopher://deming.eng.clemson.edu`

`http://deming.eng.clemson.edu`

TRADSTAT

TRADSTAT is a comprehensive online source of national trade statistics.

Keywords: Trade, Commerce, Business

Sponsor: TRADSTAT Ltd., London, UK

Audience: Importers, Exporters, Business Professionals

Profile: TRADSTAT covers over 90 percent of world trade. Every month the latest trade figures are loaded into the database from over 20 countries worldwide and all their trading partners. Trade is reported by countries in the EC, EFTA, North and South America, and the Far East. TRADSTAT gives annual trends back to 1981, and monthly reports can be produced at any time for the latest 25 months' trade. The data is made available on average three to eight weeks after the month of trade. This is often weeks, even months, ahead of the equivalent printed data.

`telnet://dialog.com`

U.S. Patent and Trademark Office Database

A database of patents issued in 1994 by the U.S. Patent and Trademark Office, including a searchable index.

Keywords: Patents, Databases, Inventions, Business

Sponsor: New York University School of Business

Audience: Inventors, General Public

Contact: questions@town.hall.org

`gopher://town.hall.org/patent`

University of Toledo Library

The library's holdings are large and wide-ranging and contain significant collections in many fields.

Keywords: Business, Great Lakes Area, Humanities, International Relations, Psychology, Science

Audience: Researchers, Students, General Public

Details: Free

Expect: Enter one of the following commands . . . , Send: DIAL MVS; Expect: dialed to mvs ####; Send: UTMOST

`telnet:/ uofto1.utoledo.edu`

University of Wisconsin at Milwaukee Library

The library's holdings are large and wide-ranging and contain significant collections in many fields.

Keywords: Art, Architecture, Business, Cartography, Geography, Geology, Urban Studies, Literature (English), Literature (American)

Audience: Researchers, Students, General Public

Details: Free

Expect: Login, Send: Lib; Expect: vDIAL prompt, Send: Library

`telnet://uwmcat.lib.uwm.edu`

University of Wisconsin at Oshkosh Library

The library's holdings are large and wide-ranging and contain significant collections in many fields.

Keywords: Business, Liberal Education, Nursing

Audience: Researchers, Students, General Public

Details: Free

Expect: Login; Send: Lib; Expect: vDIAL Prompt, Send: Library

`telnet://polk.cis.uwosh.edu`

University of Wisconsin at Platteville Library

The library's holdings are large and wide-ranging and contain significant collections in many fields.

Keywords: Business, Industry

Audience: Researchers, Students, General Public

Details: Free

Expect: Login, Send: Lib; Expect: vDIAL Prompt, Send: Library

`telnet://137.104.128.44`

University of Wisconsin at Stout Library

The library's holdings are large and wide-ranging and contain significant collections in many fields.

Keywords: Mathematics, Business, Fashion Merchandising, Home Economics, Hospitality, Tourism, Hotel Administration, Restaurant Management, Microelectronics

Audience: Researchers, Students, General Public

Details: Free

Expect: Login, Send: Lib; Expect: vDIAL Prompt, Send: Library

`telnet://lib.uwstout.edu`

University of Wisconsin Eau Claire Library

The library's holdings are large and wide-ranging and contain significant collections in many fields.

Keywords: Health Sciences, Business, Nursing, Education

Audience: Researchers, Students, General Public

Details: Free

Expect: Service Name, Send: Victor

`telnet://lib.uwec.edu`

WORLD (World News and Information)

This library contains detailed information about every country in Europe, Asia, the Pacific Rim, Africa, the Middle East, and North and South America. Designed for those who need to monitor world events, organizations, and leaders, this library provides a global view of any subject or topic.

Keywords: Business, News

Audience: Business Researchers, Analysts, Entrepreneurs

Profile: WORLD includes information from newspapers and wire services, trade and business journals, company reports, country and region background, industry and product analysis, business opportunities, and selected legal texts. News sources range from the world-renowned Christian Science Monitor, Financial Times, Reuters and Associated Press to the regionally important eastern European CTK, MTI and PAP newswires, The Toronto Star, Jerusalem Post, and Xinhua News Agency. Business and trade information include a wide variety of sources, such as EIS's European newsletters and Euroscope from Coopers and Lybrand, Canada's Maclean's, Japan's Comline Daily News Service, BNA's international dailies and the Soviet Union's SovData DiaLine servicesÑall help analyze the political and economic climate around the globe. Company information is contained in the EXTEL cards as well as ICC. Providers of country background and industry analysis include Associated Banks of Europe, Bank of America, Business International, IBC USA and the US Department of Commerce. Economic risk can be assessed with the Economist's Economic Risk Services, IBC's International Reports and International Country Risk Guide and many of Business International's Country Reports. Political risk is forecast in IBC's Political Risk Services as well as BOA's World Information Services' Country RiskOutlooks, Monitors and Forecasts.

Contact: Mead New Sales Group at (800) 227-4908 or (513) 859-5398 inside the US, or (513) 865-7981 for all inquiries outside the US.

User Info: To subscribe, contact Mead directly.

To examine the Nexis user guide, you can access it at the ftp site of the University of Texas at Austin at the URL address: ftp://ftp.cc.utexas.edu

The files are in: /pub/ref-services/LEXIS

`telnet://nex.meaddata.com`

`http://www.meaddata.com`

Yahoo Market and Investments

A comprehensive look at the current economic status, with a wide range of coverage, from brokers to stocks.

Keywords: Business, Stock Market, Investment, Economy

Sponsor: Stanford University, Palo Alto, California, USA

Audience: Investors, Economists

Contact: jerry@akebono.stanford.edu

`http://akebono.stanford.edu/yahoo/Economy/Markets_and_Investments`

Business (British)

British Online Yellow Pages

A directory of British firms and organizations; searches of the database are possible by firm, location, or product.

Keywords: Britain, Business (British)

Sponsor: British Telecom

Audience: General Public, Market Researchers

Details: Free

`telnet://sun.nsf.ac.uk`

ICC British Company Directory

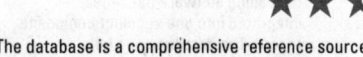

The database is a comprehensive reference source for companies registered in England, Wales, Scotland, and Northern Ireland.

Keywords: UK Companies, Business (British)

Sponsor: ICC Information Group Ltd., London, UK

Audience: Business Professionals

Profile: The database contains a record for each company included on the Index of Companies maintained by the official Companies Registration Offices in the UK Companies that have been dissolved since 1968 are listed. The total number of records in the ICC British Company Directory is over 2 million. Reference data includes name, registered number, registered address, issued and nominal-share capital, dates of incorporation and document filings at the Companies Registration Office. Document filings include latest filed annual accounts and annual returns, changes of directors or registered address, special resolutions, mergers of public (PLC) companies, winding-up orders, appointment of liquidators, and so on.

Contact: Dialog in the US at (800) 334-2564, Dialog internationally at country-specific locations.

User Info: To subscribe, contact Dialog directly.

Notes: Coverage: Current; updated weekly.

`telnet://dialog.com`

Business (US)

America

For people interested in how the United States is dealing with foreign trade policies, congressional status, and other inside information about the government that is freely distributable.

Keywords: Trade, Government (US), Congress (US), Business (International)

Audience: General Public, Researchers, Journalists, Political Scientists, Students

Contact: subscribe@xamiga.linet.org

User Info: To subscribe to the list, send an e-mail message to the URL address below, consisting of a single line reading:

SUB america YourFirstName YourLastName

To send a message to the entire list, address it to: america@xamiga.linet.org

Notes: This list has monthly postings that generally are in large batches, with posts exceeding a few hundred lines.

`mailto:subscribe@xamiga.linet.org`

Commerce Business Daily

The Commerce Business Daily is a publication that announces invitations to bid on proposals requested by the US Federal Government. This gopher is updated every business day.

Keywords: Business (US), Economics, Commerce, Trade, Government (US)

Sponsor: CNS and Softshare Government Information Systems

Audience: Economists, Business Professionals, General Public, Journalists, Students, Politicians.

Profile: Invitations via Internet email that apply only to specific companies can be arranged.

Contact: Melissa Allensworth
sshare@cscns.com
service@cscns.com

Details: Free

`gopher://cns.cscns.com/cbd/About the CBD`

Business Information

Uniform Commercial Code (UCC)

Articles 1 and 2 of the UCC, adopted with some variations in all 50 states (USA).

Keywords: Commerce, Business Information, Standards

Audience: Politicians, Marketers, Students, Retailers, Lawyers

Details: Free

http://www.law.cornell.edu/ucc/ucc.table.html

University of Northern Iowa Library

The library's holdings are large and wide-ranging and contain significant collections in many fields.

Keywords: Art, Business Information, Education, Music, Fiction

Audience: Researchers, Students, General Public

Contact: Mike Yohe
yohe@uni.edu

Details: Free

Expect: Login; Send: Public

telnet://infosys.uni.edu

Business Management

ABI/Inform

ABI/Inform is a comprehensive source for business and management information, containing abstracts from close to 1,000 publications and the full-text from over 100 publications. The database covers trends, corporate strategies and tactics, management techniques, competitive information, and product information

Keywords: Business, Business Management, Management

Sponsor: UMI, Ann Arbor, Michigan, US

Audience: General Public, Researchers, Librarians

Profile: A few of the thousands of business subjects that can searched in ABI/Inform include: company news and analysis, market conditions and strategies, employee management and compensation, international trade and investment, management styles and corporate cultures, and economic conditions and forecasts.

Contact: CDP Technologies Sales Department (800) 950-2035, ext. 400

User Info: To subscribe, contact CDP Technologies directly

telnet://cdplus@cdplus.com

Business Marketing

Alliance Marketing Systems

Develops marketing strategies for new business on those in need of turn-around. Designs advertising/marketing plans to prequalify the buying public.

Keywords: Business Marketing, Sales

Audience: Business Professionals, Marketing Professionals, Sales Executives

Details: Costs

xx@xx.xxx

Buyers' Guide to Micro Software

Buyers' Guide to Micro Software

The database contains a directory of business and professional microcomputer software available in the United States.

Keywords: Buyers' Guides, Microcomputing, Software

Sponsor: Online, Inc., Weston, CT, USA

Audience: Computer Users

Profile: Provided are directory, product, technical, and bibliographic information on leading software packages, integrated into one succinct composite record. The database can help professionals locate suitable packages compatible with specified hardware, without having to sift through large numbers of records.

The file is highly selective, listing packages rated at least "good" by the technical press; all packages from major software producers, even if negatively reviewed; and packages unique to specific business segments, with special emphasis placed on library and medical software. Each record includes directory information; technical specifications, including required hardware and operating systems; an abstracted product description, and, when available, a full citation of representative reviews.

Contact: Dialog in the US at (800) 334-2564, Dialog internationally at country-specific locations.

Details: Costs

User Info: To subscribe, contact Dialog directly.

Notes: Coverage: current; updated monthly.

telnet://dialog.com

BX-Talk

BX-Talk

BX-talk has been created for users of Builder Xcessory (BX) to discuss problems (and solutions) and ideas for using BX, which is a graphical user interface builder for Motif applications, and is sold by ICS. Please note that this list is not associated with ICS (the authors of BX) in any way.

Keywords: Builder Xcessory, Graphical User Interfaces

Audience: Graphics Experts, Computer Operators

Contact: Darci L. Chapman
bx-talk-request@qiclab.scn.rain.com

Details: Free

User Info: To subscribe to the list, send an e-mail message requesting a subscription to the URL address below.

To send a message to the entire list, address it to: bx-talk@qiclab.scn.rain.com

Notes: This list is unmoderated.

mailto:bx-talk-request@qiclab.scn.rain.com

C Programming Language

info-C

Discussions about C programming and the C programming language.

Keywords: Programming, C Programming Language

Audience: C Programmers

Contact: Mark Plotnick
info-C-request@research.att.com

Details: Free

User Info: To subscribe to the list, send an e-mail message requesting a subscription to the URL address below.

mailto:info-C-request@research.att.com

C-IBM-370

The C on IBM mainframes mailing list is a place to discuss aspects of using the C programming language on s/370-architecture computers—especially under IBM's operating systems for that environment.

Keywords: C Programming Language, Programming Languages, IBM

Audience: IBM Users, Computer Users, Computer Programmers

Contact: David Wolfskill
C-IBM-370-request@dhw68k.cts.com

Details: Free

User Info: To subscribe to the list, send an e-mail message requesting a subscription to the URL address below.

To send a message to the entire list, address it to:

C-IBM-370@dhw68k.cts.com

mailto:C-IBM-370-request@dhw68k.cts.com

C-L

Discussion of C programming.

Keywords: Programming Languages

Audience: C Programmers

Contact: George Foster, Katie Hanson
igaf400@indyvax, abh100@indycms

Details: Free

User Info: To subscribe to the list, send an e-mail message to the URL address below, consisting of a single line reading:

SUB C-L YourFirstName YourLastName

To send a message to the entire list, address it to:

C-L@indycms.iupui.edu

mailto:listserv@indycms.iupui.edu

C-SPAN (Cable-Satellite Public Affairs Network) Gopher

C-SPAN (Cable-Satellite Public Affairs Network) Gopher

Online information from C-SPAN, the public affairs television network.

Keywords: News Media, Government, Congress (US), Television

Sponsor: C-SPAN

Audience: Journalists, Government Officials, Educators (K-12), General Public

Profile: Comprehensive listings of C-SPAN's programming and coverage of events in Washington D.C. and beyond. In addition to the programming notes and schedules, this site also features online educational resources sponsored by C-SPAN, text of historic documents and speeches, and background political information on the House of Representatives and the Supreme Court.

Contact: cspanviewr@aol.com

Details: Free

gopher://c-span.org

c2man

c2man

This is a discussion of Graham Stoney's c2man program, which parses comments from C and C++ programs and produces documentation for man pages, info files, and so on.

Keywords: Computer Programs, c2man

Audience: Computer Programmers

Contact: listserv@research.canon.oz.au

User Info: To subscribe to the list, send an e-mail message to the URL address below, consisting of a single line reading:

SUB c2man YourFirstName YourLastName

To send a message to the entire list, address it to:
c2man@research.canon.oz.au

Notes: This list is archived and unmoderated.

mailto:listserv@research.canon.oz.au

Cabinetry

Utah Valley Community College Library

The library's holdings are large and wide-ranging and contain significant collections in many fields.

Keywords: Accounting, Automobiles, Cabinetry, Child Care, Drafting, Electronics, Home Building, Local History, Refrigeration, Air Conditioning

Audience: General Public, Researchers, Librarians, Document Delivery Professionals

Details: Free

Expect: Login; Send: Opub

`telnet://uvlib.uvcc.edu`

Cabot (Sebastian)

Cabot

This is the official mailing list of the New York State Institute for Sebastian Cabot Studies.

Keywords: Cabot (Sebastian)

Audience: Scholars, Students, Historians

Contact: Richard Welty
cabot-request@sol.crd.ge.com

User Info: To subscribe to the list, send an e-mail message requesting a subscription to the URL address below.

To send a message to the entire list, address it to:

cabot@sol.crd.ge.com

`mailto:cabot-request@sol.crd.ge.com`

CADC (Canadian Astronomy Data Center) Home Page

CADC (Canadian Astronomy Data Center) Home Page

The CADC maintains archives of scientific data from the Hubble Space Telescope and the Canada France Hawaii Telescope. It also serves as a distribution point for various astronomy-related software packages.

Keywords: Astronomy, Hubble Telescope

Sponsor: Dominional Astrophysical Observatory, Victoria, British Columbia, Canada

Audience: Astronomers

Contact: Dennis Crabtree
crabtree@dao.nrc.ca

`http://ucluelet.dao.nrc.ca`

CAEDS-L

CAEDS-L

A mailing list for the discussion of CAED (Computer Aided Engineering Design) products.

Keywords: Computer-Aided Design, Engineering, Computer Graphics

Audience: Engineers

Contact: netman@suvm.acs.syr.edu

Details: Free

User Info: To subscribe to the list, send an e-mail message to the URL address shown below consisting of a single line reading:

SUB caeds-l YourFirstName YourLastName

To send a message to the entire list, address it to:

CaeDS-1@suvm.ACS.SYR.EDU

`mailto:listserv@suvm.acs.syr.edu`

CAF Archive

CAF Archive

A source of information relating to Computers and Academic Freedom (CAF).

Keywords: Education, Computers, Academic Freedom

Audience: Educators, Researchers

Contact: kadie@eff.org

`http://www.eff.org/CAF/cafhome.html`

Calendars

On-this-day

Subscribers receive a daily listing of notable birthdays, events, religious holidays, astronomical events, and other items of interest. The messages are sent out in the wee hours of the morning.

Keywords: Calendars

Audience: General Public

Contact: Wayne Geiser
geiser@pictel.com

Details: Free

User Info: To subscribe to the list, send an e-mail message requesting a subscription to the URL address below.

To send a message to the entire list, address it to: geiser@pictel.com

`mailto:geiser@pictel.com`

California

alt.california

A Usenet newsgroup providing information and discussion about California and Californian lifestyles.

Keywords: California

Audience: Californians, General Public

User Info: To subscribe to this Usenet newsgroup, you need access to a newsreader.

`news:alt.california`

ba.general

A Usenet newsgroup providing general information and discussion about the San Francisco Bay area.

Keywords: California

Audience: Tourists, Visitors, Bay area Residents

User Info: To subscribe to this Usenet newsgroup, you need access to a newsreader.

`news:ba.general`

ca-Firearms

This is an announcement and discussion of firearms legislation and related issues. The ca- list is for California statewide issues; the ba- list is for the San Francisco Bay area and gets all messages sent to the ca- list. Prospective members should subscribe to one or the other, generally depending on whether or not they are SF Bay area residents.

Keywords: Firearms, Gun Control Legislation, California

Audience: Politicians, General Public, Gun Users, California Residents

Contact: Jeff Chan
ca-firearms-request@shell.portal.com

Details: Free

User Info: To subscribe to the list, send an e-mail message requesting a subscription to the URL address below.

To send a message to the entire list, address it to:

ca-firearms@shell.portal.com

`mailto:ca-firearms-request@shell.portal.com`

ca-Liberty

This is an announcement of area-based Libertarian meetings, events, activities, and so on. The ca- list is for California statewide issues; the ba- list is for the San Francisco Bay area and gets all messages sent to the ca- list. Prospective members should subscribe to one or the other, generally depending on whether or not they are SF Bay area residents.

Keywords: Libertarian Party, Politics, California

Audience: Libertarians, Political Scientists, Politicians, General Public

Contact: Jeff Chan
ca-liberty-request@shell.portal.com

Details: Free

User Info: To subscribe to the list, send an e-mail message requesting a subscription to the URL address below.

To send a message to the entire list, address it to:

ca-liberty@shell.portal.com

```
mailto:ca-liberty-
request@shell.portal.com
```

California State Senate Gopher

This is a gopher site accessing California state government records and providing links to related gophers.

Keywords: California, Government (US), Law (US State)

Sponsor: California State Senate, California, USA

Audience: Californians, General Public

Profile: The California State Senate Gopher provides access to state government records, pending bills, laws, state statistics, budgets, and related matters. The gopher also provides links to related gophers inside and outside state government.

Contact: Gopher Provider
gopher@sen.ca.gov

```
gopher://gopher.sen.ca.gov
```

California Museum of Photography: Network Exhibitions

This is a collection of digital images for educational and general use.

Keywords: Photography, Art, Education, California

Sponsor: University of California, Riverside, California, USA

Audience: Photographers, Artists, Educators (esp. K-12), Historians

Profile: The California Museum of Photography is in the process of selecting groups of images from the collections as thematic exhibitions. Instead of displays on the walls, these exhibitions comprise a group of digital images with associated text. Particular emphasis is on the utility of these images in class projects for elementary and secondary school students. However, the digital images also have potential value for more advanced scholarly research in preparation of papers in the Humanities, Social Sciences, and the Arts.

Contact: Russ Harvey
russ@cornucopia.ucr.edu

```
gopher://gopher.ucr.edu
```

California Privacy Act 1992

Text of the California Privacy Act of 1992.

Keywords: Law, California

Audience: General Public, Lawyers

Details: Free

```
gopher://wiretap.spies.com
```

CERFnet Guide

A comprehensive guide to the CERFnet (California Education and Research Federation Network), a data-communications regional network that operates throughout California. The purpose of CERFnet is to advance science and education by assisting the interchange of information among research and educational institutions.

Keywords: Internet, Science, Education, California

Audience: Internet Surfers, Researchers, Educators

Contact: CERFnet Hotline
help@cerf.net

Details: Free

Files are in: cerfnet/cerfnet_info/cerfnet_guide/

```
ftp://nic.cerf.net
```

CERFNet News

This is a mid-level network linking academic, government, and industrial research facilities throughout California.

Keywords: Education, California

Sponsor: California Education and Research Federation Network

Audience: Researchers, Students (college, graduate)

Contact: help@cerf.net

Details: Free

```
gopher://gopher.cerf.net/11/cerfnet
```

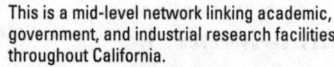

CAMIS (Center for Advanced Medical Informatics at Stanford)

CAMIS (Center for Advanced Medical Informatics at Stanford)

CAMIS is a shared computing resource supporting research activities in biomedical informatics.

Keywords: Medical Informatics, Heuristics, Health Sciences

Sponsor: Stanford University School of Medicine, Palo Alto, CA, USA

Audience: Medical Informatics, Health Science Researchers

Profile: The CAMIS gopher includes an Internet-wide title search, computing information, and technical reports for the Section on Medical Informatics (SMI) community as well as that of the Knowledge Systems Laboratory (KSL), information on the Heuristic Programming Project, pointers to various online library catalogs, and more.

Contact: Torsten_Heycke@med.stanford.edu

```
gopher://camis.stanford.edu/00/
gopherdoc
```

Canada

1991 Census of Population Documentation

This gopher provides Canadian Census information from 1991 including geographic and demographic information.

Keywords: Census Data, Canada, Demography, Geography

Audience: Canadians, Researchers, Demographers

Contact: David McCallum
carl@acadvm1.uottawa.ca

```
gopher://alpha.epas.utoronto.ca/Data
Library/Census of Population
```

1994 Federal Budget (Canada)

★★★★

This site offers full-text of Canada's federal budget. It also has a wealth of information on Canadian industry and industrial policy, including Provincial and Sectorial GATT opportunities and briefs from the Information Highway Advisory Council.

Keywords: Canada, Government (International), Industry, Foreign Trade

Sponsor: Industry Canada, Canada

Audience: Canadians, Government Officials, Businesspeople, Researchers

Contact: Tyson Macaulay
tyson@debra.dgbt.doc.ca

```
gopher://debra.dgbt.doc.ca/industry
canada documents/isc.news.releases
```

Biking in Canada

A repository of information for bicyclists, including utility programs, events, FAQs, and how-to guides; some with Canadian-specific details.

Keywords: Sports, Bicycling, Canada

Sponsor: Habitat Ecology Division at the Bedford Institute of Oceanography

Audience: Cyclists, Fitness Enthusiasts

Contact: sysop@biome.bio.ns.ca

Details: Free

```
gopher://gopher.biome.bio.dfo.ca/pub/
biking
```

A B C D E F G H I J K L M N O P Q R S T U V W X Y Z

A
B
C
D
E
F
G
H
I
J
K
L
M
N
O
P
Q
R
S
T
U
V
W
X
Y
Z

Can-Stud-Assoc

This is a mailing list for anyone who might wish to discuss Canadian postsecondary education and student associations' involvement in it.

Keywords: Canada, Education (Post-Secondary)

Audience: Canadians, Students (college)

Contact: can-stud-assoc-request@unixg.ubc.ca

Details: Free

User Info: To subscribe to the list, send an e-mail message requesting a subscription to the URL address below.

To send a message to the entire list, address it to:

can-stud-assoc@unixg.ubc.ca

mailto:can-stud-assoc-request@unixg.ubc.ca

Canada

The wiretap gopher provides access to a range of Canadian documents in full-text format in French.

Keywords: Canada, French

Audience: Canadian Citizens, Lawyers

Details: Free

gopher://wiretap.spies.com

CANADA (Canadian News and Information Library)

The Canadian News and Information Library (CANADA) contains Canadian legal news, business and company information.

Keywords: News, Analysis, Companies, Canada

Audience: Canadians

Profile: The CANADA library contains respected Canadian news publications such as *The Toronto Star*, *The Vancouver Sun*, *Ottawa Business News*, and the *Montreal Gazette*. The CANADA library also offers Canadian company profiles, country reports, and Canada's financial database, CANCORP Plus.

Contact: Mead New Sales Group at (800) 227-4908 or (513) 859-5398 inside the US, or (513) 865-7981 for all inquiries outside the US.

User Info: To subscribe, contact Mead directly.

To examine the Nexis user guide, you can access it at the ftp site of the University of Texas at Austin at the URL address: ftp://ftp.cc.utexas.edu

The files are in: /pub/ref-services/LEXIS

telnet://nex.meaddata.com

http://www.meaddata.com

Canadian Geographical WWW Index Travel

This web site provides weekly weather information.

Keywords: Weather, Travel, Canada, Geography

Sponsor: University of Manitoba, Canada

Audience: Travelers, Educators, Students

Contact: www@umanitoba.ca

Details: Free

http://www.umanitoba.ca

CCES-L

A mailing list for the national communication branch of the CFES (Canadian Federation of Engineering Students).

Keywords: Engineering, Canada

Audience: Engineers, Students

Contact: Canadian Federation of Engineering Students
cfes@jupiter.sun.csd.unb.ca

Details: Free

User Info: To subscribe to the list, send an e-mail message to the URL address below consisting of a single line reading:

SUB cces-l YourFirstName YourLastName

To send a message to the entire list, address it to: cces-l@unb.ca

mailto:listserv@unb.ca

CEC

A mailing list for CEC (Canadian Electro-Acoustics Community).

Keywords: Engineering, Acoustical Engineering, Canada, Canadian Electro-Acoustics Community

Audience: Engineers

Contact: Peter Gross
grosspa@qucdn.queensu.ca

Details: Free

User Info: To subscribe to the list, send an e-mail message to the URL address below, consisting of a single line reading:

SUB cec YourFirstName YourLastName

To send a message to the entire list, address it to:

cec@qucdn.queensu.ca

mailto:listserv@qucdn.queensu.ca

CFES-L

National communication branch of the CFES (Canadian Federation of Engineering Students).

Keywords: Engineering, Students, Canada

Audience: Engineers, Students

Contact: Canadian Federation of Engineering Students
cfes@jupiter.sun.csd.unb.ca

Details: Free

User Info: To subscribe to the list, send an e-mail message to the URL address below consiting of a single line reading:

SUB cfes-l YourFirstName YourLastName

To send a message to the entire list, address it to: CfES-L@UNB.CA

mailto:listserv@unb.ca

Freedom of Information Directory of Records (Canada)

A database compiled by the Canadian federal government listing documents available to the public under The Freedom of Information and Protection of Privacy Act. It can be searched by keyword, or browsed through a menuing system.

Keywords: Canada, Government (International), Freedom of Information Act

Sponsor: British Columbia Systems Corporation, British Columbia, Canada

Audience: Canadians, Journalists, Activists

Contact: Office of the Information and Privacy Commissione
tcphelp@bcsc02.gov.bc.ca

gopher://bcsc02.gov.bc.ca

MegaGopher

This is the gopher at the University of Montreal. It supports the software and information requirements for the MegaSequencing project. It also serves as a repository of data for organellar genome and molecular evolution research and acts as the focal point for the GDE (Genetic Data Environment) package.

Keywords: Biology, Canada

Audience: Biologists

Contact: Tim Littlejohn
tim@bch.umontreal.ca

Details: Free

gopher://megasun.bch.umontreal.ca

Natural Resources Canada (NRCan) Gopher

This site offers information on forests, energy, mining, and geomatics from the Canadian government. Also has reports from the Geological Survey of Canada and an overview of NRCan statutes, organization, and personnel. Provides links to other Canadian environmental and government gophers.

Keywords: Canada, Environment, Geology, Forestry

Sponsor: The Department of Natural Resources, Canada

Audience: Canadians, Environmentalists, Environmental Researchers, Geologists

Contact: Bob Fillmore
fillmore@emr.ca

Notes: NRCan maintains a toll-free hotline (800) 267-5166

`gopher://gopher.emr.ca`

`http://www.emr.ca/`

NLC (National Library of Canada)

A Canadian library gopher in French and English.

Keywords: Canada, Libraries, Library Science

Sponsor: National Library of Canada (NLC), Canada

Audience: Canadians, Librarians, Publishers

Profile: This site provides a gateway to Canadian library and Internet resources linking users to the National Library, which offers a bibliographic database, a list of NLC publications, and other services for libraries and publishers. It also has links to many other Canadian libraries and Internet services, as well as a large selection of general information from and about the Government of Canada and its provinces.

Contact: Nancy Brodie, Lynn Herbert

Nancy.Brodie@nlc-bnc.ca, Lynn.Herbert@nlc-bnc.ca

`gopher://gopher.nlc-bnc.ca`

North American Free Trade Agreement (NAFTA)

The agreement between the governments of Canada, the United Mexican States, and the United States of America to establish a free trade area in North America.

Keywords: Trade, US, Mexico, Canada, Free Trade, NAFTA

Audience: Journalists, Politicians, Economists, Students

Details: Free

`gopher://wiretap.spies.com/00/Gov/NAFTA`

Open Government Pilot

This web site provides information concerning the Canadian government, including information on Canadian infrastructure, industry, communications, provinces, and parliament.

Keywords: Canada, Government (International)

Sponsor: Canadian Federal Government

Audience: Canadians, Educators, Students

Details: Free

`http://debra.dgbt.doc.ca/opengov`

Open Government Project (Canada)

This site provides online audio-visual and text information on the Canadian government.

Keywords: Canada, Government

Sponsor: Directorate of Communications Development, Industry Canada, Canada

Audience: Canadians, Government Officials, Journalists

Profile: This bilingual (French/English) site has detailed information on members of the Canadian Senate and House of Commons, as well as Supreme Court rulings and biographies of the justices. It features a number of pictures, maps, and links to other Canadian information servers.

Contact: Tyson Macaulay
tyson.macaulay@crc.doc.ca

`http://debra.dgbt.doc.ca/ogp.html`

`gopher://debra.dgbt.doc.ca/open_government_project`

PEI (Prince Edward Island, Canada) Crafts Council Gopher

A gopher devoted to all manner of crafts, from weaving to glass blowing. Information includes a database of tools, services, and materials for crafts enthusiasts, as well as FAQs and pointers to other crafts resources. Also provides background on the PEI Craft Council's activities and on Prince Edward Island.

Keywords: Crafts, Hobbies, Canada

Sponsor: PEI Crafts Council, Prince Edward Island, Canada

Audience: Crafts Enthusiasts

Details: Free

`gopher://crafts-council.pe.ca`

soc.culture.canada

A Usenet newsgroup providing information and discussion about Canada and its people.

Keywords: Culture, Canada, Sociology

Audience: Sociologists, Canadians

Details: Free

User Info: To subscribe to this Usenet newsgroup, you need access to a newsreader.

`news:soc.culture.canada`

Statistics Canada Gopher

A repository of information from the National Statistical Agency of Canada.

Keywords: Statistics, Canada, Canadian Documents

Sponsor: Statistics Canada, Canada

Audience: Canadians, Researchers

Profile: Updated daily, this site allows users to search Statistics Canada documents and provides updates of upcoming statistical conferences and publications in Canada. It also allows access to Statistics Canada FTP and list servers.

Contact: Michael Thoen, Jackie Godfrey
thoemic@statcan.ca, godfrey@statcan.ca

`gopher://talon.statcan.ca`

Supreme Court of Canada

This gopher allows access to Canadian Supreme Court rulings from 1993 forward. Documents are available as full-text and searchable by keyword. This site also has information on Canadian statute and case law.

Keywords: Law (International), Canada

Sponsor: Universite de Montreal Law Gopher Project, Montreal, Canada

Audience: Lawyers, General Public

Contact: Pablo Fuentes
fuentesp@droit.umontreal.ca

`gopher://gopher.droit.umontreal.ca/English/SCC`

University of Saskatchewan Libraries

A major Canadian University library with access to library catalogs archives, and Canadian Government documents.

Keywords: Canada, Government (International)

Sponsor: University of Saskatchewan

Audience: Canadians, General Public

Profile: The University of Saskatchewan Libraries maintain online databases of their collections archives, and catalogs. The libraries are a voluminous resource for the study of Canada, Canadian government, and Canadian-American issues.

Login: sonia

`telnet://sklib.usask.ca`

Canadian Documents

Statistics Canada Gopher

A repository of information from the National Statistical Agency of Canada.

Keywords: Statistics, Canada, Canadian Documents

Sponsor: Statistics Canada, Canada

Audience: Canadians, Researchers

A B C D E F G H I J K L M N O P Q R S T U V W X Y Z

A
B
C
D
E
F
G
H
I
J
K
L
M
N
O
P
Q
R
S
T
U
V
W
X
Y
Z

Profile: Updated daily, this site allows users to search Statistics Canada documents and provides updates of upcoming statistical conferences and publications in Canada. It also allows access to Statistics Canada FTP and list servers.

Contact: Michael Thoen, Jackie Godfrey
thoemic@statcan.ca
godfrey@statcan.ca

`gopher://talon.statcan.ca`

University of Nevada, Las Vegas Library - Las Vegas, NV

★★

The library's holdings are large and wide-ranging and contain significant collections in many fields.

Keywords: Gaming, Hotel Administration, Nevadiana, Canadian Documents, Nevada State Documents

Audience: General Public, Researchers, Librarians, Document Delivery Professionals

Contact: Myoung-ja Lee Kwon
kwon@nevada.edu.

Details: Free

Expect: login; Send: library

`telnet://library.lv-lib.nevada.edu`

Canadian Electro-Acoustics Community

CEC

CEC (Canadian Electro-Acoustics Community).

Keywords: Engineering, Acoustical Engineering, Canada, Canadian Electro-Acoustics Community

Audience: Engineers

Contact: Peter Gross
grosspa@qucdn

Details: Free

User Info: To subscribe to the list, send an e-mail message to the URL address below, consisting of a single line reading:

SUB cec YourFirstName YourLastName

To send a message to the entire list, address it to:

cec@qucdn.queensu.ca

`mailto:listerv@qucdn.queensu.ca`

Canadian University Consortium on Health in International Development (CANCHID)

Canadian University Consortium on Health in International Development (CANCHID)

★

CANCHID is a multi-campus consortium that includes medical schools and other educational institutions devoted to research and projects dealing with health care issues in developing countries.

Keywords: Health, International Development

Audience: Public Health, Medicine, International Aid Agencies

Contact: Sam Lanfranco
lanfran@vm1.yorku.ca

Details: Free

User Info: To subscribe to the list, send an e-mail message to the URL address below, consisting of a single line reading:

SUB canchid YourFirstName YourLastName

To send a message to the entire list, address it to:

canchid@vm1.yorku.ca

`mailto:listserv@vm1.yorku.ca`

Canadian-American Studies

University of Maine System Library Catalog

★★

The library's holdings are large and wide-ranging and contain significant collections in many fields.

Keywords: Ucadian Studies, St. John Valley (History of), Canadian-American Studies, Geology, Aquaculture, Maine

Audience: General Public, Researchers, Librarians, Document Delivery Professionals

Contact: Elaine Albright, Marilyn Lutz

Details: Free

Expect: login, Send: ursus

`telnet://ursus.maine.edu`

Cancer

IST BioGopher

This is the gopher server of the National Institute for Cancer Research (IST) and of the Advanced Biotechnology Center of Genoa, Italy.

Keywords: Cancer, Biotechnology, Italy, Europe

Audience: Biologists, Medical Researchers

Profile: The server includes data from the Interlab Project Databases (biological materials availability in European laboratories) and the Bio-Media Bulletin Board System (biotechnology researchers, projects, fundings and products).

Contact: gophman@istge.ist.unige.it

Details: Free

`gopher://istge.ist.unige.it`

National Cancer Center, Tokyo, Japan

This is the information service for the National Cancer Center in Tokyo, Japan, as well as the entry point for the Japanese Cancer Research Resources Bank (JCRB).

Keywords: Cancer, Japan

Audience: Biologists, Medical Researchers

Contact: ncc-gopher-news@gan.ncc.go.jp

Details: Free

`gopher://ncc.go.jp`

Canopus

Canopus

Newsletter of the Space Science and Astronomy Technical Committee of the American Institute of Aeronautics and Astronautics. Its objective is to provide an insider's perspective on issues in space science and astronomy.

Keywords: Space Science, Astronomy

Sponsor: NASA (National Aeronautics and Space Administration)

Audience: Astronomers, Space Scientists

Contact: William W. L. Taylor
wtaylor@nhqvax.hq.nasa.gov

Details: Costs

User Info: To subscribe to the list, send an e-mail message to the URL address below.

`mailto:wtaylor@nhqvax.hq.nasa.gov`

Cantus

Cantus

This gopher site accesses the Gregorian Chant Database, which is maintained by the Catholic University of America.

Keywords: Gregorian Chants, Music, Liturgy

Sponsor: Catholic University of America (CUA)

Audience: Vocalists, Educators, Students

Profile: The database contains an introduction to the Cantus Gopher at the CUA, and has a searchable index.

`gopher://vmsgopher.cua.edu`

Card Games

ba-Poker

Discussion of poker as it is available to residents of and visitors to the San Franciso Bay area (broadly defined), in home games as well as in licensed card rooms. Topics include upcoming events, unusual games, strategies, comparisons of various venues, and player "networking."

Keywords: Poker, Card Games, San Francisco Bay Area

Audience: Poker Players

Contact: Martin Veneroso
ba-poker-request@netcom.com

Details: Free

User Info: To subscribe to the list, send an e-mail message requesting a subscription to the URL address below.

To send a message to the entire list, address it to: ba-poker@netcom.com

`mailto:ba-poker-request@netcom.com`

Cards

This list is for people interested in collecting, speculating, and investing in baseball, football, basketball, hockey, and other trading cards memorabilia. Discussion and want/sell lists are welcome.

Keywords: Trading Cards, Collectibiles, Memorabilia

Audience: Sports Card Collectors, Sports Card Traders, Memorabilia Collectors

Contact: Keane Arase
cards-request@tanstaafl.uchicago.edu

Details: Free

User Info: To subscribe to the list, send an e-mail message requesting a subscription to the URL address below.

To send a message to the entire list, address it to:

cards@tanstaafl.uchicago.edu

Notes: The list is open to anyone.

`mailto:cards-request@tanstaafl.uchicago.edu`

rec.gambling

Discussion of card games, gambling, and gambling sites.

Keywords: Card Games, Gambling

Audience: Card Players, Gamblers

Profile: Discussion in this group covers gambling, and card games, the rules of various card games, odds, betting, and the pros and cons of various gambling and card playing sites. The archived FAQ is a lengthy card game resource.

Contact: rec.gambling Moderator
jacobs@cs.utah.edu

Notes: The rec.gambling FAQ is accessible via anonymous ftp at soda.berkeley.edu through the path pub/rec.gambling.

`news:rCardiopulmonary Medicine`

Cardopulmonary Medicine

University of Texas Health Science Center at Tyler Library

The library's holdings are large and wide-ranging and contain significant collections in many fields.

Keywords: Biochemistry, Cardiopulmonary Medicine, Cell Biology, Family Practice, Molecular Biology

Audience: Researchers, Students, General Public

Details: Free

Expect: Username Prompt, Send: LIS

`telnet://athena.uthscsa.edu`

`ec.gambling`

Careers

CAREER (Career Library)

The LEXIS Career Library contains job and job-related information.

Keywords: Employment, Careers

Audience: Lawyers, Law Students

Profile: The LEXIS Career Library contains job and job-related information designed to assist the student and attorney in finding the right job. The Career Library contains a number of helpful directories, many of which have an "Address" feature that enables users to generate a mailing list from their answer set.

Contact: Mead New Sales Group at (800) 227-4908 or (513) 859-5398 inside the US, or (513) 865-7981 for all inquires outside the US.

Details: Costs

User Info: To subscribe, contact Mead directly.

To examine the Lexis user guide, you can access it at the ftp site of the University of Texas at Austin at the URL address: ftp://ftp.cc.utexas.edu

The files are in: /pub/res-services/LEXIS

`telnet://nex.meaddata.com`

Occupational Outlook Handbook 1992-93

An annual U.S. Department of Labor publication that provides detailed information for more than 320 occupations, including job descriptions, typical salaries, education and training requirements, working conditions, job outlook, and more.

Keywords: Careers, Employment, Labor

Sponsor: U.S. Deptartment of Labor

Audience: General Public, Job Seekers, Business Professionals

Details: Free

`gopher://umslvma.umsl.edu/11/library/govdocs/ooha`

Caribbean

amlat.mujeres

This conference serves as a forum for interchange between organizations and women's movements in Latin America and the Caribbean.

Keywords: Women, Latin America, Caribbean, Feminism

Audience: Women, Feminists, Activists

Contact: Agencia Latinoamericana de Informacion
info@alai.ec, uualai@ecuanex.ec

Details: Costs

Establish an account on the nearest APC node. Login, type c for conferences, then type: **go amlat.mujeres**.

For information on the nearest APC node, contact:
APC International Secretariat IBASE
E-mail: apcadmin@apc.org

Contact: Carlos Afonso (cafonso@ax.apc.org) or APC North American Regional Office e-mail: apcadmin@apc.org

Edie Farwell (efarwell@igc.apc.org)

`telnet://igc.apc.org`

A B C D E F G H I J K L M N O P Q R S T U V W X Y Z

A
B
C
D
E
F
G
H
I
J
K
L
M
N
O
P
Q
R
S
T
U
V
W
X
Y
Z

cread (Latin American & Caribbean Distance & Continuing Education)

This is a digest list of distance education information primarily focused on Latin America and the Caribbean.

Keywords: Latin America, Caribbean, Education (Distance)

Audience: Educators, Administrators, Faculty

Details: Free

User Info: To subscribe to the list, send an e-mail message to the URL address below consisting of a single line reading: SUB cread YourFirstName YourLastName.

To send a message to the entire list, address it to: cread@yorkvm1.bitnet

`mailto:listserv@yorkvm1.bitnet`

Latin America & Caribbean Network Gopher server

A gopher server currently under construction providing net access to Latin America and the Caribbean.

Keywords: Caribbean, Latin America

Sponsor: Lacnet Corporation

Audience: Caribbean Enthusiasts

Profile: The Latin America & Caribbean Network Gopher server is a gopher server currently under construction. When finished it will provide gopher access to gopher servers throughout Latin America and the Caribbean providing government and institutional information on various countries.

Contact: Luis Rodriguez or Javier Hidalgo lrodriguez@mia.lac.net or jhidalgo@mia.lac.net

Notes: Currently under construction.

`gopher://mia.lac.net`

Carnivorous Plants

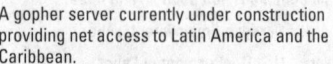

CP

Topics of interest to the group include the cultivation and propagation of CP's (carnivorous plants), field observations of CP's, sources of CP material, and CP trading between members. The discussion is not moderated, and usually consists of short messages offering plants for trade, asking CP questions and advice, relating experiences with plant propagation, and so on. The group also maintains archives of commercial plant sources and members growing lists.

Keywords: Carnivorous Plants, Botany

Audience: Horticulturists, Botanists

Contact: Rick Walker walker@hpl-opus.hpl.hp.com

User Info: To subscribe to the list, send an e-mail message to the address below consisting of a single line reading:

SUB CP YourFirstName YourLastName

To send a message to the entire list, address it to: CP@hpl-opus.hpl.hp.com

`mailto:listserv@hpl-opus.hpl.hp.com`

Carter (Hodding)

Mississippi State University Library

The library's holdings are large and wide-ranging and contain significant collections in many fields.

Keywords: History (US), Forestry, Energy, Carter (Hodding, Papers of), Mississippi

Audience: General Public, Researchers, Librarians, Document Delivery Professionals

Contact: Stephen Cunetto shc1@ra.msstate.edu

Details: Free

Expect: username, Send: msu; Expect: password, Send: library

`mailto:telnet://libserv.msstate.edn`

Cartography

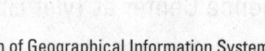

next-gis

Discussion of Geographical Information Systems (GIS) and cartography-related topics on the NeXT and other workstation computers. Some moderated reposting of comp.infosys.gis occurs as well.

Keywords: Geography, Cartography, GIS, NeXT

Audience: GIS Users, NeXT Users

Contact: Steven R. Staton sstaton@deltos.com

Details: Free

User Info: To subscribe to the list, send an e-mail message to the URL address shown below consisting of a single line reading:

SUB next-gis YourFirstName YourLastName

To send a message to the entire list, address it to: next-gis@DistributionAddress

`mailto:listserv@deltos.com`

The University of Kansas Library

The library's holdings are large and wide-ranging and contain significant collections in many fields.

Keywords: Botany, Chinese Studies, Cartography, Kansas, Opera, Ornithology, Joyce

(James), Yeats (William Butler), Walpole (Sir Robert, Collections of)

Audience: General Public, Researchers, Librarians, Document Delivery Professionals

Contact: John S. Miller

Details: Free

Expect: Username, Send: relay <cr>

`telnet://kuhub.cc.ukans.edu`

University of Wisconsin at Milwaukee Library

The library's holdings are large and wide-ranging and contain significant collections in many fields.

Keywords: Art, Architecture, Business, Cartography, Geography, Geology, Urban Studies, Literature (English), Literature (American)

Audience: Researchers, Students, General Public

Details: Free

Expect: Login, Send: Lib; Expect: vDIAL prompt, Send: Library

`telnet://uwmcat.lib.uwm.edu`

USGS (United States Geological Survey) Gopher

A gopher site covering issues related to the United State Geological Survey.

Keywords: Cartography, Geology

Sponsor: United States Geological Survey

Audience: Geologists, Cartologists

Profile: The USGS gopher was established to provide general information about USGS, information about USGS Divisions, publications, data, and briefings, USGS's Network resources, and other data on geology, hydrology, and cartography.

Contact: Gopher Operator webmaster@info.er.usgs.gov

`gopher://info.er.usgs.gov`

`telnet://libserv.msstate.edu`

Cartoons

alt.binaries.pictures.cartoons

A Usenet newsgroup devoted to cartoon illustrations.

Keywords: Cartoons

Audience: Animators, General Public

User Info: To subscribe to this Usenet newsgroup, you need access to a newsreader.

`news://alt.binaries.pictures.cartoons`

The University of Iowa Libraries

The library's holdings are large and wide-ranging and contain significant collections in many fields.

Keywords: Hunt (Leigh), Native American Studies, Typography, Railroads, Cartoons, French Revolution, NASA, Hydraulics

Audience: General Public, Researchers, Librarians, Document Delivery Professionals

Details: Free

Send <RETURN>to display a menu of available systems. Type 1 for OASIS access and press <RETURN>to display the Welcome to OASIS screen.

`telnet://oasis.uiowa.edu`

Case Law (US)

MEGA (Combined Federal/State Case Law)

The Federal/State Case Law combined library contains files that allow one-stop searching of combined federal and state case law on the LEXIS service. American Law Reports (ALR)) and Lawyers' Edition, 2d articles are also included.

Keywords: Case Law (US), Law (US State), Law (US Federal)

Audience: Lawyers

Profile: The MEGA file is a one-stop search of all available federal and state case law on the LEXIS service. The circuit-base MEGA files combine federal and state case law from federal and state courts within the geographical area defined by the federal circuit. The state-based MEGA files combine case law from the courts of the state plus case law from the federal circuit for that state and the federal district courts within the state. Two chronological files restrict combined federal and state case law searches to particular date ranges. Each MEGA file includes all available U.S. Supreme Court cases. American Law Reports (ALR)) and Lawyers' Edition, 2d (LEd2) articles are also included.

Contact: New Sales Group @ (800) 227-4908 or (513) 859-5398 inside the US, or (513) 865-7981 for all inquires outside the US.

User Info: To subscribe, contact Mead directly.

To examine the Lexis user guide, you can access it at the ftp site of the University of Texas at Austin at the URL address: ftp://ftp.cc.utexas.edu

The files are in: /pub/res-services/LEXIS

`telnet://nex.meaddata.com`

STATES (States Library)

The combined States Library contains case law, code, and agency materials from the 53 individual US state libraries (50 states plus the District of Columbia, Puerto Rico, and the Virgin Islands), all in the same library.

Keywords: Law, Analysis, Case Law, States

Audience: Lawyers

Profile: The combined States Library contains case law, code, and agency materials from the 53 individual state libraries (50 states plus the District of Columbia, Puerto Rico and the Virgin Islands), all in the same library. The States library also features many large group files which allow several individual files to be accessed in the same search. Many of the group files involve case law, including files that cover all state case law available on the LEXIS service plus ALR material and files that combine all federal and state case law available on the LEXIS service.

Contact: New Sales Group at 800-227-4908 or 513-859-5398 inside the US, or 1-513-865-7981 for all inquires outside the US.

User Info: To subscribe, contact Mead directly.

To examine the Lexis user guide, you can access it at the ftp site of the University of Texas at Austin at the URL address: ftp://ftp.cc.utexas.edu

The files are in: /pub/ref-services/LEXIS

`telnet://nex.meaddata.com`

`http://www.meaddata.com`

Catalyst

Catalyst

This is the electronic version of Catalyst, a refereed print journal for community college educators.

Keywords: Education (Adult), Education (Distance), Education (Continuing), Education (International)

Audience: Educators, Administrators, Faculty, Researchers

Details: Free

User Info: To subscribe to the journal, send an e-mail message to the URL address below, consisting of a single line reading:

SUB catalyst YourFirstName YourLastName

To send a message to the entire list, address it to: catalyst@vtvm1.bitnet

`mailto:listserv@vtvm1.cc.vt.edu`

Catholicism

AmerCath (History of American Catholicism)

This mailing list focuses on the history of American Catholicism.

Keywords: Catholicism, Christianity, Religion

Sponsor: Jefferson Community College, University of Kentucky, Louisville, KY, USA

Audience: Researchers, Educators, Students, Catholics

Profile: Since AMERCATH can be accessed internationally, it thus forms a global network of people who research and teach the history of American Catholicism. AMERCATH facilitates communication among faculty, students, and researchers.

Contact: Anne Kearney
jccannek@ukcc.uky.edu

Details: Free

User Info: To subscribe to the list, send an e-mail message to the address below, consisting of a single line reading:

Sub AmerCath YourFirstName YourLastName

To send a message to the entire list, address it to:

AmerCath@ukcc.uky.edu

`mailto:listserv@ukcc.uky.edu`

Catholic

The Catholic mailing list is a forum for Catholics who wish to discuss their discipleship to Jesus Christ in terms of the Catholic approach to Christianity. "Catholic" is loosely defined as anyone embracing the Catholic approach to Christianity whether Roman Catholic, Anglo-Catholic, or Orthodox. Discussions on ecumenism are encouraged.

Keywords: Catholicism, Ecumenism, Religion

Audience: Catholics, Priests, Theologians

Contact: Cindy Smith
cms@dragon.com

Details: Free

User Info: To subscribe to the list, send an e-mail message to the address below, consisting of a single line reading:

SUB Catholic YourFirstName YourLastName

To send a message to the entire list, address it to:

Catholic@american.edu

Notes: This list is also bi-directionally forwarded to the newsgroup bit.listserv.catholic.

`mailto:listserv@american.edu`

A
B
C
D
E
F
G
H
I
J
K
L
M
N
O
P
Q
R
S
T
U
V
W
X
Y
Z

Catholic Doctrine

This is for discussions of orthodox Catholic theology by everyone under the jurisdiction of the Holy Father, John Paul II. No attacks on the Catholic Church here, please.

Keywords: Theology, Catholocism

Audience: Catholics, Priests, Theologians

Contact: catholic-request@sarto.gaithersburg.md.us

Details: Free

User Info: To subscribe to the list, send an e-mail message requesting a subscription to the URL address below.

To send a message to the entire list, address it to:

catholic@sarto.gaithersburg.md.us

Notes: There is an archive server (containing Catholic art and magisterial documents) associated with this list. Send mail to the URL address below to get details about the archive server.

`mailto:catholic-request@sarto.gaithersburg.md.us`

Catholic University of America Gopher

★★

Gopher server of the Catholic University of America.

Keywords: Catholicism, Libraries

Sponsor: Catholic University of America

Audience: Catholics

Profile: The Catholic University of America gopher provides access to CUA's libraries and archived material as well as providing links to outside, and foreign, related gophers, and electronic resources.

`gopher://gopher.cua.edu`

Catholic-action

★

Catholic-action is a moderated list concerned with Catholic evangelism, church revitalization, and preservation of Catholic teachings, traditions, and values, and the vital effort to decapitate modernist heresy.

Keywords: Catholicism, Evangelism, Religion

Audience: Catholics, Priests

Contact: Richard Freeman rfreeman@vpnet.chi.il.us

Details: Free

User Info: To subscribe to the list, send an e-mail message requesting a subscription to the URL address below.

`mailto:rfreeman@vpnet.chi.il.us`

CAUCE-L (Canadian Association for University Continuing Education)

CAUCE-L (Canadian Association for University Continuing Education)

Provides an electronic forum for the discussion of issues (broad, narrow, practical, theoretical, controversial, or mundane) related to university continuing education.

Keywords: Education (Adult), Education (Distance), Education (Continuing)

Sponsor: Canadian Association for University Continuing Education

Audience: Educators, Administrators, Faculty

Details: Free

User Info: To subscribe to the list, send an e-mail message to the URL address below, consisting of a single line reading:

SUB cauce-l YourFirstName YourLastName

To send a message to the entire list, address it to: cauce@max.cc.uregina.ca

`mailto:listserv@max.cc.uregina.ca`

Caves

alt.caving

A Usenet newsgroup dedicated to discussions of caving and related issues, including cave locations, equipment, spelunking techniques, and other caving information.

Keywords: Spelunking, Caves

Audience: Spelunkers

User Info: To subscribe to this Usenet newsgroup, you need access to a newsreader.

`news://alt.caving`

Cavers

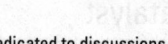

This is an information resource and forum for anyone interested in exploring caves.

Keywords: Caves, Spelunking

Audience: Cave Explorers, Spelunkers

Contact: John D. Sutter cavers-request@vlsi.bu.edu

Details: Free

User Info: To subscribe to the list, send an e-mail message requesting a subscription to the URL address below.

To send a message to the entire list, address it to:

cavers@vlsi.bu.edu

`mailto:cavers-request@vlsi.bu.edu`

CBDS-I

CBDS-I

★★

A mailing list for the discussion of CBDS (Circuit Board Design System).

Keywords: Engineering, Computer-Aided Design, Electronics

Audience: Engineers

Contact: netman@suvm.acs.syr.edu

Details: Free

User Info: To subscribe to the list, send an e-mail message to the URL address below consisting of a single line reading:

SUB cbds-l YourFirstName YourLastName

To send a message to the entire list, address it to:

cbds-l@suvm.acs.syr.edu

`mailto:listserv@suvm.acs.syr.edu`

CCES-L

CCES-L

★★

A mailing list for the national communication branch of the CFES (Canadian Federation of Engineering Students).

Keywords: Engineering, Canada

Audience: Engineers, Students

Contact: Canadian Federation of Engineering Students cfes@jupiter.sun.csd.unb.ca

Details: Free

User Info: To subscribe to the list, send an e-mail message to the URL address below consisting of a single line reading:

SUB cces-l YourFirstName YourLastName

To send a message to the entire list, address it to: cces-l@unb.ca

`mailto:listserv@unb.ca`

CCNEWS

CCNEWS

An electronic forum for campus-computing newsletter editors and other publications specialists.

Keywords: Computers, Editors, Students, Newsletters

Audience: Students (college), Editors

Profile: CCNEWS consists of a biweekly newsletter that focuses on the writing, editing, designing, and producing of campus-computing publications, and an articles abstracts published on alternating weeks that describes new contributions to the articles archive.

Contact: Wendy Rickard Bollentin
ccnews@educom.bitnet

Details: Free

User Info: To subscribe to the list, send an e-mail message to the URL address below consisting of a single line reading:

SUB ccnews YourFirstName YourLastName

To send a message to the entire list, address it to: ccnews@educom.bitnet

Inquire about needing a password.

`mailto:listserv@bitnic.cren.net`

Cd-Forum

Cd-Forum

The purpose of this list is to provide support and to discuss/share experiences about gender-related issues, including cross dressing, transvestism, and transsexualism.

Keywords: Transsexualism, Transvestism, Sexuality, Gender

Audience: Transsexuals, Transvestites

Contact: Valerie
cd-request@valis.biocad.com

Details: Free

User Info: To subscribe to the list, send an e-mail message requesting a subscription to the URL address below.

To send a message to the entire list, address it to: cd@valis.biocad.com

Notes: This list is in digest format.

`mailto:cd-request@valis.biocad.com`

CD-ROM

Amiga CD-ROM

For Amiga users who are interested in CD-ROM drives and discs.

Keywords: Computers, Amiga, CD-ROM

Audience: Computer Users

Contact: ben@ben.com

Details: Free

User Info: To subscribe to the list, send an e-mail message requesting a subscription to the URL address below.

To send a message to the entire list, address it to: cdrom-list@ben.com

`mailto:cdrom-list-request@ben.com`

CDPub

CDPub is an electronic mailing list for those engaged or interested in CD-ROM publishing in general, and in desktop CD-ROM recorders and publishing systems in particular. Topics of interest to the list include information on the various desktop publishing systems for premastering using CD-ROM media and tapes (for example, DAT), replication services, various standards of interest to publishers (for example, ISO9660, RockRidge), retrieval engines, and platform independence issues. Discussions on all platforms are welcome.

Keywords: CD-ROM, Electronic Publishing, Desktop Publishing

Audience: CD-ROM Publishers, Desktop Publishers, Publishers

Contact: CDPub-Info@knex.via.mind.org

Details: Free

User Info: To subscribe to the list, send an e-mail message requesting a subscription to the URL address below.

To send a message to the entire list, address it to: CDPub@knex.via.mind.org

`mailto:mail-server@knex.via.mind.org`

CE Software

CE Software

Technical support for CE Software Products, such as QuickKeys for the Macintosh.

Keywords: Software, Technical Support, Macintosh

Audience: Software users

Details: Free

User Info: To subscribe to the list, send an e-mail message requesting a subscription to the URL address below.

`mailto:ce_info%cedsm@uunet.uu.net`

CEC

CEC

A mailing list for the CEC (Canadian Electro-Acoustics Community).

Keywords: Engineering, Acoustical Engineering, Canada, Canadian Electro-Acoustics Community

Audience: Engineers

Contact: Peter Gross
grosspa@qucdn.queensu.ca

Details: Free

User Info: To subscribe to the list, send an e-mail message to the URL address below, consisting of a single line reading:

SUB cec YourFirstName YourLastName

To send a message to the entire list, address it to:

cec@qucdn.queensu.ca

`mailto:listserv@qucdn.queensu.ca`

CEDAR (Central European Environmental Data Request) Facility

CEDAR (Central European Environmental Data Request) Facility

This gopher site provides information about the environmental and scientific community in Central and Eastern Europe (CEE), with access to environmental information located throughout the world on various international computer networks and hosts.

Keywords: Europe, EEC, Environment

Sponsor: The International Society for Environmental Protection, and The Austrian Federal Ministry for Environment, Youth and Family (BMUJF)

Audience: Environmentalists, Educators, Students, Urban Planners

Contact: cedar-info@cedar.univie.ac.at

Notes: CEDAR Marxergasse 3/20, A-1030 Vienna, Austria Tel.: +43-1-715 58 79

`gopher://pan.cedar.univie.ac.at`

CEE Environmental Libraries Database

CEE Environmental Libraries Database

A directory of over 300 libraries and environmental information centers in Central Eastern Europe that

A B C D E F G H I J K L M N O P Q R S T U V W X Y Z

A B **C** D E F G H I J K L M N O P Q R S T U V W X Y Z

specalize in, or maintain significant collections of information about, the environment, ecology, sustainable living, or conservation. The database concentrates on six Central Eastern European countries: Bulgaria, Czech Republic, Hungary, Romania, Slovakia, and Poland.

Keywords: Central Eastern Europe, Environment, Sustainable Living, Bulgaria, Czech Republic, Hungary, Romania, Slovakia, Poland.

Sponsor: The Wladyslaw Poniecki Charitable Foundation, Inc.

Audience: Environmentalists, Green Movement, Librarians, Community Builders, Sustainable Living Specialists.

Profile: This database is the product of an Environmental Training Project (ETP) that was funded in 1992 by the US Agency for International Development as a 5-year cooperative agreement with a consortium headed by the University of Minnesota (US AID Cooperative Agreement Number EUR-0041-A-002-2020). Other members of the consortium include the University of Pittsburgh's Center for Hazardous Materials Research, The Institute for Sustainable Communities, and the World Wildlife Fund. The Wladyslaw Poniecki Charitable Foundation, Inc., was a subcontractor to the World Wildlife Fund and published the Directory of Libraries and Environmental Information Centers in Central Eastern Europe: A Locator/ Directory. This gopher database consists of an electronic version of the printed directory, subsequently modified and updated online. Access to the data is facilitated by a WAIS search engine which makes it possible to retrieve information about libraries, subject area specializations, personnel, and so on.

Contact: Doug Kahn, CEDAR
kahn@pan.cedar.univie.ac.at

```
gopher://gopher.poniecki.berkeley.edu
```

Cell Biology

University of Texas Health Science Center at Tyler Library

The library's holdings are large and wide-ranging and contain significant collections in many fields.

Keywords: Biochemistry, Cardiopulmonary Medicine, Cell Biology, Family Practice, Molecular Biology

Audience: Researchers, Students, General Public

Details: Free

Expect: Username Prompt, Send: LIS

```
telnet://athena.uthscsa.edu
```

Cell Church Discussion Group

Cell Church Discussion Group

A list for Christians who are in cell churches or in churches that are in transition to becoming cell churches, as well as anyone interested in learning more about cell churches. A cell church is a nontraditional form of church life in which small groups of Christians (cells) meet in a special way in their homes for the evangelism of the unchurched, the bonding of believers, their nurture, and ministry to one another.

Keywords: Cell Churches, Christianity, Evangelism, Religion

Audience: Christians, Theologians, Evangelists

Contact: Jon Reid
reid@cei.com

Details: Free

User Info: To subscribe to the list, send an e-mail message to the URL address below with the single word SUBSCRIBE in the body (not subject) of your message.

To send a message to the entire list, address it to: cell-church@bible.acu.edu

Notes: The group archives, FAQ, and helpful articles are available by anonymous FTP from bible.acu.edu; they can also be retrieved by sending mail to cell-church-archives@bible.acu.edu with the single word LIST for a list of files, or HELP for more information.

```
mailto:cell-church-
request@bible.acu.edu
```

Cello

Cello

A DOS-based Internet browser incorporating WWW (World Wide Web), gopher, ftp, telnet, and usenet.

Keywords: Internet Tools, Cello, DOS

Audience: Internet Surfers

Details: Free

```
ftp://fatty.law.cornell.edu
```

```
gopher://fatty.law.cornell.edu
```

```
http://fatty.law.cornell.edu/cello/
cellotop.html
```

Cello FAQ

A site containing common questions and answers about Cello, a multipurpose Internet browser that allows access to the myriad information resources of the Internet. It supports World Wide Web, Gopher, FTP, CSO/pf/qi, and Usenet News retrievals natively,

and other protocols (WAIS, Hytelnet, Telnet, and TN3270) through external clients and public gateways.

Keywords: Internet Tools, Internet Reference

Sponsor: Cornell Law School, New York, USA

Audience: Students, Computer Scientists, Researchers.

```
http://www.law.cornell.edu/cello/
cellofaq.html
```

Cellular Technology

AT&T Bell Laboratories WWW Information Page

This web site provides information on research and development at AT&T Bell Laboratories.

Keywords: Telecommunications, Technology, AT&T, Cellular Technology

Sponsor: AT&T Bell Laboratories

Audience: Engineers, Educators, Communications Specialists

Contact: webmaster@research.att.com

Details: Free

```
http://www.research.att.com
```

Celtic Culture

soc.culture.celtic

A Usenet newsgroup providing information and discussion about Irish Scottish, Britain, and Cornish culture.

Keywords: Celtic Culture, Sociology

Audience: Sociologists, Celts

Details: Free

User Info: To subscribe to this Usenet newsgroup, you need access to a newsreader.

```
news:soc.culture.celtic
```

Celtic Philology

Harvard University Library

The library's holdings are large and wide-ranging and contain significant collections in many fields.

Keywords: Afrikaans, Alchemy, Arabic Culure (History of), Celtic Philology, Congo Languages, Folklore, Hebraica, Mormonism, Numismatics, Quakers, Sanskrit, Witchcraft, Arabic Philology

Audience: General Public, Researchers, Librarians, Document Delivery Professionals

Details: Free

Expect: Mitek Server..., Send: Enter or Return; Expect: prompt, Send: hollis

`telnet://hollis.harvard.edu`

Celtic Studies

soc.cultures.celtic

This Usenet newsgroup discusses all issues related to Celtic culture, including its history, language, art, and religion.

Keywords: Celtic Studies

Sponsor: Mo dhachaidh, Edinburgh, Scotland

Audience: Anthropologists, Celtic Enthusiasts

Contact: Godfrey Nolan
godfrey@itc.icl.ie

User Info: To subscribe to this Usenet newsgroup, you need access to a newsreader.

Notes: The soc.culture.celtic FAQ is particularly large and contains many references to other online resources — it is posted to the newsgroup regularly.

`news://alt.cultures.celtic`

CEM-L

CEM-L

A mailing list for discussion surrounding the UTD (University of Texas at Dallas) Center for Engineering Mathematics.

Keywords: Engineering, Mathematics

Audience: Engineers, Mathematicians, Educators, Students

Contact: David Lippke
lippke@utdallas.edn

Details: Free

User Info: To subscribe to the list, send an e-mail message to the URL address below, consisting of a single line reading:

SUB cem-l YourFirstName YourLastName

To send a message to the entire list, address it to:

cem-l@utdallas.edu

`mailto:listserv@utdallas.edu`

Censorship

alt.censorship

A Usenet newsgroup providing information and discussion about freedom of speech and freedom of the press.

Keywords: Censorship, Freedom of Speech, Constitution (US), Activism

Audience: Press, Students, Educators, Activists

User Info: To subscribe to this Usenet newsgroup, you need access to a newsreader.

`news:alt.censorship`

Census Data

1991 Census of Population Documentation

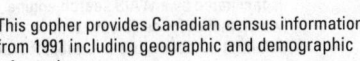

This gopher provides Canadian census information from 1991 including geographic and demographic information.

Keywords: Census Data, Canada, Demography, Geography

Audience: Canadians, Researchers, Demographers

Contact: David McCallum
carl@acadvm1.uottawa.ca

`gopher://alpha.epas.utoronto.ca/Data Library/Census of Population`

LabStat

The public database of the Bureau of Labor Statistics.

Keywords: Economics, Labor, Census Data

Sponsor: United States Government, Bureau of Labor Statistics

Audience: General Public, Statisticians, Researchers

Profile: LABSTAT provides current and historical data, as well as numerous press releases. This site is composed of individual databases (in flat file format) corresponding to each of 26 surveys.

Contact: labstat.helpdesk@bls.gov.

Details: Free

Login: anonymous; use e-mail address as password.

Notes: For each news release published by the Bureau of Labor Statistics, the two most current are stored in the /news.release directory. The documentation provides a list of the abbreviations used to identify the news releases, and a description of the sub-directories available to the user.

`ftp://stats.bls.gov`

The Texas Information Highway

Access to the public information resources of the state of Texas.

Keywords: Texas, States, Government, Census Data, Tourism

Sponsor: Texas Department of Information Resources

Audience: Texans, General Public

Profile: Still under construction as we go to press, this is a model program to make state and local information resources available to Internet users. The current collection features city, country, and state political information, including full-text of bills before the Texas state legislature. Materials related to Texas history and tourism are also provided, along with links to Texas-area user groups and other state and federal information servers.

Contact: Wayne McDilda
wayne@dir.texas.gov

`gopher://info.texas.gov`

U.S. Bureau of the Census Gopher

A gopher offering official census data and services direct from the Census Bureau.

Keywords: Census Data, Demography, Statistics

Sponsor: U.S. Census Bureau

Audience: Journalists, Government Officials, General Public

Profile: A wealth of demographic and economic data from the Census Bureau. Information available includes population estimates, financial data from state and local governments, and assorted statistical briefs. This gopher also has details on the offices, programs, and personnel of the Bureau itself, as well as links to other federal information systems and sources of Census data.

Contact: gatekeeper@census.gov

Details: Free, Images

`gopher://gopher.census.gov`

`http://www.census.gov`

Center for Biomedical Informatics, Brazil

Center for Biomedical Informatics, Brazil

The Center for Biomedical Informatics maintains a software library with 50 disks containing about 150 public-domain medical application programs for IBM-PC-compatible microcomputers.

Keywords: Health Sciences, Public Domain Software

Sponsor: Center for Biomedical Informatics, Brazil

Audience: Physicians, Nurses, Dentists, University Biomedical Researchers, Students

Details: Costs

To receive the catalogue in electronic form, send the following one-line message to infomed@ccvax.unicamp.br or infomed@bruc.bitnet: get public-domain p (for version in Portuguese) get public-domain e (for version in English). Instructions on how to acquire the software are included.

`ftp://ccsun.unicamp.br`

A
B
C
D
E
F
G
H
I
J
K
L
M
N
O
P
Q
R
S
T
U
V
W
X
Y
Z

A
B
C
D
E
F
G
H
I
J
K
L
M
N
O
P
Q
R
S
T
U
V
W
X
Y
Z

Center for Extreme Ultraviolet Astrophysics

Center for Extreme Ultraviolet Astrophysics

A department of the University of California at Berkeley devoted to research in extreme ultraviolet astronomy. It is the ground-based institution of EUVE (the Extreme Ultraviolet Explorer), a NASA satellite launched in 1992.

Keywords: Astronomy, Astrophysics, EUVE, NASA, Satellite

Sponsor: NASA and University of California at Berkeley

Audience: Astronomers, Astrophysicists

Profile: Provides access to details about the EUVE Guest Observer (EGO) Center, the EUVE Public Archive of Mission Data and Information, satellite operation information, and so on. The EUVE Guest Observer Center provides information, software, and data to EUVE Guest Observers.

Contact: egoinfo@cea.berkeley.edu, archive@cea.berkeley.edu

Details: Free

http://cea-ftp.cea.berkeley.edu/

Central Eastern Europe

CEE Environmental Libraries Database

A directory of over 300 libraries and environmental information centers in Central Eastern Europe that specalize in, or maintain significant collections of information about the environment, ecology, sustainable living, or conservation. The database concentrates on six Central Eastern European countries: Bulgaria, Czech Republic, Hungary, Romania, Slovakia, and Poland.

Keywords: Central Eastern Europe, Environment, Sustainable Living, Bulgaria, Czech Republic, Hungary, Romania, Slovakia, Poland.

Sponsor: The Wladyslaw Poniecki Charitable Foundation, Inc.

Audience: Environmentalists, Green Movement, Librarians, Community Builders, Sustainable Living Specialists.

Profile: This database is the product of an Environmental Training Project (ETP) that was funded in 1992 by the US Agency for International Development as a 5-year cooperative agreement with a consortium headed by the University of Minnesota (US AID Cooperative Agreement Number EUR-0041-A-002-

2020). Other members of the consortium include the University of Pittsburgh's Center for Hazardous Materials Research, The Institute for Sustainable Communities, and the World Wildlife Fund. The Wladyslaw Poniecki Charitable Foundation, Inc., was a subcontractor to the World Wildlife Fund and published the Directory of Libraries and Environmental Information Centers in Central Eastern Europe: A Locator/ Directory . This gopher database consists of an electronic version of the printed directory, subsequently modified and updated online. Access to the data is facilitated by a WAIS search engine which makes it possible to retrieve information about libraries, subject area specializations, personnel, and so on.

Contact: Doug Kahn, CEDAR kahn@pan.cedar.univie.ac.at

gopher://gopher.poniecki.berkeley.edu

Central Europe

Central European Environment Data Report (CEDAR) Facility

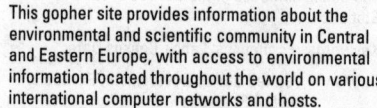

This gopher site provides information about the environmental and scientific community in Central and Eastern Europe, with access to environmental information located throughout the world on various international computer networks and hosts.

Keywords: Europe, Central Europe, Eastern Europe, Environment

Sponsor: The International Society for Environmental Protection, and The Austrian Federalorer), a NASA satellite launched in 1992.

Keywords:

Audience: Environmentalists, Educators, Students, Urban Planners, Environmental Scientists

Profile: The CEDAR Facility, established in 1991, is administered by the International Society for Environmental Protection (ISEP). The Facility is designed to provide regional groups and individuals with access to its information retrieval and higher computing resources, technical advice and database and network access support. In addition, CEDAR works to facilitate information and dialogue exchange with organizations in other parts of the world and in partner countries; and to promote training forums, including the joint development of seminars and conferences with ISEP on environmental and network topics. Finally, CEDAR develops and manages environmental reference data sets, including a US EPA bibliographic reference on hazardous waste treatment, CEDAR databases on Central and Eastern European

environmental expertise and information, and the holdings of the Regional Environmental Center Library at Budapest.

Contact: cedar-info@cedar.univie.ac.at

gopher://pan.cedar.univie.ac.at

CERRO (Central European Regional Research Organization)

CERRO provides access to information about the economic restructuring of Central Europe, including a discussion list, papers, news summaries, and pointers to other gophers in Central Europe.

Keywords: Central Europe, Economics, News

Audience: Economists, Researchers, Journalists

Contact: gunther.maier@wu-wien.ac.at

Details: Free

gopher://osiris.wu.wein.ac.at

EcoDirectory

A directory of libraries and Environmental Information Centers in Central Eastern Europe.

Keywords: Environment, Eastern Europe, Central Europe

Sponsor: The Wladyslaw Poniecki Charitable Foundation, Inc.

Audience: Environmentalists, Librarians, International Development Specialists

Profile: This database is the product of an Environmental Training Project (ETP) that was founded in 1992 by the US Agency for International Development. The project concentrated on six Central and Eastern European countries: Bulgaria, Czech Republic, Hungary, Romania, Slovakia, and Poland.

            It contains information on over 300 libraries and Environmental Information Centers in those countries. Access to the data is facilitated by a WAIS search engine that makes it possible to retrieve information about libraries, subject area specializations, personnel, and so on.

Contact: Joerg Findeisen, CEDAR findeisen@pan.cedar.univie.ac.at

gopher://gopher.poniecki.berkeley.edu

Cerebi

Cerebi

This list discusses the Cerebus comic book by Dave Sim. Anything relating to Cerebus or Sim is welcome.

Keywords: Comic Books, Sim (Dave)

Audience: Comics Enthusiasts

Contact: Christian Walters cerebi-request@tomservo.b23b.ingr.com

Details: Free

User Info: To subscribe to the list, send an e-mail message requesting a subscription to the URL address below.

To send a message to the entire list, address it to:
cerebi@tomservo.b23b.ingr.com

Notes: It's just an echo list, so anything that gets mailed is bounced to everyone.

```
mailto:cerebi-
request@tomservo.b23b.ingr.com
```

CERFnet Guide

CERFnet Guide ★

A comprehensive guide to the CERFnet (California Education and Research Federation Network), a data-communications regional network that operates throughout California. The purpose of CERFnet is to advance science and education by assisting the interchange of information among research and educational institutions.

Keywords: Internet, Science, Education, California

Audience: Internet Surfers, Researchers, Educators

Contact: CERFnet Hotline
help@cerf.net

Details: Free

Files are in: cerfnet/cerfnet_info/cerfnet_guide/

```
ftp://nic.cerf.net
```

CERFNet News

CERFNet News ★

This is a mid-level network linking academic, government, and industrial research facilities throughout California.

Keywords: Education, California

Sponsor: California Education and Research Federation Network

Audience: Researchers, Students (college, graduate)

Contact: help@cerf.net

Details: Free

```
gopher://gopher.cerf.net/11/cerfnet
```

CERT (Computer Emergency Response Team) Advisory

CERT (Computer Emergency Response Team) Advisory ★★

A major directory on computer advisory, providing access to a broad range of related resources (library catalogs, databases, and servers) via the Internet.

Keywords: Computers, Security, Computer Networking

Audience: Computer Users

Profile: Profides information on how to obtain a patch or details of a workaround for a known computer security problem. CERT works with vendors to produce a workaround or a patch for a problem, and does not publish vulnerability information until a workaround or patch is available. A CERT advisory may also be a warning about ongoing attacks to network systems.

Contact: cert@cert.org

```
ftp://cert.org/pub/cert_advisories
```

Cervantes (Miguel de)

Dartmouth College Library ★★

The library's holdings are large and wide-ranging and contain significant collections in many fields.

Keywords: American Calligraphy, Cervantes (Miguel de), Railroads, Polar Regions, Frost (Robert), Shakespeare (William), Spanish Plays

Audience: General Public, Researchers, Librarians, Document Delivery Professionals

Contact: Katharina Klemperer
kathy.klemperer@dartmouth.edu

Details: Free

Expect: login, Send: wolfpac

```
telnet://lib.dartmouth.edu
```

CEXPRESS (Computer Express Internet Superstore)

CEXPRESS (Computer Express Internet Superstore) ★

Computer Express offers over 3,000 software titles and hardware products, available for immediate delivery.

Keywords: Computer Products

Audience: Consumers

```
mailto:info@cexpress.com
```

```
gopher cexpress.com
```

```
http://cexpress.com
```

cfcp-members

cfcp-members ★

The Confederation of Future Computer Professionals (CFCP) is a group of users on the Internet who are interested enough in various fields of computers to consider computers as their future. The Confederation exists to foster education and stimulate communication.

Keywords: Internet, Computers

Audience: Internet Surfers, Computer Users

Contact: mlindsey@nyx.cs.du.edu

Details: Free

User Info: To subscribe to the list, send an e-mail message requesting a subscription to the URL address below.

```
mailto:mlindsey@nyx.cs.du.edu
```

CFD

CFD

A mailing list for the CFD (Computational Fluid Dynamics Group).

Keywords: Engineering, Fluid Dynamics

Audience: Engineers

Contact: justin@ukcc.uky.edu
justin@engr.uky.edu

Details: Free

User Info: To subscribe to the list, send an e-mail message to the URL address below, consisting of a single line reading:

SUB cfd YourFirstName YourLastName

To send a message to the entire list, address it to:

cfd@ukcc.uky.edu

```
mailto:justin@ukcc.uky.edu
```

CFES-L

CFES-L

National communication branch of the CFES (Canadian Federation of Engineering Students).

A
B
C
D
E
F
G
H
I
J
K
L
M
N
O
P
Q
R
S
T
U
V
W
X
Y
Z

Keywords: Engineering, Students, Canada

Audience: Engineers, Students

Contact: Canadian Federation of Engineering Students
cfes@jupiter.sun.csd.unb.ca

Details: Free

User Info: To subscribe to the list, send an e-mail message to the URL address below consiting of a single line reading:

SUB cfes-l YourFirstName YourLastName

To send a message to the entire list, address it to:

cfes-l@unb.ca

`mailto:listserv@unb.ca`

CGN (Christian Growth Newsletter)

CGN (Christian Growth Newsletter)

This site is intended to help Christians in personal growth, and includes testimonials and encouraging articles.

Keywords: Christianity, Religion

Audience: Christians

Contact: Laura Smith
bible@olsen.ch

`mailto:bible@olsen.ch`

Chalkhills

Chalkhills

A mailing list for the discussion of the music and records of XTC (the band).

Keywords: Pop Music, XTC

Audience: Pop Music Enthusiasts, XTC Enthusiasts

Contact: John M. Relph
chalkhills-request@presto.ig.com

Details: Free

User Info: To subscribe to the list, send an e-mail message requesting a subscription to the URL address below.

To send a message to the entire list, address it to: chalkhills@presto.ig.com

Notes: Chalkhills is moderated and distributed in a digest format.

`mailto:chalkhills-request@presto.ig.com`

Chaos Theory

Artificial Life

A forum for the accumulation and dissemination of information about all aspects of the Artificial Life enterprise. Services provided include an FTP site containing preprints and software, a bibliographic database on Artificial Life, and links to various Usenet services.

Keywords: Artificial Life, Chaos Theory

Sponsor: MITPress, Cambridge, Massachusetts, USA

Audience: Mathematical Biologists, Researchers, Theoretical Biologists

Contact: Chris Langton
cgl@santafe.edu

`http://alife.santafe.edu`

Spanky Fractal Database

This web site provides a collection of fractals and fractal-related material for free distribution on the Internet.

Keywords: Mathematics, Chaos Theory, Computer Programming, Computer Graphics

Audience: Mathematicians, Computer Programmers

Profile: Contains information on dynamical systems, software, distributed fractal generators, galleries, and databases from all over the world.

Contact: Noel Giffin
noel@triumf.ca

Details: Free

`http://spanky.triumf.ca`

Chat Groups

alt.kids-talk

A Usenet newsgroup that provides a place for the pre-collegiate to chat.

Keywords: Chat Groups, Children

Audience: Kids, Students (K-12)

User Info: To subscribe to this Usenet newsgroup, you need access to a newsreader.

`news:alt.kids-talk`

alt.romance.chat

A Usenet newsgroup providing discussion about the romantic side of love.

Keywords: Chat Groups, Romance

Audience: General Public

User Info: To subscribe to this Usenet newsgroup, you need access to a newsreader.

`news:alt.romance.chat`

k12.chat.junior

A Usenet newsgroup providing information and discussion for and about students in junior high school.

Keywords: Students, Chat Groups

Audience: Students (K-8)

Details: Free

User Info: To subscribe to this Usenet newsgroup, you need access to a newsreader.

`news:k12.chat.junior`

k12.chat.senior

A Usenet newsgroup providing information and discussion for and about students in senior high school.

Keywords: Students, Chat Groups

Audience: Students (K-12)

Details: Free

User Info: To subscribe to this Usenet newsgroup, you need access to a newsreader.

`news:k12.chat.senior`

Chaucer (Geoffrey)

Chaucer

A discussion list on the subject of Medieval English literature, especially that of Chaucer.

Keywords: Chaucer (Geoffrey), Literature (English)

Audience: Chaucer Fans, English Teachers

Contact: Dan Mosser

mosserd@vtm1.cc.vt.edu

`mailto: CHAUCER@VTM1.CC.VT.EDU`

University of Chicago Library

The library's holdings are large and wide-ranging and contain significant collections in many fields.

Keywords: English Bibles, Lincoln (Abraham), Kentucky & Ohio River Valley (History of), Balzac (Honore de), American Drama, Cromwell (Oliver), Goethe, Judaica, Italy, Chaucer (Geoffrey), Wells (Ida, Personal Papers of), Douglas (Stephen A.), Italy, Literature (Children's)

Audience: General Public, Researchers, Librarians, Document Delivery Professionals

Details: Free

Expect: ENTER CLASS, Send: LIB48 3;
Expect: CONNECTED, Send: RETURN

`telnet://olorin.uchicago.edu`

ChE Electronic Newsletter

ChE Electronic Newsletter

This newsletter contains information of interest to
chemical engineers.

Keywords: Chemical Engineering, Chemistry,
Engineering

Audience: Chemical Engineers

Contact: Martyn S. Ray

trayms@cc.curtin.edu.au

Details: Free

Inquire about needing a password.

`mailto:trayms@cc.curtin.edu.au`

Chemical Engineering

American Chemical Society

This is the gopher site of the American Chemical
Society.

Keywords: Chemistry, Chemical Engineering

Sponsor: The American Chemical Society

Audience: Chemists, Chemical Engineers

Profile: This site contains supplemental material
pages from the Journal of the American
Chemical Society. Instructions for
authors' submissions are also to be
found here, as well as general
information about the Society.

Contact: Gopher Operator
gopher@acsinfo.acs.org

Details: Free

`gopher://acsinfo.acs.org`

ChE Electronic Newsletter

This newsletter contains information of interest to
chemical engineers.

Keywords: Chemical Engineering, Chemistry,
Engineering

Audience: Chemical Engineers

Contact: Martyn S. Ray
trayms@cc.curtin.edu.au

Details: Free

Inquire about needing a password.

`mailto:trayms@cc.curtin.edu.au`

Chemistry (History of)

Purdue University Library

The library's holdings are large and wide-ranging.
They contain significant collections in many fields.

Keywords: Economics (History of), Literature
(English), Literature (American), Indiana,
Rogers (Bruce), Engineering (History of),
Aviation, Earth Science, Atmospheric
Science, Consumer Science, Family
Science, Chemistry (History of), Physics,
Veterinary Science

Audience: General Public, Researchers, Librarians,
Document Delivery Professionals

Contact: Dan Ferrer
dan@asterix.lib.purdue.edu

Details: Free

Expect: User ID prompt, Send: GUEST

`telnet://lib.cc.purdue.edu`

University of Delaware Libraries (DELCAT)

The library's holdings are large and wide-ranging
and contain significant collections in many fields.

Keywords: Literature (American), Hemingway
(Ernest), Papermaking (History of),
Chemistry (History of), Literature (Irish),
Delaware

Audience: General Public, Researchers, Librarians,
Document Delivery Professionals

Contact: Stuart Glogoff
epo27855@udacsvm.bitnet

Details: Free

Expect: prompt, Send: RETURN 2-3 times

`telnet://delcat.udel.edu or`
`delcat.acs.udel.edu`

Chemistry

American Chemical Society

This is the gopher site of the American Chemical
Society.

Keywords: Chemistry, Chemical Engineering

Sponsor: The American Chemical Society

Audience: Chemists, Chemical Engineers

Profile: This site contains supplemental material
pages from the Journal of the American
Chemical Society. Instructions for
authors' submissions are also to be
found here, as well as general
information about the Society.

Contact: Gopher Operator
gopher@acsinfo.acs.org

Details: Free

`gopher://acsinfo.acs.org`

ChE Electronic Newsletter

This newsletter contains information of interest to
chemical engineers.

Keywords: Chemical Engineering, Chemistry,
Engineering

Audience: Chemical Engineers

Contact: Martyn S. Ray

trayms@cc.curtin.edu.au

Details: Free

Inquire about needing a password.

`mailto:trayms@cc.curtin.edu.au`

Chem-Talk

A communication network for chemists, providing
dialog and conversation to help clarify articles,
illuminate new perceptions of theories, and sustain
participants' precarious journies in chemistry.

Keywords: Chemistry

Audience: Chemists, Scientists, Researchers

Contact: Manus Monroe
...!{ames,cbosgd}!pacbell!unicom!manus

Details: Free

User Info: To subscribe to the list, send an e-mail
message requesting a subscription to
the URL address below.

`mailto:...!{ames,cbosgd}!pacbell!`
`unicom!manus`

Chemical Abstracts

Worldwide coverage of the chemical sciences
literature.

Keywords: Chemistry, Engineering

Sponsor: Chemical Abstracts Service, American
Chemical Society

Audience: Researchers, Librarians, Chemists

Profile: Provides coverage of chemical sciences
literature from over 9,000 journals,
patents from 27 countries, and 2
international property organizations,
new books, conference proceedings,
and government research reports.
Updated every two weeks.

Contact: PAUL.ALBERT@NETEAST.COM

User Info: To subscribe contact Orbit-Questel
directly.

`telnet://orbit.com`

Chemical Abstracts Service Source Index

Listing of bibliographic and library holdings
information for scientific and technical primary
literature relevant to the chemical sciences.

A B C D E F G H I J K L M N O P Q R S T U V W X Y Z

Keywords: Chemistry

Sponsor: Chemical Abstracts Service, American Chemical Society

Audience: Researchers, Librarians, Chemists

Profile: Approximately 65,000 records. Titles listed in CASSI represent all publications covered by CAS since 1907. Updated quarterly.

Contact: paul.albert@neteast.com

User Info: To subscribe contact Orbit-Questel directly.

`telnet://orbit.com`

Chemical Dictionary

Companion files to the Chemical Abstracts databases.

Keywords: Chemistry

Sponsor: Chemical Abstracts Service, American Chemical Society

Audience: Researchers, Chemists, Librarians

Profile: All compounds cited in the literature from 1957 to date are contained in these files. Each of the over 11 million records contains a CAS Registry Number, the molecular formula, CAS nomenclature for a specific compound, and many common synonyms.

Contact: paul.albert@neteast.com

User Info: To subscribe contact Orbit-Questel directly.

`telnet://orbit.com`

Chemical Industry Notes

Citations to worldwide chemical business news.

Keywords: Chemistry, Business

Sponsor: Chemical Abstracts Service, American Chemical Society

Audience: Researchers, Librarians, Chemists

Profile: Contains worldwide chemical business news related to production, pricing, sales, facilities, products and processes, corporate activities, government activities, and people. Contains over 950,000 records. Update weekly.

Contact: paul.albert@neteast.com

User Info: To subscribe contact Orbit-Questel directly.

`telnet://orbit.com`

Chemistry

This directory is a compilation of information resources focused on chemistry.

Keywords: Chemistry, Science

Audience: Chemical Engineers, Chemistry Teachers, Students

Details: Free

`ftp://una.hh.lib.umich.edu/70/inetdirsstacks/chemistry:wiggins`

Chemistry Tutorial Information

This site provides chemistry tutorial information in the form of text, data, pictures, source code, and executable programs for Macintosh computers.

Keywords: Chemistry, Tutorials, Macintosh Computer, Education

Sponsor: University of Michigan

Audience: Chemistry Students (secondary, college, university)

Contact: comments@mac.archive.umich.edu

Details: Free

`gopher://plaza.aarnet.edu.au@/micros/mac/umich/misc/chemistry/00index.txt`

Imperial College Gopher Server

★★★

A gopher server pertaining to the Imperial College Chemistry Department.

Keywords: Chemistry

Sponsor: Imperial College, United Kingdom

Audience: Chemists

Profile: This gopher server provides access the Imperial College Chemistry Department's extensive online facilities. The server provides links to outside chemistry gophers, and contains files related to chemistry software, biochemistry, organic chemistry, and much more.

Contact: Gopher Operator gopher@argon.ch.ic.ac.uk

`gopher://argon.ch.ic.ac.uk`

ISIS/Draw

ISIS/Draw provides a chemical drawing package from MDL Information Systems and the American Chemical Society.

Keywords: Chemistry, Graphics

Sponsor: MDL Information Systems, Inc., ACS

Audience: Chemists, Chemistry Professors, Chemistry Students

Profile: ISIS/Draw, the premier chemical drawing package from MDL Information Systems, Inc., is now available to chemistry students and professors at a special academic price through the American Chemical Society (ACS). Used by major pharmaceutical, agrochemical, and chemical companies worldwide, ISIS/Draw has the chemical intelligence to know that a line is a bond, and a letter is an atom. It can be used to: build queries for a structure-searching

---

database; create presentation-quality sketches of chemical structures, reactions, and a wide range of other graphics; cut and paste annotated chemical structure drawings into popular word processing programs to create instructional materials and reports.

Details: Costs

Call ACS at (800) 227-5558. When placing an order, use the following catalog numbers: 2152-9-151 (Windows) or 2156-1-151 (Macintosh).

`dmg96@acs.org`

Special Chemicals Update Program

Comprehensive reports covering 32 specialty chemical industry segments.

Keywords: Chemistry, Business

Sponsor: Chemical Marketing Research Center

Audience: Librarians, Researchers, Chemists

Profile: Coverage of chemical industry segments, plus more than a dozen reports of general interest on the management of specialty chemical businesses.

Contact: paul.albert@neteast.com

User Info: To subscribe contact Orbit-Questel directly.

`telnet://orbit.com`

WWW Chemistry Sites

This is a major 'departure' site for a vast array of chemical resources. Provides a list of WWW chemistry sites at academic institutions.

Keywords: Chemistry

Audience: Chemists, Chemistry Students, Chemical Engineers

Contact: Max Kopelevich mik@chem.ucla.edu

Details: Free

`http://www.chem.ucla.edu/chempointers.html`

Chess

Chessnews

A mailing list for the discussion of chess and related events.

Keywords: Chess, Games

Audience: Chess Enthusiasts

Contact: Michael Nolan chessnews-request@tssi.com

Details: Free

User Info: To subscribe to the list, send an e-mail message requesting a subscription to the URL address below.
To send a message to the entire list, address it to: chessnews@tssi.com

Notes: The Chessnews mailing list is a repeater for the usenet newsgroup rec.games.chess. This is a bidirectional repeater. Postings originating from usenet are sent to the list, and those originating from the list are sent to re

`mailto:chessnews-request@tssi.com`

Internet Chess Library

An FTP and gopher site containing all kinds of chess-related files.

Keywords: Chess

Audience: Chess Players

Profile: The Internet Chess Library is an FTP and gopher site with archives containing all kinds of chess-related files. The library contains chess software of different types, schedules, international chess announcements, rating guides, and anything else relating to chess.

Contact: Chris Petroff

             chris@chess.uaknor.edu

`gopher://chess.uaknor.edu`

`ftp://chess.uaknor.edu`

rec.games.chess

A Usenet newsgroup providing information and discussion about chess strategies, organized computer chess playing events, and software.

Keywords: Chess, Games, Recreation

Audience: Chess Players, Game Players

User Info: To subscribe to this Usenet newsgroup, you need access to a newsreader.

`news:rec.games.chess`

Chiba University Gopher

Chiba University Gopher

The Chiba University gopher, including files from the university's library.

Keywords: Japan, Asia, Libraries

Sponsor: Chiba University, Chiba, Japan

Audience: Japan Residents, Computer Programmers, Librarians, Linguists

Contact: hasimoto@chiba-u.ac.jp

`gopher://himawari.ipc.chiba-u.ac.jp`

Chicago

The University of Illinois at Chicago Library

The library's holdings are large and wide-ranging and contain significant collections in many fields.

Keywords: Health Science, Chicago, Industry, Slavery, Abolitionism, Roosevelt (Franklin D.)

Audience: General Public, Researchers, Librarians, Document Delivery Professionals

Details: Free

             Expect: introductory screen, Send: Clear key; Expect: UIC flame screen, Send: Enter key; Expect: Logon screen, Send: DIAL PVM; Expect: PVM (Passthru) screen, Send: Type: Move cursor to NOTIS and press Enter key Response: One line message about port in use Type: Enter key

`telnet://uicvm.uic.edu`

Chicano Culture

Chicano/LatinoNet

An electronic mechanism that brings together Chicano/Latino research, as well as linguistic minority and educational research efforts being carried out at the University of California and elsewhere. It serves as a gateway between faculty, staff, and students who are engaged in research and curricular efforts in these areas.

Keywords: Culture, Race, Chicano Culture, Latino Culture

Sponsor: Chicano Studies Research Center, University of California at Los Angeles

Audience: Students, Mexican-Americans, Latinos

Contact: Richard Chabran
             Chabran@latino.sscnet.ucla.ed

Details: Free

`gopher://latino.sscnet.ucla.edu`

Mexican Culture FAQ

This is the FAQ from the soc.culture.mexican newsgroup. Provides information on Mexican culture, history, society, language, and tourism.

Keywords: Culture, Race, Chicano Culture, Latino Culture

Sponsor: News Group Moderators for soc.culture.mexican

Audience: Students, Latinos, Chicanos

Contact: News Group Moderator
             mendoza-grado@att.com

Details: Free

`ftp://ftp.mty.itesm.ms/pub/mexico/faqs`

`http://www.cis.ohio-state.edu/hypertext/faq/usenet/mexican-faq/faq.html`

Child Care

ACS Gopher

A gopher relating to the Department of Health and Human Services Administration for Children and Families. Provides access to ACS documents, the Department of Health and Human Services information, and other Federal Government documentation relating to children, families, and child care.

Keywords: Children, Child Care

Sponsor: Department of Health and Human Services Administration for Children and Families, USA

Audience: Child Care Providers

Contact: Tim Link
             linkt@gopher.acf.dhhs.gov

`gopher://spike.acf.dhhs.gov`

misc.kids

A Usenet newsgroup providing information and discussion about children and their behavior.

Keywords: Children, Child Care

Audience: Parents, Child Development Professionals, Children

Details: Free

User Info: To subscribe to this Usenet newsgroup, you need access to a newsreader.

`news:misc.kids`

UNICEF Gopher

The gopher site of the United Nations Children's Fund.

Keywords: Children, Child Care

Sponsor: United Nations

Audience: Child Care Providers, Children's Rights Activists

Profile: This gopher provides access to full-text UNICEF publications such as the State of the World's Children report and the Progress of Nations, the UNICEF Annual Report, UNICEF Features, the First Call for Children newsletter, press releases, information notes and other advocacy and information booklets, brochures, and pamphlets. The gopher also contains the full-text of the Convention on the Rights of the Child and the Declaration and Plan of Action of the 1990 World Summit for Children.

A B C D E F G H I J K L M N O P Q R S T U V W X Y Z

Contact: UNICEF Gopher Host
          rpadolina@unicef.org

`gopher://hqfaus01.unicef.org`

Utah Valley Community College Library ★★

The library's holdings are large and wide-ranging and contain significant collections in many fields.

Keywords: Accounting, Automobiles, Cabinetry, Child Care, Drafting, Electronics, Home Building, Local History, Refrigeration, Air Conditioning

Audience: General Public, Researchers, Librarians, Document Delivery Professionals

Details: Free

           Expect: Login; Send: Opub

`telnet:// uvlib.uvcc.edu`

Childbirth

Midwifery Resources on the Net ★★

A resource list for helping find information about midwifery on the Internet.

Keywords: Midwifery, Childbirth, Medicine, Nursing

Audience: Midwives, Medical professionals

Details: Free

`gopher://una.hh.lib.umich.edu`

Children

ACS Gopher ★★

A gopher relating to the Department of Health and Human Services Administration for Children and Families. Provides access to ACS documents, the Department of Health and Human Services information, and other Federal Government documentation relating to children, families, and child care.

Keywords: Children, Child Care

Sponsor: Department of Health and Human Services Administration for Children and Families, USA

Audience: Child Care Providers

Contact: Tim Link

           linkt@gopher.acf.dhhs.gov

`gopher://spike.acf.dhhs.gov`

alt.kids-talk ★

A Usenet newsgroup that provides a place for the pre-collegiate to chat.

Keywords: Chat Groups, Children

Audience: Kids, Students (K-12)

User Info: To subscribe to this Usenet newsgroup, you need access to a newsreader.

`news:alt.kids-talk`

Children's Rights ★

Contains files from the Children's Rights Council, the Central Ohio Organization, Fathers and Children for Equality, and the National Congress for Men and Children.

Keywords: Children, Law

Audience: Lawyers, Social Workers, Children's Rights Activists

Details: Free

`telnet://cwgk4.chem.cwru.edu`

FrEd Mail Foundation ★

This foundation specializes in establishing innovative and educationally rewarding collaborative projects using the Internet for the K-12 community.

Keywords: Children, Education (K-12)

Audience: Educators (K-12)

Contact: Al Rogers

           arogers@bonita.cerf.fred.org

Details: Free

`gopher://gopher.cerf.net/11/fredmail`

KIDLINK and KIDCAFE ★

This discussion group is designed to act as a structured forum for e-mail exchanges between children aged 10-15.

Keywords: Education, Children

Audience: Children

Profile: A dialog is set up each year called 'KIDS-XX' where 'XX' is the current year. Each participating child posts an e-mail message answering the following four questions before he or she can engage in the dialog: 1. Who am I? 2. What do I want to be when I grow up? 3. How do I want the world to be better when I grow up? 4. What can I do to make this happen?

KIDLINK operates the following free discussion lists and services:

- KIDLINK: discussion group for children aged 10-15.

- RESPONSE: the destination for answers to the four questions above.

- KIDCAFE: a forum for children aged 10-15. Read-only for people outside this age group.

- KIDCAFEP: a Portuguese-language version of KIDCAFE.

- KIDCAFEJ: a Japanese-language version of KIDCAFE.

- KIDCAFEN: a Scandinavian-language (Nordic) version of KIDCAFE.

- KIDFORUM: a showcase of works by kids on a series of topics specified to promote exchange between classrooms. Teachers can plan for class participation in monthly topics.

- KIDPROJ: a forum enabling teachers/youth group leaders to design projects for children through the KIDLINK network.

- KIDLEADR: an informal meeting place for exchanging ideas, networking, asking for help, requesting hello messages, and so on, for teachers, coordinators, parents, social workers, and others interested in KIDS-94.

- KIDLEADP: a Portuguese-language version of KIDLEADR.

- KIDLEADS: a Spanish-language version of KIDLEADR.

- KIDLEADN: a Scandinavian-language (Nordic) version of KIDLEADR.

Contact: Odd de Presno
           opresno@extern.uio.no

Details: Free

           For information about the projects, subscribe to the KIDLINK announcement service: send an e-mail message to: listserv@vm1.NoDak.edu with the following command in the text of your message: SUB KIDLINK Yourfirstname Yourlastname.

Notes: For more information, read the 'WHAT IS KIDLINK / KIDS-94' page at gopher://kids.ccit.duq.edu/00/about/kidlink-general.

`gopher://kids.ccit.duq.edu`

Lego Information ★★★

A web site containing pictures, sets, and instructions for building with Legos. Also discusses various ideas, activities, and history pertaining to Legos, as well as information about clubs for Lego enthusiasts.

Keywords: Construction, Toys, Children

Sponsor: Lego

Audience: Children, General Public

Contact: David Koblas
           koblas@netcom.com

`http://legowww.itek.norut.no`

misc.kids ★

A Usenet newsgroup providing information and discussion about children and their behavior.

Keywords: Children, Child Care

Audience: Parents, Child Development Professionals, Children

Details: Free

User Info: To subscribe to this Usenet newsgroup, you need access to a newsreader.

`news:misc.kids`

Pen-pals

This mailing list provides a forum for children to correspond with each other electronically. Although the list is not moderated, it is monitored for content and is managed by listproc.

Keywords: Computing, Children, Writing

Audience: Computer Users, Children, Student Writers

Contact: pen-pals-request@mainstream.com

Details: Free

User Info: To subscribe to the list, send an e-mail message requesting a subscription to the URL address below.

To send a message to the entire list, address it to: pen-pals@mainstream.com

`mailto:pen-pals@mainstream.com`

The Curiosity Club

★ ★

This web site offers both an astrophysics exploration and a playspace for young scientists

Keywords: Astronomy, Mythology, Children

Sponsor: Center for Extreme Ultraviolet Astrophysics, Berkeley, California, and The San Francisco Unified School District, San Francisco, California

Audience: Educators, Students, Astronomers,

Contact: Kasey Rios Asberry jasberry@sfsuvax1.sfsu.edu

Details: Free

`http://nisus.sfusd.k12.ca.us/`
`curiosity_club/bridge1.html`

UNICEF Gopher

★ ★ ★

The gopher site of the United Nations Children's Fund.

Keywords: Children, Child Care

Sponsor: United Nations

Audience: Child Care Providers, Children's Rights Activists

Profile: This gopher provides access to full-text UNICEF publications such as the State of the World's Children report and the Progress of Nations, the UNICEF Annual Report, UNICEF Features, the First Call for Children newsletter, press releases, information notes and other advocacy

and information booklets, brochures, and pamphlets. The gopher also contains the full-text of the Convention on the Rights of the Child and the Declaration and Plan of Action of the 1990 World Summit for Children.

Contact: UNICEF Gopher Host rpadolina@unicef.org

`gopher://hqfaus01.unicef.org`

Children's Books

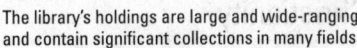

University of North Carolina at Greensboro MINERVA Library

★ ★

The library's holdings are large and wide-ranging and contain significant collections in many fields.

Keywords: Herbert (George), Film, Dickinson (Emily), Children's Books

Audience: Researchers, Students, General Public

Details: Free

Expect: Login; Send: Info or MINERVA

`telnet://steffi.acc.uncg.edu`

Chile

edista (Educación a Distancia)

★

The University Distance Program (UNIDIS) at the University of Santiago, Chile, sponsors Educación a Distancia (Education at a Distance).

Keywords: Education (Adult), Education (Distance), Education (Continuing), Chile

Sponsor: The University Distance Program (UNIDIS) at the University of Santiago, Chile

Audience: Educators, Researchers

Details: Free

User Info: To subscribe to the list, send an e-mail message to the URL address shown below consisting of a single line reading:

SUB edistaYourFirstName YourLastName

To send a message to the entire list, address it to: edista@usachvm1.bitnet

`mailto:listserv@usachvm1.bitnet`

China

INTLAW (International Law Library)

The International Law Library provides comprehensive international law materials.

Keywords: International Law, EEC, Commonwealth, China

Audience: Lawyers, International Lawyers

Profile: The International Law Library provides comprehensive international law materials. The International Law library contains federal case law, European Community materials, treaties and agreements, Commonwealth law materials, topical and professional journals, French law materials (in French), China law materials, plus relevant topical publications.

Contact: New Sales Group at (800) 227-4908 or (513) 859-5398 inside the US, or (513) 865-7981 for all inquires outside the US.

User Info: To subscribe, contact Mead directly.

To examine the Lexis user guide, you can access it at the ftp site of the University of Texas at Austin at the URL address: ftp://ftp.cc.utexas.edu

The files are in: /pub/ref-services/LEXIS

`telnet://nex.meaddata.com`

`http://www.meaddata.com`

Princeton University Library

★ ★

The library's holdings are large and wide-ranging. They contain significant collections in many fields.

Keywords: China, Japan, Classics, History (Ancient), Near Eastern Studies, Literature (American), Literature (English), Aeronautics, Middle Eastern Studies, Mormonism, Publishing

Audience: General Public, Researchers, Librarians, Document Delivery Professionals

Details: Free

Expect: Connect message, blank screen, Send: <cr>; Expect: #, Send: Call 500

`telnet://pucable.princeton.edu`

soc.culture.china

★

A Usenet newsgroup providing information and discussion about China and Chinese culture.

Keywords: China, Sociology

Audience: Sociologists, Chinese, Sinologists

Details: Free

User Info: To subscribe to this Usenet newsgroup, you need access to a newsreader.

`news:soc.culture.china`

Chinapats

Chinapats

Covers all patent applications published under the patent law of People's Republic of China.

Keywords: Patents, Intellectual Property, Trademarks

Sponsor: European Patent Office

Audience: Patent Attorneys, Patent Agents, Librarians, Researchers

Profile: English language abstracts are included for all applications filed by Chinese applicants. Contains more than 59,000 records. Updated monthly.

Contact: paul.albert@neteast.com

User Info: To subscribe contact Orbit-Questel directly.

`telnet://orbit.com`

Chinese Language

alt.chinese.text

★

A Usenet newsgroup providing information and discussion about Chinese language software.

Keywords: Chinese Language, Language Software

Audience: Chinese, Chinese Speakers, Computer Users

User Info: To subscribe to this Usenet newsgroup, you need access to a newsreader.

`news:alt.chinese.text`

Chinese Studies

The University of Kansas Library

★★

The library's holdings are large and wide-ranging and contain significant collections in many fields.

Keywords: Botany, Chinese Studies, Cartography (History of), Kansas, Opera, Ornithology, Joyce (James), Yeats (William Butler), Walpole (Sir Robert, Collections of)

Audience: General Public, Researchers, Librarians, Document Delivery Professionals

Contact: John S. Miller

Details: Free

Expect: Username, Send: relay <cr>

`telnet://kuhub.cc.ukans.edu`

Choral Singing

Chorus

★

This is the lesbian and gay chorus mailing list, formed November 1991 by John Schrag (jschrag@alias.com) and Brian Jarvis (jarvis@psych.toronto.edu). Membership includes artistic directors, singers, chorus officers, interpreters, and support staff and friends. Topics of discussion include repertoire, arrangements, staging, costuming, management, fundraising, music, events and concerts.

Keywords: Singing, Choral Singing, Homosexuality, Gay, Lesbian

Audience: Lesbian Singers, Gay Singers, Chorus Officers, Lesbians, Gays, Choral Singers

Contact: chorus-request@psych.toronto.edu

Details: Free

User Info: To subscribe to the list, send an e-mail message requesting a subscription to the URL address below.

To send a message to the entire list, address it to: chorus@psych.toronto.edu

`mailto:chorus-request@psych.toronto.edu`

`news:alt.christnet.bible`

Christianity

alt.christnet

★

This Usenet newsgroup is a gathering place for Christian ministers and users.

Keywords: Religion, Christianity, Bible, Divinity

Audience: Christians, Ministers

User Info: To subscribe to this Usenet newsgroup, you need access to a newsreader.

`news:alt.christnet`

Christian

alt.christnet.bible

★

A Usenet newsgroup providing information and discussion about bible discussion and research.

Keywords: Bible, Christian, Religion, Divinity

Audience: Biblical Scholars, Bible Readers

User Info: To subscribe to this Usenet newsgroup, you need access to a newsreader.

AmerCath (History of American Catholicism)

★

This mailing list focuses on the history of American Catholicism.

Keywords: Catholicism, Christianity, Religion

Sponsor: Jefferson Community College, University of Kentucky, Louisville, KY, USA

Audience: Researchers, Educators, Students, Catholics

Profile: Because AMERCATH can be accessed internationally, it forms a global network of people who research and teach the history of American Catholicism. AMERCATH facilitates communication among faculty, students, and researchers.

Contact: Anne Kearney jccannek@ukcc.uky.edu

Details: Free

User Info: To subscribe to the list, send an e-mail message to the address below, consisting of a single line reading:

Sub AmerCath YourFirstName YourLastName

To send a message to the entire list, address it to:

AmerCath@ukcc.uky.edu

`mailto:listserv@ukcc.uky.edu`

Bethany Christian Services

A major directory on adoption, providing access to a broad range of related resources (library catalogs, databases, and servers) via the Internet.

Keywords: Adoption, Christianity, Pregnancy, Abortion Rights

Sponsor: Bethany Christian Services, Grand Rapids, Michigan, USA

Audience: Pregnant Women

Profile: The gopher server of Bethany, a pro-life, pro-family agency reaching out to women with unplanned pregnancies and adoptive couples contains a large amount of information about national and international adoption, the adoption process, African-American adoptions, and adoption of children with special needs. Also contains information for pregnant women, such as birth father rights and responsibilities, pregnancy counceling, and so on.

Contact: gophermaster@bethany.org

`gopher://gopher.bethany.org/11`

Cell Church Discussion Group

A list for Christians who are in cell churches or in churches that are in transition to becoming cell churches, as well as anyone interested in learning more about cell churches. A cell church is a nontraditional form of church life in which small groups of Christians (cells) meet in a special way in their homes for the evangelism of the unchurched, the bonding of believers, their nurture, and ministry to one another.

Keywords: Cell Churches, Christianity, Evangelism, Religion

Audience: Christians, Theologians, Evangelists

Contact: Jon Reid reid@cei.com

Details: Free

User Info: To subscribe to the list, send an e-mail message to the URL address below with the single word SUBSCRIBE in the body (not subject) of your message.

To send a message to the entire list, address it to: cell-church@bible.acu.edu

Notes: The group archives, FAQ, and helpful articles are available by anonymous FTP from bible.acu.edu; they can also be retrieved by sending mail to cell-church-archives@bible.acu.edu with the single word LIST for a list of files, or HELP for more information.

`mailto:cell-church-request@bible.acu.edu`

CGN (Christian Growth Newsletter)

This site is intended to help Christians in personal growth, and includes testimonials and encouraging articles.

Keywords: Christianity, Religion

Audience: Christians

Contact: Laura Smith
bible@olsen.ch

`mailto:bible@olsen.ch`

Christian

The purpose of this list is to provide a nonhostile environment for discussion among Christians. Non-Christians may join the list and "listen in," but full-blown debates between Christians and non-Christians are best carried out in talk.religion.misc or soc.religion.christian.

Keywords: Christianity

Audience: Christians, Theologians

Contact: mailjc-request@grian.cps.altadena.ca.us

Details: Free

User Info: To subscribe to the list, send an e-mail message requesting a subscription to the URL address below.

To send a message to the entire list, address it to:

mailjc@grian.cps.altadena.ca.us

`mailto:mailjc-request@grian.cps.altadena.ca.us`

Christian Growth Newsletter (CGN)

Intended to help Christians in personal growth. It includes testimonies and encouraging articles.

Keywords: Christianity, Religion

Audience: Christians

Contact: Laura Smith
bible@olsen.ch

Details: Free

`mailto:bible@olsen.ch`

Ecchst-l

A discussion list for scholars of Ecclesiastical history, including those interested both in the history of the church and in the examination of theology in an historical context.

Keywords: Religion, Ecclesiastical History, Christianity, Theology

Audience: Historians, Theologians

Contact: Gregory H. Singleton
ugsingle@uxa.ecn.bgu.edu

User Info: To subscribe, send an e-mail message to the URL address below consisting of a single line reading: SUB ecchst-l YourFirstName YourLastName.

To send a message to the entire list, address it to: ecchst-l@bgu.edu

`mailto:listserv@bgu.edu`

Shakers

A forum on the United Society of Believers for those interested in the history, culture, artifacts, and beliefs of the Shakers (United Society of Believers). Discussions cover a broad range of subject matter.

Keywords: Shakers, Christianity, Religion

Audience: Shakers, Theologians

Contact: Marc Rhorer
rhorer@ukcc.uky.edu

Details: Free

User Info: To subscribe to the list, send an e-mail message to the URL address shown below consisting of a single line reading:

SUB shaker YourFirstName YourLastName

To send a message to the entire list, address it to: shaker@ukcc.uky.edu

`mailto:listserv@ukcc.uky.edu`

soc.religion.christian

A Usenet newsgroup providing information and discussion about Christianity and related issues.

Keywords: Christianity, Religion

Audience: Christians, Theologians

Details: Free

User Info: To subscribe to this Usenet newsgroup, you need access to a newsreader.

`news:soc.religion.christian`

Chromatography

Biotechnet Electronic Buyer's Guide

Biotechnet is a global computer network created specially for research biologists. It is intended to be a valuable source of information and data, a communications resource, a forum to foster the exchange of current ideas, and an international marketplace for relevant goods and service.

Keywords: Molecular Biology, Electrophoresis, Chromatography

Audience: Molecular Biologists, Chemists, Laboratory Suppliers

Profile: One of the services offered by Biotechnet is the Electronic Buyer's Guide, which is divided into five individual databases for specific product categories: Molecular Biology, Electrophoresis, Chromatography, Liquid Handling, and Instruments & Apparatus. After selecting one of the guides at the prompt, you can search through each database to find either product names and applications or the name and address of the company that manufactures the product you wish to locate.

Details: Free

Password: bguide

`telnet://biotech@biotechnet.com`

Chronic Fatigue Syndrome

Disability-Related Resources

A collection of information that includes newsletters for deaf/blind issues, electronic resources for the deaf, and a section on Chronic Fatigue Syndrome.

Keywords: Disabilities, Deafness, Blindness, Chronic Fatigue Syndrome

Sponsor: University of Washington DO-IT Program

Audience: Deaf and Disabled People, Health Care Professionals

Contact: Sheryl Burgstahler, Ph.D.
doit@u.washington.edu

`gopher://hawking.u.washington.edu`

Church (Frank)

Boise State University Library

The library's holdings are large and wide-ranging and contain significant collections in many fields.

Keywords: Jordan (Len, Senatorial Papers of), Church (Frank, Senatorial Papers of), Poetry (American)

Audience: General Public, Researchers, Librarians, Document Delivery Professionals

Contact: Dan Lester

Details: Free

Expect: login; Send: catalyst

`telnet://catalyst.idbsu.edu`

A
B
C
D
E
F
G
H
I
J
K
L
M
N
O
P
Q
R
S
T
U
V
W
X
Y
Z

Church History

University of Pennsylvania PENNINFO Library

The library's holdings are large and wide-ranging and contain significant collections in many fields.

Keywords: Church History, Spanish Inquisition, Witchcraft, Shakespeare (William), Bibles, Aristotle (Texts of), Fiction, Whitman (Walt), French Revolution, Drama (French), Literature (English), Literature (Spanish)

Audience: Researchers, Students, General Public

Contact: Al DSouza
penninfo-admin@dccs.upenn.edu
dsouza@dccs.upenn.edu

Details: Free

Expect: Login; Send: Public

`telnet://penninfo.upenn.edu`

CIA

CIA World Factbook

Annual report of CIA (Central Intelligence Agency) research in over 247 nations.

Keywords: CIA, Intelligence, Annual Reports

Audience: Governments, Lawyers, FBI

Details: Free

`gopher://marvel.loc.gov`

CILEA (Consorzio Interuniversitario Lombardo per la Elaborazione Automatica)

CILEA (Consorzio Interuniversitario Lombardo per la Elaborazione Automatica)

The gopher for the InterUniversity Computer Center, Milan, Italy, provides access to CILEA hosts, databases in Europe, CERN (European Laboratory for Particle Physics) services such as WWW and ALICE, Usenet newsgroups, PostScript documentation on various items, Italian research network information, and more.

Keywords: Informatics, Italy, Europe

Audience: Particle physicists, Researchers

Contact: Luciano Guglielm
guglielm@imicilea.cilea.it

Details: Free

`gopher://imicilea.cilea.it`

Cinema

CinemaSpace

CinemaSpace, from the Film Studies Program at UC Berkeley, is devoted to all aspects of Cinema and New Media.

Keywords: Cinema, Film, Multimedia

Sponsor: Film Studies Program at UC Berkeley

Audience: Students, Film researchers

Profile: Projects for CinemaSpace include academic papers on film and new media, film theory and critique. multimedia lectures, and sources of film clips and references to other sites.

Contact: xcohen@garnet.berkeley.edu

Details: Free

`http://remarque.berkeley.edu/~xcohen`

Circle K International

Circle K International

This list is for members and alumni of the worldwide collegiate service organization sponsored by Kiwanis International.

Keywords: Kiwanis International

Audience: Kiwanis Members

Contact: Jeffrey M. Wolff
jwolff@nyx.cs.du.edu

Details: Free

User Info: To subscribe to the list, send an e-mail message requesting a subscription to the URL address below.

`mailto:jwolff@nyx.cs.du.edu`

CIRCUITS-L

CIRCUITS-L

This list discusses all aspects of the introductory course in circuit analysis for electrical engineering undergraduates.

Keywords: Engineering, Electrical Engineering, Teaching, Electric Circuit Analysis

Audience: Engineers, Students (college)

Contact: Paul E. Gray
mailto:GRAY@MAPLE.UCS.UWPLATT.EDU

Details: Free

User Info: To subscribe to the list, send an e-mail message to the URL address below, and include: name; E-mail address; home phone, business phone, and FAX numbers (including area code); and US postal address (including ZIP code)

To send a message to the entire list, address it to:

CIRCUITS-L@UWPLATT.EDU

`mailto:CIRCUITS-REQUEST@UWPLATT.EDU`

CIS (Commonwealth of Independent States)

soc.culture.soviet

A Usenet newsgroup providing information and discussion about topics relating to Russia or the former Soviet Union.

Keywords: Russia, CIS (Commonwealth of Independent States), Communism, Sociology

Audience: Sociologists, Russians

Details: Free

User Info: To subscribe to this Usenet newsgroup, you need access to a newsreader.

`news:soc.culture.soviet`

talk.politics.soviet

A Usenet newsgroup providing information and discussion about Soviet, domestic and international politics.

Keywords: Communism, Russia, Politics, CIS (Commonwealth of Independent States)

Audience: Political Scientists

Details: Free

User Info: To subscribe to this Usenet newsgroup, you need access to a newsreader.

`news:talk.politics.soviet`

Cisco Systems

Cisco

This list is for discussion of the network products from Cisco Systems, Inc (primarily the AGS gateway, but also the ASM terminal multiplex) and any other relevant products. Discussions about operation, problems, features, topology, configuration, protocols, routing, loading, serving, and so on, are all encouraged. Other topics include vendor relations, new product announcements, availability of fixes and new features, and discussion of new requirements and desirables.

Keywords: Cisco Systems, Networks

Audience: Cisco Employees, Cisco Users, Distributors

Contact: David Wood
cisco-request@spot.colorado.edu

Details: Free

User Info: To subscribe to the list, send an e-mail message requesting a subscription to the URL address below.

To send a message to the entire list, address it to: cisco@spot.colorado.edu

```
mailto:cisco-
request@spot.colorado.edu
```

Citation Authority

Citation Authority

Legal citation authority expected to be used in the highest US appellate state courts, based on a 1985 survey (revised March 1991).

Keywords: Law (US), State Courts

Audience: Lawyers

Details: Free

Expect: login; Send: lawlib

```
gopher://liberty.uc.wlu.edu/00/
library/law/lawftp/citation.txt
```

Citizens Project

Citizens Project

A grass-roots community group in the Pikes Peak region of Colorado.

Keywords: Community, Networking, Colorado

Audience: Activists, Policymakers, Community Leaders, Government

Profile: Based in Colorado Springs, Colorado, the Citizens Project makes use of the online world in pursuit of its mission to investigate, inform, and advocate issues affecting the Pikes Peak region. It maintains an extensive gopher server, FTP site, and a ListServ (for people who have only e-mail access).

Contact: Citizens Project
citizens@cscns.com

Details: Free

User Info: To subscribe to the list, send an e-mail message to the URL address below, consisting of a single line reading:

SUB cns-citizens-pub YourFirstName YourLastName

```
mailto:listserv@cscns.com
```

City of San Carlos World Wide Web Fire Safety Tutorial

City of San Carlos World Wide Web Fire Safety Tutorial

This WWW site offers fire prevention information, with a special emphasis on preventing wildland fires. Also includes color diagram on how to create a proper firebreak.

Keywords: Disaster Relief, Safety

Sponsor: The City of San Carlos, California, USA

Audience: Students, Educators, Environmentalists, Community Groups

```
http://www.abag.ca.gov/abag/
local_gov/city/san_carlos/schome.html
```

CIUWInfo (Centrum Informacyj ny Uniwersyetu Warzawskiego)

CIUWInfo (Centrum Informacyj ny Uniwersyetu Warzawskiego)

Provides data from the Informatics Center information service of Warsaw University, Warsaw, Poland.

Keywords: Informatics, Poland

Audience: Researchers

Contact: chomac@plearn.edu.pl

Details: Free

```
gopher://chomac@plearn.edu.pl
```

Civil Liberties

ACLU Free Reading Room

A gopher site containing information relating to the ACLU (American Civil Liberties Union), including the current issue of the ACLU newsletter, Civil Liberties; a growing collection of recent public policy reports and action guides; Congressional voting records for the 103rd Congress; and an archive of news releases from the ACLU's national headquarters.

Keywords: ACLU, Civil Liberties, Congress (US), Activism

Sponsor: ACLU (American Civil Liberties Union)

Audience: Privacy Activists, Civil Libertarians, Activists

Contact: infoaclu@aclu.org

```
gopher://aclu.org
```

Civil Rights

amend2-info

Colorado voted in an amendment to their state constitution to revoke any existing gay/lesbian/bisexual civil rights legislation and prohibit the drafting of any new legislation. This moderated list is for information on the implication and issues of this amendment.

Keywords: Activists, Gay, Lesbian, Bisexual, Constitutional Amendments, Colorado, Civil Liberties

Audience: General Public, Gays, Lesbians, Bisexuals, Activists

Contact: amend2-info@cs.colorado.edu

User Info: To subscribe to the list, send an e-mail message requesting a subscription to the URL address below.

To send a message to the entire list, address it to: amend2-info@cs.colorado.edu

```
mailto:majordomo@cs.colorado.edu
```

Civil War

University of Tennessee at Chatanooga Library

The library's holdings are large and wide-ranging and contain significant collections in many fields.

Keywords: Civil War, Literature (American)

Audience: Researchers, Students, General Public

Contact: Randy Whitson
rwhitson@utcvmutc.edu

Details: Free

Expect: OK prompt; Send: Login pub1; Expect: Password; Send: Usc

```
telnet://library.utc.edu
```

Civil-L

Civil-L

A mailing list for the discussion of Civil Engineering Research and Education.

Keywords: Engineering (Civil), Computer-Aided Instruction

Audience: Engineers, Educators, Students

Contact: Eldo Hildebrand
ELDO@UNB.CA

Details: Free

User Info: To subscribe to the list, send an e-mail message to the URL address shown below consisting of a single line reading:

SUB civil-l YourFirstName YourLastName

To send a message to the entire list, address it to: CIVIL-L@UNB.CA

`mailto:listserv@unb.ca`

CJI (Computer Jobs in Israel)

CJI (Computer Jobs in Israel)

Computer Jobs in Israel (CJI) is a one-way list that will automatically send you the monthly updated computer jobs document. This list will also send you other special documents or announcements regarding finding computer work in Israel. Eventually this list will be an open, moderated list for everyone to exchange information about computer jobs in Israel.

Keywords: Israel, Computer, Jobs

Audience: Computer Users, Jews, Israelis, Israel Residents

Contact: Jacob Richman listserv@jerusalem1.datasrv.co.il

Details: Free

User Info: To subscribe to the list, send an e-mail message to the address below, consisting of a single line reading:

SUB CJI YourFirstName YourLastName

To send a message to the entire list, address it to: CJI@jerusalem1.datasrv.co.il

`mailto:listserv@jerusalem1.datasrv.co.il`

CLAIMS

CLAIMS

Provides access to over 2.3 million U.S. patents issued by the U.S. Patent and Trademark Office.

Keywords: Patents, Intellectual Property, Trademarks

Sponsor: IFI/Plenum Data Corporation

Audience: Patent Attorneys, Patent Agents, Librarians, Researchers

Profile: Chemical patents are covered from 1950 forward; mechanical and electrical patents from 1963 forward; design patents from 1980 forward.

Contact: PAUL.ALBERT@NETEAST.COM

User Info: To subscribe contact Orbit-Questel directly.

`telnet://orbit.com`

Clarissa

Clarissa

This list discusses the Nickelodeon TV show "Clarissa Explains It All."

Keywords: Television Shows, Nickelodeon

Audience: Nickelodeon Viewers, TV Viewers

Contact: Jim Lick clarissa-request@tcp.com

Details: Free

User Info: To subscribe to the list, send an e-mail message requesting a subscription to the URL address below.

To send a message to the entire list, address it to: clarissa@tcp.com

`mailto:clarissa-request@tcp.com`

Class Four Relay Magazine

Class Four Relay Magazine

A magazine by Relay Ops for the relay community.

Keywords: Relays, Magazines, Electronics

Sponsor: Carnegie Mellon University, Pittsburg, PA, USA

Audience: Relay Community

Profile: Includes articles on general questions and issues of relay usage, information for and about relay ops, discussion of policy issues and guidelines, and technical issues and new developments.

Contact: Joey J. Stanford stjs@vm.marist.edu

Details: Free

`mailto:stjs@vm.marist.edu`

Classics

History at the University of Virginia

A collection of online history resources, with particular emphasis on medieval and classical studies. Links to other systems, including the Library of Congress.

Keywords: History (World), Classics, Medieval Studies

Sponsor: University of Virginia, Charlottesville, Virginia, USA

Audience: Historians, Students (College/University)

Contact: mssbks@virginia.edu

Details: Free

`gopher://gopher.lib.virginia.edu`

Johns Hopkins University Library

The library's holdings are large and wide-ranging and contain significant collections in many fields.

Keywords: Literature (English), Economics, Classics, Drama (German), Slavery, Trade Unions, Incunabula, Bibles, Diseases (History of), Nursing (History of), Abolitionism

Audience: General Public, Researchers, Librarians, Document Delivery Professionals

Details: Free

`telnet://jhuvm.hcf.jhu.edu`

Princeton University Library

The library's holdings are large and wide-ranging. They contain significant collections in many fields.

Keywords: China, Japan, Classics, History (Ancient), Near Eastern Studies, Literature (American), Literature (English), Aeronautics, Middle Eastern Studies, Mormonism, Publishing

Audience: General Public, Researchers, Librarians, Document Delivery Professionals

Details: Free

Expect: Connect message, blank screen, Send: <cr>; Expect: #, Send: Call 500

`telnet://pucable.princeton.edu`

Cleveland FreeNet

Cleveland FreeNet

A network designed for community access and education.

Keywords: Networks, Community Access

Sponsor: The Cleveland FreeNet Project, Case Western Reserve University, Cleveland, Ohio, USA

Audience: Educators, Researchers, Students, Parents

Profile: A prototypical user-friendly city FreeNet, containing complete historical documents, an up-to-date news service, extensive info on the arts, sciences, technology, medicine, business, and education.

Notes: Registration is required, and information on registration is included.

`telnet://freenet-in-a.cwru.edu`

Cleveland Sports

Cleveland Sports

A forum for people to discuss their favorite Cleveland sports teams/personalities, and to obtain news and information about those teams that most out-of-towners couldn't get otherwise. Teams discussed include the Cleveland Indians, the Cleveland Browns, the Cleveland Cavaliers, and the teams from Ohio State University.

Keywords: Cleveland Sports, Ohio State Universiry

Audience: Cleveland Sports Enthusiasts, Sports Enthusiasts, Cleveland Residents

Contact: Richard Kowicki
aj755@cleveland.freenet.edu

Details: Free

User Info: To subscribe to the list, send an e-mail message requesting a subscription to the URL address below.

`mailto:aj755@cleveland.freenet.edu`

Climatology

Energy and Climate Information Exchange (ECIX) Newsletter

This newsletter focuses on energy and climate issues, and contains summaries of network postings, updates on national and international policy initiatives, full-length articles, information on new network resources, and a calendar of upcoming events.

Keywords: Energy, Meteorology, Climatology

Audience: Meteorologists, Geologists, Energy Researchers, Climatologists

Contact: econet@igc.org

`mailto:larris@igc.org`

Clinton (Bill)

alt.politics.clinton

A Usenet newsgroup providing information and discussion about President Bill Clinton and the White House. Perspective tends to be anti-Clinton.

Keywords: Politics (US), Clinton (Bill)

Audience: Politicians, General Public

User Info: To subscribe to this Usenet newsgroup, you need access to a newsreader.

`news:alt.politics.clinton`

Clinton's Economic Plan

The contents of US President Clinton's economic plan.

Keywords: Economics, Government (US), Clinton (Bill)

Audience: Economists, General Public

Details: Free

The data contained on the President's Economic Plan diskette is now available via anonymous FTP at cu.nih.gov. The data can be found in a directory named USDOC-OBA-INFO.

`gopher://wiretap.spies.com/11/Gov/Economic`

White House Frequently Asked Questions

This document is a good starting point for answering questions such as: How do I send e-mail to President Clinton? How do I get current news updates from the White House? Where can I get White House documents from?

Keywords: Clinton (Bill), Government (US), Politics (US), FAQs

Audience: General Public, Researchers

Details: Free

Expect: login; Send: anonymous; Expect: password; Send: your e-mail address; Expect: directory; Send: /pub/nic; Expect: file; Send: whitehouse FAQ.

`ftp://ftp.sura.net`

Clinton Watch

A regular political column devoted to a critical examination of the Clinton Administration.

Keywords: Politics, Clinton(Bill), Satire, Government (US)

Sponsor: Informatics Resource

Audience: Republicans, General Public, Citizens

Contact: clintonwatch@dolphin.gulf.net

`gopher://dolphin.gulf.net`

Clip Art

Gopher-Based ASCII Clip Art Collection

A collection of over 500 individual pictures, ranging from images of food to Star Wars, created with ASCII characters. Organized by subject, and including archives of the Usenet group alt.ascii-art. Also contains links to other ASCII collections.

Keywords: Clip Art, Design

Sponsor: Texas Tech Computer Sciences Gopher Server

Audience: Computer Users, General Public

Contact: Abdul Malik Yoosufan
gripe@cs.ttu.edu

Details: Free, Images

`gopher://cs4sun.cs.ttu.edu`

`ftp://ftp.cs.ttu.edu:/pub/asciiart`

The ASCII Bazaar

An extensive collection of ASCII art, organized by subject. Also includes FAQ files, software tools, ASCII art discussion lists, and links to other collections of ASCII art.

Keywords: Clip Art, Computer Art

Sponsor: Department of Computer and Information Sciences, University of Alabama at Birmingham, Birmingham, Alabama, USA

Audience: Computer Users, General Public

Contact: R. L. Samuell
samuell@cis.uab.edu

`gopher://twinbrook.cis.uab.edu`

Clp.x

Clp.x

Devoted to discussion of concurrent logic programming languages, concurrent constraint programming languages, semantics, proof techniques and program transformations, parallel Prolog systems, implementations, and programming techniques and idioms.

Keywords: Programming, Programming Languages, Concurrent Logic

Audience: Concurrent Logic Programmers

Contact: Jacob Levy
jlevy.pa@xerox.com

Details: Free

User Info: To subscribe to the list, send an e-mail message requesting a subscription to the URL address below.

To send a message to the entire lst, address it to: clp.x@xerox.com

`mailto:clp-request.x@xerox.com`

CMPCOM (Computers and Communications) Library

CMPCOM (Computers and Communications) Library

The Computers and Communications Library provides industry-specific sources. More than 40 full-text sources that concentrate on computers and communications are available. Full-text files can be searched in a variety of ways: as an individual file, by major-subject group file, or as a user-defined group file.

Keywords: Computers, Communications, Technology, Electronics

A
B
C
D
E
F
G
H
I
J
K
L
M
N
O
P
Q
R
S
T
U
V
W
X
Y
Z

Audience: Business Researchers, Analysts, Entrepreneurs

Profile: This library can be used to gain insight on new products and technologies being introduced; monitor industry news for high technology systems, electronics, engineering, communications, and computer hardware and software; and locate product evaluations for both the professional as well as the casual personal computer user.

Contact: Mead New Sales Group at (800) 227-4908 or (513) 859-5398 inside the US, or (513) 865-7981 for all inquiries outside the US.

User Info: To subscribe, contact Mead directly.

To examine the Nexis user guide, you can access it at the ftp site of the University of Texas at Austin at the URL address: ftp://ftp.cc.utexas.edu

The files are in: /pub/ref-services/LEXIS

`telnet://nex.meaddata.com`

`http://www.meaddata.com`

CMPGN (Campaign Library)

CMPGN (Campaign Library)

The CMPGN Library contains information and news about US Congressional, Senatorial, Gubernatorial and Presidentail elections. The media, political campaigns, and others whose responsibilities include monotoring activity on the campaign trail will find CMPGN to be a unique and comprehensive source of information for campaign research.

Keywords: Politics (US), Congress (US)

Audience: Journalists, Political Researchers

Profile: CMPGN allows searching of individual files or group files that cover topics such as candidate and incumbent profiles; Honoraria, PACs, and demographic and media profiles; Committee and Floor voting records and floor statement indexes for all House and Senate incumbents; and reputable sources of news that are known for their in-depth campaign coverage, including the Hotline, the Cook Political Report, ABC news Transcripts, Roll Call, States News Service, US Newswire, Federal News Service, and much more.

Contact: Mead New Sales Group at (800) 227-4908 or (513) 859-5398 inside the US, or (513) 865-7981 for all inquiries outside the US.

User Info: To subscribe, contact Mead directly.

To examine the Nexis user guide, you can access it at the ftp site of the University of Texas at Austin at the URL address: ftp://ftp.cc.utexas.edu

The files are in: /pub/ref-services/LEXIS

`telnet://nex.meaddata.com`

`http://www.meaddata.com`

CNI

CNI

CNI (Coalition for Networked Information) is an Internet information retrieval service. The CNI promotes the creation of and access to information resources in networked environments in order to enrich scholarship and to enhance intellectual productivity.

Keywords: Internet, Information Retrieval, CNI

Audience: Internet Surfers

Details: Free

The readme file is: CNI/info.packet/README

`ftp://ftp.cni.org/CNI (/info.packet/README)`

`gopher://ftp.cni.org`

`http://www.cni.org/CNI.homepage.html`

CNI Gopher

The gopher for CNI (Coalition for Networked Information), an Internet information retrieval service. The CNI promotes the creation of and access to information resources in networked environments in order to enrich scholarship and to enhance intellectual productivity.

Keywords: Internet, Information Retrieval, CNI

Audience: Internet Surfers

Contact: Craig A. Summerhill
Craig@cni.org

Details: Free

`gopher://gopher.cni.org`

CNI TopNode Project

Part of CNI (Coalition for Networked Information) directories and resource information service.

Keywords: Internet, Information Retrieval, CNI

Audience: Internet Surfers

Details: Free

`ftp://ftp.cni.org/CNI/projects/topnode`

`gopher://ftp.cni.org`

`http://www.cni.org/CNI.homepage.html`

CNI-Copyright Mailing List Archives

CNI-Copyright Mailing List Archives

An archive of lists related to copyright and intellectual property law.

Keywords: Copyright Law, Intellectual Property

Sponsor: CNI (The Coalition for Networked Information)

Audience: Entrepreneurs, Lawyers, Journalists

Contact: Craig Summerhill, Joan K. Lippincott
craig@cni.org, joan@cni.org

`gopher://gopher.cni.org`

CNN Headline News Gopher

CNN Headline News Gopher

Latest news as read by the CNN anchorpersons. Searchable index of subject matter.

Keywords: News Media, Politics (International), Journalism

Sponsor: CNN Newsource Service

Audience: General Public, Students, Journalists

Contact: Chet Rhodes
cr9@umail.umd.edu

Details: Free

`gopher://info.umd.edu:925/`

Coastal Marine Biology

University of Maryland, College Park

The library's holdings are large and wide-ranging and contain significant collections in many fields. Agriculture, Coastal Marine Biology, Fisheries, Water Quality, Oceanography

Keywords: Agriculture, Coastal Marine Biology, Fisheries, Water Quality, Oceanography

Audience: Researchers, Students, General Public

Contact: Janet McLeod
mcleod@umail.umd.edu

Details: Free

Expect: Login; Send: Atdu

`telnet://info.umd.edu`

CoCo

CoCo

This is a discussion related to the Tandy Color Computer (any model) OS-9 Operating System, and any other topics relating to the "CoCo," as this computer is affectionately known.

Keywords: Tandy Computers, Computers

Audience: Tandy Computer Users, Computer Users

Contact: Paul E. Campbell
pecampbe@mtus5.BITNET

Details: Free

User Info: To subscribe to the list, send an e-mail message requesting a subscription to the URL address below.

`mailto:listserv@pucc.princeton.edu`

CODES (Codes Library)

CODES (Codes Library)

The Codes Library offers access to US federal and state legislative materials, in codified, slip law, and bill form, plus federal and state regulatory materials and a statutes archive.

Keywords: Statutes, Codes, State, Federal

Audience: (US) Lawyers

Profile: The Codes library contains an extensive compilation of federal and state statutory materials, in codified as well as slip law form, from all 50 states, the District of Columbia, Puerto Rico, the Virgin Islands and the United States Code Service. The library also contains federal and state regulatory materials plus a statues archive. Pending legislation can be found with 50-state and federal fill tracking, the full text of federal bills, the Congressional Record, and the full text of bills for a growing number of states. Administrative materials include the Code of Federal Regulations, the Federal Register, 50-state regulation tracking, and the administrative codes for a selected number of states.

Contact: New Sales Group at (800) 227-4908 or (513) 859-5398 inside the US, or (513) 865-7981 for all inquires outside the US.

User Info: To subscribe, contact Mead directly.

To examine the Lexis user guide, you can access it at the ftp site of the University of Texas at Austin at the URL address: ftp://ftp.cc.utexas.edu

The files are in: /pub/ref-services/LEXIS

`telnet://nex.meaddata.com`

`http://www.meaddata.com`

Cognitive Science

(The) Observer

The central scope of the group covers the theory of autopoiesis (of Humberto Maturana and Francisco Varela) and enactive cognitive science. The extended scope includes applications of the above theoretical work and other relevant work (for example, systems theory, cognitive science, phenomenology, artificial life, and so on). This is an edited electronic newsletter issued (approximately) twice monthly.

Keywords: Autopoiesis, Systems Theory, Cognitive Science

Audience: Systems Theorists, Researchers

Contact: Randall Whitaker
rwhit@cs.umu.se

User Info: To subscribe to the list, send an e-mail message to the URL address below consisting of a single line reading:

SUB the observer YourFirstName YourLastName.

To send a message to the entire list, address it to: rwhit@cs.umu.se

`mailto:listserv@cs.umu.se`

Cognitive and Psychological Sciences on the Internet

A resource containing links to academic programs, organizations and conference lists, journals and magazines, Usenet newsgroups, discussion lists, and other general information regarding cognitive science.

Keywords: Cognitive Science, Psychology, Neuroscience

Sponsor: The Stanford University Psychology Department

Audience: Cognitive Scientists, Neuroscientists, Psychologists, Psychiatrists

Contact: Scott Mainwaring
sdm@psych.stanford.edu

`http://matia.stanford.edu/cogsci.html`

ELSNET (European Network in Language and Speech)

A web site addressing the development of language technology in Europe and abroad by helping to coordinate progress on both scientific and technological fronts.

Keywords: Linguistics, Cognitive Science, Communication

Sponsor: The University of Edinburgh Centre for Cognitive Science, Edinburgh, Scotland

Audience: Linguists, Cognitive Scientists

Contact: Ewan Klein
klein@ed.ac.uk

`http://www.cogsci.ed.ac.uk/elsnet/home.html`

COHOUSING-L

COHOUSING-L

A list for discussion of Cohousing, the name of a type of collaborative housing that has been developed primarily in Denmark since 1972 where it is known as bofoellesskaber. Cohousing is housing designed to foster community and cooperation while preserving independence. Private residences are clustered near shared facilities. The members design and manage all aspects of their community.

Keywords: Community, Housing, Cooperatives

Audience: Urban Planners, Architects, General Contractors

Contact: fholson@uci.com

Details: Free

User Info: To subscribe to the list, send an e-mail message to the address below consisting of a single line reading:

SUB COHOUSING-L YourFirstName YourLastName

To send a message to the entire list, address it to: COHOUSING-L@uci.com

`mailto:listserv@uci.com`

Coins

coins

A forum for discussions on numismatic topics, including US and world coins, paper money, tokens, and medals.

Keywords: Coins, Numismatics

Audience: Coin Collectors

Contact: Daniel J. Power
COINS-REQUEST@ISCSVAX.UNI.EDU

Details: Free

User Info: To subscribe to the list, send an e-mail message requesting a subscription to the URL address below.

To send a message to the entire list, address it to: COINS@ISCSVAX.UNI.EDU

`mailto:COINS-REQUEST@ISCSVAX.UNI.EDU`

Colby College Library

Colby College Library

The library's holdings are large and wide-ranging and contain significant collections in many fields.

Keywords: Contemporary Letters, Hardy (Thomas),James (Henry), Mann (Thomas, Collections of), Housman (A.E., Letters of), Maine Authors, Irish History (Modern)

A
B
C
D
E
F
G
H
I
J
K
L
M
N
O
P
Q
R
S
T
U
V
W
X
Y
Z

A B **C** D E F G H I J K L M N O P Q R S T U V W X Y Z

Audience: General Public, Researchers, Librarians, Document Delivery Professionals

Details: Free

Expect: login, Send: library

`telnet://library.colby.edu`

Collectibiles

Cards

This list is for people interested in collecting, speculating, and investing in baseball, football, basketball, hockey, and other trading cards and/or memorabilia. Discussion and want/sell lists are welcome.

Keywords: Trading Cards, Collectibles, Memorabilia

Audience: Sports Card Collectors, Sports Card Traders, Memorabilia Collectors

Contact: Keane Arase
cards-request@tanstaafl.uchicago.edu

Details: Free

User Info: To subscribe to the list, send an e-mail message requesting a subscription to the URL address below.

To send a message to the entire list, address it to:

cards@tanstaafl.uchicago.edu

Notes: The list is open to anyone.

`mailto:cards-request@tanstaafl.uchicago.edu`

Collections (of)

Colby College Library

The library's holdings are large and wide-ranging and contain significant collections in many fields.

Keywords: Contemporary Letters, Hardy (Thomas),James (Henry), Mann (Thomas), Collections (of), Housman (A.E., Letters of), Maine Authors, Irish History (Modern)

Audience: General Public, Researchers, Librarians, Document Delivery Professionals

Details: Free

Expect: login, Send: library

`telnet://library.colby.edu`

Georgia State University Library

The library's holdings are large and wide-ranging and contain significant collections in many fields.

Keywords: Labor (History of), Multimedia, Mercer (Johnny, Collection of)

Audience: General Public, Researchers, Librarians, Document Delivery Professionals

Contact: Phil Williams
isgpew@gsuvm1.gsu.edu

Details: Free

Expect: VM screen, Send: RETURN; Expect: CP READ, Send: DIAL VTAM, press RETURN; Expect: CICS screen, Send: PF1

`telnet://library.gsu.edu`

University of New Hampshire Videotex Library

The library's holdings are large and wide-ranging and contain significant collections in many fields.

Keywords: Dance, Folk Music, Milne (A.A., Collection of), Galway (Ireland)

Audience: Researchers, Students, General Public

Contact: Robin Tuttle
r_tuttle1@unhh.unh.edu

Details: Free

Expect: USERNAME; Send: Student (no password required). Control-z to log off.

`telnet://unhvt@unh.edu`

The University of Kansas Library

The library's holdings are large and wide-ranging and contain significant collections in many fields.

Keywords: Botany, Chinese Studies, Cartography (History of), Kansas, Opera, Ornithology, Joyce (James), Yeats (William Butler), Walpole (Sir Robert, Collections of)

Audience: General Public, Researchers, Librarians, Document Delivery Professionals

Contact: John S. Miller

Details: Free

Expect: Username, Send: relay <cr>

`telnet://kuhub.cc.ukans.edu`

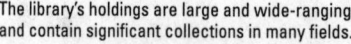

College

rec.sport.basketball.college

A Usenet newsgroup providing information and discussion about college basketball.

Keywords: Basketball, College, Sports

Audience: Basketball Fans, Sport Fans

User Info: To subscribe to this Usenet newsgroup, you need access to a newsreader.

`news:rec.sport.basketball.college`

College E-mail Addresses

College E-mail Addresses

Information on e-mail addresses at graduate offices.

Keywords: Internet, E-mail

Audience: Internet Surfers, Students, College/ University Educators

Details: Free

File is: pub/usenet/soc.college/ Admission_Office_Email_Address_List

`ftp://pit-manager.mit.edu/pub/usenet-by-group/soc.college`

`gopher://sipb.mit.edu`

rec.sport.football.college

A Usenet newsgroup providing information and discussion about college football.

Keywords: Football, College, Sports

Audience: Football Fans, Sports Fans

User Info: To subscribe to this Usenet newsgroup, you need access to a newsreader.

`news:rec.sport.football.college`

Colorado

amend2-info

Colorado voted in an amendment to their state constitution that revoke any existing gay/lesbian/ bisexual civil rights legislation and prohibit the drafting of any new legislation. This moderated list is for information on the implication and issues of this amendment.

Keywords: Activists, Gay, Lesbian, Bisexual, Constitutional Amendments, Colorado, Civil Rights

Audience: General Public, Gays, Lesbians, Bisexuals, Activists

Contact: amend2-info@cs.colorado.edu

User Info: To subscribe to the list, send an e-mail message requesting a subscription to the URL address below.

To send a message to the entire list, address it to: amend2-info@cs.colorado.edu

`mailto:majordomo@cs.colorado.edu`

Citizens Project

A grass-roots community group in the Pikes Peak region of Colorado.

Keywords: Community, Networking, Colorado

Audience: Activists, Policymakers, Community Leaders, Government

Profile: Based in Colorado Springs, Colorado, the Citizens Project makes use of the online world in pursuit of its mission to investigate, inform, and advocate issues affecting the Pikes Peak region. It maintains an extensive gopher server, FTP site, and a ListServ (for people who have only e-mail access).

Contact: Citizens Project
citizens@cscns.com

Details: Free

User Info: To subscribe to the list, send an e-mail message to the URL address below, consisting of a single line reading:

SUB cns-citizens-pub YourFirstName YourLastName

mailto:listserv@cscns.com

Colorado Document Citations

A list of publications from all Colorado statutory government agencies. The wiretap gopher provides access to a range of world documents in full-text format.

Keywords: Colorado, Government (US)

Audience: Researchers, Lawyers, Colorado Residents, Governments, historians, Researchers, General Public

Select from Menu as appropriate

telnet://pac.carl.org

Telluride Institute

This is a community organization involved in building an electronic dimension in rural Colorado. The vision of Telluride Institute includes linking rural residents to each other and outside resources, creating new opportunities for education, jobs, and arts.

Keywords: Community, Networking, Virtual Community, Rural Development, Colorado

Sponsor: The Telluride Institute, Telluride, Colorado

Audience: Activists, Policymakers, Community Leaders, Students, Colorado Residents

Profile: The Telluride Institute is a local community-based organization that produces arts, environmental, and educational events in the Telluride area of Colorado. The Institite is committed to the creation of what it calls the "InfoZone": it wants to use modern telecommunications to link together the local community and to connect to the rest of the world to exchange ideas, commerce, arts, and inspiration.

Contact: Richard Lowenberg
tellinst@CSN.ORG

Details: Free

Send an e-mail message to the URL address below asking for further information.

mailto:tellinst@csn.org

Columbia University Libraries

Columbia University Libraries

The Columbia libraries include a medical library and a mathematics library.

Keywords: Libraries, Research

Audience: General Public, Researchers

Details: Free

When connected, hit return, enter terminal type: **vt100**.

telnet://clio.cul.columbia.edu

Comedians

alt.fan.monty-python

A Usenet newsgroup providing an electronic fan club for those wacky Brits.

Keywords: Humor, Entertainment, Comedians, Satire

Audience: Monty Python Enthusiasts, General Public

User Info: To subscribe to this Usenet newsgroup, you need access to a newsreader.

news:alt.fan.monty-python

alt.fan.rush-limbaugh

A Usenet newsgroup providing information and discussion about Rush Limbaugh, a politically conservative American figure.

Keywords: Limbaugh (Rush), Politics (Conservative), Comedians

Audience: Followers of Rush Limbaugh

User Info: To subscribe to this Usenet newsgroup, you need access to a newsreader.

news:alt.fan.rush-limbaugh

Comedy

alt.peeves

A Usenet newsgroup providing information and discussion about peeves, complaints, and whining.

Keywords: Humor, Comedy

Audience: General Public, Complainers

User Info: To subscribe to this Usenet newsgroup, you need access to a newsreader.

news:alt.peeves

alt.tasteless

A Usenet newsgroup providing information and discussion about tasteless jokes.

Keywords: Humor, Comedy

Audience: General Interest, Jokers

User Info: To subscribe to this Usenet newsgroup, you need access to a newsreader.

news:alt.tasteless

Comic Books

Cerebi

This list discusses the Cerebus comic book by Dave Sim. Anything relating to Cerebus or Sim is welcome.

Keywords: Comic Books, Sim (Dave)

Audience: Comics Enthusiasts

Contact: Christian Walters
cerebi-request@tomservo.b23b.ingr.com

Details: Free

User Info: To subscribe to the list, send an e-mail message requesting a subscription to the URL address below.

To send a message to the entire list, address it to:
cerebi@tomservo.b23b.ingr.com

Notes: It's just an echo list, so anything that gets mailed is bounced to everyone.

mailto:cerebi-request@tomservo.b23b.ingr.com

comix

This list is intended for talking about non-mainstream and independent comic books. There is little talk about superheroes, and none about Marvel Mutants.

Keywords: Comic Books

Audience: Comics Enthusiasts

Contact: Elizabeth Lear Newman
comix-request@world.std.com

Details: Free

User Info: To subscribe to the list, send an e-mail message requesting a subscription to the URL address below.

To send a message to the entire list, address it to: comix@world.std.com

mailto:comix-request@world.std.com

A B C D E F G H I J K L M N O P Q R S T U V W X Y Z

A B C D E F G H I J K L M N O P Q R S T U V W X Y Z

modesty-blaise

A discussion forum on Peter O'Donnell's Modesty Blaise books and comics. Topics include character, plot, artists, and relevant articles.

Keywords: Comic Books, Comics

Audience: Modesty Blaise Enthusiasts

Contact: Thomas Gramstad
modesty-blaise-request@math.uio.no

User Info: To subscribe to the list, send an e-mail message to the URL address below consisting of a single line reading:

SUB modesty-blaise YourFirstName YourLastName

mailto: modesty-blaise-request@math.uio.no

rec.arts.comics.misc

A Usenet newsgroup providing information and discussion about comic books and graphic novels.

Keywords: Comic Books, Books

Audience: Comics Enthusiasts, Readers, Writers

Details: Free

User Info: To subscribe to this Usenet newsgroup, you need access to a newsreader.

news:rec.arts.comics.misc

Comics

disney-comics

A forum for discussion of Disney comics.

Keywords: Comics, Disney

Audience: Comics Enthusiasts, Disney

Contact: Per Starbuck
disney-comics-request@student.docs.uu.se

Details: Free

User Info: To subscribe to the list, send an e-mail message requesting a subscription to the URL address below.

To send a message to the entire list, address it to: disney-comics-request@student.docs.uu.se

mailto:disney-comics-request@student.docs.uu.se

modesty-blaise

A discussion forum on Peter O'Donnell's Modesty Blaise books and comics. Topics include character, plot, artists, and relevant articles.

Keywords: Comic Books, Comics

Audience: Modesty Blaise Enthusiasts

Contact: Thomas Gramstad
modesty-blaise-request@math.uio.no

User Info: To subscribe to the list, send an e-mail message to the URL address below consisting of a single line reading: SUB modesty-blaise YourFirstName YourLastName

mailto: modesty-blaise-request@math.uio.no

Commcoll

Commcoll

A mailing list providing a forum for faculty, staff, and administrators at two-year institutions.

Keywords: Education (Continuing), Community Colleges

Sponsor: Jefferson Community College at the University of Kentucky, Kentucky, USA

Audience: Educators, Administrators

User Info: To subscribe to the list, send an e-mail message to the URL address below consisting of a single line reading: SUB commcoll YourFirstName YourLastName.

To send a message to the entire list, address it to: commcoll@ukcc.uky.edu

mailto: listserv@ukcc.uky.edu

Commerce Business Daily

Commerce Business Daily

The Commerce Business Daily is a publication that announces invitations to bid on proposals requested by the US Federal Government. This gopher is updated every business day.

Keywords: Business (US), Economics, Commerce, Trade, Government (US)

Sponsor: CNS and Softshare Government Information Systems

Audience: Economists, Business Professionals, General Public, Journalists, Students, Politicians.

Profile: Invitations via Internet email that apply only to specific companies can be arranged.

Contact: Melissa Allensworth
sshare@cscns.com
service@cscns.com

Details: Free

gopher://cns.cscns.com/cbd/About the CBD

Ireland-Related Online Resources

This is a list of network-accessible online resources (documents, images, information, access mechanisms for off-line material, and so on) of Irish interest. Coverage includes some Bulletin Board Services, some commercial information systems such as CompuServe and commercial bibliographic services.

Keywords: Ireland, Travel, Commerce, Geography

Audience: Irish, General Public, Tourists, Businesses

Contact: fmurtagh@eso.org

http://http.hq.eso.org/~fmurtagh/ireland-resources.html

National Export Strategy

This site provides the complete text of a report presented to Congress by the Trade Promotion Coordinating Committee, describing ways to develop U.S. export promotion efforts.

Keywords: Commerce, Trade, Exports, Business

Sponsor: United States Government, Trade Promotion Coordinating Committee

Audience: Exporters, Businesspeople, Trade Specialists

Details: Free

ftp://sunny.stat-usa.gov

http://sunny.stat-usa.gov

Overseas Business Reports

Full-text of U.S. International Trade Administration reports, discussing the economic and commercial climate in various countries around the world.

Keywords: Business, Trade, Commerce

Sponsor: U.S. Government, International Trade Administration

Audience: Businesspeople, Trade Specialists, Investors

Details: Free

gopher://umslvma.umsl.edu/11/library/govdocs/obr

Trademark Act of the US

The US Trademark Act of 1946 (the "Lanham Act"), Title 15, United States Code, Sections 1051–1127.

Keywords: Trademarks, Laws (US), Government (US), Commerce

Audience: Journalists, Politicians, Students, Lawyers, Business Professionals, Designers, Marketers

Details: Free

http://www.law.cornell.edu/lanham/lanham.table.html

TRADSTAT

TRADSTAT is a comprehensive online source of national trade statistics.

Keywords: Trade, Commerce, Business

Sponsor: TRADSTAT Ltd., London, UK

Audience: Importers, Exporters, Businesses

Profile: TRADSTAT covers over 90 percent of world trade. Every month the latest trade figures are loaded into the database from over 20 countries worldwide and all their trading partners. Trade is reported by countries in the EC, EFTA, North and South America, and the Far East. TRADSTAT gives annual trends back to 1981, and monthly reports can be produced at any time for the latest 25 months' trade. The data is made available on average three to eight weeks after the month of trade. This is often weeks, even months, ahead of the equivalent printed data.

User Info: To subscribe, contact Dialog directly.

`telnet://dialog.com`

Uniform Commercial Code (UCC)

Articles 1 and 2 of the UCC, adopted with some variations in all 50 states (USA).

Keywords: Commerce, Business Info, Standards

Audience: Politicians, Marketers, Students, Retailers, Lawyers

Details: Free

`http://www.law.cornell.edu/ucc/ucc.table.html`

CommerceNet

CommerceNet

An open, internet-based infrastructure for electronic commerce, created by a coalition of Silicon Valley organizations.

Keywords: Business, Electronic Commerce

Sponsor: CommerceNet, Inc. 800 El Camino Real, Menlo Park, CA 94025.

Audience: Businesses, Commercial Internet Users, General Public

Profile: Services include basic enabling services required by virtually every user and application (generic directories, secure multimedia messaging, network access control, and payment facilities). Applications include a framework for the developmentof compelling applications and services targeted to electronic commerce among companies in the region. Applications are designed to address the varied business and community needs of CommerceNet

users; these are developed by third-party providers, in compliance with protocols established by CommerceNet. Connectivity is high-quality and affordable, with minimal on-site equipment or network expertise required of the user.

Contact: feedback@commerce.net

`http://www.commerce.net`

Commercial Real Estate

Commercial Real Estate

Users can send and receive listings on property for sale, ask and answer questions, send press releases, receive editorial material, and do networking on commercial property.

Keywords: Real Estate

Audience: Real Estate Brokers, General Public

Contact: commercial.realestate@data-base.com

Details: Free

User Info: To subscribe to the list, send an e-mail message requesting a subscription to the URL address below.

`mailto:commercial.realestate@data-base.com`

Commodore-Amiga

Commodore-Amiga

This list is for Commodore Amiga computer users. Weekly postings include hardware reviews, news briefs, system information, company progress, and information for finding out more about the Commodore and Amiga.

Keywords: Commodore-Amiga, Computers

Audience: Computer Users

Contact: subscribe@xamiga.linet.org

Details: Free

Send subscription requests to the URL address below using this format:

#commodore username@domain

`mailto:subscribe@xamiga.linet.org`

Commodore-Amiga Computers

CSAA

The Comp.Sys.Amiga.Announce mailing list has been created for those who have no access to USENET. It provides the gate between the USENET newsgroup C.S.A.A. and e-mail. This group distributes announcements of importance to people

using the Commodore brand Amiga computers. Announcements contain information on new products, disk library releases, software updates, reports of major bugs or dangerous viruses, notices of meetings or upcoming events, and so forth. A large proportion of posts announce the upload of software packages to anonymous FTP archive sites.

Keywords: Commodore-Amiga Computers, Computers

Audience: Commodore-Amiga Users

Contact: Carlos Amezaga announce-request@cs.ucdavis.edu

Details: Free

User Info: To subscribe to the list, send an e-mail message requesting a subscription to the URL address below.

To send a message to the entire list, address it to:announce@cs.ucdavis.edu

`mailto:announce-request@cs.ucdavis.edu`

Commonwealth of Independent States (CIS)

Sovokinform

CIS news, events, general information; usually in transliterated Russian.

Keywords: Commonwealth of Independent States (CIS)

Audience: Journalists, Political Scientists

Contact: burkov@drfmc.ceng.cea.fr

Details: Free

User Info: To subscribe to the list, send an e-mail message requesting a subscription to the URL address below.

To send a message to the entire list, address it to: sovokinform@drfmc.ceng.cea.fr

`mailto:burkov@drfmc.ceng.cea.fr`

Commonwealth

INTLAW (International Law Library)

The International Law Library provides comprehensive international law materials.

Keywords: International Law, EEC, Commonwealth, China

Audience: Lawyers, International Lawyers

Profile: The International Law library provides comprehensive international law materials. The International Law library contains federal case law, European Community materials, treaties and agreements, Commonwealth law

A
B
C
D
E
F
G
H
I
J
K
L
M
N
O
P
Q
R
S
T
U
V
W
X
Y
Z

A
B
C
D
E
F
G
H
I
J
K
L
M
N
O
P
Q
R
S
T
U
V
W
X
Y
Z

materials, topical and professional journals, French law materials (in French) China law materials, plus relevant topical publications.

Contact: New Sales Group at (800) 227-4908 or (513) 859-5398 inside the US, or (513) 865-7981 for all inquires outside the US.

User Info: To subscribe, contact Mead directly.

To examine the Lexis user guide, you can access it at the ftp site of the University of Texas at Austin at the URL address: ftp://ftp.cc.utexas.edu

The files are in: /pub/ref-services/LEXIS

`telnet://nex.meaddata.com`

`http://www.meaddata.com`

Communes

alt.housing.nontrad

This newsgroup is for discussion of all forms of "nontraditional housing," including cohousing and communes.

Keywords: Community, Housing, Communes

Audience: General Public, Community Activists

Details: Free

To participate in a USENET newsgroup, you need access to a "newsreader."

`news:alt.housing.nontrad`

commune

The purpose of this list is to discuss the COMMUNE protocol, a Telnet replacement.

Keywords: Communes, Telnet

Audience: Commune Protocol Users

Contact: Dan Bernstein
commune-request@stealth.acf.nyu.edu

Details: Free

User Info: To subscribe to the list, send an e-mail message requesting a subscription to the URL address below.

To send a message to the entire list, address it to:

commune-list@stealth.acf.nyu.edu

`mailto:commune-`
`request@stealth.acf.nyu.edu`

Communication

ELSNET (European Network in Language and Speech)

A web site addressing the development of language technology in Europe and abroad by helping to coordinate progress on both scientific and technological fronts.

Keywords: Linguistics, Cognitive Science, Communication

Sponsor: The University of Edinburgh Centre for Cognitive Science, Edinburgh, Scotland

Audience: Linguists, Cognitive Scientists

Contact: Ewan Klein
klein@ed.ac.uk

`http://www.cogsci.ed.ac.uk/elsnet/`
`home.html`

Journal of Technology Education

Electronic journal devoted to educational issues in technology.

Keywords: Communication, Education, Technology,

Audience: Educators

Details: Free

Send an e-mail message to the URL address below with the request: GET MISCELLA JTE-V5N1. This file will give you access information for additional issues.

`mailto:listserv@vtvm1.cc.vt.edu`

Communication and Mass Communication Resources

Communication and Mass Communication Resources

An archive of materials related to mass communications and the media.

Keywords: Mass Communications, Media, Journalism, Telecommunications, Advertising

Sponsor: The University of Iowa

Audience: Mass Communications Students and Teachers, Journalists, Broadcasting Professionals

Contact: Karla Tonella
Karla_Tonella@uiowa.edu

`gopher://iam41.arcade.uiowa.edu`

Communications

Almost 2001 Archive

Archive of transcripts of Almost 2001, a series on computer communications of the future, produced by NBC (National Broadcasting Company).

Keywords: Computers, Communications, Internet

Sponsor: The WELL (Whole Earth 'Lectronic Link)

Audience: Computer Users, Internet Surfers

Details: Free

To participate in a conference on the WELL, you must first establish an account on the WELL.To do so, start by typing: telnet://well.sf.ca.us

`gopher://gopher.well.sf.ca.us//11/`
`Communications/2001`

AM/FM

A mailing list for the AM/FM Online Edition, a monthly compilation of news stories concerning the UK radio industry.

Keywords: Radio, United Kingdom, Communications

Audience: Radio Enthusiasts (UK), Communications Specialists, Students (college, graduate)

Contact: Stephen Hebditch
listserv@orbital.demon.co.uk

User Info: To subscribe to the list, send an e-mail message to the URL addres below, consisting of a single line reading:

SUB am/fm YourFirstName YourLastName

To send a message to the entire list, address it to: AM/FM@orbital.demon.co.uk

`mailto:listserv@orbital.demon.co.uk`

CMPCOM (Computers and Communications) Library

The Computers and Communications Library provides you industry-specific sources. More than 40 full-text sources that concentrate on computers and communications are available. Full-text files can be searched in a variety of ways: as an individual file, by major-subject group file, or as a user-defined group file.

Keywords: Computers, Communications, Technology, Electronics

Audience: Business Researchers, Analysts, Entrepreneurs

Profile: This library can be used to gain insight on new products and technologies being introduced; monitor industry news for high technology systems, electronics, engineering, communications, and computer hardware and software; and locate product evaluations for both the professional as well as the casual personal computer user.

Contact: Mead New Sales Group at (800) 227-4908 or (513) 859-5398 inside the US, or (513) 865-7981 for all inquiries outside the US.

User Info: To subscribe, contact Mead directly.

To examine the Nexis user guide, you can access it at the ftp site of the University of Texas at Austin at the URL address: ftp://ftp.cc.utexas.edu

The files are in: /pub/ref-services/LEXIS

`telnet://nex.meaddata.com`

`http://www.meaddata.com`

ejcrec 'Electronic Journal of Communications/La Revue électronique de communication' ★

This journal is a quarterly bilingual (English and French) journal for the communications field broadly.

Keywords: Communications

Audience: Educators, Administrators, Communications Professionals

Details: Free

User Info: To subscribe to the journal, send an e-mail message to the URL address shown below consisting of a single line reading

Join edupage YourFirstName YourLastName

`mailto:comserve@rpitsvm.bitnet`

Electronic Communications Privacy Act of 1986 ★

This is the act to amend Title 18, United States Code, with respect to the interception of certain communications, other forms of surveillance, and for other purposes. This act affects every USENET, Bitnet, BBS, shortwave listener, TV viewer, and so on.

Keywords: Communications, Privacy, Government (US Federal), Laws (US Federal)

Audience: Journalists, Privacy Activists, Students, Politicians

Details: Free

`gopher://wiretap.spies.com/00/Gov/ecpa.act`

Newsline

An electronic newsletter describing additions to or changes in Comserve, the electronic information and discussion service for communications faculty and students.

Keywords: Communications, Comserve

Audience: Communications Students, Communications Specialists

Profile: The information includes announcements of additions to Comserve's database, new services offered through Comserve's electronic conferences, or fundamental changes in the services offered by Comserve.

Contact: Timothy Stephen, Teresa Harrison

Support@RpiecsSupport@Vm.Ecs.Rpi.Edu

User Info: To subscribe, send an e-mail message to the URL address below consisting of a single line reading:

SUB NEWSLINE YourFirstName YourLastName

`mailto:Comserve@Vm.Ecs.Rpi.Edu`

PRL

The Pirate Radio SWL list is for the distribution of questions, answers, information, and loggings of Pirate Radio Stations.

Keywords: Radio, Communications

Audience: Radio Listeners, Radio Pirates

Contact: John Brewer brewer@ace.enet.dec.com

User Info: To subscribe to the list, send an e-mail message to the URL address below, consisting of a single line reading:

SUB PRLYourFirstName YourLastName.

To send a message to the entire list, address it to: brewer@ace.enet.dec.com

`mailto:listserv@ace.enet.dec.com`

Prog-Pubs ★

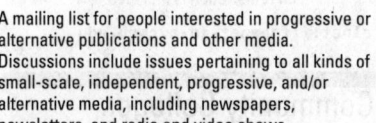

A mailing list for people interested in progressive or alternative publications and other media. Discussions include issues pertaining to all kinds of small-scale, independent, progressive, and/or alternative media, including newspapers, newsletters, and radio and video shows.

Keywords: Media, Alternative Press, Communications

Audience: Students (college/university), Independent Media Professionals

Contact: prog-pubs-request@fuggles.acc.virginia.edu

Details: Free

User Info: To subscribe to the list, send an e-mail message requesting a subscription to the URL address below.

To send a message to the entire list, address it to:prog-pubs@fuggles.acc.virginia.edu

`mailto:prog-pubs@fuggles.acc.virginia.edu`

Scit-L ★

A list for those interested in information and communications science.

Keywords: Communications, Information Sciences

Audience: Communications Specialists, Communications Students, Information Scientists

Contact: Elia Zureik Scitdoc@qucdn.queensu.ca

User Info: To subscribe to this list, send an e-mail message to the URL address below, consisting of a single line reading:

SUB scit-l YourFirstName YourLastName

To send a message to the entire list, address it to: scit-l@qucdn.queensu.ca

`mailto:listserv@qucdn.queensu.ca`

Stutt-L ★

A list for the clinical discussion of stuttering, a speech disorder.

Keywords: Communications, Speech Disorders, Disabilities

Audience: Communications Specialists, Speech Pathologists

Contact: Woody Starkweather v5002e@vm.temple.edu

User Info: To subscribe to this list, send an e-mail message to the URL address below, consisting of a single line reading:

SUB Stutt-L YourFirstName YourLastName

To send a message to the entire list, address it to: stutt-l@rm.temple.edu

`mailto:listserv@vm.temple.edu`

The Black Box Catalog

The Black Box Catalog, the industry's most complete source for data communication equipment, is now available on the Internet. The complete range of products, technical references, and application briefs are available on the Black Box World Wide Web Server.

Keywords: Communications, Networking, Telecommunication, Computers

Sponsor: Black Box Corporation, Lawrence, PA

Audience: Engineers, Network Administration, LAN Administrators, Communication Specialists

Profile: Black Box Corporation is a leading international supplier of data communications networking and related computer connectivity products. Black Box's commitment to providing effective solutions that substantially enhance the capabilities of communications systems is backed by a technical support staff that is available around the clock, a liberal 45-day return policy, and same day shipment of its 6000 products.

Contact: Webmaster webmaster@blackbox.com

Details: Costs

`http://www.blackbox.com`

Communism

Emory University Library ★★

The library's holdings are large and wide-ranging and contain significant collections in many fields.

Keywords: Health Sciences, Theology, History (US), Communism, Economics (History of), Literature (American)

Audience: General Public, Researchers, Librarians, Document Delivery Professionals

A
B
C
D
E
F
G
H
I
J
K
L
M
N
O
P
Q
R
S
T
U
V
W
X
Y
Z

Details: Free

Expect: VM screen, Send: RETURN;
Expect: CP READ, Send: DIAL VTAM,
press RETURN; Expect: CICS screen,
Send: PF1

`telnet://emuvm1.cc.emory.edu`

soc.culture.soviet

A Usenet newsgroup providing information and
discussion about topics relating to Russia or the
former Soviet Union.

Keywords: Russia, CIS (Commonwealth of
Independent States), Communism,
Sociology

Audience: Sociologists, Russians

Details: Free

User Info: To subscribe to this Usenet newsgroup,
you need access to a newsreader.

`news:soc.culture.soviet`

talk.politics.soviet

A Usenet newsgroup providing information and
discussion about Soviet politics, domestic and
international.

Keywords: Communism, Russia, Politics, CIS
(Commonwealth of Independent States)

Audience: Political Scientists

Details: Free

User Info: To subscribe to this Usenet newsgroup,
you need access to a newsreader.

`news:talk.politics.soviet`

val-l

Discussion on changes in the Communist countries,
ranging from Cuba and Vietnam to the former Soviet
Union.

Keywords: Communism, Soviet Union, Political
Science

Audience: Political Scientists

Contact: cdell@umkcax1 or
cdell@umkcvax1.bitnet

Details: Free

User Info: To subscribe to the list, send an e-mail
message to the URL address below
consisting of a single line reading:

SUB val-l YourFirstName YourLastName

To send a message to the entire list,
address it to: val-l@ucflvm.cc.ucf.edu

`mailto:listserv@ucflvm.cc.ucf.edu`

Community Access

Cleveland FreeNet

A network designed for community access and
education.

Keywords: Networks, Community Access

Sponsor: The Cleveland FreeNet Project, Case
Western Reserve University, Cleveland,
Ohio, USA

Audience: Educators, Researchers, Students,
Parents

Profile: A prototypical user-friendly city FreeNet,
containing complete historical
documents, an up-to-date news service,
extensive info on the arts, sciences,
technology, medicine, business, and
education.

Notes: Registration is required, and information
on registration is included.

`telnet://freenet-in-a.cwru.edu`

Community Colleges

Commcoll

A mailing list providing a forum for faculty, staff, and
administrators at two-year institutions.

Keywords: Education (Continuing), Community
Colleges

Sponsor: Jefferson Community College at the
University of Kentucky, Kentucky, USA

Audience: Educators, Administrators

User Info: To subscribe to the list, send an e-mail
message to the URL address below
consisting of a single line reading:

SUB commcoll YourFirstName
YourLastName.

To send a message to the entire list,
address it to: commcoll@ukcc.uky.edu

`mailto: listserv@ukcc.uky.edu`

Community Networking

Free-Net Working Papers

An FTP site with a collection of articles and papers
about community networking.

Keywords: Community Networking, Networking

Sponsor: Carleton University, National
Clearinghouse for Machine Readable
Texts

Audience: Activists, Government, General Public

Profile: Project Guttenburg's goal is to provide a
collection of 10,000 of the most used
books by the year 2001.

Contact: Jay Weston, Michael S. Hart

jweston@carleton.ca

Details: Free

Login anonymous; cd text

`ftp://alfred.carleton.ca/pub/freenet/
working.papers`

FreeNets

This resource provides extensive information about
FreeNets, which are public access Internet sites at
no-charge or for donations.

Keywords: Internet Access, Community Networking

Audience: Individuals, Communities, Libraries

Profile: FreeNets, community computing
services providing Internet access, exist
internationally and include such systems
as LA FreeNet, Buffalo FreeNet,
Cleveland FreeNet, FreeNet Erlangen-
Nuernberg, Victoria FreeNet, Vaasa
FreePort (Finland), CapAccess (D.C.),
and many more.

Details: Free

URL (gopher path) below contains
pointers to all FreeNets.

`gopher path: 1/internet/freenets
marvel.loc.gov`

Community

(The) Electronic Public Interest versus the Private Good

Statement by community networker Dave Hughes,
sounding the warning that the federal goverment
may be leaving the marketplace too much control
over who gets access to the information
infrastructure.

Keywords: Community, Networking, Government
(US)

Audience: Activists, Policymakers, Community
Leaders

Contact: Dave Hughes

dave@oldcolo.com

Details: Free

`http://nearnet.gnn.com/mag/articles/
oram/bio.hughes.html`

(The) WELL (Whole Earth 'Lectronic Link)

The WELL is a computer conferencing system, a virtual community, and an electronic coffee shop.

Keywords: Community, Networking, Computer Conferencing, Virtual Community

Sponsor: Whole Earth 'Lectronic Link

Audience: General Public, Internet Surfers

Profile: The WELL is a classic example of an online community that uses what is called 'conferencing' to bring a myriad of people together for intense interactions without them having to be connected at the same time. At the end of 1993, the WELL had about 8,000 users (about 90% from all over the USA and about 10% from other locations) and approximately 200 public discussion areas ('conferences'), and 200 private discussion areas. It is a place rich in diverse 'neighborhoods.'

Contact: The WELL Support Staff

info@well.sf.ca.us

Direct dial access through: +1 (415) 332-4335

To participate in a conference on the WELL, you must first establish an account on the WELL. To do so, start by typing: **telnet well.sf.ca.us**

telnet://well.sf.ca.us

(The) Worldwide Impact of Network Access

This is an article by community networker Felipe Rodriquez. In this statement Rodriquez argues that developed countries should help less developed countries build their information infrastructures, and that governments should not censor the content of network traffic.

Keywords: Community, Networking, Europe, Development (International)

Audience: Activists, Policymakers, Community Leaders

Contact: Felipe Rodriquez

felipe@hacktic.nl

http://nearnet.gnn.com/mag/articles/ oram/bio.rodriquez.html

alt.housing.nontrad

This newsgroup is for discussion of all forms of "nontraditional housing," including cohousing and communes.

Keywords: Community, Housing, Communes

Audience: General Public, Community Activists

Details: Free

To participate in a USENET newsgroup, you need access to a "newsreader."

news:alt.housing.nontrad

An NREN That Includes Everyone

★

In this article, community networker Tom Grundner (founder of Free-Net), advocates a National Community Network, one that treats parents looking for health-care information as researchers. He advocates expanding our definition of educational access to include people of all ages—senior citizens as well as kindergarteners.

Keywords: Community, Networking, Government (US)

Audience: Activists, Policymakers, Community Leaders

Contact: Tom Grundner

tmg@nptn.org

Details: Free

Notes: This document contains hypertext links to the NPTN (National Public Telecomputing Network).

http://nearnet.gnn.com/mag/articles/ oram/bio.grundner.html

Blacksburg Electronic Village Gopher

★★★

The Blacksburg Electronic Village is a project to link an entire town in southwestern Virginia with a 21st-century telecommunications infrastructure. This infrastructure will bring a useful set of information services and interactive communications facilities into the daily activities of citizens and businesses.

Keywords: Community, Networking, Telecommunications

Sponsor: Town of Blacksburg, Virginia, USA

Audience: Activists, Policymakers, Community Leaders, Government

Profile: This community gopher server run by the town of Blacksburg contains information about Blacksburg and how it is building its electronic infrastructure. It includes a list of Blacksburg-area BBSs, instructions for local residents to get an account on the town's BBS, and a section called "Village Schoolhouse."

Details: Costs

gopher://morse.cns.vt.edu

Citizens Project

★★★★

A grass-roots community group in the Pikes Peak region of Colorado.

Keywords: Community, Networking, Colorado

Audience: Activists, Policymakers, Community Leaders, Government

Profile: Based in Colorado Springs, Colorado, the Citizens Project makes use of the online world in pursuit of its mission to investigate, inform, and advocate issues affecting the Pikes Peak region. It maintains an extensive gopher server, FTP site, and a ListServ (for people who have only e-mail access).

Contact: Citizens Project

citizens@cscns.com

Details: Free

User Info: To subscribe to the list, send an e-mail message to the URL address below, consisting of a single line reading:

SUB cns-citizens-pub YourFirstName YourLastName

mailto:listserv@cscns.com

Civic Promise of the National Information Infrastructure (NII)

Community networker Richard Civille (founder of EcoNet and director of the Center for Civic Networking) describes several experiments in community networking.

Keywords: Community, Networking, Government (US)

Audience: Activists, Policymakers, Community Leaders, Government

Contact: Richard Civille

rciville@civicnet.org

Details: Free

http://nearnet.gnn.com/mag/articles/ oram/bio.civille.html

COHOUSING-L

★

A list for discussion of cohousing, the name of a type of collaborative housing that has been developed primarily in Denmark since 1972 where it is known as bofoellesskaber. Cohousing is housing designed to foster community and cooperation while preserving independence. Private residences are clustered near shared facilities. The members design and manage all aspects of their community.

Keywords: Community, Housing, Cooperatives

Audience: Urban Planners, Architects, General Contractors

Contact: fholson@uci.com

Details: Free

User Info: To subscribe to the list, send an e-mail message to the address below consisting of a single line reading:

SUB COHOUSING-L YourFirstName YourLastName

To send a message to the entire list, address it to: COHOUSING-L@uci.com

mailto:listserv@uci.com

A B C D E F G H I J K L M N O P Q R S T U V W X Y Z

A
B
C
D
E
F
G
H
I
J
K
L
M
N
O
P
Q
R
S
T
U
V
W
X
Y
Z

Community Networks Benefit Federal Goals

Statement by community networker Frank Odasz, founder and director of Big Sky Telegraph, a network of rural BBSs throughout Montana. In this article he makes the case that the federal goverment will benefit from the widespread rural employment of networking technology.

Keywords: Community, Networking, Rural Development, Development

Audience: Activists, Policy Analysts, Community Leaders, Government, Citizens, Rural Residents, Native Americans

Contact: Frank Odasz

franko@bigsky.dillon.mt.us,

Details: Free

`http://nearnet.gnn.com/mag/articles/oram/bio.odasz.html`

CSF: Communications for a Sustainable Future

★★★★

A gopher server for the distribution of Conflict Resolution Materials.

Keywords: Conflict Resolution, Community, Politics

Sponsor: Communications for a Sustainable Future

Audience: Activists, Policy Analysts, Community Leaders, Mediators, Lawyers

Profile: Communications for a Sustainable Future is a collective effort of several scholars. CSF does research, education, and applied work. Its main subject areas are: Intractable Conflicts and Constructive Confrontation, Environmental and Public Policy Dispute Resolution, Social/Political Conflicts, International Conflicts.

Contact: roper@csf.colorado.edu

Details: Free

`gopher://csf.colorado.edu`

ECHO

★★★★

A computer conferencing system based in New York City.

Keywords: Community, Networking, Women's Issues

Sponsor: East Coast Hang Out

Audience: Activists, Policy Makers, Community Leaders, Governments, Students, Feminists, Educators, Health-Care Professionals, Artists, Communicators, General Public

Profile: ECHO was started by Stacy Horn, as an East Coast counterpart to the WELL. ECHO makes an effort to be hospitable to women and has one of the highest percentages of women in an online community.

Contact: Stacy Horn

horn@echonyc.com,

Details: Costs

`telnet://echonyc.com`

Electronic Democracy Must Come from Us

★

Article about government policy and community networks by community networker Evelyn Pine (former national director of Computer Professionals for Social Responsibility). A short critique of the promises of electronic networking contrasted with the realities of political control.

Keywords: Community, Networking, Government (US)

Audience: Activists, Community Leaders, Governments

Contact: Evelyn Pine

evy@well.sf.ca.us

Details: Free

`http://nearnet.gnn.com/mag/articles/oram/bio.pine.html`

Leaders of Community Networking: People Who Create Online Communities

★

A WWW document with links to several important community networking resources. A brief overview of community networking is provided, as are links to statements by several leaders in the movement.

Keywords: Community, Networking, Government (US Federal)

Audience: Activists, Policymakers, Community Leaders, Government, Citizens

Details: Free

`http://nearnet.gnn.com/mag/articles/oram/introduction.html`

Networks & Communities

★★

This directory is a compilation of information resources focused on networks and communities.

Keywords: Community , Networking, Privacy

Audience: Network Developers, Community Activists, Free-net Organizers, Fundraisers

Details: Free

`ftp://una.hh.lib.umich.edu/70/inetdirsstacks/nets:sternberg`

People Using Networks Can Have an Impact on Government

★★★★

Statement by community networker Anne Fallis, who emphasizes the need for easy-to-use interfaces and inexpensive access to worldwide information. She lists many examples of local communities using networking.

Keywords: Community, Networking, Activism

Audience: Activists, Policymakers, Community Leaders, Network Users

Contact: Anne Fallis

afallis@silver.sdsmt.edu

Details: Free

`http://nearnet.gnn.com/mag/articles/oram/bio.fallis.html`

Telluride Institute

★

This is a community organization involved in building an electronic dimension in rural Colorado. The vision of Telluride Institute includes linking rural residents to each other and outside resources, creating new opportunities for education, jobs, and arts.

Keywords: Community, Networking, Virtual Community, Rural Development, Colorado

Sponsor: The Telluride Institute, Telluride, Colorado

Audience: Activists, Policymakers, Community Leaders, Students, Colorado Residents

Profile: The Telluride Institute is a local community-based organization that produces arts, environmental, and educational events in the Telluride area of Colorado. The Institte is committed to the creation of what it calls the "InfoZone": it wants to use modern telecommunications to link together the local community and to connect to the rest of the world to exchange ideas, commerce, arts, and inspiration.

Contact: Richard Lowenberg

tellinst@CSN.ORG

Details: Free

Send an e-mail message to the URL address below asking for further information.

`mailto:tellinst@csn.org`

TWICS

★★★★

This is an English-language computer conferencing system in Japan.

Keywords: Community, Networking, Computer Conferencing, Japan, Virtual Community

Sponsor: TWICS Co., Ltd.

Audience: Internationalists, General Public, Journalists, Policymakers

Profile: TWICS is a computer conferencing system that has a reputation for being a thriving electronic community. It recently obtained a full Internet connection and is currently one of the few places in Japan accesible via the Internet. Unlike a database or a gopher server, TWICS is a place to visit for interaction with actual people.

Contact: Tim Buress

twics@twics.co.jp,

Details: Free

`telnet://tanuki.twics.co.jp`

Community Service

Community Services Catalyst

This electronic journal provides information concerning community services around the country, especially those dealing with continuing education. The journal is published quarterly.

Keywords: Education (Continuing), Community Service

Sponsor: National Council on Community Services and Continuing Education (an affiliate council of the American Association of Community Colleges), USA

Audience: Educators, Administrators

User Info: To subscribe to the list, send an e-mail message to the URL address below consisting of a single line reading:

SUB catalyst YourFirstName YourLastName

To send a message to the entire list, address it to: catalyst@vtvm1.cc.vt.edu

`mailto: listserv@vtvml.cc.vt.edu`

comp.compression

comp.compression

A Usenet newsgroup providing information and discussion about data compression algorithms and theory.

Keywords: Computers, Mathematics (Algorithims)

Audience: Computer Users

User Info: To subscribe to this Usenet newsgroup, you need access to a newsreader.

`news:comp.compression`

comp.databases

comp.databases

A Usenet newsgroup providing information and discussion about databases and data management issues.

Keywords: Computing, Computer Databases

Audience: Computer Users

User Info: To subscribe to this Usenet newsgroup, you need access to a newsreader.

`news:comp.databases`

comp.graphics

comp.graphics

A Usenet newsgroup providing information and discussion about computer graphics, art, animation and more.

Keywords: Computer Graphics, Art

Audience: Computer Users

User Info: To subscribe to this Usenet newsgroup, you need access to a newsreader.

`news:comp.graphics`

comp.infosystems.gopher

comp.infosystems.gopher

A Usenet newsgroup providing information and discussion about the gopher information search tool.

Keywords: Gopher, Internet Reference, Information Retrieval

Audience: Internet Surfers

User Info: To subscribe to this Usenet newsgroup, you need access to a newsreader.

`news:comp.infosystems.gopher`

comp.infosystems.wais

comp.infosystems.wais

A Usenet newsgroup providing information and discussion about the WAIS full-text search tool.

Keywords: WAIS, Internet Reference, Information Retrieval

Audience: Internet Surfers

User Info: To subscribe to this Usenet newsgroup, you need access to a newsreader.

`news:comp.infosystems.wais`

comp.infosystems.www

comp.infosystems.www

A Usenet newsgroup providing information and discussion about the World Wide Web.

Keywords: WWW, Internet Reference, Information Retrieval

Audience: Internet Surfers

User Info: To subscribe to this Usenet newsgroup, you need access to a newsreader.

`news:comp.infosystems.www`

comp.lang.c

comp.lang.c

A Usenet newsgroup providing information and discussion about the C programming language.

Keywords: Computer Programming, Programming Languages

Audience: Computer Users, C Programmers

User Info: To subscribe to this Usenet newsgroup, you need access to a newsreader.

`news:comp.lang.c`

comp.lang.c++

comp.lang.c++

A Usenet newsgroup providing information and discussion about the object-oriented C++ programming language.

Keywords: Computers, Programming Languages

Audience: Computer Users, C++ Programmers

User Info: To subscribe to this Usenet newsgroup, you need access to a newsreader.

`news:comp.lang.c++`

comp.org.eff.talk

comp.org.eff.talk

A Usenet newsgroup organized by the EFF (Electronic Frontier Foundation) providing information and discussion about the political, social, and legal issues surrounding the Internet.

Keywords: Computers, Intellectual Property, Security, Internet

Audience: Internet Surfers

User Info: To subscribe to this Usenet newsgroup, you need access to a newsreader.

`news:comp.org.eff.talk`

A
B
C
D
E
F
G
H
I
J
K
L
M
N
O
P
Q
R
S
T
U
V
W
X
Y
Z

A
B
C
D
E
F
G
H
I
J
K
L
M
N
O
P
Q
R
S
T
U
V
W
X
Y
Z

comp.os

comp.os

A Usenet newsgroup providing information and discussion about computer operating systems. There are many categories within this group.

Keywords: Computer Systems

Audience: Computer Users

User Info: To subscribe to this Usenet newsgroup, you need access to a newsreader.

news:comp.os

comp.os.ms-windows.apps

comp.os.ms-windows.apps

A Usenet newsgroup providing information and discussion about applications in Windows.

Keywords: Computers Systems

Audience: Computer Users, Windows Users

User Info: To subscribe to this Usenet newsgroup, you need access to a newsreader.

news:comp.os.ms-windows.apps

comp.os.os2.misc

comp.os.os2.misc

A Usenet newsgroup providing information and discussion about miscellaneous topics concerning O/S2.

Keywords: Computer Systems

Audience: Computer Users, O/S2 Users

User Info: To subscribe to this Usenet newsgroup, you need access to a newsreader.

news:comp.os.os2.misc

comp.security.misc

comp.security.misc

A Usenet newsgroup providing information and discussion about security issues of computers and networks.

Keywords: Computers, Security, Firewalls

Audience: Computer Users

User Info: To subscribe to this Usenet newsgroup, you need access to a newsreader.

news:comp.security.misc

comp.sys.amiga

comp.sys.amiga

A Usenet newsgroup providing information and discussion about Amiga systems. There are many categories within this group.

Keywords: Computer Systems, Amiga Aystems

Audience: Computer Users, Amiga Users

User Info: To subscribe to this Usenet newsgroup, you need access to a newsreader.

news:comp.sys.amiga

comp.sys.apple2

comp.sys.apple2

A Usenet newsgroup providing information and discussion about Apple II systems. There are several categories within this group.

Keywords: Computer Systems, Apple Computer

Audience: Computer Users, Apple II Users

User Info: To subscribe to this Usenet newsgroup, you need access to a newsreader.

news:comp.sys.apple2

comp.sys.atari.st

comp.sys.atari.st

A Usenet newsgroup providing information and discussion about 16-bit Atari.

Keywords: Computer Systems

Audience: Computer Users, Atari Users

User Info: To subscribe to this Usenet newsgroup, you need access to a newsreader.

news:comp.sys.atari.st

comp.sys.ibm.pc

comp.sys.ibm.pc

A Usenet newsgroup providing information and discussion about the IBM PC computer. There are many categories within this group.

Keywords: Computer Systems, IBM

Audience: Computer Users, IBM Users

User Info: To subscribe to this Usenet newsgroup, you need access to a newsreader.

news:comp.sys.ibm.pc

comp.sys.mac

comp.sys.mac

A Usenet newsgroup providing information and discussion about the Macintosh computer. There are many categories within this group.

Keywords: Computer Systems, Macintosh Computers

Audience: Computer Users, Macintosh Users

User Info: To subscribe to this Usenet newsgroup, you need access to a newsreader.

news:comp.sys.mac

comp.sys.next

comp.sys.next

A Usenet newsgroup providing information and discussion about NeXT computers. There are several categories within this group.

Keywords: Computer Systems, NeXT

Audience: Computer Users, NeXT Users

User Info: To subscribe to this Usenet newsgroup, you need access to a newsreader.

news:comp.sys.next

comp.sys.sgi

comp.sys.sgi

A Usenet newsgroup providing information and discussion about Silicon Graphic systems. There are several categories within this group.

Keywords: Computer Systems

Audience: Computer Users, Silicon Graphics Users

User Info: To subscribe to this Usenet newsgroup, you need access to a newsreader.

news:comp.sys.sgi

comp.sys.sun

comp.sys.sun

A Usenet newsgroup providing information and discussion about Sun systems. There are several categories within this group.

Keywords: Computer Systems, Sun

Audience: Computer Users, Sun Users

User Info: To subscribe to this Usenet newsgroup, you need access to a newsreader.

news:comp.sys.sun

comp.text.tex

comp.text.tex ⭐

A Usenet newsgroup providing information and discussion about the TeX and LaTeX systems.

Keywords: Text Processing, Internet

Audience: Computer Users, TeX and LaTeX Users

User Info: To subscribe to this Usenet newsgroup, you need access to a newsreader.

`news:comp.text.tex`

comp.unix.aix

comp.unix.aix ⭐

A Usenet newsgroup providing information and discussion about IBM's version of UNIX.

Keywords: Computer System, Internet, UNIX

Audience: Computer Users, UNIX Users, IBM Users

User Info: To subscribe to this Usenet newsgroup, you need access to a newsreader.

`news:comp.unix.aix`

comp.unix.questions

comp.unix.questions ⭐

A Usenet newsgroup providing discussion and questions for those learning UNIX.

Keywords: Computers, UNIX

Audience: Computer Users, UNIX Users

User Info: To subscribe to this Usenet newsgroup, you need access to a newsreader.

`news:comp.unix.questions`

comp.unix.wizards

comp.unix.wizards ⭐

A Usenet newsgroup providing discussion and questions for true UNIX wizards.

Keywords: Computers, UNIX

Audience: Computer Users, Unix Users

User Info: To subscribe to this Usenet newsgroup, you need access to a newsreader.

`news:comp.unix.wizards`

comp.windows.x

comp.windows.x ⭐

A Usenet newsgroup providing information and discussion about the X Window systems.

Keywords: Computer Systems

Audience: Computer Users, Windows Users

User Info: To subscribe to this Usenet newsgroup, you need access to a newsreader.

`news:comp.windows.x`

comp.windows.x.motif

comp.windows.x.motif ⭐

A Usenet newsgroup providing information and discussion about the Motif GUI for the X Window systems.

Keywords: Computer Graphics

Audience: Computer Users, Windows Users

User Info: To subscribe to this Usenet newsgroup, you need access to a newsreader.

`news:comp.windows.x.motif`

Companies

CANADA (Canadian News and Information Library)

The Canadian News and Information Library (CANADA) contains Canadian legal news, business, and company information.

Keywords: News, Analysis, Companies, Canada

Audience: Canadians

Profile: The CANADA Library contains respected Canadian news publications such as *The Toronto Star*, *The Vancouver Sun*, *Ottawa Business News* and the *Montreal Gazette*. The CANADA Library also offers Canadian company profiles, country reports, and Canada's financial database, CANCORP Plus.

Contact: Mead New Sales Group at (800) 227-4908 or (513) 859-5398 inside the US, or (513) 865-7981 for all inquiries outside the US.

User Info: To subscribe, contact Mead directly.

To examine the Nexis user guide, you can access it at the ftp site of the University of Texas at Austin at the URL address: ftp://ftp.cc.utexas.edu

The files are in: /pub/ref-services/LEXIS

`telnet://nex.meaddata.com`

`http://www.meaddata.com`

COMPNY

The COMPNY library contains more than 75 files of business and financial information, including thousands of in-depth company and industry research reports from leading national and international investments banks and brokerage houses.

Keywords: Companies, Financials, Filings, Disclosure

Audience: Business and Financial Researchers, Analysts, Entrepreneurs and Regulators.

Profile: COMPNY includes the following types of information:

- Full-text 10-Q, 10-K, Annual Reports to Shareholders, and Proxy filings

- Extracts of filings for more than 11,000 public companies whose securities are traded on the major exchanges as well as over-the-counter

- Abstracts of S-registration statements, 13-Ds, 14-Ds, 8Ks, Form 4s, and other SEC filings updated on a daily basis

- Business news abstracts from more than 400 information sources

- Daily US economic trends and forecasts.

The materials may be searched in individual files, such as brokerage house reports, or in group files organized by subject, such as SEC filings.

Contact: Mead New Sales Group at (800) 227-4908 or (513) 859-5398 inside the US, or (513) 865-7981 for all inquiries outside the US.

User Info: To subscribe, contact Mead directly.

To examine the Nexis user guide, you can access it at the ftp site of the University of Texas at Austin at the URL address: ftp://ftp.cc.utexas.edu

The files are in: /pub/ref-services/LEXIS

`telnet://nex.meaddata.com`

`http://www.meaddata.com`

INVEST (Investment News and Information)

The INVEST library contains company and industry research reports provided through the Investext(R) database. These reports are created by industry experts who are employed for their accurate and insightful evaluation. Only the most recent 12 months of data will be displayed.

Keywords: Companies, Financials, Analysis

Audience: Business Researchers, Analysts, Entrepreneurs

Profile: INVEST is categorized by type. Selections can be made using these categories: Industry (more than 50 industries are available), State (where a

A
B
C
D
E
F
G
H
I
J
K
L
M
N
O
P
Q
R
S
T
U
V
W
X
Y
Z

specific company is located), Country (Country in which the company is located), US Broker or International Broker. The INVEST library provides an automatic display following the selection of a file. For industry reports, a menu will appear providing definitions as they relate to the industries. All remaining files will provide a confirmation of the file selected.

Contact: Mead New Sales Group at (800) 227-4908 or (513) 859-5398 inside the US, or (513) 865-7981 for all inquiries outside the US.

User Info: To subscribe, contact Mead directly.

To examine the Nexis user guide, you can access it at the ftp site of the University of Texas at Austin at the URL address: ftp://ftp.cc.utexas.edu

The files are in: /pub/ref-services/LEXIS

`telnet://nex.meaddata.com`

`http://www.meaddata.com`

MDEAFR

The Middle East and Africa (MDEAFR) library contains detailed information about every country in the Mideast and Africa. Structured for those who want to follow the unfolding events in the Gulf states, as well as in North and South Africa, this library contains a broad array of sources, including international research reports from InvestextR.

Keywords: News, Analysis, Companies, Middle East, Africa

Audience: Journalists, Businesspeople

Profile: The MDEAFR library contains a wide array of pertinent sources. Among the information sources are newspapers and wire services, trade and business journals, company reports, country and region background, industry and product analysis, business opportunities, and selected legal texts. News sources range from the world-renowned Associated Press and Christian Science Monitor to the regionally important Jerusalem Post and Africa News. Company information is contained in the EXTEL cards as well as ICC. Providers of country background and industry analysis include Associated Banks of Europe, Bank of America, Business International, IBC USA, and the US Department of Commerce. Customers interested in new business opportunities can check OPIC and Foreign Trade Opportunities (FTO).

Contact: Mead New Sales Group at (800) 227-4908 or (513) 859-5398 inside the US, or (513) 865-7981 for all inquiries outside the US.

User Info: To subscribe, contact Mead directly.

To examine the Nexis user guide, you can access it at the ftp site of the University of Texas at Austin at the URL address: ftp://ftp.cc.utexas.edu

The files are in: /pub/ref-services/LEXIS

`telnet://nex.meaddata.com`

`http://www.meaddata.com`

NEWS (General News)

The General News (NEWS) library includes more than 2,300 sources. Full-text news from national and international newspapers, magazines, newsletters, and wire services and abstract information are both available.

Keywords: News, Analysis, People, Companies

Audience: Journalists, General Public

Profile: The General News (NEWS) library contains a number of publications and wire services of general interest, as well as others that specialize in particular areas of business . The NEWS library is organized into individual files, group files by source or subject, and user-defined combination files for full-text information sources. Abstracts are also available as individual files or can be searched together in one group file. The NEWS library includes such prestigious full-text sources as the New York Times and more than more than 30 major newspapers from around the US and the world.

Contact: Mead New Sales Group at (800) 227-4908 or (513) 859-5398 inside the US, or (513) 865-7981 for all inquiries outside the US.

User Info: To subscribe, contact Mead directly.

To examine the Nexis user guide, you can access it at the ftp site of the University of Texas at Austin at the URL address: ftp://ftp.cc.utexas.edu

The files are in: /pub/ref-services/LEXIS

`telnet://nex.meaddata.com`

`http://www.meaddata.com`

NSAMER (North and South America Library)

The North and South America library contains detailed information about every country in North and South America (except the United States). The US-Canada Free Trade Agreement, the North American Free Trade Agreement, relations with Mexico and events in such countries as Brazil, Peru, and Nicaragua are among the topics covered by a variety of business, news and legal sources. International research reports from InvestextR are also included. The United States is not covered in this library.

Keywords: News, Analysis, Companies, North America, South America

Audience: Journalists, Businesspeople

Profile: The North and South America library contains a broad array of sources. Among the information sources are newspapers and wire services, trade and business journals, company reports, country and region backgrounds, industry and product analyses, business opportunities, and selected legal texts. News sources range from the world-renowned Washington Post and Christian Science Monitor to the regionally important Toronto Star and

Latin American Newsletters. Canadian Business and Maclean's represent a portion of the array of business and trade journals. Company information is contained in the EXTEL cards as well as ICC. Providers of country background and industry analyses include Associated Banks of Europe, Bank of America, Business International, IBC USA and the US Department of Commerce. Among the specialized resources are IBC's Mexico and Brazil Services as well as BI's Business Latin America. Researchers interested in new business opportunities can check OPIC and Foreign Trade Opportunities (FTO).And selected legal texts covering the US-Canada Free Trade Agreement and other international agreements planners and advisors to better assess the business climate in North and South America.

Contact: Mead New Sales Group at (800) 227-4908 or (513) 859-5398 inside the US, or (513) 865-7981 for all inquiries outside the US.

User Info: To subscribe, contact Mead directly.

To examine the Nexis user guide, you can access it at the ftp site of the University of Texas at Austin at the URL address: ftp://ftp.cc.utexas.edu

The files are in: /pub/ref-services/LEXIS

`telnet://nex.meaddata.com`

`http://www.meaddata.com`

Company Name

DIALOG Company Name Finder

This database is a search aid designed to locate company information in DIALOG databases.

Keywords: Company Name

Sponsor: Dialog Information Services, Inc., Palo Alto, CA, USA

Audience: Business Professionals, Market Researchers

Profile: Company name records are created for unique entries in the company name indexes of the DIALOG files included. Company names are shown in the form in which they appear in the original database index, including abbreviations, punctuation (commas and periods are stripped out), and spelling variations, and are limited to 46 characters. Long company names may be truncated because of the 46-character maximum.

Contact: Dialog in the US at (800) 334-2564, Dialog internationally at country-specific locations.

User Info: To subscribe, contact Dialog directly.

Notes: Coverage: Dialog databases indexing company name; updated quarterly.

`telnet://dialog.com`

Composition

Computer Music Journal Archive and World Wide Web Home Page.

This resource reinforces material available in the hardcopy version of Computer Music Journal, published by the MIT Press

Keywords: Computer Music, Composition, Synthesis, Interaction

Sponsor: The MIT Press

Audience: Computer Musicians

Profile: The archive includes the tables of contents, abstracts, and editor's notes for the last several volumes of CMJ (including the recent bibliography, diskography, and taxonomy of the field), a number of useful CM-related documents such as the full MIDI and AIFF format specifications, a lengthy reference list, the guidelines for manuscript submission, and the full-text of several recent articles.

Contact: Stephen Pope
cmj@cnmat.Berkeley.edu

Details: Free

`ftp://mitpress.mit.edu:/pub/Computer-Music-Journal`

IRCAM DSP and musical software

This site offers a variety of computer music resources.

Keywords: Computer Music, Sound Synthesis, Composition, DSP

Sponsor: IRCAM

Audience: Computer Music Researchers and Computer Musicians

Profile: Contains a list and brief description of IRCAM software (digital signal processing, voice and sound synthesis, music composition, wind instrument making, and other programs). There are also calendars of the IRCAM-EIC concerts and tours, and links to various other music servers.

Contact: Michel Fingerhut
fingerhu@ircam.fr

Details: Free

`http://www.ircam.fr`

Computational Chemistry

Theoretical Journal Abstract And Bibliographic Files

Abstract and bibliographic information for several theoretical chemistry journals.

Keywords: Theoretical Chemistry, Quantum Chemistry, Quantum Mechanics, Computational Chemistry.

Sponsor: Online, Inc., Weston, CT, US

Audience: Chemists, Librarians, Students , (College up)

Profile: Provided are directory, product, technical, and bibliographic information on leading software packages, integrating this information into one succinct composite record. The database can help professionals locate suitable packages compatible with specified hardware without sifting through large numbers of records.

Contact: Dialog in the US at (800) 334-2564, Dialog internationally at country specific locations.

Mailserv@osc.edu

Details: Free

User Info: To subscribe, contact Dialog directly.

Select Other OSC Gopher Servers then select OSC Chemistry Gopher Server

`telnet://dialog.com`

`gopher://infomeister.osc.edu`

Computational Neuroscience

Purkinje Park

A server maintained by CalTech to support the sharing of information between users of the GENESIS neural simulator, and to address topics of general interest to the Computational Neuroscience community.

Keywords: Computational Neuroscience, GENESIS, Neural Simulation.

Sponsor: Cal Tech

Audience: Neuroscientists, Computational Neuroscientists

Contact: Dave Beeman

dbeeman@smaug.bbb.caltech.edu

`http://www.bbb.caltech.edu/index.html`

Computer

CJI (Computer Jobs in Israel)

Computer Jobs in Israel (CJI) is a one-way list that will automatically send you the monthly updated computer jobs document. This list will also send you other special documents or announcements regarding finding computer work in Israel. Eventually this list will be an open, moderated list for everyone to exchange information about computer jobs in Israel.

Keywords: Israel, Computer, Jobs

Audience: Computer Users, Jews, Israelis, Israel Residents

Contact: Jacob Richman

listserv@jerusalem1.datasrv.co.il

Details: Free

User Info: To subscribe to the list, send an e-mail message to the address below, consisting of a single line reading:

SUB CJI YourFirstName YourLastName

To send a message to the entire list, address it to:
CJI@jerusalem1.datasrv.co.il

`mailto:listserv@jerusalem1.datasrv.co.il`

Georgia-Computer Systems Protection Act

Lists full text of the Georgia Computer Systems Protection Act.

Keywords: Computer, Crime

Audience: Lawyers, Computer Programmers, Computer Operators

Details: Free

`gopher://wiretap.spies.com`

Computer Administration

alpha-osf-managers

This list is intended to be a quick-turnaround trouble shooting aid for those who administer and manage DEC Alpha AXP systems running OSF/1.

Keywords: Computer Systems, Computer Administration

Sponsor: Oakridge National Laboratory

Audience: Computer Programmers

User Info: To subscribe to the list, send an e-mail message to the URL address below consisting of a single line reading: subscribe alpha-osf-managers.

Notes: Alpha-osf-managers archived at ftp/kpc.com: /pub/list/alpha-osf-managers

`mailto:majordomo@ornl.gov`

A
B
C
D
E
F
G
H
I
J
K
L
M
N
O
P
Q
R
S
T
U
V
W
X
Y
Z

cm5-Managers

This is a discussion of administrating the Thinking Machines CM5 parallel supercomputer.

Keywords: Supercomputers, Computer Administration

Audience: Supercomputer Users, Supercomputer Administrators

Contact: J. Eric Townsend
jet@nas.nasa.gov

Details: Free

User Info: To subscribe to the list, send an e-mail message to the address below, consisting of a single line reading:

SUB cm5-managers YourFirstName YourLastName

To send a message to the entire list, address it to: cm5-managers@boxer.nas.nasa.gov

mailto:listserv@boxer.nas.nasa.gov

LLTI

The Language Learning Technology International (LLTI) forum is a discussion of computer-assisted language learning.

Keywords: Language, Linguistics, Computer Aided Instruction

Audience: Linguists, Language Teachers, Language Students

Details: Free

User Info: To subscribe to the list, send an e-mail message to the URL address below, consisting of a single line reading:

SUB llti YourFirstName YourLastName

To send a message to the entire list, address it to:

llti@dartcms1.dartmouth.edu

mailto:listserv@dartcms1.dartmouth.edu

OE-CALL: Old English Computer Assisted Language Learning Newsletter

A newsletter for persons interested in computer assisted language-learning methods for teaching Old English.

Keywords: Old English, Computer-Aided Instruction

Audience: English Teachers, Educators

Contact: Clare Lees, Patrick W. Conner
mailto:u47c2@wvnvm.bitnet

Details: Free

mailto:lees@fordmurh.bitnet

Vetcai-L

Discussion of veterinary medicine computer assisted instruction.

Keywords: Veterinary Medicine, Computer Aided Instruction

Audience: Veterinarians, Medical Educators

Contact: Pat Oblander
oblandr@ksuvm.ksu.edu

User Info: To subscribe to the list, send an e-mail message to the URL address below consisting of a single line reading:

SUB vetcai'l YourFirstName YourLastName

To send a message to the entire list, address it to: vetcai-l@ksuvm.ksu.edu

mailto:listserv@ksuvm.ksu.edu

Computer Aided Learning

AskERIC Virtual Library

This gopher is part of a federally-funded system to provide public access to educational resources.

Keywords: Education (K-12), Computer-Aided Learning, Libraries, Electronic Books

Sponsor: Educational Resources Information Center (ERIC)

Audience: K-12 Teachers, Administrators

Profile: This gopher contains a wide-range of educational aids including pre-prepared lesson plans, guides to Internet resources for the classroom organized by subject, updates on conferences for educators, and archives of education-related listservs. Also allows access to outside gophers, libraries, and sources of electronic books and journals.

Contact: Nancy A. Morgan
nmorgan@ericir.syr.edu
askeric@ericir.syr.edu

gopher://ericir/syr.edu

Computer Applications

CUSSNET

Computer Users in the Social Sciences (CUSS) is a discussion group devoted to issues of interest to social workers, counselors, and human service workers of all disciplines. The discussion frequently involves computer applications in treatment, agency administration, and research. Students, faculty, community-based professionals, and casual

observers join in the discussion. Software, hardware, and ethical issues associated with their use in the human services generate lively and informative discussions.

Keywords: Social Sciences, Computers, Computer Applications

Audience: Social Workers, Human Services Workers, General Public

Contact: cussnet-request@stat.com

Details: Free

User Info: To subscribe to the list, send an e-mail message to the address below consisting of a single line reading:

SUB cussnet YourFirstName YourLastName.

To send a message to the entire list, address it to: cussnet@stat.com

mailto:listserv@stat.com

Computer Art

Art Com Magazine

A newsletter about art and technology (subjects covered include robotics, artists' software, hyperfiction) that is guest-edited by individual artists.

Keywords: Computer Art, Literature (Contemporary), Technology, Hyperfiction

Sponsor: Art Com Electronic Network

Audience: Artists, Writers

Contact: Fred Truck
fjt@well.sf.ca.us

To participate in a conference on the WELL, you must first establish an account on the WELL. To do so, start by typing: telnet://well.sf.ca.us

mailto:artcomtv@well.sf.ca.us

artist-users

A discussion group for users and potential users of software tools from Cadence Design Systems.

Keywords: Computers, Computer Art

Sponsor: Cadence Design Systems

Audience: Computer Artists

Contact: Jeff Putsch
artist-users-request@uicc.com

User Info: To subscribe to the list, send an e-mail message to the URL address below.

To send a message to the entire list, address it to: artist-users-request@uicc.com

Notes: This mailing list is bi-directionally gatewayed to the Usenet newsgroup

mailto:artist-users-request@uicc.com

Kaleidospace

This is a new web server that provides a multimedia showcase for artists, performers, CD-ROM authors, musicians, writers, animators, filmmakers, and software developers.

Keywords: Art, Computer Art, Multimedia

Audience: Artists, Performers, CD-ROM Authors, Musicians, Writers, Animators, Filmmakers, Software Developers

Profile: This site was created to support independent artists. The site has similarities to other web servers such as IUMA, but differs in that it works with all kinds of artists, and that it processes orders for the artist's material.

Contact: Jeannie Novak, Peter Markiewicz
jeannienov@aol.com,
peterm@ewald.mbi.ucla.edu

`http://kspace.com`

`http://fire.kspace.com`

NYAL (New York Art Line)

A gopher containing selected resources on the arts.

Keywords: Art, Audio-Visual Materials, Multimedia, Computer Art

Sponsor: Panix Public Access Unix & Internet Gopher Server, New York, USA

Audience: Artists, Art Enthusiasts

Profile: NYAL features a wide variety of arts resources. The primary focus of this site is visual art, particularly in the New York city area. Information includes online access to selected galleries, image archives, and New York city arts groups. Beyond visual art, information on dance, music, and techno art (with a special section on Internet art) is also available. It also features links to various electronic journals, museums, and schools.

Contact: Kenny Greenberg
kgreen@panix.com

`gopher://gopher.panix.com`

`http//gopher.panix.com/nyart/Kpage/kg`

rec.video

A Usenet newsgroup providing information and discussion about video.

Keywords: Video, Art, Film, Computer Art

Audience: Cinematographers, Video Artists

User Info: To subscribe to this Usenet newsgroup, you need access to a newsreader.

`news:rec.video`

The ASCII Bazaar

An extensive collection of ASCII art, organized by subject. Also includes FAQ files, software tools, ASCII art discussion lists, and links to other collections of ASCII art.

Keywords: Clip Art, Computer Art

Sponsor: Department of Computer and Information Sciences, University of Alabama at Birmingham, Birmingham, Alabama, USA

Audience: Computer Users, General Public

Contact: R. L. Samuell
samuell@cis.uab.edu

`gopher://twinbrook.cis.uab.edu`

Computer Communications

EFFector Online-The Electronic Frontier Foundation, Inc.

Established to make the electronic frontier truly useful and accessible to everyone, emphasizing the free and open flow of information and communication.

Keywords: Computer Communications, Electronic Media, Intellectual Property, Privacy

Audience: Computer Users, Civil Libertarians

Profile: EFFector Online presents news, information, and discussion about the world of computer-based communications media that constitute the electronic frontier. It covers issues such as freedom of speech in digital media, privacy rights, censorship, and standards of responsibility for users and operators of computer systems, as well as policy issues such as the development of a national information infrastructure, and intellectual property.

Contact: Gerard Van der Leun, Mike Godwin
gerard@eff.org
mnemonic@eff.org

Details: Free

User Info: To subscribe, send an e-mail message requesting a subscription to: request@eff.org

Notes: This takes you to the front door of the eff gopher server which contains much more information than just Effector online.

`gopher://gopher.eff.org/1`

Computer Conferencing

(The) WELL (Whole Earth 'Lectronic Link)

The WELL is a computer conferencing system, a virtual community, and an electronic coffee shop.

Keywords: Community, Networking, Computer Conferencing, Virtual Community

Sponsor: Whole Earth 'Lectronic Link

Audience: General Public, Internet Surfers

Profile: The WELL is a classic example of an online community that uses what is called "conferencing" to bring a myriad of people together for intense interactions without them having to be connected at the same time. At the end of 1993, the WELL had about 8,000 users (about 90% from all over the USA and about 10% from other locations) and approximately 200 public discussion areas ('conferences'), and 200 private discussion areas. It is a place rich in diverse 'neighborhoods.'

Contact: The WELL Support Staff
info@well.sf.ca.us

Direct dial access through: +1 (415) 332-4335

To participate in a conference on the WELL, you must first establish an account on the WELL. To do so, start by typing: telnet well.sf.ca.us

`telnet://well.sf.ca.us`

TWICS

This is an English-language computer conferencing system in Japan.

Keywords: Community, Networking, Computer Conferencing, Japan, Virtual Community

Sponsor: TWICS Co., Ltd.

Audience: Internationalists, General Public, Journalists, Policymakers

Profile: TWICS is a computer conferencing system that has a reputation for being a thriving electronic community. It recently obtained a full Internet connection and is currently one of the few places in Japan accessible via the Internet. Unlike a database or a gopher server, TWICS is a place to visit for interaction with actual people.

Contact: Tim Buress
twics@twics.co.jp,

Details: Free

`telnet://tanuki.twics.co.jp`

Computer Databases

comp.databases

A Usenet newsgroup providing information and discussion about databases and data management issues.

Keywords: Computing, Computer Databases

Audience: Computer Users

User Info: To subscribe to this Usenet newsgroup, you need access to a newsreader.

`news:comp.databases`

A B C D E F G H I J K L M N O P Q R S T U V W X Y Z

Computer Ethics

IMPACT ONLINE

The electronic version of IMPACT, the newsletter of the Social Impact group of the Boston Computer Society.

Keywords: Information Technology, Computer Ethics, Computers

Sponsor: Boston Computer Society, Boston, MA

Audience: Computer Users

Profile: The purpose of the Social Impact group is to provide a forum for the discussion of social and ethical concerns related to information technology.

Contact: Ian Wells
bcs-ssi@compass.com

Read on comp.society

You will need access to a newsreader.

`news:comp.society`

Computer Games

crossfire

To discuss the developement of the game Crossfire. The official anonymous FTP-site is ftp.ifi.uio.no in the directory /pub/crossfire. Old mails to the list are archived there. Crossfire is a multiplayer arcade and adventure game made for the X-window environment.

Keywords: Computer Games

Audience: Crossfire specialists,Computer Game Enthusiasts

Contact: Frank Tore Johansen
crossfire-request@ifi.uio.no

Details: Free

User Info: To subscribe to the list, send an e-mail message requesting a subscription to the URL address below.

To send a message to the entire list, address it to: crossfire@ifi.uio.no

`mailto:crossfire-request@ifi.uio.no`

Digital Games Review

Reviews of video and computer entertainment titles for the entire industry.

Keywords: Computer Games, Games, Video Games

Audience: Computer Game Players, Computer Game Developers

Profile: Reviews are written by computer game enthusiasts, with an eye to accessibility, enjoyment, and fun, as well as to graphics, technical sophistication, and complexity.

Contact: Dave Taylor
taylor@intuitive.com

Details: Free

`mailto:digital-games-request@intuitive.com`

Rec.arts.int-fiction

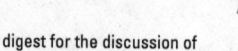

A USENET newsgroup about interactive literature and interactive computer games.

Keywords: Literature (General), Interactive Media, Computer Games

Audience: General Public, Computer Games Players

Details: Free

To participate in a USENET newsgroup, you need access to a 'newsreader'.

`news:rec.arts.int-fiction`

The Chaosium Digest

This is a weekly digest for the discussion of Chaosium's many games, including Call of Cthulhu, Elric!, Elfquest, and Pendragon.

Keywords: Computer Games

Audience: Chaosium Enthusiasts, Computer Users

Contact: appel@erzo.berkeley.edu

Details: Free

User Info: To subscribe to the list, send an e-mail message requesting a subscription to the URL address below.

To send a message to the entire list, address it to: appel@erzo.berkeley.edu

`mailto:appel@erzo.berkeley.edu`

Computer Graphics

ACM SIGGRAPH Online Bibliography Project

★ ★ ★ ★

This is a collection of computer-graphics bibliographic references.

Keywords: Multimedia, Interactive, Computer Graphics, Programming

Sponsor: Association of Computing Machinery (ACM), Special Interest Group on Computer Graphics (SIGGRAPH)

Audience: Developers, Designers, Producers, Educators, Programmers, Graphic Artists

Profile: The goal of this project is to maintain an up-to-date database of computer-graphics literature, in a format that is accessible to as many members of the computer-graphics community as possible. The database includes references from conferences and workshops worldwide and from a variety of publications dating back as far as the late-19th century. The majority of the major journals and conference proceedings from the mid-1970s to the present are listed.

Contact: bibadmin@siggraph.org

Details: Free

`ftp://siggraph.org/publications`

CAEDS-L

A mailing list for the discussion of CAED (Computer Aided Engineering Design) Products.

Keywords: Computer-Aided Design, Engineering, Computer Graphics

Audience: Engineers

Contact: netman@suvm.acs.syr.edu

Details: Free

User Info: To subscribe to the list, send an e-mail message to the URL address shown below consisting of a single line reading:

SUB caeds-l YourFirstName YourLastName

To send a message to the entire list, address it to:

caeds-1@suvm.acs.syr.edu

`mailto:listserv@suvm.acs.syr.edu`

comp.graphics

A Usenet newsgroup providing information and discussion about computer graphics, art, animation and more.

Keywords: Computer Graphics, Art

Audience: Computer Users

User Info: To subscribe to this Usenet newsgroup, you need access to a newsreader.

`news:comp.graphics`

comp.windows.x.motif

A Usenet newsgroup providing information and discussion about the Motif GUI for the X Window systems.

Keywords: Computer Graphics

Audience: Computer Users, Windows Users

User Info: To subscribe to this Usenet newsgroup, you need access to a newsreader.

`news:comp.windows.x.motif`

DISSPLA (Display Integrated Software System and Plotting Language)

News and information exchange concerning DISSPLA.

Keywords: Computer Graphics, Programming

Audience: DISSPLA Users, Computer Programmers

Profile: DISSPLA is a high-level FORTRAN graphics subroutine library designed for programmers in engineering, science and business.

Contact: Zvika Bar-Deroma
er7101@technion.technion.ac.il

Details: Free

User Info: To subscribe to the list, send an e-mail message to the URL address shown below consisting of a single line reading:

SUB disspla YourFirstName YourLastName

To send a message to the entire list, address it to: disspla@taunivm.tau.ac.il

`mailto:listserv@taunivm.tau.ac.il`

Images from Various Sources

This site serves as a link to some 35 image archives throughout the world. A wide variety of images is available, with a particularly large number of weather, geological, and biological collections from government and private sources.

Keywords: Computer Graphics, Photography, Art

Sponsor: The University of Alaska

Audience: General Public

Contact: Douglas Toelle
sxinfo@orca.alaska.edu

Details: Free, Images

`gopher://gopher.uacn.alaska.edu`

`http://info.alaska.edu:70`

INGRAFX

This E-conference is for discussion of all matters relating to information graphics.

Keywords: Computer Graphics, Graphic Design, Scientific Visualization

Audience: Graphic Designers, Cartographers, Animators

Contact: Jeremy Crampton
http://info.cern.ch/hypertext/WWW/The Project.html

User Info: To subscribe to the list, send an e-mail message to the URL address below consisting of a single line reading:

SUB ingrafx YourFirstName YourLastName

To send a message to the entire list, address it to: ingrafx@psuvm.psu.edu

`mailto:listserv@psuvm.psu.edu`

naplps-list

This is a mailing list for people interested in NAPLPS graphics.

Keywords: Computer Graphics, Art

Audience: Graphic Artists, Artists

Contact: Dave Hughes
oldcolo@goldmill.uucp

`naplps-list@oldcolo.com`

PERQ-fanatics

This mailing list is for users of PERQ graphics workstations.

Keywords: PERQ workstations, Computer Graphics

Audience: PERQ Users, Graphic Artists

Contact: perq-fanatics-request@alchemy.com

Details: Free

User Info: To subscribe to the list, send an e-mail message requesting a subscription to the URL address below.

To send a message to the entire list, address it to: perq-fanatics@alchemy.com

`mailto:perq-fanatics-request@alchemy.com`

PHOTO-CD

This list provides libraries of information on Kodak CD products or technology and closely related products.

Keywords: Photography, Photo-CD, Computer Graphics

Sponsor: Eastman Kodak, Rochester, NY

Audience: Photographers, General Public

Contact: Don Cox
listmgr@info.kodak.com

User Info: To subscribe to the list, send an e-mail message to the address below, consisting of a single line reading:

SUB photo-cd Your First Name Your Last Name

To send a message to the entire list, address it to: photo-cd@info.kodak.com

`mailto:listserv@info.kodak.com`

picasso-users

A mailing list for users of the Picasso Graphical User Interface Development System.

Keywords: Computing, Computer Graphics

Audience: Computer Users, Computer Graphic Designers, Graphics

Contact: picasso-users@postgres.berkeley.edu

Details: Free

User Info: To subscribe to the list, send an e-mail message requesting a subscription to the URL address below.

To send a message to the entire list, address it to: picasso-users@postgres.berkeley.edu

`mailto:picasso-users@postgres.berkeley.edu`

Spanky Fractal Database

This web site provides a collection of fractals and fractal-related material for free distribution on the Internet.

Keywords: Mathematics, Chaos Theory, Computer Programming, Computer Graphics

Audience: Mathematicians, Computer Programmers

Profile: Contains information on dynamical systems, software, distributed fractal generators, galleries, and databases from all over the world.

Contact: Noel Giffin
noel@triumf.ca

Details: Free

`http://spanky.triumf.ca`

VTcad-L

This E-conference is for discussion of CAD by Va Tech users. Discussion includes: CAD applications, CAD hardware, CAD networking.

Keywords: Computer Graphics, Computers

Audience: Computer Graphic Designers, Engineers, Architects

Contact: Darrell A. Early
bestuur@VTVM1.cc.vt.edu

Details: Free

User Info: To subscribe to the list, send an e-mail message to the URL address below consisting of a single line reading: SUB vtcad-L YourFirstName YourLastName

To send a message to the entire list, address it to: vtcad-L@vtvm1.cc.vt.edu

`mailto:listserv@vtvm1.cc.vt.edu`

Computer Hardware

dg-users

The mailing list is concerned with the technical details of Data General, its O/Ss, and the cornucopia of hardware they supply and support.

Keywords: Computer Hardware, Data General

A
B
C
D
E
F
G
H
I
J
K
L
M
N
O
P
Q
R
S
T
U
V
W
X
Y
Z

Audience: Computer Hardware Users

Contact: brian@ilinx.wimsey.com

User Info: To subscribe to the list, send an e-mail message requesting a subscription to the URL address below.

To send a message to the entire list, address it to: dg-users-request@ilinx.wimsey.com

```
mailto:dg-users-
request@ilinx.wimsey.com
```

numeric-interest

★

Discussion of issues of floating-point correctness and performance with respect to hardware, operating systems, languages, and standard libraries.

Keywords: Computers, Computer Hardware

Audience: Computer Users

Contact: David Hough
numeric-interest-request@validgh.com

Details: Free

User Info: To subscribe to the list, send an e-mail message requesting a subscription to the URL address below.

To send a message to the entire list, address it to: numeric-interest@validgh.com

```
mailto:numeric-interest-
request@validgh.com
```

Computer Music

Computer Music Journal Archive and World Wide Web Home Page

★★★★

This resource reinforces material available in the hardcopy version of Computer Music Journal, published by the MIT Press.

Keywords: Computer Music, Composition, Synthesis, Interaction

Sponsor: The MIT Press

Audience: Computer Musicians

Profile: The archive includes the tables of contents, abstracts, and editor's notes for the last several volumes of CMJ (including the recent bibliography, diskography, and taxonomy of the field), a number of useful CM-related documents such as the full MIDI and AIFF format specifications, a lengthy reference list, the guidelines for manuscript submission, and the full-text of several recent articles.

Contact: Stephen Pope
cmj@cnmat.Berkeley.edu

Details: Free

```
ftp://mitpress.mit.edu:/pub/Computer-
Music-Journal
```

IRCAM DSP and musical software

 ★★

This site offers a variety of computer music resources.

Keywords: Computer Music, Sound Synthesis, Composition, DSP

Sponsor: IRCAM

Audience: Computer Music Researchers and Computer Musicians

Profile: Contains a list and brief description of IRCAM software (digital signal processing, voice and sound synthesis, music composition, wind instrument making, and other programs). There are also calendars of the IRCAM-EIC concerts and tours, and links to various other music servers.

Contact: Michel Fingerhut
fingerhu@ircam.fr

Details: Free

```
http://www.ircam.fr
```

Computer Network Conferencing

Computer Network Conferencing

★

Discussions on the topic of computer network conferencing. The memo is intended to make more people aware of the present developments in the computer conferencing field as well as to put forward ideas on what should be done to formalize this work.

Keywords: Internet, Conferencing Systems

Audience: Internet Surfers

Contact: Darren Reed
avalon@coombs.anu.edu.au

Details: Free

File is: documents/rfc/rfc1324.txt

```
ftp://nic.merit.edu
```

Computer Networking

CERT (Computer Emergency Response Team) Advisory

 ★★

A major directory on computer advisory, providing access to a broad range of related resources (library catalogs, databases, and servers) via the Internet.

Keywords: Computers, Security, Computer Networking

Audience: Computer Users

Profile: Profides information on how to obtain a patch or details of a workaround for a known computer security problem. CERT works with vendors to produce a workaround or a patch for a problem, and does not publish vulnerability information until a workaround or patch is available. A CERT advisory may also be a warning about ongoing attacks to network systems.

Contact: cert@cert.org

```
ftp://cert.org/pub/cert_advisories
```

NCSA (National Center for Supercomputing Applications)

 ★★★★

A high-performance computing and communications facility and research center designed to serve the US computational science and engineering community.

Keywords: Supercomputing, Computer Networking, Computer Science, Mosaic

Sponsor: University of Illinois at Urbana-Champaign, Champaign, Illinois, USA

Audience: Students, Researchers, Computer Scientists, General Public

Contact: Systems Operator
pubs@ncsa.uiuc.edu

```
http://www.ncsa.uiuc.edu/General/
NCSAHome.html
```

The Scout Report

 ★★★★

The Scout Report is a weekly publication offered by InterNIC Information Services to the Internet community as a fast, convenient way to stay informed on network activities.

Keywords: WWW, Information Retrieval, Internet, Computer Networking

Sponsor: National Science Foundation, USA

Audience: Researchers, Students, General Public

Profile: The purpose of this resource is to combine in one place the highlights of new resource announcements and other news that occurred on the Internet during the previous week. The Report is released every Friday. Categories included each week will vary depending on content, and the report will evolve with time and with input from the networking community.

Contact: InfoGuide
scout@is.internic.net,
guide@is.internic.net

```
http://www.internic.net/scout-report
```

Computer Networks

alt.config

A Usenet newsgroup providing information and discussion about alternative subnet discussions and connectivity.

Keywords: Internet, Computer Networks, Connectivity

Audience: Network Administrators

User Info: To subscribe to this Usenet newsgroup, you need access to a newsreader.

`news:alt.config`

Computer Science Center Link

This is a newsletter about academic computing, located at the University of Maryland, College Park campus, featuring articles about networking, new trends in computing, and innovative uses of computing.

Keywords: Computer Science, Computer Networks

Sponsor: University of Maryland

Audience: Computer Students

Contact: Link Editor
yellow_pages@umail.umd.edu

Details: Free
Request a free subscription by sending e-mail to: yellow_pages@umail.umd.edu

`mailto:yellow_pages@umail.umd.edu`

Computing and Network News

A newsletter published 10 times a year for the Kansas State University community.

Keywords: Computers, Computer Networks, Computer Science

Sponsor: Kansas State University

Audience: Kansas State University Students, Educators

Contact: Betsy Edwards
betsy@ksuvm.ksu.edu

Details: Free

`mailto:editor@ksuvm.ksu.edu`

MichNet News (previously Merit Network News)

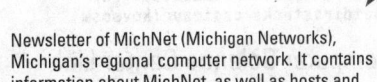

Newsletter of MichNet (Michigan Networks), Michigan's regional computer network. It contains information about MichNet, as well as hosts and services that can be reached through MichNet.

Keywords: Computer Networks, Michigan Networks

Sponsor: MichNet

Audience: Michigan Network Users, Network Users

Contact: Pat McGregor
patmcg@merit.edu

Details: Free
Contact the MichNet News at mnn-request@merit.edu. Available by anonymous FTP from the address below.

`ftp://nis.nsf.net`

Computer News

CUD (Computer Underground Digest)

USA Today of cyberspace and the computer underground. Contains information relating to the computer underground.

Keywords: Hacking, Computer News, Cyberculture

Audience: Hackers, Reality Hackers, Computer Underground Enthusiasts

Contact: Gordon Meyer, Jim Thomas
tk0jut2@niu.bitnet or
pumpcon@mindvox.phantom.com.

Details: Free

`ftp://etext.archive.umich.edu/pub/Zines/CUD`

Computer Products

CEXPRESS (Computer Express Internet Superstore)

Computer Express offers over 3,000 software titles and hardware products, available for immediate delivery.

Keywords: Computer Products

Audience: Consumers

`mailto:info@cexpress.com`

`gophercexpress.com`

`http://cexpress.com`

gateway2000

This list is a source of information about Gateway2000 products.

Keywords: Computer Products, Software, Hardware

Audience: Computer Users, Hardware Engineers, Software Engineers

Details: Free

User Info: To subscribe to the list, send an e-mail message requesting a subscription to the URL address below.

To send a message to the entire list, address it to: gateway2000@sei.cmu.edu

`gateway2000-request@sei.cmu.edu`

Hewlett-Packard Computers

This web site provides information on Hewlett Packard products, news, contacts, and services.

Keywords: Computer Products, Hewlett-Packard

Sponsor: Hewlett-Packard

Audience: Computer Users, Educators, Distributors

Contact: webmaster@www.hp.com.

Details: Free

`http://www.hp.com`

Computer Professionals

CPSR/PDX Newsletter

This is the newsletter of the Portland chapter of Computer Professionals for Social Responsibility.

Keywords: Computer Professionals, Social Responsibility

Audience: Computer Professionals

Contact: Erik Nilsson
ERIKN@Goldfish.mitron.tek.com

Details: Free

`mailto:erikn@goldfish.mitron.tek.com`

Computer Programming

comp.lang.c

A Usenet newsgroup providing information and discussion about the C programming language.

Keywords: Computer Programming, Programming Languages

Audience: Computer Users, C Programmers

User Info: To subscribe to this Usenet newsgroup, you need access to a newsreader.

`news:comp.lang.c`

PERL (Practical Extraction and Report Language)

An HTML-formatted and highly indexed PERL programming reference document.

Keywords: Programming Languages, Computer Programming

A
B
C
D
E
F
G
H
I
J
K
L
M
N
O
P
Q
R
S
T
U
V
W
X
Y
Z

A
B
C
D
E
F
G
H
I
J
K
L
M
N
O
P
Q
R
S
T
U
V
W
X
Y
Z

Audience: Computer Programmers, Students, Researchers

Contact: Larry Wall
lwall@netlabs.com

`http://www.cs.cmu.edu/Web/People/rgs/perl.html`

Python

A mailing list for discussion of and questions about all aspects of the design and use of the Python programming language.

Keywords: Computer Programming Languages

Audience: Computer Programmers, Python Language Users

Contact: Guido van Rossum
python-list-request@cwi.nl

Details: Free

User Info: To subscribe to the list, send an e-mail message requesting a subscription to the URL address below.

To send a message to the entire list, address it to: python-list@cwi.nl

Notes: The source of the latest Python release is always available by anonymous FTP from ftp.cwi.nl, in directory /pub/python.

`mailto:python-list-request@cwi.nl`

Spanky Fractal Database

This web site provides a collection of fractals and fractal-related material for free distribution on the Internet.

Keywords: Mathematics, Chaos Theory, Computer Programming, Computer Graphics

Audience: Mathematicians, Computer Programmers

Profile: Contains information on dynamical systems, software, distributed fractal generators, galleries, and databases from all over the world.

Contact: Noel Giffin
noel@triumf.ca

Details: Free

`http://spanky.triumf.ca`

UTIRC (University of Toronto Instructional and Research Computing

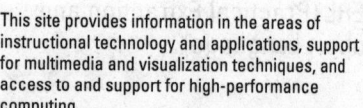

This site provides information in the areas of instructional technology and applications, support for multimedia and visualization techniques, and access to and support for high-performance computing.

Keywords: Computing, Computer Programming, Computer-Aided Design

Sponsor: University of Toronto, Division of Computing, Toronto, Canada

Audience: Programmers, Designers

Details: Free

`http://www.utirc.utoronto.ca/HTMLdocs/NewHTML/intro.html`

Computer Programs

c2man

This is a discussion of Graham Stoney's c2man program, which parses comments from C and C++ programs and produces documentation for man pages, info files, and so on.

Keywords: Computer Programs, c2man

Audience: Computer Programmers

Contact: listserv@research.canon.oz.au

User Info: To subscribe to the list, send an e-mail message to the URL address below, consisting of a single line reading:

SUB c2man YourFirstName YourLastName

To send a message to the entire list, address it to:
c2man@research.canon.oz.au

Notes: This list is archived and unmoderated.

`mailto:listserv@research.canon.oz.au`

nqthm-users

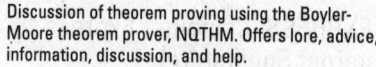

Discussion of theorem proving using the Boyler-Moore theorem prover, NQTHM. Offers lore, advice, information, discussion, and help.

Keywords: Computer Programs, NQTHM, Boyler-Moore Theorem Prover

Audience: NQTHM Theorem Users

Contact: nqthm-users-request@cli.com

Details: Free

User Info: To subscribe to the list, send an e-mail message requesting a subscription to the URL address below.

To send a message to the entire list, address it to: nqthm-users@cli.com

`mailto:nqthm-users@cli.com`

Computer Resources

DIGIT

A bimonthly publication containing information aimed at users of computing resources at the University of Colorado, Boulder.

Keywords: Computers, Computer Resources

Audience: University of Colorado Students, Computer Students

Contact: Suzanne Kincaid
kincaid@spot.colorado.edu

Details: Free

`mailto:kincaid@spot.colorado.edu`

Computer Science

alt.books.reviews

A Usenet conference devoted to reviews of books, especially science fiction and computer science books.

Keywords: Literature (General), Computer Science, Science Fiction, Book Reviews

Audience: General Public, Publishers, Educators, Librarians, Booksellers

Profile: Alt.books.reviews (a.b.r. for short) is a forum for posting reviews of books of interest to readers, school and public librarians, bookstores, publishers, teachers and professors, and others who desire an "educated opinion" of a book. This is an unmoderated newsgroup.

Contact: sbrock@csn.org.

Details: Free

To participate in a Usenet newsgroup, you need access to a newsreader.

Notes: The reviews in alt.books.reviews are archived at csn.org. Ftp to csn.org; login: anonymous; password: your complete e-mail address. At the ftp prompt, type: cd pub/alt.books.reviews

`news:alt.books.reviews`

Artificial Intelligence, Expert Sys., Virtual Reality

This directory is a compilation of information resources focused on computer science research, artificial intelligence, expert systems, and virtual reality.

Keywords: Computer Science, Artificial Intelligence, Expert Systems, Virtual Reality

Audience: Computer Scientists, Engineers

Contact: M. Kovacs

Details: Free

`ftp://una.hh.lib.umich.edu/70/inetdirstacks/csaiesvr:kovacsm`

Computer Science Center Link

This is a newsletter about academic computing, located at the University of Maryland, College Park campus, featuring articles about networking, new trends in computing, and innovative uses of computing.

Keywords: Computer Science, Computer Networks
Sponsor: University of Maryland
Audience: Computer Students
Contact: Link Editor
yellow_pages@umail.umd.edu
Details: Free

Request a free subscription by sending
e-mail to: yellow_pages@umail.umd.edu

`mailto:yellow_pages@umail.umd.edu`

Computing and Network News ★

A newsletter published 10 times a year for the
Kansas State University community.

Keywords: Computers, Computer Networks,
Computer Science
Sponsor: Kansas State University
Audience: Kansas State University Students,
Educators
Contact: Betsy Edwards
betsy@ksuvm.ksu.edu
Details: Free

`mailto:editor@ksuvm.ksu.edu`

Computists' Communique ★★★

A weekly newsletter serving professionals in
artificial intelligence, information science, and
computer science.

Keywords: Artificial Intelligence, Information
Science, Computer Science
Audience: Computer Scientists, Information
Scientists, Computists International
Members
Profile: Content is career oriented and depends
partly on contributions from members.
The moderator filters submissions,
reports and comments on industry news,
collects common knowledge about
academia and industry, and helps track
people and projects. The Communique is
only available to members of Computists
International, a networking association
for computer and information scientists.
It is an association for mutual mentoring
about grant and funding sources,
information channels, applications, text,
software publishing, and the sociology of
work.
Contact: Kenneth I. Laws
laws@ari.sri.com
Details: Costs

`mailto:laws@ari.sri.com`

ctf-discuss ★

This mailing list aims to stimulate discussion of
issues critical to the computer science community in
the United States (and, by extension, the world). The
Computer Science and Telecommunications Board
(CSTB) of the National Research Council (NRC) is

charged with identifying and initiating studies in
areas critical to the health of the field. Recently one
such study, Computing the Future, has generated a
major discussion in the community and has
motivated the establishment of this mailing list in
order to involve broader participation. This list will
be used in the future to report and discuss the
activities of the CSTB and to solicit opinions in a
variety of areas.

Keywords: Computer Science, Telecommunications
Audience: Computer Scientists, Telecommunications Experts
Contact: Dave Farber
ctf-discuss-request@cis.upenn.edu
Details: Free
User Info: To subscribe to the list, send an e-mail
message requesting a subscription to
the URL address below.

To send a message to the entire list,
address it to: ctf-discuss@cis.upenn.edu

`mailto:ctf-discuss-`
`request@cis.upenn.edu`

National Centre for Software Technology ★★

The National Centre for Software Technology (NCST)
is an autonomous R&D unit in Bombay and
Bangalore. Specialty areas of research include
graphics, CAD, real time systems, knowledge-based
systems, and software engineering.

Keywords: Computer Science, Engineering,
Computer-Aided Design
Sponsor: National Centre for Software
Technology, Bombay, India
Audience: Reseachers, Computer Scientists,
Engineers, Students
Contact: Postmaster
postmaster@saathi.ncst.ernet.in

`gopher://shakti.ncst.ernet.in`

NCSA (National Center for Supercomputing Applications) ★★★★

A high-performance computing and communications
facility and research center designed to serve the
US computational science and engineering
community.

Keywords: Supercomputing, Computer Networking,
Computer Science, Mosaic
Sponsor: University of Illinois at Urbana-
Champaign, Champaign, Illinois, USA
Audience: Students, Researchers, Computer
Scientists, General Public
Contact: Systems Operator
pubs@ncsa.uiuc.edu

`http://www.ncsa.uiuc.edu/General/`
`NCSAHome.html`

The InterNIC Home Page

This is the home page for the InterNIC networking
organization.

Keywords: WWW, Information Retrieval, Computer
Science, Internet Resources
Sponsor: National Science Foundation, USA
Audience: Reseachers, Students, General Public
Profile: The InterNIC is a collaborative project of
three organizations, which work
together to offer the Internet community
a full scope of network information
services. These services include
providing information about accessing
and using the Internet, assistance in
locating resources on the network, and
registering network components for
Internet connectivity. The overall goal of
the InterNIC is to make networking and
networked information more easily
accessible to researchers, educators,
and the general public. The term
InterNIC signifies cooperation between
Network Information Centers, or NICS.
Contact: InfoGuide
guide@internic.net
Details: InterNIC signifies cooperation between
Network Information Centers

`http://www.internic.net`

University of Puerto Rico Library ★★

The library's holdings are large and wide-ranging
and contain significant collections in many fields.

Keywords: Computer Science, Education, Nursing,
Agriculture, Economics
Audience: Researchers, Students, General Public
Details: Free

After Locator: telnet://, press Tab twice.
Type DIAL VTAM. Enter NOTIS.

Press Return. On the blank screen, type
LUUP.

`telnet://136.145.2.10`

University of Texas at Austin Library ★★

The library's holdings are large and wide-ranging
and contain significant collections in many fields.

Keywords: Music, Natural Science, Nursing,
Science Technology, Behavioral
Science, Social Work, Computer
Science, Engineering, Latin American
Studies, Middle Eastern Studies
Audience: Researchers, Students, General Public
Details: Free

Expect: Blank Screen, Send: Return;
Expect: Go, Send: Return; Expect: Enter
Terminal Type, Send: vt100

Notes: Some databases are restricted to UT
Austin users only.

`telnet://utcat.utexas.edu`

A
B
C
D
E
F
G
H
I
J
K
L
M
N
O
P
Q
R
S
T
U
V
W
X
Y
Z

Computer Specialists

Posix-ada

To discuss the Ada binding of the POSIX standard. This is the IEEE P1003.5 working group.

Keywords: Poxis, Computer Specialists

Audience: Posix Users, Software Developers

Contact: Karl Nyberg
posix-ada-request@grebyn.com

Details: Free

User Info: To subscribe to the list, send an e-mail message requesting a subscription to the URL address below.

To send a message to the entire list, address it to: posix-ada@grebyn.com

`mailto:posix-ada-request@grebyn.com`

Computer Speech Interfaces

ECTL

A list dedicated to researchers interested in Computer Speech Interfaces.

Keywords: Computer Speech Interfaces

Audience: Computer Speech Researchers

Contact: David Leip
ectl-request@snowhite.cis.uoguelph.ca

Details: Free

User Info: To subscribe to the list, send an e-mail message requesting a subscription to the URL address below.

To send a message to the entire list, address it to: ectl-request@snowhite.cis.uoguelph.ca

`mailto:ectl-request@snowhite.cis.uoguelph.ca`

Computer Systems

alpha-osf-managers

This list is intended to be a quick-turnaround trouble shooting aid for those who administer and manage DEC Alpha AXP systems running OSF/1.

Keywords: Computer Systems, Computer Administration

Sponsor: Oakridge National Laboratory

Audience: Computer Programmers

User Info: To subscribe to the list, send an e-mail message to the URL address below consisting of a single line reading:

subscribe alpha-osf-managers.

Notes: Alpha-osf-managers archived at ftp/kpc.com: /pub/list/alpha-osf-managers

`mailto:majordomo@ornl.gov`

Apple Computer Higher Education Gopher Server

This directory is maintained by Apple Computer to provide information about products from Apple Computer.

Keywords: Computer Systems, Computer-Aided Instruction, Apple Computer

Sponsor: Apple Computer, Cupertino, CA

Audience: General Public

Profile: This directory also contains promotional material, such as Apple Press Releases, extensive product information, Apple publications, regional market information, Higher Education Marketing Information and support information.

Contact: mail to:
feedback@info.hed.apple.com

`http://www.apple.com`

Apple Computer WWW Server

A web site containing information about Apple Computer. The resource is designed to provide timely product information, including press releases on Apple's technology and research. Also contains links to Freeware and Shareware sites, and includes information for developers and programmers.

Keywords: Computer Systems, Technology, Apple Computer, Shareware

Audience: General Public

`http://www.apple.com`

comp.os

A Usenet newsgroup providing information and discussion about computer operating systems. There are many categories within this group.

Keywords: Computer Systems

Audience: Computer Users

User Info: To subscribe to this Usenet newsgroup, you need access to a newsreader.

`news:comp.os`

comp.os.ms-windows.apps

A Usenet newsgroup providing information and discussion about applications in Windows.

Keywords: Computers Systems

Audience: Computer Users, Windows Users

User Info: To subscribe to this Usenet newsgroup, you need access to a newsreader.

`news:comp.os.ms-windows.apps`

comp.os.os2.misc

A Usenet newsgroup providing information and discussion about miscellaneous topics concerning O/S2.

Keywords: Computer Systems

Audience: Computer Users, O/S2 Users

User Info: To subscribe to this Usenet newsgroup, you need access to a newsreader.

`news:comp.os.os2.misc`

comp.sys.amiga

A Usenet newsgroup providing information and discussion about Amiga systems. There are many categories within this group.

Keywords: Computer Systems, Amiga Aystems

Audience: Computer Users, Amiga Users

User Info: To subscribe to this Usenet newsgroup, you need access to a newsreader.

`news:comp.sys.amiga`

comp.sys.apple2

A Usenet newsgroup providing information and discussion about Apple II systems. There are several categories within this group.

Keywords: Computer Systems, Apple Computer

Audience: Computer Users, Apple II Users

User Info: To subscribe to this Usenet newsgroup, you need access to a newsreader.

`news:comp.sys.apple2`

comp.sys.atari.st

A Usenet newsgroup providing information and discussion about 16-bit Atari.

Keywords: Computer Systems

Audience: Computer Users, Atari Users

User Info: To subscribe to this Usenet newsgroup, you need access to a newsreader.

`news:comp.sys.atari.st`

comp.sys.ibm.pc

A Usenet newsgroup providing information and discussion about the IBM PC computer. There are many categories within this group.

Keywords: Computer Systems, IBM

Audience: Computer Users, IBM Users

User Info: To subscribe to this Usenet newsgroup, you need access to a newsreader.

`news:comp.sys.ibm.pc`

comp.sys.mac ★

A Usenet newsgroup providing information and discussion about the Macintosh computer. There are many categories within this group.

Keywords: Computer Systems, Macintosh Computers

Audience: Computer Users, Macintosh Users

User Info: To subscribe to this Usenet newsgroup, you need access to a newsreader.

`news:comp.sys.mac`

comp.sys.next ★

A Usenet newsgroup providing information and discussion about NeXT computers. There are several categories within this group.

Keywords: Computer Systems, NeXT

Audience: Computer Users, NeXT Users

User Info: To subscribe to this Usenet newsgroup, you need access to a newsreader.

`news:comp.sys.next`

comp.sys.sgi ★

A Usenet newsgroup providing information and discussion about Silicon Graphic systems. There are several categories within this group.

Keywords: Computer Systems

Audience: Computer Users, Silicon Graphics Users

User Info: To subscribe to this Usenet newsgroup, you need access to a newsreader.

`news:comp.sys.sgi`

comp.sys.sun ★

A Usenet newsgroup providing information and discussion about Sun systems. There are several categories within this group.

Keywords: Computer Systems, Sun

Audience: Computer Users, Sun Users

User Info: To subscribe to this Usenet newsgroup, you need access to a newsreader.

`news:comp.sys.sun`

comp.unix.aix ★

A Usenet newsgroup providing information and discussion about IBM's version of UNIX.

Keywords: Computer Systems, Internet, UNIX

Audience: Computer Users, UNIX Users, IBM Users

User Info: To subscribe to this Usenet newsgroup, you need access to a newsreader.

`news:comp.unix.aix`

comp.windows.x ★

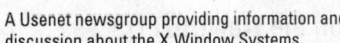

A Usenet newsgroup providing information and discussion about the X Window Systems.

Keywords: Computer Systems

Audience: Computer Users, Windows Users

User Info: To subscribe to this Usenet newsgroup, you need access to a newsreader.

`news:comp.windows.x`

Digital Equipment WWW Information Server ★★

Digital Equipment's server contains product and service information, and includes archives to public domain software. Also includes an online catalog resource for purchasing products from Digital Equipment.

Keywords: Computer Systems, Digital Equipment

Audience: Digital Equipment Users

Contact: Steve Painter
steve_painter@mro.mts.dec.com

`http://www.service.digital.com/home.html`

Digital's World Wide Web Server ★★

Digital World Wide Web server provides product and service information, back issues of the Digital Technical Journal, performance reports, buyers guides, and product catalogs.

Keywords: Digital Equipment Corporation, Computer Systems

Audience: Computer Users, Computing Consultants

Contact: Russ Jones
webmaster@pa.dec.com

Details: Free

`http://www.digital.com/home.html`

HYTELNET ★★★★

A shareware application database directory to libraries.

Keywords: Computer Systems, Libraries, Shareware

Audience: General Audience

Profile: HYTELNET is a guide to library catalogs from the Americas, Europe

Contact: Peter Scott
aa375@freenet.carleton.ca

Details: Free

Notes: HYTELNET is in English, but the interface to some international

`gopher://gophlib@gopher.yale.edu`

Info-tandem ★★

Info-tandem is an e-mail list for users of systems from Tandem Computers, Inc.

Keywords: Computer Systems, Tandem Computers

Audience: Programmers, Analysts

Contact: Scott Hazen Mueller
scott@zorch.sf-bay.org

Details: Free

User Info: To subscribe to the list, send an e-mail message requesting

`mailto:info-tandem-request@zorch.sf-bay.org`

Pcbuild ★

An open, unmoderated E-conference for discussion of PC hardware, including such topics as upgrading your PC, building your own PC, hardware problems, questions, and businesses from which to buy hardware cheaply.

Keywords: Computer Systems

Audience: PC Users

Contact: Dave Gomberg
gomberg@ucsfvm.edu

Details: Free

User Info: To subscribe to the list, send an e-mail message to the URL address below, consisting of a single line reading: SUB pcbuild YourFirstName YourLastName

To send a message to the entire list, address it to:
pcbuild@tsclion.trenton.edu

`mailto:listserv@tsclion.trenton.edu`

Posix-testing ★

A forum for discussion of issues related to testing operating systems for conformance to the various POSIX standards and proposed standards. Issues include problems related to test suites in general, testability of various features of the standards, and portability of the test suites to the many very different POSIX implementations anticipated in the near future.

Keywords: COmputer Systems

Audience: Posix Testers

Contact: Chuck Karish
posix-testing-request@mindcraft.com

Details: Free

User Info: To subscribe to the list, send an e-mail message requesting a subscription to the URL address below.

A B C D E F G H I J K L M N O P Q R S T U V W X Y Z

To send a message to the entire list, address it to: posix-testing@mindcraft.com

```
mailto:posix-testing-
request@mindcraft.com
```

Pubnet

A mailing list for the discussion of administration and use of public-access computer systems, primarily UNIX systems. The list also answers questions about setting up or running a public-access system

Keywords: Computer Systems, UNIX

Audience: Computer System Designers, UNIX Users

Contact: Chip Rosenthal
pubnet-request@chinacat.unicom.com

Details: Free

User Info: To subscribe to the list, send an e-mail message requesting a subscription to the URL address below.
To send a message to the entire list, address it to:
pubnet@chinacat.unicom.com

```
mailto:pubnet-
request@chinacat.unicom.com
```

Sun Microsystems, Inc.

This site provides a directory of Sun Microsystems products and services, including a company profile, announcements, financial statements, marketing reports, and international sales and support access.

Keywords: Computer Systems, Sun Microsystems

Sponsor: Sun Microsystems, Inc., Mountain View, California, USA

Audience: Sun Microsystems Users

Profile: Languages: English

Contact: webmaster@sun.com.

Details: Free

```
http://www.sun.com
```

Computer Technology

Current Cites

A monthly publication of the Library Technology Watch Program at the library, University of California, Berkeley.

Keywords: Computer Technology, Libraries

Sponsor: The Library, University of California, Berkeley, CA

Audience: Librarians, Computer Programmers

Profile: Over 30 journals in librarianship and computer technology are scanned for articles on optical-disk technologies,

computer networks and networking, information transfer, expert systems and artificial intelligence, and hypermedia and multimedia.

Contact: David Robison
drobison@library.berkeley.edu

Details: Free

```
telnet://melvyl.ucop.edu
```

Hot off the Tree (HOTT)

HOTT contains excerpts and abstracts of articles from trade journals, popular periodicals, online news services, and electronic bulletin boards.

Keywords: Computer Technology, Technology

Sponsor: University of California, San Diego Library's Technology Watch Information Group (TWIG)

Audience: Computer Programmers, Technology Enthusiasts, General Public

Contact: Susan Jurist
sjurist@ucsd.edu or sjurist@ucsd.bitnet

Details: Free
Available on MELVYL, the University of California online catalog. Anyone with access to telnet, can telnet MELVYL (31.0.0.13) and show hott.

```
telnet://melvyl.berkeley.edu/showhott
```

Computer Underground

High Weirdness by E-Mail

Guide to some interesting sources of information online.

Keywords: Technology, Hacking, Computer Underground

Audience: Mystics, Reality Hackers, Weirdos

Profile: This file focuses mainly on bizarre philosophies, such as Discordia and SubGenius. Contents include: offbeat religions and 'spirituality' paganism and magic, occultism, UFOs and paranormal phenomena.

Details: Free

```
ftp://etext.archive.umich.edu/pub/
Zines/Weirdness
```

Computer Users

Futurebus+ Users

This discussion group focuses on the design, implementation, integration, and operation of hardware and software related to Futurebus+.

Keywords: Computer Users, Hardware, Software

Audience: Computer Users, Software Engineers, Hardware Engineers

Contact: majordomo@theus.rain.com

Details: Free

User Info: To subscribe to the list, send an e-mail message to the URL address below consisting of a single line reading:

SUB fbus_users YourFirstName YourLastName

To send a message to the entire list, address it to:
fbus_users+@theus.rain.com

```
mailto:majordomo@theus.rain.com
```

Computer Viruses

ST viruses

This list is to provide fast and efficient help with computer viruses infecting the Atari ST/TT/Falcon only.

Keywords: Computer Viruses, Atari

Audience: Computer Users

Contact: r.c.karsmakers@stud.let.ruu.nl

Details: Free

User Info: To subscribe to the list, send an e-mail message requesting a subscription to the URL address below.

To send a message to the entire list, address it to:
r.c.karsmakers@stud.let.ruu.nl

```
mailto:r.c.karsmakers@stud.let.ruu.nl
```

Virus-L

Virus-l is a forum for the discussion of computer virus experiences, protection software, and other virus-related topics. This list includes archives and files that list a number of viruses, trojan horses, and pirated programs for the IBM PC.

Keywords: Computer Viruses, Security

Audience: Computer Users

Contact: Kenneth R. van Wyk
luken@vax1.cc.lehigh.edu

Details: Free

User Info: To subscribe to the list, send an e-mail message to the URL address below consisting of a single line reading:

SUB virus-l YourFirstName YourLastName

To send a message to the entire list, address it to: virus-l@ibml.cc.lehigh.edu

```
mailto:listserv@ibm1.cc.lehigh.edu
```

A B C D E F G H I J K L M N O P Q R S T U V W X Y Z

CBDS-I

A mailing list for the discussion of CBDS (Circuit Board Design System).

Keywords: Engineering, Computer-Aided Design, Electronics

Audience: Engineers

Contact: NETMAN@suvm.ACS.SYR.EDU

Details: Free

User Info: To subscribe to the list, send an e-mail message to the URL address below consisting of a single line reading:

SUB cbds-I YourFirstName YourLastName

To send a message to the entire list, address it to:

CbDS-L@suvm.ACS.SYR.EDU

`mailto: listserv@suvm.ACS.SYR.EDU`

Free Art For HTML Page

This web site provides copyrighted graphics for the Mosaic program.

Keywords: Computer-Aided Design, Graphics

Audience: Designers, Educators

Contact: Harlan Wallach wallach@mcs.com

Details: Free

`http://www.mcs.net/wallach/Fart/ buttons.html`

National Centre for Software Technology

The National Centre for Software Technology (NCST) is an autonomous R&D unit in Bombay and Bangalore. Specialty areas of research include graphics, CAD, real time systems, knowledge-based systems, and software engineering.

Keywords: Computer Science, Engineering, Computer-Aided Design

Sponsor: National Centre for Software Technology, Bombay, India

Audience: Reseachers, Computer Scientists, Engineers, Students

Contact: Postmaster postmaster@saathi.ncst.ernet.in

`gopher://shakti.ncst.ernet.in`

UTIRC (University of Toronto Instructional and Research Computing

This site provides information in the areas of instructional technology and applications, support for multimedia and visualization techniques, and access to and support for high-performance computing.

Keywords: Computing, Computer Programming, Computer-Aided Design

Sponsor: University of Toronto, Division of Computing, Toronto, Canada

Audience: Programmers, Designers

Details: Free

`http://www.utirc.utoronto.ca/ HTMLdocs/NewHTML/intro.html`

Civil-L

A mailing list for the discussion of civil engineering Research and Education.

Keywords: Engineering (Civil), Computer-Aided Instruction

Audience: Engineers, Educators, Students

Contact: Eldo Hildebrand eldo@unb.ca

Details: Free

User Info: To subscribe to the list, send an e-mail message to the URL address shown below consisting of a single line reading:

SUB civil-I YourFirstName YourLastName

To send a message to the entire list, address it to:

civil-I@unb.ca

`mailto:listserv@unb.ca`

Computer-Human Interactions

Loughborough University of Technology Computer-Human Interaction (LUTCHI) Research Centre

This server contains general information on computer-human interaction.

Keywords: Interface Design, Ergonomics, Computer-Human Interactions, Programming

Sponsor: Loughborough University of Technology, Leicestershire, UK

Audience: Software Developers, Software Designers, Programmers

Profile: The LUTCHI Research Centre is based within the Department of Computer Studies at the Loughborough University of Technology, Leicestershire, UK. This server contains information about LUTCHI research projects, official LUTCHI publicity releases, as well as documents, images, and movies associated with those projects.

Contact: Ben Anderson b.anderson@lut.ac.uk

Details: Free, Moderated, Image and Sound files available. Multimedia files available.

Use a World-Wide Web (Mosaic) client and open a connection to the resource.

`http://pipkin.lut.ac.uk`

Computer-Mediated Marketing Environments

Computer-Mediated Marketing Environments

A web site devoted to research aimed at understanding the ways in which computer-mediated marketing environments (CMEs), especially the Internet, are revolutionizing the way firms conduct business.

Keywords: WWW, Information Retrieval, Internet, Marketing, Business

Sponsor: Vanderbilt University, Owen Graduate School of Management, Nashville, Tennessee, USA

Audience: General Public, Entrepeneurs, Financial Planners, Marketers

Contact: Donna Hoffman, Tom Novak hoffman@colette.ogsm.vanderbilt.edu novak@moe.ogsm.vanderbilt.edu

`http://colette.ogsm.vanderbilt.edu`

Computers

Almost 2001 Archive

Archive of transcripts of Almost 2001, a series on computer communications of the future, produced by NBC (National Broadcasting Company).

Keywords: Computers, Communications, Internet

Sponsor: The WELL (Whole Earth 'Lectronic Link)

Audience: Computer Users, Internet Surfers

Details: Free, Moderated.

To participate in a conference on the WELL, you must first establish an account on the WELL. To do so, start by typing: telnet://well.sf.ca.us

`gopher://gopher.well.sf.ca.us//11/ Communications/2001`

Alspa

Discussion by users of the CP/M machines made by (now defunct) Alspa Computer, Inc.

Keywords: Computers, Alspa Computer, Inc., CP/M

Audience: CP/M Users

Contact: Brad Allen alspa-users-request@ssyx.ucsc.edu

A B C D E F G H I J K L M N O P Q R S T U V W X Y Z

Details: Free

User Info: To subscribe to the list, send an e-mail message requesting a subscription to the URL address below.

To send a message to the entire list, address it to: alspa-users@ssyx.ucsc.edu

`mailto:alspa-users-request@ssyx.ucsc.edu`

alt.bbs ★

A Usenet newsgroup providing information and discussion about computer BBS systems and software.

Keywords: BBS Systems, Cyberspace, Computers

Audience: BBS Users

User Info: To subscribe to this Usenet newsgroup, you need access to a newsreader.

`news:alt.bbs`

alt.cyberpunk ★

A Usenet newsgroup providing information and discussion about the high-tech low-life.

Keywords: Computers, Cyberspace

Audience: Hackers, Cybernauts, General Public

User Info: To subscribe to this Usenet newsgroup, you need access to a newsreader.

`news:alt.cyberpunk`

alt.folklore.computers ★

A Usenet newsgroup providing information and discussion concerning stories and anecdotes about computers.

Keywords: Computers, Folklore

Audience: Computer Users, Storytellers

User Info: To subscribe to this Usenet newsgroup, you need access to a newsreader.

`news:alt.folklore.computers`

alt.security.pgp ★

A Usenet newsgroup providing information and discussion about the Pretty Good Privacy package, a privately-developed encryption technique.

Keywords: Privacy, Encryption, Security Firewalls, Computers

Audience: Internet Surfers

User Info: To subscribe to this Usenet newsgroup, you need access to a newsreader.

`news:alt.security.pgp`

Amiga CD-ROM ★

For Amiga users who are interested in CD-ROM drives and discs.

Keywords: Computers, Amiga, CD-ROM

Audience: Computer Users

Contact: ben@ben.com

Details: Free

User Info: To subscribe to the list, send an e-mail message requesting a subscription to the URL address below.

To send a message to the entire list, address it to: cdrom-list@ben.com

`mailto:cdrom-list-request@ben.com`

AMOS ★

For the AMOS programming language on Amiga computers. Features source, bug reports, and help from users around the world, but mainly from European users. Most posts will be in English, but there are no language limitations.

Keywords: Computers, Programming Languages, AMOS, Amiga

Audience: Programmers, Computer Users

Contact: subscribe@xamiga.linet.org

Details: Free

User Info: To subscribe to the list, send an e-mail message to the URL address below, consisting of a single line reading:

SUB #amos userneame@domain

To send a message to the entire list, address it to:
subscribe@xamiga.linet.org

`mailto:subscribe@xamiga.linet.org`

ApE-info ★★

A mailing list for the discussion of the scientific visualization software package ApE, its usage, development, and implementation.

Keywords: Computers, Visualization, Science

Sponsor: Jim Lick

Audience: ApE Software Users, Computer Programmers

Contact: Jim Lick
ape-info-request@ferkel.ucsb.edu

User Info: To subscribe to the list, send an e-mail message to the URL address below.

To send a message to the entire list, address it to: ape-info@ferkel.ucsb.edu

`mailto:ape-info-request@ferkel.ucsb.edu`

Apple II Files ★

This FTP site contains the archive of files relating to Apple II computers.

Keywords: Apple Computers, Computers

Audience: Programmers, Computer Users, Apple II Users

Details: Free

`ftp://archive.umich.edu`

AppWare-info

A forum for discussion of issues relating to AppWare software. Topics include simple programming questions, tips for program efficiency, quirks of, and complaints about the environment or tools, the process of writing new ALMs or functions, third party enhancements, and any other question.

Keywords: Computers, Programming Languages

Sponsor: Novell Inc.

Audience: AppWare Users, Computer Programmers

Contact: Novell Inc.
appware-info@serius.uchicago.edu

User Info: To subscribe to the list, send an e-mail message to the URL address below.

To send a message to the entire list, address it to: appware-info@serius.uchicago.edu

`mailto:appware-info-request@serius.uchicago.edu`

`ftp://serius.uchicago.edu`

artist-users

A discussion group for users and potential users of software tools from Cadence Design Systems.

Keywords: Computers, Computer Art

Sponsor: Cadence Design Systems

Audience: Computer Artists

Contact: Jeff Putsch
artist-users-request@uicc.com

User Info: To subscribe to the list, send an e-mail message to the URL address below.

To send a message to the entire list, address it to: artist-users-request@uicc.com

Notes: This mailing list is bi-directionally gatewayed to the Usenet newsgroup

`mailto:artist-users-request@uicc.com`

att-pc+

A mailing list for users and potential users of the AT&T PC 63xx series of systems.

Keywords: Computers, AT&T Computer Systems

Audience: Computer Programmers

Contact: Bill Kennedy
bill@ssbn.wlk.com

User Info: To subscribe to the list, send an e-mail message to the URL address below.

To send a message to the entire list, address it to: att-pc+@ssbn.wlk.com

Notes: Sub-lists are maintained for MS-DOS-only and Simul-Task mailings as well as the full list for items of general interest. Membership must be requested and mail path verification is required before membership is granted.

`mailto:att-pc+@ssbn.wlk.com`

A B C D E F G H I J K L M N O P Q R S T U V W X Y Z

auc-TeX

Discussion and information exchange about the AUC TeX package, which runs under GNU Emacs.

Keywords: Computers, TeX, AUC TeX, Emacs

Audience: Computer Users

Contact: Kresten Krab Thorup
auc-tex-request@iesd.auc.dk

Details: Free

User Info: To subscribe to the list, send an e-mail message requesting a subscription to the URL address below.

To send a message to the entire list, address it to: auc-tex@iesd.auc.dk

`mailto:auc-tex-request@iesd.auc.dk`

Aviator

A mailing list for users of Aviator™, the flight-simulation program from Artificial Horizons, Inc.

Keywords: Aviation, Simulation, Computers, Flight Simulation

Audience: Software Users

Contact: Jim Hickstein
aviator@lcdwest.teradyne.com

Details: Free

User Info: To subscribe to the list, send an e-mail message requesting a subscription to the URL address below.

To send a message to the entire list, address it to:
aviator@ICDwest.Teradyne.COM

Notes: Aviator runs on Sun workstations with the GX graphics accelerator option. Its charter is simply to facilitate communication among users of Aviator. It is not intended for communication with the "providers" of Aviator. All mail received at the submission address is reflected to all the subscribers of the list.

`mailto:aviator-request@ICDwest.Teradyne.COM`

bionet.software

A Usenet newsgroup providing information and discussion about software for use in biological research.

Keywords: Computers, Biology

Audience: Students, Educators, Biologists

User Info: To subscribe to this Usenet newsgroup, you need access to a newsreader.

`news:bionet.software`

Buyer's Guide to Micro Software

★★★

The database contains a directory of business and professional microcomputer software available in the United States.

Keywords: Buyer's Guides, Microcomputers, Computers, Software

Sponsor: Online, Inc., Weston, CT, USA

Audience: Computer Users

Profile: Provided are directory, product, technical, and bibliographic information on leading software packages, integrated this information into one succinct composite record. The database can help professionals locate suitable packages compatible with specified hardware, without having to sift through large numbers of records.

The file is highly selective, listing packages rated at least "good" by the technical press; all packages from major software producers, even if negatively reviewed; and packages unique to specific business segments, with special emphasis placed on library and medical software. Each record includes directory information; technical specifications, including required hardware and operating systems; an abstracted product description; and, when available, a full citation of representative reviews.

Contact: Dialog in the US at (800) 334-2564, Dialog internationally at country-specific locations.

Details: Costs

User Info: To subscribe, contact Dialog directly.

Notes: Coverage: current; updated monthly.

`telnet://dialog.com`

CAF Archive

A source of information relating to Computers and Academic Freedom (CAF).

Keywords: Education, Computers, Academic Freedom

Audience: Educators, Researchers

Contact: kadie@eff.org
http://www.eff.org/CAF/cafhome.html

CCNEWS

★★★

An electronic forum for campus-computing newsletter editors and other publications specialists.

Keywords: Computers, Editors, Students, Newsletters

Audience: Students (college), Editors

Profile: CCNEWS consists of a biweekly newsletter that focuses on the writing, editing, designing, and producing of campus-computing publications, and an articles abstracts published on alternating weeks that describes new contributions to the articles archive.

Contact: Wendy Rickard Bollentin
ccnews@educom.bitnet

Details: Free

User Info: To subscribe to the list, send an e-mail message to the URL address below consisting of a single line reading:

SUB ccnews YourFirstName YourLastName

To send a message to the entire list, address it to: ccnews@educom.bitnet

Inquire about needing a password.

`mailto:listserv@bitnic.cren.net`

CERT (Computer Emergency Response Team) Advisory

★★

A major directory on computer advisory, providing access to a broad range of related resources (library catalogs, databases, and servers) via the Internet.

Keywords: Computers, Security, Computer Networking

Audience: Computer Users

Profile: Profides information on how to obtain a patch or details of a workaround for a known computer security problem. CERT works with vendors to produce a workaround or a patch for a problem, and does not publish vulnerability information until a workaround or patch is available. A CERT advisory may also be a warning about ongoing attacks to network systems.

Contact: cert@cert.org

`ftp://cert.org/pub/cert_advisories`

cfcp-members

The Confederation of Future Computer Professionals (CFCP) is a group of users on the Internet who are interested enough in various fields of computers to consider computers as their future. The Confederation exists to foster education and stimulate communication.

Keywords: Internet, Computers

Audience: Internet Surfers, Computer Users

Contact: mlindsey@nyx.cs.du.edu

Details: Free

User Info: To subscribe to the list, send an e-mail message requesting a subscription to the URL address below.

`mailto:mlindsey@nyx.cs.du.edu`

CMPCOM (Computers and Communications) Libraryzzzz

The Computers and Communications Library provides you industry-specific sources. More than 40 full-text sources that concentrate on computers and communications are available. Full-text files can be searched in a variety of ways: as an individual file, by major-subject group file, or as a user-defined group file.

A B C D E F G H I J K L M N O P Q R S T U V W X Y Z

A
B
C
D
E
F
G
H
I
J
K
L
M
N
O
P
Q
R
S
T
U
V
W
X
Y
Z

Keywords: Computers, Communications, Technology, Electronics

Audience: Business Researchers, Analysts, Entrepreneurs

Profile: This library can be used to gain insight on new products and technologies being introduced; monitor industry news for high technology systems, electronics, engineering, communications, and computer hardware and software; and locate product evaluations for both the professional as well as the casual personal computer user.

Contact: Mead New Sales Group at (800) 227-4908 or (513) 859-5398 inside the US, or (513) 865-7981 for all inquiries outside the US.

User Info: To subscribe, contact Mead directly.

To examine the Nexis user guide, you can access it at the ftp site of the University of Texas at Austin at the URL address: ftp://ftp.cc.utexas.edu

The files are in: /pub/ref-services/LEXIS

`telnet://nex.meaddata.com`

`http://www.meaddata.com`

CoCo

This is a discussion related to the Tandy Color Computer (any model) OS-9 Operating System, and any other topics relating to the "CoCo," as this computer is affectionately known.

Keywords: Tandy Computers, Computers

Audience: Tandy Computer Users, Computer Users

Contact: Paul E. Campbell
pecampbe@mtus5.BITNET

Details: Free

User Info: To subscribe to the list, send an e-mail message requesting a subscription to the URL address below.

`mailto:listserv@pucc.princeton.edu`

Commodore-Amiga

This list is for Commodore Amiga computer users. Weekly postings include hardware reviews, news briefs, system information, company progress, and information for finding out more about the Commodore and Amiga.

Keywords: Commodore-Amiga, Computers

Audience: Computer Users

Contact: subscribe@xamiga.linet.org

Details: Free

Send subscription requests to the URL address below using this format:

#commodore username@domain

`mailto:subscribe@xamiga.linet.org`

comp.compression

A Usenet newsgroup providing information and discussion about data compression algorithms and theory.

Keywords: Computers, Mathematics (Algorithims)

Audience: Computer Users

User Info: To subscribe to this Usenet newsgroup, you need access to a newsreader.

`news:comp.compression`

comp.lang.c++

A Usenet newsgroup providing information and discussion about the object-oriented C++ programming language.

Keywords: Computers, Programming Languages

Audience: Computer Users, C++ Programmers

User Info: To subscribe to this Usenet newsgroup, you need access to a newsreader.

`news:comp.lang.c++`

comp.org.eff.talk

A Usenet newsgroup organized by the EFF (Electronic Frontier Foundation) providing information and discussion about the political, social, and legal issues surrounding the Internet.

Keywords: Computers, Intellectual Property, Security, Internet

Audience: Internet Surfers

User Info: To subscribe to this Usenet newsgroup, you need access to a newsreader.

`news:comp.org.eff.talk`

comp.security.misc

A Usenet newsgroup providing information and discussion about security issues of computers and networks.

Keywords: Computers, Security, Firewalls

Audience: Computer Users

User Info: To subscribe to this Usenet newsgroup, you need access to a newsreader.

`news:comp.security.misc`

comp.unix.questions

A Usenet newsgroup providing discussion and questions for those learning UNIX.

Keywords: Computers, UNIX

Audience: Computer Users, UNIX Users

User Info: To subscribe to this Usenet newsgroup, you need access to a newsreader.

`news:comp.unix.questions`

comp.unix.wizards

A Usenet newsgroup providing discussion and questions for true UNIX wizards.

Keywords: Computers, UNIX

Audience: Computer Users, Unix Users

User Info: To subscribe to this Usenet newsgroup, you need access to a newsreader.

`news:comp.unix.wizards`

Computing and Network News

A newsletter published 10 times a year for the Kansas State University community.

Keywords: Computers, Computer Networks, Computer Science

Sponsor: Kansas State University

Audience: Kansas State University Students, Educators

Contact: Betsy Edwards
betsy@ksuvm.ksu.edu

Details: Free

`mailto:editor@ksuvm.ksu.edu`

Convex Customer Satisfaction Information Server

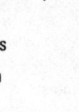

An online customer help server for Convex computer users.

Keywords: Computers, Convex Computers

Sponsor: Convex Computer Corporation

Audience: Convex Computer Users

Contact: iserv_admin@convex.com

Details: Free

Notes: Convex has its own gopher client, called "cxgopher."

`gopher://iserv.convex.com`

CSAA

The Comp.Sys.Amiga.Announce mailing list has been created for those who have no access to USENET. It provides the gate between the USENET newsgroup C.S.A.A. and e-mail. This group distributes announcements of importance to people using the Commodore brand Amiga computers. Announcements contain information on new products, disk library releases, software updates, reports of major bugs or dangerous viruses, notices of meetings or upcoming events, and so forth. A large proportion of posts announce the upload of software packages to anonymous FTP archive sites.

Keywords: Commodore-Amiga Computers, Computers

Audience: Commodore-Amiga Users

Contact: Carlos Amezaga
announce-request@cs.ucdavis.edu

Details: Free

User Info: To subscribe to the list, send an e-mail message requesting a subscription to the URL address below.

To send a message to the entire list, address it to:announce@cs.ucdavis.edu

`mailto:announce-request@cs.ucdavis.edu`

ctree

A forum for the discussion of FairCom's C-Tree, R-Tree, and D-Tree products. This mailing list is not associated with FairCom. Discussion covers virtually all hardware and operating system ports.

Keywords: Computers, FairCom

Audience: Computer Operators

Contact: Tony Olekshy
alberta!oha!ctree-request

Details: Free

User Info: To subscribe to the list, send an e-mail message requesting a subscription to the URL address below.

To send a message to the entire list, address it to: ctree

`mailto:alberta!oha!ctree-request`

CUSSNET

Computer Users in the Social Sciences (CUSS) is a discussion group devoted to issues of interest to social workers, counselors, and human service workers of all disciplines. The discussion frequently involves computer applications in treatment, agency administration, and research. Students, faculty, community-based professionals, and casual observers join in the discussion. Software, hardware, and ethical issues associated with their use in the human services generate lively and informative discussions.

Keywords: Social Sciences, Computers, Computer Applications

Audience: Social Workers, Human Services Workers, General Public

Contact: cussnet-request@stat.com

Details: Free

User Info: To subscribe to the list, send an e-mail message to the address below consisting of a single line reading:

SUB cussnet YourFirstName YourLastName.

To send a message to the entire list, address it to: cussnet@stat.com

`mailto:listserv@stat.com`

data-exp

The mail list server provides an open forum for users to discuss the Visualization Data Explorer Package. It contains three files at the moment: a. FAQ, b. summary, and c. forum.

Keywords: Computers, Software, Hardware, Visualization Data Explorer Package

Audience: Computer Users

User Info: To subscribe to the list, send an e-mail message requesting a subscription to the URL address below.

To send a message to the entire list, address it to: stein@watson.ibm.com

`mailto:stein@watson.ibm.com`

DECNEWS for Education and Research

Monthly electronic newsletter from Digital Equipment Corporation (DEC) summarizing announcements of its products, programs, and applications of interest to computer users in the academic and research communities.

Keywords: Computers, Education,

Sponsor: Digital Equipment Corp.

Audience: Computer Users, Educators, Researchers

Contact: Mary Hoffmann
decnews@mr4dec.enet.dec.com

Details: Free

User Info: To subscribe, send an e-mail message to the address below consisting of a single line reading:

SUB DECNews YourFirstName YourLastName

To send a message to the entire list, address it to:
decnews@ubvm.buffalo.edu

`mailto:listserv@ubvm.buffalo.edu`

DECnews-EDU

DECNEWS for Education and Research is a monthly electronic publication from Digital Equipment Corporation's Education Business Unit for the education and research communities worldwide.

Keywords: Education, Computers, Digital Equipment Corporation

Audience: Educators, Researchers

Contact: Anne Marie McDonald
decnews@mr4dec.enet.dec.com

Details: Free

User Info: To subscribe to the list, send an e-mail message requesting a subscription to the URL address below.

To send a message to the entire list, address it to:
decnews@mr4dec.enet.dec.com

`mailto:decnews@mr4dec.enet.dec.com`

DECnews-PR

DECnews for Press and Analysts is an Internet-based distribution of all Digital Equipment Corporation press releases. This is a one-way mailing list. There are approximately 8 press releases per week.

Keywords: DEC, Computers

Audience: Computing Consultants, Computing Analysts

Contact: Russ Jones
decnews-pr-request@pa.dec.com

User Info: To subscribe to the list, send an e-mail message requesting a subscription to the URL address below.

To send a message to the entire list, address it to: decnews-pr-request@pa.dec.com

Notes:User Info: To subscribe, send e-mail to decnews-pr@pa.dec.com with a subject line of

Subject: subscribe. Please include your name and telephone number in the body of the subscription request.

`mailto:decnews-pr-request@pa.dec.com`

DECnews-UNIX

DECnews for UNIX is published by Digital Equipment Corporation every three weeks and contains product and service information of interest to the Digital UNIX community.

Keywords: DEC, UNIX, Computers

Audience: UNIX Users

Contact: Russ Jones
decnews-unix-request@pa.dec.com

User Info: To subscribe to the list, send an e-mail message requesting a subscription to the URL address below.

To send a message to the entire list, address it to: decnews-unix-request@pa.dec.com

Notes:User Info: To subscribe, send e-mail to decnews-unix@pa.dec.com with a subject line of Subject: subscribe abstract. Please include your name and telephone number in the body of the subscription request.

`mailto:decnews-unix-request@pa.dec.com`

DECstation-managers

Fast-turnaround troubleshooting tool for managers of RISC DECstations.

Keywords: DEC, Computers

Audience: Computer Systems Analysts/ Programmers, Engineers

Contact: decstation-managers-request@ornl.gov

User Info: To subscribe to the list, send an e-mail message to the URL address shown below consisting of a single line reading:

SUB decstation-manager YourFirstName YourLastName

To send a message to the entire list, address it to: decstation-manager@msu.edu

A
B
C
D
E
F
G
H
I
J
K
L
M
N
O
P
Q
R
S
T
U
V
W
X
Y
Z

A
B
C
D
E
F
G
H
I
J
K
L
M
N
O
P
Q
R
S
T
U
V
W
X
Y
Z

`mailto:majordomo@ornl.gov`

DIGIT

A bimonthly publication containing information aimed at users of computing resources at the University of Colorado, Boulder.

Keywords: Computers, Computer Resources

Audience: University of Colorado Students, Computer Students

Contact: Suzanne Kincaid
kincaid@spot.colorado.edu

Details: Free

`mailto:kincaid@spot.colorado.edu`

dirt-users

Dirt is an X11-based UIMS.

Keywords: Computers

Audience: UIMS Users

Contact: dirt-users-request@ukc.ac.uk

User Info: To subscribe to the list, send an e-mail message requesting a subscription to the URL address below.

To send a message to the entire list, address it to: dirt-users@ukc.ac.uk

`mailto:dirt-users@ukc.ac.uk`

dist-users

This list is for discussions of issues related to the dist 3.0 package and its components: metaconfig, jmake, patch tools, and so on. The dist package was posted on comp.sources.misc (August 1993).

Keywords: dist, Computers

Audience: dist Users

Contact: Shigeya Suzuki
Raphael Manfredi

Contact: shigeya@foretune.co.jp
ram@acri.fr

User Info: To subscribe to the list, send an e-mail message to the URL address shown below consisting of a single line reading: SUB dist-users YourFirstName YourLastName

To send a message to the entire list, address it to: dist-users@msu.edu

`mailto:majordomo@foretune.co.jp`

dp-friends

This is a list for discussing Decision Power, a product of ICL Computers Limited composed of the logic programming language Prolog, the constraint handling system Chip, the database interface Seduce (runs on top of Ingres), the development environment Kegi (runs on X) and the end-user graphical display environment KHS (also runs on X).

Keywords: Computers

Audience: Computer Users

Contact: Ken Johnson
dp-friends-request@aiai.ed.ac.uk

User Info: To subscribe to the list, send an e-mail message requesting a subscription to the URL address below.

To send a message to the entire list, address it to: dp-friends-request@aiai.ed.ac.uk

`mailto:dp-friends-request@aiai.ed.ac.uk`

ESRI (Environmental Systems Research Institute)

Environmental Systems Research Institute, Inc. is the world leader in GIS technology. ARC/INFO is ESRI's powerful and flexible flagship GIS software.

Keywords: Geographic Information Systems (GIS), Environment, Software, Computers

Audience: Geographers, Environmentalists, Computer Users

Details: Costs

For product information, call (909)793-2853, X1475.

For training information, call (909)793-2853, X1585, or fax (909)793-5953.

`mailto:ajackson@esri.com`

Fam-Med

An Internet resource and discussion group on computers in family medicine.

Keywords: Medicine, Computers, Telecommunications

Sponsor: Gustavus Adolphus College, Minnesota

Audience: Health-CareProfessionals, Family Physicians

Profile: Fam-Med is an electronic conference and file area that focuses on the use of computer and telecommunication technologies in the teaching and practice of family medicine. The conference and files are accessible to anyone able to send e-mail. The discussion on Fam-Med is distributed in two ways: by an unmoderated mail echo in which all posted messages are immediately distributed to subscribers without human intervention, and by a digest where messages accumulated over several days are assembled into a single document with erroneous posts deleted.

Contact: Paul Kleeberg
paul@gac.edu

Details: Free

To join either the unmoderated list or the digest, send e-mail to the contact above. To post to Fam-Med, send e-mail to Fam-Med@GAC.Edu

`gopher://ftp.gac.edu/00/pub/E-mail-archives/fam-med/`

foxpro-l

This mailing list is designed to foster information sharing between users of the FoxPro™ database development environment now owned and distributed by Microsoft. Both new and experienced users of FoxPro are welcome to join in the discussions.

Keywords: Databases, Computers, Microsoft Corp.

Audience: Database Users, Microsoft FoxPro Users, Software Engineers

Contact: Chris O'Neill
coneill@heaven.polarbear.rankin-inlet.nt.ca

Details: Free

User Info: To subscribe to the list, send an e-mail message requesting a subscription to the URL address below.

To send a message to the entire list, address it to: foxpro-l@polarbear.rankin-inlet.nt.ca

`mailto:fileserv@polarbear.rankin-inlet.nt.ca`

General Hacking Info

Files on the topic of hacking.

Keywords: Hacking, Computers

Audience: Hackers, Computer Users

Details: Free

Expect: login,Send: anonymous;

Expect: Password,Send: Your e-mail Address

`ftp://ftp.eff.org`

GlobeTrotter

File concerning hacking from an international perspective.

Keywords: Hacking, Computers

Audience: Hackers, Computer Users

Details: Free

Expect: login,Send: anonymous;

Expect: Password,Send: Your e-mail Address

`ftp://ftp.eff.org`

Hacker's Network

File of hacking, published in Britain.

Keywords: Hacking, Computers

Audience: Hackers, Computer Users

Details: Free

Expect: login,Send: anonymous;

Expect: Password,Send: Your e-mail Address

`ftp://ftp.eff.org`

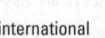

IMPACT ONLINE

The electronic version of IMPACT, the newsletter of the Social Impact group of the Boston Computer Society.

Keywords: Information Technology, Computer Ethics, Computers, Social Responsibility

Sponsor: Boston Computer Society, Boston, MA

Audience: Computer Users, Boston Residents, Information Scientists

Profile: The purpose of the Social Impact group is to provide a forum for the discussion of social and ethical concerns related to information technology.

Contact: Ian Wells
bcs-ssi@compass.com

Read on comp.society

You will need access to a newsreader.

`news:comp.society`

International Business Machines

This is IBM's main WWW server and it contains extensive links to information about the company and its products.

Keywords: Computers, Business

Audience: General Public

Profile: Industry Solutions, Products and Services, Technology information and News about the company.

Contact: mail to: askibm@www.ibm.com

`http://www.ibm.com`

Legion of Doom/Hackers Technical Journals

Technical journals of the infamous hacking ring Legion of Doom.

Keywords: Hacking, Computers

Audience: Hackers, Computer Users

Details: Free

Expect: login,Send: anonymous;

Expect: Password,Send: Your e-mail Address

`ftp://ftp.eff.org`

Microsoft FTP Site

Microsoft's file repository.

Keywords: Computers, Microsoft Corporations

Sponsor: Microsoft

Audience: Software Developers, Microsoft Product Users

Details: Free

`ftp://ftp.microsoft.com`

Nihon Sun Microsystems

This site provides a directory for Sun Microsystems in Japan. Includes the Rolling Stones Official Server WWW site, with access to Rolling Stones music, merchandise, and information. Also provides multimedia links to the Science University of Tokyo and other Asia-Pacific resources.

Keywords: Computers, Rolling Stones

Sponsor: Sun Microsystems, Inc., Tokyo, Japan

Audience: Computer Users, Rolling Stones Fans

Contact: www-admin@sun.co.jp

Details: Multimedia, Free, Sounds. Images

`http://www.sun.co.jp`

numeric-interest

Discussion of issues of floating-point correctness and performance with respect to hardware, operating systems, languages, and standard libraries.

Keywords: Computers, Computer Hardware

Audience: Computer Users

Contact: David Hough
numeric-interest-request@validgh.com

Details: Free

User Info: To subscribe to the list, send an e-mail message requesting a subscription to the URL address below.

To send a message to the entire list, address it to: numeric-interest@validgh.com

`mailto:numeric-interest-request@validgh.com`

Online Radio

Transcripts and promotional information from Online Radio, a weekly radio program of Perth's Curtin University devoted to reporting the latest developments in the computing world.

Keywords: Computers, Internet, Radio

Sponsor: Curtin University Computing Center, Perth, Australia

Audience: Computer Enthusiasts

Contact: Onno Benschop
online@info.curtin.edu.au

`gopher://ob1.curtin.edu.au`

Pc532

A mailing list for people interested in the pc532 project, a National Semiconductor NS32532-based system, offered at a low cost.

Keywords: Computers, Hardware, Software

Audience: Computer Users, Software Developers

Contact: Dave Rand
pc532-request@bungi.com

Details: Free

User Info: To subscribe to the list, send an e-mail message requesting a subscription to the URL address below.
To send a message to the entire list, address it to: pc532@bungi.com

`mailto:pc532-request@bungi.com`

Pcgeos-list

A discussion forum for users of PC/GEOS products, including GeoWorks Ensemble, GeoWorks Pro, GeoWorks POS, and third-party products. Topics include general information, tips, techniques, applications, and experiences.

Keywords: Computers, Software

Audience: Computer Users, Software Developers

Contact: listserv@pandora.sf.ca.us

Details: Free

User Info: To subscribe to the list, send an e-mail message to the URL address below, consisting of a single line reading:

SUB pcgeos-list YourFirstName YourLastName

To send a message to the entire list, address it to: pcgeos@pandora.sf.ca.us

`mailto:listserv@pandora.sf.ca.us`

Pdp8-lovers

A mailing list for owners of vintage DEC (Digital Equipment Corp.) computers, especially the PDP-8 series. Discussion topics include hardware, software, and programming techniques.

Keywords: Computers, Hardware, Software

Audience: Computer Users, Product Analysts

Contact: Robert E. Seastrom
pdp8-lovers-request@mc.lcs.mit.edu

Details: Free

User Info: To subscribe to the list, send an e-mail message requesting a subscription to the URL address below.
To send a message to the entire list, address it to: pdp8-lovers@mc.lcs.mit.edu

`mailto:pdp8-lovers@mc.lcs.mit.edu`

Prompt

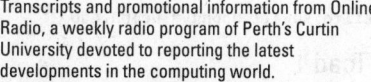

Contains news tips and briefs for the NCSU (North Carolina State University) campus community. Complementing the paper newsletter Connect, Prompt is designed to provide timely, up-to-date information concerning all platforms of computing.

A
B
C
D
E
F
G
H
I
J
K
L
M
N
O
P
Q
R
S
T
U
V
W
X
Y
Z

A B C D E F G H I J K L M N O P Q R S T U V W X Y Z

Keywords: Computers

Audience: NCSU Computer Students, Educators, Computer Users

Contact: Sarah Noell
sarah_noell@ncsu.edu

Details: Free

User Info: To subscribe to the list, send an e-mail message to the URL address below, consisting of a single line reading:

prompt YourFirstName YourLastName

To send a message to the entire list, address it to: prompt@cc.ncsu.edu

`mailto:listserv@cc.ncsu.edu`

REACH (Research and Educational Applications of Computers in the Humanities)

Newsletter of the Humanities Computing Facility of the University of California, Santa Barbara. Contains material of general interest to computing humanists, including announcements of new listservers, projects, and conferences.

Keywords: Computers

Audience: Computer Users

Contact: Eric Dahlin
HCF1DAHL@UCSBvm.bitnet

Details: Free

listserv@ucsbvm.bitnet

reach@ucsbvm.bitnet

`mailto:listserv@ucsbvm.bitnet`

SUMEX-AIM

★★★★

An FTP archive of software, demonstration programs, and various applications, especially for Macintosh computers.

Keywords: Computers, Macintosh, Software

Audience: Computer Users, Macintosh Users

Details: Free

`ftp://sumex-aim.Stanford.edu`

Texas: Computer Crimes Statute

★

Lists text of the Texas Computer Crimes Statute.

Keywords: Computers, Crime, Texas

Audience: Lawyers, Computer Programmers, Computer Operators

Details: Free

Select from menu as appropriate

`gopher://wiretap.spies.com`

The Black Box Catalog

The Black Box Catalog, the industry's most complete source for data communication equipment, is now available on the Internet. The complete range of products, technical references, and application briefs are available on the Black Box World Wide Web Server.

Keywords: Communications, Networking, Telecommunication, Computers

Sponsor: Black Box Corporation, Lawrence, PA

Audience: Engineers, Network Administration, LAN Administrators, Communication Specialists

Profile: Black Box Corporation is a leading international supplier of data communications networking and related computer connectivity products. Black Box's commitment to providing effective solutions that substantially enhance the capabilities of communications systems is backed by a technical support staff that is available around the clock, a liberal 45-day return policy, and same day shipment of its 6000 products.

Contact: Webmaster
webmaster@blackbox.com

Details: Costs

`http://www.blackbox.com`

VapourWare

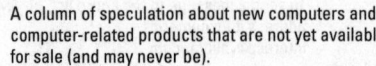

A column of speculation about new computers and computer-related products that are not yet available for sale (and may never be).

Keywords: Computers

Audience: Computer Users

Contact: Murphy Sewall
sewall@UConnVM.UConn.Edu

Details: Free

`mailto:sewall@uconnvm.uconn.edu`

VTcad-L

★

This E-conference is for discussion of CAD by Va Tech users. Discussion includes: CAD applications, CAD hardware, CAD networking.

Keywords: Computer Graphics, Computers

Audience: Computer Graphic Designers, Engineers, Architects

Contact: Darrell A. Early
bestuur@VTVM1.cc.vt.edu

Details: Free

User Info: To subscribe to the list, send an e-mail message to the URL address below consisting of a single line reading:

SUB vtcad-L YourFirstName YourLastName

To send a message to the entire list, address it to: vtcad-L@vtvm1.cc.vt.edu

`mailto:listserv@vtvm1.cc.vt.edu`

Works

Works discusses personal workstation computers, such as the Sun2, Sun3, Apollo, Silicon Graphics, and AT&T workstations. Works provides a way for interested members of the Internet community to discuss and share useful insights about these kinds of systems.

Keywords: Workstations, Computers

Audience: Workstation Users, Computer Users

Contact: Dave Steiner
steiner@rutgers.edu

Details: Free

User Info: To subscribe to the list, send an e-mail message requesting a subscription to the URL address below.

`mailto:works@rutgers.edu`

Computing

Academic Computing Training & User Support

This directory is a compilation of information resources focusing on academic computer training and user support.

Keywords: Computing, Academics

Audience: Computer Users

`ftp://una.hh.lib.umich.edu/70/`
`inetdirsstacks/acadcomp/kovacsm`

BFU (Brussels Free Universities)

★

The gopher server of the Brussels Free Universities VUB /ULB is the national entry point for EMBnet in Belgium and provides links to university library systems and EMBnet databases.

Keywords: Computing, EMBnet, Belgium, Europe

Audience: Scientists, Biologists, Biotechnologists

Contact: support@vub.ac.be

Details: Free

`gopher://gopher.vub.ac.be`

comp.databases

A Usenet newsgroup providing information and discussion about databases and data management issues.

Keywords: Computing, Computer Databases

Audience: Computer Users

User Info: To subscribe to this Usenet newsgroup, you need access to a newsreader.

`news:comp.databases`

ETHCSE-L

A mailing list for the discussion of ethical issues in software engineering, dealing with subjects of interest to professional software engineers.

Keywords: Engineering, Computing, Ethics

Audience: Engineers, Software Engineers, Researchers

Contact: Margaret Mason
MASON@UTKVml.utk.edu

Details: Free

User Info: To subscribe to the list, send an e-mail message to the URL address shown below consisting of a single line reading:

SUB ethcse-l YourFirstName YourLastName

To send a message to the entire list, address it to:

ethcse-l@utkvm1.utk.edu

`mailto: listserv@utkvm1.UTK.EDU`

High-Performance Computing Act of 1991

★★★

This is a Senate bill to provide for a coordinated federal research program to ensure continued US leadership in high-performance computing.

Keywords: Computing, Government (US Federal), Law (US Federal)

Audience: General Public, Journalists, Politicians, Scientists

Details: Free

File is: /internet/nren/hpca.1991/ gorebill.1991-txt

`ftp://nis.nsf.net`

Imperial College Department of Computing

★★

This is the home of the department of Computing, Imperial College, United Kingdom, the UKUUG (UK UNIX User Group) Archive and the DoC Information Service.

Keywords: Computing, United Kingdom, Europe

Audience: Computer Scientists

Contact: imjm@doc.ic.ac.uk

Details: Free

`gopher://src.doc.ic.ac.uk`

`http://src.doc.ic.ac.uk`

INSPEC

IINSPEC corresponds to the three Science Abstracts print publications: Physics Abstracts, Electrical and Electronics Abstracts, and Computer and Control Abstracts.

Keywords: Physics, Electronic, Computing

Sponsor: Institution of Electrical Engineers, London, UK

Audience: Physicists, Electrical Engineers, Computer Specialists

Profile: Approximately 16 percent of the database's source publications are in languages other than English, but all articles are abstracted and indexed in English. The special DIALOG online thesaurus feature is available to assist searchers in determining appropriate subject terms and codes.

Contact: Dialog in the US at (800) 334-2564, Dialog internationally at country-specific locations.

User Info: To subscribe, contact Dialog directly.

Notes: Coverage: April 1969 to the present; updated weekly.

`telnet://dialog.com`

Metacard-list

Discussion of the MetaCard product from MetaCard Corp. MetaCard is an application-development system similar to Apple's HyperCard product; it runs on a variety of popular platforms in a UNIX/X11/Motif environment.

Keywords: MetaCard, Computing, UNIX

Audience: MetaCard Users, Computer Users

Contact: metacard-list-owner@grot.starconn.com

Details: Free

Notes:User Info: To subscribe to the list, send an e-mail message requesting a subscription to the URL address below.

`mailto:metacard-list@grot.starconn.com`

Pen-pals

★

This mailing list provides a forum for children to correspond with each other electronically. Although the list is not moderated, it is monitored for content and is managed by listproc.

Keywords: Computing, Children, Writing

Audience: Computer Users, Children, Student Writers

Contact: pen-pals-request@mainstream.com

Details: Free

User Info: To subscribe to the list, send an e-mail message requesting a subscription to the URL address below.

To send a message to the entire list, address it to: pen-pals@mainstream.com

`mailto:pen-pals@mainstream.com`

picasso-users

A mailing list for users of the Picasso Graphical User Interface Development System.

Keywords: Computing, Computer Graphics

Audience: Computer Users, Computer Graphic Designers, Graphics

Contact: picasso-users@postgres.berkeley.edu

Details: Free

User Info: To subscribe to the list, send an e-mail message requesting a subscription to the URL address below.

To send a message to the entire list, address it to: picasso-users@postgres.berkeley.edu

`mailto:picasso-users@postgres.berkeley.edu`

Progress

Discussion of the Progress RDBMS (Relational Database Management System).

Keywords: Databases, Computing

Audience: Computer Users, Business Students

Contact: Progress-list-request@math.niu.edu

Details: Free

User Info: To subscribe to the list, send an e-mail message requesting a subscription to the URL address below.

To send a message to the entire list, address it to: progress-list@math.niu.edu

`mailto:Progress-list-request@math.niu.edu`

Project-management

★

The aim of the list is to discuss project-management techniques generally, as well as project-management software and programs.

Keywords: Project Management, Computing, Software

Audience: Business Professionals, Business Students

Contact: project-management-request@smtl.demon.co.uk

Details: Free

User Info: To subscribe to the list, send an e-mail message requesting a subscription to the URL address below.

To send a message to the entire list, address it to: project-management@smtl.demon.co.uk

`mailto:project-management-request@smtl.demon.co.uk`

Proof-users

Discussion of the left-associative natural language "parser proof."

A
B
C
D
E
F
G
H
I
J
K
L
M
N
O
P
Q
R
S
T
U
V
W
X
Y
Z

A
B
C
D
E
F
G
H
I
J
K
L
M
N
O
P
Q
R
S
T
U
V
W
X
Y
Z

Keywords: Computing, Programming

Audience: Computer Programmers

Contact: Craig Latta
proof-request@xcf.berkeley.edu

Details: Free

To join, e-mail proof-request@xcf.berkeley.edu with the subject line "add me".

`mailto:proof-request@xcf.berkeley.edu`

Qnx2

Discussion of all aspects of the QNX real-time operating systems. Topics include compatible hardware, available third-party software, software reviews, available PD/free software, QNX platform-specific programming discussions, and QNX and FLEET networking.

Keywords: Computing, Hardware, Software

Audience: Computer Users, Hardware/Software Designers, Product Analysts

Contact: Martin Zimmerman
camz@dlogtech.cuc.ab.ca

Details: Free

User Info: To subscribe to the list, send an e-mail message requesting a subscription to the URL address below.
To send a message to the entire list, address it to: qnx2@dlogtech.cuc.ab.ca

`mailto:qnx2@dlogtech.cuc.ab.ca`

Qnx4

A mailing list for discussion of all aspects of the QNX real-time operating systems. Topics include compatible hardware, available third-party software, software reviews, available PD/free software, QNX and FLEET networking, process control, and so on.

Keywords: Computing, Hardware, Software, Networking

Audience: Computer Users, Hardware/Software Designers, Product Analysts

Contact: Martin Zimmerman
camz@dlogtech.cuc.ab.ca

Details: Free

User Info: To subscribe to the list, send an e-mail message requesting a subscription to the URL address below.
To send a message to the entire list, address it to: qnx4@dlogtech.cuc.ab.ca

`mailto:qnx4@dlogtech.cuc.ab.ca`

soc.penpals

A Usenet newsgroup providing information and discussion for people in search of Net pals and other online correspondence.

Keywords: Computing, Writing

Audience: Computer Users, Writers

Details: Free

User Info: To subscribe to this Usenet newsgroup, you need access to a newsreader.

`news:soc.penpals`

Supercomputers

Weekly mailing list of the world's most powerful computing sites.

Keywords: Supercomputers, Computing

Audience: Supercomputer Users, computer scientists

Contact: gunter@yarrow.wt.uwa.oz.au

Details: Free

User Info: To subscribe to the list, send an e-mail message requesting a subscription to the URL address below.
To send a message to the entire list, address it to:
gunter@yarrow.wt.uwa.oz.au

`mailto:gunter@yarrow.wt.uwa.oz.au`

UTIRC (University of Toronto Instructional and Research Computing

This site provides information in the areas of instructional technology and applications, support for multimedia and visualization techniques, and access to and support for high-performance computing.

Keywords: Computing, Computer Programming, Computer-Aided Design

Sponsor: University of Toronto, Division of Computing, Toronto, Canada

Audience: Programmers, Designers

Details: Free

`http://www.utirc.utoronto.ca/`
`HTMLdocs/NewHTML/intro.html`

Computing and Network News

Computing and Network News

A newsletter published 10 times a year for the Kansas State University community.

Keywords: Computers, Computer Networks, Computer Science

Sponsor: Kansas State University

Audience: Kansas State University Students, Educators

Contact: Betsy Edwards
betsy@ksuvm.ksu.edu

Details: Free

`mailto:editor@ksuvm.ksu.edu`

Computists' Communique

Computists' Communique

A weekly newsletter serving professionals in artificial intelligence, information science, and computer science.

Keywords: Artificial Intelligence, Information Science, Computer Science

Audience: Computer Scientists, Information Scientists, Computists International Members

Profile: Content is career oriented and depends partly on contributions from members. The moderator filters submissions, reports and comments on industry news, collects common knowledge about academia and industry, and helps track people and projects. The Communique is only available to members of Computists International, a networking association for computer and information scientists. It is an association for mutual mentoring about grant and funding sources, information channels, applications, text, software publishing, and the sociology of work.

Contact: Kenneth I. Laws
laws@ari.sri.com

Details: Costs

`mailto:laws@ari.sri.com`

Comserve

Newsline

An electronic newsletter describing additions to or changes in Comserve, the electronic information and discussion service for communications faculty and students.

Keywords: Communications, Comserve

Audience: Communications Students, Communications Specialists

Profile: The information includes announcements of additions to Comserve's database, new services offered through Comserve's electronic conferences, or fundamental changes in the services offered by Comserve.

Contact: Timothy Stephen, Teresa Harrison
Support@RpiecsSupport@Vm.Ecs.Rpi.Edu

User Info: To subscribe, send an e-mail message to the URL address below consisting of a single line reading:

SUB NEWSLINE YourFirstName YourLastName

`mailto:Comserve@Vm.Ecs.Rpi.Edu`

Concrete Blonde

concrete-blonde

This list discusses the rock group Concrete Blonde and related artists and issues.

Keywords: Pop Music, Concrete Blonde

Audience: Concrete Blonde Enthusiasts, Pop Music Enthusiasts

Contact: Robert Earl
concrete-blonde-request@piggy.ucsb.edu

Details: Free

User Info: To subscribe to the list, send an e-mail message requesting a subscription to the URL address below.

To send a message to the entire list, address it to:

concrete-blonde@piggy.ucsb.edu

`mailto:concrete-blonde-request@piggy.ucsb.edu`

Concurrent Logic

Clp.x

Devoted to discussion of concurrent logic programming languages, concurrent constraint programming languages, semantics, proof techniques and program transformations, parallel Prolog systems, implementations, and programming techniques and idioms.

Keywords: Programming, Programming Languages, Concurrent Logic

Audience: Concurrent Logic Programmers

Contact: Jacob Levy
jlevy.pa@xerox.com

Details: Free

User Info: To subscribe to the list, send an e-mail message requesting a subscription to the URL address below.

To send a message to the entire lst, address it to: clp.x@xerox.com

`mailto:clp-request.x@xerox.com`

Conference about Virtual Reality (The)

Conference about Virtual Reality (The)

A conference on the WELL about cyberspace and virtual reality.

Keywords: Virtual Reality, Art, Cyberspace

Audience: Artists, Computer Programmers, Cyberpunks

Contact: Peter Rothman
avatarp@well.sf.ca.us

To participate in a conference on the WELL, you must first establish an account on the WELL. To do so, start by typing: telnet woll.sf.ca.us

`telnet://well.sf.ca.us`

Conferences

news.announce.conferences

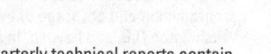

A Usenet newsgroup providing information and discussion about conferences, as well as calls for papers.

Keywords: Conferences, Papers, Writing

Audience: Writers, General Public

Details: Free

User Info: To subscribe to this Usenet newsgroup, you need access to a newsreader.

`news:news.announce.conferences`

Scholarly Communication

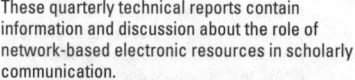

These quarterly technical reports contain information and discussion about the role of network-based electronic resources in scholarly communication.

Keywords: Education, Scholarly Communication, Conferences

Audience: Educators, Researchers

Details: Free

File is: pub/vpiej-l/reports

`ftp://borg.lib.vt.edu/pub/vpiej-1/reports`

`http://borg.lib.vt.edu/scholar.info.html`

Conferencing Systems

Computer Network Conferencing

Discussions on the topic of computer network conferencing. The memo is intended to make more people aware of the present developments in the computer conferencing field as well as to put forward ideas on what should be done to formalize this work.

Keywords: Internet, Conferencing Systems

Audience: Internet Surfers

Contact: Darren Reed
avalon@coombs.anu.edu.au

Details: Free

File is: documents/rfc/rfc1324.txt

`ftp://nic.merit.edu`

DECuserve-journal

A monthly digest of technical discussions that take place on the DECUS conferencing system, open to anyone who is interested in Digital Equipment topics, "3rd party" topics, and connectivity topics.

Keywords: DECUS, Conferencing Systems

Audience: Conferencing System Users

Contact: Sharon Frey
frey@eisner.decus.org

User Info: To subscribe to the list, send an e-mail message requesting a subscription to the URL address below.

To send a message to the entire list, address it to: frey@eisner.decus.org

`mailto:frey@eisner.decus.org`

Conflict Resolution

CSF: Communications for a Sustainable Future

A gopher server for the distribution of Conflict Resolution Materials.

Keywords: Conflict Resolution, Community, Politics

Sponsor: Communications for a Sustainable Future

Audience: Activists, Policy Analysts, Community Leaders, Mediators, Lawyers

Profile: Communications for a Sustainable Future is a collective effort of several scholars. CSF does research, education, and applied work. Its main subject areas are: Intractable Conflicts and Constructive Confrontation, Environmental and Public Policy Dispute Resolution, Social/Political Conflicts, International Conflicts.

Contact: roper@csf.colorado.edu

Details: Free

`gopher://csf.colorado.edu`

NAME (National Association for Mediation in Education) Publications and Resources List

This is a tax-exempt clearinghouse of information promoting conflict resolution, mediation, and violence prevention in schools. NAME also publishes a newsletter and has a directory of over 120 resources, including guidelines for conflict resolution, and technical assistance.

A
B
C
D
E
F
G
H
I
J
K
L
M
N
O
P
Q
R
S
T
U
V
W
X
Y
Z

Keywords: Conflict Resolution, Mediation, Education (K-12)

Sponsor: National Association for Mediation in Education, University of Massachusetts, Amherst, Massachusetts, USA

Audience: Counselors, Educators, Administrators, Parents

Contact: Clarinda Merripen
ConflictNet@agc.ipc.org

Request introductory packet from address below.

`mailto:ConflictNet@agc.ipc.org`

Congo Languages

Harvard University Library

The library's holdings are large and wide-ranging and contain significant collections in many fields.

Keywords: Afrikaans, Alchemy, Arabic Culure (History of), Celtic Philology, Congo Languages, Folklore, Hebraica, Mormonism, Numismatics, Quakers, Sanskrit, Witchcraft, Arabic Philology

Audience: General Public, Researchers, Librarians, Document Delivery Professionals

Details: Free

Expect: Mitek Server..., Send: Enter or Return; Expect: prompt, Send: hollis

`telnet://hollis.harvard.edu`

Congress (US)

ACLU Free Reading Room

A gopher site containing information relating to the ACLU (American Civil Liberties Union), including the current issue of the ACLU newsletter, Civil Liberties; a growing collection of recent public policy reports and action guides; Congressional voting records for the 103rd Congress; and an archive of news releases from the ACLU's national headquarters.

Keywords: ACLU, Civil Liberties, Congress (US), Activism

Sponsor: ACLU (American Civil Liberties Union)

Audience: Privacy Activists, Civil Libertarians, Activists

Contact: infoaclu@aclu.org

`gopher://aclu.org`

America

For people interested in how the United States is dealing with foreign trade policies, congressional status, and other inside information about the government that is freely distributable.

Keywords: Trade, Government (US), Congress (US), Business (International)

Audience: General Public, Researchers, Journalists, Political Scientists, Students

Contact: subscribe@xamiga.linet.org

User Info: To subscribe to the list, send an e-mail message to the URL address below, consisting of a single line reading:

SUB america YourFirstName YourLastName

To send a message to the entire list, address it to: america@xamiga.linet.org

Notes: This list has monthly postings that are generally in large batches, with posts exceeding a few hundred lines.

`mailto:subscribe@xamiga.linet.org`

C-SPAN (Cable-Satellite Public Affairs Network) Gopher

Online information from C-SPAN, the public affairs television network.

Keywords: News Media, Government, Congress (US), Television

Sponsor: C-SPAN

Audience: Journalists, Government Officials, Educators (K-12), General Public

Profile: Comprehensive listings of C-SPAN's programming and coverage of events in Washington D.C. and beyond. In addition to the programming notes and schedules, this site also features online educational resources sponsored by C-SPAN, text of historic documents and speeches, and background political information on the House of Representatives and the Supreme Court.

Contact: cspanviewr@aol.com

Details: Free

`gopher://c-span.org`

CMPGN (Campaign Library)

The CMPGN library contains information and news about US Congressional, Senatorial, Gubernatorial and Presidentail elections. The media, political campaigns, and others whose responsibilities include monotoring activity on the campaign trail will find CMPGN to be a unique and comprehensive source of information for campaign research.

Keywords: Politics (US), Congress (US)

Audience: Journalists, Political Researchers

Profile: CMPGN allows searching of individual files or group files that cover topics such as candidate and incumbent profiles; Honoraria, PACs, and demographic and media profiles; Committee and Floor voting records and floor statement indexes for all House and Senate incumbents; and reputable sources of news that are known for their in-depth

campaign coverage, including the Hotline, the Cook Political Report, ABC news Transcripts, Roll Call, States News Service, US Newswire, Federal News Service, and much more.

Contact: Mead New Sales Group at (800) 227-4908 or (513) 859-5398 inside the US, or (513) 865-7981 for all inquiries outside the US.

User Info: To subscribe, contact Mead directly.

To examine the Nexis user guide, you can access it at the ftp site of the University of Texas at Austin at the URL address: ftp://ftp.cc.utexas.edu

The files are in: /pub/ref-services/LEXIS

`telnet://nex.meaddata.com`

`http://www.meaddata.com`

Congressional Contact Information

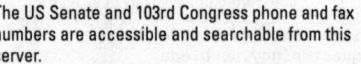

The US Senate and 103rd Congress phone and fax numbers are accessible and searchable from this server.

Keywords: Congress (US), Directories, Government (US)

Sponsor: Library of Congress

Audience: General Public, Journalists, Students, Politicians

Details: Free

`gopher://marvel.loc.gov/11/congress/directory`

Congressional Quarterly Gopher

Online Information from Congressional Quarterly (CQ), the premier journal covering events on Capitol Hill.

Keywords: Congress (US), Government (US Federal), Laws (US Federal)

Sponsor: Congressional Quarterly

Audience: Journalists, Government Officials, Educators, General Public

Profile: This gopher allows access to weekly stories and news briefs from CQ, as well as providing information on legislation before Congress, Congressional voting records, and results of recent federal elections. Also has catalogs of CQ's publications and schedules of their professional education seminars.

Contact: gopher_admin@cqalert.com

Details: Free

`gopher://gopher.cqalert.com`

GAO

Files intended to provide Congress and Administration with an overview of health problems facing the nation.

Keywords: Health, Congress (US)

Audience: US Congress, Journalists, General Public

Profile: These files concern health-care reform and human services and date from December 1992. They are provided by the government to familiarize the reader with the health issues confronting the administration.

Details: Free

Login: anonymous

Notes: ABSTRACT.FIL is a file with abstracts for each of the 28 reports.

`ftp://cu.nig.gov`

University of Tennessee at Knoxville Library

The library's holdings are large and wide-ranging and contain significant collections in many fields.

Keywords: Native American Affairs, Congress (US), Folklore, Travel (History of)

Audience: Researchers, Students, General Public

Details: Free

Expect: OK Prompt; Send: Login pub1; Expect: Password, Send: Usc

`telnet://opac.lib.utk.edu`

US House of Representatives Gopher

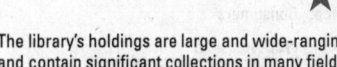

The online service of the U.S. House of Representatives.

Keywords: Congress (US), Federal Law (US), Government Records (US)

Sponsor: House Administration Committee Internet Working Group

Audience: Government Officials, Journalists, Educators (K-12), General Public

Profile: Provides access to information on members and committees of the House of Representatives, as well as full-text of bills before the House. Includes education resources on the legislative process, Congressional directories, and House schedules. Also has information for visitors (including area maps), as well as access to other federal information systems.

Contact: House Internet Working Group househlp@hr.house.gov

`gopher://gopher.house.gov`

Connectivity

alt.config

A Usenet newsgroup providing information and discussion about alternative subnet discussions and connectivity.

Keywords: Internet, Computer Networks, Connectivity

Audience: Network Administrators

User Info: To subscribe to this Usenet newsgroup, you need access to a newsreader.

`news:alt.config`

Conservation

consgis

A discussion list for those using GIS (Geographic Information Systems) in the interest of conservation.

Keywords: Conservation, Environment, GIS (Geographic Information Systems)

Audience: Geographers, Environmentalists, Cartographers

Contact: Dr. Peter August pete@edcserv.edc.uri.edu

Details: Free

User Info: To subscribe to the list, send an e-mail message to the URL address below consisting of a single line reading:

SUB consgis YourFirstName YourLastName.

To send a message to the entire list, address it to: consgis@uriacc.uri.edu

`mailto:listserv@uriacc.uri.edu`

Conspiracy

alt.conspiracy

A Usenet newsgroup providing discussion about conspiracy and paranoia.

Keywords: Conspiracy, Paranoia

Audience: Paranoid Persons, General Public

User Info: To subscribe to this Usenet newsgroup, you need access to a newsreader.

`news:alt.conspiracy`

Constitution

alt.censorship

A Usenet newsgroup providing information and discussion about freedom of speech and freedom of the press.

Keywords: Censorship, Freedom of Speech, Constitution, Activism

Audience: Press, Students, Educators, Activists

User Info: To subscribe to this Usenet newsgroup, you need access to a newsreader.

`news:alt.censorship`

Utah State Constitution

Lists full text of the Utah State Constitution 1991.

Keywords: Utah, Constitution

Audience: Utah Residents, Historians

`gopher://wiretap.spies.com`

Constitutional Amendments

Amend2-info

Colorado voted in an amendment to their state constitution which revokes any existing gay/lesbian/bisexual civil rights legislation and prohibits the drafting of any new legislation. This moderated list is for information on the implication and issues of this amendment.

Keywords: Activists, Gay, Lesbian, Bisexual, Constitutional Amendments, Colorado, Civil Rights

Audience: General Public, Gays, Lesbians, Bisexuals, Activists

Contact: amend2-info@cs.colorado.edu

User Info: To subscribe to the list, send an e-mail message requesting a subscription to the URL address below.

To send a message to the entire list, address it to: amend2-info@cs.colorado.edu

`mailto:majordomo@cs.colorado.edu`

Constitutional Law

University of Texas at Austin Tarlton Law Library

The library's holdings are large and wide-ranging and contain significant collections in many fields. British Commonwealth Law, Constitutional Law, International Law, Human Rights

Keywords: British Commonwealth Law, Constitutional Law, Law (International), Human Rights

Audience: Researchers, Students, General Public

Details: Free

Expect: Login, Send: Library

`telnet://tallons.law.utexas.edu`

A
B
C
D
E
F
G
H
I
J
K
L
M
N
O
P
Q
R
S
T
U
V
W
X
Y
Z

Construction

Architecture, Building

This directory is a compilation of information resources focused on architecture.

Keywords: Architecture, Building, Construction, AEC

Audience: Architects, Builders, Civil Engineers

Contact: J. Brown

Details: Free

```
ftp://una.hh.lib.umich.edu/70/
inetdirsstacks/archi:brown
```

Lego Information

A web site containing pictures, sets, and instructions for building with Legos. Also discusses various ideas, activities, and history pertaining to Legos, as well as information about clubs for Lego enthusiasts.

Keywords: Construction, Toys, Children

Sponsor: Lego

Audience: Children, General Public

Contact: David Koblas
koblas@netcom.com

```
http://legowww.itek.norut.no
```

Consumer Goods

Consumer News

Contains consumer information about products ranging from bargain airline tickets to personal computers.

Keywords: Consumer Goods

Audience: Consumers

Details: Free

```
gopher://gopher.cic.net/00/e-serials/
alphabetic/c/consumer-news/
AboutIndex.gz
```

```
http://gopher.cis.net
```

misc.forsale

A Usenet newsgroup providing information and discussion about items for sale.

Keywords: Consumer Goods

Audience: General Public

Details: Free

User Info: To subscribe to this Usenet newsgroup, you need access to a newsreader.

```
news:misc.forsale
```

Consumer Rights

Privacy Rights Clearinghouse (PRC)

A collection of materials related to privacy issues.

Keywords: Privacy, Legislation, Consumer Rights, Freedom of Information

Sponsor: University of San Diego

Audience: Citizens, Privacy Activists, Journalists

Profile: This site contains fact sheets (in English and Spanish) on privacy issues ranging from wiretapping to credit reporting. Also includes federal and state privacy legislation as well as related position papers and press releases.

Contact: prc@teetot.acusd.edu

Expect: Login; Send: Privacy

```
gopher://teetot.acusd.edu
```

```
telnet://teetot.acusd.edu
```

Consumer Science

Purdue University Library

The library's holdings are large and wide-ranging. They contain significant collections in many fields.

Keywords: Economics (History of), Literature (English), Literature (American), Indiana, Rogers (Bruce), Engineering (History of), Aviation, Earth Science, Atmospheric Science, Consumer Science, Family Science, Chemistry (History of), Physics, Veterinary Science

Audience: General Public, Researchers, Librarians, Document Delivery Professionals

Contact: Dan Ferrer
dan@asterix.lib.purdue.edu

Details: Free

Expect: User ID prompt, Send: GUEST

```
telnet://lib.cc.purdue.edu
```

Consumerism

misc.consumers

A Usenet newsgroup providing information and discussion about consumer interests, including product reviews.

Keywords: Consumerism

Audience: Consumers, General Public

Details: Free

User Info: To subscribe to this Usenet newsgroup, you need access to a newsreader.

```
news:misc.consumers
```

misc.wanted

A Usenet newsgroup providing information and discussion about items, excluding software, that are wanted or needed.

Keywords: Consumerism

Audience: General Public

Details: Free

User Info: To subscribe to this Usenet newsgroup, you need access to a newsreader.

```
news:misc.wanted
```

U.S. Consumer Product Safety Commission (CPSC)

The CPSC's mission is to protect the public from defective and potentially dangerous consumer products. This gopher has archives of CPSC press releases and action reports from 1990-1994, as well as a calendar of upcoming events and guidelines for reporting potentially dangerous products to the CPSC.

Keywords: Safety, Consumerism, Laws (US Federal)

Sponsor: US Consumer Product Safety Commission

Audience: Consumers, Activists

Contact: pweddle@cpsc.gov

Notes: You can call the CPSC at their toll-free hotline at (800) 638-2772.

```
gopher://cpsc.gov
```

Contemporary Letters

Colby College Library

The library's holdings are large and wide-ranging and contain significant collections in many fields.

Keywords: Contemporary Letters, Hardy (Thomas),James (Henry), Mann (Thomas, Collections of), Housman (A.E., Letters of), Maine Authors, Irish History (Modern)

Audience: General Public, Researchers, Librarians, Document Delivery Professionals

Details: Free

Expect: login, Send: library

```
telnet://library.colby.edu
```

Contemporary Music

Northwestern University Library ★★

The library's holdings are large and wide-ranging and contain significant collections in many fields.

Keywords: Africa, Wright (Frank Lloyd), Women's Studies, Art, Literature (American), Contemporary Music, Government (US State), UN Documents, Music

Audience: General Public, Researchers, Librarians, Document Delivery Professionals

Details: Free

Expect: COMMAND:, Send: DIAL VTAM

`telnet://nuacvm.acns.nwu.edu`

Convex Computers

Convex Customer Satisfaction Information Server ★

An online customer help server for Convex computer users.

Keywords: Computers, Convex Computers

Sponsor: Convex Computer Corporation

Audience: Convex Computer Users

Contact: iserv_admin@convex.com

Details: Free

Notes: Convex has its own gopher client, called "cxgopher."

`gopher://iserv.convex.com`

Cooking

rec.food.cooking ★

A Usenet newsgroup providing information and discussion about cooking.

Keywords: Food, Cooking

Audience: General Public, Cooks, Chefs

User Info: To subscribe to this Usenet newsgroup, you need access to a newsreader.

`news:rec.food.cooking`

rec.food.veg ★

A Usenet newsgroup providing information and discussion about vegetarian cooking.

Keywords: Vegetarianism, Food, Cooking

Audience: Vegetarians, Cooks, Chefs

User Info: To subscribe to this Usenet newsgroup, you need access to a newsreader.

`news:rec.food.veg`

Recipe Archive ★★★

This is an archive of recipes organized by main ingredient or title.

Keywords: Cooking, Food

Audience: General Public, Cooks, Chefs

Profile: Here are a few intriguing examples from the archive:

Advokaat: Advokaat is the Dutch word for egg cognac. It is highly recommended for A. I. (Alcohol Imbibing) meetings. This recipe is a modification of a recipe obtained in Poland. It makes a potent, superb advokaat (or egg cognac). The milk and eggs are healthy, the sugar and alcohol are not!

Berlinerkranzer: Norwegian wreath cookies are decorative holiday cookies that add quite a bright, colorful, aromatic touch to your plate of cookies.

Bouillabaisse: This recipe for Marseille-style fish soup represents a combination of several recipes derived from old Gourmets, Julia Child, the Playboy Gourmet Cookbook, and "Gee, that sounds good, let's add it.." The accompanying rouille is a garlic/hot pepper mayonnaise condiment traditional to Marseille-style fish soup.

Details: Free

gopher://calypso.oit.unc.edu/ 7waissrc%3a/ref.d/indexes.d/recipes.src

gopher://calypso.oit.unc.edu/ 7waissrc%3a/ref.d/indexes.d/ usenet-cookbook.sr

They can also be accessed through mosaic at the URL address shown below or from the calypso.oit.unc.edu gopher in the subdirectories: Internet Dog-Eared Pages (Frequently used resources)/ Search Many WAIS Indices

Notes: There are two searchable gopher indexes containing recipes that have passed through the rec.food.cooking and rec.food.recipes newsgroups. They can be found at the following URL addresses:

`ftp://gatekeeper.dec.com/pub/recipes`

The World Wide Web rec.food.recipes archive

World-Wide Web archive of recipes posted to Usenet newsgroup rec.food.recipes. Updated weekly.

Keywords: Food, Recipes, Cooking

Audience: Cooks, General Public

Contact: Amy Gale mara@kauri.vuw.ac.nz

User Info: Use a World-Wide Web (WWW) client such as lynx

`http://www.vuw.ac.nz/non-local/ recipes-archive/recipe-archive.html`

COOMBSQUEST Social Sciences and Humanities Information Facility

COOMBSQUEST Social Sciences and Humanities Information Facility ★★★★

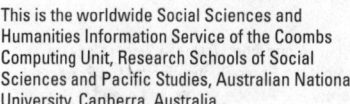

This is the worldwide Social Sciences and Humanities Information Service of the Coombs Computing Unit, Research Schools of Social Sciences and Pacific Studies, Australian National University, Canberra, Australia.

Keywords: Social Science Humanities Australia

Sponsor: Australian National University

Audience: Social Scientists, Humanists, Researchers, Educators, Students

Profile: COOMBSQUEST provides direct access to the Coombspapers Social Sciences Research Data Bank. The databank was established in December 1991 to act as the world's major electronic repository of social science and humanities papers, and other high-grade research material dealing with Australia, the Pacific region, and Southeast and Northeast Asia, Buddhism, Taoism, and other Oriental religions.

Contact: T. Matthew Ciolek tmciolek@coombs.anu.edu.au

Details: Free

`gopher://coombs.anu.edu.au`

`http://combs.anu.edu.au./ CoombsHome.html`

Cooperatives

COHOUSING-L ★

A list for discussion of cohousing, the name of a type of collaborative housing that has been developed primarily in Denmark since 1972 where it is known as bofoellesskaber. Cohousing is housing designed to foster community and cooperation while preserving independence. Private residences are clustered near shared facilities. The members design and manage all aspects of their community.

Keywords: Community, Housing, Cooperatives

Audience: Urban Planners, Architects, General Contractors

Contact: fholson@uci.com

Details: Free

User Info: To subscribe to the list, send an e-mail message to the address below consisting of a single line reading:

A B C D E F G H I J K L M N O P Q R S T U V W X Y Z

SUB COHOUSING-L YourFirstName
YourLastName

To send a message to the entire list,
address it to: COHOUSING-L@uci.com

`mailto:listserv@uci.com`

Copyright

Berne Convention Implementation Act of 1988 ★

An act to amend Title 17, United States Code, to
implement the Berne Convention for the Protection
of Literary and Artistic Works, as revised in Paris on
July 24, 1971, and for other purposes.

Keywords: Legislation (US), Government (US),
Politics (US), Copyright

Audience: Lawyers, Students, Politicians,
Journalists

Details: Free

`gopher://wiretap.spies.com/00/Gov/`
`Copyright/US.Berne.Convention.txt`

Copyright Act ★

The full text of the Copyright Act of 1976, Title 17,
United States Code, Sections 101–810.

Keywords: Politics (US), Government (US Federal),
Laws (US Federal), Copyright

Audience: Lawyers, Students, Politicians,
Journalists

Details: Free

`gopher://wiretap.spies.com/00/Gov/`
`Copyright/US.Copyright.1976.tx`

Copyright Basics ★

This information is from Circular 1 issued by the
Copyright Office, Library of Congress, January 1991.
It explains what copyright is, who can claim
copyright, the principles of copyrights, what works
are protected, how to secure a copyright, and so on.

Keywords: Copyright, Government (US Federal),
Laws (US Federal)

Audience: Lawyers, Students, Politicians,
Journalists

Details: Free

`gopher://wiretap.spies.com/00/Gov/`
`Copyright/US.Copyright.Basics.txt`

CNI-Copyright Mailing List Archives ★★

An archive of lists related to copyright and
intellectual property law.

Keywords: Copyright Law, Intellectual Property

Sponsor: CNI (The Coalition for Networked
Information)

Audience: Entrepreneurs, Lawyers, Journalists

Contact: Craig Summerhill, Joan K. Lippincott
craig@cni.org, joan@cni.org

`gopher://gopher.cni.org`

Universal Copyright Convention ★★

The Universal Copyright Convention as revised at
Paris (1971). Convention and protocols were done at
Paris on July 24, 1971. It was ratified by the
President of the United States of America on August
28, 1972.

Keywords: Copyright, Laws (US), Government (US),
Politics (US)

Audience: Lawyers, Students, Politicians,
Journalists

Details: Free

`gopher://wiretap.spies.com/00/Gov/`
`Copyright/US.Universal.Copyright.Conv`
`.txt`

Cornell Law School Gopher

Cornell Law School Gopher ★★★

A gopher server providing extensive access to
Cornell Law School's online archives.

Keywords: Law (US)

Sponsor: The Legal Information Institute

Audience: Legal Professionals, Students

Profile: The Cornell Law School Gopher provides
access to Cornell Law School's
extensive online archives. Areas
covered by the gopher include case law,
copyright law, trademark law,
commercial law, and information about
the admissions and events at the Cornell
Law school.

Contact: Thomas R. Bruce or Peter W. Martin
feedback@fatty.law.cornell.edu

`gopher://fatty.law.cornell.edu`

Cornell University Libraries

Cornell University Libraries ★★★★

This library system maintains special collections in
engineering, nuclear engineering, textile
engineering, agriculture, medicine, Africana,
entomology, hotels, ILR, mathematics, physical
sciences, and veterinary medicine.

Keywords: Libraries, Research

Audience: General Public, Researchers

Details: Free

When userid/password screen appears,
press return. When cp read appears on
the screen, type library.

`telnet://cornellc.cit.cornell.edu`

Cornucopia of Disability Information (CODI)

Cornucopia of Disability Information (CODI) ★★★

A large collection of disability-related information
available via gopher.

Keywords: Disabilities, Health

Sponsor: State University of New York (SUNY) at
Buffalo

Audience: Disabled People, Activists, Rehabilitation
Counselors, Health Care Professionals

Profile: This site provides a wide variety of
information resources concerning
people with disabilities, ranging from
legal information to a directory of
computer resources aimed at the
disabled consumer. Includes state, local,
and national information and
government documents such as the
Americans with Disabilities Act. Also has
links to many other related resources on
the Internet, such as the National
Rehabilitation Information Center.

Contact: Jay Leavitt
leavitt@ubvmsb.cc.buffalo.edu

`gopher://val-dor.cc.buffalo.edu`

Corporations

INCORPR (Corporation and Partnership Records)

The Corporation and Partnership Records (INCORP)
library contains current US corporation and
partnership filings.

Keywords: Corporations, Partnerships, Filings,
Trademarks

Audience: Corporations, Lawyers, Researchers

Profile: The INCORP library contains current
records on corporations and limited
partnerships registered with the office of
the Secretary or Department of State.
These records include information
extracted by the state's staff from
articles of incorporation, annual reports,
amendments, and other public filings.

Contact: Mead New Sales Group at (800) 227-4908
or (513) 859-5398 inside the US, or (513)
865-7981 for all inquiries outside the US.

User Info: To subscribe, contact Mead directly.

To examine the Nexis user guide, you can access it at the ftp site of the University of Texas at Austin at the URL address: ftp://ftp.cc.utexas.edu

The files are in: /pub/ref-services/LEXIS

```
telnet://nex.meaddata.com
```

```
http://www.meaddata.com
```

Corpse/Respondents

Corpse/Respondents

This is a gothic pen-pal zine in digest form with small traffic mailing list.

Keywords: Gothic Rock, Rock Music

Audience: Gothic Rock Enthusiasts

Contact: carriec@eskimo.com

Details: Free

User Info: To subscribe send an e-mail message to the URL address below with "subscribe corpse <yournameandaddress>" in the text.

```
mailto:carriec@eskimo.com
```

Correct Time

Correct Time/NBS

Correct Time/NBS tells the correct time from the National Bureau of Standards (NBS).

Keywords: Internet, Services, Correct Time

Audience: Internet Surfers

Details: Free

```
ftp://india.colorado.edu/pub
```

Cosmic Update

Cosmic Update

Internet notice identifying new computer software from the National Aeronautics and Space Administration (NASA) made available for international use.

Keywords: NASA, Software, Space

Audience: Space Scientists, Astronomers

Profile: COSLINE is a 24-hour electronic information service to COSMIC's customers. The principal feature of COSLINE is the catalog Search facility. A separate help file is available for browsing from the Search main menu option.

Contact: Pat Mortenson
service@cossack.cosmic.uga.edu

Details: Free

User Info: To subscribe, send an e-mail message requesting a subscription to the URL address below.

```
mailto:service@cossack.cosmic.uga.edu
```

Counterev-L

Counterev-L

This list is under the aegis of l'Alliance Monarchists, affiliated with l'Alliance pour la maintenance de la France en Europe, and is dedicated to promoting the cause of traditional monarchy and counterrevolution. Its principles are a government based on natural law, decentralization, subsidiarity, an economy based on the principles of distributive justice, and the defense of traditional Western values.

Keywords: Monarchy, Government (International)

Audience: Monarchists, Counterrevolutionaries

Contact: Jovan Weismiller
ae852@yfn.ysu.edu

Details: Free

User Info: To subscribe to the list, send an e-mail message requesting a subscription to the URL address below.

```
mailto:ae852@yfn.ysu.edu
```

CP

CP

Topics of interest to the group include the cultivation and propagation of CP's (carniverous plants), field observations of CP's, sources of CP material, and CP trading between members. The discussion is not moderated, and usually consists of short messages offering plants for trade, asking CP questions and advice, relating experiences with plant propagation, and so on. The group also maintains archives of commercial plant sources and members growing lists.

Keywords: Carnivorous Plants, Botany

Audience: Horticulturists, Botanists

Contact: Rick Walker
walker@hpl-opus.hpl.hp.com

User Info: To subscribe to the list, send an e-mail message to the address below consisting of a single line reading:

SUB CP YourFirstName YourLastName

To send a message to the entire list, address it to: CP@hpl-opus.hpl.hp.com

```
mailto:listserv@hpl-opus.hpl.hp.com
```

CP/M

Alspa

Discussion by users of the CP/M machines made by (now defunct) Alspa Computer, Inc.

Keywords: Computers, Alspa Computer, Inc., CP/M

Audience: CP/M Users

Contact: Brad Allen
alspa-users-request@ssyx.ucsc.edu

Details: Free

User Info: To subscribe to the list, send an e-mail message requesting a subscription to the URL address below.

To send a message to the entire list, address it to: alspa-users@ssyx.ucsc.edu

```
mailto:alspa-users-
request@ssyx.ucsc.edu
```

CPSR/PDX Newsletter

CPSR/PDX Newsletter

This is the newsletter of the Portland chapter of Computer Professionals for Social Responsibility.

Keywords: Computer Professionals, Social Responsibility

Audience: Computer Professionals

Contact: Erik Nilsson
ERIKN@Goldfish.mitron.tek.com

Details: Free

```
mailto:erikn@goldfish.mitron.tek.com
```

Crafts

PEI (Prince Edward Island, Canada) Crafts Council Gopher

A gopher devoted to all manner of crafts, from weaving to glass blowing. Information includes a database of tools, services, and materials for crafts enthusiasts, as well as FAQs and pointers to other crafts resources. Also provides background on the PEI Craft Council's activities and on Prince Edward Island.

Keywords: Crafts, Hobbies, Canada

Sponsor: PEI Crafts Council, Prince Edward Island, Canada

Audience: Crafts Enthusiasts

Details: Free

```
gopher://crafts-council.pe.ca
```

A B C D E F G H I J K L M N O P Q R S T U V W X Y Z

rec.crafts.brewing

A Usenet newsgroup providing information and discussion about making beers and meads.

Keywords: Beer, Crafts

Audience: Beer Brewers

User Info: To subscribe to this Usenet newsgroup, you need access to a newsreader.

`news:rec.crafts.brewing`

rec.photo

A Usenet newsgroup providing information and discussion about photography.

Keywords: Photography, Art, Crafts

Audience: Photographers, Artists

User Info: To subscribe to this Usenet newsgroup, you need access to a newsreader.

`news:rec.photo`

rec.woodworking

A Usenet newsgroup providing information and discussion about woodworking.

Keywords: Woodworking, Crafts, Hobbies

Audience: Woodworkers

User Info: To subscribe to this Usenet newsgroup, you need access to a newsreader.

`news:rec.woodworking`

cread (Latin American & Caribbean Distance & Continuing Education)

cread (Latin American & Caribbean Distance & Continuing Education)

This is a digest list of distance education information primarily focused on Latin America and the Caribbean.

Keywords: Latin America, Caribbean, Education (Distance)

Audience: Educators, Administrators, Faculty

Details: Free

User Info: To subscribe to the list, send an e-mail message to the URL address below consisting of a single line reading: SUB cread YourFirstName YourLastName.

To send a message to the entire list, address it to: cread@yorkvm1.bitnet

`mailto:listserv@yorkvm1.bitnet`

Creationism

talk.origins

A Usenet newsgroup providing information and discussion about evolution versus creationism.

Keywords: Evolution, Creationism, Activism

Audience: General Public, Evolutionists, Creationists, Activists

Details: Free

User Info: To subscribe to this Usenet newsgroup, you need access to a newsreader.

`news:talk.origins`

Creativity

de Bono

This is a discussion list concerning the work of Edward de Bono. Also provides help with teaching the CoRT Thinking Program, and Six Thinking Hats.

Keywords: de Bono (Edward), Education (Alternative), Creativity

Audience: Teachers, Students, Management Trainers

Contact: Rosa Casarez
Casarez@netcom.net

`mailto:casarez@netcom.com`

Creighton University Library Online Catalogue

Creighton University Library Online Catalogue

This site maintains a catalog of the Creighton University library's holdings.

Keywords: Health Sciences, Libraries

Sponsor: Creighton University, Omaha, Nebraska, USA

Audience: Health-Care Professionals, Medical Educators, Students

Details: Free

At the prompt type <lib hsl>for Health Sciences Library.

`telnet://attachpals@owl.creighton.edu`

Crew

rec.sport.rowing

A Usenet newsgroup providing information and discussion about recreational and competitive rowing. It provides information from the United States Rowing Association, the latest race results, equipment sales, coaching positions and more.

Keywords: Rowing, Crew, Sports

Audience: Rowers, Coaches, Athletes

Profile: This newsgroup covers technical, training and nutritional aspects as well as the latest race results, National Team information, equipment sales, coaching positions, information from the United States Rowing Association and more.

User Info: To subscribe to this Usenet newsgroup, you need access to a newsreader.

`news:rec.sport.rowing`

Cricket

rec.sport.cricket

A Usenet newsgroup providing information and discussion about cricket.

Keywords: Cricket, Sports

Audience: Cricket Fans, Sports Fans

User Info: To subscribe to this Usenet newsgroup, you need access to a newsreader.

`news:rec.sport.cricket`

University of Glasgow Information Service (GLANCE)

GLANCE provides subject-based information services, including an extensive section on European and world sports.

Keywords: Sports, Soccer, Motor Racing, Mountaineering, Squash, Cricket, Golf, Tennis, Europe, Scotland

Sponsor: University of Glasgow, Glasgow, Scotland

Audience: Sport Enthusiasts, Fitness Enthusiasts, Nature Lovers

Profile: Information at this site includes schedules, results, and statistics for sports such as cricket and soccer. There is also a selection of items on mountaineering.

Contact: Alan Dawson
a.dawson@uk.ac.gla.compserv

Details: Free

`gopher://govan.cent.gla.ac.uk/Subject/Sports and Rec`

Crime

Georgia-Computer Systems Protection Act

Lists full text of the Georgia Computer Systems Protection Act.

Keywords: Computer, Crime

Audience: Lawyers, Computer Programmers, Computer Operators

Details: Free

`gopher://wiretap.spies.com`

Investigators and Detectives

This resource provides information files for individuals involved with investigative research, as well as a free monthly newsletter.

Keywords: Detectives, Crime, Information Retrieval, Security

Audience: Investigators, Detectives, Information Brokers, General Public

Profile: Investigators and Detectives provides access to information covering topics such as private investigative research, strategies, sources, the art and science of investigating, theft deterrents, and electronic PI schematics and plans. Also offers a free sample of a newsletter covering various topics of interest to Private Investigators, such as techniques and strategies, security, and tracing.

Contact: Mike Enlow
menlow@Intec.win.net
michael@enlow.com

Details: Inside Secrets.

`mailto:info@enlow.com`

Texas: Computer Crimes Statute

Lists text of the Texas Computer Crimes Statute.

Keywords: Computers, Crime, Texas

Audience: Lawyers, Computer Programmers, Computer Operators

Details: Free
Select from menu as appropriate

`gopher://wiretap.spies.com`

UN Criminal Justice Country Profiles

UN profiles of world crime in 113 countries.

Keywords: Crime, UN

Sponsor: United Nations

Audience: Lawyers, Legal Professionals, Librarians, Governments

Details: Free
Select from menu as appropriate.

`gopher://uacsc2.albany.edu`

Croatia

Cro-News/SCYU-Digest

This unmoderated list is the distribution point for the news coming from Croatia. The list carries articles from Novi Vjesnik, Vecernji List, Croatia Monitor, Slobodna Dalmacija, Novi Danas, Radio Free Europe/ Radio Luxemburg bulletins, and UPI reports.

Keywords: Croatia, News Media

Audience: Croats, Journalists, General Public

Contact: Nino Margetic
cro-news-request@medphys.ucl.ac.uk

Details: Free

User Info: To subscribe to the list, send an e-mail message requesting a subscription to the URL address below.

To send a message to the entire list, address it to: cro-news@medphys.ucl.ac.uk

`mailto:cro-news-request@medphys.ucl.ac.uk`

Cro-Views

Cro-Views is an opinion service that consists of discussions relating to Croatia and other former Yugoslav republics. The main objective is to give people who cannot access the news network (for example, via <rn>command in UNIX) a chance to read and voice their own opinions about these issues.

Keywords: Croatia, News

Audience: Croats, Journalists, General Public

Contact: Joe Stojsic
Joe@Mullara.Met.UniMelb.Edu.AU

Details: Free

User Info: To subscribe to the list, send an e-mail message requesting a subscription to the URL address below.

Notes: Cro-Views is an unmoderated service, but abusive language and name-calling is not tolerated.

`mailto:Joe@Mullara.Met.UniMelb.Edu.AU`

Croatian-News/Hrvatski-Vjesnik

News from and related to Croatia, run by volunteers. These are actually two news distributions: one in Croatian (occasionally an article might be in some other South Slavic language) and one in English.

Keywords: Croatia, News

Audience: Croats, Journalists, General Public

Contact: Croatian-News-Request@Andrew.CMU.Edu, Hrvatski-Vjesnik-Zamolbe@Andrew.CMU.Edu

Details: Free

User Info: To subscribe to the list, send an e-mail message to the URL address below with the following information: your name, your e-mail address, and state/country where your account is. Please put the state/country information in the Subject: line of your letter. If you would like to receive the news in Croatian as well, please indicate that in your message. If you would prefer to receive the news in Croatian only, please send a message to the following address: Hrvatski-Vjesnik-Zamolbe@Andrew.CMU.Edu

To send a message to the entire list, address it to:Croatian-News@Andrew.CMU.Edu

`mailto:Croatian-News-Request@Andrew.CMU.Edu`

Cromwell (Oliver)

University of Chicago Library

The library's holdings are large and wide-ranging and contain significant collections in many fields.

Keywords: English Bibles, Lincoln (Abraham), Kentucky & Ohio River Valley (History of), Balzac (Honore de), American Drama, Cromwell (Oliver), Goethe, Judaica, Italy, Chaucer (Geoffrey), Wells (Ida, Personal Papers of), Douglas (Stephen A.), Italy, Literature (Children's)

Audience: General Public, Researchers, Librarians, Document Delivery Professionals

Details: Free
Expect: ENTER CLASS, Send: LIB48 3;
Expect: CONNECTED, Send: RETURN

`telnet://olorin.uchicago.edu`

Cross Cultural Studies

Anthropology, Cross Cultural Studies, & Archaeology

This directory is a compilation of information resources focused on anthropology, cross cultural studies, and archaeology.

Keywords: Anthropology, Cross Cultural Studies, Archaeology

Audience: Anthropologists, Archaeologists, Students, Educators

Contact: G. Bell

Details: Free

`ftp://una.hh.lib.umich.edu/70/ inetdirsstacks/anthro:bell`

A
B
C
D
E
F
G
H
I
J
K
L
M
N
O
P
Q
R
S
T
U
V
W
X
Y
Z

crossfire

crossfire

To discuss the developement of the game Crossfire. The official anonymous FTP-site is ftp.ifi.uio.no in the directory /pub/crossfire. Old mails to the list are archived there. Crossfire is a multiplayer arcade and adventure game made for the X-window environment.

Keywords: Computer Games

Audience: Crossfire specialists, Computer Game Enthusiasts

Contact: Frank Tore Johansen
crossfire-request@ifi.uio.no

Details: Free

User Info: To subscribe to the list, send an e-mail message requesting a subscription to the URL address below.

To send a message to the entire list, address it to: crossfire@ifi.uio.no

`mailto:crossfire-request@ifi.uio.no`

Crowes

Crowes

To provide a forum for discussion about the rock band the Black Crowes. Topics include the group's music and lyrics, as well as the band's participation with NORML, concert dates and playlists, and bootlegs (audio and video).

Keywords: Rock Music, Pop Music

Audience: Rock Music Enthusiasts, Pop Music Enthusiasts

Contact: rstewart@unex.ucla.edu

Details: Free

User Info: To subscribe, mail to the address below with the command SUBSCRIBE in the first line.

`mailto:rstewart@unex.ucla.edu`

Cryonics

cryonics

Cryonic suspension is an experimental procedure whereby patients who can no longer be kept alive with today's medical abilities are preserved at low temperatures for treatment in the future. This list is a forum for topics related to cryonics, including biochemistry of memory, low temperature biology, legal status of cryonics and cryonically suspended people, nanotechnology and cell repair machines, philosophy of identity, mass media coverage of cryonics, new research and publications, conferences, and local cryonics group meetings.

Keywords: Cryonics

Audience: Doctors, Biologists, Biochemists

Contact: Kevin Q. Brown
kqb@whscad1.att.com

Details: Free

User Info: To subscribe to the list, send an e-mail message requesting a subscription to the URL address below.

`mailto:kqb@whscad1.att.com`

CSAA

CSAA

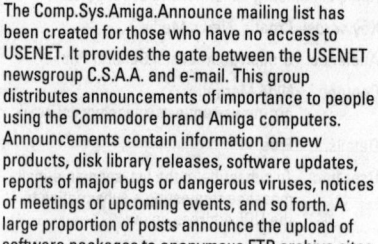

The Comp.Sys.Amiga.Announce mailing list has been created for those who have no access to USENET. It provides the gate between the USENET newsgroup C.S.A.A. and e-mail. This group distributes announcements of importance to people using the Commodore brand Amiga computers. Announcements contain information on new products, disk library releases, software updates, reports of major bugs or dangerous viruses, notices of meetings or upcoming events, and so forth. A large proportion of posts announce the upload of software packages to anonymous FTP archive sites.

Keywords: Commodore-Amiga Computers, Computers

Audience: Commodore-Amiga Users

Contact: Carlos Amezaga
announce-request@cs.ucdavis.edu

Details: Free

User Info: To subscribe to the list, send an e-mail message requesting a subscription to the URL address below.

To send a message to the entire list, address it to:announce@cs.ucdavis.edu

`mailto:announce-request@cs.ucdavis.edu`

CSF: Communications for a Sustainable Future

CSF: Communications for a Sustainable Future

A gopher server for the distribution of Conflict Resolution Materials.

Keywords: Conflict Resolution, Community, Politics

Sponsor: Communications for a Sustainable Future

Audience: Activists, Policy Analysts, Community Leaders, Mediators, Lawyers

Profile: Communications for a Sustainable Future is a collective effort of several scholars. CSF does research, education, and applied work. Its main subject areas are: Intractable Conflicts and Constructive Confrontation, Environmental and Public Policy Dispute Resolution, Social/Political Conflicts, International Conflicts.

Contact: roper@csf.colorado.edu

Details: Free

`gopher://csf.colorado.edu`

CSORG (Clearinghouse for Subject-Oriented Internet Resource Guides)

CSORG (Clearinghouse for Subject-Oriented Internet Resource Guides)

The goal of CSORG is to collect and make widely available guides to Internet resources which are subject-oriented. These guides are produced by members of the Internet community, and by SILS students who participate in the Internet Resource Discovery project.

Keywords: WWW, Information Retrieval, Internet

Sponsor: University of Michigan, School of Information and Library Studies, Michigan, USA

Audience: Reseachers, Students, General Public

Contact: Louis Rosenfeld
i-guides@umich.edu

`gopher://una.hh.lib.umich.edu/11/inetdirs`

CSU Entomology WWW Site

CSU Entomology WWW Site

A web site containing online photos of insects, entomology educational programs, and extensive Internet entomology links.

Keywords: Bioscience, Biology, Entomology

Sponsor: Colorado State University, Denver, Colorado, USA

Audience: Students, Researchers, Entomologists

Contact: Lou Bjostad
lbjostad@lamar.colorado.edu

`http://www.colostate.edu/Depts/Entomology/ent.html`

ctf-discuss

ctf-discuss

This mailing list aims to stimulate discussion of issues critical to the computer science community in the United States (and, by extension, the world). The Computer Science and Telecommunications Board (CSTB) of the National Research Council (NRC) is charged with identifying and initiating studies in areas critical to the health of the field. Recently one such study, Computing the Future, has generated a major discussion in the community and has motivated the establishment of this mailing list in order to involve broader participation. This list will be used in the future to report and discuss the activities of the CSTB and to solicit opinions in a variety of areas.

Keywords: Computer Science, Telecommunications

Audience: Computer Scientists, Telecommunications Experts

Contact: Dave Farber
ctf-discuss-request@cis.upenn.edu

Details: Free

User Info: To subscribe to the list, send an e-mail message requesting a subscription to the URL address below.

To send a message to the entire list, address it to: ctf-discuss@cis.upenn.edu

`mailto:ctf-discuss-request@cis.upenn.edu`

CTN News

CTN News

This is a list covering news on Tibet.

Keywords: Tibet, New Media

Audience: Tibetans, Journalists, General Public

Contact: ctn-editors@utcc.utoronto.ca

Details: Free

User Info: To subscribe to the list, send an e-mail message requesting a subscription to the URL address below.

To send a message to the entire list, address it to: CTN_News@utcc.utoronto.ca

`mailto:ctn-editors@utcc.utoronto.ca`

Cuba

INFOMED

Provides yearly statistical information in the form of tables (in ASCII format) listing the principal indicators of health in Cuba.

Keywords: Cuba, Health Statistics, Public Health

Sponsor: Cuban Ministry of Health

Audience: Medical Professionals, Researchers, Public Health Professionals

Details: Free

To obtain a table from the yearbook, send an electronic message to the URL address below without a subject and with the following content in the body of the message:

GET ANUARIO <name of table>

Examples of tables are CMT-11: Death rates by age group; CMT-15: Infant mortality by province, and so on. For a listing of the available tables request the help file.

`mailto:listserv@infomed.cu`

CUD (Computer Underground Digest)

CUD (Computer Underground Digest)

USA Today of cyberspace and the computer underground. Contains information relating to the computer underground.

Keywords: Hacking, Computer News, Cyberculture

Audience: Hackers, Reality Hackers, Computer Underground Enthusiasts

Contact: Gordon Meyer, Jim Thomas
tk0jut2@niu.bitnet
pumpcon@mindvox.phantom.com.

Details: Free

`ftp://etext.archive.umich.edu/pub/Zines/CUD`

Culinary (Collection of)

University of Denver Library

The library's holdings are large and wide-ranging and contain significant collections in many fields.

Keywords: Folklore Collection, Husted (Margaret), Culinary (Collection of)

Audience: Researchers, Students, General Public

Contact: Bob Stocker
bstocker@ducair.bitnet

Details: Free

Expect: Login; Send: Atdu

`telnet:// du.edu`

Cults

The Purple Thunderbolt of Spode (PURPS)

Magazine of the OTISian faith (a small but growing cult worshiping OTIS, the ancient Sumerian goddess of life) carrying news, fiction, poetry, humor, and the pure, unadulterated Secrets of the Universe to its subscribers.

Keywords: Religion, Cults

Audience: OTIS Followers

Contact: barker@acc.fau.edu

User Info: To subscribe, send an e-mail message requesting a subscription to the URL address below.

`mailto:barker@acc.fau.edu`

Cultural Studies

African Art Exhibit and Tutorial

This web site provides images of African art and an overview of African aesthetics.

Keywords: Art, Africa, Cultural Studies

Sponsor: University of Virginia

Audience: Artists, Art Students, Educators, Historians

`http://www.lib.virginia.edu`

Armadillo's World Wide Web Page

This site provides resources and instructional material for an interdisciplinary Texan culture course.

Keywords: History (US), Texas, Cultural Studies, Education

Sponsor: Rice University, Houston, Texas, USA

Audience: Educators, Students

Contact: armadillo@rice.edu

`http://chico.rice.edu/armadillo`

Culture

African Education Research Network

Various links to African studies programs at select universities, and other archived information of interest to the African studies scholar.

A B C D E F G H I J K L M N O P Q R S T U V W X Y Z

A
B
C
D
E
F
G
H
I
J
K
L
M
N
O
P
Q
R
S
T
U
V
W
X
Y
Z

Keywords: Culture, Race, Africa, African Studies

Sponsor: Ohio University, African Education Research Network

Audience: Students, African-Americans, Africans

Contact: Milton E. Ploghoft

Contact: mperdreau@ohiou.edu

Details: Free

`gopher://gopher.ohiou.edu/00/`
`dept.servers/aern`

Argentina

Mailing list for general discussion and information about Argentina, including Argentine culture and politics.

Keywords: Argentina, Politics, Culture

Sponsor: Carlos G. Mendioroz

Audience: Spanish Speakers, Students

Contact: Carlos G. Mendioroz
argentina-request@ois.db.toronto.edu

User Info: To subscribe to the list, send an e-mail message to the URL address below.

To send a message to the entire list, address it to:
argentina@ois.db.toronto.edu

`mailto:argentina-`
`request@ois.db.toronto.edu`

Black/African Related Online Information

This is a list of online information storage sites that contain a significant amount of information pertaining to Black or African people, culture, and issues around the world.

Keywords: Culture, Race, Africa, African Studies

Sponsor: AfriInfo

Audience: Students, African-Americans, Africans

Contact: McGee
mcgee@epsilon.eecs.nwu.edu

Details: Free

`ftp://ftp.netcom.com/pub/amcgee/`
`my_african_related_lists/afrisite.msg`

Chicano/LatinoNet

An electronic mechanism which brings together Chicano/Latino research, as well as linguistic minority and educational research efforts being carried out at the University of California and elsewhere. It serves as a gateway between faculty, staff, and students who are engaged in research and curricular efforts in these areas.

Keywords: Culture, Race, Chicano Culture, Latino Culture

Sponsor: Chicano Studies Research Center, University of California at Los Angeles

Audience: Students, Mexican-Americans, Latinos

Contact: Richard Chabran
Chabran@latino.sscnet.ucla.ed

Details: Free

`gopher://latino.sscnet.ucla.edu/`

Japanese Information

This web site contains extensive information on the geography, culture, law, and tourism of Japan. Includes archived Japanese newsgroup information and FAQs.

Keywords: Culture, Race, Japan, Japanese Culture

Sponsor: Nippon Telegraph and Telephone

Audience: Students, Tourists, Japanese, Japanese-Americans

Contact: Webmaster
www-admin@seraph.ntt.jp

Details: Free

`http://www.ntt.jp/japan/index.html`

Mexican Culture FAQ

This is the FAQ from the soc.culture.mexican newsgroup. Provides information on Mexican culture, history, society, language, and tourism.

Keywords: Culture, Race, Chicano Culture, Latino Culture

Sponsor: News Group Moderators for soc.culture.mexican

Audience: Students, Latinos, Chicanos

Contact: News Group Moderator
mendoza-grado@att.com

Details: Free

`ftp://ftp.mty.itesm.ms/pub/mexico/`
`faqs`

`http://www.cis.ohio-state.edu/`
`hypertext/faq/usenet/mexican-faq/`
`faq.html`

Poland-I

A mailing list devoted to discussion of Polish culture and events.

Keywords: Poland, Culture

Audience: Researchers

Contact: Micahl Prussak
michal@gs58.sp.cs.cmu.edu

Details: Free

User Info: To subscribe to the list, send an e-mail message to the URL address below, consisting of a single line reading:

SUB poland-I YourFirstName YourLastName

To send a message to the entire list, address it to: poland-1@ubvm.cc.buffalo.edu

`mailto:listserv@ubvm.cc.buffalo.edu`

Reggae Down Babylon

A collection of links to sources of information about reggae music on the World Wide Web and the Internet. Site includes reggae FAQs, and listings of reggae radio shows, lyrics, pictures, and news group archives.

Keywords: Reggae, Culture, Music

Sponsor: Reggae Down Babylon

Audience: Music Fans, Musicians, Reggae Enthusiasts

Contact: ReggaeMaster
damjohns@nyx10.cs.du.edu

Details: Free

`ftp://jammin.nosc.mil/pub/reggae`

SCS

A discussion of the culture of the former Soviet Union.

Keywords: Soviet Union, Culture

Audience: Researchers, Slavicists, General Public

Contact: John B. Harlan
ijph200@indycms.iupui.edu

Details: Free

User Info: To subscribe to the list, send an e-mail message to the URL address below consisting of a single line reading:

SUB scs YourFirstName YourLastName

To send a message to the entire list, address to: scs@indycms.iupui.edu

`mailto:listserv@indycms.iupui.edu`

slovak-I

A mailing list for discussion of Slovak culture, and so on.

Keywords: Slovakia, Culture

Audience: Researchers, Students, Slovaks

Contact: Jan George Frajkor
gfrajkor@ccs.carleton.ca

User Info: To subscribe to the list, send an e-mail message to the URL address below consisting of a single line reading:

SUB slovak-I YourFirstName YourLastName

To sen a message to the entire list, address it to: slovak-1@ubvm.cc.buffalo.edu

`mailto:listserv@ubvm.cc.buffalo.edu`

soc.culture.canada

A Usenet newsgroup providing information and discussion about Canada and its people.

Keywords: Culture, Canada, Sociology

Audience: Sociologists, Canadians

Details: Free

User Info: To subscribe to this Usenet newsgroup, you need access to a newsreader.

`news:soc.culture.canada`

Spojrzenia

A weekly E-journal devoted to Polish culture, history and politics.

Keywords: Poland, News (international), Culture

Audience: Poles, Students

Contact: Jerzy Krzystek
krzystek@u.washington.edu

Details: Free

User Info: To subscribe to the list, send an e-mail message requesting a subscription to the URL address below.

To send a message to the entire list, address it to:

spojrzenia@u.washington.edu

`mailto:krzystek@u.washington.edu`

WWW Paris

A web site created as a collaborative effort among individuals in both Paris and the United States.

Keywords: Paris, Culture, Art, Travel, French, Tourism

Audience: Students, Educators, Travelers, Researchers

Profile: Contains an extensive collection of images and text regarding all of the major monuments and museums of Paris, including maps of the Metro and the RER; calendars of events and current expositions; promotional images and text relating to local department stores; there is also a visitors' section with up-to-date tourist information on hotels, restaurants, telephones, airport schedules, a basic Paris glossary, and the latest weather images. Includes an extensive collection of links to other resources about Paris and France, and a selected bibliography of history and architecture in Paris.

Contact: Norman Barth, Eric Pouliquen
nbarth@ucsd.edu, epouliq@ucsd.edu

`http://meteora.ucsd.edu/~norman/paris`

Current Cites

Current Cites

A monthly publication of the Library Technology Watch Program at The Library, University of California, Berkeley.

Keywords: Computer Technology, Libraries

Sponsor: The Library, University of California, Berkeley, CA

Audience: Librarians, Computer Programmers

Profile: Over 30 journals in librarianship and computer technology are scanned for articles on optical-disk technologies, computer networks and networking, information transfer, expert systems and artificial intelligence, and hypermedia and multimedia.

Contact: David Robison
drobison@library.berkeley.edu

Details: Free

`telnet://melvyl.ucop.edu`

Current Contents

Current Contents

Current Contents provides access to the tables of contents from the current issues of leading domestic and international scientific journals. Every discipline within the sciences is represented. The database provides complete bibliographic information for each article, review, letter, note and editorial.

Keywords: Sciences, Scientific Journals

Sponsor: Institute for Scientific Information

Audience: General Public, Researchers, Librarians, Physicians

Contact: CDP Technologies Sales Department (800)950-2035, extension 400

User Info: To subscribe, contact CDP Technologies directly

`telnet://cdplus@cdplus.com`

Current Events

misc.headlines

A Usenet newsgroup providing information and discussion about current events and issues.

Keywords: Current Events

Audience: General Public

Details: Free

User Info: To subscribe to this Usenet newsgroup, you need access to a newsreader.

`news:misc.headlines`

Current Weather Maps and Movies

Current Weather Maps and Movies

This web site is updated hourly, and provides links to downloadable software sites instrumental in accessing interactive weather browsers. International information is available, and visual and infrared maps are supplied from satellites.

Keywords: Weather, Meteorology, Aviation

Sponsor: Michigan State University, Michigan, USA

Audience: General Public, Oceanography, Pilots

Contact: Charles Henrich
henrich@crh.cl.msu.edu

`http://rs560.cl.msu.edu/weather`

CUSSNET

CUSSNET

Computer Users in the Social Sciences (CUSS) is a discussion group devoted to issues of interest to social workers, counselors, and human service workers of all disciplines. The discussion frequently involves computer applications in treatment, agency administration, and research. Students, faculty, community-based professionals, and casual observers join in the discussion. Software, hardware, and ethical issues associated with their use in the human services generate lively and informative discussions.

Keywords: Social Sciences, Computers, Computer Applications

Audience: Social Workers, Human Services Workers, General Public

Contact: cussnet-request@stat.com

Details: Free

User Info: To subscribe to the list, send an e-mail message to the address below consisting of a single line reading:

SUB cussnet YourFirstName YourLastName.

To send a message to the entire list, address it to: cussnet@stat.com

`mailto:listserv@stat.com`

A B C D E F G H I J K L M N O P Q R S T U V W X Y Z

CVNet (Color and Vision Network)

CVNet (Color and Vision Network)

The network provides a means of communications for scientists working in biological color vision research. Members' e-mail addresses are maintained and sent to others in the network. CVNet distributes notices of jobs, meetings, and some other special announcements to all registrants. Members can post bulletins, announcements, and so on.

Keywords: Optics, Biological Research, Psychology

Sponsor: York University, North York, Ontario, Canada

Audience: Psychologists, Color/Vision Researchers

Contact: Peter K. Kaiser
cvnet@vm1.yorkU.ca

Details: Free

User Info: To subscribe, send an e-mail message requesting a subscription to the URL address below.

`mailto:cvnet@vm1.yorkU.ca`

Cyberculture

CUD (Computer Underground Digest)

USA Today of cyberspace and the computer underground. Contains information relating to the computer underground.

Keywords: Hacking, Computer News, Cyberculture

Audience: Hackers, Reality Hackers, Computer Underground Enthusiasts

Contact: Gordon Meyer, Jim Thomas
tk0jut2@niu.bitnet or
pumpcon@mindvox.phantom.com.

Details: Free

`ftp://etext.archive.umich.edu/pub/
Zines/CUD`

fringeware

A moderated mailing list devoted to cyberculture and the like.

Keywords: Cyberculture

Audience: Cyberculture Enthusiasts

Details: Free

User Info: To subscribe to the list, send an e-mail message to the URL address shown below.

To send a message to the entire list, address it to:
fringeware@illuminati.io.com

`mailto:fringeware-
request@illuminati.io.com`

FutureCulture FAQ (Frequently Asked Questions) File

List of online and offline items of interest to subscribers of FutureCulture, a mailing list on 'technoculture' or 'new edge' or 'cyberculture.'

Keywords: Technology, Cyberculture, Postmodernism, Sci-Fi, Zines

Audience: Reality Hackers, Cyberculture Enthusiasts

Profile: This list discusses cyberpunk culture, rave culture, industrial music, virtual reality, drugs, computer underground, Net sociology, and virtual communities.

Contact: Alias Datura (adatura on IRC)
adatura@uafhp.uark.edu

Details: Free

`ftp://etext.archive.umich.edu/pub`

Internet Wiretap

A resource containing electronic books, zines, and government documents, White House press releases, and links to worldwide gopher and WAIS servers.

Keywords: Electronic Media, Cyberculture, Zines

Sponsor: Internet Wiretap

Audience: Cyberculture Enthusiasts, Civil Libertarians, Educators

`gopher://wiretap.spies.com/11/`

`http://wiretap.spies.com`

Cyberpunk Games

flashlife

A mailing list for general managers of Shadowrun and other cyberpunk role-playing games to discuss rules and scenarios, ask questions, and make up answers.

Keywords: Games, Cyberpunk Games

Audience: Game Players

Details: Free

User Info: To subscribe to the list, send an e-mail message requesting a subscription to the URL address below.

To send a message to the entire list, address it to:
flashlife@netcom.com

`mailto:flashlife-request@netcom.com`

Cyberspace

alt.bbs

A Usenet newsgroup providing information and discussion about computer BBS systems & software.

Keywords: BBS Systems, Cyberspace, Computers

Audience: BBS Users

User Info: To subscribe to this Usenet newsgroup, you need access to a newsreader.

`news:alt.bbs`

alt.cyberpunk

A Usenet newsgroup providing information and discussion about the high-tech low-life.

Keywords: Computers, Cyberspace

Audience: Hackers, Cybernauts, General Public

User Info: To subscribe to this Usenet newsgroup, you need access to a newsreader.

`news:alt.cyberpunk`

Conference about Virtual Reality (The)

A conference on the WELL about cyberspace and virtual reality.

Keywords: Virtual Reality, Art, Cyberspace

Audience: Artists, Computer Programmers, Cyberpunks

Contact: Peter Rothman
avatarp@well.sf.ca.us

To participate in a conference on the WELL, you must first establish an account on the WELL. To do so, start by typing: telnet well.sf.ca.us

`telnet://well.sf.ca.us`

THINKNET

Electronic newsletter on philosophy, systems theory, interdisciplinary studies, and thoughtful conversation in cyberspace.

Keywords: Cyberspace, Systems Theory, Philosophy

Audience: Philosophers, System Theorists

Contact: Kent D. Palmer Ph.D.
Internet: palmer@world.std.com

Details: Free

User Info: To subscribe, send an e-mail message to the URL address below consisting of a single line reading:

SUB THINKNET YourFirstName YourLastName

`mailto:palmer@world.std.com`

Vigis-L

A mailing list for the discussion of Virtual Reality and GIS (Geographic Information Systems).

Keywords: Virtual Reality, Geography, GIS (Geographic Information Systems), Cyberspace

Audience: Geographers, Cartographers, Cybernauts

Contact: Tom Edwards
navanax.u.washington.edu

User Info: To subscribe to the list, send an e-mail message to the URL address below consisting of a single line reading:

SUB vigis-l YourFirstName YourLastName.

To send a message to the entire list, address it to:
vigis@uwavm.u.washington.edu

`mailto:listserv@uwavm.u.washington.edu`

Virtual Reality Space

A collection of virtual reality information, including downloadable software tools from Silicon Graphics.

Keywords: Virtual Reality, Cyberspace, Software, Silicon Graphics

Sponsor: The University of Texas, Austin, Texas, USA

Audience: Virtual Reality Enthusiasts, Programmers

Contact: Jay Ashcraft
ashcraft@ccwf.cc.utexas.edu

`gopher://ftp.cc.utexas.edu`

`ftp://cc.utexas.edu`

Cycling

Physical Education & Recreation

A collection of information on sporting and recreational activities from aikido to windsurfing.

Keywords: Sports, Recreation, Aikido, Cycling, Scuba Diving, Windsurfing

Audience: Sports Enthusiasts, Fitness Enthusiasts

Contact: ctcadmin@ctc.ctc.edu

`gopher://ctc.ctc.edu`

CYFERNET (Child, Youth, and Family Education Network)

CYFERNET (Child, Youth, and Family Education Network)

This public information service supports child, youth, and family development programs.

Keywords: Education, Networks

Sponsor: Youth Development Information Center at the National Agricultural Library

Audience: Educators, Children, Families

Profile: CYFERNET contains information useful to child, youth, and family development professionals. Features include programs for children aged 5-8 years, youth-at-risk programs, community projects, and education.

Contact: jkane@nalusda.gov

Details: Free

`gopher://ra.esusda.gov/11/CYFER-net`

Czech Republic

CEE Environmental Libraries Database

A directory of over 300 libraries and environmental information centers in Central Eastern Europe that specalize in, or maintain significant collections of information about, the environment, ecology, sustainable living, or conservation. The database concentrates on six Central Eastern European countries: Bulgaria, Czech Republic, Hungary, Romania, Slovakia, and Poland.

Keywords: Central Eastern Europe, Environment, Sustainable Living, Bulgaria, Czech Republic, Hungary, Romania, Slovakia, Poland.

Sponsor: The Wladyslaw Poniecki Charitable Foundation, Inc.

Audience: Environmentalists, Green Movement, Librarians, Community Builders, Sustainable Living Specialists.

Profile: This database is the product of an Environmental Training Project (ETP) that was funded in 1992 by the US Agency for International Development as a 5-year cooperative agreement with a consortium headed by the University of Minnesota (US AID Cooperative Agreement Number EUR-0041-A-002-2020). Other members of the consortium include the University of Pittsburgh's

Center for Hazardous Materials Research, The Institute for Sustainable Communities, and the World Wildlife Fund. The Wladyslaw Poniecki Charitable Foundation, Inc., was a subcontractor to the World Wildlife Fund and published the Directory of Libraries and Environmental Information Centers in Central Eastern Europe: A Locator/Directory . This gopher database consists of an electronic version of the printed directory, subsequently modified and updated online. Access to the data is facilitated by a WAIS search engine which makes it possible to retrieve information about libraries, subject area specializations, personnel, and so on.

Contact: Doug Kahn, CEDAR
kahn@pan.cedar.univie.ac.at

`gopher://gopher.poniecki.berkeley.edu`

EUnet Czechia

This is the information service of EUnet Czechia, the network service provider in the Czech Republic and contains information about top-level domains.

Keywords: Czech Republic

Audience: Czechs, General Public

Contact: gopher.eunet.cz

Details: Free

`http://www.eunet.cz`

Prague University of Economics Gopher Service

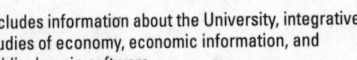

Includes information about the University, integrative studies of economy, economic information, and public domain software.

Keywords: Czech Republic, Economics, Europe

Audience: Czechs, Economists

Contact: gopher@pub.vse.cz

Details: Free

`gopher://pub.vse.cz`

University of Nebraska at Lincoln Library

The library's holdings are large and wide-ranging and contain significant collections in many fields..

Keywords: Slovak Republic, Czech Republic, Folklore, Military History, Latvia, Law (Tax), Law (US)

Audience: General Public, Researchers, Librarians, Document Delivery Professionals

Contact: Anita Cook

Details: Free

Expect: login, Send: library

`telnet://unllib.unl.edu`

A
B
C
D
E
F
G
H
I
J
K
L
M
N
O
P
Q
R
S
T
U
V
W
X
Y
Z

D

Dallas Stars

Dallas Stars

Discussion of the Dallas Stars (of the National Hockey League) and their farm clubs.

Keywords: Hockey, Sports

Audience: NHL Enthusiasts

Details: Free

User Info: To subscribe to the list, send an e-mail message requesting a subscription to the URL address below.

To send a message to the entire list, address it to: hamlet@u.washington.edu

Notes: Please include the word "DSTARS" in your subject line and include your name and preferred e-mail address in the body of your message.

`mailto:hamlet@u.washington.edu`

Dance

Arts

An umbrella arts conference on the WELL.

Keywords: Art, Music, Dance

Audience: Artists, Dancers, Musicians, Photographers

Profile: A general arts conference that includes listings of show opportunities, books, and events, as well as discussion about art and art criticism.

Contact: Tim Collins

`telnet://well.sf.ca.us`

Ballroom

Discussion of any aspect of ballroom dancing, including places to dance, special events, clubs, ballroom dance music, dances, and steps.

Keywords: Ballroom Dancing, Dancing

Audience: Ballroom Dancers

Contact: Shahrukh Merchant
ballroom-request@athena.mit.edu

Details: Free

User Info: To subscribe to the list, send an e-mail message requesting a subscription to the URL address below.

To send a message to the entire list, address it to: ballroom@athena.mit.edu

`mailto:ballroom-request@athena.mit.edu`

Folk-dancing

A discussion of folk dancing, including contra, square, western square, morris, cajun, and barn dancing.

Keywords: Dance, Folk Dance

Audience: Dancers, Folk Dancers

Contact: Terry J. Wood
tjw+@pitt.edu

Details: Free

User Info: To subscribe to the list, send an e-mail message requesting a subscription to the URL address below

To send a message to the entire list, address it to: fdml@pitt.edu

Notes: Please note that the Folk Dancing Mailing List (fdml) operates in conjunction with the Usenet newsgroup rec.folk-dancing. When subscribing to the FDML, please include several computer mail addresses and a postal mail address (or phone number).

`mailto:tjw+@pitt.edu`

Morris

A discussion list related to Morris Dancing, including Cotswold, Border, Northwest, Rapper, Longsword, Abbots Bromley, Garland, and similar forms of English dance along with the accompanying music and traditions.

Keywords: Morris Dancing, England, Dance

Audience: Morris Dancers

Details: Free

User Info: To subscribe to the list, send an e-mail message requesting subscription to the URL address below.

`mailto:morris@suvm.acs.syr.edu`

rec.arts.dance

A Usenet newsgroup providing information and discussion about all types of dance.

Keywords: Dance, Fine Arts

Audience: Dancers, Dance Enthusiasts, Choreographers

User Info: To subscribe to this Usenet newsgroup, you need access to a newsreader.

`news: rec.arts.dance`

Strathspey

A forum for the discussion of all aspects of Scottish Country Dancing, e.g. dancing technique.

Keywords: Dance, Scotland, Scottish Dance

Audience: Dancers, Dance Historians

Contact: owner-strathspey@math.uni-frankfurt.de

Details: Free

User Info: To subscribe to the list, send an e-mail message requesting a subscription to the URL address below.

To send a message to the entire list, address it to: strathspey@math.uni-frankfurt.de

`mailto:strathspey-request@math.uni-frankfurt.de`

University of New Hampshire Videotex Library

The library's holdings are large and wide-ranging and contain significant collections in many fields.

Keywords: Dance, Folk Music, Milne (A.A., Collection of), Galway (Ireland)

Audience: Researchers, Students, General Public

Contact: Robin Tuttle
r_tuttle1@unhh.unh.edu

Details: Free

Expect: USERNAME; Send: Student (no password required). Control-z to log off.

`telnet://unhvt@unh.edu`

Dante

Dartmouth Dante DatabaseLibrary

This database is focused entirely on the works of Dante.

Keywords: Dante

Audience: Dante Scholars, Educators (College, University)

Details: Free

User Info: Expect: login, Send: wolfpac

`telnet://dartmouth.edu`

Dark Shadows

dark-shadows

Dark Shadows was a daily soap opera that ran on ABC in the late Sixties (ending in 1971). It had a Gothic feel to it and featured storylines involving the supernatural.

Keywords: Television, Television Series

Audience: Horror Enthusiasts, Soap Opera Enthusiasts

Contact: Bernie Roehl
shadows-request@sunee.waterloo.ca

Details: Free

User Info: To subscribe to the list, send an e-mail message requesting a subscription to the URL address below.

To send a message to the entire list, address it to:
shadows@usunee.waterloo.ca

`news:alt.horror`

`news:rec.arts.tv.soaps`

Dartmouth College Library

Dartmouth College Library

The library's holdings are large and wide-ranging and contain significant collections in many fields.

Keywords: Calligraphy, Cervantes (Miguel de), Railroads, Polar Regions, Frost (Robert), Shakespeare (William), Spanish Plays

Audience: General Public, Researchers, Librarians, Document Delivery Professionals

Contact: Katharina Klemperer
kathy.klemperer@dartmouth.edu

Details: Free

User Info: Expect: login, Send: wolfpac

`telnet://lib.dartmouth.edu`

Data General

dg-users

The mailing list is concerned with the technical details of Data General, its O/Ss, and the cornucopia of hardware they supply and support.

Keywords: Computer Hardware, Data General

Audience: Computer Hardware Users

Contact: brian@ilinx.wimsey.com

User Info: To subscribe to the list, send an e-mail message requesting a subscription to the URL address below.

To send a message to the entire list, address it to: dg-users-request@ilinx.wimsey.com

`mailto:dg-users-request@ilinx.wimsey.com`

data-exp

data-exp

The mail list server provides an open forum for users to discuss the Visualization Data Explorer Package. It contains three files at the moment: a. FAQ, b. summary, and c. forum.

Keywords: Computing, Software, Hardware, Visualization Data Explorer Package

Audience: Computer Users

User Info: To subscribe to the list, send an e-mail message requesting a subscription to the URL address below.

To send a message to the entire list, address it to: stein@watson.ibm.com

`mailto:stein@watson.ibm.com`

Database Management

Big-DB

Discussions pertaining to large databases (generally greater than 1 million records) and large database management systems such as IMS, DB2, and CCA's Model/204.

Keywords: Databases, Database Management

Audience: Database Users, Database Managers

Contact: Fareed Asad-Harooni
big-DB@midway.uchicago.edu

Details: Free

User Info: To subscribe to the list, send an e-mail message requesting a subscription to the URL address below.

`mailto:big-DB@midway.uchicago.edu`

Databases

Barron's Guide to Accessing On-Line Bibliographic Databases

A comprehensive listing of publicly-accessible online libraries, including login instructions for each site.

Keywords: Libraries, Databases

Sponsor: University of North Texas

Audience: Researchers, Library Users, Librarians

Contact: Billy Barron
billy@unt.edu

`gopher://alf.zfn.uni-bremen.de/Allgemeine`

Big-DB

Discussions pertaining to large databases (generally greater than 1 million records) and large database management systems such as IMS, DB2, and CCA's Model/204.

Keywords: Databases, Database Management

Audience: Database Users, Database Managers

Contact: Fareed Asad-Harooni
big-DB@midway.uchicago.edu

User Info: To subscribe to the list, send an e-mail message requesting a subscription to the URL address below.

Details: Free

`mailto:big-DB@midway.uchicago.edu`

Britannica Online

This web site provides an information service for Encyclopaedia Britannica, Inc. Its database allows for keyword searches, and also includes experimental articles.

Keywords: Information Retrieval, Databases

Sponsor: Encyclopaedia Britannica, Inc.

Audience: Researchers, Educators, Students

Contact: support@eb.com

Details: Costs

`http://www.eb.com`

DIALOG Bluesheets

This database contains records representing the Bluesheet documentation issued for all databases on the DIALOG Information Retrieval Service.

Keywords: Databases

Sponsor: Dialog Information Services, Inc., Palo Alto, CA, USA

Audience: Dialog Users, Market Researchers

Profile: All databases are represented, including bibliographic files, complete-text files, menu-driven files, and gateway services. Each record represents a Bluesheet and contains traditional first-page information, including a file description, subject coverage, sources, file data, origin, and legal terms and conditions. All searchable indexes, display codes, field names, examples, sorts, limits, report fields, map fields, predefined formats, and direct record access information are included. Source information for the DIALOG Bluesheets database is derived from print Bluesheet documentation. Additional information not found on the printed Bluesheets is also included, such as the availability of DIALOG AlertSM service, Classroom Instruction Program databases, type of data in the file, document types indexed in the database represented, DIALINDEX category acronyms, and annual accession number ranges for files having accession number limits.

Contact: Dialog in the US at (800) 334-2564, Dialog internationally at country-specific locations.

User Info: To subscribe, contact Dialog directly.

Notes: Coverage: same as for all Dialog databases; updated weekly.

`telnet://dialog.com`

ERIC (Educational Resources Information Center)

ERIC is a database of short abstracts and information about education-related topics of interest to teachers and administrators.

Keywords: Education, Databases

Sponsor: (Office of Educational Research and Development), US Department of Education, Department of Education (ED)

Audience: Educators, Administrators

Profile: ERIC is the complete database on educational materials from the Educational Resources Information Center in Washington, DC. The database corresponds to two print indexes: Resources in Education, which is concerned with identifying the most significant and timely education research reports; and Current Index to Journals in Education, an index of more than 700 periodicals of interest to every segment of the teaching profession.

Details: Costs

ERIC can be accessed in a variety of ways, for example, through CARL (Colorado Alliance of Research Libraries), through the University of Saskatchewan

(Request: sklib username: sonia)

ERIC can also be accessed by WAIS if you have WAIS installed on your local computer.

`telnet://pac.carl.org`

`telnet://skdevel12.usask.ca`

foxpro-l

This mailing list is designed to foster information sharing between users of the FoxPro™ database development environment now owned and distributed by Microsoft. Both new and experienced users of FoxPro are welcome to join in the discussions.

Keywords: Databases, Computers, Microsoft Corp.

Audience: Database Users, Microsoft FoxPro Users, Software Engineers

Contact: Chris O'Neill coneill@heaven.polarbear.rankin-inlet.nt.ca

Details: Free

User Info: To subscribe to the list, send an e-mail message requesting a subscription to the URL address below.

To send a message to the entire list, address it to: foxpro-l@polarbear.rankin-inlet.nt.ca

`mailto:fileserv@polarbear.rankin-inlet.nt.ca`

GIS Master Bibliography Project

A bibliography of GIS literature encompassing journal articles, conference proceedings, books, and technical reports.

Keywords: GIS, Databases

Sponsor: Ohio State University - Department of Geography and others

Audience: GIS Users, Researchers, Students

Contact: Dr. Duane Marble marble.1@osu.edu

Details: Free

`ftp://128.146.209.34/biblio`

Internet Libraries (Gopher)

The site maintains the most current possible list of all library catalogs accessible on the Internet.

Keywords: Libraries, Databases, Internet, Information Retrieval

Audience: Reseacher, Students, Librarians

Contact: Gopherlib gopherlib@gopher.yale.edu

`gopher://yaleinfo.yale.edu`

Links to Many Databases

A collection of links to over 40 databases covering a wide variety of subjects ranging from Postmodern Culture to the 1990 Census.

Keywords: Databases, Research

Sponsor: University of Texas, Austin, Texas, USA

Audience: Researchers, General Public

Contact: remark@ftp.cc.utexas.edu

`gopher://ftp.cc.utexas.edu`

MS-Access

A list for the discussion of MS (Microsoft) Access topics, including Access Basic questions, reviews, rumors, and so on.

Keywords: Microsoft Access Program, Databases

Audience: MS-Access Users

Details: Free

User Info: To subscribe to the list, send an e-mail message requesting subscription to the URL address below.

`mailto:ms-access-request@eunet.co.at`

NASA/IPAC Extragalactic Database (NED)

Contains positions, basic data, and over 500,000 names for 250,000 extragalactic objects, as well as some 450,000 bibliographic references to 21,000 published papers, and 25,000 notes from catalogs and other publications.

A B C **D** E F G H I J K L M N O P Q R S T U V W X Y Z

A B C **D** E F G H I J K L M N O P Q R S T U V W X Y Z

Keywords: Astronomy, Databases

Sponsor: Jet Propulsory Lab/ Infrared Processing and Analysis Center

Audience: Astronomers, Scientists

Profile: Uses a VT100 or X-based interface.

Contact: G. Helou, B. Madore, M. Schmitz
ned@ipac.caltech.edu

Details: Free

User Info: Telnet to URL address below; Expect: login; Send: ned

Notes: sshare@cscns.com

service@cscns.com

`telnet://ned@ned.ipac.caltech.edu`

`ftp://ned.ipac.caltech.edu/pub/ned`

Progress

Discussion of the Progress RDBMS (Relational Database Management System).

Keywords: Databases, Computing

Audience: Computer Users, Business Students

Contact: Progress-list-request@math.niu.edu

Details: Free

User Info: To subscribe to the list, send an e-mail message requesting a subscription to the URL address below. To send a message to the entire list, address it to: progress-list@math.niu.edu

`mailto:Progress-list-request@math.niu.edu`

Research Databases and Resources by Subject

A collection of databases on over forty subjects, ranging from Anthropology to Women's Studies.

Keywords: Databases, Academic Research

Sponsor: University of California at Berkeley

Audience: Researchers, General Public

Contact: Gopher Manager

gophcom@infolib.lib.berkeley.edu

`gopher://umslvma.umsl.edu/library/Subjects/Biology/Bioformt/Biodbs <Heads Classification>`

`gopher://infolib.lib.berkeley.edu`

SABINET (South African Bibliographic and Information Network)

This gopher offers information searches from a variety of electronic databases, as well as for library locations and availability of books and periodicals.

Keywords: South Africa, Databases, Networks

Audience: South African Internet Surfers

Contact: hennie@info1.sabinet.co.za

Details: Free

`gopher://info2.sabinet.co.za`

The Tumor Gene Database

A database containing information about genes associated with tumorigenesis and cellular transformation.

Keywords: Genetics, Diseases, Biomedical Research, Databases

Sponsor: Department of Cell Biology, Baylor College of Medicine

Audience: Biomedical Researchers

Contact: David Steffen, Ph.D.
steffen@bcm.tmc.edu

`gopher://mbcr.bcm.tmc.edu`

U.S. Patent and Trademark Office Database

A database of patents issued in 1994 by the U.S. Patent and Trademark Office, including a searchable index.

Keywords: Patents, Databases, Inventions, Business

Sponsor: New York University School of Business

Audience: Inventors, General Public

Contact: questions@town.hall.org

`gopher://town.hall.org/patent`

White House Information Service

An outstanding database of current White House information, from 1992 to the present.

Keywords: White House, Politics, President (US), Database

Sponsor: Texas A & M University

Audience: General Public

Profile: Much of the older information on this site was obtained from the clinton@marist.bitnet listserv list or the alt.politics.clinton Usenet newsgroup, both of which receive the information indirectly via the MIT White House information server. Newer and current material is received directly from the MIT distribution list. The menu includes a searchable database and headings such as Domestic Affairs (Health Care, Technology, and so on), Press Briefings and Conferences, the President's Daily Schedule, and many more.

Contact: whadmin@tamu.edu

Details: Free

`gopher://tamuts.tamu.edu/11/.dir/president.dir`

Datsuns

datsun-roadsters

A mailing list for discussing any and all aspects of the owning, showing, repairing, driving, and so on, of Datsun roadsters.

Keywords: Datsuns, Automobiles

Audience: Datsun Owners, Automobile Enthusiasts

Contact: Mark J. Bradakis
datsun-roadsters-request@autox.team.net
datsun-roadsters-request@hoosier.utah.edu

Details: Free

User Info: To subscribe to the list, send an e-mail message requesting a subscription to the URL address below.

To send a message to the entire list, address it to: datsun-roadsters-request@autox.team.net

`mailto:datsun-roadsters-request@autox.team.net`

DC-MOTSS

DC-MOTSS

DC-MOTSS is a social mailing list for the gay, lesbian, and bisexual folks who live in the Washington Metropolitan Area—everything within approximately 50 miles of The Mall.

Keywords: Gays, Lesbians, Bisexuality, Washington DC

Audience: Gays, Lesbians, Bisexuals, Washington DC Residents

Contact: DC-MOTSS-request@vector.intercon.com

Details: Free

User Info: To subscribe to the list, send an e-mail message requesting a subscription to the URL address below.

To send a message to the entire list, address it to: DC-MOTSS-request@vector.intercon.com

`mailto:DC-MOTSS-request@vector.intercon.com`

DCRaves

DCRaves

One of several regional rave-related mailing lists, DCRaves covers the Washington, DC, area exclusively. Archives are available through the listserv, FTP, or gopher at american.edu.

Keywords: Raves, Washington DC

Audience: Ravers

Details: Free

User Info: To subscribe to the list, send an e-mail message to the URL address shown below consisting of a single line reading:

SUB dcraves YourFirstName YourLastName

To send a message to the entire list, address it to: dcraves@american.edu

`mailto:listserv@american.edu`

DDN (Defense Data Network)

DDN Management Bulletin ★

A means of communicating official policy, procedures, and other information of concern to management personnel at DDN facilities.

Keywords: Defense, DDN

Sponsor: DDN Network Info Center

Audience: Defense Analysts

Contact: nic@nic.ddn.mil

Details: Free

`ftp://nic.ddn.mil`

DDN New User Guide ★

Defense Data Network (DDN) guide for new users.

Keywords: Internet, Internet Guides, Defense, Security, DDN

Audience: Internet Surfers

Details: Free

File is: netinfo/nug.doc

`ftp://nic.ddn.mil/netinfo`

DDTs-Users

DDTs-Users

The DDTs-Users mailing list is for discussions of issues related to the DDTs defect-tracking software from QualTrak, including software, methods, mechanisms, techniques, general usage tips, policies, bugs, and bug workarounds.

Keywords: Software, Software Defects

Audience: Computer Users

Contact: ddts-users-request@bigbird.bu.edu

User Info: To subscribe to the list, send an e-mail message requesting a subscription to the URL address below.

To send a message to the entire list, address it to: ddts-users-request@bigbird.bu.edu

`mailto:ddts-users-request@bigbird.bu.edu`

de Bono (Edward)

de Bono ★★

This is a discussion list concerning the work of Edward de Bono. Also provides help with teaching the CoRT Thinking Program, and Six Thinking Hats.

Keywords: de Bono (Edward), Education (Alternative), Creativity

Audience: Teachers, Students, Management Trainers

Contact: Rosa Casarez

`mailto: rcasarez@mercury.sfsu.edu`

dead-runners

dead-runners ★

The Dead Runners Society is a mailing list for runners who like to talk about the psychological, philosophical, and personal aspects of running.

Keywords: Running, Sports

Audience: Runners, Athletes

Contact: Christopher Mark Conn dead-runners-request@unx.sas.com

Details: Free

User Info: To subscribe to the list, send an e-mail message requesting a subscription to the URL address below.

To send a message to the entire list, address it to: dead-runners-request@unx.sas.com

`mailto:dead-runners-request@unx.sas.com`

Deafness

Deaf Gopher ★★

Gopher menu of deaf resources in the State of Michigan.

Keywords: Disabilities, Deafness, Health

Sponsor: Michigan State University

Audience: Deaf and Disabled People, Health Care Professionals, Activists, Policy Makers, Rehabilitation Counselors, Therapists

Profile: A small but useful menu of deaf resources that includes a collection of files in essay and/or report form about a variety of historical and cultural aspects of deafness.

Contact: Gary LaPointe deafgopher@ah3.cal.msu.edu

Details: Free

`gopher://cl.msu.edu/11/msu/dept/deaf`

Disability-Related Resources ★★

A collection of information that includes newsletters for deaf/blind issues, electronic resources for the deaf, and a section on Chronic Fatigue Syndrome.

Keywords: Disabilities, Deafness, Blindness, Chronic Fatigue Syndrome

Sponsor: University of Washington DO-IT Program

Audience: Deaf and Disabled People, Health Care Professionals

Contact: Sheryl Burgstahler, Ph.D. doit@u.washington.edu

`gopher://hawking.u.washington.edu`

Deborah Harry and Blondie Information Service

Deborah Harry and Blondie Information Service ★

An information service on everything and anything regarding Deborah Harry and Blondie, including tour information, recordings/films release information, and so on.

Keywords: Rock Music, Harry (Deborah), Musical Groups

Audience: Rock Music Enthusiasts, Deborah Harry Enthusiasts

Contact: gunter@yarrow.wt.uwa.oz.au

Details: Free

User Info: To subscribe to the list, send an e-mail message requesting a subscription to the URL address below.

To send a message to the entire list, address it to: gunter@yarrow.wt.uwa.oz.au

`mailto:gunter@yarrow.wt.uwa.oz.au`

DEC

DECNEWS for Education and Research ★★★

Monthly electronic newsletter from Digital Equipment Corporation (DEC) summarizing announcements of its products, programs, and applications of interest to computer users in the academic and research communities.

Keywords: Computers, Education

Sponsor: Digital Equipment Corp.

Audience: Computer Users, Educators, Researchers

Contact: Mary Hoffmann decnews@mr4dec.enet.dec.com

Details: Free

A
B
C
D
E
F
G
H
I
J
K
L
M
N
O
P
Q
R
S
T
U
V
W
X
Y
Z

A B C D E F G H I J K L M N O P Q R S T U V W X Y Z

User Info: To subscribe, send an e-mail message to the address below consisting of a single line reading:

SUB DECNews YourFirstName YourLastName

To send a message to the entire list, address it to: DECNews@ubvm.buffalo.edu

`mailto:listserv@ubvm.buffalo.edu`

DECnews-EDU ★

DECNEWS for Education and Research is a monthly electronic publication from Digital Equipment Corporation's Education Business Unit for the education and research communities worldwide.

Keywords: Education, Computers, DEC

Audience: Educators, Researchers

Contact: Anne Marie McDonald
decnews@mr4dec.enet.dec.com

Details: Free

User Info: To subscribe to the list, send an e-mail message requesting a subscription to the URL address below.

To send a message to the entire list, address it to: decnews@mr4dec.enet.dec.com

`mailto:decnews@mr4dec.enet.dec.com`

DECnews-PR ★

DECnews for Press and Analysts is an Internet-based distribution of all Digital Equipment Corporation press releases. This is a one-way mailing list. Approximately eight press releases per week.

Keywords: DEC, Computers

Audience: Computing Consultants, Computing Analysts

Contact: Russ Jones
decnews-pr-request@pa.dec.com

User Info: To subscribe to the list, send an e-mail message requesting a subscription to the URL address below.

To send a message to the entire list, address it to: decnews-pr-request@pa.dec.com

User Info: To subscribe, send e-mail to decnews-pr@pa.dec.com with a subject line of

Subject: subscribe. Please include your name and telephone number in the body of the subscription request.

`mailto:decnews-pr-request@pa.dec.com`

DECnews-UNIX ★

DECnews for UNIX is published by Digital Equipment Corporation every three weeks and contains product and service information of interest to the Digital UNIX community.

Keywords: DEC, UNIX, Computers

Audience: UNIX Users

Contact: Russ Jones
decnews-unix-request@pa.dec.com

User Info: To subscribe to the list, send an e-mail message requesting a subscription to the URL address below.

To send a message to the entire list, address it to: decnews-unix-request@pa.dec.com

User Info: To subscribe, send e-mail to decnews-unix@pa.dec.com with a subject line of Subject: subscribe abstract. Please include your name and telephone number in the body of the subscription request.

`mailto:decnews-unix-request@pa.dec.com`

DECstation-managers ★

Fast-turnaround troubleshooting tool for managers of RISC DECstations.

Keywords: DEC, Computers

Audience: Computer Systems Analysts/ Programmers, Engineers

Contact: decstation-managers-request@ornl.gov

User Info: To subscribe to the list, send an e-mail message to the URL address shown below consisting of a single line reading:

SUB decstation-manager YourFirstName YourLastName

To send a message to the entire list, address it to: decstation-manager@msu.edu

`mailto:majordomo@ornl.gov`

DECUS

DECuserve-journal ★

A monthly digest of technical discussions that take place on the DECUS conferencing system, open to anyone who is interested in Digital Equipment topics, "3rd party" topics, and connectivity topics.

Keywords: DECUS, Conferencing System

Audience: Conferencing System Users

Contact: Sharon Frey
frey@eisner.decus.org

User Info: To subscribe to the list, send an e-mail message requesting a subscription to the URL address below.

To send a message to the entire list, address it to: frey@eisner.decus.org

`mailto:frey@eisner.decus.org`

Deed Transfers

ASSETS (Real Estate Tax Assessor and Deed Transfer Records)   ★★★

The RealEstate Tax Assessor and Deed Transfer Records (ASSETS) library contains information compiled from real property records.

Keywords: Real Estate, Property, Tax Assessor, Deed Transfers, Records

Audience: Lawyers

Profile: The ASSETS library contains a variety of real estate information, including asset ownership, property address, owner's mailing address, assessed valuation, current market value, and recent property sales and deed transfers. Information is collected from county tax assessors' and recorders' offices nationwide and compiled by TRW REDI Property Data. The ASSETS library also contains a variety of boat and aircraft registration information.

Contact: Mead New Sales Group at (800) 227-4908 or (513) 859-5398 inside the US, or (513) 865-7981 for all inquiries outside the US.

User Info: To subscribe, contact Mead directly.

To examine the Nexis user guide, you can access it at the ftp site of the University of Texas at Austin at the URL address: ftp://ftp.cc.utexas.edu

The files are in: /pub/ref-services/LEXIS

`telnet://nex.meaddata.com`

`http://www.meaddata.com`

Defense

DDN Management Bulletin   ★

A means of communicating official policy, procedures, and other information of concern to management personnel at DDN facilities.

Keywords: Defense, DDN

Sponsor: DDN Network Info Center

Audience: Defense Industry Followers

Contact: NIC@NIC.DDN.MIL

Details: Free

`ftp//nic.ddn.mil`

DDN New User Guide   ★

Defense Data Network (DDN) guide for new users.

Keywords: Internet, Internet Guides, Defense, Security

Audience: Internet Surfers

Details: Free

File is: netinfo/nug.doc

`ftp://nic.ddn.mil/netinfo`

DMS/FI Market Intelligence Reports

DMS/FI Market Intelligence Reports is the largest collection of unclassified defense and aerospace information available from any single source.

Keywords: Defense, Aerospace

Sponsor: Forecast International/DMS, Newtown, CT, USA

Audience: Defense Analysts

Profile: This file contains the most comprehensive and up-to-date full-text data and analysis for the industry and provides users with valuable information on defense budgets, aerospace and weapons programs, power systems, companies (US and international), agencies, or countries that are involved in the aerospace/defense industry. File 589 contains a great deal of information relative to civil and commercial programs. Reports provide detailed and extensive information such as forecasts, major activity, funding, inventories, location, and much more. This information is gathered from such diverse sources as government documents, civil and defense journals, manufacturers, and field interviews with key industry people. This database is vital to anyone involved in market research, business development, or program management in the aerospace/defense industry.

Contact: Dialog in the US at (800) 334-2564, Dialog internationally at country-specific locations.

User Info: To subscribe, contact Dialog directly.

Notes: Coverage: Current; updated weekly.

`telnet://dialog.com`

Jane's Defense & Aerospace News/Analysis

This file provides articles that summarize, highlight, and interpret worldwide events in the defense and aerospace industry.

Keywords: Defense, Aerospace, News Media

Sponsor: Jane's Information Group, Alexandria, VA US

Audience: Aerospace Industry Professionals

Profile: The database contains the complete text of the following publications: Jane's Defense Weekly, International Defense Review, Jane's Intelligence Review (formerly Jane's Soviet Intelligence Review), Interavia Aerospace Review, and Jane's Airport Review. File 587 also contains the complete text of DMS newsletters, which ceased publication in 1989.

Contact: Dialog in the US at (800) 334-2564, Dialog internationally at country-specific locations.

User Info: To subscribe, contact Dialog directly.

Notes: Coverage: 1982 to the present; updated weekly.

`telnet://dialog.com`

Lockheed Missiles & Space Company

A web site containing information about Lockheed Missiles and Space Company, a major aerospace and defense company specializing in the development of space systems, missiles, and other high technology products. Includes company information and press releases.

Keywords: Defense, Aerospace

Sponsor: The Lockheed Palo Alto Artificial Intelligence Center

Audience: Aerospace Industry Professionals

`http://www.lmsc.lockheed.com`

NATO

Online version of The NATO Handbook, which recommends changes for the future of the North Atlantic Treaty Organization in light of decreasing defense resources.

Keywords: NATO, Guidelines, Defense

Sponsor: The NATO Office of Information and Press

Audience: Goverment Officials, Military Personnel, Historians

Details: Free

Select from menu as appropriate.

`gopher://wiretap.spies.com`

Delaware

University of Delaware Libraries (DELCAT)

The library's holdings are large and wide-ranging and contain significant collections in many fields.

Keywords: Literature (American), Hemingway (Ernest), Papermaking (History of), Chemistry (History of), Literature (Irish), Delaware

Audience: General Public, Researchers, Librarians, Document Delivery Professionals

Contact: Stuart Glogoff
epo27855@udacsvm.bitnet

Details: Free

User Info: Expect: prompt, Send: RETURN 2-3 times

`telnet://delcat.udel.edu`

`telnet://delcat.acs.udel.edu`

Delphes European Business

Delphes European Business

This is a French database that provides information on international markets, products, industries, and companies from a European perspective.

Keywords: Business, Europe

Sponsor: Chamber of Commerce and Industry of Paris and The French Assembly of the Chambers of Commerce and Industry, Paris, France

Audience: Business Professionals, Business Analysts

Profile: Abstracts are produced by approximately 60 local organizations grouped into two networks, CCIP (Chamber of Commerce and Industry of Paris) and ACFCI (French Assembly of the Chambers of Commerce and Industry), which collect and consolidate the information into the Delphes database. Delphes contains bibliographic citations and informative abstracts from over 900 European trade journals, newspapers, and business periodicals, in French, English, Italian, German, or Spanish. Titles are in the original language; abstracts are in French. A comprehensive classification scheme in English, French, and Spanish is used to index documents covered. Geographic coverage is 45% France, 35% Europe, and 20% is devoted to other countries. In addition, about 1,000 new books, corporate and business directories, and reports are reviewed each year.

Contact: Dialog in the US at (800) 334-2564, Dialog internationally at country-specific locations.

User Info: To subscribe, contact Dialog directly.

Notes: Coverage: 1980 to the present; updated weekly.

`telnet://dialog.com`

Delphi

Delphi

Delphi is an online service provider.

Keywords: Internet

Sponsor: Delphi, NewsCorp. Technologies

Audience: Internet Users

Details: Costs

`telnet://delphi.com`

A
B
C
D
E
F
G
H
I
J
K
L
M
N
O
P
Q
R
S
T
U
V
W
X
Y
Z

A
B
C
D
E
F
G
H
I
J
K
L
M
N
O
P
Q
R
S
T
U
V
W
X
Y
Z

Democracy

Historical Documents

A collection of historical documents (with particular emphasis on freedom and democracy) ranging from the Magna Carta to Nelson Mandela's Inauguration Speech.

Keywords: History (World), Democracy

Sponsor: The Queens Borough Public Library

Audience: Historians, Activists, General Public

`gopher://vax.queens.lib.ny.us/Social Sciences/Historical Documents`

Political Platforms of the US

Full text of various documents including the Democratic platform of 1992, the Jerry Brown positions of 1992, the Libertarian platform of 1990, and more.

Keywords: Politics (US), Government (US Federal), Democracy, Libertarian Politics

Audience: Politicians, Grass-Roots Organizers, Journalists

Details: Free

`gopher://wiretap.spies.com/11/Gov/Platform`

Democratic Socialists of America
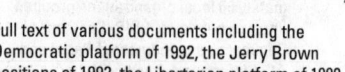

DSA-LGB

DSA-LGB is a mailing list for members of the Lesbian/Gay/Bisexual Commission of the Democratic Socialists of America, and for others interested in similar concerns.

Keywords: Democratic Socialists of America, Gay, Lesbian

Audience: Democratic Socialists, Gays, Lesbians

Contact: DSA-LGB-request@midway.uchicago.edu

User Info: To subscribe to the list, send an e-mail message requesting a subscription to the URL address below.

To send a message to the entire list, address it to: DSA-LGB-request@midway.uchicago.edu

`mailto:DSA-LGB-request@midway.uchicago.edu`

Demography

1991 Census of Population Documentation

This gopher provides Canadian Census information from 1991 including geographic and demographic information.

Keywords: Census Data, Canada, Demography, Geography

Audience: Canadians, Researchers, Demographers

Contact: David McCallum
carl@acadvm1.uottawa.ca

`gopher://alpha.epas.utoronto.ca/Data Library/Census of Population`

ANU (Australian National University) Asian-Settlements Database ★★★

A searchable database containing abstracts of theses and research studies provided by the Asian Institute of Technology, relating to issues of demography and social geography in Asia.

Keywords: Asian Studies, Demography, Geography

Sponsor: The COOMBSQUEST Social Sciences & Humanities Information Facility at ANU (Australian National University), Canberra, Australia

Audience: Asia Studies Instructors, Demographers, Geographers

Contact: Dr. T. Matthew Ciolek
coombspapers@coombs.anu.edu.au

Details: Free

`gopher://cheops.anu.edu.au/Coombs-db/ANU-Asian-Settlements.src`

`http://coombs.anu.edu.au/WWWVL-AsianStudies.html`

ANU (Australian National University) Demography and Publications Database

A WAIS database of publications on demography by researchers from Australian National University.

Keywords: Demography

Sponsor: Research Schools of Social Sciences & Pacific and Asian Studies, ANU (Australian National University), Canberra, Australia

Audience: Demographers

Contact: demography@anu.edu.au

`waissrc:/Coombs-db/ANU-Demography-Publications.src`

`gopher://cheops.anu.edu.au/7waissrc/Coombs-db/ANU-Demography-Publications.src`

U.S. Bureau of the Census Gopher

A gopher offering official Census data and services direct from the Census Bureau.

Keywords: Census, Demography, Statistics

Sponsor: U.S. Census Bureau

Audience: Journalists, Government Officials, General Public

Profile: A wealth of demographic and economic data from the Census Bureau. Information available includes population estimates, financial data from state and local governments, and assorted statistical briefs. This gopher also has details on the offices, programs, and personnel of the Bureau itself, as well as links to other federal information systems and sources of Census data.

Contact: gatekeeper@census.gov

Details: Images, Free

`gopher://gopher.census.gov`

`http://www.census.gov`

Denmark

DENet Information Server

This is the gopher of the Danish national academic network, which is located at the Danish Computer Centre for Research and Education (UNI-C).

Keywords: Education, Denmark, Libraries

Audience: Researchers, Educators

Profile: This gopher provides DENet information and statistics, UNI-C information, directory services and phone books, pointers to Danish electronic libraries and gophers, an index of major Danish FTP archives, and news in Danish.

Contact: Steen.Linden@uni-c.dk

Details: Free

`gopher://gopher.denet.dk`

Denmark's Library for Medicine and Science

Keywords: Science, Medicine, Libraries, Denmark

Audience: Scientists, Health Care Professionals, Medical Researchers

Details: Free

At the CCL>prompt type DIA ENG for English interface.

`telnet://cosmos.bib.dk`

Dentistry

Dental Information Area

A collection of dental information, including a selection of related educational software and dental informatics materials.

Keywords: Dentistry, Health Care, Informatics

Sponsor: Columbia School of Oral and Dental Surgery

Audience: Dentists, Medical Students, Health Care Professionals

Contact: Dr. John Zimmerman
jlz4@columbia.edu

`gopher://cuhsla.cpmc.columbia.edu/`
`health.sci/dental.toc`

MEDLINE

MEDLINE is a major source of bibliographic biomedical literature. The MEDLINE database encompasses information from three printed indexes (Index Medicus, Index to Dental Literature and the International Nursing Index) as well as additional information not published in the Index Medicus.

Keywords: Biomedicine, Dentistry, Nursing, Medicine

Sponsor: U.S. National Library of Medicine

Audience: Librarians, Researchers, Physicians, Students

Contact: CDP Technologies Sales Department (800)950-2035, extension 400

User Info: To subscribe, contact CDP Technologies directly

`telnet://cdplus@cdplus.com`

University of Texas Health Science Center at San Antonio Library

The library's holdings are large and wide-ranging and contain significant collections in many fields.

Keywords: Allied Health, Dentistry, Nursing, Veterinary Science, Ambulatory Care, Obstetrics/Gynecology, Pediatrics

Audience: Researchers, Students, General Public

Details: Free

User Info: Expect: Login, Send: LIS

`telnet:// athena.uthscsa.edu`

Deos-L

Deos-L

A mailing list intended to promote communication among distance educators, to disseminate information and requests about distance education around the world, and to discuss issues raised in the electronic journal DEOSNEWS.

Keywords: Education (Distance), Education (Continuing)

Sponsor: The American Center for the Study of Distance Education, Pennsylvania State University, Pennsylvania, USA

Audience: Distance Educators, Administrators

User Info: To subscribe to the list, send an e-mail message to the URL address below consisting of a single line reading:

SUB deos-l YourFirstName YourLastName

To send a message to the entire list, address it to: deos-l@psuvm.psu.edu

`mailto:listserv@psuvm.psu.edu`

deosnews (Distance Education Online Symposium)

deosnews (Distance Education Online Symposium)

The Distance Education Online Symposium publishes The American Journal of Distance Education.

Keywords: Education (Adult), Education (Distance), Education (Continuing)

Sponsor: Distance Education Online Symposium, American Center for the Study of Distance Education, Pennsylvania State University, State College, PA

Audience: Educators, Administrators, Researchers

Details: Free

User Info: To subscribe to the journal, send an e-mail message to the URL address shown below consisting of a single line reading:

SUB deosnews YourFirstName YourLastName

`mailto:listserv@psuvm.bitnet`

Department of Defense

National Technology Transfer Center (NTTC)

A federally-funded national network to apply government research to commercial applications.

Keywords: Technology, Technology Transfer, Research and Development, Business and Industry, Department of Defense, Government (US)

Sponsor: National Technology Transfer Center

Audience: Business People, Entrepreneurs, Manufactures, Technology Enthusiasts

Profile: Features state-by-state listings of agencies designed to facilitate the adaptation of new technologies to industry. Also provides updates on conferences, and a current list of Department of Defense projects soliciting private assistance from small businesses. Allows limited access to NTTC databases.

Contact: Charles Monfradi
cmonfra@nttc.edu, info@nttc.edu

`gopher://iron.nttc.edu`

`http://iridium.nttc.edu/nttc.hmtl`

Department of Justice Gopher

Department of Justice Gopher

A gopher containing online information from the Justice Department.

Keywords: Federal Laws (US), Government (US), Justice Department

Sponsor: United States Department of Justice

Audience: Lawyers, Citizens

Profile: The Department of Justice (DOJ) gopher features DOJ criminal and law enforcement statistics, as well as agency procurement requests, job listings, and press releases. Also has links to other US government online systems.

Contact: gopher@usdoj.gov

`gopher://gopher.usdoj.gov`

A B C D E F G H I J K L M N O P Q R S T U V W X Y Z

A
B
C
D
E
F
G
H
I
J
K
L
M
N
O
P
Q
R
S
T
U
V
W
X
Y
Z

Department of Labor

NLSNews Newsletter (National Longitudinal Surveys of Labor Market Experience)

Issued by the Center for Human Resource Research (Ohio State University); distributed to researchers using NLS data, as well as to other interested persons.

Keywords: Labor, Government (US), Department of Labor

Sponsor: Bureau of Labor Statistics, US Department of Labor

Audience: Statisticians, Researchers (Labor)

Profile: A typical issue contains updates on the status and availability of NLS data tapes and CD-ROMs for the six NLS cohorts (Older Men, Mature Women, Young Men, Young Women, Youth, and Children), notices to researchers of data-file or documentation errors, summaries of in-progress and completed NLS research, and other information of general interest to the NLS research community.

Contact: Gale James
james@ohsthr.bitnet

A description of the subscription service that enables users to automatically receive, as soon as it becomes available, the latest issue of the NLS Newsletter and/or error updates can be found in the file subscribe.info, available via nlserve@ohsthr.bitnet, the Center's file server.

`mailto:james@ohsthr.bitnet`

derby

derby

To discuss various aspects and strategies of horseracing, primarily dealing with, but not limited to, handicapping.

Keywords: Horseracing, Handicapping

Audience: Horseracing Enthusiasts

Contact: John Wilkes
derby-request@ekrl.com

User Info: To subscribe to the list, send an e-mail message requesting a subscription to the URL address below.

To send a message to the entire list, address it to: derby-request@ekrl.com

`mailto:derby-request@ekrl.com`

Dermatology

rxderm-l

A mailing list intended for promoting the discussion of dermatologic treatment among practicing dermatologists.

Keywords: Dermatology, Skin, Disease, Doctors

Audience: Dermatologists

Contact: A.C. Huntley
achuntley@ucdavis.edu

User Info: To subscribe to the list, send an e-mail message to the URL address below consisting of a single line reading:

SUB rxderm-l YourFirstName YourLastName. To send a message to the entire list, address it to: rxderm-l@ucdavis.edu

`mailto:listserv@ucdavis.edu`

Derwent World Patents Index

Derwent World Patents Index

Patent specifications issued by the patent offices of 33 major issuing authorities.

Keywords: Patents, Intellectual Property, Trademarks

Sponsor: Derwent Publications, Ltd.

Audience: Patent Attorneys, Patent Agents, Librarians, Researchers

Profile: Includes European Patent Office and Patent Cooperation Treaty published applications, plus Research Disclosure and International Technology Disclosure. Each patent is extensively indexed from the complete patent specifications. Abstracts are included.

Contact: paul.albert@neteast.com

User Info: To subscribe contact Orbit-Questel directly.

`telnet://orbit.com`

Deryni-L

Deryni-L

A list for readers and fans of Katernine Kurtz's novels and other works.

Keywords: Science Fiction, Kurtz (Katernine)

Audience: Science Fiction Readers

Contact: Edward J. Branley
elendil@mintir.new-orleans.la.us

User Info: To subscribe to the list, send an e-mail message requesting a subscription to the URL address below.

To send a message to the entire list, address it to: deryni-l@mintir.new-orleans.la.us

`mailto:deryni-l@mintir.new-orleans.la.us`

Design

Engineering-Design

Supports researchers at the five national Engineering Design Centres.

Keywords: Engineering, Design

Audience: Engineers, Researchers

Contact: engineering-design-request@mailbase.ac.uk

Details: Free

User Info: To subscribe to the list, send an e-mail message to the URL address shown below consiting of a single line reading:

SUB engineering-design YourFirstName YourLastName

To send a message to the entire list, address it to:

engineering-design@mailbase.ac.uk

`mailbase@mailbase.ac.uk`

Engineering; A. Park, J. Miller

This directory is a compilation of information resources focused on engineering.

Keywords: Engineering, Design

Audience: Engineers, Students, Educators

Details: Free

`ftp://una.hh.lib.umich.edu/70/inetdirstacks/engin:parkmiller`

Geodesic

A mailing list for the discussion of Buckminster Fuller's works.

Keywords: Geodesic Quantum Physics, Design, Fuller (Buckminster)

Audience: Designers, Physicists

Contact: Patrick G. Salsbury
salsbury@acsu.buffalo.edu

Details: Free

User Info: To subscribe to the list, send an e-mail message to the URL address shown below consisting of a single line reading:

SUB geodesic YourFirstName YourLastName

To send a message to the entire list, address it to:

geodesic@ubvm.cc.buffalo.edu

`mailto:listserv@ubvm.cc.buffalo.edu`

Gopher-Based ASCII Clip Art Collection

★★

A collection of over 500 individual pictures, ranging from images of food to Star Wars, created with ASCII characters. Organized by subject, and including archives of the Usenet group alt.ascii-art. Also contains links to other ASCII collections.

Keywords: Clip Art, Design

Sponsor: Texas Tech Computer Sciences Gopher Server

Audience: Computer Users, General Public

Contact: Abdul Malik Yoosufan gripe@cs.ttu.edu

Details: Free, Images

```
gopher://cs4sun.cs.ttu.edu
```

```
ftp://ftp.cs.ttu.edu:/pub/asciiart
```

Desktop Publishing

(The) DTP Direct Catalog

★

DTP Direct specializes in Macintosh hardware and software tools for desktop publishers and graphics professionals.

Keywords: Macintosh, Desktop Publishing, Graphic Design

Sponsor: InterNex Server Bureau

Audience: Graphic Designers, Artists, Desktop Publishers

Details: Free, Moderated, Image and Sound files available. Multimedia files available.

```
http://www.internex.net/DTP/home.html
```

CDPub

★

CDPub is an electronic mailing list for those engaged or interested in CD-ROM publishing in general, and in desktop CD-ROM recorders and publishing systems in particular. Topics of interest to the list include information on the various desktop publishing systems for premastering using CD-ROM media and tapes (e.g. DAT), replication services, various standards of interest to publishers (e.g. ISO9660, RockRidge), retrieval engines, and platform independence issues. Discussions on all platforms are welcome.

Keywords: CD-ROM, Electronic Publishing, Desktop Publishing

Audience: CD-ROM Publishers, Desktop Publishers, Publishers

Contact: CDPub-Info@knex.via.mind.org

Details: Free

User Info: To subscribe to the list, send an e-mail message requesting a subscription to the URL address below.

To send a message to the entire list, address it to: CDPub@knex.via.mind.org

```
mailto:mail-server@knex.via.mind.org
```

framers

 ★

This is a forum to share experiences and information about the FrameMaker desktop-publishing package from Frame Technology.

Keywords: Desktop Publishing

Audience: Desktop Publishers, Publishers

Details: Free

User Info: To subscribe to the list, send an e-mail message requesting a subscription to the URL address below.

To send a message to the entire list, address it to: framers@uunet.uu.net

```
mailto:framers-request@uunet.uu.net
```

journet

 ★★

An electronic conference for the discussion of topics of interest to journalists and journalism educators.

Keywords: Journalism, Writing, Desktop Publishing, Electronic Publishing <Standard Audience>Journalists, Writers, Publishers, Educators

Audience: Journalism, Writing, Desktop Publishing, Electronic Publishing <Standard Audience>Journalists, Writers, Publishers, Educators

Contact: George Frajkor gfrajkor@ccs.carleton.ca

User Info: To subscribe to the list, send an e-mail message to the URL address below consisting of a single line reading:

SUB journet YourFirstName YourLastName

To send a message to the entire list, address it to: journet@qucdn.queensu.ca

```
mailto:listserv@qucdn.queensu.ca
```

PAGEMAKER

 ★

The PageMaker ListServ is dedicated to the discussion of desktop publishing in general, with emphasis on the use of Aldus PageMaker. The list discusses PageMaker's use in both the PC and Macintosh realms. The list also maintains an extensive archive of help files that are extremely useful for the modern desktop publisher.

Keywords: Desktop Publishing, Aldus Pagemaker, IBM PC, Macintosh

Audience: Desktop Publishers, Computer Users

Contact: Geoff Peters gwp@cs.purdue.edu

Details: Free

User Info: To subscribe to the list, send an e-mail message to the URL address shown below consisting of a single line reading:

SUB pagemaker YourFirstName YourLastName

To send a message to the entire list, address it to: gwp@cs.purdue.edu

```
mailto:listserv@cs.purdue.edu
```

Detective Fiction

Mystery

 ★

This mailing list reviews and discusses mystery and detective fiction, including works on film, television, and radio.

Keywords: Mystery Fiction, Detective Fiction, Books

Audience: Mystery Enthusiasts

Details: Free

User Info: To subscribe to the list, send an e-mail message requesting a subscription to the URL address below.

```
mailto:mystery-request@introl.com
```

Detectives

Investigators and Detectives

 ★★★

This resource provides information files for individuals involved with investigative research, as well as a free monthly newsletter.

Keywords: Detectives, Crime, Information Retrieval, Security

Audience: Investigators, Detectives, Information Brokers, General Public

Profile: Investigators and Detectives provides access to information covering topics such as private investigative research, strategies, sources, the art and science of investigating, theft deterrents, and electronic PI schematics and plans. Also offers a free sample of a newsletter covering various topics of interest to Private Investigators, such as techniques and strategies, security, and tracing.

Contact: Mike Enlow menlow@Intec.win.net michael@enlow.com

Details: Inside Secrets.

```
mailto:info@enlow.com
```

Development

AGRIS International

 ★★★

This database serves as a comprehensive inventory of worldwide agricultural literature that reflects research results, food production, and rural development.

Keywords: Agriculture, Rural Development, Food Production, Development

Sponsor: US National Agricultural Library, Beltsville, MD, USA

Audience: Agronomists, Market Researchers

A
B
C
D
E
F
G
H
I
J
K
L
M
N
O
P
Q
R
S
T
U
V
W
X
Y
Z

Profile: Designed to help users identify problems involved in all aspects of world food supply, the file corresponds in part to Agr Index, published monthly by the Food and Agriculture Organization (FAO) of the United Nations. Subject coverage focuses on many topics; general agriculture; geography and history; education, extension, and advisory work; administration and legislation; economics, development, and rural sociology; plant production; protection of plants and stored products; forestry; animal production; aquatic sciences and fisheries;machinery and buildings; natural resources; food science; home economics; human nutrition; pollution; and more.

Contact: Dialog in the US at (800) 334-2564

Details: Costs

User Info: To subscribe, contact Dialog directly.

`telnet://dialog.com`

apngowid.meet

A conference on plans by Asia Pacific regional women's groups for the United Nations Fourth World Conference on Women to be held in Beijing in September 1995.

Keywords: Women, Asia, Pacific, Feminists, Development, United Nations, World Conference on Women

Audience: Women, Feminists, Nongovernmental Organizations

Contact: AsPac Info, Docu and Communication Committee AP-IDC@p95.f401.n751.z6.g

Details: Costs, Moderated.

Establish an account on the nearest APC node. Login, type c for conferences, then type: go apngowid.meet.

For information on the nearest APC node, contact: APC International Secretariat IBASE e-mail: apcadmin@apc.org

`http://www.igc.apc.org/igc/www.women.html`

Community Networks Benefit Federal Goals

Statement by community networker Frank Odasz, founder and director of Big Sky Telegraph, a network of rural BBSs throughout Montana. In this article he makes the case that the federal goverment will benefit from the widespread rural employment of networking technology.

Keywords: Community, Networking, Rural Development, Development

Audience: Activists, Policy Analysts, Community Leaders, Government, Citizens, Rural Residents, Native Americans

Contact: Frank Odasz franko@bigsky.dillon.mt.us,

Details: Free

`http://nearnet.gnn.com/mag/articles/oram/bio.odasz.html`

devel-l

Discussion forum on technology transfer in international development.

Keywords: Development, Technology

Sponsor: Volunteers in Technical Assistance (VITA)

Audience: Technology Professionals

Contact: vita@gmuvax.gmu.edu

Details: Free

User Info: To subscribe to the list, send an e-mail message to the URL address shown below consisting of a single line reading:

SUB devel-l YourFirstName YourLastName

`mailto:listserv@auvm.american.edu`

DevelopNet News

A monthly newsletter on technology transfer in international development.

Keywords: Nonprofits, Technology, Development

Sponsor: Volunteers in Technical Assistance

Audience: Technology Professionals

Contact: R.R. Ronkin vita@gmuvax.gmu.edu

Details: Free

User Info: To subscribe, send an e-mail message to the address below.

Inquire about needing a password.

`mailto:vita@gmuvax.gmu.edu`

Global Change Information Gateway

★★★★

This gatewas was created to address environmental data management issues raised by the US Congress, the Administration, and the advisory arms of the Federal policy community. It contains documents related to the UN conference on Environment and Development.

Keywords: UN, Environment, Development, Oceans, Atmosphere

Audience: Environmentalists, Scientists, Researchers, Environmentalists

Profile: [profile needed]????????????

Details: Free

Select from menu as appropriate.

`gopher://scilibx.ucsc.edu`

World Bank Gopher Server

 ★★★

A collection of online information from the World Bank.

Keywords: Government (International), Development, International Finance, Foreign Trade

Sponsor: The World Bank

Audience: Nongovernmental Organizations, Activists, Government Officials, Environmentalists

Profile: A collection of World Bank information including a list of publications, environmental assessments, economic reports, and updates on current projects being funded by the World Bank.

Contact: webmaster@www.worldbank.org gopher://gopher.worldbank.org

`http://www.worldbank.org`

Development (International)

(The) Worldwide Impact of Network Access

This is an article by community networker Felipe Rodriquez. In this statement Rodriquez argues that developed countries should help less developed countries build their information infrastructures, and that governments should not censor the content of network traffic.

Keywords: Community, Networking, Europe, Development (International)

Audience: Activists, Policymakers, Community Leaders

Contact: Felipe Rodriquez felipe@hacktic.nl

`http://nearnet.gnn.com/mag/articles/oram/bio.rodriquez.html`

un.wcw.doc.eng

★

This is a read-only conference comprised of official UN documents for the United Nations Fourth World Conference on Women: Action for Equality, Development and Peace, scheduled to take place at the Beijing International Convention Center, Beijing, China, from 4-15 September 1995. The documents are provided by the official Conference Secretariat, are posted as received by the UN Non-Governmental Liaison Service (NGLS).

Keywords: Women, Development (International), Peace, UN, World Conference on Women

Audience: Women, Activists, Non-Governmental Organizations, Feminists

Contact: United Nations Non-Governmental Liaison Service/Edie Farwell ngls@igc.apc.org, efarwell@igc.apc.org

Details: Costs, Moderated

User Info: Establish an account on the nearest APC node. Login, type c for conferences, then type go un.wcw.doc.eng.

For information on the nearest APC node, contact:

APC International Secretariat IBASE e-mail: apcadmin@apc.org

`telnet://igc.apc.org`

United Nations

Includes full text of UN press releases, UN Conference on Environment and Development reports, UN Development Programme documents, U.N. telephone directories.

Keywords: UN, Environment, Development (International)

Audience: Researchers, Educators, Political Scientists, Environmentalists

Details: Free

`gopher://nywork1.undp.org`

Women.dev

Conference for information about local, regional, and international development as it relates to women. The conference includes bibliographies, statements, news, articles, and announcements about development and women in Africa, South America, and South Asia.

Keywords: Women, Development (International), International Politics

Audience: Women, Activists, Non-governmental Organizations, Feminists

Details: Free, Sound files available.

User Info: Establish an account on the nearest APC node. Login, type c for conferences, then type go women.dev.

For information on the nearest APC node, contact:

APC International Secretariat IBASE e-mail: apcadmin@apc.org

Contact: Carlos Afonso (cafonso@ax.apc.org) or
APC North American Regional Office e-mail: apcadmin@apc.org
Edie Farwell (efarwell@igc.apc.org)

`telnet://igc.apc.org`

Deviance

deviants

The workings of the Great Wok and all things deviant from social norms are discussed here.

Keywords: Deviance

Audience: Curiosity Seekers, Researchers, Deviants

Contact: deviants-request@csv.warwick.ac.uk

Details: Free

User Info: To subscribe to the list, send an e-mail message requesting a subscription to the URL address below.

To send a message to the entire list, address it to: deviants-request@csv.warwick.ac.uk

`mailto:deviants-request@csv.warwick.ac.uk`

dg-users

dg-users

The mailing list is concerned with the technical details of Data General, its O/Ss, and the cornucopia of hardware they supply and support.

Keywords: Computer Hardware, Data General

Audience: Computer Hardware Users

Contact: brian@ilinx.wimsey.com

User Info: To subscribe to the list, send an e-mail message requesting a subscription to the URL address below.

To send a message to the entire list, address it to: dg-users-request@ilinx.wimsey.com

`mailto:dg-users-request@ilinx.wimsey.com`

dh.mujer

dh.mujer

The Association for Progressive Communications conference for women and human rights issues throughout the world, contains news and announcements.

Keywords: Feminism, Human Rights

Audience: Feminists, Activists

Contact: Debra Guzman hrcoord@igc.apc.org

Details: Costs

User Info.: Establish an account on the nearest APC node. Login, type c for conferences, then type go dh.mujer.

For information on the nearest APC node, contact: APC International Secretariat IBASE

e-mail: apcadmin@apc.org

`gopher://gopher.telnet://igc.apc.org`

`http://igc.apc.org`

DIALOG Company Name Finder

DIALOG Company Name Finder

This database is a search aid designed to locate company information in DIALOG databases.

Keywords: Companies

Sponsor: Dialog Information Services, Inc., Palo Alto, CA, USA

Audience: Business Professionals, Market Researchers

Profile: Company name records are created for unique entries in the company name indexes of the DIALOG files included. Company names are shown in the form in which they appear in the original database index, including abbreviations, punctuation (commas and periods are stripped out), and spelling variations, and are limited to 46 characters. Long company names may be truncated because of the 46-character maximum.

Contact: Dialog in the US at (800) 334-2564, Dialog internationally at country-specific locations.

User Info: To subscribe, contact Dialog directly.

Notes: Coverage: Dialog databases indexing company name; updated quarterly.

`telnet://dialog.com`

Dick (Philip K.)

Pkd-list

A discussion of the works and life of Philip K. Dick (1928-82), science fiction writer. Topics also include the nature of reality, consciousness, and religious experience.

Keywords: Science Fiction, Dick (Philip K.)

Audience: Philip K. Dick Readers, Science Fiction Enthusiasts

Contact: pkd-list-request@wang.com

Details: Free

User Info: To subscribe to the list, send an e-mail message requesting a subscription to the URL address below. To send a message to the entire list, address it to: pkd-list@wang.com

`mailto:pkd-list@wang.com`

Dickens (Charles)

Princeton University Online Manuscripts Catalog Library

The library's holdings are large and wide-ranging. They contain significant collections in many fields.

Keywords: Books (Antiquarian), Dickens (Charles), Disraeli (Benjamin), Eliot (George), Hardy (Thomas), Kingsley (Charles), Trollope (Anthony)

Audience: General Public, Researchers, Librarians, Document Delivery Professionals

Details: Free

A B C **D** E F G H I J K L M N O P Q R S T U V W X Y Z

User Info: Expect: VM370 logo, Send: <cr>; Expect: Welcome screen, Send: folio <cr>; Expect: Welcome screen for FOLIO, Send: <cr>; Expect: List of choices, Send: 3 <cr>; To exit: type: logoff

`telnet://pucc.princeton.edu`

Dickinson (Emily)

University of North Carolina at Greensboro MINERVA Library

★★

The library's holdings are large and wide-ranging and contain significant collections in many fields.

Keywords: Herbert (George), Film, Dickinson (Emily), Children's Books

Audience: Researchers, Students, General Public

Details: Free

User Info: Expect: Login; Send: Info or MINERVA

`telnet://steffi.acc.uncg.edu`

Dictionaries

Online-dict

A mailing list devoted to a discussion of online dictionaries and related issues including installation, modification, and maintenance of their databases, search engines, and user interfaces.

Keywords: Dictionaries, Information Technology, Lexicology

Audience: Librarians, Information Scientists, Systems Operators

Contact: Jack Lynch
jlynch@dept.english.upenn.edu

Details: Free

User Info: To subscribe, send an e-mail message to the URL address below consisting of a single line reading:

SUB online-dict YourFirstName YourLastName.

To send a message to the entire list, address it to: online-dict@dept.english.upenn.edu

`mailto:listserv@dept.english.upenn.edu`

Diet

International Food and Nutrition (INFAN) Database

★★★

A database covering all aspects of nutrition, health and food, as for example, weight control, food safety, eating patterns, and more.

Keywords: Nutrition, Health, Diet

Sponsor: Pennsylvania State University Nutrition Center

Audience: Nutritionists, Health Care Professionals, Consumers

Details: Free

To access the database, select PENpages (1), then General Information (3), and finally INFAN Database (4).

`telnet://penpages@psupen.psu.edu`

DIGIT

DIGIT

A bimonthly publication containing information aimed at users of computing resources at the University of Colorado, Boulder.

Keywords: Computing, Computer Resources

Audience: University of Colorado Students, Computer Students

Contact: Suzanne Kincaid
kincaid@spot.colorado.edu

Details: Free

`mailto:kincaid@spot.colorado.edu`

Digital Equipment Corporation

DECnews-EDU

DECNEWS for Education and Research is a monthly electronic publication from Digital Equipment Corporation's Education Business Unit for the education and research communities worldwide.

Keywords: Education, Computers, Digital Equipment Corporation

Audience: Educators, Researchers

Contact: Anne Marie McDonald
decnews@mr4dec.enet.dec.com

Details: Free

User Info: To subscribe to the list, send an e-mail message requesting a subscription to the URL address below.

To send a message to the entire list, address it to:
decnews@mr4dec.enet.dec.com

`mailto:decnews@mr4dec.enet.dec.com`

Digital's World Wide Web Server

Digital World Wide Web server provides product and service information, back issues of the Digital Technical Journal, performance reports, buyers guides and product catalogs.

Keywords: Digital Equipment Corporation, Computer Systems

Audience: Computer Users, Computing Consultants

Contact: Russ Jones
webmaster@pa.dec.com

Details: Free

`http://www.digital.com/home.html`

Digital Equipment WWW Information Server

Digital Equipment WWW Information Server

Digital Equipment's server contains product and service information, and includes archives to public domain software. Also includes an online catalog resource for purchasing products from Digital Equipment.

Keywords: Computer Systems, Digital Equipment

Audience: Digital Equipment Users

Contact: Steve Painter
steve_painter@mro.mts.dec.com

`http://www.service.digital.com/home.html`

Digital Games Review

Digital Games Review

Reviews of video and computer entertainment titles for the entire industry.

Keywords: Computer Games, Games, Video Games

Audience: Computer Game Players, Computer Game Developers

Profile: Reviews are written by computer game enthusiasts, with an eye to accessibility, enjoyment, and fun, as well as to graphics, technical sophistication, and complexity.

Contact: Dave Taylor
taylor@intuitive.com

Details: Free

`mailto:digital-games-request@intuitive.com`

DIMUND

DIMUND FTP

DIMUND (Document Image Understanding) is an Internet information retrieval service.

Keywords: Internet, Information Retrieval, DIMUND, Documents

Sponsor: Document Processing Group, University of Maryland

Audience: Internet Surfers

Contact: gopher@dimund.cfar.umd.edu

Details: Free

`gopher://dimund.umd.edu`

dinosaur

dinosaur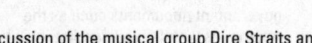

Discussion of dinosaurs and their reptilian contemporaries.

Keywords: Dinosaurs, Archosaurs

Audience: Dinosaur Enthusiasts, Paleontologists

Contact: John Matrow
          dinosaur-request@donald.WichitaKS.NCR.COM

Details: Free

User Info: To subscribe to the list, send an e-mail message requesting a subscription to the URL address below.

          To send a message to the entire list, address it to: dinosaur-request@donald.WichitaKS.NCR.COM

`mailto:dinosaur-request@donald.WichitaKS.NCR.COM`

Diogenes

Diogenes

Diogenes provides access to the US Food and Drug Administration (FDA) regulatory information needed by the health care industry.

Keywords: Food, Drugs

Sponsor: Diogenes, Rockville, MD, USA

Audience: Health Care Professionals

Profile: The database contains news stories and unpublished documents relating to the United States regulation of pharmaceuticals and medical devices. The complete text is provided for materials that are substantive and timely. Diogenes covers information relating to the Food and Drug Administration regulation of drugs and medical devices, including listings of approved products, experience reports for devices, documentation of the approval process for specific products, recall and regulatory action documentation, and more.

Contact: Dialog in the US at (800) 334-2564, Dialog internationally at country-specific locations.

User Info: To subscribe, contact Dialog directly.

Notes: Coverage: 1976 to the present; updated weekly.

`telnet://dialog.com`

Dire Straits

dire-straits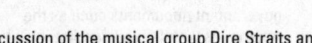

Discussion of the musical group Dire Straits and associated side projects.

Keywords: Rock Music, Dire Straits, Music

Audience: Rock Music Enthusiasts, Dire Straits Enthusiasts

Contact: Rand P. Hall
          dire-straits-request@merrimack.edu

Details: Free

User Info: To subscribe to the list, send an e-mail message requesting a subscription to the URL address below.

          To send a message to the entire list, address it to: dire-straits-request@merrimack.edu

Anonymous ftp to: merrimack.edu
(*f*=ANONYMOUS/DIRE-STRAITS)

          Mail list probably exists.

Direct

Direct

Discussion of the work of the musical artist Vangelis.

Keywords: New Age Music, Musical Groups

Audience: Musicians, Music Enthusiasts, Vangelis Fans

Contact: Keith Gregoire
          direct-request@celtech.com

User Info: To subscribe to the list, send an e-mail message requesting a subscription to the URL address below. To send a message to the entire list, address it to: direct@celtech.com

          Both bounce and daily digest modes are available; specify your preference when subscribing.

`mailto:direct-request@celtech.com`

Directories

Congressional Contact Information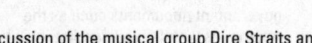

The US Senate and 103rd Congress phone and fax numbers are accessible and searchable from this server.

Keywords: Congress (US), Directories, Government (US)

Sponsor: Library of Congress

Audience: General Public, Journalists, Students, Politicians

Details: Free

`gopher://marvel.loc.gov/11/congress/directory`

Internet Resources for Earth Sciences

A document detailing Internet resources for a variety of earth science disciplines ,including GIS.

Keywords: Directory, GIS, Geology, Geography, GPS, Mapping, Earth Science

Sponsor: Bill Thoen

Audience: Earth Scientists, Researchers

Profile: A complete document detailing the types of information available in earth sciences and the mechanisms to retrieve needed information.

Contact: Bill Thoen
          bthoen@gisnet.com

Details: Free

`ftp://ftp.csn.org/COGS/ores.text`

dirt-users

dirt-users

Dirt is an X11-based UIMS.

Keywords: Computer Applications

Audience: UIMS Users

Contact: dirt-users-request@ukc.ac.uk

User Info: To subscribe to the list, send an e-mail message requesting a subscription to the URL address below.

          To send a message to the entire list, address it to: dirt-users@ukc.ac.uk

`mailto:dirt-users@ukc.ac.uk`

Disabilities

ADA-Law

A mailing list for discussion of the Americans with Disabilities Act (ADA) and other disability-related legislation both in the US and abroad.

Keywords: Disabilities, Law (US)

Audience: Disabled People, Legal Professionals

Contact: wtm@bunker.afd.olivetti.com

User Info: To subscribe to the list, send an e-mail message to the URL address below consisting of a single line reading:

          SUB ADA-Law YourFirstName YourLastName

          To send a message to the entire list, address it to: ADA-Law@vm1.nodak.edu

`mailto:listserv@vm1.nodak.edu`

A B C **D** E F G H I J K L M N O P Q R S T U V W X Y Z

A
B
C
D
E
F
G
H
I
J
K
L
M
N
O
P
Q
R
S
T
U
V
W
X
Y
Z

Americans with Disabilities Act

Gives access to the full text of the Americans with Disabilities Act (ADA) and all the related legislation.

Keywords: Disabilities

Audience: General Public, Disabled People, Differently Abled People, Politicians, Journalists, Students

Profile: The purpose of ADA is to provide a clear and comprehensive national mandate to end discrimination against individuals with disabilities and to bring them into the economic and social mainstream of American life; to provide enforceable standards addressing discrimination against individuals with disabilities; and to ensure that the federal government plays a central role in enforcing these standards on behalf of individuals with disabilities.

Details: Free

`gopher://val-dor.cc.buffalo.edu/11/.legislation/`

BlindFam

The Blindness and Family Life mailing list is devoted to a discussion of the day-to-day impact of this disability on families, and the patterns of domestic life associated with blindness.

Keywords: Blindness, Disabilities, Family

Audience: Blind People, Families, Health Care Professionals, Rehabilitation Counselors

Contact: Roger Myers, Patt Bromberger
Meyers@ab.wvnet.edu
Patt@squid.tram.com

User Info: To subscribe, send an e-mail message to the URL address below consisting of a single line reading:

SUB BlindFam YourFirstName YourLastName

To send a message to the entire list, address it to:
BlindFam@sjuvm.stjohns.edu

`mailto:listserv@sjuvm.stjohns.edu`

Cornucopia of Disability Information (CODI)

A large collection of disability-related information available via gopher.

Keywords: Disabilities, Health

Sponsor: State University of New York (SUNY) at Buffalo

Audience: Disabled People, Activists, Rehabilitation Counselors, Health Care Professionals

Profile: This site provides a wide variety of information resources concerning people with disabilities, ranging from legal information to a directory of computer resources aimed at the disabled consumer. Includes state, local, and national information and government documents such as the Americans with Disabilities Act. Also has links to many other related resources on the Internet, such as the National Rehabilitation Information Center.

Contact: Jay Leavitt
leavitt@ubvmsb.cc.buffalo.edu

`gopher://val-dor.cc.buffalo.edu`

Deaf Gopher

Gopher menu of deaf resources in the State of Michigan.

Keywords: Disabilities, Deafness, Health

Sponsor: Michigan State University

Audience: Deaf and Disabled People, Health Care Professionals, Activists, Policy Makers, Rehabilitation Counselors, Therapists

Profile: A small but useful menu of deaf resources that includes a collection of files in essay and/or report form about a variety of historical and cultural aspects of deafness.

Contact: Gary LaPointe
deafgopher@ah3.cal.msu.edu

Details: Free

`gopher://cal.msu.edu/11/msu/dept/deaf`

Disability Information

A collection of information about and links to sources of disability-related information from around the world. Includes archives of many related mailing lists and electronic newsletters, as well as legal and technical help for the disabled, and information about the Parkinson's Disease Information Exchange Network.

Keywords: Disabilities, Health, Diseases

Sponsor: Computing & Information Services at Texas A&M University, Galveston, Texas, USA

Audience: Disabled People, Rehabilitation Counselors, Health Care Professionals, Activists

Contact: Computing & Information Services at Texas A&M University
gopher@tamu.edu

`gopher://gopher.tamu.edu/.dir/disability.dir`

Disability Reading Room

Gopher menu of all kinds of reading material on disabilities.

Keywords: Disabilities, Health

Sponsor: University of Maryland

Audience: Deaf and Disabled People, Health Care Professionals, Activists, Policy Analysts, Rehabilitation Counselors, Therapists

Profile: A fascinating collection of reading material on disabilities and related issues, including first-person stories of dealing with chronic pain, detailed descriptions of laws involving the disabled, relevant press releases, and a large selection of journals on disabilities and related matters.

Contact: UMD Computer Science Center
consult@umail.umd.edu

Details: Free

`gopher://info.umd.edu`

Disability-Related Resources

A collection of information that includes newsletters for deaf/blind issues, electronic resources for the deaf, and a section on Chronic Fatigue Syndrome.

Keywords: Disabilities, Deafness, Blindness, Chronic Fatigue Syndrome

Sponsor: University of Washington DO-IT Program

Audience: Deaf and Disabled People, Health Care Professionals

Contact: Sheryl Burgstahler, Ph.D.
doit@u.washington.edu

`gopher://hawking.u.washington.edu`

Down's Syndrome

For discussion of any issue related to Down's Syndrome.

Keywords: Down's Syndrome, Disabilities

Audience: Down's Syndrome Community

Contact: wtm@bunker.afd.olivetti.com

Details: Free

User Info: To subscribe to the list, send an e-mail message to the URL address shown below consisting of a single line reading:

SUB downs-syndrome YourFirstName YourLastName

To send a message to the entire list, address it to:
downs-syndrome@vm1.nodak.edu

`mailto:listserv@vm1.nodak.edu`

Handicap

An anonymous data site containing disability-related files or programs.

Keywords: Health, Disabilities

Audience: Disabled People

Profile: There are about 40 directories with 500 files/programs covering all types of disabilities. The "Handicap BBS List" originates here.

Details: Free

Login: anonymous

`ftp://handicap.shel.isc-br.com`

History and Analysis of Disabilities Newsletter

★

Covers the history of disabilities, disabled persons, and disability issues.

Keywords: Disabilities, Disabled Persons

Sponsor: History of Disabilities Network, Centre for Independent Living, Toronto, and International Society for the History of Disabilities, Paris.

Audience: Disabled persons, Doctors, Historians

Contact: Gary Woodill
fcty731@ryerson

Details: Free

mailto:fcty7310@ryerson.bitnet

misc.handicap

★

A Usenet newsgroup providing information and discussion for and about handicapped individuals.

Keywords: Disabilities

Audience: Disabled

Details: Free

User Info: To subscribe to this Usenet newsgroup, you need access to a newsreader.

news:misc.handicap

Stutt-L

★

A list for the clinical discussion of stuttering, a speech disorder.

Keywords: Communications, Speech Disorders, Disabilities

Audience: Communications Specialists, Speech Pathologists

Contact: Woody Starkweather
v5002e@vm.temple.edu

User Info: To subscribe to this list, send an e-mail message to the URL address below, consisting of a single line reading:

SUB Stutt-L YourFirstName YourLastName

To send a message to the entire list, address it to: stutt-l@rm.temple.edu

mailto: listserv@vm.temple.edu

Women.health

★

This conference features articles, documents, news, announcements, policy statements, and other information about women's health around the world. Topics include breast cancer, ovarian cancer, alcohol, abortion, pregnancy, sterilization of women, pesticides, Quinacrine, HIV, disability.

Keywords: Women, Abortion, AIDS, Disabilities, Feminism, Health

Audience: Activists, Family Planners, Health Professionals, Non-Governmental Organizations, Women

Details: Costs

User Info.: Establish an account on the nearest APC node. Login, type c for conferences, then type go women.health. For information on the nearest APC node, contact: APC International Secretariat IBASE e-mail: apcadmin@apc.org Contact: Carlos Afonso (cafonso@ax.apc.org) or APC North American Regional Office e-mail: apcadmin@apc.org Contact: Edie Farwell (efarwell@igc.apc.org)

Notes: ALAI: Agencia Latinoamericana de Informacion e-mail message to APCadmin@apc.org

telnet://igc.apc.org

Disaster Relief

City of San Carlos World Wide Web Fire Safety Tutorial

★★

This WWW site offers fire prevention information, with a special emphasis on preventing wildland fires. Also includes color diagram on how to create a proper firebreak.

Keywords: Disaster Relief, Safety

Sponsor: The City of San Carlos, California, USA

Audience: Students, Educators, Environmentalists, Community Groups

**http://www.abag.ca.gov/abag/
local_gov/city/san_carlos/schome.html**

Tornado Warnings

★★

Gopher site providing up-to-the-minute tornado warnings for the United States.

Keywords: Disaster Relief

Sponsor: University of Illinois at Urbana-Champaign, Department of Atmospheric Sciences

Audience: Weather Forecasters, General Public, News Media

Contact: John Kemp
johnkemp@uiuc.edu

Details: Free

**gopher://wx.atmos.uiuc.edu/11/Severe/
Tornado_Warnings**

Disaster Research

Disaster Research

★

This newsletter deals with hazards and disasters. It includes articles on recent events and policy developments, plus updates on ongoing research and upcoming meetings; it also fields queries, responses, and ongoing discussion among readers.

Keywords: Disaster Research

Audience: Health Care Professionals, Public Servants

Contact: mailserv@vaxf.colorado.edu (Internet).

Details: Free

mailto:hazards@vaxf.colorado.edu

Disclosure Database

Disclosure Database

Disclosure Database provides in-depth financial information on over 12,500 companies.

Keywords: Securities, Stock Market

Sponsor: Disclosure Incorporated, Bethesda, MD, USA

Audience: Business Professionals

Profile: The information is derived from reports filed with the US Securities and Exchange Commission (SEC) by publicly owned companies. These reports provide detailed and reliable financial information on the companies included. Extracts of 10-K and 10-Q financial reports are included, as well as 20-F financial reports and registration reports for new registrants. Disclosure provides an online source of information for marketing intelligence, corporate planning, accounting research, and corporate finance. Contents of the records include management discussion and president's letter on past-year performance, footnotes to the financials, significant events, and market conditions affecting a particular company.

Contact: Dialog in the US at (800) 334-2564, Dialog internationally at country-specific locations.

User Info: To subscribe, contact Dialog directly.

Notes: Coverage: Current; updated weekly.

telnet://dialog.com

Disclosure

COMPNY

The COMPNY library contains more than 75 files of business and financial information, including thousands of in-depth company and industry research reports from leading national and international investments banks and brokerage houses.

Keywords: Companies, Financials, Filings, Disclosure

Audience: Business and Financial Researchers, Analysts, Entrepreneurs and Regulators.

Profile: COMPNY includes the following types of information: Full-text 10-Q, 10-K, Annual Reports toShareholders and Proxy filings; Extracts of filings for more than 11,000 public companies whose

A B C **D** E F G H I J K L M N O P Q R S T U V W X Y Z

A
B
C
D
E
F
G
H
I
J
K
L
M
N
O
P
Q
R
S
T
U
V
W
X
Y
Z

securities are traded on the major exchanges as well as over-the-counter Abstracts of S-registration statements, 13-Ds, 14-Ds, 8Ks, Form 4s and other SEC filings updated on a daily basis; Business news abstracts from more than 400 information sources; Daily US economic trends and forecasts.

The materials may be searched in individual files, such as brokerage house reports, or in group files organized by subject, such as SEC filings.

Contact: Mead New Sales Group at (800) 227-4908 or (513) 859-5398 inside the US, or (513) 865-7981 for all inquiries outside the US.

User Info: To subscribe, contact Mead directly.

To examine the Nexis user guide, you can access it at the ftp site of the University of Texas at Austin at the URL address: ftp://ftp.cc.utexas.edu

The files are in: /pub/ref-services/LEXIS

`telnet://nex.meaddata.com`

`http://www.meaddata.com`

Diseases

Disability Information ★★★

A collection of information about and links to sources of disability-related information from around the world. Includes archives of many related mailing lists and electronic newsletters, as well as legal and technical help for the disabled, and information about the Parkinson's Disease Information Exchange Network.

Keywords: Disabilities, Health, Diseases

Sponsor: Computing & Information Services at Texas A&M University, Galveston, Texas, USA

Audience: Disabled People, Rehabilitation Counselors, Health Care Professionals, Activists

Contact: Computing & Information Services at Texas A&M University

gopher@tamu.edu

`gopher://gopher.tamu.edu/.dir/`
`disability.dir`

Discipline and Disease Specific Sources

This database contains links to sources of Medical and Health Care information. Has disease-specific resources for AIDS, Cancer, Parkinson's Disease, and Sudden Infant Death Syndrome, among others. Also covers over 30 discipline-specific sources, ranging from anesthesiology to tropical medicine.

Keywords: Medicine, Diseases, Medical Research

Sponsor: University of Miami Biomedical Gopher Project, Miami, Florida, USA

Audience: Medical Professionals, Medical Researchers

Contact: Thomas Williams, Michael Cutherell
twilliam@mednet.med.miami.edu
mcuthere@mednet.med.miami.edu

Details: Free

`gopher://caldmed.med.miami.edu`

Institute for Molecular Virology

A unique virology resource for students, scientists, computer visualization experts, and the general public.

Keywords: Diseases, Viruses, Biology

Sponsor: University of Wisconsin-Madison, Madison, Wisconsin, USA

Audience: Virologists, Biologists, Researchers

Contact: Stephen Spencer
sspencer@rhino.bocklabs.wisc.edu

`http://www.bocklabs.wisc.edu/`
`Welcome.html`

rxderm-l

A mailing list intended for promoting the discussion of dermatologic treatment among practicing dermatologists.

Keywords: Dermatology, Skin, Disease, Doctors

Audience: Dermatologists

Contact: A.C. Huntley
achuntley@ucdavis.edu

User Info: To subscribe to the list, send an e-mail message to the URL address below consisting of a single line reading:

SUB rxderm-l YourFirstName YourLastName

To send a message to the entire list, address it to: rxderm-l@ucdavis.edu

`mailto:listserv@ucdavis.edu`

The Tumor Gene Database

A database containing information about genes associated with tumorigenesis and cellular transformation.

Keywords: Genetics, Disease, Biomedical Research, Databases

Sponsor: Department of Cell Biology, Baylor College of Medicine

Audience: Biomedical Researchers

Contact: David Steffen, Ph.D.
steffen@bcm.tmc.edu

`gopher://mbcr.bcm.tmc.edu`

Diseases (History of)

Johns Hopkins University Library

The library's holdings are large and wide-ranging and contain significant collections in many fields, including the following:

Keywords: Literature (English), Economics, Classics, Drama (German), Slavery, Trade Unions, Incunabula, Bibles, Diseases (History of), Nursing (History of), Abolitionism

Audience: General Public, Researchers, Librarians, Document Delivery Professionals

Details: Free

`telnet://jhuvm.hcf.jhu.edu`

Disk Jockeys

BPM

This list is for novice and professional DJs. Discussion often covers music releases, DJ'ing techniques, and turntable maintenance.

Keywords: Disk Jockeys, Music

Audience: Disk Jockeys, Music Enthusiasts

Contact: Simon Gatral
bpm-request@andrew.cmu.edu

Details: Free

User Info: To subscribe to the list, send an e-mail message requesting a subscription to the URL address below.

To send a message to the entire list, address it to:

bpm@andrew.cmu.edu

`mailto:bpm-request@andrew.cmu.edu`

Disney

disney-afternoon

Discussion of The Disney Afternoon and other related topics. This is a very high-volume, low-noise mailing list.

Keywords: Disney, Television

Audience: Disney Enthusiasts, Television Viewers

Contact: Stephanie da Silva
ranger-list-request@taronga.com

Details: Free, Moderated

User Info: To subscribe to the list, send an e-mail message requesting a subscription to the URL address below.

To send a message to the entire list, address it to: ranger-list-request@taronga.com

`mailto:ranger-list-`
`request@taronga.com`

disney-comics ★

A forum for discussion of Disney comics.

Keywords: Comics, Disney

Audience: Comics Enthusiasts, Disney Enthusiasts

Contact: Per Starbuck
disney-comics-
request@student.docs.uu.se

Details: Free

User Info: To subscribe to the list, send an e-mail
message requesting a subscription to
the URL address below.

To send a message to the entire list,
address it to: disney-comics-
request@student.docs.uu.se

`mailto:disney-comics-`
`request@student.docs.uu.se`

rec.arts.disney ★

A Usenet newsgroup providing information and
discussion about Disney and related topics.

Keywords: Disney

Audience: Disney Fans

Details: Free

User Info: To subscribe to this Usenet newsgroup,
you need access to a newsreader.

`news:rec.arts.disney`

Disraeli (Benjamin)

Princeton University Online Manuscripts Catalog Library ★★

The library's holdings are large and wide-ranging.
They contain significant collections in many fields.

Keywords: Books (Antiquarian), Dickens (Charles),
Disraeli (Benjamin), Eliot (George), Hardy
(Thomas), Kingsley (Charles), Trollope
(Anthony)

Audience: General Public, Researchers, Librarians,
Document Delivery Professionals

Details: Free

User Info: Expect: VM370 logo, Send: <cr>; Expect:
Welcome screen, Send: folio <cr>;
Expect: Welcome screen for FOLIO,
Send: <cr>; Expect: List of choices,
Send: 3 <cr>; To exit: type: logoff

`telnet://pucc.princeton.edu`

DISSPLA (Display Integrated Software System and Plotting Language)

DISSPLA (Display Integrated Software System and Plotting Language) ★

News and information exchange concerning
DISSPLA.

Keywords: Computer Graphics, Programming

Audience: DISSPLA Users, Computer Programmers

Profile: DISSPLA is a high-level FORTRAN
graphics subroutine library designed for
programmers in engineering, science
and business.

Contact: Zvika Bar-Deroma
er7101@technion.technion.ac.il

Details: Free

User Info: To subscribe to the list, send an e-mail
message to the URL address shown
below consisting of a single line reading:

SUB disspla YourFirstName
YourLastName

To send a message to the entire list,
address it to: disspla@taunivm.tau.ac.il

`mailto:listserv@taunivm.tau.ac.il`

Dist

Dist-users

This list is for discussions of issues related to the
dist 3.0 package and its components: metaconfig,
jmake, patch tools, and so on. The dist package was
posted on comp.sources.misc (August 1993).

Keywords: Dist, Programming, Computer
Applications

Audience: dist Users

Contact: Shigeya Suzuki, Raphael Manfredi
shigeya@foretune.co.jp
ram@acri.fr

User Info: To subscribe to the list, send an e-mail
message to the URL address shown
below consisting of a single line reading:

SUB dist-users YourFirstName
YourLastName

To send a message to the entire list,
address it to: dist-users@msu.edu

`mailto:majordomo@foretune.co.jp`

Distance Education

Distance Education

This gopher site takes advantage of New
Brunswick's advanced telecommunications
infrastructure to provide leading edge technology-
based learning environments. A computer-based
teleconferencing system forms the core of the
network complemented by computer-aided
communications, electronic data links and other
multimedia technologies.

Keywords: Education (Distance), Independent Study

Sponsor: TeleEducation New Brunswick,
Department of Advanced Education and
Labor

Audience: Educators, Students

`gopher://gopher.ollc.mta.ca`

Theater ★★

This directory is a compilation of information
resources focused on theater.

Keywords: Theater, Drama, Performing Arts

Audience: Theater Personnel, Drama Personnel,
Performers

Contact: Deborah Torres Martha Vander Kolk
dtorres@umich.edu mjvk@umich.edu

Details: Free

`ftp://una.hh.lib.umich.edu/70/`
`inetdirstacks/theater:torresmjvk`

Drama (British)

Indiana University Libraries ★★

The library's holdings are large and wide-ranging
and contain significant collections in many fields.

Keywords: Literature (English), Literature
(American), 1640-Present, British Plays
(19th-C.), Western Americana, Railway
History, Aristotle (Texts of), Lafayette
(Marquis de), Handel (G.F.), Austrian
History, Antiquarian Books, Rare Books,
French Opera (19th-C.), Drama (British) ,

Audience: General Public, Researchers, Librarians,
Document Delivery Professionals

Details: Free

Expect: User ID prompt, Send: GUEST

`telnet://iuis.ucs.indiana.edu`

A
B
C
D
E
F
G
H
I
J
K
L
M
N
O
P
Q
R
S
T
U
V
W
X
Y
Z

A
B
C
D
E
F
G
H
I
J
K
L
M
N
O
P
Q
R
S
T
U
V
W
X
Y
Z

Drama (French)

University of Pennsylvania PENNINFO Library

The library's holdings are large and wide-ranging and contain significant collections in many fields.

Keywords: Church History, Spanish Inquisition, Witchcraft, Shakespeare (William), Bibles, Aristotle (Texts of), Fiction, Whitman (Walt), French Revolution, Drama (French), Literature (English), Literature (Spanish)

Audience: Researchers, Students, General Public

Contact: Al DSouza
penninfo-admin@dccs.upenn.edu
dsouza@dccs.upenn.edu

Details: Free

User Info: Expect: Login; Send: Public

`telnet://penninfo.upenn.edu`

Drama (German)

Johns Hopkins University Library

The library's holdings are large and wide-ranging and contain significant collections in many fields.

Keywords: Literature (English), Economics, Classics, Drama (German), Slavery, Trade Unions, Incunabula, Bibles, Diseases (History of), Nursing (History of), Abolitionism

Audience: General Public, Researchers, Librarians, Document Delivery Professionals

Details: Free

`telnet://jhuvm.hcf.jhu.edu`

Drew University

Drewids

This is the mailing list for Drew University alumni to chat.

Keywords: Drew University

Audience: Drew University Alumni

Contact: drewids-approval@plts.org

Details: Free

User Info: To subscribe to the list, send an e-mail message to the URL address shown below consisting of a single line reading:

SUB drewids YourFirstName YourLastName

To send a message to the entire list, address it to: drewids@Warren.MentorG.com

Notes: There is a similar mailing list called drewids-news. When you subscribe to either, we ask that you write to the mailing list (drewids@Warren.MentorG.COM) and tell us what school and class (for example, CLA'91, THEO'66, or GRA'95) you were in.

`mailto:majordomo@Warren.MentorG.com`

Drewids-news

This is the "announcements only" version of the "drewids" (Drew University Alumni) mailing list.

Keywords: Drew University

Audience: Drew University Alumni

Contact: drewids-approval@plts.org

Details: Free

User Info: To subscribe to the list, send an e-mail message to the URL address shown below consisting of a single line reading:

SUB drewids-news YourFirstName YourLastName

To send a message to the entire list, address it to: drewids-news@Warren.MentorG.com

`mailto:majordomo@Warren.MentorG.com`

Drone On...

Drone On...

The Drone On... list is for the discussion of Spacemen 3 and resultant bands, as well as any other droning guitar bands that anyone wants to bring up.

Keywords: Rock Music, Musical Groups

Audience: Spacemen 3 Enthusiasts, Rock Music Enthusiasts

Contact: droneon-request@ucsd.edu

Details: Free

User Info: To subscribe to the list, send an e-mail message requesting a subscription to the URL address below.

To send a message to the entire list, address it to: droneon-request@ucsd.edu

`mailto:droneon-request@ucsd.edu`

Drosophila

Drosophila Information Newsletter

A quarterly electronic publication, this is an offshoot of Drosophila Information Service.

Keywords: Drosophila, Biology, Genetics

Audience: Biologists, Geneticists

Contact: Kathy Matthews
matthewk@ucs.indiana.edu

Details: Free

User Info: To subscribe, send an e-mail message to the address below consisting of a single line reading:

SUB drosophila-information-newsletter YourFirstName Your Last Name

To send a message to the entire list, address it to:

drosophila.information.newsletter@ucs.indiana.edu

`mailto:listserv@iubvm.ucs.indiana.edu`

DRT EC and Eastern Europe Business Database

DRT EC and Eastern Europe Business Database

DRTE's comprehensive full-text coverage of business and industry in the EC is combined with in-depth reporting on doing business in Eastern Europe.

Keywords: European Community, Eastern Europe

Sponsor: DRT Europe Services Brussels, Belgium

Audience: Market Analysts, Business Professionals, Market Researchers

Profile: DRTE reports provide comprehensive and detailed coverage of all EC proposals, laws and policy directions and their commercial applications, and unique, country-specific information on the regulatory framework for business development and expansion in Eastern Europe. These are continually updated to reflect the rapidly changing nature of the political and administrative structure of these emerging economies as they affect business undertakings with EC concerns.

Contact: Data-star through Dialog in the US at (800) 334-2564, Dialog internationally at country-specific locations.

User Info: To subscribe, contact Dialog directly.

Notes: Coverage: The database is updated weekly to enable it to offer exceptionally current full-text information.

`telnet://dialog.com`

Drug Regulations

Federal Food and Drug Administration

The Federal Food and Drug Administration (FDA) databank contains reports and articles related to the FDA.

Keywords: FDA, Drug Regulations, Nutrition

Sponsor: Federal Food and Drug Administration

Audience: Researchers, Nutritionists, Consumers, Health Care Providers

Profile: The topics covered include the drug and device product-approvals list, FDA federal register summaries by subject, text from drug bulletins, current information on AIDS, FDA consumer magazine index and selected articles, summaries of FDA information, text of testimony at FDA congressional hearings, and speeches given by the FDA commissioner and deputy.

Details: Free

`telnet://bbs@fdabbs.fda.gov`

Drugs

alt.drugs

★

A Usenet newsgroup providing information and discussion about the use of mind, body and behavior drugs, and about popular drug awareness.

Keywords: Drugs

Audience: Drug Users, Drug Educators

User Info: To subscribe to this Usenet newsgroup, you need access to a newsreader.

`news:alt.drugs`

Diogenes

Diogenes provides access to the US Food and Drug Administration (FDA) regulatory information needed by the health care industry.

Keywords: Food, Drugs

Sponsor: Diogenes, Rockville, MD, USA

Audience: Health Care Professionals

Profile: The database contains news stories and unpublished documents relating to the United States regulation of pharmaceuticals and medical devices. The complete text is provided for materials that are substantive and timely. Diogenes covers information relating to the Food and Drug Administration regulation of drugs and medical devices, including listings of approved products, experience reports for devices, documentation of the approval process for specific products, recall and regulatory action documentation, and more.

Contact: Dialog in the US at (800) 334-2564, Dialog internationally at country-specific locations.

User Info: To subscribe, contact Dialog directly.

Notes: Coverage: 1976 to the present; updated weekly.

`telnet://dialog.com`

Drug Information Fulltext

Drug Information Fulltext corresponds to two print publications: AHFS Drug Information, which contains information on 1,000 drugs available commercially in the United States, and the Handbook on Injectable Drugs, which covers 217 commercially available and 57 investigational drugs in use in the US.

Keywords: Drugs, Pharmaceuticals

Sponsor: American Society of Hospital Pharmacists, Washington, DC, USA

Audience: Health Care Professionals, Pharmacists

Profile: Drug Information Fulltext can be searched for information on the stability, chemistry, and pharmaco-kinetics of drugs, as well as on their action, usage, dosage, and administration. The file also covers compatibility and interactions of drugs and cautions for use.

Contact: Dialog in the US at (800) 334-2564, Dialog internationally at country-specific locations.

User Info: To subscribe, contact Dialog directly.

Notes: Coverage: Current; updated quarterly.

`telnet://dialog.com`

Drugs of the Future

Drugs of the Future contains descriptions of drugs in the earliest stages of development. It includes details about synthesis, uses, pharmacological actions, and clinical tests and also provides a monthly summary of drugs whose status has changed.

Keywords: Drugs

Sponsor: J.R. Prous, S.A., Barcelona, Spain

Audience: Health Care Professionals

Profile: The file is drawn from the prestigious print publication Drugs of the Future.

Contact: Dialog in the US at (800) 334-2564, Dialog internationally at country-specific locations.

User Info: To subscribe, contact Dialog directly.

Notes: Coverage: 1989 to the present; updated monthly.

`telnet://dialog.com`

Recreational Pharmacology Server

 ★★★★

Very extensive collection of drug FAQs, data sheets, net articles, resources, and electronic books. Complete list of Internet links to related sites.

Keywords: Pharmacology, Drugs, Neuroscience

Sponsor: University of Washington, Seattle, Washington, USA

Audience: Students, General Public, Pharmacologists, Neuroscientists

Contact: Webmaster
lamontg@u.washington.edu

Details: Free

`http://stein1.u.washington.edu:2012/pharm/pharm.html`

Drum Machines

DR-660

 ★

The DR-660 mailing list is for the discussion of practical applications of and technical matters relating to the Boss DR-660 drum machine.

Keywords: Drum Machines

Audience: Musicians

Contact: Mike Perkowitz
dr-660-request@cs.washington.edu

Details: Free

User Info: To subscribe to the list, send an e-mail message requesting a subscription to the URL address below.

To send a message to the entire list, address it to: dr-660-request@cs.washington.edu

`mailto:dr-660-request@cs.washington.edu`

DSA-LGB

DSA-LGB

DSA-LGB is a mailing list for members of the Lesbian/Gay/Bisexual Commission of the Democratic Socialists of America, and for others interested in similar concerns.

Keywords: Democratic Socialists of America, Gay, Lesbians

Audience: Democratic Socialists, Gays, Lesbians

Contact: DSA-LGB-request@midway.uchicago.edu

User Info: To subscribe to the list, send an e-mail message requesting a subscription to the URL address below.

To send a message to the entire list, address it to: DSA-LGB-request@midway.uchicago.edu

`mailto:DSA-LGB-request@midway.uchicago.edu`

A B C D E F G H I J K L M N O P Q R S T U V W X Y Z

dts-l (Dead Teachers Society Discussion List)

dts-l (Dead Teachers Society Discussion List)

This list is for broad discussions of teaching and learning.

Keywords: Education (Adult), Education (Distance), Education (Continuing)

Audience: Educators (K-12), Educational Administrators

Details: Free

User Info: To subscribe to the list, send an e-mail message to the URL address shown below consisting of a single line reading:

SUB dts-l YourFirstName YourLastName

To send a message to the entire list, address it to: dts-l @iubvm.bitnet

`mailto:listserv@iubvm.bitnet`

Dual-Personalities

Dual-Personalities

Discussion, maintenance/survival tips, and commercial offerings for the System/83 UNIX box made by the now-defunct DUAL Systems Corp. of Berkeley, as well as similar machines using the IEEE-696 bus (such as the CompuPro 8/16E with Root/Unisoft UNIX).

Keywords: UNIX

Audience: UNIX Users

Contact: dual-personalities-request@darwin.uucp

Details: Free

User Info: To subscribe to the list, send an e-mail message requesting a subscription to the URL address below.

To send a message to the entire list, address it to: dual-personalities-request@darwin.uucp

`mailto:dual-personalities-request@darwin.uucp`

Dun & Bradstreet

D&B - Duns Financial Records Plus

★★★

This database provides up to three years of comprehensive financial statements for over 650,000 private and public companies.

Keywords: Finance, Business, Dun & Bradstreet

Sponsor: Dun & Bradstreet Information Services, Parsippany, NJ, USA

Audience: Business Professionals

Profile: Information provided includes balance sheet, income statement, and 14 of the most widely used business ratios for measuring solvency, efficiency, and profitability. A company's financial position can be compared to those of others in the same industry as determined by industry norm percentages. In addition, there are over 1.2 million records included that contain company history and operations background only. DFR also contains company identification data, such as company name, address, primary and secondary SIC codes, D-U-N-S number, and number of employees. Textual paragraphs cover the history and operations background of a firm.

Notes: Coverage: Current; updated quarterly.

Contact: Dialog in the US at (800) 334-2564, Dialog internationally at country-specific locations.

Details: Costs

User Info: To subscribe, contact Dialog directly.

`telnet://dialog.com`

D&B - Dun's Electronic Business Directory

★★★

This database provides online information for over 8.9 million business and professionals throughout the US.

Keywords: Finance, Business, Dun & Bradstreet

Sponsor: Dun & Bradstreet Information Services, Parsippany, NJ, USA

Audience: Business Professionals, Business Analysts

Profile: A full directory listing is provided for each entry, including address, telephone number, SIC codes and descriptions, and number of employees. The file covers both public and private US companies of all sizes and types. Fifteen broad business categories are indexed as industry groups: agriculture, business services, communication, construction, finance, insurance, manufacturing, mining, professional services, public administration, real estate, retail, transportation, utilities, and wholesale. Data for the file is compiled and maintained primarily through Dun & Bradstreet's intensive credit interviewing process. Dun's staff of 1,300 business analysts actively interviews millions of entrepreneurs each year. This information is supplemented with data from large-volume telemarketing and direct mail campaigns.

Notes: Coverage: Current; updated quarterly.

Contact: Dialog in the US at (800) 334-2564, Dialog internationally at country-specific locations.

Details: Costs

User Info: To subscribe, contact Dialog directly.

`telnet://dialog.com`

D&B - European Dun's Market (EDMI)

This database presents detailed information on over 2.5 million businesses located in 26 European countries.

Keywords: Dun & Bradstreet, Europe, Business

Sponsor: Dun & Bradstreet Information Services, Parsippany, NJ, USA

Audience: Business Professionals

Profile: EDMI provides directory listings, sales volume and marketing data, and references to parent companies. Companies are selected for inclusion based on sales volume, national prominence, and international interest. Names, addresses, SIC codes, D-U-N-S numbers, and other data are given in each record. Both public and private companies are included.

Contact: Dialog in the US at (800) 334-2564, Dialog internationally at country-specific locations.

User Info: To subscribe, contact Dialog directly.

Notes: Coverage: Current; updated quarterly.

`telnet://dialog.com`

Dun & Bradstreet Corporation

★★

Dun and Bradstreet's home page contains examples of existing services, services in development, and business and financial information, advising and so on.

Keywords: Finance, Business, Dun & Bradstreet

Audience: General Public, Business Professionals

Profile: Files include company news, related industry information, product descriptions, and discussions of IBM's services.

`http://www.corp.dnb.com`

DVI-list

DVI-list

This mailing list is intended for discussions about Intel's DVI (Digital Video Interactive) system. These discussions cover both applications and programming with DVI.

Keywords: Interactive Computing, Multimedia

Audience: Interactive Program Developers, Computer Programmers, Multimedia Users

Contact: Andrew Patrick dvi-list-request@calvin.dgbt.doc.ca

User Info: To subscribe to the list, send an e-mail
message requesting a subscription to
the URL address below.

To send a message to the entire list,
address it to: dvi-list-
request@calvin.dgbt.doc.ca

`mailto:dvi-list-`
`request@calvin.dgbt.doc.ca`

DYNSYS-L

DYNSYS-L

The Dynamical System exchanges information
among people working in ergodic theory and
dynamical systems.

Keywords: Entropy, Systems Theory

Audience: Engineers

Details: Free

`mailto:newserv@uhcvm1.oit.uhc.edu`

A
B
C
D
E
F
G
H
I
J
K
L
M
N
O
P
Q
R
S
T
U
V
W
X
Y
Z

A
B
C
D
E
F
G
H
I
J
K
L
M
N
O
P
Q
R
S
T
U
V
W
X
Y
Z

E

e-europe

e-europe

The electronic communications network for doing business in Eastern Europe. Its purpose is to help those countries in their transition to market economies.

Keywords: Eastern Europe, Economics, Business

Audience: Business Professionals, Investors, Economists

Contact: James W. Reese
r505040@univ scvm
e-europe@pucc.princeton.edu

Details: Free

User info: To subscribe to the list, send an e-mail message to the URL address shown below consisting of a single line reading:

SUB e-europe YourFirstName YourLastName.

To send a message to the entire list, address it to: e-europe@indycms. iupui.edu

mailto:listserv@indycms.iupui.edu

E-Mail

Bbones

A list discussing the construction of e-mail backbones for organizations and campuses.

Keywords: E-mail, Networking

Audience: Internet Surfers

Contact: mail-bbones-request@yorku.ca

Details: Free

User Info: To subscribe to the list, send an e-mail message requesting a subscription to the URL address below.

To send a message to the entire list, address it to: mail-bbones@yorku.ca

mailto:mail-bbones-request@yorku.ca

College E-mail Addresses

Information on e-mail addresses at graduate offices.

Keywords: Internet, E-mail

Audience: Internet Surfers, Students, College/ University Educators

Details: Free

File is: pub/usenet/soc.college/ Admission_Office_Email_Address_List

ftp://pit-manager.mit.edu/pub/usenet-by-group/soc.college

gopher://sipb.mit.edu

E-mail 101

E-mail 101 describes how to use e-mail as well as other Internet features.

Keywords: Internet, E-mail

Audience: Internet Surfers

Details: Free

gopher://mrcnext.cso.uiuc.edu

http://mrcnext.cso.uiuc.edu

E-mail Gopher

E-mail Gopher allows the use of a gopher via e-mail.

Keywords: Internet, Services, E-mail, Gopher

Audience: Internet Surfers

Details: Free

Include the word "help" in the Email.

(This is the National Cancer Center of Japan Server)

gopher://gopher.ncc.go.jp/11/INFO/ gopher

E-mail Services

A list of services available by e-mail.

Keywords: Internet, E-mail, Services

Audience: Internet Surfers

Contact: David DeSimone
an207@cleveland.freenet.edu

Details: Free

File is: pub/docs/about-the-net/libsoft/ email_services.txt

ftp://sunsite.unc.edu/pub/docs/about-the-net/libsoft/email_services.txt

http://sunsite.unc.edu/pub/docs/ about-the-net/libsoft/ email_services.txt

E-mail Understanding

A special issue of the University of Illinois publication UIUC net describing electronic mail.

Keywords: Internet, E-mail

Audience: Internet Surfers

Details: Free

File is: doc/net/uiucnet/vol2no2.txt

ftp://ftp.cso.uiuc.edu/doc/net/ uiucnet

E-mail Usenet

E-mail Usenet allows the user to post to a newsgroup via e-mail.

Keywords: Internet, Services, E-mail, Usenet

Audience: Internet Surfers

Details: Free

`mailto://hierarchy-group-name@cs.utexas.edu`

E-mail WWW

E-mail WWW allows the user to obtain a web file via e-mail.

Keywords: Internet Services, E-mail, WWW

Audience: Internet Surfers

Details: Free

Include the words "www URL" in the e-mail.

`http://info.cern.ch/hypertext/WWW/TheProject.html`

E-mail-How To

An introductory guide to the UNIXMail System and to the procedures for sending and receiving mail, sending files by mail, and adding messages to files that are sent by mail.

Keywords: Internets Tools, Internet Guides, E-mail

Sponsor: SURAnet Network Information Center

Audience: Internet Surfers

Contact: info@sura.net

Details: Free

File is: pub/nic/network.service.guides/how.to.email.guide

`ftp://ftp.sura.net`

Educator's Guide to E-mail Lists

A guide to help educators find e-mail lists. Includes a very large list of e-mail addresses related to education.

Keywords: Education, E-mail, Internet

Sponsor: University of Massachusetts, Amherst, MA

Audience: Educators, Researchers

Contact: Prescott Smith
pgsmith@educ.umass.edu

Details: Free

`ftp://nic.umass.edu`

FAXNET

FAXNET allows the user to send faxes via e-mail.

Keywords: Internet Services, E-mail

Audience: Internet Surfers

Details: Free

Include the word "help" in the e-mail.

`mailto:info@awa.com`

Finding E-mail Addresses

Tips on finding e-mail addresses.

Keywords: Internet, E-mail

Audience: Internet Surfers

Contact: Jonathan Kamens
jib@MIT.Edu

Details: Free

File is: pub/docs/about-the-net/libsoft/email_address.txt

`ftp://sunsite.unc.edu`

Internet Phone Books

A collection of Internet phone books and e-mail directories.

Keywords: Phone Books, Internet Guides, E-mail

Sponsor: Texas Tech University

Audience: Internet Surfers, General Public

Profile: This gopher includes a number of resources for finding people on the Internet. In addition to the standard Netfind, WHOIS, and Inter-NIC services, it also has information on finding college and international e-mail addresses. Also features snail mail information from the U.S. Post Office on Zip codes, as well as an international directory of telephone area codes.

Contact: Abdul Malik Yoosufani
gripe@cs.ttu.edu

`gopher://cs4sun.cs.ttu.edu`

Internet Policy

An article entitled "What Should We Plan Given the Dilemma of the Network?" by G. Cook.

Keywords: Internet, E-mail

Audience: Internet Surfers

Details: Free

`ftp://pit-manager.mit.edu`

LIST REVIEW SERVICE

Explores e-mail distribution lists (primarily bitnet and ListServ lists).

Keywords: E-mail, Bitnet Lists, Listserv

Audience: Email Users

Profile: Akin to book and restaurant reviews, each issue begins with a narrative description of usually one week's worth of monitoring, then presents simple statistical data, such as the number of messages and lines, number of queries and nonqueries, number of subscribers and countries represented, list owner, location, and how to subscribe.

Contact: Raleigh C. Muns
srcmuns@umslvma.bitnet

Details: Free

User Info: To subscribe, send an e-mail message to the address below.

To send a message to the entire list, address it to:

listreviewservice@kentvm.kent.edu

`mailto:listserv@kentvm.kent.edu`

MetaMail

This resource contains information about MetaMail, which allows existing mail readers to read multimedia e-mail in the MIME (Multipurpose Internet Mail Extensions) format.

Keywords: Internet, E-mail

Audience: Internet Surfers

Contact: Nathaniel S. Borenstein
nsb@nsb.fv.com

Readme file is pub/nsb/README

`ftp://thumper.bellcore.com`

MIME (Multipurpose Internet Mail Extensions)

This resource contains information about the MIME (Multipurpose Internet Mail Extensions) protocol.

Keywords: Internet, E-Mail

Audience: Internet Surfers

Contact: Nathaniel S. Borenstein
nsb@nsb.fv.com

File is: documents/rfc/rfc1521.txt

`ftp://nic.merit.edu`

Netfind

Netfind is a way of finding Internet e-mail addresses.

Keywords: WWW, Information Retrieval, E-mail

Sponsor: Emory University, Georgia, USA

Audience: Reseachers, Students, General Public

Profile: This service relies on common but not universal programs, and thus may not find some people with valid addresses. The most foolproof way of finding someone's e-mail address remains to call them on the phone and ask. All Netfind sites are functionally equivalent. Multiple ones are listed here in case some are overloaded or down with technical problems.

Contact: Netfind Help
schwartz@cs.colorado.edu

`gopher://emoryu1.cc.emory.edu/11/internet/General/netfind`

news.newusers.questions

A Usenet newsgroup providing information and discussion.

Keywords: Usenet, E-mail, Internet Resources

Audience: Usenet Users, E-mail Users

Details: Free

User info: To subscribe to this Usenet newsgroup, you need access to a newsreader.

`news:news.newusers.questions`

PGP Mail

Information regarding the use of PGP (Pretty Good Privacy) mail, a public key.

Keywords: Internet, E-mail

Audience: Internet Surfers

Details: Free

`ftp://ftp.uu.net/networking/mail`

Pine E-mail

A description of the Program for Internet News and E-mail (PINE), a tool for reading, sending, and managing electronic messages.

Keywords: Internet Tools, E-mail

Audience: Internet Surfers

Details: Free

File is: mail/pine.blur

`ftp://ftp.cac.washington.edu`

E-mail-How To

E-mail-How To

An introductory guide to the UNIXMail System and to the procedures for sending and receiving mail, sending files by mail, and adding messages to files that are sent by mail.

Keywords: Internets Tools, Internet Guides, E-mail

Sponsor: SURAnet Network Information Center

Audience: Internet Surfers

Contact: info@sura.net

Details: Free

File is: pub/nic/network.service.guides/ how.to.email.guide

`ftp://ftp.sura.net`

eagles

eagles

This list provides a forum for Boy Scouts, Scouters, and former Scouts who are gay/bisexual to discuss how they can apply pressure to the BSA to change their homophobic policies.

Keywords: Boy Scouts, Gays, Lesbians

Audience: Gays, Lesbians, Boy Scouts, Former Boy Scouts

Contact: eagles-request@flash.usc.edu

Details: Free

User info: To subscribe to the list, send an e-mail message requesting a subscription to the URL address below.

To send a message to the entire list, address it to: eagles-request@flash.usc.edu

`mailto:eagles-request@flash.usc.edu`

Earth Science

Earth and Sky

This is a weekly publication of transcripts of earth science and astronomy radio programs aired daily on the Earth & Sky Radio Series, hosted by Deborah Byrd and Joel Block.

Keywords: Earth Science, Astronomy

Audience: General Public, Earth Scientists, Astronomers

Contact: majordomo@lists.utexas.edu

Details: Free

User Info: To subscribe to the list, send an e-mail message to the URL address shown below consisting of a single line reading:

SUB earth-and-sky YourFirstName YourLastName

To send a message to the entire list, address it to: earth-and-sky@lists.utexas.edu

Notes: To add yourself to the EARTHANDSKY mailing list send

subscribe EARTHANDSKY

yourname@host.domain.name in an e-mail message to:

`mailto:majordomo@lists.utexas.edu`

Internet Resources for Earth Sciences

A document detailing Internet resources for a variety of earth science disciplines ,including GIS.

Keywords: Directory, GIS, Geology, Geography, GPS, Mapping, Earth Science

Sponsor: Bill Thoen

Audience: Earth Scientists, Researchers

Profile: A complete document detailing the types of information available in earth sciences and the mechanisms to retrieve needed information.

Contact: Bill Thoen bthoen@gisnet.com

Details: Free

`ftp://ftp.csn.org/COGS/ores.text`

Purdue University Library

The library's holdings are large and wide-ranging. They contain significant collections in many fields.

Keywords: Economics (History of), Literature (English), Literature (American), Indiana, Rogers (Bruce), Engineering (History of), Aviation, Earth Science, Atmospheric Science, Consumer Science, Family Science, Chemistry (History of), Physics, Veterinary Science

Audience: General Public, Researchers, Librarians, Document Delivery Professionals

Contact: Dan Ferrer dan@asterix.lib.purdue.edu

Details: Free

User Info: Expect: User ID prompt, Send: GUEST

`telnet://lib.cc.purdue.edu`

East Asian Studies

University of Pennsylvania Library- Philadelphia Pa.

The library's holdings are large and wide-ranging and contain significant collections in many fields.

Keywords: Literature (English), Literature (American), History (World), Medieval Studies, East Asian Studies, Middle Eastern Studies, South Asian Studies, Judaica, Lithuania.

Audience: Educators, Students, Researchers

Profile: Access to the central Van Pelt Library and to most of the departmental libraries is restricted to members of the University community on weekends and holidays. Online visitors are advised to call (215) 898-7554 for information on hours and access restrictions.

Contact: Patricia Renfro, Associate Director of Libraries

Details: Free

`telnet://library.upenn.edu`

Eastern Europe

Central European Environment Data Report (CEDAR) Facility

This gopher site provides information about the environmental and scientific community in Central and Eastern Europe, with access to environmental information located throughout the world on various international computer networks and hosts.

Keywords: Europe, Central Europe, Eastern Europe, Environment

A B C D E F G H I J K L M N O P Q R S T U V W X Y Z

Sponsor: The International Society for Environmental Protection, and The Austrian Federal Ministry for Environment, Youth and Family (BMUJF)

Audience: Environmentalists, Educators, Students, Urban Planners, Environmental Scientists

Profile: The CEDAR Facility, established in 1991, is administered by the International Society for Environmental Protection (ISEP). The Facility is designed to provide regional groups and individuals with access to its information retrieval and higher computing resources, technical advice and database and network access support. In addition, CEDAR works to facilitate information and dialogue exchange with organizations in other parts of the world and in partner countries; and to promote training forums, including the joint development of seminars and conferences with ISEP on environmental and network topics. Finally, CEDAR develops and manages environmental reference data sets, including a US EPA bibliographic reference on hazardous waste treatment, CEDAR databases on Central and Eastern European environmental expertise and information, and the holdings of the Regional Environmental Center Library at Budapest.

Contact: cedar-info@cedar.univie.ac.at

`gopher://pan.cedar.univie.ac.at`

DRT EC and Eastern Europe Business Database

DRTE's comprehensive full-text coverage of business and industry in the EC is combined with in-depth reporting on doing business in Eastern Europe.

Keywords: European Community, Eastern Europe

Sponsor: DRT Europe Services Brussels, Belgium

Audience: Market Analysts, Business Professionals, Market Researchers

Profile: DRTE reports provide comprehensive and detailed coverage of all EC proposals, laws and policy directions and their commercial applications, and unique, country-specific information on the regulatory framework for business development and expansion in Eastern Europe. These are continually updated to reflect the rapidly changing nature of the political and administrative structure of these emerging economies as they affect business undertakings with EC concerns.

Contact: Data-star through Dialog in the US at (800) 334-2564, Dialog internationally at country-specific locations.

User info: To subscribe, contact Dialog directly.

Notes: Coverage: The database is updated weekly to enable it to offer exceptionally current full-text information.

`telnet://dialog.com`

e-europe

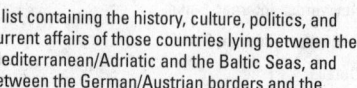

The electronic communications network for doing business in Eastern Europe. Its purpose is to help these countries in their transition to market economies.

Keywords: Eastern Europe, Economics, Business

Audience: Business Professionals, Investors, Economists

Contact: James W. Reese r505040@univ scvm or e-europe@pucc.princeton.edu

Details: Free

User info: To subscribe to the list, send an e-mail message to the URL address shown below consisting of a single line reading:

SUB e-europe YourFirstName YourLastName.

To send a message to the entire list, address it to: e-europe@indycms.iupui.edu

`mailto:listserv@indycms.iupui.edu`

EcoDirectory

A directory of Libraries and Environmental Information Centers in Central Eastern Europe.

Keywords: Environment, Eastern Europe, Central Europe

Sponsor: The Wladyslaw Poniecki Charitable Foundation, Inc.

Audience: Environmentalists, Librarians, International Development Specialists

Profile: This database is the product of an Environmental Training Project (ETP) which was founded in 1992 by the US Agency for International Development. The project concentrated on six Central and Eastern European countries: Bulgaria, Czech Republic, Hungary, Romania, Slovakia, and Poland.

It contains information on over 300 Libraries and Environmental Information Centers in those countries. Access to the data is facilitated by a WAIS search engine which makes it possible to retrieve information about libraries, subject area specializations, personnel, and so on.

Contact: Joerg Findeisen, CEDAR findeisen@pan.cedar.univie.ac.at

`gopher://gopher.poniecki.berkeley.edu`

Hungary

This discussion list circulates timely information about Hungary.

Keywords: Hungary, Eastern Europe, News

Audience: Researchers, Observers, Political Scientists

Contact: Eric Dahlin hcf2hung@iucsbuxa

Details: Free

User info: To subscribe to the list, send an e-mail message to the URL address shown below consisting of a single line reading:

SUB hungary YourFirstName YourLastName

`mailto:listserv@gwuvm.gwu.edu`

Mideur-l

A list containing the history, culture, politics, and current affairs of those countries lying between the Mediterranean/Adriatic and the Baltic Seas, and between the German/Austrian borders and the former Soviet Union.

Keywords: Soviet Union, Baltic Republics, Eastern Europe, News

Audience: Political Scientists, Researchers, Historians, General Public

Contact: Jan George Frajkor mideur-1@ubvm.cc.buffalo.edu

Details: Free

User info: To subscribe to the list, send an e-mail message to the URL address below consisting of a single line reading:

SUB mideur-l YourFirstName YourLastName

To send a message to the entire list, address it to: mideur-1@ubvm.cc.buffalo.edu

`mailto:listserv@ubvm.cc.buffalo.edu`

Pigulki

This is an English-language digest concerning the Net news from Poland.

Keywords: Poland, Eastern Europe

Audience: Poles, Poland Observers, Journalists

Contact: Marek Zielinski zielinski@acfcluster.nyu.edu

Details: Free

User info: To subscribe to the list, send an e-mail message requesting a subscription to the URL address below. To send a message to the entire list, address it to: davep@acsu.buffalo.edu

`mailto:davep@acsu.buffalo.edu`

Russian and East European Studies Home Pages

Keywords: Russia, Eastern Europe, Government, Political Science

Sponsor: University of Pittsburgh

Audience: Researchers, Politicians

Contact: Casey Palowitch
cjp@acid.library.pitt.edu

`http://www.pitt.edu/cjp/rspubl.html`

Eastern European Business

DRT EC and Eastern Europe Business Database

DRTE's comprehensive full-text coverage of business and industry in the EC is combined with in-depth reporting on doing business in Eastern Europe.

Keywords: European Community, Eastern Europe

Sponsor: DRT Europe Services Brussels, Belgium

Audience: Market Analysts, Business Profession-als, Market Researchers

Profile: DRTE reports provide comprehensive and detailed coverage of all EC proposals, laws and policy directions and their commercial applications, and unique, country-specific information on the regulatory framework for business development and expansion in Eastern Europe. These are continually updated to reflect the rapidly changing nature of the political and administrative structure of these emerging economies as they affect business undertakings with EC concerns.

Contact: Data-star through Dialog in the US at (800) 334-2564, Dialog internationally at country-specific locations.

User info: To subscribe, contact Dialog directly.

Notes: Coverage: The database is updated weekly to enable it to offer exceptionally current full-text information.

`telnet://dialog.com`

Eastern Washington University Library

Eastern Washington University Library

The library's holdings are large and wide-ranging and contain significant collections in many fields.

Keywords: Education, Music, Social Science, Behavioral Science

Audience: Researchers, Students, General Public

Details: Free

User Info: Expect: Login; Send: Lib

`telnet://wsduvm12.csc.wsu.edu`

ebikes

ebikes

New York City Bicycle discussion list.

Keywords: Bicycling, New York

Audience: Bicyclists

Contact: Danny Lieberman
ebikes-request@panix.com

Details: Free

User info: To subscribe to the list, send an e-mail message requesting a subscription to the URL address below.

To send a message to the entire list, address it to: ebikes-request@panix.com

`mailto:ebikes-request@panix.com`

EC

EC

Dedicated to discussion of the European Community (EC).

Keywords: European Community, Europe

Audience: Europeans, Researchers, General Public, Economists

Contact: John B. Harlan
ijbh200@indyvax.iupiu.edu or
ec@vm.cc.metu.edu.tr

Details: Free

User info: To subscribe to the list, send an e-mail message to the URL address shown below consisting of a single line reading:

SUB ec YourFirstName YourLastName

`mailto:listserv@linycms.iupiu.edu`

Ecclesiastical History

Ecchst-l

A discussion list for scholars of Ecclesiastical history, including those interested both in the history of the Church and in the examination of theology in an historical context.

Keywords: Religion, Ecclesiastical History, Christianity, Theology

Audience: Historians, Theologians

Contact: Gregory H. Singleton
ugsingle@uxa.ecn.bgu.edu

User info: To subscribe, send an e-mail message to the URL address below consisting of a single line reading:

SUB ecchst-l YourFirstName YourLastName.

To send a message to the entire list, address it to: ecchst-l@bgu. edu

`mailto:listserv@bgu.edu`

Echinoderm

Starnet (Echinoderm Newsletter)

The Starnet echinoderm electronic newsletter is distributed quarterly.

Keywords: Echinoderm, Starfish, Marine Biology

Audience: Marine Biologists

Contact: Win Hide
whide@matrix.bchs.uh.edu

Details: Free

User info: To subscribe to the list, send an e-mail message requesting a subscription to the URL address below.

`mailto:whide@matrix.bchs.uh.edu`

echl-news

echl-news

For people interested in discussing and following the East Coast Hockey League.

Keywords: Hockey, Sports

Audience: Hockey Enthusiasts

Contact: echl-news-request@andrew.cmu.edu

Details: Free

User info: To subscribe to the list, send an e-mail message requesting a subscription to the URL address below.

To send a message to the entire list, address it to: echl-news-request@andrew.cmu.edu

`mailto:echl-news-request@andrew.cmu.edu`

ECHO

ECHO

A computer conferencing system based in New York City.

Keywords: Community, Networking, WomenÕs Issues

Sponsor: East Coast Hang Out

A B C D E F G H I J K L M N O P Q R S T U V W X Y Z

Audience: Activists, Policy Makers, Community Leaders, Governments, Students, Feminists, Educators, Health Care Professionals, Artists, Communicators, General Public

Profile: ECHO was started by Stacy Horn, as an East Coast counterpart to the WELL. ECHO makes an effort to be hospitable to women and has one of the highest percentages of women in an online community.

Contact: Stacy Horn
horn@echonyc.com,

Details: Costs

`telnet://echonyc.com`

echoes

echoes

Info and commentary on the musical group Pink Floyd, as well as other projects members of the group have been involved with.

Keywords: Rock Music, Pink Floyd

Audience: Rock Music Enthusiasts, Pink Floyd Enthusiasts

Contact: H. W. Neff
echoes-request@fawnya.tcs.com

Details: Free

User Info: To subscribe to the list, send an e-mail message requesting a subscription to the URL address below.

To send a message to the entire list, address it to: echoes-request@fawnya.tcs.com

`mailto:echoes-request@fawnya.tcs.com`

EcoDirectory

EcoDirectory

A directory of Libraries and Environmental Information Centers in Central Eastern Europe.

Keywords: Environment, Eastern Europe, Central Europe

Sponsor: The Wladyslaw Poniecki Charitable Foundation, Inc.

Audience: Environmentalists, Librarians, International Development Specialists

Profile: This database is the product of an Environmental Training Project (ETP) which was founded in 1992 by the US Agency for International Development. The project concentrated on six Central and Eastern European countries: Bulgaria, Czech Republic, Hungary, Romania, Slovakia, and Poland.

It contains information on over 300 Libraries and Environmental Information Centers in those countries. Access to the data is facilitated by a WAIS search engine which makes it possible to retrieve information about libraries, subject area specializations, personnel, and so on.

Contact: Joerg Findeisen, CEDAR
findeisen@pan.cedar.univie.ac.at

`gopher://gopher.poniecki.berkeley.edu`

Ecology

Australian Environmental Resources Information Network (ERIN)

This gopher contains a wide range of Australian environmental information.

Keywords: Environment, Australia, Ecology

Audience: Environmentalists, Ecologists, Researchers, Australians

Profile: Coverage includes biodiversity, protected areas, terrestrial and marine environments, environmental protection and legislation, international agreements, and general information about ERIN.

Contact: gopher@erin.gov.au

Details: Free

`gopher://kaos.erin.gov.au`

`http://kaos.erin.gov.au/erin.html`

Biosis Previews

The database encompasses the entire field of life sciences and covers original research reports and reviews in biological and biomedical areas. This includes field, laboratory, clinical, experimental and theoretical work. The traditional areas of biology, including botany, zoology, and microbiology, are covered, as well as the related fields such as plant and animal science, agriculture, pharmacology, and ecology.

Keywords: Biology, Botany, Zoology, Microbiology, Plant Science, Animal Science, Agriculture, Pharmacology, Ecology, Biochemistry, Biophysics, Bioengineering

Sponsor: Biosis

Audience: Librarians, Researchers, Students, Biologists, Botanists, Zoologists, Scientists, Taxonomists

Contact: CDP Technologies Sales Department (800)950-2035, extension 400.

User info: To subscribe, contact CDP Technologies directly.

`telnet://cdplus@cdplus.com`

sci.environment

A Usenet newsgroup providing information and discussion about the environment and ecology.

Keywords: Environment, Ecology

Audience: Environmentalists, ecologists, Earth Scientists

Details: Free

User info: To subscribe to this Usenet newsgroup, you need access to a newsreader.

`news:sci.environment`

Sense of Place

An electronic environmentalists magazine. The magazine incorporates graphics and text in a format specifically designed to be read on a Macintosh screen. You must have Hypercard version 2.1 or later.

Keywords: Environment, Ecology

Audience: Environmentalists

Contact: SOP@dartmouth.edu

Details: Costs

User info: To subscribe send electronic mail to SOP@dartmouth.edu

`gopher://gopher.dartmouth.edu/1/anonftp/pub/sop`

The University of Notre Dame Library

The Library's holdings are large and wide-ranging and contain significant collections in many fields, including the following: Irish Music, Maps of Ireland, History of Botany, Ecology, Entomology, Parasitology, Aquatic Biology, History of Universities, Manuscript Studies, Paleography, Botany, Ireland

Keywords: Music (Irish), Ireland, Botany (History of), Ecology, Entomology, Parasitology, Aquatic Biology, Universities (History of), Paleography

Audience: General Public, Researchers, Librarians, Document Delivery Professionals

Details: Free

User Info: Expect: ENTER COMMAND OR HELP:, Send: library; To leave, type x on the command line and press the enter key. At the ENTER COMMAND OR HELP: prompt, type bye and press the enter key.

`telnet://irishmvs.cc.nd.edu`

Western Lands

A collection of articles and reports relating to environmental and land use issues in the Western United States.

Keywords: Environmentalism, Ecology, Forests, The Western United States

Sponsor: The Institute for Global Communications (IGC)

Audience: Environmentalists, Ecologists, Activists, Foresters, Citizens

Contact: Dan Yurman, IGC User Support
dyurman@igc.apc.com.
support@igc.apc.com

Notes: User submissions encouraged.

`gopher://gopher.igc.apc.org/11/`
`environment/forests/western.lands`

Economic Development

econ-dev

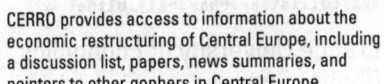

This mailing list is for sharing with economic development professionals who are helping small, innovative companies compete in the new global environment.

Keywords: Economic Development, Business

Audience: Economic Development Experts, Business Professionals

Contact: majordomo@csn.org

Details: Free

User info: To subscribe to the list, send an e-mail message to the URL address shown below consisting of a single line reading:

SUB econ-dev YourFirstName YourLastName

To send a message to the entire list, address it to: econ.dev@csn.org

`mailto:majordomo@csn.org`

Economic Policy

Economic Policy Research

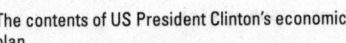

A forum for the exchange of papers and information on economic-policy research.

Keywords: Economics, Economic Policy

Audience: Economists, Policy Analysts

Details: Free

`gopher://cis.anu.edu.au`

`http://coombs.anu.edu.au/`
`CoombsHome.html`

Economics

Asian and Pacific Economic Literature

★★★

A list of economic literature covering Asia and the Pacific region.

Keywords: Asia, Pacific, Economics

Audience: Economists, Business Professionals

Details: Free

`ftp://coombs.anu.edu`

Business News—Singapore

This gopher site focuses on business in Singapore.

Keywords: Singapore, Economics, Business

Audience: Economists, Business Professionals

Details: Free

`gopher://gopher.cic.net/11/e-serials/`
`alphabetic/b/business-news`

`http://gopher.cic.net`

Business, Economics

★★

This directory is a compilation of information resources focused on business and economics.

Keywords: Business, Economics

Audience: Business Professionals, Business Students, Economists

Details: Free

`ftp://una.hh.lib.umich.edu/70/`
`inetdirsstacks/govdocs:tsangaustin`

CERRO (Central European Regional Research Organization)

★★★

CERRO provides access to information about the economic restructuring of Central Europe, including a discussion list, papers, news summaries, and pointers to other gophers in Central Europe.

Keywords: Central Europe, Economics, News

Audience: Economists, Researchers, Journalists

Contact: gunther.maier@wu-wien.ac.at

Details: Free

`gopher://osiris.wu.wein.ac.at`

Clinton's Economic Plan

★

The contents of US President Clinton's economic plan.

Keywords: Economics, Government (US), Clinton (Bill)

Audience: Economists, General Public

Details: Free

The data contained on the President's Economic Plan diskette is now available via anonymous FTP at cu.nih.gov. The data can be found in a directory named USDOC-OBA-INFO.

`gopher://wiretap.spies.com/11/Gov/`
`Economic`

Commerce Business Daily

★

The Commerce Business Daily is a publication that announces invitations to bid on proposals requested by the US Federal Government. This gopher is updated every business day.

Keywords: Business (US), Economics, Commerce, Trade, Government (US)

Sponsor: CNS and Softshare Government Information Systems

Audience: Economists, Business Professionals, General Public, Journalists, Students, Politicians.

Profile: Invitations via Internet email that apply only to specific companies can be arranged.

Contact: Melissa Allensworth
sshare@cscns.com
service@cscns.com

Details: Free

`gopher://cns.cscns.com/cbd/About the`
`CBD`

e-europe

The electronic communications network for doing business in Eastern Europe. Its purpose is to help these countries in their transition to market economies.

Keywords: Eastern Europe, Economics, Business

Audience: Business Professionals, Investors, Economists

Contact: James W. Reese
r505040@univ scvm
e-europe@pucc.princeton.edu

Details: Free

User info: To subscribe to the list, send an e-mail message to the URL address shown below consisting of a single line reading:

SUB e-europe YourFirstName YourLastName.

To send a message to the entire list, address it to: e-europe@indycms. iupui.edu

`mailto:listserv@indycms.iupui.edu`

Economic Policy Research

★

A forum for the exchange of papers and information on economic-policy research.

Keywords: Economics, Economic Policy

Audience: Economists, Policy Analysts

Details: Free

`gopher://cis.anu.edu.au`

`http://coombs.anu.edu.au/`
`CoombsHome.html`

Info-South (Latin American News)

The database provides citations and abstracts of materials relating to contemporary economic, political, and social issues in Latin America.

Keywords: International News, Economics, International Politics, Latin America

Sponsor: University of Miami, Coral Gables, FL, US

A
B
C
D
E
F
G
H
I
J
K
L
M
N
O
P
Q
R
S
T
U
V
W
X
Y
Z

Audience: General Public

Profile: Coverage includes a wide range of topics assessing the current situation in Latin America.

Contact: Dialog in the US at (800) 334-2564, Dialog internationally at country-specific locations.

User info: To subscribe, contact Dialog directly.

Notes: Coverage: 1988 to the present; updated weekly.

`telnet://dialog.com`

Internet Economics

An article entitled "Some Economics of the Internet" by Jeffrey K. Mackie-Mason.

Keywords: Economics, Internet

Audience: Internet Surfers

Contact: Jeffrey K. Mackie-Mason

Details: Free

`ftp://gopher.econ.lsa.umich.edu`

Internet Pricing

An article entitled "Pricing the Internet."

Keywords: Internet, Economics

Audience: Internet Surfers

Contact: Mackie-Mason and Varian

Details: Free

`gopher:// gopher.econ.lsa.umich.edu`

Johns Hopkins University Library

The library's holdings are large and wide-ranging and contain significant collections in many fields.

Keywords: Literature (English), Economics, Classics, Drama (German), Slavery, Trade Unions, Incunabula, Bibles, Diseases (History of), Nursing (History of), Abolitionism

Audience: General Public, Researchers, Librarians, Document Delivery Professionals

Details: Free

`telnet://jhuvm.hcf.jhu.edu`

LabStat

The public database of the Bureau of Labor Statistics.

Keywords: Economics, Labor, Census Data

Sponsor: United States Government, Bureau of Labor Statistics

Audience: General Public, Statisticians, Researchers

Profile: LABSTAT provides current and historical data, as well as numerous press releases. This site is composed of individual databases (in flat file format) corresponding to each of 26 surveys.

Contact: labstat.helpdesk@bls.gov.

Details: Free

Login: anonymous; use e-mail address as password.

Notes: For each news release published by the Bureau of Labor Statistics, the two most current are stored in the /news.release directory. The documentation provides a list of the abbreviations used to identify the news releases and a description of the sub-directories available to the user.

`ftp://stats.bls.gov`

NetEc

An electronic forum for published academic papers relating to economics.

Keywords: Economics, Business

Audience: Economists, Business People

Contact: netec@uts.mcc.ac.uk

Details: Free

User info: To subscribe to the list, send an e-mail message to the address below consisting of a single line reading:

SUB netec YourFirstName YourLastName

To send a message to the entire list, address it to: netec@hasara11.bitnet

`mailto:listserv@hasara11.bitnet`

Prague University of Economics Gopher Service

Includes information about the university, integrative studies of economy, economic information, and public domain software.

Keywords: Czech Republic, Economics, Europe

Audience: Czechs, Economists

Contact: gopher@pub.vse.cz

Details: Free

`gopher://pub.vse.cz`

The Management Archive

This is an electronic forum for management ideas and information.

Keywords: Management, Business, Economics

Audience: Managers, Business Professionals, Economists

Profile: The Archive arranges working papers, teaching materials, and so on, in directories by subject. All materials in the Archive are fully indexed and searchable. If you have material that you would like to see receive worldwide network exposure and distribution, submit them to the Archive.

Contact: Jim Goes goes@chimera.sph.umn.edu

Details: Free

User Info: Expect: login, Send: anonymous; Expect: password, Send: your e-mail address.

`ftp://chimera.sph.umn.edu`

University of Puerto Rico Library

The library's holdings are large and wide-ranging and contain significant collections in many fields.

Keywords: Computer Science, Education, Nursing, Agriculture, Economics

Audience: Researchers, Students, General Public

Details: Free

After Locator: telnet://, press Tab twice. Type DIAL VTAM. Enter NOTIS.

Press Return. On the blank screen, type LUUP.

`telnet://136.145.2.10`

University of Wisconsin Green Bay Library

The library's holdings are large and wide-ranging and contain significant collections in many fields.

Keywords: Economics, Environmental Studies, Music, Natural Science

Audience: Researchers, Students, General Public

Details: Free

User Info: Expect: Service Name, Send: Victor

`telnet://gbls2k.uwgb.edu`

Economics (History of)

Emory University Library

The library's holdings are large and wide-ranging and contain significant collections in many fields.

Keywords: Health Sciences, Theology, History (US), Communism, Economics (History of), Literature (American)

Audience: General Public, Researchers, Librarians, Document Delivery Professionals

Details: Free

User Info: Expect:VM screen, Send: RETURN; Expect: CP READ, Send: DIAL VTAM, press RETURN; Expect: CICS screen, Send: PF1

`telnet://emuvm1.cc.emory.edu`

Purdue University Library

The library's holdings are large and wide-ranging. They contain significant collections in many fields.

Keywords: Economics (History of), Literature (English), Literature (American), Indiana, Rogers (Bruce), Engineering (History of), Aviation, Earth Science, Atmospheric Science, Consumer Science, Family Science, Chemistry (History of), Physics, Veterinary Science

Audience: General Public, Researchers, Librarians, Document Delivery Professionals

Contact: Dan Ferrer
dan@asterix.lib.purdue.edu

Details: Free

User Info: Expect: User ID prompt, Send: GUEST

`telnet://lib.cc.purdue.edu`

Economy

Asia-Pacific

The database covers the business, economics, and new industries of the Pacific Rim nations, including East Asia, Southeast Asia, the Indian Subcontinent, the Middle East, Australia, and the Pacific Island nations.

Keywords: Asia, Pacific, Business, Economy

Sponsor: Aristarchus Knowledge Industries, Seattle, WA, USA

Audience: Market Researchers, Economists, Market Analysts

Profile: Records are of two types: main records consisting of abstracts or citations for journal articles and other publications; and company thesaurus records. Detailed abstracts are provided for selected journal articles, monographs, selected papers in conference proceedings, dissertations, and government documents. Shorter citations with briefer indexing are provided for a wide variety of journal articles, newspapers, government documents, and annual report publications. Asia-Pacific also includes an extensive Corporate Thesaurus subfile, which provides detailed coverage of the corporate players in the Pacific Rim, including thousands of companies traded on the stock exchanges of Southeast and East Asia.

Contact: Dialog in the US at (800) 334-2564; Dialog internationally at country-specific locations.

Details: Costs

User info: To subscribe, contact Dialog directly.

`telnet://dialog.com`

Universite de Montreal UDEMATIK Library

The library's holdings are large and wide-ranging and contain significant collections in many fields.

Keywords: Art, Architecture, Economy, Sexology, Social Law, Science, Technology, Literary Studies

Audience: Researchers, Students, General Public

Contact: Joelle or Sebastien Roy
udematik@ere.umontreal.ca
stemp@ere.umontreal.ca
roys@ere.umontreal.ca

User Info: Expect: Login; Send: Application id INFO

`telnet:// udematik.umontreal.ca`

Yahoo Market and Investments

A comprehensive look at the current economic status, with a wide range of coverage, from brokers to stocks.

Keywords: Business, Stock Market, Investment, Economy

Sponsor: Stanford University, Palo Alto, California, USA

Audience: Investors, Economists

Contact: jerry@akebono.stanford.edu

`http://akebono.stanford.edu/yahoo/`
`Economy/Markets_and_Investments`

ECTL

ECTL

A list dedicated to researchers interested in Computer Speech Interfaces.

Keywords: Computer Speech Interfaces

Audience: Computer Speech Researchers

Contact: David Leip
ectl-request@snowhite.cis.uoguelph.ca

Details: Free

User Info: To subscribe to the list, send an e-mail message requesting a subscription to the URL address below.

To send a message to the entire list, address it to: ectl-request@snowhite.cis.uoguelph.ca

`mailto:ectl-`
`request@snowhite.cis.uoguelph.ca`

ecto

ecto

Information and discussion about singer/songwriter Happy Rhodes, and other music, art, books, and films of common (or singular) interest.

Keywords: Music, Art, Rhodes (Happy)

Audience: Music Enthusiasts, Art Enthusiasts

Contact: Jessica Dembski
ecto-request@ns1.rutgers.edu

Details: Free

User Info: To subscribe to the list, send an e-mail message requesting a subscription to the URL address below.

To send a message to the entire list, address it to: ecto-request@ns1.rutgers.edu

`mailto:ecto-request@ns1.rutgers.edu`

Ecumenism

Catholic

The CATHOLIC mailing list is a forum for Catholics who wish to discuss their discipleship to Jesus Christ in terms of the Catholic approach to Christianity. "Catholic" is loosely defined as anyone embracing the Catholic approach to Christianity whether Roman Catholic, Anglo-Catholic, or Orthodox. Discussions on ecumenism are encouraged.

Keywords: Catholicism, Ecumenism, Religion

Audience: Catholics, Priests, Theologians

Contact: Cindy Smith
cms@dragon.com

Details: Free

User info: To subscribe to the list, send an e-mail message to the address below, consisting of a single line reading:

SUB Catholic YourFirstName YourLastName

To send a message to the entire list, address it to:

Catholic@american.edu

Notes: This list is also bi-directionally forwarded to the newsgroup bit.listserv.catholic.

`mailto:listserv@american.edu`

edista (Educacin a Distancia)

edista (Educacin a Distancia)

The University Distance Program (UNIDIS) at the University of Santiago, Chile, sponsors Educacin a Distancia (Education at a Distance).

Keywords: Education (Adult), Education (Distance), Education (Continuing), Chile

Sponsor: The University Distance Program (UNIDIS) at the University of Santiago, Chile

Audience: Educators, Researchers

Details: Free

User info: To subscribe to the list, send an e-mail message to the URL address shown below consisting of a single line reading:

SUB edistaYourFirstName YourLastName

To send a message to the entire list, address it to: edista@usachvm1.bitnet

`mailto:listserv@usachvm1.bitnet`

A B C D E F G H I J K L M N O P Q R S T U V W X Y Z

Editors

CCNEWS

An electronic forum for campus-computing newsletter editors and other publications specialists.

Keywords: Computers, Editors, Students, Newsletters

Audience: Students (college), Editors

Profile: CCNEWS consists of a biweekly newsletter that focuses on the writing, editing, designing, and producing of campus-computing publications, and an articles abstracts published on alternating weeks that describes new contributions to the articles archive.

Contact: Wendy Rickard Bollentin
ccnews@educom.bitnet

Details: Free

User info: To subscribe to the list, send an e-mail message to the URL address below consisting of a single line reading:

SUB ccnews YourFirstName YourLastName

To send a message to the entire list, address it to: ccnews@educom.bitnet

Inquire about needing a password.

`mailto:listserv@bitnic.cren.net`

EDNET

EDNET

This forum explores the educational potential of the Internet.

Keywords: Education, Internet

Audience: Students, Educators

Profile: This independent, unmoderated mailing-list interest group is open and free of charge to all participants. Ednet links educators with common interests, and introduces students to a number of fields and sources of information, while offering criticism and suggestions.

Contact: Prescott Smith
pgsmith@educ.umass.edu

Details: Free

User info: To subscribe to the list, send an e-mail message to the address shown below consisting of a single line reading:

SUB Ednet YourFirstName YourLastName

To send a message to the entire list, address it to:

ednet@nic.umass.edu.

`gopher://ericir.syr.edu/00/AskERIC/FullText/Lists/Messages/`

`EDNET-List/README`

`mailto:listserv@nic.umass.edu`

edpolyan (Educational Policy Analysis)

edpolyan (Educational Policy Analysis)

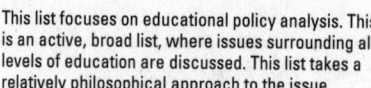

This list focuses on educational policy analysis. This is an active, broad list, where issues surrounding all levels of education are discussed. This list takes a relatively philosophical approach to the issue.

Keywords: Education (Continuing), Educational Policy

Audience: University Administrators, K-12 Educators, Postsecondary Educators

Details: Free

User info: To subscribe to the list, send an e-mail message to the URL address shown below consisting of a single line reading:

SUB edpolyan YourFirstName YourLastName

To send a message to the entire list, address it to: edpolyan@asuacad.bitnet

`mailto:listserv@asuacad.bitnet`

edpolyar (Educational Policy Analysis Archive)

edpolyar (Educational Policy Analysis Archive)

The Educational Policy Analysis Archive, an outgrowth of the edpolyan scholarly discussion list, publishes peer-reviewed articles of between 500 and 1,500 lines in length on all aspects of education policy analysis.

Keywords: Education (Continuing), Educational Policy

Audience: K-12 Educators, University Administrators, Postsecondary Educators

Details: Free, Moderated

User info: To subscribe to the archive, send an e-mail message to the URL address shown below consisting of a single line reading

SUB edpolyar YourFirstName YourLastName

`mailto:listserv@asuacad.bitnet`

edstyle (Learning Styles Theory and Research List)

edstyle (Learning Styles Theory and Research List)

This list discusses all forms of information about learning styles.

Keywords: Education (Continuing)

Audience: Educators, Educational Administrators, Researchers

Details: Free

User info: To subscribe to the list, send an e-mail message to the URL address shown below consisting of a single line reading:

SUB edstyle YourFirstName YourLastName

To send a message to the entire list, address it to: edstyle @sjuvm.bitnet

`mailto:listserv@sjuvm.bitnet`

Education (Adult)

AACIS-L (American Association for Collegiate Independent Study)

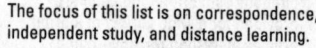

The focus of this list is on correspondence, independent study, and distance learning.

Keywords: Education (Adult), Education (Distance), Education (Continuing)

Sponsor: American Association for Collegiate Independent Study (AACIS)

Audience: Faculty Administrators

Details: Free

User info: To subscribe to the list, send an e-mail message to the URL address shown below consisting of a single line reading:

SUB aacis-l YourFirstName YourLastName

To send a message to the entire list, address it to: aacis-l@bgu.edu

`mailto:listserv@bgu.edu`

ADLTED-L (Canadian Adult Education Network)

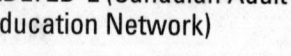

The Canadian Adult Continuing Education Network list is a broad, worldwide discussion group.

Keywords: Education (Adult), Education (Distance), Education (Continuing)

Sponsor: Canadian Adult Education Network

Audience: Researchers, Educators, Administrators, Faculty

Details: Free

User info: To subscribe to the list, send an e-mail message to the URL address shown below, consisting of a single line reading:

SUB adlted-I YourFirstName YourLastName

To send a message to the entire list, address it to: adletd-L@uregina1.bitnet

`mailto:listserv@uregina1.uregina.ca`

Adult/Distance Education

This directory is a compilation of information resources focused on adult/distance education. The directory is sponsored by The American Association for Collegiate Independent Study, and focuses on correspondence, independent study and distance learning.

Keywords: Education (Adult), Education (Distance), Education (Continuing)

Audience: Educators, Researchers

Details: Free

`ftp://una.hh.lib.umich.edu/70/ inetdirsstacks/disted:ellsworth`

AEDNET (Adult Education Network)

★★★★

This is an international electronic network for those involved in distance education.

Keywords: Education (Adult), Education (Distance), Education (Continuing)

Sponsor: Adult Education Network

Audience: Educators, Researchers, Administrators, Faculty

Details: Free

User info: To subscribe to the list, send an e-mail message to the URL address below consisting of a single line reading:

SUB aednet YourFirstName YourLastName

To send a message to the entire list, address it to: AEDNET@alpha.acast.nova.edu

`mailto:listserv@alpha.acast.nova.edu`

Altlearn (Alternative Approaches to Learning Discussion)

A discussion list that is broadly concerned with learning strategies at all levels.

Keywords: Education (Adult), Education (Distance), Education (Alternative)

Sponsor: Alternative Approaches to Learning Discussion

Audience: Educators, Administrators, Researchers

Details: Free

User info: To subscribe to the list, send an e-mail message to the URL address below, consisting of a single line reading:

SUB Altlearn YourFirstName YourLastName

To send a message to the entire list, address it to: altlearn@sjuvm.bitnet

`mailto:listserv@sjuvm.bitnet`

Asat-eva (Distance Education Evaluation Group)

★

This mailing list addresses issues in evaluating all forms of distance learning and programs.

Keywords: Education (Adult), Education (Distance), Education (Continuing)

Sponsor: Agricultural Satellite Corporation

Audience: Educators, Administrators, Researchers

Details: Free

User info: To subscribe to the list, send an e-mail message to the URL address below, consisting of a single line reading:

SUB asat-evaYourFirstName YourLastName

To send a message to the entire list, address it to: asat-eva@unlvm.unl.edu

`mailto:listserv@unlvm.unl.edu`

Catalyst

★

This is the electronic version of Catalyst, a refereed print journal for community college educators.

Keywords: Education (Adult), Education (Distance), Education (Continuing), Education (International)

Audience: Educators, Administrators, Faculty, Researchers

Details: Free, Moderated

User info: To subscribe to the journal, send an e-mail message to the URL address below, consisting of a single line reading:

SUB catalyst YourFirstName YourLastName

To send a message to the entire list, address it to: catalyst@vtvm1.bitnet

`mailto:listserv@vtvm1.cc.vt.edu`

CAUCE-L (Canadian Association for University Continuing Education)

★

Provides an electronic forum for the discussion of issues (broad, narrow, practical, theoretical, controversial, or mundane) related to university continuing education.

Keywords: Education (Adult), Education (Distance), Education (Continuing)

Sponsor: Canadian Association for University Continuing Education

Audience: Educators, Administrators, Faculty

Details: Free

User info: To subscribe to the list, send an e-mail message to the URL address below, consisting of a single line reading:

SUB cauce-l YourFirstName YourLastName

To send a message to the entire list, address it to: cauce@max.cc.uregina.ca

`mailto:listserv@max.cc.uregina.ca`

deos-l (International Discussion Forum for Distance Learning)

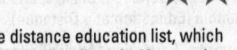

A large, diverse distance education list, which currently has 1,325 subscribers in 48 countries.

Keywords: Education (Adult), Education (Distance), Education (Continuing)

Sponsor: American Center for the Study of Distance Education

Audience: Educators, Administrators

Details: Free

User info: To subscribe to the list, send an e-mail message to the URL address shown below consisting of a single line reading:

SUB deos-l YourFirstName YourLastName

To send a message to the entire list, address it to: deos-l@psuvm.bitnet

`mailto:listserv@psuvm.bitnet`

deosnews (Distance Education Online Symposium)

The Distance Education Online Symposium publishes The American Journal of Distance Education.

Keywords: Education (Adult), Education (Distance), Education (Continuing)

Sponsor: Distance Education Online Symposium, American Center for the Study of Distance Education, Pennsylvania State University, State College, PA

Audience: Educators, Administrators, Researchers

Details: Free

User info: To subscribe to the journal, send an e-mail message to the URL address shown below consisting of a single line reading:

SUB deosnews YourFirstName YourLastName

`mailto:listserv@psuvm.bitnet`

dts-l (Dead Teachers Society Discussion List)

★

This list is for broad discussions of teaching and learning.

Keywords: Education (Adult), Education (Distance), Education (Continuing)

Audience: Educators (K-12), Educational Administrators

A B C D E F G H I J K L M N O P Q R S T U V W X Y Z

A
B
C
D
E
F
G
H
I
J
K
L
M
N
O
P
Q
R
S
T
U
V
W
X
Y
Z

Details: Free

User info: To subscribe to the list, send an e-mail message to the URL address shown below consisting of a single line reading:

SUB dts-l YourFirstName YourLastName

To send a message to the entire list, address it to: dts-l @iubvm.bitnet

`mailto:listserv@iubvm.bitnet`

edista (Educacin a Distancia) ★

The University Distance Program (UNIDIS) at the University of Santiago, Chile, sponsors Educacin a Distancia (Education at a Distance).

Keywords: Education (Adult), Education (Distance), Education (Continuing), Chile

Sponsor: The University Distance Program (UNIDIS) at the University of Santiago, Chile

Audience: Educators, Researchers

Details: Free

User info: To subscribe to the list, send an e-mail message to the URL address shown below consisting of a single line reading:

SUB edistaYourFirstName YourLastName

To send a message to the entire list, address it to: edista@usachvm1.bitnet

`mailto:listserv@usachvm1.bitnet`

hilat-l (Higher Education in Latin America) ★

Provides a means of interchange about research on higher education in Latin America. Postings are mostly in English, but are also welcome in Spanish and Portuguese.

Keywords: Education (Adult), Education (Distance), Education (Continuing), Latin America

Audience: Educators, Administrators, Faculty

Details: Free

User info: To subscribe to the list, send an e-mail message to the URL address shown below consisting of a single line reading:

SUB hilat-l YourFirstName YourLastName

To send a message to the entire list, address it to: hilat-l @bruspvm.bitnet

`mailto:listserv@bruspvm.bitnet`

horizons 'New Horizons in Adult Education'

A journal transmitted to educators around the world.

Keywords: Education (Adult), Education (Distance), Education (Continuing)

Audience: Educators, Administrators, Faculty, Researchers

Details: Free

User info: To subscribe to the journal, send an e-mail message to the URL address shown below consisting of a single line reading:

SUB horizonsYourFirstName YourLastName

`mailto:listserv@alpha.acast.nova.edu`

ipct-j 'Interpersonal Computing and Technology: An Electronic Journal for the 21st Century'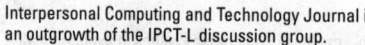

Interpersonal Computing and Technology Journal is an outgrowth of the IPCT-L discussion group.

Keywords: Education (Adult), Education (Distance), Education (Continuing), Information Technology

Sponsor: Interpersonal Computing and Technology

Audience: Educators, Administrators, Faculty

Details: Free

User info: To subscribe to the journal, send an e-mail message to the URL address shown below consisting of a single line reading:

SUB ipct-j YourFirstName YourLastName

`mailto:listserv@guvm.bitnet`

joe 'The Journal of Extension'

This is the peer-reviewed publication of the Cooperative Extension System; it covers all phases of extension education, including adult and distance education.

Keywords: Education (Adult), Education (Distance), Education (Continuing)

Audience: Educators (K-12), Faculty Administrators

Details: Free

User info: To subscribe to the journal, send an e-mail message requesting a subscription to the URL address shown below.

`mailto:almanac@joe.uwex.edu`

Jte-l 'Journal of Technology Education'

The Journal of Technology Education provides a forum for all topics relating to technology in education.

Keywords: Education (Adult), Education (Distance), Education (Continuing), Information Technology

Audience: Faculty, Administrators, Educators (K-12)

Details: Free

User info: To subscribe to the journal, send an e-mail message to the URL address below consisting of a single line reading:

SUB jte-l YourFirstName YourLastName

`mailto:listserv@vtvm1.cc.vt.edu`

Newedu-l (New Paradigms in Education List) ★

This list discusses education broadly, including delivery systems, media, collaborative learning, learning styles, and distance education.

Keywords: Education (Adult), Education (Distance), Education (Continuing)

Audience: Educators (k-12), Administrators, Researchers

Details: Free

User info: To subscribe to the list, send an e-mail message to the URL address below consisting of a single line reading:

SUB newedu-l YourFirstName YourLastName

To send a message to the entire list, address it to: newedu-l @uscvm.bitnet

`mailto:listserv@uscvm.bitnet`

POD (Professional Organizational Development) ★★★

The POD network is aimed at faculty, instructional, and organizational development in higher education.

Keywords: Education (Adult), Education (Distance), Education (Continuing)

Audience: Educators, Administrators, Researchers

Details: Free

User info: To subscribe to the list, send an e-mail message to the URL address shown below consisting of a single line reading:

SUB pod YourFirstName YourLastName

To send a message to the entire list, address it to: pod@lists.acs.ohio-state.edu

`mailto:listserv@lists.acs.ohio-state.edu`

Pubs-IAT (Institute for Academic Technology newsletter)

This newsletter shares information on publications, programs, courses, and other activities of the Institute for Academic Technology.

Keywords: Education (Adult), Education (Distance), Education (Continuing), Information Technology

Sponsor: Institute for Academic Technology

Audience: Educators, Administrators, Researchers

Details: Free

User info: To subscribe to the list, send an e-mail message to the URL address below, consisting of a single line reading:

SUB pubs-iat YourFirstName YourLastName

To send a message to the entire list, address it to: pubs-iat@gibbs.oit.unc.edu

`mailto:listserv@gibbs.oit.unc.edu`

Resodlaa (Research SIG of the Open and Distance Learning Association of Australia) ★

The purpose of this list is to foster electronic discussion, symposia, and conferences on topical issues in distance education and open-learning research.

Keywords: Education (Adult), Education (Distance), Education (Continuing), Australia

Sponsor: Research Special Interest Group (SIG) of the Open and Distance Learning Association of Australia

Audience: Educators, Administrators, Researchers

Details: Free

User info: To subscribe to the list, send an e-mail message to the URL address below, consisting of a single line reading:

SUB resodlaa YourFirstName YourLastName

To send a message to the entire list, address it to: resodlaa @usq.edu.au

`mailto:listserv@usq.edu.au`

Stlhe-l (Forum for Teaching & Learning in Higher Education) ★

This list focuses on postsecondary education teaching and learning.

Keywords: Education (Adult), Education (Distance), Education (Continuing), Education (Post Secondary)

Audience: Educators, Faculty, Administrators, Researchers

Details: Free

User info: To subscribe to the list, send an e-mail message to the URL address below, consisting of a single line reading:

SUB stlhe-l YourFirstName YourLastName

To send a message to the entire list, address it to: stlhe-l@unbvm1.bitnet

`mailto:listserv@unbvm1.bitnet`

teacheft (Teaching Effectiveness) ★

This list treats teaching effectiveness and a broad range of teaching and learning interests.

Keywords: Education (Adult), Education (Distance), Education (Continuing)

Audience: Educators, Educational Administrators, Researchers

Details: Free

User info: To subscribe to the list, send an e-mail message to the URL address shown below consisting of a single line reading:

SUB stlhe-l YourFirstName YourLastName

To send a message to the entire list, address it to: stlhe-l@wcu.bitnet

`mailto:listserv@wcu.bitnet`

teslit-l (Adult Education & Literacy Test Literature) ★

This is a sublist of tesl-l (Teaching English as a Second Language). Discussions focus primarily on issues of literacy and the teaching of English as a second language.

Keywords: Education (Adult), Education (Distance), Education (Continuing), Literacy

Audience: Educators (K-12), Educational Administrators, Researchers

Details: Free

User info: To subscribe to the list, send an e-mail message to the URL address below consisting of a single line reading:

SUB teslit-l YourFirstName YourLastName

To send a message to the entire list, address it to: teslit-l @cunyvm.bitnet

Notes: Members of teslit-l must be members of tesl-l.

`mailto:listserv@cunyvm.bitnet`

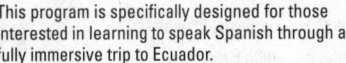

Education (Alternative)

Altlearn (Alternative Approaches to Learning Discussion) ★

A discussion list that is broadly concerned with learning strategies at all levels.

Keywords: Education (Adult), Education (Distance), Education (Alternative)

Sponsor: Alternative Approaches to Learning Discussion

Audience: Educators, Administrators, Researchers

Details: Free

User info: To subscribe to the list, send an e-mail message to the URL address below, consisting of a single line reading:

SUB Altlearn YourFirstName YourLastName

To send a message to the entire list, address it to: altlearn@sjuvm.bitnet

`mailto:listserv@sjuvm.bitnet`

de Bono

This is a discussion list concerning the work of Edward de Bono. Also provides help with teaching the CoRT Thinking Program, and Six Thinking Hats.

Keywords: de Bono (Edward), Education (Alternative), Creativity

Audience: Teachers, Students, Management Trainers

Contact: Rosa Casarez

`mailto: rcasarez@mercury.sfm.edu`

Marimed Foundation ★★

This foundation provides therapy and education to adjudicated and emotionally impaired teens. Therapies include wilderness experiences on a square-rigged sail ship, boat building, and traditional therapies.

Keywords: Education (Alternative), Sailing

Audience: Educators, Alternative Educators, Social Workers

Contact: Dr. Robert Grossman
marimed@holonet.net

Details: Free

`mailto:marimed@holonet.net`

Education (Bilingual)

Academia Latinoamericana de Espanol ★

This program is specifically designed for those interested in learning to speak Spanish through a fully immersive trip to Ecuador.

Keywords: Spanish Language, Education (Bilingual)

Sponsor: Academia Latinoamericana de Espanol, Quito, Ecuador

Audience: Researchers, Students, Language Teachers

Contact: Webmaster
webmaster@comnet.com

`http://www.comnet.com/ecuador/`
`learnSpanish.html`

Bilingual Education Network ★

This gopher site contains bilingual and bicultural, ESL (English as a Second Language), and Foreign Language resources and curriculum guidelines.

Keywords: ESL (English as a Second Language), Education (Bilingual)

Sponsor: California Department of Education, California, USA

Audience: Educators, Administrators, Parents

`gopher://goldmine.cde.ca.gov`

Felipe's Bilingual WWW Pages ★★

An interactive web site containing gopher and web links to various Latin American resources.

Keywords: Latin America, Education (Bilingual)

Sponsor: University of Texas, Texas, USA

Audience: Educators, Language Students, Translators

Contact: Felipe Campos
felipe@bongo.utexas.edu

`http://edb518ea.edb.utexas.edu`

A B C D **E** F G H I J K L M N O P Q R S T U V W X Y Z

A
B
C
D
E
F
G
H
I
J
K
L
M
N
O
P
Q
R
S
T
U
V
W
X
Y
Z

INTER-L ★

A list for members of the National Association of Foreign Student Advisors.

Keywords: Advisory, Education (Bilingual), Educational Policy

Sponsor: National Association of Foreign Student Advisors (NAFSA)

Audience: Foreign Students, NAFSA Members

Details: Free

User info: To subscribe to the list, send an e-mail message to the address below consisting of a single line reading:

`mailto:listserv@vtm1.cc.vt.edu`

KFLC-L ★

A mailing list for distributing information on the meetings and proceedings of the Kentucky Foreign Language Conferences (KFLC).

Keywords: Language, Linguistics, Education (Bilingual)

Audience: Linguists, Educators

Contact: John Greenway
engjlg@ukcc.uky.edu

User info: To subscribe, send an e-mail message to the URL address below consisting of a single line reading:

SUB kflc-l YourFirstName YourLastName.

To send a message to the entire list, address it to: kflc-l@ukcc.uky.edu

`mailto:listserv@ukcc.uky.edu`

The University of Michigan Library ★★

The library's holdings are large and wide-ranging and contain significant collections in many fields, including the following: Bilingual Education, Linguistics, Neuroscience, Michigan History, Temperance and Prohibition, African Government, Prohibition

Keywords: Education (Bilingual), Linguistics, Neuroscience, Michigan, Prohibition, Government (African)

Audience: General Public, Researchers, Librarians, Document Delivery Professionals

Details: Free

User Info: Expect: nothing, Send: <cr>

`telnet://cts.merit.edu`

Education (College/University)

soc.college ★

A Usenet newsgroup providing information and discussion about college life, activities, campus, and so on.

Keywords: Sociology, Social Science, Education (College/University)

Audience: Sociologists, Social Scientists, Educators (College/University), Students (College/University)

Details: Free

User info: To subscribe to this Usenet newsgroup, you need access to a newsreader.

`news:soc.college`

University of Minnesota Gopher Server ★★

The University of Minnesota Gopher server provides information about Minnesota University, as well as providing access to other universities' gopher servers.

Keywords: Universities, Education (College/University)

Sponsor: University of Minnesota, Minnesota, USA

Audience: Students

Contact: Gopher Development Team
gopher@boombox.micro.umn.edu

`gopher://gopher.tc.umn.edu`

Education (Continuing)

AACIS-L (American Association for Collegiate Independent Study) ★

The focus this list is on correspondence, independent study, and distance learning.

Keywords: Education (Adult), Education (Distance), Education (Continuing)

Sponsor: American Association for Collegiate Independent Study (AACIS)

Audience: Faculty Administrators

Details: Free

User Info: To subscribe to the list, send an e-mail message to the URL address shown below consisting of a single line reading:

SUB aacis-l YourFirstName YourLastName

To send a message to the entire list, address it to: aacis-l@bgu.edu

`mailto:listserv@bgu.edu`

ADLTED-L (Canadian Adult Education Network) ★

The Canadian Adult Continuing Education Network list is a broad, worldwide discussion group.

Keywords: Education (Adult), Education (Distance), Education (Continuing)

Sponsor: Canadian Adult Education Network

Audience: Researchers, Educators, Administrators, Faculty

Details: Free

User info: To subscribe to the list, send an e-mail message to the URL address shown below, consisting of a single line reading:

SUB adlted-l YourFirstName YourLastName

To send a message to the entire list, address it to: adlted-L@uregina1.bitnet

`mailto:listserv@uregina1.uregina.ca`

AEDNET (Adult Education Network) ★★★★

This is an international electronic network for those involved in distance education.

Keywords: Education (Adult), Education (Distance), Education (Continuing)

Sponsor: Adult Education Network

Audience: Educators, Researchers, Administrators, Faculty

Details: Free

User info: To subscribe to the list, send an e-mail message to the URL address below consisting of a single line reading:

SUB aednet YourFirstName YourLastName

To send a message to the entire list, address it to:
AEDNET@alpha.acast.nova.edu

`mailto:listserv@alpha.acast.nova.edu`

Adult/Distance Education ★

This directory is a compilation of information resources focused on adult/distance education. The directory is sponsored by The American Association for Collegiate Independent Study, and focuses on correspondence, independent study and distance learning.

Keywords: Education (Adult), Education (Distance), Education (Continuing)

Audience: Educators, Researchers

Details: Free

`ftp://una.hh.lib.umich.edu/70/`
`inetdirsstacks/disted:ellsworth`

Asat-eva (Distance Education Evaluation Group) ★

This mailing list addresses issues in evaluating all forms of distance learning and programs.

Keywords: Education (Adult), Education (Distance), Education (Continuing)

Sponsor: Agricultural Satellite Corporation

Audience: Educators, Administrators, Researchers

Details: Free

User info: To subscribe to the list, send an e-mail message to the URL address below, consisting of a single line reading:

SUB asat-evaYourFirstName YourLastName

To send a message to the entire list, address it to: asat-eva@unlvm.unl.edu

`mailto:listserv@unlvm.unl.edu`

Catalyst ★

This is the electronic version of Catalyst, a refereed print journal for community college educators.

Keywords: Education (Adult), Education (Distance), Education (Continuing), Education (International)

Audience: Educators, Administrators, Faculty, Researchers

Details: Free, Moderated

User info: To subscribe to the journal, send an e-mail message to the URL address below, consisting of a single line reading:

SUB catalyst YourFirstName YourLastName

To send a message to the entire list, address it to: catalyst@vtvm1.bitnet

`mailto:listserv@vtvm1.cc.vt.edu`

CAUCE-L (Canadian Association for University Continuing Education) ★

Provides an electronic forum for the discussion of issues (broad, narrow, practical, theoretical, controversial, or mundane) related to university continuing education.

Keywords: Education (Adult), Education (Distance), Education (Continuing)

Sponsor: Canadian Association for University Continuing Education

Audience: Educators, Administrators, Faculty

Details: Free

User info: To subscribe to the list, send an e-mail message to the URL address below, consisting of a single line reading:

SUB cauce-l YourFirstName YourLastName

To send a message to the entire list, address it to: cauce@max.cc.uregina.ca

`mailto:listserv@max.cc.uregina.ca`

Commcoll

A mailing list providing a forum for faculty, staff and administrators at two-year institutions.

Keywords: Education (Continuing), Community Colleges

Sponsor: Jefferson Community College at the University of Kentucky, Kentucky, USA

Audience: Educators, Administrators

User info: To subscribe to the list, send an e-mail message to the URL address below consisting of a single line reading:

SUB commcoll YourFirstName YourLastName

To send a message to the entire list, address it to: commcoll@ukcc.uky.edu

`mailto:listserv@ukcc.uky.edu`

Community Services Catalyst

This electronic journal provides information concerning community services around the country, especially those dealing with continuing education. The journal is published quarterly.

Keywords: Education (Continuing), Community Service

Sponsor: National Council on Community Services and Continuing Education (an affiliate council of the American Association of Community Colleges), USA

Audience: Educators, Administrators

User info: To subscribe to the list, send an e-mail message to the URL address below consisting of a single line reading:

SUB catalyst YourFirstName YourLastName

To send a message to the entire list, address it to: catalyst@vtvm1.cc.vt.edu

`mailto: listserv@vtvml.cc.vt.edu`

Deos-L ★★★

A mailing list intended to promote communication among distance educators, to disseminate information and requests about distance education around the world, and to discuss issues raised in the electronic journal DEOSNEWS.

Keywords: Education (Distance), Education (Continuing)

Sponsor: The American Center for the Study of Distance Education, Pennsylvania State University, Pennsylvania, USA

Audience: Distance Educators, Administrators

User info: To subscribe to the list, send an e-mail message to the URL address below consisting of a single line reading:

SUB deos-l YourFirstName YourLastName

To send a message to the entire list, address it to: deos-l@psuvm.psu.edu

`mailto:listserv@psuvm.psu.edu`

deos-l (International Discussion Forum for Distance Learning) ★★★

A large, diverse distance education list, which currently has 1,325 subscribers in 48 countries.

Keywords: Education (Adult), Education (Distance), Education (Continuing)

Sponsor: American Center for the Study of Distance Education

Audience: Educators, Administrators

Details: Free

User info: To subscribe to the list, send an e-mail message to the URL address shown below consisting of a single line reading:

SUB deos-l YourFirstName YourLastName

To send a message to the entire list, address it to: deos-l @psuvm.bitnet

`mailto:listserv@psuvm.bitnet`

deosnews (Distance Education Online Symposium) ★★★

The Distance Education Online Symposium publishes The American Journal of Distance Education.

Keywords: Education (Adult), Education (Distance), Education (Continuing)

Sponsor: Distance Education Online Symposium, American Center for the Study of Distance Education, Pennsylvania State University, State College, PA

Audience: Educators, Administrators, Researchers

Details: Free

User info: To subscribe to the journal, send an e-mail message to the URL address shown below consisting of a single line reading:

SUB deosnews YourFirstName YourLastName

`mailto:listserv@psuvm.bitnet`

dts-l (Dead Teachers Society Discussion List) ★

This list is for broad discussions of teaching and learning.

Keywords: Education (Adult), Education (Distance), Education (Continuing)

Audience: Educators K-12, Educational Administrators

Details: Free

User info: To subscribe to the list, send an e-mail message to the URL address shown below consisting of a single line reading:

SUB dts-l YourFirstName YourLastName

To send a message to the entire list, address it to: dts-l @iubvm.bitnet

`mailto:listserv@iubvm.bitnet`

A
B
C
D
E
F
G
H
I
J
K
L
M
N
O
P
Q
R
S
T
U
V
W
X
Y
Z

A
B
C
D
E
F
G
H
I
J
K
L
M
N
O
P
Q
R
S
T
U
V
W
X
Y
Z

edista (Educacin a Distancia) ★

The University Distance Program (UNIDIS) at the University of Santiago, Chile, sponsors Educacin a Distancia (Education at a Distance).

Keywords: Education (Adult), Education (Distance), Education (Continuing), Chile

Sponsor: The University Distance Program (UNIDIS) at the University of Santiago, Chile

Audience: Educators, Researchers

Details: Free

User info: To subscribe to the list, send an e-mail message to the URL address shown below consisting of a single line reading:

SUB edistaYourFirstName YourLastName

To send a message to the entire list, address it to: edista@usachvm1.bitnet

`mailto:listserv@usachvm1.bitnet`

edpolyan (Educational Policy Analysis) ★

This list focuses on educational policy analysis. This is an active, broad list, where issues surrounding all levels of education are discussed. This list takes a relatively philosophical approach to the issue.

Keywords: Education (Continuing), Educational Policy

Audience: University Administrators, K-12 Educators, Postsecondary Educators

Details: Free

User info: To subscribe to the list, send an e-mail message to the URL address shown below consisting of a single line reading:

SUB edpolyan YourFirstName YourLastName

To send a message to the entire list, address it to: edpolyan@asuacad.bitnet

`mailto:listserv@asuacad.bitnet`

edpolyar (Educational Policy Analysis Archive) ★

The Educational Policy Analysis Archive, an outgrowth of the edpolyan scholarly discussion list, publishes peer-reviewed articles of between 500 and 1,500 lines in length on all aspects of education policy analysis.

Keywords: Education (Continuing), Educational Policy

Audience: K-12 Educators, University Administrators, Postsecondary Educators

Details: Free, Moderated

User info: To subscribe to the archive, send an e-mail message to the URL address shown below consisting of a single line reading

SUB edpolyar YourFirstName YourLastName

`mailto:listserv@asuacad.bitnet`

edstyle (Learning Styles Theory and Research List) ★

This list discusses all forms of information about learning styles.

Keywords: Education (Continuing)

Audience: Educators, Educational Administrators, Researchers

Details: Free

User info: To subscribe to the list, send an e-mail message to the URL address shown below consisting of a single line reading:

SUB edstyle YourFirstName YourLastName

To send a message to the entire list, address it to: edstyle @sjuvm.bitnet

`mailto:listserv@sjuvm.bitnet`

edupage (A News Update from EDUCOM) ★★★★

A newsletter put out by EDUCOM summarizing information technology news.

Keywords: Education (Continuing), Information Technology

Sponsor: EDUCOM

Audience: Educators, Administrators

Details: Free

User info: To subscribe to the newsletter, send an e-mail message requesting a subscription to the URL address shown below and include your name, institutional affiliation, and e-mail address.

`mailto:edupage@educom.edu`

euitnews (Educational Uses of Information Technology) ★★★

EDUCOM's newsletter for the Educational Uses of Information Technology program encompasses distance learning, self-paced instruction, computer-aided instruction, video, and other information technologies for teaching and learning.

Keywords: Education (Continuing), Information Technology

Audience: Administrators, K-12 Educators

Details: Free

User info: To subscribe to the newsletter, send an e-mail message to the URL address below consisting of a single line reading:

SUB euitnews YourFirstName YourLastName

`mailto:listserv@bitnic.educom.edu`

hilat-I (Higher Education in Latin America) ★

Provides a means of interchange about research on higher education in Latin America. Postings are mostly in English, but are also welcome in Spanish and Portuguese.

Keywords: Education (Adult), Education (Distance), Education (Continuing), Latin America

Audience: Educators, Administrators, Faculty

Details: Free

User info: To subscribe to the list, send an e-mail message to the URL address shown below consisting of a single line reading:

SUB hilat-I YourFirstName YourLastName

To send a message to the entire list, address it to: hilat-I @bruspvm.bitnet

`mailto:listserv@bruspvm.bitnet`

horizons 'New Horizons in Adult Education' ★★★★

A journal transmitted to educators around the world.

Keywords: Education (Adult), Education (Distance), Education (Continuing)

Audience: Educators, Administrators, Faculty, Researchers

Details: Free

User info: To subscribe to the journal, send an e-mail message to the URL address shown below consisting of a single line reading:

SUB horizonsYourFirstName YourLastName

`mailto:listserv@alpha.acast.nova.edu`

ipct-j 'Interpersonal Computing and Technology: An Electronic Journal for the 21st Century' ★

Interpersonal Computing and Technology Journal is an outgrowth of the IPCT-L discussion group.

Keywords: Education (Adult), Education (Distance), Education (Continuing), Information Technology

Sponsor: Interpersonal Computing and Technology

Audience: Educators, Administrators, Faculty

Details: Free

User info: To subscribe to the journal, send an e-mail message to the URL address shown below consisting of a single line reading:

SUB ipct-j YourFirstName YourLastName

`mailto:listserv@guvm.bitnet`

joe 'The Journal of Extension' ★★★

This is the peer-reviewed publication of the Cooperative Extension System; it covers all phases of extension education, including adult and distance education.

Keywords: Education (Adult), Education (Distance), Education (Continuing)

Audience: Educators (K-12), Faculty Administrators

Details: Free

User info: To subscribe to the journal, send an e-mail message requesting a subscription to the URL address shown below.

`mailto:almanac@joe.uwex.edu`

Jte-l 'Journal of Technology Education' ★

The Journal of Technology Education provides a forum for all topics relating to technology in education.

Keywords: Education (Adult), Education (Distance), Education (Continuing), Information Technology

Audience: Faculty, Administrators, Educators (K-12)

Details: Free

User info: To subscribe to the journal, send an e-mail message to the URL address below consisting of a single line reading:

SUB jte-l YourFirstName YourLastName

`mailto:listserv@vtvm1.cc.vt.edu`

Newedu-l (New Paradigms in Education List) ★

This list discusses education broadly, including delivery systems, media, collaborative learning, learning styles, and distance education.

Keywords: Education (Adult), Education (Distance), Education (Continuing)

Audience: Educators (k-12), Administrators, Researchers

Details: Free

User info: To subscribe to the list, send an e-mail message to the URL address below consisting of a single line reading:

SUB newedu-l YourFirstName YourLastName

To send a message to the entire list, address it to: newedu-l @uscvm.bitnet

`mailto:listserv@uscvm.bitnet`

POD (Professional Organizational Development) ★★★

The POD network is aimed at faculty, instructional, and organizational development in higher education.

Keywords: Education (Adult), Education (Distance), Education (Continuing)

Audience: Educators, Administrators, Researchers

Details: Free

User info: To subscribe to the list, send an e-mail message to the URL address shown below consisting of a single line reading:

SUB pod YourFirstName YourLastName

To send a message to the entire list, address it to: pod@lists.acs.ohio-state.edu

`mailto:listserv@lists.acs.ohio-state.edu`

Pubs-IAT (Institute for Academic Technology newsletter) ★★★★

This newsletter shares information on publications, programs, courses, and other activities of the Institute for Academic Technology.

Keywords: Education (Adult), Education (Distance), Education (Continuing), Information Technology

Sponsor: Institute for Academic Technology

Audience: Educators, Administrators, Researchers

Details: Free

User info: To subscribe to the list, send an e-mail message to the URL address below, consisting of a single line reading:

SUB pubs-iat YourFirstName YourLastName

To send a message to the entire list, address it to: pubs-iat@gibbs.oit.unc.edu

`mailto:listserv@gibbs.oit.unc.edu`

Resodlaa (Research SIG of the Open and Distance Learning Association of Australia) ★

The purpose of this list is to foster electronic discussion, symposia, and conferences on topical issues in distance education and open-learning research.

Keywords: Education (Adult), Education (Distance), Education (Continuing), Australia

Sponsor: Research Special Interest Group (SIG) of the Open and Distance Learning Association of Australia

Audience: Educators, Administrators, Researchers

Details: Free

User info: To subscribe to the list, send an e-mail message to the URL address below, consisting of a single line reading:

SUB resodlaa YourFirstName YourLastName

To send a message to the entire list, address it to: resodlaa @usq.edu.au

`mailto:listserv@usq.edu.au`

Stlhe-l (Forum for Teaching & Learning in Higher Education) ★

This list focuses on postsecondary education teaching and learning.

Keywords: Education (Adult), Education (Distance), Education (Continuing), Education (Post Secondary)

Audience: Educators, Faculty, Administrators, Researchers

Details: Free

User info: To subscribe to the list, send an e-mail message to the URL address below consisting of a single line reading:

SUB stlhe-l YourFirstName YourLastName

To send a message to the entire list, address it to: stlhe-l@unbvm1.bitnet

`mailto:listserv@unbvm1.bitnet`

teacheft (Teaching Effectiveness) ★

This list treats teaching effectiveness and a broad range of teaching and learning interests.

Keywords: Education (Adult), Education (Distance), Education (Continuing)

Audience: Educators, Educational Administrators, Researchers

Details: Free

User info: To subscribe to the list, send an e-mail message to the URL address shown below consisting of a single line reading:

SUB stlhe-l YourFirstName YourLastName

To send a message to the entire list, address it to: stlhe-l@wcu.bitnet

`mailto:listserv@wcu.bitnet`

teslit-l (Adult Education & Literacy Test Literature) ★

This is a sublist of tesl-l (Teaching English as a Second Language). Discussions focus primarily on issues of literacy and the teaching of English as a second language.

Keywords: Education (Adult), Education (Distance), Education (Continuing), Literacy

Audience: Educators K-12, Educational Administrators, Researchers

Details: Free

User info: To subscribe to the list, send an e-mail message to the URL address below consisting of a single line reading:

SUB teslit-l YourFirstName YourLastName

To send a message to the entire list, address it to: teslit-l @cunyvm.bitnet

Notes: Members of teslit-l must be members of tesl-l.

`mailto:listserv@cunyvm.bitnet`

A B C D E F G H I J K L M N O P Q R S T U V W X Y Z

The Electronic AIR

Biweekly (nominal schedule) electronic newsletter for the Association for Institutional Research members, as well as college and university planners.

Keywords: Education (Continuing), Institutional Research

Sponsor: Association for Institutional Research (AIR)

Audience: College/University Planners, University Administrators

Contact: Larry Nelson
NELSON_L@PLU.bitnet

Details: Free

`mailto:nelson_l@plu.bitnet`

Education (Distance)

AACIS-L (American Association for Collegiate Independent Study)

The focus of this list is on correspondence, independent study, and distance learning.

Keywords: Education (Adult), Education (Distance), Education (Continuing)

Sponsor: American Association for Collegiate Independent Study (AACIS)

Audience: Faculty Administrators

Details: Free

User Info: To subscribe to the list, send an e-mail message to the URL address shown below consisting of a single line reading:

SUB aacis-l YourFirstName YourLastName

To send a message to the entire list, address it to: aacis-l@bgu.edu

`mailto:listserv@bgu.edu`

ADLTED-L (Canadian Adult Education Network)

The Canadian Adult Continuing Education Network list is a broad, worldwide discussion group.

Keywords: Education (Adult), Education (Distance), Education (Continuing)

Sponsor: Canadian Adult Education Network

Audience: Researchers, Educators, Administrators, Faculty

Details: Free

User info: To subscribe to the list, send an e-mail message to the URL address shown below, consisting of a single line reading:

SUB adlted-l YourFirstName YourLastName

To send a message to the entire list, address it to: adlted-l@uregina1.bitnet

`mailto:listserv@uregina1.uregina.ca`

Adult/Distance Education

This directory is a compilation of information resources focused on adult/distance education. The directory is sponsored by The American Association for Collegiate Independent Study, and focuses on correspondence, independent study and distance learning.

Keywords: Education (Adult), Education (Distance), Education (Continuing)

Audience: Educators, Researchers

Details: Free

`ftp://una.hh.lib.umich.edu/70/`
`inetdirsstacks/disted:ellsworth`

AEDNET (Adult Education Network)

This is an international electronic network for those involved in distance education.

Keywords: Education (Adult), Education (Distance), Education (Continuing)

Sponsor: Adult Education Network

Audience: Educators, Researchers, Administrators, Faculty

Details: Free

User info: To subscribe to the list, send an e-mail message to the URL address below consisting of a single line reading:

SUB aednet YourFirstName YourLastName

To send a message to the entire list, address it to:
AEDNET@alpha.acast.nova.edu

`mailto:listserv@alpha.acast.nova.edu`

Altlearn (Alternative Approaches to Learning Discussion)

A discussion list that is broadly concerned with learning strategies at all levels.

Keywords: Education (Adult), Education (Distance), Education (Alternative)

Sponsor: Alternative Approaches to Learning Discussion

Audience: Educators, Administrators, Researchers

Details: Free

User info: To subscribe to the list, send an e-mail message to the URL address below, consisting of a single line reading:

SUB Altlearn YourFirstName YourLastName

To send a message to the entire list, address it to: altlearn@sjuvm.bitnet

`mailto:listserv@sjuvm.bitnet`

Asat-eva (Distance Education Evaluation Group)

This mailing list addresses issues in evaluating all forms of distance learning and programs.

Keywords: Education (Adult), Education (Distance), Education (Continuing)

Sponsor: Agricultural Satellite Corporation

Audience: Educators, Administrators, Researchers

Details: Free

User info: To subscribe to the list, send an e-mail message to the URL address below, consisting of a single line reading:

SUB asat-evaYourFirstName YourLastName

To send a message to the entire list, address it to: asat-eva@unlvm.unl.edu

`mailto:listserv@unlvm.unl.edu`

Catalyst

This is the electronic version of Catalyst, a refereed print journal for community college educators.

Keywords: Education (Adult), Education (Distance), Education (Continuing), Education (International)

Audience: Educators, Administrators, Faculty, Researchers

Details: Free, Moderated

User info: To subscribe to the journal, send an e-mail message to the URL address below, consisting of a single line reading:

SUB catalyst YourFirstName YourLastName

To send a message to the entire list, address it to: catalyst@vtvm1.bitnet

`mailto:listserv@vtvm1.cc.vt.edu`

CAUCE-L (Canadian Association for University Continuing Education)

Provides an electronic forum for the discussion of issues (broad, narrow, practical, theoretical, controversial, or mundane) related to university continuing education.

Keywords: Education (Adult), Education (Distance), Education (Continuing)

Sponsor: Canadian Association for University Continuing Education

Audience: Educators, Administrators, Faculty

Details: Free

User info: To subscribe to the list, send an e-mail message to the URL address below, consisting of a single line reading:

SUB cauce-l YourFirstName YourLastName

To send a message to the entire list, address it to: cauce@max.cc.uregina.ca

`mailto:listserv@max.cc.uregina.ca`

A B C D E F G H I J K L M N O P Q R S T U V W X Y Z

cread (Latin American & Caribbean Distance & Continuing Education)

This is a digest list of distance education information primarily focused on Latin America and the Caribbean.

Keywords: Latin America, Caribbean, Education (Distance)

Audience: Educators, Administrators, Faculty

Details: Free

User info: To subscribe to the list, send an e-mail message to the URL address below consisting of a single line reading:

SUB cread YourFirstName YourLastName.

To send a message to the entire list, address it to: cread@yorkvm1.bitnet

`mailto:listserv@yorkvm1.bitnet`

Deos-L

A mailing list intended to promote communication among distance educators, to disseminate information and requests about distance education around the world, and to discuss issues raised in the electronic journal DEOSNEWS.

Keywords: Education (Distance), Education (Continuing)

Sponsor: The American Center for the Study of Distance Education, Pennsylvania State University, Pennsylvania, USA

Audience: Distance Educators, Administrators

User info: To subscribe to the list, send an e-mail message to the URL address below consisting of a single line reading:

SUB deos-l YourFirstName YourLastName

To send a message to the entire list, address it to: deos-l@psuvm.psu.edu

`mailto:listserv@psuvm.psu.edu`

deos-l (International Discussion Forum for Distance Learning)

A large, diverse distance education list, which currently has 1,325 subscribers in 48 countries.

Keywords: Education (Adult), Education (Distance), Education (Continuing)

Sponsor: American Center for the Study of Distance Education

Audience: Educators, Administrators

Details: Free

User info: To subscribe to the list, send an e-mail message to the URL address shown below consisting of a single line reading:

SUB deos-l YourFirstName YourLastName

To send a message to the entire list, address it to: deos-l@psuvm.bitnet

`mailto:listserv@psuvm.bitnet`

deosnews (Distance Education Online Symposium)

The Distance Education Online Symposium publishes The American Journal of Distance Education.

Keywords: Education (Adult), Education (Distance), Education (Continuing)

Sponsor: Distance Education Online Symposium, American Center for the Study of Distance Education, Pennsylvania State University, State College, PA

Audience: Educators, Administrators, Researchers

Details: Free

User info: To subscribe to the journal, send an e-mail message to the URL address shown below consisting of a single line reading:

SUB deosnews YourFirstName YourLastName

`mailto:listserv@psuvm.bitnet`

Distance Education

This gopher site takes advantage of New Brunswick's advanced telecommunications infrastructure to provide leading edge technology-based learning environments. A computer-based teleconferencing system forms the core of the network complemented by computer-aided communications, electronic data links and other multimedia technologies.

Keywords: Education (Distance), Independent Study

Sponsor: TeleEducation New Brunswick, Department of Advanced Education and Labor

Audience: Educators, Students, Professionals

`gopher://gopher.ollc.mta.ca`

dts-l (Dead Teachers Society Discussion List)

This list is for broad discussions of teaching and learning.

Keywords: Education (Adult), Education (Distance), Education (Continuing)

Audience: Educators K-12, Educational Administrators

Details: Free

User info: To subscribe to the list, send an e-mail message to the URL address shown below consisting of a single line reading:

SUB dts-l YourFirstName YourLastName

To send a message to the entire list, address it to: dts-l @iubvm.bitnet

`mailto:listserv@iubvm.bitnet`

edista (Educacin a Distancia)

The University Distance Program (UNIDIS) at the University of Santiago, Chile, sponsors Educacin a Distancia (Education at a Distance).

Keywords: Education (Adult), Education (Distance), Education (Continuing), Chile

Sponsor: The University Distance Program (UNIDIS) at the University of Santiago, Chile

Audience: Educators, Researchers

Details: Free

User info: To subscribe to the list, send an e-mail message to the URL address shown below consisting of a single line reading:

SUB edistaYourFirstName YourLastName

To send a message to the entire list, address it to: edista@usachvm1.bitnet

`mailto:listserv@usachvm1.bitnet`

hilat-l (Higher Education in Latin America)

Provides a means of interchange about research on higher education in Latin America. Postings are mostly in English, but are also welcome in Spanish and Portuguese.

Keywords: Education (Adult), Education (Distance), Education (Continuing), Latin America

Audience: Educators, Administrators, Faculty

Details: Free

User info: To subscribe to the list, send an e-mail message to the URL address shown below consisting of a single line reading:

SUB hilat-l YourFirstName YourLastName

To send a message to the entire list, address it to: hilat-l @bruspvm.bitnet

`mailto:listserv@bruspvm.bitnet`

horizons 'New Horizons in Adult Education'

A journal transmitted to educators around the world.

Keywords: Education (Adult), Education (Distance), Education (Continuing)

Audience: Educators, Administrators, Faculty, Researchers

Details: Free

User info: To subscribe to the journal, send an e-mail message to the URL address shown below consisting of a single line reading:

SUB horizonsYourFirstName YourLastName

`mailto:listserv@alpha.acast.nova.edu`

A
B
C
D
E
F
G
H
I
J
K
L
M
N
O
P
Q
R
S
T
U
V
W
X
Y
Z

A
B
C
D
E
F
G
H
I
J
K
L
M
N
O
P
Q
R
S
T
U
V
W
X
Y
Z

International Centre for Distance Learning ★★★

This site is a distance education database.

Keywords: Education (Distance)

Sponsor: International Centre for Distance Learning, The Open University, United Kingdom

Audience: Educators, Students, Researchers

Profile: The database is extensive, and provides information about courses, related institutions, and relevant literature, with over 30,000 entries, including the following: study skills, agriculture, fisheries, architecture, building, surveying, planning, arts, humanities and social sciences,business, services, management, economics, education and training, applied science, technology, computers, environment, pure science and mathematics, medicine, health, social welfare, law, law enforcement, regulations and standards, personal, home and family affairs

User Info: Expect: Login; Send: icdl; Send: <Country>; Password: AAA

`telnet://acsvax.open.ac.uk`

ipct-j 'Interpersonal Computing and Technology: An Electronic Journal for the 21st Century' ★

Interpersonal Computing and Technology Journal is an outgrowth of the IPCT-L discussion group.

Keywords: Education (Adult), Education (Distance), Education (Continuing), Information Technology

Sponsor: Interpersonal Computing and Technology

Audience: Educators, Administrators, Faculty

Details: Free, Moderated

User info: To subscribe to the journal, send an e-mail message to the URL address shown below consisting of a single line reading:

SUB ipct-j YourFirstName YourLastName

`mailto:listserv@guvm.bitnet`

joe 'The Journal of Extension' ★★★

This is the peer-reviewed publication of the Cooperative Extension System; it covers all phases of extension education, including adult and distance education.

Keywords: Education (Adult), Education (Distance), Education (Continuing)

Audience: Educators (K-12), Faculty Administrators

Details: Free, Moderated

User info: To subscribe to the journal, send an e-mail message requesting a subscription to the URL address shown below.

`mailto:almanac@joe.uwex.edu`

Jte-l 'Journal of Technology Education' ★

The Journal of Technology Education provides a forum for all topics relating to technology in education.

Keywords: Education (Adult), Education (Distance), Education (Continuing), Information Technology

Audience: Faculty, Administrators, Educators (K-12)

Details: Free

User info: To subscribe to the journal, send an e-mail message to the URL address below consisting of a single line reading:

SUB jte-l YourFirstName YourLastName

`mailto:listserv@vtvm1.cc.vt.edu`

Newedu-l (New Paradigms in Education List) ★

This list discusses education broadly, including delivery systems, media, collaborative learning, learning styles, and distance education.

Keywords: Education (Adult), Education (Distance), Education (Continuing)

Audience: Educators (K-12), Administrators, Researchers

Details: Free

User info: To subscribe to the list, send an e-mail message to the URL address below consisting of a single line reading:

SUB newedu-l YourFirstName YourLastName

To send a message to the entire list, address it to: newedu-l @uscvm.bitnet

`mailto:listserv@uscvm.bitnet`

POD (Professional Organizational Development) ★★★

The POD network is aimed at faculty, instructional, and organizational development in higher education.

Keywords: Education (Adult), Education (Distance), Education (Continuing)

Audience: Educators, Administrators, Researchers

Details: Free

User info: To subscribe to the list, send an e-mail message to the URL address shown below consisting of a single line reading:

SUB pod YourFirstName YourLastName

To send a message to the entire list, address it to: pod@lists.acs.ohio-state.edu

`mailto:listserv@lists.acs.ohio-state.edu`

Pubs-IAT (Institute for Academic Technology newsletter) ★★★★

This newsletter shares information on publications, programs, courses, and other activities of the Institute for Academic Technology.

Keywords: Education (Adult), Education (Distance), Education (Continuing), Information Technology

Sponsor: Institute for Academic Technology

Audience: Educators, Administrators, Researchers

Details: Free

User info: To subscribe to the list, send an e-mail message to the URL address below, consisting of a single line reading:

SUB pubs-iat YourFirstName YourLastName

To send a message to the entire list, address it to: pubs-iat@gibbs.oit.unc.edu

`mailto:listserv@gibbs.oit.unc.edu`

Resodlaa (Research SIG of the Open and Distance Learning Association of Australia) ★

The purpose of this list is to foster electronic discussion, symposia, and conferences on topical issues in distance education and open-learning research.

Keywords: Education (Adult), Education (Distance), Education (Continuing), Australia

Sponsor: Research Special Interest Group (SIG) of the Open and Distance Learning Association of Australia

Audience: Educators, Administrators, Researchers

Details: Free

User info: To subscribe to the list, send an e-mail message to the URL address below, consisting of a single line reading:

SUB resodlaa YourFirstName YourLastName

To send a message to the entire list, address it to: resodlaa @usq.edu.au

`mailto:listserv@usq.edu.au`

Stlhe-l (Forum for Teaching & Learning in Higher Education) ★

This list focuses on postsecondary education teaching and learning.

Keywords: Education (Adult), Education (Distance), Education (Continuing), Education (Post Secondary)

Audience: Educators, Faculty, Administrators, Researchers

Details: Free

User info: To subscribe to the list, send an e-mail message to the URL address below consisting of a single line reading:

SUB stlhe-l YourFirstName YourLastName

To send a message to the entire list, address it to: stlhe-l@unbvm1.bitnet

`mailto:listserv@unbvm1.bitnet`

teacheft (Teaching Effectiveness)

This list treats teaching effectiveness and a broad range of teaching and learning interests.

Keywords: Education (Adult), Education (Distance), Education (Continuing)

Audience: Educators, Educational Administrators, Researchers

Details: Free

User info: To subscribe to the list, send an e-mail message to the URL address shown below consisting of a single line reading:

SUB stlhe-l YourFirstName YourLastName

To send a message to the entire list, address it to: stlhe-l@wcu.bitnet

`mailto:listserv@wcu.bitnet`

teslit-l (Adult Education & Literacy Test Literature)

This is a sublist of tesl-l (Teaching English as a Second Language). Discussions focus primarily on issues of literacy and the teaching of English as a second language.

Keywords: Education (Adult), Education (Distance), Education (Continuing), Literacy

Audience: Educators K-12, Educational Administrators, Researchers

Details: Free

User info: To subscribe to the list, send an e-mail message to the URL address below consisting of a single line reading:

SUB teslit-l YourFirstName YourLastName

To send a message to the entire list, address it to: teslit-l @cunyvm.bitnet

Notes: Members of teslit-l must be members of tesl-l.

`mailto:listserv@cunyvm.bitnet`

University of Wisconsin Extension Program in Independent Study

★★★

A gopher containing information about courses of study at the University of Wisconsin Extension Program in Independent Study. Over fifty-five disciplines, from Arabic to Womens Studies, are represented.

Keywords: Education (Distance), Independent Study

Sponsor: University of Wisconsin Extension Program in Independent Study, Madison, Wisconsin, USA

Audience: Professionals, Educators, Students

Notes: Information is free, but fees are charged for courses. Contact the Advisor to Students at 608-263-2055, or write University of Wisconsin Extension Program in Independent Study, 104 Extension Building, 432 North Lake Street, Madison, WI 53706-1498

`gopher://gopher.uwex.edu`

Virtual Hospital

★★

The Virtual Hospital (VH) is a continuously updated medical multimedia database accessible 24 hours a day. The site provides distance learning to practicing physicians and may be used for Continuing Medical Education (CME).

Keywords: Medicine, Education (Distance)

Sponsor: The Electronic Differential Multimedia Laboratory, Department of Radiology, University of Iowa College of Medicine, USA

Audience: Biologists, Researchers, Medical Professionals, Health Care Professionals

Contact: Librarian
librarian@vh.radiology.uiowa.edu

`http://indy.radiology.uiowa.edu/`
`VirtualHospital.html`

Education (International)

Catalyst

This is the electronic version of Catalyst, a refereed print journal for community college educators.

Keywords: Education (Adult), Education (Distance), Education (Continuing), Education (International)

Audience: Educators, Administrators, Faculty, Researchers

Details: Free, Moderated

User info: To subscribe to the journal, send an e-mail message to the URL address below, consisting of a single line reading:

SUB catalyst YourFirstName YourLastName

To send a message to the entire list, address it to: catalyst@vtvm1.bitnet

`mailto:listserv@vtvm1.cc.vt.edu`

Education (K-12)

AskERIC Virtual Library

★★★★

This gopher is part of a federally-funded system to provide public access to educational resources.

Keywords: Education (K-12), Computer-Aided Learning, Libraries, Electronic Books

Sponsor: Educational Resources Information Center (ERIC)

Audience: K-12 Teachers, Administrators

Profile: This gopher contains a wide range of educational aids including pre-prepared lesson plans, guides to Internet resources for the classroom organized by subject, updates on conferences for educators, and archives of education-related listservs. Also allows access to outside gophers, libraries, and sources of electronic books and journals.

Contact: Nancy A. Morgan
nmorgan@ericir.syr.edu
askeric@ericir.syr.edu

`gopher://ericir.syr.edu`

FrEd Mail Foundation

This foundation specializes in establishing innovative and educationally rewarding collaborative projects using the Internet for the K-12 community.

Keywords: Children, Education (K-12)

Audience: Educators (K-12)

Contact: Al Rogers
arogers@bonita.cerf.fred.org

Details: Free

`gopher://gopher.cerf.net/11/fredmail`

Incomplete Guide to the Internet (K12-Netzanleitung)

An Internet guide created especially for teachers and students in grades K-12.

Keywords: Education (K-12), Internet

Audience: Educators (K-12), Students (K-12)

Contact: Chuck Farmer
cfarmer@ncsa.uiuc.edu

Details: Free

`ftp://ncsa.uiuc.edu`

K-12 School Libraries

★★

This directory is a compilation of information resources focused on K-12 Education.

Keywords: Libraries, Education (K-12)

Audience: Librarians, Educators (K-12)

`ftp://una.hh.lib.umich.edu/70/`
`inetdirstacks/k12schmed:troselius`

K12 Net

Decentralized network of school-based bulletin board systems (BBSs).

Keywords: Education (K-12), Networks

Audience: Educators (K-12), School Children

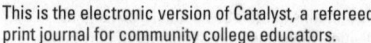

A B C D E F G H I J K L M N O P Q R S T U V W X Y Z

A B C D **E** F G H I J K L M N O P Q R S T U V W X Y Z

Profile: K12 Net provides millions of teachers, students, and parents in metropolitan and rural areas throughout the world with the ability to meet and talk with each other to discuss educational issues, exchange information, and share resources on a global scale.

Contact: Jack Crawford, Janet Murray
jack@k12net.org or jmurray@psg.com

Details: Free

`gopher://woonext.dsrd.ornl.gov/11/Docs/k12net`

NAME (National Association for Mediation in Education) Publications and Resources List ★★

This is a tax-exempt clearinghouse of information promoting conflict resolution, mediation, and violence prevention in schools. NAME also publishes a newsletter and has a directory of over 120 resources, including guidelines for conflict resolution, and technical assistance.

Keywords: Conflict Resolution, Mediation, Education (K-12)

Sponsor: National Association for Mediation in Education, University of Massachusetts, Amherst, Massachusetts, USA

Audience: Counselors, Educators, Administrators, Parents

Contact: Clarinda Merripen
ConflictNet@agc.ipc.org

Request introductory packet from address below.

`mailto:ConflictNet@agc.ipc.org`

NIH EDNET ★

EdNet is set up as a free electronic bulletin board at the Bethesda, Maryland campus of the National Institute of Health (NIH). Its purpose is to allow high school students to ask questions of NIH scientists about current research.

Keywords: NIH, Education (Post-Secondary), Education (K-12), Science

Sponsor: National Institute of Health (NIH)

Audience: Students (high school and up), Educators

Details: Free

To receive an EDNET UserÕs Guide and account, send an e-mail message with your name and mailing address to the URL address below.

`mailto:vt5@cu.nih.gov`

NWNet Internet Guide ★

An introductory guide to the Internet. Details the basic Internet tools of electronic mail, FTP (File Transfer Protocol), and Telnet. Covers types of resources found on the Internet, and how to use them. Includes information directed toward supercomputer users and the K-12 community.

Keywords: Internet, Internet Guides, Supercomputers, Education (K-12)

Sponsor: NorthWestNet

Audience: Internet Surfers, Supercomputer Users, Students (K-12)

Contact: Jonathan Kochmer
nusirg@nwnet.net

Details: Free
File is: /user-docs/nusirg/nusirg.whole-guide.ps

`ftp://ftphost.nwnet.net`

Sais-I (Science Awareness and Promotion) ★

The SAIS list creates a forum for exchanging innovative ideas about making science more appealing to students.

Keywords: Science, Education (K-12), Education (Secondary)

Audience: Students (K-12), Students (high school up), Science Teachers

Contact: Keith W. Wilson
sais@unb.ca

Details: Free

User info: To subscribe to the list, send an e-mail message to the URL address below consisting of a single line reading:

SUB sais-I YourFirstName YourLastName

To send a message to the entire list, address it to: sais-I@unb.ca

`mailto:listserv@unb.ca`

Spacelink  ★★★★

This contains information about NASA and its activities, including a large number of curricular activities for elementary and secondary science classes.

Keywords: NASA, Aeronautics, Education (K-12)

Audience: Students (K-12), Educators, General Public

Details: Free

`telnet://newuser@spacelink.msfc.nasa.gov`

Education (Post-Graduate)

The PSYCHGRAD Project and Psychology-Related Information ★★

An electronic forum for the communication and dissemination of information among psychology graduate students.

Keywords: Psychology, Education (Post-Graduate)

Sponsor: University of Ottawa, Canada

Audience: Psychologists, Psychology Graduate Students

Profile: Designed to facilitate electronic communications and networking between psychology graduate students, this site contains archives of psychology listserv groups, and directories of psychology associations, along with related electronic journals and software. Also has links to other gopher and WWW sites related to psychology.

Contact: Matthew Simpson
054340@acadvm1.uottawa.ca
054340@uottawa.bitnet

`gopher://panda1.uottawa.ca`

Education (Post-Secondary)

Can-Stud-Assoc ★

This is a mailing list for anyone who might wish to discuss Canadian post-secondary education and student associations' involvement in it.

Keywords: Canada, Education (Post-Secondary)

Audience: Canadians, Students (college)

Contact: can-stud-assoc-request@unixg.ubc.ca

Details: Free

User info: To subscribe to the list, send an e-mail message requesting a subscription to the URL address below.

To send a message to the entire list, address it to:

can-stud-assoc@unixg.ubc.ca

`mailto:can-stud-assoc-request@unixg.ubc.ca`

disted 'Journal of Distance Education and Communication'  ★★★

This online journal covers distance education broadly, including formal and informal education, geographically disadvantaged learners, and both K-12 and post-secondary education.

Keywords: Education (Adult), Education (Distance), Education (Continuing), K-12 Education (K-12), Education (Post-Secondary)

Audience: K-12 Educators, K-12 Administrators

Details: Free

User info: To subscribe to the journal, send an e-mail message to the URL address shown below consisting of a single line reading:

SUB disted YourFirstName YourLastName

`mailto:listserv@uwavm.bitnet`

don't-tell ★

The don't-tell list is for people concerned about the effects that the new military policy known as "don't ask/don't tell" will have at academic institutions, whether military or ROTC-affiliated.

Keywords: Sexuality, Military Policy, Education (Post-Secondary)

Audience: Students, Gays, Lesbians, Military Personnel, Civil Libertarians

Contact: dont-tell-request@choice.princeton.edu

Details: Free

User info: To subscribe to the list, send an e-mail message requesting a subscription to the URL address below.

To send a message to the entire list, address it to: dont-tell-request@choice.princeton.edu

`mailto:dont-tell-request@choice.princeton.edu`

NIH EDNET

★

EdNet is set up as a free electronic bulletin board at the Bethesda, Maryland campus of the National Institute of Health (NIH). Its purpose is to allow high school students to ask questions of NIH scientists about current research.

Keywords: NIH, Education (Post-Secondary), Education (K-12), Science

Sponsor: National Institute of Health (NIH)

Audience: Students (high school and up), Educators

Details: Free

To receive an EDNET User's Guide and account, send an e-mail message with your name and mailing address to the URL address below.

`mailto:vt5@cu.nih.gov`

Stlhe-I (Forum for Teaching & Learning in Higher Education)

★

This list focuses on post-secondary education teaching and learning.

Keywords: Education (Adult), Education (Distance), Education (Continuing), Education (Post Secondary)

Audience: Educators, Faculty, Administrators, Researchers

Details: Free

User info: To subscribe to the list, send an e-mail message to the URL address below consisting of a single line reading:

SUB stlhe-I YourFirstName YourLastName

To send a message to the entire list, address it to: stlhe-I@unbvm1.bitnet

`mailto:listserv@unbvm1.bitnet`

Education (Secondary)

Sais-I (Science Awareness and Promotion)

★

The SAIS list creates a forum for exchanging innovative ideas about making science more appealing to students.

Keywords: Science, Education (K-12), Education (Secondary)

Audience: Students (K-12), Students (high school up), Science Teachers

Contact: Keith W. Wilson
sais@unb.ca

Details: Free

User info: To subscribe to the list, send an e-mail message to the URL address below consisting of a single line reading:

SUB sais-I YourFirstName YourLastName

To send a message to the entire list, address it to: sais-I@unb.ca

`mailto:listserv@unb.ca`

Education

alt.usage.english

★

A Usenet newsgroup providing information and discussion about English grammar, word usages and related topics.

Keywords: Lexicology, Academia, Linguistics, Education

Audience: English Educators

User info: To subscribe to this Usenet newsgroup, you need access to a newsreader.

`news:alt.usage.english`

Armadillo's World Wide Web Page

This site provides resources and instructional material for an interdisciplinary Texan culture course.

Keywords: History (US), Texas, Cultural Studies, Education

Sponsor: Rice University, Houston, Texas, USA

Audience: Educators, Students

Contact: armadillo@rice.edu

`http://chico.rice.edu/armadillo`

CAF Archive

A source of information relating to Computers and Academic Freedom (CAF).

Keywords: Education, Computers, Academic Freedom

Audience: Educators, Researchers

Contact: kadie@eff.org

`http://www.eff.org/CAF/cafhome.html`

California Museum of Photography: Network Exhibitions

This is a collection of digital images for educational and general use.

Keywords: Photography, Art, Education

Sponsor: University of California, Riverside, California, USA

Audience: Photographers, Artists, Educators (esp. K-12), Historians

Profile: The California Museum of Photography is in the process of selecting groups of images from the collections as thematic exhibitions. Instead of displays on the walls, these exhibitions comprise a group of digital images with associated text. Particular emphasis is on the utility of these images in class projects for elementary and secondary school students. However, the digital images also have potential value for more advanced scholarly research in preparation of papers in the Humanities, Social Sciences and the Arts.

Contact: Russ Harvey
russ@cornucopia.ucr.edu

`gopher://gopher.ucr.edu`

CERFnet Guide

★

A comprehensive guide to the CERFnet (California Education and Research Federation Network), a data-communications regional network that operates throughout California. The purpose of CERFnet is to advance science and education by assisting the interchange of information among research and educational institutions.

Keywords: Internet, Science, Education, California

Audience: Internet Surfers, Researchers, Educators

Contact: CERFnet Hotline
help@cerf.net

Details: Free

Files are in: cerfnet/cerfnet_info/
cerfnet_guide/

`ftp://nic.cerf.net`

CERFNet News

★

This is a mid-level network linking academic, government, and industrial research facilities throughout California.

Keywords: Education, California

Sponsor: California Education and Research Federation Network

Audience: Researchers, Students (college, graduate)

A
B
C
D
E
F
G
H
I
J
K
L
M
N
O
P
Q
R
S
T
U
V
W
X
Y
Z

A
B
C
D
E
F
G
H
I
J
K
L
M
N
O
P
Q
R
S
T
U
V
W
X
Y
Z

Contact: help@cerf.net

Details: Free

`gopher://gopher.cerf.net/11/cerfnet`

Chemistry Tutorial Information

This site provides chemistry tutorial information in the form of text, data, pictures, source code, and executable programs for Macintosh computers.

Keywords: Chemistry, Tutorials, Macintosh, Education

Sponsor: University of Michigan

Audience: Chemistry Students (high school up)

Contact: comments@mac.archive.umich.edu

Details: Free, Images

`gopher://plaza.aarnet.edu.au@/micros/mac/umich/misc/chemistry/00index.txt`

CYFERNET (Child, Youth, and Family Education Network)

This public information service supports child, youth, and family development programs.

Keywords: Education, Networks

Sponsor: Youth Development Information Center at the National Agricultural Library

Audience: Educators, Children, Families

Profile: CYFERNET contains information useful to child, youth, and family development professionals. Features include programs for children aged 5-8 years, youth-at-risk programs, community projects, and education.

Contact: jkane@nalusda.gov

Details: Free

`gopher://ra.esusda.gov/11/CYFER-net`

DECNEWS for Education and Research ★★

Monthly electronic newsletter from Digital Equipment Corporation (DEC) summarizing announcements of its products, programs, and applications of interest to computer users in the academic and research communities.

Keywords: Computing, Education, DEC

Sponsor: Digital Equipment Corp.

Audience: Computer Users, Educators, Researchers

Contact: Mary Hoffmann
            decnews@mr4dec.enet.dec.com

Details: Free

User info: To subscribe, send an e-mail message to the address below consisting of a single line reading:

SUB DECNews YourFirstName YourLastName

To send a message to the entire list, address it to:
DECNews@ubvm.buffalo.edu

`mailto:listserv@ubvm.buffalo.edu`

DECnews-EDU ★

DECNEWS for Education and Research is a monthly electronic publication from Digital Equipment Corporation's Education Business Unit for the education and research communities worldwide.

Keywords: Education, Computers, Digital Equipment Corporation

Audience: Educators, Researchers

Contact: Anne Marie McDonald
            decnews@mr4dec.enet.dec.com

Details: Free

User info: To subscribe to the list, send an e-mail message requesting a subscription to the URL address below.

To send a message to the entire list, address it to:
decnews@mr4dec.enet.dec.com

`mailto:decnews@mr4dec.enet.dec.com`

DENet Information Server ★★★

This is the gopher of the Danish national academic network, which is located at the Danish Computer Centre for Research and Education (UNI-C).

Keywords: Education, Denmark, Libraries

Audience: Researchers, Educators

Profile: This gopher provides DENet information and statistics, UNI-C information, directory services and phone books, pointers to Danish electronic libraries and gophers, an index of major Danish FTP archives, and news in Danish.

Contact: Steen.Linden@uni-c.dk

Details: Free

`gopher://gopher.denet.dk`

Diversity U ★

Diversity University is an experiment in interactive learning.

Keywords: Education, Interactive Learning, Multimedia

Audience: Educators, Researchers

Details: Free

`gopher://erau.db.erau.edu`

Eastern Washington University Library ★★

The library's holdings are large and wide-ranging and contain significant collections in many fields.

Keywords: Education, Music, Social Science, Behavioral Science

Audience: Researchers, Students, General Public

Details: Free

User Info: Expect: Login; Send: Lib

`telnet://wsduvm12.csc.wsu.edu`

EDNET ★

This forum explores the educational potential of the Internet.

Keywords: Education, Internet

Audience: Students, Educators

Profile: This independent, unmoderated mailing-list interest group is open and free of charge to all participants. Ednet links educators with common interests, and introduces students to a number of fields and sources of information, while offering criticism and suggestions.

Contact: Prescott Smith
            pgsmith@educ.umass.edu

Details: Free

User info: To subscribe to the list, send an e-mail message to the address shown below consisting of a single line reading:

SUB Ednet YourFirstName YourLastName

To send a message to the entire list, address it to:

ednet@nic.umass.edu.

`gopher://ericir.syr.edu/00/AskERIC/FullText/Lists/Messages/`

`EDNET-List/README`

`mailto:listserv@nic.umass.edu`

Education Gopher ★

Florida Tech's gopher relating to education. Includes information on search tools, libraries, electronic texts, and selected education-related gophers and information servers.

Keywords: Education, Gopher

Audience: Educators, Researchers

Contact: Kevin Barry
            barry@sci-ed.fit.edu

Details: Free

`gopher://sci-ed.fit.edu`

Educator's Guide to E-mail Lists ★

A guide to help educators find e-mail lists. Includes a very large list of e-mail addresses related to education.

Keywords: Education, E-mail, Internet

Sponsor: University of Massachusetts, Amherst, MA

Audience: Educators, Researchers

Contact: Prescott Smith
            pgsmith@educ.umass.edu

Details: Free

`ftp://nic.umass.edu`

EDUCOM ★

A large source of information relating to education.

Keywords: Education

Audience: Educators, Researchers

Contact: inquiry@educom.edu

Details: Free

`gopher://ivory.educom.edu/11/`

ERIC (Educational Resources Information Center) ★★★

ERIC is a database of short abstracts and information about education-related topics of interest to teachers and administrators.

Keywords: Education, Databases

Sponsor: (Office of Educational Research and Development), US Department of Education

            Department of Education (ED)

Audience: Educators, Administrators

Profile: ERIC is the complete database on educational materials from the Educational Resources Information Center in Washington, DC. The database corresponds to two print indexes: Resources in Education, which is concerned with identifying the most significant and timely education research reports; and Current Index to Journals in Education, an index of more than 700 periodicals of interest to every segment of the teaching profession.

Details: Costs

            ERIC can be accessed in a variety of ways, for example, through CARL (Colorado Alliance of Research Libraries), through the University of Saskatchewan

            (Request: sklib username: sonia)

            ERIC can also be accessed by WAIS if you have WAIS installed on your local computer.

`telnet://pac.carl.org`

`telnet://skdevel12.usask.ca`

GLOSAS News (Global Systems Analysis and Simulating Association) ★

Newsletter of GLOSAS in the US, which is dedicated to global electronic education and simulation as a tool for promoting peace and the care of the natural environment.

Keywords: Education, Simulation, Peace

Audience: Educators, Environmentalists

Contact: Anton Ljutic
            anton@vax2.concordia.ca

Details: Free

User info: To subscribe, send an e-mail message to the address below consisting of a single line reading:

            SUB glosas YourFirstName YourLastName

            To send a message to the entire list, address it to: glosas@ vm/.mcgill.ca

`mailto:listserv@vm1.mcgill.ca`

Information Infrastructure and Technology Act of 1992 ★

The Information Infrastructure and Technology Act of 1992 builds on the High-Performance Computing Act. The newer bill will ensure that the technology developed by the High-Performance Computing Program is applied widely in K-12 education, libraries, health care, and industry, particularly manufacturing. It will authorize a total of $1.15 billion over the next five years.

Keywords: Government (US Federal), Law (US Federal), Information Technology, Education, Health Care

Audience: Journalists, Politicians, Scientists, Manufacturers, Educators

Details: Free

            File is: /internet/nren/iita.1992/gorebill.1992.txt

`ftp://nis.nsf.net`

IUCAA (Inter-University Centre for Astronomy and Astrophysics) ★

The IUCAA was set up to promote the growth of active groups in astronomy and astrophysics in India. The Centre runs vigorous visitor programs involving short and long-term visits of scientists from India and abroad.

Keywords: Astronomy, Astrophysics, Physics, Education

Sponsor: Centre for Astronomy and Astrophysics (IUCAA)

Audience: Researchers, Astronomers, Physicists, Students

Contact: Postmaster
            amk@iucaa.ernet.in

`http://iucaa.iucaa.ernet.in/welcome.html`

Journal of Technology Education ★

Electronic journal devoted to educational issues in technology.

Keywords: Communication, Education, Technology,

Audience: Educators

Details: Free

            Send an e-mail message to the URL address below with the request: GET MISCELLA JTE-V5N1. This file will give you access information for additional issues.

`mailto:listserv@vtvm1.cc.vt.edu`

KIDLINK and KIDCAFE ★

This discussion group is designed to act as a structured forum for e-mail exchanges between children aged 10-15.

Keywords: Education, Children

Audience: Children

Profile: A dialog is set up each year called 'KIDS-XX' where 'XX' is the current year. Each participating child posts an e-mail message answering the following four questions before he or she can engage in the dialog: 1. Who am I? 2. What do I want to be when I grow up? 3. How do I want the world to be better when I grow up? 4. What can I do to make this happen?

            KIDLINK operates the following free discussion lists and services:

            •KIDLINK: discussion group for children aged 10-15.

            •RESPONSE: the destination for answers to the four questions above.

            •KIDCAFE: a forum for children aged 10-15. Read-only for people outside this age group.

            •KIDCAFEP: a Portuguese-language version of KIDCAFE.

            •KIDCAFEJ: a Japanese-language version of KIDCAFE.

            •KIDCAFEN: a Scandinavian-language (Nordic) version of KIDCAFE.

            •KIDFORUM: a showcase of works by kids on a series of topics specified to promote exchange between classrooms. Teachers can plan for class participation in monthly topics.

            •KIDPROJ: a forum enabling teachers/youth group leaders to design projects for children through the KIDLINK network.

            •KIDLEADR: an informal meeting place for exchanging ideas, networking, asking for help, requesting hello messages, and so on, for teachers, coordinators, parents, social workers, and others interested in KIDS-94.

A
B
C
D
E
F
G
H
I
J
K
L
M
N
O
P
Q
R
S
T
U
V
W
X
Y
Z

- •KIDLEADP: a Portuguese-language version of KIDLEADR.

- •KIDLEADS: a Spanish-language version of KIDLEADR.

- •KIDLEADN: a Scandinavian-language (Nordic) version of KIDLEADR.

Contact: Odd de Presno
opresno@extern.uio.no

Details: Free

For information about the projects, subscribe to the KIDLINK announcement service: send an e-mail message to: listserv@vm1.NoDak.edu with the following command in the text of your message:

SUB KIDLINK Yourfirstname Yourlastname.

Notes: For more information, read the 'WHAT IS KIDLINK / KIDS-94' page at gopher://kids.ccit.duq.edu/00/about/kidlink-general.

`gopher://kids.ccit.duq.edu`

NCTM-L

A mailing list for the discussion of standards applying to the National Council of Teachers of Mathematics.

Keywords: Education, Mathematics

Audience: Mathematics Educators

Contact: barry@sci-ed.fit.edu

Details: Free

User info: To subscribe to this list, send an e-mail message to the URL address below, consisting of a single line reading:

SUB nctm-l YourFirstName YourLastName

To send a message to the entire list, address it to: nctm-l@sci-ed.fit.edu

`mailto:listproc@sci-ed.fit.edu`

PENPages

This easy-to-use general-interest database contains articles and brochures.

Keywords: Food, Employment, Education

Sponsor: Pennsylvania State University, PA

Audience: General Public

User Info: Expect: login; Send: your state's two-letter code (or "world" if sent from outside the USA)

`telnet://psunet.psu.edu`

Scholarly Communication

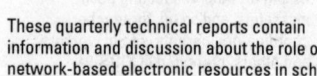

These quarterly technical reports contain information and discussion about the role of network-based electronic resources in scholarly communication.

Keywords: Education, Scholarly Communication, Conferences

Audience: Educators, Researchers

Details: Free

File is: pub/vpiej-l/reports

`ftp://borg.lib.vt.edu/pub/vpiej-1/reports`

`http://borg.lib.vt.edu/scholar.info.html`

Thailand: The Big Picture

A web site maintaining a complete list of Internet servers pertaining to and found within Thailand. General information concerning Thailand and extensive Internet connections to Thai academic institutions.

Keywords: Thailand, Education, Travel Research

Sponsor: National Electronics and Computer Center at the National Science and Technology Development Agency, USA

Audience: Researchers, Exchange Students

Contact: Trin Tantsetthi
webmaster@www.nectec.or.th

`http://www.nectec.or.th`

UNC-CH Info system

The University of North Carolina at Chapel Hill's campus-wide information server, providing access to a wide range of campus information and to electronic information services worldwide.

Keywords: Education, Internet Services

Sponsor: University of North Carolina at Chapel Hill

Audience: Educators, Researchers, Internet Surfers

Contact: info@unc.edu

Details: Free

`gopher://gibbs.oit.unc.edu`

University of Northern Iowa Library

The library's holdings are large and wide-ranging and contain significant collections in many fields.

Keywords: Art, Business Information, Education, Music, Fiction

Audience: Researchers, Students, General Public

Contact: Mike Yohe
yohe@uni.edu

Details: Free

User Info: Expect: Login; Send: Public

`telnet://infosys.uni.edu`

University of Puerto Rico Library

The library's holdings are large and wide-ranging and contain significant collections in many fields.

Keywords: Computer Science, Education, Nursing, Agriculture, Economics

Audience: Researchers, Students, General Public

Details: Free

After Locator: telnet://, press Tab twice. Type DIAL VTAM. Enter NOTIS.

Press Return. On the blank screen, type LUUP.

`telnet://136.145.2.10`

University of Puget Sound Library

The library's holdings are large and wide-ranging and contain significant collections in many fields.

Keywords: Education, Literature (General), Music, Natural Science, Theology

Audience: Researchers, Students, General Public

Details: Free

User Info: Expect: Login; Send: Library

`telnet://192.124.98.2`

University of Wisconsin Eau Claire Library

The library's holdings are large and wide-ranging and contain significant collections in many fields.

Keywords: Health Sciences, Business, Nursing, Education

Audience: Researchers, Students, General Public

Details: Free

User Info: Expect: Service Name, Send: Victor

`telnet://lib.uwec.edu`

University of Wisconsin River Falls Library

The library's holdings are large and wide-ranging and contain significant collections in many fields.

Keywords: Agriculture, Education, History (US)

Audience: Researchers, Students, General Public

Details: Free

User Info: Expect: Service Name, Send: Victor

`telnet://davee.dl.uwrf.edu`

University of Wisconsin Stevens Point Library

The library's holdings are large and wide-ranging and contain significant collections in many fields.

Keywords: Education, Environmental Studies, Ethnic Studies, History (US)

Audience: Researchers, Students, General Public

Details: Free

User Info: Expect: Login; Send: Lib; Expect: vDIAL Prompt, Send: Library

`telnet://lib.uwsp.edu`

US Department of Education Online Library

★★★

A resource for information on federal programs, including full-text of the GOALS 2000, Educate America Act, The Prisoners of Time Report, and other documents regarding education legislation, reports, and information.

Keywords: Education, Law (US)

Sponsor: US Department of Education

Audience: Educators, Students, Legislators, Researchers

`http://www.ed.gov/`

`gopher://gopher.ed.gov`

`ftp://ftp.ed.gov`

Usenet University

★

An archive of Usenet university groups that are currently active on the Internet.

Keywords: Education, Universities

Audience: University Students, Educators, Researchers

Details: Free
File is: pub/doc/uu/FAQ

`ftp://nic.funet.fi`

Virginia's PEN (Public Education Network)

★

This is a statewide educational network.

Keywords: Education, Community Networking, Virginia

Sponsor: Virginia Department of Education

Audience: Educators

Profile: Educators throughout Virginia can access PEN via a local telephone call or through a toll-free line. The network includes discussion groups, news reports, study guides, and curriculum resources. In one of the features, History OnLine, students and teachers query historical figures such as Thomas Jefferson, and historians will answer in character.

Contact: Harold Cathern
hcathern@vdoe386.vak12.edu

Details: Free

Password: Guest

`telnet://guest@vdoe386.vak12.edu`

Educational Policy

edpolyan (Educational Policy Analysis)

★

This list focuses on educational policy analysis. This is an active, broad list, where issues surrounding all levels of education are discussed. This list takes a relatively philosophical approach to the issue.

Keywords: Education (Continuing), Educational Policy

Audience: University Administrators, K-12 Educators, Postsecondary Educators

Details: Free

User info: To subscribe to the list, send an e-mail message to the URL address shown below consisting of a single line reading:

SUB edpolyan YourFirstName YourLastName

To send a message to the entire list, address it to: edpolyan@asuacad.bitnet

`mailto:listserv@asuacad.bitnet`

edpolyar (Educational Policy Analysis Archive)

★

The Educational Policy Analysis Archive, an outgrowth of the edpolyan scholarly discussion list, publishes peer-reviewed articles of between 500 and 1,500 lines in length on all aspects of education policy analysis.

Keywords: Education (Continuing), Educational Policy

Audience: K-12 Educators, University Administrators, Postsecondary Educators

Details: Free, Moderated

User info: To subscribe to the archive, send an e-mail message to the URL address shown below consisting of a single line reading:

SUB edpolyar YourFirstName YourLastName

`mailto:listserv@asuacad.bitnet`

INTER-L

★

A list for members of the National Association of Foreign Student Advisors.

Keywords: Advisory, Education (Bilingual), Educational Policy

Sponsor: National Association of Foreign Student Advisors (NAFSA)

Audience: Foreign Students, NAFSA Members

Details: Free

User info: To subscribe to the list, send an e-mail message to the address below consisting of a single line reading:

`mailto:listserv@vtm1.cc.vt.edu`

University of Wisconsin Superior Library

★★

The library's holdings are large and wide-ranging and contain significant collections in many fields.

Keywords: Educational Policy, Government (US)

Audience: Researchers, Students, General Public

Details: Free

User Info: Expect: Login, Send: Lib; Expect: vDIAL Prompt, Send: Library

`telnet://sail.uwsuper.edu`

Educators

journet

★★

An electronic conference for the discussion of topics of interest to journalists and journalism educators.

Keywords: Journalism, Writing, Desktop Publishing, Electronic Publishing

Audience: Journalists, Writers, Publishers, Educators

Contact: George Frajkor
gfrajkor@ccs.carleton.ca

User info: To subscribe to the list, send an e-mail message to the URL address below consisting of a single line reading:

SUB journet YourFirstName YourLastName

To send a message to the entire list, address it to: journet@qucdn.queensu.ca

`mailto:listserv@qucdn.queensu.ca`

Educator's Guide to E-mail Lists

Educator's Guide to E-mail Lists

★

A guide to help educators find e-mail lists. Includes a very large list of e-mail addresses related to education.

Keywords: Education, E-mail, Internet

Sponsor: University of Massachusetts, Amherst, MA

Audience: Educators, Researchers

Contact: Prescott Smith
pgsmith@educ.umass.edu

Details: Free

`ftp://nic.umass.edu`

A
B
C
D
E
F
G
H
I
J
K
L
M
N
O
P
Q
R
S
T
U
V
W
X
Y
Z

A B C D E F G H I J K L M N O P Q R S T U V W X Y Z

EDUCOM

EDUCOM

A large source of information relating to education.

Keywords: Education

Audience: Educators, Researchers

Contact: inquiry@educom.edu

Details: Free

`gopher://ivory.educom.edu/11`

edupage (A News Update from EDUCOM)

edupage (A News Update from EDUCOM)

A newsletter put out by EDUCOM summarizing information technology news.

Keywords: Education (Continuing), Information Technology

Sponsor: EDUCOM

Audience: Educators, Administrators

Details: Free

User info: To subscribe to the newsletter, send an e-mail message requesting a subscription to the URL address shown below and include your name, institutional affiliation, and e-mail address.

`mailto:edupage@educom.edu`

EEC

CEDAR (Central European Environmental Data Request) Facility

This gopher site provides information about the environmental and scientific community in Central and Eastern Europe (CEE), with access to environmental information located throughout the world on various international computer networks and hosts.

Keywords: Europe, EEC, Environment

Sponsor: The International Society for Environmental Protection, and The Austrian Federal Ministry for Environment, Youth and Family (BMUJF)

Audience: Environmentalists, Educators, Students, Urban Planners

Contact: cedar-info@cedar.univie.ac.at

Notes: CEDAR Marxergasse 3/20, A-1030 Vienna, Austria Tel.: +43-1-715 58 79

`gopher://pan.cedar.univie.ac.at`

INTLAW (International Law Library)

The International Law library provides comprehensive international law materials.

Keywords: International Law, EEC, Commonwealth, China

Audience: Lawyers, International Lawyers

Profile: The International Law library provides comprehensive international law materials. The International Law library contains federal case law, European Community materials, treaties and agreements, Commonwealth law materials, topical and professional journals, French law materials (in French), China law materials, plus relevant topical publications.

Contact: New Sales Group at 800-227-4908 or 513-859-5398 inside the US, or 1-513-865-7981 for all inquires outside the US.

User info: To subscribe, contact Mead directly.

To examine the Lexis user guide, you can access it at the ftp site of the University of Texas at Austin at the URL address: ftp://ftp.cc.utexas.edu

The files are in: /pub/ref-services/LEXIS

`telnet://nex.meaddata.com`

`http://www.meaddata.com`

EEJobs

EEJobs

Discusses and advertises positions available and positions desired in the electrical and electronic engineering fields. Discussion and tips on how to find jobs are also welcome.

Keywords: Engineering, Electrical Engineering, Employment

Audience: Engineers, Students

Contact: Jerome Grimmer st6267@aix370.siu.edu

Details: Free

User info: To subscribe to the list, send an e-mail messagel with a subject of SERVER.COMMANDS to ST6267@AIX370.SIU.EDU

In the body of the mail, type on the first line, /BBOARD SUB EEJOBS or /BBOARD SIGNON EEJOBS to be added to the EEJOBS list.

`st6267@aix370.siu.edu`

Eerie, Indiana

Eerie, Indiana

The list is for the discussion of the critically acclaimed but short-lived TV series "Eerie, Indiana" which originally aired on NBC in 1991-1992 and is now distributed internationally.

Keywords: Eerie, Indiana

Audience: Television Viewers

Contact: Corey Kirk owner-eerie-indiana@sfu.ca

Details: Free

User Info: To subscribe to the list, send an e-mail message requesting a subscription to the URL address below.

To send a message to the entire list, address it to: owner-eerie-indiana@sfu.ca

`mailto:owner-eerie-indiana@sfu.ca`

EFFector Online—The Electronic Frontier Foundation, Inc.

EFFector Online—The Electronic Frontier Foundation, Inc.

★★★

Established to make the electronic frontier truly useful and accessible to everyone, emphasizing the free and open flow of information and communication.

Keywords: Computer Communications, Electronic Media, Intellectual Property, Privacy

Audience: Computer Users, Civil Libertarians

Profile: EFFector Online presents news, information, and discussion about the world of computer-based communications media that constitute the electronic frontier. It covers issues such as freedom of speech in digital media, privacy rights, censorship, and standards of responsibility for users and operators of computer systems, as well as policy issues such as the development of a national information infrastructure, and intellectual property.

Contact: Gerard Van der Leun, Mike Godwin gerard@eff.org mnemonic@eff.org

Details: Free

User info: To subscribe, send an e-mail message requesting a subscription to: request@eff.org

Notes: This takes you to the front door of the eff gopher server which contains much more information than just Effector online.

`gopher://gopher.eff.org/1`

Ei Compendex Plus

Ei Compendex Plus

The Ei Compendex Plus database is the machine-readable version of The Engineering Index (monthly/annual), which provides abstracted information from the world's significant literature of engineering and technology.

Keywords: Engineering, Technology

Sponsor: Engineering Information Inc. (Ei), Hoboken, NJ, USA

Audience: Engineers

Profile: Ei Compendex Plus provides worldwide coverage of approximately 4,500 journals and selected government reports and books. Subjects covered include: civil, energy, environmental, geological, and biological engineering; electrical, automotive, nuclear, and aerospace engineering; and computers, robotics, and industrial robots.

Contact: Dialog in the US at (800) 334-2564, Dialog internationally at country-specific locations.

User info: To subscribe, contact Dialog directly.

Notes: Coverage: 1970 to the present; updated weekly.

`telnet://dialog.com`

EINet Galaxy

EINet Galaxy

EINet Galaxy is a guide to world-wide information and services. It includes public information as well as commercial information and services provided by EINet customers and affiliates. The information is organized by topic, and can be searched.

Keywords: WWW, Information Retrieval, Internet

Sponsor: Microelectronic and Computer Technology Corporation (MCC)

Audience: Reseachers, Students

Contact: Wayne Allen, Bruce Speyer WA@EINet.net, Speyer@EINet.net

`http://galaxy.einet.net/galaxy.html`

ejcrec 'Electronic Journal of Communications/La Revue _lectronique de communication'

ejcrec 'Electronic Journal of Communications/La Revue _lectronique de communication'

This journal is a quarterly bilingual (English and French) journal for the communications field broadly.

Keywords: Communications

Audience: Educators, Administrators, Communications Professionals

Details: Free

User info: To subscribe to the journal, send an e-mail message to the URL address shown below consisting of a single line reading:

Join edupage YourFirstName YourLastName

`mailto:comserve@rpitsvm.bitnet`

Electric

Electric Power Database

Electric Power Database provides references to research and development projects of interest to the electric power industry, and corresponds to the print Digest of Research in the Electric Utility Industry.

Keywords: Energy, Electric

Sponsor: Electric Power Research Institute (EPRI), Palo Alto, CA, USA

Audience: Engineers

Profile: The database covers US and Canadian research on 13 major categories related to issues in electric power, including hydroelectric power, fossil fuels, nuclear power, transmission, economics, advanced power systems, and environmental assessment. The records include abstracts of project summaries for past and ongoing research projects. Such projects are conducted largely by companies under contract to EPRI or to other utilities, and by EPRI itself. Research from other corporate and utility sources is also covered.

Contact: Dialog in the US at (800) 334-2564, Dialog internationally at country-specific locations.

User info: To subscribe, contact Dialog directly.

Notes: Coverage: 1972 to the present; updated monthly.

`telnet://dialog.com`

Electric Circuit Analysis

CIRCUITS-L

This list discusses all aspects of the introductory course in circuit analysis for electrical engineering undergraduates.

Keywords: Engineering, Electrical Engineering, Teaching, Electric Circuit Analysis

Audience: Engineers, Students (college)

Contact: Paul E. Gray gray@maple.ucs.uwplatt.edu

Details: Free

User info: To subscribe to the list, send an e-mail message to the URL address below, and include: name; e-mail address; home phone, business phone, and FAX numbers (including area code); and US postal address (including ZIP code)

To send a message to the entire list, address it to:

circuits-l@uwplatt.edu

`mailto:circuits-request@uwplatt.edu`

Electric Light Orchestra

Electric Light Orchestra

Discussion of the music of Electric Light Orchestra and later solo efforts by band members and former members.

Keywords: Electric Light Orchestra, Rock Music

Audience: Rock Music Enthusiasts

Contact: elo-list-request@andrew.cmu.edu

Details: Free

User Info: To subscribe to the list, send an e-mail message requesting a subscription to the URL address below.

To send a message to the entire list, address it to: elo-list-request@andrew.cmu.edu

`mailto:elo-list-request@andrew.cmu.edu`

Electric Vehicles

EV

General list for discussion of all aspects of electric vehicles.

Keywords: Electric Vehicles

Audience: Electric Vehicle Enthusiasts

Contact: Clyde Visser listserv@sjsuvm1.sjsu.edu

A B C D E F G H I J K L M N O P Q R S T U V W X Y Z

A
B
C
D
E
F
G
H
I
J
K
L
M
N
O
P
Q
R
S
T
U
V
W
X
Y
Z

User info: To subscribe to the list, send an e-mail message to the URL address below consisting of a single line reading:

SUB electric-vehicle YourFirstName YourLastName

To send a message to the entire list, address it to: electric-vehicle@sjsuvm1.sjsu.edu

`mailto:listserv@sjsuvm1.sjsu.edu`

Electrical Engineering

Adv-Eli

Adv-Eli discusses the latest advances in electrical engineering. It is sponsored by the IEEE Student Branch of Santa Maria University (Chile).

Keywords: Electrical Engineering, Engineering, Electronics

Audience: Engineers, Educators, Students

Contact: Francisco Javier Fernandez ffernand@utfsm

Details: Free

User info: To subscribe to the list, send an e-mail message to the URL address shown below consiting of a single line reading:

SUB adv-eli YourFirstName YourLastName

To send a message to the entire list, address it to: adv-eli@loa.disca.utfsm.cl

`listserv@loa.disca.utfsm.cl`

Adv-Elo

Discusses the latest advances in electronics. Sponsored by the IEEE Student Branch of Santa Maria University (Chile).

Keywords: Electrical Engineering, Engineering, Electronics, Technological Advances

Audience: Engineers, Educators, Students

Contact: Rodrigo E. Rodriguez rrodrigu@utfsm

Details: Free

User info: To subscribe to the list, send an e-mail message to the URL address shown below consiting of a single line reading:

SUB adv-elo YourFirstName YourLastName

To send a message to the entire list, address it to: adv-elo@loa.disca.utfsm.cl

`listserv@loa.disca.utfsm.cl`

CIRCUITS-L

This list discusses all aspects of the introductory course in circuit analysis for electrical engineering undergraduates.

Keywords: Engineering, Electrical Engineering, Teaching, Electric Circuit Analysis

Audience: Engineers, Students (college)

Contact: Paul E. Gray gray@maple.ucs.uwplatt.edu

Details: Free

User info: To subscribe to the list, send an e-mail message to the URL address below, and include: name; e-mail address; home phone, business phone, and FAX numbers (including area code); and US postal address (including ZIP code)

To send a message to the entire list, address it to:

circuits-l@uwplatt.edu

`mailto:circuits-request@uwplatt.edu`

EEJobs

Discusses and advertises positions available and positions desired in the electrical and electronic engineering fields. Discussion and tips on how to find jobs are also welcome.

Keywords: Engineering, Electrical Engineering, Employment

Audience: Engineers, Students

Contact: Jerome Grimmer st6267@aix370.siu.edu

Details: Free

User info: To subscribe to the list, send an e-mail messagel with a subject of SERVER.COMMANDS to st627@aix370.siu.edu

In the body of the mail, type on the first line, /BBOARD SUB EEJOBS or /BBOARD SIGNON EEJOBS to be added to the EEJOBS list.

`st6267@aix370.siu.edu`

IEEE-L

Serves as a forum for all IEEE student branch officers and members.

Keywords: Engineering, Electrical Engineering

Audience: Engineers, Electrical Engineers, Students

Contact: Paul D. Kroculick or Chas Elliot tjwo465@bingtjw.cc.binghamton.edub a0803@bingsuns.cc.binghamton.edu

Details: Free

User info: To subscribe to the list, send an e-mail message to the URL address below consisting of a single line reading:

SUB ieee-l YourFirstName YourLastName.

To send a message to the entire list, address it to: IEEE-l@bingvmb.cc.binghamton.edu

`mailto:listerv@bingvmb.cc.binghamton.edu`

Electronic

INSPEC

IINSPEC corresponds to the three Science Abstracts print publications: Physics Abstracts, Electrical and Electronics Abstracts, and Computer and Control Abstracts.

Keywords: Physics, Electronic, Computing

Sponsor: Institution of Electrical Engineers, London, UK

Audience: Physicists, Electrical Engineers, Computer Specialists

Profile: Approximately 16 percent of the database's source publications are in languages other than English, but all articles are abstracted and indexed in English. The special DIALOG online thesaurus feature is available to assist searchers in determining appropriate subject terms and codes.

Contact: Dialog in the US at (800) 334-2564, Dialog internationally at country-specific locations.

User info: To subscribe, contact Dialog directly.

Notes: Coverage: April 1969 to the present; updated weekly.

`telnet://dialog.com`

Electronic Art

ISEA (Inter-Society on Electronic Arts) Online

An online forum for discussion of topics related to ISEA-94, the 5th International Symposium on Electronic Art which will take place in Finland in August, 1994.

Keywords: Art, Electronic Art, Technology

Audience: Artists, Art Enthusiasts

Details: Free

`ftp://ftp.ncsa.uiuc.edu`

Multimedia, Telecommunications, and Art Project

A project to promote online art that will be implemented as gopher site and on the World-Wide Web.

Keywords: Multimedia, Electronic Art, Telecommunications

Sponsor: CISR (Centre for Image and Sound Research), Vancouver, B.C., Canada

Audience: Artists, Writers

Contact: Derek Dowden Derek_Dowden@mindlink.bc.ca

For more information, send an e-mail message to the URL address below.

`mailto:Derek_Dowden@mindlink.bc.ca`

OTIS (Operative Term Is Stimulate)

An image-based electronic art gallery.

Keywords: Art, Graphics, Electronic Art, Animation

Audience: Graphic Artists

Profile: OTIS is a public-access library containing hundreds of images, animations, and information files.

Within the sunsite ftp, the directory is: /pub/multimedia/pictures/OTIS. Use the bin command to insure you're in binary transfer mode.

`ftp://sunsite.unc.edu`

Electronic Books

AskERIC Virtual Library

This gopher is part of a federally-funded system to provide public access to educational resources.

Keywords: Education (K-12), Computer-Aided Learning, Libraries, Electronic Books

Sponsor: Educational Resources Information Center (ERIC)

Audience: K-12 Teachers, Administrators

Profile: This gopher contains a wide range of educational aids including pre-prepared lesson plans, guides to Internet resources for the classroom organized by subject, updates on conferences for educators, and archives of education-related listservs. Also allows access to outside gophers, libraries, and sources of electronic books and journals.

Contact: Nancy A. Morgan
nmorgan@ericir.syr.edu
askeric@ericir.syr.edu

`gopher://ericir/syr.edu`

Electronic Books

A collection of books available as ASCII text files, including classics of antiquity (Aristotle, Virgil, Sophocles, the Bible), as well as more contemporary works of fiction and nonfiction by authors ranging from Dostoevsky to Martin Luther King, Jr.

Keywords: Books, Online Books, Literature (Contemporary), Literature (General)

Sponsor: The Blacksburg Electronic Village (BEV) at Virginia Tech

Audience: General Public, Historians

Contact: BEV Gopher Administrators
gopher@gopher.vt.edu

`gopher://gopher.vt.edu`

Electronic Cafe

Electronic Cafe

A seminal art and telecommunications group that specializes in video transmission.

Keywords: Art, Video, Telecommunications

Audience: Artists

Profile: This combines performance, communication, and community outreach by making telecommunications equipment available in a cafe-style artists' space.

Contact: Kit Galloway and Sherrie Rabinowitz, 1641 18th St., Santa Monica, CA 90404, USA

`mailto:ecafe@netcom.com`

Electronic Commerce

CommerceNet

An open, internet-based infrastructure for electronic commerce, created by a coalition of Silicon Valley organizations.

Keywords: business, electronic commerce

Sponsor: CommerceNet, Inc. 800 El Camino Real, Menlo Park, CA 94025.

Audience: businesses, commercial internet users, general public

Profile: Services include basic enabling services required by virtually every user and application (generic directories, secure multimedia messaging, network access control, and payment facilities). Applications include a framework for the developmentof compelling applications and services targeted to electronic commerce among companies in the region. Applications are designed to address the varied business and community needs of CommerceNet users; these are developed by third-party providers, in compliance with protocols established by CommerceNet. Connectivity is high-quality and affordable, with minimal on-site equipment or network expertise required of the user.

Contact: feedback@commerce.net

`http://www.commerce.net`

Internet Shopping Network

A shopping network on the Infobahn

Keywords: Business, Electronic Commerce

Sponsor: Internet Shopping Network

Audience: Business Users, Commercial Internet Users, General Public

Profile: The Internet Shopping Network aims to conduct research and develop products and services that commercialize the Internet, for the purpose of retailing and mass merchandising. The stores within this network offer approximately 20,000 products from 1000 vendors.

`http://internet.net`

Telemedia, Networks, and Systems Group

A list of commercial services on the Web (and Net)

Keywords: Business, Electronic Commerce

Sponsor: MIT Laboratory for Computer Science, Cambridge, MA 02139

Audience: Business Professionals, Commercial Internet Users, General Public

Profile: This list of commercial Internet services is well-maintained and frequently updated.

Contact: hhh@mit.edu

`http://tns-www.lcs.mit.edu/commerce.html`

`http://www.directory.net`

Electronic Communications Privacy Act of 1986

Electronic Communications Privacy Act of 1986

This is the act to amend Title 18, United States Code, with respect to the interception of certain communications, other forms of surveillance, and for other purposes. This act affects every Usenet, Bitnet, BBS, shortwave listener, TV viewer, and so on.

Keywords: Communications, Privacy, Government (US Federal), Laws (US Federal)

Audience: Journalists, Privacy Activists, Students, Politicians

Details: Free

`gopher://wiretap.spies.com/00/Gov/ecpa.act`

A B C D E F G H I J K L M N O P Q R S T U V W X Y Z

Electronic Democracy Must Come from Us

Electronic Democracy Must Come from Us

★

Article about government policy and community networks by community networker Evelyn Pine (former national director of Computer Professionals for Social Responsibility). A short critique of the promises of electronic networking contrasted with the realities of political control.

Keywords: Community, Networking, Government (US)

Audience: Activists, Community Leaders, Governments

Contact: Evelyn Pine
evy@well.sf.ca.us

Details: Free

`http://nearnet.gnn.com/mag/articles/`
`oram/bio.pine.html`

Electronic Hebrew Users Newsletter (E-Hug)

Electronic Hebrew Users Newsletter (E-Hug)

★

This newsletter is electronic only, and is mandated, like the original, to cover everything relating to the use of Hebrew, Yiddish, Judesmo, and Aramaic on computers.

Keywords: Judaism, Religion, Hebrew Language

Sponsor: Berkeley Hillel Foundation

Audience: Jews, Judaism Students

Contact: Ari Davidow
well!ari@apple.com

Details: Free

User info: To subscribe, send an e-mail message to the address below consisting of a single line reading:

To send a message to the entire list,

`mailto:listserv@dartcms1.bitnet`

Electronic Media

Animals

This directory is a compilation of information resources focused on animals.

Keywords: Animals, Electronic Media

Audience: Animal Lovers, Veterinarians, Activists

Contact: Ken Boschert
ken@wudcm.wustl.edu

Details: Free

`ftp://una.hh.lib.umich.edu/70/`
`inetdirsstacks/animals:boschert`

Books Online

★★★

This web site contains hundreds of full-text online books, including many classics such as *Anna Karenina* and *The Complete Works of William Shakespeare*. Also provides links to other book resources and has a searchable index.

Keywords: Books, Electronic Media

Audience: Readers, Literary Scholars

Contact: spok@cs.cmu.edu

`gopher://calypso-2.oit.unc.edu/11/`
`sunsite.d/book.d`

`http://www.cs.cmu.edu/Web/books.html`

EFFector Online—The Electronic Frontier Foundation, Inc.

★★★

Established to make the electronic frontier truly useful and accessible to everyone, emphasizing the free and open flow of information and communication.

Keywords: Computer Communications, Electronic Media, Intellectual Property, Privacy

Audience: Computer Users, Civil Libertarians

Profile: EFFector Online presents news, information, and discussion about the world of computer-based communications media that constitute the electronic frontier. It covers issues such as freedom of speech in digital media, privacy rights, censorship, and standards of responsibility for users and operators of computer systems, as well as policy issues such as the development of a national information infrastructure, and intellectual property.

Contact: Gerard Van der Leun, Mike Godwin
gerard@eff.org mnemonic@eff.org

Details: Free

User info: To subscribe, send an e-mail message requesting a subscription to: request@eff.org

Notes: This takes you to the front door of the eff gopher server which contains much more information than just Effector online.

`gopher://gopher.eff.org/1`

GameBytes magazine

★★

This monthly electronic magazine provides reviews (with graphics) of electronic games.

Keywords: Games, Electronic Media, Entertainment

Sponsor: Game Bytes Magazine

Audience: Game Players, Computer Game Developers, Computer Graphics Designers

Contact: Ross Erickson
rwericks@ingr.com

Details: Free

`http://wcl-rs.bham.ac.uk/GameBytes`

Internet Wiretap

★★

A resource containing electronic books, zines, and government documents, White House press releases, and links to worldwide gopher and WAIS servers.

Keywords: Electronic Media, Cyberculture, Zines

Sponsor: Internet Wiretap

Audience: Cyberculture Enthusiasts, Civil Libertarians, Educators

`gopher://wiretap.spies.com/11/,`
`http://wiretap.spies.com`

Leonardo Electronic Almanac

★★★★

The Leonardo Electronic Almanac (LEA) is a monthly, edited journal and an electronic archive dedicated to providing current perspectives in the art, science and technology domains.

Keywords: Art, Multimedia, Music, Electronic Media

Sponsor: International Society for the Arts, Sciences, and Technology

Audience: New Media Artists, Researchers, Developers, Art Educators, Art Professionals

Profile: LEA is an international, interdisciplinary forum for people interested in the use of new media in contemporary artistic expression, especially involving 20th century science and technology. Material is contributed by artists, scientists, philosophers and educators. LEA is published by the MIT Press for Leonardo, the International Society for the Arts, Sciences, and Technology (ISAST).

Contact: Craig Harris
craig@well.sf.ca.us

Details: Costs, Moderated, Images, Sounds, Multimedia

`mailto:journals-orders@mit.edu`

`ftp://mitpress.mit.edu/pub/Leonardo-`
`Elec-Almanac`

News

★★

This directory is a general compilation of information resources focused on news.

Keywords: News Media, Electronic Media, Journalism

Audience: Newsreaders, Journalists, General Public

Details: Free

`ftp://una.hh.lib.umich.edu/70/`
`inetdirsstacks/news:robinson`

A B C D E F G H I J K L M N O P Q R S T U V W X Y Z

Electronic Music

Analog Heaven

The Analog Heaven mailing list caters to people interested in vintage analog electronic music equipment. Topics include items for sale, repair tips, equipment modifications, ASCII & GIF schematics, and a general discussion of new and old analog equipment. There is an FTP/Gopher site located at cs.uwp.edu with discussions on various machines, a definitive guide to Roland synths, patch editors, modification schematics, and GIFs/JPEGs of vintage synths, as well as a few sound samples of some of the gear itself.

Keywords: Music, Synthesizers, Sequencers, Analog Equipment, Electronic Music

Audience: Electronic Music Enthusiasts, Musicians

Contact: Todd Sines
analogue-request@magnus.acs.ohio-state.edu

Details: Free, Sound files available.

User info: To subscribe to the list, send an e-mail message requesting a subscription to the URL address below.

To send a message to the entire list, address it to: analogue@magnus.acs.ohio-state.edu

`mailto:analogue-request@magnus.acs.ohio-state.edu`

Space-music

This mailing list is for the discussion of artists who use primarily electronic instruments to create 'sound spaces' or sound atmospheres that fall into categories defined as 'floating,' 'cosmic,' or 'noncommercial' and demand an active listener.

Keywords: Music, Electronic Music

Audience: Electronic Music Enthusiasts

Contact: Dave Datta
space-music-request@cs.uwp.edu

Details: Free

User info: To subscribe to the list, send an e-mail message requesting a subscription to the URL address below.

To send a message to the entire list, address it to: space-music@cs.uwp.edu

`mailto:space-music-request@cs.uwp.edu`

Synth-l

Synth-l is the electronic music "gearhead" list dedicated to the discussion of the less esoteric aspects of synthesis. Discussion concentrates on the availability and capabilities of music software and hardware, but sometimes diverges to other subjects.

Keywords: Electronic Music, Music Software

Audience: Electronic Music Enthusiasts, Musicians, Software Designers

Contact: Joe McMahon
Synth-L@american.edu

Details: Free

User info: To subscribe to the list, send an e-mail message to the address shown below consisting of a single line reading:

SUB Synth-L YourFirstName YourLastName

To send a message to the entire list, address it to: Synth-L@american.edu

`mailto:listserv@american.edu`

Electronic Publications

(The) Scientist Newsletter

Electronic newsletter pertaining to science.

Keywords: Science, Electronic Publications

Audience: Scientists, Educators, Researchers, General Public

`gopher://internic.net`

The Internet Press

A guide to electronic journals about the Internet.

Keywords: Internet Guides, Electronic Publications

Audience: General Public

Profile: Publications discussed include the following: NSF Network News, Meta Magazine, Bits and Bytes, The Network Observer, HotWIRED, Scout Report, Netsurfer Digest, and The Internet Informer.

Contact: Kevin M. Savetz

User info: To subscribe to the list, send an e-mail message to the URL address below, with the subject line subscribe ipress. (Leave the body of the message blank.)

`mailto:savetz@rahul.net`

Electronic Publishing

CDPub

CDPub is an electronic mailing list for those engaged or interested in CD-ROM publishing in general, and in desktop CD-ROM recorders and publishing systems in particular. Topics of interest to the list include information on the various desktop publishing systems for premastering using CD-ROM media and tapes (e.g. DAT), replication services, various standards of interest to publishers (e.g. ISO9660, RockRidge), retrieval engines, and platform independence issues. Discussions on all platforms are welcome.

Keywords: CD-ROM, Electronic Publishing, Desktop Publishing

Audience: CD-ROM Publishers, Desktop Publishers, Publishers

Contact: CDPub-Info@knex.via.mind.org

Details: Free

User info: To subscribe to the list, send an e-mail message requesting a subscription to the URL address below.

To send a message to the entire list, address it to: CDPub@knex.via.mind.org

`mailto:mail-server@knex.via.mind.org`

Electronic Newsstand Gopher

This gopher contains tables of contents, selected full-text articles, and assorted other information from many mainstream print journals.

Keywords: Journals, Electronic Publishing, Publishing, News

Audience: News Enthusiasts, Publishers, Publishing Professionals, Journalists

Profile: This gopher was compiled with the collaboration of the American Journal of International Law, Policy Review, Technology Review, Business Week, Current History, The Economist, Foreign Affairs, National Review, The New Yorker, The New Republic, Mother Jones, among other distinguished publications.

Contact: William Love
love@enews.com

`gopher://gopher.enews.com`

journet

An electronic conference for the discussion of topics of interest to journalists and journalism educators.

Keywords: Journalism, Writing, Desktop Publishing, Electronic Publishing

Audience: Journalists, Writers, Publishers, Educators

Contact: George Frajkor
gfrajkor@ccs.carleton.ca

User info: To subscribe to the list, send an e-mail message to the URL address below consisting of a single line reading:

SUB journet YourFirstName YourLastName. To send a message to the entire list, address it to: journet@qucdn.queensu.ca

`mailto:listserv@qucdn.queensu.ca`

Electronics

Adv-Eli

Adv-Eli discusses the latest advances in electrical engineering. It is sponsored by the IEEE Student Branch of Santa Maria University (Chile).

Keywords: Electrical Engineering, Engineering, Electronics

Audience: Engineers, Educators, Students

A
B
C
D
E
F
G
H
I
J
K
L
M
N
O
P
Q
R
S
T
U
V
W
X
Y
Z

Contact: Francisco Javier Fernandez
ffernand@utfsm

Details: Free

User info: To subscribe to the list, send an e-mail message to the URL address shown below consiting of a single line reading:

SUB adv-eli YourFirstName YourLastName

To send a message to the entire list, address it to: adv-eli@loa.disca.utfsm.cl

listserv@loa.disca.utfsm.cl

Adv-Elo

Discusses the latest advances in electronics. Sponsored by the IEEE Student Branch of Santa Maria University (Chile).

Keywords: Electrical Engineering, Engineering, Electronics, Technological Advances

Audience: Engineers, Educators, Students

Contact: Rodrigo E. Rodriguez
rrodrigu@utfsm

Details: Free

User info: To subscribe to the list, send an e-mail message to the URL address shown below consiting of a single line reading:

SUB adv-elo YourFirstName YourLastName

To send a message to the entire list, address it to: adv-elo@loa.disca.utfsm.cl

listserv@loa.disca.utfsm.cl

CBDS-I ★★

A mailing list for the discussion of CBDS (Circuit Board Design System).

Keywords: Engineering, Computer-Aided Design, Electronics

Audience: Engineers

Contact: NETMAN@SUVM.ACS.SYR.EDU

Details: Free

User info: To subscribe to the list, send an e-mail message to the URL address below consisting of a single line reading:

SUB cbds-I YourFirstName YourLastName

To send a message to the entire list, address it to:

CbDS-L@SUVM.ACS.SYR.EDU

mailto: LISTSERV@SUVM.ACS.SYR.EDU

Class Four Relay Magazine ★★★

A magazine by Relay Ops for the relay community.

Keywords: Relays, Magazines, Electronics

Sponsor: Carnegie Mellon University, Pittsburg, PA, USA

Audience: Relay Community

Profile: Includes articles on general questions and issues of relay usage, information for and about relay ops, discussion of policy issues and guidelines, and technical issues and new developments.

Contact: Joey J. Stanford
stjs@vm.marist.edu

Details: Free

mailto:stjs@vm.marist.edu

CMPCOM (Computers and Communications) Library

The Computers and Communications Library provides you industry-specific sources. More than 40 full-text sources that concentrate on computers and communications are available. Full-text files can be searched in a variety of ways: as an individual file, by major-subject group file, or as a user-defined group file.

Keywords: Computers, Communications, Technology, Electronics

Audience: Business Researchers, Analysts, Entrepreneurs

Profile: This library can be used to gain insight on new products and technologies being introduced; monitor industry news for high technology systems, electronics, engineering, communications, and computer hardware and software; and locate product evaluations for both the professional as well as the casual personal computer user.

Contact: Mead New Sales Group at (800) 227-4908 or (513) 859-5398 inside the US, or (513) 865-7981 for all inquiries outside the US.

User info: To subscribe, contact Mead directly.

To examine the Nexis user guide, you can access it at the ftp site of the University of Texas at Austin at the URL address: ftp://ftp.cc.utexas.edu

The files are in: /pub/ref-services/LEXIS

telnet://nex.meaddata.com
http://www.meaddata.com

rec.radio.amateur.misc ★

A Usenet newsgroup providing information and discussion about ham radios.

Keywords: Radio, Electronics

Audience: Ham Radio Users

User info: To subscribe to this Usenet newsgroup, you need access to a newsreader.

news:rec.radio.amateur.misc

rec.radio.shortwave ★

A Usenet newsgroup providing information and discussion about shortwave radio.

Keywords: Radio, Electronics

Audience: Shortwave Radio Users

User info: To subscribe to this Usenet newsgroup, you need access to a newsreader.

news:rec.radio.shortwave

sci.electronics ★

A Usenet newsgroup providing information and discussion about circuits, theory and electrons.

Keywords: Electronics, Engineering

Audience: Electrical Engineers

Details: Free

User info: To subscribe to this Usenet newsgroup, you need access to a newsreader.

news:sci.electronics

Utah Valley Community College Library ★★

The library's holdings are large and wide-ranging and contain significant collections in many fields.

Keywords: Accounting, Automobiles, Cabinetry, Child Care, Drafting, Electronics, Home Building, Local History, Refrigeration, Air Conditioning

Audience: General Public, Researchers, Librarians, Document Delivery Professionals

Details: Free

User Info: Expect: Login; Send: Opub

telnet:// uvlib.uvcc.edu

Electrophoresis

Biotechnet Electronic Buyer's Guide ★★★

Biotechnet is a global computer network created specially for research biologists. It is intended to be a valuable source of information and data, a communications resource, a forum to foster the exchange of current ideas, and an international marketplace for relevant goods and service.

Keywords: Molecular Biology, Electrophoresis, Chromatography

Audience: Molecular Biologists, Chemists, Laboratory Suppliers

Profile: One of the services offered by Biotechnet is the Electronic Buyer's Guide, which is divided into five individual databases for specific product categories: Molecular Biology, Electrophoresis, Chromatography, Liquid Handling, and Instruments & Apparatus. After selecting one of the guides at the prompt, you can search through each database to find either product names and applications or the name and address of the company that manufactures the product you wish to locate.

Details: Free

Notes: Password: bguide

`telnet://biotech@biotechnet.com`

Eliot (George)

Princeton University Online Manuscripts Catalog Library

The library's holdings are large and wide-ranging. They contain significant collections in many fields.

Keywords: Books (Antiquarian), Dickens (Charles), Disraeli (Benjamin), Eliot (George), Hardy (Thomas), Kingsley (Charles), Trollope (Anthony)

Audience: General Public, Researchers, Librarians, Document Delivery Professionals

Details: Free

User Info: Expect: VM370 logo, Send: <cr>; Expect: Welcome screen, Send: folio <cr>; Expect: Welcome screen for FOLIO, Send: <cr>; Expect: List of choices, Send: 3 <cr>; To exit: type: logoff

`telnet://pucc.princeton.edu`

ELISA (Electronic Library Service)

ELISA (Electronic Library Service)

An information delivery service of the Library of the Australian National University.

Keywords: OPAC System, Australia

Sponsor: Australian National University

Audience: General Public

Profile: This information delivery service contains Australian mirrors of major gopher directories, and is a national entry point for Australian gopher services.

Contact: infodesk@info.anu.edu.au

Details: Free

`gopher://info.anu.edu.au`

ELSNET (European Network in Language and Speech)

ELSNET (European Network in Language and Speech)

A web site addressing the development of language technology in Europe and abroad by helping to coordinate progress on both scientific and technological fronts.

Keywords: Linguistics, Cognitive Science, Communication

Sponsor: The University of Edinburgh Centre for Cognitive Science, Edinburgh, Scotland

Audience: Linguists, Cognitive Scientists

Contact: Ewan Klein
klein@ed.ac.uk

`http://www.cogsci.ed.ac.uk/elsnet/home.html`

Emacs

auc-TeX

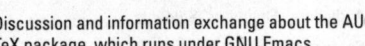

Discussion and information exchange about the AUC TeX package, which runs under GNU Emacs.

Keywords: Computers, TeX, AUC TeX, Emacs

Audience: Computer Users

Contact: Kresten Krab Thorup
auc-tex-request@iesd.auc.dk

Details: Free

User info: To subscribe to the list, send an e-mail message requesting a subscription to the URL address below.

To send a message to the entire list, address it to: auc-tex@iesd.auc.dk

`mailto:auc-tex-request@iesd.auc.dk`

NotGNU

There are three lists associated with the NotGNU Emacs editor. NotGNU-list is an interactive list dedicated to miscellaneous discussions, problems, and suggestions for NotGNU. NotGNU-announce is used for announcing new versions of NotGNU, notification of new services, bug reports, amd so on. NotGNU-distribution is a list to which new NotGNU binaries will be sent unencoded upon release.

Keywords: NotGNU, Emacs

Audience: NotGNU Users

Contact: notgnu-request@netcom.com

Details: Free

User info: To subscribe to the list, send an e-mail message requesting a subscription to the URL address below.

To send a message to the entire list, address it to: notgnu@netcom.com

`mailto:notgnu-request@netcom.com`

EMBASE

EMBASE

EMBASE is an acclaimed comprehensive index of international literature on medicine, science and pharmacology.

Keywords: Medicine, Science, Pharmacology

Sponsor: Elsevier Science Publishers

Audience: Librarians, Researchers, Students, Physicians

Contact: CDP Technologies Sales Department (800)950-2035, extension 400

User info: To subscribe, contact CDP Technologies directly

`telnet://cdplus@cdplus.com`

EMBnet (European Molecular Biology Network)

EMBnet (European Molecular Biology Network)

A group of European Internet sites which provide computational molecular biology services to both national and international researchers.

Keywords: Biology, Bioscience, Molecular Biology

Sponsor: The EC Funding Program (BRIDGE)

Audience: Biologists, Molecular Biologists, Researchers

Contact: Rodrigo Lopez, Robert Herzog
rodrigol@biotek.uio.no
rherzog@ulb.ac.be

`http://biomaster.uio.no/embnet-www.html`

EMBnet

BFU (Brussels Free Universities)

The gopher server of the Brussels Free Universities VUB /ULB is the national entry point for EMBnet in Belgium and provides links to university library systems and EMBnet databases.

Keywords: Computing, EMBnet, Belgium, Europe

Audience: Scientists, Biologists, Biotechnologists

Contact: support@vub.ac.be

Details: Free

`gopher://gopher.vub.ac.be`

A B C D E F G H I J K L M N O P Q R S T U V W X Y Z

A
B
C
D
E
F
G
H
I
J
K
L
M
N
O
P
Q
R
S
T
U
V
W
X
Y
Z

Emergency Preparedness

Disaster Research

This newsletter deals with hazards and disasters. It includes articles on recent events and policy developments, plus updates on ongoing research and upcoming meetings; it also fields queries, responses, and ongoing discussion among readers.

Keywords: Disaster Research, Emergency Preparedness

Audience: Health Care Professionals, Public Servants

Contact: mailserv@vaxf.colorado.edu (Internet).

Details: Free

`mailto:hazards@vaxf.colorado.edu`

Emory University Library

Emory University Library

The library's holdings are large and wide-ranging and contain significant collections in many fields.

Keywords: Health Sciences, Theology, History (US), Communism, Economics (History of), Literature (American)

Audience: General Public, Researchers, Librarians, Document Delivery Professionals

Details: Free

User Info: Expect: VM screen, Send: RETURN; Expect: CP READ, Send: DIAL VTAM, press RETURN; Expect: CICS screen, Send: PF1

`telnet://emuvm1.cc.emory.edu`

Employment

Academic Job Listings All Over the World

A major directory on academic institution information, providing access to a broad range of related resources (library catalogs, databases, and servers) via the Internet.

Keywords: Academia, Employment

Audience: Academics, General Public

Contact: Prentiss Riddle
cwis@rice.edu

`gopher://riceinfo.rice.edu/11/Subject/Jobs`

CAREER (Career Library)

The LEXIS Career Library contains job and job-related information.

Keywords: Employment

Audience: Lawyers, Law Students

Profile: The LEXIS Career Library contains job and job-related information designed to assist the student and attorney in finding the right job. The Career Library contains a number of helpful directories, many of which have an "Address" feature that enables users to generate a mailing list from their answer set.

Contact: Mead New Sales Group at 800-227-4908 or 513-859-5398 inside the US, or 1-513-865-7981 for all inquires outside the US.

Details: Costs

User info: To subscribe, contact Mead directly.

To examine the Lexis user guide, you can access it at the ftp site of the University of Texas at Austin at the URL address: ftp://ftp.cc.utexas.edu

The files are in: /pub/res-services/LEXIS

`telnet://nex.meaddata.com`

EEJobs

Discusses and advertises positions available and positions desired in the electrical and electronic engineering fields. Discussion and tips on how to find jobs are also welcome.

Keywords: Engineering, Electrical Engineering, Employment

Audience: Engineers, Students

Contact: Jerome Grimmer
st6267@aix370.siu.edu

Details: Free

User info: To subscribe to the list, send an e-mail messagel with a subject of SERVER.COMMANDS to st6267@aix370.siu.edu

In the body of the mail, type on the first line, /BBOARD SUB EEJOBS or /BBOARD SIGNON EEJOBS to be added to the EEJOBS list.

`mailto:st626@aix370.siu.edu`

misc.jobs.misc

A Usenet newsgroup providing information and discussion about miscellaneous available jobs.

Keywords: Employment

Audience: Job Seekers, General Public

Details: Free

User info: To subscribe to this Usenet newsgroup, you need access to a newsreader.

`news:misc.jobs.misc`

misc.jobs.offered

A Usenet newsgroup providing information and discussion about job openings, listed by subject.

Keywords: Employment

Audience: Job Seekers, General Public

Details: Free

User info: To subscribe to this Usenet newsgroup, you need access to a newsreader.

`news:misc.jobs.offered`

misc.jobs.resumes

A Usenet newsgroup providing information and discussion about resumes.

Keywords: Employment

Audience: Job Seekers, General Public

Details: Free

User info: To subscribe to this Usenet newsgroup, you need access to a newsreader.

`news:misc.jobs.resumes`

Occupational Outlook Handbook 1992-93

An annual U.S. Department of Labor publication that provides detailed information for more than 320 occupations, including job descriptions, typical salaries, education and training requirements, working conditions, job outlook, and more.

Keywords: Careers, Employment, Labor

Sponsor: U.S. Deptartment of Labor

Audience: General Public, Job Seekers, Business Professionals

Details: Free

`gopher://umslvma.umsl.edu/11/library/govdocs/ooha`

Online Career Center

The Online Career Center gopher provides access to job listings and employment information to member companies and to the public.

Keywords: Employment, Internships

Sponsor: Online Career Center

Audience: Job Seekers

Profile: Online Career Center is a not-for-profit organization funded by its member companies. It is devoted to distributing and exchanging employment and career information between its member companies, human resource professionals, and perspective employees.

Contact: OCC Operator
occ@msen.com

`gopher://gopher.msen.com`

PENPages

This easy-to-use general-interest database contains articles and brochures.

Keywords: Food, Employment, Education

Sponsor: Pennsylvania State University, PA

Audience: General Public

User Info: Expect: login; Send: your state's two-letter code (or "world" if sent from outside the USA)

`telnet://psunet.psu.edu`

Encryption

alt.security.pgp

A Usenet newsgroup providing information and discussion about the Pretty Good Privacy package, a privately-developed encryption technique.

Keywords: Privacy, Encryption, Security, Firewalls, Computers

Audience: Internet Surfers

User info: To subscribe to this Usenet newsgroup, you need access to a newsreader.

`news:alt.security.pgp`

Encyclopedia of Associations

Encyclopedia of Associations

The Encyclopedia of Associations database is a comprehensive source of detailed information on over 88,000 nonprofit membership organizations worldwide.

Keywords: Nonprofit Organizations

Sponsor: Gale Research Inc., Detroit, MI, USA

Audience: Researchers

Profile: The database corresponds to the print Encyclopedia of Associations family of publications as follows: National Organizations of the US, covering more than 23,000 American associations of national scope; International Organizations, covering some 11,000 multinational, binational, and non-US national organizations; and Regional, State, and Local Organizations, covering more than 54,000 US associations with interstate, state, intrastate, city, or local scope or membership.

Contact: Dialog in the US at (800) 334-2564, Dialog internationally at country-specific locations.

User info: To subscribe, contact Dialog directly.

Notes: Coverage: Current editions; updated semiannually.

`telnet://dialog.com`

Energy

Electric Power Database

Electric Power Database provides references to research and development projects of interest to the electric power industry, and corresponds to the print Digest of Research in the Electric Utility Industry.

Keywords: Energy, Electric

Sponsor: Electric Power Research Institute (EPRI), Palo Alto, CA, USA

Audience: Engineers

Profile: The database covers US and Canadian research on 13 major categories related to issues in electric power, including hydroelectric power, fossil fuels, nuclear power, transmission, economics, advanced power systems, and environmental assessment. The records include abstracts of project summaries for past and ongoing research projects. Such projects are conducted largely by companies under contract to EPRI or to other utilities, and by EPRI itself. Research from other corporate and utility sources is also covered.

Contact: Dialog in the US at (800) 334-2564, Dialog internationally at country-specific locations.

User info: To subscribe, contact Dialog directly.

Notes: Coverage: 1972 to the present; updated monthly.

`telnet://dialog.com`

ENERGY

The Energy News and Information (ENERGY) library consists of news, legal, and regulatory information.

Keywords: Energy, News, Law, Regulations

Audience: Energy Researchers

Profile: The ENERGY library contains more than 50 full-text sources concentrating on energy-related news and issues. Also available are decisions and orders of the United States Federal Power Commission, Federal Energy Regulatory Commission, and Nuclear Regulatory Commission. At the state level, it covers administrative decisions and orders for 17 states. Energy industry research reports from InvestextR are also available.

Contact: Mead New Sales Group at (800) 227-4908 or (513) 859-5398 inside the US, or (513) 865-7981 for all inquiries outside the US.

User info: To subscribe, contact Mead directly.

To examine the Nexis user guide, you can access it at the ftp site of the University of Texas at Austin at the URL address: ftp://ftp.cc.utexas.edu

The files are in: /pub/ref-services/LEXIS

`telnet://nex.meaddata.com`

`http://www.meaddata.com`

Energy and Climate Information Exchange (ECIX) Newsletter

This newsletter focuses on energy and climate issues, and contains summaries of network postings, updates on national and international policy initiatives, full-length articles, information on new network resources, and a calendar of upcoming events.

Keywords: Energy, Meteorology, Climatology

Audience: Meteorologists, Geologists, Energy Researchers, Climatologists

Contact: econet@igc.org

`mailto:larris@igc.org`

Energy Research in Israel Newsletter

This newsletter on Bitnet is for people interested in energy research, and is meant to allow important local and international energy information to be disseminated efficiently.

Keywords: Energy, Israel

Audience: Energy Researchers, Utility Professionals, Conservationists

Contact: Michael Wolff
WOLFF@ILNCRD.bitnet

Details: Free

User info: To subscribe, send an e-mail message to the address below consisting of a single line reading:

To send a message to the entire list,

`mailto:listserv@taunivm.bitnet`

Energy-L

A mailing list for the discussion of all relevant information on the subject of energy in Israel.

Keywords: Engineering, Energy, Israel

Audience: Engineers, Researchers

Contact: Jo van Zwaren, Dr Michael Wolff
jo%ilncrd.bitnet@cunyvm.cuny.edu
wolff@ilncrd

Details: Free

User info: To subscribe to the list, send an e-mail message to the URL addres below consisting of a single line reading:

SUB energy-l YourFirstName YourLastName

To send a message to the entire list, address it to: energy-i@taunivm.tau.ac.il

`mailto:listserv@taumivm.tau.ac.il`

A B C D E F G H I J K L M N O P Q R S T U V W X Y Z

A
B
C
D
E
F
G
H
I
J
K
L
M
N
O
P
Q
R
S
T
U
V
W
X
Y
Z

Martin Marietta Energy Systems Gopher

Information on Martin Marietta's energy projects and technologies for both government and commercial applications.

Keywords: Technology, Energy, Industry

Sponsor: Martin Marietta

Audience: Business Professionals, Entrepreneurs, Manufactures, Energy Researchers, Technology Enthusiasts

Profile: This gopher contains a list of technologies currently being developed at Martin Marietta as well as detailing facilities available to university, government, and commercial researchers. Also includes updates on employment openings, and a list of current publications.

Contact: gopher@ornl.gov

`gopher:// gopher.ornl.gov`

`http://www.ornl.gov/mmes.html`

Mississippi State University Library

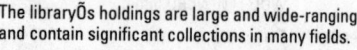

The libraryÕs holdings are large and wide-ranging and contain significant collections in many fields.

Keywords: History (US), Forestry, Energy, Carter (Hodding, Papers of), Mississippi

Audience: General Public, Researchers, Librarians, Document Delivery Professionals

Contact: Stephen Cunetto
shc1@ra.msstate.edu

Details: Free

User Info: Expect: username, Send: msu; Expect: password, Send: library

`telnet://libserv.msstate.edu`

Solstice

This file server provides state-of-the-art information on renewable energy, energy efficiency, the environment, and sustainable community development.

Keywords: Energy, Environment

Sponsor: The Center for Renewable Energy and Sustainable Technology (CREST)

Audience: Environmentalists, Urban Planners, Educators, Students

Contact: www-content@solstice.crest.org

Details: Free

Login: anonymous, Password: e-mail

`http://solstice.crest.org`

Energy and Climate Information Exchange (ECIX) Newsletter

Energy and Climate Information Exchange (ECIX) Newsletter

This newsletter focuses on energy and climate issues, and contains summaries of network postings, updates on national and international policy initiatives, full-length articles, information on new network resources, and a calendar of upcoming events.

Keywords: Energy, Meteorology, Climatology

Audience: Meteorologists, Geologists, Energy Researchers, Climatologists

Contact: econet@igc.org

`mailto:larris@igc.org`

Energy Research in Israel Newsletter

Energy Research in Israel Newsletter

This newsletter on Bitnet is for people interested in energy research, and is meant to allow important local and international energy information to be disseminated efficiently.

Keywords: Energy, Israel

Audience: Energy Researchers, Utility Professionals, Conservationists

Contact: Michael Wolff
WOLFF@ILNCRD.bitnet

Details: Free

User info: To subscribe, send an e-mail message to the address below consisting of a single line reading:

To send a message to the entire list,

`mailto:listserv@taunivm.bitnet`

Engineering

Adv-Eli

Adv-Eli discusses the latest advances in electrical engineering. It is sponsored by the IEEE Student Branch of Santa Maria University (Chile).

Keywords: Electrical Engineering, Engineering, Electronics

Audience: Engineers, Educators, Students

Contact: Francisco Javier Fernandez
ffernand@utfsm

Details: Free

User info: To subscribe to the list, send an e-mail message to the URL address shown below consiting of a single line reading:

SUB adv-eli YourFirstName YourLastName

To send a message to the entire list, address it to: adv-eli@loa.disca.utfsm.cl

`listserv@loa.disca.utfsm.cl`

Adv-Elo

Discusses the latest advances in electronics. Sponsored by the IEEE Student Branch of Santa Maria University (Chile).

Keywords: Electrical Engineering, Engineering, Electronics, Technological Advances

Audience: Engineers, Educators, Students

Contact: Rodrigo E. Rodriguez
rrodrigu@utfsm

Details: Free

User info: To subscribe to the list, send an e-mail message to the URL address shown below consiting of a single line reading:

SUB adv-elo YourFirstName YourLastName

To send a message to the entire list, address it to: adv-elo@loa.disca.utfsm.cl

`listserv@loa.disca.utfsm.cl`

Aelflow

A mailing list for the discussion of aerospace and aeronautical engineering.

Keywords: Aerospace, Aeronautics, Engineering

Sponsor: The Aerospace Engineering Fluid Group

Audience: Engineers, Educators, Students

Contact: Dr. Yakov Cohen
aer8601@technion.ac.il.edu

Details: Free

User info: To subscribe to the list, send an e-mail message to the URL address shown below consiting of a single line reading:

SUB aelflow YourFirstName YourLastName

To send a message to the entire list, address it to: aelflow@technion.ac.il ed

`listserv@technion.ac.il ed`

Aerospace Engineering

This directory is a compilation of information resources focused on aerospace engineeering.

Keywords: Aerospace, Engineering, Aviation, Space

Audience: Aerospace Engineers, Space Scientists

Profile: This is a guide to Internet resources that contain information pertaining to aerospace engineering. Originally the guide was to cover the area of aerospace engineering as applied to lower atmospheric flight. However, it is difficult to narrow the sites down to specific subject areas. As the guide evolved, sites were included with a broader scope of information. The guide is by no means comprehensive and exhaustive; there are sites that are not included and those the authors were not aware of, and they welcome suggestions. The directory lists sites on FTP, Gopher, Listserv, OPAC, Telnet, and WWW.

Details: Free

`ftp://una.hh.lib.umich.edu/70/`
`inetdirsstacks/aerospace:potsiedalq`

CAEDS-L

A mailing list for the discussion of CAED (Computer Aided Engineering Design) Products.

Keywords: Computer-Aided Design, Engineering, Computer Graphics

Audience: Engineers

Contact: NETMAN@SUVM.acs.syr.edu

Details: Free

User info: To subscribe to the list, send an e-mail message to the URL address shown below consisting of a single line reading:

SUB caeds-l YourFirstName YourLastName

To send a message to the entire list, address it to:

cae-1@suvm.acs.syr.edu

`mailto:listserv@suvm.acs.syr.edu`

CBDS-I

A mailing list for the discussion of CBDS (Circuit Board Design System).

Keywords: Engineering, Computer-Aided Design, Electronics

Audience: Engineers

Contact: netman@suv.acs.syr.edu

Details: Free

User info: To subscribe to the list, send an e-mail message to the URL address below consisting of a single line reading:

SUB cbds-I YourFirstName YourLastName

To send a message to the entire list, address it to:

cbds-l@suvm.acs.syr.edu

`mailto:listserv@suvm.acs.syr.edu`

CCES-L

A mailing list for the national communication branch of the CFES (Canadian Federation of Engineering Students).

Keywords: Engineering, Canada

Audience: Engineers, Students

Contact: Canadian Federation of EngineeringStudents cfes@jupiter.sun.csd.unb.ca

Details: Free

User info: To subscribe to the list, send an e-mail message to the URL address below consisting of a single line reading:

SUB cces-l YourFirstName YourLastName

To send a message to the entire list, address it to:

cces-l@unb.ca

`mailto:listserv@unb.ca`

CEC

CEC (Canadian Electro-Acoustics Community).

Keywords: Engineering, Acoustical Engineering, Canada, Canadian Electro-Acoustics Community

Audience: Engineers

Contact: Peter Gross grosspa@qucdn

Details: Free

User info: To subscribe to the list, send an e-mail message to the URL address below, consisting of a single line reading:

SUB cec YourFirstName YourLastName

To send a message to the entire list, address it to: cec@qucdn.queensu.ca

`mailto:listserv@qucdn.queensu.ca`

CEM-L

A mailing list for discussion surrounding the UTD (University of Texas at Dallas) Center for Engineering Mathematics.

Keywords: Engineering, Mathematics

Audience: Engineers, Mathematicians, Educators, Students

Contact: David Lippke LIPPKE@UTDALLAS

Details: Free

User info: To subscribe to the list, send an e-mail message to the URL address below, consisting of a single line reading:

SUB cem-l YourFirstName YourLastName

To send a message to the entire list, address it to: cem-l@utdallas.edu

`mailto:listserv@utdallas.edu`

CFD

CFD (Computational Fluid Dynamics Group).

Keywords: Engineering, Fluid Dynamics

Audience: Engineers

Contact: JUSTIN@UKCC.UKY.EDU justin@engr.uky.edu

Details: Free

User info: To subscribe to the list, send an e-mail message to the URL address below, consisting of a single line reading:

SUB cfd YourFirstName YourLastName

To send a message to the entire list, address it to:

cfd@ukcc.uky.edu

`mailto:justin@ukcc.uky.edu`

CFES-L

National communication branch of the CFES (Canadian Federation of Engineering Students).

Keywords: Engineering, Students, Canada

Audience: Engineers, Students

Contact: Canadian Federation of EngineeringStudents cfes@jupiter.sun.csd.unb.ca

Details: Free

User info: To subscribe to the list, send an e-mail message to the URL address below consiting of a single line reading:

SUB cfes-l YourFirstName YourLastName

To send a message to the entire list, address it to:

cfes-l@unb.ca

`mailto:listserv@unb.ca`

ChE Electronic Newsletter

This newsletter contains information of interest to chemical engineers.

Keywords: Chemical Engineering, Chemistry, Engineering

Audience: Chemical Engineers

Contact: Martyn S. Ray trayms@cc.curtin.edu.au

Details: Free

Inquire about needing a password.

`mailto:trayms@cc.curtin.edu.au`

Chemical Abstracts

Worldwide coverage of the chemical sciences literature.

Keywords: Chemistry, Engineering

Sponsor: Chemical Abstracts Service, American Chemical Society

Audience: Researchers, Librarians, Chemists

Profile: Provides coverage of chemical sciences literature from over 9,000 journals, patents from 27 countries, and 2 international property organizations, new books, conference proceedings, and government research reports. Updated every two weeks.

A B C D E F G H I J K L M N O P Q R S T U V W X Y Z

A
B
C
D
E
F
G
H
I
J
K
L
M
N
O
P
Q
R
S
T
U
V
W
X
Y
Z

Contact: paul.albert@neteast.com

User info: To subscribe contact Orbit-Questel directly.

`telnet://orbit.com`

CIRCUITS-L

This list discusses all aspects of the introductory course in circuit analysis for electrical engineering undergraduates.

Keywords: Engineering, Electrical Engineering, Teaching, Electric Circuit Analysis

Audience: Engineers, Students (college)

Contact: Paul E. Gray
mailto:gray@maple.ucs.uwplatt.edu

Details: Free

User info: To subscribe to the list, send an e-mail message to the URL address below, and include: name; e-mail address; home phone, business phone, and FAX numbers (including area code); and US postal address (including ZIP code)

To send a message to the entire list, address it to:

circuits-l@uwplatt.edu

`mailto:circuits-request@uwplatt.edu`

EEJobs

Discusses and advertises positions available and positions desired in the electrical and electronic engineering fields. Discussion and tips on how to find jobs are also welcome.

Keywords: Engineering, Electrical Engineering, Employment

Audience: Engineers, Students

Contact: Jerome Grimmer
st6267@aix370.siu.edu

Details: Free

User info: To subscribe to the list, send an e-mail messagel with a subject of SERVER.COMMANDS to st6267@aix370.siu.edu

In the body of the mail, type on the first line, /BBOARD SUB EEJOBS or / BBOARD SIGNON EEJOBS to be added to the EEJOBS list.

`st626@aix370.siu.edu`

Ei Compendex Plus

The Ei Compendex Plus database is the machine-readable version of The Engineering Index (monthly/annual), which provides abstracted information from the world's significant literature of engineering and technology.

Keywords: Engineering, Technology

Sponsor: Engineering Information Inc. (Ei), Hoboken, NJ, USA

Audience: Engineers

Profile: Ei Compendex Plus provides worldwide coverage of approximately 4,500 journals and selected government reports and books. Subjects covered include: civil, energy, environmental, geological, and biological engineering; electrical, automotive, nuclear, and aerospace engineering; and computers, robotics, and industrial robots.

Contact: Dialog in the US at (800) 334-2564, Dialog internationally at country-specific locations.

User info: To subscribe, contact Dialog directly.

Notes: Coverage: 1970 to the present; updated weekly.

`telnet://dialog.com`

Energy-L

A mailing list for the discussion of all relevant information on the subject of energy in Israel.

Keywords: Engineering, Energy, Israel

Audience: Engineers, Researchers

Contact: Jo van Zwaren, Dr Michael Wolff
jo%ilncrd.bitnet@cunyvm.cuny.edu
wolff@ilncrd

Details: Free

User info: To subscribe to the list, send an e-mail message to the URL addres below consisting of a single line reading:

SUB energy-l YourFirstName YourLastName

To send a message to the entire list, address it to: energy-l@TAUNIVM. TAU.AC.IL

`mailto:listserv@taunivm.tau.ac.il`

Engineering-Design

Supports researchers at the five national Engineering Design Centres.

Keywords: Engineering, Design

Audience: Engineers, Researchers

Contact: engineering-design-request@mailbase.ac.uk

Details: Free

User info: To subscribe to the list, send an e-mail message to the URL address shown below consiting of a single line reading:

SUB engineering-design YourFirstName YourLastName

To send a message to the entire list, address it to:

engineering-design@mailbase.ac.uk

`mail to:mailbase@mailbase.ac.uk`

Engineering; A. Park, J. Miller

This directory is a compilation of information resources focused on engineering.

Keywords: Engineering, Design

Audience: Engineers, Students, Educators

Details: Free

`ftp://una.hh.lib.umich.edu/70/`
`inetdirsstacks/engin:parkmiller`

ETHCSE-L

A mailing list for the discussion of Ethical Issues in Software Engineering, dealing with subjects of interest to professional software engineers.

Keywords: Engineering, Computing, Ethics

Audience: Engineers, Software Engineers, Researchers

Contact: Margaret Mason
mason@utkvm1.utk.edu

Details: Free

User info: To subscribe to the list, send an e-mail message to the URL address shown below consisting of a single line reading:

SUB ethcse-l YourFirstName YourLastName

To send a message to the entire list, address it to:

ethcse-l@utkvm1.utk.edu

`mailto:listerv@utkvm1.utk.edu`

IEEE-L

Serves as a forum for all IEEE student branch officers and members.

Keywords: Engineering, Electrical Engineering

Audience: Engineers, Electrical Engineers, Students

Contact: Paul D. Kroculick or Chas Elliot
tjw0465@bingtjw.cc.binghamton.edu
ba08034@bingsuns.cc.binghamton.edu

Details: Free

User info: To subscribe to the list, send an e-mail message to the URL address below consisting of a single line reading:

SUB ieee-l YourFirstName YourLastName. To send a message to the entire list, address it to:

iee-l@bingvmb.cc.binghamton.edu

`mailto:listserv@bingvb.cc.binghamton.edu`

IHS International Standards and Specifications

The database contains references to industry standards, and military and federal specifications and standards covering all aspects of engineering and related disciplines.

Keywords: Engineering, Military Specifications, Federal Standards

Sponsor: Information Handling Services, Englewood, CO, US

Audience: Engineers, Military Hisorians, Lawyers

Profile: The file includes 90% of the world's most referenced standards from over 70 domestic, foreign, and international standardizing bodies. Also included is the world's largest commercially available collection of unclassified active and historical US military and federal specifications and standards.

Contact: Dialog in the US at (800) 334-2564, Dialog internationally at country-specific locations.

User info: To subscribe, contact Dialog directly.

Notes: Coverage: Current; updated weekly for MILSPECS, every two months.

`telnet://dialog.com`

National Centre for Software Technology

The National Centre for Software Technology (NCST) is an autonomous R&D unit in Bombay and Bangalore. Specialty areas of research include graphics, CAD, real time systems, knowledge-based systems, and software engineering.

Keywords: Computer Science, Engineering, Computer-Aided Design

Sponsor: National Centre for Software Technology, Bombay, India

Audience: Reseachers, Computer Scientists, Engineers, Students

Contact: Postmaster postmaster@saathi.ncst.ernet.in

`gopher://shakti.ncst.ernet.in`

sci.electronics

A Usenet newsgroup providing information and discussion about circuits, theory and electrons.

Keywords: Electronics, Engineering

Audience: Electrical Engineers

Details: Free

User info: To subscribe to this Usenet newsgroup, you need access to a newsreader.

`news:sci.electronics`

University of Texas at Austin Library

The library's holdings are large and wide-ranging and contain significant collections in many fields. Music, Natural Science, Nursing, Science Technology, Behavioral Science, Social Work, Computer Science, Engineering, Latin American Studies, Middle Eastern Studies

Keywords: Music, Natural Science, Nursing, Science Technology, Behavioral Science, Social Work, Computer Science, Engineering, Latin American Studies, Middle Eastern Studies

Audience: Researchers, Students, General Public

Details: Free

User Info: Expect: Blank Screen, Send: Return; Expect: Go, Send: Return; Expect: Enter Terminal Type, Send: vt100

note: Some databases are restricted to UT Austin users only.

`telnet://utcat.utexas.edu`

US Army Corps of Engineers

This site provides information on the organization, programs, news, facilities, and activities of the US Army Corps of Engineers.

Keywords: Military, Engineering

Sponsor: Cold Regions Research and Engineering Laboratory, under

Audience: Military Personnel, Engineers, Researchers

Contact: www@usace.mil

Details: Free

`http://www.usace.mil/usace.html`

Engineering (Biomedical)

sci.engr.biomed

A Usenet newsgroup providing information and discussion about the field of biomedical engineering.

Keywords: Biomedicine, Engineering (Biomedical)

Audience: Engineers (Biomedical), Biomedical Researchers

Details: Free

User info: To subscribe to this Usenet newsgroup, you need access to a newsreader.

`news:sci.engr.biomed`

Engineering (Chemical)

chem-eng

This is an electronic newsletter on chemical engineering.

Keywords: Engineering (Chemical)

Audience: Chemical Engineers, Chemists, Engineers

Contact: Martyn Ray trayms@cc.curtin.edu.au

Details: Free

User info: To subscribe to the list, send an e-mail message requesting a subscription to the URL address below.

`mailto:trayms@cc.curtin.edu.au`

Engineering (Civil)

Civil-L

A mailing list for the discussion of Civil Engineering Research and Education.

Keywords: Engineering (Civil), Computer-Aided Instruction

Audience: Engineers, Educators, Students

Contact: Eldo Hildebrand ELDO@UNB.CA

Details: Free

User info: To subscribe to the list, send an e-mail message to the URL address shown below consisting of a single line reading:

SUB civil-l YourFirstName YourLastName

To send a message to the entire list, address it to:

civil-l@unb.ca

`mailto:listserv@unb.ca`

Engineering (Electrical)

af

A mailing list for discussion of AudioFile, a client/server, network-transparent, device-independent audio system.

Keywords: Audio Electronics, Electrical Engineering

Audience: Audio Enthusiasts, Electrical Engineers

Contact: af-request@crl.dec.com

User info: To subscribe to the list, send an e-mail message to the URL address below.

To send a message to the entire list, address it to: af@crl.dec.com

`mailto:af-request@crl.dec.com`

Engineering (History of)

Purdue University Library

The library's holdings are large and wide-ranging. They contain significant collections in many fields.

Keywords: Economics (History of), Literature (English), Literature (American), Indiana, Rogers (Bruce), Engineering (History of), Aviation, Earth Science, Atmospheric Science, Consumer Science, Family Science, Chemistry (History of), Physics, Veterinary Science

Audience: General Public, Researchers, Librarians, Document Delivery Professionals

Contact: Dan Ferrer dan@asterix.lib.purdue.edu

A B C D E F G H I J K L M N O P Q R S T U V W X Y Z

Details: Free

User Info: Expect: User ID prompt, Send: GUEST

`telnet://lib.cc.purdue.edu`

Engineering (Mechanical)

MECH-L

A mailing list for the discussion of mechanical engineering.

Keywords: Engineering (Mechanical)

Audience: Engineers, Mechanical Engineers

Contact: S. Nomura
b470ssn@utarlvm1.uta.edu

Details: Free

User info: To subscribe to the list, send an e-mail message to the URL address below consisting of a single line reading:

SUB mech-l YourFirstName YourLastName

To send a message to the entire list, address it to: mech-l@utarlvm1.uta.edu

`mailto:listserv@utarlvm1.uta.edu`

England

Morris

A discussion list related to Morris Dancing, including Cotswold, Border, Northwest, Rapper, Longsword, Abbots Bromley, Garland, and similar forms of English dance along with the accompanying music and traditions.

Keywords: Morris Dancing, England, Dance

Audience: Morris Dancers

Details: Free

User info: To subscribe to the list, send an e-mail message requesting subscription to the URL address below.

`mailto:morris@suvm.acs.syr.edu`

English

The English Server

A large and eclectic collection of humanities resources.

Keywords: Humanities, Academia, English, Popular Culture, Feminism

Sponsor: Carnegie Mellon University English Department, Pittsburgh, Pennsylvania, USA

Audience: General Public, University Students, Educators (College/University), Researchers (Humanities)

Profile: Contains archives of conventional humanities materials, such as historical documents and classic books in electronic form. Also offers more unusual and hard-to-find resources, particularly in the field of popular culture and media. Features access to many humanities and culture-related online journals such as Bad Subjects, FineArt Forum, and Postmodern Culture. Also has links to a wide variety of related Internet sites and resources.

Contact: Geoff Sauer
postmaster@english-server.hss.cmu.

`gopher://english-server.hss.cmu.edu`

`http://english-server.hss.cmu.edu`

English Bibles

University of Chicago Library

The library's holdings are large and wide-ranging and contain significant collections in many fields.

Keywords: English Bibles, Lincoln (Abraham), Kentucky & Ohio River Valley (History of), Balzac (Honore de), American Drama, Cromwell (Oliver), Goethe, Judaica, Italy, Chaucer (Geoffrey), Wells (Ida, Personal Papers of), Douglas (Stephen A.), Italy, Literature (Children's)

Audience: General Public, Researchers, Librarians, Document Delivery Professionals

Details: Free

User Info: Expect: ENTER CLASS, Send: LIB48 3; Expect: CONNECTED, Send: RETURN

`telnet://olorin.uchicago.edu`

Entering the WWW

Entering the WWW

An article entitled "Entering the World-Wide Web: A Guide to Cyberspace."

Keywords: Internet Tools, WWW

Sponsor: Honolulu Community College

Audience: Internet Surfers

Contact: Kevin Hughes
kevinh@pulua.hcc.hawaii.edu

Details: Free

`http://www.hcc.hawaii.edu/guide/www.guide.html`

Entertainment

alt.fan.monty-python

A Usenet newsgroup providing an electronic fan club for those wacky Brits.

Keywords: Humor, Entertainment, Comedy, Satire

Audience: Monty Python Enthusiasts, General Public

User info: To subscribe to this Usenet newsgroup, you need access to a newsreader.

`news:alt.fan.monty-python`

ENTERT (Entertainment News Library)

The Entertainment News library contains sources of information about the entertainment industry, including broadcasting, cable TV, theater, television, books, movies, ballet and dance, video, radio, music, and the record industry.

Keywords: Entertainment, News

Audience: Business Researchers, Analysts, Entrepreneurs

Profile: ENTERT includes the full text of publications such as Variety, Daily Variety, Communications Daily and People, as well as documents about entertainment-related topics from premier NEXIS sources such as the Los Angeles Times and USA Today. Additionally, ENTERT has the premier source database covering the entertainment industry, BASELINE, which provides daily updates of the financial status of movies, background on actors and details on works in production.

Contact: Mead New Sales Group at (800) 227-4908 or (513) 859-5398 inside the US, or (513) 865-7981 for all inquiries outside the US.

User info: To subscribe, contact Mead directly.

To examine the Nexis user guide, you can access it at the ftp site of the University of Texas at Austin at the URL address: ftp://ftp.cc.utexas.edu

The files are in: /pub/ref-services/LEXIS

`telnet://nex.meaddata.com`

`http://www.meaddata.com`

Film and Video

This directory is a compilation of information resources focused on film and video.

Keywords: Film, Video, Entertainment

Audience: Students, Producers, Artists

Details: Free

`ftp://una.hh.lib.umich.edu/70/inetdirsstacks/filmvideo:woodgarlock`

GameBytes magazine

This monthly electronic magazine provides reviews (with graphics) of electronic games.

Keywords: Games, Electronic Media, Entertainment

Sponsor: Game Bytes Magazine

Audience: Game Players, Computer Game Developers, Computer Graphics Designers

Contact: Ross Erickson
rwericks@ingr.com

Details: Free

`http://wcl-rs.bham.ac.uk/GameBytes`

Zarf's List of Interactive Games on the Web

A list containing links to games and toys that can be played on the Internet.

Keywords: Games, Toys, Entertainment, Recreation

Sponsor: Carnegie Mellon University, School of Computer Science, Pittsburgh, Pennsylvania, USA

Audience: General Public, Game Players, Kids

Contact: Andrew Plotkin
zarf@cs.cmu.edu, apli@andrew.cmu.edu

`http://www.cs.cmu.edu/:8001/afs/ cs.cmu.edu/user/zarf/www/games.html`

Entomology

AGRICOLA

The AGRICOLA database of the National Agricultural Library (NAL) provides comprehensive coverage of worldwide journal literature and monographs on agriculture and related subjects.

Keywords: Agriculture, Animal Studies, Botany, Entomology

Sponsor: US National Agricultural Library, Beltsville, MD, USA

Audience: Agronomists, Botanists, Chemists, Entomologists

Profile: Related subjects include: animal studies, botany, chemistry, entomology, fertilizers, forestry, hydroponics, soils, and more.

Contact: Dialog in the US at (800) 334-2564, Dialog internationally at country-specific locations.

User info: To subscribe, contact Dialog directly.

Notes: Coverage: 1970 to the present; updated monthly.

`telnet://dialog.com`

CSU Entomology WWW Site

A web site containing online photos of insects, entomology educational programs, and extensive Internet entomology links.

Keywords: Bioscience, Biology, Entomology

Sponsor: Colorado State University, Denver, Colorado, USA

Audience: Students, Researchers, Entomologists

Contact: Lou Bjostad
lbjostad@lamar.colorado.edu

`http://www.colostate.edu/Depts/ Entomology/ent.html`

McGill University, Montreal Canada, INFOMcGILL Library

The library's holdings are large and wide-ranging and contain significant collections in many fields.

Keywords: Architecture, Entomology, Biology, Science (History of), Medicine (History of), Napolean, Shakespeare (William)

Audience: Researchers, Students, General Public

Contact: Roy Miller
ccrmmus@mcgillm (Bitnet)
ccrmmus@musicm.mcgill.ca (Internet)

User Info: Expect: VM logo; Send: Enter; Expect: prompt; Send: PF3 or type INFO

`telnet://vm1.mcgill.ca`

The University of Notre Dame Library

The library's holdings are large and wide-ranging and contain significant collections in many fields.

Keywords: Music (Irish), Ireland, Botany (History of), Ecology, Entomology, Parasitology, Aquatic Biology, Universities (History of), Paleography

Audience: General Public, Researchers, Librarians, Document Delivery Professionals

Details: Free

User Info: Expect: ENTER COMMAND OR HELP:, Send: library; To leave, type x on the command line and press the enter key. At the ENTER COMMAND OR HELP: prompt, type bye and press the enter key.

`telnet://irishmvs.cc.nd.edu`

Entropy

DYNSYS-L

The Dynamical System exchanges information among people working in ergodic theory and dynamical systems.

Keywords: Entropy, Systems Theory

Audience: Engineers

Details: Free

`mailto:newserv@uncvm1.oit.unc.edu`

ENVIRN (Environment Library)

ENVIRN (Environment Library)

The Environment (ENVIRN) Library contains a variety of environment-related news and legal information.

Keywords: News, Analysis, Law, Environment

Audience: Environmental Researchers, Business Professionals

Profile: The ENVIRN library contains a combination of environmental information that can provide critical insight into environmental hazards, EPA ratings, specific company investigations, evaluations on potentially hazardous chemicals, and parties responsible for cleanup of specific hazardous sites. Additionally, ENVIRN provides a wealth of environment-related information—legislation, regulations, and court and agency decisions at both the federal and state levels; news; the Environmental Law Reporter, and American Law Reports.

Contact: Mead New Sales Group at (800) 227-4908 or (513) 859-5398 inside the US, or (513) 865-7981 for all inquiries outside the US.

User info: To subscribe, contact Mead directly.

To examine the Nexis user guide, you can access it at the ftp site of the University of Texas at Austin at the URL address: ftp://ftp.cc.utexas.edu

The files are in: /pub/ref-services/LEXIS

`telnet://nex.meaddata.com`

`http://www.meaddata.com`

Enviroethics

Enviroethics

A mailing list for the scholarly discussion of environmental ethics and philosophy.

Keywords: Environment, Environmental Studies

Audience: Environmental Researchers, Environmental Scientists, Environmentalists

Contact: Clare Palmer, Ian Tilsed
C.A. Palmer@greenwich.ac.uk, I.J. Tilsed@exeter.ac.uk

A
B
C
D
E
F
G
H
I
J
K
L
M
N
O
P
Q
R
S
T
U
V
W
X
Y
Z

A
B
C
D
E
F
G
H
I
J
K
L
M
N
O
P
Q
R
S
T
U
V
W
X
Y
Z

User info: To subscribe, send an e-mail message to the URL address below consisting of a single line reading:

join enviroethics YourFirstName YourLastName

To obtain a list of archived files, send an e-mail message with the body 'index enviroethics' to the same address.

`mailto:mailbase@mailbase.ac.uk`

Environment

Activ-L

A mailing list for the discussion of peace, empowerment, justice and environmental issues.

Keywords: Peace, Justice, Environment, Activism

Audience: Activists, Students

Contact: Rich Winkel
harelb@math.cornell.edu

User info: To subscribe to the list, send an e-mail message to the URL address below consisting of a single line reading:

SUB activ-l YourFirstName YourLastName

To send a message to the entire list, address it to: active-l@mizzou1.miss ouri.edu

`mailto:listserv@mizzou1.missouri.edu`

Australian Environmental Resources Information Network (ERIN)

This gopher contains a wide range of Australian environmental information.

Keywords: Environment, Australia, Ecology

Audience: Environmentalists, Ecologists, Researchers, Australians

Profile: Coverage includes biodiversity, protected areas, terrestrial and marine environments, environmental protection and legislation, international agreements, and general information about ERIN.

Contact: gopher@erin.gov.au

Details: Free

`gopher://kaos.erin.gov.au`

`http://kaos.erin.gov.au/erin.html`

CEDAR (Central European Environmental Data Request) Facility

This gopher site provides information about the environmental and scientific community in Central and Eastern Europe (CEE), with access to environmental information located throughout the world on various international computer networks and hosts.

Keywords: Europe, EEC, Environment

Sponsor: The International Society for Environmental Protection, and The Austrian Federal Ministry for Environment, Youth and Family (BMUJF)

Audience: Environmentalists, Educators, Students, Urban Planners

Contact: cedar-info@cedar.univie.ac.at

Notes: CEDAR Marxergasse 3/20, A-1030 Vienna, Austria Tel.: +43-1-715 58 79

`gopher://pan.cedar.univie.ac.at`

CEE Environmental Libraries Database

A directory of over 300 libraries and environmental information centers in Central Eastern Europe that specalize in, or maintain significant collections of information about, the environment, ecology, sustainable living, or conservation. The database concentrates on six Central Eastern European countries: Bulgaria, Czech Republic, Hungary, Romania, Slovakia, and Poland.

Keywords: Central Eastern Europe, Environment, Sustainable Living, Bulgaria, Czech Republic, Hungary, Romania, Slovakia, Poland.

Sponsor: The Wladyslaw Poniecki Charitable Foundation, Inc.

Audience: Environmentalists, Green Movement, Librarians, Community Builders, Sustainable Living Specialists.

Profile: This database is the product of an Environmental Training Project (ETP) that was funded in 1992 by the US Agency for International Development as a 5-year cooperative agreement with a consortium headed by the University of Minnesota (US AID Cooperative Agreement Number EUR-0041-A-002-2020). Other members of the consortium include the University of Pittsburgh's Center for Hazardous Material Research, The Institute for Sustainable Communi-ties, and the World Wildlife Fund. The Wladyslaw Poniecki Charitable Foundation, Inc., was a subcontractor to the World Wildlife Fund and published the Directory of Libraries and Environmental Information Centers in Central Eastern Europe: A Locator/ Directory . This gopher database consists of an electronic version of the printed directory, subsequently modified

and updated online. Access to the data is facilitated by a WAIS search engine which makes it possible to retrieve information about libraries, subject area specializations, personnel, and so on.

Contact: Doug Kahn, CEDAR
kahn@pan.cedar.univie.ac.at

`gopher://gopher.poniecki.berkeley.edu`

Central European Environment Data Report (CEDAR) Facility

This gopher site provides information about the environmental and scientific community in Central and Eastern Europe, with access to environmental information located throughout the world on various international computer networks and hosts.

Keywords: Europe, Central Europe, Eastern Europe, Environment

Sponsor: The International Society for Environmental Protection, and The Austrian Federal Ministry for Environment, Youth and Family (BMUJF)

Audience: Environmentalists, Educators, Students, Urban Planners, Environmental Scientists

Profile: The CEDAR Facility, established in 1991, is administered by the International Society for Environmental Protection (ISEP). The Facility is designed to provide regional groups and individuals with access to its information retrieval and higher computing resources, technical advice and database and network access support. In addition, CEDAR works to facilitate information and dialogue exchange with organizations in other parts of the world and in partner countries; and to promote training forums, including the joint development of seminars and conferences with ISEP on environmental and network topics. Finally, CEDAR develops and manages environmental reference data sets, including a US EPA bibliographic reference on hazardous waste treatment, CEDAR databases on Central and Eastern European environmental expertise and information, and the holdings of the Regional Environmental Center Library at Budapest.

Contact: cedar-info@cedar.univie.ac.at

`gopher://pan.cedar.univie.ac.at`

consgis

A discussion list for those using GIS (Geographic Information Systems) in the interest of conservation.

Keywords: Conservation, Environment, GIS (Geographic Information Systems)

Audience: Geographers, Environmentalists, Cartographers

Contact: Dr. Peter August
pete@edcserv.edc.uri.edu

Details: Free

User info: To subscribe to the list, send an e-mail message to the URL address below consisting of a single line reading:

SUB consgis YourFirstName YourLastName.

To send a message to the entire list, address it to: consgis@uriacc.uri.edu

`mailto:listserv@uriacc.uri.edu`

EcoDirectory

A directory of Libraries and Environmental Information Centers in Central Eastern Europe.

Keywords: Environment, Eastern Europe, Central Europe

Sponsor: The Wladyslaw Poniecki Charitable Foundation, Inc.

Audience: Environmentalists, Librarians, International Development Specialists

Profile: This database is the product of an Environmental Training Project (ETP) which was founded in 1992 by the US Agency for International Development. The project concentrated on six Central and Eastern European countries: Bulgaria, Czech Republic, Hungary, Romania, Slovakia, and Poland.

It contains information on over 300 Libraries and Environmental Information Centers in those countries. Access to the data is facilitated by a WAIS search engine which makes it possible to retrieve information about libraries, subject area specializations, personnel, and so on.

Contact: Joerg Findeisen, CEDAR findeisen@pan.cedar.univie.ac.at

`gopher://gopher.poniecki.berkeley.edu`

ENVIRN (Environment Library)

The Environment (ENVIRN) Library contains a variety of environment-related news and legal information.

Keywords: News, Analysis, Law, Environment

Audience: Environmental Researchers, Business Professionals

Profile: The ENVIRN library contains a combination of environmental information that can provide critical insight into environmental hazards, EPA ratings, specific company investigations, evaluations on potentially hazardous chemicals, and parties responsible for cleanup of specific hazardous sites. Additionally, ENVIRN provides a wealth of environment-related information—legislation, regulations, and court and agency decisions at both the federal and state levels; news; the Environmental Law Reporter, and American Law Reports.

Contact: Mead New Sales Group at (800) 227-4908 or (513) 859-5398 inside the US, or (513) 865-7981 for all inquiries outside the US.

User info: To subscribe, contact Mead directly.

To examine the Nexis user guide, you can access it at the ftp site of the University of Texas at Austin at the URL address: ftp://ftp.cc.utexas.edu

The files are in: /pub/ref-services/LEXIS

`telnet://nex.meaddata.com`

`http://www.meaddata.com`

Enviroethics

A mailing list for the scholarly discussion of environmental ethics and philosophy.

Keywords: Environment, Environmental Studies

Audience: Environmental Researchers, Environmental Scientists, Environmentalists

Contact: Clare Palmer, Ian Tilsed C.A. Palmer@greenwich.ac.uk, I.J. Tilsed@exeter.ac.uk

User info: To subscribe, send an e-mail message to the URL address below consisting of a single line reading:

join enviroethics YourFirstName YourLastName

To obtain a list of archived files, send an e-mail message with the body 'index enviroethics' to the same address.

`mailto:mailbase@mailbase.ac.uk`

ESRI (Environmental Systems Research Institute)

Environmental Systems Research Institute, Inc. is the world leader in GIS technology. ARC/INFO is ESRI's powerful and flexible flagship GIS software.

Keywords: Geographic Information Systems (GIS), Environment, Software, Computers

Audience: Geographers, Environmentalists, Computer Users

Details: Costs

For product information, call (909)793-2853, X1475.

For training information, call (909)793-2853, X1585, or fax (909)793-5953.

`mailto:ajackson@esri.com`

GIS-L

A forum for the discussion of all issues pertaining to GIS (Geographic Information Systems), including hydrological modeling, environmental issues, and available software packages.

Keywords: Geography, Environment, GIS (Geographical Information Systems)

Audience: Geographers, Cartographers

Contact: David Mark dmark@acsu.buffalo.edu

User info: To subscribe to the list, send an e-mail message to the URL address below consisting of a single line reading:

SUB gis-l YourFirstName YourLastName

To send a message to the entire list, address it to: gis-l@ubvm.cc.buffalo.edu

`mailto:listserv@ubvm.cc.buffalo.edu`

Global Change Information Gateway

This gateway was created to address environmental data management issues raised by the US Congress, the Administration, and the advisory arms of the Federal policy community. It contains documents related to the UN conference on Environment and Development.

Keywords: United Nations, Environment, Development, Oceans, Atmosphere

Audience: Environmentalists, Scientists, Researchers

Details: Free

Notes: Select from menu as appropriate.

`gopher://scilibx.ucsc.edu`

National Oceanic & Atmospheric Administration (NOAA) Office of Environmental Safety and Health, Department of Energy

The NOAA catalog provides keyword access to sources of environmental information in the US. Gopher for resources pertaining to health and environmental safety.

Keywords: Environment, Oceans, Atmospheric Science, Health, Environmental Safety

Sponsor: National Oceanic & Atmospheric Administration (NOAA)

Department of Energy (USA)

Audience: Environmental Scientists, Researchers, Environmentalists, Epidemiologists, Public Health Officials

Details: Free

`gopher://scilibx.ucsc.edu`

`gopher://gopher.ns.doc.gov`

NativeNet

Provides information about and discusses issues relating to indigenous people around the world, including threats to their cultures and habitats (e.g. rainforests).

Keywords: Indigenous People, Environment, Anthroplogy

Audience: Anthropologists, Environmentalists, Indigenous People

Contact: Gary S. Trujillo gst@gnosys.svle.ma.us

A
B
C
D
E
F
G
H
I
J
K
L
M
N
O
P
Q
R
S
T
U
V
W
X
Y
Z

Details: Free

User info: To subscribe to the list, send an e-mail message requesting a subscription to the URL address below.

`mailto:gst@gnosys.svle.ma.us`

Natural Resources Canada (NRCan) Gopher

This site offers information on forests, energy, mining, and geomatics from the Canadian government. Also has reports from the Geological Survey of Canada and an overview of NRCan statutes, organization, and personnel. Provides links to other Canadian environmental and government gophers.

Keywords: Canada, Environment, Geology, Forestry

Sponsor: The Department of Natural Resources, Canada

Audience: Canadians, Environmentalists, Environmental Researchers, Geologists

Contact: Bob Fillmore
fillmore@emr.ca

Notes: NRCan maintains a toll-free hotline - 1-800-267-5166

`gopher://gopher.emr.ca`

`http://www.emr.ca/`

sci.environment

A Usenet newsgroup providing information and discussion about the environment and ecology.

Keywords: Environment, Ecology

Audience: Environmentalists, ecologists, Earth Scientists

Details: Free

User info: To subscribe to this Usenet newsgroup, you need access to a newsreader.

`news:sci.environment`

Sense of Place

An electronic environmentalists magazine. The magazine incorporates graphics and text in a format specifically designed to be read on a Macintosh screen. You must have Hypercard version 2.1 or later.

Keywords: Environment, Ecology

Audience: Environmentalists

Contact: SOP@dartmouth.edu

Details: Costs

User info: To subscribe send electronic mail to SOP@dartmouth.edu

`gopher://gopher.dartmouth.edu/1/anonftp/pub/sop`

Solstice

★★★★

This file server provides state-of-the-art information on renewable energy, energy efficiency, the environment, and sustainable community development.

Keywords: Energy, Environment

Sponsor: The Center for Renewable Energy and Sustainable Technology (CREST)

Audience: Environmentalists, Urban Planners, Educators, Students

Contact: www-content@solstice.crest.org

Details: Free

Login: anonymous, Password: e-mail

`http://solstice.crest.org/`

South Florida Environmental Reader

Newsletter distributing information on the environment of South Florida.

Keywords: Environment, Florida

Audience: Environmentalists

Contact: aem@mthvax.cs.miami.edu

Details: Free

User info: To subscribe to the list, send an e-mail messgae requesting a subscription to the URL address below.

To send a mesage to the entire USL, address it to: sfer@mthvax.cs.miami.edu

`mail to:sfer-requesti@mthvax.cs.miami.edu`

United Nations

★★★

Includes full text of UN press releases, UN Conference on Environment and Development reports, UN Development Programme documents, U.N. telphone directories.

Keywords: UN, Environment, Development (International)

Audience: Researchers, Educators, Political Scientists, Environmentalists

Details: Free

`gopher://nywork1.undp.org`

US/Mexico Border Discussion List

★★

This group provides a forum for the discussion of issues pertaining to the US/Mexico border environment.

Keywords: Mexico, Environment, Latin American Culture

Sponsor: The US Environmental Protection Agency

Audience: Activists, Environmentalists, Urban Planners

Details: Free

User info: To subscribe to the list, send a message to the URL address below consisting of a single line reading:

SUB us_mexborder YourFirstName YourLastName

To send a message to the entire list, address it to: us_mexborder@unixmail.rtpnc.epa.gov

`mailto:
listserver@unixmail.rtpnc.epa.gov`

Environmental Health

Safety (Environmental Health and Safety Discussion List)

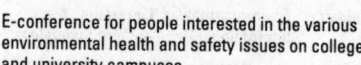

E-conference for people interested in the various environmental health and safety issues on college and university campuses.

Keywords: Environmental Health, Safety, Health

Audience: Students (College/University), Educators (college/University)

Contact: Ralph Stuart, Dayna Flath
rstuart@moose.uvm.edu
dmf@uvmvm.uvm.edu

Details: Free

User info: To subscribe to the list, send an e-mail message to the URL address below, consisting of a single line reading:

SUB safety YourFirstName YourLastName

To send a message to the entire list, address it to: safety@uvmvm.uvm.edu

`mailto:listserv@uvmvm.uvm.edu`

Environmental Policies

US Department of the Interior

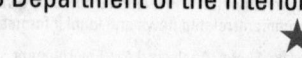

This resource contains Internet links to the Bureau of Indian Affairs, Bureau of Land Management, Bureau of Reclamation, National Biological Survey, National Park Service, and the US Fish and Wildlife Service.

Keywords: Government (US), Environmental Policies

Sponsor: US Department of the Interior Survey, Office of Public Affairs

Audience: Biologists, Geologists, Researchers, Environmentalists

`http://info.er.usgs.gov/doi/doi.html`

Environmental Safety

National Oceanic & Atmospheric Administration (NOAA)
Office of Environmental Safety and Health, Department of Energy

The NOAA catalog provides keyword access to sources of environmental information in the US. Gopher for resources pertaining to health and environmental safety.

Keywords: Environment, Oceans, Atmospheric Science, Health, Environmental Safety

Sponsor: National Oceanic & Atmospheric Administration (NOAA)

Department of Energy (USA)

Audience: Environmental Scientists, Researchers, Environmentalists, Epidemiologists, Public Health Officials

Details: Free

`gopher://scilibx.ucsc.edu`

`gopher://gopher.ns.doc.gov`

Office of Environmental Safety and Health, Department of Energy

Gopher for resources pertaining to health and environmental safety.

Keywords: Health, Environmental Safety

Sponsor: Department of Energy (US)

Audience: Epidemiologists, Public Health Policymakers, General Public

Details: Free

`gopher://gopher.ns.doc.gov`

Environmental Studies

Enviroethics

A mailing list for the scholarly discussion of environmental ethics and philosophy.

Keywords: Environment, Environmental Studies

Audience: Environmental Researchers, Environmental Scientists, Environmentalists

Contact: Clare Palmer, Ian Tilsed
C.A.Palmer@greenwich.ac.uk, I.J.Tilsed@exeter.ac.uk

User info: To subscribe, send an e-mail message to the URL address below consisting of a single line reading:

join enviroethics YourFirstName YourLastName

To obtain a list of archived files, send an e-mail message with the body 'index enviroethics' to the same address.

`mailto:mailbase@mailbase.ac.uk`

Solid Waste Recycling

The text of an eight-lesson correspondence class designed to teach the basics of setting up a successful recycling program.

Keywords: Recycling, Environmental Studies

Sponsor: University of Wisconsin

Audience: Environmentalists, Educators, Students

Contact: Judy Faber
faber@engr.wisc.edu

`gopher://wissago.uwex.edu/11/uwex/course/recycling`

University of Wisconsin Green Bay Library

The library's holdings are large and wide-ranging and contain significant collections in many fields.

Keywords: Economics, Environmental Studies, Music, Natural Science

Audience: Researchers, Students, General Public

Details: Free

User Info: Expect: Service Name, Send: Victor

`telnet://gbls2k.uwgb.edu`

University of Wisconsin Stevens Point Library

The library's holdings are large and wide-ranging and contain significant collections in many fields.

Keywords: Education, Environmental Studies, Ethnic Studies, History (US)

Audience: Researchers, Students, General Public

Details: Free

User Info: Expect: Login; Send: Lib; Expect: vDIAL Prompt, Send: Library

`telnet://lib.uwsp.edu`

Environmentalism

Western Lands

A collection of articles and reports relating to environmental and land use issues in the Western United States.

Keywords: Environmentalism, Ecology, Forests, The Western United States

Sponsor: The Institute for Global Communications (IGC)

Audience: Environmentalists, Ecologists, Activists, Foresters, Citizens

Contact: Dan Yurman, IGC User Support
dyurman@igc.apc.com
support@igc.apc.com

Notes: User submissions encouraged.

`gopher://gopher.igc.apc.org/11/environment/forests/western.lands`

Enzymes

REBASE (Restriction Enzyme Database)

The Restriction Enzyme Database contains both data and literature citations. It can be searched for enzyme names, species, authors, journals, and recognition sequences.

Keywords: Physiology, Enzymes

Sponsor: New England Biolabs

Audience: Scientists, Molecular Biologists

Contact: Richard Roberts
roberts@cshl.org

Details: Free

`gopher://gopher.gdb.org/77/.INDEX/rebase`

EPPD-L

EPPD-L

Engineering and Public Policy Discussion List.

Keywords: Engineering, Public Policy

Audience: Engineers

Contact: Ken Sollows
listserv@unb.ca

Details: Free

User info: To subscribe to the list, send an e-mail message to the URL address shown below consiting of a single line reading:

SUB eppd-l YourFirstName YourLastName

To send a message to the entire list, address it to:

EPPD-L@UNB.CA

`"Contact the Moderator" (ie: ContactŌs Email)`

Equestrians

rec.equestrian

A Usenet newsgroup providing information and discussion about all things pertaining to horses.

Keywords: Horses, Equestrians, Animals, Sports

A
B
C
D
E
F
G
H
I
J
K
L
M
N
O
P
Q
R
S
T
U
V
W
X
Y
Z

A
B
C
D
E
F
G
H
I
J
K
L
M
N
O
P
Q
R
S
T
U
V
W
X
Y
Z

Audience: Horse Riders, Horse Trainers, Horse Owners

User info: To subscribe to this Usenet newsgroup, you need access to a newsreader.

`news:rec.equestrian`

Equine Research

The University of Minnesota Library System (LUMINA) ★★

The library's holdings are large and wide-ranging and contain significant collections in many fields.

Keywords: Immigration (History of), Ethnic Studies, Horticulture, Equine Research, Botanical Taxonomy, Quantum Physics, Native American Studies, Holmes (Sherlock)

Audience: General Public, Researchers, Librarians, Document Delivery Professionals

Contact: Craig D. Rice
cdr@acc.stolaf.edu

Details: Free

`telnet://lumina.lib.umn.edu`

Ergonomics

HFS-L ★★

Human Factors and Ergonomics Society, Virginia Tech Chapter.

Keywords: Ergonomics, Physical Therapy

Audience: Researchers, Physical Therapists, Designers

Contact: Cortney Vargo
CORTV@VTVM1.CC.VT.EDU

Details: Free

User info: To subscribe to the list, send an e-mail message to the URL address shown below consiting of a single line reading:

SUB hfs-l YourFirstName YourLastName

To send a message to the entire list, address it to: hfs-l@vtvm1.cc.vt.edu

`listserv@vtvm1.cc.vt.edu`

Loughborough University of Technology Computer-Human Interaction (LUTCHI) Research Centre ★★★★

This server contains general information on computer-human interaction.

Keywords: Interface Design, Ergonomics, Computer-Human Interactions, Programming

Sponsor: Loughborough University of Technology, Leicestershire, UK

Audience: Software Developers, Software Designers, Programmers

Profile: The LUTCHI Research Centre is based within the Department of Computer Studies at the Loughborough University of Technology, Leicestershire, UK. This server contains information about LUTCHI research projects, official LUTCHI publicity releases, as well as documents, images, and movies associated with those projects.

Contact: Ben Anderson
B.Anderson@lut.ac.uk

Details: Free, Moderated, Image and Sound files available. Multimedia files available.

Use a World-Wide Web (Mosaic) client and open a connection to the resource.

`http://pipkin.lut.ac.uk`

ERIC (Educational Resources Information Center)

ERIC (Educational Resources Information Center) ★★★

ERIC is a database of short abstracts and information about education-related topics of interest to teachers and administrators.

Keywords: Education, Databases

Sponsor: (Office of Educational Research and Development), US Department of Education

Department of Education (ED)

Audience: Educators, Administrators

Profile: ERIC is the complete database on educational materials from the Educational Resources Information Center in Washington, DC. The database corresponds to two print indexes: Resources in Education, which is concerned with identifying the most significant and timely education research reports; and Current Index to Journals in Education, an index of more than 700 periodicals of interest to every segment of the teaching profession.

Details: Costs

ERIC can be accessed in a variety of ways, for example, through CARL (Colorado Alliance of Research Libraries), through the University of Saskatchewan

(Request: sklib username: sonia)

ERIC can also be accessed by WAIS if you have WAIS installed on your local computer.

`telnet://pac.carl.org`

`telnet://skdevel12.usask.ca`

Erofile

Erofile ★

This newsletter provides reviews of the latest books associated with French and Italian studies in fields such as literary criticism, cultural studies, film studies, pedagogy, and software.

Keywords: Italian Studies, French Studies, Book Reviews

Audience: French Students, Italian Students, Book Reviewers

Details: Free

`mailto:erofile@ucsbuxa.ucsb.edu`

Esbdc-l

Esbdc-l ★★

A mailing list intended to facilitate discussion between small business development centers, focusing on such topics as performance standards, business behavior, products, specific industry information access, deficit reduction plans, and private cost sharing.

Keywords: Business, Small Business

Sponsor: Association of Small Business Development Centers, USA

Audience: State Officials, Educators, Certified Public Accountants, Investors

User info: To subscribe to the list, send an e-mail message to the URL address below consisting of a single line reading:

SUB esbdc-l YourFirstName YourLastName

To send a message to the entire list, address it to: esbdc-l@ferris.bitnet

`mailto:listserv@ferris.bitnet`

ESL (English as a Second Language)

Bilingual Education Network ★

This gopher site contains bilingual and bicultural, ESL (English as a Second Language), and Foreign Language resources and curriculum guidelines.

Keywords: ESL (English as a Second Language), Education (Bilingual)

Sponsor: California Department of Education, California, USA

Audience: Educators, Administrators, Parents

`gopher://goldmine.cde.ca.gov`

ESRI (Environmental Systems Research Institute)

ESRI (Environmental Systems Research Institute)

Environmental Systems Research Institute, Inc. is the world leader in GIS technology. ARC/INFO is ESRIŌs powerful and flexible flagship GIS software.

Keywords: Geographic Information Systems (GIS), Environment, Software, Computers

Audience: Geographers, Environmentalists, Computer Users

Details: Costs

For product information, call (909)793-2853, X1475.

For training information, call (909)793-2853, X1585, or fax (909)793-5953.

`mailto:ajackson@esri.com`

Essence

Essence

A description of Essence, an Internet resource discovery system based on semantic file indexing.

Keywords: Internet Tools, Essence (Internet Resource Directory)

Sponsor: University of Colorado, Boulder, CO

Audience: Internet Surfers

Contact: Darren R. Hardy, Michael F. Schwartz
hardy@cs.colorado.edu
schwartz@cs.colorado.edu

Details: Free

File is: pub/cs/distribs/essence/README

`ftp://.cs.colorado.edu`

Estonia

Balt-L

A forum devoted to communications to and about the Baltic Republics of Lithuania, Latvia, and Estonia.

Keywords: Lithuania, Latvia, Estonia, Baltic Republics

Audience: Researchers, Baltic Nationals

Contact: Jean-Michel Thizy
jmyhg@uottawa.edu

Details: Free

User info: To subscribe to the list, send an e-mail message to the URL address below, consisting of a single line reading:

SUB balt-l YourFirstName YourLastName

`mailto:listserv@ubvm.cc.buffalo.edu`

Ethics

ETHCSE-L

A mailing list for the discussion of Ethical Issues in Software Engineering, dealing with subjects of interest to professional software engineers.

Keywords: Engineering, Computing, Ethics

Audience: Engineers, Software Engineers, Researchers

Contact: Margaret Mason
mason@utkvml.utk.edu

Details: Free

User info: To subscribe to the list, send an e-mail message to the URL address shown below consisting of a single line reading:

SUB ethcse-l YourFirstName YourLastName

To send a message to the entire list, address it to:

ethsce-l@utkvm1.utk.edu

`mailto:listserv@utkvm1.utk.edu`

misc.legal

A Usenet newsgroup providing information and discussion about law and ethics.

Keywords: Law, Ethics

Audience: Lawyers, Legal Professionals, General Public

Details: Free

User info: To subscribe to this Usenet newsgroup, you need access to a newsreader.

`news:misc.legal`

Mother Jones

A web site containing online electronic issues of Mother Jones magazine (and Zine), making possible instant electronic feedback to the publishers regarding articles.

Keywords: Zines, Ethics, Public Policy, Activism

Sponsor: Mother Jones

Audience: Students, General Public

Contact: Webserver
webserver@mojones.com

`http://www.mojones.com/motherjones.html`

---

talk.religion.misc

A Usenet newsgroup providing information and discussion about religious, ethical, and moral implications.

Keywords: Religion, Ethics

Audience: General Public, Researchers, Students

Details: Free

User info: To subscribe to this Usenet newsgroup, you need access to a newsreader.

`news:talk.religion.misc`

Ethnic Studies

Geneology

A large collection of geneology resources for both beginners and specialists. Includes archives of geneology lists, FAQs, helper software, and specific geneological information for a number of national and ethnic groups.

Keywords: Geneology, Ethnic Studies

Sponsor: Go M-Link at the University of Michigan

Audience: Geneologists, General Public, Researchers

Contact: Sue Davidsen
davidsen@umich.edu

`gopher://vienna.hh.lib.umich.edu`

The University of Minnesota Library System (LUMINA)

The library's holdings are large and wide-ranging and contain significant collections in many fields.

Keywords: Immigration (History of), Ethnic Studies, Horticulture, Equine Research, Botanical Taxonomy, Quantum Physics, Native American Studies, Holmes (Sherlock)

Audience: General Public, Researchers, Librarians, Document Delivery Professionals

Contact: Craig D. Rice
cdr@acc.stolaf.edu

Details: Free

`telnet://lumina.lib.umn.edu`

University of Wisconsin Stevens Point Library

The library's holdings are large and wide-ranging and contain significant collections in many fields.

Keywords: Education, Environmental Studies, Ethnic Studies, History (US)

Audience: Researchers, Students, General Public

Details: Free

User Info: Expect: Login; Send: Lib; Expect: vDIAL Prompt, Send: Library

`telnet://lib.uwsp.edu`

A B C D E F G H I J K L M N O P Q R S T U V W X Y Z

A
B
C
D
E
F
G
H
I
J
K
L
M
N
O
P
Q
R
S
T
U
V
W
X
Y
Z

Ethnicity

POS302-L

A discussion list created for the "Race, Ethnicity, and Social Inequality" seminar offered at Illinois State University (spring 1994). The general purposes of the list are to create an e-mail audience for the written work of enrolled students and to invite a broad audience to participate in the seminar.

Keywords: Race, Ethnicity, Minorities

Audience: Ethnic Studies Students, Sociologists, Educators

Details: Free

User info: To subscribe to the list, send an e-mail message to the URL address below, consisting of a single line reading:

SUB pos302-l YourFirstName YourLastName

To send a message to the entire list, address it to: pos302-l@ilstu.edu

`mailto:listserv@ilstu.edu`

Ethnomusicology Research Digest

Ethnomusicology Research Digest

For subscribers with a professional interest in ethnomusicology, including news, discussion, queries, bibliographies, and archives. Subscription by permission only.

Keywords: Musicians, Ethnomusicology

Audience: Ethnomusicologists, Educators, Librarians, Researchers, Students

Contact: Karl Signell signell@umdd.umd.edu

Details: Free

User info: To subscribe, send an e-mail message to the address below consisting of a single line reading:

SUB ethmus-l YourFirstName YourLastName

To send a message to the entire list, address it to: ethmus-l@umdd.vmd.edu

`mailto:listserv@umdd.umd.edu`

Ethnomusicology

Ethnomusicology Research Digest

For subscribers with a professional interest in ethnomusicology, including news, discussion, queries, bibliographies, and archives. Subscription by permission only.

Keywords: Musicians, Ethnomusicology

Audience: Ethnomusicologists, Educators, Librarians, Researchers, Students

Contact: Karl Signell signell@umdd.umd.edu

Details: Free

User info: To subscribe, send an e-mail message to the address below consisting of a single line reading:

SUB ethmus-l YourFirstName YourLastName

To send a message to the entire list, address it to: ethmus-l@umdd.vmd.edu

`mailto:listserv@umdd.umd.edu`

Etiquette

Net Etiquette Guide

Guidelines and netiquette for the Net user.

Keywords: Internet, Etiquette, Netiquette

Sponsor: SURAnet Network Information Center

Audience: Internet Surfers

Contact: info@sura.net

Details: Free

File is: pub/nic/internet.literature/netiquette.txt

`ftp://ftp.sura.net`

euitnews (Educational Uses of Information Technology)

euitnews (Educational Uses of Information Technology)

EDUCOM's newsletter for the Educational Uses of Information Technology program encompasses distance learning, self-paced instruction, computer-aided instruction, video, and other information technologies for teaching and learning.

Keywords: Education (Continuing), Information Technology

Audience: Administrators, K-12 Educators

Details: Free

User info: To subscribe to the newsletter, send an e-mail message to the URL address below consisting of a single line reading:

SUB euitnews YourFirstName YourLastName

`mailto:listserv@bitnic.educom.edu`

EUnet

EUnet

A global Internet Service Provider with national providers in almost 30 countries. Applications such as customer support, remote diagnosis, software development tools, and product information are available through this net.

Keywords: Internet

Sponsor: EUnet Information Services

Audience: Internet Surfers

Contact: info@eu.net

Details: Free

`http://www.eu.net`

EUnet Czechia

EUnet Czechia

This is the information service of EUnet Czechia, the network service provider in the Czech Republic and contains information about top-level domains.

Keywords: Czech Republic

Audience: Czechs, General Public

Contact: gopher.eunet.cz

Details: Free

`http://www.eunet.cz`

Euromath

Euromath Center Gopher Server

A gopher server providing information about the Euromath Center, the Euromath Project, and related activities.

Keywords: Europe, Mathematics, Euromath

Sponsor: University of Copenhagen

Audience: Mathematicians, Europeans

Contact: Klaus Harbo emc@euromath.dk

Details: Free

`gopher://laurel.euromath.dk`

Europe

(The) Worldwide Impact of Network Access

This is an article by community networker Felipe Rodriquez. In this statement Rodriquez argues that developed countries should help less developed countries build their information infrastructures, and that governments should not censor the content of network traffic.

Keywords: Community, Networking, Europe, Development (International)

Audience: Activists, Policymakers, Community Leaders

Contact: Felipe Rodriquez
felipe@hacktic.nl

`http://nearnet.gnn.com/mag/articles/oram/bio.rodriquez.html`

Agence FrancePresse International French Wire

Agence FrancePresse International French Wire provides full-text articles in French relating to national, international, business, and sports news.

Keywords: News Media, Europe, Third World, French

Sponsor: Agence FrancePresse, Paris, France

Audience: Market Researchers, Journalists, Francophiles

Profile: Agence FrancePresse distributes its French service worldwide, including Western and Eastern Europe, Canada, northern and western Africa, the Middle East, Vietnam, French Guiana, the West Indies, and the French Pacific islands. Agence FrancePresse International French Wire has extensive coverage of the European countries, including every aspect of economic, political, and general business news. It also provides excellent industrial and market news from both developed countries and from the Third World.

Coverage: September 1991 to the present; updated daily.

Contact: Dialog in the US at (800) 334-2564; Dialog internationally at country-specific locations.

Details: Costs

Notes: To subscribe, contact Dialog directly.

`telnet://dialog.com`

ASTRA-UG

A mailing list for the discussion of Italian and European GIS.

Keywords: (Geographical Information Systems), Europe, Italy

Audience: Geographers, Cartographers, Europeans

Details: Free

User info: To subscribe to the list, send an e-mail mesage to the URL address below, consisting of a single line reading:

SUB ASTRA-UG YourFirstName YourLastName

`astra-ug@icnucevm`

BFU (Brussels Free Universities)

The gopher server of the Brussels Free Universities VUB /ULB is the national entry point for EMBnet in Belgium and provides links to university library systems and EMBnet databases.

Keywords: Computing, EMBnet, Belgium, Europe

Audience: Scientists, Biologists, Biotechnologists

Contact: support@vub.ac.be

Details: Free

`gopher://gopher.vub.ac.be`

CEDAR (Central European Environmental Data Request) Facility

This gopher site provides information about the environmental and scientific community in Central and Eastern Europe (CEE), with access to environmental information located throughout the world on various international computer networks and hosts.

Keywords: Europe, EEC, Environment

Sponsor: The International Society for Environmental Protection, and The Austrian Federal Ministry for Environment, Youth and Family (BMUJF)

Audience: Environmentalists, Educators, Students, Urban Planners

Contact: cedar-info@cedar.univie.ac.at

Notes: CEDAR Marxergasse 3/20, A-1030 Vienna, Austria Tel.: +43-1-715 58 79

`gopher://pan.cedar.univie.ac.at`

Central European Environment Data Report (CEDAR) Facility

This gopher site provides information about the environmental and scientific community in Central and Eastern Europe, with access to environmental information located throughout the world on various international computer networks and hosts.

Keywords: Europe, Central Europe, Eastern Europe, Environment

Sponsor: The International Society for Environmental Protection, and The Austrian Federal Ministry for Environment, Youth and Family (BMUJF)

Audience: Environmentalists, Educators, Students, Urban Planners, Environmental Scientists

Profile: The CEDAR Facility, established in 1991, is administered by the International Society for Environmental Protection (ISEP). The Facility is designed to provide regional groups and individuals with access to its information retrieval and higher computing resources, technical advice and database and network access support. In addition, CEDAR works to facilitate information and dialogue exchange with organizations in other parts of the world and in partner countries; and to promote training forums, including the joint development of seminars and conferences with ISEP on environmental and network topics. Finally, CEDAR develops and manages environmental reference data sets, including a US EPA bibliographic reference on hazardous waste treatment, CEDAR databases on Central and Eastern European environmental expertise and information, and the holdings of the Regional Environmental Center Library at Budapest.

Contact: cedar-info@cedar.univie.ac.at

`gopher://pan.cedar.univie.ac.at`

CILEA (Consorzio Interuniversitario Lombardo per la Elaborazione Automatica)

The gopher for the InterUniversity Computer Center, Milan, Italy, provides access to CILEA hosts, databases in Europe, CERN (European Laboratory for Particle Physics) services such as WWW and ALICE, Usenet newsgroups, PostScript documentation on various items, Italian research network information, and more.

Keywords: Informatics, Italy, Europe

Audience: Particle physicists, Researchers

Contact: Luciano Guglielm
guglielm@imicilea.cilea.it

Details: Free

`gopher://imicilea.cilea.it`

D&B - European Dun's Market (EDMI)

This database presents detailed information on over 2.5 million businesses located in 26 European countries.

Keywords: Dun & Bradstreet, Europe, Business

Sponsor: Dun & Bradstreet Information Services, Parsippany, NJ, USA

Audience: Business Professionals, Business Analysts

Profile: EDMI provides directory listings, sales volume and marketing data, and references to parent companies. Companies are selected for inclusion based on sales volume, national prominence, and international interest. Names, addresses, SIC codes, D-U-N-S numbers, and other data are given in each record. Both public and private companies are included.

A B C D E F G H I J K L M N O P Q R S T U V W X Y Z

A
B
C
D
E
F
G
H
I
J
K
L
M
N
O
P
Q
R
S
T
U
V
W
X
Y
Z

Contact: Dialog in the US at (800) 334-2564, Dialog internationally at country-specific locations.

User info: To subscribe, contact Dialog directly.

Notes: Coverage: Current; updated quarterly.

`telnet://dialog.com`

Delphes European Business

This is a French database that provides information on international markets, products, industries, and companies from a European perspective.

Keywords: Business, Europe

Sponsor: Chamber of Commerce and Industry of Paris and The French Assembly of the Chambers of Commerce and Industry, Paris, France

Audience: Business Professionals, Business Analysts

Profile: Abstracts are produced by approximately 60 local organizations grouped into two networks, CCIP (Chamber of Commerce and Industry of Paris) and ACFCI (French Assembly of the Chambers of Commerce and Industry), which collect and consolidate the information into the Delphes database. Delphes contains bibliographic citations and informative abstracts from over 900 European trade journals, newspapers, and business periodicals, in French, English, Italian, German, or Spanish. Titles are in the original language; abstracts are in French. A comprehensive classification scheme in English, French, and Spanish is used to index documents covered. Geographic coverage is 45% France, 35% Europe, and 20% is devoted to other countries. In addition, about 1,000 new books, corporate and business directories, and reports are reviewed each year.

Contact: Dialog in the US at (800) 334-2564, Dialog internationally at country-specific locations.

User info: To subscribe, contact Dialog directly.

Notes: Coverage: 1980 to the present; updated weekly.

`telnet://dialog.com`

EC

Dedicated to discussion of the European Community (EC).

Keywords: European Community, Europe

Audience: Europeans, Researchers, General Public, Economists

Contact: John B. Harlan
             ijbh200@indyvax.iupiu.edu
             ec@vm.cc.metu.edu.tr

Details: Free

User info: To subscribe to the list, send an e-mail message to the URL address shown below consisting of a single line reading:

             SUB ec YourFirstName YourLastName

`mailto:listserv@linycms.iupiu.edu`

Euromath Center Gopher Server

A gopher server providing information about the Euromath Center, the Euromath Project, and related activities.

Keywords: Europe, Mathematics, Euromath

Sponsor: University of Copenhagen

Audience: Mathematicians, Europeans

Contact: Klaus Harbo
             emc@euromath.dk

Details: Free

`gopher://laurel.euromath.dk`

EUROPE (European News Library)

The Europe library contains detailed information about every country in Eastern, Central and Western Europe.

Keywords: Business, Europe

Audience: Business Researchers, Analysts, Entrepreneurs, Regulatory Agencies

Profile: EUROPE is designed for those who need to monitor countries of the European Community, the European Free Trade Association, or emerging European market economies. This library includes a wide array of sources: Among the information sources are: newspapers and wire services, trade and business journals, company reports, country and region background, industry and product analyses, business opportunities, and selected legal texts. News sources range from the world-renowned Financial Times and Reuters to the regionally important PAP and CTK newswires. EIS's European newsletters and Euroscipe from Coopers and Lybrand help analyze the legal and business environment in Western Europe. Company information is contained in the EXTEL cards as well as ICC.

Contact: Mead New Sales Group at (800) 227-4908 or (513) 859-5398 inside the US, or (513) 865-7981 for all inquiries outside the US.

User info: To subscribe, contact Mead directly.

             To examine the Nexis user guide, you can access it at the ftp site of the University of Texas at Austin at the URL address: ftp://ftp.cc.utexas.edu

             The files are in: /pub/ref-services/LEXIS

`telnet://nex.meaddata.com`

`http://www.meaddata.com`

European Patents Fulltext

European Patents Fulltext contains the complete text of European published applications and patents and European PCT published applications.

Keywords: Patents, Europe, Law (International)

Sponsor: European Patent Office, Vienna, Austria

Audience: Patent Researchers

Profile: It contains bibliographic, administrative, and legal information from the European Patent Registry. Records have abstracts, patent specifications including all claims, and the search report, including cited patents and other references.

Contact: Dialog in the US at (800) 334-2564, Dialog internationally at country-specific locations.

User info: To subscribe, contact Dialog directly.

Notes: Coverage: 1978 to the present; updated weekly.

`telnet://dialog.com`

European Root Gopher

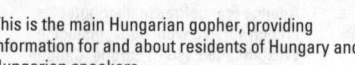

A root gopher server and registry for European gophers run by the Swedish University Network to serve European users.

Keywords: Europe, Gophers

Sponsor: Swedish University Computer Network (SUNET)

Audience: European Internet Surfers

Contact: gopher-info@sunic.sunet.se

Details: Free

`gopher://gopher@sunet.se`

Hungarian Gopher—Hollosi Information Exchange (HIX)

This is the main Hungarian gopher, providing information for and about residents of Hungary and Hungarian speakers.

Keywords: Hungary, Europe

Sponsor: Stanford University, Palo Alto, CA

Audience: Hungarian Internet Surfers

Contact: hollosi@andrea.standford.edu

Details: Free

`gopher://hix.elte.hu`

ICGEBnet

This is the information server of the International Centre for Genetic Engineering and Molecular Biology (ICGEB), Trieste, Italy.

Keywords: Molecular Biology, Biotechnology, Italy, Europe

Audience: Molecular Biotechnologists, Molecular Biologists

Profile: The primary purpose of the ICGEB computer resource is to disseminate the best of currently available computational technology to the molecular biologists of the ICGEB research community.

Contact: postmaster@icgeb.trieste.it

Details: Free

`gopher://icgeb.trieste.it`

ICTP (International Centre for Theoretical Physics) ★

ICTP's gopher disseminates information regarding the many scientific activities carried out at ICTP (Trieste, Italy). Information is also provided on the scientific publications, courses, and other services offered by ICS (International Centre for Science and High Technology) and TWAS (Third World Academy of Sciences) at Trieste.

Keywords: Theoretical Physics, Italy, Europe

Audience: Physicists

Profile: Topics include programming techniques, theoretical aspects, Icon in relation to other languages, applications of Icon, implementation issues, porting, and bugs.

Contact: admin@ictp.trieste.it

Details: Free

`gopher://gopher.ictp.trieste.it`

`http://gopher.ictp.trieste.it`

Imperial College Department of Computing ★★

This is the home of the department of Computing, Imperial College, United Kingdom, the UKUUG (UK UNIX User Group) Archive and the DoC Information Service.

Keywords: Computing, United Kingdom, Europe

Audience: Computer Scientists

Contact: imjm@doc.ic.ac.uk

Details: Free

`gopher://src.doc.ic.ac.uk`

`http://src.doc.ic.ac.uk`

Information Services in Germany ★

This gopher is an informal entry point for Germany, together with some hints to specialties in German information systems.

Keywords: Germany, Information, Europe

Audience: German Internet Surfers

Contact: lange@rz.tu-clausthal.de

Details: Free

`gopher://gopher.tu-clausthal.de`

IST BioGopher ★

This is the gopher server of the National Institute for Cancer Research (IST) and of the Advanced Biotechnology Center of Genoa, Italy.

Keywords: Cancer, Biotechnology, Italy, Europe

Audience: Biologists, Medical Researchers

Profile: The server includes data from the Interlab Project Databases (biological materials availability in European laboratories) and the Bio-Media Bulletin Board System (biotechnology researchers, projects, fundings and products).

Contact: gophman@istge.ist.unige.it

Details: Free

`gopher://istge.ist.unige.it`

Lysator's Gopher Service ★

Lysator is the name of the Academic Computer Society at Linkoping University, Linkoping, Sweden. It relies on voluntary efforts by students, and any service of activity runs as long as they think it is fun—content always reflects their personal interests.

Keywords: Sweden, Students, Europe

Audience: Swedish Students

Contact: Lars Aronsson@lysator.liu.se

Details: Free

`gopher://gopher.lysator.liu.se`

`http://dla.ucop.edu`

Maastricht Treaty ★

The file contains the text of the latest edition of the Treaty on European Union, also known as the Maastricht Treaty, signed on February 7, 1992.

Keywords: Europe, European Union, Maastricht Treaty

Audience: Politicians, Historians, Europeans, Political Scientists, General Public

Details: Free

Select from menu as appropriate.

`gopher://wiretap.spies.com`

NORDUnet region Root Gopher ★

The Nordic University and Research Network is a collaboration by the national research networks in Denmark, Finland, Iceland, Norway, and Sweden. It provides the national research and education communities with an efficient networking service that ensures the coherence of the national networks and connects these to similar networks in the rest of Europe and the world.

Keywords: Nordic University, Europe

Audience: Nordic Internet Surfers

Contact: hostmaster@nic.nordu.net

Details: Free

`gopher://gopher.nordu.net`

OLIS (Oxford University Library Information Service) Gopher ★★

OLIS is a network of libraries. It contains all the books from the English, Modern Languages, Social Studies, and Hooke libraries. It also contains books and journals cataloged since September 1988 in the Bodleian and Dependant libraries and the Taylor Institution. Books can be searched in any OLIS library from any location.

Keywords: Libraries, United Kingdom, Europe

Audience: Library Users

Contact: jose@olis.lib.ox.ac.uk

Details: Free

`gopher://gopher.lib.ox.ac.uk/00/Info/OLIS`

Prague University of Economics Gopher Service ★★

Includes information about the University, integrative studies of economy, economic information, and public domain software.

Keywords: Czech Republic, Economics, Europe

Audience: Czechs, Economists

Contact: gopher@pub.vse.cz

Details: Free

`gopher://pub.vse.cz`

RIPE Network Coordination Centre Gopher ★

RIPE (Reseaux IP Europeens) is a collaborative organization open to all European Internet service providers. RIPE coordinates the operation of a pan-European IP network. In November 1993, more than 500,000 hosts throughout Europe were reachable via networks coordinated by RIPE.

Keywords: Europe, Networks

Audience: European Internet Surfers

Contact: ncc@ripe.net

Details: Free

`gopher://gopher.ripe.net`

soc.culture.europe ★

A Usenet newsgroup providing information and discussion about all aspects of Europe.

Keywords: Europe, Sociology

Audience: Sociologists, Europeans

Details: Free

User info: To subscribe to this Usenet newsgroup, you need access to a newsreader.

`news:soc.culture.europe`

A B C D E F G H I J K L M N O P Q R S T U V W X Y Z

A
B
C
D
E
F
G
H
I
J
K
L
M
N
O
P
Q
R
S
T
U
V
W
X
Y
Z

SURFnet—KB InfoServer

InfoService is a joint project by SURFnet (National Network Organization for Research and Higher Education) and the Koninklijke Bibliotheek (National Library of the Netherlands).

Keywords: Netherlands, Networks, Europe

Audience: European Internet Surfers

Contact: infoservices@surfnet.nl

Details: Free

`gopher://gopher.nic.surfnet.nl`

Swiss Scientific Supercomputing Center (CSCS) Info Server ★

The Centro Svizzero di Calcolo Scientifico (CSCS) info server is the national scientific computing center in Switzerland.

Keywords: Switzerland, Supercomputing, Europe

Audience: Swiss Internet Surfers

Contact: mgay@cscs.ch

Details: Free

`gopher://pobox.cscs.ch`

University of Glasgow Information Service (GLANCE) ★★★★

GLANCE provides subject-based information services, including an extensive section on European and world sports.

Keywords: Sports, Soccer, Motor Racing, Mountaineering, Squash, Cricket, Golf, Tennis, Europe, Scotland

Sponsor: University of Glasgow, Glasgow, Scotland

Audience: Sport Enthusiasts, Fitness Enthusiasts, Nature Lovers

Profile: Information at this site includes schedules, results, and statistics for sports such as cricket and soccer. There is also a selection of items on mountaineering.

Contact: Alan Dawson A.Dawson@uk.ac.gla.compserv

Details: Free

`gopher://govan.cent.gla.ac.uk/Subject/Sports and Rec`

EUROPE (European News Library)

EUROPE (European News Library)

The Europe library contains detailed information about every country in Eastern, Central and Western Europe.

Keywords: Business, Europe

Audience: Business Researchers, Analysts, Entrepreneurs, Regulatory Agencies

Profile: EUROPE is designed for those who need to monitor countries of the European Community, the European Free Trade Association, or emerging European market economies. This library includes a wide array of sources: Among the information sources are: newspapers and wire services, trade and business journals, company reports, country and region background, industry and product analyses, business opportunities, and selected legal texts. News sources range from the world-renowned Financial Times and Reuters to the regionally important PAP and CTK newswires. EIS's European newsletters and Euroscipe from Coopers and Lybrand help analyze the legal and business environment in Western Europe. Company information is contained in the EXTEL cards as well as ICC.

Contact: Mead New Sales Group at (800) 227-4908 or (513) 859-5398 inside the US, or (513) 865-7981 for all inquiries outside the US.

User info: To subscribe, contact Mead directly.

To examine the Nexis user guide, you can access it at the ftp site of the University of Texas at Austin at the URL address: ftp://ftp.cc.utexas.edu

The files are in: /pub/ref-services/LEXIS

`telnet://nex.meaddata.com`

`http://www.meaddata.com`

European Community

DRT EC and Eastern Europe Business Database

DRTE's comprehensive full-text coverage of business and industry in the EC is combined with in-depth reporting on doing business in Eastern Europe.

Keywords: European Community, Eastern Europe.

Sponsor: DRT Europe Services Brussels, Belgium

Audience: Market Analysts, Business Professionals, Market Researchers

Profile: DRTE reports provide comprehensive and detailed coverage of all EC proposals, laws and policy directions and their commercial applications, and unique, country-specific information on the regulatory framework for business development and expansion in Eastern Europe. These are continually updated to reflect the rapidly changing nature of the political and administrative structure of these emerging economies as they affect business undertakings with EC concerns.

Contact: Data-star through Dialog in the US at (800) 334-2564, Dialog internationally at country-specific locations.

User info: To subscribe, contact Dialog directly.

Notes: Coverage: The database is updated weekly to enable it to offer exceptionally current full-text information.

`telnet://dialog.com`

EC ★

Dedicated to discussion of the European Community (EC).

Keywords: European Community, Europe

Audience: Europeans, Researchers, General Public, Economists

Contact: John B. Harlan ijbh200@indyvax.iupui.edu ec@vm.cc.metu.edu.tr

Details: Free

User info: To subscribe to the list, send an e-mail message to the URL address shown below consisting of a single line reading:

SUB ec YourFirstName YourLastName

`mailto:listserv@linycms.iupui.edu`

INTNAT (International Library)

The International library contains all French treaties, conventions and agreements that are effective today, as well as decisions from the Cour Europenne des Droits de l'Homme and the Cour de Justice des Communautes Europennes plus the Journal Officiel des Communautes Europenne.

Keywords: French Law, European Community

Audience: International Lawyers

Profile: The International library contains all French treaties, conventions and agreements published before 1958 that are in effect today, as well as decisions from the European Court of Human Rights (Cour Europeenne des Droits del'Homme), the European Court of Justice (Cour de Justice des Communautes Europeennes) and the Journal Officiel des Communautes Europeenne, the daily record of the European Community.

Contact: New Sales Group at 800-227-4908 or 513-859-5398 inside the US, or 1-513-865-7981 for all inquires outside the US.

User info: To subscribe, contact Mead directly.

To examine the Lexis user guide, you can access it at the ftp site of the University of Texas at Austin at the URL address: ftp://ftp.cc.utexas.edu

The files are in: /pub/ref-services/LEXIS

`telnet://nex.meaddata.com`

`http://www.meaddata.com`

European Documents

University of Hawaii Library

The library's holdings are large and wide-ranging and contain significant collections in many fields.

Keywords: Asia, European Documents, Book Arts, Hawaii

Audience: General Public, Researchers, Librarians, Document Delivery Professionals

Details: Free

User Info: Expect: enter class, Send: LIB

`telnet://starmaster.uhcc.hawaii.edu`

European Patents Fulltext

European Patents Fulltext

European Patents Fulltext contains the complete text of European published applications and patents and European PCT published applications.

Keywords: Patents, Europe, Law (International)

Sponsor: European Patent Office, Vienna, Austria

Audience: Patent Researchers

Profile: It contains bibliographic, administrative, and legal information from the European Patent Registry. Records have abstracts, patent specifications including all claims, and the search report, including cited patents and other references.

Contact: Dialog in the US at (800) 334-2564, Dialog internationally at country-specific locations.

User info: To subscribe, contact Dialog directly.

Notes: Coverage: 1978 to the present; updated weekly.

`telnet://dialog.com`

European Root Gopher

European Root Gopher

A root gopher server and registry for European gophers run by the Swedish University Network to serve European users.

Keywords: Europe, Gophers

Sponsor: Swedish University Computer Network (SUNET)

Audience: European Internet Surfers

Contact: gopher-info@sunic.sunet.se

Details: Free

`gopher://gopher@sunet.se`

European Space Agency

European Space Agency

A major directory on aeronautics, providing access to a broad range of related resources (library catalogs, databases, and servers) via the Internet.

Keywords: Space Science, Aeronautics

Audience: Space Science Researchers

Profile: The home page of the European Space Agency, including information about ESA's mission, specific ESA programs (Science, Manned Spaceflight and Microgravity, Earth Observation, Telecommunications, Launchers), and issues related to the space and aeronautics industry.

Contact: webmaster@esa.it

`http://www.esrin.esa.it`

European Union

Maastricht Treaty

The file contains the text of the latest edition of the Treaty on European Union, also known as the Maastricht Treaty, signed on February 7, 1992.

Keywords: Europe, European Union, Maastricht Treaty

Audience: Politicians, Historians, Europeans, Political Scientists, General Public

Details: Free

Select from menu as appropriate.

`gopher://wiretap.spies.com`

EUVE

Center for Extreme Ultraviolet Astrophysics

A department of the University of California at Berkeley devoted to research in extreme ultraviolet astronomy. It is the ground-based institution of EUVE (the Extreme Ultraviolet Explorer), a NASA satellite launched in 1992.

Keywords: Astronomy, Astrophysics, EUVE, NASA, Satellite

Sponsor: NASA and University of California at Berkeley

Audience: Astronomers, Astrophysicists

Profile: Provides access to details about the EUVE Guest Observer (EGO) Center, the EUVE Public Archive of Mission Data and Information, satellite operation information, and so on. The EUVE Guest Observer Center provides information, software, and data to EUVE Guest Observers.

Contact: egoinfo@cea.berkeley.edu
archive@cea.berkeley.edu

Details: Free

`http://cea-ftp.cea.berkeley.edu`

EV

EV

General list for discussion of all aspects of electric vehicles.

Keywords: Electric Vehicles

Audience: Electric Vehicle Enthusiasts

Contact: Clyde Visser
listserv@sjsuvm1.sjsu.edu

User info: To subscribe to the list, send an e-mail message to the URL address below consisting of a single line reading:

SUB electric-vehicle YourFirstName YourLastName

To send a message to the entire list, address it to: electric-vehicle@sjsuvm1.sjsu.edu

`mailto:listserv@sjsuvm1.sjsu.edu`

Evangelism

Catholic-action

Catholic-action is a moderated list concerned with Catholic evangelism, church revitalization, and preservation of Catholic teachings, traditions and values, and the vital effort to decapitate modernist heresy.

Keywords: Catholicism, Evangelism, Religion

Audience: Catholics, Priests

Contact: Richard Freeman
rfreeman@vpnet.chi.il.us

Details: Free

User info: To subscribe to the list, send an e-mail message requesting a subscription to the URL address below.

`mailto:rfreeman@vpnet.chi.il.us`

A B C D E F G H I J K L M N O P Q R S T U V W X Y Z

A
B
C
D
E
F
G
H
I
J
K
L
M
N
O
P
Q
R
S
T
U
V
W
X
Y
Z

Cell Church Discussion Group ★

A list for Christians who are in cell churches or in churches that are in transition to becoming cell churches, as well as anyone interested in learning more about cell churches. A cell church is a nontraditional form of church life in which small groups of Christians (cells) meet in a special way in their homes for the evangelism of the unchurched, the bonding of believers, their nurture, and ministry to one another.

Keywords: Cell Churches, Christianity, Evangelism, Religion

Audience: Christians, Theologians, Evangelists

Contact: Jon Reid
reid@cei.com

Details: Free

User info: To subscribe to the list, send an e-mail message to the URL address below with the single word SUBSCRIBE in the body (not subject) of your message.

To send a message to the entire list, address it to: cell-church@bible.acu.edu

Notes: The group archives, FAQ, and helpful articles are available by anonymous FTP from bible.acu.edu; they can also be retrieved by sending mail to cell-church-archives@bible.acu.edu with the single word LIST for a list of files, or HELP for more information.

`mailto:cell-church-request@bible.acu.edu`

Evolution

talk.origins ★

A Usenet newsgroup providing information and discussion about evolution versus creationism.

Keywords: Evolution, Creationism, Activism

Audience: General Public, Evolutionists, Creationists, Activists

Details: Free

User info: To subscribe to this Usenet newsgroup, you need access to a newsreader.

`news:talk.origins`

Executive Branch

EXEC (Executive Branch News US)

The EXEC library contains information and news about the Executive Branch of the Federal Government. From the Department of Agriculture to the White House, this file is a comprehensive source of information that will be especially useful to those whose responsibilities include monitoring federal regulations, Agency and Department activity, and the people and issues involved.

Keywords: News, Legislation, Regulation, Politics, Executive Branch

Audience: Journalists, Lobbyists, Business Executives, Analysts, Entrepreneurs

Profile: The EXEC library allows the searching of individual files or group files that cover topics such as the Federal Register and Code of Federal Regulations; public laws; proposed treasury regulation; and over 50 news sources, including BNAÕs Daily Report for Executives, the Dept. of State Dispatch, ABC News transcripts, Federal News Service Daybook, Government Executive, MacNeil/Lehrer Newshour, New Leader, National Review, the Washington Post, the Washington Times, Presidential Documents, and many others.

Contact: Mead New Sales Group at (800) 227-4908 or (513) 859-5398 inside the US, or (513) 865-7981 for all inquiries outside the US.

User info: To subscribe, contact Mead directly.

To examine the Nexis user guide, you can access it at the ftp site of the University of Texas at Austin at the URL address: ftp://ftp.cc.utexas.edu

The files are in: /pub/ref-services/LEXIS

`telnet://nex.meaddata.com, http://www.meaddata.com`

Experimental Stock Market Data

Experimental Stock Market Data ★★★

This is an experimental page that provides a link to the latest stock market information.

Keywords: Stock Market, Investments, Finance

Audience: General Public, Investors, Stock Brokers

Profile: This site is updated automatically, to reflect the current day's closing information. Provides general market news and quotes for selected stocks, although prices are not guaranteed. Also includes recent prices for many mutual funds, as well as technical analysis charts for a large number of stocks and mutual funds.

Contact: Mark Torrance
stockmaster@ai.mit.edu

Details: Free

`http://www.ai.mit.edu/stocks.html`

Expert Systems

Artificial Intelligence, Expert Sys., Virtual Reality

This directory is a compilation of information resources focused on computer science research, artificial intelligence, expert systems, and virtual reality.

Keywords: Computer Science, Artificial Intelligence, Expert Systems, Virtual Reality

Audience: Computer Scientists, Engineers

Details: Free

`ftp://una.hh.lib.umich.edu/70/inetdirsstacks/csaiesvr:kovacsm`

Exports

ITRADE (International Trade Library)

The International Trade library contains materials related to the importing of goods and services, exporting of goods and services, licensing of intellectual property, payment of taxes, or investment and banking at the international level.

Keywords: Law, Import, Exports, International Banking

Audience: Lawyers

Profile: ITRADE contains a comprehensive collection of federal case law, statutes, regulations, and agency decisions all related to the importing of goods and services, exporting of goods and services, licensing of intellectual property, payment of taxes, or investment and banking at the international level.

Contact: New Sales Group at 800-227-4908 or 513-859-5398 inside the US, or 1-513-865-7981 for all inquires outside the US.

User info: To subscribe, contact Mead directly.

To examine the Lexis user guide, you can access it at the ftp site of the University of Texas at Austin at the URL address: ftp://ftp.cc.utexas.edu

The files are in: /pub/ref-services/LEXIS

`telnet://nex.meaddata.com`

`http://www.meaddata.com`

National Export Strategy ★★

This site provides the complete text of a report presented to Congress by the Trade Promotion Coordinating Committee, describing ways to develop U.S. export promotion efforts.

Keywords: Commerce, Trade, Exports, Business

Sponsor: United States Government, Trade Promotion Coordinating Committee

Audience: Exporters, Business Professionals, Trade Specialists

Details: Free

`ftp://sunny.stat-usa.gov`

`http://sunny.stat-usa.gov`

PIERS Exports (US Ports)

Keywords: Trade, Exports, Maritime

Sponsor: The Journal of Commerce/PIERS, New York, NY, USA

Audience: Importers, Exporters, Business, Trade Specialists

Profile: Principal applications include identification of new sources of supply, monitoring exports of products whose details are lost in traditional government reports, and identification of potential trade partners. PIERS covers virtually all maritime movements in and out of the continental US and Puerto Rico. Details on each individual shipment are stored in the database.

Contact: Dialog in the US at (800) 334-2564, Dialog internationally at country specific locations.

User info: To subscribe, contact Dialog directly.

Notes: Coverage: current 15 months, excluding data in file 571.

`telnet://dialog.com`

EXPRESS Information Modeling Language

EXPRESS-Users

Discussion of topics pertaining to the EXPRESS information modeling language, such as information sources, how to download information, information modeling techniques, and sample models.

Keywords: Programming, EXPRESS Information Modeling Language

Audience: EXPRESS Programmers

Contact: Steve Clark, Charlie Lindahl EXPRESS-users-request@cme.nist.gov

Details: Free

User info: To subscribe to the list, send an e-mail message requesting a subscription to the URL address below.

`mailto:EXPRESS-users-request@cme.nist.gov`

Extraterrestrial Life

alt.alien.visitors

A Usenet newsgroup providing information and discussion about space aliens on Earth and related stories.

Keywords: UFOs, Aliens, Extraterrestrial Life

Audience: Alien Enthusiasts

User info: To subscribe to this Usenet newsgroup, you need access to a newsreader.

`news:alt.alien.visitors`

Extraterrestrials

A forum for academics, scientists and others interested in questions about the existence of intelligent life in the universe.

Keywords: Astronomy, Extraterrestrial Life, Space

Sponsor: University of Kent at Canterbury, United Kingdom

Audience: Scientists, Astronomers, General Public

Contact: Dr. Peter Moore pgm@ukc.ac.uk

User info: To subscribe to the list, send an e-mail message to the URL address shown below consisting of a single line reading:

SUB extraterrestrials YourFirstName YourLastName

To send a message to the entire list, address it to: extraterrestrials@mailbase.ac.uk

`mailbase@mailbase.ac.uk`

The University of California Search for Extraterrestrial Civilizations

A web site containing information on the UC Berkeley SETI Program, SERENDIP (Search for Extraterrestrial Radio Emmisions from Nearby Developed Intelligent Populations), an ongoing scientific research effort aimed at detecting radio signals from extraterrestrial civilizations. Details about the program and updates on current research activities are also accessible.

Keywords: Extraterrestrial Life, Astronomy, Aliens

Audience: Astronomers, Physicists, Students, Educators, Engineers, General Public

Contact: Dan Werthimer sereninfo@ssl.berkeley.edu

Details: Free

If Mosaic is available, use the http address below. Otherwise, please send a request for information to the contact address provided.

`http://sereninfo.ssl.berkeley.edu`

A B C D E F G H I J K L M N O P Q R S T U V W X Y Z

A
B
C
D
E
F
G
H
I
J
K
L
M
N
O
P
Q
R
S
T
U
V
W
X
Y
Z

FairCom

ctree

A forum for the discussion of FairCom's C-Tree, R-Tree, and D-Tree products. This mailing list is not associated with FairCom. Discussion covers virtually all hardware and operating system ports.

Keywords: Computers, FairCom

Audience: Computer Operators

Contact: Tony Olekshy
alberta!oha!ctree-request

Details: Free

User Info: To subscribe to the list, send an e-mail message requesting a subscription to the URL address below.

To send a message to the entire list, address it to: ctree

mailto:alberta!oha!ctree-request

Fam-Med

Fam-Med

An Internet resource and discussion group on computers in family medicine.

Keywords: Medicine, Computers, Telecommunications

Sponsor: Gustavus Adolphus College, Minnesota

Audience: Health Care Professionals, Family Physicians

Profile: Fam-Med is an electronic conference and file area that focuses on the use of computer and telecommunication technologies in the teaching and practice of family medicine. The conference and files are accessible to anyone able to send e-mail. The discussion on Fam-Med is distributed in two ways: by an unmoderated mail echo in which all posted messages are immediately distributed to subscribers without human intervention, and by a digest where messages accumulated over several days are assembled into a single document with erroneous posts deleted.

Contact: Paul Kleeberg
Paul@GAC.Edu

Details: Free

To join either the unmoderated list or the digest, send e-mail to the contact above. To post to Fam-Med, send e-mail to Fam-Med@GAC.Edu

gopher://ftp.gac.edu/00/pub/E-mail-archives/fam-med/

Family

BlindFam

The Blindness and Family Life mailing list is devoted to a discussion of the day-to-day impact of this disability on families, and the patterns of domestic life associated with blindness.

Keywords: Blindness, Disabilities, Family

Audience: Blind People, Families, Health Care Professionals, Rehabilitation Counselors

Contact: Roger Myers, Patt Bromberger
Meyers@ab.wvnet.edu,
Patt@squid.tram.com

User Info: To subscribe, send an e-mail message to the URL address below consisting of a single line reading:

SUB BlindFam YourFirstName YourLastName.

To send a message to the entire list, address it to:
BlindFam@sjuvm.stjohns.edu

mailto:listserv@sjuvm.stjohns.edu

National Family Database— MAPP

This database contains family sociological and health data, including research briefs, bibliographies, census data, program ideas, reference materials, media materials, and publications.

Keywords: Sociology, Family, Health

Sponsor: Department of Agriculture Economics and Rural Sociology, Pennsylvania State University

Audience: Sociologists, Public Health Policymakers, Health Care Providers

To access the database select PENpages (1), then General Information (3) and finally Information on MAPP - National Family Database (5)

telnet://penpages@psupen.psu.edu

Family and Legal Status (INPADOC)

Family and Legal Status (INPADOC)

The database includes a listing of patents issued in 56 countries and patenting organizations.

Keywords: Patents, Technlogy

Sponsor: European Patent Office (EPO), Vienna, Austria

A
B
C
D
E
F
G
H
I
J
K
L
M
N
O
P
Q
R
S
T
U
V
W
X
Y
Z

Audience: Patent Researchers, Inventors

Profile: INPADOC contains bibliographic data consisting of title, inventor, and assignee for most patents. In addition, this file brings together information on priority-application numbers, countries and dates, and equivalent patents (for instance, patent families) for patents. This file also contains the legal status information for patents in some countries.

Contact: Dialog in the US at (800) 334-2564, Dialog internationally at country-specific locations.

User Info: To subscribe, contact Dialog directly.

Notes: Coverage: April 1968 to the present; updated weekly.

`telnet://dialog.com`

Family Practice

University of Texas Health Science Center at Tyler Library

The library's holdings are large and wide-ranging and contain significant collections in many fields.

Keywords: Biochemistry, Cardiopulmonary Medicine, Cell Biology, Family Practice, Molecular Biology

Audience: Researchers, Students, General Public

Details: Free

User Info: Expect: Username Prompt, Send: LIS

`telnet://athena.uthscsa.edu`

Family Science

Purdue University Library

The library's holdings are large and wide-ranging. They contain significant collections in many fields.

Keywords: Economics (History of), Literature (English), Literature (American), Indiana, Rogers (Bruce), Engineering (History of), Aviation, Earth Science, Atmospheric Science, Consumer Science, Family Science, Chemistry (History of), Physics, Veterinary Science

Audience: General Public, Researchers, Librarians, Document Delivery Professionals

Contact: Dan Ferrer
dan@asterix.lib.purdue.edu

Details: Free

User Info: Expect: User ID prompt, Send: GUEST

`telnet://lib.cc.purdue.edu`

FAQs

Internet Services FAQ

General information and answers to frequently asked questions (FAQs) about the Internet.

Keywords: Internet, Internet Guides, FAQs

Audience: Internet Surfers

Details: Free

User Info: File is: pub/usenet/news.answers/internet-services/faq

`ftp://rtfm.mit.edu`

Sci.space.news

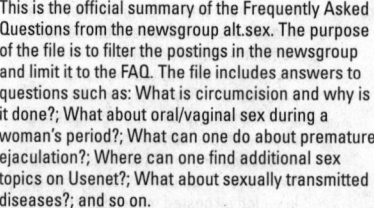

Keywords: Space, FAQs

Audience: Space Flight Enthusiasts

Profile: This newsgroup carries recent information about the world's space programs. Reading the FAQ set is recommended before asking questions on the other sci.space. groups.

Contact: Peter Yee
yee@atlas.arc.nasa.gov

Details: Free, Moderated

To participate in a Usenet newsgroup you need access to a newsreader.

`news:sci.space.news`

Sex FAQ

This is the official summary of the Frequently Asked Questions from the newsgroup alt.sex. The purpose of the file is to filter the postings in the newsgroup and limit it to the FAQ. The file includes answers to questions such as: What is circumcision and why is it done?; What about oral/vaginal sex during a woman's period?; What can one do about premature ejaculation?; Where can one find additional sex topics on Usenet?; What about sexually transmitted diseases?; and so on.

Keywords: Sex, FAQ

Audience: General Public

Contact: David Johnson, Snugglebunny
superdj@cs.mcgill.ca

Details: Free

`ftp://pit-manager.mit.edu/pub/usenet/news.answers/alt-sex/faq`

White House Frequently Asked Questions

This document is a good starting point for answering questions such as: How do I send e-mail to President Clinton? How do I get current news updates from the White House? Where can I get White House documents from?

Keywords: Clinton (Bill), Government (US), Politics (US), FAQs

Audience: General Public, Researchers

Details: Free

User Info: Expect: login; Send: anonymous; Expect: password; Send: your e-mail address; Expect: directory; Send: /pub/nic; Expect: file; Send: whitehouse FAQ.

`ftp://ftp.sura.net`

WWW FAQ

Answers to frequently-asked questions (FAQs) about World Wide Web (WWW), an Internet access tool.

Keywords: Internet Tools, WWW, FAQs

Audience: Internet Surfers

Details: Free

`ftp://info.cern.ch`

Farming

agmodels-l

A forum for the discussion of agricultural simulation models of all types. Issues include plant growth, micro-meteorology, soil hydrology, transport, farm economy, and farm systems.

Keywords: Agriculture, Farming

Audience: Agronomists

Contact: Jerome Pier
jp@unl.edu

User Info: To subscribe to the list, send an e-mail message to the URL address below consisting of a single line reading:

SUB agmodels-l YourFirstName YourLastName.

To send a message to the entire list, address it to: agmodels-l@unl.edu

`mailto:listserv@unl.edu`

Agriculture

This directory is a compilation of information resources focused on agriculture.

Keywords: Agriculture, Farming

Audience: Farmers, Agronomists, Agriculturalists

Contact: Wilfred Drew
drewwe@snymorva.cs.snymor.edu

Details: Free

`ftp://una.hh.lib.umich.edu`

`gopher://snymorvb.cs.snymor.edu`

`gopher://SNYMORVB.cs.snymor.edu`

Fashion Industry

alt.fashion

A Usenet newsgroup providing information and discussion about all facets of the fashion industry.

Keywords: Fashion Industry, Style

Audience: Designers, General Public

User Info: To subscribe to this Usenet newsgroup, you need access to a newsreader.

`news:alt.fashion`

Fashion Photography Conference

A conference on the WELL about photography; topics range from products and technical information to aesthetics and fashion photography.

Keywords: Photography, Fashion Industry

Audience: Photographers, Fashion Enthusiasts

Contact: Ralph E. Bedwell
ralf@well.sf.ca.us

To participate in a conference on the WELL, you must first establish an account on the WELL. To do so, start by typing: telnet well.sf.ca.us

`telnet://well.sf.ca.us`

Fashion Merchandising

University of Wisconsin at Stout Library

The library's holdings are large and wide-ranging and contain significant collections in many fields.

Keywords: Mathematics, Business, Fashion Merchandising, Home Economics, Hospitality, Tourism, Hotel Administration, Restaurant Management, Microelectronics

Audience: Researchers, Students, General Public

Details: Free

User Info: Expect: Login, Send: Lib; Expect: vDIAL Prompt, Send: Library

`telnet://lib.uwstout.edu`

FAX

SupraFAX

This list was created to help people who are using the SupraFAX v.32bis modem.

Keywords: Modem, FAX

Audience: Modem Users, FAX Users

Contact: David Tiberio
subscribe@xamiga.linet.org

Details: Free

User Info: To subscribe to the list, send an e-mail message requesting a subscription to the URL address below. To send a message to the entire list, address it to: subscribe@xamiga.linet.org

`mailto:subscribe@xamiga.linet.org`

FAXNET

FAXNET

FAXNET allows the user to send faxes via e-mail.

Keywords: Internet Services, E-mail

Audience: Internet Surfers, E-mail Users

Details: Free

User Info: Include the word "help" in the e-mail.

`mailto:info@awa.com`

FDA

Federal Food and Drug Administration

The Federal Food and Drug Administration (FDA) databank contains reports and articles related to the FDA.

Keywords: FDA, Drug Regulations, Nutrition

Sponsor: Federal Food and Drug Administration

Audience: Researchers, Nutritionists, Consumers, Health Care Providers

Profile: The topics covered include the drug and device product-approvals list, FDA federal register summaries by subject, text from drug bulletins, current information on AIDS, FDA consumer magazine index and selected articles, summaries of FDA information, text of testimony at FDA congressional hearings, and speeches given by the FDA commissioner and deputy.

Details: Free

`telnet://bbs@fdabbs.fda.gov`

Seafood Internet Network

A mailing list to facilitate information exchange about the HACCP Alliance and the implementation of the FDA seafood HACCP program.

Keywords: Food, FDA

Audience: Seafood Industry Professionals

Contact: Robert J. Price
rjprice@dale.ucdavis.edu

User Info: To subscribe , send an e-mail message to: listproc@ucdavis.edu Leave the subject blank and place in the body of the note: subscribe seafood YourFirstName YourLastName

`mailto:seafood@ucdavis.edu`

Federal Databases

GPO Gateway to Government Act of 1992: Senator Al Gore

A bill to establish an electronic gateway in the Government Printing Office (GPO) to provide public access to a wide range of Federal databases containing public information stored electronically.

Keywords: Government (US Federal), Federal Databases

Audience: General Public, Journalists, Politicians

Details: Free

User Info: File is: /pub/nic/NREN/GPO.bill.6-92

`ftp://ftp.sura.net`

A Grant Getter's Guide to the Internet

A summary of Internet-accessible information regarding federal grants.

Keywords: Grants, Federal Register (US), Federal Databases

Sponsor: University of Idaho, Moscow, Idaho, USA

Audience: Researchers, Scientists, Public Health Professionals, Students

Profile: This site is intended to provide federal grant information on the Internet. The focus is federal grant resources, including those sponsored by the National Institute of Health (NIH), the National Science Foundation (NSF), and the National Telecommunications and Information Administration (NTIA). This server also includes supplemental education-related information. This guide is searchable by keyword and contains pointers to such grant sources as the Federal Register, the National Science Foundation, the National Institutes of Health, and the Catalog of Federal Domestic Assistance. This same site allows direct access to many of the systems mentioned in the guide.

Contact: James Kearney, Marty Zimmerman
jkearney@raven.csrv.uidaho.edu,
martyz@uidaho.edu

`gopher://gopher.uidaho.edu/Science, Research, & Grant Information/Grant Information`

A B C D E F G H I J K L M N O P Q R S T U V W X Y Z

Questions and Answers about the GPO Gateway to Government Act

Questions and answers dealing with the bill GPO Gateway to Government Act of 1992. Questions such as, "What will the gateway do?," "Why is this gateway needed?," "What types of Information will be available through the Gateway?," and more.

Keywords: Laws (US Federal), Government (US Federal), Federal Databases

Audience: General Public, Journalists, Politicians

Details: Free

File is: /pub/nic/NREN/GPO.questions

`ftp://ftp.sura.net`

Federal Documents (US)

Miscellaneous Federal Documents

This directory includes documents such as the Civil Rights Act of 1991, the Computer Fraud and Abuse Act, the High-Performance Computing Senate Report, and more.

Keywords: Government (US Federal), Federal Documents (US)

Audience: Politicians, Journalists, Students (high school and up)

Details: Free

`gopher://wiretap.spies.com/11/Gov/US-Docs`

The Old Dominion University Library

The library's holdings are large and wide-ranging and contain significant collections in many fields.

Keywords: Virginia, Federal Documents (US)

Audience: General Public, Researchers, Librarians, Document Delivery Professionals

Details: Free

`telnet://geac.lib.odu.edu`

Federal Government (US)

FinanceNet (National Performance Review)

FinanceNet is intended to act as a forum for discussing the "reinvention" of government, to make it more cost effective and efficient.

Keywords: Finance, Federal Documents (US), Federal Register (US), Federal Government (US)

Sponsor: National Performance Review (NPR)

Audience: Government Officials, Journalists, Financial Analysts

Profile: FinanceNet is associated with Vice President Al Gore's National Performance Review (NPR). Available resources include text of Congressional testimony, agency reports, publications and announcements of upcoming events, all related to the improvement of federal money-managing and government accounting. It also has links to a number of other federal systems, including the NPR, Congressional Quarterly, and the Federal Register.

Contact: B. Preston Rich or Linda L.Hoogeveen Preston.Rich@nsf.gov or lhoog@tmn.com

Details: Free

Notes: Send a blank message to info@financenet.gov to receive more information about this project.

`gopher://gopher.financenet.gov`

`http://www.financenet.gov`

U.S. Army Area Handbooks

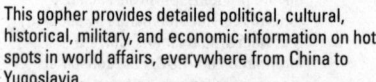

This gopher provides detailed political, cultural, historical, military, and economic information on hot spots in world affairs, everywhere from China to Yugoslavia.

Keywords: Military (US), Politics (International), Federal Government (US)

Sponsor: The Thomas Jefferson Library at the University of Missouri at St. Louis , St. Louis, Missouri, USA

Audience: Journalists, Government Officials, Travelers/Tourists

Profile: The Army Area Handbooks, which provide a comprehensive overview of several important countries including Japan, China, Israel, Egypt, South Korea, and Somalia, are only one of the many government resources available at this site. Other full-text documents include the proposed 1995 federal budget, the CIA world fact book, the NAFTA agreement, health care proposals currently before Congress, and statistics for the U.S. industrial outlook. Also has links to many federal gophers and information systems.

Contact: Joe Rottman rottman@umslvma.umsl.edu

Details: Free

`gopher://umslvma.umsl.edu/11/library/govdocs`

Federal Law (US)

Publications of the Office of Environment, Safety and Health

A collection of government safety information including updates, bulletins, and hazard alerts. Topics are diverse, covering everything from 'Employee Hit on Head by Falling Steel Wheel' to 'New Regulations to Control the Speed of Bloodborne Diseases.'

Keywords: Safety, Government (US), Federal Laws (US)

Sponsor: U.S. Department of Energy

Audience: Government Officials, General Public

Details: Free

`gopher://dewey.tis.inel.gov`

US House of Representatives Gopher

The online service of the U.S. House of Representatives.

Keywords: Congress (US), Federal Law (US), Government Records (US)

Sponsor: House Administration Committee Internet Working Group

Audience: Government Officials, Journalists, Educators (K-12), General Public

Profile: Provides access to information on members and committees of the House of Representatives, as well as full text of bills before the House. Includes education resources on the legislative process, Congressional directories, and House schedules. Also has information for visitors (including area maps), as well as access to other federal information systems.

Contact: House Internet Working Group househlp@hr.house.gov

`gopher://gopher.house.gov`

Federal Register

CODES (Codes Library)

The Codes Library offers access to US federal and state legislative materials, in codified, slip law, and bill form, plus federal and state regulatory materials and a statutes archive.

Keywords: Statutes, Codes, State, Federal Registry

Audience: (US) Lawyers

Profile: The Codes Library contains an extensive compilation of federal and state statutory materials, in codified as well as slip law form, from all 50 states, the District of Columbia, Puerto Rico, the Virgin Islands and the United States Code Service. The library also contains federal and state regulatory materials plus a statues archive. Pending legislation can be found with 50-state and federal fill tracking, the full text of federal bills, the Congressional Record, and the full text of bills for a growing number of states. Administrative materials include the Code of Federal Regulations, the Federal Register, 50-state regulation tracking, and the administrative codes for a selected number of states.

Contact: New Sales Group at (800) 227-4908 or (513) 859-5398 inside the US, or (513) 865-7981 for all inquires outside the US.

User Info: To subscribe, contact Mead directly.

To examine the Lexis user guide, you can access it at the ftp site of the University of Texas at Austin at the URL address: ftp://ftp.cc.utexas.edu

The files are in: /pub/ref-services/LEXIS

`telnet://nex.meaddata.com`

`http://www.meaddata.com`

A Grant Getter's Guide to the Internet

A summary of Internet-accessible information regarding federal grants.

Keywords: Grants, Federal Register, Federal Databases (US)

Sponsor: University of Idaho, Moscow, Idaho, USA

Audience: Researchers, Scientists, Public Health Professionals, Students

Profile: This site is intended to provide federal grant information on the Internet. The focus is federal grant resources, including those sponsored by the National Institute of Health (NIH), the National Science Foundation (NSF), and the National Telecommunications and Information Administration (NTIA). This server also includes supplemental education-related information. This guide is searchable by keyword and

contains pointers to such grant sources as the Federal Register, the National Science Foundation, the National Institutes of Health, and the Catalog of Federal Domestic Assistance. This same site allows direct access to many of the systems mentioned in the guide.

Contact: James Kearney, Marty Zimmerman
jkearney@raven.csrv.uidaho.edu
martyz@uidaho.edu

`gopher://gopher.uidaho.edu/Science, Research, & Grant Information/Grant Information`

Internet Federal Register (IFR)

The full text of the US Federal Register.

Keywords: Federal Register, Government (US Federal), Law (US Federal)

Sponsor: Counterpoint Publishing

Audience: General Public, Journalists, Students, Politicians, Citizens

Contact: fedreg@internet.com

Details: Costs

`gopher://gopher.internet.com`

Federal Standards

IHS International Standards and Specifications

The database contains references to industry standards, and military and federal specifications and standards covering all aspects of engineering and related disciplines.

Keywords: Engineering, Military Specifications, Federal Standards

Sponsor: Information Handling Services, Englewood, CO, US

Audience: Engineers, Military Hisorians, Lawyers

Profile: The file includes 90% of the world's most referenced standards from over 70 domestic, foreign, and international standardizing bodies. Also included is the world's largest commercially available collection of unclassified active and historical US military and federal specifications and standards.

Contact: Dialog in the US at (800) 334-2564, Dialog internationally at country-specific locations.

User Info: To subscribe, contact Dialog directly.

Notes: Coverage: Current; updated weekly for MILSPECS, every two months.

`telnet://dialog.com`

FEDSEC (Federal Securities Library)

FEDSEC (Federal Securities Library)

The US Federal Securities library covers federal case law, Securities Exchanges Commission (SEC) materials, Commodities Futures Trading Commion (CFTC) materials and other legal and legislative materials relevant to the securities industry, as well as company information, news and analysis.

Keywords: Law, Filings, Securities, SEC

Audience: Lawyers, Bankers, Stock Brokers

Profile: The Federal Securities library contains over 60 separately searchable files covering federal case law: Securities Exchange Commion (SEC) no-action letters, decisions, orders, releases, and SEC filings (both full text and abstracts); Commodities Futures Trading Commion (CFTC) decisions, orders, releases; legislative materials; statutory and regulatory materials; selected RICO, class derivative, and collateralized mortgage obligations case law, rules and regulations; Federal Reserve Board materials; AICPA annual reports and accounting & audit literature files; Standard & Poors company information; state administrative decisions, orders, and releases; and company news and analysis information.

Contact: New Sales Group at (800) 227-4908 or 513-859-5398 inside the US, or 1-513-865-7981 for all inquires outside the US.

User Info: To subscribe, contact Mead directly.

To examine the Lexis user guide, you can access it at the ftp site of the University of Texas at Austin at the URL address: ftp://ftp.cc.utexas.edu

The files are in /pub/ref-services/LEXIS

`telnet://nex.meaddata.com`

`http://www.meaddata.com`

FEDTAX (Federal Tax Library)

FEDTAX (Federal Tax Library)

The Federal Tax Library offerers a comprehensive, up-to-date collection of tax-related materials, including case law, agency materials, legislative and regulatory materials, and so on.

Keywords: Law, Analysis, Tax

Audience: Lawyers

A B C D E F G H I J K L M N O P Q R S T U V W X Y Z

Profile: The Federal Tax Library offers a comprehensive, up-to-date collection of tax-related materials. This library includes federal and state tax case law, Internal Revenue Service rulings and releases, state tax administrative decisions and rulings, the Internal Revenue Code, federal tax regulations, international news and treaties, tax looseleaf services, tax periodicals, tax law reviews, tax dailies, pending state legislation, and state property records.

Contact: New Sales Group at (800) 227-4908 or (513) 859-5398 inside the US, or (513) 865-7981 for all inquires outside the US.

User Info: To subscribe, contact Mead directly.

To examine the Lexis user guide, you can access it at the ftp site of the University of Texas at Austin at the URL address: ftp://ftp.cc.utexas.edu

The files are in: /pub/ref-services/LEXIS

`telnet://nex.meaddata.com`

`http://www.meaddata.com`

FedWorld Bulletin Board

FedWorld Bulletin Board

A BBS run by the National Technical Information Service, with many databases of government documents, job announcements, and connections to other federal government online services.

Keywords: US Federal Government, Government Documents

Sponsor: US National Technical Information Service

Audience: General Public, Researchers

Profile: This is the place to begin any kind of search for US federal government records and publications. The GateWay option connects you to the Library of Congress, Supreme Court opinions, government job listing, the various Federal Reserve Banks, Congressional Bills and studies, and so on.

To establish an account: Expect: login, Send: new

Notes: Mail to sysop once you have an account.

`telnet://fedworld.gov`

Felipe's Bilingual WWW Pages

Felipe's Bilingual WWW Pages

An interactive web site containing gopher and web links to various Latin American resources.

Keywords: Latin America, Education (Bilingual)

Sponsor: University of Texas, Texas, USA

Audience: Educators, Language Students, Translators

Contact: Felipe Campos
felipe@bongo.utexas.edu

`http://edb518ea.edb.utexas.edu`

Feminism

alt.feminism

A Usenet newsgroup providing information and discussion about feminism.

Keywords: Feminism, Women's Studies, Abortion, Activism

Audience: Women, General Public

User Info: To subscribe to this Usenet newsgroup, you need access to a newsreader.

`news:alt.feminism`

Amazons International

An electronic digest newsletter for and about Amazons (physically and psychologically strong, assertive women who are challenging traditional ideas about gender roles, femininity, and the female physique).

Keywords: Gender, Amazons, Feminism

Audience: Women, Feminists, Writers, Art Historians

Profile: The digest is dedicated to the image of the female hero in fiction and in fact, as it is expressed in art and literature, in the physiques and feats of female athletes,and in sexual values and practices; it also provides information, discussion, and a supportive environment for these values and issues.

Contact: Thomas Gramstad
amazons-request@math.uio.no

Details: Free

User Info: To subscribe to the list, send an e-mail message requesting a subscription to the URL address below.

To send a message to the entire list, address it to: amazons@math.uio.no

`mailto:amazons-request@math.uio.no`

amlat.mujeres

This conference serves as a forum for interchange between organizations and women's movements in Latin America and the Caribbean.

Keywords: Women, Latin America, Caribbean, Feminism

Audience: Women, Feminists, Activists

Contact: Agencia Latinoamericana de Informacion
info@alai.ec, uualai@ecuanex.ec

Details: Costs

Establish an account on the nearest APC node. Login, type c for conferences, then type: go amlat.mujeres.

For information on the nearest APC node, contact:
APC International Secretariat IBASE
E-mail: apcadmin@apc.org

`telnet://igc.apc.org`

apngowid.meet

A conference on plans by Asia Pacific regional women's groups for the United Nations Fourth World Conference on Women to be held in Beijing in September 1995.

Keywords: Women, Asia, Pacific, Feminists, Development, United Nations, World Conference on Women

Audience: Women, Feminism, Nongovernmental Organizations

Contact: AsPac Info, Docu and Communication Committee
AP-IDC@p95.f401.n751.z6.g

Details: Costs, Moderated

Establish an account on the nearest APC node. Login, type c for conferences, then type: go apngowid.meet.

For information on the nearest APC node, contact: APC International Secretariat IBASE E-mail: apcadmin@apc.org

`http://www.igc.apc.org/igc/www.women.html`

dh.mujer

The primary Association for Progressive Communications conference for women and human rights issues throughout the world, contains news and announcements.

Keywords: Women's Issues, Feminism, Human Rights

Audience: Feminists, Activists

Contact: Debra Guzman
hrcoord@igc.apc.org

Details: Costs

Establish an account on the nearest APC node. Login, type c for conferences, then type go dh.mujer.

For information on the nearest APC node, contact: APC International Secretariat IBASE E-mail: apcadmin@apc.org

Contact: Carlos Afonso (cafonso@ax.apc.org) or APC North American Regional Office
E-mail: apcadmin@apc.org
Edie Farwell (efarwell@igc.apc.org)

`gopher://gopher.telnet://igc.apc.org`

`http://igc.apc.org`

The English Server

A large and eclectic collection of humanities resources.

Keywords: Humanities, Academia, English, Popular Culture, Feminism

Sponsor: Carnegie Mellon University English Department, Pittsburgh, Pennsylvania, USA

Audience: General Public, University Students, Educators (College/University), Researchers (Humanities)

Profile: Contains archives of conventional humanities materials, such as historical documents and classic books in electronic form. Also offers more unusual and hard-to-find resources, particularly in the field of popular culture and media. Features access to many humanities and culture-related online journals such as Bad Subjects, FineArt Forum, and Postmodern Culture. Also has links to a wide variety of related Internet sites and resources.

Contact: Geoff Sauer
postmaster@english-server.hss.cmu.

`gopher://english-server.hss.cmu.edu`

`http://english-server.hss.cmu.edu`

Forum for Women's Issues

A forum for issues relating to women.

Keywords: Women, General Interest, Feminism

Audience: Women

Contact: Reva Basch
reva@well.sf.ca.us

Details: Free

To participate in a conference on the WELL, you must first establish an account on the WELL. To do so, start by typing: telnet://well.sf.ca.us

`telnet://well.sf.ca.us`

hr.women

A conference on human rights issues pertaining to women.

Keywords: Women, Feminism, Human Rights

Audience: Women, Feminists, Activists

Contact: Jillaine Smith
jillaine@igc.apc.org

Details: Costs

Establish an account on the nearest APC node. Login, type c for conferences, then type go hr.women.

For information on the nearest APC node, contact: APC International Secretariat IBASE E-mail: apcadmin@apc.org

Contact: Carlos Afonso (cafonso@ax.apc.org) or APC North American Regional Office
E-mail: apcadmin@apc.org
Edie Farwell (efarwell@igc.apc.org)

`telnet://igc.apc.org`

InforM Women's Studies Database

A gopher- or FTP-accessible archive of documents, opportunities, and resources pertaining to women's studies and women's issues.

Keywords: Women's Studies, Feminism, Women

Audience: Women, Women's Studies Students, Women's Studies Educators, Other Women's Issues Observers

Profile: This women's studies database is an easily navigable archive of files on women's studies and women's issues. It includes information such as health, employment opportunities, political issues, gender issues in the workplace and in education, reproductive rights, sex discrimination, sexual harassment, violence, work and family, women and computers, feminist film reviews, and poetry. InforM contains a compilation of electronic forums (listservs and newsgroups) for the discussion of male/female relations, societal problems, and for women of diverse cultures and sexual persuasions.

Contact: Paula Gaber
Gaber@info.umd.edu

Details: Free

Gopher or telnet to Inform.umd.edu, select Educational Resources/Women's Studies/. Or FTP to Inform.umd.edu, log in as anonymous, then cd /inforM/Educational_Resources/WomensStudies/

This source is also accessible through gopher, ftp, or telnet.

`gopher://inform.umd.edu`

`http://inform.umd.edu/welcome.html`

Notable Women

A database listing some important and notable women through the ages. Available for online searching by keyword, or as a full-text file.

Keywords: Women's Studies, History (Women's), Feminism

Sponsor: Estrella Mountain Community College (Arizona)

Audience: Women's Studies Educators, Historians, Researchers, Feminists

Contact: EMC Gopher Team
root@gopher.emc.maricopa.edu

`gopher://gopher.emc.maricopa.edu`

Women's Studies and Resources

A collection of materials related to women's studies and issues.

Keywords: Women's Studies, Feminism

Sponsor: Peripatetic Eclectic Gopher (PEG) at UC Irvine

Audience: Women, Feminists, Activists, Women's Studies Educators and Students

Profile: Contains bibliographies, listserv archives, conference announcements, and other resources related to women's studies. Also has links to other groups and sites related to women's issues.

Contact: Calvin Boyer
cjboyer@uci.edu

`gopher://peg.cwis.uci.edu`

Women.forum

Conference for discussion of women's issues.

Keywords: Women, Feminism, Women's Issues

Audience: Women, Feminists

Contact: Corina Hughes
corina@igc.apc.org

Details: Costs

User Info.: Establish an account on the nearest APC node. Login, type c for conferences, then type go women.forum. For information on the nearest APC node, contact: APC International Secretariat IBASE E-mail: apcadmin@apc.org Contact: Carlos Afonso (cafonso@ax.apc.org) or APC North American Regional Office E-mail: apcadmin@apc.org Contact: Edie Farwell (efarwell@igc.apc.org)

Notes: ALAI: Agencia Latinoamericana de Informacion E-mail message to APCadmin@apc.org

`telnet://igc.apc.org`

Women.health

This conference features articles, documents, news, announcements, policy statements, and other information about women's health around the world. Topics include breast cancer, ovarian cancer, alcohol, abortion, pregnancy, sterilization of women, pesticides, Quinacrine, HIV, disability.

Keywords: Women, Abortion, AIDS, Disability, Feminism, Health

Audience: Activists, Family Planners, Health Professionals, Non-Governmental Organizations, Women

A B C D E F G H I J K L M N O P Q R S T U V W X Y Z

A
B
C
D
E
F
G
H
I
J
K
L
M
N
O
P
Q
R
S
T
U
V
W
X
Y
Z

Details:	Costs
	Establish an account on the nearest APC node. Login, type c for conferences, then type go women.health. For information on the nearest APC node, contact: APC International Secretariat IBASE E-mail: apcadmin@apc.org Contact: Carlos Afonso (cafonso@ax.apc.org) or APC North American Regional Office E-mail: apcadmin@apc.org Contact: Edie Farwell (efarwell@igc.apc.org)
Notes:	ALAI: Agencia Latinoamericana de Informacion e-mail message to APCadmin@apc.org

`telnet://igc.apc.org`

Women.news

★

This conference features news and action alerts about women and women's issues around the world, including human rights, feminism, health, sexual abuse, workers, population, abortion, activism, development, and peace.

Keywords: Feminism, Gender, Women

Audience: Women, Feminists, Activists

Contact: Debra Guzman, Sue VanHattum
hrcoord@igc.apc.org or
suev@igc.apc.org

Details: Free
Establish an account on the nearest APC node. Login, type c for conferences, then type go women.news. For information on the nearest APC node, contact: APC International Secretariat IBASE E-mail: apcadmin@apc.org

Contact: Carlos Afonso (cafonso@ax.apc.org) or APC North American Regional Office E-mail: apcadmin@apc.org or Edie Farwell (efarwell@igc.apc.org)

Notes: Alai: Agencia Latinoamericana De Informacion E-mail message to APCadmin@apc.org

`telnet://igc.apc.org`

Fen

rec.arts.anime

★

A Usenet newsgroup providing information and discussion about Japanese animation fen.

Keywords: Animation, Fen, Japan

Audience: Animators

Details: Free

User Info: To subscribe to this Usenet newsgroup, you need access to a newsreader.

`news:rec.arts.anime`

Fiction

Online BookStore (OBS)

 ★★★

Offers full text (fiction and nonfiction) in a variety of electronic formats, free and for a fee.

Keywords: Online Books, Books, ShareWord, Fiction, Nonfiction Books

Sponsor: Editorial Inc./OBS

Audience: General Public, Reading Enthusiasts

Profile: Started in 1992, the OBS offers a variety of full-text titles.

Contact: Laura Fillmore
laura@editorial.com

Details: Costs, Moderated, Images, Multimedia

User Info: To subscribe to the list, send an e-mail message requesting a subscription to the URL address below.

`mailto:laura@editorial.com`

University of Northern Iowa Library

 ★★

The library's holdings are large and wide-ranging and contain significant collections in many fields.

Keywords: Art, Business Information, Education, Music, Fiction

Audience: Researchers, Students, General Public

Contact: Mike Yohe
yohe@uni.edu

Details: Free

User Info: Expect: Login; Send: Public

`telnet://infosys.uni.edu`

University of Pennsylvania PENNINFO Library

 ★★

The library's holdings are large and wide-ranging and contain significant collections in many fields.

Keywords: Church History, Spanish Inquisition, Witchcraft, Shakespeare (William), Bibles, Aristotle (Texts of), Fiction, Whitman (Walt), French Revolution, Drama (French), Literature (English), Literature (Spanish)

Audience: Researchers, Students, General Public

Contact: Al DSouza
penninfo-admin@dccs.upenn.edu
dsouza@dccs.upenn.edu

Details: Free

User Info: Expect: Login; Send: Public

`telnet://penninfo.upenn.edu`

Filings

BKRTCY (Bankruptcy Library)

The Federal Bankruptcy library is a comprehensive collection of primary and secondary legal research materials pertaining to bankruptcy issues.

Keywords: Law, Filings, Bankruptcy

Audience: Lawyers, Bankers

Profile: The Federal Bankruptcy library is a comprehensive collection of primary and secondary legal research materials that includes case law, rules, statutory and regulatory materials, legal publications, accounting literature and other resources pertaining to bankruptcy issues.

Contact: New Sales Group at (800) 227-4908 or (513) 859-5398 inside the US, or (513) 865-7981 for all inquires outside the US.

User Info: To subscribe, contact Mead directly.
To examine the Lexis user guide, you can access it at the ftp site of the University of Texas at Austin at the URL address: ftp://ftp.cc.utexas.edu
The files are in /pub/ref-services/LEXIS

`telnet://nex.meaddata.com`

`http://www.meaddata.com`

COMPNY

The COMPNY library contains more than 75 files of business and financial information, including thousands of in-depth company and industry research reports from leading national and international investments banks and brokerage houses.

Keywords: Companies, Financials, Filings, Disclosure

Audience: Business and Financial Researchers, Analysts, Entrepreneurs and Regulators.

Profile: COMPNY includes the following types of information:

- Full-text 10-Q, 10-K, Annual Reports to Shareholders and Proxy filings.

- Extracts of filings for more than 11,000 public companies whose securities are traded on the major exchanges as well as over-the-counter.

- Abstracts of S-registration statements, 13-Ds, 14-Ds, 8Ks, Form 4s and other SEC filings updated on a daily basis.

- Business news abstracts from more than 400 information sources.

- Daily US economic trends and forecasts.

The materials may be searched in individual files, such as brokerage house reports, or in group files organized by subject, such as SEC filings.

Contact: Mead New Sales Group at (800) 227-4908 or (513) 859-5398 inside the US, or (513) 865-7981 for all inquiries outside the US.

User Info: To subscribe, contact Mead directly.

To examine the Nexis user guide, you can access it at the ftp site of the University of Texas at Austin at the URL address: ftp://ftp.cc.utexas.edu

The files are in: /pub/ref-services/LEXIS

`telnet://nex.meaddata.com`

`http://www.meaddata.com`

FEDSEC (Federal Securities Library)

★★★★

The US Federal Securities library covers federal case law, Securities Exchanges Commission (SEC) materials, Commodities Futures Trading Commision (CFTC) materials and other legal and legislative materials relevant to the securities industry, as well as company information, news and analysis.

Keywords: Law, Filings, Securities, SEC

Audience: Lawyers, Bankers, Stockbrokers

Profile: The Federal Securities library contains over 60 separately searchable files covering federal case law: Securities Exchange Commision (SEC) no-action letters, decisions, orders, releases, and SEC filings (both full text and abstracts); Commodities Futures Trading Commision (CFTC) decisions, orders, releases; legislative materials; statutory and regulatory materials; selected RICO, class derivative, and collateralized mortgage obligations case law, rules and regulations; Federal Reserve Board materials; AICPA annual reports and accounting and audit literature files; Standard & Poors company information; state administrative decisions, orders, and releases; and company news and analysis information.

Contact: New Sales Group at (800) 227-4908 or 513-859-5398 inside the US, or 1-513-865-7981 for all inquires outside the US.

User Info: To subscribe, contact Mead directly.

To examine the Lexis user guide, you can access it at the ftp site of the University of Texas at Austin at the URL address: ftp://ftp.cc.utexas.edu

The files are in: /pub/ref-services/LEXIS

`telnet://nex.meaddata.com`

`http://www.meaddata.com`

INCORPR (Corporation and Partnership Records)

The Corporation and Partnership Records (INCORP) library contains current US corporation and partnership filings.

Keywords: Corporations, Partnerships, Filings, Trademarks

Audience: Corporations, Lawyers, Researchers

Profile: The INCORP library contains current records on corporations and limited partnerships registered with the office of the Secretary or Department of State. These records include information extracted by the state's staff from articles of incorporation, annual reports, amendments, and other public filings.

Contact: Mead New Sales Group at (800) 227-4908 or (513) 859-5398 inside the US, or (513) 865-7981 for all inquiries outside the US.

User Info: To subscribe, contact Mead directly.

To examine the Nexis user guide, you can access it at the ftp site of the University of Texas at Austin at the URL address: ftp://ftp.cc.utexas.edu

The files are in: /pub/ref-services/LEXIS

`telnet://nex.meaddata.com`

`http://www.meaddata.com`

NAARS (National Automated Accounting Research System)

The National Automated Accounting Research System (NAARS) library, provided as a service by agreement with the American Institute of Certified Public Accountants (AICPA) contains a variety of accounting information.

Keywords: Accounting, Auditing, Filings, Publications

Audience: Accountants

Profile: The NAARS library contains annual reports of public corporations and accounting literature and publications for the accounting professional. Annual reports are annotated with descriptive terms assigned by the AICPA. These terms allow the user to search for annual report footnotes that illustrate one or more recognized accounting practices.

Contact: Mead New Sales Group at (800) 227-4908 or (513) 859-5398 inside the US, or (513) 865-7981 for all inquiries outside the US.

User Info: To subscribe, contact Mead directly.

To examine the Nexis user guide, you can access it at the ftp site of the University of Texas at Austin at the URL address: ftp://ftp.cc.utexas.edu

The files are in: /pub/ref-services/LEXIS

`telnet://nex.meaddata.com`

`http://www.meaddata.com`

SEC (Securities and Exchange Commission) EDGAR (Electronic Data Gathering, Analysis and Retrieval) System

Provides free access to 1994 SEC filings for approximately 2,300 companies.

Keywords: Securities, Filings, SEC, Stock Market

Sponsor: New York University School of Business

Audience: Business Professionals, Investors

Profile: This expanding project aims to make available current, public SEC filings that are filed electronically. The system is searchable by company name and is updated and indexed daily. Many types of SEC forms, including 10-K and 10-Q financial reports, are available in a number of different electronic formats. The site also provides some explanatory documentation on the EDGAR program and on the types of SEC forms and information available to the public.

Contact: Ajit Kambil
piotr@edgar.stern.nyu.edu

Details: Free

`ftp://town.hall.org/edgar`

`http://www.town.hall.org`

Film

alt.cult-movies

A Usenet newsgroup providing information and discussion about popular movies.

Keywords: Film, Popular Culture

Audience: Movie Watchers, Critics

User Info: To subscribe to this Usenet newsgroup, you need access to a newsreader.

`news:alt.cult-movies`

ANIME-L

This discussion list covers animation news, with a special emphasis on Japanese "animedia."

Keywords: Animation, Film, Japan

Audience: Animation Enthusiasts, Animators

Details: Free

User Info: To subscribe to the list, send an e-mail message to the address below, consisting of a single line reading:

Sub anime-l YourFirstName YourLastName

To send a message to the entire list, address it to: anime-l@vtvm1.bitnet

`mailto:listserv@vtvm1.cc.vt.edu`

CinemaSpace

CinemaSpace, from the Film Studies Program at UC Berkeley, is devoted to all aspects of Cinema and New Media.

Keywords: Cinema, Film, Multimedia

Sponsor: Film Studies Program at UC Berkeley

Audience: Students, Film researchers

A
B
C
D
E
F
G
H
I
J
K
L
M
N
O
P
Q
R
S
T
U
V
W
X
Y
Z

A B C D E F G H I J K L M N O P Q R S T U V W X Y Z

Profile: Projects for CinemaSpace include academic papers on film and new media, film theory and critique, multimedia lectures, and sources of film clips and references to other sites.

Contact: xcohen@garnet.berkeley.edu

Details: Free

`http://remarque.berkeley.edu/~xcohen`

Film and Video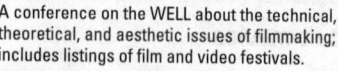

This directory is a compilation of information resources focused on film and video.

Keywords: Film, Video, Entertainment

Audience: Students, Producers, Artists

Details: Free

`ftp://una.hh.lib.umich.edu/70/`
`inetdirsstacks/filmvideo:woodgarlock`

Filmmaking Conference

A conference on the WELL about the technical, theoretical, and aesthetic issues of filmmaking; includes listings of film and video festivals.

Keywords: Film, Filmmaking, Video

Audience: Filmmakers

Contact: Sandy Santra
trevor@well.sf.ca.us

Details: Costs

To participate in a conference on the WELL, you must first establish an account on the WELL. To do so, start by typing: telnet well.sf.ca.us

`telnet://well.sf.ca.us`

Iowa State University ★★

The library's holdings contain significant collections in many fields.

Keywords: Agriculture, Veterinary Medicine, Statistics, Labor, Soil Conservation, Film

Audience: General Public, Researchers, Librarians, Document Delivery Professionals

Details: Free

User Info: Expect: DIAL, Send: LIB

`telnet://isn.iastate.edu`

National Broadcasting Society— Alpha Epsilon Rho

Forum for mass media professionals to share experiences and ideas.

Keywords: Film, Television, Radio, Mass Media

Sponsor: National Broadcasting Society-Alpha Epsilon Rho

Audience: Journalists, Students, Educators, Broadcasting Professionals

---

Contact: Reg Gamar
regbc@cunyvm.bitnet

Details: Free

User Info: To subscribe to the list, send an e-mail message to the address shown below consisting of a single line reading:

SUB NBS-AER YourFirstName YourLastName

To send a message to the entire list, address it to: nbs-aer@cunyvm.bitnet

`mailto:listserv@cunyvm.bitnet`

news: aus.films

Discussion of films and the film industry from an Australian perspective.

Keywords: Film, Australia

Audience: Australia Enthusiasts, Film Enthusiasts

Details: Free

User Info: To subscribe to a Usenet newsgroup, you need access to a "newsreader."

`news:aus.films`

rec.arts.movies

A Usenet newsgroup providing information and discussion about films and film making.

Keywords: Film

Audience: Film Enthusiasts, Filmmakers

Details: Free

User Info: To subscribe to this Usenet newsgroup, you need access to a newsreader.

`news:rec.arts.movies`

rec.arts.sf.starwars

A Usenet newsgroup providing information and discussion about the popular Star Wars trilogy.

Keywords: Science Fiction, Film

Audience: Star Wars Enthusiasts, Movie Viewers

User Info: To subscribe to this Usenet newsgroup, you need access to a newsreader.

`news:rec.arts.sf.starwars`

rec.arts.startrek.misc

A Usenet newsgroup providing general information and discussion about all aspects of Star Trek, including its various television and film reviews.

Keywords: Television, Film

Audience: Trekkies, Television Viewers, Movie Viewers

User Info: To subscribe to this Usenet newsgroup, you need access to a newsreader.

`news:rec.arts.startrek.misc`

---

rec.video

A Usenet newsgroup providing information and discussion about video.

Keywords: Video, Art, Film, Computer Art

Audience: Cinematographers, Video Artists

User Info: To subscribe to this Usenet newsgroup, you need access to a newsreader.

`news:rec.video`

Theater, Film & Television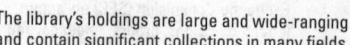

This directory is a compilation of information resources focused on theater, film & television.

Keywords: Theater, Film, Television

Audience: Theater Personnel, Film Personnel, Television Personnel

Details: Free

`ftp://una.hh.lib.umich.edu/70/`
`inetdirsstacks/filmtv:robinson`

University of North Carolina at Greensboro MINERVA Library ★★

The library's holdings are large and wide-ranging and contain significant collections in many fields.

Keywords: Herbert (George), Film, Dickinson (Emily), Children's Books

Audience: Researchers, Students, General Public

Details: Free

User Info: Expect: Login; Send: Info or MINERVA

`telnet://steffi.acc.uncg.edu`

Filmmaking

Filmmaking Conference

A conference on the WELL about the technical, theoretical, and aesthetic issues of filmmaking; includes listings of film and video festivals.

Keywords: Film, Filmmaking, Video

Audience: Filmmakers

Contact: Sandy Santra
trevor@well.sf.ca.us

Details: Costs

To participate in a conference on the WELL, you must first establish an account on the WELL. To do so, start by typing: telnet well.sf.ca.us

`telnet://well.sf.ca.us`

FINALE

FINALE Discussion List

Discussion list targeted towards people who use the FINALE music notation program.

Keywords: Music Notation, FINALE

Sponsor: CODA

Audience: FINALE Program Users

Profile: The music notation program FINALE (for Macintosh and Windows) provides the basis for the chief discussion on this list. Other CODA products, as well as various notation programs, are also suitable topics.

Contact: Henry Howey
mus_heh@SHSU.edu

Details: Free

User Info: To subscribe to the list, send an e-mail message to the URL address below, consisting of a single line reading:

SUB finale YourFirstName YourLastName

`mail to: listserv@shsu.edu`

Finance

Banking News Library

The Banking News library provides you specific banking industry sources. More than 40 full-text and selected full-text sources which focus on the banking related news and issues.

Keywords: Banking, Finance, Regulation

Audience: Journalists, Banking Industry Analysts

Profile: This library contains news, Investext Industry Reports, and legal/regulatory information. Also included in an abstract files is the Financial Industry Information Service (FINIS). The S&L file includes documents from newspapers and magazines which are specific to the S&L.

Contact: Mead New Sales Group at (800) 227-4908 or (513) 859-5398 inside the US, or (513) 865-7981 for all inquiries outside the US.

User Info: To subscribe, contact Mead directly.

To examine the Nexis user guide, you can access it at the ftp site of the University of Texas at Austin at the URL address: ftp://fp.cc.utexas.edu

The files are in: /pub/ref-services/LEXIS

`telnet://nex.meaddata.com`

`http://www.meaddata.com`

Budget of the United States (1994)

Provides the full text of the 1994 budget of the United States.

Keywords: Budget, Government (US), Finance

Audience: Politicians, Lawyers, Journalists, Economists, Students, US Citizens

Details: Free

Notes: This document is over one megabyte in size and thus takes a couple of minutes to load onto the screen.

`gopher:// wiretap.spies.com/00/Gov/ US-Gov/budget.94`

Business Wire

The database contains the unedited text of news releases from over 10,000 diverse news sources: companies, public relations firms, government agencies, political organizations, colleges and universities, and research institutes.

Keywords: Business, Finance, and Industry

Sponsor: Business Wire, San Francisco, CA, USA

Audience: Business Analysts, Market Researchers, General Public

Profile: Approximately 90% of all releases carried by Business Wire are business/financial, covering essentially every category of business and industry. News releases include all information on earnings, dividend announcements, mergers and acquisitions, major contract awards, new products, new security offerings, takeovers, restructurings, and more. Business Wire transmits the full, unedited text of these releases, complete with financial statements and other details that are not generally made available by the press. In addition, all releases carry the name and telephone number of a contact person within that company. Also contained are news on other subjects, such as entertainment, travel, sports, politics, medicine and science, and lifestyles.

Contact: Dialog in the US at (800) 334-2564, Dialog internationally at country specific locations.

Details: Costs

User Info: To subscribe, contact Dialog directly.

`telnet://dialog.com`

COMPNY

The COMPNY library contains more than 75 files of business and financial information, including thousands of in-depth company and industry research reports from leading national and international investments banks and brokerage houses.

Keywords: Companies, Finance, Filings, Disclosure

Audience: Business and Financial Researchers, Analysts, Entrepreneurs and Regulators.

Profile: COMPNY includes the following types of information:
- Full-text 10-Q, 10-K, Annual Reports to Shareholders and Proxy filings.
- Extracts of filings for more than 11,000 public companies whose securities are traded on the major exchanges as well as over-the-counter.
- Abstracts of S-registration statements, 13-Ds, 14-Ds, 8Ks, Form 4s and other SEC filings updated on a daily basis.
- Business news abstracts from more than 400 information sources.
- Daily US economic trends and forecasts.

The materials may be searched in individual files, such as brokerage house reports, or in group files organized by subject, such as SEC filings.

Contact: Mead New Sales Group at (800) 227-4908 or (513) 859-5398 inside the US, or (513) 865-7981 for all inquiries outside the US.

User Info: To subscribe, contact Mead directly.

To examine the Nexis user guide, you can access it at the ftp site of the University of Texas at Austin at the URL address: ftp://ftp.cc.utexas.edu

The files are in: /pub/ref-services/LEXIS

`telnet://nex.meaddata.com`

`http://www.meaddata.com`

INVEST (Investment News and Information)

The INVEST library contains company and industry research reports provided through the Investext(R) database. These reports are created by industry experts who are employed for their accurate and insightful evaluation. Only the most recent 12 months of data will be displayed.

Keywords: Companies, Finance, Analysis

Audience: Business Researchers, Analysts, Entrepreneurs

Profile: INVEST is categorized by type. Selections can be made using these categories: Industry (more than 50 industries are available), State (where a specific company is located), Country (Country in which the company is located), US Broker or International Broker. The INVEST library provides an automatic display following the selection of a file. For industry reports, a menu will appear providing definitions as they relate to the industries. All remaining files will provide a confirmation of the file selected.

Contact: Mead New Sales Group at (800) 227-4908 or (513) 859-5398 inside the US, or (513) 865-7981 for all inquiries outside the US.

A
B
C
D
E
F
G
H
I
J
K
L
M
N
O
P
Q
R
S
T
U
V
W
X
Y
Z

User Info: To subscribe, contact Mead directly.

To examine the Nexis user guide, you can access it at the ftp site of the University of Texas at Austin at the URL address: ftp://ftp.cc.utexas.edu

The files are in: /pub/ref-services/LEXIS

`telnet://nex.meaddata.com`

`http://www.meaddata.com`

D&B - Duns Financial Records Plus

 ★★★

This database provides up to three years of comprehensive financial statements for over 650,000 private and public companies.

Keywords: Finance, Business, Dun & Bradstreet

Sponsor: Dun & Bradstreet Information Services, Parsippany, NJ, USA

Audience: Business Professionals

Profile: Information provided includes balance sheet, income statement, and 14 of the most widely used business ratios for measuring solvency, efficiency, and profitability. A company's financial position can be compared to those of others in the same industry as determined by industry norm percentages. In addition, there are over 1.2 million records included that contain company history and operations background only. DFR also contains company identification data, such as company name, address, primary and secondary SIC codes, D-U-N-S number, and number of employees. Textual paragraphs cover the history and operations background of a firm. Coverage: Current; updated quarterly.

Contact: Dialog in the US at (800) 334-2564, Dialog internationally at country-specific locations.

Details: Costs

User Info: To subscribe, contact Dialog directly.

`telnet://dialog.com`

D&B - Dun's Electronic Business Directory

★★★

Keywords: Finance, Business, Dun & Bradstreet

Sponsor: Dun & Bradstreet Information Services, Parsippany, NJ, USA

Audience: Business Professionals, Business Analysts

Profile: A full directory listing is provided for each entry, including address, telephone number, SIC codes and descriptions, and number of employees. The file covers both public and private US companies of all sizes and types. Fifteen broad business categories are indexed as industry groups: agriculture, business services, communication, construction, finance, insurance, manufacturing, mining, professional services, public

administration, real estate, retail, transportation, utilities, and wholesale. Data for the file is compiled and maintained primarily through Dun & Bradstreet's intensive credit interviewing process. Dun's staff of 1,300 business analysts actively interviews millions of entrepreneurs each year. This information is supplemented with data from large-volume telemarketing and direct mail campaigns. Coverage: Current; updated quarterly.

Contact: Dialog in the US at (800) 334-2564, Dialog internationally at country-specific locations.

Details: Costs

User Info: To subscribe, contact Dialog directly.

`telnet://dialog.com`

Dun & Bradstreet Corporation

 ★★

Dun and Bradstreet's home page contains examples of existing services, services in development, and business and financial information, advising and so on.

Keywords: Finance, Business

Audience: General Public, Business Professionals

Profile: Files include company news, related industry information, product descriptions, and discussions of IBM's services.

`http://www.corp.dnb.com`

Experimental Stock Market Data

 ★★★

This is an experimental page that provides a link to the latest stock market information.

Keywords: Stock Market, Investments, Finance

Audience: General Public, Investors, Stock Brokers

Profile: This site is updated automatically, to reflect the current day's closing information. Provides general market news and quotes for selected stocks, although prices are not guaranteed. Also includes recent prices for many mutual funds, as well as technical analysis charts for a large number of stocks and mutual funds.

Contact: Mark Torrance stockmaster@ai.mit.edu

Details: Free

`http://www.ai.mit.edu/stocks.html`

FinanceNet (National Performance Review)

 ★★★★

FinanceNet is intended to act as a forum for discussing the "reinvention" of government, to make it more cost effective and efficient.

Keywords: Finance, Federal Documents (US), Federal Register (US), Federal Government (US)

Sponsor: National Performance Review (NPR)

Audience: Government Officials, Journalists, Financial Analysts

Profile: FinanceNet is associated with Vice President Al Gore's National Performance Review (NPR). Available resources include text of Congressional testimony, agency reports, publications and announcements of upcoming events, all related to the improvement of federal money-managing and government accounting. It also has links to a number of other federal systems, including the NPR, Congressional Quarterly, and the Federal Register.

Contact: B. Preston Rich or Linda L.Hoogeveen Preston.Rich@nsf.gov or lhoog@tmn.com

Details: Free

Notes: Send a blank message to info@financenet.gov to receive more information about this project.

`gopher://gopher.financenet.gov`

`http://www.financenet.gov/`

misc.invest

 ★

A Usenet newsgroup providing information and discussion about how to invest money.

Keywords: Investments, Finance

Audience: General Public

Details: Free

User Info: To subscribe to this Usenet newsgroup, you need access to a newsreader.

`news:misc.invest`

Stock Market Secrets

 ★

Publication of a stock market-related daily commentary. Questions are answered on a wide variety of investment and financial topics.

Keywords: Stock Market, Investments, Finance

Audience: Investors, Stock Brokers, Financial Advisors

Contact: smi-request@world.std.com

Details: Free, Moderated

User Info: To subscribe to the list, send an e-mail message requesting a subscription to the URL address below. To send a message to the entire list, address it to: smi@world.std.com

`mailto:smi-request@world.std.com`

US General Accounting Office Transitional Reports

A major directory on accounting, providing access to a broad range of related resources (library catalogs, databases, and servers) via the Internet.

Keywords: Government (US), Finance

Audience: Politicians, Government Workers

Profile: Contains full-text documents of the Transitional Reports for the U.S. General Accounting Office. Reports includes Budget Issues, Investment, Government Management Issues, Financial Management Issues, Health Care Reform, National Security Issues, International Trade Issues, and so on.

Contact: kh3@cu.nih.gov

`gopher://thor.ece.uc.edu`

Finding E-mail Addresses

Finding E-mail Addresses

Tips on finding e-mail addresses.

Keywords: Internet, E-mail

Audience: Internet Surfers

Contact: Jonathan Kamens
jib@MIT.Edu

Details: Free
File is pub/docs/about-the-net/libsoft/ email_address.txt

`ftp://sunsite.unc.edu`

Finding Resources on the Internet

Finding Resources on the Internet

A collection of help files introducing the new user to Internet utilities and resources.

Keywords: Internet Reference, Information Retrieval

Sponsor: Proper Publishing

Audience: Internet Surfers

Contact: info@proper.com

`gopher://proper.com`

Fine Arts

Art-support

A UK Mailbase forum for the discussion of art-related matters.

Keywords: Art, Fine Arts

Audience: Artists, Art Enthusiasts, Art Students
Login guest; password mailbase

`gopher://mailbase@mailbase.ac.uk`

`mailto:art-support-request@mailbase.ac.uk`

`telnet://mailbase.ac.uk`

HypArt

This is the site of an International collaborative art project.

Keywords: Art, Fine Art

Sponsor: University of Hamburg

Audience: Artists, Designers

Contact: rosenfeld@rrz.uni-hamburg.de

Details: Free

`http://rzsun01.rrz.uni-hamburg.de/ cgi-bin/HypArt.sh`

Internet Art Gallery

An online art collection in the form of JPEG files, including the works of 85 artists ranging from Dali to Van Eyck.

Keywords: Art, Fine Art, Art History

Sponsor: New York State Education Department

Audience: Artists, Art Students, Art Teachers, General Public

Contact: Steve Richter, George Casler
steve@unix5.nysed.gov,
gcasler@unix5.nysed.gov

`gopher://unix5.nysed.gov`

rec.arts.fin

A Usenet newsgroup providing information and discussion about the visual arts. Discussions range from archival materials to Ansel Adams, Mary Cassat, and Andy Warhol.

Keywords: Art, Fine Art

Audience: Artists, Art Educators, Art Professionals

User Info: To subscribe to this Usenet newsgroup, you need access to a newsreader.

`news:rec.arts.fin`

rec.arts.dance

A Usenet newsgroup providing information and discussion about all types of dance.

Keywords: Dance, Fine Arts

Audience: Dancers, Dance Enthusiasts, Choreographers

User Info: To subscribe to this Usenet newsgroup, you need access to a newsreader.

`news: rec.arts.dance`

Rosen Sculpture Exhibition

This web site contains various examples of sculpture movements.

Keywords: Art, Fine Arts

Sponsor: Visual Resources Curator of the Department of Art at Appalachian State University, Boone, North Carolina, USA

Audience: Art Educators, Art Students

`http://www.acs.appstate.edu/art`

FineArt Forum

FineArt Forum

A monthly newsletter that includes listings of art and technology events, showcases, conferences, and jobs.

Keywords: Art, Multimedia

Sponsor: The International Society for the Arts, Sciences, and Technology

Audience: Art Educators, Art Professionals, Artists

Profile: Published by the National Science Foundation Engineering Research Center for Computational Field Simulation, Mississippi State University. FineArt Forum has provided timely information to a large international audience since 1988. The subscriber list consists of individuals working in the realm where art, science, and technology converge. Issues provide information about conferences and competitions, calls for presentations and research, and notices about performances. FineArt_Online is both an archive of FineArt Forum, ISEA News, Leonardo Electronic News, and a variety of longer postings. In January 1994 it began posting an online gallery.

Contact: Paul Brown
brown@erc.msstate.edu

User Info: To subscribe, send e-mail to: brown@erc.msstate.edu, with the message SUB FAST; also give your name, postal address, and e-mail address.

`http://www.msstate.edu/ Fineart_Online/home.html`

A B C D E F G H I J K L M N O P Q R S T U V W X Y Z

A
B
C
D
E
F
G
H
I
J
K
L
M
N
O
P
Q
R
S
T
U
V
W
X
Y
Z

Finger (Internet Database)

Finger Database

This service allows access to a database facility via finger.

Keywords: Internet Services, Finger

Audience: Internet Surfers

Contact: http://www.usyd.edu.au

Details: Free

```
http://www-nsrutgers.edu/htbin/finger
```

Firearms

ba-Firearms

This is an announcement and discussion of firearms legislation and related issues. The ca- list is for California statewide issues; the ba- list is for the San Francisco Bay Area and gets all messages sent to the ca- list. Prospective members should subscribe to one or the other, generally depending on whether or not they are SF Bay Area residents.

Keywords: Firearms, Gun Control Legislation, San Francisco Bay Area

Audience: Politicians, General Public, Gun Users, San Francisco Bay Area Residents

Contact: Jeff Chan
ba-firearms-request@shell.portal.com

Details: Free

User Info: To subscribe to the list, send an e-mail message requesting a subscription to the URL address below.

To send a message to the entire list, address it to:
ba-firearms@shell.portal.com

```
mailto:ba-firearms-
request@shell.portal.com
```

ca-Firearms

This is an announcement and discussion of firearms legislation and related issues. The ca- list is for California statewide issues; the ba- list is for the San Francisco Bay Area and gets all messages sent to the ca- list. Prospective members should subscribe to one or the other, generally depending on whether or not they are SF Bay Area residents.

Keywords: Firearms, Gun Control Legislation, California

Audience: Politicians, General Public, Gun Users, California Residents

Contact: Jeff Chan
ca-firearms-request@shell.portal.com

Details: Free

User Info: To subscribe to the list, send an e-mail message requesting a subscription to the URL address below.

To send a message to the entire list, address it to:
ca-firearms@shell.portal.com

```
mailto:ca-firearms-
request@shell.portal.com
```

rec.guns

A Usenet newsgroup providing information and discussion about firearms.

Keywords: Firearms, Weapons

Audience: Gun Users

User Info: To subscribe to this Usenet newsgroup, you need access to a newsreader.

```
news:rec.guns
```

Firewalls

comp.security.misc

A Usenet newsgroup providing information and discussion about security issues of computers and networks.

Keywords: Computers, Security, Firewalls

Audience: Computer Users

User Info: To subscribe to this Usenet newsgroup, you need access to a newsreader.

```
news:comp.security.misc
```

Systems Operators, firewalls

A mailing list to discuss the issues involved in setting up and maintaining Internet security firewall systems.

Keywords: Security, Internet Security, Firewalls

Audience: Security Workers, Network Administrator, System Operators

Contact: Brent Chapman
Brent@GreatCircle.com

Details: Free

User Info: To subscribe to the list, send an e-mail message consisting of a single line reading:

SUB firewalls YourFirstName YourLastName

```
mailto:majordomo@greatcircle.com
```

Fish

alt.aquaria

A Usenet newsgroup providing information and discussion about the aquarium as a hobby.

Keywords: Aquariums, Fish, Hobbies

Audience: Aquarium Keepers, Fish Lovers

User Info: To subscribe to this Usenet newsgroup, you need access to a newsreader.

```
news:alt.aquaria
```

FINS (Fish Information Service)

This site provides information on issues relating to fish, including aquarium-building tips, diseases, clubs, newsgroups, movies, and fish trivia from Woods Hole Oceanographic Institute.

Keywords: Fish, Oceanography

Sponsor: Active Window Productions

Audience: Fish Enthusiasts, Ichthyologists

Details: Free

```
http://www.actwin.com/fish/index.html
```

rec.aquaria

A Usenet newsgroup providing information and discussion about pet fish and aquaria.

Keywords: Fish, Aquatic Sciences

Audience: Fish Enthusiasts

Details: Free

User Info: To subscribe to this Usenet newsgroup, you need access to a newsreader.

```
news:rec.aquaria
```

Fisheries

University of Maryland, College Park

The library's holdings are large and wide-ranging and contain significant collections in many fields.

Keywords: Agriculture, Coastal Marine Biology, Fisheries, Water Quality, Oceanography

Audience: Researchers, Students, General Public

Contact: Janet McLeod
mcleod@umail.umd.edu

Details: Free

User Info: Expect: Login; Send: Atdu

```
telnet://info.umd.edu
```

wildnet (Computing and Statistics in Fishers & Wildlife Biology)

This mailing list was established for the exchange of ideas, questions, and solutions in the area of fisheries and wildlife biology computing and statistics.

Keywords: Wildlife, Fisheries, Statistics

Audience: Wildlife Biologists, Environmentalists, Statisticians

Contact: Eric Woodsworth
woodsworth@sask.usask.ca

Details: Free

User Info: To subscribe to the list, send an e-mail message requesting a subscription to the URL address below.

To send a message to the entire list, address it to: wildnet@tribune.usask.ca

```
mailto:wildnet-
request@tribune.usask.ca
```

Fitness

Biking

Information on biking events and maintenance, including an FAQ from rec.bicycles.

Keywords: Sports, Bicycling, Fitness

Audience: Bicyclists, Fitness Enthusiasts

Contact: Joern Yngve Dahl-Stamnes
dahls@fysel.unit.no

Details: Free

```
ftp://ugle.unit.no/local/biking
```

GolfData OnLine

A web site sampling of the information on the subscriber service GolfData OnLine. Provides numerous links to other sites which may be of interest to golfers.

Keywords: Golf, Sports, Fitness

Audience: Golfers, Sports Fans

Contact: david@gdol.com

Notes: GolfData Online is a paid subscriber electronic bulletin board service for golf enthusiasts. More information about how to subscribe can be obtained by accessing the address below.

```
http://www.gdol.com
```

Open Computing Facilty (OCF) Gopher, Sports Section ★★★★

A gopher server offering access to information about a number of sporting activities.

Keywords: Sports, Fitness

Sponsor: Open Computing Facility, University of California, Berkeley

Audience: Sports Fans, Fitness Enthusiasts

Profile: This gopher has information on various sports, including football, cricket, skiing, windsurfing, and basketball, as well as links to WWW. Resources include schedules for some professional and collegiate sports, as well as FAQs and other miscellaneous information.

Contact: general-manager@ocf.berkeley.edu

Details: Free

```
gopher://gopher.ocf.berkeley.edu/11/
gopherspace
```

The Wellness List

This list is founded for the purpose of discussing issues concerning Health/Nutrition/Wellness/Life Expectancy/Physical Fitness, and the books, experiences, and solutions recommended by the participants.

Keywords: Health, Nutrition, Fitness

Audience: Doctors, Nutritionists, General Public

Profile: This resource provides announcements of and reviews of books that include solutions, nutrition related position papers, requests for information, recommendations of participants, healthy recipes, nutrition and fitness related product announcements, and general discussion of related issues. Health professionals, authors, and nutritionists are encouraged to subscribe and share their knowledge with the participants.

Contact: George Rust, Wellnessmart
george@wellnessmart.com,
info@wellnessmart.com

User Info: To subscribe send an e-mail message to the URL address below consisting of a single line reading: subscribe wellnesslist

```
mailto:majordomo@wellnessmart.com
```

FL-Raves (Florida Raves)

FL-Raves (Florida Raves) ★

One of several regional rave-related mailing lists, this covers the state of Florida. Discussions tend to be social; Floridians may want to check out SERaves as well.

Keywords: Raves, Florida

Audience: Ravers, Florida Residents

Details: Free

User Info: To subscribe to the list, send an e-mail message requesting a subscription to the URL address below.

To send a message to the entire list, address it to:
flraves@cybernet.cse.fau.edu

```
mailto:flraves-
request@cybernet.cse.fau.edu
```

Flags

flags ★

A discussion about all kinds of flags, including (inter)national, (un)official, political, religious, movements' flags, and others. Topics include the analysis of symbols and colors used on flags, and the history of particular flags.

Keywords: Flags

Audience: Historians

Contact: Giuseppe Bottasini
bottasini@cesi.it

Details: Free

User Info: To subscribe to the list, send an e-mail message requesting a subscription to the URL address below.

To send a message to the entire list, address it to: flags@cesi.it

```
mailto:bottasi@cesi.it
```

flamingo

flamingo ★

This list discusses the series 'Parker Lewis' (formerly 'Parker Lewis Can't Lose') on the Fox television network.

Keywords: Television, Fox Television

Audience: Television Viewers

Details: Free

User Info: To subscribe to the list, send an e-mail message requesting a subscription to the URL address below.

To send a message to the entire list, address it to:
flamingo@lenny.corp.sgi.com

```
mailto:flamingo-request@lenny.corp.
sgi.com
```

flashlife

flashlife ★

A mailing list for general managers of Shadowrun and other cyberpunk role-playing games to discuss rules and scenarios, ask questions, and make up answers.

Keywords: Games, Cyberpunk Games, Role Playing

Audience: Game Players, Cyberpunks

Details: Free

User Info: To subscribe to the list, send an e-mail message requesting a subscription to the URL address below.

To send a message to the entire list, address it to: flashlife@netcom.com

```
mailto:flashlife-request@netcom.com
```

Flight Simulation

Aviator ★

A mailing list for users of Aviator™, the flight-simulation program from Artificial Horizons, Inc.

Keywords: Aviation, Simulation, Computers, Flight Simulation

Audience: Compueter Games Users

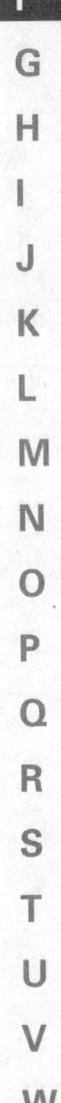

A
B
C
D
E
F
G
H
I
J
K
L
M
N
O
P
Q
R
S
T
U
V
W
X
Y
Z

Contact: Jim Hickstein
           aviator@ICDwest.Teradyne.COM

Details: Free

User Info: To subscribe to the list, send an e-mail
            message requesting a subscription to
            the URL address below.

            To send a message to the entire list,
            address it to:
            aviator@ICDwest.Teradyne.COM

Notes: Aviator runs on Sun workstations with
           the GX graphics accelerator option. Its
           charter is simply to facilitate
           communication among users of Aviator.
           It is not intended for communication with
           the "providers" of Aviator. All mail
           received at the submission address is
           reflected to all the subscribers of the list.

```
mailto:aviator-
request@ICDwest.Teradyne.COM
```

Florida

Florida State University System Library

The library's holdings are large and wide-ranging and contain significant collections in many fields.

Keywords: Florida, Latin America, Judaica,
            Literature (Children's), Marine
            Engineering, Law (Brazilian), Law
            (British)

Audience: General Public, Researchers, Librarians,
            Document Delivery Professionals

Details: Free

User Info: Expect: Command ==>, Send: dial vtam;
            Expect: LUIS User Menu, Send: Your
            Catalog choice; To log off: Send: %off

```
telnet://nervm.nerdc.ufl.edu
```

South Florida Environmental Reader

★

Newsletter distributing information on the environment of South Florida.

Keywords: Environment, Florida

Audience: Environmentalists

Contact: aem@mthvax.cs.miami.edu

Details: Free

User Info: To subscribe to the list, send an e-mail
            messgae requesting a subscription to
            the URL address below.

            To send a mesage to the entire USL,
            address it to: sfer@mthvax.cs.miami.edu

```
mail to:sfer-
requesti@mthvax.cs.miami.edu
```

Fluid Dynamics

CFD

CFD (Computational Fluid Dynamics Group).

Keywords: Engineering, Fluid Dynamics

Audience: Engineers

Contact: JUSTIN@UKCC.UKY.EDU
            justin@engr.uky.edu

Details: Free

User Info: To subscribe to the list, send an e-mail
            message to the URL address below,
            consisting of a single line reading:

            SUB cfd YourFirstName YourLastName

            To send a message to the entire list,
            address it to:
            cfd@UKCC.UKY.EDU

```
justin@UKCC.UKY.EDU
```

FM-10

FM-10

★

A discussion of modifications, enhancements, and uses of the Ramsey FM-10 and other BA-1404 based FM stereo broadcasters; some discussion of the FM pirate radio, as well.

Keywords: Radio, Broadcasting

Audience: Broadcasters, Radio Broadcasters

Details: Free

User Info: To subscribe to the list, send an e-mail
            message requesting a subscription to
            the URL address below.

            To send a message to the entire list,
            address it to: fm-10@dg-rtp.dg.com

```
mailto:fm-10-request@dg-rtp.dg.com
```

fogelberg

fogelberg

★

A discussion of the work of recording artist Dan Fogelberg.

Keywords: Music, Musicians

Audience: Dan Fogelberg Enthusiasts

Contact: ai411@yfn.ysu.edu

Details: Free

User Info: To subscribe to the list, send an e-mail
            message requesting a subscription to
            the URL address below.

            To send a message to the entire list,
            address it to: fogelberg@yfn.ysu.edu

```
mailto:ai411@yfn.ysu.edu
```

Folk Dance

Folk-dancing

A discussion of folk dancing, including contra, square, western square, morris, cajun, and barn dancing.

Keywords: Dance, Folk Dance

Audience: Dancers, Folk Dancers

Contact: Terry J. Wood
            tjw+@pitt.edu

Details: Free

User Info: To subscribe to the list, send an e-mail
            message requesting a subscription to
            the URL address below.

            To send a message to the entire list,
            address it to: fdml@pitt.edu

Notes: Please note that the Folk Dancing
            Mailing List (fdml) operates in
            conjunction with the Usenet newsgroup
            rec.folk-dancing. When subscribing to
            the FDML, please include several
            computer mail addresses and a postal
            mail address (or phone number).

```
mailto:tjw+@pitt.edu
```

Folk Music

Folk music

★

This discussion list deals with the music of the recent wave of American singer/songwriters. List traffic includes tour schedules, reviews, album and release information.

Keywords: Folk Music, Music

Audience: Folk Musicians, Musicians, Folk Music
            Enthusiasts

Contact: Alan Rowoth
            listserv@nysernet.org

Details: Free

User Info: To subscribe to the list, send an e-mail
            message to the URL address below
            consisting of a single line reading:

            SUB folk_music YourFirstName
            YourLastName

            To send a message to the entire list,
            address it to: folk_music@nysernet.org

```
mailto:listserv@nysernet.org
```

University of New Hampshire Videotex Library

The library's holdings are large and wide-ranging and contain significant collections in many fields.

Keywords: Dance, Folk Music, Milne (A.A.,
            Collection of), Galway (Ireland)

Audience: Researchers, Students, General Public

Contact: Robin Tuttle
r_tuttle1@unhh.unh.edu

Details: Free

User Info: Expect: USERNAME; Send: Student (no
password required). Control-z to log off.

`telnet://unhvt@unh.edu`

Folklore

alt.folklore.computers

A Usenet newsgroup providing information and
discussion concerning stories and anecdotes about
computers.

Keywords: Computers, Folklore

Audience: Computer Users, Storytellers

User Info: To subscribe to this Usenet newsgroup,
you need access to a newsreader.

`news:alt.folklore.computers`

alt.folklore.urban

A Usenet newsgroup providing information and
discussion about urban legends and urban myths.

Keywords: Urban Studies, Folklore

Audience: Story Tellers, General Public

User Info: To subscribe to this Usenet newsgroup,
you need access to a newsreader.

`news:alt.folklore.urban`

Harvard University Library

The library's holdings are large and wide-ranging
and contain significant collections in many fields.

Keywords: Afrikaans, Alchemy, Arabic Culure
(History of), Celtic Philology, Congo
Languages, Folklore, Hebraica,
Mormonism, Numismatics, Quakers,
Sanskrit, Witchcraft, Arabic Philology

Audience: General Public, Researchers, Librarians,
Document Delivery Professionals

Details: Free

User Info: Expect: Mitek Server..., Send: Enter or
Return; Expect: prompt, Send: hollis

`telnet://hollis.harvard.edu`

University of Nebraska at Lincoln Library

The library's holdings are large and wide-ranging
and contain significant collections in many fields.

Keywords: Slovak Republic, Czech Republic,
Folklore, Military History, Latvia, Law
(Tax), Law (US)

Audience: General Public, Researchers, Librarians,
Document Delivery Professionals

Contact: Anita Cook

Details: Free

User Info: Expect: login, Send: library

`telnet://unllib.unl.edu`

University of Tennessee at Knoxville Library

The library's holdings are large and wide-ranging
and contain significant collections in many fields.

Keywords: Native American Affairs, Congress (US),
Folklore, Travel (History of)

Audience: Researchers, Students, General Public

Details: Free

User Info: Expect: OK Prompt; Send: Login pub1;
Expect: Password, Send: Usc

`telnet://opac.lib.utk.edu`

Folklore Collection

University of Denver Library

The library's holdings are large and wide-ranging
and contain significant collections in many fields.

Keywords: Folklore Collection, Husted (Margaret,
Culinary Collection of)

Audience: Researchers, Students, General Public

Contact: Bob Stocker
bstocker@ducair.bitnet

Details: Free

User Info: Expect: Login; Send: Atdu

`telnet:// du.edu`

Food

Diogenes

Diogenes provides access to the US Food and Drug
Administration (FDA) regulatory information needed
by the health care industry.

Keywords: Food, Drugs

Sponsor: Diogenes, Rockville, MD, USA

Audience: Health Care Professionals

Profile: The database contains news stories and
unpublished documents relating to the
United States regulation of pharmaceuticals and medical devices. The complete
text is provided for materials that are
substantive and timely. Diogenes covers
information relating to the Food and Drug
Administration regulation of drugs and
medical devices, including listings of
approved products, experience reports
for devices, documentation of the
approval process for specific products,
recall and regulatory action documentation, and more.

Contact: Dialog in the US at (800) 334-2564, Dialog
internationally at country-specific
locations.

User Info: To subscribe, contact Dialog directly.

Notes: Coverage: 1976 to the present; updated
weekly.

`telnet://dialog.com`

PENPages

This easy-to-use general-interest database contains
articles and brochures.

Keywords: Food, Employment, Education

Sponsor: Pennsylvania State University, PA

Audience: General Public

User Info: Expect: login; Send: your state's two-
letter code (or "world" if sent from
outside the USA)

`telnet://psunet.psu.edu`

rec.food.cooking

A Usenet newsgroup providing information and
discussion about cooking.

Keywords: Food, Cooking

Audience: General Public, Cooks, Chefs

User Info: To subscribe to this Usenet newsgroup,
you need access to a newsreader.

`news:rec.food.cooking`

rec.food.veg

A Usenet newsgroup providing information and
discussion about vegetarian cooking.

Keywords: Vegetarianism, Food, Cooking

Audience: Vegetarians, Cooks, Chefs

User Info: To subscribe to this Usenet newsgroup,
you need access to a newsreader.

`news:rec.food.veg`

Recipe Archive

This is an archive of recipes organized by main
ingredient or title.

Keywords: Cooking, Food

Audience: General Public, Cooks, Chefs

Profile: Here are a few intriguing examples from
the archive:

Advokaat: Advokaat is the Dutch word
for egg cognac. It is highly recommended for A. I. (Alcohol Imbibing)
meetings. This recipe is a modification of
a recipe obtained in Poland. It makes a
potent, superb advokaat (or egg
cognac). The milk and eggs are healthy,
the sugar and alcohol are not!

Berlinerkranzer: Norwegian wreath
cookies are decorative holiday cookies
that add quite a bright, colorful, aromatic
touch to your plate of cookies.

A B C D E F G H I J K L M N O P Q R S T U V W X Y Z

Bouillabaisse: This recipe for Marseille-style fish soup represents a combination of several recipes derived from old Gourmets, Julia Child, the Playboy Gourmet Cookbook, and "Gee, that sounds good, let's add it.." The accompanying rouille is a garlic/hot pepper mayonnaise condiment traditional to Marseille-style fish soup.

Details: Free

gopher://calypso.oit.unc.edu/ 7waissrc%3a/ref.d/indexes.d/recipes.src

gopher://calypso.oit.unc.edu/ 7waissrc%3a/ref.d/indexes.d/ usenet-cookbook.sr

They can also be accessed through MOSAIC at the URL address shown below or from the calypso.oit.unc.edu gopher in the subdirectories: Internet Dog-Eared Pages (Frequently used resources)/Search Many WAIS Indices

Notes: There are two searchable gopher Indexes containing recipes that have passed through the rec.food.cooking and rec.food.recipes newsgroups. They can be found at the following URL addresses:

`ftp://gatekeeper.dec.com/pub/recipes`

Seafood Internet Network

A mailing list to facilitate information exchange about the HACCP Alliance and the implementation of the FDA seafood HACCP program.

Keywords: Food, FDA

Audience: Seafood Industry Professionals

Contact: Robert J. Price
rjprice@dale.ucdavis.edu

User Info: To subscribe , send an e-mail message to: listproc@ucdavis.edu Leave the subject blank and place in the body of the note: subscribe seafood YourFirstName YourLastName

`mailto:seafood@ucdavis.edu`

The World Wide Web rec.food.recipes archive

World Wide Web archive of recipes posted to Usenet newsgroup rec.food.recipes. Updated weekly.

Keywords: Food, Recipes, Cooking

Audience: Cooks, General Public

Contact: Amy Gale
mara@kauri.vuw.ac.nz

User Info: Use a World-Wide Web (WWW) client such as lynx

`http://www.vuw.ac.nz/non-local/ recipes-archive/recipe-archive.html`

VEGCNY-L (Vegetarians in Central New York area)

VegCNY-L is an open discussion list intended to serve those people living in the Central New York area who are vegetarians, as well as those who are interested in vegetarianism.

Keywords: Vegetarianism, New York, Food

Audience: Vegetarians

Contact: Chuck Goelzer Lyons
cgl1@cornell.edu

Details: Free

User Info: To subscribe to the list, send an e-mail message to the URL address below consisting of a single line reading:

SUB VEGCNY-L YourFirstName Your:LastName

To send a message to the entire list, address it to: VEGCNY-L@cornell.edu

`mailto:listserv@cornell.edu`

veggie (Vegetarian Issues Discussion List)

Veggie is an open list for the discussion of vegetarianism.

Keywords: Vegetarianism, Food

Audience: Vegetarians

Details: Free

User Info: To subscribe to the list, send an e-mail message to the URL address below consisting of a single line reading:

SUB veggie YourFirstName YourLastName

`mailto:listserv@gibbs.oit.unc.edu`

veggies

Vegetarian matters in Britain.

Keywords: Vegetarianism, Britain, Food

Audience: Vegetarians

Details: Free

User Info: To subscribe to the list, send an e-mail message requesting a subscription to the URL address below.

To send a message to the entire list, address it to: veggies@ncl.ak.uk

`mailto:veggies-request@ncl.ac.uk`

veglife (Vegetarian Life List)

Veglife (formerly Granola) provides a supportive atmosphere for the discussion of issues related to the vegetarian lifestyle.

Keywords: Vegetarianism, Food

Audience: Vegetarians

Contact: Darrell A. Early, Charles Goelzer Lyons

Details: Free

User Info: To subscribe to the list, send an e-mail message to the URL address below consisting of a single line reading:

SUB veglife YourFirstName YourLastName

To send a message to the entire list, address it to: veglife@vtvml.cc.vt.edu

`mailto:listserv@vtvm1.cc.vt.edu`

Food Production

AGRIS International

This database serves as a comprehensive inventory of worldwide agricultural literature that reflects research results, food production, and rural development.

Keywords: Agriculture, Rural Development, Food Production, Development

Sponsor: US National Agricultural Library, Beltsville, MD, USA

Audience: Agronomists, Market Researchers

Profile: Designed to help users identify problems involved in all aspects of world food supply, the file corresponds in part to Agr Index, published monthly by the Food and Agriculture Organization (FAO) of the United Nations. Subject coverage focuses on many topics, general agriculture; geography and history; education, extension, and advisory work; administration and legislation; economics, development, and rural sociology; plant production; protection of plants and stored products; forestry; animal production; aquatic sciences and fisheries; machinery and buildings; natural resources; food science; home economics; human nutrition; pollution; and more.

Contact: Dialog in the US at (800) 334-2564

Details: Costs

User Info: To subscribe, contact Dialog directly.

`telnet://dialog.com`

Food Industry Investext

The world's largest database of company, industry, topical, and geographic analysis.

Keywords: Food Production, Agriculture Industry

Sponsor: Thomson Financial Networks, Boston, MA, US

Audience: Business Professionals, Market Researchers

Profile: The database is composed of more than 320,000 full-text reports written by analysts at 180 investment banks and research firms worldwide. The research can be used for a wide range of business intelligence activities, including competitive analysis, evaluation of companies, and strategic planning. Coverage includes 14,000 companies worldwide and 53 industry groups.

Contact: Dialog in the US at (800) 334-2564, Dialog internationally at country-specific locations.

User Info: To subscribe, contact Dialog directly.

Notes: Coverage: July 1982 to the present; updated daily.

`telnet://dialog.com`

Football

NFL Scores, Schedules, and Point Spreads

Information on National Football League (NFL) football scores, schedules, and point spreads.

Keywords: Professional Sports, Sports, Football, NFL

Audience: Football Fans

Contact: office@world.std.com

Details: Free

`gopher://world.std.com/News and Weather`

Professional Sports Schedules

Sports schedules for major professional sports.

Keywords: Sports, Baseball, Hockey, Football, Basketball

Sponsor: Colorado University, Boulder, CO

Audience: Sports Fans, Football Fans, Hockey Fans, Baseball Enthusiasts, Basketball Enthusiasts

Profile: The Colorado University gopher maintains an interactive online database of schedules for all major US professional sports teams (NBA, NFL, NHL, MLB). The database is indexed by both team name and dates of games, and can be searched accordingly.

Contact: gopher@gopher.colorado.edu

Details: Free

`gopher://gopher.colorado.edu/11/professional/sports/schedules`

rec.sport.football.college

A Usenet newsgroup providing information and discussion about college football.

Keywords: Football, College, Sports

Audience: Football Fans, Sports Fans

User Info: To subscribe to this Usenet newsgroup, you need access to a newsreader.

`news:rec.sport.football.college`

rec.sport.football.pro

A Usenet newsgroup providing information and discussion about pro football.

Keywords: Football, Sports

Audience: Football Enthusiasts

User Info: To subscribe to this Usenet newsgroup, you need access to a newsreader.

`news:rec.sport.football.pro`

Usenet Sports Groups Archived

An archive for Usenet groups, including many related to sports ranging from football to table tennis.

Keywords: Sports, Skydiving, Volleyball, Football, Scuba Diving, Table Tennis

Sponsor: Massachusetts Institute of Technology, Boston, MA

Audience: Sports Enthusiasts

Contact: ftp-bugs@rtfm.mit.edu

Details: Free

`ftp://rtfm.mit.edu/pub/usenet`

Wiretap Sports Archives

Sports articles, including information on soccer in the US and Canada, rules for soccer and Australian football, and some rather dated material on American football.

Keywords: Sports, Football, Soccer

Sponsor: The Internet Wiretap Library

Audience: Sports Enthusiasts

Details: Free

`gopher://wiretap.spies.com/library/article/sports`

Ford

Fordnatics

This unmoderated forum discusses high-performance Fords or Ford-powered vehicles, focusing on modifications and driving techniques for competition or track use.

Keywords: Automobiles, Fords

Audience: Automobile Enthusiasts, Ford Drivers, Racers

Details: Free

User Info: To subscribe to the list, send an e-mail message requesting a subscription to the URL address below.

   To send a message to the entire list, address it to:
   fordnatics@freud.arc.nasa.gov

`mailto:fordnatics-request@freud.arc.nasa.gov`

Mustangs

A forum for the discussion of technical issues, problems, solutions, and modifications relating to late-model (1980 and later) Ford Mustangs.

Keywords: Ford, Automobiles

Audience: Ford Owners

Details: Free

User Info: To subscribe to the list, send an e-mail message requesting a subscription to the URL address below.

`mailto:mustangs-request@cup.hp.com`

Foreign Trade

1994 Federal Budget (Canada)

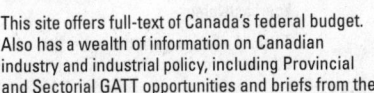

This site offers full-text of Canada's federal budget. Also has a wealth of information on Canadian industry and industrial policy, including Provincial and Sectorial GATT opportunities and briefs from the Information Highway Advisory Council.

Keywords: Canada, Government (International), Industry, Foreign Trade

Sponsor: Industry Canada, Canada

Audience: Canadians, Government Officials, Business Professionals, Researchers

Contact: Tyson Macaulay
   tyson@debra.dgbt.doc.ca

`gopher://debra.dgbt.doc.ca/industry canada documents/isc.news.releases`

World Bank Gopher Server

A collection of online information from the World Bank.

Keywords: Government (International), Development, International Finance, Foreign Trade

Sponsor: The World Bank

Audience: Nongovernmental Organizations, Activists, Government Officials, Environmentalists

Profile: A collection of World Bank information including a list of publications, environmental assessments, economic reports, and updates on current projects being funded by the World Bank.

Contact: webmaster@www.worldbank.org

`gopher://gopher.worldbank.org`

`http://www.worldbank.org`

A B C D E F G H I J K L M N O P Q R S T U V W X Y Z

A B C D E F G H I J K L M N O P Q R S T U V W X Y Z

Forestry

FMDSS-L (Forest Management Decision Support Systems)

This is a forum for the rapid exchange of information, ideas, and opinions related to the topics of DSS (decision support systems) and information systems for forest-management planning.

Keywords: Forest Management, Forestry

Audience: Foresters

Contact: Tom Moore
listserv@pnfi.forestry.ca

Details: Free

User Info: To subscribe to the list, send an e-mail message to the URL address below consisting of a single line reading:

SUB fmdss-l YourFirstName YourLastName

To send a message to the entire list, address it to: fmdss-l@pnfi.forestry.ca

`mailto:listserv@pnfi.forestry.ca`

Mississippi State University Library

The library's holdings are large and wide-ranging and contain significant collections in many fields.

Keywords: History (US), Forestry, Energy, Carter (Hodding, Papers of), Mississippi

Audience: General Public, Researchers, Librarians, Document Delivery Professionals

Contact: Stephen Cunetto
shc1@ra.msstate.edu

Details: Free

User Info: Expect: username, Send: msu; Expect: password, Send: library

`telnet://libserv.msstate.edu`

Natural Resources Canada (NRCan) Gopher

This site offers information on forests, energy, mining, and geomatics from the Canadian government. Also has reports from the Geological Survey of Canada and an overview of NRCan statutes, organization, and personnel. Provides links to other Canadian environmental and government gophers.

Keywords: Canada, Environment, Geology, Forestry

Sponsor: The Department of Natural Resources, Canada

Audience: Canadians, Environmentalists, Environmental Researchers, Geologists

Contact: Bob Fillmore
fillmore@emr.ca

Notes: NRCan maintains a toll-free hotline - 1-(800) 267-5166

`gopher://gopher.emr.ca`

`http://www.emr.ca`

Forests

Western Lands

A collection of articles and reports relating to environmental and land use issues in the Western United States.

Keywords: Environmentalism, Ecology, Forests, The Western United States

Sponsor: The Institute for Global Communications (IGC)

Audience: Environmentalists, Ecologists, Activists, Foresters, Citizens

Contact: Dan Yurman, IGC User Support
dyurman@igc.apc.com.,
support@igc.apc.com

Notes: User submissions encouraged.

`gopher://gopher.igc.apc.org/11/ environment/forests/western.lands`

Four Wheel Drive

Offroad

Discusses and shares experiences with four-wheel and off-road adventures, including driving tips, vehicle modifications, and anything else related to four-wheeling. This list is specifically designed for four-wheel-drive vehicle owners, users, or enthusiasts. Discussions center around technical and mechanical matters, driving techniques, and trip reports.

Keywords: Four Wheel Drive

Audience: Off Road Driving Enthusiasts, Four Wheel Drive Enthusiasts

Contact: Stefan Roth
offroad-request@ai.gtri.gatech.edu

Details: Free

User Info: To subscribe to the list, send an e-mail message requesting a subscription to the URL address below.

To send a message to the entire list, address it to: offroad@ai.gtri.gatech.edu

`mailto:offroad-request@ai.gtri.gatech.edu`

Fox Television

flamingo

This list discusses the series 'Parker Lewis' (formerly 'Parker Lewis Can't Lose') on the Fox television network.

Keywords: Television, Fox Television

Audience: Television Viewers

Details: Free

User Info: To subscribe to the list, send an e-mail message requesting a subscription to the URL address below.

To send a message to the entire list, address it to:
flamingo@lenny.corp.sgi.com

`mailto:flamingo-request@lenny.corp. sgi.com`

Melrose-place

Discussion of the Fox television show Melrose Place.

Keywords: Melrose Place, Fox Television, Television Series

Audience: Melrose Place Fans, Television Viewers

Details: Free

User Info: To subscribe to the list, send an e-mail message requesting a subscription to the URL address below.

`mailto:melrose-place-request@ferkel.ucsb.edu`

foxpro-l

foxpro-l

This mailing list is designed to foster information sharing between users of the FoxPro™ database development environment now owned and distributed by Microsoft. Both new and experienced users of FoxPro are welcome to join in the discussions.

Keywords: Databases, Computers, Microsoft Corp.

Audience: Database Users, Microsoft FoxPro Users, Software Engineers

Contact: Chris O'Neill
coneill@heaven.polarbear.rankin-inlet.nt.ca

Details: Free

User Info: To subscribe to the list, send an e-mail message requesting a subscription to the URL address below.

To send a message to the entire list, address it to: foxpro-l@polarbear.rankin-inlet.nt.ca

`mailto:fileserv@polarbear.rankin-inlet.nt.ca`

framers

framers

This is a forum to share experiences and information about the FrameMaker desktop-publishing package from Frame Technology.

Keywords: Desktop Publishing

Audience: Desktop Publishers, Publishers

Details: Free

User Info: To subscribe to the list, send an e-mail message requesting a subscription to the URL address below.

To send a message to the entire list, address it to: framers@uunet.uu.net

`mailto:framers-request@uunet.uu.net`

France

france-foot

Discussions of the French football (soccer) scene. Results and news are posted regularly.

Keywords: Soccer, Sports, France, Football

Audience: Soccer Enthusiasts, French Sports Enthusiasts

Contact: Vincent Habchi, Kent Hedlundh dvlkhh@cs.umu.se

Details: Free

User Info: To subscribe to the list, send an e-mail message requesting a subscription to the URL address below.

To send a message to the entire list, address it to: france-foot@inf.enst.fr

`mailto:france-foot-request@inf.enst.fr`

soc.culture.french

A Usenet newsgroup providing information and discussion about French culture and history.

Keywords: France, Sociology

Audience: Sociologists, Francophiles

Details: Free

User Info: To subscribe to this Usenet newsgroup, you need access to a newsreader.

`news:soc.culture.french`

Fraud

Scifraud

Scifraud is dedicated to the discussion of fraud in science.

Keywords: Science, Fraud

Audience: Scientists

Contact: Al Higgins, Mike Ramundo ach13@albnyvms.bitnet sysmrr@albnyvm1.bitnet

Details: Free

User Info: To subscribe to the list, send an e-mail message to the URL address below consisting of a single line reading:

SUB scifraud YourFirstName YourLastName

To send a message to the entire list, address it to: scifraud@uacs2.albany.edu

`mailto:listserv@uacsc2.albany.edu`

freaks

freaks

This mailing list focuses on Marillion and related rock groups.

Keywords: Music, Rock Music

Audience: Marillion Enthusiasts

Details: Free

User Info: To subscribe to the list, send an e-mail message requesting a subscription to the URL address below.

To send a message to the entire list, address it to:freaks@bnf.com

`mailto:freaks-request@bnf.com`

FrEd Mail Foundation

FrEd Mail Foundation

This foundation specializes in establishing innovative and educationally rewarding collaborative projects using the Internet for the K-12 community.

Keywords: Children, Education (K-12)

Audience: Educators (K-12)

Contact: Al Rogers arogers@bonita.cerf.fred.org

Details: Free

`gopher://gopher.cerf.net/11/fredmail`

Free Art For HTML Page

Free Art For HTML Page

This web site provides copyrighted graphics for the MOSAIC program.

Keywords: Computer-Aided Design, Graphics

Audience: Designers, Educators

Contact: Harlan Wallach wallach@mcs.com

Details: Free

`http://www.mcs.net/wallach/Fart/buttons.html`

Free for All

Free for All

An experiment in a networked hypermedia group bulletin board.

Keywords: Internet, Group Communications, Multimedia

Audience: Internet Surfers,Multimedia Enthusiasts

Details: Free, Multimedia

`http://south.ncsa.uiuc.edu/Free.html`

Free Software

GNUs Bulletin: Newsletter of the Free Software Foundation

Bringing you news about the GNU Project, the Free Software Foundation is dedicated to eliminating restrictions on copying, redistribution, understanding, and modification of computer programs.

Keywords: Software, Shareware, Free Software

Sponsor: Free Software Foundation

Audience: Computer Programmers, Computer Users

Contact: Leonard H. Tower, Jr. tower@ai.mit.edu

Details: Free

news:gnu.announce

`mailto:info-gnu-request@prep.ai.mit.edu`

Free Trade

North American Free Trade Agreement (NAFTA)

The agreement among the governments of Canada, the United Mexican States, and the United States of America to establish a free trade area in North America.

Keywords: Trade, US, Mexico, Canada, Free Trade, NAFTA

Audience: Journalists, Politicians, Economists, Students

Details: Free

`gopher://wiretap.spies.com/00/Gov/NAFTA`

A B C D E F G H I J K L M N O P Q R S T U V W X Y Z

A
B
C
D
E
F
G
H
I
J
K
L
M
N
O
P
Q
R
S
T
U
V
W
X
Y
Z

freedom

freedom

Mailing list of people organizing against the Idaho Citizens Alliance antigay ballot initiative.

Keywords: Gay Rights, Activism, Gays

Audience: Gays, Lesbians, Bisexuals, Idaho Citizens, Activists

Details: Free

User Info: To subscribe to the list, send an e-mail message to the URL address shown below consisting of a single line reading:

SUB freedom YourFirstName YourLastName.

To send a message to the entire list, address it to: freedom@idbsu.idbsu.edu

`mailto:listserv@idbsu.idbsu.edu`

Freedom of Information

Freedom of Information Act (FOIA): Guide to Use

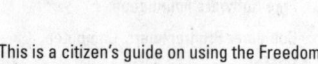

This is a citizen's guide on using the Freedom of Information Act and the Privacy Act of 1974 to request government records.

Keywords: Privacy, Freedom of Information, Government (US Federal)

Audience: Journalists, Privacy Activists, Students, Politicians, US Citizens

Details: Free

`gopher://wiretap.spies.com/00/Gov/foia.cit`

Freedom of Information Directory of Records (Canada)

A database compiled by the Canadian federal government listing documents available to the public under The Freedom of Information and Protection of Privacy Act. It can be searched by keyword, or browsed through a menuing system.

Keywords: Canada, Government (International), Freedom of Information Act

Sponsor: British Columbia Systems Corporation, British Columbia, Canada

Audience: Canadians, Journalists, Activists

Contact: Office of the Information and Privacy Commissioner tcphelp@bc02.gov.bc.ca

`gopher://bcsc02.gov.bc.ca`

Privacy Rights Clearinghouse (PRC)

A collection of materials related to privacy issues.

Keywords: Privacy, Legislation, Consumer Rights, Freedom of Information

Sponsor: University of San Diego

Audience: Citizens, Privacy Activists, Journalists

Profile: This site contains fact sheets (in English and Spanish) on privacy issues ranging from wiretapping to credit reporting. Also includes federal and state privacy legislation as well as related position papers and press releases.

Contact: prc@teetot.acusd.edu

User Info: Expect: Login; Send: Privacy

`gopher://teetot.acusd.edu`

`telnet://teetot.acusd.edu`

Freedom of Speech

alt.censorship

A Usenet newsgroup providing information and discussion about freedom of speech and freedom of the press.

Keywords: Censorship, Freedom of Speech, Constitution (US), Activism

Audience: Press, Students, Educators, Activists

User Info: To subscribe to this Usenet newsgroup, you need access to a newsreader.

`news:alt.censorship`

Free Net Working Papers

Free-Net Working Papers

An FTP site with a collection of articles and papers about community networking.

Keywords: Community Networking, Networking

Sponsor: Carleton University, National Clearinghouse for Machine Readable Texts

Audience: Activists, Government, General Public

Profile: Project Guttenburg's goal is to provide a collection of 10,000 of the most used books by the year 2001.

Contact: Jay Weston, Michael S. Hart jweston@carleton.ca

Details: Free

Login anonymous; cd text

`ftp://alfred.carleton.ca/pub/freenet/working.papers`

FreeNets

FreeNets

This resource provides extensive information about FreeNets, which are public access Internet sites at no charge or for donations.

Keywords: Internet Access, Community Networking

Audience: Individuals, Communities, Libraries

Profile: FreeNets, community computing services providing Internet access, exist internationally and include such systems as LA FreeNet, Buffalo FreeNet, Cleveland FreeNet, FreeNet Erlangen-Nuernburg, Victoria FreeNet, Vaasa FreePort (Finland), CapAccess (D.C.), and many more.

Details: Free

URL (gopher path) below contains pointers to all FreeNets.

`gopher path: 1/internet/freenets marvel.loc.gov`

Freeware

info-GNU-MSDOS

This electronic conference is for the GNUISH MS-DOS Development Group.

Keywords: Shareware, Freeware, MS-DOS Computers

Audience: MS-DOS Users, GNUISH MS-DOS Developers

Contact: David J. Camp david@wubios.wustl.edu

Details: Free

User Info: To subscribe to the list, send an e-mail message to the URL address below consisting of a single line reading:

SUB info-GNU-MSDOS YourFirstName YourLastName

`mailto:listserv@wugate.wustl.edu`

French

Agence FrancePresse International French Wire

Agence FrancePresse International French Wire provides full-text articles in French relating to national, international, business, and sports news.

Keywords: News, Europe, Third World, French

Sponsor: Agence FrancePresse, Paris, France

Audience: Market Researchers, Journalists, Francophiles

Profile: Agence FrancePresse distributes its French service worldwide, including Western and Eastern Europe, Canada, northern and western Africa, the Middle East, Vietnam, French Guiana, the West Indies, and the French Pacific islands. Agence FrancePresse International French Wire has extensive coverage of the European countries, including every aspect of economic, political, and general business news. It also provides excellent industrial and market news from both developed countries and from theThird World.
Coverage: September 1991 to the present; updated daily.

Contact: Dialog in the US at (800) 334-2564; Dialog internationally at country-specific locations.

Details: Costs

User Info: To subscribe, contact Dialog directly.

`telnet://dialog.com`

Canada

The wiretap gopher provides access to a range of Canadian documents in full-text format in French.

Keywords: Canada, French

Audience: Canadian Citizens, Lawyers

Details: Free

`gopher://wiretap.spies.com`

WWW Paris

A web site created as a collaborative effort among individuals in both Paris and the United States.

Keywords: Paris, Culture, Art, Travel, French, Tourism

Audience: Students, Educators, Travelers, Researchers

Profile: Contains an extensive collection of images and text regarding all of the major monuments and museums of Paris, including maps of the Metro and the RER; calendars of events and current expositions; promotional images and text relating to local department stores; there is also a visitors' section with up-to-date tourist information on hotels, restaurants, telephones, airport schedules, a basic Paris glossary, and the latest weather images. Includes an extensive collection of links to other resources about Paris and France, and a selected bibliography of history and architecture in Paris.

Contact: Norman Barth, Eric Pouliquen nbarth@ucsd.edu, epouliq@ucsd.edu

`http://meteora.ucsd.edu/~norman/paris`

French Law

INTNAT (International Library)

The International library contains all French treaties, conventions and agreements that are effective today, as well as decisions from the Cour Europ_enne des Droits de l'Homme and the Cour de Justice des Communautes Europ_ennes plus the Journal Officiel des Communautes Europ_enne.

Keywords: French Law, European Community

Audience: International Lawyers

Profile: The International library contains all French treaties, conventions and agreements published before 1958 that are in effect today, as well as decisions from the European Court of Human Rights (Cour Europeenne des Droits de l'Homme), the European Court of Justice (Cour de Justice des Communautes Europeennes) and the Journal Officiel des Communautes Europeenne, the daily record of the European Community.

Contact: New Sales Group at (800) 227-4908 or 513-859-5398 inside the US, or 1-513-865-7981 for all inquires outside the US.

User Info: To subscribe, contact Mead directly.

To examine the Lexis user guide, you can access it at the ftp site of the University of Texas at Austin at the URL address: ftp://ftp.cc.utexas.edu

The files are in: /pub/ref-services/LEXIS

`telnet://nex.meaddata.com`

`http://www.meaddata.com`

French Opera (19th-C.)

Indiana University Libraries

The library's holdings are large and wide-ranging and contain significant collections in many fields.

Keywords: Literature (English), Literature (American), 1640-Present, British Plays (19th-C.), Western Americana, Railway History, Aristotle (Texts of), Lafayette (Marquis de), Handel (G.F.), Austrian History, Antiquarian Books, Rare Books, French Opera (19th-C.), Drama (British) ,

Audience: General Public, Researchers, Librarians, Document Delivery Professionals

Details: Free

User Info: Expect: User ID prompt, Send: GUEST

`telnet://iuis.ucs.indiana.edu`

French Revolution

The University of Iowa Libraries

The library's holdings are large and wide-ranging and contain significant collections in many fields.

Keywords: Hunt (Leigh), Native American Studies, Typography, Railroads, Cartoons, French Revolution, NASA, Hydraulics

Audience: General Public, Researchers, Librarians, Document Delivery Professionals

Details: Free

Send <RETURN>to display a menu of available systems. Type 1 for OASIS access and press <RETURN>to display the Welcome to OASIS screen.

`telnet://oasis.uiowa.edu`

University of Pennsylvania PENNINFO Library

The library's holdings are large and wide-ranging and contain significant collections in many fields.

Keywords: Church History, Spanish Inquisition, Witchcraft, Shakespeare (William), Bibles, Aristotle (Texts of), Fiction, Whitman (Walt), French Revolution, Drama (French), Literature (English), Literature (Spanish)

Audience: Researchers, Students, General Public

Contact: Al DSouza penninfo-admin@dccs.upenn.edu dsouza@dccs.upenn.edu

Details: Free

User Info: Expect: Login; Send: Public

`telnet://penninfo.upenn.edu`

French Studies

Erofile

This newsletter provides reviews of the latest books associated with French and Italian studies in fields such as literary criticism, cultural studies, film studies, pedagogy, and software.

Keywords: Italian Studies, French Studies, Book Reviews

Audience: French Students, Italian Students, Book Reviewers

Details: Free

`mailto:erofile@ucsbuxa.ucsb.edu`

A B C D E F G H I J K L M N O P Q R S T U V W X Y Z

Friends of Ohio State

Friends of Ohio State

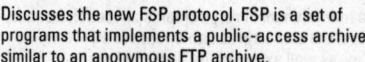

A forum for alumni and other friends of Ohio State University.

Keywords: Ohio

Audience: Ohio State University Alumni

Contact: Jerry Canterbury
antivirus@aol.com

Details: Free

User Info: To subscribe to the list, send an e-mail message requesting a subscription to the URL address below.

To send a message to the entire list, address it to: antivirus@aol.com

mailto:antivirus@aol.com

fringeware

fringeware

A moderated mailing list devoted to cyberculture and the like.

Keywords: Cyberculture

Audience: Cyberculture Enthusiasts

Details: Free, Moderated

User Info: To subscribe to the list, send an e-mail message to the URL address shown below.

To send a message to the entire list, address it to: fringeware@illuminati.io.com

mailto:fringeware-request@illuminati.io.com

Frost (Robert)

Dartmouth College Library

The library's holdings are large and wide-ranging and contain significant collections in many fields.

Keywords: American Calligraphy, Cervantes (Miguel de), Railroads, Polar Regions, Frost (Robert), Shakespeare (William), Spanish Plays

Audience: General Public, Researchers, Librarians, Document Delivery Professionals

Contact: Katharina Klemperer
kathy.klemperer@dartmouth.edu

Details: Free

User Info: Expect: login, Send: wolfpac

telnet://lib.dartmouth.edu

FSP Protocol

fsp-discussion

Discusses the new FSP protocol. FSP is a set of programs that implements a public-access archive similar to an anonymous FTP archive.

Keywords: FSP Protocol, Public Access Archives

Audience: Computer Users

Details: Free

User Info: To subscribe to the list, send an e-mail message requesting a subscription to the URL address below.

To send a message to the entire list, address it to: fsp-discussion@germany.eu.net

mailto:listmaster@germany.eu.net

fsuucp

fsuucp

The FSUUCP mailing list is for the discussion of bug hunting, feature proposing, and announcements of the availability and release dates of FSUUCP, an MS-DOS UUCP mail news package.

Keywords: Software, Shareware

Audience: Students, Computer Users

Details: Free

User Info: To subscribe to the list, send an e-mail message requesting a subscription to the URL address below.

To send a message to the entire list, address it to: fsuucp@polyslo.calpoly.edu

mailto:fsuucp-request@polyslo.calpoly.edu

FTP

FTP FAQ

Common questions and answers about FTP (File Transfer Protocol), FTP sites, and anonymous FTP. General information for the novice FTP user.

Keywords: FTP, Internet Tools

Audience: Students, Computer Scientists, Researchers

Contact: Perry Rovers
perry.rovers@kub.nl

ftp://ftp.ifh.de/pub/FAQ/ftp.faq

FTP-How To

A short guide to using anonymous FTP, an Internet access tool.

Keywords: Internet Tools, FTP

Sponsor: SURAnet Network Information Center

Audience: Internet Surfers

Contact: info@sura.net

Details: Free

File is: pub/nic/network.service.guides/how.to.ftp.guide

ftp://ftp.sura.net

FTP Setup

Tips on using FTP, an Internet access tool.

Keywords: Internet Tools, FTP

Sponsor: Carnegie Mellon University, Pittsburgh, PA

Audience: Internet Surfers

Details: Free

File is: pub/tech_tips/anonymous_ftp

ftp://cert.org

Fuller (Buckminster)

Geodesic

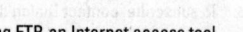

A mailing list for the discussion of Buckminster Fuller's works.

Keywords: Geodesic Quantum Physics, Design, Fuller (Buckminster)

Audience: Designers, Physicists

Contact: Patrick G. Salsbury
salsbury@acsu.buffalo.edu

Details: Free

User Info: To subscribe to the list, send an e-mail message to the URL address shown below consisting of a single line reading:

SUB geodesic YourFirstName YourLastName

To send a message to the entire list, address it to: geodesic@ubvm.cc.buffalo.edu

mailto: listserv@ubvm.cc.buffalo.edu

Funding

Research (Funding Support List)

The Research list is for people (primarily at educational institutions) interested in applying for funding support from various sources.

Keywords: Grants, Funding

Audience: Educators (College, Graduate)

Profile: This list assists faculty in locating sources of support from government agencies, corporations, and foundations. It also forwards information regarding the latest news from potential sponsors such as the National Science Foundation and the National Institutes of Health, and provides information on upcoming international seminars on various topics ranging from medicine to artificial intelligence.

Contact: Eleanor Cicinsky
v2153a@vm.temple.edu

User Info: To subscribe to the list, send an e-mail message to the address below consisting of a single line reading:

SUB research YourFirstName YourLastName

To send a message to the entire list, address it to: research@vm.temple.edu

`mailto:listserv@vm.temple.edu`

Funet Sports Information

Funet Sports Information

 ★★★★

An FTP archive of information on various sports with links to the archive at wuarchive.wustl.edu.

Keywords: Sports, Hockey, Football, Basketball, Baseball

Sponsor: Finnish Academic and Research Network (FUNET)

Audience: Sports Enthusiasts

Profile: A fairly extensive archive of information on both American (NBA, MLB, NHL, NFL) and worldwide sports (soccer, ice hockey, motor racing, and so on). Includes FAQs for various sports, statistics, pictures, and some sports games for the PC.

Contact: Jari Pullinen
sports-adm@nic.funet.fi

Details: Free, Images

`gopher://ftp.funet.fi/pub/sports`

Funk Music

Funky Music

 ★★

This mailing list covers funk and funk-influenced music, including hip-hop, house party, soul, and rhythm and blues.

Keywords: Musical Genres, Funk Music

Audience: Musicians, Funk Music Enthusiasts

Details: Free

User Info: To subscribe to the list, send an e-mail message requesting a subscription to the URL address below. To send a message to the entire list, address it to: funky-music@mit.edu

`mailto:funky-music-request@mit.edu`

Fusion

fusion

 ★

Fusion is an e-mail redistribution of Usenet sci.physics.fusion newsgroup for sites/users lacking access to Usenet.

Keywords: Physics, Fusion, Science

Audience: Physicists, Scientists

Details: Free

User Info: To subscribe to the list, send an e-mail message requesting a subscription to the URL address below.

To send a message to the entire list, address it to: fusion@zorch.sf-bay.org

`mailto:fusion-request@zorch.sf-bay.org`

Futurebus+ Users

Futurebus+ Users

 ★

This discussion group focuses on the design, implementation, integration, and operation of hardware and software related to Futurebus+.

Keywords: Computer Users, Hardware, Software

Audience: Computer Users, Software Engineers, Hardware Engineers

Contact: majordomo@theus.rain.com

Details: Free

User Info: To subscribe to the list, send an e-mail message to the URL address below consisting of a single line reading:

SUB fbus_users YourFirstName YourLastName

To send a message to the entire list, address it to:
fbus_users+@theus.rain.com

`mailto:majordomo@theus.rain.com`

FutureCulture FAQ (Frequently Asked Questions) File

FutureCulture FAQ (Frequently Asked Questions) File

 ★★★

List of online and offline items of interest to subscribers of FutureCulture, a mailing list on 'technoculture' or 'new edge' or 'cyberculture.'

Keywords: Technology, Cyberculture, Postmodernism, Sci-Fi, Zines

Audience: Reality Hackers, Cyberculture Enthusiasts

Profile: This list discusses cyberpunk culture, rave culture, industrial music, virtual reality, drugs, computer underground, Net sociology, and virtual communities.

Contact: Alias Datura (adatura on IRC)
adatura@uafhp.uark.edu

Details: Free

`ftp://etext.archive.umich.edu/pub`

Fuzzy Logic

fuzzy-mail

 ★

Discussion of fuzzy logic, fuzzy sets. It is linked with the NAFIPS-L list and the comp.ai.fuzzy newsgroup.

Keywords: Fuzzy Logic

Audience: Programmers

Contact: listserv@vexpert.dbai.tuwien.ac.at

Details: Free, Moderated

User Info: To subscribe to the list, send an e-mail message to the URL address below consisting of a single line reading:

SUB fuzzy-mail YourFirstName YourLastName

To send a message to the entire list, address it to: fuzzy-mail@vexpert.dbai.tuwien.ac.at

`mailto:listserv@vexpert.dbai.tuwien.ac.at`

fuzzy-ramblings

fuzzy-ramblings

 ★

Discussion of the British girl-group "We've Got a Fuzzbox and We're Going to Use It!"

Keywords: Music

Audience: Musicians, Music Enthusiasts

Details: Free

User Info: To subscribe to the list, send an e-mail message requesting a subscription to the URL address below.

To send a message to the entire list, address it to: fuzzy-ramblings@piggy.ucsb.edu

`mailto:fuzzy-ramblings-request@piggy.ucsb.edu`

fwake-l

fwake-l

 ★★

A conference and forum for a broad discussion of James Joyce's *Finnegan's Wake*.

Keywords: Joyce (James), Literature (Irish), Writing

Audience: Writers, Joyce Scholars, Literary Critics, Literary Theorists

A B C D E F G H I J K L M N O P Q R S T U V W X Y Z

User Info: To subscribe to the list, send an e-mail message to the URL address below consisting of a single line reading:

SUB fwake-l YourFirstName YourLastName

`mailto:listserv@irlearn.ucd.ie`

FYI on Questions and Answers to Commonly asked New Internet User Questions

FYI on Questions and Answers to Commonly asked New Internet User Questions

Answers to questions commonly asked by new Internet users.

Keywords: Internet, Internet Resources

Sponsor: Xylogics, Inc. and SRI International

Audience: Internet Surfers

Contact: Gary Scott Malkin or April N. Marine
gmalkin@Xylogics.com
april@nisc.sri.com

Details: Free

User Info: File is: documents/fyi/RFC_1594.txt

`ftp://nic.merit.edu`

G

gaelic-l

Gaelic-L

A multidisciplinary discussion list that facilitates the exchange of news, views, and information in Scottish Gaelic, Irish, and Manx.

Keywords: Scottish Gaelic, Irish, Manx, Linguistics

Audience: Linguists

Contact: Marion Gunn
mgunn@irlearn.ucd.ie or
caoimhin@smo.ac.uk
lss203@cs.napier.ac.uk

Details: Free

User Info: To subscribe to the list, send an e-mail message to the URL address shown below, consisting of a single line reading:

SUB gaelic-l YourFirstName YourLastName

To send a message to the entire list, address it to: gaelic-l@irlearn.ucd.ie

mailto:listserv@irlearn.ucd.ie

Galway (Ireland)

The Complete Guide to Galway

This is a detailed guide to the city of Galway (past and present), covering tourist sites, industry, local transportation, folklore, history, entertainment, drinking and dining. This web site includes maps, photographs and illustrations.

Keywords: Galway (Ireland), Tourism, Travel

Audience: Irish, Tourists, Historians, Businesses

Contact: Joe Desbonnet
joe@epona.physics.ucg.ie

http://wombatix.physics.ucg.ie/ galway/galway.html

University of New Hampshire Videotex Library

The library's holdings are large and wide-ranging and contain significant collections in many fields.

Keywords: Dance, Folk Music, Milne (A.A., Collection of), Galway (Ireland)

Audience: Researchers, Students, General Public

Contact: Robin Tuttle
r_tuttle1@unhh.unh.edu

Details: Free

Expect: USERNAME; Send: Student (no password required). Control-z to log off.

telnet://unhvt@unh.edu

Gambling

rec.gambling

Discussion of card games, gambling, and gambling sites.

Keywords: Cards, Gambling

Audience: Card Players, Gamblers

Profile: Discussion in this group covers gambling and card games, the rules of various card games, odds, betting, and the pros and cons of various gambling and card playing sites. The archived FAQ is a lengthy card game resource.

Contact: rec.gambling Moderator
jacobs@cs.utah.edu

Notes: The rec.gambling FAQ is accessible via anonymous ftp at soda.berkeley.edu through the path pub/rec.gambling.

news:rec.gambling

University of Nevada, Las Vegas Library - Las Vegas, NV

The library's holdings are large and wide-ranging and contain significant collections in many fields.

Keywords: Gambling, Hotel Administration, Nevadiana, Canadian Documents, Nevada State Documents

Audience: General Public, Researchers, Librarians, Document Delivery Professionals

Contact: Myoung-ja Lee Kwon
kwon@nevada.edu.

Details: Free

Expect: login; Send: library

telnet://library.lv-lib.nevada.edu

Game Theory

Pd-games

A mailing list for people interested in game theory, especially Prisoner's Dilemma types of problems. Discussions include purely technical issues and questions, as well as specific scientific applications and the political and ideological aspects and consequences of game theory.

Keywords: Game Theory, Mathematics

Audience: Game Theorists, Mathematicians

Contact: Thomas Gramstad
pd-games-request@math.uio.no

Details: Free

User Info: To subscribe to the list, send an e-mail message requesting a subscription to the URL address below.

To send a message to the entire list, address it to: pd-games@math.uio.no

mailto:pd-games-request@math.uio.no

A B C D E F **G** H I J K L M N O P Q R S T U V W X Y Z

Games

ars magica

A mailing list for the discussion of White Wolf's role-playing game, Ars Magica.

Keywords: Role-Playing, Games

Audience: Role-playing Enthusiasts, Game Players

Contact: ars-magica-request@soda.berkeley.edu

User Info: To subscribe to the list, send an e-mail message to the URL address below.

To send a message to the entire list, address it to: ars-magica-request@soda.berkeley.edu

Also available upon request as a nightly digest.

`mailto:ars-magica-request@soda.berkeley.edu`

Chessnews

A mailing list for the discussion of chess and related events.

Keywords: Chess, Games

Audience: Chess Enthusiasts

Contact: Michael Nolan
chessnews-request@tssi.com

Details: Free

User Info: To subscribe to the list, send an e-mail message requesting a subscription to the URL address below.

To send a message to the entire list, address it to: chessnews@tssi.com

Notes: The Chessnews mailing list is a repeater for the USENET newsgroup rec.games.chess. This is a bi-directional repeater. Postings originating from USENET are sent to the list, and those originating from the list are sent to re

`mailto:chessnews-request@tssi.com`

Digital Games Review

Reviews of video and computer entertainment titles for the entire industry.

Keywords: Computer Games, Games, Video Games

Audience: Computer Game Players, Computer Game Developers

Profile: Reviews are written by computer game enthusiasts, with an eye to accessibility, enjoyment, and fun, as well as to graphics, technical sophistication, and complexity.

Contact: Dave Taylor
taylor@intuitive.com

Details: Free

`mailto:digital-games-request@intuitive.com`

flashlife

A mailing list for general managers of Shadowrun and other cyberpunk role-playing games to discuss rules and scenarios, ask questions, and make up answers.

Keywords: Games, Cyberpunk Games

Audience: Game Players

Details: Free

User Info: To subscribe to the list, send an e-mail message requesting a subscription to the URL address below.

To send a message to the entire list, address it to: flashlife@netcom.com

`mailto:flashlife-request@netcom.com`

GameBytes magazine

This monthly electronic magazine provides reviews (with graphics) of electronic games.

Keywords: Games, Electronic Media, Entertainment

Sponsor: Game Bytes Magazine

Audience: Game Players, Computer Game Developers, Computer Graphic Designers

Contact: Ross Erickson
rwericks@ingr.com

Details: Free

`http://wcl-rs.bham.ac.uk/GameBytes`

Internet Hunt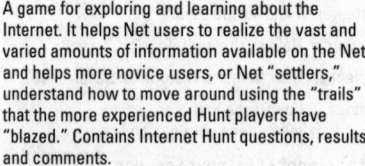

A game for exploring and learning about the Internet. It helps Net users to realize the vast and varied amounts of information available on the Net and helps more novice users, or Net "settlers," understand how to move around using the "trails" that the more experienced Hunt players have "blazed." Contains Internet Hunt questions, results, and comments.

Keywords: Internet, Internet Guides, Games

Sponsor: CICnet

Audience: Internet Surfers

Contact: Rick Gates
rgates@nic.cic.net

Details: Free

`gopher://gopher.cic.net`

MUD

A discussion list for the exchange of information about new and recommended Multiuser Dungeons and Dragons (MUDs).

Keywords: MUDs, Games

Audience: MUD Users

Contact: Joseph Wisdom
jwisdom@gnu.ai.mit.edu

Details: Free

User Info: To subscribe to the list, send an e-mail message requesting subscription to the URL address below.

`mailto:jwisdom@gnu.ai.mit.edu`

Nero Ashbury

Nero is a live-action, medieval role-playing game with a plot line and characters that continue from one adventure to the next. Nero has been successful in New England for over six years and is growing rapidly.

Keywords: Medieval Studies, Role-Playing, Games

Audience: General Public, Role-Playing Enthusiasts

Contact: lsonko@pearl.tufts.edu

Details: Free

User Info: To subscribe to the list, send an e-mail message requesting a subscription to the URL address below.

`mailto:lsonko@pearl.tufts.edu`

rec.gambling

A Usenet newsgroup providing information and discussion about gambling.

Keywords: Games, Gambling, Recreation

Audience: Gamblers

User Info: To subscribe to this Usenet newsgroup, you need access to a newsreader.

`news:rec.gambling`

rec.games.board

A Usenet newsgroup providing hints and discussion about board games.

Keywords: Games, Recreation

Audience: Game Players

User Info: To subscribe to this Usenet newsgroup, you need access to a newsreader.

`news:rec.games.board`

rec.games.chess

A Usenet newsgroup providing information and discussion about chess strategies, organized computer chess playing events, and software.

Keywords: Chess, Games, Recreation

Audience: Chess Players, Game Players

User Info: To subscribe to this Usenet newsgroup, you need access to a newsreader.

`news:rec.games.chess`

rec.games.programmer

A Usenet newsgroup providing information and discussion about adventure game programming.

Keywords: Games, Programming, Video Games

Audience: Programmers

User Info: To subscribe to this Usenet newsgroup, you need access to a newsreader.

`news:rec.games.programmer`

rec.games.video.arcade

A Usenet newsgroup providing information and discussion about video games.

Keywords: Games, Video Games

Audience: Game Players

User Info: To subscribe to this Usenet newsgroup, you need access to a newsreader.

`news:rec.games.video.arcade`

rec.puzzles

A Usenet newsgroup providing information and discussion about math puzzles and brain teasers.

Keywords: Games, Puzzles, Recreation

Audience: General Public

User Info: To subscribe to this Usenet newsgroup, you need access to a newsreader.

`news:rec.puzzles`

Zarf's List of Interactive Games on the Web

A list containing links to games and toys that can be played on the Internet.

Keywords: Games, toys, entertainment, recreation

Sponsor: Carnegie Mellon University, School of Computer Science, Pittsburgh, Pennsylvania, USA

Audience: General Public, Game Players, Kids

Contact: Andrew Plotkin zarf@cs.cmu.edu, apli@andrew.cmu.edu

`http://www.cs.cmu.edu/:8001//afs/ cs.cmu.edu/user/zarf/www/games.html`

GAO

GAO

 ★★★

Files intended to provide Congress and Administration with an overview of health problems facing the nation.

Keywords: Health, Congress (US)

Audience: US Congress, Journalists, General Public

Profile: These files concern health-care reform and human services and date from December 1992. They are provided by the government to familiarize the reader with the health issues confronting the administration.

Details: Free

Notes: Login: anonymous ABSTRACT.FIL is a file with abstracts for each of the 28 reports.

`ftp://cu.nig.gov`

Gardening

alt.bonsai

A Usenet newsgroup providing information and discussion about Bonsai gardening.

Keywords: Bonsai Trees, Japan, Gardening, Landscaping

Audience: Gardeners, Bonsai Enthusiasts

User Info: To subscribe to this Usenet newsgroup, you need access to a newsreader.

`news:alt.bonsai`

rec.gardens

A Usenet newsgroup providing information and discussion about gardening.

Keywords: Gardening, Landscaping

Audience: Gardeners

User Info: To subscribe to this Usenet newsgroup, you need access to a newsreader.

`news:rec.gardens`

Gateway2000

Gateway2000

★

This list is a source of information about Gateway2000 products.

Keywords: Computer Products, Software, Hardware

Audience: Computer Users, Hardware Engineers, Software Engineers

Details: Free

User Info: To subscribe to the list, send an e-mail message requesting a subscription to the URL address below.

To send a message to the entire list, address it to: gateway2000@sei.cmu.edu

`gateway2000-request@sei.cmu.edu`

Gay Rights

Amend2-discuss

★★

A mailing list for discussion of the implications and issues surrounding the passage of Colorado's Amendment 2, which revokes any existing homosexual civil rights legislation and prohibits the drafting of any new legislation.

Keywords: Activism, Gay Rights, Lesbians, Bisexuality

Audience: Gay Rights Activists

Contact: amend2-mod@cs.colorado.edu

User Info: To subscribe to the list, send an e-mail message to the URL address below, consisting of a single line reading:

subscribe amend2-discuss

`mailto:majordomo@cs.colorado.edu`

freedom

Mailing list of people organizing against the Idaho Citizens Alliance antigay ballot initiative.

Keywords: Gay Rights, Activism, Gays

Audience: Gays, Lesbians, Bisexuals, Idaho Citizens, Activists

Details: Free

User Info: To subscribe to the list, send an e-mail message to the URL address shown below, consisting of a single line reading:

SUB freedom YourFirstName YourLastName.

To send a message to the entire list, address it to: freedom@idbsu.idbsu.edu

`mailto:listserv@idbsu.idbsu.edu`

Qn

A mailing list for Queer Nation activists and for anyone interested in Queer Nation, an activist group devoted to furthering gay rights. The purpose of qn is to network among various Queer Nation chapters, to discuss actions and tactics to bring about Queer Liberation.

Keywords: Homosexuality, Gay Rights, Activism

Audience: Gay Rights Activists, Political Activists

Contact: Roger Klorese qn-request@queernet.org

Details: Free

User Info: To subscribe to the list, send an e-mail message requesting a subscription to the URL address below.

To send a message to the entire list, address it to: qn@queernet.org

`mailto:qn-request@queernet.org`

Stonewall25

A mailing list for discussion and planning of the "Stonewall 25," an international gay/lesbian/bisexual rights march in New York City on Sunday, June 26, 1994, and the events accompanying it.

Keywords: Gay Rights, Lesbian, Bisexual, Activism

Audience: Gays, Lesbians, Bisexuals, Activists

Contact: stonewall25-request@queernet.org

Details: Free

User Info: To subscribe to the list, send an e-mail message requesting a subscription to the URL address below.

To send a message to the entire list, address it to: stonewall25@queernet.org

`mailto:stonewall25-request@queernet.org`

A B C D E F **G** H I J K L M N O P Q R S T U V W X Y Z

A
B
C
D
E
F
G
H
I
J
K
L
M
N
O
P
Q
R
S
T
U
V
W
X
Y
Z

Gays

AUGLBC-I

The American University Gay, Lesbian, and Bisexual Community (AUGLBC) is a support group for lesbian, gay, bisexual, transsexual, and supportive students. The group is also connected with the International Gay and Lesbian Youth Organization (known as IGLYO).

Keywords: Gays, Lesbians, Bisexuals, Transsexuality, Sexuality

Audience: Gays, Lesbians, Bisexuals, Transsexuals, Students (college)

Contact: Erik G. Paul

User Info: To subscribe to the list, send an e-mail message to the URL address below, consisting of a single line reading:

SUB AUGLBC-I YourFirstName YourLastName

To send a message to the entire list, address it to: AUGLBC-I@american.edu

`mailto:listserv@american.edu`

AusGBLF

An Australian-based mailing list for gays, bisexuals, lesbians, and friends.

Keywords: Australia, Gays, Lesbians, Bisexuality

Audience: Gays, Lesbians, Bisexuals

Contact: zglc@minyos.xx.rmit.oz.au

Details: Free

User Info: To subscribe to the list, send an e-mail message requesting a subscription to the URL address below.

To send a message to the entire list, address it to: ausgblf@minyos.xx.rmit.oz.au

`mailto:ausgblf-request@minyos.xx.rmit.oz.au`

Bears

A mailing list in digest format for gay and bisexual men who are bears themselves and for those who enjoy the company of bears. The definition of a "bear" encompasses men who are variously cuddly, furry, perhaps stocky, or bearded. Mail.bears is designed to be a forum to bring together folks with similar interests for conversation, friendship, and sharing of experiences.

Keywords: Gays, Bisexuality

Audience: Gays, Bisexuals

Contact: Steve Dyer, Brian Gollum
bears-request@spdcc.COM

Details: Free

User Info: To subscribe to the list, send an e-mail message requesting a subscription to the URL address below.

To send a message to the entire list, address it to: bears@spdcc.COM

`mailto:bears-request@spdcc.COM`

Chorus

This is the lesbian and gay chorus mailing list, formed November 1991 by John Schrag (jschrag@alias.com) and Brian Jarvis (jarvis@psych.toronto.edu). Membership includes artistic directors, singers, chorus officers, interpreters, and support staff and friends. Topics of discussion include repertoire, arrangements, staging, costuming, management, fundraising, music, events, and concerts.

Keywords: Singing, Choral Singing, Homosexuality, Gays, Lesbians

Audience: Lesbian Singers, Gay Singers, Chorus Officers, Lesbians, Gays, Choral Singers

Contact: chorus-request@psych.toronto.edu

Details: Free

User Info: To subscribe to the list, send an e-mail message requesting a subscription to the URL address below.

To send a message to the entire list, address it to: chorus@psych.toronto.edu

`mailto:chorus-request@psych.toronto.edu`

DC-MOTSS

DC-MOTSS is a social mailing list for the gay, lesbian, and bisexual folks who live in the Washington Metropolitan Area—everything within approximately 50 miles of The Mall.

Keywords: Gays, Lesbians, Bisexuality, Washington DC

Audience: Gays, Lesbians, Bisexuals, Washington DC Residents

Contact: DC-MOTSS-request@vector.intercon.com

Details: Free

User Info: To subscribe to the list, send an e-mail message requesting a subscription to the URL address below.

To send a message to the entire list, address it to: DC-MOTSS-request@vector.intercon.com

`mailto:DC-MOTSS-request@vector.intercon.com`

DSA-LGB

DSA-LGB is a mailing list for members of the Lesbian/Gay/Bisexual Commission of the Democratic Socialists of America, and for others interested in similar concerns.

Keywords: Democratic Socialists of America, Gays, Lesbians

Audience: Democratic Socialists, Gays, Lesbians

Contact: DSA-LGB-request@midway.uchicago.edu

User Info: To subscribe to the list, send an e-mail message requesting a subscription to the URL address below.

To send a message to the entire list, address it to: DSA-LGB-request@midway.uchicago.edu

`mailto:DSA-LGB-request@midway.uchicago.edu`

eagles

This list provides a forum for Boy Scouts, Scouters, and former Scouts who are gay/bisexual to discuss how they can apply pressure to the BSA to change their homophobic policies.

Keywords: Boy Scouts, Gays, Lesbians

Audience: Gays, Lesbians, Boy Scouts, Former Boy Scouts

Contact: eagles-request@flash.usc.edu

Details: Free

User Info: To subscribe to the list, send an e-mail message requesting a subscription to the URL address below.

To send a message to the entire list, address it to: eagles-request@flash.usc.edu

`mailto:eagles-request@flash.usc.edu`

gay-libn

A network for gay, lesbian, and bisexual librarians.

Keywords: Libraries, Gays, Lesbians, Bisexuality

Audience: Librarians, Gays, Lesbians, Bisexuals

Details: Free

User Info: To subscribe to the list, send an e-mail message to the URL address below, consisting of a single line reading:

SUB gay-libn YourFirstName YourLastName

To send a message to the entire list, address it to: gay-libn@vm.usc.edu

`mailto:listserv@vm.usc.edu`

gaynet

This list covers gay, lesbian, and bisexual concerns (with a focus on college campuses), including outreach programs, political action, AIDS education, school administration issues, social programs, and support group exchanges.

Keywords: Gays, Lesbians

Audience: Gays, Lesbians, Bisexuals, Students

Contact: Roger B.A. Klorese
gaynet-approval@queernet.org

Details: Free

User Info: To subscribe to the list, send an e-mail message to the URL address below, consisting of a single line reading:

SUB gaynet YourFirstName YourLastName

To send a message to the entire list, address it to: gaynet@queernet.org

`mailto:majordomo@queernet.org`

Ne-social-motss

Announcements of lesbian/gay/bisexual social events and other happenings in the Northeastern US.

Keywords: Social Events, Lesbians, Gays, Bisexuality

Audience: Lesbians, Gays, Bisexuals

Contact: ne-social-motss-request@plts.org

Details: Free

User Info: To subscribe to the list, send an e-mail message requesting a subscription to the URL address below.

`mailto:ne-social-motss-request@plts.org`

NJ-motss

Mailing list for gay, lesbian, and bisexual issues in New Jersey.

Keywords: Gays, Lesbians, Bisexuality, New Jersey

Audience: Gays, Lesbians, Bisexuals

Contact: majordomo@plts.org

Details: Free

User Info: To subscribe to the list, send an e-mail message to the URL address shown below, consisting of a single line reading:

SUB NJ-motss YourFirstName YourLastName

To send a message to the entire list, address it to: NJ-motss@plts.org

`mailto: majordomo@plts.org`

NJ-motss-announce

Announcements of interests to New Jersey's gay, lesbian, and bisexual population.

Keywords: Gays, Lesbians, Bisexuality, New Jersey

Audience: Gays, Lesbians, Bisexuals

Contact: majordomo@plts.org

Details: Free

User Info: To subscribe to the list, send an e-mail message to the URL address shown below, consisting of a single line reading:

SUB NJ-motss-announce YourFirstName YourLastName

To send a message to the entire list, address it to: NJ-motss-announce@plts.org

`mailto:majordomo@plts.org`

noglstp

This list is sponsored by the National Organization of Gay and Lesbian Scientists and Technical Professionals, Inc. (a 501-C3 organization). National office is in Pasadena, CA and can be reached at (818) 791-7689 or P.O. Box 91803, Pasadena, CA 90019. There is also a newsletter that is available to membership.

Keywords: Gays, Lesbians, Scientists, Technical Professionals

Audience: Gay Scientists, Lesbian Scientists

Contact: noglstp-request@elroy.jpl.nasa.gov

Details: Free

User Info: To subscribe to the list, send an e-mail message requesting a subscription to the URL address below.

To send a message to the entire list, address it to: noglstp@elroy.jpl.nasa.gov

`mailto:noglstp-request@elroy.jpl.nasa.gov`

Oh-motss

The oh-motss (Ohio Members of the Same Sex) mailing list is for open discussion of lesbian, gay, and bisexual issues in and affecting Ohio. The mailing list is not moderated. It is open to all, regardless of location or sexuality. The subscriber list is known only to the list owner.

Keywords: Gays, Lesbians, Ohio

Audience: Gays, Lesbians

Contact: oh-motss-request@cps.udayton.edu

Details: Free

User Info: To subscribe to the list, send an e-mail message requesting a subscription to the URL address below.

To send a message to the entire list, address it to: oh-motss@cps.udayton.edu

`mailto:oh-motss-request@cps.udayton.edu`

OUTIL (Out in Linguistics)

The list is open to lesbian, gay, bisexual, transsexual linguists and their friends. The only requirement is that you be willing to be out to everyone on the list. The purposes of the group are to be visible and to gather occasionally to enjoy one another's company.

Keywords: Linguistics, Gays, Lesbians, Bisexuals, Transsexuality

Audience: Linguists, Gays, Lesbians, Bisexuality, Transsexuals

Contact: Arnold Zwicky outil-request@csli.stanford.edu

Details: Free

User Info: To subscribe to the list, send an e-mail message requesting a subscription to the URL address below.

To send a message to the entire list, address it to: outil@csli.stanford.edu

`mailto:outil-request@csli.stanford.edu`

soc.motss

A Usenet newsgroup providing information and discussion about homosexuality.

Keywords: Homosexuality, Gays, Lesbians, Bisexuality

Audience: Gays, Lesbians, Bisexuals

Details: Free

User Info: To subscribe to this Usenet newsgroup, you need access to a newsreader.

`news:soc.motss`

GC-L

GC-L

Project for international business and management curricula.

Keywords: Business, Management, Linguistics

Sponsor: Global Classroom

Audience: Linguists, Language Teachers, Language Students, International Business Professionals

Details: Free

User Info: To subscribe to the list, send an e-mail message to the address below, consisting of a single line reading:

SUB gc-l YourFirstName YourLastName

To send a message to the entire list, address it: gc-l@uriacc.uri.edu

`mailto:listserv@uriacc.uri.edu`

Gegstaff

Gegstaff

All topics relating to sexuality and gender in geography.

Keywords: Geography, Sexuality

Audience: Geographers, Sex Enthusiasts

Details: Free

User Info: To subscribe to the list, send an e-mail message to the URL address shown below, consisting of a single line reading:

A
B
C
D
E
F
G
H
I
J
K
L
M
N
O
P
Q
R
S
T
U
V
W
X
Y
Z

SUB gegstaff YourFirstName YourLastName

To send a message to the entire list, address it to: gegstaff@ukcc.uky.edu

`mailto:listserv@ukcc.uky.edu`

Gender

Amazons International

An electronic digest newsletter for and about Amazons (physically and psychologically strong, assertive women who are challenging traditional ideas about gender roles, femininity, and the female physique).

Keywords: Gender, Amazons, Feminism

Audience: Women, Feminists, Writers, Art Historians

Profile: The digest is dedicated to the image of the female hero in fiction and in fact, as it is expressed in art and literature, in the physiques and feats of female athletes, and in sexual values and practices; it also provides information, discussion, and a supportive environment for these values and issues.

Contact: Thomas Gramstad amazons-request@math.uio.no

Details: Free

User Info: To subscribe to the list, send an e-mail message requesting a subscription to the URL address below.

To send a message to the entire list, address it to: amazons@math.uio.no

`mailto:amazons-request@math.uio.no`

BITHRY-L

This list is for the theoretical discussion of bisexuality and gender issues. It is not a social group, a support group, or an announcement or news forum.

Keywords: Bisexuality, Gender

Audience: Bisexuals

Contact: Elaine Brennan listserv@brownvm.brown.edu

Details: Free

User Info: To subscribe to the list, send an e-mail message to the URL address below, consisting of a single line reading:

SUB bithry-l YourFirstName YourLastName

To send a message to the entire list, address it to: bithry-l@brownvm.brown.edu

`mailto:listserv@brownvm.brown.edu`

Cd-Forum

The purpose of this list is to provide support and to discuss/share experiences about gender-related issues, including cross dressing, transvestism, and transsexualism.

Keywords: Transsexualism, Transvestism, Sexuality, Gender

Audience: Transsexuals, Transvestites

Contact: Valerie cd-request@valis.biocad.com

Details: Free

User Info: To subscribe to the list, send an e-mail message requesting a subscription to the URL address below.

To send a message to the entire list, address it to: cd@valis.biocad.com

Notes: This list is in digest format.

`mailto:cd-request@valis.biocad.com`

soc.men

A Usenet newsgroup providing information and discussion about men, their problems, and their relationships.

Keywords: Men's Movement, Gender

Audience: Men, Activists

Details: Free

User Info: To subscribe to this Usenet newsgroup, you need access to a newsreader.

`news:soc.men`

Women.news

This conference features news and action alerts about women and women's issues around the world — including human rights, feminism, health, sexual abuse, workers, population, abortion, activism, development, and peace.

Keywords: Feminism, Gender, Women

Audience: Women, Feminists, Activists

Contact: Debra Guzman, Sue VanHattum hrcoord@igc.apc.org suev@igc.apc.org

Details: Free

User Info: Establish an account on the nearest APC node. Login, type c for conferences, then type go women.news.

For information on the nearest APC node, contact: APC International Secretariat IBASE

E-mail: apcadmin@apc.org

`telnet://igc.apc.org`

Geneology

Geneology

A large collection of geneology resources for both beginners and specialists. Includes archives of geneology lists, FAQs, helper software, and specific geneological information for a number of national and ethnic groups.

Keywords: Geneology, Ethnic Studies

Sponsor: Go M-Link at the University of Michigan

Audience: Geneologists, General Public, Researchers

Contact: Sue Davidsen davidsen@umich.edu

`gopher://vienna.hh.lib.umich.edu`

General Hacking Info

General Hacking Info

Files on the topic of hacking.

Keywords: Hacking, Computers

Audience: Hackers, Computer Users

Details: Free

Expect: login, Send: anonymous;

Expect: Password, Send: Your e-mail Address

`ftp://ftp.eff.org`

GENESIS

Purkinje Park

A server maintained by CalTech to support the sharing of information between users of the GENESIS neural simulator, and to address topics of general interest to the Computational Neuroscience community.

Keywords: Computational Neuroscience, GENESIS, Neural Simulation.

Sponsor: Cal Tech

Audience: Neuroscientists, Computational Neuroscientists

Contact: Dave Beeman dbeeman@smaug.bbb.caltech.edu

`http://www.bbb.caltech.edu/index.html`

Genetics

bionet.molbio.genbank.updates

A Usenet newsgroup providing information and discussion about the GenBank Nucleic acid database.

Keywords: Molecular Biology, Biology, Genetics

Audience: Molecular Biologists, Researchers

User Info: To subscribe to this Usenet newsgroup, you need access to a newsreader.

`news:bionet.molbio.genbank.updates`

Drosophila Information Newsletter

A quarterly electronic publication; this is an offshoot of Drosophila Information Service.

Keywords: Drosophila, Biology, Genetics

Audience: Biologists, Geneticists

Contact: Kathy Matthews
MATTHEWK@UCS.INDIANA.EDU

Details: Free

User Info: To subscribe, send an e-mail message to the address below, consisting of a single line reading:

SUB drosophila-information-newsletter YourFirstName Your Last Name

To send a message to the entire list, address it to: drosophila.information. newsletter@ucs.indiana.edu

`mailto:listserv@iubvm.ucs.indiana.edu`

GenBank

The GenBank database provides a collection of nucleotide sequences as well as relevant bibliographic and biological annotation.

Keywords: Genetics, Medicine, Molecular Biology

Sponsor: National Center for Biotechnology Information (NCBI) at the National Library of Medicine (NLM)

Audience: Geneticists, Scientists, Molecular Biologists

Profile: DNA sequence entries are rated by specialized indexers in the Division of Library Operations. Over 325,000 articles per year from 3,400 journals are scanned for sequence data. They are supplemented by journals in plant and veterinary sciences through a collaboration with the National Agricultural Library. These records join the direct submission data stream and submissions from the European Molecular Biology Laboratory (EMBL) Data Library and the DNA Database of Japan (DDBJ).

Contact: info@ncbi.nlm.nih.gov

Details: Free

Send direct submissions to gb-sub@ncbi.nlm.nih.gov and updates and changes to existing GenBank records to update@ncbi.nlm.nih.gov For help in retrieval by e-mail send an e-mail message with the word "help" in the the body of the message to retrieve@ncbi.nlm.hih.gov

`gopher://gopher.nih.gov/77/gopherlib/`
`indices/genbank/index`

Johns Hopkins Genetic Databases

This gopher provides electronic access to documents pertaining to computational biology and a number of different genetic databases.

Keywords: Genetics, Molecular Biology, Medicine, Biology

Sponsor: Johns Hopkins University

Audience: Geneticists, Researchers, Scientists, Molecular Biologists

Profile: The databases accessible from this entry point include GenBank, Swiss-Prot, PDB, PIR, LiMB, TFD, AAtDB, ACEDB, CompoundKB, PROSITE EC Enzyme Database, NRL_3D Protein-Sequence-Structure Database, Eukaryotic Promoter Database (EPD), Cloning Vector Database, Expressed Sequence Tag Database (ESTDB), Online Mendelian Inheritance Man (OMIM), Sequence Analysis Bibliographic Reference Data Bank (Seqanalref), and Database Taxonomy (GenBank, Swiss-Prot). The gopher also provides direct links to other gophers with information relevant to biology.

Contact: Dan Jacobson
danj@mail.gdb.org

Details: Free

`gopher://merlot.welch.jhu.edu`

MGD (Mouse Genome Database)

This site provides a comprehensive database of genetic information on the laboratory mouse.

Keywords: Biology, Genetics

Sponsor: The Jackson Laboratory

Audience: Biologists, Researchers, Educators, Students

Contact: mgi-help@informatics.jax.org

Details: Free

Notes: Contact Mouse Genome Informatics User Support by telephone at (207) 288-3371, X 1900, or by FAX at (207) 288-2516.

`http://www.informatics.jax.org/`
`mgd.html`

The Tumor Gene Database

A database containing information about genes associated with tumorigenesis and cellular transformation.

Keywords: Genetics, Diseases, Biomedical Research, Databases

Sponsor: Department of Cell Biology, Baylor College of Medicine

Audience: Biomedical Researchers

Contact: David Steffen, Ph.D.
steffen@bcm.tmc.edu

`gopher://mbcr.bcm.tmc.edu`

GENFED (General Federal Library)

GENFED (General Federal Library)

The General Federal library is a comprehensive collection of federal legal materials of a general nature, including case law, legislative and regulatory materials, administrative decisions, court rules, and publications.

Keywords: Law (US Case), Law (US Federal)

Audience: Lawyers

Profile: The General Federal library is a comprehensive collection of federal legal materials of a general nature. Case law from all federal courts is available. Legislative materials include the United States Codes Service, United States Public Laws, pending federal legislation, legislative histories, and the Congressional Record. Regulatory materials include the Code of Federal Regulstions and the Federal Register. Administrative decisions, court rules, circuit summaries, sentencing guidelines, and legal publications are also available.

Contact: New Sales Group at 800-227-4908 or 513-859-5398 inside the US, or 1-513-865-7981 for all inquiries outside the US.

Details: Costs

User Info: To subscribe, contact Mead directly.

To examine the Lexis user guide, you can access it at the ftp site of the University of Texas at Austin at the URL address: ftp://ftp.cc.utexas.edu

The files are in: /pub/res-services/LEXIS

`telnet://nex.meaddata.com`

A
B
C
D
E
F
G
H
I
J
K
L
M
N
O
P
Q
R
S
T
U
V
W
X
Y
Z

Genius

Mensatalk

A discussion group for members of Mensa.

Keywords: Mensa, Genius

Audience: Mensa Members

Details: Free

User Info: To subscribe to the list, send an e-mail message requesting a subscription to the URL address below.

`mailto:mensatalk-request@psg.com`

GENMED (General Medical Information)

GENMED (General Medical Information)

The General Medical Information (GENMED) library contains a variety of medical care and treatment, toxicology, and hospital administration materials.

Keywords: Medicine, Toxicology, Hospital, Treatment

Audience: Medical Professionals

Profile: The GENMED library contains full-text medical journals and newsletters, as well as drug information, disease, and trauma reviews, Physicians Data Query cancer information, and medical administration journals. GENMED also offers a gateway to the MEDLINE database.

Contact: Mead New Sales Group at (800) 227-4908 or (513) 859-5398 inside the US, or (513) 865-7981 for all inquiries outside the US.

User Info: To subscribe, contact Mead directly.

To examine the Nexis user guide, you can access it at the ftp site of the University of Texas at Austin at the URL address: ftp://ftp.cc.utexas.edu

The files are in: /pub/ref-services/LEXIS

`telnet://nex.meaddata.com`

`http://www.meaddata.com`

Geodesic Quantum Physics

Geodesic

A mailing list for the discussion of Buckminster Fuller's works.

Keywords: Geodesic Quantum Physics, Design, Fuller (Buckminster)

Audience: Designers, Physicists

Contact: Patrick G. Salsbury
salsbury@acsu.buffalo.edu

Details: Free

User Info: To subscribe to the list, send an e-mail message to the URL address shown below consisting of a single line reading:

SUB geodesic YourFirstName YourLastName

To send a message to the entire list, address it to: geodesic@ubvm.cc. buffalo.edu

`mailto:LISTSERV@UBVM.CC.BUFFALO.EDU`

Geographic Information and Analysis Laboratory (GIAL)

Geographic Information and Analysis Laboratory (GIAL)

Server distributing a variety of information related to geography and GIS.

Keywords: Architecture, Geography, GIS, NCGIA

Sponsor: SUNY-Buffalo and the National Center for Geographic Information and Analysis (NCGIA)

Audience: Geographers, GIS Professionals, Researchers, Students

Contact: Brandon Plewe, Reginald O. Carroll, Patricia M. Baumgarten
plewe@geog.buffalo.edu
carrol@geog.buffalo.edu
pmb@geog.buffalo.edu

Details: Free

Images

Notes: Check out the You-are-here server!

`http://zia.geog.buffalo.edu/`

Geography

1991 Census of Population Documentation

This gopher provides Canadian Census information from 1991 including geographic and demographic information.

Keywords: Census Data, Canada, Demography, Geography

Audience: Canadians, Researchers, Demographers

Contact: David McCallum
carl@acadvm1.uottawa.ca

`gopher://alpha.epas.utoronto.ca/Data Library/Census of Population`

ACDGIS-L

GIS discussions for German speakers.

Keywords: Germany, Geographic Information Systems, Geography

Audience: Germans, Geographers, Cartographers

Details: Costsost

Inquire through wigeoarn@awiwuw11.bitnet

`mailto:acdgis-l@awiwuw11.bitnet`

ANU (Australian National University) Asian-Settlements Database

A searchable database containing abstracts of theses and research studies provided by the Asian Institute of Technology, relating to issues of demography and social geography in Asia.

Keywords: Asian Studies, Demography, Geography

Sponsor: The COOMBSQUEST Social Sciences & Humanities Information Facility at ANU (Australian National University), Canberra, Australia

Audience: Asia Studies Instructors, Demographers, Geographers

Contact: Dr. T. Matthew Ciolek
coombspapers@coombs.anu.edu.au

Details: Free

`gopher://cheops.anu.edu.au/Coombs-db/ ANU-Asian-Settlements.src`

`http://coombs.anu.edu.au/WWWVL- AsianStudies.html`

Canadian Geographical WWW Index Travel

This web site provides weekly weather information.

Keywords: Weather, Travel, Canada, Geography

Sponsor: University of Manitoba, Canada

Audience: Travelers, Educators, Students

Contact: www@umanitoba.ca

Details: Free

`http://www.umanitoba.ca`

Gegstaff

All topics relating to sexuality and gender in geography.

Keywords: Geography, Sexuality

Audience: Geographers, Sex Enthusiasts

Details: Free

User Info: To subscribe to the list, send an e-mail message to the URL address shown below, consisting of a single line reading:

SUB gegstaff YourFirstName YourLastName

To send a message to the entire list, address it to: gegstaff@ukcc.uky.edu

`mailto:listserv@ukcc.uky.edu`

Geographic Information and Analysis Laboratory (GIAL)

Server distributing a variety of information related to geography and GIS.

Keywords: Geography, GIS, NCGIA

Sponsor: SUNY-Buffalo and the National Center for Geographic Information and Analysis (NCGIA)

Audience: Geographers, GIS Professionals, Researchers, Students

Contact: Brandon Plewe, Reginald O. Carroll, Patricia M. Baumgarten
plewe@geog.buffalo.edu,
carrol@geog.buffalo.edu,
pmb@geog.buffalo.edu

Details: Free

Images

Notes: Check out the You-are-here server!

`http://zia.geog.buffalo.edu`

GIS-L

A forum for the discussion of all issues pertaining to GIS (Geographic Information Systems), including hydrological modeling, environmental issues, and available software packages.

Keywords: Geography, Environment, GIS (Geographic Information Systems)

Audience: Geographers, Cartographers

Contact: David Mark
dmark@acsu.buffalo.edu

User Info: To subscribe to the list, send an e-mail message to the URL address below, consisting of a single line reading:

SUB gis-l YourFirstName YourLastName.

To send a message to the entire list, address it to: gis-l@ubvm.cc.buffalo.edu

`mailto:listserv@ubvm.cc.buffalo.edu`

gis-t

A mailing list for the discussion of GIS (Geographic Information Systems) and transportation.

Keywords: Geography, Transportation, GIS (Geographic Information Systems)

Audience: Geographers, Cartographers

Contact: Jay Sandhu
jsandhu@esri.com

User Info: To subscribe to the list, send an e-mail message to the URL address below, consisting of a single line reading:

SUB gis-t YourFirstName YourLastName.

To send a message to the entire list, address it to: gis-t@esri.com

`mailto:listserv@esri.com`

Internet GIS and RS Information Sites

This document contains a lengthy listing of GIS and remote sensing sites on the Internet.

Keywords: GIS, Remote Sensing, Image Processing, Geography

Sponsor: Queen's University Department of Geography

Audience: Researchers, General Public

Contact: Michael McDermott
mcdermom@gisdog.gis.queensu.ca

Details: Free

Notes: ASCII version also available from the same FTP site.

`ftp://gis.queensu.ca/pub/gis/docs/gissites.html`

Internet Resources for Earth Sciences

A document detailing Internet resources for a variety of earth science disciplines including GIS.

Keywords: Directory, GIS, Geology, Geography, GPS, Mapping, Earth Science

Sponsor: Bill Thoen

Audience: Earth Scientists, Researchers

Profile: A complete document detailing the types of information available in earth sciences and the mechanisms to retrieve needed information.

Contact: Bill Thoen
bthoen@gisnet.com

Details: Free

`ftp://ftp.csn.org/COGS/ores.text`

Ireland-Related Online Resources

This is a list of network-accessible online resources (documents, images, information, access mechanisms for offline material, and so on) of Irish interest. Coverage includes some Bulletin Board services, some commercial information systems such as CompuServe and commercial bibliographic services.

Keywords: Ireland, Travel, Commerce, Geography

Audience: Irish, General Public, Tourists, Businesses

Contact: fmurtagh@eso.org

`http://http.hq.eso.org/~fmurtagh/ireland-resources.html`

MAPINFO-L

A mailing list for the discussion of MapInfo.

Keywords: Geographic Information Systems

Audience: Geographers, Cartographers

Contact: Bill Thoen
bthoen@gisnet.com

Details: Free

User Info: To subscribe to the list, send an e-mail message to the URL address below, consisting of a single line reading:

SUB mapinfo-l YourFirstName YourLastName

`mapinfo-l@csn.org`

next-gis

Discussion of Geographical Information Systems (GIS) and cartography-related topics on the NeXT and other workstation computers. Some moderated reposting of comp.infosys.gis occurs as well.

Keywords: Geography, Cartography, GIS, NeXT

Audience: GIS Users, NeXT Users

Contact: Steven R. Staton
sstaton@deltos.com

Details: Free

User Info: To subscribe to the list, send an e-mail message to the URL address shown below, consisting of a single line reading:

SUB next-gis YourFirstName YourLastName

To send a message to the entire list, address it to: next-gis@DistributionAddress

`mailto:listserv@deltos.com`

Sahel-NAFR

This site contains information about a database of composite satellite images of Sahel and North Africa (known as the Sahelian and NW Africa 14-Day NDVI Composites). The images come from a pilot program defined between the U.S. Geological Survey and the U.S. Agency for International Development (AID) to develop and test a near-real-time monitoring procedure using satellite remote sensing and Geographic Information System technologies in grasshopper and locust control programs in West Africa. Also contains an appendix with information about the Senegalese Grasshoppers.

Keywords: Geology, Geography, GIS (Geographic Information Systems)

Sponsor: U.S. Geological Survey and U.S. Agency for International Development (AID)

Audience: Geologists, Geographers

`http://sun1.cr.usgs.gov/glis/hyper/guide/sahel_nafr`

A B C D E F G H I J K L M N O P Q R S T U V W X Y Z

A B C D E F **G** H I J K L M N O P Q R S T U V W X Y Z

Ulgis-L

A mailing list for the discussion of user interfaces and GIS (Geographic Information Systems).

Keywords: Geography, GIS (Geographic Information Systems)

Audience: Geographers, Cartographers

Contact: David Mark
dmark@acsu.buffalo.edu

User Info: To subscribe to the list, send an e-mail message to the URL address below, consisting of a single line reading:

SUB uigis-l YourFirstName YourLastName.

To send a message to the entire list, address it to: uigis@ubvm.cc.buffalo.edu

`mailto:listserv@ubvm.cc.buffalo.edu`

United States Geographic Name Server

A database searchable by city name or zip code, this server provides geographic data including population, longitude and latitude, elevation, county, state, and zip codes.

Keywords: Geography, GIS (Geographical Information Systems)

Audience: Geographers, General Public

Contact: pubgopher@pluto.cc.brandeis.edu

`gopher://pluto.cc.brandeis.edu`

United States Geological Survey Home Page

USGS server dedicated to all aspects of geography and geographic data.

Keywords: USGS, GIS, Geography

Sponsor: United States Geological Survey

Audience: Geographers, GIS Professionals, Researchers, Students

Profile: Probably the most comprehensive geography/GIS server on the net. Features include a GIS tutorial, descriptions (and examples) of available USGS data products, access to online spatial data, and more.

Contact: webmaster@info.er.usgs.gov

Details: Free, Images, Sounds, Multimedia

Notes: The USGS maintains many servers; this page contains links to most of them, such as EROS Data Center, GLIS, and others.

`http://info.er.usgs.gov/USGSHome.html`

University of Michigan Library

The library's holdings are large and wide-ranging and contain significant collections in many fields.

Keywords: Asia, Astronomy, Transportation, Lexicology, Math, Zoology, Geography

Audience: Researchers, Students, General Public

Contact: info@merit.edu

Details: Free

Expect: Which Host; Send: Help

`telnet:// cts.merit.edu`

University of Wisconsin at Milwaukee Library

The library's holdings are large and wide-ranging and contain significant collections in many fields.

Keywords: Art, Architecture, Business, Cartography, Geography, Geology, Urban Studies, Literature (English), Literature (American)

Audience: Researchers, Students, General Public

Details: Free

Expect: Login, Send: Lib; Expect: vDIAL prompt, Send: Library

`telnet://uwmcat.lib.uwm.edu`

Vietnam

This file in the CIA World Factbook provides geographical, political, and cultural information about Vietnam.

Keywords: Vietnam, Geography

Sponsor: Central Intelligence Agency

Audience: Educators, Students, Travellers, Vietnamese Americans

Contact: Ephraim Vishniac
ephraim@think.com

Details: Free

`gopher://info.und.edu`

vigis-l

A mailing list for the discussion of Virtual Reality and GIS (Geographic Information Systems).

Keywords: Virtual Reality, Geography, GIS (Geographic Information Systems), Cyberspace

Audience: Geographers, Cartographers, Cybernauts

Contact: Tom Edwards
navanax.u.washington.edu

User Info: To subscribe to the list, send an e-mail message to the URL address below, consisting of a single line reading:

SUB vigis-l YourFirstName YourLastName.

To send a message to the entire list, address it to: vigis@uwavm.u.washington.edu

`mailto:listserv@uwavm.u.washington.edu`

Geology

Internet Resources for Earth Sciences

A document detailing Internet resources for a variety of earth science disciplines, including GIS.

Keywords: Directory, GIS, Geology, Geography, GPS, Mapping, Earth Science

Sponsor: Bill Thoen

Audience: Earth Scientists, Researchers

Profile: A complete document detailing the types of information available in earth sciences and the mechanisms to retrieve needed information.

Contact: Bill Thoen
bthoen@gisnet.com

Details: Free

`Ftp://ftp.csn.org/COGS/ores.text`

Natural Resources Canada (NRCan) Gopher

This site offers information on forests, energy, mining, and geomatics from the Canadian government. Also has reports from the Geological Survey of Canada and an overview of NRCan statutes, organization, and personnel. Provides links to other Canadian environmental and government gophers.

Keywords: Canada, Environment, Geology, Forestry

Sponsor: The Department of Natural Resources, Canada

Audience: Canadians, Environmentalists, Environmental Researchers, Geologists

Contact: Bob Fillmore
fillmore@emr.ca

Notes: NRCan maintains a toll-free hotline - 1-800-267-5166

`gopher://gopher.emr.ca`

`http://www.emr.ca`

Sahel-NAFR

This site contains information about a database of composite satellite images of Sahel and North Africa (known as the Sahelian and NW Africa 14-Day NDVI Composites). The images come from a pilot program defined between the U.S. Geological Survey and the U.S. Agency for International Development (AID) to develop and test a near-real-time monitoring procedure using satellite remote sensing and Geographic Information System technologies in grasshopper and locust control programs in West Africa. Also contains an appendix with information about the Senegalese Grasshoppers.

Keywords: Geology, Geography, GIS (Geographic Information Systems)

Sponsor: U.S. Geological Survey and U.S. Agency for International Development (AID)

Audience: Geologists, Geographers

`http://sun1.cr.usgs.gov/glis/hyper/guide/sahel_nafr`

University of Maine System Library Catalog

The library's holdings are large and wide-ranging and contain significant collections in many fields.

Keywords: Ucadian Studies, St. John Valley (History of), Canadian-American Studies, Geology, Aquaculture, Maine

Audience: General Public, Researchers, Librarians, Document Delivery Professionals

Contact: Elaine Albright, Marilyn Lutz

Details: Free

Expect: login, Send: ursus

`telnet://ursus.maine.edu`

University of Rochester Library

The library's holdings are large and wide-ranging and contain significant collections in many fields.

Keywords: Architecture, Art History, Photography, Literature (Asian), Lasers, Geology, Statistics, Optics, Medieval Studies

Audience: Researchers, Students, General Public

Details: Free

User Info: Expect: Login; Send: Library

`telnet://128.151.226.71`

University of Tulsa Library

The library's holdings are large and wide-ranging and contain significant collections in many fields.

Keywords: Literature (American), Petroleum, Geology

Audience: Researchers, Students, General Public

Details: Free

User Info: Expect: Username Prompt, Send: LIAS

`telnet://vax2.utulsa.edu`

University of Utah Library

The library's holdings are large and wide-ranging and contain significant collections in many fields.

Keywords: Western America, Middle Eastern Studies, Geology, Mining

Audience: Researchers, Students, General Public

Details: Free

Expect: Command Line, Send: Dial Unis

`telnet://lib.utah.edu`

University of Wisconsin at Milwaukee Library

The library's holdings are large and wide-ranging and contain significant collections in many fields.

Keywords: Art, Architecture, Business, Cartography, Geography, Geology, Urban Studies, Literature (English), Literature (American)

Audience: Researchers, Students, General Public

Details: Free

Expect: Login, Send: Lib; Expect: vDIAL prompt, Send: Library

`telnet://uwmcat.lib.uwm.edu`

US Geological Survey Server

This resource containis publications, USGS research programs, technology transfer partnerships, and fact sheets about geology.

Keywords: Biology, Geology, Natural Science

Sponsor: US Geological Survey

Audience: Biologists, Geologists, Researchers, Naturalists

Contact: Systems Operator webmaster@info.er.usgs.gov

`http://info.er.usgs.gov`

USGS (United States Geological Survey) Gopher

The library's holdings are large and wide-ranging ...

A gopher site covering issues related to the United State Geological Survey.

Keywords: Cartography, Geology

Sponsor: United States Geological Survey

Audience: Geologists, Cartologists

Profile: The USGS gopher was established to provide general information about USGS, information about USGS Divisions, publications, data, and briefings, USGS's Network resources, and other data on geology, hydrology, and cartography.

Contact: Gopher Operator webmaster@info.er.usgs.gov

`gopher://info.er.usgs.gov`

Georgetown University Medical Center Online Catalogue

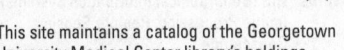

Georgetown University Medical Center Online Catalogue

This site maintains a catalog of the Georgetown University Medical Center library's holdings.

Keywords: Medicine, Library

Sponsor: Georgetown University, Washington, DC

Audience: Medical Professionals, Educators, Students

Contact: Jane Banks banksj@gumedlib2.georgetown.edu

Details: Free

The password is dahlgren, then enter netguest, hit RETURN several times and select option 1.

`telnet://medlib@gumedlib.georgetown.edu`

Georgia State University Library

Georgia State University Library

The library's holdings are large and wide-ranging and contain significant collections in many fields.

Keywords: Labor (History of), Multimedia, Mercer (Johnny, Collection of)

Audience: General Public, Researchers, Librarians, Document Delivery Professionals

Contact: Phil Williams isgpew@gsuvm1.gsu.edu

Details: Free

Expect: VM screen, Send: RETURN; Expect: CP READ, Send: DIAL VTAM, press RETURN; Expect: CICS screen, Send: PF1

`telnet://library.gsu.edu`

Georgia-Computer Systems Protection Act

Georgia-Computer Systems Protection Act

Lists full text of the Georgia Computer Systems Protection Act.

Keywords: Computer, Crime

Audience: Lawyers, Computer Programmers, Computer Operators

Details: Free

`gopher://wiretap.spies.com`

A B C D E F **G** H I J K L M N O P Q R S T U V W X Y Z

A
B
C
D
E
F
G
H
I
J
K
L
M
N
O
P
Q
R
S
T
U
V
W
X
Y
Z

Geoscience

Geoscience at Texas A&M University

General server with info on all aspects of GIS and remote sensing, especially GPS.

Keywords:	GIS (Geographical Information Systems), Image Processing, Remote Sensing, Geoscience
Sponsor:	Texas A&M University - Department of Agricultural Engineering
Audience:	Researchers, GIS and IP professionals, Students
Contact:	Hal Mueller hmueller@diamond.tamu.edu
Details:	Free
	Images
Notes:	Contains links to related Univeristy of Texas gophers and WWW servers.

`http://ageninfo.tamu.edu/geoscience.html`

Meetings Calendar (Geosciences)

A collection of meetings and conferences in the geosciences, with a special emphasis on meteorology. The entries are sorted by date and some contain links to Calls for Papers.

Keywords:	Geosciences, Meteorology
Sponsor:	Freie Universit Berlin, Germany
Audience:	Researchers, Meteorologists
Contact:	Dennis Schulze dennis@bibo.met.fu-berlin.de
Details:	Free
Notes:	If there is a conference you want to have included in this list, send an e-mail to dennis@bibo.met.fu-berlin.de

`http://www.met.fu-berlin.de/konferenzen/index.html`

Germany

9nov89-l

A discussion list relating to recent events in the former German Democratic Republic.

Keywords:	German Democratic Republic, Germany, Berlin Wall
Audience:	Researchers, Political Scientists
Contact:	Axel Mahler axel@avalanche.cs.tu-berlin.de
User Info:	To subscribe to the list, send an e-mail message to the URL address shown below, consisting of a single line reading:

SUB 9nov89-l YourFirstName YourLastName

To send a message to the entire list, address it to: 9nov89-1@tubvm.cs.tu.berlin.de

`mailto:listserv@tubvm.cs.tu-berlin.de`

ACDGIS-L

GIS discussions for German speakers.

Keywords:	Germany, Geographic Information Systems, Geography
Audience:	Germans, Geographers, Cartographers
Details:	Costsost
	Inquire through wigeoarn@awiwuw11.bitnet

`mailto:acdgis-l@awiwuw11.bitnet`

Germany

Full text in German of various German laws and codes.

Keywords:	German, Law
Sponsor:	Berlin University, Berlin, Germany
Audience:	Lawyers, Historians, Germans
Details:	Free
	Select from menu as appropriate.

`gopher://gate1.zedat.fu-berlin.de`

Hoppenstedt Directory of German Companies

This directory covers 50,000 German companies with sales exceeding 2 million DM or with a minimum of 20 employees.

Keywords:	German Companies, International Business, Germany
Sponsor:	Hoppenstedt Wirtschaftsdatenbank, Darmstadt, Germany
Audience:	Business Professionals, International Market, Researchers, Germans
Profile:	Records include current company address, line of business, number of employees, sales, capital stock, branches and subsidiaries, and a listing of executives and directors with positions in the company. The file is bilingual; users can view the records in either German or English.
Contact:	Dialog in the US at (800) 334-2564; Dialog internationally at country-specific locations.
User Info:	To subscribe, contact Dialog directly.
Notes:	Coverage: 1973 to the present; updated semiannually.

`telnet://dialog.com`

Information Services in Germany

This gopher is an informal entry point for Germany, together with some hints to specialties in German information systems.

Keywords:	Germany, Information, Europe
Audience:	German Internet Surfers
Contact:	lange@rz.tu-clausthal.de
Details:	Free

`gopher://gopher.tu-clausthal.de`

soc.culture.german

A Usenet newsgroup providing information and discussion about German Culture.

Keywords:	Germany, Sociology
Audience:	Sociologists, Germans
Details:	Free
User Info:	To subscribe to this Usenet newsgroup, you need access to a newsreader.

`news:soc.culture.german`

Gerontology

AgeLine

The AgeLine database is produced by the American Association of Retired Persons (AARP) and provides bibliographic coverage of social gerontology—the study of aging in social, psychological, health-related, and economic contexts.

Keywords:	Gerontology, Retired, Public Policy, Aging
Sponsor:	American Association of Retired Persons, Washington, DC, USA
Audience:	Retired Persons, Health Care Providers, Researchers
Profile:	AgeLine covers the delivery of health care for the older population and its associated costs and policies, as well as public policy, employment, and consumer issues. Literature covered is of interest to researchers, health professionals, service planners, policy makers, employers, older adults and their families, and consumer advocates.
Coverage:	1978 to the present (selected coverage back to 1966); updated bimonthly.
Contact:	Dialog in the US at (800) 334-2564; Dialog internationally at country-specific locations.
Details:	Costs
	There is no print equivalent of the database. To subscribe, contact Dialog directly.

`telnet://dialog.com`

Gifts

The Branch Mall, an Electronic Shopping Mall

Branch Information Services offers shopping to customers and leases storefronts and electronic catalogs to vendors.

Keywords: Mall, Shopping, Gifts, Advertising, Mailorder

Sponsor: Branch Information Services

Audience: Consumers, Merchants

Contact: Jon Zeeff
jon@branch.com

Details: Free

Notes: Free for consumers.

`http://branch.com`

GIS (Geographical Information Systems)

ACDGIS-L

GIS discussions for German speakers.

Keywords: Germany, Geographical Information Systems, Geography

Audience: Germans, Geographers, Cartographers

Details: Costsost
Inquire through wigeoarn@awiwuw11.bitnet

`mailto:acdgis-l@awiwuw11.bitnet`

ASTRA-UG

A mailing list for the discussion of Italian and European GIS

Keywords: GIS (Geographical Information Systems), Europe, Italy

Audience: Geographers, Cartographers, Europeans

Details: Free

User Info: To subscribe to the list, send an e-mail mesage to the URL address below, consisting of a single line reading:
SUB ASTRA-UG YourFirstName YourLastName

`astra-ug@icnucevm`

consgis

A discussion list for those using GIS (Geographic Information Systems) in the interest of conservation.

Keywords: Conservation, Environment, GIS (Geographical Information Systems)

Audience: Geographers, Environmentalists, Cartographers

Contact: Dr. Peter August
pete@edcserv.edc.uri.edu

Details: Free

User Info: To subscribe to the list, send an e-mail message to the URL address below, consisting of a single line reading:
SUB consgis YourFirstName YourLastName.
To send a message to the entire list, address it to: consgis@uriacc.uri.edu

`mailto:listserv@uriacc.uri.edu`

ESRI (Environmental Systems Research Institute)

Environmental Systems Research Institute, Inc. is the world leader in GIS technology. ARC/INFO is ESRI's powerful and flexible flagship GIS software.

Keywords: GIS (Geographical Information Systems), Environment, Software, Computers

Audience: Geographers, Environmentalists, Computer Users

Details: Costs
For product information, call (909)793-2853, X1475.
For training information, call (909)793-2853, X1585, or fax (909)793-5953.

`mailto:ajackson@esri.com`

Geographic Information and Analysis Laboratory (GIAL)

Server distributing a variety of information related to geography and GIS.

Keywords: Geography, GIS (Geographical Information Systems), NCGIA

Sponsor: SUNY-Buffalo and the National Center for Geographic Information and Analysis (NCGIA)

Audience: Geographers, GIS Professionals, Researchers, Students

Contact: Brandon Plewe, Reginald O. Carroll, Patricia M. Baumgarten
plewe@geog.buffalo.edu,
carrol@geog.buffalo.edu,
pmb@geog.buffalo.edu

Details: Free, Images

Notes: Check out the You-are-here server!

`http://zia.geog.buffalo.edu/`

Geoscience at Texas A&M University

General server with info on all aspects of GIS and remote sensing, especially GPS.

Keywords: GIS (Geographical Information Systems), Image Processing, Remote Sensing, Geoscience

Sponsor: Texas A&M University - Department of Agricultural Engineering

Audience: Researchers, GIS and IP professionals, Students

Contact: Hal Mueller
hmueller@diamond.tamu.edu

Details: Free

Images

Notes: Contains links to related Univeristy of Texas gophers and WWW servers.

`http://ageninfo.tamu.edu/
geoscience.html`

GIS Master Bibliography Project

A bibliography of GIS literature encompassing journal articles, conference proceedings, books, and technical reports.

Keywords: GIS (Geographical Information Systems), Databases

Sponsor: Ohio State University - Department of Geography and others

Audience: GIS Users, Researchers, Students

Contact: Dr. Duane Marble
marble.1@osu.edu

Details: Free

`ftp://128.146.209.34/biblio`

GIS-L

A forum for the discussion of all issues pertaining to GIS (Geographical Information Systems), including hydrological modeling, environmental issues, and available software packages.

Keywords: Geography, Environment, GIS (Geographic Information Systems)

Audience: Geographers, Cartographers

Contact: David Mark
dmark@acsu.buffalo.edu

User Info: To subscribe to the list, send an e-mail message to the URL address below, consisting of a single line reading:
SUB gis-l YourFirstName YourLastName.
To send a message to the entire list, address it to: gis-l@ubvm.cc.buffalo.edu

`mailto:listserv@ubvm.cc.buffalo.edu`

GIS-L and comp.infosystems.gis FAQ

HTML and/or ASCII document describing all aspects of GIS on the Internet.

Keywords: GIS (Geographical Information Systems), Usenet

Audience: GIS Users

Profile: Contains information on data sources, formats, software info, and pointers to other Internet GIS info sources.

Contact: Lisa Nyman
lnyman@census.gov

A B C D E F **G** H I J K L M N O P Q R S T U V W X Y Z

Details: Free

Notes: ASCII version also available.

`http://www.cencus.gov/geo/gis/faqindex.html`

`ftp://ftp.cencus.gov/pub/geo/gis-faq.txt`

GIS-T

A mailing list for the discussion of GIS (Geographical Information Systems) and transportation.

Keywords: Geography, Transportation, GIS (Geographical Information Systems)

Audience: Geographers, Cartographers

Contact: Jay Sandhu
jsandhu@esri.com

User Info: To subscribe to the list, send an e-mail message to the URL address below, consisting of a single line reading:

SUB gis-t YourFirstName YourLastName.

To send a message to the entire list, address it to: gis-t@esri.com

`mailto:listserv@esri.com`

ingr-en

A mailing list for the discussion of Intergraph products .

Keywords: GIS (Geographical Information Systems), Intergraph

Audience: Geographers, Cartographers

Contact: Dusan Blasko
blasko@svfnov.tuke.sk

User Info: To subscribe to the list, send an e-mail message to the URL address below, consisting of a single line reading:

SUB ingr-en YourFirstName YourLastName.

To send a message to the entire list, address it to: ingr-en@ccsun.tuke.sk

`mailto:listserv@ccsun.tuke.sk`

Internet GIS and RS Information Sites

This document contains a lengthy listing of GIS and remote sensing sites on the Internet.

Keywords: GIS (Geographical Information Systems), Remote Sensing, Image Processing, Geography

Sponsor: Queen's University Department of Geography

Audience: Researchers, General Public

Contact: Michael McDermott
mcdermom@gisdog.gis.queensu.ca

Details: Free

Notes: ASCII version also available from the same FTP site.

`ftp://gis.queensu.ca/pub/gis/docs/gissites.html`

Internet Resources for Earth Sciences

A document detailing Internet resources for a variety of earth science disciplines, including GIS.

Keywords: Directory, GIS, Geology, Geography, GPS, Mapping, Earth Science

Sponsor: Bill Thoen

Audience: Earth Scientists, Researchers

Profile: A complete document detailing the types of information available in earth sciences and the mechanisms to retrieve needed information.

Contact: Bill Thoen
bthoen@gisnet.com

Details: Free

`ftp://ftp.csn.org/COGS/ores.text`

Internet Resources for Geographic Information and GIS

An HTML document with information on all aspects of GIS.

Keywords: GIS

Sponsor: Bates College- Department of Classical and Romance Languages

Audience: GIS Professionals

Contact: Neel Smith
nsmith@abacus.bates.edu

Details: Free

`http://abacus.bates.edu/~nsmith/General/Resources-GIS.html`

ITRE Home Page

A server dealing with transportation research and some GIS-related discussion.

Keywords: GIS, Transportation

Sponsor: University of North Carolina Institute for Transportation Research and Education

Audience: GIS Professionals, Transportation Professionals

Profile: The ITRE server address GIS issues regarding transportation, a different flavor than will be found on most servers on the Net. Also features image mapping examples.

Contact: Jay Novello
jay@itre.uncecs.edu

Details: Free, Images, Multimedia

`http://itre.uncecs.edu/`

mapinfo-l

A mailing list for the discussion of MapInfo Software.

Keywords: GIS (Geographic Information Systems)

Audience: Geographers, Cartographers

Contact: Bill Thoen
bthoen@gisnet.com

`mailto:mapinfo-l-request@csn.org`

next-gis

Discussion of Geographical Information Systems (GIS) and cartography-related topics on the NeXT and other workstation computers. Some moderated reposting of comp.infosys.gis occurs as well.

Keywords: Geography, Cartography, GIS, NeXT

Audience: GIS Users, NeXT Users

Contact: Steven R. Staton
sstaton@deltos.com

Details: Free

User Info: To subscribe to the list, send an e-mail message to the URL address shown below, consisting of a single line reading:

SUB next-gis YourFirstName YourLastName

To send a message to the entire list, address it to: next-gis@DistributionAddress

Details: Free

User Info: To subscribe to the list, send an e-mail message to the URL address below, consisting of a single line reading:

SUB mapinfo-l YourFirstName YourLastName

`mailto:listserv@deltos.com`

rrl

A mailing list for the discussion of GIS (Geographic Information Systems) in the United Kingdom.

Keywords: GIS (Geographic Information Systems), United Kingdom

Audience: Geographers, Cartographers

Contact: rrl@uk.ac.leicester

`mailto:rrl@uk.ac.leicester`

Sahel-NAFR

This site contains information about a database of composite satellite images of Sahel and North Africa (known as the Sahelian and NW Africa 14-Day NDVI Composites). The images come from a pilot program defined between the U.S. Geological Survey and the U.S. Agency for International Development (AID) to develop and test a near-real-time monitoring procedure using satellite remote sensing and Geographic Information System technologies in grasshopper and locust control programs in West Africa. Also contains an appendix with information about the Senegalese Grasshoppers.

Keywords: Geology, Geography, GIS (Geographic Information Systems)

Sponsor: U.S. Geological Survey and U.S. Agency for International Development (AID)

Audience: Geologists, Geographers

`http://sun1.cr.usgs.gov/glis/hyper/guide/sahel_nafr`

UIgis-L

A mailing list for the discussion of user interfaces and GIS (Geographic Information Systems).

Keywords: Geography, GIS (Geographic Information Systems)

Audience: Geographers, Cartographers

Contact: David Mark
dmark@acsu.buffalo.edu

User Info: To subscribe to the list, send an e-mail message to the URL address below, consisting of a single line reading:

SUB uigis-l YourFirstName YourLastName.

To send a message to the entire list, address it to: uigis@ubvm.cc.buffalo.edu

`mailto:listserv@ubvm.cc.buffalo.edu`

United States Geographic Name Server

A database searchable by city name or zip code, this server provides geographic data including population, longitude and latitude, elevation, county, state, and zip codes.

Keywords: Geography, GIS (Geographical Information Systems)

Audience: Geographers, General Public

Contact: pubgopher@pluto.cc.brandeis.edu

`gopher://pluto.cc.brandeis.edu`

United States Geological Survey Home Page

★★★★

USGS server dedicated to all aspects of geography and geographic data.

Keywords: USGS, GIS, Geography

Sponsor: United States Geological Survey

Audience: Geographers, GIS Professionals, Researchers, Students

Profile: Probably the most comprehensive geography/GIS server on the net. Features include a GIS tutorial, descriptions (and examples) of available USGS data products, access to online spatial data, and more.

Contact: webmaster@info.er.usgs.gov

Details: Free, Images, Sounds, Multimedia

Notes: The USGS maintains many servers; this page contains links to most of them, such as EROS Data Center, GLIS and others.

`http://info.er.usgs.gov/USGSHome.html`

The University of Minnesota Remote Sensing Lab

General information about remote sensing and GIS.

Keywords: GIS, Remote Sensing, Image Processing

Sponsor: University of Minnesota, Department of Forest Resources

Audience: Researchers, GIS and IP professionals, Students

Profile: The RSL server contains information regarding all aspects of image process and GIS. Some features include: home of the GIS Jobs Clearinghouse, archives of ESRI-L, IMAGRS-L and TGIS-L, and the NBS CPSU WWW server.

Contact: Stephen Lime
sdlime@torpedo.forestry.umn.edu

Details: Free, Images

Notes: The RSL also maintains a companion gopher server and anonymous FTP site for the GIS Jobs Clearinghouse.

`http://walleye.forestry.umn.edu/0/www/main.html`

vigis-l

A mailing list for the discussion of Virtual Reality and GIS (Geographic Information Systems).

Keywords: Virtual Reality, Geography, GIS (Geographic Information Systems), Cyberspace

Audience: Geographers, Cartographers, Cybernauts

Contact: Tom Edwards
navanax.u.washington.edu

User Info: To subscribe to the list, send an e-mail message to the URL address below, consisting of a single line reading:

SUB vigis-l YourFirstName YourLastName.

To send a message to the entire list, address it to:
vigis@uwavm.u.washington.edu

`mailto:listserv@uwavm.u.washington.edu`

Germany

Full text in German of various German laws and codes.

Keywords: German, Law

Sponsor: Berlin University, Berlin, Germany

Audience: Lawyers, Historians, Germans

Details: Free

Select from menu as appropriate.

`gopher://gate1.zedat.fu-berlin.de`

Glass

Massachusetts Institute of Technology Library

The library's holdings are large and wide-ranging and contain significant collections in many fields.

Keywords: Aeronautics (History of), Linguistics, Mathematics (History of), Microscopy, Spectroscopy, Aeronautics, Mathematics, Glass

Audience: General Public, Researchers, Librarians, Document Delivery Professionals

Details: Free

Expect: Mitek Server..., Send: Enter or Return; Expect: prompt, Send: hollis

`telnet://library.mit.edu`

Global Change Information Gateway

Global Change Information Gateway

This gatewas was created to address environmental data management issues raised by the US Congress, the Administration, and the advisory arms of the Federal policy community. It contains documents related to the UN conference on Environment and Development.

Keywords: United Nations, Environment, Development, Oceans, Atmosphere

Audience: Environmentalists, Scientists, Researchers, Environmentalists

Details: Free

Select from menu as appropriate.

`gopher://scilibx.ucsc.edu`

Global Internet

Global Internet

A full-service Internet provider, offering superior quality Internet access and value-added services to business professionals, researchers, and educational communities.

Keywords: Internet, Finance

Sponsor: Global Internet, Palo Alto, CA (415)855-1700

Audience: Internet Users, Business Professionals, Financial Analysts, Publishers

Details: Costs

`mailto:sales@gi.net`

A B C D E F **G** H I J K L M N O P Q R S T U V W X Y Z

A
B
C
D
E
F
G
H
I
J
K
L
M
N
O
P
Q
R
S
T
U
V
W
X
Y
Z

Global News

News of Earth

Newsletter covering global news.

Keywords: Global News, News

Audience: General Public

Profile: News of Earth consists of: NewsE-A Analysis, an analysis of global news; NewsE-B Bulletins, late-breaking global news; NewsE-C Commentary, a commentary on global news; NewsE-D Distribution, global news monitored from shortwave radio broadcasts; and, the continuation of JBH Online (Online-L), published from 1987 through 1990 (Issues 1-213); NewsE-I Interviews, interviews on global issues; NewsE-L Letters, news and reaction from readers; NewsE-S Supplements, containing additional news and information from electronic and print sources. News of Earth supplements continues JBH News (JBHNewsL), published in 1990 (issues 1-4). NewsE is a "superlist" that includes all components listed above.

Contact: John B. Harlan
jbharlan@indyvax.iupui.edu

Details: Free

User Info: To subscribe, send an e-mail message to the URL address below, consisting of a single line reading:

SUB NEWSE-x (where x is A, B, C, D, I, L or S) YourFirstName YourLastName

To send a message to the entire list, address it to: newse@indyvax.iupui.edu

`mailto:listserv@Indyvax.iupui.edu`

GlobeTrotter

GlobeTrotter

File concerning hacking from an international perspective.

Keywords: Hacking, Computers

Audience: Hackers, Computer Users

Details: Free

Expect: login,Send: anonymous;
Password,Send: Your e-mail Address

`ftp://ftp.eff.org`

GLOSAS News (Global Systems Analysis and Simulating Association)

GLOSAS News (Global Systems Analysis and Simulating Association)

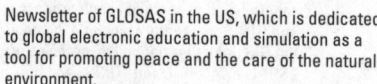

Newsletter of GLOSAS in the US, which is dedicated to global electronic education and simulation as a tool for promoting peace and the care of the natural environment.

Keywords: Education, Simulation, Peace

Audience: Educators, Environmentalists

Contact: Anton Ljutic
anton@vax2.concordia.ca

Details: Free

User Info: To subscribe, send an e-mail message to the address below, consisting of a single line reading:

SUB glosas YourFirstName YourLastName

Address it to: glosas@vm/.mcgill.ca

To send a message to the entire list,

`mailto:listserv@vm1.mcgill.ca`

GNUs Bulletin: Newsletter of the Free Software Foundation

GNUs Bulletin: Newsletter of the Free Software Foundation

Bringing you news about the GNU Project, the Free Software Foundation is dedicated to eliminating restrictions on copying, redistribution, understanding, and modification of computer programs.

Keywords: Software, Shareware

Sponsor: Free Software Foundation

Audience: Computer Programmers, Computer Users

Contact: Leonard H. Tower, Jr.
tower@ai.mit.edu

Details: Free

`mailto:info-gnu-request@prep.ai.mit.edu`

God

alt.atheism

A Usenet newsgroup providing information and discussion about atheism.

Keywords: Religion, Divinity, God

Audience: Philosophers, Clergy, Atheists

User Info: To subscribe to this Usenet newsgroup, you need access to a newsreader.

`news:alt.atheism`

Goethe

University of Chicago Library

The library's holdings are large and wide-ranging and contain significant collections in many fields.

Keywords: English Bibles, Lincoln (Abraham), Kentucky & Ohio River Valley (History of), Balzac (Honore de), American Drama, Cromwell (Oliver), Goethe, Judaica, Italy, Chaucer (Geoffrey), Wells (Ida, Personal Papers of), Douglas (Stephen A.), Italy, Literature (Children's)

Audience: General Public, Researchers, Librarians, Document Delivery Professionals

Details: Free

Expect: ENTER CLASS, Send: LIB48 3; Expect: CONNECTED, Send: RETURN

`telnet://olorin.uchicago.edu`

Gold in Networks

Gold in Networks

An introductory guide to the Internet.

Keywords: Internet, Internet Guide

Sponsor: Ohio State University

Audience: Internet Surfers

Contact: J. Martin
nic@osu.edu

Details: Free

File is: documents/fyi/fyi_1o.txt

`ftp://nic.merit.edu`

Golf

GolfData OnLine

A web site sampling of the information on the subscriber service GolfData OnLine. Provides numerous links to other sites that may be of interest to golfers.

Keywords: Golf, Sports, Fitness

Audience: Golfers, Sports Fans

Contact: david@gdol.com

Notes: GolfData Online is a paid subscriber electronic bulletin board service for golf enthusiasts. More information about how to subscribe can be obtained by accessing the address below.

`http://www.gdol.com`

University of Glasgow Information Service (GLANCE) ★★★★

GLANCE provides subject-based information services, including an extensive section on European and world sports.

Keywords: Sports, Soccer, Motor Racing, Mountaineering, Squash, Cricket, Golf, Tennis, Europe, Scotland

Sponsor: University of Glasgow, Glasgow, Scotland

Audience: Sport Enthusiasts, Fitness Enthusiasts, Nature Lovers

Profile: Information at this site includes schedules, results, and statistics for sports such as cricket and soccer. There is also a selection of items on mountaineering.

Contact: Alan Dawson
A.Dawson@uk.ac.gla.compserv

Details: Free

`gopher://govan.cent.gla.ac.uk/Subject/Sports and Rec`

Gopher

comp.infosystems.gopher

A Usenet newsgroup providing information and discussion about the gopher information search tool.

Keywords: Gopher, Internet Reference, Information Retrieval

Audience: Internet Surfers

User Info: To subscribe to this Usenet newsgroup, you need access to a newsreader.

`news:comp.infosystems.gopher`

E-mail Gopher

E-mail Gopher allows the use of a gopher via e-mail.

Keywords: Internet, Services, e-mail, Gopher

Audience: Internet Surfers

Details: Free
Include the word "help" in the Email.

`gopher://gopher.ncc.go.jp/11/INFO/gopher`

Education Gopher

Florida Tech's gopher relating to education. Includes information on search tools, libraries, electronic texts, and selected education-related gophers and information servers.

Keywords: Education, Gopher

Audience: Educators, Researchers

Contact: Kevin Barry
barry@sci-ed.fit.edu

Details: Free

`gopher://sci-ed.fit.edu`

European Root Gopher

A root gopher server and registry for European gophers run by the Swedish University Network to serve European users.

Keywords: Europe, Gophers

Sponsor: Swedish University Computer Network (SUNET)

Audience: European Internet Surfers

Contact: gopher-info@sunic.sunet.se

Details: Free

`gopher://gopher@sunet.se`

French Language Gophers (Les Gophers Francophones) ★★★

A gopher site providing links to over 50 gopher servers in the French-speaking world. Most sites are located in either Canada, Switzerland, or France.

Keywords: Gopher, French Language, French Studies

Sponsor: National Capitol Freenet, Canada

Audience: French Students, Francophiles

Contact: gopher@jussieu.fr

`gopher://freenet.carleton.ca/Les Gopher francophones/`

Gopher

A guide to using gopher, an Internet access tool that locates and retrieves resources using a graph of menus.

Keywords: Internet Tools, Gopher

Audience: Internet Surfers

Contact: gopher@boombox.micro.umn.edu

Details: Free
File is: pub/gopher/00README

`ftp://boombox.micro.umn.edu`

Gopher-Based ASCII Clip Art Collection ★★

A collection of over 500 individual pictures, ranging from images of food to Star Wars, created with ASCII characters. Organized by subject, and including archives of the Usenet group alt.ascii-art. Also contains links to other ASCII collections.

Keywords: Clip Art, Design, ASCII, Gopher

Sponsor: Texas Tech Computer Sciences Gopher Server

Audience: Computer Users, General Public

Contact: Abdul Malik Yoosufan
gripe@cs.ttu.edu

Details: Free, Images

`gopher://cs4sun.cs.ttu.edu`

`ftp://ftp.cs.ttu.edu:/pub/asciiart`

Gopher Demo

A session demonstrating gopher at the University of Minnesota.

Keywords: Internet Tools, Gopher

Audience: Internet Surfers

`gopher://gopher.micro.umn.edu`

Gopher FAQ

Answers to frequently asked questions (FAQs) about gophers from the USENET newsgroup comp.infosystems.gopher

Keywords: Internet Tools, Gopher

Audience: Internet Surfers

Contact: Paul Lindner
lindner@boombox.micro.umn.edu

Details: Free
File is: pub/usenet/news.answers/gopher-faq

`ftp://pit-manager.mit.edu`

Gopher Jewels ★★★★

A searchable catalog of outstanding gopher sites worldwide.

Keywords: Gopher, Internet Tools

Audience: Internet Surfers, Researchers

Profile: Gopher Jewels, indexed by subject and searchable through WAIS, allows access to more than 2,000 gopher sites. The main server also has archives of the Gopher Jewels listserv, and extensive help and FAQ files on the uses of gopher. It is also available as a WWW site.

Contact: David Riggins
david.riggins@tpoint.comgopherjewels-comment@einet.net

Details: Free

`gopher://cwis.usc.edu/11/Other_Gophers_and_Information_Resources/Gopher_Jewels`

`http://galaxy.einet.net/gopher/gopher.html`

Gopher Sites

A list of worldwide gopher sites (sorted by domain structure) available on the Internet.

Keywords: Internet Tools, Gopher

Sponsor: Washington & Lee University, Lexington, VA, USA

Audience: Internet Surfers

Details: Free
File is: pub/lawlib/veronica.gopher.sites

`ftp://liberty.uc.wlu.edu`

A
B
C
D
E
F
G
H
I
J
K
L
M
N
O
P
Q
R
S
T
U
V
W
X
Y
Z

Gopher Telnet Demo

A Telnet session demonstrating the use of gopher.

Keywords: Internet Tools, Gopher

Audience: Internet Surfers

Details: Free

```
telnet: //
gopher@consultant.micro.umn.ed
```

Gopher/Veronica-How To

A special issue of the University of Illinois publication describing gopher and Veronica.

Keywords: Internet Tools, Gopher, Veronica

Sponsor: University of Illinois, Urbana, IL

Audience: Internet Surfers

Details: Free

File is: doc/net/uiucnet/vol6no1.txt

```
ftp://ftp.cso.uiuc.edu
```

LIST Gopher

★★★

This is a library-related service that enables users to obtain information by using their e-mail accounts.

Keywords: Mailing Lists, Listserv, Libraries, Gopher

Sponsor: North Carolina State University, Raleigh, North Carolina, USA

Audience: Librarians, Library Users, E-mail Users

Profile: LISTGopher enables users to search library-related LISTSERV archives through the Gopher interface. Users enter their e-mail address, the list they want to search, and the keyword(s) they wish to find. LISTGopher then sends the results of their search to the user's e-mail address. Currently, only library-related archives are supported, but more archive types may be added in the future.

Contact: Eric Lease Morgan, Systems Librarian eric_morgan@ncsu.edu

```
http://ericmorgan.lib.ncsu.edu/staff/
morgan/morgan.html
```

```
gopher://dewey.lib.ncsu.edu /library/
disciplines/library/listgopher
```

Gothic Rock

Corpse/Respondents

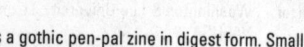

This is a gothic pen-pal zine in digest form. Small traffic mailing list.

Keywords: Gothic Rock, Rock Music

Audience: Gothic Rock Enthusiasts

Contact: carriec@eskimo.com

Details: Free

User Info: To subscribe, send an e-mail message to the URL address below, with "subscribe corpse <yournameandaddress>" in the text.

```
mailto:carriec@eskimo.com
```

Government

alt.politics.election

A Usenet newsgroup organized to help people in the process of running for office.

Keywords: Politics (US), Government

Audience: Politicians, Campaign Managers

User Info: To subscribe to this Usenet newsgroup, you need access to a newsreader.

```
news:alt.politics.election
```

Amnesty International

A site containing information about Amnesty International, an organization focused strictly and specifically on human rights around the world.

Keywords: Government, Human Rights, Politics (International), Activism

Sponsor: Amnesty International

Audience: Students, Activists

Contact: Catherine Hampton ariel@netcom.com

```
ftp://ftp.netcom.com/pub/ariel/
```

```
http:www/human.rights/
amnesty.international/ai.html
```

BUSREF (Business Reference)

The Business Refernce (BUSREF) library contains a variety of reference materials covering business and industry.

Keywords: News, Reference, Business, Government

Audience: Businessmen

Profile: The BUSREF library contains company directories, reference publications, information on business opportunities, and biographical information on political candidates, Congressional members, celebrities, and international decision makers.

Contact: Mead New Sales Group at (800) 227-4908 or (513) 859-5398 inside the US, or (513) 865-7981 for all inquiries outside the US.

User Info: To subscribe, contact Mead directly.

To examine the Nexis user guide, you can access it at the ftp site of the University of Texas at Austin at the URL address: ftp://ftp.cc.utexas.edu

The files are in: /pub/ref-services/LEXIS

```
telnet://nex.meaddata.com
```

```
http://www.meaddata.com
```

C-SPAN (Cable-Satellite Public Affairs Network) Gopher

Online information from C-SPAN, the public affairs television network.

Keywords: News Media, Government, Congress (US), Television

Sponsor: C-SPAN

Audience: Journalists, Government Officials, Educators (K-12), General Public

Profile: Comprehensive listings of C-SPAN's programming and coverage of events in Washington D.C. and beyond. In addition to the programming notes and schedules, this site also features online educational resources sponsored by C-SPAN, text of historic documents and speeches, and background political information on the House of Representatives and the Supreme Court.

Contact: cspanviewr@aol.com

Details: Free

```
gopher://c-span.org
```

Open Government Project (Canada)

★★★★

This site provides online audio-visual and text information on the Canadian government.

Keywords: Canada, Government

Sponsor: Directorate of Communications Development, Industry Canada, Canada

Audience: Canadians, Government Officials, Journalists

Profile: This bilingual (French/English) site has detailed information on members of the Canadian Senate and House of Commons, as well as Supreme Court rulings and biographies of the justices. It features a number of pictures, maps, and links to other Canadian information servers.

Contact: Tyson Macaulay tyson.macaulay@crc.doc.ca

```
http://debra.dgbt.doc.ca/ogp.html
```

```
gopher://debra.dgbt.doc.ca/
open_government_project
```

Russian and East European Studies Home Pages

Keywords: Russia, Eastern Europe, Government, Political Science

Sponsor: University of Pittsburgh

Audience: Researchers, Politicians

Contact: Casey Palowitch cjp@acid.library.pitt.edu

```
http://www.pitt.edu/cjp/rspubl.html
```

The Texas Information Highway

Access to the public information resources of the state of Texas.

Keywords: Texas, States, Government, Census, Tourism

Sponsor: Texas Department of Information Resources

Audience: Texans, General Public

Profile: Still under construction as we go to press, this is a model program to make state and local information resources available to Internet users. The current collection features city, country, and state political information, including full-text of bills before the Texas state legislature. Materials related to Texas history and tourism are also provided, along with links to Texas-area user groups and other state and federal information servers.

Contact: Wayne McDilda
wayne@dir.texas.gov

`gopher://info.texas.gov`

Government (African)

The University of Michigan Library

The library's holdings are large and wide-ranging and contain significant collections in many fields.

Keywords: Education (Bilingual), Linguistics, Neuroscience, Michigan, Prohibition, Government (African)

Audience: General Public, Researchers, Librarians, Document Delivery Professionals

Details: Free

Expect: nothing, Send: <cr>

`telnet://cts.merit.edu`

Government (International)

1994 Federal Budget (Canada)

This site offers full-text of Canada's federal budget. Also has a wealth of information on Canadian industry and industrial policy, including Provincial and Sectorial GATT opportunities and briefs from the Information Highway Advisory Council.

Keywords: Canada, Government (International), Industry, Foreign Trade

Sponsor: Industry Canada, Canada

Audience: Canadians, Government Officials, Businesspeople, Researchers

Contact: Tyson Macaulay
tyson@debra.dgbt.doc.ca

`gopher://debra.dgbt.doc.ca/industry
canada documents/isc.news.releases`

Counterev-L

This list is under the aegis of l'Alliance Monarchists, affiliated with l'Alliance pour la maintenance de la France en Europe, and is dedicated to promoting the cause of traditional monarchy and counterrevolution. Its principles are a government based on natural law, decentralization, subsidiarity, an economy based on the principles of distributive justice, and the defense of traditional Western values.

Keywords: Monarchy, Government (International)

Audience: Monarchists, Counterrevolutionaries

Contact: Jovan Weismiller
ae852@yfn.ysu.edu

Details: Free

User Info: To subscribe to the list, send an e-mail message requesting a subscription to the URL address below.

`mailto:ae852@yfn.ysu.edu`

Freedom of Information Directory of Records (Canada)

A database compiled by the Canadian federal government listing documents available to the public under The Freedom of Information and Protection of Privacy Act. It can be searched by keyword, or browsed through a menuing system.

Keywords: Canada, Government (International), Freedom of Information Act

Sponsor: British Columbia Systems Corporation, British Columbia, Canada

Audience: Canadians, Journalists, Activists

Contact: Office of the Information and Privacy Commissioner
TCPHELP@BCSC02.GOV.BC.CA

`gopher://bcsc02.gov.bc.ca`

Government Docs (US & World)

A large and eclectic collection of documents, ranging from the Laws of William the Conqueror to the North American Free Trade Agreement (NAFTA). Particular strengths include 20th century American political documents and international treaties and covenants.

Keywords: Government (International), History (World), Politics (International)

Sponsor: The Internet Wiretap

Audience: Researchers, Historians, Political Scientists, Journalists

Contact: gopher@wiretap.spies.com

`gopher://wiretap.spies.com/Gov`

Open Government Pilot

This web site provides information concerning the Canadian government, including information on Canadian infrastructure, industry, communications, provinces, and parliament.

Keywords: Canada, Government (International)

Sponsor: Canadian Federal Government

Audience: Canadians, Educators, Students

Details: Free

`http://debra.dgbt.doc.ca/opengov`

UN Resolutions

List of selected US and world government documents and UN resolutions.

Keywords: Government (International), United Nations, Government (US)

Sponsor: United Nations

Audience: Historians, Internationalists, Political Scientists

Details: Free

`gopher://wiretap.spies.com`

University of Saskatchewan Libraries

A major Canadian University library with access to library catalogs archives, and Canadian Government documents.

Keywords: Canada, Government (International)

Sponsor: University of Saskatchewan

Audience: Canadians, General Public

Profile: The University of Saskatchewan Libraries maintain online databases of their collections archives, and catalogs. The libraries are a voluminous resource for the study of Canada, Canadian government, and Canadian-American issues.

Login: sonia

`telnet://sklib.usask.ca`

World Bank Gopher Server

A collection of online information from the World Bank.

Keywords: Government (International), Development, International Finance, Foreign Trade

Sponsor: The World Bank

Audience: Nongovernmental Organizations, Activists, Government Officials, Environmentalists

Profile: A collection of World Bank information including a list of publications, environmental assessments, economic reports, and updates on current projects being funded by the World Bank.

Contact: webmaster@www.worldbank.org

`gopher://gopher.worldbank.org`

`http://www.worldbank.org`

A B C D E F **G** H I J K L M N O P Q R S T U V W X Y Z

Government (US)

America

For people interested in how the United States is dealing with foreign trade policies, congressional status, and other inside information about the government that is freely distributable.

Keywords: Foreign Trade, Government (US), Congress (US), Business (US)

Audience: General Public, Researchers, Journalists, Political Scientists, Students

Contact: subscribe@xamiga.linet.org

User Info: To subscribe to the list, send an e-mail message to the URL address below, consisting of a single line reading:

SUB america YourFirstName YourLastName

To send a message to the entire list, address it to: america@xamiga.linet.org

Notes: This list has monthly postings that are generally in large batches, with posts exceeding a few hundred lines.

`mailto:subscribe@xamiga.linet.org`

Americans with Disabilities Act

Gives access to the full text of the Americans with Disabilities Act (ADA) and all the related legislation.

Keywords: Disabilities, Legislation (US), Government (US)

Audience: General Public, Disabled People, Differently Abled People, Politicians, Journalists, Students

Profile: The purpose of ADA is to provide a clear and comprehensive national mandate to end discrimination against individuals with disabilities and to bring them into the economic and social mainstream of American life; to provide enforceable standards addressing discrimination against individuals with disabilities; and to ensure that the federal government plays a central role in enforcing these standards on behalf of individuals with disabilities.

Details: Free

`gopher://val-dor.cc.buffalo.edu/11/.legislation/`

An NREN That Includes Everyone

In this article, community networker Tom Grundner (founder of Free-Net) advocates a National Community Network— one that treats parents looking for health-care information as researchers. He advocates expanding our definition of educational access to include people of all ages— senior citizens as well as kindergarteners.

Keywords: Community, Networking, Government (US)

Audience: Activists, Policymakers, Community Leaders

Contact: Tom Grundner
tmg@nptn.org

Details: Free

Notes: This document contains hypertext links to the NPTN (National Public Telecomputing Network).

`http://nearnet.gnn.com/mag/articles/oram/bio.grundner.html`

Berne Convention Implementation Act of 1988

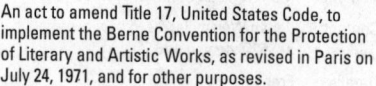

An act to amend Title 17, United States Code, to implement the Berne Convention for the Protection of Literary and Artistic Works, as revised in Paris on July 24, 1971, and for other purposes.

Keywords: Legislation (US), Government (US), Politics (US), Copyright

Audience: Lawyers, Students, Politicians, Journalists

Details: Free

`gopher://wiretap.spies.com/00/Gov/Copyright/US.Berne.Convention.txt`

Bibliographies of US Senate Hearings

The US Senate produces a series of committee hearings, prints, and publications as part of the legislative process. The Documents department at North Carolina State University contains files for the 99th through 103rd Congresses, which can also be searched through a WAIS searchable database.

Keywords: Senate (US), Politics (US), Legislation (US), Bibliographies, Government (US)

Audience: General Public, Journalists, Students, Politicians, US Citizens

Contact: Jack McGeachy
Jack_McGeachy@ncsu.edu

Details: Free

`gopher://dewey.lib.ncsu.edu/11/library/disciplines/government/senate`

Budget of the United States (1994)

Provides the full text of the 1994 budget of the United States.

Keywords: Budget, Government (US), Finance

Audience: Politicians, Lawyers, Journalists, Economists, Students, US Citizens

Details: Free

Notes: This document is over one megabyte in size and thus takes a couple of minutes to load onto the screen.

`gopher:// wiretap.spies.com/00/Gov/US-Gov/budget.94`

California State Senate Gopher

This is a gopher site accessing California State government records and providing links to related gophers.

Keywords: California, Government (US), Law (US State)

Sponsor: California State Senate, California, USA

Audience: Californians, General Public

Profile: The California State Senate Gopher provides access to state government records, pending bills, laws, state statistics, budgets, and related matters. The gopher also provides links to related gophers inside and outside state government.

Contact: Gopher Provider
gopher@sen.ca.gov

`gopher://gopher.sen.ca.gov`

Civic Promise of the National Information Infrastructure (NII)

Community networker Richard Civille (founder of EcoNet and director of the Center for Civic Networking) describes several experiments in community networking.

Keywords: Community, Networking, Government (US)

Audience: Activists, Policymakers, Community Leaders, Government

Contact: Richard Civille
rciville@civicnet.org

Details: Free

`http://nearnet.gnn.com/mag/articles/oram/bio.civille.html`

Clinton Watch

A regular political column devoted to a critical examination of the Clinton Administration.

Keywords: Politics, Clinton(Bill), Satire, Government (US)

Sponsor: Informatics Resource

Audience: Republicans, General Public, Citizens

Contact: clintonwatch@dolphin.gulf.net

`gopher://dolphin.gulf.net`

Clinton's Economic Plan

The contents of US President Clinton's economic plan.

Keywords: Economics, Government (US), Clinton (Bill)

Audience: Economists, General Public

Details: Free

The data contained on the President's Economic Plan diskette is now available via anonymous FTP at cu.nih.gov. The data can be found in a directory named USDOC-OBA-INFO.

`gopher://wiretap.spies.com/11/Gov/Economic`

Colorado Document Citations

A list of publications from all Colorado statutory government agencies.

The wiretap gopher provides access to a range of world documents in full-text format.

Keywords: Colorado, Government (US)

Audience: Researchers, Lawyers, Colorado Residents, Governments, historians, Researchers, General Public

Select from menu as appropriate.

`telnet://pac.carl.org`

Commerce Business Daily

The Commerce Business Daily is a publication that announces invitations to bid on proposals requested by the US Federal Government. This gopher is updated every business day.

Keywords: Business (US), Economics, Commerce, Trade, Government (US)

Sponsor: CNS and Softshare Government Information Systems

Audience: Economists, Business Professionals, General Public, Journalists, Students, Politicians.

Profile: Invitations via Internet e-mail that apply only to specific companies can be arranged.

Contact: Melissa Allensworth
sshare@cscns.com
service@cscns.com

Details: Free

`gopher://cns.cscns.com/cbd/About the CBD`

Congressional Contact Information

The US Senate and 103rd Congress phone and fax numbers are accessible and searchable from this server.

Keywords: Congress (US), Directories, Government (US)

Sponsor: Library of Congress

Audience: General Public, Journalists, Students, Politicians

Details: Free

`gopher://marvel.loc.gov/11/congress/directory`

Department of Justice Gopher

★ ★ ★

A gopher containing online information from the Justice Department.

Keywords: Federal Law (US), Government (US), Justice Department

Sponsor: United States Department of Justice

Audience: Lawyers, Citizens

Profile: The Department of Justice (DOJ) gopher features DOJ criminal and law enforcement statistics, as well as agency procurement requests, job listings, and press releases. Also has links to other US government online systems.

Contact: gopher@usdoj.gov

`gopher://gopher.usdoj.gov`

Electronic Democracy Must Come from Us

★

Article about government policy and community networks by community networker Evelyn Pine (former national director of Computer Professionals for Social Responsibility). A short critique of the promises of electronic networking contrasted with the realities of political control.

Keywords: Community, Networking, Government (US)

Audience: Activists, Community Leaders, Governments

Contact: Evelyn Pine
evy@well.sf.ca.us

Details: Free

`http://nearnet.gnn.com/mag/articles/oram/bio.pine.html`

(The) Electronic Public Interest versus the Private Good

★

Statement by community networker Dave Hughes, sounding the warning that the federal goverment may be leaving to the marketplace too much control over who gets access to the Information infrastructure.

Keywords: Community, Networking, Government (US)

Audience: Activists, Policymakers, Community Leaders

Contact: Dave Hughes
dave@oldcolo.com

Details: Free

`http://nearnet.gnn.com/mag/articles/oram/bio.hughes.html`

National Technology Transfer Center (NTTC)

★ ★

A federally-funded national network to apply government research to commercial applications.

Keywords: Technology, Technology Transfer, Research and Development, Business and Industry, Department of Defense, Government (US)

Sponsor: National Technology Transfer Center

Audience: Business People, Entrepreneurs, Manufactures, Technology Enthusiasts

Profile: Features state-by-state listings of agencies designed to facilitate the adaptation of new technologies to industry. Also provides updates on conferences, and a current list of Department of Defense projects soliciting private assistance from small businesses. Allows limited access to NTTC databases.

Contact: Charles Monfradi
cmonfra@nttc.edu, info@nttc.edu

`gopher://iron.nttc.edu`

`http://iridium.nttc.edu/nttc.hmtl`

NLSNews Newsletter (National Longitudinal Surveys of Labor Market Experience)

Issued by the Center for Human Resource Research (Ohio State University); distributed to researchers using NLS data, as well as to other interested persons.

Keywords: Labor, Government (US), Department of Labor

Sponsor: Bureau of Labor Statistics, US Department of Labor

Audience: Statisticians, Researchers (Labor)

Profile: A typical issue contains updates on the status and availability of NLS data tapes and CD-ROMs for the six NLS cohorts (Older Men, Mature Women, Young Men, Young Women, Youth, and Children), notices to researchers of data-file or documentation errors, summaries of in-progress and completed NLS research, and other information of general interest to the NLS research community.

Contact: Gale James
james@ohsthr.bitnet

A description of the subscription service that enables users to automatically receive, as soon as it becomes available, the latest issue of the NLS Newsletter and/or error updates can be found in the file subscribe.info, available via nlserve@ohsthr.bitnet, the Center's file server.

`mailto:james@ohsthr.bitnet`

Park Rangers

★

This list is primarily for anyone working or interested in working as a ranger (general, interpretive, and so on) for the US National Park Service, but rangers from state and county agencies and from other countries are also welcome. The group discusses numerous topics related to this profession.

A
B
C
D
E
F
G
H
I
J
K
L
M
N
O
P
Q
R
S
T
U
V
W
X
Y
Z

Keywords: US National Park Service, Government (US)

Audience: Park Rangers

Contact: Cynthia Dorminey
60157903@wsuvm1.csc.wsu.edu

Details: Free

User Info: To subscribe to the list, send an e-mail message requesting a subscription to the URL address below.

To send a message to the entire list, address it to: 60157903@wsuvm1.csc.wsu.edu

`mailto:60157903@wsuvm1.csc.wsu.edu`

Publications of the Office of Environment, Safety and Health

 ★★★

A collection of government safety information including updates, bulletins, and hazard alerts. Topics are diverse, covering everything from "Employee Hit on Head by Falling Steel Wheel" to "New Regulations to Control the Speed of Bloodborne Diseases."

Keywords: Safety, Government (US), Federal Laws (US)

Sponsor: U.S. Department of Energy

Audience: Government Officials, General Public

Details: Free

`gopher://dewey.tis.inel.gov`

PVS (Project Vote Smart)

★★

A gopher site containing Federal political information from PVS.

Keywords: Politics, Government (US)

Sponsor: Project Vote Smart, Corvallis, Oregon, USA

Audience: Voters, General Public

Profile: PVS is a volunteer organization dedicated to providing voters with factual information about candidates for Federal office. Currently, the gopher offers background information, including detailed profiles and legislative analysis of Senators and Representatives for all 50 states.

Contact: pvs@neu.edu

Notes: For more information on Project Vote Smart, call their toll free hotline at 1-800-622-SMART. Or write to: Project Vote Smart, 129 NW Fourth St. #240, Corvallis, OR 97330

`gopher://gopher.neu.edu`

Trademark Act of the US

 ★

The US Trademark Act of 1946 (the "Lanham Act"), Title 15, United States Code, Sections 1051_1127.

Keywords: Trademarks, Laws (US), Government (US), Commerce

Audience: Journalists, Politicians, Students, Lawyers, Business Professionals, Designers, Marketers

Details: Free

`http://www.law.cornell.edu/lanham/lanham.table.html`

UN Resolutions

 ★

List of selected US and world government documents and UN resolutions.

Keywords: Government (International), United Nations, Government (US)

Sponsor: United Nations

Audience: Historians, Internationalists, Political Scientists

Details: Free

`gopher://wiretap.spies.com`

Universal Copyright Convention

 ★★

The Universal Copyright Convention as revised at Paris (1971). Convention and protocols were done at Paris on July 24, 1971. It was ratified by the President of the United States of America on August 28, 1972.

Keywords: Copyright, Laws (US), Government (US), Politics (US)

Audience: Lawyers, Students, Politicians, Journalists

Details: Free

`gopher://wiretap.spies.com/00/Gov/Copyright/US.Universal.Copyright.Conv.txt`

University of Wisconsin Superior Library

 ★★

The library's holdings are large and wide-ranging and contain significant collections in many fields.

Keywords: Educational Policy, Government (US)

Audience: Researchers, Students, General Public

Details: Free

Expect: Login, Send: Lib; Expect: vDIAL Prompt, Send: Library

`telnet://sail.uwsuper.edu`

US Department of the Interior

 ★★

This resource contains Internet links to the Bureau of Indian Affairs, Bureau of Land Management, Bureau of Reclamation, National Biological Survey, National Park Service, and the US Fish and Wildlife Service.

Keywords: Government (US), Environmental Policies

Sponsor: US Department of the Interior Survey, Office of Public Affairs

Audience: Biologists, Geologists, Researchers, Environmentalists

`http://info.er.usgs.gov/doi/doi.html`

US General Accounting Office Transitional Reports

 ★★★

A major directory on accounting, providing access to a broad range of related resources (library catalogs, databases, and servers) via the Internet.

Keywords: Government (US), Finance

Audience: Politicians, Government Workers

Profile: Contains full-text documents of the Transitional Reports for the U.S. General Accounting Office. Reports includes Budget Issues, Investment, Government Management Issues, Financial Management Issues, Health Care Reform, National Security Issues, International Trade Issues, and so on.

Contact: kh3@cu.nih.gov

`gopher://thor.ece.uc.edu`

War Powers Resolution of 1973

 ★

A joint resolution concerning the war powers of Congress and the President resolved by the Senate and the House of Representatives of the United States of America in Congress.

Keywords: War, Law (International), Government (US)

Audience: Politicians, Students, Lawyers, Historians

Details: Free

`gopher://wiretap.spies.com/00/Gov/warpower.act`

White House Frequently Asked Questions

 ★★★★

This document is a good starting point for answering questions such as: How do I send e-mail to President Clinton? How do I get current news updates from the White House? Where can I get White House documents from?

Keywords: Clinton (Bill), Government (US), Politics (US), FAQs

Audience: General Public, Researchers

Details: Free

Expect: login; Send: anonymous; Expect: password; Send: your e-mail address; Expect: directory; Send: /pub/nic; Expect: file; Send: whitehouse FAQ.

`ftp://ftp.sura.net`

Government (US Federal/State)

Congressional Quarterly Gopher

Online Information from Congressional Quarterly (CQ), the premier journal covering events on Capitol Hill.

Keywords: Congress (US), Government (US Federal), Laws (US Federal)

Sponsor: Congressional Quarterly

Audience: Journalists, Government Officials, Educators, General Public

Profile: This gopher allows access to weekly stories and news briefs from CQ, as well as providing information on legislation before Congress, Congressional voting records, and results of recent federal elections. Also has catalogs of CQ's publications and schedules of their professional education seminars.

Contact: gopher_admin@cqalert.com

Details: Free

`gopher://gopher.cqalert.com`

Copyright Act ★

The full text of the Copyright Act of 1976, Title 17, United States Code, Sections 101_810.

Keywords: Politics (US), Government (US Federal), Laws (US Federal), Copyright

Audience: Lawyers, Students, Politicians, Journalists

Details: Free

`gopher://wiretap.spies.com/00/Gov/Copyright/US.Copyright.1976.tx`

Copyright Basics ★

This information is from Circular 1 issued by the Copyright Office, Library of Congress, January 1991. It explains what copyright is, who can claim copyright, the principles of copyrights, what works are protected, how to secure a copyright, and so on.

Keywords: Copyright, Government (US Federal), Laws (US Federal)

Audience: Lawyers, Students, Politicians, Journalists

Details: Free

`gopher://wiretap.spies.com/00/Gov/Copyright/US.Copyright.Basics.txt`

Electronic Communications Privacy Act of 1986 ★

This is the act to amend Title 18, United States Code, with respect to the interception of certain communications, other forms of surveillance, and for other purposes. This act affects every USENET, Bitnet, BBS, shortwave listener, TV viewer, and so on.

Keywords: Communications, Privacy, Government (US Federal), Laws (US Federal)

Audience: Journalists, Privacy Activists, Students, Politicians

Details: Free

`gopher://wiretap.spies.com/00/Gov/ecpa.act`

Freedom of Information Act (FOIA): Guide to Use ★

This is a citizen's guide on using the Freedom of Information Act and the Privacy Act of 1974 to request government records.

Keywords: Privacy, Freedom of Information, Government (US Federal)

Audience: Journalists, Privacy Activists, Students, Politicians, US Citizens

Details: Free

`gopher://wiretap.spies.com/00/Gov/foia.cit`

GPO Gateway to Government Act of 1992: Senator Al Gore ★

A bill to establish an electronic gateway in the Government Printing Office (GPO) to provide public access to a wide range of Federal databases containing public information stored electronically.

Keywords: Government (US Federal), Federal Databases

Audience: General Public, Journalists, Politicians

Details: Free

File is: /pub/nic/NREN/GPO.bill.6-92

`ftp://ftp.sura.net`

Government-Sponsored Electronic Bulletin Boards ★★★★

A list of U.S. Government-sponsored electronic bulletin boards (BBSs) for various agencies and departments.

Keywords: Government (US Federal), Law (US Federal), BBS

Sponsor: United States Government

Audience: General Public, Researchers

Profile: EBBs provide a wide and ever-changing assortment of government information, including text files, statistics, software, and graphics. Some of the information is also available in printed form, but much is not. Depository librarians may find government-sponsored EBBs useful in answering reference questions and in obtaining electronic versions of government publications, regardless of whether those publications were distributed to depository libraries.

Details: Free

`gopher://gopher.ncsu.edu`

High-Performance Computing Act of 1991 ★★★

This is a Senate bill to provide for a coordinated federal research program to ensure continued US leadership in high-performance computing.

Keywords: Computing, Government (US Federal), Law (US Federal)

Audience: General Public, Journalists, Politicians, Scientists

Details: Free

File is: /internet/nren/hpca.1991/gorebill.1991-txt

`ftp://nis.nsf.net`

Historical Documents of the US ★

A large sample of US historical documents, from the Fundamental Orders of 1639 to the Vietnam Era Documents, including World War II documents, Federalist papers, and more.

Keywords: Historical Documents (US), Government (US Federal), Law (US Federal)

Audience: Historians, Journalists, Students, Politicians

Details: Free

`gopher://wiretap.spies.com/11/Gov/US-History`

Information Infrastructure and Technology Act of 1992 ★

The Information Infrastructure and Technology Act of 1992 builds on the High-Performance Computing Act. The newer bill will ensure that the technology developed by the High-Performance Computing Program is applied widely in K-12 education, libraries, health care, and industry, particularly manufacturing. It will authorize a total of $1.15 billion over the next five years.

Keywords: Government (US Federal), Law (US Federal), Information Technology, Education, Health Care

Audience: Journalists, Politicians, Scientists, Manufacturers, Educators

Details: Free

File is: /internet/nren/iita.1992/gorebill.1992.txt

`ftp://nis.nsf.net`

Internet Federal Register (IFR) ★★★★

The full text of the US Federal Register.

Keywords: Federal Register, Government (US Federal), Law (US Federal)

Sponsor: Counterpoint Publishing

Audience: General Public, Journalists, Students, Politicians, Citizens

Contact: fedreg@internet.com

Details: Costs

`gopher://gopher.internet.com`

A B C D E F **G** H I J K L M N O P Q R S T U V W X Y Z

A
B
C
D
E
F
G
H
I
J
K
L
M
N
O
P
Q
R
S
T
U
V
W
X
Y
Z

Leaders of Community Networking: People Who Create Online Communities

A WWW document with links to several important community networking resources. A brief overview of community networking is provided, as are links to statements by several leaders in the movement.

Keywords: Community, Networking, Government (US Federal)

Audience: Activists, Policymakers, Community Leaders, Government, Citizens

Details: Free

`http://nearnet.gnn.com/mag/articles/oram/introduction.html`

Miscellaneous Federal Documents

This directory includes documents such as the Civil Rights Act of 1991, the Computer Fraud and Abuse Act, the High-Performance Computing Senate Report, and more.

Keywords: Government (US Federal), Federal Documents (US)

Audience: Politicians, Journalists, Students (high school up)

Details: Free

`gopher://wiretap.spies.com/11/Gov/US-Docs`

Patent Act of the US

This resource contains full-text documentation regarding the US Patent Act (Title 35, United States Code, Sections 1 - 376).

Keywords: Patents, Laws (US Federal), Government (US Federal)

Audience: Journalists, Politicians, Economists, Lawyers, Scientists

Details: Free

`http://fatty.law.cornell.edu/patent/patent.overview.html`

Political Platforms of the US

Full text of various documents including the Democratic platform of 1992, the Jerry Brown positions of 1992, the Libertarian platform of 1990, and more.

Keywords: Politics (US), Government (US Federal), Democracy, Libertarian Politics

Audience: Politicians, Grass-Roots Organizers, Journalists

Details: Free

`gopher://wiretap.spies.com/11/Gov/Platform`

Privacy Act of 1974

The act that regulates the maintenance of privacy and protection of records on individuals.

Keywords: Privacy, Laws (US Federal), Government (US Federal)

Audience: Journalists, Politicians, Lawyers

Details: Free
Choose from menu as appropriate.

`gopher://wiretap.spies.com/00/Gov/privacy.act`

Northwestern University Library

The library's holdings are large and wide-ranging and contain significant collections in many fields.

Keywords: Africa, Wright (Frank Lloyd), Women's Studies, Art, Literature (American), Contemporary Music, Government (US State), UN Documents, Music

Audience: General Public, Researchers, Librarians, Document Delivery Professionals

Details: Free

Expect: COMMAND:, Send: DIAL VTAM

`telnet://nuacvm.acns.nwu.edu`

Questions and Answers about the GPO Gateway to Government Act

Questions and answers dealing with the bill GPO Gateway to Government Act of 1992. Questions such as, "What will the gateway do?", "Why is this gateway needed?", "What types of information will be available through the gateway?", and more.

Keywords: Laws (US Federal), Government (US Federal), Federal Databases

Audience: General Public, Journalists, Politicians

Details: Free
File is: /pub/nic/NREN/GPO.questions

`ftp://ftp.sura.net`

Government Documents

FedWorld Bulletin Board

A BBS run by the National Technical Information Service, with many databases of government documents, job announcements, and connections to other federal government online services.

Keywords: US Federal Government, Government Documents

Sponsor: US National Technical Information Service

Audience: General Public, Researchers

Profile: This is the place to begin any kind of search for US federal government records and publications. The GateWay option connects you to the Library of Congress, Supreme Court opinions, government job listing, the various Federal Reserve Banks, Congressional Bills and studies, and so on.

To establish an account: Expect: login, Send: new

Notes: Mail to sysop once you have an account.

`telnet://fedworld.gov`

Government Docs (US & World)

A large and eclectic collection of documents, ranging from the Laws of William the Conqueror to the North American Free Trade Agreement (NAFTA). Particular strengths include 20th century American political documents and international treaties and covenants.

Keywords: Government (International), Government Documents, History (World), Politics (International)

Sponsor: The Internet Wiretap

Audience: Researchers, Historians, Political Scientists, Journalists

Contact: gopher@wiretap.spies.com

`gopher://wiretap.spies.com/Gov`

US House of Representatives Gopher

The online service of the U.S. House of Representatives.

Keywords: Congress (US), Federal Law (US), Government Documents

Sponsor: House Administration Committee Internet Working Group

Audience: Government Officials, Journalists, Educators (K-12), General Public

Profile: Provides access to information on members and committees of the House of Representatives, as well as full-text of bills before the House. Includes education resources on the legislative process, Congressional directories, and House schedules. Also has information for visitors (including area maps), as well as access to other federal information systems.

Contact: House Internet Working Group househlp@hr.house.gov

`gopher://gopher.house.gov`

GRANOLA (Vegetarian Discussion List)

GRANOLA (Vegetarian Discussion List)

A ListServ for discussion of vegetarian issues, including everything from recipes to animal rights.

Keywords: Health, Nutrition, Vegetarian, Recipes

Audience: Vegetarians, Nutritionists, Health Professionals

Details: Free

User Info: To subscribe to the list, send an e-mail message to the URL address shown below, consisting of a single line reading:

SUB granola YourFirstName YourLastName

`mailto:listserv@gitvm1.bitnet`

Grants

A Grant Getter's Guide to the Internet

★★★★

A summary of Internet-accessible information regarding federal grants.

Keywords: Grants, Federal Register (US), Federal Databases (US)

Sponsor: University of Idaho, Moscow, Idaho, USA

Audience: Researchers, Scientists, Public Health Professionals, Students

Profile: This site is intended to provide federal grant information on the Internet. The focus is federal grant resources, including those sponsored by the National Institute of Health (NIH), the National Science Foundation (NSF), and the National Telecommunications and Information Administration (NTIA). This server also includes supplemental education-related information. This guide is searchable by keyword and contains pointers to such grant sources as the Federal Register, the National Science Foundation, the National Institutes of Health, and the Catalog of Federal Domestic Assistance. This same site allows direct access to many of the systems mentioned in the guide.

Contact: James Kearney, Marty Zimmerman jkearney@raven.csrv.uidaho.edu, martyz@uidaho.edu

`gopher://gopher.uidaho.edu/Science, Research, & Grant Information/Grant Information`

National Institutes of Health Gopher

Provides access to a broad range of National Institutes of Health (NIH) resources (library catalogues, databases) via the Internet.

Keywords: Health, AIDS, Molecular Biology, Grants

Sponsor: National Institutes of Health

Audience: Health Professionals, Molecular Biologists, Researchers

Profile: This gopher provides access to NIH resources, including institute phone books and calendars, library catalogs, molecular biology databases, the full text of the NIH Guide for Grants and Contracts, files containing AIDS and cancer information, and more.

Contact: gopher@gopher.nih.gov

Details: Free

Expect: Login; Enter: Gopher

`telnet://gopher.nih.gov`

`gopher://gopher.nih.gov`

`gopher://odie.niaid.nih.gov`

NIH Grant Line (Drgline Bulletin Board)

The purpose of the NIH Grant Line is to make program and policy information from the Public Health Service (PHS) agencies rapidly available to the biomedical research community.

Keywords: Biomedical Research, NIH, Grants

Sponsor: The National Institute of Health

Audience: Scientists, Researchers, Students

Profile: Most of the research opportunity information available on this bulletin board is derived from the weekly publication "NIH Guide for Grants and Contracts," and consists of notices, RFAs, RFPs (announcements of availability), numbered program announcements, and statements of PHS policy. The information found on the NIH Grant Line is grouped into three main sections: (1) short news flashes that appear without any prompting shortly after you have logged on, (2) bulletins that are for reading, and (3) files that are intended mainly for downloading. The E-Guide is available for electronic transmission each week. The material consists predominantly of statements about the research interests of the PHS agencies, institutes, and national centers that have funds to support research in the extramural community. Currently under development are two new files: one will be a monthly listing of new NIH Awards, and the other will be an order form to obtain NIH publications from DRG's Office of Grants Inquiries.

Details: Free

To access the NIH Grant Line, telnet to the URL address below and when a message has been received that the connection is open, type: ,GEN1 (the comma is mandatory). At the INITIALS? prompt, type BB5 and at the ACCOUNT? prompt, type CCS2

The NIH Guide to Grants and Contracts can also be accessed through gopher://helix.nih.gov/11/res/nih-guide

`telnet://wylbur.cu.nih.gov`

Research (Funding Support List)

The Research list is for people (primarily at educational institutions) interested in applying for funding support from various sources.

Keywords: Grants, Funding

Audience: Educators (College, Graduate)

Profile: This list assists faculty in locating sources of support from government agencies, corporations, and foundations. It also forwards information regarding the latest news from potential sponsors such as the National Science Foundation and the National Institutes of Health, and provides information on upcoming international seminars on various topics ranging from medicine to artificial intelligence.

Contact: Eleanor Cicinsky v2153a@vm.temple.edu

User Info: To subscribe to the list, send an e-mail message to the address below consisting of a single line reading:

SUB research YourFirstName YourLastName.

To send a message to the entire list, address it to: research@vm.temple.edu

`mailto:listserv@vm.temple.edu`

Graphical User Interfaces

BX-Talk

BX-talk has been created for users of Builder Xcessory (BX) to discuss problems (and solutions) and ideas for using BX, which is a graphical user interface builder for Motif applications, and is sold by ICS. Please note that this list is not associated with ICS (the authors of BX) in any way.

Keywords: Builder Xcessory, Graphical User Interfaces

Audience: Graphics Experts, Computer Operators

Contact: Darci L. Chapman bx-talk-request@qiclab.scn.rain.com

Details: Free

A B C D E F G H I J K L M N O P Q R S T U V W X Y Z

A B C D E F **G** H I J K L M N O P Q R S T U V W X Y Z

User Info:	To subscribe to the list, send an e-mail message requesting a subscription to the URL address below.
	To send a message to the entire list, address it to: bx-talk@qiclab.scn.rain.com
Notes:	This list is unmoderated.

`mailto:bx-talk-request@qiclab.scn.rain.com`

Graphic Arts

Williams College Library

The library's holdings are large and wide-ranging and contain significant collections in many fields.

Keywords:	Americana, Graphic Arts, Printing (History of), Performing Arts, Printing
Audience:	General Public, Researchers, Librarians, Document Delivery Professionals
Contact:	Jim Cubit
Details:	Free
Expect:	Mitek Server..., Send: Enter or Return; Expect: prompt, Send: hollis

`telnet://library.williams.edu`

Graphic Design

(The) DTP Direct Catalog

DTP Direct specializes in Macintosh hardware and software tools for desktop publishers and graphics professionals.

Keywords:	Macintosh, Desktop Publishing, Graphic Design
Sponsor:	InterNex Server Bureau
Audience:	Graphic Designers, Artists, Desktop Publishers
Details:	Free, Moderated, Image, and Sound files available. Multimedia files available.

`http://www.internex.net/DTP/home.html`

INGRAFX

This E-conference is for discussion of all matters relating to information graphics.

Keywords:	Computer Graphics, Graphic Design, Scientific Visualization
Audience:	Graphic Designers, Cartographers, Animators
Contact:	Jeremy Crampton http://info.cern.ch/hypertext/WWW/The Project.html

User Info:	To subscribe to the list, send an e-mail message to the URL address below, consisting of a single line reading:
	SUB ingrafx YourFirstName YourLastName
	To send a message to the entire list, address it to: ingrafx@psuvm.psu.edu

`mailto:listserv@psuvm.psu.edu`

Graphics

Free Art For HTML Page

This web site provides copyrighted graphics for the Mosaic program.

Keywords:	Computer-Aided Design, Graphics
Audience:	Designers, Educators
Contact:	Harlan Wallach wallach@mcs.com
Details:	Free

`http://www.mcs.net/wallach/Fart/buttons.html`

ISIS/Draw

ISIS/Draw provides a chemical drawing package from MDL Information Systems and The American Chemical Society (ACS).

Keywords:	Chemistry, Graphics
Sponsor:	ACS and MDL Information Systems, Inc.
Audience:	Chemists, Chemistry Professors, Chemistry Students
Profile:	ISIS/Draw, the premier chemical drawing package from MDL Information Systems, Inc., is now available to chemistry students and professors at a special academic price through the American Chemical Society (ACS). Used by major pharmaceutical, agrochemical, and chemical companies worldwide, ISIS/Draw has the chemical intelligence to know that a line is a bond, and a letter is an atom. It can be used to: build queries for a structure-searching database; create presentation-quality sketches of chemical structures, reactions, and a wide range of other graphics; cut and paste annotated chemical structure drawings into popular word processing programs to create instructional materials and reports.
Details:	Costs
	Call ACS at 1-800-227-5558. When placing an order, use the following catalog numbers: 2152-9-151 (Windows) or 2156-1-151 (Macintosh).

`dmg96@acs.org`

OTIS (Operative Term Is Stimulate)

An image-based electronic art gallery.

Keywords:	Art, Graphics, Electronic Art, Animation
Audience:	Graphic Artists
Profile:	OTIS is a public-access library containing hundreds of images, animations, and information files.
	Within the sunsite ftp, the directory is: /pub/multimedia/pictures/OTIS. Use the bin command to ensure you're in binary transfer mode.

`ftp://sunsite.unc.edu`

UWP Music Archive (named for the host machine's location: the University of Wisconsin—Parkside)

An extensive repository of files relating to a diverse array of music genres: rock, folk, classical, and so on.

Keywords:	Music, Lyrics, Graphics
Sponsor:	University of Wisconsin—Parkside
Audience:	Musicians, Music Enthusiasts, Musicologists
Profile:	This FTP archive contains a music database, artist discographies, essays about music and particular works, hundreds of image files (mostly .GIF and .JPEG format) of musicians—including album covers and posters, a lyrics archive, and the ever-popular 'Beginner's Introduction to Classical Music.'
Contact:	Dave Datta datta@ftp.uwp.edu
User Info:	Select "Music Archives" from the gopher top-level menu.
Notes:	Also accessible through CMU's "English Server" gopher server. (q.v.)

`gopher://gopher.uwp.edu`

Great Lakes Area

University of Toledo Library

The library's holdings are large and wide-ranging and contain significant collections in many fields.

Keywords:	Business, Great Lakes Area, Humanities, International Relations, Psychology, Science
Audience:	Researchers, Students, General Public
Details:	Free
Expect:	Enter one of the following commands . . . , Send: DIAL MVS; Expect: dialed to mvs ####; Send: UTMOST

`telnet:/ uofto1.utoledo.edu`

Greece

soc.culture.greek

A Usenet newsgroup providing information and discussion about Greek culture.

Keywords: Greece, Sociology

Audience: Sociologists, Greeks

Details: Free

User Info: To subscribe to this Usenet newsgroup, you need access to a newsreader.

`news:soc.culture.greek`

Gregorian Chants

Cantus

This gopher site accesses the Gregorian Chant Database, which is maintained by the Catholic University of America.

Keywords: Gregorian Chants, Music, Liturgy

Sponsor: Catholic University of America (CUA)

Audience: Vocalists, Educators, Students

Profile: The database contains an introduction to the Cantus Gopher at the CUA, and has a searchable index.

`gopher://vmsgopher.cua.edu`

Group Communications

Free for All

An experiment in a networked hypermedia group bulletin board.

Keywords: Internet, Group Communications, Multimedia

Audience: Internet Surfers, Multimedia Enthusiasts

Details: Free, Mm

`http://south.ncsa.uiuc.edu/Free.html`

Hypermedia/Internet

A guide to hypermedia and the Internet.

Keywords: Internet, Group Communications, Hypermedia

Sponsor: Australian National University

Audience: Internet Surfers

Contact: David Geoffrey Green
David.Green@anu.edu.au

Details: Free

`http://life.anu.edu.au`

irc (Internet Relay Chat)

A multiuser, multichannel chatting network. It enables people all over the Internet to "talk" to one another interactively.

Keywords: Internet, Group Communications

Audience: Internet Surfers

Details: Free

User Info: Readme file is: irc/README

`ftp://cs.bu.edu`

Guidelines

NATO

Online version of The NATO Handbook, which recommends changes for the future of the North Atlantic Treaty Organization in light of decreasing defense resources.

Keywords: NATO, Guidelines, Defense

Sponsor: The NATO Office of Information and Press

Audience: Governent Officials, Military Personnel, Historians

Details: Free
Select from menu as appropriate.

`gopher://wiretap.spies.com`

Guitar

alt.guitar

A Usenet newsgroup providing information and discussion about guitar playing.

Keywords: Guitar, Musical Instruments

Audience: Guitarists

User Info: To subscribe to this Usenet newsgroup, you need access to a newsreader.

`news:alt.guitar`

Gun Control Legislation

BA-Firearms

This is an announcement and discussion of firearms legislation and related issues. The ca- list is for California statewide issues; the ba- list is for the San Francisco Bay Area and gets all messages sent to the ca- list. Prospective members should subscribe to one or the other, generally depending on whether or not they are SF Bay Area residents.

Keywords: Firearms, Gun Control Legislation, San Francisco Bay Area

Audience: Politicians, General Public, Gun Users, San Francisco Bay Area Residents

Contact: Jeff Chan
ba-firearms-request@shell.portal.com

Details: Free

User Info: To subscribe to the list, send an e-mail message requesting a subscription to the URL address below.

To send a message to the entire list, address it to: ba-firearms@shell.portal.com

`mailto:ba-firearms-request@shell.portal.com`

ca-Firearms

This is an announcement and discussion of firearms legislation and related issues. The ca- list is for California statewide issues; the ba- list is for the San Francisco Bay Area and gets all messages sent to the ca- list. Prospective members should subscribe to one or the other, generally depending on whether or not they are SF Bay Area residents.

Keywords: Firearms, Gun Control Legislation, California

Audience: Politicians, General Public, Gun Users, California Residents

Contact: Jeff Chan
ca-firearms-request@shell.portal.com

Details: Free

User Info: To subscribe to the list, send an e-mail message requesting a subscription to the URL address below.

To send a message to the entire list, address it to: ca-firearms@shell.portal.com

`mailto:ca-firearms-request@shell.portal.com`

GUTENBERG Listserver

GUTENBERG Listserver

A mailing list providing information about Project Gutenberg.

Keywords: Project Gutenberg, Literature (General), Reference

Sponsor: National Clearinghouse for Machine Readable Texts

Audience: General Public, Researchers, Educators, Students

Contact: Michael S. Hart
gutnberg@vmd.cso.uiuc.edu

Details: Free

User Info: To subscribe to the list, send an e-mail message to the URL address shown below, consisting of a single line reading:

SUB GUTNBERG YourFirstName YourLastName

`mailto:listserv@vmd.cso.uiuc.edu`

A B C D E F G H I J K L M N O P Q R S T U V W X Y Z

A
B
C
D
E
F
G
H
I
J
K
L
M
N
O
P
Q
R
S
T
U
V
W
X
Y
Z

H

Hacking

CUD (Computer Underground Digest) ★

USA Today of cyberspace and the computer underground. Contains information relating to the computer underground.

Keywords: Hacking, Computer News, Cyberculture

Audience: Hackers, Reality Hackers, Computer Underground Enthusiasts

Contact: Gordon Meyer, Jim Thomas tk0jut2@niu.bitnet or pumpcon@mindvox.phantom.com.

Details: Free

`ftp://etext.archive.umich.edu/pub/Zines/CUD`

General Hacking Info ★

Files on the topic of hacking.

Keywords: Hacking, Computers

Audience: Hackers, Computer Users

Details: Free

Notes: Expect: login,Send: anonymous; Expect: Password,Send: Your E-mail Address

`ftp://ftp.eff.org`

GlobeTrotter ★

File concerning hacking from an international perspective.

Keywords: Hacking, Computers

Audience: Hackers, Computer Users

Details: Free

Notes: Expect: login,Send: anonymous; Expect: Password,Send: Your E-mail Address

`ftp://ftp.eff.org`

Hacker's Network ★

File of hacking, published in Britain.

Keywords: Hacking, Computers

Audience: Hackers, Computer Users

Details: Free

Notes: Expect: login,Send: anonymous; Expect: Password,Send: Your E-mail Address

`ftp://ftp.eff.org`

High Weirdness by E-Mail ★★★

Guide to some interesting sources of information online.

Keywords: Technology, Hacking, Computer Underground

Audience: Mystics, Hackers, Computer Users

Profile: This file focuses mainly on bizarre philosophies, such as Discordia and SubGenius. Contents include: offbeat religions and 'spirituality' paganism and magic, occultism, UFOs, and paranormal phenomena.

Details: Free

`ftp://etext.archive.umich.edu/pub/Zines/Weirdness`

Legion of Doom/Hackers Technical Journals ★

Technical journals of the infamous hacking ring Legion of Doom.

Keywords: Hacking, Computers

Audience: Hackers, Computer Users

Details: Free

Notes: Expect: login,Send: anonymous; Expect: Password,Send: Your E-mail Address

`ftp://ftp.eff.org`

Haiti

Summit of the Americas Internet Gopher ★

A gopher containing supporting materials for the Summit of the Americas, a meeting of the Western Hemisphere's democratically elected heads of state, to be held in Miami in December of 1994.

Keywords: American Studies, International Relations, Haiti, Latin America

Sponsor: The Florida University Latin American and Caribbean Center

Audience: Government Officials, Journalists, NGOs, General Public

Contact: Rene Ramos summit@SERVAX.FIU.EDU

`gopher://summit.fiu.edu`

Hamill (Peter)

Ph7

A mailing list for discussions about Peter Hamill and related rock groups.

Keywords: Rock Music, Hamill (Peter)

Audience: Musicians, Rock Music Enthusiasts

Contact: ph7-request@bnf.com

User Info: To Subscribe to the list, send an e-mail message requesting a subscription to the URL address below.

To send a message to the entire list, address it to: ph7@bnf.com

`mailto:ph7-request@bnf.com`

Handel (G.F.)

Indiana University Libraries

The library's holdings are large and wide-ranging and contain significant collections in many fields.

Keywords: Literature (English), Literature (American), 1640-Present, British Plays (19th-C.), Western Americana, Railway History, Aristotle (Texts of), Lafayette (Marquis de), Handel (G.F.), Austrian History, Antiquarian Books, Rare Books, French Opera (19th-C.), Drama (British)

Audience: General Public, Researchers, Librarians, Document Delivery Professionals

Details: Free

Notes: Expect: User ID prompt, Send: GUEST

`telnet://iuis.ucs.indiana.edu`

Handicap

Handicap

An anonymous data site containing disability-related files or programs.

Keywords: Health, Disability

Audience: Disabled People

Profile: There are about 40 directories with 500 files/programs covering all types of disabilities. The "Handicap BBS List" originates here.

Details: Free

Notes: Login: anonymous

`ftp://handicap.shel.isc-br.com`

Handicapping

derby

To discuss various aspects and strategies of horseracing, primarily dealing with, but not limited to, handicapping.

Keywords: Horseracing, Handicapping

Audience: Horseracing Enthusiasts

Contact: John Wilkes
derby-request@ekrl.com

User Info: To Subscribe to the list, send an e-mail message requesting a subscription to the URL address below. To send a message to the entire list, address it to: derby-request@ekrl.com

`mailto:derby-request@ekrl.com`

Hardware

data-exp

The mail list server provides an open forum for users to discuss the Visualization Data Explorer Package. It contains three files at the moment: a. FAQ, b. summary, and c. forum.

Keywords: Computing, Software, Hardware, Visualization Data Explorer Package

Audience: Computer Users

User Info: To Subscribe to the list, send an e-mail message requesting a subscription to the URL address below.

To send a message to the entire list, address it to: stein@watson.ibm.com

`mailto:stein@watson.ibm.com`

Futurebus+ Users

This discussion group focuses on the design, implementation, integration, and operation of hardware and software related to Futurebus+.

Keywords: Computer Users, Hardware, Software

Audience: Computer Users, Software Engineers, Hardware Engineers

Contact: majordomo@theus.rain.com

Details: Free

User Info: To Subscribe to the list, send an e-mail message to the URL address below consisting of a single line reading:

SUB fbus_users YourFirstName YourLastName

To send a message to the entire list, address it to: fbus_users+@theus.rain.com

`mailto:majordomo@theus.rain.com`

gateway2000

This list is a source of information about Gateway2000 products.

Keywords: Computer Products, Software, Hardware

Audience: Computer Users, Hardware Engineers, Software Engineers

Details: Free

User Info: To Subscribe to the list, send an e-mail message requesting a subscription to the URL address below.

To send a message to the entire list, address it to: gateway2000@sei.cmu.edu

`gateway2000-request@sei.cmu.edu`

Pc532

A mailing list for people interested in the pc532 project, a National Semiconductor NS32532-based system, offered at a low cost.

Keywords: Computers, Hardware, Software

Audience: Computer Users, Software Developers

Contact: Dave Rand
pc532-request@bungi.com

Details: Free

User Info: To Subscribe to the list, send an e-mail message requesting a subscription to the URL address below.

To send a message to the entire list, address it to: pc532@bungi.com

`mailto:pc532-request@bungi.com`

Pdp8-lovers

A mailing list for owners of vintage DEC (Digital Equipment Corp.) computers, especially the PDP-8 series. Discussion topics include hardware, software, and programming techniques.

Keywords: Computers, Hardware, Software

Audience: Computer Users, Product Analysts

Contact: Robert E. Seastrom
pdp8-lovers-request@mc.lcs.mit.edu

Details: Free

User Info: To Subscribe to the list, send an e-mail message requesting a subscription to the URL address below.

To send a message to the entire list, address it to: pdp8-lovers@mc.lcs.mit.edu

`mailto:pdp8-lovers@mc.lcs.mit.edu`

Qnx2

Discussion of all aspects of the QNX real-time operating systems. Topics include compatible hardware, available third-party software, software reviews, available PD/free software, QNX platform-specific programming discussions, and QNX and FLEET networking.

Keywords: Computing, Hardware, Software

Audience: Computer Users, Hardware/Software Designers, Product Analysts

Contact: Martin Zimmerman
camz@dlogtech.cuc.ab.ca

Details: Free

User Info: To Subscribe to the list, send an e-mail message requesting a subscription to the URL address below.

To send a message to the entire list, address it to: qnx2@dlogtech.cuc.ab.ca

`mailto:qnx2@dlogtech.cuc.ab.ca`

Qnx4

A mailing list for discussion of all aspects of the QNX real-time operating systems. Topics include compatible hardware, available third-party software, software reviews, available PD/free software, QNX and FLEET networking, process control, and so on.

Keywords: Computing, Hardware, Software, Networking

Audience: Computer Users, Hardware/Software Designers, Product Analysts

Contact: Martin Zimmerman
camz@dlogtech.cuc.ab.ca

Details: Free

User Info: To Subscribe to the list, send an e-mail message requesting a subscription to the URL address below.

To send a message to the entire list, address it to: qnx4@dlogtech.cuc.ab.ca

`mailto:qnx4@dlogtech.cuc.ab.ca`

Hardy (Thomas)

Colby College Library

The library's holdings are large and wide-ranging and contain significant collections in many fields.

Keywords: Contemporary Letters, Hardy (Thomas),James (Henry), Mann (Thomas, Collections of), Housman (A.E., Letters of), Maine Authors, Irish History (Modern)

Audience: General Public, Researchers, Librarians, Document Delivery Professionals

Details: Free

Notes: Expect: login, Send: library

`telnet://library.colby.edu`

Princeton University Online Manuscripts Catalog Library

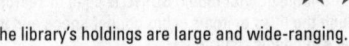

The library's holdings are large and wide-ranging. They contain significant collections in many fields.

Keywords: Books (Antiquarian), Dickens (Charles), Disraeli (Benjamin), Eliot (George), Hardy (Thomas), Kingsley (Charles), Trollope (Anthony)

Audience: General Public, Researchers, Librarians, Document Delivery Professionals

Details: Free

Notes: Expect: VM370 logo, Send: <cr>; Expect: Welcome screen, Send: folio <cr>; Expect: Welcome screen for FOLIO, Send: <cr>; Expect: List of choices, Send: 3 <cr>; To exit: type: logoff

`telnet://pucc.princeton.edu`

Harper (Roy)

Stormcock

For general discussion and news concerning the music of Roy Harper, a folk-rock musician with a conscience. Recommendations and news concerning similar artists are encouraged.

Keywords: Rock Music, Music, Harper (Roy)

Audience: Music Fans

Contact: Paul Davison
stormcock-request@qmw.ac.uk

Details: Free

User Info: To Subscribe to the list, send an e-mail message to the address shown below consisting of a single line reading:

SUB stormcock YourFirstName YourLastName

To send a message to the entire list, address it to: stormcock@qmw.ac.uk

`mailto: listserv@qmw.ac.uk`

Harry (Deborah)

Deborah Harry and Blondie Information Service

An information service on everything and anything regarding Deborah Harry and Blondie, including tour information, recordings/films release information, and so on.

Keywords: Rock Music, Harry (Deborah), Musical Groups

Audience: Rock Music Enthusiasts, Deborah Harry Enthusiasts

Contact: gunter@yarrow.wt.uwa.oz.au

Details: Free

User Info: To Subscribe to the list, send an e-mail message requesting a subscription to the URL address below.

To send a message to the entire list, address it to: gunter@yarrow.wt. uwa.oz.au

`mailto:gunter@yarrow.wt.uwa.oz.au`

Harvard Biosciences Online Journals

Harvard Biosciences Online Journals

A resource containing selected online journals and periodicals in biology and medicine. Includes peer-reviewed e-journals, journal indexes, and databases.

Keywords: Biology, Bioscience, Molecular Biology

Sponsor: Harvard Biolabs, Harvard University, Cambridge, Massachusetts, USA

Audience: Biologists, Molecular Biologists, Researchers

Contact: Keith Robinson, Steve Brenner
krobinson@nucleus.harvard.edu
s.e.brenner@bioc.cam.ac.uk

`http://golgi.harvard.edu/ journals.html`

Harvard Medical Gopher

Harvard Medical Gopher

This gopher site accesses information from Harvard Medical School. Provides bibliographic information from Harvard Medical Library, basic science and clinical resources, and public health and government statistics.

Keywords: Medicine, Libraries, Health Care

Sponsor: Harvard Medical School, Cambridge, Massachusetts, USA

Audience: Physicians, Health Care Professionals, Educators, Students

Contact: gopher@warren.med.harvard.edu

Details: Free

`gopher://gopher.med.harvard.edu`

Harvard University Library

Harvard University Library

The library's holdings are large and wide-ranging and contain significant collections in many fields.

Keywords: Afrikaans, Alchemy, Arabic Culture (History of), Celtic Philology, Congo Languages, Folklore, Hebraica, Mormonism, Numismatics, Quakerism, Sanskrit, Witchcraft, Arabic Philology

Audience: General Public, Researchers, Librarians, Document Delivery Professionals

Details: Free

Notes: Expect: Mitek Server..., Send: Enter or Return; Expect: prompt, Send: hollis

`telnet://hollis.harvard.edu`

Hawaii

Hawaii FYI

A state information system providing a wide range of free legal information.

Keywords: Hawaii, Law (US)

Audience: Hawaiians, Lawyers

Details: Free

`telnet://fyi.uhcc.hawaii.edu`

University of Hawaii Library

The library's holdings are large and wide-ranging and contain significant collections in many fields.

Keywords: Asia, European Documents, Book Arts, Hawaii

A
B
C
D
E
F
G
H
I
J
K
L
M
N
O
P
Q
R
S
T
U
V
W
X
Y
Z

A B C D E F G H I J K L M N O P Q R S T U V W X Y Z

Audience: General Public, Researchers, Librarians, Document Delivery Professionals

Details: Free

Notes: Expect: enter class, Send: LIB

`telnet://starmaster.uhcc.hawaii.edu`

Health

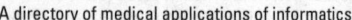

(The) Center for Biomedical Informatics of the State University of Campinas, Brazil

★★

A directory of medical applications of informatics.

Keywords: Health, Medicine, Informatics

Sponsor: State University of Campinas, Brazil

Audience: Medical Professionals, Medical Educators, Medical Researchers

Profile: Designed to foster educational and practical uses of computers in medicine and the health sciences by providing free international access to resources.

Contact: Renato M.E. Sabbatini
sabbatini@ccvax.unicamp.br

Details: Free

`ftp://ccsun.unicamp.br`

AIDS Treatment News

★★★

A newsletter on AIDS treatment.

Keywords: AIDS, Health, Medicine

Sponsor: IGC (Institute for Global Communications)

Audience: AIDS Researchers, Health Workers, AIDS Sufferers

Profile: This newsletter contains interviews, reports on new and existing treatment modalities, announcements of clinical drug testing trial, and more.

Contact: atn@igc.apc.org

Details: Free

`gopher://odie.niaid.nih.gov/11/aids`

AIDS/HIV Information

★★

A clearinghouse for AIDS/HIV-related information. Contains Internet connections to WWW and gopher servers, and archives of AIDS server FAQs, including an archive of AIDS treatment news.

Keywords: AIDS, Medicine, Health

Sponsor: Queer Resources Directory, USA

Audience: AIDS Sufferers, Gays, Activists

Contact: QRD Staff
QRDstaff@vector.casti.com

Details: AIDS Treatment News

`http://vector.casti.com/QRD/.html/AIDS.html`

Alternative Medicine, the Definitive Guide

A one-stop reference covering common health problems and leading alternative therapies.

Keywords: Alternative Medicine, Medicine, Health, Health Care

Sponsor: Future Medicine Publishing, Inc.

Audience: General Public, Health Care Professionals

Profile: Spanning a global effort of 4 years, and including input from nearly 400 health-care professionals, this one-stop reference offers 1100 pages of in-depth explanations to 43 of the leading alternative therapies. In addition to covering over 200 of the most common health problems, the site offers a wide range of choices for maintaining and regaining your health, highlighted with graphic illustrations. This is truly the "Voice of Alternative Medicine."

Details: Costs

`mailto:FutureMd@CRL.com`

AMALGAME

A resource containing Macintosh demos and XFCN PrintZ files on the subject of health.

Keywords: Health

Sponsor: University of Montreal

Audience: Medical Researchers

Contact: benoit@medent.umontreal.ca

Details: Free

`ftp://amalgame.Medent.Umontreal.Ca`

Archive of Biology Software and Data

The main area of concentration of this archive is molecular biology. It contains software for the Macintosh, MS-DOS, VAX-VMS, and UNIX platforms.

Keywords: Health, Biology, Molecular Biology

Sponsor: Indiana University

Audience: Biologists, Students

Contact: archive@bio.indiana.edu

Details: Free

Notes: It is recommended that the file Archive.doc be transferred and read first. This file gives considerable information about and instructions for using the archive.

`ftp://ftp.bio.indiana.edu`

Biomedical Computer Laboratory (BCL)

A resource for biomedical computing.

Keywords: Health, Biomedical Computing, Biology, Medicine

Sponsor: Washington University School of Medicine

Audience: Medical Researchers, Biologists

Profile: A significant portion of the activities at BCL are supported by the National Center for Research Resources' Biomedical Research Technology Program (BRTP), which promotes the application of advances in computer science and technology, engineering, mathematics, and the physical sciences to research problems in biology and medicine by supporting the development of advanced research technologies.

Contact: Kenneth W. Clark
info@wubcl.wustl.edu

Details: Free

Notes: Expect: login; Send: anonymous

Investigators wishing to explore the possibility of interactions with BCL at Washington University should send e-mail (preferred).

`ftp://wubcl.wustl.edu`

BOING (Bio-Oriented INternet Gophers)

A searchable gopher index, BOING is used to search through the titles of items in bio-gopher space and to access the items returned.

Keywords: Biology, Health, Medicine

Audience: Health Professionals, Biomedical Researchers, Students (college, graduate)

Details: Free

`gopher://gopher.gdb.org`

Canadian University Consortium on Health in International Development (CANCHID)

★

CANCHID is a multi-campus consortium that includes medical schools and other educational institutions devoted to research and projects dealing with health care issues in developing countries.

Keywords: Health, International Development

Audience: Public Health, Medicine, International Aid Agencies

Contact: Sam Lanfranco
lanfran@vm1.yorku.ca

Details: Free

User Info: To Subscribe to the list, send an e-mail message to the URL address below, consisting of a single line reading:

SUB canchid YourFirstName YourLastName

To send a message to the entire list, address it to: canchid@vm1.yorku.ca

`mailto:listserv@vm1.yorku.ca`

Cornucopia of Disability Information (CODI)

 ★★★

A large collection of disability-related information available via gopher.

Keywords: Disabilities, Health

Sponsor: State University of New York (SUNY) at Buffalo

Audience: Disabled People, Activists, Rehabilitation Counselors, Health Care Professionals

Profile: This site provides a wide variety of information resources concerning people with disabilities, ranging from legal information to a directory of computer resources aimed at the disabled consumer. Includes state, local, and national information and government documents such as the Americans with Disabilities Act. Also has links to many other related resources on the Internet, such as the National Rehabilitation Information Center.

Contact: Jay Leavitt leavitt@ubvmsb.cc.buffalo.edu

`gopher://val-dor.cc.buffalo.edu`

Deaf Gopher

★★

Gopher menu of deaf resources in the state of Michigan.

Keywords: Disabilities, Deafness, Health

Sponsor: Michigan State University

Audience: Deaf and Disabled People, Health Care Professionals, Activists, Policy Makers, Rehabilitation Counselors, Therapists

Profile: A small but useful menu of deaf resources that includes a collection of files in essay and/or report form about a variety of historical and cultural aspects of deafness.

Contact: Gary LaPointe deafgopher@ah3.cal.msu.edu

Details: Free

`gopher://cl.msu.edu/11/msu/dept/deaf`

Disability Information

 ★★★

A collection of information about and links to sources of disability-related information from around the world. Includes archives of many related mailing lists and electronic newsletters, as well as legal and technical help for the disabled, and information about the Parkinson's Disease Information Exchange Network.

Keywords: Disabilities, Health, Diseases

Sponsor: Computing & Information Services at Texas A&M University, Galveston, Texas, USA

Audience: Disabled People, Rehabilitation Counselors, Health Care Professionals, Activists

Contact: Computing & Information Services at Texas A&M University gopher@tamu.edu

`gopher://gopher.tamu.edu/.dir/disability.dir`

Disability Reading Room

 ★★★

Gopher menu of all kinds of reading material on disabilities.

Keywords: Disabilities, Health

Sponsor: University of Maryland

Audience: Deaf and Disabled People, Health Care Professionals, Activists, Policy Analysts, Rehabilitation Counselors, Therapists

Profile: A fascinating collection of reading material on disabilities and related issues, including first-person stories of dealing with chronic pain, detailed descriptions of laws involving the disabled, relevant press releases, and a large selection of journals on disabilities and related matters.

Contact: UMD Computer Science Center consult@umail.umd.edu

Details: Free

`gopher://info.umd.edu`

GAO

 ★★★

Files intended to provide Congress and Administration with an overview of health problems facing the nation.

Keywords: Health, Congress (US)

Audience: US Congress, Journalists, General Public

Profile: These files concern health-care reform and human services and date from December 1992. They are provided by the government to familiarize the reader with the health issues confronting the administration.

Details: Free

Notes: Login: anonymous ABSTRACT.FIL is a file with abstracts for each of the 28 reports.

`ftp://cu.nig.gov`

GRANOLA (Vegetarian Discussion List)

★

A ListServ for discussion of vegetarian issues, including everything from recipes to animal rights.

Keywords: Health, Nutrition, Vegetarian, Recipes

Audience: Vegetarians, Nutritionists, Health Professionals

Details: Free

User Info: To Subscribe to the list, send an e-mail message to the URL address shown below consisting of a single line reading:

SUB granola YourFirstName YourLastName

`mailto:listserv@gitvm1.bitnet`

Handicap

 ★

An anonymous data site containing disability-related files or programs.

Keywords: Health, Disability

Audience: Disabled People

Profile: There are about 40 directories with 500 files/programs covering all types of disabilities. The "Handicap BBS List" originates here.

Details: Free

Notes: Login: anonymous

`ftp://handicap.shel.isc-br.com`

Health News Daily

 ★★★

The database contains all the daily news and full-text articles from Health News Daily, a publication from F-D-C Reports, Inc.

Keywords: Health, Pharmacology, Medical Research, News

Sponsor: F-D-C Reports, Inc., Chevy Chase, MD, US

Audience: Health Professionals, Market Researchers, Pharmacists

Profile: The database provides specialized, in-depth business, scientific, regulatory, and legal news. Timely coverage of pharmacy and pharmaceuticals is given, as well as coverage of medical devices and diagnostics, medical research, cosmetics, health policy, provider payment policies, and cost containment in national health care.

Coverage: 1990 to the present; updated daily.

Contact: Dialog in the US at (800) 334-2564, Dialog internationally at country-specific locations.

Details: Costs

User Info: To Subscribe, contact Dialog directly.

`telnet://dialog.com`

Health Periodicals Database

This source covers a broad range of health subjects and issues.

Keywords: Health, Biotechnology, Medicine, Nutrition

Sponsor: Information Access Company, Foster City, CA, US

Audience: Health Professionals, Dieticians, Librarians

A
B
C
D
E
F
G
H
I
J
K
L
M
N
O
P
Q
R
S
T
U
V
W
X
Y
Z

Profile: The database provides indexing and full text of journals covering a broad range of health subjects and issues including: prenatal care, dieting, drug abuse, AIDS, biotechnology, cardiovascular disease, environment, public health, safety, paramedical professions, sports medicine, substance abuse, toxicology, and much more.

Contact: Dialog in the US at (800) 334-2564, Dialog internationally at country-specific locations.

User Info: To Subscribe, contact Dialog directly.

Notes: Coverage: 1988 to the present; updated weekly.

`telnet://dialog.com`

Health Planning and Administration

The database contains references to nonclinical literature on many aspects of health care.

Keywords: Health, Health Care

Sponsor: US National Library of Medicine, Bethesda, MD, US

Audience: Healthcare professionals

Profile: Coverage includes: health care planning and facilities, health insurance, and the aspects of financial management, personnel administration, manpower planning, and licensure and accreditation that apply to the delivery of health care.

Contact: Dialog in the US at (800) 334-2564, Dialog internationally at country-specific locations.

User Info: To Subscribe, contact Dialog directly.

Notes: Coverage: 1975 to the present; updated monthly.

`telnet://dialog.com`

HICNet Newsletter (MEDNEWS - The Health InfoCom Newsletter)

Usually published once a week, this is a large newsletter that is broken up into multiple sections to facilitate network movement.

Keywords: Health, Medical News

Audience: Health Professionals

Contact: David Dodell
ddodell@stjhmc.fidonet.org

Details: Free

User Info: To Subscribe, send an e-mail message to the address below consisting of a single line reading:

SUB mednews YourFirstName YourLastName

To send a message to the entire list, address it to: mednews@asuacad.bitnet

`mailto:listserv@asuacad.bitnet`

International Food and Nutrition (INFAN) Database

A database covering all aspects of nutrition, health and food, as for example, weight control, food safety, eating patterns, and more.

Keywords: Nutrition, Health, Diet

Sponsor: Pennsylvania State University Nutrition Center

Audience: Nutritionists, Health Care Professionals, Consumers

Details: Free

To access the database, select PENpages (1), then General Information (3), and finally INFAN Database (4).

`telnet://penpages@psupen.psu.edu`

National Family Database— MAPP

This database contains family sociological and health data, including research briefs, bibliographies, census data, program ideas, reference materials, media materials, and publications.

Keywords: Sociology, Family, Health

Sponsor: Department of Agriculture Economics and Rural Sociology, Pennsylvania State University

Audience: Sociologists, Public Health Policymakers, Health Care Providers

To access the database select PENpages (1), then General Information (3) and finally Information on MAPP - National Family Database (5)

`telnet://penpages@psupen.psu.edu`

National Institutes of Health Gopher

Provides access to a broad range of National Institutes of Health (NIH) resources (library catalogues, databases) via the Internet.

Keywords: Health, AIDS, Molecular Biology, Grants

Sponsor: National Institutes of Health

Audience: Health Professionals, Molecular Biologists, Researchers

Profile: This gopher provides access to NIH resources, including institute phone books and calendars, library catalogs, molecular biology databases, the full text of the NIH Guide for Grants and Contracts, files containing AIDS and cancer information and more.

Contact: gopher@gopher.nih.gov

Details: Free

Notes: Expect: Login; Enter: Gopher

`telnet://gopher.nih.gov`

`gopher://gopher.nih.gov`

`gopher://odie.niaid.nih.gov`

National Library of Medicine Gopher World Health Organization (WHO)

This gopher provides information about the National Library of Medicine, the world's largest single-topic library.

Keywords: Medicine, Health, World Health

Sponsor: National Library of Medicine, Massachusetts

World Health Organization, Geneva, Switzerland

Audience: Health-care Professionals, Medical Professionals, Researchers

Profile: The National Library of Medicine (NLM) cares for over 4.5 million holdings (including books, journals, reports, manuscripts, and audio-visual items). The NLM offers extensive online information services dealing with clinical care, toxicology, environmental health, and basic biomedical research. It has several active research and development components, including an extramural grants program, houses an extensive history of medicine collection, and provides several programs designed to improve the nation's medical library system.

Contact: R. P. C. Rodgers
rodgers@nlm.nih.gov
akazawa@who.ch

Details: Free

`gopher://el-gopher.med.utah.edu`

`gopher://gopher.who.ch`

National Oceanic & Atmospheric Administration (NOAA) Office of Environmental Safety and Health, Department of Energy

The NOAA catalog provides keyword access to sources of environmental information in the US. Gopher for resources pertaining to health and environmental safety.

Keywords: Environment, Oceans, Atmospheric Science, Health, Environmental Safety

Sponsor: National Oceanic & Atmospheric Administration (NOAA)

Department of Energy (USA)

Audience: Environmental Scientists, Researchers, Environmentalists, Epidemiologists, Public Health Officials

Details: Free

`gopher://scilibx.ucsc.edu`

`gopher://gopher.ns.doc.gov`

Office of Environmental Safety and Health, Department of Energy

★★★★

Gopher for resources pertaining to health and environmental safety.

Keywords: Health, Environmental Safety

Sponsor: Department of Energy (US)

Audience: Epidemiologists, Public Health Policymakers, General Public

Details: Free

`gopher://gopher.ns.doc.gov`

Prion (Prion Research Digest)

★

Prion Infection Digest discusses current research on prion (slow virus) infection. The Prion Digest was formed as a reference point for the discussion and sharing of current research into prion infection.

Keywords: Prion, Health

Audience: Medical Researchers, Health-care Professionals

Contact: Chris Swanson
prion-request@stolaf.edu

Details: Free

User Info: To Subscribe to the list, send an e-mail message requesting a subscription to the URL address below.

To send a message to the entire list, address it to: prion@stolaf.edu

`mailto:prion-request@stolaf.edu`

Safety (Environmental Health and Safety Discussion List)

★

E-conference for people interested in the various environmental health and safety issues on college and university campuses.

Keywords: Environmental Health, Safety, Health

Audience: Students (College/University), Educators (college/University)

Contact: Ralph Stuart, Dayna Flath
rstuart@moose.uvm.edu
dmf@uvmvm.uvm.edu

Details: Free

User Info: To Subscribe to the list, send an e-mail message to the URL address below, consisting of a single line reading:

SUB safety YourFirstName YourLastName

To send a message to the entire list, address it to: safety@uvmvm.uvm.edu

`mailto:listserv@uvmvm.uvm.edu`

table.abortion

★

A Usenet newsgroup providing information and discussion about all sides of the abortion issue.

Keywords: Abortion, Women's Issues, Health

Audience: Women, Activists, Health Care Professionals

Details: Free

User Info: To Subscribe to this Usenet newsgroup, you need access to a newsreader.

`news:table.abortion`

The Wellness List

This list is founded for the purpose of discussing issues concerning Health/Nutrition/Wellness/Life Expectancy/Physical Fitness, and the books, experiences, and solutions recommended by the participants.

Keywords: Health, Nutrition, Fitness

Audience: Doctors, Nutritionists, General Public

Profile: This resource provides announcements of and reviews of books that include solutions, nutrition-related position papers, requests for information, recommendations of participants, healthy recipes, nutrition and fitness related product announcements, and general discussion of related issues. Health professionals, authors, and nutritionists are encouraged to subscribe and share their knowledge with the participants.

Contact: George Rust, Wellnessmart
george@wellnessmart.com,
info@wellnessmart.com

User Info: To Subscribe send an e-mail message to the URL address below consisting of a single line reading: subscribe wellnesslist

`mailto:majordomo@wellnessmart.com`

University of Pennsylvania School of Medicine Library

★★

The library's holdings are large and wide-ranging and contain significant collections in many fields.

Keywords: Health Care, Nursing, History, Health

Audience: Researchers, Students, General Public

Details: Free

Notes: Expect: Login; Send: Public

`telnet://penninfo.upenn.edu`

Women.health

★

This conference features articles, documents, news, announcements, policy statements, and other information about women's health around the world. Topics include breast cancer, ovarian cancer, alcohol, abortion, pregnancy, sterilization of women, pesticides, Quinacrine, HIV, and disability.

Keywords: Women, Abortion, AIDS, Disability, Feminism, Health

Audience: Activists, Family Planners, Health Professionals, Non-Governmental Organizations, Women

Details: Costs

User Info: Establish an account on the nearest APC node. Login, type c for conferences, then type go women.health. For information on the nearest APC node, contact: APC International Secretariat IBASE
E-mail: apcadmin@apc.org

`telnet://igc.apc.org`

World Health Organization (WHO)

★★★

This gopher provides access to the databases of the WHO.

Keywords: World Health Organization, Health, Medicine, Non-governmental organizations

Sponsor: World Health Organization, Geneva, Switzerland

Audience: Medical Professionals, Researchers

Contact: akazawa@who.ch

Details: Free

`gopher://gopher.who.ch`

Health Care

Accri-l

★★

A mailing list providing information on anesthesia and critical care resources available via the Internet.

Keywords: Health Care, Medical Treatment, Medicine

Audience: Health Care Professionals, Health Care Providers

Contact: A.J. Wright
meds002@uabdpo.dpo.uab.edu

User Info: To Subscribe, send an e-mail message to the URL address below consisting of a single line reading:

SUB accri-l YourFirstName YourLastName

To send a message to the entire list, address it to: accri-l@uabdpo.dpo.uab.edu

`mailto:listserv@uabdpo.dpo.uab.edu`

Act-up

★★

A mailing list for discussion of the work being done by various Act-Up chapters worldwide.

Keywords: AIDS, Health Care, Activism

Audience: AIDS Activists, Health Science Researchers

A
B
C
D
E
F
G
H
I
J
K
L
M
N
O
P
Q
R
S
T
U
V
W
X
Y
Z

A B C D E F G H I J K L M N O P Q R S T U V W X Y Z

Contact: Lenard Diggins
act-up-request@world.std.com

User Info: To Subscribe to theist list, send an e-mail message to the URL address below.

To send a message to the entire list, address it to: act-up-request@world.std.com

`mailto:act-up-request@world.std.com`

Alternative Medicine, the Definitive Guide

A one stop reference covering common health problems and leading alternative therapies.

Keywords: Alternative Medicine, Medicine, Health, Health Care

Sponsor: Future Medicine Publishing, Inc.

Audience: General Public, Health Care Professionals

Profile: Spanning a global effort of 4 years and input from nearly 400 health-care professionals, this one-stop reference offers 1100 pages of in-depth explanations to 43 of the leading alternative therapies. In addition to covering over 200 of the most common health problems, a wide range of choices to maintaining and regaining your health are highlighted with graphic illustrations. This is truly the "Voice of Alternative Medicine."

Details: Costs

`URL:FutureMd@CRL.com`

Dental Information Area

A collection of dental information, including a selection of related educational software and dental informatics materials.

Keywords: Dentistry, Health Care, Informatics

Sponsor: Columbia School of Oral and Dental Surgery

Audience: Dentists, Medical Students, Health Care Professionals

Contact: Dr. John Zimmerman
jlz4@columbia.edu

`gopher://cuhsla.cpmc.columbia.edu/health.sci/dental.toc`

Harvard Medical Gopher

This gopher site accesses information from Harvard Medical School. Provides bibliographic information from Harvard Medical Library, basic science and clinical resources, and public health and government statistics.

Keywords: Medicine, Libraries, Health Care

Sponsor: Harvard Medical School, Cambridge, Massachusetts, USA

Audience: Physicians, Health Care Professionals, Educators, Students

Contact: gopher@warren.med.harvard.edu

Details: Free

`gopher://gopher.med.harvard.edu`

Health and Clinical Information & Bioethics Online Service

A collection of gopher links to servers offering a wide variety of health information.

Keywords: Medicine, Medical Treatment, Health Care

Sponsor: Medical College of Wisconsin (MCW) InfoScope, Wisconsin, USA

Audience: Health Care Professionals, Health Care Providers

Profile: Links include the National Institutes of Health, MedNews Digest, Family Medicine list archives, and full-text of national health plans. Also features the Bioethics Online Service, which provides updates, journal abstracts, alerts, and a forum for discussing medical ethics. Site specific information on MCW physicians and surgeons is also available.

Contact: Dieta Murra
mcw-info@its.mcw.edu

`gopher://post.its.mcw.edu`

Health Planning and Administration

The database contains references to nonclinical literature on many aspects of health care.

Keywords: Health, Health Care

Sponsor: US National Library of Medicine, Bethesda, MD, US

Audience: Healthcare professionals

Profile: Coverage includes: health care planning and facilities, health insurance, and the aspects of financial management, personnel administration, manpower planning, and licensure and accreditation that apply to the delivery of health care.

Contact: Dialog in the US at (800) 334-2564, Dialog internationally at country-specific locations.

User Info: To Subscribe, contact Dialog directly.

Notes: Coverage: 1975 to the present; updated monthly.

`telnet://dialog.com`

Information Infrastructure and Technology Act of 1992

The Information Infrastructure and Technology Act of 1992 builds on the High-Performance Computing Act. The newer bill will ensure that the technology developed by the High-Performance Computing Program is applied widely in K-12 education, libraries, health care, and industry, particularly manufacturing. It will authorize a total of $1.15 billion over the next five years.

Keywords: Government (US Federal), Law (US Federal), Information Technology, Education, Health Care

Audience: Journalists, Politicians, Scientists, Manufacturers, Educators

Details: Free

File is: /internet/nren/iita.1992/gorebill.1992.txt

`ftp://nis.nsf.net`

Marshall University School of Medicine (MUSOM) RuralNet Gopher

★★★

A gopher server dedicated to the improvement of rural health care.

Keywords: Rural Development, Health Care, Medical Treatment, Bioinformatics

Sponsor: Marshall University School of Medicine

Audience: Health Care Professionals, Medical Students, Rural Residents

Profile: A collection of health care resources, with particular emphasis on rural health care. Includes listings of clinical resources by subject area, information on state and federal rural health care initiatives, and links to local and national health and education services.

Contact: Mike McCarthy, Andy Jarrell
mmccarth@muvms6.wvnet.edu
jarrell@musom01.mu.wvnet.edu

`gopher://ruralnet.mu.wvnet.edu`

New York State Department of Health Gopher

An electronic guide to health information from the state of New York.

Keywords: Health Care, Statistics, Health Sciences, New York

Sponsor: New York State Department of Health

Audience: Health Care Professionals, Health Care Consumers

Profile: Information provided includes health statistics for New York State, lists of health care providers, facilities, and publications, as well as New York State Department of Health press releases.

Contact: nyhealth@albnydh2.bitnet

`gopher://gopher.health.state.ny.us`

NIBNews - A Monthly Electronic Bulletin About Medical Informatics

Disseminates information about Brazilian and Latin American activities, people, information, events, publications, software, and so on, involving computer applications in health care, medicine, and biology.

Keywords: Health Care, Biology, Brazil, Latin America, South America, Medicine

Audience: Health Care Professionals, Biologists

Contact: Renato M. E. Sabbatini
SABBATINI@BRUC.BITNET

Details: Free
E-mail a short notice to

`mailto:sabbatini@ccvax.unicamp.br`

sci.med

A Usenet newsgroup providing information and discussion about medicine and its related products.

Keywords: Medicine, Health Care

Audience: Medical Professionals

Details: Free

User Info: To Subscribe to this Usenet newsgroup, you need access to a newsreader.

`news:sci.med`

sci.med.physics

A Usenet newsgroup providing information and discussion about physics in medical testing and care.

Keywords: Physics, Medical Research, Health Care

Audience: Physicists, Medical Researchers, Medical Practitioners, Health Care Professionals

Details: Free

User Info: To Subscribe to this Usenet newsgroup, you need access to a newsreader.

`news:sci.med.physics`

Stanford Medical Center Gopher

This gopher allows extensive access to the Stanford Medical Center's archives.

Keywords: Medicine, Health Care, Health Sciences

Sponsor: Stanford Medical Center, Palo Alto, California, USA

Audience: Health Care Professionals, Health Science Researchers

Contact: Stanford Medical Center
gopher@medisg.stanford.edu

`gopher://med.stanford.edu`

University of Pennsylvania School of Medicine Library

The library's holdings are large and wide-ranging and contain significant collections in many fields.

Keywords: Health Care, Nursing, History, Health

Audience: Researchers, Students, General Public

Details: Free

Notes: Expect: Login; Send: Public

`telnet://penninfo.upenn.edu`

Health News Daily

Health News Daily

The database contains all the daily news and full-text articles from Health News Daily, a publication from F-D-C Reports, Inc.

Keywords: Health, Pharmacology, Medical Research, News

Sponsor: F-D-C Reports, Inc., Chevy Chase, MD, US

Audience: Health Professionals, Market Researchers, Pharmacists

Profile: The database provides specialized, in-depth business, scientific, regulatory, and legal news. Timely coverage of pharmacy and pharmaceuticals is given, as well as coverage of medical devices and diagnostics, medical research, cosmetics, health policy, provider payment policies, and cost containment in national health care.

Coverage: 1990 to the present; updated daily.

Contact: Dialog in the US at (800) 334-2564, Dialog internationally at country-specific locations.

Details: Costs

User Info: To Subscribe, contact Dialog directly.

`telnet://dialog.com`

Health Periodicals Database

Health Periodicals Database

This source covers a broad range of health subjects and issues.

Keywords: Health, Biotechnology, Medicine, Nutrition

Sponsor: Information Access Company, Foster City, CA, US

Audience: Health Professionals, Dieticians, Librarians

Profile: The database provides indexing and full text of journals covering a broad range of health subjects and issues including: prenatal care, dieting, drug abuse, AIDS, biotechnology, cardiovascular disease, environment, public health, safety, paramedical professions, sports medicine, substance abuse, toxicology, and much more.

Contact: Dialog in the US at (800) 334-2564, Dialog internationally at country-specific locations.

User Info: To Subscribe, contact Dialog directly.

Notes: Coverage: 1988 to the present; updated weekly.

`telnet://dialog.com`

Health Sciences

CAMIS (Center for Advanced Medical Informatics at Stanford)

CAMIS is a shared computing resource supporting research activities in biomedical informatics.

Keywords: Medical Informatics, Heuristics, Health Sciences

Sponsor: Stanford University School of Medicine, Palo Alto, CA, USA

Audience: Medical Informatics, Health Science Researchers

Profile: The CAMIS gopher includes an Internet-wide title search, computing information, and technical reports for the Section on Medical Informatics (SMI) community as well as that of the Knowledge Systems Laboratory (KSL), information on the Heuristic Programming Project, pointers to various online library catalogs, and more.

Contact: Torsten_Heycke@med.stanford.edu

`gopher://camis.stanford.edu/00/gopherdoc`

Center for Biomedical Informatics, Brazil

The Center for Biomedical Informatics maintains a software library with 50 disks containing about 150 public-domain medical application programs for IBM-PC-compatible microcomputers.

Keywords: Health Sciences, Public Domain Software

Sponsor: Center for Biomedical Informatics, Brazil

A
B
C
D
E
F
G
H
I
J
K
L
M
N
O
P
Q
R
S
T
U
V
W
X
Y
Z

Audience: Physicians, Nurses, Dentists, University Biomedical Researchers, Students

Details: Costs

To receive the catalogue in electronic form, send the following one-line message to infomed@ccvax.unicamp.br or infomed@bruc.bitnet: get public-domain p (for version in Portuguese) get public-domain e (for version in English). Instructions on how to acquire the software are included.

`ftp://ccsun.unicamp.br`

Creighton University Library Online Catalogue

This site maintains a catalog of the Creighton University library's holdings.

Keywords: Health Sciences, Libraries

Sponsor: Creighton University, Omaha, Nebraska, USA

Audience: Health Care Professionals, Medical Educators, Students

Details: Free

At the prompt type <lib hsl>for Health Sciences Library.

`telnet://attachpals@owl.creighton.edu`

Emory University Library

The library's holdings are large and wide-ranging and contain significant collections in many fields.

Keywords: Health Sciences, Theology, History (US), Communism, Economics (History of), Literature (American)

Audience: General Public, Researchers, Librarians, Document Delivery Professionals

Details: Free

Notes: Expect: READ, Send: DIAL VTAM, press RETURN; Expect: CICS screen, Send: PF1

`telnet://emuvm1.cc.emory.edu`

New York State Department of Health Gopher

An electronic guide to health information from the state of New York.

Keywords: Health Care, Statistics, Health Sciences, New York

Sponsor: New York State Department of Health

Audience: Health Care Professionals, Health Care Consumers

Profile: Information provided includes health statistics for New York State, lists of health care providers, facilities, and publications, as well as New York State Department of Health press releases.

Contact: nyhealth@albnydh2.bitnet

`gopher://gopher.health.state.ny.us`

NIH (National Institute of Health)

This server is a network-based computer service operated by the Division of Computer Research and Technology (DCRT) to distribute information for and about the NIH (National Institutes of Health).

Keywords: NIH, Health Sciences, Biomedical Research, Medicine

Sponsor: Division of Computer Research and Technology (DCRT), National Institute of Health

Audience: Scientists, Biomedical Researchers, Health CareProfessionals, General Public

Profile: This server provides Internet access to information about NIH health and clinical issues (including CancerNet and a variety of AIDS information), NIH-funded grants and research projects, and a variety of research resources in support of NIH and worldwide biomedical researchers. For example, the major molecular biology databases (GenBank, SWISSPROT, PIR, PDB, TFD, Prosite, LiMB) can be accessed through keyword searches from this gopher.

Details: Free

`gopher://gopher.nih.gov`

Stanford Medical Center Gopher

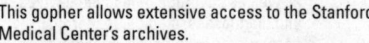

This gopher allows extensive access to the Stanford Medical Center's archives.

Keywords: Medicine, Health Care, Health Sciences

Sponsor: Stanford Medical Center, Palo Alto, California, USA

Audience: Health Care Professionals, Health Science Researchers

Contact: Stanford Medical Center gopher@medisg.stanford.edu

`gopher://med.stanford.edu`

The National Library of Medicine (NLM) Online Catalog System

Catalog of library holdings.

Keywords: Medicine, Health Sciences, Biomedicine, Rare Books

Sponsor: National Library of Medicine

Audience: Health Professionals, Medical Educators, Students

Profile: The National Library of Medicine (NLM) is the world's largest biomedical library with a collection of over 4.9 million items. NLM is a national resource for all US health sciences libraries and fills over a quarter of a million interlibrary loan requests each year for these libraries. The library is open to the public, but its collection is designed primarily for health professionals. The library collects materials comprehensively in all major areas of the health sciences. Housed within the library is one of the world's finest medical history collections of pre-1914 medical texts, rare medical texts, manu-scripts, and incunabula.

Contact: ref@nlm.nih.gov

Details: Free

The NLM can be accessed also through the WWW at http://www.nlm.nih.gov

`telnet://locator@locator.nlm.nih.gov`

The University of Illinois at Chicago Library

The library's holdings are large and wide-ranging and contain significant collections in many fields.

Keywords: Health Science, Chicago, Industry, Slavery, Abolitionism, Roosevelt (Franklin D.)

Audience: General Public, Researchers, Librarians, Document Delivery Professionals

Details: Free

Notes: Expect: introductory screen, Send: Clear key; Expect: UIC flame screen, Send: Enter key; Expect: Logon screen, Send: DIAL PVM; Expect: PVM (Passthru) screen, Send: Type: Move cursor to NOTIS and press Enter key Response: One line message about port in use Type: Enter key

`telnet://uicvm.uic.edu`

University of Texas at Galveston (Medical Branch) Library

The library's holdings are large and wide-ranging and contain significant collections in many fields.

Keywords: Health Sciences, Biomedicine, Nursing

Audience: Researchers, Students, General Public

Details: Free

Notes: Expect: Login, Send: Library

`telnet://ibm.gal.utexas.edu`

University of Wisconsin Eau Claire Library

The library's holdings are large and wide-ranging and contain significant collections in many fields.

Keywords: Health Sciences, Business, Nursing, Education

Audience: Researchers, Students, General Public

Details: Free

Notes: Expect: Service Name, Send: Victor

`telnet://lib.uwec.edu`

Health Statistics

INFOMED

Provides yearly statistical information in the form of tables (in ASCII format) listing the principal indicators of health in Cuba.

Keywords: Cuba, Health Statistics, Public Health

Sponsor: Cuban Ministry of Health

Audience: Medical Professionals, Researchers, Public Health Professionals

Details: Free

To obtain a table from the yearbook, send an electronic message to the URL address below without a subject and with the following content in the body of the message:

GET ANUARIO <name of table>

Examples of tables are CMT-11: Death rates by age group; CMT-15: Infant mortality by province, and so on. For a listing of the available tables request the help file.

`mailto:listserv@infomed.cu`

Hebraica

Harvard UniversityLibrary

The library's holdings are large and wide-ranging and contain significant collections in many fields.

Keywords: Afrikaans, Alchemy, Arabic Culture (History of), Celtic Philology, Congo Languages, Folklore, Hebraica, Mormonism, Numismatics, Quakerism, Sanskrit, Witchcraft, Arabic Philology

Audience: General Public, Researchers, Librarians, Document Delivery Professionals

Details: Free

Notes: Expect: Mitek Server..., Send: Enter or Return; Expect: prompt, Send: hollis

`telnet://hollis.harvard.edu`

Hebrew Language

Electronic Hebrew Users Newsletter (E-Hug)

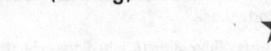

This newsletter is electronic only, and is mandated, like the original, to cover everything relating to the use of Hebrew, Yiddish, Judesmo, and Aramaic on computers.

Keywords: Judaism, Religion, Hebrew Language

Sponsor: Berkeley Hillel Foundation

Audience: Jews, Judaism Students

Contact: Ari Davidow
well!ari@apple.com

Details: Free

User Info: To Subscribe, send an e-mail message to the address below consisting of a single line reading:

SUB e-hug YourFirstName YourLastName

To send a message to the entire list, address it to: e-hug@dartcms1.bitnet

`mailto:listserv@dartcms1.bitnet`

NYIsrael Project of NYSERnet

Large repository of historical and cultural information as well as software, mailing lists, and images relating to Judaism, Jews, the Hebrew language, and Israel.

Keywords: Judaism, Jews, Hebrew Language, Israel

Sponsor: The New York Israel Project, NYSERNet, Inc.

Audience: Jewish Organizations

Profile: The purpose of this project is to create a network of diverse Jewish organizations worldwide that can communicate electronically and share information with one another.

Contact: Avrum Goodblatt
goodblat@israel.nysernet.org

Details: Free

`gopher://israel.nysernet.org`

Hemingway (Ernest)

Papa

A mailing list devoted to discussion of the life and works of Ernest Hemingway.

Keywords: Hemingway (Ernest), Literature (American)

Audience: Ernest Hemingway Readers

Contact: Dave Gross
dgross@polyslo.calpoly.edu

Details: Free

User Info: To Subscribe to the list, send an e-mail message requesting a subscription to the URL address below. To send a message to the entire list, address it to: dgross@polyslo.calpoly.edu

`mailto:dgross@polyslo.calpoly.edu`

University of Delaware Libraries (DELCAT)

The library's holdings are large and wide-ranging and contain significant collections in many fields.

Keywords: Literature (American), Hemingway (Ernest), Papermaking (History of), Chemistry (History of), Literature (Irish), Delaware

Audience: General Public, Researchers, Librarians, Document Delivery Professionals

Contact: Stuart Glogoff
epo27855@udacsvm.bitnet

Details: Free

Notes: Expect: prompt, Send: RETURN 2-3 times

`telnet://delcat.udel.edu`

`telnet://delcat.acs.udel.edu`

Herbert (George)

University of North Carolina at Greensboro MINERVA Library

The library's holdings are large and wide-ranging and contain significant collections in many fields.

Keywords: Herbert (George), Film, Dickinson (Emily), Children's Books

Audience: Researchers, Students, General Public

Details: Free

Notes: Expect: Login; Send: Info or MINERVA

`telnet://steffi.acc.uncg.edu`

Herzegovina

BosNet

BosNet is a group/forum run by volunteers. Its goals are to present and distribute information relevant to the events in/about the Republic of Bosnia-Herzegovina (RB&H) and to initiate and coordinate various initiatives, and so on.

Keywords: Bosnia, Herzegovina

Audience: Bosnians, Political Scientists, Students

Contact: listproc@cu23.crl.aecl.ca

Details: Free, Moderated

User Info: To Subscribe to the list, send an e-mail message requesting a subscription to the URL address below. To send a message to the entire list, address it to: BosNet@cu23.crl.aecl.ca

Notes: The contributions/opinions presented on BosNet do not necessarily reflect the personal opinions of the moderator or the member(s) of the Editorial Board. To participate in a discussion on a specific topic related to RB&H, please consider Usenet newsgroup soc.culture.bosnia-herzegovina.

`mailto:listproc@cu23.crl.aecl.ca`

A B C D E F G H I J K L M N O P Q R S T U V W X Y Z

A
B
C
D
E
F
G
H
I
J
K
L
M
N
O
P
Q
R
S
T
U
V
W
X
Y
Z

Heuristics

CAMIS (Center for Advanced Medical Informatics at Stanford)

CAMIS is a shared computing resource supporting research activities in biomedical informatics.

Keywords: Medical Informatics, Heuristics, Health Sciences

Sponsor: Stanford University School of Medicine, Palo Alto, CA, USA

Audience: Medical Informatics, Health Science Researchers

Profile: The CAMIS gopher includes an Internet-wide title search, computing information, and technical reports for the Section on Medical Informatics (SMI) community as well as that of the Knowledge Systems Laboratory (KSL), information on the Heuristic Programming Project, pointers to various online library catalogs, and more.

Contact: Torsten_Heycke@med.stanford.edu

`gopher://camis.stanford.edu/00/`
`gopherdoc`

Hewlett-Packard

Hewlett-Packard Computers

This web site provides information on Hewlett Packard products, news, contacts, and services.

Keywords: Computer Products, Hewlett-Packard

Sponsor: Hewlett-Packard

Audience: Computer Users, Educators, Distributors

Contact: webmaster@www.hp.com.

Details: Free

`http://www.hp.com`

HFS-L

HFS-L

★★

Human Factors and Ergonomics Society Virginia Tech Chapter.

Keywords: Ergonomics, Physical Therapy

Audience: Researchers, Physical Therapists, Designers

Contact: Cortney Vargo
courtv@vtvm1.cc.vt.edu

Details: Free

User Info: To Subscribe to the list, send an e-mail message to the URL address shown below consiting of a single line reading:

SUB hfs-l YourFirstName YourLastName

To send a message to the entire list, address it to: hfs-l@vtm1.cc.vt.edu

`mailto:listserv@vtm1.cc.vt.edu`

HICNet Newsletter (MEDNEWS - The Health InfoCom Newsletter)

HICNet Newsletter (MEDNEWS - The Health InfoCom Newsletter)

Usually published once a week, this is a large newsletter that is broken up into multiple sections to facilitate network movement.

Keywords: Health, Medical News

Audience: Health Professionals

Contact: David Dodell
ddodell@stjhmc.fidonet.org

Details: Free

User Info: To Subscribe, send an e-mail message to the address below consisting of a single line reading:

SUBhicnet YourFirstName YourLastName

To send a message to the entire list, address it to: hicnet@asvacad.bitnet

`mailto:listserv@asuacad.bitnet`

High Weirdness by E-Mail

High Weirdness by E-Mail

Guide to some interesting sources of information online.

Keywords: Technology, Hacking, Computer Underground

Audience: Mystics, Hackers, Internet Surfers

Profile: This file focuses mainly on bizarre philosophies, such as Discordia and SubGenius. Contents include: offbeat religions and 'spirituality' paganism and magic, occultism, UFOs, and paranormal phenomena.

Details: Free

`ftp://etext.archive.umich.edu/pub/`
`Zines/Weirdness`

High-Performance Computing Act of 1991

High-Performance Computing Act of 1991

This is a Senate bill to provide for a coordinated federal research program to ensure continued US leadership in high-performance computing.

Keywords: Computing, Government (US Federal), Law (US Federal)

Audience: General Public, Journalists, Politicians, Scientists

Details: Free

File is internet/nren/hpca.1991/
gorebill.1991-txt

`ftp://nis.nsf.net`

Highlands and Islands of Scotland

Highlands and Islands of Scotland

This web site provides information on Scotland, including business, leisure, culture, Gaelic language, tourism, distance education, and work opportunities.

Keywords: Scotland, Travel

Sponsor: British Telecom, United Kingdom

Audience: Travelers, Educators, Students

Contact: webmaster@nsa.bt.co.uk

Details: Free

`http://nsa.bt.co.uk/nsa.html`

hilat-l (Higher Education in Latin America)

hilat-l (Higher Education in Latin America)

★

Provides a means of interchange about research on higher education in Latin America. Postings are mostly in English, but are also welcome in Spanish and Portuguese.

Keywords: Education (Adult), Education (Distance), Education (Continuing), Latin America

Audience: Educators, Administrators, Faculty

Details: Free

User Info: To Subscribe to the list, send an e-mail message to the URL address shown below consisting of a single line reading:

SUB hilat-l YourFirstName YourLastName

To send a message to the entire list, address it to: hilat-l @bruspvm.bitnet

`mailto:listserv@bruspvm.bitnet`

Hispanic

Latin American Database Historic World Documents

International legal files covering 33 nations and article citations from publications relating to Hispanic legal systems. The wiretap gopher provides access to a range of world documents in full-text format.

Keywords: Hispanic, Law, International Law, International Documents

Audience: General Public, Hispanics, Lawyers

Profile: The database includes two files, 1) LAWL containing legislation from 33 nations, mostly Spanish speaking 2) HISS containing Hispanic Legal Article citations.

Details: Free

Select from menu as appropriate.

`gopher://marvel.loc.gov`

Historic Preservation

Archaeology, Historic Preservation

This directory is a compilation of information resources focused on archaeology, historic preservation, and heritage conservation.

Keywords: Archaeology, Historic Preservation

Audience: Archaeologists, Historians, Architects

Details: Free

`ftp://una.hh.lib.umich.edu/70/
inetdirsstacks/archpres:stott`

Historical Documents

Historical Documents

A collection of historical documents (with particular emphasis on freedom and democracy) ranging from the Magna Carta to Nelson Mandela's Inauguration Speech.

Keywords: History (World), Democracy, Historical Documents

Sponsor: The Queens Borough Public Library

Audience: Historians, Activists, General Public

`gopher://vax.queens.lib.ny.us/Social
Sciences/Historical Documents`

Historic World Documents

The wiretap gopher provides access to a range of world documents in full-text format.

Keywords: Historical Documents, Treaties, History (World)

Audience: Governments, Historians, Researchers, General Public

Details: Free

Select from Menu as appropriate

`gopher://wiretap.spies.com`

Historical Documents of the US

A large sample of US historical documents, from the Fundamental Orders of 1639 to the Vietnam Era Documents, including World War II documents, Federalist papers, and more.

Keywords: Historical Document, Government (US Federal), Law (US Federal)

Audience: Historians, Journalists, Students, Politicians

Details: Free

`gopher://wiretap.spies.com/11/Gov/US-
History`

University of North Carolina at Wilmington SEABOARD Library

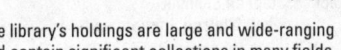

The library's holdings are large and wide-ranging and contain significant collections in many fields.

Keywords: Marine Biology, Historical Documents

Audience: Researchers, Students, General Public

Contact: Eddy Cavenaugh
cavenaughd@uncwil.bitnet
cavenaughd@vxc.uncwil.edu

Details: Free

Notes: Expect: Login; Send: Info

`telnet://vxc.uncwil.edu`

History

British National Register of Archives

A multi-volume electronic guide to accessing a wide-variety of archival materials and repositories in the United Kingdom.

Keywords: United Kingdom, History, Business (British), Information Retrieval

Sponsor: Coombspapers Social Sciences Research Data Bank at ANU (Australian National University).

Audience: Researchers, Anglophiles, Archivists

Contact: Dr. T. Matthew Ciolek
tmciolek@coombs.anu.edu.au

`gopher://coombs.anu.edu.au`

`ftp:/coombs.anu.edu.au/coombspapers/
otherarchives/uk-nra-archives/`

`http://coombs.anu.edu.au/
CoombsHome.html`

University of Pennsylvania School of Medicine Library

The library's holdings are large and wide-ranging and contain significant collections in many fields.

Keywords: Health Care, Nursing, History, Health

Audience: Researchers, Students, General Public

Details: Free

Notes: Expect: Login; Send: Public

`telnet://penninfo.upenn.edu`

History (20th Century)

Vwar-L

An electronic conference on issues relating to the Vietnam War.

Keywords: History (20th Century), History (US), Vietnam

Audience: Historians

Contact: Lydia Fish
fishlm@snybufva.cs.snybuf.edu

User Info: To Subscribe to the list, send an e-mail message to the URL address below consisting of a single line reading:

SUB vwar-l YourFirstName YourLastName

To send a message to the entire list, address it to: vwar-l@ubvm.cc. buffalo.edu

`mailto: listserv@ubvm.cc.buffalo.edu`

History (Ancient)

Princeton University Library

The library's holdings are large and wide-ranging. They contain significant collections in many fields.

Keywords: China, Japan, Classics, History (Ancient), Near Eastern Studies, Literature (American), Literature (English), Aeronautics, Middle Eastern Studies, Mormonism, Publishing

A B C D E F G H I J K L M N O P Q R S T U V W X Y Z

Audience: General Public, Researchers, Librarians, Document Delivery Professionals

Details: Free

Notes: Expect: Connect message, blank screen, Send: <cr>; Expect: #, Send: Call 500

`telnet://pucable.princeton.edu`

History (Jewish)

US Holocaust Memorial Museum

The web site of the newly-opened (April, 1993) US Holocaust Memorial Museum in Washington D.C.

Keywords: Jews, Jewish Politics, Holocaust, History (Jewish)

Audience: Jews, Holocaust Researchers, Israelis, Students

Profile: This resource contains files on educational programs, general information about the Holocaust Research Institute, a contact list for the Association of Holocaust Organizations, and a searchable archive of related materials.

`http://www.ushmm.org`

History (US)

Armadillo's World Wide Web Page

This site provides resources and instructional material for an interdisciplinary Texan culture course.

Keywords: History (US), Texas, Cultural Studies, Education

Sponsor: Rice University, Houston, Texas, USA

Audience: Educators, Students

Contact: armadillo@rice.edu

`http://chico.rice.edu/armadillo`

Emory University Library

The library's holdings are large and wide-ranging and contain significant collections in many fields.

Keywords: Health Sciences, Theology, History (US), Communism, Economics (History of), Literature (American)

Audience: General Public, Researchers, Librarians, Document Delivery Professionals

Details: Free

Notes: Expect: VM screen, Send: RETURN; Expect: CP READ, Send: DIAL VTAM, press RETURN; Expect: CICS screen, Send: PF1

`telnet://emuvm1.cc.emory.edu`

Mississippi State University Library

The library's holdings are large and wide-ranging and contain significant collections in many fields.

Keywords: History (US), Forestry, Energy, Carter (Hodding, Papers of), Mississippi

Audience: General Public, Researchers, Librarians, Document Delivery Professionals

Contact: Stephen Cunetto
shc1@ra.msstate.edu

Details: Free

Notes: Expect: username, Send: msu; Expect: password, Send: library

`telnet://libserv.msstate.edu`

U.S. Civil War Reading List

A major directory on abolitionism, providing access to a broad range of resources (library catalogs, databases, and servers) via the Internet.

Keywords: History (US), Abolitionism

Audience: General Public, Historians

Profile: The Suggested Civil War Reading List contains 61 books, several of them with multiple volumes, as well as an 11-hour documentary film and a CD of Civil War era songs. The material is sorted into general categories: General Histories of the War, Causes of the War and History to 1861, Slavery and Southern Society, Reconstruction, Biographies and Autobiographies, Source Documents and official Records, Unit Histories and Soldiers' Reminiscences, Fiction, Specific Battles and Campaigns, Strategies and Tactics, The Experience of Soldiers.

Contact: Stephen Schmidt
whale@leland.Stanford.edu

`http://www.cis.ohio-state.edu/`
`hypertext/faq/usenet/civil-war-usa/`
`reading-list/faq.html`

University of Colorado at Boulder Library

The library's holdings are large and wide-ranging and contain significant collections in many fields.

Keywords: Numismatics, Human Rights, Literature (Children's), Labor Archives, History (US)

Audience: Researchers, Students, General Public

Contact: Donna Pattee
pattee@spot.colorado.edu

Details: Free

Notes: Expect: Login; Send: Culine

`telnet:// culine.colorado.edu`

University of Southern Colorado Library

The library's holdings are large and wide-ranging and contain significant collections in many fields.

Keywords: History (US)

Audience: Researchers, Students, General Public

Details: Free

Notes: Expect: OK Prompt, Send: Login Pub1; Expect: Password: usc

`telnet://starburst.uscolo.edu`

University of Wisconsin River Falls Library

The library's holdings are large and wide-ranging and contain significant collections in many fields.

Keywords: Agriculture, Education, History (US)

Audience: Researchers, Students, General Public

Details: Free

Notes: Expect: Service Name, Send: Victor

`telnet://davee.dl.uwrf.edu`

University of Wisconsin Stevens Point Library

The library's holdings are large and wide-ranging and contain significant collections in many fields.

Keywords: Education, Environmental Studies, Ethnic Studies, History (US)

Audience: Researchers, Students, General Public

Details: Free

Notes: Expect: Login; Send: Lib; Expect: vDIAL Prompt, Send: Library

`telnet://lib.uwsp.edu`

Vwar-L

An electronic conference on issues relating to the Vietnam War.

Keywords: History (20th Century), History (US), Vietnam

Audience: Historians

Contact: Lydia Fish
fishlm@snybufva.cs.snybuf.edu

User Info: To Subscribe to the list, send an e-mail message to the URL address below consisting of a single line reading:

SUB vwar-l YourFirstName YourLastName

To send a message to the entire list, address it to: vwar-l@ubvm.cc. buffalo.edu

`mailto: listserv@ubvm.cc.buffalo.edu`

History (Women's)

Notable Women

A database listing some important and notable women through the ages. Available for online searching by keyword, or as a full-text file.

Keywords: Women's Studies, History (Women's), Feminism

Sponsor: Estrella Mountain Community College (Arizona)

Audience: Women's Studies Educators, Historians, Researchers, Feminists

Contact: EMC Gopher Team
root@gopher.emc.maricopa.edu

`gopher://gopher.emc.maricopa.edu`

History (World)

Government Docs (US & World)

A large and eclectic collection of documents, ranging from the Laws of William the Conqueror to the North American Free Trade Agreement (NAFTA). Particular strengths include 20th century American political documents and international treaties and covenants.

Keywords: Government (International), History (World), Politics (International)

Sponsor: The Internet Wiretap

Audience: Researchers, Historians, Political Scientists, Journalists

Contact: gopher@wiretap.spies.com

`gopher://wiretap.spies.com/Gov`

Historic World Documents

The wiretap gopher provides access to a range of world documents in full-text format.

Keywords: Historical Documents, Treaties, History (World)

Audience: Governments, Historians, Researchers, General Public

Details: Free

Notes: Select from Menu as appropriate

`gopher://wiretap.spies.com`

Historical Documents

A collection of historical documents (with particular emphasis on freedom and democracy) ranging from the Magna Carta to Nelson Mandela's Inauguration Speech.

Keywords: History (World), Democracy, Historical Documents

Sponsor: The Queens Borough Public Library

Audience: Historians, Activists, General Public

`gopher://vax.queens.lib.ny.us/Social Sciences/Historical Documents`

History at the University of Virginia

A collection of online history resources, with particular emphasis on medieval and classical studies. Links to other systems, including the Library of Congress.

Keywords: History (World), Classics, Medieval Studies

Sponsor: University of Virginia, Charlottesville, Virginia, USA

Audience: Historians, Students (College/University)

Contact: mssbks@virginia.edu

Details: Free

`gopher://gopher.lib.virginia.edu`

History Discussion Forum

This mailing list is a general starting point for the discussion of history; subscribers include professional historians, graduate students, and history enthusiasts.

Keywords: History (World)

Sponsor: Penn State University

Audience: Historians, History Enthusiasts

User Info: To Subscribe to the list, send an e-mail message requesting a subscription to the URL address below consisting of a single line reading:

SUB history YourFirstName YourLastName

To send a message to the entire list, address it to: history@psuvm.psu.edu

`mailto:listserv@psuvm.psu.edu`

`news:bit.listserv.history`

HNSource

HNSource is an extensive collection of history resources.

Keywords: History (World)

Sponsor: Academic Computer Service and the Department of History of the University of Kansas

Audience: Historians, Researchers, Librarians, Students

Profile: HNSource provides information, announcements, guides, references, and links to related Internet resources, including FTP sites, WAIS sites, OPACs, and gophers

Contact: Lynn Nelson
lhnelson@ukanvm.bitnet

Notes: telnet: Expect: login; Send: history.

`http://history.cc.ukans.edu/history/WWW_history_main.html`

`telnet:history.cc.ukans.edu`

soc.history

A Usenet newsgroup providing information and discussion about historical issues.

Keywords: History (World)

Audience: Historians

Details: Free

User Info: To Subscribe to this Usenet newsgroup, you need access to a newsreader.

`news:soc.history`

UCSB Library Reference Guide

A list of art references including indexes, dictionaries, bilbiographies and biographical materials.

Keywords: Art, History (World), Libraries

Sponsor: University of California at Santa Barbara

Audience: Artists, Historians, Librarians

`gopher://ucsbuxa.ucsb.edu`

UN Development Program

Provides a detailed history of the UN and its development, as well as an outline of UN Internet programs.

Keywords: United Nations, History (World)

Sponsor: United Nations

Audience: General Public, Historians, Internationalists, Researchers

Details: Free

`gopher://nywork1.undp.org`

University of Pennsylvania Library- Philadelphia Pa.

The library's holdings are large and wide-ranging and contain significant collections in many fields.

Keywords: Literature (English), Literature (American), History (World), Medieval Studies, East Asian Studies, Middle Eastern Studies, South Asian Studies, Judaica, Lithuania

Audience: Educators, Students, Researchers

Profile: Access to the central Van Pelt Library and to most of the departmental libraries is restricted to members of the University community on weekends and holidays. Online visitors are advised to call (215) 898-7554 for information on hours and access restrictions.

A B C D E F G H I J K L M N O P Q R S T U V W X Y Z

A B C D E F G **H** I J K L M N O P Q R S T U V W X Y Z

Contact: Patricia Renfro, Associate Director of Libraries

Details: Free

`telnet://library.upenn.edu`

World Constitutions ★

A list of world constitutions, containing the constitutions of more than 18 nations including Basic Law of Germany 1949; Constitution of Macedonia (in former Yugoslavia); Magna Carta.

Keywords: Law (International), History (World), Politics (International)

Audience: Researchers, Lawyers, Historians

Details: Free

`gopher://wiretap.spies.com`

History and Analysis of Disabilities Newsletter

History and Analysis of Disabilities Newsletter ★

Covers the history of disabilities, disabled persons, and disability issues.

Keywords: Disabilities, Disabled Persons

Sponsor: History of Disabilities Network, Centre for Independent Living, Toronto, and International Society for the History of Disabilities, Paris.

Audience: Disabled persons, Doctors, Historians

Contact: Gary Woodill
fcty7310@ryerson.bitnet

Details: Free

`mailto:fcty7310@ryerson.bitnet`

Hitchhiker's Guide

Hitchhiker's Guide ★

A narrative of what the Internet has to offer.

Keywords: Internet, Internet Guides

Sponsor: University of Illinois, Urbana, IL

Audience: Internet Surfers

Contact: Ed Krol
krol@uxc.cso.uiuc.ed

Details: Free

File is: documents/rfc/rfc1118.txt

`ftp://nic.merit.edu`

HIV

AIDS Treatment News

A newsletter on AIDS treatment.

Keywords: AIDS, HIV, Health, Medicine

Sponsor: IGC (Institute for Global Communications)

Audience: AIDS Researchers, Health Workers, AIDS Sufferers

Profile: This newsletter contains interviews, reports on new and existing treatment modalities, announcements of clinical drug testing trial, and more.

Contact: atn@igc.apc.org

Details: Free

`gopher://odie.niaid.nih.gov/11/aids`

Hobbies

alt.aquaria ★

A Usenet newsgroup providing information and discussion about the aquarium as a hobby.

Keywords: Aquariums, Fish, Hobbies

Audience: Aquarium Keepers, Fish Lovers

User Info: To Subscribe to this Usenet newsgroup, you need access to a newsreader.

`news:alt.aquaria`

Model-horse ★

Discussion of the model-horse hobby. All aspects of showing (live and photo), collecting, re-making/re-painting for all breeds are discussed. All ages and levels of experience welcome.

Keywords: Model Horses, Hobbies

Audience: Model Horse Collectors

Details: Free

User Info: To Subscribe to the list, send an e-mail message requesting a subscription to the URL address below.

`mailto:model-horse-request@qiclab.scn.rain.com`

PEI (Prince Edward Island, Canada) Crafts Council Gopher ★★

A gopher devoted to all manner of crafts, from weaving to glass blowing. Information includes a database of tools, services, and materials for crafts enthusiasts, as well as FAQs and pointers to other crafts resources. Also provides background on the PEI Craft Council's activities and on Prince Edward Island.

Keywords: Crafts, Hobbies, Canada

Sponsor: PEI Crafts Council, Prince Edward Island, Canada

Audience: Crafts Enthusiasts

Details: Free

`gopher://crafts-council.pe.ca`

rec.collecting.cards

A Usenet newsgroup providing information and discussion about collecting sports and other trading cards.

Keywords: Trading Cards, Hobbies

Audience: Card Collectors

User Info: To Subscribe to this Usenet newsgroup, you need access to a newsreader.

`news:rec.collecting.cards`

rec.woodworking ★

A Usenet newsgroup providing information and discussion about woodworking.

Keywords: Woodworking, Crafts, Hobbies

Audience: Woodworkers

User Info: To Subscribe to this Usenet newsgroup, you need access to a newsreader.

`news:rec.woodworking`

Hockey

American Hockey League

This list is for people interested in discussing and following the activities of The American Hockey League.

Keywords: Sports, Hockey, American Hockey League

Audience: Hockey Enthusiasts, Sports Enthusiasts

Contact: ahl-news-request@andrew.cmu.edu

Details: Free

User Info: To Subscribe to the list, send an e-mail message requesting a subscription to the URL address below.

To send a message to the entire list, address it to: ahl-news@andrew.cmu.edu

`mailto:ahl-news-request@andrew.cmu.edu`

Blues (St. Louis Blues)

Provides information, game reports, stats, discussion, and so on, on the St. Louis Blues of the National Hockey League.

Keywords: Hockey, Sports

Audience: Hockey Enthusiasts

Contact: Joe Ashkar
blues@medicine.wustl.edu

User Info: To Subscribe to the list, send an e-mail message requesting a subscription to the URL address below.

To send a message to the entire list, address it to: blues@medicine.wustl.edu

`mailto:blues@medicine.wustl.edu`

Boston Bruins

This list is for discussion of the Boston Bruins of the National Hockey League and their farm teams. Also available as a digest.

Keywords: Hockey, Sports, Boston

Audience: Hockey Enthusiasts, Boston Residents, Sports Enthusiasts

Contact: Garry Knox
bruins-request@cristal.umd.edu

Details: Free

User Info: To Subscribe to the list, send an e-mail message requesting a subscription to the URL address below.

To send a message to the entire list, address it to: bruins@cristal.umd.edu

`mailto:bruins-request@cristal.umd.edu`

Dallas Stars

Discussion of the Dallas Stars (of the National Hockey League) and their farm clubs.

Keywords: Hockey, Sports

Audience: NHL Enthusiasts

Details: Free

User Info: To Subscribe to the list, send an e-mail message requesting a subscription to the URL address below. To send a message to the entire list, address it to: hamlet@u.washington.edu

Notes: Please include the word "DSTARS" in your subject line and include your name and preferred e-mail address in the body of your message.

`mailto:hamlet@u.washington.edu`

echl-news

For people interested in discussing and following the East Coast Hockey League.

Keywords: Hockey, Sports

Audience: Hockey Enthusiasts

Contact: echl-news-request@andrew.cmu.edu

Details: Free

User Info: To Subscribe to the list, send an e-mail message requesting a subscription to the URL address below.

To send a message to the entire list, address it to: echl-news-request@andrew.cmu.edu

`mailto:echl-news-request@andrew.cmu.edu`

mda

Discussion of the Mighty Ducks of Anaheim of the National Hockey League, including statistics and game summaries.

Keywords: Hockey, Sports

Audience: Ice Hockey Fans

Contact:

Details: Free

User Info: To Subscribe to the list, send an e-mail message to the URL address below, consisting of a single line reading:

SUB mda YourFirstName YourLastName

To send a message to the entire list, address it to: mda@macsch.com

`mailto:mda@macsch.com`

New York Islanders

A discussion of the New York Islanders hockey team, with emphasis on the current season.

Keywords: Hockey, Sports, New York

Audience: New York Islanders Fans, Ice Hockey Fans

Contact: David Strauss
dss2k@virginia.edu

Details: Free

User Info: To Subscribe to the list, send an e-mail message requesting a subscription to the URL address below.

`mailto:dss2k@virginia.edu`

NHL Goalie Stats

A mailing list for the distribution of information regarding NHL goalie statistics.

Keywords: Hockey, Sports Statistics

Audience: Hockey Enthusiasts

Profile: Weekday reports of goalie statistics from the National Hockey League.

Contact: dfa@triple-i.com

Details: Free

User Info: To Subscribe to the list, send an e-mail message requesting a subscription to the URL address below.

To send a message to the entire list, address it to: dfa@triple-i.com

`mailto:dfa@triple-i.com`

Professional Sports Schedules

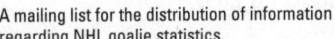

Sports schedules for major professional sports.

Keywords: Sports, Baseball, Hockey, Football, Basketball

Sponsor: Colorado University, Boulder, CO

Audience: Sports Fans, Football Fans, Hockey Fans, Baseball Enthusiasts, Basketball Enthusiasts

Profile: The Colorado University gopher maintains an interactive online database of schedules for all major US professional sports teams (NBA, NFL, NHL, MLB). The database is indexed by both team name and dates of games, and can be searched accordingly.

Contact: gopher@gopher.colorado.edu

Details: Free

`gopher://gopher.colorado.edu/11/professional/sports/schedules`

Quebec Nordiques

A mailing list to discuss topics concerning the National Hockey League's Quebec Nordiques.

Keywords: Hockey, Quebec (Canada), Sports

Audience: Hockey Enthusiasts

Contact: Danny J. Sohier
nords-request@badaboum.ulaval.ca

Details: Free

User Info: To Subscribe to the list, send an e-mail message requesting a subscription to the URL address below.

To send a message to the entire list, address it to: nords@badaboum.ulaval.ca

`mailto:nords@badaboum.ulaval.ca`

rec.sport.hockey

A Usenet newsgroup providing information and discussion about hockey.

Keywords: Hockey, Sports

Audience: Hockey Fans, Sports Fans

User Info: To Subscribe to this Usenet newsgroup, you need access to a newsreader.

`news:rec.sport.hockey`

Holmes (Sherlock)

The University of Minnesota Library System (LUMINA)

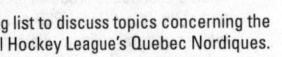

The library's holdings are large and wide-ranging and contain significant collections in many fields.

Keywords: Immigration (History of), Ethnic Studies, Horticulture, Equine Research, Botanical Taxonomy, Quantum Physics, Native American Studies, Holmes (Sherlock)

Audience: General Public, Researchers, Librarians, Document Delivery Professionals

Contact: Craig D. Rice
cdr@acc.stolaf.edu

Details: Free

`telnet://lumina.lib.umn.edu`

A B C D E F G H I J K L M N O P Q R S T U V W X Y Z

A
B
C
D
E
F
G
H
I
J
K
L
M
N
O
P
Q
R
S
T
U
V
W
X
Y
Z

Holocaust

The Israel Information Service

A gopher server containing information on Israel.

Keywords: Israel, Middle East, Political Science, Anti-Semitism, Holocaust, Archaeology

Sponsor: Israeli Foreign Ministry

Audience: Israelis, Jews, Tourists, General Public

Profile: This server features updates on the Middle East peace process, including text of the latest Israel-PLO accord, as well as general political, diplomatic, cultural, and economic information on the state of Israel. Also includes archives on archaeology in Israel, anti-Semitism and the Holocaust, and current excerpts from Israeli newspapers.

Contact: Chaim Shacham shacham@israel-info.gov.il

`gopher://israel-info.gov.il`

US Holocaust Memorial Museum

The web site of the newly-opened (April, 1993) US Holocaust Memorial Museum in Washington D.C.

Keywords: Jews, Jewish Politics, Holocaust, History (Jewish)

Audience: Jews, Holocaust Researchers, Israelis, Students

Profile: This resource contains files on educational programs, general information about the Holocaust Research Institute, a contact list for the Association of Holocaust Organizations, and a searchable archive of related materials.

`http://www.ushmm.org`

Home Building

Utah Valley Community College Library

The library's holdings are large and wide-ranging and contain significant collections in many fields.

Keywords: Accounting, Automobiles, Cabinetry, Child Care, Drafting, Electronics, Home Building, Local History, Refrigeration, Air Conditioning

Audience: General Public, Researchers, Librarians, Document Delivery Professionals

Details: Free

Notes: Expect: Login; Send: Opub

`telnet:// uvlib.uvcc.edu`

Home Economics

misc.consumers.house

A Usenet newsgroup providing information and discussion about owning and maintaining your house.

Keywords: Home Economics, Housing

Audience: Home Owners, General Public

Details: Free

User Info: To Subscribe to this Usenet newsgroup, you need access to a newsreader.

`news:misc.consumers.house`

University of Wisconsin at Stout Library

The library's holdings are large and wide-ranging and contain significant collections in many fields.

Keywords: Mathematics, Business, Fashion Merchandising, Home Economics, Hospitality, Tourism, Hotel Administration, Restaurant Management, Microelectronics

Audience: Researchers, Students, General Public

Details: Free

Notes: Expect: Login, Send: Lib; Expect: vDIAL Prompt, Send: Library

`telnet://lib.uwstout.edu`

Hong Kong

Hong Kong Law

Lists the basic Hong Kong Law (1990) and Hong Kong Bill of Rights Ordinance (1991).

Keywords: Hong Kong, Law (International)

Audience: Lawyers, Sinologists

Details: Free

`gopher://marvel.loc.gov`

soc.culture.hongkong

A Usenet newsgroup providing information and discussion about Hong Kong and its people.

Keywords: Hong Kong, Sociology

Audience: Sociologists

Details: Free

User Info: To Subscribe to this Usenet newsgroup, you need access to a newsreader.

`news:soc.culture.hongkong`

Hongkongiana

Hong Kong Polytechnic Library System

An index to journal articles about Hong Kong, published in selected Hong Kong periodicals beginning in 1986. The online version is written in English.

Keywords: Hong Kong, Hongkongiana

Sponsor: Hong Kong Polytechnic Library, Hong Kong

Audience: Sinologists, General Public

Details: Free

Notes: Expect: Username, Send: Library

`telnet://library.hkp.hk`

Hoppenstedt Directory of German Companies

Hoppenstedt Directory of German Companies

This directory covers 50,000 German companies with sales exceeding 2 million DM or with a minimum of 20 employees.

Keywords: German Companies, International Business, Germany

Sponsor: Hoppenstedt Wirtschaftsdatenbank, Darmstadt, Germany

Audience: Business Professionals, International Market, Researchers, Germans

Profile: Records include current company address, line of business, number of employees, sales, capital stock, branches and subsidiaries, and a listing of executives and directors with positions in the company. The file is bilingual; users can view the records in either German or English.

Contact: Dialog in the US at (800) 334-2564, Dialog internationally at country-specific locations.

User Info: To Subscribe, contact Dialog directly.

Notes: Coverage: 1973 to the present; updated semiannually.

`telnet://dialog.com`

horizons 'New Horizons in Adult Education'

horizons 'New Horizons in Adult Education'

 ★★★★

A journal transmitted to educators around the world.

Keywords: Education (Adult), Education (Distance), Education (Continuing)

Audience: Educators, Administrators, Faculty, Researchers

Details: Free

User Info: To Subscribe to the journal, send an e-mail message to the URL address shown below consisting of a single line reading:

SUB horizonsYourFirstName YourLastName

`mailto:listserv@alpha.acast.nova.edu`

Horseracing

derby

★

To discuss various aspects and strategies of horseracing, primarily dealing with, but not limited to, handicapping.

Keywords: Horseracing, Handicapping

Audience: Horseracing Enthusiasts

Contact: John Wilkes
derby-request@ekrl.com

User Info: To Subscribe to the list, send an e-mail message requesting a subscription to the URL address below.

To send a message to the entire list, address it to: derby-request@ekrl.com

`mailto:derby-request@ekrl.com`

Horses

rec.equestrian

★

A Usenet newsgroup providing information and discussion about all things pertaining to horses.

Keywords: Horses, Equestrians, Animals, Sports

Audience: Horse Riders, Horse Trainers, Horse Owners

User Info: To Subscribe to this Usenet newsgroup, you need access to a newsreader.

`news:rec.equestrian`

Horticulture

The University of Minnesota Library System (LUMINA)

★★

The library's holdings are large and wide-ranging and contain significant collections in many fields.

Keywords: Immigration (History of), Ethnic Studies, Horticulture, Equine Research, Botanical Taxonomy, Quantum Physics, Native American Studies, Holmes (Sherlock)

Audience: General Public, Researchers, Librarians, Document Delivery Professionals

Contact: Craig D. Rice
cdr@acc.stolaf.edu

Details: Free

`telnet://lumina.lib.umn.edu`

hospex

hospex

★

A bulletin board for people interested in being hosts to foreign visitors.

Keywords: Travel, Hospitality

Audience: International Travelers, General Public

Contact: hospex@plearn.edu.p1

Details: Free

User Info: To Subscribe to the list, send an e-mail message to the URL address shown below consisting of a single line reading:

SUB hospex YourFirstName YourLastName

`mailto:listserv@plearn.bitnet`

Hospital Administration

GENMED (General Medical Information)

The General Medical Information (GENMED) library contains a variety of medical care and treatment, toxicology, and hospital administration materials.

Keywords: Medicine, Toxicology, Hospital Administration, Treatment

Audience: Medical Professionals

Profile: The GENMED library contains full-text medical journals and newsletters, as well as drug information, disease and trauma reviews, Physicians Data Query cancer information, and medical administration journals. GENMED also offers a gateway to the MEDLINE database.

Contact: Mead New Sales Group at (800) 227-4908 or (513) 859-5398 inside the US, or (513) 865-7981 for all inquiries outside the US.

User Info: To Subscribe, contact Mead directly.

To examine the Nexis user guide, you can access it at the ftp site of the University of Texas at Austin at the URL address: ftp://ftp.cc.utexas.edu

The files are in: /pub/ref-services/LEXIS

`telnet://nex.meaddata.com`

`http://www.meaddata.com`

Vetadm-L

 ★

A discussion group for those involved in veterinary hospital administration.

Keywords: Hospital Administration, Veterinary Hospitals

Audience: Veterinarians

Contact: Joel Hammond
joel@tamvet.bitnet

Details: Free

User Info: To Subscribe to the list, send an e-mail message to the URL address below consisting of a single line reading:

SUB vetadm-l YourFirstName YourLastName

To send a message to the entire list, address it to: vetadm-l@tamvml.tamu.edu

`mailto:listserv@tamvm1.tamu.edu`

Hospitality

University of Wisconsin at Stout Library

★★

The library's holdings are large and wide-ranging and contain significant collections in many fields.

Keywords: Mathematics, Business, Fashion Merchandising, Home Economics, Hospitality, Tourism, Hotel Administration, Restaurant Management, Microelectronics

Audience: Researchers, Students, General Public

Details: Free

Notes: Expect: Login, Send: Lib; Expect: vDIAL Prompt, Send: Library

`telnet://lib.uwstout.edu`

A B C D E F G **H** I J K L M N O P Q R S T U V W X Y Z

Hot Air Balloons

Balloon

This is a list for balloonists of any sort. Discussion covers all types of balloons, be they hot air or gas, commercial or sport, and just about anything related to ballooning.

Keywords: Ballooning, Hot Air Balloons

Audience: Balloonists

Contact: Phil Herbert
balloon-request@lut.ac.uk

User Info: To Subscribe to the list, send an e-mail message requesting a subscription to the URL address below.

To send a message to the entire list, address it to: balloon@lut.ac.uk

`mailto:balloon-request@lut.ac.uk`

Hot off the Tree (HOTT)

Hot off the Tree (HOTT)

HOTT contains excerpts and abstracts of articles from trade journals, popular periodicals, online news services, and electronic bulletin boards.

Keywords: Computer Technology, Technology

Sponsor: University of California, San Diego library's Technology Watch Information Group (TWIG)

Audience: Computer Programmers, Technology Enthusiasts, General Public

Contact: Susan Jurist
sjurist@ucsd.edu or sjurist@ucsd.bitnet

Details: Free

Available on MELVYL, the University of California online catalog. Anyone with access to telnet, can telnet MELVYL (31.0.0.13) and show hott.

`telnet://melvyl.berkeley.edu/showhott`

Hotel Administration

University of Nevada, Las Vegas Library - Las Vegas, NV

The library's holdings are large and wide-ranging and contain significant collections in many fields.

Keywords: Gaming, Hotel Administration, Nevadiana, Canadian Documents, Nevada State Documents

Audience: General Public, Researchers, Librarians, Document Delivery Professionals

Contact: Myoung-ja Lee Kwon
kwon@nevada.edu.

Details: Free

Notes: Expect: login; Send: library

`telnet://library.lv-lib.nevada.edu`

University of Wisconsin at Stout Library

The library's holdings are large and wide-ranging and contain significant collections in many fields.

Keywords: Mathematics, Business, Fashion Merchandising, Home Economics, Hospitality, Tourism, Hotel Administration, Restaurant Management, Microelectronics

Audience: Researchers, Students, General Public

Details: Free

Notes: Expect: Login, Send: Lib; Expect: vDIAL Prompt, Send: Library

`telnet://lib.uwstout.edu`

Housing

alt.housing.nontrad

This newsgroup is for discussion of all forms of "nontraditional housing," including cohousing and communes

Keywords: Community, Housing, Communes

Audience: General Public, Community Activists

Details: Free

To participate in a Usenet newsgroup, you need access to a Ònewsreader.Ò

`news:alt.housing.nontrad`

COHOUSING-L

A list for discussion of Cohousing, the name of a type of collaborative housing that has been developed primarily in Denmark since 1972 where it is known as bofoellesskaber. Cohousing is housing designed to foster community and cooperation while preserving independence. Private residences are clustered near shared facilities. The members design and manage all aspects of their community.

Keywords: Community, Housing, Cooperatives

Audience: Urban Planners, Architects, General Contractors

Contact: fholson@uci.com

Details: Free

User Info: To Subscribe to the list, send an e-mail message to the address below consisting of a single line reading:

SUB COHOUSING-L YourFirstName YourLastName

To send a message to the entire list, address it to: COHOUSING-L@uci.com

`mailto:listserv@uci.com`

misc.consumers.house

A Usenet newsgroup providing information and discussion about owning and maintaining your house.

Keywords: Home Economics, Housing

Audience: Home Owners, General Public

Details: Free

User Info: To Subscribe to this Usenet newsgroup, you need access to a newsreader.

`news:misc.consumers.house`

Housman (A.E.)

Colby College Library

The library's holdings are large and wide-ranging and contain significant collections in many fields.

Keywords: Contemporary Letters, Hardy (Thomas), James (Henry), Mann (Thomas, Collections of), Housman (A.E., Letters of), Maine Authors, Irish History (Modern)

Audience: General Public, Researchers, Librarians, Document Delivery Professionals

Details: Free

Notes: Expect: login, Send: library

`telnet://library.colby.edu`

hr.women

hr.women

A conference on human rights issues pertaining to women.

Keywords: Women's Issues, Feminists, Human Rights

Audience: Women, Feminists, Activists

Contact: Jillaine Smith
jillaine@igc.apc.org

Details: Costs

User Info: Establish an account on the nearest APC node. Login, type c for conferences, then type go hr.women. For information on the nearest APC node, contact: APC International Secretariat IBASE E-mail: apcadmin@apc.org

`telnet://igc.apc.org`

HTML FAQ

HTML FAQ

Common questions and answers about HTML (Hypertext Markup Language). The FAQ covers the practices of creating new documents specifically for the WWW format, as well as transforming existing materials into WWW documents.

Keywords: WWW, Internet Reference, Information Retrieval

Audience: Students, Computer Scientists, Researchers

Contact: Iain O'Cain
ec@umcc.umich.edu

`http://www.umcc.umich.edu/~ec/www/html_faq.html`

Hubble Telescope

CADC (Canadian Astronomy Data Center) Home Page

The CADC maintains archives of scientific data from the Hubble Space Telescope and the Canada France Hawaii Telescope. It also serves as a distribution point for various astronomy-related software packages.

Keywords: Astronomy, Hubble Telescope

Sponsor: Dominional Astrophysical Observatory, Victoria, British Columbia, Canada

Audience: Astronomers

Contact: Dennis Crabtree
crabtree@dao.nrc.ca

`http://ucluelet.dao.nrc.ca`

Sci.astro.hubble

Information about all subjects concerning NASA's Hubble space telescope.

Keywords: Hubble Telescope, Astronomy, Space, NASA, Stargazing, Telescopes

Audience: Astronomers, General Public, Science Teachers, Stargazers

Contact: Paul A. Scowen
scowen@wfpc3.la.asu.edu

Details: Free, Moderated, Images

User Info: To Subscribe to this Usenet newsgroup, you need access to a newsreader.

`news:sci.astro.hubble`

Human Behavior

MBI, Music and the Brain Information Center Database (MuSICA)

The intent of this resource is to establish a comprehensive database of scientific research on music.

Keywords: Music Resources, Human Behavior, Neurology

Sponsor: Music and the Brain Information Center

Audience: Researchers, Scientists

Profile: MuSICA maintains a data base of scientific research (references and abstracts) on music as related to behavior, the brain and allied fields, in order to foster interdisciplinary knowledge. Topics include the auditory system; human and animal behavior; creativity; the neuropsychology of music and the human brain; the effects of music on behavior and physiology; music education, medicine, performance, and therapy; neurobiology; perception and psychophysics. Citations and abstracts are excerpted from the following journals: The Bulletin of the Council for Research in Music Education, The Journal of Research in Music Education, Music Perception, Psychology of Music, Psychomusicology.

Contact: Norman Weinberger, Gordon Shaw
mbic@mila.ps.uci.edu

Details: Free

Expect login: Send mbi Expect password: Send nammbi

`telnet://mila.ps.uci.edu`

Political Analysis and Research Cooperation (PARC) News Bulletin

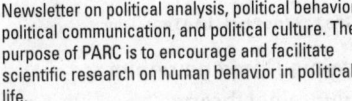

Newsletter on political analysis, political behavior, political communication, and political culture. The purpose of PARC is to encourage and facilitate scientific research on human behavior in political life.

Keywords: Politics (US), Human Behavior

Audience: Political Scientists, Political Analysts

Contact: Tom Bryde
kusftb@vms2.uni-c.dk

Details: Free

User Info: To Subscribe, send an e-mail message to the URL address below.

`mailto:kusftb@vms2.uni-c.dk`

Human Communications

CRTNet (Communication Research and Theory Network)

All topics related to human communications.

Keywords: Communications, Sociology, Human Communications

Audience: Sociologists, Psychologists, Therapists

`mailto:listserv@psuvm.bitnet`

Human Rights

Amnesty International

A site containing information about Amnesty International, an organization focused strictly and specifically on human rights around the world.

Keywords: Government, Human Rights, Politics (International), Activism

Sponsor: Amnesty International

Audience: Students, Activists

Contact: Catherine Hampton
ariel@netcom.com

`ftp://ftp.netcom.com/pub/ariel`

`http://www/human.rights/amnesty.international/ai.html`

dh.mujer

The primary Association for Progressive Communications conference for women and human rights issues throughout the world, contains news and announcements.

Keywords: Women's Issues, Feminism, Human Rights

Audience: Feminists, Activists

Contact: Debra Guzman
hrcoord@igc.apc.org

Details: Costs

User Info: Establish an account on the nearest APC node. Login, type c for conferences, then type go dh.mujer. For information on the nearest APC node, contact: APC International Secretariat IBASE E-mail: apcadmin@apc.org

A B C D E F G **H** I J K L M N O P Q R S T U V W X Y Z

A B C D E F G H I J K L M N O P Q R S T U V W X Y Z

Contact: Carlos Afonso (cafonso@ax.apc.org) or
APC North American Regional Office
E-mail: apcadmin@apc.org
Contact: Edie Farwell
(efarwell@igc.apc.org)

`gopher://gopher.telnet://igc.apc.org`

`http://igc.apc.org`

hr.women

A conference on human rights issues pertaining to women.

Keywords: Women's Issues, Feminists, Human Rights

Audience: Women, Feminists, Activists

Contact: Jillaine Smith
jillaine@igc.apc.org

Details: Costs

User Info: Establish an account on the nearest APC node. Login, type c for conferences, then type go hr.women. For information on the nearest APC node, contact: APC International Secretariat IBASE E-mail: apcadmin@apc.org

`telnet://igc.apc.org`

University of Colorado at Boulder Library

The library's holdings are large and wide-ranging and contain significant collections in many fields.

Keywords: Numismatics, Human Rights, Literature (Children's), Labor Archives, History (US)

Audience: Researchers, Students, General Public

Contact: Donna Pattee
pattee@spot.colorado.edu

Details: Free

Expect: Login; Send: Culine

`telnet:// culine.colorado.edu`

University of Texas at Austin Tarlton Law Library

The library's holdings are large and wide-ranging and contain significant collections in many fields.

Keywords: British Commonwealth Law, Constitutional Law, Law (International), Human Rights

Audience: Researchers, Students, General Public

Details: Free

Notes: Expect: Login, Send: Library

`telnet://tallons.law.utexas.edu`

Humanities

The English Server

A large and eclectic collection of humanities resources.

Keywords: Humanities, Academia, English, Popular Culture, Feminism

Sponsor: Carnegie Mellon University English Department, Pittsburgh, Pennsylvania, USA

Audience: General Public, University Students, Educators (College/University), Researchers (Humanities)

Profile: Contains archives of conventional humanities materials, such as historical documents and classic books in electronic form. Also offers more unusual and hard-to-find resources, particularly in the field of popular culture and media. Features access to many humanities and culture-related online journals such as Bad Subjects, FineArt Forum, and Postmodern Culture. Also has links to a wide variety of related Internet sites and resources.

Contact: Geoff Sauer
postmaster@english-server.hss.cmu.

`gopher://english-server.hss.cmu.edu`

`http://english-server.hss.cmu.edu/`

University of Toledo Library

The library's holdings are large and wide-ranging and contain significant collections in many fields.

Keywords: Business, Great Lakes Area, Humanities, International Relations, Psychology, Science

Audience: Researchers, Students, General Public

Details: Free

Notes: Expect: Enter one of the following commands . . . , Send: DIAL MVS; Expect: dialed to mvs ####; Send: UTMOST

`telnet://uofto1.utoledo.edu`

Virginia Commonwealth University Library

The library's holdings are large and wide-ranging and contain significant collections in many fields.

Keywords: Art, Biology, Humanities, Journalism, Music, Urban Planning

Audience: Researchers, Students, General Public

Details: Free

Notes: Expect: Login; Send: Opub

`telnet://vcuvm1.ucc.vcu.edu`

Humor

alt.callahans

A Usenet newsgroup providing information and discussion about Callahan's bar for puns and fellowship.

Keywords: Humor, Word Play

Audience: Punsters, Comedians

User Info: To Subscribe to this Usenet newsgroup, you need access to a newsreader.

`news:alt.calahans`

alt.fan.monty-python

A Usenet newsgroup providing an electronic fan club for those wacky Brits.

Keywords: Humor, Entertainment, Comedy, Satire

Audience: Monty Python Enthusiasts, General Public

User Info: To Subscribe to this Usenet newsgroup, you need access to a newsreader.

`news:alt.fan.monty-python`

alt.peeves

A Usenet newsgroup providing information and discussion about peeves, complaints, and whining.

Keywords: Humor, Comedy

Audience: General Public, Complainers

User Info: To Subscribe to this Usenet newsgroup, you need access to a newsreader.

`news:alt.peeves`

alt.religion.kibology

A Usenet newsgroup consisting of followers of a god named Kibo, who is, in fact, a human being living in Boston. This newsgroup is highly humorous and hardly religious.

Keywords: Satire, Humor, Religion

Audience: Kibologists

User Info: To Subscribe to this Usenet newsgroup, you need access to a newsreader.

`news:alt.religion.kibology`

alt.tasteless

A Usenet newsgroup providing information and discussion about tasteless jokes.

Keywords: Humor, Comedy

Audience: General Interest, Jokers

User Info: To Subscribe to this Usenet newsgroup, you need access to a newsreader.

`news:alt.tasteless`

rec.humor

A Usenet newsgroup providing information and discussion about jokes.

Keywords: Jokes, Humor

Audience: General Public, Jokers

User Info: To Subscribe to this Usenet newsgroup, you need access to a newsreader.

`news:rec.humor`

talk.bizarre

A Usenet newsgroup providing information and discussion about the unusual, the bizarre, and the curious.

Keywords: Humor

Audience: General Public

Details: Free

User Info: To Subscribe to this Usenet newsgroup, you need access to a newsreader.

`news:talk.bizarre`

Hungary

agora

A forum for Hungarian speakers to discuss a wide variety of subjects.

Keywords: Hungary

Audience: Hungarian Speakers

Contact: Zoli Fekete
fekete@bcvms.bc.edu,
agora@world.std.com

Details: Free

Notes: Inquiries and contributions to the list can be sent to the personal address of the contact above (place word AGORA in the subject field), or to the world.std.com address below (place word $SEGIT in the subject field).

`mailto:agora@world.std.com`

CEE Environmental Libraries Database

A directory of over 300 libraries and environmental information centers in Central Eastern Europe that specalize in, or maintain significant collections of information about, the environment, ecology, sustainable living, or conservation.

Keywords: Central Eastern Europe, Environment, Sustainable Living, Bulgaria, Czech Republic, Hungary, Romania, Slovakia, Poland.

Sponsor: The Wladyslaw Poniecki Charitable Foundation, Inc.

Audience: Environmentalists, Green Movement, Librarians, Community Builders, Sustainable Living Specialists.

Profile: This database is the product of an Environmental Training Project (ETP) that was funded in 1992 by the US Agency for International Development as a 5-year cooperative agreement with a consortium headed by the University of Minnesota (US AID Cooperative Agreement Number EUR-0041-A-002-2020). Other members of the consortium include the University of Pittsburgh's Center for Hazardous Materials Research, The Institute for Sustainable Communities, and the World Wildlife Fund. The Wladyslaw Poniecki Charitable Foundation, Inc., was a subcontractor to the World Wildlife Fund and published the Directory of Libraries and Environmental Information Centers in Central Eastern Europe: A Locator/Directory . This gopher database consists of an electronic version of the printed directory, subsequently modified and updated online. Access to the data is facilitated by a WAIS search engine which makes it possible to retrieve information about libraries, subject area specializations, personnel, and so on.

Contact: Doug Kahn, CEDAR
kahn@pan.cedar.univie.ac.at

`gopher://gopher.poniecki.berkeley.edu`

Hungarian Gopher-Hollosi Information Exchange (HIX)

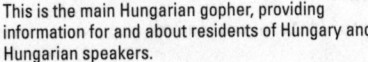

This is the main Hungarian gopher, providing information for and about residents of Hungary and Hungarian speakers.

Keywords: Hungary, Europe

Sponsor: Stanford University, Palo Alto, CA

Audience: Hungarian Internet Surfers

Contact: hollosi@andrea.standford.edu

Details: Free

`gopher://hix.elte.hu`

Hungary

This discussion list circulates timely information about Hungary.

Keywords: Hungary, Eastern Europe, News

Audience: Researchers, Observers, Political Scientists

Contact: Eric Dahlin
hcf2hung@iucsbuxa

Details: Free

User Info: To Subscribe to the list, send an e-mail message to the URL address shown below consisting of a single line reading:

SUB hungary YourFirstName YourLastName

`mailto:listserv@gwuvm.gwu.edu`

HungerWeb

HungerWeb

This web site focuses on the political, economic, agricultural, and ethical implications of world hunger.

Keywords: World Health, Activism

Sponsor: Oxfam

Audience: Activists, Financial Planners

Contact: Daniel Zalik
Daniel_Zalik@cs.brown.edu

Details: Free

`http://www.hunger.brown.edu/oxfam`

Hunt (Leigh)

The University of Iowa Libraries

The library's holdings are large and wide-ranging and contain significant collections in many fields.

Keywords: Hunt (Leigh), Native American Studies, Typography, Railroads, Cartoons, French Revolution, NASA, Hydraulics

Audience: General Public, Researchers, Librarians, Document Delivery Professionals

Details: Free

Send <RETURN>to display a menu of available systems. Type 1 for OASIS access and press <RETURN>to display the Welcome to OASIS screen.

`telnet://oasis.uiowa.edu`

Husted (Margaret, Culinary Collections of)

University of Denver Library

The library's holdings are large and wide-ranging and contain significant collections in many fields.

Keywords: Folklore Collection, Husted (Margaret, Culinary Collection of)

Audience: Researchers, Students, General Public

Contact: Bob Stocker
bstocker@ducair.bitnet

Details: Free

Notes: Expect: Login; Send: Atdu

`telnet://du.edu`

A B C D E F G **H** I J K L M N O P Q R S T U V W X Y Z

A B C D E F G H I J K L M N O P Q R S T U V W X Y Z

Hydraulics

The University of Iowa Libraries

The library's holdings are large and wide-ranging and contain significant collections in many fields.

Keywords: Hunt (Leigh), Native American Studies, Typography, Railroads, Cartoons, French Revolution, NASA, Hydraulics

Audience: General Public, Researchers, Librarians, Document Delivery Professionals

Details: Free

Send <RETURN>to display a menu of available systems. Type 1 for OASIS access and press <RETURN>to display the Welcome to OASIS screen.

`telnet://oasis.uiowa.edu`

HypArt

HypArt

This is the site of an International collaborative art project.

Keywords: This is the site of an International collaborative art project.

Sponsor: University of Hamburg

Audience: Artists, Designers

Contact: rosenfeld@rrz.uni-hamburg.de

Details: Free

`http://rzsun01.rrz.uni-hamburg.de/ cgi-bin/HypArt.sh`

Hyperfiction

alt.hypertext

A Usenet newsgroup devoted to hyperfiction and hypertext documents. Postings range from information about and reviews of both recent hyperfiction and recent nonfiction hypertext documents, to information and/or reviews of software for creating hypertext.

Keywords: Literature (General), Hyperfiction, Hypertext

Audience: General Public, Writers, Computer Programmers

Details: Free

User Info: To subscribe to this Usenet newsgroup, you need access to a newsreader.

`news:alt.hypertext`

Art Com Magazine

A newsletter about art and technology (subjects covered include robotics, artists' software, hyperfiction) that is guest-edited by individual artists.

Keywords: Computer Art, Literature (Contemporary), Technology, Hyperfiction

Sponsor: Art Com Electronic Network

Audience: Artists, Writers

Contact: Fred Truck
fjt@well.sf.ca.us

User Info: To participate in a conference on the WELL, you must first establish an account on the WELL. To do so, start by typing: telnet://well.sf.ca.us

`mailto:artcomtv@well.sf.ca.us`

Hypermedia

Hypermedia/Internet

A guide to hypermedia and the Internet.

Keywords: Internet, Group Communications, Hypermedia

Sponsor: Australian National University

Audience: Internet Surfers

Contact: David Geoffrey Green
David.Green@anu.edu.au

Details: Free

`http:// life.anu.edu.au`

Hypertext

alt.hypertext

A Usenet newsgroup devoted to hyperfiction and hypertext documents. Postings range from information about and reviews of both recent hyperfiction and recent nonfiction hypertext documents, to information and/or reviews of software for creating hypertext.

Keywords: Literature (General), Hyperfiction, Hypertext

Audience: General Public, Writers, Computer Programmers

Details: Free

User Info: To subscribe to this Usenet newsgroup, you need access to a newsreader.

`news:alt.hypertext`

HYTELNET

HYTELNET

Keywords: Computer Systems, Libraries, Shareware

Audience: General Audience

Profile: HYTELNET is a guide to library catalogs all over the world

Contact: Peter Scott
aa375@freenet.carleton.ca

Details: Free

Notes: HYTELNET is in English, but the interface to some international

`gopher://gopher.yale.edu/11/libraries`

I.S.P.O.B. Bulletin YSSTI (Yugoslav System for Scientific and Technology Information)

I.S.P.O.B. Bulletin YSSTI (Yugoslav System for Scientific and Technology Information)

The participants in this system can exchange news about the operations and development of YSSTI.

Keywords: Technology, Yugoslavia, Science

Sponsor: Institute of Information Sciences, University of Maribor, Yugoslavia

Audience: Technology Professionals, Librarians

Contact: Davor Sostaric
davor%rcum@yubgef51.bitnet

User Info: Subscribe by sending an e-mail with a single line containing:

SUBSCRIBE P.O.B. to addresses POB%RCUM@YUBGEF51.bitnet

mailto:pob%rcum@yubgef51.bitnet

IBM

C-IBM-370

The C on IBM mainframes mailing list is a place to discuss aspects of using the C programming language on s/370-architecture computers—especially under IBM's operating systems for that environment.

Keywords: C Language, Programming Languages, IBM

Audience: IBM Users, Computer Users, Computer Programmers

Contact: David Wolfskill
C-IBM-370-request@dhw68k.cts.com

Details: Free

User Info: To subscribe to the list, send an e-mail message requesting a subscription to the URL address below.

To send a message to the entire list, address it to: C-IBM-370@dhw68k.cts.com

mailto:C-IBM-370-request@dhw68k.cts.com

comp.sys.ibm.pc

A Usenet newsgroup providing information and discussion about the IBM PC computer. There are many categories within this group.

Keywords: Computer Systems, IBM

Audience: Computer Users, IBM Users

User Info: To subscribe to this Usenet newsgroup, you need access to a newsreader.

news:comp.sys.ibm.pc

PAGEMAKER

The PageMaker ListServ is dedicated to the discussion of desktop publishing in general, with emphasis on the use of Aldus PageMaker. The list discusses PageMaker's use in both the PC and Macintosh realms. The list also maintains an extensive archive of help files that are extremely useful for the modern desktop publisher.

Keywords: Desktop Publishing, Aldus Pagemaker, Macintosh

Audience: Desktop Publishers, Computer Users

Contact: Geoff Peters
gwp@cs.purdue.edu

Details: Free

User Info: To subscribe to the list, send an e-mail message to the URL address shown below, consisting of a single line reading:

SUB pagemaker YourFirstName YourLastName.

To send a message to the entire list, address it to: gwp@cs.purdue.edu

mailto:listserv@cs.purdue.edu

ICC British Company Directory

ICC British Company Directory

The database is a comprehensive reference source for companies registered in England, Wales, Scotland, and Northern Ireland.

Keywords: United Kingdom, Business (British)

Sponsor: ICC Information Group Ltd., London, UK

Audience: Business Professionals, Business Analysts

Profile: The database contains a record for each company included on the Index of Companies maintained by the official Companies Registration Offices in the UK. Companies that have been dissolved since 1968 are also listed. The total number of records in the ICC British Company Directory is over 2 million. Reference data includes name, registered number, registered address, issued and nominal-share capital, dates of incorporation and document filings at the Companies Registration Office. Document filings include latest filed annual accounts and annual returns, changes of directors or registered address, special resolutions, mergers of public (PLC) companies, winding-up orders, appointment of liquidators, and so on.

Contact: Dialog in the US at (800) 334-2564; Dialog internationally at country-specific locations.

User Info: To subscribe, contact Dialog directly.

Notes: Coverage: Current; updated weekly.

`telnet://dialog.com`

Ice Hockey

Funet Sports Information

An FTP archive of information on various sports with links to the archive at wuarchive.wustl.edu.

Keywords: Sports, Professional Sports, Ice Hockey, Motor Racing, NFL, NHL, NBA, MLB

Sponsor: Finnish Academic and Research Network (FUNET)

Audience: Sports Enthusiasts

Profile: A fairly extensive archive of information on both American (NBA, MLB, NHL, NFL) and worldwide sports (soccer, ice hockey, motor racing, and so on). Includes FAQs for various sports, statistics, pictures, and some sports games for the PC.

Contact: Jari Pullinen sports-adm@nic.funet.fi

Details: Free, Images

`gopher://ftp.funet.fi/pub/sports`

OlymPuck

★

This list is for the discussion of Olympic ice hockey. Discussions concerning players, coaches, teams, and games are welcome and encouraged. Related topics, such as the interaction between the Olympic competition and college or NHL hockey, are also discussed.

Keywords: Olympics, Ice Hockey, NHL

Audience: Ice Hockey Players, Olympics Enthusiasts, Ice Hockey Fans

Details: Free

User Info: To subscribe to the list, send an e-mail message to the URL address below, consisting of a single line reading:

SUB olympuck YourFirstName YourLastName

To send a message to the entire list, address it to: olympuck@maine.maine.edu

`mailto:listserv@ maine.maine.edu`

ICGEBnet

ICGEBnet

★★★

This is the information server of the International Centre for Genetic Engineering and Molecular Biology (ICGEB), Trieste, Italy.

Keywords: Molecular Biology, Biotechnology, Italy, Europe

Audience: Molecular Biotechnologists, Molecular Biologists

Profile: The primary purpose of the ICGEB computer resource is to disseminate the best of currently available computational technology to the molecular biologists of the ICGEB research community.

Contact: postmaster@icgeb.trieste.it

Details: Free

`gopher://icgeb.trieste.it`

Icon Programming Language

Icon-group

★

Discussion of topics related to the Icon programming language

Keywords: Icon Programming Language, Programming Language String Processing

Audience: Icon Programmers, Computer Programmers

Profile: Icon is a high-level, general purpose programming language emphazing string and structure processing. Topics include programming techniques, theoretical aspects, Icon in relation to other languages, applications of Icon, implementation issues, porting, and bugs.

Contact: Bill Mitchell (Internet) whm@arizona.edu

Details: Free

User Info: To subscribe to the list, send an e-mail message requesting a subscription to the URL address below.

`mailto:Icon-group-request@arizona.edu.`

ICTP (International Centre for Theoretical Physics)

ICTP (International Centre for Theoretical Physics)

★★★

ICTP's gopher disseminates information regarding the many scientific activities carried out at ICTP (Trieste, Italy). Information is also provided on the scientific publications, courses, and other services offered by ICS (International Centre for Science and High Technology) and TWAS (Third World Academy of Sciences) at Trieste.

Keywords: Theoretical Physics, Italy, Europe, Physics

Audience: Physicists

Profile: Topics include programming techniques, theoretical aspects, Icon in relation to other languages, applications of Icon, implementation issues, porting, and bugs.

Contact: admin@ictp.trieste.it

Details: Free

`gopher://gopher.ictp.trieste.it`

`http://gopher.ictp.trieste.it`

IEEE-L

IEEE-L

★

Serves as a forum for all IEEE student branch officers and members.

Keywords: Engineering, Electrical Engineering

Audience: Engineers, Electrical Engineers, Students

Details: Free

User Info: To subscribe to the list, send an e-mail message to the URL address below, consisting of a single line reading:

SUB ieee-l YourFirstName YourLastName.

To send a message to the entire list, address it to: iee-l@bingvmb.cc.binghamton.edu

`mailto:listserv@bingvmb.cc.binghamton.edu`

IHOUSE-L International Voice Newsletter Prototype List

IHOUSE-L International Voice Newsletter Prototype List

★

Contains articles of interest to international students and scholars, professors, administrators, and other interested staff and groups (on- and off-campus).

Keywords: International Visitors, Washington University

Sponsor: International Office of Washington University, St. Louis MO

Audience: International Students

Contact: Doyle Cozadd c73221dc@wuvmdwastl.edu

Details: Free

User Info: To subscribe, send an e-mail message to the address below, consisting of a single line reading:

SUB ihousel@Your First Name Your Last Name

To send a message to the entire list, Address it to: ihouse-l@wnvmd 8tl.con

`mailto:listserv@wuvmd.wustl.edu`

IHS International Standards and Specifications

IHS International Standards and Specifications

The database contains references to industry standards, and military and federal specifications and standards covering all aspects of engineering and related disciplines.

Keywords: Engineering, Military Specifications, Federal Standards

Sponsor: Information Handling Services, Englewood, CO, US

Audience: Engineers, Military Hisyorians, Lawyers, Business Professionals

Profile: The file includes 90 percent of the world's most referenced standards from over 70 domestic, foreign, and international standardizing bodies. Also included is the world's largest commercially available collection of unclassified active and historical US military and federal specifications and standards.

Contact: Dialog in the US at (800) 334-2564; Dialog internationally at country-specific locations.

User Info: To subscribe, contact Dialog directly.

Notes: Coverage: Current; updated weekly for MILSPECS, every two months.

`telnet://dialog.com`

Illinois

Illinois Legislation

This directory contains several Illinois Department of Nuclear Safety Statues and Regulations.

Keywords: Nuclear Safety, Law, Illinois

Audience: Lawyers, General Public, Activists

Details: Free

`gopher://wiretap.spies.com`

Image Processing

Geoscience at Texas A&M University

General server with info on all aspects of GIS and remote sensing, especially GPS.

Keywords: GIS, Image Processing, Remote Sensing, Geoscience, GPS

Sponsor: Texas A&M University - Department of Agricultural Engineering

Audience: Researchers, GIS and IP professionals, Students

Contact: Hal Mueller
hmueller@diamond.tamu.edu

Details: Free, Images

Notes: Contains links to related Univeristy of Texas gophers and WWW servers.

`http://ageninfo.tamu.edu/geoscience.html`

Internet GIS and RS Information Sites

This document contains a lengthy listing of GIS and remote sensing sites on the Internet.

Keywords: GIS, Remote Sensing, Image Processing, Geography

Sponsor: Queen's University Department of Geography

Audience: Researchers, General Public

Contact: Michael McDermott
mcdermom@gisdog.gis.queensu.ca

Details: Free

Notes: ASCII version also available from the same FTP site.

`ftp://gis.queensu.ca/pub/gis/docs/gissites.html`

The University of Minnesota Remote Sensing Lab

General information about remote sensing and GIS.

Keywords: GIS, Remote Sensing, Image Processing

Sponsor: University of Minnesota, Department of Forest Resources

Audience: Researchers, GIS and IP professionals, Students

Profile: The RSL server contains information regarding all aspects of image process and GIS. Some features include: home of the GIS Jobs Clearinghouse, archives of ESRI-L, IMAGRS-L, and TGIS-L, and the NBS CPSU WWW server.

Contact: Stephen Lime
sdlime@torpedo.forestry.umn.edu

Details: Free, Images

Notes: The RSL also maintains a companion gopher server and anonymous FTP site for the GIS Jobs Clearinghouse.

`http://walleye.forestry.umn.edu/0/www/main.html`

Images from Various Sources

Images from Various Sources

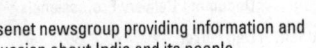

This site serves as a link to some 35 image archives throughout the world. A wide variety of images is available, with a particularly large number of weather, geological, and biological collections from government and private sources.

Keywords: Computer Graphics, Photography, Art

Sponsor: The University of Alaska

Audience: General Public

Contact: Douglas Toelle
sxinfo@orca.alaska.edu

Details: Free, Images

The ancient science of life that originated in India. This mailing list provides information about ayurveda, such as lectures, workshops, and stores that sell ayurvedic herbs.

Keywords: Spirituality, Ayurveda, India

Audience: General Public, Religion Students

Contact: ayurveda-request@netcom.com

Details: Free

User Info: To subscribe to the list, send an e-mail message requesting a subscription to the URL address below.

To send a message to the entire list, address it to: ayurveda@netcom.com

`mailto:ayurveda-request@netcom.com`

soc.culture.indian

A Usenet newsgroup providing information and discussion about India and its people.

Keywords: India, Sociology

Audience: Sociologists, Students

Details: Free

User Info: To subscribe to this Usenet newsgroup, you need access to a newsreader.

`news:soc.culture.indian`

Indiana

Eerie, Indiana

The list is for the discussion of the critically acclaimed but short-lived TV series "Eerie, Indiana," which originally aired on NBC in 1991-1992 and is now distributed internationally.

Keywords: Eerie, Indiana

Audience: Television Viewers

Contact: Corey Kir
owner-eerie-indiana@sfu.ca

A B C D E F G H I J K L M N O P Q R S T U V W X Y Z

A
B
C
D
E
F
G
H
I
J
K
L
M
N
O
P
Q
R
S
T
U
V
W
X
Y
Z

Details: Free

User Info: To subscribe to the list, send an e-mail message requesting a subscription to the URL address below.

To send a message to the entire list, address it to: owner-eerie-indiana@sfu.ca

```
mailto:owner-eerie-indiana@sfu.ca
```

Indiana University Libraries

The library's holdings are large and wide-ranging and contain significant collections in many fields.

Keywords: Literature (English), Literature (American), 1640-Present, British Plays (19th-C.), Western Americana, Railway History, Aristotle (Texts of), Lafayette (Marquis de), Handel (G.F.), Austrian History, Antiquarian Books, Rare Books, French Opera (19th-C.), Drama (British),

Audience: General Public, Researchers, Librarians, Historians

Details: Free

Expect: User ID prompt, Send: GUEST

```
telnet://iuis.ucs.indiana.edu
```

Purdue University Library

The library's holdings are large and wide-ranging. They contain significant collections in many fields.

Keywords: Economics (History of), Literature (English), Literature (American), Indiana, Rogers (Bruce), Engineering (History of), Aviation, Earth Science, Atmospheric Science, Consumer Science, Family Science, Chemistry (History of), Physics, Veterinary Science

Audience: General Public, Researchers, Librarians, Document Delivery Professionals

Contact: Dan Ferrer
dan@asterix.lib.purdue.edu

Details: Free

Expect: User ID prompt, Send: GUEST

```
telnet://lib.cc.purdue.edu
```

Indigenous People

Indigenous

A collection of various online resources about indigenous peoples.

Keywords: Indigenous Peoples, Anthropology

Audience: Reseachers, Anthropologists, Native Americans

Details: Free

```
ftp://netcom.com
```

NativeNet

Provides information about and discusses issues relating to indigenous people around the world, including threats to their cultures and habitats (e.g. rainforests).

Keywords: Indigenous People, Environment, Anthroplogy

Audience: Anthropologists, Environmentalists, Indigenous People

Contact: Gary S. Trujillo
gst@gnosys.svle.ma.us

Details: Free

User Info: To subscribe to the list, send an e-mail message requesting a subscription to the URL address below.

```
mailto:gst@gnosys.svle.ma.us
```

Industry

1994 Federal Budget (Canada)

This site offers full-text of Canada's federal budget. Also has a wealth of information on Canadian industry and industrial policy, including Provincial and Sectorial GATT opportunities and briefs from the Information Highway Advisory Council.

Keywords: Canada, Government (International), Industry, Foreign Trade

Sponsor: Industry Canada, Canada

Audience: Canadians, Government Officials, Businesspeople, Researchers

Contact: Tyson Macaulay
tyson@debra.dgbt.doc.ca

```
gopher://debra.dgbt.doc.ca/industry
canada documents/isc.news.releases
```

MARKET (Markets and Industries News and Information)

The Markets and Industries News and Information (MARKET) library contains sources covering developments in a wide variety of markets and industries.

Keywords: News, Analysis, Industry, Marketing

Audience: Businesspeople, Researchers

Profile: The MARKET library contains a wide selection of sources ranging from trade and industry sources to InvestextR industry reports to company profiles. To round out the offering, MARKET also covers advertising, marketing, public opinion polls, market research, public relations, sales and selling, promotions, consumer attitudes, trends and behaviors, demographics, product announcements, and product reviews. In addition, Predicasts Overview of Markets and Technology (PROMT), Marketing and Advertising Reference

Service (MARS), US and International Forecast Databases (UFRCST and IFRCST), and the US Time Series (USTIME), all from Information Access Company, are available.

Contact: Mead New Sales Group at (800) 227-4908 or (513) 859-5398 inside the US, or (513) 865-7981 for all inquiries outside the US.

User Info: To subscribe, contact Mead directly.

To examine the Nexis user guide, you can access it at the ftp site of the University of Texas at Austin at the URL address: ftp://ftp.cc.utexas.edu

The files are in: /pub/ref-services/LEXIS

```
telnet://nex.meaddata.com
```

```
http://www.meaddata.com
```

Martin Marietta Energy Systems Gopher

Information on Martin Marietta's energy projects and technologies for both government and commercial applications.

Keywords: Technology, Energy, Industry

Sponsor: Martin Marietta

Audience: Businesspeople, Entrepreneurs, Manufactures, Energy Researchers, Technology Enthusiasts

Profile: This gopher contains a list of technologies currently being developed at Martin Marietta, as well as detailing facilities available to university, government, and commercial researchers. Also includes updates on employment openings, and a list of current publications.

Contact: gopher@ornl.gov

```
gopher://gopher.ornl.gov
```

```
http://www.ornl.gov/mmes.html
```

Tecbase- Sandia National Laboratory

A catalog of technologies, developed at Sandia National Laboratories, which have potential commercial applications.

Keywords: Technology, Information Technology, Industry

Sponsor: Sandia National Laboratory

Audience: Business People, Entrepreneurs, Manufactures, Technicians

Contact: TechTransfer@ccsmtp.sandia.gov

```
gopher://somnet.sandia.gov/Tecbase
```

The University of Illinois at Chicago Library

The library's holdings are large and wide-ranging and contain significant collections in many fields.

Keywords: Health Science, Chicago, Industry, Slavery, Abolitionism, Roosevelt (Franklin D.)

Audience: General Public, Researchers, Librarians, Document Delivery Professionals

Details: Free

Expect: introductory screen, Send: Clear key; Expect: UIC flame screen, Send: Enter key; Expect: Logon screen, Send: DIAL PVM; Expect: PVM (Passthru) screen, Send: Type: Move cursor to NOTIS and press Enter key Response: One line message about port in use Type: Enter key

`telnet://uicvm.uic.edu`

University of Wisconsin at Platteville Library

The library's holdings are large and wide-ranging and contain significant collections in many fields.

Keywords: Business, Industry

Audience: Researchers, Students, General Public

Details: Free

Expect: Login, Send: Lib; Expect: vDIAL Prompt, Send: Library

`telnet://137.104.128.44`

Infectious Diseases

National Institute for Allergy & Infectious Disease (NIAID)

This is a resource into other databases for searching many medical fields, such as the NIAID network userlist or a databank of AIDS-related information.

Keywords: Medicine, Infectious Diseases, Allergies

Sponsor: NIAID

Audience: Health-care Professionals, Researchers, Students

Contact: Brent Sessions
sessions@odie.niaid.nih.gov

Details: Free

`gopher://gopher.niaid.nih.gov/1`

Infiniti Automobiles

nissan

Discusses Nissan and Infiniti automobiles, with the exception of the Sentra SE-R, NX2000, and G20, which are served by the se-r list.

Keywords: Nissan Automobiles, Infiniti Automobiles

Audience: Nissan Owners, Nissan Enthusiasts

Contact: Rich Siegel
nissan-request@world.std.com

Details: Free

User Info: To subscribe to the list, send an e-mail message requesting a subscription to the URL address below.

To send a message to the entire list, address it to: nissan@world.std.com

`mailto:nissan-request@world.std.com`

info-Ada

info-Ada

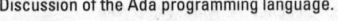

Discussion of the Ada programming language.

Keywords: Programming, Ada (Programming Language)

Audience: Programmers

Contact: Karl A. Nyberg
Karl@grebyn.com

Details: Free

User Info: To subscribe to the list, send an e-mail message requesting a subscription to the URL address below.

`mailto:info-Ada-request@sei.cmu.edu`

info-C

info-C

Discussions about C programming and the C programming language.

Keywords: Programming, C (Programming Language)

Audience: Programmers

Contact: Mark Plotnick
info-C-request@research.att.com

Details: Free

User Info: To subscribe to the list, send an e-mail message requesting a subscription to the URL address below.

`mailto:info-C-request@research.att.com`

info-GNU-MSDOS

info-GNU-MSDOS

This electronic conference is for the GNUISH MS-DOS Development Group.

Keywords: Shareware, Freeware, MS-DOS Computers

Audience: MS-DOS Users, GNUISH MS-DOS Developers

Contact: David J. Camp
david@wubios.wustl.edu

Details: Free

User Info: To subscribe to the list, send an e-mail message to the URL address below, consisting of a single line reading:

SUB info-GNU-MSDOS YourFirstName YourLastName

`mailto:listserv@wugate.wustl.edu`

info-M2

info-M2

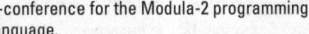

E-conference for the Modula-2 programming language.

Keywords: Programming Languages, Modula-2 (Programming Language)

Audience: Programmers

Contact: Thomas Habernoll
postmast@ucf1vm.cc.ucf.edu (USA);
habernol@tubvm.cs.tu-berlin.de (Europe)

Details: Free

User Info: To subscribe to the list, send an e-mail message to the URL address below, consisting of a single line reading:

SUB info-M2 YourFirstName YourLastName

To send a message to the entire list, address it to: info-M2@ucf1vm.cc.ucf.edu

`mailto:listserv@ucf1vm.cc.ucf.edu`

info-Pascal

info-Pascal

Discussions of any Pascal implementation, from mainframe to micro, for Pascal program users.

Keywords: Programming, Pascal

Audience: Pascal Programmers, Pascal Users

Contact: Hernan Lobos *Mitzio*
hlobos@utfsm.bitnet

A B C D E F G H I J K L M N O P Q R S T U V W X Y Z

Details: Free

User Info: To subscribe to the list, send an e-mail message requesting a subscription to the URL address below

`info-Pascal@brl.mil`

Info-South (Latin American News)

Info-South (Latin American News)

The database provides citations and abstracts of materials relating to contemporary economic, political, and social issues in Latin America.

Keywords: International News, Economics, International Politics, Latin America

Sponsor: University of Miami, Coral Gables, FL, US

Audience: General Public

Profile: Coverage includes a wide range of topics assessing the current situation in Latin America.

Contact: Dialog in the US at (800) 334-2564; Dialog internationally at country-specific locations.

User Info: To subscribe, contact Dialog directly.

Notes: Coverage: 1988 to the present; updated weekly.

`telnet://dialog.com`

Info-tandem

Info-tandem

Info-tandem is an e-mail list for users of systems from Tandem Computers, Inc.

Keywords: Computer Systems, Tandem Computers

Audience: Programmers, Analysts, Tandem Computer Users

Contact: Scott Hazen Mueller scott@zorch.sf-bay.org

Details: Free

User Info: To subscribe to the list, send an e-mail message requesting

`mailto:info-tandem-request@zorch.sf-bay.org`

info-UNIX

info-UNIX

Info-UNIX is intended for Question/Answer discussion, where "novice" system administrators

information and discussion about the gopher information search tool.

Keywords: Gopher, Internet Reference, Information Retrieval

Audience: Internet Surfers

User Info: To subscribe to this Usenet newsgroup, you need access to a newsreader.

`news:comp.infosystems.gopher`

Information Retrieval

comp.infosystems.wais

A Usenet newsgroup providing information and discussion about the WAIS full-text search tool.

Keywords: WAIS, Internet Reference, Information Retrieval

Audience: Internet Surfers

User Info: To subscribe to this Usenet newsgroup, you need access to a newsreader.

`news:comp.infosystems.wais`

comp.infosystems.www

A Usenet newsgroup providing information and discussion about the World Wide Web.

Keywords: WWW, Internet Reference, Information Retrieval

Audience: Internet Surfers

User Info: To subscribe to this Usenet newsgroup, you need access to a newsreader.

`news:comp.infosystems.www`

Computer-Mediated Marketing Environments

A web site devoted to research aimed at understanding the ways in which computer-mediated marketing environments (CMEs), especially the Internet, are revolutionizing the way firms conduct business.

Keywords: WWW, Information Retrieval, Internet, Marketing, Business

Sponsor: Vanderbilt University, Owen Graduate School of Management, Nashville, Tennessee, USA

Audience: General Public, Entrepeneurs, Financial Planners, Marketers

Contact: Donna Hoffman, Tom Novak hoffman@colette.ogsm.vanderbilt.edu, novak@moe.ogsm.vanderbilt.edu

`http://colette.ogsm.vanderbilt.edu`

CSORG (Clearinghouse for Subject-Oriented Internet Resource Guides)

The goal of CSORG is to collect and make widely available guides to Internet resources that are subject-oriented. These guides are produced by members of the Internet community and by SILS students who participate in the Internet Resource Discovery project.

Keywords: WWW, Information Retrieval, Internet

Sponsor: University of Michigan, School of Information and Library Studies, Michigan, USA

Audience: Reseachers, Students, General Public

Contact: Louis Rosenfeld i-guides@umich.edu

`gopher://una.hh.lib.umich.edu/11/inetdirs`

DIMUND

DIMUND (Document Image Understanding) is an Internet information retrieval service.

Keywords: Internet, Information Retrieval, DIMUND, Documents

Sponsor: Document Processing Group, University of Maryland

Audience: Internet Surfers

Contact: gopher@dimund.cfar.umd.edu

Details: Free

`gopher:// dimund.umd.edu`

DIMUND FTP

DIMUND (Document Image Understanding) information service FTP archives. Provides access to selected documents.

Keywords: Internet, Information Retrieval, DIMUND, Documents

Sponsor: Document Processing Group, University of Maryland

Audience: Internet Surfers

Contact: gopher@dimund.cfar.umd.edu

Details: Free

`ftp://dimund.umd.edu`

Doc Center

A hard-copy document-delivery service for government and industry specifications and standards.

Keywords: Internet, Information Retrieval

Audience: Internet Surfers, Document Delivery Professionals

Details: Costs

`http://www.service.com/doccenter/home.html`

EINet Galaxy

EINet Galaxy is a guide to world-wide information and services. It includes public information as well as commercial information and services provided by EINet customers and affiliates. The information is organized by topic, and can be searched.

Keywords: WWW, Information Retrieval, Internet

Sponsor: Microelectronic and Computer Technology Corporation (MCC)

Audience: Reseachers, Students

Contact: Wayne Allen, Bruce Speyer WA@EINet.net, Speyer@EINet.net

`http://galaxy.einet.net/galaxy.html`

Finding Resources on the Internet

A collection of help files introducing the new user to Internet utilities and resources.

Keywords: Internet Reference, Information Retrieval

Sponsor: Proper Publishing

Audience: Internet Surfers

Contact: info@proper.com

`gopher://proper.com`

HTML FAQ

Common questions and answers about HTML (Hypertext Markup Language). The FAQ covers the practices of creating new documents specifically for the WWW format, as well as transforming existing materials into WWW documents.

Keywords: WWW, Internet Reference, Information Retrieval

Audience: Students, Computer Scientists, Researchers

Contact: Iain O'Cain ec@umcc.umich.edu

`http://www.umcc.umich.edu/~ec/www/html_faq.html`

Internet Libraries (Gopher)

The site maintains the most current possible list of all library catalogs accessible on the Internet.

Keywords: Libraries, Databases, Internet, Information Retrieval

Audience: Reseacher, Students, Librarians

Contact: Gopherlib gopherlib@gopher.yale.edu

`gopher://yaleinfo.yale.edu`

Internet Multicasting

Answers to frequently asked questions (FAQs) about the Internet Multicasting Service.

Keywords: Internet, Information Retrieval

Audience: Internet Surfers

Details: Free, Sound files available.
Include "send FAQ" in the e-mail.

`mailto: info@radio.com`

Internet Sound

Internet Sound contains various documents and programs regarding sound.

Keywords: Internet, Information Retrieval

Audience: Internet Surfers

Contact: Guido van Rossum ftp://ftp.cwi.nl/pub/audio/INDEX ftp://ftp.cwi.nl/pub/audio/index.html

Details: Free, Sound files available.
The index is: pub/audio/INDEX

`ftp://ftp.cwi.nl`

Internet Tools HTML

An HTML version of a list summarizing Internet tools for network information retrieval (NIR) and computer-mediated communication (CMC) forums; it is useful in a WWW server.

Keywords: Internet Tools, Information Retrieval

Audience: Internet Surfers

Contact: John December decemj@rpi.edu

Details: Free
Files are located in pub/communications. Read the internet-tools.readme first.

`ftp://ftp.rpi.edu`

Investigators and Detectives

This resource provides information files for individuals involved with investigative research, as well as a free monthly newsletter.

Keywords: Detectives, Crime, Information Retrieval, Security

Audience: Investigators, Detectives, Information Brokers, General Public

Profile: Investigators and Detectives provides access to information covering topics such as private investigative research, strategies, sources, the art and science of investigating, theft deterrents, and electronic PI schematics and plans. Also offers a free sample of a newsletter covering various topics of interest to Private Investigators, such as techniques and strategies, security, and tracing.

Contact: Mike Enlow menlow@Intec.win.net, michael@enlow.com

Details: Inside Secrets.

`mailto:info@enlow.com`

Library Special

Library Special collections on the Internet.

Keywords: Internet, Information Retrieval

Audience: Internet Surfers

Details: Free

`ftp://dla.ucop.edu/pub`

`http://dla.ucop.edu`

LOCIS (LIBRARY Of CONGRESS INFORMATION SYSTEM)

The Library of Congress (LC) telnet service is a Campus-Wide Information System that combines the vast collection of information available about the Library, with easy access to diverse electronic resources over the Internet. Its goal is to serve the staff of the LC, as well as the U.S. Congress and constituents throughout the world.

Keywords: Information Retrieval, Libraries

Sponsor: Library of Congress, Washington, D.C., USA

Audience: Reseachers, Students, Librarians

Contact: LC MARVEL Design Team lcmarvel@loc.gov

Notes: The Library of Congress (LC) Machine-Assisted Realization of the Virtual Electronic Library (MARVEL) also exists as a gopher site: gopher://marvel.loc.gov

`telnet://locis.loc.gov`

Multicast Backbone

Live audio and video multicast virtual network on top of the Internet.

Keywords: Internet, Information Retrieval

Audience: Internet Surfers

Details: Free, Sound files available.

`ftp://venera.isi.edu`

`http://venera.isi.edu`

Netfind

Netfind is a way of finding Internet e-mail addresses.

Keywords: WWW, Information Retrieval, E-mail

Sponsor: Emory University, Georgia, USA

Audience: Reseachers, Students, General Public

Profile: This service relies on common but not universal programs, and thus may not find some people with valid addresses. The most foolproof way of finding someone's e-mail address remains to call them on the phone and ask. All Netfind sites are functionally equivalent.

A
B
C
D
E
F
G
H
I
J
K
L
M
N
O
P
Q
R
S
T
U
V
W
X
Y
Z

Multiple ones are listed here in case some are overloaded or down with technical problems.

Contact: Netfind Help
schwartz@cs.colorado.edu

`gopher://emoryu1.cc.emory.edu/11/`
`internet/General/netfind`

NIR Archives

Archives of the NIR (Networked Information Retrieval) service.

Keywords: Internet, Information Retrieval

Audience: Internet Surfers

Details: Free

Files are in: pub/lists/nir

`ftp:// mailbase.ac.uk`

NIR Gopher

The gopher for the NIR (Networked Information Retrieval) service.

Keywords: Internet, Information Retrieval, NIR

Audience: Internet Surfers

Details: Free

`gopher:// mailbase.ac.auk /11/lists-`
`k-o/nic`

Retrieval Success

Succesfull stories of using the Internet for reference. In each case, a librarian used Internet resources to answer reference questions. In many cases, particularly for the smaller libraries, the Internet provided information that would otherwise have been inaccessible.

Keywords: Internet, Information Retrieval

Audience: Internet Surfers

Contact: Karen Schneider
kgs@panix.com

Details: Free

File is: pub/lists/unite/files/internet-stories.txt

`ftp://mailbase.ac.uk`

Searching Gopherspace with Veronica

A resource which conducts Veronica searches over restricted areas of the Internet.

Keywords: WWW, Information Retrieval, Internet

Audience: Reseachers, Students, General Public

`gopher://gopher.well.sf.ca.us/11/`
`outbound/veronica.search`

The InterNIC Home Page

This is the home page for the InterNIC networking organization.

Keywords: WWW, Information Retrieval, Computer Science, Internet Resources

Sponsor: National Science Foundation, USA

Audience: Reseachers, Students, General Public

Profile: The InterNIC is a collaborative project of three organizations, which work together to offer the Internet community a full scope of network information services. These services include providing information about accessing and using the Internet, assistance in locating resources on the network, and registering network components for Internet connectivity. The overall goal of the InterNIC is to make networking and networked information more easily accessible to researchers, educators, and the general public. The term InterNIC signifies cooperation between Network Information Centers, or NICS.

Contact: InfoGuide
guide@internic.net

Details: InterNIC signifies cooperation between Network Information Centers

`http://www.internic.net`

The Scout Report

The Scout Report is a weekly publication offered by InterNIC Information Services to the Internet community as a fast, convenient way to stay informed on network activities.

Keywords: WWW, Information Retrieval, Internet, Computer Networking

Sponsor: National Science Foundation, USA

Audience: Researchers, Students, General Public

Profile: The purpose of this resource is to combine in one place the highlights of new resource announcements and other news that occurred on the Internet during the previous week. The Report is released every Friday. Categories included each week will vary depending on content, and the report will evolve with time and with input from the networking community.

Contact: InfoGuide
scout@is.internic.net
guide@is.internic.net

`http://www.internic.net/scout-report`

The Wired Librarian

A collection of online resources designed to help library professionals and users keep abreast of current developments in library science and information studies. Includes links to many library and information systems associations and services.

Keywords: Library Science, Libraries, Information Retrieval

Sponsor: Davidson Library, University of California, Santa Barbara, California, USA

Audience: Librarians, Library Users

Contact: Andrea L. Duda
duda@library.ucsb.edu

`gopher://ucsbuxa.ucsb.edu`

UNITE Archive

The User Network Interface to Everything (UNITE) discussion list. The list is a focus for discussion on the concept of a total solution interface with user-friendly, desktop-integrated access to all network services.

Keywords: Internet, Information Retrieval, Interface Design

Audience: Internet Surfers

Contact: George Munroe, Jill Foster
unite-request@mailbase.ac.uk

Details: Free

Files are in: pub/lists/unite

`ftp://mailbase.ac.uk`

Veronica FAQ

A gopher containing common questions and answers about Veronica, a title search and retrieval system for use with the Internet Gopher.

Keywords: Internet Reference, Information Retrieval, Veronica

Audience: Students, Computer Scientists, Researchers

`gopher://pogonip.scs.unr.edu/00/`
`veronica/veronica-faq`

WAIS, Inc.

WAIS, Inc. provides interactive on line publishing systems and services to organizations that publish information over the Internet. The organization's three main goals are: to develop the Internet as a viable means for distributing information electronically; to improve the nature and quality of information available over networks; and to offer better methods to access that information.

Keywords: WWW, Information Retrieval, Publishing, Internet Tools

Sponsor: WAIS, Inc.

Audience: Researchers, Students, General Public, Publishers

Contact: Webmaster
webmaster@wais.com

`http://server.wais.com/`

World Wide Web FAQ

A web site containing common questions and answers about WWW, a distributed hypermedia system first developed by CERN.

Keywords: WWW, Internet Reference, Information Retrieval

Audience: Students, Computer Scientists, Researchers

Contact: Thomas Boutell, Nathan Torkington
boutell@netcom.com,
nathan.torckington@vuw.ac.nz

`http://sunsite.unc.edu/boutell/faq/www_faq.html`

World Wide Web Worm (WWWW)

WWWW provides a mechanism to search the WWW in a multitude of ways. It also provides lists of all Home pages and of all URLs cited anywhere. This site contains an exhaustive list of WWW servers nationally and internationally.

Keywords: WWW, Information Retrieval, Internet

Sponsor: University of Colorado at Boulder, Department of Computer Science, Boulder, Colorado, USA

Audience: Researchers, Students, General Public

Contact: Oliver McBryan
mcbryan@cs.colorado.edu

`http://www.cs.colorado.edu/home/mcbryan/WWWW.html`

Information Sciences

Computists' Communique

A weekly newsletter serving professionals in artificial intelligence, information science, and computer science.

Keywords: Artificial Intelligence, Information Science, Computer Science

Audience: Computer Scientists, Information Scientists, Computists International Members

Profile: Content is career-oriented and depends partly on contributions from members. The moderator filters submissions, reports and comments on industry news, collects common knowledge about academia and industry, and helps track people and projects. The Communique is only available to members of Computists International, a networking association for computer and information scientists. It is an association for mutual mentoring about grant and funding sources, information channels, applications, text, software publishing, and the sociology of work.

Contact: Kenneth I. Laws
laws@ari.sri.com

Details: Costs, Moderated

`mailto:laws@ari.sri.com`

I.S.P.O.B. Bulletin YSSTI (Yugoslav System for Scientific and Technology Information)

The participants in this system can exchange news about the operations and development of YSSTI.

Keywords: Information Sciences, Yugoslavia

Sponsor: Institute of Information Sciences, University of Maribor, Yugoslavia

Audience: Information Scientists

Contact: Davor Sostaric
davor%rcum@yubgef51.bitnet

Subscribe by sending an e-mail with a single line containing:

SUBSCRIBE P.O.B. to addresses
POB%RCUM@YUBGEF51.bitnet

`mailto:pob%rcum@yubgef51.bitnet`

Scit-L

A list for those interested in information and communications science.

Keywords: Communications, Information Sciences

Audience: Communications Specialists, Communications Students, Information Scientists

Contact: Elia Zureik
Scitdoc@qucdn.queensu.ca

User Info: To subscribe to this list, send an e-mail message to the URL address below, consisting of a single line reading:

SUB scit-l YourFirstName YourLastName

To send a message to the entire list, address it to: scit-l@qucdn.queensu.ca

`mailto: listserv@qucdn.queensu.ca`

Information Services in Germany

Information Services in Germany

This gopher is an informal entry point for Germany, together with some hints to specialties in German information systems.

Keywords: Germany, Europe

Audience: Germans Internet Surfers

Contact: lange@rz.tu-clausthal.de

Details: Free

`gopher://gopher.tu-clausthal.de`

Information Sources

Information Sources

These compiled resources provide information describing the Internet and computer-mediated communication technologies, as well as information on related applications, culture, discussion forums, and bibliographies.

Keywords: Internet, Networking

Audience: Internet Surfers, Computer-Mediated Communication Researchers, Librarians

User Info: Files are located in: pub/communications.

Contact: John December
decemj@rpi.edu

Details: Free

`ftp://ftp.rpi.edu`

`http://www.rpi.edu/Internet/Guides/decemj/icmc/top.html`

Information Technology

edupage (A News Update from EDUCOM)

A newsletter put out by EDUCOM summarizing information technology news.

Keywords: Education (Continuing), Information Technology

Sponsor: EDUCOM

Audience: Educators, Administrators

Details: Free

User Info: To subscribe to the newsletter, send an e-mail message requesting a subscription to the URL address shown below, and include your name, institutional affiliation, and e-mail address.

`mailto:edupage@educom.edu`

euitnews (Educational Uses of Information Technology)

EDUCOM's newsletter for the Educational Uses of Information Technology program encompasses distance learning, self-paced instruction, computer-aided instruction, video, and other information technologies for teaching and learning.

Keywords: Education (Continuing), Information Technology

Audience: Administrators, K-12 Educators

Details: Free

A B C D E F G H I J K L M N O P Q R S T U V W X Y Z

A
B
C
D
E
F
G
H
I
J
K
L
M
N
O
P
Q
R
S
T
U
V
W
X
Y
Z

User Info: To subscribe to the newsletter, send an e-mail message to the URL address below, consisting of a single line reading:

SUB euitnews YourFirstName YourLastName

`mailto:listserv@bitnic.educom.edu`

IMPACT ONLINE ★

The electronic version of IMPACT, the newsletter of the Social Impact group of the Boston Computer Society.

Keywords: Information Technology, Computer Ethics, Social Responsibility

Sponsor: Boston Computer Society, Boston, MA

Audience: Computer Users, Boston Residents, Information Scientists

Profile: The purpose of the Social Impact group is to provide a forum for the discussion of social and ethical concerns related to information technology.

Contact: Ian Wells
bcs-ssi@compass.com

Notes: Read on comp.society

You will need access to a newsreader.

`news:comp.society`

Information Infrastructure and Technology Act of 1992 ★

The Information Infrastructure and Technology Act of 1992 builds on the High-Performance Computing Act. The newer bill will ensure that the technology developed by the High-Performance Computing Program is applied widely in K-12 education, libraries, health care, and industry, particularly manufacturing. It will authorize a total of $1.15 billion over the next five years.

Keywords: Government (US Federal), Law (US Federal), Information Technology, Education

Audience: Journalists, Politicians, Scientists, Manufacturers, Educators

Details: Free

File is: /internet/nren/iita.1992/gorebill.1992.txt

`ftp://nis.nsf.net`

ipct-j 'Interpersonal Computing and Technology: An Electronic Journal for the 21st Century' ★

Interpersonal Computing and Technology Journal is an outgrowth of the IPCT-L discussion group.

Keywords: Education (Adult), Education (Distance), Education (Continuing), Information Technology

Sponsor: Interpersonal Computing and Technology

Audience: Educators, Administrators, Faculty

Details: Free, Moderated

User Info: To subscribe to the journal, send an e-mail message to the URL address shown below, consisting of a single line reading:

SUB ipct-j YourFirstName YourLastName

`mailto:listserv@guvm.bitnet`

Jte-l 'Journal of Technology Education' ★

The Journal of Technology Education provides a forum for all topics relating to technology in education.

Keywords: Education (Adult), Education (Distance), Education (Continuing), Information Technology

Audience: Faculty, Administrators, Educators (K-12)

Details: Free

User Info: To subscribe to the journal, send an e-mail message to the URL address shown below, consisting of a single line reading:

SUB jte-l YourFirstName YourLastName

`mailto:listserv@vtvm1.cc.vt.edu`

Online-dict

A mailing list devoted to a discussion of online dictionaries and related issues including installation, modification, and maintenance of their databases, search engines, and user interfaces.

Keywords: Dictionaries, Information Technology, Lexicology

Audience: Librarians, Information Scientists, Systems Operators

Contact: Jack Lynch
jlynch@dept.english.upenn.edu

Details: Free

User Info: To subscribe, send an e-mail message to the URL address below, consisting of a single line reading:

SUB online-dict YourFirstName YourLastName.

To send a message to the entire list, address it to: online-dict@dept.english.upenn.edu

`mailto:listserv@dept.english.upenn.edu`

Pubs-IAT (Institute for Academic Technology newsletter) ★★★★

This newsletter shares information on publications, programs, courses, and other activities of the Institute for Academic Technology.

Keywords: Education (Adult), Education (Distance), Education (Continuing), Information Technology

Sponsor: Institute for Academic Technology

Audience: Educators, Administrators, Researchers

Details: Free

User Info: To subscribe to the list, send an e-mail message to the URL address below, consisting of a single line reading:

SUB pubs-iat YourFirstName YourLastName

To send a message to the entire list, address it to: pubs-iat@gibbs.oit.unc.edu

`mailto:listserv@gibbs.oit.unc.edu`

Tecbase- Sandia National Laboratory ★★

A catalog of technologies, developed at Sandia National Laboratories, which have potential commercial applications.

Keywords: Technology, Information Technology, Industry

Sponsor: Sandia National Laboratory

Audience: Business People, Entrepreneurs, Manufactures, Technicians

Contact: TechTransfer@ccsmtp.sandia.gov

`gopher://somnet.sandia.gov/Tecbase`

INGR-EN

INGR-EN ★★

A mailing list for the discussion of Intergraph products.

Keywords: Geographic Information Systems, Intergraph (GIS)

Audience: Geographers, Cartographers

Contact: Dusan Blasko
blasko@svfnov.tuke.sk

Details: Free

User Info: To subscribe to the list, send an e-mail message to the URL address below, consisting of a single line reading:

SUB ingr-en YourFirstName YourLastName

`ingr-en@ccsun.tuke.sk`

INGRAFX

INGRAFX ★★

This E-conference is for discussion of all matters relating to information graphics.

Keywords: Computer Graphics, Graphic Design, Scientific Visualization

Audience: Graphic Designers, Cartographers, Animators

Contact: Jeremy Crampton
http://info.cern.ch/hypertext/WWW/The
Project.html

User Info: To subscribe to the list, send an e-mail
message to the URL address below,
consisting of a single line reading:

SUB ingrafx YourFirstName
YourLastName

To send a message to the entire list,
address it to: ingrafx@psuvm.psu.edu

`mailto:listserv@psuvm.psu.edu`

INPADOC/INPANEW

INPADOC/INPANEW

Patent documents issued by more than fifty national
and international patent offices.

Keywords: Patents, Intellectual Property,
Trademarks

Sponsor: European Patent Office

Audience: Patent Attorneys, Patent Agents,
Librarians, Researchers

Profile: Bibliographic information is searchable,
including inventor names, assignees,
international patent classification codes,
and in most cases, titles, as well as
complete publications and application
data. Contains approximately 20 million
records. Updated weekly.

Contact: PAUL.ALBERT@NETEAST.COM

User Info: To subscribe, contact Orbit-Questel
directly.

`telnet://orbit.com`

Insect Biology

SOCINSCT (Social Insect Biology Research List)

SOCINSCT is dedicated to communication among
investigators active in the discipline of social insect
biology.

Keywords: Biology, Insect Biology, Zoology,
Entomology

Audience: Biologists, Researchers

Profile: It is restricted to discussions of research
at the university level. Social insects
(bees, wasps, ants, and termites) are the
main interest, but information can
include any area of sociobiology, or
solitary bees and wasps. Such areas
could include: orientation, navigation,
adaptation/selection/evolution,
superorganism concept, behavior,
physiology and biochemistry,
pheromones, flight and energetics,
taxonomy and systematics, ecology,
genetics, pollination, and nectar/pollen

biology. Announcements of meetings
and professional opportunities, requests
for research help, sharing of literature
references, sharing research topics, and
discussion of ideas are welcome.

Contact: Erik Seielstad
erik@acspr1.acs.brockport.edu

Details: Free

User Info: To subscribe to the list, send an e-mail
message to the address below,
consisting of a single line reading:

SUB socinsct YourFirstName
YourLastName

To send message to the entire list,
address it to: socinsct@albany.edu

`mailto:listserv@albany.edu`

Insider Trading

Insider Trading Monitor

The database contains the transaction details of all
insider-trading filings .

Keywords: Insider Trading, Securities

Sponsor: Invest/Net, Inc., Ft. Lauderdale, FL US

Audience: Stockbrokers , Media

Profile: This source contains the transaction
details of all insider-trading filings,
(ownership changes) received by the US
Securities and Exchange Commission
(SEC) since January 1984. The
ownership of securities by over 100,000
officers, directors, and major
shareholders (10 percent or more) in
over 8,500 US public companies is
covered in the file.

Contact: Dialog in the US at (800) 334-2564; Dialog
internationally at country-specific
locations.

User Info: To subscribe, contact Dialog directly.

Notes: Coverage: April 1984 to the present;
updated daily.

`telnet://dialog.com`

insoft-l

insoft-l

This list discusses techniques for developing new
software and for converting existing software, as
well as internationalization tools, announcements of
internationalized public-domain software and of
foreign-language versions of commercial software,
calls for papers, conference announcements, and
references to documentation related to the
internationalization of software.

Keywords: Programming, Software Internationalization

Sponsor: Center for Computing and Information
Services, Technical University of Brno

Audience: Software Developers, Computer
Professionals

Contact: insoft-l-request@cis.vutbr.cs

Details: Free, Moderated

User Info: To subscribe to the list, send an e-mail
message to the URL address below,
consisting of a single line reading:

SUB insoft-l YourFirstName
YourLastName

To send a message to the entire list,
address it to: insoft-l@cis.vutbr.cs

`mailto:listserv@cis.vutbr.cs`

INSPEC

INSPEC

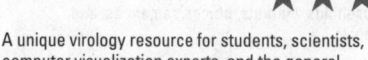

IINSPEC corresponds to the three Science Abstracts
print publications: Physics Abstracts, Electrical and
Electronics Abstracts, and Computer and Control
Abstracts.

Keywords: Physics, Electronics, Computing

Sponsor: Institution of Electrical Engineers,
London, UK

Audience: Physicists, Electrical Engineers,
Computer Specialists

Profile: Approximately 16 percent of the
database's source publications are in
languages other than English, but all
articles are abstracted and indexed in
English. The special DIALOG online
thesaurus feature is available to assist
searchers in determining appropriate
subject terms and codes.

Contact: Dialog in the US at (800) 334-2564; Dialog
internationally at country-specific
locations.

User Info: To subscribe, contact Dialog directly.

Notes: Coverage: April 1969 to the present;
updated weekly.

`telnet://dialog.com`

Institute for Molecular Virology

Institute for Molecular Virology

A unique virology resource for students, scientists,
computer visualization experts, and the general
public.

Keywords: Disease, Viruses, Biology, Medicine

Sponsor: University of Wisconsin-Madison,
Madison, Wisconsin, USA

Audience: Virologists, Biologists, Researchers,
Medical Students, Medical Researchers

Contact: Stephen Spencer
sspencer@rhino.bocklabs.wisc.edu

`http://www.bocklabs.wisc.edu/`
`Welcome.html`

A B C D E F G H I J K L M N O P Q R S T U V W X Y Z

A
B
C
D
E
F
G
H
I
J
K
L
M
N
O
P
Q
R
S
T
U
V
W
X
Y
Z

Institutional Real Estate Newsline

Institutional Real Estate Newsline

Five-page fax briefing with articles regarding institutional real estate, life insurance company, banks, pension fund, real estate investment trust, and commercial mortgage backed securities markets.

Keywords: Real Estate, Investments, Insurance

Sponsor: Institutional Real Estate

Audience: Investors

Details: Costs

`mailto:IREI@crl.com`

Institutional Research

The Electronic AIR

Biweekly (nominal schedule) electronic newsletter for the Association for Institutional Research members, as well as college and university planners.

Keywords: Education (Continuing), Institutional Research

Sponsor: Association for Institutional Research (AIR)

Audience: College/University Planners, University Administrators

Contact: Larry Nelson NELSON_L@PLU.bitnet

Details: Free

`mailto:nelson_l@plu.bitnet`

Institutions

AltInst

A mailing list for proposing and critiquing alternative institutions and ways of life. Topics include alternative ways to run conversations, countries, households, markets, offices, romances, and schools.

Keywords: Institutions, Alternative Management

Audience: General Public

Contact: Robin Hanson AltInst-request@cs.cmu.edu

Details: Free

User Info: To subscribe to the list, send an e-mail message requesting a subscription to the URL address below.

To send a message to the entire list, address it to: AltInst@cs.cmu.edu

Notes: AltInst is open to people from any political persuasion, but general political flaming/discussion is forbidden.

`mailto:AltInst-request@cs.cmu.edu`

Insurance

Insurance Periodicals Index

The database indexes and abstracts 35 of the most respected and widely read insurance industry journals and magazines.

Keywords: Insurance Industry, Law

Sponsor: NILS Publishing Company, Chatsworth, CA, US

Audience: Insurance Brokers, Industry Professionals, Lawyers, Researchers

Profile: The subject coverage of the publications indexed includes the following major groupings: AIDS, alcohol abuse, asbestos, automobile insurance, aviation insurance, banks, bonds, catastrophes, crime, disability insurance, drug abuse, financial services, health insurance, insurance agents and brokers, legislation, liability insurance, life insurance, Lloyds, loss control, marketing, pensions, pollution, product liability, property insurance, rates, regulation, risk management, tort reform, uninsured motorists, workers' compensation, and so on.

Contact: Dialog in the US at (800) 334-2564, Dialog internationally at country-specific locations.

User Info: To subscribe, contact Dialog directly.

Notes: Coverage: 1984 to the present; updated biweekly.

`telnet://dialog.com`

Institutional Real Estate Newsline

Five-page fax briefing with articles regarding institutional real estate, life insurance company, banks, pension fund, real estate investment trust and commercial mortgage backed securities markets.

Keywords: Real Estate, Investments, Insurance

Sponsor: Institutional Real Estate

Audience: Investors

Details: Costs

`mailto:IREI@crl.com`

INSURE (Insurance)

The Insurance (INSURE) library contains specific full-text and abstract news and legal information sources focusing on the insurance industry.

Keywords: News, Analysis, Law, Insurance

Audience: Insurance Professionals, Lawyers, Industry Researchers

Profile: The INSURE library contains leading insurance industry news sources, legal and regulatory materials from NILS Publishing Company's INSURLAW, analyst reports on the insurance industry from InvestextR, and insurance company financial reports. Federal and state case law and federal regulations are also available.

Contact: Mead New Sales Group @ (800) 227-4908 or (513) 859-5398 inside the US, or (513) 865-7981 for all inquiries outside the US.

User Info: To subscribe, contact Mead directly.

Notes: To examine the Nexis user guide, you can access it at the ftp site of the University of Texas at Austin at the URL address: ftp://ftp.cc.utexas.edu

The files are in: /pub/res-services/LEXIS

`telnet://nex.meaddata.com`

Intellectual Property

Chinapats

Covers all patent applications published under the patent law of People's Republic of China.

Keywords: Patents, Intellectual Property, Trademarks

Sponsor: European Patent Office

Audience: Patent Attorneys, Patent Agents, Librarians, Researchers

Profile: English language abstracts are included for all applications filed by Chinese applicants. Contains more than 59,000 records. Updated monthly.

Contact: PAUL.ALBERT@NETEAST.COM

User Info: To subscribe, contact Orbit-Questel directly.

`telnet://orbit.com`

CLAIMS

Provides access to over 2.3 million U.S. patents issued by the U.S. Patent and Trademark Office.

Keywords: Patents, Intellectual Property, Trademarks

Sponsor: IFI/Plenum Data Corporation

Audience: Patent Attorneys, Patent Agents, Librarians, Researchers

Profile: Chemical patents are covered from 1950 forward; mechanical and electrical patents from 1963 forward; design patents from 1980 forward.

Contact: PAUL.ALBERT@NETEAST.COM

User Info: To subscribe, contact Orbit-Questel directly.

`telnet://orbit.com`

CNI-Copyright Mailing List Archives

An archive of lists related to copyright and intellectual property law.

Keywords: Copyright Law, Intellectual Property

Sponsor: CNI (The Coalition for Networked Information)

Audience: Entrepreneurs, Lawyers, Journalists

Contact: Craig Summerhill, Joan K. Lippincott craig@cni.org, joan@cni.org

`gopher://gopher.cni.org`

comp.org.eff.talk

A Usenet newsgroup organized by the EFF (Electronic Frontier Foundation) providing information and discussion about the political, social, and legal issues surrounding the Internet.

Keywords: Computers, Intellectual Property, Security, Internet

Audience: Internet Surfers

User Info: To subscribe to this Usenet newsgroup, you need access to a newsreader.

`news:comp.org.eff.talk`

Derwent World Patents Index

Patent specifications issued by the patent offices of 33 major issuing authorities.

Keywords: Patents, Intellectual Property, Trademarks

Sponsor: Derwent Publications, Ltd.

Audience: Patent Attorneys, Patent Agents, Librarians, Researchers

Profile: Includes European Patent Office and Patent Cooperation Treaty published applications, plus Research Disclosure and International Technology Disclosure. Each patent is extensively indexed from the complete patent specifications. Abstracts are included.

Contact: PAUL.ALBERT@NETEAST.COM

User Info: To subscribe, contact Orbit-Questel directly.

`telnet://orbit.com`

EFFector Online—The Electronic Frontier Foundation, Inc.

Established to make the electronic frontier truly useful and accessible to everyone, emphasizing the free and open flow of information and communication.

Keywords: Computer Communications, Electronic Media, Intellectual Property, Privacy

Audience: Computer Users, Civil Libertarians

Profile: EFFector Online presents news, information, and discussion about the world of computer-based communications media that constitute the electronic frontier. It covers issues such as freedom of speech in digital media, privacy rights, censorship, and standards of responsibility for users and operators of computer systems, as well as policy issues such as the development of a national information infrastructure, and intellectual property.

Contact: Gerard Van der Leun, Mike Godwin gerard@eff.org mnemonic@eff.org

Details: Free

User Info: To subscribe, send an e-mail message requesting a subscription to: request@eff.org

Notes: This takes you to the front door of the eff gopher server, which contains much more information than just EFFector online.

`gopher://gopher.eff.org/1`

INPADOC/INPANEW

Patent documents issued by more than fifty national and international patent offices.

Keywords: Patents, Intellectual Property, Trademarks

Sponsor: European Patent Office

Audience: Patent Attorneys, Patent Agents, Librarians, Researchers

Profile: Bibliographic information is searchable, including inventor names, assignees, international patent classification codes, and in most cases, titles, as well as complete publications and application data. Contains approximately 20 million records. Updated weekly.

Contact: PAUL.ALBERT@NETEAST.COM

User Info: To subscribe, contact Orbit-Questel directly.

`telnet://orbit.com`

JAPIO

Comprehensive source of unexamined Japanese patent applications.

Keywords: Patents, Intellectual Property, Trademarks

Sponsor: Japan Patent Information Organization

Audience: Patent Attorneys, Patent Agents, Librarians, Researchers

Profile: More than 2.8 million records covering all technologies. Unique features include English-language abstracts for many Japanese patent applications

Contact: PAUL.ALBERT@NETEAST.COM

User Info: To subscribe, contact Orbit-Questel directly.

`telnet://orbit.com`

Legal Status

Records thousands of types of actions that can affect the legal status of a patent document after it is published and after the patent is granted.

Keywords: Patents, Intellectual Property, Trademarks

Sponsor: European Patent Office

Audience: Patent Attorneys, Patent Agents, Librarians, Researchers

Profile: Information about the disposition of patent applications published under the Patent Cooperation Treaty by the World Intellectual Property Organizations is included as well. Contains more than 8 million records. Updated weekly.

Contact: PAUL.ALBERT@NETEAST.COM

User Info: To subscribe, contact Orbit-Questel directly.

`telnet://orbit.com`

US Patents

Complete patent information of all claims of U.S. patents issued since 1971.

Keywords: Patents, Intellectual Property, Trademarks

Sponsor: Derwent, Inc.

Audience: Patent Attorneys, Patent Agents, Librarians, Researchers

Profile: Includes complete front page information, plus all claims of US patents issued since 1971. Merged file contains approximately 1.4 million records. Updated weekly.

Contact: PAUL.ALBERT@NETEAST.COM

User Info: To subscribe, contact Orbit-Questel directly.

`telnet://orbit.com`

Intelligence

Africa in the CIA World Fact Book

A gopher site containing geographial and political information about individual countries in Africa.

Keywords: Africa, Intelligence, Project Gutenberg

Sponsor: Project Gutenberg

Audience: Africans, General Public

`gopher://hoshi.cic.sfu.ca/11/dlam/cia/Africa`

CIA World Factbook

Annual report of CIA (Central Intelligence Agency) research in over 247 nations.

Keywords: CIA, Intelligence, Annual Reports

A
B
C
D
E
F
G
H
I
J
K
L
M
N
O
P
Q
R
S
T
U
V
W
X
Y
Z

Audience: Governments, Lawyers, FBI

Details: Free

`gopher://marvel.loc.gov`

INTER-L

INTER-L

A list for members of the National Association of Foreign Student Advisors.

Keywords: Education (Bilingual), Educational Policy

Sponsor: National Association of Foreign Student Advisors (NAFSA)

Audience: Foreign Students, NAFSA Members

Details: Free

User Info: To subscribe to the list, send an e-mail, message to the address below, consisting of a single line reading:

??missing line here??

`mailto:listserv@vtm1.cc.vt.edu`

Interaction

Computer Music Journal Archive and World Wide Web Home Page.

★★★★

This resource reinforces material available in the hardcopy version of Computer Music Journal, published by the MIT Press

Keywords: Computer Music, Composition, Synthesis, Interaction

Sponsor: The MIT Press

Audience: Computer Musicians

Profile: The archive includes the tables of contents, abstracts, and editor's notes for the last several volumes of CMJ (including the recent bibliography, diskography, and taxonomy of the field), a number of useful CM-related documents such as the full MIDI and AIFF format specifications, a lengthy reference list, the guidelines for manuscript submission, and the full-text of several recent articles.

Contact: Stephen Pope
cmj@cnmat.Berkeley.edu

Details: Free

`ftp://mitpress.mit.edu:/pub/Computer-Music-Journal`

Interactive

ACM SIGGRAPH Online Bibliography Project

 ★★★★

This is a collection of computer-graphics bibliographic references.

Keywords: Multimedia, Interactive, Computer Graphics, Programming

Sponsor: Association of Computing Machinery (ACM), Special Interest Group on Computer Graphics (SIGGRAPH)

Audience: Developers, Designers, Producers, Educators, Programmers, Graphic Artists

Profile: The goal of this project is to maintain an up-to-date database of computer-graphics literature in a format that is accessible to as many members of the computer-graphics community as possible. The database includes references from conferences and workshops worldwide and from a variety of publications dating back as far as the late-19th century. The majority of the major journals and conference proceedings from the mid-1970s to the present are listed.

Contact: bibadmin@siggraph.org

Details: Free, Moderated, Multimedia

`ftp://siggraph.org/publications`

DVI-list

This mailing list is intended for discussions about Intel's DVI (Digital Video Interactive) system. These discussions cover both applications and programming with DVI.

Keywords: Interactive Computing

Audience: Interactive Program Developers

Contact: Andrew Patrick
dvi-list-request@calvin.dgbt.doc.ca

User Info: To subscribe to the list, send an e-mail message requesting a subscription to the URL address below.

To send a message to the entire list, address it to: dvi-list-request@calvin.dgbt.doc.ca

`mailto:dvi-list-request@calvin.dgbt.doc.ca`

Interactive

A conference on Arts Wire about interactive art that includes a library of artists' statements about artworks, texts, and publications, as well as discussion.

Keywords: Art, Interactive Art

Sponsor: New York Foundation for the Arts

Audience: Artists, Writers

Contact: Anna Couey, Judy Malloy
couey@tmn.com, jmalloy@tmn.com

`telnet://tmn.com`

NIC (Nucleus for Interactive Computing)

 ★★★★

WWW-based system for interactive computing.

Keywords: Multimedia, Interactive Computing, Interface Design, Scripting Laguages, Programming

Sponsor: BYU Interactive Software Systems Lab

Audience: Software Developers, Educators

Profile: NIC is a system for interactive computing that combines a data model, a user interface model, and a scripting language to create flexible and powerful user interfaces. Documentation still under construction is located here.

Contact: Dan Olsen
olsen@cs.byu.edu

Details: Free, Moderated, Image, and Sound files available. Multimedia files available.

Use a World Wide Web (Mosaic) client and open a connection to the resource.

`ftp://issl.cs.byu.edu/docs/NIC/home.html`

Interactive Learning

Diversity U

Diversity University is an experiment in interactive learning.

Keywords: Education, Interactive Learning, Multimedia

Audience: Educators, Researchers

Details: Free

`gopher://erau.db.erau.edu`

Interactive Frog Dissection Kit

An interactive simulation of the dissection of a computer-generated frog.

Keywords: Biology, Simulation, Interactive Learning

Sponsor: Lawrence Berkeley Laboratory-Whole Frog Project, Berkeley, California, USA

Audience: Students, Educators, Biologists

Contact: David Robertson
dwrobertson@lbl.gov

Notes: Copyrighted (commercial uses require permission)

`http://george.1b1.gov/ITG.hm.pg.docs/dissect/info.html`

Interactive Media

Index to Multimedia Information Sources

This site provides a guide to multimedia on the Web, including lists of software, companies, research, publications, conferences, archives, and galleries.

Keywords: Multimedia, Interactive Media

Audience: Multimedia Users, Educators

Contact: Simon Gibbs
simon.gibbs@gmd.de

Details: Free

`http://cui_www.unige.ch/OSG/`
`MultimediaInfo/index.html`

Rec.arts.int-fiction

A Usenet newsgroup about interactive literature and interactive computer games.

Keywords: Literature (General), Interactive Media, Computer Games

Audience: General Public, Computer Games Players

Details: Free

To participate in a Usenet newsgroup, you need access to a newsreader.

`news:rec.arts.int-fiction`

rec.arts.movies movie database (Cardiff WWW front-end)

An extensive, interactive database covering over 32,000 movies, with more than 370,000 filmography entries, from early cinema to current releases.

Keywords: Movies, Television, Popular Culture, Interactive Media

Audience: Movie Buffs

Profile: A WWW front-end to the rec.arts.movies movie database, complete with form-filling interfaces to add new data and to rate movies (on a scale from 1 through 10). The database includes filmographies for actors, directors, writers, composers, cinematographers, editors, production designers, costume designers, and producers; plot summaries; character names; movie ratings; year of release; running times; movie trivia; quotes; goofs; soundtracks; personal trivia and Academy Award information.

Contact: Rob Hartill
Robert.Hartill@cm.cf.ac.uk

Details: Free

`http://www.cm.cf.ac.uk/Movies`

`http://www.msstate.edu/Movies,`

Interactivity

INTERCUL

A study of international communication.

Keywords: Languages (international)

Audience: Linguists, Language Teachers, Language Students

Details: Free

User Info: To subscribe to the list, send an e-mail message to the address below, consisting of a single line reading:

??missing line?????

`mailto:listserv@vm.its.rpi.edu`

Interface Design

Loughborough University of Technology Computer-Human Interaction (LUTCHI) Research Centre

This server contains general information on computer-human interaction.

Keywords: Interface Design, Ergonomics, Computer-Human Interactions, Programming

Sponsor: Loughborough University of Technology, Leicestershire, UK

Audience: Software Developers, Software Designers, Programmers

Profile: The LUTCHI Research Centre is based within the Department of Computer Studies at the Loughborough University of Technology, Leicestershire, UK. This server contains information about LUTCHI research projects, official LUTCHI publicity releases, as well as documents, images, and movies associated with those projects.

Contact: Ben Anderson
B.Anderson@lut.ac.uk

Details: Free, Moderated, Image, and Sound files available. Multimedia files available.

Use a World-Wide Web (Mosaic) client and open a connection to the resource.

`http://pipkin.lut.ac.uk`

NIC (Nucleus for Interactive Computing)

WWW-based system for interactive computing.

Keywords: Multimedia, Interactive Computing, Interface Design, Scripting Languages, Programming

Sponsor: BYU Interactive Software Systems Lab

Audience: Software Developers, Educators

Profile: NIC is a system for interactive computing that combines a data model, a user interface model, and a scripting language to create flexible and powerful user interfaces. Documentation still under construction is located here.

Contact: Dan Olsen
olsen@cs.byu.edu

Details: Free, Moderated, Image, and Sound files available. Multimedia files available.

Use a World Wide Web (Mosaic) client and open a connection to the resource.

`ftp://issl.cs.byu.edu/docs/NIC/`
`home.html`

UNITE Archive

The User Network Interface to Everything (UNITE) discussion list. The list is a focus for discussion on the concept of a total solution interface with user-friendly, desktop-integrated access to all network services.

Keywords: Internet, Information Retrieval, Interface Design

Audience: Internet Surfers

Contact: George Munroe, Jill Foster
unite-request@mailbase.ac.uk

Details: Free

Files are in: pub/lists/unite

`ftp://mailbase.ac.uk`

Intergraph

INGR-EN

A mailing list for the discussion of Intergraph products.

Keywords: Geographic Information Systems, Intergraph

Audience: Geographers, Cartographers

Contact: Dusan Blasko
blasko@svfnov.tuke.sk

Details: Free

User Info: To subscribe to the list, send an e-mail message to the URL address below, consisting of a single line reading:

SUB ingr-en YourFirstName YourLastName

`ingr-en@ccsun.tuke.sk`

A B C D E F G H I J K L M N O P Q R S T U V W X Y Z

Sidebar alphabet: A B C D E F G H **I** J K L M N O P Q R S T U V W X Y Z

International Banking

ITRADE (International Trade Library)

 ★ ★ ★

The International Trade library contains materials related to the importing of goods and services, exporting of goods and services, licensing of intellectual property, payment of taxes, or investment and banking at the international level.

Keywords: Law, Imports, International Banking

Audience: Lawyers, Bankers, International Lawyers

Profile: ITRADE contains a comprehensive collection of federal case law, statutes, regulations, and agency decisions all related to the importing of goods and services, exporting of goods and services, licensing of intellectual property, payment of taxes, or investment and banking at the international level.

Contact: New Sales Group at 800-227-4908 or 513-859-5398 inside the US, or (513)-865-7981 for all inquires outside the US.

User Info: To subscribe, contact Mead directly.

Notes: To examine the Lexis user guide, you can access it at the ftp site of the University of Texas at Austin at the URL address: ftp://ftp.cc.utexas.edu

The files are in: /pub/ref-services/LEXIS

`telnet://nex.meaddata.com`

`http://www.meaddata.com`

International Business Machines

International Business Machines

This is IBM's main WWW server and it contains extensive links to information about the company and its products.

Keywords: Computers, Business

Audience: General Public

Profile: Contains: Industry, Solutions, Products and Services, Technology information and News about the company.

Contact: mail to: askibm@www.ibm.com

`http://www.ibm.com`

International Business

Hoppenstedt Directory of German Companies

 ★ ★ ★

This directory covers 50,000 German companies with sales exceeding 2 million DM or with a minimum of 20 employees.

Keywords: German Companies, International Business, Germany

Sponsor: Hoppenstedt Wirtschaftsdatenbank, Darmstadt, Germany

Audience: Business Professionals, International Market, Researchers, Germans

Profile: Records include current company address, line of business, number of employees, sales, capital stock, branches and subsidiaries, and a listing of executives and directors with positions in the company. The file is bilingual; users can view the records in either German or English.

Contact: Dialog in the US at (800) 334-2564; Dialog internationally at country-specific locations.

User Info: To subscribe, contact Dialog directly.

Notes: Coverage: 1973 to the present; updated semiannually.

`telnet://dialog.com`

Infomat International Business

 ★ ★ ★

The database provides concise English-language abstracts of business news articles appearing in over 600 international business newspapers and journals from more than 20 countries.

Keywords: International Business, International News

Sponsor: Information Access Company, Foster City, CA

Audience: Business Professionals

Profile: Abstracts included are selected to meet the specific information requests of Infomat's client companies, which are major players in key industries, such as biotechnology, communications/ telecommunications, construction/civil engineering, electronics, financial services, food and beverages, and others.

Contact: Dialog in the US at (800) 334-2564; Dialog internationally at country-specific locations.

User Info: To subscribe, contact Dialog directly.

Notes: Coverage: April 1984 to the present; updated weekly.

`telnet://dialog.com`

International Centre for Distance Learning

International Centre for Distance Learning

 ★ ★ ★

This site is a distance education database.

Keywords: Education (Distance)

Sponsor: International Centre for Distance Learning, The Open University, United Kingdom

Audience: Educators, Students, Researchers

Profile: The database is extensive, and provides information about courses, related institutions, and relevant literature, with over 30,000 entries, including the following: study skills, agriculture, fisheries, architecture, building, surveying, planning, arts, humanities and social sciences, business, services, management, economics, education and training, applied science, technology, computers, environment, pure science and mathematics, medicine, health, social welfare, law, law enforcement, regulations and standards, personal, home, and family affairs

Expect: Login; Send: icdl; Send: <Country>; Password: AAA

`telnet://acsvax.open.ac.uk`

International Communication

Voice of America and Worldnet

 ★ ★ ★

A gopher server for the Voice of America and Worldnet. Includes full-text transcripts of VOA news reports, press releases, and announcements.

Keywords: US Government Publications, News Media, Radio, International Communication

Sponsor: United States Information Agency

Audience: Journalists, Government Officials, General Public

Contact: info@voa.gov, letters-usa@VOA.GOV (For correspondence from inside the U.S.)

`gopher://gopher.voa.gov`

International Court of Justice Historical Documents

International Court of Justice Historical Documents

This gopher offers full-text documents from the International Court of Justice, and contains a searchable index.

Keywords: Judicial Process, Law (International)

Audience: Lawyers, Legal Scholars, Legal Professionals, Law Students

Notes: File is in Foreign and International Law/ International Court of Justice Historical Documents

`gopher://fatty.law.cornell.edu`

International Development

Canadian University Consortium on Health in International Development (CANCHID)

CANCHID is a multi campus consortium that includes medical schools and other educational institutions devoted to research and projects dealing with health care issues in developing countries.

Keywords: Health, International Development

Audience: Public Health, Medicine, International Aid Agencies

Contact: Sam Lanfranco
lanfran@vm1.yorku.ca

Details: Free

User Info: To subscribe to the list, send an e-mail message to the URL address below, consisting of a single line reading:

SUB canchid YourFirstName YourLastName

To send a message to the entire list, address it to: canchid@vm1.yorku.ca

`mailto:listserv@vm1.yorku.ca`

International Documents

Historic World Documents

The wiretap gopher provides access to a range of world documents in full-text format.

Keywords: International Documents, Treaties, History (World)

Audience: Governments, Historians, Researchers, General Public

Details: Free

Select from menu as appropriate.

`gopher://wiretap.spies.com`

Latin American Database Historic World Documents

International legal files covering 33 nations and article citations from publications relating to Hispanic legal systems. The wiretap gopher provides access to a range of world documents in full-text format.

Keywords: Hispanic, Law, International Law, International Documents

Audience: General Public, Hispanics, Lawyers

Profile: The database includes two files, 1) LAWL containing legislation from 33 nations, mostly Spanish speaking 2) HISS containing Hispanic Legal Article citations.

Details: Free

Select from menu as appropriate.

`gopher://marvel.loc.gov`

International Finance

American Banker Full Text

This database corresponds to the authoritative print publication American Banker.

Keywords: Banking, International Finance, International Trade

Sponsor: American Banker-Bond Buyer, New York, NY, USA

Audience: Financial Analysts, Bankers

Profile: Specific coverage is given to local, regional, and international financial services, technology applications, legal commentary and court actions, international trade, government regulations, Washington events, marketing of financial services, general economic overviews, personnel issues, and profiles and movements of industry personnel. Statistical rankings of all types of financial institutions (from thrifts to commercial banks, US and worldwide) are included beginning with the October 1987 editions. Other special features include quarterly bank earnings, results of American Banker surveys, and the complete text of speeches and articles by the industry professionals that are unavailable in the printed paper.

Contact: Dialog in the US at (800) 334-2564; Dialog internationally at country-specific locations.

Details: Costs

User Info: To subscribe, contact Dialog directly.

`telnet://dialog.com`

World Bank Gopher Server

A collection of online information from the World Bank.

Keywords: Government (International), Development, International Finance, Foreign Trade

Sponsor: The World Bank

Audience: Nongovernmental Organizations, Activists, Government Officials, Environmentalists

Profile: A collection of World Bank information, including a list of publications, environmental assessments, economic reports, and updates on current projects being funded by the World Bank.

Contact: webmaster@www.worldbank.org

`gopher://gopher.worldbank.org`

`http://www.worldbank.org`

International Food and Nutrition (INFAN) Database

International Food and Nutrition (INFAN) Database

A database covering all aspects of nutrition, health and food, including weight control, food safety, eating patterns, and more.

Keywords: Nutrition, Health, Diet

Sponsor: Pennsylvania State University Nutrition Center

Audience: Nutritionists, Health-Care Professionals, Consumers

Details: Free

To access the database, select PENpages (1), then General Information (3), and finally INFAN Database (4).

`telnet://penpages@psupen.psu.edu`

International Law

INTLAW (International Law Library)

The International Law Library provides comprehensive international law materials.

Keywords: International Law, EEC, Commonwealth, China

Audience: Lawyers, International Lawyers

Profile: The International Law Library provides comprehensive international law materials. The International Law Library contains federal case law, European Community materials, treaties and agreements, Commonwealth law

A B C D E F G H I J K L M N O P Q R S T U V W X Y Z

materials, topical and professional journals, French law materials (in French) China law materials, plus relevant topical publications.

Contact: New Sales Group at 800-227-4908 or 513-859-5398 inside the US, or (513)-865-7981 for all inquires outside the US.

User Info: To subscribe, contact Mead directly.

To examine the Lexis user guide, you can access it at the ftp site of the University of Texas at Austin at the URL address: ftp://ftp.cc.utexas.edu

The files are in: /pub/ref-services/LEXIS

`telnet://nex.meaddata.com`

`http://www.meaddata.com`

Latin American Database Historic World Documents

International legal files covering 33 nations and article citations from publications relating to Hispanic legal systems. The wiretap gopher provides access to a range of world documents in full-text format.

Keywords: Hispanic, Law, International Law, International Documents

Audience: General Public, Hispanics, Lawyers

Profile: The database includes two files, 1) LAWL containing legislation from 33 nations, mostly Spanish speaking 2) HISS containing Hispanic Legal Article citations.

Details: Free

Select from menu as appropriate.

`gopher://marvel.loc.gov`

International News

Info-South (Latin American News)

The database provides citations and abstracts of materials relating to contemporary economic, political, and social issues in Latin America.

Keywords: International News, Economics, International Politics, Latin America

Sponsor: University of Miami, Coral Gables, FL, US

Audience: General Public

Profile: Coverage includes a wide range of topics assessing the current situation in Latin America.

Contact: Dialog in the US at (800) 334-2564; Dialog internationally at country-specific locations.

User Info: To subscribe, contact Dialog directly.

Notes: Coverage: 1988 to the present; updated weekly.

`telnet://dialog.com`

Infomat International Business

The database provides concise English-language abstracts of business news articles appearing in over 600 international business newspapers and journals from more than 20 countries.

Keywords: International Business, International News

Sponsor: Information Access Company, Foster City, CA, US

Audience: Business Professionals

Profile: Abstracts included are selected to meet the specific information requests of Infomat's client companies that are major players in key industries, such as biotechnology, communications/telecommunications, construction/civil engineering, electronics, financial services, food and beverages, and others.

Contact: Dialog in the US at (800) 334-2564; Dialog internationally at country-specific locations.

User Info: To subscribe, contact Dialog directly.

Notes: Coverage: April 1984 to the present; updated weekly.

`telnet://dialog.com`

International Politics

Women.dev

Conference for information about local, regional, and international development as it relates to women. The conference includes bibliographies, statements, news, articles, and announcements about development and women in Africa, South America, and South Asia.

Keywords: Women, Development (International), International Politics

Audience: Women, Activists, Non-governmental Organizations, Feminists

Details: Sound files available, Free.

User Info: Establish an account on the nearest APC node. Login, type c for conferences, then type go women.dev.

For information on the nearest APC node, contact:

APC International Secretariat

IBASE

E-mail: apcadmin@apc.org

Contact: Carlos Afonso (cafonso@ax.apc.org)

or

APC North American Regional Office

E-mail: apcadmin@apc.org

Contact: Edie Farwell (efarwell@igc.apc.org)

Notes: Alai: Agencia Latinoamericana De Informacion

E-mail message to APCadmin@apc.org

`telnet://igc.apc.org`

International Relations

Summit of the Americas Internet Gopher

A gopher containing supporting materials for the Summit of the Americas, a meeting of the Western Hemisphere's democratically elected heads of state, to be held in Miami in December of 1994.

Keywords: American Studies, International Relations, Haiti, Latin America

Sponsor: The Florida University Latin American and Caribbean Center

Audience: Government Officials, Journalists, NGOs, General Public

Contact: Rene Ramos summit@SERVAX.FIU.EDU

`gopher://summit.fiu.edu`

University of Toledo Library

The library's holdings are large and wide-ranging and contain significant collections in many fields.

Keywords: Business, Great Lakes Area, Humanities, International Relations, Psychology, Science

Audience: Researchers, Students, General Public

Details: Free

Expect: Enter one of the following commands . . . , Send: DIAL MVS; Expect: dialed to mvs ####; Send: UTMOST

`telnet:// uofto1.utoledo.edu`

International Research

Research on Demand

A resource for the provision of market information, strategic information location, product information, and national and international business information.

Keywords: Market Research, Internet Research, Legal Research, International Research

Audience: Marketing Specialists, Lawyers, Public Relations Experts, Business Professionals, Researchers, Writers, Producers

Profile: This resource has special access to unique information resources worldwide. Areas of particular information access include the former Soviet Union, Europe, and the US. Information access also includes access to all the major online systems, including Dialog, BRS, Orbit, DataStar, and so on. Current Awareness Services include research information gathered from the Internet.

Details: Costs

User Info: To subscribe, send an e-mail message to the URL address below. In the body of your message, state the nature of your inquiry.

Notes: Contact ROD directly in the US at: (800) 227-0750; outside the US at: (510) 841-1145.

`mailto:rod@holonet.net`

International Trade

American Banker Full Text ★★★★

This database corresponds to the authoritative print publication American Banker.

Keywords: Banking, International Finance, International Trade

Sponsor: American Banker-Bond Buyer, New York, NY, USA

Audience: Financial Analysts, Bankers

Profile: Specific coverage is given to local, regional, and international financial services, technology applications, legal commentary and court actions, international trade, government regulations, Washington events, marketing of financial services, general economic overviews, personnel issues, and profiles and movements of industry personnel. Statistical rankings of all types of financial institutions (from thrifts to commercial banks, US and worldwide) are included beginning with the October 1987 editions. Other special features include quarterly bank earnings, results

of American Banker surveys, and the complete text of speeches and articles by the industry professionals that are unavailable in the printed paper.

Contact: Dialog in the US at (800) 334-2564; Dialog internationally at country-specific locations.

Details: Costs

User Info: To subscribe, contact Dialog directly.

`telnet://dialog.com`

International Visitors

IHOUSE-L International Voice Newsletter Prototype List ★

Contains articles of interest to international students and scholars, professors, administrators, and other interested staff and groups (on- and off-campus).

Keywords: International Visitors, Washington University

Sponsor: International Office of Washington University, St. Louis MO

Audience: International Students

Contact: Doyle Cozadd C73221DC@WUVMD

Details: Free

User Info: To subscribe, send an e-mail message to the address below, consisting of a single line reading:

SUB: house-l Your First Name Your Last Name

To send a message to the entire list,

`mailto:listserv@wuvmd.wustl.edu`

Internet

AARNet Guide

This is the Australian Network Sites and Resources Guide.

Keywords: Internet, Internet Guide

Sponsor: Australian Academic and Research Network

Audience: Internet Surfers

Details: Free

Files are in: pub/resource-guide

`ftp://aarnet.edu.au/pub/resource-guide`

Agricultural Guide ★

A specialized guide, entitled "Not Just Cows," to the Internet/Bitnet resources in agriculture and related science.

Keywords: Agriculture, Internet

Sponsor: University of North Carolina

Audience: Internet Surfers

Contact: Wilfred Drew

Details: Free

File is: pub/docs/about-the-net/libsoft/agguide.dos

`ftp://sunsite.unc.edu/pub/docs/about-the-net/libsoft/agguide.dos`

`gopher://sunsite.unc.edu`

`http://sunsite.unc.edu/pub/docs/about-the-net/libsoft/agguide.dos`

Alex Description

An NIR (Network Information Retrieval) description of Alex, an Internet access tool.

Keywords: Internet Tools, Internet, Alex

Audience: Internet Surfers

Details: Free

File is: usr0/anon/doc/NIR.Tool

`ftp://alex.sp.cs.cmu.edu/usr0/anon/doc/NIR.Tool`

Almost 2001 Archive

Archive of transcripts of Almost 2001, a series on computer communications of the future, produced by NBC (National Broadcasting Company).

Keywords: Computers, Communications, Internet

Sponsor: The WELL (Whole Earth 'Lectronic Link)

Audience: Computer Users, Internet Surfers

Details: Free, Moderated

To participate in a conference on the WELL, you must first establish an account on the WELL.To do so, start by typing: telnet://well.sf.ca.us

`gopher://gopher.well.sf.ca.us//11/Communications/2001`

alt.config

A Usenet newsgroup providing information and discussion about alternative subnet discussions and connectivity.

Keywords: Internet, Computer Networks, Connectivity

Audience: Network Administrators

User Info: To subscribe to this Usenet newsgroup, you need access to a newsreader.

`news:alt.config`

Best of the Web '94

This web site highlights those places which were judged as the best sites (based on the criteria of quality, versatility, and power) on the World Wide Web.

A B C D E F G H I J K L M N O P Q R S T U V W X Y Z

A B C D E F G H I J K L M N O P Q R S T U V W X Y Z

Keywords: Internet, WWW

Audience: Internet Surfers

Contact: Brandon Plewe
plewe@acsu.buffalo.edu

Details: Free

`http://wings.buffalo.edu/contest`

Big Dummy's Guide

A comprehensive guide to the Internet for people with little or no experience with network communications.

Keywords: Internet

Sponsor: Electronic Frontier Foundation

Audience: Internet Surfers

Contact: Shari Steele
ssteele@eff.org

Details: Free

Big Dummy's Guide to the Internet is available in: /pub/Net_info/Big_Dummy, in several versions. The basic text version is bigdummy.txt

`ftp://ftp.eff.org`

bit.general

A Usenet newsgroup providing information and discussion about Bitnet or Usenet. Contained in the bit. category are many bit.listserv discussion lists.

Keywords: Internet, News

Audience: General Public, Internet Surfers

User Info: To subscribe to this Usenet newsgroup, you need access to a newsreader.

`news:bit.general`

CERFnet Guide

A comprehensive guide to the CERFnet (California Education and Research Federation Network), a data-communications regional network that operates throughout California. The purpose of CERFnet is to advance science and education by assisting the interchange of information among research and educational institutions.

Keywords: Internet, Science, Education, California

Audience: Internet Surfers, Researchers, Educators

Contact: CERFnet Hotline
help@cerf.net

Details: Free

Files are in: cerfnet/cerfnet_info/ cerfnet_guide/

`ftp://nic.cerf.net`

cfcp-members

The Confederation of Future Computer Professionals (CFCP) is a group of users on the Internet who are interested enough in various fields of computers to consider computers as their future. The Confederation exists to foster education and stimulate communication.

Keywords: Internet, Computers

Audience: Internet Surfers, Computer Users

Contact: mlindsey@nyx.cs.du.edu

Details: Free

User Info: To subscribe to the list, send an e-mail message requesting a subscription to the URL address below.

`mailto:mlindsey@nyx.cs.du.edu`

CNI

CNI (Coalition for Networked Information) is an Internet information retrieval service. The CNI promotes the creation of and access to information resources in networked environments in order to enrich scholarship and to enhance intellectual productivity.

Keywords: Internet, Information Retrieval, CNI

Audience: Internet Surfers

Details: Free

The readme file is: CNI/info.packet/ README

`ftp://ftp.cni.org/CNI (/info.packet/ README)`

`gopher://ftp.cni.org`

`http://www.cni.org/CNI.homepage.html`

CNI Gopher

The gopher for CNI (Coalition for Networked Information), an Internet information retrieval service. The CNI promotes the creation of and access to information resources in networked environments in order to enrich scholarship and to enhance intellectual productivity.

Keywords: Internet, Information Retrieval, CNI

Audience: Internet Surfers

Contact: Craig A. Summerhill
Craig@cni.org

Details: Free

`gopher://gopher.cni.org`

CNI TopNode Project

Part of CNI (Coalition for Networked Information) directories and resource information service.

Keywords: Internet, Information Retrieval, CNI

Audience: Internet Surfers

Details: Free

`ftp://ftp.cni.org/CNI/projects/ topnode`

`gopher://ftp.cni.org`

`http://www.cni.org/CNI.homepage.html`

College E-mail Addresses

Information on e-mail addresses at graduate offices.

Keywords: Internet, E-mail

Audience: Internet Surfers, Students, College/ University Educators

Details: Free

File is: pub/usenet/soc.college/ Admission_Office_Email_Address_List

`ftp://pit-manager.mit.edu/pub/usenet- by-group/soc.college`

`gopher://sipb.mit.edu`

comp.org.eff.talk

A Usenet newsgroup organized by the EFF (Electronic Frontier Foundation) providing information and discussion about the political, social, and legal issues surrounding the Internet.

Keywords: Computers, Intellectual Property, Security, Internet

Audience: Internet Surfers

User Info: To subscribe to this Usenet newsgroup, you need access to a newsreader.

`news:comp.org.eff.talk`

comp.text.tex

A Usenet newsgroup providing information and discussion about the TeX and LaTeX systems.

Keywords: Text Processing, Internet

Audience: Computer Users, TeX and LaTeX Users

User Info: To subscribe to this Usenet newsgroup, you need access to a newsreader.

`news:comp.text.tex`

comp.unix.aix

A Usenet newsgroup providing information and discussion about IBM's version of UNIX.

Keywords: Computer System, Internet, UNIX

Audience: Computer Users, UNIX Users, IBM Users

User Info: To subscribe to this Usenet newsgroup, you need access to a newsreader.

`news:comp.unix.aix`

Computer Network Conferencing ★

Discussions on the topic of computer network conferencing. The memo is intended to make more people aware of the present developments in the computer conferencing field, as well as to put forward ideas on what should be done to formalize this work.

Keywords: Internet, Conferencing Systems

Audience: Internet Surfers

Contact: Darren Reed
avalon@coombs.anu.edu.au

Details: Free

File is: documents/rfc/rfc1324.txt

`ftp://nic.merit.edu`

Computer-Mediated Marketing Environments ★★

A web site devoted to research aimed at understanding the ways in which computer-mediated marketing environments (CMEs), especially the Internet, are revolutionizing the way firms conduct business.

Keywords: WWW, Information Retrieval, Internet, Marketing, Business

Sponsor: Vanderbilt University, Owen Graduate School of Management, Nashville, Tennessee, USA

Audience: General Public, Entrepeneurs, Financial Planners, Marketers

Contact: Donna Hoffman, Tom Novak
hoffman@colette.ogsm.vanderbilt.edu,
novak@moe.ogsm.vanderbilt.edu

`http://colette.ogsm.vanderbilt.edu`

Correct Time/NBS ★

Correct Time/NBS tells the correct time from the National Bureau of Standards (NBS).

Keywords: Internet, Services, Correct Time

Audience: Internet Surfers

Details: Free

`ftp://india.colorado.edu/pub (Bogus site!)`

CSORG (Clearinghouse for Subject-Oriented Internet Resource Guides) ★★★

The goal of CSORG is to collect and make widely available guides to Internet resources that are subject-oriented. These guides are produced by members of the Internet community, and by SILS students who participate in the Internet Resource Discovery project.

Keywords: WWW, Information Retrieval, Internet

Sponsor: University of Michigan, School of Information and Library Studies, Michigan, USA

Audience: Reseachers, Students, General Public

Contact: Louis Rosenfeld
i-guides@umich.edu

`gopher://una.hh.lib.umich.edu/11/inetdirs`

DDN New User Guide ★

Defense Data Network (DDN) guide for new users.

Keywords: Internet, Internet Guides, Defense, Security

Audience: Internet Surfers

Details: Free

File is: netinfo/nug.doc

`ftp://nic.ddn.mil/netinfo`

Delphi

Delphi is an online service provider.

Keywords: Internet

Sponsor: Delphi, NewsCorp. Technologies

Audience: Internet Users

Details: Costs

`telnet://delphi.com`

DIMUND

DIMUND (Document Image Understanding) is an Internet information retrieval service.

Keywords: Internet, Information Retrieval, DIMUND, Documents

Sponsor: Document Processing Group, University of Maryland

Audience: Internet Surfers

Contact: gopher@dimund.cfar.umd.edu

Details: Free

`gopher:// dimund.umd.edu`

DIMUND FTP ★

DIMUND (Document Image Understanding) information service FTP archives. Provides access to selected documents.

Keywords: Internet, Information Retrieval, DIMUND, Documents

Sponsor: Document Processing Group, University of Maryland

Audience: Internet Surfers

Contact: gopher@dimund.cfar.umd.edu

Details: Free

`ftp://dimund.umd.edu`

Doc Center ★★★

A hard-copy document-delivery service for government and industry specifications and standards.

Keywords: Internet, Information Retrieval

Audience: Internet Surfers, Document Delivery Professionals

Details: Costs

`http://www.service.com/doccenter/home.html`

E-mail 101 ★

E-mail 101 describes how to use e-mail as well as other Internet features.

Keywords: Internet, E-mail

Audience: Internet Surfers

Details: Free

`gopher://mrcnext.cso.uiuc.edu`

`http://mrcnext.cso.uiuc.edu`

E-mail Gopher ★

E-mail Gopher allows the use of a gopher via e-mail.

Keywords: Internet, Services, E-mail, Gopher

Audience: Internet Surfers

Details: Free

Include the word "help" in the e-mail.

`gopher://gopher.ncc.go.jp/11/INFO/gopher`

`(This is the National Cancer Center of Japan Server)`

E-mail Services ★

A list of services available by e-mail.

Keywords: Internet, E-mail, Services

Audience: Internet Surfers

Contact: David DeSimone
an207@cleveland.freenet.edu

Details: Free

File is: pub/docs/about-the-net/libsoft/email_services.txt

`ftp://sunsite.unc.edu/pub/docs/about-the-net/libsoft/email_services.txt`

`http://sunsite.unc.edu/pub/docs/about-the-net/libsoft/email_services.txt`

E-mail Understanding ★

A special issue of the University of Illinois publication UIUC net describing electronic mail.

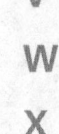

A
B
C
D
E
F
G
H
I
J
K
L
M
N
O
P
Q
R
S
T
U
V
W
X
Y
Z

Keywords: Internet, E-mail

Audience: Internet Surfers

Details: Free

File is: doc/net/uiucnet/vol2no2.txt

`ftp://ftp.cso.uiuc.edu/doc/net/uiucnet`

E-mail Usenet

E-mail Usenet enables the user to post to a newsgroup via e-mail.

Keywords: Internet, Services, E-mail, Usenet

Audience: Internet Surfers

Details: Free

`mailto://hierarchy-group-name@cs.utexas.edu`

EDNET

This forum explores the educational potential of the Internet.

Keywords: Education, Internet

Audience: Students, Educators

Profile: This independent, unmoderated mailing-list interest group is open and free of charge to all participants. Ednet links educators with common interests, and introduces students to a number of fields and sources of information, while offering criticism and suggestions.

Contact: Prescott Smith
pgsmith@educ.umass.edu

Details: Free

User Info: To subscribe to the list, send an e-mail message to the address shown below, consisting of a single line reading:

SUB Ednet YourFirstName YourLastName

To send a message to the entire list, address it to: ednet@nic.umass.edu.

`gopher://ericir.syr.edu/00/AskERIC/FullText/Lists/Messages/EDNET-List/README`

`mailto:listserv@nic.umass.edu`

Educator's Guide to E-mail Lists

A guide to help educators find e-mail lists. Includes a very large list of e-mail addresses related to education.

Keywords: Education, E-mail, Internet

Sponsor: University of Massachusetts, Amherst, MA

Audience: Educators, Researchers

Contact: Prescott Smith
pgsmith@educ.umass.edu

Details: Free

`ftp://nic.umass.edu`

EINet Galaxy

EINet Galaxy is a guide to world-wide information and services. It includes public information as well as commercial information and services provided by EINet customers and affiliates. The information is organized by topic, and can be searched.

Keywords: WWW, Information Retrieval, Internet

Sponsor: Microelectronic and Computer Technology Corporation (MCC)

Audience: Researchers, Students

Contact: Wayne Allen, Bruce Speyer
WA@EINet.net
Speyer@EINet.net

`http://galaxy.einet.net/galaxy.html`

EUnet

A global Internet Service Provider with national providers in almost 30 countries. Applications such as customer support, remote diagnosis, software development tools, and product information are available through this net.

Keywords: Internet

Sponsor: EUnet Information Services

Audience: Internet Surfers

Contact: info@eu.net

Details: Free

`http://www.eu.net`

Finding E-mail Addresses

Tips on finding e-mail addresses.

Keywords: Internet, E-mail

Audience: Internet Surfers

Contact: Jonathan Kamens
jib@MIT.Edu

Details: Free

File is: pub/docs/about-the-net/libsoft/email_address.txt

`ftp://sunsite.unc.edu`

Free for All

An experiment in a networked hypermedia group bulletin board.

Keywords: Internet, Group Communications, Multimedia

Audience: Internet Surfers, Multimedia Enthusiasts

Details: Free, Multimedia

`http://south.ncsa.uiuc.edu/Free.html`

FYI on Questions and Answer Answers to Commonly asked New Internet User Questions

Answers to questions commonly asked by new Internet users.

Keywords: Internet, Internet Resources

Sponsor: Xylogics, Inc., and SRI International

Audience: Internet Surfers

Profile: File is: documents/fyi/RFC_1594.txt

Contact: Gary Scott Malkin, April N. Marine
gmalkin@Xylogics.com or
april@nisc.sri.com

Details: Free

`ftp://nic.merit.edu`

Global Internet

A full-service Internet provider, offering superior quality Internet access and value-added services to business professionals, researchers, and educational communities.

Keywords: Internet, Finance

Sponsor: Global Internet, Palo Alto, CA (415)855-1700

Audience: Internet Users, Business Professionals, Financial Analysts, Publishers

Details: Costs

`mailto:sales@gi.net`

Gold in Networks

An introductory guide to the Internet.

Keywords: Internet

Sponsor: Ohio State University

Audience: Internet Surfers

Contact: J. Martin
nic@osu.edu

Details: Free

File is: documents/fyi/fyi_1o.txt

`ftp://nic.merit.edu`

Hitchhiker's Guide

A narrative of what the Internet has to offer.

Keywords: Internet

Sponsor: University of Illinois, Urbana, IL

Audience: Internet Surfers

Contact: Ed Krol
krol@uxc.cso.uiuc.ed

Details: Free

File is: documents/rfc/rfc1118.txt

`ftp://nic.merit.edu`

Details: Free

`ftp://nic.umass.edu`

Hypermedia/Internet

A guide to hypermedia and the Internet.

Keywords: Internet, Group Communications, Hypermedia

Sponsor: Australian National University

Audience: Internet Surfers

Contact: David Geoffrey Green
David.Green@anu.edu.au

Details: Free

`http:// life.anu.edu.au`

Incomplete Guide to the Internet (K12-Netzanleitung)

An Internet guide created especially for teachers and students in grades K-12.

Keywords: Education (K-12), Internet

Audience: Educators (K-12), Students (K-12)

Contact: Chuck Farmer
cfarmer@ncsa.uiuc.edu

Details: Free

`ftp://ncsa.uiuc.edu`

Infopop

A WINHELP (hypertext) guide to the Internet, CompuServe, BBS systems, and more.

Keywords: Internet, Internet Guides

Sponsor: Fenwick Library, George Mason University, Fairfax, VA

Audience: Internet Surfers

Contact: Wally Grotophorst
wallyg@fen1.gmu.edu

Details: Free

Read the file: library/readme

`ftp://ftp.gmu.edu`

Information Sources

These compiled resources provide information describing the Internet and computer-mediated communication technologies, as well as information on related applications, culture, discussion forums, and bibliographies.

Keywords: Internet, Networking

Audience: Internet Surfers, Computer-Mediated Communication Researchers

Contact: John December
decemj@rpi.edu

Details: Free

`ftp://ftp.rpi.edu`

`http://www.rpi.edu/Internet/Guides/`
`decemj/icmc/top.html`

Internet Browsers

A list of sources for Internet browsers and client software.

Keywords: Internet, Internet Tools

Sponsor: ANU Bioinformatics Hypermedia Service

Audience: Internet Surfers

Contact: David Green
David Green@anu.edu.au

Details: Free

`http://life.anu.edu.au/links/`
`syslib.html`

Internet Companion

A beginner's guide to global networking.

Keywords: Internet, Internet Guides

Sponsor: Software Tool & Die

Audience: Internet Surfers

Contact: staff@world.std.com

Details: Free

Files are in: OBS/
The.Internet.Companion

`ftp://world.std.com`

Internet Cruise

A computer-based tutorial for new and experienced Internet "navigators." Provides an introduction to Internet resources as diverse as: supercomputing, minorities, multimedia, cooking, and so on. Also provides information about the tools needed to access those resources.

Keywords: Internet, Internet Guides

Sponsor: Merit Network Information Center, Ann Arbor, MI

Audience: Internet Surfers

Contact: Steve Burdick, Laura Kelleher, Mark Davis-Craig
cruise2feedback@merit.edu

Details: Free

File is located in: /internet/resources

`ftp://nic.merit.edu`

Internet Economics

An article entitled "Some Economics of the Internet," by Jeffrey K. Mackie-Mason.

Keywords: Economics, Internet

Audience: Internet Surfers

Contact: Jeffrey K. Mackie-Mason

Details: Free

`ftp://gopher.econ.lsa.umich.edu`

Internet Growth

Contains figures showing the growth of the Internet, derived from historical figures and published by Mark Lottor and Marten Terpstra.

Keywords: Internet

Sponsor: Electronic Frontier Foundation

Audience: Internet Surfers

Details: Free

Files are in: matrix/growth/internet

`ftp://tic.com`

Internet Hunt

A game for exploring and learning about the Internet. It helps Net users to realize the vast and varied amounts of information available on the Net and helps more novice users, or Net "settlers," understand how to move around using the "trails" that the more experienced Hunt players have "blazed." Contains Internet Hunt questions, results, and comments.

Keywords: Internet, Games

Sponsor: CICnet

Audience: Internet Surfers

Contact: Rick Gates
rgates@nic.cic.net

Details: Free

`gopher://gopher.cic.net`

Internet Information Listing

A comprehensive collection of Internet information and utilities. Includes a listing of Internet providers, a large collection of guide books (NSF Resource Guide, Zen and the Art of the Internet, Big Dummy's Guide, and others), as well as specific help files for Internet utilities such as FTP, Telnet, and IRC. This site also features access to many popular gopher destinations.

Keywords: Internet, Internet Guides

Sponsor: Phantom Access Technologies, Inc.

Audience: Internet Surfers

Contact: root@phantom.com

`gopher://mindvox.phantom.com`

Internet Libraries (Gopher)

The site maintains the most current possible list of all library catalogs accessible on the Internet.

Keywords: Libraries, Databases, Internet, Information Retrieval

Audience: Reseacher, Students, Librarians

Contact: Gopherlib
gopherlib@gopher.yale.edu

`gopher://yaleinfo.yale.edu`

A B C D E F G H I J K L M N O P Q R S T U V W X Y Z

Internet Monthly Reports

Monthly communications to the Internet Research Group.

Keywords: Internet, Internet Guides

Sponsor: Merit Network Information Center Services

Audience: Internet Surfers

Details: Free

Index is: internet/newsletters/ INDEX.internet.monthly.report

`ftp://nic.merit.edu`

Internet Multicasting

Answers to frequently asked questions (FAQs) about the Internet Multicasting Service.

Keywords: Internet, Information Retrieval

Audience: Internet Surfers

Details: Free, Sound

Include "send FAQ" in the e-mail.

`mailto:info@radio.com`

Internet Policy

An article entitled "What Should We Plan Given the Dilemma of the Network?" by G. Cook.

Keywords: Internet, E-mail

Audience: Internet Surfers

Details: Free

`ftp://pit-manager.mit.edu`

Internet Pricing

An article entitled "Pricing the Internet."

Keywords: Internet, Economics

Audience: Internet Surfers

Details: Free

`gopher://gopher.econ.lsa.umich.edu`

Internet Public Subsidies

An article entitled "The Economic Case for Public Subsidy of the Internet."

Keywords: Internet, Economics

Audience: Internet Surfers

Details: Free

`gopher://ssugopher.sonoma.edu`

Internet Services FAQ

General information and answers to frequently asked questions (FAQs) about the Internet.

Keywords: Internet, Internet Guides, FAQs

Audience: Internet Surfers

Details: Free

User Info: File is: pub/usenet/news.answers/ internet-services/faq

`ftp://rtfm.mit.edu`

Internet Sound

Internet Sound contains various documents and programs regarding sound.

Keywords: Internet, Information Retrieval

Audience: Internet Surfers

User Info: ftp://ftp.cwi.nl/pub/audio/INDEX
ftp://ftp.cwi.nl/pub/audio/index.html

The index is: pub/audio/INDEX

Details: Free, Sound

`ftp://ftp.cwi.nl`

Internet Statistics

The latest statistical information about the Internet from the National Science Foundation.

Keywords: Internet

Sponsor: Merit Network Information Center

Audience: Internet Surfers

Details: Free

Index is: nsfnet/statistics/ INDEX.statistics

`ftp://nic.merit.edu`

Internet Systems UNITE

A list of tools for use on the Internet, by UNITE (User Network Interface to Everything).

Keywords: Internet, Internet Tools

Audience: Internet Surfers

Contact: unite-request@mailbase.ac.uk

Details: Free

File is: pub/lists/unite/files/systems-list.txt

`ftp://mail.base.ac.uk`

Internet Tools EARN

A guide to network research tools by the European Academic Research Network (EARN).

Keywords: Internet, Internet Tools

Audience: Internet Surfers

Contact: listserv@earncc.bitnet

Details: Free

Document is:earn/earn-resource-tool-guide.txt

`ftp://ns.ripe.net`

Internet Tools NIR

A status report on Networked Information Retrieval (NIR) tools and groups.

Keywords: Internet, Internet Tools

Sponsor: Joint IETF/RARE/CNI Networked Information Retrieval Working Group

Audience: Internet Surfers

Contact: Jill Foster
jill foster@newcastle.ac.uk

Details: Free

User Info: File is: pub/lists/nir/files/nir.status.report

`ftp://mail.base.ac.uk`

Internet Tools Summary

A list summarizing Internet tools for Network Information Retrieval (NIR) and computer-mediated communication (CMC) forums.

Keywords: Internet, Internet Tools

Audience: Internet Surfers

Contact: John December
decemj@rpi.edu

Details: Free

User Info: Files are located in: pub/communications. Read the internet-tools.readme first.

`ftp://ftp.rpi.edu`

InterNIC Directory Services (White Pages)

This web site provides free access to X.500, WHOIS, and Netfind white pages on the Internet.

Keywords: WWW, Internet, Internet Tools

Sponsor: National Science Foundation, USA

Audience: General Public, Students

Contact: Database Administrator
admin@ds.internic.net

`http://ds.internic.net/ds/dspgwp.html`

irc (Internet Relay Chat)

A multiuser, multichannel chatting network. It enables people all over the Internet to "talk" to one another interactively.

Keywords: Internet, Group Communications

Audience: Internet Surfers

Details: Free

User Info: Readme file is: irc/README

`ftp://cs.bu.edu`

Library Resources

A specialized guide to library resources on the Internet, with a focus on strategies for selection and use.

Keywords: Libraries, Internet

Audience: Internet Surfers, Researchers

User Info: File is: pub/internet/libcat-guide

`ftp://dla.ucop.edu/pub/internet/libcat-guide`

Library Special

Library Special collections on the Internet.

Keywords: Internet, Information Retrieval

Audience: Internet Surfers

Details: Free

`ftp://dla.ucop.edu/pub`

`http://dla.ucop.edu`

Merit Network Information Center Services

This site provides a large collection of Internet guides and information.

Keywords: Internet, Internet Guides, Internet Tools

Sponsor: Merit Network, Inc.

Audience: Internet Surfers

Profile: This site serves as a clearinghouse for many Internet guides, documents, and utilities. It includes Internet FAQs, bibliographies, glossaries, and user guides such as Zen and the Art of the Internet and The Internet Companion. It also has archives of various Internet documents listing service providers, acceptable use policies, and resources. Many software programs for navigating the Internet are also available here for a wide variety of platforms

Contact: nic-info@nic.merit.edu

`gopher://nic.merit.edu`

`ftp://nic.merit.edu`

MetaMail

This resource contains information about MetaMail, which allows existing mail readers to read multimedia e-mail in the MIME (Multipurpose Internet Mail Extensions) format.

Keywords: Internet, E-mail

Audience: Internet Surfers

Contact: Nathaniel S. Borenstein
nsb@nsb.fv.com

Readme file is pub/nsb/README

`ftp://thumper.bellcore.com`

MIME (Multipurpose Internet Mail Extensions)

This resource contains information about the MIME (Multipurpose Internet Mail Extensions) protocol.

Keywords: Internet, E-Mail

Audience: Internet Surfers

Contact: Nathaniel S. Borenstein
nsb@nsb.fv.com

File is: documents/rfc/rfc1521.txt

`ftp://nic.merit.edu`

MIT Media Lab

Online documents available through the ACCESS service that the MIT Media Laboratory is providing to sponsors using the File Transfer Protocol (FTP).

Keywords: Internet, Multimedia

Audience: Internet Surfers

Details: Free, Multimedia

`ftp://media-lab.media.mit.edu`

Multicast Backbone

Live audio and video multicast virtual network on top of the Internet.

Keywords: Internet, Information Retrieval

Audience: Internet Surfers

Details: Free, Sound

`ftp://venera.isi.edu`

`http://venera.isi.edu`

Multimedia Index

A list of multimedia information sources on the Internet.

Keywords: Internet, Multimedia

Sponsor: Centre Universitaire d'Informatique, University of Geneva

Audience: Internet Surfers

Contact: Oscar Nierstrasz
oscar@cui.unige.ch

Details: Free, Multimedia

`http://cui_www.unige.ch`

Multimedia Lab BU

Information about the Multimedia Lab at Boston University (BU), investigating issues surrounding the contruction of general-purpose distributed multimedia information systems (DMISs).

Keywords: Internet, Multimedia

Sponsor: Boston University

Audience: Internet Surfers

Contact: T.D.C. Little
tdcl@spiderman.bu.edu

Details: Free, Multimedia

`http://spiderman.bu.edu`

Multimedia Survey

A survey of distributed multimedia research, standards, and products by RARE (Associated Networks for European Research).

Keywords: Internet, Multimedia

Audience: Internet Surfers

Details: Free, Multimedia files available.

`ftp://ftp.ed.ac.uk/pub/mmsurvey`

Neci-announce

This is the announcement forum of New England Community Internet, an organization dedicated to making Usenet and Internet accessible to the public without economic or technical barriers. The group is developing ways to bring IP connectivity at low cost into homes and nonprofit organizations.

Keywords: Internet, Usenet

Audience: Internet Surfers, Usenet Users

Contact: neci-announce-request@pioneer.ci.net

Details: Free

User Info: To subscribe to the list, send an e-mail message requesting a subscription to the URL address below.

`mailto:neci-announce-request@pioneer.ci.net`

Neci-digest

This is the daily discussion forum of New England Community Internet, an organization dedicated to making Usenet and Internet accessible to the public without economic or technical-expertise barriers. The group is developing ways to bring IP connectivity at low cost into homes and nonprofit organizations.

Keywords: Internet, Usenet

Audience: Internet Surfers, Usenet Users

Contact: neci-digest-request@pioneer.ci.net

Details: Free

User Info: To subscribe to the list, send an e-mail message requesting a subscription to the URL address below.

`mailto:neci-digest-request@pioneer.ci.net`

Neci-discuss

This is the general discussion forum of New England Community Internet, an organization dedicated to making Usenet and Internet accessible to the public without economic or technical-expertise barriers. The group is developing ways to bring IP connectivity at low cost into homes and nonprofit organizations.

A
B
C
D
E
F
G
H
I
J
K
L
M
N
O
P
Q
R
S
T
U
V
W
X
Y
Z

A
B
C
D
E
F
G
H
I
J
K
L
M
N
O
P
Q
R
S
T
U
V
W
X
Y
Z

Keywords: Internet, Usenet

Audience: Internet Surfers, Usenet Users

Contact: neci-discuss-request@pioneer.ci.net

Details: Free

User Info: To subscribe to the list, send an e-mail message requesting a subscription to the URL address below.

Notes: To get a daily digestified version, subscribe to neci-digest. To receive organizational announcements only, subscribe to neci-announce.

`mailto:neci-discuss-request@pioneer.ci.net`

Net Etiquette Guide

Guidelines and Netiquette for the Net user.

Keywords: Internet, Etiquette, Netiquette

Sponsor: SURAnet Network Information Center

Audience: Internet Surfers

Contact: info@sura.net

Details: Free

File is: pub/nic/internet.literature/netiquette.txt

`ftp://ftp.sura.net`

Net-News

A newsletter devoted to library and information resources on the Internet.

Keywords: Information, Libraries, Networking, Internet

Sponsor: Metronet

Audience: Librarians, Researchers

Contact: Dana Noonan

noonan@msus1.msus.edu

Details: Free

Send e-mail request to noonan@msus1.msus.edu or metronet@vz.acs.umn.edu

`gopher://noonan@msus1.msus.edu`

NetCom

NetCom is an Internet provider. It has produced "Net Cruiser" software for Windows.

Keywords: Internet

Audience: Internet Users

Details: Costs

`Netcom@netcom.com`

New User's Questions

Answers to commonly asked questions by new Internet users.

Keywords: Internet, Internet Guides

Sponsor: Xylogics, Inc., and SRI International

Audience: Internet Surfers

Contact: Gary Scott Malkin, April N. Marine
gmalkin@Xylogics.COM
april@nisc.sri.com

Details: Free

File is: documents/fyi/fyi_04.txt

`ftp://nic.merit.edu`

NIR Archives

Archives of the NIR (Networked Information Retrieval) service.

Keywords: Internet, Information Retrieval

Audience: Internet Surfers

Details: Free

Files are in: pub/lists/nir

`ftp:// mailbase.ac.uk`

NIR Gopher

The gopher for the NIR (Networked Information Retrieval) service.

Keywords: Internet, Information Retrieval, NIR

Audience: Internet Surfers

Details: Free

`gopher:// mailbase.ac.auk /11/lists-k-o/nic`

NSF Resource Guide

A guide to Internet resources from the NSF (National Science Foundation).

Keywords: Internet, Internet Guides

Audience: Internet Surfers

Details: Free

Read the overview in: resource-guide/overview

`ftp://ds.internic.net`

NWNet Internet Guide

An introductory guide to the Internet. Details the basic Internet tools of electronic mail, FTP (File Transfer Protocol), and Telnet. Covers types of resources found on the Internet, and how to use them. Includes information directed toward supercomputer users and the K-12 community.

Keywords: Internet, Internet Guides, Supercomputers, Education (K-12)

Sponsor: NorthWestNet

Audience: Internet Surfers, Supercomputer Users, Students (K-12)

Contact: Jonathan Kochmer
nusirg@nwnet.net

Details: Free

File is: /user-docs/nusirg/nusirg.whole-guide.ps

`ftp://ftphost.nwnet.net`

NYSERNet Internet Guide

A comprehensive guide to the Internet from the New York State Education and Research Network (NYSERNet). NYSERNet provides access to specialized databases and online libraries, as well as to supercomputing and parallel-processing facilities throughout the US and to many national networks.

Keywords: Internet, Internet Guides, New York, Supercomputers

Sponsor: NYSERNet K-12 Networking Interest Group

Audience: Internet Surfers

Contact: info@nysernet.org

Details: Free

`ftp://nysernet.org`

Ogphre - SunSITE

A collection of Internet resources organized by subject. Particular strengths include agriculture, religious texts, poetry, creative writing, and US politics. The ftp site has a set of more general Internet guides.

Keywords: Agriculture, Politics (US), Religion, Internet

Sponsor: The University of North Carolina - Chapel Hill and Sun Microsystems, USA

Audience: General Public, Internet Surfers, Researchers

Contact: Darlene Fladager, Elizabeth Lyons
Darlene_Fladager@unc.edu,
Elizabeth_Lyons@unc.edu

`gopher://sunsite.unc.edu`

`ftp://sunsite.unc.edu`

Online Radio

Transcripts and promotional information from Online Radio, a weekly radio program of Perth's Curtin University devoted to reporting the latest developments in the computing world.

Keywords: Computers, Internet, Radio

Sponsor: Curtin University Computing Center, Perth, Australia

Audience: Computer Enthusiasts

Contact: Onno Benschop
online@info.curtin.edu.au

`gopher://ob1.curtin.edu.au`

ORA-NEWS

Announcements from O'Reilly & Associates, publishers of books about the Internet, UNIX, and other open systems. Other products and services include The Global Network Navigator (an interactive online magazine) and Internet in a Box. It's gatewayed to the biz.oreilly.announce Usenet newsgroup.

Keywords: Internet, UNIX, Usenet

Audience: Internet Surfers, Usenet Users, UNIX Users

Contact: listown@online.ora.com

Details: Free, Moderated

User Info: To subscribe to the list, send an e-mail message requesting a subscription to the URL address below.

To send a message to the entire list, address it to: ora-news@online.ora.com

`mailto:listproc@online.ora.com`

ParNET

To discuss the installation, use, and modification of ParNET, an Amiga<->Amiga networking program.

Keywords: Internet

Audience: ParNet Users

Contact: Ben Jackson
parnet-list@ben.com

Details: Free

User Info: To subscribe to the list, send an e-mail message requesting a subscription to the URL address below.

To send a message to the entire list, address it to: parnet-list@ben.com

`mailto:parnet-list-request@ben.com`

PGP Mail

Information regarding the use of PGP (Pretty Good Privacy) mail, a public key.

Keywords: Internet, E-mail

Audience: Internet Surfers

Details: Free

`ftp://ftp.uu.net/networking/mail`

Privacy

An archive about identity, privacy, and anonymity on the Internet, from the Usenet newsgroup alt.privacy.

Keywords: Privacy, Internet

Audience: Internet Surfers

Details: Free
File is: pub/nic/internet.literature/netiquette.txt

`ftp://pit-manager.mit.edu`

PSI

PSI is an Internet service provider.

Keywords: Internet

Sponsor: PSI

Audience: Internet Users

Details: Costs

`telnet://psi.com`

Retrieval Success

Succesfull stories of using the Internet for reference. In each case, a librarian used Internet resources to answer reference questions. In many cases, particularly for the smaller libraries, the Internet provided information that would otherwise have been inaccessible.

Keywords: Internet, Information Retrieval

Audience: Internet Surfers

Contact: Karen Schneider
kgs@panix.com

Details: Free
File is: pub/lists/unite/files/internet-stories.txt

`ftp://mailbase.ac.uk`

Searching Gopherspace with Veronica

A resource that conducts Veronica searches over restricted areas of the Internet.

Keywords: WWW, Information Retrieval, Internet

Audience: Reseachers, Students, General Public

`gopher://gopher.well.sf.ca.us/11/outbound/veronica.search`

Singapore DMC

The Digital Media Center (DMC) home page contains links related to contents about Singapore, the National Computer Board (NCB), and various other National IT (Information Technology) projects.

Keywords: Internet, Networking

Audience: Internet Surfers

Contact: shaopin@ncb.gov.sg
kianjin@ncb.gov.sg

Details: Free

`http://king.ncb.gov.sg`

Smiley Faces Dictionary

An unofficial list of more than 200 smilies.

Keywords: Internet, Smiley

Audience: Internet Surfers

Details: Free

User Info: File is: /pub/smiley-dictionary

`http://ftp.gsfc.nasa.gov`

Surfing the Internet

An introductory guide to "surfing," or finding information on the Internet.

Keywords: Internet, Internet Guides, Surfing (internet)

Audience: Internet Surfers

Details: Free

`ftp://rtfm.mit.edu`

The Scout Report

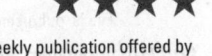

The Scout Report is a weekly publication offered by InterNIC Information Services to the Internet community as a fast, convenient way to stay informed on network activities.

Keywords: WWW, Information Retrieval, Internet, Computer Networking

Sponsor: National Science Foundation, USA

Audience: Researchers, Students, General Public

Profile: The purpose of this resource is to combine in one place the highlights of new resource announcements and other news which occurred on the Internet during the previous week. The Report is released every Friday. Categories included each week will vary depending on content, and the report will evolve with time and with input from the networking community.

Contact: InfoGuide
scout@is.internic.net,
guide@is.internic.net

`http://www.internic.net/scout-report`

The World Wide Web Acronym Server

This web site is a guide to acronyms and abbreviations used on

Keywords: Internet, Lexicography

Audience: Internet Surfers

Contact: Peter Flynn
pflynn@curia.ucc.ie

Details: Free

`http://curia.ucc.ie/info/net/acronyms/acro.html`

UNITE Archive

The User Network Interface to Everything (UNITE) discussion list. The list is a focus for discussion on the concept of a total solution interface with user-friendly, desktop-integrated, access to all network services.

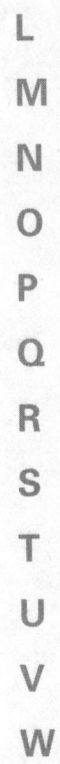

A
B
C
D
E
F
G
H
I
J
K
L
M
N
O
P
Q
R
S
T
U
V
W
X
Y
Z

Keywords: Internet, Information Retrieval, Interface Design

Audience: Internet Surfers

Contact: George Munroe, Jill Foster
unite-request@mailbase.ac.uk

Details: Free

Files are in: pub/lists/unite

`ftp://mailbase.ac.uk`

Usenet Repository ★

Regular informational postings and FAQs from various newsgroups on the Usenet, grouped into archives by newsgroup.

Keywords: Internet, Networking, Usenet

Audience: Internet Surfers

Details: Free

File is: pub/usenet-by-group

`ftp://pit-manager.mit.edu`

What is the Internet? ★

An introductory guide to the Internet.

Keywords: Internet

Sponsor: University of Illinois and Merit Network, Inc.

Audience: Internet Surfers

Contact: Ed Krol , Ellen Hoffman
e-krol@uiuc.edu or ellen@merit.edu

Details: Free

File is: documents/fyi/fyi_20.txt

`ftp://nic.merit.edu`

World Wide Web Worm (WWWW) ★★★★

WWWW provides a mechanism to search the WWW in a multitude of ways. It also provides lists of all Home pages and of all URLs cited anywhere. This site contains an exhaustive list of WWW servers nationally and internationally.

Keywords: WWW, Information Retrieval, Internet

Sponsor: University of Colorado at Boulder, Department of Computer Science, Boulder, Colorado, USA

Audience: Researchers, Students, General Public

Contact: Oliver McBryan
mcbryan@cs.colorado.edu

`http://www.cs.colorado.edu/home/mcbryan/WWWW.html`

Zen and the Art of the Internet ★

A beginner's guide to the Internet.

Keywords: Internet

Audience: Internet Surfers

Contact: Brendan Kehoe
guide-bugs@cs.widener.edu

Details: Free

User Info: File is: /net/zen/zen-1.0.txt

`ftp://csn.org`

Internet Access

FreeNets ★★★

This resource provides extensive information about FreeNets, which are public access Internet sites at no-charge or for donations.

Keywords: Internet Access, Community Networking

Audience: Individuals, Communities, Libraries

Profile: FreeNets, community computing services providing Internet access, exist internationally and include such systems as LA FreeNet, Buffalo FreeNet, Cleveland FreeNet, FreeNet Erlangen-Nuernburg, Victoria FreeNet, Vaasa FreePort (Finland), CapAccess (D.C.), and many more.

Details: Free

The URL (gopher path) below, contains pointers to all FreeNets.

`gopher path: 1/internet/freenets marvel.loc.gov`

Internet Art Gallery

Internet Art Gallery ★★

An online art collection in the form of JPEG files, including the works of 85 artists ranging from Dali to Van Eyck.

Keywords: Art, Fine Art, Art History

Sponsor: New York State Education Department

Audience: Artists, Art Students, Art Teachers, General Public

Contact: Steve Richter, George Casler
steve@unix5.nysed.gov,
gcasler@unix5.nysed.gov

`gopher://unix5.nysed.gov`

Internet Browsers

Internet Browsers ★★

A list of sources for Internet browsers and client software.

Keywords: Internet, Internet Tools

Sponsor: ANU Bioinformatics Hypermedia Service

Audience: Internet Surfers

Contact: David Green
David Green@anu.edu.au

Details: Free

`http://life.anu.edu.au/links/syslib.html`

Internet Chess Library

Internet Chess Library

An FTP and gopher site containing all kinds of chess-related files.

Keywords: Chess

Audience: Chess Players

Profile: The Internet Chess Library is an FTP and gopher site with archives containing all kinds of chess-related files. The library contains chess software of different types, schedules, international chess announcements, rating guides, and anything else relating to chess.

Contact: Chris Petroff
chris@chess.uaknor.edu

`gopher://chess.uaknor.edu`

`ftp://chess.uaknor.edu`

Internet Companion

Internet Companion ★

A beginner's guide to global networking.

Keywords: Internet, Internet Guides

Sponsor: Software Tool & Die

Audience: Internet Surfers

Contact: staff@world.std.com

Details: Free

User Info: Files are in: OBS/The.Internet.Companion

`ftp://world.std.com`

Internet Cruise

Internet Cruise ★

A computer-based tutorial for new and experienced Internet "navigators." Provides an introduction to Internet resources as diverse as: supercomputing, minorities, multimedia, cooking, and so on. Also provides information about the tools needed to access those resources.

Keywords: Internet, Internet Guides

Sponsor: Merit Network Information Center, Ann Arbor, MI

Audience: Internet Surfers

Contact: Steve Burdick, Laura Kelleher, Mark
             Davis-Craig
             cruise2feedback@merit.edu

Details: Free

User Info: File is located in: /internet/resources

`ftp://nic.merit.edu`

Internet Directories

The McKinley Group

A resource for the location of US and international
data, to assist in the preparation of Geographic
Information Systems (GIS). Specializes also in
locating copies of old advertisements from
anywhere in the world.

Keywords: Internet Publishing, Internet Directories,
             Internet Marketing, Internet Research

Audience: Management Information Specialists,
             Market Researchers, Lawyers

Profile: Provision of strategic information to
             assist organizations and businesses in
             targeting their markets more effectively.
             Specializes in obtaining hard-to-locate
             information for the creation of
             Geographic Information Systems.
             Resource include old advertisements
             from newspapers and magazines
             worldwide.

Details: Costs

User Info: To subscribe, send an e-mail message to
             the URL address below. In the body of
             your message, state the nature of your
             inquiry.

`mailto:mckinley@holonet.net`

Internet Economics

Internet Economics

An article entitled "Some Economics of the
Internet," by Jeffrey K. Mackie-Mason.

Keywords: Economics, Internet

Audience: Internet Surfers

Contact: Jeffrey K. Mackie-Mason

Details: Free

`ftp://gopher.econ.lsa.umich.edu`

Internet FAQs and Guides

Internet FAQs and Guides

A collection of introductory Internet information,
including guides to netiquette, jargon, and utilities,
such as ftp and telnet.

Keywords: Internet Resources

Sponsor: University of Wisconsin - Stevens Point

Audience: Internet Surfers

Contact: Peter Zuge
             gopher@worf.uwsp.edu

`gopher://nt2.uwsp.edu`

Internet Federal Register (IFR)

Internet Federal Register (IFR)

The full text of the US Federal Register.

Keywords: Federal Register, Government (US
             Federal), Law (US Federal)

Sponsor: Counterpoint Publishing

Audience: General Public, Journalists, Students,
             Politicians, Citizens

Contact: fedreg@internet.com

Details: Costs

`gopher://gopher.internet.com`

Internet GIS and RS Information Sites

Internet GIS and RS Information Sites

This document contains a lengthy listing of GIS and
remote sensing sites on the Internet.

Keywords: GIS, Remote Sensing, Image Processing,
             Geography

Sponsor: Queen's University Department of
             Geography

Audience: Researchers, General Public

Contact: Michael McDermott
             mcdermom@gisdog.gis.queensu.ca

Details: Free

Notes: ASCII version also available from the
             same FTP site.

`ftp://gis.queensu.ca/pub/gis/docs/gissites.html`

Internet Guides

AARNet Guide

This is the Australian Network Sites and Resources
Guide.

Keywords: Internet, Internet Guide

Sponsor: Australian Academic and Research
             Network

Audience: Internet Surfers

Details: Free

             Files are in: pub/resource-guide

`ftp://aarnet.edu.au/pub/resource-guide`

DDN New User Guide

Defense Data Network (DDN) guide for new users.

Keywords: Internet, Internet Guides, Defense,
             Security

Audience: Internet Surfers

Details: Free

             File is: netinfo/nug.doc

`ftp://nic.ddn.mil/netinfo`

E-mail-How To

An introductory guide to the e-Mail System and to
the procedures for sending and receiving mail,
sending files by mail, and adding messages to files
that are sent by mail.

Keywords: Internets Tools, Internet Guides, E-mail

Sponsor: SURAnet Network Information Center

Audience: Internet Surfers

Contact: info@sura.net

Details: Free

             File is: pub/nic/network.service.guides/
             how.to.email.guide

`ftp://ftp.sura.net`

Infopop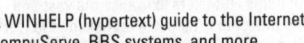

A WINHELP (hypertext) guide to the Internet,
CompuServe, BBS systems, and more.

Keywords: Internet, Internet Guides

Sponsor: Fenwick Library, George Mason
             University, Fairfax, VA

Audience: Internet Surfers

Contact: Wally Grotophorst
             wallyg@fen1.gmu.edu

Details: Free

User Info: Read the file: library/readme

`ftp://ftp.gmu.edu`

Internet Companion

A beginner's guide to global networking.

Keywords: Internet, Internet Guides

Sponsor: Software Tool & Die

Audience: Internet Surfers

Contact: staff@world.std.com

Details: Free

             Files are in: OBS/
             The.Internet.Companion

`ftp://world.std.com`

A B C D E F G H I J K L M N O P Q R S T U V W X Y Z

Internet Cruise ★

A computer-based tutorial for new and experienced Internet "navigators." Provides an introduction to Internet resources as diverse as: supercomputing, minorities, multimedia, cooking, and so on. Also provides information about the tools needed to access those resources.

Keywords: Internet, Internet Guides

Sponsor: Merit Network Information Center, Ann Arbor, MI

Audience: Internet Surfers

Contact: Steve Burdick, Laura Kelleher, Mark Davis-Craig cruise2feedback@merit.edu

Details: Free

User Info: File is located in: /internet/resources

`ftp://nic.merit.edu`

Internet Growth ★

Contains figures showing the growth of the Internet, derived from historical figures and published by Mark Lottor and Marten Terpstra.

Keywords: Internet, Internet Guides

Sponsor: Electronic Frontier Foundation

Audience: Internet Surfers

Details: Free

User Info: Files are in: matrix/growth/internet

`ftp://tic.com`

Internet Hunt ★

A game for exploring and learning about the Internet. It helps Net users to realize the vast and varied amounts of information available on the Net and helps more novice users, or Net "settlers," understand how to move around using the "trails" that the more experienced Hunt players have "blazed." Contains Internet Hunt questions, results, and comments.

Keywords: Internet, Internet Guides, Games

Sponsor: CICnet

Audience: Internet Surfers

Contact: Rick Gates rgates@nic.cic.net

Details: Free

`gopher://gopher.cic.net`

Internet Information Listing ★★★★

A comprehensive collection of Internet information and utilities. Includes a listing of Internet providers, a large collection of guide books (NSF Resource Guide, Zen and the Art of the Internet, Big Dummy's Guide, and others), as well as specific help files for Internet utilities such as FTP, Telnet, and IRC. This site also features access to many popular gopher destinations.

Keywords: Internet Guides

Sponsor: Phantom Access Technologies, Inc.

Audience: Internet Surfers

Contact: root@phantom.com

`gopher://mindvox.phantom.com`

Internet Monthly Reports ★

Monthly communications to the Internet Research Group.

Keywords: Internet, Internet Guides

Sponsor: Merit Network Information Center Services

Audience: Internet Surfers

Details: Free

Index is: internet/newsletters/ INDEX.internet.monthly.report

`ftp://nic.merit.edu`

Internet Phone Books ★★★

A collection of Internet phone books and e-mail directories.

Keywords: Phone Books, Internet Guides, E-mail

Sponsor: Texas Tech University

Audience: Internet Surfers, General Public

Profile: This gopher includes a number of resources for finding people on the Internet. In addition to the standard Netfind, WHOIS, and Inter-NIC services, it also has information on finding college and international e-mail addresses. Also features snail mail information from the U.S. Post Office on ZIP codes, as well as an international directory of telephone area codes.

Contact: Abdul Malik Yoosufani gripe@cs.ttu.edu

`gopher://cs4sun.cs.ttu.edu`

Internet Services FAQ ★

General information and answers to frequently asked questions (FAQs) about the Internet.

Keywords: Internet, Internet Guides, FAQs

Audience: Internet Surfers

Details: Free

User Info: File is: pub/usenet/news.answers/ internet-services/faq

`ftp://rtfm.mit.edu`

Internet Statistics ★

The latest statistical information about the Internet from the National Science Foundation.

Keywords: Internet, Internet Guides

Sponsor: Merit Network Information Center

Audience: Internet Surfers

Details: Free

Index is: /nsfnet/statistics/INDEX.statistics

`ftp://nic.merit.edu`

Librarian's Internet Reference

Electronic version of "Internet Connections: A Librarian's Guide to Dial-Up Access and Use," written by Engle, Mary E, and Marilyn Lutz, William Jones, Jr., and Genevieve Engel.

Keywords: Internet Guides, Librarianship

Audience: Librarians

Contact: Mary Engle Mary_Engle@ucop.edu

`gopher://gopher.poniecki.berkeley.edu`

`Poniecki Foundation/Internet Guides`

Merit Network Information Center Services ★★

This site provides a large collection of Internet guides and information.

Keywords: Internet, Internet Guides, Internet Tools

Sponsor: Merit Network, Inc.

Audience: Internet Surfers

Profile: This site serves as a clearinghouse for many Internet guides, documents, and utilities. It includes Internet FAQs, bibliographies, glossaries, and user guides such as Zen and the Art of the Internet and The Internet Companion. It also has archives of various Internet documents listing service providers, acceptable use policies, and resources. Many software programs for navigating the Internet are also available here for a wide variety of platforms

Contact: nic-info@nic.merit.edu

`gopher://nic.merit.edu`

`ftp://nic.merit.edu`

New User's Questions ★

Answers to commonly asked questions by new Internet users.

Keywords: Internet, Internet Guides

Sponsor: Xylogics, Inc., and SRI International

Audience: Internet Surfers

Contact: Gary Scott Malkin, April N. Marine gmalkin@Xylogics.COM april@nisc.sri.com

Details: Free File is: documents/fyi/fyi_04.txt

`ftp://nic.merit.edu`

NSF Resource Guide

A guide to Internet resources from the NSF (National Science Foundation).

Keywords: Internet, Internet Guides

Audience: Internet Surfers

Details: Free

Read the overview in: resource-guide/overview

`ftp://ds.internic.net`

NWNet Internet Guide ★

An introductory guide to the Internet. Details the basic Internet tools of electronic mail, FTP (File Transfer Protocol), and Telnet. Covers types of resources found on the Internet, and how to use them. Includes information directed toward supercomputer users and the K-12 community.

Keywords: Internet, Internet Guides, Supercomputers, Education (K-12)

Sponsor: NorthWestNet

Audience: Internet Surfers, Supercomputer Users, Students (K-12)

Contact: Jonathan Kochmer
nusirg@nwnet.net

Details: Free

File is: /user-docs/nusirg/nusirg.whole-guide.ps

`ftp://ftphost.nwnet.net`

NYSERNet Internet Guide ★

A comprehensive guide to the Internet from the New York State Education and Research Network (NYSERNet). NYSERNet provides access to specialized databases and online libraries, as well as to supercomputing and parallel-processing facilities throughout the US and to many national networks.

Keywords: Internet, Internet Guides, New York, Supercomputers

Sponsor: NYSERNet K-12 Networking Interest Group

Audience: Internet Surfers

Contact: info@nysernet.org

Details: Free

`ftp://nysernet.org`

Surfing the Internet ★

An introductory guide to "surfing," or finding information on the Internet.

Keywords: Internet, Internet Guides, Surfing (internet)

Audience: Internet Surfers

Details: Free

`ftp://rtfm.mit.edu`

The Internet Press ★★★

A guide to electronic journals about the Internet.

Keywords: Internet Guides, Electronic Publications

Audience: General Public

Profile: Publications discussed include the following: NSF Network News, Meta Magazine, Bits and Bytes, The Network Observer, HotWIRED, Scout Report, Netsurfer Digest, and The Internet Informer.

Contact: Kevin M. Savetz

User Info: To subscribe to the list, send an e-mail message to the URL address below, with the subject line subscribe ipress. (Leave the body of the message blank.)

`mailto:savetz@rahul.net`

Usenet What Is? ★

An article entitled "What Is Usenet?"

Keywords: Internet Guides, Internet Tools, Usenet

Audience: Internet Surfers

Details: Free

File is: pub/usenet/news.answers/what-is/usenet/part1

`ftp://rtfm.mit.edu`

Usenet World ★

A special issue of the Amateur Computerist newsletter about Usenet.

Keywords: Internet Guides, Internet Tools, Usenet

Audience: Internet Surfers

Details: Free

File is: doc/misc/acn/acn4-5.txt

`ftp://wuarchive.wustl.edu`

Internet Hunt

Internet Hunt ★

A game for exploring and learning about the Internet. It helps Net users to realize the vast and varied amounts of information available on the Net and helps more novice users, or Net "settlers," understand how to move around using the "trails" that the more experienced Hunt players have "blazed." Contains Internet Hunt questions, results, and comments.

Keywords: Internet, Internet Guides, Games

Sponsor: CICnet

Audience: Internet Surfers

Contact: Rick Gates
rgates@nic.cic.net

Details: Free

`gopher://gopher.cic.net`

Internet Information Listing

Internet Information Listing ★★★★

A comprehensive collection of Internet information and utilities. Includes a listing of Internet providers, a large collection of guide books (NSF Resource Guide, Zen and the Art of the Internet, Big Dummy's Guide, and others), as well as specific help files for Internet utilities such as FTP, Telnet, and IRC. This site also features access to many popular gopher destinations.

Keywords: Internet, Internet Guides

Sponsor: Phantom Access Technologies, Inc.

Audience: Internet Surfers

Contact: root@phantom.com

`gopher://mindvox.phantom.com`

Internet Libraries (Gopher)

Internet Libraries (Gopher) ★★★

The site maintains the most current possible list of all library catalogs accessible on the Internet.

Keywords: Libraries, Databases, Internet, Information Retrieval

Audience: Reseacher, Students, Librarians

Contact: Gopherlib
gopherlib@gopher.yale.edu

`gopher://yaleinfo.yale.edu`

Internet Marketing

The McKinley Group ★★★

A resource for the location of US and international data, to assist in the preparation of Geographic Information Systems (GIS). Specializes also in locating copies of old advertisements from anywhere in the world.

Keywords: Internet Publishing, Internet Directories, Internet Marketing, Internet Research

Audience: Management Information Specialists, Market Researchers, Lawyers

Profile: Provision of strategic information to assist organizations and businesses in targeting their markets more effectively. Specializes in obtaining hard-to-locate information for the creation of Geographic Information Systems. Resource include old advertisements from newspapers and magazines worldwide.

Details: Costs

To subscribe, send an e-mail message to the URL address below.

`mailto:mckinley@holonet.net`

A B C D E F G H I J K L M N O P Q R S T U V W X Y Z

Internet Monthly Reports

Internet Monthly Reports

Monthly communications to the Internet Research Group.

Keywords: Internet, Internet Guides

Sponsor: Merit Network Information Center Services

Audience: Internet Surfers

Details: Free

User Info: internet/newsletters/ INDEX.internet.monthly.report

`ftp://nic.merit.edu`

Internet Multicasting

Internet Multicasting

Answers to frequently asked questions (FAQs) about the Internet Multicasting Service.

Keywords: Internet, Information Retrieval

Audience: Internet Surfers

Details: Free, Sound Files Available.

Include "send FAQ" in the e-mail.

`mailto: info@radio.com`

Internet Nonprofit Center

Internet Nonprofit Center

A clearinghouse of information for nonprofit organizations and those interested in donating to them. Includes annual reports, directories, financial information, and brochures of selected nonprofit organizations, as well as volunteer opportunities and advice for potential donors. The Internet Nonprofit Center is currently located on EnviroLink Network, a gopher dedicated to environmental causes.

Keywords: Nonprofit Organizations, Philanthropy

Sponsor: American Institute of Philanthropy, USA, and The Internet Nonprofit Center, Brooklyn, New York, USA

Audience: Activists, Philanthropists

Contact: Cliff Landesman clandesm@panix.com

`gopher://envirolink.org`

Internet Phone Books

Internet Phone Books

A collection of Internet phone books and e-mail directories.

Keywords: Phone Books, Internet Guides, E-mail

Sponsor: Texas Tech University

Audience: Internet Surfers, General Public

Profile: This gopher includes a number of resources for finding people on the Internet. In addition to the standard Netfind, WHOIS, and Inter-NIC services, it also has information on finding college and international e-mail addresses. Also features snail mail information from the U.S. Post Office on ZIP codes, as well as an international directory of telephone area codes.

Contact: Abdul Malik Yoosufani gripe@cs.ttu.edu

`gopher://cs4sun.cs.ttu.edu`

Internet Policy

Internet Policy

An article entitled "What Should We Plan Given the Dilemma of the Network?" by G. Cook.

Keywords: Internet, E-mail

Audience: Internet Surfers

Details: Free

`ftp://pit-manager.mit.edu`

Internet Pricing

Internet Pricing

An article entitled "Pricing the Internet."

Keywords: Internet, Economics

Audience: Internet Surfers

Contact: Mackie-Mason and Varian

Details: Free

`gopher:// gopher.econ.lsa.umich.edu`

Internet Public Subsidies

Internet Public Subsidies

An article entitled "The Economic Case for Public Subsidy of the Internet."

Keywords: Internet, Pricing

Audience: Internet Surfers

Contact: Sandra Schickele

Details: Free

`gopher://ssugopher.sonoma.edu`

Internet Publishing

The McKinley Group

A resource for the location of US and international data, to assist in the preparation of Geographic Information Systems (GIS). Specializes also in locating copies of old advertisements from anywhere in the world.

Keywords: Internet Publishing, Internet Directories, Internet Marketing, Internet Research

Audience: Management Information Specialists, Market Researchers, Lawyers

Profile: Provision of strategic information to assist organizations and businesses in targeting their markets more effectively. Specializes in obtaining hard-to-locate information for the creation of Geographic Information Systems. Resource include old advertisements from newspapers and magazines worldwide.

Details: Costs

To subscribe, send an e-mail message to the URL address below. In the body of your message, state the nature of your inquiry.

`mailto:mckinley@holonet.net`

Internet Reference

Cello FAQ

A site containing common questions and answers about Cello, a multipurpose Internet browser that allows access to the myriad information resources of the Internet. It supports World Wide Web, Gopher, FTP, CSO/pf/qi, and Usenet News retrievals natively, and other protocols (WAIS, Hytelnet, Telnet, and TN3270) through external clients and public gateways.

Keywords: Internet Tools, Internet Reference

Sponsor: Cornell Law School, New York, USA

Audience: Students, Computer Scientists, Researchers.

`http://www.law.cornell.edu/cello/ cellofaq.html`

comp.infosystems.gopher

A Usenet newsgroup providing information and discussion about the gopher information search tool.

Keywords: Gopher, Information Retrieval

Audience: Internet Surfers

User Info: To subscribe to this Usenet newsgroup, you need access to a newsreader.

`news:comp.infosystems.gopher`

comp.infosystems.wais

A Usenet newsgroup providing information and discussion about the WAIS full-text search tool.

Keywords: WAIS, Information Retrieval

Audience: Internet Surfers

User Info: To subscribe to this Usenet newsgroup, you need access to a newsreader.

`news:comp.infosystems.wais`

comp.infosystems.www

A Usenet newsgroup providing information and discussion about the World Wide Web.

Keywords: WWW, Information Retrieval

Audience: Internet Surfers

User Info: To subscribe to this Usenet newsgroup, you need access to a newsreader.

`news:comp.infosystems.www`

Finding Resources on the Internet

A collection of help files introducing the new user to Internet utilities and resources.

Keywords: Internet Reference, Information Retrieval

Sponsor: Proper Publishing

Audience: Internet Surfers

Contact: info@proper.com

`gopher://proper.com`

FTP FAQ

Common questions and answers about FTP (File Transfer Protocol), FTP sites, and anonymous FTP. General information for the novice FTP user.

Keywords: FTP, Internet Guides

Audience: Students, Computer Scientists, Researchers

Contact: Perry Rovers
perry.rovers@kub.nl

`ftp://ftp.ifh.de/pub/FAQ/ftp.faq`

HTML FAQ

Common questions and answers about HTML (Hypertext Markup Language). The FAQ covers the practices of creating new documents specifically for the WWW format, as well as transforming existing materials into WWW documents.

Keywords: WWW, Internet Reference, Information Retrieval

Audience: Students, Computer Scientists, Researchers

Contact: Iain O'Cain
ec@umcc.umich.edu

`http://www.umcc.umich.edu/~ec/www/html_faq.html`

Lynx FAQ

A resource providing common questions and answers about Cello, a distributed hypertext browser with full WWW capabilities.

Keywords: Internet Reference

Sponsor: University of Kansas, Distributed Computing Group, Kansas, USA

Audience: Students, Computer Scientists, Researchers

Contact: Garrett Blythe, Lou Montulli
doslynx@falcon.cc.ukans.edu, montulli@mcom.com, lynx-help@ukanaix.cc.ukans.edu

`http://ftp2.cc.ukans.edu/about_lynx`

`http://ftp2.cc.ukans.edu/lynx_help`

`http://ftp2.cc.ukans.edu/lynx_writeup`

NCSA Mosaic FAQ

Common questions and answers about NCSA Mosaic, a network information browser (more technically, a World Wide Web Client) that allows one to retrieve documents from the World Wide Web system. There are versions of Mosaic available for Microsoft Windows on IBM PC-compatible machines, the X Window System on UNIX computers, and for the Apple Macintosh.

Keywords: Internet Reference

Sponsor: National Center for Supercomputing Applications at the University of Illinois at Urbana-Champaign, Illinois, USA

Audience: Students, Computer Scientists, Researchers

Contact: Software Development Group
softdev@ncsa.uiuc.edu

`http://www.ncsa.uiuc.edu/SDG/Software/MacMosaic/FAQ/FAQ-mac.html`

Veronica FAQ

A gopher containing common questions and answers about Veronica, a title search and retrieval system for use with the Internet Gopher.

Keywords: Internet Reference, Information Retrieval, Veronica

Audience: Students, Computer Scientists, Researchers

`gopher://pogonip.scs.unr.edu/00/veronica/veronica-faq`

WAIS FAQ

★ ★

Common questions and answers about WAIS (Wide Area Information Servers), a networked full-text retrieval system.

Keywords: Internet Reference

Sponsor: Thinking Machines, Apple Computer, Dow Jones, and KPMG Peat Marwick

Audience: Students, Computer Scientists, Researchers

Contact: Aydin Edguer
edguer.ces.cwru.edu

`ftp://rtfm.mit.edu/pub/usenet-by-group/news.answers/wais-faq/getting-started`

World Wide Web FAQ

A web site containing common questions and answers about WWW, a distributed hypermedia system first developed by CERN.

Keywords: WWW, Internet Reference, Information Retrieval

Audience: Students, Computer Scientists, Researchers

Contact: Thomas Boutell, Nathan Torkington
boutell@netcom.com, nathan.torckington@vuw.ac.nz

`http://sunsite.unc.edu/boutell/faq/www_faq.html`

Internet Research

Research on Demand

A resource for the provision of market information, strategic information location, product information, and national and international business information.

Keywords: Market Research, Internet Research, Legal Research, International Research

Audience: Marketing Specialists, Lawyers, Public Relations Experts, Business Professionals, Researchers, Writers, Producers

Profile: This resource has special access to unique information resources worldwide. Areas of particular information access include the former Soviet Union, Europe, and the US. Information access also includes access to all the major online systems, including Dialog, BRS, Orbit, DataStar, and so on. Current Awareness Services include research information gathered from the Internet.

Details: Costs

User Info: To subscribe, send an e-mail message to the URL address below. In the body of your message, state the nature of your inquiry.

Notes: Contact ROD directly in the US at: (800) 227-0750; outside the US at: (510) 841-1145.

`mailto:rod@holonet.net`

A
B
C
D
E
F
G
H
I
J
K
L
M
N
O
P
Q
R
S
T
U
V
W
X
Y
Z

A B C D E F G H I J K L M N O P Q R S T U V W X Y Z

The McKinley Group

A resource for the location of US and international data, to assist in the preparation of Geographic Information Systems (GIS). Specializes also in locating copies of old advertisements from anywhere in the world.

Keywords: Internet Publishing, Internet Directories, Internet Marketing, Internet Research

Audience: Management Information Specialists, Market Researchers, Lawyers

Profile: Provision of strategic information to assist organizations and businesses in targeting their markets more effectively. Specializes in obtaining hard-to-locate information for the creation of Geographic Information Systems. Resource include old advertisements from newspapers and magazines worldwide.

Details: Costs

To subscribe, send an e-mail message to the URL address below. In the body of your message, state the nature of your inquiry.

`mailto:mckinley@holonet.net`

Internet Resources

FYI on Questions and Answer Answers to Commonly asked New Internet User Questions

Answers to questions commonly asked by new Internet users.

Keywords: Directories, Internet Resources

Sponsor: Xylogics, Inc., and SRI International

Audience: Internet Surfers

Profile: File is: documents/fyi/RFC_1594.txt

Contact: Gary Scott Malkin, April N. Marine gmalkin@Xylogics.com or april@nisc.sri.com

Details: Free

`ftp://nic.merit.edu`

Internet FAQs and Guides

A collection of introductory Internet information, including guides to netiquette, jargon, and utilities, such as ftp and telnet.

Keywords: Internet Resources

Sponsor: University of Wisconsin - Stevens Point

Audience: Internet Surfers

Contact: Peter Zuge gopher@worf.uwsp.edu

`gopher://nt2.uwsp.edu`

Music

This directory is a general compilation of information resources focused on music.

Keywords: Internet Resources, Music

Audience: Musicians, Music Enthusiasts

Details: Free

`ftp://una.hh.lib.umich.edu/70/ inetdirsstacks/music:robinson`

news.announce.newgroups

A Usenet newsgroup providing information and discussion about creating a new newsgroup, changing active newsgroups, and how to access new Usenet groups.

Keywords: Usenet, Internet Resources

Audience: Usenet Users

Details: Free

User Info: To subscribe to this Usenet newsgroup, you need access to a newsreader.

`news:news.announce.newgroups`

news.answers

A Usenet newsgroup providing information and discussion about periodic Usenet articles.

Keywords: Usenet, Internet Resources

Audience: Usenet Users

Details: Free

User Info: To subscribe to this Usenet newsgroup, you need access to a newsreader.

`news:news.answers`

news.groups

A Usenet newsgroup providing information and discussion about lists of existing newsgroups.

Keywords: Usenet, Internet Resources

Audience: Usenet Users

Details: Free

User Info: To subscribe to this Usenet newsgroup, you need access to a newsreader.

`news:news.groups`

news.lists

A Usenet newsgroup providing information and discussion about news-related statistics and lists.

Keywords: Usenet, Internet Resources

Audience: Usenet Users

Details: Free

User Info: To subscribe to this Usenet newsgroup, you need access to a newsreader.

`news:news.lists`

news.newusers.questions

A Usenet newsgroup providing information and discussion about how

Keywords: Usenet, E-mail, Internet Resources

Audience: Usenet Users, E-mail Users

Details: Free

User Info: To subscribe to this Usenet newsgroup, you need access to a newsreader.

`news:news.newusers.questions`

The InterNIC Home Page

This is the home page for the InterNIC networking organization.

Keywords: WWW, Information Retrieval, Computer Science, Internet Resources

Sponsor: National Science Foundation, USA

Audience: Researchers, Students, General Public

Profile: The InterNIC is a collaborative project of three organizations, which work together to offer the Internet community a full scope of network information services. These services include providing information about accessing and using the Internet, assistance in locating resources on the network, and registering network components for Internet connectivity. The overall goal of the InterNIC is to make networking and networked information more easily accessible to researchers, educators, and the general public. The term InterNIC signifies cooperation between Network Information Centers, or NICS.

Contact: InfoGuide guide@internic.net

Details: InterNIC signifies cooperation between Network Information Centers

`http://www.internic.net`

Internet Resources for Earth Sciences

Internet Resources for Earth Sciences

A document detailing Internet resources for a variety of earth science disciplines, including GIS.

Keywords: Directory, GIS, Geology, Geography, GPS, Mapping, Earth Science

Sponsor: Bill Thoen

Audience: Earth Scientists, Researchers

Profile: A complete document detailing the types of information available in earth sciences and the mechanisms to retrieve needed information.

Contact: Bill Thoen

bthoen@gisnet.com

Details: Free

```
ftp://ftp.csn.org/COGS/ores.text
```

Internet Resources for Geographic Information and GIS

Internet Resources for Geographic Information and GIS

An HTML document with information on all aspects of GIS.

Keywords: GIS, Geography

Sponsor: Bates College - Department of Classical and Romance Languages

Audience: GIS Professionals

Contact: Neel Smith
            nsmith@abacus.bates.edu

Details: Free

```
http://abacus.bates.edu/~nsmith/
General/Resources-GIS.html
```

Internet Security

firewalls

A mailing list to discuss the issues involved in setting up and maintaining Internet security firewall systems.

Keywords: Security, Internet Security, Firewalls

Audience: Security Workers

Contact: Brent Chapman
            Brent@GreatCircle.com

Details: Free

User Info: To subscribe to the list, send an e-mail message consisting of a single line reading:

            SUB firewalls YourFirstName YourLastName

```
mailto:majordomo@greatcircle.com
```

Internet Services FAQ

Internet Services FAQ

General information and answers to frequently asked questions (FAQs) about the Internet.

Keywords: Internet, Internet Guides, FAQs

Audience: Internet Surfers

Details: Free

User Info: File is: pub/usenet/news.answers/
            internet-services/faq

```
ftp://rtfm.mit.edu
```

Internet Services

E-mail WWW

E-mail WWW allows the user to obtain a web file via e-mail.

Keywords: Internet Services, E-mail, WWW

Audience: Internet Surfers

Details: Free
            Include the words "www URL" in the e-mail.

```
http://info.cern.ch/hypertext/WWW/
TheProject.html
```

FAXNET

FAXNET allows the user to send faxes via e-mail.

Keywords: Internet Services, E-mail

Audience: Internet Surfers

Details: Free
            Include the word "help" in the e-mail.

```
mailto:info@awa.com
```

Finger Database

This service allows access to a database facility via finger.

Keywords: Internet Services, Finger (Internet Database)

Audience: Internet Surfers

Contact: http://www.usyd.edu.au

Details: Free

```
finger://help@dir.su.oz.au
```

Knowbot

Knowbot provides a uniform user interface to heterogenous remote information services.

Keywords: Internet Services, Knowbot

Audience: Internet Surfers

Details: Free
            Login; Send: email address

```
telnet://info.cnri.reston.va.us
```

MarketBase Gopher

An online catalog of goods and services dedicated to providing a forum where buyers and sellers meet to electronically exchange the attributes of products and services. Free access is provided to product purchasers.

Keywords: Internet Services, MarketBase

Audience: Internet Surfers

Contact: help@mb.com

Details: Free

```
gopher://mb.com
```

UNC-CH Info system

The University of North Carolina at Chapel Hill's campus-wide information server, providing access to a wide range of campus information and to electronic information services worldwide.

Keywords: Education, Internet Services

Sponsor: University of North Carolina at Chapel Hill

Audience: Educators, Researchers, Internet Surfers

Contact: info@unc.edu

Details: Free

```
gopher://gibbs.oit.unc.edu
```

Internet Shopping Network

Internet Shopping Network

A shopping network on the Infobahn.

Keywords: Business, Electronic Commerce

Sponsor: Internet Shopping Network

Audience: Business Users, General Public

Profile: The Internet Shopping Network aims to conduct research and develop products and services that commercialize the Internet, for the purpose of retailing and mass merchandising. The stores within this network offer approximately 20,000 products from 1000 vendors.

```
http://www.internet.net
```

Internet Sound

Internet Sound

Internet Sound contains various documents and programs regarding sound.

Keywords: Internet, Information Retrieval

Audience: Internet Surfers

Contact: Guido van Rossum
            ftp://ftp.cwi.nl/pub/audio/INDEX
            ftp://ftp.cwi.nl/pub/audio/index.html

Details: Free, Sound files available.
            The index is: pub/audio/INDEX

```
ftp://ftp.cwi.nl
```

A B C D E F G H I J K L M N O P Q R S T U V W X Y Z

A
B
C
D
E
F
G
H
I
J
K
L
M
N
O
P
Q
R
S
T
U
V
W
X
Y
Z

Internet Statistics

Internet Statistics

⭐

The latest statistical information about the Internet from the National Science Foundation.

Keywords: Internet, Internet Guides
Sponsor: Merit Network Information Center
Audience: Internet Surfers
Details: Free
Index is: /nsfnet/statistics/INDEX.statistics

`ftp://nic.merit.edu`

Internet Systems UNITE

Internet Systems UNITE

⭐

A list of tools for use on the Internet, by UNITE (User Network Interface to Everything).

Keywords: Internet, Internet Tools
Audience: Internet Surfers
Contact: unite-request@mailbase.ac.uk
Details: Free
User Info: File is: pub/lists/unite/files/systems-list.txt

`ftp://mail.base.ac.uk`

Internet Tools

Alex Description

⭐

An NIR (Network Information Retrieval) description of Alex, an Internet access tool.

Keywords: Internet Tools, Internet, Alex
Audience: Internet Surfers
Details: Free
File is: usr0/anon/doc/NIR.Tool

`ftp://alex.sp.cs.cmu.edu/usr0/anon/doc/NIR.Tool`

Arachnophilia: Florida Institute of Technology's WWW server.

⭐⭐

Provides pointers to information resources and search tools around the Web. Specifically for use by educators and researchers.

Keywords: Internet Tools
Audience: Educators, Researchers
Contact: www@sci-ed.fit.edu
Details: Free

`http://sci-ed.fit.edu`

Archie

⭐

A description of Archie, an electronic directory service for the Internet, which allows the user to find files remotely.

Keywords: Internet Tools, Archie
Sponsor: Computing Centre, McGill University, Montreal, Quebec, Canada
Audience: Internet Surfers
Contact: archie-group@archie.mcgill.ca
Details: Free
File is: pub/archie/doc/whatis.archie

`ftp://archie.ans.net`

Archie Demo

⭐

A Telnet demonstration of Archie, an Internet access tool.

Keywords: Internet Tools, Archie
Audience: Internet Surfers
Details: Free

`telnet://archie@archie.ans.net`
`(login; Send: archie)`

Archie Hypertext Servers

⭐

A list of hypertext Archie servers around the world.

Keywords: Internet Tools, Archie
Sponsor: NEXOR
Audience: Internet Surfers
Contact: Martijn Koster m.koster@nexor.co.uk
Details: Free

`http://web.nexor.co.uk.archie.html`

Archie Manual

⭐

A reference manual for Archie, an Internet access tool.

Keywords: Internet Tools, Archie
Audience: Internet Surfers
Contact: R. Rodgers, Nelson N. Beebe, A. Emtage rodgers@maxwell.mmwb.ucsf.edu, beebe@math.utah.edu
Details: Free
File is: pub/archie/doc/archie.man.txt

`ftp://archie.ans.net`

Cello

⭐

A DOS-based Internet browser incorporating WWW (World-Wide Web), Gopher, FTP, Telnet, and usenet.

Keywords: Internet Tools, Cello, DOS
Audience: Internet Surfers

Details: Free

`ftp://fatty.law.cornell.edu`

`gopher://fatty.law.cornell.edu`

`http://fatty.law.cornell.edu`

Cello FAQ

⭐⭐⭐⭐

A site containing common questions and answers about Cello, a multipurpose Internet browser which allows access to the myriad information resources of the Internet. It supports World Wide Web, Gopher, FTP, CSO/pf/qi, and Usenet News retrievals natively, and other protocols (WAIS, Hytelnet, Telnet, and TN3270) through external clients and public gateways.

Keywords: Internet Tools, Internet Reference
Sponsor: Cornell Law School, New York, USA
Audience: Students, Computer Scientists, Researchers.

`http://www.law.cornell.edu/cello/cellofaq.html`

Entering the WWW

⭐

An article entitled "Entering the World-Wide Web: A Guide to Cyberspace."

Keywords: Internet Tools, WWW
Sponsor: Honolulu Community College
Audience: Internet Surfers
Contact: Kevin Hughes kevinh@pulua.hcc.hawaii.edu
Details: Free

`http://www.hcc.hawaii.edu/guide/www.guide.html`

E-mail-How To

⭐

An introductory guide to the UNIXMail System and to the procedures for sending and receiving mail, sending files by mail, and adding messages to files that are sent by mail.

Keywords: Internets Tools, Internet Guides, E-mail
Sponsor: SURAnet Network Information Center
Audience: Internet Surfers
Contact: info@sura.net
Details: Free
File is: pub/nic/network.service.guides/how.to.email.guide

`ftp://ftp.sura.net`

Essence

⭐

A description of Essence, an Internet resource discovery system based on semantic file indexing.

Keywords: Internet Tools, Essence (Internet Resource Directory)
Sponsor: University of Colorado, Boulder, CO

Audience: Internet Surfers

Contact: Darren R. Hardy, Michael F. Schwartz
            hardy@cs.colorado.edu or
            schwartz@cs.colorado.edu

Details: Free

            File is: pub/cs/distribs/essence/README

`ftp://.cs.colorado.edu`

FTP-How To

A short guide to using anonymous FTP, an Internet access tool.

Keywords: Internet Tools, FTP

Sponsor: SURAnet Network Information Center

Audience: Internet Surfers

Contact: info@sura.net

Details: Free

            File is: pub/nic/network.service.guides/
            how.to.ftp.guide

`ftp://ftp.sura.net`

FTP Setup

Tips on using FTP, an Internet access tool.

Keywords: Internet Tools, FTP

Sponsor: Carnegie Mellon University, Pittsburgh,
            PA

Audience: Internet Surfers

Details: Free

            File is: pub/tech_tips/anonymous_ftp

`ftp://cert.org`

Gopher

A guide to using gopher, an Internet access tool that locates and retrieves resources using a graph of menus.

Keywords: Internet Tools, Gopher

Audience: Internet Surfers

Contact: gopher@boombox.micro.umn.edu

Details: Free

            File is: pub/gopher/00README

`ftp://boombox.micro.umn.edu`

Gopher Demo

A session demonstrating gopher at the University of Minnesota.

Keywords: Internet Tools, Gopher

Audience: Internet Surfers

`gopher:// gopher.micro.umn.edu`

Gopher FAQ

Answers to frequently asked questions (FAQs) about gophers from the Usenet newsgroup comp.infosystems.gopher

Keywords: Internet Tools, Gopher

Audience: Internet Surfers

Contact: Paul Lindner
            lindner@boombox.micro.umn.edu

Details: Free

            File is: pub/usenet/news.answers/
            gopher-faq

`ftp://pit-manager.mit.edu`

Gopher Jewels

A searchable catalog of outstanding gopher sites worldwide.

Keywords: Gopher, Internet Tools

Audience: Internet Surfers, Researchers

Profile: Gopher Jewels, indexed by subject and
            searchable through WAIS, allows
            access to more than 2,000 gopher sites.
            The main server also has archives of the
            Gopher Jewels listserv, and extensive
            help and FAQ files on the uses of gopher.
            It is also available as a WWW site.

Contact: David Riggins
            david.riggins@tpoint.com
            gopherjewels-comment@einet.net

Details: Free

`gopher://cwis.usc.edu/11/`
`Other_Gophers_and_Information_Resources/`
`Gopher_Jewels`

`http://galaxy.einet.net/gopher/`
`gopher.html`

Gopher Sites

A list of worldwide gopher sites (sorted by domain structure) available on the Internet.

Keywords: Internet Tools, Gopher

Sponsor: Washington & Lee University, Lexington,
            VA

Audience: Internet Surfers

Details: Free

            File is: pub/lawlib/veronica.gopher.sites

`ftp://liberty.uc.wlu.edu`

Gopher Telnet Demo

A Telnet session demonstrating the use of gopher.

Keywords: Internet Tools, Gopher

Audience: Internet Surfers

Details: Free

`telnet: //`
`gopher@consultant.micro.umn.ed`

Gopher/Veronica-How To

A special issue of the University of Illinois publication describing gopher and Veronica.

Keywords: Internet Tools, Gopher, Veronica

Sponsor: University of Illinois, Urbana, IL

Audience: Internet Surfers

Details: Free

            File is: doc/net/uiucnet/vol6no1.txt

`ftp://ftp.cso.uiuc.edu`

Hytelnet

A hypertext database of publicly accessible Internet sites.

Keywords: Internet Tools, Hytelnet

Audience: Internet Surfers

Profile: Hytelnet currently lists over 1,400 sites,
            including libraries, campus-wide
            information systems, Gopher, WAIS, and
            WWW systems, and Freenets.

Contact: Earl Fogel
            earl.fogel@usask.ca

Details: Free

            File is: pub/hytelnet/README

`ftp://ftp.usask.ca`

Internet Browsers

A list of sources for Internet browsers and client software.

Keywords: Internet, Internet Tools

Sponsor: ANU Bioinformatics Hypermedia Service

Audience: Internet Surfers

Contact: David Green

            David Green@anu.edu.au

Details: Free

`http://life.anu.edu.au/links/`
`syslib.html`

Internet Systems UNITE

A list of tools for use on the Internet, by UNITE (User Network Interface to Everything).

Keywords: Internet, Internet Tools

Audience: Internet Surfers

Contact: unite-request@mailbase.ac.uk

Details: Free

            File is: pub/lists/unite/files/systems-
            list.txt

`ftp://mail.base.ac.uk`

A B C D E F G H I J K L M N O P Q R S T U V W X Y Z

A
B
C
D
E
F
G
H
I
J
K
L
M
N
O
P
Q
R
S
T
U
V
W
X
Y
Z

Internet Tools EARN

A guide to network research tools by the European Academic Research Network (EARN).

Keywords: Internet, Internet Tools

Audience: Internet Surfers

Contact: listserv@earncc.bitnet

Details: Free

User Info: The file is: earn/earn-resource-tool-guide.txt

`ftp://ns.ripe.net`

Internet Tools HTML

An html version of a list summarizing Internet tools for network information retrieval (NIR) and computer-mediated communication (CMC) forums; it is useful in a WWW server.

Keywords: Internet Tools, Information Retrieval

Audience: Internet Surfers

Contact: John December
decemj@rpi.edu

Details: Free

User Info: Files are located in pub/communications. Read the internet-tools.readme first.

`ftp://ftp.rpi.edu`

Internet Tools NIR

A status report on networked information retrieval (NIR): tools and groups.

Keywords: Internet, Internet Tools

Sponsor: Joint IETF/RARE/CNI Networked Information Retrieval Working Group

Audience: Internet Surfers

Contact: Jill Foster
Jill Foster@newcastle.ac.uk

Details: Free

User Info: File is: pub/lists/nir/files/nir.status.report

`ftp://mail.base.ac.uk`

Internet Tools Summary

A list summarizing Internet tools for network information retrieval (NIR) and computer-mediated communication (CMC) forums.

Keywords: Internet, Internet Tools

Audience: Internet Surfers

Contact: John December
decemj@rpi.edu

Details: Free

User Info: Files are located in: pub/communications. Read the internet-tools.readme first.

`ftp://ftp.rpi.edu`

InterNIC Directory Services (White Pages)

This web site provides free access to X.500, WHOIS, and Netfind white pages on the Internet.

Keywords: WWW Information, Internet, Internet Tools

Sponsor: National Science Foundation, USA

Audience: General Public, Students

Contact: Database Administrator
admin@ds.internic.net

`http://ds.internic.net/ds/dspgwp.html`

Jughead

Jonzy's Universal Gopher Hierarchy Excavation and Display (Jughead) gets menu information from various gopher servers.

Keywords: Internet Tools

Sponsor: University of Utah Computer Center

Audience: Internet Surfers

Contact: Rhett "Jonzy" Jones
jonzy@cc.utah.edu

Details: Free

User Info: File is: pub/gopher/Unix/GopherTools/jughead/jughead.ReadMe

`ftp:// boombox.micro.umn`

List Serv

A mailing list server for group communication.

Keywords: Internet Tools, ListServ

Audience: Internet Surfers

Details: Free

`mailto:listserv@uacsc2.albany`

Merit Network Information Center Services

This site provides a large collection of Internet guides and information.

Keywords: Internet, Internet Guides, Internet Tools

Sponsor: Merit Network, Inc.

Audience: Internet Surfers

Profile: This site serves as a clearinghouse for many Internet guides, documents, and utilities. It includes Internet FAQs, bibliographies, glossaries, and user guides such as Zen and the Art of the Internet and The Internet Companion. It also has archives of various Internet documents listing service providers, acceptable use policies, and resources. Many software programs for navigating the Internet are also available here for a wide variety of platforms

Contact: nic-info@nic.merit.edu

`gopher://nic.merit.edu`

`ftp://nic.merit.edu`

Mosaic Home Page

This is the welcome page to the National Center for Supercomputing Applications (NCSA) World Wide Web server, which features the Mosaic application. Mosaic provides a network-distributed hypermedia system for information discovery. It is Internet-based and is free for academic, research, and internal commercial use.

Keywords: Internet Tools, Mosaic, WWW

Audience: Internet Surfers

Contact: mosaic-x@ncsa.uiuc.edu

Details: Free

`http://www.ncsa.uiuc.edu/SDG/`
`Software/Mosaic/NCSAMosaicHome.html`

Netfind

Netfind is a service for locating individuals on the Internet.

Keywords: Internet Tools

Sponsor: University of Colorado, Boulder, CO

Audience: Internet Surfers

Contact: Michael F. Schwartz, Panagiotis G. Tsirigotis
schwartz@cs.colorado.edu
panos@cs.colorado.edu

Details: Free

User Info: File is: pub/cs/distribs/netfind/README

`ftp://ftp.cs.colorado.edu`

Pine E-mail

A description of the Program for Internet News and E-mail (PINE), a tool for reading, sending, and managing electronic messages.

Keywords: Internet Tools, E-mail

Audience: Internet Surfers

Details: Free

User Info: File is: mail/pine.blur

`ftp://ftp.cac.washington.edu`

Ping

With Ping, a user requests an "echo" from an Internet host to check status. It is useful for checking to see if a host or gateway is up and functioning.

Keywords: Internet Tools, Ping

Audience: Internet Surfers

Details: Free

User Info: File is: utils/ping/README

`ftp://vixen.cso.uiuc.edu/utils/ping/`
`README`

Prospero

A guide to using Prospero, an Internet access tool that provides a user-centered view of remote files.

Keywords: Internet Tools, Prospero

Audience: Internet Surfers

Contact: info-prospero@ISI.EDU

Details: Free

User Info: Files are in: pub/prospero/doc

`ftp://prospero.isi.edu`

Telnet Access to WWW (World Wide Web)

A server providing free public access to WWW written in both English and Hebrew.

Keywords: WWW, Internet Tools, Jerusalem

Sponsor: Hebrew University of Jerusalem

Audience: Internet Surfers

Contact: RASHTY@www.huji.ac.il
Expect: Username; Send: WWW

`telnet://www.huji.ac.il`

Telnet-How To

An introduction to telnet, an Internet access tool.

Keywords: Internet Tools, Telnet

Sponsor: SURAnet Network Information Center

Audience: Internet Surfers

Contact: info@sura.net

Details: Free

User Info: File is: pub/nic/network.service.guides/how.to.telnet.guide

`ftp://ftp.sura.net`

The Virtual Tourist - WWW Information ★★★

This site constitutes an attempt to catalogue and organize WWW sites by geographic location.

Keywords: WWW, Internet Tools

Sponsor: The State University of New York at Buffalo, Buffalo, New York, USA

Audience: Internet Surfers, General Public

Profile: Using CERN's master list of WWW servers, this Mosiac-accessible site is centered around an interactive world map that displays WWW/NIR sites within countries and regions. Multimedia Virtual Tourist guides are available for some countires, providing political, cultural, and historical information.

Contact: Brandon Plewe
plewe@acsu.buffalo.edu

`http://wings.buffalo.edu/world`

Usenet What Is?

An article entitled "What Is Usenet?"

Keywords: Internet Guides, Internet Tools, Usenet

Audience: Internet Surfers

Details: Free

User Info: File is: pub/usenet/news.answers/what-is/usenet/part1

`ftp://rtfm.mit.edu`

Usenet World

A special issue of the Amateur Computerist newsletter about Usenet.

Keywords: Internet Guides, Internet Tools, Usenet

Audience: Internet Surfers

Details: Free

User Info: File is: doc/misc/acn/acn4-5.txt

`ftp://wuarchive.wustl.edu`

Veronica Introduction

Veronica (Very Easy Rodent-Oriented Net-wide Index to Computerized Archives) is an Internet access tool that locates titles of gopher items by keyword search.

Keywords: Internet Tools, Veronica

Audience: Internet Surfers

Details: Free

User Info: File is pub/com.archives/bionet.software/veronica

`ftp://cs.dal.ca`

WAIS

WAIS (Wide Area Information Servers) is an Internet access tool that retrieves resources by searching indexes of databases.

Keywords: Internet Tools, WAIS

Audience: Internet Surfers

Details: Free

User Info: Read wais/README first.

`ftp://think.com`

WAIS, Inc.

WAIS, Inc. provides interactive online publishing systems and services to organizations that publish information over the Internet. The organization's three main goals are: to develop the Internet as a viable means for distributing information electronically; to improve the nature and quality of information available over networks; and to offer better methods to access that information.

Keywords: WWW, Information Retrieval, Publishing, Internet Tools

Sponsor: WAIS, Inc.

Audience: Researchers, Students, General Public, Publishers

Contact: Webmaster
webmaster@wais.com

`http://server.wais.com/`

Whois

Whois is an Internet access tool that provides information on registered network names.

Keywords: Internet Tools, Whois

Sponsor: SRI International Telecommunication Sciences Center

Audience: Internet Surfers

Contact: Nancy C. Fischer
fischer@sri-nic

Details: Free

User Info: File is: documents/rfc/rfc0954.txt

`ftp://nic.merit.edu`

World-Wide Web (WWW)

World-Wide Web (WWW) is an Internet access tool that retrieves resources through a hypertext browser of databases.

Keywords: Internet Tools, WWW

Sponsor: CERN (European Laboratory for Particle Physics)

Audience: Internet Surfers

Details: Free

User Info: Documents and guides are in: pub/www/doc

`http://info.cern.ch`

World-Wide Web Demo

A Telnet session demonstrating the World-Wide Web (WWW), an Internet access tool.

Keywords: Internet Tools, WWW

Audience: Internet Surfers

Details: Free
No surname is needed.

`telnet://info.cern.ch`

WWW Catalog

A catalog for World-Wide Web (WWW), an Internet access tool.

Keywords: Internet Tools, WWW

Sponsor: Centre Universitaire d'Informatique, University of Geneva

Audience: Internet Surfers

Details: Free

`http://cui_www.unige.ch`

A B C D E F G H **I** J K L M N O P Q R S T U V W X Y Z

A
B
C
D
E
F
G
H
I
J
K
L
M
N
O
P
Q
R
S
T
U
V
W
X
Y
Z

WWW FAQ

Answers to frequently-asked questions (FAQs) about World-Wide Web (WWW), an Internet access tool.

Keywords: Internet Tools, WWW, FAQs

Audience: Internet Surfers

Details: Free

`ftp://info.cern.ch`

X.500

A catalog of available X.500 Implementations, a globally distributed Internet directory service.

Keywords: Internet Tools, X.500

Sponsor: SRI International and Lawrence Berkeley Laboratory

Audience: Internet Surfers

Contact: Ruth Lang, Russ Wright

rlang@nisc.sri.com or wright@lbl.gov

Details: Free
File is: documents/fyi/fyi_11.txt

`ftp://nic.merit.edu`

World-Wide Web Book

A book describing the WWW (World-Wide Web) project.

Keywords: Internet Tools, WWW

Audience: Internet Surfers

Details: Free

`ftp://emx.cc.utexas.edu`

Internet Wiretap

Internet Wiretap

A resource containing electronic books, zines, and government documents, White House press releases, and links to worldwide gopher and WAIS servers.

Keywords: Electronic Media, Cyberculture, Zines

Sponsor: Internet Wiretap

Audience: Cyberculture Enthusiasts, Civil Libertarians, Educators

`gopher://wiretap.spies.com/11/`

`http://wiretap.spies.com`

InterNIC Directory Services (White Pages)

InterNIC Directory Services (White Pages)

This Web site provides free access to X.500, WHOIS, and Netfind white pages on the Internet.

Keywords: WWW Information, Internet, Internet Tools

Sponsor: National Science Foundation, USA

Audience: General Public, Students

Contact: Database Administrator admin@ds.internic.net

`http://ds.internic.net/ds/dspgwp.html`

Internships

Online Career Center

The Online Career Center gopher provides access to job listings and employment information to member companies and to the public.

Keywords: Employment, Internships

Sponsor: Online Career Center

Audience: Job Seekers

Profile: Online Career Center is a not-for-profit organization funded by its member companies. It is devoted to distributing and exchanging employment and career information between its member companies, human resource professionals, and perspective employees.

Contact: OCC Operator occ@msen.com

`gopher://gopher.msen.com`

Interpretation

LANTRA-L

A discussion of interpretation and translation.

Keywords: Interpretation, Translation, Language, Linguistics

Audience: Linguists, Interpreters, Translators

Details: Free

`mailto:listserv@searn.bitnet`

InterText

InterText

A network-distributed bimonthly literary magazine.

Keywords: Literature (Contemporary), Journals

Audience: General Public, Writers

Profile: InterText publishes all kinds of material, ranging from mainstream stories to fantasy to horror to science fiction to humor. InterText publishes in both ASCII and PostScript formats, and reaches over 1,000 readers worldwide.

Contact: Jason Snel jsnell@ocf.berkeley.edu

Details: Free

Select OCF On-Line Library; then select Fiction; then select InterText

Notes: The ASCII version runs approximately 150 KB per issue; if you have tight file gateways, the issue can be split up and squeezed through if need be. The PostScript version runs approximately 500 KB. If you would like to see back issues of InterText, you can FTP them from: network.ucsd.edu(128.54.16.3) in/ intertext. Login as anonymous, with your e-mail address as your password.

`gopher://ocf.berkeley.edu`

INTLAW (International Law Library)

INTLAW (International Law Library)

The International Law Library provides comprehensive international law materials.

Keywords: International Law, EEC, Commonwealth, China

Audience: Lawyers, International Lawyers

Profile: The International Law Library provides comprehensive international law materials. The International Law Library contains federal case law, European Community materials, treaties and agreements, Commonwealth law materials, topical and professional journals, French law materials (in French) China law materials, plus relevant topical publications.

Contact: New Sales Group at (800) 227-4908 or 513-859-5398 inside the US, or (513) 865-7981 for all inquires outside the US.

User Info: To subscribe, contact Mead directly.

To examine the Lexis user guide, you can access it at the ftp site of the University of Texas at Austin at the URL address: ftp://ftp.cc.utexas.edu

The files are in: /pub/ref-services/LEXIS

`telnet://nex.meaddata.com`

`http://www.meaddata.com`

INTNAT (International Library)

INTNAT (International Library)

The International Library contains all French treaties, conventions, and agreements that are in effect today, as well as decisions from the Cour Européenne des Droits de l'Homme and the Cour de Justice des Communautes Européennes, and the Journal Officiel des Communautes Européenne.

Keywords: French Law, European Community

Audience: International Lawyers

Profile: The International Library contains all French treaties, conventions, and agreements published before 1958 that are in effect today, as well as decisions from the European Court of Human Rights (Cour Europeenne des Droits de l'Homme), the European Court of Justice (Cour de Justice des Communautes Europeennes) and the Journal Officiel des Communautes Europeenne, the daily record of the European Community.

Contact: New Sales Group at 800-227-4908 or 513-859-5398 inside the US, or (513)-865-7981 for all inquires outside the US.

User Info: To subscribe, contact Mead directly.

To examine the Lexis user guide, you can access it at the ftp site of the University of Texas at Austin at the URL address: ftp://ftp.cc.utexas.edu

The files are in: /pub/ref-services/LEXIS

`telnet://nex.meaddata.com`

`http://www.meaddata.com`

Inventions

Derwent World Patents Index

Derwent World Patents Index and Derwent World Patents Index Latest contain data from nearly 3 million inventions represented in more than 6 million patent documents from 33 patent-issuing authorities around the world.

Keywords: Patents, Inventions

Sponsor: Derwent Publications, Ltd., London, UK

Audience: Science Researchers

Profile: In addition to bibliographic information, the basic patent record includes the full abstract (for new patents issued from 1981 to the present), informative title, International Patent Classification codes, and Derwent subject codes. These files also provide access to equivalent patents, grouped together by patent family in the basic patent record. The use of manual and fragmentation codes is restricted to Derwent subscribers, in accordance with their subscription level.

Pharmaceutical patents are included from 1963 to the present, agricultural chemical patents from 1965 to the present, and polymer and plastics patents from 1966 to the present. Coverage of all chemical patents began in 1970; coverage of all patents, irrespective of subject, began in 1974.

Contact: Dialog in the US at (800) 334-2564, Dialog internationally at country-specific locations.

User Info: To subscribe, contact Dialog directly.

Notes: Coverage: 1963 to the present; updated weekly (file 351) and monthly (file 350).

`telnet://dialog.com`

INVEST (Investment News and Information)

The INVEST library contains company and industry research reports provided through the Investext(R) database. These reports are created by industry experts who are employed for their accurate and insightful evaluation. Only the most recent 12 months of data will be displayed.

Keywords: Companies, Financials, Analysis

Audience: Business Researchers, Analysts, Entrepreneurs

Profile: INVEST is categorized by type. Selections can be made using these categories: Industry (more than 50 industries are available), State (where a specific company is located), Country (Country in which the company is located), and US Broker or International Broker. The INVEST library provides an automatic display following the selection of a file. For industry reports, a menu will appear providing definitions as they relate to the industries. All remaining files will provide a confirmation of the file selected.

Contact: Mead New Sales Group at (800) 227-4908 or (513) 859-5398 inside the US, or (513) 865-7981 for all inquiries outside the US.

User Info: To subscribe, contact Mead directly.

To examine the Nexis user guide, you can access it at the ftp site of the University of Texas at Austin at the URL address: ftp://ftp.cc.utexas.edu

The files are in: /pub/ref-services/LEXIS

`telnet://nex.meaddata.com`

`http://www.meaddata.com`

LEXPAT (Patents US)

The LEXPAT library contains the full text of US patents issued since 1975, the US Patent and Trademark Office Manual of Classification, and the Index to US Patent Classification. The approximately 1,500 patents added to the library each week appear online within four days of their issue.

Keywords: Patents, Inventors, Assignees, Litigants

Audience: Lawyers, Business Researchers, Analysts, Entrepreneurs

Profile: LEXPAT may be searched by individual files for the full text of utility, design, or plant patents, or you can combine the files in one 'omni' search. The Manual, Index, and Class files can be used to supplement your full-text patent searches. LEXPAT is a valuable tool for both patent professionals and for anyone who needs to access to technical information. More than 80 percent of the information contained in patents is unavailable in any other form.

Contact: Mead New Sales Group at (800) 227-4908 or (513) 859-5398 inside the US, or (513) 865-7981 for all inquiries outside the US.

User Info: To subscribe, contact Mead directly.

To examine the Nexis user guide, you can access it at the ftp site of the University of Texas at Austin at the URL address: ftp://ftp.cc.utexas.edu

The files are in: /pub/ref-services/LEXIS

`telnet://nex.meaddata.com`

`http://www.meaddata.com`

U.S. Patent and Trademark Office Database

A database of patents issued in 1994 by the U.S. Patent and Trademark Office, including a searchable index.

Keywords: Patents, Databases, Inventions, Business

Sponsor: New York University School of Business

Audience: Inventors, General Public

Contact: questions@town.hall.org

`gopher://town.hall.org/patent`

A
B
C
D
E
F
G
H
I
J
K
L
M
N
O
P
Q
R
S
T
U
V
W
X
Y
Z

Investigators and Detectives

Investigators and Detectives

This resource provides information files for individuals involved with investigative research, as well as a free monthly newsletter.

Keywords:	Detectives, Crime, Information Retrieval, Security
Audience:	Investigators, Detectives, Information Brokers, General Public
Profile:	Investigators and Detectives provides access to information covering topics such as private investigative research, strategies, sources, the art and science of investigating, theft deterrents, and electronic PI schematics and plans. Also offers a free sample of a newsletter covering various topics of interest to Private Investigators, such as techniques and strategies, security, and tracing.
Contact:	Mike Enlow menlow@Intec.win.net, michael@enlow.com
Details:	Inside Secrets.

`mailto:info@enlow.com`

Investments

Experimental Stock Market Data

★★★

This is an experimental page that provides a link to the latest stock market information.

Keywords:	Stock Market, Investments, Finance
Audience:	General Public, Investors, Stock Brokers
Profile:	This site is updated automatically to reflect the current day's closing information. Provides general market news and quotes for selected stocks, although prices are not guaranteed. Also includes recent prices for many mutual funds, as well as technical analysis charts for a large number of stocks and mutual funds.
Contact:	Mark Torrance stockmaster@ai.mit.edu
Details:	Free

`http://www.ai.mit.edu/stocks.html`

Institutional Real Estate Newsline

Five-page fax briefing with articles regarding institutional real estate, life insurance company, banks, pension fund, real estate investment trust and commercial mortgage backed securities markets.

Keywords:	Real Estate, Investments, Insurance
Sponsor:	Institutional Real Estate
Audience:	Investors
Details:	Costs

`mailto:IREI@crl.com`

misc.invest

★

A Usenet newsgroup providing information and discussion about how to invest money.

Keywords:	Investments, Finance
Audience:	General Public
Details:	Free
User Info:	To subscribe to this Usenet newsgroup, you need access to a newsreader.

`news:misc.invest`

misc.invest.real-estate

★

A Usenet newsgroup providing information and discussion about property investments.

Keywords:	Investments, Real Estate
Audience:	General Public
Details:	Free
User Info:	To subscribe to this Usenet newsgroup, you need access to a newsreader.

`news:misc.invest.real-estate`

Stock Market Secrets

★

Publication of a stock market-related daily commentary. Questions are answered on a wide variety of investment and financial topics.

Keywords:	Stock Market, Investments, Finance
Audience:	Investors, Stock Brokers, Financial Advisors
Contact:	smi-request@world.std.com
Details:	Free, Moderated
User Info:	To subscribe to the list, send an e-mail message requesting a subscription to the URL address below.
	To send a message to the entire list, address it to: smi@world.std.com

`mailto:smi-request@world.std.com`

Yahoo Market and Investments

A comprehensive look at the current economic status, with a wide range of coverage, from brokers to stocks.

Keywords:	Business, Stock Market, Investment, Economy
Sponsor:	Stanford University, Palo Alto, California, USA
Audience:	Investors, Economists
Contact:	jerry@akebono.stanford.edu

`http://akebono.stanford.edu/yahoo/`
`Economy/Markets_and_Investments`

Iowa State University

Iowa State University

The library's holdings contain significant collections in many fields.

Keywords:	Agriculture, Veterinary Medicine, Statistics, Labor, Soil Conservation, Film
Audience:	General Public, Researchers, Librarians, Document Delivery Professionals
Details:	Free
	Expect: DIAL, Send: LIB

`telnet://isn.iastate.edu`

ipct-j 'Interpersonal Computing and Technology: An Electronic Journal for the 21st Century'

ipct-j 'Interpersonal Computing and Technology: An Electronic Journal for the 21st Century'

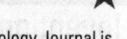

Interpersonal Computing and Technology Journal is an outgrowth of the IPCT-L discussion group.

Keywords:	Education (Adult), Education (Distance), Education (Continuing), Information Technology
Sponsor:	Interpersonal Computing and Technology
Audience:	Educators, Administrators, Faculty
Details:	Free, Moderated
User Info:	To subscribe to the journal, send an e-mail message to the URL address shown below, consisting of a single line reading:
	SUB ipct-j YourFirstName YourLastName

`mailto:listserv@guvm.bitnet`

Iran

soc.culture.iranian

A Usenet newsgroup providing information and discussion about Iran and Iranian culture.

Keywords: Iran, Sociology

Audience: Sociologists, Iranians

Details: Free

User Info: To subscribe to this Usenet newsgroup, you need access to a newsreader.

`news:soc.culture.iranian`

irc

irc (Internet Relay Chat)

A multiuser, multichannel chatting network. It allows people all over the Internet to "talk" to one another interactively.

Keywords: Internet, Group Communications

Audience: Internet Surfers

Details: Free

User Info: Readme file is: irc/README

`ftp://cs.bu.edu`

Operlist

A discussion list for everything having to do with IRC (Internet Relay Chat). Its main purpose is irc routing discussions, protocol discussions, and announcements of new versions of IRC clients and servers.

Keywords: irc

Audience: irc Users

Contact: Helen Trillian Rose
operlist-request@eff.org

Details: Free

User Info: To subscribe to the list, send an e-mail message requesting a subscription to the URL address below.

To send a message to the entire list, address it to: operlist@eff.org

`mailto:operlist@eff.org`

IRCAM DSP and musical software

IRCAM DSP and musical software

This site offers a variety of computer music resources.

Keywords: Computer Music, Sound Synthesis, Composition, DSP

Sponsor: IRCAM

Audience: Electronic Music Enthusiasts

Profile: Contains a list and brief description of IRCAM software (digital signal processing, voice and sound synthesis, music composition, wind instrument making, and other programs). There are also calendars of the IRCAM-EIC concerts and tours, and links to various other music servers.

Contact: Michel Fingerhut
fingerhu@ircam.fr

Details: Free

`http://www.ircam.fr`

Ireland

Ireland-Related Online Resources

This is a list of network-accessible online resources (documents, images, information, access mechanisms for offline material, and so on) of Irish interest. Coverage includes some Bulletin Board services, some commercial information systems such as CompuServe, and commercial bibliographic services.

Keywords: Ireland, Travel, Commerce, Geography

Audience: Irish, General Public, Tourists, Businesses

Contact: fmurtagh@eso.org

`http://http.hq.eso.org/~fmurtagh/ireland-resources.html`

The University of Notre Dame Library

The library's holdings are large and wide-ranging and contain significant collections in many fields.

Keywords: Music (Irish), Ireland, Botany (History of), Ecology, Entomology, Parasitology, Aquatic Biology, Universities (History of), Paleography

Audience: General Public, Researchers, Librarians, Document Delivery Professionals

Details: Free

Expect: ENTER COMMAND OR HELP:, Send: library; To leave, type x on the command line and press the Enter key. At the ENTER COMMAND OR HELP: prompt, type bye and press the Enter key.

`telnet://irishmvs.cc.nd.edu`

Irish

gaelic-l

A multidisciplinary discussion list that facilitates the exchange of news, views, and information in Scottish Gaelic, Irish, and Manx.

Keywords: Scottish Gaelic, Irish, Manx, Language

Audience: Linguists

Contact: Marion Gunn
mgunn@irlearn.ucd.ie or
caoimhin@smo.ac.uk
lss203@cs.napier.ac.uk

Details: Free

User Info: To subscribe to the list, send an e-mail message to the URL address shown below, consisting of a single line reading:

SUB gaelic-l YourFirstName YourLastName

To send a message to the entire list, address it to: gaelic-l@irlearn.ucd.ie

`mailto:listserv@irlearn.ucd.ie`

Irish History (Modern)

Colby College Library

The library's holdings are large and wide-ranging and contain significant collections in many fields.

Keywords: Contemporary Letters, Hardy (Thomas), James (Henry), Mann (Thomas, Collections of), Housman (A.E., Letters of), Maine Authors, Irish History (Modern)

Audience: General Public, Researchers, Librarians, Document Delivery Professionals

Details: Free

Expect: login, Send: library

`telnet://library.colby.edu`

Iron

Materials Business File

Covers all commercial aspects of iron and steel, non-ferrous metals and non-metallic materials.

Keywords: Materials Science, Business, Iron, Steel

Sponsor: Materials Information, a joint information service of ASM International and the Institute of Materials

Audience: Materials Scientists, Researchers

Profile: Articles are abstracted from over 2,000 worldwide technical and trade journals to create more than 65,000 records. Update monthly.

Contact: PAUL.ALBERT@NETEAST.COM

User Info: To subscribe, contact Orbit-Questel directly.

`telnet://orbit.com`

IRVL-I (Institute for Research on Visionary Leadership)

IRVL-I (Institute for Research on Visionary Leadership)

The Forum for Research on Visionary Leadership provides continuing substantive discourse on visionary leadership and networked archiving of digests of dialogue.

Keywords: Leadership

Sponsor: Institute for Visionary Leadership

Audience: Administrators

Contact: estepp@byrd.mu.wvnet.edu or m034050@marshall

User Info: To subscribe to the list, send an e-mail message to the address below, consisting of a single line reading:

SUB irvl-I YourFirstName YourLastName.

To send a message to the entire list, address it to: irvl-I@byrd.mu.wvnet.edu

`mailto: listserv@byrd.mu.wvnet.edu`

ISEA (Inter-Society on Electronic Arts) Online

ISEA (Inter-Society on Electronic Arts) Online

An online forum for discussion of topics related to ISEA-94, the 5th International Symposium on Electronic Art that will take place in Finland in August, 1994.

Keywords: Art, Electronic Art, Technology

Audience: Artists, Art Enthusiasts

Details: Free

`ftp://ftp.ncsa.uiuc.edu`

ISIS/Draw

ISIS/Draw

ISIS/Draw provides a chemical drawing package from the American Chemical Society (ACS).

Keywords: Chemistry, Graphics

Sponsor: (ACS) and MDL Information Systems, Inc.

Audience: Chemists, Chemistry Professors, Chemistry Students

Profile: ISIS/Draw, the premier chemical drawing package from MDL Information Systems, Inc., is now available to chemistry students and professors at a special academic price through the American Chemical Society (ACS). Used by major pharmaceutical, agrochemical, and chemical companies worldwide, ISIS/Draw has the chemical intelligence to know that a line is a bond, and a letter is an atom. It can be used to: build queries for a structure-searching database; create presentation-quality sketches of chemical structures, reactions, and a wide range of other graphics; cut and paste annotated chemical structure drawings into popular word processing programs to create instructional materials and reports.

Details: Costs

Call ACS at 1-800-227-5558. When placing an order, use the following catalog numbers: 2152-9-151 (Windows) or 2156-1-151 (Macintosh).

`dmg96@acs.org`

Islam

MSA

A mailing list to meet the communication needs of Muslim Student Associations (MSA) in North America. Issues related to Islam and MSAs are discussed.

Keywords: Islam, Muslim Student Associations

Audience: Muslim

Details: Free

User Info: To subscribe to the list, send an e-mail message requesting subscription to the URL address below.

`mailto:msa-request@htm3.ee.queensu.ca`

MSA-Net

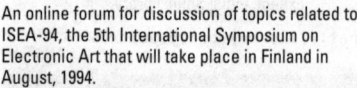

A mailing list intended to meet the communication needs of Muslim Student Associations (MSA) in North America, and to discuss issues related to Islam and MSAs are discussed.

Keywords: Islam, Muslim Associations

Audience: Muslims

Contact: Aalim Fevens msa-request@htm3.ee.queensu.ca

User Info: To subscribe to the list, send an e-mail message

Notes: Members must be Muslim.

`mailto:msa-request@htm3.ee.queensu.ca`

Israel

CJI (Computer Jobs in Israel)

Computer Jobs in Israel (CJI) is a one-way list that will automatically send you the monthly updated computer jobs document. This list will also send you other special documents or announcements regarding finding computer work in Israel. Eventually this list will be an open, moderated list for everyone to exchange information about computer jobs in Israel.

Keywords: Israel, Computer, Jobs

Audience: Computer Users, Jews, Israelis, Israel Residents

Contact: Jacob Richman listserv@jerusalem1.datasrv.co.il

Details: Free

User Info: To subscribe to the list, send an e-mail message to the address below, consisting of a single line reading:

SUB CJI YourFirstName YourLastName

To send a message to the entire list, address it to:
CJI@jerusalem1.datasrv.co.il

`mailto:listserv@jerusalem1.datasrv.co.il`

Energy Research in Israel Newsletter

This newsletter on Bitnet is for people interested in energy research, and is meant to allow important local and international energy information to be disseminated efficiently.

Keywords: Energy, Israel

Audience: Energy Researchers, Utility Professionals, Conservationists

Contact: Michael Wolff

WOLFF@ILNCRD.bitnet

Details: Free

User Info: To subscribe, send an e-mail message to the address below, consisting of a single line reading:

???missing line????

To send a message to the entire list,

`mailto:listserv@taunivm.bitnet`

Energy-L

A mailing list for the discussion of all relevant information on the subject of energy in Israel.

Keywords: Engineering, Energy, Israel

Audience: Engineers, Researchers

Contact: Jo van Zwaren Dr Michael Wolff JO%ILNCRD.BITNET@CUNYVM.CUNY. EDU WOLFF@ILNCRD

Details: Free

User Info: To subscribe to the list, send an e-mail message to the URL addres below, consisting of a single line reading:

SUB energy-l YourFirstName YourLastName

To send a message to the entire list, address it to: energy-l@TAUNIVM.TAU.AC.IL

`mailto:LISTSERV@TAUNIVM.TAU.AC.IL`

Israel-mideast

This discussion group provides information on and analysis of Israel and the Middle East. Includes news flashes, Israeli leaders briefings, editorials and articles translated from the Israeli press, background papers, press communiques, and economic, environmental and cultural updates.

Keywords: Israel, Middle East, Politics

Sponsor: Israel Information Center, Jerusalem

Audience: General Public, Students

Contact: Israel Information Service ask@israel-info.gov.il

User Info: To subscribe to the list, send an e-mail message to the address below, consisting of a single line reading:

SUB israel mideast YourFirstName YourLastName.

To send a message to the entire list, address it to: israel mideast@vm.tau.ac.il

`mailto:listserv@vm.tau.ac.il`

Jerusalem-One Network

A gopher site covering issues concerned with Jews, Jewish politics, and history.

Keywords: Judaism, Israel, Politics (International)

Audience: Political Activists, Holocaust Researchers, Jews, Israelis

Profile: The Jerusalem-One Network was established in May 1993 by the Jewish International Communications Network (JICN), a branch of the Jewish International Association Against Assimilation. Entries include The Jewish Electronic Library, The Holocaust Archives, and JUNK (the Jewish student University Network)

`gopher://jerusalem1.datasrv.co.il`

jewishnt

A mailing list for the discussion of all things concerning the establishment of the Global Jewish Information Network

Keywords: Judaism, Jews, Israel, Religion

Sponsor: The Global Jewish Information Network Project

Audience: Jews, Israelis, Political Activists

Contact: Dov Winder viner@bguvm.bgu.ac.il

User Info: To subscribe to the list, send an e-mail message to the URL address below, consisting of a single line reading:

SUB jewishnt

`mailto: listserv@bguvm.bgu.ac.il`

Judaica

A mailing list for the discussion of Jewish and Near Eastern Studies.

Keywords: Judaica, Israel, Middle Eastern Studies, Religion

Audience: Judaica Scholars, Jews, Middle East Scholars

Contact: Tzvee Zahavy maic@uminn1.bitnet

User Info: To subscribe to the list, send an e-mail message to the URL address below, consisting of a single line reading:

SUB judaica

`mailto:listserv@vm1.spcs.umn.edu`

Material Science in Israel Newsletter

Newsletter on bitnet for people interested in material sciences, established to allow important local and international information to be disseminated efficiently and rapidly to all interested parties.

Keywords: Material Science, Israel

Audience: Material Scientists

Contact: Michael Wolff WOLFF@ILNCRD.bitnet

Details: Free

User Info: To subscribe to the list, send an e-mail message to the URL address below, consisting of a single line reading:

SUB YourFirstName YourLastName

To send a message to the entire list, address it to: @taunivmbitnet

`mailto:listserv@taunivmbitnet`

Medical and Biological Research in Laboratories Institutions (Israel)

A descriptive listing of medical research and diagnostic laboratories in Israel. This site also has information on medical research being carried out in Israeli universities and hospitals.

Keywords: Medical Research, Biological Research, Israel

Audience: Medical Researchers, Biomedical Researchers, Medical Professionals

Profile: MATIMOP, The Israeli Industry Center for Health Care Research And Development, is a non-profit service organization, founded by an Israeli association of hospitals, universities, and other medical researchers, aiming their activities at promoting cooperation of Israeli entrepreneurs and manufacturers with qualified business firms abroad. This gopher details specific medical and biological research projects in progress in every department of every major Israeli health care institution: including universities, The General Federation of Labour, public hospitals, government-municipal hospitals, government hospitals, as well as medical and biological research in the Israeli laboratories and research institutes.

Contact: rdinfo@matimop.org.il

`gopher://gopher.matimop.org.il`

NYIsrael Project of NYSERnet

Large repository of historical and cultural information as well as software, mailing lists, and images relating to Judaism, Jews, the Hebrew language, and Israel.

Keywords: Judaism, Jews, Hebrew Language, Israel

Sponsor: The New York Israel Project, NYSERNet, Inc.

Audience: Jewish Organizations

Profile: The purpose of this project is to create a network of diverse Jewish organizations worldwide that can communicate electronically and share information with one another.

Contact: Avrum Goodblatt goodblat@israel.nysernet.org

Details: Free

`gopher://israel.nysernet.org`

Shamash, The New York - Israel Project

This site is designed to facilitate communications between Jews and Jewish organizations through the medium of the Internet. Information includes archives of Jewish lists, updates of community Jewish events in New York and beyond, a Jewish

A B C D E F G H **I** J K L M N O P Q R S T U V W X Y Z

white pages, and a section on the Holocaust. It also has Hebrew software and access to other Jewish and Israeli information servers.

Keywords: Judaism, Israel, New York

Sponsor: New York - Israel Project (Nysernet), New York, USA

Audience: Jews, Jewish Organizations

Contact: Avrum Goodblatt, Chaim Dworkin
goodblat@israel.nysernet.org,
chaim@israel.nysernet.org.

`gopher://nysernet.org`

The Israel Information Service

A gopher server containing information on Israel.

Keywords: Israel, Middle East, Political Science, Anti-Semitism, Holocaust, Archaeology

Sponsor: Israeli Foreign Ministry

Audience: Israelis, Jews, Tourists, General Public

Profile: This server features updates on the Middle East peace process, including text of the latest Israel-PLO accord, as well as general political, diplomatic, cultural, and economic information on the state of Israel. Also includes archives on archaeology in Israel, anti-Semitism and the Holocaust, and current excerpts from Israeli newspapers.

Contact: Chaim Shacham
shacham@israel-info.gov.il

`gopher://israel-info.gov.il`

IST BioGopher

IST BioGopher

This is the gopher server of the National Institute for Cancer Research (IST) and of the Advanced Biotechnology Center of Genoa, Italy.

Keywords: Cancer, Biotechnology, Italy, Europe

Audience: Biologists, Medical Researchers

Profile: The server includes data from the Interlab Project Databases (biological materials availability in European laboratories) and the Bio-Media Bulletin Board System (biotechnology researchers, projects, fundings, and products).

Contact: gophman@istge.ist.unige.it

Details: Free

`gopher://istge.ist.unige.it`

Italian Studies

Erofile

This newsletter provides reviews of the latest books associated with French and Italian studies in fields such as literary criticism, cultural studies, film studies, pedagogy, and software.

Keywords: Italian Studies, French Studies, Book Reviews

Audience: French Students, Italian Students, Book Reviewers

Details: Free

`mailto:erofile@ucsbuxa.ucsb.edu`

Italy

ASTRA-UG

A mailing list for the discussion of Italian and European GIS.

Keywords: Geographic Information Systems, Europe, Italy

Audience: Geographers, Cartographers, Europeans

Details: Free

User Info: To subscribe to the list, send an e-mail mesage to the URL address below, consisting of a single line reading:

SUB ASTRA-UG YourFirstName YourLastName

`astra-ug@icnucevm`

CILEA (Consorzio Interuniversitario Lombardo per la Elaborazione Automatica)

The gopher for the InterUniversity Computer Center, Milan, Italy, provides access to CILEA hosts, databases in Europe, CERN (European Laboratory for Particle Physics) services such as WWW and ALICE, Usenet newsgroups, PostScript documentation on various items, Italian research network information, and more.

Keywords: Informatics, Italy, Europe

Audience: Particle physicists, Researchers

Contact: Luciano Guglielm
guglielm@imicilea.cilea.it

Details: Free

`gopher://imicilea.cilea.it`

ICGEBnet

This is the information server of the International Centre for Genetic Engineering and Molecular Biology (ICGEB), Trieste, Italy.

Keywords: Molecular Biology, Biotechnology, Italy, Europe

Audience: Molecular Biotechnologists, Molecular Biologists

Profile: The primary purpose of the ICGEB computer resource is to disseminate the best of currently available computational technology to the molecular biologists of the ICGEB research community.

Contact: postmaster@icgeb.trieste.it

Details: Free

`gopher://icgeb.trieste.it`

ICTP (International Centre for Theoretical Physics)

ICTP's gopher disseminates information regarding the many scientific activities carried out at ICTP (Trieste, Italy). Information is also provided in the scientific publications, courses, and other services offered by ICS (International Centre for Science and High Technology) and TWAS (Third World Academy of Sciences) at Trieste.

Keywords: Theoretical Physics, Italy, Europe

Audience: Physicists

Profile: Topics include programming techniques, theoretical aspects, applications, implementation issues, porting, and bugs of Icon.

Contact: admin@ictp.trieste.it

Details: Free

`gopher://gopher.ictp.trieste.it`

`http://gopher.ictp.trieste.it`

IST BioGopher

This is the gopher server of the National Institute for Cancer Research (IST) and of the Advanced Biotechnology Center of Genoa, Italy.

Keywords: Cancer, Biotechnology, Italy, Europe

Audience: Biologists, Medical Researchers

Profile: The server includes data from the Interlab Project Databases (biological materials availability in European laboratories) and the Bio-Media Bulletin Board System (biotechnology researchers, projects, fundings, and products).

Contact: gophman@istge.ist.unige.it

Details: Free

`gopher://istge.ist.unige.it`

LANGIT

A forum for members of the Italian Linguistics Center (Centri Linguistici Italian).

Keywords: Italy, Linguistics

Audience: Linguists, Educators, Students

Details: Free

User Info: To subscribe to the list, send an e-mail message to the address below.

`mailto:listserv@icineca.bitnet`

soc.culture.italian

A Usenet newsgroup providing information and discussion about the Italian people and their culture.

Keywords: Italy, Sociology

Audience: Sociologists, Italians

Details: Free

User Info: To subscribe to this Usenet newsgroup, you need access to a newsreader.

`news:soc.culture.italian`

University of Chicago Library

The library's holdings are large and wide-ranging and contain significant collections in many fields, including the following:

Keywords: English Bibles, Lincoln (Abraham), Kentucky & Ohio River Valley (History of), Balzac (Honore de), American Drama, Cromwell (Oliver), Goethe, Judaica, Italy, Chaucer (Geoffrey), Wells (Ida, Personal Papers of), Douglas (Stephen A.), Italy, Literature (Children's)

Audience: General Public, Researchers, Librarians, Document Delivery Professionals

Details: Free

Expect: ENTER CLASS, Send: LIB48 3; Expect: CONNECTED, Send: RETURN

`telnet://olorin.uchicago.edu`

ITRADE (International Trade Library)

ITRADE (International Trade Library)

The International Trade Library contains materials related to the import and export of goods and services, licensing of intellectual property, payment of taxes, or investment and banking at the international level.

Keywords: Law, Import, Export, International Banking

Audience: Lawyers

Profile: ITRADE contains a comprehensive collection of federal case law, statutes, regulations, and agency decisions all related to the importing of goods and services, exporting of goods and services, licensing of intellectual property, payment of taxes, or investment and banking at the international level.

Contact: New Sales Group at 800-227-4908 or 513-859-5398 inside the US, or (513)-865-7981 for all inquires outside the US.

User Info: To subscribe, contact Mead directly.

To examine the Lexis user guide, you can access it at the ftp site of the University of Texas at Austin at the URL address: ftp://ftp.cc.utexas.edu

The files are in: /pub/ref-services/LEXIS

`telnet://nex.meaddata.com`

`http://www.meaddata.com`

ITRE Home Page

ITRE Home Page

A server dealing with transportation research and some GIS-related discussion.

Keywords: GIS, Transportation

Sponsor: University of North Carolina Institute for Transportation Research and Education

Audience: GIS Professionals, Transportation Professionals

Profile: The ITRE server address GIS issues regarding transportation, a different flavor than will be found on most servers on the Net. Also features image mapping examples.

Contact: Jay Novello
jay@itre.uncecs.edu

Details: Free, Images, Multimedia

`http://itre.uncecs.edu/`

IUCAA (Inter-University Centre for Astronomy and Astrophysics)

IUCAA (Inter-University Centre for Astronomy and Astrophysics)

The IUCAA was set up to promote the growth of active groups in astronomy and astrophysics in India. The Centre runs vigorous visitor programs involving short and long-term visits of scientists from India and abroad.

Keywords: Astronomy, Astrophysics, Physics, Education

Sponsor: Centre for Astronomy and Astrophysics (IUCAA)

Audience: Reseachers, Astronomers, Physicists, Students

Contact: Postmaster
amk@iucaa.ernet.in

`http://iucaa.iucaa.ernet.in/`
`welcome.html`

A
B
C
D
E
F
G
H
I
J
K
L
M
N
O
P
Q
R
S
T
U
V
W
X
Y
Z

A
B
C
D
E
F
G
H
I
J
K
L
M
N
O
P
Q
R
S
T
U
V
W
X
Y
Z

James (Henry)

Colby College Library

The library's holdings are large and wide-ranging and contain significant collections in many fields.

Keywords: Contemporary Letters, Hardy (Thomas),James (Henry), Mann (Thomas, Collections of), Housman (A.E., Letters of), Maine Authors, Irish History (Modern)

Audience: General Public, Researchers, Librarians, Document Delivery Professionals

Details: Free

User Info: Expect: login, Send: library

`telnet://library.colby.edu`

Jane's Defense & Aerospace News/Analysis

Jane's Defense & Aerospace News/Analysis

This file provides articles that summarize, highlight, and interpret worldwide events in the defense and aerospace industry.

Keywords: Defense, Aerospace, News Media

Sponsor: Jane's Information Group, Alexandria, VAAUS

Audience: Aerospace Industry Professionals

Profile: The database contains the complete text of the following publications: Jane's Defense Weekly, International Defense Review, Jane's Intelligence Review (formerly Jane's Soviet Intelligence Review), Interavia Aerospace Review, and Jane's Airport Review. File 587 also contains the complete text of DMS newsletters, which ceased publication in 1989.

Contact: Dialog in the US at (800) 334-2564, Dialog internationally at country-specific locations.

User Info: To subscribe, contact Dialog directly.

Notes: Coverage: 1982 to the present; updated weekly.

`telnet://dialog.com`

Japan

alt.bonsai

A Usenet newsgroup providing information and discussion about Bonsai gardening.

Keywords: Bonsai Trees, Japan, Gardening, Landscaping

Audience: Gardeners, Bonsai Enthusiasts

User Info: To subscribe to this Usenet newsgroup, you need access to a newsreader.

`news:alt.bonsai`

ANIME-L

This discussion list covers animation news, with a special emphasis on Japanese "animedia."

Keywords: Animation, Film, Japan

Audience: Animation Enthusiasts, Animators

Details: Free

User Info: To subscribe to the list, send an e-mail message to the address below, consisting of a single line reading:

Sub anime-l YourFirstName YourLastName

To send a message to the entire list, address it to: anime-l@vtvm1.bitnet

`mailto:listserv@vtvm1.cc.vt.edu`

Chiba University Gopher

The Chiba University gopher, including files from the university's library.

Keywords: Japan, Asia, Libraries

Sponsor: Chiba University, Chiba, Japan

Audience: Japan Residents, Computer Programmers, Librarians, Linguists

Contact: hasimoto@chiba-u.ac.jp

`gopher://himawari.ipc.chiba-u.ac.jp`

Japanese Information

This web site contains extensive information on the geography, culture, law, and tourism of Japan. Includes archived Japanese newsgroup information and FAQs.

Keywords: Cultural Studies, Race, Japan

Sponsor: Nippon Telegraph and Telephone

Audience: Students, Tourists, Japanese, Japanese-Americans

Contact: Webmaster www-admin@seraph.ntt.jp

Details: Free

`http://www.ntt.jp/japan/index.html`

JAPIO

Comprehensive source of unexamined Japanese patent applications.

Keywords: Patents, Intellectual Property, Trademarks, Japan

Sponsor: Japan Patent Information Organization

Audience: Patent Attorneys, Patent Agents, Librarians, Researchers

A
B
C
D
E
F
G
H
I
J
K
L
M
N
O
P
Q
R
S
T
U
V
W
X
Y
Z

Profile: More than 2.8 million records covering all technologies. Unique features include English-language abstracts for many Japanese patent applications.

Contact: paul.albert@neteast.com

User Info: To subscribe, contact Orbit-Questel directly.

`telnet://orbit.com`

National Cancer Center, Tokyo, Japan

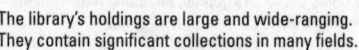

This is the information service for the National Cancer Center in Tokyo, Japan, as well as the entry point for the Japanese Cancer Research Resources Bank (JCRB).

Keywords: Cancer, Japan

Audience: Biologists, Medical Researchers

Contact: ncc-gopher-news@gan.ncc.go.jp

Details: Free

`gopher://ncc.go.jp`

Princeton University Library

★★

The library's holdings are large and wide-ranging. They contain significant collections in many fields.

Keywords: China, Japan, Classics, History (Ancient), Near Eastern Studies, Literature (American), Literature (English), Aeronautics, Middle Eastern Studies, Mormonism, Publishing

Audience: General Public, Researchers, Librarians, Document Delivery Professionals

Details: Free

User Info: Expect: Connect message, blank screen, Send: <cr>; Expect: #, Send: Call 500

`telnet://pucable.princeton.edu`

rec.arts.anime

★

A Usenet newsgroup providing information and discussion about Japanese animation fen.

Keywords: Animation, Fen, Japan

Audience: Animators

Details: Free

User Info: To Subscribe to this Usenet newsgroup, you need access to a newsreader.

`news:rec.arts.anime`

soc.culture.japan

★

A Usenet newsgroup providing information and discussion about Japan and the Japanese culture.

Keywords: Japan, Sociology

Audience: Sociologists, Japanese

Details: Free

User Info: To Subscribe to this Usenet newsgroup, you need access to a newsreader.

`news:soc.culture.japan`

TWICS

★★★★

This is an English-language computer conferencing system in Japan.

Keywords: Community Networking, Networking, Japan, Virtual Community

Sponsor: TWICS Co., Ltd.

Audience: Internationalists, General Public, Journalists, Policy Makers

Profile: TWICS is a computer conferencing system that has a reputation for being a thriving electronic community. This system maintains a full Internet connection. Unlike a database or a gopher server, TWICS allows real-time online interaction with actual people.

Contact: Tim Buress twics@twics.co.jp,

Details: Free

`telnet://tanuki.twics.co.jp`

Jerusalem

Telnet Access to WWW (World Wide Web)

★★

A server providing free public access to WWW, written in both English and Hebrew.

Keywords: WWW, Internet Tools, Jerusalem

Sponsor: Hebrew University of Jerusalem

Audience: Internet Surfers

Contact: rashty@www.huji.ac.il

User Info: Expect: Username; Send: WWW

`telnet://www.huji.ac.il`

Jerusalem-One Network

Jerusalem-One Network

★★★

A gopher site covering issues concerned with Jews, Jewish politics, and history.

Keywords: Judaism, Israel, Politics (International)

Audience: Political Activists, Holocaust Researchers, Jews, Israelis

Profile: The Jerusalem-One Network was established in May 1993 by the Jewish International Communications Network (JICN), a branch of the Jewish International Association Against Assimilation. Entries include The Jewish Electronic Library, The Holocaust Archives, and JUNK (the Jewish student University Network)

`gopher://jerusalem1.datasrv.co.il`

Jewish Politics

US Holocaust Memorial Museum

The web site of the newly-opened (April, 1993) US Holocaust Memorial Museum in Washington D.C.

Keywords: Jews, Jewish Politics, Holocaust, History (Jewish)

Audience: Jews, Holocaust Researchers, Israelis, Students

Profile: This resource contains files on educational programs, general information about the Holocaust Research Institute, a contact list for the Association of Holocaust Organizations, and a searchable archive of related materials.

`http://www.ushmm.org`

Jobs

CJI (Computer Jobs in Israel)

★

Computer Jobs in Israel (CJI) is a one-way list that will automatically send you the monthly updated computer jobs document. This list will also send you other special documents or announcements regarding finding computer work in Israel. Eventually this list will be an open, moderated list for everyone to exchange information about computer jobs in Israel.

Keywords: Israel, Computer, Jobs

Audience: Computer Users, Jews, Israelis, Israel Residents

Contact: Jacob Richman listserv@jerusalem1.datasrv.co.il

Details: Free

User Info: To subscribe to the list, send an e-mail message to the address below, consisting of a single line reading:

SUB CJI YourFirstName YourLastName

To send a message to the entire list, address it to: CJI@jerusalem1.datasrv.co.il

`mailto:listserv@jerusalem1.datasrv.co.il`

joe 'The Journal of Extension'

joe 'The Journal of Extension'

★★★

This is the peer-reviewed publication of the Cooperative Extension System; it covers all phases of extension education, including adult and distance education.

Keywords: Education (Adult), Education (Distance), Education (Continuing)

Audience: Educators (K-12), Faculty Administrators

Details: Free, Moderated

User Info: To subscribe to the journal, send an e-mail message requesting a subscription to the URL address shown below.

`mailto:almanac@joe.uwex.edu`

Johns Hopkins Genetic Databases

Johns Hopkins Genetic Databases

This gopher provides electronic access to documents pertaining to computational biology and a number of different genetic databases.

Keywords: Genetics, Molecular Biology, Medicine, Biology

Sponsor: Johns Hopkins University

Audience: Geneticists, Researchers, Scientists, Molecular Biologists

Profile: The databases accessible from this entry point include GenBank, Swiss-Prot, PDB, PIR, LiMB, TFD, AAtDB, ACEDB, CompoundKB, PROSITE EC Enzyme Database, NRL_3D Protein-Sequence-Structure Database, Eukaryotic Promoter Database (EPD), Cloning Vector Database, Expressed Sequence Tag Database (ESTDB), Online Mendelian Inheritance Man (OMIM), Sequence Analysis Bibliographic Reference Data Bank (Seqanalref), and Database Taxonomy (GenBank, Swiss-Prot). The gopher also provides direct links to other gophers with information relevant to biology.

Contact: Dan Jacobson
             danj@mail.gdb.org

Details: Free

`gopher://merlot.welch.jhu.edu`

Johns Hopkins University Library

Johns Hopkins University Library

The library's holdings are large and wide-ranging and contain significant collections in many fields.

Keywords: Literature (English), Economics, Classics, Drama (German), Slavery, Trade Unions, Incunabula, Bibles, Diseases (History of), Nursing (History of), Abolitionism

Audience: General Public, Researchers, Librarians, Document Delivery Professionals

Details: Free

`telnet://jhuvm.hcf.jhu.edu`

Jokes

rec.humor

A Usenet newsgroup providing information and discussion about jokes.

Keywords: Jokes, Humor

Audience: General Public, Jokers

User Info: To Subscribe to this Usenet newsgroup, you need access to a newsreader.

`news:rec.humor`

Jordan (Len, Senatorial Papers of)

Boise State University Library

The library's holdings are large and wide-ranging and contain significant collections in many fields.

Keywords: Jordan (Len, Senatorial Papers of), Church (Frank, Senatorial Papers of), Poetry (American)

Audience: General Public, Researchers, Librarians, Document Delivery Professionals

Details: Free

User Info: Expect: login; Send: catalyst

`telnet://catalyst.idbsu.edu`

Journal of Technology Education

Journal of Technology Education

Electronic journal devoted to educational issues in technology.

Keywords: Communication, Education, Technology

Audience: Educators

Details: Free

             Send an e-mail message to the URL address below with the request: GET miscella jte-v5n1. This file will give you access information for additional issues.

`mailto:listserv@vtvm1.cc.vt.edu`

Journalism

CNN Headline News Gopher

Latest news as read by the CNN anchorpersons. Searchable index of subject matter.

Keywords: News Media, Politics (International), Journalism

Sponsor: CNN Newsource Service

Audience: General Public, Students, Journalists

Contact: Chet Rhodes
             cr9@umail.umd.edu

Details: Free

`gopher://info.umd.edu:925/`

Communication and Mass Communication Resources

An archive of materials related to mass communications and the media.

Keywords: Mass Communications, Media, Journalism, Telecommunications, Advertising

Sponsor: The University of Iowa

Audience: Mass Communications Students and Teachers, Journalists, Broadcasting Professionals

Contact: Karla Tonella
             Karla_Tonella@uiowa.edu

`gopher://iam41.arcade.uiowa.edu`

Journet

An electronic conference for the discussion of topics of interest to journalists and journalism educators.

Keywords: Journalism, Writing, Desktop Publishing, Electronic Publishing

Audience: Journalists, Writers, Publishers, Educators

Contact: George Frajkor
             gfrajkor@ccs.carleton.ca

User Info: To subscribe to the list, send an e-mail message to the URL address below consisting of a single line reading:

             SUB journet YourFirstName YourLastName

             To send a message to the entire list, address it to: journet@qucdn.queensu.ca

`mailto:listserv@qucdn.queensu.ca`

News

This directory is a general compilation of information resources focused on news.

Keywords: News Media, Electronic Media, Journalism

Audience: Newsreaders, Journalists, General Public

Details: Free

`ftp://una.hh.lib.umich.edu/70/`
`inetdirsstacks/news:robinson`

ViewPoints

Newsletter of the Visual Communication Division of the Association of Educators in Journalism and Mass Communication.

A B C D E F G H I **J** K L M N O P Q R S T U V W X Y Z

Keywords: Journalism, Mass Communication, Visual Communication

Audience: Educators, Photographers, Desktop Publishers

Contact: Paul Lester
lester@fullerton.edu

Details: Free

`mailto:lester@fullerton.edu`

Virginia Commonwealth University Library

The library's holdings are large and wide-ranging and contain significant collections in many fields.

Keywords: Art, Biology, Humanities, Journalism, Music, Urban Planning

Audience: Researchers, Students, General Public

Details: Free

User Info: Expect: Login; Send: Opub

`telnet://vcuvm1.ucc.vcu.edu`

Journals

Electronic Newsstand Gopher

This gopher contains tables of contents, selected full-text articles, and assorted other information from many mainstream print journals.

Keywords: Journals, Electronic Publishing, Publishing, News

Audience: News Enthusiasts, Publishers, Publishing Professionals, Journalists

Profile: This gopher was compiled with the collaboration of the American Journal of International Law, Policy Review, Technology Review, Business Week, Current History, The Economist, Foreign Affairs, National Review, The New Yorker, The New Republic, Mother Jones, among other distinguished publications.

Contact: William Love
love@enews.com

`gopher://gopher.enews.com`

InterText

A network-distributed bimonthly literary magazine.

Keywords: Literature (Contemporary), Journals

Audience: General Public, Writers

Profile: InterText publishes all kinds of material, ranging from mainstream stories to fantasy to horror to science fiction to humor. InterText publishes in both ASCII and PostScript formats, and reaches over 1,000 readers worldwide.

Contact: Jason Snell
jsnell@ocf.berkeley.edu

Details: Free
Select OCF On-Line Library; then select Fiction; then select InterText

Notes: The ASCII version runs approximately 150K per issue; if you have tight file gateways, the issue can be split up and squeezed through if need be. The PostScript version runs approximately 500K. If you would like to see back issues of InterText, you can FTP them from: network.ucsd.edu(128.54.16.3) in/ intertext. Login as anonymous, with your e-mail address as your password.

`gopher://ocf.berkeley.edu`

LAWREV (Law Review Library)

The Law Review library contains law reviews, American Bar Association publications, American Institute of Certified Public Accountants periodicals, and other materials. The present focus concentrates on both state and national issues of legal significance.

Keywords: US Law, Analysis, Law Reviews, Journals

Audience: Lawyers

Profile: The Law Review library currently consists of over 70 law reviews, several American Bar Association publicatons and American Institute of Certified Public Accountants periodicals, an Environmental Law Institute publication, ALR and LEd2d articles, two leading legal indices and a number of Warren Gorham & Lamont tax journals. The present focus concentrates on both state and national issues of legal significance.

Contact: New Sales Group at 800-227-4908 or 513-859-5398 inside the US, or 1-513-865-7981 for all inquires outside the US.

User Info: To subscribe, contact Mead directly.

To examine the Lexis user guide, you can access it at the ftp site of the University of Texas at Austin at the URL address: ftp://ftp.cc.utexas.edu

The files are in: /pub/ref-services/LEXIS

`telnet://nex.meaddata.com`

`http://www.meaddata.com`

Journey-L

Journey-L

Information and discussion of the rock band Journey and any of the band members' outside projects.

Keywords: Musical Groups, Rock Music

Audience: Rock Music Fans

Contact: Hunter Goatley or Britt Pierce
journey-l@wkuvx1.wku.edu

User Info: To subscribe to the list, send an e-mail message to the URL address below, with the body text subscribe journey-l. To subscribe to the digest version, send the message to : journey-l-digest-request@wkuvx1.wku.edu

`mailto:journey-l-request@wkuvx1.wku.edu`

Joyce (James)

fwake-l

A conference and forum for a broad discussion of James Joyce's Finnegan's Wake.

Keywords: Joyce (James), Literature (Irish), Authors, Writing

Audience: Writers, Joyce Scholars, Literary Critics, Literary Theorists

User Info: To Subscribe to the list, send an e-mail message to the URL address below consisting of a single line reading:

SUB fwake-l

`mailto:listserv@irlearn.ucd.ie`

The University of Kansas Library

The library's holdings are large and wide-ranging and contain significant collections in many fields.

Keywords: Botany, Chinese Studies, Cartography (History of), Kansas, Opera, Ornithology, Joyce (James), Yeats (William Butler), Walpole (Sir Robert, Collections of)

Audience: General Public, Researchers, Librarians, Document Delivery Professionals

Contact: John S. Miller

Details: Free

User Info: Expect: Username, Send: relay <cr>

`telnet://kuhub.cc.ukans.edu`

Jte-l 'Journal of Technology Education'

Jte-l 'Journal of Technology Education'

The Journal of Technology Education provides a forum for all topics relating to technology in education.

Keywords: Education (Adult), Education (Distance), Education (Continuing), Information Technology

Audience: Faculty, Administrators, Educators (K-12)

Details: Free

User Info: To subscribe to the journal, send an e-mail message to the URL address below consisting of a single line reading:

SUB jte-l YourFirstName YourLastName

`mailto:listserv@vtvm1.cc.vt.edu`

Judaica

Florida State University System Library

The library's holdings are large and wide-ranging and contain significant collections in many fields.

Keywords: Florida, Latin America, Judaica, Literature (Children's), Marine Engineering, Law (Brazilian), Law (British)

Audience: General Public, Researchers, Librarians, Document Delivery Professionals

Details: Free

User Info: Expect: Command ==>, Send: dial vtam; Expect: LUIS User Menu, Send: Your Catalog choice; To log off: Send: %off

`telnet://nervm.nerdc.ufl.edu`

Judaica

A mailing list for the discussion of Jewish and Near Eastern Studies.

Keywords: Judaica, Israel, Middle Eastern Studies, Religion

Audience: Judaica Scholars, Jews, Middle East Scholars

Contact: Tzvee Zahavy
maic@uminn1.bitnet

User Info: To subscribe to the list, send an e-mail message to the URL address below consisting of a single line reading:

SUB judaica YourFirstName YourLastName

`mailto:listserv@vm1.spcs.umn.edu`

University of Chicago Library

The library's holdings are large and wide-ranging and contain significant collections in many fields.

Keywords: English Bibles, Lincoln (Abraham), Kentucky & Ohio River Valley (History of), Balzac (Honore de), American Drama, Cromwell (Oliver), Goethe, Judaica, Italy, Chaucer (Geoffrey), Wells (Ida, Personal Papers of), Douglas (Stephen A.), Italy, Literature (Children's)

Audience: General Public, Researchers, Librarians, Document Delivery Professionals

Details: Free

User Info: Expect: ENTER CLASS, Send: LIB48 3; Expect: CONNECTED, Send: RETURN

`telnet://olorin.uchicago.edu`

University of Pennsylvania Library- Philadelphia Pa.

The library's holdings are large and wide-ranging and contain significant collections in many fields.

Keywords: Literature (English), Literature (American), History (World), Medieval Studies, East Asian Studies, Middle Eastern Studies, South Asian Studies, Judaica, Lithuania.

Audience: Educators, Students, Researchers

Profile: Access to the central Van Pelt Library and to most of the departmental libraries is restricted to members of the University community on weekends and holidays. Online visitors are advised to call (215) 898-7554 for information on hours and access restrictions.

Contact: Patricia Renfro, Associate Director of Libraries

Details: Free

`telnet://library.upenn.edu`

Judaism

Electronic Hebrew Users Newsletter (E-Hug)

This newsletter is electronic only, and is mandated, like the original, to cover everything relating to the use of Hebrew, Yiddish, Judesmo, and Aramaic on computers.

Keywords: Judaism, Religion, Hebrew Language

Sponsor: Berkeley Hillel Foundation

Audience: Jews, Judaism Students

Contact: Ari Davidow
well!ari@apple.com

Details: Free

User Info: To subscribe, send an e-mail message to the address below consisting of a single line reading:

To send a message to the entire list,

`mailto:listserv@dartcms1.bitnet`

Jerusalem-One Network ★★★

A gopher site covering issues concerned with Jews, Jewish politics, and history.

Keywords: Judaism, Israel, Politics (International)

Audience: Political Activists, Holocaust Researchers, Jews, Israelis

Profile: The Jerusalem-One Network was established in May 1993 by the Jewish International Communications Network (JICN), a branch of the Jewish International Association Against Assimilation. Entries include The Jewish Electronic Library, The Holocaust Archives, and JUNK (the Jewish student University Network)

`gopher://jerusalem1.datasrv.co.il`

jewishnt

A mailing list for the discussion of all things concerning the establishment of the Global Jewish Information Network

Keywords: Judaism, Israel, Religion

Sponsor: The Global Jewish Information Network Project

Audience: Jews, Israelis, Political Activists

Contact: Dov Winder
viner@bguvm.bgu.ac.il

User Info: To subscribe to the list, send an e-mail message to the URL address below consisting of a single line reading:

SUB jewishnt YourFirstName YourLastName

`mailto:listserv@bguvm.bgu.ac.il`

NYIsrael Project of NYSERnet

Large repository of historical and cultural information as well as software, mailing lists, and images relating to Judaism, Jews, the Hebrew language, and Israel.

Keywords: Judaism, Jews, Hebrew Language, Israel

Sponsor: The New York Israel Project, NYSERNet, Inc.

Audience: Jewish Organizations

Profile: The purpose of this project is to create a network of diverse Jewish organizations worldwide that can communicate electronically and share information with one another.

Contact: Avrum Goodblatt
goodblat@israel.nysernet.org

Details: Free

`gopher://israel.nysernet.org`

Shamash, The New York - Israel Project

This site is designed to facilitate communications between Jews and Jewish organizations through the medium of the Internet. Information includes archives of Jewish lists, updates of community Jewish events in New York and beyond, a Jewish white pages, and a section on the Holocaust. It also has Hebrew software and access to other Jewish and Israeli information servers.

Keywords: Judaism, Israel, New York

Sponsor: New York - Israel Project (Nysernet), New York, USA

Audience: Jews, Jewish Organizations

Contact: Avrum Goodblatt, Chaim Dworkin
goodblat@israel.nysernet.org, chaim@israel.nysernet.org.

`gopher://nysernet.org`

A B C D E F G H I J K L M N O P Q R S T U V W X Y Z

A
B
C
D
E
F
G
H
I
J
K
L
M
N
O
P
Q
R
S
T
U
V
W
X
Y
Z

soc.culture.jewish

A Usenet newsgroup providing information and discussion about Jewish culture and religion.

Keywords: Judaism, Sociology

Audience: Sociologists, Jews, Jewish Organizations

Details: Free

User Info: To Subscribe to this Usenet newsgroup, you need access to a newsreader.

`news:soc.culture.jewish`

US Holocaust Memorial Museum

The web site of the newly-opened (April, 1993) US Holocaust Memorial Museum in Washington D.C.

Keywords: Jews, Jewish Politics, Holocaust, History (Jewish)

Audience: Holocaust Researchers, Israelis, Students

Profile: This resource contains files on educational programs, general information about the Holocaust Research Institute, a contact list for the Association of Holocaust Organizations, and a searchable archive of related materials.

`http://www.ushmm.org`

Judicial Process

International Court of Justice Historical Documents

This gopher offers full-text documents from the International Court of Justice, and contains a searchable index.

Keywords: Judicial Process, Judgments, Judges, Law (International)

Audience: Lawyers, Legal Scholars, Legal Professionals, Law Students

File is in Foreign and International Law/ International Court of Justice Historical Documents/

`gopher://fatty.law.cornell.edu`

Law and Politics Book Review

Reviews books of interest to political scientists studying US law, the courts, and the judicial process. Reviews are commissioned by the editor.

Keywords: Political Science, Law, Judicial Process

Audience: Political Scientists, Lawyers

Details: Free, Moderated

User Info: To subscribe, send an e-mail message to the address below consisting of a single line reading:

To send a message to the entire list, address it to: listserv@umcvmb.bitnet

`mailto:listserv@umcvmb.bitnet`

LEGNEW (Legal News)

The Legal News Library provides general news information about the domestic legal industry and legal profession.

Keywords: Law (US), Judicial Process, Supreme Court (US)

Audience: Business Researchers, Analysts, Entrepreneurs

Profile: Included are sources which cover materials on law firm management, bar association journals and a hot file of case list summaries on recently decided US Supreme Court cases. LEGNEW is organized very simply. There are individual files, group files, and user-defined combination files.

Contact: Mead New Sales Group at (800) 227-4908 or (513) 859-5398 inside the US, or (513) 865-7981 for all inquiries outside the US.

User Info: To Subscribe, contact Mead directly.

To examine the Nexis user guide, you can access it at the ftp site of the University of Texas at Austin at the URL address: ftp://ftp.cc.utexas.edu

The files are in: /pub/ref-services/LEXIS

`telnet://nex.meaddata.com`

`http://www.meaddata.com`

Supreme Court Decisions (Project Hermes)

US Supreme Court decisions available online as part of 'Project Hermes.'

Keywords: Supreme Court, Judiciary, Law

Sponsor: Case Western Reserve University

Audience: General Public, Lawyers, Students

Profile: Project Hermes was started in May 1990 by the US Supreme Court as an experiment in disseminating its opinions electronically. Starting with the 1993 calendar year, the US Supreme Court began disseminating opinions electronically on an official basis. Each decision consists of a syllabus (summarizing the ruling), the opinion, and optional concurrent and dissenting opinions.

Contact: Peter W. Martin martin@law.mail.cornell.edu

Details: Free

Anonymous ftp: Expect: login; Send: anonymous; Expect: password; Send: your e-mail address

`ftp://cwru.edu`

`gopher://marvel.loc.gov`

Supreme Court Judges

Biographies from the sitting Justices, and a few former Justices.

Keywords: Judiciary, Supreme Court, Judges, Biography

Audience: General Public, Lawyers, Judges, Journalists

Details: Free

`gopher://info.umd.edu`

VRDCT (Jury Verdicts Library)

The Verdicts library aids litigation preparation by providing quick and convenient access to selected online verdict and settlement information for civil cases nationwide. Case information covered includes verdict and settlement amounts, expert witnesses, case summaries and counsel data.

Keywords: Judicial Process, Law

Audience: Lawyers

Profile: The Verdicts library aids litigation preparation by providing quick and convenient access to selected online verdict and settlement information for civil cases nationwide. Case information covered includes verdict and settlement amounts, expert witnesses, case summaries and counsel data.

Contact: New Sales Group at 800-227-4908 or 513-859-5398 inside the US, or 1-513-865-7981 for all inquires outside the US.

User Info: To Subscribe, contact Mead directly.

To examine the Lexis user guide, you can access it at the ftp site of the University of Texas at Austin at the URL address: ftp://ftp.cc.utexas.edu

The files are in: /pub/ref-services/LEXIS

`telnet://nex.meaddata.com`

`http://www.meaddata.com`

Jughead

Jughead

Jonzy's Universal Gopher Hierarchy Excavation and Display (Jughead) gets menu information from various gopher servers.

Keywords: Internet Tools

Sponsor: University of Utah Computer Center

Audience: Internet Surfers

Contact: Rhett "Jonzy" Jones jonzy@cc.utah.edu

Details: Free

File is: pub/gopher/Unix/GopherTools/ jughead/jughead.ReadMe

`ftp://boombox.micro.umn`

Jury

VRDCT (Jury Verdicts Library)

The Verdicts library aids litigation preparation by providing quick and convenient access to selected online verdict and settlement information for civil cases nationwide. Case information covered includes verdict and settlement amounts, expert witnesses, case summaries and counsel data.

Keywords: Judicial Process, Law

Audience: Lawyers

Profile: The Verdicts library aids litigation preparation by providing quick and convenient access to selected online verdict and settlement information for civil cases nationwide. Case information covered includes verdict and settlement amounts, expert witnesses, case summaries and counsel data.

Contact: New Sales Group at 800-227-4908 or 513-859-5398 inside the US, or 1-513-865-7981 for all inquires outside the US.

User Info: To Subscribe, contact Mead directly.

To examine the Lexis user guide, you can access it at the ftp site of the University of Texas at Austin at the URL address: ftp://ftp.cc.utexas.edu

The files are in: /pub/ref-services/LEXIS

`telnet://nex.meaddata.com`

`http://www.meaddata.com`

Justice

Activ-L

A mailing list for the discussion of peace, empowerment, justice, and environmental issues.

Keywords: Peace, Justice, Environment, Activism

Audience: Activists, Students

Contact: Rich Winkel
harelb@math.cornell.edu

User Info: To Subscribe to the list, send an e-mail message to the URL address below consisting of a single line reading:

SUB activ-l YourFirstName YourLastName.

To send a message to the entire list, address it to: active-l@mizzou1.missouri.edu

`mailto:listserv@mizzou1.missouri.edu`

Justice Department

Department of Justice Gopher

A gopher containing online information from the Justice Department.

Keywords: Federal Law (US), Government (US), Justice Department

Sponsor: United States Department of Justice

Audience: Lawyers, Citizens

Profile: The Department of Justice (DOJ) gopher features DOJ criminal and law enforcement statistics, as well as agency procurement requests, job listings, and press releases. Also has links to other US government online systems.

Contact: gopher@usdoj.gov

`gopher://gopher.usdoj.gov`

A
B
C
D
E
F
G
H
I
J
K
L
M
N
O
P
Q
R
S
T
U
V
W
X
Y
Z

A
B
C
D
E
F
G
H
I
J
K
L
M
N
O
P
Q
R
S
T
U
V
W
X
Y
Z

K-12 Education

disted 'Journal of Distance Education and Communication'

This online journal covers distance education broadly, including formal and informal education, geographically disadvantaged learners, and both K-12 and postsecondary education.

Keywords: Education (Adult), Education (Distance), Education (Continuing), K-12 Education (K-12), Education (Post-Secondary)

Audience: K-12 Educators, K-12 Administrators

Details: Free

To subscribe to the journal, send an e-mail message to the URL address shown below consisting of a single line reading:

SUB disted YourFirstName YourLastName

`mailto:listserv@uwavm.bitnet`

K-12 School Libraries

This directory is a compilation of information resources focused on K-12 Education.

Keywords: Libraries, Education (K-12)

Audience: Librarians, Educators (K-12)

`ftp://una.hh.lib.umich.edu/70/ inetdirsstacks/k12schmed:troselius`

k12.chat.junior

A Usenet newsgroup providing information and discussion for and about students in junior high school.

Keywords: Students, Chat Groups

Audience: Students (K-8)

Details: Free

To subscribe to this Usenet newsgroup, you need access to a newsreader.

`news:k12.chat.junior`

k12.chat.senior

A Usenet newsgroup providing information and discussion for and about students in senior high school.

Keywords: Students, Chat Groups

Audience: Students (K-12)

Details: Free

To subscribe to this Usenet newsgroup, you need access to a newsreader.

`news:k12.chat.senior`

K12 Net

Decentralized network of school-based bulletin board systems (BBSs).

Keywords: Education (K-12), Networks

Audience: Educators (K-12), School Children

Profile: K12 Net provides millions of teachers, students, and parents in metropolitan and rural areas throughout the world with the ability to meet and talk with each other to discuss educational issues, exchange information, and share resources on a global scale.

Contact: Jack Crawford, Janet Murray jack@k12net.org or jmurray@psg.com

Details: Free

`gopher://woonext.dsrd.ornl.gov/11/ Docs/k12net`

Kaleidospace

Kaleidospace

This is a new web server that provides a multimedia showcase for artists, performers, CD-ROM authors, musicians, writers, animators, filmmakers, and software developers.

Keywords: Art, Computer Art, Multimedia

Audience: Artists, Performers, CD-ROM Authors, Musicians, Writers, Animators, Filmmakers, Software Developers

Profile: This site was created to support independent artists. The site has similarities to other web servers, such as IUMA, but differs in that it works with all types of artists, and that it processes orders for the artist's material.

Contact: Jeannie Novak, Peter Markiewicz jeannienov@aol.com peterm@ewald.mbi.ucla.edu

`http://kspace.com`

`http://fire.kspace.com`

Kansas

The University of Kansas Library

The library's holdings are large and wide-ranging and contain significant collections in many fields.

Keywords: Botany, Chinese Studies, Cartography (History of), Kansas, Opera, Ornithology, Joyce (James), Yeats (William Butler), Walpole (Sir Robert, Collections of)

Audience: General Public, Researchers, Librarians, Document Delivery Professionals

A
B
C
D
E
F
G
H
I
J
K
L
M
N
O
P
Q
R
S
T
U
V
W
X
Y
Z

Contact: John S. Miller

Details: Free

Expect: Username, Send: relay <cr>

`telnet://kuhub.cc.ukans.edu`

Kentucky and Ohio River Valley (History of)

University of Chicago Library

The library's holdings are large and wide-ranging and contain significant collections in many fields.

Keywords: English Bibles, Lincoln (Abraham), Kentucky & Ohio River Valley (History of), Balzac (Honore de), American Drama, Cromwell (Oliver), Goethe, Judaica, Italy, Chaucer (Geoffrey), Wells (Ida, Personal Papers of), Douglas (Stephen A.), Italy, Literature (Children's)

Audience: General Public, Researchers, Librarians, Document Delivery Professionals

Details: Free

Expect: ENTER CLASS, Send: LIB48 3; Expect: CONNECTED, Send: RETURN

`telnet://olorin.uchicago.edu`

KFLC-L

KFLC-L

A mailing list for distributing information on the meetings and proceedings of the Kentucky Foreign Language Conferences (KFCL).

Keywords: Language, Linguistics, Education (Bilingual)

Audience: Linguists, Educators

Contact: John Greenway
engjlg@ukcc.uky.edu

To subscribe, send an e-mail message to the URL address below consisting of a single line reading:

SUB kflc-l YourFirstName YourLastName.

To send a message to the entire list, address it to: kflc-l@ukcc.uky.edu

`mailto:listserv@ukcc.uky.edu`

KIDLINK and KIDCAFE

KIDLINK and KIDCAFE

This discussion group is designed to act as a structured forum for e-mail exchanges between children aged 10-15.

Keywords: Education, Children

Audience: Children

Profile: A dialog is set up each year called 'KIDS-XX' where 'XX' is the current year. Each participating child posts an e-mail message answering the following four questions before he or she can engage in the dialog: 1. Who am I? 2. What do I want to be when I grow up? 3. How do I want the world to be better when I grow up? 4. What can I do to make this happen?

KIDLINK operates the following free discussion lists and services:

- KIDLINK: discussion group for children aged 10-15.

- RESPONSE: the destination for answers to the four questions above.

- KIDCAFE: a forum for children aged 10-15. Read-only for people outside this age group.

- KIDCAFEP: a Portuguese-language version of KIDCAFE.

- KIDCAFEJ: a Japanese-language version of KIDCAFE.

- KIDCAFEN: a Scandinavian-language (Nordic) version of KIDCAFE.

- KIDFORUM: a showcase of works by kids on a series of topics specified to promote exchange between classrooms. Teachers can plan for class participation in monthly topics.

- KIDPROJ: a forum enabling teachers/ youth group leaders to design projects for children through the KIDLINK network.

- KIDLEADR: an informal meeting place for exchanging ideas, networking, asking for help, requesting hello messages, etc., for teachers, coordinators, parents, social workers, and others interested in KIDS-94.

- KIDLEADP: a Portuguese-language version of KIDLEADR.

- KIDLEADS: a Spanish-language version of KIDLEADR.

- KIDLEADN: a Scandinavian-language (Nordic) version of KIDLEADR.

Contact: Odd de Presno|
opresno@extern.uio.no

Details: Free

For information about the projects, subscribe to the KIDLINK announcement service: send an e-mail message to: listserv@vm1.NoDak.edu with the following command in the text of your message:

SUB KIDLINK Yourfirstname Yourlastname.

Notes: For more information, read the 'WHAT IS KIDLINK / KIDS-94' page at gopher:// kids.ccit.duq.edu/00/about/kidlink-general.

`gopher://kids.ccit.duq.edu`

Kinesiology

Biomch-L

This list is intended for members of the International, European, American, Canadian, and other Societies of Biomechanics, and for members of ISEK (International Society of Electrophysiological Kinesiology), as well as for all others with an interest in the general field of biomechanics and human or animal movement.

Keywords: Biomechanics, Kinesiology, Movement

Sponsor: International Society of Biomechanics

Audience: Kinesiologists

Contact: Ton van den Bogert
listserv@nic.surfnet.nl

Details: Free

To subscribe to the list, send an e-mail message to the URL address below, consisting of a single line reading:

SUB biomch-l YourFirstName YourLastName

To send a message to the entire list, address it to: biomch-l@nic.surfnet.nl

Notes: To obtain technical help, send the command send biomch-l guide to listserv@hearn or listserv@nic.surfnet.nl.

`mailto:listserv@nic.surfnet.nl`

Kingsley (Charles)

Princeton University Online Manuscripts Catalog Library

The library's holdings are large and wide-ranging. They contain significant collections in many fields.

Keywords: Books (Antiquarian), Dickens (Charles), Disraeli (Benjamin), Eliot (George), Hardy (Thomas), Kingsley (Charles), Trollope (Anthony)

Audience: General Public, Researchers, Librarians, Document Delivery Professionals

Details: Free

Expect: VM370 logo, Send: <cr>; Expect: Welcome screen, Send: folio <cr>; Expect: Welcome screen for FOLIO, Send: <cr>; Expect: List of choices, Send: 3 <cr>; To exit: type: logoff

`telnet://pucc.princeton.edu`

Kites

(The) Kites FTP Archive

Files pertaining to kites and kite-flying.

Keywords: Kites, Recreation

Sponsor: University of Hawaii

Audience: Kite Enthusiasts, Aeronautical Engineers

Contact: Kevin Mayeshiro
            kevin@ftp.hawaii.edu

Details: Free, Moderated, Images

`ftp://ftp.hawaii.edu/pub/rec.kites`

Kiwanis International

Circle K International

This list is for members and alumni of the worldwide
collegiate service organization sponsored by
Kiwanis International.

Keywords: Kiwanis International

Audience: Kiwanis Members

Contact: Jeffrey M. Wolff
            jwolff@nyx.cs.du.edu

Details: Free

            To subscribe to the list, send an e-mail
            message requesting a subscription to
            the URL address below.

`mailto:jwolff@nyx.cs.du.edu`

Knowbot

Knowbot

Knowbot provides a uniform user interface to
heterogenous remote information services.

Keywords: Internet Services, Knowbot

Audience: Internet Surfers

Details: Free

            Login; Send: email address

`telnet://info.cnri.reston.va.us`

Knowledge Representation

nl-kr

This E-conference is open to discussion of any topic
related to the understanding and generation of
natural language and knowledge representation as
subfields of artificial intelligence.

Keywords: Programming Languages, Natural
            Language, Knowledge Representation,
            Linguistics

Audience: Computer Programmers

Contact: Christopher Welty
            weltyc@cs.rpi.edu

Details: Free, Moderated

            To subscribe to the list, send an e-mail
            message requesting a subscription to
            the URL address below.

`mailto:nl-kr-request@cs.rpi.edu`

Korea

soc.culture.korean

A Usenet newsgroup providing information and
discussion about Korea's culture and its people.

Keywords: Korea, Sociology

Audience: Sociologists, Koreans

Details: Free

            To subscribe to this Usenet newsgroup,
            you need access to a newsreader

`news:soc.culture.korean`

Kurtz (Katernine)

Deryni-L

A list for readers and fans of Katernine Kurtz's novels
and other works.

Keywords: Science Fiction, Kurtz (Katernine)

Audience: Science Fiction Enthusiasts

Contact: Edward J. Branley
            elendil@mintir.new-orleans.la.us

User Info: To subscribe to the list, send an e-mail
            message requesting a subscription to
            the URL address below.

            To send a message to the entire list,
            address it to: deryni-l@mintir.new-
            orleans.la.us

`mailto:deryni-l@mintir.new-`
`orleans.la.us`

A
B
C
D
E
F
G
H
I
J
K
L
M
N
O
P
Q
R
S
T
U
V
W
X
Y
Z

L

Labor

Iowa State University

The library's holdings contain significant collections in many fields.

Keywords: Agriculture, Veterinary Medicine, Statistics, Labor, Soil Conservation, Film

Audience: General Public, Researchers, Librarians, Document Delivery Professionals

Details: Free

Expect: DIAL, Send: LIB

`telnet://isn.iastate.edu`

LabStat

The public database of the Bureau of Labor Statistics.

Keywords: Economics, Labor, Census Data

Sponsor: United States Government, Bureau of Labor Statistics

Audience: General Public, Statisticians, Researchers

Profile: LABSTAT provides current and historical data, as well as numerous press releases. This site is composed of individual databases (in flat file format) corresponding to each of 26 surveys.

Contact: labstat.helpdesk@bls.gov.

Details: Free

Login: anonymous; use e-mail address as password.

Notes: For each news release published by the Bureau of Labor Statistics, the two most current are stored in the /news.release directory. The documentation provides a list of the abbreviations used to identify the news releases, and a description of the sub-directories available to the user.

`ftp://stats.bls.gov`

NLSNews Newsletter (National Longitudinal Surveys of Labor Market Experience)

This newsletter issued by the Center for Human Resource Research (Ohio State University); distributed to researchers using NLS data, as well as to other interested persons.

Keywords: Labor, Government (US), Department of Labor

Sponsor: Bureau of Labor Statistics, US Department of Labor

Audience: Statisticians, Researchers (Labor)

Profile: A typical issue contains updates on the status and availability of NLS data tapes and CD-ROMs for the six NLS cohorts (Older Men, Mature Women, Young Men, Young Women, Youth, and Children), notices to researchers of data-file or documentation errors, summaries of in-progress and completed NLS research, and other information of general interest to the NLS research community.

Contact: Gale James
james@ohsthr.bitnet

A description of the subscription service that enables users to automatically receive, as soon as it becomes available, the latest issue of the NLS Newsletter and error updates can be found in the file subscribe.info, available via nlserve@ohsthr.bitnet, the Center's file server.

`mailto:james@ohsthr.bitnet`

Occupational Outlook Handbook 1992-93

An annual U.S. Department of Labor publication that provides detailed information for more than 320 occupations, including job descriptions, typical salaries, education and training requirements, working conditions, job outlook, and more.

Keywords: Careers, Employment, Labor

Sponsor: U.S. Deptartment of Labor

Audience: General Public, Job Seekers, Business Professionals

Details: Free

`gopher://umslvma.umsl.edu/11/library/govdocs/ooha`

Labor (History of)

Georgia State University Library

The library's holdings are large and wide-ranging and contain significant collections in many fields.

Keywords: Labor (History of), Multimedia, Mercer (Johnny, Collection of)

Audience: General Public, Researchers, Librarians, Document Delivery Professionals

Contact: Phil Williams
isgpew@gsuvm1.gsu.edu

Details: Free

Expect: VM screen, Send: RETURN; Expect: CP READ, Send: DIAL VTAM, press RETURN; Expect: CICS screen, Send: PF1

`telnet://library.gsu.edu`

A B C D E F G H I J K **L** M N O P Q R S T U V W X Y Z

Labor Archives

University of Colorado at Boulder Library

The library's holdings are large and wide-ranging and contain significant collections in many fields.

Keywords: Numismatics, Human Rights, Literature (Children's), Labor Archives, History (US)

Audience: Researchers, Students, General Public

Contact: Donna Pattee
pattee@spot.colorado.edu

Details: Free

Expect: Login; Send: Culine

`telnet://culine.colorado.edu`

Laboratory Primate Newsletter

Laboratory Primate Newsletter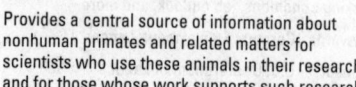

Provides a central source of information about nonhuman primates and related matters for scientists who use these animals in their research and for those whose work supports such research.

Keywords: Primatology, Psychology

Audience: Primate Researchers, Psychologists

Contact: Judith E. Schrier
primate@brownvm.brown.edu

Details: Free

`mailto:listserv@brownvm.brown.edu`

Lafayette (Marquis de)

Indiana University Libraries

The library's holdings are large and wide-ranging and contain significant collections in many fields.

Keywords: Literature (English), Literature (American), 1640-Present, British Plays (19th-C.), Western Americana, Railway History, Aristotle (Texts of), Lafayette (Marquis de), Handel (G.F.), Austrian History, Antiquarian Books, Rare Books, French Opera (19th-C.), Drama (British),

Audience: General Public, Researchers, Librarians, Document Delivery Professionals

Details: Free

Expect: User ID prompt, Send: GUEST

`telnet://iuis.ucs.indiana.edu`

Land Records

University of New Mexico UNMinfo Library

The library's holdings are large and wide-ranging and contain significant collections in many fields.

Keywords: Photography (History of), Architecture, Native American Affairs, Land Records

Audience: Researchers, Students, General Public

Contact: Art St. George
stgeorge@unmb.bitnet

Details: Free

Expect: Login; Send: Unminfo

`telnet://unminfo.unm.edu`

Landscaping

alt.bonsai

A Usenet newsgroup providing information and discussion about bonsai gardening.

Keywords: Bonsai Trees, Japan, Gardening, Landscaping

Audience: Gardeners, Bonsai Enthusiasts

User Info: To subscribe to this Usenet newsgroup, you need access to a newsreader.

`news:alt.bonsai`

rec.gardens

A Usenet newsgroup providing information and discussion about gardening.

Keywords: Gardening, Landscaping

Audience: Gardeners

User Info: To subscribe to this Usenet newsgroup, you need access to a newsreader.

`news:rec.gardens`

Lang-Lucid

Lang-Lucid

Discussions on all subjects related to the programming language Lucid, including language design issues, implementations for personal computers, implementations for parallel machines, language extensions, programming environments, products, bug reports, and bug fixes/workarounds.

Keywords: Programming, Programming Languages

Audience: Lucid Programmers

Contact: R. Jagannathan
lang-lucid-request@csl.sri.com

Details: Free

User Info: To subscribe to the list, send an e-mail message requesting a subscription to the URL address below.

`mailto:lang-lucid-request@csl.sri.com`

LANGIT

LANGIT

A forum for members of the Italian Linguistics Center (Centri Linguistici Italian).

Keywords: Italy, Linguistics

Audience: Linguists, Educators, Students

Details: Free

User Info: To subscribe to the list, send an e-mail message to the URL address below.

`mailto:listserv@icineca.bitnet`

Language

Academia Latinoamericana de Espanol

This program is specifically designed for those interested in learning to speak Spanish through a fully immersive trip to Ecuador.

Keywords: Spanish, Language, Education (Bilingual)

Sponsor: Academia Latinoamericana de Espanol, Quito, Ecuador

Audience: Reseachers, Students, Language Teachers

Contact: Webmaster
webmaster@comnet.com

`http://www.comnet.com/ecuador/learnSpanish.html`

gaelic-l

A multidisciplinary discussion list that facilitates the exchange of news, views, and information in Scottish Gaelic, Irish, and Manx.

Keywords: Scottish Gaelic, Irish, Manx, Language

Audience: Linguists

Contact: Marion Gunn
mgunn@irlearn.ucd.ie or
caoimhin@smo.ac.uk
lss203@cs.napier.ac.uk

Details: Free

User Info: To subscribe to the list, send an e-mail message to the URL address shown below consisting of a single line reading:

SUB gaelic-I YourFirstName YourLastName

To send a message to the entire list, address it to: gaelic-I@irlearn.ucd.ie

`mailto:listserv@irlearn.ucd.ie`

GC-L ★

Project for international business and management curricula.

Keywords: Business, Management, Language

Sponsor: Global Classroom

Audience: Linguists, Language Teachers, Language Students, International Business Educators

Details: Free

User Info: To subscribe to the list, send an e-mail message to the address below consisting of a single line reading:

`mailto:listserv@uriacc.uri.edu`

INTERCUL ★

A study of international communication.

Keywords: Languages (international)

Audience: Linguists, Language Teachers, Language Students

Details: Free

`mailto:listserv@vm.its.rpi.edu`

KFLC-L

A mailing list for distributing information on the meetings and proceedings of the Kentucky Foreign Language Conferences (KFCL).

Keywords: Language, Linguistics, Education (Bilingual)

Audience: Linguists, Educators

Contact: John Greenway engjlg@ukcc.uky.edu

User Info: To subscribe, send an e-mail message to the URL address below consisting of a single line reading:

SUB kflc-I YourFirstName YourLastName.

To send a message to the entire list, address it to: kflc-I@ukcc.uky.edu

`mailto:listserv@ukcc.uky.edu`

Lantra-L ★

A discussion of interpretation and translation.

Keywords: Interpretation, Translation, Linguistics

Audience: Linguists, Interpreters, Translators

User Info: To subscribe to the list, send and e-mail message to the URL address below consisting of a single line reading:

SUB lantra-I Your First Name Your Last Name

To send a message to the entire list, address it to: kabtra-I@search.bitnet

Details: Free

`mailto:listserv@searn.bitnet`

LINGUIST ★

A discussion of language and linguistics.

Keywords: Language, Linguistics

Audience: Linguists, Language Teachers, Language Students

Details: Free

User Info: To subscribe to the list, send an e-mail message to the address shown below consisting of a single line reading:

SUB linguist Your First Name Your Last Name

`mailto:listserv@tamvmi.bitnet`

LLTI ★

The Language Learning Technology International (LLTI) forum is a discussion of computer-assisted language learning.

Keywords: Linguistics, Computer-Aided Instruction

Audience: Linguists, Language Teachers, Language Students

Details: Free

User Info: To subscribe to the list, send an e-mail message to the URL address below, consisting of a single line reading:

SUB llti YourFirstName YourLastName

To send a message to the entire list, address it to: llti@dartcms1.dartmouth.edu

`mailto:listserv@dartcms1.dartmouth.edu`

LTEST ★

A discussion of language-testing research and practice.

Keywords: Linguistics, Translations

Audience: Linguists, Language Teachers, Language Students

Details: Free

User Info: To subscribe to the list, send an e-mail message to the URL address below, consisting of a single line reading:

SUB Ltest YourFirstName YourLastName

To send a message to the entire list, address it to:ltest@uclan1.bitnet

`mailto:listserv@uclan1.bitnet`

Russian ★

This list is dedicated to the discussion of Russian-language issues, including Russian language, linguistics, grammar, translations, and literature.

Keywords: Language, Literature (Russian), Linguistics

Audience: Slavicists, Linguists, Translators

Contact: Andrew Wollert ispajw@asuacad russian@asuvm.inre.asu.edu

Details: Free

User Info: To subscribe to the list, send an e-mail message requesting subscription to the URL address below.

`russian@asuvm.inre.asu.edu`

The Human Languages Page ★★★

This site provides language resources from around the world, including dictionaries, language tutorials, and spoken samples of languages.

Keywords: Language, Linguistics

Audience: Linguists, Educators, Students

Profile: Languages covered include Esperanto, Gaelic, Arabic, Hindi, and Kanji. Also provides link to the Gutenberg Project (electronic texts) and to the Library of Congress.

Contact: Tyler Jones tjones@willamette.edu.

Details: Free

`http://www.willamette.edu/~tjones/Language-Page.html`

Language Software

alt.chinese.text ★

A Usenet newsgroup providing information and discussion about Chinese language software.

Keywords: Chinese Language, Language Software

Audience: Chinese, Chinese Speakers, Computer Users

User Info: To subscribe to this Usenet newsgroup, you need access to a newsreader.

`news:alt.chinese.text`

Lasers

University of Rochester Library ★★

The library's holdings are large and wide-ranging and contain significant collections in many fields.

Keywords: Architecture, Art History, Photography, Literature (Asian), Lasers, Geology, Statistics, Optics, Medieval Studies

A B C D E F G H I J K **L** M N O P Q R S T U V W X Y Z

Audience: Researchers, Students, General Public

Details: Free

Expect: Login; Send: Library

`telnet://128.151.226.71`

Latin America

amlat.mujeres

This conference serves as a forum for interchange between organizations and women's movements in Latin America and the Caribbean.

Keywords: Women, Latin America, Caribbean, Feminism

Audience: Women, Feminists, Activists

Contact: Agencia Latinoamericana de Informacion
info@alai.ec, uualai@ecuanex.ec

Details: Costs

Establish an account on the nearest APC node. Login, type c for conferences, then type: **go amlat.mujeres**

For information on the nearest APC node, contact:

APC International Secretariat IBASE E-mail: apcadmin@apc.org

Contact: Carlos Afonso (cafonso@ax.apc.org) or APC North American Regional Office E-mail: apcadmin@apc.org
Edie Farwell (efarwell@igc.apc.org)

`telnet://igc.apc.org`

cread (Latin American & Caribbean Distance & Continuing Education)

This is a digest list of distance education information primarily focused on Latin America and the Caribbean.

Keywords: Latin America, Caribbean, Education (Distance)

Audience: Educators, Administrators, Faculty

Details: Free

User Info: To subscribe to the list, send an e-mail message to the URL address below consisting of a single line reading:

SUB cread YourFirstName YourLastName.

To send a message to the entire list, address it to: cread@yorkvm1.bitnet

`mailto:listserv@yorkvm1.bitnet`

Felipe's Bilingual WWW Pages

An interactive web site containing gopher and web links to various Latin American resources.

Keywords: Latin America, Education (Bilingual)

Sponsor: University of Texas, Texas, USA

Audience: Educators, Language Students, Translators

Contact: Felipe Campos
felipe@bongo.utexas.edu

`http://edb518ea.edb.utexas.edu`

Florida State University System Library

The library's holdings are large and wide-ranging and contain significant collections in many fields.

Keywords: Florida, Latin America, Judaica, Literature (Children's), Marine Engineering, Law (Brazilian), Law (British)

Audience: General Public, Researchers, Librarians, Document Delivery Professionals

Details: Free

Expect: Command ==>, Send: dial vtam; Expect: LUIS User Menu, Send: Your Catalog choice; To log off: Send: %off

`telnet://nervm.nerdc.ufl.edu`

hilat-l (Higher Education in Latin America)

Provides a means of interchange about research on higher education in Latin America. Postings are mostly in English, but are also welcome in Spanish and Portuguese.

Keywords: Education (Adult), Education (Distance), Education (Continuing), Latin America

Audience: Educators, Administrators, Faculty

Details: Free

User Info: To subscribe to the list, send an e-mail message to the URL address shown below consisting of a single line reading:

SUB hilat-l YourFirstName YourLastName

To send a message to the entire list, address it to: hilat-l @bruspvm.bitnet

`mailto:listserv@bruspvm.bitnet`

Info-South (Latin American News)

The database provides citations and abstracts of materials relating to contemporary economic, political, and social issues in Latin America.

Keywords: International News, Economics, International Politics, Latin America

Sponsor: University of Miami, Coral Gables, FL, US

Audience: General Public

Profile: Coverage includes a wide range of topics assessing the current situation in Latin America.

Contact: Dialog in the US at (800) 334-2564, Dialog internationally at country-specific locations.

User Info: To subscribe, contact Dialog directly.

Notes: Coverage: 1988 to the present; updated weekly.

`telnet://dialog.com`

Latin America & Caribbean Network Gopher server

A Gopher server currently under construction providing Internet access to Latin America and the Caribbean.

Keywords: Caribbean, Latin America

Sponsor: Lacnet Corporation

Audience: Caribbean Enthusiasts

Profile: The Latin America & Caribbean Network Gopher server is a gopher server currently under construction. When finished it will provide gopher access to gopher servers throughout Latin America and the Caribbean providing government and institutional information on various countries.

Contact: Luis Rodriguez or Javier Hidalgo
lrodriguez@mia.lac.net
jhidalgo@mia.lac.net

Notes: Currently under construction.

`gopher://mia.lac.net`

Latin American Database Historic World Documents

International legal files covering 33 nations and article citations from publications relating to Hispanic legal systems. The wiretap gopher provides access to a range of world documents in full-text format.

Keywords: Latin America, Law (International), International Documents, Latin America

Audience: General Public, Hispanics, Lawyers

Profile: The database includes two files, LAWL containing legislation from 33 nations, mostly Spanish speaking, and HISS containing Hispanic Legal Article citations.

Details: Free

Notes: Select from menu as appropriate.

`gopher://marvel.loc.gov`

NIBNews - A Monthly Electronic Bulletin About Medical Informatics

Disseminates information about Brazilian and Latin American activities, people, information, events, publications, software, and so on, involving computer applications in health care, medicine, and biology.

Keywords: Health Care, Biology, Brazil, Latin America, South America, Medicine

Audience: Health-Care Professionals, Biologists

Contact: Renato M. E. Sabbatini
SABBATINI@BRUC.BITNET

Details: Free

E-mail a short notice to

`mailto:sabbatini@ccvax.unicamp.br`

Summit of the Americas Internet Gopher

A gopher containing supporting materials for the Summit of the Americas, a meeting of the Western Hemisphere's democratically elected heads of state, to be held in Miami in December of 1994.

Keywords: American Studies, International Relations, Haiti, Latin America

Sponsor: The Florida University Latin American and Caribbean Center

Audience: Government Officials, Journalists, NGOs, General Public

Contact: Rene Ramos
summit@SERVAX.FIU.EDU

`gopher://summit.fiu.edu`

Latin American Studies

University of Texas at Austin Library ★★

The library's holdings are large and wide-ranging and contain significant collections in many fields.

Keywords: Music, Natural Science, Nursing, Science Technology, Behavioral Science, Social Work, Computer Science, Engineering, Latin American Studies, Middle Eastern Studies

Audience: Researchers, Students, General Public

Details: Free

Expect: Blank Screen, Send: Return; Expect: Go, Send: Return; Expect: Enter Terminal Type, Send: vt100

Notes: Some databases are restricted to UT Austin users only.

`telnet://utcat.utexas.edu`

Latino Culture

Chicano/LatinoNet ★★★

An electronic mechanism that brings together Chicano/Latino research, as well as linguistic minority and educational research efforts being carried out at the University of California and elsewhere. It serves as a gateway between faculty, staff, and students who are engaged in research and curricular efforts in these areas.

Keywords: Culture, Race, Chicano Culture, Latino Culture

Sponsor: Chicano Studies Research Center, University of California at Los Angeles

Audience: Students, Mexican-Americans, Latinos

Contact: Richard Chabran
Chabran@latino.sscnet.ucla.ed

Details: Free

`gopher://latino.sscnet.ucla.edu`

Mexican Culture FAQ  ★★★

This is the FAQ from the soc.culture.mexican newsgroup. Provides information on Mexican culture, history, society, language, and tourism.

Keywords: Culture, Race, Chicano Culture, Latino Culture

Sponsor: News Group Moderators for soc.culture.mexican

Audience: Students, Latinos, Chicanos

Contact: News Group Moderator
mendoza-grado@att.com

Details: Free

`ftp://ftp.mty.itesm.ms/pub/mexico/faqs`

`http://www.cis.ohio-state.edu/hypertext/faq/usenet/mexican-faq/faq.html`

US/Mexico Border Discussion List ★★

This group provides a forum for the discussion of issues pertaining to the US/Mexico border environment.

Keywords: Mexico, Environment, Latino Culture

Sponsor: The US Environmental Protection Agency

Audience: Activists, Environmentalists, Urban Planners

Details: Free

User Info: To subscribe to the list, send a message to the URL address below consisting of a single line reading:

SUB us_mexborder YourFirstName YourLastName

To send a message to the entire list, address it to: us_mexborder@unixmail.rtpnc.epa.gov

`mailto:listserver@unixmail.rtpnc.epa.gov`

Latvia

Balt-L ★

A forum devoted to communications to and about the Baltic Republics of Lithuania, Latvia, and Estonia.

Keywords: Lithuania, Latvia, Estonia, Baltic Republics

Audience: Researchers, Baltic Nationals

Contact: Jean-Michel Thizy
jmyhg@uottawa.edu

Details: Free

User Info: To subscribe to the list, send an e-mail message to the URL address below, consisting of a single line reading:

SUB balt-l YourFirstName YourLastName

`mailto:listserv@ubvm.cc.buffalo.edu`

University of Nebraska at Lincoln Library ★★

The library's holdings are large and wide-ranging and contain significant collections in many fields.

Keywords: Slovak Republic, Czech Republic, Folklore, Military History, Latvia, Law (Tax), Law (US)

Audience: General Public, Researchers, Librarians, Document Delivery Professionals

Contact: Anita Cook

Details: Free

Expect: login, Send: library

`telnet://unllib.unl.edu`

Law

BKRTCY (Bankruptcy Library)

The Federal Bankruptcy library is a comprehensive collection of primary and secondary legal research materials pertaining to bankruptcy issues.

Keywords: Law, Filings, Bankruptcy

Audience: Lawyers, Bankers

Profile: The Federal Bankruptcy library is a comptrehensive collection of primary and secondary legal research materials that includes case law, rules, statutory and regulatory materials, legal publications, accounting literature and other resources pertaining to bankruptcy issues.

Contact: New Sales Group at (800) 227-4908 or 513-859-5398 inside the US, or 1-513-865-7981 for all inquires outside the US.

User Info: To subscribe, contact Mead directly.

To examine the Lexis user guide, you can access it at the ftp site of the University of Texas at Austin at the URL address: ftp://ftp.cc.utexas.edu

The files are in: pub/ref-services/LEXIS

`telnet://nex.meaddata.com`

`http://www.meaddata.com`

A
B
C
D
E
F
G
H
I
J
K
L
M
N
O
P
Q
R
S
T
U
V
W
X
Y
Z

California Privacy Act 1992

Text of the California Privacy Act of 1992.

Keywords: Law, California

Audience: General Public, Lawyers

Details: Free

`gopher://wiretap.spies.com`

Children's Rights

Contains files from the Children's Rights Council, the Central Ohio Organization, Fathers and Children for Equality, and the National Congress for Men and Children.

Keywords: Children, Law

Audience: Lawyers, Social Workers, Children's Rights Activists

Details: Free

`telnet://cwgk4.chem.cwru.edu`

ENERGY

The Energy News and Information (ENERGY) library consists of news, legal, and regulatory information.

Keywords: Energy, News, Law, Regulations

Audience: Energy Researchers

Profile: The ENERGY library contains more than 50 full-text sources concentrating on energy-related news and issues. Also available are decisions and orders of the United States Federal Power Commission, Federal Energy Regulatory Commission, and Nuclear Regulatory Commission. At the state level, it covers administrative decisions and orders for 17 states. Energy industry research reports from InvestextR are also available.

Contact: Mead New Sales Group at (800) 227-4908 or (513) 859-5398 inside the US, or (513) 865-7981 for all inquiries outside the US.

User Info: To subscribe, contact Mead directly.

To examine the Nexis user guide, you can access it at the ftp site of the University of Texas at Austin at the URL address: ftp://ftp.cc.utexas.edu

The files are in: pub/ref-services/LEXIS

`telnet://nex.meaddata.com`

`http://www.meaddata.com`

ENVIRN (Environment Library)

The Environment (ENVIRN) Library contains a variety of environment-related news and legal information.

Keywords: News, Analysis, Law, Environment

Audience: Environmental Researchers, Businesspeople

Profile: The ENVIRN Library contains a combination of environmental information that can provide critical insight into environmental hazards, EPA ratings, specific company investigations, evaluations on potentially hazardous chemicals, and parties responsible for cleanup of specific hazardous sites. Additionally, ENVIRN provides a wealth of environment-related informationÑlegislation, regulations, and court and agency decisions at both the federal and state levels; news; the Environmental Law Reporter, and American Law Reports.

Contact: Mead New Sales Group at (800) 227-4908 or (513) 859-5398 inside the US, or (513) 865-7981 for all inquiries outside the US.

User Info: To subscribe, contact Mead directly.

To examine the Nexis user guide, you can access it at the ftp site of the University of Texas at Austin at the URL address: ftp://ftp.cc.utexas.edu

The files are in: /pub/ref-services/LEXIS

`telnet://nex.meaddata.com`

`http://www.meaddata.com`

FEDSEC (Federal Securities Library)

The US Federal Securities library covers federal case law, Securities Exchanges Commission (SEC) materials, Commodities Futures Trading Commision (CFTC) materials and other legal and legislative materials relevant to the securities industry, as well as company information, news and analysis.

Keywords: Law, Filings, Securities, SEC

Audience: Lawyers, Bankers, Stockbrokers

Profile: The Federal Securities library contains over 60 separately searchable files covering federal case law: Securities Exchange Commision (SEC) no-action letters, decisions, orders, releases, and SEC filings (both full text and abstracts); Commodities Futures Trading Commision (CFTC) decisions, orders, releases; legislative materials; statutory and regulatory materials; selected RICO, class derivative, and collateralized mortgage obligations case law, rules and regulations; Federal Reserve Board materials; AICPA annual reports and accounting & audit literature files; Standard & Poors company information; state administrative decisions, orders, and releases; and company news and analysis information.

Contact: New Sales Group at (800) 227-4908 or 513-859-5398 inside the US, or 1-513-865-7981 for all inquires outside the US.

User Info: To subscribe, contact Mead directly.

To examine the Lexis user guide, you can access it at the ftp site of the University of Texas at Austin at the URL address: ftp://ftp.cc.utexas.edu

The files are in: pub/ref-services/LEXIS

`telnet://nex.meaddata.com`

`http://www.meaddata.com`

FEDTAX (Federal Tax Library)

The Federal Tax library offers a comprehensive, up-to-date collection of tax-related materials, including case law, agency materials, legislative and regulatory materials, and more.

Keywords: Law, Analysis, Tax

Audience: Lawyers

Profile: This library includes federal and state tax case law, Internal Revenue Service rulings and releases, state tax administrative decisions and rulings, the Internal Revenue Code, federal tax regulations, international news and treaties, tax looseleaf services, tax periodicals, tax law reviews, tax dailies, pending state legislation, and state property records.

Contact: New Sales Group at (800) 227-4908 or 513-859-5398 inside the US, or 1-513-865-7981 for all inquires outside the US.

User Info: To subscribe, contact Mead directly.

To examine the Lexis user guide, you can access it at the ftp site of the University of Texas at Austin at the URL address: ftp://ftp.cc.utexas.edu
The files are in: pub/ref-services/LEXIS

`telnet://nex.meaddata.com`

`http://www.meaddata.com`

Germany

Full text in German of various German laws and codes.

Keywords: German, Law

Sponsor: Berlin University, Berlin, Germany

Audience: Lawyers, Historians, Germans

Details: Free

Select from menu as appropriate.

`gopher://gate1.zedat.fu-berlin.de`

Illinois Legislation

This directory contains several Illinois Department of Nuclear Safety Statues and Regulations.

Keywords: Nuclear Safety, Law, Illinois

Audience: Lawyers

Details: Free

`gopher://wiretap.spies.com`

Hawaii FYI

A state information system providing a wide range of free legal information.

Keywords: Hawaii, Law

Audience: Hawaiians, Lawyers

Details: Free

`telnet://fyi.uhcc.hawaii.edu`

Hong Kong Law

Lists the basic Hong Kong Law (1990) and Hong Kong Bill of Rights Ordinance (1991).

Keywords: Hong Kong, Law

Audience: Lawyers, Sinologists

Details: Free

`gopher://marvel.loc.gov`

Insurance Periodicals Index

The database indexes and abstracts 35 of the most respected and widely read insurance industry journals and magazines.

Keywords: Insurance Industry, Law

Sponsor: NILS Publishing Company, Chatsworth, CA, US

Audience: Insurance Brokers

Profile: The subject coverage of the publications indexed includes the following major groupings: AIDS, alcohol abuse, asbestos, automobile insurance, aviation insurance, banks, bonds, catastrophes, crime, disability insurance, drug abuse, financial services, health insurance, insurance agents and brokers, legislation, liability insurance, life insurance, Lloyds, loss control, marketing, pensions, pollution, product liability, property insurance, rates, regulation, risk management, tort reform, uninsured motorists, workers' compensation, and more.

Contact: Dialog in the US at (800) 334-2564, Dialog internationally at country-specific locations.

User Info: To subscribe, contact Dialog directly.

Notes: Coverage: 1984 to the present; updated biweekly.

`telnet://dialog.com`

INSURE (Insurance)

The Insurance (INSURE) library contains specific full-text and abstract news and legal information sources focusing on the insurance industry.

Keywords: News, Analysis, Law, Insurance

Audience: Insurance Professionals, Lawyers

Profile: The INSURE library contains leading insurance industry news sources, legal and regulatory materials from NILS Publishing Company's INSURLAW, analyst reports on the insurance industry from InvestextR, and insurance company financial reports. Federal and state case law and federal regulations are also available.

Contact: Mead New Sales Group @ (800) 227-4908 or (513) 859-5398 inside the US, or (513) 865-7981 for all inquiries outside the US.

User Info: To subscribe, contact Mead directly.

To examine the Nexis user guide, you can access it at the ftp site of the University of Texas at Austin at the URL address: ftp://ftp.cc.utexas.edu The files are in: /pub/res-services/LEXIS

`telnet://nex.meaddata.com`

ITRADE (International Trade Library)

The International Trade Library contains materials related to the importing of goods and services, exporting of goods and services, licensing of intellectual property, payment of taxes, or investment and banking at the international level.

Keywords: Law, Import, Export, International Banking

Audience: Lawyers

Profile: ITRADE contains a comprehensive collection of federal case law, statutes, regulations, and agency decisions all related to the importing of goods and services, exporting of goods and services, licensing of intellectual property, payment of taxes, or investment and banking at the international level.

Contact: New Sales Group at (800) 227-4908 or 513-859-5398 inside the US, or 1-513-865-7981 for all inquires outside the US.

User Info: To subscribe, contact Mead directly.

To examine the Lexis user guide, you can access it at the ftp site of the University of Texas at Austin at the URL address: ftp://ftp.cc.utexas.edu
The files are in: /pub/ref-services/LEXIS

`telnet://nex.meaddata.com`

`http://www.meaddata.com`

Latin American Database Historic World Documents

International legal files covering 33 nations and article citations from publications relating to Hispanic legal systems. The wiretap gopher provides access to a range of world documents in full-text format.

Keywords: Hispanic, Law, International Law, International Documents

Audience: General Public, Hispanics, Lawyers

Profile: The database includes two files, 1) LAWL containing legislation from 33 nations, mostly Spanish speaking 2) HISS containing Hispanic Legal Article citations.

Details: Free

Select from menu as appropriate.

`gopher://marvel.loc.gov`

Law and Politics Book Review

Reviews books of interest to political scientists studying US law, the courts, and the judicial process. Reviews are commissioned by the editor.

Keywords: Political Science, Law, Judicial Process

Audience: Political Scientists, Lawyers

Details: Free, Moderated

User Info: To send a message to the entire list, address it to: listserv@umcvmb.bitnet

`mailto:listserv@umcvmb.bitnet`

Maryland

System provides access to a wide range of state information, including the policies and activities of members of Maryland's congress and voting district data.

Keywords: Maryland, Law, Voting

Audience: Maryland Residents, Lawyers

Details: Free

Select from menu as appropriate.

`gopher://info.umd.edu`

misc.legal

A Usenet newsgroup providing information and discussion about law and ethics.

Keywords: Law, Ethics

Audience: Lawyers, Legal Professionals, General Public

Details: Free

User Info: To subscribe to this Usenet newsgroup, you need access to a newsreader.

`news:misc.legal`

Multilateral Treaties

An experimental program to make available to the Internet community the text of a wide variety of multilateral conventions, even those that have not yet been ratified.

Keywords: Multilateral, Treaty, Law

Sponsor: The Fletcher School of Law and Diplomacy, Cornell University, Ithaca, NY

A B C D E F G H I J K L M N O P Q R S T U V W X Y Z

A
B
C
D
E
F
G
H
I
J
K
L
M
N
O
P
Q
R
S
T
U
V
W
X
Y
Z

Audience: Government Officials, Researchers, Lawyers

Profile: Almost all treaties listed are available in print form. The program will enable access to even very recent conventions. Primary focus is on Environmental and human rights issues but other fields are also included. The conventions coming out of the 1992 United Nations Conference on the Environment and Development have NOT been included as they are available elsewhere through CIESIN. Those Treaties covered include: Convention on International Trade in Endangered Species of Wild Fa; Montreal Protocol on Substances that Depleate the Ozone Layer; The Berne Convention for the Protection of Literary and Artistic Works; Agreement on the Rescue of Astronauts; the return of Astronauts

Contact: Peter Scott Director, Multilaterals Project, Fletcher School of Law and Diplomacy
pstott@pearl.tufts.edu
pstott@icg.apc.org

Details: Free

Select from menu as appropriate

`gopher://gopher.law.cornell.edu/11/foreign/fletcher-cat`

New Mexico LegalNet

The system makes legal resources available, including state motor vehicle and corporation databases, court dockets, border trade information, and country and city data.

Keywords: Law, New Mexico

Audience: New Mexico Residents, Lawyers, Private Investigators

Contact: inettgen@technet.nm.org

Details: Costs

`telnet://technet.nm.org`

Ohio

Provides access to Ohio State Supreme Court Opinions and Ohio 8th District Court Opinions.

Keywords: Ohio, Law

Sponsor: Case Western University Freenet, Youngstown University Freenet

Audience: Lawyers, General Public, Ohio Residents

Details: Free

`telnet://ytn.ysu.edu`

STATES (States Library)

The combined States Library contains case law, code and agency materials from the 53 individual US state libraries (50 states plus the District of Columbia, Puerto Rico and the Virgin Islands), all in the same library.

Keywords: Law, Analysis, Case, States

Audience: Lawyers

Profile: The States Library features many large group files which allow several individual files to be accessed in the same search. Many of the group files involve case law, including files that cover all state case law available on the LEXIS service plus ALR material and files that combine all federal and state case law available on the LEXIS service.

Contact: New Sales Group at (800) 227-4908 or 513-859-5398 inside the US, or 1-513-865-7981 for all inquires outside the US.

User Info: To subscribe, contact Mead directly.

To examine the Lexis user guide, you can access it at the ftp site of the University of Texas at Austin at the URL address: ftp://ftp.cc.utexas.edu

The files are in: pub/ref-services/LEXIS

`telnet://nex.meaddata.com`

`http://www.meaddata.com`

Supreme Court Decisions

Full text of Supreme Court decisions issued since 1989, as well as brief biographies of Supreme Court justices.

Keywords: Supreme Court, Law

Audience: Legal Professionals, Educators, Researchers

`gopher://info.umd.edu`

Supreme Court Decisions (Project Hermes)

US Supreme Court decisions available online as part of 'Project Hermes.'

Keywords: Supreme Court, Judiciary, Law

Sponsor: Case Western Reserve University

Audience: General Public, Lawyers, Students

Profile: Project Hermes was started in May 1990 by the US Supreme Court as an experiment in disseminating its opinions electronically. Starting with the 1993 calendar year, the US Supreme Court began disseminating opinions electronically on an official basis. Each decision consists of a syllabus (summarizing the ruling), the opinion, and optional concurrent and dissenting opinions.

Contact: Peter W. Martin
martin@law.mail.cornell.edu

Details: Free

Anonymous ftp: Expect: login; Send: anonymous; Expect: password; Send: your e-mail address

`ftp://cwru.edu`
`gopher://marvel.loc.gov`

Uniform Code of Military Justice

The files in this directory contain the US Uniform Code of Military Justice.

Keywords: Military, Law

Audience: Journalists, Politicians, Students, Military Personnel

Details: Free

`gopher://wiretap.spies.com/00/Gov/UCMJ`

Law (Brazilian)

Florida State University System Library

The library's holdings are large and wide-ranging and contain significant collections in many fields.

Keywords: Florida, Latin America, Judaica, Literature (Children's), Marine Engineering, Law (Brazilian), Law (British)

Audience: General Public, Researchers, Librarians, Document Delivery Professionals

Details: Free

Expect: Command ==>, Send: dial vtam; Expect: LUIS User Menu, Send: Your Catalog choice; To log off: Send: %off

`telnet://nervm.nerdc.ufl.edu`

Law (British)

Florida State University System Library

The library's holdings are large and wide-ranging and contain significant collections in many fields.

Keywords: Florida, Latin America, Judaica, Literature (Children's), Marine Engineering, Law (Brazilian), Law (British)

Audience: General Public, Researchers, Librarians, Document Delivery Professionals

Details: Free

Expect: Command ==>, Send: dial vtam; Expect: LUIS User Menu, Send: Your Catalog choice; To log off: Send: %off

`telnet://nervm.nerdc.ufl.edu`

Law (International)

European Patents Fulltext

European Patents Fulltext contains the complete text of European published applications and patents and European PCT published applications.

Keywords: Patents, Europe, Law (International)

Sponsor: European Patent Office, Vienna, Austria

Audience: Patent Researchers

Profile: It contains bibliographic, administrative, and legal information from the European Patent Registry. Records have abstracts, patent specifications including all claims, and the search report, including cited patents and other references.

Contact: Dialog in the US at (800) 334-2564, Dialog internationally at country-specific locations.

User Info: To subscribe, contact Dialog directly.

Notes: Coverage: 1978 to the present; updated weekly.

`telnet://dialog.com`

International Court of Justice Historical Documents

This gopher offers full-text documents from the International Court of Justice, and contains a searchable index.

Keywords: Judicial Process, Judgments, Judges, Law (International)

Audience: Lawyers, Legal Scholars, Legal Professionals, Law Students

File is in Foreign and International Law/ International Court of Justice Historical Documents/

`gopher://fatty.law.cornell.edu`

Law and Courts Preprint Archive

An online archive of papers dealing with American and international legal issues presented at major conferences since August 1993.

Keywords: Law (US), Law (International), Legislation, Political Science

Sponsor: American Political Science Association

Audience: Lawyers, Legal Professionals

Contact: Professor Herbert Jacob mzltov@nwu.edu

`gopher://gopher.nwu.edu`

Pre-Law, Legislation, Court Decisions

A collection of legal information including court decisions on abortion, a directory of US Judges, US Supreme Court rulings, and some primary documents relating to US and International law.

Keywords: Law (US Federal), Law, Law (International)

Sponsor: Skidmore College Gopher Project, New York, USA

Audience: Lawyers, Legal Professionals

Contact: Leo Geoffrion, Peggy Seiden ldg@skidmore.edu, pseiden@skidmore.edu

`gopher://grace.skidmore.edu/readings/ social-sciences/law`

Supreme Court of Canada

This gopher allows access to Canadian Supreme Court rulings from 1993 forward. Documents are available as full-text and searchable by keyword. This site also has information on Canadian statute and case law.

Keywords: Law (International), Canada

Sponsor: Universite de Montreal Law Gopher Project, Montreal, Canada

Audience: Lawyers, General Public

Contact: Pablo Fuentes fuentesp@droit.umontreal.ca

`gopher://gopher.droit.umontreal.ca/ English/SCC`

University of Texas at Austin Tarlton Law Library

The library's holdings are large and wide-ranging and contain significant collections in many fields.

Keywords: British Commonwealth Law, Constitutional Law, Law (International), Human Rights

Audience: Researchers, Students, General Public

Details: Free

Expect: Login, Send: Library

`telnet://tallons.law.utexas.edu`

War Powers Resolution of 1973

A joint resolution concerning the war powers of Congress and the President resolved by the Senate and the House of Representatives of the United States of America in Congress.

Keywords: War, Law (International), Government (US)

Audience: Politicians, Students, Lawyers, Historians

Details: Free

`gopher://wiretap.spies.com/00/Gov/ warpower.act`

World Constitutions

A list of world constitutions, containing the constitutions of more than 18 nations including Basic Law of Germany 1949; Constitution of Macedonia (in former Yugoslavia); Magna Carta.

Keywords: Law (International), History (World), Politics (International)

Audience: Researchers, Lawyers, Historians

Details: Free

`gopher://wiretap.spies.com`

Law (Tax)

University of Nebraska at Lincoln Library

The library's holdings are large and wide-ranging and contain significant collections in many fields.

Keywords: Slovak Republic, Czech Republic, Folklore, Military History, Latvia, Law (Tax), Law (US)

Audience: General Public, Researchers, Librarians, Document Delivery Professionals

Contact: Anita Cook

Details: Free

Expect: login, Send: library

`telnet://unllib.unl.edu`

Law (US)

ADA-Law

A mailing list for discussion of the Americans with Disabilities Act (ADA) and other disability-related legislation both in the US and abroad.

Keywords: Disabilities, Law (US)

Audience: Disabled People, Legal Professionals

Contact: wtm@bunker.afd.olivetti.com

User Info: To subscribe to the list, send an e-mail message to the URL address below consisting of a single line reading:

SUB ADA-Law YourFirstName YourLastName

To send a message to the entire list, address it to: ADA-Law@vm1.nodak.edu

`mailto:listserv@vm1.nodak.edu`

California State Senate Gopher

This is a gopher site accessing California State government records and providing links to related gophers.

Keywords: California, Government (US), Law (US State)

Sponsor: California State Senate, California, USA

Audience: Californians, General Public

Profile: The California State Senate Gopher provides access to state government records, pending bills, laws, state statistics, budgets, and related matters. The gopher also provides links to related gophers inside and outside state government.

Contact: Gopher Provider
            gopher@sen.ca.gov

gopher://gopher.sen.ca.gov

Citation Authority

Legal citation authority expected to be used in the highest US appellate state courts, based on a 1985 survey (revised March 1991).

Keywords: Law (US), State Courts

Audience: Lawyers

Details: Free

            Expect: login; Send: lawlib

gopher://liberty.uc.wlu.edu/00/
library/law/lawftp/citation.txt

Cornell Law School Gopher

A gopher server providing extensive access to Cornell Law School's online archives.

Keywords: Law (US)

Sponsor: The Legal Information Institute

Audience: Legal Professionals, Students

Profile: The Cornell Law School Gopher provides access to Cornell Law School's extensive online archives. Areas covered by the gopher include case law, copyright law, trademark law, commercial law, and information about the admissions and events at the Cornell Law school.

Contact: Thomas R. Bruce or Peter W. Martin
            feedback@fatty.law.cornell.edu

gopher://fatty.law.cornell.edu

Law and Courts Preprint Archive

An online archive of papers dealing with American and international legal issues presented at major conferences since August 1993.

Keywords: Law (US), Law (International), Legislation, Political Science

Sponsor: American Political Science Association

Audience: Lawyers, Legal Professionals

Contact: Professor Herbert Jacob
            mzltov@nwu.edu

gopher://gopher.nwu.edu

LEGNEW (Legal News)

The Legal News Library provides general news information about the domestic legal industry and legal profession.

Keywords: Law (US), Justicial Process, Supreme Court (US)

Audience: Business Researchers, Analysts, Entrepreneurs

Profile: Included are sources which cover materials on law firm management, bar association journals and a hot file of case list summaries on recently decided US Supreme Court cases. LEGNEW is organized very simply. There are individual files, group files, and user-defined combination files.

Contact: Mead New Sales Group at (800) 227-4908 or (513) 859-5398 inside the US, or (513) 865-7981 for all inquiries outside the US.

User Info: To subscribe, contact Mead directly.

            To examine the Nexis user guide, you can access it at the ftp site of the University of Texas at Austin at the URL address: ftp://ftp.cc.utexas.edu
            The files are in: /pub/ref-services/LEXIS

telnet://nex.meaddata.com

http://www.meaddata.com

MEGA (Combined Federal/State Case Law)

The Federal/State Case Law combined library contains files that allow one-stop searching of combined federal and state case law on the LEXIS service. American Law Reports (ALR)) and Lawyers' Edition, 2d articles are also included.

Keywords: Case Law (US), Law (US State), Law (US Federal)

Audience: Lawyers

Profile: The MEGA file is a one-stop search of all available federal and state case law on the LEXIS service. The circuit-base MEGA files combine federal and state case law from federal and state courts within the geographical area defined by the federal circuit. The state-based MEGA files combine case law from the courts of the state plus case law from the federal circuit for that state and the federal district courts within the state. Two chronological files restrict combined federal and state case law searches to particular date ranges. Each MEGA file includes all available U.S. Supreme Court cases. American Law Reports (ALR)) and Lawyers' Edition, 2d (LEd2) articles are also included.

Contact: New Sales Group @ (800) 227-4908 or 513-859-5398 inside the US, or 1-513-865-7981 for all inquires outside the US.

User Info: To subscribe, contact Mead directly.

            To examine the Lexis user guide, you can access it at the ftp site of the University of Texas at Austin at the URL address: ftp://ftp.cc.utexas.edu
            The files are in: /pub/res-services/LEXIS

telnet://nex.meaddata.com

Pre-Law, Legislation, Court Decisions

A collection of legal information including court decisions on abortion, a directory of US Judges, US Supreme Court rulings, and some primary documents relating to US and International law.

Keywords: Law (US Federal), Law (US State), Law (International)

Sponsor: Skidmore College Gopher Project, New York, USA

Audience: Lawyers, Legal Professionals

Contact: Leo Geoffrion, Peggy Seiden
            ldg@skidmore.edu,
            pseiden@skidmore.edu

gopher://grace.skidmore.edu/readings/
social-sciences/law

LAWREV (Law Review Library)

The Law Review Library contains law reviews, American Bar Association publications, American Institute of Certified Public Accountants periodicals, and other materials. The present focus concentrates on both state and national issues of legal significance.

Keywords: Law (US), Analysis, Journals

Audience: Lawyers

Profile: The Law Review Library currently consists of over 70 law reviews, several American Bar Association publicatons and American Institute of Certified Public Accountants periodicals, an Environmental Law Institute publication, ALR and LEd2d articles, two leading legal indices and a number of Warren Gorham & Lamont tax journals. The present focus concentrates on both state and national issues of legal significance.

Contact: New Sales Group at (800) 227-4908 or 513-859-5398 inside the US, or 1-513-865-7981 for all inquires outside the US.

User Info: To subscribe, contact Mead directly.

            To examine the Lexis user guide, you can access it at the ftp site of the University of Texas at Austin at the URL address: ftp://ftp.cc.utexas.edu

            The files are in: pub/ref-services/LEXIS

telnet://nex.meaddata.com

University of Nebraska at Lincoln Library

The library's holdings are large and wide-ranging and contain significant collections in many fields.

Keywords: Slovak Republic, Czech Republic, Folklore, Military History, Latvia, Law (Tax), Law (US)

Audience: General Public, Researchers, Librarians, Document Delivery Professionals

Contact: Anita Cook

Details: Free

      Expect: login, Send: library

`telnet://unllib.unl.edu`

US Department of Education Online Library

A resource for information on federal programs, including full-text of the GOALS 2000, Educate America Act, The Prisoners of Time Report, and other documents regarding education legislation, reports, and information.

Keywords: Education, Law (US)

Sponsor: US Department of Education

Audience: Educators, Students, Legislators, Researchers

`http://www.ed.gov`

`gopher://gopher.ed.gov`

`ftp://ftp.ed.gov`

Law (US Case)

GENFED (General Federal Library)

The General Federal Library is a comprehensive collection of federal legal materials of a general nature, including case law, legislative and regulatory materials, administrative decisions, court rules, and publications.

Keywords: Law (US Case), Law (US Federal)

Audience: Lawyers

Profile: Case law from all federal courts is available. Legislative materials include the United States Codes Service, United States Public Laws, pending federal legislation, legislative histories, and the Congressional Record. Regulatory materials include the Code of Federal Regulstions and the Federal Register. Administrative decisions, court rules, circuit summaries, sentencing guidelines, and legal publications are also available.

Contact: New Sales Group at (800) 227-4908 or 513-859-5398 inside the US, or 1-513-865-7981 for all inquiries outside the US.

Details: Costs

User Info: To subscribe, contact Mead directly.

    To examine the Lexis user guide, you can access it at the ftp site of the University of Texas at Austin at the URL address: ftp://ftp.cc.utexas.edu

    The files are in: pub/res-services/LEXIS

`telnet://nex.meaddata.com`

Law (US Federal)

GENFED (General Federal Library)

The General Federal Library is a comprehensive collection of federal legal materials of a general nature, including case law, legislative and regulatory materials, administrative decisions, court rules, and publications.

Keywords: Law (US Case), Law (US Federal)

Audience: Lawyers

Profile: Case law from all federal courts is available. Legislative materials include the United States Codes Service, United States Public Laws, pending federal legislation, legislative histories, and the Congressional Record. Regulatory materials include the Code of Federal Regulstions and the Federal Register. Administrative decisions, court rules, circuit summaries, sentencing guidelines, and legal publications are also available.

Contact: New Sales Group at (800) 227-4908 or 513-859-5398 inside the US, or 1-513-865-7981 for all inquiries outside the US.

Details: Costs

User Info: To subscribe, contact Mead directly.

    To examine the Lexis user guide, you can access it at the ftp site of the University of Texas at Austin at the URL address: ftp://ftp.cc.utexas.edu

The files are in: /pub/res-services/LEXIS

`telnet://nex.meaddata.com`

Government-Sponsored Electronic Bulletin Boards

A list of U.S. Government-sponsored electronic bulletin boards (BBSs) for various agencies and departments.

Keywords: Government (US Federal), Law (US Federal), BBS

Sponsor: United States Government

Audience: General Public, Researchers

Profile: EBBs provide a wide and ever-changing assortment of government information, including text files, statistics, software, and graphics. Some of the information is also available in printed form but much is not. Depository librarians may find government- sponsored EBBs useful in answering reference questions and in obtaining electronic versions of government publications, regardless of whether those publications were distributed to depository libraries.

Details: Free

`gopher://gopher.ncsu.edu`

High-Performance Computing Act of 1991

This is a Senate bill to provide for a coordinated federal research program to ensure continued US leadership in high-performance computing.

Keywords: Computing, Government (US Federal), Law (US Federal)

Audience: General Public, Journalists, Politicians, Scientists

Details: Free

    File is: /internet/nren/hpca.1991/ gorebill.1991-txt

`ftp://nis.nsf.net`

Historical Documents of the US

A large sample of US historical documents, from the Fundamental Orders of 1639 to the Vietnam Era Documents, including World War II documents, Federalist papers, and more.

Keywords: Historical Documents (US), Government (US Federal), Law (US Federal)

Audience: Historians, Journalists, Students, Politicians

Details: Free

`gopher://wiretap.spies.com/11/Gov/US-History`

Information Infrastructure and Technology Act of 1992

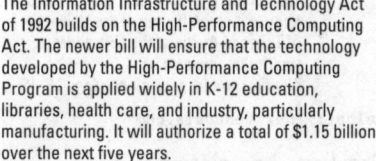

The Information Infrastructure and Technology Act of 1992 builds on the High-Performance Computing Act. The newer bill will ensure that the technology developed by the High-Performance Computing Program is applied widely in K-12 education, libraries, health care, and industry, particularly manufacturing. It will authorize a total of $1.15 billion over the next five years.

Keywords: Government (US Federal), Law (US Federal), Information Technology, Education, Health Care

Audience: Journalists, Politicians, Scientists, Manufacturers, Educators

Details: Free

    File is: /internet/nren/iita.1992/ gorebill.1992.txt

`ftp://nis.nsf.net`

Internet Federal Register (IFR)

The full text of the US Federal Register.

Keywords: Federal Register, Government (US Federal), Law (US Federal)

Sponsor: Counterpoint Publishing

Audience: General Public, Journalists, Students, Politicians, Citizens

A B C D E F G H I J K L M N O P Q R S T U V W X Y Z

Contact: fedreg@internet.com

Details: Costs

gopher://gopher.internet.com

MEGA (Combined Federal/State Case Law)

The Federal/State Case Law combined library contains files that allow one-stop searching of combined federal and state case law on the LEXIS service. American Law Reports (ALR)) and Lawyers' Edition, 2d articles are also included.

Keywords: Case Law (US), Law (US), Law (US Federal)

Audience: Lawyers

Profile: The MEGA file is a one-stop search of all available federal and state case law on the LEXIS service. The circuit-base MEGA files combine federal and state case law from federal and state courts within the geographical area defined by the federal circuit. The state-based MEGA files combine case law from the courts of the state plus case law from the federal circuit for that state and the federal district courts within the state. Two chronological files restrict combined federal and state case law searches to particular date ranges. Each MEGA file includes all available U.S. Supreme Court cases. American Law Reports (ALR)) and Lawyers' Edition, 2d (LEd2) articles are also included.

Contact: New Sales Group @ (800) 227-4908 or 513-859-5398 inside the US, or 1-513-865-7981 for all inquires outside the US.

User Info: To subscribe, contact Mead directly.

To examine the Lexis user guide, you can access it at the ftp site of the University of Texas at Austin at the URL address: ftp://ftp.cc.utexas.edu The files are in: pub/res-services/LEXIS

telnet://nex.meaddata.com

Pre-Law, Legislation, Court Decisions

A collection of legal information including court decisions on abortion, a directory of US Judges, US Supreme Court rulings, and some primary documents relating to US and International law.

Keywords: Law (US Federal), Law (US), Law (International)

Sponsor: Skidmore College Gopher Project, New York, USA

Audience: Lawyers, Legal Professionals

Contact: Leo Geoffrion, Peggy Seiden ldg@skidmore.edu, pseiden@skidmore.edu

gopher://grace.skidmore.edu/readings/social-sciences/law

Law and Courts Preprint Archive

Law and Courts Preprint Archive

An online archive of papers dealing with American and international legal issues presented at major conferences since August 1993.

Keywords: Law (US), Law (International), Legislation, Political Science

Sponsor: American Political Science Association

Audience: Lawyers, Legal Professionals

Contact: Professor Herbert Jacob mzltov@nwu.edu

gopher://gopher.nwu.edu

http://www.meaddata.com

Laws

Congressional Quarterly Gopher

Online Information from Congressional Quarterly (CQ), the premier journal covering events on Capitol Hill.

Keywords: Congress (US), Government (US Federal), Laws

Sponsor: Congressional Quarterly

Audience: Journalists, Government Officials, Educators, General Public

Profile: This gopher allows access to weekly stories and news briefs from CQ, as well as providing information on legislation before Congress, Congressional voting records, and results of recent federal elections. Also has catalogs of CQ's publications and schedules of their professional education seminars.

Contact: gopher_admin@cqalert.com

Details: Free

gopher://gopher.cqalert.com

Copyright Act

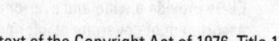

The full text of the Copyright Act of 1976, Title 17, United States Code, Sections 101_810.

Keywords: Politics (US), Government (US Federal), Laws, Copyright

Audience: Lawyers, Students, Politicians, Journalists

Details: Free

gopher://wiretap.spies.com/00/Gov/Copyright/US.Copyright.1976.tx

Copyright Basics

This information is from Circular 1 issued by the Copyright Office, Library of Congress, January 1991. It explains what copyright is, who can claim copyright, the principles of copyrights, what works are protected, how to secure a copyright, and more.

Keywords: Copyright, Government (US Federal), Laws

Audience: Lawyers, Students, Politicians, Journalists

Details: Free

gopher://wiretap.spies.com/00/Gov/Copyright/US.Copyright.Basics.txt

Department of Justice Gopher

A gopher containing online information from the Justice Department.

Keywords: Laws, Government (US), Justice Department

Sponsor: United States Department of Justice

Audience: Lawyers, Citizens

Profile: The Department of Justice (DOJ) gopher features DOJ criminal and law enforcement statistics, as well as agency procurement requests, job listings, and press releases. Also has links to other US government online systems.

Contact: gopher@usdoj.gov

gopher://gopher.usdoj.gov

Electronic Communications Privacy Act of 1986

This is the act to amend Title 18, United States Code, with respect to the interception of certain communications, other forms of surveillance, and for other purposes. This act affects every Usenet, Bitnet, BBS, shortwave listener, TV viewer, and so on.

Keywords: Communications, Privacy, Government (US Federal), Laws

Audience: Journalists, Privacy Activists, Students, Politicians

Details: Free

gopher://wiretap.spies.com/00/Gov/ecpa.act

Patent Act of the US

This resource contains full-text documentation regarding the US Patent Act (Title 35, United States Code, Sections 1 - 376).

Keywords: Patents, Laws, Government (US Federal)

Audience: Journalists, Politicians, Economists, Lawyers, Scientists

Details: Free

http://fatty.law.cornell.edu/patent/patent.overview.html

Privacy Act of 1974

The act that regulates the maintenance of privacy and protection of records on individuals.

Keywords: Privacy, Laws, Government (US Federal)

Audience: Journalists, Politicians, Lawyers

Details: Free
Choose from menu as appropriate.

`gopher://wiretap.spies.com/00/Gov/privacy.act`

Questions and Answers about the GPO Gateway to Government Act ⭐

Questions and answers dealing with the bill GPO Gateway to Government Act of 1992. Questions such as, "What will the gateway do?," "Why is this gateway needed?," "What types of Information will be available through the Gateway?," and more.

Keywords: Laws (US Federal), Government (US Federal), Federal Databases

Audience: General Public, Journalists, Politicians

Details: Free
File is: pub/nic/NREN/GPO.questions

`ftp://ftp.sura.net`

Trademark Act of the US ⭐

The US Trademark Act of 1946 (the "Lanham Act"), Title 15, United States Code, Sections 1051_1127.

Keywords: Trademarks, Laws, Government (US), Commerce

Audience: Journalists, Politicians, Students, Lawyers, Business Professionals, Designers, Marketers

Details: Free

`http://www.law.cornell.edu/lanham/lanham.table.html`

Universal Copyright Convention ⭐⭐

The Universal Copyright Convention as revised at Paris (1971). Convention and protocols were done at Paris on July 24, 1971. It was ratified by the President of the United States of America on August 28, 1972.

Keywords: Copyright, Laws, Government (US), Politics (US)

Audience: Lawyers, Students, Politicians, Journalists

Details: Free

`gopher://wiretap.spies.com/00/Gov/Copyright US.Universal.Copyright.Conv.txt`

U.S. Consumer Product Safety Commission (CPSC) ⭐⭐⭐

The CPSC's mission is to protect the public from defective and potentially dangerous consumer products. This gopher has archives of CPSC press releases and action reports from 1990-1994, as well as a calendar of upcoming events and guidelines for reporting potentially dangerous products to the CPSC.

Keywords: Safety, Consumerism, Laws

Sponsor: US Consumer Product Safety Commission

Audience: Consumers, Activists

Contact: pweddle@cpsc.gov

Notes: You can call the CPSC at their toll-free hotline at (800) 638-2772.

`gopher://cpsc.gov`

Leaders of Community Networking: People Who Create Online Communities

Leaders of Community Networking: People Who Create Online Communities ⭐

A WWW document with links to several important community networking resources. A brief overview of community networking is provided, as are links to statements by several leaders in the movement.

Keywords: Community, Networking, Government (US Federal)

Audience: Activists, Policymakers, Community Leaders, Government, Citizens

Details: Free

`http://nearnet.gnn.com/mag/articles/oram/introduction.html`

Leadership

IRVL-I (Institute for Research on Visionary Leadership) ⭐⭐

The Forum for Research on Visionary Leadership provides continuing substantive discourse on visionary leadership and networked archiving of digests of dialogue.

Keywords: Leadership

Sponsor: Institute for Visionary Leadership

Audience: Administrators

Contact: estepp@byrd.mu.wvnet.edu or m034050@marshall

User Info: To subscribe to the list, send an e-mail message to the address below consisting of a single line reading:

SUB irvl-I YourFirstName YourLastName

To send a message to the entire list, address it to: irvl-l@byrd.mu.wvnet.edu

`mailto: listserv@byrd.mu.wvnet.edu`

Legal Research

Research on Demand ⭐⭐⭐

A resource for the provision of market information, strategic information location, product information, and national and international business information.

Keywords: Market Research, Internet Research, Legal Research, International Research

Audience: Marketing Specialists, Lawyers, Public Relations Experts, Business Professionals, Researchers, Writers, Producers

Profile: This resource has special access to unique information resources worldwide. Areas of particular information access include the former Soviet Union, Europe, and the US. Information access also includes access to all the major online systems, including Dialog, BRS, Orbit, DataStar, and so on. Current Awareness Services include research information gathered from the Internet.

Details: Costs

User Info: To subscribe, send an e-mail message to the URL address below. In the body of your message, state the nature of your inquiry.

Notes: Contact ROD directly in the US at: (800) 227-0750; outside the US at: (510) 841-1145.

`mailto:rod@holonet.net`

Legal Status

Legal Status ⭐⭐⭐

Records thousands of types of actions that can affect the legal status of a patent document after it is published and after the patent is granted.

Keywords: Patents, Intellectual Property, Trademarks

Sponsor: European Patent Office

Audience: Patent Attorneys, Patent Agents, Librarians, Researchers

Profile: Information about the disposition of patent applications published under the Patent Cooperation Treaty by the World

A B C D E F G H I J K L M N O P Q R S T U V W X Y Z

Intellectual Property Organizations is included as well. Contains more than 8 million records. Updated weekly.

Contact: paul.albert@neteast.com

User Info: To subscribe contact Orbit-Questel directly.

`telnet://orbit.com`

Legion of Doom/Hackers Technical Journals

Legion of Doom/Hackers Technical Journals

Technical journals of the infamous hacking ring Legion of Doom.

Keywords: Hacking, Computers

Audience: Hackers, Computer Users

Details: Free

User Info: Expect: login,Send: anonymous; Expect: Password,Send: Your E-mail Address

`ftp://ftp.eff.org`

Legislation

Americans with Disabilities Act

Gives access to the full text of the Americans with Disabilities Act (ADA) and all the related legislation.

Keywords: Disabled People, Differently Abled People, Legislation, Government

Audience: General Public, Disabled People, Differently Abled People, Politicians, Journalists, Students

Profile: The purpose of ADA is to provide a clear and comprehensive national mandate to end discrimination against individuals with disabilities and to bring them into the economic and social mainstream of American life; to provide enforceable standards addressing discrimination against individuals with disabilities; and to ensure that the federal government plays a central role in enforcing these standards on behalf of individuals with disabilities.

Details: Free

`gopher://val-dor.cc.buffalo.edu/11/ .legislation`

Berne Convention Implementation Act of 1988

An act to amend Title 17, United States Code, to implement the Berne Convention for the Protection of Literary and Artistic Works, as revised in Paris on July 24, 1971, and for other purposes.

Keywords: Legislation, Government (US), Politics (US), Copyright

Audience: Lawyers, Students, Politicians, Journalists

Details: Free

`gopher://wiretap.spies.com/00/Gov/ Copyright/US.Berne.Convention.txt`

Bibliographies of US Senate Hearings

The US Senate produces a series of committee hearings, prints, and publications as part of the legislative process. The Documents department at North Carolina State University contains files for the 99th through 103rd Congresses, which can also be searched through a WAIS searchable database.

Keywords: Senate (US), Politics (US), Legislation, Bibliographies, Government (US)

Audience: General Public, Journalists, Students, Politicians, US Citizens

Contact: Jack McGeachy
Jack_McGeachy@ncsu.edu

Details: Free

`gopher://dewey.lib.ncsu.edu/11/ library/disciplines/government/senate`

EXEC (Executive Branch News US)

The EXEC library contains information and news about the Executive Branch of the Federal Government. From the Department of Agriculture to the White House, this file is a comprehensive source of information that will be especially useful to those whose responsibilities include monitoring federal regulations, Agency and Department activity, and the people and issues involved.

Keywords: News, Legislation, Regulation, Politics, Executive Branch

Audience: Journalists, Lobbyists, Business Executives, Analysts, Entrepreneurs

Profile: The EXEC library allows the searching of individual files or group files that cover topics such as the Federal Register and Code of Federal Regulations; public laws; proposed treasury regulation; and over 50 news sources, including BNA's Daily Report for Executives, the Dept. of State Dispatch, ABC News transcripts, Federal News Service Daybook, Government Executive, MacNeil/Lehrer Newshour, New Leader, National Review, the Washington Post, the Washington Times, Presidential Documents, and many others.

Contact: Mead New Sales Group at (800) 227-4908 or (513) 859-5398 inside the US, or (513) 865-7981 for all inquiries outside the US.

User Info: To subscribe, contact Mead directly.

To examine the Nexis user guide, you can access it at the ftp site of the University of Texas at Austin at the URL address: ftp://ftp.cc.utexas.edu

The files are in: /pub/ref-services/LEXIS

`telnet://nex.meaddata.com`

`http://www.meaddata.com`

Law and Courts Preprint Archive

An online archive of papers dealing with American and international legal issues presented at major conferences since August 1993.

Keywords: Law (US), Law (International), Legislation, Political Science

Sponsor: American Political Science Association

Audience: Lawyers, Legal Professionals

Contact: Professor Herbert Jacob
mzltov@nwu.edu

`gopher://gopher.nwu.edu`

Privacy Rights Clearinghouse (PRC)

A collection of materials related to privacy issues.

Keywords: Privacy, Legislation, Consumer Rights, Freedom of Information

Sponsor: University of San Diego

Audience: Citizens, Privacy Activists, Journalists

Profile: This site contains fact sheets (in English and Spanish) on privacy issues ranging from wiretapping to credit reporting. Also includes federal and state privacy legislation as well as related position papers and press releases.

Contact: prc@teetot.acusd.edu

Expect: Login; Send: Privacy

`gopher:// teetot.acusd.edu`

`telnet://teetot.acusd.edu`

Legislation (Australian)

Australia

Full-text versions of Australian legislation.

Keywords: Australia, Legislation (Australian)

Audience: Australian Citizens, Environmentalists, Governments

Details: Free

Select from menu as appropriate

`gopher://wiretap.spies.com`

LEGNEW (Legal News)

LEGNEW (Legal News)

The Legal News Library provides general news information about the domestic legal industry and legal profession.

Keywords: Law (US), Judicial Process, Supreme Court (US)

Audience: Business Researchers, Analysts, Entrepreneurs

Profile: Included are sources which cover materials on law firm management, bar association journals and a hot file of case list summaries on recently decided US Supreme Court cases. LEGNEW is organized very simply. There are individual files, group files, and user-defined combination files.

Contact: Mead New Sales Group at (800) 227-4908 or (513) 859-5398 inside the US, or (513) 865-7981 for all inquiries outside the US.

User Info: To subscribe, contact Mead directly.

To examine the Nexis user guide, you can access it at the ftp site of the University of Texas at Austin at the URL address: ftp://ftp.cc.utexas.edu The files are in: /pub/ref-services/LEXIS

`telnet://nex.meaddata.com`

`http://www.meaddata.com`

Lego Information

Lego Information

A web site containing pictures, sets, and Instructions for building with Legos. Also discusses various ideas, activities, and history pertaining to Legos, as well as information about clubs for Lego enthusiasts.

Keywords: Construction, Toys, Children

Sponsor: Lego

Audience: Children, General Public

Contact: David Koblas koblas@netcom.com

`http://legowww.itek.norut.no`

Leonardo Electronic Almanac

Leonardo Electronic Almanac

★★★★

The Leonardo Electronic Almanac (LEA) is a monthly, edited journal and an electronic archive dedicated to providing current perspectives in the art, science, and technology domains.

Keywords: Art, Multimedia, Music, Electronic Media

Sponsor: International Society for the Arts, Sciences, and Technology

Audience: New Media Artists, Researchers, Art Educators, Art Professionals

Profile: LEA is an international, interdisciplinary forum for people interested in the use of new media in contemporary artistic expression, especially involving 20th century science and technology. Material is contributed by artists, scientists, philosophers and educators. LEA is published by the MIT Press for Leonardo, the International Society for the Arts, Sciences, and Technology (ISAST).

Contact: Craig Harris craig@well.sf.ca.us

Details: Costs, Moderated, Images, Sounds, Multimedia

`mail to:journals-orders@mit.edu`

`ftp://mitpress.mit.edu/pub/Leonardo-Elec-Almanac`

Lesbians

amend2-discuss

A mailing list for discussion of the implications and issues surrounding the passage of Colorado's Amendment 2, which revokes any existing homosexual civil rights legislation and prohibits the drafting of any new legislation.

Keywords: Activism, Gay Rights, Lesbians, Bisexuality

Audience: Gay Rights Activists

Contact: amend2-mod@cs.colorado.edu

User Info: To subscribe to the list, send an e-mail message to the URL address below consisting of a single line reading:

subscribe amend2-discuss

`mailto:majordomo@cs.colorado.edu`

amend2-info

Colorado voted in an amendment to their state constitution which revokes any existing gay/lesbian/bisexual civil rights legislation and prohibits the drafting of any new legislation. This moderated list is for information on the implication and issues of this amendment.

Keywords: Activists, Gays, Lesbians, Bisexuality, Constitutional Amendments, Colorado, Civil Rights

Audience: General Public, Gays, Lesbians, Bisexuals, Activists

Contact: amend2-info@cs.colorado.edu

User Info: To subscribe to the list, send an e-mail message requesting a subscription to the URL address below.

To send a message to the entire list, address it to: amend2-info@cs.colorado.edu

`mailto:majordomo@cs.colorado.edu`

AUGLBC-I

The American University Gay, Lesbian, and Bisexual Community (AUGLBC) is a support group for lesbian, gay, bisexual, transsexual, and supportive students. The group is also connected with the International Gay and Lesbian Youth Organization (known as IGLYO).

Keywords: Gays, Lesbians, Bisexuality, Transsexuality, Sexuality

Audience: Gays, Lesbians, Bisexuals, Transsexuals, Students (college)

Contact: Erik G. Paul

User Info: To subscribe to the list, send an e-mail message to the URL address below, consisting of a single line reading:

SUB AUGLBC-I YourFirstName YourLastName

To send a message to the entire list, address it to: AUGLBC-I@american.edu

`mailto:listserv@american.edu`

AusGBLF

An Australian-based mailing list for gays, bisexuals, lesbians, and friends.

Keywords: Australia, Gays, Lesbians, Bisexuality

Audience: Gays, Lesbians, Bisexuals

Contact: zglc@minyos.xx.rmit.oz.au

Details: Free

User Info: To subscribe to the list, send an e-mail message requesting a subscription to the URL address below.

To send a message to the entire list, address it to: ausgblf@minyos.xx.rmit.oz.au

`mailto:ausgblf-request@minyos.xx.rmit.oz.au`

ba-Sappho

Ba-Sappho is a San Francisco Bay Area lesbian mailing list intended for local networking and announcements. BA-Sappho is not a discussion group.

Keywords: Lesbians, San Francisco Bay Area

Audience: Lesbians

Contact: ba-sappho-request@labrys.mti.sgi.com

Details: Free

A B C D E F G H I J K L M N O P Q R S T U V W X Y Z

A B C D E F G H I J K L M N O P Q R S T U V W X Y Z

User Info: To subscribe to the list, send an e-mail message requesting a subscription to the URL address below.

To send a message to the entire list, address it to: ba-sappho@labrys.mti.sgi.com

`mailto:ba-sappho-request@labrys.mti.sgi.com`

Chorus ★

This is the lesbian and gay chorus mailing list, formed November 1991 by John Schrag (jschrag@alias.com) and Brian Jarvis (jarvis@psych.toronto.edu). Membership includes artistic directors, singers, chorus officers, interpreters, and support staff and friends. Topics of discussion include repertoire, arrangements, staging, costuming, management, fundraising, music, events, and concerts.

Keywords: Singing, Choral Singing, Homosexuality, Gays, Lesbians

Audience: Lesbian Singers, Gay Singers, Chorus Officers, Lesbians, Gays, Choral Singers

Contact: chorus-request@psych.toronto.edu

Details: Free

User Info: To subscribe to the list, send an e-mail message requesting a subscription to the URL address below.

To send a message to the entire list, address it to: chorus@psych.toronto.edu

`mailto:chorus-request@psych.toronto.edu`

DC-MOTSS ★

DC-MOTSS is a social mailing list for the gay, lesbian, and bisexual folks who live in the Washington Metropolitan Area—everything within approximately 50 miles of The Mall.

Keywords: Gays, Lesbians, Bisexuality, Washington DC

Audience: Gays, Lesbians, Bisexuals, Washington DC Residents

Contact: DC-MOTSS-request@vector.intercon.com

Details: Free

User Info: To subscribe to the list, send an e-mail message requesting a subscription to the URL address below.

To send a message to the entire list, address it to: DC-MOTSS-request@vector.intercon.com

`mailto:DC-MOTSS-request@vector.intercon.com`

DSA-LGB

DSA-LGB is a mailing list for members of the Lesbian/Gay/Bisexual Commission of the Democratic Socialists of America, and for others interested in similar concerns.

Keywords: Democratic Socialists of America, Gays, Lesbians

Audience: Democratic Socialists, Gays, Lesbians

Contact: DSA-LGB-request@midway.uchicago.edu

User Info: To subscribe to the list, send an e-mail message requesting a subscription to the URL address below.

To send a message to the entire list, address it to: DSA-LGB-request@midway.uchicago.edu

`mailto:DSA-LGB-request@midway.uchicago.edu`

eagles ★

This list provides a forum for Boy Scouts, Scouters, and former Scouts who are gay/bisexual to discuss how they can apply pressure to the BSA to change their homophobic policies.

Keywords: Boy Scouts, Gays, Lesbians

Audience: Gays, Lesbians, Boy Scouts, Former Boy Scouts

Contact: eagles-request@flash.usc.edu

Details: Free

User Info: To subscribe to the list, send an e-mail message requesting a subscription to the URL address below.

To send a message to the entire list, address it to: eagles-request@flash.usc.edu

`mailto:eagles-request@flash.usc.edu`

gay-libn ★

A network for gay, lesbian, and bisexual librarians.

Keywords: Libraries, Gays, Lesbians, Bisexual

Audience: Librarians, Gays, Lesbians, Bisexuals

Details: Free

User Info: To subscribe to the list, send an e-mail message to the URL address below consisting of a single line reading:

SUB gay-libn YourFirstName YourLastName

To send a message to the entire list, address it to: gay-libn@vm.usc.edu

`mailto:listserv@vm.usc.edu`

gaynet ★

This list covers gay, lesbian, and bisexual concerns (with a focus on college campuses), including outreach programs, political action, AIDS education, school administration issues, social programs, and support group exchanges.

Keywords: Gays, Lesbians

Audience: Gays, Lesbians, Bisexuals, Students

Contact: Roger B.A. Klorese gaynet-approval@queernet.org

Details: Free

User Info: To subscribe to the list, send an e-mail message to the URL address below consisting of a single line reading:

SUB gaynet YourFirstName YourLastName

To send a message to the entire list, address it to: gaynet@queernet.org

`mailto:majordomo@queernet.org`

Moms ★

Moms is a list for lesbian mothers.

Keywords: Lesbian, Parenting

Audience: Lesbian Mothers, Lesbians

Contact: moms-request@qiclab.scn.rain.com

Details: Free

User Info: To subscribe to the list, send an e-mail message requesting subscription to the URL address below.

`mailto:moms-request@qiclab.scn.rain.com`

Ne-social-motss ★

Announcements of lesbian/gay/bisexual social events and other happenings in the Northeastern US.

Keywords: Social Events, Lesbian, Gay, Bisexuality

Audience: Lesbians, Gays, Bisexuals

Contact: ne-social-motss-request@plts.org

Details: Free

User Info: To subscribe to the list, send an e-mail message requesting a subscription to the URL address below.

`mailto:ne-social-motss-request@plts.org`

NJ-motss ★

Mailing list for gay, lesbian, and bisexual issues in New Jersey.

Keywords: Gay, Lesbian, Bisexuality, New Jersey

Audience: Gays, Lesbians, Bisexuals

Contact: majordomo@plts.org

Details: Free

User Info: To subscribe to the list, send an e-mail message to the URL address shown below consisting of a single line reading:

SUB NJ-motss YourFirstName YourLastName

To send a message to the entire list, address it to: NJ-motss@plts.org

`mailto:majordomo@plts.org`

NJ-motss-announce

Announcements of interests to New Jersey's gay, lesbian, and bisexual population.

Keywords: Gay, Lesbian, Bisexuality, New Jersey

Audience: Gays, Lesbians, Bisexuals

Contact: majordomo@plts.org

Details: Free

User Info: To subscribe to the list, send an e-mail message to the URL address shown below consisting of a single line reading:

SUB NJ-motss-announce YourFirstName YourLastName

To send a message to the entire list, address it to: NJ-motss-announce@plts.org

`mailto:majordomo@plts.org`

noglstp

This list is sponsored by the National Organization of Gay and Lesbian Scientists and Technical Professionals, Inc. (a 501-C3 organization). National office is in Pasadena, CA and can be reached at (818) 791-7689 or p.o. Box 91803, Pasadena, CA 90019. There is also a newsletter that is available to membership.

Keywords: Gay, Lesbian, Scientists, Technical Professionals

Audience: Gay Scientists, Lesbian Scientists

Contact: noglstp-request@elroy.jpl.nasa.gov

Details: Free

User Info: To subscribe to the list, send an e-mail message requesting a subscription to the URL address below.

To send a message to the entire list, address it to: noglstp@elroy.jpl.nasa.gov

`mailto:noglstp-request@elroy.jpl.nasa.gov`

Oh-motss

The Oh-motss (Ohio Members of the Same Sex) mailing list is for open discussion of lesbian, gay, and bisexual issues in and affecting Ohio. The mailing list is not moderated. It is open to all, regardless of location or sexuality. The subscriber list is known only to the list owner.

Keywords: Gays, Lesbian, Ohio

Audience: Gays, Lesbians

Contact: oh-motss-request@cps.udayton.edu

Details: Free

User Info: To subscribe to the list, send an e-mail message requesting a subscription to the URL address below.

To send a message to the entire list, address it to: oh-motss@cps.udayton.edu

`mailto:oh-motss-request@cps.udayton.edu`

OUTIL (Out in Linguistics)

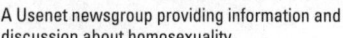

The list is open to lesbian, gay, bisexual, transsexual linguists, and their friends. The only requirement is that you be willing to be out to everyone on the list. The purposes of the group are to be visible and to gather occasionally to enjoy one another's company.

Keywords: Linguistics, Gays, Lesbians, Bisexuals, Transsexuals

Audience: Linguists, Gays, Lesbians, Bisexuals, Transsexuals

Contact: Arnold Zwicky outil-request@csli.stanford.edu

Details: Free

User Info: To subscribe to the list, send an e-mail message requesting a subscription to the URL address below.

To send a message to the entire list, address it to: outil@csli.stanford.edu

`mailto:outil-request@csli.stanford.edu`

soc.motss

A Usenet newsgroup providing information and discussion about homosexuality.

Keywords: Homosexuality, Gays, Lesbians, Bisexuals

Audience: Gays, Lesbians, Bisexuals

Details: Free

User Info: To subscribe to this Usenet newsgroup, you need access to a newsreader.

`news:soc.motss`

Stonewall25

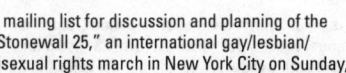

A mailing list for discussion and planning of the "Stonewall 25," an international gay/lesbian/bisexual rights march in New York City on Sunday, June 26, 1994, and the events accompanying it.

Keywords: Gay Rights, Lesbian, Bisexual, Activism

Audience: Gays, Lesbians, Bisexuals, Activists

Contact: stonewall25-request@queernet.org

Details: Free

User Info: To subscribe to the list, send an e-mail message requesting a subscription to the URL address below.

To send a message to the entire list, address it to: stonewall25@queernet.org

`mailto:stonewall25-request@queernet.org`

Lexicography

The World Wide Web Acronym Server

This web site is a guide to acronyms and abbreviations.

Keywords: Internet, Lexicography

Audience: Internet Surfers

Contact: Peter Flynn pflynn@curia.ucc.ie

Details: Free

`http://curia.ucc.ie/info/net/acronyms/acro.html`

Lexicology

alt.usage.english

A Usenet newsgroup providing information and discussion about English grammar, word usages, and related topics.

Keywords: Lexicology, Academia, Linguistics, Education

Audience: English Educators

User Info: To subscribe to this Usenet newsgroup, you need access to a newsreader.

`news:alt.usage.english`

Online-dict

A mailing list devoted to a discussion of online dictionaries and related issues including installation, modification, and maintenance of their databases, search engines, and user interfaces.

Keywords: Dictionaries, Information Technology, Lexicology

Audience: Librarians, Information Scientists, Systems Operators

Contact: Jack Lynch jlynch@dept.english.upenn.edu

Details: Free

User Info: To subscribe, send an e-mail message to the URL address below consisting of a single line reading:

SUB online-dict YourFirstName YourLastName

To send a message to the entire list, address it to: online-dict@dept.english.upenn.edu

`mailto:listserv@dept.english.upenn.edu`

A B C D E F G H I J K L M N O P Q R S T U V W X Y Z

A
B
C
D
E
F
G
H
I
J
K
L
M
N
O
P
Q
R
S
T
U
V
W
X
Y
Z

Style Sheets from the Online Writers' Workshop.

This gopher provides information and examples on how to write bibliographies using three formats: MLA (Modern Language Association), Old-MLA, and APA (American Psychological Association).

Keywords: Bibliographies, Writing, Lexicology

Sponsor: University of Illinois at Urbana-Champaign

Audience: Writers, Students (High School/College/University)

Contact: Dr. Michael Pemberton
michaelp@ux1.cso.uiuc

`gopher://gopher.uiuc.edu`

University of Michigan Library

The library's holdings are large and wide-ranging and contain significant collections in many fields.

Keywords: Asia, Astronomy, Transportation, Lexicology, Mathematics, Zoology, Geography

Audience: Researchers, Students, General Public

Contact: info@merit.edu

Details: Free

Expect: Which Host; Send: Help

`telnet://cts.merit.edu`

LEXPAT (Patents US)

LEXPAT (Patents US)

The LEXPAT library contains the full text of US patents issued since 1975, the US Patent and Trademark Office Manual of Classification, and the Index to US Patent Classification. The approximately 1,500 patents added to the library each week appear online within four days of their issue.

Keywords: Patents, Inventors, Assignees, Litigants

Audience: Lawyers, Business Researchers, Analysts, Entrepreneurs

Profile: LEXPAT may be searched by individual files for the full text of utility, design or plant patents, or you can combine the files in one 'omni' search. The Manual, Index and Class files can be used to supplement your full-text patent searches. LEXPAT is a valuable tool for both patent professionals and for anyone who needs to access to technical information. More than 80 percent of the information contained in patents is unavailable in any other form.

Contact: Mead New Sales Group at (800) 227-4908 or (513) 859-5398 inside the US, or (513) 865-7981 for all inquiries outside the US.

User Info: To subscribe, contact Mead directly.

To examine the Nexis user guide, you can access it at the ftp site of the University of Texas at Austin at the URL address: ftp://ftp.cc.utexas.edu
The files are in: /pub/ref-services/LEXIS

`telnet://nex.meaddata.com`

`http://www.meaddata.com`

Liberal Education

University of Wisconsin at Oshkosh Library

The library's holdings are large and wide-ranging and contain significant collections in many fields.

Keywords: Business, Liberal Education, Nursing

Audience: Researchers, Students, General Public

Details: Free

Expect: Login; Send: Lib; Expect: vDIAL Prompt, Send: Library

`telnet://polk.cis.uwosh.edu`

Libertarian Politics

alt.politics.libertarian

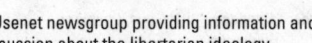

A Usenet newsgroup providing information and discussion about the libertarian ideology.

Keywords: Libertarian Politics

Audience: Libertarians, Politicians

User Info: To subscribe to this Usenet newsgroup, you need access to a newsreader.

`news:alt.politics.libertarian`

ca-Liberty

This is an announcement of area-based Libertarian meetings, events, activities, etc. The ca- list is for California statewide issues; the ba- list is for the San Francisco Bay Area and gets all messages sent to the ca- list. Prospective members should subscribe to one or the other, generally depending on whether or not they are SF Bay Area residents.

Keywords: Libertarian Politics, California

Audience: Libertarians, Political Scientists, Politicians, General Public

Contact: Jeff Chan
ca-liberty-request@shell.portal.com

Details: Free

User Info: To subscribe to the list, send an e-mail message requesting a subscription to the URL address below.

To send a message to the entire list, address it to:
ca-liberty@shell.portal.com

`mailto:ca-liberty-request@shell.portal.com`

Political Platforms of the US

Full text of various documents including the Democratic platform of 1992, the Jerry Brown positions of 1992, the Libertarian platform of 1990, and more.

Keywords: Politics (US), Government (US Federal), Democracy, Libertarian Politics

Audience: Politicians, Grass-Roots Organizers, Journalists

Details: Free

`gopher://wiretap.spies.com/11/Gov/Platform`

Librarianship

Librarian's Internet Reference

Electronic version of 'Internet Connections: A Librarian's Guide to Dial-Up Access and Use,' written by Mary E. Engle, and Marilyn Lutz, William Jones, Jr., and Genevieve Engel.

Keywords: Internet Guides, Librarianship

Audience: Librarians

Contact: Mary Engle
Mary_Engle@ucop.edu

`gopher://gopher.poniecki.berkeley.edu`
`Poniecki Foundation/Internet Guides`

Newsletter on Serials Pricing Issues

The focus of this newsletter is the pricing of library serials.

Keywords: Serials Pricing, Librarianship

Audience: Librarians, Publishers

Profile: Contributions include examples of titles considered to be overpriced, as well as of publishers' actions to keep prices down, strategies for coping with serials price increases, information about libraries' evaluation and cancellation policies and procedures, announcements of and reports from relevant meetings, and other news of serials prices.

Contact: Marcia Tuttle
tuttle@unc.bitnet

Details: Free

User Info: To subscribe, send an e-mail message to the URL address shown below consisting of a single line reading:

SUB serials_pricing YourFirstName YourLastName

`mailto:listserv@uncvx1.Bitnet`

Libraries

AskERIC Virtual Library

★★★★

This gopher is part of a federally-funded system to provide public access to educational resources.

Keywords: Education (K-12), Computer-Aided Learning, Libraries, Electronic Books

Sponsor: Educational Resources Information Center (ERIC)

Audience: K-12 Teachers, Administrators

Profile: This gopher contains a wide-range of educational aids including pre-prepared lesson plans, guides to Internet resources for the classroom organized by subject, updates on conferences for educators, and archives of education-related listservs. Also allows access to outside gophers, libraries, and sources of electronic books and journals.

Contact: Nancy A. Morgan
nmorgan@ericir.syr.edu
askeric@ericir.syr.edu

`gopher://ericir/syr.edu`

Barron's Guide to Accessing On-Line Bibliographic Databases

★★

A comprehensive listing of publicly-accessible online libraries, including login instructions for each site.

Keywords: Libraries, Databases

Sponsor: University of North Texas

Audience: Researchers, Library Users, Librarians

Contact: Billy Barron
billy@unt.edu

`gopher://alf.zfn.uni-bremen.de/Allgemeine`

BRIDGE

★

An online public access catalogue, the PALS-based catalogue provides access to the collections of two institutions, St. Boniface University and the Manitoba General Hospital.

Keywords: Medicine, Libraries

Sponsor: St. Boniface University, and the Manitoba General Hospital Libraries

Audience: Health Professionals, Students, Medical Educators

Details: Free

`telnet://BE@umopac.umanitoba.ca`

Brown University Library

★★★★

The Brown libraries contain approximately 1.5 million volumes, including historical archives of early American imprints and the biomedical engineering holdings.

Keywords: Libraries, Research

Audience: General Public, Researchers

Contact: Howard Pasternick
blips15@brownvm.brown.edu

Details: Free

At the Brown logon screen: tab to command field, Enter Dial Josiah, tab to Josiah choice on the screen.

`telnet://brownvm.brown.edu`

`telnet://library.brown.edu`

Catholic University of America Gopher

★★

Gopher server of the Catholic University of America

Keywords: Catholicism, Libraries

Sponsor: Catholic University of America

Audience: Catholics

Profile: The Catholic University of America gopher provides access to CUA's libraries and archived material as well as providing links to outside, and foreign, related gophers, and electronic resources.

`gopher://gopher.cua.edu`

Chiba University Gopher

The Chiba University gopher, including files from the university's library.

Keywords: Japan, Asia, Libraries

Sponsor: Chiba University, Chiba, Japan

Audience: Japan Residents, Computer Programmers, Librarians, Linguists

Contact: hasimoto@chiba-u.ac.jp

`gopher://himawari.ipc.chiba-u.ac.jp`

Columbia University Libraries

★★★★

The Columbia libraries include a medical library and a mathematics library.

Keywords: Libraries, Research

Audience: General Public, Researchers

Details: Free

When connected, hit return, enter terminal type: vt100.

`telnet://clio.cul.columbia.edu`

Cornell University Libraries

★★★★

This library system maintains special collections in engineering, nuclear engineering, textile engineering, agriculture, medicine, Africana, entomology, hotels, ILR, mathematics, physical sciences, and veterinary medicine.

Keywords: Libraries, Research

Audience: General Public, Researchers

Details: Free

When userid/password screen appears, press return. When cp read appears on the screen, type library.

`telnet://cornellc.cit.cornell.edu`

Creighton University Library Online Catalogue

★★★★

This site maintains a catalog of the Creighton University library's holdings.

Keywords: Health Sciences, Libraries

Sponsor: Creighton University, Omaha, Nebraska, USA

Audience: Health-Care Professionals, Medical Educators, Students

Details: Free

At the prompt type <lib hsl>for Health Sciences Library.

`telnet://attachpals@owl.creighton.edu`

Current Cites

★★★

A monthly publication of the Library Technology Watch Program at The Library, University of California, Berkeley.

Keywords: Computer Technology, Libraries

Sponsor: The Library, University of California, Berkeley, CA

Audience: Librarians, Computer Programmers

Profile: Over 30 journals in librarianship and computer technology are scanned for articles on optical-disk technologies, computer networks and networking, information transfer, expert systems and artificial intelligence, and hypermedia and multimedia.

Contact: David Robison
drobison@library.berkeley.edu

Details: Free

`telnet://melvyl.ucop.edu`

Denmark's Library for Medicine and Science

★

Keywords: Science, Medicine, Libraries, Denmark

Audience: Scientists, Health-Care Professionals, Medical Researchers

Details: Free

At the CCL>prompt type DIA ENG for English interface.

`telnet://cosmos.bib.dk`

gay-libn

★

A network for gay, lesbian, and bisexual librarians.

Keywords: Libraries, Gays, Lesbians, Bisexuality

Audience: Librarians, Gays, Lesbians, Bisexuals

Details: Free

User Info: To subscribe to the list, send an e-mail message to the URL address below consisting of a single line reading:

SUB gay-libn YourFirstName YourLastName

To send a message to the entire list, address it to: gay-libn@vm.usc.edu

`mailto:listserv@vm.usc.edu`

Georgetown University Medical Center Online Catalogue

This site maintains a catalog of the Georgetown University Medical Center library's holdings.

Keywords: Medicine, Libraries

Sponsor: Georgetown University, Washington, DC

Audience: Medical Professionals, Educators, Students

Contact: Jane Banks
banksj@gumedlib2.georgetown.edu

Details: Free

The password is dahlgren, then enter netguest, hit RETURN several times and select option 1.

`telnet://medlib@gumedlib.georgetown.edu`

Harvard Medical Gopher

This gopher site accesses information from Harvard Medical School. Provides bibliographic information from Harvard Medical Library, basic science and clinical resources, and public health and government statistics.

Keywords: Medicine, Libraries, Health Care

Sponsor: Harvard Medical School, Cambridge, Massachusetts, USA

Audience: Physicians, Health-Care Professionals, Educators, Students

Contact: gopher@warren.med.harvard.edu

Details: Free

`gopher://gopher.med.harvard.edu`

HYTELNET

A shareware application database directory to libraries.

Keywords: Computer Systems, Libraries, Shareware

Audience: General Audience

Profile: HYTELNET is a guide to library catalogs from the Americas, Europe

Contact: Peter Scott
aa375@freenet.carleton.ca

Details: Free

Notes: HYTELNET is in English, but the interface to some international

`gopher://gophlib@gopher.yale.edu`

Internet Libraries (Gopher)

The site maintains the most current possible list of all library catalogs accessible on the Internet.

Keywords: Libraries, Databases, Internet, Information Retrieval

Audience: Reseacher, Students, Librarians

Contact: Gopherlib
gopherlib@gopher.yale.edu

`gopher://yaleinfo.yale.edu`

K-12 School Libraries

This directory is a compilation of information resources focused on K-12 Education.

Keywords: Libraries, Education (K-12)

Audience: Librarians, Educators (K-12)

`ftp://una.hh.lib.umich.edu/70/
inetdirsstacks/k12schmed:troselius`

Library Resources

A specialized guide to library resources on the Internet, with a focus on strategies for selection and use.

Keywords: Libraries, Internet, Internet Guide

Audience: Internet Surfers, Researchers

File is: pub/internet/libcat-guide

`ftp://dla.ucop.edu/pub/internet/
libcat-guide`

Library Special

Library special collections on the Internet.

Keywords: Internet, Information Retrieval

Audience: Internet Surfers

Details: Free

`ftp://dla.ucop.edu/pub`

`http://dla.ucop.edu`

LIST Gopher

This is a library-related service that allows users to obtain information by using their e-mail accounts.

Keywords: Mailing Lists, Listserv, Libraries, Gopher

Sponsor: North Carolina State University, Raleigh, North Carolina, USA

Audience: Librarians, Library Users, e-mail Users

Profile: LISTGopher allows users to search library-related LISTSERV archives through the Gopher interface. Users enter their Email address, the list they want to search, and the keyword(s) they wish to find. LISTGopher then send the results of their search to the user's e-mail address. Currently, only library-related archives are supported, but more archive types may be added in the future.

Contact: Eric Lease Morgan, Systems Librarian
eric_morgan@ncsu.edu

`http://ericmorgan.lib.ncsu.edu/staff/
morgan/morgan.html`

`gopher://dewey.lib.ncsu.edu /library/
disciplines/library/listgopher`

LOCIS (LIBRARY Of CONGRESS INFORMATION SYSTEM)

The Library of Congress (LC) telnet service is a Campus-Wide Information System that combines the vast collection of information available about the Library with easy access to diverse electronic resources over the Internet. Its goal is to serve the staff of LC, as well as the U.S. Congress and it's constituents.

Keywords: Information Retrieval, Libraries

Sponsor: Library of Congress, Washington, D.C., USA

Audience: Reseachers, Students, Librarians

Contact: LC MARVEL Design Team
lcmarvel@loc.gov

Notes: The Library of Congress (LC) Machine-Assisted Realization of the Virtual Electronic Library (MARVEL) also exists as a gopher site: gopher://marvel.loc.gov

`telnet://locis.loc.gov`

Medical College of Ohio Library Online Catalogue

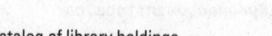

A catalog of library holdings.

Keywords: Medicine, Libraries

Sponsor: Medical College of Ohio

Audience: Health Professionals, Medical Researchers, Educators, Students

Details: Free

`telnet://library@136.247.10.14`

Medical College of Wisconsin Library Online Catalogue

A catalog of library holdings.

Keywords: Medicine, Library

Sponsor: Medical College of Wisconsin

Audience: Health Professionals, Medical Researchers, Educators, Students

Details: Free

`telnet://ils.lib.mcw.edu`

Montefiore Medical Center Library Online Catalog ★

A catalog of library holdings.

Keywords: Medicine, Libraries

Sponsor: Montefiore Medical Center at Albert Einstein College of Medicine, New York

Audience: Health-care Professionals, Medical Researchers, Educators, Students

Details: Free

After Telnetting, hit RETURN twice, then select 0 on main menu. Select 2 on locations menu. To exit, hit the Telnet escape key.

`telnet://lis.aecom.yu.edu`

National Institute of Health Library Online Catalog ★★★★

This entry point provides access to the books and journal holdings in the NIH Library. Journal articles are not included.

Keywords: NIH, Medicine, Science, Libraries

Sponsor: National Institute of Health (NIH)

Audience: Scientists, Researchers, Educators, Health-care Professionals

Details: Free

`telnet://nih-library.ncrr.nih.gov`

Net-News ★★★

A newsletter devoted to library and information resources on the Internet.

Keywords: Information, Libraries, Networking, Internet

Sponsor: Metronet

Audience: Librarians, Researchers

Contact: Dana Noonan
noonan@msus1.msus.edu

Details: Free

Send email request to noonan@msus1.msus.edu or metronet@vz.acs.umn.edu

`gopher://noonan@msus1.msus.edu`

NLC (National Library of Canada) ★★★★

A Canadian library gopher in French and English.

Keywords: Canada, Libraries, Library Science

Sponsor: National Library of Canada (NLC), Canada

Audience: Canadians, Librarians, Publishers

Profile: This site provides a gateway to Canadian library and Internet resources linking users to the National Library, which offers a bibliographic database, a list of NLC publications, and other services for libraries and publishers. It also has links to many other Canadian libraries and Internet services, as well as a large selection of general information from and about the Government of Canada and its provinces.

Contact: Nancy Brodie, Lynn Herbert
Nancy.Brodie@nlc-bnc.ca,
Lynn.Herbert@nlc-bnc.ca

`gopher://gopher.nlc-bnc.ca`

OLIS (Oxford University Library Information Service) Gopher ★★

OLIS is a network of libraries. It contains all the books from the English, Modern Languages, Social Studies, and Hooke libraries. It also contains books and journals cataloged since September 1988 in the Bodleian and Dependant libraries and the Taylor Institution. Books can be searched in any OLIS library from any location.

Keywords: Libraries, United Kingdom, Europe

Audience: Library Users

Contact: jose@olis.lib.ox.ac.uk

Details: Free

`gopher://gopher.lib.ox.ac.uk/00/Info/OLIS`

The Wired Librarian ★★

A collection of online resources designed to help library professionals and users keep abreast of current developments in library science and information studies. Includes links to many library and information systems associations and services.

Keywords: Libraries, Information Retrieval

Sponsor: Davidson Library, University of California, Santa Barbara, California, USA

Audience: Librarians, Library Users

Contact: Andrea L. Duda
duda@library.ucsb.edu

`gopher://ucsbuxa.ucsb.edu`

UCSB Library Reference Guide ★★

A list of art references including indexes, dictionaries, bilbiographies, and biographical materials.

Keywords: Art, History (World), Libraries

Sponsor: University of California at Santa Barbara

Audience: Artists, Historians, Librarians

`gopher://ucsbuxa.ucsb.edu`

University of Texas Health Science Center (UTHSCSA) Biomedical Library Information System ★★

Keywords: Medicine, Libraries

Sponsor: Audie L. Murphy Memorial Veterans' Administration Hospital, San Antonio, TX

Audience: Medical Professionals, Medical Educators, Students

Details: Free

`telnet://lis@athena.uthscsa.edu`

University of Wales College of Medicine Library Online Catalog ★★

Keywords: Medicine, Libraries

Sponsor: University of Wales, United Kingdom

Audience: Health Care Professionals, Medical Educators, Students

Details: Free

Expect: login, Send: 'janet'; Expect: password; Send: 'janet'

`telnet://sun.nsf.ac.uk`

Vetlib-L (Veterinary Medicine Librarians List) ★

Vetlib-L is an E-mail discussion group for librarians in schools and colleges of veterinary medicine worldwide.

Keywords: Veterinary Medicine, Libraries

Sponsor: Virginia Polytechnic Institute and State University

Audience: Veterinarians, Librarians

Contact: Victoria T. Kok, James Powell
kok@vtvm1.cc.vt.edu or
jpowell@vtvm1.cc.vt.edu

Details: Free

User Info: To subscribe to the list, send an e-mail message to the URL address below consisting of a single line reading:

vetlib-l YourFirstName YourLastName

To send a message to the entire list, address it to: vetlib-l@vtvm1.cc.vt.edu

`mailto:listserv@vtvm1.cc.vt.edu`

Yale Directory of Internet Libraries ★★★

An online directory of international library catalogs with continuing links to many servers, including several with Internet access tools.

A
B
C
D
E
F
G
H
I
J
K
L
M
N
O
P
Q
R
S
T
U
V
W
X
Y
Z

A
B
C
D
E
F
G
H
I
J
K
L
M
N
O
P
Q
R
S
T
U
V
W
X
Y
Z

Keywords: Libraries

Sponsor: Yale University, New Haven, Connecticut, USA

Audience: General Audience

Profile: The Yale Directory of Internet Libraries is a comprehensive listing of international libraries that provide information about the subject area strengths of many of its entries.

`gopher://gophlib@gopher.yale.edu`

Library of Congress, Astronomy, Astrophysics, and Physics Resources

Library of Congress, Astronomy, Astrophysics, and Physics Resources

Pointers to important remote databases relating to astronomy and physics.

Keywords: Astronomy, Astrophysics, NASA

Sponsor: Library of Congress, Washington, DC

Audience: Astronomers, Educators (Post-Secondary), Physicists, Students

Profile: The Library of Congress has pointers to many important remote databases including Astronomy, Astrophysics, and Physics Journals, the Aerospace Directory from Rice University, The American Astronomical Society, The Astronomical Internet Resources Directory, The Cold Fusion Bibliography, The Electromagnetic Wave Research Institute of NRC (Florence, Italy), LANL Physics Information, The Lunar/Planetary Institute Database of Geology, Geophysics, and Astronomy, The NASA Extragalactic Database, The NASA Network Applications and Information Center (NAIC), The National Institute of Standards and Technology (NIST), The Physics Resource Directory from University of California, Irvine, and The Space Telescope Electronic Information System (STEIS).

Contact: lcmarvel@seq1.loc.gov

Details: Costs

User info: Can be accessible via telnet:// marvel.loc.gov (login: marvel).

`gopher://marvel.loc.gov/11/global/ sci/astro`

Limbaugh (Rush)

alt.fan.rush-limbaugh

A Usenet newsgroup providing information and discussion about Rush Limbaugh, a politically conservative American figure.

Keywords: Limbaugh (Rush), Politics (Conservative), Comedians

Audience: Followers of Rush Limbaugh

User Info: To subscribe to this Usenet newsgroup, you need access to a newsreader.

`news:alt.fan.rush-limbaugh`

Lincoln (Abraham)

University of Chicago Library

The library's holdings are large and wide-ranging and contain significant collections in many fields.

Keywords: English Bibles, Lincoln (Abraham), Kentucky & Ohio River Valley (History of), Balzac (Honore de), American Drama, Cromwell (Oliver), Goethe, Judaica, Italy, Chaucer (Geoffrey), Wells (Ida, Personal Papers of), Douglas (Stephen A.), Italy, Literature (Children's)

Audience: General Public, Researchers, Librarians, Document Delivery Professionals

Details: Free

Expect: ENTER CLASS, Send: LIB48 3;
Expect: CONNECTED, Send: RETURN

`telnet://olorin.uchicago.edu`

Linguistics

alt.usage.english

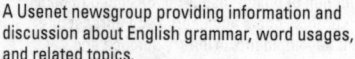

A Usenet newsgroup providing information and discussion about English grammar, word usages, and related topics.

Keywords: Lexicology, Academia, Linguistics, Education

Audience: English Educators

User Info: To subscribe to this Usenet newsgroup, you need access to a newsreader.

`news:alt.usage.english`

ELSNET (European Network in Language and Speech)

A web site addressing the development of language technology in Europe and abroad by helping to coordinate progress on both scientific and technological fronts.

Keywords: Linguistics, Cognitive Science, Communication

Sponsor: The University of Edinburgh Centre for Cognitive Science, Edinburgh, Scotland

Audience: Linguists, Cognitive Scientists

Contact: Ewan Klein
klein@ed.ac.uk

`http://www.cogsci.ed.ac.uk/elsnet/ home.html`

KFLC-L

A mailing list for distributing information on the meetings and proceedings of the Kentucky Foreign Language Conferences (KFCL).

Keywords: Language, Linguistics, Education (Bilingual)

Audience: Linguists, Educators

Contact: John Greenway
engjlg@ukcc.uky.edu

User Info: To subscribe, send an e-mail message to the URL address below consisting of a single line reading:

SUB kflc-l YourFirstName YourLastName

To send a message to the entire list, address it to: kflc-l@ukcc.uky.edu

`mailto:listserv@ukcc.uky.edu`

LANGIT

A forum for members of the Italian Linguistics Center (Centri Linguistici Italian).

Keywords: Italy, Linguistics

Audience: Linguists, Educators, Students

Details: Free

User Info: To subscribe to the list, send an e-mail message to the address below.

`mailto:listserv@icineca.bitnet`

Lantra-I

A discussion of interpretation and translation.

Keywords: Interpretation, Translation, Language, Linguistics

Audience: Linguists, Interpreters, Translators

Details: Free

User Info: To subscribe to the list send an e-mail message the the URL address below consisting of a single line reading:

SUB landra-I Your First Name Your Last Name

To send a message to the entire list, address it to: lantra-I@search.bitnet

`mailto:listserv@searn.bitnet`

Linguist

A discussion of language and linguistics.

Keywords: Language, Linguistics

Audience: Linguists, Language Teachers, Language Students

Details: Free

User Info: To subscribe to the list, send an e-mail message to the URL address shown below consisting of a single line reading:

SUB linguist Your First Name Your Last Name

`mailto:listserv@tamvmi.bitnet`

LLTI

The Language Learning Technology International (LLTI) forum is a discussion of computer-assisted language learning.

Keywords: Linguistics, Computer-Aided Instruction

Audience: Linguists, Language Teachers, Language Students

Details: Free

User Info: To subscribe to the list, send an e-mail message to the URL address below, consisting of a single line reading:

SUB llti YourFirstName YourLastName

To send a message to the entire list, address it to:
llti@dartcms1.dartmouth.edu

`mailto:listserv@dartcms1.dartmouth.edu`

LTEST

A discussion of language-testing research and practice.

Keywords: Linguistics

Audience: Linguists, Language Teachers, Language Students

Details: Free

User Info: To subscribe to the list, send an e-mail message to the URL address below, consisting of a single line reading:

SUB Ltest YourFirstName YourLastName

To send a message to the entire list, address it to: ltest@uclan1.bitnet

`mailto:listserv@uclan1.bitnet`

Massachusetts Institute of Technology Library

The library's holdings are large and wide-ranging and contain significant collections in many fields.

Keywords: Aeronautics (History of), Linguistics, Mathematics (History of), Microscopy, Spectroscopy, Aeronautics, Mathematics, Glass

Audience: General Public, Researchers, Librarians, Document Delivery Professionals

Details: Free

Expect: Mitek Server..., Send: Enter or Return; Expect: prompt, Send: hollis

`telnet://library.mit.edu`

MEDTEXT-L

A discussion of medieval text, including philology, codicology, and technology.

Keywords: Medieval, Philology, Linguistics

Audience: Linguists, Language Teachers, Language Students, Historians

Details: Free

User Info: To subscribe to the list, send an e-mail message to the URL address below consisting of a single line reading:

medtext-l YourFirstName YourLastName

To send a message to the entire list, address it to: medtext-l@uiucvmd.bitnet

`mailto:listserv@uiucvmd.bitnet`

nl-kr

This E-conference is open to discussion of any topic related to the understanding and generation of natural language and knowledge representation as subfields of artificial intelligence.

Keywords: Programming Languages, Natural Language, Knowledge Representation, Linguistics

Audience: Computer Programmers

Contact: Christopher Welty
weltyc@cs.rpi.edu

Details: Free, Moderated

User Info: To subscribe to the list, send an e-mail message requesting a subscription to the URL address below.

`mailto:nl-kr-request@cs.rpi.edu`

OUTIL (Out in Linguistics)

The list is open to lesbian, gay, bisexual, transsexual linguists, and their friends. The only requirement is that you be willing to be out to everyone on the list. The purposes of the group are to be visible and to gather occasionally to enjoy one another's company.

Keywords: Linguistics, Gays, Lesbians, Bisexuals, Transsexuals

Audience: Linguists, Gays, Lesbians, Bisexuals, Transsexuals

Contact: Arnold Zwicky
outil-request@csli.stanford.edu

Details: Free

User Info: To subscribe to the list, send an e-mail message requesting a subscription to the URL address below.

To send a message to the entire list, address it to: outil@csli.stanford.edu

`mailto:outil-request@csli.stanford.edu`

Russian

This list is dedicated to the discussion of Russian-language issues, including Russian language, linguistics, grammar, translations, and literature.

Keywords: Language, Literature (Russian), Linguistics

Audience: Slavicists, Linguists, Translators

Contact: Andrew Wollert
ispajw@asuacad
russian@asuvm.inre.asu.edu

Details: Free

User Info: To subscribe to the list, send an e-mail message requesting subscription to the URL address below.

`russian@asuvm.inre.asu.edu`

The Human Languages Page

This site provides language resources from around the world, including dictionaries, language tutorials, and spoken samples of languages.

Keywords: Languages, Linguistics

Audience: Linguists, Educators, Students

Profile: Languages covered include Esperanto, Gaelic, Arabic, Hindi, and Kanji. Also provides link to the Gutenberg Project (electronic texts) and to the Library of Congress.

Contact: Tyler Jones
tjones@willamette.edu.

Details: Free

`http://www.willamette.edu/~tjones/Language-Page.html`

The University of Michigan Library

The library's holdings are large and wide-ranging and contain significant collections in many fields.

Keywords: Education (Bilingual), Linguistics, Neuroscience, Michigan, Prohibition, Government (African)

Audience: General Public, Researchers, Librarians, Document Delivery Professionals

Details: Free

Expect: nothing, Send: <cr>

`telnet://cts.merit.edu`

Links to Many Databases

Links to Many Databases

A collection of links to over 40 databases covering a wide variety of subjects ranging from Postmodern Culture to the 1990 Census.

Keywords: Databases, Research

Sponsor: University of Texas, Austin, Texas, USA

Audience: Researchers, General Public

Contact: remark@ftp.cc.utexas.edu

`gopher://ftp.cc.utexas.edu`

A
B
C
D
E
F
G
H
I
J
K
L
M
N
O
P
Q
R
S
T
U
V
W
X
Y
Z

ListServ

LIST Gopher

This is a library-related service that allows users to obtain information by using their e-mail accounts.

Keywords: Mailing Lists, Listserv, Libraries, Gopher

Sponsor: North Carolina State University, Raleigh, North Carolina, USA

Audience: Librarians, E-mail Users

Profile: LISTGopher allows users to search library-related LISTSERV archives through the Gopher interface. Users enter their Email address, the list they want to search, and the keyword(s) they wish to find. LISTGopher then send the results of their search to the user's Email address. Currently, only library-related archives are supported, but more archive types may be added in the future.

Contact: Eric Lease Morgan, Systems Librarian
eric_morgan@ncsu.edu

`http://ericmorgan.lib.ncsu.edu/staff/morgan/morgan.html`

`gopher://dewey.lib.ncsu.edu /library/disciplines/library/listgopher`

LIST REVIEW SERVICE

Explores e-mail distribution lists (primarily bitnet and List Serv lists).

Keywords: Bitnet, ListServ

Audience: Email Users

Profile: Akin to book and restaurant reviews, each issue begins with a narrative description of usually one weeks worth of monitoring, then presents simple statistical data, such as the number of messages and lines, number of queries and nonqueries, number of subscribers and countries represented, list owner, location, and how to subscribe.

Contact: Raleigh C. Muns
srcmuns@umslvma.bitnet

Details: Free

User Info: To subscribe, send an e-mail message to the address below consisting of a single line reading:

SUB listreviewservice Your First Name Your Last Name

To send a message to the entire list, address it to:
listreviewservice@kentvm.kent.edu

`mailto:listserv@kentvm.kent.edu`

ListServ

A mailing list server for group communication.

Keywords: Internet Tools, ListServ

Audience: Internet Surfers

Details: Free

`mailto:listserv@uacsc2.albany`

Literacy

teslit-l (Adult Education & Literacy Test Literature)

This is a sublist of tesl-l (Teaching English as a Second Language). Discussions focus primarily on issues of literacy and the teaching of English as a second language.

Keywords: Education (Adult), Education (Distance), Education (Continuing), Literacy

Audience: K-12 Educators, Administrators, Researchers

Details: Free

User Info: To subscribe to the list, send an e-mail message to the URL address below consisting of a single line reading:

SUB teslit-l YourFirstName YourLastName

To send a message to the entire list, address it to: teslit-l @cunyvm.bitnet

Notes: Members of teslit-l must be members of tesl-l.

`mailto:listserv@cunyvm.bitnet`

Literary Criticism

PMC-MOO

A real-time, text-based, virtual-reality environment in which subscribers to Postmodern Culture can interact and participate in live conferences.

Keywords: Literature (Contemporary), Postmodern Culture, Literary Criticism

Audience: General Public, Writers, Literary Critics, Literary Theorists, Researchers

Profile: In addition to providing Postmodern Culture's subscribers with the opportunity to interact and to participate in live conferences, PMC-MOO provides access to texts generated by the journal and by PMC-TALK, as well as the opportunity to experience (or to help design) programs that simulate object lessons in postmodern theory. PMC-MOO is based on the LambdaMOO program, freeware by Pavel Curtis.

Contact: pmc@unity.ncsu.edu

Notes: If your Internet account is on a UNIX machine and you have access to the Emacs editior (type 'man emacs' or 'help emacs' or simply 'emacs' at your command prompt to find out, or ask your user-services people). You can connect to PMC-MOO using a customized Emacs client available from our FTP site. This client provides text-buffering, multiple windows, and many features superior to an unmediated Telnet connection. To retrieve the Emacs client, perform the following ftp transfer: ftp ftp.ncsu.edu; login: ftp; password: [your e-mail address]; cd pub/docs/pmc/pmc-talk; get PMC-MOO.doc; get mud.el; bin; get mud.elc; quit.

`telnet://dewey.lib.ncsu.edu`

Postmodern Culture

Postmodern Culture is a peer-reviewed electronic journal of interdisciplinary criticism on contemporary literature, theory, and culture.

Keywords: Literature (Contemporary), Postmodern Culture, Literary Criticism

Sponsor: Oxford University Press

Audience: General Public, Writers, Literary Critics, Literary Theorists, Researchers

Profile: All back issues of Postmodern Culture are always available; previous issues have included: Andrew Ross, Hacking Away at the Counter-Culture, Bell Hooks, Postmodern Blackness, Laura Kipnis, Marx: The Video (A Politics of Revolting Bodies), Kathy Acker, Dead Doll Humility' and Obsession, Neil Larsen, Postmodernism and Imperialism: Theory and Politics in Latin America, Patrick O'Donnell, His Master's Voice: On William Gaddis's JR, Greg Ulmer, Grammatology Hypemedia, Charles Bernstein, The Second War and Postmodern Memory, Allison Fraiberg, Of AIDS, Cyborgs, and Other Indiscretions: Resurfacing the Body in the Postmodern (with a response by David Porush), Stuart Moulthrop, You Say You Want a Revolution: Hypertext and the Laws of Media, Bob Perelman, The Marginalization of Poetry

Details: Costs

User Info: To subscribe to the list, send an e-mail message requesting a subscription to the URL address below.

`mailto:pmc@ncsvm.cc.ncsu.edu`

Literary Studies

Universite de Montreal UDEMATIK Library

The library's holdings are large and wide-ranging and contain significant collections in many fields.

Keywords: Art, Architecture, Economy, Sexology, Social Law, Science, Technology, Literary Studies

Audience: Researchers, Students, General Public

Contact: Joelle or Sebastien Roy
udematik@ere.umontreal.ca or
stemp@ere.umontreal.ca or
roys@ere.umontreal.ca

Expect: Login; Send: Application id INFO

`telnet://udematik.umontreal.ca`

Literate Programming

Litprog

A network list dealing with topics related to literate programming, both general (is literate programming compatible with writing portable programs), and particular (is it possible to use CWEB with ANSI C).

Keywords: Programming, Literate Programming

Audience: Computer Programmers

Contact: George D. Greenwade
bed_gdg@shsu.edu

Details: Free

User Info: To subscribe to the list, send an e-mail message to the URL address shown below consisting of a single line reading:

SUB litprog YourFirstName YourLastName

To send a message to the entire list, address it to: litprog @shsu.edu

Notes: This list is open to novices and seasoned literate programmers.

`mailto:listserv@shsu.edu`

Literature (American)

Emory University Library

The library's holdings are large and wide-ranging and contain significant collections in many fields.

Keywords: Health Sciences, Theology, History (US), Communism, Economics (History of), Literature (American)

Audience: General Public, Researchers, Librarians, Document Delivery Professionals

Details: Free

Expect: VM screen, Send: RETURN; Expect: CP READ, Send: DIAL VTAM, press RETURN; Expect: CICS screen, Send: PF1

`telnet://emuvm1.cc.emory.edu`

Indiana University Libraries

The library's holdings are large and wide-ranging and contain significant collections in many fields.

Keywords: Literature (English), Literature (American), 1640-Present, British Plays (19th-C.), Western Americana, Railway History, Aristotle (Texts of), Lafayette (Marquis de), Handel (G.F.), Austrian History, Antiquarian Books, Rare Books, French Opera (19th-C.), Drama (British),

Audience: General Public, Researchers, Librarians, Document Delivery Professionals

Details: Free

Expect: User ID prompt, Send: GUEST

`telnet://iuis.ucs.indiana.edu`

Northwestern University Library

The library's holdings are large and wide-ranging and contain significant collections in many fields.

Keywords: Africa, Wright (Frank Lloyd), Women's Studies, Art, Literature (American), Contemporary Music, Government (US State), UN Documents, Music

Audience: General Public, Researchers, Librarians, Document Delivery Professionals

Details: Free

Expect: COMMAND: Send: DIAL VTAM

`telnet://nuacvm.acns.nwu.edu`

Papa

A mailing list devoted to discussion of the life and works of Ernest Hemingway.

Keywords: Hemingway (Ernest), Literature (American)

Audience: Ernest Hemingway Readers

Contact: Dave Gross
dgross@polyslo.calpoly.edu

Details: Free

User Info: To subscribe to the list, send an e-mail message requesting a subscription to the URL address below.

To send a message to the entire list, address it to:
dgross@polyslo.calpoly.edu

`mailto:dgross@polyslo.calpoly.edu`

Princeton University Library

The library's holdings are large and wide-ranging. They contain significant collections in many fields.

Keywords: China, Japan, Classics, History (Ancient), Near Eastern Studies, Literature (American), Literature (English), Aeronautics, Middle Eastern Studies, Mormonism, Publishing

Audience: General Public, Researchers, Librarians, Document Delivery Professionals

Details: Free

Expect: Connect message, blank screen, Send: <cr>; Expect: #, Send: Call 500

`telnet://pucable.princeton.edu`

Purdue University Library

The library's holdings are large and wide-ranging. They contain significant collections in many fields.

Keywords: Economics (History of), Literature (English), Literature (American), Indiana, Rogers (Bruce), Engineering (History of), Aviation, Earth Science, Atmospheric Science, Consumer Science, Family Science, Chemistry (History of), Physics, Veterinary Science

Audience: General Public, Researchers, Librarians, Document Delivery Professionals

Contact: Dan Ferrer
dan@asterix.lib.purdue.edu

Details: Free

Expect: User ID prompt, Send: GUEST

`telnet://lib.cc.purdue.edu`

University of Delaware Libraries (DELCAT)

The library's holdings are large and wide-ranging and contain significant collections in many fields.

Keywords: Literature (American), Hemingway (Ernest), Papermaking (History of), Chemistry (History of), Literature (Irish), Delaware

Audience: General Public, Researchers, Librarians, Document Delivery Professionals

Contact: Stuart Glogoff
epo27855@udacsvm.bitnet

Details: Free

Expect: prompt, Send: RETURN 2-3 times

`telnet://delcat.udel.edu`

`telnet://delcat.acs.udel.edu`

University of Pennsylvania Library- Philadelphia Pa.

The library's holdings are large and wide-ranging and contain significant collections in many fields.

Keywords: Literature (English), Literature (American), History (World), Medieval Studies, East Asian Studies, Middle Eastern Studies, South Asian Studies, Judaica, Lithuania.

Audience: Educators, Students, Researchers

Profile: Access to the central Van Pelt Library and to most of the departmental libraries is restricted to members of the University community on weekends and

A B C D E F G H I J K L M N O P Q R S T U V W X Y Z

A B C D E F G H I J K L M N O P Q R S T U V W X Y Z

holidays. Online visitors are advised to call (215) 898-7554 for information on hours and access restrictions.

Contact: Patricia Renfro, Associate Director of Libraries

Details: Free

`telnet://library.upenn.edu`

University of Tennessee at Chatanooga Library

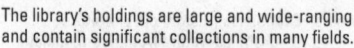

The library's holdings are large and wide-ranging and contain significant collections in many fields.

Keywords: Civil War, Literature (American)

Audience: Researchers, Students, General Public

Contact: Randy Whitson
rwhitson@utcvmutc.edu

Details: Free

Expect: OK prompt; Send: Login pub1; Expect: Password, Send: Usc

`telnet://library.utc.edu`

University of Tennessee at Memphis Library

The library's holdings are large and wide-ranging and contain significant collections in many fields.

Keywords: Tennessee, Literature (American)

Audience: Researchers, Students, General Public

Details: Costs

Expect: Username Prompt, Send: Harvey

`telnet://utmem1.utmem.edu`

University of Tulsa Library

The library's holdings are large and wide-ranging and contain significant collections in many fields.

Keywords: Literature (American), Petroleum, Geology

Audience: Researchers, Students, General Public

Details: Free

Expect: Username Prompt, Send: LIAS

`telnet://vax2.utulsa.edu`

University of Wisconsin at Milwaukee Library

The library's holdings are large and wide-ranging and contain significant collections in many fields.

Keywords: Art, Architecture, Business, Cartography, Geography, Geology, Urban Studies, Literature (English), Literature (American)

Audience: Researchers, Students, General Public

Details: Free

Expect: Login, Send: Lib; Expect: vDIAL prompt, Send: Library

`telnet://uwmcat.lib.uwm.edu`

Literature (Asian)

University of Rochester Library

The library's holdings are large and wide-ranging and contain significant collections in many fields.

Keywords: Architecture, Art History, Photography, Literature (Asian), Lasers, Geology, Statistics, Optics, Medieval Studies

Audience: Researchers, Students, General Public

Details: Free

Expect: Login; Send: Library

`telnet://128.151.226.71`

Literature (Children's)

Florida State University System Library

The library's holdings are large and wide-ranging and contain significant collections in many fields.

Keywords: Florida, Latin America, Judaica, Literature (Children's), Marine Engineering, Law (Brazilian), Law (British)

Audience: General Public, Researchers, Librarians, Document Delivery Professionals

Details: Free

Expect: Command ==>, Send: dial vtam; Expect: LUIS User Menu, Send: Your Catalog choice; To log off: Send: %off

`telnet://nervm.nerdc.ufl.edu`

University of Chicago Library

The library's holdings are large and wide-ranging and contain significant collections in many fields.

Keywords: English Bibles, Lincoln (Abraham), Kentucky & Ohio River Valley (History of), Balzac (Honore de), American Drama, Cromwell (Oliver), Goethe, Judaica, Italy, Chaucer (Geoffrey), Wells (Ida, Personal Papers of), Douglas (Stephen A.), Italy, Literature (Children's)

Audience: General Public, Researchers, Librarians, Document Delivery Professionals

Details: Free

Expect: ENTER CLASS, Send: LIB48 3; Expect: CONNECTED, Send: RETURN

`telnet://olorin.uchicago.edu`

University of Colorado at Boulder Library

The library's holdings are large and wide-ranging and contain significant collections in many fields.

Keywords: Numismatics, Human Rights, Literature (Children's), Labor Archives, History (US)

Audience: Researchers, Students, General Public

Contact: Donna Pattee
pattee@spot.colorado.edu

Details: Free

Expect: Login; Send: Culine

`telnet://culine.colorado.edu`

Literature (Contemporary)

ACEN (Art Com Electronic Network)

A conference on the WELL for art, technology, and text-based artworks.

Keywords: Art, Literature (Contemporary), Multimedia

Sponsor: Art Com Electronic Network

Audience: Artists, Musicians, Writers

Profile: Started in 1986, ACEN is a seminal art BBS that includes actual artworks, discussion on topics such as software as art, and on line published works by John Cage, Fred Truck, Jim Rosenberg, Judy Malloy, and others.

Contact: Carl Loeffler
artcomtv@well.sf.ca.us

To participate in a conference on the WELL, you must first establish an account on the WELL. To do so, start by typing: `telnet://well.sf.ca.us`

`telnet://well.sf.ca.us`

Art Com Magazine

A newsletter about art and technology (subjects covered include robotics, artists' software, hyperfiction) that is guest-edited by individual artists.

Keywords: Computer Art, Literature (Contemporary), Technology, Hyperfiction

Sponsor: Art Com Electronic Network

Audience: Artists, Writers

Contact: Fred Truck
fjt@well.sf.ca.us

To participate in a conference on the WELL, you must first establish an account on the WELL. To do so, start by typing: `telnet://well.sf.ca.us`

`mailto:artcomtv@well.sf.ca.us`

Electronic Books

A collection of books available as ASCII text files, including classics of antiquity (Aristotle, Virgil, Sophocles, the Bible), as well as more contemporary works of fiction and nonfiction by authors ranging from Dostoevsky to Martin Luther King, Jr.

Keywords: Books, Online Books, Literature (Contemporary), Literature (General)

Sponsor: The Blacksburg Electronic Village (BEV) at Virginia Tech

Audience: General Public, Historians

Contact: BEV Gopher Administrators
gopher@gopher.vt.edu

`gopher://gopher.vt.edu`

InterText

A network-distributed bimonthly literary magazine.

Keywords: Literature (Contemporary), Journals

Audience: General Public, Writers

Profile: InterText publishes all kinds of material, ranging from mainstream stories to fantasy to horror to science fiction to humor. InterText publishes in both ASCII and PostScript formats, and reaches over 1,000 readers worldwide.

Contact: Jason Snell
jsnell@ocf.berkeley.edu

Details: Free

Select OCF On-Line Library; then select Fiction; then select InterText

Notes: The ASCII version runs approximately 150K per issue; if you have tight file gateways, the issue can be split up and squeezed through if need be. The PostScript version runs approximately 500K. If you would like to see back issues of InterText, you can FTP them from: network.ucsd.edu(128.54.16.3) in/ intertext. Login as anonymous, with your e-mail address as your password.

`gopher://ocf.berkeley.edu`

PMC-MOO

A real-time, text-based, virtual-reality environment in which subscribers to Postmodern Culture can interact and participate in live conferences.

Keywords: Literature (Contemporary), Postmodern Culture, Literary Criticism

Audience: General Public, Writers, Literary Critics, Literary Theorists, Researchers

Profile: In addition to providing Postmodern Culture's subscribers with the opportunity to interact and to participate in live conferences, PMC-MOO provides access to texts generated by the journal and by PMC-TALK, as well as the opportunity to experience (or to help design) programs that simulate object lessons in postmodern theory. PMC-

MOO is based on the LambdaMOO program, freeware by Pavel Curtis.

Contact: pmc@unity.ncsu.edu

Notes: If your Internet account is on a UNIX machine and you have access to the Emacs editior (type 'man emacs' or 'help emacs' or simply 'emacs' at your command prompt to find out, or ask your user-services people). You can connect to PMC-MOO using a customized Emacs client available from our FTP site. This client provides text-buffering, multiple windows, and many features superior to an unmediated Telnet connection. To retrieve the Emacs client, perform the following ftp transfer: ftp ftp.ncsu.edu; login: ftp; password: [your e-mail address]; cd pub/docs/pmc/pmc-talk; get PMC-MOO.doc; get mud.el; bin; get mud.elc; quit.

`telnet://dewey.lib.ncsu.edu`

Postmodern Culture

Postmodern Culture is a peer-reviewed electronic journal of interdisciplinary criticism on contemporary literature, theory, and culture.

Keywords: Literature (Contemporary), Postmodern Culture, Literary Criticism

Sponsor: Oxford University Press

Audience: General Public, Writers, Literary Critics, Literary Theorists, Researchers

Profile: All back issues of Postmodern Culture are always available; previous issues have included: Andrew Ross, Hacking Away at the Counter-Culture, Bell Hooks, Postmodern Blackness, Laura Kipnis, Marx: The Video (A Politics of Revolting Bodies), Kathy Acker, Dead Doll Humility' and Obsession, Neil Larsen, Postmodernism and Imperialism: Theory and Politics in Latin America, Patrick O'Donnell, His Master's Voice: On William Gaddis's JR, Greg Ulmer, Grammatology Hypemedia, Charles Bernstein, The Second War and Postmodern Memory, Allison Fraiberg, Of AIDS, Cyborgs, and Other Indiscretions: Resurfacing the Body in the Postmodern (with a response by David Porush), Stuart Moulthrop, You Say You Want a Revolution: Hypertext and the Laws of Media, Bob Perelman, The Marginalization of Poetry

Details: Costs

User Info: To subscribe to the list, send an e-mail message requesting a subscription to the URL address below.

`mailto:pmc@ncsvm.cc.ncsu.edu`

Literature (English)

Chaucer

A discussion list on the subject of Medieval English literature, especially that of Chaucer.

Keywords: Chaucer (Geoffrey), Literature (English)

Audience: Chaucer Fans, English Teachers

Contact: Dan Mosser
mosserd@vtm1.cc.vt.edu

`mailto:chaucer@vtm1.cc.vt.edu`

Indiana University Libraries

The library's holdings are large and wide-ranging and contain significant collections in many fields.

Keywords: Literature (English), Literature (American), 1640-Present, British Plays (19th-C.), Western Americana, Railway History, Aristotle (Texts of), Lafayette (Marquis de), Handel (G.F.), Austrian History, Antiquarian Books, Rare Books, French Opera (19th-C.), Drama (British),

Audience: General Public, Researchers, Librarians, Document Delivery Professionals

Details: Free

Expect: User ID prompt, Send: GUEST

`telnet://iuis.ucs.indiana.edu`

Johns Hopkins University Library

The library's holdings are large and wide-ranging and contain significant collections in many fields.

Keywords: Literature (English), Economics, Classics, Drama (German), Slavery, Trade Unions, Incunabula, Bibles, Diseases (History of), Nursing (History of), Abolitionism

Audience: General Public, Researchers, Librarians, Document Delivery Professionals

Details: Free

`telnet://jhuvm.hcf.jhu.edu`

Princeton University Library

The library's holdings are large and wide-ranging. They contain significant collections in many fields.

Keywords: China, Japan, Classics, History (Ancient), Near Eastern Studies, Literature (American), Literature (English), Aeronautics, Middle Eastern Studies, Mormonism, Publishing

Audience: General Public, Researchers, Librarians, Document Delivery Professionals

Details: Free

Expect: Connect message, blank screen, Send: <cr>; Expect: #, Send: Call 500

`telnet://pucable.princeton.edu`

Purdue University Library

The library's holdings are large and wide-ranging. They contain significant collections in many fields.

Keywords: Economics (History of), Literature (English), Literature (American), Indiana, Rogers (Bruce), Engineering (History of), Aviation, Earth Science, Atmospheric

A
B
C
D
E
F
G
H
I
J
K
L
M
N
O
P
Q
R
S
T
U
V
W
X
Y
Z

A B C D E F G H I J K L M N O P Q R S T U V W X Y Z

Science, Consumer Science, Family Science, Chemistry (History of), Physics, Veterinary Science

Audience: General Public, Researchers, Librarians, Document Delivery Professionals

Contact: Dan Ferrer
dan@asterix.lib.purdue.edu

Details: Free

Expect: User ID prompt, Send: GUEST

`telnet://lib.cc.purdue.edu`

University of Pennsylvania Library- Philadelphia Pa.

The library's holdings are large and wide-ranging and contain significant collections in many fields.

Keywords: Literature (English), Literature (American), History (World), Medieval Studies, East Asian Studies, Middle Eastern Studies, South Asian Studies, Judaica, Lithuania.

Audience: Educators, Students, Researchers

Profile: Access to the central Van Pelt Library and to most of the departmental libraries is restricted to members of the University community on weekends and holidays. Online visitors are advised to call (215) 898-7554 for information on hours and access restrictions.

Contact: Patricia Renfro, Associate Director of Libraries

Details: Free

`telnet://library.upenn.edu`

University of Pennsylvania PENNINFO Library

The library's holdings are large and wide-ranging and contain significant collections in many fields.

Keywords: Church History, Spanish Inquisition, Witchcraft, Shakespeare (William), Bibles, Aristotle (Texts of), Fiction, Whitman (Walt), French Revolution, Drama (French), Literature (English), Literature (Spanish)

Audience: Researchers, Students, General Public

Contact: Al DSouza
penninfo-admin@dccs.upenn.edu
dsouza@dccs.upenn.edu

Details: Free

Expect: Login; Send: Public

`telnet://penninfo.upenn.edu`

University of Wisconsin at Milwaukee Library

The library's holdings are large and wide-ranging and contain significant collections in many fields.

Keywords: Art, Architecture, Business, Cartography, Geography, Geology, Urban Studies, Literature (English), Literature (American)

Audience: Researchers, Students, General Public

Details: Free

Expect: Login, Send: Lib; Expect: vDIAL prompt, Send: Library

`telnet://uwmcat.lib.uwm.edu`

Literature (General)

alt.books.reviews

A Usenet conference devoted to reviews of books, especially science fiction and computer science books.

Keywords: Literature (General), Computer Science, Science Fiction, Book Reviews

Audience: General Public, Publishers, Educators, Librarians, Booksellers

Profile: Alt.books.reviews (a.b.r. for short) is a forum for posting reviews of books of interest to readers, school and public librarians, bookstores, publishers, teachers and professors, and others who desire an "educated opinion" of a book. This is an unmoderated newsgroup.

Contact: sbrock@csn.org.

Details: Free

To participate in a Usenet newsgroup, you need access to a newsreader

Notes: The reviews in alt.books.reviews are archived at csn.org. FTP to csn.org; login: anonymous; password: your complete
e-mail address. At the FTP prompt, type:
`cd pub/alt.books.reviews`

`news:alt.books.reviews`

alt.hypertext

A USENET newsgroup devoted to hyperfiction and hypertext documents. Postings range from information about and reviews of both recent hyperfiction and recent nonfiction hypertext documents, to information reviews of software for creating hypertext.

Keywords: Literature (General), Hyperfiction, Hypertext

Audience: General Public, Writers, Computer Programmers

Details: Free

To participate in a USENET newsgroup, you need access to a newsreader.

`news:alt.hypertext`

Electronic Books

A collection of books available as ASCII text files, including classics of antiquity (Aristotle, Virgil, Sophocles, the Bible), as well as more contemporary works of fiction and nonfiction by authors ranging from Dostoevsky to Martin Luther King, Jr.

Keywords: Books, Online Books, Literature (Contemporary), Literature (General)

Sponsor: The Blacksburg Electronic Village (BEV) at Virginia Tech

Audience: General Public, Historians

Contact: BEV Gopher Administrators
gopher@gopher.vt.edu

`gopher://gopher.vt.edu`

GUTENBERG Listserver

A mailing list providing information about Project Gutenberg.

Keywords: Project Gutenberg, Literature (General), Reference

Sponsor: National Clearinghouse for Machine Readable Texts

Audience: General Public, Researchers, Educators, Students

Contact: Michael S. Hart
gutnberg@vmd.cso.uiuc.edu

Details: Free

User Info: To subscribe to the list, send an e-mail message to the URL address shown below consisting of a single line reading:

SUB GUTNBERG YourFirstName YourLastName

`mailto:listserv@vmd.cso.uiuc.edu`

Project Gutenberg

The purpose of Project Gutenberg is to encourage the creation and distribution of English-language electronic texts.

Keywords: Literature (General), Reference

Sponsor: National Clearinghouse for Machine Readable Texts

Audience: General Public, Researchers, Educators, Students

Profile: Contents include: Project Gutenberg's goal is to provide a collection of 10,000 of the most used books by the year 2001, and to reduce the effective costs to the user to a price of approximately one cent per book, plus the cost of media and of shipping and handling. Thus it is hoped that the entire cost of libraries of this nature will be about US$100, plus the price of the disks and CD-ROMS and mailing. Project Gutenberg assists in the selection of hardware and software as well as in their installation and use. It also assists in scanning, spelling checkers, proofreading, etc.

Contact: Michael S. Hart
hart@vmd.cso.uiuc.edu

Details: Costs

Login anonymous; cd text

`ftp://mrcnext.cso.uiuc.edu`

Rec.arts.int-fiction

A Usenet newsgroup about interactive literature and interactive computer games.

Keywords: Literature (General), Interactive Media, Computer Games

Audience: General Public, Computer Games Players

Details: Free

To participate in a USENET newsgroup, you need access to a newsreader.

`news:rec.arts.int-fiction`

rec.arts.poems

A Usenet newsgroup providing information and discussion about poetry.

Keywords: Poetry, Literature (General)

Audience: Poets, Poetry Readers

User Info: To subscribe to this Usenet newsgroup, you need access to a newsreader.

`news:rec.arts.poems`

University of Puget Sound Library

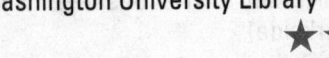

The library's holdings are large and wide-ranging and contain significant collections in many fields.

Keywords: Education, Literature (General), Music, Natural Science, Theology

Audience: Researchers, Students, General Public

Details: Free

Expect: Login; Send: Library

`telnet://192.124.98.2`

Literature (German)

Washington University Library

The library's holdings are large and wide-ranging and contain significant collections in many fields.

Keywords: Technology, Literature (German), Social Science, Behavioral Science

Audience: Researchers, Students, General Public

Contact: services@wugate.wustl.edu

Details: Free

Expect: Login; Send: Services

`telnet://wugate.wustl.edu`

Literature (Irish)

fwake-l

A conference and forum for a broad discussion of James Joyce's *Finnegan's Wake*.

Keywords: Joyce (James), Literature (Irish), Authors, Writing

Audience: Writers, Joyce Scholars, Literary Critics, Literary Theorists

User Info: To subscribe to the list, send an e-mail message to the URL address below consisting of a single line reading:

SUB fwake-l

`mailto:listserv@irlearn.ucd.ie`

University of Delaware Libraries (DELCAT)

The library's holdings are large and wide-ranging and contain significant collections in many fields.

Keywords: Literature (American), Hemingway (Ernest), Papermaking (History of), Chemistry (History of), Literature (Irish), Delaware

Audience: General Public, Researchers, Librarians, Document Delivery Professionals

Contact: Stuart Glogoff
epo27855@udacsvm.bitnet

Details: Free

Expect: prompt, Send: RETURN 2-3 times

`telnet://delcat.udel.edu`

`delcat.acs.udel.edu`

Literature (Russian)

Russian

This list is dedicated to the discussion of Russian-language issues, including Russian language, linguistics, grammar, translations, and literature.

Keywords: Language, Literature (Russian), Linguistics

Audience: Slavicists, Linguists, Translators

Contact: Andrew Wollert
ispajw@asuacad
russian@asuvm.inre.asu.edu

Details: Free

User Info: To subscribe to the list, send an e-mail message requesting subscription to the URL address below.

`russian@asuvm.inre.asu.edu`

Literature (Spanish)

University of Pennsylvania PENNINFO Library

The library's holdings are large and wide-ranging and contain significant collections in many fields.

Keywords: Church History, Spanish Inquisition, Witchcraft, Shakespeare (William), Bibles, Aristotle (Texts of), Fiction, Whitman (Walt), French Revolution, Drama (French), Literature (English), Literature (Spanish)

Audience: Researchers, Students, General Public

Contact: Al DSouza
penninfo-admin@dccs.upenn.edu
dsouza@dccs.upenn.edu

Details: Free

Expect: Login; Send: Public

`telnet://penninfo.upenn.edu`

Lithuania

Balt-L

A forum devoted to communications to and about the Baltic Republics of Lithuania, Latvia, and Estonia.

Keywords: Lithuania, Latvia, Estonia, Baltic Republics

Audience: Researchers, Baltic Nationals

Contact: Jean-Michel Thizy
jmyhg@uottawa.edu

Details: Free

User Info: To subscribe to the list, send an e-mail message to the URL address below, consisting of a single line reading:

SUB balt-l YourFirstName YourLastName

`mailto:listserv@ubvm.cc.buffalo.edu`

University of Pennsylvania Library- Philadelphia Pa.

The library's holdings are large and wide-ranging and contain significant collections in many fields.

Keywords: Literature (English), Literature (American), History (World), Medieval Studies, East Asian Studies, Middle Eastern Studies, South Asian Studies, Judaica, Lithuania.

Audience: Educators, Students, Researchers

Profile: Access to the central Van Pelt Library and to most of the departmental libraries is restricted to members of the University community on weekends and holidays. Online visitors are advised to call (215) 898-7554 for information on hours and access restrictions.

A B C D E F G H I J K L M N O P Q R S T U V W X Y Z

Contact: Patricia Renfro, Associate Director of Libraries

Details: Free

`telnet://library.upenn.edu`

Litigants

LEXPAT (Patents US)

The LEXPAT library contains the full text of US patents issued since 1975, the US Patent and Trademark Office Manual of Classification, and the Index to US Patent Classification. The approximately 1,500 patents added to the library each week appear online within four days of their issue.

Keywords: Patents, Inventors, Assignees, Litigants

Audience: Lawyers, Business Researchers, Analysts, Entrepreneurs

Profile: LEXPAT may be searched by individual files for the full text of utility, design or plant patents, or you can combine the files in one 'omni' search. The Manual, Index and Class files can be used to supplement your full-text patent searches. LEXPAT is a valuable tool for both patent professionals and for anyone who needs to access to technical information. More than 80 percent of the information contained in patents is unavailable in any other form.

Contact: Mead New Sales Group at (800) 227-4908 or (513) 859-5398 inside the US, or (513) 865-7981 for all inquiries outside the US.

User Info: To subscribe, contact Mead directly.

To examine the Nexis user guide, you can access it at the ftp site of the University of Texas at Austin at the URL address: ftp://ftp.cc.utexas.edu The files are in: /pub/ref-services/LEXIS

`telnet://nex.meaddata.com`

`http://www.meaddata.com`

Liturgy

Cantus

This gopher site accesses the Gregorian Chant Database, which is maintained by the Catholic University of America.

Keywords: Gregorian Chants, Music, Liturgy

Sponsor: Catholic University of America (CUA)

Audience: Vocalists, Educators, Students

Profile: The database contains an introduction to the Cantus Gopher at the CUA, and has a searchable index.

`gopher://vmsgopher.cua.edu`

Lockheed Missiles & Space Company

Lockheed Missiles & Space Company

A web site containing information about Lockheed Missiles and Space Company, a major aerospace and defense company specializing in the development of space systems, missiles and other high technology products. Includes company information and press releases.

Keywords: Defense, Aerospace

Sponsor: The Lockheed Palo Alto Artificial Intelligence Center

Audience: Aerospace Engineers, Defense Analysts

`http://www.lmsc.lockheed.com`

Loughborough University of Technology Computer-Human Interaction (LUTCHI) Research Centre

Loughborough University of Technology Computer-Human Interaction (LUTCHI) Research Centre

This server contains general information on computer-human interaction.

Keywords: Interface Design, Ergonomics, Computer-Human Interactions, Programming

Sponsor: Loughborough University of Technology, Leicestershire, UK

Audience: Software Developers, Software Designers, Programmers

Profile: The LUTCHI Research Centre is based within the Department of Computer Studies at the Loughborough University of Technology, Leicestershire, UK. This server contains information about LUTCHI research projects, official publicity releases, as well as documents, images, and movies associated with those projects.

Contact: Ben Anderson B.Anderson@lut.ac.uk

Details: Free, Moderated, Image, Sound, and Multimedia.

Use a World Wide Web (Mosaic) client and open a connection to the resource.

`http://pipkin.lut.ac.uk`

Lower Rio Grande Valley (History of)

University of Texas-Pan American Library

The library's holdings are large and wide-ranging and contain significant collections in many fields.

Keywords: Lower Rio Grande Valley (History of), Mexican-American Studies

Audience: Researchers, Students, General Public

Details: Free

Expect: Username Prompt, Send: packey

`telnet://panam2.panam.edu`

Lynx FAQ

Lynx FAQ

A resource providing common questions and answers about Cello, a distributed hypertext browser with full WWW capabilities.

Keywords: Internet Reference FAQs

Sponsor: University of Kansas, Distributed Computing Group, Kansas, USA

Audience: Students, Computer Scientists, Researchers

Contact: Garrett Blythe, Lou Montulli doslynx@falcon.cc.ukans.edu montulli@mcom.com lynx-help@ukanaix.cc.ukans.edu

`http://ftp2.cc.ukans.edu/about_lynx`

`http://ftp2.cc.ukans.edu/lynx_help`

`http://ftp2.cc.ukans.edu/lynx_writeup`

Lyrics

UWP Music Archive (named for the host machine's location: the University of Wisconsin—Parkside)

An extensive repository of files relating to a diverse array of music genres: rock, folk, classical, etc.

Keywords: Music, Lyrics, Graphics

Sponsor: University of Wisconsin—Parkside

Audience: Musicians, Music Enthusiasts, Musicologists

Profile: This FTP archive contains a music database, artist discographies, essays about music and particular works, hundreds of image files (mostly .GIF and

.JPEG format) of musicians Ñ including album covers and posters, a lyrics archive and the ever-popular 'Beginner's Introduction to Classical Music.'

Contact: Dave Datta
datta@ftp.uwp.edu

User Info: Select Music Archives from the gopher top-level menu.

Notes: Also accessible through CMU's "English Server" gopher server. (q.v.)

`gopher://gopher.uwp.edu`

Lysator's Gopher Service

Lysator's Gopher Service

Lysator is the name of the Academic Computer Society at Linkoping University, Linkoping, Sweden. It relies on voluntary efforts by students, and any service of activity runs as long as they think it is fun—content always reflects their personal interests.

Keywords: Sweden, Europe

Audience: Swedish Students

Contact: Lars Aronsson@lysator.liu.se

Details: Free

`gopher://gopher.lysator.liu.se`

`http://dla.ucop.edu`

A
B
C
D
E
F
G
H
I
J
K
L
M
N
O
P
Q
R
S
T
U
V
W
X
Y
Z

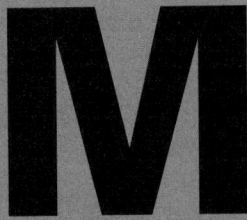

Maastricht Treaty

Maastricht Treaty

The file contains the text of the latest edition of the Treaty on European Union, also known as the Maastricht Treaty, signed on February 7, 1992.

Keywords: Europe, European Community, Maastricht Treaty

Audience: Politicians, Historians, Europeans, Political Scientists, General Public

Details: Free

Select from menu as appropriate.

`gopher://wiretap.spies.com`

Macintosh Computer

(The) DTP Direct Catalog

DTP Direct specializes in Macintosh hardware and software tools for desktop publishers and graphics professionals.

Keywords: Macintosh Computer, Desktop Publishing, Graphic Design

Sponsor: InterNex Server Bureau

Audience: Graphic Designers, Artists, Desktop Publishers

Details: Free, Moderated, Image, Sound, and Multimedia files available.

`http://www.internex.net/DTP/home.html`

CE Software

Technical support for CE Software Products, such as QuickKeys for the Macintosh.

Keywords: Software, Technical Support, Macintosh Computer

Audience: Software users

Details: Free

User Info: To Subscribe to the list, send an e-mail message requesting a subscription to the URL address below.

`mailto:ce_info%cedsm@uunet.uu.net`

Chemistry Tutorial Information

This site provides chemistry tutorial information in the form of text, data, pictures, source code, and executable programs for Macintosh computers.

Keywords: Chemistry, Tutorials, Macintosh Computer, Education

Sponsor: University of Michigan

Audience: Chemistry Students (high school up)

Contact: comments@mac.archive.umich.edu

Details: Free, Image files available.

`gopher://plaza.aarnet.edu.au@/micros/mac/umich/misc/chemistry/00index.txt`

comp.sys.mac

A Usenet newsgroup providing information and discussion about the Macintosh computer. There are many categories within this group.

Keywords: Computer Systems, Macintosh Computer

Audience: Computer Users, Macintosh Users

Details: To subscribe to this Usenet newsgroup, you need access to a newsreader.

`news:comp.sys.mac`

PAGEMAKER

The PageMaker ListServ is dedicated to the discussion of desktop publishing in general, with emphasis on the use of Aldus PageMaker. The list discusses PageMaker's use in both the PC and Macintosh realms. The list also maintains an extensive archive of help files that are extremely useful for the modern desktop publisher.

Keywords: Desktop Publishing, Aldus Pagemaker, IBM PC, Macintosh Computer

Audience: Desktop Publishers, Computer Users

Contact: Geoff Peters
gwp@cs.purdue.edu

Details: Free

User Info: To Subscribe to the list, send an e-mail message to the URL address shown below consisting of a single line reading:

SUB pagemaker YourFirstName YourLastName.

To send a message to the entire list, address it to:

gwp@cs.purdue.edu

`mailto:listserv@cs.purdue.edu`

SUMEX-AIM

An FTP archive of software, demonstration programs, and various applications, especially for Macintosh computers.

Keywords: Computers, Macintosh Computer, Software

Audience: Computer Users, Macintosh Users

Details: Free

`ftp://sumex-aim.Stanford.edu`

Magazines

(The) Electric Eclectic

A multimedia magazine delivered online that includes pictures, sounds, and text.

A B C D E F G H I J K L **M** N O P Q R S T U V W X Y Z

Keywords: Magazines, Multimedia

Audience: General Public

`mailto:ee-discuss-request@eitech.cm`

Class Four Relay Magazine

A magazine by Relay Ops for the relay community.

Keywords: Relays, Magazines, Electronics

Sponsor: Carnegie Mellon University, Pittsburgh, PA, USA

Audience: Relay Community

Profile: Includes articles on general questions and issues of relay usage, information for and about relay ops, discussion of policy issues and guidelines, and technical issues and new developments.

Contact: Joey J. Stanford
stjs@vm.marist.edu

Details: Free

`mailto:stjs@vm.marist.edu`

Mailing Lists

LIST Gopher

This is a library-related service that allows users to obtain information by using their e-mail accounts.

Keywords: Mailing Lists, Listserv, Libraries, Gopher

Sponsor: North Carolina State University, Raleigh, North Carolina, USA

Audience: Librarians, Library Users, Email Users

Profile: LISTGopher allows users to search library-related LISTSERV archives through the Gopher interface. Users enter their e-mail address, the list they want to search, and the keyword(s) they want to find. LISTGopher then send the results of their search to the user's Email address. Currently, only library-related archives are supported, but more archive types may be added in the future.

Contact: Eric Lease Morgan, Systems Librarian
eric_morgan@ncsu.edu
http://ericmorgan.lib.ncsu.edu/staff/morgan/morgan.html

`gopher://dewey.lib.ncsu.edu/library/`
`disciplines/library/listgopher`

MLoL

The MLoL (Musical List of Lists) is a list of music-related mailing lists available on the Internet.

Keywords: Music, Mailing Lists

Audience: Musicians, General Public

Details: Free

User Info: To Subscribe to the list, send an e-mail message requesting a subscription to the URL address below.

`mailto:mlol-request@wariat.org`

Newlists

This is a mailing list clearing house for new mailing lists. Subscribers will get announcements of new lists that are mailed to this list.

Keywords: Mailing Lists

Audience: Internet Surfers

Contact: Marty Hoag
info@vm1.nodak.edu

Details: Free

User Info: To Subscribe to the list, send an e-mail message requesting a subscription to the URL address below.

`mailto:info@vm1.nodak.edu`

Maine

University of Maine System Library Catalog

The library's holdings are large and wide-ranging and contain significant collections in many fields.

Keywords: Ucadian Studies, St. John Valley (History of), Canadian-American Studies, Geology, Aquaculture, Maine

Audience: General Public, Researchers, Librarians, Document Delivery Professionals

Contact: Elaine Albright, Marilyn Lutz

Details: Free

Notes: Expect: login, Send: ursus

`telnet://ursus.maine.edu`

Maine Authors

Colby College Library

The library's holdings are large and wide-ranging and contain significant collections in many fields.

Keywords: Contemporary Letters, Hardy (Thomas),James (Henry), Mann (Thomas, Collections of), Housman (A.E., Letters of), Maine Authors, Irish History (Modern)

Audience: General Public, Researchers, Librarians, Document Delivery Professionals

Details: Free

Notes: Expect: login, Send: library

`telnet://library.colby.edu`

Malls

The Branch Mall, an Electronic Shopping Mall

Branch Information Services offers shopping to customers and leases storefronts and electronic catalogs to vendors.

Keywords: Malls, Shopping, Gifts, Advertising

Sponsor: Branch Information Services

Audience: Consumers, Merchants

Contact: Jon Zeeff
jon@branch.com

Details: Free

Notes: Free for consumers.

`http://branch.com`

Management

ABI/Inform

ABI/Inform is a comprehensive source for business and management information, containing abstracts from close to 1,000 publications and the full-text from over 100 publications. The database covers trends, corporate strategies and tactics, management techniques, competitive information and product information

Keywords: Business, Business Management, Management

Sponsor: UMI, Ann Arbor, Michigan, US

Audience: General Public, Researchers, Librarians

Profile: A few of the thousands of business subjects that can searched in ABI/Inform include: company news and analysis, market conditions and strategies, employee management and compensation, international trade and investment, management styles and corporate cultures, and economic conditions and forecasts.

Contact: CDP Technologies Sales Department (800)950-2035, extension 400

User Info: To Subscribe, contact CDP Technologies directly

`telnet://cdplus@cdplus.com`

Asian Pacific Business and Marketing Resources

A forum on business and marketing in the Pacific Rim region.

Keywords: Asia, Pacific, Business, Management

Audience: Business Professionals, Market Researchers

Details: Free

`gopher://hoshi.cic.sfu.ca/11/dlam/`
`business/forum`

GC-L

Project for international business and management curricula.

Keywords: Business, Management, Language

Sponsor: Global Classroom

Audience: Linguists, Language Teachers, Language Students, International Business Educators

Details: Free

User Info: To Subscribe to the list, send an e-mail message to the address below consisting of a single line reading:

`mailto:listserv@uriacc.uri.edu`

The Management Archive

This is an electronic forum for management ideas and information.

Keywords: Management, Business, Economics

Audience: Managers, Business Professionals, Economists

Profile: The Archive arranges working papers, teaching materials, and so on, in directories by subject. All materials in the Archive are fully indexed and searchable. If you have material that you would like to see receive worldwide network exposure and distribution, submit them to the Archive.

Contact: Jim Goes
goes@chimera.sph.umn.edu

Details: Free

Notes: Expect: login, Send: anonymous; Expect: password, Send: your e-mail address.

`ftp://chimera.sph.umn.edu`

Total Quality Management Gopher

A collection of materials relating to the elimination of defects through comprehensive quality control in industry, government, and universities.

Keywords: Quality Control, Management, Business

Sponsor: The Clemson University Department of Industrial Engineering, Clemson, South Carolina, USA

Audience: Managers, Administrators

Contact: quality@eng.clemson.edu

`gopher://deming.eng.clemson.edu`

`http://deming.eng.clemson.edu`

Mann (Thomas)

Colby College Library

The library's holdings are large and wide-ranging and contain significant collections in many fields.

Keywords: Contemporary Letters, Hardy (Thomas),James (Henry), Mann (Thomas, Collections of), Housman (A.E., Letters of), Maine Authors, Irish History (Modern)

Audience: General Public, Researchers, Librarians, Document Delivery Professionals

Details: Free

Notes: Expect: login, Send: library

`telnet://library.colby.edu`

Manx

gaelic-l

A multidisciplinary discussion list that facilitates the exchange of news, views, and information in Scottish Gaelic, Irish, and Manx.

Keywords: Scottish Gaelic, Irish, Manx, Language

Audience: Linguists

Contact: Marion Gunn
mgunn@irlearn.ucd.ie or
caoimhin@smo.ac.uk
lss203@cs.napier.ac.uk

Details: Free

User Info: To Subscribe to the list, send an e-mail message to the URL address shown below consisting of a single line reading:

SUB gaelic-l YourFirstName YourLastName

To send a message to the entire list, address it to:

gaelic-l@irlearn.ucd.ie

`mailto:listserv@irlearn.ucd.ie`

MapInfo-l

MapInfo-l

A mailing list for the discussion of MapInfo Software.

Keywords: GIS (Geographic Information Systems)

Audience: Geographers, Cartographers

Contact: Bill Thoen
bthoen@gisnet.com

`mailto:mapinfo-1-request@csn.org`

Mapping

Internet Resources for Earth Sciences

A document detailing Internet resources for a variety of earth science disciplines, including GIS.

Keywords: Directory, GIS, Geology, Geography, GPS, Mapping, Earth Science

Sponsor: Bill Thoen

Audience: Earth Scientists, Researchers

Profile: A complete document detailing the types of information available in earth sciences and the mechanisms to retrieve needed information.

Contact: Bill Thoen
bthoen@gisnet.com

Details: Free

`ftp://ftp.csn.org/COGS/ores.text`

Marimed Foundation

Marimed Foundation

This foundation provides therapy and education to adjudicated and emotionally impaired teens. Therapies include wilderness experiences on a square-rigged sail ship, boat building, and traditional therapies.

Keywords: Education (Alternative), Sailing

Audience: Educators, Social Workers

Contact: Dr. Robert Grossman
marimed@holonet.net

Details: Free

`mailto:marimed@holonet.net`

Marine Biology

Starnet (Echinoderm Newsletter)

The Starnet echinoderm electronic newsletter is distributed quarterly.

Keywords: Echinoderm, Starfish, Marine Biology

Audience: Marine Biologists

Contact: Win Hide
whide@matrix.bchs.uh.edu

Details: Free

User Info: To Subscribe to the list, send an e-mail message requesting a subscription to the URL address below.

`mailto:whide@matrix.bchs.uh.edu`

A B C D E F G H I J K L **M** N O P Q R S T U V W X Y Z

University of North Carolina at Wilmington SEABOARD Library

 ★★

The library's holdings are large and wide-ranging and contain significant collections in many fields.

Keywords: Marine Biology, Historical Documents

Audience: Researchers, Students, General Public

Contact: Eddy Cavenaugh
cavenaughd@uncwil.bitnet
cavenaughd@vxc.uncwil.edu

Details: Free

Notes: Expect: Login; Send: Info

`telnet://vxc.uncwil.edu`

Marine Engineering

Florida State University System Library

★★

The library's holdings are large and wide-ranging and contain significant collections in many fields.

Keywords: Florida, Latin America, Judaica, Literature (Children's), Marine Engineering, Law (Brazilian), Law (British)

Audience: General Public, Researchers, Librarians, Document Delivery Professionals

Details: Free

Notes: Expect: Command ==>, Send: dial vtam; Expect: LUIS User Menu, Send: Your Catalog choice; To log off: Send: %off

`telnet://nervm.nerdc.ufl.edu`

Maritime Industry

PIERS Imports (US Ports)

PIERS (Port Import Export Reporting Service) Imports (US Ports), produced by The Journal of Commerce, is a compilation of manifests of vessels loading or discharging cargo at approximately 120 US seaports.

Keywords: Trade, Imports, Maritime Industry

Sponsor: The Journal of Commerce/PIERS, New York, NY, USA

Audience: Business Professionals

Profile: The principal applications of this information include: identification of new sources of supply for imports, monitoring imports of products whose details are lost in traditional government reports, and identification of potential trade partners.

Contact: Dialog in the US at (800) 334-2564, Dialog internationally at country specific locations.

User Info: To Subscribe, contact Dialog directly.

Notes: Coverage: current 15 months, updated monthly.

`telnet://dialog.com`

Research Ship Schedules and Information

 ★★★

A gopher providing information on research and deep water vessels from more than 45 countries. Includes detailed ship specifications, some with deck plans and photographs available as GIF files. Also has cruise schedules for US ships, as well as some from other countries.

Keywords: Oceanography, Transportation, Maritime Industry, Travel

Sponsor: University of Delaware (The OCEANIC Ocean Information Center), Newark, Delaware, USA

Audience: Oceanographers, General Public

Contact: Ocean Information Center, University of Delaware, College of Marine Studies
oceanic@diu.cms.udel.edu

Details: Free, Images

`gopher://diu.cms.udel.edu`

MARKET (Markets and Industries News and Information)

MARKET (Markets and Industries News and Information)

 ★★★★

The Markets and Industries News and Information (MARKET) library contains sources covering developments in a wide variety of markets and industries.

Keywords: News, Analysis, Industry, Marketing

Audience: Business Professionals, Researchers

Profile: The MARKET library contains a wide selection of sources ranging from trade and industry sources to InvestextR industry reports to company profiles. To round out the offering, MARKET also covers advertising, marketing, public opinion polls, market research, public relations, sales and selling, promotions, consumer attitudes, trends and behaviors, demographics, product announcements and product reviews. In addition, Predicasts Overview of Markets and Technology (PROMT), Marketing and Advertising Reference Service (MARS), US and International Forecast Databases (UFRCST and IFRCST) and the US Time Series (USTIME), all from Information Access Company, are available.

Contact: Mead New Sales Group at (800) 227-4908 or (513) 859-5398 inside the US, or (513) 865-7981 for all inquiries outside the US.

User Info: To Subscribe, contact Mead directly.

To examine the Nexis user guide, you can access it at the ftp site of the University of Texas at Austin at the URL address: ftp://ftp.cc.utexas.edu

The files are in: /pub/ref-services/LEXIS

`telnet://nex.meaddata.com`

`http://www.meaddata.com`

Market Conditions

Business Dateline

 ★★★

The database contains the full text of articles from more than 350 local and regional business publications from throughout the United States and Canada.

Keywords: Business, Regional Business, Market Conditions

Sponsor: UMI, Louisville, KY, USA

Audience: Business Analysts, Market Researchers, Writers

Profile: Sources include city business journals, daily newspapers, regional business magazines, and wire services. Subjects include city economic conditions, new product announcements, manufacturing methods, executive profiles, quality control, company histories, market conditions, service industries, regulations, litigation, and legislation.

Contact: Dialog in the US at (800) 334-2564, Dialog internationally at country specific locations.

Details: Costs

User Info: To Subscribe, contact Dialog directly.

`telnet://dialog.com`

Market Research

Research on Demand

 ★★★

A resource for the provision of market information, strategic information location, product information, and national and international business information.

Keywords: Market Research, Internet Research, Legal Research, International Research

Audience: Marketing Specialists, Lawyers, Public Relations Experts, Business Professionals, Researchers, Writers, Producers

Profile: This resource has special access to unique information resources worldwide. Areas of particular information access include the former Soviet Union, Europe, and the US. Information access also includes access to all the major online systems, including Dialog, BRS, Orbit, DataStar, and so on. Current Awareness Services include research information gathered from the Internet.

Details: Costs

User Info: To Subscribe, send an e-mail message to the URL address below. In the body of your message, state the nature of your inquiry.

Notes: Contact ROD directly in the US at: (800) 227-0750; outside the US at: (510) 841-1145.

`mailto:rod@holonet.net`

Marketing

MarketBase Gopher

An online catalog of goods and services dedicated to providing a forum where buyers and sellers meet to electronically exchange the attributes of products and services. Free access is provided to product purchasers.

Keywords: Internet Services, Marketing

Audience: Internet Surfers

Contact: help@mb.com

Details: Free

`gopher://mb.com`

Computer-Mediated Marketing Environments

A web site devoted to research aimed at understanding the ways in which computer-mediated marketing environments (CMEs), especially the Internet, are revolutionizing the way firms conduct business.

Keywords: WWW, Information Retrieval, Internet, Marketing, Business

Sponsor: Vanderbilt University, Owen Graduate School of Management, Nashville, Tennessee, USA

Audience: General Public, Entrepeneurs, Financial Planners, Marketers

Contact: Donna Hoffman, Tom Novak hoffman@colette.ogsm.vanderbilt.edu, novak@moe.ogsm.vanderbilt.edu

`http://colette.ogsm.vanderbilt.edu`

MARKET (Markets and Industries News and Information)

The Markets and Industries News and Information (MARKET) library contains sources covering developments in a wide variety of markets and industries.

Keywords: News, Analysis, Industry, Marketing

Audience: Business Professionals, Researchers

Profile: The MARKET library contains a wide selection of sources ranging from trade and industry sources to InvestextR industry reports to company profiles. To round out the offering, MARKET also covers advertising, marketing, public

---

opinion polls, market research, public relations, sales and selling, promotions, consumer attitudes, trends and behaviors, demographics, product announcements and product reviews. In addition, Predicasts Overview of Markets and Technology (PROMT), Marketing and Advertising Reference Service (MARS), US and International Forecast Databases (UFRCST and IFRCST) and the US Time Series (USTIME), all from Information Access Company, are available.

Contact: Mead New Sales Group at (800) 227-4908 or (513) 859-5398 inside the US, or (513) 865-7981 for all inquiries outside the US.

User Info: To Subscribe, contact Mead directly.

To examine the Nexis user guide, you can access it at the ftp site of the University of Texas at Austin at the URL address: ftp://ftp.cc.utexas.edu

The files are in: /pub/ref-services/LEXIS

`telnet://nex.meaddata.com`

`http://www.meaddata.com`

Marshall University School of Medicine (MUSOM) RuralNet Gopher

Marshall University School of Medicine (MUSOM) RuralNet Gopher

A gopher server dedicated to the improvement of rural health care.

Keywords: Rural Development, Health Care, Medical Treatment, Bioinformatics

Sponsor: Marshall University School of Medicine

Audience: Health Care Professionals, Medical Students

Profile: A collection of health care resources, with particular emphasis on rural health care. Includes listings of clinical resources by subject area, information on state and federal rural health care initiatives, and links to local and national health and education services.

Contact: Mike McCarthy, Andy Jarrell mmccarth@muvms6.wvnet.edu jarrell@musom01.mu.wvnet.edu

`gopher://ruralnet.mu.wvnet.edu`

Martial Arts

Aikido Information

An FTP site containing aikido dojo addresses from around the world, plus a calendar of events, FAQs, and lists of books and periodicals related to aikido.

Keywords: Aikido, Martial Arts, Sports

Sponsor: University of California at San Diego, San Diego, CA, USA

Audience: Aikido Enthusiasts, Martial Artists

Contact: aikido@cs.ucsd.edu

Details: Free

`ftp://cs.ucsd.edu/pub/aikido`

aikido-l

A discussion group and information exchange on the Japanese martial art Aikido.

Keywords: Aikido, Martial Arts

Sponsor: Gerry Santoro

Audience: Aikido Enthusiasts

Contact: aikido-l-request@psuvm.psu.edu

User Info: To Subscribe to the list, send an e-mail message to the URL address below consisting of a single line reading:

SUB aikido-l YourFirstName YourLastName.

To send a message to the entire list, address it to: aikido-l@psuvm.psu.edu

`mailto:listserv@psuvm.psu.edu`

rec.martial-arts

A Usenet newsgroup providing information and discussion about martial arts.

Keywords: Martial Arts

Audience: Martial Artists

User Info: To Subscribe to this Usenet newsgroup, you need access to a newsreader.

`news:rec.martial-arts`

Martin Marietta Energy Systems Gopher

Martin Marietta Energy Systems Gopher

Information on Martin Marietta's energy projects and technologies for both government and commercial applications.

Keywords: Technology, Energy, Industry

Sponsor: Martin Marietta

Audience: Business Professionals, Entrepreneurs, Manufactures, Energy Researchers, Technology Professionals

Profile: This gopher contains a list of technologies currently being developed at Martin Marietta as well as detailing facilities available to university, government, and commercial researchers. Also includes updates on employment openings, and a list of current publications.

A B C D E F G H I J K L **M** N O P Q R S T U V W X Y Z

Contact: gopher@ornl.gov

`gopher:// gopher.ornl.gov`

`http://www.ornl.gov/mmes.html`

Maryland

Maryland ★

System provides access to a wide range of state information, including the policies and activities of members of Maryland's congress and voting district data.

Keywords: Maryland, Law (US State), Voting

Audience: Maryland Residents, Lawyers

Details: Free

User Info: Select from menu as appropriate.

`gopher://info.umd.edu`

Mass Media

Communication and Mass Communication Resources ★★

An archive of materials related to mass communications and the media.

Keywords: Mass Media, Media, Journalism, Telecommunications, Advertising

Sponsor: The University of Iowa

Audience: Mass Communications Students and Teachers, Journalists, Broadcasting Professionals

Contact: Karla Tonella
Karla_Tonella@uiowa.edu

`gopher://iam41.arcade.uiowa.edu`

National Broadcasting Society— Alpha Epsilon Rho ★

Forum for mass media professionals to share experiences and ideas.

Keywords: Film, Television, Radio, Mass Media

Sponsor: National Broadcasting Society-Alpha Epsilon Rho

Audience: Journalists, Students, Educators, Broadcasting Professionals

Contact: Reg Gamar
regbc@cunyvm.bitnet

Details: Free

User Info: To Subscribe to the list, send an e-mail message to the address shown below consisting of a single line reading:

SUB NBS-AER YourFirstName YourLastName

To send a message to thhe entire list, address it to: nbs-aer@cunyvm.bitnet

`mailto:listserv@cunyvm.bitnet`

ViewPoints ★

Newsletter of the Visual Communication Division of the Association of Educators in Journalism and Mass Communication.

Keywords: Journalism, Mass Media, Visual Communication

Audience: Educators, Photographers, Desktop Publishers

Contact: Paul Lester
lester@fullerton.edu

Details: Free

`mailto:lester@fullerton.edu`

Massachusetts Institute of Technology Library

Massachusetts Institute of Technology Library ★

The library's holdings are large and wide-ranging and contain significant collections in many fields.

Keywords: Aeronautics (History of), Linguistics, Mathematics (History of), Microscopy, Spectroscopy, Aeronautics, Mathematics, Glass

Audience: General Public, Researchers, Librarians, Document Delivery Professionals

Details: Free

User Info: Expect: Mitek Server..., Send: Enter or Return; Expect: prompt, Send: hollis

`telnet://library.mit.edu`

Material Science

Material Science in Israel Newsletter ★

Newsletter on bitnet, for people interested in material sciences, established to allow important local and international information to be disseminated efficiently and rapidly to all interested parties.

Keywords: Material Science, Israel

Audience: Material Scientists

Contact: Michael Wolff
wolff@ilncrd.bitnet

Details: Free

User Info: To Subscribe to the list, send an e-mail message to the URL address below, consisting of a single line reading:

SUB YourFirstName YourLastName

To send a message to the entire list, address it to: @taunivmbitnet

`mailto:listserv@taunivmbitnet`

Materials Business File

Covers all commercial aspects of iron and steel, non-ferrous metals and non-metallic materials.

Keywords: Material Science, Business, Iron, Steel

Sponsor: Materials Information, a joint information service of ASM International and the Institute of Materials

Audience: Material Scientists, Researchers

Profile: Articles are abstracted from over 2,000 worldwide technical and trade journals to create more than 65,000 records. Update monthly.

Contact: paul.albert@neteast.com

User Info: To Subscribe contact Orbit-Questel directly.

`telnet://orbit.com`

METADEX

International literature covering metals and alloys.

Keywords: Material Science, Metals, Alloys

Sponsor: Materials Information, a joint information service of ASM International and the Institute of Materials

Audience: Material Scientists, Researchers

Profile: Contains more than 925,000 records from the international literature on metals and alloys concerning processes, properties, materials classes, applications, specific alloy designations, intermetallic compounds and metallurgical systems. Updated monthly.

Contact: paul.albert@neteast.com

User Info: To Subscribe contact Orbit-Questel directly.

`telnet://orbit.com`

PIRA - Paper, Printing and Publishing, Packaging, and Nonwovens Abstracts

Coverage of all aspects of paper, pulp, nonwovens, printing, publishing and packaging.

Keywords: Material Science, Paper, Printing, Publishing, Packaging, Nonwovens

Sponsor: PIRA International

Audience: Material Scientists, Researchers

Profile: File contains more than 300,000 records. Special applications: company and market profiles, product and trade name searches, research and technology trends. Updated biweekly.

Contact: paul.albert@neteast.com

User Info: To Subscribe contact Orbit-Questel directly.

`telnet://orbit.com`

RAPRA Abstracts

Coverage on technical and commercial aspects of the rubber, plastics, and polymer composites industries.

Keywords: Material Science, Rubbers, Plastics, Polymers

Sponsor: Rapra Technology, Ltd.

Audience: Material Scientists, Researchers

Profile: This unique source of information covers the world's polymer literature including journals, conference proceedings, books, specifications, reports and trade literature. Contains over 375,000 records. Updated biweekly.

Contact: paul.albert@neteast.com

User Info: To Subscribe contact Orbit-Questel directly.

`telnet://orbit.com`

Mathematical Biology

Smbnet (Society for Mathematical Biology Digest)

Keywords: Mathematical Biology, Biology

Audience: Mathematical Biologists, Biologists

Contact: Ray Mejia

Details: Free

User Info: To Subscribe to the list, send an e-mail message to the URL address below consisting of a single line reading:

SUB smbnet YourFirstName YourLastName

To send a message to the entire list, address it to: smbnet@fconvx.ncifcrf.gov

`mailto:listserv@fconvx.ncifcrf.gov`

Mathematics (Algorithms)

comp.compression

A Usenet newsgroup providing information and discussion about data compression algorithms and theory.

Keywords: Computers, Mathematics (Algorithms)

Audience: Computer Users

User Info: To Subscribe to this Usenet newsgroup, you need access to a newsreader.

`news:comp.compression`

Mathematics

alife

The alife mailing list is for communications regarding artificial life, a formative interdisciplinary field involving computer science, the natural sciences, mathematics, and medicine.

Keywords: Artificial Life, Science, Mathematics

Sponsor: UCLA

Audience: Scientists, Biologists, Mathematicians

Contact: alife-request@cognet.ucla.edu

User Info: To Subscribe to the list, send an e-mail message to the URL address below.

To send a message to the entire list, address it to: alife@cognet.ucla.edu

`mailto:alife-request@cognet.ucla.edu`

Anneal

A mailing list for the discussion of simulated annealing techniques and analysis, as well as related issues such as stochastic optimization, Boltzmann machines, and metricity of NP-complete move spaces.

Keywords: Mathematics, Simulation, Annealing

Sponsor: UCLA

Audience: Mathematicians, Physicists

Contact: Daniel R. Greening
anneal-request@cs.ucla.edu

User Info: To Subscribe to the list, send an e-mail message to the URL address below.

To send a message to the entire list, address it to: anneal@cs.ucla.edu

Notes: Membership is restricted to those doing active research in simulated annealing or related areas.

`mailto:anneal-request@cs.ucla.edu`

CEM-L

A mailing list for discussion surrounding the UTD (University of Texas at Dallas) Center for Engineering Mathematics.

Keywords: Engineering, Mathematics

Audience: Engineers, Mathematicians, Educators, Students

Contact: David Lippke
lippke@utdallas

Details: Free

User Info: To Subscribe to the list, send an e-mail message to the URL address below, consisting of a single line reading:

SUB cem-l YourFirstName YourLastName

To send a message to the entire list, address it to: CEM-L@UTDALLAS.EDU

`mailto:listserv@utdallas.edu`

Euromath Center Gopher Server

A gopher server providing information about the Euromath Center, the Euromath Project, and related activities.

Keywords: Europe, Mathematics, Euromath

Sponsor: University of Copenhagen

Audience: Mathematicians, Europeans

Contact: Klaus Harbo
emc@euromath.dk

Details: Free

`gopher://laurel.euromath.dk`

Massachusetts Institute of Technology Library

The library's holdings are large and wide-ranging and contain significant collections in many fields.

Keywords: Aeronautics (History of), Linguistics, Mathematics (History of), Microscopy, Spectroscopy, Aeronautics, Mathematics, Glass

Audience: General Public, Researchers, Librarians, Document Delivery Professionals

Details: Free

Notes: Expect: Mitek Server..., Send: Enter or Return; Expect: prompt, Send: hollis

`telnet://library.mit.edu`

NCTM-L

A mailing list for the discussion of standards applying to the National Council of Teachers of Mathematics.

Keywords: Education, Mathematics

Audience: Mathematics Educators

Contact: barry@sci-ed.fit.edu

Details: Free

User Info: To Subscribe to this list, send an e-mail message to the URL address below, consisting of a single line reading:

SUB nctm-l YourFirstName YourLastName.

To send a message to the entire list, address it to: nctm-l@sci-ed.fit.edu

`mailto:listproc@sci-ed.fit.edu`

Pd-games

A mailing list for people interested in game theory, especially Prisoner's Dilemma types of problems. Discussions include purely technical issues and questions, as well as specific scientific applications and the political and ideological aspects and consequences of game theory.

Keywords: Game Theory, Mathematics

Audience: Game Theorists, Mathematicians

Contact: Thomas Gramstad
pd-games-request@math.uio.no

Details: Free

User Info: To Subscribe to the list, send an e-mail message requesting a subscription to the URL address below.

To send a message to the entire list, address it to: pd-games@math.uio.no

`mailto:pd-games-request@math.uio.no`

sci.math

A Usenet newsgroup providing information and discussion about mathematics.

Keywords: Mathematics

Audience: Mathematicians

Details: Free

To subscribe to this Usenet newsgroup, you need access to a newsreader.

`news:sci.math`

Spanky Fractal Database

★★★★

This Web site provides a collection of fractals and fractal-related material for free distribution on the Internet.

Keywords: Mathematics, Chaos Theory, Computer Programming, Computer Graphics

Audience: Mathematicians, Computer Programmers

Profile: Contains information on dynamical systems, software, distributed fractal generators, galleries, and databases from all over the world.

Contact: Noel Giffin
noel@triumf.ca

Details: Free

`http://spanky.triumf.ca`

Statlib

★★★

Statlib is an archive of statistics-related materials.

Keywords: Statistics, Mathematics

Audience: Statisticians, Mathematicians

Profile: This archive contains a large collection of statistics software data. The directory lists the source to entire statistics packages, the collection of applied statistics algorithms, the archives of the s-new mailing list, and more.

Contact: statlib@lib.stat.cmu.edu

Details: Free

`ftp://lib.stat.cmu.edu`

University of Michigan Library

★★

The library's holdings are large and wide-ranging and contain significant collections in many fields.

Keywords: Asia, Astronomy, Transportation, Lexicology, Mathamatics, Zoology, Geography

Audience: Researchers, Students, General Public

Contact: info@merit.edu

Details: Free

Notes: Expect: Which Host; Send: Help

`telnet://cts.merit.edu`

University of Wisconsin at Stout Library

★★

The library's holdings are large and wide-ranging and contain significant collections in many fields.

Keywords: Mathematics, Business, Fashion Merchandising, Home Economics, Hospitality, Tourism, Hotel Administration, Restaurant Management, Microelectronics

Audience: Researchers, Students, General Public

Details: Free

Notes: Expect: Login, Send: Lib; Expect: vDIAL Prompt, Send: Library

`telnet://lib.uwstout.edu`

May (Julian)

Milieu

★

Discussion of the works of Julian May, notably the Saga of the Exiles and the Galactic Milieu Trilogy.

Keywords: May (Julian), Science Fiction

Audience: Julian May Readers

Contact: milieu-request@yoyo.cc.monash.edu.au

Details: Free

User Info: To subscribe to the list, send an e-mail message requesting a subscription to the URL address below.

`mailto:milieu-request@yoyo.cc.monash.edu.au`

Mazda Miata

Miata

★

An open forum for Mazda Miata owners.

Keywords: Mazda Miata, Automobiles

Audience: Automobile Owners

Details: Free

User Info: To Subscribe to the list, send an e-mail message requesting subscription to the URL address below.

`mailto:miata-request@jhunix.hcf.jhu.edu`

MBI, Music and the Brain Information Center Database (MuSICA)

MBI, Music and the Brain Information Center Database (MuSICA)

★★★★

The intent of this resource is to establish a comprehensive database of scientific research on music.

Keywords: Music Resources, Human Behavior, Neurology

Sponsor: Music and the Brain Information Center

Audience: Researchers, Scientists

Profile: MuSICA maintains a data base of scientific research (references and abstracts) on music as related to behavior, the brain and allied fields, in order to foster interdisciplinary knowledge. Topics include the auditory system; human and animal behavior; creativity; the neuropsychology of music and the human brain; the effects of music on behavior and physiology; music education, medicine, performance, and therapy; neurobiology; perception and psychophysics. Citations and abstracts are excerpted from the following journals: The Bulletin of the Council for Research in Music Education, The Journal of Research in Music Education, Music Perception, Psychology of Music, Psychomusicology.

Contact: Norman Weinberger, Gordon Shaw
mbic@mila.ps.uci.edu

Details: Free

Expect login: Send mbi Expect password: Send nammbi

`telnet://mila.ps.uci.edu`

McDonnell Douglas Aerospace

McDonnell Douglas Aerospace

★★

A Web site providing information about McDonnell Douglas, including a company profile and related discussion about technology.

Keywords: Aerospace, Space, Aviation, Technology

Audience: Aerospace Engineers

Contact: mail to: Zook@pat.mdc.com

`http://pat.mdc.com`

McGill University, Montreal Canada, INFOMcGILL Library

McGill University, Montreal Canada, INFOMcGILL Library

The library's holdings are large and wide-ranging and contain significant collections in many fields.

Keywords: Architecture, Entomology, Biology, Science (History of), Medicine (History of), Napolean, Shakespeare (William)

Audience: Researchers, Students, General Public

Contact: Roy Miller
ccrmmus@mcgillm (Bitnet) or
ccrmmus@musicm.mcgill.ca (Internet)

Notes: Expect: VM logo; Send: Enter; Expect: prompt; Send: PF3 or type INFO

`telnet://vm1.mcgill.ca`

mda

mda

Discussion of the Mighty Ducks of Anaheim of the National Hockey League, including statistics and game summaries.

Keywords: Hockey, Sports

Audience: Hockey Enthusiasts, Hockey Players

Details: Free

User Info: To Subscribe to the list, send an e-mail message to the URL address below, consisting of a single line reading:

SUB mda YourFirstName YourLastName

To send a message to the entire list, address it to: mda@macsch.com

`mailto:mda@macsch.com`

MDEAFR

MDEAFR

The Middle East and Africa (MDEAFR) library contains detailed information about every country in the Mideast and Africa. Structured for those who want to follow the unfolding events in the Gulf states, as well as in North and South Africa, this library contains a broad array of sources, including international research reports from InvestextR.

Keywords: News, Analysis, Companies, Middle East, Africa

Audience: Journalists, Business Professionals

Profile: The MDEAFR library contains a wide array of pertinent sources. Among the information sources are newspapers and wire services, trade and business journals, company reports, country and region background, industry and product analysis, business opportunities, and selected legal texts. News sources range from the world-renowned Associated Press and Christian Science Monitor to the regionally important Jerusalem Post and Africa News. Company information is contained in the EXTEL cards as well as ICC. Providers of country background and industry analysis include Associated Banks of Europe, Bank of America, Business International, IBC USA, and the US Department of Commerce. Customers interested in new business opportunities can check OPIC and Foreign Trade Opportunities (FTO).

Contact: Mead New Sales Group at (800) 227-4908 or (513) 859-5398 inside the US, or (513) 865-7981 for all inquiries outside the US.

User Info: To Subscribe, contact Mead directly.

To examine the Nexis user guide, you can access it at the ftp site of the University of Texas at Austin at the URL address: ftp://ftp.cc.utexas.edu

The files are in: /pub/ref-services/LEXIS

`telnet://nex.meaddata.com`

`http://www.meaddata.com`

MECH-L

MECH-L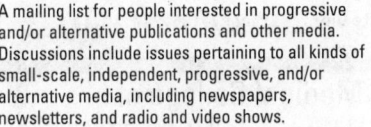

A mailing list for the discussion of mechanical engineering.

Keywords: Mechanical Engineering

Audience: Engineers, Mechanical Engineers

Contact: S. Nomura
b470ssn@utarlvm1.uta.edu

Details: Free

User Info: To Subscribe to the list, send an e-mail message to the URL address below consisting of a single line reading:

SUB mech-l YourFirstName YourLastName.

To send a message to the entire list, address it to: mech-l@utarlvm1.uta.edu

`mailto:listserv@utarlvm1.uta.edu`

Media

Communication and Mass Communication Resources

An archive of materials related to mass communications and the media.

Keywords: Mass Communications, Media, Journalism, Telecommunications, Advertising

Sponsor: The University of Iowa

Audience: Mass Communications Students and Teachers, Journalists, Broadcasting Professionals

Contact: Karla Tonella
karla_tonella@uiowa.edu

`gopher://iam41.arcade.uiowa.edu`

Prog-Pubs

A mailing list for people interested in progressive and/or alternative publications and other media. Discussions include issues pertaining to all kinds of small-scale, independent, progressive, and/or alternative media, including newspapers, newsletters, and radio and video shows.

Keywords: Media, Alternative Press, Communications

Audience: Students (college/university), Independent Media Professionals

Contact: prog-pubs-request@fuggles.acc.virginia.edu

Details: Free

User Info: To Subscribe to the list, send an e-mail message requesting a subscription to the URL address below.

To send a message to the entire list, address it to:prog-pubs@fuggles.acc.virginia.edu

`mailto:prog-pubs@fuggles.acc.virginia.edu`

Mediation

NAME (National Association for Mediation in Education) Publications and Resources List

This is a tax-exempt clearinghouse of information promoting conflict resolution, mediation, and violence prevention in schools. NAME also publishes a newsletter and has a directory of over 120 resources, including guidelines for conflict resolution, and technical assistance.

Keywords: Conflict Resolution, Mediation, Education (K-12)

Sponsor: National Association for Mediation in Education, University of Massachusetts, Amherst, Massachusetts, USA

A
B
C
D
E
F
G
H
I
J
K
L
M
N
O
P
Q
R
S
T
U
V
W
X
Y
Z

Audience: Counselors, Educators, Administrators, Parents

Contact: Clarinda Merripen
conflictnet@agc.ipc.org

Request introductory packet from address below.

```
mailto:conflictnet@agc.ipc.org
```

Medical College of Ohio Library Online Catalogue

Medical College of Ohio Library Online Catalogue ★★

Catalog of library holdings.

Keywords: Medicine, Libraries

Sponsor: Medical College of Ohio

Audience: Health Professionals, Medical Researchers, Educators, Students

Details: Free

```
telnet://library@136.247.10.14
```

Medical College of Wisconsin Library Online Catalogue

Medical College of Wisconsin Library Online Catalogue ★★

Catalog of library holdings.

Keywords: Medicine, Libraries

Sponsor: Medical College of Wisconsin

Audience: Health Professionals, Medical Researchers, Educators, Students

Details: Free

```
telnet://ils.lib.mcw.edu
```

Medical Informatics

CAMIS (Center for Advanced Medical Informatics at Stanford)

CAMIS is a shared computing resource supporting research activities in biomedical informatics.

Keywords: Medical Informatics, Heuristics, Health Sciences

Sponsor: Stanford University School of Medicine, Palo Alto, CA, USA

Audience: Medical Informatics, Health Science Researchers

Profile: The CAMIS gopher includes an Internet-wide title search, computing information, and technical reports for the Section on Medical Informatics (SMI) community as well as that of the Knowledge Systems Laboratory (KSL), information on the Heuristic Programming Project, pointers to various online library catalogs, and more.

Contact: torsten_heycke@med.stanford.edu

```
gopher://camis.stanford.edu/00/
gopherdoc
```

Medical News

HICNet Newsletter (MEDNEWS - The Health InfoCom Newsletter)  ★★★

Usually published once a week, this is a large newsletter that is broken up into multiple sections to facilitate network movement.

Keywords: Health, Medical News

Audience: Health Professionals

Contact: David Dodell
ddodell@stjhmc.fidonet.org

Details: Free

```
mailto:listserv@asuacad.bitnet
```

Medical Research

Discipline and Disease Specific Sources

This database contains links to sources of Medical and Health Care information. Has disease-specific resources for AIDS, Cancer, Parkinson's Disease, and Sudden Infant Death Syndrome, among others. Also covers over 30 discipline-specific sources, ranging from anesthesiology to tropical medicine.

Keywords: Medicine, Diseases, Medical Research

Sponsor: University of Miami Biomedical Gopher Project, Miami, Florida, USA

Audience: Medical Professionals, Medical Researchers, Medical Practitioners

Contact: Thomas Williams, Michael Cutherell
twilliam@mednet.med.miami.edu
mcuthere@mednet.med.miami.edu

Details: Free

```
gopher://caldmed.med.miami.edu
```

Health News Daily  ★★★

The database contains all the daily news and full-text articles from Health News Daily, a publication from F-D-C Reports, Inc.

Keywords: Health, Pharmacology, Medical Research, News

Sponsor: F-D-C Reports, Inc., Chevy Chase, MD, US

Audience: Health Professionals, Pharmaceutical Industry, Market Researchers

Profile: The database provides specialized, in-depth business, scientific, regulatory, and legal news. Timely coverage of pharmacy and pharmaceuticals is given, as well as coverage of medical devices and diagnostics, medical research, cosmetics, health policy, provider payment policies, and cost containment in national health care.

Coverage: 1990 to the present; updated daily.

Contact: Dialog in the US at (800) 334-2564, Dialog internationally at country-specific locations.

Details: Costs

User Info: To Subscribe, contact Dialog directly.

```
telnet://dialog.com
```

Medical and Biological Research in Laboratories Institutions (Israel) ★★

A descriptive listing of medical research and diagnostic laboratories in Israel. This site also has information on medical research being carried out in Israeli universities and hospitals.

Keywords: Medical Research, Biological Research, Israel

Audience: Medical Researchers, Biomedical Researchers, Medical Professionals

Profile: MATIMOP, The Israeli Industry Center for Health Care Research And Development, is a non-profit service organization, founded by an Israeli association of hospitals, universities, and other medical researchers, aiming their activities at promoting cooperation of Israeli entrepreneurs and manufacturers with qualified business firms abroad. This gopher details specific medical and biological research projects in progress in every department of every major Israeli health care institution: including universities, The General Federation of Labour, public hospitals, government-municipal hospitals, government hospitals, as well as medical and biological research in the Israeli laboratories and research institutes.

Contact: rdinfo@matimop.org.il

```
gopher://gopher.matimop.org.il
```

Poisons Information Database ★★

Directories of antivenoms, toxicologists, poison control centers, and poisons from around the world.

Keywords: Medical Research, Bioscience

Sponsor: Venom and Toxin Research Group, Department of Anatomy, National University of Singapore, Singapore

Audience: Biologists, Researchers, Medical Professionals, Toxicologists

Contact: Professor P. Gopalkrishnakone
antgopal@leonis.nus.sg

```
http://biomed.nus.sg/PID/PID.html
```

sci.med.physics

A Usenet newsgroup providing information and discussion about physics in medical testing and care.

Keywords: Physics, Medical Research, Health Care

Audience: Physicists, Medical Researchers, Medical Practitioners, Health Care Professionals

Details: Free

User Info: To Subscribe to this Usenet newsgroup, you need access to a newsreader.

`news:sci.med.physics`

Medical Treatment

Accri-I

A mailing list providing information on anesthesia and critical care resources available via the Internet.

Keywords: Health Care, Medical Treatment, Medicine

Audience: Health Care Professionals, Health Care Providers

Contact: A.J. Wright
meds002@uabdpo.dpo.uab.edu

User Info: To Subscribe, send an e-mail message to the URL address below consisting of a single line reading:

SUB accri-I YourFirstName YourLastName.

To send a message to the entire list, address it to: accri-I@uabdpo.dpo.uab.edu

`mailto:listserv@uabdpo.dpo.uab.edu`

Health and Clinical Information & Bioethics Online Service

A collection of gopher links to servers offering a wide variety of health information.

Keywords: Medicine, Medical Treatment, Health Care

Sponsor: Medical College of Wisconsin (MCW) InfoScope, Wisconsin, USA

Audience: Health Care Professionals, Health Care Providers

Profile: Links include the National Institutes of Health, MedNews Digest, Family Medicine list archives, and full-text of national health plans. Also features the Bioethics Online Service, which provides updates, journal abstracts, alerts, and a forum for discussing medical ethics. Site specific information on MCW physicians and surgeons is also available.

Contact: Dieta Murra
mcw-info@its.mcw.edu

`gopher://post.its.mcw.edu`

Marshall University School of Medicine (MUSOM) RuralNet Gopher

A gopher server dedicated to the improvement of rural health care.

Keywords: Rural Development, Health Care, Medical Treatment, Bioinformatics

Sponsor: Marshall University School of Medicine

Audience: Health Care Professionals, Medical Students

Profile: A collection of health care resources, with particular emphasis on rural health care. Includes listings of clinical resources by subject area, information on state and federal rural health care initiatives, and links to local and national health and education services.

Contact: Mike McCarthy, Andy Jarrell
mmccarth@muvms6.wvnet.edu
jarrell@musom01.mu.wvnet.edu

`gopher://ruralnet.mu.wvnet.edu`

Medicine

(The) Center for Biomedical Informatics of the State University of Campinas, Brazil

A directory of medical applications of informatics.

Keywords: Health, Medicine, Informatics

Sponsor: State University of Campinas, Brazil

Audience: Medical Professionals, Medical Educators, Medical Researchers

Profile: Designed to foster educational and practical uses of computers in medicine and the health sciences by providing free international access to resources.

Contact: Renato M.E. Sabbatini
sabbatini@ccvax.unicamp.br

Details: Free

`ftp://ccsun.unicamp.br`

Accri-I

A mailing list providing information on anesthesia and critical care resources available via the Internet.

Keywords: Health Care, Medical Treatment, Medicine

Audience: Health Care Professionals, Health Care Providers

Contact: A.J. Wright
meds002@uabdpo.dpo.uab.edu

User Info: To Subscribe, send an e-mail message to the URL address below consisting of a single line reading:

SUB accri-I YourFirstName YourLastName.

To send a message to the entire list, address it to: accri-I@uabdpo.dpo.uab.edu

`mailto:listserv@uabdpo.dpo.uab.edu`

Aids

A forum for the discussion of AIDS, predominantly from a medical perspective, but also with some discussion of political and social issues.

Keywords: AIDS, Medicine, Politics, Society

Sponsor: UCLA

Audience: AIDS Researchers, AIDS Activists, Health Care Providers

Contact: Daniel R. Greening
aids-request@cs.ucla.edu

User Info: To Subscribe to the list, send an e-mail message to the URL address below.

To send a message to the entire list, address it to: aids@cs.ucla.edu

`mailto:aids-request@cs.ucla.edu`

AIDS Treatment News

A newsletter on AIDS treatment.

Keywords: AIDS, HIV, Health, Medicine

Sponsor: IGC (Institute for Global Communications)

Audience: AIDS Researchers, Health Workers, AIDS Sufferers

Profile: This newsletter contains interviews, reports on new and existing treatment modalities, announcements of clinical drug testing trial, and more.

Contact: atn@igc.apc.org

Details: Free

`gopher://odie.niaid.nih.gov/11/aids`

AIDS/HIV Information

A clearinghouse for AIDS/HIV-related information. Contains Internet connections to WWW and gopher servers, and archives of AIDS server FAQ's, including an archive of AIDS treatment news.

Keywords: AIDS, Medicine, Health

Sponsor: Queer Resources Directory, USA

Audience: AIDS Sufferers, Gays, Students, Activists

Contact: QRD Staff
QRDstaff@vector.casti.com

Details: AIDS Treatment News

`http://vector.casti.com/QRD/.html/AIDS.html`

A
B
C
D
E
F
G
H
I
J
K
L
M
N
O
P
Q
R
S
T
U
V
W
X
Y
Z

AIDSLINE

 ★★★

The AIDSLINE database is a bibliography of research and clinical information as well as health policy issues concerning AIDS. The citations in AIDSLINE are primarily derived from MEDLINE, Health Planning & Administration, CancerLit, CATLINE, AVLINE, the meeting abstracts from the International Conferences on AIDS, the Symposia on Non-human Models of AIDS, and AIDS-related abstracts from the Annual Meetings of the American Society of Microbiology.

Keywords: AIDS, Medicine

Sponsor: U.S. National Library of Medicine

Audience: AIDS Researchers, Epidemiologists, Clinicians, AIDS Sufferers

Contact: CDP Technologies Sales Department (800)950-2035, extension 400

User Info: To Subscribe, contact CDP Technologies directly

`telnet://cdplus@cdplus.com`

Allied and Alternative Medicine (AMED)

 ★★★★

The Allied and Alternative Medicine database covers the fields of contemporary and alternative medicine.

Keywords: Medicine, Alternative Medicine

Sponsor: Medical Information Service, British Library, Boston Spa, West Yorkshire, UK

Audience: Doctors, Nurses, Health Care Providers, Medical Practitioners, Health Care Industry, General Public

Profile: The AMED database will be of interest to all those who need to know more about alternatives to conventional medicine, such as doctors, nurses and other medical practitioners, therapists, health care libraries, specialist colleges, self-help groups, and the pharmaceutical industry. Coverage includes acupuncture, homeopathy, hypnosis, chiropractic, osteopathy, psychotherapy, diet therapy, herbalism, holistic treatment, traditional Chinese medicine, occupational therapy, physiotherapy, rehabilitation, ayurvedic medicine, reflexology, iridology, moxibustion, meditation, yoga, healing research, and the Alexander Technique.

Contact: Data-star through Dialog in the US at (800) 334-2564; Dialog internationally at country-specific locations.

Details: Costs

User Info: To Subscribe, contact Dialog directly.

`telnet://dialog.com`

Alternative Medicine, the Definitive Guide

A one-stop reference covering common health problems and leading alternative therapies.

Keywords: Alternative Medicine, Medicine, Health, Health Care

Sponsor: Future Medicine Publishing, Inc.

Audience: General Public, Health Care Professionals

Profile: Spanning a global effort of 4 years and input from nearly 400 Health Care professionals, this one stop reference offers 1100 pages of in-depth explanations to 43 of the leading alternative therapies. In addition to covering over 200 of the most common health problems, a wide range of choices to maintaining and regaining your health are highlighted with graphic illustrations. This is truly the "Voice of Alternative Medicine."

Details: Costs

`FutureMd@CRL.com`

Biomedical Computer Laboratory (BCL)

 ★★★

A resource for biomedical computing.

Keywords: Health, Biomedical Computing, Biology, Medicine

Sponsor: Washington University School of Medicine

Audience: Medical Researchers, Biologists

Profile: A significant portion of the activities at BCL are supported by the National Center for Research Resources' Biomedical Research Technology Program (BRTP), which promotes the application of advances in computer science and technology, engineering, mathematics, and the physical sciences to research problems in biology and medicine by supporting the development of advanced research technologies.

Contact: Kenneth W. Clark info@wubcl.wustl.edu

Details: Free

Notes: Expect: login; Send: anonymous

Notes: Investigators wishing to explore the possibility of interactions with BCL at Washington University should send e-mail (preferred).

`ftp://wubcl.wustl.edu`

BOING (Bio-Oriented INternet Gophers)

 ★★★★

A searcheable gopher index, BOING is used to search through the titles of items in bio-gopher space and to access the items returned.

Keywords: Biological Sciences, Health, Medicine

Audience: Health Professionals, Biomedical Researchers, Students (college, graduate)

Details: Free

`gopher://gopher.gdb.org`

BRIDGE

 ★

An online public access catalogue, the PALS-based catalog provides access to the collections of two institutions, St. Boniface University and the Manitoba General Hospital.

Keywords: Medicine, Library

Sponsor: St. Boniface University, and the Manitoba General Hospital Libraries

Audience: Health Professionals, Students, Medical Educators

Details: Free

`telnet://BE@umopac.umanitoba.ca`

Denmark's Library for Medicine and Science

 ★★

Keywords: Science, Medicine, Libraries, Denmark

Audience: Scientists, Health Care Professionals, Medical Researchers

Details: Free

At the CCL>prompt type DIA ENG for English interface.

`telnet://cosmos.bib.dk`

Discipline and Disease Specific Sources

This database contains links to sources of Medical and Health Care information. Has disease-specific resources for AIDS, Cancer, Parkinson's Disease, and Sudden Infant Death Syndrome, among others. Also covers over 30 discipline-specific sources, ranging from anesthesiology to tropical medicine.

Keywords: Medicine, Diseases, Medical Research

Sponsor: University of Miami Biomedical Gopher Project, Miami, Florida, USA

Audience: Medical Professionals, Medical Researchers, Medical Practitioners

Contact: Thomas Williams, Michael Cutherell twilliam@mednet.med.miami.edu, mcuthere@mednet.med.miami.edu

Details: Free

`gopher://caldmed.med.miami.edu`

EMBASE

 ★★★★

EMBASE is an acclaimed comprehensive index of international literature on medicine, science and pharmacology.

Keywords: Medicine, Science, Pharmacology

Sponsor: Elsevier Science Publishers

Audience: Librarians, Researchers, Students, Physicians

Contact: CDP Technologies Sales Department (800)950-2035, extension 400

User Info: To Subscribe, contact CDP Technologies directly

`telnet://cdplus@cdplus.com`

Fam-Med

An Internet resource and discussion group on computers in family medicine.

Keywords: Medicine, Computers, Telecommunications

Sponsor: Gustavus Adolphus College, Minnesota

Audience: Health CareProfessionals, Family Physicians

Profile: Fam-Med is an electronic conference and file area that focuses on the use of computer and telecommunication technologies in the teaching and practice of family medicine. The conference and files are accessible to anyone able to send e-mail. The discussion on Fam-Med is distributed in two ways: by an unmoderated mail echo in which all posted messages are immediately distributed to subscribers without human intervention, and by a digest where messages accumulated over several days are assembled into a single document with erroneous posts deleted.

Contact: Paul Kleeberg
paul@gac.edu

Details: Free

To join either the unmoderated list or the digest, send e-mail to the contact above. To post to Fam-Med, send e-mail to fam-med@gac.edu

`gopher://ftp.gac.edu/00/pub/e-mail-archives/fam-med/`

GenBank

The GenBank database provides a collection of nucleotide sequences as well as relevant bibliographic and biological annotation.

Keywords: Genetics, Medicine, Molecular Biology

Sponsor: National Center for Biotechnology Information (NCBI) at the National Library of Medicine (NLM)

Audience: Geneticists, Scientists, Molecular Biologists

Profile: DNA sequence entries are rated by specialized indexers in the Division of Library Operations. Over 325,000 articles per year from 3,400 journals are scanned for sequence data. They are supplemented by journals in plant and veterinary sciences through a collaboration with the National Agricultural Library. These records join the direct submission data stream and submissions from the European Molecular Biology Laboratory (EMBL) Data Library and the DNA Database of Japan (DDBJ).

Contact: info@ncbi.nlm.nih.gov

Details: Free

Send direct submissions to gb-sub@ncbi.nlm.nih.gov and updates and changes to existing GenBank records to update@ncbi.nlm.nih.gov

For help in retrieval by e-mail send an e-mail message with the word "help" in the the body of the message to retrieve@ncbi.nlm.hih.gov

`gopher://gopher.nih.gov/77/gopherlib/indices/genbank/index`

GENMED (General Medical Information)

The General Medical Information (GENMED) library contains a variety of medical care and treatment, toxicology, and hospital administration materials.

Keywords: Medicine, Toxicology, Hospital, Treatment

Audience: Medical Professionals

Profile: The GENMED library contains full-text medical journals and newsletters, as well as drug information, disease and trauma reviews, Physicians Data Query cancer information, and medical administration journals. GENMED also offers a gateway to the MEDLINE database.

Contact: Mead New Sales Group at (800) 227-4908 or (513) 859-5398 inside the US, or (513) 865-7981 for all inquiries outside the US.

User Info: To Subscribe, contact Mead directly.

To examine the Nexis user guide, you can access it at the ftp site of the University of Texas at Austin at the URL address: ftp://ftp.cc.utexas.edu

The files are in: /pub/ref-services/LEXIS

`telnet://nex.meaddata.com`

`http://www.meaddata.com`

Georgetown University Medical Center Online Catalogue

This site maintains a catalog of the Georgetown University Medical Center library's holdings.

Keywords: Medicine, Library

Sponsor: Georgetown University, Washington, DC

Audience: Medical Professionals, Educators, Students

Contact: Jane Banks
banksj@gumedlib2.georgetown.edu

Details: Free

The password is dahlgren, then enter netguest, hit RETURN several times and select option 1.

`telnet://medlib@gumedlib.georgetown.edu`

Harvard Medical Gopher

This gopher site accesses information from Harvard Medical School. Provides bibliographic information from Harvard Medical Library, basic science and clinical resources, and public health and government statistics.

Keywords: Medicine, Libraries, Health Care

Sponsor: Physicians, Health Care Professionals, Educators, Students <Standard Producer>Harvard Medical School, Cambridge, Massachusetts, USA

Audience: Physicians, Health Care Professionals, Educators, Students <Standard Producer>Harvard Medical School, Cambridge, Massachusetts, USA

Contact: gopher@warren.med.harvard.edu

Details: Free

`gopher://gopher.med.harvard.edu`

Health and Clinical Information & Bioethics Online Service

A collection of gopher links to servers offering a wide variety of health information.

Keywords: Medicine, Medical Treatment, Health Care

Sponsor: Medical College of Wisconsin (MCW) InfoScope, Wisconsin, USA

Audience: Health Care Professionals, Health Care Providers

Profile: Links include the National Institutes of Health, MedNews Digest, Family Medicine list archives, and full-text of national health plans. Also features the Bioethics Online Service, which provides updates, journal abstracts, alerts, and a forum for discussing medical ethics. Site specific information on MCW physicians and surgeons is also available.

Contact: Dieta Murra
mcw-info@its.mcw.edu

`gopher://post.its.mcw.edu`

Health Periodicals Database

This source covers a broad range of health subjects and issues.

Keywords: Health, Biotechnology, Medicine, Nutrition

Sponsor: Information Access Company, Foster City, CA, US

Audience: Health Professionals, Dieticians, Librarians

Profile: The database provides indexing and full text of journals covering a broad range of health subjects and issues including: prenatal care, dieting, drug abuse, AIDS, biotechnology, cardiovascular disease, environment, public health, safety, paramedical professions, sports medicine, substance abuse, toxicology, and much more.

A B C D E F G H I J K L **M** N O P Q R S T U V W X Y Z

A
B
C
D
E
F
G
H
I
J
K
L
M
N
O
P
Q
R
S
T
U
V
W
X
Y
Z

Contact:	Dialog in the US at (800) 334-2564, Dialog internationally at country-specific locations.
User Info:	To Subscribe, contact Dialog directly.
Notes:	Coverage: 1988 to the present; updated weekly.

`telnet://dialog.com`

Johns Hopkins Genetic Databases

 ★★★

This gopher provides electronic access to documents pertaining to computational biology and a number of different genetic databases.

Keywords:	Genetics, Molecular Biology, Medicine, Biology
Sponsor:	Johns Hopkins University
Audience:	Geneticists, Researchers, Scientists, Molecular Biologists
Profile:	The databases accessible from this entry point include GenBank, Swiss-Prot, PDB, PIR, LiMB, TFD, AAtDB, ACEDB, CompoundKB, PROSITE EC Enzyme Database, NRL_3D Protein-Sequence-Structure Database, Eukaryotic Promoter Database (EPD), Cloning Vector Database, Expressed Sequence Tag Database (ESTDB), Online Mendelian Inheritance Man (OMIM), Sequence Analysis Bibliographic Reference Data Bank (Seqanalref), and Database Taxonomy (GenBank, Swiss-Prot). The gopher also provides direct links to other gophers with information relevant to biology.
Contact:	Dan Jacobson danj@mail.gdb.org
Details:	Free

`gopher://merlot.welch.jhu.edu`

Medical College of Ohio Library Online Catalogue

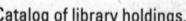 ★★

Catalog of library holdings.

Keywords:	Medicine, Libraries
Sponsor:	Medical College of Ohio
Audience:	Health Professionals, Medical Researchers, Educators, Students
Details:	Free

`telnet://library@136.247.10.14`

Medical College of Wisconsin Library Online Catalogue

 ★★

Catalog of library holdings.

Keywords:	Medicine, Libraries
Sponsor:	Medical College of Wisconsin
Audience:	Health Professionals, Medical Researchers, Educators, Students
Details:	Free

`telnet://ils.lib.mcw.edu`

MEDLARS (MEDical Literature Analysis and Retrieval System)

 ★★★★

MEDLARS is the computerized system of databases and databanks pertinent to biomedical research and patient care, including MEDLINE, the largest and one of the most-used biomedical databases ever.

Keywords:	Medicine, MEDLINE, Biomedical Research
Sponsor:	National Library of Medicine
Audience:	Health Care Providers, Scientists, Biomedical Researchers
Profile:	The computer files can be searched either to produce a list of publications (bibliographic citations) or to retrieve factual information on a specific question. MEDLARS comprises two computer subsystems, ELHISS and TOXNET (TOXicology data NETwork), on which reside over 40 online databases containing about 16 million references. MEDLINE is the largest database and corresponds to three print indexes: Index Medicus, Index to Dental Literature, and Internatonal Nursing Index.
Details:	Costs
User Info:	To Subscribe to the service, send e-mail requesting an account to: medlars@nlm.nih.gov
	An account is needed for entry and a fee is charged for use. Many university library computers have free link to the MEDLINE database.

`telnet://medlars.nlm.nih.gov`

MEDLINE

 ★★★

MEDLINE is a major source of bibliographic biomedical literature. The MEDLINE database encompasses information from three printed indexes (Index Medicus, Index to Dental Literature and the International Nursing Index) as well as additional information not published in the Index Medicus.

Keywords:	Biomedicine, Dentistry, Nursing, Medicine
Sponsor:	U.S. National Library of Medicine
Audience:	Librarians, Researchers, Physicians, Students
Contact:	CDP Technologies Sales Department (800)950-2035, extension 400
User Info:	To Subscribe, contact CDP Technologies directly

`telnet://cdplus@cdplus.com`

Midwifery Resources on the Net

 ★★

A resource list for helping find information about midwifery on the Internet.

Keywords:	Midwifery, Childbirth, Medicine, Nursing
Audience:	Midwives, Medical professionals
Details:	Free

`gopher://una.hh.lib.umich.edu`

Montefiore Medical Center Library Online Catalog

 ★

Catalog of library holdings.

Keywords:	Medicine, Libraries
Sponsor:	Montefiore Medical Center at Albert Einstein College of Medicine, New York
Audience:	Health Care Professionals, Medical Researchers, Educators, Students
Details:	Free
	After Telnetting, hit RETURN twice, then select 0 on main menu. Select 2 on locations menu.To exit, hit the Telnet escape key.

`telnet://lis.aecom.yu.edu`

National Institute for Allergy & Infectious Disease (NIAID)

★

This is a resource into other databases for searching many medical fields, such as the NIAID network userlist or a databank of AIDS-related information.

Keywords:	Medicine, Infectious Diseases, Allergies
Sponsor:	NIAID
Audience:	Health Care Professionals, Researchers, Students
Contact:	Brent Sessions sessions@odie.niaid.nih.gov
Details:	Free

`gopher://gopher.niaid.nih.gov/1`

National Institute of Health Library Online Catalog

 ★★★★

This entry point provides access to the books and journal holdings in the NIH Library. Journal articles are not included.

Keywords:	NIH, Medicine, Science, Libraries
Sponsor:	National Institute of Health (NIH)
Audience:	Scientists, Researchers, Educators, Health Care Professionals
Details:	Free

`telnet://nih-library.ncrr.nih.gov`

National Library of Medicine Gopher
World Health Organization (WHO)

 ★★★★

This gopher provides information about the National Library of Medicine, the world's largest single-topic library.

Keywords:	Medicine, Health, World Health
Sponsor:	National Library of Medicine, Massachusetts
	World Health Organization, Geneva, Switzerland

Audience: Health Care Professionals, Medical Professionals, Researchers

Profile: The National Library of Medicine (NLM) cares for over 4.5 million holdings (including books, journals, reports, manuscripts, and audio-visual items). The NLM offers extensive online information services dealing with clinical care, toxicology, environmental health, and basic biomedical research, It has several active research and development components, including an extramural grants program, houses an extensive history of medicine collection, and provides several programs designed to improve the nation's medical library system.

Contact: R. P. C. Rodgers
rodgers@nlm.nih.gov

akazawa@who.ch

Details: Free

`gopher://el-gopher.med.utah.edu`

`gopher://gopher.who.ch`

NIBNews - A Monthly Electronic Bulletin About Medical Informatics

Disseminates information about Brazilian and Latin American activities, people, information, events, publications, software, and more, involving computer applications in health care, medicine, and biology.

Keywords: Health Care, Biology, Brazil, Latin America, South America, Medicine

Audience: Health Care Professionals, Biologists

Contact: Renato M. E. Sabbatini
sabbatini@bruc.bitnet

Details: Free
E-mail a short notice to

`mailto:sabbatini@ccvax.unicamp.br`

NIH (National Institute of Health)

★★★★

This server is a network-based computer service operated by the Division of Computer Research and Technology (DCRT) to distribute information for and about the NIH (National Institutes of Health).

Keywords: NIH, Health Sciences, Biomedical Research, Medicine

Sponsor: Division of Computer Research and Technology (DCRT), National Institute of Health

Audience: Scientists, Biomedical Researchers, Health CareProfessionals, General Public

Profile: This server provides Internet access to information about NIH health and clinical issues (including CancerNet and a variety of AIDS information), NIH-funded grants and research projects, and a variety of research resources in support of NIH and worldwide biomedical researchers. For example, the major molecular biology databases (GenBank, SWISSPROT, PIR, PDB, TFD, Prosite, LiMB) can be accessed through keyword searches from this gopher.

Details: Free

`gopher://gopher.nih.gov`

sci.med

A Usenet newsgroup providing information and discussion about medicine and its related products.

Keywords: Medicine, Health Care

Audience: Medical Professionals

Details: Free

User Info: To Subscribe to this Usenet newsgroup, you need access to a newsreader.

`news:sci.med`

South East Florida AIDS Information Network (SEFAIN)

★

Contains a wide range of information on AIDS research(ers), organizations, and services in searchable databases.

Keywords: AIDS, Medicine

Sponsor: This project is sponsored in part by the National Library of Medicine

Audience: Medical Professionals, Scientists, Educators, Health Care Providers

Details: Free
Select L on main menu, then select 1 on next menu

`telnet://library@callcat.med.miami.edu`

Stanford Medical Center Gopher

★★

This gopher allows extensive access to the Stanford Medical Center's archives.

Keywords: Medicine, Health Care, Health Sciences

Sponsor: Stanford Medical Center, Palo Alto, California, USA

Audience: Health Care Professionals, Health Science Researchers

Contact: Stanford Medical Center
gopher@medisg.stanford.edu

`gopher://med.stanford.edu`

The National Library of Medicine (NLM) Online Catalog System

★★★★

Catalog of library holdings.

Keywords: Medicine, Health Sciences, Biomedicine, Rare Books

Sponsor: National Library of Medicine

Audience: Health Professionals, Medical Educators, Students

Profile: The National Library of Medicine (NLM) is the world's largest biomedical library with a collection of over 4.9 million items. NLM is a national resource for all US health sciences libraries and fills over a quarter of a million interlibrary loan requests each year for these libraries. The library is open to the public, but its collection is designed primarily for health professionals. The library collects materials comprehensively in all major areas of the health sciences. Housed within the library is one of the world's finest medical history collections of pre-1914 and rare medical texts, manuscripts, and incunabula.

Contact: ref@nlm.nih.gov

Details: Free
The NLM can be accessed also through the WWW at http://www.nlm.nih.gov

`telnet://locator@locator.nlm.nih.gov`

University of Texas Health Science Center (UTHSCSA) Biomedical Library Information System

★★

Keywords: Medicine, Libraries

Sponsor: Audie L. Murphy Memorial Veterans' Administration Hospital, San Antonio, TX

Audience: Medical Professionals, Medical Educators, Students

Details: Free

`telnet://lis@athena.uthscsa.edu`

University of Wales College of Medicine Library Online Catalog

★★

Keywords: Medicine, Libraries

Sponsor: University of Wales, United Kingdom

Audience: Health Care Professionals, Medical Educators, Students

Details: Free

Notes: Expect: login, Send: 'janet'; Expect: password; Send: 'janet'

`telnet://sun.nsf.ac.uk`

A
B
C
D
E
F
G
H
I
J
K
L
M
N
O
P
Q
R
S
T
U
V
W
X
Y
Z

Virtual Hospital

The Virtual Hospital (VH) is a continuously updated medical multimedia database accessible 24 hours a day. The site provides distance learning to practicing physicians and may be used for Continuing Medical Education (CME).

Keywords: Medicine, Education (Distance)

Sponsor: The Electronic Differential Multimedia Laboratory, Department of Radiology, University of Iowa College of Medicine, USA

Audience: Biologists, Researchers, Medical Professionals, Health Care Professionals

Contact: Librarian
librarian@vh.radiology.uiowa.edu

`http://indy.radiology.uiowa.edu/`
`VirtualHospital.html`

Washington University-St. Louis Medical Library & MembersLibrary

The library's holdings are large and wide-ranging and contain significant collections in many fields.

Keywords: Medicine, Science, Technology

Audience: Researchers, Students, General Public

Details: Free

Notes: Expect: Destination Code Prompt, Send: Catalog

`telnet://mcftcp.wustl.edu`

World Health Organization (WHO)

This gopher provides access to the databases of the WHO.

Keywords: World Health Organization, Health, Medicine, Non-governmental organizations

Sponsor: World Health Organization, Geneva, Switzerland

Audience: Medical Professionals, Researchers

Contact: akazawa@who.ch

Details: Free

`gopher://gopher.who.ch`

Medicine (History of)

McGill University, Montreal Canada, INFOMcGILL Library

The library's holdings are large and wide-ranging and contain significant collections in many fields.

Keywords: Architecture, Entomology, Biology, Science (History of), Medicine (History of), Napolean, Shakespeare (William)

Audience: Researchers, Students, General Public

Contact: Roy Miller
ccrmmus@mcgillm (Bitnet) or
ccrmmus@musicm.mcgill.ca (Internet)

Notes: Expect: VM logo; Send: Enter; Expect: prompt; Send: PF3 or type INFO

`telnet:// vm1.mcgill.ca`

University of Maryland System Library

The library's holdings are large and wide-ranging and contain significant collections in many fields.

Keywords: Medicine (History of), Nursing, Pharmacology, Microbiology, Aquaculture, Aquatic Chemistry, Toxicology

Audience: General Public, Researchers, Librarians, Document Delivery Professionals

Contact: Ron Larsen

Details: Free

Notes: Expect: Available Services menu; Send: PAC

`telnet://victor.umd.edu`

Medieval Studies

History at the University of Virginia

A collection of online history resources, with particular emphasis on medieval and classical studies. Links to other systems, including the Library of Congress.

Keywords: History (World), Classics, Medieval Studies

Sponsor: University of Virginia, Charlottesville, Virginia, USA

Audience: Historians, Students (College/University)

Contact: mssbks@virginia.edu

Details: Free

`gopher://gopher.lib.virginia.edu`

MEDTEXT-L

A discussion of medieval text, including philology, codicology, and technology.

Keywords: Medieval, Philology, Linguistics

Audience: Linguists, Language Teachers, Language Students, Historians

Details: Free

User Info: To Subscribe to the list, send an e-mail message to the URL address below consisting of a single line reading:

medtext-l YourFirstName YourLastName

To send a message to the entire list, address it to: medtext-l@uiucvmd.bitnet

`mailto:listserv@uiucvmd.bitnet`

Nero Ashbury

Nero is a live-action, medieval role-playing game with a plot line and characters that continue from one adventure to the next. Nero has been successful in New England for over six years and is growing rapidly.

Keywords: Medieval Studies, Role-Playing, Games

Audience: General Public, Role-Playing Enthusiasts

Contact: lsonko@pearl.tufts.edu

Details: Free

User Info: To Subscribe to the list, send an e-mail message requesting a subscription to the URL address below.

`mailto:lsonko@pearl.tufts.edu`

rec.org.sca

A Usenet newsgroup providing information and discussion about medieval re-enactments.

Keywords: SCA (Society For Creative Anachronism), Medieval Studies

Audience: General Public

User Info: To Subscribe to this Usenet newsgroup, you need access to a newsreader.

`news:rec.org.sca`

University of Pennsylvania Library- Philadelphia Pa.

The library's holdings are large and wide-ranging and contain significant collections in many fields.

Keywords: Literature (English), Literature (American), History (World), Medieval Studies, East Asian Studies, Middle Eastern Studies, South Asian Studies, Judaica, Lithuania

Audience: Educators, Students, Researchers

Profile: Access to the central Van Pelt Library and to most of the departmental libraries is restricted to members of the University community on weekends and holidays. Online visitors are advised to call (215) 898-7554 for information on hours and access restrictions.

Contact: Patricia Renfro, Associate Director of Libraries

Details: Free

`telnet://library.upenn.edu`

University of Rochester Library

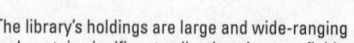

The library's holdings are large and wide-ranging and contain significant collections in many fields.

Keywords: Architecture, Art History, Photography, Literature (Asian), Lasers, Geology, Statistics, Optics, Medieval Studies

Audience: Researchers, Students, General Public

Details: Free

Notes: Expect: Login; Send: Library

`telnet://128.151.226.71`

Audience: Researchers, Students, General Public

Meetings Calendar (Geosciences)

Meetings Calendar (Geosciences)

A collection of meetings and conferences in the geosciences, with a special emphasis on meteorology. The entries are sorted by date and some contain links to Calls for Papers.

Keywords: Geosciences, Meteorology

Sponsor: Freie Universit_t Berlin, Germany

Audience: Researchers, Meteorologists

Contact: Dennis Schulze
dennis@bibo.met.fu-berlin.de

Details: Free

Notes: If there is a conference you want to have included in this list, send an e-mail to dennis@bibo.met.fu-berlin.de

`http://www.met.fu-berlin.de/`
`konferenzen/index.html`

MEGA (Combined Federal/ State Case Law)

MEGA (Combined Federal/State Case Law)

The Federal/State Case Law combined library contains files that allow one-stop searching of combined federal and state case law on the LEXIS service. American Law Reports (ALR)) and Lawyers' Edition, 2d articles are also included.

Keywords: Case Law (US), Law (US State), Law (US Federal)

Audience: Lawyers

Profile: The MEGA file is a one-stop search of all available federal and state case law on the LEXIS service. The circuit-base MEGA files combine federal and state case law from federal and state courts within the geographical area defined by the federal circuit. The state-based MEGA files combine case law from the courts of the state plus case law from the federal circuit for that state and the federal district courts within the state. Two chronological files restrict combined federal and state case law searches to particular date ranges. Each MEGA file includes all available U.S. Supreme Court cases. American Law Reports (ALR) and Lawyers' Edition, 2d (LEd2) articles are also included.

Contact: New Sales Group @ 800-227-4908 or 513-859-5398 inside the US, or 1-513-865-7981 for all inquires outside the US.

User Info: To Subscribe, contact Mead directly.

To examine the Lexis user guide, you can access it at the ftp site of the University of Texas at Austin at the URL address: ftp://ftp.cc.utexas.edu

The files are in: /pub/res-services/LEXIS

`telnet://nex.meaddata.com`

MegaGopher

MegaGopher

This is the gopher at the University of Montreal. It supports the software and information requirements for the MegaSequencing project. It also serves as a repository of data for organellar genome and molecular evolution research and acts as the focal point for the GDE (Genetic Data Environment) package.

Keywords: Biology, Canada

Audience: Biologists

Contact: Tim Littlejohn
tim@bch.umontreal.ca

Details: Free

`gopher://megasun.bch.umontreal.ca`

Melrose Place

Melrose-place

Discussion of the Fox television show Melrose Place.

Keywords: Melrose Place, Fox Television, Television Series

Audience: Melrose Place Enthusiasts, Television Viewers

Details: Free

User Info: To Subscribe to the list, send an e-mail message requesting a subscription to the URL address below.

`mailto:melrose-place-request@ferkel.`
`ucsb.edu`

MELVYL Library System

MELVYL Library System

MELVYL is the University of California's catalog of books and periodicals for the university and the California State Library. It also permits access to database systems around the world.

Keywords: Libraries, Databases, OPACS, Internet Surfers

Audience: General Interest, Students, Teachers, Librarians

Producer: University of California

Contact: Genny Engel, MELVYL System Users Services
email:gen@dla.ucop.edu

Profile: The MELVYL system is a centralized information system that can be reached from terminals in libraries at all nine campuses of the University of California. The system can also be reached by any terminal microcomputer with dialup access to UC computers connected to the MELVYL system. The MELVYL system includes a library catalog database, a periodicals database, article citation databases, and other files. A large number of other libraries and database systems are also accessible from MELVYL.

Details: Free

Notes: All these databases are searched using the same basic commands.

`telnet://melvyl.ucop.edu`

Memorabilia

Cards

This list is for people interested in collecting, speculating, and investing in baseball, football, basketball, hockey, and other trading cards and/or memorabilia. Discussion and want/sell lists are welcome.

Keywords: Trading Cards, Collectibiles, Memorabilia

Audience: Sports Card Collectors, Sports Card Traders, Memorabilia Collectors

Contact: Keane Arase
cards-request@tanstaafl.uchicago.edu

Details: Free

User Info: To Subscribe to the list, send an e-mail message requesting a subscription to the URL address below.

To send a message to the entire list, address it to: cards@tanstaafl.uchicago.edu

Notes: The list is open to anyone.

`mailto:cards-request@tanstaafl.`
`uchicago.edu`

Sports-cards

For people interested in collection, speculation and investing in baseball, football, basketball, hockey, and other trading cards and/or memorabilia. Discussion and want/sell lists are welcome.

Keywords: Memorabilia, Sports, Trading Cards

Audience: Collectors, Sports Card Traders

Contact: Keane Arase
cards-request@tanstaafl.uchicago.edu

Details: Free

User Info: To Subscribe to the list, send an e-mail message requesting a subscription to the URL address below.

To send a message to the entire list, address it to: cards@tanstaafl.uchicago.edu

`mailto:cards-`
`request@tanstaafl.uchicago.edu`

A B C D E F G H I J K L M N O P Q R S T U V W X Y Z

Men

Men ★

This digested mailing list discusses men's issues.

Keywords: Men, General Interest

Audience: General Public

Contact: mail-men-request@summit.novell.com

Details: Free

User Info: To Subscribe to the list, send an e-mail message requesting a subscription to the URL address below.

`mailto:mail-men-request@summit.novell.com`

soc.men ★

A Usenet newsgroup providing information and discussion about men, their problems, and their relationships.

Keywords: Men, Gender

Audience: Men, Activists

Details: Free

User Info: To Subscribe to this Usenet newsgroup, you need access to a newsreader.

`news:soc.men`

Mensa

Mensatalk ★

A discussion group for members of Mensa.

Keywords: Mensa, Genius

Audience: Mensa Members

Details: Free

User Info: To Subscribe to the list, send an e-mail message requesting a subscription to the URL address below.

`mailto:mensatalk-request@psg.com`

Mercer (Johnny, Collection of)

Georgia State University Library ★★

The library's holdings are large and wide-ranging and contain significant collections in many fields.

Keywords: Labor (History of), Multimedia, Mercer (Johnny, Collection of)

Audience: General Public, Researchers, Librarians, Document Delivery Professionals

Contact: Phil Williams
isgpew@gsuvm1.gsu.edu

Details: Free

Notes: Expect: VM screen, Send: RETURN; Expect: CP READ, Send: DIAL VTAM, press RETURN; Expect: CICS screen, Send: PF1

`telnet://library.gsu.edu`

Merit Network Information Center Services

Merit Network Information Center Services ★★

This site provides a large collection of Internet guides and information.

Keywords: Internet, Internet Guides, Internet Tools

Sponsor: Merit Network, Inc.

Audience: Internet Surfers

Profile: This site serves as a clearinghouse for many Internet guides, documents, and utilities. It includes Internet FAQs, bibliographies, glossaries, and user guides such as Zen and the Art of the Internet and The Internet Companion. It also has archives of various Internet documents listing service providers, acceptable use policies, and resources. Many software programs for navigating the Internet are also available here for a wide variety of platforms

Contact: nic-info@nic.merit.edu

`gopher://nic.merit.edu`

`ftp://nic.merit.edu`

MetaCard

Metacard-list ★

Discussion of the MetaCard product from MetaCard Corp. MetaCard is an application-development system similar to Apple's HyperCard product; it runs on a variety of popular platforms in a UNIX/X11/Motif environment.

Keywords: MetaCard, Computing, UNIX

Audience: Computer Users

Contact: metacard-list-owner@grot.starconn.com

Details: Free

User Info: To Subscribe to the list, send an e-mail message requesting a subscription to the URL address below.

`mailto:metacard-list@grot.starconn.com`

Metals

METADEX

International literature covering metals and alloys.

Keywords: Material Science, Metals, Alloys

Sponsor: Materials Information, a joint information service of ASM International and the Institute of Materials

Audience: Material Scientists, Researchers

Profile: Contains more than 925,000 records from the international literature on metals and alloys concerning processes, properties, materials classes, applications, specific alloy designations, intermetallic compounds and metallurgical systems. Updated monthly.

Contact: paul.albert@neteast.com

User Info: To Subscribe contact Orbit-Questel directly.

`telnet://orbit.com`

MetaMail

MetaMail ★★

This resource contains information about MetaMail, which allows existing mail readers to read multimedia e-mail in the MIME (Multipurpose Internet Mail Extensions) format.

Keywords: Internet, E-mail

Audience: Internet Surfers

Contact: Nathaniel S. Borenstein
nsb@nsb.fv.com

Readme file is pub/nsb/readme

`ftp://thumper.bellcore.com`

Meteorology

Current Weather Maps and Movies ★★★

This web site is updated hourly, and provides links to downloadable software sites instrumental in accessing interactive weather browsers. International information is available, and visual and infrared maps are supplied from satellites.

Keywords: Weather, Meteorology, Aviation

Sponsor: Michigan State University, Michigan, USA

Audience: General Public, Oceanography, Pilots

Contact: Charles Henrich
henrich@crh.cl.msu.edu

`http://rs560.cl.msu.edu/weather`

A B C D E F G H I J K L **M** N O P Q R S T U V W X Y Z

Energy and Climate Information Exchange (ECIX) Newsletter

This newsletter focuses on energy and climate issues, and contains summaries of network postings, updates on national and international policy initiatives, full-length articles, information on new network resources, and a calendar of upcoming events.

Keywords: Energy, Meteorology, Climatology

Audience: Meteorologists, Geologists, Energy Researchers, Climatologists

Contact: econet@igc.org

`mailto:larris@igc.org`

Meetings Calendar (Geosciences)

A collection of meetings and conferences in the geosciences, with a special emphasis on meteorology. The entries are sorted by date and some contain links to Calls for Papers.

Keywords: Geosciences, Meteorology

Sponsor: Freie Universit_t Berlin, Germany

Audience: Researchers, Meteorologists

Contact: Dennis Schulze dennis@bibo.met.fu-berlin.de

Details: Free

Notes: If there is a conference you want to have included in this list, send an e-mail to dennis@bibo.met.fu-berlin.de

`http://www.met.fu-berlin.de/ konferenzen/index.html`

Weather-users

Weather-users is a mailing list for developers of programs that access the Weather Underground database at the University of Michigan.

Keywords: Weather, Programming, Meteorology

Audience: Programmers

Contact: Scott Hazen Mueller scott@zorch.sf-bay.org

Details: Free

User Info: To Subscribe to the list, send an e-mail message

`mailto:weather-users-request@zorch.sf-bay.org`

Meteorology Students

A discussion of meteorology, with particular emphasis on student-related topics, such as scholarships, summer schools, conferences, and university meteorology programs.

Keywords: Metereology

Audience: Meteorology Students

Contact: dennis@metw3.met.fu-berlin.de

Details: Free

User Info: To Subscribe to the list, send an e-mail message requesting a subscription to the URL address below.

`mailto:dennis@metw3.met.fu-berlin.de`

Mexican Culture FAQ

Mexican Culture FAQ

This is the FAQ from the soc.culture.mexican newsgroup. Provides information on Mexican culture, history, society, language, and tourism.

Keywords: Cultural Studies, Race, Chicano Culture, Latino Culture

Sponsor: News Group Moderators for soc.culture.mexican

Audience: Students, Hispanics

Contact: News Group Moderator mendoza-grado@att.com

Details: Free

`ftp://ftp.mty.itesm.ms/pub/mexico/ faqs`

`http://www.cis.ohio-state.edu/ hypertext/faq/usenet/mexican-faq/ faq.html`

Mexican-American Studies

University of Texas-Pan American Library

The library's holdings are large and wide-ranging and contain significant collections in many fields.

Keywords: Lower Rio Grande Valley (History of), Mexican-American Studies

Audience: Researchers, Students, General Public

Details: Free

Notes: Expect: Username Prompt, Send: packey

`telnet://panam2.panam.edu`

Mexico

North American Free Trade Agreement (NAFTA)

The agreement between the governments of Canada, the United Mexican States, and the United States of America to establish a free trade area in North America.

Keywords: Trade, US, Mexico, Canada, Free Trade, NAFTA

Audience: Journalists, Politicians, Economists, Students

Details: Free

`gopher://wiretap.spies.com/00/Gov/ NAFTA`

US/Mexico Border Discussion List

This group provides a forum for the discussion of issues pertaining to the US/Mexico border environment.

Keywords: Mexico, Environment, Latino Culture

Sponsor: The US Environmental Protection Agency

Audience: Activists, Environmentalists, Urban Planners

Details: Free

User Info: To Subscribe to the list, send a message to the URL address below consisting of a single line reading:

SUB us_mexborder YourFirstName YourLastName.

To send a message to the entire list, address it to: us_mexborder@unixmail.rtpnc.epa.gov

`mailto: listserver@unixmail.rtpnc.epa.gov`

MGD (Mouse Genome Database)

MGD (Mouse Genome Database)

This site provides a comprehensive database of genetic information on the laboratory mouse.

Keywords: Biology, Genetics

Sponsor: The Jackson Laboratory

Audience: Biologists, Researchers, Educators, Students

Contact: mgi-help@informatics.jax.org

Details: Free

User Info: Contact Mouse Genome Informatics User Support by telephone at (207) 288-3371, X 1900, or by FAX at (207) 288-2516.

`http://www.informatics.jax.org/ mgd.html`

Miata

Miata

An open forum for Mazda Miata owners.

Keywords: Mazda Miata, Automobiles

Audience: Automobile Owners

A B C D E F G H I J K L M N O P Q R S T U V W X Y Z

A B C D E F G H I J K L **M** N O P Q R S T U V W X Y Z

Details: Free

User Info: To Subscribe to the list, send an e-mail message requesting subscription to the URL address below.

`mailto:miata-request@jhunix.hcf.jhu.edu`

Michigan

MichNet News (previously Merit Network News) ⭐

Newsletter of MichNet (Michigan Networks), Michigan's regional computer network. It contains information about MichNet, as well as hosts and services that can be reached through MichNet.

Keywords: Computer Networks, Michigan

Sponsor: MichNet

Audience: Network Developers

Contact: Pat McGregor
patmcg@merit.edu

Details: Free

Contact the MichNet News at mnn-request@merit.edu. Available by anonymous FTP from the address below.

`ftp://nis.nsf.net`

The University of Michigan Library ⭐⭐

The library's holdings are large and wide-ranging and contain significant collections in many fields. Bilingual Education, Linguistics, Neuroscience, Michigan History, Temperance and Prohibition, African Government, Prohibition

Keywords: Education (Bilingual), Linguistics, Neuroscience, Michigan, Prohibition, Government (African)

Audience: General Public, Researchers, Librarians, Document Delivery Professionals

Details: Free

Notes: Expect: nothing, Send: <cr>

`telnet://cts.merit.edu`

Microbiology

Biosis Previews

The database encompasses the entire field of life sciences and covers original research reports and reviews in biological and biomedical areas. This includes field, laboratory, clinical, experimental and theoretical work. The traditional areas of biology, including botany, zoology, and microbiology, are covered, as well as the related fields such as plant and animal science, agriculture, pharmacology, and ecology.

Keywords: Biology, Botany, Zoology, Microbiology, Plant Science, Animal Science, Agriculture, Pharmacology, Ecology, Biochemistry, Biophysics, Bioengineering

Sponsor: Biosis

Audience: Librarians, Researchers, Students, Biologists, Botanists, Zoologists, Scientists, Taxonomists

Contact: CDP Technologies Sales Department (800)950-2035, extension 400

User Info: To Subscribe, contact CDP Technologies directly

`telnet:\\cdplus@cdplus.com`

University of Maryland System Library ⭐⭐

The library's holdings are large and wide-ranging and contain significant collections in many fields.

Keywords: Medicine (History of), Nursing, Pharmacology, Microbiology, Aquaculture, Aquatic Chemistry, Toxicology

Audience: General Public, Researchers, Librarians, Document Delivery Professionals

Contact: Ron Larsen

Details: Free

Notes: Expect: Available Services menu; Send: PAC

`telnet://victor.umd.edu`

vetmicro ⭐

Discussion group for veterinary microbiology.

Keywords: Veterinary Microbiology, Veterinary Medicine, Microbiology

Audience: Veterinarians

Contact: James T. Case, Bill Cohen
jcase@ucdcvdls.bitnet or
bcohen@ucdcvdls.bitnet

Details: Free

User Info: To Subscribe to the list, send an e-mail message to the URL address below consisting of a single line reading:

SUB vetmicro YourFirstName YourLastName

To send a message to the entire list, address it to: vetmicro@ucdavis.edu

`mailto:listserv@ucdavis.edu`

Microcomputing

Buyer's Guide to Micro Software ⭐⭐⭐

The database contains a directory of business and professional microcomputer software available in the United States.

Keywords: Buyer's Guides, Microcomputing, Computers, Software

Sponsor: Online, Inc., Weston, CT, USA

Audience: Computer Users

Profile: Provided are directory, product, technical, and bibliographic information on leading software packages, integrated this information into one succinct composite record. The database can help professionals locate suitable packages compatible with specified hardware, without having to sift through large numbers of records.

The file is highly selective, listing packages rated at least "good" by the technical press; all packages from major software producers, even if negatively reviewed; and packages unique to specific business segments, with special emphasis placed on library and medical software. Each record includes directory information; technical specifications, including required hardware and operating systems; an abstracted product description; and, when available, a full citation of representative reviews.

Contact: Dialog in the US at (800) 334-2564, Dialog internationally at country-specific locations.

Details: Costs

User Info: To Subscribe, contact Dialog directly.

Notes: Coverage: current; updated monthly.

`telnet://dialog.com`

MICnews ⭐

Microcomputer and advanced workstation computing news relevant to the computing populace at the University of California, Los Angeles (UCLA).

Keywords: Microcomputing, Advanced Workshops

Sponsor: Microcomputer Information Center, UCLA

Audience: UCLA Students

Contact: Bob Cooper
csmibob@mvs.oac.ucla.edu

Details: Free

User Info: To Subscribe to the list, send an e-mail message to the URL address below, consisting of a single line reading:

SUB micnews YourFirstName YourLastName

To send a message to the entire list, address it to:
micnews@uclacn1.ucla.edu

`mailto:listserv@uslach1.edu`

Output ⭐

Newsletter of the Florida State University (FSU) Computing Center. Includes topics such as networking, microcomputing, mainframe computing, and supercomputing on campus, including use of computers in classroom and research computing at FSU.

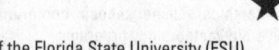

Keywords: Networking, Microcomputing, Supercomputing

Audience: FSU Computer Science Students, Computer Users

Contact: Suzanne C. Nelson
nelson@avm.cc.fsu.edu

Details: Free

Send your request addressed to the Editor.

`mailto:nelson@avm.cc.fsu.edu`

Microelectronics

University of Wisconsin at Stout Library

The library's holdings are large and wide-ranging and contain significant collections in many fields.

Keywords: Mathematics, Business, Fashion Merchandising, Home Economics, Hospitality, Tourism, Hotel Administration, Restaurant Management, Microelectronics

Audience: Researchers, Students, General Public

Details: Free

Notes: Expect: Login, Send: Lib; Expect: vDIAL Prompt, Send: Library

`telnet://lib.uwstout.edu`

Microscopy

Massachusetts Institute of Technology Library

The library's holdings are large and wide-ranging and contain significant collections in many fields.

Keywords: Aeronautics (History of), Linguistics, Mathematics (History of), Microscopy, Spectroscopy, Aeronautics, Mathematics, Glass

Audience: General Public, Researchers, Librarians, Document Delivery Professionals

Details: Free

Notes: Expect: Mitek Server..., Send: Enter or Return; Expect: prompt, Send: hollis

`telnet://library.mit.edu`

Microsoft Corporation

foxpro-l

This mailing list is designed to foster information sharing between users of the FoxPro database development environment now owned and distributed by Microsoft. Both new and experienced users of FoxPro are welcome to join in the discussions.

Keywords: Databases, Computers, Microsoft Corporation

Audience: Database Users, Microsoft FoxPro Users, Software Engineers

Contact: Chris O'Neill
coneill@heaven.polarbear.rankin-inlet.nt.ca

Details: Free

User Info: To Subscribe to the list, send an e-mail message requesting a subscription to the URL address below.

To send a message to the entire list, address it to: foxpro-l@polarbear.rankin-inlet.nt.ca

`mailto:fileserv@polarbear.rankin-inlet.nt.ca`

Microsoft Corporation World Wide Web Server

This system has been set up to provide lay and technical information for the public about Microsoft and its products.

Keywords: Microsoft, Windows, MS-DOS, Chicago

Sponsor: Microsoft Corporation

Audience: Computer Users, Microsoft Product Users, Computer Programmers, Investors

Profile: The Microsoft Knowledge Base and Software Library is accessible here. Information can be obtained on Windows NT Server, Developer Network News, Windows News, and also Windows Sockets Information. There are sections on Windows 4 (Chicago), Microsoft's new 32-bit TCP/IP VxD stack, a "What's New" page, current employment opportunities at Microsoft, recent speeches given by Microsoft Corporation's CEO Bill Gates, as well as current financial information about Microsoft.

Contact: Email: www@microsoft.com

Details: Free, Images

Notes: The information contained on this server is copyrighted, and may not be distributed, downloaded, modified, reused, reposted, or otherwise used outside the scope of a WWW client without the express written permission of Microsoft Corporation.

`http://www.microsoft.com`

`gopher://gopher.microsoft.com`

`ftp://ftp.microsoft.com`

MS-Access

A list for the discussion of MS (Microsoft) Access topics, including Access Basic questions, reviews, rumors, and so on.

Keywords: Microsoft Corporation, Databases

Audience: Computer Users, Database Managers

Details: Free

User Info: To Subscribe to the list, send an e-mail message requesting subscription to the URL address below.

`mailto:ms-access-request@eunet.co.at`

Middle East

Israel-mideast

This discussion group provides information on and analysis of Israel and the Middle East. Includes news flashes, briefings by Israeli leaders, editorials and articles translated from the Israeli press, background papers, press communiques and economic, environmental and cultural updates.

Keywords: Israel, Middle East, Politics

Sponsor: Israel Information Center, Jerusalem

Audience: General Public, Students

Contact: Israel Information Service
ask@israel-info.gov.il

User Info: To Subscribe to the list, send an e-mail message to the address below consisting of a single line reading:

SUB israel mideast YourFirstName YourLastName

To send a message to the entire list, address it to: israel mideast@vm.tau.ac.il

`mailto:listserv@vm.tau.ac.il`

MDEAFR

The Middle East and Africa (MDEAFR) library contains detailed information about every country in the Mideast and Africa. Structured for those who want to follow the unfolding events in the Gulf states, as well as in North and South Africa, this library contains a broad array of sources, including international research reports from InvestextR.

Keywords: Analysis, Companies, Middle East, Africa

Audience: Journalists, Business Professionals

Profile: The MDEAFR library contains a wide array of pertinent sources. Among the information sources are newspapers and wire services, trade and business journals, company reports, country and region background, industry and product analysis, business opportunities, and selected legal texts. News sources range from the world-renowned Associated Press and Christian Science Monitor to the regionally important Jerusalem Post and Africa News. Company information is contained in the EXTEL cards as well as ICC. Providers of country background and industry analysis include Associated Banks of Europe, Bank of America, Business International, IBC USA, and the US Department of Commerce. Customers interested in new business opportunities can check OPIC and Foreign Trade Opportunities (FTO).

A B C D E F G H I J K L **M** N O P Q R S T U V W X Y Z

A B C D E F G H I J K L **M** N O P Q R S T U V W X Y Z

Contact: Mead New Sales Group at (800) 227-4908 or (513) 859-5398 inside the US, or (513) 865-7981 for all inquiries outside the US.

User Info: To Subscribe, contact Mead directly.

To examine the Nexis user guide, you can access it at the ftp site of the University of Texas at Austin at the URL address: ftp://ftp.cc.utexas.edu

The files are in: /pub/ref-services/LEXIS

`telnet://nex.meaddata.com`

`http://www.meaddata.com`

talk.politics.mideast

A Usenet newsgroup providing information and discussion about Middle Eastern topics.

Keywords: Middle East, Middle Eastern Studies, Politics (Middle Eastern)

Audience: Political Scientists

Details: Free

User Info: To Subscribe to this Usenet newsgroup, you need access to a newsreader.

`news:talk.politics.mideast`

The Israel Information Service

★★★

A gopher server containing information on Israel.

Keywords: Israel, Middle East, Political Science, Anti-Semitism, Holocaust, Archaeology

Sponsor: Israeli Foreign Ministry

Audience: Israelis, Jews, Tourists, General Public

Profile: This server features updates on the Middle East peace process, including text of the latest Israel-PLO accord, as well as general political, diplomatic, cultural and economic information on the state of Israel. Also includes archives on archaeology in Israel, anti-Semitism and the Holocaust, and current excerpts from Israeli newspapers.

Contact: Chaim Shacham
shacham@israel-info.gov.il

`gopher://israel-info.gov.il`

Middle Eastern Studies

Judaica

A mailing list for the discussion of Jewish and Near Eastern Studies.

Keywords: Judaica, Israel, Middle Eastern Studies, Religion

Audience: Judaica Scholars, Jews, Middle East Scholars

Contact: Tzvee Zahavy
maic@uminn1.bitnet

User Info: To Subscribe to the list, send an e-mail message to the URL address below consisting of a single line reading:

SUB judaica

`mailto:listserv@vm1.spcs.umn.edu`

Princeton University Library

The library's holdings are large and wide-ranging. They contain significant collections in many fields. China, Japan, Classics, Ancient History, Near East Studies, Literature, Aeronautics, Middle East, Mormon History, Publishing

Keywords: China, Japan, Classics, History (Ancient), Near Eastern Studies, Literature (American), Literature (English), Aeronautics, Middle Eastern Studies, Mormonism, Publishing

Audience: General Public, Researchers, Librarians, Document Delivery Professionals

Details: Free

Notes: Expect: Connect message, blank screen, Send: <cr>; Expect: #, Send: Call 500

`telnet://pucable.princeton.edu`

soc.culture.arabic

A Usenet newsgroup providing information and discussion about Arabic culture and technologies.

Keywords: Sociology, Middle Eastern Studies

Audience: Sociologists

Details: Free

User Info: To Subscribe to this Usenet newsgroup, you need access to a newsreader.

`news:soc.culture.arabic`

talk.politics.mideast

A Usenet newsgroup providing information and discussion about Middle Eastern topics.

Keywords: Middle East, Middle Eastern Studies, Politics (Middle Eastern)

Audience: Political Scientists

Details: Free

User Info: To Subscribe to this Usenet newsgroup, you need access to a newsreader.

`news:talk.politics.mideast`

University of Pennsylvania Library- Philadelphia Pa.

The library's holdings are large and wide-ranging and contain significant collections in many fields.

Keywords: Literature (English), Literature (American), History (World), Medieval Studies, East Asian Studies, Middle Eastern Studies, South Asian Studies, Judaica, Lithuania.

Audience: Educators, Students, Researchers

Profile: Access to the central Van Pelt Library and to most of the departmental libraries is restricted to members of the University community on weekends and holidays. Online visitors are advised to call (215) 898-7554 for information on hours and access restrictions.

Contact: Patricia Renfro, Associate Director of Libraries

Details: Free

`telnet://library.upenn.edu`

University of Texas at Austin Library

The library's holdings are large and wide-ranging and contain significant collections in many fields.

Keywords: Music, Natural Science, Nursing, Science Technology, Behavioral Science, Social Work, Computer Science, Engineering, Latin American Studies, Middle Eastern Studies

Audience: Researchers, Students, General Public

Details: Free

Notes: Expect: Blank Screen, Send: Return; Expect: Go, Send: Return; Expect: Enter Terminal Type, Send: vt100

Note: Some databases are restricted to UT Austin users only.

`telnet://utcat.utexas.edu`

University of Utah Library

The library's holdings are large and wide-ranging and contain significant collections in many fields.

Keywords: Western America, Middle Eastern Studies, Geology, Mining

Audience: Researchers, Students, General Public

Details: Free

Notes: Expect: Command Line, Send: Dial Unis

`telnet://lib.utah.edu`

Mideur-I

Mideur-L

A list containing the history, culture, politics, and current affairs of those countries lying between the Mediterranean/Adriatic and the Baltic Seas, and between the German/Austrian borders and the former Soviet Union.

Keywords: Soviet Union, Baltic Republics, Eastern Europe, News

Audience: Political Scientists, Researchers, Historians, General Public

Contact: Jan George Frajkor
mideur-1@ubvm.cc.buffalo.edu

Details: Free

User Info: To Subscribe to the list, send an e-mail message to the URL address below consisting of a single line reading:

SUB mideur-l YourFirstName YourLastName

To send a message to the entire list, address it to: mideur-1@ubvm.cc.buffalo.edu

`mailto:listserv@ubvm.cc.buffalo.edu`

MIDI

Alternate Tuning Mailing List

This mailing list is intended for exchanging ideas relevant to alternate tunings.

Keywords: Musical Instruments, MIDI

Sponsor: Mills College

Audience: Musicians

Profile: This list deals with just intonation, paratactical tunings, experimental music instrument design, non-standard equal temperaments, MIDI tuning system exclusive specifications, concert postings, non-Western tunings, and the experimental tunings of such people as Harry Partch, Lou Harrison, Martin Bartlett, James Tenney and others.

Contact: Greg Higgs
Higgs@Mills.edu

Details: Free

User Info: To Subscribe to the list, send an e-mail message to the URL address below, consisting of a single line reading:

SUB tuning YourFirstName YourLastName

`listproc@varese.mills.edu`

Midwifery

Midwifery Resources on the Net

A resource list for helping find information about midwifery on the Internet.

Keywords: Midwifery, Childbirth, Medicine, Nursing

Audience: Midwives, Medical professionals

Details: Free

`gopher://una.hh.lib.umich.edu`

Migration

Migra-list

Mailing list on international migration.

Keywords: Migration

Sponsor: US Immigration and Naturalization Service

Audience: Politicians, General Public

Contact: Maurizio Oliva
moliva@cc.utah.edu

Details: Free

`mailto:migra-list@cc.utah.edu`

Milieu

Milieu

Discussion of the works of Julian May, notably the Saga of the Exiles, and the Galactic Milieu Trilogy.

Keywords: May (Julian), Science Fiction

Audience: Julian May Readers

Contact: milieu-request@yoyo.cc.monash.edu.au

Details: Free

User Info: To Subscribe to the list, send an e-mail message requesting subscription to the URL address below.

`mailto:milieu-request@yoyo.cc.monash.edu.au`

Military (US)

Uniform Code of Military Justice

The files in this directory contain the US Uniform Code of Military Justice.

Keywords: Military, Law

Audience: Journalists, Politicians, Students, Military Personnel

Details: Free

`gopher://wiretap.spies.com/00/Gov/UCMJ`

U.S. Army Area Handbooks

This gopher provides detailed political, cultural, historical, military, and economic information on hot spots in world affairs, everywhere from China to Yugoslavia.

Keywords: Military (US), Politics (International), Federal Government (US)

Sponsor: The Thomas Jefferson Library at the University of Missouri at St. Louis , St. Louis, Missouri, USA

Audience: Journalists, Government Officials, Travelers/Tourists

Profile: The Army Area Handbooks, which provide a comprehensive overview of several important countries including Japan, China, Israel, Egypt, South Korea, and Somalia, are only one of the many government resources available at this site. Other full-text documents include the proposed 1995 federal budget, the

CIA world fact book, the NAFTA agreement, health care proposals currently before Congress, and statistics for the U.S. industrial outlook. Also has links to many federal gophers and information systems.

Contact: Joe Rottman
rottman@umslvma.umsl.edu

Details: Free

`gopher://umslvma.umsl.edu/11/library/govdocs`

US Army Corps of Engineers

This site provides information on the organization, programs, news, facilities, and activities of the US Army Corps of Engineers.

Keywords: Military, Engineering

Sponsor: Cold Regions Research and Engineering Laboratory

Audience: Military Personnel, Engineers, Researchers

Contact: www@usace.mil

Details: Free

`http://www.usace.mil/usace.html`

Military History

University of Nebraska at Lincoln Library

The library's holdings are large and wide-ranging and contain significant collections in many fields.

Keywords: Slovak Republic, Czech Republic, Folklore, Military History, Latvia, Law (Tax), Law (US)

Audience: General Public, Researchers, Librarians, Document Delivery Professionals

Contact: Anita Cook

Details: Free

Expect: login, **Send:** library

`telnet://unllib.unl.edu`

Military Policy

dont-tell

The dont-tell list is for people concerned about the effects that the new military policy known as "don't ask/don't tell" will have at academic institutions, whether military or ROTC-affiliated.

Keywords: Sexuality, Military Policy, Education (Post-Secondary)

Audience: Students, Gays, Lesbians, Military Personnel, Civil Libertarians

Contact: dont-tell-request@choice.princeton.edu

A
B
C
D
E
F
G
H
I
J
K
L
M
N
O
P
Q
R
S
T
U
V
W
X
Y
Z

Details: Free

User Info: To subscribe to the list, send an e-mail message requesting a subscription to the URL address below.

To send a message to the entire list, address it to: dont-tell-request@choice.princeton.edu

`mailto:dont-tell-request@choice.princeton.edu`

Military Science

sci.military

A Usenet newsgroup providing information and discussion about science and the military.

Keywords: Military Science

Audience: Military Personnel, Military Historians

Details: Free

User Info: To Subscribe to this Usenet newsgroup, you need access to a newsreader.

`news:sci.military`

Military Specifications

IHS International Standards and Specifications

The database contains references to industry standards, and military and federal specifications and standards covering all aspects of engineering and related disciplines.

Keywords: Engineering, Military Specifications, Federal Standards

Sponsor: Information Handling Services, Englewood, CO, US

Audience: Engineers, Military Hisorians, Lawyers

Profile: The file includes 90% of the world's most referenced standards from over 70 domestic, foreign, and international standardizing bodies. Also included is the world's largest commercially available collection of unclassified active and historical US military and federal specifications and standards.

Contact: Dialog in the US at (800) 334-2564, Dialog internationally at country-specific locations.

User Info: To Subscribe, contact Dialog directly.

Notes: Coverage: Current; updated weekly for MILSPECS, every two months.

`telnet://dialog.com`

Milne (A.A.)

University of New Hampshire Videotex Library

The library's holdings are large and wide-ranging and contain significant collections in many fields.

Keywords: Dance, Folk Music, Milne (A.A., Collection of), Galway (Ireland)

Audience: Researchers, Students, General Public

Contact: Robin Tuttle r_tuttle1@unhh.unh.edu

Details: Free

Notes: Expect: USERNAME; Send: Student (no password required). Control-z to log off.

`telnet://unhvt@unh.edu`

MIME (Multipurpose Internet Mail Extensions)

MIME (Multipurpose Internet Mail Extensions)

This resource contains information about the MIME (Multipurpose Internet Mail Extensions) protocol.

Keywords: Internet, E-Mail

Audience: Internet Surfers

Contact: Nathaniel S. Borenstein nsb@nsb.fv.com

User Info: File is: documents/rfc/rfc1521.txt

`ftp://nic.merit.edu`

Mind

Mind-L

A discussion group for people interested in mind-altering techniques, as well as mind machines. Related topics include smart nutrients, hypnosis, relaxation techniques, and subliminal tapes/videos. Does not cover hallucinatory drugs.

Keywords: Mind, Pschiatry, Psychology

Audience: Pschologists, Psychiatrists

Details: Free

User Info: To Subscribe to the list, send an e-mail message requesting subscription to the URL address below.

`mailto:mind-l-request@asylum.sf.ca.us`

Miniatures

Miniatures

The Miniatures Digest is a mailing list for discussion of the painting, sculpting, converting, and displaying of miniature figurines, generally for war games or fantasy role-playing games.

Keywords: Miniatures, Role-Playing

Audience: Miniature Figurine Collectors

Contact: minimallist-request@cs.unc.edu

Details: Free

User Info: To Subscribe to the list, send an e-mail message requesting subscription to the URL address below.

`mailto:minilist@cs.unc.edu`

Miniaturized Plants

Bonsai

This list has been set up to facilitate discussion of the art and craft of bonsai (the Oriental art of miniaturizing trees and plants into forms that mimic nature) and related art forms.

Keywords: Bonsai, Ornamental Plants, Miniaturized Plants

Audience: Bonsai Enthusiasts, Horticulturists, Ornamental Plant Enthusiasts, Nursery Owners

Contact: Dan@foghorn.pass.wayne.edu

Details: Free

User Info: To Subscribe to the list, send an e-mail message to the URL address below, consisting of a single line reading:

SUB bonsai YourFirstName YourLastName

To send a message to the entire list, address it to: bonsai@cms.cc.wayne.edu

Notes: Everyone interested, whether novice or professional, is invited to subscribe.

`mailto:listserv@cms.cc.wayne.edu`

Mining

University of Utah Library

The library's holdings are large and wide-ranging and contain significant collections in many fields.

Keywords: Western America, Middle Eastern Studies, Geology, Mining

Audience: Researchers, Students, General Public

Details: Free

Notes: Expect: Command Line, Send: Dial Unis

`telnet://lib.utah.edu`

Minor League

Minors ★

Issues affecting minor league baseball, including new stadium standards, minor league franchise status and changes, road trips and groups, schedules, team and league status, players and teams to watch, and collectibles.

Keywords: Baseball Enthusiasts

Audience: Baseball Enthusiasts

Details: Free

User Info: To Subscribe to the list, send an e-mail message requesting subscription to the URL address below.

`mailto:minors-request@medrant.apple.com`

Minorities

POS302-L ★

A discussion list created for the "Race, Ethnicity, and Social Inequality" seminar offered at Illinois State University (spring 1994). The general purposes of the list are to create an e-mail audience for the written work of enrolled students and to invite a broad audience to participate in the seminar.

Keywords: Race, Ethnicity, Minorities

Audience: Ethnic Studies Students, Sociologists, Educators

Details: Free

User Info: To Subscribe to the list, send an e-mail message to the URL address below, consisting of a single line reading:

SUB pos302-l YourFirstName YourLastName

To send a message to the entire list, address it to: pos302-l@ilstu.edu

`mailto:listserv@ilstu.edu`

soc.culture.african.american ★

A Usenet newsgroup providing information and discussion about African American culture.

Keywords: African American Studies, Sociology, Minorities

Audience: Sociologists

Details: Free

User Info: To Subscribe to this Usenet newsgroup, you need access to a newsreader.

`news:soc.culture.african.american`

Miracles

Miracles ★

This list provides daily readings from: A Course in Miracles and other selected readings from teachers, lecturers, and Course in Miracles Centers to provide additional reflection, inspiration, and avenues of practical application.

Keywords: Miracles

Audience: General Public

Contact: perry.sills@EBayperrys@spiritlead. Sun.COM

Details: Free

User Info: To Subscribe to the list, send an e-mail message requesting subscription to the URL address below.

`mailto:perry@spiritlead.Sun.COM`

misc.consumers

misc.consumers ★

A Usenet newsgroup providing information and discussion about consumer interests, including product reviews.

Keywords: Consumerism

Audience: Consumers, General Public

Details: Free

User Info: To Subscribe to this Usenet newsgroup, you need access to a newsreader.

`news:misc.consumers`

misc.consumers.house ★

A Usenet newsgroup providing information and discussion about owning and maintaining your house.

Keywords: Home Economics, Housing

Audience: Home Owners, General Public

Details: Free

User Info: To Subscribe to this Usenet newsgroup, you need access to a newsreader.

`news:misc.consumers.house`

misc.forsale

misc.forsale ★

A Usenet newsgroup providing information and discussion about items for sale.

Keywords: Consumerism

Audience: General Public

Details: Free

User Info: To Subscribe to this Usenet newsgroup, you need access to a newsreader.

`news:misc.forsale`

misc.handicap

misc.handicap ★

A Usenet newsgroup providing information and discussion for and about handicapped individuals.

Keywords: Disabilities

Audience: Differently Abled People, Disabled

Details: Free

User Info: To Subscribe to this Usenet newsgroup, you need access to a newsreader.

`news:misc.handicap`

misc.headlines

misc.headlines ★

A Usenet newsgroup providing information and discussion about current events and issues.

Keywords: Current Events

Audience: General Public

Details: Free

User Info: To Subscribe to this Usenet newsgroup, you need access to a newsreader.

`news:misc.headlines`

misc.invest

misc.invest ★

A Usenet newsgroup providing information and discussion about how to invest money.

Keywords: Investments, Finance

Audience: General Public

Details: Free

User Info: To Subscribe to this Usenet newsgroup, you need access to a newsreader.

`news:misc.invest`

misc.invest.real-estate

misc.invest.real-estate ★

A Usenet newsgroup providing information and discussion about property investments.

Keywords: Investments, Real Estate

A B C D E F G H I J K L **M** N O P Q R S T U V W X Y Z

Audience: General Public

Details: Free

User Info: To Subscribe to this Usenet newsgroup, you need access to a newsreader.

`news:misc.invest.real-estate`

misc.jobs.misc

misc.jobs.misc

A Usenet newsgroup providing information and discussion about miscellaneous available jobs.

Keywords: Employment

Audience: Job Seekers, General Public

Details: Free

User Info: To Subscribe to this Usenet newsgroup, you need access to a newsreader.

`news:misc.jobs.misc`

misc.jobs.offered

misc.jobs.offered

A Usenet newsgroup providing information and discussion about job openings, listed by subject.

Keywords: Employment

Audience: Job Seekers, General Public

Details: Free

User Info: To Subscribe to this Usenet newsgroup, you need access to a newsreader.

`news:misc.jobs.offered`

misc.jobs.resumes

misc.jobs.resumes

A Usenet newsgroup providing information and discussion about resumes.

Keywords: Employment

Audience: Job Seekers, General Public

Details: Free

User Info: To Subscribe to this Usenet newsgroup, you need access to a newsreader.

`news:misc.jobs.resumes`

misc.kids

misc.kids

A Usenet newsgroup providing information and discussion about children and their behavior.

Keywords: Children, Child Care

Audience: Parents, Child Development Professionals, Children

Details: Free

User Info: To Subscribe to this Usenet newsgroup, you need access to a newsreader.

`news:misc.kids`

misc.legal

misc.legal

A Usenet newsgroup providing information and discussion about law and ethics.

Keywords: Law, Ethics

Audience: Lawyers, Legal Professionals, General Public

Details: Free

User Info: To Subscribe to this Usenet newsgroup, you need access to a newsreader.

`news:misc.legal`

misc.wanted

misc.wanted

A Usenet newsgroup providing information and discussion about items, excluding software, that are wanted or needed.

Keywords: Consumerism

Audience: General Public

Details: Free

User Info: To Subscribe to this Usenet newsgroup, you need access to a newsreader.

`news:misc.wanted`

Miscellaneous Federal Documents

Miscellaneous Federal Documents

This directory includes documents such as the Civil Rights Act of 1991, the Computer Fraud and Abuse Act, the High-Performance Computing Senate Report, and more.

Keywords: Government (US Federal), Federal Documents (US)

Audience: Politicians, Journalists, Students (high school up)

Details: Free

`gopher://wiretap.spies.com/11/Gov/US-Docs`

Mississippi State University Library

Mississippi State University Library

The library's holdings are large and wide-ranging and contain significant collections in many fields.

Keywords: History (US), Forestry, Energy, Carter (Hodding, Papers of), Mississippi

Audience: General Public, Researchers, Librarians, Document Delivery Professionals

Contact: Stephen Cunetto
shc1@ra.msstate.edu

Details: Free

User Info: Expect: username, Send: msu; Expect: password, Send: library

`telnet://libserv.msstate.edu`

MIT Media Lab

MIT Media Lab

Online documents available through the ACCESS service that the MIT Media Laboratory is providing to sponsors using the File Transfer Protocol (FTP).

Keywords: Internet, Multimedia

Audience: Internet Surfers

Details: Free, Multimedia

`ftp://media-lab.media.mit.edu`

MLoL

MLoL

The MLoL (Musical List of Lists) is a list of music-related mailing lists available on the Internet.

Keywords: Music, Mailing Lists

Audience: Musicians, General Public

Details: Free

User Info: To Subscribe to the list, send an e-mail message requesting a subscription to the URL address below.

`mailto:mlol-request@wariat.org`

Model Horses

Model-horse

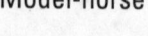

Discussion of the model-horse hobby. All aspects of showing (live and photo), collecting, re-making/re-painting for all breeds are discussed. All ages and levels of experience welcome.

Keywords: Model Horses, Hobbies

Audience: Model Horse Collectors

Details: Free

User Info: To Subscribe to the list, send an e-mail message requesting a subscription to the URL address below.

`mailto:model-horse-request@qiclab.scn.rain.com`

Modem

SupraFAX

This list was created to help people who are using the SupraFAX v.32bis modem.

Keywords: Modem, FAX

Audience: Modem Users, FAX Users

Contact: David Tiberio
subscribe@xamiga.linet.org

Details: Free

User Info: To Subscribe to the list, send an e-mail message requesting a subscription to the URL address below.

   To send a message to the entire list, address it to: subscribe@xamiga.linet.org

`mailto:subscribe@xamiga.linet.org`

Modern Dance

OMD (Orchestral Manoeuvres In The Dark)

The OMD list is a forum for discussions about the English pop band Orchestral Manoevres In The Dark, which often incorporate modern dance elements into its music. The discussions are not moderated but they should have something to do with the band or with ex-band members.

Keywords: OMD, Modern Dance

Audience: OMD Enthusiasts

Contact: Dave Datta
omd-request@cs.uwp.edu

Details: Free

User Info: To Subscribe to the list, send an e-mail message requesting a subscription to the URL address below.

   To send a message to the entire list, address it to: omd@cs.uwp.edu

Notes: The list is available as a daily digest and reflector. Archives are stored at ftp.uwp.edu.

`mailto:omd-request@cs.uwp.edu`

modesty-blaise

modesty-blaise

A discussion forum on Peter O'Donnell's Modesty Blaise books and comics. Topics include character, plot, artists, and relevant articles.

Keywords: Comic Books, Comics, O'Donnell (Peter)

Audience: Modesty Blaise Enthusiasts

Contact: Thomas Gramstad
modesty-blaise-request@math.uio.no

User Info: To Subscribe to the list, send an e-mail message to the URL address below consisting of a single line reading:

   SUB modesty-blaise YourFirstName YourLastName

`mailto: modesty-blaise-request@math.uio.no`

Modula-2 (Programming Language)

info-M2

E-conference for the Modula-2 programming language.

Keywords: Programming Languages, Modula-2 (Programming Language)

Audience: Modula-2 Programmers

Contact: Thomas Habernoll
postmast@ucf1vm.cc.ucf.edu (USA);
habernol@tubvm.cs.tu-berlin.de (Europe)

Details: Free

User Info: To Subscribe to the list, send an e-mail message to the URL address below consisting of a single line reading:

   SUB info-M2 YourFirstName YourLastName

   To send a message to the entire list, address it to: info-M2@ucf1vm.cc.ucf.edu

`mailto:listserv@ucf1vm.cc.ucf.edu`

Molecular Biology

Archive of Biology Software and Data

The main area of concentration of this archive is molecular biology. It contains software for the Macintosh, MS-DOS, VAX-VMS, and UNIX.

Keywords: Health, Biology, Molecular Biology

Sponsor: Indiana University

Audience: Biologists, Students

Contact: archive@bio.indiana.edu

Details: Free

Notes: It is recommended that the file Archive.doc be transferred and read first. This file gives considerable information about and instructions for using the archive.

`ftp://ftp.bio.indiana.edu`

Bioinformatics

This gopher server provides data and software related to bioinformatics, including public-domain software for biology and mirror storage for the main databases of the Human Genome Project and Molecular Biology.

Keywords: Bioinformatics, Biology, Molecular Biology

Sponsor: Weizmann Institute of Science, Israel

Audience: Scientists, Biologists

Contact: lsprilus@weizmann.weizmann.ac.il

Details: Free

`gopher://bioinformatics.weizmann.ac.il`

`http://bioinformatics.weizman.act.il`

bionet.molbio.genbank.updates

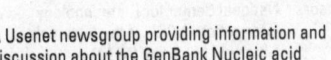

A Usenet newsgroup providing information and discussion about the GenBank Nucleic acid database.

Keywords: Molecular Biology, Biology, Genetics

Audience: Molecular Biologists, Researchers

User Info: To Subscribe to this Usenet newsgroup, you need access to a newsreader.

`news:bionet.molbio.genbank.updates`

Biotechnet Electronic Buyer's Guide

Biotechnet is a global computer network created specially for research biologists. It is intended to be a valuable source of information and data, a communications resource, a forum to foster the exchange of current ideas, and an international marketplace for relevant goods and service.

Keywords: Molecular Biology, Electrophoresis, Chromatography

Audience: Molecular Biologists, Chemists, Laboratory Suppliers

Profile: One of the services offered by Biotechnet is the Electronic Buyer's Guide, which is divided into five individual databases for specific product categories: Molecular Biology, Electrophoresis, Chromatography, Liquid Handling, and Instruments & Apparatus. After selecting one of the guides at the prompt, you can search through each database to find either product names and applications or the name and address of the company that manufactures the product you wish to locate.

A B C D E F G H I J K L **M** N O P Q R S T U V W X Y Z

A
B
C
D
E
F
G
H
I
J
K
L
M
N
O
P
Q
R
S
T
U
V
W
X
Y
Z

Details: Free

Password: bguide

`telnet://biotech@biotechnet.com`

EMBnet (European Molecular Biology Network)

 ★★★★

A group of European Internet sites which provide computational molecular biology services to both national and international researchers.

Keywords: Biology, Bioscience, Molecular Biology

Sponsor: The EC Funding Program (BRIDGE)

Audience: Biologists, Molecular Biologists, Researchers

Contact: Rodrigo Lopez, Robert Herzog
rodrigol@biotek.uio.no
rherzog@ulb.ac.be

`http://biomaster.uio.no/embnet-www.html`

GenBank

 ★★★★

The GenBank database provides a collection of nucleotide sequences as well as relevant bibliographic and biological annotation.

Keywords: Genetics, Medicine, Molecular Biology

Sponsor: National Center for Biotechnology Information (NCBI) at the National Library of Medicine (NLM)

Audience: Geneticists, Scientists, Molecular Biologists

Profile: DNA sequence entries are rated by specialized indexers in the Division of Library Operations. Over 325,000 articles per year from 3,400 journals are scanned for sequence data. They are supplemented by journals in plant and veterinary sciences through a collaboration with the National Agricultural Library. These records join the direct submission data stream and submissions from the European Molecular Biology Laboratory (EMBL) Data Library and the DNA Database of Japan (DDBJ).

Contact: info@ncbi.nlm.nih.gov

Details: Free

Send direct submissions to gb-sub@ncbi.nlm.nih.gov and updates and changes to existing GenBank records to update@ncbi.nlm.nih.gov

For help in retrieval by e-mail send an e-mail message with the word "help" in the the body of the message to retrieve@ncbi.nlm.nih.gov

`gopher://gopher.nih.gov/77/gopherlib/indices/genbank/index`

Harvard Biosciences Online Journals

 ★★★★

A resource containing selected online journals and periodicals in biology and medicine. Includes peer-reviewed e-journals, journal indexes, and databases.

Keywords: Biology, Bioscience, Molecular Biology

Sponsor: Harvard Biolabs, Harvard University, Cambridge, Massachusetts, USA

Audience: Biologists, Molecular Biologists, Researchers

Contact: Keith Robinson, Steve Brenner
krobinson@nucleus.harvard.edu
s.e.brenner@bioc.cam.ac.uk

`http://golgi.harvard.edu/journals.html`

ICGEBnet

★

This is the information server of the International Centre for Genetic Engineering and Molecular Biology (ICGEB), Trieste, Italy.

Keywords: Molecular Biology, Biotechnology, Italy, Europe

Audience: Molecular Biotechnologists, Molecular Biologists

Profile: The primary purpose of the ICGEB computer resource is to disseminate the best of currently available computational technology to the molecular biologists of the ICGEB research community.

Contact: postmaster@icgeb.trieste.it

Details: Free

`gopher://icgeb.trieste.it`

Johns Hopkins Genetic Databases

 ★★★

This gopher provides electronic access to documents pertaining to computational biology and a number of different genetic databases.

Keywords: Genetics, Molecular Biology, Medicine, Biology

Sponsor: Johns Hopkins University

Audience: Geneticists, Researchers, Scientists, Molecular Biologists

Profile: The databases accessible from this entry point include GenBank, Swiss-Prot, PDB, PIR, LiMB, TFD, AAtDB, ACEDB, CompoundKB, PROSITE EC Enzyme Database, NRL_3D Protein-Sequence-Structure Database, Eukaryotic Promoter Database (EPD), Cloning Vector Database, Expressed Sequence Tag Database (ESTDB), Online Mendelian Inheritance Man (OMIM), Sequence Analysis Bibliographic Reference Data Bank (Seqanalref), and Database Taxonomy (GenBank, Swiss-Prot). The gopher also provides direct links to other gophers with information relevant to biology.

Contact: Dan Jacobson
danj@mail.gdb.org

Details: Free

`gopher://merlot.welch.jhu.edu`

National Institutes of Health Gopher

 ★★★★

Provides access to a broad range of National Institutes of Health (NIH) resources (library catalogues, databases) via the Internet.

Keywords: Health, AIDS, Molecular Biology, Grants

Sponsor: National Institutes of Health

Audience: Health Professionals, Molecular Biologists, Researchers

Profile: This gopher provides access to NIH resources, including institute phone books and calendars, library catalogs, molecular biology databases, the full text of the NIH Guide for Grants and Contracts, files containing AIDS and cancer information and more.

Contact: gopher@gopher.nih.gov

Details: Free

Notes: Expect: Login; Enter: Gopher

`telnet://gopher.nih.gov`

`gopher://gopher.nih.gov`

`gopher://odie.niaid.nih.gov`

University of Texas Health Science Center at Tyler Library

 ★★

The library's holdings are large and wide-ranging and contain significant collections in many fields.

Keywords: Biochemistry, Cardiopulmonary Medicine, Cell Biology, Family Practice, Molecular Biology

Audience: Researchers, Students, General Public

Details: Free

Notes: Expect: Username Prompt, Send: LIS

`telnet://athena.uthscsa.edu`

Moms

Moms

 ★

Moms is a list for lesbian mothers.

Keywords: Lesbians, Parenting

Audience: Lesbians

Contact: moms-request@qiclab.scn.rain.com

Details: Free

User Info: To Subscribe to the list, send an e-mail message requesting subscription to the URL address below.

`mailto:moms-request@qiclab.scn.rain.com`

Monarchy

Counterev-L

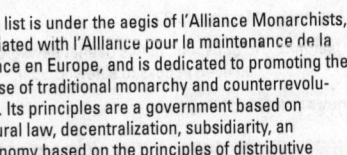

This list is under the aegis of l'Alliance Monarchists, affiliated with l'Alliance pour la maintenance de la France en Europe, and is dedicated to promoting the cause of traditional monarchy and counterrevolution. Its principles are a government based on natural law, decentralization, subsidiarity, an economy based on the principles of distributive justice, and the defense of traditional Western values.

Keywords: Monarchy, Government (International)

Audience: Monarchists, Counterrevolutionaries

Contact: Jovan Weismiller
ae852@yfn.ysu.edu

Details: Free

User Info: To Subscribe to the list, send an e-mail message requesting a subscription to the URL address below.

`mailto:ae852@yfn.ysu.edu`

Montefiore Medical Center Library Online Catalog

Montefiore Medical Center Library Online Catalog

Catalog of library holdings.

Keywords: Medicine, Libraries

Sponsor: Montefiore Medical Center at Albert Einstein College of Medicine, New York

Audience: Health Care Professionals, Medical Researchers, Educators, Students

Details: Free
After Telnetting, hit RETURN twice, then select 0 on main menu. Select 2 on locations menu.To exit, hit the Telnet escape key.

`telnet://lis.aecom.yu.edu`

Moon Travel Handbooks

Moon Travel Handbooks

Moon Publications' gopher features a travel newsletter, as well as excerpts and ordering information for their travel guides.

Keywords: Travel, Books

Sponsor: Moon Publications

Audience: International Travelers, General Public

Contact: gopher@moon.com

Notes: Also see Moon Publications' hypertext exhibit, Big Island of Hawaii Handbook, at http://bookweb.cwis.uci.edu:8042.

`gopher://gopher.moon.com`

Mormonism

Harvard University Library

The library's holdings are large and wide-ranging and contain significant collections in many fields.

Keywords: Afrikaans, Alchemy, Arabic Culure (History of), Celtic Philology, Congo Languages, Folklore, Hebraica, Mormonism, Numismatics, Quakers, Sanskrit, Witchcraft, Arabic Philology

Audience: General Public, Researchers, Librarians, Document Delivery Professionals

Details: Free

Notes: Expect: Mitek Server..., Send: Enter or Return; Expect: prompt, Send: hollis

`telnet://hollis.harvard.edu`

Princeton University Library

The library's holdings are large and wide-ranging. They contain significant collections in many fields.

Keywords: China, Japan, Classics, History (Ancient), Near Eastern Studies, Literature (American), Literature (English), Aeronautics, Middle Eastern Studies, Mormonism, Publishing

Audience: General Public, Researchers, Librarians, Document Delivery Professionals

Details: Free

Notes: Expect: Connect message, blank screen, Send: <cr>; Expect: #, Send: Call 500

`telnet://pucable.princeton.edu`

Morphology

Qmlist (Quantitative Morphology List)

This is an open, unmoderated mailing list to support researchers and clinicians in the field of quantitative morphology.

Keywords: Morphology

Audience: Morphologists, Biologists

Contact: Dean Pentcheff
dean2@tbone.biol.scarolina.edu

Details: Free

User Info: To Subscribe to the list, send an e-mail message to the URL address below, consisting of a single line reading:

SUB qmlist YourFirstName YourLastName

To send a message to the entire list, address it to:
qmlist@tbone.biol.scarolina.edu

`mailto:listserv@tbone.biol.scarolina.edu`

Morris Dancing

Morris

A discussion list related to Morris Dancing, including Cotswold, Border, Northwest, Rapper, Longsword, Abbots Bromley, Garland, and similar forms of English dance along with the accompanying music and traditions.

Keywords: Morris Dancing, England, Dance

Audience: Morris Dancers

Details: Free

User Info: To Subscribe to the list, send an e-mail message requesting subscription to the URL address below.

`mailto:morris@suvm.acs.syr.edu`

Mosaic

Mosaic Home Page

This is the welcome page to the National Center for Supercomputing Applications (NCSA) World Wide Web server, which features the Mosaic application. Mosaic provides a network-distributed hypermedia system for information discovery. It is Internet-based and is free for academic, research, and internal commercial use.

Keywords: Internet Tools, Mosaic, WWW

Audience: Internet Surfers

Contact: mosaic-x@ncsa.uiuc.edu

Details: Free

`http://www.ncsa.uiuc.edu/sdg/ software/mosaic/hcsamosaichome.html`

NCSA (National Center for Supercomputing Applications)

A high-performance computing and communications facility and research center designed to serve the US computational science and engineering community.

Keywords: Supercomputing, Computer Networking, Computer Science, Mosaic

Sponsor: University of Illinois at Urbana-Champaign, Champaign, Illinois, USA

Audience: Students, Researchers, Computer Scientists, General Public

Contact: Systems Operator
pubs@ncsa.uiuc.edu

`http://www.ncsa.uiuc.edu/general/ hcsamome.html`

A
B
C
D
E
F
G
H
I
J
K
L
M
N
O
P
Q
R
S
T
U
V
W
X
Y
Z

A B C D E F G H I J K L **M** N O P Q R S T U V W X Y Z

Mother Jones

Mother Jones

A web site containing online electronic issues of Mother Jones magazine (and Zine), making possible instant electronic feedback to the publishers regarding articles.

Keywords: Zines, Ethics, Public Policy, Activism

Sponsor: Mother Jones

Audience: Students, General Public

Contact: Webserver
webserver@mojones.com

`http://www.mojones.com/motherjones.html`

Motor Racing

Funet Sports Information

An FTP archive of information on various sports with links to the archive at wuarchive.wustl.edu.

Keywords: Sports, Hockey, Motor Racing

Sponsor: Finnish Academic and Research Network (FUNET)

Audience: Sports Enthusiasts

Profile: A fairly extensive archive of information on both American (NBA, MLB, NHL, NFL) and worldwide sports (soccer, ice hockey, motor racing, and so on). Includes FAQs for various sports, statistics, pictures, and some sports games for the PC.

Contact: Jari Pullinen
sports-adm@nic.funet.fi

Details: Free, Images

`gopher://ftp.funet.fi/pub/sports`

University of Glasgow Information Service (GLANCE)

GLANCE provides subject-based information services, including an extensive section on European and world sports.

Keywords: Sports, Soccer, Motor Racing, Mountaineering, Squash, Cricket, Golf, Tennis, Europe, Scotland

Sponsor: University of Glasgow, Glasgow, Scotland

Audience: Sport Enthusiasts, Fitness Enthusiasts, Nature Lovers

Profile: Information at this site includes schedules, results, and statistics for sports such as cricket and soccer. There is also a selection of items on mountaineering.

Contact: Alan Dawson
a.dawson@uk.ac.gla.compserv

Details: Free

`gopher://govan.cent.gla.ac.uk/subject/sports and rec`

Motorcycles

BMW Motorcycles

This is a discussion of all years and models of BMW motorcycles.

Keywords: BMW Motorcycles, Motorcycles

Audience: Motorcycle Enthusiasts, BMW Enthusiasts

Contact: bmw-request@rider.cactus.org

Details: Free

User Info: To Subscribe to the list, send an e-mail message requesting a subscription to the URL address below.

To send a message to the entire list, address it to: bmw@rider.cactus.org

`mailto:bmw-request@rider.cactus.org`

Brit-Iron

The purpose of this list is to provide a friendly forum in which riders, owners, and admirers of British motorcycles can share information and experiences. A list of parts sources and shops that repair these classic machines is maintained. All makes are welcome, from AJS to Vellocette.

Keywords: Motorcycles

Audience: British Motorcycle Enthusiasts, Motorcycle Enthusiasts

Contact: cstringe@indiana.edu

Details: Free

User Info: To Subscribe to the list, send an e-mail message requesting a subscription to the URL address below.

To send a message to the entire list, address it to: brit-iron@indiana.edu

`mailto:brit-iron@indiana.edu`

Nedod

Discussion of events, technical issues, and just plain social exchange related to motorcycling in the New England area of the US.

Keywords: Motorcycles, New England

Audience: Motorcycle Enthusiasts

Contact: cookson@mbunix.mitre.org

User Info: To Subscribe to the list, send an e-mail message requesting a subscription to the URL address below.

`mailto:nedod-request@mbunix.mitre.org`

rec.motorcycles

A Usenet newsgroup providing information and discussion about motorcycles and related products.

Keywords: Motorcycles

Audience: Motorcycle Riders

User Info: To Subscribe to this Usenet newsgroup, you need access to a newsreader.

`news:rec.motorcycles`

Mountaineering

University of Glasgow Information Service (GLANCE)

GLANCE provides subject-based information services, including an extensive section on European and world sports.

Keywords: Sports, Soccer, Motor Racing, Mountaineering, Squash, Cricket, Golf, Tennis, Europe, Scotland

Sponsor: University of Glasgow, Glasgow, Scotland

Audience: Sport Enthusiasts, Fitness Enthusiasts, Nature Lovers

Profile: Information at this site includes schedules, results, and statistics for sports such as cricket and soccer. There is also a selection of items on mountaineering.

Contact: Alan Dawson
a.dawson@uk.ac.gla.compserv

Details: Free

`gopher://govan.cent.gla.ac.uk/Subject/Sports and Rec`

Movement

Biomch-L

This list is intended for members of the International, European, American, Canadian, and other Societies of Biomechanics, and for members of ISEK (International Society of Electrophysiological Kinesiology), as well as for all others with an interest in the general field of biomechanics and human or animal movement.

Keywords: Biomechanics, Kinesiology, Movement

Sponsor: International Society of Biomechanics

Audience: Kinesiologists

Contact: Ton van den Bogert
listserv@nic.surfnet.nl

Details: Free

User Info: To Subscribe to the list, send an e-mail message to the URL address below, consisting of a single line reading:

SUB biomch-l YourFirstName
YourLastName

To send a message to the entire list,
address it to: biomch-l@nic.surfnet.nl

Notes: To obtain technical help, send the
command send biomch-l guide to
listserv@hearn or listserv@nic.surfnet.nl.

`mailto:listserv@nic.surfnet.nl`

Movies

rec.arts.movies movie database

An extensive FTP database covering over 32,000
movies, with more than 370,000 filmography entries,
from early cinema to current releases.

Keywords: Movies, Television, Popular Culture

Audience: Movie Buffs

Profile: Interfaces to search the database
include Unix, MS-DOS and Amiga (and
Windows and Mac versions are in
development). The database includes
filmographies for actors, directors,
writers, composers, cinematographers,
editors, production designers, costume
designers and producers; plot
summaries; character names; movie
ratings; year of release; running times;
movie trivia; quotes; goofs; soundtracks;
personal trivia and Academy Award
information.

Contact: Col Needham
cn@ibmpcug.co.uk

Details: Free

`ftp://cathouse.org/pub/cathouse/`
`movies/database`

rec.arts.movies movie database (Cardiff WWW front-end)

An extensive, interactive database covering over
32,000 movies, with more than 370,000 filmography
entries, from early cinema to current releases.

Keywords: Movies, Television, Popular Culture,
Interactive Media

Audience: Movie Buffs

Profile: A WWW front-end to the rec.arts.movies
movie database, complete with form-
filling interfaces to add new data and to
rate movies (on a scale from 1 through
10). The database includes filmographies
for actors, directors, writers, composers,
cinematographers, editors, production
designers, costume designers and
producers; plot summaries; character
names; movie ratings; year of release;
running times; movie trivia; quotes;
goofs; soundtracks; personal trivia and
Academy Award information.

Contact: Rob Hartill
Robert.Hartill@cm.cf.ac.uk

Details: Free

`http://www.cm.cf.ac.uk/movies`

`http://www.msstate.edu/movies`

MR2-Interest

Mr2-interest

Discussion of Toyota MR2s, old and new.

Keywords: Automobiles

Audience: Automobile Owners

Details: Free

User Info: To Subscribe to the list, send an e-mail
message requesting subscription to the
URL address below.

`mailto:mr2-interest-request@validgh.`
`com`

MS-Access

MS-Access

A list for the discussion of MS (Microsoft) Access
topics, including Access Basic questions, reviews,
rumors, and so on.

Keywords: Microsoft Corporation, Databases

Audience: Computer Users, Database Managers

Details: Free

User Info: To Subscribe to the list, send an e-mail
message requesting subscription to the
URL address below.

`mailto:ms-access-request@eunet.co.at`

MS-DOS Computers

info-GNU-MSDOS

This electronic conference is for the GNUISH MS-
DOS Development Group.

Keywords: Shareware, Freeware, MS-DOS
Computers

Audience: MS-DOS Users, GNUISH MS-DOS
Developers

Contact: David J. Camp
david@wubios.wustl.edu

Details: Free

User Info: To Subscribe to the list, send an e-mail
message to the URL address below
consisting of a single line reading:

SUB info-GNU-MSDOS YourFirstName
YourLastName

`mailto:listserv@wugate.wustl.edu`

Microsoft Corporation World Wide Web Server

This system has been set up to provide lay and
technical information for the public about Microsoft
and its products.

Keywords: Microsoft, Windows, MS-DOS, Chicago

Sponsor: Microsoft Corporation

Audience: Computer Users, Microsoft Product
Users, Computer Programmers,
Investors

Profile: The Microsoft Knowledge Base and
Software Library is accessible here.
Information can be obtained on
Windows NT Server, Developer Network
News, Windows News, and also
Windows Sockets Information. There are
sections on Windows 4 (Chicago),
Microsoft's new 32-bit TCP/IP VxD stack,
a "What's New" page, current
employment opportunities at Microsoft,
recent speeches given by Microsoft
Corporation's CEO Bill Gates, as well as
current financial information about
Microsoft.

Contact: Email: www@microsoft.com

Details: Free, Images

Notes: The information contained on this server
is copyrighted, and may not be
distributed, downloaded, modified,
reused, reposted, or otherwise used
outside the scope of a WWW client
without the express written permission
of Microsoft Corporation.

`http://www.microsoft.com`

`gopher://gopher.microsoft.com`

`ftp://ftp.microsoft.com`

MSA-Net

MSA-Net

A mailing list intended to meet the communication
needs of Muslim Student Associations (MSA) in
North America, and to discuss issues related to
Islam and MSAs are discussed.

Keywords: Islam, Muslim Student Associations

Audience: Muslims

Contact: Aalim Fevens
msa-request@htm3.ee.queensu.ca

User Info: To Subscribe to the list, send an e-mail
message

Notes: Members must be Muslim.

`mailto:msa-request@htm3.ee.queensu.ca`

Mt. Xinu

Mtxinu-users

Discussion and bug fixes for users of the 4.3+NFS
release from the Mt. Xinu folks.

Keywords: Mt. Xinu Computing

Audience: Computer Users

A
B
C
D
E
F
G
H
I
J
K
L
M
N
O
P
Q
R
S
T
U
V
W
X
Y
Z

A
B
C
D
E
F
G
H
I
J
K
L
M
N
O
P
Q
R
S
T
U
V
W
X
Y
Z

Details: Free

User Info: To Subscribe to the list, send an e-mail message requesting subscription to the URL address below.

`mailto:mtxinu-users-request@nike.cair.du.edu`

Muchomedia Conference

Muchomedia Conference

A conference on the WELL about multimedia with topics ranging from products and software to multimedia for beginners.

Keywords: Multimedia, Art

Audience: Artists, Computer Programmers, Producers

Contact: Douglas Crockford
crock@well.sf.ca.us

Notes: To participate in a conference on the WELL, you must first establish an account on the WELL. To do so, start by typing: telnet well.sf.ca.us

`telnet://well.sf.ca.us`

MUDs

MUD

A discussion list for the exchange of information about new and recommended Multiuser Dungeons and Dragons (MUDs).

Keywords: MUDs, Games

Audience: MUD Users

Contact: Joseph Wisdom
jwisdom@gnu.ai.mit.edu

Details: Free

User Info: To Subscribe to the list, send an e-mail message requesting subscription to the URL address below.

`mailto:jwisdom@gnu.ai.mit.edu`

Multicasting

Multicast

Discussion of multicast and broadcast issues in an open systems interconnection environment.

Keywords: Multicasting, Broadcasting

Audience: Multicasters, Broadcasting Professionals

Details: Free

User Info: To Subscribe to the list, send an e-mail message requesting subscription to the URL address below.

`mailto:multicast-request@arizona.edu`

Multicast Backbone

Live audio and video multicast virtual network on top of the Internet.

Keywords: Internet, Information Retrieval, Multitaskingg

Audience: Internet Surfers

Details: Free; sound files available.

`ftp://venera.isi.edu`

`http://venera.isi.edu`

Multilateral Treaties

Multilateral Treaties

An experimental program to make available to the Internet community the text of a wide variety of multilateral conventions, even those which have not yet been ratified.

Keywords: Treaties, Law (International)

Sponsor: The Fletcher School of Law and Diplomacy, Cornell University, Ithaca, NY

Audience: Government Officials, Researchers, Lawyers

Profile: Almost all treaties listed are available in print form. The program will enable access to even very recent conventions. Primary focus is on Environmental and human rights issues but other fields are also included. The conventions coming out of the 1992 United Nations Conference on the Environment and Development have NOT been included as they are available elsewhere through CIESIN. Those Treaties covered include: Convention on International Trade in Endangered Species of Wild Fa; Montreal Protocol on Substances that Depleate the Ozone Layer; The Berne Convention for the Protection of Literary and Artistic Works; Agreement on the Rescue of Astronauts; the return of Astronauts

Contact: Peter Scott Director, Multilaterals Project, Fletcher School of Law and Diplomacy
pstott@pearl.tufts.edu
pstott@icg.apc.org

Details: Free

Notes: Select from menu as appropriate

`gopher://gopher.law.cornell.edu/11/foreign/fletcher-cat`

Multimedia

(The) Electric Eclectic

A multimedia magazine delivered online that includes pictures, sounds, and text.

Keywords: Magazines, Multimedia

Audience: General Public

`mailto:ee-discuss-request@eitech.cm`

ACEN (Art Com Electronic Network)

A conference on the WELL for art, technology, and text-based artworks.

Keywords: Art, Literature (Contemporary), Multimedia

Sponsor: Art Com Electronic Network

Audience: Artists, Musicians, Writers

Profile: Started in 1986, ACEN is a seminal art BBS that includes actual artworks, discussion on topics such as software as art, and on line published works by John Cage, Fred Truck, Jim Rosenberg, Judy Malloy, and others.

Contact: Carl Loeffler
artcomtv@well.sf.ca.us

To participate in a conference on the WELL, you must first establish an account on the WELL. To do so, start by typing: telnet://well.sf.ca.us

`telnet://well.sf.ca.us`

ACM SIGGRAPH Online Bibliography Project

This is a collection of computer-graphics bibliographic references.

Keywords: Multimedia, Interactive, Computer Graphics, Programming

Sponsor: Association of Computing Machinery (ACM), Special Interest Group on Computer Graphics (SIGGRAPH)

Audience: Developers, Designers, Producers, Educators, Programmers, Graphic Artists

Profile: The goal of this project is to maintain an up-to-date database of computer-graphics literature, in a format that is accessible to as many members of the computer-graphics community as possible. The database includes references from conferences and workshops worldwide and from a variety of publications dating back as far as the late-19th century. The majority of the major journals and conference proceedings from the mid-1970s to the present are listed.

Contact: bibadmin@siggraph.org

Details: Free, Moderated, Multimedia

`ftp://siggraph.org/publications`

CinemaSpace

CinemaSpace, from the Film Studies Program at UC Berkeley, is devoted to all aspects of Cinema and New Media.

Keywords: Cinema, Film, Multimedia

Sponsor: Film Studies Program at UC Berkeley

Audience: Students, Film researchers

Profile: Projects for CinemaSpace include academic papers on film and new media, film theory and critique. multimedia lectures, and sources of film clips and references to other sites.

Contact: xcohen@garnet.berkeley.edu

Details: Free

`http://remarque.berkeley.edu/~xcohen`

Diversity U

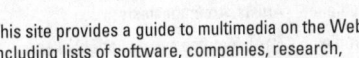

Diversity University is an experiment in interactive learning.

Keywords: Education, Interactive Learning, Multimedia

Audience: Educators, Researchers

Details: Free

`gopher://erau.db.erau.edu`

FineArt Forum

A monthly newsletter that includes listings of art and technology events, showcases, conferences, and jobs.

Keywords: Art, Multimedia

Sponsor: The International Society for the Arts, Sciences, and Technology

Audience: Art Educators, Art Professionals, Artists

Profile: Published by the National Science Foundation Engineering Research Center for Computational Field Simulation, Mississippi State University. FineArt Forum has provided timely information to a large international audience since 1988. The subscriber list consists of individuals working in the realm where art, science, and technology converge. Issues provide information about conferences and competitions, calls for presentations and research, and notices about performances. FineArt_Online is both an archive of FineArt Forum, ISEA News, Leonardo Electronic News, and a variety of longer postings. In January 1994 it began posting an online gallery.

Contact: Paul Brown brown@erc.msstate.edu

User Info: To Subscribe, send e-mail to: brown@erc.msstate.edu, with the message

SUB FAST; also give your name, postal address, and e-mail address.

`http://www.msstate.edu/ fineart_online/home.html`

Free for All

An experiment in a networked hypermedia group bulletin board.

Keywords: Internet, Group Communications, Multimedia

Audience: Internet Surfers, Multimedia Enthusiasts

Details: Free, Multimedia

`http://south.ncsa.uiuc.edu/free.html`

Georgia State University Library

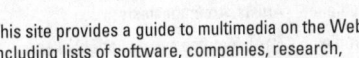

The library's holdings are large and wide-ranging and contain significant collections in many fields.

Keywords: Labor (History of), Multimedia, Mercer (Johnny, Collection of)

Audience: General Public, Researchers, Librarians, Document Delivery Professionals

Contact: Phil Williams isgpew@gsuvm1.gsu.edu

Details: Free

Notes: Expect: VM screen, Send: RETURN; Expect: CP READ, Send: DIAL VTAM, press RETURN; Expect: CICS screen, Send: PF1

`telnet://library.gsu.edu`

Index to Multimedia Information Sources

This site provides a guide to multimedia on the Web, including lists of software, companies, research, publications, conferences, archives, and galleries.

Keywords: Multimedia, Interactive Media

Audience: Designers, Educators

Contact: Simon Gibbs simon.gibbs@gmd.de

Details: Free

`http://cui_www.unige.ch/osg/ multimediainfo/index.html`

Kaleidospace

This is a new Web server that provides a multimedia showcase for artists, performers, CD-ROM authors, musicians, writers, animators, filmmakers and software developers.

Keywords: Art, Computer Art, Multimedia

Audience: Artists, Performers, CD-ROM Authors, Musicians, Writers, Animators, Filmmakers, Software Developers

Profile: This site was created to support independent artists. The site has similarities to other web servers such as IUMA, but differs in that it works with all kinds of artists, and that it processes orders for the artist's material.

Contact: Jeannie Novak, Peter Markiewicz jeannienov@aol.com peterm@ewald.mbi.ucla.edu

`http://kspace.com`

`http://fire.kspace.com`

Leonardo Electronic Almanac

The Leonardo Electronic Almanac (LEA) is a monthly, edited journal and an electronic archive dedicated to providing current perspectives in the art, science and technology domains.

Keywords: Art, Multimedia, Music, Electronic Media

Sponsor: International Society for the Arts, Sciences, and Technology

Audience: New Media Artists, Researchers, Developers, Art Educators, Art Professionals

Profile: LEA is an international, interdisciplinary forum for people interested in the use of new media in contemporary artistic expression, especially involving 20th century science and technology. Material is contributed by artists, scientists, philosophers and educators. LEA is published by the MIT Press for Leonardo, the International Society for the Arts, Sciences, and Technology (ISAST).

Contact: Craig Harris craig@well.sf.ca.us

Details: Costs, Moderated, Images, Sounds, Multimedia

`mail to:journals-orders@mit.edu`

`ftp://mitpress.mit.edu/pub/Leonardo- Elec-Almanac`

MIT Media Lab

Online documents available through the ACCESS service that the MIT Media Laboratory is providing to sponsors using the File Transfer Protocol (FTP).

Keywords: Internet, Multimedia

Audience: Internet Surfers

Details: Free, Multimedia

`ftp://media-lab.media.mit.edu`

Muchomedia Conference

A conference on the WELL about multimedia with topics ranging from products and software to multimedia for beginners.

Keywords: Multimedia, Art

Audience: Artists, Computer Programmers, Producers

Contact: Douglas Crockford crock@well.sf.ca.us

Notes: To participate in a conference on the WELL, you must first establish an account on the WELL. To do so, start by typing: telnet well.sf.ca.us

`telnet://well.sf.ca.us`

Multimedia Index

A list of multimedia information sources on the Internet.

A
B
C
D
E
F
G
H
I
J
K
L
M
N
O
P
Q
R
S
T
U
V
W
X
Y
Z

A
B
C
D
E
F
G
H
I
J
K
L
M
N
O
P
Q
R
S
T
U
V
W
X
Y
Z

Keywords: Internet, Multimedia

Sponsor: Centre Universitaire d'Informatique, University of Geneva

Audience: Internet Surfers

Contact: Oscar Nierstrasz
oscar@cui.unige.ch

Details: Free, Multimedia

`http://cui_www.unige.ch`

Multimedia Lab BU ★

Information about the Multimedia Lab at Boston University (BU), investigating issues surrounding the contruction of general purpose distributed multimedia information systems (DMISs).

Keywords: Internet, Multimedia

Sponsor: Boston University

Audience: Internet Surfers

Contact: T.D.C. Little
tdcl@spiderman.bu.edu

Details: Free, Multimedia

`http://spiderman.bu.edu`

Multimedia Survey ★

A survey of distributed multimedia research, standards, and products by RARE (Associated Networks for European Research).

Keywords: Internet, Multimedia

Audience: Internet Surfers

Details: Free, Multimedia

`ftp://ftp.ed.ac.uk/pub/mmsurvey`

Multimedia, Telecommunications, and Art Project ★★

A project to promote online art that will be implemented as gopher site and on the World Wide Web.

Keywords: Multimedia, Electronic Art, Telecommunications

Sponsor: CISR (Centre for Image and Sound Research), Vancouver, BC, Canada

Audience: Artists, Writers

Contact: Derek Dowden
Derek_Dowden@mindlink.bc.ca

For more information, send an e-mail message to the URL address below.

`mailto:Derek_Dowden@mindlink.bc.ca`

NIC (Nucleus for Interactive Computing) ★★★★

WWW-based system for interactive computing.

Keywords: Multimedia, Interactive Computing, Interface Design, Scripting Laguages, Programming

Sponsor: BYU Interactive Software Systems Lab

Audience: Software Developers, Educators

Profile: NIC is a system for interactive computing that combines a data model, a user interface model, and a scripting language to create flexible and powerful user interfaces. Documentation still under construction is located here.

Contact: Dan Olsen
olsen@cs.byu.edu

Details: Free, Moderated, Image, Sound and Multimedia files available.

Use a World Wide Web (Mosaic) client and open a connection to the resource.

`ftp://issl.cs.byu.edu/docs/NIC/home.html`

NYAL (New York Art Line) ★★

A gopher containing selected resources on the arts.

Keywords: Art, Audio-Visual Materials, Multimedia, Computer Art

Sponsor: Panix Public Access Unix & Internet Gopher Server, New York, USA

Audience: Artists, Art Enthusiasts

Profile: NYAL features a wide variety of arts resources. The primary focus of this site is visual art, particularly in the New York city area. Information includes online access to selected galleries, image archives, and New York city arts groups. Beyond visual art, information on dance, music, and techno art (with a special section on Internet art) is also available. It also features links to various electronic journals, museums, and schools.

Contact: Kenny Greenberg
kgreen@panix.com

`gopher://gopher.panix.com`

`http//gopher.panix.com/nyart/Kpage/kg`

Museums

Smithsonian Online

Located on America Online (with partial access by ftp), this allows online access to the Institution's resources.

Keywords: Museums, Art Exhibitions

Sponsor: Smithsonian Institution, Washington DC

Audience: Educators, Students, General Public

Profile: Smithsonian Online includes resources for teachers and students in the form of bulletin boards about Smithsonian museums, photographs, listings of events in Washington and other communities, and excerpts from Smithsonian and Air & Space/ Smithsonian.

`ftp://photo1.si.edu`

UC Berkeley Museum of Paleontology and the WWW Subway

This web site provides a multimedia museum display from UC Berkeley's Museum of Paleontology. Also features an interactive Subway, a tool linking users to other museums and WWW sites around the world.

Keywords: WWW, Museums, Paleontology

Sponsor: University of California at Berkeley, Museum of Paleontology, Berkeley, California, USA

Audience: Paleontologists, Internet Surfers, General Public

Contact: David Polly, Robert Guralnick
davip@ucmp1.berkeley.edu
robg@fossil.berkeley.edu

`http://ucmp1.berkeley.edu/subway.html`

Music

alt.music.alternative ★

A Usenet newsgroup providing information and discussion about alternative music.

Keywords: Music

Audience: Alternative Music Listeners

User Info: To Subscribe to this Usenet newsgroup, you need access to a newsreader.

`news:alt.music.alternative`

Analog Heaven ★

The Analog Heaven mailing list caters to people interested in vintage analog electronic music equipment. Topics include items for sale, repair tips, equipment modifications, ASCII & GIF schematics, and a general discussion of new and old analog equipment. There is an FTP/Gopher site located at cs.uwp.edu with discussions on various machines, a definitive guide to Roland synths, patch editors, modification schematics, and GIFs/JPEGs of vintage synths, as well as a few sound samples of some of the gear itself.

Keywords: Music, Synthesizers, Sequencers, Analog Equipment, Electronic Music

Audience: Electronic Music Enthusiasts, Musicians

Contact: Todd Sines
analogue-request@magnus.acs.ohio-state.edu

Details: Free; sound files available.

User Info: To Subscribe to the list, send an e-mail message requesting a subscription to the URL address below.

To send a message to the entire list, address it to:
analogue@magnus.acs.ohio-state.edu

`mailto:analogue-request@magnus.acs.ohio-state.edu`

Arts

An umbrella arts conference on the WELL.

Keywords: Art, Music, Dance

Audience: Artists, Dancers, Musicians, Photographers

Profile: A genereal arts conference that includes listings of show opportunities, books, and events, as well as discussion about art and art criticism.

Contact: Tim Collins

`telnet://well.sf.ca.us`

Arts Wire

A national communications network for the arts located on the Meta Network.

Keywords: Art, Writing, Activism, Music

Sponsor: New York Foundation for the Arts

Audience: Art Activists, Art Organizations, Artists, Composers, Foundations, Government Arts Agencies, Writers

Profile: Arts Wire provides immediate access to news, information, and dialogue on conditions affecting the arts and artists, as well as private conferences for organizations. Core features include Money, a searcable resource of grant deadlines; Hotwire, a summary of arts news; and conferences about new music, interactive art, literature, AIDS, and Latino art.

Contact: Judy Malloy
artswire@tmn.com

`telnet://tmn.com`

AusRave (Australian Raves) ★

A regional rave-related mailing list covering the Australian continent. AusRave contains both discussions and informational postings.

Keywords: Music, Raves, Australia

Audience: Ravers (Australian)

Contact: Simon Rumble
ausrave@lsupoz.apana.org.au

Details: Free, Moderated

User Info: To Subscribe to the list, send an e-mail message requesting a subscription to the URL address below.

To send a message to the entire list, address it to:
ausrave@lsupoz.apana.org.au

Notes: The mailing list Best of AusRave provides information only

Postings to AusRave are not archived, but the list does have an FTP site at: elecsun4.elec.uow.edu.au

`mailto:ausrave-request@lsupoz.apana.org.au`

Bagpipe ★

A mailing list of people interested in any topic related to bagpipes, most generally defined as any instrument where air is forced manually from a bellows or bag through drones and/or over reeds. All manner of Scottish, Irish, English, and other instruments are discussed.

Keywords: Music, Bagpipes

Audience: Bagpipe Enthusiasts

Contact: pipes-request@sunapee.dartmouth.edu

Details: Free

User Info: To Subscribe to the list, send an e-mail message requesting a subscription to the URL address below.

To send a message to the entire list, address it to:
pipes@sunapee.dartmouth.edu

`mailto:pipes-request@sunapee.dartmouth.edu`

Bel Canto ★

A mailing list for the discussion of the music, lyrics, and shows of the group Bel Canto, and solo projects of group members, or even the work of related artists if appropriate.

Keywords: Music, Pop Groups

Audience: Music Enthusiasts

Contact: dewy-fields-request@ifi.uio.no

Details: Free

User Info: To Subscribe to the list, send an e-mail message requesting a subscription to the URL address below.

To send a message to the entire list, address it to: dewy-fields@ifi.uio.no

`mailto:dewy-fields-request@ifi.uio.no`

Beloved ★

A mailing list for the discussion of the Beloved, an English pop group with strong ambient and techno influences.

Keywords: Music, Pop Groups

Audience: Music Enthusiasts

Contact: Jyrki Sarkkinen
beloved-request@phoenix.oulu.fi

Details: Free

User Info: To Subscribe to the list, send an e-mail message requesting a subscription to the URL address below.

To send a message to the entire list, address it to: beloved@phoenix.oulu.fi

`mailto:beloved-request@phoenix.oulu.fi`

Best-of-AusRave (Australian Raves) ★

A regional rave-related mailing list covering the Australian continent, for people who want Australian rave information without the side discussions and social chatter from the regular list.

Keywords: Music, Raves, Australia

Audience: Ravers (Australian)

Contact: Simon Rumble
best-of-ausrave-request@lsupoz.apana.org.au

Details: Free, Moderated

User Info: To Subscribe to the list, send an e-mail message to the URL address below, consisting of a single line reading:

SUB ausrave YourFirstName YourLastName

To send a message to the entire list, address it to: best-of-ausrave@lsupoz.apana.org.au

`mailto:best-of-ausrave-request@lsupoz.apana.org.au`

Blues-L ★

A mailing list for the discussion of Blues music and the culture surrounding the genre of the Blues.

Keywords: Blues, Music

Audience: Blues Enthusiasts

Contact: listserv@brownvm.brown.edu

Details: Free

User Info: To Subscribe to the list, send an e-mail message to the URL address below, consisting of a single line reading:

SUB blues-l YourFirstName YourLastName

To send a message to the entire list, address it to:
blues-l@brownvm.brown.edu

Notes: To receive the list in digest form: once you get acknowledgment from the listserver that you are on the list, send another message to the URL address below with the message: SET BLUES-L DIG

`mailto:listserv@brownvm.brown.edu`

BPM ★

This list is for novice and professional DJs. Discussion often covers music releases, DJ'ing techniques, and turntable maintenance.

Keywords: Disk Jockeys, Music

Audience: Disk Jockeys, Music Enthusiasts

Contact: Simon Gatrall
bpm-request@andrew.cmu.edu

Details: Free

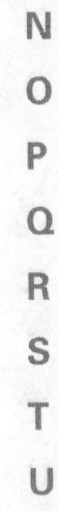

User Info: To Subscribe to the list, send an e-mail message requesting a subscription to the URL address below.

To send a message to the entire list, address it to: bpm@andrew.cmu.edu

`mailto:bpm-request@andrew.cmu.edu`

Cantus

This gopher site accesses the Gregorian Chant Database, which is maintained by the Catholic University of America.

Keywords: Gregorian Chants, Music, Liturgy

Sponsor: Catholic University of America (CUA)

Audience: Vocalists, Educators, Students

Profile: The database contains an introduction to the Cantus Gopher at the CUA, and has a searchable index.

`gopher://vmsgopher.cua.edu`

dire-straits

Discussion of the musical group Dire Straits and associated side projects.

Keywords: Rock Music, Dire Straits, Music

Audience: Rock Music Enthusiasts, Dire Straits Enthusiasts

Contact: Rand P. Hall dire-straits-request@merrimack.edu

Details: Free

User Info: To subscribe to the list, send an e-mail message requesting a subscription to the URL address below.

To send a message to the entire list, address it to: dire-straits-request@merrimack.edu

`Anonymous ftp to: merrimack.edu (Ä=ANONYMOUS/DIRE-STRAITS)`

`Mail list probably exists.`

Drake University

The library's holdings are large and wide-ranging and contain significant collections in many fields.

Keywords: Music, Pharmacology, Theology

Audience: General Public, Researchers, Librarians, Document Delivery Professionals

Details: Free, Moderated

Send: COWLES to access the main library, and LAWLIB to access the Law Library. To leave the system, enter CTRL-Z

`telnet://lib.drake.edu`

Eastern Washington University Library

The library's holdings are large and wide-ranging and contain significant collections in many fields.

Keywords: Education, Music, Social Science, Behavioral Science

Audience: Researchers, Students, General Public

Details: Free

Notes: Expect: Login; Send: Lib

`telnet://wsduvm12.csc.wsu.edu`

ecto

Information and discussion about singer/songwriter Happy Rhodes, and other music, art, books, and films of common (or singular) interest.

Keywords: Music, Art, Rhodes (Happy)

Audience: Music Enthusiasts, Art Enthusiasts

Contact: Jessica Dembski ecto-request@ns1.rutgers.edu

Details: Free

User Info: To subscribe to the list, send an e-mail message requesting a subscription to the URL address below.

To send a message to the entire list, address it to: ecto-request@ns1.rutgers.edu

`mailto:ecto-request@ns1.rutgers.edu`

fogelberg

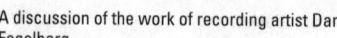

A discussion of the work of recording artist Dan Fogelberg.

Keywords: Music, Musicians

Audience: Dan Fogelberg Enthusiasts

Contact: ai411@yfn.ysu,edu

Details: Free

User Info: To Subscribe to the list, send an e-mail message requesting a subscription to the URL address below.

To send a message to the entire list, address it to: fogelberg@yfn.ysu.edu

`mailto:ai411@yfn.ysu.edu`

Folk music

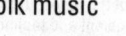

This discussion list deals with the music of the recent wave of American singer/songwriters. List traffic includes tour schedules, reviews, album and release information.

Keywords: Folk Music, Music

Audience: Folk Musicians, Musicians, Folk Music Fans

Contact: Alan Rowoth listserv@nysernet.org

Details: Free

User Info: To Subscribe to the list, send an e-mail message to the URL address below consisting of a single line reading:

SUB folk_music YourFirstName YourLastName

To send a message to the entire list, address it to: folk_music@nysernet.org

`mailto:listserv@nysernet.org`

freaks

This mailing list focuses on Marillion and related rock groups.

Keywords: Music, Rock Music

Audience: Marillion Enthusiasts

Details: Free

User Info: To Subscribe to the list, send an e-mail message requesting a subscription to the URL address below.

To send a message to the entire list, address it to:freaks@bnf.com

`mailto:freaks-request@bnf.com`

fuzzy-ramblings

Discussion of the British girl-group "We've Got a Fuzzbox and We're Going to Use It!"

Keywords: Music

Audience: Musicians, Music Enthusiasts

Details: Free

User Info: To Subscribe to the list, send an e-mail message requesting a subscription to the URL address below.

To send a message to the entire list, address it to: fuzzy-ramblings@piggy.ucsb.edu

`mailto:fuzzy-ramblings-request@piggy.ucsb.edu`

Impulse

This is the online site of Impulse Magazine, a monthly comprehensive journal of contemporary music news, reviews, information, and opinion.

Keywords: Music (Contemporary)

Sponsor: Impulse Magazine

Audience: Musicians, Music Fans

Contact: Bill Paige impulse@dsigroup.com

Details: Free

User Info: To Subscribe, send a message to the URL address below with the message: subscribe impulse

`mailto:impulse@dsigroup.com`

Leonardo Electronic Almanac

The Leonardo Electronic Almanac (LEA) is a monthly, edited journal and an electronic archive dedicated to providing current perspectives in the art, science and technology domains.

Keywords: Art, Multimedia, Music, Electronic Media

Sponsor: International Society for the Arts, Sciences, and Technology

Audience: New Media Artists, Researchers, Developers, Art Educators, Art Professionals

A
B
C
D
E
F
G
H
I
J
K
L
M
N
O
P
Q
R
S
T
U
V
W
X
Y
Z

Profile: LEA is an international, interdisciplinary forum for people interested in the use of new media in contemporary artistic expression, especially involving 20th century science and technology. Material is contributed by artists, scientists, philosophers and educators. LEA is published by the MIT Press for Leonardo, the International Society for the Arts, Sciences, and Technology (ISAST).

Contact: Craig Harris
craig@well.sf.ca.us

Details: Costs, Moderated, Images, Sounds, Multimedia

```
mail to:journals-orders@mit.edu
```

```
ftp: //mitpress.mit.edu/pub/Leonardo-
Elec-Almanac
```

Middle-eastern-music

⭐

Discussion of music from the Middle East.

Keywords: Middle Eastern Music, Music, Middle East

Audience: Music Enthusiasts, Musicians

Details: Free

User Info: To Subscribe to the list, send an e-mail message requesting a subscription to the URL address below.

```
mailto:middle-eastern-music-
request@nic.funet.fi
```

MLoL

⭐

The MLoL (Musical List of Lists) is a list of music-related mailing lists available on the Internet.

Keywords: Music, Mailing Lists

Audience: Musicians, General Public

Details: Free

User Info: To Subscribe to the list, send an e-mail message requesting a subscription to the URL address below.

```
mailto:mlol-request@wariat.org
```

Music

⭐⭐

This directory is a general compilation of information resources focused on music.

Keywords: Internet Resources, Music

Audience: Musicians, Music Enthusiasts

Details: Free

```
ftp://una.hh.lib.umich.edu/70/
inetdirsstacks/music:robinson
```

mw-raves

⭐

One of several rave-related lists, MW-Raves (Midwest Raves) covers the Midwestern US. Postings are usually informational, but discussions of scene-related issues can also be expected.

Keywords: Raves, Music

Audience: Ravers

Contact: Andy Crosby
mw-raves-request@engin.umich.edu

Details: Free

User Info: To Subscribe to the list, send an e-mail message to the URL address below consisting of a single line reading:

SUB mw-raves YourFirstName YourLastName.

To send a message to the entire list, address it to: mw-raves@csd.uwm.edu

```
mailto:mw-raves@csd.uwm.edu
```

NetJam

⭐

NetJam provides a means for people to collaborate on musical compositions by sending Musical Instrument Digital Interface (MIDI) and other files to each other.

Keywords: Music, Musicians

Audience: Musicians

Contact: Craig Latta
netjam-request@xcf.berkeley.edu

Details: Free

User Info: To Subscribe to the list, send an e-mail message requesting a subscription to the URL address below.

```
mailto:netjam-
request@xcf.berkeley.edu
```

Network-Audio-Bits

⭐

A bimonthly electronic magazine that features reviews and news of current music in rock, pop, new age, jazz, funk, folk, and other genres—including major-label and independent recording artists.

Keywords: Music Reviews, Music

Audience: Music Fans, General Public

Contact: Michael A. Murphy
murph@maine.bitnet

Details: Free

User Info: To Subscribe to the list, send an e-mail message requesting a subscription to the URL address below.

```
mailto:murph@maine.bitnet
```

NewMusNet

A place on the Arts Wire to discuss issues concerning composers, performers, and presenters of new music and to access information about new music.

Keywords: Music, New Music

Audience: Composers, Musicians, Performers

Contact: Pauline Oliveros
oliveros@tmn.com

```
telnet://tmn.com
```

On-u

⭐

This mailing list encourages discussions related to Adrian Sherwood's On-U Sound label and to the artists who record on it, including Tack>>Head, Gary Clail, The Dub Syndicate, African Head Charge, Bim Sherman and Mark Stewart.

Keywords: Music, Musicians

Audience: Musicians, Music Fans

Contact: Ben Golding
on-u-request@connect.com.au

Details: Free

User Info: To Subscribe to the list, send an e-mail message requesting a subscription to the URL address below.

To send a message to the entire list, address it to: on-u@connect.com.au

```
mailto:on-u@connect.com.au
```

Queen

⭐

A mailing list to discuss the rock group Queen.

Keywords: Music, Rock Music

Audience: Queen Fans, Music Fans, Musicians

Contact: Dan Blanchard
qms-request@uiuc.edu

Details: Free

User Info: To Subscribe to the list, send an e-mail message requesting a subscription to the URL address below.

To send a message to the entire list, address it to: qms@uiuc.edu

```
mailto:qms-request@uiuc.edu
```

rec.music.cd

⭐

A Usenet newsgroup providing information and discussion about Compact Discs.

Keywords: Music, Audio Electronics

Audience: Compact Disc Users

User Info: To Subscribe to this Usenet newsgroup, you need access to a newsreader.

```
news:rec.music.cd
```

rec.music.classical

⭐

A Usenet newsgroup providing information and discussion about classical music.

Keywords: Music

Audience: Classical Music Listeners

User Info: To Subscribe to this Usenet newsgroup, you need access to a newsreader.

```
news:rec.music.classical
```

A
B
C
D
E
F
G
H
I
J
K
L
M
N
O
P
Q
R
S
T
U
V
W
X
Y
Z

A
B
C
D
E
F
G
H
I
J
K
L
M
N
O
P
Q
R
S
T
U
V
W
X
Y
Z

rec.music.gdead

A Usenet newsgroup providing information and discussion about the Grateful Dead.

Keywords: Music, Popular Culture

Audience: Grateful Dead Listeners

User Info: To Subscribe to this Usenet newsgroup, you need access to a newsreader.

`news:rec.music.gdead`

rec.music.makers

A Usenet newsgroup providing information and discussion about music-making.

Keywords: Musical Instruments, Music

Audience: Performers, Music Listeners

User Info: To Subscribe to this Usenet newsgroup, you need access to a newsreader.

`news:rec.music.makers`

rec.music.makers.synth

A Usenet newsgroup providing information and discussion about synthesizers.

Keywords: Music, Audio Electronics

Audience: Synthesizer Users

User Info: To Subscribe to this Usenet newsgroup, you need access to a newsreader.

`news:rec.music.makers.synth`

Reggae Down Babylon

A collection of links to sources of information about reggae music on the World Wide Web and the Internet. Site includes reggae FAQs, and listings of reggae radio shows, lyrics, pictures, and news group archives.

Keywords: Reggae, Culture, Music

Sponsor: Reggae Down Babylon

Audience: Music Fans, Musicians, Reggae Enthusiasts

Contact: ReggaeMaster
damjohns@nyx10.cs.du.edu

Details: Free

`ftp://jammin.nosc.mil/pub/reggae`

Soundtracks

Discussions and reviews of new and older soundtracks (musical and technical aspects). Information about availability of specific soundtracks on different formats in different parts of the world.

Keywords: Music, Recordings

Audience: Audio Enthusiasts, Music Researchers

Contact: Michel Hafner
soundtracks-request@ifi.unizh.ch

User Info: To Subscribe to the list, send an e-mail message requesting a subscription to the URL address below.

To send a message to the entire list, address it to: soundtracks@ifi.unizh.ch

`mailto:soundtracks-request@ifi.unizh.ch`

Space-music

This mailing list is for the discussion of artists who use primarily electronic instruments to create 'sound spaces' or sound atmospheres that fall into categories defined as 'floating,' 'cosmic,' or 'noncommercial' and demand an active listener.

Keywords: Music, Electronic Music

Audience: Electronic Music Enthusiasts

Contact: Dave Datta
space-music-request@cs.uwp.edu

Details: Free

User Info: To Subscribe to the list, send an e-mail message requesting a subscription to the URL address below.

To send a message to the entire list, address it to: space-music@cs.uwp.edu

`mailto:space-music-request@cs.uwp.edu`

Stormcock

For general discussion and news concerning the music of Roy Harper, a folk-rock musician with a conscience. Recommendations and news concerning similar artists are encouraged.

Keywords: Rock Music, Music, Harper (Roy)

Audience: Music Fans

Contact: Paul Davison
stormcock-request@qmw.ac.uk

Details: Free

User Info: To Subscribe to the list, send an e-mail message to the address shown below consisting of a single line reading:

SUB stormcock YourFirstName YourLastName

To send a message to the entire list, address it to: stormcock@qmw.ac.uk

`mailto: listserv@qmw.ac.uk`

University of Northern Iowa Library

The library's holdings are large and wide-ranging and contain significant collections in many fields.

Keywords: Art, Business Information, Education, Music, Fiction

Audience: Researchers, Students, General Public

Contact: Mike Yohe
yohe@uni.edu

Details: Free

Expect: Login; Send: Public

`telnet://infosys.uni.edu`

University of Puget Sound Library

The library's holdings are large and wide-ranging and contain significant collections in many fields.

Keywords: Education, Literature (General), Music, Natural Science, Theology

Audience: Researchers, Students, General Public

Details: Free

Notes: Expect: Login; Send: Library

`telnet://192.124.98.2`

University of Texas at Austin Library

The library's holdings are large and wide-ranging and contain significant collections in many fields.

Keywords: Music, Natural Science, Nursing, Science Technology, Behavioral Science, Social Work, Computer Science, Engineering, Latin American Studies, Middle Eastern Studies

Audience: Researchers, Students, General Public

Details: Free

Notes: Expect: Blank Screen, Send: Return; Expect: Go, Send: Return; Expect: Enter Terminal Type, Send: vt100

Notes: Some databases are restricted to UT Austin users only.

`telnet://utcat.utexas.edu`

University of Wisconsin Green Bay Library

The library's holdings are large and wide-ranging and contain significant collections in many fields.

Keywords: Economics, Environmental Studies, Music, Natural Science

Audience: Researchers, Students, General Public

Details: Free

Notes: Expect: Service Name, Send: Victor

`telnet://gbls2k.uwgb.edu`

UWP Music Archive (named for the host machine's location: the University of Wisconsin-Parkside)

An extensive repository of files relating to a diverse array of music

genres: rock, folk, classical, and so on.

Keywords: Music, Lyrics, Graphics

Sponsor: University of Wisconsin-Parkside

Audience: Musicians, Music Enthusiasts, Musicologists

Profile: This FTP archive contains a music database, artist discographies, essays about music and particular works, hundreds of image files (mostly .GIF and .JPEG format) of musicians—including album covers and posters, a lyrics archive and the ever-popular 'Beginner's Introduction to Classical Music.'

Contact: Dave Datta
datta@ftp.uwp.edu

User Info: Select "Music Archives" from the gopher top-level menu.

Notes: Also accessible through CMU's "English Server" gopher server. (q.v.)

`gopher://gopher.uwp.edu`

Virginia Commonwealth University Library

The library's holdings are large and wide-ranging and contain significant collections in many fields.

Keywords: Art, Biology, Humanities, Journalism, Music, Urban Planning

Audience: Researchers, Students, General Public

Details: Free

Notes: Expect: Login; Send: Opub

`telnet://vcuvm1.ucc.vcu.edu`

Music Research

Music

This directory is a general compilation of information resources focused on music.

Keywords: Internet Resources, Music Research

Audience: Musicians, Music Enthusiasts

Details: Free

`ftp://una.hh.lib.umich.edu/70/
inetdirsstacks/music:robinson`

Music-research

This list provides an effective, efficient means of bringing together musicologists, music analysts, computer scientists, and others working on applications of computers in music research.

Keywords: Music Research, Music

Audience: Music Researchers, Musicians, Musicologists

Details: Free

To subscribe to the list, send an e-mail message requesting subscription to the URL address below.

`mailto:music-research-
request@prg.oxford.ac.uk`

Northwestern University Library

The library's holdings are large and wide-ranging and contain significant collections in many fields.

Keywords: Africa, Wright (Frank Lloyd), Women's Studies, Art, Literature (American), Music Research, Government (US State), UN Documents, Music

Audience: General Public, Researchers, Librarians, Document Delivery Professionals

Details: Free

Expect: COMMAND:, Send: DIAL VTAM

`telnet://nuacvm.acns.nwu.edu`

Music (Irish)

The University of Notre Dame Library

The library's holdings are large and wide-ranging and contain significant collections in many fields.

Keywords: Music (Irish), Ireland, Botany (History of), Ecology, Entomology, Parasitology, Aquatic Biology, Universities (History of), Paleography

Audience: General Public, Researchers, Librarians, Document Delivery Professionals

Details: Free

Notes: Expect: ENTER COMMAND OR HELP:, Send: library; To leave, type x on the command line and press the enter key. At the ENTER COMMAND OR HELP: prompt, type bye and press the enter key.

`telnet://irishmvs.cc.nd.edu`

Music Library Association Mailing List

Music Library Association Mailing List

This is a mail distribution service for the Music Library Association (MLA).

Keywords: Music, Libraries, Bibliography

Sponsor: Indiana University

Audience: Music Librarians

Profile: The services provided for the MLA include mail distribution, mail archiving, and file/document serving. This is a list server implementation, and the list managers intend that these services be used for various activities of the MLA that can benefit by wide-scale distribution, such as announcements of deadlines for NOTES and the MLA Newsletter, news items, general inquiries about MLA activities, and so on.

Contact: Ralph Papkhian
Papakhi@iubvm.ucs.Indiana.edu

Details: Free

User Info: To Subscribe to the list, send an e-mail message to the URL address below, consisting of a single line reading:

SUB mla-u YourFirstName YourLastName

`mailto:listserv@iubvm.ucs.indiana.edu`

Music Notation

FINALE Discussion List

Discussion list targeted towards people who use the FINALE music notation program.

Keywords: Music Notation, FINALE

Sponsor: CODA

Audience: FINALE Program Users

Profile: The music notation program FINALE (for Macintosh and Windows) provides the basis for the chief discussion on this list. Other CODA products, as well as various notation programs, are also suitable topics.

Contact: Henry Howey
mus_heh@SHSU.edu

Details: Free

To send a message to the list, send an e-mail message to the URL address below, consisting of a single line reading:

SUB finale YourFirstName YourLastName

`mail to:listserv@shsu.edu`

Music Resources

MBI, Music and the Brain Information Center Database (MuSICA)

The intent of this resource is to establish a comprehensive database of scientific research on music.

Keywords: Music Resources, Human Behavior, Neurology

Sponsor: Music and the Brain Information Center

Audience: Researchers, Scientists

Profile: MuSICA maintains a data base of scientific research (references and abstracts) on music as related to behavior, the brain and allied fields, in order to foster interdisciplinary knowledge. Topics include the auditory system; human and animal behavior; creativity; the neuropsychology of music and the human brain; the effects of music on behavior and physiology; music education, medicine, performance, and therapy; neurobiology; perception and psychophysics. Citations and abstracts are excerpted from the following

A
B
C
D
E
F
G
H
I
J
K
L
M
N
O
P
Q
R
S
T
U
V
W
X
Y
Z

journals: The Bulletin of the Council for Research in Music Education, The Journal of Research in Music Education, Music Perception, Psychology of Music, Psychomusicology.

Contact: Norman Weinberger, Gordon Shaw
mbic@mila.ps.uci.edu

Details: Free

Expect login: Send mbi Expect password: Send nammbi

`telnet://mila.ps.uci.edu`

University of California Santa Barbara Virtual Library

This source provides detailed lists of internet music resources.

Keywords: Music Resources

Sponsor: University of California at Santa Barbara

Audience: Musicians

Profile: This site contains lists pointing to music resources on the internet, including ftp sites, gopher servers, newsgroups, and list servers.

Details: Free

Path is The Subject Collections/The Arts Collections/Music

`gopher://ucsbuxa.ucsb.edu`

Music Reviews

Network-Audio-Bits

A bimonthly electronic magazine that features reviews and news of current music in rock, pop, new age, jazz, funk, folk, and other genres—including major-label and independent recording artists.

Keywords: Music Reviews, Music

Audience: Music Fans, General Public

Contact: Michael A. Murphy
murph@maine.bitnet

Details: Free

User Info: To Subscribe to the list, send an e-mail message requesting a subscription to the URL address below.

`mailto:murph@maine.bitnet`

Music Software

Synth-I

Synth-I is the electronic music "gearhead" list dedicated to the discussion of the less esoteric aspects of synthesis. Discussion concentrates on the availability and capabilities of music software and hardware, but sometimes diverges to other subjects.

Keywords: Electronic Music, Music Software

Audience: Electronic Music Enthusiasts, Musicians, Software Designers

Contact: Joe McMahon
Synth-L@american.edu

Details: Free

User Info: To Subscribe to the list, send an e-mail message to the address shown below consisting of a single line reading:

SUB Synth-L YourFirstName YourLastName

To send a message to the entire list, address it to: Synth-L@american.edu

`mailto:listserv@american.edu`

Musical Genres

alt.music.progressive

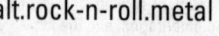

A Usenet newsgroup providing information and discussion about progressive music, including the groups Marillion, Asia, King Crimson, and many others.

Keywords: Musical Genres, Pop Culture

Audience: Progressive Music Listeners

User Info: To Subscribe to this Usenet newsgroup, you need access to a newsreader.

`news:alt.music.progressive`

alt.rap

A Usenet newsgroup providing information and discussion for fans of rap music, including talk about rap performers, new albums, concerts and other aspects of rap.

Keywords: Musical Genres

Audience: Rap Listeners, Rappers

User Info: To Subscribe to this Usenet newsgroup, you need access to a newsreader.

`news:alt.rap`

alt.rock-n-roll

A Usenet newsgroup providing information and general discussion about Rock & Roll.

Keywords: Musical Genres

Audience: Music Listeners

User Info: To Subscribe to this Usenet newsgroup, you need access to a newsreader.

`news:alt.rock-n-roll`

alt.rock-n-roll.metal

A Usenet newsgroup providing information and discussion about heavy metal music.

Keywords: Musical Genres

Audience: Heavy Metal Listeners

User Info: To Subscribe to this Usenet newsgroup, you need access to a newsreader.

`news:alt.rock-n-roll.metal`

Funky Music

This mailing list covers funk and funk-influenced music, including hip-hop, house party, soul, and rhythm and blues.

Keywords: Musical Genres, Funk Music

Audience: Musicians, Funk Music Enthusiasts

Details: Free

User Info: To Subscribe to the list, send an e-mail message requesting a subscription to the URL address below.

To send a message to the entire list, address it to: funky-music@mit.edu

`mailto:funky-music-request@mit.edu`

rec.music.folk

A Usenet newsgroup providing information and discussion about folk music.

Keywords: Musical Genres

Audience: Folk Music Listeners

User Info: To Subscribe to this Usenet newsgroup, you need access to a newsreader.

`news:rec.music.folk`

Musical Groups

Direct

Discussion of the work of the musical artist Vangelis.

Keywords: New Age Music, Musical Groups

Audience: Musicians, Music Enthusiasts, Vangelis Fans

Contact: Keith Gregoire
direct-request@celtech.com

User Info: To Subscribe to the list, send an e-mail message requesting a subscription to the URL address below.

To send a message to the entire list, address it to: direct@celtech.com

Both bounce and daily digest modes are available; specify your preference when subscribing.

`mailto:direct-request@celtech.com`

Journey-L

Information and discussion of the rock band Journey and any of the band members' outside projects.

Keywords: Musical Groups, Rock & Roll

Audience: Rock Music Fans

Contact: Hunter Goatley or Britt Pierce
journey-l@wkuvx1.wku.edu

User Info: To Subscribe to the list, send an e-mail message to the URL address below, with the body text subscribe journey-l.

To Subscribe to the digest version, send the message to : journey-l-digest-request@wkuvx1.wku.edu

`mailto:journey-l-request@wkuvx1.wku.edu`

Prince

A mailing list devoted to discussing the musician formerly named Prince and related artists.

Keywords: Prince, Musical Groups

Audience: Musicians, Music Students, Music Fans

Contact: prince-request@icpsr.umich.edu

Details: Free

User Info: To Subscribe to the list, send an e-mail message requesting a subscription to the URL address below.

To send a message to the entire list, address it to: prince-request@icpsr.umich.edu

`mailto:prince@icpsr.umich.edu`

rec.music.beatles

A Usenet newsgroup providing information and discussion about the Beatles.

Keywords: Musical Groups, Popular Culture

Audience: Beatles Listeners

User Info: To Subscribe to this Usenet newsgroup, you need access to a newsreader.

`news:rec.music.beatles`

rec.music.phish

A Usenet newsgroup providing information and discussion about the band Phish.

Keywords: Musical Groups, Popular Culture

Audience: Phish Listeners

User Info: To Subscribe to this Usenet newsgroup, you need access to a newsreader.

`news:rec.music.phish`

The Beastie Boys' Web Page

This web site features video, audio, magazine articles, lyrics, a discography, and other assorted information relating to the Beastie Boys.

Keywords: Musical Groups, Rap Music

Audience: Beastie Boys Fans

Contact: irogers@ezmail.ucs.indiana.edu

`http://www.nando.net/music/gm`

The Ultimate Gopher for Rush Fans

A collection of lyrics, articles, press releases, concert updates, newsletters, and reviews concerning the musical group Rush.

Keywords: Musical Groups, Rush, Rock & Roll

Sponsor: syrinx.umd.edu

Audience: Rock Music Enthusiasts, Rush Enthusiasts

Contact: jlang.syrinx.umd.edu

`gopher://syrinx.umd.edu`

Musical Instruments

alt.guitar

A Usenet newsgroup providing information and discussion about guitar playing.

Keywords: Guitar, Musical Instruments

Audience: Guitarists

User Info: To Subscribe to this Usenet newsgroup, you need access to a newsreader.

`news:alt.guitar`

Alternate Tuning Mailing List

This mailing list is intended for exchanging ideas relevant to alternate tunings.

Keywords: Musical Instruments, MIDI

Sponsor: Mills College

Audience: Musicians

Profile: This list deals with just intonation, paratactical tunings, experimental music instrument design, non-standard equal temperaments, MIDI tuning system exclusive specifications, concert postings, non-Western tunings, and the experimental tunings of such people as Harry Partch, Lou Harrison, Martin Bartlett, James Tenney and others.

Contact: Greg Higgs
Higgs@Mills.edu

Details: Free

User Info: To Subscribe to the list, send an e-mail message to the URL address below, consisting of a single line reading:

SUB tuning YourFirstName YourLastName

`listproc@varese.mills.edu`

rec.music.makers

A Usenet newsgroup providing information and discussion about music-making.

Keywords: Musical Instruments, Music

Audience: Performers, Music Listeners

User Info: To Subscribe to this Usenet newsgroup, you need access to a newsreader.

`news:rec.music.makers`

rec.music.makers.guitar

A Usenet newsgroup providing information and discussion about guitars and guitar playing.

Keywords: Musical Instruments

Audience: Guitar Listeners, Guitar Players

User Info: To Subscribe to this Usenet newsgroup, you need access to a newsreader.

`news:rec.music.makers.guitar`

Musicals

Musicals

This forum is intended for the general discussion of musical theater, in all forms, but related non-musical theater topics are welcome, too.

Keywords: Musicals, Theater

Audience: Music, Theater Enthusiasts

Details: Free

User Info: To Subscribe to the list, send an e-mail message requesting a subscription to the URL address below.

`mailto:musicals-request@world.std.com`

Musicians

Ethnomusicology Research Digest

For subscribers with a professional interest in ethnomusicology, including news, discussion, queries, bibliographies, and archives. Subscription by permission only.

Keywords: Musicians, Ethnomusicology, Music Research

Audience: Ethnomusicologists, Educators, Librarians, Researchers, Students

Contact: Karl Signell
signell@umdd.umd.edu

Details: Free

User Info: To Subscribe, send an e-mail message to the address below consisting of a single line reading:

SUB ethmus-l YourFirstName YourLastName

To send a message to the entire list, address it to: ethmus-l@umdd.vmd.edu

`mailto:listserv@umdd.umd.edu`

A B C D E F G H I J K L M N O P Q R S T U V W X Y Z

A B C D E F G H I J K L **M** N O P Q R S T U V W X Y Z

NetJam

NetJam provides a means for people to collaborate on musical compositions by sending Musical Instrument Digital Interface (MIDI) and other files to each other.

Keywords: Music, Musicians

Audience: Musicians

Contact: Craig Latta
netjam-request@xcf.berkeley.edu

Details: Free

User Info: To Subscribe to the list, send an e-mail message requesting a subscription to the URL address below.

`mailto:netjam-request@xcf.berkeley.edu`

On-u

This mailing list encourages discussions related to Adrian Sherwood's On-U Sound label and to the artists who record on it, including Tack>>Head, Gary Clail, The Dub Syndicate, African Head Charge, Bim Sherman and Mark Stewart.

Keywords: Music, Musicians

Audience: Musicians, Music Fans

Contact: Ben Golding
on-u-request@connect.com.au

Details: Free

User Info: To Subscribe to the list, send an e-mail message requesting a subscription to the URL address below.

To send a message to the entire list, address it to: on-u@connect.com.au

`mailto:on-u@connect.com.au`

MSA-Net

A mailing list intended to meet the communication needs of Muslim Student Associations (MSA) in North America, and to discuss issues related to Islam and MSAs are discussed.

Keywords: Islam, Muslim Student Associations

Audience: Muslims

Contact: Aalim Fevens
msa-request@htm3.ee.queensu.ca

User Info: To Subscribe to the list, send an e-mail message

Notes: Members must be Muslim.

`mailto:msa-request@htm3.ee.queensu.ca`

Mustangs

Mustangs

A forum for the discussion of technical issues, problems, solutions, and modifications relating to late-model (1980 and later) Ford Mustangs.

Keywords: Automobiles

Audience: Automobile Owners

Details: Free

User Info: To Subscribe to the list, send an e-mail message requesting a subscription to the URL address below.

`mailto:mustangs-request@cup.hp.com`

mw-raves

mw-raves

One of several rave-related lists, MW-Raves (Midwest Raves) covers the Midwestern US. Postings are usually informational, but discussions of scene-related issues can also be expected.

Keywords: Raves, Music

Audience: Ravers

Contact: Andy Crosby
mw-raves-request@engin.umich.edu

Details: Free

User Info: To Subscribe to the list, send an e-mail message to the URL address below consisting of a single line reading:

SUB mw-raves YourFirstName YourLastName.

To send a message to the entire list, address it to: mw-raves@csd.uwm.edu

`mailto:mw-raves@csd.uwm.edu`

Mutual Funds

NETworth (The Internet Resource for Individual Investors)

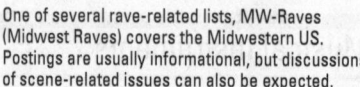

This is an interactive WWW site, providing information about mutual fund performance, prospecti, and promotional information.

Keywords: Mutual Funds, Investments, Finance

Sponsor: Galt Technologies, Inc.

Audience: Investors

Profile: This WWW site provides registered users free quotes on over 4500 mutual funds; also available is the Morningstar Analysis, financial newsletters, educational forums, financial databases, mutual fund industry news, press releases, and a clipping service.

Contact: Email: admin@atlas.galt.com

Details: Free, I

Notes: For additional information, you can call NETworth at (800)420-GALT

`http://networth.galt.com/www/home/start.html`

Mycoplasma

vetmycop

Veterinary mycoplasma discussion group.

Keywords: Veterinary Medicine, Mycoplasma

Audience: Veterinarians

Contact: James T. Case, Bill Cohen
jcase@ucdcvdls.bitnet or
bcohen@ucdcvdls.bitnet

Details: Free

User Info: To Subscribe to the list, send an e-mail message to the URL address below consisting of a single line reading:

SUB vetmycop YourFirstName YourLastName

To send a message to the entire list, address it to: vetmycop@ucdavis.edu

`mailto:listserv@ucdavis.edu`

Mystery

Mystery

This mailing list reviews and discusses mystery and detective fiction, including works on film, television, and radio.

Keywords: Mystery Fiction, Detective Fiction, Books

Audience: Mystery Enthusiasts

Details: Free

User Info: To Subscribe to the list, send an e-mail message requesting a subscription to the URL address below.

`mailto:mystery-request@introl.com`

Mythology

The Curiosity Club

This web site offers both an astrophysics exploration and a playspace for young scientists

Keywords: Astronomy, Mythology, Children

Sponsor: Center for Extreme Ultraviolet Astrophysics, Berkeley, California, and The San Francisco Unified School District, San Francisco, California

Audience: Educators, Students, Astronomers,

Contact: Kasey Rios Asberry
jasberry@sfsuvax1.sfsu.edu

Details: Free

`http://nisus.sfusd.k12.ca.us/curiosity_club/bridge1.html`

N

NA-net

NA-net

This mailing list is a forum for discussions on the subject of numerical analysis.

Keywords: Numerical Analysis

Audience: Numerical Analysts

User Info: To subscribe to the list, send an e-mail message requesting a subscription to the URL address below.

`mailto:na.join@na-net.ornl.gov`

NAARS (National Automated Accounting Research System)

NAARS (National Automated Accounting Research System)

The National Automated Accounting Research System (NAARS) library, provided as a service by agreement with the American Institute of Certified Public Accountants (AICPA) contains a variety of accounting information.

Keywords: Accounting, Auditing, Filings, Publishing

Audience: Accountants

Profile: The NAARS library contains annual reports of public corporations and accounting literature and publications for the accounting professional. Annual reports are annotated with descriptive terms assigned by the AICPA. These terms allow the user to search for annual report footnotes that illustrate one or more recognized accounting practices.

Contact: Mead New Sales Group at (800) 227-4908 or (513) 859-5398 inside the US, or (513) 865-7981 for all inquiries outside the US.

User Info: To subscribe, contact Mead directly.

To examine the Nexis user guide, you can access it at the ftp site of the University of Texas at Austin at the URL address: ftp://ftp.cc.utexas.edu

The files are in: /pub/ref-services/LEXIS

`telnet://nex.meaddata.com`

`http://www.meaddata.com`

NAFTA

North American Free Trade Agreement (NAFTA)

The agreement between the governments of Canada, the United Mexican States, and the United States of America to establish a free trade area in North America.

Keywords: Trade, US, Mexico, Canada, Free Trade, NAFTA

Audience: Journalists, Politicians, Economists, Students

Details: Free

`gopher://wiretap.spies.com/00/gov/nafta`

NAME (National Association for Mediation in Education) Publications and Resources List

NAME (National Association for Mediation in Education) Publications and Resources List

This is a tax-exempt clearinghouse of information promoting conflict resolution, mediation, and violence prevention in schools. NAME also publishes a newsletter and has a directory of over 120 resources, including guidelines for conflict resolution, and technical assistance.

Keywords: Conflict Resolution, Mediation, Education (K-12)

Sponsor: National Association for Mediation in Education, University of Massachusetts, Amherst, Massachusetts, USA

Audience: Counselors, Educators, Administrators, Parents

Contact: Clarinda Merripen ConflictNet@agc.ipc.org

Notes: Request introductory packet from address below.

`mailto:conflictnet@agc.ipc.org`

naplps-list

naplps-list

This is a mailing list for people interested in NAPLPS graphics.

Keywords: Computer Graphics, Art

Audience: Graphic Artists

Contact: Dave Hughes oldcolo@goldmill.uucp naplps-list@oldcolo.com

Napolean

McGill University, Montreal Canada, INFOMcGILL Library

⭐

The library's holdings are large and wide-ranging and contain significant collections in many fields.

Keywords:	Architecture, Entomology, Biology, Science (History of), Medicine (History of), Napolean, Shakespeare (William)
Audience:	Researchers, Students, General Public
Contact:	Roy Miller ccrmmus@mcgillm (Bitnet) ccrmmus@musicm.mcgill.ca (Internet)
User Info:	Expect: VM logo; Send: Enter; Expect: prompt; Send: PF3 or type INFO

`telnet://vm1.mcgill.ca`

NASA

Center for Extreme Ultraviolet Astrophysics

 ⭐⭐⭐

A department of the University of California at Berkeley devoted to research in extreme ultraviolet astronomy. It is the ground-based institution of EUVE (the Extreme Ultraviolet Explorer), a NASA satellite launched in 1992.

Keywords:	Astronomy, Astrophysics, EUVE, NASA, Satellite
Sponsor:	NASA and University of California at Berkeley
Audience:	Astronomers, Astrophysicists
Profile:	Provides access to details about the EUVE Guest Observer (EGO) Center, the EUVE Public Archive of Mission Data and Information, satellite operation information, and so on. The EUVE Guest Observer Center provides information, software, and data to EUVE Guest Observers.
Contact:	egoinfo@cea.berkeley.edu archive@cea.berkeley.edu
Details:	Free

`http://cea-ftp.cea.berkeley.edu`

Cosmic Update

 ⭐⭐⭐

Internet notice identifying new computer software from the National Aeronautics and Space Administration (NASA) made available for international use.

Keywords:	NASA, Software, Space
Audience:	Space Scientists, Astronomers

Profile:	COSLINE is a 24-hour electronic information service to COSMIC's customers. The principal feature of COSLINE is the catalog Search facility. A separate help file is available for browsing from the Search main menu option.
Contact:	Pat Mortenson service@cossack.cosmic.uga.edu
Details:	Free
User Info:	To subscribe, send an e-mail message requesting a subscription to the URL address below.

`mailto:service@cossack.cosmic.uga.edu`

Library of Congress, Astronomy, Astrophysics, and Physics Resources

 ⭐⭐⭐⭐

Pointers to important remote databases relating to astronomy and physics.

Keywords:	Astronomy, Astrophysics, NASA
Sponsor:	Library of Congress, Washington, DC
Audience:	Astronomers, Educators (Post-Secondary), Physicists, Students
Profile:	The Library of Congress has pointers to many important remote databases including Astronomy, Astrophysics, and Physics Journals, the Aerospace Directory from Rice University, The American Astronomical Society, The Astronomical Internet Resources Directory, The Cold Fusion Bibliography, The Electromagnetic Wave Research Institute of NRC (Florence, Italy), LANL Physics Information, The Lunar/Planetary Institute Database of Geology, Geophysics, and Astronomy, The NASA Extragalactic Database, The NASA Network Applications and Information Center (NAIC), The National Institute of Standards and Technology (NIST), The Physics Resource Directory from University of California, Irvine, and The Space Telescope Electronic Information System (STEIS).
Contact:	lcmarvel@seq1.loc.gov
Details:	Costs
User info:	Can be accessible via telnet://marvel.loc.gov (login: marvel).

`gopher://marvel.loc.gov/11/global/sci/astro`

NASA Ames SPACE Archive

 ⭐

This archive contains information about NASA projects. It also has an online CD-ROM jukebox with a rotating selection of NASA mission CD-ROMs.

Keywords:	NASA, Space
Sponsor:	NASA Ames Research Center
Audience:	General Public, Scientists, Technical Writers, Science Teachers

---

Profile:	This site has access to general space information, including the texts of the press release kits for the space shuttle missions and other NASA press releases. There are also weather images from satellites and other sources in the /pub/weather directory. The /pub/cdrom directory contains information about which NASA mission CD-ROMs are currently mounted.
Contact:	Peter Yee yee@atlas.arc.nasa.gov
User Info:	Expect: login, Send: anonymous; Expect: password, Send: your Internet address

`ftp://explorer.arc.nasa.gov`

NASA/IPAC Extragalactic Database (NED)

 ⭐⭐⭐

Contains positions, basic data, and over 500,000 names for 250,000 extragalactic objects, as well as some 450,000 bibliographic references to 21,000 published papers, and 25,000 notes from catalogs and other publications.

Keywords:	Astronomy, Databases
Sponsor:	Jet Propulsory Lab/ Infrared Processing and Analysis Center
Audience:	Astronomers, Scientists
Profile:	Uses a VT100 or X-based interface.
Contact:	G. Helou, B. Madore, M. Schmitz ned@ipac.caltech.edu
Details:	Free
User Info:	Telnet to URL address below; Expect: login; Send: ned
Notes:	sshare@cscns.com service@cscns.com

`telnet://ned@ned.ipac.caltech.edu`

`ftp://ned.ipac.caltech.edu/pub/ned`

NSSDC (National Space Science Data Center)'s Online Data & Information Service

 ⭐⭐⭐

The NSSDC (National Space Science Data Center) is the NASA facility charged with archiving the data from all of NASA's science missions.

Keywords:	Space, Astrophysics, Software, NASA, Science
Sponsor:	NASA
Audience:	Scientists, Space Scientists, Astronomers, Engineers
Profile:	This resource contains information about NASA's missions and analysis of their data.
Details:	Free
User Info:	Expect: Login, Send: nssdc See the menu entries in your particular area of interest.

`telnet://nssdc.gsfc.nasa.gov`

Sci.astro.hubble

Information about all subjects concerning NASA's Hubble space telescope.

Keywords: Hubble Telescope, Astronomy, Space, NASA, Stargazing, Telescopes

Audience: Astronomers, General Public, Science Teachers, Stargazers

Contact: Paul A. Scowen
scowen@wfpc3.la.asu.edu

Details: Free, Moderated, Images

User Info: To subscribe to this Usenet newsgroup, you need access to a newsreader.

`news:sci.astro.hubble`

Spacelink

This contains information about NASA and its activities, including a large number of curricular activities for elementary and secondary science classes.

Keywords: NASA, Aeronautics, Education (K-12)

Audience: Students (K-12), Educators, General Public

Details: Free

`telnet://`
`newuser@spacelink.msfc.nasa.gov`

The University of Iowa Libraries

The library's holdings are large and wide-ranging and contain significant collections in many fields.

Keywords: Hunt (Leigh), Native American Studies, Typography, Railroads, Cartoons, French Revolution, NASA, Hydraulics

Audience: General Public, Researchers, Librarians, Document Delivery Professionals

Details: Free

Send <RETURN>to display a menu of available systems. Type 1 for OASIS access and press <RETURN>to display the Welcome to OASIS screen.

`telnet://oasis.uiowa.edu`

National Broadcasting Society—Alpha Epsilon Rho

National Broadcasting Society—Alpha Epsilon Rho

Forum for mass media professionals to share experiences and ideas.

Keywords: Film, Television, Radio, Mass Media

Sponsor: National Broadcasting Society-Alpha Epsilon Rho

Audience: Journalists, Students, Educators, Broadcasting Professionals

Contact: Reg Gamar
regbc@cunyvm.bitnet

Details: Free

User Info: To subscribe to the list, send an e-mail message to the address shown below consisting of a single line reading:

SUB NBS-AER YourFirstName YourLastName

To send a message to the entire list, address it to: nbs-aer@cunyvm.bitnet

`mailto:listserv@cunyvm.bitnet`

National Cancer Center, Tokyo, Japan

National Cancer Center, Tokyo, Japan

This is the information service for the National Cancer Center in Tokyo, Japan, as well as the entry point for the Japanese Cancer Research Resources Bank (JCRB).

Keywords: Cancer, Japan

Audience: Biologists, Medical Researchers

Contact: ncc-gopher-news@gan.ncc.go.jp

Details: Free

`gopher://ncc.go.jp`

National Centre for Software Technology

National Centre for Software Technology

The National Centre for Software Technology (NCST) is an autonomous R&D unit in Bombay and Bangalore. Specialty areas of research include graphics, CAD, real time systems, knowledge-based systems, and software engineering.

Keywords: Computer Science, Engineering, Computer-Aided Design

Sponsor: National Centre for Software Technology, Bombay, India

Audience: Reseachers, Computer Scientists, Engineers, Students

Contact: Postmaster
postmaster@saathi.ncst.ernet.in

`gopher://shakti.ncst.ernet.in`

National Collegiate Athletic Association

Pac-10-Sports

This mailing list is dedicated to discussing sports of all types that are played competitively within the Pac-10 Athletic Conference.

Keywords: Pac-10 Sports, National Collegiate Athletic Association, Sports

Audience: Pac-10 Sports Fans

Contact: Cliff Slaughterbeck
crs@u.washington.edu

Details: Free

User Info: To subscribe to the list, send an e-mail message requesting a subscription to the URL address below.

To send a message to the entire list, address it to: crs@u.washington.edu

`mailto:crs@u.washington.edu`

National Export Strategy

National Export Strategy

This site provides the complete text of a report presented to Congress by the Trade Promotion Coordinating Committee, describing ways to develop U.S. export promotion efforts.

Keywords: Commerce, Foreign Trade, Exports, Business

Sponsor: United States Government, Trade Promotion Coordinating Committee

Audience: Exporters, Business Professionals, Trade Specialists

Details: Free

`ftp://sunny.stat-usa.gov`

`http://sunny.stat-usa.gov`

National Family Database—MAPP

National Family Database—MAPP

This database contains family sociological and health data, including research briefs, bibliographies, census data, program ideas, reference materials, media materials, and publications.

Keywords: Sociology, Family, Health

Sponsor: Department of Agriculture Economics and Rural Sociology, Pennsylvania State University

A
B
C
D
E
F
G
H
I
J
K
L
M
N
O
P
Q
R
S
T
U
V
W
X
Y
Z

A
B
C
D
E
F
G
H
I
J
K
L
M
N
O
P
Q
R
S
T
U
V
W
X
Y
Z

Audience: Sociologists, Public Health Officials, Health Care Providers

User Info: To access the database select PENpages (1), then General Information (3) and finally Information on MAPP - National Family Database (5)

`telnet://penpages@psupen.psu.edu`

National Hockey League (NHL)

Blues (St. Louis Blues)

Provides information, game reports, stats, discussion, and so on, on the St. Louis Blues of the National Hockey League.

Keywords: Hockey, Sports, National Hockey League (NHL)

Audience: Hockey Enthusiasts

Contact: Joe Ashkar
blues@medicine.wustl.edu

User Info: To subscribe to the list, send an e-mail message requesting a subscription to the URL address below.

To send a message to the entire list, address it to: blues@medicine.wustl.edu

`mailto:blues@medicine.wustl.edu`

Boston Bruins

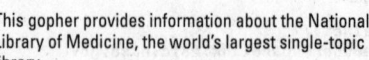

This list is for discussion of the Boston Bruins of the National Hockey League and their farm teams. Also available as a digest.

Keywords: Boston Bruins, Hockey (Ice), National Hockey League (NHL)

Audience: Hockey Enthusiasts, Boston Residents, Sports Enthusiasts

Contact: Garry Knox
bruins-request@cristal.umd.edu

Details: Free

User Info: To subscribe to the list, send an e-mail message requesting a subscription to the URL address below.

To send a message to the entire list, address it to: bruins@cristal.umd.edu

`mailto:bruins-request@cristal.umd.edu`

NHL Goalie Stats

Keywords: Hockey, National Hockey League (NHL), Sports Statistics

Audience: Hockey Enthusiasts

Profile: Weekday reports of goalie statistics from the National Hockey League.

Contact: dfa@triple-i.com

Details: Free

User Info: To subscribe to the list, send an e-mail message requesting a subscription to the URL address below.

To send a message to the entire list, address it to: dfa@triple-i.com

`mailto:dfa@triple-i.com`

National Institute for Allergy & Infectious Disease (NIAID)

National Institute for Allergy & Infectious Disease (NIAID)

This is a resource into other databases for searching many medical fields, such as the NIAID network user list or a databank of AIDS-related information.

Keywords: Medicine, Infectious Diseases, Allergies

Sponsor: NIAID

Audience: Health Care Professionals, Researchers, Students

Contact: Brent Sessions
sessions@odie.niaid.nih.gov

Details: Free

`gopher://gopher.niaid.nih.gov/1`

National Institute of Health Library Online Catalog

National Institute of Health Library Online Catalog

This entry point provides access to the books and journal holdings in the NIH Library. Journal articles are not included.

Keywords: NIH, Medicine, Science, Libraries

Sponsor: National Institute of Health (NIH)

Audience: Scientists, Researchers, Educators, Health Care Professionals

Details: Free

`telnet://nih-library.ncrr.nih.gov`

National Institutes of Health Gopher

National Institutes of Health Gopher

Provides access to a broad range of National Institutes of Health (NIH) resources (library catalogues, databases) via the Internet.

Keywords: Health, AIDS, Molecular Biology, Grants

Sponsor: National Institutes of Health

Audience: Health Care Professionals, Molecular Biologists, Researchers

Profile: This gopher provides access to NIH resources, including institute phone books and calendars, library catalogs, molecular biology databases, the full text of the NIH Guide for Grants and Contracts, files containing AIDS and cancer information and more.

Contact: gopher@gopher.nih.gov

Details: Free

User Info: Expect: Login; Enter: Gopher

`telnet://gopher.nih.gov`

`gopher://gopher.nih.gov`

`gopher://odie.niaid.nih.gov`

National Library of Medicine Gopher

National Library of Medicine Gopher

This gopher provides information about the National Library of Medicine, the world's largest single-topic library.

Keywords: Medicine, Health, World Health

Sponsor: National Library of Medicine, Massachusetts

World Health Organization, Geneva, Switzerland

Audience: Health Care Professionals, Medical Professionals, Researchers

Profile: The National Library of Medicine (NLM) cares for over 4.5 million holdings (inncluding books, journals, reports, manuscripts, and audio-visual items). The NLM offers extensive online information services dealing with clinical care, toxicology, environmental health, and basic biomedical research, It has several active research and development components, including an extramural grants program, houses an extensive history of medicine collection, and provides several programs designed to improve the nation's medical library system.

Contact: R. P. C. Rodgers
rodgers@nlm.nih.gov
akazawa@who.ch

Details: Free

`gopher://el-gopher.med.utah.edu`

`gopher://gopher.who.ch`

User Info: To subscribe to the list, send an e-mail message requesting a subscription to the URL address below.

To send a message to the entire list, address it to: dfa@triple-i.com

`mailto:dfa@triple-i.com`

National Oceanic & Atmospheric Administration (NOAA)

National Oceanic & Atmospheric Administration (NOAA)

 ★★★★

The NOAA catalog provides keyword access to sources of environmental information in the US. Gopher for resources pertaining to health and environmental safety.

Keywords: Environment, Oceans, Atmospheric Science, Health, Environmental Safety

Sponsor: National Oceanic & Atmospheric Administration (NOAA), Department of Energy (USA)

Audience: Researchers, Environmentalists, Epidemiologists, Public Health Officials

Details: Free

`gopher://scilibx.ucsc.edu`

`gopher://gopher.ns.doc.gov`

National Performance Review (NPR)

National Performance Review (NPR)

 ★★★

The Report of the National Performance Review, from the task force led by Vice President Gore, titled 'From Red Tape to Results: Creating a Government that Works Better and Costs Less,' Sept. 7, 1993.

Keywords: President, US Politics, White House

Audience: Political Scientists, General Public

Profile: On March 3, 1993, President Clinton asked Vice President Gore to lead the effort to effect real change in the federal government. Gore's NPR Task Force overview and accompanying reports make specific recommendations for: reducing costs and waste, changing the way government operates, and making government more responsive and effective.

Details: Free

`gopher://cyfer.esusda.gov/11/ace/policy/npr/nat`

National Science Foundation Center for Biological Timing

National Science Foundation Center for Biological Timing

 ★★★

This gopher accesses investigative research pertaining to various aspects of biological timing. The goal of this gopher is to make the museum's collections information available over the Internet. This server contains names of virus families/groups and members now available online from the Australian National University's Bio-Informatics Facility.

Keywords: Biology, Vertebrates

Sponsor: Reasearch School of Biological Research, Australian National University, Canberra, Australia

Audience: Biologists, Educators, Researchers

Profile: The center combines the efforts of several universities pertaining to research in biological timing. This includes Vistudies, the internal timing mechanisms that control cycles of sleep and waking, hormone pulsatility, neural excitability, and reproductive rhythmicity. Investigators are involved with research from behavior testing to molecular genetics.

The center also supports educational and outreach programs to industry, universities and high schools. The center also hosts an annual scientific symposium and a number of mini-symposia.

Details: Free

`gopher://gopher.virginia.edu/11/pubs/biotimin`

National Technology Transfer Center (NTTC)

National Technology Transfer Center (NTTC)

 ★★

A federally-funded national network to apply government research to commercial applications.

Keywords: Technology, Research and Development, Business, Industry, Department of Defense, Government (US)

Sponsor: National Technology Transfer Center

Audience: Business Professionals, Entrepreneurs, Manufacturers, Technology Professionals

Profile: Features state-by-state listings of agencies designed to facilitate the adaptation of new technologies to industry. Also provides updates on conferences, and a current list of Department of Defense projects soliciting private assistance from small businesses. Allows limited access to NTTC databases.

Contact: Charles Monfradi cmonfra@nttc.edu, info@nttc.edu

`gopher://iron.nttc.edu`

`http://iridium.nttc.edu/nttc.hmtl`

Native American Affairs

University of New Mexico Unminfo Library

 ★★

The library's holdings are large and wide-ranging and contain significant collections in many fields.

Keywords: Photography (History of), Architecture, Native American Affairs, Land Records

Audience: Researchers, Students, General Public

Contact: Art St. George stgeorge@unmb.bitnet

Details: Free

User Info: Expect: Login; Send: Unminfo

`telnet://unminfo.unm.edu`

University of Tennessee at Knoxville Library

 ★★

The library's holdings are large and wide-ranging and contain significant collections in many fields.

Keywords: Native American Affairs, Congress (US), Folklore, Travel (History of)

Audience: Researchers, Students, General Public

Details: Free

User Info: Expect: OK Prompt; Send: Login pub1; Expect: Password, Send: Usc

`telnet://opac.lib.utk.edu`

Native American Studies

The University of Iowa Libraries

 ★★

The library's holdings are large and wide-ranging and contain significant collections in many fields.

Keywords: Hunt (Leigh), Native American Studies, Typography, Railroads, Cartoons, French Revolution, NASA, Hydraulics

Audience: General Public, Researchers, Librarians, Document Delivery Professionals

A B C D E F G H I J K L M **N** O P Q R S T U V W X Y Z

Details: Free

Send <RETURN>to display a menu of available systems. Type 1 for OASIS access and press <RETURN>to display the Welcome to OASIS screen.

`telnet://oasis.uiowa.edu`

The University of Minnesota Library System (LUMINA)

The library's holdings are large and wide-ranging and contain significant collections in many fields.

Keywords: Immigration (History of), Ethnic Studies, Horticulture, Equine Research, Botanical Taxonomy, Quantum Physics, Native American Studies, Holmes (Sherlock)

Audience: General Public, Researchers, Librarians, Document Delivery Professionals

Contact: Craig D. Rice
cdr@acc.stolaf.edu

Details: Free

`telnet://lumina.lib.umn.edu`

NativeNet

NativeNet

Provides information about and discusses issues relating to indigenous people around the world, including threats to their cultures and habitats (e.g. rainforests).

Keywords: Indigenous People, Environment, Anthroplogy

Audience: Anthropologists, Environmentalists, Indigenous People

Contact: Gary S. Trujillo
gst@gnosys.svle.ma.us

Details: Free

User Info: To subscribe to the list, send an e-mail message requesting a subscription to the URL address below.

`mailto:gst@gnosys.svle.ma.us`

NATO

NATO

Online version of The NATO Handbook, which recommends changes for the future of the North Atlantic Treaty Organization in light of decreasing defense resources.

Keywords: NATO, Guidelines, Defense

Sponsor: The NATO Office of Information and Press

Audience: Government Officials, Military Personnel, Historians

Details: Free

Select from menu as appropriate.

`gopher://wiretap.spies.com`

Natural History

Smithsonian Institution Natural History Gopher

The Smithsonian Natural History Gopher Server provides access to data associated with the Institutions museum collections (natural history and anthropology).

Keywords: Smithsonian, Natural History, Anthropology

Sponsor: Museum of Natural History, Smithsonian Institution, Washington, DC.

Audience: Anthropologists, Biologists, Natural History Scientists, Researchers

Profile: With over 120 million collections and 135 professional scientists, the National Museum of Natural History is one of the worlds largest museums devoted to natural history and anthropology. This server provides access to data associated with the collections, and to information and tools for the study of the natural world. The Department of Vertebrate Zoology includes checklists of known species names. Currently the Mammal Species of the World have been posted. Plans to expand this to include Amphibians, Fishes, and so on, are under way.

Contact: Don Gourley
don@smithson.si.edu

Details: Free

`gopher://nmnhgoph.si.edu`

Natural Language

nl-kr

This E-conference is open to discussion of any topic related to the understanding and generation of natural language and knowledge representation as subfields of artificial intelligence.

Keywords: Programming Languages, Natural Language, Knowledge Representation, Linguistics

Audience: Computer Programmers

Contact: Christopher Welty
weltyc@cs.rpi.edu

Details: Free, Moderated

User Info: To subscribe to the list, send an e-mail message requesting a subscription to the URL address below.

`mailto:nl-kr-request@cs.rpi.edu`

Natural Resources Canada (NRCan) Gopher

Natural Resources Canada (NRCan) Gopher

This site offers information on forests, energy, mining, and geomatics from the Canadian government. Also has reports from the Geological Survey of Canada and an overview of NRCan statutes, organization, and personnel. Provides links to other Canadian environmental and government gophers.

Keywords: Canada, Environment, Geology, Forestry

Sponsor: The Department of Natural Resources, Canada

Audience: Canadians, Environmentalists, Geologists

Contact: Bob Fillmore
fillmore@emr.ca

Notes: NRCan maintains a toll-free hotline (800) 267-5166

`gopher://gopher.emr.ca`

`http://www.emr.ca`

Natural Science

University of Puget Sound Library

The library's holdings are large and wide-ranging and contain significant collections in many fields.

Keywords: Education, Literature (General), Music, Natural Science, Theology

Audience: Researchers, Students, General Public

Details: Free

User Info: Expect: Login; Send: Library

`telnet://192.124.98.2`

University of Texas at Austin Library

The library's holdings are large and wide-ranging and contain significant collections in many fields.

Keywords: Music, Natural Science, Nursing, Science Technology, Behavioral Science, Social Work, Computer Science, Engineering, Latin American Studies, Middle Eastern Studies

Audience: Researchers, Students, General Public

Details: Free

User Info: Expect: Blank Screen, Send: Return; Expect: Go, Send: Return; Expect: Enter Terminal Type, Send: vt100

Note: Some databases are restricted to UT Austin users only.

`telnet://utcat.utexas.edu`

University of Wisconsin Green Bay Library

The library's holdings are large and wide-ranging and contain significant collections in many fields.

Keywords: Economics, Environmental Studies, Music, Natural Science

Audience: Researchers, Students, General Public

Details: Free

User Info: Expect: Service Name, Send: Victor

`telnet://gbls2k.uwgb.edu`

US Geological Survey Server

This resource containis publications, USGS research programs, technology transfer partnerships, and fact sheets about geology.

Keywords: Biology, Geology, Natural Science

Sponsor: US Geological Survey

Audience: Biologists, Geologists, Researchers, Naturalists

Contact: Systems Operator
webmaster@info.er.usgs.gov

`http://info.er.usgs.gov`

Navy

Navnews

Contains official news and information about fleet operations and exercises, personnel policies, budget actions, and more. This is the same news service that is distributed through Navy circuits to ships at sea and to shore commands around the world. Subscriptions to NAVNEWS by e-mail are available at no charge to anyone with a mailbox on any network reachable through the Internet.

Keywords: Navy, News

Sponsor: The Navy Internal Relations Activity, Washington, DC

Audience: Navy Personnel, Sailors, General Public

Contact: navnews@nctamslant.navy.mil

Details: Free

User Info: To subscribe to the list, send an e-mail message requesting a subscription to the URL address below.

`mailto:navnews@nctamslant.navy.mil`

NBA

Funet Sports Information

An FTP archive of information on various sports with links to the archive at wuarchive.wustl.edu.

Keywords: Sports, Professional Sports, Ice Hockey, Motor Racing, NFL, NHL, NBA, MLB

Sponsor: Finnish Academic and Research Network (FUNET)

Audience: Sports Enthusiasts

Profile: A fairly extensive archive of information on both American (NBA, MLB, NHL, NFL) and worldwide sports (soccer, ice hockey, motor racing, and so on). Includes FAQs for various sports, statistics, pictures, and some sports games for the PC.

Contact: Jari Pullinen
sports-adm@nic.funet.fi

Details: Free, Images

`gopher://ftp.funet.fi/pub/sports`

NCGIA

Geographic Information and Analysis Laboratory (GIAL)

Server distributing a variety of information related to geography and GIS.

Keywords: Geography, GIS, NCGIA

Sponsor: SUNY-Buffalo and the National Center for Geographic Information and Analysis (NCGIA)

Audience: Geographers, GIS Professionals, Researchers, Students

Contact: Brandon Plewe, Reginald O. Carroll, Patricia M. Baumgarten
plewe@geog.buffalo.edu
carrol@geog.buffalo.edu
pmb@geog.buffalo.edu

Details: Free, Images

Notes: Check out the You-are-here server!

`http://zia.geog.buffalo.edu/`

NCSA (National Center for Supercomputing Applications)

NCSA (National Center for Supercomputing Applications)

A high-performance computing and communications facility and research center designed to serve the US computational science and engineering community.

Keywords: Supercomputing, Computing, Computer Science, Mosaic

Sponsor: University of Illinois at Urbana-Champaign, Champaign, Illinois, USA

Audience: Students, Researchers, Computer Scientists, General Public

Contact: Systems Operator
pubs@ncsa.uiuc.edu

`http://www.ncsa.uiuc.edu/General/NCSAHome.html`

NCSA Mosaic FAQ

NCSA Mosaic FAQ

Common questions and answers about NCSA Mosaic, a network information browser (more technically, a World Wide Web Client) that allows one to retrieve documents from the World Wide Web system. There are versions of Mosaic available for Microsoft Windows on IBM PC-compatible machines, the X Window System on UNIX computers, and for the Apple Macintosh.

Keywords: Internet Reference

Sponsor: National Center for Supercomputing Applications at the University of Illinois at Urbana-Champaign, Illinois, USA

Audience: Students, Computer Scientists, Researchers

Contact: Software Development Group
softdev@ncsa.uiuc.edu

`http://www.ncsa.uiuc.edu/SDG/Software/MacMosaic/FAQ/FAQ-mac.html`

NCTM-L

NCTM-L

A mailing list for the discussion of standards applying to the National Council of Teachers of Mathematics.

Keywords: Education, Mathematics

Audience: Mathematicians

Contact: barry@sci-ed.fit.edu

Details: Free

User Info: To subscribe to this list, send an e-mail message to the URL address below, consisting of a single line reading:

SUB nctm-l YourFirstName YourLastName

To send a message to the entire list, address it to: nctm-l@sci-ed.fit.edu

`mailto:listproc@sci-ed.fit.edu`

Ncube

Ncube

Exchange of information among people using Ncube parallel computers.

Keywords: Ncube, Parallel Computers

Audience: Ncube Users

Contact: David Krumme
ncube-users-request@cs.tufts.edu

Details: Free

A
B
C
D
E
F
G
H
I
J
K
L
M
N
O
P
Q
R
S
T
U
V
W
X
Y
Z

User Info: To subscribe to the list, send an e-mail message requesting a subscription to the URL address below.

```
mailto:ncube-users-
request@cs.tufts.edu
```

Ne-social-motss

Ne-social-motss

Announcements of lesbian/gay/bisexual social events and other happenings in the Northeastern US.

Keywords: Social Events, Lesbian, Gay, Bisexuality

Audience: Lesbians, Gays, Bisexuals

Contact: ne-social-motss-request@plts.org

Details: Free

User Info: To subscribe to the list, send an e-mail message requesting a subscription to the URL address below.

```
mailto:ne-social-motss-
request@plts.org
```

Near Eastern Studies

Princeton University Library

★★

The library's holdings are large and wide-ranging. They contain significant collections in many fields.

Keywords: China, Japan, Classics, History (Ancient), Near Eastern Studies, Literature (American), Literature (English), Aeronautics, Middle Eastern Studies, Mormonism, Publishing

Audience: General Public, Researchers, Librarians, Document Delivery Professionals

Details: Free

User Info: Expect: Connect message, blank screen, Send: <cr>; Expect: #, Send: Call 500

```
telnet://pucable.princeton.edu
```

NEARnet

NEARnet Newsletter

★

A quarterly publication for users of NEARnet and others who are interested in academic and research networking. The newsletter contains articles about NEARnet services, member organizations, and plans for the future.

Keywords: Networking, NEARnet

Audience: Computer Users, Students

Contact: nearnet-staff@nic.near.net

Details: Free

Available through anonymous FTP at (nic.near.net) in the directory newsletters.

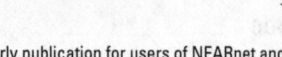

```
mailto:nearnet-staff@nic.near.net
```

Neci-announce

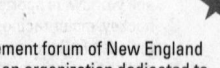

Neci-announce

★

This is the announcement forum of New England Community Internet, an organization dedicated to making Usenet and Internet accessible to the public without economic or technical barriers. The group is developing ways to bring IP connectivity at low cost into homes and nonprofit organizations.

Keywords: Internet, Usenet

Audience: Internet Surfers, Usenet Users

Contact: neci-announce-request@pioneer.ci.net

Details: Free

User Info: To subscribe to the list, send an e-mail message requesting a subscription to the URL address below.

```
mailto:neci-announce-
request@pioneer.ci.net
```

Neci-digest

Neci-digest

★

This is the daily discussion forum of New England Community Internet, an organization dedicated to making Usenet and Internet accessible to the public without economic or technical-expertise barriers. The group is developing ways to bring IP connectivity at low cost into homes and nonprofit organizations.

Keywords: Internet, Usenet

Audience: Internet Surfers, Usenet Users

Contact: neci-digest-request@pioneer.ci.net

Details: Free

User Info: To subscribe to the list, send an e-mail message requesting a subscription to the URL address below.

```
mailto:neci-digest-
request@pioneer.ci.net
```

Neci-discuss

Neci-discuss

★

This is the general discussion forum of New England Community Internet, an organization dedicated to making Usenet and Internet accessible to the public without economic or technical-expertise barriers. The group is developing ways to bring IP connectivity at low cost into homes and nonprofit organizations.

Keywords: Internet, Usenet

Audience: Internet Surfers, Usenet Users

Contact: neci-discuss-request@pioneer.ci.net

Details: Free

User Info: To subscribe to the list, send an e-mail message requesting a subscription to the URL address below.

Notes: To get a daily digestified version, subscribe to neci-digest. To receive organizational announcements only, subscribe to neci-announce.

```
mailto:neci-discuss-
request@pioneer.ci.net
```

Nedod

Nedod

Discussion of events, technical issues, and just plain social exchange related to motorcycling in the New England area of the US.

Keywords: Motorcycles, New England

Audience: Motorcycle Enthusiasts

Contact: cookson@mbunix.mitre.org

User Info: To subscribe to the list, send an e-mail message requesting a subscription to the URL address below.

```
mailto:nedod-request@mbunix.mitre.org
```

NERaves (Northeast Raves)

NERaves (Northeast Raves)

One of several regional rave-related mailing lists, NE-Raves covers the Northeastern US.

Keywords: Raves

Audience: Ravers

Details: Free

User Info: To subscribe to the list, send an e-mail message to the URL address below consisting of a single line reading:

SUB neraves YourFirstName YourLastName

To send a message to the entire list, address it to: neraves@umdd.umd.edu

```
mailto:listserv@umdd.umd.edu
```

Nerdnosh

Nerdnosh

This is a virtual campfire gathering of storytellers. Bring us your tired, your family fables, your journals of yesterday and your imprints on tomorrow.

Keywords: Storytelling

Audience: Storytellers, General Public

Contact: Timothy Bowden
urder@clovis.felton.ca.us

Details: Free

User Info: To subscribe to the list, send an e-mail message requesting a subscription to the URL address below, consisting of a single line reading:

SUB nerdnosh YourFirstName YourLastName

To send a message to the entire list, address it to: nerdnosh@clovis.felton.ca.us

`mailto:listserv@clovis.felton.ca.us`

Nero Ashbury

Nero Ashbury

★

Nero is a live-action, medieval role-playing game with a plot line and characters that continue from one adventure to the next. Nero has been successful in New England for over six years and is growing rapidly.

Keywords: Medieval Studies, Role-Playing, Games

Audience: General Public, Role-Playing Enthusiasts

Contact: lsonko@pearl.tufts.edu

Details: Free

User Info: To subscribe to the list, send an e-mail message requesting a subscription to the URL address below.

`mailto:lsonko@pearl.tufts.edu`

Net-News

Net-News

★★★

A newsletter devoted to library and information resources on the Internet.

Keywords: Information Science, Libraries, Networking, Internet

Sponsor: Metronet

Audience: Librarians, Researchers

Contact: Dana Noonan
noonan@msus1.msus.edu

Details: Free

User Info: Send email request to noonan@msus1.msus.edu metronet@vz.acs.umn.edu

`gopher://noonan@msus1.msus.edu`

Netblazer

Netblazer-users

★

Provides an unmoderated forum for discussions among users of Telebit NetBlazer products. Topics include known problems and workarounds, features discussions, and configuration advice.

Keywords: Telebit Computer Products, Netblazer

Audience: Telebit Netblazer Users

Contact: netblazer-users-request@telebit.com

Details: Free

User Info: To subscribe to the list, send an e-mail message requesting a subscription to the URL address below.

`mailto:netblazer-users-request@telebit.com`

NetCom

NetCom

★

NetCom is an Internet provider. It has produced "Net Cruiser" software for Windows.

Keywords: Internet

Audience: Internet Users

Details: Costs

`Netcom@netcom.com`

NetEc

NetEc

★★★

An electronic forum for published academic papers relating to economics.

Keywords: Economics, Business

Audience: Economists, Business Professionals

Contact: netec@uts.mcc.ac.uk

Details: Free

User Info: To subscribe to the list, send an e-mail message to the address below consisting of a single line reading:

SUB netec YourFirstName YourLastName

To send a message to the entire list, address it to: netec@hasara11.bitnet

`mailto:listserv@hasara11.bitnet`

Netfind

Netfind

★

Netfind is a service for locating individuals on the Internet.

Keywords: Internet Tools

Sponsor: University of Colorado, Boulder, CO

Audience: Internet Surfers

Profile: This service relies on common but not universal programs, and thus may not find some people with valid addresses. The most foolproof way of finding someone's e-mail address remains to call them on the phone and ask. All Netfind sites are functionally equivalent. Multiple ones are listed here in case some are overloaded or down with technical problems.

Contact: Michael F. Schwartz, Panagiotis G. Tsirigotis
schwartz@cs.colorado.edu
panos@cs.colorado.edu

Details: Free

User Info: File is pub/cs/distribs/netfind/readme

`ftp://ftp.cs.colorado.edu`

`gopher://emoryu1.cc.emory.edu/11/internet/General/netfind`

Netherlands

SURFnet—KB InfoServer

InfoService is a joint project by SURFnet (National Network Organization for Research and Higher Education) and the Koninklijke Bibliotheek (National Library of the Netherlands).

Keywords: Netherlands, Networks, Europe

Audience: European Internet Surfers

Contact: infoservices@surfnet.nl

Details: Free

`gopher://gopher.nic.surfnet.nl`

Netiquette

Net Etiquette Guide

★

Guidelines and Netiquette for the Net user.

Keywords: Internet, Etiquette, Netiquette

Sponsor: SURAnet Network Information Center

Audience: Internet Surfers

Contact: info@sura.net

Details: Free

User Info: File is: pub/nic/internet.literature/netiquette.txt

`ftp://ftp.sura.net`

A
B
C
D
E
F
G
H
I
J
K
L
M
N
O
P
Q
R
S
T
U
V
W
X
Y
Z

NetJam

NetJam

NetJam provides a means for people to collaborate on musical compositions by sending Musical Instrument Digital Interface (MIDI) and other files to each other.

Keywords: Music, Musicians

Audience: Musicians

Contact: Craig Latta
netjam-request@xcf.berkeley.edu

Details: Free

User Info: To subscribe to the list, send an e-mail message requesting a subscription to the URL address below.

`mailto:netjam-`
`request@xcf.berkeley.edu`

NetMonth

NetMonth

An independant guide to Bitnet.

Keywords: Bitnet, Networking

Audience: Computer Users, Internet Surfers

Contact: Philip Baczewski
nmonthed@vm.marist.edu

Details: Costs

User Info: To subscribe, send an e-mail message to the address below, consisting of a single line reading:

netmonth YourFirstName YourLastName

To send a message to the entire list, address it to: netmonth@vm.marist.edu

`mailto:listserv@vm.marist.edu`

NetVet Veterinary Resources

NetVet Veterinary Resources

An Internet server for veterinary and animal resources.

Keywords: Veterinary Medicine, Animal Welfare, Animals

Sponsor: Washington University, St. Louis, Division of Comparative Medicine

Audience: Veterinarians, Animal Lovers

Profile: A collection of veterinary and animal-related computer resources that includes archives of animal legislation and regulation, listings for colleges of Veterinary Medicine, conference information, and animal-related databases, including the Electronic Zoo. Also has links to other animal and veterinary-related systems.

Contact: Dr. Ken Boshert
ken@wudcm.wustl.edu

`gopher://netvet.wustl.edu`

`http://netvet.wustl.edu/`

Network-Audio-Bits

Network-Audio-Bits

A bimonthly electronic magazine that features reviews and news of current music in rock, pop, new age, jazz, funk, folk, and other genres—including major-label and independent recording artists.

Keywords: Music Reviews, Music

Audience: Music Enthusiasts, General Public

Contact: Michael A. Murphy
murph@maine.bitnet

Details: Free

User Info: To subscribe to the list, send an e-mail message requesting a subscription to the URL address below.

`mailto:murph@maine.bitnet`

Network Servers

The FARNET Gazette

This short monthly electronic newsletter is of interest to network service providers with a research and education focus.

Keywords: Network Servers

Audience: Network Service Providers

Contact: Laura Breeden
breeden@farnet.org

Details: Free

`mailto:gazette-request@farnet.org`

Network Time Protocol

ntp

Discussion of the Network Time Protocol.

Keywords: Network Time Protocol

Audience: Network Time Protocol Users

Contact: ntp-request@trantor.umd.edu

User Info: To subscribe to the list, send an e-mail message requesting a subscription to the URL address below.

To send a message to the entire list, address it to: ntp@trantor.umd.edu

`mailto:ntp-request@trantor.umd.edu`

Networking

(The) Electronic Public Interest versus the Private Good

Statement by community networker Dave Hughes, sounding the warning that the federal goverment may be leaving to the marketplace too much control over who gets access to the Information infrastructure.

Keywords: Community, Networking, Government (US)

Audience: Activists, Policymakers, Community Leaders

Contact: Dave Hughes
dave@oldcolo.com

Details: Free

`http://nearnet.gnn.com/mag/articles/`
`oram/bio.hughes.html`

(The) WELL (Whole Earth 'Lectronic Link)

The WELL is a computer conferencing system, a virtual community, and an electronic coffee shop.

Keywords: Community, Networking, Computer Conferencing, Virtual Community

Sponsor: Whole Earth 'Lectronic Link

Audience: General Public, Internet Surfers

Profile: The WELL is a classic example of an online community that uses what is called "conferencing" to bring a myriad of people together for intense interactions without them having to be connected at the same time. At the end of 1993, the WELL had about 8,000 users (about 90% from all over the USA and about 10% from other locations) and approximately 200 public discussion areas ('conferences'), and 200 private discussion areas. It is a place rich in diverse 'neighborhoods.'

Contact: The WELL Support Staff
info@well.sf.ca.us

Direct dial access through:
(415) 332-4335

To participate in a conference on the WELL, you must first establish an account on the WELL. To do so, start by typing: telnet well.sf.ca.us

`telnet://well.sf.ca.us`

(The) Worldwide Impact of Network Access

★

This is an article by community networker Felipe Rodriquez. In this statement Rodriquez argues that developed countries should help less developed countries build their information infrastructures, and that governments should not censor the content of network traffic.

Keywords: Community, Networking, Europe, Development (International)

Audience: Activists, Policymakers, Community Leaders

Contact: Felipe Rodriquez
felipe@hacktic.nl

`http://nearnet.gnn.com/mag/articles/`
`oram/bio.rodriquez.html`

An NREN That Includes Everyone

★

In this article, community networker Tom Grundner (founder of Free-Net), advocates a National Community Network, one that treats parents looking for Health Care information as researchers. He advocates expanding our definition of educational access to include people of all ages—senior citizens as well as kindergarteners.

Keywords: Community, Networking, Government (US)

Audience: Activists, Policymakers, Community Leaders

Contact: Tom Grundner
tmg@nptn.org

Details: Free

Notes: This document contains hypertext links to the NPTN (National Public Telecomputing Network).

`http://nearnet.gnn.com/mag/articles/`
`oram/bio.grundner.html`

Blacksburg Electronic Village Gopher

★★★

The Blacksburg Electronic Village is a project to link an entire town in southwestern Virginia with a 21st-century telecommunications infrastructure. This infrastructure will bring a useful set of information services and interactive communications facilities into the daily activities of citizens and businesses.

Keywords: Community, Networking, Telecommunications

Sponsor: Town of Blacksburg, Virginia, USA

Audience: Activists, Policymakers, Community Leaders, Government

Profile: This community gopher server run by the town of Blacksburg contains information about Blacksburg and how it is building its electronic infrastructure. It includes a list of Blacksburg-area BBSs, instructions for local residents to get an account on the town's BBS, and a section called "Village Schoolhouse."

Details: Costs, Moderated

`gopher://morse.cns.vt.edu`

Citizens Project

 ★★★★

A grass-roots community group in the Pikes Peak region of Colorado.

Keywords: Community, Networking, Colorado

Audience: Activists, Policymakers, Community Leaders, Government

Profile: Based in Colorado Springs, Colorado, the Citizens Project makes use of the online world in pursuit of its mission to investigate, inform, and advocate issues affecting the Pikes Peak region. It maintains an extensive gopher server, FTP site, and a ListServ (for people who have only e-mail access).

Contact: Citizens Project
citizens@cscns.com

Details: Free

User Info: To subscribe to the list, send an e-mail message to the URL address below, consisting of a single line reading:

SUB cns-citizens-pub YourFirstName YourLastName

`mailto:listserv@cscns.com`

Civic Promise of the National Information Infrastructure (NII)

★

Community networker Richard Civille (founder of EcoNet and director of the Center for Civic Networking) describes several experiments in community networking.

Keywords: Community, Networking, Government (US)

Audience: Activists, Policymakers, Community Leaders, Government

Contact: Richard Civille
rciville@civicnet.org

Details: Free

`http://nearnet.gnn.com/mag/articles/`
`oram/bio.civille.html`

Community Networks Benefit Federal Goals

★

Statement by community networker Frank Odasz, founder and director of Big Sky Telegraph, a network of rural BBSs throughout Montana. In this article he makes the case that the federal government will benefit from the widespread rural employment of networking technology.

Keywords: Community, Networking, Rural Development, Development

Audience: Activists, Policy Analysts, Community Leaders, Government, Citizens, Rural Residents, Native Americans

Contact: Frank Odasz
franko@bigsky.dillon.mt.us,

Details: Free

`http://nearnet.gnn.com/mag/articles/`
`oram/bio.odasz.html`

ECHO

 ★★★★

A computer conferencing system based in New York City.

Keywords: Community, Networking, Women's Issues

Sponsor: East Coast Hang Out

Audience: Activists, Policy Makers, Community Leaders, Governments, Students, Feminists, Educators, Health Care Professionals, Artists, Communicators, General Public

Profile: ECHO was started by Stacy Horn, as an East Coast counterpart to the WELL. ECHO makes an effort to be hospitable to women and has one of the highest percentages of women in an online community.

Contact: Stacy Horn
horn@echonyc.com,

Details: Costs

`telnet://echonyc.com`

Electronic Democracy Must Come from Us

★

Article about government policy and community networks by community networker Evelyn Pine (former national director of Computer Professionals for Social Responsibility). A short critique of the promises of electronic networking contrasted with the realities of political control.

Keywords: Community, Networking, Government (US)

Audience: Activists, Community Leaders, Governments

Contact: Evelyn Pine
evy@well.sf.ca.us

Details: Free

`http://nearnet.gnn.com/mag/articles/`
`oram/bio.pine.html`

Free-Net Working Papers

 ★★★★

An FTP site with a collection of articles and papers about community networking.

Keywords: Community Networking, Networking

Sponsor: Carleton University, National Clearinghouse for Machine Readable Texts

Audience: Activists, Government, General Public

Profile: Project Guttenburg's goal is to provide a collection of 10,000 of the most used books by the year 2001.

Contact: Jay Weston, Michael S. Hart
jweston@carleton.ca

Details: Free

Login anonymous; cd text

`ftp://alfred.carleton.ca/pub/freenet/`
`working.papers`

A
B
C
D
E
F
G
H
I
J
K
L
M
N
O
P
Q
R
S
T
U
V
W
X
Y
Z

A
B
C
D
E
F
G
H
I
J
K
L
M
N
O
P
Q
R
S
T
U
V
W
X
Y
Z

Information Sources

These compiled resources provide information describing the Internet and computer-mediated communication technologies, as well as information on realated applications, culture, discussion forums, and bibliographies.

Keywords: Internet, Networking

Audience: Internet Surfers, Computer-Mediated Communication Researchers

Profile: Files are located in: pub/communications.

Contact: John December
decemj@rpi.edu

Details: Free

`ftp://ftp.rpi.edu`

`http://www.rpi.edu/Internet/Guides/decemj/icmc/top.html`

Leaders of Community Networking: People Who Create Online Communities

A WWW document with links to several important community networking resources. A brief overview of community networking is provided, as are links to statements by several leaders in the movement.

Keywords: Community, Networking, Government (US Federal)

Audience: Activists, Policymakers, Community Leaders, Government, Citizens

Details: Free

`http://nearnet.gnn.com/mag/articles/oram/introduction.html`

NEARnet Newsletter

A quarterly publication for users of NEARnet and others who are interested in academic and research networking. The newsletter contains articles about NEARnet services, member organizations, and plans for the future.

Keywords: Networking, NEARnet

Audience: Network Users, Students (high school up)

Contact: nearnet-staff@nic.near.net

Details: Free
Available through anonymous FTP at (nic.near.net) in the directory newsletters.

`mailto:nearnet-staff@nic.near.net`

Net-News

A newsletter devoted to library and information resources on the Internet.

Keywords: Information, Libraries, Networking, Internet

Sponsor: Metronet

Audience: Librarians, Researchers

Contact: Dana Noonan
noonan@msus1.msus.edu

Details: Free
Send email request to noonan@msus1.msus.edu or metronet@vz.acs.umn.edu

`gopher://noonan@msus1.msus.edu`

NetMonth

An independant guide to Bitnet.

Keywords: Bitnet, Networking

Audience: Computer Users, Internet Surfers

Contact: Philip Baczewski
nmonthed@vm.marist.edu

Details: Costs

User Info: To subscribe, send an e-mail message to the address below, consisting of a single line reading:
netmonth YourFirstName YourLastName
To send a message to the entire list, address it to: netmonth@vm.marist.edu

`mailto:listserv@vm.marist.edu`

Networks & Communities

This directory is a compilation of information resources focused on networks and communities.

Keywords: Community , Networking, Privacy

Audience: Network Developers, Community Activists, Free-Net Organizers, Fundraisers

Details: Free

`ftp://una.hh.lib.umich.edu/70/inetdirsstacks/nets:sternberg`

Output

Newsletter of the Florida State University (FSU) Computing Center. Includes topics such as networking, microcomputing, mainframe computing, and supercomputing on campus, including use of computers in classroom and research computing at FSU.

Keywords: Networking, Microcomputing, Supercomputing

Audience: FSU Computer Science Students, Computer Users

Contact: Suzanne C. Nelson
nelson@avm.cc.fsu.edu

Details: Free
Send your request addressed to the Editor.

`mailto:nelson@avm.cc.fsu.edu`

People Using Networks Can Have an Impact on Government

Statement by community networker Anne Fallis, who emphasizes the need for easy-to-use interfaces and inexpensive access to worldwide information. She lists many examples of local communities using networking.

Keywords: Community, Networking, Activism

Audience: Activists, Policymakers, Community Leaders, Network Users

Contact: Anne Fallis
afallis@silver.sdsmt.edu

Details: Free

`http://nearnet.gnn.com/mag/articles/oram/bio.fallis.html`

Polish Archives

Information about Polish Internet gophers and Polish electronic journals.

Keywords: Poland, Telecommunications, Networking

Audience: Historians, Poles

Contact: Darek Milewski
Milewski@poniecki.berkeley.edu

User Info: To subscribe, send an e-mail message requesting a subscription to the URL address below.

`gopher://gopher.poniecki.berkeley.edu`

Qnx4

A mailing list for discussion of all aspects of the QNX real-time operating systems. Topics include compatible hardware, available third-party software, software reviews, available PD/free software, QNX and FLEET networking, process control, and so on.

Keywords: Computing, Hardware, Software, Networking

Audience: Computer Users, Hardware/Software Designers, Product Analysts

Contact: Martin Zimmerman
camz@dlogtech.cuc.ab.ca

Details: Free

User Info: To subscribe to the list, send an e-mail message requesting a subscription to the URL address below.
To send a message to the entire list, address it to: qnx4@dlogtech.cuc.ab.ca

`mailto:qnx4@dlogtech.cuc.ab.ca`

Singapore DMC

The Digital Media Center (DMC) home page contains links related to contents about Singapore, the National Computer Board (NCB), and various other National IT (Information Technology) projects.

Keywords: Internet, Networking

Audience: Internet Surfers

Contact: shaopin@ncb.gov.sg
            kianjin@ncb.gov.sg

Details: Free

http://king.ncb.gov.sg

Telluride Institute

This is a community organization involved in building an electronic dimension in rural Colorado. The vision of Telluride Institute includes linking rural residents to each other and outside resources, creating new opportunities for education, jobs, and arts.

Keywords: Community, Networking, Virtual Community, Rural Development, Colorado

Sponsor: The Telluride Institute, Telluride, Colorado

Audience: Activists, Policymakers, Community Leaders, Students, Colorado Residents

Profile: The Telluride Institute is a local community-based organization that produces arts, environmental, and educational events in the Telluride area of Colorado. The Institite is committed to the creation of what it calls the "InfoZone": it wants to use modern telecommunications to link together the local community and to connect to the rest of the world to exchange ideas, commerce, arts, and inspiration.

Contact: Richard Lowenberg
            tellinst@CSN.ORG

Details: Free

            Send an e-mail message to the URL address below asking for further information.

mailto:tellinst@csn.org

The Black Box Catalog

The Black Box Catalog, the industry's most complete source for data communication equipment, is now available on the Internet. The complete range of products, technical references, and application briefs are available on the Black Box World Wide Web Server.

Keywords: Communications, Networking, Telecommunication, Computers

Sponsor: Black Box Corporation, Lawrence, PA

Audience: Engineers, Network Administration, LAN Administrators, Communication Specialists

Profile: Black Box Corporation is a leading international supplier of data communications networking and related computer connectivity products. Black Box's commitment to providing effective solutions that substantially enhance the capabilities of communications systems is backed by a technical support staff that is available around the clock, a liberal 45-day return policy, and same day shipment of its 6000 products.

Contact: Webmaster
            webmaster@blackbox.com

Details: Costs

http://www.blackbox.com

TWICS

This is an English-language computer conferencing system in Japan.

Keywords: Community, Networking, Computer Conferencing, Japan, Virtual Community

Sponsor: TWICS Co., Ltd.

Audience: Internationalists, General Public, Journalists, Policymakers

Profile: TWICS is a computer conferencing system that has a reputation for being a thriving electronic community. It recently obtained a full Internet connection and is currently one of the few places in Japan accesible via the Internet. Unlike a database or a gopher server, TWICS is a place to visit for interaction with actual people.

Contact: Tim Buress
            twics@twics.co.jp,

Details: Free

telnet://tanuki.twics.co.jp

Usenet Repository

Regular informational postings and FAQs from various newsgroups on the Usenet, grouped into archives by newsgroup.

Keywords: Internet, Networking, Usenet

Audience: Internet Surfers

Details: Free

File is: pub/Usenet-by-group

ftp://pit-manager.mit.edu

Women's Wire

Women's Wire is an online interactive network focusing on women's issues and interests.

Keywords: Networking, Women's Issues, Online Services

Audience: Women, Internet Users

Profile: This service acts as an international clearinghouse for resources and networking on a broad range of topics including news, politics, careers, education, parenting, health, and arts. Provides e-mail and access to thousands of resources, including Usenet newsgroups.

Details: Costs

            Access via an easy-to-use graphical interface for Macintosh and Windows platforms, or a text-based interface for DOS and Unix platforms. Local access numbers available throughout the US and in most countries.

mailto:info@wwire.net

Networks

Cisco

This list is for discussion of the network products from Cisco Systems, Inc (primarily the AGS gateway, but also the ASM terminal multiplex) and any other relevant products. Discussions about operation, problems, features, topology, configuration, protocols, routing, loading, serving, and so on, are all encouraged. Other topics include vendor relations, new product announcements, availability of fixes and new features, and discussion of new requirements and desirables.

Keywords: Cisco Systems, Networks

Audience: Cisco Employees, Cisco Users, Distributors

Contact: David Wood
            cisco-request@spot.colorado.edu

Details: Free

User Info: To subscribe to the list, send an e-mail message requesting a subscription to the URL address below.

            To send a message to the entire list, address it to: cisco@spot.colorado.edu

mailto:cisco-request@spot.colorado.edu

Cleveland FreeNet

A network designed for community access and education.

Keywords: Networks, Community Access

Sponsor: The Cleveland FreeNet Project, Case Western Reserve University, Cleveland, Ohio, USA

Audience: Educators, Researchers, Students, Parents

Profile: A prototypical user-friendly city FreeNet, containing complete historical documents, an up-to-date news service, extensive info on the arts, sciences, technology, medicine, business, and education.

Notes: Registration is required, and information on registration is included.

telnet://freenet-in-a.cwru.edu

CYFERNET (Child, Youth, and Family Education Network)

This public information service supports child, youth, and family development programs.

Keywords: Education, Networks

Sponsor: Youth Development Information Center at the National Agricultural Library

Audience: Educators, Children, Families

A
B
C
D
E
F
G
H
I
J
K
L
M
N
O
P
Q
R
S
T
U
V
W
X
Y
Z

A
B
C
D
E
F
G
H
I
J
K
L
M
N
O
P
Q
R
S
T
U
V
W
X
Y
Z

Profile: CYFERNET contains information useful to child, youth, and family development professionals. Features include programs for children aged 5-8 years, youth-at-risk programs, community projects, and education.

Contact: jkane@nalusda.gov

Details: Free

`gopher://ra.esusda.gov/11/CYFER-net`

K12 Net

Decentralized network of school-based bulletin board systems (BBSs).

Keywords: Education (K-12), Networks

Audience: Educators (K-12), School Children

Profile: K12 Net provides millions of teachers, students, and parents in metropolitan and rural areas throughout the world with the ability to meet and talk with each other to discuss educational issues, exchange information, and share resources on a global scale.

Contact: Jack Crawford, Janet Murray
jack@k12net.org
jmurray@psg.com

Details: Free

`gopher://woonext.dsrd.ornl.gov/11/Docs/k12net`

Networks & Communities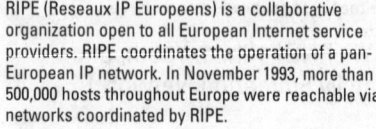

This directory is a compilation of information resources focused on networks and communities.

Keywords: Community , Networking, Privacy

Audience: Network Developers, Community Activists, Free-net Organizers, Fundraisers

Details: Free

`ftp://una.hh.lib.umich.edu/70/inetdirsstacks/nets:sternberg`

RIPE Network Coordination Centre Gopher

RIPE (Reseaux IP Europeens) is a collaborative organization open to all European Internet service providers. RIPE coordinates the operation of a pan-European IP network. In November 1993, more than 500,000 hosts throughout Europe were reachable via networks coordinated by RIPE.

Keywords: Europe, Networks

Audience: European Internet Surfers

Contact: ncc@ripe.net

Details: Free

`gopher://gopher.ripe.net`

SABINET (South African Bibliographic and Information Network)

This gopher offers information searches from a variety of electronic databases, as well as for library locations and availability of books and periodicals.

Keywords: South Africa, Databases, Networks

Audience: South African Internet Surfers

Contact: hennie@info1.sabinet.co.za

Details: Free

`gopher://info2.sabinet.co.za`

SURFnet—KB InfoServer

InfoService is a joint project by SURFnet (National Network Organization for Research and Higher Education) and the Koninklijke Bibliotheek (National Library of the Netherlands).

Keywords: Netherlands, Networks, Europe

Audience: European Internet Surfers

Contact: infoservices@surfnet.nl

Details: Free

`gopher://gopher.nic.surfnet.nl`

Virginia's PEN (Public Education Network)

This is a statewide educational network.

Keywords: Education, Networks, Virginia

Sponsor: Virginia Department of Education

Audience: Educators

Profile: Educators throughout Virginia can access PEN via a local telephone call or through a toll-free line. The network includes discussion groups, news reports, study guides, and curriculum resources. In one of the features, History OnLine, students and teachers query historical figures such as Thomas Jefferson, and historians will answer in character.

Contact: Harold Cathernh
hcathern@vdoe386.vak12.edu

Details: Free

Password: Guest

`telnet://guest@vdoe386.vak12ed.edu`

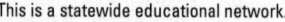

Neural Networks

Neuron

This is a moderated list (in digest form) that deals with all aspects of neural networks (and any type of network or neuromorphic system). Topics include both connectionist models (artificial neural networks) and biological systems ("wetware").

Keywords: Neural Networks, Biological Research

Audience: Neuroscientists, Neurobiologists

Contact: Peter Marvit
neuron-request@cattell.psych.upenn.edu

Details: Free, Moderated

User Info: To subscribe to the list, send an e-mail message requesting a subscription to the URL address below.

Notes: Back issues and limited software are available via FTP from cattell.psych.upenn.edu. The Digest is gatewayed to Usenet's comp.ai.neural-nets.

`mailto:neuron-request@cattell.psych.upenn.edu`

Neural Simulation

Purkinje Park

A server maintained by CalTech to support the sharing of information between users of the GENESIS neural simulator, and to address topics of general interest to the Computational Neuroscience community.

Keywords: Computational Neuroscience, GENESIS, Neural Simulation.

Sponsor: Cal Tech

Audience: Neuroscientists, Computational Neuroscientists

Contact: Dave Beeman
dbeeman@smaug.bbb.caltech.edu

`http://www.bbb.caltech.edu/index.html`

Neurobiology

Neurosciences Internet Resource Guide

A comprehensive Internet resource addressing biological, chemical, medical, engineering, and computer science aspects of neurobiology.

Keywords: Neurobiology, Neuroscience, Brain Research

Sponsor: The University of Michigan School of Information and Library

Audience: Neuroscientists, Neurobiologists

Profile: This resource provides links to journal articles, tutorials on neuroimaging and neurobiology, moderated newsgroups, and international forums, all of which address issues surrounding the field of neuroscience.

Contact: Sheryl Cormicle, Steve Bonario
sherylc@sils.umich.edu
sbonario@umich.edu

`http://http2.sils.umich.edu/Public/nirg/nirg1.html`

Neurology

MBI, Music and the Brain Information Center Database (MuSICA)

The intent of this resource is to establish a comprehensive database of scientific research on music.

Keywords: Music Resources, Human Behavior, Neurology

Sponsor: Music and the Brain Information Center

Audience: Researchers, Scientists

Profile: MuSICA maintains a data base of scientific research (references and abstracts) on music as related to behavior, the brain and allied fields, in order to foster interdisciplinary knowledge. Topics include the auditory system; human and animal behavior; creativity; the neuropsychology of music and the human brain; the effects of music on behavior and physiology; music education, medicine, performance, and therapy; neurobiology; perception and psychophysics. Citations and abstracts are excerpted from the following journals: The Bulletin of the Council for Research in Music Education, The Journal of Research in Music Education, Music Perception, Psychology of Music, Psychomusicology.

Contact: Norman Weinberger, Gordon Shaw
mbic@mila.ps.uci.edu

Details: Free
Expect login: Send mbi Expect password: Send nammbi

`telnet://mila.ps.uci.edu`

Neuroscience

Cognitive and Psychological Sciences on the Internet

A resource containing links to academic programs, organizations and conference lists, journals and magazines, Usenet newsgroups, discussion lists, and other general information regarding cognitive science.

Keywords: Cognitive Science, Psychology, Neuroscience

Sponsor: The Stanford University Psychology Department

Audience: Cognitive Scientists, Neuroscientists, Psychologists, Psychiatrists

Contact: Scott Mainwaring
sdm@psych.stanford.edu

`http://matia.stanford.edu/cogsci.html`

Neurosciences Internet Resource Guide

A comprehensive Internet resource addressing biological, chemical, medical, engineering, and computer science aspects of neurobiology.

Keywords: Neurobiology, Neuroscience, Brain Research

Sponsor: The University of Michigan School of Information and Library

Audience: Neuroscientists, Neurobiologists

Profile: This resource provides links to journal articles, tutorials on neuroimaging and neurobiology, moderated newsgroups, and international forums, all of which address issues surrounding the field of neuroscience.

Contact: Sheryl Cormicle, Steve Bonario
sherylc@sils.umich.edu
sbonario@umich.edu

`http://http2.sils.umich.edu/Public/nirg/nirg1.html`

Recreational Pharmacology Server

Very extensive collection of drug FAQs, data sheets, net articles, resources, and electronic books. Complete list of Internet links to related sites.

Keywords: Pharmacology, Drugs, Neuroscience

Sponsor: University of Washington, Seattle, Washington, USA

Audience: Students, General Public, Pharmacologists, Neuroscientists

Contact: Webmaster
lamontg@u.washington.edu

Details: Free

`http://stein1.u.washington.edu:2012/pharm/pharm.html`

The University of Michigan Library

The library's holdings are large and wide-ranging and contain significant collections in many fields.

Keywords: Education (Bilingual), Linguistics, Neuroscience, Michigan, Prohibition, Government (African)

Audience: General Public, Researchers, Librarians, Document Delivery Professionals

Details: Free

User Info: Expect: nothing, Send: <cr>

`telnet://cts.merit.edu`

Nevada

University of Nevada at Reno Library

The library's holdings are large and wide-ranging and contain significant collections in many fields.

Keywords: Basque Studies, Nevada , UN Army Map Service, Patents

Audience: General Public, Researchers, Librarians, Document Delivery Professionals

Details: Free

User Info: Expect: login, Send: wolfpac

`telnet://wolfpac.lib.unr.edu`

Nevada State Documents

University of Nevada, Las Vegas Library - Las Vegas, NV

The library's holdings are large and wide-ranging and contain significant collections in many fields.

Keywords: Gaming, Hotel Administration, Canadian Documents, Nevada State Documents

Audience: General Public, Researchers, Librarians, Document Delivery Professionals

Contact: Myoung-ja Lee Kwon
kwon@nevada.edu.

Details: Free

User Info: Expect: login; Send: library

`telnet://library.lv-lib.nevada.edu`

New Age Music

Direct

Discussion of the work of the musical artist Vangelis.

Keywords: New Age Music, Musical Groups

Audience: Musicians, Music Enthusiasts, Vangelis Fans

Contact: Keith Gregoire
direct-request@celtech.com

User Info: To subscribe to the list, send an e-mail message requesting a subscription to the URL address below.

To send a message to the entire list, address it to: direct@celtech.com

Both bounce and daily digest modes are available; specify your preference when subscribing.

`mailto:direct-request@celtech.com`

A B C D E F G H I J K L M N O P Q R S T U V W X Y Z

New England

Nedod

Discussion of events, technical issues, and just plain social exchange related to motorcycling in the New England area of the US.

Keywords: Motorcycles, New England

Audience: Motorcycle Enthusiasts

Contact: cookson@mbunix.mitre.org

User Info: To subscribe to the list, send an e-mail message requesting a subscription to the URL address below.

`mailto:nedod-request@mbunix.mitre.org`

New Jersey

NJ-motss

Mailing list for gay, lesbian, and bisexual issues in New Jersey.

Keywords: Gay, Lesbian, Bisexuality, New Jersey

Audience: Gays, Lesbians, Bisexuals

Contact: majordomo@plts.org

Details: Free

User Info: To subscribe to the list, send an e-mail message to the URL address shown below consisting of a single line reading:

SUB NJ-motss YourFirstName YourLastName

To send a message to the entire list, address it to: NJ-motss@plts.org

`mailto:majordomo@plts.org`

NJ-motss-announce

Announcements of interests to New Jersey's gay, lesbian, and bisexual population.

Keywords: Gay, Lesbian, Bisexuality, New Jersey

Audience: Gays, Lesbians, Bisexuals

Contact: majordomo@plts.org

Details: Free

User Info: To subscribe to the list, send an e-mail message to the URL address shown below consisting of a single line reading:

SUB NJ-motss-announce YourFirstName YourLastName

To send a message to the entire list, address it to: NJ-motss-announce@plts.org

`mailto:majordomo@plts.org`

New Media

CTN News

This is a list covering news on Tibet.

Keywords: Tibet, New Media

Audience: Tibetans, Journalists, General Public

Contact: ctn-editors@utcc.utoronto.ca

Details: Free

User Info: To subscribe to the list, send an e-mail message requesting a subscription to the URL address below.

To send a message to the entire list, address it to: CTN_ News@utcc.utoronto.ca

`mailto:ctn-editors@utcc.utoronto.ca`

New Mexico

New Mexico LegalNet

The system makes legal resources available, including state motor vehicle and corporation databases, court dockets, border trade information, and country and city data.

Keywords: Law, New Mexico

Audience: New Mexico Residents, Lawyers, Private Investigators

Contact: inettgen@technet.nm.org

Details: Costs

`telnet://technet.nm.org`

New Music

NewMusNet

A place on the Arts Wire to discuss issues concerning composers, performers, and presenters of new music and to access information about new music.

Keywords: Music, New Music

Audience: Composers, Musicians, Performers

Contact: Pauline Oliveros
oliveros@tmn.com

`telnet://tmn.com`

New Orleans

New-orleans

A list for discussing any and all aspects of the city of New Orleans. History, politics, culture, food, restaurants, music, entertainment, Mardi Gras, and so on, are all fair game.

Keywords: New Orleans, Travel

Audience: New Orleans Residents, Travelers/ Tourists

Contact: Edward J. Branley

elendil@mintir.new-orleans.la.us

User Info: To subscribe to the list, send an e-mail message requesting a subscription to the URL address below.

`mailto:mail-server@mintir.new-orleans.la.us`

Neworl-dig

This is a digest version of the New Orleans mailing list. It is distributed on a monthly basis, and includes articles from the New Orleans list, minus the "noise."

Keywords: New Orleans, Travel

Audience: New Orleans Residents, New Orleans Visitors

Contact: Edward J. Branley
elendil@mintir.new-orleans.la.us

Details: Free

User Info: To subscribe to the list, send an e-mail message requesting a subscription to the URL address below.

`mailto:mail-server@mintir.new-orleans.la.us`

New Testament

Bible (King James Version)

The Bible (King James Version) includes the complete text of the modern Thomas Nelson revision of the 1769 edition of the King James version of the Bible.

Keywords: Bible, Religious Text, Old Testament, New Testament

Sponsor: Thomas Nelson Publishers, Nashville, TN, USA

Audience: Christians, Theologians, Historians, Moralists

Profile: The King James version originated from translations ordered by King James of England in 1604 at the Hampton Court Conference. Both the Old and New Testaments are included in this version. Records in the database represent both chapters and verses.

Contact: Dialog in the US at (800) 334-2564, Dialog internationally at country specific locations.

Details: Costs

User Info: To subscribe, contact Dialog directly.

`telnet://dialog.com`

New User's Questions

New User's Questions

Answers to commonly asked questions by new Internet users.

Keywords: Internet, Internet Guides

Sponsor: Xylogics, Inc., and SRI International

Audience: Internet Surfers

Contact: Gary Scott Malkin, April N. Marine
gmalkin@Xylogics.COM
april@nisc.sri.com

Details: Free

Notes: File is: documents/fyi/fyi_04.txt

`ftp://nic.merit.edu`

New York Islanders

New York Islanders

A discussion of the New York Islanders hockey team, with emphasis on the current season.

Keywords: Hockey, Sports, New York

Audience: Ice Hockey Enthusiasts

Contact: David Strauss
dss2k@virginia.edu

Details: Free

User Info: To subscribe to the list, send an e-mail message requesting a subscription to the URL address below.

`mailto:dss2k@virginia.edu`

New York

BTHS-ENews-l

This list provides an open forum for students, teachers, and alumni of Brooklyn Technical High School.

Keywords: New York

Audience: Teachers, Students, Educators

Contact: listserv@Cornell.edu

Details: Free

User Info: To subscribe to the list, send an e-mail message to the URL address below, consisting of a single line reading:

SUB BTHS-ENews-l YourFirstName YourLastName

To send a message to the entire list, address it to: BTHS-ENews-l@Cornell.edu

`mailto:listserv@Cornell.edu`

ebikes

New York City Bicycle discussion list.

Keywords: Bicycling, New York

Audience: Bicyclists

Contact: Danny Lieberman
ebikes-request@panix.com

Details: Free

User Info: To subscribe to the list, send an e-mail message requesting a subscription to the URL address below.

To send a message to the entire list, address it to: ebikes-request@panix.com

`mailto:ebikes-request@panix.com`

Information about New York City

Facts about New York City, including information on museums, restaurants, hotels, bars, and other areas of interest to New Yorkers and visitors alike.

Keywords: New York, Travel

Sponsor: City University of New York (CUNY)

Audience: New York City Residents, Tourists, General Public

Contact: Anil Khullar
gopher@netops.gc.cuny.edu

Notes: Still under construction, some items are incomplete

`gopher://timesq.gc.cuny.edu`

New York Islanders

A discussion of the New York Islanders hockey team, with emphasis on the current season.

Keywords: Hockey, New York Islanders, New York

Audience: New York Islanders Fans, Ice Hockey Fans

Contact: David Strauss
dss2k@virginia.edu

Details: Free

User Info: To subscribe to the list, send an e-mail message requesting a subscription to the URL address below.

`mailto:dss2k@virginia.edu`

New York State Department of Health Gopher

An electronic guide to health information from the state of New York.

Keywords: Health Care, Statistics, Health Sciences, New York

Sponsor: New York State Department of Health

Audience: Health Care Professionals, General Public

Profile: Information provided includes health statistics for New York State, lists of health care providers, facilities, and publications, as well as New York State Department of Health press releases.

Contact: nyhealth@albnydh2.bitnet

`gopher://gopher.health.state.ny.us`

NYSERNet Internet Guide

A comprehensive guide to the Internet from the New York State Education and Research Network (NYSERNet). NYSERNet provides access to specialized databases and online libraries, as well as to supercomputing and parallel-processing facilities throughout the US and to many national networks.

Keywords: Internet, Internet Guides, New York, Supercomputers

Sponsor: NYSERNet K-12 Networking Interest Group

Audience: Internet Surfers

Contact: info@nysernet.org

Details: Free

`ftp://nysernet.org`

Shamash, The New York - Israel Project

This site is designed to facilitate communications between Jews and Jewish organizations through the medium of the Internet. Information includes archives of Jewish lists, updates of community Jewish events in New York and beyond, a Jewish white pages, and a section on the Holocaust. It also has Hebrew software and access to other Jewish and Israeli information servers.

Keywords: Judaism, Israel, New York

Sponsor: New York - Israel Project (Nysernet), New York, USA

Audience: Jews, Jewish Organizations

Contact: Avrum Goodblatt, Chaim Dworkin
goodblat@israel.nysernet.org
chaim@israel.nysernet.org.

`gopher://nysernet.org`

A B C D E F G H I J K L M N O P Q R S T U V W X Y Z

A
B
C
D
E
F
G
H
I
J
K
L
M
N
O
P
Q
R
S
T
U
V
W
X
Y
Z

VEGCNY-L (Vegetarians in Central New York area)

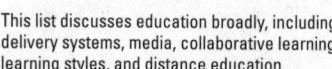

VegCNY-L is an open discussion list intended to serve those people living in the Central New York area who are vegetarians, as well as those who are interested in vegetarianism.

Keywords: Vegetarianism, New York, Food

Audience: Vegetarians

Contact: Chuck Goelzer Lyons
cgl1@cornell.edu

Details: Free

User Info: To subscribe to the list, send an e-mail message to the URL address below consisting of a single line reading:

SUB VEGCNY-L YourFirstName Your:LastName

To send a message to the entire list, address it to: VEGCNY-L@cornell.edu

`mailto:listserv@cornell.edu`

Newedu-l (New Paradigms in Education List)

Newedu-l (New Paradigms in Education List)

This list discusses education broadly, including delivery systems, media, collaborative learning, learning styles, and distance education.

Keywords: Education (Adult), Education (Distance), Education (Continuing)

Audience: Educators (k-12), Administrators, Researchers

Details: Free

User Info: To subscribe to the list, send an e-mail message to the URL address below consisting of a single line reading:

SUB newedu-l YourFirstName YourLastName

To send a message to the entire list, address it to: newedu-l @uscvm.bitnet

`mailto:listserv@uscvm.bitnet`

Newlists

Newlists

This is a mailing list clearing house for new mailing lists. Subscribers will get announcements of new lists that are mailed to this list.

Keywords: Mailing Lists

Audience: Internet Surfers

Contact: Marty Hoag
info@vm1.nodak.edu

Details: Free

User Info: To subscribe to the list, send an e-mail message requesting a subscription to the URL address below.

`mailto:info@vm1.nodak.edu`

NewMusNet

NewMusNet

A place on the Arts Wire to discuss issues concerning composers, performers, and presenters of new music and to access information about new music.

Keywords: Music, New Music

Audience: Composers, Musicians, Performers

Contact: Pauline Oliveros
oliveros@tmn.com

`telnet://tmn.com`

Neworl-dig

Neworl-dig

This is a digest version of the New Orleans mailing list. It is distributed on a monthly basis, and includes articles from the New Orleans list, minus the "noise."

Keywords: New Orleans, Travel

Audience: New Orleans Residents, Travelers/ Tourists

Contact: Edward J. Branley
elendil@mintir.new-orleans.la.us

Details: Free

User Info: To subscribe to the list, send an e-mail message requesting a subscription to the URL address below.

`mailto:mail-server@mintir.new-orleans.la.us`

News

Agence FrancePresse International French Wire

Agence FrancePresse International French Wire provides full-text articles in French relating to national, international, business, and sports news.

Keywords: News, Europe, Third World, French

Sponsor: Agence FrancePresse, Paris, France

Audience: Market Researchers, Journalists, Francophiles

Profile: Agence FrancePresse distributes its French service worldwide, including Western and Eastern Europe, Canada, northern and western Africa, the Middle East, Vietnam, French Guiana, the West Indies, and the French Pacific islands. Agence FrancePresse International French Wire has extensive coverage of the European countries, including every aspect of economic, political, and general business news. It also provides excellent industrial and market news from both developed countries and from theThird World.

Coverage: September 1991 to the present; updated daily.

Contact: Dialog in the US at (800) 334-2564; Dialog internationally at country-specific locations.

Details: Costs

User Info: To subscribe, contact Dialog directly.

`telnet://dialog.com`

bit.general

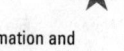

A Usenet newsgroup providing information and discussion about Bitnet or Usenet. Contained in the bit. category are many bit.listserv discussion lists.

Keywords: Internet, News

Audience: General Public, Internet Surfers

User Info: To subscribe to this Usenet newsgroup, you need access to a newsreader.

`news:bit.general`

BUSREF (Business Reference)

The Business Refernce (BUSREF) library contains a variety of reference materials covering business and industry.

Keywords: News, Reference, Business, Government

Audience: Businessmen

Profile: The BUSREF library contains company directories, reference publications, information on business opportunities, and biographical information on political candidates, Congressional members, celebrities, and international decision makers.

Contact: Mead New Sales Group at (800) 227-4908 or (513) 859-5398 inside the US, or (513) 865-7981 for all inquiries outside the US.

User Info: To subscribe, contact Mead directly.

To examine the Nexis user guide, you can access it at the ftp site of the University of Texas at Austin at the URL address: ftp://ftp.cc.utexas.edu

The files are in: /pub/ref-services/LEXIS

`telnet://nex.meaddata.com`

`http://www.meaddata.com`

CANADA (Canadian News and Information Library)

The Canadian News and Information library (CANADA) contains Canadian legal news, business and company information.

Keywords: News, Analysis, Companies, Canada

Audience: Canadians

Profile: The CANADA library contains respected Canadian news publications such as The Toronto Star, The Vancouver Sun, Ottawa Business News and the Montreal Gazette. The CANADA library also offers Canadian company profiles, country reports, and Canada's financial database, CANCORP Plus.

Contact: Mead New Sales Group at (800) 227-4908 or (513) 859-5398 inside the US, or (513) 865-7981 for all inquiries outside the US.

User Info: To subscribe, contact Mead directly.

To examine the Nexis user guide, you can access it at the ftp site of the University of Texas at Austin at the URL address: ftp://ftp.cc.utexas.edu

The files are in: /pub/ref-services/LEXIS

`telnet://nex.meaddata.com`

`http://www.meaddata.com`

CERRO (Central European Regional Research Organization)

CERRO provides access to information about the economic restructuring of Central Europe, including a discussion list, papers, news summaries, and pointers to other gophers in Central Europe.

Keywords: Central Europe, Economics, News

Audience: Economists, Researchers, Journalists

Contact: gunther.maier@wu-wien.ac.at

Details: Free

`gopher://osiris.wu.wein.ac.at`

Cro-Views

Cro-Views is an opinion service that consists of discussions relating to Croatia and other former Yugoslav republics. The main objective is to give people who cannot access the news network (e.g. via <rn>command in UNIX) a chance to read and voice their own opinions about these issues.

Keywords: Croatia, News

Audience: Croats, Journalists, General Public

Contact: Joe Stojsic
Joe@Mullara.Met.UniMelb.Edu.AU

Details: Free

User Info: To subscribe to the list, send an e-mail message requesting a subscription to the URL address below.

Notes: Cro-Views is an unmoderated service, but abusive language and name-calling is not tolerated.

`mailto:Joe@Mullara.Met.UniMelb.Edu.AU`

Croatian-News/Hrvatski-Vjesnik

News from and related to Croatia, run by volunteers. These are actually two news distributions: one in Croatian (occasionally an article might be in some other South Slavic language) and one in English.

Keywords: Croatia, News

Audience: Croats, Journalists, General Public

Contact: Croatian-News-Request@Andrew.CMU.Edu, Hrvatski-Vjesnik-Zamolbe@Andrew.CMU.Edu

Details: Free

User Info: To subscribe to the list, send an e-mail message to the URL address below with the following information: your name, your e-mail address, and state/country where your account is. Please put the state/country information in the Subject line of your letter. If you would like to receive the news in Croatian as well, please indicate that in your message. If you would prefer to receive the news in Croatian only, please send a message to the following address: Hrvatski-Vjesnik-Zamolbe@Andrew.CMU.Edu

To send a message to the entire list, address it to:Croatian-News@Andrew.CMU.Edu

`mailto:Croatian-News-Request@Andrew.CMU.Edu`

Electronic Newsstand Gopher

This gopher contains tables of contents, selected full-text articles, and assorted other information from many mainstream print journals.

Keywords: Journals, Electronic Publishing, Publishing, News

Audience: News Enthusiasts, Publishers, Publishing Professionals, Journalists

Profile: This gopher was compiled with the collaboration of the American Journal of International Law, Policy Review, Technology Review, Business Week, Current History, The Economist, Foreign Affairs, National Review, The New Yorker, The New Republic, Mother Jones, among other distinguished publications.

Contact: William Love
love@enews.com

`gopher://gopher.enews.com`

ENERGY

The Energy News and Information (ENERGY) library consists of news, legal, and regulatory information.

Keywords: Energy, News, Law, Regulations

Audience: Energy Researchers

Profile: The ENERGY library contains more than 50 full-text sources concentrating on energy-related news and issues. Also available are decisions and orders of the United States Federal Power Commission, Federal Energy Regulatory Commission, and Nuclear Regulatory Commission. At the state level, it covers administrative decisions and orders for 17 states. Energy industry research reports from InvestextR are also available.

Contact: Mead New Sales Group at (800) 227-4908 or (513) 859-5398 inside the US, or (513) 865-7981 for all inquiries outside the US.

User Info: To subscribe, contact Mead directly.

To examine the Nexis user guide, you can access it at the ftp site of the University of Texas at Austin at the URL address: ftp://ftp.cc.utexas.edu

The files are in: /pub/ref-services/LEXIS

`telnet://nex.meaddata.com`

`http://www.meaddata.com`

ENTERT (Entertainment News Library)

The Entertainment News library contains sources of information about the entertainment industry, including broadcasting, cable TV, theater, television, books, movies, ballet and dance, video, radio, music, and the record industry.

Keywords: Entertainment, News

Audience: Business Researchers, Analysts, Entrepreneurs

Profile: ENTERT includes the full text of publications such as Variety, Daily Variety, Communications Daily and People, as well as documents about entertainment-related topics from premier NEXIS sources such as the Los Angeles Times and USA Today. Additionally, ENTERT has the premier source database covering the entertainment industry, BASELINE, which provides daily updates of the financial status of movies, background on actors and details on works in production.

Contact: Mead New Sales Group at (800) 227-4908 or (513) 859-5398 inside the US, or (513) 865-7981 for all inquiries outside the US.

User Info: To subscribe, contact Mead directly.

To examine the Nexis user guide, you can access it at the ftp site of the University of Texas at Austin at the URL address: ftp://ftp.cc.utexas.edu

The files are in: /pub/ref-services/LEXIS

`telnet://nex.meaddata.com`

`http://www.meaddata.com`

ENVIRN (Environment Library)

The Environment (ENVIRN) Library contains a variety of environment-related news and legal information.

Keywords: News, Analysis, Law, Environment

A
B
C
D
E
F
G
H
I
J
K
L
M
N
O
P
Q
R
S
T
U
V
W
X
Y
Z

Audience: Environmental Researchers, Business Professionals

Profile: The ENVIRN library contains a combination of environmental information that can provide critical insight into environmental hazards, EPA ratings, specific company investigations, evaluations on potentially hazardous chemicals, and parties responsible for cleanup of specific hazardous sites. Additionally, ENVIRN provides a wealth of environment-related information— legislation, regulations, and court and agency decisions at both the federal and state levels; news; the Environmental Law Reporter, and American Law Reports.

Contact: Mead New Sales Group at (800) 227-4908 or (513) 859-5398 inside the US, or (513) 865-7981 for all inquiries outside the US.

User Info: To subscribe, contact Mead directly.

To examine the Nexis user guide, you can access it at the ftp site of the University of Texas at Austin at the URL address: ftp://ftp.cc.utexas.edu

The files are in: /pub/ref-services/LEXIS

`telnet://nex.meaddata.com`

`http://www.meaddata.com`

EXEC (Executive Branch News US)

★

The EXEC library contains information and news about the Executive Branch of the Federal Government. From the Department of Agriculture to the White House, this file is a comprehensive source of information that will be especially useful to those whose responsibilities include monitoring federal regulations, Agency and Department activity, and the people and issues involved.

Keywords: News, Legislation, Regulation, Politics, Executive Branch

Audience: Journalists, Lobbyists, Business Executives, Analysts, Entrepreneurs

Profile: The EXEC library allows the searching of individual files or group files that cover topics such as the Federal Register and Code of Federal Regulations; public laws; proposed treasury regulation; and over 50 news sources, including BNA's Daily Report for Executives, the Dept. of State Dispatch, ABC News transcripts, Federal News Service Daybook, Government Executive, MacNeil/Lehrer Newshour, New Leader, National Review, the Washington Post, the Washington Times, Presidential Documents, and many others.

Contact: Mead New Sales Group at (800) 227-4908 or (513) 859-5398 inside the US, or (513) 865-7981 for all inquiries outside the US.

User Info: To subscribe, contact Mead directly.

To examine the Nexis user guide, you can access it at the ftp site of the University of Texas at Austin at the URL address: ftp://ftp.cc.utexas.edu

The files are in: /pub/ref-services/LEXIS

`telnet://nex.meaddata.com`

`http://www.meaddata.com`

Health News Daily

★ ★ ★

The database contains all the daily news and full-text articles from Health News Daily, a publication from F-D-C Reports, Inc.

Keywords: Health, Pharmacology, Medical Research, News

Sponsor: F-D-C Reports, Inc., Chevy Chase, MD, US

Audience: Health Professionals, Pharmaceutical Industry, Market Researchers

Profile: The database provides specialized, in-depth business, scientific, regulatory, and legal news. Timely coverage of pharmacy and pharmaceuticals is given, as well as coverage of medical devices and diagnostics, medical research, cosmetics, health policy, provider payment policies, and cost containment in national health care.

Coverage: 1990 to the present; updated daily.

Contact: Dialog in the US at (800) 334-2564, Dialog internationally at country-specific locations.

Details: Costs

User Info: To subscribe, contact Dialog directly.

`telnet://dialog.com`

Hungary

★

This discussion list circulates timely information about Hungary.

Keywords: Hungary, Eastern Europe, News

Audience: Researchers, Observers, Political Scientists

Contact: Eric Dahlin
hcf2hung@iucsbuxa

Details: Free

User Info: To subscribe to the list, send an e-mail message to the URL address shown below consisting of a single line reading:

SUB hungary YourFirstName YourLastName

`mailto:listserv@gwuvm.gwu.edu`

INSURE (Insurance)

★

The Insurance (INSURE) library contains specific full-text and abstract news and legal information sources focusing on the insurance industry.

Keywords: News, Analysis, Law, Insurance

Audience: Insurance Professionals, Lawyers

Profile: The INSURE library contains leading insurance industry news sources, legal and regulatory materials from NILS Publishing Company's INSURLAW, analyst reports on the insurance industry from InvestextR, and insurance company financial reports. Federal and state case law and federal regulations are also available.

Contact: Mead New Sales Group @ (800) 227-4908 or (513) 859-5398 inside the US, or (513) 865-7981 for all inquiries outside the US.

User Info: To subscribe, contact Mead directly.

To examine the Nexis user guide, you can access it at the ftp site of the University of Texas at Austin at the URL address: ftp://ftp.cc.utexas.edu The files are in: /pub/res-services/LEXIS

`telnet://nex.meaddata.com`

MARKET (Markets and Industries News and Information)

★

The Markets and Industries News and Information (MARKET) library contains sources covering developments in a wide variety of markets and industries.

Keywords: News, Analysis, Industry, Marketing

Audience: Business Professionals, Researchers

Profile: The MARKET library contains a wide selection of sources ranging from trade and industry sources to InvestextR industry reports to company profiles. To round out the offering, MARKET also covers advertising, marketing, public opinion polls, market research, public relations, sales and selling, promotions, consumer attitudes, trends and behaviors, demographics, product announcements and product reviews. In addition, Predicasts Overview of Markets and Technology (PROMT), Marketing and Advertising Reference Service (MARS), US and International Forecast Databases (UFRCST and IFRCST) and the US Time Series (USTIME), all from Information Access Company, are available.

Contact: Mead New Sales Group at (800) 227-4908 or (513) 859-5398 inside the US, or (513) 865-7981 for all inquiries outside the US.

User Info: To subscribe, contact Mead directly.

To examine the Nexis user guide, you can access it at the ftp site of the University of Texas at Austin at the URL address: ftp://ftp.cc.utexas.edu

The files are in: /pub/ref-services/LEXIS

`telnet://nex.meaddata.com`

`http://www.meaddata.com`

User Info: To subscribe, contact Mead directly.

To examine the Nexis user guide, you can access it at the ftp site of the University of Texas at Austin at the URL address: ftp://ftp.cc.utexas.edu

The files are in: /pub/ref-services/LEXIS

`telnet://nex.meaddata.com`

`http://www.meaddata.com`

MDEAFR

The Middle East and Africa (MDEAFR) library contains detailed information about every country in the Mideast and Africa. Structured for those who want to follow the unfolding events in the Gulf states, as well as in North and South Africa, this library contains a broad array of sources, including international research reports from InvestextR.

Keywords: News, Analysis, Companies, Middle East, Africa

Audience: Journalists, Business Professionals

Profile: The MDEAFR library contains a wide array of pertinent sources. Among the information sources are newspapers and wire services, trade and business journals, company reports, country and region background, industry and product analysis, business opportunities, and selected legal texts. News sources range from the world-renowned Associated Press and Christian Science Monitor to the regionally important Jerusalem Post and Africa News. Company information is contained in the EXTEL cards as well as ICC. Providers of country background and industry analysis include Associated Banks of Europe, Bank of America, Business International, IBC USA, and the US Department of Commerce. Customers interested in new business opportunities can check OPIC and Foreign Trade Opportunities (FTO).

Contact: Mead New Sales Group at (800) 227-4908 or (513) 859-5398 inside the US, or (513) 865-7981 for all inquiries outside the US.

User Info: To subscribe, contact Mead directly.

To examine the Nexis user guide, you can access it at the ftp site of the University of Texas at Austin at the URL address: ftp://ftp.cc.utexas.edu

The files are in: /pub/ref-services/LEXIS

`telnet://nex.meaddata.com`

`http://www.meaddata.com`

Mideur-l

A list containing the history, culture, politics, and current affairs of those countries lying between the Mediterranean/Adriatic and the Baltic Seas, and between the German/Austrian borders and the former Soviet Union.

Keywords: Soviet Union, Baltic Republics, Eastern Europe, News

Audience: Political Scientists, Researchers, Historians, General Public

Contact: Jan George Frajkor mideur-1@ubvm.cc.buffalo.edu

Details: Free

User Info: To subscribe to the list, send an e-mail message to the URL address below consisting of a single line reading:

SUB mideur-l YourFirstName YourLastName

To send a message to the entire list, address it to: mideur-1@ubvm.cc.buffalo.edu

`mailto:listserv@ubvm.cc.buffalo.edu`

News

This directory is a general compilation of information resources focused on news.

Keywords: News Media, Electronic Media, Journalism

Audience: Newsreaders, Journalists, General Public

Details: Free

`ftp://una.hh.lib.umich.edu/70/ inetdirsstacks/news:robinson`

NEWS (General News)

The General News (NEWS) library includes more than 2,300 sources. Full-text news from national and international newspapers, magazines, newsletters, and wire services and abstract information are both available.

Keywords: News, Analysis, People, Companies

Audience: Journalists, General Public

Profile: The General News (NEWS) library contains a number of publications and wire services of general interest, as well as others that specialize in particular areas of business . The NEWS library is organized into individual files, group files by source or subject, and user-defined combination files for full-text information sources. Abstracts are also available as individual files or can be searched together in one group file. The NEWS library includes such prestigious full-text sources as the New York Times and more than more than 30 major newspapers from around the US and the world.

Contact: Mead New Sales Group at (800) 227-4908 or (513) 859-5398 inside the US, or (513) 865-7981 for all inquiries outside the US.

User Info: To subscribe, contact Mead directly.

To examine the Nexis user guide, you can access it at the ftp site of the University of Texas at Austin at the URL address: ftp://ftp.cc.utexas.edu

The files are in: /pub/ref-services/LEXIS

`telnet://nex.meaddata.com`

`http://www.meaddata.com`

News of Earth

Newsletter covering global news.

Keywords: Global News, News

Audience: General Public

Profile: News of Earth consists of: NewsE-A Analysis, an analysis of global news; NewsE-B Bulletins, late-breaking global news; NewsE-C Commentary, a commentary on global news; NewsE-D Distribution, global news monitored from shortwave radio broadcasts; and, the continuation of JBH Online (Online-L), published from 1987 through 1990 (Issues 1-213); NewsE-I Interviews, interviews on global issues; NewsE-L Letters, news and reaction from readers; NewsE-S Supplements, containing additional news and information from electronic and print sources. News of Earth supplements continues JBH News (JBHNewsL), published in 1990 (issues 1-4). NewsE is a "superlist" that includes all components listed above.

Contact: John B. Harlan jbharlan@indyvax.iupui.edu

Details: Free

User Info: To subscribe, send an e-mail message to the URL address below consisting of a single line reading:

SUB NEWSE-x (where x is A, B, C, D, I, L or S) YourFirstName YourLastName

To send a message to the entire list, address it to: newse@indyvax.iupui.edu

`mailto:listserv@Indyvax.iupui.edu`

NewsCommando

This makes available synergies discerned in, and created from, print news media (up to a 12-year time span). The depth of insight possible using the information-mosaic method can be staggering. A form of an electronic magazine, NewsCommando serves as a reference tool, allows access to Medline, PaperChase, or other searches, and, in many ways, is the poor man's IdeaFisher/IdeaBank.

Keywords: NewsCommando, News

Audience: NewsCommando Users

Contact: Lance Sanders starkid@ddsw1.mcs.com

Details: Free

Articles will be deposited in your mailbox with a "NewsCom/Vol.#" Subject header. Most will be in excess of 20K. Please group-save them to a file for later reading.

`mailto:starkid@ddsw1.mcs.com`

Novice MZT

Novize MZT (News of Ministry for Science and Technology of the Republic of Slovenia) provides easy, accessible news about science, development, universities, and innovative activities to individuals and institutions in research and development areas. Published at least once monthly.

Keywords: Slovenia, Science, Technology, News

Audience: Slovenians, Scientists, Technocrats

Contact: Novice-mzt@krpan.arnes.si or Novice.mzt@uni-lj.si

A B C D E F G H I J K L M **N** O P Q R S T U V W X Y Z

User Info: To subscribe to the list, send an e-mail message requesting a subscription to the URL address below.

To send a message to the entire list, address it to: Novice-mzt@krpan.arnes.si

```
mailto:Novice-MZT@krpan.arnes.si
```

NSAMER (North and South America Library)

The North and South America library contains detailed information about every country in North and South America (except the United States). The US-Canada Free Trade Agreement, the North American Free Trade Agreement, relations with Mexico and events in such countries as Brazil, Peru, and Nicaragua are among the topics covered by a variety of business, news and legal sources. International research reports from InvestextR are also included. The United States is not covered in this library.

Keywords: News, Analysis, Companies, North America, South America

Audience: Journalists, Business Professionals

Profile: The North and South America library contains a broad array of sources. Among the information sources are newspapers and wire services, trade and business journals, company reports, country and region backgrounds, industry and product analyses, business opportunities, and selected legal texts. News sources range from the world-renowned Washington Post and Christian Science Monitor to the regionally important Toronto Star and Latin American Newsletters. Canadian Business and Maclean's represent a portion of the array of business and trade journals. Company information is contained in the EXTEL cards as well as ICC. Providers of country background and industry analyses include Associated Banks of Europe, Bank of America, Business International, IBC USA and the US Department of Commerce. Among the specialized resources are IBC's Mexico and Brazil Services as well as BI's Business Latin America. Researchers interested in new business opportunities can check OPIC and Foreign Trade Opportunities (FTO).And selected legal texts covering the US-Canada Free Trade Agreement and other international agreements planners and advisors to better assess the business climate in North and South America.

Contact: Mead New Sales Group at (800) 227-4908 or (513) 859-5398 inside the US, or (513) 865-7981 for all inquiries outside the US.

User Info: To subscribe, contact Mead directly.

To examine the Nexis user guide, you can access it at the ftp site of the University of Texas at Austin at the URL address: ftp://ftp.cc.utexas.edu

The files are in: /pub/ref-services/LEXIS

```
telnet://nex.meaddata.com
```

```
http://www.meaddata.com
```

SPORTS (Sports News)

The Sports News (SPORTS) library contains a variety of sports-related news and information.

Keywords: News, Analysis, Sports, Biographies

Audience: Sports Enthusiasts, Journalists

Profile: The SPORTS library is a specialized news library that contains the full text of Sports Illustrated and The Sporting News and selected sports-related stories from many major US newspapers and wire services. Biographical information and 1992 Olympic facts are also part of this library.

Contact: Mead New Sales Group at (800) 227-4908 or (513) 859-5398 inside the US, or (513) 865-7981 for all inquiries outside the US.

User Info: To subscribe, contact Mead directly.

To examine the Nexis user guide, you can access it at the ftp site of the University of Texas at Austin at the URL address: ftp://ftp.cc.utexas.edu

The files are in: /pub/ref-services/LEXIS

```
telnet://nex.meaddata.com
```

```
http://www.meaddata.com
```

TOPNWS (Top News)

The Top News (TOPNWS) library contains today's news today for selected key sources from around the world.

Keywords: News, Analysis

Audience: Journalists, General Public

Profile: In the Top News (TOPNWS) library newswires are collected and updated every 60 minutes. Newspapers and other daily publications are updated throughout the day on the day of publication. Transcripts are updated within three hours of broadcast. Two weeks worth of data from more than 40 major publications may be searched as individual files or in specialized group files. The TODAY group file contains today's published information from all sources. the 2WEEK group file expands the window of current information from all sources to two weeks. Specialized section files, designed to be like sections of a newspaper, contain stories from each publication that pertain to the section or topic selected.

Contact: Mead New Sales Group at (800) 227-4908 or (513) 859-5398 inside the US, or (513) 865-7981 for all inquiries outside the US.

User Info: To subscribe, contact Mead directly.

To examine the Nexis user guide, you can access it at the ftp site of the University of Texas at Austin at the URL address: ftp://ftp.cc.utexas.edu

The files are in: /pub/ref-services/LEXIS

```
telnet://nex.meaddata.com
```

```
http://www.meaddata.com
```

United Press International News—Sports

Full text of UPI stories and articles.

Keywords: Sports, News

Sponsor: United Press International (UPI)

Audience: Sports Enthusiasts

Profile: This gopher allows access to daily UPI news feeds, including sports news. The most current articles available tend to run three to five days behind. This delay is compensated for by UPIs far-ranging coverage of national and international sporting news. Indexed, with back articles from 1992 onwards available.

Contact: UPI clarinews@clarinet.com

Details: Free

```
gopher://mrfrosty.micro.umn.edu./UPI-
data/Today/sports
```

WORLD (World News and Information)

This library contains detailed information about every country in Europe, Asia, the Pacific Rim, Africa, the Middle East, and North and South America. Designed for those who need to monitor world events, organizations, and leaders, this library provides a global view of any subject or topic.

Keywords: Business, News

Audience: Business Researchers, Analysts, Entrepreneurs

Profile: WORLD includes information from newspapers and wire services, trade and business journals, company reports, country and region background, industry and product analysis, business opportunities, and selected legal texts. News sources range from the world-renowned Christian Science Monitor, Financial Times, Reuters and Associated Press to the regionally important eastern European CTK, MTI and PAP newswires, The Toronto Star, Jerusalem Post, and Xinhua News Agency. Business and trade information include a wide variety of sources, such as EIS's European newsletters and Euroscope from Coopers and Lybrand, Canada's Maclean's, Japan's Comline Daily News Service, BNA's international dailies and the Soviet Union's SovData DiaLine services—all help analyze the political and economic climate around the globe. Company information is contained in the EXTEL cards as well as ICC. Providers of country background and industry analysis include Associated Banks of Europe, Bank of America, Business International, IBC USA and the US Department of Commerce. Economic risk can be assessed with the Economist's Economic Risk Services, IBC's International Reports and International Country Risk Guide and many of

Business International's Country Reports. Political risk is forecast in IBC's Political Risk Services as well as BOA's World Information Services' Country RiskOutlooks, Monitors and Forecasts.

Contact: Mead New Sales Group at (800) 227-4908 or (513) 859-5398 inside the US, or (513) 865-7981 for all inquiries outside the US.

User Info: To subscribe, contact Mead directly.

To examine the Nexis user guide, you can access it at the ftp site of the University of Texas at Austin at the URL address: ftp://ftp.cc.utexas.edu

The files are in: /pub/ref-services/LEXIS

`telnet://nex.meaddata.com`

`http://www.meaddata.com`

News (International)

Spojrzenia

A weekly E-journal devoted to Polish culture, history and politics.

Keywords: Poland, News (International), Culture

Audience: Poles, Students

Contact: Jerzy Krzystek
krzystek@u.washington.edu

Details: Free

User Info: To subscribe to the list, send an e-mail message requesting a subscription to the URL address below. To send a message to the entire list, address it to:

spojrzenia@u.washington.edu

`mailto:krzystek@u.washington.edu`

Sri Lanka Net (SLNet)

A moderated mailing list that carries news and other articles about Sri Lanka.

Keywords: Sri Lanka, News (International)

Audience: Sri Lankans, Students

Contact: pkd@fed.frb.gov
slnetad@ganu.colorado.edu

Details: Free, Moderated

User Info: To subscribe to the list, send an e-mail message requesting a subscription to the URL address below.

To send a message to the entire list, address it to:
slnetad@ganu.colorado.edu

`mailto:pkd@fed.frb.gov`

`mailto:slnetad@ganu.colorado.edu`

News Media

Africa-n

A moderated mailing list dedicated to the exchange of news and information on Africa, including correspondence from many sources worldwide.

Keywords: News Media, Africa

Audience: Africans, Students

Contact: Faraz Rabbani
frabbani@epas.utoronto.ca

User Info: To subscribe to the list, send an e-mail message to the URL address below consisting of a single line reading:

SUB africa-n YourFirstName YourLastName

To send a message to the entire list, address it to: africa-n@utoronto.bitnet

`mailto:listserv@utoronto.bitnet`

C-SPAN (Cable-Satellite Public Affairs Network) Gopher

Online information from C-SPAN, the public affairs television network.

Keywords: News Media, Government, Congress (US), Television

Sponsor: C-SPAN

Audience: Journalists, Government Officials, Educators (K-12), General Public

Profile: Comprehensive listings of C-SPAN's programming and coverage of events in Washington D.C. and beyond. In addition to the programming notes and schedules, this site also features online educational resources sponsored by C-SPAN, text of historic documents and speeches, and background political information on the House of Representatives and the Supreme Court.

Contact: cspanviewr@aol.com

Details: Free

`gopher://c-span.org`

CNN Headline News Gopher

Latest news as read by the CNN anchorpersons. Searchable index of subject matter.

Keywords: News Media, Politics (International), Journalism

Sponsor: CNN Newsource Service

Audience: General Public, Students, Journalists

Contact: Chet Rhodes
cr9@umail.umd.edu

Details: Free

`gopher://info.umd.edu:925/`

Cro-News/SCYU-Digest

This unmoderated list is the distribution point for the news coming from Croatia. The list carries articles from Novi Vjesnik, Vecernji List, Croatia Monitor, Slobodna Dalmacija, Novi Danas, Radio Free Europe/Radio Luxemburg bulletins, and UPI reports.

Keywords: Croatia, News Media

Audience: Croats, Journalists, General Public

Contact: Nino Margetic
cro-news-request@medphys.ucl.ac.uk

Details: Free

User Info: To subscribe to the list, send an e-mail message requesting a subscription to the URL address below.

To send a message to the entire list, address it to: cro-news@medphys.ucl.ac.uk

`mailto:cro-news-request@medphys.ucl.ac.uk`

Jane's Defense & Aerospace News/Analysis

This file provides articles that summarize, highlight, and interpret worldwide events in the defense and aerospace industry.

Keywords: Defense, Aerospace, News Media

Sponsor: Jane's Information Group, Alexandria, VA US

Audience: Aerospace Industry Professionals

Profile: The database contains the complete text of the following publications: Jane's Defense Weekly, International Defense Review, Jane's Intelligence Review (formerly Jane's Soviet Intelligence Review), Interavia Aerospace Review, and Jane's Airport Review. File 587 also contains the complete text of DMS newsletters, which ceased publication in 1989.

Contact: Dialog in the US at (800) 334-2564, Dialog internationally at country-specific locations.

User Info: To subscribe, contact Dialog directly.

Notes: Coverage: 1982 to the present; updated weekly.

`telnet://dialog.com`

Navnews

Contains official news and information about fleet operations and exercises, personnel policies, budget actions, and more. This is the same news service that is distributed through Navy circuits to ships at sea and to shore commands around the world. Subscriptions to NAVNEWS by e-mail are available at no charge to anyone with a mailbox on any network reachable through the Internet.

Keywords: Navy, News

Sponsor: The Navy Internal Relations Activity, Washington, DC

A
B
C
D
E
F
G
H
I
J
K
L
M
N
O
P
Q
R
S
T
U
V
W
X
Y
Z

Audience: Navy Personnel, Sailors, General Public

Contact: navnews@nctamslant.navy.mil

Details: Free

User Info: To subscribe to the list, send an e-mail message requesting a subscription to the URL address below.

`mailto:navnews@nctamslant.navy.mil`

News

This directory is a general compilation of information resources focused on news.

Keywords: News, Electronic Media, Journalism

Audience: Newsreaders, Journalists, General Public

Details: Free

`ftp://una.hh.lib.umich.edu/70/`
`inetdirsstacks/news:robinson`

Voice of America and Worldnet

A gopher server for the Voice of America and Worldnet. Includes full-text transcripts of VOA news reports, press releases, and announcements.

Keywords: US Government Publications, News Media, Radio, International Communication

Sponsor: United States Information Agency

Audience: Journalists, Government Officials, General Public

Contact: info@voa.gov, letters-usa@VOA.GOV (for correspondence from inside the U.S.)

`gopher://gopher.voa.gov`

Hot Wired

This is WIRED Magazine's online service.

Keywords: Postmodern Culture, News Media

Sponsor: WIRED Magazine

Audience: Internet Surfers, Internet Users, General Public

Profile: Features interactive forums on a variety of issues. Also includes archives and reprints of WIRED articles, as well as articles produced specifically for the online environment.

Contact: Hot Wired
info@wired.com

`http://www:hotwired.com`

News, Weather, and Travel Advisories

News, Weather, and Travel Advisories

A major directory of news, weather, and travel advisories, providing access to a broad range of related resources (library catalogues, databases, and servers) via the Internet.

Keywords: Travel, Weather, Aviation

Sponsor: Kennesaw State College, Georgia, USA

Audience: General Public, Travelers/Tourists

Profile: This collection includes CNN news sources, the National Weather Service Forecast, and the US State Department Travel Advisory, among other sources.

Details: Free

`gopher://kscsuna1.kennesaw.edu`

news.announce.conferences

news.announce.conferences

A Usenet newsgroup providing information and discussion about conferences, as well as calls for papers.

Keywords: Conferences, Paper, Writing

Audience: Writers, General Public

Details: Free

User Info: To subscribe to this Usenet newsgroup, you need access to a newsreader.

`news:news.announce.conferences`

news.announce.newgroups

news.announce.newgroups

A Usenet newsgroup providing information and discussion about creating a new newsgroup, changing active newsgroups, and how to access new Usenet groups.

Keywords: Usenet, Internet Resources

Audience: Usenet Users

Details: Free

User Info: To subscribe to this Usenet newsgroup, you need access to a newsreader.

`news:news.announce.newgroups`

news.answers

news.answers

A Usenet newsgroup providing information and discussion about periodic Usenet articles.

Keywords: Usenet, Internet Resources

Audience: Usenet Users

Details: Free

User Info: To subscribe to this Usenet newsgroup, you need access to a newsreader.

`news:news.answers`

news.groups

news.groups

A Usenet newsgroup providing information and discussion about lists of existing newsgroups.

Keywords: Usenet, Internet Resources

Audience: Usenet Users

Details: Free

User Info: To subscribe to this Usenet newsgroup, you need access to a newsreader.

`news:news.groups`

news.lists

news.lists

A Usenet newsgroup providing information and discussion about news-related statistics and lists.

Keywords: Usenet, Internet Resources

Audience: Usenet Users

Details: Free

User Info: To subscribe to this Usenet newsgroup, you need access to a newsreader.

`news:news.lists`

news.newusers.questions

news.newusers.questions

A Usenet newsgroup providing information and discussion about Usenet news groups.

Keywords: Usenet, E-mail, Internet Resources

Audience: Usenet Users, E-mail Users

Details: Free

User Info: To subscribe to this Usenet newsgroup, you need access to a newsreader.

`news:news.newusers.questions`

news.aus.films

news.aus.films

Discussion of films and the film industry from an Australian perspective.

Keywords: Film, Australia

Audience: Australia Enthusiasts, Film Enthusiasts

Details: Free

User Info: To subscribe to a Usenet newsgroup, you need access to a "newsreader."

`news:aus.films`

Newsbrief

Newsbrief

Provides a variety of information and feature articles, primarily for campus users.

Keywords: Information Technology

Sponsor: Office of Information Technology at the University of North Carolina, Chapel Hill (UNC Chapel Hill)

Audience: Students, Educators

Contact: Karen C. Blansfield, Judy Hallman karen@rhumba.acs.unc.edu

Details: Free

User Info: To subscribe, send an e-mail message to the URL address below consisting of a single line reading:

SUB newsbrief YourFirstName YourLastName

To send a message to the entire list, address it to: newsbrief@uncvm1.bitnet

`mailto:listserv@uncvm1.bitnet`

NewsCommando

NewsCommando

This makes available synergies discerned in, and created from, print news media (up to a 12-year time span). The depth of insight possible using the information-mosaic method can be staggering. A form of an electronic magazine, NewsCommando serves as a reference tool, allows access to Medline, PaperChase, or other searches, and, in many ways, is the poor man's IdeaFisher/IdeaBank.

Keywords: NewsCommando, News

Audience: NewsCommando Users

Contact: Lance Sanders starkid@ddsw1.mcs.com

Details: Free

User Info: Articles will be deposited in your mailbox with a "NewsCom/Vol.#" Subject header. Most will be in excess of 20K. Please group-save them to a file for later reading.

`mailto:starkid@ddsw1.mcs.com`

Newsletter on Serials Pricing Issues

Newsletter on Serials Pricing Issues

The focus of this newsletter is the pricing of library serials.

Keywords: Serials Pricing, Librarianship

Audience: Librarians, Publishing Professionals

Profile: Contributions include examples of titles considered to be overpriced, as well as of publishers' actions to keep prices down, strategies for coping with serials price increases, information about libraries' evaluation and cancellation policies and procedures, announcements of and reports from relevant meetings, and other news of serials prices.

Contact: Marcia Tuttle tuttle@unc.bitnet

Details: Free

User Info: To subscribe, send an e-mail message to the URL address shown below consisting of a single line reading:

SUB serials_pricing YourFirstName YourLastName

`mailto:listserv@uncvx1.bitnet`

Newsletters

CCNEWS

An electronic forum for campus-computing newsletter editors and other publications specialists.

Keywords: Computers, Editors, Students, Newsletters

Audience: Students (college), Editors

Profile: CCNEWS consists of a biweekly newsletter that focuses on the writing, editing, designing, and producing of campus-computing publications, and an articles abstracts published on alternating weeks that describes new contributions to the articles archive.

Contact: Wendy Rickard Bollentin ccnews@educom.bitnet

Details: Free

User Info: To subscribe to the list, send an e-mail message to the URL address below consisting of a single line reading:

SUB ccnews YourFirstName YourLastName

To send a message to the entire list, address it to: ccnews@educom.bitnet

Inquire about needing a password.

`mailto:listserv@bitnic.cren.net`

Newsline

Newsline

An electronic newsletter describing additions to or changes in Comserve, the electronic information and discussion service for communications faculty and students.

Keywords: Communications, Comserve

Audience: Communications Students, Communications Specialists

Profile: The information includes announcements of additions to Comserve's database, new services offered through Comserve's electronic conferences, or fundamental changes in the services offered by Comserve.

Contact: Timothy Stephen, Teresa Harrison Support@Rpiecs Support@Vm.Ecs.Rpi.Edu

User Info: To subscribe, send an e-mail message to the URL address below consisting of a single line reading:

SUB newsline YourFirstName YourLastName

`mailto:Comserve@Vm.Ecs.Rpi.Edu`

NeXT

comp.sys.next

A Usenet newsgroup providing information and discussion about NeXT computers. There are several categories within this group.

Keywords: Computer Systems, NeXT

Audience: Computer Users, NeXT Users

User Info: To subscribe to this Usenet newsgroup, you need access to a newsreader.

`news:comp.sys.next`

next-gis

Discussion of Geographical Information Systems (GIS) and cartography-related topics on the NeXT and other workstation computers. Some moderated reposting of comp.infosys.gis occurs as well.

Keywords: Geography, Cartography, GIS, NeXT

Audience: GIS Users, NeXT Users

A B C D E F G H I J K L M N O P Q R S T U V W X Y Z

Contact: Steven R. Staton
sstaton@deltos.com

Details: Free

User Info: To subscribe to the list, send an e-mail message to the URL address shown below consisting of a single line reading:

SUB next-gis YourFirstName YourLastName

To send a message to the entire list, address it to: next-gis@DistributionAddress

`mailto:listserv@deltos.com`

NeXT-icon

Distribute and receive 64 x 64 or 48 x 48 pixel icons, (2-, 12-, 24- and/or 32-bit), compatible with the NeXT Computer's NeXTSTEP software. Nearly all mail is in NeXTmail format.

Keywords: NeXT, NeXT-icon

Audience: NeXT Users

Contact: Timothy Reed
next-icon-request@bmt.gun.com

Details: Free

User Info: To subscribe to the list, send an e-mail message requesting a subscription to the URL address below.

To send a message to the entire list, address it to: next-icon@bmt.gun.com

`mailto:next-icon-request@bmt.gun.com`

NeXT-Med

NeXT-Med is open to end users and developers interested in medical solutions using NeXT computers and/or 486 systems running NeXTSTEP. Discussions on any topic related to NeXT use in the medical industry or related to health care is encouraged.

Keywords: NeXT, NeXT-Med

Audience: NeXT Users, NeXT Developers

Contact: next-med-request@ms.uky.edu

Details: Free

User Info: To subscribe to the list, send an e-mail message requesting a subscription to the URL address below.

To send a message to the entire list, address it to: next-med@ms.uky.edu

`mailto:next-med@ms.uky.edu`

NFL

Funet Sports Information

★★★★

An FTP archive of information on various sports with links to the archive at wuarchive.wustl.edu.

Keywords: Sports, Professional Sports, Ice Hockey, Motor Racing, NFL, NHL, NBA, MLB

Sponsor: Finnish Academic and Research Network (FUNET)

Audience: Sports Enthusiasts

Profile: A fairly extensive archive of information on both American (NBA, MLB, NHL, NFL) and worldwide sports (soccer, ice hockey, motor racing, and so on). Includes FAQs for various sports, statistics, pictures, and some sports games for the PC.

Contact: Jari Pullinen
sports-adm@nic.funet.fi

Details: Free, Images

`gopher://ftp.funet.fi/pub/sports`

NFL Scores, Schedules, and Point Spreads

★

Information on National Football League (NFL) football scores, schedules, and point spreads.

Keywords: Sports, Football, NFL

Audience: Football Enthusiasts

Contact: office@world.std.com

Details: Free

`gopher://world.std.com/News and Weather`

NHL

Dallas Stars

★

Discussion of the Dallas Stars (of the National Hockey League) and their farm clubs.

Keywords: Hockey, NHL

Audience: NHL Enthusiasts

Details: Free

User Info: To subscribe to the list, send an e-mail message requesting a subscription to the URL address below.

To send a message to the entire list, address it to: hamlet@u.washington.edu

Notes: Please include the word "DSTARS" in your subject line and include your name and preferred e-mail address in the body of your message.

`mailto:hamlet@u.washington.edu`

Funet Sports Information

★★★★

An FTP archive of information on various sports with links to the archive at wuarchive.wustl.edu.

Keywords: Sports, Professional Sports, Ice Hockey, Motor Racing, NFL, NHL, NBA, MLB

Sponsor: Finnish Academic and Research Network (FUNET)

Audience: Sports Enthusiasts

Profile: A fairly extensive archive of information on both American (NBA, MLB, NHL, NFL) and worldwide sports (soccer, ice hockey, motor racing, and so on). Includes FAQs for various sports, statistics, pictures, and some sports games for the PC.

Contact: Jari Pullinen
sports-adm@nic.funet.fi

Details: Free, Images

`gopher://ftp.funet.fi/pub/sports`

NHL Goalie Stats

★

A mailing list for the distribution of information regarding goalie stats.

Keywords: Hockey

Audience: Hockey Enthusiasts

Profile: Weekday reports of goalie statistics from the National Hockey League.

Contact: dfa@triple-i.com

Details: Free

User Info: To subscribe to the list, send an e-mail message requesting a subscription to the URL address below. To send a message to the entire list, address it to: dfa@triple-i.com

`mailto:dfa@triple-i.com`

OlymPuck

★

This list is for the discussion of Olympic ice hockey. Discussions concerning players, coaches, teams, and games are welcome and are encouraged. Related topics, such as the interaction between the Olympic competition and college or NHL hockey, are also discussed.

Keywords: Olympics, Ice Hockey, NHL

Audience: Ice Hockey Players, Olympics Enthusiasts, Ice Hockey Fans

Details: Free

User Info: To subscribe to the list, send an e-mail message to the URL address below, consisting of a single line reading:

SUB olympuck YourFirstName YourLastName

To send a message to the entire list, address it to: olympuck@maine.maine.edu

`mailto:listserv@maine.maine.edu`

NIBNews - A Monthly Electronic Bulletin About Medical Informatics

NIBNews - A Monthly Electronic Bulletin About Medical Informatics

Disseminates information about Brazilian and Latin American activities, people, information, events, publications, software, and so on, involving computer applications in health care, medicine, and biology.

Keywords: Health Care, Biology, Brazil, Latin America, South America, Medicine

Audience: Health Care Professionals, Biologists

Contact: Renato M. E. Sabbatini
sabbatini@bruc.bitnet

Details: Free

`mailto:sabbatini@ccvax.unicamp.br`

NIC (Nucleus for Interactive Computing)

NIC (Nucleus for Interactive Computing)

★★★★

WWW-based system for interactive computing.

Keywords: Multimedia, Interactive Computing, Interface Design, Scripting Languages, Programming

Sponsor: BYU Interactive Software Systems Lab

Audience: Software Developers, Educators

Profile: NIC is a system for interactive computing that combines a data model, a user interface model, and a scripting language to create flexible and powerful user interfaces. Documentation still under construction is located here.

Contact: Dan Olsen
olsen@cs.byu.edu

Details: Free, Moderated; Sound, Image and Multimedia files available.

Use a World Wide Web (Mosaic) client and open a connection to the resource.

`ftp://issl.cs.byu.edu/docs/NIC/home.html`

Nickelodeon

Clarissa

This list discusses the Nickelodeon TV show "Clarissa Explains It All."

Keywords: Television Shows, Nickelodeon

Audience: Nickelodeon Viewers, TV Viewers

Contact: Jim Lick
clarissa-request@tcp.com

Details: Free

User Info: To subscribe to the list, send an e-mail message requesting a subscription to the URL address below.

To send a message to the entire list, address it to: clarissa@tcp.com

`mailto:clarissa-request@tcp.com`

NIH (National Institute of Health)

National Institute of Health Library Online Catalog

This entry point provides access to the books and journal holdings in the NIH Library. Journal articles are not included.

Keywords: NIH, Medicine, Science, Libraries

Sponsor: National Institute of Health (NIH)

Audience: Scientists, Researchers, Educators, Health Care Professionals

Details: Free

`telnet://nih-library.ncrr.nih.gov`

NIH (National Institute of Health)

This server is a network-based computer service operated by the Division of Computer Research and Technology (DCRT) to distribute information for and about the NIH (National Institutes of Health).

Keywords: NIH, Health Sciences, Biomedical Research, Medicine

Sponsor: Division of Computer Research and Technology (DCRT), National Institute of Health

Audience: Scientists, Biomedical Researchers, Health CareProfessionals, General Public

Profile: This server provides Internet access to information about NIH health and clinical issues (including CancerNet and a variety of AIDS information), NIH-funded grants and research projects, and a variety of research resources in support of NIH and worldwide biomedical researchers. For example, the major molecular biology databases (GenBank, SWISSPROT, PIR, PDB, TFD, Prosite, LiMB) can be accessed through keyword searches from this gopher.

Details: Free

`gopher://gopher.nih.gov`

NIH EDNET

EdNet is set up as a free electronic bulletin board at the Bethesda, Maryland campus of the National Institute of Health (NIH). Its purpose is to allow high school students to ask questions of NIH scientists about current research.

Keywords: NIH, Education (Post Secondary), Education (K-12), Science

Sponsor: National Institute of Health (NIH)

Audience: Students, Educators

Details: Free

User Info: To receive an EDNET User's Guide and account, send an e-mail message with your name and mailing address to the URL address below.

`mailto:vt5@cu.nih.gov`

NIH Grant Line (Drgline Bulletin Board)

The purpose of the NIH Grant Line is to make program and policy information from the Public Health Service (PHS) agencies rapidly available to the biomedical research community.

Keywords: Biomedical Research, NIH, Grants

Sponsor: The National Institute of Health

Audience: Scientists, Researchers, Students

Profile: Most of the research opportunity information available on this bulletin board is derived from the weekly publication "NIH Guide for Grants and Contracts,", and consists of notices, RFAs, RFPs (announcements of availability), numbered program announcements, and statements of PHS policy. The information found on the NIH Grant Line is grouped into three main sections: (1) short news flashes that appear without any prompting shortly after you have logged on, (2) bulletins that are for reading, and (3) files that are intended mainly for downloading. The E-Guide is available for electronic transmission each week. The material consists predominantly of statements about the research interests of the PHS agencies, institutes, and national centers that have funds to support research in the extramural community. Currently under development are two new files: one will be a monthly listing of new NIH Awards, and the other will be an order form to obtain NIH publications from DRG's Office of Grants Inquiries.

Details: Free

User Info: To access the NIH Grant Line, telnet to the URL address below and when a message has been received that the connection is open, type: ,GEN1 (the comma is mandatory). At the INITIALS? prompt, type BB5 and at the ACCOUNT? prompt, type CCS2

The NIH Guide to Grants and Contracts can also be accessed through gopher://helix.nih.gov/11/res/nih-guide

`telnet://wylbur.cu.nih.gov`

A
B
C
D
E
F
G
H
I
J
K
L
M
N
O
P
Q
R
S
T
U
V
W
X
Y
Z

Nihon Sun Microsystems

Nihon Sun Microsystems

This site provides a directory for Sun Microsystems in Japan. Includes the Rolling Stones Official Server WWW site, with access to Rolling Stones music, merchandise, and information. Also provides multimedia links to the Science University of Tokyo and other Asia-Pacific resources.

Keywords: Rolling Stones

Sponsor: Sun Microsystems, Inc., Tokyo, Japan

Audience: Computer Users, Rolling Stones Enthusiasts

Contact: www-admin@sun.co.jp

Details: Multimedia, Free, Sounds, Images

`http://www.sun.co.jp`

NIR

NIR Archives

Archives of the NIR (Networked Information Retrieval) service.

Keywords: Internet, Information Retrieval

Audience: Internet Surfers

Details: Free

Notes: Files are in: pub/lists/nir

`ftp:// mailbase.ac.uk`

NIR Gopher

The gopher for the NIR (Networked Information Retrieval) service.

Keywords: Internet, Information Retrieval, NIR

Audience: Internet Surfers

Details: Free

`gopher:// mailbase.ac.auk /11/lists-k-o/nic`

Nissan Automobiles

nissan

Discusses Nissan and Infiniti automobiles, with the exception of the Sentra SE-R, NX2000, and G20, which are served by the SE-R list.

Keywords: Nissan Automobiles, Infiniti Automobiles

Audience: Automobiles Owners, Automobiles Enthusiasts

Contact: Rich Siegel
nissan-request@world.std.com

Details: Free

User Info: To subscribe to the list, send an e-mail message requesting a subscription to the URL address below.

To send a message to the entire list, address it to: nissan@world.std.com

`mailto:nissan-request@world.std.com`

NJ-motss

NJ-motss

Mailing list for gay, lesbian, and bisexual issues in New Jersey.

Keywords: Gay, Lesbian, Bisexuality, New Jersey

Audience: Gays, Lesbians, Bisexuals

Contact: majordomo@plts.org

Details: Free

User Info: To subscribe to the list, send an e-mail message to the URL address shown below consisting of a single line reading:

SUB NJ-motss YourFirstName YourLastName

To send a message to the entire list, address it to: NJ-motss@plts.org

`mailto: majordomo@plts.org`

NJ-motss-announce

NJ-motss-announce

Announcements of interests to New Jersey's gay, lesbian, and bisexual population.

Keywords: Gays, Lesbians, Bisexuality, New Jersey

Audience: Gays, Lesbians, Bisexuals

Contact: majordomo@plts.org

Details: Free

User Info: To subscribe to the list, send an e-mail message to the URL address shown below consisting of a single line reading:

SUB NJ-motss-announce YourFirstName YourLastName

To send a message to the entire list, address it to: NJ-motss-announce@plts.org

`mailto:majordomo@plts.org`

nl-kr

nl-kr

This E-conference is open to discussion of any topic related to the understanding and generation of natural language and knowledge representation as subfields of artificial intelligence.

Keywords: Programming Languages, Natural Language, Knowledge Representation, Linguistics

Audience: Computer Scientists

Contact: Christopher Welty
weltyc@cs.rpi.edu

Details: Free, Moderated

User Info: To subscribe to the list, send an e-mail message requesting a subscription to the URL address below.

`mailto:nl-kr-request@cs.rpi.edu`

NLC (National Library of Canada)

NLC (National Library of Canada)

A Canadian library gopher in French and English.

Keywords: Canada, Libraries, Library Science

Sponsor: National Library of Canada (NLC), Canada

Audience: Canadians, Librarians, Publishing Professionals

Profile: This site provides a gateway to Canadian library and Internet resources linking users to the National Library, which offers a bibliographic database, a list of NLC publications, and other services for libraries and publishers. It also has links to many other Canadian libraries and Internet services, as well as a large selection of general information from and about the Government of Canada and its provinces.

Contact: Nancy Brodie, Lynn Herbert
Nancy.Brodie@nlc-bnc.ca,
Lynn.Herbert@nlc-bnc.ca

`gopher://gopher.nlc-bnc.ca`

NLSNews Newsletter (National Longitudinal Surveys of Labor Market Experience)

NLSNews Newsletter (National Longitudinal Surveys of Labor Market Experience)

Issued by the Center for Human Resource Research (Ohio State University); distributed to researchers using NLS data, as well as to other interested persons.

Keywords: Labor, Government (US), Department of Labor

Sponsor: Bureau of Labor Statistics, US Department of Labor

Audience: Statisticians, Researchers

Profile: A typical issue contains updates on the status and availability of NLS data tapes and CD-ROMs for the six NLS cohorts (Older Men, Mature Women, Young Men, Young Women, Youth, and Children), notices to researchers of data-file or documentation errors, summaries of in-progress and completed NLS research, and other information of general interest to the NLS research community.

Contact: Gale James
james@ohsthr.bitnet

Notes: A description of the subscription service that enables users to automatically receive, as soon as it becomes available, the latest issue of the NLS Newsletter and/or error updates can be found in the file subscribe.info, available via nlserve@ohsthr.bitnet, the Center's file server.

`mailto:james@ohsthr.bitnet`

noglstp

noglstp

This list is sponsored by the National Organization of Gay and Lesbian Scientists and Technical Professionals, Inc. (a 501-C3 organization). National office is in Pasadena, CA and can be reached at (818) 791-7689 or p.o. Box 91803, Pasadena, CA 90019. There is also a newsletter that is available to membership.

Keywords: Gays, Lesbians, Scientists, Technical Professionals

Audience: Gays, Lesbians, Support

Contact: noglstp-request@elroy.jpl.nasa.gov

Details: Free

User Info: To subscribe to the list, send an e-mail message requesting a subscription to the URL address below.

To send a message to the entire list, address it to: noglstp@elroy.jpl.nasa.gov

`mailto:noglstp-`
`request@elroy.jpl.nasa.gov`

Non Serviam

Non Serviam

Non Serviam is an electronic newsletter centered on the philosophy of Max Stirner, author of Der Einzige und Sein Eigentum (The Ego and Its Own) and on his dialectical egoism. The contents, however, are decided by the individual contributors and the editor.

Keywords: Stirner (Max), Non Serviam, Philosophy

Audience: Max Stirner Enthusiasts

Contact: Svein Olav Nyberg
solan@math.uio.no

Details: Free

User Info: To subscribe to the list, send an e-mail message requesting a subscription to the URL address below.

To send a message to the entire list, address it to: solan@math.uio.no

`mailto:solan@math.uio.no`

Non-Governmental Organizations

World Health Organization (WHO)

This gopher provides access to the databases of the WHO.

Keywords: World Health Organization, Health, Medicine, Non-governmental organizations

Sponsor: World Health Organization, Geneva, Switzerland

Audience: Medical Professionals, Researchers

Contact: akazawa@who.ch

Details: Free

`gopher://gopher.who.ch`

Nonfiction Books

Online BookStore (OBS)

Offers full text (fiction and nonfiction) in a variety of electronic formats, free and for a fee.

Keywords: Online Books, Books, ShareWord, Fiction, Nonfiction Books

Sponsor: Editorial Inc./OBS

Audience: General Public, Reading Enthusiasts

Profile: Started in 1992, the OBS offers a variety of full-text titles.

Contact: Laura Fillmore
laura@editorial.com

Details: Costs, Moderated, Images, Multimedia

User Info: To subscribe to the list, send an e-mail message requesting a subscription to the URL address below.

`http://marketplace.com/0/obs`

Nonprofit Organizations

DevelopNet News

A monthly newsletter on technology transfer in international development.

Keywords: Nonprofits, Technology, Development

Sponsor: Volunteers in Technical Assistance

Audience: Technology Professionals, International Development Specialists

Contact: R.R. Ronkin
vita@gmuvax.gmu.edu

Details: Free

User Info: To subscribe, send an e-mail message to the address below. Inquire about needing a password.

`mailto:vita@gmuvax.gmu.edu`

Encyclopedia of Associations

The Encyclopedia of Associations database is a comprehensive source of detailed information on over 88,000 nonprofit membership organizations worldwide.

Keywords: Nonprofit Organizations

Sponsor: Gale Research Inc., Detroit, MI, USA

Audience: Researchers

Profile: The database corresponds to the print Encyclopedia of Associations family of publications as follows: National Organizations of the US, covering more than 23,000 American associations of national scope; International Organizations, covering some 11,000 multinational, binational, and non-US national organizations; and Regional, State, and Local Organizations, covering more than 54,000 US associations with interstate, state, intrastate, city, or local scope or membership.

Contact: Dialog in the US at (800) 334-2564, Dialog internationally at country-specific locations.

User Info: To subscribe, contact Dialog directly.

Notes: Coverage: Current editions; updated semiannually.

`telnet://dialog.com`

Internet Nonprofit Center

A clearinghouse of information for nonprofit organizations and those interested in donating to them. Includes annual reports, directories, financial information, and brochures of selected nonprofit organizations, as well as volunteer opportunities and advice for potential donors. The Internet Nonprofit Center is currently located on EnviroLink Network, a gopher dedicated to environmental causes.

Keywords: Nonprofit Organizations, Philanthropy

Sponsor: American Institute of Philanthropy, USA, and The Internet Nonprofit Center, Brooklyn, New York, USA

Audience: Activists, Philanthropists

Contact: Cliff Landesman
clandesm@panix.com

`gopher://envirolink.org`

A B C D E F G H I J K L M **N** O P Q R S T U V W X Y Z

Nordic Skiing

nordic-skiing

Discussion of Nordic skiing sports. This includes cross-country, biathlon, ski-orienteering, ski jumping, Nordic combined, telemark, and backcountry.

Keywords: Nordic Skiing

Audience: Skiers

Contact: Mitch Collinsworth
nordic-ski-request@graphics.cornell.edu

Details: Free

User Info: To subscribe to the list, send an e-mail message requesting a subscription to the URL address below.

To send a message to the entire list, address it to: nordic-ski@graphics.cornell.edu

`mailto:nordic-ski-`
`request@graphics.cornell.edu`

Nordic University

NORDUnet region Root Gopher

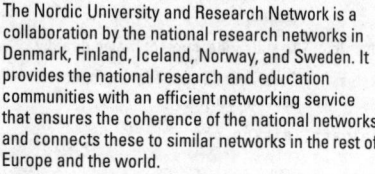

The Nordic University and Research Network is a collaboration by the national research networks in Denmark, Finland, Iceland, Norway, and Sweden. It provides the national research and education communities with an efficient networking service that ensures the coherence of the national networks and connects these to similar networks in the rest of Europe and the world.

Keywords: Nordic University, Europe

Audience: Internet Surfers

Contact: hostmaster@nic.nordu.net

Details: Free

`gopher://gopher.nordu.net`

North America

NSAMER (North and South America Library)

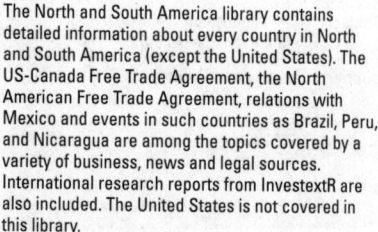

The North and South America library contains detailed information about every country in North and South America (except the United States). The US-Canada Free Trade Agreement, the North American Free Trade Agreement, relations with Mexico and events in such countries as Brazil, Peru, and Nicaragua are among the topics covered by a variety of business, news and legal sources. International research reports from InvestextR are also included. The United States is not covered in this library.

Keywords: News, Analysis, Companies, North America, South America

---

Audience: Journalists, Business Professionals

Profile: The North and South America library contains a broad array of sources. Among the information sources are newspapers and wire services, trade and business journals, company reports, country and region backgrounds, industry and product analyses, business opportunities, and selected legal texts. News sources range from the world-renowned Washington Post and Christian Science Monitor to the regionally important Toronto Star and Latin American Newsletters. Canadian Business and Maclean's represent a portion of the array of business and trade journals. Company information is contained in the EXTEL cards as well as ICC. Providers of country background and industry analyses include Associated Banks of Europe, Bank of America, Business International, IBC USA and the US Department of Commerce. Among the specialized resources are IBC's Mexico and Brazil Services as well as BI's Business Latin America. Researchers interested in new business opportunities can check OPIC and Foreign Trade Opportunities (FTO).And selected legal texts covering the US-Canada Free Trade Agreement and other international agreements planners and advisors to better assess the business climate in North and South America.

Contact: Mead New Sales Group at (800) 227-4908 or (513) 859-5398 inside the US, or (513) 865-7981 for all inquiries outside the US.

User Info: To subscribe, contact Mead directly.

To examine the Nexis user guide, you can access it at the ftp site of the University of Texas at Austin at the URL address: ftp://ftp.cc.utexas.edu

The files are in: /pub/ref-services/LEXIS

`telnet://nex.meaddata.com`

`http://www.meaddata.com`

North American Free Trade Agreement (NAFTA)

North American Free Trade Agreement (NAFTA)

The agreement between the governments of Canada, the United Mexican States, and the United States of America to establish a free trade area in North America.

Keywords: Foreign Trade, Mexico, Canada, Free Trade, NAFTA

Audience: Journalists, Politicians, Economists, Students

Details: Free

`gopher://wiretap.spies.com/00/Gov/`
`NAFTA`

North Carolina

Newsbrief

Provides a variety of information and feature articles, primarily for campus users.

Keywords: University of North Carolina, North Carolina; Information Technology

Sponsor: Office of Information Technology at the University of North Carolina, Chapel Hill (UNC Chapel Hill)

Audience: Students, Educators

Contact: Karen C. Blansfield, Judy Hallman
karen@rhumba.acs.unc.edu

Details: Free

User Info: To subscribe, send an e-mail message to the URL address below consisting of a single line reading:

To send a message to the entire list,

`mailto:listserv@uncvm1.bitnet`

University of North Carolina at Chapel Hill Info Library

The library's holdings are large and wide-ranging and contain significant collections in many fields.

Keywords: North Carolina; Southern Historical Collection, Rare Books; Books (Antiquarian)

Audience: Researchers, Students, General Public

Contact: Judy Hallman
hallman@unc.bitnet

Details: Free

User Info: Expect: Login; Send: Info

`telnet://info.oit.unc.edu`

Northwestern University Library

Northwestern University Library

The library's holdings are large and wide-ranging and contain significant collections in many fields.

Keywords: Africa, Wright (Frank Lloyd), Women's Studies, Art, Literature (American), Contemporary Music, Government (US State), UN Documents, Music

Audience: General Public, Researchers, Librarians, Document Delivery Professionals

Details: Free

User Info: Expect: COMMAND:, Send: DIAL VTAM

`telnet://nuacvm.acns.nwu.edu`

Norway

NORWEAVE

Building on the success of NORWAVES, NORWEAVE is an additional e-mail service for Norwegians and friends of Norway. The aim of NORWEAVE is to create a network of people in Norway and abroad who can help each other exchange information and establish contacts across geographical boundaries.

Keywords: Norway

Audience: Norwegians, Travelers/Tourists

Contact: listserv@nki.no

Details: Free

User Info: To subscribe to the list, send an e-mail message to the URL address shown below consisting of a single line reading:

SUB norweave YourFirstName YourLastName

To send a message to the entire list, address it to: norweave@nki.no

`mailto:listserv@nki.no`

Notable Women

Notable Women

A database listing some important and notable women through the ages. Available for online searching by keyword, or as a full-text file.

Keywords: Women's Studies, History (Women's), Feminism

Sponsor: Estrella Mountain Community College (Arizona)

Audience: Women's Studies Educators, Historians, Researchers, Feminists

Contact: EMC Gopher Team root@gopher.emc.maricopa.edu

`gopher://gopher.emc.maricopa.edu`

NotGNU

NotGNU

There are three lists associated with the NotGNU Emacs editor. NotGNU-list is an interactive list dedicated to miscellaneous discussions, problems, and suggestions for NotGNU. NotGNU-announce is used for announcing new versions of NotGNU, notification of new services, bug reports, amd so on. NotGNU-distribution is a list to which new NotGNU binaries will be sent unencoded upon release.

Keywords: NotGNU, Emacs

Audience: NotGNU Users

Contact: notgnu-request@netcom.com

Details: Free

User Info: To subscribe to the list, send an e-mail message requesting a subscription to the URL address below.

To send a message to the entire list, address it to: notgnu@netcom.com

`mailto:notgnu-request@netcom.com`

Novice MZT

Novice MZT

Novize MZT (News of Ministry for Science and Technology of the Republic of Slovenia) provides easy, accessible news about science, development, universities, and innovative activities to individuals and institutions in research and development areas. Published at least once monthly.

Keywords: Slovenia, Science, Technology, News

Audience: Slovenians, Scientists, Technocrats

Contact: Novice-mzt@krpan.arnes.si or Novice.mzt@uni-lj.si

User Info: To subscribe to the list, send an e-mail message requesting a subscription to the URL address below.

To send a message to the entire list, address it to: Novice-mzt@krpan.arnes.si

`mailto:Novice-MZT@krpan.arnes.si`

NPLC

NPLC

This list was set up to establish a network for rapid communication among researchers in the field of plant lipids. Announcements for example (of post-doc positions) to the field can be posted. The list can also be used to query coworkers regarding techniques, resources, and so on.

Keywords: Plant Lipids

Audience: Researchers

Contact: Walid Tout tout@genesys.cps.msu.edu

Details: Free

User Info: To subscribe to the list, send an e-mail message requesting a subscription to the URL address below.

To send a message to the entire list, address it to: nplc@genesys.cps.msu.edu

`mailto:NPLC@genesys.cps.msu.edu`

NQTHM

nqthm-users

Discussion of theorem proving using the Boyler-Moore theorem prover, NQTHM. Offers lore, advice, information, discussion, and help.

Keywords: Computer Programs, NQTHM, Boyler-Moore Theorem Prover

Audience: NQTHM Theorem Users

Contact: nqthm-users-request@cli.com

Details: Free

User Info: To subscribe to the list, send an e-mail message requesting a subscription to the URL address below.

To send a message to the entire list, address it to: nqthm-users@cli.com

`mailto:nqthm-users@cli.com`

NSAMER (North and South America Library)

NSAMER (North and South America Library)

The North and South America library contains detailed information about every country in North and South America (except the United States). The US-Canada Free Trade Agreement, the North American Free Trade Agreement, relations with Mexico and events in such countries as Brazil, Peru, and Nicaragua are among the topics covered by a variety of business, news and legal sources. International research reports from InvestextR are also included. The United States is not covered in this library.

Keywords: News, Analysis, Companies, North America, South America

Audience: Journalists, Business Professionals

Profile: The North and South America library contains a broad array of sources. Among the information sources are newspapers and wire services, trade and business journals, company reports, country and region backgrounds, industry and product analyses, business opportunities, and selected legal texts. News sources range from the world-renowned Washington Post and Christian Science Monitor to the regionally important Toronto Star and Latin American Newsletters. Canadian Business and Maclean's represent a portion of the array of business and trade journals. Company information is contained in the EXTEL cards as well as ICC. Providers of country background and industry analyses include Associated Banks of Europe, Bank of America, Business International, IBC USA and the US Department of Commerce. Among the specialized resources are IBC's Mexico and Brazil Services as well as BI's Business Latin America. Researchers interested in new business opportunities can check OPIC and Foreign Trade Opportunities (FTO).And selected legal texts covering the US-Canada Free Trade Agreement and other international agreements planners and advisors to better assess the business climate in North and South America.

A
B
C
D
E
F
G
H
I
J
K
L
M
N
O
P
Q
R
S
T
U
V
W
X
Y
Z

Contact: Mead New Sales Group at (800) 227-4908 or (513) 859-5398 inside the US, or (513) 865-7981 for all inquiries outside the US.

User Info: To subscribe, contact Mead directly.

To examine the Nexis user guide, you can access it at the ftp site of the University of Texas at Austin at the URL address: ftp://ftp.cc.utexas.edu

The files are in: /pub/ref-services/LEXIS

`telnet://nex.meaddata.com`

`http://www.meaddata.com`

NSF Resource Guide

NSF Resource Guide

A guide to Internet resources from the NSF (National Science Foundation).

Keywords: Internet, Internet Guides

Audience: Internet Surfers

Details: Free

Note: Read the overview in: resource-guide/overview

`ftp://ds.internic.net`

NSSDC (National Space Science Data Center)'s Online Data & Information Service

NSSDC (National Space Science Data Center)'s Online Data & Information Service

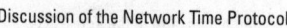

The NSSDC (National Space Science Data Center) is the NASA facility charged with archiving the data from all of NASA's science missions.

Keywords: Space, Science, Astrophysics, Software, NASA, Science

Sponsor: NASA

Audience: Scientists, Space Scientists, Astronomers, Engineers

Profile: This resource contains information about NASA's missions and analysis of their data.

Details: Free

User Info: Expect: Login, Send: nssdc

See the menu entries in your particular area of interest.

`telnet://nssdc.gsfc.nasa.gov`

NTIS FedWorld

NTIS FedWorld

This is a growing list of web servers, ftp, gopher, and telnet sites organized by NTIS categories.

Keywords: NTIS FedWorld

Audience: General Public, Researchers, Business Professionals, Politicians

Contact: Bob Bunge webmaster@fedworld.gov

`http://www.fedworld.gov`

`telnet://fedworld.gov`

`ftp://ftp.fedworld.gov`

ntp

ntp

Discussion of the Network Time Protocol.

Keywords: Network Time Protocol

Audience: Network Time Protocol Users

Contact: ntp-request@trantor.umd.edu

User Info: To subscribe to the list, send an e-mail message requesting a subscription to the URL address below.

To send a message to the entire list, address it to: ntp@trantor.umd.edu

`mailto:ntp-request@trantor.umd.edu`

Nuclear Medicine

nucmed

A discussion of nuclear medicine and related issues. Of particular concern is the format of digital images.

Keywords: Nuclear Medicine

Audience: Medical Researchers, Doctors

Contact: Trevor Cradduck trevorc@uwovax.uwo.ca

Details: Free

User Info: To subscribe to the list, send an e-mail message requesting a subscription to the URL address below.

To send a message to the entire list, address it to: nucmed@uwovax.uwo.ca

`mailto:nucmed-request@uwovax.uwo.ca`

Nuclear Safety

Illinois Legislation

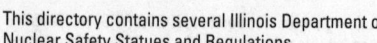

This directory contains several Illinois Department of Nuclear Safety Statues and Regulations.

Keywords: Nuclear Safety, Law, Illinois

Audience: Lawyers

Details: Free

`gopher://wiretap.spies.com`

numeric-interest

numeric-interest

Discussion of issues of floating-point correctness and performance with respect to hardware, operating systems, languages, and standard libraries.

Keywords: Computer Hardware

Audience: Computer Users

Contact: David Hough numeric-interest-request@validgh.com

Details: Free

User Info: To subscribe to the list, send an e-mail message requesting a subscription to the URL address below.

To send a message to the entire list, address it to: numeric-interest@validgh.com

`mailto:numeric-interest-request@validgh.com`

Numerical Analysis

NA-net

This mailing list is a forum for discussions on the subject of numerical analysis.

Keywords: Numerical Analysis

Audience: Numerical Analysts

User Info: To subscribe to the list, send an e-mail message requesting a subscription to the URL address below.

`mailto:na.join@na-net.ornl.gov`

Numismatics

coins

A forum for discussions on numismatic topics, including US and world coins, paper money, tokens, and medals.

Keywords: Coins, Numismatics

Audience: Coin Collectors

Contact: Daniel J. Power
coins-request@iscsvax.uni.edu

Details: Free

User Info: To subscribe to the list, send an e-mail message requesting a subscription to the URL address below.

To send a message to the entire list, address it to: coins@iscsvax.uni.edu

`mailto:coins-request@iscsvax.uni.edu`

Harvard University Library

The library's holdings are large and wide-ranging and contain significant collections in many fields.

Keywords: Afrikaans, Alchemy, Arabic Culure (History of), Celtic Philology, Congo Languages, Folklore, Hebraica, Mormonism, Numismatics, Quakers, Sanskrit, Witchcraft, Arabic Philology

Audience: General Public, Researchers, Librarians, Document Delivery Professionals

Details: Free

User Info: Expect: Mitek Server..., Send: Enter or Return; Expect: prompt, Send: hollis

`telnet://hollis.harvard.edu`

University of Colorado at Boulder Library

The library's holdings are large and wide-ranging and contain significant collections in many fields.

Keywords: Numismatics, Human Rights, Literature (Children's), Labor Archives, History (US)

Audience: Researchers, Students, General Public

Contact: Donna Pattee
pattee@spot.colorado.edu

Details: Free

User Info: Expect: Login; Send: Culine

`telnet://culine.colorado.edu`

Nursing

Johns Hopkins University Library

The library's holdings are large and wide-ranging and contain significant collections in many fields.

Keywords: Literature (English), Economics, Classics, Drama (German), Slavery, Trade Unions, Incunabula, Bibles, Diseases (History of), Nursing, Abolitionism

Audience: General Public, Researchers, Librarians, Document Delivery Professionals

Details: Free

`telnet://jhuvm.hcf.jhu.edu`

MEDLINE

MEDLINE is a major source of bibliographic biomedical literature. The MEDLINE database encompasses information from three printed indexes (Index Medicus, Index to Dental Literature and the International Nursing Index) as well as additional information not published in the Index Medicus.

Keywords: Biomedicine, Dentistry, Nursing, Medicine

Sponsor: U.S. National Library of Medicine

Audience: Librarians, Researchers, Physicians, Students

Contact: CDP Technologies Sales Department (800)950-2035, extension 400

User Info: To subscribe, contact CDP Technologies directly

`telnet://cdplus@cdplus.com`

Midwifery Resources on the Net

A resource list for helping find information about midwifery on the Internet.

Keywords: Midwifery, Childbirth, Medicine, Nursing

Audience: Midwives, Medical professionals

Details: Free

`gopher://una.hh.lib.umich.edu`

University of Maryland SystemLibrary

The library's holdings are large and wide-ranging and contain significant collections in many fields.

Keywords: Medicine (History of), Nursing, Pharmacology, Microbiology, Aquaculture, Aquatic Chemistry, Toxicology

Audience: General Public, Researchers, Librarians, Document Delivery Professionals

Contact: Ron Larsen

Details: Free

User Info: Expect: Available Services menu; Send: PAC

`telnet://victor.umd.edu`

University of Pennsylvania School of Medicine Library

The library's holdings are large and wide-ranging and contain significant collections in many fields.

Keywords: Health Care, Nursing, History, Health

Audience: Researchers, Students, General Public

Details: Free

User Info: Expect: Login; Send: Public

`telnet://penninfo.upenn.edu`

University of Puerto Rico Library

The library's holdings are large and wide-ranging and contain significant collections in many fields.

Keywords: Computer Science, Education, Nursing, Agriculture, Economics

Audience: Researchers, Students, General Public

Details: Free

After Locator: telnet://, press Tab twice. Type DIAL VTAM. Enter NOTIS.

Press Return. On the blank screen, type LUUP.

`telnet://136.145.2.10`

University of Texas at Austin Library

The library's holdings are large and wide-ranging and contain significant collections in many fields.

Keywords: Music, Natural Science, Nursing, Science Technology, Behavioral Science, Social Work, Computer Science, Engineering, Latin American Studies, Middle Eastern Studies

Audience: Researchers, Students, General Public

Details: Free

User Info: Expect: Blank Screen, Send: Return; Expect: Go, Send: Return; Expect: Enter Terminal Type, Send: vt100

note: Some databases are restricted to UT Austin users only.

`telnet://utcat.utexas.edu`

University of Texas at Galveston (Medical Branch) Library

The library's holding's are large and wide-ranging and contain significant collections in many fields.

Keywords: Health Sciences, Biomedicine, Nursing

Audience: Researchers, Students, General Public

Details: Free

User Info: Expect: Login, Send: Library

`telnet://ibm.gal.utexas.edu`

University of Texas Health Science Center at San Antonio Library

The library's holdings are large and wide-ranging and contain significant collections in many fields.

Keywords: Allied Health, Dentistry, Nursing, Veterinary Science, Ambulatory Care, Obstetrics/Gynecology, Pediatrics

Audience: Researchers, Students, General Public

Details: Free

User Info: Expect: Login, Send: LIS

`telnet://athena.uthscsa.edu`

A B C D E F G H I J K L M N O P Q R S T U V W X Y Z

A B C D E F G H I J K L M N O P Q R S T U V W X Y Z

University of Wisconsin at Oshkosh Library

The library's holdings are large and wide-ranging and contain significant collections in many fields.

Keywords: Business, Liberal Education, Nursing

Audience: Researchers, Students, General Public

Details: Free

User Info: Expect: Login; Send: Lib; Expect: vDIAL Prompt, Send: Library

`telnet://polk.cis.uwosh.edu`

University of Wisconsin Eau Claire Library

The library's holdings are large and wide-ranging and contain significant collections in many fields.

Keywords: Health Sciences, Business, Nursing, Education

Audience: Researchers, Students, General Public

Details: Free

User Info: Expect: Service Name, Send: Victor

`telnet://lib.uwec.edu`

Nutrition

Federal Food and Drug Administration

The Federal Food and Drug Administration (FDA) databank contains reports and articles related to the FDA.

Keywords: FDA, Drug Regulations, Nutrition

Sponsor: Federal Food and Drug Administration

Audience: Researchers, Nutritionists, Consumers, Health Care Providers

Profile: The topics covered include the drug and device product-approvals list, FDA federal register summaries by subject, text from drug bulletins, current information on AIDS, FDA consumer magazine index and selected articles, summaries of FDA information, text of testimony at FDA congressional hearings, and speeches given by the FDA commissioner and deputy.

Details: Free

`telnet://bbs@fdabbs.fda.gov`

GRANOLA (Vegetarian Discussion List)

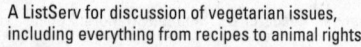

A ListServ for discussion of vegetarian issues, including everything from recipes to animal rights.

Keywords: Health, Nutrition, Vegetarian, Recipes

Audience: Vegetarians, Nutritionists, Health Professionals

Details: Free

User Info: To subscribe to the list, send an e-mail message to the URL address shown below consisting of a single line reading:

SUB granola YourFirstName YourLastName

`mailto:listserv@gitvm1.bitnet`

Health Periodicals Database

This source covers a broad range of health subjects and issues.

Keywords: Health, Biotechnology, Medicine, Nutrition

Sponsor: Information Access Company, Foster City, CA, US

Audience: Health Professionals, Dieticians, Librarians

Profile: The database provides indexing and full text of journals covering a broad range of health subjects and issues including: prenatal care, dieting, drug abuse, AIDS, biotechnology, cardiovascular disease, environment, public health, safety, paramedical professions, sports medicine, substance abuse, toxicology, and much more.

Contact: Dialog in the US at (800) 334-2564, Dialog internationally at country-specific locations.

User Info: To subscribe, contact Dialog directly.

Notes: Coverage: 1988 to the present; updated weekly.

`telnet://dialog.com`

International Food and Nutrition (INFAN) Database

A database covering all aspects of nutrition, health and food, as for example, weight control, food safety, eating patterns, and more.

Keywords: Nutrition, Health, Diet

Sponsor: Pennsylvania State University Nutrition Center

Audience: Nutritionists, Health Care Professionals, Consumers

Details: Free

To access the database, select PENpages (1), then General Information (3), and finally INFAN Database (4).

`telnet://penpages@psupen.psu.edu`

The Wellness List

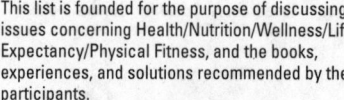

This list is founded for the purpose of discussing issues concerning Health/Nutrition/Wellness/Life Expectancy/Physical Fitness, and the books, experiences, and solutions recommended by the participants.

Keywords: Health, Nutrition, Fitness

Audience: Doctors, Nutritionists, General Public

Profile: This resource provides announcements of and reviews of books that include solutions, nutrition related position papers, requests for information, recommendations of participants, healthy recipes, nutrition and fitness related product announcements, and general discussion of related issues. Health professionals, authors, and nutritionists are encouraged to subscribe and share their knowledge with the participants.

Contact: George Rust, Wellnessmart eorge@wellnessmart.com info@wellnessmart.com

User Info: To subscribe send an e-mail message to the URL address below consisting of a single line reading:

subscribe wellnesslist

`mailto:majordomo@wellnessmart.com`

NW-Raves (Northwest Raves)

NW-Raves (Northwest Raves)

One of several regional rave-related mailing lists, NW-Raves covers the northwestern US and western Canada. No archives are available.

Keywords: Raves

Audience: Ravers

Contact: Pat Lui nw-raves-request@wimsey.bc.ca

Details: Free

User Info: To subscribe to the list, send an e-mail message requesting a subscription to the URL address below.

To send a message to the entire list, address it to: nw-raves@wimsey.bc.ca

`mailto:nw-raves-request@wimsey.bc.ca`

NWNet Internet Guide

NWNet Internet Guide

An introductory guide to the Internet. Details the basic Internet tools of electronic mail, FTP (File Transfer Protocol), and Telnet. Covers types of resources found on the Internet, and how to use them. Includes information directed toward supercomputer users and the K-12 community.

Keywords: Internet, Internet Guides, Supercomputing, Education (K-12)

Sponsor: NorthWestNet

Audience: Internet Surfers, Computer Users, Students (K-12)

Contact: Jonathan Kochmer nusirg@nwnet.net

Details: Free

File is: /user-docs/nusirg/nusirg.whole-guide.ps

`ftp://ftphost.nwnet.net`

NYAL (New York Art Line)

NYAL (New York Art Line)

A gopher containing selected resources on the arts.

Keywords: Art, Audio-Visual Materials, Multimedia, Computer Art

Sponsor: Panix Public Access Unix & Internet Gopher Server, New York, USA

Audience: Artists, Art Enthusiasts

Profile: NYAL features a wide variety of arts resources. The primary focus of this site is visual art, particularly in the New York city area. Information includes online access to selected galleries, image archives, and New York city arts groups. Beyond visual art, information on dance, music, and techno art (with a special section on Internet art) is also available. It also features links to various electronic journals, museums, and schools.

Contact: Kenny Greenberg
            kgreen@panix.com

`gopher://gopher.panix.com`

`http://gopher.panix.com/nyart
/Kpage/kg`

NYIsrael Project of NYSERnet

NYIsrael Project of NYSERnet

Large repository of historical and cultural information as well as software, mailing lists, and images relating to Judaism, Jews, the Hebrew language, and Israel.

Keywords: Judaism, Hebrew Language, Israel

Sponsor: The New York Israel Project, NYSERNet, Inc.

Audience: Jewish Organizations

Profile: The purpose of this project is to create a network of diverse Jewish organizations worldwide that can communicate electronically and share information with one another.

Contact: Avrum Goodblatt
            goodblat@israel.nysernet.org

Details: Free

`gopher://israel.nysernet.org`

NYSERNet Internet Guide

NYSERNet Internet Guide

A comprehensive guide to the Internet from the New York State Education and Research Network (NYSERNet). NYSERNet provides access to specialized databases and online libraries, as well as to supercomputing and parallel-processing facilities throughout the US and to many national networks.

Keywords: Internet, Internet Guides, New York, Supercomputers

Sponsor: NYSERNet K-12 Networking Interest Group

Audience: Internet Surfers

Contact: info@nysernet.org

Details: Free

`ftp://nysernet.org`

A
B
C
D
E
F
G
H
I
J
K
L
M
N
O
P
Q
R
S
T
U
V
W
X
Y
Z

O

Object-Oriented Programming

BETA ★

A discussion forum for BETA users. BETA is a modern object-oriented programming language.

Keywords: Programming Languages, Object-Oriented Programming, BETA

Audience: Programmers

Contact: Elmer Soerensen Sandvad
usergroup-request@mjolner.dk

Details: Free, Moderated

User Info: To subscribe to the list, send an e-mail message requesting a subscription to the URL address below. To send a message to the entire list, address it to: usergroup@mjolner.dk

`mailto:usergroup-request@mjolner.dk`

Objectivism

Objectivism ★

A mailing list where students of Objectivism can discuss their ideas, issues, exchange news, and so on. Any issue that may have some relevance to Objectivists is appropriate here.

Keywords: Objectivism

Audience: Objectivists, Philosophers

Contact: Paul Vixie
objectivism-request@vix.com

Details: Free

User Info: To subscribe to the list, send an e-mail message requesting a subscription to the URL address below. To send a message to the entire list, address it to: objectivism@vix.com

`mailto:objectivism-request@vix.com`

Obstetrics/Gynecology

University of Texas Health Science Center at San Antonio Library ★★

The library's holdings are large and wide-ranging and contain significant collections in many fields.

Keywords: Allied Health, Dentistry, Nursing, Veterinary Science, Ambulatory Care, Obstetrics/Gynecology, Pediatrics

Audience: Researchers, Students, General Public

Details: Free

User Info: Expect: Login, Send: LIS

`telnet:// athena.uthscsa.edu`

Occupational Outlook Handbook 1992-93

Occupational Outlook Handbook 1992-93 ★★★

An annual U.S. Department of Labor publication that provides detailed information for more than 320 occupations, including job descriptions, typical salaries, education and training requirements, working conditions, job outlook, and more.

Keywords: Careers, Employment, Labor

Sponsor: U.S. Department of Labor

Audience: General Public, Job Seekers, Business Professionals

Details: Free

`gopher://umslvma.umsl.edu/11/library/govdocs/ooha`

Oceanography

FINS (Fish Information Service) ★

This site provides information on issues relating to fish, including aquarium-building tips, diseases, clubs, newsgroups, movies, and fish trivia from Woods Hole Oceanographic Institute.

Keywords: Fish, Oceanography

Sponsor: Active Window Productions

Audience: Fish Enthusiasts, Ichthyologists

Details: Free

`http://www.actwin.com/fish/index.html`

Research Ship Schedules and Information ★★★

A gopher providing information on research and deep water vessels from more than 45 countries. Includes detailed ship specifications, some with deck plans and photographs available as GIF files. Also has cruise schedules for US ships, as well as some from other countries.

Keywords: Oceanography, Transportation, Maritime Industry, Travel

Sponsor: University of Delaware (The OCEANIC Ocean Information Center), Newark, Delaware, USA

Audience: Oceanographers, General Public

Contact: Ocean Information Center, University of Delaware, College of Marine Studies
oceanic@diu.cms.udel.edu

Details: Free, Images

`gopher://diu.cms.udel.edu`

A
B
C
D
E
F
G
H
I
J
K
L
M
N
O
P
Q
R
S
T
U
V
W
X
Y
Z

University of Maryland, College Park

The library's holdings are large and wide-ranging and contain significant collections in many fields.

Keywords: Agriculture, Coastal Marine Biology, Fisheries, Water Quality, Oceanography

Audience: Researchers, Students, General Public

Contact: Janet McLeod
            mcleod@umail.umd.edu

Details: Free

User Info: Expect: Login; Send: Atdu

`telnet://info.umd.edu`

Oceans

Global Change Information Gateway

This gateway was created to address environmental data management issues raised by the US Congress, the Administration, and the advisory arms of the Federal policy community. It contains documents related to the UN conference on Environment and Development.

Keywords: UN, Environment, Development, Oceans, Atmosphere

Audience: Environmentalists, Scientists, Researchers, Environmentalists

Details: Free

            Select from menu as appropriate.

`gopher://scilibx.ucsc.edu`

National Oceanic & Atmospheric Administration (NOAA)
Office of Environmental Safety and Health, Department of Energy

The NOAA catalog provides keyword access to sources of environmental information in the US. Gopher for resources pertaining to health and environmental safety.

Keywords: Environment, Oceans, Atmospheric Science, Health, Environmental Safety

Sponsor: National Oceanic & Atmospheric Administration (NOAA)
            Department of Energy (USA)

Audience: Environmental Scientists, Researchers, Environmentalists, Epidemiologists, Public Health Officials

Details: Free

`gopher://scilibx.ucsc.edu`

`gopher://gopher.ns.doc.gov`

ODA

ODA

A mailing list for topics related to the ISO 8613 standard for Office Document Architecture and Office Document Interchange Format.

Keywords: Office Document Architecture

Audience: Office Document Architects

Contact: Les Gondor
            utzoo!trigraph!oda-request

Details: Free

User Info: To subscribe to the list, send an e-mail message requesting a subscription to the URL address below. To send a message to the entire list, address it to: utzoo!@trigraph!oda-request

`mailto:utzoo!trigraph!oda-request`

OE-CALL: Old English Computer-Assisted Language Learning Newsletter

OE-CALL: Old English Computer-Assisted Language Learning Newsletter

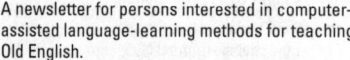

A newsletter for persons interested in computer-assisted language-learning methods for teaching Old English.

Keywords: Old English, Computer Assisted Instruction

Audience: English Teachers, Educators

Contact: Clare Lees, Patrick W. Conner
            mailto:u47c2@wvnvm.bitnet

Details: Free

`mailto:lees@fordmurh.bitnet`

Office Document Architecture

ODA

A mailing list for topics related to the ISO 8613 standard for Office Document Architecture and Office Document Interchange Format.

Keywords: Office Document Architecture

Audience: Architects

Contact: Les Gondor
            utzoo!trigraph!oda-request

Details: Free

User Info: To subscribe to the list, send an e-mail message requesting a subscription to the URL address below. To send a message to the entire list, address it to: utzoo!@trigraph!oda-request

`mailto:utzoo!trigraph!oda-request`

Office of Environmental Safety and Health, Department of Energy

Office of Environmental Safety and Health, Department of Energy

Gopher for resources pertaining to health and environmental safety.

Keywords: Health, Environmental Safety

Sponsor: Department of Energy (US)

Audience: Epidemiologists, Public Health Officials, General Public

Details: Free

`gopher://gopher.ns.doc.gov`

Offroad

Offroad

Discusses and shares experiences with four-wheel and off-road adventurers, including driving tips, vehicle modifications, and anything else related to four-wheeling. This list is specifically designed for four-wheel-drive vehicle owners, users, or enthusiasts. Discussions center around technical and mechanical matters, driving techniques, and trip reports.

Keywords: Autmobils

Audience: Automobile Enthusiasts

Contact: Stefan Roth
            offroad-request@ai.gtri.gatech.edu

Details: Free

User Info: To subscribe to the list, send an e-mail message requesting a subscription to the URL address below. To send a message to the entire list, address it to: offroad@ai.gtri.gatech.edu

`mailto:offroad-request@ai.gtri.gatech.edu`

Oglasna Deska

Oglasna Deska

Oglasna Deska (bulletin board) consists of transcripts taken from SLON, which is a nickname for a Decnet connecting several computers in Slovenia. There is a conference similar to a Usenet newsgroup running under SLON and the articles and replies are occasionally saved and sent to the world. The topics cover a wide area.

Keywords: Slovenia, SLON, Usenet

Audience: Slovenians, Croatians, Serbians

Contact: Dean Mozetic
oglasna-deska@krpan.arnes.si

Details: Free

User Info: To subscribe to the list, send an e-mail message requesting a subscription to the URL address below. To send a message to the entire list, address it to: oglasna-deka@krpan.arnes.si

Notes: The topics covered are equivalent to Usenet newsgroups such as politics, automobiles, humor, computer networks, climbing, and miscellaneous investments.

`mailto:oglasna-deska@krpan.arnes.si`

Ogphre - SunSITE

Ogphre - SunSITE

A collection of Internet resources organized by subject. Particular strengths include agriculture, religious texts, poetry, creative writing, and US politics. The ftp site has a set of more general Internet guides.

Keywords: Agriculture, Politics (US), Religion, Internet, Poetry

Sponsor: The University of North Carolina - Chapel Hill and Sun Microsystems, USA

Audience: General Public, Internet Surfers, Researchers

Contact: Darlene Fladager, Elizabeth Lyons
Darlene_Fladager@unc.edu
Elizabeth_Lyons@unc.edu

`gopher://sunsite.unc.edu`

`ftp://sunsite.unc.edu`

Ohio

Oh-motss

The oh-motss (Ohio Members of the Same Sex) mailing list is for open discussion of lesbian, gay, and bisexual issues in and affecting Ohio. The mailing list is not moderated. It is open to all, regardless of location or sexuality. The subscriber list is known only to the list owner.

Keywords: Gays, Lesbians, Ohio, Bisexuality

Audience: Gays, Lesbians

Contact: oh-motss-request@cps.udayton.edu

Details: Free

User Info: To subscribe to the list, send an e-mail message requesting a subscription to the URL address below. To send a message to the entire list, address it to: oh-motss@cps.udayton.edu

`mailto:oh-motss-request@cps.udayton.edu`

Ohio

Provides access to Ohio State Supreme Court Opinions and Ohio 8th District Court Opinions.

Keywords: Ohio, Law

Sponsor: Case Western University Freenet, Youngstown University Freenet

Audience: Lawyers, General Public, Ohio Residents

Details: Free

`telnet://ytn.ysu.edu`

Cleveland Sports

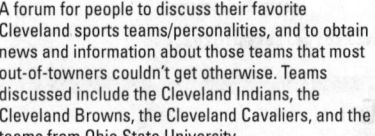

A forum for people to discuss their favorite Cleveland sports teams/personalities, and to obtain news and information about those teams that most out-of-towners couldn't get otherwise. Teams discussed include the Cleveland Indians, the Cleveland Browns, the Cleveland Cavaliers, and the teams from Ohio State University.

Keywords: Cleveland, Sports, Ohio State Universiry

Audience: Cleveland Sports Enthusiasts, Sports Enthusiasts, Cleveland Residents

Contact: Richard Kowicki
aj755@cleveland.freenet.edu

Details: Free

User Info: To subscribe to the list, send an e-mail message requesting a subscription to the URL address below.

`mailto:aj755@cleveland.freenet.edu`

Friends of Ohio State

A forum for alumni and other friends of Ohio State University.

Keywords: Ohio

Audience: Ohio State University Alumni

Contact: Jerry Canterbury
antivirus@aol.com

Details: Free

User Info: To subscribe to the list, send an e-mail message requesting a subscription to the URL address below. To send a message to the entire list, address it to: antivirus@aol.com

`mailto:antivirus@aol.com`

Old English

OE-CALL: Old English Computer-Assisted Language Learning Newsletter

A newsletter for persons interested in computer-assisted language-learning methods for teaching Old English.

Keywords: Old English, Computer Assisted Instruction

Audience: English Teachers, Educators

Contact: Clare Lees, Patrick W. Conner
mailto:u47c2@wvnvm.bitnet

Details: Free

`mailto:lees@fordmurh.bitnet`

Old Testament

Bible (King James Version)

The Bible (King James Version) includes the complete text of the modern Thomas Nelson revision of the 1769 edition of the King James version of the Bible.

Keywords: Bible, Religion, Christianity

Sponsor: Thomas Nelson Publishers, Nashville, TN, USA

Audience: Christians, Theologians, Historians, Moralists

Profile: The King James version originated from translations ordered by King James of England in 1604 at the Hampton Court Conference. Both the Old and New Testaments are included in this version. Records in the database represent both chapters and verses.

Contact: Dialog in the US at (800) 334-2564, Dialog internationally at country-specific locations.

Details: Costs

User Info: To subscribe, contact Dialog directly.

`telnet://dialog.com`

Olympics

Olympic Games 1994 at Lillehammer

News, results, and updates every 15 minutes, as well as archive images, from the 1994 Winter Olympic Games at Lillehammer, Norway.

Keywords: Olympics, Sports, Winter Games

Sponsor: Sun Microsystem, Skrivervik Data AS, Oslonett AS, Norsk Telegrambyra

A
B
C
D
E
F
G
H
I
J
K
L
M
N
O
P
Q
R
S
T
U
V
W
X
Y
Z

A
B
C
D
E
F
G
H
I
J
K
L
M
N
O
P
Q
R
S
T
U
V
W
X
Y
Z

Audience: General Public, Journalists, Skiers, Skaters, Winter Sports Fans

Profile: This server offers news and results on all the Olympic events in Lillehammer plus a chronological list of all events, a complete schedule day by day, and a very large archive of images. Also flash messages from NTB, a Norwegian news wire, and the opportunity to search in the NTB database.

Contact: oslonett@oslonett.no

`http://www.sun.com`

OlymPuck

★

This list is for the discussion of Olympic ice hockey. Discussions concerning players, coaches, teams, and games are welcome and are encouraged. Related topics, such as the interaction between the Olympic competition and college or NHL hockey, are also discussed.

Keywords: Olympics, Hockey

Audience: Hockey Players, Olympics Enthusiasts, Hockey Enthusiasts

Details: Free

User Info: To subscribe to the list, send an e-mail message to the URL address below, consisting of a single line reading:

TAB olympuck YourFirstName YourLastName

To send a message to the entire list, address it to: olympuck@maine.maine.edu

`mailto:listserv@maine.maine.edu`

rec.sport.olympics

★

A Usenet newsgroup providing information and discussion about the summer Olympics Games.

Keywords: Olympics, Summer Sports

Audience: Olympic Enthusiasts

User Info: To subscribe to this Usenet newsgroup, you need access to a newsreader.

`news:rec.sport.olympics`

OMD

OMD (Orchestral Manoeuvres In The Dark)

★

The OMD list is a forum for discussions about the English pop band Orchestral Manoeuvres In The Dark, which often incorporate modern dance elements into its music. The discussions are not moderated but they should have something to do with the band or with ex-band members.

Keywords: Modern Dance, Pop Music

Audience: Pop Music Enthusiasts

Contact: Dave Datta omd-request@cs.uwp.edu

Details: Free

User Info: To subscribe to the list, send an e-mail message requesting a subscription to the URL address below. To send a message to the entire list, address it to: omd@cs.uwp.edu

Notes: The list is available as a daily digest and reflector. Archives are stored at ftp.uwp.edu.

`mailto:omd-request@cs.uwp.edu`

On-this-day

On-this-day

★

Subscribers receive a daily listing of notable birthdays, events, religious holidays, astronomical events, and other items of interest.

Keywords: Calendars

Audience: General Public

Contact: Wayne Geiser geiser@pictel.com

Details: Free

User Info: To subscribe to the list, send an e-mail message requesting a subscription to the URL address below. To send a message to the entire list, address it to: geiser@pictel.com

`mailto:geiser@pictel.com`

On-u

On-u

★

This mailing list encourages discussions related to Adrian Sherwood's On-U Sound label and to the artists who record on it, including Tack>>Head, Gary Clail, The Dub Syndicate, African Head Charge, Bim Sherman and Mark Stewart.

Keywords: Music, Musicians

Audience: Musicians, Music Enthusiasts

Contact: Ben Golding on-u-request@connect.com.au

Details: Free

User Info: To subscribe to the list, send an e-mail message requesting a subscription to the URL address below. To send a message to the entire list, address it to: on-u@connect.com.au

`mailto:on-u@connect.com.au`

Online Books

Electronic Books

A collection of books available as ASCII text files, including classics of antiquity (Aristotle, Virgil, Sophocles, the Bible), as well as more contemporary works of fiction and nonfiction by authors ranging from Dostoevsky to Martin Luther King, Jr.

Keywords: Books, Online Books, Literature (Contemporary), Literature (General)

Sponsor: The Blacksburg Electronic Village (BEV) at Virginia Tech

Audience: General Public, Historians

Contact: BEV Gopher Administrators gopher@gopher.vt.edu

`http://marketplace.com/0/OBS`

Online BookStore (OBS)

Offers full text (fiction and nonfiction) in a variety of electronic formats, free and for a fee.

Keywords: Online Books, Books, ShareWord, Fiction, Nonfiction Books

Sponsor: Editorial Inc./OBS

Audience: General Public, Reading Enthusiasts

Profile: Started in 1992, the OBS offers a variety of full-text titles.

Contact: Laura Fillmore laura@editorial.com

Details: Costs, Moderated, Images, Multimedia

User Info: To subscribe to the list, send an e-mail message requesting a subscription to the URL address below.

`http://marketplace.com/0/obs`

Online Career Center

Online Career Center

The Online Career Center gopher provides access to job listings and employment information to member companies and to the public.

Keywords: Employment, Internships

Sponsor: Online Career Center

Audience: Job Seekers

Profile: Online Career Center is a not-for-profit organization funded by its member companies. It is devoted to distributing and exchanging employment and career information between its member companies, human resource professionals, and prospective employees.

Contact: OCC Operator occ@msen.com

`gopher://gopher.msen.com`

Online Radio

Online Radio

Transcripts and promotional information from Online Radio, a weekly radio program of Perth's Curtin University devoted to reporting the latest developments in the computing world.

Keywords: Computing, Internet, Radio

Sponsor: Curtin University Computing Center, Perth, Australia

Audience: Computer Users

Contact: Onno Benschop
online@info.curtin.edu.au

`gopher://ob1.curtin.edu.au`

Online Services

Women's Wire

Women's Wire is an online interactive network focusing on women's issues and interests.

Keywords: Networking, Women's Issues, Online Services

Audience: Women, Internet Users

Profile: This service acts as an international clearinghouse for resources and networking on a broad range of topics including news, politics, careers, education, parenting, health, and arts. Provides e-mail and access to thousands of resources, including Usenet newsgroups.

Details: Costs

Access via an easy-to-use graphical interface for Macintosh and Windows platforms, or a text-based interface for DOS and Unix platforms. Local access numbers available throughout the US and in most countries.

`mailto:info@wwire.net`

Online-dict

Online-dict

A mailing list devoted to a discussion of online dictionaries and related issues including installation, modification, and maintenance of their databases, search engines, and user interfaces.

Keywords: Dictionaries, Information Technology, Lexicology

Audience: Librarians, Information Scientists, Systems Operators

Contact: Jack Lynch
jlynch@dept.english.upenn.edu

Details: Free

User Info: To subscribe, send an e-mail message to the URL address below consisting of a single line reading:

SUB online-dict YourFirstName YourLastName.

To send a message to the entire list, address it to: online-dict@dept.english.upenn.edu

`mailto:listserv@dept.english.upenn.edu`

OPACS

ELISA (Electronic Library Service)

An information delivery service of the Library of the Australian National University.

Keywords: OPAC System, Australia

Sponsor: Australian National University

Audience: General Public

Profile: This information delivery service contains Australian mirrors of major gopher directories, and is a national entry point for Australian gopher services.

Contact: infodesk@info.anu.edu.au

Details: Free

`gopher://info.anu.edu.au`

OLIS (Oxford University Library Information Service) Gopher

OLIS is a network of libraries. It contains all the books from the English, Modern Languages, Social Studies, and Hooke libraries. It also contains books and journals cataloged since September 1988 in the Bodleian and Dependant libraries and the Taylor Institution. Books can be searched in any OLIS library from any location.

Keywords: Libraries, United Kingdom, Europe, IPACS

Audience: Researchers

Contact: jose@olis.lib.ox.ac.uk

Details: Free

`gopher://gopher.lib.ox.ac.uk/00/Info/OLIS`

Hytelnet

A hypertext database of publicly accessible Internet sites.

Keywords: Internet Tools, Hytelnet

Audience: Internet Surfers

Profile: Hytelnet currently lists over 1,400 sites, including libraries, campus-wide information systems, Gopher, WAIS, and WWW systems, and Freenets.

Contact: Earl Fogel
earl.fogel@usask.ca

Details: Free

Notes: File is: pub/hytelnet/README

`ftp://ftp.usask.ca`

LOCIS (LIBRARY Of CONGRESS INFORMATION SYSTEM)

The Library of Congress (LC) telnet service is a Campus-Wide Information System that combines the vast collection of information available about the Library, with easy access to diverse electronic resources over the Internet. Its goal is to serve the staff of LC, as well as the U.S. Congress and constituents throughout the world.

Keywords: Information Retrieval, Libraries

Sponsor: Library of Congress, Washington, D.C., USA

Audience: Reseachers, Students, Librarians

Contact: LC MARVEL Design Team
lcmarvel@loc.gov

Notes: The Library of Congress (LC) Machine-Assisted Realization of the Virtual Electronic Library (MARVEL) also exists as a gopher site: gopher://marvel.loc.gov

`telnet://locis.loc.gov`

MELVYL Library System

MELVYL is the University of California's catalog of books and periodicals for the university and the California State Library. It also permits access to database systems around the world.

Keywords: Libraries, Databases, OPACS, Internet Surfers

Audience: General Interest, Students, Teachers, Librarians

Producer: University of California

Contact: Genny Engel, MELVYL System Users Services
email:gen@dla.ucop.edu

Profile: The MELVYL system is a centralized information system that can be reached from terminals in libraries at all nine campuses of the University of California. The system can also be reached by any terminal microcomputer with dialup access to UC computers connected to the MELVYL system. The MELVYL system includes a library catalog database, a periodicals database, article citation databases, and other files. A large number of other libraries and database systems are also accessible from MELVYL.

Details: Free

Notes: All these databases are searched using the same basic commands.

`telnet://melvyl.ucop.edu`

A
B
C
D
E
F
G
H
I
J
K
L
M
N
O
P
Q
R
S
T
U
V
W
X
Y
Z

A
B
C
D
E
F
G
H
I
J
K
L
M
N
O
P
Q
R
S
T
U
V
W
X
Y
Z

OLIS (Oxford University Library Information Service) Gopher

OLIS is a network of libraries. It contains all the books from the English, Modern Languages, Social Studies, and Hooke libraries. It also contains books and journals cataloged since September 1988 in the Bodleian and Dependant libraries and the Taylor Institution. Books can be searched in any OLIS library from any location.

Keywords: Libraries, United Kingdom, Europe
Audience: Library Users
Contact: jose@olis.lib.ox.ac.uk
Details: Free

`gopher://gopher.lib.ox.ac.uk/00/Info/OLIS`

Yale Directory of Internet Libraries

An online directory of international library catalogs with

Keywords: Libraries
Sponsor: Yale University, New Haven, Connecticut, USA
Audience: General Audience
Profile: The Yale Directory of Internet Libraries is a comprehensive
Notes: The Yale Directory of Internet Libraries is in English, but the

`gopher://gophlib@gopher.yale.edu`

Open Computing Facility (OCF) Gopher, Sports Section

Open Computing Facilty (OCF) Gopher, Sports Section

A gopher server offering access to information about a number of sporting activities.

Keywords: Sports, Fitness
Sponsor: Open Computing Facility, University of California, Berkeley
Audience: Sports Enthusiasts, Fitness Enthusiasts
Profile: This gopher has information on various sports, including football, cricket, skiing, windsurfing, and basketball, as well as links to WWW. Resources include schedules for some professional and collegiate sports, as well as FAQs and other miscellaneous information.

Contact: general-manager@ocf.berkeley.edu
Details: Free

`gopher://gopher.ocf.berkeley.edu/11/gopherspace`

Open Government Pilot

Open Government Pilot

This web site provides information concerning the Canadian government, including information on Canadian infrastructure, industry, communications, provinces, and parliament.

Keywords: Canada, Government (International)
Sponsor: Canadian Federal Government
Audience: Canadians, Educators, Students
Details: Free

`http://debra.dgbt.doc.ca/opengov`

Open Government Project (Canada)

Open Government Project (Canada)

This site provides online audio-visual and text information on the Canadian government.

Keywords: Canada, Government (International)
Sponsor: Directorate of Communications Development, Industry Canada, Canada
Audience: Canadians, Government Officials, Journalists
Profile: This bilingual (French/English) site has detailed information on members of the Canadian Senate and House of Commons, as well as Supreme Court rulings and biographies of the justices. It features a number of pictures, maps, and links to other Canadian information servers.
Contact: Tyson Macaulay tyson.macaulay@crc.doc.ca

`http://debra.dgbt.doc.ca/ogp.html`

`gopher://debra.dgbt.doc.ca/open_government_project`

Opera

The University of Kansas Library

The library's holdings are large and wide-ranging and contain significant collections in many fields.

Keywords: Botany, Chinese Studies, Cartography (History of), Kansas, Opera, Ornithology, Joyce (James), Yeats (William Butler), Walpole (Sir Robert, Collections of)

Audience: General Public, Researchers, Librarians, Document Delivery Professionals
Contact: John S. Miller
Details: Free
User Info: Expect: Username, Send: relay <cr>

`telnet://kuhub.cc.ukans.edu`

Operating Systems

Bugs-386bsd

This list is for 386bsd bugs, patches, and ports.

Keywords: Operating Systems, 386bsd
Audience: Computer Operators, Computer Scientists, Computer Engineers
Contact: bugs-386bsd-request@ms.uky.edu
Details: Free
User Info: To subscribe to the list, send an e-mail message requesting a subscription to the URL address below. To send a message to the entire list, address it to:

bugs-386bsd@ms.uky.edu

Notes: Requirement to join: an interest in actively working on 386bsd to improve the operating system for use by yourself and others.

`mailto:bugs-386bsd-request@ms.uky.edu`

Std-UNIX

Discussion of UNIX standards, particularly the IEEE P1003 Portable Operating System Environment draft standard.

Keywords: UNIX, Operating Systems
Audience: UNIX Users
Contact: Sean Eric Fagan sef@uunet.uu.net
Details: Free, Moderated
User Info: To subscribe to the list, send an e-mail message requesting a subscription to the URL address below.

`mailto:sef@uunet.uu.net`

UNIX-wizards

Distribution list for people maintaining UNIX machines.

Keywords: UNIX, Operating Systems
Audience: UNIX System Administrators
Contact: Mike Muuss mike@brl.mil
Details: Free
User Info: To subscribe to the list, send an e-mail message requesting a subscription to the URL address below.

`mailto:UNIX-wizards-request@brl.mil`

Operlist

Operlist ★

A discussion list for everything having to do with IRC (Internet Relay Chat). Its main purpose is irc routing discussions, protocol discussions, and announcements of new versions of IRC clients and servers.

Keywords: irc

Audience: irc Users

Contact: Helen Trillian Rose
operlist-request@eff.org

Details: Free

User Info: To subscribe to the list, send an e-mail message requesting a subscription to the URL address below. To send a message to the entire list, address it to: operlist@eff.org

`mailto:operlist@eff.org`

Optics

CVNet (Color and Vision Network) ★

The network provides a means of communications for scientists working in biological color and/or vision research. Members' e-mail addresses are maintained and sent to others in the network. CVNet distributes notices of jobs, meetings, and some other special announcements to all registrants. Members can post bulletins, announcements, and so on.

Keywords: Optics, Biological Research, Psychology

Sponsor: York University, North York, Ontario, Canada

Audience: Psychologists, Color/Vision Researchers

Contact: Peter K. Kaiser
cvnet@vm1.yorkU.ca

Details: Free

User Info: To subscribe, send an e-mail message requesting a subscription to the URL address below.

`mailto:cvnet@vm1.yorkU.ca`

University of Rochester Library ★★

The library's holdings are large and wide-ranging and contain significant collections in many fields.

Keywords: Architecture, Art History, Photography, Literature (Asian), Lasers, Geology, Statistics, Optics, Medieval Studies

Audience: Researchers, Students, General Public

Details: Free

User Info: Expect: Login; Send: Library

`telnet://128.151.226.71`

ORA-NEWS

ORA-NEWS ★

Announcements from O'Reilly & Associates, publishers of books about the Internet, UNIX and other open systems. Other products and services include The Global Network Navigator (an interactive online magazine) and Internet in a Box. It's gatewayed to the biz.oreilly.announce Usenet newsgroup.

Keywords: Internet, UNIX, Usenet

Audience: Internet Surfers, Usenet Users, UNIX Users

Contact: listown@online.ora.com

Details: Free, Moderated

User Info: To subscribe to the list, send an e-mail message requesting a subscription to the URL address below. To send a message to the entire list, address it to: ora-news@online.ora.com

`mailto:listproc@online.ora.com`

Oregon

Oregon-news ★

Mailing list of people organizing against the Oregon Citizens' Alliance. This list will carry news of lawsuits, rallies, events, votes, and so on, that take place in the state of Oregon.

Keywords: Oregon

Audience: Oregonians, Activists

Contact: oregon-news-request@vector.intercon.com

Details: Free

User Info: To subscribe to the list, send an e-mail message requesting a subscription to the URL address below. To send a message to the entire list, address it to: oregon-news@vector.intercon.com

`mailto:oregon-news-request@vector.intercon.com`

Orienteering

Orienteering ★

Discusses all aspects of the sport of orienteering.

Keywords: Orienteering

Audience: Orienteering Enthusiasts

Contact: Mitch Collinsworth
orienteering-request@graphics.cornell.edu

Details: Free

User Info: To subscribe to the list, send an e-mail message requesting a subscription to the URL address below. To send a message to the entire list, address it to: orienteering@graphics.cornell.edu

`mailto:orienteering@graphics.cornell.edu`

Origami

Origami ★

This unmoderated mailing list is for discussion of all facets of origami, the Japanese art of paper folding. Topics include bibliographies, folding techniques, display ideas, descriptions of new folds, creativity, materials, organizations, computer representations of folds, and so on.

Keywords: Origami

Audience: Origami Enthusiasts

Contact: origami-l-request@nstn.ns.ca

Details: Free

Archives available by anonymous ftp from rugcis.rug.nl Start ftp: ftp rugcis.rug.nl

User Info: Expect: blogin, Send: anonymous; Expect: password, Send: your Internet address. Change dir: cd origami.

`mailto:origami-l-request@nstn.ns.ca`

Ornithology

The University of Kansas Library ★★

The library's holdings are large and wide-ranging and contain significant collections in many fields.

Keywords: Botany, Chinese Studies, Cartography (History of), Kansas, Opera, Ornithology, Joyce (James), Yeats (William Butler), Walpole (Sir Robert, Collections of)

Audience: General Public, Researchers, Librarians, Document Delivery Professionals

Contact: John S. Miller

Details: Free

User Info: Expect: Username, Send: relay <cr>

`telnet://kuhub.cc.ukans.edu`

TitNeT Titnews Titnotes ★★★

The network of the International Tit Society (TITS),

Keywords: Ornithology, Birds

Sponsor: International Tit Society

Audience: Bird Watchers

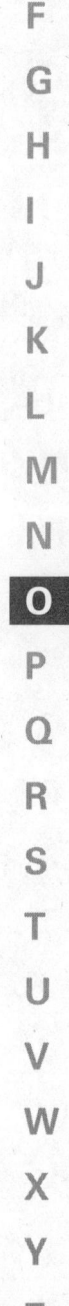

A
B
C
D
E
F
G
H
I
J
K
L
M
N
O
P
Q
R
S
T
U
V
W
X
Y
Z

Profile: The network of the International Tit Society (TITS), Titnet posts three formal series: 1) TITNET is the listing of e-mail subscribers, and includes their e-mail addresses, institutional affiliations, and research interests. 2) TITNEWS is the forum for exchange concerning academic activities, and consists of single-topic issues and multiple announcements. 3) TITNOTES is the forum for exchange of information about tits (and other hole-nesting birds).

Contact: Jack P. Hailman
jhailman@vms.macc.wisc.edu.

Details: Free

User Info: To subscribe, send an e-mail message requesting a subscription to the URL address below. Provide: (1) Full name, (2) e-mail address, (3) institutional affiliation, (4) species studied, and (5) topics studied.

`mailto:jhailman@vms.macc.wisc.edu`

titnet (Paridae and Hole-nesting Bird Discussion List)

Promotes communication among scientists working on tits (Paridae) and other hole-nesting birds.

Keywords: Birds, Ornithology

Audience: Bird Watchers

Profile: Titnet is a publication listing e-mail addresses of conference members. Titnews contains announcements and discussions of activities such as bibliographic systems and hence serves as the e-mail newsletter. Titnotes contains material on the biology of the birds and hence serves as a kind of e-mail journal.

Contact: Jack P. Hailman
jhailman@macc.wisc.edu

Details: Free

User Info: To subscribe to the list, send an e-mail message requesting a subscription to the URL address below. To send a message to the entire list, address it to: jhailman@macc.wisc.edu

Notes: Send (1) full name, (2) mailing address, which is forwarded to Dr. Ficken for PARUS INTERNATIONAL, (3) e-mail address(es), (4) species studied, and (5) types of studies (population dynamics, general ecology, vocalizations, nesting, behavior, and so on.).

`mailto:jhailman@macc.wisc.edu`

OTIS (Operative Term Is Stimulate)

OTIS (Operative Term Is Stimulate)

An image-based electronic art gallery.

Keywords: Art, Graphics, Electronic Art, Animation

Audience: Graphic Artists

Profile: OTIS is a public-access library containing hundreds of images, animations, and information files.

Within the sunsite ftp, the directory is: /pub/multimedia/pictures/OTIS. Use the bin command to insure you're in binary transfer mode.

`ftp://sunsite.unc.edu`

Our-kids

Our-kids

Support for parents and others regarding care, diagnoses, and therapy for young children with developmental delays, whether or not otherwise diagnosed (e.g. CP, PDD, sensory integrative dysfunction, and so on). The name "our-kids" avoids labeling those who are, first and foremost, the special little ones in our lives.

Keywords: Parenting

Audience: Parents, Child Development Professionals

Contact: our-kids-request@oar.net

Details: Free

User Info: To subscribe to the list, send an e-mail message requesting a subscription to the URL address below. To send a message to the entire list, address it to: our-kids@oar.net

`mailto:our-kids-request@oar.net`

OUTIL (Out in Linguistics)

OUTIL (Out in Linguistics)

The list is open to lesbian, gay, bisexual and transsexual linguists and their friends. The only requirement is that you be willing to be "out" to everyone on the list. The purposes of the group are to be visible and to gather occasionally to enjoy one another's company.

Keywords: Linguistics, Gays, Lesbians, Bisexuals, Transsexuals

Audience: Linguists, Gays, Lesbians, Bisexuals, Transsexuals

Contact: Arnold Zwicky
outil-request@csli.stanford.edu

Details: Free

User Info: To subscribe to the list, send an e-mail message requesting a subscription to the URL address below. To send a message to the entire list, address it to: outil@csli.stanford.edu

`mailto:outil-request@csli.stanford.edu`

Output

Output

Newsletter of the Florida State University (FSU) Computing Center. Includes topics such as networking, microcomputing, mainframe computing, and supercomputing on campus, including use of computers in classroom and research computing at FSU.

Keywords: Networking, Microcomputing, Supercomputing

Audience: FSU Computer Science Students, Computer Users

Contact: Suzanne C. Nelson
nelson@avm.cc.fsu.edu

Details: Free

Send your request addressed to the editor.

`mailto:nelson@avm.cc.fsu.edu`

Overseas Business Reports

Overseas Business Reports

Full-text of U.S. International Trade Administration reports, discussing the economic and commercial climate in various countries around the world.

Keywords: Business, Foreign Trade, Commerce

Sponsor: U.S. Government, International Trade Administration

Audience: Business Professionals, Trade Specialists, Investors

Details: Free

`gopher://umslvma.umsl.edu/11/library/govdocs/obr`

Oysters

Oysters

For discussion of the British folk-rock band The Oyster Band and related topics.

Keywords: Folk Music

Audience: Folk Music Enthusiasts

Contact: oysters-request@blowfish.taligent.com

Details: Free

User Info: To subscribe to the list, send an e-mail message requesting a subscription to the URL address below. To send a message to the entire list, address it to: oysters@blowfish.taligent.com

`mailto:oysters-request@blowfish.taligent.com`

P

Pac-10 Sports

Pac-10-Sports

This mailing list is dedicated to discussing sports of all types that are played competitively within the Pac-10 Athletic Conference.

Keywords: Sports

Audience: Sports Enthusiasts

Contact: Cliff Slaughterbeck
crs@u.washington.edu

Details: Free

User Info: To subscribe to the list, send an e-mail message requesting a subscription to the URL address that follows.

To send a message to the entire list, address it to: crs@u.washington.edu

`mailto:crs@u.washington.edu`

Pacific

Apngowid.meet

A conference on plans by Asia Pacific regional women's groups for the United Nations Fourth World Conference on Women to be held in Beijing in September 1995.

Keywords: Women, Asia, Pacific, Feminists, Development, United Nations, World Conference on Women

Audience: Women, Feminists, Nongovernmental Organizations

Contact: AsPac Info, Docu and Communication Committee
AP-IDC@p95.f401.n751.z6.g

Details: Costs, Moderated

Establish an account on the nearest APC node. Login, type c for conferences, then type: go apngowid.meet.

For information on the nearest APC node, contact: APC International Secretariat IBASE

E-mail: apcadmin@apc.org

E-mail message to APCadmin@apc.org

`http://www.igc.apc.org/igc/`
`www.women.html`

Asia-Pacific

The database covers the business, economics, and new industries of the Pacific Rim nations, including East Asia, Southeast Asia, the Indian Subcontinent, the Middle East, Australia, and the Pacific Island nations.

Keywords: Asia, Pacific, Business, Economy

Sponsor: Aristarchus Knowledge Industries, Seattle, WA, USA

Audience: Market Researchers, Economists, Market Analysts

Profile: Records are of two types: main records consisting of abstracts or citations for journal articles and other publications; and company thesaurus records. Detailed abstracts are provided for selected journal articles, monographs, selected papers in conference proceedings, dissertations, and government documents. Shorter citations with briefer indexing are provided for a wide variety of journal articles, newspapers, government documents, and annual report publications. Asia-Pacific also includes an extensive Corporate Thesaurus subfile, which provides detailed coverage of the corporate players in the Pacific Rim, including thousands of companies traded on the stock exchanges of Southeast and East Asia.

Contact: Dialog in the US at (800) 334-2564; Dialog internationally at country-specific locations.

Details: Costs

User Info: To subscribe, contact Dialog directly.

`telnet://dialog.com`

Asian and Pacific Economic Literature

A list of economic literature covering Asia and the Pacific region.

Keywords: Asia, Pacific, Economics

Audience: Economists, Business Professionals

Details: Free

`ftp://coombs.anu.edu`

Asian Pacific Business and Marketing Resources

A forum on business and marketing in the Pacific Rim region.

Keywords: Asia, Pacific, Business, Management

Audience: Business Professionals, Market Researchers

Details: Free

`gopher://hoshi.cic.sfu.ca/11/dlam/`
`business/forum`

Packaging

PIRA - Paper, Printing and Publishing, Packaging, and Nonwovens Abstracts

Coverage of all aspects of paper, pulp, nonwovens, printing, publishing and packaging.

Keywords: Material Science, Paper, Printing, Publishing, Packaging, Nonwovens

Sponsor: PIRA International

Audience: Materials Scientists, Researchers

Profile: File contains more than 300,000 records. Special applications: company and market profiles, product and trade name searches, research and technology trends. Updated biweekly.

Contact: paul.albert@neteast.com

User Info: To subscribe, contact Orbit-Questel directly.

`telnet://orbit.com`

Pagan

Pagan

Discusses the religions, philosophy, and other aspects of paganism.

Keywords: Paganism, Religion

Audience: Pagans

Contact: Stacey Greenstein
pagan-request@drycas.club.cc.cmu.edu

Details: Free

User Info: To subscribe to the list, send an e-mail message requesting a subscription to the URL address that follows.

User Info: To send a message to the entire list, address it to:
pagan@drycas.club.cc.cmu.edu

`mailto:pagan-`
`request@drycas.club.cc.cmu.edu`

Paganism

alt.pagan

A Usenet newsgroup providing information and discussion about paganism and religion.

Keywords: Paganism, Religion

Audience: Cults, Worshippers, Religion Students

User Info: To subscribe to this Usenet newsgroup, you need access to a newsreader.

`news:alt.pagan`

Pagan

Discusses the religions, philosophy, and other aspects of paganism.

Keywords: Paganism, Religion

Audience: Pagans

Contact: Stacey Greenstein
pagan-request@drycas.club.cc.cmu.edu

Details: Free

User Info: To subscribe to the list, send an e-mail message requesting a subscription to the URL address that follows.

To send a message to the entire list, address it to:
pagan@drycas.club.cc.cmu.edu

`mailto:pagan-`
`request@drycas.club.cc.cmu.edu`

PAGEMAKER

PAGEMAKER

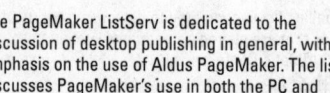

The PageMaker ListServ is dedicated to the discussion of desktop publishing in general, with emphasis on the use of Aldus PageMaker. The list discusses PageMaker's use in both the PC and Macintosh realms. The list also maintains an extensive archive of help files that are extremely useful for the modern desktop publisher.

Keywords: Desktop Publishing, Aldus Pagemaker, IBM PC, Macintosh

Audience: Desktop Publishers, Computer Users

Contact: Geoff Peters
gwp@cs.purdue.edu

Details: Free

User Info: To subscribe to the list, send an e-mail message to the URL address shown that follows consisting of a single line reading:

SUB pagemaker YourFirstName YourLastName.

To send a message to the entire list, address it to: gwp@cs.purdue.edu

`mailto:listserv@cs.purdue.edu`

Pakistan

soc.culture.pakistan

A Usenet newsgroup providing information and discussion about Pakistani people and their culture.

Keywords: Pakistan, Sociology

Audience: Sociologists, Pakistanis

Details: Free

User Info: To subscribe to this Usenet newsgroup, you need access to a newsreader.

`news:soc.culture.pakistan`

Paleography

The University of Notre Dame Library

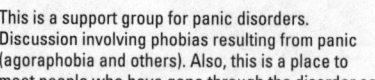

The library's holdings are large and wide-ranging and contain significant collections in many fields.

Keywords: Music (Irish), Ireland, Botany (History of), Ecology, Entomology, Parasitology, Aquatic Biology, Universities (History of), Paleography

Audience: General Public, Researchers, Librarians, Document Delivery Professionals

Details: Free

User Info: Expect: ENTER COMMAND OR HELP:, Send: library; To leave, type x on the command line and press Enter. At the ENTER COMMAND OR HELP: prompt, type bye and press Enter.

`telnet://irishmvs.cc.nd.edu`

Paleontology

UC Berkeley Museum of Paleontology and the WWW Subway

This web site provides a multimedia museum display from UC Berkeley's Museum of Paleontology. Also features an interactive Subway, a tool linking users to other museums and WWW sites around the world.

Keywords: WWW, Museums, Paleontology

Sponsor: University of California at Berkeley, Museum of Paleontology, Berkeley, California, USA

Audience: Paleontologists, Internet Surfers, General Public

Contact: David Polly, Robert Guralnick
davip@ucmp1.berkeley.edu
robg@fossil.berkeley.edu

Details: Subway

`http://ucmp1.berkeley.edu/subway.html`

Panic

Panic

This is a support group for panic disorders. Discussion involving phobias resulting from panic (agoraphobia and others). Also, this is a place to meet people who have gone through the disorder as well.

Keywords: Agoraphobia

Audience: Panic Disorder Sufferers

Contact: Panic-Request@gnu.ai.mit.edu

Details: Free

User Info: To subscribe to the list, send an e-mail message requesting a subscription to the URL address that follows.

To send a message to the entire list, address it to: panic@gnu.ai.mit.edu

`mailto:Panic-Request@gnu.ai.mit.edu`

Papa

Papa

A mailing list devoted to the discussion of the life and works of Ernest Hemingway.

Keywords: Hemingway (Ernest), Literature (American)

Audience: Ernest Hemingway Enthusiasts

Contact: Dave Gross
dgross@polyslo.calpoly.edu

Details: Free

User Info: To subscribe to the list, send an e-mail message requesting a subscription to the URL address that follows.

To send a message to the entire list, address it to: dgross@polyslo.calpoly.edu

`mailto:dgross@polyslo.calpoly.edu`

Paper

PIRA - Paper, Printing and Publishing, Packaging, and Nonwovens Abstracts

Coverage of all aspects of paper, pulp, nonwovens, printing, publishing, and packaging.

Keywords: Material Science, Paper, Printing, Publishing, Packaging, Nonwovens

Sponsor: PIRA International

Audience: Material Scientists, Researchers

Profile: File contains more than 300,000 records. Special applications: company and market profiles, product and trade name searches, research and technology trends. Updated biweekly.

Contact: paul.albert@neteast.com

User Info: To subscribe contact, Orbit-Questel directly.

`telnet://orbit.com`

Papermaking (History of)

University of Delaware Libraries (DELCAT)

The library's holdings are large and wide-ranging and contain significant collections in many fields.

Keywords: Literature (American), Hemingway (Ernest), Papermaking (History of), Chemistry (History of), Literature (Irish), Delaware

Audience: General Public, Researchers, Librarians, Document Delivery Professionals

Contact: Stuart Glogoff
epo27855@udacsvm.bitnet

Details: Free

User Info: Expect: prompt, Send: RETURN 2-3 times

`telnet://delcat.udel.edu or delcat.acs.udel.edu`

Papers (of)

Mississippi State University Library

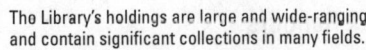

The Library's holdings are large and wide-ranging and contain significant collections in many fields.

Keywords: History (US), Forestry, Energy, Carter (Hodding, Papers of), Mississippi

Audience: General Public, Researchers, Librarians, Document Delivery Professionals

Contact: Stephen Cunetto
shc1@ra.msstate.edu

Details: Free

User Info: Expect: username, Send: msu; Expect: password, Send: library

`telnet://libserv.msstate.edu`

Papers

news.announce.conferences

A Usenet newsgroup providing information and discussion about conferences, as well as calls for papers.

Keywords: Conferences, Papers, Writing

Audience: Writers, General Public

Details: Free

User Info: To subscribe to this Usenet newsgroup, you need access to a newsreader.

`news:news.announce.conferences`

Parallel Computers

Ncube

Exchange of information among people using Ncube parallel computers.

Keywords: Ncube, Parallel Computers

Audience: Ncube Users

Contact: David Krumme
ncube-users-request@cs.tufts.edu

Details: Free

User Info: To subscribe to the list, send an e-mail message requesting a subscription to the URL address that follows.

`mailto:ncube-users-request@cs.tufts.edu`

Paranoia

alt.conspiracy

A Usenet newsgroup providing discussion about conspiracy and paranoia.

Keywords: Conspiracy, Paranoia

Audience: Paranoid Persons, General Public

User Info: To subscribe to this Usenet newsgroup, you need access to a newsreader.

`news:alt.conspiracy`

Parasitology

The University of Notre Dame Library

The library's holdings are large and wide-ranging and contain significant collections in many fields.

Keywords: Music (Irish), Ireland, Botany (History of), Ecology, Entomology, Parasitology, Aquatic Biology, Universities (History of), Paleography

Audience: General Public, Researchers, Librarians, Document Delivery Professionals

Details: Free

User Info: Expect: ENTER COMMAND OR HELP:, Send: library; To leave, type x on the command line and press Enter. At the ENTER COMMAND OR HELP: prompt, type bye and press Enter.

`telnet://irishmvs.cc.nd.edu`

Parenting

ADD-parents

A mailing list intended to provide support and information to parents of children with Attention Deficit/Hyperactivity Disorder.

Keywords: Parenting, ADD (Attention Deficit/Hyperactivity Disorder)

Audience: Parents, Educators, Health Care Providers

Contact: add-parents-request@mv.mv.com

User Info: To subscribe to the list, send an e-mail message to the URL address that follows.

To send a message to the entire list, address it to: add-parents@mv.mv.com

`mailto:add-parents-request@mv.mv.com`

A B C D E F G H I J K L M N O **P** Q R S T U V W X Y Z

A
B
C
D
E
F
G
H
I
J
K
L
M
N
O
P
Q
R
S
T
U
V
W
X
Y
Z

Moms

Moms is a list for lesbian mothers.

Keywords: Lesbian, Parenting

Audience: Lesbian Mothers, Lesbians

Contact: moms-request@qiclab.scn.rain.com

Details: Free

User Info: To subscribe to the list, send an e-mail message requesting a subscription to the URL address that follows.

`mailto:moms-request@qiclab.scn.rain.com`

Our-kids

Support for parents and others regarding care, diagnoses, and therapy for young children with developmental delays, whether or not otherwise diagnosed (that is, CP, PDD, sensory integrative dysfunction, and so on). The name "our-kids" avoids labeling those who are, first and foremost, the special little ones in our lives.

Keywords: Parenting

Audience: Parents, Child Development Professionals

Contact: our-kids-request@oar.net

Details: Free

User Info: To subscribe to the list, send an e-mail message requesting a subscription to the URL address that follows.

To send a message to the entire list, address it to: our-kids@oar.net

`mailto:our-kids-request@oar.net`

Paris

WWW Paris

A web site created as a collaborative effort among individuals in both Paris and the United States.

Keywords: Paris, Culture, Art, Travel, French, Tourism

Audience: Students, Educators, Travelers, Researchers

Profile: Contains an extensive collection of images and text regarding all of the major monuments and museums of Paris, including maps of the Metro and the RER; calendars of events and current expositions; promotional images and text relating to local department stores; there is also a visitors' section with up-to-date tourist information about hotels, restaurants, telephones, airport schedules, a basic Paris glossary, and the latest weather images. Includes an extensive collection of links to other resources about Paris and France, and a selected bibliography of history and architecture in Paris.

Contact: Norman Barth, Eric Pouliquen
nbarth@ucsd.edu
epouliq@ucsd.edu

`http://meteora.ucsd.edu/~norman/paris`

Park Rangers

Park Rangers

This list is primarily for anyone working or interested in working as a ranger (general, interpretive, and so on) for the US National Park Service. However, rangers from state and county agencies and from other countries are also welcome. The group discusses numerous topics related to this profession.

Keywords: US National Park Service, Government (US)

Audience: Park Rangers

Contact: Cynthia Dorminey
60157903@wsuvm1.csc.wsu.edu

Details: Free

User Info: To subscribe to the list, send an e-mail message requesting a subscription to the URL address that follows.

To send a message to the entire list, address it to: 60157903@wsuvm1.csc.wsu.edu

`mailto:60157903@wsuvm1.csc.wsu.edu`

ParNET

ParNET

To discuss the installation, use, and modification of ParNET, an Amiga<->Amiga networking program.

Keywords: Internet

Audience: ParNet Users

Contact: Ben Jackson
parnet-list@ben.com

Details: Free

User Info: To subscribe to the list, send an e-mail message requesting a subscription to the URL address that follows.

To send a message to the entire list, address it to: parnet-list@ben.com

`mailto:parnet-list-request@ben.com`

Partners

Partners

Advises the administration of Carnegie Mellon University, Pittsburgh, PA, through the vice-president of Human Resources (who reads the list), of developments in domestic-partnership benefits and makes recommendations about university policy regarding benefits.

Keywords: Domestic Partnerships

Audience: Carnegie Mellon Community

Contact: partners-request@cs.cmu.edu

Details: Free

User Info: To subscribe to the list, send an e-mail message requesting a subscription to the URL address that follows.

To send a message to the entire list, address it to: partners@cs.cmu.edu

`mailto:partners@cs.cmu.edu`

Partnerships

INCORPR (Corporation and Partnership Records)

The Corporation and Partnership Records (INCORP) library contains current US corporation and partnership filings.

Keywords: Corporations, Partnerships, Filings, Trademarks

Audience: Corporations, Lawyers, Researchers

Profile: The INCORP library contains current records on corporations and limited partnerships registered with the office of the Secretary or Department of State. These records include information extracted by the state's staff from articles of incorporation, annual reports, amendments, and other public filings.

Contact: Mead New Sales Group at (800) 227-4908 or (513) 859-5398 inside the US, or (513) 865-7981 for all inquiries outside the US.

User Info: To subscribe, contact Mead directly.

Notes: To examine the Nexis user guide, you can access it at the ftp site of the University of Texas at Austin at the URL address: ftp://ftp.cc.utexas.edu

The files are in: /pub/ref-services/LEXIS

`telnet://nex.meaddata.com`

`http://www.meaddata.com`

Pascal

info-Pascal

Discussions of any Pascal implementation, from mainframe to micro, for Pascal program users.

Keywords: Programming, Pascal

Audience: Pascal Programmers

Contact: Hernan Lobos *Mitzio*
hlobos@utfsm.bitnet

Details: Free

User Info: To subscribe to the list, send an e-mail message requesting a subscription to the URL address that follows.

`info-Pascal@brl.mil`

Patents

Chinapats

Covers all patent applications published under the patent law of People's Republic of China.

Keywords: Patents, Intellectual Property, Trademarks

Sponsor: European Patent Office

Audience: Patent Attorneys, Patent Agents, Librarians, Researchers

Profile: English language abstracts are included for all applications filed by Chinese applicants. Contains more than 59,000 records. Updated monthly.

Contact: paul.albert@neteast.com

User Info: To subscribe, contact Orbit-Questel directly.

`telnet://orbit.com`

CLAIMS

Provides access to over 2.3 million U.S. patents issued by the U.S. Patent and Trademark Office.

Keywords: Patents, Intellectual Property, Trademarks

Sponsor: IFI/Plenum Data Corporation

Audience: Patent Attorneys, Patent Agents, Librarians, Researchers

Profile: Chemical patents are covered from 1950 forward; mechanical and electrical patents from 1963 forward; design patents from 1980 forward.

Contact: paul.albert@neteast.com

User Info: To subscribe, contact Orbit-Questel directly.

`telnet://orbit.com`

Derwent World Patents Index

Derwent World Patents Index and Derwent World Patents Index Latest contain data from nearly 3 million inventions represented in more than 6 million patent documents from 33 patent-issuing authorities around the world.

Keywords: Patents, Inventions

Sponsor: Derwent Publications, Ltd., London, UK

Audience: Science Researchers

Profile: In addition to bibliographic information, the basic patent record includes the full abstract (for new patents issued from 1981 to the present), informative title, International Patent Classification codes, and Derwent subject codes. These files also provide access to equivalent patents, grouped together by patent family in the basic patent record. The use of manual and fragmentation codes is restricted to Derwent subscribers, in accordance with their subscription level.

Pharmaceutical patents are included from 1963 to the present, agricultural chemical patents from 1965 to the present, and polymer and plastics patents from 1966 to the present. Coverage of all chemical patents began in 1970; coverage of all patents, irrespective of subject, began in 1974.

Contact: Dialog in the US at (800) 334-2564, Dialog internationally at country-specific locations.

User Info: To subscribe, contact Dialog directly.

Notes: Coverage: 1963 to the present; updated weekly (file 351) and monthly (file 350).

`telnet://dialog.com`

Derwent World Patents Index/API Merged

Patents covering petroleum processes, fuels, lubricants, petrochemicals, pipelines, tankers, storage, pollution control, synthetic fuels, synthesis gas, C1 chemistry, and other technologies.

Keywords: Petroleum, Patents

Sponsor: Derwent Publications, Ltd. and the American Petroleum Institute Central Abstracting and Indexing Service

Audience: Researchers, Librarians

Profile: Unique features include patent family searching, petrochemical patents searching, deep chemical/petroleum indexing.

Contact: paul.albert@neteast.com

User Info: To subscribe, contact Orbit-Questel directly.

`telnet://orbit.com`

European Patents Fulltext

European Patents Fulltext contains the complete text of European published applications and patents and European PCT published applications.

Keywords: Patents, Europe, Law (International)

Sponsor: European Patent Office, Vienna, Austria

Audience: Patent Researchers

Profile: It contains bibliographic, administrative, and legal information from the European Patent Registry. Records have abstracts, patent specifications including all claims, and the search report, including cited patents and other references.

Contact: Dialog in the US at (800) 334-2564, Dialog internationally at country-specific locations.

User Info: To subscribe, contact Dialog directly.

Notes: Coverage: 1978 to the present; updated weekly.

`telnet://dialog.com`

Family and Legal Status (INPADOC)

The database includes a list of patents issued in 56 countries and patenting organizations.

Keywords: Patents, Technlogy

Sponsor: European Patent Office (EPO), Vienna, Austria

Audience: Patent Researchers, Inventors

Profile: INPADOC contains bibliographic data consisting of title, inventor, and assignee for most patents. In addition, this file brings together information about priority-application numbers, countries and dates, and equivalent patents (that is, patent families) for patents. This file also contains the legal status information for patents in some countries.

Contact: Dialog in the US at (800) 334-2564, Dialog internationally at country-specific locations.

User Info: To subscribe, contact Dialog directly.

Notes: Coverage: April 1968 to the present; updated weekly.

`telnet://dialog.com`

IMSWorld Patents International

The database provides an analysis of the product patent position of more than 1,000 pharmaceutical compounds, either marketed or in active R&D.

Keywords: Patents, Pharmaceuticals

Sponsor: IMSWorld Publications, Ltd., London, UK

Audience: Patent Researchers

Profile: Each record includes an evaluated entry for all international patents, estimated patent expiration dates, therapeutic class, laboratory code, patent number issued by country, published application number by country, extensions to patent terms for the US and Japan where granted, and US marketing exclusivity information if applicable.

Contact: Dialog in the US at (800) 334-2564, Dialog internationally at country-specific locations.

User Info: To subscribe, contact Dialog directly.

Notes: Coverage: Current; updated monthly.

`telnet://dialog.com`

INPADOC/INPANEW

Patent documents issued by more than fifty national and international patent offices.

Keywords: Patents, Intellectual Property, Trademarks

Sponsor: European Patent Office

Audience: Patent Attorneys, Patent Agents, Librarians, Researchers

Profile: Bibliographic information is searchable, including inventor names, assignees, international patent classification codes, and in most cases, titles, as well as complete publications and application data. Contains approximately 20 million records. Updated weekly.

Contact: paul.albert@neteast.com

User Info: To subscribe, contact Orbit-Questel directly.

`telnet://orbit.com`

JAPIO

Comprehensive source of unexamined Japanese patent applications.

Keywords: Patents, Intellectual Property, Trademarks

Sponsor: Japan Patent Information Organization

Audience: Patent Attorneys, Patent Agents, Librarians, Researchers

Profile: More than 2.8 million records covering all technologies. Unique features include English-language abstracts for many Japanese patent applications

Contact: paul.albert@neteast.com

User Info: To subscribe, contact Orbit-Questel directly.

`telnet://orbit.com`

Legal Status

Records thousands of types of actions that can affect the legal status of a patent document after it is published and after the patent is granted.

Keywords: Patents, Intellectual Property, Trademarks

Sponsor: European Patent Office

Audience: Patent Attorneys, Patent Agents, Librarians, Researchers

Profile: Information about the disposition of patent applications published under the Patent Cooperation Treaty by the World Intellectual Property Organizations is included as well. Contains more than 8 million records. Updated weekly.

Contact: paul.albert@neteast.com

User Info: To subscribe, contact Orbit-Questel directly.

`telnet://orbit.com`

LEXPAT (Patents US)

The LEXPAT library contains the full text of US patents issued since 1975, the US Patent and Trademark Office Manual of Classification, and the Index to US Patent Classification. The approximately 1,500 patents added to the library each week appear online within four days of their issue.

Keywords: Patents, Inventors, Assignees, Litigants

Audience: Lawyers, Business Researchers, Analysts, Entrepreneurs

Profile: LEXPAT may be searched by individual files for the full text of utility, design or plant patents, or you can combine the files in one 'omni' search. The Manual, Index and Class files can be used to supplement your full-text patent searches. LEXPAT is a valuable tool for both patent professionals and for anyone who needs to access to technical information. More than 80 percent of the information contained in patents is unavailable in any other form.

Contact: Mead New Sales Group at (800) 227-4908 or (513) 859-5398 inside the US, or (513) 865-7981 for all inquiries outside the US.

User Info: To subscribe, contact Mead directly.

To examine the Nexis user guide, you can access it at the ftp site of the University of Texas at Austin at the following URL address: ftp://ftp.cc.utexas.edu

The files are in: /pub/ref-services/LEXIS

`telnet://nex.meaddata.com`

`http://www.meaddata.com`

Patent Act of the US

This resource contains full-text documentation regarding the US Patent Act (Title 35, United States Code, Sections 1 - 376).

Keywords: Patents, Laws (US Federal), Government (US Federal)

Audience: Journalists, Politicians, Economists, Lawyers, Scientists

Details: Free

`http://fatty.law.cornell.edu/patent/patent.overview.html`

U.S. Patent and Trademark Office Database

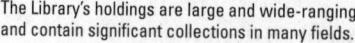

A database of patents issued in 1994 by the U.S. Patent and Trademark Office, including a searchable index.

Keywords: Patents, Databases, Inventions, Business

Sponsor: New York University School of Business

Audience: Inventors, General Public

Contact: questions@town.hall.org

`gopher://town.hall.org/patent`

University of Nevada at Reno Library

The Library's holdings are large and wide-ranging and contain significant collections in many fields.

Keywords: Basque Studies, Nevada , UN Army Map Service, Patents

Audience: General Public, Researchers, Librarians, Document Delivery Professionals

Details: Free

User Info: Expect: login, Send: wolfpac

`telnet://wolfpac.lib.unr.edu`

US Patents

Complete patent information of all claims of U.S. patents issued since 1971.

Keywords: Patents, Intellectual Property, Trademarks

Sponsor: Derwent, Inc.

Audience: Patent Attorneys, Patent Agents, Librarians, Researchers

Profile: Includes complete front page information, plus all claims of US patents issued since 1971. Merged file contains approximately 1.4 million records. Updated weekly.

Contact: paul.albert@neteast.com

User Info: To subscribe, contact Orbit-Questel directly.

`telnet://orbit.com`

PB-Cle-Raves

PB-Cle-Raves

One of several regional rave-related mailing lists, PB-Cle-Raves covers the Pittsburgh, PA, and Cleveland, OH, metropolitan areas exclusively.

Keywords: Raves

Audience: Ravers

Contact: Joe LeSesne
pb-cle-raves-request@telerama.lm.com

Details: Free

User Info: To subscribe to the list, send an e-mail message requesting a subscription to the URL address that follows.

To send a message to the entire list, address it to: pb-cle-raves@telerama.lm.com

`mailto:pb-cle-raves-request@telerama.lm.com`

Pc532

Pc532

A mailing list for people interested in the pc532 project, a National Semiconductor NS32532-based system, offered at a low cost.

Keywords: Computers, Hardware, Software

Audience: Computer Users, Software Developers

Contact: Dave Rand
pc532-request@bungi.com

Details: Free

User Info: To subscribe to the list, send an e-mail message requesting a subscription to the URL address that follows.

To send a message to the entire list, address it to: pc532@bungi.com

`mailto:pc532-request@bungi.com`

Pcbuild

Pcbuild ⭐

An open, unmoderated E-conference for discussion of PC hardware, including such topics as upgrading your PC, building your own PC, hardware problems, questions, and businesses from which to buy hardware cheaply.

Keywords: Computer Systems

Audience: PC Users

Contact: Dave Gomberg
gomberg@ucsfvm.edu

Details: Free

User Info: To subscribe to the list, send an e-mail message to the URL address that follows, consisting of a single line reading:

SUB pcbuild YourFirstName YourLastName

To send a message to the entire list, address it to: pcbuild@tsclion.trenton.edu

`mailto:listserv@tsclion.trenton.edu`

Pcgeos-list

Pcgeos-list ⭐

A discussion forum for users of PC/GEOS products, including GeoWorks Ensemble, GeoWorks Pro, GeoWorks POS, and third-party products. Topics include general information, tips, techniques, applications, and experiences.

Keywords: Computers, Software

Audience: Computer Users, Software Developers

Contact: listserv@pandora.sf.ca.us

Details: Free

User Info: To subscribe to the list, send an e-mail message to the URL address that follows, consisting of a single line reading:

SUB pcgeos-list YourFirstName YourLastName

To send a message to the entire list, address it to: pcgeos@pandora.sf.ca.us

`mailto:listserv@pandora.sf.ca.us`

Pd-games

Pd-games ⭐

A mailing list for people interested in game theory, especially Prisoner's Dilemma types of problems. Discussions include purely technical issues and questions, as well as specific scientific applications and the political and ideological aspects and consequences of game theory.

Keywords: Game Theory, Mathematics

Audience: Game Theorists, Mathematicians

Contact: Thomas Gramstad
pd-games-request@math.uio.no

Details: Free

User Info: To subscribe to the list, send an e-mail message requesting a subscription to the URL address that follows.

To send a message to the entire list, address it to: pd-games@math.uio.no

`mailto:pd-games-request@math.uio.no`

Pdp8-lovers

Pdp8-lovers ⭐

A mailing list for owners of vintage DEC (Digital Equipment Corp.) computers, especially the PDP-8 series. Discussion topics include hardware, software, and programming techniques.

Keywords: Computers, Hardware, Software

Audience: Computer Users, Product Analysts

Contact: Robert E. Seastrom
pdp8-lovers-request@mc.lcs.mit.edu

Details: Free

User Info: To subscribe to the list, send an e-mail message requesting a subscription to the URL address that follows.

To send a message to the entire list, address it to: pdp8-lovers@mc.lcs.mit.edu

`mailto:pdp8-lovers@mc.lcs.mit.edu`

Peace

activ-l ⭐⭐

A mailing list for discussion of peace, empowerment, justice, and environmental issues.

Keywords: Peace, Justice, Environment, Activism

Audience: Activists, Students

Contact: Rich Winkel
harelb@math.cornell.edu

User Info: To subscribe to the list, send an e-mail message to the URL address that follows, consisting of a single line reading:

SUB activ-l YourFirstName YourLastName.

To send a message to the entire list, address it to: active-l@mizzou1.missouri.edu

`mailto:listserv@mizzou1.missouri.edu`

GLOSAS News (Global Systems Analysis and Simulating Association) ⭐

Newsletter of GLOSAS in the US, which is dedicated to global electronic education and simulation as a tool for promoting peace and the care of the natural environment.

Keywords: Education, Simulation, Peace

Audience: Educators, Environmentalists

Contact: Anton Ljutic
anton@vax2.concordia.ca

Details: Free

User Info: To subscribe, send an e-mail message to the address that follows.

`mailto:listserv@vm1.mcgill.ca`

un.wcw.doc.eng ⭐

This is a read-only conference comprised of official UN documents for the United Nations Fourth World Conference on Women: Action for Equality, Development and Peace, scheduled to take place at the Beijing International Convention Center, Beijing, China, from 4-15 September 1995. The documents are provided by the official Conference Secretariat, are posted as received by the UN Non-Governmental Liaison Service (NGLS).

Keywords: Women, Development (International), Peace, UN, World Conference on Women

Audience: Women, Activists, Non-Governmental Organizations, Feminists

Contact: United Nations Non-Governmental Liaison Service/Edie Farwell
ngls@igc.apc.org
efarwell@igc.apc.org

Details: Costs, Moderated

User Info: Establish an account on the nearest APC node. Login, type c for conferences, then type go un.wcw.doc.eng.

For information about the nearest APC node, contact: APC International Secretariat IBASE

E-mail: apcadmin@apc.org

E-mail message to APCadmin@apc.org

`telnet://igc.apc.org`

un.wcw.doc.fra

This is a read-only conference comprised of official UN documents for the United Nations Fourth World Conference on Women: Action for Equality, Development and Peace, scheduled to take place at the Beijing International Convention Center, Beijing, China, from 4-15 September 1995. The documents are provided by the official Conference Secretariat, are posted as received by the UN Non-Governmental Liaison Service (NGLS).

Keywords: Women, Development (International), Peace, UN, World Conference on Women

Audience: Women, Activists, Non-Governmental Organizations, Feminists

Contact: United Nations Non-Governmental Liaison Service/Edie Farwell ngls@igc.apc.org or efarwell@igc.apc.org

Details: Costs, Moderated

User Info: Establish an account on the nearest APC node. Login, type c for conferences, then type go un.wcw.doc.fra. For information on the nearest APC node, contact: APC International Secretariat IBASE

E-mail: apcadmin@apc.org

E-mail message to APCadmin@apc.org

`telnet://igc.apc.org`

Pediatrics

University of Texas Health Science Center at San Antonio Library

The library's holdings are large and wide-ranging and contain significant collections in many fields.

Keywords: Allied Health, Dentistry, Nursing, Veterinary Science, Ambulatory Care, Obstetrics/Gynecology, Pediatrics

Audience: Researchers, Students, General Public

Details: Free

User Info: Expect: Login, Send: LIS

`telnet://athena.uthscsa.edu`

PEI (Prince Edward Island, Canada) Crafts Council Gopher

PEI (Prince Edward Island, Canada) Crafts Council Gopher

A gopher devoted to all manner of crafts, from weaving to glass blowing. Information includes a database of tools, services, and materials for crafts enthusiasts, as well as FAQs and pointers to other crafts resources. Also provides background on the PEI Craft Council's activities and on Prince Edward Island.

Keywords: Crafts, Hobbies, Canada

Sponsor: PEI Crafts Council, Prince Edward Island, Canada

Audience: Crafts Enthusiasts

Details: Free

`gopher://crafts-council.pe.ca`

Pen-pals

Pen-pals

This mailing list provides a forum for children to correspond with each other electronically. Although the list is not moderated, it is monitored for content and is managed by listproc.

Keywords: Computing, Children, Writing

Audience: Computer Users, Children, Student Writers

Contact: pen-pals-request@mainstream.com

Details: Free

User Info: To subscribe to the list, send an e-mail message requesting a subscription to the URL address that follows.

To send a message to the entire list, address it to: pen-pals@mainstream.com

`mailto:pen-pals@mainstream.com`

Pennsylvania

PennInfo

PennInfo is a menu-based campus-wide information system whose design offers both the novice and the experienced user access to information of interest to the University of Pennsylvania community. PennInfo currently contains more than 3,500 documents, posted by approximately 70 providers of information. A sampling of the content in PennInfo includes: University of Pennsylvania facts, available grants, fellowships, and research resources; and the entire Penn course register and course timetable.

Keywords: Pennsylvania

Sponsor: University of Pennsylvania

Audience: Researchers, Educators

Details: Free

`telnet://penninfo.upenn.edu`

PENPages

PENPages

This easy-to-use, general-interest database contains articles and brochures.

Keywords: Food, Employment, Education

Sponsor: Pennsylvania State University, PA

Audience: General Public

Notes: Expect: login; Send: your state's two-letter code (or "world" if sent from outside the USA)

`telnet://psunet.psu.edu`

People

NEWS (General News)

The General News (NEWS) library includes more than 2,300 sources. Full-text news from national and international newspapers, magazines, newsletters, and wire services and abstract information are both available.

Keywords: News, Analysis, People, Companies

Audience: Journalists, General Public

Profile: The General News (NEWS) library contains a number of publications and wire services of general interest, as well as others that specialize in particular areas of business . The NEWS library is organized into individual files, group files by source or subject, and user-defined combination files for full-text information sources. Abstracts are also available as individual files or can be searched together in one group file. The NEWS library includes such prestigious full-text sources as the New York Times and more than more than 30 major newspapers from around the US and the world.

Contact: Mead New Sales Group at (800) 227-4908 or (513) 859-5398 inside the US, or (513) 865-7981 for all inquiries outside the US.

User Info: To subscribe, contact Mead directly.

To examine the Nexis user guide, you can access it at the ftp site of the University of Texas at Austin at the following URL address: ftp://ftp.cc.utexas.edu

The files are in: /pub/ref-services/LEXIS

`telnet://nex.meaddata.com`

`http://www.meaddata.com`

People Using Networks Can Have an Impact on Government

People Using Networks Can Have an Impact on Government

Statement by community networker Anne Fallis, who emphasizes the need for easy-to-use interfaces and inexpensive access to worldwide information. She lists many examples of local communities using networking.

Keywords: Community, Networking, Activism

Audience: Activists, Policymakers, Community Leaders, Network Users

Contact: Anne Fallis
afallis@silver.sdsmt.edu

Details: Free

`http://nearnet.gnn.com/mag/articles/`
`oram/bio.fallis.html`

Performing Arts

Theater

This directory is a compilation of information resources focused on theater.

Keywords: Theater, Drama, Performing Arts

Audience: Theater Personnel, Drama Personnel, Performers

Contact: Deborah Torres, Martha Vander Kolk
dtorres@umich.edu
mjvk@umich.edu

Details: Free

`ftp://una.hh.lib.umich.edu/70/`
`inetdirsstacks/theater:torresmjvk`

Williams College Library

The library's holdings are large and wide-ranging and contain significant collections in many fields.

Keywords: Americana, Graphic Arts, Printing (History of), Performing Arts, Printing

Audience: General Public, Researchers, Librarians, Document Delivery Professionals

Contact: Jim Cubit

Details: Free

User Info: Expect: Mitek Server..., Send: Enter or Return; Expect: prompt, Send: hollis

`telnet://library.williams.edu`

Periodicals

Book Review Index

This database contains references to more than 2.5 million citations to reviews of approximately 1.5 million distinct book and periodical titles.

Keywords: Book Reviews, Periodicals, Publications

Sponsor: Gale Research, Inc., Detroit, MI, USA

Audience: Publishing Professionals, Authors

Profile: The database covers every review published since 1969 in nearly 500 periodicals and newspapers. Each record includes the author and title of the work being reviewed, journal name, date of review, and page number. Document type indications are also included if the work is a periodical; a reference work; a children's book, periodical, or reference book; or a young adult book, periodical, or reference book. Book Review Index corresponds to the print publication of the same name. Periodicals indexed range from the Harvard Business Review to the Center for Children's Books: Bulletin, and from the American Scholar to Psychology Today. General interest magazines such as Ms., Time, The New Yorker, and Atlantic are covered, as are specialized periodicals like Flying, Yachting, and National Genealogical Society Quarterly.

Contact: Dialog in the US at (800) 334-2564, Dialog internationally at country specific locations.

Details: Costs

User Info: To subscribe, contact Dialog directly.

`telnet://dialog.com`

PERL (Practical Extraction and Report Language)

PERL (Practical Extraction and Report Language)

An HTML-formatted and highly indexed PERL programming reference document.

Keywords: Programming Languages, Computer Programming

Audience: Computer Programmers, Students, Researchers

Contact: Larry Wall
lwall@netlabs.com

`http://www.cs.cmu.edu/Web/People/rgs/`
`perl.html`

PERQ workstations

PERQ-fanatics

This mailing list is for users of PERQ graphics workstations.

Keywords: PERQ workstations, Computer Graphics

Audience: PERQ Users, Graphic Artists

Contact: perq-fanatics-request@alchemy.com

Details: Free

User Info: To subscribe to the list, send an e-mail message requesting a subscription to the URL address that follows.

To send a message to the entire list, address it to: perq-fanatics@alchemy.com

`mailto:perq-fanatics-`
`request@alchemy.com`

Personal Papers

University of Chicago Library

The library's holdings are large and wide-ranging and contain significant collections in many fields.

Keywords: English Bibles, Lincoln (Abraham), Kentucky & Ohio River Valley (History of), Balzac (Honore de), American Drama, Cromwell (Oliver), Goethe, Judaica, Italy, Chaucer (Geoffrey), Wells (Ida, Personal Papers of), Douglas (Stephen A.), Italy, Literature (Children's)

Audience: General Public, Researchers, Librarians, Document Delivery Professionals

Details: Free

Expect: ENTER CLASS, Send: LIB48 3; Expect: CONNECTED, Send: RETURN

`telnet://olorin.uchicago.edu`

Personals

alt.personals.ads

A Usenet newsgroup providing a forum for singles.

Keywords: Personals, Singles

Audience: Singles

User Info: To subscribe to this Usenet newsgroup, you need access to a newsreader.

`news:alt.personals.ads`

A B C D E F G H I J K L M N O P Q R S T U V W X Y Z

Peru

Peru

A mailing list for the discussion of Peruvian culture and other issues.

Keywords: Peru, South America

Audience: Peruvians, Educators, Researchers

Contact: Herbert Koller
owner-peru@cs.sfsu.edu

Details: Free

User Info: To subscribe to the list, send an e-mail message requesting a subscription to the URL address that follows.

To send a message to the entire list, address it to: owner-peru@cs.sfsu.edu

Notes: This mailing list is simply an echo site, so all posts get bounced from that address to all the people subscribed.

`mailto:owner-peru@cs.sfsu.edu`

Petroleum

API Energy Business News Index (APIBIZ)

Worldwide coverage of commercial, financial, marketing, and regulatory information affecting the petroleum and energy industries.

Keywords: Petroleum, Business

Sponsor: The American Petroleum Institute - Central Abstracting and Information Services

Audience: Researchers, Librarians

Profile: Twenty-two major news and economics publications are the primary sources for worldwide coverage of information affecting the petroleum and energy industries. Contains more than 600,000 records. Updated weekly.

Contact: paul.albert@neteast.com

User Info: To subscribe, contact Orbit-Questel directly.

`telnet://orbit.com`

Derwent World Patents Index/ API Merged

Patents covering petroleum processes, fuels, lubricants, petrochemicals, pipelines, tankers, storage, pollution control, synthetic fuels, synthesis gas, C1 chemistry, and other technologies.

Keywords: Petroleum, Patents

Sponsor: Derwent Publications, Ltd. and the American Petroleum Institute Central Abstracting and Indexing Service

Audience: Researchers, Librarians

Profile: Unique features include patent family searching, petrochemical patents searching, deep chemical/petroleum indexing.

Contact: paul.albert@neteast.com

User Info: To subscribe, contact Orbit-Questel directly.

`telnet://orbit.com`

TULSA (Petroleum Abstracts)

References and abstracts to literature and patents related to oil and natural gas exploration, development and production.

Keywords: Petroleum

Sponsor: Petroleum Abstracts, a division of the University of Tulsa

Audience: Researchers, Librarians

Profile: More than 500,000 references. Includes such areas as logging, well drilling, well completion and servicing, petroleum geology, exploration geophysics and geochemistry, oil and gas production, reservoir studies and recovery methods, pollution, alternative fuels, and transportation and storage. Updated weekly.

Contact: paul.albert@neteast.com

User Info: To subscribe, contact Orbit-Questel directly.

`telnet://orbit.com`

University of Tulsa Library

The library's holdings are large and wide-ranging and contain significant collections in many fields.

Keywords: Literature (American), Petroleum, Geology

Audience: Researchers, Students, General Public

Details: Free

Expect: Username Prompt, Send: LIAS

`telnet://vax2.utulsa.edu`

Pets

rec.pets

A Usenet newsgroup providing information and discussion about pets and pet care.

Keywords: Pets, Animals

Audience: Pet Owners

User Info: To subscribe to this Usenet newsgroup, you need access to a newsreader.

`news:rec.pets`

rec.pets.cats

A Usenet newsgroup providing information and discussion about domestic cats.

Keywords: Pets, Animals

Audience: Cat Owners

User Info: To subscribe to this Usenet newsgroup, you need access to a newsreader.

`news:rec.pets.cats`

rec.pets.dogs

A Usenet newsgroup providing information and discussion about dogs.

Keywords: Pets, Animals

Audience: Dog Owners

User Info: To subscribe to this Usenet newsgroup, you need access to a newsreader.

`news:rec.pets.dogs`

PGP Mail

PGP Mail

Information regarding the use of PGP (Pretty Good Privacy) mail, a public key.

Keywords: Internet, e-mail

Audience: Internet Surfers

Details: Free

`ftp://ftp.uu.net/networking/mail`

Ph7

Ph7

A mailing list for discussions about Peter Hamill and related rock groups.

Keywords: Rock Music, Hamill (Peter)

Audience: Musicians, Rock Music Enthusiasts

Contact: ph7-request@bnf.com

User Info: To subscribe to the list, send an e-mail message requesting a subscription to the URL address that follows.

To send a message to the entire list, address it to: ph7@bnf.com

`mailto:ph7-request@bnf.com`

Pharmaceutical Development

IMSWorld R&D Focus

The database provides information on worldwide pharmaceutical development.

Keywords: Pharmaceutical Development

Sponsor: IMSWorld Publications, Ltd., London, UK

Audience: Pharmacists, Health Care Professionals

Profile: All aspects of drug development are covered, from product discovery to launch. This R&D monitoring database is useful for tracking pharmaceutical products in 48 countries. R&D Focus includes two types of records: 1) profile records that include for each drug the generic name, laboratory code, CAS Registry Number, chemical name, synonyms, therapeutic indications, patents issued, development history, latest stage of worldwide development, commercial potential, and company activity. 2) Drug News records that provide a "quick alert" news service covering international research and pharmaceutical development.

Contact: Dialog in the US at (800) 334-2564, Dialog internationally at country-specific locations.

Details: Costs

User Info: To subscribe, contact Dialog directly.

`telnet://dialog.com`

Pharmaceuticals

IMSWorld Patents International

The database provides an analysis of the product patent position of more than 1,000 pharmaceutical compounds, either marketed or in active R&D.

Keywords: Patents, Pharmaceuticals

Sponsor: IMSWorld Publications, Ltd., London, UK

Audience: Patent Researchers

Profile: Each record includes an evaluated entry for all international patents, estimated patent expiration dates, therapeutic class, laboratory code, patent number issued by country, published application number by country, extensions to patent terms for the US and Japan where granted, and US marketing exclusivity information if applicable.

Contact: Dialog in the US at (800) 334-2564, Dialog internationally at country-specific locations.

User Info: To subscribe, contact Dialog directly.

Notes: Coverage: Current; updated monthly.

`telnet://dialog.com`

Pharmacology

Biosis Previews

The database encompasses the entire field of life sciences and covers original research reports and reviews in biological and biomedical areas. This includes field, laboratory, clinical, experimental and theoretical work. The traditional areas of biology, including botany, zoology, and microbiology are covered, as well as the related fields such as plant and animal science, agriculture, pharmacology, and ecology.

Keywords: Biology, Botany, Zoology, Microbiology, Plant Science, Animal Science, Agriculture, Pharmacology, Ecology, Biochemistry, Biophysics, Bioengineering

Sponsor: Biosis

Audience: Librarians, Researchers, Students, Biologists, Botanists, Zoologists, Scientists, Taxonomists

Contact: CDP Technologies Sales Department (800) 950-2035, extension 400.

User Info: To subscribe, contact CDP Technologies directly.

`telnet://cdplus@cdplus.com`

Drake University

The library's holdings are large and wide-ranging and contain significant collections in many fields.

Keywords: Music, Pharmacology, Theology

Audience: General Public, Researchers, Librarians, Document Delivery Professionals

Details: Free, Moderated

User Info: COWLES to access the main library, and LAWLIB to access the Law Library. To leave the system, enter Ctrl+Z.

`telnet://lib.drake.edu`

EMBASE

EMBASE is an acclaimed comprehensive index of international literature on medicine, science, and pharmacology.

Keywords: Medicine, Science, Pharmacology

Sponsor: Elsevier Science Publishers

Audience: Librarians, Researchers, Students, Physicians

Contact: CDP Technologies Sales Department (800) 950-2035, extension 400

User Info: To subscribe, contact CDP Technologies directly.

`telnet://cdplus@cdplus.com`

Health News Daily

The database contains all the daily news and full-text articles from Health News Daily, a publication from F-D-C Reports, Inc.

Keywords: Health, Pharmacology, Medical Research, News

Sponsor: F-D-C Reports, Inc., Chevy Chase, MD, US

Audience: Health Professionals, Pharmaceutical Industry, Market Researchers

Profile: The database provides specialized, in-depth business, scientific, regulatory, and legal news. Timely coverage of pharmacy and pharmaceuticals is given, as well as coverage of medical devices and diagnostics, medical research, cosmetics, health policy, provider payment policies, and cost containment in national health care.

Coverage: 1990 to the present; updated daily.

Contact: Dialog in the US at (800) 334-2564, Dialog internationally at country-specific locations.

Details: Costs

User Info: To subscribe, contact Dialog directly.

`telnet://dialog.com`

Recreational Pharmacology Server

Very extensive collection of drug FAQs, data sheets, net articles, resources, and electronic books. Complete list of Internet links to related sites.

Keywords: Pharmacology, Drugs, Neuroscience

Sponsor: University of Washington, Seattle, Washington, USA

Audience: Students, General Public, Pharmacologists, Neuroscientists

Contact: Webmaster lamontg@u.washington.edu

Details: Free

`http://stein1.u.washington.edu:2012/pharm/pharm.html`

University of Maryland System Library

The library's holdings are large and wide-ranging and contain significant collections in many fields.

Keywords: Medicine (History of), Nursing, Pharmacology, Microbiology, Aquaculture, Aquatic Chemistry, Toxicology

Audience: General Public, Researchers, Librarians, Document Delivery Professionals

Contact: Ron Larsen

Details: Free

User Info: Expect:Available Services menu; Send: PAC

`telnet://victor.umd.edu`

A B C D E F G H I J K L M N O **P** Q R S T U V W X Y Z

University of the Pacific Library

The library's holdings are large and wide-ranging and contain significant collections in many fields.

Keywords: Pharmacology, Americana (Western)

Audience: Researchers, Students, General Public

Details: Free

User Info: Expect: Login, Send: Library

`telnet://pacificat.lib.uop.edu`

Pharmacy

Svhp-I

A restricted discussion group on veterinary pharmacy issues.

Keywords: Veterinary Pharmacy, Pharmacy, Veterinary Science

Audience: Veterinarians, Veterinary Pharmacists

Contact: Doug Kemp
vetpharm@uga.cc.uga.edu

Details: Free

User Info: To subscribe to the list, send an e-mail message to the URL address shown that follows, consisting of a single line reading:

SUB svhp-I YourFirstName YourLastName

To send a message to the entire list, address it to: svhp-I@uga.cc.uga.edu

`mailto:listserv@uga.cc.uga.edu`

Philanthropy

Internet Nonprofit Center

A clearinghouse of information for nonprofit organizations and those interested in donating to them. Includes annual reports, directories, financial information, and brochures of selected nonprofit organizations, as well as volunteer opportunities and advice for potential donors. The Internet Nonprofit Center is currently located on EnviroLink Network, a gopher dedicated to environmental causes.

Keywords: Nonprofit Organizations, Philanthropy

Sponsor: American Institute of Philanthropy, USA, and The Internet Nonprofit Center, Brooklyn, New York, USA

Audience: Activists, Philanthropists

Contact: Cliff Landesman
clandesm@panix.com

`gopher://envirolink.org`

Philology

MEDTEXT-L

A discussion of medieval text, including philology, codicology, and technology.

Keywords: Medieval, Philology, Linguistics

Audience: Linguists, Language Teachers, Language Students, Historians

Details: Free

User Info: To subscribe to the list, send an e-mail message to the URL address that follows, consisting of a single line reading:

medtext-I YourFirstName YourLastName

To send a message to the entire list, address it to: medtext-I@uiucvmd.bitnet

`mailto:listserv@uiucvmd.bitnet`

Philosophy

Non Serviam

Non Serviam is an electronic newsletter centered on the philosophy of Max Stirner, author of Der Einzige und Sein Eigentum (The Ego and Its Own) and on his dialectical egoism. The contents, however, are decided by the individual contributors and the editor.

Keywords: Max Stirner, Non Serviam, Philosophy

Audience: Max Stirner Fans

Contact: Svein Olav Nyberg
solan@math.uio.no

Details: Free

User Info: To subscribe to the list, send an e-mail message requesting a subscription to the URL address that follows.

To send a message to the entire list, address it to: solan@math.uio.no

`mailto:solan@math.uio.no`

Principia Cybernetica Newsletter

Newsletter for participants in the Principia Cybernetica Project (PCP), as well as for people interested in keeping informed about the project.

Keywords: Philosophy, Worldview

Audience: Philosophers

Profile: PCP is a computer-supported collaborative attempt to develop an integrated evolutionary-systemic philosophy or world view. Its contributors are distributed over several continents and maintain contact primarily through electronic mail (mailing list PRNCYB-L), as well as through annual meetings, the printed (and electronic) newsletter, and postal mail. PCP focuses on the clear formulation of basic concepts and principles of the cybernetic approach.

Contact: Cliff Joslyn, Francis Heylighen
fheyligh@vnet3.vub.ac.be
cjoslyn@bingvaxu.cc.binghamton.edu

Details: Free

Send a 1- to 2- page letter, giving your address and affiliations and motivating your interest in the Project to the List owner (C. Joslyn).

`mailto:cjoslyn@bingvaxu.cc.binghamton.edu`

talk.religion.newage

A Usenet newsgroup providing information and discussion about esoteric and minority religions and philosophies.

Keywords: Religion, Philosophy

Audience: General Public, Researchers, Students

Details: Free

User Info: To subscribe to this Usenet newsgroup, you need access to a newsreader.

`news:talk.religion.newage`

The Electronic Journal of Analytic Philosophy Humanities

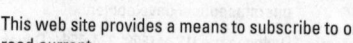

This web site provides a means to subscribe to or read current

Keywords: Philosophy

Sponsor: University of Indiana, Indiana, USA

Audience: Philosophers, Researchers, Educators, Students

Contact: ejap@phil.indiana.edu

Details: Free

User Info: To subscribe, send an e-mail message to: ejap@phil.indiana.edu

`http://www.phil.indiana.edu/ejap/ejap.html`

THINKNET

Electronic newsletter on philosophy, systems theory, interdisciplinary studies, and thoughtful conversation in cyberspace.

Keywords: Cyberspace, Systems Theory, Philosophy

Audience: Philosophers, System Theorists

Contact: Kent D. Palmer Ph.D.
Internet: palmer@world.std.com

Details: Free

User Info: To subscribe, send an e-mail message to the URL address that follows, consisting of a single line reading:

SUB THINKNET YourFirstName YourLastName

`mailto:palmer@world.std.com`

Phone Books

Internet Phone Books

A collection of Internet phone books and e-mail directories.

Keywords: Phone Books, Internet Guides, E-mail

Sponsor: Texas Tech University

Audience: Internet Surfers, General Public

Profile: This gopher includes a number of resources for finding people on the Internet. In addition to the standard Netfind, WHOIS, and Inter-NIC services, it also has information on finding college and international e-mail addresses. Also features snail mail information from the U.S. Post Office on Zip codes, as well as an international directory of telephone area codes.

Contact: Abdul Malik Yoosufani
gripe@cs.ttu.edu

`gopher://cs4sun.cs.ttu.edu`

Photography

3D

A open mailing list for discussion of 3D stereo photography.

Keywords: Photography

Audience: Photographers

Contact: John Bercovitz
JHBercovitz@lbl.gov

User Info: To subscribe to the list, send an e-mail message to the URL address that follows.

To send a message to the entire list, address it to: 3d@lbl.gov

`mailto:3d-request@lbl.gov`

California Museum of Photography: Network Exhibitions

This is a collection of digital images for educational and general use.

Keywords: Photography, Art, Education

Sponsor: University of California, Riverside, California, USA

Audience: Photographers, Artists, Educators, Historians

Profile: The California Museum of Photography is in the process of selecting groups of images from the collections as thematic exhibitions. Instead of displays on the walls, these exhibitions comprise a group of digital images with associated text. Particular emphasis is on the utility of these images in class projects for elementary and secondary school students. However, the digital images also have potential value for more advanced scholarly research in preparation of papers in the Humanities, Social Sciences, and the Arts.

Contact: Russ Harvey
russ@cornucopia.ucr.edu

`gopher://gopher.ucr.edu`

Fashion Photography Conference

A conference on the WELL about photography; topics range from products and technical information to aesthetics and fashion photography.

Keywords: Photography, Fashion

Audience: Photographers, Fashion Enthusiasts

Contact: Ralph E. Bedwell
ralf@well.sf.ca.us

Details: To participate in a conference on the WELL, you must first establish an account on the WELL. To do so, start by typing: telnet well.sf.ca.us

`telnet://well.sf.ca.us`

Images from Various Sources

This site serves as a link to some 35 image archives throughout the world. A wide variety of images is available, with a particularly large number of weather, geological, and biological collections from government and private sources.

Keywords: Computer Graphics, Photography, Art

Sponsor: The University of Alaska

Audience: General Public

Contact: Douglas Toelle
sxinfo@orca.alaska.edu

Details: Free, Images

`gopher://gopher.uacn.alaska.edu`

`http://info.alaska.edu:70`

PHOTO-CD

This list provides libraries of information about Kodak CD products or technology and closely related products.

Keywords: Photography, Computer Graphics

Sponsor: Eastman Kodak, Rochester, NY

Audience: Photographers, General Public

Contact: Don Cox
listmgr@info.kodak.com

User Info: To subscribe to the list, send an e-mail message to the address that follows, consisting of a single line reading:

Notes: SUB photo-cd Your First Name Your Last Name

To send a message to the entire list, address it to: photo-cd@info.kodak.com

`mailto:listserv@info.kodak.com`

rec.photo

A Usenet newsgroup providing information and discussion about photography.

Keywords: Photography, Art, Crafts

Audience: Photographers, Artists

User Info: To subscribe to this Usenet newsgroup, you need access to a newsreader.

`news:rec.photo`

University of Rochester Library

The library's holdings are large and wide-ranging and contain significant collections in many fields.

Keywords: Architecture, Art History, Photography, Literature (Asian), Lasers, Geology, Statistics, Optics, Medieval Studies

Audience: Researchers, Students, General Public

Details: Free

User Info: Expect: Login; Send: Library

`telnet://128.151.226.71`

Photography (History of)

University of New Mexico UNMinfo Library

The library's holdings are large and wide-ranging and contain significant collections in many fields.

Keywords: Photography (History of), Architecture, Native American Affairs, Land Records

Audience: Researchers, Students, General Public

Contact: Art St. George
stgeorge@unmb.bitnet

Details: Free

User Info: Expect: Login; Send: Unminfo

`telnet://unminfo.unm.edu`

Physical Education & Recreation

Physical Education & Recreation

A collection of information on sporting and recreational activities from aikido to windsurfing.

A B C D E F G H I J K L M N O P Q R S T U V W X Y Z

Keywords: Sports, Recreation, Aikido, Cycling, Scuba Diving, Windsurfing

Audience: Sports Enthusiasts, Fitness Enthusiasts

Contact: ctcadmin@ctc.ctc.edu

`gopher://ctc.ctc.edu`

Physical Therapy

HFS-L

Human Factors and Ergonomics Society Virginia Tech Chapter.

Keywords: Ergonomics, Physical Therapy

Audience: Researchers, Physical Therapists, Designers

Contact: Cortney Vargo
CORTV@VTVM1.CC.VT.EDU

Details: Free

User Info: To subscribe to the list, send an e-mail message to the URL address shown that follows consisting of a single line reading:

SUB hfs-l YourFirstName YourLastName

To send a message to the entire list, address it to: hfs-l@tvm1.cc.vt.edu

`listser@vtm1.cc.vt.edu`

Physics

(The) Physics Information Network

Distributes papers and software related to the American Institute of Physics and the journal Computers in Physics.

Keywords: Physics

Sponsor: American Instiute of Physics (AIP)

Audience: Physicists

Details: Free

User Info: To subscribe to the list, send an e-mail message requesting a subscription to the URL address that follows.

To send a message to the entire list, address it to: admin@pinet.aip.org

`mailto:admin@pinet.aip.org`

Astronomical Publications Resources (APR)

★★★★

Contains pointers to many relevant resources available through the Internet.

Keywords: Astronomy, Astrophysics, Physics

Sponsor: Space Telescope Science Institute

Audience: Astronomers, Physicists, Students (college, graduate), Educators

---

Profile: APR is a useful starting point to most of the astronomical publication resources available online. It is conviently divided by type of access (gopher, wais, www, telnet, ftp). As of January 1994, resources include:

- Astrophysics Preprints[MD]SISSA
- ADC Documents
- NOAO News
- NRAO Preprint Database
- STECF Newsletter
- STELAR ApJ, ApJS, AJ, PASP, A&A, A&AS, MNRAS, and JGR Abstracts
- STScI Preprint Database
- IAU Circulars Astronomical Union
- CfA Index of ApJ, AJ, PASP
- DIRA2 Database
- Electronic Journal of Astron. Soc. of the Atlantic

Contact: rrpss@stsci.edu

Details: Free, Moderated

`http://stsci.edu/net-publications.html`

`gopher://stsci.edu`

fusion

★

Fusion is an e-mail redistribution of Usenet sci.physics.fusion newsgroup for sites/users lacking access to Usenet.

Keywords: Physics, Fusion, Science

Audience: Physicists, Scientists

Details: Free

User Info: To subscribe to the list, send an e-mail message requesting a subscription to the URL address that follows.

To send a message to the entire list, address it to: fusion@zorch.sf-bay.org

`mailto:fusion-request@zorch.sf-bay.org`

INSPEC

IINSPEC corresponds to the three Science Abstracts print publications: Physics Abstracts, Electrical and Electronics Abstracts, and Computer and Control Abstracts.

Keywords: Physics, Electronic, Computing

Sponsor: Institution of Electrical Engineers, London, UK

Audience: Physicists, Electrical Engineers, Computer Specialists

Profile: Approximately 16 percent of the database's source publications are in languages other than English, but all articles are abstracted and indexed in English. The special DIALOG online thesaurus feature is available to assist searchers in determining appropriate subject terms and codes.

Contact: Dialog in the US at (800) 334-2564, Dialog internationally at country-specific locations.

User Info: To subscribe, contact Dialog directly.

Notes: Coverage: April 1969 to the present; updated weekly.

`telnet://dialog.com`

IUCAA (Inter-University Centre for Astronomy and Astrophysics)

★

The IUCAA was set up to promote the growth of active groups in astronomy and astrophysics in India. The Centre runs vigorous visitor programs involving short and long-term visits of scientists from India and abroad.

Keywords: Astronomy, Astrophysics, Physics, Education

Sponsor: Centre for Astronomy and Astrophysics (IUCAA)

Audience: Reseachers, Astronomers, Physicists, Students

Contact: Postmaster
amk@iucaa.ernet.in

`http://iucaa.iucaa.ernet.in/welcome.html`

Physics

★

A newly created digest covering current developments in theoretical and experimental physics. Topics might include particle physics, plasma physics, or astrophysics.

Keywords: Physics, Astrophysics, Plasma Physics

Audience: Physicists, Astrophysicists

Contact: Mike Miskulin
physics-request@qedqcd.rye.ny.us

Details: Free

User Info: To subscribe to the list, send an e-mail message requesting a subscription to the URL address that follows.

To send a message to the entire list, address it to: physics@qedqcd.rye.ny.u

`mailto:physics-request@qedqcd.rye.ny.us`

PPPL (The Princeton Plasma Physics Laboratory)

★

This web site provides an overview of the projects, mission, physical plant, and history of the PPPL.

Keywords: Physics, Research

Sponsor: U.S. Department of Energy (DOE)

Audience: Physicists, Educators, Students

Contact: Anthony R. De Meo or Jack A. Mervine
pppl_info@pppl.gov
webmaster@pppl.gov

Details: Free

`http://www.pppl.gov`

Purdue University Library ★★

The library's holdings are large and wide-ranging. They contain significant collections in many fields.

Keywords: Economics (History of), Literature (English), Literature (American), Indiana, Rogers (Bruce), Engineering (History of), Aviation, Earth Science, Atmospheric Science, Consumer Science, Family Science, Chemistry (History of), Physics, Veterinary Science

Audience: General Public, Researchers, Librarians, Document Delivery Professionals

Contact: Dan Ferrer
dan@asterix.lib.purdue.edu

Details: Free

Notes: Expect: User ID prompt, Send: GUEST

`telnet://lib.cc.purdue.edu`

Quantum Physics/High Energy Physics ★★★★

A resource containing extensive internet links to international academic and research institutions specializing in high-energy physics. Online links to journals, abstracts, and conference information.

Keywords: Physics, Quantum Physics, Research

Sponsor: Swiss Academic and Research Network, Switzerland

Audience: Students, Physicists, Researchers

Contact: Ingrid Graf
rikv8@cernvm.cern.ch

`http://www.cern.ch/physics/hep.html`

Quark Background Material ★

Background material describing the nature of and current research into quarks and other elementary particles..

Keywords: Quark, Physics

Sponsor: Fermi National Accelerator Laboratory

Audience: Physicists, Students, Researchers

Contact: Webmaster
webmaster@fnal.gov

Details: Free

`http://fnnews.fnal.gov/top_background.html`

sci.med.physics ★

A Usenet newsgroup providing information and discussion about physics in medical testing and care.

Keywords: Physics, Medical Research, Health Care

Audience: Physicists, Medical Researchers, Medical Practitioners, Health Care Professionals

Details: Free

User Info: To subscribe to this Usenet newsgroup, you need access to a newsreader.

`news:sci.med.physics`

sci.physics ★

A Usenet newsgroup providing information and discussion about physical laws and properties.

Keywords: Physics

Audience: Physicists

Details: Free

User Info: To subscribe to this Usenet newsgroup, you need access to a newsreader.

`news:sci.physics`

Physiology

REBASE (Restriction Enzyme Database) ★

The Restriction Enzyme Database contains both data and literature citations. It can be searched for enzyme names, species, authors, journals, and recognition sequences.

Keywords: Physiology, Enzymes

Sponsor: New England Biolabs

Audience: Scientists, Molecular Biologists

Contact: Richard Roberts
roberts@cshl.org

Details: Free

`gopher://gopher.gdb.org/77/.INDEX/rebase`

picasso-users

picasso-users ★

A mailing list for users of the Picasso Graphical User Interface Development System.

Keywords: Computing, Computer Graphics

Audience: Computer Users, Computer Graphic Designers

Contact: picasso-users@postgres.berkeley.edu

Details: Free

User Info: To subscribe to the list, send an e-mail message requesting a subscription to the URL address that follows.

To send a message to the entire list, address it to: picasso-users@postgres.berkeley.edu

`mailto:picasso-users@postgres.berkeley.edu`

PIERS Imports (US Ports)

PIERS Imports (US Ports)

PIERS (Port Import Export Reporting Service) Imports (US Ports), produced by The Journal of Commerce, is a compilation of manifests of vessels loading or discharging cargo at approximately 120 US seaports.

Keywords: Trade, Imports, Maritime

Sponsor: The Journal of Commerce/PIERS, New York, NY, USA

Audience: Business Professionals

Profile: The principal applications of this information include: identification of new sources of supply for imports, monitoring imports of products whose details are lost in traditional government reports, and identification of potential trade partners.

Contact: Dialog in the US at (800) 334-2564, Dialog internationally at country specific locations.

User Info: To subscribe, contact Dialog directly.

Notes: Coverage: current 15 months, updated monthly.

`telnet://dialog.com`

Pigulki

Pigulki ★

This is an English-language digest concerning the Net news from Poland.

Keywords: Poland, Eastern Europe

Audience: Poles, Poland Observers, Journalists

Contact: Marek Zielinski
zielinski@acfcluster.nyu.edu

Details: Free

User Info: To subscribe to the list, send an e-mail message requesting a subscription to the URL address that follows.

To send a message to the entire list, address it to: davep@acsu.buffalo.edu

`mailto:davep@acsu.buffalo.edu`

Pine E-mail

Pine E-mail ★

A description of the Program for Internet News and E-mail (PINE), a tool for reading, sending, and managing electronic messages.

Keywords: Internet Tools, e-mail

Audience: Internet Surfers

A B C D E F G H I J K L M N O P Q R S T U V W X Y Z

A
B
C
D
E
F
G
H
I
J
K
L
M
N
O
P
Q
R
S
T
U
V
W
X
Y
Z

Details: Free

User Info: File is mail/pine.blur

`ftp://ftp.cac.washington.edu`

Ping

Ping

With Ping, a user requests an "echo" from an Internet host to check status. It is useful for checking to see if a host or gateway is up and functioning.

Keywords: Internet Tools, Ping

Audience: Internet Surfers

Details: Free

User Info: File is: utils/ping/README

`ftp://vixen.cso.uiuc.edu/utils/ping/README`

Pink Floyd

echoes

Info and commentary on the musical group Pink Floyd, as well as other projects members of the group have been involved with.

Keywords: Rock Music, Pink Floyd

Audience: Rock Music Enthusiasts, Pink Floyd Enthusiasts

Contact: H. W. Neff
             echoes-request@fawnya.tcs.com

Details: Free

User Info: To subscribe to the list, send an e-mail message requesting a subscription to the URL address that follows.

             To send a message to the entire list, address it to: echoes-request@fawnya.tcs.com

`mailto:echoes-request@fawnya.tcs.com`

Pipes

Pipes

A forum for discussing the moderate use and appreciation of fine tobacco, including cigars, pipes, quality cigarettes, pipe making and carving, snuff, publications, and related topics.

Keywords: Pipes, Tobacco, Smoking

Audience: Smokers, Researchers, Market Analysts

Contact: Steve Masticola
             masticol@scr.siemens.com

Details: Free, Moderated

User Info: To subscribe to the list, send an e-mail message requesting a subscription to the URL address that follows.

             To send a message to the entire list, address it to: masticol@scr.siemens.com

`mailto:masticol@scr.siemens.com`

PIRA - Paper, Printing and Publishing, Packaging, and Nonwovens Abstracts

PIRA - Paper, Printing and Publishing, Packaging, and Nonwovens Abstracts

Coverage of all aspects of paper, pulp, nonwovens, printing, publishing and packaging.

Keywords: Material Science, Paper, Printing, Publishing, Packaging, Nonwovens

Sponsor: PIRA International

Audience: Material Scientists, Researchers

Profile: File contains more than 300,000 records. Special applications: company and market profiles, product and trade name searches, research and technology trends. Updated biweekly.

Contact: paul.albert@neteast.com

User Info: To subscribe, contact Orbit-Questel directly.

`telnet://orbit.com`

Pisma Bralcev

Pisma Bralcev

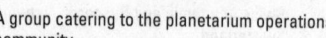

An edited mailing list that publishes readers' opinions, questions, inquiries for help, answers, and so on, in Slovene. Also includes travel tips and book reviews.

Keywords: Slovenia

Audience: Slovenians

Contact: Andrej Brodnik
             Pisma-Bralcev@krpan.arnes.si

Details: Free

User Info: To subscribe to the list, send an e-mail message requesting a subscription to the URL address that follows.

             To send a message to the entire list, address it to: pisma-bralcev@krpan.arnes.si

`mailto:Pisma-Bralcev@krpan.arnes.si`

`mailto:Pisma.Bralcev@uni-lj.si`

Pkd-list

Pkd-list

A discussion of the works and life of Philip K. Dick (1928-82), science fiction writer. Topics also include the nature of reality, consciousness, and religious experience.

Keywords: Science Fiction, Dick (Philip K.)

Audience: Philip K. Dick Readers, Science Fiction Readers

Contact: pkd-list-request@wang.com

Details: Free

User Info: To subscribe to the list, send an e-mail message requesting a subscription to the URL address that follows.

             To send a message to the entire list, address it to: pkd-list@wang.com

`mailto:pkd-list@wang.com`

Planetariums

Sci.astro.planetarium

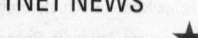

A group catering to the planetarium operations community.

Keywords: Astronomy, Planetariums

Audience: Educators, Astronomers, Planetarium Operators

Details: Free

User Info: To subscribe to this Usenet newsgroup, you need access to a newsreader.

`news:sci.astro.planetarium`

Planning

SCUP BITNET NEWS

Designed to promote the mission of the society and support its activities. Society for College and University Planning (SCUP) Bitnet News provides frequent and timely exchange of information among members as well as nonmembers interested in higher-education planning through the use of bitnet.

Keywords: Planning, University Planning

Sponsor: Society for College and University Planning

Audience: Planners

Profile: Contents of the newsletter are selected on the basis of interest and value to the membership. Particular attention is given to information that advances the state-of-the-art in planning; improves the understanding and application of the tools, techniques, processes and strategies of planning; advances the professional development of the membership; and widens the base of support for planning in higher education.

Contact: Joanne E. MacRae
USERTD8Q@UMICHUM.bitnet

Details: Free

Send an electronic mail note to the editor (Joanne Cate: budlao@uccvma) or the associate editor (Betsey Creekmore: pa94858@utkvm1)

```
mailto:Joanne Cate:
budlao@uccvma.bitnet
```

SCUPMA-L: Society of College and University Planners, Mid-Atlantic Region

This newsletter contains short news pieces and announcements about events of interest to the membership.

Keywords: Planning, University Planning

Audience: University Planners

Contact: Debbie Furlong
OPIR1@AUVM.bitnet

Details: Free

Contact Debbie Furlong at OPIR1@AUVM.bitnet

```
mailto:opir1@auvm.bitnet
```

Plant Lipids

NPLC

This list was set up to establish a network for rapid communication among researchers in the field of plant lipids. Announcements for example (of post-doc positions) to the field can be posted. The list can also be used to query coworkers regarding techniques, resources, and so on.

Keywords: Plant Lipids

Audience: Plant Lipid Researchers

Contact: Walid Tout
tout@genesys.cps.msu.edu

Details: Free

User Info: To subscribe to the list, send an e-mail message requesting a subscription to the URL address that follows.

To send a message to the entire list, address it to:
nplc@genesys.cps.msu.edu

```
mailto:NPLC@genesys.cps.msu.edu
```

Plant Science

Biosis Previews

The database encompasses the entire field of life sciences and covers original research reports and reviews in biological and biomedical areas. This includes field, laboratory, clinical, experimental and theoretical work. The traditional areas of biology, including botany, zoology, and microbiology are covered, as well as the related fields such as plant and animal science, agriculture, pharmacology, and ecology.

Keywords: Biology, Botany, Zoology, Microbiology, Plant Science, Animal Science, Agriculture, Pharmacology, Ecology, Biochemistry, Biophysics, Bioengineering

Sponsor: Biosis

Audience: Librarians, Researchers, Students, Biologists, Botanists, Zoologists, Scientists, Taxonomists

Contact: CDP Technologies Sales Department (800) 950-2035, extension 400

User Info: To subscribe, contact CDP Technologies directly

```
telnet://cdplus@cdplus.com
```

Plasma Physics

Physics

A newly created digest covering current developments in theoretical and experimental physics. Topics might include particle physics, plasma physics, or astrophysics.

Keywords: Physics, Astrophysics, Plasma Physics

Audience: Physicists, Astrophysicists

Contact: Mike Miskulin
physics-request@qedqcd.rye.ny.us

Details: Free

User Info: To subscribe to the list, send an e-mail message requesting a subscription to the URL address that follows.

To send a message to the entire list, address it to: physics@qedqcd.rye.ny.u

```
mailto:physics-
request@qedqcd.rye.ny.us
```

Plastics

RAPRA Abstracts

Coverage on technical and commercial aspects of the rubber, plastics, and polymer composites industries.

Keywords: Material Science, Rubbers, Plastics, Polymers

Sponsor: Rapra Technology, Ltd.

Audience: Materials Scientists, Researchers

Profile: This unique source of information covers the world's polymer literature including journals, conference proceedings, books, specifications, reports and trade literature. Contains over 375,000 records. Updated biweekly.

Contact: paul.albert@neteast.com

User Info: To subscribe, contact Orbit-Questel directly.

```
telnet://orbit.com
```

POD (Professional Organizational Development)

POD (Professional Organizational Development)

The POD network is aimed at faculty, instructional, and organizational development in higher education.

Keywords: Education (Adult), Education (Distance), Education (Continuing)

Audience: Educators, Administrators, Researchers

Details: Free

User Info: To subscribe to the list, send an e-mail message to the URL address shown that follows, consisting of a single line reading:

SUB pod YourFirstName YourLastName

To send a message to the entire list, address it to: pod@lists.acs.ohio-state.edu

```
mailto:listserv@lists.acs.ohio-
state.edu
```

Poetry

Poetry Conference

A conference on the WELL about poetry that includes original works.

Keywords: Poetry

Audience: Poets, Writers

Contact: Ron Buck, Sarah Randolph
macbeth@well.sf.ca.us,
stfr@well.sf.ca.us

Details: To participate in a conference on the WELL, you must first establish an account on the WELL. To do so, start by typing: telnet well.sf.ca.us

```
telnet://well.sf.ca.us
```

A
B
C
D
E
F
G
H
I
J
K
L
M
N
O
P
Q
R
S
T
U
V
W
X
Y
Z

A B C D E F G H I J K L M N O **P** Q R S T U V W X Y Z

rec.arts.poems

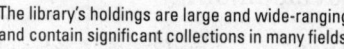

A Usenet newsgroup providing information and discussion about poetry.

Keywords: Poetry, Literature (General)

Audience: Poets, Poetry Readers

User Info: To subscribe to this Usenet newsgroup, you need access to a newsreader.

`news:rec.arts.poems`

Poetry (American)

Boise State University Library

The library's holdings are large and wide-ranging and contain significant collections in many fields.

Keywords: Jordan (Len, Senatorial Papers of), Church (Frank, Senatorial Papers of), Poetry (American)

Audience: General Public, Researchers, Librarians, Document Delivery Professionals

Contact: Dan Lester

Details: Free

User Info: Expect: login; Send: catalyst

`telnet://catalyst.idbsu.edu`

Poisons Information Database

Poisons Information Database

Directories of antivenoms, toxicologists, poison control centers, and poisons from around the world.

Keywords: Medical Research, Bioscience

Sponsor: Venom and Toxin Research Group, Department of Anatomy, National University of Singapore, Singapore

Audience: Biologists, Researchers, Medical Professionals, Toxicologists

Contact: Professor P. Gopalkrishnakone antgopal@leonis.nus.sg

`http://biomed.nus.sg/PID/PID.html`

Poker

ba-Poker

Discussion of poker as it is available to residents of and visitors to the San Franciso Bay area (broadly defined), in home games as well as in licensed card rooms. Topics include upcoming events, unusual games, strategies, comparisons of various venues, and player "networking."

Keywords: Poker, Card Games, San Francisco Bay Area

Audience: Poker Players

Contact: Martin Veneroso ba-poker-request@netcom.com

Details: Free

User Info: To subscribe to the list, send an e-mail message requesting a subscription to the URL address that follows.

To send a message to the entire list, address it to: ba-poker@netcom.com

`mailto:ba-poker-request@netcom.com`

Poland

CEE Environmental Libraries Database

A directory of over 300 libraries and environmental information centers in Central Eastern Europe that specalize in, or maintain significant collections of information about, the environment, ecology, sustainable living, or conservation. The database concentrates on six Central Eastern European countries: Bulgaria, Czech Republic, Hungary, Romania, Slovakia, and Poland.

Keywords: Central Eastern Europe, Environment, Sustainable Living, Bulgaria, Czech Republic, Hungary, Romania, Slovakia, Poland.

Sponsor: The Wladyslaw Poniecki Charitable Foundation, Inc.

Audience: Environmentalists, Green Movement, Librarians, Community Builders, Sustainable Living Specialists.

Profile: This database is the product of an Environmental Training Project (ETP) that was funded in 1992 by the US Agency for International Development as a 5-year cooperative agreement with a consortium headed by the University of Minnesota (US AID Cooperative Agreement Number EUR-0041-A-002-2020). Other members of the consortium include the University of Pittsburgh's Center for Hazardous Materials Research, The Institute for Sustainable Communities, and the World Wildlife Fund. The Wladyslaw Poniecki Charitable Foundation, Inc., was a subcontractor to the World Wildlife Fund and published the Directory of Libraries and Environmental Information Centers in Central Eastern Europe: A Locator/Directory. This gopher database consists of an electronic version of the printed directory, subsequently modified and updated online. Access to the data is facilitated by a WAIS search engine which makes it possible to retrieve information about libraries, subject area specializations, personnel, and so on.

Contact: Doug Kahn, CEDAR kahn@pan.cedar.univie.ac.at

`gopher://gopher.poniecki.berkeley.edu`

CIUWInfo (Centrum Informacyj ny Uniwersyetu Warszawskiego)

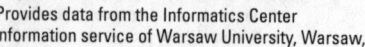

Provides data from the Informatics Center information service of Warsaw University, Warsaw, Poland.

Keywords: Informatics, Poland

Audience: Researchers

Contact: chomac@plearn.edu.pl

Details: Free

`gopher://chomac@plearn.edu.pl`

Donosy

Distribution of a news bulletin from Poland.

Keywords: Poland

Audience: Poles

Contact: Przemek Klosowski przemek@ndcvx.cc.nd.edu

User Info: To subscribe to the list, send an e-mail message to the URL that follows, consisting of a single line reading:

SUB donosy YourFirstName YourLastName.

To send a message to the entire list, address it to: donosy@fuw.edu.pl

`mailto:listproc@fuw.edu.pl`

Pigulki

This is an English-language digest concerning the Net news from Poland.

Keywords: Poland, Eastern Europe

Audience: Poles, Journalists

Contact: Marek Zielinski zielinski@acfcluster.nyu.edu

Details: Free

User Info: To subscribe to the list, send an e-mail message requesting a subscription to the URL address that follows.

To send a message to the entire list, address it to: davep@acsu.buffalo.edu

`mailto:davep@acsu.buffalo.edu`

Poland-l

A mailing list devoted to discussion of Polish culture and events.

Keywords: Poland

Audience: Researchers

Contact: Micahl Prussak michal@gs58.sp.cs.cmu.edu

Details: Free

User Info: To subscribe to the list, send an e-mail message to the URL address that follows, consisting of a single line reading:

SUB poland-l YourFirstName YourLastName

User Info: To send a message to the entire list, address it to: poland-1@ubvm.cc.buffalo.edu

`mailto:listserv@ubvm.cc.buffalo.edu`

Polish Archives

Information about Polish Internet gophers and Polish electronic journals.

Keywords: Poland, Telecommunications, Networking

Audience: Historians, Poles

Contact: Darek Milewski
Milewski@poniecki.berkeley.edu

User Info: To subscribe, send an e-mail message requesting a subscription to the URL address that follows.

`gopher://gopher.poniecki.berkeley.edu`

Spojrzenia

A weekly E-journal devoted to Polish culture, history, and politics.

Keywords: Poland, News (international), Culture

Audience: Poles, Students

Contact: Jerzy Krzystek
krzystek@u.washington.edu

Details: Free

User Info: To subscribe to the list, send an e-mail message requesting a subscription to the URL address that follows.

To send a message to the entire list, address it to: spojrzenia@u.washington.edu

`mailto:krzystek@u.washington.edu`

wroclaw

Distribution of information from weekly Polish bulletin called Society Journal.

Keywords: Poland

Audience: Polish Speakers, Researchers, General Public

Contact: Pawel Misiak
misiak@plwrtu11

Details: Free

User Info: To subscribe to the list, send an e-mail message to the URL address shown that follows, consisting of a single line reading:

SUB wroclaw YourFirstName YourLastName

To send a message to the entire list, address it to: wroclaw@plearn.edu.p1

`mailto:listserv@plearn.edu.p1`

Polar Regions

Dartmouth College Library

The library's holdings are large and wide-ranging and contain significant collections in many fields.

Keywords: American Calligraphy, Cervantes (Miguel de), Railroads, Polar Regions, Frost (Robert), Shakespeare (William), Spanish Plays

Audience: General Public, Researchers, Librarians, Document Delivery Professionals

Contact: Katharina Klemperer
kathy.klemperer@dartmouth.edu

Details: Free

User Info: Expect: login, Send: wolfpac

`telnet://lib.dartmouth.edu`

Police

Police

A mailing list for people interested in the music of the rock group The Police and its members: Sting, Stewart Copeland, and Andy Summers.

Keywords: Police, Sting

Audience: Rock Music Enthusiast

Contact: Pete Ashdown
owner-police@xmission.com

Details: Free

User Info: To subscribe to the list, send an e-mail message to the URL address shown that follows consisting of a single line reading:

SUB police YourFirstName YourLastName.

To send a message to the entire list, address it to: police@xmission.com

`mailto:majordomo@xmission.com`

Political Analysis and Research Cooperation (PARC) News Bulletin

Political Analysis and Research Cooperation (PARC) News Bulletin

Newsletter on political analysis, political behavior, political communication, and political culture. The purpose of PARC is to encourage and facilitate scientific research on human behavior in political life.

Keywords: Politics (US), Human Behavior

Audience: Political Scientists, Political Analysts

Contact: Tom Bryder
kusftb@vms2.uni-c.dk

Details: Free

User Info: To subscribe, send an e-mail message to the URL address that follows.

`mailto:kusftb@vms2.uni-c.dk`

Political Platforms of the US

Political Platforms of the US

Full text of various documents including the Democratic platform of 1992, the Jerry Brown positions of 1992, the Libertarian platform of 1990, and more.

Keywords: Politics (US), Government (US Federal), Democracy, Libertarian Politics

Audience: Politicians, Grass-Roots Organizers, Journalists

Details: Free

`gopher://wiretap.spies.com/11/Gov/Platform`

Political Science

Law and Courts Preprint Archive

An online archive of papers dealing with American and international legal issues presented at major conferences since August 1993.

Keywords: Law (US), Law (International), Legislation, Political Science

Sponsor: American Political Science Association

Audience: Lawyers, Legal Professionals

Contact: Professor Herbert Jacob
mzltov@nwu.edu

`gopher://gopher.nwu.edu`

Law and Politics Book Review

Reviews books of interest to political scientists studying US law, the courts, and the judicial process. Reviews are commissioned by the editor.

Keywords: Political Science, Law, Judicial Process

Audience: Political Scientists, Lawyers

Details: Free, Moderated

User Info: To subscribe, send an e-mail message to the address that follows, consisting of a single line reading:

To send a message to the entire list, address it to:

listserv@umcvmb.bitnet

`mailto:listserv@umcvmb.bitnet`

A B C D E F G H I J K L M N O P Q R S T U V W X Y Z

POSCIM

This mailing list is intended as a forum for those researching, teaching, or studying political science, as well as for politicians.

Keywords: Political Science

Audience: Political Scientists, Educators, Politicians, Researchers

Contact: Markus Schlegel
ups500@vm.gmd.de

Details: Free

User Info: To subscribe to the list, send an e-mail message to the URL address that follows, consisting of a single line reading:

SUB POSCIM YourFirstName YourLastName

To send a message to the entire list, address it to: ups500@vm.gmd.de

`mailto:listserv@vm.gmd.de`

Russian and East European Studies Home Pages

Keywords: Russia, Eastern Europe, Government, Political Science

Sponsor: University of Pittsburgh

Audience: Researchers, Politicians

Contact: Casey Palowitch
cjp@acid.library.pitt.edu

`http://www.pitt.edu/cjp/rspubl.html`

South African Specific Items

A selection of primarily political information on South Africa. Includes ANC (African National Congress) policy statements, as well as an A-Z of South African political figures and the latest issues of South Africa Watch Magazine. Also has weather information and links to gopher and ftp sites in South Africa.

Keywords: South Africa, Political Science

Audience: South Africans, Political Analysts, General Public

Contact: John Dovey
pjcd@maties.sun.ac.za

`gopher://lib.sun.ac.za`

The Israel Information Service

A gopher server containing information on Israel.

Keywords: Israel, Middle East, Political Science, Anti-Semitism, Holocaust, Archaeology

Sponsor: Israeli Foreign Ministry

Audience: Israelis, Jews, Tourists, General Public

Profile: This server features updates on the Middle East peace process, including text of the latest Israel-PLO accord, as well as general political, diplomatic, cultural and economic information on the state of Israel. Also includes archives on archaeology in Israel, anti-Semitism and the Holocaust, and current excerpts from Israeli newspapers.

Contact: Chaim Shacham
shacham@israel-info.gov.il

`gopher://israel-info.gov.il`

val-l

Discussion on changes in the Communist countries, ranging from Cuba and Vietnam to the former Soviet Union.

Keywords: Communism, Soviet Union, Political Science

Audience: Political Scientists

Contact: cdell@umkcax1 or
cdell@umkcvax1.bitnet

Details: Free

User Info: To subscribe to the list, send an e-mail message to the URL address that follows, consisting of a single line reading:

SUB val-l YourFirstName YourLastName

To send a message to the entire list, address it to: val-l@ucflvm.cc.ucf.edu

`mailto:listserv@ucflvm.cc.ucf.edu`

Politics

Aids

A forum for the discussion of AIDS, predominantly from a medical perspective, but also with some discussion of political and social issues.

Keywords: AIDS, Medicine, Politics, Society

Sponsor: UCLA

Audience: AIDS Researchers, AIDS Activists, Health Care Providers

Contact: Daniel R. Greening
aids-request@cs.ucla.edu

User Info: To subscribe to the list, send an e-mail message to the URL address that follows.

To send a message to the entire list, address it to: aids@cs.ucla.edu

`mailto:aids-request@cs.ucla.edu`

alt.politics.libertarian

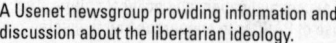

A Usenet newsgroup providing information and discussion about the libertarian ideology.

Keywords: Libertarian Party, Politics

Audience: Libertarians, Politicians

User Info: To subscribe to this Usenet newsgroup, you need access to a newsreader.

`news:alt.politics.libertarian`

Argentina

Mailing list for general discussion and information about Argentina, including Argentine culture and politics.

Keywords: Argentina, Politics, Culture

Sponsor: Carlos G. Mendioroz

Audience: Spanish Speakers, Students

Contact: Carlos G. Mendioroz
argentina-request@ois.db.toronto.edu

User Info: To subscribe to the list, send an e-mail message to the URL address that follows.

To send a message to the entire list, address it to:
argentina@ois.db.toronto.edu

`mailto:argentina-request@ois.db.toronto.edu`

ARlist

An open, unmoderated mailing list to provide a forum for discussing action research and its use in a variety of disciplines and situations. Topics include philosophical and methodological issues in action research, the use of action research for evaluation, actual case studies, and discourse on increasing the rigor of action research.

Keywords: Activism, Research, Politics

Audience: Activists, Researchers

Profile: Arlist is an open unmoderated mailing list to provide a forum for discussing action research and its use in a variety of disciplines and situations. It is usually (but perhaps not always) cyclic, participative, and qualitative.

Contact: Bob Dick
arlist@psych.psy.uq.oz.au

Details: Free

User Info: To subscribe to the list, send an e-mail message to the URL address that follows.

To send a message to the entire list, address it to: arlist@psych.psy.uq.oz.au

`mailto:arlist-request@psych.psy.uq.oz.au`

`ftp://psych.psy.uq.oz.au/dir/lists/arlist`

ba-Liberty

This is an announcement of local Libertarian meetings, events, activities, and so on. The ca- list is for California statewide issues; the ba- list is for the San Francisco Bay Area and it gets all messages sent to the ca- list. Prospective members should subscribe to one or the other, generally depending on whether or not they are SF Bay Area residents.

Keywords: Libertarian Party, Politics, San Francisco Bay Area

Audience: Libertarians, Political Scientists, Politicians, General Public

Contact: Jeff Chan
ba-liberty-request@shell.portal.com

Details: Free

User Info: To subscribe to the list, send an e-mail message requesting a subscription to the URL address that follows.

To send a message to the entire list, address it to: ba-liberty@shell.portal.com

`mailto:ba-liberty-`
`request@shell.portal.com`

Clinton Watch

A regular political column devoted to a critical examination of the Clinton Administration.

Keywords: Politics, Clinton(Bill), Satire, Government (US)

Sponsor: Informatics Resource

Audience: Republicans, General Public, Citizens

Contact: clintonwatch@dolphin.gulf.net

`gopher://dolphin.gulf.net`

CSF: Communications for a Sustainable Future

A gopher server for the distribution of Conflict Resolution Materials.

Keywords: Conflict Resolution, Community, Politics

Sponsor: Communications for a Sustainable Future

Audience: Activists, Policy Analysts, Community Leaders, Mediators, Lawyers

Profile: Communications for a Sustainable Future is a collective effort of several scholars. CSF does research, education, and applied work. Its main subject areas are: Intractable Conflicts and Constructive Confrontation, Environmental and Public Policy Dispute Resolution, Social/Political Conflicts, International Conflicts.

Contact: roper@csf.colorado.edu

Details: Free

`gopher://csf.colorado.edu`

EXEC (Executive Branch News US)

The EXEC library contains information and news about the Executive Branch of the Federal Government. From the Department of Agriculture to the White House, this file is a comprehensive source of information that will be especially useful to those whose responsibilities include monitoring federal regulations, Agency and Department activity, and the people and issues involved.

Keywords: News, Legislation, Regulation, Politics, Executive Branch

Audience: Journalists, Lobbyists, Business Executives, Analysts, Entrepreneurs

Profile: The EXEC library allows the searching of individual files or group files that cover topics such as the Federal Register and Code of Federal Regulations; public laws; proposed treasury regulation; and over 50 news sources, including BNA's Daily Report for Executives, the Dept. of State Dispatch, ABC News transcripts, Federal News Service Daybook, Government Executive, MacNeil/Lehrer Newshour, New Leader, National Review, the Washington Post, the Washington Times, Presidential Documents, and many others.

Contact: Mead New Sales Group at (800) 227-4908 or (513) 859-5398 inside the US, or (513) 865-7981 for all inquiries outside the US.

User Info: To subscribe, contact Mead directly.

To examine the Nexis user guide, you can access it at the ftp site of the University of Texas at Austin at the URL address: ftp://ftp.cc.utexas.edu

The files are in: /pub/ref-services/LEXIS

`telnet://nex.meaddata.com`

`http://www.meaddata.com`

Israel-mideast

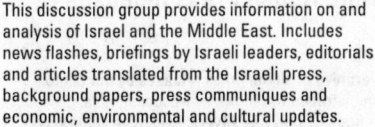

This discussion group provides information on and analysis of Israel and the Middle East. Includes news flashes, briefings by Israeli leaders, editorials and articles translated from the Israeli press, background papers, press communiques and economic, environmental and cultural updates.

Keywords: Israel, Middle East, Politics

Sponsor: Israel Information Center, Jerusalem

Audience: General Public, Students

Contact: Israel Information Service
ask@israel-info.gov.il

User Info: To subscribe to the list, send an e-mail message to the address that follows, consisting of a single line reading:

SUB israel mideast YourFirstName YourLastName.

To send a message to the entire list, address it to: israel mideast@vm.tau.ac.il

`mailto:listserv@vm.tau.ac.il`

National Performance Review (NPR)

The Report of the National Performance Review, from the task force led by Vice President Gore, titled "From Red Tape to Results: Creating a Government that Works Better and Costs Less," Sept. 7, 1993.

Keywords: President, Politics, White House

Audience: Political Scientists, General Public

Profile: On March 3, 1993, President Clinton asked Vice President Gore to lead the effort to effect real change in the federal government. Gore's NPR Task Force overview and accompanying reports make specific recommendations for: reducing costs and waste, changing the way government operates, and making government more responsive and effective.

Details: Free

`gopher://cyfer.esusda.gov/11/ace/`
`policy/npr/nat`

Presidential Documents

This gopher provides access to the full text of Presidential Proclamations, Executive Orders, Notices, Memoranda, and Determinations dating from December 23, 1992. The documents are listed sequentially by date and number (that is, Proclamation 6520 of December 23, 1992).

Keywords: Politics, President (US), White House, Documents

Audience: General Public

Details: Free

Select from menu presented (you will probably follow the following path: Internet Services/US Government/ Presidential Documents.)

`gopher://jupiter.cc.gettysborg.edu`

PVS (Project Vote Smart)

A gopher site containing Federal political information from PVS.

Keywords: Politics, Government (US)

Sponsor: Project Vote Smart, Corvallis, Oregon, USA

Audience: Voters, General Public

Profile: PVS is a volunteer organization dedicated to providing voters with factual information about candidates for Federal office. Currently, the gopher offers background information, including detailed profiles and legislative analysis of Senators and Representatives for all 50 states.

Contact: pvs@neu.edu

Notes: For more information on Project Vote Smart, call their toll free hotline at 1-800-622-SMART. Or write to: Project Vote Smart, 129 NW Fourth St. #240, Corvallis, OR 97330

`gopher://gopher.neu.edu`

talk.politics.soviet

A Usenet newsgroup providing information and discussion about Soviet politics, domestic and international.

Keywords: Communism, Russia, Politics, CIS (Commonwealth of Independent States)

Audience: Political Scientists

A B C D E F G H I J K L M N O P Q R S T U V W X Y Z

A
B
C
D
E
F
G
H
I
J
K
L
M
N
O
P
Q
R
S
T
U
V
W
X
Y
Z

Details: Free

User Info: To subscribe to this Usenet newsgroup, you need access to a newsreader.

`news:talk.politics.soviet`

Technology Initiatives for the Clinton/Gore Administration

This is a 40-page text of the press release from the Clinton administration on technology initiatives, dated February 22, 1993.

Keywords: Politics, President, White House, Technology

Audience: General Public, Journalists

Details: Free

E-mail to the ListServ and include the following in the body of the message: get cni-bigideas.whouse.paper

`mailto:listserv@cni.org`

The Frog Farm

A forum devoted to the discussion of claiming, exercising, and defending rights in America, past, present, and future. The main topics are issues that involve a free people and their public servants.

Keywords: Rights, Politics

Audience: Activists

Contact: schirado@lab.cc.wmich.edu

User Info: To subscribe to the list, send an e-mail message requesting a subscription to the URL address that follows.

To send a message to the entire list, address it to: schirado@lab.cc.wmich.edu

`mailto:schirado@lab.cc.wmich.edu`

UN Rules

Standards, guidelines, and international instruments promulgated by the UN.

Keywords: Politics, UN, Standards

Sponsor: United Nations Justice Network (UNCJIN)

Audience: Lawyers, General Public, International-ists

Details: Free

Select from menu as appropriate.

`gopher://uacsc2.albany.edu`

White House Information Service

An outstanding database of current White House information, from 1992 to the present.

Keywords: White House, Politics, President (US), Database

Sponsor: Texas A & M University

Audience: General Public

Profile: Much of the older information on this site was obtained from the clinton@marist.bitnet listserv list or the alt.politics.clinton Usenet newsgroup, both of which receive the information indirectly via the MIT White House information server. Newer and current material is received directly from the MIT distribution list. The menu includes a searchable database and headings such as Domestic Affairs (Health Care, Technology, and so on), Press Briefings and Conferences, the President's Daily Schedule, and many more.

Contact: whadmin@tamu.edu

Details: Free

`gopher://tamuts.tamu.edu/11/.dir/president.dir`

White House Phone Numbers

A list of names, addresses, e-mail addresses and telephone and fax numbers of the President, First Lady, Vice President, and all the members of the Cabinet.

Keywords: White House, President, Politics

Audience: General Public

Details: Free

`ftp://nifty.andrew.cmu.edu/pub/QRD/info/govt/cabinet`

White House Press Releases

An archive of all the press releases by the Clinton administration organized as Miscellaneous, Briefings by Dee Dee Myers, Executive Orders, Remarks during Photo Opportunities, Remarks of Bill Clinton, Briefings by George Stephanopolous.

Keywords: White House, Politics, President (US)

Audience: General Public

Details: Free

`gopher://wiretap.spies.com/11/Clinton`

Politics (Conservative)

alt.fan.rush-limbaugh

A Usenet newsgroup providing information and discussion about Rush Limbaugh, a politically conservative American figure.

Keywords: Limbaugh (Rush), Politics (Conservative), Comedians

Audience: Followers of Rush Limbaugh

User Info: To subscribe to this Usenet newsgroup, you need access to a newsreader.

`news:alt.fan.rush-limbaugh`

Politics (International)

Amnesty International

A site containing information about Amnesty International, an organization focused strictly and specifically on human rights around the world.

Keywords: Government, Human Rights, Politics (International), Activism

Sponsor: Amnesty International

Audience: Students, Activists

Contact: Catherine Hampton
             ariel@netcom.com

`ftp://ftp.netcom.com/pub/ariel/www/human.rights/amnesty.international/ai.html`

CNN Headline News Gopher

Latest news as read by the CNN anchorpersons. Searchable index of subject matter.

Keywords: News Media, Politics (International), Journalism

Sponsor: CNN Newsource Service

Audience: General Public, Students, Journalists

Contact: Chet Rhodes
             cr9@umail.umd.edu

Details: Free

`gopher://info.umd.edu:925/`

Government Docs (US & World)

A large and eclectic collection of documents, ranging from the Laws of William the Conqueror to the North American Free Trade Agreement (NAFTA). Particular strengths include 20th century American political documents and international treaties and covenants.

Keywords: Government (International), History (World), Politics (International)

Sponsor: The Internet Wiretap

Audience: Researchers, Historians, Political Scientists, Journalists

Contact: gopher@wiretap.spies.com

`gopher://wiretap.spies.com/Gov`

Jerusalem-One Network

A gopher site covering issues concerned with Jews, Jewish politics and history.

Keywords: Judaism, Israel, Politics (International)

Audience: Political Activists, Holocaust Researchers, Jews, Israelis

Profile: The Jerusalem-One Network was established in May 1993 by the Jewish International Communications Network (JICN), a branch of the Jewish International Association Against Assimilation. Entries include The Jewish Electronic Library, The Holocaust Archives, and JUNK (the Jewish student University Network)

`gopher://jerusalem1.datasrv.co.il`

U.S. Army Area Handbooks

This gopher provides detailed political, cultural, historical, military, and economic information on hot spots in world affairs, everywhere from China to Yugoslavia.

Keywords: Military (US), Politics (International), Federal Government (US)

Sponsor: The Thomas Jefferson Library at the University of Missouri at St. Louis , St. Louis, Missouri, USA

Audience: Journalists, Government Officials, Travelers/Tourists

Profile: The Army Area Handbooks, which provide a comprehensive overview of several important countries including Japan, China, Israel, Egypt, South Korea, and Somalia, are only one of the many government resources available at this site. Other full-text documents include the proposed 1995 federal budget, the CIA world fact book, the NAFTA agreement, health care proposals currently before Congress, and statistics for the U.S. industrial outlook. Also has links to many federal gophers and information systems.

Contact: Joe Rottman rottman@umslvma.umsl.edu

Details: Free

`gopher://umslvma.umsl.edu/11/library/govdocs`

Various Treaties

Provides access to a range of treaties in full-text format.

Keywords: Treaties, Politics (International)

Audience: Governments, Researchers, Lawyers

Details: Free

Select from menu as appropriate

`gopher://wiretap.spies.com`

World Constitutions

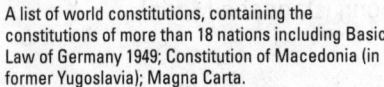

A list of world constitutions, containing the constitutions of more than 18 nations including Basic Law of Germany 1949; Constitution of Macedonia (in former Yugoslavia); Magna Carta.

Keywords: Law (International), History (World), Politics (International)

Audience: Researchers, Lawyers, Historians

Details: Free

`gopher://wiretap.spies.com`

Politics (Middle Eastern)

talk.politics.mideast

A Usenet newsgroup providing information and discussion about Middle Eastern topics.

Keywords: Middle East, Middle Eastern Studies, Politics (Middle Eastern)

Audience: Political Scientists

Details: Free

User Info: To subscribe to this Usenet newsgroup, you need access to a newsreader.

`news:talk.politics.mideast`

Politics (US)

alt.politics.clinton

A Usenet newsgroup providing information and discussion about President Bill Clinton and the White House. Perspective tends to be anti-Clinton.

Keywords: Politics (US), Clinton (Bill)

Audience: Politicians, General Public

User Info: To subscribe to this Usenet newsgroup, you need access to a newsreader.

`news:alt.politics.clinton`

alt.politics.election

A Usenet newsgroup organized to help people in the process of running for office.

Keywords: Politics (US), Government

Audience: Politicians, Campaign Managers

User Info: To subscribe to this Usenet newsgroup, you need access to a newsreader.

`news:alt.politics.election`

Berne Convention Implementation Act of 1988

An act to amend Title 17, United States Code, to implement the Berne Convention for the Protection of Literary and Artistic Works, as revised in Paris on July 24, 1971, and for other purposes.

Keywords: Legislation (US), Government (US), Politics (US), Copyright

Audience: Lawyers, Students, Politicians, Journalists

Details: Free

`gopher://wiretap.spies.com/00/Gov/Copyright/US.Berne.Convention.txt`

Bibliographies of US Senate Hearings

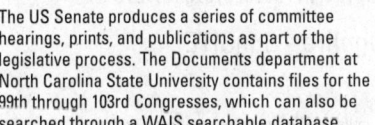

The US Senate produces a series of committee hearings, prints, and publications as part of the legislative process. The Documents department at North Carolina State University contains files for the 99th through 103rd Congresses, which can also be searched through a WAIS searchable database.

Keywords: Senate (US), Politics (US), Legislation (US), Bibliographies, Government (US)

Audience: General Public, Journalists, Students, Politicians, US Citizens

Contact: Jack McGeachy Jack_McGeachy@ncsu.edu

Details: Free

`gopher://dewey.lib.ncsu.edu/11/library/disciplines/government/senate`

CMPGN (Campaign Library)

The CMPGN library contains information and news about US Congressional, Senatorial, Gubernatorial and Presidentail elections. The media, political campaigns, and others whose responsibilities include monotoring activity on the campaign trail will find CMPGN to be a unique and comprehensive source of information for campaign research.

Keywords: Politics (US), Congress (US)

Audience: Journalists, Political Researchers

Profile: CMPGN allows searching of individual files or group files that cover topics such as candidate and incumbent profiles; Honoraria, PACs, and demographic and media profiles; Committee and Floor voting records and floor statement indexes for all House and Senate incumbents; and reputable sources of news that are known for their in-depth campaign coverage, including the Hotline, the Cook Political Report, ABC news Transcripts, Roll Call, States News Service, US Newswire, Federal News Service, and much more.

Contact: Mead New Sales Group at (800) 227-4908 or (513) 859-5398 inside the US, or (513) 865-7981 for all inquiries outside the US.

User Info: To subscribe, contact Mead directly.

To examine the Nexis user guide, you can access it at the ftp site of the University of Texas at Austin at the URL address: ftp://ftp.cc.utexas.edu

The files are in: /pub/ref-services/LEXIS

`telnet://nex.meaddata.com`

`http://www.meaddata.com`

Copyright Act

The full text of the Copyright Act of 1976, Title 17, United States Code, Sections 101_810.

Keywords: Politics (US), Government (US Federal), Laws (US Federal), Copyright

A B C D E F G H I J K L M N O P Q R S T U V W X Y Z

Audience: Lawyers, Students, Politicians, Journalists

Details: Free

```
gopher://wiretap.spies.com/00/Gov/
Copyright/US.Copyright.1976.tx
```

Ogphre - SunSITE

A collection of Internet resources organized by subject. Particular strengths include agriculture, religious texts, poetry, creative writing, and US politics. The ftp site has a set of more general Internet guides.

Keywords: Agriculture, Politics (US), Religion, Internet

Sponsor: The University of North Carolina - Chapel Hill and Sun Microsystems, USA

Audience: General Public, Internet Surfers, Researchers

Contact: Darlene Fladager, Elizabeth Lyons Darlene_Fladager@unc.edu, Elizabeth_Lyons@unc.edu

```
gopher://sunsite.unc.edu
```

```
ftp://sunsite.unc.edu
```

Political Analysis and Research Cooperation (PARC) News Bulletin

Newsletter on political analysis, political behavior, political communication, and political culture. The purpose of PARC is to encourage and facilitate scientific research on human behavior in political life.

Keywords: Politics (US), Human Behavior

Audience: Political Scientists, Political Analysts

Contact: Tom Bryder kusftb@vms2.uni-c.dk

Details: Free

User Info: To subscribe, send an e-mail message to the URL address that follows.

```
mailto:kusftb@vms2.uni-c.dk
```

Political Platforms of the US

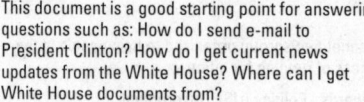

Full text of various documents including the Democratic platform of 1992, the Jerry Brown positions of 1992, the Libertarian platform of 1990, and more.

Keywords: Politics (US), Government (US Federal), Democracy, Libertarian Party

Audience: Politicians, Grass-Roots Organizers, Journalists

Details: Free

```
gopher://wiretap.spies.com/11/Gov/
Platform
```

Speeches and Addresses in the US

Includes the Clinton State of the Union Speech of 1993, Kennedy's Inaugural Speech, Martin Luther King's "I Have a Dream" speech, and so forth.

Keywords: Politics (US), Rhetoric

Audience: Journalists, Writers, Politicians, Students

Details: Free
           Choose from menu presented.

```
gopher://wiretap.spies.com/11/Gov/US-
Speech
```

Universal Copyright Convention

The Universal Copyright Convention as revised at Paris (1971). Convention and protocols were done at Paris on July 24, 1971. It was ratified by the President of the United States of America on August 28, 1972.

Keywords: Copyright, Laws (US), Government (US), Politics (US)

Audience: Lawyers, Students, Politicians, Journalists

Details: Free

```
gopher://wiretap.spies.com/00/Gov/
Copyright/
US.Universal.Copyright.Conv.txt
```

White House Frequently Asked Questions

This document is a good starting point for answering questions such as: How do I send e-mail to President Clinton? How do I get current news updates from the White House? Where can I get White House documents from?

Keywords: Clinton (Bill), Government (US), Politics (US), FAQs

Audience: General Public, Researchers

Details: Free

Expect: login; Send: anonymous; Expect: password; Send: your e-mail address; Expect: directory; Send: /pub/nic; Expect: file; Send: whitehouse FAQ.

```
ftp://ftp.sura.net
```

Polymers

RAPRA Abstracts

Coverage on technical and commercial aspects of the rubber, plastics, and polymer composites industries.

Keywords: Material Science, Rubbers, Plastics, Polymers

Sponsor: Rapra Technology, Ltd.

Audience: Materials Scientists, Researchers

Profile: This unique source of information covers the world's polymer literature including journals, conference proceedings, books, specifications, reports and trade literature. Contains over 375,000 records. Updated biweekly.

Contact: paul.albert@neteast.com

User Info: To subscribe, contact Orbit-Questel directly.

```
telnet://orbit.com
```

Pop Groups

Bel Canto

A mailing list for the discussion of the music, lyrics, and shows of the group Bel Canto, and solo projects of group members, or even the work of related artists if appropriate.

Keywords: Music, Pop Groups

Audience: Music Enthusiasts

Contact: dewy-fields-request@ifi.uio.no

Details: Free

User Info: To subscribe to the list, send an e-mail message requesting a subscription to the URL address that follows.
           To send a message to the entire list, address it to: dewy-fields@ifi.uio.no

```
mailto:dewy-fields-request@ifi.uio.no
```

Beloved

A mailing list for the discussion of the Beloved, an English pop group with strong ambient and techno influences.

Keywords: Music, Pop Groups

Audience: Music Enthusiasts

Contact: Jyrki Sarkkinen beloved-request@phoenix.oulu.fi

Details: Free

User Info: To subscribe to the list, send an e-mail message requesting a subscription to the URL address that follows.
           To send a message to the entire list, address it to: beloved@phoenix.oulu.fi

```
mailto:beloved-
request@phoenix.oulu.fi
```

Pop Music

Bong (Depeche Mode)

Bong is for the discussion of the mostly electronic band Depeche Mode and related projects like Recoil. Depeche Mode incorporate synth-pop, industrial dance, Kraftwerkian electro, ambient, techno, and rock influences in a dark blend of innovative alternative music.

Keywords: Depeche Mode, Pop Music

Audience: Pop Music Enthusiasts, Depeche Mode Enthusiasts, Musicians

Contact: Colin Smiley
bong-request@lestat.compaq.com

Details: Free

User Info: To subscribe to the list, send an e-mail message requesting a subscription to the URL address that follows.

To send a message to the entire list, address it to: bong@lestat.compaq.com

`mailto:bong-request@lestat.compaq.com`

Chalkhills

A mailing list for the discussion of the music and records of XTC (the band).

Keywords: Pop Music, XTC

Audience: Pop Music Enthusiasts, XTC Enthusiasts

Contact: John M. Relph
chalkhills-request@presto.ig.com

Details: Free, Moderated

User Info: To subscribe to the list, send an e-mail message requesting a subscription to the URL address that follows.

To send a message to the entire list, address it to: chalkhills@presto.ig.com

Notes: Chalkhills is moderated and distributed in a digest format.

`mailto:chalkhills-request@presto.ig.com`

concrete-blonde

This list discusses the rock group Concrete Blonde and related artists and issues.

Keywords: Pop Music, Concrete Blonde

Audience: Concrete Blonde Enthusiasts, Pop Music Enthusiasts

Contact: Robert Earl
concrete-blonde-request@piggy.ucsb.edu

Details: Free

User Info: To subscribe to the list, send an e-mail message requesting a subscription to the URL address that follows.

To send a message to the entire list, address it to: concrete-blonde@piggy.ucsb.edu

`mailto:concrete-blonde-request@piggy.ucsb.edu`

Crowes

To provide a forum for discussion about the rock band the Black Crowes. Topics include the group's music and lyrics, as well as the band's participation with NORML, concert dates and playlists, and bootlegs (audio and video).

Keywords: Rock Music, Pop Music

Audience: Rock Music Enthusiasts, Pop Music Enthusiasts

Contact: rstewart@unex.ucla.edu

Details: Free

User Info: To subscribe, mail to the address that follows with the command SUBSCRIBE in the first line.

`mailto:rstewart@unex.ucla.edu`

Popular Culture

alt.cult-movies

A Usenet newsgroup providing information and discussion about popular movies.

Keywords: Film, Popular Culture

Audience: Movie Watchers, Critics

User Info: To subscribe to this Usenet newsgroup, you need access to a newsreader.

`news:alt.cult-movies`

Popular Culture

This directory is a compilation of information resources focused on popular culture.

Keywords: Popular Culture

Audience: Popular Culture Enthusiasts, Internet Surfers, Students

Details: Free

`ftp://una.hh.lib.umich.edu/70/
inetdirsstacks/popcult:robinson`

rec.arts.movies movie database

An extensive FTP database covering over 32,000 movies, with more than 370,000 filmography entries, from early cinema to current releases.

Keywords: Movies, Television, Popular Culture

Audience: Movie Buffs

Profile: Interfaces to search the database include Unix, MS-DOS and Amiga (and Windows and Mac versions are in development). The database includes filmographies for actors, directors, writers, composers, cinematographers, editors, production designers, costume designers and producers; plot summaries; character names; movie ratings; year of release; running times; movie trivia; quotes; goofs; soundtracks; personal trivia and Academy Award information.

Contact: Col Needham
cn@ibmpcug.co.uk

Details: Free

`ftp://cathouse.org/pub/cathouse/
movies/database`

rec.arts.movies movie database (Cardiff WWW front-end)

An extensive, interactive database covering over 32,000 movies, with more than 370,000 filmography entries, from early cinema to current releases.

Keywords: Movies, Television, Popular Culture, Interactive Media

Audience: Movie Buffs

Profile: A WWW front-end to the rec.arts.movies movie database, complete with form-filling interfaces to add new data and to rate movies (on a scale from 1 through 10). The database includes filmographies for actors, directors, writers, composers, cinematographers, editors, production designers, costume designers and producers; plot summaries; character names; movie ratings; year of release; running times; movie trivia; quotes; goofs; soundtracks; personal trivia and Academy Award information.

Contact: Rob Hartill
Robert.Hartill@cm.cf.ac.uk

Details: Free

`http://www.cm.cf.ac.uk/Movies`

`http://www.msstate.edu/Movies`

rec.music.beatles

A Usenet newsgroup providing information and discussion about the Beatles.

Keywords: Musical Groups, Popular Culture

Audience: Beatles Listeners

User Info: To subscribe to this Usenet newsgroup, you need access to a newsreader.

`news:rec.music.beatles`

rec.music.gdead

A Usenet newsgroup providing information and discussion about the Grateful Dead.

Keywords: Music, Popular Culture

Audience: Grateful Dead Listeners

User Info: To subscribe to this Usenet newsgroup, you need access to a newsreader.

`news:rec.music.gdead`

rec.music.phish

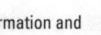

A Usenet newsgroup providing information and discussion about the band Phish.

Keywords: Musical Groups, Popular Culture

Audience: Phish Listeners

User Info: To subscribe to this Usenet newsgroup, you need access to a newsreader.

`news:rec.music.phish`

A
B
C
D
E
F
G
H
I
J
K
L
M
N
O
P
Q
R
S
T
U
V
W
X
Y
Z

A B C D E F G H I J K L M N O P Q R S T U V W X Y Z

alt.music.progressive

A Usenet newsgroup providing information and discussion about progressive music, including the groups Marillion, Asia, King Crimson, and many others.

Keywords: Musical Genres, Popular Culture

Audience: Progressive Music Listeners

User Info: To subscribe to this Usenet newsgroup, you need access to a newsreader.

`news:alt.music.progressive`

soc.culture.usa

A Usenet newsgroup providing information and discussion about the culture of the United States.

Keywords: Americana, Sociology, Popular Culture

Audience: Sociologists, General Public

Details: Free

User Info: To subscribe to this Usenet newsgroup, you need access to a newsreader.

`news:soc.culture.usa`

The English Server

A large and eclectic collection of humanities resources.

Keywords: Humanities, Academia, English, Popular Culture, Feminism

Sponsor: Carnegie Mellon University English Department, Pittsburgh, Pennsylvania, USA

Audience: General Public, University Students, Educators (College/University), Researchers (Humanities)

Profile: Contains archives of conventional humanities materials, such as historical documents and classic books in electronic form. Also offers more unusual and hard-to-find resources, particularly in the field of popular culture and media. Features access to many humanities and culture-related online journals such as Bad Subjects, FineArt Forum, and Postmodern Culture. Also has links to a wide variety of related Internet sites and resources.

Contact: Geoff Sauer
postmaster@english-server.hss.cmu.

`gopher://english-server.hss.cmu.edu`

`http://english-server.hss.cmu.edu`

Porsche

Porschephiles

This list is for people who own, operate, work on, or covet various models of Porsche automobiles. Discussion topics include features, functionality, and purchasing advice.

Keywords: Porsche, Automobiles, Sports Cars

Audience: Automobile Enthusiasts

Contact: porschephiles-request@tta.com

Details: Free

User Info: To subscribe to the list, send an e-mail message requesting a subscription to the URL address that follows.

To send a message to the entire list, address it to: porschephiles@tta.com

`mailto:porschephiles-request@tta.com`

Portuguese

Brasil

This is a mailing list for general discussion about and information on Brazil. Portuguese is the main language of discussion.

Keywords: Brazil, Portuguese

Audience: Brazilians, Portuguese Speakers

Contact: B. R. Araujo Neto
bras-net-request@cs.ucla.edu

Details: Free

User Info: To subscribe to the list, send an e-mail message requesting a subscription to the URL address that follows. Include your name, e-mail, phone number, address, and topics of interest.

To send a message to the entire list, address it to: bras-net@cs.ucla.edu

`mailto:bras-net-request@cs.ucla.edu`

POS302-L

POS302-L

A discussion list created for the "Race, Ethnicity, and Social Inequality" seminar offered at Illinois State University (spring 1994). The general purposes of the list are to create an e-mail audience for the written work of enrolled students and to invite a broad audience to participate in the seminar.

Keywords: Race, Ethnic Studies, Minorities

Audience: Ethnic Studies, Students, Sociologists, Educators

Details: Free

User Info: To subscribe to the list, send an e-mail message to the URL address that follows, consisting of a single line reading:

SUB pos302-l YourFirstName YourLastName

To send a message to the entire list, address it to: pos302-l@ilstu.edu

`mailto:listserv@ilstu.edu`

POSCIM

POSCIM

This mailing list is intended as a forum for those researching, teaching, or studying political science, as well as for politicians.

Keywords: Political Science

Audience: Political Scientists, Educators, Politicians, Researchers

Contact: Markus Schlegel
ups500@vm.gmd.de

Details: Free

User Info: To subscribe to the list, send an e-mail message to the URL address that follows, consisting of a single line reading:

SUB POSCIM YourFirstName YourLastName

To send a message to the entire list, address it to: ups500@vm.gmd.de

`mailto:listserv@vm.gmd.de`

Posix-ada

Posix-ada

To discuss the Ada binding of the POSIX standard. This is the IEEE P1003.5 working group.

Keywords: Poxis, Computer Specialists

Audience: Posix Users, Software Developers

Contact: Karl Nyberg
posix-ada-request@grebyn.com

Details: Free

User Info: To subscribe to the list, send an e-mail message requesting a subscription to the URL address that follows.

To send a message to the entire list, address it to: posix-ada@grebyn.com

`mailto:posix-ada-request@grebyn.com`

Posix-testing

Posix-testing

A forum for discussion of issues related to testing operating systems for conformance to the various POSIX standards and proposed standards. Issues include problems related to test suites in general, testability of various features of the standards, and portability of the test suites to the many very different POSIX implementations anticipated in the near future.

Keywords: COmputer Systems

Audience: Posix Testers

Contact: Chuck Karish
posix-testing-request@mindcraft.com

Details: Free

User Info: To subscribe to the list, send an e-mail message requesting a subscription to the URL address that follows.

To send a message to the entire list, address it to: posix-testing@mindcraft.com

`mailto:posix-testing-request@mindcraft.com`

Postal Services

POP

★

This list provides an organized source of information for discussion of the Post Office Protocol (POP2 and POP3 - described in RFCs 918, 937, 1081, and 1082) and implementations thereof. Its motivation was the lack of easily obtained knowledge of available POP2 and POP3 servers and clients.

Keywords: Postal Services

Audience: Postal Service Workers

Contact: Andy S. Poling
pop-request@jhunix.hcf.jhu.edu

Details: Free

User Info: To subscribe to the list, send an e-mail message requesting a subscription to the URL address that follows.

To send a message to the entire list, address it to: pop@jhunix.hcf.jhu.edu

`mailto:pop-request@jhunix.hcf.jhu.edu`

Postmodern Culture

PMC-MOO

★

A real-time, text-based, virtual-reality environment in which subscribers to Postmodern Culture can interact and participate in live conferences.

Keywords: Literature (Contemporary), Postmodern Culture, Literary Criticism

Audience: General Public, Writers, Literary Theorists, Researchers

Profile: In addition to providing Postmodern Culture's subscribers with the opportunity to interact and to participate in live conferences, PMC-MOO provides access to texts generated by the journal and by PMC-TALK, as well as the opportunity to experience (or to help design) programs that simulate object lessons in postmodern theory. PMC-MOO is based on the LambdaMOO program, freeware by Pavel Curtis.

Contact: pmc@unity.ncsu.edu

Notes: If your Internet account is on a UNIX machine and you have access to the Emacs editior (type 'man emacs' or 'help emacs' or simply 'emacs' at your command prompt to find out, or ask your user-services people). You can connect to PMC-MOO using a customized Emacs client available from our FTP site. This client provides text-buffering, multiple windows, and many features superior to an unmediated Telnet connection.

To retrieve the Emacs client, perform the following ftp transfer: ftp ftp.ncsu.edu; login: ftp; password: [your e-mail address]; cd pub/docs/pmc/pmc-talk; get PMC-MOO.doc; get mud.el; bin; get mud.elc; quit.

`telnet://dewey.lib.ncsu.edu`

Postmodern Culture

 ★★★★

Postmodern Culture is a peer-reviewed electronic journal of interdisciplinary criticism on contemporary literature, theory, and culture.

Keywords: Literature (Contemporary), Postmodern Culture, Literary Criticism

Sponsor: Oxford University Press

Audience: General Public, Writers, Critics, Literary Theorists, Researchers

Profile: All back issues of Postmodern Culture are always available; previous issues have included:

- Andrew Ross, Hacking Away at the Counter-Culture

- Bell Hooks, Postmodern Blackness

- Laura Kipnis, Marx: The Video (A Politics of Revolting Bodies)

- Kathy Acker, Dead Doll Humility' and Obsession

- Neil Larsen, Postmodernism and Imperialism: Theory and Politics in Latin America

- Patrick O'Donnell, His Master's Voice: On William Gaddis's JR

- Greg Ulmer, Grammatology Hypemedia

- Charles Bernstein, The Second War and Postmodern Memory

- Allison Fraiberg, Of AIDS, Cyborgs, and Other Indiscretions: Resurfacing the Body in the Postmodern (with a response by David Porush)

- Stuart Moulthrop, You Say You Want a Revolution: Hypertext and the Laws of Media

- Bob Perelman, The Marginalization of Poetry

Details: Costs

User Info: To subscribe to the list, send an e-mail message requesting a subscription to the URL address that follows.

`mailto:pmc@ncsvm.cc.ncsu.edu`

WIRED Online

 ★★★

This is WIRED Magazine's gopher server.

Keywords: Postmodern Culture, News Media

Sponsor: WIRED Magazine

Audience: Internet Surfers, Internet Users, General Public

Profile: Features full-text of WIRED back issues, including the Net Surf column devoted to Internet exploration. Also has archives of the HotWIRED weekly mailing list, some guides to getting started surfing the net, general information about WIRED magazine, and an archive of material on the proposed Clipper federal encryption standard.

Contact: WIRED Online department, WIRED Magazine
online@wired.com, info@wired.com

`gopher://gopher.wired.com`

Postmodernism

FutureCulture FAQ (Frequently Asked Questions) File

 ★★★

List of online and offline items of interest to subscribers of FutureCulture, a mailing list on 'technoculture' or 'new edge' or 'cyberculture.'

Keywords: Technology, Cyberculture, Postmodernism, Sci-Fi, Zines

Audience: Reality Hackers, Cyberculture Enthuasists

Profile: This list discusses cyberpunk culture, rave culture, industrial music, virtual reality, drugs, computer underground, Net sociology, and virtual communities.

Contact: Alias Datura (adatura on IRC)
adatura@uafhp.uark.edu

Details: Free

`ftp://etext.archive.umich.edu/pub`

Power Boating

The Nautical Bookshelf

Catalog and ordering information for Nautical Bookshelf's collection of books on sailing and other water sports.

Keywords: Boating, Power Boating, Sailing, Sports

Sponsor: Nautical Bookshelf

Audience: Boating Enthusiasts, Sailors

Contact: staff@nautical.com

`gopher://gopher.nautical.com`

A
B
C
D
E
F
G
H
I
J
K
L
M
N
O
P
Q
R
S
T
U
V
W
X
Y
Z

Poxis

Posix-ada

To discuss the Ada binding of the POSIX standard. This is the IEEE P1003.5 working group.

Keywords: Poxis, Computer Specialists

Audience: Posix Users, Software Developers

Contact: Karl Nyberg
posix-ada-request@grebyn.com

Details: Free

User Info: To subscribe to the list, send an e-mail message requesting a subscription to the URL address that follows.

To send a message to the entire list, address it to: posix-ada@grebyn.com

`mailto:posix-ada-request@grebyn.com`

PPPL (The Princeton Plasma Physics Laboratory)

PPPL (The Princeton Plasma Physics Laboratory)

This web site provides an overview of the projects, mission, physical plant and history of the PPPL.

Keywords: Physics, Research

Sponsor: U.S. Department of Energy (DOE)

Audience: Physicists, Educators, Students

Contact: Anthony R. De Meo or Jack A. Mervine
pppl_info@pppl.gov
webmaster@pppl.gov

Details: Free

`http://www.pppl.gov`

Prague University of Economics Gopher Service

Prague University of Economics Gopher Service

Includes information about the University, integrative studies of economy, economic information, and public domain software.

Keywords: Czech Republic, Economics, Europe

Audience: Czechs, Economists

Contact: gopher@pub.vse.cz

Details: Free

`gopher://pub.vse.cz`

Pre-Law, Legislation, Court Decisions

Pre-Law, Legislation, Court Decisions

A collection of legal information including court decisions on abortion, a directory of US Judges, US Supreme Court rulings, and some primary documents relating to US and International law.

Keywords: Law (US Federal), Law (US State), Law (International)

Sponsor: Skidmore College Gopher Project, New York, USA

Audience: Lawyers, Legal Professionals

Contact: Leo Geoffrion, Peggy Seiden
ldg@skidmore.edu
pseiden@skidmore.edu

`gopher://grace.skidmore.edu/readings/social-sciences/law`

Pregnancy

Bethany Christian Services

A major directory on adoption, providing access to a broad range of related resources (library catalogs, databases, and servers) through the Internet.

Keywords: Adoption, Christianity, Pregnancy, Abortion Rights

Sponsor: Bethany Christian Services, Grand Rapids, Michigan, USA

Audience: Pregnant Women

Profile: The gopher server of Bethany, a pro-life, pro-family agency reaching out to women with unplanned pregnancies and adoptive couples. Contains a large amount of information about national and international adoption, the adoption process, African-American adoptions, and adoption of children with special needs. Also contains information for pregnant women, such as birth father rights and responsibilities, pregnancy counceling, and so on.

Contact: gophermaster@bethany.org

`gopher://gopher.bethany.org/11`

President

National Performance Review (NPR)

The Report of the National Performance Review, from the task force led by Vice President Gore, titled 'From Red Tape to Results: Creating a Government that Works Better and Costs Less,' Sept. 7, 1993.

Keywords: President, Politics, White House

Audience: Political Scientists, General Public

Profile: On March 3, 1993, President Clinton asked Vice President Gore to lead the effort to effect real change in the federal government. Gore's NPR Task Force overview and accompanying reports make specific recommendations for: reducing costs and waste, changing the way government operates, and making government more responsive and effective.

Details: Free

`gopher://cyfer.esusda.gov/11/ace/policy/npr/nat`

Technology Initiatives for the Clinton/Gore Administration

This is a 40-page text of the press release from the Clinton administration on technology initiatives, dated February 22, 1993.

Keywords: Politics, President, White House, Technology

Audience: General Public, Journalists

Details: Free

E-mail to the ListServ and include the following in the body of the message: get cni-bigideas.whouse.paper

`mailto:listserv@cni.org`

White House Phone Numbers

A list of names, addresses, e-mail addresses and telephone and fax numbers of the President, First Lady, Vice President, and all the members of the Cabinet.

Keywords: White House, President, Politics

Audience: General Public

Details: Free

`ftp://nifty.andrew.cmu.edu/pub/QRD/info/govt/cabinet`

President (US)

Presidential Documents

This gopher provides access to the full text of Presidential Proclamations, Executive Orders, Notices, Memoranda, and Determinations dating from December 23, 1992. The documents are listed sequentially by date and number (that is, Proclamation 6520 of December 23, 1992).

Keywords: Politics, President (US), White House, Documents

Audience: General Public

Details: Free

Select from menu presented (probably you will follow the following path: Internet Services/US Government/Presidential Documents.

`gopher://jupiter.cc.gettysborg.edu`

White House Information Service

An outstanding database of current White House information, from 1992 to the present.

Keywords: White House, Politics, President (US), Database

Sponsor: Texas A & M University

Audience: General Public

Profile: Much of the older information on this site was obtained from the clinton@marist.bitnet listserv list or the alt.politics.clinton Usenet newsgroup, both of which receive the information indirectly via the MIT White House information server. Newer and current material is received directly from the MIT distribution list. The menu includes a searchable database and headings such as Domestic Affairs (Health Care, Technology, and so on), Press Briefings and Conferences, the President's Daily Schedule, and many more.

Contact: whadmin@tamu.edu

Details: Free

`gopher://tamuts.tamu.edu/11/.dir/president.dir`

White House Press Releases

★★★★

An archive of all the press releases by the Clinton administration organized as Miscellaneous, Briefings by Dee Dee Myers, Executive Orders, Remarks during Photo Opportunities, Remarks of Bill Clinton, Briefings by George Stephanopolous.

Keywords: White House, Politics, President (US)

Audience: General Public

Details: Free

`gopher://wiretap.spies.com/11/Clinton`

Pricing

Internet Public Subsidies

★

An article entitled "The Economic Case for Public Subsidy of the Internet."

Keywords: Internet, Pricing

Audience: Internet Surfers

Contact: Sandra Schickele

Details: Free

`gopher://ssugopher.sonoma.edu`

Primates

Primate-talk (Primate Discussion List)

★★★

Forum for the discussion of primatology and related subjects.

Keywords: Primates, Primatology, Veterinary Medicine

Audience: Primatologists, Veterinarians

Profile: This list is open to any e-mail user with an interest in primatology. Subject matter ranges from, but is not limited to, news items, meeting announcements, research issues, information requests, veterinary/husbandry topics, job notices, animal exchange information, and book reviews.

Contact: Larry Jacobsen
jacobsen@pimate.wisc.edu

Details: Free

User Info: To subscribe to the list, send an e-mail message requesting a subscription to the URL address that follows.

`mailto:primate-talk-request@primate.wisc.edu`

WRPRCC

★★★

Keywords: Primates, Wisconsin

Sponsor: Wisconsin Regional Primate Research Center

Audience: Primatologists, Zoologists

Contact: jacobsen@primate.wisc.edu

Details: Free

User Info: Expect: Login; enter: wiscinfo; choose: UW-Madison Information Servers Wisconsin Primate Research Center Server

`gopher://gopher.primate.wisc.edu`

Primatology

Laboratory Primate Newsletter

★

Provides a central source of information about nonhuman primates and related matters for scientists who use these animals in their research and for those whose work supports such research.

Keywords: Primatology, Psychology

Audience: Primate Researchers, Psychologists

Contact: Judith E. Schrier
primate@brownvm.brown.edu

Details: Free

`mailto:listserv@brownvm.brown.edu`

Primate-talk (Primate Discussion List)

★★★

Forum for the discussion of primatology and related subjects.

Keywords: Primates, Primatology, Veterinary Medicine

Audience: Primatologists, Veterinarians

Profile: This list is open to any e-mail user with an interest in primatology. Subject matter ranges from, but is not limited to, news items, meeting announcements, research issues, information requests, veterinary/husbandry topics, job notices, animal exchange information, and book reviews.

Contact: Larry Jacobsen
jacobsen@pimate.wisc.edu

Details: Free

User Info: To subscribe to the list, send an e-mail message requesting a subscription to the URL address that follows.

`mailto:primate-talk-request@primate.wisc.edu`

Prince

Prince

★

A mailing list devoted to discussing the musician formerly named Prince and related artists.

Keywords: Musical Groups, Rock Music

Audience: Musicians, Music Students, Music Enthusiasts

Contact: prince-request@icpsr.umich.edu

Details: Free

User Info: To subscribe to the list, send an e-mail message requesting a subscription to the URL address that follows.

To send a message to the entire list, address it to: prince-request@icpsr.umich.edu

`mailto:prince@icpsr.umich.edu`

Princeton University Library

Princeton University Library

★★

The library's holdings are large and wide-ranging. They contain significant collections in many fields.

Keywords: China, Japan, Classics, History (Ancient), Near Eastern Studies, Literature (American), Literature (English), Aeronautics, Middle Eastern Studies, Mormonism, Publishing

Audience: General Public, Researchers, Librarians, Document Delivery Professionals

A B C D E F G H I J K L M N O **P** Q R S T U V W X Y Z

Details: Free

User Info: Expect: Connect message, blank screen, Send: <cr>; Expect: #, Send: Call 500

`telnet://pucable.princeton.edu`

Princeton University Online Manuscripts Catalog Library

Princeton University Online Manuscripts Catalog Library

★★

The library's holdings are large and wide-ranging. They contain significant collections in many fields.

Keywords: Books (Antiquarian), Dickens (Charles), Disraeli (Benjamin), Eliot (George), Hardy (Thomas), Kingsley (Charles), Trollope (Anthony)

Audience: General Public, Researchers, Librarians, Document Delivery Professionals

Details: Free

User Info: Expect: VM370 logo, Send: <cr>; Expect: Welcome screen, Send: folio <cr>; Expect: Welcome screen for FOLIO, Send: <cr>; Expect: List of choices, Send: 3 <cr>; To exit: type: logoff

`telnet://pucc.princeton.edu`

Principia Cybernetica Newsletter

Principia Cybernetica Newsletter

★★★

Newsletter for participants in the Principia Cybernetica Project (PCP), as well as for people interested in keeping informed about the project.

Keywords: Philosophy, Worldview

Audience: Philosophers

Profile: PCP is a computer-supported collaborative attempt to develop an integrated evolutionary-systemic philosophy or world view. Its contributors are distributed over several continents and maintain contact primarily through electronic mail (mailing list PRNCYB-L), as well as through annual meetings, the printed (and electronic) newsletter, and postal mail. PCP focuses on the clear formulation of basic concepts and principles of the cybernetic approach.

Contact: Cliff Joslyn, Francis Heylighen fheyligh@vnet3.vub.ac.be

cjoslyn@bingvaxu.cc.binghamton.edu

Details: Free

Send a 1- to 2- page letter, giving your address and affiliations and motivating your interest in the Project to the List owner (C. Joslyn).

`mailto:cjoslyn@bingvaxu.cc.binghamton.edu`

Printing

PIRA - Paper, Printing and Publishing, Packaging, and Nonwovens Abstracts

Coverage of all aspects of paper, pulp, nonwovens, printing, publishing and packaging.

Keywords: Material Science, Paper, Printing, Publishing, Packaging

Sponsor: PIRA International

Audience: Material Scientists, Researchers

Profile: File contains more than 300,000 records. Special applications: company and market profiles, product and trade name searches, research and technology trends. Updated biweekly.

Contact: paul.albert@neteast.com

User Info: To subscribe, contact Orbit-Questel directly.

`telnet://orbit.com`

Prion (Prion Research Digest)

Prion (Prion Research Digest)

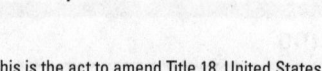

Prion Infection Digest discusses current research on prion (slow virus) infection. The Prion Digest was formed as a reference point for the discussion and sharing of current research into prion infection.

Keywords: Prion, Health

Audience: Medical Researchers, Health-care Professionals

Contact: Chris Swanson prion-request@stolaf.edu

Details: Free

User Info: To subscribe to the list, send an e-mail message requesting a subscription to the URL address that follows.

To send a message to the entire list, address it to: prion@stolaf.edu

`mailto:prion-request@stolaf.edu`

Privacy

alt.security.pgp

★

A Usenet newsgroup providing information and discussion about the Pretty Good Privacy package, a privately-developed encryption technique.

Keywords: Privacy, Encryption, Security Firewalls, Computers

Audience: Internet Surfers

User Info: To subscribe to this Usenet newsgroup, you need access to a newsreader.

`news:alt.security.pgp`

EFFector Online—The Electronic Frontier Foundation, Inc.

Established to make the electronic frontier truly useful and accessible to everyone, emphasizing the free and open flow of information and communication.

Keywords: Computer Communications, Electronic Media, Intellectual Property, Privacy

Audience: Computer Users, Civil Libertarians

Profile: EFFector Online presents news, information, and discussion about the world of computer-based communications media that constitute the electronic frontier. It covers issues such as freedom of speech in digital media, privacy rights, censorship, and standards of responsibility for users and operators of computer systems, as well as policy issues such as the development of a national information infrastructure, and intellectual property.

Contact: Gerard Van der Leun, Mike Godwin gerard@eff.org mnemonic@eff.org

Details: Free

User Info: To subscribe, send an e-mail message requesting a subscription to: request@eff.org

Notes: This takes you to the front door of the eff gopher server which contains much more information than just Effector online.

`gopher://gopher.eff.org/1`

Electronic Communications Privacy Act of 1986

★

This is the act to amend Title 18, United States Code, with respect to the interception of certain communications, other forms of surveillance, and for other purposes. This act affects every Usenet, Bitnet, BBS, shortwave listener, TV viewer, and so on.

Keywords: Communications, Privacy, Government (US Federal), Laws (US Federal)

Audience: Journalists, Privacy Activists, Students, Politicians

Details: Free

`gopher://wiretap.spies.com/00/Gov/ecpa.act`

Freedom of Information Act (FOIA): Guide to Use

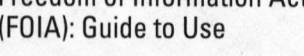

This is a citizen's guide on using the Freedom of Information Act and the Privacy Act of 1974 to request government records.

Keywords: Privacy, Freedom of Information, Government (US Federal)

Audience: Journalists, Privacy Activists, Students, Politicians, US Citizens

Details: Free

`gopher://wiretap.spies.com/00/Gov/`
`foia.cit`

Networks & Communities

This directory is a compilation of information resources focused on networks and communities.

Keywords: Community , Networking, Privacy

Audience: Network Developers, Community Activists, Free-net Organizers, Fundraisers

Details: Free

`ftp://una.hh.lib.umich.edu/70/`
`inetdirsstacks/nets:sternberg`

Privacy

An archive about identity, privacy, and anonymity on the Internet, from the Usenet newsgroup alt.privacy.

Keywords: Privacy, Internet

Audience: Internet Surfers

Details: Free

Notes: File is: pub/nic/internet.literature/ netiquette.txt

`ftp://pit-manager.mit.edu`

Privacy Act of 1974

The act that regulates the maintenance of privacy and protection of records on individuals.

Keywords: Privacy, Law (US Federal), Government (US Federal)

Audience: Journalists, Politicians, Lawyers

Details: Free

User Info: Choose from menu as appropriate.

`gopher://wiretap.spies.com/00/Gov/`
`privacy.act`

Privacy Rights Clearinghouse (PRC)

A collection of materials related to privacy issues.

Keywords: Privacy, Legislation, Consumer Rights, Freedom of Information

Sponsor: University of San Diego

Audience: Citizens, Privacy Activists, Journalists

Profile: This site contains fact sheets (in English and Spanish) on privacy issues ranging from wiretapping to credit reporting. Also includes federal and state privacy legislation as well as related position papers and press releases.

Contact: prc@teetot.acusd.edu

User Info: Expect: Login; Send: Privacy

`gopher://teetot.acusd.edu`

`telnet://teetot.acusd.edu`

PRL

PRL

The Pirate Radio SWL list is for the distribution of questions, answers, information, and loggings of Pirate Radio Stations.

Keywords: Radio, Communications

Audience: Radio Broadcasters, Radio Pirates

Contact: John Brewer brewer@ace.enet.dec.com

User Info: To subscribe to the list, send an e-mail message to the URL address that follows, consisting of a single line reading:

SUB PRLYourFirstName YourLastName

To send a message to the entire list, address it to: brewer@ace.enet.dec.com

`mailto:listserv@ace.enet.dec.com`

Professional Sports

Funet Sports Information

An FTP archive of information on various sports with links to the archive at wuarchive.wustl.edu.

Keywords: Sports, Professional Sports, Ice Hockey, Motor Racing, NFL, NHL, NBA, MLB

Sponsor: Finnish Academic and Research Network (FUNET)

Audience: Sports Enthusiasts

Profile: A fairly extensive archive of information on both American (NBA, MLB, NHL, NFL) and worldwide sports (soccer, ice hockey, motor racing, and so on). Includes FAQs for various sports, statistics, pictures, and some sports games for the PC.

Contact: Jari Pullinen sports-adm@nic.funet.fi

Details: Free, Images

`gopher://ftp.funet.fi/pub/sports`

NFL Scores, Schedules, and Point Spreads

Information on National Football League (NFL) football scores, schedules, and point spreads.

Keywords: Professional Sports, Sports, Football, NFL

Audience: Football Fans

Contact: office@world.std.com

Details: Free

`gopher://world.std.com/News and`
`Weather`

Professional Sports Schedules

Sports schedules for major professional sports.

Keywords: Sports, Baseball, Hockey, Football, Basketball, Professional Sports

Sponsor: Colorado University, Boulder, CO

Audience: Sports Enthusiasts, Football Enthusiasts, Hockey Enthusiasts, Baseball Enthusiasts, Basketball Enthusiasts

Profile: The Colorado University gopher maintains an interactive online database of schedules for all major US professional sports teams (NBA, NFL, NHL, MLB). The database is indexed by both team name and dates of games, and can be searched accordingly.

Contact: gopher@gopher.colorado.edu

Details: Free

`gopher://gopher.colorado.edu/11/`
`professional/sports/schedules`

Prog-Pubs

Prog-Pubs

A mailing list for people interested in progressive and/or alternative publications and other media. Discussions include issues pertaining to all kinds of small-scale, independent, progressive, and/or alternative media, including newspapers, newsletters, and radio and video shows.

Keywords: Media, Alternative Press, Communications

Audience: Students (College/University), Media Professionals

Contact: prog-pubs-request@fuggles.acc. virginia.edu

Details: Free

User Info: To subscribe to the list, send an e-mail message requesting a subscription to the URL address that follows.

To send a message to the entire list, address it to:prog-pubs@fuggles.acc.virginia.edu

`mailto:prog-`
`pubs@fuggles.acc.virginia.edu`

Programming

ABC

Discussion of the ABC Programming Language and its implementations.

Keywords: Programming, ABC Programming Language

Audience: Programmers

Contact: Steven Pemberton abc-list-request@cwi.nl

A B C D E F G H I J K L M N O P Q R S T U V W X Y Z

Details: Free

User Info: To subscribe to the list, send an e-mail message requesting a subscription to the URL address that follows.

To send a message to the entire list, address it to: ABC@cwi.nl

`mailto:abc-list-request@cwi.nl`

ACM SIGGRAPH Online Bibliography Project

★★★★

This is a collection of computer-graphics bibliographic references.

Keywords: Multimedia, Interactive, Computer Graphics, Programming

Sponsor: Association of Computing Machinery (ACM), Special Interest Group on Computer Graphics (SIGGRAPH)

Audience: Developers, Designers, Producers, Educators, Programmers, Graphic Artists

Profile: The goal of this project is to maintain an up-to-date database of computer-graphics literature, in a format that is accessible to as many members of the computer-graphics community as possible. The database includes references from conferences and workshops worldwide and from a variety of publications dating back as far as the late-19th century. The majority of the major journals and conference proceedings from the mid-1970s to the present are listed.

Contact: bibadmin@siggraph.org

Details: Free, Moderated, Multimedia

`ftp://siggraph.org/publications`

Ada-sw

A list for users who access and contribute software to the Ada Repository on SIMTEL20.

Keywords: Programming, Ada

Audience: Programmers

Details: Free

User Info: To subscribe to the list, send an e-mail message requesting a subscription to the URL address that follows.

To send a message to the entire list, address it to Ada-sw@wsmr-simtel20.army.mil

`mailto:ada-sw-request@wsmr-simtel20.army.mil`

APL-L

A discussion of the APL language, its implementation, application, and use. Contributions on teaching APL are particularly welcome.

Keywords: Programming, Programming Languages, APL

Audience: Programmers

Contact: David G. Macneil dgm@unb.cat4327@unb.ca

Details: Free

User Info: To subscribe to the list, send an e-mail message to the URL address that follows, consisting of a single line reading:

SUB APL-L YourFirstName YourLastName

To send a message to the entire list, address it to: APL-L@cis.vutbr.cs

`mailto:listserv@unb.ca`

BETA

A discussion forum for BETA users. BETA is a modern object-oriented programming language.

Keywords: Programming, Object-Oriented Programming, BETA

Audience: Programmers

Contact: Elmer Soerensen Sandvad usergroup-request@mjolner.dk

Details: Free, Moderated

User Info: To subscribe to the list, send an e-mail message requesting a subscription to the URL address that follows.

To send a message to the entire list, address it to: usergroup@mjolner.dk

`mailto:usergroup-request@mjolner.dk`

Clp.x

Devoted to discussion of concurrent logic programming languages, concurrent constraint programming languages, semantics, proof techniques and program transformations, parallel Prolog systems, implementations, and programming techniques and idioms.

Keywords: Programming, Programming Languages, Concurrent Logic

Audience: Concurrent Logic Programmers

Contact: Jacob Levy jlevy.pa@xerox.com

Details: Free

User Info: To subscribe to the list, send an e-mail message requesting a subscription to the URL address that follows.

To send a message to the entire lst, address it to: clp.x@xerox.com

`mailto:clp-request.x@xerox.com`

DISSPLA (Display Integrated Software System and Plotting Language)

News and information exchange concerning DISSPLA.

Keywords: Computer Graphics, Programming

Audience: DISSPLA Users, Computer Programmers

Profile: DISSPLA is a high-level FORTRAN graphics subroutine library designed for programmers in engineering, science and business.

Contact: Zvika Bar-Deroma er7101@technion.technion.ac.il

Details: Free

User Info: To subscribe to the list, send an e-mail message to the URL address shown that follows, consisting of a single line reading:

SUB disspla YourFirstName YourLastName

To send a message to the entire list, address it to: disspla@taunivm.tau.ac.il

`mailto:listserv@taunivm.tau.ac.il`

EXPRESS-Users

Discussion of topics pertaining to the EXPRESS information modeling language, such as information sources, how to download information, information modeling techniques, and sample models.

Keywords: Programming, EXPRESS Information Modeling Language

Audience: EXPRESS Programmers

Contact: Steve Clark, Charlie Lindahl EXPRESS-users-request@cme.nist.gov

Details: Free

User Info: To subscribe to the list, send an e-mail message requesting a subscription to the URL address that follows.

`mailto:EXPRESS-users-request@cme.nist.gov`

Icon-group

Discussion of topics related to the Icon programming language

Keywords: Programming, Icon Programming Language, Programming Language, String Processing

Audience: Icon Programmers

Profile: Icon is a high-level, general purpose programming language emphazing string and structure processing. Topics include programming techniques, theoretical aspects, Icon in relation to other languages, applications of Icon, implementation issues, porting, and bugs.

Contact: Bill Mitchell whm@arizona.edu

Details: Free

User Info: To subscribe to the list, send an e-mail message requesting a subscription to the URL address that follows.

`mailto:Icon-Group-Request@arizona.edu.`

A B C D E F G H I J K L M N O P Q R S T U V W X Y Z

info-Ada ★

Discussion of the Ada programming language.

Keywords: Programming, Ada (Programming Language)

Audience: Programmers

Contact: Karl A. Nyberg
Karl@grebyn.com

Details: Free

User Info: To subscribe to the list, send an e-mail message requesting a subscription to the URL address that follows

`mailto:info-Ada-request@sei.cmu.edu`

info-C ★

Discussions about C programming and the C programming language.

Keywords: Programming, C (Programming Language)

Audience: C Programmers

Contact: Mark Plotnick
info-C-request@research.att.com

Details: Free

User Info: To subscribe to the list, send an e-mail message requesting a subscription to the URL address that follows.

`mailto:info-C-`
`request@research.att.com`

info-M2 ★

E-conference for the Modula-2 programming language.

Keywords: Programming, Modula-2 (Programming Language)

Audience: Modula-2 Programmers

Contact: Thomas Habernoll
postmast@ucf1vm.cc.ucf.edu (USA)
habernol@tubvm.cs.tu-berlin.de (Europe)

Details: Free

User Info: To subscribe to the list, send an e-mail message to the URL address that follows, consisting of a single line reading:

SUB info-M2 YourFirstName YourLastName

To send a message to the entire list, address it to: info-M2@ucf1vm.cc.ucf.edu

`mailto:listserv@ucf1vm.cc.ucf.edu`

info-Pascal ★

Discussions of any Pascal implementation, from mainframe to micro, for Pascal program users.

Keywords: Programming, Pascal

Audience: Pascal Programmers, Pascal Users

Contact: Hernan Lobos *Mitzio*
hlobos@utfsm.bitnet

Details: Free

User Info: To subscribe to the list, send an e-mail message requesting a subscription to the following URL address.

`info-Pascal@brl.mil`

insoft-l ★

This list discusses techniques for developing new software and for converting existing software, as well as internationalization tools, announcements of internationalized public-domain software and of foreign-language versions of commercial software, calls for papers, conference announcements, and references to documentation related to the internationalization of software.

Keywords: Programming, Software Internationalization

Sponsor: Center for Computing and Information Services, Technical University of Brno

Audience: Software Developers

Contact: insoft-l-request@cis.vutbr.cs

Details: Free, Moderated

User Info: To subscribe to the list, send an e-mail message to the URL address that follows, consisting of a single line reading:

SUB insoft-l YourFirstName YourLastName

To send a message to the entire list, address it to: insoft-l@cis.vutbr.cs

`mailto:listserv@cis.vutbr.cs`

Lang-Lucid ★

Discussions on all aspects related to the programming language Lucid, including language design issues, implementations for personal computers, implementations for parallel machines, language extensions, programming environments, products, bug reports, and bug fixes/workarounds.

Keywords: Programming, Programming Languages

Audience: Lucid Programmers

Contact: R. Jagannathan
lang-lucid-request@csl.sri.com

Details: Free

User Info: To subscribe to the list, send an e-mail message requesting a subscription to the URL address that follows.

`mailto:lang-lucid-request@csl.sri.com`

Litprog ★

A network list dealing with topics related to literate programming, both general (is literate programming compatible with writing portable programs), and particular (is it possible to use CWEB with ANSIC).

Keywords: Programming, Literate Programming

Audience: Computer Programmers

Contact: George D. Greenwade
bed_gdg@shsu.edu

Details: Free

User Info: To subscribe to the list, send an e-mail message to the URL address that follows, consisting of a single line reading:

SUB listprog YourFirstName YourLastName

To send a message to the entire list, address it to: listprog @shsu.edu

Notes: This list is open to novices and seasoned literate programmers.

`mailto:listserv@shsu.edu`

Loughborough University of Technology Computer-Human Interaction (LUTCHI) Research Centre ★★★★

This server contains general information on computer-human interaction.

Keywords: Interface Design, Ergonomics, Computer-Human Interactions, Programming

Sponsor: Loughborough University of Technology, Leicestershire, UK

Audience: Software Developers, Software Designers, Programmers

Profile: The LUTCHI Research Centre is based within the Department of Computer Studies at the Loughborough University of Technology, Leicestershire, UK. This server contains information about LUTCHI research projects, official LUTCHI publicity releases, as well as documents, images, and movies associated with those projects.

Contact: Ben Anderson
B.Anderson@lut.ac.uk

Details: Free, Moderated, Sound, Image, and Multimedia files available.

Use a World-Wide Web (Mosaic) client and open a connection to the resource.

`http://pipkin.lut.ac.uk`

NIC (Nucleus for Interactive Computing) ★★★★

WWW-based system for interactive computing.

Keywords: Multimedia, Interactive Computing, Interface Design, Scripting Laguages, Programming

Sponsor: BYU Interactive Software Systems Lab

Audience: Software Developers, Educators

Profile: NIC is a system for interactive computing that combines a data model, a user interface model, and a scripting language to create flexible and powerful user interfaces. Documentation still under construction is located here.

A
B
C
D
E
F
G
H
I
J
K
L
M
N
O
P
Q
R
S
T
U
V
W
X
Y
Z

A B C D E F G H I J K L M N O P Q R S T U V W X Y Z

Contact: Dan Olsen
olsen@cs.byu.edu

Details: Free, Moderated, Sound, Image, and Multimedia files available.

Use a World Wide Web (Mosaic) client and open a connection to the resource.

`ftp://issl.cs.byu.edu/docs/NIC/home.html`

Proof-users

Discussion of the left-associative natural language "parser proof".

Keywords: Computing, Programming

Audience: Computer Programmers

Contact: Craig Latta
proof-request@xcf.berkeley.edu

Details: Free

To join, e-mail proof-request@xcf.berkeley.edu with the subject line "add me".

`mailto:proof-request@xcf.berkeley.edu`

rec.games.programmer

A Usenet newsgroup providing information and discussion about adventure game programming.

Keywords: Games, Programming, Video Games

Audience: Programmers

User Info: To subscribe to this Usenet newsgroup, you need access to a newsreader.

`news:rec.games.programmer`

Simula

An electronic conference for discussion of the SIMULA programming language.

Keywords: Programming, SIMULA

Audience: SIMULA Programmers

Details: Free

User Info: To subscribe to the list, send an e-mail message to the URL address that follows, consisting of a single line reading:

SUB Simula YourFirstName YourLastName

To send a message to the entire list, address it to: Simula@bitnic.educom.edu

`mailto:listserv@bitnic.educom.edu`

Weather-users

Weather-users is a mailing list for developers of programs that access the Weather Underground database at the University of Michigan.

Keywords: Weather, Programming, Meteorology

Audience: Programmers

Contact: Scott Hazen Mueller
scott@zorch.sf-bay.org

Details: Free

User Info: To subscribe to the list, send an e-mail message

`mailto:weather-users-request@zorch.sf-bay.org`

Programming Languages

AMOS

For the AMOS programming language on Amiga computers. Features source, bug reports, and help from users around the world, but mainly from European users. Most posts will be in English, but there are no language limitations.

Keywords: Computers, Programming Languages, AMOS, Amiga

Audience: Programmers, Computer Users

Contact: subscribe@xamiga.linet.org

Details: Free

User Info: To subscribe to the list, send an e-mail message to the URL address that follows, consisting of a single line reading:

SUB #amos userneame@domain

To send a message to the entire list, address it to: subscribe@xamiga.linet.org

`mailto:subscribe@xamiga.linet.org`

APL-L

Discussion of the APL language, its implementation, application, and use. Contributions on teaching APL are particularly welcome.

Keywords: Programming, Programming Languages, APL

Audience: Programmers

Contact: David G. Macneil
dgm@unb.cat4327@unb.ca

Details: Free

User Info: To subscribe to the list, send an e-mail message to the URL address that follows, consisting of a single line reading:

SUB APL-L YourFirstName YourLastName

To send a message to the entire list, address it to: APL-L@cis.vutbr.cs

`mailto:listserv@unb.ca`

AppWare-info

A forum for discussion of issues relating to AppWare software. Topics include simple programming questions, tips for program efficiency, quirks of, and complaints about the environment or tools, the process of writing new ALMs or functions, third party enhancements, and any other question.

Keywords: Computers, Programming Languages

Sponsor: Novell Inc.

Audience: AppWare Users, Computer Programmers

Contact: Novell Inc.
appware-info@serius.uchicago.edu

User Info: To subscribe to the list, send an e-mail message to the URL address that follows.

To send a message to the entire list, address it to: appware-info@serius.uchicago.edu

`mailto:appware-info-request@serius.uchicago.edu`

`ftp://serius.uchicago.edu`

C-IBM-370

The C on IBM mainframes mailing list is a place to discuss aspects of using the C programming language on s/370-architecture computers—especially under IBM's operating systems for that environment.

Keywords: C Language, Programming Languages, IBM

Audience: IBM Users, Computer Users, Computer Programmers

Contact: David Wolfskill
C-IBM-370-request@dhw68k.cts.com

Details: Free

User Info: To subscribe to the list, send an e-mail message requesting a subscription to the URL address that follows.

To send a message to the entire list, address it to: C-IBM-370@dhw68k.cts.com

`mailto:C-IBM-370-request@dhw68k.cts.com`

C-L

Discussion of C programming.

Keywords: Programming Languages

Audience: C Programmers

Contact: George Foster, Katie Hanson
igaf400@indyvax, abh100@indycms

Details: Free

User Info: To subscribe to the list, send an e-mail message to the URL address that follows, consisting of a single line reading:

SUB C-L YourFirstName YourLastName

To send a message to the entire list, address it to: C-L@indycms.iupui.edu

`mailto:listserv@indycms.iupui.edu`

Clp.x

Devoted to discussion of concurrent logic programming languages, concurrent constraint programming languages, semantics, proof techniques and program transformations, parallel Prolog systems, implementations, and programming techniques and idioms.

Keywords: Programming, Programming Languages, Concurrent Logic

Audience: Concurrent Logic Programmers

Contact: Jacob Levy
jlevy.pa@xerox.com

Details: Free

User Info: To subscribe to the list, send an e-mail message requesting a subscription to the URL address that follows.

To send a message to the entire lst, address it to: clp.x@xerox.com

`mailto:clp-request.x@xerox.com`

comp.lang.c

A Usenet newsgroup providing information and discussion about the C programming language.

Keywords: Computer Programming, Programming Languages

Audience: Computer Users, C Programmers

User Info: To subscribe to this Usenet newsgroup, you need access to a newsreader.

`news:comp.lang.c`

comp.lang.c++

A Usenet newsgroup providing information and discussion about the object-oriented C++ programming language.

Keywords: Computers, Programming Languages

Audience: Computer Users, C++ Programmers

User Info: To subscribe to this Usenet newsgroup, you need access to a newsreader.

`news:comp.lang.c++`

Icon-group

Discussion of topics related to the Icon programming language

Keywords: Programming, Icon Programming Language, Programming Language, String Processing

Audience: Icon Programmers

Profile: Icon is a high-level, general purpose programming language emphasizing string and structure processing. Topics include programming techniques, theoretical aspects, Icon in relation to other languages, applications of Icon, implementation issues, porting, and bugs.

Contact: Bill Mitchell
whm@arizona.edu

Details: Free

User Info: To subscribe to the list, send an e-mail message requesting a subscription to the URL address that follows.

`mailto:Icon-Group-Request@arizona.edu.`

Lang-Lucid

Discussions on all aspects related to the programming language Lucid, including language design issues, implementations for personal computers, implementations for parallel machines, language extensions, programming environments, products, bug reports, and bug fixes/workarounds.

Keywords: Programming, Programming Languages

Audience: Lucid Programmers

Contact: R. Jagannathan
lang-lucid-request@csl.sri.com

Details: Free

User Info: To subscribe to the list, send an e-mail message requesting a subscription to the URL address that follows.

`mailto:lang-lucid-request@csl.sri.com`

nl-kr

This E-conference is open to discussion of any topic related to the understanding and generation of natural language and knowledge representation as subfields of artificial intelligence.

Keywords: Programming Languages, Natural Language, Knowledge Representation, Linguistics

Audience: Computer Programmers

Contact: Christopher Welty
weltyc@cs.rpi.edu

Details: Free, Moderated

User Info: To subscribe to the list, send an e-mail message requesting a subscription to the URL address that follows.

`mailto:nl-kr-request@cs.rpi.edu`

PERL (Practical Extraction and Report Language)

An HTML-formatted and highly indexed PERL programming reference document.

Keywords: Programming Languages, Computer Programming

Audience: Computer Programmers, Students, Researchers

Contact: Larry Wall
lwall@netlabs.com

`http://www.cs.cmu.edu/Web/People/rgs/perl.html`

Progress

Progress

Discussion of the Progress RDBMS (Relational Database Management System).

Keywords: Databases, Computing

Audience: Computer Users, Business Students

Contact: Progress-list-request@math.niu.edu

Details: Free

User Info: To subscribe to the list, send an e-mail message requesting a subscription to the URL address that follows.

To send a message to the entire list, address it to: progress-list@math.niu.edu

`mailto:Progress-list-request@math.niu.edu`

Prohibition

The University of Michigan Library

The Library's holdings are large and wide-ranging and contain significant collections in many fields.

Keywords: Education (Bilingual), Linguistics, Neuroscience, Michigan, Prohibition, Government (African)

Audience: General Public, Researchers, Librarians, Document Delivery Professionals

Details: Free

Expect: nothing, Send: <cr>

`telnet://cts.merit.edu`

Project Gutenberg

Africa in the CIA World Fact Book

A gopher site containing geographial and political information about individual countries in Africa.

Keywords: Africa, Intelligence, Project Gutenberg

Sponsor: Project Gutenberg

Audience: Africans, General Public

`gopher://hoshi.cic.sfu.ca/11/dlam/cia/Africa`

GUTENBERG Listserver

A mailing list providing information about Project Gutenberg.

Keywords: Project Gutenberg, Literature (General), Reference

Sponsor: National Clearinghouse for Machine Readable Texts

A B C D E F G H I J K L M N O P Q R S T U V W X Y Z

A
B
C
D
E
F
G
H
I
J
K
L
M
N
O
P
Q
R
S
T
U
V
W
X
Y
Z

Audience:	General Public, Researchers, Educators, Students
Contact:	Michael S. Hart gutnberg@vmd.cso.uiuc.edu
Details:	Free
User Info:	To subscribe to the list, send an e-mail message to the following URL address consisting of a single line reading: SUB GUTNBERG YourFirstName YourLastName

`mailto:listserv@vmd.cso.uiuc.edu`

Project Gutenberg

The purpose of Project Gutenberg is to encourage the creation and distribution of English-language electronic texts.

Keywords:	Literature (General), Reference
Sponsor:	National Clearinghouse for Machine Readable Texts
Audience:	General Public, Researchers, Educators, Students
Profile:	Contents include: Project Gutenberg's goal is to provide a collection of 10,000 of the most used books by the year 2001, and to reduce the effective costs to the user to a price of approximately one cent per book, plus the cost of media and of shipping and handling. Thus it is hoped that the entire cost of libraries of this nature will be about US$100, plus the price of the disks and CD-ROMS and mailing. Project Gutenberg assists in the selection of hardware and software as well as in their installation and use. It also assists in scanning, spelling checkers, proofreading, and so on.
Contact:	Michael S. Hart hart@vmd.cso.uiuc.edu
Details:	Costs
User Info:	Login anonymous; cd text

`ftp://mrcnext.cso.uiuc.edu`

Project Management

Project-management

The aim of the list is to discuss project-management techniques generally, as well as project-management software and programs.

Keywords:	Project Management, Computing, Software
Audience:	Business Professionals, Business Students
Contact:	project-management-request@smtl.demon.co.uk
Details:	Free

User Info:	To subscribe to the list, send an e-mail message requesting a subscription to the URL address that follows. To send a message to the entire list, address it to: project-management@smtl.demon.co.uk

`mailto:project-management-request@smtl.demon.co.uk`

Prompt

Prompt

Contains news tips and briefs for the NCSU (North Carolina State University) campus community. Complementing the paper newsletter Connect, Prompt is designed to provide timely, up-to-date information concerning all platforms of computing.

Keywords:	Computing
Audience:	NCSU Computer Students, Educators, Computer Users
Contact:	Sarah Noell sarah_noell@ncsu.edu
Details:	Free
User Info:	To subscribe to the list, send an e-mail message to the URL address that follows, consisting of a single line reading: prompt YourFirstName YourLastName To send a message to the entire list, address it to: prompt@cc.ncsu.edu

`mailto:listserv@cc.ncsu.edu`

Proof-users

Proof-users

Discussion of the left-associative natural language "parser proof".

Keywords:	Computing, Programming
Audience:	Computer Programmers
Contact:	Craig Latta proof-request@xcf.berkeley.edu
Details:	Free
	To join, e-mail proof-request@xcf.berkeley.edu with the subject line "add me".

`mailto:proof-request@xcf.berkeley.edu`

Property

ASSETS (Real Estate Tax Assessor and Deed Transfer Records)

The RealEstate Tax Assessor and Deed Transfer Records (ASSETS) library contains information compiled from real property records.

Keywords:	Real Estate, Property, Tax Assessor, Deed Transfers, Records
Audience:	Lawyers
Profile:	The ASSETS library contains a variety of real estate information, including asset ownership, property address, owner's mailing address, assessed valuation, current market value, and recent property sales and deed transfers. Information is collected from county tax assessors' and recorders' offices nationwide and compiled by TRW REDI Property Data. The ASSETS library also contains a variety of boat and aircraft registration information.
Contact:	Mead New Sales Group at (800) 227-4908 or (513) 859-5398 inside the US, or (513) 865-7981 for all inquiries outside the US.
User Info:	To subscribe, contact Mead directly. To examine the Nexis user guide, you can access it at the ftp site of the University of Texas at Austin at the URL address: ftp://ftp.cc.utexas.edu The files are in: /pub/ref-services/LEXIS

`telnet://nex.meaddata.com`

`http://www.meaddata.com`

Prospero

Prospero

A guide to using Prospero, an Internet access tool that provides a user-centered view of remote files.

Keywords:	Internet Tools, Prospero
Audience:	Internet Surfers
Contact:	info-prospero@ISI.EDU
Details:	Free
Notes:	Files are in: pub/prospero/doc

`ftp://prospero.isi.edu`

PSI

PSI

PSI is an Internet service provider.

Keywords: Internet

Sponsor: PSI

Audience: Internet Users

Details: Costs

`telnet://psi.com`

Psychiatry

PsycINFO

PsycINFO is a leading research database providing bibliographic access to the international literature in psychology, as well as the related behavioral and social sciences.

Keywords: Psychology, Psychiatry, Behavior

Sponsor: American Psychological Association

Audience: Social workers, Psychologists, Psychiatrists, Librarians, Students

Contact: CDP Technologies Sales Department (800)950-2035, extension 400

User Info: To subscribe, contact CDP Technologies directly

`telnet://cdplus@cdplus.com`

Psychology

Cognitive and Psychological Sciences on the Internet

A resource containing links to academic programs, organizations and conference lists, journals and magazines, Usenet newsgroups, discussion lists, and other general information regarding cognitive science.

Keywords: Cognitive Science, Psychology, Neuroscience

Sponsor: The Stanford University Psychology Department

Audience: Cognitive Scientists, Neuroscientists, Psychologists, Psychiatrists

Contact: Scott Mainwaring sdm@psych.stanford.edu

`http://matia.stanford.edu/cogsci.html`

CVNet (Color and Vision Network)

The network provides a means of communications for scientists working in biological color and/or vision research. Members' e-mail addresses are maintained and sent to others in the network. CVNet distributes notices of jobs, meetings, and some other special announcements to all registrants. Members can post bulletins, announcements, and so on.

Keywords: Optics, Biological Research, Psychology

Sponsor: York University, North York, Ontario, Canada

Audience: Psychologists, Color/Vision Researchers

Contact: Peter K. Kaiser cvnet@vm1.yorkU.ca

Details: Free

User Info: To subscribe, send an e-mail message requesting a subscription to the URL address that follows.

`mailto:cvnet@vm1.yorkU.ca`

Laboratory Primate Newsletter

Provides a central source of information about nonhuman primates and related matters for scientists who use these animals in their research and for those whose work supports such research.

Keywords: Primatology, Psychology

Audience: Primate Researchers, Psychologists

Contact: Judith E. Schrier PRIMATE@BROWNVM.brown.edu

Details: Free

`mailto:listserv@brownvm.brown.edu`

PsycINFO

PsycINFO is a leading research database providing bibliographic access to the international literature in psychology, as well as the related behavioral and social sciences.

Keywords: Psychology, Psychiatry, Behavior

Sponsor: American Psychological Association

Audience: Social workers, Psychologists, Psychiatrists, Librarians, Students

Contact: CDP Technologies Sales Department (800) 950-2035, extension 400

User Info: To subscribe, contact CDP Technologies directly

`telnet://cdplus@cdplus.com`

The PSYCHGRAD Project and Psychology-Related Information

An electronic forum for the communication and dissemination of information among psychology graduate students.

Keywords: Psychology, Education (Post-Graduate)

Sponsor: University of Ottawa, Canada

Audience: Psychologists, Psychology Graduate Students

Profile: Designed to facilitate electronic communications and networking between psychology graduate students, this site contains archives of psychology listserv groups, and directories of psychology associations, along with related electronic journals and software. Also has links to other gopher and WWW sites related to psychology.

Contact: Matthew Simpson 054340@acadvm1.uottawa.ca 054340@uottawa.bitnet

`gopher://panda1.uottawa.ca`

University of Toledo Library

The library's holdings are large and wide-ranging and contain significant collections in many fields.

Keywords: Business, Great Lakes Area, Humanities, International Relations, Psychology, Science

Audience: Researchers, Students, General Public

Details: Free

User Info: Expect: Enter one of the following commands . . . , Send: DIAL MVS; Expect: dialed to mvs ####; Send: UTMOST

`telnet://uofto1.utoledo.edu`

Psychotherapy

alt.sexual.abuse.recovery

A Usenet newsgroup providing information and discussion about sexual abuse recovery and helping others deal with traumatic experiences.

Keywords: Sexual Abuse, Psychotherapy

Audience: Victims

User Info: To subscribe to this Usenet newsgroup, you need access to a newsreader.

`news:alt.sexual.abuse.recovery`

Public Access Archives

fsp-discussion

Discusses the new FSP protocol. FSP is a set of programs that implements a public-access archive similar to an anonymous-FTP archive.

Keywords: FSP Protocol, Public Access Archives

Audience: Computer Users

Details: Free

User Info: To subscribe to the list, send an e-mail message requesting a subscription to the URL address that follows.

To send a message to the entire list, address it to: fsp-discussion@germany.eu.net

`mailto:listmaster@germany.eu.net`

A B C D E F G H I J K L M N O P Q R S T U V W X Y Z

A B C D E F G H I J K L M N O **P** Q R S T U V W X Y Z

Public Domain Software

Center for Biomedical Informatics, Brazil ⭐

The Center for Biomedical Informatics maintains a software library with 50 disks containing about 150 public-domain medical application programs for IBM-PC-compatible microcomputers.

Keywords: Health Sciences, Public Domain Software

Sponsor: Center for Biomedical Informatics, Brazil

Audience: Physicians, Nurses, Dentists, University Biomedical Researchers, Students

Details: Costs

User Info: To receive the catalogue in electronic form, send the following one-line message to infomed@ccvax.unicamp.br or infomed@bruc.bitnet: get public-domain p (for version in Portuguese) get public-domain e (for version in English). Instructions on how to acquire the software are included.

`ftp://ccsun.unicamp.br`

Public Health

INFOMED ⭐

Provides yearly statistical information in the form of tables (in ASCII format) listing the principal indicators of health in Cuba.

Keywords: Cuba, Health Statistics, Public Health

Sponsor: Cuban Ministry of Health

Audience: Medical Professionals, Researchers, Public Health Professionals

Details: Free

User Info: To obtain a table from the yearbook, send an electronic message to the URL address that follows without a subject and with the following content in the body of the message:

GET ANUARIO <name of table>

Notes: Examples of tables are CMT-11: Death rates by age group; CMT-15: Infant mortality by province, and so on. For a listing of the available tables request the help file.

`mailto:listserv@infomed.cu`

Public Policy

AgeLine

The AgeLine database is produced by the American Association of Retired Persons (AARP) and provides bibliographic coverage of social gerontology—the study of aging in social, psychological, health-related, and economic contexts.

Keywords: Gerontology, Retired, Public Policy, Aging

Sponsor: American Association of Retired Persons, Washington, DC, USA

Audience: Retired Persons, Health Care Providers, Researchers

Profile: AgeLine covers the delivery of health care for the older population and its associated costs and policies, as well as public policy, employment, and consumer issues. Literature covered is of interest to researchers, health professionals, service planners, policy makers, employers, older adults and their families, and consumer advocates.

Coverage: 1978 to the present (selected coverage back to 1966); updated bimonthly.

Contact: Dialog in the US at (800) 334-2564; Dialog internationally at country-specific locations.

Details: Costs

User Info: There is no print equivalent of the database. To subscribe, contact Dialog directly.

`telnet://dialog.com`

EPPD-L

Engineering and Public Policy Discussion List.

Keywords: Engineering, Public Policy

Audience: Engineers

Contact: Ken Sollows
listserv@unb.ca

Details: Free

User Info: To subscribe to the list, send an e-mail message to the URL address shown that follows, consiting of a single line reading:

SUB eppd-l YourFirstName YourLastName

To send a message to the entire list, address it to: eppd-l@unb.ca

Mother Jones

A web site containing online electronic issues of Mother Jones magazine (and Zine), making possible instant electronic feedback to the publishers regarding articles.

Keywords: Zines, Ethics, Public Policy, Activism

Sponsor: Mother Jones

Audience: Students, General Public

Contact: Webserver
webserver@mojones.com

`http://www.mojones.com/motherjones.html`

Publications

Book Review Index

This database contains references to more than 2.5 million citations to reviews of approximately 1.5 million distinct book and periodical titles.

Keywords: Book Reviews, Periodicals, Publications

Sponsor: Gale Research, Inc., Detroit, MI, USA

Audience: Publishing Professionals, Authors

Profile: The database covers every review published since 1969 in nearly 500 periodicals and newspapers. Each record includes the author and title of the work being reviewed, journal name, date of review, and page number. Document type indications are also included if the work is a periodical; a reference work; a children's book, periodical, or reference book; or a young adult book, periodical, or reference book. Book Review Index corresponds to the print publication of the same name. Periodicals indexed range from the Harvard Business Review to the Center for Children's Books: Bulletin, and from the American Scholar to Psychology Today. General interest magazines such as Ms., Time, The New Yorker, and Atlantic are covered, as are specialized periodicals like Flying, Yachting, and National Genealogical Society Quarterly.

Contact: Dialog in the US at (800) 334-2564, Dialog internationally at country specific locations.

Details: Costs

User Info: To subscribe, contact Dialog directly.

`telnet://dialog.com`

Books In Print

This is the major source of information on books currently published and in-print in the United States.

Keywords: Books, Publications

Sponsor: R.R. Bowker, New York, NY, US

Audience: General Public, Writers, Researchers

Profile: The database provides the record of forthcoming books, books in-print, and books out-of-print. Scientific, technical, medical, scholarly, and popular works, as well as childrens books, are included in the file. The file corresponds to several print publications: Books in Print, Subject Guide to Books in Print, Books in Print Supplement, Paperbound Books in Print, Forthcoming Books, Law Books in Print, Subject Guide to Forthcoming Books, and Scientific and Technical

Books & Serials in Print. Records in Books In Print include basic bibliographic information (author, title, publisher, date), as well as L.C. card number, International Standard Book Number (ISBN), and price.

Contact: Dialog in the US at (800) 334-2564, Dialog internationally at country specific locations.

User Info: To subscribe, contact Dialog directly.

`telnet://dialog.com`

NAARS (National Automated Accounting Research System)

The National Automated Accounting Research System (NAARS) library, provided as a service by agreement with the American Institute of Certified Public Accountants (AICPA) contains a variety of accounting information.

Keywords: Accounting, Auditing, Filings, Publications

Audience: Accountants

Profile: The NAARS library contains annual reports of public corporations and accounting literature and publications for the accounting professional. Annual reports are annotated with descriptive terms assigned by the AICPA. These terms allow the user to search for annual report footnotes that illustrate one or more recognized accounting practices.

Contact: Mead New Sales Group at (800) 227-4908 or (513) 859-5398 inside the US, or (513) 865-7981 for all inquiries outside the US.

User Info: To subscribe, contact Mead directly.

To examine the Nexis user guide, you can access it at the ftp site of the University of Texas at Austin at the URL address: ftp://ftp.cc.utexas.edu

The files are in: /pub/ref-services/LEXIS

`telnet://nex.meaddata.com`

`http://www.meaddata.com`

Publications of the Office of Environment, Safety and Health

A collection of government safety information including updates, bulletins, and hazard alerts. Topics are diverse, covering everything from 'Employee Hit on Head by Falling Steel Wheel' to 'New Regulations to Control the Speed of Bloodborne Diseases.'

Keywords: Safety, Government (US), Federal Laws (US), Publications

Sponsor: U.S. Department of Energy

Audience: Government Officials, General Public

Details: Free

`gopher://dewey.tis.inel.gov`

Quanta

An electronically distributed science fiction magazine that is published monthly. Each issue contains short fiction, articles, and editorials by authors from around the world and across the Net.

Keywords: Science Fiction, Writing, Publications

Audience: Science Fiction Enthusiasts, Writers

Contact: da1n@andrew.cmu.edu

Details: Free

User Info: To subscribe to the list, send an e-mail message requesting a subscription to the URL address that follows.

To send a message to the entire list, address it to: da1n@andrew.cmu.edu

`mailto:da1n@andrew.cmu.edu`

Scholarly Publishing

Transcript of a paper entitled 'Model University Policy Regarding Faculty Publication in Scientific and Technical Scholarly Journals: A Background Paper and Review of the Issues.'

Keywords: Publications, Scholarly Communication

Sponsor: Triangle Research Libraries Network, Durham, Raleigh, and Chapel Hill, North Carolina

Audience: Educators, Publishers

Details: Free

File is: pub/docs/about-the-net/trln-copyright-paper

`ftp://sunsite.unc.edu`

Publishers

journet

An electronic conference for the discussion of topics of interest to journalists and journalism educators.

Keywords: Journalism, Writing, Desktop Publishing, Electronic Publishing

Audience: Journalists, Writers, Publishers, Educators

Contact: George Frajkor gfrajkor@ccs.carleton.ca

User Info: To subscribe to the list, send an e-mail message to the URL address that follows, consisting of a single line reading:

SUB journet YourFirstName YourLastName

To send a message to the entire list, address it to: journet@qucdn.queensu.ca

`mailto:listserv@qucdn.queensu.ca`

Publishing

Electronic Newsstand Gopher

This gopher contains tables of contents, selected full-text articles, and assorted other information from many mainstream print journals.

Keywords: Journals, Electronic Publishing, Publishing, News

Audience: News Enthusiasts, Publishers, Publishing Professionals, Journalists

Profile: This gopher was compiled with the collaboration of the American Journal of International Law, Policy Review, Technology Review, Business Week, Current History, The Economist, Foreign Affairs, National Review, The New Yorker, The New Republic, Mother Jones, among other distinguished publications.

Contact: William Love love@enews.com

`gopher://gopher.enews.com`

PIRA - Paper, Printing and Publishing, Packaging, and Nonwovens Abstracts

Coverage of all aspects of paper, pulp, nonwovens, printing, publishing, and packaging.

Keywords: Material Science, Paper, Printing, Publishing, Packaging

Sponsor: PIRA International

Audience: Materials Scientists, Researchers

Profile: File contains more than 300,000 records. Special applications: company and market profiles, product and trade name searches, research and technology trends. Updated biweekly.

Contact: paul.albert@neteast.com

User Info: To subscribe contact Orbit-Questel directly.

`telnet://orbit.com`

Princeton University Library

The library's holdings are large and wide-ranging. They contain significant collections in many fields.

Keywords: China, Japan, Classics, History (Ancient), Near Eastern Studies, Literature (American), Literature (English), Aeronautics, Middle Eastern Studies, Mormonism, Publishing

Audience: General Public, Researchers, Librarians, Document Delivery Professionals

Details: Free

Expect: Connect message, blank screen, Send: <cr>; Expect: #, Send: Call 500

`telnet://pucable.princeton.edu`

Publishing

This directory is a compilation of information resources focused on publishing.

Keywords: Publishing, Books

Audience: Publishing Professionals, Book Readers, Book Sellers

Details: Free

`ftp://una.hh.lib.umich.edu/70/`
`inetdirsstacks/publishing:robinson`

The MIT Press Online Catalogs

A descriptive listing of recent books and current journals published by the MIT Press.

Keywords: Academia, Books, Publishing, Technology

Sponsor: The MIT Press, Cambridge, Massachusetts, USA.

Audience: Reseachers, Scholars, University Students, Technical Professionals

Profile: Contains a keyword-searchable index of books published in the years 1993 to 1994, as well as current journals covering computational and cognitive sciences, architecture, photography, art and literary theory, economics, environmental science, and linguistics.

Contact: ehling@mitpress.mit.edu

Notes: Coverage: 1993 to present; updated semiannually. MIT Press can also be accessed by calling (800) 356-0343.

`http://www-mitpress.mit.edu`

`gopher://gopher.mit.edu`

WAIS, Inc.

WAIS, Inc. provides interactive on-line publishing systems and services to organizations whcih publish information over the Internet. The organization's three main goals are: to develop the Internet as a viable means for distributing information electronically; to improve the nature and quality of information available over networks; and to offer better methods to access that information.

Keywords: WWW, Information Retrieval, Publishing, Internet Tools

Sponsor: WAIS, Inc.

Audience: Researchers, Students, General Public, Publishers

Contact: Webmaster webmaster@wais.com

`http://server.wais.com`

Pubnet

Pubnet

A mailing list for the discussion of administration and use of public-access computer systems, primarily UNIX systems. The list also answers questions about setting up or running a public-access system

Keywords: Computer Systems, UNIX

Audience: Computer System Designers, UNIX Users

Contact: Chip Rosenthal pubnet-request@chinacat.unicom.com

Details: Free

User Info: To subscribe to the list, send an e-mail message requesting a subscription to the URL address that follows.

To send a message to the entire list, address it to:
pubnet@chinacat.unicom.com

`mailto:pubnet-`
`request@chinacat.unicom.com`

Pubs-IAT (Institute for Academic Technology newsletter)

Pubs-IAT (Institute for Academic Technology newsletter)

This newsletter shares information on publications, programs, courses, and other activities of the Institute for Academic Technology.

Keywords: Education (Adult), Education (Distance), Education (Continuing), Information Technology

Sponsor: Institute for Academic Technology

Audience: Educators, Administrators, Researchers

Details: Free

User Info: To subscribe to the list, send an e-mail message to the URL address that follows, consisting of a single line reading:

SUB pubs-iat YourFirstName YourLastName

To send a message to the entire list, address it to: pubs-iat@gibbs.oit.unc.edu

`mailto:listserv@gibbs.oit.unc.edu`

Purdue University Library

Purdue University Library

The library's holdings are large and wide-ranging. They contain significant collections in many fields.

Keywords: Economics (History of), Literature (English), Literature (American), Indiana, Rogers (Bruce), Engineering (History of), Aviation, Earth Science, Atmospheric Science, Consumer Science, Family Science, Chemistry (History of), Physics, Veterinary Science

Audience: General Public, Researchers, Librarians, Document Delivery Professionals

Contact: Dan Ferrer dan@asterix.lib.purdue.edu

Details: Free

Expect: User ID prompt, Send: GUEST

`telnet://lib.cc.purdue.edu`

Purkinje Park

Purkinje Park

A server maintained by CalTech to support the sharing of information between users of the GENESIS neural simulator, and to address topics of general interest to the Computational Neuroscience community.

Keywords: Computational Neuroscience, GENESIS, Neural Simulation.

Sponsor: Cal Tech

Audience: Neuroscientists, Computational Neuroscientists

Contact: Dave Beeman dbeeman@smaug.bbb.caltech.edu

`http://www.bbb.caltech.edu/index.html`

Puzzles

rec.puzzles

A Usenet newsgroup providing information and discussion about math puzzles and brain teasers.

Keywords: Games, Puzzles, Recreation

Audience: General Public

User Info: To subscribe to this Usenet newsgroup, you need access to a newsreader.

`news:rec.puzzles`

PVS (Project Vote Smart)

PVS (Project Vote Smart)

A gopher site containing Federal political information from PVS.

Keywords: Politics, Government (US)

Sponsor: Project Vote Smart, Corvallis, Oregon, USA

Audience: Voters, General Public

Profile: PVS is a volunteer organization
            dedicated to providing voters with
            factual information about candidates for
            Federal office. Currently, the gopher
            offers background information, including
            detailed profiles and legislative analysis
            of Senators and Representatives for all
            50 states.

Contact: pvs@neu.edu

Notes: For more information on Project Vote
            Smart, call their toll free hotline at
            1-800-622-SMART. Or write to: Project
            Vote Smart, 129 NW Fourth St. #240,
            Corvallis, OR 97330

`gopher://gopher.neu.edu`

Python

Python

A mailing list for discussion of and questions about
all aspects of the design and use of the Python
programming language.

Keywords: Computer Programming Languages

Audience: Computer Programmers, Python
            Language Users

Contact: Guido van Rossum
            python-list-request@cwi.nl

Details: Free

User Info: To subscribe to the list, send an e-mail
            message requesting a subscription to
            the URL address that follows.

            To send a message to the entire list,
            address it to: python-list@cwi.nl

Notes: The source of the latest Python release
            is always available by anonymous FTP
            from ftp.cwi.nl, in directory /pub/python.

`mailto:python-list-request@cwi.nl`

A
B
C
D
E
F
G
H
I
J
K
L
M
N
O
P
Q
R
S
T
U
V
W
X
Y
Z

A
B
C
D
E
F
G
H
I
J
K
L
M
N
O
P
Q
R
S
T
U
V
W
X
Y
Z

Q

Qmlist (Quantitative Morphology List)

Qmlist (Quantitative Morphology List)

This is an open, unmoderated mailing list to support researchers and clinicians in the field of quantitative morphology.

Keywords: Morphology

Audience: Morphologists, Biologists

Contact: Dean Pentcheff
dean2@tbone.biol.scarolina.edu

Details: Free

User Info: To subscribe to the list, send an e-mail message to the URL address below, consisting of a single line reading:

SUB qmlist YourFirstName YourLastName

To send a message to the entire list, address it to:
qmlist@tbone.biol.scarolina.edu

mailto:listserv@tbone.biol.scarolina.edu

Qn

Qn

A mailing list for Queer Nation activists and for anyone interested in Queer Nation, an activist group devoted to furthering gay rights. The purpose of QN is to network among various Queer Nation chapters, to discuss actions and tactics to bring about Queer Liberation.

Keywords: Homosexuality, Gay Rights, Activism

Audience: Gay Rights Activists, Political Activists

Contact: Roger Klorese
qn-request@queernet.org

Details: Free

User Info: To subscribe to the list, send an e-mail message requesting a subscription to the URL address below.

To send a message to the entire list, address it to: qn@queernet.org

mailto:qn-request@queernet.org

Qnx2

Qnx2

Discussion of all aspects of the QNX real-time operating systems. Topics include compatible hardware, available third-party software, software reviews, available public domain or free software, QNX platform-specific programming discussions, and QNX and FLEET networking.

Keywords: Computing, Hardware, Software

Audience: Computer Users, Hardware/Software Designers, Product Analysts

Contact: Martin Zimmerman
camz@dlogtech.cuc.ab.ca

Details: Free

User Info: To subscribe to the list, send an e-mail message requesting a subscription to the URL address below.

To send a message to the entire list, address it to: qnx2@dlogtech.cuc.ab.ca

mailto:qnx2@dlogtech.cuc.ab.ca

Qnx4

Qnx4

A mailing list for discussion of all aspects of the QNX real-time operating systems. Topics include compatible hardware, available third-party software, software reviews, available PD/free software, QNX and FLEET networking, process control, and so on.

Keywords: Computing, Hardware, Software, Networking

Audience: Computer Users, Hardware/Software Designers, Product Analysts

Contact: Martin Zimmerman
camz@dlogtech.cuc.ab.ca

Details: Free

User Info: To subscribe to the list, send an e-mail message requesting a subscription to the URL address below.

To send a message to the entire list, address it to: qnx4@dlogtech.cuc.ab.ca

mailto:qnx4@dlogtech.cuc.ab.ca

Quakerism

Quaker FTP Archive at ClarkNet

This archive contains extensive writings concerning contemporary Quaker life.

Keywords: Quakerism, Religion

Sponsor: Clark Internet Services

Audience: Quakers

Contact: George Amoss
daruma@clark.net

ftp://ftp.clark.net/pub/quaker

ftp://ftp.univie.ac.at/archive/faq/ Quaker-faq

Harvard University Library

The library's holdings are large and wide-ranging and contain significant collections in many fields.

Keywords: Afrikaans, Alchemy, Arabic Culture (History of), Celtic Philology, Congo Languages, Folklore, Hebraica, Mormonism, Numismatics, Quakerism, Sanskrit, Witchcraft, Arabic Philology

Audience: General Public, Researchers, Librarians, Document Delivery Professionals

Details: Free

User Info: Expect: Mitek Server..., Send: Enter or Return; Expect: prompt, Send: hollis

`telnet://hollis.harvard.edu`

Quality Control

Total Quality Management Gopher

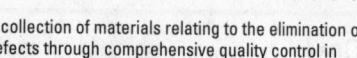

A collection of materials relating to the elimination of defects through comprehensive quality control in industry, government, and universities.

Keywords: Quality Control, Management, Business

Sponsor: The Clemson University Department of Industrial Engineering, Clemson, South Carolina, USA

Audience: Managers, Administrators

Contact: quality@eng.clemson.edu

`gopher://deming.eng.clemson.edu`

`http://deming.eng.clemson.edu`

Quanta

Quanta

⭐

An electronically distributed science fiction magazine that is published monthly. Each issue contains short fiction, articles, and editorials by authors from around the world and across the Net.

Keywords: Science Fiction, Writing, Publications

Audience: Science Fiction Enthusiasts, Writers

Contact: da1n@andrew.cmu.edu

Details: Free

User Info: To subscribe to the list, send an e-mail message requesting a subscription to the URL address below. To send a message to the entire list, address it to: da1n@andrew.cmu.edu

`mailto:da1n@andrew.cmu.edu`

Quantum Chemistry

Theoretical Journal Abstract And Bibliographic Files

⭐

Abstract and bibliographic information for several theoretical chemistry journals. Coverage includes: Theoretical Chemistry, Quantum Chemistry, Quantum Mechanics, Computational Chemistry.

Keywords: Theoretical Chemistry, Quantum Chemistry, Computational Chemistry.

Sponsor: Online, Inc., Weston, CT, US

Audience: Chemists, Librarians, Students (College/ Graduate)

Profile: Provided are directory, product, technical, and bibliographic information on leading software packages, integrating this information into one succinct composite record. The database can help professionals locate suitable packages compatible with specified hardware without sifting through large numbers of records.

Contact: Dialog in the US at (800) 334-2564, Dialog internationally at country-specific locations.

Details: Free

User Info: To subscribe, contact Dialog directly.

`telnet://dialog.com`

Quantum Physics

Quantum Physics/High Energy Physics

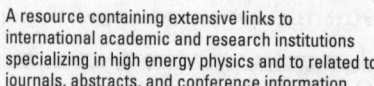

A resource containing extensive links to international academic and research institutions specializing in high energy physics and to related to journals, abstracts, and conference information.

Keywords: Physics, Quantum Physics, Research

Sponsor: Swiss Academic and Research Network, Switzerland

Audience: Students, Physicists, Researchers

Contact: Ingrid Graf rikv8@cernvm.cern.ch

`http://www.cern.ch/Physics/HEP.html`

The University of Minnesota Library System (LUMINA)

⭐⭐

The library's holdings are large and wide-ranging and contain significant collections in many fields.

Keywords: Immigration (History of), Ethnic Studies, Horticulture, Equine Research, Botanical Taxonomy, Quantum Physics, Native American Studies, Holmes (Sherlock)

Audience: General Public, Researchers, Librarians, Document Delivery Professionals

Contact: Craig D. Rice cdr@acc.stolaf.edu

Details: Free

`telnet://lumina.lib.umn.edu`

Quarks

Quark Background Material

Background material describing the nature of and current research into quarks and other elementary particles.

Keywords: Quarks, Physics

Sponsor: Fermi National Accelerator Laboratory

Audience: Physicists, Students, Researchers

Contact: webmaster@fnal.gov

Details: Free

`http://fnnews.fnal.gov/ top_background.html`

Quattro

Quattro

A mailing list for discussions pertaining to Audi automobiles, especially the AWD (all wheel drive) Quattro models. It also includes news, opinions, maintenance procedures, and parts sources.

Keywords: Automobiles

Audience: Automobile Enthusiasts

Contact: David Tahajian quattro-request@aries.east.sun.com

Details: Free

User Info: To subscribe to the list, send an e-mail message requesting a subscription to the URL address below.

To send a message to the entire list, address it to: quattro@aries.east.sun.com

`mailto:quattro- request@aries.east.sun.com`

Quebec

Rezo, bulletin irregulomadaire du RQSS

E-newsletter of RQSS (Regroupement Quebecois des Sciences Sociales), open to anyone interested in social science research in Quebec and/or about Quebec.

Keywords: Quebec, Social Science

Audience: Social Scientists

Contact: Pierre J. Hamel HAMEL@INRS-URB.UQUEBEC.CA

Details: Free

User Info: To subscribe, send an e-mail message to the URL address below, consisting of a single line reading:

SUB rezo YourFirstName YourLastName

To send a message to the entire list, address it to: rezo@uquebec.ca

`mailto:listserv@uquebec.ca`

Quebec Nordiques

Quebec Nordiques

A mailing list to discuss topics concerning the National Hockey League's Quebec Nordiques.

Keywords: Hockey, Sports

Audience: Hockey Enthusiasts

Contact: Danny J. Sohier
nords-request@badaboum.ulaval.ca

Details: Free

User Info: To subscribe to the list, send an e-mail message requesting a subscription to the URL address below.

To send a message to the entire list, address it to:
nords@badaboum.ulaval.ca

`mailto:nords@badaboum.ulaval.ca`

Queen

Queen

A mailing list to discuss the rock group Queen.

Keywords: Music, Rock Music

Audience: Queen Fans, Music Fans, Musicians

Contact: Dan Blanchard
qms-request@uiuc.edu

Details: Free

User Info: To subscribe to the list, send an e-mail message requesting a subscription to the URL address below.

To send a message to the entire list, address it to: qms@uiuc.edu

`mailto:qms-request@uiuc.edu`

Questions and Answers about the GPO Gateway to Government Act

Questions and Answers about the GPO Gateway to Government Act

Questions and answers dealing with the bill GPO Gateway to Government Act of 1992. Questions such as, "What will the gateway do?," "Why is this gateway needed?," "What types of information will be available through the Gateway?," and more.

Keywords: Laws (US Federal), Government (US Federal), Federal Databases

Audience: General Public, Journalists, Politicians

Details: Free

File is: /pub/nic/NREN/GPO.questions

`ftp://ftp.sura.net`

Quotations

Quotations

A mailing list for the sharing of quotations.

Keywords: Quotations

Audience: General Public

Contact: Jason R. Newquist
jrnewquist@ucdavis.ucdavis.edu

User Info: To subscribe, send an e-mail message to: listproc@ucdavis.edu. Leave the subject blank and place in the body of the note: subscribe quotations YourFirstName YourLastName

`mailto:quotations@ucdavis.edu`

Quotecom Home Page

Quotecom Home Page

QuoteCom is a service dedicated to providing financial market data to Intenet users.

Keywords: Investments, Securities, Finance

Audience: Investors

Producer: QuoteCom, Inc.

Contact: Chris Cooper
Email:chris@quote.com
staff@quote.com
support@quote.com

Profile: This site offers many financial services for a fee. You can register for their free service, which allows you to get up to five quotes per day. Other services available after subscribing include bar charts on historical data, S&P's Stock Guide database, S&P's MarketScope Alerts, Hoover company profiles, historical data, Canadian market data, European market data, and more.

User Info: No services are available without registering. Free services are limited to five quotes per day. Basic service costs $9.95 per month.

Notes: Most of QuoteCom's data is proprietary, and is protected by copyrights of the various providers.

`http://www.quote.com`

A
B
C
D
E
F
G
H
I
J
K
L
M
N
O
P
Q
R
S
T
U
V
W
X
Y
Z

A
B
C
D
E
F
G
H
I
J
K
L
M
N
O
P
Q
R
S
T
U
V
W
X
Y
Z

Race

African Education Research Network

Various links to African studies programs at select universities, and other archived information of interest to the African studies scholar.

Keywords: Culture, Race, Africa, African Studies

Sponsor: Ohio University, African Education Research Network

Audience: Students, African-Americans, Africans

Contact: Milton E. Ploghoft
mperdreau@ohiou.edu

Details: Free

`gopher://gopher.ohiou.edu/00/`
`dept.servers/aern`

Black/African Related Online Information

This is a list of online information storage sites that contain a significant amount of information pertaining to Black or African people, culture, and issues around the world.

Keywords: Culture, Race, Africa, African Studies

Sponsor: AfriInfo

Audience: Students, African-Americans, Africans

Contact: McGee
mcgee@epsilon.eecs.nwu.edu

Details: Free

`ftp://ftp.netcom.com/pub/amcgee/`
`my_african_related_lists/afrisite.msg`

Chicano/LatinoNet

An electronic mechanism which brings together Chicano/Latino research, as well as linguistic minority and educational research efforts being carried out at the University of California and elsewhere. It serves as a gateway between faculty, staff, and students who are engaged in research and curricular efforts in these areas.

Keywords: Culture, Race, Chicano Culture, Latino Culture

Sponsor: Chicano Studies Research Center, University of California at Los Angeles

Audience: Students, Mexican-Americans, Latinos

Contact: Richard Chabran
Chabran@latino.sscnet.ucla.ed

Details: Free

`gopher://latino.sscnet.ucla.edu`

Japanese Information

This web site contains extensive information on the geography, culture, law, and tourism of Japan. Includes archived Japanese newsgroup information and FAQs.

Keywords: Culture, Race, Japan, Japanese Culture

Sponsor: Nippon Telegraph and Telephone

Audience: Students, Tourists, Japanese, Japanese-Americans

Contact: Webmaster
www-admin@seraph.ntt.jp

Details: Free

`http://www.ntt.jp/japan/index.html`

Mexican Culture FAQ

This is the FAQ from the soc.culture.mexican newsgroup. Provides information on Mexican culture, history, society, language, and tourism.

Keywords: Culture, Race, Chicano Culture, Latino Culture

Sponsor: News Group Moderators for soc.culture.mexican

Audience: Students, Latinos, Chicanos

Contact: News Group Moderator
mendoza-grado@att.com

Details: Free

`ftp://ftp.mty.itesm.ms/pub/mexico/`
`faqs`

`http://www.cis.ohio-state.edu/`
`hypertext/faq/usenet/mexican-faq/`
`faq.html`

POS302-L

A discussion list created for the "Race, Ethnicity, and Social Inequality" seminar offered at Illinois State University (spring 1994). The general purposes of the list are to create an e-mail audience for the written work of enrolled students and to invite a broad audience to participate in the seminar.

Keywords: Race, Ethnicity, Minorities

Audience: Ethnic Studies Students, Sociologists, Educators

Details: Free

User Info: To subscribe to the list, send an e-mail message to the URL address below, consisting of a single line reading:

SUB pos302-l YourFirstName YourLastName

To send a message to the entire list, address it to: pos302-l@ilstu.edu

`mailto:listserv@ilstu.edu`

A B C D E F G H I J K L M N O P Q **R** S T U V W X Y Z

Radio

AM/FM

A mailing list for the AM/FM Online Edition, a monthly compilation of news stories concerning the UK radio industry.

Keywords: Radio, United Kingdom, Communications

Audience: Radio Enthusiasts (UK), Communications Specialists, Students (college, graduate)

Contact: Stephen Hebditch
listserv@orbital.demon.co.uk

User Info: To subscribe to the list, send an e-mail message to the URL addres below, consisting of a single line reading:

SUB am/fm YourFirstName YourLastName

To send a message to the entire list, address it to: AM/FM@orbital.demon.co.uk

`mailto:listserv@orbital.demon.co.uk`

FM-10

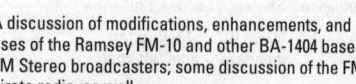

A discussion of modifications, enhancements, and uses of the Ramsey FM-10 and other BA-1404 based FM Stereo broadcasters; some discussion of the FM pirate radio, as well.

Keywords: Radio, Broadcasting

Audience: Broadcasters, Radio Broadcasters

Details: Free

User Info: To subscribe to the list, send an e-mail message requesting a subscription to the URL address below. To send a message to the entire list, address it to: fm-10@dg-rtp.dg.com

`mailto:fm-10-request@dg-rtp.dg.com`

National Broadcasting Society— Alpha Epsilon Rho

Forum for mass media professionals to share experiences and ideas.

Keywords: Film, Television, Radio, Mass Media

Sponsor: National Broadcasting Society-Alpha Epsilon Rho

Audience: Journalists, Students, Educators, Broadcasting Professionals

Contact: Reg Gamar
regbc@cunyvm.bitnet

Details: Free

User Info: To subscribe to the list, send an e-mail message to the address shown below consisting of a single line reading:

SUB NBS-AER YourFirstName YourLastName

To send a message to the entire list, address it to: nbs-aer@cunyvm.bitnet

`mailto:listserv@cunyvm.bitnet`

Online Radio

Transcripts and promotional information from Online Radio, a weekly radio program of Perth's Curtin University devoted to reporting the latest developments in the computing world.

Keywords: Computers, Internet, Radio

Sponsor: Curtin University Computing Center, Perth, Australia

Audience: Computer Enthusiasts

Contact: Onno Benschop
online@info.curtin.edu.au

`gopher://ob1.curtin.edu.au`

PRL

The Pirate Radio SWL list is for the distribution of questions, answers, information, and loggings of Pirate Radio Stations.

Keywords: Radio, Communications

Audience: Radio Listeners, Radio Pirates

Contact: John Brewer
brewer@ace.enet.dec.com

User Info: To subscribe to the list, send an e-mail message to the URL address below, consisting of a single line reading:

SUB PRLYourFirstName YourLastName.

To send a message to the entire list, address it to: brewer@ace.enet.dec.com

`mailto:listserv@ace.enet.dec.com`

rec.radio.amateur.misc

A Usenet newsgroup providing information and discussion about ham radios.

Keywords: Radio, Electronics

Audience: Ham Radio Operators

User Info: To subscribe to this Usenet newsgroup, you need access to a newsreader.

`news:rec.radio.amateur.misc`

rec.radio.shortwave

A Usenet newsgroup providing information and discussion about shortwave radio.

Keywords: Radio, Electronics

Audience: Shortwave Radio Users

User Info: To subscribe to this Usenet newsgroup, you need access to a newsreader.

`news:rec.radio.shortwave`

Voice of America and Worldnet

A gopher server for the Voice of America and Worldnet. Includes full-text transcripts of VOA news reports, press releases, and announcements.

Keywords: US Government Publications, News Media, Radio, International Communication

Sponsor: United States Information Agency

Audience: Journalists, Government Officials, General Public

Contact: info@voa.gov, letters-usa@VOA.GOV (for correspondence from inside the U.S.)

`gopher://gopher.voa.gov`

Railroads

Dartmouth College Library

The library's holdings are large and wide-ranging and contain significant collections in many fields.

Keywords: American Calligraphy, Cervantes (Miguel de), Railroads, Polar Regions, Frost (Robert), Shakespeare (William), Spanish Plays

Audience: General Public, Researchers, Librarians, Document Delivery Professionals

Contact: Katharina Klemperer
kathy.klemperer@dartmouth.edu

Details: Free

Expect: login, Send: wolfpac

`telnet://lib.dartmouth.edu`

rec.railroad

A Usenet newsgroup providing information and discussion about railroads.

Keywords: Railroads, Transportation

Audience: Railroad Enthusiast

User Info: To subscribe to this Usenet newsgroup, you need access to a newsreader.

`news:rec.railroad`

The University of Iowa Libraries

The library's holdings are large and wide-ranging and contain significant collections in many fields.

Keywords: Hunt (Leigh), Native American Studies, Typography, Railroads, Cartoons, French Revolution, NASA, Hydraulics

Audience: General Public, Researchers, Librarians, Document Delivery Professionals

Details: Free

Send <RETURN>to display a menu of available systems. Type 1 for OASIS access and press <RETURN>to display the Welcome to OASIS screen.

`telnet://oasis.uiowa.edu`

TRANS (The Transportation Library)

The Transportation Library contains federal transportation case law, statutes and agency decisions.

Keywords: Transportation Law, US Government Regulations, Aviation Industry, Railroads, Trucking Industry

Audience: Lawyers

Profile: The Transportation Library contains federal transportation case law, statutes and agency decisions. The major emphasis of the library is on three modes of transportation (aviation, railroad and trucking) and how those modes are regulated by the federal government. Agency decisions are provided from the Interstate Commerce Commission, Department of Transportation and the National Transportation Safety Board (NTSB).

Contact: New Sales Group at 800-227-4908 or 513-859-5398 inside the US, or 1-513-865-7981 for all inquires outside the US.

User Info: To subscribe, contact Mead directly.

To examine the Lexis user guide, you can access it at the ftp site of the University of Texas at Austin at the URL address: ftp://ftp.cc.utexas.edu

The files are in: /pub/res-services/LEXIS

`telnet://nex.meaddata.com`

Railway History

Indiana University Libraries ★★

The library's holdings are large and wide-ranging and contain significant collections in many fields.

Keywords: Literature (English), Literature (American), 1640-Present, British Plays (19th-C.), Western Americana, Railway History, Aristotle (Texts of), Lafayette (Marquis de), Handel (G.F.), Austrian History, Antiquarian Books, Rare Books, French Opera (19th-C.), Drama (British) ,

Audience: General Public, Researchers, Librarians, Document Delivery Professionals

Details: Free

Expect: User ID prompt, Send: GUEST

`telnet://iuis.ucs.indiana.edu`

Rap Music

The Beastie Boys' Web Page

This web site features video, audio, magazine articles, lyrics, a discography, and other assorted information relating to the Beastie Boys.

Keywords: Musical Groups, Rap Music

Audience: Beastie Boys Fans

Contact: irogers@ezmail.ucs.indiana.edu

`http://www.nando.net/music/gm`

RAPRA Abstracts

RAPRA Abstracts

Coverage on technical and commercial aspects of the rubber, plastics, and polymer composites industries.

Keywords: Material Science, Rubbers, Plastics, Polymers

Sponsor: Rapra Technology, Ltd.

Audience: Material Scientists, Researchers

Profile: This unique source of information covers the world's polymer literature including journals, conference proceedings, books, specifications, reports and trade literature. Contains over 375,000 records. Updated biweekly.

Contact: paul.albert@neteast.com
To subscribe contact Orbit-Questel directly.

`telnet://orbit.com`

Rare Books

Indiana University Libraries ★★

The library's holdings are large and wide-ranging and contain significant collections in many fields.

Keywords: Literature (English), Literature (American), 1640-Present, British Plays (19th-C.), Western Americana, Railway History, Aristotle (Texts of), Lafayette (Marquis de), Handel (G.F.), Austrian History, Antiquarian Books, Rare Books, French Opera (19th-C.), Drama (British) ,

Audience: General Public, Researchers, Librarians, Document Delivery Professionals

Details: Free

Expect:User ID prompt, Send: GUEST

`telnet://iuis.ucs.indiana.edu`

The National Library of Medicine (NLM) Online Catalog System ★★★★

Catalog of library holdings.

Keywords: Medicine, Health Sciences, Biomedicine, Rare Books

Sponsor: National Library of Medicine

Audience: Health Professionals, Medical Educators, Students

Profile: The National Library of Medicine (NLM) is the world's largest biomedical library with a collection of over 4.9 million items. NLM is a national resource for all US health sciences libraries and fills over a quarter of a million interlibrary loan requests each year for these libraries. The library is open to the public, but its collection is designed primarily for health professionals. The library collects materials comprehensively in all major areas of the health sciences. Housed within the library is one of the world's finest medical history collections of pre-1914 and rare medical texts, manuscripts, and incunabula.

Contact: ref@nlm.nih.gov

Details: Free

The NLM can be accessed also through the WWW at http://www.nlm.nih.gov

`telnet://locator@locator.nlm.nih.gov`

University of North Carolina at Chapel Hill Info Library ★★

The library's holdings are large and wide-ranging and contain significant collections in many fields.

Keywords: North Carolina; Southern Historical Collection, Rare Books

Audience: Researchers, Students, General Public

Contact: Judy Hallman
hallman@unc.bitnet

Details: Free

Expect: Login; Send: Info

`telnet://info.oit.unc.edu`

Rascal Aviation Archives

Rascal Aviation Archives ★★

A major directory on aeronautics, providing access to a broad range of related resources (library catalogues, databases, and servers) via the Internet.

Keywords: Aeronautics, Aviation

Audience: Aviators, Aeronautical Engineers

Contact: rdd@rascal.ics.utexas.edu

`ftp://rascal.ics.utexas.edu/ explore-me/Aviation-stuff`

Raves

AusRave (Australian Raves) ★

A regional rave-related mailing list covering the Australian continent. AusRave contains both discussions and informational postings.

Keywords: Music, Raves, Australia

A B C D E F G H I J K L M N O P Q **R** S T U V W X Y Z

A B C D E F G H I J K L M N O P Q **R** S T U V W X Y Z

Audience: Ravers (Australian)

Contact: Simon Rumble
ausrave@lsupoz.apana.org.au

Details: Free, Moderated

User Info: To subscribe to the list, send an e-mail message requesting a subscription to the URL address below. To send a message to the entire list, address it to: ausrave@lsupoz.apana.org.au

Notes: The mailing list Best of AusRave provides information only

Postings to AusRave are not archived, but the list does have an FTP site at: elecsun4.elec.uow.edu.au

`mailto:ausrave-request@lsupoz.apana.org.au`

Best-of-AusRave (Australian Raves)

A regional rave-related mailing list covering the Australian continent, for people who want Australian rave information without the side discussions and social chatter from the regular list.

Keywords: Music, Raves, Australia

Audience: Ravers (Australian)

Contact: Simon Rumble
best-of-ausrave-request@lsupoz.apana.org.au

Details: Free, Moderated

User Info: To subscribe to the list, send an e-mail message to the URL address below, consisting of a single line reading:

SUB ausrave YourFirstName YourLastName

To send a message to the entire list, address it to: best-of-ausrave@lsupoz.apana.org.au

`mailto:best-of-ausrave-request@lsupoz.apana.org.au`

DCRaves

One of several regional rave-related mailing lists, DCRaves covers the Washington, DC, area exclusively. Archives are available through the listserv, FTP, or gopher at american.edu.

Keywords: Raves, Washington DC

Audience: Rave Enthusiasts

Details: Free

User Info: To subscribe to the list, send an e-mail message to the URL address shown below consisting of a single line reading:

SUB dcraves YourFirstName YourLastName

To send a message to the entire list, address it to: dcraves@american.edu

`mailto:listserv@american.edu`

FL-Raves (Florida Raves)

One of several regional rave-related mailing lists, this covers the state of Florida. Discussions tend to be social; Floridians may want to check out SERaves as well.

Keywords: Raves

Audience: Ravers, Florida Residents

Contact: Steve Smith

Details: Free

User Info: To subscribe to the list, send an e-mail message requesting a subscription to the URL address below. To send a message to the entire list, address it to: flraves@cybernet.cse.fau.edu

`mailto:flraves-request@cybernet.cse.fau.edu`

mw-raves

One of several rave-related lists, MW-Raves (Midwest Raves) covers the Midwestern US. Postings are usually informational, but discussions of scene-related issues can also be expected.

Keywords: Raves, Music

Audience: Ravers

Contact: Andy Crosby
mw-raves-request@engin.umich.edu

Details: Free

User Info: To subscribe to the list, send an e-mail message to the URL address below consisting of a single line reading:

SUB mw-raves YourFirstName YourLastName

To send a message to the entire list, address it to: mw-raves@csd.uwm.edu

`mailto:mw-raves@csd.uwm.edu`

NERaves (Northeast Raves)

One of several regional rave-related mailing lists, NE-Raves covers the Northeastern US.

Keywords: Raves

Audience: Ravers

Details: Free

User Info: To subscribe to the list, send an e-mail message to the URLaddress below consisting of a single line reading:

SUB neraves YourFirstName YourLastName

To send a message to the entire list, address it to: neraves@umdd.umd.edu

`mailto:listserv@umdd.umd.edu`

NW-Raves (Northwest Raves)

One of several regional rave-related mailing lists, NW-Raves covers the northwestern US and western Canada. No archives are available.

Keywords: Raves

Audience: Ravers

Contact: Pat Lui
nw-raves-request@wimsey.bc.ca

Details: Free

User Info: To subscribe to the list, send an e-mail message requesting a subscription to the URL address below. To send a message to the entire list, address it to: nw-raves@wimsey.bc.ca

`mailto:nw-raves-request@wimsey.bc.ca`

PB-Cle-Raves

One of several regional rave-related mailing lists, PB-Cle-Raves covers the Pittsburgh, PA, and Cleveland, OH, metropolitan areas exclusively.

Keywords: Raves

Audience: Ravers

Contact: Joe LeSesne
pb-cle-raves-request@telerama.lm.com

Details: Free

User Info: To subscribe to the list, send an e-mail message requesting a subscription to the URL address below. To send a message to the entire list, address it to: pb-cle-raves@telerama.lm.com

`mailto:pb-cle-raves-request@telerama.lm.com`

REACH (Research and Educational Applications of Computers in the Humanities)

REACH (Research and Educational Applications of Computers in the Humanities)

Newsletter of the Humanities Computing Facility of the University of California, Santa Barbara. Contains material of general interest to computing humanists, including announcements of new listservers, projects, and conferences.

Keywords: Computing

Audience: Computer Users

Contact: Eric Dahlin
hcf1dahl@ucsbvm.bitnet

Details: Free

User Info: listserv@ucsbvm.bitnet

reach@ucsbvm.bitnet

`mailto:listserv@ucsbvm.bitnet`

Real Estate

ASSETS (Real Estate Tax Assessor and Deed Transfer Records)

The RealEstate Tax Assessor and Deed Transfer Records (ASSETS) library contains information compiled from real property records.

Keywords: Real Estate, Property, Tax Assessor, Deed Transfers, Records

Audience: Lawyers

Profile: The ASSETS library contains a variety of real estate information, including asset ownership, property address, owner's mailing address, assessed valuation, current market value, and recent property sales and deed transfers. Information is collected from county tax assessors' and recorders' offices nationwide and compiled by TRW REDI Property Data. The ASSETS library also contains a variety of boat and aircraft registration information.

Contact: Mead New Sales Group at (800) 227-4908 or (513) 859-5398 inside the US, or (513) 865-7981 for all inquiries outside the US.

User Info: To subscribe, contact Mead directly. To examine the Nexis user guide, you can access it at the ftp site of the University of Texas at Austin at the URL address: ftp.cc.utexas.edu

The files are in: /pub/ref-services/LEXIS

`telnet://nex.meaddata.com`

`http://www.meaddata.com`

Commercial Real Estate

Users can send and receive listings on property for sale, ask and answer questions, send press releases, receive editorial material, and do networking on commercial property.

Keywords: Real Estate

Audience: Real Estate Brokers, General Public

Contact: commercial.realestate@data-base.com

Details: Free

User Info: To subscribe to the list, send an e-mail message requesting a subscription to the URL address below.

`mailto:commercial.realestate@data-base.com`

Institutional Real Estate Newsline

Five-page fax briefing with articles regarding institutional real estate, life insurance company, banks, pension fund, real estate investment trust and commercial mortgage backed securities markets.

Keywords: Real Estate, Investments, Insurance

Sponsor: Institutional Real Estate

Audience: Investors

Details: Costs

`mailto:IREI@crl.com`

misc.invest.real-estate

A Usenet newsgroup providing information and discussion about property investments.

Keywords: Investments, Real Estate

Audience: General Public

Details: Free

User Info: To subscribe to this Usenet newsgroup, you need access to a newsreader.

`news:misc.invest.real-estate`

REBASE (Restriction Enzyme Database)

REBASE (Restriction Enzyme Database)

The Restriction Enzyme Database contains both data and literature citations. It can be searched for enzyme names, species, authors, journals, and recognition sequences.

Keywords: Physiology, Enzymes

Sponsor: New England Biolabs

Audience: Scientists, Molecular Biologists

Contact: Richard Roberts roberts@cshl.org

Details: Free

`gopher://gopher.gdb.org/77/.INDEX/rebase`

rec.aquaria

rec.aquaria

A Usenet newsgroup providing information and discussion about pet fish and aquaria.

Keywords: Fish, Aquatic Sciences

Audience: Fish Enthusiasts

Details: Free

User Info: To subscribe to this Usenet newsgroup, you need access to a newsreader.

`news:rec.aquaria`

rec.arts.anime

rec.arts.anime

A Usenet newsgroup providing information and discussion about Japanese animation fen.

Keywords: Animation, Fen, Japan

Audience: Animators

Details: Free

User Info: To subscribe to this Usenet newsgroup, you need access to a newsreader.

`news:rec.arts.anime`

rec.arts.books

rec.arts.books

A Usenet newsgroup providing information and discussion about a wide variety of books.

Keywords: Books

Audience: Readers, Writers

Details: Free

User Info: To subscribe to this Usenet newsgroup, you need access to a newsreader.

`news:rec.arts.books`

rec.arts.comics.misc

rec.arts.comics.misc

A Usenet newsgroup providing information and discussion about comic books and graphic novels.

Keywords: Comic Books, Books

Audience: Comics Enthusiasts, Readers, Writers

Details: Free

User Info: To subscribe to this Usenet newsgroup, you need access to a newsreader.

`news:rec.arts.comics.misc`

rec.arts.dance

rec.arts.dance

A Usenet newsgroup providing information and discussion about all types of dance.

Keywords: Dance, Fine Arts

Audience: Dancers, Dance Enthusiasts, Choreographers

User Info: To subscribe to this Usenet newsgroup, you need access to a newsreader.

`news: rec.arts.dance`

A B C D E F G H I J K L M N O P Q R S T U V W X Y Z

rec.arts.disney

rec.arts.disney

A Usenet newsgroup providing information and discussion about Disney and related topics.

Keywords: Disney

Audience: Disney Enthusiasts

Details: Free

User Info: To subscribe to this Usenet newsgroup, you need access to a newsreader.

news:rec.arts.disney

rec.arts.fin

rec.arts.fin

A Usenet newsgroup providing information and discussion about the visual arts. Discussions range from archival materials to Ansel Adams, Mary Cassat and Andy Warhol.

Keywords: Art, Fine Art

Audience: Artists, Art Educators, Art Professionals

User Info: To subscribe to this Usenet newsgroup, you need access to a newsreader.

news:rec.arts.fin

Rec.arts.int-fiction

Rec.arts.int-fiction

A USENET newsgroup about interactive literature and interactive computer games.

Keywords: Literature (General), Interactive Media, Computer Games

Audience: General Public, Computer Games Players

Details: Free

To participate in a USENET newsgroup, you need access to a 'newsreader'.

news:rec.arts.int-fiction

rec.arts.movies

rec.arts.movies

A Usenet newsgroup providing information and discussion about films and film making.

Keywords: Film

Audience: Film Enthusiasts, Filmmakers

Details: Free

User Info: To subscribe to this Usenet newsgroup, you need access to a newsreader.

news:rec.arts.movies

rec.arts.movies movie database

rec.arts.movies movie database

An extensive FTP database covering over 32,000 movies, with more than 370,000 filmography entries, from early cinema to current releases.

Keywords: Movies, Television, Popular Culture

Audience: Film Enthusiasts

Profile: Interfaces to search the database include Unix, MS-DOS and Amiga (and Windows and Mac versions are in development). The database includes filmographies for actors, directors, writers, composers, cinematographers, editors, production designers, costume designers and producers; plot summaries; character names; movie ratings; year of release; running times; movie trivia; quotes; goofs; soundtracks; personal trivia and Academy Award information.

Contact: Col Needham
cn@ibmpcug.co.uk

Details: Free

ftp://cathouse.org/pub/cathouse/movies/database

rec.arts.movies movie database (Cardiff WWW front-end)

rec.arts.movies movie database (Cardiff WWW front-end)

An extensive, interactive database covering over 32,000 movies, with more than 370,000 filmography entries, from early cinema to current releases.

Keywords: Movies, Television, Popular Culture, Interactive Media

Audience: Film Enthusiasts

Profile: A WWW front-end to the rec.arts.movies movie database, complete with form-filling interfaces to add new data and to rate movies (on a scale from 1 through 10). The database includes filmographies for actors, directors, writers, composers, cinematographers, editors, production designers, costume designers and producers; plot summaries; character names; movie ratings; year of release; running times; movie trivia; quotes; goofs; soundtracks; personal trivia and Academy Award information.

Contact: Rob Hartill
Robert.Hartill@cm.cf.ac.uk

Details: Free

http://www.cm.cf.ac.uk/Movies

http://www.msstate.edu/Movies

rec.arts.poems

rec.arts.poems

A Usenet newsgroup providing information and discussion about poetry.

Keywords: Poetry, Literature (General)

Audience: Poets, Poetry Readers

User Info: To subscribe to this Usenet newsgroup, you need access to a newsreader.

news:rec.arts.poems

rec.arts.sf.starwars

rec.arts.sf.starwars

A Usenet newsgroup providing information and discussion about the popular Star Wars trilogy.

Keywords: Science Fiction, Film

Audience: Star Wars Enthusiasts, Movie Viewers

User Info: To subscribe to this Usenet newsgroup, you need access to a newsreader.

news:rec.arts.sf.starwars

rec.arts.sf.tv

rec.arts.sf.tv

A Usenet newsgroup providing information and discussion about science fiction television programs.

Keywords: Science Fiction, Television

Audience: Science Fiction Enthusiasts, Television Viewers

User Info: To subscribe to this Usenet newsgroup, you need access to a newsreader.

news:rec.arts.sf.tv

rec.arts.sf.written

rec.arts.sf.written

A Usenet newsgroup providing information and discussion about science fiction publications.

Keywords: Science Fiction

Audience: Science Fiction Readers

User Info: To subscribe to this Usenet newsgroup, you need access to a newsreader.

`news:rec.arts.sf.written`

rec.arts.startrek.current

rec.arts.startrek.current

A Usenet newsgroup providing information and discussion about current Star Trek (The Next Generation) episodes and characters.

Keywords: Television, Science Fiction

Audience: Trekkies, Television Viewers

User Info: To subscribe to this Usenet newsgroup, you need access to a newsreader.

`news:rec.arts.startrek.current`

rec.arts.startrek.misc

rec.arts.startrek.misc

A Usenet newsgroup providing general information and discussion about all aspects of Star Trek, including its various television and film reviews.

Keywords: Television, Film

Audience: Trekkies, Television Viewers, Film Enthusiasts

User Info: To subscribe to this Usenet newsgroup, you need access to a newsreader.

`news:rec.arts.startrek.misc`

rec.arts.tv

rec.arts.tv

A Usenet newsgroup providing information and discussion about past and present TV shows and related trivia.

Keywords: Television, Trivia

Audience: General Public, Television Viewers, Trivia Enthusiasts

User Info: To subscribe to this Usenet newsgroup, you need access to a newsreader.

`news:rec.arts.tv`

rec.arts.tv.soaps

rec.arts.tv.soaps

A Usenet newsgroup providing information and discussion about television soap operas.

Keywords: Television

Audience: Television Viewers, Soap Opera Enthusiasts

User Info: To subscribe to this Usenet newsgroup, you need access to a newsreader.

`news:rec.arts.tv.soaps`

rec.arts.tv.uk

rec.arts.tv.uk

A Usenet newsgroup providing information and discussion about television shows in the United Kingdom.

Keywords: Television, United Kingdom

Audience: Television Viewers, British

User Info: To subscribe to this Usenet newsgroup, you need access to a newsreader.

`news:rec.arts.tv.uk`

rec.audio

rec.audio

A Usenet newsgroup providing information and discussion about audio products, including troubleshooting advice.

Keywords: Audio Electronics, Stereo Electronics

Audience: Stereo Owners, Music Listeners

User Info: To subscribe to this Usenet newsgroup, you need access to a newsreader.

`news:rec.audio`

rec.autos.driving

rec.autos.driving

 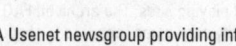 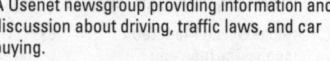

A Usenet newsgroup providing information and discussion about driving, traffic laws, and car buying.

Keywords: Automobiles

Audience: Drivers, Automobile Buyers

User Info: To subscribe to this Usenet newsgroup, you need access to a newsreader.

`news:rec.autos.driving`

rec.autos.sport

rec.autos.sport

A Usenet newsgroup providing information and discussion about automobile competition.

Keywords: Automobiles, Automobile Racing, Sports

Audience: Automobile Racing Enthusiasts

User Info: To subscribe to this Usenet newsgroup, you need access to a newsreader.

`news:rec.autos.sports`

rec.autos.tech

rec.autos.tech

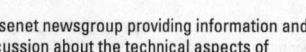

A Usenet newsgroup providing information and discussion about the technical aspects of automobiles.

Keywords: Automobiles, Technology

Audience: Automobile Mechanics

User Info: To subscribe to this Usenet newsgroup, you need access to a newsreader.

`news:rec.autos.tech`

rec.autos.vw

rec.autos.vw

A Usenet newsgroup providing information and discussion about Volkswagon products.

Keywords: Automobiles

Audience: Volkswagon Drivers

User Info: To subscribe to this Usenet newsgroup, you need access to a newsreader.

`news:rec.autos.vw`

rec.backcountry

rec.backcountry

A Usenet newsgroup providing information and discussion about wilderness, backpacking, and camping.

Keywords: Recreation, Sports

Audience: Campers, Backpackers, Wilderness Enthusiasts

User Info: To subscribe to this Usenet newsgroup, you need access to a newsreader.

`news:rec.backcountry`

rec.boats

rec.boats

A Usenet newsgroup providing information and discussion about boating, gear, places to sail, clubs, repairs, and racing.

A B C D E F G H I J K L M N O P Q **R** S T U V W X Y Z

A

B

C

D

E

F

G

H

I

J

K

L

M

N

O

P

Q

R

S

T

U

V

W

X

Y

Z

Keywords: Sailing, Sports

Audience: Sailors, Boating Enthusiasts

User Info: To subscribe to this Usenet newsgroup, you need access to a newsreader.

news:rec.boats

rec.collecting.cards

rec.collecting.cards

A Usenet newsgroup providing information and discussion about collecting sports and other trading cards.

Keywords: Trading Cards, Hobbies

Audience: Card Collectors

User Info: To subscribe to this Usenet newsgroup, you need access to a newsreader.

news:rec.collecting.cards

rec.crafts.brewing

rec.crafts.brewing

A Usenet newsgroup providing information and discussion about making beers and meads.

Keywords: Beer, Crafts

Audience: Beer Brewers

User Info: To subscribe to this Usenet newsgroup, you need access to a newsreader.

news:rec.crafts.brewing

rec.equestrian

rec.equestrian

A Usenet newsgroup providing information and discussion about all things pertaining to horses.

Keywords: Horses, Equestrians, Animals, Sports

Audience: Horse Enthusiasts, Horse Trainers, Horse Owners

User Info: To subscribe to this Usenet newsgroup, you need access to a newsreader.

news:rec.equestrian

rec.food.cooking

rec.food.cooking

A Usenet newsgroup providing information and discussion about cooking.

Keywords: Food, Cooking

Audience: General Public, Cooks, Chefs

User Info: To subscribe to this Usenet newsgroup, you need access to a newsreader.

news:rec.food.cooking

rec.food.veg

rec.food.veg

A Usenet newsgroup providing information and discussion about vegetarian cooking.

Keywords: Vegetarianism, Food, Cooking

Audience: Vegetarians, Cooks, Chefs

User Info: To subscribe to this Usenet newsgroup, you need access to a newsreader.

news:rec.food.veg

rec.gambling

rec.gambling

Discussion of card games, gambling, and gambling sites.

Keywords: Cards, Gambling

Audience: Card Players, Gamblers

Profile: Discussion in this group covers gambling, and card games, the rules of various card games, odds, betting, and the pros and cons of various gambling and card playing sites. The archived FAQ is a lengthy card game resource.

Contact: rec.gambling Moderator
jacobs@cs.utah.edu

Notes: The rec.gambling FAQ is accessible via anonymous ftp at soda.berkeley.edu through the path pub/rec.gambling.

news:rec.gambling

rec.games.board

rec.games.board

A Usenet newsgroup providing hints and discussion about board games.

Keywords: Games, Recreation

Audience: Game Players

User Info: To subscribe to this Usenet newsgroup, you need access to a newsreader.

news:rec.games.board

rec.games.chess

rec.games.chess

A Usenet newsgroup providing information and discussion about chess strategies, organized computer chess playing events, and software.

Keywords: Chess, Games, Recreation

Audience: Chess Players, Game Players

User Info: To subscribe to this Usenet newsgroup, you need access to a newsreader.

news:rec.games.chess

rec.games.programmer

rec.games.programmer

A Usenet newsgroup providing information and discussion about adventure game programming.

Keywords: Games, Programming, Video Games

Audience: Programmers

User Info: To subscribe to this Usenet newsgroup, you need access to a newsreader.

news:rec.games.programmer

rec.games.video.arcade

rec.games.video.arcade

A Usenet newsgroup providing information and discussion about video games.

Keywords: Games, Video Games

Audience: Game Players

User Info: To subscribe to this Usenet newsgroup, you need access to a newsreader.

news:rec.games.video.arcade

rec.gardens

rec.gardens ★

A Usenet newsgroup providing information and discussion about gardening.

Keywords: Gardening, Landscaping

Audience: Gardeners

User Info: To subscribe to this Usenet newsgroup, you need access to a newsreader.

`news:rec.gardens`

rec.guns

rec.guns ★

A Usenet newsgroup providing information and discussion about firearms.

Keywords: Firearms, Weapons

Audience: Gun Users

User Info: To subscribe to this Usenet newsgroup, you need access to a newsreader.

`news:rec.guns`

rec.humor

rec.humor ★

A Usenet newsgroup providing information and discussion about jokes.

Keywords: Jokes, Humor

Audience: General Public, Jokers

User Info: To subscribe to this Usenet newsgroup, you need access to a newsreader.

`news:rec.humor`

rec.martial-arts

rec.martial-arts ★

A Usenet newsgroup providing information and discussion about martial arts.

Keywords: Martial Arts

Audience: Martial Artist Enthusiasts

User Info: To subscribe to this Usenet newsgroup, you need access to a newsreader.

`news:rec.martial-arts`

rec.motorcycles

rec.motorcycles ★

A Usenet newsgroup providing information and discussion about motorcycles and related products.

Keywords: Motorcycles

Audience: Motorcycle Enthusiasts

User Info: To subscribe to this Usenet newsgroup, you need access to a newsreader.

`news:rec.motorcycles`

rec.music.beatles

rec.music.beatles ★

A Usenet newsgroup providing information and discussion about the Beatles.

Keywords: Musical Groups, Popular Culture

Audience: Beatles Enthusiasts

User Info: To subscribe to this Usenet newsgroup, you need access to a newsreader.

`news:rec.music.beatles`

rec.music.cd

rec.music.cd ★

A Usenet newsgroup providing information and discussion about Compact Discs.

Keywords: Music, Audio Electronics

Audience: Compact Disc Users

User Info: To subscribe to this Usenet newsgroup, you need access to a newsreader.

`news:rec.music.cd`

rec.music.classical

rec.music.classical ★

A Usenet newsgroup providing information and discussion about classical music.

Keywords: Music

Audience: Classical Music Listeners

User Info: To subscribe to this Usenet newsgroup, you need access to a newsreader.

`news:rec.music.classical`

rec.music.folk

rec.music.folk ★

A Usenet newsgroup providing information and discussion about folk music.

Keywords: Musical Genres

Audience: Folk Music Enthusiasts

User Info: To subscribe to this Usenet newsgroup, you need access to a newsreader.

`news:rec.music.folk`

rec.music.gdead

rec.music.gdead ★★

A Usenet newsgroup providing information and discussion about the Grateful Dead.

Keywords: Music, Popular Culture

Audience: Grateful Dead Enthusiasts

User Info: To subscribe to this Usenet newsgroup, you need access to a newsreader.

`news:rec.music.gdead`

rec.music.makers

rec.music.makers ★

A Usenet newsgroup providing information and discussion about music-making.

Keywords: Musical Instruments, Music

Audience: Performers, Musicians

User Info: To subscribe to this Usenet newsgroup, you need access to a newsreader.

`news:rec.music.makers`

rec.music.makers.guitar

rec.music.makers.guitar ★

A Usenet newsgroup providing information and discussion about guitars and guitar playing.

Keywords: Musical Instruments

Audience: Guitar Players

User Info: To subscribe to this Usenet newsgroup, you need access to a newsreader.

`news:rec.music.makers.guitar`

A B C D E F G H I J K L M N O P Q R S T U V W X Y Z

A B C D E F G H I J K L M N O P Q R S T U V W X Y Z

rec.music.makers.synth

rec.music.makers.synth ★

A Usenet newsgroup providing information and discussion about synthesizers.

Keywords: Music, Audio Electronics

Audience: Musicians

User Info: To subscribe to this Usenet newsgroup, you need access to a newsreader.

news:rec.music.makers.synth

rec.music.phish

rec.music.phish ★

A Usenet newsgroup providing information and discussion about the band Phish.

Keywords: Musical Groups, Popular Culture

Audience: Phish Enthusiasts

User Info: To subscribe to this Usenet newsgroup, you need access to a newsreader.

news:rec.music.phish

rec.org.sca

rec.org.sca ★

A Usenet newsgroup providing information and discussion about medieval re-enactments.

Keywords: SCA (Society For Creative Anachronism), Medieval Studies

Audience: General Public

User Info: To subscribe to this Usenet newsgroup, you need access to a newsreader.

news:rec.org.sca

rec.pets

rec.pets ★

A Usenet newsgroup providing information and discussion about pets and pet care.

Keywords: Pets, Animals

Audience: Pet Owners

User Info: To subscribe to this Usenet newsgroup, you need access to a newsreader.

news:rec.pets

rec.pets.cats

rec.pets.cats ★

A Usenet newsgroup providing information and discussion about domestic cats.

Keywords: Pets, Animals

Audience: Cat Owners

User Info: To subscribe to this Usenet newsgroup, you need access to a newsreader.

news:rec.pets.cats

rec.pets.dogs

rec.pets.dogs ★

A Usenet newsgroup providing information and discussion about dogs.

Keywords: Pets, Animals

Audience: Dog Owners

User Info: To subscribe to this Usenet newsgroup, you need access to a newsreader.

news:rec.pets.dogs

rec.photo

rec.photo ★

A Usenet newsgroup providing information and discussion about photography.

Keywords: Photography, Art, Crafts

Audience: Photographers

User Info: To subscribe to this Usenet newsgroup, you need access to a newsreader.

news:rec.photo

rec.puzzles

rec.puzzles ★

A Usenet newsgroup providing information and discussion about math puzzles and brain teasers.

Keywords: Games, Puzzles, Recreation

Audience: General Public

User Info: To subscribe to this Usenet newsgroup, you need access to a newsreader.

news:rec.puzzles

rec.radio.amateur.misc

rec.radio.amateur.misc ★

A Usenet newsgroup providing information and discussion about ham radios.

Keywords: Radio, Electronics

Audience: Ham Radio Operators

User Info: To subscribe to this Usenet newsgroup, you need access to a newsreader.

news:rec.radio.amateur.misc

rec.radio.shortwave

rec.radio.shortwave ★

A Usenet newsgroup providing information and discussion about shortwave radio.

Keywords: Radio, Electronics

Audience: Shortwave Radio Users

User Info: To subscribe to this Usenet newsgroup, you need access to a newsreader.

news:rec.radio.shortwave

rec.railroad

rec.railroad ★

A Usenet newsgroup providing information and discussion about railroads.

Keywords: Railroads, Transportation

Audience: Railroad Enthusiast

User Info: To subscribe to this Usenet newsgroup, you need access to a newsreader.

news:rec.railroad

rec.scuba

rec.scuba ★

A Usenet newsgroup providing information and discussion about scuba equipment and techniques.

Keywords: Scuba Sports, Travel, Recreation

Audience: Scuba Divers

User Info: To subscribe to this Usenet newsgroup, you need access to a newsreader.

news:scuba

rec.skiing

rec.skiing ★

A Usenet newsgroup providing information and discussion about skiing.

Keywords: Sports, Recreation, Skiing

Audience: Skiers

User Info: To subscribe to this Usenet newsgroup, you need access to a newsreader.

`news:rec.skiing`

rec.sport.baseball

rec.sport.baseball ★

A Usenet newsgroup providing information and discussion about professional baseball.

Keywords: Baseball, Sports

Audience: Baseball Fans, Sports Fans

User Info: To subscribe to this Usenet newsgroup, you need access to a newsreader.

`news:rec.sport.baseball`

rec.sport.basketball.college

rec.sport.basketball.college ★

A Usenet newsgroup providing information and discussion about college basketball.

Keywords: Basketball, Sports

Audience: Basketball Enthusiasts, Sport Enthusiasts

User Info: To subscribe to this Usenet newsgroup, you need access to a newsreader.

`news:rec.sport.basketball.college`

rec.sport.basketball.pro

rec.sport.basketball.pro ★

A Usenet newsgroup providing information and discussion about professional basketball.

Keywords: Basketball, Sports

Audience: Basketball Fans, Sports Enthusiasts

User Info: To subscribe to this Usenet newsgroup, you need access to a newsreader.

`news:rec.sport.basketball.pro`

rec.sport.cricket

rec.sport.cricket ★

A Usenet newsgroup providing information and discussion about cricket.

Keywords: Cricket, Sports

Audience: Cricket Fans, Sports Enthusiasts

User Info: To subscribe to this Usenet newsgroup, you need access to a newsreader.

`news:rec.sport.cricket`

rec.sport.football.college

rec.sport.football.college ★

A Usenet newsgroup providing information and discussion about college football.

Keywords: Football, Sports

Audience: Football Enthusiasts, Sports Enthusiasts

User Info: To subscribe to this Usenet newsgroup, you need access to a newsreader.

`news:rec.sport.football.college`

rec.sport.football.pro

rec.sport.football.pro ★

A Usenet newsgroup providing information and discussion about pro football.

Keywords: Football, Sports

Audience: Football Enthusiasts

User Info: To subscribe to this Usenet newsgroup, you need access to a newsreader.

`news:rec.sport.football.pro`

rec.sport.hockey

rec.sport.hockey ★

A Usenet newsgroup providing information and discussion about hockey.

Keywords: Hockey, Sports

Audience: Hockey Fans, Sports Fans

User Info: To subscribe to this Usenet newsgroup, you need access to a newsreader.

`news:rec.sport.hockey`

rec.sport.olympics

rec.sport.olympics ★

A Usenet newsgroup providing information and discussion about the summer Olympics Games.

Keywords: Olympic Games, Summer Sports

Audience: Olympic Enthusiasts

User Info: To subscribe to this Usenet newsgroup, you need access to a newsreader.

`news:rec.sport.olympics`

rec.sport.pro-wrestling

rec.sport.pro-wrestling ★

A Usenet newsgroup providing information and discussion about professional wrestling.

Keywords: Wrestling, Sports

Audience: Wrestling Fans, Sports Fans

User Info: To subscribe to this Usenet newsgroup, you need access to a newsreader.

`news:rec.sport.pro-wrestling`

rec.sport.rowing

rec.sport.rowing ★

A Usenet newsgroup providing information and discussion about recreational and competitive rowing. It provides information from the United States Rowing Association, the latest race results, equipment sales, coaching positions and more.

Keywords: Rowing, Crew, Sports

Audience: Rowers, Coaches, Athletes

Profile: This newsgroup covers technical, training and nutritional aspects as well as the latest race results, National Team information, equipment sales, coaching positions, information from the United States Rowing Association and more.

User Info: To subscribe to this Usenet newsgroup, you need access to a newsreader.

`news:rec.sport.rowing`

rec.sport.soccer

rec.sport.soccer ★

A Usenet newsgroup providing information and discussion about soccer.

A
B
C
D
E
F
G
H
I
J
K
L
M
N
O
P
Q
R
S
T
U
V
W
X
Y
Z

Keywords: Soccer, Sports

Audience: Soccer Enthusiasts, Sports Enthusiasts

User Info: To subscribe to this Usenet newsgroup, you need access to a newsreader.

`news:rec.sport.soccer`

rec.sport.tennis

rec.sport.tennis

A Usenet newsgroup providing information and discussion about tennis.

Keywords: Tennis, Sports

Audience: Tennis Players, Sports Enthusiasts

User Info: To subscribe to this Usenet newsgroup, you need access to a newsreader.

`news:rec.sport.tennis`

rec.travel

rec.travel

A Usenet newsgroup providing information and discussion about travel.

Keywords: Travel

Audience: Travelers

User Info: To subscribe to this Usenet newsgroup, you need access to a newsreader.

`news:rec.travel`

rec.video

rec.video

A Usenet newsgroup providing information and discussion about video.

Keywords: Video, Art, Film, Computer Art

Audience: Cinematographers, Video Artists

User Info: To subscribe to this Usenet newsgroup, you need access to a newsreader.

`news:rec.video`

rec.video.satellite

rec.video.satellite

A Usenet newsgroup providing information and discussion about satellite television.

Keywords: Television

Audience: Television Viewers

User Info: To subscribe to this Usenet newsgroup, you need access to a newsreader.

`news:rec.video.satellite`

rec.woodworking

rec.woodworking

A Usenet newsgroup providing information and discussion about woodworking.

Keywords: Woodworking, Crafts, Hobbies

Audience: Woodworkers

User Info: To subscribe to this Usenet newsgroup, you need access to a newsreader.

`news:rec.woodworking`

Recipes

GRANOLA (Vegetarian Discussion List)

A ListServ for discussion of vegetarian issues, including everything from recipes to animal rights.

Keywords: Health, Nutrition, Vegetarian, Recipes

Audience: Vegetarians, Nutritionists, Health Professionals

Details: Free

User Info: To subscribe to the list, send an e-mail message to the URL address shown below consisting of a single line reading:

SUB granola YourFirstName YourLastName

`mailto:listserv@gitvm1.bitnet`

Recipe Archive

This is an archive of recipes organized by main ingredient or title.

Keywords: Cooking, Food, Recipes

Audience: General Public, Cooks, Chefs

Profile: Here are a few intriguing examples from the archive:

Advokaat: Advokaat is the Dutch word for egg cognac. It is highly recommended for A. I. (Alcohol Imbibing) meetings. This recipe is a modification of a recipe obtained in Poland. It makes a potent, superb advokaat (or egg cognac). The milk and eggs are healthy, the sugar and alcohol are not!

Berlinerkranzer: Norwegian wreath cookies are decorative holiday cookies that add quite a bright, colorful, aromatic touch to your plate of cookies.

Bouillabaisse: This recipe for Marseille-style fish soup represents a combination of several recipes derived from old Gourmets, Julia Child, the Playboy Gourmet Cookbook, and "Gee, that sounds good, let's add it.." The accompanying rouille is a garlic/hot pepper mayonnaise condiment traditional to Marseille-style fish soup.

Details: Free

gopher://calypso.oit.unc.edu/ 7waissrc%3a/ref.d/indexes.d/recipes.src

gopher://calypso.oit.unc.edu/ 7waissrc%3a/ref.d/indexes.d/ usenet-cookbook.sr

They can also be accessed through mosaic at the URL address shown below or from the calypso.oit.unc.edu gopher in the subdirectories: Internet Dog-Eared Pages (Frequently used resources)/ Search Many WAIS Indices

Notes: There are two searchable gopher indexes containing recipes that have passed through the rec.food.cooking and rec.food.recipes newsgroups. They can be found at the following URL addresses:

`ftp://gatekeeper.dec.com/pub/recipes`

The World Wide Web rec.food.recipes archive

World Wide Web archive of recipes posted to Usenet newsgroup rec.food.recipes. Updated weekly.

Keywords: Food, Recipes, Cooking

Audience: Cooks, General Public

Contact: Amy Gale
mara@kauri.vuw.ac.nz

User Info: Use a World-Wide Web (WWW) client such as lynx

`http://www.vuw.ac.nz/non-local/ recipes-archive/recipe-archive.html`

Recordings

Soundtracks

Discussions and reviews of new and older soundtracks (musical and technical aspects). Information about availability of specific soundtracks on different formats in different parts of the world.

Keywords: Music, Recordings

Audience: Audio Enthusiasts, Music Researchers

Contact: Michel Hafner
soundtracks-request@ifi.unizh.ch

User Info: To subscribe to the list, send an e-mail message requesting a subscription to the URL address below. To send a message to the entire list, address it to: soundtracks@ifi.unizh.ch

`mailto:soundtracks- request@ifi.unizh.ch`

Recreation

(The) Kites FTP Archive

★

Files pertaining to kites and kite-flying.

Keywords: Kites, Recreation

Sponsor: University of Hawaii

Audience: Kite Enthusiasts, Aeronautical Engineers

Contact: Kevin Mayeshiro

kevin@ftp.hawaii.edu

Details: Free, Moderated, Images

`ftp://ftp.hawaii.edu/pub/rec.kites`

Physical Education & Recreation

★★

A collection of information on sporting and recreational activities from aikido to windsurfing.

Keywords: Sports, Recreation, Aikido, Cycling, Scuba Diving, Windsurfing

Audience: Sports Enthusiasts, Fitness Enthusiasts

Contact: ctcadmin@ctc.ctc.edu

`gopher://ctc.ctc.edu`

rec.backcountry

★

A Usenet newsgroup providing information and discussion about wilderness, backpacking, and camping.

Keywords: Recreation, Sports

Audience: Campers, Backpackers, Wilderness Enthusiasts

User Info: To subscribe to this Usenet newsgroup, you need access to a newsreader.

`news:rec.backcountry`

rec.gambling

★

A Usenet newsgroup providing information and discussion about gambling.

Keywords: Games, Gambling, Recreation

Audience: Gamblers

User Info: To subscribe to this Usenet newsgroup, you need access to a newsreader.

`news:rec.gambling`

rec.games.board

★

A Usenet newsgroup providing hints and discussion about board games.

Keywords: Games, Recreation

Audience: Game Players

User Info: To subscribe to this Usenet newsgroup, you need access to a newsreader.

`news:rec.games.board`

rec.games.chess

★

A Usenet newsgroup providing information and discussion about chess strategies, organized computer chess playing events, and software.

Keywords: Chess, Games, Recreation

Audience: Chess Players, Game Players

User Info: To subscribe to this Usenet newsgroup, you need access to a newsreader.

`news:rec.games.chess`

rec.puzzles

★

A Usenet newsgroup providing information and discussion about math puzzles and brain teasers.

Keywords: Games, Puzzles, Recreation

Audience: General Public

User Info: To subscribe to this Usenet newsgroup, you need access to a newsreader.

`news:rec.puzzles`

rec.scuba

★

A Usenet newsgroup providing information and discussion about scuba equipment and techniques.

Keywords: Scuba Sports, Travel, Recreation

Audience: Scuba Divers

User Info: To subscribe to this Usenet newsgroup, you need access to a newsreader.

`news:scuba`

rec.skiing

★

A Usenet newsgroup providing information and discussion about skiing.

Keywords: Sports, Recreation, Skiing

Audience: Skiers

User Info: To subscribe to this Usenet newsgroup, you need access to a newsreader.

`news:rec.skiing`

Zarf's List of Interactive Games on the Web

A list containing links to games and toys that can be played on the Internet.

Keywords: Games, Toys, Entertainment, Recreation

Sponsor: Carnegie Mellon University, School of Computer Science, Pittsburgh, Pennsylvania, USA

Audience: General Public, Game Players, Kids

Contact: Andrew Plotkin

zarf@cs.cmu.edu, apli@andrew.cmu.edu

`http://www.cs.cmu.edu/afs/cs.cmu.edu/ user/zarf/www/games.html`

Recreational Pharmacology Server

Recreational Pharmacology Server

★★★★

Very extensive collection of drug FAQs, data sheets, net articles, resources, and electronic books. Complete list of Internet links to related sites.

Keywords: Pharmacology, Drugs, Neuroscience

Sponsor: University of Washington, Seattle, Washington, USA

Audience: Students, General Public, Neuroscientists, Pharmacists

Contact: Webmaster

lamontg@u.washington.edu

Details: Free

`http://stein1.u.washington.edu:2012/ pharm/pharm.html`

Recycling

Solid Waste Recycling

★★

The text of an eight-lesson correspondence class designed to teach the basics of setting up a successful recycling program.

Keywords: Recycling, Environmental Studies

Sponsor: University of Wisconsin

Audience: Environmentalists, Educators, Students

Contact: Judy Faber

faber@engr.wisc.edu

`gopher://wissago.uwex.edu/11/uwex/ course/recycling`

Reference

BUSREF (Business Reference)

The Business Refernce (BUSREF) library contains a variety of reference materials covering business and industry.

Keywords: News, Reference, Business, Government

Audience: Businessmen

Profile: The BUSREF library contains company directories, reference publications, information on business opportunities, and biographical information on political candidates, Congressional members, celebrities, and international decision makers.

Contact: Mead New Sales Group at (800) 227-4908 or (513) 859-5398 inside the US, or (513) 865-7981 for all inquiries outside the US.

A B C D E F G H I J K L M N O P Q R S T U V W X Y Z

A
B
C
D
E
F
G
H
I
J
K
L
M
N
O
P
Q
R
S
T
U
V
W
X
Y
Z

User Info: To subscribe, contact Mead directly.

To examine the Nexis user guide, you can access it at the ftp site of the University of Texas at Austin at the URL address: ftp://ftp.cc.utexas.edu

The files are in: /pub/ref-services/LEXIS

`telnet://nex.meaddata.com`

`http://www.meaddata.com`

GUTENBERG Listserver

A mailing list providing information about Project Gutenberg.

Keywords: Project Gutenberg, Literature (General), Reference

Sponsor: National Clearinghouse for Machine Readable Texts

Audience: General Public, Researchers, Educators, Students

Contact: Michael S. Hart
            gutnberg@vmd.cso.uiuc.edu

Details: Free

User Info: To subscribe to the list, send an e-mail message to the URL address shown below consisting of a single line reading:

SUB GUTNBERG YourFirstName YourLastName

`mailto:listserv@vmd.cso.uiuc.edu`

Project Gutenberg

★★★★

The purpose of Project Gutenberg is to encourage the creation and distribution of English-language electronic texts.

Keywords: Literature (General), Reference

Sponsor: National Clearinghouse for Machine Readable Texts

Audience: General Public, Researchers, Educators, Students

Profile: Contents include:

Project Gutenberg's goal is to provide a collection of 10,000 of the most used books by the year 2001, and to reduce the effective costs to the user to a price of approximately one cent per book, plus the cost of media and of shipping and handling. Thus it is hoped that the entire cost of libraries of this nature will be about US$100, plus the price of the disks and CD-ROMS and mailing. Project Gutenberg assists in the selection of hardware and software as well as in their installation and use. It also assists in scanning, spelling checkers, proofreading, and so on.

Contact: Michael S. Hart
            hart@vmd.cso.uiuc.edu

Details: Costs

Login anonymous; cd text

`ftp://mrcnext.cso.uiuc.edu`

Refrigeration

Utah Valley Community College Library

The library's holdings are large and wide-ranging and contain significant collections in many fields.

Keywords: Accounting, Automobiles, Cabinetry, Child Care, Drafting, Electronics, Home Building, Local History, Refrigeration, Air Conditioning

Audience: General Public, Researchers, Librarians, Document Delivery Professionals

Details: Free

Expect: Login; Send: Opub

`telnet://uvlib.uvcc.edu`

Reggae

Reggae Down Babylon

A collection of links to sources of information about reggae music on the World Wide Web and the Internet. Site includes reggae FAQs, and listings of reggae radio shows, lyrics, pictures, and news group archives.

Keywords: Reggae, Music, Cultural Studies

Sponsor: Reggae Down Babylon

Audience: Music Enthusiasts, Musicians

Contact: ReggaeMaster
            damjohns@nyx10.cs.du.edu

Details: Free

`ftp://jammin.nosc.mil/pub/reggae`

Regional Business

Business Dateline

The database contains the full text of articles from more than 350 local and regional business publications from throughout the United States and Canada.

Keywords: Business, Regional Business, Market Conditions

Sponsor: UMI, Louisville, KY, USA

Audience: Business Analysts, Market Researchers, Writers

Profile: Sources include city business journals, daily newspapers, regional business magazines, and wire services. Subjects include city economic conditions, new product announcements, manufacturing methods, executive profiles, quality control, company histories, market conditions, service industries, regulations, litigation, and legislation.

Contact: Dialog in the US at (800) 334-2564, Dialog internationally at country specific locations.

Details: Costs

User Info: To subscribe, contact Dialog directly.

`telnet://dialog.com`

Regulations

Banking News Library

The Banking News library provides you specific banking industry sources. More than 40 full-text and selected full-text sources which focus on the banking related news and issues.

Keywords: Banking, Financial News, Regulation

Audience: Journalists, Banking Industry Analysts

Profile: This library contains news, Investext Industry Reports, and legal/ regulatory information. Also included in an abstract file is the Financial Industry Information Service (FINIS). The S&L file includes documents from newspapers and magazines which are specific to the S&L crisis.

Contact: Mead New Sales Group at (800) 227-4908 or (513) 859-5398 inside the US, or (513) 865-7981 for all inquiries outside the US.

User Info: To subscribe, contact Mead directly.

To examine the Nexis user guide, you can access it at the ftp site of the University of Texas at Austin at the URL address: ftp://ftp.cc.utexas.edu

The files are in: /pub/ref-services/LEXIS

`telnet://nex.meaddata.com`

`http://www.meaddata.com`

ENERGY

The Energy News and Information (ENERGY) library consists of news, legal, and regulatory information.

Keywords: Energy, News, Law, Regulations

Audience: Energy Researchers

Profile: The ENERGY library contains more than 50 full-text sources concentrating on energy-related news and issues. Also available are decisions and orders of the United States Federal Power Commission, Federal Energy Regulatory Commission, and Nuclear Regulatory Commission. At the state level, it covers administrative decisions and orders for 17 states. Energy industry research reports from InvestextR are also available.

Contact: Mead New Sales Group at (800) 227-4908 or (513) 859-5398 inside the US, or (513) 865-7981 for all inquiries outside the US.

User Info: To subscribe, contact Mead directly.

To examine the Nexis user guide, you can access it at the ftp site of the University of Texas at Austin at the URL address: ftp://ftp.cc.utexas.edu

The files are in: /pub/ref-services/LEXIS

`telnet://nex.meaddata.com`

`http://www.meaddata.com`

EXEC (Executive Branch News US)

The EXEC library contains information and news about the Executive Branch of the Federal Government. From the Department of Agriculture to the White House, this file is a comprehensive source of information that will be especially useful to those whose responsibilities include monitoring federal regulations, Agency and Department activity, and the people and issues involved.

Keywords: News, Legislation, Regulation, Politics, Executive Branch

Audience: Journalists, Lobbyists, Business Executives, Analysts, Entrepreneurs

Profile: The EXEC library allows the searching of individual files or group files that cover topics such as the Federal Register and Code of Federal Regulations; public laws; proposed treasury regulation; and over 50 news sources, including BNA's Daily Report for Executives, the Dept. of State Dispatch, ABC News transcripts, Federal News Service Daybook, Government Executive, MacNeil/Lehrer Newshour, New Leader, National Review, the Washington Post, the Washington Times, Presidential Documents, and many others.

Contact: Mead New Sales Group at (800) 227-4908 or (513) 859-5398 inside the US, or (513) 865-7981 for all inquiries outside the US.

User Info: To subscribe, contact Mead directly.

To examine the Nexis user guide, you can access it at the ftp site of the University of Texas at Austin at the URL address: ftp://ftp.cc.utexas.edu

The files are in: /pub/ref-services/LEXIS

`telnet://nex.meaddata.com`

`http://www.meaddata.com`

Relays

Class Four Relay Magazine

A magazine by Relay Ops for the relay community.

Keywords: Relays, Magazines, Electronics

Sponsor: Carnegie Mellon University, Pittsburg, PA, USA

Audience: Relay Community

Profile: Includes articles on general questions and issues of relay usage, information for and about relay ops, discussion of policy issues and guidelines, and technical issues and new developments.

Contact: Joey J. Stanford
stjs@vm.marist.edu

Details: Free

`mailto:stjs@vm.marist.edu`

Religion

alt.atheism
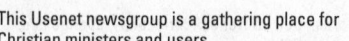

A Usenet newsgroup providing information and discussion about atheism.

Keywords: Religion, Divinity, God

Audience: Philosophers, Clergy, Atheists

User Info: To subscribe to this Usenet newsgroup, you need access to a newsreader.

`news:alt.atheism`

alt.christnet

This Usenet newsgroup is a gathering place for Christian ministers and users.

Keywords: Religion, Christianity, Bible, Divinity

Audience: Christians, Ministers

User Info: To subscribe to this Usenet newsgroup, you need access to a newsreader.

`news:alt.christnet`

alt.christnet.bible

A Usenet newsgroup providing information and discussion about bible discussion and research.

Keywords: Bible, Christian, Religion, Divinity

Audience: Biblical Scholars, Bible Readers

User Info: To subscribe to this Usenet newsgroup, you need access to a newsreader.

`news:alt.christnet.bible`

alt.pagan

A Usenet newsgroup providing information and discussion about paganism and religion.

Keywords: Paganism, Religion

Audience: Cults, Worshippers, Religion Students

User Info: To subscribe to this Usenet newsgroup, you need access to a newsreader.

`news:alt.pagan`

alt.religion.kibology

A Usenet newsgroup consisting of followers of a god named Kibo, who is, in fact, a human being living in Boston. This newsgroup is highly humorous and hardly religious.

Keywords: Satire, Humor, Religion

Audience: Kibologists

User Info: To subscribe to this Usenet newsgroup, you need access to a newsreader.

`news:alt.religion.kibology`

AmerCath (History of American Catholicism)

This mailing list focuses on the history of American Catholicism.

Keywords: Catholicism, Christianity, Religion

Sponsor: Jefferson Community College, University of Kentucky, Louisville, KY, USA

Audience: Researchers, Educators, Students, Catholics

Profile: Since AMERCATH can be accessed internationally, it thus forms a global network of people who research and teach the history of American Catholicism. AMERCATH facilitates communication among faculty, students, and researchers.

Contact: Anne Kearney
jccannek@ukcc.uky.edu

Details: Free

User Info: To subscribe to the list, send an e-mail message to the address below, consisting of a single line reading:

Sub AmerCath YourFirstName YourLastName

To send a message to the entire list, address it to:

AmerCath@ukcc.uky.edu

`mailto:listserv@ukcc.uky.edu`

ANU (Australian National University) Buddhism Database

A searchable database of messages from the BUDDHA-L listserv, an academic forum for the discussion of Buddhism. It currently contains archives for messages posted in 1993-94.

Keywords: Religion, Asian Studies, Buddhism

Sponsor: COOMBSQUEST Social Sciences & Humanities Information Facility at ANU (Australian National University), Canberra, Australia

A B C D E F G H I J K L M N O P Q R S T U V W X Y Z

A
B
C
D
E
F
G
H
I
J
K
L
M
N
O
P
Q
R
S
T
U
V
W
X
Y
Z

Audience: Buddhists, Religious Studies Instructors, Asian Studies Educators

Contact: Dr. T.Matthew Ciolek
              coombspapers@coombs.anu.edu.au

gopher://cheops.anu.edu.au/Coombs-db/
ANU-Buddha-1.src

http://coombs.anu.edu.au/
WWWVL-AsianStudies.html

Bible (King James Version)

The Bible (King James Version) includes the complete text of the modern Thomas Nelson revision of the 1769 edition of the King James version of the Bible.

Keywords: Bible, Religious Text, Old Testament, New Testament

Sponsor: Thomas Nelson Publishers, Nashville, TN, USA

Audience: Christians, Theologians, Historians, Moralists

Profile: The King James version originated from translations ordered by King James of England in 1604 at the Hampton Court Conference. Both the Old and New Testaments are included in this version. Records in the database represent both chapters and verses.

Contact: Dialog in the US at (800) 334-2564, Dialog internationally at country specific locations.

Details: Costs

User Info: To subscribe, contact Dialog directly.

telnet://dialog.com

Catholic

The CATHOLIC mailing list is a forum for Catholics who wish to discuss their discipleship to Jesus Christ in terms of the Catholic approach to Christianity. "Catholic" is loosely defined as anyone embracing the Catholic approach to Christianity whether Roman Catholic, Anglo-Catholic, or Orthodox. Discussions on ecumenism are encouraged.

Keywords: Catholicism, Ecumenism, Religion

Audience: Catholics, Priests, Theologians

Contact: Cindy Smith
              cms@dragon.com

Details: Free

User Info: To subscribe to the list, send an e-mail message to the address below, consisting of a single line reading:

              SUB Catholic YourFirstName YourLastName

              To send a message to the entire list, address it to: Catholic@american.edu

Notes: This list is also bi-directionally forwarded to the newsgroup bit.listserv.catholic.

mailto:listserv@american.edu

Catholic-action

Catholic-action is a moderated list concerned with Catholic evangelism, church revitalization, and preservation of Catholic teachings, traditions and values, and the vital effort to decapitate modernist heresy.

Keywords: Catholicism, Evangelism, Religion

Audience: Catholics, Priests

Contact: Richard Freeman
              rfreeman@vpnet.chi.il.us

Details: Free

User Info: To subscribe to the list, send an e-mail message requesting a subscription to the URL address below.

mailto:rfreeman@vpnet.chi.il.us

Cell Church Discussion Group

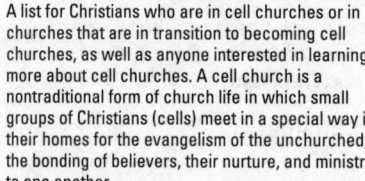

A list for Christians who are in cell churches or in churches that are in transition to becoming cell churches, as well as anyone interested in learning more about cell churches. A cell church is a nontraditional form of church life in which small groups of Christians (cells) meet in a special way in their homes for the evangelism of the unchurched, the bonding of believers, their nurture, and ministry to one another.

Keywords: Cell Churches, Christianity, Evangelism, Religion

Audience: Christians, Theologians, Evangelists

Contact: Jon Reid
              reid@cei.com

Details: Free

User Info: To subscribe to the list, send an e-mail message to the URL address below with the single word SUBSCRIBE in the body (not subject) of your message. To send a message to the entire list, address it to: cell-church@bible.acu.edu

Notes: The group archives, FAQ, and helpful articles are available by anonymous FTP from bible.acu.edu; they can also be retrieved by sending mail to cell-church-archives@bible.acu.edu with the single word LIST for a list of files, or HELP for more information.

mailto:cell-church-
request@bible.acu.edu

CGN (Christian Growth Newsletter)

This site is intended to help Christians in personal growth, and includes testimonials and encouraging articles.

Keywords: Christianity, Religion

Audience: Christians

Contact: Laura Smith
              bible@olsen.ch

mailto:bible@olsen.ch

Christian Growth Newsletter (CGN)

Intended to help Christians in personal growth. It includes testimonies and encouraging articles.

Keywords: Christianity, Religion

Audience: Christians

Contact: Laura Smith
              bible@olsen.ch

Details: Free

mailto:bible@olsen.ch

Ecchst-l

A discussion list for scholars of Ecclesiastical history, including those interested both in the history of the Church and in the examination of theology in an historical context.

Keywords: Religion, Ecclesiastical History, Christianity, Theology

Audience: Historians, Theologians

Contact: Gregory H. Singleton
              ugsingle@uxa.ecn.bgu.edu

User Info: To subscribe, send an e-mail message to the URL address below consisting of a single line reading:

              SUB ecchst-l YourFirstName YourLastName.

              ??????missing info?????

              To send a message to the entire list, address it to: ecchst-l@bgu.edu

mailto:listserv@bgu.edu

Electronic Hebrew Users Newsletter (E-Hug)

This newsletter is electronic only, and is mandated, like the original, to cover everything relating to the use of Hebrew, Yiddish, Judesmo, and Aramaic on computers.

Keywords: Judaism, Religion, Hebrew Language

Sponsor: Berkeley Hillel Foundation

Audience: Jews, Judaism Students

Contact: Ari Davidow
              well!ari@apple.com

Details: Free

User Info: To subscribe, send an e-mail message to the address below consisting of a single line reading:

              To send a message to the entire list,

mailto:listserv@dartcms1.bitnet

jewishnt

A mailing list for the discussion of all things concerning the establishment of the Global Jewish Information Network

Keywords: Judaism, Jews, Israel, Religion

Sponsor: The Global Jewish Information Network Project

Audience: Jews, Israelis, Political Activists

Contact: Dov Winder
viner@bguvm.bgu.ac.il

User Info: To subscribe to the list, send an e-mail message to the URL address below consisting of a single line reading:

SUB jewishnt

`mailto: listserv@bguvm.bgu.ac.il`

Judaica

A mailing list for the discussion of Jewish and Near Eastern Studies.

Keywords: Judaica, Israel, Middle Eastern Studies, Religion

Audience: Judaica Scholars, Jews, Middle East Scholars

Contact: Tzvee Zahavy
maic@uminn1.bitnet

User Info: To subscribe to the list, send an e-mail message to the URL address below consisting of a single line reading:

SUB judaica

`mailto:listserv@vm1.spcs.umn.edu`

Ogphre - SunSITE

A collection of Internet resources organized by subject. Particular strengths include agriculture, religious texts, poetry, creative writing, and US politics. The ftp site has a set of more general Internet guides.

Keywords: Agriculture, Politics (US), Religion, Internet

Sponsor: The University of North Carolina - Chapel Hill and Sun Microsystems, USA

Audience: General Public, Internet Surfers, Researchers

Contact: Darlene Fladager, Elizabeth Lyons
Darlene_Fladager@unc.edu,
Elizabeth_Lyons@unc.edu

`gopher://sunsite.unc.edu, ftp://
sunsite.unc.edu`

Pagan

Discusses the religions, philosophy, and other aspects of paganism.

Keywords: Paganism, Religion

Audience: Pagans

Contact: Stacey Greenstein
pagan-request@drycas.club.cc.cmu.edu

Details: Free

User Info: To subscribe to the list, send an e-mail message requesting a subscription to the URL address below. To send a message to the entire list, address it to: pagan@drycas.club.cc.cmu.edu

`mailto:pagan-
request@drycas.club.cc.cmu.edu`

Quaker FTP Archive at ClarkNet

Extensive writings concerning contemporary Quaker life.

Keywords: Quakerism, Religion

Sponsor: Clark Internet Services

Audience: Quakers

Contact: George Amoss
daruma@clark.net

`ftp://ftp.clark.net/pub/quaker`

ftp://ftp.univie.ac.at/archive/faq/Quaker-faq

Shakers

A forum on the United Society of Believers for those interested in the history, culture, artifacts, and beliefs of the Shakers (United Society of Believers). Discussions cover a broad range of subject matter.

Keywords: Shakers, Christianity, Religion

Audience: Shakers, Theologians

Contact: Marc Rhorer
rhorer@ukcc.uky.edu

Details: Free

User Info: To subscribe to the list, send an e-mail message to the URL address shown below consisting of a single line reading:

SUB shaker YourFirstName YourLastName

To send a message to the entire list, address it to: shaker@ukcc.uky.edu

`mailto:listserv@ukcc.uky.edu`

soc.religion.christian

A Usenet newsgroup providing information and discussion about Christianity and related issues.

Keywords: Christianity, Religion

Audience: Christians, Theologians

Details: Free

User Info: To subscribe to this Usenet newsgroup, you need access to a newsreader.

`news:soc.religion.christian`

talk.religion.misc

A Usenet newsgroup providing information and discussion about religious, ethical, and moral implications.

Keywords: Religion, Ethics

Audience: General Public, Researchers, Students

Details: Free

User Info: To subscribe to this Usenet newsgroup, you need access to a newsreader.

`news:talk.religion.misc`

talk.religion.newage

A Usenet newsgroup providing information and discussion about esoteric and minority religions and philosophies.

Keywords: Religion, Philosophy

Audience: General Public, Researchers, Students

Details: Free

User Info: To subscribe to this Usenet newsgroup, you need access to a newsreader.

`news:talk.religion.newage`

The Purple Thunderbolt of Spode (PURPS)

Magazine of the OTISian faith (a small but growing cult worshiping OTIS, the ancient Sumerian goddess of life) carrying news, fiction, poetry, humor, and the pure, unadulterated Secrets of the Universe to its subscribers.

Keywords: Religion, Cults

Audience: OTIS Followers

Contact: barker@acc.fau.edu

User Info: To subscribe, send an e-mail message requesting a subscription to the URL address below.

`mailto:barker@acc.fau.edu`

Remote Sensing

Geoscience at Texas A&M University

General server with info on all aspects of GIS and remote sensing, especially GPS.

Keywords: GIS, Image Processing, Remote Sensing, Geoscience, GPS

Sponsor: Texas A&M University - Department of Agricultural Engineering

Audience: Researchers, GIS and IP professionals, Students

Contact: Hal Mueller
hmueller@diamond.tamu.edu

Details: Free

Images

Notes: Contains links to related Univeristy of Texas gophers and WWW servers.

`http://ageninfo.tamu.edu/
geoscience.html`

A B C D E F G H I J K L M N O P Q R S T U V W X Y Z

A B C D E F G H I J K L M N O P Q R S T U V W X Y Z

Internet GIS and RS Information Sites

This document contains a lengthy listing of GIS and remote sensing sites on the Internet.

Keywords: GIS, Remote Sensing, Image Processing, Geography

Sponsor: Queen's University Department of Geography

Audience: Researchers, General Public

Contact: Michael McDermott
mcdermom@gisdog.gis.queensu.ca

Details: Free

Notes: ASCII version also available from the same FTP site.

`ftp://gis.queensu.ca/pub/gis/docs/gissites.html`

The University of Minnesota Remote Sensing Lab

General information about remote sensing and GIS.

Keywords: GIS, Remote Sensing, Image Processing

Sponsor: University of Minnesota, Department of Forest Resources

Audience: Researchers, GIS and IP professionals, Students

Profile: The RSL server contains information regarding all aspects of image process and GIS. Some features include: home of the GIS Jobs Clearinghouse, archives of ESRI-L, IMAGRS-L and TGIS-L and the NBS CPSU WWW server.

Contact: Stephen Lime
sdlime@torpedo.forestry.umn.edu

Details: Free, Images

Notes: The RSL also maintains a companion gopher server and anonymous FTP site for the GIS Jobs Clearinghouse.

`http://walleye.forestry.umn.edu/0/www/main.html`

Research and Development

ARlist

An open, unmoderated mailing list to provide a forum for discussing action research and its use in a variety of disciplines and situations. Topics include philosophical and methodological issues in action research, the use of action research for evaluation, actual case studies, and discourse on increasing the rigor of action research.

Keywords: Activism, Research, Politics

Audience: Activists, Researchers

Profile: Arlist is an open unmoderated mailing list to provide a forum for discussing action research and its use in a variety of disciplines and situations. It is usually (but perhaps not always) cyclic, participative, and qualitative.

Contact: Bob Dick
arlist@psych.psy.uq.oz.au

Details: Free

User Info: To subscribe to the list, send an e-mail message to the URL address below. To send a message to the entire list, address it to: arlist@psych.psy.uq.oz.au

`mailto:arlist-request@psych.psy.uq.oz.au`

`ftp://psych.psy.uq.oz.au/dir/lists/arlist`

Brown University Library

The Brown libraries contain approximately 1.5 million volumes, including historical archives of early American imprints and the biomedical engineering holdings.

Keywords: Libraries, Research

Audience: General Public, Researchers

Contact: Howard Pasternick
blips15@brownvm.brown.edu

Details: Free
At the Brown logon screen: tab to command field, Enter Dial Josiah, tab to Josiah choice on the screen.

`telnet://brownvm.brown.edu`

`telnet://library.brown.edu`

Columbia University Libraries

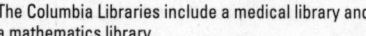

The Columbia Libraries include a medical library and a mathematics library.

Keywords: Libraries, Research

Audience: General Public, Researchers

Details: Free
When connected, hit return, enter terminal type: vt100.

`telnet://clio.cul.columbia.edu`

Cornell University Libraries

This library system maintains special collections in engineering, nuclear engineering, textile engineering, agriculture, medicine, Africana, entomology, hotels, ILR, mathematics, physical sciences, and veterinary medicine.

Keywords: Libraries, Research

Audience: General Public, Researchers

Details: Free
When userid/password screen appears, press return. When cp read appears on the screen, type library.

`telnet://cornellc.cit.cornell.edu`

DENet Information Server

This is the gopher of the Danish national academic network, which is located at the Danish Computer Centre for Research and Education (UNI-C).

Keywords: Research, Education, Denmark

Audience: Researchers, Educators

Profile: This gopher provides DENet information and statistics, UNI-C information, directory services and phone books, pointers to Danish electronic libraries and gophers, an index of major Danish FTP archives, and news in Danish.

Contact: Steen.Linden@uni-c.dk

Details: Free

`gopher://gopher.denet.dk`

Links to Many Databases

A collection of links to over 40 databases covering a wide variety of subjects ranging from Postmodern Culture to the 1990 Census.

Keywords: Databases, Research

Sponsor: University of Texas, Austin, Texas, USA

Audience: Researchers, General Public

Contact: remark@ftp.cc.utexas.edu

`gopher://ftp.cc.utexas.edu`

PPPL (The Princeton Plasma Physics Laboratory)

★

This web site provides an overview of the projects, mission, physical plant and history of the PPPL.

Keywords: Physics, Research

Sponsor: U.S. Department of Energy (DOE)

Audience: Physicists, Educators, Students

Contact: Anthony R. De Meo or Jack A. Mervine
pppl_info@pppl.gov, or
webmaster@pppl.gov

Details: Free

`http://www.pppl.gov`

Quantum Physics/High Energy Physics

A resource containing extensive internet links to international academic and research institutions specializing in high energy physics. Online links to journals, abstracts, and conference information.

Keywords: Physics, Quantum Physics, Research

Sponsor: Swiss Academic and Research Network, Switzerland

Audience: Students, Physicists, Researchers

Contact: Ingrid Graf
rikv8@cernvm.cern.ch

`http://www.cern.ch/Physics/HEP.html`

Thailand: The Big Picture

A web site maintaining a complete list of Internet servers pertaining to and found within Thailand. General information concerning Thailand and extensive Internet connections to Thai academic institutions.

Keywords: Thailand, Education, Travel, Research

Sponsor: National Electronics and Computer Center at the National Science and Technology Development Agency, USA

Audience: Researchers, Exchange Students

Contact: Trin Tantsetthi
webmaster@www.nectec.or.th

`http://www.nectec.or.th`

National Technology Transfer Center (NTTC)

A federally-funded national network to apply government research to commercial applications.

Keywords: Technology, Technology Transfer, Research and Development, Business and Industry, Department of Defense, Government (US)

Sponsor: National Technology Transfer Center

Audience: Business People, Entrepreneurs, Manufactures, Technology Enthusiasts

Profile: Features state-by-state listings of agencies designed to facilitate the adaptation of new technologies to industry. Also provides updates on conferences, and a current list of Department of Defense projects soliciting private assistance from small businesses. Allows limited access to NTTC databases.

Contact: Charles Monfradi
cmonfra@nttc.edu, info@nttc.edu

`gopher://iron.nttc.edu`

`http://iridium.nttc.edu/nttc.hmtl`

Research Databases and Resources by Subject

A collection of databases on over forty subjects, ranging from Anthropology to Women's Studies.

Keywords: Databases, Academic Research

Sponsor: University of California at Berkeley

Audience: Researchers, General Public

Contact: Gopher Manager
gophcom@infolib.lib.berkeley.edu

`gopher://umslvma.umsl.edu/Library/`
`Subjects/Biology/Bioformt/Biodbs`

`gopher://infolib.lib.berkeley.edu`

Research (Funding Support List)

The Research list is for people (primarily at educational institutions) interested in applying for funding support from various sources.

Keywords: Grants, Funding

Audience: Educators (College, University)

Profile: This list assists faculty in locating sources of support from government agencies, corporations, and foundations. It also forwards information regarding the latest news from potential sponsors such as the National Science Foundation and the National Institutes of Health, and provides information on upcoming international seminars on various topics ranging from medicine to artificial intelligence.

Contact: Eleanor Cicinsky
v2153a@vm.temple.edu

User Info: To subscribe to the list, send an Email message to the address below consisting of a single line reading:

SUB research YourFirstName YourLastName

To send a message to the entire list, address it to: research@vm.temple.edu

`mailto:listserv@vm.temple.edu`

Research on Demand

A resource for the provision of market information, strategic information location, product information, and national and international business information.

Keywords: Market Research, Internet Research, Legal Research, International Research

Audience: Marketing Specialists, Lawyers, Public Relations Experts, Business Professionals, Researchers, Writers, Producers

Profile: This resource has special access to unique information resources worldwide. Areas of particular information access include the former Soviet Union, Europe, and the US. Information access also includes access to all the major online systems, including Dialog, BRS, Orbit, DataStar, and so on. Current Awareness Services include research information gathered from the Internet.

Details: Costs

User Info: To subscribe, send an e-mail message to the URL address below. In the body of your message, state the nature of your inquiry.

Notes: Contact ROD directly in the US at: (800) 227-0750; outside the US at: (510) 841-1145.

`mailto:rod@holonet.net`

Research Ship Schedules and Information

A gopher providing information on research and deep water vessels from more than 45 countries. Includes detailed ship specifications, some with deck plans and photographs available as GIF files. Also has cruise schedules for US ships, as well as some from other countries.

Keywords: Oceanography, Transportation, Maritime Industry, Travel

Sponsor: University of Delaware (The OCEANIC Ocean Information Center), Newark, Delaware, USA

Audience: Oceanographers, General Public

Contact: Ocean Information Center, University of Delaware of Delaware, College of Marine Studies
oceanic@diu.cms.udel.edu

Details: Free, Images

`gopher://diu.cms.udel.edu`

Resodlaa (Research SIG of the Open and Distance Learning Association of Australia)

The purpose of this list is to foster electronic discussion, symposia, and conferences on topical issues in distance education and open-learning research.

Keywords: Education (Adult), Education (Distance), Education (Continuing), Australia

Sponsor: Research Special Interest Group (SIG) of the Open and Distance Learning Association of Australia

Audience: Educators, Administrators, Researchers

Details: Free

User Info: To subscribe to the list, send an e-mail message to the URL address below, consisting of a single line reading:

SUB resodlaa YourFirstName YourLastName

To send a message to the entire list, address it to: resodlaa @usq.edu.au

`mailto:listserv@usq.edu.au`

Restaurant Management

University of Wisconsin at Stout Library

The library's holdings are large and wide-ranging and contain significant collections in many fields.

Keywords: Mathematics, Business, Fashion Merchandising, Home Economics, Hospitality, Tourism, Hotel Administration, Restaurant Management, Microelectronics

A
B
C
D
E
F
G
H
I
J
K
L
M
N
O
P
Q
R
S
T
U
V
W
X
Y
Z

Audience: Researchers, Students, General Public

Details: Free

Expect:Login, Send: Lib; Expect: vDIAL Prompt, Send: Library

`telnet://lib.uwstout.edu`

Retirement

AgeLine

The AgeLine database is produced by the American Association of Retired Persons (AARP) and provides bibliographic coverage of social gerontology—the study of aging in social, psychological, health-related, and economic contexts.

Keywords: Gerontology, Retirement, Public Policy, Aging

Sponsor: American Association of Retired Persons, Washington, DC, USA

Audience: Retired Persons, Health Care Providers, Researchers

Profile: AgeLine covers the delivery of health care for the older population and its associated costs and policies, as well as public policy, employment, and consumer issues. Literature covered is of interest to researchers, health professionals, service planners, policy makers, employers, older adults and their families, and consumer advocates.

Coverage: 1978 to the present (selected coverage back to 1966); updated bimonthly.

Contact: Dialog in the US at (800) 334-2564; Dialog internationally at country-specific locations.

Details: Costs

There is no print equivalent of the database. To subscribe, contact Dialog directly.

`telnet://dialog.com`

Retrieval Success

Retrieval Success

Succesful stories of using the Internet for reference. In each case, a librarian used Internet resources to answer reference questions. In many cases, particularly for the smaller libraries, the Internet provided information that would otherwise have been inaccessible.

Keywords: Internet, Information Retrieval

Audience: Internet Surfers

Contact: Karen Schneider
kgs@panix.com

Details: Free

File is: pub/lists/unite/files/internet-stories.txt

`ftp://mailbase.ac.uk`

Rezo, bulletin irregulomadaire du RQSS

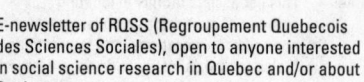

Rezo, bulletin irregulomadaire du RQSS

E-newsletter of RQSS (Regroupement Quebecois des Sciences Sociales), open to anyone interested in social science research in Quebec and/or about Quebec.

Keywords: Quebec, Social Science

Audience: Social Scientists

Contact: Pierre J. Hamel
hamel@inrs-urb.uquebec.ca

Details: Free

User Info: To subscribe, send an e-mail message to the URL address below, consisting of a single line reading:

SUB rezo YourFirstName YourLastName

To send a message to the entire list, address it to: rezo@uquebec.ca

`mailto:listserv@uquebec.ca`

Rhetoric

Speeches and Addresses in the US

Includes the Clinton State of the Union Speech of 1993, Kennedy's Inaugural Speech, Martin Luther King's "I Have a Dream" speech, and more.

Keywords: Politics (US), Rhetoric

Audience: Journalists, Writers, Politicians, Students

Details: Free

Choose from menu presented.

`gopher://wiretap.spies.com/11/Gov/US-Speech`

Rhodes (Happy)

ecto

Information and discussion about singer/songwriter Happy Rhodes, and other music, art, books, and films of common (or singular) interest.

Keywords: Music, Art, Rhodes (Happy)

Audience: Music Enthusiasts, Art Enthusiasts

Contact: Jessica Dembski
ecto-request@ns1.rutgers.edu

Details: Free

User Info: To subscribe to the list, send an e-mail message requesting a subscription to the URL address below. To send a message to the entire list, address it to: ecto-request@ns1.rutgers.edu

`mailto:ecto-request@ns1.rutgers.edu`

Rights

The Frog Farm

A forum devoted to the discussion of claiming, exercising, and defending rights in America, past, present, and future. The main topics are issues that involve a free people and their public servants.

Keywords: Rights, Politics

Audience: Activists

Contact: schirado@lab.cc.wmich.edu

User Info: To subscribe to the list, send an e-mail message requesting a subscription to the URL address below. To send a message to the entire list, address it to: schirado@lab.cc.wmich.edu

`mailto:schirado@lab.cc.wmich.edu`

RIPE Network Coordination Centre Gopher

RIPE Network Coordination Centre Gopher

RIPE (Reseaux IP Europeens) is a collaborative organization open to all European Internet service providers. RIPE coordinates the operation of a pan-European IP network. In November 1993, more than 500,000 hosts throughout Europe were reachable via networks coordinated by RIPE.

Keywords: Europe, Networks

Audience: Internet Surfers

Contact: ncc@ripe.net

Details: Free

`gopher://gopher.ripe.net`

Rock Music

Backstreets

Discussion of Bruce Springsteen's music.

Keywords: Rock Music, Springsteen (Bruce)

Audience: Bruce Springsteen Fans

Contact: Kevin Kinder
backstreets-request@virginia.edu

Details: Free

User Info: To subscribe to the list, send an e-mail message requesting a subscription to the URL address below. To send a message to the entire list, address it to: backstreets@virginia.edu

`mailto:backstreets-request@virginia.edu`

Corpse/Respondents ★

This is a gothic pen-pal zine in digest form. Small traffic mailing list.

Keywords: Gothic Rock, Rock Music

Audience: Gothic Rock Enthusiasts

Contact: carriec@eskimo.com

Details: Free

User Info: To subscribe send an e-mail message to the URL address below with "subscribe corpse <yournameandaddress>" in the text.

`mailto:carriec@eskimo.com`

Crowes ★

To provide a forum for discussion about the rock band the Black Crowes. Topics include the group's music and lyrics, as well as the band's participation with NORML, concert dates and playlists, and bootlegs (audio and video).

Keywords: Rock Music, Pop Music

Audience: Rock Music Enthusiasts, Pop Music Enthusiasts

Contact: rstewart@unex.ucla.edu

Details: Free

User Info: To subscribe, mail to the address below with the command SUBSCRIBE in the first line.

`mailto:rstewart@unex.ucla.edu`

Deborah Harry and Blondie Information Service ★

An information service on everything and anything regarding Deborah Harry and Blondie, including tour information, recordings/films release information, and so on.

Keywords: Rock Music, Harry (Deborah)

Audience: Rock Music Enthusiasts, Deborah Harry Enthusiasts

Contact: gunter@yarrow.wt.uwa.oz.au

Details: Free

User Info: To subscribe to the list, send an e-mail message requesting a subscription to the URL address below. To send a message to the entire list, address it to: gunter@yarrow.wt.uwa.oz.au

`mailto:gunter@yarrow.wt.uwa.oz.au`

dire-straits ★

Discussion of the musical group Dire Straits and associated side projects.

Keywords: Rock Music, Dire Straits, Music

Audience: Rock Music Enthusiasts, Dire Straits Enthusiasts

Contact: Rand P. Hall
dire-straits-request@merrimack.edu

Details: Free

User Info: To subscribe to the list, send an e-mail message requesting a subscription to the URL address below. To send a message to the entire list, address it to: dire-straits-request@merrimack.edu

`Anonymous ftp to: merrimack.edu (f=ANONYMOUS/DIRE-STRAITS)`

Dokken/Lynch Mob ★

Articles, questions and discussions on Dokken and Lynch Mob.

Keywords: Rock Music, Dokken, Lynch Mob

Audience: Rock Music Enthusiasts

Contact: Kirsten DeNoyelles
kydeno00@ukpr.uky.edu

Details: Free

User Info: To subscribe to the list, send an e-mail message requesting a subscription to the URL address below. To send a message to the entire list, address it to: kydeno00@ukpr.uky.edu

`mailto:kydeno00@ukpr.uky.edu`

Drone On... ★

The Drone On... list is for the discussion of Spacemen 3 and resultant bands, as well as any other droning guitar bands that anyone wants to bring up.

Keywords: Rock Music, Spacemen 3

Audience: Spacemen 3 Enthusiasts, Rock Music Enthusiasts

Contact: droneon-request@ucsd.edu

Details: Free

User Info: To subscribe to the list, send an e-mail message requesting a subscription to the URL address below. To send a message to the entire list, address it to: droneon-request@ucsd.edu

`mailto:droneon-request@ucsd.edu`

echoes ★

Info and commentary on the musical group Pink Floyd, as well as other projects members of the group have been involved with.

Keywords: Rock Music, Pink Floyd

Audience: Rock Music Enthusiasts, Pink Floyd Enthusiasts

Contact: H. W. Neff
echoes-request@fawnya.tcs.com

Details: Free

User Info: To subscribe to the list, send an e-mail message requesting a subscription to the URL address below. To send a message to the entire list, address it to: echoes-request@fawnya.tcs.com

`mailto:echoes-request@fawnya.tcs.com`

Electric Light Orchestra ★

Discussion of the music of Electric Light Orchestra and later solo efforts by band members and former members.

Keywords: Electric Light Orchestra, Rock Music

Audience: Rock Music Enthusiasts

Contact: elo-list-request@andrew.cmu.edu

Details: Free

User Info: To subscribe to the list, send an e-mail message requesting a subscription to the URL address below. To send a message to the entire list, address it to: elo-list-request@andrew.cmu.edu

`mailto:elo-list-request@andrew.cmu.edu`

freaks ★

This mailing list focuses on Marillion and related rock groups.

Keywords: Music, Rock Music

Audience: Marillion Enthusiasts

Details: Free

User Info: To subscribe to the list, send an e-mail message requesting a subscription to the URL address below. To send a message to the entire list, address it to:freaks@bnf.com

`mailto:freaks-request@bnf.com`

Journey-L ★★

Information and discussion of the rock band Journey and any of the band members' outside projects.

Keywords: Musical Groups, Rock Music

Audience: Rock Music Fans

Contact: Hunter Goatley or Britt Pierce
journey-l@wkuvx1.wku.edu

User Info: To subscribe to the list, send an e-mail message to the URL address below, with the body text subscribe journey-l. To subscribe to the digest version, send the message to : journey-l-digest-request@wkuvx1.wku.edu

`mailto:journey-l-request@wkuvx1.wku.edu`

A
B
C
D
E
F
G
H
I
J
K
L
M
N
O
P
Q
R
S
T
U
V
W
X
Y
Z

Ph7

A mailing list for discussions about Peter Hamill and related rock groups.

Keywords: Rock Music, Hamill (Peter)

Audience: Musicians, Rock Music Enthusiasts

Contact: ph7-request@bnf.com

User Info: To subscribe to the list, send an e-mail message requesting a subscription to the URL address below. To send a message to the entire list, address it to: ph7@bnf.com

`mailto:ph7-request@bnf.com`

Queen

A mailing list to discuss the rock group Queen.

Keywords: Music, Rock Music

Audience: Queen Fans, Music Fans, Musicians

Contact: Dan Blanchard
qms-request@uiuc.edu

Details: Free

User Info: To subscribe to the list, send an e-mail message requesting a subscription to the URL address below. To send a message to the entire list, address it to: qms@uiuc.edu

`mailto:qms-request@uiuc.edu`

Stormcock

For general discussion and news concerning the music of Roy Harper, a folk-rock musician with a conscience. Recommendations and news concerning similar artists are encouraged.

Keywords: Rock Music, Music, Harper (Roy)

Audience: Music Fans

Contact: Paul Davison
stormcock-request@qmw.ac.uk

Details: Free

User Info: To subscribe to the list, send an e-mail message to the address shown below consisting of a single line reading:

SUB stormcock YourFirstName YourLastName

To send a message to the entire list, address it to: stormcock@qmw.ac.uk

`mailto: listserv@qmw.ac.uk`

The Ultimate Gopher for Rush Fans

A collection of lyrics, articles, press releases, concert updates, newsletters, and reviews concerning the musical group Rush.

Keywords: Musical Groups, Rush, Rock Music

Sponsor: syrinx.umd.edu

Audience: Rock Music Enthusiasts, Rush Enthusiasts

Contact: jlang.syrinx.umd.edu

`gopher://syrinx.umd.edu`

Rogers (Bruce)

Purdue University Library

The library's holdings are large and wide-ranging. They contain significant collections in many fields.

Keywords: Economics (History of), Literature (English), Literature (American), Indiana, Rogers (Bruce), Engineering (History of), Aviation, Earth Science, Atmospheric Science, Consumer Science, Family Science, Chemistry (History of), Physics, Veterinary Science

Audience: General Public, Researchers, Librarians, Document Delivery Professionals

Contact: Dan Ferrer
dan@asterix.lib.purdue.edu

Details: Free

Expect: User ID prompt, Send: GUEST

`telnet://lib.cc.purdue.edu`

Role-Playing Games

ars magica

A mailing list for the discussion of White Wolf's role-playing game, Ars Magica.

Keywords: Role-Playing Games, Games

Audience: Role-playing Enthusiasts, Game Players

Contact: ars-magica-request@soda.berkeley.edu

User Info: To subscribe to the list, send an e-mail message to the URL address below. To send a message to the entire list, address it to: ars-magica-request@soda.berkeley.edu

Also available upon request as a nightly digest.

`mailto:ars-magica-request@soda.berkeley.edu`

Miniatures

The Miniatures Digest is a mailing list for discussion of the painting, sculpting, converting, and displaying of miniature figurines, generally for war games or fantasy role-playing games.

Keywords: Miniatures, Role-Playing Games

Audience: Miniature Figurine Entusiasts

Contact: minimallist-request@cs.unc.edu

Details: Free

Notes:User Info: To subscribe to the list, send an e-mail message requesting subscription to the URL address below.

`mailto:minilist@cs.unc.edu`

Nero Ashbury

Nero is a live-action, medieval role-playing game with a plot line and characters that continue from one adventure to the next. Nero has been successful in New England for over six years and is growing rapidly.

Keywords: Medieval Studies, Role-Playing Games

Audience: General Public, Role-Playing Enthusiasts

Contact: lsonko@pearl.tufts.edu

Details: Free

User Info: To subscribe to the list, send an e-mail message requesting a subscription to the URL address below.

`mailto:lsonko@pearl.tufts.edu`

Rolling Stones

Nihon Sun Microsystems

This site provides a directory for Sun Microsystems in Japan. Includes the Rolling Stones Official Server WWW site, with access to Rolling Stones music, merchandise, and information. Also provides multimedia links to the Science University of Tokyo and other Asia-Pacific resources.

Keywords: Computers, Rolling Stones

Sponsor: Sun Microsystems, Inc., Tokyo, Japan

Audience: Computer Users, Rolling Stones Fans

Contact: www-admin@sun.co.jp

Details: Multimedia, Free, Sounds, Images

`http://www.sun.co.jp`

Romance

alt.romance.chat

A Usenet newsgroup providing discussion about the romantic side of love.

Keywords: Chat Groups, Romance

Audience: General Public

User Info: To subscribe to this Usenet newsgroup, you need access to a newsreader.

`news:alt.romance.chat`

Romania

CEE Environmental Libraries Database

A directory of over 300 libraries and environmental information centers in Central Eastern Europe that specialize in, or maintain significant collections of information about, the environment, ecology, sustainable living, or conservation. The database concentrates on six Central Eastern European countries: Bulgaria, Czech Republic, Hungary, Romania, Slovakia, and Poland.

Keywords: Central Eastern Europe, Environment, Sustainable Living, Bulgaria, Czech Republic, Hungary, Romania, Slovakia, Poland.

Sponsor: The Wladyslaw Poniecki Charitable Foundation, Inc.

Audience: Environmentalists, Green Movement, Librarians, Community Builders, Sustainable Living Specialists.

Profile: This database is the product of an Environmental Training Project (ETP) that was funded in 1992 by the US Agency for International Development as a 5-year cooperative agreement with a consortium headed by the University of Minnesota (US AID Cooperative Agreement Number EUR-0041-A-002-2020). Other members of the consortium include the University of Pittsburgh's Center for Hazardous Materials Research, The Institute for Sustainable Communities, and the World Wildlife Fund. The Wladyslaw Poniecki Charitable Foundation, Inc., was a subcontractor to the World Wildlife Fund and published the Directory of Libraries and Environmental Information Centers in Central Eastern Europe: A Locator/Directory . This gopher database consists of an electronic version of the printed directory, subsequently modified and updated online. Access to the data is facilitated by a WAIS search engine which makes it possible to retrieve information about libraries, subject area specializations, personnel, and so on.

Contact: Doug Kahn, CEDAR
kahn@pan.cedar.univie.ac.at

`gopher://gopher.poniecki.berkeley.edu`

Roosevelt (Franklin D.)

The University of Illinois at Chicago Library

The library's holdings are large and wide-ranging and contain significant collections in many fields.

Keywords: Health Science, Chicago, Industry, Slavery, Abolitionism, Roosevelt (Franklin D.)

Audience: General Public, Researchers, Librarians, Document Delivery Professionals

Details: Free

Expect:introductory screen, Send: Clear key; Expect: UIC flame screen, Send: Enter key; Expect: Logon screen, Send: DIAL PVM; Expect: PVM (Passthru) screen, Send: Type: Move cursor to NOTIS and press Enter key Response: One line message about port in use Type: Enter key

`telnet://uicvm.uic.edu`

Rosen Sculpture Exhibition

Rosen Sculpture Exhibition

This web site contains various examples of sculpture movements.

Keywords: Art, Fine Arts

Sponsor: Visual Resources Curator of the Department of Art at Appalachian State University, Boone, North Carolina, USA

Audience: Art Educators, Art Students

`http://www.acs.appstate.edu/art`

Rowing

rec.sport.rowing

A Usenet newsgroup providing information and discussion about recreational and competitive rowing. It provides information from the United States Rowing Association, the latest race results, equipment sales, coaching positions and more.

Keywords: Rowing, Crew, Sports

Audience: Rowers, Coaches, Athletes

Profile: This newsgroup covers technical, training and nutritional aspects as well as the latest race results, National Team information, equipment sales, coaching positions, information from the United States Rowing Association and more.

User Info: To subscribe to this Usenet newsgroup, you need access to a newsreader.

`news:rec.sport.rowing`

rrl

rrl

A mailing list for the discussion of GIS (Geographic Information Systems) in the United Kingdom.

Keywords: GIS (Geographical Information Systems), United Kingdom

Audience: Geographers, Cartographers

Contact: rrl@uk.ac.leicester

`mailto:rrl@uk.ac.leicester`

Rubber

RAPRA Abstracts

Coverage on technical and commercial aspects of the rubber, plastics, and polymer composites industries.

Keywords: Material Science, Rubbers, Plastics, Polymers

Sponsor: Rapra Technology, Ltd.

Audience: Material Scientists, Researchers

Profile: This unique source of information covers the world's polymer literature including journals, conference proceedings, books, specifications, reports and trade literature. Contains over 375,000 records. Updated biweekly.

Contact: paul.albert@neteast.com
To subscribe contact Orbit-Questel directly.

`telnet://orbit.com`

Running

dead-runners

The Dead Runners Society is a mailing list for runners who like to talk about the psychological, philosophical, and personal aspects of running.

Keywords: Running, Sports

Audience: Runners

Contact: Christopher Mark Conn
dead-runners-request@unx.sas.com

Details: Free

User Info: To subscribe to the list, send an e-mail message requesting a subscription to the URL address below. To send a message to the entire list, address it to: dead-runners-request@unx.sas.com

`mailto:dead-runners-request@unx.sas.com`

Rural Development

AGRIS International

This database serves as a comprehensive inventory of worldwide agricultural literature that reflects research results, food production, and rural development.

A
B
C
D
E
F
G
H
I
J
K
L
M
N
O
P
Q
R
S
T
U
V
W
X
Y
Z

Keywords: Agriculture, Rural Development, Food Production, Development

Sponsor: US National Agricultural Library, Beltsville, MD, USA

Audience: Agronomists, Market Researchers

Profile: Designed to help users identify problems involved in all aspects of world food supply, the file corresponds in part to Agr Index, published monthly by the Food and Agriculture Organization (FAO) of the United Nations. Subject coverage focuses on many topics, general agriculture; geography and history; education, extension, and advisory work; administration and legislation; economics, development, and rural sociology; plant production; protection of plants and stored products; forestry; animal production; aquatic sciences and fisheries;machinery and buildings; natural resources; food science; home economics; human nutrition; pollution; and more.

Contact: Dialog in the US at (800) 334-2564

Details: Costs

User Info: To subscribe, contact Dialog directly.

`telnet://dialog.com`

Community Networks Benefit Federal Goals

Statement by community networker Frank Odasz, founder and director of Big Sky Telegraph, a network of rural BBSs throughout Montana. In this article he makes the case that the federal goverment will benefit from the widespread rural employment of networking technology.

Keywords: Community, Networking, Rural Development, Development

Audience: Activists, Policy Analysts, Community Leaders, Government, Citizens, Rural Residents, Native Americans

Contact: Frank Odasz
franko@bigsky.dillon.mt.us,

Details: Free

`http://nearnet.gnn.com/mag/articles/oram/bio.odasz.html`

Marshall University School of Medicine (MUSOM) RuralNet Gopher

★★★

A gopher server dedicated to the improvement of rural health care.

Keywords: Rural Development, Health Care, Medical Treatment, Bioinformatics

Sponsor: Marshall University School of Medicine

Audience: Health Care Professionals, Medical Students, Rural Residents

Profile: A collection of health care resources, with particular emphasis on rural health care. Includes listings of clinical resources by subject area, information on state and federal rural health care initiatives, and links to local and national health and education services.

Contact: Mike McCarthy, Andy Jarrell
mmccarth@muvms6.wvnet.edu,
jarrell@musom01.mu.wvnet.edu

`gopher://ruralnet.mu.wvnet.edu`

Telluride Institute

★

This is a community organization involved in building an electronic dimension in rural Colorado. The vision of Telluride Institute includes linking rural residents to each other and outside resources, creating new opportunities for education, jobs, and arts.

Keywords: Community, Networking, Virtual Community, Rural Development, Colorado

Sponsor: The Telluride Institute, Telluride, Colorado

Audience: Activists, Policymakers, Community Leaders, Students, Colorado Residents

Profile: The Telluride Institute is a local community-based organization that produces arts, environmental, and educational events in the Telluride area of Colorado. The Institite is committed to the creation of what it calls the "InfoZone": it wants to use modern telecommunications to link together the local community and to connect to the rest of the world to exchange ideas, commerce, arts, and inspiration.

Contact: Richard Lowenberg
tellinst@CSN.ORG

Details: Free

Send an e-mail message to the URL address below asking for further information.

`mailto:tellinst@csn.org`

Rush

The Ultimate Gopher for Rush Fans

★★

A collection of lyrics, articles, press releases, concert updates, newsletters, and reviews concerning the musical group Rush.

Keywords: Musical Groups, Rush, Rock & Roll

Sponsor: syrinx.umd.edu

Audience: Rock Music Enthusiasts, Rush Enthusiasts

Contact: jlang.syrinx.umd.edu

`gopher://syrinx.umd.edu`

Russia

Russian

This list is dedicated to the discussion of Russian-language issues, including Russian language, linguistics, grammar, translations, and literature.

Keywords: Language, Literature (Russian), Linguistics

Audience: Slavicists, Linguists, Translators

Contact: Andrew Wollert
ispajw@asuacad
russian@asuvm.inre.asu.edu

Details: Free

User Info: To subscribe to the list, send an e-mail message requesting subscription to the URL address below.

`russian@asuvm.inre.asu.edu`

Russian and East European Studies Home Pages

Keywords: Russia, Eastern Europe, Government, Political Science

Sponsor: University of Pittsburgh

Audience: Researchers, Politicians

Contact: Casey Palowitch
cjp@acid.library.pitt.edu

`http://www.pitt.edu/cjp/rspubl.html`

soc.culture.soviet

A Usenet newsgroup providing information and discussion about topics relating to Russia or the former Soviet Union.

Keywords: Russia, CIS (Commonwealth of Independent States), Communism, Sociology

Audience: Sociologists, Russians

Details: Free

User Info: To subscribe to this Usenet newsgroup, you need access to a newsreader.

`news:soc.culture.soviet`

talk.politics.soviet

A Usenet newsgroup providing information and discussion about Soviet politics, domestic and international.

Keywords: Communism, Russia, Politics, CIS (Commonwealth of Independent States)

Audience: Political Scientists

Details: Free

User Info: To subscribe to this Usenet newsgroup, you need access to a newsreader.

`news:talk.politics.soviet`

rxderm-l

rxderm-l

A mailing list intended for promoting the discussion of dermatologic treatment among practicing dermatologists.

Keywords: Dermatology, Skin, Disease, Doctors

Audience: Dermatologists

Contact: A.C. Huntley
achuntley@ucdavis.edu

User Info: To subscribe to the list, send an e-mail message to the URL address below consisting of a single line reading:

SUB rxderm-l YourFirstName YourLastName. To send a message to the entire list, address it to: rxderm-l@ucdavis.edu

mailto:
listserv@ucdavis.edu

A
B
C
D
E
F
G
H
I
J
K
L
M
N
O
P
Q
R
S
T
U
V
W
X
Y
Z

A
B
C
D
E
F
G
H
I
J
K
L
M
N
O
P
Q
R
S
T
U
V
W
X
Y
Z

S

SABINET (South African Bibliographic and Information Network)

SABINET (South African Bibliographic and Information Network)

This gopher offers information searches from a variety of electronic databases, as well as for library locations and availability of books and periodicals.

Keywords: South Africa, Databases, Networks

Audience: South African Internet Surfers

Contact: hennie@info1.sabinet.co.za

Details: Free

`gopher://info2.sabinet.co.za`

Safety

City of San Carlos World Wide Web Fire Safety Tutorial

This WWW site offers fire prevention information, with a special emphasis on preventing wildland fires. Also includes color diagram on how to create a proper firebreak.

Keywords: Disaster Relief, Safety

Sponsor: The City of San Carlos, California, USA

Audience: Students, Educators, Environmentalists, Community Groups

`http://www.abag.ca.gov/abag/local_gov/city/san_carlos/schome.html`

Publications of the Office of Environment, Safety, and Health

A collection of government safety information including updates, bulletins, and hazard alerts. Topics are diverse, covering everything from "Employee Hit on Head by Falling Steel Wheel" to "New Regulations to Control the Speed of Bloodborne Diseases."

Keywords: Safety, Government (US), Federal Laws (US)

Sponsor: U.S. Department of Energy

Audience: Government Officials, General Public

Details: Free

`gopher://dewey.tis.inel.gov`

Safety (Environmental Health and Safety Discussion List)

E-conference for people interested in the various environmental health and safety issues on college and university campuses.

Keywords: Environmental Health, Safety, Health

Audience: Students (College/University), Educators (college/University)

Contact: Ralph Stuart, Dayna Flath
rstuart@moose.uvm.edu
dmf@uvmvm.uvm.edu

Details: Free

User Info: To subscribe to the list, send an e-mail message to the URL address below, consisting of a single line reading:

SUB safety YourFirstName YourLastName

To send a message to the entire list, address it to: safety@uvmvm.uvm.edu

`mailto:listserv@uvmvm.uvm.edu`

U.S. Consumer Product Safety Commission (CPSC)

The CPSC's mission is to protect the public from defective and potentially dangerous consumer products. This gopher has archives of CPSC press releases and action reports from 1990-1994, as well as a calendar of upcoming events and guidelines for reporting potentially dangerous products to the CPSC.

Keywords: Safety, Consumerism, Laws (US Federal)

Sponsor: US Consumer Product Safety Commission

Audience: Consumers, Activists

Contact: pweddle@cpsc.gov

Notes: You can call the CPSC at their toll-free hotline at (800) 638-2772.

`gopher://cpsc.gov`

Sahel-NAFR

Sahel-NAFR

This site contains information about a database of composite satellite images of Sahel and North Africa (known as the Sahelian and NW Africa 14-Day NDVI Composites). The images come from a pilot program defined between the U.S. Geological Survey and the U.S. Agency for International Development (AID) to develop and test a near-real-time monitoring procedure using satellite remote sensing and Geographic Information System technologies in grasshopper and locust control programs in West Africa. Also contains an appendix with information about the Senegalese Grasshoppers.

Keywords: Geology, Geography, GIS (Geographic Information Systems)

Sponsor: U.S. Geological Survey and U.S. Agency for International Development (AID)

Audience: Geologists, Geographers

`http://sun1.cr.usgs.gov/glis/hyper/guide/sahel_nafr`

Sailing

Marimed Foundation

This foundation provides therapy and education to adjudicated and emotionally impaired teens. Therapies include wilderness experiences on a square-rigged sail ship, boat building, and traditional therapies.

Keywords: Education (Alternative), Sailing

Audience: Educators, Alternative Educators, Social Workers

Contact: Dr. Robert Grossman
marimed@holonet.net

Details: Free

`mailto:marimed@holonet.net`

rec.boats

A Usenet newsgroup providing information and discussion about boating, gear, places to sail, clubs, repairs, and racing.

Keywords: Sailing, Sports

Audience: Sailors, Boating Enthusiasts

User Info: To subscribe to this Usenet newsgroup, you need access to a newsreader.

`news:rec.boats`

The Nautical Bookshelf

Catalog and ordering information for Nautical Bookshelf's collection of books on sailing and other water sports.

Keywords: Boating, Power Boating, Sailing, Sports

Sponsor: Nautical Bookshelf

Audience: Boating Enthusiasts, Sailors

Contact: staff@nautical.com

`gopher://gopher.nautical.com`

Sais-l (Science Awareness and Promotion)

Sais-l (Science Awareness and Promotion)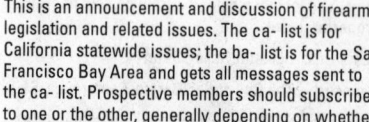

The SAIS list creates a forum for exchanging innovative ideas about making science more appealing to students.

Keywords: Science, Education (K-12), Education (Secondary)

Audience: Students (K-12), Students (high school up), Science Teachers

Contact: Keith W. Wilson
sais@unb.ca

Details: Free

User Info: To subscribe to the list, send an e-mail message to the URL address below consisting of a single line reading:

SUB sais-l YourFirstNameYourLastName

To send a message to the entire list, address it to: sais-l@unb.ca

`mailto:listserv@unb.ca`

Sales

Alliance Marketing Systems

Develops marketing strategies for new business on those in need of turn-around. Designs advertising/marketing plans to prequalify the buying public.

Keywords: Business Marketing, Sales

Audience: Business Professionals, Marketing Professionals, Sales Executives

Details: Costs

`xx@xx.xxx`

San Francisco Bay Area

ba-Firearms

This is an announcement and discussion of firearms legislation and related issues. The ca- list is for California statewide issues; the ba- list is for the San Francisco Bay Area and gets all messages sent to the ca- list. Prospective members should subscribe to one or the other, generally depending on whether or not they are Bay Area residents.

Keywords: Firearms, Gun Control Legislation, San Francisco Bay Area

Audience: Politicians, General Public, Gun Users, San Francisco Bay Area Residents

Contact: Jeff Chan
ba-firearms-request@shell.portal.com

Details: Free

User Info: To subscribe to the list, send an e-mail message requesting a subscription to the URL address below. To send a message to the entire list, address it to: ba-firearms@shell.portal.com

`mailto:ba-firearms-request@shell.portal.com`

ba-Liberty

This is an announcement of local Libertarian meetings, events, activities, and so on. The ca- list is for California statewide issues; the ba- list is for the San Francisco Bay Area and it gets all messages sent to the ca- list. Prospective members should subscribe to one or the other, generally depending on whether or not they are Bay Area residents.

Keywords: Libertarian Party, Politics, San Francisco Bay Area

Audience: Libertarians, Political Scientists, Politicians, General Public

Contact: Jeff Chan
ba-liberty-request@shell.portal.com

Details: Free

User Info: To subscribe to the list, send an e-mail message requesting a subscription to the URL address below. To send a message to the entire list, address it to: ba-liberty@shell.portal.com

`mailto:ba-liberty-request@shell.portal.com`

ba-Poker

Discussion of poker as it is available to residents of and visitors to the San Franciso Bay Area (broadly defined), in home games as well as in licensed card rooms. Topics include upcoming events, unusual games, strategies, comparisons of various venues, and player "networking."

Keywords: Poker, Card Games, San Francisco Bay Area

Audience: Poker Players

Contact: Martin Veneroso
ba-poker-request@netcom.com

Details: Free

User Info: To subscribe to the list, send an e-mail message requesting a subscription to the URL address below. To send a message to the entire list, address it to: ba-poker@netcom.com

`mailto:ba-poker-request@netcom.com`

ba-Sappho

Ba-Sappho is a San Francisco Bay Area lesbian mailing list intended for local networking and announcements. BA-Sappho is not a discussion group.

Keywords: Lesbians, San Francisco Bay Area

Audience: Lesbians

Contact: ba-sappho-request@labrys.mti.sgi.com

Details: Free

User Info: To subscribe to the list, send an e-mail message requesting a subscription to the URL address below. To send a message to the entire list, address it to: ba-sappho@labrys.mti.sgi.com

`mailto:ba-sappho-request@labrys.mti.sgi.com`

ba-Volleyball

This list is used for announcements about San Francisco Bay Area volleyball events, clinics, tournaments, and so on.

Keywords: Volleyball, San Francisco Bay Area

Audience: Volleyball Enthusiasts

Contact: ba-volleyball-request@klerk.cup.hp.com

User Info: To subscribe to the list, send an e-mail message requesting a subscription to the URL address below. To send a message to the entire list, address it to: ba-volleyball@klerk.cup.hp.com

```
mailto:ba-volleyball-
request@klerk.cup.hp.com
```

Sanskrit

Harvard University Library

The library's holdings are large and wide-ranging and contain significant collections in many fields.

Keywords: Afrikaans, Alchemy, Arabic Culure (History of), Celtic Philology, Congo Languages, Folklore, Hebraica, Mormonism, Numismatics, Quakers, Sanskrit, Witchcraft, Arabic Philology

Audience: General Public, Researchers, Librarians, Document Delivery Professionals

Details: Free

User Info: Expect: Mitek Server..., Send: Enter or Return; Expect: prompt, Send: hollis

```
telnet://hollis.harvard.edu
```

Satellite

Center for Extreme Ultraviolet Astrophysics
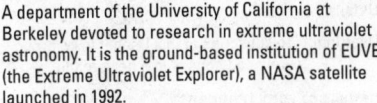

A department of the University of California at Berkeley devoted to research in extreme ultraviolet astronomy. It is the ground-based institution of EUVE (the Extreme Ultraviolet Explorer), a NASA satellite launched in 1992.

Keywords: Astronomy, Astrophysics, EUVE, NASA, Satellite

Sponsor: NASA and University of California at Berkeley

Audience: Astronomers, Astrophysicists

Profile: Provides access to details about the EUVE Guest Observer (EGO) Center, the EUVE Public Archive of Mission Data and Information, satellite operation information, and so on. The EUVE Guest Observer Center provides information, software, and data to EUVE Guest Observers.

Contact: egoinfo@cea.berkeley.edu, archive@cea.berkeley.edu

Details: Free

```
http://cea-ftp.cea.berkeley.edu/
```

Satire

alt.fan.monty-python

A Usenet newsgroup providing an electronic fan club for those wacky Brits.

Keywords: Humor, Entertainment, Comedians, Satire

Audience: Monty Python Enthusiasts, General Public

User Info: To subscribe to this Usenet newsgroup, you need access to a newsreader.

```
news:alt.fan.monty-python
```

alt.religion.kibology

A Usenet newsgroup consisting of followers of a god named Kibo, who is, in fact, a human being living in Boston. This newsgroup is highly humorous and hardly religious.

Keywords: Satire, Humor, Religion

Audience: Kibologists

User Info: To subscribe to this Usenet newsgroup, you need access to a newsreader.

```
news:alt.religion.kibology
```

Clinton Watch

A regular political column devoted to a critical examination of the Clinton Administration.

Keywords: Politics, Clinton(Bill), Satire, Government (US)

Sponsor: Informatics Resource

Audience: Republicans, General Public, Citizens

Contact: clintonwatch@dolphin.gulf.net

```
gopher://dolphin.gulf.net
```

SCA (Society For Creative Anachronism)

rec.org.sca

A Usenet newsgroup providing information and discussion about medieval reenacts.

Keywords: SCA (Society For Creative Anachronism), Medieval Studies

Audience: General Public

User Info: To subscribe to this Usenet newsgroup, you need access to a newsreader.

```
news:rec.org.sca
```

Scandinavia

soc.culture.nordic

A Usenet newsgroup providing information and discussion about Nordic culture.

Keywords: Scandinavla, Sociology

Audience: Sociologists

Details: Free

User Info: To subscribe to this Usenet newsgroup, you need access to a newsreader.

```
news:soc.culture.nordic
```

Scholarly Communication

Scholarly Communication

These quarterly technical reports contain information and discussion about the role of network-based electronic resources in scholarly communication.

Keywords: Education, Scholarly Communication, Conferences

Audience: Educators, Researchers

Details: Free

File is: pub/vpiej-l/reports

```
ftp://borg.lib.vt.edu/pub/vpiej-1/
reports
```

```
http://borg.lib.vt.edu/
scholar.info.html
```

Scholarly Publishing

Transcript of a paper entitled 'Model University Policy Regarding Faculty Publication in Scientific and Technical Scholarly Journals: A Background Paper and Review of the Issues.'

Keywords: Publications, Scholarly Communication

Sponsor: Triangle Research Libraries Network, Durham, Raleigh, and Chapel Hill, North Carolina

Audience: Educators, Publishers

Details: Free

File is: pub/docs/about-the-net/trln-copyright-paper

```
ftp://sunsite.unc.edu
```

A B C D E F G H I J K L M N O P Q R S T U V W X Y Z

Scholarly Publishing

Scholarly Publishing

Transcript of a paper entitled 'Model University Policy Regarding Faculty Publication in Scientific and Technical Scholarly Journals: A Background Paper and Review of the Issues.'

Keywords: Publications, Scholarly Communication

Sponsor: Triangle Research Libraries Network, Durham, Raleigh, and Chapel Hill, North Carolina

Audience: Educators, Publishers

Details: Free

File is: pub/docs/about-the-net/trln-copyright-paper

`ftp://sunsite.unc.edu`

Sci-Fi

FutureCulture FAQ (Frequently Asked Questions) File

List of online and offline items of interest to subscribers of FutureCulture, a mailing list on 'technoculture' or 'new edge' or 'cyberculture.'

Keywords: Technology, Cyberculture, Postmodernism, Sci-Fi, Zines

Audience: Reality Hackers, Cyberculture Enthuasists

Profile: This list discusses cyberpunk culture, rave culture, industrial music, virtual reality, drugs, computer underground, Net sociology, and virtual communities.

Contact: Alias Datura (adatura on IRC) adatura@uafhp.uark.edu

Details: Free

`ftp://etext.archive.umich.edu/pub`

sci.astro

sci.astro

A Usenet newsgroup providing information and discussion about astronomy.

Keywords: Astronomy, Space

Audience: Astronomers

User Info: To subscribe to this Usenet newsgroup, you need access to a newsreader.

`news:sci.astro`

Sci.astro.fits

Sci.astro.fits

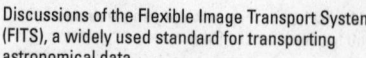

Discussions of the Flexible Image Transport System (FITS), a widely used standard for transporting astronomical data.

Keywords: Astronomy

Audience: Astronomers

Details: Free, Images

User Info: To subscribe to this Usenet newsgroup, you need access to a newsreader.

`news:sci.astro.fits`

Sci.astro.hubble

Sci.astro.hubble

Information about all subjects concerning NASA's Hubble space telescope.

Keywords: Hubble Telescope, Astronomy, Space, NASA, Stargazing, Telescopes

Audience: Astronomers, General Public, Science Teachers, Stargazers

Contact: Paul A. Scowen scowen@wfpc3.la.asu.edu

Details: Free, Moderated, Images

User Info: To subscribe to this Usenet newsgroup, you need access to a newsreader.

`news:sci.astro.hubble`

Sci.astro.planetarium

Sci.astro.planetarium

A group catering to the planetarium operations community.

Keywords: Astronomy, Planetariums

Audience: Educators, Astronomers, Planetarium Operators

Details: Free

User Info: To subscribe to this Usenet newsgroup, you need access to a newsreader.

`news:sci.astro.planetarium`

sci.electronics

sci.electronics

A Usenet newsgroup providing information and discussion about circuits, theory and electrons.

Keywords: Electronics, Engineering

Audience: Electrical Engineers

Details: Free

User Info: To subscribe to this Usenet newsgroup, you need access to a newsreader.

`news:sci.electronics`

sci.engr.biomed

sci.engr.biomed

A Usenet newsgroup providing information and discussion about the field of biomedical engineering.

Keywords: Biomedicine, Engineering (Biomedical)

Audience: Engineers (Biomedical), Biomedical Researchers

Details: Free

User Info: To subscribe to this Usenet newsgroup, you need access to a newsreader.

`news:sci.engr.biomed`

sci.environment

sci.environment

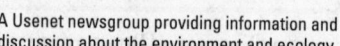

A Usenet newsgroup providing information and discussion about the environment and ecology.

Keywords: Environment, Ecology

Audience: Environmentalists, ecologists, Earth Scientists

Details: Free

User Info: To subscribe to this Usenet newsgroup, you need access to a newsreader.

`news:sci.environment`

sci.math

sci.math

A Usenet newsgroup providing information and discussion about mathematics.

Keywords: Mathematics

Audience: Mathematicians

Details: Free

User Info: To subscribe to this Usenet newsgroup, you need access to a newsreader.

`news:sci.math`

sci.med

sci.med ★

A Usenet newsgroup providing information and discussion about medicine and its related products.

Keywords: Medicine, Health Care

Audience: Medical Professionals

Details: Free

User Info: To subscribe to this Usenet newsgroup, you need access to a newsreader.

`news:sci.med`

sci.med.physics

sci.med.physics ★

A Usenet newsgroup providing information and discussion about physics in medical testing and care.

Keywords: Physics, Medical Research, Health Care

Audience: Physicists, Medical Researchers, Medical Practitioners, Health Care Professionals

Details: Free

User Info: To subscribe to this Usenet newsgroup, you need access to a newsreader.

`news:sci.med.physics`

sci.military

sci.military ★

A Usenet newsgroup providing information and discussion about science and the military.

Keywords: Military Science

Audience: Military Personnel, Military Historians

Details: Free

User Info: To subscribe to this Usenet newsgroup, you need access to a newsreader.

`news:sci.military`

sci.physics

sci.physics ★

A Usenet newsgroup providing information and discussion about physical laws and properties.

Keywords: Physics

Audience: Physicists

Details: Free

User Info: To subscribe to this Usenet newsgroup, you need access to a newsreader.

`news:sci.physics`

Sci.space

Sci.space ★

A wide variety of discussions about space flight.

Keywords: Space, Space Flight

Audience: Space Enthusiasts, General Public

Details: Free

To participate in a Usenet newsgroup you need access to a "newsreader."

`news:sci.space.news`

`news:sci.space.science`

Sci.space.news

Sci.space.news ★

Keywords: Space, FAQs

Audience: Space Flight Enthusiasts

Profile: This newsgroup carries recent information about the world's space programs. Reading the FAQ set is recommended before asking questions on the other sci.space. groups.

Contact: Peter Yee
yee@atlas.arc.nasa.gov

Details: Free, Moderated

To participate in a Usenet newsgroup you need access to a newsreader.

`news:sci.space.news`

Sci.space.science

Sci.space.science ★

A place for technical discussions about space exploration and research.

Keywords: Space Exploration, Space

Audience: Space Enthusiasts, Space Professionals

Contact: george william herbert
gwh@crl.com gwh@soda.berkeley.edu
gwh@isu.isunet.edu

Details: Free, Moderated

User Info: To participate in a Usenet newsgroup you need access to a newsreader.

`news:sci.space.science`

Science

(The) Scientist Newsletter

Electronic newsletter pertaining to science.

Keywords: Science, Electronic Publications

Audience: Scientists, Educators, Researchers, General Public

`gopher://internic.net`

alife

The alife mailing list is for communications regarding artificial life, a formative interdisciplinary field involving computer science, the natural sciences, mathematics, and medicine.

Keywords: Artificial Life, Science, Mathematics

Sponsor: UCLA

Audience: Scientists, Biologists, Mathematicians

Contact: alife-request@cognet.ucla.edu

User Info: To subscribe to the list, send an e-mail message to the URL address below. To send a message to the entire list, address it to: alife@cognet.ucla.edu

`mailto:alife-request@cognet.ucla.edu`

ANU (Australian National University) Vietnam-SciTech-L Database

A WAIS databases of information on the development of science and technology in Vietnam

Keywords: Vietnam, Science, Technology

Sponsor: Australia Vietnam Science-Technology Link

Audience: Vietnamese

Contact: Vern Weitzel
vern@coombs.anu.edu.au

`waissrc:/Coombs-db/ANU-Vietnam-SciTech-L.src`

`gopher://cheops.anu.edu.au/7waissrc/Coombs-db/ANU-Vietnam-SciTech-L.src`

ApE-info

A mailing list for the discussion of the scientific visualization software package ApE, its usage, development, and implementation.

Keywords: Computers, Visualization, Science

Sponsor: Jim Lick

Audience: ApE Software Users, Computer Programmers

Details: Free

User Info: To subscribe to this Usenet newsgroup, you need access to a newsreader.

`news:sci.physics`

A B C D E F G H I J K L M N O P Q R S T U V W X Y Z

A
B
C
D
E
F
G
H
I
J
K
L
M
N
O
P
Q
R
S
T
U
V
W
X
Y
Z

Contact: Jim Lick
            ape-info-request@ferkel.ucsb.edu

User Info: To subscribe to the list, send an e-mail
            message to the URL address below. To
            send a message to the entire list,
            address it to: ape-info@ferkel.ucsb.edu

`mailto:ape-info-`
`request@ferkel.ucsb.edu`

Aquatic Sciences and Fisheries

This database is a comprehensive database on the
science, technology, and management of marine and
freshwater environments.

Keywords: Aquatic, Science

Sponsor: US National Oceanic and Atmospheric
            Administration (NOAA)/Cambridge
            Scientific Abstracts, Bethesda, MD, US

Audience: Marine Biologists, Environmentalists

Profile: The database corresponds to the print
            Aquatic Sciences and Fisheries
            Abstracts, Part 1: Biological Sciences
            and Living Resources, Part 2: Ocean
            Technology, Policy, and Non-Living
            Resources, and Part 3: Aquatic Pollution
            and Environmental Quality. ASFA
            includes citations to 5,000 primary
            journals, monographs, conference
            proceedings, and technical reports.

Contact: Dialog in the US at (800) 334-2564, Dialog
            internationally at country specific
            locations.

User Info: To subscribe, contact Dialog directly.

`telnet://dialog.com`

CERFnet Guide

A comprehensive guide to the CERFnet (California
Education and Research Federation Network), a
data-communications regional network that
operates throughout California. The purpose of
CERFnet is to advance science and education by
assisting the interchange of information among
research and educational institutions.

Keywords: Internet, Science, Education, California

Audience: Internet Surfers, Researchers, Educators

Contact: CERFnet Hotline
            help@cerf.net

Details: Free

            Files are in: cerfnet/cerfnet_info/
            cerfnet_guide/

`ftp://nic.cerf.net`

Chemistry

★★

This directory is a compilation of information
resources focused on chemistry.

Keywords: Chemistry, Science

Audience: Chemical Engineers, Chemistry
            Teachers, Students

Details: Free

`ftp://una.hh.lib.umich.edu/7`/
`inetdirsstacks/chemistry:wiggins`

Current Contents

Current Contents provides access to the tables of
contents from the current issues of leading domestic
and international scientific journals. Every discipline
within the sciences is represented. The database
provides complete bibliographic information for
each article, review, letter, note and editorial.

Keywords: Sciences, Scientific Journals

Sponsor: Institute for Scientific Information

Audience: General Public, Researchers, Librarians,
            Physicians

Contact: CDP Technologies Sales Department
            (800)950-2035, extension 400

User Info: To subscribe, contact CDP Technologies
            directly

`telnet://cdplus@cdplus.com`

Denmark's Library for Medicine and Science

Keywords: Science, Medicine, Libraries, Denmark

Audience: Scientists, Health Care Professionals,
            Medical Researchers

Details: Free

            At the CCL>prompt, type DIA ENG for
            English interface.

`telnet://cosmos.bib.dk`

EMBASE

EMBASE is an acclaimed comprehensive index of
international literature on medicine, science and
pharmacology.

Keywords: Medicine, Science, Pharmacology

Sponsor: Elsevier Science Publishers

Audience: Librarians, Researchers, Students,
            Physicians

Contact: CDP Technologies Sales Department
            (800) 950-2035, extension 400.

User Info: To subscribe, contact CDP Technologies
            directly.

`telnet:\\cdplus@cdplus.com`

fusion

Fusion is an e-mail redistribution of Usenet
sci.physics.fusion newsgroup for sites/users lacking
access to Usenet.

Keywords: Physics, Fusion, Science

Audience: Physicists, Scientists

Details: Free

User Info: To subscribe to the list, send an e-mail
            message requesting a subscription to
            the URL address below. To send a
            message to the entire list, address it to:
            fusion@zorch.sf-bay.org

`mailto:fusion-request@zorch.`
`sf-bay.org`

National Institute of Health Library Online Catalog

This entry point provides access to the books and
journal holdings in the NIH Library. Journal articles
are not included.

Keywords: NIH, Medicine, Science, Libraries

Sponsor: National Institute of Health (NIH)

Audience: Scientists, Researchers, Educators,
            Health Care Professionals

Details: Free

`telnet://nih-library.ncrr.nih.gov`

NIH EDNET

★

EdNet is set up as a free electronic bulletin board at
the Bethesda, Maryland campus of the National
Institute of Health (NIH). Its purpose is to allow high
school students to ask questions of NIH scientists
about current research.

Keywords: NIH, Education (Post-Secondary),
            Education (K-12), Science

Sponsor: National Institute of Health (NIH)

Audience: Students (high school and up), Educators

Details: Free

            To receive an EDNET User's Guide and
            account, send an e-mail message with
            your name and mailing address to the
            URL address below.

`mailto:vt5@cu.nih.gov`

Novice MZT

Novize MZT (News of Ministry for Science and
Technology of the Republic of Slovenia) provides
easy, accessible news about science, development,
universities, and innovative activities to individuals
and institutions in research and development areas.
Published at least once monthly.

Keywords: Slovenia, Science, Technology, News

Audience: Slovenians, Scientists, Technocrats

Contact: Novice-mzt@krpan.arnes.si or
            Novice.mzt@uni-lj.si

User Info: To subscribe to the list, send an e-mail
            message requesting a subscription to
            the URL address below. To send a
            message to the entire list, address it to:
            Novice-mzt@krpan.arnes.si

`mailto:Novice-MZT@krpan.arnes.si`

NSSDC's (National Space Science Data Center) Online Data & Information Service

The NSSDC (National Space Science Data Center) is
the NASA facility charged with archiving the data
from all of NASA's science missions.

Keywords: Space, Astrophysics, Software, NASA,
            Science

Sponsor: NASA

Audience: Scientists, Space Scientists, Astronomers, Engineers

Profile: This resource contains information about NASA's missions and analysis of their data.

Details: Free

User Info: Expect: Login, Send: nssdc

See the menu entries in your particular area of interest.

`telnet://nssdc.gsfc.nasa.gov`

Sais-l (Science Awareness and Promotion)

The SAIS list creates a forum for exchanging innovative ideas about making science more appealing to students.

Keywords: Science, Education (K-12), Education (Secondary)

Audience: Students (K-12), Students (high school up), Science Teachers

Contact: Keith W. Wilson
sais@unb.ca

Details: Free

User Info: To subscribe to the list, send an e-mail message to the URL address below consisting of a single line reading:

SUB sais-l YourFirstName YourLastName

To send a message to the entire list, address it to: sais-l@unb.ca

`mailto:listserv@unb.ca`

Scifaq-l

A mailing list to facilitate access to Usenet FAQ documents. It is available to people who have access to local Usenet distributions via NETNEWS or some other medium but do not have USETNET feeds per se. The list contains the latest releases of all Usenet FAQs relating to topics in science.

Keywords: Science

Audience: Usenet Users, Scientists

Profile: The sci.answers newsgroup is moderated, and therefore the gateway between it and the scifaq-l mailing list has been made one-way, from Usenet into the list. The list itself is not moderated, and can be used for relevant discussion or distribution of FAQ-like documents by e-mail subscribers.

Contact: Una Smith
smith-una@yale.edu

Details: Free

User Info: To subscribe to the list, send an e-mail message to the URL address below consisting of a single line reading:

SUB scifaq-l YourFirstName YourLastName

To send a message to the entire list, address it to: scifaq-l@yalevm.cis.yale.edu

`mailto:listserv@yalevm.cis.yale.edu`

Scifraud

Scifraud is dedicated to the discussion of fraud in science.

Keywords: Science, Fraud

Audience: Scientists

Contact: Al Higgins, Mike Ramundo
ach13@albnyvms.bitnet
sysmrr@albnyvm1.bitnet

Details: Free

User Info: To subscribe to the list, send an e-mail message to the URL address below consisting of a single line reading:

SUB scifraud YourFirstName YourLastName

To send a message to the entire list, address it to: scifraud@uacs2.albany.edu

`mailto:listserv@uacsc2.albany.edu`

Universite de Montreal UDEMATIK Library

The library's holdings are large and wide-ranging and contain significant collections in many fields.

Keywords: Art, Architecture, Economy, Sexology, Social Law, Science, Technology, Literary Studies

Audience: Researchers, Students, General Public

Contact: Joelle or Sebastien Roy
udematik@ere.umontreal.ca
stemp@ere.umontreal.ca
roys@ere.umontreal.ca

User Info: Expect: Login; Send: Application id INFO

`telnet://udematik.umontreal.ca`

University of Toledo Library

The library's holdings are large and wide-ranging and contain significant collections in many fields.

Keywords: Business, Great Lakes Area, Humanities, International Relations, Psychology, Science

Audience: Researchers, Students, General Public

Details: Free

User Info: Expect: Enter one of the following commands . . . , Send: DIAL MVS; Expect: dialed to mvs ####; Send: UTMOST

`telnet://uofto1.utoledo.edu`

Washington University-St. Louis Medical Library & MembersLibrary

The library's holdings are large and wide-ranging and contain significant collections in many fields.

Keywords: Medicine, Science, Technology

Audience: Researchers, Students, General Public

Details: Free

User Info: Expect: Destination Code Prompt, Send: Catalog

`telnet://mcftcp.wustl.edu`

Science Fiction

alt.books.reviews

A Usenet conference devoted to reviews of books, especially science fiction and computer science books.

Keywords: Literature (General), Computer Science, Science Fiction, Book Reviews

Audience: General Public, Publishers, Educators, Librarians, Booksellers

Profile: Alt.books.reviews (a.b.r. for short) is a forum for posting reviews of books of interest to readers, school and public librarians, bookstores, publishers, teachers and professors, and others who desire an "educated opinion" of a book. This is an unmoderated newsgroup.

Contact: sbrock@csn.org.

Details: Free

To participate in a Usenet newsgroup, you need access to a "newsreader"

Notes: The reviews in alt.books.reviews are archived at csn.org. FTP to csn.org; login: anonymous; password: your complete e-mail address. At the ftp prompt, type: cd pub/alt.books.reviews

`news:alt.books.reviews`

Deryni-L

A list for readers and fans of Katernine Kurtz's novels and other works.

Keywords: Science Fiction, Kurtz (Katernine)

Audience: Science Fiction Enthusiasts

Contact: Edward J. Branley
elendil@mintir.new-orleans.la.us

User Info: To subscribe to the list, send an e-mail message requesting a subscription to the URL address below. To send a message to the entire list, address it to: deryni-l@mintir.new-orleans.la.us

`mailto:deryni-l@mintir.new-orleans.la.us`

Milieu

Discussion of the works of Julian May, notably the Saga of the Exiles, and the Galactic Milieu Trilogy.

Keywords: May (Julian), Science Fiction

Audience: Julian May Readers

Contact: milieu-request@yoyo.cc.monash.edu.au

A B C D E F G H I J K L M N O P Q R **S** T U V W X Y Z

Details: Free

Notes: To subscribe to the list, send an e-mail
            message requesting subscription to the
            URL address below.

`mailto:milieu-`
`request@yoyo.cc.monash.edu.au`

Pkd-list

A discussion of the works and life of Philip K. Dick
(1928-82), science fiction writer. Topics also include
the nature of reality, consciousness, and religious
experience.

Keywords: Science Fiction, Dick (Philip K.)

Audience: Philip K. Dick Readers, Science Fiction
            Enthusiasts

Contact: pkd-list-request@wang.com

Details: Free

User Info: To subscribe to the list, send an e-mail
            message requesting a subscription to
            the URL address below. To send a
            message to the entire list, address it to:
            pkd-list@wang.com

`mailto:pkd-list@wang.com`

Quanta ★

An electronically distributed science fiction
magazine that is published monthly. Each issue
contains short fiction, articles, and editorials by
authors from around the world and across the Net.

Keywords: Science Fiction, Writing, Publications

Audience: Science Fiction Enthusiasts, Writers

Contact: da1n@andrew.cmu.edu

Details: Free

User Info: To subscribe to the list, send an e-mail
            message requesting a subscription to
            the URL address below. To send a
            message to the entire list, address it to:
            da1n@andrew.cmu.edu

`mailto:da1n@andrew.cmu.edu`

rec.arts.sf.starwars ★

A Usenet newsgroup providing information and
discussion about the popular Star Wars trilogy.

Keywords: Science Fiction, Film

Audience: Star Wars Enthusiasts, Movie Viewers

User Info: To subscribe to this Usenet newsgroup,
            you need access to a newsreader.

`news:rec.arts.sf.starwars`

rec.arts.sf.tv ★

A Usenet newsgroup providing information and
discussion about science fiction television
programs.

Keywords: Science Fiction, Television

Audience: Science Fiction Enthusiasts, Television
            Viewers

User Info: To subscribe to this Usenet newsgroup,
            you need access to a newsreader.

`news:rec.arts.sf.tv`

rec.arts.sf.written ★

A Usenet newsgroup providing information and
discussion about science fiction publications.

Keywords: Science Fiction

Audience: Science Fiction Readers

User Info: To subscribe to this Usenet newsgroup,
            you need access to a newsreader.

`news:rec.arts.sf.written`

rec.arts.startrek.current ★

A Usenet newsgroup providing information and
discussion about current Star Trek (The Next
Generation) episodes and characters.

Keywords: Television, Science Fiction

Audience: Trekkies, Television Viewers

User Info: To subscribe to this Usenet newsgroup,
            you need access to a newsreader.

`news:rec.arts.startrek.current`

Star Trek Resources on the Internet ★★★

This extensive resource contains information on
mailing lists, news archives, other Internet
resources addressing the culture surounding Star
Trek fans.

Keywords: Science Fiction, Television

Audience: General Public, Trekkies, Television
            Viewers

Contact: Brigitte Jellinek
            bjelli@cosy.sbg.ac.at

`http://www.cosy.sbg.ac.at/rec/`
`startrek/star_trek_resources.html`

Science (History of)

McGill University, Montreal Canada, INFOMcGILL Library

The library's holdings are large and wide-ranging
and contain significant collections in many fields.

Keywords: Architecture, Entomology, Biology,
            Science (History of), Medicine (History
            of), Napolean, Shakespeare (William)

Audience: Researchers, Students, General Public

Contact: Roy Miller
            ccrmmus@mcgillm (Bitnet)
            ccrmmus@musicm.mcgill.ca (Internet)

User Info: Expect: VM logo; Send: Enter; Expect:
            prompt; Send: PF3 or type INFO

`telnet://vm1.mcgill.ca`

Science Technology

University of Texas at Austin Library ★★

The library's holdings are large and wide-ranging
and contain significant collections in many fields.

Keywords: Music, Natural Science, Nursing,
            Science Technology, Behavioral
            Science, Social Work, Computer
            Science, Engineering, Latin American
            Studies, Middle Eastern Studies

Audience: Researchers, Students, General Public

Details: Free

User Info: Expect: Blank Screen, Send: Return;
            Expect: Go, Send: Return; Expect: Enter
            Terminal Type, Send: vt100

Notes: Some databases are restricted to UT
            Austin users only.

`telnet://utcat.utexas.edu`

Scientific Journals

Current Contents

Current Contents provides access to the tables of
contents from the current issues of leading domestic
and international scientific journals. Every discipline
within the sciences is represented. The database
provides complete bibliographic information for
each article, review, letter, note, and editorial.

Keywords: Sciences, Scientific Journals

Sponsor: Institute for Scientific Information

Audience: General Public, Researchers, Librarians,
            Physicians

Contact: CDP Technologies Sales Department
            (800) 950-2035, extension 400.

User Info: To subscribe, contact CDP Technologies
            directly.

`telnet://cdplus@cdplus.com`

Scientific Research

Washington State University at Puyallup Library ★★

The library's holdings are large and wide-ranging
and contain significant collections in many fields.

Keywords: Agriculture, Scientific Research

Audience: Researchers, Students, General Public

Details: Free

User Info: Expect: Login; Send: Lib

`telnet://wsuvm1.cscwsu.edu`

Scientific Visualization

INGRAFX

This E-conference is for discussion of all matters relating to information graphics.

Keywords: Computer Graphics, Graphic Design, Scientific Visualization

Audience: Graphic Designers, Cartographers, Animators

Contact: Jeremy Crampton
http://info.cern.ch/hypertext/WWW/The Project.html

User Info: To subscribe to the list, send an e-mail message to the URL address below consisting of a single line reading:

SUB ingrafx YourFirstName YourLastName

To send a message to the entire list, address it to: ingrafx@psuvm.psu.edu

`mailto:listserv@psuvm.psu.edu`

Scientists

noglstp

★

This list is sponsored by the National Organization of Gay and Lesbian Scientists and Technical Professionals, Inc. (a 501-C3 organization). National office is in Pasadena, CA and can be reached at (818) 791-7689 or P.O. Box 91803, Pasadena, CA 90019. There is also a newsletter that is available to membership.

Keywords: Gay, Lesbian, Scientists, Technical Professionals

Audience: Gay Scientists, Lesbian Scientists

Contact: noglstp-request@elroy.jpl.nasa.gov

Details: Free

User Info: To subscribe to the list, send an e-mail message requesting a subscription to the URL address below. To send a message to the entire list, address it to: noglstp@elroy.jpl.nasa.gov

`mailto:noglstp-request@elroy.jpl.nasa.gov`

Scit-L

Scit-L

★

A list for those interested in information and communications science.

Keywords: Communications, Information Sciences

Audience: Communications Specialists, Communications Students, Information Scientists

---

Contact: Elia Zureik
Scitdoc@qucdn.queensu.ca

User Info: To subscribe to this list, send an e-mail message to the URL address below, consisting of a single line reading:

SUB scit-l YourFirstName YourLastName

To send a message to the entire list, address it to: scit-l@qucdn.queensu.ca

`mailto:listserv@qucdn.queensu.ca`

Scotland

Highlands and Islands of Scotland

★★

This web site provides information on Scotland, including business, leisure, culture, Gaelic language, tourism, distance education, and work opportunities.

Keywords: Scotland, Travel

Sponsor: British Telecom, United Kingdom

Audience: Travelers, Educators, Students

Contact: webmaster@nsa.bt.co.uk

Details: Free

`http://nsa.bt.co.uk/nsa.html`

Strathspey

★

A forum for the discussion of all aspects of Scottish Country Dancing, for example, dancing technique.

Keywords: Dance, Scotland, Scottish Dance

Audience: Dancers, Dance Historians

Contact: owner-strathspey@math.uni-frankfurt.de

Details: Free

User Info: To subscribe to the list, send an e-mail message requesting a subscription to the URL address below. To send a message to the entire list, address it to: strathspey@math.uni-frankfurt.de

`mailto:strathspey-request@math.uni-frankfurt.de`

University of Glasgow Information Service (GLANCE)

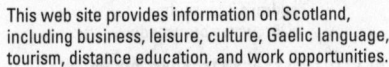 ★★★★

GLANCE provides subject-based information services, including an extensive section on European and world sports.

Keywords: Sports, Soccer, Motor Racing, Mountaineering, Squash, Cricket, Golf, Tennis, Europe, Scotland

Sponsor: University of Glasgow, Glasgow, Scotland

Audience: Sport Enthusiasts, Fitness Enthusiasts, Nature Lovers

Profile: Information at this site includes schedules, results, and statistics for sports such as cricket and soccer. There is also a selection of items on mountaineering.

Contact: Alan Dawson
A.Dawson@uk.ac.gla.compserv

Details: Free

`gopher://govan.cent.gla.ac.uk/Subject/Sports and Rec`

Scottish Dance

Strathspey

★

A forum for the discussion of all aspects of Scottish Country Dancing, for example, dancing technique.

Keywords: Dance, Scotland, Scottish Dance

Audience: Dancers, Dance Historians

Contact: owner-strathspey@math.uni-frankfurt.de

Details: Free

User Info: To subscribe to the list, send an e-mail message requesting a subscription to the URL address below. To send a message to the entire list, address it to: strathspey@math.uni-frankfurt.de

`mailto:strathspey-request@math.uni-frankfurt.de`

Scottish Gaelic

Gaelic-L

★

A multidisciplinary discussion list that facilitates the exchange of news, views, and information in Scottish Gaelic, Irish, and Manx.

Keywords: Scottish Gaelic, Irish, Manx, Linguistics

Audience: Linguists

Contact: Marion Gunn
mgunn@irlearn.ucd.ie
caoimhin@smo.ac.uk
lss203@cs.napier.ac.uk

Details: Free

User Info: To subscribe to the list, send an e-mail message to the URL address shown below consisting of a single line reading:

SUB gaelic-l YourFirstName YourLastName

To send a message to the entire list, address it to: gaelic-l@irlearn.ucd.ie

`mailto:listserv@irlearn.ucd.ie`

Scripting Languages

NIC (Nucleus for Interactive Computing)

 ★★★★

WWW-based system for interactive computing.

Keywords: Multimedia, Interactive Computing, Interface Design, Scripting Laguages, Programming

Sponsor: BYU Interactive Software Systems Lab

Audience: Software Developers, Educators

Profile: NIC is a system for interactive computing that combines a data model, a user interface model, and a scripting language to create flexible and powerful user interfaces. Documentation still under construction is located here.

Contact: Dan Olsen
olsen@cs.byu.edu

Details: Free, Moderated; Sound, Image, and Multimedia files available.

Use a World Wide Web (Mosaic) client and open a connection to the resource.

```
ftp://issl.cs.byu.edu/docs/NIC/
home.html
```

Scuba Diving

Physical Education & Recreation ★★

A collection of information on sporting and recreational activities from aikido to windsurfing.

Keywords: Sports, Recreation, Aikido, Cycling, Scuba Diving, Windsurfing

Audience: Sports Enthusiasts, Fitness Enthusiasts

Contact: ctcadmin@ctc.ctc.edu

```
gopher://ctc.ctc.edu
```

rec.scuba ★

A Usenet newsgroup providing information and discussion about scuba equipment and techniques.

Keywords: Scuba Sports, Travel, Recreation

Audience: Scuba Divers

User Info: To subscribe to this Usenet newsgroup, you need access to a newsreader.

```
news:scuba
```

Scuba-d ★

Digest of the Usenet rec.scuba newsgroup.

Keywords: Scuba Diving

Audience: Scuba Divers

Contact: Catherine Yang, Nick Simicich
cyang@brownvm.brown.edu
njs@watson.ibm.com

Details: Free

User Info: To subscribe to the list, send an e-mail message to the URL address below consisting of a single line reading:

SUB scuba-d YourFirstName YourLastName

To send a message to the entire list, address it to: scuba-d@brownvm.brown.edu

```
mailto:listserv@brownvm.brown.edu
```

Scuba-l (Scuba Diving Mailing List) ★

Mailing list for discussion of all aspects of scuba diving.

Keywords: Scuba Diving

Audience: Scuba Divers

Contact: Catherine Yang
cyang@brownvm.brown.edu

Details: Free

User Info: To subscribe to the list, send an e-mail message to the URL address below consisting of a single line reading:

SUB scuba-l YourFirstName YourLastName

To send a message to the entire list, address it to: scuba-l@brownvm.brown.edu

```
mailto:listserv@brownvm.brown.edu
```

Usenet Sports Groups Archived ★

An archive for Usenet groups, including many related to sports ranging from football to table tennis.

Keywords: Sports, Skydiving, Volleyball, Football, Scuba Diving, Table Tennis

Sponsor: Massachusetts Institute of Technology, Boston, MA

Audience: Sports Enthusiasts

Contact: ftp-bugs@rtfm.mit.edu

Details: Free

```
ftp://rtfm.mit.edu/pub/usenet
```

SCUP BITNET NEWS

SCUP BITNET NEWS ★★★

Designed to promote the mission of the society and support its activities. Society for College and University Planning (SCUP) Bitnet News provides frequent and timely exchange of information among members as well as nonmembers interested in higher-education planning through the use of bitnet.

Keywords: Planning, University Planning

Sponsor: Society for College and University Planning

Audience: Planners

Profile: Contents of the newsletter are selected on the basis of interest and value to the membership. Particular attention is given to information that advances the state-of-the-art in planning; improves the understanding and application of the tools, techniques, processes and strategies of planning; advances the professional development of the membership; and widens the base of support for planning in higher education.

Contact: Joanne E. MacRae
usertd8q@umichum.bitnet

Details: Free

Send an electronic mail note to the editor (Joanne Cate: budlao@uccvma.bitnet) or the associate editor (Betsey Creekmore: pa94858@utkvm1)

```
mailto:Joanne Cate:
budlao@uccvma.bitnet
```

SCUPMA-L: Society of College and University Planners, Mid-Atlantic Region

SCUPMA-L: Society of College and University Planners, Mid-Atlantic Region ★★★

This newsletter contains short news pieces and announcements about events of interest to the membership.

Keywords: Planning, University Planning

Audience: University Planners

Contact: Debbie Furlong
OPIR1@AUVM.bitnet

Details: Free

Contact: Debbie Furlong at OPIR1@AUVM.bitnet

```
mailto:opir1@auvm.bitnet
```

Seafood Internet Network

Seafood Internet Network ★★

A mailing list to facilitate information exchange about the HACCP Alliance and the implementation of the FDA seafood HACCP program.

Keywords: Food, FDA

Audience: Seafood Industry Professionals

Contact: Robert J. Price
rjprice@dale.ucdavis.edu

User Info: To subscribe, send an e-mail message to: listproc@ucdavis.edu. Leave the subject blank and place in the body of the note:

subscribe seafood YourFirstName YourLastName

```
mailto:seafood@ucdavis.edu
```

Searching Gopherspace with Veronica

Searching Gopherspace with Veronica

A resource which conducts Veronica searches over restricted areas of the Internet.

Keywords: WWW, Information Retrieval, Internet

Audience: Researchers, Students, General Public

```
gopher://gopher.well.sf.ca.us/11/
outbound/veronica.search
```

Securities

Disclosure Database

Disclosure Database provides in-depth financial information on over 12,500 companies.

Keywords: Securities, Stock Market

Sponsor: Disclosure Incorporated, Bethesda, MD, USA

Audience: Business Professionals

Profile: The information is derived from reports filed with the US Securities and Exchange Commission (SEC) by publicly owned companies. These reports provide detailed and reliable financial information on the companies included. Extracts of 10-K and 10-Q financial reports are included, as well as 20-F financial reports and registration reports for new registrants. Disclosure provides an online source of information for marketing intelligence, corporate planning, accounting research, and corporate finance. Contents of the records include management discussion and president's letter on past-year performance, footnotes to the financials, significant events, and market conditions affecting a particular company.

Contact: Dialog in the US at (800) 334-2564, Dialog internationally at country-specific locations.

User Info: To subscribe, contact Dialog directly.

Notes: Coverage: Current; updated weekly.

```
telnet://dialog.com
```

FEDSEC (Federal Securities Library)

The US Federal Securities library covers federal case law, Securities Exchanges Commission (SEC) materials, Commodities Futures Trading Commision (CFTC) materials and other legal and legislative materials relevant to the securities industry, as well as company information, news and analysis.

Keywords: Law, Filings, Securities

Audience: Lawyers, Bankers, Stockbrokers

Profile: The Federal Securities library contains over 60 separately searchable files covering federal case law: Securities Exchange Commission (SEC) no-action letters, decisions, orders, releases, and SEC filings (both full text and abstracts); Commodities Futures Trading Commision (CFTC) decisions, orders, releases; legislative materials; statutory and regulatory materials; selected RICO, class derivative, and collateralized mortgage obligations case law, rules and regulations; Federal Reserve Board materials; AICPA annual reports and accounting & audit literature files; Standard & Poors company information; state administrative decisions, orders, and releases; and company news and analysis information.

Contact: New Sales Group at (800) 227-4908 or 513-859-5398 inside the US, or 1-513-865-7981 for all inquires outside the US.

User Info: To subscribe, contact Mead directly.

To examine the Lexis user guide, you can access it at the ftp site of the University of Texas at Austin at the URL address: ftp://ftp.cc.utexas.edu. The files are in: pub/ref-services/LEXIS

```
telnet://nex.meaddata.com
```

```
http://www.meaddata.com
```

Insider Trading Monitor

The database contains the transaction details of all insider-trading filings.

Keywords: Insider Trading, Securities

Sponsor: Invest/Net, Inc., Ft. Lauderdale, FL US

Audience: Stockbrokers , Media

Profile: This source contains the transaction details of all insider-trading filings, (ownership changes) received by the US Securities and Exchange Commission (SEC) since January 1984. The ownership of securities by over 100,000 officers, directors, and major shareholders (10% or more) in over 8,500 US public companies is covered in the file.

Contact: Dialog in the US at (800) 334-2564, Dialog internationally at country-specific locations.

User Info: To subscribe, contact Dialog directly.

Notes: Coverage: April 1984 to the present; updated daily.

```
telnet://dialog.com
```

SEC (Securities and Exchange Commission) EDGAR (Electronic Data Gathering, Analysis and Retrieval) System

Provides free access to 1994 SEC filings for approximately 2,300 companies.

Keywords: Securities, Filings, Stock Market

Sponsor: New York University School of Business

Audience: Business Professionals, Investors

Profile: This expanding project aims to make available current, public SEC filings that are filed electronically. The system is searchable by company name and is updated and indexed daily. Many types of SEC forms, including 10-K and 10-Q financial reports, are available in a number of different electronic formats. The site also provides some explanatory documentation on the EDGAR program and on the types of SEC forms and information available to the public.

Contact: Ajit Kambil
piotr@edgar.stern.nyu.edu

Details: Free

```
ftp://town.hall.org/edgar
```

```
http://www.town.hall.org
```

Security

CERT (Computer Emergency Response Team) Advisory

A major directory on computer advisory, providing access to a broad range of related resources (library catalogs, databases, and servers) via the Internet.

Keywords: Computers, Security, Computer Networking

Audience: Computer Users

Profile: Profides information on how to obtain a patch or details of a workaround for a known computer security problem. CERT works with vendors to produce a workaround or a patch for a problem, and does not publish vulnerability information until a workaround or patch is available. A CERT advisory may also be a warning about ongoing attacks to network systems.

Contact: cert@cert.org

```
ftp://cert.org/pub/cert_advisories
```

comp.org.eff.talk

A Usenet newsgroup organized by the EFF (Electronic Frontier Foundation) providing information and discussion about the political, social, and legal issues surrounding the Internet.

Keywords: Computers, Intellectual Property, Security, Internet

Audience: Internet Surfers

User Info: To subscribe to this Usenet newsgroup, you need access to a newsreader.

```
news:comp.org.eff.talk
```

A B C D E F G H I J K L M N O P Q R **S** T U V W X Y Z

comp.security.misc

A Usenet newsgroup providing information and discussion about security issues of computers and networks.

Keywords: Computers, Security, Firewalls

Audience: Computer Users

User Info: To subscribe to this Usenet newsgroup, you need access to a newsreader.

`news:comp.security.misc`

DDN New User Guide

Defense Data Network (DDN) guide for new users.

Keywords: Internet, Internet Guides, Defense, Security

Audience: Internet Surfers

Details: Free

File is: netinfo/nug.doc

`ftp://nic.ddn.mil/netinfo`

firewalls

A mailing list to discuss the issues involved in setting up and maintaining Internet security firewall systems.

Keywords: Security, Internet Security, Firewalls

Audience: Security Workers

Contact: Brent Chapman
Brent@GreatCircle.com

Details: Free

User Info: To subscribe to the list, send an e-mail message consisting of a single line reading:

SUB firewalls YourFirstName YourLastName

`mailto:majordomo@greatcircle.com`

Investigators and Detectives

This resource provides information files for individuals involved with investigative research, as well as a free monthly newsletter.

Keywords: Detectives, Crime, Information Retrieval, Security

Audience: Investigators, Detectives, Information Brokers, General Public

Profile: Investigators and Detectives provides access to information covering topics such as private investigative research, strategies, sources, the art and science of investigating, theft deterrents, and electronic PI schematics and plans. Also offers a free sample of a newsletter covering various topics of interest to Private Investigators, such as techniques and strategies, security, and tracing.

Contact: Mike Enlow
menlow@Intec.win.net,
michael@enlow.com

Details: Inside Secrets.

`mailto:info@enlow.com`

Security

A forum for discussion of the field of security in general, be it electronic, physical, or computer-related.

Keywords: Security

Audience: Security Workers

Contact: Hobbit@aim.rutgers.edu

Details: Free

User Info: To subscribe to the list, send an e-mail message requesting a subscription to the URL address below.

`mailto:security-request@aim.rutgers.edu.`

Virus-L

Virus-L is a forum for the discussion of computer virus experiences, protection software, and other virus-related topics. This list includes archives and files that list a number of viruses, trojan horses, and pirated programs for the IBM PC.

Keywords: Computer Viruses, Security

Audience: Computer Users

Contact: Kenneth R. van Wyk
luken@vax1.cc.lehigh.edu

Details: Free

User Info: To subscribe to the list, send an e-mail message to the URL address below consisting of a single line reading:

SUB virus-l YourFirstName YourLastName

To send a message to the entire list, address it to: virus-l@ibml.cc.lehigh.edu

`mailto:listserv@ibm1.cc.lehigh.edu`

Senate (US)

Bibliographies of US Senate Hearings

The US Senate produces a series of committee hearings, prints, and publications as part of the legislative process. The Documents department at North Carolina State University contains files for the 99th through 103rd Congresses, which can also be searched through a WAIS searchable database.

Keywords: Senate (US), Politics (US), Legislation (US), Bibliographies, Government (US)

Audience: General Public, Journalists, Students, Politicians, US Citizens

Contact: Jack McGeachy
Jack_McGeachy@ncsu.edu

Details: Free

`gopher://dewey.lib.ncsu.edu/11/library/disciplines/government/senate`

Senatorial (Papers of)

Boise State University Library

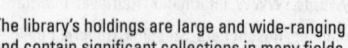

The library's holdings are large and wide-ranging and contain significant collections in many fields.

Keywords: Jordan (Len, Senatorial Papers of), Church (Frank, Senatorial Papers of), Poetry (American)

Audience: General Public, Researchers, Librarians, Document Delivery Professionals

Contact: Dan Lester

Details: Free

User Info: Expect: login; Send: catalyst

`telnet://catalyst.idbsu.edu`

Sense of Place

Sense of Place

An electronic environmentalists magazine. The magazine incorporates graphics and text in a format specifically designed to be read on a Macintosh screen. You must have Hypercard version 2.1 or later.

Keywords: Environment, Ecology

Audience: Environmentalists

Contact: SOP@dartmouth.edu

Details: Costs, Images

User Info: To subscribe send electronic mail to: SOP@dartmouth.edu

`gopher://gopher.dartmouth.edu/1/anonftp/pub/sop`

Sequencers

Analog Heaven

The Analog Heaven mailing list caters to people interested in vintage analog electronic music equipment. Topics include items for sale, repair tips, equipment modifications, ASCII & GIF schematics, and a general discussion of new and old analog equipment. There is an FTP/Gopher site located at cs.uwp.edu with discussions on various machines, a definitive guide to Roland synths, patch editors, modification schematics, and GIFs/JPEGs of vintage synths, as well as a few sound samples of some of the gear itself.

Keywords: Music, Synthesizers, Sequencers, Analog Equipment, Electronic Music

Audience: Electronic Music Enthusiasts, Musicians

Contact: Todd Sines
analogue-request@magnus.acs.ohio-state.edu

Details: Free; sound files available.

User Info: To subscribe to the list, send an e-mail message requesting a subscription to the URL address below. To send a message to the entire list, address it to: analogue@magnus.acs.ohio-state.edu

`mailto:analogue-request@magnus.acs.ohio-state.edu`

Serials Pricing

Newsletter on Serials Pricing Issues

⭐⭐⭐

The focus of this newsletter is the pricing of library serials.

Keywords: Serials Pricing, Librarianship

Audience: Librarians, Publishers

Profile: Contributions include examples of titles considered to be overpriced, as well as of publishers' actions to keep prices down, strategies for coping with serials price increases, information about libraries' evaluation and cancellation policies and procedures, announcements of and reports from relevant meetings, and other news of serials prices.

Contact: Marcia Tuttle
tuttle@unc.bitnet

Details: Free

User Info: To subscribe, send an e-mail message to the URL address shown below consisting of a single line reading:

SUB serials_pricing YourFirstName YourLastName

`mailto:listserv@uncvx1.Bitnet`

Services

Correct Time/NBS

⭐

Correct Time/NBS tells the correct time from the National Bureau of Standards (NBS).

Keywords: Internet, Services, Correct Time

Audience: Internet Surfers

Details: Free

`ftp://india.colorado.edu/pub (Bogus site!)`

E-mail Gopher

⭐

E-mail Gopher allows the use of a gopher via e-mail.

Keywords: Internet, Services, E-mail, Gopher

Audience: Internet Surfers

Details: Free
Include the word "help" in the Email.

`gopher://gopher.ncc.go.jp/11/INFO/gopher`

(This is the National Cancer Center of Japan Server)

E-mail Services

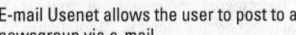

A list of services available by e-mail.

Keywords: Internet, E-mail, Services

Audience: Internet Surfers

Contact: David DeSimone
an207@cleveland.freenet.edu

Details: Free
File is: pub/docs/about-the-net/libsoft/email_services.txt

`ftp://sunsite.unc.edu/pub/docs/about-the-net/libsoft/email_services.txt`

`http://sunsite.unc.edu/pub/docs/about-the-net/libsoft/email_services.txt`

E-mail Usenet

⭐

E-mail Usenet allows the user to post to a newsgroup via e-mail.

Keywords: Internet, Services, E-mail, Usenet

Audience: Internet Surfers

Details: Free

`mailto://hierarchy-group-name@cs.utexas.edu`

Settlements

VRDCT (Jury Verdicts Library)

The Verdicts Library aids litigation preparation by providing quick and convenient access to selected online verdict and settlement information for civil cases nationwide. Case information covered includes verdict and settlement amounts, expert witnesses, case summaries, and counsel data.

Keywords: Jury, Verdicts, Judgments, Settlements

Audience: Lawyers

Profile: The Verdicts library aids litigation preparation by providing quick and convenient access to selected online verdict and settlement information for civil cases nationwide. Case information covered includes verdict and settlement amounts, expert witnesses, case summaries and counsel data.

Contact: New Sales Group at (800) 227-4908 or (513) 859-5398 inside the US, or (513) 865-7981 for all inquires outside the US.

User Info: To subscribe, contact Mead directly.
To examine the Lexis user guide, you can access it at the ftp site of the University of Texas at Austin at the URL address: ftp://ftp.cc.utexas.edu. The files are in: pub/ref-services/LEXIS

`telnet://nex.meaddata.com`

`http://www.meaddata.com`

Sex

alt.sex

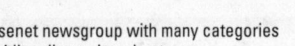

A Usenet newsgroup with many categories providing discussion about sex.

Keywords: Sex

Audience: Adults

User Info: To subscribe to this Usenet newsgroup, you need access to a newsreader.

`news:alt.sex`

Sex FAQ

⭐

This is the official summary of the Frequently Asked Questions from the newsgroup alt.sex. The purpose of the file is to filter the postings in the newsgroup and limit it to the FAQ. The file includes answers to questions such as: What is circumcision and why is it done?, What can one do about premature ejaculation?, Where can one find additional sex topics on Usenet?, What about sexually transmitted diseases?, and more.

Keywords: Sex, FAQ

Audience: General Public

Contact: David Johnson, Snugglebunny
superdj@cs.mcgill.ca

Details: Free

`ftp://pit-manager.mit.edu/pub/usenet/news.answers/alt-sex/faq`

Sexology

Universite de Montreal UDEMATIK Library

The library's holdings are large and wide-ranging and contain significant collections in many fields.

Keywords: Art, Architecture, Economy, Sexology, Social Law, Science, Technology, Literary Studies

Audience: Researchers, Students, General Public

Contact: Joelle or Sebastien Roy
udematik@ere.umontreal.ca
stemp@ere.umontreal.ca
roys@ere.umontreal.ca

User Info: Expect: Login; Send: Application id INFO

`telnet://udematik.umontreal.ca`

A B C D E F G H I J K L M N O P Q R S T U V W X Y Z

A
B
C
D
E
F
G
H
I
J
K
L
M
N
O
P
Q
R
S
T
U
V
W
X
Y
Z

Sexual Abuse

alt.sexual.abuse.recovery

A Usenet newsgroup providing information and discussion about sexual abuse recovery and helping others deal with traumatic experiences.

Keywords: Sexual Abuse, Psychotherapy

Audience: Victims of Sexual Abuse

User Info: To subscribe to this Usenet newsgroup, you need access to a newsreader.

`news:alt.sexual.abuse.recovery`

Sexual Orientation

Alternates

A mailing list for people who advocate and practice an open sexual lifestyle. Its members are primarily bisexual people and their significant others. It serves as a forum and support group for adult men and women who espouse their freedom of choice and imagination in human sexual relations, no matter what their orientaion.

Keywords: Sexuality, Bisexuality, Sexual Orientation

Audience: Bisexuals, General Public

Contact: alternates-request@ns1.rutgers.edu

User Info: To subscribe to the list, send an e-mail message requesting a subscription to the URL address below. To send a message to the entire list, address it to: alternates@ns1.rutgers.edu

`mailto:alternates-request@ns1.rutgers.edu`

Bisexu-L

This list is for the discussion of issues of bisexuality and the civilized exchange of relevant ideas, opinions, and experiences between members of all orientations. There is no discrimination on the basis of orientation, religion, gender, race, and so on.

Keywords: Bisexuality, Sexual Orientation

Audience: Bisexuals, General Public

Contact: Bill Sklar
listserv@brownvm.brown.edu

Details: Free

User Info: To subscribe to the list, send an e-mail message to the URL address below, consisting of a single line reading:

SUB Bisexu-L YourFirstName YourLastName

To send a message to the entire list, address it to: bisexu-l@brownvm.brown.edu

`mailto:listserv@brownvm.brown.edu`

Sexuality

Alternates

A mailing list for people who advocate and practice an open sexual lifestyle. Its members are primarily bisexual people and their significant others. It serves as a forum and support group for adult men and women who espouse their freedom of choice and imagination in human sexual relations, no matter what their orientaion.

Keywords: Sexuality, Bisexuality, Sexual Orientation

Audience: Bisexuals, General Public

Contact: alternates-request@ns1.rutgers.edu

User Info: To subscribe to the list, send an e-mail message requesting a subscription to the URL address below. To send a message to the entire list, address it to: alternates@ns1.rutgers.edu

`mailto:alternates-request@ns1.rutgers.edu`

AUGLBC-I

The American University Gay, Lesbian, and Bisexual Community (AUGLBC) is a support group for lesbian, gay, bisexual, transsexual, and supportive students. The group is also connected with the International Gay and Lesbian Youth Organization (known as IGLYO).

Keywords: Gay, Lesbian, Bisexual, Transsexual, Sexuality

Audience: Gays, Lesbians, Bisexuals, Transsexuals, Students (college)

Contact: Erik G. Paul

User Info: To subscribe to the list, send an e-mail message to the URL address below, consisting of a single line reading:

SUB AUGLBC-I YourFirstName YourLastName

To send a message to the entire list, address it to: AUGLBC-I@american.edu

`mailto:listserv@american.edu`

Cd-Forum

The purpose of this list is to provide support and to discuss/share experiences about gender-related issues, including cross dressing, transvestism, and transsexualism.

Keywords: Transsexualism, Transvestism, Sexuality, Gender

Audience: Transsexuals, Transvestites

Contact: Valerie
cd-request@valis.biocad.com

Details: Free

User Info: To subscribe to the list, send an e-mail message requesting a subscription to the URL address below. To send a message to the entire list, address it to: cd@valis.biocad.com

Notes: This list is in digest format.

`mailto:cd-request@valis.biocad.com`

dont-tell

The don't-tell list is for people concerned about the effects that the new military policy known as "don't ask/don't tell" will have at academic institutions, whether military or ROTC-affiliated.

Keywords: Sexuality, Military Policy, Education (Post-Secondary)

Audience: Students, Gays, Lesbians, Military Personnel, Civil Libertarians

Contact: dont-tell-request@choice.princeton.edu

Details: Free

User Info: To subscribe to the list, send an e-mail message requesting a subscription to the URL address below. To send a message to the entire list, address it to: dont-tell-request@choice.princeton.edu

`mailto:dont-tell-request@choice.princeton.edu`

gegstaff

All topics relating to sexuality and gender in geography.

Keywords: Geography, Sexuality

Audience: Geographers, Sex Enthusiasts

Details: Free

User Info: To subscribe to the list, send an e-mail message to the URL address shown below consisting of a single line reading:

SUB gegstaff YourFirstName YourLastName

To send a message to the entire list, address it to: gegstaff@ukcc.uky.edu

`mailto:listserv@ukcc.uky.edu`

Shakers

Shakers

A forum on the United Society of Believers for those interested in the history, culture, artifacts, and beliefs of the Shakers (United Society of Believers). Discussions cover a broad range of subject matter.

Keywords: Shakers, Christianity, Religion

Audience: Shakers, Theologians

Contact: Marc Rhorer
rhorer@ukcc.uky.edu

Details: Free

User Info: To subscribe to the list, send an e-mail message to the URL address shown below consisting of a single line reading:

SUB shaker YourFirstName YourLastName

To send a message to the entire list, address it to: shaker@ukcc.uky.edu

`mailto:listserv@ukcc.uky.edu`

Shakespeare (William)

Dartmouth College Library

The library's holdings are large and wide-ranging and contain significant collections in many fields.

Keywords: American Calligraphy, Cervantes (Miguel de), Railroads, Polar Regions, Frost (Robert), Shakespeare (William), Spanish Plays

Audience: General Public, Researchers, Librarians, Document Delivery Professionals

Contact: Katharina Klemperer kathy.klemperer@dartmouth.edu

Details: Free

User Info: Expect: login, Send: wolfpac

`telnet://lib.dartmouth.edu`

McGill University, Montreal Canada, INFOMcGILL Library

The library's holdings are large and wide-ranging and contain significant collections in many fields.

Keywords: Architecture, Entomology, Biology, Science (History of), Medicine (History of), Napolean, Shakespeare (William)

Audience: Researchers, Students, General Public

Contact: Roy Miller ccrmmus@mcgillm (Bitnet) ccrmmus@musicm.mcgill.ca (Internet)

User Info: Expect: VM logo; Send: Enter; Expect: prompt; Send: PF3 or type INFO

`telnet:// vm1.mcgill.ca`

University of Pennsylvania PENNINFO Library

The library's holdings are large and wide-ranging and contain significant collections in many fields.

Keywords: Church History, Spanish Inquisition, Witchcraft, Shakespeare (William), Bibles, Aristotle (Texts of), Fiction, Whitman (Walt), French Revolution, Drama (French), Literature (English), Literature (Spanish)

Audience: Researchers, Students, General Public

Contact: Al DSouza penninfo-admin@dccs.upenn.edu dsouza@dccs.upenn.edu

Details: Free

User Info: Expect: Login; Send: Public

`telnet://penninfo.upenn.edu`

Shamash, The New York - Israel Project

Shamash, The New York - Israel Project

This site is designed to facilitate communications between Jews and Jewish organizations through the medium of the Internet. Information includes archives of Jewish lists, updates of community Jewish events in New York and beyond, a Jewish white pages, and a section on the Holocaust. It also has Hebrew software and access to other Jewish and Israeli information servers.

Keywords: Judaism, Israel, New York

Sponsor: New York - Israel Project (Nysernet), New York, USA

Audience: Jews, Jewish Organizations

Contact: Avrum Goodblatt, Chaim Dworkin goodblat@israel.nysernet.org chaim@israel.nysernet.org.

`gopher://nysernet.org`

Shareware

Apple Computer WWW Server

A web site containing information about Apple Computer. The resource is designed to provide timely product information, including press releases on Apple's technology and research. Also contains links to Freeware and Shareware sites, and includes information for developers and programmers.

Keywords: Computer Systems, Technology, Apple Computer, Shareware

Audience: General Public

`http://www.apple.com`

fsuucp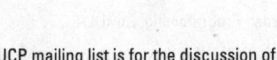

The FSUUCP mailing list is for the discussion of bug hunting, feature proposing, and announcements of the availability and release dates of FSUUCP, an MS-DOS UUCP/mail/ news package.

Keywords: Software, Shareware

Audience: Students, Computer Users

Details: Free

User Info: To subscribe to the list, send an e-mail message requesting a subscription to the URL address below. To send a message to the entire list, address it to: fsuucp@polyslo.calpoly.edu

`mailto:fsuucp-request@polyslo.calpoly.edu`

GNUs Bulletin: Newsletter of the Free Software Foundation

Bringing you news about the GNU Project, the Free Software Foundation is dedicated to eliminating restrictions on copying, redistribution, understanding, and modification of computer programs.

Keywords: Software, Shareware, Free Software

Sponsor: Free Software Foundation

Audience: Computer Programmers, Computer Users

Contact: Leonard H. Tower, Jr. tower@ai.mit.edu

Details: Free

`mailto:info-gnu-request@prep.ai.mit.edu`

HYTELNET

A shareware application database directory to libraries.

Keywords: Computer Systems, Libraries, Shareware

Audience: General Audience

Profile: HYTELNET is a guide to library catalogs from the Americas, Europe

Contact: Peter Scott aa375@freenet.carleton.ca

Details: Free

Notes: HYTELNET is in English, but the interface to some international

`gopher://gophlib@gopher.yale.edu`

info-GNU-MSDOS

This electronic conference is for the GNUISH MS-DOS Development Group.

Keywords: Shareware, Freeware, MS-DOS Computers

Audience: MS-DOS Users, GNUISH MS-DOS Developers

Contact: David J. Camp david@wubios.wustl.edu

Details: Free

User Info: To subscribe to the list, send an e-mail message to the URL address below consisting of a single line reading:

SUB info-GNU-MSDOS YourFirstName YourLastName

`mailto:listserv@wugate.wustl.edu`

A B C D E F G H I J K L M N O P Q R **S** T U V W X Y Z

A
B
C
D
E
F
G
H
I
J
K
L
M
N
O
P
Q
R
S
T
U
V
W
X
Y
Z

ShareWord

Online BookStore (OBS)

Offers full text (fiction and nonfiction) in a variety of electronic formats, free and for a fee.

Keywords: Online Books, Books, ShareWord, Fiction, Nonfiction Books

Sponsor: Editorial Inc./OBS

Audience: General Public, Reading Enthusiasts

Profile: Started in 1992, the OBS offers a variety of full-text titles.

Contact: Laura Fillmore
laura@editorial.com

Details: Costs, Moderated, Images, Multimedia

User Info: To subscribe to the list, send an e-mail message requesting a subscription to the URL address below.

`mailto:laura@editorial.com`

Shopping

The Branch Mall, an Electronic Shopping Mall

Branch Information Services offers shopping to customers and leases storefronts and electronic catalogs to vendors.

Keywords: Mall, Shopping, Gifts, Advertising, Mailorder

Sponsor: Branch Information Services

Audience: Consumers, Merchants

Contact: Jon Zeeff
jon@branch.com

Details: Free

Notes: Free for consumers.

`http://branch.com`

Shortwave Radio

Drake-R8

To discuss and share experiences, technical issues, problems, and so on, related to the Drake R8 shortwave receiver.

Keywords: Shortwave Radio

Audience: Shortwave Radio Users

Contact: Mik Butler
mik@hpsesuka.pwd.hp.com

User Info: To subscribe to the list, send an e-mail message requesting a subscription to the URL address below. To send a message to the entire list, address it to: mik@hpsesuka.pwd.hp.com

`mailto:mik@hpsesuka.pwd.hp.com`

Silicon Graphics

Virtual Reality Space

A collection of virtual reality information, including downloadable software tools from Silicon Graphics.

Keywords: Virtual Reality, Cyberspace, Software, Silicon Graphics

Sponsor: The University of Texas, Austin, Texas, USA

Audience: Virtual Reality Enthusiasts, Programmers

Contact: Jay Ashcraft
ashcraft@ccwf.cc.utexas.edu

`gopher://ftp.cc.utexas.edu`

`ftp://cc.utexas.edu`

Sim (Dave)

Cerebi

This list discusses the Cerebus comic book by Dave Sim. Anything relating to Cerebus or Sim is welcome.

Keywords: Comic Books, Sim (Dave)

Audience: Comics Enthusiasts

Contact: Christian Walters
cerebi-request@tomservo.b23b.ingr.com

Details: Free

User Info: To subscribe to the list, send an e-mail message requesting a subscription to the URL address below. To send a message to the entire list, address it to: cerebi@tomservo.b23b.ingr.com

Notes: It's just an echo list, so anything that gets mailed is bounced to everyone.

`mailto:cerebi-request@tomservo.b23b.ingr.com`

SIMULA

Simula

An electronic conference for discussion of the SIMULA programming language.

Keywords: Programming, SIMULA

Audience: SIMULA Programmers

Details: Free

User Info: To subscribe to the list, send an e-mail message to the URL address below consisting of a single line reading:

SUB Simula YourFirstName YourLastName

To send a message to the entire list, address it to: Simula@bitnic.educom.edu

`mailto:listserv@bitnic.educom.edu`

Simulation

Anneal

A mailing list for the discussion of simulated annealing techniques and analysis, as well as related issues such as stochastic optimization, Boltzmann machines, and metricity of NP-complete move spaces.

Keywords: Mathematics, Simulation, Annealing

Sponsor: UCLA

Audience: Mathematicians, Physicists

Contact: Daniel R. Greening
anneal-request@cs.ucla.edu

User Info: To subscribe to the list, send an e-mail message to the URL address below. To send a message to the entire list, address it to: anneal@cs.ucla.edu

Notes: Membership is restricted to those doing active research in simulated annealing or related areas.

`mailto:anneal-request@cs.ucla.edu`

Aviator

A mailing list for users of Aviator™, the flight-simulation program from Artificial Horizons, Inc.

Keywords: Aviation, Simulation, Computers, Flight Simulation

Audience: Software Users

Contact: Jim Hickstein
aviator@ICDwest.Teradyne.COM

Details: Free

User Info: To subscribe to the list, send an e-mail message requesting a subscription to the URL address below. To send a message to the entire list, address it to: aviator@ICDwest.Teradyne.COM

Notes: Aviator runs on Sun workstations with the GX graphics accelerator option. Its charter is simply to facilitate communication among users of Aviator. It is not intended for communication with the "providers" of Aviator. All mail received at the submission address is reflected to all the subscribers of the list.

`mailto:aviator-request@ICDwest.Teradyne.COM`

GLOSAS News (Global Systems Analysis and Simulating Association)

Newsletter of GLOSAS in the US, which is dedicated to global electronic education and simulation as a tool for promoting peace and the care of the natural environment.

Keywords: Education, Simulation, Peace

Audience: Educators, Environmentalists

Contact: Anton Ljutic
anton@vax2.concordia.ca

Details: Free

`mailto:listserv@vm1.mcgill.ca`

Interactive Frog Dissection Kit

An interactive simulation of the dissection of a computer-generated frog.

Keywords: Biology, Simulation, Interactive Learning

Sponsor: Lawrence Berkeley Laboratory-Whole Frog Project, Berkeley, California, USA

Audience: Students, Educators, Biologists

Contact: David Robertson
dwrobertson@lbl.gov

Notes: Copyrighted (commercial uses require permission)

`http://george.1b1.gov/ITG.hm.pg.docs/ dissect/info.html`

Singapore

Business News—Singapore

This gopher site focuses on business in Singapore.

Keywords: Singapore, Economics, Business

Audience: Economists, Business Professionals

Details: Free

`gopher://gopher.cic.net/11/e-serials/ alphabetic/b/business-news`

`http://gopher.cic.net`

Singapore DMC

Singapore DMC

The Digital Media Center (DMC) home page contains links related to contents about Singapore, the National Computer Board (NCB), and various other National IT (Information Technology) projects.

Keywords: Internet, Networking

Audience: Internet Surfers

Contact: shaopin@ncb.gov.sg
kianjin@ncb.gov.sg

Details: Free

`http://king.ncb.gov.sg`

Singing

Chorus

This is the lesbian and gay chorus mailing list, formed November 1991 by John Schrag (jschrag@aliac.com) and Brian Jarvis (jarvis@psych.toronto.edu). Membership includes artistic directors, singers, chorus officers, interpreters, and support staff and friends. Topics of discussion include repertoire, arrangements, staging, costuming, management, fundraising, music, events, and concerts.

Keywords: Singing, Choral Singing, Homosexuality, Gay, Lesbian

Audience: Lesbian Singers, Gay Singers, Chorus Officers, Lesbians, Gays, Choral Singers

Contact: chorus-request@psych.toronto.edu

Details: Free

User Info: To subscribe to the list, send an e-mail message requesting a subscription to the URL address below. To send a message to the entire list, address it to: chorus@psych.toronto.edu

`mailto:chorus- request@psych.toronto.edu`

Singles

alt.personals.ads

A Usenet newsgroup providing a forum for singles.

Keywords: Personals, Singles

Audience: Singles

User Info: To subscribe to this Usenet newsgroup, you need access to a newsreader.

`news:alt.personals.ads`

Soc.singles

A Usenet newsgroup for single people discussing their activities and social events.

Keywords: Singles

Audience: Single People

To participate in a Usenet newsgroup you need access to a 'newsreader.'

`news:soc.singles`

Skiing

rec.skiing

A Usenet newsgroup providing information and discussion about skiing.

Keywords: Sports, Recreation, Skiing

Audience: Skiers

User Info: To subscribe to this Usenet newsgroup, you need access to a newsreader.

`news:rec.skiing`

Skiing in Utah

An FTP site maintaining information on skiing sites in Utah, Idaho, and Wyoming.

Keywords: Sports, Skiing

Sponsor: Utah University

Audience: Skiers

Details: Free

`ftp://ski.utah.edu/skiing`

Skin

rxderm-l

A mailing list intended for promoting the discussion of dermatologic treatment among practicing dermatologists.

Keywords: Dermatology, Skin, Disease, Doctors

Audience: Dermatologists

Contact: A.C. Huntley
achuntley@ucdavis.edu

User Info: To subscribe to the list, send an e-mail message to the URL address below consisting of a single line reading:

SUB rxderm-l YourFirstName YourLastName

To send a message to the entire list, address it to: rxderm-l@ucdavis.edu

`mailto:listserv@ucdavis.edu`

Skydiving

Base-Jumping

An open discussion of fixed-object skydiving. Topics include equipment, sites, packing techniques, and publications.

Keywords: Skydiving

Audience: Skydivers

Contact: base-request@lunatix.lex.ky.us

Details: Free

User Info: To subscribe to the list, send an e-mail message requesting a subscription to the URL address below. To send a message to the entire list, address it to: base@lunatix.lex.ky.us

Notes: Membership is open to anyone who has made at least one base jump or skydive.

`mailto:base-request@lunatix.lex.ky.us`

A B C D E F G H I J K L M N O P Q R S T U V W X Y Z

A
B
C
D
E
F
G
H
I
J
K
L
M
N
O
P
Q
R
S
T
U
V
W
X
Y
Z

Usenet Sports Groups Archived

An archive for Usenet groups, including many related to sports ranging from football to table tennis.

Keywords: Sports, Skydiving, Volleyball, Football, Scuba Diving, Table Tennis

Sponsor: Massachusetts Institute of Technology, Boston, MA

Audience: Sports Enthusiasts

Contact: ftp-bugs@rtfm.mit.edu

Details: Free

`ftp://rtfm.mit.edu/pub/usenet`

Slavery

Johns Hopkins University Library

★★

The library's holdings are large and wide-ranging and contain significant collections in many fields.

Keywords: Literature (English), Economics, Classics, Drama (German), Slavery, Trade Unions, Incunabula, Bibles, Diseases (History of), Nursing (History of), Abolitionism

Audience: General Public, Researchers, Librarians, Document Delivery Professionals

Details: Free

`telnet://jhuvm.hcf.jhu.edu`

The University of Illinois at Chicago Library

★★

The library's holdings are large and wide-ranging and contain significant collections in many fields.

Keywords: Health Science, Chicago, Industry, Slavery, Abolitionism, Roosevelt (Franklin D.)

Audience: General Public, Researchers, Librarians, Document Delivery Professionals

Details: Free

User Info: Expect: introductory screen, Send: Clear key; Expect: UIC flame screen, Send: Enter key; Expect: Logon screen, Send: DIAL PVM; Expect: PVM (Passthru) screen, Send: Type: Move cursor to NOTIS and press Enter key Response: One line message about port in use Type: Enter key

`telnet://uicvm.uic.edu`

SLON

Oglasna Deska

Oglasna Deska (bulletin board) consists of transcripts taken from SLON, which is a nickname for a Decnet connecting several computers in Slovenia. There is a conference similar to a Usenet newsgroup running under SLON and the articles and replies are occasionally saved and sent to the world. The topics cover a wide area.

Keywords: Slovenia, SLON, Usenet Newsgroup

Audience: Slovenians, Croatians, Serbians

Contact: Dean Mozetic
Oglasna-Deska@krpan.arnes.si

Details: Free

User Info: To subscribe to the list, send an e-mail message requesting a subscription to the URL address below. To send a message to the entire list, address it to: oglasna-deka@krpan.arnes.si

Notes: The topics covered are equivalent to Usenet newsgroups such as politics, automobiles, humor, computer networks, climbing, and miscellaneous investments.

`mailto:Oglasna-Deska@krpan.arnes.si`

Slovak Republic

University of Nebraska at Lincoln Library

★★

The library's holdings are large and wide-ranging and contain significant collections in many fields.

Keywords: Slovak Republic, Czech Republic, Folklore, Military History, Latvia, Law (Tax), Law (US)

Audience: General Public, Researchers, Librarians, Document Delivery Professionals

Contact: Anita Cook

Details: Free

User Info: Expect: login, Send: library

`telnet://unllib.unl.edu`

Slovakia

CEE Environmental Libraries Database

A directory of over 300 libraries and environmental information centers in Central Eastern Europe that specalize in, or maintain significant collections of information about, the environment, ecology, sustainable living, or conservation. The database concentrates on six Central Eastern European countries: Bulgaria, Czech Republic, Hungary, Romania, Slovakia, and Poland.

Keywords: Central Eastern Europe, Environment, Sustainable Living, Bulgaria, Czech Republic, Hungary, Romania, Slovakia, Poland.

Sponsor: The Wladyslaw Poniecki Charitable Foundation, Inc.

Audience: Environmentalists, Green Movement, Librarians, Community Builders, Sustainable Living Specialists.

Profile: This database is the product of an Environmental Training Project (ETP) that was funded in 1992 by the US Agency for International Development as a 5-year cooperative agreement with a consortium headed by the University of Minnesota (US AID Cooperative Agreement Number EUR-0041-A-002-2020). Other members of the consortium include the University of Pittsburgh's Center for Hazardous Materials Research, The Institute for Sustainable Communities, and the World Wildlife Fund. The Wladyslaw Poniecki Charitable Foundation, Inc., was a subcontractor to the World Wildlife Fund and published the Directory of Libraries and Environmental Information Centers in Central Eastern Europe: A Locator/ Directory . This gopher database consists of an electronic version of the printed directory, subsequently modified and updated online. Access to the data is facilitated by a WAIS search engine which makes it possible to retrieve information about libraries, subject area specializations, personnel, and so on.

Contact: Doug Kahn, CEDAR
kahn@pan.cedar.univie.ac.at

`gopher://gopher.poniecki.berkeley.edu`

slovak-l

A mailing list for discussion of Slovak culture, and more.

Keywords: Slovakia, Culture

Audience: Researchers, Students, Slovaks

Contact: Jan George Frajkor
gfrajkor@ccs.carleton.ca

User Info: To subscribe to the list, send an e-mail message to the URL address below consisting of a single line reading:

SUB slovak-l YourFirstName YourLastName

To send a message to the entire list, address it to: slovak-1@ubvm.cc.buffalo.edu

`mailto:listserv@ubvm.cc.buffalo.edu`

Slovenia

Novice MZT

Novize MZT (News of Ministry for Science and Technology of the Republic of Slovenia) provides easy, accessible news about science, development, universities, and innovative activities to individuals and institutions in research and development areas. Published at least once monthly.

Keywords: Slovenia, Science, Technology, News

Audience: Slovenians, Scientists, Technocrats

Contact: Novice-mzt@krpan.arnes.si or
Novice.mzt@uni-lj.si

User Info: To subscribe to the list, send an e-mail message requesting a subscription to the URL address below. To send a message to the entire list, address it to: Novice-mzt@krpan.arnes.si

```
mailto:Novice-MZT@krpan.arnes.si
```

Oglasna Deska

Oglasna Deska (bulletin board) consists of transcripts taken from SLON, which is a nickname for a Decnet connecting several computers in Slovenia. There is a conference similar to a Usenet newsgroup running under SLON and the articles and replies are occasionally saved and sent to the world. The topics cover a wide area.

Keywords: Slovenia, SLON, Usenet Newsgroup

Audience: Slovenians, Croatians, Serbians

Contact: Dean Mozetic
Oglasna-Deska@krpan.arnes.si

Details: Free

User Info: To subscribe to the list, send an e-mail message requesting a subscription to the URL address below. To send a message to the entire list, address it to: oglasna-deka@krpan.arnes.si

Notes: The topics covered are equivalent to Usenet newsgroups such as politics, automobiles, humor, computer networks, climbing, and miscellaneous investments.

```
mailto:Oglasna-Deska@krpan.arnes.si
```

Pisma Bralcev

An edited mailing list that publishes readers' opinions, questions, inquiries for help, answers, and so on, in Slovene. Also includes travel tips and book reviews.

Keywords: Slovenia

Audience: Slovenians

Contact: Andrej Brodnik
Pisma-Bralcev@krpan.arnes.si

Details: Free

User Info: To subscribe to the list, send an e-mail message requesting a subscription to the URL address below. To send a message to the entire list, address it to: pisma-bralcev@krpan.arnes.si

```
mailto:Pisma-Bralcev@krpan.arnes.si
mailto:Pisma.Bralcev@uni-lj.si
```

Small Business

Esbdc-l

A mailing list intended to facilitate discussion between small business development centers, focusing on such topics as performance standards, business behavior, products, specific industry information access, deficit reduction plans, and private cost sharing.

Keywords: Business, Small Business

Sponsor: Association of Small Business Development Centers, USA

Audience: State Officials, Educators, Certified Public Accountants, Investors

User Info: To subscribe to the list, send an e-mail message to the URL address below consisting of a single line reading:

SUB esbdc-l YourFirstName YourLastName

To send a message to the entire list, address it to: esbdc-l@ferris.bitnet

```
mailto:listserv@ferris.bitnet
```

Smbnet (Society for Mathematical Biology Digest)

Smbnet (Society for Mathematical Biology Digest)

Keywords: Mathematical Biology, Biology

Audience: Mathematical Biologists, Biologists

Contact: Ray Mejia

Details: Free

User Info: To subscribe to the list, send an e-mail message to the URL address below consisting of a single line reading:

SUB smbnet YourFirstName YourLastName

To send a message to the entire list, address it to: smbnet@fconvx.ncifcrf.gov

```
mailto:listserv@fconvx.ncifcrf.gov
```

Smiley Faces Dictionary

Smiley Faces Dictionary

An unofficial list of more than 200 smilies.

Keywords: Internet, Smiley

Audience: Internet Surfers

Details: Free

User Info: File is pub/smiley-dictionary

```
http://ftp.gsfc.nasa.gov
```

Smithsonian

Smithsonian Institution Natural History Gopher

The Smithsonian Natural History Gopher server provides access to data associated with the Institutions museum collections (natural history and anthropology).

Keywords: Smithsonian, Natural History, Anthropology

Sponsor: Museum of Natural History, Smithsonian Institution, Washington, DC.

Audience: Anthropologists, Biologists, Natural History Scientists, Researchers

Profile: With over 120 million collections and 135 professional scientists, the National Museum of Natural History is one of the worlds largest museums devoted to natural history and anthropology. This server provides access to data associated with the collections, and to information and tools for the study of the natural world. The Department of Vertebrate Zoology includes checklists of known species names. Currently the Mammal Species of the World have been posted. Plans to expand this to include Amphibians, Fishes, and so on. are under way.

Contact: Don Gourley
don@smithson.si.edu

Details: Free

```
gopher://nmnhgoph.si.edu
```

Smithsonian Online

Located on America Online (with partial access by ftp), this allows online access to the Institution's resources.

Keywords: Museums, Art Exhibitions, Smithsonian

Sponsor: Smithsonian Institution, Washington DC

Audience: Educators, Students, General Public

A B C D E F G H I J K L M N O P Q R S T U V W X Y Z

A B C D E F G H I J K L M N O P Q R **S** T U V W X Y Z

Profile: Smithsonian Online includes resources for teachers and students in the form of bulletin boards about Smithsonian museums, photographs, listings of events in Washington and other communities, and excerpts from Smithsonian and Air & Space/ Smithsonian.

`ftp://photo1.si.edu`

Smoking

Pipes

A forum for discussing the moderate use and appreciation of fine tobacco, including cigars, pipes, quality cigarettes, pipe making and carving, snuff, publications, and related topics.

Keywords: Pipes, Tobacco, Smoking

Audience: Smokers, Researchers, Market Analysts

Contact: Steve Masticola
masticol@scr.siemens.com

Details: Free, Moderated

User Info: To subscribe to the list, send an e-mail message requesting a subscription to the URL address below. To send a message to the entire list, address it to: masticol@scr.siemens.com

`mailto:masticol@scr.siemens.com`

soc.history

soc.history

A Usenet newsgroup providing information and discussion about historical issues.

Keywords: History (World)

Audience: Historians

Details: Free

User Info: To subscribe to this Usenet newsgroup, you need access to a newsreader.

`news:soc.history`

soc.men

soc.men

A Usenet newsgroup providing information and discussion about men, their problems, and their relationships.

Keywords: Men's Movement, Gender

Audience: Men, Activists

Details: Free

User Info: To subscribe to this Usenet newsgroup, you need access to a newsreader.

`news:soc.men`

soc.motss

soc.motss

A Usenet newsgroup providing information and discussion about homosexuality.

Keywords: Homosexuality, Gays, Lesbians, Bisexuals

Audience: Gays, Lesbians, Bisexuals

Details: Free

User Info: To subscribe to this Usenet newsgroup, you need access to a newsreader.

`news:soc.motss`

soc.penpals

soc.penpals

A Usenet newsgroup providing information and discussion for people in search of Net pals and other online correspondence.

Keywords: Computing, Writing

Audience: Computer Users, Writers

Details: Free

User Info: To subscribe to this Usenet newsgroup, you need access to a newsreader.

`news:soc.penpals`

soc.religion.christian

soc.religion.christian

A Usenet newsgroup providing information and discussion about Christianity and related issues.

Keywords: Christianity, Religion

Audience: Christians, Theologians

Details: Free

User Info: To subscribe to this Usenet newsgroup, you need access to a newsreader.

`news:soc.religion.christian`

Soc.singles

Soc.singles

A Usenet newsgroup for single people discussing their activities and social events.

Keywords: Singles

Audience: Single People

To participate in a Usenet newsgroup you need access to a 'newsreader.'

`news:soc.singles`

Soccer

france-foot

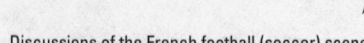

Discussions of the French football (soccer) scene. Results and news are posted regularly.

Keywords: Soccer, Sports, France, Football

Audience: Soccer Enthusiasts, French Sports Enthusiasts

Contact: Vincent Habchi, Kent Hedlundh
dvlkhh@cs.umu.se

Details: Free

User Info: To subscribe to the list, send an e-mail message requesting a subscription to the URL address below. To send a message to the entire list, address it to: france-foot@inf.enst.fr

`mailto:france-foot-request@inf.enst.fr`

rec.sport.soccer

A Usenet newsgroup providing information and discussion about soccer.

Keywords: Soccer, Sports

Audience: Soccer Fans, Sports Fans

User Info: To subscribe to this Usenet newsgroup, you need access to a newsreader.

`news:rec.sport.soccer`

University of Glasgow Information Service (GLANCE)

GLANCE provides subject-based information services, including an extensive section on European and world sports.

Keywords: Sports, Soccer, Motor Racing, Mountaineering, Squash, Cricket, Golf, Tennis, Europe, Scotland

Sponsor: University of Glasgow, Glasgow, Scotland

Audience: Sport Enthusiasts, Fitness Enthusiasts, Nature Lovers

Profile: Information at this site includes schedules, results, and statistics for sports such as cricket and soccer. There is also a selection of items on mountaineering.

Contact: Alan Dawson
A.Dawson@uk.ac.gla.compserv

Details: Free

`gopher://govan.cent.gla.ac.uk/`
`Subject/Sports and Rec`

Wiretap Sports Archives

Sports articles, including information on soccer in the US and Canada, rules for soccer and Australian football, and some rather dated material on American football.

Keywords: Sports, Football, Soccer

Sponsor: The Internet Wiretap Library

Audience: Sports Enthusiasts

Details: Free

`gopher://wiretap.spies.com/library/`
`article/sports`

Social and Behavioral Science

soc.bi

A Usenet newsgroup providing information and discussion about bisexuality.

Keywords: Bisexuality, Social and Behavioral Science

Audience: Bisexuals, Bisexual Activists, Sociologists, Social Scientists

Details: Free

User Info: To subscribe to this Usenet newsgroup, you need access to a newsreader.

`news:soc.bi`

Social Events

Ne-social-motss

Announcements of lesbian/gay/bisexual social events and other happenings in the Northeastern US.

Keywords: Social Events, Lesbian, Gay, Bisexuality

Audience: Lesbians, Gays, Bisexuals

Contact: ne-social-motss-request@plts.org

Details: Free

User Info: To subscribe to the list, send an e-mail message requesting a subscription to the URL address below.

`mailto:ne-social-motss-`
`request@plts.org`

Social Law

Universite de Montreal UDEMATIK Library

The library's holdings are large and wide-ranging and contain significant collections in many fields.

Keywords: Art, Architecture, Economy, Sexology, Social Law, Science, Technology, Literary Studies

Audience: Researchers, Students, General Public

Contact: Joelle or Sebastien Roy
udematik@ere.umontreal.ca
stemp@ere.umontreal.ca
roys@ere.umontreal.ca

User Info: Expect: Login; Send: Application id INFO

`telnet://udematik.umontreal.ca`

Social Responsibility

CPSR/PDX Newsletter

This is the newsletter of the Portland chapter of Computer Professionals for Social Responsibility.

Keywords: Computer Professionals, Social Responsibility

Audience: Computer Professionals

Contact: Erik Nilsson
erin@goldfish.mitron.tek.com

Details: Free

`mailto:erikn@goldfish.mitron.tek.com`

Social Science

CUSSNET

Computer Users in the Social Sciences (CUSS) is a discussion group devoted to issues of interest to social workers, counselors, and human service workers of all disciplines. The discussion frequently involves computer applications in treatment, agency administration, and research. Students, faculty, community-based professionals, and casual observers join in the discussion. Software, hardware, and ethical issues associated with their use in the human services generate lively and informative discussions.

Keywords: Social Sciences, Computers, Computer Applications

Audience: Social Workers, Human Services Workers, General Public

Contact: cussnet-request@stat.com

Details: Free

User Info: To subscribe to the list, send an e-mail message to the address below consisting of a single line reading:

SUB cussnet YourFirstName YourLastName

To send a message to the entire list, address it to: cussnet@stat.com

`mailto:listserv@stat.com`

Eastern Washington University Library

The library's holdings are large and wide-ranging and contain significant collections in many fields.

Keywords: Education, Music, Social Science, Behavioral Science

Audience: Researchers, Students, General Public

Details: Free

User Info: Expect: Login; Send: Lib

`telnet://wsduvm12.csc.wsu.edu`

Rezo, bulletin irregulomadaire du RQSS

E-newsletter of RQSS (Regroupement Quebecois des Sciences Sociales) is open to anyone interested in social science research in Quebec and/or about Quebec.

Keywords: Quebec, Social Science

Audience: Social Scientists

Contact: Pierre J. Hamel
HAMEL@INRS-URB.UQUEBEC.CA

Details: Free

User Info: To subscribe, send an e-mail message to the URL address below, consisting of a single line reading:

SUB rezo YourFirstName YourLastName

To send a message to the entire list, address it to: rezo@uquebec.ca

`mailto:listserv@uquebec.ca`

soc.college

A Usenet newsgroup providing information and discussion about college life, activities, campus, and so on.

Keywords: Sociology, Social Science, Education (College/University)

Audience: Sociologists, Social Scientists, Educators (College/University), Students (College/University)

Details: Free

User Info: To subscribe to this Usenet newsgroup, you need access to a newsreader.

`news:soc.college`

Washington University Library

The library's holdings are large and wide-ranging and contain significant collections in many fields.

Keywords: Technology, Literature (German), Social Science, Behavioral Science

Audience: Researchers, Students, General Public

Contact: services@wugate.wustl.edu

Details: Free

User Info: Expect: Login; Send: Services

`telnet://wugate.wustl.edu`

A
B
C
D
E
F
G
H
I
J
K
L
M
N
O
P
Q
R
S
T
U
V
W
X
Y
Z

Social Science and Humanities—Australia

COOMBSQUEST Social Sciences and Humanities Information Facility

This is the worldwide Social Sciences and Humanities Information Service of the Coombs Computing Unit, Research Schools of Social Sciences and Pacific Studies, Australian National University, Canberra, Australia.

Keywords: Social Science Humanities Australia

Sponsor: Australian National University

Audience: Social Scientists, Humanists, Researchers, Educators, Students

Profile: COOMBSQUEST provides direct access to the Coombspapers Social Sciences Research Data Bank. The databank was established in December 1991 to act as the world's major electronic repository of social science and humanities papers, and other high-grade research material dealing with Australia, the Pacific region, and Southeast and Northeast Asia, Buddhism, Taoism, and other Oriental religions.

Contact: T. Matthew Ciolek
tmciolek@coombs.anu.edu.au

Details: Free

`gopher://coombs.anu.edu.au`

`http://combs.anu.edu.au./CoombsHome.html`

Social Work

University of Texas at Austin Library

The library's holdings are large and wide-ranging and contain significant collections in many fields.

Keywords: Music, Natural Science, Nursing, Science Technology, Behavioral Science, Social Work, Computer Science, Engineering, Latin American Studies, Middle Eastern Studies

Audience: Researchers, Students, General Public

Details: Free

User Info: Expect: Blank Screen, Send: Return; Expect: Go, Send: Return; Expect: Enter Terminal Type, Send: vt100

Note: Some databases are restricted to UT Austin users only.

`telnet://utcat.utexas.edu`

Society

Aids

A forum for the discussion of AIDS, predominantly from a medical perspective, but also with some discussion of political and social issues.

Keywords: AIDS, Medicine, Politics, Society

Sponsor: UCLA

Audience: AIDS Researchers, AIDS Activists, Health Care Providers

Contact: Daniel R. Greening
aids-request@cs.ucla.edu

User Info: To subscribe to the list, send an e-mail message to the URL address below. To send a message to the entire list, address it to: aids@cs.ucla.edu

`mailto:aids-request@cs.ucla.edu`

SOCINSCT (Social Insect Biology Research List)

SOCINSCT (Social Insect Biology Research List)

SOCINSCT is dedicated to communication among investigators active in the discipline of social insect biology.

Keywords: Biology, Insect Biology

Audience: Biologists, Researchers (college, graduate)

Profile: It is restricted to discussions of research at the university level. Social insects (bees, wasps, ants, and termites) are the main interest but information can include any area of sociobiology, or solitary bees and wasps. Such areas could include: orientation, navigation, adaptation/selection/evolution, superorganism concept, behavior, physiology and biochemistry, pheromones, flight and energetics, taxonomy and systematics, ecology, genetics, pollination, and nectar/pollen biology. Announcements of meetings and professional opportunities, requests for research help, sharing of literature references, sharing research topics and discussion of ideas are welcome.

Contact: Erik Seielstad
erik@acspr1.acs.brockport.edu

Details: Free

User Info: To subscribe to the list, send an e-mail message to the address below consisting of a single line reading:

SUB socinsct YourFirstName YourLastName

To send message to the entire list, address it to: socinsct@albany.edu

`mailto:listserv@albany.edu`

Sociology

CRTNet (Communication Research and Theory Network)

All topics related to human communications.

Keywords: Communications, Sociology, Human Communications

Audience: Sociologists, Psychologists, Therapists

Contact: Tom Benson
t3b@psuvm.psu.edu

`mailto:listserv@psuvm.bitnet`

National Family Database—MAPP

This database contains family sociological and health data, including research briefs, bibliographies, census data, program ideas, reference materials, media materials, and publications.

Keywords: Sociology, Family, Health

Sponsor: Department of Agriculture Economics and Rural Sociology, Pennsylvania State University

Audience: Sociologists, Public Health Policymakers, Health Care Providers

To access the database select PENpages (1), then General Information (3) and finally Information on MAPP - National Family Database (5)

`telnet://penpages@psupen.psu.edu`

soc.college

A Usenet newsgroup providing information and discussion about college life, activities, campus, and so on.

Keywords: Sociology, Social Science, Education (College/University)

Audience: Sociologists, Social Scientists, Educators (College/University), Students (College/University)

Details: Free

User Info: To subscribe to this Usenet newsgroup, you need access to a newsreader.

`news:soc.college`

soc.culture.african.american

A Usenet newsgroup providing information and discussion about African American culture.

Keywords: African American Studies, Sociology, Minorities

Audience: Sociologists

Details: Free

User Info: To subscribe to this Usenet newsgroup, you need access to a newsreader.

news:soc.culture.african.american

soc.culture.arabic

⭐

A Usenet newsgroup providing information and discussion about Arabic culture and technologies.

Keywords: Sociology, Middle Eastern Studies

Audience: Sociologists

Details: Free

User Info: To subscribe to this Usenet newsgroup, you need access to a newsreader.

news:soc.culture.arabic

soc.culture.asian.american

⭐

A Usenet newsgroup providing information and discussion about Asian American culture.

Keywords: Asian American Studies, Sociology

Audience: Sociologists

Details: Free

User Info: To subscribe to this Usenet newsgroup, you need access to a newsreader.

news:soc.culture.asian.american

soc.culture.british

⭐

A Usenet newsgroup providing information and discussion about Britain and British culture.

Keywords: Sociology, United Kingdom

Audience: Sociologists

Details: Free

User Info: To subscribe to this Usenet newsgroup, you need access to a newsreader.

news:soc.culture.british

soc.culture.canada

⭐

A Usenet newsgroup providing information and discussion about Canada and its people.

Keywords: Culture, Canada, Sociology

Audience: Sociologists, Canadians

Details: Free

User Info: To subscribe to this Usenet newsgroup, you need access to a newsreader.

news:soc.culture.canada

soc.culture.celtic

⭐

A Usenet newsgroup providing information and discussion about Irish Scottish, Britain, and Cornish culture.

Keywords: Celtic Culture, Sociology

Audience: Sociologists, Celts

Details: Free

User Info: To subscribe to this Usenet newsgroup, you need access to a newsreader.

news:soc.culture.celtic

soc.culture.china

⭐

A Usenet newsgroup providing information and discussion about China and Chinese culture.

Keywords: China, Sociology

Audience: Sociologists, Chinese, Sinologists

Details: Free

User Info: To subscribe to this Usenet newsgroup, you need access to a newsreader.

news:soc.culture.china

soc.culture.europe

⭐

A Usenet newsgroup providing information and discussion about all aspects of Europe.

Keywords: Europe, Sociology

Audience: Sociologists, Europeans

Details: Free

User Info: To subscribe to this Usenet newsgroup, you need access to a newsreader.

news:soc.culture.europe

soc.culture.french

⭐

A Usenet newsgroup providing information and discussion about French culture and history.

Keywords: France, Sociology

Audience: Sociologists, Francophiles

Details: Free

User Info: To subscribe to this Usenet newsgroup, you need access to a newsreader.

news:soc.culture.french

soc.culture.german

⭐

A Usenet newsgroup providing information and discussion about German culture.

Keywords: Germany, Sociology

Audience: Sociologists, Germans

Details: Free

User Info: To subscribe to this Usenet newsgroup, you need access to a newsreader.

news:soc.culture.german

soc.culture.greek

⭐

A Usenet newsgroup providing information and discussion about Greek culture.

Keywords: Greece, Sociology

Audience: Sociologists, Greeks

Details: Free

User Info: To subscribe to this Usenet newsgroup, you need access to a newsreader.

news:soc.culture.greek

soc.culture.hongkong

⭐

A Usenet newsgroup providing information and discussion about Hong Kong and its people.

Keywords: Hong Kong, Sociology

Audience: Sociologists

Details: Free

User Info: To subscribe to this Usenet newsgroup, you need access to a newsreader.

news:soc.culture.hongkong

soc.culture.indian

⭐

A Usenet newsgroup providing information and discussion about India and its people.

Keywords: India, Sociology

Audience: Sociologists

Details: Free

User Info: To subscribe to this Usenet newsgroup, you need access to a newsreader.

news:soc.culture.indian

soc.culture.iranian

⭐

A Usenet newsgroup providing information and discussion about Iran and Iranian culture.

Keywords: Iran, Sociology

Audience: Sociologists, Iranians

Details: Free

User Info: To subscribe to this Usenet newsgroup, you need access to a newsreader.

news:soc.culture.iranian

soc.culture.italian

⭐

A Usenet newsgroup providing information and discussion about the Italian people and their culture.

Keywords: Italy, Sociology

Audience: Sociologists, Italians

Details: Free

User Info: To subscribe to this Usenet newsgroup, you need access to a newsreader.

news:soc.culture.italian

soc.culture.japan

⭐

A Usenet newsgroup providing information and discussion about Japan and the Japanese culture.

Keywords: Japan, Sociology

A B C D E F G H I J K L M N O P Q R S T U V W X Y Z

Audience: Sociologists, Japanese

Details: Free

User Info: To subscribe to this Usenet newsgroup, you need access to a newsreader.

news:soc.culture.japan

soc.culture.jewish

A Usenet newsgroup providing information and discussion about Jewish culture and religion.

Keywords: Judaism, Sociology

Audience: Sociologists, Jews, Jewish Organizations

Details: Free

User Info: To subscribe to this Usenet newsgroup, you need access to a newsreader.

news:soc.culture.jewish

soc.culture.korean

A Usenet newsgroup providing information and discussion about Korea's culture and its people.

Keywords: Korea, Sociology

Audience: Sociologists, Koreans

Details: Free

User Info: To subscribe to this Usenet newsgroup, you need access to a newsreader

news:soc.culture.korean

soc.culture.nordic

A Usenet newsgroup providing information and discussion about Nordic culture.

Keywords: Scandinavia, Sociology

Audience: Sociologists

Details: Free

User Info: To subscribe to this Usenet newsgroup, you need access to a newsreader.

news:soc.culture.nordic

soc.culture.pakistan

A Usenet newsgroup providing information and discussion about Pakistani people and their culture.

Keywords: Pakistan, Sociology

Audience: Sociologists, Pakistanis

Details: Free

User Info: To subscribe to this Usenet newsgroup, you need access to a newsreader.

news:soc.culture.pakistan

soc.culture.soviet

A Usenet newsgroup providing information and discussion about topics relating to Russia or the former Soviet Union.

Keywords: Russia, CIS (Commonwealth of Independent States), Communism, Sociology

Audience: Sociologists, Russians

Details: Free

User Info: To subscribe to this Usenet newsgroup, you need access to a newsreader.

news:soc.culture.soviet

soc.culture.spain

A Usenet newsgroup providing information and discussion about culture on the Iberian peninsula.

Keywords: Spain, Sociology

Audience: Sociologists, Spaniards, Spain Enthusiasts

Details: Free

User Info: To subscribe to this Usenet newsgroup, you need access to a newsreader.

news:soc.culture.spain

soc.culture.taiwan

A Usenet newsgroup providing information and discussion about Taiwanese people and their culture.

Keywords: Taiwan, Sociology

Audience: Sociologists, Taiwanese

Details: Free

User Info: To subscribe to this Usenet newsgroup, you need access to a newsreader.

news:soc.culture.taiwan

soc.culture.turkish

A Usenet newsgroup providing information and discussion about Turkish people and culture.

Keywords: Turkey, Sociology

Audience: Sociologists, Turks

Details: Free

User Info: To subscribe to this Usenet newsgroup, you need access to a newsreader.

news:soc.culture.turkish

soc.culture.usa

A Usenet newsgroup providing information and discussion about the culture of the United States.

Keywords: Americana, Sociology, Popular Culture

Audience: Sociologists, General Public

Details: Free

User Info: To subscribe to this Usenet newsgroup, you need access to a newsreader.

news:soc.culture.usa

soc.culture.vietnamese

A Usenet newsgroup providing information and discussion about the people and culture of Vietnam.

Keywords: Vietnam, Sociology

Audience: Sociologists, Vietnamese

Details: Free

User Info: To subscribe to this Usenet newsgroup, you need access to a newsreader.

news:soc.culture.vietnamese

soc.culture.yugoslavia

A Usenet newsgroup providing information and discussion about the people and culture of Yugoslavia.

Keywords: Yugoslavia, Sociology

Audience: Sociologists, Yugoslavians

Details: Free

User Info: To subscribe to this Usenet newsgroup, you need access to a newsreader.

news:soc.culture.yugoslavia

Software

Biosym

For users of Biosym Technologies software, including the products InsightII, Discover, Dmol, Homology, Delphi, and Polymer. The list is not run by Biosym.

Keywords: Biosym Technologies Software, Software

Audience: Software Users

Contact: Reinhard Doelz
dibug-request@comp.bioz.unibas.ch

Details: Free

User Info: To subscribe to the list, send an e-mail message requesting a subscription to the URL address below. To send a message to the entire list, address it to: dibug@comp.bioz.unibas.ch

mailto:dibug-request@comp.bioz.unibas.ch

Buyer's Guide to Micro Software

The database contains a directory of business and professional microcomputer software available in the United States.

Keywords: Buyer's Guides, Microcomputers, Computers, Software

Sponsor: Online, Inc., Weston, CT, USA

Audience: Computer Users

Profile: Provided are directory, product, technical, and bibliographic information on leading software packages, integrated this information into one succinct composite record. The database can help professionals locate suitable packages compatible with specified hardware, without having to sift through large numbers of records.

The file is highly selective, listing packages rated at least "good" by the technical press; all packages from major software producers, even if negatively reviewed; and packages unique to specific business segments, with special emphasis placed on library and medical software. Each record includes directory information; technical specifications, including required hardware and operating systems; an abstracted product description; and, when available, a full citation of representative reviews.

Contact: Dialog in the US at (800) 334-2564, Dialog internationally at country-specific locations.

Details: Costs

User Info: To subscribe, contact Dialog directly.

Notes: Coverage: current; updated monthly.

`telnet://dialog.com`

CE Software

Technical support for CE Software Products, such as QuickKeys for the Macintosh.

Keywords: Software, Technical Support, Macintosh

Audience: Software users

Details: Free

User Info: To subscribe to the list, send an e-mail message requesting a subscription to the URL address below.

`mailto:ce_info%cedsm@uunet.uu.net`

Cosmic Update

Internet notice identifying new computer software from the National Aeronautics and Space Administration (NASA) made available for international use.

Keywords: NASA, Software, Space

Audience: Space Scientists, Astronomers

Profile: COSLINE is a 24-hour electronic information service to COSMIC's customers. The principal feature of COSLINE is the catalog Search facility. A separate help file is available for browsing from the Search main menu option.

Contact: Pat Mortenson
service@cossack.cosmic.uga.edu

Details: Free

User Info: To subscribe, send an e-mail message requesting a subscription to the URL address below.

`mailto:service@cossack.cosmic.uga.edu`

data-exp

The mail list server provides an open forum for users to discuss the Visualization Data Explorer Package. It contains three files at the moment: a. FAQ, b. summary, and c. forum.

Keywords: Computers, Software, Hardware, Visualization Data Explorer Package

Audience: Computer Users

User Info: To subscribe to the list, send an e-mail message requesting a subscription to the URL address below. To send a message to the entire list, address it to: stein@watson.ibm.com

`mailto:stein@watson.ibm.com`

DDTs-Users

The DDTs-Users mailing list is for discussions of issues related to the DDTs defect-tracking software from QualTrak, including software, methods, mechanisms, techniques, general usage tips, policies, bugs, and bug workarounds.

Keywords: Software, Software Defects

Audience: Computer Users, DDTs Administrators

Contact: DDTs-Users-request@BigBird.BU.EDU

User Info: To subscribe to the list, send an e-mail message requesting a subscription to the URL address below. To send a message to the entire list, address it to: DDTs-Users-request@BigBird.BU.EDU

`mailto:DDTs-Users-request@BigBird.BU.EDU`

ESRI (Environmental Systems Research Institute)

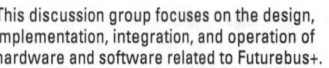

Environmental Systems Research Institute, Inc. is the world leader in GIS technology. ARC/INFO is ESRI's powerful and flexible flagship GIS software.

Keywords: Geographic Information Systems (GIS), Environment, Software, Computers

Audience: Geographers, Environmentalists, Computer Users

Details: Costs

For product information, call (909) 793-2853, X1475.

For training information, call (909) 793-2853, X1585, or fax (909) 793-5953.

`mailto:ajackson@esri.com`

fsuucp

The FSUUCP mailing list is for the discussion of bug hunting, feature proposing, and announcements of the availability and release dates of FSUUCP, an MS-DOS UUCP/mail/ news package.

Keywords: Software, Shareware

Audience: Students, Computer Users

Details: Free

User Info: To subscribe to the list, send an e-mail message requesting a subscription to the URL address below. To send a message to the entire list, address it to: fsuucp@polyslo.calpoly.edu

`mailto:fsuucp-request@polyslo.calpoly.edu`

Futurebus+ Users

This discussion group focuses on the design, implementation, integration, and operation of hardware and software related to Futurebus+.

Keywords: Computer Users, Hardware, Software

Audience: Computer Users, Software Engineers, Hardware Engineers

Contact: majordomo@theus.rain.com

Details: Free

User Info: To subscribe to the list, send an e-mail message to the URL address below consisting of a single line reading:

SUB fbus_users YourFirstName YourLastName

To send a message to the entire list, address it to:
fbus_users+@theus.rain.com

`mailto:majordomo@theus.rain.com`

gateway2000

This list is a source of information about Gateway2000 products.

Keywords: Computer Products, Software, Hardware

Audience: Computer Users, Hardware Engineers, Software Engineers

Details: Free

User Info: To subscribe to the list, send an e-mail message requesting a subscription to the URL address below. To send a message to the entire list, address it to: gateway2000@sei.cmu.edu

`gateway2000-request@sei.cmu.edu`

GNUs Bulletin: Newsletter of the Free Software Foundation

Bringing you news about the GNU Project, the Free Software Foundation is dedicated to eliminating restrictions on copying, redistribution, understanding, and modification of computer programs.

Keywords: Software, Shareware, Free Software

Sponsor: Free Software Foundation

Audience: Computer Programmers, Computer Users

Contact: Leonard H. Tower, Jr.
tower@ai.mit.edu

Details: Free

news:gnu.announce

`mailto:info-gnu-request@prep.ai.mit.edu`

A B C D E F G H I J K L M N O P Q R S T U V W X Y Z

NSSDC's (National Space Science Data Center) Online Data & Information Service

The NSSDC (National Space Science Data Center) is the NASA facility charged with archiving the data from all of NASA's science missions.

Keywords: Space, Astrophysics, Software, NASA, Science

Sponsor: NASA

Audience: Scientists, Space Scientists, Astronomers, Engineers

Profile: This resource contains information about NASA's missions and analysis of their data.

Details: Free

User Info: Expect: Login, Send: nssdc

See the menu entries in your particular area of interest.

`telnet://nssdc.gsfc.nasa.gov`

Pc532

A mailing list for people interested in the pc532 project, a National Semiconductor NS32532-based system, offered at a low cost.

Keywords: Computers, Hardware, Software

Audience: Computer Users, Software Developers

Contact: Dave Rand
pc532-request@bungi.com

Details: Free

User Info: To subscribe to the list, send an e-mail message requesting a subscription to the URL address below. To send a message to the entire list, address it to: pc532@bungi.com

`mailto:pc532-request@bungi.com`

Pcgeos-list

A discussion forum for users of PC/GEOS products, including GeoWorks Ensemble, GeoWorks Pro, GeoWorks POS, and third-party products. Topics include general information, tips, techniques, applications, and experiences.

Keywords: Computers, Software

Audience: Computer Users, Software Developers

Contact: listserv@pandora.sf.ca.us

Details: Free

User Info: To subscribe to the list, send an e-mail message to the URL address below, consisting of a single line reading:

SUB pcgeos-list YourFirstName YourLastName

To send a message to the entire list, address it to: pcgeos@pandora.sf.ca.us

`mailto:listserv@pandora.sf.ca.us`

Pdp8-lovers

A mailing list for owners of vintage DEC (Digital Equipment Corp.) computers, especially the PDP-8 series. Discussion topics include hardware, software, and programming techniques.

Keywords: Computers, Hardware, Software

Audience: Computer Users, Product Analysts

Contact: Robert E. Seastrom
pdp8-lovers-request@mc.lcs.mit.edu

Details: Free

User Info: To subscribe to the list, send an e-mail message requesting a subscription to the URL address below. To send a message to the entire list, address it to: pdp8-lovers@mc.lcs.mit.edu

`mailto:pdp8-lovers@mc.lcs.mit.edu`

Project-management

The aim of the list is to discuss project-management techniques generally, as well as project-management software and programs.

Keywords: Project Management, Computing, Software

Audience: Business Professionals, Business Students

Contact: project-management-request@smtl.demon.co.uk

Details: Free

User Info: To subscribe to the list, send an e-mail message requesting a subscription to the URL address below. To send a message to the entire list, address it to: project-management@smtl.demon.co.uk

`mailto:project-management-request@smtl.demon.co.uk`

Qnx2

Discussion of all aspects of the QNX real-time operating systems. Topics include compatible hardware, available third-party software, software reviews, available PD/free software, QNX platform-specific programming discussions, and QNX and FLEET networking.

Keywords: Computing, Hardware, Software

Audience: Computer Users, Hardware/Software Designers, Product Analysts

Contact: Martin Zimmerman
camz@dlogtech.cuc.ab.ca

Details: Free

User Info: To subscribe to the list, send an e-mail message requesting a subscription to the URL address below. To send a message to the entire list, address it to: qnx2@dlogtech.cuc.ab.ca

`mailto:qnx2@dlogtech.cuc.ab.ca`

Qnx4

A mailing list for discussion of all aspects of the QNX real-time operating systems. Topics include compatible hardware, available third-party software, software reviews, available PD/free software, QNX and FLEET networking, process control, and more.

Keywords: Computing, Hardware, Software, Networking

Audience: Computer Users, Hardware/Software Designers, Product Analysts

Contact: Martin Zimmerman
camz@dlogtech.cuc.ab.ca

Details: Free

User Info: To subscribe to the list, send an e-mail message requesting a subscription to the URL address below. To send a message to the entire list, address it to: qnx4@dlogtech.cuc.ab.ca

`mailto:qnx4@dlogtech.cuc.ab.ca`

SUMEX-AIM

An FTP archive of software, demonstration programs, and various applications, especially for Macintosh computers.

Keywords: Computers, Macintosh, Software

Audience: Computer Users, Macintosh Users

Details: Free

`ftp://sumex-aim.Stanford.edu`

Virtual Reality Space

A collection of virtual reality information, including downloadable software tools from Silicon Graphics.

Keywords: Virtual Reality, Cyberspace, Software, Silicon Graphics

Sponsor: The University of Texas, Austin, Texas, USA

Audience: Virtual Reality Enthusiasts, Programmers

Contact: Jay Ashcraft
ashcraft@ccwf.cc.utexas.edu

`gopher://ftp.cc.utexas.edu`

`ftp://cc.utexas.edu`

Software Defects

DDTs-Users

The DDTs-Users mailing list is for discussions of issues related to the DDTs defect-tracking software from QualTrak, including software, methods, mechanisms, techniques, general usage tips, policies, bugs, and bug workarounds.

Keywords: Software, Software Defects

Audience: Computer Users, DDTs Administrators

Contact: DDTs-Users-request@BigBird.BU.EDU

User Info: To subscribe to the list, send an e-mail message requesting a subscription to the URL address below. To send a message to the entire list, address it to: DDTs-Users-request@bigbird.bu.edu

```
mailto:DDTs-Users-
request@bigbird.bu.edu
```

Software Internationalization

insoft-l

This list discusses techniques for developing new software and for converting existing software, as well as internationalization tools, announcements of internationalized public-domain software and of foreign-language versions of commercial software, calls for papers, conference announcements, and references to documentation related to the internationalization of software.

Keywords: Programming, Software Internationa-lization

Sponsor: Center for Computing and Information Services, Technical University of Brno

Audience: Software Developers

Contact: insoft-l-request@cis.vutbr.cs

Details: Free, Moderated

User Info: To subscribe to the list, send an e-mail message to the URL address below consisting of a single line reading:

SUB insoft-l YourFirstName YourLastName

To send a message to the entire list, address it to: insoft-l@cis.vutbr.cs

```
mailto:listserv@cis.vutbr.cs
```

Soil Conservation

Iowa State University

The library's holdings contain significant collections in many fields.

Keywords: Agriculture, Veterinary Medicine, Statistics, Labor, Soil Conservation, Film

Audience: General Public, Researchers, Librarians, Document Delivery Professionals

Details: Free

User Info: Expect: DIAL, Send: LIB

```
telnet://isn.iastate.edu
```

Solid Waste Recycling

Solid Waste Recycling

The text of an eight-lesson correspondence class designed to teach the basics of setting up a successful recycling program.

Keywords: Recycling, Environmental Studies

Sponsor: University of Wisconsin

Audience: Environmentalists, Educators, Students

Contact: Judy Faber
faber@engr.wisc.edu

```
gopher://wissago.uwex.edu/11/uwex/
course/recycling
```

Solstice

Solstice

This file server provides state-of-the-art information on renewable energy, energy efficiency, the environment, and sustainable community development.

Keywords: Energy, Environment

Sponsor: The Center for Renewable Energy and Sustainable Technology (CREST)

Audience: Environmentalists, Urban Planners, Educators, Students

Contact: www-content@solstice.crest.org

Details: Free

Login: anonymous, Password: e-mail

```
http://solstice.crest.org
```

Sound Synthesis

IRCAM DSP and musical software

This site offers a variety of computer music resources.

Keywords: Computer Music, Sound Synthesis, Composition, DSP

Sponsor: IRCAM

Audience: Computer Music Researchers and Computer Musicians

Profile: Contains a list and brief description of IRCAM software (digital signal processing, voice and sound synthesis, music composition, wind instrument making, and other programs). There are also calendars of the IRCAM-EIC concerts and tours, and links to various other music servers.

Contact: Michel Fingerhut
fingerhu@ircam.fr

Details: Free

```
http://www.ircam.fr
```

Soundtracks

Soundtracks

Discussions and reviews of new and older soundtracks (musical and technical aspects). Information about availability of specific soundtracks on different formats in different parts of the world.

Keywords: Music, Recordings

Audience: Audio Enthusiasts, Music Researchers

Contact: Michel Hafner
soundtracks-request@ifi.unizh.ch

User Info: To subscribe to the list, send an e-mail message requesting a subscription to the URL address below. To send a message to the entire list, address it to: soundtracks@ifi.unizh.ch

```
mailto:soundtracks-
request@ifi.unizh.ch
```

South Africa

SABINET (South African Bibliographic and Information Network)

This gopher offers information searches from a variety of electronic databases, as well as for library locations and availability of books and periodicals.

Keywords: South Africa, Databases, Networks

Audience: South African Internet Surfers

Contact: hennie@info1.sabinet.co.za

Details: Free

```
gopher://info2.sabinet.co.za
```

South Africa

A major directory on Africa, providing access to a broad range of related resources (library catalogs, databases, and servers) via the Internet.

Keywords: Africa, South Africa

Audience: General Public

Profile: South Africa's home page, containing information about different regions and major cities, weather conditions, vital statistics, and information about the University of South Africa.

Contact: Aleksandar Radovanovic
radova@osprey.unisa.ac.za

```
http://osprey.unisa.ac.za/0/docs/
south-africa.html
```

A B C D E F G H I J K L M N O P Q R **S** T U V W X Y Z

A B C D E F G H I J K L M N O P Q R S T U V W X Y Z

South African Specific Items

A selection of primarily political information on South Africa. Includes ANC (African National Congress) policy statements, as well as an A-Z of South African political figures and the latest issues of South Africa Watch Magazine. Also has weather information and links to gopher and FTP sites in South Africa.

Keywords: South Africa, Political Science

Audience: South Africans, Political Analysts, General Public

Contact: John Dovey
pjcd@maties.sun.ac.za

gopher://lib.sun.ac.za

South America

NIBNews - A Monthly Electronic Bulletin About Medical Informatics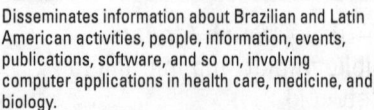

Disseminates information about Brazilian and Latin American activities, people, information, events, publications, software, and so on, involving computer applications in health care, medicine, and biology.

Keywords: Health Care, Biology, Brazil, Latin America, South America, Medicine

Audience: Health Care Professionals, Biologists

Contact: Renato M. E. Sabbatini
sabbatini@bruc.bitnet

Details: Free

E-mail a short notice to:

mailto:sabbatini@ccvax.unicamp.br

NSAMER (North and South America Library)

The North and South America library contains detailed information about every country in North and South America (except the United States). The US-Canada Free Trade Agreement, the North American Free Trade Agreement, relations with Mexico and events in such countries as Brazil, Peru, and Nicaragua are among the topics covered by a variety of business, news and legal sources. International research reports from InvestextR are also included. The United States is not covered in this library.

Keywords: News, Analysis, Companies, North America, South America

Audience: Journalists, Business Professionals

Profile: The North and South America library contains a broad array of sources. Among the information sources are newspapers and wire services, trade and business journals, company reports, country and region backgrounds, industry and product analyses, business opportunities, and selected legal texts. News sources range from the world-renowned Washington Post and Christian Science Monitor to the regionally important Toronto Star and Latin American Newsletters. Canadian Business and Maclean's represent a portion of the array of business and trade journals. Company information is contained in the EXTEL cards as well as ICC. Providers of country background and industry analyses include Associated Banks of Europe, Bank of America, Business International, IBC USA and the US Department of Commerce. Among the specialized resources are IBC's Mexico and Brazil Services as well as BI's Business Latin America. Researchers interested in new business opportunities can check OPIC and Foreign Trade Opportunities (FTO).And selected legal texts covering the US-Canada Free Trade Agreement and other international agreements planners and advisors to better assess the business climate in North and South America.

Contact: Mead New Sales Group at (800) 227-4908 or (513) 859-5398 inside the US, or (513) 865-7981 for all inquiries outside the US.

User Info: To subscribe, contact Mead directly.

To examine the Nexis user guide, you can access it at the ftp site of the University of Texas at Austin at the URL address: ftp://ftp.cc.utexas.edu. The files are in pub/ref-services/LEXIS

telnet://nex.meaddata.com

http://www.meaddata.com

Peru

A mailing list for the discussion of Peruvian culture and other issues.

Keywords: Peru, South America

Audience: Peruvians, Educators, Researchers

Contact: Herbert Koller
owner-peru@cs.sfsu.edu

Details: Free

User Info: To subscribe to the list, send an e-mail message requesting a subscription to the URL address below. To send a message to the entire list, address it to: owner-peru@cs.sfsu.edu

Notes: This mailing list is simply an echo site, so all posts get bounced from that address to all the people subscribed.

mailto:owner-peru@cs.sfsu.edu

South Asian Studies

University of Pennsylvania Library- Philadelphia Pa.

The library's holdings are large and wide-ranging and contain significant collections in many fields.

Keywords: Literature (English), Literature (American), History (World), Medieval Studies, East Asian Studies, Middle Eastern Studies, South Asian Studies, Judaica, Lithuania.

Audience: Educators, Students, Researchers

Profile: Access to the central Van Pelt Library and to most of the departmental libraries is restricted to members of the University community on weekends and holidays. Online visitors are advised to call (215) 898-7554 for information on hours and access restrictions.

Contact: Patricia Renfro, Associate Director of Libraries

Details: Free

telnet://library.upenn.edu

South East Florida AIDS Information Network (SEFAIN)

South East Florida AIDS Information Network (SEFAIN)

Contains a wide range of information on AIDS research(ers), organizations, and services in searchable databases.

Keywords: AIDS, Medicine

Sponsor: This project is sponsored in part by the National Library of Medicine

Audience: Medical Professionals, Scientists, Educators, Health Care Providers

Details: Free

Select L on main menu, then select 1 on next menu

**telnet://
library@callcat.med.miami.edu**

South Florida Environmental Reader

South Florida Environmental Reader

Newsletter distributing information on the environment of South Florida.

Keywords: Environment, Florida

Audience: Environmentalists

Contact: aem@mthvax.cs.miami.edu

Details: Free

User Info: To subscribe to the list, send an e-mail message requesting a subscription to the URL address below.

To send a mesage to the entire USL, address it to: sfer@mthvax.cs.miami.edu

```
mail to:sfer-
requesti@mthvax.cs.miami.edu
```

Soviet Union

Mideur-l ★

A list containing the history, culture, politics, and current affairs of those countries lying between the Mediterranean/Adriatic and the Baltic Seas, and between the German/Austrian borders and the former Soviet Union.

Keywords: Soviet Union, Baltic Republics, Eastern Europe, News

Audience: Political Scientists, Researchers, Historians, General Public

Contact: Jan George Frajkor mideur-1@ubvm.cc.buffalo.edu

Details: Free

User Info: To subscribe to the list, send an e-mail message to the URL address below consisting of a single line reading:

SUB mideur-l YourFirstName YourLastName

To send a message to the entire list, address it to: mideur-1@ubvm.cc.buffalo.edu

```
mailto:listserv@ubvm.cc.buffalo.edu
```

SCS ★

A discussion of the culture of the former Soviet Union.

Keywords: Soviet Union, Culture

Audience: Researchers, Slavicists, General Public

Contact: John B. Harlan ijph200@indycms.iupui.edu

Details: Free

User Info: To subscribe to the list, send an e-mail message to the URL address below consisting of a single line reading:

SUB scs YourFirstName YourLastName

To send a message to the entire list, address to: scs@indycms.iupui.edu

```
mailto:listserv@indycms.iupui.edu
```

val-l ★

Discussion on changes in the Communist countries, ranging from Cuba and Vietnam to the former Soviet Union.

Keywords: Communism, Soviet Union, Political Science

Audience: Political Scientists

Contact: cdell@umkcax1 or cdell@umkcvax1.bitnet

Details: Free

User Info: To subscribe to the list, send an e-mail message to the URL address below consisting of a single line reading:

SUB val-l YourFirstName YourLastName

To send a message to the entire list, address it to: val-l@ucflvm.cc.ucf.edu

```
mailto:listserv@ucflvm.cc.ucf.edu
```

Sovokinform

Sovokinform ★

CIS news, events, general information; usually in transliterated Russian.

Keywords: Commonwealth of Independent States (CIS)

Audience: Journalists, Political Scientists

Contact: burkov@drfmc.ceng.cea.fr

Details: Free

User Info: To subscribe to the list, send an e-mail message requesting a subscription to the URL address below. To send a message to the entire list, address it to: sovokinform@drfmc.ceng.cea.fr

```
mailto:burkov@drfmc.ceng.cea.fr
```

Space

Aerospace Engineering

This directory is a compilation of information resources focused on aerospace engineeering.

Keywords: Aerospace, Engineering, Aviation, Space

Audience: Aerospace Engineers, Space Scientists

Profile: This is a guide to Internet resources that contain information pertaining to aerospace engineering. Originally the guide was to cover the area of aerospace engineering as applied to lower atmospheric flight. However, it is difficult to narrow the sites down to specific subject areas. As the guide evolved, sites were included with a broader scope of information. The guide is by no means comprehensive and exhaustive; there are sites that are not included and those the authors were not aware of, and they welcome suggestions. The directory lists sites on FTP, Gopher, Listserv, OPAC, Telnet, Usenet, and WWW.

Details: Free

```
ftp://una.hh.lib.umich.edu/70/
inetdirsstacks/aerospace:potsiedalq
```

Astronomy

This directory is a compilation of information resources focused on astronomy.

Keywords: Astronomy, Stars, Astrophysics, Space

Audience: Astronomers, Astrophysicists, Space Enthusiasts

Contact: A. Park, J. Miller

Details: Free

```
ftp://una.hh.lib.umich.edu/70/
inetdirsstacks/astron:parkmiller
```

Cosmic Update

Internet notice identifying new computer software from the National Aeronautics and Space Administration (NASA) made available for international use.

Keywords: NASA, Software, Space

Audience: Space Scientists, Astronomers

Profile: COSLINE is a 24-hour electronic information service to COSMIC's customers. The principal feature of COSLINE is the catalog Search facility. A separate help file is available for browsing from the Search main menu option.

Contact: Pat Mortenson service@cossack.cosmic.uga.edu

Details: Free

User Info: To subscribe, send an e-mail message requesting a subscription to the URL address below.

```
mailto:service@cossack.cosmic.uga.edu
```

Extraterrestrials

A forum for academics, scientists and others interested in questions about the existence of intelligent life in the universe.

Keywords: Astronomy, Extraterrestrial Life, Space

Sponsor: University of Kent at Canterbury, United Kingdom

Audience: Scientists, Astronomers, General Public

Contact: Dr. Peter Moore pgm@ukc.ac.uk

User Info: To subscribe to the list, send an e-mail message to the URL address shown below consisting of a single line reading:

SUB extraterrestrials YourFirstName YourLastName

To send a message to the entire list, address it to: extraterrestrials@mailbase.ac.uk

```
mailbase@mailbase.ac.uk
```

A B C D E F G H I J K L M N O P Q R **S** T U V W X Y Z

A B C D E F G H I J K L M N O P Q R **S** T U V W X Y Z

McDonnell Douglas Aerospace

A web site providing information about McDonnell Douglas, including a company profile and related discussion about technology.

Keywords: Aerospace, Space, Aviation, Technology

Audience: Aerospace Engineers

Contact: mail to:
Zook@pat.mdc.com

`http://pat.mdc.com`

NASA Ames SPACE Archive

This archive contains information about NASA projects. It also has an online CD-ROM jukebox with a rotating selection of NASA mission CD-ROMs.

Keywords: NASA, Space, Space Science

Sponsor: NASA Ames Research Center

Audience: General Public, Scientists, Technical Writers, Science Teachers

Profile: This site has access to general space information, including the texts of the press release kits for the space shuttle missions and other NASA press releases. There are also weather images from satellites and other sources in the pub/Weather directory. The pub/cdrom directory contains information about which NASA mission CD-ROMs are currently mounted.

Contact: Peter Yee
yee@atlas.arc.nasa.gov

User Info:User Info: Expect: login, Send: anonymous; Expect: password, Send: your Internet address

`ftp://explorer.arc.nasa.gov`

NSSDC (National Space Science Data Center)'s Online Data & Information Service

The NSSDC (National Space Science Data Center) is the NASA facility charged with archiving the data from all of NASA's science missions.

Keywords: Space, Astrophysics, Software, NASA, Science

Sponsor: NASA

Audience: Scientists, Space Scientists, Astronomers, Engineers

Profile: This resource contains information about NASA's missions and analysis of their data.

Details: Free

Expect: Login, Send: nssdc

See the menu entries in your particular area of interest.

`telnet://nssdc.gsfc.nasa.gov`

sci.astro

A Usenet newsgroup providing information and discussion about astronomy.

Keywords: Astronomy, Space

Audience: Astronomers

User Info: To subscribe to this Usenet newsgroup, you need access to a newsreader.

`news:sci.astro`

Sci.astro.hubble

Information about all subjects concerning NASA's Hubble space telescope.

Keywords: Hubble Telescope, Astronomy, Space, NASA, Stargazing, Telescopes

Audience: Astronomers, General Public, Science Teachers, Stargazers

Contact: Paul A. Scowen
scowen@wfpc3.la.asu.edu

Details: Free, Moderated, Images

User Info: To subscribe to this Usenet newsgroup, you need access to a newsreader.

`news:sci.astro.hubble`

Sci.space

A wide variety of discussions about space flight.

Keywords: Space, Space Flight

Audience: Space Enthusiasts, General Public

Details: Free

To participate in a Usenet newsgroup you need access to a newsreader.

`news:sci.space.news`

`news:sci.space.science`

Sci.space.news

Keywords: Space, FAQs

Audience: Space Flight Enthusiasts

Profile: This newsgroup carries recent information about the world's space programs. Reading the FAQ set is recommended before asking questions on the other sci.space. groups.

Contact: Peter Yee
yee@atlas.arc.nasa.gov

Details: Free, Moderated

To participate in a Usenet newsgroup you need access to a newsreader.

`news:sci.space.news`

Sci.space.science

A place for technical discussions about space exploration and research.

Keywords: Space Exploration, Space

Audience: Space Enthusiasts, Space Professionals

Contact: george william herbert
gwh@crl.com
gwh@soda.berkeley.edu
gwh@isu.isunet.edu

Details: Free, Moderated

User Info: To participate in a Usenet newsgroup you need access to a newsreader.

`news:sci.space.science`

Space Exploration

Sci.space.science

A place for technical discussions about space exploration and research.

Keywords: Space Exploration, Space

Audience: Space Enthusiasts, Space Professionals

Contact: george william herbert
gwh@crl.com
gwh@soda.berkeley.edu
gwh@isu.isunet.edu

Details: Free, Moderated

User Info: To participate in a Usenet newsgroup you need access to a "newsreader."

`news:sci.space.science`

Space Flight

Sci.space

A wide variety of discussions about space flight.

Keywords: Space, Space Flight

Audience: Space Enthusiasts, General Public

Details: Free

To participate in a Usenet newsgroup you need access to a newsreader.

`news:sci.space.news`

`news:sci.space.science`

Space Science

Canopus

Newsletter of the Space Science and Astronomy Technical Committee of the American Institute of Aeronautics and Astronautics. Its objective is to provide an insider's perspective on issues in space science and astronomy.

Keywords: Space Science, Astronomy

Sponsor: NASA (National Aeronautics and Space Administration)

Audience: Astronomers, Space Scientists

Contact: William W. L. Taylor
wtaylor@nhqvax.hq.nasa.gov

Details: Costs

User Info: To subscribe to the list, send an e-mail message to the URL address below.

`mailto:wtaylor@nhqvax.hq.nasa.gov`

European Space Agency

A major directory on aeronautics, providing access to a broad range of related resources (library catalogs, databases, and servers) via the Internet.

Keywords: Space Science, Aeronautics

Audience: Space Science Researchers

Profile: The home page of the European Space Agency, including information about ESA's mission, specific ESA programs (Science, Manned Spaceflight and Microgravity, Earth Observation, Telecommunications, Launchers), and issues related to the space and aeronautics industry.

Contact: webmaster@esa.it

`http://www.esrin.esa.it`

NASA Ames SPACE Archive

This archive contains information about NASA projects. It also has an online CD-ROM jukebox with a rotating selection of NASA mission CD-ROMs.

Keywords: NASA, Space, Space Science

Sponsor: NASA Ames Research Center

Audience: General Public, Scientists, Technical Writers, Science Teachers

Profile: This site has access to general space information, including the texts of the press release kits for the space shuttle missions and other NASA press releases. There are also weather images from satellites and other sources in the pub/Weather directory. The pub/cdrom directory contains information about which NASA mission CD-ROMs are currently mounted.

Contact: Peter Yee
yee@atlas.arc.nasa.gov

User Info:User Info: Expect: login, Send: anonymous; Expect: password, Send: your Internet address

`ftp://explorer.arc.nasa.gov`

Ssi_mail

A moderated list for topics related to Space Studies Institute programs—past, present, and future.

Keywords: Space Studies, Space Science, Aeronautics

Audience: Space Students, Space Scientists

Contact: Mitchell James
mjames@link.com
mitchellj@aol.com

Details: Free, Moderated

User Info: To subscribe to the list, send an e-mail message requesting a subscription to the URL address below. To send a message to the entire list, address it to: ssi_mail@link.com

Notes: Archives available.

`mailto:listprocessor@link.com`

Space Studies

Ssi_mail

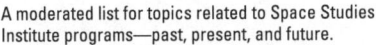

A moderated list for topics related to Space Studies Institute programs—past, present, and future.

Keywords: Space Studies, Space Science, Aeronautics

Audience: Space Students, Space Scientists

Contact: Mitchell James
mjames@link.com
mitchellj@aol.com

Details: Free, Moderated

User Info: To subscribe to the list, send an e-mail message requesting a subscription to the URL address below. To send a message to the entire list, address it to: ssi_mail@link.com

Notes: Archives available.

`mailto:listprocessor@link.com`

Spacelink

Spacelink

This contains information about NASA and its activities, including a large number of curricular activities for elementary and secondary science classes.

Keywords: NASA, Aeronautics, Education (K-12)

Audience: Students (K-12), Educators, General Public

Details: Free

`telnet://`
`newuser@spacelink.msfc.nasa.gov`

Spacemen 3

Drone On...

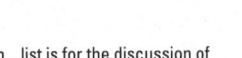

The Drone On... list is for the discussion of Spacemen 3 and resultant bands, as well as any other droning guitar bands that anyone wants to bring up.

Keywords: Rock Music, Spacemen 3

Audience: Spacemen 3 Enthusiasts, Rock Music Enthusiasts

Contact: droneon-request@ucsd.edu

Details: Free

User Info: To subscribe to the list, send an e-mail message requesting a subscription to the URL address below. To send a message to the entire list, address it to: droneon-request@ucsd.edu

`mailto:droneon-request@ucsd.edu`

Space-music

Space-music

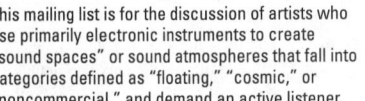

This mailing list is for the discussion of artists who use primarily electronic instruments to create "sound spaces" or sound atmospheres that fall into categories defined as "floating," "cosmic," or "noncommercial," and demand an active listener.

Keywords: Music, Electronic Music

Audience: Electronic Music Enthusiasts

Contact: Dave Datta
space-music-request@cs.uwp.edu

Details: Free

User Info: To subscribe to the list, send an e-mail message requesting a subscription to the URL address below. To send a message to the entire list, address it to: space-music@cs.uwp.edu

`mailto:space-music-request@cs.uwp.edu`

Spain

soc.culture.spain

A Usenet newsgroup providing information and discussion about culture on the Iberian peninsula.

Keywords: Spain, Sociology

Audience: Sociologists, Spaniards, Spain Enthusiasts

Details: Free

User Info: To subscribe to this Usenet newsgroup, you need access to a newsreader.

`news:soc.culture.spain`

Spanish

Academia Latinoamericana de Espanol

This program is specifically designed for those interested in learning to speak Spanish through a fully immersive trip to Ecuador.

A B C D E F G H I J K L M N O P Q R **S** T U V W X Y Z

Keywords: Spanish, Language, Education (Bilingual)

Sponsor: Academia Latinoamericana de Espanol, Quito, Ecuador

Audience: Reseachers, Students, Language Teachers

Contact: Webmaster

webmaster@comnet.com

`http://www.comnet.com/ecuador/`
`learnSpanish.html`

Spanish Inquisition

University of Pennsylvania PENNINFO Library

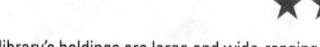

The library's holdings are large and wide-ranging and contain significant collections in many fields.

Keywords: Church History, Spanish Inquisition, Witchcraft, Shakespeare (William), Bibles, Aristotle (Texts of), Fiction, Whitman (Walt), French Revolution, Drama (French), Literature (English), Literature (Spanish)

Audience: Researchers, Students, General Public

Contact: Al DSouza
penninfo-admin@dccs.upenn.edu
dsouza@dccs.upenn.edu

Details: Free

User Info: Expect: Login; Send: Public

`telnet://penninfo.upenn.edu`

Spanish Plays

Dartmouth College Library

The library's holdings are large and wide-ranging and contain significant collections in many fields.

Keywords: American Calligraphy, Cervantes (Miguel de), Railroads, Polar Regions, Frost (Robert), Shakespeare (William), Spanish Plays

Audience: General Public, Researchers, Librarians, Document Delivery Professionals

Contact: Katharina Klemperer
kathy.klemperer@dartmouth.edu

Details: Free

User Info: Expect: login, Send: wolfpac

`telnet://lib.dartmouth.edu`

Spanky Fractal Database

Spanky Fractal Database

This web site provides a collection of fractals and fractal-related material for free distribution on the Internet.

Keywords: Mathematics, Chaos Theory, Computer

Programming, Computer Graphics

Audience: Mathematicians, Computer Programmers

Profile: Contains information on dynamical systems, software, distributed fractal generators, galleries, and databases from all over the world.

Contact: Noel Giffin
noel@triumf.ca

Details: Free

`http://spanky.triumf.ca`

Special Chemicals Update Program

Special Chemicals Update Program

Comprehensive reports covering 32 specialty chemical industry segments.

Keywords: Chemistry, Business

Sponsor: Chemical Marketing Research Center

Audience: Librarians, Researchers, Chemists

Profile: Coverage of chemical industry segments, plus more than a dozen reports of general interest on the management of specialty chemical businesses.

Contact: PAUL.ALBERT@NETEAST.COM

User Info: To subscribe, contact Orbit-Questel directly.

`telnet://orbit.com`

Spectroscopy

Massachusetts Institute of Technology Library

The library's holdings are large and wide-ranging and contain significant collections in many fields.

Keywords: Aeronautics (History of), Linguistics, Mathematics (History of), Microscopy, Spectroscopy, Aeronautics, Mathematics, Glass

Audience: General Public, Researchers, Librarians, Document Delivery Professionals

Details: Free

User Info: Expect: Mitek Server..., Send: Enter or Return; Expect: prompt, Send: hollis

`telnet://library.mit.edu`

Speech Disorders

Stutt-L

A list for the clinical discussion of stuttering, a speech disorder.

Keywords: Communications, Speech Disorders, Disabilities

Audience: Communications Specialists, Speech Pathologists

Contact: Woody Starkweather
v5002e@vm.temple.edu

User Info: To subscribe to this list, send an e-mail message to the URL address below, consisting of a single line reading:

SUB Stutt-L YourFirstName YourLastName

To send a message to the entire list, address it to: stutt-l@rm.temple.edu

`mailto:listserv@vm.temple.edu`

Speeches and Addresses in the US

Speeches and Addresses in the US

Includes the Clinton State of the Union Speech of 1993, Kennedy's Inaugural Speech, Martin Luther King's "I Have a Dream" speech, and more.

Keywords: Politics (US), Rhetoric

Audience: Journalists, Writers, Politicians, Students

Details: Free

Choose from menu presented.

`gopher://wiretap.spies.com/11/Gov/US-`
`Speech`

Spelunking

alt.caving

A Usenet newsgroup dedicating to discussions of caving and related issues, including cave locations, equipment, spelunking techniques, and other caving information.

Keywords: Spelunking, Caves

Audience: Spelunkers

User Info: To subscribe to this Usenet newsgroup, you need access to a newsreader.

`news://alt.caving`

Cavers

This is an information resource and forum for anyone interested in exploring caves.

Keywords: Caves, Spelunking

Audience: Cave Explorers, Spelunkers

Contact: John D. Sutter
cavers-request@vlsi.bu.edu

Details: Free

User Info: To subscribe to the list, send an e-mail message requesting a subscription to the URL address below. To send a message to the entire list, address it to: cavers@vlsi.bu.edu

`mailto:cavers-request@vlsi.bu.edu`

Spirituality

Ayurveda

Ayurveda is the ancient science of life that originated in India. This mailing list provides information about ayurveda, such as lectures, workshops, and stores that sell ayurvedic herbs.

Keywords: Spirituality, Ayurveda, India

Audience: General Public

Contact: ayurveda-request@netcom.com

Details: Free

User Info: To subscribe to the list, send an e-mail message requesting a subscription to the URL address below. To send a message to the entire list, address it to: ayurveda@netcom.com

`mailto:ayurveda-request@netcom.com`

Spojrzenia

Spojrzenia

A weekly E-journal devoted to Polish culture, history and politics.

Keywords: Poland, News (international), Culture

Audience: Poles, Students

Contact: Jerzy Krzystek
krzystek@u.washington.edu

Details: Free

User Info: To subscribe to the list, send an e-mail message requesting a subscription to the URL address below. To send a message to the entire list, address it to: spojrzenia@u.washington.edu

`mailto:krzystek@u.washington.edu`

Sports

Aikido Information

An FTP site containing aikido dojo addresses from around the world, plus a calendar of events, FAQs, and lists of books and periodicals related to aikido.

Keywords: Aikido, Martial Arts, Sports

Sponsor: University of California at San Diego, San Diego, CA, USA

Audience: Aikido Enthusiasts, Martial Artists

Contact: aikido@cs.ucsd.edu

Details: Free

`ftp://cs.ucsd.edu/pub/aikido`

American Hockey League

This list is for people interested in discussing and following the activities of the American Hockey League.

Keywords: Sports, Hockey, American Hockey League

Audience: Hockey Enthusiasts, Sports Enthusiasts

Contact: ahl-news-request@andrew.cmu.edu

Details: Free

User Info: To subscribe to the list, send an e-mail message requesting a subscription to the URL address below. To send a message to the entire list, address it to: ahl-news@andrew.cmu.edu

`mailto:ahl-news-request@andrew.cmu.edu`

Biking

Information on biking events and maintenance, including an FAQ from rec.bicycles.

Keywords: Sports, Bicycling, Fitness

Audience: Bicyclists, Fitness Enthusiasts

Contact: Joern Yngve Dahl-Stamnes
dahls@fysel.unit.no

Details: Free

`ftp://ugle.unit.no/local/biking`

Biking in Canada

A repository of information for bicyclists, including utility programs, events, FAQs, and how-to guides; some with Canadian-specific details.

Keywords: Sports, Bicycling, Canada

Sponsor: Habitat Ecology Division at the Bedford Institute of Oceanography

Audience: Cyclists, Fitness Enthusiasts

Contact: sysop@biome.bio.ns.ca

Details: Free

`gopher://gopher.biome.bio.dfo.ca/pub/biking`

Blues (St. Louis Blues)

Provides information, game reports, stats, discussion, and so on, on the St. Louis Blues of the National Hockey League.

Keywords: Hockey, Sports, National Hockey League

Audience: Hockey Enthusiasts

Contact: Joe Ashkar
blues@medicine.wustl.edu

User Info: To subscribe to the list, send an e-mail message requesting a subscription to the URL address below. To send a message to the entire list, address it to: blues@medicine.wustl.edu

`mailto:blues@medicine.wustl.edu`

Cleveland Sports

A forum for people to discuss their favorite Cleveland sports teams/personalities, and to obtain news and information about those teams that most out-of-towners couldn't get otherwise. Teams discussed include the Cleveland Indians, the Cleveland Browns, the Cleveland Cavaliers, and the teams from Ohio State University.

Keywords: Cleveland, Sports, Ohio State Universiry

Audience: Cleveland Sports Enthusiasts, Sports Enthusiasts, Cleveland Residents

Contact: Richard Kowicki
aj755@cleveland.freenet.edu

Details: Free

User Info: To subscribe to the list, send an e-mail message requesting a subscription to the URL address below.

`mailto:aj755@cleveland.freenet.edu`

dead-runners

The Dead Runners Society is a mailing list for runners who like to talk about the psychological, philosophical, and personal aspects of running.

Keywords: Running, Sports

Audience: Runners

Contact: Christopher Mark Conn
dead-runners-request@unx.sas.com

Details: Free

User Info: To subscribe to the list, send an e-mail message requesting a subscription to the URL address below. To send a message to the entire list, address it to: dead-runners-request@unx.sas.com

`mailto:dead-runners-request@unx.sas.com`

dragnet

To discuss strip drag racing from a participant's viewpoint.

Keywords: Drag Racing, Sports

Audience: Drag Racers

A B C D E F G H I J K L M N O P Q R S T U V W X Y Z

Contact: dragnet-request@chiller.compaq.com

User Info: To subscribe to the list, send an e-mail message requesting a subscription to the URL address below. To send a message to the entire list, address it to: dragnet-request@chiller.compaq.com

`mailto:dragnet-request@chiller.compaq.com`

echl-news

For people interested in discussing and following the East Coast Hockey League.

Keywords: Hockey, Sports

Audience: Hockey Enthusiasts

Contact: echl-news-request@andrew.cmu.edu

Details: Free

User Info: To subscribe to the list, send an e-mail message requesting a subscription to the URL address below. To send a message to the entire list, address it to: echl-news-request@andrew.cmu.edu

`mailto:echl-news-request@andrew.cmu.edu`

france-foot

Discussions of the French football (soccer) scene. Results and news are posted regularly.

Keywords: Soccer, Sports, France, Football

Audience: Soccer Enthusiasts, French Sports Enthusiasts

Contact: Vincent Habchi, Kent Hedlundh dvlkhh@cs.umu.se

Details: Free

User Info: To subscribe to the list, send an e-mail message requesting a subscription to the URL address below. To send a message to the entire list, address it to: france-foot@inf.enst.fr

`mailto:france-foot-request@inf.enst.fr`

Funet Sports Information

An FTP archive of information on various sports with links to the archive at wuarchive.wustl.edu.

Keywords: Sports, Professional Sports, Ice Hockey, Motor Racing, NFL, NHL, NBA, MLB

Sponsor: Finnish Academic and Research Network (FUNET)

Audience: Sports Enthusiasts

Profile: A fairly extensive archive of information on both American (NBA, MLB, NHL, NFL) and worldwide sports (soccer, ice hockey, motor racing, and so on). Includes FAQs for various sports, statistics, pictures, and some sports games for the PC.

Contact: Jari Pullinen sports-adm@nic.funet.fi

Details: Free, Images

`gopher://ftp.funet.fi/pub/sports`

GolfData OnLine

A web site sampling of the information on the subscriber service GolfData OnLine. Provides numerous links to other sites which may be of interest to golfers.

Keywords: Golf, Sports, Fitness

Audience: Golfers, Sports Fans

Contact: david@gdol.com

Notes: GolfData Online is a paid subscriber electronic bulletin board service for golf enthusiasts. More information about how to subscribe can be obtained by accessing the address below.

`http://www.gdol.com`

mda

Discussion of the Mighty Ducks of Anaheim of the National Hockey League, including statistics and game summaries.

Keywords: Hockey, Sports

Audience: Ice Hockey Fans

Details: Free

User Info: To subscribe to the list, send an e-mail message to the URL address below, consisting of a single line reading:

SUB mda YourFirstName YourLastName

To send a message to the entire list, address it to: mda@macsch.com

`mailto:mda@macsch.com`

NFL Scores, Schedules, and Point Spreads

Information on National Football League (NFL) football scores, schedules, and point spreads.

Keywords: Professional Sports, Sports, Football, NFL

Audience: Football Fans

Contact: office@world.std.com

Details: Free

`gopher://world.std.com/News and Weather`

Olympic Games 1994 at Lillehammer

News, results, and updates every 15 minutes, as well as archive images, from the 1994 Winter Olympic Games at Lillehammer, Norway.

Keywords: Olympics, Sports, Winter Games

Sponsor: Sun Microsystem, Skrivervik Data AS, Oslonett AS, Norsk Telegrambyra

Audience: General Public, Journalists, Skiers, Skaters, Winter Sports Fans

Profile: This server offers news and results on all the Olympic events in Lillehammer plus a chronological list of all events, a complete schedule day by day, and a very large archive of images. Also flash messages from NTB, a Norwegian news wire, and the opportunity to search in the NTB database.

Contact: oslonett@oslonett.no

`http://www.sun.com`

Open Computing Facilty (OCF) Gopher, Sports Section

A gopher server offering access to information about a number of sporting activities.

Keywords: Sports, Fitness

Sponsor: Open Computing Facility, University of California, Berkeley

Audience: Sports Fans, Fitness Enthusiasts

Profile: This gopher has information on various sports, including football, cricket, skiing, windsurfing, and basketball, as well as links to WWW. Resources include schedules for some professional and collegiate sports, as well as FAQs and other miscellaneous information.

Contact: general-manager@ocf.berkeley.edu

Details: Free

`gopher://gopher.ocf.berkeley.edu/11/gopherspace`

Pac-10-Sports

This mailing list is dedicated to discussing sports of all types that are played competitively within the Pac-10 Athletic Conference.

Keywords: Pac-10 Sports, National Collegiate Athletic Association, Sports

Audience: Pac-10 Sports Fans

Contact: Cliff Slaughterbeck crs@u.washington.edu

Details: Free

User Info: To subscribe to the list, send an e-mail message requesting a subscription to the URL address below. To send a message to the entire list, address it to: crs@u.washington.edu

`mailto:crs@u.washington.edu`

Physical Education & Recreation

A collection of information on sporting and recreational activities from aikido to windsurfing.

Keywords: Sports, Recreation, Aikido, Cycling, Scuba Diving, Windsurfing

Audience: Sports Enthusiasts, Fitness Enthusiasts

Contact: ctcadmin@ctc.ctc.edu

`gopher://ctc.ctc.edu`

Professional Sports Schedules ★

Sports schedules for major professional sports.

Keywords: Sports, Baseball, Hockey, Football, Basketball

Sponsor: Colorado University, Boulder, CO

Audience: Sports Fans, Football Fans, Hockey Fans, Baseball Enthusiasts, Basketball Enthusiasts

Profile: The Colorado University gopher maintains an interactive online database of schedules for all major US professional sports teams (NBA, NFL, NHL, MLB). The database is indexed by both team name and dates of games, and can be searched accordingly.

Contact: gopher@gopher.colorado.edu

Details: Free

`gopher://gopher.colorado.edu/11/ professional/sports/schedules`

Quebec Nordiques ★

A mailing list to discuss topics concerning the National Hockey League's Quebec Nordiques.

Keywords: Hockey, Quebec (Canada), Sports

Audience: Hockey Enthusiasts

Contact: Danny J. Sohier nords-request@badaboum.ulaval.ca

Details: Free

User Info: To subscribe to the list, send an e-mail message requesting a subscription to the URL address below. To send a message to the entire list, address it to: nords@badaboum.ulaval.ca

`mailto:nords@badaboum.ulaval.ca`

rec.autos.sport ★

A Usenet newsgroup providing information and discussion about automobile competition.

Keywords: Automobiles, Automobile Racing, Sports

Audience: Automobile Racing Enthusiasts

User Info: To subscribe to this Usenet newsgroup, you need access to a newsreader.

`news:rec.autos.sports`

rec.backcountry ★

A Usenet newsgroup providing information and discussion about wilderness, backpacking, and camping.

Keywords: Recreation, Sports

Audience: Campers, Backpackers, Wilderness Enthusiasts

User Info: To subscribe to this Usenet newsgroup, you need access to a newsreader.

`news:rec.backcountry`

rec.boats ★

A Usenet newsgroup providing information and discussion about boating, gear, places to sail, clubs, repairs, and racing.

Keywords: Sailing, Sports

Audience: Sailors, Boating Enthusiasts

User Info: To subscribe to this Usenet newsgroup, you need access to a newsreader.

`news:rec.boats`

rec.equestrian ★

A Usenet newsgroup providing information and discussion about all things pertaining to horses.

Keywords: Horses, Equestrians, Animals, Sports

Audience: Horse Riders, Horse Trainers, Horse Owners

User Info: To subscribe to this Usenet newsgroup, you need access to a newsreader.

`news:rec.equestrian`

rec.skiing ★

A Usenet newsgroup providing information and discussion about skiing.

Keywords: Sports, Recreation, Skiing

Audience: Skiers

User Info: To subscribe to this Usenet newsgroup, you need access to a newsreader.

`news:rec.skiing`

rec.sport.baseball ★

A Usenet newsgroup providing information and discussion about professional baseball.

Keywords: Baseball, Sports

Audience: Baseball Fans, Sports Fans

User Info: To subscribe to this Usenet newsgroup, you need access to a newsreader.

`news:rec.sport.baseball`

rec.sport.basketball.college ★

A Usenet newsgroup providing information and discussion about college basketball.

Keywords: Basketball, College, Sports

Audience: Basketball Fans, Sport Fans

User Info: To subscribe to this Usenet newsgroup, you need access to a newsreader.

`news:rec.sport.basketball.college`

rec.sport.basketball.pro ★

A Usenet newsgroup providing information and discussion about professional basketball.

Keywords: Basketball, Sports

Audience: Basketball Fans, Sports Fans

User Info: To subscribe to this Usenet newsgroup, you need access to a newsreader.

`news:rec.sport.basketball.pro`

rec.sport.cricket ★

A Usenet newsgroup providing information and discussion about cricket.

Keywords: Cricket, Sports

Audience: Cricket Fans, Sports Fans

User Info: To subscribe to this Usenet newsgroup, you need access to a newsreader.

`news:rec.sport.cricket`

rec.sport.football.college ★

A Usenet newsgroup providing information and discussion about college football.

Keywords: Football, College, Sports

Audience: Football Fans, Sports Fans

User Info: To subscribe to this Usenet newsgroup, you need access to a newsreader.

`news:rec.sport.football.college`

rec.sport.football.pro ★

A Usenet newsgroup providing information and discussion about pro football.

Keywords: Football, Sports

Audience: Football Enthusiasts

User Info: To subscribe to this Usenet newsgroup, you need access to a newsreader.

`news:rec.sport.football.pro`

rec.sport.hockey ★

A Usenet newsgroup providing information and discussion about hockey.

Keywords: Hockey, Sports

Audience: Hockey Fans, Sports Fans

User Info: To subscribe to this Usenet newsgroup, you need access to a newsreader.

`news:rec.sport.hockey`

rec.sport.pro-wrestling ★

A Usenet newsgroup providing information and discussion about professional wrestling.

Keywords: Wrestling, Sports

Audience: Wrestling Fans, Sports Fans

User Info: To subscribe to this Usenet newsgroup, you need access to a newsreader.

`news:rec.sport.pro-wrestling`

A
B
C
D
E
F
G
H
I
J
K
L
M
N
O
P
Q
R
S
T
U
V
W
X
Y
Z

rec.sport.rowing

A Usenet newsgroup providing information and discussion about recreational and competitive rowing. It provides information from the United States Rowing Association, the latest race results, equipment sales, coaching positions, and more.

Keywords: Rowing, Crew, Sports

Audience: Rowers, Coaches, Athletes

Profile: This newsgroup covers technical, training and nutritional aspects as well as the latest race results, National Team information, equipment sales, coaching positions, information from the United States Rowing Association and more.

User Info: To subscribe to this Usenet newsgroup, you need access to a newsreader.

`news:rec.sport.rowing`

rec.sport.soccer

A Usenet newsgroup providing information and discussion about soccer.

Keywords: Soccer, Sports

Audience: Soccer Fans, Sports Fans

User Info: To subscribe to this Usenet newsgroup, you need access to a newsreader.

`news:rec.sport.soccer`

rec.sport.tennis

A Usenet newsgroup providing information and discussion about tennis.

Keywords: Tennis, Sports

Audience: Tennis Fans, Sports Fans

User Info: To subscribe to this Usenet newsgroup, you need access to a newsreader.

`news:rec.sport.tennis`

Skiing in Utah

An FTP site maintaining information on skiing sites in Utah, Idaho, and Wyoming.

Keywords: Sports, Skiing

Sponsor: Utah University

Audience: Skiers

Details: Free

`ftp://ski.utah.edu/skiing`

SPORTS (Sports News)

The Sports News (SPORTS) library contains a variety of sports-related news and information.

Keywords: News, Analysis, Sports, Biographies

Audience: Sports Enthusiasts, Journalists

Profile: The SPORTS library is a specialized news library that contains the full text of Sports Illustrated and The Sporting News and selected sports-related stories from many major US newspapers and wire services. Biographical information and 1992 Olympic facts are also part of this library.

Contact: Mead New Sales Group at (800) 227-4908 or (513) 859-5398 inside the US, or (513) 865-7981 for all inquiries outside the US.

User Info: To subscribe, contact Mead directly.

To examine the Nexis user guide, you can access it at the ftp site of the University of Texas at Austin at the URL address: ftp://ftp.cc.utexas.edu. The files are in: /pub/ref-services/LEXIS

`telnet://nex.meaddata.com`

`http://www.meaddata.com`

Sports-cards

For people interested in collection, speculation and investing in baseball, football, basketball, hockey, and other trading cards and memorabilia. Discussion and want/sell lists are welcome.

Keywords: Memorabilia, Sports, Trading Cards

Audience: Collectors, Sports Card Traders

Contact: Keane Arase cards-request@tanstaafl.uchicago.edu

Details: Free

User Info: To subscribe to the list, send an e-mail message requesting a subscription to the URL address below. To send a message to the entire list, address it to: cards@tanstaafl.uchicago.edu

`mailto:cards-request@tanstaafl.uchicago.edu`

The Nautical Bookshelf

Catalog and ordering information for Nautical Bookshelf's collection of books on Sailing and other water sports.

Keywords: Boating, Power Boating, Sailing, Sports

Sponsor: Nautical Bookshelf

Audience: Boating Enthusiasts, Sailors

Contact: staff@nautical.com

`gopher://gopher.nautical.com`

Think Wind

An FTP site for information on windsurfing, with FAQs, pictures, details about destinations, and threads from rec.windsurfing.

Keywords: Sports, Windsurfing

Audience: Windsurfers

Contact: phansen@lemming.uvm.edu

Details: Free, Images

`ftp://lemming.uvm.edu/rec.windsurfing`

United Press International News - Sports

Full text of UPI stories and articles.

Keywords: Sports, News

Sponsor: United Press International (UPI)

Audience: Sports Enthusiasts

Profile: This gopher allows access to daily UPI news feeds, including sports news. The most current articles available tend to run three to five days behind. This delay is compensated for by UPIs far-ranging coverage of national and international sporting news. Indexed, with back articles from 1992 onwards available.

Contact: UPI clarinews@clarinet.com

Details: Free

`gopher://mrfrosty.micro.umn.edu./UPI-data/Today/sports`

University of Glasgow Information Service (GLANCE)

GLANCE provides subject-based information services, including an extensive section on European and world sports.

Keywords: Sports, Soccer, Motor Racing, Mountaineering, Squash, Cricket, Golf, Tennis, Europe, Scotland

Sponsor: University of Glasgow, Glasgow, Scotland

Audience: Sport Enthusiasts, Fitness Enthusiasts, Nature Lovers

Profile: Information at this site includes schedules, results, and statistics for sports such as cricket and soccer. There is also a selection of items on mountaineering.

Contact: Alan Dawson A.Dawson@uk.ac.gla.compserv

Details: Free

`gopher://govan.cent.gla.ac.uk/Subject/Sports and Rec`

Usenet Sports Groups Archived

An archive for Usenet groups, including many related to sports ranging from football to table tennis.

Keywords: Sports, Skydiving, Volleyball, Football, Scuba Diving, Table Tennis

Sponsor: Massachusetts Institute of Technology, Boston, MA

Audience: Sports Enthusiasts

Contact: ftp-bugs@rtfm.mit.edu

Details: Free

`ftp://rtfm.mit.edu/pub/usenet`

Velo News Experimental Tour de France Web Page

This web site provides background information on the Tour de France, including press coverage from this year's race.

Keywords: Bicycles, Sports

Sponsor: Velo News

Audience: Bicyclists, Sports Fans

Contact: VeloNews@aol.com

`http://cob.fsu.edu/velonews/`

Wiretap Sports Archives

Sports articles, including information on soccer in the US and Canada, rules for soccer and Australian football, and some rather dated material on American football.

Keywords: Sports, Football, Soccer

Sponsor: The Internet Wiretap Library

Audience: Sports Enthusiasts

Details: Free

`gopher://wiretap.spies.com/library/article/sports`

Sports Cars

Porschephiles

This list is for people who own, operate, work on, or covet various models of Porsche automobiles. Discussion topics include features, functionality, and purchasing advice.

Keywords: Porsche, Automobiles, Sports Cars

Audience: Porsche Owners, Sports Car Owners, Automobile Mechanics

Contact: porschephiles-request@tta.com

Details: Free

User Info: To subscribe to the list, send an e-mail message requesting a subscription to the URL address below. To send a message to the entire list, address it to: porschephiles@tta.com

`mailto:porschephiles-request@tta.com`

Sports Statistics

NHL Goalie Stats

A list of NHL goalie statistics.

Keywords: Hockey, National Hockey League (NHL), Sports Statistics

Audience: Hockey Enthusiasts

Profile: Weekday reports of goalie statistics from the National Hockey League.

Contact: dfa@triple-i.com

Details: Free

User Info: To subscribe to the list, send an e-mail message requesting a subscription to the URL address below. To send a message to the entire list, address it to: dfa@triple-i.com

`mailto:dfa@triple-i.com`

Sports-cards

Sports-cards

For people interested in collection, speculation and investing in baseball, football, basketball, hockey, and other trading cards and/or memorabilia. Discussion and want/sell lists are welcome.

Keywords: Memorabilia, Sports, Trading Cards

Audience: Collectors, Sports Card Traders

Contact: Keane Arase
cards-request@tanstaafl.uchicago.edu

Details: Free

User Info: To subscribe to the list, send an e-mail message requesting a subscription to the URL address below. To send a message to the entire list, address it to: cards@tanstaafl.uchicago.edu

`mailto:cards-request@tanstaafl.uchicago.edu`

Springsteen (Bruce)

Backstreets

Discussion of Bruce Springsteen's music.

Keywords: Rock Music, Springsteen (Bruce)

Audience: Bruce Springsteen Fans

Contact: Kevin Kinder
backstreets-request@virginia.edu

Details: Free

User Info: To subscribe to the list, send an e-mail message requesting a subscription to the URL address below. To send a message to the entire list, address it to: backstreets@virginia.edu

`mailto:backstreets-request@virginia.edu`

Squash

University of Glasgow Information Service (GLANCE)

GLANCE provides subject-based information services, including an extensive section on European and world sports.

Keywords: Sports, Soccer, Motor Racing, Mountaineering, Squash, Cricket, Golf, Tennis, Europe, Scotland

Sponsor: University of Glasgow, Glasgow, Scotland

Audience: Sport Enthusiasts, Fitness Enthusiasts, Nature Lovers

Profile: Information at this site includes schedules, results, and statistics for sports such as cricket and soccer. There is also a selection of items on mountaineering.

Contact: Alan Dawson
A.Dawson@uk.ac.gla.compserv

Details: Free

`gopher://govan.cent.gla.ac.uk/Subject/Sports and Rec`

Sri Lanka

Sri Lanka Net (SLNet)

A moderated mailing list that carries news and other articles about Sri Lanka.

Keywords: Sri Lanka, News (International)

Audience: Sri Lankans, Students

Contact: pkd@fed.frb.gov
slnetad@ganu.colorado.edu

Details: Free, Moderated

User Info: To subscribe to the list, send an e-mail message requesting a subscription to the URL address below. To send a message to the entire list, address it to: slnetad@ganu.colorado.edu

`mailto:pkd@fed.frb.gov`

`mailto:slnetad@ganu.colorado.edu`

ST Viruses

ST viruses

This list is to provide fast and efficient help with computer viruses infecting the Atari ST/TT/Falcon only.

Keywords: Computer Viruses, Atari

Audience: Computer Users

Contact: r.c.karsmakers@stud.let.ruu.nl

Details: Free

User Info: To subscribe to the list, send an e-mail message requesting a subscription to the URL address below. To send a message to the entire list, address it to: r.c.karsmakers@stud.let.ruu.nl

`mailto:r.c.karsmakers@stud.let.ruu.nl`

A B C D E F G H I J K L M N O P Q R S T U V W X Y Z

St. John Valley (History of)

University of Maine System Library Catalog

The library's holdings are large and wide-ranging and contain significant collections in many fields.

Keywords: Ucadian Studies, St. John Valley (History of), Canadian-American Studies, Geology, Aquaculture, Maine

Audience: General Public, Researchers, Librarians, Document Delivery Professionals

Contact: Elaine Albright, Marilyn Lutz

Details: Free

User Info: Expect: login, Send: ursus

```
telnet://ursus.maine.edu
```

St. Petersburg

St. Petersburg Business News

Contains a digest of business information extracted from Russian and St. Petersburg morning newspapers, stock exchange reports, reports from the News own correspondents.

Keywords: Business, St. Petersburg

Audience: Russians, Business

Contact: Elena Artemova
esa@cfea.ecc.spb.su
spbeac@sovamsu.sovusa.com

Details: Costs

User Info: To send a message to the entire list, address it to:

```
mailto:listserv@sovamsu.sovusa.com
```

Stagecraft

Stagecraft

This list is for the discussion of all aspects of stage work, including special effects, sound effects, sound reinforcement, stage management, set design and building, lighting, design, company management, hall management, hall design, and show production.

Keywords: Theater, Drama

Audience: Stage Producers

Contact: Brad Davis
stagecraft-request@zinc.com

User Info: To subscribe to the list, send an Email message requesting a subscription to the URL address below. To send a message to the entire list, address it to: stagecraft@zinc.com

Notes: Also contains archives of list discussions.

```
mailto:stagecraft-request@zinc.com
```

Standards

UN Rules

Standards, guidelines and international instruments promulgated by the UN.

Keywords: Politics, UN, Standards

Sponsor: United Nations Justice Network (UNCJIN)

Audience: Lawyers, General Public, Internationalists

Details: Free

Select from Menu as appropriate

```
gopher://uacsc2.albany.edu
```

Uniform Commercial Code (UCC)

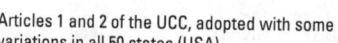

Articles 1 and 2 of the UCC, adopted with some variations in all 50 states (USA).

Keywords: Commerce, Business Info, Standards

Audience: Politicians, Marketers, Students, Retailers, Lawyers

Details: Free

```
http://www.law.cornell.edu/ucc/
ucc.table.html
```

Stanford Medical Center Gopher

Stanford Medical Center Gopher

This gopher allows extensive access to the Stanford Medical Center's archives.

Keywords: Medicine, Health Care, Health Sciences

Sponsor: Stanford Medical Center, Palo Alto, California, USA

Audience: Health Care Professionals, Health Science Researchers

Contact: Stanford Medical Center
gopher@medisg.stanford.edu

```
gopher://med.stanford.edu
```

Starfish

Starnet (Echinoderm Newsletter)

The Starnet echinoderm electronic newsletter is distributed quarterly.

Keywords: Echinoderm, Starfish, Marine Biology

Audience: Marine Biologists

Contact: Win Hide
whide@matrix.bchs.uh.edu

Details: Free

User Info: To subscribe to the list, send an e-mail message requesting a subscription to the URL address below.

```
mailto:whide@matrix.bchs.uh.edu
```

Stargazing

Sci.astro.hubble

Information about all subjects concerning NASA's Hubble space telescope.

Keywords: Hubble Telescope, Astronomy, Space, NASA, Stargazing, Telescopes

Audience: Astronomers, General Public, Science Teachers, Stargazers

Contact: Paul A. Scowen
scowen@wfpc3.la.asu.edu

Details: Free, Moderated, Images

User Info: To subscribe to this Usenet newsgroup, you need access to a newsreader.

```
news:sci.astro.hubble
```

Stars

Astronomy

This directory is a compilation of information resources focused on astronomy.

Keywords: Astronomy, Stars, Astrophysics, Space

Audience: Astronomers, Astrophysicists, Space Enthusiasts

Contact: A. Park, J. Miller

Details: Free

```
ftp://una.hh.lib.umich.edu/70/
inetdirsstacks/astron:parkmiller
```

State Courts

Citation Authority

Legal citation authority expected to be used in the highest US appellate state courts, based on a 1985 survey (revised March 1991).

Keywords: Law (US), State Courts

Audience: Lawyers

Details: Free

User Info: Expect: login; Send: lawlib

`gopher://liberty.uc.wlu.edu/00/library/law/lawftp/citation.txt`

State Small Business Profiles

State Small Business Profiles

This site contains Small Business Administration reports, which provide statistics on the small business sector in each state.

Keywords: Business, Statistics, United States

Sponsor: U.S. Government, Small Business Administration, in conjunction with the Reference Department of the Thomas Jefferson Library of the University of Missouri-St. Louis

Audience: Business Professionals, Researchers

Profile: The 1993 State Business Profiles bring together an array of statistics on the small business sector in each state. Included is data on small business income and employment trends; women-owned and minority-owned businesses; business closings and formations; and state exports.

Contact: Raleigh Muns
srcmuns@umslvma.umsl.edu

Details: Free

Notes: For additional information you can call the Small Business Administration toll free at 1-800-359-2777, or the SBA District Office in Washington, D.C. at (202) 205-6600.

`gopher://umslvma.umsl.edu/11/library/govdocs/states`

States

CODES (Codes Library)

The Codes Library offers access to US federal and state legislative materials, in codified, slip law, and bill form, plus federal and state regulatory materials and a statutes archive.

Keywords: Statutes, Codes, State, Federal

Audience: (US) Lawyers

Profile: The Codes library contains an extensive compilation of federal and state statutory materials, in codified as well as slip law form, from all 50 states, the District of Columbia, Puerto Rico, the Virgin Islands and the United States Code Service. The library also contains federal and state regulatory materials plus a statues archive. Pending legislation can be found with 50-state and federal fill tracking, the full text of federal bills, the Congressional Record, and the full text of bills for a growing number of states. Administrative materials include the Code of Federal Regulations, the Federal Register, 50-state regulation tracking, and the administrative codes for a selected number of states.

Contact: New Sales Group at (800) 227-4908 or (513) 859-5398 inside the US, or 1-513-865-7981 for all inquires outside the US.

User Info: To subscribe, contact Mead directly.

To examine the Lexis user guide, you can access it at the ftp site of the University of Texas at Austin at the URL address: ftp://ftp.cc.utexas.edu. The files are in: pub/ref-services/LEXIS

`telnet://nex.meaddata.com`

`http://www.meaddata.com`

STATES (States Library)

The combined States Library contains case law, code and agency materials from the 53 individual US state libraries (50 states plus the District of Columbia, Puerto Rico and the Virgin Islands), all in the same library.

Keywords: Law, Analysis, Case, States

Audience: Lawyers

Profile: The combined States Library contains case law, code and agency materials from the 53 individual state libraries (50 states plus the District of Columbia, Puerto Rico and the Virgin Islands), all in the same library. The States Library also features many large group files which allow several individual files to be accessed in the same search. Many of the group files involve case law, including files that cover all state case law available on the LEXIS service plus ALR material and files that combine all federal and state case law available on the LEXIS service.

Contact: New Sales Group at (800) 227-4908 or (513) 859-5398 inside the US, or 1-513-865-7981 for all inquires outside the US.

User Info: To subscribe, contact Mead directly.

To examine the Lexis user guide, you can access it at the ftp site of the University of Texas at Austin at the URL address: ftp://ftp.cc.utexas.edu. The files are in: pub/ref-services/LEXIS

`telnet://nex.meaddata.com`

`http://www.meaddata.com`

The Texas Information Highway

Access to the public information resources of the state of Texas.

Keywords: Texas, States, Government, Census, Tourism

Sponsor: Texas Department of Information Resources

Audience: Texans, General Public

Profile: Still under construction as we go to press, this is a model program to make state and local information resources available to Internet users. The current collection features city, country, and state political information, including full-text of bills before the Texas state legislature. Materials related to Texas history and tourism are also provided, along with links to Texas-area user groups and other state and federal information servers.

Contact: Wayne McDilda
wayne@dir.texas.gov

`gopher://info.texas.gov`

Statistics

Iowa State University

The library's holdings contain significant collections in many fields.

Keywords: Agriculture, Veterinary Medicine, Statistics, Labor, Soil Conservation, Film

Audience: General Public, Researchers, Librarians, Document Delivery Professionals

Details: Free

User Info: Expect: DIAL, Send: LIB

`telnet://isn.iastate.edu`

New York State Department of Health Gopher

An electronic guide to health information from the state of New York.

Keywords: Health Care, Statistics, Health Sciences, New York

Sponsor: New York State Department of Health

Audience: Health Care Professionals, Health Care Consumers

Profile: Information provided includes health statistics for New York State, lists of health care providers, facilities, and publications, as well as New York State Department of Health press releases.

Contact: nyhealth@albnydh2.bitnet

`gopher://gopher.health.state.ny.us`

A B C D E F G H I J K L M N O P Q R S T U V W X Y Z

State Small Business Profiles

This site contains Small Business Administration reports, which provide statistics on the small business sector in each state.

Keywords: Business, Statistics, United States

Sponsor: U.S. Government, Small Business Administration, in conjunction with the Reference Department of the Thomas Jefferson Library of the University of Missouri-St. Louis

Audience: Business Professionals, Researchers

Profile: The 1993 State Business Profiles bring together an array of statistics on the small business sector in each state. Included is data on small business income and employment trends; women-owned and minority-owned businesses; business closings and formations; and state exports.

Contact: Raleigh Muns
srcmuns@umslvma.umsl.edu

Details: Free

Notes: For additional information you can call the Small Business Administration toll free at (800) 359-2777, or the SBA District Office in Washington, D.C. at (202) 205-6600.

`gopher://umslvma.umsl.edu/11/library/govdocs/states`

Statistics Canada Gopher

A repository of information from the National Statistical Agency of Canada.

Keywords: Statistics, Canada, Canadian Documents

Sponsor: Statistics Canada, Canada

Audience: Canadians, Researchers

Profile: Updated daily, this site allows users to search Statistics Canada documents and provides updates of upcoming statistical conferences and publications in Canada. It also allows access to Statistics Canada FTP and list servers.

Contact: Michael Thoen, Jackie Godfrey
thoemic@statcan.ca
godfrey@statcan.ca

`gopher://talon.statcan.ca`

Statlib

Statlib is an archive of statistics-related materials.

Keywords: Statistics, Mathematics

Audience: Statisticians, Mathematicians

Profile: This archive contains a large collection of statistics software data. The directory lists the source to entire statistics packages, the collection of applied statistics algorithms, the archives of the s-new mailing list, and more.

Contact: statlib@lib.stat.cmu.edu

Details: Free

`ftp://lib.stat.cmu.edu`

U.S. Bureau of the Census Gopher

A gopher offering official Census data and services direct from the Census Bureau.

Keywords: Census, Demography, Statistics

Sponsor: U.S. Census Bureau

Audience: Journalists, Government Officials, General Public

Profile: A wealth of demographic and economic data from the Census Bureau. Information available includes population estimates, financial data from state and local governments, and assorted statistical briefs. This gopher also has details on the offices, programs, and personnel of the Bureau itself, as well as links to other federal information systems and sources of Census data.

Contact: gatekeeper@census.gov

Details: Free, Images

`gopher://gopher.census.gov`

`http://www.census.gov (CHECK)`

University of Rochester Library

The library's holdings are large and wide-ranging and contain significant collections in many fields.

Keywords: Architecture, Art History, Photography, Literature (Asian), Lasers, Geology, Statistics, Optics, Medieval Studies

Audience: Researchers, Students, General Public

Details: Free

User Info: Expect: Login; Send: Library

`telnet://128.151.226.71`

Wildnet (Computing and Statistics in Fishers & Wildlife Biology)

★

This mailing list was established for the exchange of ideas, questions, and solutions in the area of fisheries and wildlife biology computing and statistics.

Keywords: Wildlife, Fisheries, Statistics

Audience: Wildlife Biologists, Environmentalists, Statisticians

Contact: Eric Woodsworth
woodsworth@sask.usask.ca

Details: Free

User Info: To subscribe to the list, send an e-mail message requesting a subscription to the URL address below. To send a message to the entire list, address it to: wildnet@tribune.usask.ca

`mailto:wildnet-request@tribune.usask.ca`

Statutes

CODES (Codes Library)

The Codes library offers access to US federal and state legislative materials, in codified, slip law, and bill form, plus federal and state regulatory materials and a statutes archive.

Keywords: Statutes, Codes, State, Federal

Audience: (US) Lawyers

Profile: The Codes library contains an extensive compilation of federal and state statutory materials, in codified as well as slip law form, from all 50 states, the District of Columbia, Puerto Rico, the Virgin Islands and the United States Code Service. The library also contains federal and state regulatory materials plus a statues archive. Pending legislation can be found with 50-state and federal fill tracking, the full text of federal bills, the Congressional Record, and the full text of bills for a growing number of states. Administrative materials include the Code of Federal Regulations, the Federal Register, 50-state regulation tracking, and the administrative codes for a selected number of states.

Contact: New Sales Group at (800) 227-4908 or (513) 859-5398 inside the US, or (513) 865-7981 for all inquires outside the US.

User Info: To subscribe, contact Mead directly.

To examine the Lexis user guide, you can access it at the ftp site of the University of Texas at Austin at the URL address: ftp://ftp.cc.utexas.edu. The files are in: pub/ref-services/LEXIS

`telnet://nex.meaddata.com`

`http://www.meaddata.com`

Std-UNIX

Std-UNIX

Discussion of UNIX standards, particularly the IEEE P1003 Portable Operating System Environment draft standard.

Keywords: UNIX, Operating Systems

Audience: UNIX Users

Contact: Sean Eric Fagan
sef@uunet.uu.net

Details: Free, Moderated

User Info: To subscribe to the list, send an e-mail message requesting a subscription to the URL address below.

`mailto:sef@uunet.uu.net`

Stealth

Stealth

Discussion of anything related to Dodge Stealth and Mitsubishi 3000GT cars.

Keywords: Automobile

Audience: Car Enthusiasts

Contact: stealth-request%jim.uucp@wupost.wustl.edu

Details: Free

User Info: Expect: Username prompt, Send: tcucat

User Info: To subscribe to the list, send an e-mail message requesting a subscription to the URL address below. To send a message to the entire list, address it to: stealth-request96jim.uucp@wupost.wustl.edu

`mailto:stealth-request%jim.uucp@wupost.wustl.edu`

Steel

Materials Business File

Covers all commercial aspects of iron and steel, non-ferrous metals and non-metallic materials.

Keywords: Material Science, Business, Iron, Steel

Sponsor: Material Information, a joint information service of ASM International and the Institute of Materials

Audience: Materials Scientists, Researchers

Profile: Articles are abstracted from over 2,000 worldwide technical and trade journals to create more than 65,000 records. Update monthly.

Contact: paul.albert@neteast.com

User Info: To subscribe contact Orbit-Questel directly.

`telnet://orbit.com`

Stereo Electronics

rec.audio

A Usenet newsgroup providing information and discussion about audio products, including troubleshooting advice.

Keywords: Audio Electronics, Stereo Electronics

Audience: Stereo Owners, Music Listeners

User Info: To subscribe to this Usenet newsgroup, you need access to a newsreader.

`news:rec.audio`

Stlhe-l (Forum for Teaching & Learning in Higher Education)

Stlhe-l (Forum for Teaching & Learning in Higher Education)
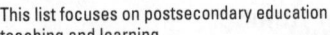

This list focuses on postsecondary education teaching and learning.

Keywords: Education (Adult), Education (Distance), Education (Continuing), Education (Post Secondary)

Audience: Educators, Faculty, Administrators, Researchers

Details: Free

User Info: To subscribe to the list, send an e-mail message to the URL address below consisting of a single line reading:

SUB stlhe-l YourFirstName YourLastName

To send a message to the entire list, address it to: stlhe-l@unbvm1.bitnet

`mailto:listserv@unbvm1.bitnet`

Stock Market

Disclosure Database

Disclosure Database provides in-depth financial information on over 12,500 companies.

Keywords: Securities, Stock Market

Sponsor: Disclosure Incorporated, Bethesda, MD, USA

Audience: Business Professionals

Profile: The information is derived from reports filed with the US Securities and Exchange Commission (SEC) by publicly owned companies. These reports provide detailed and reliable financial information on the companies included. Extracts of 10-K and 10-Q financial reports are included, as well as 20-F financial reports and registration reports for new registrants. Disclosure provides an online source of information for marketing intelligence, corporate planning, accounting research, and corporate finance. Contents of the records include management discussion and president's letter on past-year performance, footnotes to the financials, significant events, and market conditions affecting a particular company.

Contact: Dialog in the US at (800) 334-2564, Dialog internationally at country-specific locations.

User Info: To subscribe, contact Dialog directly.

Notes: Coverage: Current; updated weekly.

`telnet://dialog.com`

Experimental Stock Market Data

This is an experimental page that provides a link to the latest stock market information.

Keywords: Stock Market, Investments, Finance

Audience: General Public, Investors, Stock Brokers

Profile: This site is updated automatically, to reflect the current day's closing information. Provides general market news and quotes for selected stocks, although prices are not guaranteed. Also includes recent prices for many mutual funds, as well as technical analysis charts for a large number of stocks and mutual funds.

Contact: Mark Torrance stockmaster@ai.mit.edu

Details: Free

`http://www.ai.mit.edu/stocks.html`

SEC (Securities and Exchange Commission) EDGAR (Electronic Data Gathering, Analysis and Retrieval) System

Provides free access to 1994 SEC filings for approximately 2,300 companies.

Keywords: Securities, Filings, SEC, Stock Market

Sponsor: New York University School of Business

Audience: Business Professionals, Investors

Profile: This expanding project aims to make available current, public SEC filings that are filed electronically. The system is searchable by company name and is updated and indexed daily. Many types of SEC forms, including 10-K and 10-Q financial reports, are available in a number of different electronic formats. The site also provides some explanatory documentation on the EDGAR program and on the types of SEC forms and information available to the public.

Contact: Ajit Kambil piotr@edgar.stern.nyu.edu

Details: Free

`ftp://town.hall.org/edgar`

`http://www.town.hall.org`

Stock Market Secrets

Publication of a stock market-related daily commentary. Questions are answered on a wide variety of investment and financial topics.

Keywords: Stock Market, Investments, Finance

Audience: Investors, Stock Brokers, Financial Advisors

Contact: smi-request@world.std.com

A B C D E F G H I J K L M N O P Q R **S** T U V W X Y Z

A
B
C
D
E
F
G
H
I
J
K
L
M
N
O
P
Q
R
S
T
U
V
W
X
Y
Z

Details: Free, Moderated

User Info: To subscribe to the list, send an e-mail message requesting a subscription to the URL address below.

To send a message to the entire list, address it to: smi@world.std.com

`mailto:smi-request@world.std.com`

Yahoo Market and Investments

 ★★★

A comprehensive look at the current economic status, with a wide range of coverage, from brokers to stocks.

Keywords: Business, Stock Market, Investment, Economy

Sponsor: Stanford University, Palo Alto, California, USA

Audience: Investors, Economists

Contact: jerry@akebono.stanford.edu

`http://akebono.stanford.edu/yahoo/`
`Economy/Markets_and_Investments`

Stonewall25

Stonewall25

★

A mailing list for discussion and planning of the "Stonewall 25," an international gay/lesbian/bisexual rights march in New York City on Sunday, June 26, 1994, and the events accompanying it.

Keywords: Gay Rights, Lesbian, Bisexual, Activism

Audience: Gays, Lesbians, Bisexuals, Activists

Contact: stonewall25-request@queernet.org

Details: Free

User Info: To subscribe to the list, send an e-mail message requesting a subscription to the URL address below. To send a message to the entire list, address it to: stonewall25@queernet.org

`mailto:stonewall25-`
`request@queernet.org`

Stormcock

Stormcock

★

For general discussion and news concerning the music of Roy Harper, a folk-rock musician with a conscience. Recommendations and news concerning similar artists are encouraged.

Keywords: Rock Music, Music, Harper (Roy)

Audience: Music Fans

Contact: Paul Davison
stormcock-request@qmw.ac.uk

Details: Free

User Info: To subscribe to the list, send an e-mail message to the address shown below consisting of a single line reading:

SUB stormcock YourFirstName YourLastName

To send a message to the entire list, address it to: stormcock@qmw.ac.uk

`mailto:listserv@qmw.ac.uk`

Storytelling

Nerdnosh

 ★

This is a virtual campfire gathering of storytellers. Bring us your tired, your family fables, your journals of yesterday, and your imprints on tomorrow.

Keywords: Storytelling

Audience: Storytellers, General Public

Contact: Timothy Bowden
urder@clovis.felton.ca.us

Details: Free

User Info: To subscribe to the list, send an e-mail message requesting a subscription to the URL address below, consisting of a single line reading:

SUB nerdnosh YourFirstName YourLastName

To send a message to the entire list, address it to:
nerdnosh@clovis.felton.ca.us

`mailto:listserv@clovis.felton.ca.us`

String Processing

Icon-group

 ★

Discussion of topics related to the Icon programming language.

Keywords: Programming, Icon Programming Language, Programming Language, String Processing

Audience: Icon Programmers

Profile: Icon is a high-level, general purpose programming language emphazing string and structure processing. Topics include programming techniques, theoretical aspects, Icon in relation to other languages, applications of Icon, implementation issues, porting, and bugs.

Contact: Bill Mitchell
whm@arizona.edu

Details: Free

User Info: To subscribe to the list, send an e-mail message requesting a subscription to the URL address below.

`mailto:Icon-Group-`
`Request@arizona.edu.`

Students

CCNEWS

 ★★★

An electronic forum for campus-computing newsletter editors and other publications specialists.

Keywords: Computers, Editors, Students, Newsletters

Audience: Students (college), Editors

Profile: CCNEWS consists of a biweekly newsletter that focuses on the writing, editing, designing, and producing of campus-computing publications, and an articles abstracts published on alternating weeks that describes new contributions to the articles archive.

Contact: Wendy Rickard Bollentin
CCNEWS@EDUCOM.BITNET

Details: Free

User Info: To subscribe to the list, send an e-mail message to the URL address below consisting of a single line reading:

SUB ccnews YourFirstName YourLastName

To send a message to the entire list, address it to: ccnews@educom.bitnet

Inquire about needing a password.

`mailto:listserv@bitnic.cren.net`

CFES-L

National communication branch of the CFES (Canadian Federation of Engineering Students).

Keywords: Engineering, Students, Canada

Audience: Engineers, Students

Contact: Canadian Federation of Engineering Students
cfes@jupiter.sun.csd.unb.ca

Details: Free

User Info: To subscribe to the list, send an e-mail message to the URL address below consiting of a single line reading:

SUB cfes-l YourFirstName YourLastName

To send a message to the entire list, address it to: cfes-l@unb.ca

`mailto:listserv@unb.ca`

k12.chat.junior

 ★

A Usenet newsgroup providing information and discussion for and about students in junior high school.

Keywords: Students, Chat Groups

Audience: Students (K-8)

Details: Free

User Info: To subscribe to this Usenet newsgroup, you need access to a newsreader.

`news:k12.chat.junior`

k12.chat.senior

A Usenet newsgroup providing information and discussion for and about students in senior high school.

Keywords: Students, Chat Groups

Audience: Students (K-12)

Details: Free

User Info: To subscribe to this Usenet newsgroup, you need access to a newsreader.

`news:k12.chat.senior`

Lysator's Gopher Service

Lysator is the name of the Academic Computer Society at Linkoping University, Linkoping, Sweden. It relies on voluntary efforts by students, and any service of activity runs as long as they think it is fun—content always reflects their personal interests.

Keywords: Sweden, Students, Europe

Audience: Swedish Students

Contact: Lars Aronsson@lysator.liu.se

Details: Free

`gopher://gopher.lysator.liu.se`

`http://dla.ucop.edu`

Style

alt.fashion

A Usenet newsgroup providing information and discussion about all facets of the fashion industry.

Keywords: Fashion Industry, Style

Audience: Designers, General Public

User Info: To subscribe to this Usenet newsgroup, you need access to a newsreader.

`news:alt.fashion`

Style Sheets from the Online Writers' Workshop

Style Sheets from the Online Writers' Workshop

This gopher provides information and examples on how to write bibliographies using three formats: MLA (Modern Language Association), Old-MLA, and APA (American Psychological Association).

Keywords: Bibliographies, Writing, Lexicology

Sponsor: University of Illinois at Urbana-Champaign

Audience: Writers, Students (High School/College/University)

Contact: Dr. Michael Pemberton michaelp@ux1.cso.uiuc

`gopher://gopher.uiuc.edu`

Subways

Subway Navigator (City Subway Routes)

This service help you find a route in the subway systems of some cities in the world. Estimated times of departure/arrival are also given.

Keywords: Subways, Transit, Travel

Audience: Subway Riders, International Travelers

Profile: Cities covered are:

Frankfurt, Germany

Hong Kong

Lille, France

Lyon, France

Madrid, Spain

Marseille, France

Montreal, Canada

Munich, Germany

New York City, NY, USA*

Paris, France

Toulouse, France

*The network includes all NYCTA (New-York City Transit Authority) subway stations.

Contact: Pierre.David@prism.uvsq.fr

Details: Free

`gopher://gopher.jussieu.fr/11/metro`

`telnet://vishnu.jussieu.fr`

Summer Sports

rec.sport.olympics

A Usenet newsgroup providing information and discussion about the summer Olympics Games.

Keywords: Olympic Games, Summer Sports

Audience: Olympic Enthusiasts

User Info: To subscribe to this Usenet newsgroup, you need access to a newsreader.

`news:rec.sport.olympics`

Summit of the Americas Internet Gopher

Summit of the Americas Internet Gopher

A gopher containing supporting materials for the Summit of the Americas, a meeting of the Western Hemisphere's democratically elected heads of state, to be held in Miami in December of 1994.

Keywords: American Studies, International Relations, Haiti, Latin America

Sponsor: The Florida University Latin American and Caribbean Center

Audience: Government Officials, Journalists, NGOs, General Public

Contact: Rene Ramos summit@SERVAX.FIU.EDU

`gopher://summit.fiu.edu`

Sun

comp.sys.sun

A Usenet newsgroup providing information and discussion about Sun systems. There are several categories within this group.

Keywords: Computer Systems, Sun

Audience: Computer Users, Sun Users

User Info: To subscribe to this Usenet newsgroup, you need access to a newsreader.

`news:comp.sys.sun`

Sun Microsystems, Inc.

Sun Microsystems, Inc.

This site provides a directory of Sun Microsystems products and services, including a company profile, announcements, financial statements, marketing reports, and international sales and support access.

Keywords: Computer Systems, Sun Microsystems

Sponsor: Sun Microsystems, Inc., Mountain View, California, USA

Audience: Sun Microsystems Users

Profile: Languages: English

Contact: webmaster@sun.com.

Details: Free

`http://www.sun.com`

A
B
C
D
E
F
G
H
I
J
K
L
M
N
O
P
Q
R
S
T
U
V
W
X
Y
Z

A
B
C
D
E
F
G
H
I
J
K
L
M
N
O
P
Q
R
S
T
U
V
W
X
Y
Z

Supercomputers

cm5-Managers

This is a discussion of administrating the Thinking Machines CM5 parallel supercomputer.

Keywords: Supercomputers, Computer Administration

Audience: Supercomputer Users, Supercomputer Administrators

Contact: J. Eric Townsend
jet@nas.nasa.gov

Details: Free

User Info: To subscribe to the list, send an e-mail message to the address below, consisting of a single line reading:

SUB cm5-managers YourFirstName YourLastName

To send a message to the entire list, address it to: cm5-managers@boxer.nas.nasa.gov

`mailto:listserv@boxer.nas.nasa.gov`

NWNet Internet Guide

An introductory guide to the Internet. Details the basic Internet tools of electronic mail, FTP (File Transfer Protocol), and Telnet. Covers types of resources found on the Internet, and how to use them. Includes information directed toward supercomputer users and the K-12 community.

Keywords: Internet, Internet Guides, Supercomputers, Education (K-12)

Sponsor: NorthWestNet

Audience: Internet Surfers, Supercomputer Users, Students (K-12)

Contact: Jonathan Kochmer
nusirg@nwnet.net

Details: Free

File is user-docs/nusirg/nusirg.whole-guide.ps

`ftp://ftphost.nwnet.net`

NYSERNet Internet Guide

A comprehensive guide to the Internet from the New York State Education and Research Network (NYSERNet). NYSERNet provides access to specialized databases and online libraries, as well as to supercomputing and parallel-processing facilities throughout the US and to many national networks.

Keywords: Internet, Internet Guides, New York, Supercomputers

Sponsor: NYSERNet K-12 Networking Interest Group

Audience: Internet Surfers

Contact: info@nysernet.org

Details: Free

`ftp://nysernet.org`

Supercomputers

Weekly mailing list of the world's most powerful computing sites.

Keywords: Supercomputers, Computing

Audience: Supercomputer Users, Computer Scientists

Contact: gunter@yarrow.wt.uwa.oz.au

Details: Free

User Info: To subscribe to the list, send an e-mail message requesting a subscription to the URL address below. To send a message to the entire list, address it to: gunter@yarrow.wt.uwa.oz.au

`mailto:gunter@yarrow.wt.uwa.oz.au`

Supercomputing

NCSA (National Center for Supercomputing Applications)

★★★★

A high-performance computing and communications facility and research center designed to serve the US computational science and engineering community.

Keywords: Supercomputing, Computer Networking, Computer Science, Mosaic

Sponsor: University of Illinois at Urbana-Champaign, Champaign, Illinois, USA

Audience: Students, Researchers, Computer Scientists, General Public

Contact: Systems Operator
pubs@ncsa.uiuc.edu

`http://www.ncsa.uiuc.edu/General/NCSAHome.html`

Output

Newsletter of the Florida State University (FSU) Computing Center. Includes topics such as networking, microcomputing, mainframe computing, and supercomputing on campus, including use of computers in classroom and research computing at FSU.

Keywords: Networking, Microcomputing, Supercomputing

Audience: FSU Computer Science Students, Computer Users

Contact: Suzanne C. Nelson
nelson@avm.cc.fsu.edu

Details: Free

Send your request addressed to the Editor.

`mailto:nelson@avm.cc.fsu.edu`

Swiss Scientific Supercomputing Center (CSCS) Info Server

The Centro Svizzero di Calcolo Scientifico (CSCS) info server is the national scientific computing center in Switzerland.

Keywords: Switzerland, Supercomputing, Europe

Audience: Swiss Internet Surfers

Contact: mgay@cscs.ch

Details: Free

`gopher://pobox.cscs.ch`

SupraFAX

SupraFAX

This list was created to help people who are using the SupraFAX v.32bis modem.

Keywords: Modem, FAX

Audience: Modem Users, FAX Users

Contact: David Tiberio
subscribe@xamiga.linet.org

Details: Free

User Info: To subscribe to the list, send an e-mail message requesting a subscription to the URL address below. To send a message to the entire list, address it to: subscribe@xamiga.linet.org

`mailto:subscribe@xamiga.linet.org`

Supreme Court

Supreme Court Decisions

Full text of Supreme Court decisions issued since 1989, as well as brief biographies of Supreme Court justices.

Keywords: Supreme Court, Law

Audience: Legal Professionals, Educators, Researchers

`gopher://info.umd.edu`

Supreme Court Decisions (Project Hermes)

US Supreme Court decisions available online as part of 'Project Hermes.'

Keywords: Supreme Court, Judiciary, Law

Sponsor: Case Western Reserve University

Audience: General Public, Lawyers, Students

Profile: Project Hermes was started in May 1990 by the US Supreme Court as an experiment in disseminating its opinions electronically. Starting with the 1993 calendar year, the US Supreme Court began disseminating opinions electronically on an official basis. Each decision consists of a syllabus (summarizing the ruling), the opinion, and optional concurrent and dissenting opinions.

Contact: Peter W. Martin
martin@law.mail.cornell.edu

Details: Free

Anonymous ftp: Expect: login; Send: anonymous; Expect: password; Send: your e-mail address

`ftp://cwru.edu`

`gopher://marvel.loc.gov`

Supreme Court Judges

★

Biographies from the sitting Justices, and a few former Justices.

Keywords: Judiciary, Supreme Court, Judges, Biography

Audience: General Public, Lawyers, Judges, Journalists

Details: Free

`gopher://info.umd.edu`

Supreme Court (US)

LEGNEW (Legal News)

The Legal News Library provides general news information about the domestic legal industry and legal profession.

Keywords: Law (US), Justice, Supreme Court (US)

Audience: Business Researchers, Analysts, Entrepreneurs

Profile: Included are sources which cover materials on law firm management, bar association journals and a hot file of case list summaries on recently decided US Supreme Court cases. LEGNEW is organized very simply. There are individual files, group files, and user-defined combination files.

Contact: Mead New Sales Group at (800) 227-4908 or (513) 859-5398 inside the US, or (513) 865-7981 for all inquiries outside the US.

User Info: To subscribe, contact Mead directly.

To examine the Nexis user guide, you can access it at the ftp site of the University of Texas at Austin at the URL address: ftp://ftp.cc.utexas.edu. The files are in pub/ref-services/LEXIS.

`telnet://nex.meaddata.com`

`http://www.meaddata.com`

Supreme Court of Canada

Supreme Court of Canada

 ★★

This gopher allows access to Canadian Supreme Court rulings from 1993 forward. Documents are available as full-text and searchable by keyword. This site also has information on Canadian statute and case law.

Keywords: Law (International), Canada

Sponsor: Universite de Montreal Law Gopher Project, Montreal, Canada

Audience: Lawyers, General Public

Contact: Pablo Fuentes
fuentesp@droit.umontreal.ca

`gopher://gopher.droit.umontreal.ca/English/SCC`

Surfing (Internet)

Surfing the Internet

 ★

An introductory guide to "surfing," or finding information on the Internet.

Keywords: Internet, Internet Guides, Surfing (internet)

Audience: Internet Surfers

Details: Free

`ftp://rtfm.mit.edu`

SURFnet—KB InfoServer

SURFnet—KB InfoServer

InfoService is a joint project by SURFnet (National Network Organization for Research and Higher Education) and the Koninklijke Bibliotheek (National Library of the Netherlands).

Keywords: Netherlands, Networks, Europe

Audience: European Internet Surfers

Contact: infoservices@surfnet.nl

Details: Free

`gopher://gopher.nic.surfnet.nl`

Sustainable Living

CEE Environmental Libraries Database

A directory of over 300 libraries and environmental information centers in Central Eastern Europe that specalize in, or maintain significant collections of information about, the environment, ecology, sustainable living, or conservation. The database concentrates on six Central Eastern European countries: Bulgaria, Czech Republic, Hungary, Romania, Slovakia, and Poland.

Keywords: Central Eastern Europe, Environment, Sustainable Living, Bulgaria, Czech Republic, Hungary, Romania, Slovakia, Poland.

Sponsor: The Wladyslaw Poniecki Charitable Foundation, Inc.

Audience: Environmentalists, Green Movement, Librarians, Community Builders, Sustainable Living Specialists.

Profile: This database is the product of an Environmental Training Project (ETP) that was funded in 1992 by the US Agency for International Development as a 5-year cooperative agreement with a consortium headed by the University of Minnesota (US AID Cooperative Agreement Number EUR-0041-A-002-2020). Other members of the consortium include the University of Pittsburgh's Center for Hazardous Materials Research, The Institute for Sustainable Communities, and the World Wildlife Fund. The Wladyslaw Poniecki Charitable Foundation, Inc., was a subcontractor to the World Wildlife Fund and published the Directory of Libraries and Environmental Information Centers in Central Eastern Europe: A Locator/Directory . This gopher database consists of an electronic version of the printed directory, subsequently modified and updated online. Access to the data is facilitated by a WAIS search engine which makes it possible to retrieve information about libraries, subject area specializations, personnel, and so on.

Contact: Doug Kahn, CEDAR
kahn@pan.cedar.univie.ac.at

`gopher://gopher.poniecki.berkeley.edu`

Svhp-I

Svhp-I

 ★

A restricted discussion group on veterinary pharmacy issues.

Keywords: Veterinary Pharmacy, Pharmacy, Veterinary Science

Audience: Veterinarians, Veterinary Pharmacists

Contact: Doug Kemp
vetpharm@uga.cc.uga.edu

A B C D E F G H I J K L M N O P Q R **S** T U V W X Y Z

Details: Free

User Info: To subscribe to the list, send an e-mail message to the URL address shown below consisting of a single line reading:

SUB svhp-l YourFirstName YourLastName

To send a message to the entire list, address it to: svhp-l@uga.cc.uga.edu

`mailto:listserv@uga.cc.uga.edu`

Sweden

Lysator's Gopher Service ★

Lysator is the name of the Academic Computer Society at Linkoping University, Linkoping, Sweden. It relies on voluntary efforts by students, and any service of activity runs as long as they think it is fun; content always reflects their personal interests.

Keywords: Sweden, Students, Europe

Audience: Swedish Students

Contact: Lars Aronsson@lysator.liu.se

Details: Free

`gopher://gopher.lysator.liu.se`

`http://dla.ucop.edu`

Swiss Scientific Supercomputing Center (CSCS) Info Server

Swiss Scientific Supercomputing Center (CSCS) Info Server ★

The Centro Svizzero di Calcolo Scientifico (CSCS) info server is the national scientific computing center in Switzerland.

Keywords: Switzerland, Supercomputing, Europe

Audience: Swiss Internet Surfers

Contact: mgay@cscs.ch

Details: Free

`gopher://pobox.cscs.ch`

Switzerland

Swiss Scientific Supercomputing Center (CSCS) Info Server ★

The Centro Svizzero di Calcolo Scientifico (CSCS) info server is the national scientific computing center in Switzerland.

Keywords: Switzerland, Supercomputing, Europe

Audience: Swiss Internet Surfers

Contact: mgay@cscs.ch

Details: Free

`gopher://pobox.cscs.ch`

Synth-l

Synth-l ★

Synth-l is the electronic music "gearhead" list dedicated to the discussion of the less esoteric aspects of synthesis. Discussion concentrates on the availability and capabilities of music software and hardware, but sometimes diverges to other subjects.

Keywords: Electronic Music, Music Software

Audience: Electronic Music Enthusiasts, Musicians, Software Designers

Contact: Joe McMahon
            Synth-L@american.edu

Details: Free

User Info: To subscribe to the list, send an e-mail message to the address shown below consisting of a single line reading:

SUB Synth-L YourFirstName YourLastName

To send a message to the entire list, address it to: Synth-L@american.edu

`mailto:listserv@american.edu`

Synthesis

Computer Music Journal Archive and World Wide Web Home Page. ★★★★

This resource reinforces material available in the hardcopy version of Computer Music Journal, published by the MIT Press.

Keywords: Computer Music, Composition, Synthesis, Interaction

Sponsor: The MIT Press

Audience: Computer Musicians

Profile: The archive includes the tables of contents, abstracts, and editor's notes for the last several volumes of CMJ (including the recent bibliography, diskography, and taxonomy of the field), a number of useful CM-related documents such as the full MIDI and AIFF format specifications, a lengthy reference list, the guidelines for manuscript submission, and the full-text of several recent articles.

Contact: Stephen Pope
            cmj@cnmat.Berkeley.edu

Details: Free

`ftp://mitpress.mit.edu:/pub/Computer-Music-Journal`

Contact: mgay@cscs.ch

Details: Free

`gopher://pobox.cscs.ch`

Synthesizers

Analog Heaven ★

The Analog Heaven mailing list caters to people interested in vintage analog electronic music equipment. Topics include items for sale, repair tips, equipment modifications, ASCII & GIF schematics, and a general discussion of new and old analog equipment. There is an FTP/Gopher site located at cs.uwp.edu with discussions on various machines, a definitive guide to Roland synths, patch editors, modification schematics, and GIFs/JPEGs of vintage synths, as well as a few sound samples of some of the gear itself.

Keywords: Music, Synthesizers, Sequencers, Analog Equipment, Electronic Music

Audience: Electronic Music Enthusiasts, Musicians

Contact: Todd Sines
            analogue-request@magnus.acs.ohio-state.edu

Details: Free, Sound

User Info: To subscribe to the list, send an e-mail message requesting a subscription to the URL address below. To send a message to the entire list, address it to: analogue@magnus.acs.ohio-state.edu

`mailto:analogue-request@magnus.acs.ohio-state.edu`

Systems Administration

info-UNIX

Info-UNIX is intended for Question/Answer discussion, where "novice" Systems Administrators can pose questions.

Keywords: UNIX (Opersting Systems), Systems Administration

Audience: UNIX Systems Administrators

Contact: Mike Muuss
            mike@brl.mil

User Info: To subscribe to the list, send an e-mail message requesting a subscription to the URL address below.

`mailto:info-UNIX@brl.mil`

Systems Theory

(The) Observer

The central scope of the group covers the theory of autopoiesis (of Humberto Maturana and Francisco Varela) and enactive cognitive science. The extended scope includes applications of the above theoretical work and other relevant work (e.g. systems theory, cognitive science, phenomenology, artificial life, and so on). This is an edited electronic newsletter issued (approximately) twice monthly.

Keywords: Autopoiesis, Systems Theory, Cognitive Science

Audience: Systems Theorists, Researchers

Contact: Randall Whitaker
rwhit@cs.umu.se

User Info: To subscribe to the list, send an e-mail message to the URL address below consisting of a single line reading:

SUB the observer YourFirstName YourLastName

To send a message to the entire list, address it to: rwhit@cs.umu.se

mailto: listserv@cs.umu.se

DYNSYS-L

The Dynamical System exchanges information among people working in ergodic theory and dynamical systems.

Keywords: Entropy, Systems Theory

Audience: Engineers

Details: Free

newserv@uhcvm1.oit.uhc.edu

THINKNET

Electronic newsletter on philosophy, systems theory, interdisciplinary studies, and thoughtful conversation in cyberspace.

Keywords: Cyberspace, Systems Theory, Philosophy

Audience: Philosophers, System Theorists

Contact: Kent D. Palmer Ph.D.
Internet: palmer@world.std.com

Details: Free

User Info: To subscribe, send an e-mail message to the URL address below consisting of a single line reading:

SUB THINKNET YourFirstName YourLastName

mailto:palmer@world.std.com

A
B
C
D
E
F
G
H
I
J
K
L
M
N
O
P
Q
R
S
T
U
V
W
X
Y
Z

A
B
C
D
E
F
G
H
I
J
K
L
M
N
O
P
Q
R
S
T
U
V
W
X
Y
Z

T

Table Tennis

Usenet Sports Groups Archived

An archive for Usenet groups, including many related to sports ranging from football to table tennis.

Keywords: Sports, Skydiving, Volleyball, Football, Scuba Diving, Table Tennis

Sponsor: Massachusetts Institute of Technology, Boston, MA

Audience: Sports Enthusiasts

Contact: ftp-bugs@rtfm.mit.edu

Details: Free

`ftp://rtfm.mit.edu/pub/usenet`

table.abortion

table.abortion

A Usenet newsgroup providing information and discussion about all sides of the abortion issue.

Keywords: Abortion, Women's Issues, Health

Audience: Women, Activists, Health Care Professionals

Details: Free

User Info: To subscribe to this Usenet newsgroup, you need access to a newsreader.

`news:table.abortion`

Taiwan

soc.culture.taiwan

A Usenet newsgroup providing information and discussion about Taiwanese people and their culture.

Keywords: Taiwan, Sociology

Audience: Sociologists, Taiwanese

Details: Free

User Info:User Info: To subscribe to this Usenet newsgroup, you need access to a newsreader.

`news:soc.culture.taiwan`

talk.bizarre

talk.bizarre

A Usenet newsgroup providing information and discussion about the unusual, the bizarre, and the curious.

Keywords: Humor

Audience: General Public

Details: Free

User Info: To subscribe to this Usenet newsgroup, you need access to a newsreader.

`news:talk.bizarre`

talk.origins

talk.origins

A Usenet newsgroup providing information and discussion about evolution versus creationism.

Keywords: Evolution, Creationism, Activism

Audience: General Public, Evolutionists, Creationists, Activists

Details: Free

User Info: To subscribe to this Usenet newsgroup, you need access to a newsreader.

`news:talk.origins`

talk.politics.mideast

talk.politics.mideast

A Usenet newsgroup providing information and discussion about Middle Eastern topics.

Keywords: Middle East, Middle Eastern Studies, Politics (International)

Audience: Political Scientists

Details: Free

User Info: To subscribe to this Usenet newsgroup, you need access to a newsreader.

`news:talk.politics.mideast`

talk.politics.soviet

talk.politics.soviet

A Usenet newsgroup providing information and discussion about Soviet politics, domestic and international.

Keywords: Communism, Russia, Politics, Commonwealth of Independent States (CIS)

Audience: Political Scientists

Details: Free

User Info: To subscribe to this Usenet newsgroup, you need access to a newsreader.

`news:talk.politics.soviet`

A B C D E F G H I J K L M N O P Q R **S** T U V W X Y Z

talk.religion.misc

talk.religion.misc

A Usenet newsgroup providing information and discussion about religious, ethical, and moral implications.

Keywords: Religion, Ethics

Audience: General Public, Researchers, Students

Details: Free

User Info: To subscribe to this Usenet newsgroup, you need access to a newsreader.

`news:talk.religion.misc`

talk.religion.newage

talk.religion.newage

A Usenet newsgroup providing information and discussion about esoteric and minority religions and philosophies.

Keywords: Religion, Philosophy

Audience: General Public, Researchers, Students

Details: Free

User Info: To subscribe to this Usenet newsgroup, you need access to a newsreader.

`news:talk.religion.newage`

Tandem Computers

Info-tandem

Info-tandem is an e-mail list for users of systems from Tandem Computers, Inc.

Keywords: Computer Systems, Tandem Computers

Audience: Programmers, Analysts

Contact: Scott Hazen Mueller
scott@zorch.sf-bay.org

Details: Free

User Info: To subscribe to the list, send an e-mail message requesting

`mailto:info-tandem-request@zorch.sf-bay.org`

Tandy Computers

CoCo

This is a discussion related to the Tandy Color Computer (any model) OS-9 Operating System, and any other topics relating to the "CoCo," as this computer is affectionately known.

Keywords: Tandy Computers, Computers

Audience: Tandy Computer Users, Computer Users

Contact: Paul E. Campbell
pecampbe@mtus5.BITNET

Details: Free

User Info: To subscribe to the list, send an e-mail message requesting a subscription to the URL address below.

`mailto:listserv@pucc.princeton.edu`

Tax

FEDTAX (Federal Tax Library)

The Federal Tax library offers a comprehensive, up-to-date collection of tax-related materials, including case law, agency materials, legislative and regulatory materials, and so on.

Keywords: Law, Analysis, Tax

Audience: Lawyers

Profile: The Federal Tax library offers a comprehensive, up-to-date collection of tax-related materials. This library includes federal and state tax case law, Internal Revenue Service rulings and releases, state tax administrative decisions and rulings, the Internal Revenue Code, federal tax regulations, international news and treaties, tax looseleaf services, tax periodicals, tax law reviews, tax dailies, pending state legislation, and state property records.

Contact: New Sales Group at 800-227-4908 or 513-859-5398 inside the US, or 1-513-865-7981 for all inquires outside the US.

User Info: To subscribe, contact Mead directly.

To examine the Lexis user guide, you can access it at the ftp site of the University of Texas at Austin at the URL address: ftp://ftp.cc.utexas.edu

The files are in: /pub/ref-services/LEXIS

`telnet://nex.meaddata.com`

`http://www.meaddata.com`

Tax Assessor

ASSETS (Real Estate Tax Assessor and Deed Transfer Records)

The Real Estate Tax Assessor and Deed Transfer Records (ASSETS) library contains information compiled from real property records.

Keywords: Real Estate, Property, Taxes

Audience: Lawyers

Profile: The ASSETS library contains a variety of real estate information, including asset ownership, property address, owner's mailing address, assessed valuation, current market value, and recent property sales and deed transfers. Information is collected from county tax assessors' and recorders' offices nationwide and compiled by TRW REDI Property Data. The ASSETS library also contains a variety of boat and aircraft registration information.

Contact: Mead New Sales Group at (800) 227-4908 or (513) 859-5398 inside the US, or (513) 865-7981 for all inquiries outside the US.

User Info: To subscribe, contact Mead directly.

To examine the Nexis user guide, you can access it at the ftp site of the University of Texas at Austin at the URL address: ftp://ftp.cc.utexas.ed

The files are in: /pub/ref-services/LEXIS

`telnet://nex.meaddata.com`

`http://www.meaddata.com`

taxacom

taxacom

Discussion list on biological systematics.

Keywords: Biology

Audience: Biologists

Contact: James H. Beach
beach@huh.harvard.edu

Details: Free

User Info: To subscribe to the list, send an e-mail message to the URL address below, consisting of a single line reading:

SUB taxacom YourFirstName YourLastName

To send a message to the entire list, address it to:
taxacom@harvarda.harvard.edu

`mailto:listserv@harvarda.harvard.edu`

teacheft (Teaching Effectiveness)

teacheft (Teaching Effectiveness)

This list treats teaching effectiveness and a broad range of teaching and learning interests.

Keywords: Education (Adult), Education (Distance), Education (Continuing)

Audience: Educators, Educational Administrators, Researchers

Details: Free

User Info: To subscribe to the list, send an e-mail message to the URL address shown below consisting of a single line reading:

SUB stlhe-l YourFirstName YourLastName

To send a message to the entire list, address it to: stlhe-l@wcu.bitnet

`mailto:listserv@wcu.bitnet`

Teaching

CIRCUITS-L

This list discusses all aspects of the introductory course in circuit analysis for electrical engineering undergraduates.

Keywords: Engineering, Electrical Engineering, Teaching, Electric Circuit Analysis

Audience: Engineers, Students (college)

Contact: Paul E. Gray
mailto:GRAY@MAPLE.UCS.UWPLATT.EDU

Details: Free

User Info: To subscribe to the list, send an e-mail message to the URL address below, and include: name; e-mail address; home phone, business phone, and FAX numbers (including area code); and US postal address (including ZIP code)

To send a message to the entire list, address it to:

circuits-l@uwplatt.edu

`mailto:circuits-request@uwplatt.edu`

Technical Professionals

noglstp

This list is sponsored by the National Organization of Gay and Lesbian Scientists and Technical Professionals, Inc. (a 501-C3 organization). National office is in Pasadena, CA and can be reached at (818) 791-7689 or P.O. Box 91803, Pasadena, CA 90019. There is also a newsletter that is available to members.

Keywords: Gay, Lesbian, Scientists, Technical Professionals

Audience: Gay Scientists, Lesbian Scientists

Contact: noglstp-request@elroy.jpl.nasa.gov

Details: Free

User Info: To subscribe to the list, send an e-mail message requesting a subscription to the URL address below.

To send a message to the entire list, address it to: noglstp@elroy.jpl.nasa.gov

`mailto:noglstp-request@elroy.jpl.nasa.gov`

Technical Writing

techwr-l (Technical Writing List)

This is a mailing list for technical communicators. It concerns anything related to any facet of technical communication (practice, research, teaching).

Keywords: Technical Writing

Audience: Technical Writers, Educators, Editors

Contact: Eric J. Ray
ejray@okway.okstate.edu

Details: Free

User Info: To subscribe to the list, send an e-mail message to the URL address below consisting of a single line reading:

SUB techwr-l YourFirstName YourLastName

To send a message to the entire list, address it to:
techwr-l@vm1.ucc.okstate.edu

Notes: Digest version available.

`mailto:listserv@vm1.ucc.okstate.edu`

Technology

alt.artcom

A Usenet newsgroup providing information and discussion about contemporary art and technology. Discussion ranges from GIF files to Australian alternative cinema.

Keywords: Art, Technology

Audience: Artists, Writers

User Info: To subscribe to this Usenet newsgroup, you need access to a newsreader.

`news:alt.artcom`

ANU (Australian National University) Vietnam-SciTech-L Database

A WAIS databases of information on the development of science and technology in Vietnam

Keywords: Vietnam, Science, Technology

Sponsor: Australia Vietnam Science-Technology Link

Audience: Vietnamese

Contact: Vern Weitzel
vern@coombs.anu.edu.au

`waissrc:/Coombs-db/ANU-Vietnam-SciTech-L.src`

`gopher://cheops.anu.edu.au/7waissrc/Coombs-db/ANU-Vietnam-SciTech-L.src`

Apple Computer WWW Server

A web site containing information about Apple Computer. The resource is designed to provide timely product information, including press releases on Apple's technology and research. Also contains links to Freeware and Shareware sites, and includes information for developers and programmers.

Keywords: Computer Systems, Technology, Apple Computer, Shareware

Audience: General Public

`http://www.apple.com`

Art Com Magazine

A newsletter about art and technology (subjects covered include robotics, artists' software, hyperfiction) that is guest-edited by individual artists.

Keywords: Computer Art, Literature (Contemporary), Technology, Hyperfiction

Sponsor: Art Com Electronic Network

Audience: Artists, Writers

Contact: Fred Truck
fjt@well.sf.ca.us

To participate in a conference on the WELL, you must first establish an account on the WELL. To do so, start by typing: telnet://well.sf.ca.us

`mailto:artcomtv@well.sf.ca.us`

AT&T Bell Laboratories WWW Information Page

This web site provides information on research and development at AT&T Bell Laboratories.

Keywords: Telecommunications, Technology, AT&T, Cellular Technology

Sponsor: AT&T Bell Laboratories

Audience: Engineers, Educators, Communications Specialists

Contact: webmaster@research.att.com

Details: Free

`http://www.research.att.com`

CMPCOM (Computers and Communications) Library

The Computers and Communications Library provides you industry-specific sources. More than 40 full-text sources that concentrate on computers and communications are available. Full-text files can be searched in a variety of ways: as an individual file, by major-subject group file, or as a user-defined group file.

Keywords: Computers, Communications, Technology, Electronics

Audience: Business Researchers, Analysts, Entrepreneurs

A B C D E F G H I J K L M N O P Q R S T U V W X Y Z

A B C D E F G H I J K L M N O P Q R S **T** U V W X Y Z

Profile: This library can be used to gain insight on new products and technologies being introduced; monitor industry news for high technology systems, electronics, engineering, communications, and computer hardware and software; and locate product evaluations for both the professional as well as the casual personal computer user.

Contact: Mead New Sales Group at (800) 227-4908 or (513) 859-5398 inside the US, or (513) 865-7981 for all inquiries outside the US.

User Info: To subscribe, contact Mead directly.

To examine the Nexis user guide, you can access it at the ftp site of the University of Texas at Austin at the URL address: ftp://ftp.cc.utexas.edu

The files are in: /pub/ref-services/LEXIS

`telnet://nex.meaddata.com`

`http://www.meaddata.com`

devel-l

Discussion forum on technology transfer in international development.

Keywords: Development, Technology

Sponsor: Volunteers in Technical Assistance (VITA)

Audience: Technical Professionals

Contact: vita@gmuvax.gmu.edu

Details: Free

User Info: To subscribe to the list, send an e-mail message to the URL address shown below consisting of a single line reading:

SUB devel-l YourFirstName YourLastName

`mailto:listserv@auvm.american.edu`

DevelopNet News

A monthly newsletter on technology transfer in international development.

Keywords: Nonprofits, Technology, Development

Sponsor: Volunteers in Technical Assistance

Audience: Technology Professionals

Contact: R.R. Ronkin
vita@gmuvax.gmu.edu

Details: Free

User Info: To subscribe, send an e-mail message to the address below.

Inquire about needing a password.

`mailto:vita@gmuvax.gmu.edu`

Ei Compendex Plus

The Ei Compendex Plus database is the machine-readable version of The Engineering Index (monthly/annual), which provides abstracted information from the world's significant literature of engineering and technology.

Keywords: Engineering, Technology

Sponsor: Engineering Information Inc. (Ei), Hoboken, NJ, USA

Audience: Engineers

Profile: Ei Compendex Plus provides worldwide coverage of approximately 4,500 journals and selected government reports and books. Subjects covered include: civil, energy, environmental, geological, and biological engineering; electrical, automotive, nuclear, and aerospace engineering; and computers, robotics, and industrial robots.

Contact: Dialog in the US at (800) 334-2564, Dialog internationally at country-specific locations. User Info: To subscribe, contact Dialog directly. Notes: Coverage 1970 to the present; updated weekly.

`telnet://dialog.com`

Family and Legal Status (INPADOC)

The database includes a listing of patents issued in 56 countries and patenting organizations.

Keywords: Patents, Technlogy

Sponsor: European Patent Office (EPO), Vienna, Austria

Audience: Patent Researchers, Inventors

Profile: INPADOC contains bibliographic data consisting of title, inventor, and assignee for most patents. In addition, this file brings together information on priority-application numbers, countries and dates, and equivalent patents (i.e. patent families) for patents. This file also contains the legal status information for patents in some countries.

Contact: Dialog in the US at (800) 334-2564, Dialog internationally at country-specific locations.

User Info: To subscribe, contact Dialog directly.

Notes: Coverage: April 1968 to the present; updated weekly.

`telnet://dialog.com`

FutureCulture FAQ (Frequently Asked Questions) File

List of online and offline items of interest to subscribers of FutureCulture, a mailing list on 'technoculture' or 'new edge' or 'cyberculture.'

Keywords: Technology, Cyberculture, Postmodernism, Sci-Fi, Zines

Audience: Reality Hackers, Cyberculture Enthuasists

Profile: This list discusses cyberpunk culture, rave culture, industrial music, virtual reality, drugs, computer underground, Net sociology, and virtual communities.

Contact: Alias Datura (adatura on IRC)
adatura@uafhp.uark.edu

Details: Free

`ftp://etext.archive.umich.edu/pub`

High Weirdness by E-Mail

Guide to some interesting sources of information online.

Keywords: Technology, Hacking, Computer Underground

Audience: Mystics, Reality Hackers, Weirdos

Profile: This file focuses mainly on bizarre philosophies, such as Discordia and SubGenius. Contents include: offbeat religions and 'spirituality' paganism and magic, occultism, UFOs and paranormal phenomena.

Details: Free

`ftp://etext.archive.umich.edu/pub/Zines/Weirdness`

Hot off the Tree (HOTT)

HOTT contains excerpts and abstracts of articles from trade journals, popular periodicals, online news services, and electronic bulletin boards.

Keywords: Computer Technology, Technology

Sponsor: University of California, San Diego Library's Technology Watch Information Group (TWIG)

Audience: Computer Programmers, Technology Enthusiasts, General Public

Contact: Susan Jurist
sjurist@ucsd.edu or sjurist@ucsd.bitnet

Details: Free

Available on MELVYL, the University of California online catalog. Anyone with access to telnet, can telnet MELVYL (31.0.0.13) and show hott.

`telnet://melvyl.berkeley.edu/showhott`

ISEA (Inter-Society on Electronic Arts) Online

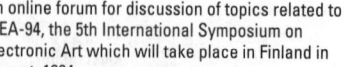

An online forum for discussion of topics related to ISEA-94, the 5th International Symposium on Electronic Art which will take place in Finland in August, 1994.

Keywords: Art, Electronic Art, Technology

Audience: Artists, Art Enthusiasts

Details: Free

`ftp://ftp.ncsa.uiuc.edu`

Journal of Technology Education

Electronic journal devoted to educational issues in technology.

Keywords: Communication, Education, Technology,

Audience: Educators

Details: Free

Send an e-mail message to the URL address below with the request: GET MISCELLA JTE-V5N1. This file will give you access information for additional issues.

`mailto:listserv@vtvm1.cc.vt.edu`

Martin Marietta Energy Systems Gopher

Information on Martin Marietta's energy projects and technologies for both government and commercial applications.

Keywords: Technology, Energy, Industry

Sponsor: Martin Marietta

Audience: Business Professionals, Entrepreneurs, Manufactures, Energy Researchers, Technology Enthusiasts

Profile: This gopher contains a list of technologies currently being developed at Martin Marietta as well as detailing facilities available to university, government, and commercial researchers. Also includes updates on employment openings, and a list of current publications.

Contact: gopher@ornl.gov

`gopher://gopher.ornl.gov`

`http://www.ornl.gov/mmes.html`

McDonnell Douglas Aerospace

A web site providing information about McDonnell Douglas, including a company profile and related discussion about technology.

Keywords: Aerospace, Space, Aviation, Technology

Audience: Aerospace Engineers

Contact: mail to: Zook@pat.mdc.com

`http://pat.mdc.com`

National Technology Transfer Center (NTTC)

A federally-funded national network to apply government research to commercial applications.

Keywords: Technology, Technology Transfer, Research and Development, Business and Industry, Department of Defense, Government (US)

Sponsor: National Technology Transfer Center

Audience: Business People, Entrepreneurs, Manufactures, Technology Enthusiasts

Profile: Features state-by-state listings of agencies designed to facilitate the adaptation of new technologies to industry. Also provides updates on conferences, and a current list of Department of Defense projects soliciting private assistance from small businesses. Allows limited access to NTTC databases.

Contact: Charles Monfradi cmonfra@nttc.edu, info@nttc.edu

`gopher://iron.nttc.edu`

`http://iridium.nttc.edu/nttc.hmtl`

Novice MZT

Novize MZT (News of Ministry for Science and Technology of the Republic of Slovenia) provides easy, accessible news about science, development, universities, and innovative activities to individuals and institutions in research and development areas. Published at least once monthly.

Keywords: Slovenia, Science, Technology, News

Audience: Slovenians, Scientists, Technocrats

Contact: Novice-mzt@krpan.arnes.si or Novice.mzt@uni-lj.si

User Info: To subscribe to the list, send an e-mail message requesting a subscription to the URL address below.

To send a message to the entire list, address it to: Novice-mzt@krpan.arnes.si

`mailto:Novice-MZT@krpan.arnes.si`

rec.autos.tech

A Usenet newsgroup providing information and discussion about the technical aspects of automobiles.

Keywords: Automobiles, Technology

Audience: Automobile Users

User Info: To subscribe to this Usenet newsgroup, you need access to a newsreader.

`news:rec.autos.tech`

Tecbase- Sandia National Laboratory

A catalog of technologies developed at Sandia National Laboratories that have potential commercial applications.

Keywords: Technology, Information Technology, Industry

Sponsor: Sandia National Laboratory

Audience: Business Professionals, Entrepreneurs, Manufacturers, Technicians

Contact: TechTransfer@ccsmtp.sandia.gov

`gopher://somnet.sandia.gov/Tecbase`

Technology Initiatives for the Clinton/Gore Administration

This is a 40-page text of the press release from the Clinton Administration on technology initiatives, dated February 22, 1993.

Keywords: Politics, President (US), White House, Technology

Audience: General Public, Journalists

Details: Free

Send e-mail to the URL address below and include the following in the body of the message:

get cni-bigideas.whouse.paper

`mailto:listserv@cni.org`

The MIT Press Online Catalogs

A descriptive listing of recent books and current journals published by the MIT Press.

Keywords: Academia, Books, Publishing, Technology

Sponsor: The MIT Press, Cambridge, Massachusetts, USA.

Audience: Reseachers, Scholars, University Students, Technical Professionals

Profile: Contains a keyword-searchable index of books published in the years 1993 to 1994, as well as current journals covering computational and cognitive sciences, architecture, photography, art and literary theory, economics, environmental science, and linguistics.

Contact: ehling@mitpress.mit.edu

Notes: Coverage: 1993 to present; updated semiannually. MIT Press can also be accessed by calling (800) 356-0343.

`http://www-mitpress.mit.edu`

`gopher://gopher.mit.edu`

Universite de Montreal UDEMATIK Library

The library's holdings are large and wide-ranging and contain significant collections in many fields.

Keywords: Art, Architecture, Economy, Sexology, Social Law, Science, Technology, Literary Studies

Audience: Researchers, Students, General Public

Contact: Joelle or Sebastien Roy udematik@ere.umontreal.ca or stemp@ere.umontreal.ca or roys@ere.umontreal.ca

User Info: Expect: Login; Send: Application id INFO

`telnet://udematik.umontreal.ca`

Washington University Library

The library's holdings are large and wide-ranging and contain significant collections in many fields.

A B C D E F G H I J K L M N O P Q R S **T** U V W X Y Z

A
B
C
D
E
F
G
H
I
J
K
L
M
N
O
P
Q
R
S
T
U
V
W
X
Y
Z

Keywords: Technology, Literature (German), Social Science, Behavioral Science

Audience: Researchers, Students, General Public

Contact: services@wugate.wustl.edu

Details: Free

User Info: Expect: Login; Send: Services

`telnet://wugate.wustl.edu`

Washington University-St. Louis Medical Library & MembersLibrary

The library's holdings are large and wide-ranging and contain significant collections in many fields.

Keywords: Medicine, Science, Technology

Audience: Researchers, Students, General Public

Details: Free

User Info: Expect: Destination Code Prompt, Send: Catalog

`telnet://mcftcp.wustl.edu`

Technological Advances

Adv-Elo

Discusses the latest advances in electronics. Sponsored by the IEEE Student Branch of Santa Maria University (Chile).

Keywords: Electrical Engineering, Engineering, Electronics, Technological Advances

Audience: Engineers, Educators, Students

Contact: Rodrigo E. Rodriguez
rrodrigu@utfsm

Details: Free

User Info: To subscribe to the list, send an e-mail message to the URL address shown below consiting of a single line reading:

SUB adv-elo YourFirstName YourLastName

To send a message to the entire list, address it to: adv-elo@loa.disca.utfsm.cl

`listserv@loa.disca.utfsm.cl`

Technology Transfer

National Technology Transfer Center (NTTC)

A federally-funded national network to apply government research to commercial applications.

Keywords: Technology, Research and Development, Business and Industry, Department of Defense, Government (US)

Sponsor: National Technology Transfer Center

Audience: Business People, Entrepreneurs, Manufactures, Technology Enthusiasts

Profile: Features state-by-state listings of agencies designed to facilitate the adaptation of new technologies to industry. Also provides updates on conferences, and a current list of Department of Defense projects soliciting private assistance from small businesses. Allows limited access to NTTC databases.

Contact: Charles Monfradi
cmonfra@nttc.edu, info@nttc.edu

`gopher://iron.nttc.edu`

`http://iridium.nttc.edu/nttc.hmtl`

techwr-l (Technical Writing List)

techwr-l (Technical Writing List)

This is a mailing list for technical communicators. It concerns anything related to any facet of technical communication (practice, research, teaching).

Keywords: Technical Writing

Audience: Technical Writers, Educators, Editors

Contact: Eric J. Ray
ejray@okway.okstate.edu

Details: Free

User Info: To subscribe to the list, send an e-mail message to the URL address below consisting of a single line reading:

SUB techwr-l YourFirstName YourLastName

To send a message to the entire list, address it to:
techwr-l@vm1.ucc.okstate.edu

Notes: Digest version available.

`mailto:listserv@vm1.ucc.okstate.edu`

Telebit Computer Products

Netblazer-users

Provides an unmoderated forum for discussions among users of Telebit NetBlazer products. Topics include known problems and workarounds, features discussions, and configuration advice.

Keywords: Telebit Computer Products, Netblazer

Audience: Telebit Netblazer Users

Contact: netblazer-users-request@telebit.com

Details: Free

User Info: To subscribe to the list, send an e-mail message requesting a subscription to the URL address below.

`mailto:netblazer-users-request@telebit.com`

Telecommunications

AT&T Bell Laboratories WWW Information Page

This web site provides information on research and development at AT&T Bell Laboratories.

Keywords: Telecommunications, Technology, AT&T, Cellular Technology

Sponsor: AT&T Bell Laboratories

Audience: Engineers, Educators, Communications Specialists

Contact: webmaster@research.att.com

Details: Free

`http://www.research.att.com`

The Black Box Catalog

The Black Box Catalog, the industry's most complete source for data communication equipment, is now available on the Internet. The complete range of products, technical references, and application briefs are available on the Black Box World Wide Web Server.

Keywords: Communications, Networking, Telecommunication, Computers

Sponsor: Black Box Corporation, Lawrence, PA

Audience: Engineers, Network Administration, LAN Administrators, Communication Specialists

Profile: Black Box Corporation is a leading international supplier of data communications networking and related computer connectivity products. Black Box's commitment to providing effective solutions that substantially enhance the capabilities of communications systems is backed by a technical support staff that is available around the clock, a liberal 45-day return policy, and same day shipment of its 6000 products.

Contact: Webmaster
webmaster@blackbox.com

Details: Costs

`http://www.blackbox.com`

Blacksburg Electronic Village Gopher

The Blacksburg Electronic Village is a project to link an entire town in Southwestern Virginia with a 21st-century telecommunications infrastructure. This infrastructure will bring a useful set of information services and interactive communications facilities into the daily activities of citizens and businesses.

Keywords: Community Networking, Networking, Telecommunications

Sponsor: Town of Blacksburg, Virginia, USA

Audience: Activists, Policymakers, Community Leaders, Government

Profile: This community gopher server run by the town of Blacksburg contains information about Blacksburg and how it is building its electronic infrastructure. It includes a list of Blacksburg-area BBSs, instructions for local residents to get an account on the town's BBS, and a section called "Village Schoolhouse."

Details: Costs, Moderated

`gopher://morse.cns.vt.edu`

Communication and Mass Communication Resources

An archive of materials related to mass communications and the media.

Keywords: Mass Communications, Media, Journalism, Telecommunications, Advertising

Sponsor: The University of Iowa

Audience: Mass Communications Students and Teachers, Journalists, Broadcasting Professionals

Contact: Karla Tonella
Karla_Tonella@uiowa.edu

`gopher://iam41.arcade.uiowa.edu`

ctf-discuss

This mailing list aims to stimulate discussion of issues critical to the computer science community in the United States (and, by extension, the world). The Computer Science and Telecommunications Board (CSTB) of the National Research Council (NRC) is charged with identifying and initiating studies in areas critical to the health of the field. Recently one such study, Computing the Future, has generated a major discussion in the community and has motivated the establishment of this mailing list in order to involve broader participation. This list will be used in the future to report and discuss the activities of the CSTB and to solicit opinions in a variety of areas.

Keywords: Computer Science, Telecommunications

Audience: Computer Scientists, Telecommunications Experts

Contact: Dave Farber
ctf-discuss-request@cis.upenn.edu

Details: Free

User Info: To subscribe to the list, send an e-mail message requesting a subscription to the URL address below.

To send a message to the entire list, address it to: ctf-discuss@cis.upenn.edu

`mailto:ctf-discuss-`
`request@cis.upenn.edu`

Electronic Cafe

A seminal art and telecommunications group that specializes in video transmission.

Keywords: Art, Video, Telecommunications

Audience: Artists

Profile: This combines performance, communication, and community outreach by making telecommunications equipment available in a cafe-style artists' space.

Contact: Kit Galloway and Sherrie Rabinowitz, 1641 18th St., Santa Monica, CA 90404, USA

`mailto:ecafe@netcom.com`

Fam-Med

An Internet resource and discussion group on computers in family medicine.

Keywords: Medicine, Computers, Telecommunications

Sponsor: Gustavus Adolphus College, Minnesota

Audience: Health CareProfessionals, Family Physicians

Profile: Fam-Med is an electronic conference and file area that focuses on the use of computer and telecommunication technologies in the teaching and practice of family medicine. The conference and files are accessible to anyone able to send e-mail. The discussion on Fam-Med is distributed in two ways: by an unmoderated mail echo in which all posted messages are immediately distributed to subscribers without human intervention, and by a digest where messages accumulated over several days are assembled into a single document with erroneous posts deleted.

Contact: Paul Kleeberg
Paul@GAC.Edu

Details: Free

To join either the unmoderated list or the digest, send e-mail to the contact above. To post to Fam-Med, send e-mail to Fam-Med@GAC.Edu

`gopher://ftp.gac.edu/00/pub/e-mail-`
`archives/fam-med/`

Multimedia, Telecommunications, and Art Project

A project to promote online art that will be implemented as gopher site and on the World-Wide Web.

Keywords: Multimedia, Electronic Art, Telecommunications

Sponsor: CISR (Centre for Image and Sound Research), Vancouver, B.C., Canada

Audience: Artists, Writers

Contact: Derek Dowden
Derek_Dowden@mindlink.bc.ca

For more information, send an e-mail message to the URL address below.

`mailto:Derek_Dowden@mindlink.bc.ca`

Polish Archives

Information about Polish Internet gophers and Polish electronic journals.

Keywords: Poland, Telecommunications, Networking

Audience: Historians, Poles

Contact: Darek Milewski
Milewski@poniecki.berkeley.edu

User Info: To subscribe, send an e-mail message requesting a subscription to the URL address below.

`gopher://gopher.poniecki.berkeley.edu`

Telecom Archives

All of the back issues of Telecom Digest are on file here. Includes many other online articles and resources topical to the telecommunications industry.

Keywords: Telecommunications

Audience: Telecommunications Experts, Researchers, Communications Specialists

Contact: Patrick Townson
telecom-request@eecs.nwu.edu

`http://lcs.mit.edu/telecom-archives`

Telecomputing

The Teleputing Hotline And Field Computing Source Letter

A leading voice in covering telephone connections worldwide. Plans to expand coverage of a worldwide revolution called Field Computing.

Keywords: Business, Telecomputing, Telecommunications

Audience: Industry, Telecommunications Experts, Business Professionals

Profile: Field Computing involves linking workers outside the office -in sales, repair, and delivery functions- to central computer systems with handheld terminals and wireless data networks. The Teleputing Hotline has covered this trend since its inception.

Contact: Dana Blankenhorn
MCI: 409-8960 GEnie: nb.atl CompuServe

Details: Costs

User Info: To subscribe to the list, send an e-mail message requesting a subscription to the URL address below.

`mailto:sfer`
`request@mthvax.cs.miami.edu`

Telemedia, Networks, and Systems Group

Telemedia, Networks, and Systems Group

A list of commercial services on the Web (and Net)

Keywords: Business, Electronic Commerce

Sponsor: MIT Laboratory for Computer Science, Cambridge, MA 02139

Audience: Business Professionals, Commercial Internet Users, General Public

Profile: This list of commercial Internet services is well-maintained and frequently updated.

Contact: hhh@mit.edu

`http://tns-www.lcs.mit.edu/commerce.html`

`http://tns-www.lcs.mit.edu`

Telescopes

Sci.astro.hubble

★

Information about all subjects concerning NASA's Hubble space telescope.

Keywords: Hubble Telescope, Astronomy, Space, NASA, Stargazing, Telescopes

Audience: Astronomers, General Public, Science Teachers, Stargazers

Contact: Paul A. Scowen scowen@wfpc3.la.asu.edu

Details: Free, Moderated, Images

User Info: To subscribe to this Usenet newsgroup, you need access to a newsreader.

`news:sci.astro.hubble`

Television

30something

★★

A mailing list for discussion of the TV show 30something.

Keywords: Television, Baby Boomer Culture

Audience: Television Viewers, Baby Boomers

Contact: Marc Rouleau 30something-request@fuggles.acc.virginia.edu

User Info: To subscribe to the list, send an e-mail message to the URL address below. To send a message to the entire list, address it to: 30something@fuggles.acc.virginia.edu

`mailto:30something-request@fuggles.acc.virginia.edu`

C-SPAN (Cable-Satellite Public Affairs Network) Gopher

★★★

Online information from C-SPAN, the public affairs television network.

Keywords: News Media, Government, Congress (US), Television

Sponsor: C-SPAN

Audience: Journalists, Government Officials, Educators (K-12), General Public

Profile: Comprehensive listings of C-SPAN's programming and coverage of events in Washington D.C. and beyond. In addition to the programming notes and schedules, this site also features online educational resources sponsored by C-SPAN, text of historic documents and speeches, and background political information on the House of Representatives and the Supreme Court.

Contact: cspanviewr@aol.com

Details: Free

`gopher://c-span.org`

Clarissa

★

This list discusses the Nickelodeon TV show "Clarissa Explains It All."

Keywords: Television, Nickelodeon

Audience: Nickelodeon Viewers, TV Viewers

Contact: Jim Lick clarissa-request@tcp.com

Details: Free

User Info: To subscribe to the list, send an e-mail message requesting a subscription to the URL address below.

To send a message to the entire list, address it to: clarissa@tcp.com

`mailto:clarissa-request@tcp.com`

disney-afternoon

★

Discussion of the Disney Afternoon and other related topics. This is a very high-volume, low-noise mailing list.

Keywords: Disney, Television

Audience: Disney Enthusiasts, Television Viewers

Contact: Stephanie da Silva ranger-list-request@taronga.com

Details: Free, M

User Info: To subscribe to the list, send an e-mail message requesting a subscription to the URL address below.

To send a message to the entire list, address it to: ranger-list-request@taronga.com

`mailto:ranger-list-request@taronga.com`

dark-shadows

★

Dark Shadows was a daily soap opera that ran on ABC in the late Sixties (ending in 1971). It had a Gothic feel to it and featured storylines involving the supernatural.

Keywords: Dark Shadows, Television

Audience: Horror Enthusiasts, Soap Opera Enthusiasts

Contact: Bernie Roehl shadows-request@sunee.waterloo.ca

Details: Free

User Info: To subscribe to the list, send an e-mail message requesting a subscription to the URL address below.

To send a message to the entire list, address it to: shadows@usunee.waterloo.ca

`news:alt.horror`
`news:rec.arts.tv.soaps`

flamingo

★

This list discusses the series 'Parker Lewis' (formerly 'Parker Lewis Can't Lose') on the Fox television network.

Keywords: Television, Television

Audience: Television Viewers, 'Parker Lewis' Enthusiasts'

Details: Free

User Info: To subscribe to the list, send an e-mail message requesting a subscription to the URL address below.

To send a message to the entire list, address it to: flamingo@lenny.corp.sgi.com

`mailto:flamingo-request@lenny.corp.sgi.com`

Melrose-place

★

Discussion of the Fox television show Melrose Place.

Keywords: Melrose Place, Fox Television, Television

Audience: Melrose Place Fans, Television Viewers

Details: Free

User Info: To subscribe to the list, send an e-mail message requesting a subscription to the URL address below.

`mailto:melrose-place-request@ferkel.ucsb.edu`

National Broadcasting Society— Alpha Epsilon Rho

★

Forum for mass media professionals to share experiences and ideas.

Keywords: Film, Television, Radio, Mass Media

Sponsor: National Broadcasting Society-Alpha Epsilon Rho

Audience: Journalists, Students, Educators, Broadcasting Professionals

Contact: Reg Gamar
regbc@cunyvm.bitnet

Details: Free

User Info: To subscribe to the list, send an e-mail message to the address shown below consisting of a single line reading:

SUB NBS-AER YourFirstName YourLastName

To send a message to the entire list, address it to: nbs-aer@cunyvm.bitnet

`mailto:listserv@cunyvm.bitnet`

rec.arts.movies movie database

An extensive FTP database covering over 32,000 movies, with more than 370,000 filmography entries, from early cinema to current releases.

Keywords: Movies, Television, Popular Culture

Audience: Movie Buffs

Profile: Interfaces to search the database include Unix, MS-DOS and Amiga (and Windows and Mac versions are in development). The database includes filmographies for actors, directors, writers, composers, cinematographers, editors, production designers, costume designers and producers; plot summaries; character names; movie ratings; year of release; running times; movie trivia; quotes; goofs; soundtracks; personal trivia and Academy Award information.

Contact: Col Needham
cn@ibmpcug.co.uk

Details: Free

`ftp://cathouse.org/pub/cathouse/movies/database`

rec.arts.movies movie database (Cardiff WWW front-end)

An extensive, interactive database covering over 32,000 movies, with more than 370,000 filmography entries, from early cinema to current releases.

Keywords: Movies, Television, Popular Culture, Interactive Media

Audience: Movie Buffs

Profile: A WWW front-end to the rec.arts.movies movie database, complete with form-filling interfaces to add new data and to rate movies (on a scale from 1 through 10). The database includes filmographies for actors, directors, writers, composers, cinematographers, editors, production designers, costume designers and producers; plot summaries; character names; movie ratings; year of release; running times; movie trivia; quotes; goofs; soundtracks; personal trivia and Academy Award information.

Contact: Rob Hartill
Robert.Hartill@cm.cf.ac.uk

Details: Free

`http://www.cm.cf.ac.uk/Movies`

`http://www.msstate.edu/Movies`

rec.arts.sf.tv

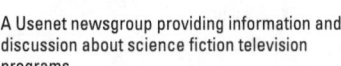

A Usenet newsgroup providing information and discussion about science fiction television programs.

Keywords: Science Fiction, Television

Audience: Science Fiction Enthusiasts, Television Viewers

User Info: To subscribe to this Usenet newsgroup, you need access to a newsreader.

`news:rec.arts.sf.tv`

rec.arts.startrek.current

A Usenet newsgroup providing information and discussion about current Star Trek (The Next Generation) episodes and characters.

Keywords: Television, Science Fiction

Audience: Trekkies, Television Viewers

User Info: To subscribe to this Usenet newsgroup, you need access to a newsreader.

`news:rec.arts.startrek.current`

rec.arts.startrek.misc

A Usenet newsgroup providing general information and discussion about all aspects of Star Trek, including its various television and film reviews.

Keywords: Television, Film

Audience: Trekkies, Television Viewers, Movie Viewers

User Info: To subscribe to this Usenet newsgroup, you need access to a newsreader.

`news:rec.arts.startrek.misc`

rec.arts.tv

A Usenet newsgroup providing information and discussion about past and present TV shows and related trivia.

Keywords: Television, Trivia

Audience: General Public, Television Viewers, Trivia Enthusiasts

User Info: To subscribe to this Usenet newsgroup, you need access to a newsreader.

`news:rec.arts.tv`

rec.arts.tv.soaps

A Usenet newsgroup providing information and discussion about television soap operas.

Keywords: Television

Audience: Television Viewers, Soap Opera Viewers

User Info: To subscribe to this Usenet newsgroup, you need access to a newsreader.

`news:rec.arts.tv.soaps`

rec.arts.tv.uk

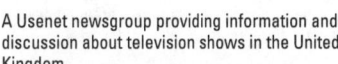

A Usenet newsgroup providing information and discussion about television shows in the United Kingdom.

Keywords: Television, United Kingdom

Audience: Television Viewers, British

User Info: To subscribe to this Usenet newsgroup, you need access to a newsreader.

`news:rec.arts.tv.uk`

rec.video.satellite

A Usenet newsgroup providing information and discussion about satellite television.

Keywords: Television

Audience: Satellite Television Watchers

User Info: To subscribe to this Usenet newsgroup, you need access to a newsreader.

`news:rec.video.satellite`

Star Trek Resources on the Internet

This extensive resource contains information on mailing lists, news archives, other Internet resources addressing the culture surounding Star Trek fans.

Keywords: Science Fiction, Television

Audience: General Public, Trekkers, Television Viewers

Contact: Brigitte Jellinek
bjelli@cosy.sbg.ac.at

`http://www.cosy.sbg.ac.at/rec/startrek/star_trek_resources.html`

Theater, Film & Television

This directory is a compilation of information resources focused on theater, film, and television.

Keywords: Theater, Film, Television

Audience: Entertainment Prols, Actors

Details: Free

`ftp://una.hh.lib.umich.edu/70/inetdirstacks/filmtv:robinson`

A B C D E F G H I J K L M N O P Q R S **T** U V W X Y Z

Telluride Institute

Telluride Institute

This is a community organization involved in building an electronic dimension in rural Colorado. The vision of Telluride Institute includes linking rural residents to each other and outside resources, creating new opportunities for education, jobs, and arts.

Keywords: Community Networking, Virtual Community, Rural Development, Colorado

Sponsor: The Telluride Institute, Telluride, Colorado

Audience: Activists, Policy Makers, Community Leaders, Students, Colorado Residents

Profile: The Telluride Institute is a local community-based organization that produces arts, environmental, and educational events in the Telluride area of Colorado. The Institite is committed to the creation of what it calls the "InfoZone": it wants to use modern telecommunications to link together the local community and to connect to the rest of the world to exchange ideas, commerce, arts, and inspiration.

Contact: Richard Lowenberg
tellinst@csn.org

Details: Free

Send an e-mail message to the URL address below asking for further information.

`mailto:tellinst@csn.org`

Telnet Access to WWW (World Wide Web)

Telnet Access to WWW (World Wide Web)

A server providing free public access to WWW written in both English and Hebrew.

Keywords: WWW, Internet Tools, Jerusalem

Sponsor: Hebrew University of Jerusalem

Audience: Internet Surfers

Contact: rashty@www.huji.ac.il

User Info: Expect: Username; Send: WWW

`telnet://www.huji.ac.il`

Telnet

commune

The purpose of this list is to discuss the COMMUNE protocol, a Telnet replacement.

Keywords: Commune Protocol, Telnet

Audience: Commune Protocol Users

Contact: Dan Bernstein
commune-request@stealth.acf.nyu.edu

Details: Free

User Info: To subscribe to the list, send an e-mail message requesting a subscription to the URL address below.

To send a message to the entire list, address it to:

commune-list@stealth.acf.nyu.edu

`mailto:commune-request@stealth.acf.nyu.edu`

Telnet-How To

An introduction to telnet, an Internet access tool.

Keywords: Internet Tools, Telnet

Sponsor: SURAnet Network Information Center

Audience: Internet Surfers

Contact: info@sura.net

Details: Free

File is: pub/nic/network.service.guides/how.to.telnet.guide

`ftp://ftp.sura.net`

Tennessee

University of Tennessee at Memphis Library

The library's holdings are large and wide-ranging and contain significant collections in many fields.

Keywords: Tennessee, Literature (American)

Audience: Researchers, Students, General Public

Details: Costs

User Info: Expect: Username Prompt, Send: Harvey

`telnet://utmem1.utmem.edu`

Tennis

rec.sport.tennis

A Usenet newsgroup providing information and discussion about tennis.

Keywords: Tennis, Sports

Audience: Tennis Fans, Sports Fans

User Info: To subscribe to this Usenet newsgroup, you need access to a newsreader.

`news:rec.sport.tennis`

University of Glasgow Information Service (GLANCE)

GLANCE provides subject-based information services, including an extensive section on European and world sports.

Keywords: Sports, Soccer, Motor Racing, Mountaineering, Squash, Cricket, Golf, Tennis, Europe, Scotland

Sponsor: University of Glasgow, Glasgow, Scotland

Audience: Sport Enthusiasts, Fitness Enthusiasts, Nature Lovers

Profile: Information at this site includes schedules, results, and statistics for sports such as cricket and soccer. There is also a selection of items on mountaineering.

Contact: Alan Dawson
A.Dawson@uk.ac.gla.compserv

Details: Free

`gopher://govan.cent.gla.ac.uk/Subject/Sports and Rec`

teslit-l (Adult Education & Literacy Test Literature)

teslit-l (Adult Education & Literacy Test Literature)

This is a sublist of tesl-l (Teaching English as a Second Language). Discussions focus primarily on issues of literacy and the teaching of English as a second language.

Keywords: Education (Adult), Education (Distance), Education (Continuing), Literacy

Audience: K-12 Educators, Administrators, Researchers

Details: Free

User Info: To subscribe to the list, send an e-mail message to the URL address below consisting of a single line reading:

SUB teslit-l YourFirstName YourLastName

To send a message to the entire list, address it to: teslit-l @cunyvm.bitnet

Notes: Members of teslit-l must be members of tesl-l.

`mailto:listserv@cunyvm.bitnet`

TeX

auc-TeX

Discussion and information exchange about the AUC TeX package, which runs under GNU Emacs.

Keywords: Computers, TeX, AUC TeX, Emacs

Audience: Computer Users

Contact: Kresten Krab Thorup
            auc-tex-request@iesd.auc.dk

Details: Free

User Info: To subscribe to the list, send an e-mail
            message requesting a subscription to
            the URL address below.

            To send a message to the entire list,
            address it to: auc-tex@iesd.auc.dk

`mailto:auc-tex-request@iesd.auc.dk`

Texas

Armadillo's World Wide Web Page

This site provides resources and instructional
material for an interdisciplinary Texan culture
course.

Keywords: History (US), Texas, Cultural Studies,
            Education

Sponsor: Rice University, Houston, Texas, USA

Audience: Educators, Students

Contact: armadillo@rice.edu

`http://chico.rice.edu/armadillo`

Texas: Computer Crimes Statute

Lists text of the Texas Computer Crimes Statute.

Keywords: Computing, Crime, Texas

Audience: Lawyers, Computer Programmers

Details: Free

            Select from menu as appropriate

`gopher://wiretap.spies.com`

The Texas Information Highway

★★

Access to the public information resources of the
state of Texas.

Keywords: Texas, Travel, Government, Census, Pata

Sponsor: Texas Department of Information
            Resources

Audience: Texans, General Public

Profile: Still under construction as we go to
            press, this is a model program to make
            state and local information resources
            available to Internet users. The current
            collection features city, country, and
            state political information, including full-
            text of bills before the Texas state
            legislature. Materials related to Texas
            history and tourism are also provided,
            along with links to Texas-area user
            groups and other state and federal
            information servers.

Contact: Wayne McDilda
            wayne@dir.texas.gov

`gopher://info.texas.gov`

Text Processing

comp.text.tex

A Usenet newsgroup providing information and
discussion about the TeX and LaTeX systems.

Keywords: Text Processing, Internet

Audience: Computer Users, TeX and LaTeX Users

User Info: To subscribe to this Usenet newsgroup,
            you need access to a newsreader.

`news:comp.text.tex`

Thailand

Thailand: The Big Picture

A web site maintaining a complete list of Internet
servers pertaining to and found within Thailand.
General information concerning Thailand and
extensive Internet connections to Thai academic
institutions.

Keywords: Thailand, Education, Travel

Sponsor: National Electronics and Computer
            Center at the National Science and
            Technology Development Agency, USA

Audience: Researchers, Exchange Students

Contact: Trin Tantsetthi
            webmaster@www.nectec.or.th

`http://www.nectec.or.th`

Theater

Musicals

This forum is intended for the general discussion of
musical theater, in all forms, but related non-musical
theater topics are welcome, too.

Keywords: Musicals, Theater

Audience: Musical Theater Enthusiasts

Details: Free

User Info: To subscribe to the list, send an e-mail
            message requesting a subscription to
            the URL address below.

`mailto:musicals-request@world.std.com`

Stagecraft

This list is for the discussion of all aspects of stage
work, including special effects, sound effects, sound
reinforcement, stage management, set design and
building, lighting, design, company management, hall
management, hall design, and show production.

Keywords: Theater, Drama

Audience: Stage Producers

Contact: Brad Davis
            stagecraft-request@zinc.com

User Info: To subscribe to the list, send an Email
            message requesting a subscription to
            the URL address below. To send a
            message to the entire list, address it to:
            stagecraft@zinc.com

Notes: Also contains archives of list
            discussions.

`mailto:stagecraft-request@zinc.com`

Theater

This directory is a compilation of information
resources focused on theater.

Keywords: Theater, Drama, Performing Arts

Audience: Theater Personnel, Drama Personnel,
            Performers

Contact: Deborah Torres, Martha Vander Kolk
            dtorres@umich.edu
            mjvk@umich.edu

Details: Free

`ftp://una.hh.lib.umich.edu/70/`
`inetdirsstacks/theater:torresmjvk`

Theater, Film & Television

This directory is a compilation of information
resources focused on theater, film, and television.

Keywords: Theater, Film, Television

Audience: Theater Personnel, Film Personnel,
            Television Personnel

Details: Free

`ftp://una.hh.lib.umich.edu/70/`
`inetdirsstacks/filmtv:robinson`

Theology

Catholic Doctrine

This is for discussions of orthodox Catholic theology
by everyone under the jurisdiction of the Holy Father,
John Paul II. No attacks on the Catholic Church
here, please.

Keywords: Catholic Doctrine, Theology

Audience: Catholics, Priests, Theologians

Contact: catholic-
            request@sarto.gaithersburg.md.us

Details: Free, Moderated

User Info: To subscribe to the list, send an e-mail
            message requesting a subscription to
            the URL address below.

            To send a message to the entire list,
            address it to:

            catholic@sarto.gaithersburg.md.us

Notes: There is an archive server (containing
            Catholic art and magisterial documents)
            associated with this list. Send mail to the
            URL address below to get details about
            the archive server.

`mailto:catholic-`
`request@sarto.gaithersburg.md.us`

A B C D E F G H I J K L M N O P Q R S **T** U V W X Y Z

A
B
C
D
E
F
G
H
I
J
K
L
M
N
O
P
Q
R
S
T
U
V
W
X
Y
Z

Drake University

The Library's holdings are large and wide-ranging and contain significant collections in many fields.

Keywords: Music, Pharmacology, Theology

Audience: General Public, Researchers, Librarians, Document Delivery Professionals

Details: Free, Moderated

Send: COWLES to access the main library, and LAWLIB to access the Law Library. To leave the system, enter CTRL-Z

`telnet://lib.drake.edu`

Ecchst-I

A discussion list for scholars of Ecclesiastical history, including those interested both in the history of the Church and in the examination of theology in an historical context.

Keywords: Religion, Ecclesiastical History, Christianity, Theology

Audience: Historians, Theologians

Contact: Gregory H. Singleton
ugsingle@uxa.ecn.bgu.edu

User Info: To subscribe, send an e-mail message to the URL address below consisting of a single line reading:

SUB ecchst-I YourFirstName YourLastName.

To send a message to the entire list, address it to: ecchst-I@bgu.edu

`mailto:listserv@bgu.edu`

Emory University Library

The library's holdings are large and wide-ranging and contain significant collections in many fields.

Keywords: Health Sciences, Theology, History (US), Communism, Economics (History of), Literature (American)

Audience: General Public, Researchers, Librarians, Document Delivery Professionals

Details: Free

User Info: Expect: VM screen, Send: RETURN; Expect: CP READ, Send: DIAL VTAM, press RETURN; Expect: CICS screen, Send: PF1

`telnet://emuvm1.cc.emory.edu`

University of Puget Sound Library

The library's' holdings are large and wide-ranging and contain significant collections in many fields.

Keywords: Education, Literature (General), Music, Natural Science, Theology

Audience: Researchers, Students, General Public

Details: Free

User Info: Expect: Login; Send: Library

`telnet://192.124.98.2`

Theoretical Chemistry

Theoretical Journal Abstract And Bibliographic Files

Abstract and bibliographic information for several theoretical chemistry journals.

Keywords: Theoretical Chemistry, Quantum Chemistry, Quantum Mechanics, Computational Chemistry

Sponsor: Springer-Verlag, and Wiley

Audience: Chemists, Librarians, Students , (College/University)

Contact: Dialog in the US at (800) 334-2564, Dialog internationally at country specific locations.

Mailserv@osc.edu

Details: Free

User Info: To subscribe, contact Dialog directly.

Select: "Other OSC Gopher Servers," then select "OSC Chemistry Gopher Server."

`telnet://dialog.com`

`gopher://infomeister.osc.edu.`

Theoretical Physics

ICTP (International Centre for Theoretical Physics)

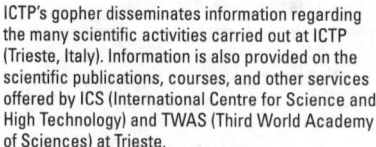

ICTP's gopher disseminates information regarding the many scientific activities carried out at ICTP (Trieste, Italy). Information is also provided on the scientific publications, courses, and other services offered by ICS (International Centre for Science and High Technology) and TWAS (Third World Academy of Sciences) at Trieste.

Keywords: Theoretical Physics, Italy, Europe

Audience: Physicists

Profile: Topics include programming techniques, theoretical aspects, Icon in relation to other languages, applications of Icon, implementation issues, porting, and bugs.

Contact: admin@ictp.trieste.it

Details: Free

`gopher://gopher.ictp.trieste.it`

`http://gopher.ictp.trieste.it`

Think Wind

Think Wind

An FTP site for information on windsurfing, with FAQs, pictures, details about destinations, and threads from rec.windsurfing.

Keywords: Sports, Windsurfing

Audience: Windsurfers

Contact: phansen@lemming.uvm.edu

Details: Free, Images

`ftp://lemming.uvm.edu/rec.windsurfing`

THINKNET

THINKNET

Electronic newsletter on philosophy, systems theory, interdisciplinary studies, and thoughtful conversation in cyberspace.

Keywords: Cyberspace, Systems Theory, Philosophy

Audience: Philosophers, System Theorists

Contact: Kent D. Palmer Ph.D.
palmer@world.std.com

Details: Free

User Info: To subscribe, send an e-mail message to the URL address below consisting of a single line reading:

SUB THINKNET YourFirstName YourLastName

`mailto:palmer@world.std.com`

Third World

Agence FrancePresse International French Wire

Agence FrancePresse International French Wire provides full-text articles in French relating to national, international, business, and sports news.

Keywords: News Media, Europe, Third World, French

Sponsor: Agence FrancePresse, Paris, France

Audience: Market Researchers, Journalists, Francophiles

Profile: Agence FrancePresse distributes its French service worldwide, including Western and Eastern Europe, Canada, northern and western Africa, the Middle East, Vietnam, French Guiana, the West Indies, and the French Pacific islands. Agence FrancePresse International French Wire has extensive coverage of the European countries, including every aspect of economic, political, and general business news. It also provides excellent industrial and market news from both developed countries and from theThird World.

Coverage: September 1991 to the present; updated daily.

Contact: Dialog in the US at (800) 334-2564; Dialog internationally at country-specific locations.

Details: Costs

User Info: To subscribe, contact Dialog directly.

`telnet://dialog.com`

Tibet

CTN News

This is a list covering news on Tibet.

Keywords: Tibet, New Media

Audience: Tibetans, Journalists, General Public

Contact: ctn-editors@utcc.utoronto.ca

Details: Free

User Info: To subscribe to the list, send an e-mail message requesting a subscription to the URL address below.

To send a message to the entire list, address it to: CTN_News@utcc.utoronto.ca

`mailto:ctn-editors@utcc.utoronto.ca`

TitNeT Titnews Titnotes

TitNeT Titnews Titnotes

The network of the International Tit Society (TITS),

Keywords: Ornithology, Birds

Sponsor: International Tit Society

Audience: Bird Watchers

Profile: The network of the International Tit Society (TITS), Titnet posts three formal series: 1) TITNET is the listing of e-mail subscribers, and includes their e-mail addresses, institutional affiliations, and research interests. 2) TITNEWS is the forum for exchange concerning academic activities, and consists of single-topic issues and multiple announcements. 3) TITNOTES is the forum for exchange of information about tits (and other hole-nesting birds).

Contact: Jack P. Hailman
jhailman@vms.macc.wisc.edu.

Details: Free

User Info: To subscribe, send an e-mail message requesting a subscription to the URL address below. Provide: (1) Full name, (2) e-mail address, (3) institutional affiliation, (4) species studied, and (5) topics studied.

`mailto:jhailman@vms.macc.wisc.edu`

titnet (Paridae and Hole-nesting Bird Discussion List)

titnet (Paridae and Hole-nesting Bird Discussion List)

Promotes communication among scientists working on tits (Paridae) and other hole-nesting birds.

Keywords: Birds, Ornithology

Audience: Bird Watchers

Profile: Titnet is a publication listing e-mail addresses of conference members. Titnews contains announcements and discussions of activities such as bibliographic systems and hence serves as the e-mail newsletter. Titnotes contains material on the biology of the birds and hence serves as a kind of e-mail journal.

Contact: Jack P. Hailman
jhailman@macc.wisc.edu

Details: Free

User Info: To subscribe to the list, send an e-mail message requesting a subscription to the URL address below.

To send a message to the entire list, address it to: jhailman@macc.wisc.edu

Notes: Send (1) full name, (2) mailing address, which is forwarded to Dr. Ficken for PARUS INTERNATIONAL, (3) e-mail address(es), (4) species studied, and (5) types of studies (population dynamics, general ecology, vocalizations, nesting, behavior, and so on).

`mailto:jhailman@macc.wisc.edu`

Tobacco

Pipes

A forum for discussing the moderate use and appreciation of fine tobacco, including cigars, pipes, quality cigarettes, pipe making and carving, snuff, publications, and related topics.

Keywords: Pipes, Tobacco, Smoking

Audience: Smokers, Researchers, Market Analysts

Contact: Steve Masticola
masticol@scr.siemens.com

Details: Free, M

User Info: To subscribe to the list, send an e-mail message requesting a subscription to the URL address below. To send a message to the entire list, address it to: masticol@scr.siemens.com

`mailto:masticol@scr.siemens.com`

TOPNWS (Top News)

TOPNWS (Top News)

The Top News (TOPNWS) library contains today's news today for selected key sources from around the world.

Keywords: News Media, Analysis

Audience: Journalists, General Public

Profile: In the Top News (TOPNWS) library newswires are collected and updated every 60 minutes. Newspapers and other daily publications are updated throughout the day on the day of publication. Transcripts are updated within three hours of broadcast. Two weeks' worth of data from more than 40 major publications may be searched as individual files or in specialized group files. The TODAY group file contains today's published information from all sources. the 2WEEK group file expands the window of current information from all sources to two weeks. Specialized section files, designed to be like sections of a newspaper, contain stories from each publication that pertain to the section or topic selected.

Contact: Mead New Sales Group at (800) 227-4908 or (513) 859-5398 inside the US, or (513) 865-7981 for all inquiries outside the US.

User Info: To subscribe, contact Mead directly.

To examine the Nexis user guide, you can access it at the ftp site of the University of Texas at Austin at the URL address: ftp://ftp.cc.utexas.edu

The files are in: /pub/ref-services/LEXIS

`telnet://nex.meaddata.com`

`http://www.meaddata.com`

Tornado Warnings

Tornado Warnings

Gopher site providing up-to-the-minute tornado warnings for the United States.

Keywords: Disaster Relief, Weather

Sponsor: University of Illinois at Urbana-Champaign, Department of Atmospheric Sciences.

Audience: Meteorologists

Contact: John Kemp
johnkemp@uiuc.edu

Details: Free

`gopher://wx.atmos.uiuc.edu/11/Severe/Tornado_Warnings`

A B C D E F G H I J K L M N O P Q R S **T** U V W X Y Z

Total Quality Management Gopher

Total Quality Management Gopher

A collection of materials relating to the elimination of defects through comprehensive quality control in industry, government, and universities.

Keywords: Quality Control, Management, Business

Sponsor: The Clemson University Department of Industrial Engineering, Clemson, South Carolina, USA

Audience: Managers, Administrators

Contact: quality@eng.clemson.edu

`gopher://deming.eng.clemson.edu`

`http://deming.eng.clemson.edu`

Tourism

The Complete Guide to Galway

This is a detailed guide to the city of Galway (past and present), covering tourist sites, industry, local transportation, folklore, history, entertainment, drinking and dining. This web site includes maps, photographs, and illustrations.

Keywords: Galway (Ireland), Tourism, Travel

Audience: Irish, Tourists, Historians, Businesses

Contact: Joe Desbonnet
joe@epona.physics.ucg.ie

`http://wombatix.physics.ucg.ie/galway/galway.html`

The Texas Information Highway

Access to the public information resources of the state of Texas.

Keywords: Texas, Government, Census, Data, Travel

Sponsor: Texas Department of Information Resources

Audience: Texans, General Public

Profile: Still under construction as we go to press, this is a model program to make state and local information resources available to Internet users. The current collection features city, county, and state political information, including full-text of bills before the Texas State Legislature. Materials related to Texas history and tourism are also provided, along with links to Texas user groups and other state and federal information servers.

Contact: Wayne McDilda
wayne@dir.texas.gov

`gopher://info.texas.gov`

University of Wisconsin at Stout Library

The library's holdings are large and wide-ranging and contain significant collections in many fields.

Keywords: Mathematics, Business, Fashion Merchandising, Home Economics, Hospitality, Tourism, Hotel Administration, Restaurant Management, Microelectronics

Audience: Researchers, Students, General Public

Details: Free

User Info: Expect: Login, Send: Lib; Expect: vDIAL Prompt, Send: Library

`telnet://lib.uwstout.edu`

WWW Paris

A web site created as a collaborative effort among individuals in both Paris and the United States.

Keywords: Paris, Culture, Art, Travel, French, Tourism

Audience: Students, Educators, Travelers, Researchers

Profile: Contains an extensive collection of images and text regarding all of the major monuments and museums of Paris, including maps of the Metro and the RER; calendars of events and current expositions; promotional images and text relating to local department stores; there is also a visitors' section with up-to-date tourist information on hotels, restaurants, telephones, airport schedules, a basic Paris glossary, and the latest weather images. Includes an extensive collection of links to other resources about Paris and France, and a selected bibliography of history and architecture in Paris.

Contact: Norman Barth, Eric Pouliquen
nbarth@ucsd.edu, epouliq@ucsd.edu

`http://meteora.ucsd.edu/~norman/paris`

Toxicology

GENMED (General Medical Information)

The General Medical Information (GENMED) library contains a variety of medical care and treatment, toxicology, and hospital administration materials.

Keywords: Medicine, Toxicology, Hospital, Treatment

Audience: Medical Professionals

Profile: The GENMED library contains full-text medical journals and newsletters, as well as drug information, disease and trauma reviews, Physicians Data Query cancer information, and medical administration journals. GENMED also offers a gateway to the MEDLINE database.

Contact: Mead New Sales Group at (800) 227-4908 or (513) 859-5398 inside the US, or (513) 865-7981 for all inquiries outside the US.

User Info: To subscribe, contact Mead directly.

To examine the Nexis user guide, you can access it at the ftp site of the University of Texas at Austin at the URL address: ftp://ftp.cc.utexas.edu

The files are in: /pub/ref-services/LEXIS

`telnet://nex.meaddata.com`

`http://www.meaddata.com`

University of Maryland System Library

The library's holdings are large and wide-ranging and contain significant collections in many fields.

Keywords: Medicine (History of), Nursing, Pharmacology, Microbiology, Aquaculture, Aquatic Chemistry, Toxicology

Audience: General Public, Researchers, Librarians, Document Delivery Professionals

Contact: Ron Larsen

Details: Free

User Info: Expect: Available Services menu; Send: PAC

`telnet://victor.umd.edu`

vettox-l (Veterinary Toxicology Discussion List)

A list dedicated to diagnostic toxicology, established at the University of California.

Keywords: Veterinary Medicine, Toxicology

Audience: Veterinarians, Toxicologists

Profile: This list is restricted to those in the practice of diagnostic toxicology, although it will not be an edited list. The goals are to provide an atmosphere of cooperation among those in the field of diagnostic toxicology and to seek solutions to the many challenges that arise during a disease investigation.

Contact: James T. Case, Bill Cohen
jcase@ucdcvdls.bitnet or bcohen@ucdcvdls.bitnet

Details: Free

User Info: To subscribe to the list, send an e-mail message to the URL address below consisting of a single line reading:

SUB vettox-l YourFirstName YourLastName

To send a message to the entire list, address it to: vettox-l@ucdavis.edu

`mailto:listserv@ucdavis.edu`

Toys

Lego Information

A web site containing pictures, sets, and instructions for building with Legos. Also discusses various ideas, activities, and history pertaining to Legos, as well as information about clubs for Lego enthusiasts.

Keywords: Construction, Toys, Children

Sponsor: Lego

Audience: Children, General Public

Contact: David Koblas
koblas@netcom.com

`http://legowww.itek.norut.no`

Zarf's List of Interactive Games on the Web

A list containing links to games and toys that can be played on the Internet.

Keywords: Games, toys, entertainment, recreation

Sponsor: Carnegie Mellon University, School of Computer Science, Pittsburgh, Pennsylvania, USA

Audience: General Public, Game Players, Kids

Contact: Andrew Plotkin
zarf@cs.cmu.edu, apli@andrew.cmu.edu

`http://www.cs.cmu.edu/afs/cs.cmu.edu/user/zarf/www/games.html`

Trade Unions

Johns Hopkins University Library

The library's holdings are large and wide-ranging and contain significant collections in many fields.

Keywords: Literature (English), Economics, Classics, Drama (German), Slavery, Trade Unions, Incunabula, Bibles, Diseases (History of), Nursing (History of), Abolitionism

Audience: General Public, Researchers, Librarians, Document Delivery Professionals

Details: Free

`telnet://jhuvm.hcf.jhu.edu`

Trade

America

For people interested in how the United States is dealing with foreign trade policies, congressional status, and other inside information about the government that is freely distributable.

Keywords: Trade, Government (US), Congress (US), Business (US)

Audience: General Public, Researchers, Journalists, Political Scientists, Students

Contact: subscribe@xamiga.linet.org

User Info: To subscribe to the list, send an e-mail message to the URL address below, consisting of a single line reading:

SUB america YourFirstName YourLastName

To send a message to the entire list, address it to: america@xamiga.linet.org

Notes: This list has monthly postings that are generally in large batches, with posts exceeding a few hundred lines.

`mailto:subscribe@xamiga.linet.org`

Commerce Business Daily

The Commerce Business Daily is a publication that announces invitations to bid on proposals requested by the US Federal Government. This gopher is updated every business day.

Keywords: Business (US), Economics, Commerce, Trade, Government (US)

Sponsor: CNS and Softshare Government Information Systems

Audience: Economists, Business Professionals, General Public, Journalists, Students, Politicians.

Profile: Invitations via Internet email that apply only to specific companies can be arranged.

Contact: Melissa Allensworth
sshare@cscns.com

service@cscns.com

Details: Free

`gopher://cns.cscns.com/cbd/About the CBD`

National Export Strategy

This site provides the complete text of a report presented to Congress by the Trade Promotion Coordinating Committee, describing ways to develop U.S. export promotion efforts.

Keywords: Commerce, Trade, Exports, Business

Sponsor: United States Government, Trade Promotion Coordinating Committee

Audience: Exporters, Business Professionals, Trade Specialists

Details: Free

`ftp://sunny.stat-usa.gov`

`http://sunny.stat-usa.gov`

North American Free Trade Agreement (NAFTA)

The agreement between the governments of Canada, the United Mexican States, and the United States of America to establish a free trade area in North America.

Keywords: Trade, US, Mexico, Canada, Free Trade, NAFTA

Audience: Journalists, Politicians, Economists, Students

Details: Free

`gopher://wiretap.spies.com/00/Gov/NAFTA`

Overseas Business Reports

Full-text of U.S. International Trade Administration reports, discussing the economic and commercial climate in various countries around the world.

Keywords: Business, Trade, Commerce

Sponsor: U.S. Government, International Trade Administration

Audience: Business Professionals, Trade Specialists, Investors

Details: Free

`gopher://umslvma.umsl.edu/11/library/govdocs/obr`

PIERS Exports (US Ports)

PIERS (Port Import Export Reporting Service) imports (US Ports), produced by The Journal of Commerce, is a compilation of manifests of vessels loading or discharging caro at approximately 120 US seaports

Keywords: Trade, Exports, Maritime

Sponsor: The Journal of Commerce/PIERS, New York, NY, USA

Audience: Importers, Exporters, Business, Trade Specialists

Profile: Principal applications include identification of new sources of supply, monitoring exports of products whose details are lost in traditional government reports, and identification of potential trade partners. PIERS covers virtually all maritime movements in and out of the continental US and Puerto Rico. Details on each individual shipment are stored in the database.

Contact: Dialog in the US at (800) 334-2564, Dialog internationally at country specific locations.

User Info: To subscribe, contact Dialog directly.

Notes: Coverage: current 15 months, excluding data in file 571.

`telnet://dialog.com`

A B C D E F G H I J K L M N O P Q R S **T** U V W X Y Z

PIERS Imports (US Ports)

PIERS (Port Import Export Reporting Service) Imports (US Ports), produced by The Journal of Commerce, is a compilation of manifests of vessels loading or discharging cargo at approximately 120 US seaports.

Keywords: Trade, Imports, Maritime

Sponsor: The Journal of Commerce/PIERS, New York, NY, USA

Audience: Business Professionals

Profile: The principal applications of this information include: identification of new sources of supply for imports, monitoring imports of products whose details are lost in traditional government reports, and identification of potential trade partners.

Contact: Dialog in the US at (800) 334-2564, Dialog internationally at country specific locations.

User Info: To subscribe, contact Dialog directly.

Notes: Coverage: current 15 months, updated monthly.

`telnet://dialog.com`

TRADSTAT

TRADSTAT is a comprehensive online source of national trade statistics.

Keywords: Trade, Commerce, Business

Sponsor: TRADSTAT Ltd., London, UK

Audience: Importers, Exporters, Businesses

Profile: TRADSTAT covers over 90 percent of world trade. Every month the latest trade figures are loaded into the database from over 20 countries worldwide and all their trading partners. Trade is reported by countries in the EC, EFTA, North and South America, and the Far East. TRADSTAT gives annual trends back to 1981, and monthly reports can be produced at any time for the latest 25 months' trade. The data is made available on average three to eight weeks after the month of trade. This is often weeks, even months, ahead of the equivalent printed data.

User Info: To subscribe, contact Dialog directly.

`telnet://dialog.com`

Trademarks

Chinapats

Covers all patent applications published under the patent law of People's Republic of China.

Keywords: Patents, Intellectual Property, Trademarks

Sponsor: European Patent Office

Audience: Patent Attorneys, Patent Agents, Librarians, Researchers

Profile: English language abstracts are included for all applications filed by Chinese applicants. Contains more than 59,000 records. Updated monthly.

Contact: PAUL.ALBERT@NETEAST.COM

User Info: To subscribe contact Orbit-Questel directly.

`telnet://orbit.com`

CLAIMS

Provides access to over 2.3 million U.S. patents issued by the U.S. Patent and Trademark Office.

Keywords: Patents, Intellectual Property, Trademarks

Sponsor: IFI/Plenum Data Corporation

Audience: Patent Attorneys, Patent Agents, Librarians, Researchers

Profile: Chemical patents are covered from 1950 forward; mechanical and electrical patents from 1963 forward; design patents from 1980 forward.

Contact: paul.albert@neteast.com

User Info: To subscribe contact Orbit-Questel directly.

`telnet://orbit.com`

Derwent World Patents Index

Patent specifications issued by the patent offices of 33 major issuing authorities.

Keywords: Patents, Intellectual Property, Trademarks

Sponsor: Derwent Publications, Ltd.

Audience: Patent Attorneys, Patent Agents, Librarians, Researchers

Profile: Includes European Patent Office and Patent Cooperation Treaty published applications, plus Research Disclosure and International Technology Disclosure. Each patent is extensively indexed from the complete patent specifications. Abstracts are included.

Contact: paul.albert@neteast.com

User Info: To subscribe contact Orbit-Questel directly.

`telnet://orbit.com`

INCORPR (Corporation and Partnership Records)

The Corporation and Partnership Records (INCORP) library contains current US corporation and partnership filings.

Keywords: Corporations, Partnerships, Filings, Trademarks

Audience: Corporations, Lawyers, Researchers

Profile: The INCORP library contains current records on corporations and limited partnerships registered with the office of the Secretary or Department of State. These records include information extracted by the state's staff from articles of incorporation, annual reports, amendments, and other public filings.

Contact: Mead New Sales Group at (800) 227-4908 or (513) 859-5398 inside the US, or (513) 865-7981 for all inquiries outside the US.

User Info: To subscribe, contact Mead directly.

To examine the Nexis user guide, you can access it at the ftp site of the University of Texas at Austin at the URL address: ftp://ftp.cc.utexas.edu

The files are in: /pub/ref-services/LEXIS

`telnet://nex.meaddata.com`

`http://www.meaddata.com`

INPADOC/INPANEW

Patent documents issued by more than 50 national and international patent offices.

Keywords: Patents, Intellectual Property, Trademarks

Sponsor: European Patent Office

Audience: Patent Attorneys, Patent Agents, Librarians, Researchers

Profile: Bibliographic information is searchable, including inventor names, assignees, international patent classification codes, and in most cases, titles, as well as complete publications and application data. Contains approximately 20 million records. Updated weekly.

Contact: PAUL.ALBERT@NETEAST.COM

User Info: To subscribe contact Orbit-Questel directly.

`telnet://orbit.com`

JAPIO

Comprehensive source of unexamined Japanese patent applications.

Keywords: Patents, Intellectual Property, Trademarks

Sponsor: Japan Patent Information Organization

Audience: Patent Attorneys, Patent Agents, Librarians, Researchers

Profile: More than 2.8 million records covering all technologies. Unique features include English-language abstracts for many Japanese patent applications

Contact: paul.albert@neteast.com

User Info: To subscribe contact Orbit-Questel directly.

`telnet://orbit.com`

Legal Status

Records thousands of types of actions that can affect the legal status of a patent document after it is published and after the patent is granted.

Keywords: Patents, Intellectual Property, Trademarks Sponsor: European Patent Office Audience: Patent Atto

neys, Pa   ent   Agents,   Librarians,

Researcher   Profile: Information about the di position

f   patent   applicati

ns published under the Patent Cooperation Treaty by the World Intellectual Property Organizations is included as well. Contains more than 8 million records. Updated weekly.

Contact: PAUL.ALBERT@NETEAST.COM

User Info: To subscribe contact Orbit-Questel directly.

`telnet://orbit.com`

Trademark Act of the US

★

The US Trademark Act of 1946 (The Lanham Act), Title 15, United States Code, Sections 1051_1127.

Keywords: Trademarks, Laws (US), Government (US), Commerce

Audience: Journalists, Politicians, Students, Lawyers, Business Professionals, Designers, Marketers

Details: Free

`http://www.law.cornell.edu/lanham/lanham.table.html`

US Patents

Complete patent information of all claims of U.S. patents issued since 1971.

Keywords: Patents, Intellectual Property, Trademarks

Sponsor: Derwent, Inc.

Audience: Patent Attorneys, Patent Agents, Librarians, Researchers

Profile: Includes complete front page information, plus all claims of US patents issued since 1971. Merged file contains approximately 1.4 million records. Updated weekly.

Contact: PAUL.ALBERT@NETEAST.COM

User Info: To subscribe contact Orbit-Questel directly.

`telnet://orbit.com`

Trading Cards

Cards

★

This list is for people interested in collecting, speculating, and investing in baseball, football, basketball, hockey, and other trading cards and/or memorabilia. Discussion and want/sell lists are welcome.

Keywords: Trading Cards, Collectibiles, Memorabilia

Audience: Sports Card Collectors, Sports Card Traders, Memorabilia Collectors

Contact: Keane Arase
cards-request@tanstaafl.uchicago.edu

Details: Free

User Info: To subscribe to the list, send an e-mail message requesting a subscription to the URL address below.

To send a message to the entire list, address it to:

cards@tanstaafl.uchicago.edu

Notes: The list is open to anyone.

`mailto:cards-request@tanstaafl.uchicago.edu`

rec.collecting.cards

★

A Usenet newsgroup providing information and discussion about collecting sports and other trading cards.

Keywords: Trading Cards, Hobbies

Audience: Card Collectors

User Info: To subscribe to this Usenet newsgroup, you need access to a newsreader.

`news:rec.collecting.cards`

Sports-cards

★

For people interested in collection, speculation and investing in baseball, football, basketball, hockey, and other trading cards and/or memorabilia. Discussion and want/sell lists are welcome.

Keywords: Memorabilia, Sports, Trading Cards

Audience: Collectors, Sports Card Traders

Contact: Keane Arase
cards-request@tanstaafl.uchicago.edu

Details: Free

User Info: To subscribe to the list, send an e-mail message requesting a subscription to the URL address below. To send a message to the entire list, address it to: cards@tanstaafl.uchicago.edu

`mailto:cards-request@tanstaafl.uchicago.edu`

Translation

Lantra-L

★

A discussion of interpretation and translation.

Keywords: Interpretation, Translation, Language, Linguistics

Audience: Linguists, Interpreters, Translators

Details: Free

`mailto:listserv@searn.bitnet`

Transportation

gis-t

A mailing list for the discussion of GIS (Geographic Information Systems) and transportation.

Keywords: Geography, Transportation, GIS (Geographic Information Systems)

Audience: Geographers, Cartographers

Contact: Jay Sandhu
jsandhu@esri.com

User Info: To subscribe to the list, send an e-mail message to the URL address below consisting of a single line reading:

SUB gis-t YourFirstName YourLastName

To send a message to the entire list, address it to: gis-t@esri.com

`mailto:listserv@esri.com`

ITRE Home Page

A server dealing with transportation research and some GIS-related discussion.

Keywords: GIS, Transportation

Sponsor: University of North Carolina Institute for Transportation Research and Education

Audience: GIS Professionals, Transportation Professionals

Profile: The ITRE server address GIS issues regarding transportation, a different flavor than will be found on most servers on the Net. Also features image mapping examples.

Contact: Jay Novello
jay@itre.uncecs.edu

Details: Free

Images

Multimedia

`http://itre.uncecs.edu`

A B C D E F G H I J K L M N O P Q R S T U V W X Y Z

rec.railroad

A Usenet newsgroup providing information and discussion about railroads.

Keywords: Railroads, Transportation

Audience: Railroad Enthusiast

User Info: To subscribe to this Usenet newsgroup, you need access to a newsreader.

`news:rec.railroad`

Research Ship Schedules and Information

A gopher providing information on research and deep water vessels from more than 45 countries. Includes detailed ship specifications, some with deck plans and photographs available as GIF files. Also has cruise schedules for US ships, as well as some from other countries.

Keywords: Oceanography, Transportation, Maritime Industry, Travel

Sponsor: University of Delaware (The OCEANIC Ocean Information Center), Newark, Delaware, USA

Audience: Oceanographers, General Public

Contact: Ocean Information Center, University of Delawareof Delaware, College of Marine Studies
oceanic@diu.cms.udel.edu

Details: Free

Images

`gopher://diu.cms.udel.edu`

Subway Navigator (city subway routes)

This service helps you find a route in the subway systems of some cities in the world. Estimated times of departure/arrival are also given.

Keywords: Subways, Transit, Travel

Audience: Subway Riders, International Travelers

Profile: Cities covered are:

- Montreal, Canada
- Paris, France
- Hong Kong
- Lille, France
- Toulouse, France
- Madrid, Spain
- Lyon, France
- Frankfurt, Germany
- New York City, NY, USA*
- Marseille, France
- Munich, Germany

*The network includes all NYCTA (New-York City Transit Authority) subway stations.

Contact: Pierre.David@prism.uvsq.fr

Details: Free

`gopher://gopher.jussieu.fr/11/metro`

`telnet://vishnu.jussieu.fr`

University of Michigan Library

The library's holdings are large and wide-ranging and contain significant collections in many fields.

Keywords: Asia, Astronomy, Transportation, Lexicology, Math, Zoology, Geography

Audience: Researchers, Students, General Public

Contact: info@merit.edu

Details: Free

User Info: Expect: Which Host; Send: Help

`telnet://cts.merit.edu`

Transportation Law

TRANS (The Transportation Library)

The Transportation Library contains federal transportation case law, statutes, and agency decisions.

Keywords: Transportation Law, US Government Regulations, Aviation Industry, Railroad Industry, Trucking Industry

Audience: Lawyers

Profile: The Transportation library contains federal transportation case law, statutes and agency decisions. The major emphasis of the library is on three modes of transportation (aviation, railroad and trucking) and how those modes are regulated by the federal government. Agency decisions are provided from the Interstate Commerce Commission, Department of Transportation and the National Transportation Safety Board (NTSB).

Contact: New Sales Group at 800-227-4908 or 513-859-5398 inside the US, or 1-513-865-7981 for all inquires outside the US.

User Info: To subscribe, contact Mead directly.

To examine the Lexis user guide, you can access it at the ftp site of the University of Texas at Austin at the URL address: ftp://ftp.cc.utexas.edu

The files are in: /pub/res-services/LEXIS

`telnet://nex.meaddata.com`

Transsexualism

AUGLBC-I

The American University Gay, Lesbian, and Bisexual Community (AUGLBC) is a support group for lesbian, gay, bisexual, transsexual, and supportive students. The group is also connected with the International Gay and Lesbian Youth Organization (known as IGLYO).

Keywords: Gays, Lesbians, Bisexuality, Transsexuality, Sexuality

Audience: Gays, Lesbians, Bisexuals, Transsexuals, Students (College)

Contact: Erik G. Paul

User Info: To subscribe to the list, send an e-mail message to the URL address below, consisting of a single line reading:

SUB AUGLBC-I YourFirstName YourLastName

To send a message to the entire list, address it to: AUGLBC-I@american.edu

`mailto:listserv@american.edu`

Cd-Forum

The purpose of this list is to provide support and to discuss/share experiences about gender-related issues, including cross dressing, transvestism, and transsexualism.

Keywords: Transsexualism, Transvestism, Sexuality, Gender

Audience: Transsexuals, Transvestites

Contact: Valerie
cd-request@valis.biocad.com

Details: Free

User Info: To subscribe to the list, send an e-mail message requesting a subscription to the URL address below.

To send a message to the entire list, address it to: cd@valis.biocad.com

Notes: This list is in digest format.

`mailto:cd-request@valis.biocad.com`

OUTIL (Out in Linguistics)

The list is open to lesbian, gay, bisexual, transsexual linguists and their friends. The only requirement is that you be willing to be out to everyone on the list. The purposes of the group are to be visible and to gather occasionally to enjoy one another's company.

Keywords: Linguistics, Gays, Lesbians, Bisexuals, Transsexuals

Audience: Linguists, Gays, Lesbians, Bisexuals, Transsexuals

Contact: Arnold Zwicky
outil-request@csli.stanford.edu

Details: Free

User Info: To subscribe to the list, send an e-mail message requesting a subscription to the URL address below.

To send a message to the entire list, address it to: outil@csli.stanford.edu

`mailto:outil-request@csli.stanford.edu`

Travel

The Avid Explorer

A web site providing travel and destination information, including links to a number of other sources of travel information on the Internet.

Keywords: Travel

Sponsor: Explore! Cruises & Expeditions

Audience: General Public

Contact: Richard Reavis
webmaster@explore.com

`http://www.explore.com`

Canadian Geographical WWW Index Traveler

This web site provides weekly weather information.

Keywords: Weather, Travel, Canada, Geography

Sponsor: University of Manitoba, Canada

Audience: Travelers, Educators, Students

Contact: www@umanitoba.ca

Details: Free

`http://www.umanitoba.ca`

The Complete Guide to Galway

This is a detailed guide to the city of Galway (past and present), covering tourist sites, industry, local transportation, folklore, history, entertainment, drinking and dining. This web site includes maps, photographs and illustrations.

Keywords: Galway (Ireland), Tourism, Travel

Audience: Irish, Tourists, Historians, Businesses

Contact: Joe Desbonnet
joe@epona.physics.ucg.ie

`http://wombatix.physics.ucg.ie/galway/galway.htmlCanadian Geographical WWW Index Travel`

Highlands and Islands of Scotland

This web site provides information on Scotland, including business, leisure, culture, Gaelic language, tourism, distance education, and work opportunities.

Keywords: Scotland, Travel

Sponsor: British Telecom, United Kingdom

Audience: Travelers, Educators, Students

Contact: webmaster@nsa.bt.co.uk

Details: Free

`http://nsa.bt.co.uk/nsa.html`

hospex

A bulletin board for people interested in being hosts to foreign visitors.

Keywords: Travel

Audience: International Travelers, General Public

Contact: hospex@plearn.edu.p1

Details: Free

User Info: To subscribe to the list, send an e-mail message to the URL address shown below consisting of a single line reading:

SUB hospex YourFirstName YourLastName

`mailto:listserv@plearn.bitnet`

Information About Alaska

This collection contains information on Alaska's government and politics, as well as historical documents about Alaska's neighbors, Russia, and Canada. It also has cultural information, including literature and sports in the Land of the Midnight Sun.

Keywords: Alaska, Travel

Sponsor: University of Alaska Computer Network (UACN), Alaska, USA

Audience: Alaskans, Travelers, General Public

Contact: Douglas Toelle
sxinfo@orca.alaska.edu

`gopher://info.alaska.edu`

Information about New York City

Facts about New York City, including information on museums, restaurants, hotels, bars, and other areas of interest to New Yorkers and visitors alike.

Keywords: New York, Travel

Sponsor: City University of New York (CUNY)

Audience: New York City Residents, Tourists, General Public

Contact: Anil Khullar
gopher@netops.gc.cuny.edu

Notes: Still under construction, some items are incomplete

`gopher://timesq.gc.cuny.edu`

Ireland-Related Online Resources

This is a list of network-accessible online resources (documents, images, information, access mechanisms for off-line material, and so on) of Irish interest. Coverage includes some Bulletin Board services, some commercial information systems such as CompuServe and commercial bibliographic services.

Keywords: Ireland, Travel, Commerce, Geography

Audience: Irish, General Public, Tourists, Businesses

Contact: fmurtagh@eso.org

`http://http.hq.eso.org/~fmurtagh/ireland-resources.html`

Moon Travel Handbooks

Moon Publications' gopher features a travel newsletter, as well as excerpts and ordering information for their travel guides.

Keywords: Travel, Books

Sponsor: Moon Publications

Audience: International Travelers, General Public

Contact: gopher@moon.com

Notes: Also see Moon Publications' hypertext exhibit, Big Island of Hawaii Handbook, at http://bookweb.cwis.uci.edu:8042.

`gopher://gopher.moon.com`

New-orleans

A list for discussing any and all aspects of the city of New Orleans. History, politics, culture, food, restaurants, music, entertainment, Mardi Gras, and so on, are all fair game.

Keywords: New Orleans, Travel

Audience: New Orleans Residents, New Orleans Visitors

Contact: Edward J. Branley
elendil@mintir.new-orleans.la.us

User Info: To subscribe to the list, send an e-mail message requesting a subscription to the URL address below.

`mailto:mail-server@mintir.new-orleans.la.us`

Neworl-dig

This is a digest version of the New Orleans mailing list. It is distributed on a monthly basis, and includes articles from the New Orleans list, minus the "noise."

Keywords: New Orleans, Travel

Audience: New Orleans Residents, New Orleans Visitors

Contact: Edward J. Branley
elendil@mintir.new-orleans.la.us

Details: Free

User Info: To subscribe to the list, send an e-mail message requesting a subscription to the URL address below.

`mailto:mail-server@mintir.new-orleans.la.us`

A B C D E F G H I J K L M N O P Q R S **T** U V W X Y Z

News, Weather, and Travel Advisories

A major directory of news, weather, and travel advisories, providing access to a broad range of related resources (library catalogues, databases, and servers) via the Internet.

Keywords: Travel, Weather, Aviation

Sponsor: Kennesaw State College, Georgia, USA

Audience: General Public, Travellers

Profile: This collection includes CNN news sources, the National Weather Service Forecast, and the US State Department Travel Advisory, among other sources.

Details: Free

`gopher://kscsuna1.kennesaw.edu`

rec.scuba

A Usenet newsgroup providing information and discussion about scuba equipment and techniques.

Keywords: Scuba Sports, Travel, Recreation

Audience: Scuba Divers

User Info: To subscribe to this Usenet newsgroup, you need access to a newsreader.

`news:scuba`

rec.travel

A Usenet newsgroup providing information and discussion about travel.

Keywords: Travel

Audience: Travelers

User Info: To subscribe to this Usenet newsgroup, you need access to a newsreader.

`news:rec.travel`

Research Ship Schedules and Information

A gopher providing information on research and deep water vessels from more than 45 countries. Includes detailed ship specifications, some with deck plans and photographs available as GIF files. Also has cruise schedules for US ships, as well as some from other countries.

Keywords: Oceanography, Transportation, Maritime Industry, Travel

Sponsor: University of Delaware (The OCEANIC Ocean Information Center), Newark, Delaware, USA

Audience: Oceanographers, General Public

Contact: Ocean Information Center, University of Delawareof Delaware, College of Marine Studies
oceanic@diu.cms.udel.edu

Details: Free, Images

`gopher://diu.cms.udel.edu`

Subway Navigator (city subway routes)

This service helps you find a route in the subway systems of some cities in the world. Estimated times of departure/arrival are also given.

Keywords: Subways, Transportation, Travel

Audience: Subway Riders, International Travelers

Profile: Cities covered are:
- Montreal, Canada
- Paris, France
- Hong Kong
- Lille, France
- Toulouse, France
- Madrid, Spain
- Lyon, France
- Frankfurt, Germany
- New York City, NY, USA*
- Marseille, France
- Munich, Germany

*The network includes all NYCTA (New-York City Transit Authority) subway stations

Contact: Pierre.David@prism.uvsq.fr

Details: Free

`gopher://gopher.jussieu.fr/11/metro`

`telnet://vishnu.jussieu.fr`

The Texas Information Highway

Access to the public information resources of the state of Texas.

Keywords: Texas, Government, Census, Data, Travel

Sponsor: Texas Department of Information Resources

Audience: Texans, General Public

Profile: Still under construction as we go to press, this is a model program to make state and local information resources available to Internet users. The current collection features city, county, and state political information, including full-text of bills before the Texas State Legislature. Materials related to Texas history and tourism are also provided, along with links to Texas user groups and other state and federal information servers.

Contact: Wayne McDilda
wayne@dir.texas.gov

`gopher://info.texas.gov`

Thailand: The Big Picture

A web site maintaining a complete list of Internet servers pertaining to and found within Thailand. General information concerning Thailand and extensive Internet connections to Thai academic institutions.

Keywords: Thailand, Education, Travel

Sponsor: National Electronics and Computer Center at the National Science and Technology Development Agency, USA

Audience: Researchers, Exchange Students

Contact: Trin Tantsetthi
webmaster@www.nectec.or.th

`http://www.nectec.or.th`

Travelnet

Internet users can gain access here to travel related products and public service announcements pertaining to travel and tourism.

Keywords: Travel

Audience: Tourists, Travel Agents

Producer: TravelWeb

Profile: Travelnet is a system staffed by professional travel agents who provide accurate and timely information on travel related products. Travelnet also provides travel related news and announcements of general interest free as a public service announcement pertaining to countries globally.

Access Info: World Wide Web

Notes: The information contained on this server is copyright and cannot be modified, reposted, or otherwise used outside the policies of the TravelWeb without the permission of the TravelWeb Corporation. The TravelWeb is a resource and referral system only pertaining to travel related products.

`mailto:Travelnet@cruzio.com`

WWW Paris

A web site created as a collaborative effort among individuals in both Paris and the United States.

Keywords: Paris, Culture, Art, Travel, French, Tourism

Audience: Students, Educators, Travelers, Researchers

Profile: Contains an extensive collection of images and text regarding all of the major monuments and museums of Paris, including maps of the Metro and the RER; calendars of events and current expositions; promotional images and text relating to local department stores; there is also a visitors' section with up-to-date tourist information on hotels, restaurants, telephones, airport schedules, a basic Paris glossary, and the latest weather images. Includes an extensive collection of links to other resources about Paris and France, and a selected bibliography of history and architecture in Paris.

Contact: Norman Barth, Eric Pouliquen
nbarth@ucsd.edu, epouliq@ucsd.edu

`http://meteora.ucsd.edu/~norman/paris`

Travel (History of)

University of Tennessee at Knoxville Library

The library's holdings are large and wide-ranging and contain significant collections in many fields.

Keywords: Native American Affairs, Congress (US), Folklore, Travel (History of)

Audience: Researchers, Students, General Public

Details: Free

User Info: Expect: OK Prompt; Send: Login pub1; Expect: Password, Send: Usc

`telnet://opac.lib.utk.edu`

Treaties

Historic World Documents

The wiretap gopher provides access to a range of world documents in full-text format.

Keywords: International Documents, Treaties, History (World)

Audience: Governments, Historians, Researchers, General Public

Details: Free

Select from Menu as appropriate

`gopher://wiretap.spies.com`

Multilateral Treaties

An experimental program to make available to the Internet community the text of a wide variety of multilateral conventions, even those which have not yet been ratified.

Keywords: Multilateral, Treaty, Law

Sponsor: The Fletcher School of Law and Diplomacy, Cornell University, Ithaca, NY

Audience: Government Officials, Researchers, Lawyers

Profile: Almost all treaties listed are available in print form. The program will enable access to even very recent conventions. Primary focus is on Environmental and human rights issues but other fields are also included. The conventions coming out of the 1992 United Nations Conference on the Environment and Development have NOT been included as they are available elsewhere through CIESIN. Those Treaties covered include: Convention on International Trade in Endangered Species of Wild Fa; Montreal Protocol on Substances that Depleate the Ozone Layer; The Berne Convention for the Protection of Literary and Artistic Works; Agreement on the Rescue of Astronauts; the return of Astronauts

Contact: Peter Scott Director, Multilaterals Project, Fletcher School of Law and Diplomacy
pstott@pearl.tufts.edu
pstott@icg.apc.org

Details: Free

Select from menu as appropriate

`gopher://gopher.law.cornell.edu/11/foreign/fletcher-cat`

Various Treaties

Provides access to a range of treaties in full-text format.

Keywords: Treaties, Politics (International)

Audience: Governments, Researchers, Lawyers

Details: Free

Select from menu as appropriate

`gopher://wiretap.spies.com`

Treatment

GENMED (General Medical Information)

The General Medical Information (GENMED) library contains a variety of medical care and treatment, toxicology, and hospital administration materials.

Keywords: Medicine, Toxicology, Hospital, Treatment

Audience: Medical Professionals

Profile: The GENMED library contains full-text medical journals and newsletters, as well as drug information, disease and trauma reviews, Physicians Data Query cancer information, and medical administration journals. GENMED also offers a gateway to the MEDLINE database.

Contact: Mead New Sales Group at (800) 227-4908 or (513) 859-5398 inside the US, or (513) 865-7981 for all inquiries outside the US.

User Info: To subscribe, contact Mead directly.

To examine the Nexis user guide, you can access it at the ftp site of the University of Texas at Austin at the URL address: ftp://ftp.cc.utexas.edu

The files are in: /pub/ref-services/LEXIS

`telnet://nex.meaddata.com`

`http://www.meaddata.com`

Trekkers

Star Trek Resources on the Internet

This extensive resource contains information on mailing lists, news archives, other Internet resources addressing the culture surounding Star Trek fans.

Keywords: Science Fiction, Television, Trekkers

Audience: General Public, Trekkers, Television Viewers

Contact: Brigitte Jellinek
bjelli@cosy.sbg.ac.at

`http://www.cosy.sbg.ac.at/rec/startrek/star_trek_resources.html`

Trivia

rec.arts.tv

A Usenet newsgroup providing information and discussion about past and present TV shows and related trivia.

Keywords: Television, Trivia

Audience: General Public, Television Viewers, Trivia Enthusiasts

User Info: To subscribe to this Usenet newsgroup, you need access to a newsreader.

`news:rec.arts.tv`

Trollope (Anthony)

Princeton University Online Manuscripts Catalog Library

The library's holdings are large and wide-ranging. They contain significant collections in many fields.

Keywords: Books (Antiquarian), Dickens (Charles), Disraeli (Benjamin), Eliot (George), Hardy (Thomas), Kingsley (Charles), Trollope (Anthony)

Audience: General Public, Researchers, Librarians, Document Delivery Professionals

Details: Free

User Info: Expect: VM370 logo, Send: <cr>; Expect: Welcome screen, Send: folio <cr>; Expect: Welcome screen for FOLIO, Send: <cr>; Expect: List of choices, Send: 3 <cr>; To exit: type: logoff

`telnet://pucc.princeton.edu`

A B C D E F G H I J K L M N O P Q R S **T** U V W X Y Z

A
B
C
D
E
F
G
H
I
J
K
L
M
N
O
P
Q
R
S
T
U
V
W
X
Y
Z

Trucking Industry

TRANS (The Transportation Library)

The Transportation Library contains federal transportation case law, statutes and agency decisions.

Keywords: Transportation Law, US Government Regulations, Aviation, Railroads, Trucking Industry

Audience: Lawyers

Profile: The Transportation library contains federal transportation case law, statutes and agency decisions. The major emphasis of the library is on three modes of transportation (aviation, railroad and trucking) and how those modes are regulated by the federal government. Agency decisions are provided by the Interstate Commerce Commission, Department of Transportation and the National Transportation Safety Board (NTSB).

Contact: New Sales Group at 800-227-4908 or 513-859-5398 inside the US, or 1-513-865-7981 for all inquires outside the US.

User Info: To subscribe, contact Mead directly.

To examine the Lexis user guide, you can access it at the ftp site of the University of Texas at Austin at the URL address: ftp://ftp.cc.utexas.edu

The files are in: /pub/res-services/LEXIS

`telnet://nex.meaddata.com`

TULSA (Petroleum Abstracts)

TULSA (Petroleum Abstracts)

References and abstracts to literature and patents related to oil and natural gas exploration, development and production.

Keywords: Petroleum

Sponsor: Petroleum Abstracts, a division of the University of Tulsa

Audience: Researchers, Librarians

Profile: More than 500,000 references. Includes such areas as logging, well drilling, well completion and servicing, petroleum geology, exploration geophysics and geochemistry, oil and gas production, reservoir studies and recovery methods, pollution, alternative fuels, and transportation and storage. Updated weekly.

Contact: paul.albert@neteast.com

User Info: To subscribe contact Orbit-Questel directly.

`telnet://orbit.com`

Turkey

soc.culture.turkish

A Usenet newsgroup providing information and discussion about Turkish people and culture.

Keywords: Turkey, Sociology

Audience: Sociologists, Turks

Details: Free

User Info: To subscribe to this Usenet newsgroup, you need access to a newsreader.

`news:soc.culture.turkish`

Tutorials

Chemistry Tutorial Information

This site provides chemistry tutorial information in the form of text, data, pictures, source code, and executable programs for Macintosh computers.

Keywords: Chemistry, Tutorials, Macintosh, Education

Sponsor: University of Michigan

Audience: Chemistry Students (high school up)

Contact: comments@mac.archive.umich.edu

Details: Free, Images

`gopher://plaza.aarnet.edu.au@/micros/`
`mac/umich/misc/chemistry/00index.txt`

TWICS

TWICS

This is an English-language computer conferencing system in Japan.

Keywords: Community Networking, Japan, Virtual Community

Sponsor: TWICS Co., Ltd.

Audience: Internationalists, General Public, Journalists, Policy Makers

Profile: TWICS is a computer conferencing system that has a reputation for being a thriving electronic community. This system maintains a full Internet connection. Unlike a database or a gopher server, TWICS enables real-time online interaction with actual people.

Contact: Tim Buress
twics@twics.co.jp,

Details: Free

`telnet://tanuki.twics.co.jp`

Typography

The University of Iowa Libraries

The library's holdings are large and wide-ranging and contain significant collections in many fields.

Keywords: Hunt (Leigh), Native American Studies, Typography, Railroads, Cartoons, French Revolution, NASA, Hydraulics

Audience: General Public, Researchers, Librarians, Document Delivery Professionals

Details: Free

Send <RETURN>to display a menu of available systems. Type 1 for OASIS access and press <RETURN>to display the Welcome to OASIS screen.

`telnet://oasis.uiowa.edu`

U

UC Berkeley Museum of Paleontology and the WWW Subway

UC Berkeley Museum of Paleontology and the WWW Subway

This web site provides a multimedia museum display from UC Berkeley's Museum of Paleontology. Also features an interactive Subway, a tool linking users to other museums and WWW sites around the world.

Keywords: WWW, Museums, Paleontology

Sponsor: University of California at Berkeley, Museum of Paleontology, Berkeley, California, USA

Audience: Paleontologists, Internet Surfers, General Public

Contact: David Polly, Robert Guralnick
davip@ucmp1.berkeley.edu
robg@fossil.berkeley.edu

Details: Subway

`http://ucmp1.berkeley.edu/subway.html`

Ucadian Studies

University of Maine System Library Catalog

The library's holdings are large and wide-ranging and contain significant collections in many fields.

Keywords: Ucadian Studies, St. John Valley (History of), Canadian-American Studies, Geology, Aquaculture, Maine

Audience: General Public, Researchers, Librarians, Document Delivery Professionals

Contact: Elaine Albright, Marilyn Lutz

Details: Free

User Info: Expect: login, Send: ursus

`telnet://ursus.maine.edu`

UCSB Library Reference Guide

UCSB Library Reference Guide

A list of art references including indexes, dictionaries, bibliographies, and biographical materials.

Keywords: Art, History (World), Libraries

Sponsor: University of California at Santa Barbara

Audience: Artists, Historians, Librarians

`gopher://ucsbuxa.ucsb.edu`

UFOs

alt.alien.visitors

A Usenet newsgroup providing information and discussion about space aliens on Earth and related stories.

Keywords: UFOs, Aliens, Extraterrestrial Life

Audience: Alien Enthusiasts

User Info: To subscribe to this Usenet newsgroup, you need access to a newsreader.

`news:alt.alien.visitors`

UIgis-L

UIgis-L

A mailing list for the discussion of user interfaces and GIS (Geographic Information Systems).

Keywords: Geography, GIS (Geographic Information Systems)

Audience: Geographers, Cartographers

Contact: David Mark
dmark@acsu.buffalo.edu

User Info: To subscribe to the list, send an e-mail message to the URL address below consisting of a single line reading:

SUB uigis-l YourFirstName YourLastName

To send a message to the entire list, address it to: uigis@ubvm.cc.buffalo.edu

`mailto:listserv@ubvm.cc.buffalo.edu`

UN Army Map Service

University of Nevada at Reno Library

The library's holdings are large and wide-ranging and contain significant collections in many fields.

Keywords: Basque Studies, Nevada , UN Army Map Service, Patents

Audience: General Public, Researchers, Librarians, Document Delivery Professionals

Details: Free

User Info: Expect: login, Send: wolfpac

`telnet://wolfpac.lib.unr.edu`

UN Documents

Northwestern University Library

The library's holdings are large and wide-ranging and contain significant collections in many fields.

Keywords: Africa, Wright (Frank Lloyd), Women's Studies, Art, Literature (American), Contemporary Music, Government (US State), UN Documents, Music

Audience: General Public, Researchers, Librarians, Document Delivery Professionals

Details: Free

User Info: Expect: COMMAND:, Send: DIAL VTAM

`telnet://nuacvm.acns.nwu.edu`

UNC-CH Info system

UNC-CH Info system

The University of North Carolina at Chapel Hill's campus-wide information server, providing access to a wide range of campus information and to electronic information services worldwide.

Keywords: Education, Internet Services

Sponsor: University of North Carolina at Chapel Hill

Audience: Educators, Researchers, Internet Surfers

Contact: info@unc.edu

Details: Free

`gopher://gibbs.oit.unc.edu`

UNICEF Gopher

UNICEF Gopher

The gopher site of the United Nations Children's Fund.

Keywords: Children, Child Care

Sponsor: United Nations

Audience: Child Care Providers, Children's Rights Activists

Profile: This gopher provides access to full-text UNICEF publications such as the State of the World's Children report and the Progress of Nations, the UNICEF Annual Report, UNICEF Features, the First Call for Children newsletter, press releases, information notes and other advocacy and information booklets, brochures and pamphlets. The Gopher also contains the full-text of the Convention on the Rights of the Child and the Declaration and Plan of Action of the 1990 World Summit for Children.

Contact: UNICEF Gopher Host rpadolina@unicef.org

`gopher://hqfaus01.unicef.org`

Uniform Code of Military Justice

Uniform Code of Military Justice

The files in this directory contain the US Uniform Code of Military Justice.

Keywords: Military, Law

Audience: Journalists, Politicians, Students, Military Personnel

Details: Free

`gopher://wiretap.spies.com/00/Gov/UCMJ`

Uniform Commercial Code (UCC)

Uniform Commercial Code (UCC)

Articles 1 and 2 of the UCC, adopted with some variations in all 50 states (USA).

Keywords: Commerce, Business Info, Standards

Audience: Politicians, Marketers, Students, Retailers, Lawyers

Details: Free

`http://www.law.cornell.edu/ucc/ucc.table.html`

Unions

Women.labr

This conference features news, announcements, articles, and other information pertaining to the status of women workers in Europe, Latin America and the Caribbean, and Asia.

Keywords: Women, Unions

Audience: Women, Activists, Unions

Details: Costs

User Info.: Establish an account on the nearest APC node. Login, type c for conferences, then type go women.labr. For information on the nearest APC node, contact: APC International Secretariat IBASE E-mail: apcadmin@apc.org Contact: Carlos Afonso (cafonso@ax.apc.org) or APC North American Regional Office E-mail: apcadmin@apc.org Contact: Edie Farwell (efarwell@igc.apc.org)

Notes: ALAI: Agencia Latinoamericana de Informacion E-mail message to APCadmin@apc.org

`telnet://igc.apc.org`

UNITE Archive

UNITE Archive

The User Network Interface to Everything (UNITE) discussion list. The list is a focus for discussion on the concept of a total solution interface with user-friendly, desktop-integrated, access to all network services.

Keywords: Internet, Information Retrieval, Interface Design

Audience: Internet Surfers

Contact: George Munroe, Jill Foster unite-request@mailbase.ac.uk

Details: Free

Files are in: pub/lists/unite

`ftp://mailbase.ac.uk`

United Kingdom

AM/FM

A mailing list for the AM/FM Online Edition, a monthly compilation of news stories concerning the UK radio industry.

Keywords: Radio, United Kingdom, Communications

Audience: Radio Enthusiasts (UK), Communications Specialists, Students (college, graduate)

Contact: Stephen Hebditch listserv@orbital.demon.co.uk

User Info: To subscribe to the list, send an E-mail message to the URL addres below, consisting of a single line reading:

SUB am/fm YourFirstName YourLastName

To send a message to the entire list, address it to: AM/FM@orbital.demon.co.uk

`mailto:listserv@orbital.demon.co.uk`

British National Register of Archives

A multi-volume electronic guide to accessing a wide-variety of archival materials and

repositories in the United Kingdom.

Keywords: United Kingdom, History, Business, Information Retrieval

Sponsor: Coombspapers Social Sciences Research Data Bank at ANU (Australian National University).

Audience: Researchers, Anglophiles

Contact: Dr. T. Matthew Ciolek
tmciolek@coombs.anu.edu.au

`gopher://coombs.anu.edu.au`

`ftp:/coombs.anu.edu.au/coombspapers/otherarchives/uk-nra-archives/`

`http://coombs.anu.edu.au/CoombsHome.html`

Imperial College Department of Computing ★★

This is the home of the department of Computing, Imperial College, United Kingdom, the UKUUG (UK UNIX User Group) Archive and the DoC Information Service.

Keywords: Computing, United Kingdom, Europe

Audience: Computer Scientists

Contact: imjm@doc.ic.ac.uk

Details: Free

`gopher://src.doc.ic.ac.uk`

`http://src.doc.ic.ac.uk`

OLIS (Oxford University Library Information Service) Gopher ★★

OLIS is a network of libraries. It contains all the books from the English, Modern Languages, Social Studies, and Hooke libraries. It also contains books and journals cataloged since September 1988 in the Bodleian and Dependant libraries and the Taylor Institution. Books can be searched in any OLIS library from any location.

Keywords: Libraries, United Kingdom, Europe

Audience: Library Users

Contact: jose@olis.lib.ox.ac.uk

Details: Free

`gopher://gopher.lib.ox.ac.uk/00/Info/OLIS`

rec.arts.tv.uk ★

A Usenet newsgroup providing information and discussion about television shows in the United Kingdom.

Keywords: Television, United Kingdom

Audience: Television Viewers, British

User Info: To subscribe to this Usenet newsgroup, you need access to a newsreader.

`news:rec.arts.tv.uk`

rrl ★★

A mailing list for the discussion of GIS (Geographic Information Systems) in the United Kingdom.

Keywords: GIS (Geographic Information Systems), United Kingdom

Audience: Geographers, Cartographers

Contact: rrl@uk.ac.leicester

`mailto:rrl@uk.ac.leicester`

soc.culture.british ★

A Usenet newsgroup providing information and discussion about Britain and British culture.

Keywords: Sociology, United Kingdom

Audience: Sociologists

Details: Free

User Info: To subscribe to this Usenet newsgroup, you need access to a newsreader.

`news:soc.culture.british`

United Nations

Global Change Information Gateway ★★★★

This gateways was created to address environmental data management issues raised by the US Congress, the Administration, and the advisory arms of the Federal policy community. It contains documents related to the UN conference on Environment and Development.

Keywords: UN, Environment, Development, Oceans, Atmosphere

Audience: Environmentalists, Scientists, Researchers, Environmentalists

Profile: [profile needed]

Details: Free
Select from menu as appropriate.

`gopher://scilibx.ucsc.edu`

UN Criminal Justice Country Profiles ★

UN profiles of world crime in 113 countries.

Keywords: Crime, UN

Sponsor: United Nations

Audience: Lawyers, Legal Professionals, Librarians, Governments

Details: Free
Select from menu as appropriate.

`gopher://uacsc2.albany.edu`

UN Development Program ★

Provides a detailed history of the UN and its development, as well as an outline of UN Internet programs.

Keywords: United Nations, History (World)

Sponsor: United Nations

Audience: General Public, Historians, International-ists, Researchers

Details: Free

`gopher://nywork1.undp.org`

UN Rules ★

Standards, guidelines and international instruments promulgated by the UN.

Keywords: Politics, UN, Standards

Sponsor: United Nations Justice Network (UNCJIN)

Audience: Lawyers, General Public, International-ists

Details: Free
Select from Menu as appropriate

`gopher://uacsc2.albany.edu`

UN Resolutions ★

List of selected US and world government documents and UN resolutions.

Keywords: Government (International), United Nations, Government (US)

Sponsor: United Nations

Audience: Historians, Internationalists, Political Scientists

Details: Free

`gopher://wiretap.spies.com`

un.wcw.doc.eng ★

This is a read-only conference comprised of official UN documents for the United Nations Fourth World Conference on Women: Action for Equality, Development and Peace, scheduled to take place at the Beijing International Convention Center, Beijing, China, from 4-15 September 1995. The documents are provided by the official Conference Secretariat, are posted as received by the UN Non-Governmental Liaison Service (NGLS).

Keywords: Women, Development (International), Peace, UN, World Conference on Women

Audience: Women, Activists, Non-Governmental Organizations, Feminists

Contact: United Nations Non-Governmental Liaison Service/Edie Farwell
ngls@igc.apc.org, efarwell@igc.apc.org

Details: Costs, Moderated

User Info: Establish an account on the nearest APC node. Login, type c for conferences, then type go un.wcw.doc.eng.

For information on the nearest APC node, contact:
APC International Secretariat IBASE
E-mail: apcadmin@apc.org

`telnet://igc.apc.org`

A B C D E F G H I J K L M N O P Q R S T **U** V W X Y Z

A B C D E F G H I J K L M N O P Q R S T **U** V W X Y Z

un.wcw.doc.fra

This is a read-only conference comprised of official UN documents for the United Nations Fourth World Conference on Women: Action for Equality, Development and Peace, scheduled to take place at the Beijing International Convention Center, Beijing, China, from 4-15 September 1995. The documents are provided by the official Conference Secretariat, are posted as received by the UN Non-Governmental Liaison Service (NGLS).

Keywords: Women, Development (International), Peace, UN, World Conference on Women

Audience: Women, Activists, Non-Governmental Organizations, Feminists

Contact: United Nations Non-Governmental Liaison Service/Edie Farwell ngls@igc.apc.org or efarwell@igc.apc.org

Details: Costs, Moderated

User Info.: Establish an account on the nearest APC node. Login, type c for conferences, then type go un.wcw.doc.fra. For information on the nearest APC node, contact: APC International Secretariat IBASE E-mail: apcadmin@apc.org Contact: Carlos Afonso (cafonso@ax.apc.org) or APC North American Regional Office E-mail: apcadmin@apc.org Contact: Edie Farwell (efarwell@igc.apc.org)

Notes: ALAI: Agencia Latinoamericana de Informacion E-mail message to APCadmin@apc.org

`telnet://igc.apc.org`

United Nations

Includes full text of UN press releases, UN Conference on Environment and Development reports, UN Development Programme documents, U.N. telephone directories.

Keywords: UN, Environment, Development (International)

Audience: Researchers, Educators, Political Scientists, Environmentalists

Details: Free

`gopher://nywork1.undp.org`

United Press International News - Sports

United Press International News - Sports

Full text of UPI stories and articles.

Keywords: Sports, News Media

Sponsor: United Press International (UPI)

Audience: Sports Enthusiasts

Profile: This gopher allows access to daily UPI news feeds, including sports news. The most current articles available tend to run three to five days behind. This delay is compensated for by UPIs far-ranging coverage of national and international sporting news. Indexed, with back articles from 1992 onwards available.

Contact: UPI

Contact: clarinews@clarinet.com

Details: Free

`gopher://mrfrosty.micro.umn.edu./UPI-data/Today/sports`

United States

State Small Business Profiles

This site contains Small Business Administration reports, which provide statistics on the small business sector in each state.

Keywords: Business, Statistics, Federal Government (US)

Sponsor: U.S. Government, Small Business Administration, in conjunction with the Reference Department of the Thomas Jefferson Library of the University of Missouri-St. Louis

Audience: Business Professionals, Researchers

Profile: The 1993 State Business Profiles bring together an array of statistics on the small business sector in each state. Included is data on small business income and employment trends; women-owned and minority-owned businesses; business closings and formations; and state exports.

Contact: Raleigh Muns srcmuns@umslvma.umsl.edu

Details: Free

Notes: For additional information you can call the Small Business Administration toll free at 1-800-359-2777, or the SBA District Office in Washington, D.C. at (202) 205-6600.

`gopher://umslvma.umsl.edu/11/library/govdocs/states`

United States Geographic Name Server

United States Geographic Name Server

A database searchable by city name or ZIP code, this server provides geographic data including population, longitude and latitude, elevation, county, state, and ZIP codes.

Keywords: Geography, GIS (Geographical Information Systems)

Audience: Geographers, General Public

Contact: pubgopher@pluto.cc.brandeis.edu

`gopher://pluto.cc.brandeis.edu`

United States Geological Survey Home Page

United States Geological Survey Home Page

USGS server dedicated to all aspects of Geography and geographic data.

Keywords: GIS, Geography

Sponsor: United States Geological Survey

Audience: Geographers, GIS Professionals, Researchers, Students

Profile: Probably the most comprehensive geography/GIS server on the net. Features include a GIS tuturial, descriptions (and examples) of available USGS data products, access to online spatial data and more.

Contact: webmaster@info.er.usgs.gov

Details: Free, Images, Sounds, Multimedia

Notes: The USGS maintains many servers, this page contains links to most of them, such as EROS Data Center, GLIS and others.

`http://info.er.usgs.gov/USGSHome.html`

Universal Copyright Convention

Universal Copyright Convention

The Universal Copyright Convention as revised at Paris (1971). Convention and protocols were done at Paris on July 24, 1971. It was ratified by the President of the United States of America on August 28, 1972.

Keywords: Copyright, Laws (US), Government (US), Politics (US)

Audience: Lawyers, Students, Politicians, Journalists

Details: Free

`gopher://wiretap.spies.com/00/Gov/Copyright/US.Universal.Copyright.Conv.txt`

Universite de Montreal UDEMATIK Library

Universite de Montreal UDEMATIK Library

The library's holdings are large and wide-ranging and contain significant collections in many fields.

Keywords: Art, Architecture, Economics, Sexology, Social Law, Science, Technology, Literary Studies

Audience: Researchers, Students, General Public

Contact: Joelle or Sebastien Roy
udematik@ere.umontreal.ca
stemp@ere.umontreal.ca
roys@ere.umontreal.ca

User Info: Expect: Login; Send: Application id INFO

`telnet://udematik.umontreal.ca`

Universities

University of Minnesota Gopher Server

The University of Minnesota gopher server provides information about the University of Minnesota, as well as providing access to other universitygopher servers.

Keywords: Universities, Education (College/University)

Sponsor: University of Minnesota, Minnesota, USA

Audience: Students

Contact: Gopher Development Team
gopher@boombox.micro.umn.edu

`gopher://gopher.tc.umn.edu`

Usenet University

An archive of Usenet university groups that are currently active on the Internet.

Keywords: Education, Universities

Audience: University Students, Educators, Researchers

Details: Free

User Info: File is: pub/doc/uu/FAQ

`ftp://nic.funet.fi`

Universities (History of)

The University of Notre Dame Library

The library's holdings are large and wide-ranging and contain significant collections in many fields.

Keywords: Music (Irish), Ireland, Botany (History of), Ecology, Entomology, Parasitology, Aquatic Biology, Universities (History of), Paleography

Audience: General Public, Researchers, Librarians, Document Delivery Professionals

Details: Free

User Info: Expect: ENTER COMMAND OR HELP:, Send: library; To leave, type x on the command line and press the enter key. At the ENTER COMMAND OR HELP: prompt, type bye and press the enter key.

`telnet://irishmvs.cc.nd.edu`

University of California Santa Barbara Virtual Library

University of California Santa Barbara Virtual Library

This source provides detailed lists of internet music resources.

Keywords: Music Resources

Sponsor: University of California at Santa Barbara

Audience: Musicians

Profile: This site contains lists pointing to music resources on the internet, including ftp sites, gopher servers, newsgroups, and list servers.

Details: Free

Path is The Subject Collections/The Arts Collections/Music

`gopher://ucsbuxa.ucsb.edu`

University of Chicago Library

University of Chicago Library

The library's holdings are large and wide-ranging and contain significant collections in many fields.

Keywords: Lincoln (Abraham), Kentucky & Ohio River Valley (History of), Balzac (Honore de), American Drama, Cromwell (Oliver), Goethe, Judaica, Italy, Chaucer (Geoffrey), Wells (Ida, Personal Papers of), Douglas (Stephen A.), Italy, Literature (Children's)

Audience: General Public, Researchers, Librarians, Document Delivery Professionals

Details: Free

User Info: Expect: ENTER CLASS, Send: LIB48 3; Expect: CONNECTED, Send: RETURN

`telnet://olorin.uchicago.edu`

University of Colorado at Boulder Library

University of Colorado at Boulder Library

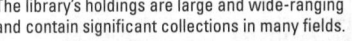

The library's holdings are large and wide-ranging and contain significant collections in many fields.

Keywords: Numismatics, Human Rights, Literature (Children's), Labor Archives, History (US)

Audience: Researchers, Students, General Public

Contact: Donna Pattee
pattee@spot.colorado.edu

Details: Free

User Info: Expect: Login; Send: Culine

`telnet://culine.colorado.edu`

University of Delaware Libraries (DELCAT)

University of Delaware Libraries (DELCAT)

The library's holdings are large and wide-ranging and contain significant collections in many fields.

Keywords: Literature (American), Hemingway (Ernest), Papermaking (History of), Chemistry (History of), Literature (Irish), Delaware

Audience: General Public, Researchers, Librarians, Document Delivery Professionals

Contact: Stuart Glogoff
epo27855@udacsvm.bitnet

Details: Free

User Info: Expect: prompt, Send: RETURN 2-3 times

`telnet://delcat.udel.edu`

`telnet://delcat.acs.udel.edu`

University of Denver Library

University of Denver Library

The library's holdings are large and wide-ranging and contain significant collections in many fields.

Keywords: Folklore Husted (Margaret, Culinary Collection of)

Audience: Researchers, Students, General Public

Contact: Bob Stocker
bstocker@ducair.bitnet

Details: Free

User Info: Expect: Login; Send: Atdu

`telnet://du.edu`

University of Glasgow Information Service (GLANCE)

University of Glasgow Information Service (GLANCE)

GLANCE provides subject-based information services, including an extensive section on European and world sports.

Keywords: Sports, Soccer, Motor Racing, Mountaineering, Squash, Cricket, Golf, Tennis, Europe, Scotland

Sponsor: University of Glasgow, Glasgow, Scotland

Audience: Sports Enthusiasts, Fitness Enthusiasts, Nature Lovers

Profile: Information at this site includes schedules, results, and statistics for sports such as cricket and soccer. There is also a selection of items on mountaineering.

Contact: Alan Dawson
A.Dawson@uk.ac.gla.compserv

Details: Free

`gopher://govan.cent.gla.ac.uk/`
`Subject/Sports and Rec`

University of Hawaii Library

University of Hawaii Library

The library's holdings are large and wide-ranging and contain significant collections in many fields.

Keywords: Asia, European Documents, Book Arts, Hawaii

Audience: General Public, Researchers, Librarians, Document Delivery Professionals

Details: Free

User Info: Expect: enter class, Send: LIB

`telnet://starmaster.uhcc.hawaii.edu`

University of Maine System Library Catalog

University of Maine System Library Catalog

The library's holdings are large and wide-ranging and contain significant collections in many fields.

Keywords: Ucadian Studies, St. John Valley (History of), Canadian-American Studies, Geology, Aquaculture, Maine

Audience: General Public, Researchers, Librarians, Document Delivery Professionals

Details: Free

User Info: Expect: login, Send: ursus

`telnet://ursus.maine.edu`

University of Maryland SystemLibrary

University of Maryland SystemLibrary

The library's holdings are large and wide-ranging and contain significant collections in many fields.

Keywords: Medicine (History of), Nursing, Pharmacology, Microbiology, Aquaculture, Aquatic Chemistry, Toxicology

Audience: General Public, Researchers, Librarians, Document Delivery Professionals

Details: Free

User Info: Expect: Available Services menu; Send: PAC

`telnet://victor.umd.edu`

University of Maryland, College Park

University of Maryland, College Park

The library's holdings are large and wide-ranging and contain significant collections in many fields.

Keywords: Agriculture, Coastal Marine Biology, Fisheries, Water Quality, Oceanography

Audience: Researchers, Students, General Public

Contact: Janet McLeod
mcleod@umail.umd.edu

Details: Free

User Info: Expect: Login; Send: Atdu

`telnet://info.umd.edu`

University of Michigan Library

University of Michigan Library

The library's holdings are large and wide-ranging and contain significant collections in many fields.

Keywords: Asia, Astronomy, Transportation, Lexicology, Mathematics, Zoology, Geography

Audience: Researchers, Students, General Public

Contact: info@merit.edu

Details: Free

User Info: Expect: Which Host; Send: Help

`telnet://cts.merit.edu`

University of Minnesota Gopher Server

University of Minnesota Gopher Server

The University of Minnesota gopher server provides information about Minnesota University, as well as providing access to other university gopher servers.

Keywords: Universities, Education (College/University)

Sponsor: University of Minnesota, Minnesota, USA

Audience: Students

Contact: Gopher Development Team
gopher@boombox.micro.umn.edu

`gopher://gopher.tc.umn.edu`

University of Nebraska at Lincoln Library

University of Nebraska at Lincoln Library

The library's holdings are large and wide-ranging and contain significant collections in many fields.

Keywords: Slovak Republic, Czech Republic, Folklore, Military History, Latvia, Law (Tax), Law (US)

Audience: General Public, Researchers, Librarians, Document Delivery Professionals

Details: Free

User Info: Expect: login, Send: library

`telnet://unllib.unl.edu`

University of Nevada at Reno Library

University of Nevada at Reno Library

The library's holdings are large and wide-ranging and contain significant collections in many fields.

Keywords: Basque Studies, Nevada , United Nations, Patents

Audience: General Public, Researchers, Librarians, Document Delivery Professionals

Details: Free

User Info: Expect: login, Send: wolfpac

`telnet://wolfpac.lib.unr.edu`

University of Nevada, Las Vegas Library - Las Vegas, NV

University of Nevada, Las Vegas Library - Las Vegas, NV

The library's holdings are large and wide-ranging and contain significant collections in many fields.

Keywords: Gambling, Hotel Administration, Nevadiana, Canadian Documents, Nevada State Documents

Audience: General Public, Researchers, Librarians, Document Delivery Professionals

Contact: Myoung-Ja Lee Kwon
kwon@nevada.edu.

Details: Free

User Info: Expect: login; Send: library

`telnet://library.lv-lib.nevada.edu`

University of New Hampshire Videotex Library

University of New Hampshire Videotex Library

The library's holdings are large and wide-ranging and contain significant collections in many fields.

Keywords: Dance, Folk Music, Milne (A.A., Collection of), Galway (Ireland)

Audience: Researchers, Students, General Public

Contact: Robin Tuttle
r_tuttle1@unhh.unh.edu

Details: Free

User Info: Expect: USERNAME; Send: Student (no password required). Control-z to log off.

`telnet://unhvt@unh.edu`

University of New Mexico Unminfo Library

University of New Mexico Unminfo Library

The library's holdings are large and wide-ranging and contain significant collections in many fields.

Keywords: Photography (History of), Architecture, Native American Affairs, Land Records

Audience: Researchers, Students, General Public

Contact: Art St. George
stgeorge@unmb.bitnet

Details: Free

User Info: Expect: Login; Send: Unminfo

`telnet://unminfo.unm.edu`

University of North Carolina at Chapel Hill Info Library

University of North Carolina at Chapel Hill Info Library

The library's holdings are large and wide-ranging and contain significant collections in many fields.

Keywords: North Carolina, Rare Books, Books (Antiquarian)

Audience: Researchers, Students, General Public

Contact: Judy Hallman
hallman@unc.bitnet

Details: Free

User Info: Expect: Login; Send: Info

`telnet://info.oit.unc.edu`

University of North Carolina; Chapel Hill

Newsbrief

Provides a variety of information and feature articles, primarily for campus users.

Keywords: University of North Carolina; Chapel Hill, North Carolina; Information Technology

Sponsor: Office of Information Technology at the University of North Carolina, Chapel Hill (UNC Chapel Hill)

Audience: Students, Educators

Contact: Karen C. Blansfield, Judy Hallman
karen@rhumba.acs.unc.edu

Details: Free

User Info: To subscribe, send an E-mail message to the URL address below consisting of a single line reading:

To send a message to the entire list,

`mailto:listserv@uncvm1.bitnet`

University of North Carolina at Greensboro MINERVA Library

University of North Carolina at Greensboro MINERVA Library

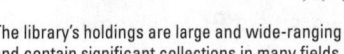

The library's holdings are large and wide-ranging and contain significant collections in many fields.

Keywords: Herbert (George), Film, Dickinson (Emily), Literature (Children's)

Audience: Researchers, Students, General Public

Details: Free

User Info: Expect: Login; Send: Info or MINERVA

`telnet://steffi.acc.uncg.edu`

University of North Carolina at Wilmington SEABOARD Library

University of North Carolina at Wilmington SEABOARD Library

The library's holdings are large and wide-ranging and contain significant collections in many fields.

Keywords: Marine Biology, Historical Documents

Audience: Researchers, Students, General Public

Contact: Eddy Cavenaugh
cavenaughd@uncwil.bitnet
cavenaughd@vxc.uncwil.edu

Details: Free

User Info: Expect: Login; Send: Info

`telnet://vxc.uncwil.edu`

A
B
C
D
E
F
G
H
I
J
K
L
M
N
O
P
Q
R
S
T
U
V
W
X
Y
Z

University of Northern Iowa Library

University of Northern Iowa Library

The library's holdings are large and wide-ranging and contain significant collections in many fields.

Keywords: Art, Business Information, Education, Music, Fiction

Audience: Researchers, Students, General Public

Contact: Mike Yohe
yohe@uni.edu

Details: Free

User Info: Expect: Login; Send: Public

`telnet://infosys.uni.edu`

University of Pennsylvania Library- Philadelphia Pa.

University of Pennsylvania Library- Philadelphia Pa.

The library's holdings are large and wide-ranging and contain significant collections in many fields.

Keywords: Literature (English), Literature (American), History (World), Medieval Studies, East Asian Studies, Middle Eastern Studies, South Asian Studies, Judaica, Lithuania.

Audience: Educators, Students, Researchers

Profile: Access to the central Van Pelt Library and to most of the departmental libraries is restricted to members of the University community on weekends and holidays. Online visitors are advised to call (215) 898-7554 for information on hours and access restrictions.

Details: Free

`telnet://library.upenn.edu`

University of Pennsylvania PENNINFO Library

University of Pennsylvania PENNINFO Library

The library's holdings are large and wide-ranging and contain significant collections in many fields.

Keywords: Church History, Spanish Inquisition, Witchcraft, Shakespeare (William), Bibles, Aristotle (Texts of), Fiction, Whitman (Walt), French Revolution, Drama (French), Literature (English), Literature (Spanish)

Audience: Researchers, Students, General Public

Contact: Al DSouza
penninfo-admin@dccs.upenn.edu
dsouza@dccs.upenn.edu

Details: Free

User Info: Expect: Login; Send: Public

`telnet://penninfo.upenn.edu`

University of Pennsylvania School of Medicine Library

University of Pennsylvania School of Medicine Library

The library's holdings are large and wide-ranging and contain significant collections in many fields.

Keywords: Health Care, Nursing, History, Health

Audience: Researchers, Students, General Public

Details: Free

User Info: Expect: Login; Send: Public

`telnet://penninfo.upenn.edu`

University of Puerto Rico Library

University of Puerto Rico Library

The library's holdings are large and wide-ranging and contain significant collections in many fields.

Keywords: Computer Science, Education, Nursing, Agriculture, Economics

Audience: Researchers, Students, General Public

Details: Free

After Locator: telnet://, press Tab twice. Type DIAL VTAM. Enter NOTIS. Press Return. On the blank screen, type LUUP.

`telnet://136.145.2.10`

University of Puget Sound Library

University of Puget Sound Library

The library's' holdings are large and wide-ranging and contain significant collections in many fields.

Keywords: Education, Literature (General), Music, Natural Science, Theology

Audience: Researchers, Students, General Public

Details: Free

User Info: Expect: Login; Send: Library

`telnet://192.124.98.2`

University of Rochester Library

University of Rochester Library

The library's holdings are large and wide-ranging and contain significant collections in many fields.

Keywords: Architecture, Art History, Photography, Literature (Asian), Lasers, Geology, Statistics, Optics, Medieval Studies

Audience: Researchers, Students, General Public

Details: Free

User Info: Expect: Login; Send: Library

`telnet://128.151.226.71`

University of Saskatchewan Libraries

University of Saskatchewan Libraries

A major Canadian University library with access to library catalogs archives, and Canadian Government documents.

Keywords: Canada, Government (International)

Sponsor: University of Saskatchewan

Audience: Canadians, General Public

Profile: The University of Saskatchewan Libraries maintain online databases of their collections archives, and catalogs. The libraries are a voluminous resource for the study of Canada, Canadian government, and Canadian-American issues.

Notes: Login: sonia

`telnet://sklib.usask.ca`

University of Southern Colorado Library

University of Southern Colorado Library

The library's holdings are large and wide-ranging and contain significant collections in many fields.

Keywords: History (US)

Audience: Researchers, Students, General Public

Details: Free

User Info: Expect: OK Prompt, Send: Login Pub1; Expect: Password: usc

`telnet://starburst.uscolo.edu`

University of Tennessee at Chatanooga Library

University of Tennessee at Chatanooga Library

The library's holdings are large and wide-ranging and contain significant collections in many fields.

Keywords: Civil War, Literature (American)

Audience: Researchers, Students, General Public

Contact: Randy Whitson
rwhitson@utcvmutc.edu

Details: Free

User Info: Expect: OK prompt; Send: Login pub1;
Expect: Password, Send: Usc

`telnet://library.utc.edu`

University of Tennessee at Knoxville Library

University of Tennessee at Knoxville Library

The library's holdings are large and wide-ranging and contain significant collections in many fields.

Keywords: Native American Affairs, Congress (US),
Folklore, Travel (History of)

Audience: Researchers, Students, General Public

Details: Free

User Info: Expect: OK Prompt; Send: Login pub1;
Expect: Password, Send: Usc

`telnet://opac.lib.utk.edu`

University of Tennessee at Memphis Library

University of Tennessee at Memphis Library

The library's holdings are large and wide-ranging and contain significant collections in many fields.

Keywords: Tennessee, Literature (American)

Audience: Researchers, Students, General Public

Details: Costs

User Info: Expect: Username Prompt; Send: Harvey

`telnet://utmem1.utmem.edu`

University of Texas at Austin Library

University of Texas at Austin Library

The library's holdings are large and wide-ranging and contain significant collections in many fields.

Keywords: Music, Natural Science, Nursing,
Science Technology, Behavioral
Science, Social Work, Computer
Science, Engineering, Latin American
Studies, Middle Eastern Studies

Audience: Researchers, Students, General Public

Details: Free

User Info: Expect: Blank Screen, Send: Return;
Expect: Go, Send: Return; Expect: Enter
Terminal Type, Send: vt100

Note: Some databases are restricted to
UT Austin users only.

`telnet://utcat.utexas.edu`

University of Texas at Austin Tarlton Law Library

University of Texas at Austin Tarlton Law Library

The library's holdings are large and wide-ranging and contain significant collections in many fields.

Keywords: British Commonwealth Law, Constitutional Law, Law (International), Human
Rights

Audience: Researchers, Students, General Public

Details: Free

User Info: Expect: Login, Send: Library

`telnet://tallons.law.utexas.edu`

University of Texas at Galveston (Medical Branch) Library

University of Texas at Galveston (Medical Branch) Library

The library's holding's are large and wide-ranging and contain significant collections in many fields.

Keywords: Health Sciences, Biomedicine, Nursing

Audience: Researchers, Students, General Public

Details: Free

User Info: Expect: Login, Send: Library

`telnet://ibm.gal.utexas.edu`

University of Texas Health Science Center (UTHSCSA) Biomedical Library Information System

University of Texas Health Science Center (UTHSCSA) Biomedical Library Information System

Keywords: Medicine, Libraries

Sponsor: Audie L. Murphy Memorial Veterans'
Administration Hospital, San Antonio, TX

Audience: Medical Professionals, Students

Details: Free

`telnet://lis@athena.uthscsa.edu`

University of Texas Health Science Center at San Antonio Library

University of Texas Health Science Center at San Antonio Library

The library's holdings are large and wide-ranging and contain significant collections in many fields.

Keywords: Dentistry, Nursing, Veterinary Science,
Ambulatory Care, Obstetrics/
Gynecology, Pediatrics

Audience: Researchers, Students, General Public

Details: Free

User Info: Expect: Login, Send: LIS

`telnet://athena.uthscsa.edu`

University of Texas Health Science Center at Tyler Library

University of Texas Health Science Center at Tyler Library

The library's holdings are large and wide-ranging and contain significant collections in many fields.

Keywords: Biochemistry, Cardiopulmonary
Medicine, Cell Biology, Molecular
Biology

A
B
C
D
E
F
G
H
I
J
K
L
M
N
O
P
Q
R
S
T
U
V
W
X
Y
Z

Audience: Researchers, Students, General Public

Details: Free

User Info: Expect: Username Prompt, Send: LIS

`telnet://athena.uthscsa.edu`

University of Texas Southwestern Medical Center Library

University of Texas Southwestern Medical Center Library

The library's holdings are large and wide-ranging and contain significant collections in many fields.

Keywords: Biomedical Science

Audience: Researchers, Students, General Public

Details: Free

User Info: Expect: Login, Send: Tlntutsw; Expect: Password, Send: Library

`telnet://library.swmed.edu`

University of Texas-Pan American Library

University of Texas-Pan American Library

The library's holdings are large and wide-ranging and contain significant collections in many fields.

Keywords: Lower Rio Grande Valley (History of), Mexican-American Studies

Audience: Researchers, Students, General Public

Details: Free

User Info: Expect: Username Prompt, Send: packey

`telnet://panam2.panam.edu`

University of the Pacific Library

University of the Pacific Library

The library's holdings are large and wide-ranging and contain significant collections in many fields.

Keywords: Pharmacology, Americana (Western)

Audience: Researchers, Students, General Public

Details: Free

User Info: Expect: Login, Send: Library

`telnet://pacificat.lib.uop.edu`

University of Toledo Library

University of Toledo Library

The library's holdings are large and wide-ranging and contain significant collections in many fields.

Keywords: Business, Great Lakes Area, Humanities, International Relations, Psychology, Science

Audience: Researchers, Students, General Public

Details: Free

User Info: Expect: Enter one of the following commands . . . , Send: DIAL MVS; Expect: dialed to mvs ####; Send: UTMOST

`telnet://uofto1.utoledo.edu`

University of Tulsa Library

University of Tulsa Library

The library's holdings are large and wide-ranging and contain significant collections in many fields.

Keywords: Literature (American), Petroleum, Geology

Audience: Researchers, Students, General Public

Details: Free

User Info: Expect: Username Prompt, Send: LIAS

`telnet://vax2.utulsa.edu`

University of Utah Library

University of Utah Library

The library's holdings are large and wide-ranging and contain significant collections in many fields.

Keywords: Western America, Middle Eastern Studies, Geology, Mining

Audience: Researchers, Students, General Public

Details: Free

User Info: Expect: Command Line, Send: Dial Unis

`telnet://lib.utah.edu`

University of Wales College of Medicine Library Online Catalog

University of Wales College of Medicine Library Online Catalog

Keywords: Medicine, Libraries

Sponsor: University of Wales, United Kingdom

Audience: Health Care Professionals, Students

Details: Free

User Info: Expect: login, Send: 'janet'; Expect: password; Send: 'janet'

`telnet://sun.nsf.ac.uk`

University of Wisconsin at Milwaukee Library

University of Wisconsin at Milwaukee Library

The library's holdings are large and wide-ranging and contain significant collections in many fields.

Keywords: Art, Architecture, Business, Cartography, Geography, Geology, Urban Studies, Literature (English), Literature (American)

Audience: Researchers, Students, General Public

Details: Free

User Info: Expect: Login, Send: Lib; Expect: vDIAL prompt, Send: Library

`telnet://uwmcat.lib.uwm.edu`

University of Wisconsin at Oshkosh Library

University of Wisconsin at Oshkosh Library

The library's holdings are large and wide-ranging and contain significant collections in many fields.

Keywords: Business, Liberal Education, Nursing

Audience: Researchers, Students, General Public

Details: Free

User Info: Expect: Login; Send: Lib; Expect: vDIAL Prompt, Send: Library

`telnet://polk.cis.uwosh.edu`

University of Wisconsin at Platteville Library

University of Wisconsin at Platteville Library

The library's holdings are large and wide-ranging and contain significant collections in many fields.

Keywords: Business, Industry

Audience: Researchers, Students, General Public

Details: Free

User Info: Expect: Login, Send: Lib; Expect: vDIAL Prompt, Send: Library

`telnet://137.104.128.44`

University of Wisconsin at Stout Library

University of Wisconsin at Stout Library

The library's holdings are large and wide-ranging and contain significant collections in many fields.

Keywords: Mathematics, Business, Fashion Merchandising, Home Economics, Hospitality, Tourism Industry, Hotel Administration, Restaurant Management, Microelectronics

Audience: Researchers, Students, General Public

Details: Free

User Info: Expect: Login, Send: Lib; Expect: vDIAL Prompt, Send: Library

`telnet://lib.uwstout.edu`

University of Wisconsin Eau Claire Library

University of Wisconsin Eau Claire Library

The library's holdings are large and wide-ranging and contain significant collections in many fields.

Keywords: Health Sciences, Business, Nursing, Education

Audience: Researchers, Students, General Public

Details: Free

User Info: Expect: Service Name, Send: Victor

`telnet://lib.uwec.edu`

University of Wisconsin Extension Program in Independent Study

University of Wisconsin Extension Program in Independent Study

A gopher containing information about courses of study at the University of Wisconsin Extension Program in Independent Study. Over fifty-five disciplines, from Arabic to Womens Studies, are represented.

Keywords: Education (Distance), Independent Study

Sponsor: University of Wisconsin Extension Program in Independent Study, Madison, Wisconsin, USA

Audience: Professionals, Educators, Students

Notes: Information is free, but fees are charged for courses. Contact the Advisor to Students at 608-263-2055, or write University of Wisconsin Extension Program in Independent Study, 104 Extension Building, 432 North Lake Street, Madison, WI 53706-1498

`gopher://gopher.uwex.edu`

University of Wisconsin Green Bay Library

University of Wisconsin Green Bay Library

The library's holdings are large and wide-ranging and contain significant collections in many fields.

Keywords: Economics, Environmental Studies, Music, Natural Science

Audience: Researchers, Students, General Public

Details: Free

User Info: Expect: Service Name, Send: Victor

`telnet://gbls2k.uwgb.edu`

University of Wisconsin River Falls Library

University of Wisconsin River Falls Library

The library's holdings are large and wide-ranging and contain significant collections in many fields.

Keywords: Agriculture, Education, History (US)

Audience: Researchers, Students, General Public

Details: Free

User Info: Expect: Service Name, Send: Victor

`telnet://davee.dl.uwrf.edu`

University of Wisconsin Stevens Point Library

University of Wisconsin Stevens Point Library

The library's holdings are large and wide-ranging and contain significant collections in many fields.

Keywords: Education, Environmental Studies, Ethnic Studies, History (US)

Audience: Researchers, Students, General Public

Details: Free

User Info: Expect: Login, Send: Lib; Expect: vDIAL Prompt, Send: Library

`telnet://lib.uwsp.edu`

University of Wisconsin Superior Library

University of Wisconsin Superior Library

The library's holdings are large and wide-ranging and contain significant collections in many fields.

Keywords: Educational Policy, Government (US)

Audience: Researchers, Students, General Public

Details: Free

User Info: Expect: Login, Send: Lib; Expect: vDIAL Prompt, Send: Library

`telnet://sail.uwsuper.edu`

University Planning

SCUP BITNET NEWS

Designed to promote the mission of the society and support its activities. Society for College and University Planning (SCUP) Bitnet News provides frequent and timely exchange of information among members as well as nonmembers interested in higher-education planning through the use of bitnet.

Keywords: University Planning

Sponsor: Society for College and University Planning

Audience: Planners

Profile: Contents of the newsletter are selected on the basis of interest and value to the membership. Particular attention is given to information that advances the state-of-the-art in planning; improves the understanding and application of the tools, techniques, processes and strategies of planning; advances the professional development of the membership; and widens the base of support for planning in higher education.

Contact: Joanne E. MacRae USERTD8Q@UMICHUM.bitnet

Details: Free

Send an electronic mail note to the editor (Joanne Cate: budlao@uccvma) or the associate editor (Betsey Creekmore: pa94858@utkvm1)

`mailto:Joanne Cate: budlao@uccvma.bitnet`

A B C D E F G H I J K L M N O P Q R S T **U** V W X Y Z

A
B
C
D
E
F
G
H
I
J
K
L
M
N
O
P
Q
R
S
T
U
V
W
X
Y
Z

SCUPMA-L: Society of College and University Planners, Mid-Atlantic Region

This newsletter contains short news pieces and announcements about events of interest to the membership.

Keywords: University Planning

Audience: University Planners

Contact: Debbie Furlong
OPIR1@AUVM.bitnet

Details: Free

`mailto:opir1@auvm.bitnet`

UNIX (Operating System)

comp.unix.aix

A Usenet newsgroup providing information and discussion about IBM's version of UNIX.

Keywords: Computer Systems, Internet, UNIX

Audience: Computer Users, UNIX Users, IBM Users

User Info: To subscribe to this Usenet newsgroup, you need access to a newsreader.

`news:comp.unix.aix`

comp.unix.questions

A Usenet newsgroup providing discussion and questions for those learning UNIX.

Keywords: Computers, UNIX

Audience: Computer Users, UNIX Users

User Info: To subscribe to this Usenet newsgroup, you need access to a newsreader.

`news:comp.unix.questions`

comp.unix.wizards

A Usenet newsgroup providing discussion and questions for true UNIX wizards.

Keywords: UNIX

Audience: Computer Users, Unix Users

User Info: To subscribe to this Usenet newsgroup, you need access to a newsreader.

`news:comp.unix.wizards`

DECnews-UNIX

DECnews for UNIX is published by Digital Equipment Corporation every three weeks and contains product and service information of interest to the Digital UNIX community.

Keywords: DEC, UNIX

Audience: UNIX Users

Contact: Russ Jones
decnews-unix-request@pa.dec.com

User Info: To subscribe to the list, send an e-mail message requesting a subscription to the URL address below.

To send a message to the entire list, address it to: decnews-unix-request@pa.dec.com

To subscribe, send e-mail to decnews-unix@pa.dec.com with a subject line of Subject: subscribe abstract. Please include your name and telephone number in the body of the subscription request.

`mailto:decnews-unix-request@pa.dec.com`

Dual-Personalities

Discussion, maintenance/survival tips, and commercial offerings for the System/83 UNIX box made by the now-defunct DUAL Systems Corp. of Berkeley, as well as similar machines using the IEEE-696 bus (such as the CompuPro 8/16E with Root/Unisoft UNIX).

Keywords: UNIX

Audience: UNIX Users

Contact: dual-personalities-request@darwin.uucp

Details: Free

User Info: To subscribe to the list, send an e-mail message requesting a subscription to the URL address below.

To send a message to the entire list, address it to: dual-personalities-request@darwin.uucp

`mailto:dual-personalities-request@darwin.uucp`

info-UNIX

Info-UNIX is intended for Question/Answer discussion, where "novice" systems administrators can pose questions.

Keywords: UNIX (Operating System), Systems Administration

Audience: UNIX Systems Administrators

Contact: Mike Muuss
mike@brl.mil

User Info: To subscribe to the list, send an e-mail message requesting a subscription to the URL address below.

`mailto:info-UNIX@brl.mil`

Metacard-list

Discussion of the MetaCard product from MetaCard Corp. MetaCard is an application-development system similar to Apple's HyperCard product; it runs on a variety of popular platforms in a UNIX/X11/Motif environment.

Keywords: MetaCard, Computing, UNIX

Audience: MetaCard Users, Computer Users

Contact: metacard-list-owner@grot.starconn.com

Details: Free

User Info: To subscribe to the list, send an e-mail message requesting a subscription to the URL address below.

`mailto:metacard-list@grot.starconn.com`

ORA-NEWS

Announcements from O'Reilly & Associates, publishers of books about the Internet, UNIX, and other open systems. Other products and services include The Global Network Navigator (an interactive online magazine) and Internet in a Box. It's gatewayed to the biz.oreilly.announce Usenet newsgroup.

Keywords: Internet, UNIX, Usenet

Audience: Internet Surfers, Usenet Users, UNIX Users

Contact: listown@online.ora.com

Details: Free, Moderated

User Info: To subscribe to the list, send an e-mail message requesting a subscription to the URL address below.

To send a message to the entire list, address it to: ora-news@online.ora.com

`mailto:listproc@online.ora.com`

Pubnet

A mailing list for the discussion of administration and use of public-access computer systems, primarily UNIX systems. The list also answers questions about setting up or running a public-access system

Keywords: Computer Systems, UNIX

Audience: Computer System Designers, UNIX Users

Contact: Chip Rosenthal
pubnet-request@chinacat.unicom.com

Details: Free

User Info: To subscribe to the list, send an e-mail message requesting a subscription to the URL address below. To send a message to the entire list, address it to: pubnet@chinacat.unicom.com

`mailto:pubnet-request@chinacat.unicom.com`

Std-UNIX

Discussion of UNIX standards, particularly the IEEE P1003 Portable Operating System Environment draft standard.

Keywords: UNIX, Operating Systems

Audience: UNIX Users

Contact: Sean Eric Fagan
sef@uunet.uu.net

Details: Free, Moderated

User Info: To subscribe to the list, send an e-mail message requesting a subscription to the URL address below.

`mailto:sef@uunet.uu.net`

UNIX-wizards

Distribution list for people maintaining UNIX machines.

Keywords: UNIX, Operating Systems

Audience: UNIX System Administrators

Contact: Mike Muuss
mike@brl.mil

Details: Free

User Info: To subscribe to the list, send an e-mail message requesting a subscription to the URL address below.

`mailto:UNIX-wizards-request@brl.mil`

Urban Planning

Virginia Commonwealth University Library

The library's holdings are large and wide-ranging and contain significant collections in many fields.

Keywords: Art, Biology, Humanities, Journalism, Music, Urban Planning

Audience: Researchers, Students, General Public

Details: Free

User Info: Expect: Login; Send: Opub

`telnet://vcuvm1.ucc.vcu.edu`

Urban Studies

alt.folklore.urban

A Usenet newsgroup providing information and discussion about urban legends and urban myths.

Keywords: Urban Studies, Folklore

Audience: Story Tellers, General Public

User Info: To subscribe to this Usenet newsgroup, you need access to a newsreader.

`news:alt.folklore.urban`

University of Wisconsin at Milwaukee Library

The library's holdings are large and wide-ranging and contain significant collections in many fields.

Keywords: Art, Architecture, Business, Cartography, Geography, Geology, Urban Studies, Literature (English), Literature (American)

Audience: Researchers, Students, General Public

Details: Free

User Info: Expect: Login, Send: Lib; Expect: vDIAL prompt, Send: Library

`telnet://uwmcat.lib.uwm.edu`

US

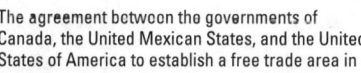

North American Free Trade Agreement (NAFTA)

The agreement between the governments of Canada, the United Mexican States, and the United States of America to establish a free trade area in North America.

Keywords: Trade, Government (US), Mexico, Canada, Free Trade, NAFTA

Audience: Journalists, Politicians, Economists, Students

Details: Free

`gopher://wiretap.spies.com/00/Gov/NAFTA`

U.S. Army Area Handbooks

U.S. Army Area Handbooks

This gopher provides detailed political, cultural, historical, military, and economic information on hot spots in world affairs, everywhere from China to Yugoslavia.

Keywords: Military (US), Politics (International), Government (US Federal)

Sponsor: The Thomas Jefferson Library at the University of Missouri at St. Louis , St. Louis, Missouri, USA

Audience: Journalists, Government Officials, Travelers/Tourists

Profile: The Army Area Handbooks, which provide a comprehensive overview of several important countries including Japan, China, Israel, Egypt, South Korea, and Somalia, are only one of the many government resources available at this site. Other full-text documents include the proposed 1995 federal budget, the CIA world fact book, the NAFTA agreement, health care proposals currently before Congress, and statistics for the U.S. industrial outlook. Also has links to many federal gophers and information systems.

Contact: Joe Rottman
rottman@umslvma.umsl.edu

Details: Free

`gopher://umslvma.umsl.edu/11/library/govdocs`

US Army Corps of Engineers

US Army Corps of Engineers

This site provides information on the organization, programs, news, facilities, and activities of the US Army Corps of Engineers.

Keywords: Military, Engineering

Sponsor: Cold Regions Research and Engineering Laboratory, under

Audience: Military Personnel, Engineers, Researchers

Contact: www@usace.mil

Details: Free

`http://www.usace.mil/usace.html`

US Bureau of the Census Gopher

U.S. Bureau of the Census Gopher

A gopher offering official Census data and services directly from the Census Bureau.

Keywords: Census Data, Demography, Statistics

Sponsor: US Census Bureau

Audience: Journalists, Government Officials, General Public

Profile: A wealth of demographic and economic data from the Census Bureau. Information available includes population estimates, financial data from state and local governments, and assorted statistical briefs. This gopher also has details on the offices, programs, and personnel of the Bureau itself, as well as links to other federal information systems and sources of Census data.

Contact: gatekeeper@census.gov

Details: Free, Images

`gopher://gopher.census.gov`

`http://www.census.gov`

US Civil War Reading List

U.S. Civil War Reading List

A major directory on abolitionism, providing access to a broad range of resources (library catalogs, databases, and servers) via the Internet.

Keywords: History (US), Abolitionism

Audience: General Public, Historians

A
B
C
D
E
F
G
H
I
J
K
L
M
N
O
P
Q
R
S
T
U
V
W
X
Y
Z

A
B
C
D
E
F
G
H
I
J
K
L
M
N
O
P
Q
R
S
T
U
V
W
X
Y
Z

Profile: The Suggested Civil War Reading List contains 61 books, several of them with multiple volumes, as well as an 11-hour documentary film and a CD of Civil War era songs. The material is sorted into general categories: General Histories of the War, Causes of the War and History to 1861, Slavery and Southern Society, Reconstruction, Biographies and Autobiographies, Source Documents and Official Records, Unit Histories and Soldiers' Reminiscences, Fiction, Specific Battles and Campaigns, Strategies and Tactics, The Experience of Soldiers.

Contact: Stephen Schmidt
whale@leland.Stanford.edu

```
http://www.cis.ohio-state.edu/
hypertext/faq/usenet/civil-war-usa/
reading-list/faq.html
```

US Consumer Product Safety Commission (CPSC)

U.S. Consumer Product Safety Commission (CPSC)
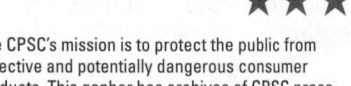 ★★★

The CPSC's mission is to protect the public from defective and potentially dangerous consumer products. This gopher has archives of CPSC press releases and action reports from 1990-1994, as well as a calendar of upcoming events and guidelines for reporting potentially dangerous products to the CPSC.

Keywords: Safety, Consumerism, Federal Law (US)

Sponsor: US Consumer Product Safety Commission

Audience: Consumers, Activists

Contact: pweddle@cpsc.gov

Notes: You can call the CPSC at their toll-free hotline at (800) 638-2772.

```
gopher://cpsc.gov
```

US Department of Education Online Library

US Department of Education Online Library
 ★★★

A resource for information on federal programs, including full-text of the GOALS 2000, Educate America Act, The Prisoners of Time Report, and other documents regarding education legislation, reports, and information.

Keywords: Education, Law (US)

Sponsor: US Department of Education

Audience: Educators, Students, Legislators, Researchers

```
http://www.ed.gov
```
```
gopher://gopher.ed.gov
```
```
ftp://ftp.ed.gov
```

US Department of the Interior

US Department of the Interior
 ★★

This resource contains Internet links to the Bureau of Indian Affairs, Bureau of Land Management, Bureau of Reclamation, National Biological Survey, National Park Service, and the US Fish and Wildlife Service.

Keywords: Government (US), Environmental Policies

Sponsor: US Department of the Interior Survey, Office of Public Affairs

Audience: Biologists, Geologists, Researchers, Environmentalists

```
http://info.er.usgs.gov/doi/doi.html
```

US Federal Government

FedWorld Bulletin Board

A BBS run by the National Technical Information Service, with many databases of government documents, job announcements, and connections to other federal government online services.

Keywords: US Federal Government, Government Documents

Sponsor: US National Technical Information Service

Audience: General Public, Researchers

Profile: This is the place to begin any kind of search for US federal government records and publications. The GateWay option connects you to the Library of Congress, Supreme Court opinions, government job listing, the various Federal Reserve Banks, Congressional Bills and studies, etc.

To establish an account: Expect: login, Send: new

Notes: Mail to sysop once you have an account

```
telnet://fedworld.gov
```

US General Accounting Office Transitional Reports

US General Accounting Office Transitional Reports
 ★★★

A major directory on accounting, providing access to a broad range of related resources (library catalogs, databases, and servers) via the Internet.

Keywords: Government (US), Finance

Audience: Politicians, Government Workers

Profile: Contains full-text documents of the Transitional Reports for the U.S. General Accounting Office. Reports includes Budget Issues, Investment, Government Management Issues, Financial Management Issues, Health Care Reform, National Security Issues, International Trade Issues, etc.

Contact: kh3@cu.nih.gov

```
gopher://thor.ece.uc.edu
```

US Geological Survey Server

US Geological Survey Server
 ★★

This resource containis publications, USGS research programs, technology transfer partnerships, and fact sheets about geology.

Keywords: Biology, Geology, Natural Science

Sponsor: US Geological Survey

Audience: Biologists, Geologists, Researchers, Naturalists

Contact: Systems Operator
webmaster@info.er.usgs.gov

```
http://info.er.usgs.gov
```

US Government

NTIS FedWorld

Keywords: US Government, Federal Databases

Audience: General Public, Researchers, Business Professionals, Politicians

Contact: Bob Bunge
webmaster@fedworld.gov

```
http://www.fedworld.gov
```
```
telnet://fedworld.gov
```
```
ftp://ftp.fedworld.gov
```

US Government Publications

Voice of America and Worldnet
 ★★★

A gopher server for the Voice of America and Worldnet. Includes full-text transcripts of VOA news reports, press releases, and announcements.

Keywords: US Government Publications, News Media, Radio, International Communication

Sponsor: United States Information Agency

Audience: Journalists, Government Officials, General Public

Contact: info@voa.gov, letters-usa@VOA.GOV (for correspondence from inside the U.S.)

`gopher://gopher.voa.gov`

US Government Regulations

TRANS (The Transportation Library)

The Transportation Library contains federal transportation case law, statutes and agency decisions.

Keywords: Transportation Law, US Government Regulations, Aviation, Railroad, Trucking Industry

Audience: Lawyers

Profile: The Transportation library contains federal transportation case law, statutes and agency decisions. The major emphasis of the library is on three modes of transportation (aviation, railroad and trucking) and how those modes are regulated by the federal government. Agency decisions are provided from the Interstate Commerce Commission, Department of Transportation and the National Transportation Safety Board (NTSB).

Contact: New Sales Group at 800-227-4908 or 513-859-5398 inside the US, or 1-513-865-7981 for all inquires outside the US.

User Info: To subscribe, contact Mead directly.

To examine the Lexis user guide, you can access it at the ftp site of the University of Texas at Austin at the URL address: ftp://ftp.cc.utexas.edu

The files are in: /pub/res-services/LEXIS

`telnet://nex.meaddata.com`

US Holocaust Memorial Museum

US Holocaust Memorial Museum

The web site of the newly-opened (April, 1993) US Holocaust Memorial Museum in Washington D.C.

Keywords: Judaism, Jewish Politics, Holocaust, History (Jewish)

Audience: Jews, Holocaust Researchers, Israelis, Students

Profile: This resource contains files on educational programs, general information about the Holocaust Research Institute, a contact list for the Association of Holocaust Organizations, and a searchable archive of related materials.

`http://www.ushmm.org`

US House of Representatives Gopher

US House of Representatives Gopher

The online service of the U.S. House of Representatives.

Keywords: Congress (US), Federal Law (US), Government Records (US)

Sponsor: House Administration Committee Internet Working Group

Audience: Government Officials, Journalists, Educators (K-12), General Public

Profile: Provides access to information on members and committees of the House of Representatives, as well as full-text of bills before the House. Includes education resources on the legislative process, Congressional directories, and House schedules. Also has information for visitors (including area maps), as well as access to other federal information systems.

Contact: House Internet Working Group househlp@hr.house.gov

`gopher://gopher.house.gov`

US Law

LAWREV (Law Review Library)

The Law Review Library contains law reviews, American Bar Association publications, American Institute of Certified Public Accountants periodicals, and other materials. The present focus concentrates on both state and national issues of legal significance.

Keywords: US Law, Analysis, Law Reviews, Journals

Audience: Lawyers

Profile: The Law Review library currently consists of over 70 law reviews, several American Bar Association publicatons and American Institute of Certified Public Accountants periodicals, an Environmental Law Institute publication, ALR and LEd2d articles, two leading legal indices and a number of Warren Gorham & Lamont tax journals. The present focus concentrates on both state and national issues of legal significance.

Contact: New Sales Group at 800-227-4908 or 513-859-5398 inside the US, or 1-513-865-7981 for all inquires outside the US.

User Info: To subscribe, contact Mead directly.

To examine the Lexis user guide, you can access it at the ftp site of the University of Texas at Austin at the URL address: ftp://ftp.cc.utexas.edu

The files are in: /pub/ref-services/LEXIS

`telnet://nex.meaddata.com`

`http://www.meaddata.com`

US National Park Service

Park Rangers

★

This list is primarily for anyone working or interested in working as a ranger (general, interpretive, and so on) for the US National Park Service, but rangers from state and county agencies and from other countries are also welcome. The group discusses numerous topics related to this profession.

Keywords: US National Park Service, Government (US)

Audience: Park Rangers

Contact: Cynthia Dorminey 60157903@wsuvm1.csc.wsu.edu

Details: Free

User Info: To subscribe to the list, send an e-mail message requesting a subscription to the URL address below. To send a message to the entire list, address it to: 60157903@wsuvm1.csc.wsu.edu

`mailto:60157903@wsuvm1.csc.wsu.edu`

US Patents

US Patents

Complete patent information of all claims of U.S. patents issued since 1971.

Keywords: Patents, Intellectual Property, Trademarks

Sponsor: Derwent, Inc.

Audience: Patent Attorneys, Patent Agents, Librarians, Researchers

Profile: Includes complete front page information, plus all claims of US patents issued since 1971. Merged file contains approximately 1.4 million records. Updated weekly.

Contact: paul.albert@neteast.com

User Info: To subscribe contact Orbit-Questel directly.

`telnet://orbit.com`

A B C D E F G H I J K L M N O P Q R S T **U** V W X Y Z

US Patent and Trademark Office Database

U.S. Patent and Trademark Office Database

A database of patents issued in 1994 by the U.S. Patent and Trademark Office, including a searchable index.

Keywords: Patents, Databases, Inventions, Business

Sponsor: New York University School of Business

Audience: Inventors, General Public

Contact: questions@town.hall.org

`gopher://town.hall.org/patent`

US/Mexico Border Discussion List

US/Mexico Border Discussion List

This group provides a forum for the discussion of issues pertaining to the US/Mexico border environment.

Keywords: Mexico, Environment, Latin American Culture

Sponsor: The US Environmental Protection Agency

Audience: Activists, Environmentalists, Urban Planners

Details: Free

User Info: To subscribe to the list, send a message to the URL address below consisting of a single line reading:

SUB us_mexborder YourFirstName YourLastName

To send a message to the entire list, address it to:
us_mexborder@unixmail.rtpnc.epa.gov

`mailto: listserver@unixmail.rtpnc.epa.gov`

USDA Agricultural Extension Service

USDA Agricultural Extension Service

Includes information from the USDA (United States Department of Agriculture) Extension Service, National Agriculture Library, and Americans Communicating Electronically (ACE)

Keywords: Agriculture

Audience: Farmers, Agriculturalists, Educators

Profile: [profile needed]

Details: Free

`gopher://cyfer.esusda.gov`

Usenet

E-mail Usenet

E-mail Usenet allows the user to post to a newsgroup via e-mail.

Keywords: Internet, Services, E-mail, Usenet

Audience: Internet Surfers

Details: Free

`mailto://hierarchy-group-name@cs.utexas.edu`

GIS-L and comp.infosystems.gis FAQ

HTML and ASCII document describing all aspects of GIS on the Internet.

Keywords: GIS, USENET

Audience: GIS Users

Profile: Contains information on data sources, formats, software info and pointers to other Internet GIS info sources.

Contact: Lisa Nyman
lnyman@census.gov

Details: Free
WWW and FTP

Notes: ASCII version also available.

`http://www.cencus.gov/geo/gis/faqindex.html`

`ftp://ftp.cencus.gov/pub/geo/gis-faq.txt`

Neci-announce

This is the announcement forum of New England Community Internet, an organization dedicated to making Usenet and Internet accessible to the public without economic or technical barriers. The group is developing ways to bring IP connectivity at low cost into homes and nonprofit organizations.

Keywords: Internet, Usenet

Audience: Internet Surfers, Usenet Users

Contact: neci-announce-request@pioneer.ci.net

Details: Free

User Info: To subscribe to the list, send an e-mail message requesting a subscription to the URL address below.

`mailto:neci-announce-request@pioneer.ci.net`

Neci-digest

This is the daily discussion forum of New England Community Internet, an organization dedicated to making Usenet and Internet accessible to the public without economic or technical-expertise barriers. The group is developing ways to bring IP connectivity at low cost into homes and nonprofit organizations.

Keywords: Internet, Usenet

Audience: Internet Surfers, Usenet Users

Contact: neci-digest-request@pioneer.ci.net

Details: Free

User Info: To subscribe to the list, send an e-mail message requesting a subscription to the URL address below.

`mailto:neci-digest-request@pioneer.ci.net`

Neci-discuss

This is the general discussion forum of New England Community Internet, an organization dedicated to making Usenet and Internet accessible to the public without economic or technical-expertise barriers. The group is developing ways to bring IP connectivity at low cost into homes and nonprofit organizations.

Keywords: Internet, Usenet

Audience: Internet Surfers, Usenet Users

Contact: neci-discuss-request@pioneer.ci.net

Details: Free

User Info: To subscribe to the list, send an e-mail message requesting a subscription to the URL address below.

Notes: To get a daily digestified version, subscribe to neci-digest. To receive organizational announcements only, subscribe to neci-announce.

`mailto:neci-discuss-request@pioneer.ci.net`

news.announce.newgroups

A Usenet newsgroup providing information and discussion about creating a new newsgroup, changing active newsgroups, and how to access new Usenet groups.

Keywords: Usenet, Internet Resources

Audience: Usenet Users

Details: Free

User Info: To subscribe to this Usenet newsgroup, you need access to a newsreader.

`news:news.announce.newgroups`

news.answers

A Usenet newsgroup providing information and discussion about periodic Usenet articles.

Keywords: Usenet, Internet Resources

Audience: Usenet Users

Details: Free

User Info: To subscribe to this Usenet newsgroup, you need access to a newsreader.

`news:news.answers`

news.groups

A Usenet newsgroup providing information and discussion about lists of existing newsgroups.

Keywords: Usenet, Internet Resources

Audience: Usenet Users

Details: Free

User Info: To subscribe to this Usenet newsgroup, you need access to a newsreader.

`news:news.groups`

news.lists

A Usenet newsgroup providing information and discussion about news-related statistics and lists.

Keywords: Usenet, Internet Resources

Audience: Usenet Users

Details: Free

User Info: To subscribe to this Usenet newsgroup, you need access to a newsreader.

`news:news.lists`

news.newusers.questions

Keywords: Usenet, E-mail, Internet Resources

Audience: Usenet Users, E-mail Users

Details: Free

User Info: To subscribe to this Usenet newsgroup, you need access to a newsreader.

`news:news.newusers.questions`

ORA-NEWS

Announcements from O'Reilly & Associates, publishers of books about the Internet, UNIX and other open systems. Other products and services include The Global Network Navigator (an interactive online magazine) and Internet in a Box. It's gatewayed to the biz.oreilly.announce Usenetnewsgroup.

Keywords: Internet, UNIX, Usenet

Audience: Internet Surfers, Usenet Users, UNIX Users

Contact: listown@online.ora.com

Details: Free, Moderated

User Info: To subscribe to the list, send an e-mail message requesting a subscription to the URL address below. To send a message to the entire list, address it to: ora-news@online.ora.com

`mailto:listproc@online.ora.com`

Usenet Repository

Regular informational postings and FAQs from various newsgroups on the Usenet, grouped into archives by newsgroup.

Keywords: Internet, Networking, Usenet

Audience: Internet Surfers

Details: Free

File is: pub/usenet-by-group

`ftp://pit-manager.mit.edu`

Usenet Sports Groups Archived

An archive for Usenet groups, including many related to sports ranging from football to table tennis.

Keywords: Sports, Skydiving, Volleyball, Football, Scuba, Table Tennis, Usenet

Sponsor: Massachusetts Institute of Technology, Boston, MA

Audience: Sports Enthusiasts

Contact: ftp-bugs@rtfm.mit.edu

Details: Free

`ftp://rtfm.mit.edu/pub/usenet`

Usenet University

An archive of Usenet university groups that are currently active on the Internet.

Keywords: Education, Universities

Audience: University Students, Educators, Researchers

Details: Free

File is: pub/doc/uu/FAQ

`ftp://nic.funet.fi`

Usenet What Is?

An article entitled "What Is Usenet?"

Keywords: Internet Guides, Internet Tools, Usenet

Audience: Internet Surfers

Details: Free

File is: pub/usenet/news.answers/what-is/usenet/part1

`ftp://rtfm.mit.edu`

Usenet World

A special issue of the Amateur Computerist newsletter about Usenet.

Keywords: Internet Guides, Internet Tools, Usenet

Audience: Internet Surfers

Details: Free

File is: doc/misc/acn/acn4-5.txt

`ftp://wuarchive.wustl.edu`

Usenet Newsgroup

Oglasna Deska

Oglasna Deska (Bulletin Board) consists of transcripts taken from SLON, which is a nickname for a Decnet connecting several computers in Slovenia. There is a conference similar to a Usenet newsgroup running under SLON and the articles and replies are occasionally saved and sent to the world. The topics cover a wide area.

Keywords: Slovenia, SLON, Usenet Newsgroup

Audience: Slovenians, Croatians, Serbians

Contact: Dean Mozetic
Oglasna-Deska@krpan.arnes.si

Details: Free

User Info: To subscribe to the list, send an e-mail message requesting a subscription to the URL address below. To send a message to the entire list, address it to: oglasna-deka@krpan.arnes.si

Notes: The topics covered are equivalent to Usenet newsgroups such as politics, automobiles, humor, computer networks, climbing, and miscellaneous investments.

`mailto:Oglasna-Deska@krpan.arnes.si`

USGS

United States Geological Survey Home Page

USGS server dedicated to all aspects of Geography and geographic data.

Keywords: USGS, GIS, Geography

Sponsor: United States Geological Survey

Audience: Geographers, GIS Professionals, Researchers, Students

Profile: Probably the most comprehensive geography/GIS server on the net. Features include a GIS tutorial, descriptions (and examples) of available USGS data products, access to online spatial data and more.

Contact: webmaster@info.er.usgs.gov

Details: Free, Images, Sounds, Multimedia

Notes: The USGS maintains many servers, this page contains links to most of them, such as EROS Data Center, GLIS and others.

`http://info.er.usgs.gov/USGSHome.html`

USGS (United States Geological Survey) Gopher

A gopher site covering issues related to the United State Geological Survey.

Keywords: Cartography, Geology, USGS

A B C D E F G H I J K L M N O P Q R S T U V W X Y Z

Sponsor: United States Geological Survey

Audience: Geologists, Cartologists

Profile: The USGS gopher was established to provide general information about USGS, information about USGS Divisions, publications, data, and briefings, USGS's Network resources, and other data on geology, hydrology, and cartography.

Contact: Gopher Operator
webmaster@info.er.usgs.gov

`gopher://info.er.usgs.gov`

Utah

Utah State Constitution

Lists full text of the Utah State Constitution 1991.

Keywords: Utah, Constitution

Audience: Utah Residents, Historians

`gopher://wiretap.spies.com`

Utah State Constitution

Utah State Constitution

Lists full text of the Utah State Constitution 1991.

Keywords: Utah, Constitution

Audience: Utah Residents, Historians

`gopher://wiretap.spies.com`

Utah Valley Community College Library

Utah Valley Community College Library

The library's holdings are large and wide-ranging and contain significant collections in many fields.

Keywords: Accounting, Automobiles, Cabinetry, Child Care, Drafting, Electronics, Home Building, Refrigeration, Air Conditioning

Audience: General Public, Researchers, Librarians, Document Delivery Professionals

Details: Free

User Info: Expect: Login; Send: Opub

`telnet://uvlib.uvcc.edu`

UTIRC (University of Toronto Instructional and Research Computing

UTIRC (University of Toronto Instructional and Research Computing

This site provides information in the areas of instructional technology and applications, support for multimedia and visualization techniques, and access to and support for high-performance computing.

Keywords: Computing, Computer Programming, Computer-Aided Design

Sponsor: University of Toronto, Division of Computing, Toronto, Canada

Audience: Programmers, Designers

Details: Free

`http://www.utirc.utoronto.ca/
htmldocs/hewhtml/intro.html`

UWP Music Archive (named for the host machine's location: the University of Wisconsin—Parkside)

UWP Music Archive (named for the host machine's location: the University of Wisconsin—Parkside)

An extensive repository of files relating to a diverse array of music genres: rock, folk, classical, and more.

Keywords: Music, Lyrics, Graphics

Sponsor: University of Wisconsin—Parkside

Audience: Musicians, Music Enthusiasts, Musicologists

Profile: This FTP archive contains a music database, artist discographies, essays about music and particular works, hundreds of image files (mostly .GIF and .JPEG format) of musicians—including album covers and posters, a lyrics archive and the ever-popular "Beginner's Introduction to Classical Music."

Contact: Dave Datta
datta@ftp.uwp.edu

User Info: Select "Music Archives" from the gopher top-level menu.

Notes: Also accessible through CMU's "English Server" gopher server. (q.v.)

`gopher://gopher.uwp.edu`

V

Val-L

val-l

Discussion on changes in the Communist countries, ranging from Cuba and Vietnam to the former Soviet Union.

Keywords: Communism, Soviet Union, Political Science

Audience: Political Scientists

Contact: cdell@umkcax1 or cdell@umkcvax1.bitnet

Details: Free

User Info: To subscribe to the list, send an e-mail message to the URL address below consisting of a single line reading:

SUB val-l YourFirstName YourLastName

To send a message to the entire list, address it to: val-l@ucflvm.cc.ucf.edu

`mailto:listserv@ucflvm.cc.ucf.edu`

VapourWare

VapourWare

A column of speculation about new computers and computer-related products that are not yet available for sale (and may never be).

Keywords: Computers

Audience: Computer Users

Contact: Murphy Sewall sewall@uconnvm.uconn.edu

Details: Free

`mailto:sewall@uconnvm.uconn.edu`

Various Treaties

Various Treaties

Provides access to a range of treaties in full-text format.

Keywords: Treaties, Politics (International)

Audience: Governments, Researchers, Lawyers

Details: Free

`gopher://wiretap.spies.com`

Vegetarianism

GRANOLA (Vegetarian Discussion List)

A ListServ for discussion of vegetarian issues, including everything from recipes to animal rights.

Keywords: Health, Nutrition, Vegetarian, Recipes

Audience: Vegetarians, Nutritionists, Health Professionals

Details: Free

User Info: To subscribe to the list, send an e-mail message to the URL address shown below consisting of a single line reading:

SUB granola YourFirstName YourLastName

`mailto:listserv@gitvm1.bitnet`

rec.food.veg

A Usenet newsgroup providing information and discussion about vegetarian cooking.

Keywords: Vegetarianism, Food, Cooking

Audience: Vegetarians, Cooks, Chefs

User Info: To subscribe to this Usenet newsgroup, you need access to a newsreader.

`news:rec.food.veg`

VEGCNY-L (Vegetarians in Central New York area)

VegCNY-L is an open discussion list intended to serve those people living in the Central New York area who are vegetarians, as well as those who are interested in vegetarianism.

Keywords: Vegetarianism, New York, Food

Audience: Vegetarians

Contact: Chuck Goelzer Lyons cgl1@cornell.edu

Details: Free

User Info: To subscribe to the list, send an e-mail message to the URL address below consisting of a single line reading:

SUB VEGCNY-L YourFirstName YourLastName

To send a message to the entire list, address it to: VEGCNY-L@cornell.edu

`mailto:listserv@cornell.edu`

A
B
C
D
E
F
G
H
I
J
K
L
M
N
O
P
Q
R
S
T
U
V
W
X
Y
Z

veggie (Vegetarian Issues Discussion List)

Veggie is an open list for the discussion of vegetarianism.

Keywords: Vegetarianism, Food

Audience: Vegetarians

Details: Free

User Info: To subscribe to the list, send an e-mail message to the URL address below consisting of a single line reading:

SUB veggie YourFirstName YourLastName

To send a message to the entire list address it to: veggie@gibbs.oit.unc.edu

`mailto:listserv@gibbs.oit.unc.edu`

veggies

A list for the discussion of vegetarian matters in Britain.

Keywords: Vegetarianism, Britain, Food

Audience: Vegetarians

Details: Free

User Info: To subscribe to the list, send an e-mail message requesting a subscription to the URL address below.

To send a message to the entire list, address it to: veggies@ncl.ak.uk

`mailto:veggies-request@ncl.ac.uk`

veglife (Vegetarian Life List)

Veglife (formerly Granola) provides a supportive atmosphere for the discussion of issues related to the vegetarian lifestyle.

Keywords: Vegetarianism, Food

Audience: Vegetarians

Contact: Darrell A. Early, Charles Goelzer Lyons

Details: Free

User Info: To subscribe to the list, send an e-mail message to the URL address below consisting of a single line reading:

SUB veglife YourFirstName YourLastName

To send a message to the entire list, address it to: veglife@vtvml.cc.vt.edu

`mailto:listserv@vtvm1.cc.vt.edu`

Velo News Experimental Tour de France Web Page

Velo News Experimental Tour de France Web Page

This web site provides background information on the Tour de France, including press coverage from this year's race.

Keywords: Bicycles, Sports

Sponsor: Velo News

Audience: Bicyclists, Sports Fans

Contact: VeloNews@aol.com

`http://cob.fsu.edu/velonews`

Verdicts

VRDCT (Jury Verdicts Library)

The Verdicts Library aids litigation preparation by providing quick and convenient access to selected online verdict and settlement information for civil cases nationwide. Case information covered includes verdict and settlement amounts, expert witnesses, case summaries, and counsel data.

Keywords: Jury, Verdicts, Judgments, Settlements

Audience: Lawyers

Contact: New Sales Group at 800-227-4908 or 513-859-5398 inside the US, or 1-513-865-7981 for all inquires outside the US.

User Info: To subscribe, contact Mead directly.

To examine the Lexis user guide, you can access it at the ftp site of the University of Texas at Austin at the URL address: ftp://ftp.cc.utexas.edu

The files are in: /pub/ref-services/LEXIS

`telnet://nex.meaddata.com`

`http://www.meaddata.com`

Veronica

Gopher/Veronica-How To

A special issue of the University of Illinois publication describing gopher and Veronica.

Keywords: Internet Tools, Gopher, Veronica

Sponsor: University of Illinois, Urbana, IL

Audience: Internet Surfers

Details: Free

File is: doc/net/uiucnet/vol6nol.txt

`ftp://ftp.cso.uiuc.edu`

Veronica FAQ

A gopher containing common questions and answers about Veronica, a title search and retrieval system for use with the Internet gopher.

Keywords: Internet Reference, Information Retrieval, Veronica

Audience: Students, Computer Scientists, Researchers

`gopher://pogonip.scs.unr.edu/00/veronica/veronica-faq`

Veronica Introduction

Veronica (Very Easy Rodent-Oriented Net-wide Index to Computerized Archives) is an Internet access tool that locates titles of gopher items by keyword search.

Keywords: Internet Tools, Veronica

Audience: Internet Surfers

Details: Free

File is: pub/comp.archives/bionet.software/veronica

`ftp://cs.dal.ca`

Vertebrates

National Science Foundation Center for Biological Timing Vertebrate Museum and Virus Gopher Server

This gopher accesses investigative research pertaining to various aspects of biological timing. The goal of this gopher is to make the Museum's collection information available over the Internet. This server contains names of virus families/groups and members now available online from the Australian National University's bio-informatics facility.

Keywords: Biology, Vertebrates

Sponsor: Reasearch School of Biological Research, Australian National University, Canberra, Australia

Audience: Biologists, Educators, Researchers

Profile: The center combines the efforts of several universities pertaining to research in biological timing. This includes Vistudies, the internal timing mechanisms that control cycles of sleep and waking, hormone pulsatility, neural excitability, and reproductive rhythmicity. Investigators are involved with research from behavior testing to molecular genetics.

The center also supports educational and outreach programs to industry, universities and high schools. The center also hosts an annual scientific symposium and a number of mini-symposia.

Details: Free

`gopher://gopher.virginia.edu/11/pubs/biotimin`

Vertebrate Museum

The goal of this gopher is to make museum collection information about vertebrates available over the Internet.

Keywords: Vertebrates, Biology

Sponsor: The Museum of Vertebrate Zoology, University of California at Berkeley

Audience: Natural Scientists, Biologists, Researchers

Details: Free

`gopher://ucmp1.berkeley.edu`

Veterinary Hospitals

Vetadm-L

A discussion group for those involved in veterinary hospital administration.

Keywords: Veterinary Hospitals

Audience: Veterinarians

Contact: Joel Hammond
joel@tamvet.bitnet

Details: Free

User Info: To subscribe to the list, send and e-mail message to the URL address below consisting of a single line reading:

SUB vetadm-l YourFirstName YourLastName

To send a message to the entire list, address it to: vetadm-l@tamvml.tamu.edu

`mailto:listserv@tamvm1.tamu.edu`

Vethis-L (Veterinary Hospital Information Systems)

Vethis-L provides a forum for the exchange of information on veterinary hospital information systems.

Keywords: Veterinary Hospitals

Audience: Veterinarians

Profile: Because of the interrelationship between veterinary hospitals and diagnostic laboratories, topics of mutual interest can be discussed here. The forum was created in response to initiatives by members of the American Association of Veterinary Medical Colleges (AAVMC) and the American Academy of Veterinary Informatics (AAVI).

Contact: Ron Smith
r-smith19@uiuc.edu

Details: Free

User Info: To subscribe to the list, send an e-mail message to the URL address below consisting of a single line reading:

SUB vethis-l YourFirstName YourLastName

To send a message to the entire list, address it to: vethis-l@vmd.cso.uiuc.edu

`mailto:listserv@vmd.cso.uiuc.edu`

Veterinary Medicine

Iowa State University

The library's holdings contain significant collections in many fields.

Keywords: Agriculture, Veterinary Medicine, Statistics, Labor, Soil Conservation, Film

Audience: General Public, Researchers, Librarians, Document Delivery Professionals

Details: Free

Expect: DIAL, Send: LIB

`telnet://isn.iastate.edu`

NetVet Veterinary Resources

An Internet server for veterinary and animal resources.

Keywords: Veterinary Medicine, Animal Welfare, Animals

Sponsor: Washington University, St. Louis, Division of Comparative Medicine

Audience: Veterinarians, Animal Lovers

Profile: A collection of veterinary and animal-related computer resources that includes archives of animal legislation and regulation, listings for colleges of Veterinary Medicine, conference information, and animal-related databases, including the Electronic Zoo. Also has links to other animal and veterinary-related systems.

Contact: Dr. Ken Boshert
ken@wudcm.wustl.edu

`gopher://netvet.wustl.edu`

`http://netvet.wustl.edu/`

Primate-talk (Primate Discussion List)

Forum for the discussion of primatology and related subjects.

Keywords: Primates, Primatology, Veterinary Medicine

Audience: Primatologists, Veterinarians

Profile: This list is open to any e-mail user with an interest in primatology. Subject matter ranges from, but is not limited to, news items, meeting announcements, research issues, information requests, veterinary/husbandry topics, job notices, animal exchange information, and book reviews.

Contact: Larry Jacobsen
jacobsen@pimate.wisc.edu

Details: Free

User Info: To subscribe to the list, send an e-mail message requesting a subscription to the URL address below.

`mailto:primate-talk-request@primate.wisc.edu`

Svhp-l

A restricted discussion group on veterinary pharmacy issues.

Keywords: Veterinary Pharmacy, Pharmacy, Veterinary Science

Audience: Veterinarians, Veterinary Pharmacists

Contact: Doug Kemp
vetpharm@uga.cc.uga.edu

Details: Free

User Info: To subscribe to the list, send an e-mail message to the URL address shown below consisting of a single line reading:

SUB svhp-l YourFirstName YourLastName

To send a message to the entire list, address it to: svhp-l@uga.cc.uga.edu

`mailto:listserv@uga.cc.uga.edu`

vetcai-l

Discussion of veterinary medicine computer-assisted instruction.

Keywords: Veterinary Medicine, Computer-Aided Instruction

Audience: Veterinarians, Medical Educators

Contact: Pat Oblander
oblandr@ksuvm.ksu.edu

User Info: To subscribe to the list, send an e-mail message to the URL address below consisting of a single line reading:

SUB vetcai-l YourFirstName YourLastName

To send a message to the entire list, address it to: vetcai-l@ksuvm.ksu.edu

`mailto:listserv@ksuvm.ksu.edu`

vetimm-l

Discussion group for veterinary immunology.

Keywords: Veterinary Medicine, Immunology

Audience: Veterinarians

A B C D E F G H I J K L M N O P Q R S T U V W X Y Z

A B C D E F G H I J K L M N O P Q R S T U V W X Y Z

Details: Free

User Info: To subscribe to the list, send an e-mail message to the URL address below consisting of a single line reading:

SUB vetimm-l YourFirstName YourLastName

To send a message to the entire list, address it to: vetimm-l@ucdavis.edu

`mailto:listserv@ucdavis.edu`

vetinfo (Discussion of Veterinary Informatics)

 ★★★

This list has been created to stimulate discussion in the area of informatics, with special reference to the field of veterinary medicine.

Keywords: Veterinary Medicine, Informatics

Audience: Veterinarians

Profile: Related topics include clinical decision support systems, laboratory information management, imaging, disease nomenclature and coding systems, expert systems, and knowledge bases. Discussions related to specific hardware and software implementations are welcome, as are approaches to specific challenges in veterinary informatics.

Contact: James T. Case, Bill Cohen jcase@ucdcvdls.bitnet

Details: Free

User Info: To subscribe to the list, send an e-mail message to the URL address below consisting of a single line reading:

SUB vetinfo YourFirstName YourLastName

To send a message to the entire list, address it to: vetinfo@ucdavis.edu

`mailto:listserv@ucdavis.edu`

Vetlib-L (Veterinary Medicine Librarians List)

★

Vetlib-L is an E-mail discussion group for librarians in schools and colleges of veterinary medicine worldwide.

Keywords: Veterinary Medicine, Libraries

Sponsor: Virginia Polytechnic Institute and State University

Audience: Veterinarians, Librarians

Contact: Victoria T. Kok, James Powell kok@vtvm1.cc.vt.edu or jpowell@vtvm1.cc.vt.edu

Details: Free

User Info: To subscribe to the list, send an e-mail message to the URL address below consisting of a single line reading:

SUB vetlib-l YourFirstName YourLastName

To send a message to the entire list, address it to: vetlib-l@vtvm1.cc.vt.edu

`mailto:listserv@vtvm1.cc.vt.edu`

Vetmed-L (Veterinary Medicine Discussion List)

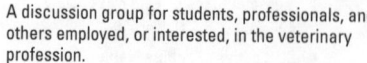 ★

A discussion group for students, professionals, and others employed, or interested, in the veterinary profession.

Keywords: Veterinary Medicine

Audience: Veterinarians, Students (college, graduate), Animal Lovers

Contact: Harold Pritchett, Doug Kemp, Jean Snow harold@uga.cc.uga.edu or vetpharm@uga.cc.uga.edu or jean@uga.cc.uga.edu

Details: Free

User Info: To subscribe to the list, send an e-mail message to the URL address below consisting of a single line reading:

SUB vetmed-l YourFirstName YourLastName

To send a message to the entire list, address it to: vetmed-l@uga.cc.uga.edu

`mailto:listserv@uga.cc.uga.edu`

vetmicro

★

A discussion group about veterinary microbiology.

Keywords: Veterinary Medicine, Microbiology

Audience: Veterinarians

Contact: James T. Case, Bill Cohen jcase@ucdcvdls.bitnet or bcohen@ucdcvdls.bitnet

Details: Free

User Info: To subscribe to the list, send an e-mail message to the URL address below consisting of a single line reading:

SUB vetmicro YourFirstName YourLastName

To send a message to the entire list, address it to: vetmicro@ucdavis.edu

`mailto:listserv@ucdavis.edu`

vetmycop

★

A veterinary mycoplasma discussion group.

Keywords: Veterinary Medicine, Mycoplasma

Audience: Veterinarians

Contact: James T. Case, Bill Cohen jcase@ucdcvdls.bitnet or bcohen@ucdcvdls.bitnet

Details: Free

User Info: To subscribe to the list, send an e-mail message to the URL address below consisting of a single line reading:

SUB vetmycop YourFirstName YourLastName

To send a message to the entire list, address it to: vetmycop@ucdavis.edu

`mailto:listserv@ucdavis.edu`

Vettox-L (Veterinary Toxicology Discussion List)

 ★★★

A list dedicated to diagnostic toxicology, established at the University of California.

Keywords: Veterinary Medicine, Toxicology

Audience: Veterinarians, Toxicologists

Profile: This list is restricted to those in the practice of diagnostic toxicology, although it will not be an edited list. The goals are to provide an atmosphere of cooperation among those in the field of diagnostic toxicology and to seek solutions to the many challenges that arise during a disease investigation.

Contact: James T. Case, Bill Cohen jcase@ucdcvdls.bitnet or bcohen@ucdcvdls.bitnet

Details: Free

User Info: To subscribe to the list, send an e-mail message to the URL address below consisting of a single line reading:

SUB vettox-l YourFirstName YourLastName

To send a message to the entire list, address it to: vettox-l@ucdavis.edu

`mailto:listserv@ucdavis.edu`

Veterinary Science

Agriculture, Veterinary Science & Zoology

This directory is a compilation of information resources focused on agriculture, veterinary science, and zoology.

Keywords: Agriculture, Veterinary Science, Zoology

Audience: Farmers, Agronomists, Veterinarians, Zoologists

Details: Free

`ftp://una.hh.lib.umich.edu/70/inetdirsstacks/agvetzoo:haas`

Purdue University Library

 ★★

The library's holdings are large and wide-ranging. They contain significant collections in many fields.

Keywords: Economics (History of), Literature (English), Literature (American), Indiana, Rogers (Bruce), Engineering (History of), Aviation, Earth Science, Atmospheric Science, Consumer Science, Family Science, Chemistry (History of), Physics, Veterinary Science

Audience: General Public, Researchers, Librarians, Document Delivery Professionals

Contact: Dan Ferrer
dan@asterix.lib.purdue.edu

Details: Free

Expect: User ID prompt, Send: GUEST

`telnet://lib.cc.purdue.edu`

Svhp-l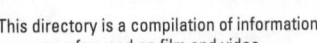

A restricted discussion group on veterinary pharmacy issues.

Keywords: Veterinary Pharmacy, Pharmacy, Veterinary Science

Audience: Veterinarians, Veterinary Pharmacists

Contact: Doug Kemp
vetpharm@uga.cc.uga.edu

Details: Free

User Info: To subscribe to the list, send an e-mail message to the URL address shown below consisting of a single line reading:

SUB svhp-l YourFirstName YourLastName

To send a message to the entire list, address it to: svhp-l@uga.cc.uga.edu

`mailto:listserv@uga.cc.uga.edu`

University of Texas Health Science Center at San Antonio Library

The library's holdings are large and wide-ranging and contain significant collections in many fields.

Keywords: Allied Health, Dentistry, Nursing, Veterinary Science, Ambulatory Care, Obstetrics/Gynecology, Pediatrics

Audience: Researchers, Students, General Public

Details: Free

Expect: Login, Send: LIS

`telnet:// athena.uthscsa.edu`

Victims

Victim Help

A discussion list for the purpose of sharing experiences/research in the broad field of victimization and trauma. Assistance of victims of crime or trauma and those who work with them is a primary focus of this group as is helping them to locate workshops and other resources.

Keywords: Victims, Victimization, Violence

Audience: Victims (of crime trauma), Psychologists, Police, Educators

Contact: Dr. R. Casarez

`rcasarez@mercury.sfsu.edu`

Video

Electronic Cafe

A seminal art and telecommunications group that specializes in video transmission.

Keywords: Art, Video, Telecommunications

Audience: Artists

Profile: This combines performance, communication, and community outreach by making telecommunications equipment available in a cafe-style artists' space.

Contact: Kit Galloway and Sherrie Rabinowitz, 1641 18th St., Santa Monica, CA 90404, USA

`mailto:ecafe@netcom.com`

Film and Video

This directory is a compilation of information resources focused on film and video.

Keywords: Film, Video, Entertainment

Audience: Students, Producers, Artists

Details: Free

`ftp://una.hh.lib.umich.edu/70/`
`inetdirsstacks/filmvideo:woodgarlock`

Filmmaking Conference

A conference on the WELL about the technical, theoretical, and aestheic issues of filmmaking; includes listings of film and video festivals.

Keywords: Film, Filmmaking, Video

Audience: Filmmakers, Film/Video Enthusiasts

Contact: Sandy Santra
trevor@well.sf.ca.us

Details: Costs

To participate in a conference on the WELL, you must first establish an account on the WELL. To do so, start by typing: telnet well.sf.ca.us

`telnet://well.sf.ca.us`

rec.video

A Usenet newsgroup providing information and discussion about video.

Keywords: Video, Art, Film, Computer Art

Audience: Cinematographers, Video Artists

User Info: To subscribe to this Usenet newsgroup, you need access to a newsreader.

`news:rec.video`

Video Games

Digital Games Review

Reviews of video and computer entertainment titles for the entire industry.

Keywords: Computer Games, Games, Video Games

Audience: Computer Game Players, Computer Game Developers

Profile: Reviews are written by computer game enthusiasts, with an eye to accessibility, enjoyment, and fun, as well as to graphics, technical sophistication, and complexity.

Contact: Dave Taylor
taylor@intuitive.com

Details: Free

`mailto:digital-games-`
`request@intuitive.com`

rec.games.programmer

A Usenet newsgroup providing information and discussion about adventure game programming.

Keywords: Games, Programming, Video Games

Audience: Programmers

User Info: To subscribe to this Usenet newsgroup, you need access to a newsreader.

`news:rec.games.programmer`

rec.games.video.arcade

A Usenet newsgroup providing information and discussion about video games.

Keywords: Games, Video Games

Audience: Game Players

User Info: To subscribe to this Usenet newsgroup, you need access to a newsreader.

`news:rec.games.video.arcade`

Vietnam

ANU (Australian National University) Vietnam-SciTech-L Database

A WAIS database of information on the development of science and technology in Vietnam

Keywords: Vietnam, Science, Technology

Sponsor: Australia Vietnam Science-Technology Link

A
B
C
D
E
F
G
H
I
J
K
L
M
N
O
P
Q
R
S
T
U
V
W
X
Y
Z

Audience: Vietnamese, Scientists, Technology Professionals

Contact: Vern Weitzel
vern@coombs.anu.edu.au

`waissrc:/Coombs-db/ANU-Vietnam-SciTech-L.src`

`gopher://cheops.anu.edu.au/7waissrc/Coombs-db/ANU-Vietnam-SciTech-L.src`

soc.culture.vietnamese

A Usenet newsgroup providing information and discussion about the people and culture of Vietnam.

Keywords: Vietnam, Sociology

Audience: Sociologists, Vietnamese

Details: Free

User Info: To subscribe to this Usenet newsgroup, you need access to a newsreader.

`news:soc.culture.vietnamese`

Vietnam

This file (in the CIA World Factbook) provides geographical, political, and cultural information about Vietnam.

Keywords: Vietnam, Geography

Sponsor: Central Intelligence Agency

Audience: Educators, Students,Travellers, Vietnamese Americans

Contact: Ephraim Vishniac
ephraim@think.com

Details: Free

`gopher://info.und.edu`

Vwar-I

An electronic conference on issues relating to the Vietnam War.

Keywords: History (20th Century), History (US), Vietnam

Audience: Historians

Contact: Lydia Fish
fishlm@snybufva.cs.snybuf.edu

User Info: To subscribe to the list, send an e-mail message to the URL address below consisting of a single line reading:

SUB vwar-I YourFirstName YourLastName

To send a message to the entire list, address it to: vwar-l@ubvm.cc.buffalo.edu

`mailto:listserv@ubvm.cc.buffalo.edu`

ViewPoints

ViewPoints

Newsletter of the Visual Communication Division of the Association of Educators in Journalism and Mass Communication.

Keywords: Journalism, Mass Communication, Visual Communication

Audience: Educators, Photographers, Desktop Publishers

Contact: Paul Lester
lester@fullerton.edu

Details: Free

`mailto:lester@fullerton.edu`

vigis-I

Vigis-L

A mailing list for the discussion of Virtual Reality and GIS (Geographic Information Systems).

Keywords: Virtual Reality, Geography, GIS (Geographic Information Systems), Cyberspace

Audience: Geographers, Cartographers, Cybernauts

Contact: Tom Edwards
navanax.u.washington.edu

User Info: To subscribe to the list, send an e-mail message to the URL address below consisting of a single line reading:

SUB vigis-I YourFirstName YourLastName.

To send a message to the entire list, address it to: vigis@uwavm.u.washington.edu

`mailto:listserv@uwavm.u.washington.edu`

Virginia Commonwealth University Library

Virginia Commonwealth University Library

The library's holdings are large and wide-ranging and contain significant collections in many fields.

Keywords: Art, Biology, Humanities, Journalism, Music, Urban Planning

Audience: Researchers, Students, General Public

Details: Free

Expect: Login; Send: Opub

`telnet://vcuvm1.ucc.vcu.edu`

Virginia

The Old Dominion University Library

The library's holdings are large and wide-ranging and contain significant collections in many fields.

Keywords: Virginia, Federal Documents (US)

Audience: General Public, Researchers, Librarians, Document Delivery Professionals

Details: Free

`telnet://geac.lib.odu.edu`

Virginia's PEN (Public Education Network)

This is a statewide educational network.

Keywords: Education, Community Networking, Virginia

Sponsor: Virginia Department of Education

Audience: Educators

Profile: Educators throughout Virginia can access PEN via a local telephone call or through a toll-free line. The network includes discussion groups, news reports, study guides, and curriculum resources. In one of the features, History OnLine, students and teachers query historical figures such as Thomas Jefferson, and historians will answer in character.

Contact: Harold Cathern
hcathern@vdoe386.vak12.edu

Details: Free

Password: Guest

`telnet://guest@vdoe386.vak12ed.edu`

Virtual Community

(The) WELL (Whole Earth 'Lectronic Link)

The WELL is a computer conferencing system, a virtual community, and an electronic coffee shop.

Keywords: Community, Networking, Computer Conferencing, Virtual Community

Sponsor: Whole Earth 'Lectronic Link

Audience: General Public, Internet Surfers

Profile: The WELL is a classic example of an online community that uses what is called "conferencing" to bring a myriad of people together for intense interactions without them having to be connected at the same time. At the end of 1993, the WELL had about 8,000 users (about 90% from all over the USA and about 10% from other locations) and approximately 200 public discussion areas ('conferences'), and 200 private discussion areas. It is a place rich in diverse 'neighborhoods.'

Contact: The WELL Support Staff
             info@well.sf.ca.us

             Direct dial access through:
             +1 (415) 332-4335

             To participate in a conference on the
             WELL, you must first establish an
             account on the WELL. To do so, start by
             typing: telnet well.sf.ca.us

`telnet://well.sf.ca.us`

Telluride Institute

This is a community organization involved in building
an electronic dimension in rural Colorado. The vision
of Telluride Institute includes linking rural residents
to each other and to outside resources, creating
new opportunities for education, jobs, and arts.

Keywords: Community Networking, Virtual
             Community, Rural Development,
             Colorado

Sponsor: The Telluride Institute, Telluride,
             Colorado

Audience: Activists, Policy Makers, Community
             Leaders, Students, Colorado Residents

Profile: The Telluride Institute is a local
             community-based organization that
             produces arts, environmental, and
             educational events in the Telluride area
             of Colorado. The Institite is committed to
             the creation of what it calls the
             "InfoZone": it wants to use modern
             telecommunications to link together the
             local community and to connect to the
             rest of the world to exchange ideas,
             commerce, arts, and inspiration.

Contact: Richard Lowenberg
             tellinst@csn.org

Details: Free

Notes: Send an e-mail message to the URL
             address below asking for further
             information.

`mailto:tellinst@csn.org`

TWICS

★★★★

This is an English-language computer conferencing
system in Japan.

Keywords: Community Networking, Japan, Virtual
             Community

Sponsor: TWICS Co., Ltd.

Audience: Internationalists, General Public,
             Journalists, Policy Makers

Profile: TWICS is a computer conferencing
             system that has a reputation for being a
             thriving electronic community. The
             system maintains a full Internet
             connection. Unlike a database or a
             gopher server, TWICS allows real-time
             online interaction with actual people.

Contact: Tim Buress
             twics@twics.co.jp

Details: Free

`telnet://tanuki.twics.co.jp`

Virtual Hospital

Virtual Hospital

★★

The Virtual Hospital (VH) is a continuously updated
medical multimedia database accessible 24 hours a
day. The site provides distance learning to practicing
physicians and may be used for Continuing Medical
Education (CME).

Keywords: Medicine, Education (Distance)

Sponsor: The Electronic Differential Multimedia
             Laboratory, Department of Radiology,
             University of Iowa College of Medicine,
             USA

Audience: Biologists, Researchers, Medical
             Professionals, Health Care Professionals

Contact: Librarian
             librarian@vh.radiology.uiowa.edu

`http://indy.radiology.uiowa.edu/`
`VirtualHospital.html`

Virtual Reality

Artificial Intelligence, Expert Sys., Virtual Reality

This directory is a compilation of information
resources focused on computer science research,
artificial intelligence, expert systems, and virtual
reality.

Keywords: Computer Science, Artificial Intelligence,
             Expert Systems, Virtual Reality

Audience: Computer Scientists, Engineers

Contact: M. Kovacs

Details: Free

`ftp://una.hh.lib.umich.edu/70/`
`inetdirsstacks/csaiesvr:kovacsm`

Conference about Virtual Reality (The)

A conference on the WELL about cyberspace and
virtual reality.

Keywords: Virtual Reality, Art, Cyberspace

Audience: Artists, Computer Programmers,
             Cyberpunks

Contact: Peter Rothman
             avatarp@well.sf.ca.us

             To participate in a conference on the
             WELL, you must first establish an
             account on the WELL. To do so, start by
             typing: telnet well.sf.ca.us

`telnet://well.sf.ca.us`

Vigis-L

★★

A mailing list for the discussion of Virtual Reality and
GIS (Geographic Information Systems).

Keywords: Virtual Reality, Geography, GIS
             (Geographic Information Systems),
             Cyberspace

Audience: Geographers, Cartographers,
             Cybernauts

Contact: Tom Edwards
             navanax.u.washington.edu

User Info: To subscribe to the list, send an e-mail
             message to the URL address below
             consisting of a single line reading:

             SUB vigis-l YourFirstName
             YourLastName.

             To send a message to the entire list,
             address it to: vigis@uwavm.u.washin
             gton.edu

`mailto:listserv@uwavm.u.washington.edu`

Virtual Reality Space

★★★

A collection of virtual reality information, including
downloadable software tools from Silicon Graphics.

Keywords: Virtual Reality, Cyberspace, Software,
             Silicon Graphics

Sponsor: The University of Texas, Austin, Texas,
             USA

Audience: Virtual Reality Enthusiasts, Programmers

Contact: Jay Ashcraft
             ashcraft@ccwf.cc.utexas.edu

`gopher://ftp.cc.utexas.edu`

`ftp://cc.utexas.edu`

Virus-L

Virus-L

★

Virus-L is a forum for the discussion of computer
virus experiences, protection software, and other
virus-related topics. It includes archives and files
that list a number of viruses, trojan horses, and
pirated programs for the IBM PC.

Keywords: Computer Viruses, Security

Audience: Computer Users

Contact: Kenneth R. van Wyk
             luken@vax1.cc.lehigh.edu

Details: Free

User Info: To subscribe to the list, send an e-mail
             message to the URL address below
             consisting of a single line reading:

             SUB virus-l YourFirstName
             YourLastName

             To send a message to the entire list,
             address it to: virus-l@ibml.cc.lehigh.edu

`mailto:listserv@ibm1.cc.lehigh.edu`

A B C D E F G H I J K L M N O P Q R S T U V W X Y Z

Viruses

Institute for Molecular Virology

A unique virology resource for students, scientists, computer visualization experts, and the general public.

Keywords: Disease, Viruses, Biology

Sponsor: University of Wisconsin-Madison, Madison, Wisconsin, USA

Audience: Virologists, Biologists, Researchers

Contact: Stephen Spencer
sspencer@rhino.bocklabs.wisc.edu

`http://www.bocklabs.wisc.edu/`
`Welcome.html`

Virus Gopher Server

This server contains names of virus families/groups and members now available online from the Australian National University's bioinformatics facility.

Keywords: Viruses, Bioinformation, Biology

Sponsor: Research School of Biological Research, Australian National University, Canberra, Australia

Audience: Researchers, Biologists, Health Professionals

Details: Free

`gopher://life.anu.edu.au`

Visual Communication

ViewPoints

Newsletter of the Visual Communication Division of the Association of Educators in Journalism and Mass Communication.

Keywords: Journalism, Mass Communication, Visual Communication

Audience: Educators, Photographers, Desktop Publishers

Contact: Paul Lester
lester@fullerton.edu

Details: Free

`mailto:lester@fullerton.edu`

Visual Impairment

Blind News Digest

This is a moderated mailing list in digest format that deals with all aspects of visual impairment and blindness.

Keywords: Blindness, Disabilities

Audience: Blind People, Health Care Providers, Therapists

Contact: wtm@bunker.afd.olivetti.com

Details: Free, Moderated

User Info: To subscribe to the list, send the message SUB BlindNws YourFirstName YourLastName to listserv@vm1.nodak.edu or send e-mail requesting a subscription to wtm@bunker.afd.olivetti.com

`mailto:wtm@bunker.afd.olivetti.com`

Visualization Data Explorer Package

data-exp

The mail list server provides an open forum for users to discuss the Visualization Data Explorer Package. It contains three files: a. FAQ, b. summary, and c. forum.

Keywords: Computing, Software, Hardware, Visualization Data Explorer Package

Audience: Computer Users

User Info: To subscribe to the list, send an e-mail message requesting a subscription to the URL address below.

To send a message to the entire list, address it to: stein@watson.ibm.com

`mailto:stein@watson.ibm.com`

Visualization

ApE-info

A mailing list for the discussion of the scientific visualization software package ApE, its usage, development, and implementation.

Keywords: Computers, Visualization, Science

Audience: ApE Software Users, Computer Programmers

Contact: Jim Lick
ape-info-request@ferkel.ucsb.edu

User Info: To subscribe to the list, send an e-mail message to the URL address below. To send a message to the entire list, address it to: ape-info@ferkel.ucsb.edu

`mailto:ape-info-`
`request@ferkel.ucsb.edu`

Voice of America and Worldnet

Voice of America and Worldnet

A gopher server for the Voice of America and Worldnet. It includes full-text transcripts of VOA news reports, press releases, and announcements.

Keywords: US Government Publications, News Media, Radio, International Communication

Sponsor: United States Information Agency

Audience: Journalists, Government Officials, General Public

Contact: info@voa.gov, letters-usa@voa.gov (for correspondence from inside the U.S.)

`gopher://gopher.voa.gov`

Volleyball

ba-Volleyball

This list is used for announcements about San Francisco Bay Area volleyball events, clinics, tournaments, and so on.

Keywords: Volleyball, San Francisco Bay Area, Sports

Audience: Volleyball Enthusiasts

Contact: ba-volleyball-request@klerk.cup.hp.com

User Info: To subscribe to the list, send an e-mail message requesting a subscription to the URL address below.

To send a message to the entire list, address it to: ba-volleyball@klerk.cup.hp.com

`mailto:ba-volleyball-`
`request@klerk.cup.hp.com`

Usenet Sports Groups Archived

An archive for Usenet groups, including many related to sports ranging from football to table tennis.

Keywords: Sports, Skydiving, Volleyball, Football, Scuba Diving, Table Tennis

Sponsor: Massachusetts Institute of Technology, Boston, MA

Audience: Sports Enthusiasts

Contact: ftp-bugs@rtfm.mit.edu

Details: Free

`ftp://rtfm.mit.edu/pub/usenet`

Voting

Maryland

System provides access to a wide range of state information, including the policies and activities of members of Maryland's congress and voting district data.

Keywords: Maryland, Law, Voting

Audience: Maryland Residents, Lawyers

Details: Free

           Select from menu as appropriate.

`gopher://info.umd.edu`

VRDCT (Jury Verdicts Library)

VRDCT (Jury Verdicts Library)

The Verdicts Library aids litigation preparation by providing quick and convenient access to selected online verdict and settlement information for civil cases nationwide. Case information covered includes verdict and settlement amounts, expert witnesses, case summaries and counsel data.

Keywords: Judicial Process, Law

Audience: Lawyers

Contact: New Sales Group at 800-227-4908 or 513-859-5398 inside the US, or 1-513-865-7981 for all inquires outside the US.

User Info: To subscribe, contact Mead directly.

           To examine the Lexis user guide, you can access it at the ftp site of the University of Texas at Austin at the URL address: ftp://ftp.cc.utexas.eduThe files are in: /pub/ref-services/LEXIS

`telnet://nex.meaddata.com`

`http://www.meaddata.com`

VTcad-L

VTcad-L

This E-conference is for discussion of CAD by Va Tech users. Discussion includes: CAD applications, CAD hardware, CAD networking.

Keywords: Computer Graphics, Computer Aided Design

Audience: Computer Graphic Designers, Engineers, Architects

Contact: Darrell A. Early bestuur@VTVM1.cc.vt.edu

Details: Free

User Info: To subscribe to the list, send an e-mail message to the URL address below consisting of a single line reading:

           SUB vtcad-l YourFirstName YourLastName

           To send a message to the entire list, address it to: vtcad-l@vtvm1.cc.vt.edu

`mailto:listserv@vtvm1.cc.vt.edu`

A
B
C
D
E
F
G
H
I
J
K
L
M
N
O
P
Q
R
S
T
U
V
W
X
Y
Z

W

WAIS

comp.infosystems.wais

A Usenet newsgroup providing information and discussion about the WAIS full-text search tool.

Keywords: WAIS, Internet Reference, Information Retrieval

Audience: Internet Surfers

To subscribe to this Usenet newsgroup, you need access to a newsreader.

`news:comp.infosystems.wais`

WAIS

WAIS (Wide Area Information Servers) is an Internet access tool that retrieves resources by searching indexes of databases.

Keywords: Internet Tools, WAIS

Audience: Internet Surfers

Details: Free

Read wais/README first.

`http://www.wais.com`

WAIS FAQ

Common questions and answers about WAIS (Wide Area Information Servers), a networked full-text retrieval system.

Keywords: Internet Reference, WAIS

Sponsor: Thinking Machines, Apple Computer, Dow Jones, and KPMG Peat Marwick

Audience: Students, Computer Scientists, Researchers

Contact: Aydin Edguer
edguer.ces.cwru.edu

`ftp://rtfm.mit.edu/pub/usenet-by-group/news.answers/wais-faq/getting-started`

WAIS, Inc.

WAIS, Inc. provides interactive on-line publishing systems and services to organizations that publish information over the Internet. The organization's three main goals are to develop the Internet as a viable means for distributing information electronically; to improve the nature and quality of information available over networks; and to offer better methods to access that information.

Keywords: WWW, Information Retrieval, Publishing, Internet Tools, WAIS

Sponsor: WAIS, Inc.

Audience: Researchers, Students, General Public, Publishers

Contact: Webmaster
webmaster@wais.com

`http://server.wais.com/`

Walpole (Sir Robert)

The University of Kansas Library

The library's holdings are large and wide ranging and contain significant collections in many fields.

Keywords: Botany, Chinese Studies, Cartography (History of), Kansas, Opera, Ornithology, Joyce (James), Yeats (William Butler), Walpole (Sir Robert)

Audience: General Public, Researchers, Librarians, Document Delivery Professionals

Contact: John S. Miller

Details: Free

Expect: Username, Send: relay <cr>

`telnet://kuhub.cc.ukans.edu`

War

War Powers Resolution of 1973

A joint resolution concerning the war powers of Congress and the President resolved by the Senate and the House of Representatives of the United States of America in Congress.

Keywords: War, Law (International), Government (US)

Audience: Politicians, Students, Lawyers, Historians

Details: Free

`gopher://wiretap.spies.com/00/Gov/warpower.act`

Washington DC

DC-MOTSS

DC-MOTSS is a social mailing list for the gay, lesbian, and bisexual folks who live in the Washington Metropolitan Area—everything within approximately 50 miles of The Mall.

Keywords: Gay, Lesbian, Bisexual, Washington DC

Audience: Gays, Lesbians, Bisexuals, Washington DC Residents

Contact: DC-MOTSS-request@vector.intercon.com

Details: Free

To subscribe to the list, send an e-mail message requesting a subscription to the URL address below.

To send a message to the entire list, address it to DC-MOTSS-request@vector.intercon.com

`mailto:DC-MOTSS-request@vector.intercon.com`

A
B
C
D
E
F
G
H
I
J
K
L
M
N
O
P
Q
R
S
T
U
V
W
X
Y
Z

DCRaves

★

One of several regional rave-related mailing lists, DCRaves covers the Washington, DC area exclusively. Archives are available through the listserv, FTP, or gopher at american.edu.

Keywords: Raves, Washington DC

Audience: Rave Enthusiasts

Details: Free

To subscribe to the list, send an e-mail message to the URL address shown below consisting of a single line reading:

SUB dcraves YourFirstName YourLastName

To send a message to the entire list, address it to dcraves@american.edu

`mailto:listserv@american.edu`

Washington State University at Puyallup Library

Washington State University at Puyallup Library

★★

The library's holdings are large and wide-ranging and contain significant collections in many fields.

Keywords: Agriculture, Scientific Research

Audience: Researchers, Students, General Public

Details: Free

Expect: Login; Send: Lib

`telnet://wsuvm1.cscwsu.edu`

Washington University

IHOUSE-L International Voice Newsletter Prototype List

★

Contains articles of interest to international students and scholars, professors, administrators, and other interested staff and groups (on- and off-campus).

Keywords: International Visitors, Washington University

Sponsor: International Office of Washington University, St. Louis, MO

Audience: International Students

Contact: Doyle Cozadd
C73221DC@WUVMD

Details: Free

`mailto:listserv@wuvmd.wustl.edu`

Washington University Library

★★

The library's holdings are large and wide ranging and contain significant collections in many fields.

Keywords: Technology, Literature (German), Social Science, Behavioral Science, Washington University

Audience: Researchers, Students, General Public

Contact: services@wugate.wustl.edu

Details: Free

Expect: Login; Send: Services

`telnet://wugate.wustl.edu`

Washington University-St. Louis Medical Library & Members Library

★★

The library's holdings are large and wide-ranging and contain significant collections in many fields.

Keywords: Medicine, Science, Technology, Washington University

Audience: Researchers, Students, General Public

Details: Free

Expect: Destination Code Prompt, Send: Catalog

`telnet://mcftcp.wustl.edu`

Water Quality

University of Maryland, College Park

★★

The library's holdings are large and wide ranging and contain significant collections in many fields

Keywords: Agriculture, Coastal Marine Biology, Fisheries, Water Quality, Oceanography

Audience: Researchers, Students, General Public

Contact: Janet McLeod

mcleod@umail.umd.edu

Details: Free

Expect: Login; Send: Atdu

`telnet://info.umd.edu`

Weapons

rec.guns

★

A Usenet newsgroup providing information and discussion about firearms.

Keywords: Firearms, Weapons

Audience: Gun Users

To subscribe to this Usenet newsgroup, you need access to a newsreader.

`news:rec.guns`

Weather

Canadian Geographical WWW Index Travel

This web site provides weekly weather information.

Keywords: Weather, Travel, Canada, Geography

Sponsor: University of Manitoba, Canada

Audience: Travelers, Educators, Students

Contact: www@umanitoba.ca

Details: Free

`http://www.umanitoba.ca`

Current Weather Maps and Movies

This web site is updated hourly, and provides links to downloadable software sites instrumental in accessing interactive weather browsers. International information is available, and visual and infrared maps are supplied from satellites.

Keywords: Weather, Meteorology, Aviation

Sponsor: Michigan State University, Michigan, USA

Audience: General Public, Oceanography, Pilots

Contact: Charles Henrich
henrich@crh.cl.msu.edu

`http://rs560.cl.msu.edu/weather`

News, Weather, and Travel Advisories

A major directory of news, weather, and travel advisories, providing access to a broad range of related resources (library catalogues, databases, and servers) via the Internet.

Keywords: Travel, Weather, Aviation

Sponsor: Kennesaw State College, Georgia, USA

Audience: General Public, Travellers

Profile: This collection includes CNN news sources, the National Weather Service forecast, and the US State Department Travel Advisory, among other sources.

Details: Free

`gopher://kscsuna1.kennesaw.edu`

Weather-users

Weather-users is a mailing list for developers of programs that access the Weather Underground database at the University of Michigan.

Keywords: Weather, Programming, Meteorology

Audience: Programmers

Contact: Scott Hazen Mueller
scott@zorch.sf-bay.org

Details: Free

To subscribe to the list, send an e-mail message.

```
mailto:weather-users-
request@zorch.sf-bay.org
```

Wells (Ida)

University of Chicago Library

The library's holdings are large and wide ranging and contain significant collections in many fields.

Keywords: English Bibles, Lincoln (Abraham), Kentucky & Ohio River Valley (History of), Balzac (Honore de), American Drama, Cromwell (Oliver), Goethe, Judaica, Italy, Chaucer (Geoffrey), Wells (Ida), Douglas (Stephen A.), Italy, Literature (Children's)

Audience: General Public, Researchers, Librarians, Document Delivery Professionals

Details: Free

Expect: ENTER CLASS, Send: LIB48 3; Expect: CONNECTED, Send: RETURN

```
telnet://olorin.uchicago.edu
```

Western America

Indiana University Libraries

The library's holdings are large and wide-ranging and contain significant collections in many fields.

Keywords: Literature (English), Literature (American), 1640-Present, British Plays (19th-C.), Western Americana, Railway History, Aristotle (Texts of), Lafayette (Marquis de), Handel (G.F.), Austrian History, Antiquarian Books, Rare Books, French Opera (19th-C.), Drama (British) ,

Audience: General Public, Researchers, Librarians, Document Delivery Professionals

Details: Free

Expect: User ID prompt, Send: GUEST

```
telnet://iuis.ucs.indiana.edu
```

University of Utah Library

The library's holdings are large and wide-ranging and contain significant collections in many fields.

Keywords: Western America, Middle Eastern Studies, Geology, Mining

Audience: Researchers, Students, General Public

Details: Free

Expect: Command Line, Send: Dial Unis

```
telnet://lib.utah.edu
```

Western Lands

Western Lands

A collection of articles and reports relating to environmental and land use issues in the western United States.

Keywords: Environmentalism, Ecology, Forests, The Western United States

Sponsor: The Institute for Global Communications (IGC)

Audience: Environmentalists, Ecologists, Activists, Foresters, Citizens

Contact: Dan Yurman, IGC User Support
dyurman@igc.apc.com
support@igc.apc.com

Notes: User submissions encouraged.

```
gopher://gopher.igc.apc.org/11/
environment/forests/western.lands
```

What is the Internet?

What is the Internet?

An introductory guide to the Internet.

Keywords: Internet, Internet Guide

Sponsor: University of Illinois and Merit Network, Inc.

Audience: Internet Surfers

Contact: Ed Krol , Ellen Hoffman
e-krol@uiuc.edu or ellen@merit.edu

Details: Free

File is: documents/fyi/fyi_20.txt

```
ftp://nic.merit.edu
```

White House

National Performance Review (NPR)

The Report of the National Performance Review, from the task force led by Vice President Gore, titled "From Red Tape to Results: Creating a Government that Works Better and Costs Less," Sept. 7, 1993.

Keywords: President, Politics, White House

Audience: Political Scientists, General Public

Profile: On March 3, 1993, President Clinton asked Vice President Gore to lead the effort to effect real change in the federal government. Gore's NPR Task Force overview and accompanying reports make specific recommendations for reducing costs and waste, changing the way government operates, and making government more responsive and effective.

Details: Free

```
gopher://cyfer.esusda.gov/11/ace/
policy/npr/nat
```

Presidential Documents

This gopher provides access to the full text of Presidential Proclamations, Executive Orders, Notices, Memoranda, and Determinations dating from December 23, 1992. The documents are listed sequentially by date and number (e.g. Proclamation 6520 of December 23, 1992).

Keywords: Politics, President (US), White House, Documents

Audience: General Public

Details: Free

Select from menu presented (probably you will follow the following path: Internet Services/US Government/ Presidential Documents).

```
gopher://jupiter.cc.gettysborg.edu
```

Technology Initiatives for the Clinton/Gore Administration

This is a 40-page text of the press release from the Clinton administration on technology initiatives, dated February 22, 1993.

Keywords: Politics, President, White House, Technology

Audience: General Public, Journalists

Details: Free

E-mail to the ListServ and include the following in the body of the message: get cni-bigideas.whouse.paper

```
mailto:listserv@cni.org
```

White House Frequently Asked Questions

This document is a good starting point for answering questions such as: How do I send e-mail to President Clinton? How do I get current news updates from the White House? Where can I get White House documents from?

Keywords: Clinton (Bill), Government (US), Politics (US), FAQs, White House

Audience: General Public, Researchers

Details: Free

Expect: login; Send: anonymous; Expect: password; Send: your e-mail address; Expect: directory; Send: /pub/nic; Expect: file; Send: whitehouse FAQ.

```
ftp://ftp.sura.net
```

White House Information Service

An outstanding database of current White House information, from 1992 to the present.

Keywords: White House, Politics, President (US), Database

A B C D E F G H I J K L M N O P Q R S T U V W X Y Z

A B C D E F G H I J K L M N O P Q R S T U V **W** X Y Z

Sponsor: Texas A & M University

Audience: General Public

Profile: Much of the older information on this site was obtained from the clinton@marist.bitnet listserv list or the alt.politics.clinton Usenet newsgroup, both of which receive the information indirectly via the MIT White House information server. Newer and current material is received directly from the MIT distribution list. The menu includes a searchable database and headings such as Domestic Affairs (Health Care, Technology, etc.), Press Briefings and Conferences, the President's Daily Schedule, and many more.

Contact: whadmin@tamu.edu

Details: Free

`gopher://tamuts.tamu.edu/11/.dir/president.dir`

White House Phone Numbers

A list of names, addresses, e-mail addresses, and telephone and fax numbers of the President, First Lady, Vice President, and all the members of the Cabinet.

Keywords: White House, President, Politics

Audience: General Public

Details: Free

`ftp://nifty.andrew.cmu.edu/pub/QRD/info/govt/cabinet`

White House Press Releases

★★★★

An archive of all the press releases by the Clinton administration organized as Miscellaneous, Briefings by Dee Dee Myers, Executive Orders, Remarks during Photo Opportunities, Remarks of Bill Clinton, and Briefings by George Stephanopolous.

Keywords: White House, Politics, President (US)

Audience: General Public

Details: Free

`gopher://wiretap.spies.com/11/Clinton`

Whitman (Walt)

University of Pennsylvania PENNINFO Library

The library's holdings are large and wide-ranging and contain significant collections in many fields.

Keywords: Church History, Spanish Inquisition, Witchcraft, Shakespeare (William), Bibles, Aristotle (Texts of), Fiction, Whitman (Walt), French Revolution, Drama (French), Literature (English), Literature (Spanish)

Audience: Researchers, Students, General Public

Contact: Al DSouza
penninfo-admin@dccs.upenn.edu
dsouza@dccs.upenn.edu

Details: Free

Expect: Login; Send: Public

`telnet://penninfo.upenn.edu`

Whois

Whois

Whois is an Internet access tool that provides information on registered network names.

Keywords: Internet Tools

Sponsor: SRI International Telecommunication Sciences Center

Audience: Internet Surfers

Contact: Nancy C. Fischer
fischer@sri-nic

Details: Free

File is: documents/rfc/rfc0954.txt

`ftp://nic.merit.edu`

Wildlife

wildnet (Computing and Statistics in Fisheries & Wildlife Biology)

This mailing list was established for the exchange of ideas, questions, and solutions in the area of fisheries and wildlife biology computing and statistics.

Keywords: Wildlife, Fisheries, Statistics

Audience: Wildlife Biologists, Environmentalists, Statisticians

Contact: Eric Woodsworth
woodsworth@sask.usask.ca

Details: Free

To subscribe to the list, send an e-mail message requesting a subscription to the URL address below. To send a message to the entire list, address it to: wildnet@tribune.usask.ca

`mailto:wildnet-request@tribune.usask.ca`

The Wilderness Society

This WWW site provides access to a collection of fact sheets about America's national parks, forests, wildlife refuges, Bureau of Land Management lands, and other natural places.

Keywords: US National Park Service, Nature, Environment, Wildlife

Sponsor: Internet Multicasting Service and the Wilderness Society

Profile: Fact sheets are included for the following subjects: the Adirondacks, America's Public Lands, Ancient Forests of the Pacific Northwest, the Arctic National Wildlife Refuge, Below-cost Timber Sales, the California Desert, Endangered Species, the Everglades, Forest Fires And Forest Health, the Grand Canyon, the General Mining Law of 1872, Grazing On Public Lands, Lifelands, National Park Concessions, the National Wilderness Preservation System, the Northern Forest, the Tongass National Forest, Wetlands, Yellowstone National Park, and Yosemite National Park.

Contact: email: questions@radio.com

Details: Free, Images

`http://town.hall.org/environment/wild_soc/wilderness.html`

Williams College Library

Williams College Library

The library's holdings are large and wide-ranging and contain significant collections in many fields.

Keywords: Americana, Graphic Arts, Printing (History of), Performing Arts, Printing

Audience: General Public, Researchers, Librarians, Document Delivery Professionals

Contact: Jim Cubit

Details: Free

Expect: Mitek Server..., Send: Enter or Return; Expect: prompt, Send: hollis

`telnet://library.williams.edu`

Windows

Microsoft Corporation World Wide Web Server

This system has been set up to provide lay and technical information for the public about Microsoft and its products.

Keywords: Microsoft, Windows, MS-DOS, Chicago

Sponsor: Microsoft Corporation

Audience: Computer Users, Microsoft Product Users, Computer Programmers, Investors

Profile: The Microsoft Knowledge Base and Software Library is accessible here. Information can be obtained on Windows NT Server, Developer Network News, Windows News, and also Windows Sockets Information. There are sections on Windows 4 (Chicago), Microsoft's new 32-bit TCP/IP VxD stack, a "What's New" page, current employment opportunities at Microsoft, recent speeches given by Microsoft Corporation's CEO Bill Gates, as well as current financial information about Microsoft.

Contact: email: www@microsoft.com

Details: Free, Images

Notes: The information contained on this server is copyrighted, and may not be distributed, downloaded, modified, reused, reposted, or otherwise used outside the scope of a WWW client without the express written permission of Microsoft Corporation.

`http://www.microsoft.com`

`gopher://gopher.microsoft.com`

`ftp://ftp.microsoft.com`

Windsurfing

Physical Education & Recreation

A collection of information on sporting and recreational activities from aikido to windsurfing.

Keywords: Sports, Recreation, Aikido, Cycling, Scuba Diving, Windsurfing

Audience: Sports Enthusiasts, Fitness Enthusiasts

Contact: ctcadmin@ctc.ctc.edu

`gopher://ctc.ctc.edu`

Think Wind

An FTP site for information on windsurfing, with FAQs, pictures, details about destinations, and threads from rec.windsurfing.

Keywords: Sports, Windsurfing

Audience: Windsurfers

Contact: phansen@lemming.uvm.edu

Details: Free, Images

`ftp://lemming.uvm.edu/rec.windsurfing`

Winter Games

Olympic Games 1994 at Lillehammer

News, results, and updates every 15 minutes, as well as archive images, from the 1994 Winter Olympic Games at Lillehammer, Norway.

Keywords: Olympics, Sports, Winter Games

Sponsor: Sun Microsystem, Skrivervik Data AS, Oslonett AS, Norsk Telegrambyra

Audience: General Public, Journalists, Skiers, Skaters, Winter Sports Fans

Profile: This server offers news and results on all the Olympic events in Lillehammer plus a chronological list of all events, a complete schedule day by day, and a very large archive of images. Also flash messages from NTB, a Norwegian news wire, and the opportunity to search in the NTB database.

Contact: oslonett@oslonett.no

`http://www.sun.com`

WIRED Online

WIRED Online

This is WIRED Magazine's gopher server.

Keywords: Postmodern Culture, News Media

Sponsor: WIRED Magazine

Audience: Internet Surfers, Internet Users, General Public

Profile: Features full-text of WIRED back issues, including the Net Surf column devoted to Internet exploration. Also has archives of the HotWIRED weekly mailing list, some guides to getting started surfing the net, general information about WIRED magazine, and an archive of material on the proposed Clipper federal encryption standard.

Contact: WIRED Online department, WIRED Magazine online@wired.com, info@wired.com

`gopher://gopher.wired.com`

Wiretap Sports Archives

Wiretap Sports Archives

Sports articles, including information on soccer in the US and Canada, rules for soccer and Australian football, and some rather dated material on American football.

Keywords: Sports, Football, Soccer

Sponsor: The Internet Wiretap Library

Audience: Sports Enthusiasts

Details: Free

`gopher://wiretap.spies.com/library/article/sports`

Wisconsin

WRPRCC

Keywords: Primates, Wisconsin

Sponsor: Wisconsin Regional Primate Research Center

Audience: Primatologists, Zoologists

Contact: jacobsen@primate.wisc.edu

Details: Free

Expect: Login; enter: wiscinfo; choose: UW-Madison Information Servers Wisconsion Primate Research Center Server

`gopher://gopher.primate.wisc.edu`

Witchcraft

Harvard University Library

The library's holdings are large and wide ranging and contain significant collections in many fields.

Keywords: Afrikaans, Alchemy, Arabic Culure (History of), Celtic Philology, Congo Languages, Folklore, Hebraica, Mormonism, Numismatics, Quakers, Sanskrit, Witchcraft, Arabic Philology

Audience: General Public, Researchers, Librarians, Document Delivery Professionals

Details: Free

Expect: Mitek Server..., Send: Enter or Return; Expect: prompt, Send: hollis

`telnet://hollis.harvard.edu`

University of Pennsylvania PENNINFO Library

The library's holdings are large and wide-ranging and contain significant collections in many fields.

Keywords: Church History, Spanish Inquisition, Witchcraft, Shakespeare (William), Bibles, Aristotle (Texts of), Fiction, Whitman (Walt), French Revolution, Drama (French), Literature (English), Literature (Spanish)

Audience: Researchers, Students, General Public

Contact: Al DSouza penninfo-admin@dccs.upenn.edu dsouza@dccs.upenn.edu

Details: Free

Expect: Login; Send: Public

`telnet://penninfo.upenn.edu`

Women

amlat.mujeres

This conference serves as a forum for interchange between organizations and women's movements in Latin America and the Caribbean.

Keywords: Women, Latin America, Caribbean, Feminism

Audience: Women, Feminists, Activists

Contact: Carlos Afonso (cafonso@ax.apc.org) or APC North American Regional Office

E-mail: apcadmin@apc.org

A B C D E F G H I J K L M N O P Q R S T U V **W** X Y Z

Edie Farwell (efarwell@igc.apc.org)

Agencia Latinoamericana de Informacion
info@alai.ec
uualai@ecuanex.ec

Establish an account on the nearest APC node. Login, type c for conferences, then type: go amlat.mujeres.

Details: Costs

For information on the nearest APC node, contact APC International Secretariat IBASE

E-mail: apcadmin@apc.org

`telnet://igc.apc.org`

apngowid.meet

A conference on plans by Asia Pacific regional women's groups for the United Nations Fourth World Conference on Women to be held in Beijing in September 1995.

Keywords: Women, Asia, Pacific, Feminists, Development, United Nations, World Conference on Women

Audience: Women, Feminists, Nongovernmental Organizations

Contact: AsPac Info, Docu and Communication Committee
AP-IDC@p95.f401.n751.z6.g

Carlos Afonso (cafonso@ax.apc.org) or APC North American Regional Office

E-mail: apcadmin@apc.org

Edie Farwell (efarwell@igc.apc.org)

Details: Costs, Moderated

Establish an account on the nearest APC node. Login, type c for conferences, then type go apngowid.meet.

For information on the nearest APC node, contact APC International Secretariat IBASE

E-mail: apcadmin@apc.org

`http://www.igc.apc.org/igc/www.women.html`

Forum for Women's Issues

A forum for issues relating to women.

Keywords: Women, General Interest, Feminists

Audience: Women

Contact: Reva Basch
reva@well.sf.ca.us

Details: Free

To participate in a conference on the WELL, you must first establish an account on the WELL.

To do so, start by typing: telnet://well.sf.ca.us

`telnet://well.sf.ca.us`

hr.women

A conference on human rights issues pertaining to women.

Keywords: Women, Feminists, Human Rights

Audience: Women, Feminists, Activists

Contact: Jillaine Smith
jillaine@igc.apc.org

Carlos Afonso (cafonso@ax.apc.org) or APC North American Regional Office

E-mail: apcadmin@apc.org

Edie Farwell (efarwell@igc.apc.org)

Details: Costs

User Info.: Establish an account on the nearest APC node. Login, type c for conferences, then type go hr.women.

For information on the nearest APC node, contact: APC International Secretariat IBASE

E-mail: apcadmin@apc.org

`telnet://igc.apc.org`

InforM Women's Studies Database

A gopher- or FTP-accessible archive of documents, opportunities, and resources pertaining to women's studies and women's issues.

Keywords: Women's Studies, Feminism, Women

Audience: Women, Women's Studies Students, Women's Studies Educators, Other Women's Issues Observers

Profile: This women's studies database is an easily navigable archive of files on women's studies and women's issues. It includes information such as health, employment opportunities, political issues, gender issues in the workplace and in education, reproductive rights, sex discrimination, sexual harassment, violence, work and family, women and computers, feminist film reviews, and poetry. InforM contains a compilation of electronic forums (listservs and newsgroups) for the discussion of male/female relations and societal problems, and for women of diverse cultures and sexual persuasions.

Contact: Paula Gaber
Gaber@info.umd.edu

Details: Free

Gopher or telnet to Inform.umd.edu, select Educational Resources/Women's Studies/. Or FTP to Inform.umd.edu, log in as anonymous, then cd /inforM/ Educational_Resources/ WomensStudies/

This source is also accessible via gopher, FTP, or Telnet.

`gopher://inform.umd.edu`

`http://inform.umd.edu/welcome.html`

un.wcw.doc.eng

This is a read-only conference comprised of official UN documents for the United Nations Fourth World Conference on Women: Action for Equality, Development and Peace, scheduled to take place at the Beijing International Convention Center, Beijing, China, from 4-15 September 1995. The documents are provided by the official Conference Secretariat, and posted as received by the UN Non-Governmental Liaison Service (NGLS).

Keywords: Women, Development (International), Peace, UN, World Conference on Women

Audience: Women, Activists, Non-Governmental Organizations, Feminists

Contact: United Nations Non-Governmental Liaison Service/Edie Farwell
ngls@igc.apc.org
efarwell@igc.apc.org

Carlos Afonso (cafonso@ax.apc.org) or APC North American Regional Office

E-mail: apcadmin@apc.org

Edie Farwell (efarwell@igc.apc.org)

Details: Costs, Moderated

User Info.: Establish an account on the nearest APC node. Login, type c for conferences, then type go un.wcw.doc.eng.

For information on the nearest APC node, contact: APC International Secretariat IBASE

E-mail: apcadmin@apc.org

`telnet://igc.apc.org`

un.wcw.doc.fra

This is a read-only conference comprised of official UN documents for the United Nations Fourth World Conference on Women: Action for Equality, Development and Peace, scheduled to take place at the Beijing International Convention Center, Beijing, China, from 4-15 September 1995. The documents are provided by the official Conference Secretariat, are posted as received by the UN Non-Governmental Liaison Service (NGLS).

Keywords: Women, Development (International), Peace, UN, World Conference on Women

Audience: Women, Activists, Non-Governmental Organizations, Feminists

Contact: United Nations Non-Governmental Liaison Service/Edie Farwell

ngls@igc.apc.org or efarwell@igc.apc.org

Carlos Afonso (cafonso@ax.apc.org) or APC North American Regional Office

E-mail: apcadmin@apc.org

Edie Farwell (efarwell@igc.apc.org)

Details: Costs, Moderated

User Info.:   Establish an account on the nearest APC node. Login, type c for conferences, then type go un.wcw.doc.fra.

For information on the nearest APC node, contact: APC International Secretariat IBASE

E-mail: apcadmin@apc.org

`telnet://igc.apc.org`

Women.dev

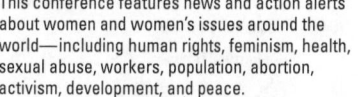

Conference for information about local, regional, and international development as it relates to women. The conference includes bibliographies, statements, news, articles, and announcements about development and women in Africa, South America, and South Asia.

Keywords: Women, Development (International), International Politics

Audience: Women, Activists, Non-governmental Organizations, Feminists

Contact: Carlos Afonso (cafonso@ax.apc.org) or APC North American Regional Office

E-mail: apcadmin@apc.org

Edie Farwell (efarwell@igc.apc.org)

Details: Subway, Free

User Info: Establish an account on the nearest APC node. Login, type c for conferences, then type go women.dev.

For information on the nearest APC node, contact: APC International Secretariat IBASE

E-mail: apcadmin@apc.org

`telnet://igc.apc.org`

Women.forum

Conference for discussion of women's issues.

Keywords: Women, Feminism, Women's Issues

Audience: Women, Feminists

Contact: Corina Hughes corina@igc.apc.org

Carlos Afonso (cafonso@ax.apc.org) or APC North American Regional Office

E-mail: apcadmin@apc.org

Edie Farwell (efarwell@igc.apc.org)

Details: Costs

User Info: Establish an account on the nearest APC node. Login, type c for conferences, then type go women.forum.

For information on the nearest APC node, contact: APC International Secretariat IBASE

E-mail: apcadmin@apc.org

`telnet://igc.apc.org`

Women.health

This conference features articles, documents, news, announcements, policy statements, and other information about women's health around the world. Topics include breast cancer, ovarian cancer, alcohol, abortion, pregnancy, sterilization of women, pesticides, Quinacrine, HIV, and disabilities.

Keywords: Women, Abortion, AIDS, Disability, Feminism, Health

Audience: Activists, Family Planners, Health Professionals, Non-Governmental Organizations, Women

Contact: Carlos Afonso (cafonso@ax.apc.org) or APC North American Regional Office

E-mail: apcadmin@apc.org

Edie Farwell (efarwell@igc.apc.org)

Details: Costs

User Info: Establish an account on the nearest APC node. Login, type c for conferences, then type go women.health.

For information on the nearest APC node, contact: APC International Secretariat IBASE

E-mail: apcadmin@apc.org

`telnet://igc.apc.org`

Women.labr

This conference features news, announcements, articles, and other information pertaining to the status of women workers in Europe, Latin America and the Caribbean, and Asia.

Keywords: Women, Unions

Audience: Women, Activists, Unions

Contact: Carlos Afonso (cafonso@ax.apc.org) or APC North American Regional Office

E-mail: apcadmin@apc.org

Edie Farwell (efarwell@igc.apc.org)

Details: Costs

User Info: Establish an account on the nearest APC node. Login, type c for conferences, then type go women.labr.

For information on the nearest APC node, contact: APC International Secretariat IBASE

E-mail: apcadmin@apc.org

`telnet://igc.apc.org`

Women.news

This conference features news and action alerts about women and women's issues around the world—including human rights, feminism, health, sexual abuse, workers, population, abortion, activism, development, and peace.

Keywords: Feminism, Gender, Women

Audience: Women, Feminists, Activists

Contact: Debra Guzman, Sue VanHattum hrcoord@igc.apc.org or suev@igc.apc.org

Carlos Afonso (cafonso@ax.apc.org) or APC North American Regional Office

E-mail: apcadmin@apc.org

Edie Farwell (efarwell@igc.apc.org)

Details: Free

User Info: Establish an account on the nearest APC node. Login, type c for conferences, then type go women.news.

For information on the nearest APC node, contact: APC International Secretariat IBASE

E-mail: apcadmin@apc.org

`telnet://igc.apc.org`

Women's Issues

Abortion and Reproductive Rights

A major directory on abortion, providing access to a broad range of related resources (library catalogs, databases, and servers) via the Internet.

Keywords: Abortion Rights, Activism, Women's Issues

Sponsor: The WELL Computer Conference System

Audience: Activists, Feminists

Profile: Choice-Net Report is a weekly update on reproductive rights issues distributed through E-mail; Women's Wire; gopher.WELL.com; Usenet groups alt.activism, talk.abortion; and soc.women, and other Internet channels.

Details: Free

`http://gopher.well.sf.ca.us`

dh.mujer

The primary Association for Progressive Communications conference for women and human rights issues throughout the world. Contains news and announcements.

Keywords: Women's Issues, Feminism, Human Rights

Audience: Feminists, Activists

Contact: Debra Guzman
hrcoord@igc.apc.org

Carlos Afonso (cafonso@ax.apc.org) or APC North American Regional Office

E-mail: apcadmin@apc.org

Edie Farwell (efarwell@igc.apc.org)

Details: Costs

User Info: Establish an account on the nearest APC node. Login, type c for conferences, then type go dh.mujer.

For information on the nearest APC node, contact: APC International Secretariat IBASE

E-mail: apcadmin@apc.org

`gopher://gopher.telnet://igc.apc.org (FREE)`

`http://igc.apc.org (FREE)`

ECHO

★★★★

A computer conferencing system based in New York City.

Keywords: Community, Networking, Women's Issues

Sponsor: East Coast Hang Out

Audience: Activists, Policy Makers, Community Leaders, Governments, Students, Feminists, Educators, Health-Care Professionals, Artists, Communicators, General Public

Contact: Stacy Horn
horn@echonyc.com,

Profile: ECHO was started by Stacy Horn as an East Coast counterpart to the WELL. ECHO makes an effort to be hospitable to women and has one of the highest percentages of women in an online community.

Details: Costs

`telnet://echonyc.com`

table.abortion

A Usenet newsgroup providing information and discussion about all sides of the abortion issue.

Keywords: Abortion, Women's Issues, Health

Audience: Women, Activists, Health-Care Professionals

Details: Free

To subscribe to this Usenet newsgroup, you need access to a newsreader.

`news:table.abortion`

Women's Wire

Women's Wire is an online interactive network focusing on women's issues and interests.

Keywords: Networking, Women's Issues, Online Services

Audience: Women, Internet Users

Profile: This service acts as an international clearinghouse for resources and networking on a broad range of topics including news, politics, careers, education, parenting, health, and arts. Provides e-mail and access to thousands of resources, including Usenet newsgroups.

Details: Costs

Access via an easy-to-use graphical interface for Macintosh and Windows platforms, or a text-based interface for DOS and Unix platforms. Local access numbers available throughout the US and in most countries.

`mailto:info@wwire.net`

Women's Studies

alt.feminism

A Usenet newsgroup providing information and discussion about feminism.

Keywords: Feminism, Women's Studies, Abortion, Activitism

Audience: Women, General Public

To subscribe to this Usenet newsgroup, you need access to a newsreader.

`news:alt.feminism`

InforM Women's Studies Database

★★★★

A gopher- or FTP-accessible archive of documents, opportunities, and resources pertaining to women's studies and women's issues.

Keywords: Women's Studies, Feminism, Women

Audience: Women, Women's Studies Students, Women's Studies Educators, Other Women's Issues Observers

Profile: This women's studies database is an easily navigable archive of files on women's studies and women's issues. It includes information such as health, employment opportunities, political issues, gender issues in the workplace and in education, reproductive rights, sex discrimination, sexual harassment, violence, work and family, women and computers, feminist film reviews, and poetry. InforM contains a compilation of electronic forums (listservs and newsgroups) for the discussion of male/female relations, societal problems, and for women of diverse cultures and sexual persuasions.

Contact: Paula Gaber

Gaber@info.umd.edu

Details: Free

Gopher or telnet to Inform.umd.edu, select Educational Resources/Women's Studies/. Or FTP to Inform.umd.edu, log in as anonymous, then cd /inforM/Educational_Resources/WomensStudies/

This source is also accessible via gopher, FTP, or Telnet.

`gopher://inform.umd.edu`

`http://inform.umd.edu/welcome.html`

Northwestern University Library

★★

The library's holdings are large and wide ranging and contain significant collections in many fields.

Keywords: Africa, Wright (Frank Lloyd), Women's Studies, Art, Literature (American), Contemporary Music, Government (US State), UN Documents, Music

Audience: General Public, Researchers, Librarians, Document Delivery Professionals

Details: Free

Expect: COMMAND:, Send: DIAL VTAM

`telnet://nuacvm.acns.nwu.edu`

Notable Women

★★★

A database listing some important and notable women through the ages. Available for online searching by keyword, or as a full-text file.

Keywords: Women's Studies, History (Women's), Feminism

Sponsor: Estrella Mountain Community College (Arizona)

Audience: Women's Studies Educators, Historians, Researchers, Feminists

Contact: EMC Gopher Team
root@gopher.emc.maricopa.edu

`gopher://gopher.emc.maricopa.edu`

Women's Studies and Resources

★★★

A collection of materials related to women's studies and issues.

Keywords: Women's Studies, Feminism

Sponsor: Peripatetic Eclectic Gopher (PEG) at UC Irvine

Audience: Women, Feminists, Activists, Women's Studies Educators and Students

Profile: Contains bibliographies, listserv archives, conference announcements, and other resources related to women's studies. Also has links to other groups and sites related to women's issues.

Contact: Calvin Boyer
cjboyer@uci.edu

`gopher://peg.cwis.uci.edu`

Woodworking

rec.woodworking

A Usenet newsgroup providing information and discussion about woodworking.

Keywords: Woodworking, Crafts, Hobbies

Audience: Woodworkers

To subscribe to this Usenet newsgroup, you need access to a newsreader.

`news:rec.woodworking`

Word Play

alt.callahans

A Usenet newsgroup providing information and discussion about Callahan's bar Members share puns and fellowship.

Keywords: Humor, Word Play

Audience: Punsters, Comedians

To subscribe to this Usenet newsgroup, you need access to a newsreader.

`news:alt.calahans`

Workstations

Works

Works discusses personal workstation computers, such as the Sun2, Sun3, Apollo, Silicon Graphics, and AT&T workstations. Works provides a way for interested members of the Internet community to discuss and share useful insights about these kinds of systems.

Keywords: Workstations, Computers

Audience: Workstation Users, Computer Users

Contact: Dave Steiner
steiner@rutgers.edu

Details: Free

To subscribe to the list, send an E-mail message requesting a subscription to the URL address below.

`mailto:works@rutgers.edu`

WORLD (World News and Information)

WORLD (World News and Information)

This library contains detailed information about every country in Europe, Asia, the Pacific Rim, Africa, the Middle East, and North and South America. Designed for those who need to monitor world events, organizations, and leaders, this library provides a global view of any subject or topic.

Keywords: Business, News

Audience: Business Researchers, Analysts, Entrepreneurs

Profile: WORLD includes information from newspapers and wire services, trade and business journals, company reports, national and regional background, industry and product analysis, business opportunities, and selected legal texts. News sources range from the world-renowned Christian Science Monitor, Financial Times, Reuters and Associated Press to the regionally important eastern European CTK, MTI and PAP newswires, The Toronto Star, Jerusalem Post, and Xinhua News Agency. Business and trade information include a wide variety of sources, such as EIS's European newsletters and Euroscope from Coopers and Lybrand, Canada's Maclean's, Japan's Comline Daily News Service, BNA's international dailies, and the Soviet Union's SovData DiaLine services—all of which help analyze the political and economic climate around the globe. Company information is contained in the EXTEL cards as well as ICC. Providers of national background and industry analysis include Associated Banks of Europe, Bank of America, Business International, IBC USA, and the US Department of Commerce. Economic risk can be assessed with the Economist's Economic Risk Services, IBC's International Reports and International Country Risk Guide, and many of Business International's Country Reports. Political risk is forecast in IBC's Political Risk Services as well as BOA's World Information Services' Country RiskOutlooks, Monitors, and Forecasts.

Contact: Mead New Sales Group at (800) 227-4908 or (513) 859-5398 inside the U.S., or (513) 865-7981 for all inquiries outside the U.S.

To subscribe, contact Mead directly.

To examine the Nexis user guide, you can access it at the ftp site of the University of Texas at Austin at the URL address: ftp://ftp.cc.utexas.edu

The files are in /pub/ref-services/LEXIS

`telnet://nex.meaddata.com`

`http://www.meaddata.com`

World Bank Gopher Server

World Bank Gopher Server

A collection of online information from the World Bank.

Keywords: Government (International), Development, International Finance, Foreign Trade

Sponsor: The World Bank

Audience: Nongovernmental Organizations, Activists, Government Officials, Environmentalists

Profile: A collection of World Bank information including a list of publications, environmental assessments, economic reports, and updates on current projects being funded by the World Bank.

Contact: webmaster@www.worldbank.org

`gopher://gopher.worldbank.org`

`http://www.worldbank.org`

World Conference on Women

apngowid.meet

A conference on plans by Asia Pacific regional women's groups for the United Nations Fourth World Conference on Women to be held in Beijing in September 1995.

Keywords: Women, Asia, Pacific, Feminists, Development, United Nations, World Conference on Women

Audience: Women, Feminists, Nongovernmental Organizations

Contact: AsPac Info, Docu and Communication Committee
AP-IDC@p95.f401.n751.z6.g

Details: Costs, Moderated

Establish an account on the nearest APC node. Login, type c for conferences, then type: go apngowid.meet.

For information on the nearest APC node, contact: APC International Secretariat IBASE

E-mail: apcadmin@apc.org

Contact: Carlos Afonso (cafonso@ax.apc.org) or APC North American Regional Office

E-mail: apcadmin@apc.org

Edie Farwell (efarwell@igc.apc.org)

`http://www.igc.apc.org/igc/www.women.html`

A B C D E F G H I J K L M N O P Q R S T U V **W** X Y Z

A
B
C
D
E
F
G
H
I
J
K
L
M
N
O
P
Q
R
S
T
U
V
W
X
Y
Z

un.wcw.doc.eng

This is a read-only conference comprised of official UN documents for the United Nations Fourth World Conference on Women: Action for Equality, Development and Peace, scheduled to take place at the Beijing International Convention Center, Beijing, China, from 4-15 September 1995. The documents are provided by the official Conference Secretariat, are posted as received by the UN Non-Governmental Liaison Service (NGLS).

Keywords: Women, Development (International), Peace, UN, World Conference on Women

Audience: Women, Activists, Non-Governmental Organizations, Feminists

Contact: United Nations Non-Governmental Liaison Service/Edie Farwell
ngls@igc.apc.org
efarwell@igc.apc.org

Details: Costs, Moderated

User Info: Establish an account on the nearest APC node. Login, type c for conferences, then type go un.wcw.doc.eng. For information on the nearest APC node, contact: APC International Secretariat IBASE

E-mail: apcadmin@apc.org

Contact: Carlos Afonso (cafonso@ax.apc.org) or APC North American Regional Office

E-mail: apcadmin@apc.org

Edie Farwell (efarwell@igc.apc.org)

`telnet://igc.apc.org`

un.wcw.doc.fra

This is a read-only conference comprised of official UN documents for the United Nations Fourth World Conference on Women: Action for Equality, Development and Peace, scheduled to take place at the Beijing International Convention Center, Beijing, China, from 4-15 September 1995. The documents are provided by the official Conference Secretariat, are posted as received by the UN Non-Governmental Liaison Service (NGLS).

Keywords: Women, Development (International), Peace, UN, World Conference on Women

Audience: Women, Activists, Non-Governmental Organizations, Feminists

Contact: United Nations Non-Governmental Liaison Service/Edie Farwell

ngls@igc.apc.org or
efarwell@igc.apc.org

Details: Costs, Moderated

User Info: Establish an account on the nearest APC node. Login, type c for conferences, then type go un.wcw.doc.fra. For information on the nearest APC node, contact: APC International Secretariat IBASE

E-mail: apcadmin@apc.org

Contact: Carlos Afonso
(cafonso@ax.apc.org) or APC North American Regional Office

E-mail: apcadmin@apc.org

Contact: Edie Farwell
(efarwell@igc.apc.org)

`telnet://igc.apc.org`

World Constitutions

World Constitutions

A list of world constitutions, containing the constitutions of more than 18 nations including Basic Law of Germany 1949; Constitution of Macedonia (in former Yugoslavia); and Magna Carta.

Keywords: Law (International), History (World), Politics (International)

Audience: Researchers, Lawyers, Historians

Details: Free

`gopher://wiretap.spies.com`

World Cycling Championship 1994

World Cycling Championship 1994

This web site contains information about events surrounding the 1994 World Cycling Championship.

Keywords: Bicycles

Audience: Bicyclists, Sports Fans

`http://www-worldbike.iunet.it/`

World Health

HungerWeb

This web site focuses on the political, economic, agricultural, and ethical implications of world hunger.

Keywords: World Health, Activism

Sponsor: Oxfam

Audience: Activists, Financial Planners

Contact: Daniel Zalik
Daniel_Zalik@cs.brown.edu

Details: Free

`http://www.hunger.brown.edu/oxfam`

National Library of Medicine Gopher
World Health Organization (WHO)

This gopher provides information about the National Library of Medicine, the world's largest single-topic library.

Keywords: Medicine, Health, World Health

Sponsor: National Library of Medicine, Massachusetts

World Health Organization, Geneva, Switzerland

Audience: Health-care Professionals, Medical Professionals, Researchers

Profile: The National Library of Medicine (NLM) cares for over 4.5 million holdings (including books, journals, reports, manuscripts, and audio-visual items). The NLM offers extensive online information services dealing with clinical care, toxicology, environmental health, and basic biomedical research. It has several active research and development components, including an extramural grants program, houses an extensive history of medicine collection, and provides several programs designed to improve the nation's medical library system.

Contact: R. P. C. Rodgers
rodgers@nlm.nih.gov

akazawa@who.ch

Details: Free

`gopher://el-gopher.med.utah.edu`

`gopher://gopher.who.ch`

World Health Organization (WHO)

This gopher provides access to the databases of the WHO.

Keywords: World Health, Health, Medicine, Non-governmental organizations

Sponsor: World Health Organization, Geneva, Switzerland

Audience: Medical Professionals, Researchers

Contact: akazawa@who.ch

Details: Free

`gopher://gopher.who.ch`

World Wide Web (WWW)

WebCrawler (The)

The WebCrawler is a tool for searching the Web.

Keywords: Robots, WWW, Internet Access

Sponsor: The Department of Computer Science and Engineering, University of Washington, Seattle, WA, USA

Audience: Internet Surfers

Profile: The WebCrawler is a tool for searching the Web. It operates by traversing the Web and either building an index for later use, or by searching in real-time for a query. The index built by the WebCrawler is available for searching via the WebCrawler Search Page.

Contact: Brian Pinkerton

User Info: email: bp@cs.washington.edu

Details: Free

```
http://www.biotech.washington.edu/
WebCrawler/WebQuery.html
```

World Wide Web (WWW)

World Wide Web (WWW) is an Internet access tool which retrieves resources through a hypertext browser of databases.

Keywords: Internet Tools, World Wide Web (WWW)

Sponsor: CERN (European Laboratory for Particle Physics)

Audience: Internet Surfers

Details: Free

Documents and guides are in: pub/www/doc

```
ftp://info.cern.ch
```

World Wide Web Book

A book describing the WWW (World Wide Web) project.

Keywords: Internet Tools, World Wide Web (WWW)

Audience: Internet Surfers

Details: Free

```
ftp://emx.cc.utexas.edu
```

World Wide Web Demo

A Telnet session demonstrating the World Wide Web (WWW), an Internet access tool.

Keywords: Internet Tools, World Wide Web (WWW)

Audience: Internet Surfers

Details: Free

No surname is needed

```
telnet://info.cern.ch
```

World Wide Web FAQ

A web site containing common questions and answers about WWW, a distributed hypermedia system first developed by CERN.

Keywords: World Wide Web (WWW), Internet Reference, Information Retrieval

Audience: Students, Computer Scientists, Researchers

Contact: Thomas Boutell, Nathan Torkington
boutell@netcom.com
nathan.torckington@vuw.ac.nz

```
http://sunsite.unc.edu/boutell/faq/
www_faq.html
```

World Wide Web Worm (WWWW)

WWWW provides a mechanism to search the WWW in a multitude of ways. It also provides lists of all Home pages and of all URLs cited anywhere. This site contains an exhaustive list of WWW servers nationally and internationally.

Keywords: World Wide Web, (WWW), Information Retrieval, Internet

Sponsor: University of Colorado at Boulder, Department of Computer Science, Boulder, Colorado, USA

Audience: Researchers, Students, General Public

Contact: Oliver McBryan
mcbryan@cs.colorado.edu

```
http://www.cs.colorado.edu/home/
mcbryan/WWWW.html
```

Worldview

Principia Cybernetica Newsletter

Newsletter for participants in the Principia Cybernetica Project (PCP), as well as for people interested in keeping informed about the project.

Keywords: Philosophy, Worldview

Audience: Philosophers

Profile: PCP is a computer-supported collaborative attempt to develop an integrated evolutionary-systemic philosophy or world view. Its contributors are distributed over several continents and maintain contact primarily through electronic mail (mailing list PRNCYB-L), as well as through annual meetings, the printed (and electronic) newsletter, and postal mail. PCP focuses on the clear formulation of basic concepts and principles of the cybernetic approach.

Contact: Cliff Joslyn, Francis Heylighen
fheyligh@vnet3.vub.ac.be
cjoslyn@bingvaxu.cc.binghamton.edu

Details: Free

Send a 1- to 2-page letter, giving your address and affiliations and explaining your interest in the Project to the List owner (C. Joslyn).

```
mailto:cjoslyn@bingvaxu.cc.binghamton.edu
```

Wrestling

rec.sport.pro-wrestling

A Usenet newsgroup providing information and discussion about professional wrestling.

Keywords: Wrestling, Sports

Audience: Wrestling Fans, Sports Fans

To subscribe to this Usenet newsgroup, you need access to a newsreader.

```
news:rec.sport.pro-wrestling
```

Wright (Frank Lloyd)

Northwestern University Library

The library's holdings are large and wide ranging and contain significant collections in many fields.

Keywords: Africa, Wright (Frank Lloyd), Women's Studies, Art, Literature (American), Contemporary Music, Government (US State), UN Documents, Music

Audience: General Public, Researchers, Librarians, Document Delivery Professionals

Details: Free

Expect: COMMAND:, Send: DIAL VTAM

```
telnet://nuacvm.acns.nwu.edu
```

Writing

Arts Wire

A national communications network for the arts located on the Meta Network.

Keywords: Art, Writing, Activism, Music

Sponsor: New York Foundation for the Arts

Audience: Art Activists, Art Organizations, Artists, Composers, Foundations, Government Arts Agencies, Writers

Profile: Arts Wire provides immediate access to news, information, and dialogue on conditions affecting the arts and artists, as well as private conferences for organizations. Core features include Money, a searchable resource of grant deadlines; Hotwire, a summary of arts news; and conferences about new music, interactive art, literature, AIDS, and Latino art.

Contact: Judy Malloy
artswire@tmn.com

```
telnet://tmn.com
```

A
B
C
D
E
F
G
H
I
J
K
L
M
N
O
P
Q
R
S
T
U
V
W
X
Y
Z

fwake-l

A conference and forum for a broad discussion of James Joyce's Finnegan's Wake

Keywords: Joyce (James), Literature (Irish), Authors, Writing

Audience: Writers, Joyce Scholars, Literary Critics, Literary Theorists

To subscribe to the list, send an e-mail message to the URL address below consisting of a single line reading: SUB fwake-l

`mailto:listserv@irlearn.ucd.ie`

journet

An electronic conference for the discussion of topics of interest to journalists and journalism educators.

Keywords: Journalism, Writing, Desktop Publishing, Electronic Publishing

Audience: Journalists, Writers, Publishers, Educators

Contact: George Frajkor
gfrajkor@ccs.carleton.ca

To subscribe to the list, send an e-mail message to the URL address below consisting of a single line reading:

SUB journet YourFirstName YourLastName

To send a message to the entire list, address it to: journet@qucdn.queensu.ca

`mailto:listserv@qucdn.queensu.ca`

news.announce.conferences

A Usenet newsgroup providing information and discussion about conferences, as well as calls for papers.

Keywords: Conferences, Papers, Writing

Audience: Writers, General Public

Details: Free

To subscribe to this Usenet newsgroup, you need access to a newsreader.

`news:news.announce.conferences`

Pen-pals

This mailing list provides a forum for children to correspond with each other electronically. Although the list is not moderated, it is monitored for content and is managed by listproc.

Keywords: Computing, Children, Writing

Audience: Computer Users, Children, Student Writers

Contact: pen-pals-request@mainstream.com

Details: Free

To subscribe to the list, send an e-mail message requesting a subscription to the URL address below. To send a message to the entire list, address it to: pen-pals@mainstream.com

`mailto:pen-pals@mainstream.com`

Quanta

An electronically distributed science fiction magazine that is published monthly. Each issue contains short fiction, articles, and editorials by authors from around the world and across the Net.

Keywords: Science Fiction, Writing, Publications

Audience: Science Fiction Enthusiasts, Writers

Contact: da1n@andrew.cmu.edu

Details: Free

To subscribe to the list, send an e-mail message requesting a subscription to the URL address below.

To send a message to the entire list, address it to: da1n@andrew.cmu.edu

`mailto:da1n@andrew.cmu.edu`

soc.penpals

A Usenet newsgroup providing information and discussion for people in search of Net pals and other online correspondence.

Keywords: Computing, Writing

Audience: Computer Users, Writers

Details: Free

To subscribe to this Usenet newsgroup, you need access to a newsreader.

`news:soc.penpals`

Style Sheets from the Online Writers' Workshop

This gopher provides information and examples on how to write bibliographies using three formats: MLA (Modern Language Association), Old-MLA, and APA (American Psychological Association).

Keywords: Bibliographies, Writing, Lexicology

Sponsor: University of Illinois at Urbana-Champaign

Audience: Writers, Students (High School/College/University)

Contact: Dr. Michael Pemberton
michaelp@ux1.cso.uiuc

`gopher://gopher.uiuc.edu`

---

wroclaw

wroclaw

Distribution of information from weekly Polish bulletin called Society Journal.

Keywords: Poland

Audience: Polish Speakers, Researchers, General Public

Contact: Pawel Misiak
misiak@plwrtu11

Details: Free

To subscribe to the list, send an e-mail message to the URL address shown below consisting of a single line reading:

SUB wroclaw YourFirstName YourLastName

To send a message to the entire list, address it to: wroclaw@plearn.edu.p1

`mailto:listserv@plearn.edu.p1`

WRPRCC

WRPRCC

Keywords: Primates, Wisconsin

Sponsor: Wisconsin Regional Primate Research Center

Audience: Primatologists, Zoologists

Contact: jacobsen@primate.wisc.edu

Details: Free

Expect: Login; enter: wiscinfo; choose: UW-Madison Information Servers Wisconsion Primate Research Center Server

`gopher://gopher.primate.wisc.edu`

WWW

Best of the Web '94

This web site highlights those places which were judged as the best sites (based on the criteria of quality, versatility, and power) on the World Wide Web.

Keywords: Internet, WWW

Audience: Internet Surfers

Contact: Brandon Plewe
plewe@acsu.buffalo.edu

Details: Free

`http://wings.buffalo.edu/contest`

comp.infosystems.www

A Usenet newsgroup providing information and discussion about the World Wide Web.

Keywords: WWW, Internet Reference, Information Retrieval

Audience: Internet Surfers

> To subscribe to this Usenet newsgroup, you need access to a newsreader.

`news:comp.infosystems.www`

Computer-Mediated Marketing Environments

A web site devoted to research aimed at understanding the ways in which computer-mediated marketing environments (CMEs), especially the Internet, are revolutionizing the way firms conduct business.

Keywords: WWW, Information Retrieval, Internet, Marketing, Business

Sponsor: Vanderbilt University, Owen Graduate School of Management, Nashville, Tennessee, USA

Audience: General Public, Entrepeneurs, Financial Planners, Marketers

Contact: Donna Hoffman, Tom Novak
hoffman@colette.ogsm.vanderbilt.edu
novak@moe.ogsm.vanderbilt.edu

`http://colette.ogsm.vanderbilt.edu`

CSORG (Clearinghouse for Subject-Oriented Internet Resource Guides)

The goal of CSORG is to collect subject-oriented guides to Internet resources and make them widely available. These guides are produced by members of the Internet community, and by SILS students who participate in the Internet Resource Discovery project.

Keywords: WWW, Information Retrieval, Internet

Sponsor: University of Michigan, School of Information and Library Studies, Michigan, USA

Audience: Reseachers, Students, General Public

Contact: Louis Rosenfeld
i-guides@umich.edu

`gopher://una.hh.lib.umich.edu/11/inetdirs`

E-mail WWW

E-mail WWW allows the user to obtain a web file via E-mail.

Keywords: Internet Services, E-mail, WWW

Audience: Internet Surfers

Details: Free
Include the words "www URL" in the e-mail.

`http://info.cern.ch/hypertext/WWW/TheProject.html`

EINet Galaxy

EINet Galaxy is a guide to world wide information and services. It includes public information as well as commercial information and services provided by EINet customers and affiliates. The information is organized by topic, and can be searched.

Keywords: WWW, Information Retrieval, Internet

Sponsor: Microelectronic and Computer Technology Corporation (MCC)

Audience: Reseachers, Students

Contact: Wayne Allen, Bruce Speyer
WA@EINet.net, Speyer@EINet.net

`http://galaxy.einet.net/galaxy.html`

Entering the WWW

An article entitled "Entering the World-Wide Web: A Guide to Cyberspace."

Keywords: Internet Tools, WWW

Sponsor: Honolulu Community College

Audience: Internet Surfers

Contact: Kevin Hughes
kevinh@pulua.hcc.hawaii.edu

Details: Free

`http://www.hcc.hawaii.edu/guide/www.guide.html`

HTML FAQ

Common questions and answers about HTML (Hypertext Markup Language). The FAQ covers the practices of creating new documents specifically for the WWW format, as well as transforming existing materials into WWW documents.

Keywords: WWW, Internet Reference, Information Retrieval

Audience: Students, Computer Scientists, Researchers

Contact: Iain O'Cain
ec@umcc.umich.edu

`http://www.umcc.umich.edu/~ec/www/html_faq.html`

Mosaic Home Page

This is the welcome page to the National Center for Supercomputing Applications (NCSA) World-Wide Web server, which features the Mosaic application. Mosaic provides a network-distributed hypermedia system for information discovery. It is Internet-based and is free for academic research and internal commercial use.

Keywords: Internet Tools, Mosaic, WWW

Audience: Internet Surfers

Contact: mosaic-x@ncsa.uiuc.edu

Details: Free

`http://www.ncsa.uiuc.edu/SDG/Software/Mosaic/NCSAMosaicHome.html`

Netfind

Netfind is a way of finding Internet e-mail addresses.

Keywords: WWW, Information Retrieval, E-mail

Sponsor: Emory University, Georgia, USA

Audience: Reseachers, Students, General Public

Profile: This service relies on common but not universal programs, and thus may not find some people with valid addresses. The most foolproof way of finding someone's e-mail address remains to call them on the phone and ask. All Netfind sites are functionally equivalent. Multiple ones are listed here in case some are overloaded or down with technical problems.

Contact: Netfind Help
schwartz@cs.colorado.edu

`gopher://emoryu1.cc.emory.edu/11/internet/General/netfind`

Searching Gopherspace with Veronica

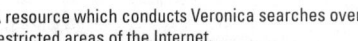

A resource which conducts Veronica searches over restricted areas of the Internet.

Keywords: WWW, Information Retrieval, Internet

Audience: Reseachers, Students, General Public

`gopher://gopher.well.sf.ca.us/11/outbound/veronica.search`

Telnet Access to WWW (World-Wide Web)

A server providing free public access to WWW written in both English and Hebrew.

Keywords: WWW, Internet Tools, Jerusalem

Sponsor: Hebrew University of Jerusalem

Audience: Internet Surfers

Contact: RASHTY@www.huji.ac.il

Expect: Username; Send: WWW

`telnet://www.huji.ac.il`

The InterNIC Home Page

This is the home page for the InterNIC networking organization.

Keywords: WWW, Information Retrieval, Computer Science, Internet Resources

Sponsor: National Science Foundation, USA

Audience: Reseachers, Students, General Public

A B C D E F G H I J K L M N O P Q R S T U V **W** X Y Z

A
B
C
D
E
F
G
H
I
J
K
L
M
N
O
P
Q
R
S
T
U
V
W
X
Y
Z

Profile: The InterNIC is a collaborative project of three organizations, which work together to offer the Internet community a full scope of network information services. These services include providing information about accessing and using the Internet, assistance in locating resources on the network, and registering network components for Internet connectivity. The overall goal of the InterNIC is to make networking and networked information more easily accessible to researchers, educators, and the general public. The term InterNIC signifies cooperation between Network Information Centers, or NICS.

Contact: InfoGuide
guide@internic.net

Details: InterNIC signifies cooperation between Network Information Centers

`http://www.internic.net`

The Scout Report

The Scout Report is a weekly publication offered by InterNIC Information Services to the Internet community as a fast, convenient way to stay informed on network activities.

Keywords: WWW, Information Retrieval, Internet, Computer Networking

Sponsor: National Science Foundation, USA

Audience: Researchers, Students, General Public

Profile: The purpose of this resource is to combine in one place the highlights of new resource announcements and other news which occurred on the Internet during the previous week. The Report is released every Friday. Categories included each week will vary depending on content, and the report will evolve with time and with input from the networking community.

Contact: InfoGuide
scout@is.internic.net
guide@is.internic.net

`http://www.internic.net/scout-report`

The Virtual Tourist - WWW Information

This site constitutes an attempt to catalogue and organize WWW sites by geographic location.

Keywords: WWW, Internet Tools

Sponsor: The State University of New York at Buffalo, Buffalo, New York, USA

Audience: Internet Surfers, General Public

Profile: Using CERN's master list of WWW servers, this Mosiac-accessible site is centered around an interactive world map which displays WWW/NIR sites within countries and regions. Multimedia Virtual Tourist guides are available for some countires, providing political, cultural, and historical information.

Contact: Brandon Plewe
plewe@acsu.buffalo.edu

`http://wings.buffalo.edu/world`

UC Berkeley Museum of Paleontology and the WWW Subway

This web site provides a multimedia museum display from UC Berkeley's Museum of Paleontology. Also features an interactive Subway—a tool linking users to other museums and WWW sites around the world.

Keywords: WWW, Museums, Paleontology

Sponsor: University of California at Berkeley, Museum of Paleontology, Berkeley, California, USA

Audience: Paleontologists, Internet Surfers, General Public

Contact: David Polly, Robert Guralnick
davip@ucmp1.berkeley.edu
robg@fossil.berkeley.edu

Details: Subway

`http://ucmp1.berkeley.edu/subway.html`

WAIS, Inc.

WAIS, Inc. provides interactive online publishing systems and services to organizations that publish information over the Internet. The organization's three main goals are to develop the Internet as a viable means for distributing information electronically; to improve the nature and quality of information available over networks; and to offer better methods to access that information.

Keywords: WWW, Information Retrieval, Publishing, Internet Tools, WAIS

Sponsor: WAIS, Inc.

Audience: Researchers, Students, General Public, Publishers

Contact: Webmaster
webmaster@wais.com

`http://server.wais.com/`

World-Wide Web (WWW)

World-Wide Web (WWW) is an Internet access tool which retrieves resources through a hypertext browser of databases.

Keywords: Internet Tools, WWW

Sponsor: CERN (European Laboratory for Particle Physics)

Audience: Internet Surfers

Details: Free

Documents and guides are in pub/www/doc

`ftp://info.cern.ch`

World-Wide Web Book

A book describing the WWW (World-Wide Web) project.

Keywords: Internet Tools, WWW

Audience: Internet Surfers

Details: Free

`ftp://emx.cc.utexas.edu`

World-Wide Web Demo

A Telnet session demonstrating the World-Wide Web (WWW), an Internet access tool.

Keywords: Internet Tools, WWW

Audience: Internet Surfers

Details: Free
No surname is needed

`telnet://info.cern.ch`

World Wide Web FAQ

A web site containing common questions and answers about WWW, a distributed hypermedia system first developed by CERN.

Keywords: WWW, Internet Reference, Information Retrieval

Audience: Students, Computer Scientists, Researchers

Contact: Thomas Boutell, Nathan Torkington
boutell@netcom.com
nathan.torckington@vuw.ac.nz

`http://sunsite.unc.edu/boutell/faq/www_faq.html`

World-Wide Web Worm (WWWW)

WWWW provides a mechanism to search the WWW in a multitude of ways. It also provides lists of all Home pages and of all URLs cited anywhere. This site contains an exhaustive list of WWW servers nationally and internationally.

Keywords: WWW, Information Retrieval, Internet

Sponsor: University of Colorado at Boulder, Department of Computer Science, Boulder, Colorado, USA

Audience: Researchers, Students, General Public

Contact: Oliver McBryan
mcbryan@cs.colorado.edu

`http://www.cs.colorado.edu/home/mcbryan/WWWW.html`

WWW Catalog

A catalog for World-Wide Web (WWW), an Internet access tool.

Keywords: Internet Tools, WWW

Sponsor: Centre Universitaire d'Informatique, University of Geneva

Audience: Internet Surfers

Details: Free

`http://cui_www.unige.ch`

WWW FAQ

Answers to frequently asked questions (FAQs) about World-Wide Web (WWW), an Internet access tool.

Keywords: Internet Tools, WWW, FAQs

Audience: Internet Surfers

Details: Free

`ftp://info.cern.ch`

WWW Biological Science Servers

WWW Biological Science Servers

A web site containing Internet links to many gopher servers and other web sites pertaining to bioscience.

Keywords: Bioscience, Biology

Sponsor: U.S. Department of the Interior Survey

Audience: Biologists, Researchers

Contact: Systems Operator
           webmaster@info.er.usgs.gov

`http://info.er.usgs.gov/network/`
`science/biology/index.html`

WWW Chemistry Sites

WWW Chemistry Sites

This is a major departure site for a vast array of chemical resources. Provides a list of WWW chemistry sites at academic institutions.

Keywords: Chemistry

Audience: Chemists, Chemistry Students, Chemical Engineers

Contact: Max Kopelevich
           mik@chem.ucla.edu

Details: Free

`http://www.chem.ucla.edu/`
`chempointers.html`

WWW Information

InterNIC Directory Services (White Pages)

This web site provides free access to X.500, WHOIS, and Netfind white pages on the Internet.

Keywords: WWW Information, Internet, Internet Tools

Sponsor: National Science Foundation, USA

Audience: General Public, Students

Contact: Database Administrator
           admin@ds.internic.net

`http://ds.internic.net/ds/dspgwp.html`

WWW Paris

WWW Paris

A web site created as a collaborative effort among individuals in both Paris and the United States.

Keywords: Paris, Culture, Art, Travel, French, Tourism

Audience: Students, Educators, Travelers, Researchers

Profile: Contains an extensive collection of images and text regarding all of the major monuments and museums of Paris, including maps of the Metro and the RER; calendars of events and current expositions; and promotional images and text relating to local department stores. There is also a visitors' section with up-to-date tourist information on hotels, restaurants, telephones, airport schedules, a basic Paris glossary, and the latest weather images. Includes an extensive collection of links to other resources about Paris and France, and a selected bibliography of history and architecture in Paris.

Contact: Norman Barth, Eric Pouliquen
           nbarth@ucsd.edu
           epouliq@ucsd.edu

`http://meteora.ucsd.edu/~norman/paris`

A
B
C
D
E
F
G
H
I
J
K
L
M
N
O
P
Q
R
S
T
U
V
W
X
Y
Z

A
B
C
D
E
F
G
H
I
J
K
L
M
N
O
P
Q
R
S
T
U
V
W
X
Y
Z

X.500

X.500

A catalog of available X.500 Implementations, a globally distributed Internet directory service.

Keywords: Internet Tools, X.500

Sponsor: SRI International and Lawrence Berkeley Laboratory

Audience: Internet Surfers

Contact: Ruth Lang, Russ Wright
rlang@nisc.sri.com or wright@lbl.gov

Details: Free

File is: documents/fyi/fyi_11.txt

`ftp://nic.merit.edu`

XTC

Chalkhills

A mailing list for the discussion of the music and records of XTC (the band).

Keywords: Pop Music, Musical Groups

Audience: Pop Music Enthusiasts, XTC Enthusiasts

Contact: John M. Relph
chalkhills-request@presto.ig.com

Details: Free, Moderated

To subscribe to the list, send an e-mail message requesting a subscription to the URL address below.

To send a message to the entire list, address it to: chalkhills@presto.ig.com

Notes: Chalkhills is moderated and distributed in a digest format.

`mailto:chalkhills-`
`request@presto.ig.com`

A
B
C
D
E
F
G
H
I
J
K
L
M
N
O
P
Q
R
S
T
U
V
W
X
Y
Z

Y

Yahoo Market and Investments

Yahoo Market and Investments

A comprehensive look at the current economic status, with a wide range of coverage, from brokers to stocks.

Keywords: Business, Stock Market, Investments, Economics

Sponsor: Stanford University, Palo Alto, California, USA

Audience: Investors, Economists

Contact: jerry@akebono.stanford.edu

http://akebono.stanford.edu/yahoo/ Economy/Markets_and_Investments

Yale Directory of Internet Libraries

Yale Directory of Internet Libraries

An online directory of international library catalogs containing links to many servers, including several with Internet access tools.

Keywords: Libraries, Internet, Resources

Sponsor: Yale University, New Haven, Connecticut, USA

Audience: General Audience

Profile: The Yale Directory of Internet Libraries is a comprehensive listing of international libraries that provides information about the subject area strengths of many of its entries.

gopher://gophlib@gopher.yale.edu

Yeats (William Butler)

The University of Kansas Library

The library's holdings are large and wide-ranging and contain significant collections in many fields.

Keywords: Botany, Chinese Studies, Cartography (History of), Kansas, Opera, Ornithology, Joyce (James), Yeats (William Butler), Walpole (Sir Robert, Collections of)

Audience: General Public, Researchers, Librarians, Document Delivery Professionals

Contact: John S. Miller

Details: Free

Expect: Username, Send: relay <cr>

telnet://kuhub.cc.ukans.edu

Yugoslavia

I.S.P.O.B. Bulletin YSSTI (Yugoslav System for Scientific and Technology Information)

The participants in this system can exchange news about the operations and development of YSSTI.

Keywords: Information Sciences, Yugoslavia

Sponsor: Institute of Information Sciences, University of Maribor, Yugoslavia

Audience: Information Scientists

Contact: Davor Sostaric davor%rcum@yubgef51.bitnet

Subscribe by sending an e-mail with a single line containing:

SUBSCRIBE P.O.B. to addresses POB%RCUM@YUBGEF51.bitnet

mailto:pob%rcum@yubgef51.bitnet

soc.culture.yugoslavia

A Usenet newsgroup providing information and discussion about the people and culture of Yugoslavia.

Keywords: Yugoslavia, Sociology

Audience: Sociologists, Yugoslavians

Details: Free

To subscribe to this Usenet newsgroup, you need access to a newsreader.

news:soc.culture.yugoslavia

Z

Zarf's List of Interactive Games on the Web

Zarf's List of Interactive Games on the Web

A list containing links to games and toys that can be played on the Internet.

Keywords: Games, Toys, Entertainment, Recreation

Sponsor: Carnegie Mellon University, School of Computer Science, Pittsburgh, Pennsylvania, USA

Audience: General Public, Game Players, Kids

Contact: Andrew Plotkin
zarf@cs.cmu.edu, apli@andrew.cmu.edu

`http://www.cs.cmu.edu/:800/afs/`
`cs.cmu.edu/user/zarf/www/games.html`

Zen and the Art of the Internet

Zen and the Art of the Internet

A beginner's guide to the Internet.

Keywords: Internet, Internet Guide

Audience: Internet Surfers

Contact: Brendan Kehoe
guide-bugs@cs.widener.edu

Details: Free

User Info: File is: /net/zen/zen-1.0.txt

`ftp://csn.org`

'Zines

FutureCulture FAQ (Frequently Asked Questions) File

List of online and offline items of interest to subscribers of FutureCulture, a mailing list on 'technoculture' or 'new edge' or 'cyberculture.'

Keywords: Technology, Cyberculture, Postmodernism, Sci-Fi, Zines

Audience: Reality Hackers, Cyberculture Enthuasists

Profile: This list discusses cyberpunk culture, rave culture, industrial music, virtual reality, drugs, computer underground, Net sociology, and virtual communities.

Contact: Alias Datura (adatura on IRC)
adatura@uafhp.uark.edu

Details: Free

`ftp://etext.archive.umich.edu/pub`

Internet Wiretap

A resource containing electronic books, zines, and government documents, White House press releases, and links to worldwide gopher and WAIS servers.

Keywords: Electronic Media, Cyberculture, Zines

Sponsor: Internet Wiretap

Audience: Cyberculture Enthusiasts, Civil Librarians, Educators

`gopher://wiretap.spies.com/11/`

`http://wiretap.spies.com`

Mother Jones

A web site containing online electronic issues of Mother Jones magazine (and Zine), making possible instant electronic feedback to the publishers regarding articles.

Keywords: Zines, Ethics, Public Policy, Activism

Sponsor: Mother Jones

Audience: Students, General Public

Contact: Webserver
webserver@mojones.com

`http://www.mojones.com/`
`motherjones.html`

Zoology

Agriculture, Veterinary Science & Zoology

This directory is a compilation of information resources focused on agriculture, veterinary science, and zoology.

Keywords: Agriculture, Veterinary Science, Zoology

Audience: Farmers, Agronomists, Veterinarians, Zoologists

Details: Free

`ftp://una.hh.lib.umich.edu/70/`
`inetdirsstacks/agvetzoo:haas`

Biosis Previews

The database encompasses the entire field of life sciences and covers original research reports and reviews in biological and biomedical areas. This includes field, laboratory, clinical, experimental and theoretical work. The traditional areas of biology, including botany, zoology and microbiology are covered, as well as the related fields such as plant and animal science, agriculture, pharmacology and ecology.

Keywords: Biology, Botany, Zoology, Microbiology, Plant Science, Animal Science, Agriculture, Pharmacology, Ecology, Biochemistry, Biophysics, Bio-engineering

A
B
C
D
E
F
G
H
I
J
K
L
M
N
O
P
Q
R
S
T
U
V
W
X
Y
Z

Sponsor: Biosis

Audience: Librarians, Researchers, Students, Biologists, Botanists, Zoologists, Scientists, Taxonomists

Contact: CDP Technologies Sales Department (800)950-2035, extension 400.

To subscribe, contact CDP Technologies directly.

`telnet://cdplus@cdplus.com`

University of Michigan Library

★★

The library's holdings are large and wide-ranging and contain significant collections in many fields, including the following:

Keywords: Asia, Astronomy, Transportation, Lexicology, Math, Zoology, Geography

Audience: Researchers, Students, General Public

Contact: info@merit.edu

Details: Free

Expect: Which Host; Send: Help

`telnet://cts.merit.edu`

APPENDIX

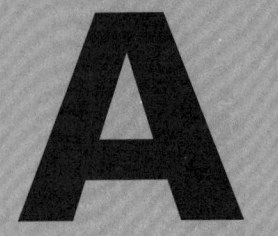

A

Keywords

ABC Programming Language
Abolitionism
Abortion
Abortion Rights
Academia
Academics
Accounting
ACLU
Acoustical Engineering
Activism
Ada (Programming Language)
ADD (Attention Deficit/Hyperactivity Disorder)
Adoption
APC (Advanced Product Centers)
Advanced Workshops
Advertising
Advisory (Student)
Aeronautics
Aeronautics (History of)
Aerospace
Aerospace Engineering
Africa
African American Studies
African Studies
Afrikaans
Aging
Agoraphobia
Agriculture
AIDS
Aikido
Air Conditioning
Airplanes
Alaska
Alchemy
Aldus PageMaker
Alex
Aliens
Allergies
Alloys
Alspa Computer
Alternative Management
Alternative Medicine
Alternative Press
Ambulatory Care
American Drama
American Studies
Americana
Americana (Western)
Amiga
Analog Equipment
Analysis

Animal Rights
Animal Science
Animal Studies
Animal Welfare
Animals
Animation
Annealing
Annual Reports
Anthropology
Anti-Semitism
Antiquarian Books
APL
Apple Computer
Aquaculture
Aquariums
Aquatic Biology
Aquatic Chemistry
Aquatic Science
Arabic Culture (History of)
Arabic Philology
Archaeology
Archie
Architecture
Archosaurs
Argentina
Aristotle (Texts of)
Art
Art Exhibitions
Art History
Artificial Intelligence
Artificial Life
ASCII
Asia
Asian American Studies
Asian Studies
Assignees
Astronomy
Astrophysics
AT&T
Atari
Atmosphere
Atmospheric Science
AUC TeX
Audio Electronics
Audio Reproduction
Audio-Visual Materials
Auditing
Australia
Austrian History
Autocrossing
Automobiles
Autopoiesis

Aviation
Aviation Industry
Ayurveda
Baby Boomer Culture
Bagpipes
Balloon Art
Ballooning
Ballroom Dancing
Baltic Republics
Balzac (Honore de)
Banking
Bankruptcy
Baseball
Basketball
Basque Studies
BBS
Beer
Behavior
Behavioral Science
Belgium
Berlin Wall
BETA
Bibles
Bibliographies
Bicycling
Biochemistry
Biodiversity
Bioengineering
Biographies
Bioinformatics
Biological Research
Biological Sciences
Biology
Biomechanics
Biomedical Computing
Biomedical Research
Biomedical Science
Biomedicine
Biophysics
Bioscience
Biosym Technologies Software
Biotechnology
Birds
Bisexuality
Bitnet
Blindness
Blues
BMW
Boating
Bonsai Trees
Book Arts
Books

Books (Antiquarian)
Bosnia
Boston
Botanical Taxonomy
Botany
Botany (History of)
Boy Scouts
Boyler-Moore Theorem Prover
Brain Research
Brazil
Britain
British Commonwealth Law
Broadcasting
Buddhism
Builder Xcessory
Building
Bulgaria
Business
Business (British)
Business (International)
Business (US)
Business Information
Business Management
Business Marketing
Buyers' Guides
C (Programming Language)
c2man
Cabinetry
Cabot (Sebastian)
Calendars
California
Canada
Canadian Documents
Canadian-American Studies
Cancer
Card Games
Cardiopulmonary Medicine
Cards
Careers
Caribbean
Carnivorous Plants
Carter (Hodding, Papers of)
Cartography
Cartography (History of)
Cartoons
Catholicism
Caves
CD-ROM
Cell Biology
Cell Churches
Cello
Cellular Technology

Celtic Studies
Celtic Philology
Censorship
Census Data
Central Europe
Cervantes (Miguel de)
Chaos Theory
Chat Groups
Chaucer (Geoffrey)
Chemical Engineering
Chemistry
Chemistry (History of)
Chess
Chicago
Chicano Culture
Child Care
Childbirth
Children
Chile
China
Chinese Language
Chinese Studies
Choral Singing
Christianity
Chromatography
Church (Frank)
Church History
CIA
Cinema
CIS (Commonwealth of Independent States)
Cisco Systems
Civil Liberties
Civil Rights
Civil War
Classics
Cleveland
Climatology
Clinton (Bill)
Clip Art
CNI
Coastal Marine Biology
Cognitive Science
Coins
Collectibles
Colorado
Comedians
Comedy
Comic Books
Comics
Commerce
Commodore-Amiga Computers
Commonwealth

Economics (History of)

Economy

Ecumenism

Education

Education (Adult)

Education (Alternative)

Education (Bilingual)

Education (College/University)

Education (Continuing)

Education (Distance)

Education (International)

Education (K-12)

Education (Post-Graduate)

Education (Post-Secondary)

Education (Secondary)

Educational Policy

EEC

Electric Vehicles

Electrical Engineering

Electronic Art

Electronic Books

Electronic Media

Electronic Music

Electronic Publishing

Electronics

Electrophoresis

Eliot (George)

Emacs

EMBnet

Emergency Preparedness

Employment

Encryption

Energy

Engineering

Engineering (History of)

England

English Bibles

Entertainment

Entomology

Entropy

Environment

Environmental Health

Environmental Policies

Environmental Safety

Environmental Studies

Enzymes

Equestrians

Equine Research

Ergonomics

ESL (English as a Second Language)

Essence (Internet Resource Directory)

Estonia

Ethics

Ethnic Studies

Ethnomusicology

Etiquette

Euromath

Europe

European Community

European Documents

Evangelism

Evolution

Executive Branch

Expert Systems

Exports

EXPRESS Information Modeling Language

Extraterrestrial Life

FairCom

Family

Family Practice

Family Science

FAQs (Frequently Asked Questions)

Farm Economics

Fashion

Fashion Industry

Fashion Merchandising

FAX

FDA

Federal

Federal Databases

Federal Documents (US)

Federal Government (US)

Federal Law (US)

Federal Register

Federal Standards

Feminism

Fen

Fiction

Filings

Film

Filmmaking

FINALE

Finance

Fine Arts

Finger (Internet Database)

Firearms

Firewalls

Fish

Fisheries

Fitness

Flags

Flight Simulation

Florida

Fluid Dynamics

Folk Dance

Folk Music

Folklore

Food

Food Production

Football

Ford

Foreign Trade

Forest Management

Forestry

Fox Television

France

Fraud

Free Software

Free Trade

Freedom of Information

Freedom of Speech

Freeware

French

French Language

French Law

French Opera (19th-C.)

French Revolution

French Studies

Frost (Robert)

FSP Protocol

FTP

Fuller (Buckminster)

Funding

Funk Music

Fusion

Fuzzy Logic

Galway (Ireland)

Gambling

Game Theory

Games

Gardening

Gay Rights

Gays

Gender

Geneology

GENESIS

Genetics

Genius

Geodesic Quantum Physics

GIS (Geographic Information Systems)

Geography

Geology

Geoscience

German

German Companies

German Democratic Republic

Germany

Gerontology

Gifts

GIS

Glass

Global News

God

Goethe

Golf

Gopher

Gophers

Gothic Rock

Government

Government (African)

Government (International)

Government (US Federal)

Government (US)

Government Documents

Government Records (US)

GPS

Grants

Graphic Arts

Graphic Design

Graphical User Interfaces

Graphics

Great Lakes Area

Greece

Gregorian Chants

Group Communications

Guidelines

Guitar

Gun Control Legislation

Hacking

Haiti

Hamill (Peter)

Handel (G.F.)

Handicapping

Hardware

Hardy (Thomas)

Harper (Roy)

Harry (Deborah)

Hawaii

Health

Health Care

Health Insurance

Health Sciences

Health Statistics

Hebraica

Hebrew Language

Hemingway (Ernest)

Herbert (George)

Herzegovina

Heuristics

Hewlett-Packard

Hispanic

Historic Preservation

Historical Documents

History

History (20th Century)

History (Ancient)

History (Jewish)

History (US)

History (Women's)

History (World)

Hobbies

Hockey

Holmes (Sherlock)

Holocaust

Home Building

Home Economics

Homosexuality

Hong Kong

Hongkongiana

Horseracing

Horses

Horticulture

Hospital Administration

Hospitality

Hot Air Balloons

Hotel Administration

Housing

Housman (A.E., Letters of)

Hubble Telescope

Human Behavior

Human Communications

Human Rights

Humanities

Humor

Hungary

Hunt (Leigh)

Husted (Margaret, Culinary Collection of)

Hydraulics

Hyperfiction

Hypermedia

Hypertext

Hytelnet

IBM

Icon Programming Language

Illinois

Image Processing

Imaging

Immigration (History of)

Immunology

Imports

Incunabula

Independent Study

India

Indiana

Indigenous Peoples

Industry

Infectious Diseases

Informatics

Information Retrieval

Information Science

Information Technology

Insect Biology

Insider Trading

Institutional Research

Institutions

Insurance Industry

Intellectual Property

Intelligence

Interactive Computing

Interactive Learning

Interactive Media

Interactivity

Interface Design

Intergraph

International Banking

International Business

International Communication

International Development

International Documents

International Finance

International Law

International News

International Politics

International Relations

International Research

International Visitors

Internet

Internet Access

Internet Business

Internet Directories

Internet Guide

Internet Guides

Internet Marketing

Internet Publishing

Internet Reference

Internet Research

Internet Resources

Internet Security

Internet Services

Internet Tools

Internships

Interpretation

Military

Military (US)

Military History

Military Policy

Military Science

Military Specifications

Milne (A.A., Collection of)

Mind

Miniatures

Miniaturized Plants

Mining

Minor League

Minorities

Miracles

Mississippi

MLB

Model Horses

Modem

Modern Dance

Modula-2 (Programming Language)

Molecular Biology

Monarchy

Mormonism

Morphology

Morris Dancing

Mosaic

Motor Racing

Motorcycles

Mountaineering

Movement

Movies

MS-DOS

Mt. Xinu

MUDs

Multicasting

Multilateral Treaties

Multimedia

Museums

Music

Music (Contemporary)

Music (Irish)

Music Notation

Music Resources

Music Reviews

Music Software

Musical Genres

Musical Groups

Musical Instruments

Musicals

Musicians

Muslim Associations

Muslim Student Associations

Mutual Funds

Mycoplasma

Mystery Fiction

Mythology

NAFTA

Napolean

NASA

National Collegiate Athletic Association

Native American Affairs

Native American Studies

NATO

Natural History

Natural Language

Natural Science

Navy

NBA

NCGIA

Ncube

Near Eastern Studies

NEARnet

Netblazer

Netherlands

Netiquette

Network Servers

Network Time Protocol

Networking

Networks

Neural Networks

Neural Simulation

Neurobiology

Neurology

Neuroscience

Nevada

Nevada State Documents

Nevadiana

New Age Music

New England

New Jersey

New Media

New Mexico

New Music

New Orleans

New Testament

New York

News (International)

News Media

NewsCommando

Newsletters

NeXT

NeXT-icon

NeXT-Med

NFL

NHL

Nickelodeon

NIH

NIR

Nissan Automobiles

Non Serviam

Non-governmental organizations

Nonfiction Books

Nonprofit Organizations

Nonprofits

Nordic Skiing

Nordic University

North America

Norway

NotGNU

NQTHM

Nuclear Medicine

Nuclear Safety

Numerical Analysis

Numismatics

Nursing

Nursing (History of)

Nutrition

Object-Oriented Programming

Objectivism

Obstetrics/Gynecology

Oceanography

Oceans

Office Document Architecture

Ohio

Old English

Old Testament

Olympics

OMD

Online Books

Online Services

OPAC System

Opera

Operating Systems

Optics

Oregon

Orienteering

Origami

Ornithology

Pacific

Packaging

Paganism

Pakistan

Paleography

Paleontology

Panic Disorders

Paper

APPENDIX B

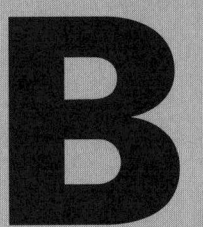

Audience Fields

Academics
Accountants
Activists
Actors
Administrators
Adoptees
Adoptive Parents
Adults
Advertisers
Aeronautical Engineers
Aerospace Engineers
Africans
Agricultural Economists
Agriculturalists
Agronomists
Aids Activists
Aids Researchers
Aids Sufferers
Aikido Enthusiasts
Alaskans
Alien Enthusiasts
Alternative Music Listeners
Amiga Users
Anglophiles
Animal Lovers
Animation Enthusiasts
Animators
Anthropologists
APC-Open Members
Ape Software Users
Apple II Users
AppWare Users
Aquarium Keepers
Archaeologists
Architects
Architectural Historians
Archivists
Art Activists
Art Educators
Art Enthusiasts
Art Historians
Art Organizations
Art Professionals
Art Students
Arts Community
Asian Studies Educators
Astronomers
Astrophysicists
Atari Users
Atheists

Athletes
Audio Enthusiasts
Australia Enthusiasts
Australians
Autocross Drivers
Automobile Buyers
Automobile Enthusiasts
Automobile Mechanics
Automobile Owners
Automobile Racers
Automobile Racing Enthusiasts
Aviators
Baby Boomers
Backpackers
Balloon Artists
Balloonists
Ballroom Dancers
Baltic Nationals
Bankers
Banking Industry Analysts
Baseball Enthusiasts
Basketball Enthusiasts
Bay Area Residents
BBS Users
Beastie Boys Enthusiasts
Beatles Listeners
Beer Brewers
Beer Enthusiasts
Bible Readers
Biblical Scholars
Bicycling Enthusiasts
Bicyclists
Biochemists
Biologists
Biomedical Researchers
Biotechnologists
Bird Watchers
Bisexuals
Blind People
Blues Enthusiasts
BMW Enthusiasts
Boating Enthusiasts
Bonsai Enthusiasts
Book Readers
Book Reviewers
Booksellers
Bosnians
Boston Residents
Botanists
Boy Scouts

Brazilians

Brewers

British

British Automobile Enthusiasts

British Motorcycle Enthusiasts

Broadcasters

Broadcasting Professionals

Bruce Springsteen Fans

Buddhists

Builders

Business Analysts

Business Professionals

Business Researchers

Business Students

Californians

Cambridge

Campaign Managers

Campers

Canadians

Card Collectors

Card Players

Caribbean Enthusiasts

Carnegie Mellon Community

Cartographers

Cartologists

Cat Owners

Catholics

Cave Explorers

CD-ROM Authors

CD-ROM Publishers

Celtic Enthusiasts

Celts

Certified Public Accountants

Chaosium Enthusiasts

Chaucer Fans

Chefs

Chemical Engineers

Chemistry Students (High School Up)

Chemistry Teachers

Chemists

Chess Players

Child Care Providers

Child Development Professionals

Children

Children's Rights Activists

Chinese

Choral Singers

Choreographers

Christians

Cinematographers

Cisco Employees

Cisco Users

Citizens

Civil Engineers

Civil Libertarians

Classical Music Listeners

Clergy

Cleveland Residents

Climatologists

Clinicians

Coaches

Cognitive Scientists

Coin Collectors

Collectors

College/University Educators

College/University Planners

Color/Vision Researchers

Colorado Residents

Comedians

Comics Enthusiasts

Commodore-Amiga Users

Commune Protocol Users

Communications Specialists

Communications Students

Community Activists

Community Builders

Community Groups

Community Leaders

Compact Disc Users

Complainers

Composers

Computational Neuroscientists

Computer Engineers

Computer Game Developers

Computer Game Players

Computer Graphic Designers

Computer Hardware Users

Computer Professionals

Computer Programmers

Computer Scientists

Computer Specialists

Computer Speech Researchers

Computer Students

Computer System Designers

Computer Systems Analysts/Programmers

Computer Underground Enthusiasts

Computer Users

Computer-Mediated Communication Researchers

Computing Analysts

Computing Consultants

Computists International Members

Concrete Blonde Enthusiasts

Concurrent Logic Programmers

Conferencing System Users

Conservationists

Consumers

Convex Computer Users

Cooks

Corporations

Counselors

Counterrevolutionaries

CP/M Users

Crafts Enthusiasts

Creationists

Cricket Fans

Critics

Croatians

Crossfire Specialists

Cult Members

Curiosity Seekers

Cyberculture Enthusiasts

Cybernauts

Cyberpunks

Cyclists

Czechs

Dan Fogelberg Enthusiasts

Dancers

Dante Scholars

Database Managers

Deaf and Disabled People

Deborah Harry Enthusiasts

Defense Analysts

Democratic Socialists

Demographers

Dentists

Depeche Mode Enthusiasts

Dermatologists

Designers

Desktop Publishers

Detectives

Deviants

Dialog Subscribers

Dieticians

Differently Abled People

Digital Equipment Users

Dire Straits Enthusiasts

Disabled People

Disk Jockeys

Disney Enthusiasts

Dist Users

Distance Educators

Distributors

Doctors

Document Delivery Professionals

Dog Owners

Down's Syndrome Community

Drag Racers

Dramatists

Drew University Alumni

Drivers

Drug Educators

Drug Users

E-Mail Users

Earth Scientists

Ecologists

Economists

Editors

Educational Administrators

Educators

Educators (College/University)

Educators (K-12)

Electric Vehicle-Drivers

Electrical Engineers

Electronic Music Enthusiasts

Energy Researchers

Engineers

English Teachers

Entomologists

Entrepreneurs

Environmentalists

Epidemiologists

Ernest Hemingway Enthusiasts

Ethnic Studies Students

Ethnomusicologists

Europeans

Evangelists

Evolutionists

Exchange Students

Exporters

Express Programmers

Faculty Administrators

Family Physicians

Family Planners

Farmers

Fashion Enthusiasts

Fax Users

Feminists

Film Enthusiasts

Filmmakers

Finale Program Users

Financial Analysts

Fish Enthusiasts

Fitness Enthusiasts

Florida Residents

Folk Dancers

Folk Music Enthusiasts

Folk Musicians

Football Enthusiasts

Foreign Students

Foresters

Former Boy Scouts

Francophiles

FreeNet Organizers

French Students

Fundraisers

Funk Music Enthusiasts

Gamblers

Game Players

Game Theorists

Gardeners

Gay Rights Activists

Gays

Geneologists

General Public

Geneticists

Geographers

Geologists

Germans

GIS Professionals

GIS Users

Gnuish Ms-Dos Developers

Golfers

Gothic Rock Enthusiasts

Government Officials

Graphic Artists

Graphic Designers

Grass-Roots Organizers

Grateful Dead Enthusiasts

Greeks

Guitar Players

Gun Users

Hackers

Ham Radio Operators

Hardware/Software Designers

Hawaiians

Health Care Professionals

Health Care Providers

Health Science Researchers

Heavy Metal Listeners

Hispanics

Historians

Hockey Enthusiasts

Hockey Players

Holocaust Researchers

Home Owners

Horse Owners

Horse Trainers

Horseracing Enthusiasts

Horticulturists

Humanists

Hungarian Speakers

IBM Users

Ichthyologists

Icon Programmers

Idaho Residents

Importers

Indigenous People

Information Brokers

Information Scientists

Insurance Industry Professionals

International Aid Agencies

International Lawyers

Internationalists

Internet Surfers

Interpreters

Inventors

Investigators

Investors

Iranians

IRC Users

Irish

Israelis

Italian Students

Italians

Japanese

Jewish Organizations

Jews

Job Seekers

Jokers

Journalism

Journalists

Joyce Scholars

Judaica Scholars

Judges

Julian May Readers

Kansas State University Students

Kibologists

Kinesiologists

Kite Enthusiasts

Kiwanis Members

Koreans

Laboratory Suppliers

Language Students

Language Teachers

Law Students

Lawyers

Legal Professionals

Legal Scholars

Legislators

Lesbians

Libertarians

Librarians

Linguists
Literary Theorists
Lobbyists
Lucid Programmers
Macintosh Users
Management Trainers
Managers
Manufacturers
Marillion Enthusiasts
Marine Biologists
Market Analysts
Market Researchers
Marketing Specialists
Martial Arts Enthusiasts
Maryland Residents
Massachusetts Residents
Material Scientists
Mathematical Biologists
Mathematicians
Max Stirner Enthusiasts
Mechanical Engineers
Media Professionals
Mediators
Medical Professionals
Medical Researchers
Medical Students
Melrose Place Enthusiasts
Memorabilia Collectors
Mensa Members
Merchants
Meteorologists
Microsoft Product Users
Middle East Scholars
Middlesex Alumni
Middlesex Students
Midwives
Military Historians
Military Personnel
Miniature Figurine Collectors
Ministers
Model Horse Collectors
Modem Users
Modesty Blaise Enthusiasts
Modula-2 Programmers
Molecular Biologists
Molecular Biotechnologists
Monarchists
Monty Python Enthusiasts
Moralists
Morphologists
Morris Dancers
Motorcycle Enthusiasts

MUD Users
Multicasters
Multimedia Users
Music Enthusiasts
Music Librarians
Music Researchers
Music Students
Musicians
Muslims
Mystery Enthusiasts
Mystics
Nafsa Members
Native Americans
Natural History Scientists
Natural Scientists
Naturalists
Nature Lovers
Navy Personnel
NCSU Computer Students
Ncube Users
Network Administrators
Network Developers
Network Service Providers
Network Time Protocol Users
Neurobiologists
Neuroscientists
New Media Artists
New Mexico Residents
New Orleans Residents
New York Residents
News Enthusiasts
Newscommando Users
Next Developers
Next Users
Norwegians
Notgnu Users
Nqthm Theorem Users
Numerical Analysts
Nursery Owners
Nurses
Nutritionists
O/S2 Users
Objectivists
Oceanographers
Ohio Residents
Ohio State University Alumni
Olympics Enthusiasts
OMD Enthusiasts
Oregonians
Orienteering Enthusiasts
Origami Enthusiasts
Ornamental Plant Enthusiasts

Otis Followers
Oyster Band Enthusiasts
Pagans
Pakistanis
Paleontologists
Panic Disorder Sufferers
Paranoid Persons
Parents
Park Rangers
Parnet Users
Particle Physicists
Pascal Programmers
Patent Agents
Patent Attorneys
Patent Researchers
Perq Users
Peruvians
Pet Owners
Pharmacists
Philanthropists
Philip K. Dick Readers
Philosophers
Phish Enthusiasts
Photographers
Physical Therapists
Physicians
Physicists
Pink Floyd Enthusiasts
Planetarium Operators
Planners
Poetry Readers
Poets
Poker Players
Poles
Policy Makers
Polish Speakers
Political Activists
Political Analysts
Political Researchers
Political Scientists
Politicians
Pop Music Enthusiasts
Popular Culture Enthusiasts
Portuguese Speakers
Posix Users
Postal Service Workers
Pregnant Women
Press
Priests
Primatologists
Privacy Activists
Private Investigators

Programmers

Progressive Music Enthusiasts

Psychiatrists

Psychologists

Public Health Officials

Public Health Professionals

Public Relations Experts

Public Servants

Publishing Professionals

Punsters

Python Language Users

Quakers

Queen Enthusiasts

Radio Broadcasters

Radio Listeners

Railroad Enthusiasts

Rap Enthusiasts

Rappers

Ravers

Readers

Real Estate Brokers

Regulatory Agencies

Rehabilitation Counselors

Religion Students

Republicans

Researchers

Retailers

Retirees

Rock Music Enthusiasts

Role-Playing Enthusiasts

Rolling Stones Enthusiasts

Rowers

Runners

Rush Enthusiasts

Rush Limbaugh Enthusiasts

Russians

Sailors

Sales Professionals

San Francisco Bay Area Residents

Satellite Television Watchers

Scholars

School Children

Science Fiction Readers

Science Teachers

Scientists

Scuba Divers

Securities

Security Workers

Serbians

Sex Researchers

Sex Therapists

Shakers

Shortwave Radio Users

Silicon Graphics Users

Simula Programmers

Singles

Sinologists

Skaters

Skiers

Skydivers

Slavicists

Slovaks

Slovenians

Smokers

Soap Opera Enthusiasts

Soccer Enthusiasts

Social Scientists

Social Workers

Sociologists

Software Designers

Software Developers

South Africans

Space Scientists

Spacemen 3 Enthusiasts

Spaniards

Spanish Speakers

Speech Pathologists

Spelunkers

Sports Card Collectors

Sports Enthusiasts

Sri Lankans

Stage Producers

Star Wars Enthusiasts

State Officials

Statisticians

Stereo Enthusiasts

Stock Brokers

Stockmarket

Storytellers

Students

Students (College/University)

Students (K-12)

Subway Riders

Sun Microsystems Users

Supercomputer Administrators

Systems Operators

Systems Theorists

Taiwanese

Tandy Computer Users

Taxonomists

Teachers

Technical Professionals

Technical Writers

Technicians

Technocrats

Technology Professionals

Telebit Netblazer Users

Telecommunications Experts

Television Professionals

Television Viewers

Tennis Players

Texans

Theologians

Theoretical Biologists

Therapists

Tibetans

Tourists

Toxicologists

Translators

Transportation Professionals

Transsexuals

Transvestites

Travelers/Tourists

Trekkies

Trivia Enthusiasts

Turks

UCLA Students

UIMs Users

Unions

University Administrators

University Biomedical Researchers

University of Colorado Students

University Planners

University Students

Unix System Administrators

Unix Users

Urban Planners

US Citizens

US Congress

USA

Usenet Users

Utah Residents

Utility Professionals

Vangelis Fans

Vegetarians

Veterinarians

Veterinary Pharmacists

Victims of Sexual Abuse

Video Artists

Vietnamese

Vietnamese Americans

Virologists

Virtual Reality Enthusiasts

Visitors

Vocalists

Volkswagon Drivers

Volleyball Enthusiasts
Voters
Washington DC Residents
Wilderness Enthusiasts
Wildlife Biologists
Windows Users
Windsurfers
Winter Sports Fans
Women
Women's Studies Educators
Women's Studies Students
Woodworkers
Workstation Users
Wrestling Fans
Writers
XTC Enthusiasts
Yugoslavians
Zoologists

Appendix

C

Internet Service Providers

Following is an updated and expanded list of commercial Internet account providers. The providers listed below run businesses that provide electronic accounts through which you can access the Internet. These include many nonprofit community computing services known as *free-nets*.

Commercial Online Data Vendors

It is important to know about the existence of the major online systems such as Dialog, Nexis/Lexis, Orbit, and CD Plus, that are accessible over the Internet. These private online worlds are complementary to the information available over the Internet, although many are quite costly to access and require specially learned research skills to handle their specific search protocols.

These online systems have been building extraordinary archives of information going back decades in many cases. The following is a chart of the major online system providers. You will need to contact them directly to set up a password to their systems and to find out about the availability of online training.

Provider	Phone	E-mail Address
Dialog (Dialog Information Systems)	telnet://dialog.com	(800) 334-2564
DataStar (Dialog Information Systems)	(800) 334-2564	telnet://dialog.com
Dow Jones News Retrieval (Mead Data)	(800) 227-4908 (513) 859-5398	telnet://nex.meaddata.co
Lexis (Mead Data)	(800) 227-4908 (513) 859-5398	telnet://nex.meaddata.com
BRS (CD Plus)	(800) 950-2035	staff@cdplus.com
Orbit Questel, Inc.	(703) 442-0900	telonet://orbit.com

Private Network Providers with their own Worlds of Information

In addition to actual Internet Access Providers, there are private network providers in the United States, and in other countries, that offer a variety of services including their own worlds of information and proprietary user environments." Some of these maintain and make available elaborate and specialized databases for access by their subscribers. They generally are closed systems, with only e-mail access to the Internet. However, technologies are being developed by which the private and the public Internet can be made seamless. The following provides basic contact information for the major providers that fall in to this category.

America Online provides access to a wide variety of media and reference sources, popular newspapers, magazines, and vendor support. Chat lines are also a major offering (715,000+ subscribers). For more information, call (800) 827-6364.

CompuServe has over 2000 separate resources with many of the largest forums available online. In addition to an array of financial and professional services, CompuServe provides a wide diversity of entertainment services, and a growing shopping service that also offers graphics (1.5 million subscribers). For more information, call (800) 848-8199.

Delphi offers a comprehensive selection of news, reference resources, and computer information as well as full gateway access to the Internet. Special-interest groups, conferences, and online games are major features of this service (200,000 subscribers). For more information, call (800) 544-4005 or contact Delphi via e-mail at info@delphi.com

GEnie provides a large menu of news and information services, special-interest groups, games, and databases. GEnie's RoundTables (RTs) provide discussion areas devoted to specific topics; file libraries, bulletin boards, and real-time chat (RTC) are special features of this service (150,000+ subscribers). For more information, contact GEnie at (800) 638-9636.

Prodigy is a "family-oriented" service providing shopping, travel, and personal finance, and specializing in up-to-the-minute information such as news, sports, and weather. Prodigy also offers a large collection of shareware programs (1.2 million subscribers).

Ziffnet is an online service with information on buying, using, supporting, and understanding personal computer products. Ziffnet is a major resource for technical support. For more information, contact Ziffnet at (800) 635-6225.

Appendix

D

Glossary of Terms, Acronyms, and the Language of the Internet

We are indebted to Hans J. Rocke, University of California at Davis, for his initial work in compiling this glossary.

A

Absolute address   An address that indicates, in machine language code, the exact storage location where data or machine instructions are to be found.

access To find or store information in memory or on a peripheral device such as a magnetic tape or disk drive. To communicate in some way with a device.

Access method   Any of the data-management techniques available to the user for transferring data from memory to an input/output device, or vice versa.

Access time   The time interval between the instant at which data is requested to be retrieved or stored, and the instant at which the operation is carried out.

address   A location on a disk or in memory within which a specific piece of information can be stored, or the number assigned to that location. See also absolute address, indirect address.

ADMD   Administrative Management Domain.

Anonymous FTP   An access command that enables Internet users to retrieve files from various servers without actually having accounts on those servers. A copy of the anonymous FTP list enables users to determine the location of files available on the Internet.

Application   A computer program that is applied to performing a specific task.

Archie   An information agent that conducts searches against data stored at various anonymous FTP sites, and indexes them for easy access by users.

Archive

1.   The storage of files (often in archived and compressed form) for future use, or the storage area that holds those files.

2.   To create an archive, to move a file into an archive, or to bundle multiple files together into a larger archive or library file.

ARPA   Advanced Research Projects Agency of the United States Department of Defense.

Artificial intelligence   Computer programs that perform functions, often by imitation, that are normally associated with human reasoning and knowledge.

ASCII   (American Standard Code For Information Interchange) A character encoding standard that uses 7 of the 8 bits of a byte to define the codes for 128 characters (27). For example, in ASCII the number 7 is treated as a character and is encoded as 00010111. Because a byte can have a total of 256 possible values (28), there are an additional 128 possible characters that can be encoded into a byte, but there is no formal ASCII standard for those additional 128 characters. Most IBM-compatible personal computers do use an IBM extended character set that includes international characters, line and box drawing characters, Greek letters, and mathematical symbols.

ASR   (Automatic Send and Receive) Having the capability to receive data and produce it on a printer or to send it through a keyboard.

Asynchronous Having a variable time interval between characters, bits, or events.

Automation   The implementation of several processes by automatic means.

B

Backbone   A single-protocol connection among different systems. Each system has a gateway to the common backbone protocol.

Bandwidth   The difference (in hertz) between the upper and lower limits of wave frequencies transmitted over a communications channel.

Baud   In communications, a unit of transmission speed of digital signals. It is the reciprocal of the length in seconds of the shortest element of the digital code. Generally a baud will equate to a bit (of data) per second.

BBS   (Bulletin Board System) BBSs began as computers running software that permitted people dial-up access, the capability to store messages for other dial-up users, and to retrieve messages left for them. BBSs were the source of the concept of electronic discussion groups, because people could leave and retrieve messages around individual topics.

The concept of the BBS was transferred to the Internet, the software was modified, and now hundreds of Usenet and ListServ discussion groups operate on the same principles: a topic is stated, and people interested in the topic send and receive messages, and conduct discussions from all around the world.

Many programs now archive the discussions so that newcomers can retrieve threads of conversation that took place before they joined a discussion.

Bit   Contraction of binary and digit. A bit is the smallest unit of information that a computer can work with. Each bit is either a one or a zero. Often computers work with chunks of bits rather than one bit at a time; the smallest chunk of bits a computer usually works with consists of 8 bits, or a byte.

Bitmapping   A digital representation of an image in which all dots or pixels making up the image correspond to specifically assigned bits in memory.

BITNET   (Because It's Time Network) A low-cost, low-speed network that was developed to satisfy a need for providing distributed network access beyond the limits of the original ARPAnet network.

Block   Physical data consisting of a fixed number of characters or records, and moved as a unit during transmission.

Body/subject   The body of an e-mail message is the actual text of a message. The subject is a special field that gives the content of a message. Many SMTP programs take advantage of the Subject line to provide sorting capabilities. Through the clever use of Subject lines, an e-mail handling facility can perform as a small but useful database.

Boolean   A system of logic devised by George Boole using a series of symbolic terms such as and, or, and not to express the relationship of data elements to one another.

Bounced message   An e-mail message might not reach its destination for any of several reasons. The address might have been typed incorrectly, the Domain Name Server might not recognize an alias, the recipient's computer might be down for maintenance, and so on. In such cases, a message is sent back to the sender to inform them that their message has not been delivered. Sometimes, the information provided in the header reveals why the message was undelivered.

Byte Eight bits. A byte is simply a chunk of 8 ones and zeros. For example 01000001 is a byte. A byte is equal to one column in a file written in character format.

C

CCA

1. Common Cryptographic Architecture; IBM encryption software for MVS and DOS applications.

2. Compatible Communications Architecture; network equipment technology protocol for transmitting asynchronous data over X.25 networks. (See X.25.)

3. Communications Control Architecture; a US Navy network that includes an ISDN backbone called bits.

CCITT (Consultative Committee Of International Telephone And Telegraph) Part of the International Telecommunications Union, a UN treaty organization, setting international standards for worldwide telecommunication, for example, X.25. (see X.25.)

CD-ROM Compact Disk Read Only Memory.

Cello A WWW browser that works under Microsoft Windows and enables people with a connection to the Internet to follow Hypertext (or Hypermedia) links to files and information services all over the world. It displays both regular text files and files that are written in HTML format, and will translate different Internet services such as Gopher, News, and FTP into a format that appears to the user as if it were a hypertext document. It was written by Thomas Bruce of the Legal Information Institute at Cornell Law School. (Extracted from the Cello FAQ.)

You also can use Cello and the WWW-HTML hypertext markup standard to build local hypertext systems on LANs, on single machines, and so on. Cello also permits the post-processing of any file for which you've set up an association in the Windows File Manager—for example, if you download an uncompressed Microsoft Word file from an FTP site, and the appropriate association exists in File Manager, Cello will run MS-Word on it for you. This same capability is used to view graphics and listen to sound files you get from the Net.

Chains In Hypertext, linking randomly located material by means of address information included within the stored item, which cites the location of the succeeding and preceding item in the sequence. Chains permit users to traverse the Internet via links within documents to their origin, or cited materials. The links of the chain provide navigation information, and the user merely needs to click on a link to be moved to a (possibly remote) document whose address is contained in the link.

Channel Any communications pathway between two computers or between a terminal and a computer. It might refer to the physical medium, such as coaxial cable, or to a specific carrier frequency (subchannel) within a larger channel or wireless medium.

Character encoding scheme A method of encoding characters including alphabetic characters (a-z, uppercase and lowercase), numbers 0-9, punctuation and other marks (for example, comma, period, space, &, *), and various control characters (for example, Tab, carriage return, linefeed) using binary numbers. For a computer to print a capital A or a number 7

on the computer screen, for instance, you must have a way to tell the computer that a particular group of bits represents an A or a 7. Standards, commonly called "character sets," exist to establish that a particular byte stands for an A and a different byte stands for a 7. A common standard for representing characters in bytes is known as ASCII.

Character format Any file format in which information is encoded as characters using only a standard character encoding → scheme. A file written in "character format" contains only those bytes that are prescribed in the encoding scheme as corresponding to the characters in the scheme (for example, alphabetic and numeric characters, punctuation marks, and spaces). A file written in the ASCII character format would store the number "7" in eight bits (for instance, one byte) 00010111. A file written in EBCDIC would store the number "7" in eight bits as 11110111.

Client The user of a network service; also used to describe a computer that relies upon another computer for some of all of its resources.

Client server

1. Architecture in which the client is the requesting machine (PC or workstation) and the server is the supplying machine (LAN file server, mini or mainframe). The client provides the user interface and performs some or most of the application processing. The server maintains the databases and processes requests from the client to extract data from or update the database. The server also controls the application's integrity and security.

2. Request/supply relationship between programs. Applications can be designed, whether running within the same computer or in multiple computers, in which one program (the client) requests data from another program (the server). In X-window, for example, the server is software that manages the display screen, and the client is the application that asks the server to display something.

Column A single vertical column in a data file that is one byte in length. Fixed-format data files traditionally are described as being arranged in lines and columns. In a fixed-format file, column locations describe the locations of variables.

Compatibility The capability of one device to interconnect or share programs or data with another by means of having the same code, speed, and signal level.

Compress To reduce the size of a file considerably by removing redundant information. Compressed files are more economical to transmit through the Internet or to store. To use the file, it must be exploded, or reconstituted.

Connect time The time during which an operator is in contact with a computer online. This is different from compute time, in which the operator actually is utilizing the computer's resources.

CREN (Corporation for Research and Educational Networking) A merger of BITNET and CSNET networks.

Cyberspace A term coined by William Gibson in his novel Neuromancer that refers to a futuristic computer network that people use by plugging their brains into it.

D

DASD Direct Access Storage Device.

Data

1. A general term for any collection of information, facts, numbers, letters, or symbols that refer to or describe an object, idea, condition, situation, or other factors.

2. Name of an android in Star Trek-The Next Generation.

Data network A telecommunications network built specifically for data transmission, rather than for voice transmission.

database A set of organized data stored in or available to a computer that can be used by the computer or its operator to perform various tasks. The database is not the program; rather it's the information with which the program will work.

Datagram The basic unit of information passed across the Internet. It consists of a source and destination address along with data. Large messages are broken into a sequence of IP datagrams.

Decryption Encoding a message to its original meaningful form by means of a key.

Document delivery A service that provides printed copies (full-text) of articles, reports, and publications, usually by subscription. Some services are connected to the Internet.

Domain A part of the naming hierarchy. Syntactically, a domain name consists of a sequence of names or other words separated by periods (for example, @prep.ai.mit.edu).

Domain name server A computer table that lists the IP numeric addresses of computers on the Internet, and their given common name. Generally, it is easier to remember a computer site by name, but the network stores the numerical address. Domain Name Servers keep track of which name belongs to which numerical address.

Domain Name System (DNS) A global naming system for use in UNIX networking for general-purpose, name-to-resource mapping. While in the Internet the network information center manages the higher-echelon domain names, the bulk of the management is decentralized to the lower-echelon sub-domains. Each name server in an Internet community is responsible for a personal piece of the global name hierarchy over which it has authority.

DOS (disk operating system) Any of a number of widely used operating systems, so-called because a primary function they provide is the control of auxiliary storage in the form of disks.

Download To transmit data from one central computer to another device or to a remote terminal.

Driver A program that controls (drives) the operation of a device or interface. The driver program interprets the computer data, providing the commands and signals required by the device or interface. The driver can output directly to the device or interface, or can provide paper output.

Duplex Pertaining to a transmission system where data can be received and transmitted. Half duplex can only transmit or receive. Full duplex can transmit and receive simultaneously.

E

E-mail   See electronic mail.

Electronic mail   A message service using electronics and telecommunications to deliver hard- or soft-copy information. These can take the form of text-only messages or of images that include text in font form and graphic material.

Emotives   The communication of emotional nuance to a written communication which is otherwise communicated by tone of voice in verbal communication. It is, for example, difficult to convey sarcasm or tongue-in-cheek comments in written fashion. To replicate that capability, a series of emotive symbols (frequently called smileys because they resemble smiling faces, tilted on their side (:-)) have developed. Emotives can convey happiness, sadness, pouting, tongue-in-cheek, and a variety of other nuances that usually are conveyed by tone of voice and body language.

Encryption   An algorithm designed to protect the interpretation and use of intellectual property in electronic files against unauthorized use.

End user   The person or organization who will directly use a particular set of information or a device.

Error   Any discrepancy between the theoretically correct behavior or values in a computer and the actual behavior or values. Most computers have routines specifically designed to detect the presence of errors.

Escape (Esc)   A control code that indicates that the next code has a different meaning than it would usually have.

Ethernet   A communications protocol developed by Xerox Corporation, widely used for local area networks.

F

FAQ (frequently asked questions) Novices to the Internet commonly face the same problems as their predecessors, and ask similar questions. FAQs are files containing the answers to the most frequently asked questions. FAQs have been expanded to cover a range of topics, so a user may find FAQ files on specific non-Internet related topics.

File   A physical unit of storage on a computer disk or tape.

File server   A computer that stores files on the Internet, and makes such files available for access by one of the various Internet access tools.

File transfer protocol (FTP)   A reliable method of transferring files over the Internet.

Finger   A software application whose purpose is to query information files about individual Internet users. The user places information regarding his phone number, address, or affiliation in a file, and the finger software retrieves such files upon request.

Firewall   A security program created to prevent incoming access from the Internet to a closed network system.

Firmware   Software that is stored in read-only memory (ROM). Firmware functions are not programmable by the user.

Fixed format   A file structure consisting of physical records of a constant size within which the precise location of each variable is based on the column location and width of the variable.

Flame   This is a pejorative term, signifying a breach of netiquette. Flaming can be losing ones temper, or it can mean calling into question someones personal opinions or observation. If you type your e-mail messages in all caps, you might inadvertently be accused of flaming.

FreeNet   An organization whose purpose is to provide access to the Internet to as many people as possible. The first such effort was established by the highly-successful Cleveland FreeNet. Such networks make Internet resources available to the public by providing access at affordable charges. They also frequently provide support and aid in connecting to and navigating across the Internet.

FTP   See file transfer protocol.

Full-text   Referring to a database that contains entire documents as opposed to citations or abstracts.

G

Gate-keeping system   A method of facilitating as well as controlling the process of gathering, organizing, filtering, distributing, and exchanging information in various formats between sources and users.

Gateway   The electronic communications node that connects the individual user with specific mainframes or networks.

Glitch   A sudden temporary mishap, error, or malfunction in mechanical, electrical, or electronic equipment.

GOPHER   A software tool developed at the University of Minnesota. GOPHER enables multiple platform types running a customizable client to access a centralized server that provides coherent translation of information in myriad forms. It also enables a user to retrieve information available from thousands of GOPHER servers, anonymous FTP connections, publicly accessible Telnet connections, World-Wide Web servers, Novell networks, WAIS servers, and many more sources throughout the world.

GOPHER is a menu-driven system. Each gopher server has links to other GOPHER servers so that one can seamlessly bounce from one server to another with no perceived change of environments. GOPHER'S down side is in finding the proper resource. Hundreds of GOPHERS now exist, each with numerous submenus. Somewhere buried in some gopher server on the other side of the world might be an important resource for which you have been looking. Unfortunately, there is no easy way to know about that resource unless you start a lengthy and time-consuming GOPHER tour.

H

Handshake   A protocol wherein a transmitting device sends a signal, and then the receiving device sends a ready signal before the transmission continues.

Hard-wired   Pertaining to the direct wiring of a terminal to a computer system (or any device to any device), as opposed to devices that communicate through telephone lines or wireless media.

Header   Part of an e-mail message generated by the transmission protocols that provide information about who originated a message, when it was posted, its pathway of travel across the Internet, and certain machine identifications along the way.

Hierarchical file   A file containing information that is organized in subordinate levels or with a relational structure.

Host   A system or subsystem in a network that performs actual processing operations against a database, and with which other network devices communicate.

Host computer   The computer and associated database that run as a separate entity, but can be accessed through the network.

Host site   The location (station) that receives communications from the other points in the network, performs operations on them through a host computer, and sends communications back to other points.

HTML (Hypertext Mark-up Language)   In practical terms, HTML is a collection of styles used to define the various components of a World-Wide Web document. Used in WWW documents to embed style information (fonts, font sizes, and layout), graphics, and hypertext links (URLs) to other Internet files and resources.

HTTP (Hypertext Terminal Protocol)   Used as a prefix in a URL, this string of letters tells the application that the address that follows is accessible as a WWW server. (See also URLs.)

Hypertext   A term coined by Ted Nelson (Xanadu) to describe a form of relationships that is nonlinear. Most text is intended to be read one paragraph at a time in a serial fashion. Given electronic capabilities, it is possible to link one paragraph with another one in a different location, perhaps even on an entirely different computer. Hypertext describes these more fluid relationships.

I

IF (interactive facsimiles)   A computer function that merges voice with facsimile transmissions to be carried over the Internet.

Indirect address   An instruction that references an address specified in the content of another address.

Information Agent   A software application whose purpose is to act on behalf of a database, updating it from information it retrieves from other databases. Archie and Veronica are examples of Information Agents.

Input

1. The process of entering data through a keyboard or terminal or other device.
2. The material that is entered through a keyboard or other device.

Intelligence   The capability of a device to make computational and evaluative decisions under the control of a program.

Interactive

1. Relating to the capability of a device or procedure that enables an operator to make decisions that influence the outcome of a procedure in process.
2. Pertaining to a device that enables an operator to input data or commands and then responds in some way to the operator.

Interface   The point and manner in which two separate systems or devices connect and interact with one another.

Internet Yellow Pages

1. A directory of Internet resources maintained in database format by a non-profit institution, for the benefit of the Internet community.

2. The New Riders publication that makes available directory information in printed form.

Internet   A concatenation of many individual TCP/IP campus, state, regional, and national networks (such as NSFnet, ARPAnet, and MILnet) into one single logical network all sharing a common addressing scheme.

IP   Internet Protocol.

IP address   The Internet protocol numerical address assigned to each computer on the network, so that its location and activities can be distinguished from other computers.

ISDN   Integrated Services Digital Network.

K

Kernel   The level of an operating system or networking system that contains the system-level commands or all of the functions hidden from the user. In a UNIX system, the kernel is a program that contains the device drivers, the memory management routines, the scheduler, and system calls. This program is always running while the system is operating.

L

LAN   local area network.

Laser   Light amplification by stimulated emission of radiation.

ListServ   A feature of e-mail that enables a single message to be "served" or delivered to many addresses simultaneously. The recipients e-mail address must appear on a distribution "list" in order to receive these reflected messages.

Local area network (LAN)   A collection of devices and communication channels that connects a group of computers and peripheral devices together so that they can communicate with each other. Typically, local area networks occupy a single building or office area.

Log

1. A record of operations on a file, indicating actions, such as file creation, modification, errors, and other data.

2. To sign on (log on) or off (log off) a computer system or area. Log on procedures might require operator passwords, or might be accomplished simply by designating the desired area.

M

Majordomo   Majordomo is a set of programs written in Perl that automate operation of multiple mailing lists. Majordomo automatically handles routine requests to subscribe or unsubscribe; it also has "closed lists" that route all subscription requests to a "list owner" for approval. It also supports "moderated lists" that send all messages to the list owner for approval before they're sent to subscribers.

MAPI   Message Application Programming Interface.

MD   Management domain.

MELVYL®   A centralized information system for all nine campuses of the University of California. It includes a library catalog database, a periodicals database, article citation databases, and other files and can be accessed through UC lines or the Internet.

Memory   The internal storage capacity of a computer system. Memory generally is located on some magnetic device such as disk, drum, or core. Data is stored in digitally encoded bytes, and manipulated as needed during calculation processes. The amount of memory a computer has directly affects its capability to perform complex functions.

MHS   Message Handling System.

MILNET   Military network.

MIME   (Multipurpose Internet Mail Extensions)   A code to specify the format of Internet messages, identifying text, program, mail-message, image, audio, video, and multipart (mixed media) files.

Mode   A particular condition or state under which a computer or other device can operate, such as an insert mode, a communications mode, or a binary mode. Operations or commands can take on different meanings in different modes.

Modem (Modulator/demodulator)   Connects computers at remote sites to the telephone system by converting data from the host computer into electronic signals, which are transmitted through the network to the target computer where another modem converts them back into machine-readable data. Modems can send as well as receive data, enabling computers to "converse" with one another.

MOSAIC

1. A free Macintosh client browser for World Wide Web servers. The program can access linked data on Internet servers through many protocols: Archie, gopher, wide area information servers, ftp (file transfer protocol), Telnet, and network news transfer protocol. The program requires system 7 and MacTCP 2.0.2. Mosaic is available through anonymous ftp from `ftp.ncsa.uiuc.edu` in the directory /MAC/mosaic.

2. Netware for Mac developed by Novell Inc. Allows users to share non-PostScript printers connected to the PC portion of a Netware network. The software intercepts the PostScript print job and translates it into PCL (printer control language) before sending it to the Netware server's print services.

3. Acronym for Macro-Connectionist Organization System For Artificial Intelligence Computation. This expert system has two medical applications, one for the diagnosis of kidney graft rejections, and one for the management of hypertension.

4. A program containing a Trojan horse strain that destroys the directories of all available unlocked hard and floppy disks, including the one on which it resides. Even unmounted but available SCSI hard disks are mounted and destroyed by the Trojan.

Mouse   A hand-held input device, similar to a keyboard, but limited to such interactions with graphics images on the screen as pointing, clicking, and dragging.

MUD (Multi-User Dungeon)   Games have been an important (and sometimes controversial) part of distributed networks. MUDs are sophisticated forms of Dungeons and Dragons in which many individuals can play the game simultaneously, confronting each other in the virtual dungeon made by the software.

MUDs have serious purposes, too. Programming solutions to problems involving multiple simultaneous access (a situation that comes up in many standard workgroup and collaborative applications) are thoroughly tested in such environments.

Multiplex   To transmit simultaneously two or more messages over the same communications channel to different receivers.

MX Record (Mail Exchange Record)   One of the components through which e-mail that is addressed to you actually gets to you. The MX Record tells domain name servers about routing and location instructions.

N

Network   Two or more computers linked together physically or through telecommunications for the purpose of electronically sharing resources such as computer files, programs, and peripheral devices.

Network control program (NCP)   A program within the software of a data processing system that controls the performance of a telecommunications network.

Network file system (NFS)   A process for mounting magnetic disks on a network so that disks not physically attached to a computer appear as if they were physically attached.

Node   A branching or exchange point in a network.

Noise   Unwanted signal or signals on an electrical circuit.

Noise immunity   The capability of a device to accept valid signals while rejecting invalid signals.

Non-switched line   A communications link permanently installed between two points.

NREN   (National Research and Education Network)   Fiber-optic (improved capacity and transmission speed) network to link all education facilities, including grade schools and libraries, higher education institutions, and government organizations.

NSFNET The National Science Foundation Network   The national backbone network, funded by the National Science Foundation and operated by the Merit Corporation, used to interconnect regional (mid-level) networks, such as WestNet, to one another.

Null modem   The communications cable used in hardwiring.

Numeric database   A database primarily containing numbers.

O

OCR   See Optical Character Recognition.

Octet   The grouping of eight numbers in a pair and two triplets as used in the domain name system; for example. 35.222.222.

Offline   Pertaining to a device or function that is not electronically connected to the main device. Media transmission from an offline device must be by means of manually carried material (disk or tape) or through telephone lines.

Online   Pertaining to devices that are electronically connected to the computer. Generally, an online device is treated as if it were an integral part of the computer system.

Online Public Access Catalog (OPAC)   A database of bibliographic records to which the public has access, reflecting the material owned by a library or a consortium of libraries.

OPAC   Online Public Access Catalog.

Operating system   The program or set of programs that control a computer's operations and monitor the functions of the other programs.

Optical Character Recognition (OCR)   A method of converting graphic symbols (particularly alphanumeric) to electronic signals by means of a reading device that recognizes character shapes. Until recently, material prepared for optical character recognition had to be typed in a specific format and with a specific type element.

Optical disk   A rigid, plastic disk, 4 3/4" in diameter, with an embedded metallic underside on which data are recorded permanently by laser (ROM, read-only-memory). Also known as compact disk, CD, or CD-ROM. Digital information is recorded on a master disk with a strong laser beam. Copies are made by "stamping" 4 3/4 inch disks. They are read by a weaker laser beam. It is a high-density storage medium, with a capacity of 600 MB.

Optical scanner   A device that uses light to scan and convert text, graphics, or other visual images into digitized data that can be read by a computer.

OSI Open System Interconnection.

P

Packet   An addressed data unit of convenient size for transmission through a network.

Parallel interface A data transmission technique in which a group of binary digits (bits) are transferred simultaneously over multiple lines. Usually, eight bits that correspond to a character are transferred as a single operation.

Parameter

1. A designation for the format of type, as requested by command codes or system defaults. Line length, page depth, typeface, and leading are examples of parameters. Commands that take place as they are entered and do not maintain their effect (such as extra leading, cancel escapement, and so on) are not parameters.

2. (program parameter) A constant or variable that remains unchanged in a subroutine, and fully or partly specifies a process to be performed during the subroutine.

3. (hardware parameter) a parameter characteristic of a machine that establishes certain limitations or capabilities of the machine. For instance, a parameter of a typesetter might be its ability to process 160 lines per minute.

Parity   The transmission of data so that all codes have either an even or an odd number of one-bits. Even parity means that one bit has been added to the codes with an odd number of one-bits so that the total is even, and odd parity means that all the even codes have a bit added so that they have an odd number of one-bits.

Parity check   A method of verifying the accuracy of a transmitted bit pattern by examining the code to determine whether its value is odd or even.

Password   An identification number keyed by the operator and checked by the computer before the database may be accessed.

Pay-by-the-drink   A method of charging the user every time a file is accessed, based on the number of connect time units elapsed and records inspected. This is in contrast to paying a subscription or license fee that permits repeated and unlimited access to the files and records for the duration of the stipulated period of time.

Peripheral   A device that is external to the system processor but operates under the processor's control, such as a line printer or a communications signal.

Platform   A manufacturer's operating system for functions that have not been standardized in the industry and require intermediary programs to interpret the commands across different systems.

Port   A communications channel between a computer and another device, such as a terminal, modem, or printer.

POP (Post Office Protocol)   A software application that enables individual e-mail users (POP clients) to retrieve mail from a central mail depository (POP server).

PostScript   Software made by Adobe for desktop publishing. A page description language that many laser printers understand. The next step is a PostScript-based non-application-specific document-interchange software that will allow searching and indexing.

PPP (Point-to-Point Protocol)   Like SLIP, PPP is a software application that allows a computer to use Internet protocols to become a terminal node on the Internet. PPP requires a high-speed modem and standard telephone line.

Printer   A peripheral device connected to a computer to render images on paper in black and white or color. Pigments can be transferred from a ribbon pressed against the print surface by an array of wires (matrix or impact printer), heated to sputtering and directed through tiny holes (ink jet) or electrostatically attached to a metal drum and transferred to paper by the xerographic method (laser).

Printout   Display of file contents in text or graphics form on paper.

Program   Series of instructions to direct the computer to perform specific tasks in a certain order.

Prompt   An on-screen processing technique that questions or "prompts" the user of a computer system for responses.

Protocol   The proper procedure and sequence of events for data transmission of a particular input device, with regard to code structure, identification of the text stream, and code recognition.

Q

Query   A data message structured so as to elicit a response from a computer.

R

RAM   Random Access Memory.

Random access   Access to data, information, or files without observing any particular order.

Random Access Memory (RAM)   A form of volatile memory that allows data (such as documents) to be stored randomly and retrieved directly by an address location. The system accesses the addressed material, with no need to read through intervening data. Information can be retrieved more speedily from random access memory than from serial media such as tape.

Raw data   Data that has not been processed, reorganized, or manipulated.

Read-only memory (ROM)   Memory that is programmed at the time of manufacture. It can be accessed only and cannot be erased. Non-volatile, read-only memory holds its contents after the power is shut off. It can be used to contain an operating system, language translators, and other "permanent" software.

Real time   Pertaining to the performance of a computer in such a way that the operator receives responses quickly enough so that there is no effective delay in the operator's activity.

Remote   Pertaining to communication with a device located at some distance from the central device, but connected in some way, with cables, wires, or telephone hookup.

Rich text format (RTF)   A text exchange standard proposed by apple to provide an application independent file format including fonts, tab positions, rulers, line breaks, hyphenation, paragraph spacing, embedded objects, such as pictures and sounds, and special text styles.

ROM   Read-only memory.

Router   A dedicated computer that sends packets from one place to another, paying attention to the current state of the network.

RS-232 Port   A standard plug with 25 pins, used to connect computers and I/O devices.

RTF   Rich text format.

S

Screen   The display surface of a video terminal or cathode ray tube.

Scroll   A function available on most video terminals where the display image seems to move up and down (or left and right) on the screen to provide incremental viewing of material earlier or later in the file.

Search The electronic comparison of character strings entered by the operator with those contained in files or databases, arranged in Boolean logic expressions.

Server A network computer that shares its resources, such as files and printer, with other computers; for example, Network file system (NFS).

SFQL Structured Full-Text Query Language.

SGML Standard Generalized Markup Language.

Sign on To connect with a remote computer by providing identification details and performing appropriate procedures.

Signal The electrical quantity that coveys data from one point to another.

Signature

1. One of the requirements for a fully-functional Internet is to provide unique signatures with which to identify individuals (for example, for the purpose of verifying authorization to move funds.) A number of cryptographic solutions to individual signatures have been proposed, most of which depend on a unique encoding pattern that is known only to a single individual.

2. In e-mail, a piece of text that identifies the sender of an e-mail message. Some people develop elaborate and attractive signatures by which their messages are personalized.

Simplex A modem that either sends or receives information but cannot do both during one transmission.

Simultaneous transmission The transmission of data in two directions at one, both sending and receiving, by the same device.

Site license Authorization (usually subject to a fee) to have multiple copies for simultaneous use within a specified organization or location.

SLIP (Serial Line Internet Protocol) A software application that allows a computer to use Internet protocols to become a terminal node on the Internet. SLIP requires a high-speed modem and standard telephone line.

Smiley Symbols by which one can tell the emotional timbre of a given e-mail message. Smileys, such as :), provide emotive qualities in a shorthand fashion.

SMTP (Simple Mail Transport Protocol) The protocol by which e-mail messages are managed by computers on the Internet. It provides the possibility of designing e-mail servers and e-mail clients. Many of the popular e-mail handling programs, such as Eudora, take advantage of the SMTP protocol to make e-mailing easy and efficient.

Software A term coined to contrast computer programs with the hardware of a computer system. Software is a stored set of instructions that governs the operation of a computer system and makes the hardware run.

Stand-alone Referring to a device that is capable of performing the functions for which it is designed without the aid of or connection to another, smarter device. The stand-alone device can receive media from another device for processing.

Standard Generalized Markup Language (SGML) Enables data to move between media by describing documents by their structural elements rather than their visual format and thus permitting further analysis or reuse by various application programs.

Star A network configuration in which a central controller communicates directly with each device or station. A diagram of this configuration looks like a star.

Station One of the input or output points of a communications system or of a multi-user computer.

Stop bit In asynchronous communication, a marker following each character.

String A sequence of entities, such as characters or commands.

Structured Query Language (SQL) A data access language designed to work with relational databases. First used on IBMs dB2, SQL (pronounced sequel) became a de facto standard in the mid-1980s.

Surfing The enjoyable act of browsing for files and interesting gems of information on the Internet. This should be contrasted with the more goal-oriented activity of finding a particular piece of information. The aim of *The New Riders Official Internet Yellow Pages* is to facilitate the latter without limiting any of the pleasure of the former.

Synchronous Occurring concurrently and with a regular or predictable time relationship. In transmission, referring to the capability of the sending and the receiving devices to run continuously at the same frequency.

System A machine or devices using various hardware and software to accomplish certain tasks. Commonly composed of a central processor, with one or more input or output devices, and capable of making decisions about the material that is being processed. Various fields of computer technology tend to define "system" in slightly different ways.

T

TCP/IP Transmission Control Protocol/Internet Protocol

Telecommunication The transmission of signals by telegraph, radio, satellite, or some other means that does not involve physical connection between the sending and receiving devices.

Teleprocessing Computer operations carried out through long- distance communications network.

Teletext A generic term for one-way information retrieval systems that broadcast digitally encoded text and graphics to remote users. Teletext users request pages of transmitted data by means of a keyboard.

TELNET The Internet standard protocol for remote terminal connection service. TELNET enables a user at one site to interact with a remote time-sharing system at another site as if the user's terminal were connected directly to the remote computer.

Terminal A device (usually with a video display) on which an operator can communicate with or receive communication from a computer.

Terminal emulation A software capability in which a computer or terminal can be made to simulate the characteristics of another terminal for communications compatibility.

Terminal server A small, specialized networked computer that connects many terminals to a LAN through one network connection. Any user on the network can then connect to various network hosts.

Text A series of words or characters having some meaning to the reader, as opposed to command codes or instructions.

Throughput The net speed of a device or system, including input, output, and processing speeds together. The throughput speed may be slower than the inherent input or output speeds because input might be slowed by simultaneous output, or vice versa, or input and output might have to take place serially.

Timesharing The use of a computer for two or more purposes during the same time interval. The computer shares its attention among the devices by means of some monitoring program.

Token sharing network A communications network designed so that all computer devices (stations) on the network are connected to a common channel, called a *bus*. A group of bits (a token) is passed from station to station to give each station in turn the opportunity to transmit data.

Transmission Control Protocol (TCP) A set of protocols, resulting from ARPA efforts, used by the Internet to support services such as remote login (TELNET), file transfer (FTP) and mail (SMTP).

Transparent Pertaining to a process that is thoroughly compatible with another process so that a user is not necessarily aware that there is more than one process or function involved. A computer program that can be added to an existing program without retraining or reeducating its users is transparent to the original program.

Tree

1. (tree structure) An arrangement of data in a hierarchical form, with each group of data containing subgroups that present more detail.

2. A network configuration in which a central controller communicates to a number of other devices or stations, each of which in turn communicates to another group of devices or stations in an hierarchy.

U

UNIX A computer operating system developed by Bell Laboratories, written in the C programming language, and distinguished by its portability to different computers. It's widely used in graphics workstations.

Upload The function of sending a file from one computer and transferring it to another. Download, on the other hand, refers to the transfer of a file from another computer onto your own.

URL Uniform Resource Locator.

Usenet   An Internet system of discussion groups, some of which may contain thousands of members, and others a mere handful. Most Usenet discussions are archived so that Internet users can query the archives and download threads of discussion centered on specific topics.

User friendly   A characterization of computer products that are easy to learn or to use.

V

Value-added   Enhancement of documents or data to increase their usefulness, such as gatekeeping and validation (for instance, by peer review), and substantive and copy editing by publishers. Libraries add value by selection, cataloging, archiving, and providing access. Electronic publishing adds value by providing full-text searching, audio, video, animation, large data sets, reducing the time required for publication, and ease of access from workstations.

Veronica   An information agent that is used to conduct searches against data stored on various Gopher servers.

Video Display Terminal (VDT)   An operator station that includes a display screen as part of its hardware. VDTs at one time were called CRTs (cathode ray tubes).

Virtual library   Extends resources through access to bibliographic databases, full-text files, images, and other information in electronic format.

Voice grade   Referring to the capability of a data transmission circuit to permit a transfer rate of up to 2400 bits per second (BAUD). A voice-grade circuit uses analog phone lines identical to standard telephone equipment, and encodes digital data into tones for transmission.

W

WAIS   Wide Area Information Server.

Wide Area Information Server (WAIS)   A method of searching indexed text. You can take a hundred files on the topic of numerical analysis and index them into one SRC file. New resources are announced in a special indexed database called "directory-of-servers," which solves the gopher problem mentioned earlier.

Wide Area Network (WAN)   A network spanning hundreds or thousands of miles, in contrast to a local area network.

World Wide Web (WWW)   Hypertext that goes beyond gopher by displaying menus and beyond WAIS by allowing pointers and chains within the text. Hypertext links can lead you down a fruitful path or to a dead end.

X

X.25   CCITT standard (1976) for the protocols and message formats that define the interface between a terminal and a packet switching network.

X.400   Global electronic messaging architecture.

Z

Z39.50   Application-layer protocol standard developed by the American National Standards Institute in 1992 for computer-to-computer information retrieval. A number of companies and universities are using it to develop interoperable search-and-retrieval software products for accessing the Internet. The open systems interconnection (OSI) model defines z39.50, but because OSI is not built into the UNIX operating system like TCP/IP, z39.50 was adapted to run over TCP/IP for the Internet.

APPENDIX

E

Further Readings

Badget, Tom, and Corey Sandler, *Welcome to... Internet: From Mystery to Mastery,* MIS: Press, NY, a subsidiary of Holt and Co., Inc., 1993, ISBN 1-55828-308-0

Blackman, Josh, *The Legal Researcher's Internet Directory, 1993/1994*, Legal Research of New York, Brooklyn, NY, 1993

Braun, Eric, *The Internet Directory,* Fawcett Columbine, New York, NY, 1994, ISBN 0 449 90898-4

Cronin, Mary J., *Doing Business on the Internet; How the Electronic Highway is Transforming American Companies,* Van Nostrand Reinhold, New York, NY, an International Thomson Publishing Company, 1994, ISBN 0-442-01770-7

Crowe, Elizabeth Powell, *The Electronic Traveller: Exploring Alternative Online Systems,* Windcrest/McGraw-Hill, New York, NY, 1994, ISBN 0-8306-4498-9

Dern, Daniel. *The Internet Guide for New Users.* New York, NY: McGraw-Hill, 1993.

Engst, Adam C., *Internet Starter Kit; Everything You Need to Get on the Internet,* Hayden Books, Division of Prentice Hall Computer Publishing, Indianapolis, IN, 1993, ISBN 1-56830-064-6

Engst, Adam, *Internet Starter Kit for Macintosh,* 2nd Edition, Hayden Books, Division of Prentice Hall Computer Publishing, Indianapolis, IN, 1994, ISBN 1-56830-111-1

Estrada, Susan. *Connecting to the Internet: An OReilly Buyers Guide.* Sebastopol, CA: OReilly & Associates, 1993

Fahey, Tom, *net.speak: the internet dictionary,* Hayden Publishing, a division of Prentice Hall, Indianapolis, IN, 1994, ISBN 1-56830-095-6

Fisher, Sharon, *Riding the Internet Highway; Deluxe Edition,* New Riders Publishing, Indianapolis, IN, 1994, ISBN 1-56205-315-9

Fraase, Michael. *The Mac Internet Tour Guide: Cruising the Internet the Easy Way.* Chapel Hill, NC: Ventana Press, 1993.

Gibbs, Mark, and Richard Smith, *Navigating the Internet,* Sams Publishing, a division of Prentice Hall Publishing, 1993, ISBN 0-672-30362-0

Gibbs, Mark and Richard Smith, *Navigating the Internet: Deluxe Edition,* Sams Publishing, a division of Prentice Hall Publishing, Indianapolis, 1994, ISBN 0-672-30485-6

Gilster, Paul, *The Internet Navigator; The Essential Guide to Network Exploration for the Individual Dial-Up User,* Foreword by Vinton G. Cerf, John Wiley & Sons, New York, NY, 1993, ISBN 0-471-59782-1

Hesslop, Brent. *The Instant Internet Guide: Hands on Global Networking.* New York, NY: McGraw-Hill, 1994

Kehoe, Brendan. *Zen & The Art of the Internet.* New York, NY: Prentice Hall, 1992

Kennedy, Joyce Lain, and Thomas J. Morrow, *Electronic Job Search Revolution; Win With the New Technology That's Reshaping Today's Job Market,* John Wiley & Sons, Inc., New York, 1994, ISBN 0-471-59820-8

Kent, Peter, *The Complete Idiot's Guide to the Internet,* Sams Publishing, a division of Prentice Hall Publishing, Indianapolis, IN, 1994, ISBN 0-672-30519-4

Kochmer, Jonathan, and NorthWestNet, *Internet Passport; NorthWestNet's Guide to Our World Online,* NorthWestNet and Nortwest Academia Computing Consortium, Inc., Bellevue, WA, 1993, 4th Edition, ISBN 0-9635281-0-6

Krol, Ed, *The Whole Internet; User's Guide & Catalog,* O'Reilly & Associates, Inc., Sebastopol, CA, 1992, ISBN 1-56592-025-2

LaQuey, Tracy, and Jeanne C. Ryer, *The Internet Plus Companion; A Beginner's Start-Up Kit for Global Networking,* Foreword by Vice President Al Gore, Addison-Wesley, Boston, MA, 1993, ISBN 0-201-62719-1

Lawley, Elizabeth Lane and Craig Summerhill, *Internet Primer for Information Professionals: Basic Guide to Internet Networking Technology,* Mecklermedia, Westport, 1993, ISBN 0-88736-831-X

Library of Congress; Office for Subject Cataloging Policy Collection and Services, *LC Classification Outline,* Library of Congress, Washington, 1990, 6th edition, ISBN 0-8444-0684-8

Lynch, Daniel and Marshall T. Rose. *Internet System Handbook.* Reading, MA: Addison-Wesley, 1993

Magid, Larry, *Everybody's Online,* Random House, New York, 1993, ISBN O-679-748-82-2

Magid, Larry, *Cruising Online,* Random House, New York, 1994, ISBN 0-679-751-556

Malamud, Carl. *Exploring the Internet: A Technical Travelogue.* New York, NY: Prentice Hall, 1992

Marine, April (Editor). *Internet: Getting Started.* Menlo Park, CA: SRI International, 1992

Marine, April (Editor). *Internet: Getting Started.* Englewood Cliffs, NJ: Prentice Hall, 1994

Newby, Gregory B., *Directory of Directories on the Internet; A Guide to Information Sources,* Meckler, Westport, CT, 1994, ISBN 0-88736-768-2

Otte, Peter, *The Information Superhighway: Beyond the Internet,* Que Corporation, Indianapolis, IN, 1994, ISBN 1-56529-825-X

Pfaffenberger, Bryan, *Que's Computer User's Dictionary*, Que Corporation, Indianapolis, IN, 1993, 4th Edition, ISBN 1-56529-604-4

Que Development Group Staff. *The Hitchhikers Guide to Internet*. Indianapolis, ID: Que, 1993

Resnick, Rosalind and Dave Taylor, *The Internet Business Guide,* Sams Publishing, a division of Prentice-Hall, Indianapolis, IN, 1994, ISBN 0-672-30530-5

Rittner, Don, *Ecolinking; Everyone's Guide to Online Environmental Information*, Peachpit Press, Berkeley, CA, 1992, ISBN 0-938151-35-5

Rugge, Sue and Alfred Glossbrenner, *The Information Broker's Handbook*, Windcrest/McGraw-Hill, New York, NY, 1992, ISBN 0-8306-3797-4

Savetz, Kevin, *Your Internet Consultant: The FAQs of Life Online*, Sams Publishing, Indianapolis,IN, 1994, ISBN 0-672-30520-8

Tweney, Dylan, *The Traveler's Guide to the Information Highway*, Ziff Davis Press, Emeryville, CA, 1994, ISBN 1-56276-206-0

Woods, Lamont and Dana Blankenhorn, *Bulletin Board Systems for Business*, John Wiley & Sons, New York, NY, 1992, ISBN 0-471-55348-4

Appendix

F

A Whimsical Tour of the Internet

Following is a whimsical guided tour of the Internet—just another way of enticing you to discover the riches that await you on the Internet!

You can start your online day by accessing the world's first random URL generator! Use your favorite WWW browser to click on an image and be taken to a random URL. You never know where you'll end up!

```
http://kuhttp.cc.ukans.edu/cwis/
organizations/kucia/uroulette/
uroulette.html
```

Then you can look for

- An almanac entry:

```
<finger://copi@oddjob.uchicago.edu>
```

- A verse from the Bible:

```
<telnet://138.26.65.78:7777>
```

- A virtual fortune cookie

```
<telnet://astro.temple.edu:12345> or
<telnet://argo.temple.edu:12345>
```

With your morning coffee you can

- Read the headlines from USA Today:

```
<telnet://freenet-in-
[a,b,c].cwru.edu>
```

```
<telnet://visitor@yfn.ysu.edu>
```

- Peruse the Electronic Newsstand:

```
<gopher://gopher.cic.net:70/11/e-
serials>
```

- See how your stocks have been doing:

```
<telnet://guest@a2i.rahul.net>
```

- Look for a new job at the Online Career Center:

```
<gopher://garnet.msen.com:9062/1>
```

- Find out about scholarship and minority assistance programs:

```
<telnet://fedix.fie.com>
```

If you're feeling scholarly, you can check out

- The Library of Congress:

```
<gopher://marvel.loc.gov:70/1>
```

- The Colorado Alliance of Research Libraries:

```
<telnet://pac.carl.org>
```

- HYTELNET, which gives access to hundreds of libraries all around the world:

```
<telnet://access.usask.ca>
```

- An online dictionary:

```
<telnet://cs.indiana.edu:2627, or
<telnet://guest@wombat.doc.ic.ac.uk>
```

Science and Math types can use

- The Scientist, a biweekly newsletter:

```
<ftp://ds.internic.net/pub/the-
scientist>
```

- The Math Gopher, for software, lesson plans, and access to other systems:

```
<gopher://archives.math.utk.edu:70>
```

- NASA Headline News:

```
<finger://nasanews@space.mit.edu>
```

- An online periodic table of elements:

```
<telnet://camms2.caos.kun.nl:2034>
```

For the publisher in you, here are some favorite starting points

- CMU list of Book Publishers & Retailers On-Line:

```
<http://www.cs.cmu.edu:8001/web/
booksellers.html>
```

- CMU list of On-Line Books:

```
<http://www.cs.cmu.edu:8001/web/
books.html>
```

- The Digital Media Center:

```
<http://160.96.7.121/
```

- The World Wide Web Virtual Library's Commercial Services:

```
<http://info.cern.ch/hypertext/
DataSources/bySubject/Yellow/
Overview.html>
```

- The World Wide Web Virtual Library, literature maintained by the Internet Book Information Center:

```
<http://sunsite.unc.edu/ibic/IBIC-
homepage.html>
```

For the academic in you, you can visit the University Press:

```
<gopher://geneva.acs.uci.edu:1070/11/
franklin/Libraries/publishers>
```

For the geographer in you, visit the map site at Delorme Mapping:

`<http://www.delorme.com/home.htm>`

For the bookworm in you, try Online BookStore (OBS):

`<http://marketplace.com/0/obs/obshome.html>`

Or try Project Gutenberg:

`<http://info.cern.ch/roeber/Misc/Gutenberg.html>` or `<http://med-amsa.bu.edu/Gutenberg/Welcome.html>`

To peruse periodicals and magazines, try

- The Electronic Newsstand:

`<gopher://internet.com:2001/11/>`

- Global Network Navigator (GNN):

`<http://nearnet.gnn.com/gnn.html>`

- Wired Magazine:

`<http://www.wired.com/>`

If you've ever dreamed of visiting far away museums, now's your chance!

- Scrolls from the Dead Sea: an Exhibit at the Library of Congress, Washington, D.C.:

`<http://sunsite.unc.edu/expo/deadsea.scrolls.exhibit/intro.html>`

- The Louvre:

`<http://mistral.enst.fr/~pioch/louvre/>`

Desperate to go downtown in the middle of the night!

- Downtown Anywhere:

`<http://www.awa.com/>`

Want to join a few societies? Try starting with:

- The Internet Society:

`<http://info.isoc.org/home.html>`

- The International Society for Arts, Science and Technology, ISAST

`< leonardo@garnet.berkeley.edu>`

Interested in finding out what's going on in the cyberspace marketplace?

- Marketplace:

`<http://marketplace.com/>`

If you're a history buff, there are:

- Databases:

`<telnet://ukanaix.cc.ukans.edu history>`

- Documents and archives:

`<ftp://byrd.mu.wvnet.edu/pub/history>`

If you want the latest shareware for your MS-DOS, Macintosh, UNIX, Amiga, Apple2, Apollo, or other computer, try one of the enormous software archives on the Internet!

- Shareware depositories:

`<ftp://archive.umich.edu>`

`<ftp://sumex-aim.stanford.edu>`

`<ftp://oak.oakland.edu>`

To see what's been shaking, there's earthquake information at:

`<finger://quake@geophys.washington.edu>`

And the USGS offers land use maps of the United States at:

`<telnet://guest@glis.cr.usgs.gov>`

For legal information try:

- Supreme Court Rulings

`<ftp://ftp.cwru.edu/hermes>`

- Law libraries, offering information by state or subject:

`<telnet://liberty.uc.wlu.edu lawlib>` and `<ftp://sulaw.law.su.oz.au/pub/law>`

- Hypertext access to legal documents:

`<telnet://www.LAW.indiana.edu www>` or `<telnet://fatty.LAW.cornell.edu www>`

For health and clinical information, there's the National Institute of Health:

`<gopher://gopher.nih.gov:70/11/clin>`

Handicapped and disabled users can access medical information, disability assistance, equipment, services, and software at:

`<ftp://handicap.shel.isc-br.com>`

If you're 'Hollywood' inclined, you can get access to a database of actors, directors, and cinematographers:

`<mailto://movie@ibmpcug.co.uk "HELP">`

Home shoppers can access catalogs and place orders for CDs, books, software, and video tapes through home shopping:

`<telnet://columbia.ilc.com cas>`

`<telnet://holonet.net cdc>`

`<telnet://books.com>`

`<telnet://netmark.com>`

If you're a music lover, you can get

- Guitar chords in tablature form:

`<ftp://ftp.nevada.edu/pub/guitar>`

- Lyrics:

`<ftp://ftp.uwp.edu/pub/music>`

- Billboard charts:

`<finger://buckmr@rpi.edu>`

- Cyber-Sleaze reports on pop stars:

`<gopher://metaverse.com`

If its food from the gods that you're looking for, try accessing Mythology and Folklore in the EINet galaxy catalog. This resource includes pointers to The Gateway of Darkness, books about mythology online, and more.

`<http://www.einet.net/galaxy/Arts-and-Humanities/Religion/Mythology-and-Folklore.html>`

If you're hungry, you can access recipe archives:

`<ftp://gatekeeper.dec.com/pub/recipes>`

`<ftp://mthvax.cs.miami.edu/pub/recipes`, `<ftp://ftp.neosoft.com/pub/rec.food/recipes>` or

`<ftp://cs.ubc.ca/pub/local/RECIPES>`

And if you're thirsty, you can take a look at the HomeBrew archives:

`<ftp://mthvax.cs.miami.edu/Home brewDigest`

If you want to taste the spirit of New York or the spirit of San Francisco, think of becoming a subscriber to:

- ECHO:

`phiber@echonyc.com (212) 255-3839`

- The WELL:

`telnet://well.sf.ca.us and login as`

`guest. VOICE: +1-415-332-4335`

If you want to play games with partners around the world, your choices include

- Bolo:

`<telnet://gwis.circ.gwu.edu:1234>`

- Go:

`<telnet://hellspark.wharton.upenn.`
`edu:6969>`

- Diplomacy:

`<mailto://judge@morrolan.eff.org>`

`<mailto://judge@dipvax.dsto.gov.au>`

`<mailto://judge@shrike.und.ac.za>`

`<mailto://judge@u.washington.edu>`

- Tetris, Moria, Nethack, MUDs, Text
  Adventures, and others:

`<telnet://castor.tat.physik.uni-`
`tuebingen.de GAMES>`

Sports fans can get:

- NBA schedules: ·

`<telnet://culine.colorado.edu:859>`

- NHL schedules:

`<telnet://culine.colorado.edu:860>`

- MLB schedules:

`<telnet://culine.colorado.edu:862>`

- NFL schedules:

`<telnet://culine.colorado.edu:863>`

  and a variety of others

`<finger://copi@oddjob.uchicago.edu>`

For access to US Government information, there's the FedWorld Gateway, providing access to scores of government databases:

`<telnet://fedworld.doc.gov>`

And of course, last but not least, you can even find love on the Internet !

`>- mailto://perfect@match.com "SEND`
`FORM"`

And there's much, much more!

Appendix

G

Making Your Voice Heard

Making Your Voice Heard

Application to List an Internet Resource

The cooperative nature of the Internet environment is one of its strongest features. If you have discovered a resource that is particularly useful to you and it is not in *The New Riders Official Internet Yellow Pages*, you can call it to the attention of the authors, who will endeavor to qualify it for listing in a subsequent edition.

You can make your recommendation by filling in this form and e-mailing or FAXing it to us.

You can e-mail or FAX your recommendation to:

YP@McKinley.com   or   FAX (510) 841-6311

The McKinley Group, Inc., 2421 Fourth St. #D, Berkeley, CA 94710, USA

(Please use a separate form for each entry that you are recommending.)

I would like to recommend the following Internet resource.

Title: _____

Brief Description: _____

_____

_____

_____

Why do you particularly like this resource?

_____

_____

_____

_____

Please supply as much of the following information as possible.

Keywords (up to 4): _____

Producer: _____

Audience (up to 3): _____

Contact Name: _____

Contact's e-mail: _____

URL (up to 3 as appropriate) _____

_____

_____

_____

Profile (up to 10 lines): _____

_____

_____

_____

_____

_____

_____

_____

_____

_____

Your Name: _____

Affiliation: _____

E-mail Address: _____

Telephone: _____

FAX: _____

Snail Mail: _____

_____

_____

_____

Making Your Voice Heard

Notification to Correct a Listing

The volatility of electronic networks is such that addresses and contents change very quickly. To report changes or errors to a listing, please bring them to our attention using the form supplied here.

You may e-mail or FAX the revised information to: YP@McKinley.com
or   FAX (510) 841-6311

The McKinley Group, Inc., 2421 Fourth St. #D, Berkeley, CA 94710, USA

(Please use a separate form for each entry that you are submitting.)

I would like to point out the following error/change in the Internet resource listing found in the Second Edition of *New Riders' Official Internet Yellow Pages*.

Title of Listing: _____

Page Number the Listing Can be Found on: _____

General Observation about this Listing: _____

URL (Confirmation): _____

Correct Information

(Insert Your Changes by the appropriate Field)

Title: _____

Short Description: _____

Keywords: _____

Sponsor: _____

Audience: _____

Profile: _____

_____

_____

_____

_____

_____

_____

_____

_____

_____

Details: _____

Notes: _____

_____

_____

URL: _____

_____

_____

Your Name: _____

Affiliation: _____

E-mail Address: _____

Or SnailMail Address: _____

Telephone: _____

FAX: _____

Date: _____

Making Your Product or Service Known

Application to List an Advertisement

Advertisements are being accepted for the New Riders' Official Internet Yellow Pages as long as they conform to the basic template format as set here.

Each line can be a maximum of 48 characters long (9 point type size).

Title: _____

Brief Description (up to 3 lines): _____

Keywords (2 or up to 4): _____

Sponsor: _____

Contact Name: _____

E-mail: _____

Phone: _____

Profile (up to 10 lines): _____

_____

_____

_____

_____

_____

_____

_____

_____

_____

_____

Details: P (Product) S (Service) IP (Can be ordered over the Internet

Access Info: (up to 2 lines) _____

_____

Notes:(up to 2 lines) _____

_____

URL: _____

Please fill in the form and return it by fax or e-mail. You will be contacted regarding payment and placement of your advertisement in the next edition.

Costs: $600 per template for 2 placements in the directory; $200 for each additional placement.

Placement: Your ad will automatically be placed in alphabetical order under the two keywords you assign.

Prices are subject to change without notice.

I am interested in advertising, please send further details. _____

I have submitted an ad template, please contact me regarding placement of my ad and payment. _____

Send this form by e-mail or FAX to:

E-mail: yp@mckinley.com

FAX: (510) 841-6311

Appendix

H

Internet Ads

Index

B

C

D

E

F

G

H

M

N

Q

R

S

T

U

X

Y

Z

New Riders' Official
Internet Yellow Pages
REGISTRATION CARD

Fill out this card to receive information about future Internet books and other New Riders titles!

Name _____ **Title** _____

Company _____

Address _____

City/State/ZIP _____

I bought this book because: _____

_____

I purchased this book from:

☐ A bookstore (Name _____)

☐ A software or electronics store (Name _____)

☐ A mail order (Name of Catalog _____)

I purchase this many computer books each year:

☐ 1–5   ☐ 6 or more

I currently use these applications: _____

_____

_____

_____

I found these chapters to be the most informative: _____

_____

I found these chapters to be the least informative: _____

_____

Additional comments: _____

_____

☐ I would like to see my name in print! You may use my name and quote me in future New Riders products and promotions. My daytime phone number is: _____

New Riders Publishing 201 West 103rd Street • Indianapolis, Indiana 46290 USA